'Never Despair'

EARLIER VOLUMES OF THIS BIOGRAPHY

Volume I. Youth, 1874–1900 *by Randolph S. Churchill*
  Volume I. Companion (in two parts)
Volume II. Young Statesman, 1900–1914 *by Randolph S. Churchill*
  Volume II. Companion (in three parts)
Volume III. 1914–1916 *by Martin Gilbert*
  Volume III. Companion (in two parts)
Volume IV. 1917–1922 *by Martin Gilbert*
  Volume IV. Companion (in three parts)
Volume V. 1922–1939 *by Martin Gilbert*
  Volume V. Companion 'The Exchequer Years' 1922–1929
  Volume V. Companion 'The Wilderness Years' 1929–1935
  Volume V. Companion 'The Coming of War' 1936–1939
Volume VI. 1939–1941, 'Finest Hour' *by Martin Gilbert*
Volume VII. 1941–1945, 'Road to Victory' *by Martin Gilbert*

OTHER BOOKS BY MARTIN GILBERT

The Appeasers (*with Richard Gott*)
The European Powers, 1900–1945
The Roots of Appeasement
Recent History Atlas, 1860–1960
British History Atlas
American History Atlas
Jewish History Atlas
First World War Atlas
Russian Imperial History Atlas
Soviet History Atlas
The Arab–Israeli Conflict, Its History in Maps
Sir Horace Rumbold, Portrait of a Diplomat
Churchill, A Photographic Portrait
Jerusalem Illustrated History Atlas
Jerusalem, Rebirth of a City
Exile and Return, The Struggle for Jewish Statehood
Children's Illustrated Bible Atlas
Auschwitz and the Allies
The Macmillan Atlas of the Holocaust
The Jews of Hope, the Plight of Soviet Jewry Today
Shcharansky, Hero of our Time
The Holocaust, the Jewish Tragedy

Editions of documents
Britain and Germany Between the Wars
Plough My Own Furrow, the Life of Lord Allen of Hurtwood
Servant of India, Diaries of the Viceroy's Private Secretary, 1905–1910

'NEVER DESPAIR'

WINSTON S. CHURCHILL
1945–1965

by
Martin Gilbert

HEINEMANN : LONDON

William Heinemann Ltd
Michelin House, 81 Fulham Road, London SW3 6RB

LONDON   MELBOURNE   JOHANNESBURG
AUCKLAND

434 29182 X
First published 1988
© 1988 C & T Publications Ltd

Printed and bound in Great Britain by
Richard Clay Ltd, Bungay, Suffolk

Contents

PART ONE: VICTORY
1945

Chapter

1	'AN IRON CURTAIN IS DRAWN DOWN'	3
2	'SOME FORM OF GESTAPO'	28
3	PRELUDE TO POTSDAM	42
4	ELECTIONEERING	46
5	'TERMINAL', THE POTSDAM CONFERENCE	60
6	DEFEAT	105

PART TWO: IN OPPOSITION
1945–1951

7	'NOW THERE IS THE TUMBLE!'	123
8	ITALIAN INTERLUDE	132
9	'VAIN REPININGS'	159
10	THE FULTON SPEECH	180
11	VIRGINIA, WASHINGTON, NEW YORK	207
12	'VICTORY BLEAK AND DISAPPOINTING'	221
13	CHARTWELL, 'THE CORPSE' AND THE WAR MEMOIRS	255
14	'FULTON STILL HOLDS ITS OWN!'	275
15	'"SCUTTLE", EVERYWHERE, IS THE ORDER OF THE DAY'	292
16	FAMILY, FRIENDS AND FEARS	304
17	'OUR BATTERED SHORES'	318
18	BRITAIN, 'THE VITAL LINK BETWEEN THEM ALL'	338
19	'GRINDING AND GNAWING PEACE'	356
20	THE DREAM	364

21 MARRAKECH, 1947   376
22 'MY EXPERIENCE, WHICH IS UNIQUE...'   396
23 WRITING THE MEMOIRS, 1948   412
24 'HARD, *HARD* WORKING WONDERFUL PAPA'   426
25 'POOR OLD BRITAIN...'   448
26 PEACE, AND THE ATOMIC BOMB   461
27 THOUGHTS, AND PLANS, AT SEVENTY-FOUR   479
28 AN ELECTION LOST   500
29 'NO EXTINCT VOLCANO HE'   515
30 KOREA, AND THE 'FRONT AGAINST COMMUNISM'   535
31 'NEW, STRANGE, GATHERING DANGERS'   560
32 RETURN TO MARRAKECH, 1950   576
33 'SUCH AWFUL HAZARDS'   590
34 'IT IS ONLY THE TRUTH THAT WOUNDS'   609
35 TOWARDS THE GENERAL ELECTION   630

PART THREE: SECOND PREMIERSHIP
1951–1955

36 PRIME MINISTER FOR THE SECOND TIME   653
37 TRANSATLANTIC JOURNEY, JANUARY 1952   672
38 1952: 'A VOLCANIC FLASH'   696
39 'THE ZEST IS DIMINISHED'   725
40 RENEWED VIGOUR   737
41 TOWARDS SEVENTY-EIGHT, AND BEYOND   759
42 RETURN TO THE UNITED STATES   786
43 STALIN'S DEATH   805
44 THE CALL FOR A SUMMIT   827
45 STROKE   846
46 RECOVERY   858
47 STAYING ON: 'I MAY ... HAVE AN INFLUENCE'   893
48 THE BERMUDA CONFERENCE, DECEMBER 1953   916
49 'UNIMAGINABLE HORRORS'   943
50 TO RESIGN OR NOT TO RESIGN   975
51 SUMMER 1954: RETURN TO WASHINGTON   992
52 DISPUTES ON THE ROAD TO MOSCOW   1018
53 'NO INTENTION OF ABANDONING MY POST'   1042
54 PRIME MINISTER AT EIGHTY   1068
55 DECISION TO RESIGN   1085

56 THE CHALLENGE OF THE HYDROGEN BOMB   1089
57 'A NEW CHANCE'   1102
58 RESIGNATION   1117

PART FOUR: FINAL DECADE
1955–1965

59 IN RETIREMENT   1131
60 'DETERMINED TO PERSEVERE'   1144
61 NEW STRENGTH, AND A NEW BOOK   1172
62 'A TEMPLE OF PEACE'   1199
63 TRAVELS AND REFLECTIONS   1242
64 'THE CLOSING DAYS OR YEARS OF LIFE'   1276
65 GOOD TIMES AND BAD   1312
66 LAST YEARS   1340

    EPILOGUE   1360

Maps   1367
Index   1377

Maps

between pages 1367 and 1376

1   The withdrawal of the Western Allies, July 1945
2   Eastern Europe and the 'Iron Curtain'
3   Poland's western frontier
4   Poland's eastern frontier
5   Venezia Giulia
6   Turkey and the Straits
7   The Dardanelles and the Bosphorus
8   Churchill's European journeys
9   Marrakech and the Canary Islands
10 The French Riviera

11 The journey to Potsdam, 1945   page 55

Illustrations

Jacket: front

Churchill at Chartwell on his eighty-first birthday, 30 November 1955

Section 1

1 Churchill and his wife leaving St Paul's Cathedral, 14 May 1945 (*Press Association Ltd*)

2 Electioneering, 26 May 1945 (*Press Association Ltd*)

3 In the ruins of Hitler's Chancellery, 16 July 1945 (*Imperial War Museum*)

4 Reviewing British troops, Berlin, 21 July 1945 (*Albums of Field Marshal Earl Alexander of Tunis*)

5 At Potsdam with Stalin and Truman, 17 July 1945 (*Signal Corps Photo*)

6 On his way to Buckingham Palace to resign, 26 July 1945 (*Associated Press Ltd*)

7 On his way to St Margaret's, Westminster, to give thanks for the victory over Japan, 15 August 1945 (*Keystone Press Agency Ltd*)

8 At Metz, 14 July 1946 (*Interpress, Paris*)

9 In the United States, with General Eisenhower, 8 March 1946 (*Charles T. Mayer*)

10 With his son Randolph and his daughter Mary at an American war cemetery in Belgium, 15 July 1946 (*Photo Helminger*)

11 With Bill Deakin and Sarah Churchill at Marrakech, January 1948 (*Churchill photograph collection*)

12 In his study at Chartwell working on his war memoirs, 29 April 1947 (*Life Photo by N. R. Farbman*)

13 With the Duchess of Kent, May 1948 (*Photo by A. Poklewski-Koziell*)

14 With Clementine Churchill on holiday at Madeira, January 1950 (*Foto-Perestrello's, Madeira*)

15   On his son Randolph's election platform, Devonport, 9 February
     1950 (*Life Photo by Mark Kauffman*)

                              Section 2

16   Re-elected, 26 October 1951 (*P. A.–Reuter Photo*)
17   Leaving Buckingham Palace, Prime Minister once more, 27
     October 1951 (*Sport and General Press Agency Ltd*)
18   In Washington with President Truman, 5 January 1952 (*White
     House photograph*)
19   Anthony Eden, Churchill, Dean Acheson and President Truman,
     Washington, 5 January 1952 (*White House photograph*)
20   With the Queen, Princess Anne and Prince Charles at Balmoral,
     30 September 1952, a photograph taken by Princess Margaret
     (*National Trust*)
21   Arriving in Jamaica with Christopher Soames and John Colville,
     9 January 1953 (*Churchill photograph collection*)
22   With the Soviet Ambassador, Andrei Gromyko, at 10 Downing
     Street, 16 April 1953 (*Keystone Press Agency Ltd*)
23   At Margate, less than four months after his stroke, speaking at
     the Conservative Party Conference, 10 October 1953 (*Keystone
     Press Agency Ltd*)
24   The Queen and the Duke of Edinburgh leave 10 Downing Street,
     4 April 1955 (*United Press International UK Ltd*)
25   Speaking at Harrow, on becoming the first Freeman of the Bor-
     ough, 24 November 1955, a sequence of four photographs (*United
     Press International UK Ltd*)

                              Section 3

26   At Chartwell, with his dog Rufus
27   On his eighty-first birthday at Chartwell, with his racehorse
     Gibraltar (*photograph by Vivienne, Camera Press London*)
28   With Anthony Eden, leaving 10 Downing Street, 15 February
     1956 (*United Press International UK Ltd*)
29   With British troops in West Germany, 18 May 1956 (*Headquarters
     Northern Army Group, Public Relations Photo Section*)
30   With his daughter Sarah, and his host Emery Reves, in the South
     of France (*Reves Collection, Dallas Museum of Art*)
31   In the South of France (*Paul Maze*)
32   In the South of France, working on his last literary task (*photo-
     graph by Emery Reves, Reves Collection, Dallas Museum of Art*)

33 Golden Wedding, 13 September 1958 (*United Press International UK Ltd*)

34 With President Eisenhower at Gettysburg, 6 May 1959 (*Churchill photograph collection*)

35 Anthony Montague Browne (*Cunard Line, Photograph by George V. Bigelow*)

36 On board *Christina*, Capri, 27 July 1959 (*United Press International UK Ltd*)

37 At Chartwell, playing bezique, 1964 (*Paris-Match*)

38 Family mourners watch as Churchill's coffin leaves St Paul's Cathedral, 30 January 1965 (*Topix*)

Jacket: back

Churchill in 1946, painting in the studio at Chartwell

One of Churchill's pigs, drawn after his signature when writing to his wife (this one is from his letter of 11 March 1957)

For Susie

Preface

THIS volume spans Winston Churchill's life from the defeat of
Germany in 1945 to his death nearly twenty years later. It covers
Churchill's meetings with Truman and Stalin at the Potsdam Conference, his 'Caretaker' Government in the summer of 1945, his six years
as Leader of the Opposition, his second premiership, from October
1951 to April 1955, and the final decade from his resignation until his
death in 1965.

As with each of the preceding volumes of the biography, I am grateful to Her Majesty The Queen, who graciously gave me permission to
seek guidance on various points from the Royal Archives, and to make
use of the letters which both she and her father sent to Churchill on
many occasions. I should also like to thank, for his guidance on a
number of historical matters relating to Her Majesty, her Private Secretary, Kenneth B. Scott.

I am grateful to Her Majesty Queen Elizabeth The Queen Mother
for permission to reproduce extracts from her letters to Churchill; and
to her Principal Private Secretary, Lieutenant-Colonel Sir Martin
Gilliat, for his help. I am also grateful to His Royal Highness The
Prince Philip, Duke of Edinburgh, for his personal recollections of
Churchill, and for permission to reproduce extracts from the letter
which he sent to Lady Churchill following Churchill's last dinner as
Prime Minister.

For help in answering my various queries relating to the Royal
Archives I should like to thank Oliver Everett, Librarian, Windsor
Castle; Sheila de Bellaigue, Deputy Registrar; Miss Pamela Clark,
Assistant Registrar, and the other members of the staff of the Royal
Archives for their courtesy over many years. I should also like to
thank Sir Oliver Millar, Surveyor of the Queen's Pictures.

I am grateful to the Editor of *The Times*, for allowing me to make
two appeals for recollections and materials through his letter columns,
the first in 1968 and the second in 1983; and to the late Roy Plomley,

for encouraging me to make a similar appeal on Desert Island Discs. The response to these appeals was substantial, bringing me information about many episodes which would otherwise have gone unrecorded.

Churchill's grandson, Winston S. Churchill MP, has also made material available to me, including the letters sent to his grandfather from Her Majesty The Queen.

In the late autumn of 1968, following Randolph Churchill's death, I was asked to continue the work which he had taken up to the outbreak of the First World War. In doing so, I was fortunate to be able to make use of three interviews which he had conducted for the last phase of the biography, the first with Harold Macmillan (later Earl of Stockton), the second with Jock Colville (later Sir John Colville), the third with Emery Reves. I have also been able to use the notes which Randolph Churchill made of various meetings with his father after he had been asked, in 1961, to write this biography.

During the course of my researches, I was also helped considerably by Churchill's daughter Sarah, Lady Audley, and by his daughter Lady Soames, who not only made available to me material from her mother's archive, and her own, but has always been most encouraging to me in my task, as was her husband Lord Soames.

Since October 1968, when I began preliminary work collecting material for this volume, I was able to talk to many of Churchill's colleagues and contemporaries who had worked with him during the post-war years. All those to whom I spoke were most generous of their time and recollections, as well as providing me with a considerable amount of historical material in the form of diaries, letters and documents. In the last months of 1968 I was fortunate to have a number of talks with Field Marshal Earl Alexander of Tunis. Earl Mountbatten of Burma gave me many vivid memories at a luncheon in London in 1975. I was later to have several talks with the Earl of Avon.

I am also grateful to Marshal of the Royal Air Force Sir Arthur Harris, for his help both in 1969 and again in 1984, a few months before his death; and to the Earl of Stockton for his help and encouragement over many years.

Five members of Churchill's wartime and post-war Private Office have been exceptionally helpful in providing me with personal recollections, with documents from their private archive, and with comments and suggestions. In this regard, I am indebted to Sir John Colville, Sir David Hunt, Anthony Montague Browne, Sir John Peck and Sir David Pitblado, each of whom saw Churchill at close quarters during his years as Prime Minister. Anthony Montague Browne also gave me invaluable guidance for the years from 1955 to 1965, during which he was Churchill's Private Secretary, guide and friend. Lady Sargant (formerly Mrs Anthony Montague Browne) has also been of considerable assistance to me in the portrayal of Churchill's last years, when she saw so much of him.

Churchill's secretaries of the war and post-war years have likewise been extremely generous of both time and recollections. For their indispensable help, I should like to thank Mrs Kathleen Hill, Mrs F. Nel (Elizabeth Layton), Mrs M. Spicer-Walker (Marion Holmes), Miss Elizabeth Gilliatt, Mrs R. G. Shillingford (Lettice Marston), Lady Onslow (Jo Sturdee), Lady Williams of Elvel (Jane Portal) and Miss Doreen Pugh. I am also grateful to Mrs James R. Bonar (Lorraine Bonar) for her recollections of Churchill's visit to Miami in 1946, during which time she was enlisted as one of his secretaries. On all matters relating to Lady Churchill and to Chartwell, I am grateful, as in previous volumes, to Miss Grace Hamblin.

I have been considerably helped for many years by Sir William Deakin, who has discussed with me many of the controversial episodes in these pages, both from his personal recollections of his work with Churchill on the war memoirs, and from the perspective of one who was the first to study in detail the voluminous official and hitherto secret files of Churchill's wartime premiership. Bill Deakin's friendship has been a high point in my work since its very first days when, in October 1962, I was taken on by Randolph Churchill as a research assistant.

Another of those who were prominent in the preparation of Churchill's war memoirs, Denis Kelly, has likewise given me the considerable benefit of his recollections of so much time spent working at Churchill's side and on his behalf. I am also grateful to Eileen Wood, the daughter of Charles Carlyle Wood, for having made available to me a considerable quantity of material relating to her father's work for Churchill on both *The Second World War* and *A History of the English-Speaking Peoples*. In completing the latter work, Churchill was principally assisted after 1953 by Alan Hodge, whose widow, Jane Aiken Hodge, gave me the benefit of her recollections, both of her husband's work with Churchill, and of her own meetings with him.

In the last years of his life, Churchill was frequently the guest of Emery and Wendy Reves at Roquebrune, in the South of France. I am grateful to both of them; Emery Reves for his vivid recollections of negotiating the foreign rights of Churchill's post-war books, and Wendy Reves for her equally vivid memories of Churchill's visits to their villa, La Pausa, known affectionately by Churchill as 'Pausaland'.

Many others who worked with Churchill during the years covered by this volume, or who came in contact with him officially or socially,

have given me their recollections and answered my queries in person
or in correspondence. Their willingness to help is greatly appreciated.
In this regard I should like to thank the Rt Hon. Julian Amery MP,
Lord Annan, Paul Beards, Sir Isaiah Berlin, Natalie Bevan, Sir Francis
Boyd, Lord Boyd-Carpenter, Graham Buckley, Desmond Bungey,
David Butler, Lord Caccia, Alan Campbell-Johnson, Major Lord
Desmond Chichester, George Christ, Lady Creswell, Lady Cromer,
John Crookshank, John Davenport, Viscount De L'Isle VC, Piers
Dixon, Neville Duke, Harold Edwards, His Excellency Eliahu Elath,
Desmond Flower, Alastair Forbes, Donald Forbes, Lord Fraser of
Kilmorack, Ronald Golding, Professor Albert Goodwin, Leslie
Graham-Dixon, Kay Halle, Sir William Hayter, Lady Hayter, Jane
Hoare-Temple, the Rt Hon. David Howell MP, Lieutenant-General Sir
Ian Jacob, Professor James Joll, Sir John Langford-Holt, James
Lees-Milne, Kenneth Lindsay, Miss Bella Lobban, Sir Donald Mac-
Dougall, Sir Steuart Mitchell, Charles J. V. Murphy, Yitzhak Navon,
Philip Newman, Sir John Plumb, the Rt Hon. J. Enoch Powell, John
Profumo, Hugh Pullar, Sir Denis Rickett, Professor Charles G. Rob,
Lady Rowan, Sir Anthony Royle, Cecil de Sausmarez, Sir Herbert
Seddon, Barbara Sharpe, Lord Sherfield, Robert Shillingford, David
Stirling, Sir John Stow, Sir Charles Taylor, W. E. Tucker, Sir Ian
Turbott, Colonel A. H. G. Wathen, Herman Wouk, Lord Wilson of
Rievaulx, Peter Woodard, Lord Wyatt of Weeford, Mrs E. L. Young
and Count Stefan Zamoyski.

It would have been impossible to prepare such a substantial amount
of material for publication without the help and guidance of many
experts, archivists and custodians of archives, all of whom have been
exceptionally generous of their time in answering my queries over
many years. I am most grateful for the assistance given by J. C. Allen,
Home Office; Barbara Anderson, Archivist, John Fitzgerald Kennedy
Library; Phyllis Arnell, Ministry of Agriculture, Fisheries and Food;
Larry Arnn; His Excellency Yehuda Avner; R. Bailey, Curator,
Chequers; Orly Bat Carmel; Kate Bateman, Reference Librarian,
United States Information Service, London; P. Beaven, Army Histor-
ical Branch, Ministry of Defence; Judith Blacklaw, Whitehall Library,
Ministry of Defence; Dr Peter Boyle; Jean Broome, Curator, Chart-
well; Hinda Cantor; Julian Challis; Paula Chesterman, Manager,
Punch Library Services; Meg Clarke, Loans Desk, Library and Re-
cords Department, Foreign and Commonwealth Office; Michael
Comay; C. R. H. Cooper, Search Department, Public Record Office;
Gordon Cowan, Managing Editor, *Daily Mail*; Humphry Crum
Ewing; Giles Curry; George H. Curtis, Harry S. Truman Library,
Independence, Missouri; Norman Davies, Registrar, General Dental

Council; G. R. Deakin; Aenid de Vine Hunt; John Doble; the Marquess of Donegall; Sally Downes, Assistant Public Relations Manager, the Jockey Club; Dr Michael Dunnill; Cemal Feridun Erkin; Aurelius Fernandez, Press Attaché, United States Information Service; Jane Flink, Director of External Relations, Winston Churchill Memorial and Library in the United States; M. Floess, Assistant to the Cultural Attaché, Swiss Embassy, London; Dr Otto Frei, *Neue Zürcher Zeitung*; Tuvia Frilling, Director, Ben-Gurion Archives; His Excellency Rahmi Kamil Gümrükçüoglu; Paul A. Hachey, Assistant Curator, Beaverbrook Art Gallery; Joe Haines; Professor D. W. Hamlyn; Dr Philip Hanson; J. Harding, Army Historical Branch, Ministry of Defence; Ian Hillwood; Edythe M. Holbrook; Warren M. Hollrah, Museum Manager and College Archivist, Winston Churchill Memorial and Library in the United States; Alistair Horne; Myra Janner; Dr Martin Johnstone; Vladimir Khanzhenkov, Counsellor, Embassy of the Union of Soviet Socialist Republics, London; C. Laken, Information Officer, Royal Netherlands Embassy, London; Richard M. Langworth, the International Churchill Society; David T. Leaker, Winston Churchill Society of Edmonton; Adrian Liddell Hart; W. M. Liesching; Robert Linsley, Secretary, Carlton Club; Major J. Locke, Regimental Headquarters, Coldstream Guards; Professor R. R. H. Lovell; Commander Shane Lyons, R.N., Ministry of Defence; Barb MacDonald, Beaverbrook Art Gallery, Fredericton, New Brunswick; Marilyn McLennan, Reference Library, Canada House; Joan McPherson, Library and Records Department, Foreign and Commonwealth Office; Larry Mandel, Embassy of the United States of America, London; Stephen Marks; John E. Marshall, Vice President for Development, Westminster College, Fulton, Missouri; Jane Masini; Ann Mavroleon; Michael Mayne, Dean of Westminster; Charles E. Menagh; R. A. L. Morant, Chief Executive Officer, The Winston Churchill Memorial Trust, Canberra; Kenneth Murphy, Archivist, *Guardian*; L. R. Muray, Diplomatic Correspondent, *Liverpool Daily Post*; Lord Napier and Ettrick; Elizabeth Ollard, Library Assistant, Royal Academy of Arts; Peter Olney, Curator of Birds, the Zoological Society of London; Nigel Owens, Home Office; Alan Palmer; Bill Phillips, Executive Director, British Technion Society; Mudgie Phipps; Professor Monte Poen; C. C. Pond, Public Information Office, House of Commons; Peter Quennell; Tim Radford, *Guardian*; Robert Rhodes James MP; Michael Rose; Frank E. Rosenfelt, Vice Chairman of the Board, Metro-Goldwyn-Mayer, United Artists; Jenny Rosser; Professor John P. Rossi; Edmund L. de Rothschild; John Sacher; Mrs Christian de Sausmarez; Marion Scheinberger, Chef du Secteur Europe 1, Comité International de la Croix-Rouge, Geneva; Eileen Schlesinger; Susanne

Schumacher, Chef du Service des Archives, Comité International de la Croix-Rouge, Geneva; Erich Segal; Kevin Selly, *Financial Times*; Michael Sherbourne; Lord Sieff; Professor David C. Smith; Professor Denis Smith; Dr Bethel Solomons; Miss P. S. Tay; Edward Thomas; Edwin A. Thompson, Director, Records Declassification Division, National Archives and Records Service, Washington, DC; Nancy Tuckerman; Cornelius M. Ulman; Vicki Vinson, Curatorial Assistant, the Wendy and Emery Reves Collection, Dallas Museum of Art; Ann Wasley, Reform Club; Gordon Wasserman; Bill West; Joan West, Conservative Central Office; Michael Whelan; John E. Wickman, Director, Dwight D. Eisenhower Library, Abilene, Kansas; Charles Wirz, Institut et Musée Voltaire, Geneva; Derek Wyatt; and Benedict K. Zobrist, Director, Harry S. Truman Library, Independence, Missouri.

On military, naval and air matters, I have been guided once more by Dr Christopher Dowling, Keeper of the Department of Education and Publications, Imperial War Museum.

No historian of British policy in the Second World War, or of the post-war Attlee and Churchill premierships, can work without the documents available for research at the Public Record Office, Kew. My own indebtedness to the Keeper of the Public Record Office, G. H. Martin, and to his staff, particularly those of the Search Rooms and the Stacks, is immense. I am also grateful to Elizabeth Forbes, of the Cabinet Office Historical Section, to her successor, Miss P. M. Andrews, and to the Staff at Hepburn House.

As with each of the previous volumes of the biography, I am grateful to the Chartwell Trust for giving me access to Churchill's papers, and to Lady Soames for access to the papers of Lady Spencer-Churchill, as well as to the owners, curators and custodians of several other sets of private papers for allowing me access, and for permission to reproduce in this volume material from the papers of the Earl of Avon, Lord Beaverbrook, Lorraine Bonar, Lord Boothby, Desmond Bungey, Alan Campbell-Johnson, Viscount Camrose, Viscount Cecil of Chelwood, Major-General Chater, the Hon. Randolph Churchill, Sir John Colville, Harry Crookshank, Admiral of the Fleet Viscount Cunningham of Hyndhope, Lord Dalton, John Davenport, the 17th Earl of Derby, Piers Dixon, Sir Pierson Dixon, Lady Juliet Duff, Dwight D. Eisenhower, Alderman Donald Forbes, Leslie Graham-Dixon, Pamela Harriman, Sir James Hawkey, Lady Hayter, Jane Hoare-Temple, Denis Kelly, Sir John Langford-Holt, James Lees-Milne, Sir Shane Leslie, Bella Lobban, Daniel Longwell, the 11th Marquess of Lothian, the Countess of Lytton, Sir Edward Marsh, Sir John Martin, Charles V. Murphy, Gilbert Murray, the Earl of Oxford and Asquith

(H. H. Asquith), Sir John Peck, Sir Richard Pim, Doreen Pugh, Hugh Pullar, Lord Quickswood, Emery Reves, the 5th Marquess of Salisbury, Lady Sargant, Sir Hugh Seddon, Robert Shillingford, Lord Soames, Lady Soames, Major-General Sir Edward Louis Spears, Lady Spencer-Churchill, Marian Walker Spicer, the Earl of Stockton (Harold Macmillan), Sir Charles Taylor, Harry S. Truman, Dr Chaim Weizmann, C. C. Wood and Herman Wouk.

I should also like to thank, for their help in access to material, F. Bartlett Watt; the BBC Written Archive Centre; the Butler library, Columbia University, New York; the Custodian of Chequers; the Dwight D. Eisenhower Library; the English-Speaking Union; Harrow School; the International Committee of the Red Cross; the Government of Israel State Archives; the National Trust; the House of Orange-Nassau Archive; the Royal Academy; the Harry S. Truman Library; and Westminster College, Fulton, Missouri.

I have indicated in the footnotes all printed sources used in this volume, and am grateful to their publishers for permission to quote from them. These sources are:

Dean Acheson, *Present at the Creation, My Years in the State Department*, New York, 1969;

Lord Avon, *The Eden Memoirs, The Reckoning*, London 1965;

Lord Birkenhead, *The Life of Lord Halifax*, London 1965;

Sir James Bisset, *Commodore*, London 1961;

Lord Boothby, *Boothby, Recollections of a Rebel*, London 1978;

Lord Boothby, *My Yesterday, Your Tomorrow*, London 1962;

General Sir Tom Bridges, *Alarms & Excursions*, London 1938 (with a Foreword by Winston S. Churchill);

Arthur Bryant (editor), *Triumph in the West 1943–1946*, London 1959;

Harry C. Butcher, *Three Years with Eisenhower*, New York 1946;

D. E. Butler, *The British General Election of 1951*, London 1952;

David Butler and Anne Sloman, *British Political Facts 1900–1975*, 4th edition, London 1975;

Lord Butler, *The Art of the Possible, the Memoirs of Lord Butler*, London 1971;

Feridun Cemal Erkin, *Les Relations Turco-Soviétiques et la question des Détroits*, Ankara 1968;

Randolph S. Churchill (editor), *The Sinews of Peace, Post-War Speeches by Winston S. Churchill*, London 1948;

Randolph S. Churchill (editor), *Europe Unite, Speeches 1947 and 1948 by Winston S. Churchill*, London 1950;

Randolph S. Churchill (editor), *In the Balance, Speeches 1949 and 1950 by Winston S. Churchill*, London 1951;

Randolph S. Churchill (editor), *Stemming the Tide, Speeches 1951 and 1952 by Winston S. Churchill*, London 1953;

Randolph S. Churchill (editor), *The Unwritten Alliance, Speeches 1953 to 1959 by Winston S. Churchill*, London 1961;

Sarah Churchill, *Keep on Dancing*, London 1981;

Winston S. Churchill, *My Early Life*, London 1930;

Winston S. Churchill, *Marlborough, His Life and Times*, volume 1, London 1934; volume 4, London 1938;

Winston S. Churchill, *Thoughts and Adventures*, London 1932;

Winston S. Churchill, *The Second World War*, volume 1, London 1948; volume 2, London 1949; volume 3, London 1950; volume 4, London 1951; volume 5, London 1952; volume 6, London 1954;

Winston S. Churchill, *The Second World War and an Epilogue on the Years 1945 to 1957*, London 1959;

Winston S. Churchill, *A History of the English-Speaking Peoples*, volume 1, London 1956; volume 2, London 1956; volume 3, London 1957; volume 4, London 1958;

Kenneth Clark, *Another Part of the Wood, A Self-Portrait*, London 1974;

Kenneth Clark, *The Other Half*, London 1977;

John Colville, *Footprints in Time*, London 1976;

John Colville, *The Fringes of Power, Downing Street Diaries 1939–1955*, London 1985;

Colin R. Coote, *The Other Club*, London 1971;

Richard Crossman (editor), *The God That Failed*, London 1950;

Richard Crossman, *The Diaries of a Cabinet Minister, 1964–1970*, London 1975;

David Dilks (editor), *The Diaries of Sir Alexander Cadogan, OM, 1938–1945*, London 1971;

Benjamin Disraeli, *Coningsby*, London 1844;

William Y. Darling, *Hades, the Ladies*, London 1933;

Piers Dixon, *Double Diploma, The Life of Sir Pierson Dixon*, London 1968;

Charles Eade (editor), *Victory, War Speeches by the Right Hon. Winston S. Churchill, OM, CH, MP, 1945*, London 1946;

Robert T. Elson *The World of 'Time Inc.', The Intimate History of a Publishing Enterprise, 1941–1960*, New York 1973;

Peter Evans, *Ari, The Life and Times of Aristotle Socrates Onassis*, London 1986;

Foreign Relations of the United States, 1946, volume 6, Washington 1976;

Foreign Relations of the United States, 1948, volume 3, Washington 1974;

Walter Graebner, *My dear Mister Churchill*, London 1965;

Kay Halle (editor), *The Irrepressible Churchill*, London 1985;

Richard Harrity and Ralph G. Martin, *Man of the Century, Churchill*, New York 1962;

R. F. Harrod, *The Prof, A Personal Memoir of Lord Cherwell*, London 1959;

John Harvey (editor), *The War Diaries of Sir Oliver Harvey, 1941–1945*, London 1978;

Sir William Hayter, *A Double Life*, London 1974;

Roy Howells, *Simply Churchill*, London 1965;

James C. Humes, *Churchill, Speaker of the Century*, London 1980;

David Hunt, *On the Spot, An Ambassador Remembers*, London 1975;

Ralph Ingersoll, *Top Secret*, New York 1946;

Lord Ismay, *The Memoirs of General the Lord Ismay*, London 1960;

Norman McGowan, *My Years with Churchill*, London 1958;

Harold Macmillan, *Tides of Fortune*, London 1969;

Reginald Maudling, *Memoirs*, London 1978;

Paul Maze, *A Frenchman in Khaki*, London 1934;

Lord Moran, *The Struggle for Survival*, London 1966;

R. A. L. Morant, *The Winston Churchill Memorial Trust, Origins and Development*, Canberra 1983;

Malcolm Muggeridge, *Like It Was*, London 1981;

Nigel Nicolson (editor), *Harold Nicolson Diaries and Letters 1939–1945*, London 1967;

Nigel Nicolson (editor), *Harold Nicolson Diaries and Letters 1945–1962*, London 1968;

J. W. Pickersgill and D. F. Forster, *The Mackenzie King Record*, volume 3, 1945–1946; and volume 4, 1947–1948, Toronto 1970;

Monte Poen (editor), *Letters Home by Harry Truman*, New York 1984;

Peter Quennell, *The Wanton Chase, An Autobiography from 1939*, London 1980;

Robert Rhodes James (editor), *Chips, The Diaries of Sir Henry Channon*, London 1967;

Robert Rhodes James, *Anthony Eden*, London 1986;

A.L. Rowse, *Memories of Men and Women*, London 1980;

Vasily Rozanov, *Apocalypse of our Time*, 1918;

Anthony Seldon, *Churchill's Indian Summer*, London 1981;

Evelyn Shuckburgh, *Descent to Suez, Diaries 1951–56*, London 1986;

Ethel Snowden, *Through Bolshevik Russia*, London 1920;

Mary Soames, *Clementine Churchill*, London 1979;

Mary Soames, *A Churchill Family Album*, London 1982;

James Stuart (Viscount Stuart of Findhorn), *Within the Fringe, An Autobiography*, London 1967;

A. J. P. Taylor, *Beaverbrook*, London 1972;

H. de Watteville, *Dictionary of National Biography*, Oxford 1937 (entry for Field Marshal Sir Henry Wilson);

Sir John Wheeler-Bennett (editor), *Action This Day, Working with Churchill*, London 1968;
Peter Willett, *Makers of the Modern Thoroughbred*, London 1984;
Harold Wilson, *The Labour Government 1964–1970, A Personal Record*, London 1971;
Harold Wilson, *Memoirs 1916–1964*, London 1986;
Frederick Woods, *A Bibliography of the Works of Sir Winston Churchill, KG, OM, CH*, London 1963 (revised 1969);
Philip Ziegler, *Mountbatten*, London 1985.

I am also grateful for permission to quote from the following newspapers, magazines and journals:
Atlantic Advocate; *Birmingham Post*; *Chicago Sun*; *Daily Express*; *Daily Herald*; *Daily Mirror*; *Daily Mail*; *Dawn*; *Europe Today*; *Evening Standard*; *Finest Hour* (the Journal of the International Churchill Society); *Independent*; *Manchester Guardian*; *Miami Daily News*; *Modern Age*; *Neue Zürcher Zeitung*; *New York Herald Tribune*; *New York Journal-American*; *New York Times*; *Newsweek*; *Observer*; *Pravda*; *Sunday Dispatch*; *Sunday Express*; *Sunday Telegraph*; *Sunday Times*; *The Times*; *The Times Literary Supplement*; *Tribune*; *Woman's Own*; and *Yorkshire Post*.

W. Roger Smith, of William Heinemann Limited, has helped in the tracking down of several elusive queries. Elaine Donaldson scrutinized the typescript in its last phase, much to its benefit. On particular points of fact, I was helped in the proof stage by Michael A. Bentley, Manager, Claridge's; Anthea Carver; Jeremy Carver; Terry Charman, Department of Printed Books, Imperial War Museum; Anna Girvan, Reference Librarian, United States Embassy, London; Dr Joseph Heller; Jane Masini; Captain Milewski, Polish Institute, London; Daniel Palm, Claremont Institute, California; Denis Richards; John Sacher; Christopher Sear, Public Information Office, House of Commons; Neil Somerville, Senior Assistant, BBC Written Archives Centre; Miss Wright, Reading Room, National Army Museum; and the Manager, Hôtel de Paris, Monte Carlo.

The maps were drawn, as for earlier volumes, by the cartographer Terry Bicknell, to whom I am most grateful. For help in proof reading, I should like to thank, as hitherto, both John Cruesemann and Lloyd Thomas, as well as Larry P. Arnn, Piers Dixon, Sir David Hunt and Michael Sherbourne. Until his last days, Sir John Colville, who had read the book in typescript, also gave the proofs the benefit of his thorough scrutiny, and answered my many queries. In the final weeks, I was helped in preparing the index by Paul Myer, Major Arthur Farrand Radley, Jane Steiner and Jessica Wyman. The last phase of the typing was undertaken by Angela Wharton.

For their willingness to house the Churchill papers for the duration of my work on them between 1968 and 1987, I would like to thank Bodley's Librarian, and the Staff of the Bodleian Library, Oxford, in particular David Vaisey, Keeper of Western Manuscripts, who allowed me to use their own much needed space.

I must once more express my particular appreciation to the Warden and Fellows of Merton College, Oxford, who for twenty years have been exceptionally tolerant of a usually absent colleague.

Indispensable help in the financial aspects of the work was provided, when most needed, by Philip M. Hawley; by the Rockefeller Foundation, which in 1985 awarded me one of the annual Humanities Fellowships; and by the Churchill Society for the Advancement of Parliamentary Democracy, of Toronto, Chairman Professor McCormack Smyth, and F. Bartlett Watt, President, who first sent me material relevant to this final volume during the course of our early correspondence more than sixteen years ago.

The typing of this volume in all its stages was done by Sue Rampton, whose work has been of the highest standard, and deeply appreciated. For more than two years, the correspondence work was typed by Brenda Harry, to whom I am most grateful. I was also frequently assisted, and most ably helped, by my son David, and, in the last month of preparation of the typescript, by my daughter Natalie. Special thanks are also due to Christine Ashby.

More than seventeen years have passed since I received the first help, on the indexing of Volume 3, from my then assistant, now my wife, Susie. Her help since then has been of increasing and all-encompassing value, and indispensable. The contented reader of this volume, as of its predecessors, owes much to her criticisms, her suggestions and her guidance on all aspects of the work; her contribution to the biography is best acknowledged by the volumes themselves, and by these final words with which the work is ended.

Merton College,   Martin Gilbert
Oxford
8 February 1988

Part One
Victory

1

'An iron curtain is drawn down'

TIRED by the celebrations and concerns of victory, Churchill slept late into the morning of 9 May 1945. He awoke to news of the capture of Rangoon, 'the splendid close of the Burma campaign', as he telegraphed that day to Admiral Mountbatten.[1] After the liberation of Burma, the struggle against Japan would continue, in the Pacific, in Indo-China, in China, and in due course on mainland Japan, but, Churchill wrote to his constituency Chairman, Sir James Hawkey, 'our greatest and most deadly foe is thrown to the ground'.[2]

After lunching in bed, Churchill set off by car, together with his daughter Mary, for the United States, Soviet and French Embassies. 'At the Russian Embassy,' noted his Private Office, 'the Prime Minister made a short speech and toasts were drunk. At the other Embassies, the arrangements were less formal but equally cordial.'[3] As he drove on to the French Embassy, Churchill's progress was witnessed by a large crowd, among which was the writer Peter Quennell, who later recalled: 'Around him, their horses hooves ringing over the tarmac, mounted policemen slowly cantered. Although his cherubic face shone, and he waved his hat and his cigar, he had a remote and visionary look, an air of magnificent self-absorption, as he rode in triumph high above the crowd.'[4]

In Moscow, Clementine Churchill was at the end of her long, exhausting, but equally triumphal tour of the Soviet hospitals which had been helped by her Red Cross fund. That noon, as Russia celebrated victory, she telegraphed to Churchill: 'We all assembled here drinking

[1] Prime Minister's Personal Telegram, T.854/5, OZ 2969, 9 May 1945: Churchill papers, 20/218.

[2] 'Private', 9 May 1945: Hawkey papers.

[3] Private Office diary, 9 May 1945. Churchill was also accompanied on this drive by his Principal Private Secretary, John Martin.

[4] Peter Quennell, *The Wanton Chase, An Autobiography from 1939*, London 1980, page 57.

champagne at twelve o'clock, send you greetings on Victory Day.'[1]

Among those whom Churchill remembered on that first day of peace in Europe were three former French Prime Ministers whom he had known before the war, and who had been held by the Germans for possible use as hostages: Léon Blum, Edouard Daladier and Paul Reynaud. 'I send you my warmest congratulations on your liberation,' Churchill telegraphed. 'I need not tell you how often my thoughts were with you during the long years of your captivity nor how glad I am to be able to rejoice with you on this day of victory.'[2] Churchill also telegraphed that day to Harry Hopkins, whose visit to him in January 1941 had marked the start of a close harmony of interests and activity. 'Among all those in the Grand Alliance,' Churchill telegraphed, 'warriors or statesmen, who struck deadly blows at the enemy and brought peace nearer, you will ever hold an honoured place.'[3]

That night Churchill dined alone with his daughter Mary. He then appeared, as he had done on the night of May 8, on the balcony of the Ministry of Health, overlooking Whitehall. The crowd was equally large, and to its cheers he declared: 'London, like a great rhinoceros, a great hippopotamus, saying, "Let them do their worst, London can take it." London could take anything.' He wished to thank the Londoners, he said, 'for never having failed in the long, monstrous days and in the long nights black as hell'.[4]

Returning to No. 10 Annexe at Storey's Gate, his principal home since the Blitz of 1940, Churchill worked until the early hours of the morning. Among the telegrams which he sent was one to President Truman in which he praised the 'valiant and magnanimous deeds' of the United States, first under Roosevelt and then, since Roosevelt's 'death in action', under Truman. These deeds, Churchill declared, 'will forever stir the hearts of Britons in all quarters of the world in which they dwell, and will I am certain lead to even closer affections and ties than those that have been fanned into flame by the two World Wars through which we have passed with harmony and elevation of mind'.[5]

Churchill had already telegraphed to Truman that day about

---

[1] Moscow Telegram No. 1801, 9 May 1945: Churchill papers, 20/204. The other signatories were Doctor Kolesnikov, Lidya Kislova, Mabel Johnson, Professor Sarkisov and Grace Hamblin (Clementine Churchill's personal secretary.)

[2] Prime Minister's Personal Telegram, T.836/5, 9 May 1945: Churchill papers, 20/218.

[3] Prime Minister's Personal Telegram, T.846/5, Foreign Office No. 4765 to Washington, 9 May 1945: Churchill papers, 20/218.

[4] Speech of 9 May 1945: Charles Eade (editor), *Victory, War Speeches by the Right Hon. Winston S. Churchill, OM, CH, MP, 1945*, London 1946, pages 129–30.

[5] Prime Minister to President No. 39, Prime Minister's Personal Telegram, T.851/5, 9 May 1945: Churchill papers, 20/218. On 10 May 1945 it was announced that 150,000 Americans had been killed in action in the European war.

the need for a meeting of the three heads of Government. 'In the meantime,' he noted, 'it is my present intention to adhere to our interpretation of the Yalta Agreements and to stand firmly on our present announced attitude towards all questions at issue.'[1] One of these questions was the control of the Italian province of Venezia Giulia, into parts of which Marshal Tito's Yugoslav partisan forces had marched, but where the Allied forces under Field Marshal Alexander were in almost complete control. Tito's forces had, however, entered the southern part of the Austrian province of Carinthia. 'Trouble brewing with Yugoslavia,' noted the First Sea Lord, Admiral Sir Andrew Cunningham, in his diary on May 10. 'Tito refusing to give way and occupying up to the Isonzo River and beyond. Also crossing the borders of Austria.'[2] To Tito, Churchill telegraphed that day, about Alexander's armies: 'It would be a great mistake I am sure for you to make an attack upon him. In such circumstances he has already the fullest authority to reply.' This 'trial of strength', Churchill suggested, should be 'reserved for the Peace Table'.[3]

That night, Churchill was due to broadcast to the nation. 'I shall be listening to you tonight my darling,' Clementine Churchill telegraphed from Moscow, 'and thinking of you and the glorious five years of your service to the nation and to the world.'[4]

The first days of victory in Europe coincided with the news that fifteen Polish leaders, approved by Britain as possible members of a future Polish Government, had been arrested by the Soviet authorities and taken to Moscow, not as political negotiators, but as prisoners. 'I do not see what we can do now in this interlude of joy-making,' Churchill minuted to the Deputy Under-Secretary of State at the Foreign Office, Sir Orme Sargent, on May 10. 'Obviously this is a most grave question between the victorious States,' Churchill added: 'I do not feel I can say anything more to Stalin at the moment; but it may be a speech should be made in Parliament in the near future.'[5] To Anthony Eden, who was then in San Francisco discussing the future of the United Nations World Organization, Churchill telegraphed on May 11:

Today there are announcements in the newspapers of the large withdrawals

[1] Prime Minister to President No. 31, Prime Minister's Personal Telegram, T.835/5, 9 May 1945: Churchill papers, 20/218.
[2] Cunningham diary, 10 May 1945: Cunningham papers.
[3] Prime Minister's Personal Telegram, T.867/5, 10 May 1945: Churchill papers, 20/218.
[4] Moscow Telegram No. 1803, 10 May 1945: Churchill papers, 20/204.
[5] Prime Minister's Personal Minute, M.458/5, 10 May 1945: Churchill papers, 20/209.

of American troops now to begin month by month. What are we to do? Great pressure will soon be put on us at home to demobilise partially. In a very short time our armies will have melted, but the Russians may remain with hundreds of divisions in possession of Europe from Lübeck to Trieste, and to the Greek frontier on the Adriatic. All these things are far more vital than the amendments to a World Constitution which may well never come into being till it is superseded after a period of appeasement by a third World War.[1]

In a second telegram to Eden on May 11, Churchill discussed two possible months for the General Election, June and October. June, he wrote, was thought by 'general consensus' to be better for the Conservative Party; October would leave Government 'paralysed' for too long and would result in the 'many questions requiring settlement' in the international sphere being 'looked at from Party angles'. Eden had earlier been in favour of June, Churchill reminded him. 'On the other hand,' Churchill added, 'the Russian peril, which I regard as enormous, could be better faced if we remain united.'[2]

Churchill set out his anxieties about Soviet policy, and the future of Europe, in a telegram to Truman, stressing the need to reach an immediate 'understanding' with Russia. The telegram, as sent on May 12, began:

I am profoundly concerned about the European situation. I learn that half the American Air Force in Europe has already begun to move to the Pacific theatre. The newspapers are full of the great movements of the American armies out of Europe. Our armies also are, under previous arrangements, likely to undergo a marked reduction. The Canadian Army will certainly leave. The French are weak and difficult to deal with. Anyone can see that in a very short space of time our armed power on the Continent will have vanished, except for moderate forces to hold down Germany.

Meanwhile what is to happen about Russia? I have always worked for friendship with Russia, but, like you, I feel deep anxiety because of their misinterpretation of the Yalta decisions, their attitude towards Poland, their overwhelming influence in the Balkans, excepting Greece, the difficulties they make about Vienna, the combination of Russian power and the territories under their control or occupied, coupled with the Communist technique in so many other countries, and above all their power to maintain very large armies in the field for a long time. What will be the position in a year or two, when the British and American Armies have melted and the French has not yet been formed on any major scale, when we may have a handful of divisions, mostly French, and when Russia may choose to keep two or three hundred on active service?

[1] Prime Minister's Personal Telegram, T.875/5, 'Personal and Top Secret', 11 May 1945: Churchill papers, 20/218. Churchill sent a copy of this telegram to Truman (Prime Minister to President No. 41, Prime Minister's Personal Telegram T.877/5, 'Personal and Top Secret', 11 May 1945: Churchill papers, 20/218).
[2] Prime Minister's Personal Telegram, T.874/5, 'Personal, Private and Top Secret', 11 May 1945: Churchill papers, 20/218.

Churchill's telegram continued:

An iron curtain is drawn down upon their front. We do not know what is going on behind. There seems little doubt that the whole of the regions east of the line Lübeck–Trieste–Corfu will soon be completely in their hands. To this must be added the further enormous area conquered by the American armies between Eisenach and the Elbe, which will, I suppose, in a few weeks be occupied, when the Americans retreat, by the Russian power. All kinds of arrangements will have to be made by General Eisenhower to prevent another immense flight of the German population westward as this enormous Muscovite advance into the centre of Europe takes place. And then the curtain will descend again to a very large extent, if not entirely. Thus a broad band of many hundreds of miles of Russian-occupied territory will isolate us from Poland.

Meanwhile the attention of our peoples will be occupied in inflicting severities upon Germany, which is ruined and prostrate, and it would be open to the Russians in a very short time to advance if they chose to the waters of the North Sea and the Atlantic.

Only ten days before Churchill used the phrase 'Iron Curtain' in this telegram to Truman, it had been used by the German Foreign Minister, Count Schwerin von Krosigk, in a broadcast to the German people. The broadcast, made on May 2, had been reported in *The Times* on the following day, the Count telling his listeners: 'In the East the iron curtain behind which, unseen by the eyes of the world, the work of destruction goes on, is moving steadily forward.' [1]

Churchill ended his 'iron curtain' telegram:

Surely it is vital now to come to an understanding with Russia, or see where we are with her, before we weaken our armies mortally or retire to the zones of occupation. This can only be done by a personal meeting. I should be most grateful for your opinion and advice. Of course we may take the view that Russia will behave impeccably, and no doubt that offers the most convenient solution. To sum up, this issue of a settlement with Russia before our strength has gone seems to me to dwarf all others. [2]

On the most immediate cause of tension, Venezia Giulia, Churchill had received from President Truman what he described to Alexander as a 'most robust and encouraging telegram'. [3] 'I must regard this as

[1] *The Times*, 3 May 1945. A considerable literature has been built up around the phrase 'Iron Curtain'. In 1918 the Russian émigré philosopher Vasiliy Rozanov wrote in his book *Apocalyse of our Time*: 'With a rumble and a roar, an iron curtain is descending on Russian history.' In 1920 Ethel Snowden, returning from Soviet Russia, described that country, in her book *Through Bolshevik Russia*, as being behind an 'iron curtain'. The phrase had later been used by Hitler's Minister of Propaganda, Dr Goebbels, when he referred on 25 February 1945 to 'ein eiserner Vorhang'.

[2] Prime Minister to President No. 44, Prime Minister's Personal Telegram, T.895/5, 'Personal and Top Secret', 12 May 1945: Cabinet papers, 120/186.

[3] Prime Minister's Personal Telegram, T.897/5, 'Personal and Top Secret', 12 May 1945: Churchill papers, 20/218.

one of the most far-sighted, sure-footed and resolute telegrams which it has ever been my fortune to read,' Churchill informed Lord Halifax, the British Ambassador in Washington.[1] In the telegram, Truman commented on reports that Tito had 'no intention' of abandoning the territory he had occupied in Venezia Giulia. 'I have come to the conclusion,' Truman wrote, 'that we must decide now whether we should uphold the fundamental principles of territorial settlement by orderly process against force, intimidation or blackmail.'

The problem, Truman told Churchill, 'is essentially one of deciding whether our two countries are going to permit our Allies to engage in uncontrolled land grabbing or tactics which are all too reminiscent of those of Hitler and Japan.' It was therefore Truman's wish that Alexander should obtain 'complete and exclusive control' of Trieste and Pola, the line of communication through Gorizia and Monfalcone, and an area 'sufficiently to the east of this line to permit proper administrative control'. Truman also suggested that Stalin be informed of the Anglo-American view. 'If we stand firm on this issue,' Truman's telegram ended, 'as we are doing on Poland, we can hope to avoid a host of other similar encroachments.'[2]

In a telegram to Eden on that day Churchill stressed the need to keep before Stalin the Polish situation, including the plight of the fifteen prisoners. This should be done, Churchill explained, 'by a vigorous press campaign and by the outspokenness which will no doubt be in any case necessary in Parliament'.[3]

Truman's telegram of May 12 confirmed a harmony of Anglo-American interests towards Russia which had not existed during Roosevelt's wartime Presidency. It was an exchange, Churchill told Truman, 'which shows how gravely we both view the situation', and he added: 'If it is handled firmly before our strength is dispersed, Europe may be saved another bloodbath. Otherwise the whole fruits of our victory may be cast away and none of the purposes of World Organization to prevent territorial aggression and future wars will be attained.'[4]

*   *   *

[1] Prime Minister's Personal Telegram, T.900/5, 'Personal and Top Secret', 12 May 1945: Churchill papers, 20/218.

[2] President to Prime Minister No. 34, 'Personal and Top Secret', 12 May 1945: Churchill papers, 20/218.

[3] Prime Minister's Personal Telegram, T.902/5, No. 647 to San Francisco, 12 May 1945: Churchill papers, 20/219.

[4] Prime Minister to President No. 45, Prime Minister's Personal Telegram, T.899/5, 'Personal and Top Secret', 12 May 1945: Churchill papers, 20/218.

Clementine Churchill now prepared to return to London. 'I know of the international difficulties which have not been surmounted,' she wrote to Stalin on May 11, before leaving Moscow, 'but I know also of my Husband's resolve & confidence that a complete understanding between the English Speaking World & the Soviet Union will be achieved and maintained as this is the only hope of the World.' [1]

Early on the morning of May 12 Clementine Churchill reached Northolt. 'Winston was determined to go and meet her himself,' their daughter Mary has recorded, 'but he did not leave Storey's Gate quite in time, and Skymaster had to make a few extra tours round the airfield to allow a loving but tardy Winston to be on the tarmac to welcome home his Clemmie.' [2]

From Northolt, Churchill and his wife drove to Chequers. The principal problem confronting Churchill there was that of the date of the General Election. He had already spoken to his principal Conservative Party colleagues on May 11, about whether the General Election should be held that summer, or in October, or postponed until the defeat of Japan, possibly not for another year or even more. James Stuart, the Chief Whip, suggested a summer election, on either June 28 or July 5. 'Even though you may be in Conference with Allies,' Stuart wrote, 'this does not put me off:—I feel it might encourage the country to give you fresh strength.'

R. A. Butler preferred an October election. 'I think it essential,' he wrote, 'that the Prime Minister should stand before the British public as a believer in a *National* broadbased Govt and should not appear to desire to go for a khaki or coupon election in the interests of his Party just after his great success in defeating Germany.' [3] Harry Crookshank was equally emphatic for avoiding a summer election. 'Anything which looks like either cashing in on the Victory, or kicking out Labour,' he wrote, 'will in my view enormously damage the Tory party in the short run, at the Election, and in the long run all through the new Parliament if we get the majority.'

Duncan Sandys took a different view. 'We should offer to go on as a Coalition until the end of the Japanese war,' he wrote. 'If this is refused, we should have an immediate June election.' J. J. Llewellyn, in similar vein, suggested that Churchill should write to Attlee '& say that if there could be a continuance of the present Government for a period of, say, two years that would be the best solution'. If that 'could not be achieved', Llewellyn added, 'then there is so much un-settlement in the position that there is no alternative but to seek a

[1] Letter of 11 May 1945: Mary Soames, *Clementine Churchill*, London 1979, page 377.
[2] Mary Soames, *Clementine Churchill*, page 378.
[3] Notes of 11 May 1945: Churchill papers, 2/549.

mandate from the people immediately'. This was also Oliver Stanley's view.[1]

On the following day, May 12, Clementine Churchill wrote to her husband—they were both at Chequers:

Winston,

As you wished, I have had a conversation with Leslie Rowan and have since reflected on this vexed question of the date for a General Election.

I feel that the interests of the country would be best served if the present Government could continue until the end of the war with Japan. I understand that you have suggested this to your Labour colleagues, but that they are unwilling to continue for so long? Could you not approach them again and try all your powers of persuasion? If, however, they persist in their refusal, I think if I were you I would then hold the Election when it suits you best. I do not see why you should be pinned down to October just because that is what the Labour Party want. But if it suits you best to have it in June, I feel it would be necessary to make a public announcement that you had asked your colleagues to continue until the end of the Japanese war, but that as they could not see their way to serve for so long, you think the next most appropriate date is the conclusion of the war in Europe.

Were you able to consult Anthony Eden before he left for San Francisco?

CSC.[2]

Churchill had indeed consulted Eden before the latter's departure. 'When you left you were in favour of June,' Churchill had telegraphed to Eden on May 11.[3] 'I agree that a June election would probably be better for our party than an October one,' Eden answered by telegram on May 12, 'though Labour party will no doubt blame us for ending the coalition which the nation I believe would like to retain for a while yet. But any advantage they might derive from this would be lost as the campaign developed.'[4] Eden's telegram, Churchill replied that same day, 'is in general harmony with my own opinion and most of us here'.[5]

That weekend, at a meeting of Conservative Central Office Area Agents, 'the majority view', Ralph Assheton wrote to Churchill, 'was in favour of an early election. There were only one or two who thought an advantage would be gained by postponing it until the autumn.'[6] That same weekend, Colonel P. B. Blair, Political Secretary to the

[1] Notes of 11 May 1945: Churchill papers, 2/549.

[2] Letter of 12 May 1945: Churchill papers, 2/549.

[3] Prime Minister's Personal Telegram, T.874/5, 'Personal, Private and Top Secret', 11 May 1945: Churchill papers, 2/550.

[4] Telegram No. 261 from San Francisco, 'Most Immediate', 'Top Secret', 'Decypher Yourself', 12 May 1945: Churchill papers, 2/550.

[5] Prime Minister's Personal Telegram, T.900/5, 'Personal and Top Secret', 12 May 1945: Churchill papers, 2/550.

[6] Letter of 15 May 1945: Churchill papers, 2/549.

Scottish Whip, warned James Stuart, who at once sent the warning on to Churchill: 'As regards the Service vote, from the purely Party point of view I should think that it would be best to have the Election as soon as possible, otherwise time will be given for the Labour Party to distribute propaganda among the Services, for instance to the effect that while Mr Churchill was everything that was good in wartime he will not do in peace time.' [1]

At Chequers on May 12, for the first time since 1940, all Churchill's children were together, Randolph having just arrived by air from Italy. Churchill worked that day until nearly four in the morning on his broadcast for the Monday evening. After further work on the speech during Sunday morning, he drove back to London for the Thanksgiving Service at St Paul's. 'The service was impressive but long,' noted the Conservative MP, Henry Channon. 'Winston was all smiles and Mrs Churchill, safely back from Russia, bowing and gracious.' [2]

From St Paul's, Churchill returned to 10 Downing Street for a meeting of the War Cabinet. The one topic for discussion was the continued presence of Yugoslav troops in Venezia Giulia and southern Austria. 'PM very thrilled,' Admiral Cunningham noted in his diary, 'at getting Truman's support over Yugoslavia.' The 'general opinion' of the War Cabinet, Cunningham added, was 'that we must stand up to Russia now or never'. [3]

During the War Cabinet discussion, Churchill pointed out that Truman's offer to delay the departure of American armies and air forces from Europe 'at any rate for a few weeks' might delay Britain's own redeployment to the Far East, 'with the result that some delay might be imposed on projected operations in South East Asia', as well as delaying the British plans to begin European demobilization six weeks after the end of the war in Europe. 'He believed, however,' the minutes recorded, 'that if the Governments of the United Kingdom and the United States took a firm line over the situation in Venezia Giulia and southern Austria, it would not in the event prove necessary to use force against the Yugoslav troops in these areas.' [4]

If Tito should take 'hostile action', Truman telegraphed to

---

[1] Letter of 14 May 1945: Churchill papers, 2/549.
[2] Channon diary, 13 May 1945: Robert Rhodes James (editor), *Chips, The Diaries of Sir Henry Channon*, London 1967, page 406.
[3] Cunningham diary, 13 May 1945: Cunningham papers.
[4] War Cabinet No. 60 of 1945, 5 p.m., 13 May 1945, Confidential Annex: Cabinet papers, 65/52.

Churchill on the following day, 'and attack our Allied Forces any-where, I would expect Field Marshal Alexander to use as many troops of all nationalities in his Command as are necessary'.[1]

On the night of May 13 Churchill broadcast from Downing Street. 'It was five years ago on Thursday last,' he began, 'that His Majesty the King commissioned me to form a National Government of all parties to carry on our affairs,' and he added: 'Five years is a long time in human life, especially when there is no remission for good conduct.' During a short survey of Britain's part in the war, Churchill had harsh words for the Republic of Ireland:

Owing to the action of the Dublin Government, so much at variance with the temper and instinct of thousands of Southern Irishmen who hastened to the battle-front to prove their ancient valour, the approaches which the South-ern Irish ports and airfields could so easily have guarded were closed by the hostile aircraft and U-boats.

This was indeed a deadly moment in our life, and if it had not been for the loyalty and friendship of Northern Ireland we should have been forced to come to close quarters or perish for ever from the earth. However, with a restraint and poise to which, I say, history will find few parallels, His Majesty's Government never laid a violent hand upon them, though at times it would have been quite easy and quite natural, and we left the Dublin Government to frolic with the Germans and later with the Japanese repre-sentatives to their hearts' content.

In the course of his broadcast, Churchill had words of praise for 'the Russian people, always holding many more troops on their front than we could', and also of recognition of 'the immense superiority of the power used by the United States in the rescue of France and the defeat of Germany'. Of the Anglo-American relationship, Churchill gave the view of those who 'may say', as he himself indeed believed: 'It would be an ill day for all the world and for the pair of them if they did not go on working together and marching together and sail-ing together and flying together, whenever something has to be done for the sake of freedom and fair play all over the world. That is the great hope of the future.'

Churchill then spoke, without mentioning Stalin, the Soviet Union or Communism, of his fears for that future:

On the continent of Europe we have yet to make sure that the simple and honourable purposes for which we entered the war are not brushed aside or overlooked in the months following our success, and that the words 'freedom', 'democracy' and 'liberation' are not distorted from their true meaning as we have understood them. There would be little use in punishing the Hitlerites

[1] President to Prime Minister No. 37, 'Personal and Top Secret', 14 May 1945: Churchill papers, 20/219.

for their crimes if law and justice did not rule, and if totalitarian or police governments were to take the place of the German invaders.

We seek nothing for ourselves. But we must make sure that those causes which we fought for find recognition at the peace table in facts as well as words, and above all we must labour that the World Organization which the United Nations are creating at San Francisco does not become an idle name, does not become a shield for the strong and a mockery for the weak.

It is the victors who must search their hearts in their glowing hours, and be worthy by their nobility of the immense forces that they wield.

Churchill continued with a reference to Japan, which he described as 'harassed and failing, but still a people of a hundred millions, for whose warriors death has few terrors'. Australia, New Zealand and Canada 'were and are directly menaced by this evil power'. They had come to Britain's aid 'in our dark times, and we must not leave un-finished any task which concerns their safety and their future'. Chur-chill ended:

I told you hard things at the beginning of these last five years; you did not shrink, and I should be unworthy of your confidence and generosity if I did not still cry: Forward, unflinching, unswerving, indomitable, till the whole task is done and the whole world is safe and clean.

One phrase in Churchill's broadcast struck many listeners as par-ticularly personal. 'I wish I could tell you tonight that all our toils and troubles were over,' he said. 'Then indeed I could end my five years' service happily, and if you thought you had had enough of me and that I ought to be put out to grass I tell you I would take it with the best grace.' This was not, however, to be, for, as Churchill went on:

... on the contrary, I must warn you, as I did when I began this five years' task—and no one knew then that it would last so long—that there is still a lot to do, and that you must be prepared for further efforts of mind and body and further sacrifices to great causes if you are not to fall back into the rut of inertia, the confusion of aim and 'the craven fear of being great'.[1] You must not weaken in any way in your alert and vigilant frame of mind. Though holiday rejoicing is necessary to the human spirit, yet it must add to the strength and resilience with which every man and woman turns again to the work they have to do, and also to the outlook and watch they have to keep on public affairs.[2]

The Soviet Union had agreed in 1943 to enter the war against

---

[1] 'Pray God our greatness may not fail, Thro' craven fears of being great', Alfred Lord Tenny-son, *Hands All Round*, first published in 1885.

[2] Broadcast of 13 May 1945: BBC Written Archives Centre, Library No. 8473–7.

Japan once Germany had been defeated. A Soviet declaration of war, Churchill telegraphed to Lord Halifax on May 14, was desired 'at the earliest moment', but should not 'be purchased at the cost of concessions prejudicing a reign of freedom and justice in Central Europe or the Balkans'.[1] Truman's firm telegram, Churchill warned Field Marshal Smuts that day, 'may result in a show-down with Russia on questions like the sovereignty and independence of Austria, Yugoslavia, Czechoslovakia and Poland'.[2] As to when the British General Election would be, 'Every rational argument points to a speedy election,' Churchill telegraphed to Eden on May 14, 'except the tremendous weight of unity in foreign affairs and especially towards Russia.'[3]

During May 14 Churchill commented, on a telegram from Alexander about fresh efforts by France to take over parts of north-western Italy: 'This is another instance of that "landgrabbing" on which the President animadverts in his No. 34.' The matter should be taken up 'at once', diplomatically. It was at the Peace Conference that France 'will have the opportunity of making her claims', Churchill added, 'and we must not forget that she was on our side, and in what shameful conditions she was attacked by Mussolini'.[4]

A second minute on May 14 concerned the Allies' reluctance to allow Admiral Doenitz, and those under him, among them General Busch, to give orders to the German population.[5] These orders were to tell the Germans to obey Allied instructions for the surrender of arms and the handing over of institutions and installations. 'It is of high importance,' Churchill wrote to the Deputy Under-Secretary of State at the Foreign Office, Sir Orme Sargent, 'that the surrender of the German people should be completed through agencies which have authority over them.' His minute continued:

I neither know nor care about Doenitz. He may be a war criminal. He used submarines to sink ships, though with nothing like the success of the First Sea Lord or Admiral King. The question for us is, has he any power to get the Germans to lay down their arms and hand them over quickly without any more loss of life? We cannot go running round into every German slum and argue with every German that it is his duty to surrender or we will shoot him. There must be some kind of force which will give orders which they will obey. Once they obey, we can do what we like to carry through unconditional surrender.

[1] Prime Minister's Personal Telegram, T.918/5, 'Personal and Top Secret', 14 May 1945: Churchill papers, 20/219.
[2] Prime Minister's Personal Telegram, T.915/5, 14 May 1945: Churchill papers, 20/225.
[3] Prime Minister's Personal Telegram, T.921/5, 'Personal and Private', 14 May 1945: Churchill papers, 20/219.
[4] Prime Minister's Personal Minute, M.473/5 (for the Chiefs of Staff Committee), 14 May 1945: Churchill papers, 20/209.
[5] Busch was then Commanding the German forces in the West.

I deprecate the raising of these grave constitutional issues at a time when the only question is to avoid sheer chaos. You seem to be startled at General Busch giving orders. The orders seem to be to get the Germans to do exactly what we want them to do. We will never be able to rule Germany apart from the Germans, unless you are prepared to let every miserable little German schoolchild lay its weary head upon your already overburdened lap. Sometimes there are great advantages in letting things slide for a while. In a few days when we have arrived at solutions to the more important questions requiring action and possibly gunfire, we will find a great many things will settle down. We can then lay down the great principles applicable to the qualities of vast communities.

It must of course be remembered that, if Doenitz is a useful tool to us, that will have to be written off against his war atrocities for being in command of submarines.

'Do you want to have a handle with which to manipulate this conquered people,' Churchill ended, 'or just have to thrust your hands into an agitated ant-heap?' [1]

Returning from leave on May 14, one of Churchill's Private Secretaries, Jock Colville, noted in his diary: 'The volume of work is if anything more pressing than when I left. Victory has brought no respite. The PM looks tired and has to fight for the energy to deal with the problems confronting him.' Churchill went to bed that night, at 2.30 a.m., 'leaving almost untouched', Colville wrote, 'the voluminous weight of paper which awaits his decision'. Colville added: 'He told me that he doubted if he had the strength to carry on.' [2]

'Our brief rejoicings and celebrations are over,' Churchill told the House of Commons on May 15, 'and we must now turn again to many difficulties and unpleasant tasks, including, especially, the defeat of Japan.' [3] The principal 'unpleasant task' on May 15 remained the future of Istria. With Truman's approval, Churchill telegraphed that day to Stalin: 'Yugoslav occupation and administration of the whole province would be in contradiction with the principle, which we seek to maintain, that the fate of the province must not be decided by conquest and by one-sided establishment of sovereignty by military occupation.' [4]

[1] Prime Minister's Personal Minute, M.474/5, 14 May 1945: Churchill papers, 20/209.
[2] Colville diary, 14 May 1945: John Colville, *The Fringes of Power, Downing Street Diaries 1939–1955*, London 1985, page 599.
[3] House of Commons, 15 May 1945: *Hansard*, column 2268.
[4] Prime Minister's Personal Telegram, T.939A/5, 'Personal and Top Secret', Foreign Office No. 2624 to Moscow, 15 May 1945: Churchill papers, 20/219.

One problem which seemed to threaten positive action in Istria was a report from Alexander concerning the low morale of his troops, including the United States forces under his command, and their possible unwillingness to fight Tito's forces. This report had upset Churchill. 'I supported you,' Churchill telegraphed to Alexander on May 16, 'as I always have, in the very strong line you took with Tito at the outset. I was angry at the rebuffs you received from him. I was surprised that you did not welcome more ardently the all-powerful backing I have been gathering for you.' Churchill added: 'I should have thought that you would have found it possible to give plain assurances to the Combined Chiefs of Staff about the moral state of your Command which would enable the joint policy of the two Governments to be carried out.' That policy, Churchill told Alexander, was concerned with more than the local issue of Istria. In Churchill's words:

If the Western Allies cannot now resist land-grabbing and other encroachments by Tito, and have to put up with some weak compromise, this may well breed a danger far greater than we now face at the head of the Adriatic. I am very anxious about the general attitude of the Russians, especially if they feel they have only war-wearied armies and trembling administrations in front of them.

Truman's 'magnificent message' of May 12, Churchill added, 'sets forth the case in all its strength and gives us hope that the United States will not sail away and leave us to face the overwhelming might of Russia without any adequate solemn settlement. If we do not show will-power at this time, we shall be driven from pillar to post.'

Churchill was confident that a show of determination would avert a clash of forces. 'I do not believe,' he told Alexander, 'that Tito or Russia behind him will provoke a major collision while the American armies are in Europe.'[1]

Alexander hastened to try to reassure Churchill about the morale of his troops. 'I am sure our soldiers will obey orders,' he wrote, 'but I doubt that they will re-enter battle, this time against the Yugoslavs, with the same enthusiasm as they did against the hated Germans.' In sending this telegram to Eden, who was then in Washington, Churchill commented: 'I am sorry Alexander should show himself thus meekly. I hope he will make matters clear to the Combined Chiefs of Staff. One has never expected war-worn troops to turn to a new task "with enthusiasm", but our experience at Athens was that once firing has begun they soon warm up, provided the cause is one which on examination can be proved to be right.'[2]

[1] Prime Minister's Personal Telegram, T.940/5, 'Private and Confidential, Personal and Top Secret', 'Through Special Channel', 16 May 1945: Churchill papers, 20/219.
[2] Prime Minister's Personal Telegram, T.942/5, 'Personal', 'Top Secret', Foreign Office Telegram No. 5029 to Washington, 16 May 1945: Churchill papers, 20/219.

Churchill's telegram to Eden crossed with a telegram from Alexander to Churchill, in which the Field Marshal reported: 'Pressure is already having its effect, and latest reports indicate that Yugoslav Forces west of Isonzo are withdrawing behind the river.'[1] 'Always count on me,' Churchill replied, 'should trouble come.'[2] At the same time, in a minute to the Secretary of State for Air, Sir Archibald Sinclair, Churchill instructed: 'No weakening of the Air Force in Italy or demobilization must take place at present.'[3] As a first fruit of these pressures, Tito withdrew all Yugoslav troops from Austria.[4]

On the morning of May 16, Churchill and the British Chiefs of Staff spent an hour and a half with General Eisenhower. Churchill began the meeting by offering Eisenhower his own warmest congratulations 'on the great victory won by the Allied forces under his command'. Churchill added: 'Few people knew what a very great part General Eisenhower himself had played in the achievement of this victory. Under his guidance the Allied armies had achieved brilliant results and he [the Prime Minister] did not think that anyone else could have controlled and directed the vast Allied war machine in North-West Europe as had General Eisenhower. In particular, we were deeply grateful to him for the consideration he had shown in his handling of the British army under his command.'

Speaking of the occupation of Germany by the Allied forces, Churchill told the Chiefs of Staff and Eisenhower:

... his policy towards Germany could be summed up in two words—'disarm' and 'dig'. He did not think that the Allies should assume full responsibility for Germany but should be responsible only for seeing that she was never in a position to start another world war. German problems should be dealt with by the Germans. The first task would be to ward off starvation and the Germans must be made to grow their own food and, if necessary, helped to do so. Unless this were done, we might well be faced with Buchenwald conditions on a vast scale, affecting millions instead of thousands, and this would inevitably have repercussions in Great Britain. He would not be averse to making use of suitably qualified Germans to reorganise and handle internal German problems. Some of the German generals already in our hands, who had suitable qualifications and whom the German people would obey, might be used for this purpose.

The British policy to 'destroy enemy equipment', Churchill added, was not one of which he approved. 'He did not agree with this policy,' the

[1] MA/1099, 'Strictly personal', 16 May 1945: Churchill papers, 20/219.
[2] Prime Minister's Personal Telegram, T.958/5, 'Personal and Top Secret', 17 May 1945: Churchill papers, 20/219.
[3] Prime Minister's Personal Minute, M.490/5, 17 May 1945: Churchill papers, 20/209.
[4] The withdrawal took place on 20 May 1945.

minutes recorded, 'and thought we should save all enemy equipment we could as we might well require it to equip the liberated peoples.'[1]

In his diary, Field Marshal Brooke recorded some of Churchill's remarks:

A series of good catch words such as:—'When the eagles are silent the parrots begin to jabber.' 'Let the Germans find all the mines they have buried and dig them up. Why should they not? Pigs are used to find olives.' We had to remind him that truffles were what pigs hunted for! We were then told that the children in Russia were taught a creed:—

'I love Lenin.
Lenin was poor, therefore I love poverty.
Lenin went hungry, therefore I can go hungry.
Lenin was often cold, therefore I shall not ask for warmth.'

'Christianity with a tomahawk,' said Winston![2]

In pondering the distribution of Honours for war work, Churchill was anxious to give due recognition to those at Bletchley and elsewhere who had been responsible for decrypting the most secret source of German intelligence, Enigma, and in interpreting its messages. For almost five years these Enigma decrypts, 'Boniface', as it was called in secret Government circles, had been at the centre of his war direction, and of British strategy. 'My admiration for the work of your Organization cannot be made public,' Churchill minuted to 'C', General Sir Stuart Menzies, its Chief. 'Nevertheless,' he wrote, it 'rises from knowledge and constant use of all that has been done.' Churchill's minute continued:

The services rendered, the incredible difficulties surmounted, and the advantages gained in the whole course and conduct of the war, cannot be over-estimated. Everyone who has taken part, working at such a ceaseless strain, deserves the most cordial expression of approval. Will you, within the secret circle, convey to all possible my compliments and gratitude to a large band of devoted and patriotic workers.[3]

'Pray give me a good list of Honours for your people,' Churchill minuted later that day to Menzies, and he added: 'They cannot of course

[1] Staff Conference, Chiefs of Staff Committee No. 130 of 1945, 11.30 a.m., 16 May 1945: Cabinet papers, 79/33.
[2] Brooke diary, 16 May 1945: Arthur Bryant, *Triumph in the West 1943–1946*, London 1959, page 469.
[3] Prime Minister's Personal Minute, M.495/5A, 'Top Secret', 19 May 1945: Churchill papers, 20/209.

be awarded in one batch, and it may be necessary to mix the names in other lists. But let me know the numbers of all ranks that you consider outstanding.'[1]

The political future of the Coalition seemed to be more assured when, on May 18, Clement Attlee went to see Churchill at No. 10 Annexe, and, as Jock Colville noted in his diary, was 'favourably disposed' to trying to persuade the Labour Party to continue with a national Government until the defeat of Japan. 'He has Ernest Bevin with him in this,' Colville added.[2] Another senior Labour Minister, A. V. Alexander, the First Lord of the Admiralty, was also in favour of maintaining the Coalition, and had expressed his view in a public speech. Herbert Morrison had also told Churchill of his 'willingness to carry on' until the end of the session.[3]

As a result of their meeting on May 18, Churchill sent Attlee a letter, with identical letters to the leaders of the Liberal Party and the Liberal National Party, proposing that 'If you should decide to stand on with us, all united together, until the Japanese surrender is compelled, let us discuss means of taking the nation's opinion—for example, a referendum—on the issue whether in these conditions the life of this Parliament should be further prolonged.' 'On this basis,' Churchill added, 'we could work together with all the energy and comradeship which has marked our long and honourable association.'[4]

At three o'clock that afternoon Attlee went to see Churchill at the Annexe, bringing with him Churchill's letter. 'I of course presumed,' Churchill wrote four weeks later, 'that he had in the interval, as leader, discussed the position with his own colleagues. It was not for me to communicate with them separately at such a moment. Mr Attlee again did not personally demur in any way to the letter, but proposed an addition which was certainly an improvement.'

Attlee asked Churchill if, after his words: 'It would give me great relief if you and your friends were found resolved to carry on with us until a decisive victory had been gained over Japan' he could add the words: 'In the meanwhile we should do our utmost to implement the

[1] Prime Minister's Personal Minute, M.497/5, 'Top Secret', 19 May 1945: Churchill papers 20/209. One of those who was honoured for his work at the head of Signals Intelligence was Commander Edward Wilfrid Harry Travis, described in Who's Who as 'Director of a Department in the Foreign Office'. The work done by Travis was no less vital to the Enigma triumph than that of Menzies. He was awarded a Knighthood in the Foreign Office list, also the United States Medal for Merit and the Légion d'Honneur, of which he was a Chevalier. He died in 1956.
[2] Colville diary, 18 May 1945: The Fringes of Power, page 600.
[3] As reported by Attlee in a press statement, published in The Times on 13 June 1945.
[4] Letter of 18 May 1945: Churchill papers, 20/194.

proposals for social security and full employment contained in the White Paper which we have laid before Parliament.'

Attlee then handed Churchill this amendment, which was in Attlee's own handwriting. Churchill's account continued:

I gladly agreed, as this was always our intention, and inserted these exact words in the letter. He made no other suggestions. The additional words proposed by Mr Attlee were communicated to Sir Archibald Sinclair of the Liberal Party, and to Mr Ernest Brown of the Liberal National Party. I asked Mr Attlee whether Mr Bevin was in agreement with him, and he said this was so. The matter then seemed to be completed. [1]

Attlee took Churchill's letter with him to the Labour Party Conference at Blackpool. For three days Churchill heard no more. On Saturday May 19 he was at Chartwell, his country home in Kent, 'so pleased' with the house, Colville noted, 'that he stayed' until the evening, reaching Chequers only in time for a late dinner. [2]

'The PM can't get the political prospect out of his head,' Colville wrote from Chequers on Sunday May 20, 'and all day the conversation was on a coming election, occasionally varied with fears of the Russian peril or a diatribe against those who wish to treat all leading Germans as war criminals and to leave none with authority to administer that battered and disordered land.' [3]

On the evening of May 21, Attlee telephoned Churchill from Blackpool with the text of his reply. To Churchill's amazement, it was a rejection of the proposal, which Attlee, Bevin, Morrison and Alexander had hitherto supported, to maintain the Coalition until the defeat of Japan. 'My colleagues and I,' Attlee telephoned, 'do not believe that it would be possible to lay aside political controversy now that the expectation of an election has engaged the attention of the country.' [4] 'Winston was hurt,' Harold Macmillan noted in his diary, 'at the unnecessarily waspish and even offensive tone of Attlee's reply.' [5]

Attlee's rejection had reached Churchill while he was with his son Randolph and Harold Macmillan. 'They think,' wrote Colville in his diary, 'they have manoeuvred skilfully, by placing on the Labour Party

[1] Prime Minister's statement, 12 June 1945: *The Times*, 13 June 1945.
[2] Colville diary, 19 May 1945: *The Fringes of Power*, page 600.
[3] Colville diary, 20 May 1945: *The Fringes of Power*, page 600.
[4] Churchill's letter and Attlee's reply were both published in full in *The Times* on 22 May 1946. 'An early General Election has long seemed likely,' stated the leading article that day. 'The decision of the Labour Party conference at Blackpool yesterday, recorded in Mr Attlee's letter to the Prime Minister, has made it certain.' The leading article added: 'It is as difficult to imagine the peace-making being conducted without the services of Mr Churchill himself and Mr Eden, as it is to envisage the mobilization of the nation for peace without Mr Bevin'. *The Times* envisaged that the outcome of the election could be 'another coalition while the emergency lasts'.
[5] Macmillan diary, 21 May 1945: Harold Macmillan *Tides of Fortune*, London 1969, page 26.

the onus of refusing to continue and of preferring faction to unity at a time when great dangers still remain.' But not so Churchill himself. 'I don't think the PM is quite happy about this,' Colville noted, 'but for all the other Tory politicians the time has now passed "when none were for the party and all were for the state". The most assiduous intriguer and hard-working electioneer is Lord Beaverbrook.' [1]

The Labour Party's decision not to maintain the Coalition until the defeat of Japan was as decisive as its decision almost exactly five years earlier not to agree to a Coalition if Neville Chamberlain were to remain as Prime Minister. Just as the decision of May 1940 led to Churchill's premiership, so the decision of May 1945 led to the break-up of the wartime Government.

'I propose to tender my resignation to the King tomorrow, May 23, at noon,' Churchill wrote to Attlee on May 22. 'Should the King, after duly considering the matter, invite me to form a new Government,' Churchill added, 'without, alas, so many to whom I have become attached—there will be many things to be settled between us. Thus we should have to settle the Dissolution Honours List, which in this case will, I presume, be published simultaneously with the Birthday Honours, but I think in a separate List. We should have also to settle about the broadcasts, which will require an inter-party meeting.' [2]

Following the Labour Party's negative response, Churchill wrote what Colville called an 'admirable' letter to the King, ' "for the archives" he said'. [3] The letter read:

Mr Churchill, with his humble duty to the King, has the honour to submit certain letters which have passed between him and the Leaders of the other Parties in the National Government, with the formation of which Your Majesty entrusted Mr Churchill on May 10, 1940.

During the last four or five months, as Mr Churchill has from time to time informed Your Majesty, Parliament, the Government, and even the work of the Cabinet, have been to some extent affected by the probabilities of an Election taking place at the close of the German War, as well as by the uncertainties as to when that event would occur and in what form. Mr Churchill had cherished a somewhat vain hope that his Labour and Liberal colleagues would have been willing to make a new and solemn agreement to continue the Party truce and collaboration until the end of the Japanese War, which now looms so formidable upon distant horizons. He has not however been able to persuade them to take this course, upon which he has lavished his utmost endeavours. The only course prescribed by Mr Attlee is that the Administration should continue to work together until October, when the Labour Ministers would leave the Government, apparently

---

[1] Colville diary, 21 May 1945: *The Fringes of Power*, page 601.
[2] 'Private and Confidential', 22 May 1945: Churchill papers, 20/194.
[3] Colville diary, 22 May 1945: *The Fringes of Power*, page 601.

irrespective of what the world situation might then be. Mr Churchill sees insuperable objections to this proposal. By it we should be condemned to between four and five months of uncertainty and electioneering hanging over the whole business of Government and Administration, both at home and abroad.

Churchill's letter continued:

Your Majesty's affairs are now in a much better posture than they were when the National Government was formed, but at the same time all that has been gained at such sacrifice and hazard may all be thrown away and new dangers of a serious character appear in view. The whole vast process of transformation of industry from war to peace, and of demobilizing the Armies while at the same time forming the largest possible forces to be sent to the Far East, as well as that of getting our trade and industry on the move again, constitutes a task which, though not so deadly as some which we have surmounted, is in some respects more difficult because more complicated.

Mr Churchill feels that this task can only be undertaken by a united Government possessing the undisputed confidence of the people, and actuated by true Ministerial harmony and agreement such as Your Majesty has the right to expect in any Administration which may be formed during Your Reign. Mr Churchill cannot feel that he could assure Your Majesty that conditions of amity and singlemindedness would prevail in the present Administration during the political disturbances which the approach of a General Election entails. It would be no service to the nation to go forward with a pretence of union which had in fact lapsed with the attainment of complete victory over Germany. Mr Churchill is convinced that he could not himself conscientiously continue to head such an Administration in the circumstances which he has outlined.

He therefore asks Your Majesty to accord him an audience at some time convenient to Your Majesty tomorrow morning, in order that he may tender his resignation of the various Offices which he now holds, and thus bring the present not inglorious Administration to a dignified end in accordance with the highest constitutional traditions and practice.

And with his humble duty remains Your Majesty's faithful & devoted servant and subject

Winston S. Churchill [1]

At noon on Wednesday May 23, Churchill went to Buckingham Palace, where, in an audience with King George VI, he tendered his resignation. 'Then there was a pause,' Colville noted in his diary, 'as the PM was anxious to emphasize to the public that the King has the right to decide for whom he shall send.' [2] From Buckingham Palace, Churchill therefore returned to No. 10 Annexe, where he lunched alone with his wife. Then, driving back to Buckingham Palace at four o'clock that afternoon, he was invited by the King to form a new

[1] Letter of 22 May 1945: Royal Archives.
[2] Colville diary, 23 May 1945: *The Fringes of Power*, page 601.

administration. He had been Leader of the Grand Coalition, as he liked to describe it, for five years and thirteen days.

That night Churchill dined alone with his wife. After dinner, he discussed the formation of the new Government with Anthony Eden, and with the Chief Whip, James Stuart. These talks continued throughout the next two days, May 24 and May 25. Stuart later recalled:

It was an interesting though tiresome jigsaw puzzle, which involved me day and night until it was solved. We never let up except to go to bed for four hours or so between 4 a.m. and 8.30 a.m. and we completed the job in two days and nights—or, more precisely, about two and a half eighteen-hour working days.

The PM seldom left his bed, eating his meals off a tray beside him. When he wished me to do so I joined him, eating at a small table near the bed. At the end of it all, I remember his saying to me, 'Well, that's it and all done by telephone from my bed. Think of poor old Mr Gladstone with all those letters he had to write.'

While this was true enough, I couldn't help saying, while laughing also, 'I agree, but I haven't seen much of my bed.' I got the immediate disarming answer, 'I am so sorry, my dear, I am afraid you have had an awful time. You must get off to bed at once.' Then as an afterthought: 'But you will be back here at half past nine in the morning to tidy up details, won't you?' I told him not to worry. [1]

Among the new appointments, Brendan Bracken replaced A. V. Alexander as First Lord of the Admiralty, and Harold Macmillan replaced Sir Archibald Sinclair as Secretary of State for Air. To Sinclair, his friend for thirty years and leader of the Liberal Party, Churchill wrote on May 26:

My dear Archie,

I grieve more than I can say that you are separating yourselves from the Government of the country in these months when there is so much to gain or lose. Particularly I grieve to separate from you. But alas, we are all the puppets of fate.

I do not wish to embark upon controversy, but I think it will be shown that the Liberal Party have made a crowning mistake in allying themselves with the forces of Socialism and trying to beat down to a minimum those which stand for freedom. The course you are forced to take is the most likely one to lead to political confusion and partisanship which it will not be easy to repair. I do not think the Liberal scheme of doing as much harm as possible to the new Government in the hopes of making a good bargain with the other side will be successful or be greeted with respect. No mercy will be shown you by the Socialists however much harm you may do to the national causes, which I think will draw up in very strong array. We shall do our

---

[1] Viscount Stuart of Findhorn recollections: James Stuart (Viscount Stuart of Findhorn), *Within the Fringe, An Autobiography*, London 1967, page 137.

utmost to carry on the business of the country successfully, and I am strongly of opinion that its confidence will be given to us.

I need scarcely say that however things go, it will make no difference to our life-long friendship. I am happy to think that you have conducted the mighty Air Power through all the course of this 5-years World War.

Yours always,

WSC [1]

'You know what it means to me,' Churchill wrote to Ernest Bevin, 'not to have your aid in these terrible times,' and he added: 'We must hope for re-union when Party passions are less strong.' [2]

The last of the ministerial appointments were completed during the morning of May 26, after which Churchill and his wife drove to his constituency, for Churchill's first speech of what was now an election campaign. 'The great victory in Europe has been won,' he declared. 'Enormous problems lie before us. A shattered continent is torn by passions and hatred such as have rarely been known in history. We are very close to that continent and its interests are an essential part of our interests.' The new administration had been dubbed a 'Caretaker' Government. 'No doubt they chose that,' he said, 'and we adopt it, because it means that we shall take very good care of everything that affects the welfare of Britain and of all classes in Britain.' [3]

That night, at Chequers, Churchill's principal guest was Joseph Davies, a former United States Ambassador in Moscow. Davies supported a meeting between Stalin and Truman, with Churchill excluded, before the inevitable tripartite meeting. Churchill replied that the United States was 'as fully concerned and committed' as Britain in the confrontation with Soviet ambitions and actions in eastern and south-eastern Europe, and objected to the 'implicit idea' of any such meeting 'that the new disputes now opening with the Soviets lay between Britain and Russia'. [4] It was not until 3.45 a.m. that this conversation ended. [5] When, two days later, Churchill was asked if Davies should be encouraged to contact 'Bevin & Co.', Churchill minuted: 'Certainly *not* repeat *not*, nor anyone else.' [6]

On May 27 Churchill saw Joseph Davies again before luncheon, and in a note for Eden set out the position which he had adopted during their discussion:

It must be remembered that Britain and the United States are united at this time upon the same ideologies, namely, freedom, and the principles set out in the

[1] 'Private', 26 May 1945: Churchill papers, 20/194.
[2] Letter dated 27 May 1945 (final manuscript draft): Churchill papers, 20/207.
[3] Speech of 26 May 1945: Churchill papers, 9/169.
[4] Winston S. Churchill, *The Second World War*, volume 6, London 1954, page 502.
[5] Private Office Diary, 26 May 1945: Lieutenant-Commander C. R. Thompson papers.
[6] Manuscript note, 28 May 1945: Churchill papers, 20/197.

American Constitution and humbly reproduced with modern variations in the Atlantic Charter. The Soviet Government have a different philosophy, namely, Communism, and use to the full the methods of police government, which they are applying in every State which has fallen a victim to their liberating arms.

The Prime Minister cannot readily bring himself to accept the idea that the position of the United States is that Britain and Soviet Russia are just two foreign Powers, six of one and half a dozen of the other, with whom the troubles of the late war have to be adjusted. Except in so far as force is concerned, there is no equality between right and wrong. The great causes and principles for which Britain and the United States have suffered and triumphed are not mere matters of the balance of power. They in fact involve the salvation of the world.

Churchill's note continued, of himself:

The Prime Minister has, for many years now gone by, striven night and day to obtain a real friendship between the peoples of Russia and those of Great Britain, and, as far as he was entitled to do so, of the United States. It is his resolve to persevere against the greatest difficulties in this endeavour. He does not by any means despair of a happy solution conferring great advantages upon Soviet Russia, and at the same time securing the sovereign independence and domestic liberties of the many States and nations which have now been overrun by the Red Army.

The freedom, independence, and sovereignty of Poland was a matter for which the British people went to war, ill-prepared as they were. It has now become a matter of honour with the nation and Empire, which is now better armed.

The rights of Czechoslovakia are very dear to the hearts of the British people.

The position of the Magyars in Hungary has been maintained over many centuries and many misfortunes, and must ever be regarded as a precious European entity. Its submergence in the Russian flood could not fail to be either the source of future conflicts or the scene of a national obliteration horrifying to every generous heart.

Austria, with its culture and its historic capital of Vienna, ought to be a free centre for the life and progress of Europe.

The Balkan countries, which are the survivors of so many centuries of war, have built up hard civilizations of their own. Yugoslavia is at present dominated by the Communist-trained leader Tito, whose power has been mainly gained by the advances of the British and American armies in Italy. Rumania and Bulgaria are largely swamped by the fact of their proximity to Soviet Russia and their having taken the wrong side in several wars. Nevertheless these countries have a right to live.

As for Greece, by hard fighting by Greeks and by the British Army the right has been obtained for the Greek people to express at an early approaching election, without fear of obstruction, on the basis of universal suffrage and secret ballot, their free, unfettered choice of régime and Government.

Churchill's note ended:

The Prime Minister cannot feel it would be wise to dismiss all these topics in the desire to placate the imperialistic demands of Soviet Communist Russia. Much as he hopes that a good, friendly, and lasting arrangement may be made and that the World Organization will come into being and act with some reality, the Prime Minister is sure that the great causes involved in the above epitome of some of the European relationships cannot be ignored. He therefore urges (a) a meeting at the earliest moment, and (b) that the three major Powers shall be invited thereto as equals. He emphasizes the fact that Great Britain would not be able to attend any meeting of a different character, and that of course the resulting controversy would compel him to defend in public the policy to which His Majesty's Government is vowed. [1]

In a telegram to Truman about his talks with Davies, Churchill was emphatic in stating 'at once that I should not be prepared to attend a meeting which was a continuation of a conference between you and Marshal Stalin', and he added: 'I consider that at this Victory Meeting, at which subjects of the gravest consequence are to be discussed, we three should meet simultaneously and on equal terms.' [2] The opportunity to do so had already arisen, for on May 27 it was Stalin who suggested that he, Churchill and Truman should meet together in Berlin. This Churchill accepted with alacrity; telling Stalin: 'I am very anxious to meet you soon.' [3] But in view of the fears which he had expressed, not for the first time, in his note of May 27, Churchill also minuted that day for the Chiefs of Staff Committee that the process of demobilization should not be too hasty. 'I do not wish to be left alone with no troops at all,' he wrote, 'and great Russian masses free to do whatever they choose in Europe.' [4]

The Soviet threat was uppermost in Churchill's mind. As in the pre-war years, he was convinced that a weak policy would only encourage the use and triumph of force. It would be necessary at the Berlin meeting, he minuted to Eden on May 28, 'to raise the great question of police government versus free government, it always being understood that the intermediate States must not pursue a hostile policy to Russia'. [5] 'I am sure,' Churchill telegraphed to Field Marshal Smuts that same day, 'that any sign that we can be bluffed and pushed about would have a deadly effect upon the future of Europe, which I

---

[1] 'Note by the Prime Minister on Mr Davies' message', enclosed with Prime Minister's Personal Minute, M.529/5, 'Private and Confidential', 28 May 1945: Churchill's papers, 20/209.

[2] Prime Minister to President No. 60, Prime Minister's Personal Telegram, T.1027/5, 'Personal and Top Secret', 31 May 1945: Churchill papers, 20/220.

[3] Prime Minister's Personal Telegram, T.1016/5, 'Personal and Top Secret', 29 May 1945: Churchill papers, 20/220.

[4] Prime Minister's Personal Minute, D.145/5, 27 May 1945: Churchill papers, 20/209.

[5] Prime Minister's Personal Minute, M.532/5, 28 May 1945: Churchill papers, 20/209.

regard with as much anxiety as I did before the outbreak of the war.'[1]

On the afternoon of May 28 Churchill gave a party at 10 Downing Street for the outgoing members of the Coalition Government, both Ministers and Under-Secretaries. 'The PM seemed deeply moved,' Hugh Dalton later recalled, 'and I, too, felt the emotion of this moment. I had a few minutes alone with him. I spoke as in my letter. I said that these had been proud and imperishable years, in which we had all worked together. I thanked him for all the support and encouragement he had given me. He said: "You and all the others have always been exceedingly kind to me, and I should like to thank you for all you've done."' Dalton's account continued:

A little later, standing behind the Cabinet table, now draped as a buffet, he addressed us, with tears visibly running down his cheeks. He said that we had all come together, and had stayed together, as a united band of friends, in a very trying time. History would recognise this. 'The light will shine on every helmet.' He was sure that, if ever such another mortal danger threatened, we would all do the same again. (I wondered whether this meant anything. If so, it could only have meant Russia. Probably it was only a phrase.) He went on to say that, when he went to meet Stalin and Truman, he wanted to take with him 'My good friend, Clem Attlee' to show that, whatever happened in the election, we were a United Nation.

Attlee and Sinclair made very brief replies, and then Wolmer[2] suggested that we might all be photographed. This was done in the garden of No. 10. It had begun to rain, the business took some time and the PM said 'We'd better finish this or my political opponents will say that this is a conspiracy on my part to give them all rheumatism!' Then we dispersed.[3]

From the Downing Street party Churchill drove to Buckingham Palace, for a meeting of the Privy Council, and kissed hands on his reappointment as Prime Minister and First Lord of the Treasury. The Caretaker Government had begun.

---

[1] Prime Minister's Personal Telegram, T.1008/5, No. 284 to San Francisco, 'Top Secret and Personal', 28 May 1945: Churchill papers, 20/220.

[2] From 1942 to 1945 Wolmer had been Minister of Economic Warfare.

[3] Hugh Dalton, diary, 28 May 1945: Dalton papers. In the margin of his diary, Dalton later amended this phrase to read: 'The light of history will shine on all your helmets.'

2
'Some form of Gestapo'

ON 29 May 1945 the House of Commons met, for the first time
in five years, with the Labour Party in Opposition. It was Churchill's first full day as Prime Minister of a predominantly Conservative
administration. During Question Time he announced that 307,210
British Commonwealth and Empire soldiers, sailors and airmen had
been killed in the period from September 1939 to the end of February
1945. This contrasted, he pointed out, with the 996,230 deaths in the
First World War. But a further 60,585 deaths among the civil population as a result of German air raids had to be added to the Second
World War figure.[1]

In answer to a question as to whether Britain might not consider
'retaking possession' of the former kingdom of Hanover 'to secure
strategic control' of the approaches to Britain, Churchill replied: 'We
are not seeking to enlarge our boundaries as a result of this war. We
have fought it for great principles, and in the satisfaction of those
principles we shall find our reward.'[2]

For Churchill, one of those 'great principles' remained the refusal
to surrender to force or to the threat of force, a principle much in his
mind on May 29, when he learned that Alexander did not wish to
dislodge Marshal Tito's forces from the Istrian port of Pola. 'We do
not seem to be looking at the situation from the same angle,' Churchill
telegraphed to Alexander that evening. 'I regard it as of first importance not to back down before Tito's encroachments or to give the

---

[1] In a further House of Commons statement on 5 June 1945, Churchill gave the number of
Merchant Navy deaths as 30,589, with a further 4,690 missing and still unaccounted for.

[2] House of Commons, 29 May 1945: *Hansard*, columns 24 and 25. Three days later, when
Churchill learned of a proposal to acquire Masirah Island (off the Arabian coast) as a permanent
Royal Air Force base, he minuted to Eden: 'I do not approve of our breaking our principle of
no acquisition for the sake of this small island. We may find ourselves weakened in much larger
and more important matters if we do.' Prime Minister's Personal Minute, M.555/5, 1 June
1945: Churchill papers, 20/209.

impression to the Balkans or to Russia that we are unable in the last resort to use force. I am sure that if we begin giving way at this juncture there is no limit to which we shall not be pushed.' Pola had been included in the area to be under Allied control 'on the express instructions of President Truman himself', Churchill explained, 'and it is of paramount importance that we should keep in exact step, both politically and militarily, with the United States in all our dealings with Tito'. If Pola were omitted from the Allied area, Churchill warned, the United States 'might lose interest in the main operations which you have now almost prepared. This would indeed be a disaster for us, who are not strong enough to carry the matter through alone.'

Churchill then expressed his hope that Alexander would make 'every preparation to attack Pola at the earliest moment', presumably from the sea. 'I hope the above,' he ended, 'will have made my policy clear to you.'[1] To Truman, in a telegram on June 2, Churchill reported that Alexander was ready to move forward to 'eject the enemy from their positions'. Churchill added: 'The fact that the Russians have so far remained quiescent is important. If we once let it be thought that there is no point beyond which we cannot be pushed about, there will be no future for Europe except another war more terrible than anything that the world has yet seen. But by showing a firm front in circumstances and a locality which are favourable to us, we may reach a satisfactory and solid foundation for peace and justice.'

In this telegram, Churchill stressed that he did not think 'that we shall get through this business by bluff', and he added: 'It is my great hope that you will act in the spirit of your No. 34.[2] The humiliation which we shall take if we do not settle this matter in accordance with our just and disinterested requirements may well be fatal to the future of the great causes you set forth so powerfully in your message.'[3]

Another area where Churchill was worried, even angered, by Allied weakness was north-west Italy, where French troops had remained in occupation, and were refusing to withdraw. On May 30 Churchill minuted for the Chiefs of Staff Committee: 'I do not like telegrams about Field Marshal Alexander being given orders to withdraw his troops from disputed areas to avoid the risk of clashes. Why do not the others, who are wrong-doers, withdraw their troops to avoid the risk of clashes?'[4]

In yet another sphere Churchill opposed what he saw as weakness:

---

[1] Prime Minister's Personal Telegram, T.1021/5, 'Personal and Top Secret', 'Through Special Channel', 29 May 1945: Churchill papers, 20/220.

[2] Truman's telegram to Churchill of 12 May 1945.

[3] Prime Minister to President No. 64, Prime Minister's Personal Telegram, T.1039/5, 'Personal and Top Secret', 2 June 1945: Cabinet papers, 120/186.

[4] Prime Minister's Personal Minute, D.147/5, 30 May 1945: Churchill papers, 20/209.

this time a War Office fear that the Soviet Union might object to the employment of Polish troops in the British Zone of Occupation of Germany. 'We need these men desperately,' Churchill minuted to Eden and Sir James Grigg on May 31, 'and I cannot see what the Russians have to say to it any more than we are consulted by them when they deport a few hundred thousand people to Siberia.'[1]

Much on Churchill's mind that day was 'the impending retreat', as he described it to Eden, of United States forces from the central zone in Germany. 'I am greatly concerned about this,' Churchill added.[2] The Americans, however, were determined to abide by their earlier decision to withdraw to the agreed line by July 15, if not sooner. 'If the Russian frontier advances to Eisenach,' Churchill minuted to Eden on June 1, 'we shall rue the day, and so will the Americans, and you may live to see the evil consequences.'[3]

On May 31, Churchill invited David Stirling to lunch, to listen to a plan which Stirling, until recently a prisoner-of-war, had devised for a combined British and American Commando activity, based on Chungking, to forestall the onward march of the Chinese Communists. The only other guests were Randolph and his four-year-old son Winston. Stirling later recalled:

One of the highlights of lunch with three generations of the Churchill family was young Winston from behind the sofa planting an accurate shot with a cushion upon his grandfather's face and lighted cigar as he entered the room. Then he disappeared behind the sofa, so that the old boy, whilst exonerating me, presumed it was Randolph who had thrown it, until the giggles from the sofa revealed the real culprit.[4]

Briefly, in the first week of June, Britain took independent military action in the Levant, insisting that French forces then in occupation of Damascus should withdraw, leaving Syria under its independent Arab government. British forces, landing at Beirut, marched eastwards towards the Syrian capital, under the command of General Paget. 'As soon as you are master of the situation,' Churchill telegraphed to Paget on June 3, 'you should show full consideration to the French. We are very intimately linked with France in Europe, and your greatest triumph will be to produce a peace without rancour. Pray ask for advice on any point you may need, apart from military operations.' Churchill added: 'In view of reports that French soldiers have been killed, pray take the utmost pains to protect them.'[5] To the Syrian

[1] Prime Minister's Personal Minute, M.548/5, 31 May 1945: Churchill papers, 20/209.
[2] Prime Minister's Personal Minute, M.546/5, 31 May 1945: Premier papers, 3/194/4, folio 9.
[3] Prime Minister's Personal Minute, M.554/5, 1 June 1945: Premier papers, 3/194/4, folio 5.
[4] David Stirling recollections: letter to the author, 4 December 1986.
[5] Prime Minister's Personal Telegram, T.1051/5, 'Personal', OZ 3522, 3 June 1945: Churchill papers, 20/220.

President, whom he had met in Cairo in February 1945, Churchill telegraphed that day: 'Now that we have come to your aid, I hope you will not make our task harder by fury and exaggeration. The French have got to have fair treatment as well as you, and we British, who do not covet anything that you possess, expect from you that moderation and helpfulness which are due to our disinterested exertions.'[1]

The British intervention was effective. On June 3 French forces withdrew from Damascus, to be replaced in the city by a British detachment. But on the following day Paget reported the imminent arrival in the eastern Mediterranean of the French battleship *Jeanne d'Arc*. 'Why do we not arrest her and turn her back on the high seas under threat of superior force?' Churchill minuted to Brendan Bracken, his new First Lord of the Admiralty, on June 4. His minute continued:

Probably only a few minutes' firing would be necessary and this would be far less bloody than shooting at the little boats when they try to pull ashore. The above is only my opinion and you may well have in mind a plan less likely to cause serious bloodshed. All the same, there is nothing like turning people back on the high seas and I do not think they will be very determined to go on if a few shells are sent across their bows. You must ring me up by 10 o'clock tomorrow. I am, of course, presuming that you have got the necessary cruisers on the spot. Remember Nelson's dictum 'Only numbers can annihilate'; but please do not annihilate.[2]

For some days, Churchill had been concerned about the difficulties of administering Germany with a hostile local population. 'I am alarmed by the winter prospect in Germany,' he telegraphed to Field Marshal Montgomery on June 4. 'I expect they will do everything you tell them,' he added, 'and hold you responsible that they are fed.' Churchill sought direct German participation in the maintenance of life and order. 'I wonder myself,' he told Montgomery, 'whether anything but German responsibility can secure the full German effort. It would not be thought a good ending to the war if you had a Buchenwald in Germany this winter, with millions instead of thousands dying.' He had also objected to the treatment of captured senior officers. 'I did not like,' he told Montgomery, 'to see the German admirals and generals, with whom we had recently made arrangements, being made to stand with their hands above their heads. Nor did I like to see the infantry component of the 11th Armoured Division used in this particular task.'[3]

---

[1] Prime Minister's Personal Telegram, T.1052/5, Foreign Office No. 377 to Beirut, 3 June 1945: Churchill papers, 20/220.

[2] Prime Minister's Personal Minute, M.569/5, 4 June 1945: Churchill papers, 20/209.

[3] Prime Minister's Personal Telegram, T.1065/5, No. 98873, 'Personal and Secret, Private and Confidential', 4 June 1945: Churchill papers, 20/220.

A great worry to Churchill in the first week of the Caretaker Government was the intended withdrawal of United States troops from those areas of Czechoslovakia and eastern Germany which it had been agreed, before May 8, should eventually fall within the Soviet sphere of military occupation. 'I view with profound misgivings,' Churchill telegraphed to Truman on June 4, 'the retreat of the American Army to our line of occupation in the central sector, thus bringing Soviet power into the heart of Western Europe and the descent of an iron curtain between us and everything to the Eastward. I hoped that this retreat, if it has to be made, would be accompanied by the settlement of many great things which would be the true foundation of world peace.' Nothing 'really important' had yet been settled, Churchill added, 'and you and I will have to bear great responsibility for the future'.[1]

Throughout the weekend at Chequers, Churchill had worked on his party political broadcast for the evening of June 4. When the script of the broadcast was ready, he showed it to his wife, who, as their daughter Mary later recalled, 'begged Winston to delete the odious and invidious reference to the Gestapo. But he would not heed her.'[2] This reference, as spoken by Churchill, appeared in the following section of his remarks:

No Socialist Government conducting the entire life and industry of the country could afford to allow free, sharp, or violently-worded expressions of public discontent. They would have to fall back on some form of Gestapo, no doubt very humanely directed in the first instance. And this would nip opinion in the bud; it would stop criticism as it reared its head, and it would gather all the power to the supreme party and the party leaders, rising like stately pinnacles above their vast bureaucracies of Civil Servants, no longer servants and no longer civil. And where would the ordinary simple folk—the common people, as they like to call them in America—where would they be, once this mighty organism had got them in its grip?

There were other references to British Socialism which were hardly less hostile and injudicious. In the first such reference he told his listeners:

My friends, I must tell you that a Socialist policy is abhorrent to the British ideas of freedom. Although it is now put forward in the main by people who have a good grounding in the Liberalism and Radicalism of the early part of this century, there can be no doubt that Socialism is inseparably interwoven with Totalitarianism and the abject worship of the State. It is not alone that property, in all its forms, is struck at, but that

---

[1] Prime Minister to President No. 72, Prime Minister's Personal Telegram, T.1060/5, 'Personal and Top Secret', 4 June 1945: Cabinet papers, 120/186.

[2] Mary Soames, *Clementine Churchill*, page 382.

liberty, in all its forms, is challenged by the fundamental conceptions of Socialism.

A few minutes later Churchill declared:

How is an ordinary citizen or subject of the King to stand up against this formidable machine, which, once it is in power, will prescribe for every one of them where they are to work; what they are to work at; where they may go and what they may say; what views they are to hold and within what limits they may express them; where their wives are to go to queue up for the State ration; and what education their children are to receive to mould their views of human liberty and conduct in the future?

Shortly before the 'Gestapo' reference, Churchill warned his listeners: 'Socialism is, in its essence, an attack not only upon British enterprise, but upon the right of the ordinary man or woman to breathe freely without having a harsh, clumsy, tyrannical hand clapped across their mouths and nostrils. A Free Parliament—look at that—a Free Parliament is odious to the Socialist doctrinaire.'

At the start of his speech, Churchill had explained why there was to be an election at all:

My sincere hope was that we could have held together until the war against Japan was finished. On the other hand, there was a high duty to consult the people after all these years. I could only be relieved of that duty by the full agreement of the three parties, further fortified, perhaps, by a kind of official Gallup Poll, which I am sure would have resulted in an overwhelming request that we should go on to the end and finish the job. That would have enabled me to say at once, 'There will be no election for a year,' or words to that effect.

I know that many of my Labour colleagues would have been glad to carry on. On the other hand, the Socialist Party as a whole had been for some time eager to set out upon the political warpath, and when large numbers of people feel like that it is not good for their health to deny them the fight they want. We will therefore give it to them to the best of our ability.

Churchill then spoke of Party politics as the necessary, if regrettable, pass to which the nation had come:

Party, my friends, has always played a great part in our affairs. Party ties have been considered honourable bonds, and no one could doubt that when the German war was over and the immediate danger to this country, which had led to the Coalition, had ceased, conflicting loyalties would arise. Our Socialist and Liberal friends felt themselves forced, therefore, to put party before country. They have departed, and we have been left to carry the nation's burden.

In the final third of his speech, Churchill turned to what a Conservative Government would do: control monopolies; bring home the soldiers 'who have borne the brunt of the war' and make sure that they had 'food, homes, and work' to return to; form a new army to 'go out and finish off, at the side of our American brothers, the Japanese tyrants at the other end of the world'; buy food and raw materials overseas; and pursue the Conservative's Four-Year Plan of economic recovery, 'with all its hopes and benefits, and with all the patient work that it means to pass it into law and bring it into action'.

Having set out this plan, Churchill turned again to attack the Labour Party. 'What a mad thing it would be,' he said, 'to slash across this whole great business of resettlement and reorganization with these inflaming controversies of Socialistic agitation! How foolish to plunge us into the bitter political and party fighting which must accompany the attempt to impose a vast revolutionary change on the whole daily life and structure of Britain!' Then, in his final minutes, Churchill told his listeners:

On with the forward march! Leave these Socialist dreamers to their Utopias or their nightmares. Let us be content to do the heavy job that is right on top of us. And let us make sure that the cottage home to which the warrior will return is blessed with modest but solid prosperity, well fenced and guarded against misfortune, and that Britons remain free to plan their lives for themselves and for those they love.[1]

Contrary to 'general supposition', Jock Colville later wrote, neither Bracken nor Beaverbrook had been involved in the writing of Churchill's speech, which, Colville added, 'aroused widespread criticism and did not really go down well, at any rate with the educated classes'. Colville added: 'For the first time he was speaking against the clock, which made him hurry unduly.'[2]

Some Conservatives were pleased with Churchill's speech. 'It was heavy pounding, certainly,' wrote Henry Channon in his diary, 'and today the Labour boys seemed very depressed and dejected by Winston's trouncing.'[3] 'If I may say so,' wrote Viscount Margesson, Churchill's former Secretary of State for War, 'I thought your broadcast was a beauty and so did others to whom I have spoken today.'[4] From

---

[1] Broadcast of 4 June 1945: BBC Written Archives Centre, Library No. 8922–5.

[2] John Colville, *Fringes of Power*, page 606. That weekend, Churchill's guests at Chequers had included his son Randolph, his friend Lord Cherwell, and Desmond Morton, whose hostility to all forms of Communism had been instrumental in 1943 in delaying Britain's support for the Yugoslav partisans led by Tito. Randolph Churchill and Morton had both stayed overnight on the Sunday ('List of Guests for Weekend June 1–4, 1945': Chequers Trust).

[3] Channon diary, 5 June 1945: Robert Rhodes James (editor), *Chips*, page 408.

[4] Letter of 5 June 1945, 'My dear Prime Minister': Churchill papers, 23/16. On 6 June 1945 Churchill appointed Margesson (who had been Conservative Chief Whip from 1935 to 1940) as one of a three-man Committee to 'interpret points in the Party Declaration' and to suggest answers to questions on it 'which may crop up during the General Election'. The other Committee members were Lord Swinton (Chairman) and Sir James Edmondson MP. ('Minute by the Prime Minister', 6 June 1945: Churchill papers, 23/16.)

Sir Edward Grigg, the British Minister resident in Cairo, came a telegram from GHQ Middle East. 'I see that your observations on the
meaning of a socialist state,' Grigg wrote, 'and particularly on its
certain need in due course of a gestapo are being ridiculed by our
opponents as scare-mongering. I hesitate to suggest how you should
dispose of this nonsense, but I feel very strongly that a reminder of the
way in which many people dismissed your warning about German
rearmament as scare-mongering would impress the troops out here
and a lot of other non-political voters.'[1]

From Churchill's daughter Sarah, still at her Royal Air Force photographic interpretation unit at Medmenham, came words of praise
and warning:

I enjoyed the speech last night, and thought you dealt with the reasons
and regrets for having a general election, and the desertion of the Liberals
and Labour, *perfectly*. Of course I loved 'no longer servants and no longer
civil'. You ask me if I felt influenced? If I were thinking Labour, I doubt it
would have made me vote Conservative; but it would have started me thinking along completely new lines about Socialism. Which is very good! You see
the people I know who are Labour, don't vote Labour for ideals or belief,
but simply because life has been hard for them, often an unequal struggle,
and they think that only by voting Labour will their daily struggle become
easier. So in that respect your speech was a bombshell, because they are all
decent people who want an easier and gayer life; but certainly wouldn't
tolerate any form of totalitarianism.

On the other hand I am not quite sure they will understand how what you
say would really be so. Because Socialism as practised in the war, did no one
any harm, and quite a lot of people good. The children of this country have
never been so well fed or healthy, what milk there was, was shared equally,
the rich didn't die because their meat ration was no larger than the poor;
and there is no doubt that this common sharing and feeling of sacrifice was
one of the strongest bonds that unified us. So why, they say, cannot this
common feeling of sacrifice be made to work as effectively in peace? Don't
think I am a rebel! But I thought that as this morning there is not very much
to do, I would try and put down what I hear and see, of what the people I
live and work with feel.

I doubt very much if one will convert any intelligent thinking Socialist
from his views. For rightly or wrongly he has thought them out and thinks
them right. But I am worried about the vast unthinking or only superficially
thinking public who I repeat are Labour because they believe that only by
voting that way will inequalities of opportunity, the privilege of class and
money be curbed. I doubt they think any deeper than that, nor do I believe
they believe in the pipe dream of a completely equal world. But they do
want more, a lot more of everything than they have hitherto had.

[1] MR/33, IZ 6159, 12 June 1945: Churchill papers, 20/221.

Well then, you say, 'What about my Four Year Plan?' It is a wonderful plan, wise and generous, possible, and the most progressive yet produced. But you know they have forgotten about it! It hasn't been plugged enough. 'What is the Four Year Plan?' quite a few people have said to me! I tell them and they say 'Oh yes, I do remember *something* about it'. But Beveridge still holds the limelight. Will you or someone be repeating carefully over the radio what it is all about again? I expect of course you will. Or can one buy it cheaply in a pamphlet?

There is one more thing, have you the time to read it? Housing! Obviously the greatest domestic issue in about 18 months. The strongest card in the Socialists' hand is, I feel, that we can't do it.[1]

On Tuesday June 5 Churchill lunched with the King at Buckingham Palace. He then went to the House of Commons to answer a Private Notice Question on Syria and the Levant. It was when the French had shelled Damascus—'this open and crowded city'—on May 29 and May 30, and four hundred civilians had been killed, that Britain had decided to intervene, he said, 'to preserve calm, to prevent misunderstandings and to bring the two sides together'. It was not Britain's intention 'to steal the property of anybody in this war'.[2] 'You have acted with great propriety and discretion,' Churchill telegraphed to General Paget two days later, 'and you have my approval for everything you have done.'[3]

On June 6 Churchill worked in bed for much of the day. Writing to the Chancellor of the Exchequer, Sir John Anderson, about a Party Political broadcast Anderson was to make, Churchill suggested: 'You should answer Mr Attlee, especially stressing the danger of inflation from Socialism.' Anderson should also 'give more space', Churchill wrote, 'to the reasons which led you to stay with the Government'.[4]

In the House of Commons on June 6, Herbert Morrison described Lord Beaverbrook and Brendan Bracken as 'Companions of the Bath', a 'sly allusion', noted Henry Channon, 'to Winston's bathing habits, which have long amused the inner coterie'.[5] That evening, Churchill

---

[1] Letter beginning 'My darling Papa', 5 June 1945, marked by Churchill, 'Keep in my private papers': Churchill papers, 1/387.

[2] House of Commons, 5 June 1945: *Hansard*, columns 689–94.

[3] Prime Minister's Personal Telegram, T.1084/5, OZ 3589, 7 June 1945: Churchill papers, 20/220.

[4] Prime Minister's Personal Minute, M.570/5, 6 June 1945: Churchill papers, 2/548. Anderson had been a National MP for the Scottish Universities since 1938.

[5] Channon diary, 6 June 1945: Robert Rhodes James (editor), *Chips*, page 408.

worked on the Conservative Party declaration of policy with the Chairman of the Conservative Party Organization, Ralph Assheton. 'Later,' noted his Private Office diary, 'they were joined by Lord Beaverbrook and Mr Bracken.' Churchill went to bed that night at 3.30 a.m.[1] In the early hours of the following day, June 8, 'after reading the morning papers', Churchill went to bed at 3.15.[2]

In the last week of May, Churchill was sent the typescript of a book of memoirs written by his detective, Inspector W. H. Thompson, who proposed resigning his position as detective inspector on June 16, in order to take up a job in connection with the licensing of drivers. On June 8, John Martin, his Principal Private Secretary, wrote to Churchill:

> On your instructions I have been through the typescript of this book and am satisfied that it contains much which it would be quite improper for anyone who has worked here as a member of your staff to publish, certainly at the present time. I have consulted the new Commissioner of Police who agrees 'that publication of this sort of reminiscences, so soon after the event, is undesirable and that a self denying ordinance should apply to Police Officers who are in close contact with the Prime Minister or other members of the Government'.[3]

John Martin had sent Churchill each of the extracts about himself. 'I see no harm in these extracts,' Churchill replied.[4] But the matter was not apparently as simple as Churchill thought. On June 11, John Martin wrote to Clementine Churchill:

> I am sorry that the PM sees no harm in it. It is the sort of thing from which we have done our best to protect him for five years.
>
> There is also the wider Service point of view on which I know that Sir Edward Bridges feels strongly. We are anxious to maintain a certain code of behaviour in these matters and if Inspector Thompson can lift the veil it will be difficult to prevent others from doing the same.[5]

Clementine Churchill supported John Martin's opposition to the publication of Thompson's memoirs, writing to her husband:

> I have read the pages marked by John Martin. There is no harm in them; in fact they are very friendly. But this record could not have been written

[1] Private Office diary, 6 June 1945: Thompson papers.
[2] Private Office diary, 7 June 1945: Thompson papers.
[3] 'Prime Minister', 8 June 1945: Churchill papers, 1/65.
[4] Note by Churchill, undated: Churchill papers, 1/65.
[5] 'Mrs Churchill', 'Private', 11 June 1945: Churchill papers, 1/65.

except by someone in your immediate entourage, and is the result of a careful diary, kept from day to day. I was interested to read the account as it brought back to me many incidents I had forgotten.

I well understand your good natured wish to help Inspector Thompson. But there are a considerable number of people who have daily access to you, who have the opportunity of observing details of your private life, and who could make a colourful narrative and raise a considerable sum of money by publishing their reminiscences. I imagine they would all feel disgusted with Inspector Thompson for having taken advantage of his position in this way, and they might also sense a good deal of favouritism if his memoirs were allowed to be published. Clearly one could not allow any number of people to publish such a book.

I have made this minute as unbiased and fair as possible, but you should of course take into account the fact that I have a poor opinion of Inspector Thompson. If you think he is hard up, I think it would be far better to make him a substantial gift in money than to allow this book to go forward.[1]

John Martin sent Clementine Churchill's minute to the Prime Minister, with a covering note which proved decisive in halting the publication of the detective's book. His note read:

I think I ought to say how disgusted all of us in the Private Office would be at the publication of such a book. We know what a privilege it has been to serve you and we have always been conscious that this privilege carried with it the responsibility of a decent reticence. The Press have constantly pressed for information about the intimate details of your private life as Prime Minister; but for five years we have done our best to protect you from this sort of inquisitiveness.[2]

Sir Edward Bridges having expressed his own 'strong views on the subject', as Martin told Churchill, the book was dead, for the time being at least.[3]

The needs of the Election had begun to fill up more and more of Churchill's time. On June 9, reading a list which Ralph Assheton had prepared of Ministers who would travel about the country giving elec-

---

[1] 'Proofs of Inspector Thompson's Book', initialled 'CSC', 12 June 1945: Churchill papers, 1/65.

[2] 'Prime Minister', 13 June 1945: Churchill papers, 1/65.

[3] *I Was Churchill's Shadow* by Ex-Detective-Inspector W. H. Thompson was eventually published in 1951. Two years later, Thompson published a second book, *Sixty Minutes with Winston Churchill*. Before the Second World War he had published a volume of reminiscences of the 1920s, *Guard from the Yard*. Other books published in Churchill's lifetime by members of his staff were Elizabeth Nel, *Mr Churchill's Secretary* and Norman McGowan, *My Years with Churchill* (McGowan had become Churchill's valet in 1949).

tion speeches, Churchill minuted: 'Many of these Ministers can make the same speech with variations again and again, and they will not be nationally reported.' It was more difficult for him, 'who have to try to say something new every time'. Surely, Churchill asked, there were one or two backbenchers who could do something, 'Profumo, for instance, or Randolph, who is long-experienced in politics and is capable of full-dress engagements, the audiences of which he will draw. I do not want him taken away more than two or three days from his work in Preston. But he is capable of holding the largest audiences.' [1]

On June 11 Churchill presided over a meeting of his Chiefs of Staff Committee. 'Winston gave a long and very gloomy review of the situation in Europe,' Field Marshal Brooke noted in his diary, and he set down Churchill's particular cause of concern:

The Russians were farther west than they had ever been except once. They were all-powerful in Europe. At any time that it took their fancy they could march across the rest of Europe and drive us back into our island. They had a two-to-one superiority over our forces, and the Americans were returning home. The quicker they went home, the sooner they would be required here again. He finished up by saying that never in his life had he been more worried by the European situation than at present. [2]

Throughout June 13 Churchill worked at No. 10 Annexe on his second broadcast, helped first by his son-in-law Duncan Sandys, and then by his son Randolph. [3] During his speech, as his daughter Sarah had suggested, Churchill elaborated on the Four-Year Plan. 'I announced this to the nation two years ago,' he explained, 'under the simple watchword of food, work, and homes. Of this extensive plan as yet only education and family allowances stand on the Statute-book, and they have yet to be carried into full effect. But we have left social insurance, industrial injuries insurance, and the national health service to be shaped by Parliament and made to play a dynamic part in the life and security of every family and home.' In this Four-Year Plan, Churchill added, there was also, 'and I hope there still is, a wide

---

[1] Prime Minister's Personal Minute, M.581/5, 9 June 1945: Churchill papers, 2/545. John Profumo, who had risen during the war to the rank of Brigadier, had been in 1940, aged twenty-five, the youngest Member of Parliament. He had voted against Neville Chamberlain in the division of 8 May 1940, which precipitated the emergence of Churchill as Prime Minister. Randolph Churchill had been elected unopposed in 1940, as part of the wartime electoral truce. 'In the event,' Profumo writes, 'I felt unable to accept any of these suggestions because I had an enormous constituency, Kettering, including Corby (Stewart & Lloyd etc.), a major part of the boot and shoe industry and large chunks of Co-op Wholesale factories, and had only really got in because it was a war-time by-election. The result was predictable.' (John Profumo recollections: letter to the author, 17 July 1986.) Profumo, defeated in 1945, was re-elected in 1950.

[2] Brooke diary, 11 June 1945: Arthur Bryant, *Triumph in the West*, pages 470–1.

[3] Private Office diary, 13 June 1945: Thompson papers.

measure of agreement between the Conservative and National Government on the one hand and the parties which are against them at the polls'.

Both at home and abroad, Churchill told his listeners, there was four years' work to be done: 'That is the reason why I have censured in the most severe terms the Socialist effort to drag their long-term fads and wavy Utopias across the practical path of need and duty. I denounce the scheme of the making of a Socialist Britain at this time while we are in such difficulties, and in danger of losing much that we have gained at so great a cost.'

Churchill then returned, albeit in a slightly modified tone, to the charges against Socialism which he had made in his first election broadcast a week earlier. Men like Sir Stafford Cripps and Herbert Morrison had shown, he said, 'by their public statements that they would use any majority they might obtain to stifle or greatly curtail the rights of Parliament to criticize such vast transformations of our British life'. If and when the plans to which they were 'publicly and irrevocably committed' came into force in their entirety, Churchill warned, 'and we had a complete Socialist system, all effective and healthy opposition and the natural change of parties in office from time to time would necessarily come to an end, and a political police would be required to enforce an absolute and permanent system upon the nation'.

Returning to social reform, Churchill introduced a pledge on free milk for the very poor, and free milk for the under-fives, with the sentence: 'If our wealth and enterprise are not cracked and spoiled by the fetters of authoritarian Socialism, there lie open vast possibilities of social endeavour in this vital sphere.'

There was also a lyrical passage with a personal touch. 'In my old age,' he said, 'I naturally look ahead. The whole theme of motherhood and family life, with those sweet affections which illuminate it, must be the fountain spring alike of present happiness and future survival.'

Churchill ended his broadcast with another theme on which his daughter Sarah had written to him, housing. He would not hesitate, he declared, 'to use war-time expedients' to repair war-damaged houses and to make up the wartime delay in construction.[1] 'It is on the provision of homes,' he ended, 'that all the other plans which I have mentioned turn. Every method, public or private, for houses, permanent or temporary, will be employed, and all obstructions, from whatever quarter they come, be they price-rings, monopoly, or any

[1] Sarah Churchill had written in her letter of 5 June 1945: 'A disciplined united nation with the resources of all branches, civil and military combined, launched "Mulberry", "Pluto", "Overlord". Why could we not in the same manner launch a housing drive?'

other form of obstacle, will be dealt with by the whole power of Parliament and the nation.' [1]

Churchill's broadcast was not universally approved. 'Miss Watson, one of the staff at No. 10, met me in the passage,' Lord Moran noted in his diary. 'She feels that neither of the two broadcasts is the true PM; there was no "vim" in them. "You know, Lord Moran, his heart isn't in this election."' [2]

---

[1] Broadcast speech of 13 June 1945: Charles Eade (compiler), *Victory: War Speeches by the Right Hon. Winston S. Churchill, OM, CH, MP, 1945*, London 1946, pages 193–9.

[2] Lord Moran diary, 14 June 1945: *The Struggle for Survival*, London 1966, pages 253–4. When Churchill had become Prime Minister in May 1940, Miss E. M. Watson was the only female secretary in the Private Secretaries' office at 10 Downing Street. She had been there since Lloyd George's Premiership. Her main task was to assemble material for the answers to Parliamentary questions, and to reply to letters from the general public. She continued to work for Churchill until her retirement in 1945.

3

Prelude to Potsdam

O N 6 June 1945 Churchill had set out for General Ismay his thoughts on the Three Power Conference, set for mid-July, and the third such meeting, after the Teheran Conference of November 1943 and the Yalta Conference of February 1945. 'The Press should not be allowed at the place of the Conference,' Churchill wrote, 'but only photographers like last time.' An 'échelon' of his Map Room would be needed. For the code word of the conference, 'I propose "Terminal".' The 'key' to all these arrangements, Churchill commented, 'is that we are there in Berlin by right on terms of absolute equality and not the guests of the Russians'.[1] 'I could not accept,' Churchill telegraphed to Truman on June 9, 'as at Yalta, the principle that we go to Berlin, over which it is agreed we are to have triple or with the French quadruple parity, merely as guests of the Soviet Government and Armies.'[2] 'PM at the Cabinet spoke for about an hour about the menace of the Russians,' Admiral Cunningham wrote in his diary on June 10, and he added: 'He is very gloomy about it.'[3]

On June 11 the Istrian dispute at least had taken a positive turn with Tito's agreement to remain behind the lines indicated by Alexander, and to withdraw from Pola. Also that day, after considerable British pressure, the French Government agreed to withdraw its troops from north-western Italy, where, for some weeks, it had seemed as if they might insist upon annexation of the region to France. 'On the whole,' Churchill telegraphed to Truman that day, 'the Levant, Venezia Giulia plus Pola, and Western Italy are not encouraging for land-

---

[1] Prime Minister's Personal Minute, D.148/5, 'Top Secret', 9 June 1945: Cabinet papers, 120/186.
[2] Prime Minister to President No. 82, Prime Minister's Personal Telegram, T.1103/5, 'Personal and Top Secret', 9 June 1945: Cabinet papers, 120/186.
[3] Cunningham diary, 10 June 1945: Cunningham papers.

grabbers but they are a proof to you and me applicable to far larger spheres that the motto holds "United we stand".' [1]

Churchill was still hoping, as he minuted to Sir Orme Sargent on June 11, 'that the retreat of the American centre to the Occupation Line can be staved off till The Three meet, and I take the view that large movements to enable France to assume her agreed part of her zone will stimulate the Russian demand to occupy the heart of Germany. Of course, at any moment the Americans may give way to the Russian demand, and we shall have to conform.' [2]

That evening Churchill gave a dinner at No. 10 Annexe to General Eisenhower. 'A cheerful party,' wrote Admiral Cunningham in his diary, 'but the PM rather gloomy about Russia. He has always wanted to use the Anglo-American retirement to their own Zones as a lever to extract similar treatment for us in Berlin and Vienna from the Russians; but the Americans will not go along with him.' The American argument, Cunningham noted, was that 'having entered into engagements about the Zones, they must keep to them, and that that is a better way of dealing with the Russians'. [3] The American troop withdrawals began nine days later, simultaneously, at Churchill's insistence, with Soviet troop withdrawals from the agreed area of the British zone in Austria. [4]

On June 14 Churchill told the House of Commons that Attlee would be accompanying him to the final conference, 'in case anyone says "Why are you committing yourself to something for which you have no authority, when in the ballot box there may be something which strips you of your authority?" There will be my right hon. Friend, and we have always in these last few years thought alike on the foreign situation and agreed together.' Churchill continued, as recorded by *Hansard*:

Then there will be an opportunity for it to be shown that, although Governments may change and parties may quarrel, yet on some of the main essentials of foreign affairs we stand together. That is, I am sure, doing no disadvantage to the party opposite; on the contrary—

Mr Cocks: Is the right hon. Gentleman going to take the Gestapo with him?

[1] Prime Minister to President No. 84, Prime Minister's Personal Telegram, T.1111/5, 'Personal and Top Secret', 11 June 1945: Churchill papers, 20/221.

[2] Prime Minister's Personal Minute, M.593/5, 11 June 1945: Churchill papers, 20/209.

[3] Cunningham diary, 11 June 1945: Cunningham papers. On the following day, when Eisenhower was presented with the Freedom of the City of London, Churchill made a short speech warmly praising Eisenhower's wartime generalship (Recording: BBC Written Archives Centre, Library No. T.8741).

[4] Prime Minister's Personal Telegram, T.1133/5, to Stalin: Churchill papers, 20/221.

The Prime Minister: I hope that we shall be in a position, in a short time, to nip the project in the bud.[1]

Planning for the 'Terminal' Conference began at the highest level. 'I feel very strongly,' Churchill telegraphed to Stalin on June 17, 'and I am sure you will agree, that on this occasion the Russian, American and British Delegations should each have separate enclaves, and that they should make their own arrangements for accommodation, food, transport, guards, communications etc.' The British Delegation would also require the use of an airfield as near as possible to its Delegation's area, but could, 'if convenient, share an airfield with the Americans'.[2]

On June 21 news reached London of the end of Japanese resistance in Okinawa, after eighty-two days' fighting, during which Japanese suicide bombers had made 1,900 attacks in a desperate attempt to hold the island. From Moscow that day came news of an ominous kind: of the fifteen Polish leaders arrested while negotiating outside Warsaw, under Soviet safe-conducts, in the last weeks of the war, twelve had been given long prison sentences. That same day, the Allied Reparations Commission held its first meeting in Moscow. 'Terminal' and the British General Election were both less than a month away. 'I have toyed meanwhile,' Churchill minuted to the Chiefs of Staff Committee on June 23, 'with the idea of putting off the meeting on account of British political turmoil. Upon reflection, however, I have decided it must go forward as originally planned.'[3]

On June 23 Churchill drafted a telegram, which in the end he did not send, to Stalin. Its subject was Istria, which in a telegram two days earlier Stalin claimed had been conquered by Tito's forces. 'Our joint idea in the Kremlin in October,' Churchill recalled, 'was that the Yugoslav business should work out around 50–50 Russian and British influence. In fact it is at present more like 90–10, and even in that poor 10 we have been subjected to violent pressure by Marshal Tito. So violent was this pressure that the United States and His Majesty's Government had to put in motion many hundreds of thousands of troops in order to prevent themselves from being attacked by Marshal Tito.' Churchill's draft continued:

Great cruelties have been inflicted by the Yugoslavs on the Italians in this

[1] House of Commons, 14 June 1945: *Hansard*, columns 1788–9. Seymour Cocks had been a Labour MP since 1929 and was a member of the Labour Party's Advisory Committee on International Affairs.

[2] Prime Minister's Personal Telegram, T.1153/5, 'Personal and Top Secret', 17 June 1945: Cabinet papers, 120/186.

[3] Prime Minister's Personal Minute, D.156/5, 23 June 1945: Cabinet papers, 120/186.

part of the world, particularly in Trieste and Fiume, and generally they have shown a disposition to grasp all the territory into which their light forces have penetrated. The movement of these light forces could not have been made unless you for your part had made immense and welcome advances from the East and in the North, and unless Field-Marshal Alexander had held twenty-seven enemy divisions on his front in Italy and finally reduced them to surrender. I do not consider that it can be said that Marshal Tito has conquered all this territory. It has been conquered by the movements of far greater forces both in the West and in the East which compelled the strategic retreat of the Germans from the Balkans.

Britain 'did not see', Churchill added, 'why we should be pushed about everywhere, especially by people we have helped, and helped before you were able to make any contact with them'.[1]

Churchill then referred to the frontier line which he had twice already, in messages to Truman, described as an Iron Curtain. 'It seems to me,' his draft telegram to Stalin ended, 'that a Russianised frontier running from Lübeck through Eisenach to Trieste and down to Albania is a matter which requires a very great deal of argument conducted between good friends. These are just the things we have to talk over together at our meeting, which is not long now.'[2]

In a note for Eden, written on June 23 to help Eden with an election broadcast, Churchill commented: 'The gulf between Britain and Russia is unbridgeable except by friendly diplomatic relations. The similarity and unity which we have with the United States will grow and it is indispensable to our safety.'[3]

[1] The first British mission to Tito was parachuted into German-occupied Yugoslavia in April 1943 (Operation 'Typical'). The first Soviet mission did not reach Tito until several months later. One of the two officers with the first British mission was Captain Deakin, who before the war had been Churchill's Literary Assistant.

[2] Draft telegram, 23 June 1945: Churchill papers, 20/221.

[3] Prime Minister's Personal Minute, Unnumbered, 23 June 1945: Churchill papers, 2/548.

4

Electioneering

O N June 17 1945 Churchill drove down to Chequers with his
Principal Private Secretary, John Martin. It was Martin's last
weekend before returning to the Colonial Office. 'The Election is absorbing most interest here,' Martin wrote to his wife on June 17. 'On
the way out to Chequers last night the PM's car was slowed down in
a traffic jam just outside the White City where crowds were coming
away from the greyhound races. Immediately he was surrounded by
an extremely enthusiastic mob—smiling and waving and cheering—
not a sign of unfriendliness or opposition. It was a remarkable demonstration and these were very much the "common people".'[1]

Churchill was tired: on June 18 he worked in bed all the morning
and did not get up until the afternoon when, as his Private Office
noted, 'he read for some time in the garden'. His only dinner guest
was Lord Cherwell.[2] 'Ismay said PM was thinking of going to Biarritz
for a holiday from 4th until the 14th July,' Admiral Cunningham
noted in his diary that day, and added: 'He certainly needs one. He
looked very tired when Eisenhower was over here.'[3]

On June 19 Churchill again spent most of the day in bed. That
night, Margesson and Beaverbrook were his dinner guests.[4] 'PM still
down at Chequers,' the Permanent Under-Secretary at the Foreign
Office, Sir Alexander Cadogan, noted in his diary, 'and quiet, so far
as I was concerned.'[5] On June 20 Churchill returned to London, for
a midday Cabinet and lunch with the King.[6] From Randolph that

[1] John Martin, letter of 17 June 1945: Martin papers.
[2] Private Office diary, 18 June 1945: Thompson papers.
[3] Cunningham diary, 18 June 1945: Cunningham papers. From 1940 to 1945 Ismay was head
of Churchill's Defence Office.
[4] Private Office diary, 19 June 1945: Thompson papers.
[5] Cadogan diary, 19 June 1945: David Dilks (editor), *The Diaries of Sir Alexander Cadogan,
OM, 1938–1945*, London 1971, page 754.
[6] Private Office diary, 20 June 1945: Thompson papers.

day came news of the start of the election campaign in Lancashire: 'On the whole,' Randolph wrote, 'I am fairly confident.'[1]

Throughout the afternoon of June 20 Churchill prepared his third, and his shortest, election broadcast. 'Papa broadcasts tonight,' Clementine Churchill wrote to their daughter Mary. 'He is very low, poor Darling. He thinks he has lost his "touch" & he grieves about it.'[2]

In the first part of his broadcast, which lasted less than eighteen minutes, Churchill again spoke of life under Socialism, when 'the central Government is to plan for all our lives and tell us exactly where we are to go and what we are to do, and any resistance to their commands will be punished'. Recalling the rearmament debates of a decade earlier, he declared: 'I have given you my warnings in the past and they were not listened to.' The executive authority under a Socialist government, he told his listeners a few minutes later, 'could not allow itself to be challenged or defeated at any time in any form of Parliament they might allow'.

In the closing moments of his speech, Churchill raised what quickly became known as the 'Laski controversy'. Harold Laski was the Chairman of the Labour Party National Executive. On June 14, after it had been announced that Attlee would be going to the Tripartite Conference with Churchill, Laski had stated in public: 'It is of course essential that if Mr Attlee attends this gathering he shall do so in the role of an observer only.'[3] Churchill had challenged this at once, writing to Attlee on June 15:

His Majesty's Government must of course bear the responsibility for all decisions, but my idea was that you should come as a friend and counsellor, and help us on all the subjects on which we have been so long agreed, and have been known to be agreed by public declaration. In practice I thought the British delegation would work just as they did at San Francisco except that, as I have already stated, you would not have official responsibility to the Crown otherwise than as a Privy Counsellor.

'Merely to come as a mute observer,' Churchill had added, 'would, I think, be derogatory to your position as Leader of your Party, and I

[1] Letter 'My dearest Papa', 20 June 1945: Churchill papers, 1/387.

[2] Letter of 20 June 1945: Mary Soames, *Clementine Churchill*, page 383.

[3] The *Daily Herald* of 15 June 1945 reported, under the heading 'Laski Says': 'Professor Harold Laski made the following statement last night as Chairman of the Labour Party: "It is, of course, essential that if Mr Attlee attends this gathering he shall do so in the role of an observer only. Obviously it is desirable that the leader of the Party which may shortly be elected to govern the country should know what is said, discussed and agreed, at this vitally important meeting. On the other hand, the Labour Party cannot be committed to any decisions arrived at, for the Three-Power Conference will be discussing matters which have not been debated either in the Party Executive or at meetings of the Parliamentary Labour Party."'

should not have a right to throw this burden upon you in such circumstances.'[1] Attlee had accepted Churchill's offer on the basis proposed by Churchill. There had never been any suggestion, he replied, that he should go as a mere observer.[2] Laski, however, had twice more repeated that it was the Labour Party's National Executive, not the Party Leader, who could alone determine the Party's foreign policy position. Churchill now, in his broadcast of June 21, raised the 'Laski controversy' as a warning and a spectre:

It was my conception that I should enjoy Mr Attlee's counsel at every stage of the discussions, and that what he said and agreed to he would naturally stand by. And from what I knew of him and his views over these last five years I did not expect there would arise in foreign affairs a single issue which could not be reconciled in an agreeable manner. In accepting my invitation Mr Attlee showed that he shared this hopeful opinion.

However, a new figure has leaped into notoriety. The situation has now been complicated and darkened by the repeated intervention of Professor Laski, chairman of the Socialist Party Executive. He has reminded all of us, including Mr Attlee, that the final determination on all questions of foreign policy rests, so far as the Socialist Party is concerned, with this dominating Socialist Executive.

Professor Laski has declared on several occasions, three at least, that there is no identity of purpose between the coalition foreign policy of the last five years, as continued by the present National Government, and the foreign policy of the powerful backroom organizations, over one of which he presides.

My friends, the British people have always hitherto wanted to have their affairs conducted by men they know, and that the men should work under the scrutiny and with the approval of the House of Commons. Now it seems we must refer to an obscure committee and be governed by unrepresentative persons, and that they will share the secrets and give the orders to the so-called responsible Ministers of the Crown, who will appear on the front Socialist bench of Parliament if they are returned and deliver orations upon which they have been instructed not from their own heart and conscience, not even from their constituencies, but from these dim conclaves below.

'I confidently believe,' Churchill ended, 'that the British democracy, with their long-trained common sense and innate love of independence, even while they are still struggling forward out of the exhaustion and sacrifices inseparable from hard-won victory, will ward off these dangers and make their way steadfastly towards something that can justly be called "hearth and home" in the land of hope and glory.'[3]

This third broadcast, like its predecessors, had a mixed reception. *The Times* described it as a 'hard-hitting onslaught upon Utopia as

---

[1] Letter of 15 June 1945: Churchill papers, 2/552.
[2] Letter of 15 June 1945 (from the House of Commons): Churchill papers, 2/552.
[3] Broadcast speech of 21 June 1945: BBC Written Archives Centre: Library No. 9025.

the theoretic Socialist sees it'.[1] Others were less impressed. 'You know I have an admiration for Winston amounting to idolatry,' Vita Sackville-West wrote to her husband, Harold Nicolson, 'so I am dreadfully distressed by the badness of his broadcast Election speeches. What has gone wrong with him? They are confused, woolly, unconstructive and so wordy that it is impossible to pick out any concrete impression from them. If I were a wobbler, they would tip me over to the other side. Archie Sinclair and Stafford Cripps were both infinitely better. I mind about this.'[2]

On June 22 Churchill set off for Chequers in an open car. Three times the car stopped for him to make a short speech, first at Uxbridge, then at High Wycombe, and finally at Princes Risborough. At Chequers on June 23, Churchill worked in bed all day, until 6.30 p.m., when he sat in the garden. After dinner he saw a film, and then went to bed. Among his letters on June 23 was one to Eden, who was preparing his own election broadcast. Churchill commented: 'There is nothing immoral in nationalization so long as you pay the people who owned the property originally in a fair way.'[3] The Socialist view, Churchill added, was that if they could plan British industry for a single year 'they would produce a new world. Our view is they could land us all in bankruptcy.'[4]

To Mackenzie King, who had just been re-elected Prime Minister of Canada, Churchill telegraphed on June 23: 'Although at times to British eyes things got rather mixed, I was always confident that Canada would stand by you as the pilot who weathered the storm. You and I, both being in the last lap of public life, can afford to be very bold in defence of the main causes for which we have fought.'[5]

That weekend, at Chequers, Churchill's only guest was his brother Jack, who was recovering from a heart attack. John Peck was the

---

[1] Leading article, 'Election Survey': *The Times*, 22 June 1945.

[2] Letter of 22 June 1945: Nigel Nicolson (editor), *Harold Nicolson Diaries and Letters 1939–1945*, London 1967, page 472.

[3] Ten days later Churchill minuted to Lord Margesson, with a copy to Randolph Churchill: 'It would seem in our interest that the Labour programme of nationalization should be stated at its highest as this will alarm more new voters than it will attract. The fact that the original full programme has been whittled away successively by the Labour leaders shows that they feel the weight of our criticism. This criticism should however continue to be directed at the original announcements by the Labour Party, which they would certainly carry into effect if they had the power.' (Prime Minister's Personal Minute, M.673/5, 'Confidential', 2 July 1945: Churchill papers, 20/209.)

[4] Prime Minister's Personal Minute, Unnumbered, 23 June 1945: Churchill papers, 2/548.

[5] Prime Minister's Personal Telegram, T.1187/5, 'Secret', 'Private', 23 June 1945: Churchill papers, 20/197. Mackenzie King had first become Prime Minister in 1921 (to 1930). He was Prime Minister again from 1935 to 1948. He died in 1950. Like Churchill, he had been born in 1874.

Private Secretary on duty, with his ADC Commander Thompson and Frank Sawyers his valet in attendance as usual. Churchill's luncheon guests on June 24 were the Attorney-General Sir David Maxwell-Fyfe, Lord Cherwell and Duncan and Diana Sandys.[1]

During the weekend Churchill prepared for an election tour which had been organized for him by Conservative Central Office. Sir Alexander Cadogan, who went down to Chequers late in the afternoon of June 24 to discuss possible Anglo-French negotiations on Syria, between Georges Bidault and Anthony Eden, noted in his diary:

A beautiful evening and the country looked lovely—far lovelier than California. PM lying on lawn sunning himself, in Siren suit and 10-gallon hat. Cherwell there. Difficult to get PM down to business. He excited by his tour and his reception everywhere. Nervous about his voice, and started talking in stage whisper, but he soon forgot about it. Eventually got him to settle some things—most important being that we might press Bidault to come here to meet A. on Levant.

At 8.30 Sawyers appeared and said 'It's 8.30.' PM said 'My God, Sawyers! What have you been doing?' But we sat on. Went in at 8.45. Bathed and changed. Dinner about 9.15. Only PM, Cherwell, Jack Churchill (who looks awful), Peck and Tommy. Cold roast beef, mince pie and flaming brandy and lots of champagne, port and cognac. A damned bad film, after, ended at 1 and I to bed at 1.15.[2]

At ten in the morning of June 25 Churchill left Chequers in an open car, accompanied by his daughter Sarah, for a four-day election tour. 'On all four days of this tour,' his Private Office diary recorded, 'there were enormous crowds on the roads and in the streets and the programme got later and later.'[3] On the first evening Churchill was joined by his wife, who remained with him for the rest of the tour, using a special train as their living, working and sleeping accommodation. On June 26, in Manchester, they were joined by Randolph. During that single day, Churchill addressed meetings in eleven cities, starting at Crewe and ending at Leeds, where Jock Colville replaced John Peck as the duty Private Secretary. On June 27 Churchill addressed ten meetings, from Bradford to Preston. 'Vast crowds and tremendous reception,' Jock Colville noted in his diary.[4] From Preston, Churchill went on in his train to Glasgow, where, as Colville later recalled, 'he made about ten speeches to deafening applause', then drove to Edinburgh 'along roads thronged with cheering men, women and children'.[5]

[1] Private Office diary, 24 June 1945: Thompson papers.
[2] Cadogan diary, 24 June 1945: David Dilks (editor), *The Diaries of Sir Alexander Cadogan*, page 756.
[3] Private Office diary, 25 June 1945: Thompson papers.
[4] Colville diary, 27 June 1945: Colville papers.
[5] Colville recollections: John Colville, *The Fringes of Power*, page 609.

On June 28 Churchill addressed six meetings, including one in Glasgow and one in Edinburgh. 'So glad you are in Scotland,' telegraphed the Chief Whip, James Stuart. 'My best wishes for a victory which will satisfy you and give you all you require for the future.'[1] That night Churchill travelled south again, telling Colville 'that nobody who had seen the enthusiasm of the crowds could be doubtful of the result of the election'. Colville replied that he would agree with that 'if it were a Presidential election'.[2]

It was while he was in Scotland that Churchill learned of the death of Eden's elder son, Simon, a Pilot Officer in the Royal Air Force, killed in action in Burma on June 23. Churchill wrote at once, in a message telephoned to London: 'I am profoundly grieved about your new anxiety, and greatly admire your courage, bearing blow on blow. Clemmie and I send our deepest sympathy to you and Beatrice.'[3]

Returning to London on the morning of June 29, Churchill told Field Marshal Brooke that if, as a result of the Election, he got in again, he would ask Brooke to remain as Chief of the Imperial General Staff, 'to carry out the reorganization of the Army'.[4] That same day, as he prepared for his ten-day holiday in France, Churchill received a letter from Sir Arthur Harris, Commander-in-Chief Bomber Command. 'I trust you bask in sunshine,' Harris wrote, '& will return here well rested to take up the further tasks which I am confident the confidence of the country will consign to you.'[5]

On June 30 John Martin said goodbye to Churchill, after five years in his Private Office, four of them as Principal Private Secretary.[6] That night Churchill gave his fourth and final election broadcast. He spoke of his tour, and of how he had been 'profoundly moved by the kindness and confidence with which I was everywhere received'. To the British soldiers, sailors and airmen listening overseas, Churchill declared: 'There is no truth in stories now being put about that you can vote for my political opponents at this election, whether they be Labour or Liberal, without at the same time voting for my dismissal from power. This you should not hesitate to do if you think it right and best for the country. All that I ask is that you should do it with your eyes open.'

---

[1] Telegram dated 28 June 1945: Churchill papers, 20/200.

[2] Colville diary, 28 June 1945: Colville papers.

[3] 'Prime Minister to Mr Eden', 'scrambled to London', 28 June 1945: Churchill papers, 20/197. Simon Eden would have been twenty-one that November.

[4] Brooke diary, 29 June 1945: Arthur Bryant, *Triumph in the West*, page 472.

[5] Letter, 'My dear Prime Minister', 28 June 1945: Churchill papers, 2/141.

[6] Martin, who returned to the Colonial Office (from which he had been seconded in 1940), was subsequently Deputy Under-Secretary of State (1956–65) and High Commissioner in Malta (1965–67). He was knighted in 1952.

Churchill then referred once more to the 'Laski controversy'. Laski, he declared, had shown himself 'the master of forces too strong for Mr Attlee to challenge by any counter-action'. The Labour Party National Executive Committee, of which Laski was Chairman, had the power to require 'the submission of Ministers to its will'. Such arrangements, he added, 'are abhorrent to the methods hitherto pursued in British public life. They strike at the root of our Parliamentary institutions, and, if they continue unabated, they will be one of the gravest changes in the constitutional history of England and of Britain.'

Churchill ended this final broadcast with what he called 'the issues which are at stake':

Many anxious eyes are turned towards us. A failure by Great Britain to produce a strong, coherent, resolute Government, supported by a substantial and solid majority in Parliament, would alter the entire balance, not only of tortured Europe but of the whole world, now struggling to rise again and bring order out of chaos.

If our country dissolves into faction and party politics, we shall cease to fill the place won for us by our policy and our victories afloat and ashore, we shall cease to fill that place in the councils of the nations which so much blood and sacrifice has gained.

Without our effective aid, the world itself might go once again astray. Without our influence upon other nations, now so high, we should lose the confidence we have won during the war from the self-governing Dominions of our Empire and Commonwealth. In an incredibly short space of time we might then by our own folly fall to the rank of a secondary Power.

I have an invincible confidence in the genius of Britain. I believe in the instinctive wisdom of our well-tried democracy. I am sure they will speak now in ringing tones, and that their decision will vindicate the hopes of our friends in every land and will enable us to march in the vanguard of the United Nations in majestic enjoyment of our fame and power.[1]

'Better than the previous three, but not exciting' was Colville's comment.[2] '*Very* good, I thought,' Cadogan wrote in his diary, and he added: 'Dignified and forceful. Very little controversy, and no mud!'[3]

There were two sentences in Churchill's draft which he had deleted at the last moment: a question and its answer concerning the 'primary task' of the conclusion of a 'just peace'. 'Has the Labour Party in its ranks,' he had intended to ask, 'men with the same ability and experience for this task as those who are to be found in the ranks of the National Government, especially Mr Anthony Eden to whom the

[1] Broadcast speech, 30 June 1945: Charles Eade (compiler), *Victory*, pages 206–11.
[2] Colville diary, 30 June 1945: Colville papers.
[3] Cadogan diary, 30 June 1945: David Dilks (editor), *The Diaries of Sir Alexander Cadogan*, page 757.

country owes a great debt for his success in the international field during these last few years?' Churchill's intended answer: 'With all respect to my colleagues in the late Government, I say that it has not.' [1]

On the afternoon of July 2 Churchill set off for a five-hour election tour of London, passing through Fulham and Putney to Richmond, then back through Brentford, Chiswick, Shepherd's Bush, Holland Park and Ladbroke Grove where, his Private Office diary noted, 'the crowds were rowdy and there was some stone-throwing'. [2] From Ladbroke Grove he went on to Marylebone, Camden Town, the Holloway Road, Kingsway, the Aldwych, the Strand and Trafalgar Square, and to Whitehall, reaching the Annexe at ten in the evening. That night he dined in bed.

On July 3 Churchill sent his Cabinet colleagues a memorandum, in which he called on them to make 'an intensive effort' during the period between Polling Day on July 5 and the announcement of the election result on July 26. These efforts, he urged, should include 'an intensive drive forward with the housing programme as a military operation in which all controls are to be used and special brigades of demobilized men enlisted for two years at exceptionally favourable terms, to go from one part of the country to another getting the thing started'. The building of houses, he declared, 'is to be handled exactly with the energy that would have been put into any of the battles we have won. Nothing is to stand in the way.'

Other priorities in this Cabinet Paper were the export drive, the securing of adequate supplies of coal 'to meet the demand of next winter' and preparation of legislation for both a National Insurance scheme and a National Health Service. [3]

On the evening of July 3, Churchill and Lord Margesson drove to Walthamstow. 'I drove for about two miles with them,' Peter Woodard later recalled, 'through a milling and rather hostile crowd.' [4] Churchill was to address a crowd of 20,000 at Walthamstow Stadium. He was almost prevented from making his speech, however, as Mary Churchill later recalled, 'because the heckling and booing were so intense'. [5] Everyone had 'a perfect right' to cheer or to boo as much as they liked, he said, and he added: 'The winners cheer and the beaten boo.' Towards the end of his speech, in which he stressed the

---

[1] Speech notes, 30 June 1945: Churchill papers, 9/209.

[2] Private Office diary, 2 July 1945: Thompson papers.

[3] Cabinet Paper No. 58 of 1945, 'Programme for July, 1945', 'Secret', 3 July 1945: Churchill papers, 23/14.

[4] Peter Woodard recollections: letter to the author, 20 December 1968. Woodard, a Lieutenant in the Royal Naval Volunteer Reserve, was standing as a Conservative against Attlee in Limehouse (he was defeated by 8,398 votes to 1,618).

[5] Mary Soames, *Clementine Churchill*, page 383.

Conservative Party's determination to build houses, Churchill described his opponents, in the stadium and beyond, as 'the booing party' and he declared:

Where I think the booing party are making such a mistake is dragging all this stuff across the practical tasks we have to fulfil. They are spoiling the tasks that have to be done in order to carry out their nightmares. They have no chance of carrying them out. They are going to be defeated at this election in a most decisive manner. (Cheers) Their exhibition here shows very clearly the sort of ideas they have of free speech. (Cheers)

That should be a great warning to the British people as a whole to make no error on Thursday next and vote against men who to mental confusion would not hesitate to add civic disorder in such a way as to prevent the exercise of the British right of free speech which has always been adopted.

After his speech, in replying to the vote of thanks, Churchill told the vast crowd: 'I give my entire forgiveness to the booers. They have this to take away with them—I am sure they are going to get a thrashing such as their party has never received since it was born.' [1]

Returning from Walthamstow to No. 10 Annexe at ten o'clock that evening, Churchill at once sent Attlee a letter, reiterating his charge concerning the power of the Labour National Executive Committee over the Parliamentary Labour Party: it was the Executive Committee, Churchill reiterated, that was 'the controlling body'. By 'way of illustration', he went on, 'the constitution would apparently enable the Executive Committee to call upon a Labour Prime Minister to appear before them and criticise his conduct of the Peace negotiations. How he could defend his actions without the disclosure of confidential information I fail to see.'

The controversy on 'these very important issues' could not be cleared up, Churchill ended, 'until the public has a statement signed jointly by yourself and the Chairman of the Executive Committee regarding the use of these powers in the future'. [2]

This challenge was sent by messenger to Attlee's house at Stanmore. Although it arrived late that night, Attlee replied to it at once. His reply, typed by himself, read:

Dear Prime Minister,

Your messenger with your letter only arrived at my house shortly before 11.30 p.m., when it had already been sent to the Press. I must, therefore, apologise to you for sending my reply to the Press before my letter will have actually reached you.

I am surprised that you, who are apparently becoming acquainted with

[1] Speech of 3 July 1945: Churchill papers, 9/170.
[2] 'Dear Attlee', 3 July 1945: Churchill papers, 2/552.

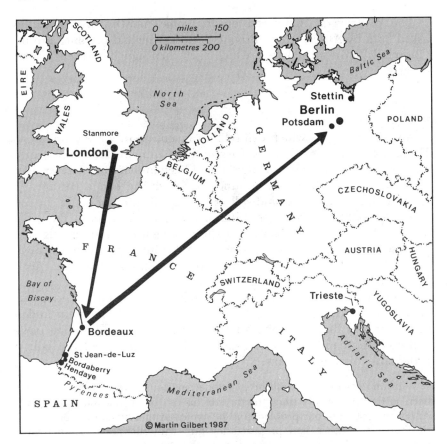

THE JOURNEY TO POTSDAM, 1945

the Constitution of the Labour Party for the first time, should on the authority of an unnamed informant seek to attach to its provisions meanings other than those accepted by myself and others who have spent years of service in the Labour Party.

Much of your trouble is due to your not understanding the distinction between the Labour Party and the Parliamentary Labour Party. This leads you to confuse the organizational work of the Party with the actions of the Parliamentary Labour Party.

Despite my very clear statement you proceed to exercise your imagination by importing into a right to be consulted a power to challenge actions and conduct. With regard to your final paragraph I think that you underestimate the intelligence of the public and I do not share your belief.

Yours sincerely

C. R. Attlee [1]

[1] 'Dear Prime Minister', 3 July 1945: Churchill papers, 2/552.

The controversy simmered on for some months, with Colville asked both by Attlee, whose Private Secretary he had become, and by Churchill, to draft the letters which each then signed and sent to the other.[1]

Among the letters which Churchill was sent on July 3 was one from Horatia Seymour, a friend of Clementine Churchill for many years. Throughout the inter-war years she had been among the most regular guests at Chartwell, in the grounds of which she had a cottage. A Liberal all her life, she would still be voting Liberal; nor could she see how she could tell 'our 300 Liberal candidates' to stand down in favour of a Conservative Party 'whose judgement and intelligence were so grievously at fault in the years before 1939'. Horatia Seymour added: 'No one taught me more about that than *you*, dear Winston!'[2]

At noon on July 4, the day before Polling Day, Churchill took the chair at a meeting of the Chiefs of Staff Committee. The point under discussion was Britain's Far Eastern policy, once Singapore had been captured from the Japanese. Brooke, who had prepared the policy proposals, noted in his diary:

Winston very tired after all his electioneering tours. He said he had never been so tired physically since the days of his escape during the Boer War.[3] At last we got on to our problem and he confessed that he had not even read the paper which we had prepared for him with such care. I, therefore, proposed that I should run over the suggestions on the map for him. He was delighted with this idea. How much he understood, and really understood, in his exhausted state it is hard to tell. However, I got him to accept the plan in principle, to authorize our sending the paper to the Americans and to pass the telegrams to the Dominion Prime Ministers for their co-operation.[4]

That evening Churchill went on a final election tour of London. At Tooting Bec a squib was thrown at him, all but exploding in his face. When the father of the young man who had thrown the squib wrote to Churchill to apologize, Churchill replied: 'I think your son

---

[1] Sir John Colville recollections: notes for the author, September 1987.

[2] 'My dear Winston', 3 July 1945: Churchill papers, 1/386.

[3] Churchill had escaped from a Boer prisoner-of-war camp on 12 December 1899, reaching Durban, and safety, two weeks later. During the first part of his journey he was hidden in a consignment of bales of wool on their way by train to the Portuguese port of Lourenço Marques.

[4] Brooke diary, 4 July 1945: Arthur Bryant, *Triumph in the West*, page 465.

ran a very great risk by an utterly foolish action. If the squib had actually exploded in my face, it might have hurt my eyes very much and I could not have been answerable for what the crowds would have done to him. However, all's well that ends well. I certainly hope his career will not be damaged and that he will be a real help to old England in the end.'[1]

On Polling Day, July 5, Churchill worked in bed during the morning, lunched with Field Marshal Alexander, toured his constituency during the afternoon, and returned at 7 p.m. to No. 10 Annexe, where he dined in bed. After dinner, Beaverbrook and Bracken were with him when he received accounts of Polling Day in different constituencies. Also with him that night were his daughter Diana and her husband Duncan Sandys. That day, in a note for the Cabinet on manpower, Churchill urged the immediate demobilization of all women. 'Women ought not to be treated the same as men,' his note began, and he went on to explain that, whereas in 1918 the demobilization of men in the wrong sequence had caused 'gravest disaster', women 'do not mutiny or cause disturbances, and the sooner they are back at their homes the better'. All women should be 'free to retire as soon as possible from the Services and those who like to stay will be found sufficient to do the necessary jobs'.[2]

To enable the Service vote to be counted, there was to be a three-week delay between Polling Day and the announcement of the result.

On the night of July 6 Churchill dined with his daughter Mary at No. 10 Annexe. Then, on July 7, after an audience with the King at Windsor, he flew with his wife and Mary, Lord Moran and Jock Colville, two secretaries, Mrs Hill and Miss Sturdee, and his detective, to Bordeaux, then drove south to Hendaye, near the Spanish border, to the Château de Bordaberry, lent to him by a hospitable Canadian, Brigadier-General Brutinel, who owned the Château Margaux vineyard. Here, Churchill had his first ten days' rest since he had become Prime Minister five years earlier.

On his first afternoon at Bordaberry, Churchill drove to nearby St Jean de Luz, where he was the guest of the British Consul at Bordeaux, Bryce Nairn, and his wife Margaret. Nairn had been the Consul at Marrakech when Churchill convalesced there in January 1944, after

[1] Letter of 7 July 1945: Churchill papers, 20/194.
[2] 'Man-power', 'Secret', Cabinet Paper No. 62 of 1945, 5 July 1945: Churchill papers, 23/14.

the Teheran Conference. His wife was a gifted painter. While his hosts bathed in the sea, Churchill set up his easel, prepared his palette, and began painting. He returned to Bordaberry at nine that night, for dinner. Then, on July 9, returned to St Jean de Luz to paint again, but a thunderstorm brought this second expedition to an abrupt end.

Even on holiday, as Churchill later wrote, 'the mystery of the ballot boxes and their contents had an ugly trick of knocking on the door and peering in at the windows'. When the palette was spread, however, he added, 'and I had a paint-brush in my hand it was easy to drive these intruders away'.[1]

'Winston at first was low and tired,' his daughter Mary recalled, 'but the magic of painting soon laid hold of him, absorbing him for hours on end, and banishing disturbing thoughts of either the present or the future.'[2]

On July 10 Churchill again returned to St Jean de Luz, to complete the painting which had been interrupted by the previous day's thunderstorm. On July 11, at lunch, there was some singing, followed by a word game, both prompted by Churchill's doctor, Lord Moran, who noted in his diary:

I hummed something out of *The Mikado*; the PM's eyes brightened, he began to sing refrain after refrain from that opera. He sang, with great gusto, 'A Wandering Minstrel I'. He loved the words and the tunes. And Mary in her eager way joined in. Then I asked him about some game they had played at Chartwell, and soon we were saying, 'I have a cat', to be asked by one's neighbour, 'What kind of cat?' Whereupon one had to find adjectives beginning with the letter chosen, a tame cat, a timid cat, a troublesome cat, a tabby cat and so on until no more adjectives would come into your head and you were counted out, and only those with a full vocabulary were left in. Winston searched his store-house of words as earnestly as if he were writing for posterity. This went on until ten minutes to four, when the PM went off to the Nairns to paint.[3]

Returning to St Jean de Luz, Churchill went on a boat along the river Nivelle, where, with Mrs Nairn, he spent the rest of the afternoon and evening painting a house near the river.[4] On the morning of July 12 Churchill bathed in the sea at Hendaye. That afternoon he watched an exhibition of Basque dances, to which the local wartime Resistance leaders and other local dignitaries had been invited. 'Hot and boring', was his verdict.[5] Then, before dinner, he bathed again.

On Friday July 13 the pattern of relaxation was repeated: a bathe in

[1] Winston S. Churchill, *The Second World War*, volume 6, page 531.
[2] Mary Soames, *Clementine Churchill*, page 383.
[3] Lord Moran diary, 11 July 1945: Moran, *The Struggle for Survival*, pages 262–3.
[4] Private Office diary, 11 July 1945: Thompson papers.
[5] Moran diary, 12 July 1945: *The Struggle for Survival*, pages 263–5.

the sea before lunch, and painting on the river Nivelle, with Margaret Nairn. There was also a visit to the house which he was painting, owned by an Englishwoman, Mrs Cunliffe-Owen. After dinner at Bordaberry, Churchill went into Hendaye, where, as his Private Office diary noted, he was 'loudly cheered by the crowd and where there was also some dancing of the Fandango'.[1] On July 14 he again bathed before lunch, when, Jock Colville later recalled:

The Prime Minister floated, like a benevolent hippo, in the middle of a large circle of protective French policemen who had duly donned bathing suits for the purpose. His British detective had also been equipped by the thoughtful authorities at Scotland Yard for such aquatic duties. Round and round this circle swam a persistent French Countess, a notorious collaborateuse who hoped by speaking to Winston Churchill to escape the fate which the implacable resistance were probably planning for her. It reminded me of the mediaeval practice of 'touching for the King's evil'. The encircling gendarmes, patiently treading water, thwarted her plot. . . .[2]

That afternoon, Churchill again painted on the Nivelle with Margaret Nairn, who, for her part, not only painted the same house, but also managed to finish a portrait of her fellow artist.

While at Bordaberry on July 14, Churchill sent a single telegram and dictated a single official minute. The telegram was to Montgomery, now Commander-in-Chief, British Army of Occupation, and it read: 'Please see that no establishments in which research and development has been carried on by the Germans are destroyed. Much of the apparatus there could be used by our own engineers and scientists.'[3] The minute was to the Chancellor of the Exchequer, Sir John Anderson, and urged 'a ruthless combing of the Services so that releases may be adequate to meet our civilian and export needs without affecting our front-line fighting effort in the war against Japan'.[4] While still at Potsdam, Churchill had asked Truman, about the atomic bomb test which was to take place in the New Mexico desert: 'Let me know if it is a plop or a flop'. While still at Bordaberry, Churchill received Truman's reply: 'It's a plop'.[5]

On the morning of July 15 Churchill left Bordaberry by car for the three-hour drive to Bordeaux. Clementine Churchill and Jock Colville were to return later that same day to London. Churchill and his daughter Mary flew from Bordeaux to Berlin, a flight of four and a half hours. The ten-day respite was over. 'Terminal' had begun.

[1] Private Office diary, 13 July 1945.
[2] Colville recollections: *The Fringes of Power*, page 610.
[3] Prime Minister's Personal Telegram, T.1236/5, OZ 4397, 'Top Secret and Personal', 14 July 1945: Churchill papers, 20/222.
[4] Prime Minister's Personal Minute, M.686/5, 14 July 1945: Churchill papers, 20/209.
[5] Sir John Colville recollections: notes for the author, September 1987.

5

'Terminal', The Potsdam Conference

CHURCHILL landed at Berlin at six o'clock local time on the evening of Sunday 15 July 1945. At the airport he inspected a British guard of honour, then drove direct to his villa at No. 23 Ringstrasse. Montgomery, Alexander, Eden and Attlee were there to greet him.

Churchill's first three official minutes written from Berlin concerned British domestic issues. The first was about the possibility of not fully gathering in the harvest owing to lack of labour. 'The utmost efforts must be made to prevent such a catastrophe,' he wrote. 'The Army should help. The return of Italian prisoners should be delayed on one pretext or another.'[1]

In the second 'Terminal' minute, Churchill reversed his view that there should be no 'large importation' of German prisoners, telling the Secretary of State for War, Sir James Grigg, that there would be 'a good case for using them to clear up the war damage in England, and to help with building, the harvest and agriculture generally'. If the manpower shortage in Britain proved to be greater than expected, 'we must be forced into a measure which otherwise is disagreeable'.[2]

Churchill's third minute of July 15 concerned groups of so-called Vigilantes who were setting themselves up in Britain to maintain law and order. Such 'lawlessness', Churchill told Sir John Anderson, 'should not be allowed.[3] The law officers and the police should consider

---

[1] Prime Minister's Personal Minute, M('Ter') 1/5, 'Secret', 15 July 1945: Churchill papers, 20/209.

[2] Prime Minister's Personal Minute, M('Ter') 2/5, 15 July 1945: Churchill papers, 20/209.

[3] In the absence of Churchill and Attlee at Potsdam, Sir John Anderson, the Chancellor of the Exchequer, was in charge of the Government.

all means of putting an end to these pranks', and the newspapers should be induced 'as far as possible' to curtail their publicity.[1]

On his first evening in Berlin, Churchill dined alone with Eden. He had hoped to see Truman after dinner—it would have been their first meeting—but the President was said to be 'fully engaged'.[2] That night Marian Holmes, one of Churchill's secretaries, noted in her diary: 'PM wandered into the office about 1 a.m. and looked at some pictures on the wall. He said he could paint those kind of scenes until the cows came home and do them much better what's more.'[3]

On July 16 Churchill and Truman met for the first time, at Truman's Berlin residence, four hundred yards from Churchill's. The two men were together for two hours. 'When Papa at length emerged,' Mary Churchill wrote to her mother, 'we decided to walk home. He told me he liked the President immensely—they talk the same language. He says he is sure he can work with him. I nearly wept for joy and thankfulness, it seemed like divine providence. Perhaps it is FDR's legacy. I can see Papa is relieved and confident.'[4]

Churchill later wrote, in his memoirs, of how he had been impressed with Truman's 'gay, precise, sparkling manner and obvious power of decision'.[5] 'PM delighted with Pres' was Sir Alexander Cadogan's comment.[6]

That afternoon Churchill drove to the ruins of Hitler's Chancellery, which he was shown over by Russian guides. 'The city was nothing but a chaos of ruins,' he later wrote. In the square in front of the Chancellery a large number of Germans had gathered. 'When I got out of the car and walked about among them, except for one old man who shook his head disapprovingly, they all began to cheer. My hate had died with their surrender and I was much moved by their demonstrations, and also by their haggard looks and threadbare clothes.'[7] Richard Pim, the head of his Map Room, later recalled how, as Churchill looked over the ruins of the bunker, he remarked: 'This is what would have happened to us if *they* had won the war. We would have been the bunker.'[8]

That night Churchill dined alone with General Marshall. He was

---

[1] Prime Minister's Personal Minute, M('Ter') 3/5, circulated to the Cabinet as Cabinet Paper No. 83 of 1945, 'The Vigilantes', 15 July 1945: Churchill papers, 20/209 (Minute) and 23/14 (Cabinet paper).

[2] Private Office diary, 15 July 1945: Thompson papers.

[3] Marian Holmes diary, 15 July 1945: Marian Walker Spicer papers.

[4] Letter of 16 July 1945: Mary Soames, *Clementine Churchill*, page 384.

[5] Winston S. Churchill, *The Second World War*, volume 6, page 545.

[6] Cadogan diary, 16 July 1945: David Dilks (editor), *The Diaries of Sir Alexander Cadogan*, pages 762–3.

[7] Winston S. Churchill, *The Second World War*, volume 6, page 545.

[8] Sir Richard Pim recollections: in conversation with the author, 1975.

also sent that day a letter from his son, 'just to wish you good luck at Potsdam'. Randolph added: 'Everyone seems to be taking a very cautious line about the Election now that it is all over. But I shall be surprised if your majority is less than 80.'[1]

On the morning of July 17 Churchill continued his sightseeing with a visit to Frederick II's Summer Palace at Sans Souci, accompanied by Attlee. He and Attlee then lunched together at Churchill's residence on the Ringstrasse. Their American lunch guest was United States Secretary for War, Henry Stimson, who put in front of Churchill a sheet of paper on which was written: 'Babies satisfactorily born.' Churchill had no idea what this meant. 'It means,' Stimson explained, 'that the experiment in the Mexican desert has come off. The atomic bomb is a reality.'[2]

The lunch over, Churchill left the Ringstrasse for the Cecilienhof, and the first Plenary meeting of the Potsdam Conference. At Stalin's suggestion, Truman took the Chair. 'They were glad to welcome him to their deliberations,' said Churchill, 'and it was their earnest desire to continue to pursue in his company the high aims which the three great Allied Powers had sought to achieve throughout the bitter years of the war in Europe. He confidently believed that their mutual understanding and friendship would grow closer and more firm as they went forward together in common study of the difficult problems which awaited their consideration.' These sentiments, commented Stalin, 'were fully shared by himself and all members of the Russian Delegation'.

Truman then made two proposals, first that Italy should join the United Nations, and second that the Foreign Ministers not only of Britain, Russia and the United States but also of China and France, should draft the peace treaties and boundary settlements of Europe. Churchill was doubtful about both these suggestions. Although Britain had suffered heavy naval losses in the Mediterranean, he said, she had much goodwill to Italy, and had provided fourteen ships which Russia claimed from the Italian Fleet. But the British people 'would not easily forget Italy's conduct in declaring war on the British Commonwealth in the hour of her greatest peril, when French resistance was on the point of collapse; nor could they forget the long struggle which we had had against Italy in North Africa in the period before the United States came into the war'.

---

[1] 'My dearest Papa', 'Personal', 16 July 1945: Churchill papers, 2/1.

[2] Winston S. Churchill, *The Second World War*, volume 6, pages 272–3. The first atomic bomb test had taken place in the United States desert state of New Mexico. 'Had I known that Tube Alloys were progressing so fast,' Churchill wrote to Lord Cherwell on 10 January 1953, 'it would have affected my judgement about the date of the General Election.' ('Secret', 10 January 1953: Churchill papers, 4/379.)

For his part, Stalin was doubtful about asking China to join the Council of Foreign Ministers. Why should she deal with questions which were primarily European ones? And why have this new body at all? We had the European Advisory Commission, and we had agreed at Yalta to regular meetings of the three Foreign Secretaries. Another organization would only complicate matters, and anyway when would the Peace Conference be held?

Truman argued that as China was a member of the World Security Council she ought to have a say in the European settlement. The new United Nations organization would, he said, leave little scope for meetings of the Foreign Secretaries of the 'Big Three'.

To Churchill all this seemed somewhat premature, and he feared a dissolution of the Grand Alliance. A world organization, he warned, open to all and all-forgiving, might be both diffuse and powerless. Free elections in Poland were more to the point. It was this practical problem that still lay before them. He attached 'great importance', Churchill told Stalin and Truman, 'to the early holding of free elections in Poland which would truly reflect the wishes of the Polish people'.[1]

Churchill's reference to free elections in Poland was the first reference at Potsdam to one of the principal purposes of the meeting, and to the unresolved legacy of Yalta. At that point, and with no further discussion, the first Plenary meeting came to an end.

Remaining at the Cecilienhof, Churchill had a private conversation with Stalin. No notes were taken, but that evening Churchill's interpreter, Major Birse, set down from memory what he recalled of the talk.

The first topic was Japan. As he was leaving Moscow, Stalin told Churchill, 'an unaddressed message had been delivered to him through the Japanese Ambassador. It was assumed that the message was intended for either Stalin, or the Soviet President, Kalinin, or other members of the Soviet Government. It was from the Emperor of Japan, who stated that "unconditional surrender" could not be accepted by Japan but that, if it was not insisted upon, "Japan might be prepared to compromise with regard to other terms". According to the message, the Emperor was making this suggestion "in the interests of all people concerned".'

Stalin then told Churchill that he had not spoken of the message 'to anyone except the Prime Minister', but that he wanted to bring it up at the next session of the Conference.

When Churchill suggested that Stalin should send Truman a note on the subject 'in order to warn him before the next Session', Stalin

[1] 'P (Terminal) 1st Meeting', 5 p.m., 17 July 1945: Cabinet papers, 99/38.

pointed out that 'he did not wish the President to think that the Soviet Government wanted to act as an intermediary, but he would have no objection if the Prime Minister mentioned it to the President'.

Churchill agreed to do so, pointing out 'that he also did not wish the President to feel that we were not at one with the United States in their aim of achieving complete victory over Japan'. America had helped Britain 'enormously' in the war against Germany, and Britain intended 'to help her now to the full'. At the same time people in America, Churchill told Stalin, 'were beginning to doubt the need for "unconditional surrender"'. They were saying: was it worth while having the pleasure of killing ten million Japanese at the cost of one million Americans and British?'

Stalin remarked that the Japanese realized the Allied strength and were 'very frightened'. Unconditional surrender in practice could be seen 'here in Berlin and the rest of Germany'.

Churchill next asked Stalin 'Where was Germany?' to which Stalin replied that Germany 'was nowhere and everywhere'. Stalin then told Churchill 'that he could not understand German upbringing. The Germans were like sheep and had always needed a man who could give them orders. They never thought for themselves.'

Churchill agreed, telling Stalin 'that the Germans had always believed in a symbol. If a Hohenzollern had been allowed to reign after the last war, there would have been no Hitler. They certainly were like sheep.'

The need for a symbol, Stalin said, 'applied only to the Germans', and to illustrate 'the German sense of justice' he then told Churchill of an incident which had recently occurred in Berlin. 'An SS man had fired at a Russian soldier from a house. Soviet troops immediately surrounded the house. A crowd of Germans approached the troops and said they had heard that, in retaliation, their rations would be stopped for a week. Instead of stopping their rations they offered 40 or 50 hostages. When the Russians refused the hostages, the Germans immediately entered the building and seized the SS man and handed him over.'

Stalin then told Churchill that he had 'taken to smoking cigars'. If a photograph of Stalin smoking a cigar could be 'flashed across the world', Churchill replied, 'it would cause an immense sensation'.

On the subject of working late hours, Stalin told Churchill that he had become 'so accustomed to working at night that, now that the need had passed, he could not get to sleep before 4 a.m.'.

During their discussion, Churchill thanked Stalin 'for the welcome which Mrs Churchill had received during her visit to Russia'. The visit had been 'a great pleasure to him', Stalin replied. Churchill then spoke of 'the women workers in Stalingrad whom Mrs Churchill had seen and who had said they were glad to work hard as they were reconstructing the city for their husbands, who would soon be coming home'. Stalin, Birse noted 'appeared to be touched'.

Churchill then said that Britain 'welcomed Russia as a Great Power and in particular as a Naval Power. The more ships that sailed the seas the greater chance there was for better relations.' He also 'wanted good relations', Stalin replied. As regards Russia's fleet 'it was still a small one, nevertheless, great or small, it could be of benefit to Great Britain'.

As their discussion came to an end, Churchill asked Stalin 'whether in future he should call him Premier, Marshal or Generalissimo'. Stalin replied 'that he hoped the Prime Minister would call him Marshal as he always had done in the past'.

Stalin then said 'that there were several questions he would like to discuss with the Prime Minister', and it was agreed that they should meet again, at Stalin's house, on the following evening.[1]

Returning to his villa, Churchill was shown a note from Beaverbrook, in which he referred to Conservative pessimism at the outcome of the Election. 'The Socialists are holding a mass demonstration on the night of July 26th,' Beaverbrook wrote, 'whereas the Tories show no such festive disposition.' The Conservative newspapers were 'frankly hostile' to the administration. 'The only asset the Tories have got,' Beaverbrook added, 'is in Berlin anyway.'[2]

That night Churchill dined alone with Eden, and then worked for a while.[3]

Writing in his diary that night, Eden was critical of Churchill's performance at the first Plenary meeting. 'W was very bad,' was his first comment, and he added: 'He had read no brief & was confused & woolly & verbose about new Council of Foreign Ministers. We had an anti-Chinese tirade from him. Americans not a little exasperated.' Neither he, Pierson Dixon nor Sir Alexander Cadogan had ever seen Churchill 'worse', Eden wrote, and of their dinner together he noted: 'Dined alone with him & again urged him not to give up our few cards without return. But he is again under Stalin's spell. He kept repeating "I like that man" & I am full of admiration of Stalin's handling of him. I told him I was, hoping that would move him. It did a little!'[4]

[1] 'Record of private talk between the Prime Minister and Generalissimo Stalin after the Plenary Session on July 17th 1945 at Potsdam', 'Top Secret', 17 July 1945: Premier papers, 3/430/7, folios 6–10. (Initialled by Churchill, 'WSC', 18 iii.)

[2] 'Following for Prime Minister from Beaverbrook', 'Sent by bag to Terminal, 3 p.m. 17/7', 17 July 1945: Churchill papers, 2/548.

[3] Private Office diary, 17 July 1945: Thompson papers.

[4] Eden diary, 17 July 1945: Robert Rhodes James, *Anthony Eden*, London 1986, page 307.

One result of Churchill's work on July 17 was a Minute to several of his Ministers in London, seeking the demobilization of as many doctors as possible, 'in order to ensure adequate medical attention for civilians in the coming winter'.[1] 'Papa is well,' Mary Churchill reported to her mother, 'although experiencing tiresome bouts of indigestion every now and then.'[2]

'Mary is a great help to me,' Churchill telegraphed to his wife on July 18. 'The first two days of intense heat,' he reported, 'have been followed by grey skies and a drop of fifteen degrees.' His telegram continued: 'Everything has opened well so far but of course we have not reached any of the serious issues. We are besieged in our impenetrable compound by a host of reporters who are furious at not being able to over-run us. It is impossible to conduct grave affairs except in silence and secrecy.'[3]

At one o'clock on July 18 President Truman came to Churchill's villa for lunch. After inspecting a guard of honour, he was introduced to Churchill's staff, before lunching alone with the Prime Minister. Their meeting lasted for nearly two hours, without anyone else present. As soon as the lunch was over, Churchill prepared a note of the discussion.[4] Their first topic was the atom bomb. 'The President showed me the telegrams about the recent experiment,' Churchill wrote, 'and asked what I thought should be done about telling the Russians. He seemed determined to do this, but asked about the timing, and said he thought that the end of the Conference would be best. I replied that if he were resolved to tell, it might well be better to hang it on to the experiment, which was a new fact on which he and we had only just had knowledge. Therefore he would have good answer to any question, "why did you not tell us this before?" He seemed impressed with this idea, and will consider it.'

Churchill went on to tell Truman that 'on behalf of His Majesty's Government I did not resist his proposed disclosure of the simple fact that we have this weapon. He reiterated his resolve at all costs to refuse to divulge any particulars.'[5]

Truman then asked Churchill how Britain and America should

[1] Prime Minister's Personal Minute, M('Ter') 6/5, 17 July 1945: Churchill papers, 20/209.
[2] Letter of 17 July 1945: Mary Soames, *Clementine Churchill*, page 385.
[3] 'Target' No. 75. 'Top Secret', 'Personal', 18 July 1945: Baroness Spencer-Churchill papers.
[4] 'PM's Conversation with President Truman, July 18, 1945 (Potsdam)', 'Copy to 1. The King, 2. Mr Attlee, 3. Mr Bevin, 4. Sir Edward Bridges': Premier papers, 3/430/8, folio 31. Churchill's note about his talk with Truman was dictated at 6.30 that evening, after his return from the second Plenary meeting (Private Office diary, 18 July 1945).
[5] This section of the discussion was not printed for the Cabinet, as were the subsequent sections, but given a limited circulation to Eden, Sir John Anderson (the Minister responsible for all matters concerning the atom bomb), Lord Cherwell and General Ismay (for the Chiefs of Staff Committee).

handle the Russian request for the division of the German fleet. 'I said, speaking personally,' Churchill noted, 'my view was that we should welcome the Russians on to the broad waters and do it in a manner which was wholehearted and gracious. This would affect the view we took of the Dardanelles, Kiel Canal, the mouth of the Baltic, and Port Arthur. I found it hard to deny the Russians the right to keep their third of the fleet afloat if they needed it. We British should not have any use for our third of the warships.' This was also Truman's view. The Americans, he said, 'would take their share, but it would be of no use to them'.

Churchill then 'made it clear that the case of the U-boats must be considered separately, as they were nasty things to have knocking about in large numbers'. Truman 'seemed to agree'.

In Churchill's view, the question of Russia's share of the German fleet 'should be handled in connection with the general layout in Central Europe'. Were 'all these States which had passed into Russian control', he asked, 'to be free and independent, or not? Of course they could not pursue a policy hostile to Russia.' To this point, Truman 'attached great importance'. He 'evidently intends', Churchill noted, 'to press with severity the need of their true independence in accordance with free, full and unfettered elections'. Truman also 'seemed to agree' with Churchill's point 'that everything should be settled as a whole, and not piecemeal'. When Churchill mentioned Persia, Turkey and Greece in this context, Truman 'seemed to be in full accord'.

The next topic over lunch was finance, and Britain's indebtedness. 'I spoke of the melancholy position of Great Britain,' Churchill noted, 'who had spent more than one-half her foreign investments in the time when we were all alone for the common cause, and now emerged from the War the only nation with a great external debt of £3,000 millions.' Churchill then explained to Truman the way in which this debt 'had grown up for war purposes through buying supplies from India, Egypt, etc. with no Lease-Lend[1] arrangement; and that it would impose upon us an annual exportation without any compensatory import to nourish the wages fund'. Truman 'followed this attentively', Churchill noted, 'and with sympathy', telling Churchill of the 'immense debt' owed by the United States to Great Britain 'for having held the fort at the beginning'. In Truman's own words, as recorded by Churchill: 'If you had gone down like France, we might well be fighting the Germans on the American coast at the present time.' It was this, Truman went on, that 'justified the United States in

---

[1] Also known as Lend-Lease, the principle had been established by Bill No. 1776, passed by the Senate in March 1941, and described by Churchill as a 'monument of generous and far-sighted statesmanship' (House of Commons, 12 March 1941).

regarding these matters as above the purely financial plane'. Churchill then told Truman that he had told 'the Election crowds' that Britain was living 'to a large extent upon American imported food, etc., for which we could not pay, and we had no intention of being kept by any country, however near to us in friendship'.

It was clear, Churchill told Truman, that Britain would have to ask for help 'to become a growing concern again. Until we got our wheels turning properly once more, we could be of little use to world security or any of the high purposes of San Francisco.'

He would 'do his very utmost', Truman replied, but of course Churchill 'knew all the difficulties he might have in his own country'. Truman's attitude, Churchill commented, 'was most warm and comforting in these matters'.

Churchill now raised the question of the war against Japan, and of Stalin's remarks to him on the previous evening. 'I said that the Japanese war might end much quicker than had been expected,' Churchill recorded, 'and that the eighteen months period which we had taken as a working rule required to be reviewed. Also, Stage III might be upon us in a few months, or perhaps even earlier.' Truman told Churchill that he also thought 'the war might come to a speedy end'. Churchill then 'imparted to the President the disclosure, about the offer from the Mikado, made to me by Marshal Stalin the night before; and I told him he was quite free to talk it over with the Marshal, as I had informed him at the Marshal's express desire'.

Churchill then explained that Stalin had not wished to transmit this information direct to Truman 'for fear he might think the Russians were trying to influence him towards peace'. In the same way, Churchill would 'abstain from saying anything which would indicate that we were in any way reluctant to go on with the war against Japan as long as the United States thought fit'. He dwelt, however, 'upon the tremendous cost in American life and, to a smaller extent, in British life which would be involved in enforcing "unconditional surrender" upon the Japanese'. It was for Truman to consider whether 'unconditional surrender' might not be expressed 'in some other way, so that we got all the essentials for future peace and security, and yet left the Japanese some show of saving their military honour and some assurance of their national existence, after they had complied with all safeguards necessary for the conqueror'. Truman countered by saying 'that he did not think the Japanese had any military honour after Pearl Harbor', to which Churchill, as he noted, contented himself with saying 'that at any rate they had something for which they were ready to face certain death in very large numbers, and this might not be so important to us as it was to them'. Truman then became what

Churchill described as 'quite sympathetic', speaking, as Stimson had done earlier, 'of the terrible responsibilities that rested upon him in regard to unlimited effusion of American blood'.

Churchill's own impression was that there was 'no question of a rigid insistence upon the phrase "unconditional surrender", apart from the essentials necessary for world peace and future security, and for the punishment of a guilty and treacherous nation'. It had been 'evident' to Churchill, in his conversations with Stimson, Marshall and now Truman, 'that they are searching their hearts on this subject, and that we have no need to press it. We know of course that the Japanese are ready to give up all conquests made in this war.'

The next subject was raised by Truman, who told Churchill of the 'great difficulties' which he had to face in regard to those British airfields, especially in Africa, 'which the Americans had built at enormous cost'. What Truman wanted was that Britain should 'meet' America on this, 'and arrange a fair plan for common use'. Churchill accepted Truman's proposal with alacrity, telling the President 'that, if I continued to be responsible, I should like to re-open the Air question as regards communications with him personally'. Truman 'welcomed' this, whereupon Churchill commented that it would be 'a great pity' if the Americans got 'worked up' about bases and air traffic, 'and set themselves to make a win of it at all costs'. Churchill continued:

> We must come to the best arrangements in our common interest. As to the airfields and other bases, President Roosevelt knew well that I wished to go much further, and would like to have a reciprocal arrangement, including naval and Air, all over the world between our two countries. Britain, though a smaller Power than the United States, had much to give. Why should an American battleship calling at Gibraltar not find the torpedoes to fit her tubes, and the shells to fit her guns deposited there? Why should we not share facilities for defence all over the world? We could add 50 per cent to the mobility of the American Fleet.

Churchill's language, Truman replied, 'was very near to his own heart'. But any such plans would have to be 'fitted in, in some way', as part of the method of carrying out the policy of the United Nations. 'I said that was alright,' Churchill replied, 'so long as the facilities were shared between Britain and the United States. There was nothing in it if they were made common to everybody.' A man might make a proposal of marriage to a young lady, Churchill explained, but 'it was not much use if he were told that she would always be a sister to him. I wanted, under whatever form or cloak, a continuation of the present war-time system of reciprocal facilities between Britain and the United States in regard to bases and fuelling points in their possession.'

The President, Churchill noted, 'seemed in full accord with this, if it could be presented in a suitable fashion, and did not appear to take crudely the form of a military alliance *à deux*. These last were not his words, but are my impression of his mind.'

Encouraged by this, Churchill went on 'with my long-cherished idea of keeping the organization of the Combined Chiefs of Staff in being, at any rate until the world calmed down after the great storm and until there was a world structure of such proved strength and capacity that we could safely confide ourselves to it'. Truman was replying to him 'in an encouraging way', Churchill noted, 'when we were interrupted by his officers reminding him that he must now start off to see Marshal Stalin'.

As he left, Truman told Churchill 'that this had been the most enjoyable luncheon he had had for many years', and how earnestly he hoped that Churchill's relations with Roosevelt 'would be continued between him and me'. Churchill added of this meeting with Truman: 'He invited personal friendship and comradeship, and used many expressions at intervals in our discussion which I could not easily hear unmoved. He seems a man of exceptional character and ability, with an outlook exactly along the lines of Anglo-American relations as they have developed, simple and direct methods of speech, and a great deal of self-confidence and resolution.'

'Let us hope,' Churchill added, 'that further developments at this Conference and hereafter will vindicate these hopeful notes.' [1]

Churchill's hopes were not entirely fulfilled. At a meeting of the Combined Chiefs of Staff that afternoon, some bitterness was expressed, particularly by Sir Alan Brooke, at Britain being excluded from the strategic discussion on the Pacific war. 'The United States Chiefs of Staff would be glad,' General Marshall remarked, 'to give the British Chiefs of Staff timely information of United States plans and intentions and to hear their comments. But they felt bound to retain freedom to decide ultimately what should be done.' The Combined Chiefs of Staff agreed, at the end of the discussion, that 'with respect to the strategic control of the war against Japan', the United States Chiefs of Staff would consult the British Chiefs of Staff on matters of general strategy, 'on the understanding that in the event of disagreement, the final decision on the action to be taken will lie with the United States Chiefs of Staff'. [2]

---

[1] 'Summarized note of the Prime Minister's conversation with President Truman, at luncheon, July 18, 1945', 'Top Secret', 18 July 1945: Premier papers, 3/430/8, folios 16–29.

[2] Combined Chiefs of Staff, 195th Meeting, Babelsberg (Potsdam), 2.30 pm., 18 July 1945: Cabinet papers, 120/186. The United States Chiefs of Staff were General of the Army G. C. Marshall, Fleet Admiral E. J. King and General of the Army H. H. Arnold. The British Chiefs of Staff were Field Marshal Sir Alan Brooke, Marshal of the Royal Air Force Sir Charles Portal and Admiral of the Fleet Sir Andrew Cunningham.

At four o'clock that afternoon, Churchill left his villa for the second Plenary session of the Conference. The meeting, which lasted nearly two and a half hours, began with Churchill raising an issue which was not on the agenda: the Press. At the Teheran conference, Churchill pointed out, it had been very difficult for the Press to get near the meeting-place, and at Yalta it had been impossible. But now, immediately outside the delegation area, there were 180 journalists 'prowling around in a state of furious indignation. They carried very powerful weapons and were making a great outcry in the world Press about the lack of facilities accorded to them.'

Stalin asked who had let the journalists in. They were not within the delegation area, Churchill explained, but mostly in Berlin. The Conference could only do its work in quiet and secrecy, he said, and this must be protected at all costs. Churchill then offered to see the Press men himself and explain why they had to be excluded and why nothing could be divulged until the Conference ended. He hoped that Truman would also see them. 'The plumage of the Press needed to be smoothed down,' Churchill commented. If the importance of secrecy and quiet for those engaged in the Conference were explained to them, 'they would take their exclusion with a good grace'.

Stalin asked what the journalists wanted. Truman explained that each of the three leaders had his own representative to stand between him and the Press. They had agreed to exclude them and matters should be left as they were. Churchill 'submitted to the majority', as he later recalled, 'but I thought and still think that a public explanation would have been better'.

The three Foreign Secretaries, Eden, Molotov and Byrnes, then produced their plan for drafting the European peace treaties. The Council would still consist of the Foreign Ministers of the five Powers enumerated by the President, but only those who had signed the articles of surrender imposed on the enemy State concerned would draw up the terms of settlement. This was accepted by Stalin, Truman and Churchill, but Churchill was concerned at an American proposal to submit the terms to the United Nations, pointing out that if this meant consulting every member of the United Nations it would be a lengthy and laborious process. Byrnes replied that the Allies were so bound by the United Nations Declaration, but both he and Stalin admitted that reference to the United Nations could only be made after the five Powers had agreed among themselves. 'I left it at that,' Churchill later recalled.

The next question on the agenda was Germany. But none of the issues to be decided—the exact powers of the Control Council, economic questions and the disposal of the Nazi fleet—were ready for discussion. 'What,' Churchill asked, 'is meant by Germany?' 'What she has become after the war,' said Stalin. 'The Germany of 1937,' said Truman. Stalin said it was impossible to get away from the war. The country no longer existed. There were no definite frontiers, no frontier guards, no troops, merely four occupied zones. At length it was agreed, as Truman wished, to take the Germany of 1937 as a starting-point.

The discussion then turned to Poland, with Stalin proposing the immediate transfer to the Lublin Poles 'of all stocks, assets, and all other property belonging to Poland which is still at the disposal of the Polish Government in London, in whatever form this property may be and no matter where or at whose disposal this property may prove to be at the present moment'. He also wanted the Polish armed forces, including the Navy and Merchant Marine, to be subordinated to the Lublin Poles.

Churchill could not accept these proposals. The burden of them, he explained, lay on British shoulders. When their homeland had been overrun and they had been driven from France many Poles had found shelter in Britain. There was no worthwhile property belonging to the Polish Government in London, but there was in London and in Canada about £20,000,000 in Polish gold. This had been frozen by us, since it was an asset of the Central Bank of Poland. It was not the property of the Polish Government in London and they had no power to draw upon it. There was of course the Polish Embassy in London, which was open and available for a Polish Ambassador as soon as the new Polish Government cared to send one—'and the sooner the better'.

The Polish Government, Churchill explained, had been financed during its five and a half years in the United Kingdom by the British Government: 'we had paid the Poles about £120,000,000 to finance their Army and diplomatic service, and to enable them to look after Poles who had sought refuge on our shores from the German scourge'. When Britain had disavowed the Polish Government in London and recognized the new Provisional Polish Government in Warsaw, it had been arranged that three months' salary should be paid to all employees and that they should then be dismissed. It would have been 'improper', Churchill noted, to have dismissed them without this payment, and the expense had fallen upon Great Britain.

Churchill then asked to speak of an important matter, 'because our position with regard to it was unique'—the demobilization or transfer to their homeland of the Polish forces that had fought with Britain in the war. When France fell Britain had evacuated all Poles who wished to come—about 45,000 men—and built up from these men, and from others who had come through Switzerland and elsewhere, a Polish Army, which had finally reached the strength of some five divisions. There were now about 30,000 Polish troops in Germany, and a Polish Corps of three divisions in Italy 'in a highly excited state of mind and grave moral distress'. This army, totalling, from front to rear, more than 180,000 men, had fought 'with great bravery and good discipline', both in Germany and, on an even larger scale, in Italy. There they had suffered severe losses and had held their positions 'as steadfastly as any troops on the Italian front'. The honour of the British was thus involved. These Polish troops, Churchill added, had 'fought gallantly side by side with ours at a time when trained troops had been scarce. Many had died,' and even if Churchill had not given pledges in Parliament, Britain would wish 'to treat them honourably'.

Stalin said he agreed with this, and Churchill, continuing, said that British policy was to persuade as many as possible, not only of the soldiers but also of the civilian employees of the late Polish Government, to go back to their country. 'But we must have a little time to get over our difficulties.'

There had been 'great improvements' in Poland in the last two months, Churchill told the Conference; he 'cordially hoped for the success of the new Government, which, although not all we could wish, marked a great advance and was the result of patient work by the three Great Powers'. He had told the House of Commons that if there were Polish soldiers who had fought at our side and did not want to go back, Britain would take them into the British Empire. Of course, the better the conditions in Poland the more Poles would go back, and it would help if the new Polish Government would assure their livelihood and freedom 'and would not victimise them for their former allegiance'. Churchill hoped, as he explained to Stalin, that, with continued improvement in Poland, 'most of these people would return and become good citizens of the land of their fathers, which had been liberated by the bravery of Russian armies'.

In reply, Stalin said he appreciated Britain's problems. Britain had sheltered the former rulers of Poland, and in spite of Britain's hospitality they had caused many difficulties. But the London Polish Government still existed. They had means of continuing their activities in the Press and elsewhere, and they had their agents. 'This made a bad impression on all the Allies.'

'We must face facts,' Churchill answered. The London Government was 'liquidated' in the official and diplomatic sense, but it was impossible to stop its individual members living and talking to people, including journalists and former sympathizers. Moreover, 'we had to be careful about the Polish Army, for if the situation was mishandled there might be a mutiny'. Churchill then asked Stalin to put 'his trust and confidence' in the British Government and give it 'reasonable time'. In return, 'everything possible should be done to make Poland an encouraging place for the Poles to go back to'.

According to Truman, there were no fundamental differences between Churchill and Stalin. Churchill had asked for a reasonable amount of time, and Stalin had undertaken to drop any of his proposals which would complicate the issue. The 'best thing', in Truman's view, was for the Foreign Secretaries to discuss these points; 'but he hoped the Yalta agreement would be carried out as soon as possible'.

Stalin then suggested referring the whole matter to the Foreign Secretaries.

'Including elections,' said Churchill.

'The Provisional Government have never refused to hold free elections,' Stalin replied.[1]

The second Plenary session of the Potsdam Conference was over. 'It went so efficiently,' Sir Alexander Cadogan wrote to his wife that evening, 'that we got through our agenda by about six—much to the PM's annoyance, as he wanted to go on talking at random and was most disappointed—just like a child with its toy taken away from it. But Truman closed the proceedings!'[2]

Returning to his villa, Churchill sat in the garden dictating a note about his midday discussion with Truman, and then, at 8.20 p.m., left for a dinner with Stalin. The gift that he took with him for the Marshal was a box of cigars. The two men dined alone, except for their respective interpreters, Birse and Pavlov. The discussion, which lasted nearly five hours, was recorded by Birse.

Speaking of the British General Election, Stalin 'suggested that the Prime Minister would have a majority of about 80.[3] He thought the Labour Party would receive 220–230 votes. The Prime Minister was not sure how the soldiers had voted, but the Marshal said that an Army preferred a strong Government and would therefore vote for the Conservatives.'[4]

It was not only Churchill's future that was discussed over the dinner table. Two years later Churchill's interpreter, Major Birse, recalled, in a note prepared for Churchill's war memoirs:

I can recall Mr Churchill asking Stalin who would succeed him. Stalin

[1] 'P (Terminal) 2nd Meeting', 5 p.m., 18 July 1945: Cabinet papers, 99/38.
[2] Letter of 18 July 1945: Cadogan diary, David Dilks (editor), *The Diaries of Sir Alexander Cadogan*, pages 765–6.
[3] This had also been Randolph Churchill's estimate.
[4] 'Record of a private talk between the Prime Minister and Generalissimo Stalin at dinner on July 18, 1945, at Potsdam', 'Top Secret', 18 July 1945: Premier papers, 3/430/6, folios 45–52.

gave no name, but said the succession had been settled for thirty years ahead. . . . At dinner, Stalin, next to whom I sat, remarked that he had great admiration for General Marshall. He went on to say that we, in the British Army, also had first class generals. Somehow he got on to the subject, for only a moment, of education and manners: in Russia, he said, people lacked both and still had a long way to go.[1]

Talking about Japan, Stalin showed Churchill the Soviet Government's answer to the Emperor's message, in which the Soviet Government stated that as the Emperor's message had been in general terms and contained no concrete proposals, 'the Soviet Government could take no action'. It was evident from Stalin's further remarks, Churchill added, that Russsia intended to attack Japan 'soon after August 8'; Stalin had told him, 'it might be a fortnight later'.

The conversation then turned to the sea: 'it was his policy', Churchill said, 'to welcome Russia as a great power on the sea. He wished to see Russian ships sailing across the oceans of the world. Russia had been like a giant with his nostrils pinched: this referred to the narrow exits from the Baltic and the Black Sea.' Churchill then brought up the question of Turkey and the Dardanelles; the Turks, he said, 'were very frightened'. Stalin then explained that the Turks had approached the Russians with regard to a treaty of alliance. In reply the Russians had said that there could be a treaty only if neither side had any claims. Russia, however, claimed Kars and Ardahan, in eastern Turkey, which had been taken away from Russia at the end of the First World War. The Turks then said that they could not discuss this claim. Russia then raised the question of the Montreux Convention.[2] Turkey said she could not discuss it, so Russia replied that she could not discuss a treaty of alliance.

In reply, Churchill said that he personally would support an amendment to the Montreux Convention, 'throwing out Japan, and giving Russia access to the Mediterranean'. He repeated 'that he welcomed Russia's appearance on the oceans'. This referred not only to the Dardanelles, he said, but also to the Kiel Canal, which should have a regime like the Suez Canal, and also to the warm waters of the Pacific. 'This was not out of gratitude for anything Russia had done,' Churchill explained, 'but his settled policy.'

Stalin then raised the question of the German fleet. A share of it would be 'most useful for Russia', he said, 'who had suffered severe losses at sea'. He was grateful to Churchill for the ships delivered in connection with the surrender of the Italian navy, 'but he would like his share of the German ships'.

[1] 'Potsdam, July 1945', note dated 12 June 1947: Churchill papers, 4/391A.
[2] Signed in 1936, limiting the passage of warships through the Dardanelles to the Allied and Associated Powers of 1918.

During the dinner, Stalin spoke of Greek 'aggression' on her Bulgarian and Albanian frontiers. There were elements in Greece, he said, 'which were stirring up trouble'. Churchill at once replied 'that he would send orders to Greece to prevent any fighting'. What he wanted to know was 'what was going to happen to Hungary'. When last he and Stalin had met, at Yalta in February, 'he was looking forward to the Russians reaching Budapest. They were now far beyond that stage.' Stalin replied 'that in all the countries liberated by the Red Army, the Russian policy was to see a strong, independent, sovereign State. He was against Sovietization of any of those countries. They would have free elections, and all except Fascist parties would participate.'

Turning to Yugoslavia, Churchill spoke of Britain's 'difficulties' there, where Britain had 'no material ambitions, but there had been the 50–50 arrangement. It was now 99–1 against Britain.' Stalin at once protested 'that it was 90 per cent British, 10 per cent Yugoslavian, and 0 per cent Russian interests'. In reply to Churchill's remarks, Stalin declared that Marshal Tito 'had the partisan mentality and had done several things he ought not to have done. The Soviet Government often did not know what Marshal Tito was about to do.'

Roumania and Bulgaria then came under discussion. 'He had been "hurt",' Stalin said, 'by the American demand for a change of government in Roumania and Bulgaria. He was not meddling in Greek affairs, so he thought it was unjust of the Americans to make the present demand.' Churchill replied that he had not previously seen the American proposals. In the case of countries 'where there had been an émigré government', Stalin explained, 'he had found it necessary to assist in the creation of a home government. This of course did not apply in the case of Roumania and Bulgaria. Everything was peaceful in those two countries.' Churchill then asked Stalin why the Soviet Government had given an award to King Michael of Roumania. Because, said Stalin, the King had acted 'bravely and wisely' at the time of the *coup d'état*.[1]

Churchill then told Stalin 'of the anxiety felt by some people with

---

[1] On 23 August 1944 King Michael of Roumania (born 1921, reigned 1927–30 and 1940–47) masterminded a royal coup against Roumania's fascist dictator, General Ion Antonescu. The General and his brother, Mihai (who was Foreign Minister) were arrested. King Michael then appointed a coalition government and ordered his army to cease fighting Soviet troops. German Stukas then bombed Bucharest, concentrating on the palace. On 26 August 1944 King Michael declared war on Germany; over the following eight months the Roumanians suffered 150,000 casualties. In March 1945, under pressure from the Soviet Deputy Foreign Minister, Andrei Vyshinsky, the King appointed a 'National Democratic Front' government of Agrarians and Communists, and was honoured by the award of the highest Soviet decoration, the 'Order of Victory', for his initiative of August 1944. He was, however, forced to abdicate, and to leave the country, on 30 December 1947.

regard to Russia's intentions. He drew a line from the North Cape
to Albania, and named the capitals east of that line which were in
Russian hands. It looked as if Russia were rolling on westwards.'
Stalin replied that he had 'no such intention'. On the contrary, he
was withdrawing troops from the West. 'Two million men
would be demobilized and sent home within the next four months.
Further demobilization was only a question of adequate railway
transport.'

Stalin then told Churchill that Russian losses during the war had
amounted to five million killed and missing. The Germans had mobilized eighteen million men apart from industry, and the Russians
twelve million.

Churchill then told Stalin that he hoped that agreement would be
reached 'both as regards the questions connected with frontiers of all
the European countries as well as Russia's access to the seas, including
the division of the German fleet, before the Conference ended'. The
Three Powers gathered round the table 'were the strongest the world
had ever seen, and it was their task to maintain the peace of the
world'.

It was agreed, Churchill said, that although 'satisfactory to us', the
German defeat 'had been a great tragedy'. But 'the Germans were
like sheep'. Churchill and Stalin then swapped stories to illustrate
this, Churchill, as Birse's notes recorded, telling 'the story of young
Lieutenant Tirpitz'.[1] Stalin spoke of his experience in Germany in
1907, 'when two hundred Germans missed a Communist meeting because there was no one to take their railway tickets at the station barrier'.[2]

Stalin then apologized to Churchill 'for not having officially thank-
ed Great Britain for her help in the way of supplies during the War.
This would be done.' In reply, Churchill spoke 'of the great part Lord
Beaverbrook had played in this connection'.

At one moment during dinner, in answer to a question from Churchill, Stalin explained the working of Collective and State farms. Both
men agreed 'that both in Russia and Britain there was no fear of unemployment'. Stalin told Churchill that Russia was ready to talk
about Anglo-Russian trade. The best publicity for Soviet Russia
abroad, Churchill said, 'would be the happiness and well-being of her
people'. Stalin then spoke 'of the continuity of Soviet policy. If

[1] The son of Grand-Admiral Tirpitz, he was captured on 28 August 1914, during one of the
first naval engagements of the war. Lady Churchill was later to prize greatly his letter of condolence to her on Churchill's death.
[2] Stalin had travelled through Germany in 1907, on his way to the 7th Congress of the
Russian Social Democrat Congress, held in London.

anything were to happen to him, there would be good men ready to step into his shoes. He was thinking thirty years ahead.'[1]

To one of the British diplomats present, William Hayter, 'Churchill was tired and below his form'.[2] He did do his utmost, however, to master the topics in time for each session; indeed, in preparation for the afternoon Plenary session on July 19, he worked in bed throughout the morning, then lunched alone, reading the documents.

The third Plenary session began that afternoon at four o'clock, when Churchill 'refuted' Stalin's information regarding provocative acts by the Greeks on the northern Greek frontier.[3] The discussion then turned to the Soviet request for one third of the German navy. 'PM: Disposed to divide as part of a satisfactory settlement,' another of the British diplomats present, Pierson Dixon, noted in his diary. 'Proposes sinking of large part of U-boats and keeping of smaller proportion to be equally divided. His consent to Russian demand conditioned by this.'[4] No firm decision was reached, 'it being understood', as Eden reported to London, 'that a decision was dependent on a satisfactory general settlement of the main issues outstanding at the Conference'.[5]

Of the next subject under discussion, Spain, the Soviet delegation had put in a paper to the Plenary, suggesting that the United Nations should be recommended to break off relations with Franco and to support the democratic forces in Spain and enable the Spanish people to establish such a regime 'as would respond to their will'.

In response, Churchill said that although he and the British people had 'no love for Franco and would not lift a finger to support him', he would be against breaking off relations, with all the attendant difficulties, 'especially as Franco's position was already fast weakening'. To take this action would in his view serve to rally the Spanish people 'more firmly round the present regime'. Moreover, as a question of principle, 'he was opposed to interfering in the internal affairs of a nation that had been neither at war with us nor liberated by us'.

Truman then told the Plenary that although he had 'no liking for

---

[1] 'Record of a private talk between the Prime Minister and Generalissimo Stalin at dinner on July 18, 1945, at Potsdam', 'Top Secret', 18 July 1945: Premier papers, 3/430/6, folios 45–52.
[2] Sir William Hayter recollections: Sir William Hayter, *A Double Life*, page 75.
[3] 'Target' No. 121. 'Terminal to Foreign Office', 20 July 1945: Premier papers, 3/430, folio 9.
[4] Pierson Dixon diary, 19 July 1945: Piers Dixon (editor), *Double Diploma, The Life of Sir Pierson Dixon*, London 1968, pages 156–7.
[5] 'Target' No. 121, 'Terminal to Foreign Office', 20 July 1945: Premier papers, 3/420, folio 9.

Franco', it was for Spain to settle her own affairs. Stalin, however, argued that the Franco regime had been imposed on the Spanish people by Hitler and Mussolini and was 'a grave danger to Europe'. If, however, breaking off relations was too severe a measure, he suggested an announcement as part of a general declaration at the end of the Conference, 'to show the Spanish people and the world that the three heads of Government were against the Franco regime'.

After considerable discussion the meeting decided to leave the subject for the moment 'as there seemed no chance of agreement', and to proceed to the next item.

The next item was about Yugoslavia. The British Delegation had submitted a paper suggesting that, as the Tito–Subasic Agreement was not being fully carried out, the Three Powers should issue a statement to say that 'in view of the Yalta Declaration' they expected the undertakings contained in the Agreement to be implemented in the near future. Stalin maintained, however, that complaints about Yugoslavia 'could not be discussed without the presence of representatives of the Yugoslav Government'. The suggestion that Tito and Subasic should be invited was therefore discussed, but was rejected after Truman had said it was his wish at this Conference 'only to discuss matters of world affairs which could be settled between the three heads of Government'. Accordingly Churchill agreed that, 'although the Yugoslav question could not be dropped, he would not press it for the moment'.

The British Delegation had circulated a paper asking that equipment taken from British companies in Roumania should be returned and that no more should be taken. After preliminary discussion in which Stalin attempted to refute some of the arguments in the British paper and said that the matter could be dealt with through the normal diplomatic channels, and after Truman had explained the United States interests, Churchill's suggestion that this Roumania dispute should be referred to the Foreign Secretaries was adopted.[1]

That evening, Truman was host at a dinner for Churchill and Stalin. Attlee was also a guest. Among the toasts was one from Churchill: 'The Leader of the British Opposition—whoever he may be.' Truman was 'not quite the genial host that FDR was', Sir Alexander Cadogan wrote home, 'and the entertainment didn't go with a bang, but it was quite pleasant and ended about 10.45, so again I got to bed early'.[2] Churchill, too, was in bed soon after midnight.[3]

*   *   *

[1] 'Target' No. 121, 'Terminal to Foreign Office', 20 July 1945: Premier papers, 3/430, folio 10.
[2] Letter of 20 July 1945: Cadogan diary, David Dilks (editor), *The Diaries of Sir Alexander Cadogan*, page 767.
[3] Private Office diary, 19 July 1945: Thompson papers.

On the morning of Friday July 20, Churchill again visited the Palace of Sans Souci, then lunched with Cherwell and James Byrnes. He also sent a letter to President Truman, thanking him for two gifts which he had received from the President on the previous day:

My dear Truman,
    (If you will allow me to address you thus.)
    I am delighted with your charming and invaluable present of the 3 suitcases. They are indeed a practical souvenir of our meeting. The clock also stood on my bed-table, and I consulted it when I woke during the night. It speaks in darkness.
    What a pleasure it is to me to find so splendid a comrade and colleague, and now I hope that our work will continue together till the dark days of world tragedy have passed away![1]

That afternoon, at the fourth Plenary session, Truman submitted a paper advocating a friendly treatment of Italy. 'He was resisted by both Churchill and Stalin,' Pierson Dixon noted in his diary, 'though for different reasons: Churchill simply thought that Italy had behaved ignobly during the war and that it was too early to be unnecessarily lenient; Stalin would not do a deal on Italy unless his Satellites were also well treated.'[2]
Churchill told the fourth Plentary session:

... our position in the Italian story was not quite the same as that of either of his two colleagues present. We had been attacked by Italy in June 1940. We had suffered very heavy losses in the Mediterranean fighting, especially that on the North African shore, to which Italy had brought German troops, and in Egypt. We had also had grievous losses in warships and merchant ships in the Mediterranean. Unaided, we had had to undertake the Abyssinian campaign, and had replaced the Emperor on his throne.
    Special detachments of Italian aircraft had been sent to bomb London, and it must also be remembered that Italy had made a most dastardly and utterly unprovoked attack upon Greece. Moreover, just before the war began, she had seized Albania by a most lawless act. All these things had happened while we had been alone. It could not therefore be denied that we had suffered grievously at the hands of the Italian State. Nor could we acquit the Italian people entirely of their responsibility for these acts, any more than we could acquit the German people for the actions taken by them under the yoke of Hitler. Nevertheless, we had endeavoured to keep alive the idea of a revival of Italy as one of the important powers of Europe and the Mediterranean.

---

[1] 'Private', 20 July 1945: Churchill papers, 2/536. A note on Churchill's copy of this letter states, 'Mrs Churchill has seen'.
[2] Pierson Dixon diary, 20 July 1945: Piers Dixon (editor), *Double Diploma, The Life of Sir Pierson Dixon*, page 158.

He only said this, Churchill explained, 'to show on the one hand the injuries that we had received at Italian hands, and on the other the broad manner in which we approached the future of Italy, and in order to show that we were not hostile to the Italian people. He therefore came forward now on behalf of His Majesty's Government to make it clear that we wished to do what was best for the future. He was anxious to join, in principle, with President Truman and Premier Stalin in making a gesture of friendship and comfort to the Italian people, who had suffered terribly and had aided the Allies in expelling the Germans from their land.'

Speaking of Austria, Churchill told Stalin 'that it was high time that we were allowed to occupy our zone and move into Vienna'. In Germany, he pointed out, Britain and the Americans 'had retired long distances into the allotted zones; but we were still prevented from moving into ours in Austria'.

Stalin accepted Churchill's appeal; there was now 'no objection', he said, to the Allied armies occupying the zones allotted to them in Vienna and Austria.[1]

On the morning of Saturday July 21, the two British leaders, Churchill and Attlee, each in his own jeep, drove along the lines of cheering British troops, assembled for a Victory Parade. 'It struck me,' John Peck later recalled, 'and perhaps others as well, although nothing was said, as decidedly odd that Winston Churchill, the great war leader but for whom we should never have been in Berlin at all, got a markedly less vociferous cheer than Mr Attlee; who, however great his contribution in the Coalition, had not hitherto made any marked personal impact upon the fighting forces.'[2]

Churchill then took the salute, after which he opened a 'Winston Club' for British troops. 'This morning's parade,' Churchill told them, 'brings back to my mind a great many moving incidents of these last long, fierce years. Now you are here in Berlin, and I find you established in this great centre which, as a volcano, erupted smoke and fire all over Europe. Twice in our generation as in bygone times the German fury has been unleashed on her neighbours. Now it is we who take our place in the occupation of this country.'[3]

Returning to Potsdam, Churchill inspected the 2nd US Armoured Division, before lunching with Alexander, Montgomery and Admiral

[1] 'P (Terminal) 4th Meeting', 4 p.m., 20 July 1945: Cabinet papers, 99/38.
[2] John Peck recollections: Sir John Peck, 'Bull and Benediction', typescript, page 283.
[3] Speech of 21 July 1945: Charles Eade (compiler), *Victory*, pages 216–17.

King. That afternoon, at the fifth Plenary session, Churchill told Stalin that the situation in Vienna and Austria was 'unsatisfactory'; Britain had not even now been allowed to take up her zone in Vienna or in Austria, although three or four months had passed since discussions started, and we had reached a deadlock. In reply, Stalin informed the Conference that he had agreed 'the previous day' to the recommendations of the European Advisory Commission, so that the way was 'now free' to fix the date for the entry of the British and American troops into their zones; 'so far as he was concerned this could start at once'.[1]

The discussion then turned to Poland. In a memorandum submitted to the Conference, the Soviet delegation had argued that Poland's western frontier should run to the west of Swinemünde, as far as the Oder river, leaving the city of Stettin on the Polish side, then up the river Oder to the confluence with the Western Neisse, and from there along its course to Czechoslovakia.

It was Truman who protested that this movement of the Polish frontier so far westward was the equivalent of giving Poland a zone of occupation of her own in Germany. But the agreement to divide Germany into four zones of occupation, British, American, French and Soviet, was based upon the 1937 frontiers. The frontier now proposed for Poland was far further to the west.

He wished it to be 'clearly understood', declared Truman, 'that Germany should be occupied in accordance with the zones stated at Yalta', but Stalin replied that the Germans had fled from the eastern regions which Poland now intended to occupy. Churchill replied, as the minutes recorded:

. . . if that was the case, how was it possible for the Germans who had fled to be fed in the regions to which they had gone, since according to Premier Stalin's view, the produce of the regions which they had left would no longer be available for feeding Germany as a whole. He had been told that if the plan of the Polish provisional Government, which he understood was being put forward by the Soviet Government, were carried out in full, one quarter of the arable land available within the 1937 frontiers of Germany would be alienated. This was important from the point of view of food supply and of reparations.

As for the population questions, he understood that there were some 3–4 million Poles who would have to be moved into the suggested area of Poland from east of the Curzon Line; whereas if the full Polish plan for Poland's western frontier were implemented, there would be some $8\frac{1}{4}$ million (he thought the figure given by the United States Delegation was 9 million) Germans who would have to be moved out into Germany. Apart from the

[1] 'Target' No. 134, 'Top Secret', 21 July 1945: Premier papers, 3/430.

question of the wholesale movement of population, he thought that this figure would mean bringing a wholly disproportionate number of Germans into a greatly reduced Germany.

According to his own information, Churchill added, not all the Germans had fled; 'there were other figures to show that some $2\frac{1}{2}$ million remained'. Stalin disputed this, telling his colleagues:

Most of these Germans had fled to the west of the German lines during the battle, and some of them to the Koenigsberg area. They had got wind of the rumour that the Russians were in Koenigsberg[1] and they preferred Russian to Polish rule. Not a single German, therefore, remained in the area from which it was suggested that Poland should get her accessions of territory; there only remained Poles. The Germans had quit their lands between the Oder and the Vistula, and the Poles were cultivating them. It would, therefore, be unlikely that the Poles would agree to the Germans returning to cultivate these lands.

Churchill continued to argue against so drastic a transfer of German territory to Poland, telling Stalin:

... he was deeply concerned to support compensation for Poland, at the expense of Germany, for what was being taken from her (in his view quite properly) east of the Curzon Line. But he thought that there should be a balance between what Poland lost and received. Poland was now claiming vastly greater compensation than what she had been called upon to give up. He could not feel that it would be for the good of Europe that such an exaggerated movement of population should take place. If there were now three to four million Poles east of the Curzon Line, then room should be made for three or four million Poles to occupy territories to the west of Poland's pre-war frontiers.

A movement of population even on this scale would cause a great shock to the people of Great Britain. But a move of $8\frac{1}{4}$ million people would be more than he could defend. Compensation should bear some relation to loss. Nor would it be good for Poland itself to acquire so much additional territory. If the Germans had run away from the territory in question, they should be allowed to go back. The Poles had no right to pursue a policy which might well involve a catastrophe in the feeding of Germany.

If enough food could not be found to feed the Germans who had moved westward, Churchill warned, 'we should be faced with conditions in our zone of occupation such as had existed in the German concentration camps, only on a scale a thousand times greater'. The British Government did not in any case admit 'that territory in the east of Germany overrun during the war could now be regarded as having become Polish territory'.

---

[1] Also spelt Königsberg; now, as annexed by the Soviet Union in 1945, known as Kaliningrad.

These territories 'were now inhabited by Poles', said Stalin. These Poles were 'cultivating the land and producing bread. It was impossible to compel the Poles to produce bread and to give it away to the Germans.' Churchill protested that these were not normal times. The Poles were apparently selling Silesian coal to Sweden while Great Britain was facing a greater fuel shortage than at any time during the war. Britain took her stand on the 'general principle' that food and fuel from the Germany of the 1937 frontiers should be available for all Germans within them, irrespective of the zone in which they lived.

Stalin asked who was to produce the coal. The Germans were not producing it, he said, 'but the Poles were'. The German proprietors of the Silesian coalfield had fled. If they came back 'the Poles would probably hang them'. Churchill then reminded Stalin of his remark at a previous meeting about not allowing Allied policy 'to be governed by memories of injuries or by feelings of retribution', and asked Stalin to realize 'that we were faced with having a large number of Germans dumped in our area, who could not be fed unless they got food from the area which the Poles had occupied'.

Stalin said that the remarks he had made on the previous day 'did not apply to war criminals'. 'Not all the $8\frac{1}{4}$ millions who had fled were war criminals,' Churchill answered. Stalin replied that he meant the German owners of the Silesian coalmines, who had fled. Russia herself was short of coal and was buying it from Poland.

Truman now intervened to support Churchill. It seemed, he said, to be an 'accomplished fact' that the eastern area of Germany had been given to Poland, but it could not be treated separately when it came to reparations and supplies. He was quite ready to discuss Poland's western boundary, even though it could only be settled at the Peace Conference, but 'he would not be prepared to see sections of Germany given away piecemeal'.

Stalin persisted that only the Poles could cultivate these areas. The Russians were short of labour and there were no Germans. We could either stop all production or let the Poles do it. The Poles had lost a valuable coal basin to Russia, and had taken the Silesian coal basin, 'which they were now working'. Churchill pointed out that Poles had always worked in the Silesian mines, and he did not object to their doing so, 'as agents of the Russian Government', but 'he did object to Silesia being treated as though it was already part of Poland'. Stalin persisted that it was impossible to 'upset' the present state of affairs. The Germans themselves had been short of labour. As the Russians advanced into Germany they had found enterprises employing forcibly deported Italians, Bulgarians, and other nationalities, including Russians and Ukrainians. When the Red Army arrived, these foreign labourers had gone home. Great numbers of men had been mobilized in Germany, and most of them had either been killed or were in captivity. The vast German industries had used few German workers, but depended on foreign labour, 'which had now melted away'. These enterprises must either be closed down or Poles 'must be given a chance to work them'. What had happened was not the result of deliberate policy, but of 'a spontaneous course of events'. Only the Germans were to blame for this.

Stalin agreed that the Polish Government's proposals would make difficulties for Germany. 'And for the British too,' Churchill interjected. But Stalin said 'he was not averse to making additional difficulties for the Germans; indeed it was our policy to make difficulties for them and to make it impossible for them to aggress again. It was better to make difficulties for the Germans than for the Poles. Moreover, the less industry there was in Germany the more markets would be open to British trade.' [1]

Britain did not wish, replied Churchill, 'to be faced with masses of starving people in Germany'.

For the first time at Potsdam, Clement Attlee now intervened, and did so to support Churchill's argument, telling Stalin that 'pending final settlement, the resources of the whole of Germany within the 1937 frontiers would have to be treated as available for distribution, as might prove necessary, to the existing population of 1937 Germany. If a part of Germany was now arbitrarily annexed to Poland, the result would be to put a very heavy burden on the countries occupying the western and southern zones of Germany. The resources of the eastern area should be made available for the population in the west. . . .'

Truman supported Attlee. The unanimity of the Western Allies was complete. The Conference than adjourned, after agreeing to continue the discussion of Germany's eastern frontier on the following day. [2]

That night, Churchill dined with Stalin and Truman. The dinner was a short one by Conference standards, scarcely two hours, and Churchill was in bed before midnight. [3]

On the morning of Sunday July 22, Churchill received a visitor who brought startling information: Stimson was his visitor, and the information was a detailed account of the first atomic bomb test in

[1] 'P (Terminal) 5th Meeting', 5 p.m., 21 July 1945: Cabinet papers, 99/38.
[2] 'P (Terminal) 5th Meeting', 5 p.m., 21 July 1945: Cabinet papers, 99/38.
[3] Private Office diary, 21 July 1945: Thompson papers.

New Mexico. Inside a one-mile circle, Stimson told him, the devastation had been absolute. Churchill then went to see Truman; they spoke together for almost an hour. With Truman were General Marshall and Admiral Leahy. 'Up to this moment,' Churchill later recalled, 'we had shaped our ideas towards an assault upon the homeland of Japan by terrific air bombing and by the invasion of very large armies.' Churchill added:

We had contemplated the desperate resistance of the Japanese fighting to the death with Samurai devotion, not only in pitched battles, but in every cave and dug-out. I had in my mind the spectacle of Okinawa island, where many thousands of Japanese, rather than surrender, had drawn up in line and destroyed themselves by hand-grenades after their leaders had solemnly performed the rite of hara-kiri. To quell the Japanese resistance man by man and conquer the country yard by yard might well require the loss of a million American lives and half that number of British—or more if we could get them there: for we were resolved to share the agony.

Now all this nightmare picture had vanished. In its place was the vision—fair and bright indeed it seemed—of the end of the whole war in one or two violent shocks. I thought immediately myself of how the Japanese people, whose courage I had always admired, might find in the apparition of this almost supernatural weapon an excuse which would save their honour and release them from their obligation of being killed to the last fighting man.

Moreover, we should not need the Russians. The end of the Japanese war no longer depended upon the pouring in of their armies for the final and perhaps protracted slaughter. We had no need to ask favours of them.[1]

Following his talk with Truman, Marshall and Leahy, Churchill returned to his villa for lunch. The sixth Plenary session took place that afternoon. Once more the future of Poland dominated the discussion, as it had at Yalta five months earlier, and in Moscow in October 1944. Churchill now 'repeated and emphasized' the principal reasons why Britain 'could not accept' the Polish territorial demands:

  (i) The final decision on all boundary questions could only be reached at the Peace Conference. (Stalin said he agreed with this.)
 (ii) It would not be advantageous for the Polish nation to take over so large an area as they were now asking for.
(iii) It would rupture the economic unity of Germany, and throw too heavy a burden on the Powers occupying the western zones, particularly as to food and fuel.
 (iv) The British had grave moral scruples about vast movements of population. We could accept a transfer of Germans from Eastern Germany

---

[1] Winston S. Churchill, *The Second World War*, volume 6, pages 552–3.

equal in number to the Poles from Eastern Poland transferred from east of the Curzon Line—say two to three millions; but a transfer of eight or nine million Germans, which was what the Polish request involved, was too many and would be entirely wrong.

(v) The information about the number of Germans in the disputed areas was not agreed. The Soviet Government said that they had all gone. The British Government believed that great numbers, running into millions, were still there. We of course had not been able to check these figures on the spot, but we must accept them until they were shown to be wrong.

Stalin would not accept Churchill's arguments. Germany could get enough fuel from the Ruhr and the Rhineland, he insisted. There were 'no Germans left' in the territory which the Poles had occupied.

Truman said he 'could not understand the urgency of the matter'. It should be remitted to the Foreign Ministers for further discussion, and for eventual settlement at the Peace Conference, whenever that might be. But Churchill protested that the question of Poland's western frontier was indeed urgent, and he went on to explain why:

The local position would remain unremedied. The Poles, who had assigned to themselves, or had been assigned, this area would be digging themselves in and making themselves masters. He therefore very much hoped that some decision could be reached at the Conference, or at least that we should know just where we stood in this matter. He could see no advantage in the Poles being invited to the Council of Foreign Ministers in London to discuss this matter, if the Three Powers had been unable to agree at the present Conference. In the meantime, the whole burden of the fuel and food problems would remain, and would fall particularly on the British, as their zone had poor supplies of food and the largest population to sustain.

Suppose, Churchill went on, that the Council of Foreign Ministers, after hearing the Poles, could not agree—'and it appeared unlikely that they would'—the winter would be coming on with all its difficulties and it would be impossible to settle the matter without another meeting of the heads of Governments. Why not have a line which the Polish authorities could provisionally occupy as Poles, 'and agree that west of that line any Poles would be working as the agents of the Soviet Government?'

Churchill, Stalin and Truman then agreed that the new Poland should advance its western frontier 'to what might be called the line of the Oder'. The difference between Stalin and Churchill was how far this extension should reach. The words 'line of the Oder' had been used at Teheran, but, as Churchill pointed out, he had only used those words as a general expression, and this 'line of the Oder' could not be properly explained without a map. What would happen, he asked, if the Foreign Secretaries met in September and discussed Poland and again reached a deadlock 'just when the winter was upon us?' Berlin, for instance, used to get some of its fuel from Silesia.

Stalin 'interjected' to say that the coal came from Saxony. 'Some 40 per cent of the hard coal for Berlin had come from Silesia,' Churchill answered.

At this point Truman read out the crucial passage of the Yalta Declaration, namely:

The three heads of Government consider that the Eastern frontier of Poland should follow the Curzon Line, with digressions from it in some regions of five to eight kilometres in favour of Poland. They recognise that Poland must receive substantial accessions of territory in the North and West. They feel that the opinion of the new Polish Provisional Government of National Unity should be sought in due course on the extent of these accessions, and that the final delimitation of the Western frontier of Poland should thereafter await the Peace Conference.

This, said Truman, was what President Roosevelt, Stalin and Churchill had decided, and he himself was in complete accord with it. Five countries were now occupying Germany instead of four. It would have been easy enough to have agreed upon a zone for Poland, but 'he did not like the way that the Poles had occupied this area without consulting the "Big Three"'. He understood Stalin's difficulties, and he understood Churchill's. It was 'the way in which this action had been taken' that mattered.

At Teheran, said Stalin, Roosevelt and Churchill had both wanted the frontier to run along the river Oder to where the Eastern Neisse joined it, while Stalin had insisted on the far more western line of the Western Neisse. Moreover, Roosevelt and Churchill had planned to leave Stettin and Breslau on the German side of the frontier.

It was Churchill who now proposed inviting the Poles to Potsdam. This was accepted by Stalin and Truman, and the invitations were sent to Warsaw that same afternoon.

The discussion then turned to the fate of Italy's former colonies: Italian Somaliland, Eritrea, Cyrenaica and Tripolitania. 'Who had found them?' asked Stalin. 'The British Army,' Churchill told Stalin, 'through heavy losses and indisputable victories had conquered them.' Berlin 'had also been taken by the Red Army' was Stalin's riposte, to which Churchill replied:

We had suffered heavy losses, although these were nothing like so great as had unhappily been those of the valiant Soviet Armies. We came out of this war as the greatest debtor in the world; there was, also, no possibility of ever regaining sufficient Naval equality with the United States. During the war we had only built one capital ship in spite of the fact that so far as he could remember, we had lost 10 or 12. Nevertheless, in spite of these losses, we had made no territorial claims. For us there was no Königsberg, no Baltic States, nothing.

It was, therefore, with a sense of perfect rectitude and complete disinterestedness that we approached this matter. As to the Italian Colonies, we had said in the House of Commons, that Italy had lost them. That meant that she had no claim of right, but it did not at all preclude that at the final peace settlement Italy should have some of her Colonies restored to her on certain conditions.

At present Britain held these colonies, Churchill added. 'He wondered who wanted them; if there were any claimant at the table they should come forward.' The United States did not want them, answered Truman, as 'they already had enough poor Italians in the United States'. Britain had 'wondered if any of these countries would do for the Jews', Churchill remarked, 'but it appeared that the Jews were not very smitten with this suggestion'.

Later in the discussion, Churchill clashed with Stalin over a Soviet proposal for a Russian military base at the Dardanelles. 'It was also proposed,' Churchill protested, 'that no one was to have anything to do with the passage of vessels through the Straits except Russia and Turkey. He felt certain that Turkey would never agree to such a condition.' The discussion continued, as recorded in the minutes:

M. MOLOTOV said that such treaties had previously existed between Russia and Turkey.

MR CHURCHILL asked what previous treaties there had been which gave Russia military bases in the Straits.

M. MOLOTOV mentioned the Russian–Turkish Treaties of 1805 and 1833.

MR CHURCHILL said that he must ask for the opportunity to look up these ancient treaties. He would only say for the present that the Russian proposals went far beyond his earlier discussions with Premier Stalin, and he would not be prepared to press their acceptance on Turkey.

It was agreed to defer consideration of the Russian proposals to a later meeting.[1]

Commenting on the minutes of the sixth Plenary session, which he read on the morning of July 23, Admiral Cunningham noted in his diary: 'The PM is certainly keeping his end up but Truman is holding back and not giving him much support.'[2]

That night, in a thunderstorm, a lime tree outside Churchill's villa

---

[1] 'P (Terminal) 6th Meeting', 5 p.m., 22 July 1945: Cabinet papers, 99/38.
[2] Cunningham diary, 23 July 1945: Cunningham papers.

blew over, cracking the water mains as it fell. Churchill, deprived of his bath, commented to Cadogan that it was a 'most unwarranted act of Providence'.[1]

Churchill worked in bed on the morning of Monday July 23. One of his minutes that morning was to Ismay, whom he asked: 'What is being done with German rifles?' adding, 'It is a great mistake to destroy rifles. If possible, at least a couple of million should be preserved for Britain.'[2] To Eden, Churchill minuted that morning, after a talk with Byrnes: 'It is quite clear that the United States did not at the present time desire Russian participation in the war against Japan.'[3] And in a second minute to Eden, he wrote of how he was 'much disturbed' to read in the newspapers of the expulsion of Germans from Czechoslovakia. 'Of course there must be an exodus,' Churchill wrote, 'but it should be conducted with due regard to the repercussions in other countries.'[4]

At lunch on July 23 Churchill entertained the British Chiefs of Staff. 'PM now most optimistic,' Admiral Cunningham noted, 'and placing great faith in the new bomb. He now thinks it a good thing that the Russians should know about it and it may make them a little more humble.'[5] At a Staff Conference on July 23, Churchill asked the Chiefs of Staff, in preparing their case against the cut-back in American military supplies if the Lend-Lease agreements were to come to an end, to make their case more 'convincing' by including specific examples 'of where the shoe was pinching'.[6]

That afternoon, at the seventh Plenary Meeting, the first item to be discussed was Turkey, Churchill, who spoke first, reiterating 'that he could not support the fortification of the Straits by a Russian base, and he could not press the Turks to agree to this'. Stalin replied that on the previous day 'Mr Churchill had said that Russia had frightened Turkey, and that one of the main reasons was the concentration of too many Russian troops in Bulgaria. The information cited by Mr Churchill was out of date. He did not know how he had been informed by the Turks, but he was bound to say that Russia had far fewer troops in Bulgaria

[1] Cadogan diary, 23 July 1945: David Dilks (editor), *The Diaries of Sir Alexander Cadogan*, pages 769–70.
[2] Prime Minister's Personal Minute, D ('Ter') 6/5, 23 July 1945: Churchill papers, 20/209.
[3] Prime Minister's Personal Minute, M ('Ter') 11/5, 23 July 1945: Churchill papers, 20/209.
[4] Prime Minister's Personal Minute, M ('Ter') 14/5, 'Secret', 23 July 1945: Churchill papers, 20/209.
[5] Cunningham diary, 23 July 1945: Cunningham papers.
[6] Staff Conference, Chiefs of Staff Committee, 'COS (Terminal) 9th Meeting', 1.30 p.m., 23 July 1945: Cabinet papers, 120/186.

than the British had in Greece.' The discussion then continued:

MR CHURCHILL asked how many British troops Premier Stalin thought were in Greece.

PREMIER STALIN said 5 Divisions.

MR CHURCHILL said that we had only 2 Divisions—the 4th British and the 4th Indian Divisions.

PREMIER STALIN enquired whether there were any armoured divisions.

MR CHURCHILL said there was none. Speaking from memory, we had about 40,000 men in Greece. Field Marshal Alexander was here, and would be able to give a more accurate figure, if his own had been mistaken. (Later in the meeting Field Marshal Alexander confirmed Mr Churchill's statement.)

PREMIER STALIN said that he entirely accepted Mr Churchill's figures. The Russians had 30,000 men in Bulgaria. If required, the Chief of the Russian General Staff would make a report on this. There was therefore nothing for the Turks to be afraid of, particularly as the Turks had 20 to 23 Divisions on the frontier.

Stalin now spoke of the Soviet–Turkish frontier. Perhaps, he said, it was the 'suggested restoration of the pre-war frontier of Czarist Russia' which had frightened the Turks. 'He, Premier Stalin, bore in mind that Kars was part of Armenia, and Ardahan was part of Georgia. These questions of the restoration of frontiers would not have arisen if the Turks had not asked for an alliance. An alliance meant that Russia undertook to defend the Turkish frontiers in the same way as Turkey undertook to defend the Russian frontiers. Russia considered the existing frontier in the area of Kars and Ardahan to be incorrect, and had told Turkey that this must be rectified. If the Turks did not want this rectified then the question of an alliance would be dropped.'

Stalin then asked Churchill if he thought that a Soviet naval base in the Dardanelles would be acceptable to Turkey, to which Churchill replied that he thought it would be 'unacceptable'. He 'strongly suggested', however, a revision of the pre-war Montreux Convention 'with the object of securing to Russia free and unrestricted navigation through the Straits between the Black Sea and the Aegean Sea—by both merchant ships and warships, whether in peace or war'. He hoped that Stalin 'would consider this alternative rather than press for a Russian base near Constantinople'. Churchill added: 'The Kiel Canal should certainly be free and open, and guaranteed by the Great Powers. He also attached great importance to the freedom of navigation on the Rhine and the Danube.'

Stalin then turned to the Soviet request for territory in East Prussia, up to and including the port of Königsberg. Truman, who spoke first, said that 'he raised no objection to Russia acquiring a piece of German territory'. Churchill then referred to a speech he had made in the House of Commons on 15 December 1944 'in which he had mentioned that the Soviet Government desired to have the ice-free port of Königsberg, and that the Polish frontier would run to the south of this port. He had made it clear that His Majesty's Government were in sympathy with this wish.' Churchill continued:

The only question which now arose was what he might describe as the legal question of transference. At present the Soviet draft involved an admission by us all that East Prussia no longer existed, and that Königsberg and the territory around it was under the authority of the Allied Control Commission for Germany, and that Lithuania was now one of the Soviet Republics. All these were really matters for the final peace settlement. But so far as His Majesty's Government were concerned, we were ready to support the Soviet wish that the Peace Treaty should make provision for the USSR acquiring the port of Königsberg.

Mr Churchill said that he had made this statement as one of principle. He had not examined the exact line on the map, and this would be a question which would have to be examined at the Peace Conference. But he would like to assure Premier Stalin of our continuing support of the Russian position in this part of the world when the Peace Conference came.

It was at the end of this seventh Plenary session that Churchill explained that it would be necessary for him and Attlee to return to London on July 25 'so that they might be there when the results of the General Election were announced on 26th July'. He therefore proposed 'that they should leave soon after midday on 25th July and return during the afternoon of 27th July. It would be possible, therefore, to hold a Plenary Meeting during the morning of 25th July; and representatives of the British Government should be back in time to attend a Plenary Meeting in the late afternoon of 27th July.' [1]

That night it was Churchill's turn to give the banquet for the other two leaders. With Stalin came Molotov, Marshal Zhukov and General Antonov. In one of the toasts, Stalin spoke of how necessary it was for Russia to join America and Britain in the war against Japan 'and then', as Admiral Cunningham noted, 'in front of all the waitresses and stewards toasted our next meeting in Seoul or Tokyo'. [2] Churchill's own account of the evening gave a picture of Stalin both relaxed and never losing a chance to maintain the Soviet national interest:

To lighten the proceedings we changed places from time to time, and the President sat opposite me. I had another very friendly talk with Stalin, who

---

[1] 'P (Terminal) 7th Meeting', 5 p.m., 23 July 1945: Cabinet papers, 99/38.
[2] Cunningham diary, 23 July 1945: Cunningham papers.

was in the best of tempers and seemed to have no inkling of the momentous information about the new bomb the President had given me. He spoke with enthusiasm about the Russian intervention against Japan, and seemed to expect a good many months of war, which Russia would wage on an ever-increasing scale, governed only by the Trans-Siberian Railway.

Then a very odd thing happened. My formidable guest got up from his seat with the bill-of-fare card in his hand and went round the table collecting the signatures of many of those who were present. I never thought to see him as an autograph-hunter! When he came back to me I wrote my name as he desired, and we both looked at each other and laughed. Stalin's eyes twinkled with mirth and good-humour.

I have mentioned before how the toasts at these banquets were always drunk by the Soviet representatives out of tiny glasses, and Stalin had never varied from this practice. But now I thought I would take him on a step. So I filled a small-sized claret glass with brandy for him and another for myself. I looked at him significantly. We both drained our glasses at a stroke and gazed approvingly at one another. After a pause Stalin said, 'If you find it impossible to give us a fortified position in the Marmara, could we not have a base at Dedeagatch?' I contented myself with saying, 'I will always support Russia in her claim to the freedom of the seas all the year round.'[1]

That night, Lord Moran noted, Churchill put a telephone call through to Lord Beaverbrook in London. Did Beaverbrook still believe, as he had done on Polling Day, that the Conservatives would get a majority of a hundred, Churchill asked. 'The figure of a hundred was not sacrosanct,' Beaverbrook replied, 'but, broadly speaking, he had not altered his estimate. The PM would have a comfortable majority.'[2]

On the morning of July 24 Churchill joined President Truman at the Berlin 'White House' for a meeting of the Combined Chiefs of Staff, who presented their final report.[3] Churchill then raised with Truman the question of the future of Lend-Lease. As a result of agreements reached early in the war, he explained, 'many British units were equipped with United States equipment and no provision had been made to replace this equipment from British sources. To make

[1] Winston S. Churchill, *The Second World War*, volume 6, page 579. The Greek port of Dedeagatch is on the Aegean Sea, near the border with Turkey.

[2] Moran diary, 23 July 1945: Moran, *The Struggle for Survival*, pages 280–3. 'At Potsdam I used to go each evening to Winston's village at Babelsberg,' Field Marshal Alexander later recalled. 'Anthony Eden used to come in. Winston would say: "What do the Party say now about the election result?" And Anthony would reply: "They still think we'll get in by a majority of about seventy."' (Field Marshal Earl Alexander of Tunis, recollections: in conversation with the author, 28 December 1968.)

[3] 'J.S (Terminal) 11 (Final)', 23 July 1945: Cabinet papers, 99/39.

such provision would take time and he hoped very much that the President would be able to make it possible for him to pass smoothly from this position of dependence on the United States to one in which British forces could be independent.' Churchill went on to explain to Truman his fear 'that a rigid interpretation of an undertaking to maintain the British war-making capacity only in so far as it was connected with the prosecution of the war against Japan, would place him in great difficulties. He hoped also that the rules applied to the supply of Lend-Lease equipment would not be held to limit British sovereign rights over British equipment. He must be free to give British equipment, for example, to the Belgians, if His Majesty's Government felt that this was desirable, and he hoped that this would not result in the drying up of equivalent supplies from the United States.'

Truman replied that he was 'striving' to give the Lend-Lease Act 'the broadest interpretation possible'. He must, however, ask Churchill 'to be patient as he wished to avoid any embarrassment with Congress over the interpretation of the Act and it might be necessary for him to ask for additional legislation in order to clear the matter up'.[1]

After a short talk alone with Truman, Churchill walked back to his own villa for lunch. After lunching alone, he saw Alexander for a few moments, and then, in an attempt to come to a preliminary agreement on Poland before the Plenary session, he received eight members of the new Polish Government, led by Boleslaw Bierut and Edward Morawski.

Churchill began the discussion by reminding the Poles that Britain had entered the war in September 1939 because Poland had been invaded: 'We had always taken the greatest interest in Poland and would not be satisfied unless Poland emerged from the war strong and independent with worthy territory to live in.' Churchill continued:

We had exerted ourselves greatly during the past year to ensure that Poland should enjoy such a position. Our relations with Soviet Russia were warm and friendly. We wanted Poland to be friendly to the Russians but also independent of them. We could not tolerate a Poland that plotted against Soviet Russia, who had the right to have a friendly Poland on her frontiers. A hostile Poland would be a disaster for Russia. There was, however, little danger of that. Although many Poles hated Russia the great majority were now agreed that it was essential to them to live in friendship with their eastern neighbour.

Britain had always been the champion of 'a strong and independent Poland', Churchill reiterated, but she was not a supporter of the frontiers which Poland had now been offered, 'and apparently wished

---

[1] 'Minutes of the 1st (and only) Plenary Session Between the United States and Great Britain, Held At 2 Kaiser Strasse, Babelsberg, Germany', 11.30 a.m., 24 July 1945: Cabinet papers, 99/39.

to take'. Casting his mind back to the discussions at Teheran and Yalta, Churchill told Bierut and his fellow Poles:

We had thought in terms rather of a frontier that might extend to the Oder in some places but would not follow its whole length. Now Poland was claiming a frontier on the Western Neisse. It was a mistake for countries to be guided purely by territorial appetite. The frontiers now claimed by Poland would involve the loss by Germany of one quarter of the arable land she possessed in 1937. It would mean the movement of from eight to nine million persons, whereas the total number of Poles displaced from east of the Curzon Line amounted to only three to four millions. The idea of such great shiftings of population came as a shock to the Western democracies.

The Poles should keep within the limits necessary to give Poland an adequate home. Their present claims would not constitute a lasting and final arrangement. They would not receive the blessing of Great Britain nor probably of the Western democracies as a whole. It was dangerous for a country to bite off more than it could chew.

In opposing the Oder–Neisse Line, Churchill said, Britain was 'not moved in any way by ill-will towards Poland', but was 'convinced that there was a danger that the Poles might go too far in pressing towards the West just as they had once pressed too far to the East'.

It was not only the territorial issue but also the political issue 'which troubled us', Churchill told Bierut, and he went on to explain:

There were other matters which troubled us. If British opinion were to be reassured about developments in Poland it was essential that the elections that were to be held should be genuinely free and unfettered, and that all the main democratic parties should have full opportunity to participate and make their programmes known.

It would be asked what was the definition of democratic parties. He did not take the view that only Communists were democrats. It was easy to call everyone who was not a Communist a Fascist beast. But between these two extremes there lay great and powerful forces which were neither one nor the other and had no intention of being one or the other.

Surely it was to Poland's advantage that the basis of political life should be widened to include as many as possible of these moderate elements instead of branding with the stigmas of war all those who did not fit the pre-conceived definitions of the extremists.

Churchill then appealed for an all-Party government as the basis for a truly democratic Poland, telling Bierut:

Anyone with power could now in the present distracted state of Europe strike at his opponents and condemn them, but the result was merely that the moderate elements were excluded from political life. It took all sorts to make a country. Could Poland afford to divide herself? She should seek a unity as broad as possible so that she might join hands with the West as well as with her Russian friends.

For example, it would be important that the Christian Democrat Party and all those sections of the National Democrat Party not compromised by active collaboration with the enemy should take part in the elections. M. Popiel should be given full opportunity to revive his party and to take part in the restoration of Polish political life.[1]

We should also expect that the press, and naturally our Embassy, should enjoy full freedom to see and report what was happening in Poland before and during the elections.

Only by pursuing a policy of tolerance and even, on occasion, mutual forgiveness could Poland preserve the regard and support of the Western democracies, and especially of Great Britain, who had something to give and also something to withhold.

Bierut made no reply to Churchill's appeal for political democracy. Instead, he spoke only of the territorial aspects. 'Poland did not claim more than she had lost,' he said. 'To satisfy her claims it would be necessary to shift only $1\frac{1}{2}$ million Germans (inclusive of those in East Prussia), who were all that remained.' Poland needed new territory 'to settle four million Poles from east of the Curzon Line, and some three million who would return from abroad'. She would have less territory than before the war. 'She had lost valuable agricultural land round Vilna, and valuable forests (Poland was always poor in timber) as well as the oil-fields of Galicia.' Before the war some 800,000 Polish farm hands had already migrated as seasonal workers to Eastern Germany. A majority of the population in the areas claimed, especially in Silesia, 'were really Poles, though attempts had been made to Germanise them'. These territories were 'historically' Polish. East Prussia still retained 'a large Polish population in the Masurians'.

Churchill interrupted Bierut's territorial survey to point out 'that there was no dispute about the cession to Poland of East Prussia south and west of Königsberg', to which Bierut replied by speaking of the Oder–Neisse line. 'It would be found,' he said, 'that the boundary they proposed was the shortest possible frontier line between Poland and Germany. It would give Poland just compensation for her losses and her contribution to Allied victory.' The Poles, Bierut ended, believed

---

[1] Karol Popiel, Chairman of the Christian Labour Party, had been Minister of State in the Polish Government in exile in London. On 24 August 1945 the Labour Government spokesman for Foreign Affairs informed the House of Commons that Popiel had returned from London to Poland and had been given 'more than reasonable facilities for organizing and restoring his party'. A year earlier, Popiel had supported a Polish Government in exile plan to induce the United States to attempt to secure for Poland the city of Lvov and the oil district of Eastern Galicia.

that the British people 'would sympathise with their wish that Poland's wrongs should be righted'.

Hitherto, Churchill noted, 'it had been impossible for us to find out for ourselves how matters stood in Poland, since it was a closed area. Could we not send people with full freedom to move about in Poland and tell us what was happening there?'

Bierut made no reply, and in a final comment Churchill 'repeated his warning', as the minutes noted, 'that though he was in favour of ample compensation for Poland, he thought the Poles were ill-advised to ask for as much territory as they were now seeking'.[1]

Bierut agreed to see Churchill again on the following morning. Churchill then returned yet again to the Cecilienhof, for the eighth Plenary session. Churchill contrasted Russia's unrestricted access, should she want it, as an observer of the political process in Italy, with the situation confronting the British military and diplomatic representatives in Roumania and Bulgaria, adding forcefully that Stalin 'would be astonished to read the catalogue of incidents to our missions in Bucharest and Sofia. They were not free to go abroad. An iron curtain had been rung down.'

These, said Stalin, 'were fairy tales', but Churchill assured him that they were not; he had confirmed them, he said, 'from our diplomatic representative and our military representative[2] at Bucharest, whom he had known personally for many years. The conditions of our mission there had been most painful, and had caused great distress. It was not for him to say what were the experiences of the United States representatives. But when our people went out in motor cars, they were closely followed wherever they went, and every movement they made was supervised. Moreover, great delay had been imposed upon the aircraft used for our Mission.'

Stalin then proposed a formula 'about the four satellite countries' which he wanted to be agreed to by Churchill and Truman. The formula read: 'The three Governments agreed to consider, each separately, in the immediate future, the question of the establishing of diplomatic relations with Finland, Roumania, Bulgaria and Hungary.' After Truman had said that he saw 'no objection' to this, the discussion continued:

MR CHURCHILL said that he was not sure that he understood where we stood in this matter. Was there not a risk that we were covering up with

---

[1] 'Conversations with the representatives of the Polish Provisional Government, 24th July to 1st August 1945', 'Meeting at the Prime Minister's Residence, Potsdam', 3.15 p.m., 24 July 1945: Cabinet papers, 99/38.

[2] Air Vice-Marshal Stevenson, who from 1938 to 1941 had been Director of Home Operations, Air Ministry.

words a real difference of view between us? He had understood President Truman to say that he was not prepared to recognise the present Governments of Roumania and Bulgaria. Had he understood the position correctly?

PRESIDENT TRUMAN said that the present arrangement committed them to examine separately the question of the recognition of these countries.

MR CHURCHILL feared that verbal agreement would make for difficulties, if the underlying difference was not resolved. An impression would be created that we intended to recognise these countries speedily.

PREMIER STALIN suggested that the President himself should say which Governments he was prepared to recognise. He did not accept Mr Churchill's point of view. The fact that it was intended to prepare Peace Treaties with these countries (as shown in the new paragraph suggested by the United States Delegation at the Foreign Secretaries' Meeting) meant that recognition of these countries was imminent.

Returning to the question of the Dardanelles, Stalin again put forward the Soviet request for a naval base, to which Churchill replied 'that an international guarantee would be more than a substitute for the erection of fortifications'. The question of a guarantee, Stalin commented, 'was not yet ripe'. The Turks 'were more likely to agree to an international guarantee', Churchill commented, 'than to a large fort being erected near Constantinople'. 'Very likely,' was Stalin's reply, 'but he was not sure.'

Churchill then raised the question of the Ukrainians being held in British prisoner-of-war camps in Italy, former soldiers in German military units, whom Russia now wished to see repatriated, under the agreement concluded at Yalta. 'These 10,000,' Churchill pointed out, 'were in the process of being sifted by the Russian Mission at Rome and that Mission had been given full access to the camp. The personnel in the camp were said to be mainly non-Soviet Ukrainians and included numbers of Poles who, so far as we could find out, had not been domiciled within the 1939 frontiers of Russia. Six hundred and sixty-five of these prisoners wished to return to Russia and their wish would immediately be fulfilled. We would also hand over immediately any others who would go without the use of force.' The question of 'how much force could be used', Churchill added, 'was one that must be fully considered and very carefully handled'.

Under the agreement which they had signed, Stalin declared, each side was bound 'not to raise any obstacle to the return to their native land of anybody who wished to go'.

Churchill replied that Stalin should send the Soviet General 'who was concerned with these matters' to discuss them at Field Marshal Alexander's headquarters in Italy. Stalin agreed, telling Churchill 'that the matter could be regarded as disposed of'.

To Truman's suggestion that 'as the Prime Minister was going away to England for two days' a communiqué should be drawn up on the decisions made so far, Churchill agreed, commenting 'that it was wise to put the fish in the basket as they were caught'.[1]

There was also a message to be sent to Japan, offering her 'an opportunity to end the war'. What had happened to Germany, the message read, 'stands forth in awful clarity as an example to the people of Japan'. The 'full application' of Allied military power, 'backed by our resolve, will mean the inevitable and complete destruction of the Japanese forces, and just as inevitably the utter devastation of the Japanese homeland'. It was now for Japan to decide 'whether she will continue to be controlled' by those who had brought Japan 'to the threshold of annihilation', or whether she would follow 'the path of reason'.

The Big Three then set out their 'terms', adding that there were no alternatives, and that 'We shall brook no delay'. The influence and authority of those who had 'deceived and misled' the people of Japan would have to be 'eliminated for all time'. The Japanese forces would have to be 'completely disarmed'. Japanese sovereignty would be limited to the four main islands of Japan 'and such minor islands as we determine'. Freedom of speech, of religion and of thought, 'as well as respect for fundamental human rights', would be established. In return, Japan would be allowed to maintain 'such industries as will sustain her economy' and would be permitted 'eventual participation in world trade relations'. The message ended:

> We call upon the Government of Japan to proclaim now the unconditional surrender of all the Japanese armed forces, and to provide proper and adequate assurances of their good faith in such action. The alternative for Japan is complete and utter destruction.[2]

As soon as this eighth Plenary session ended, Churchill later recalled, 'we all got up from the round table and stood about in twos or threes before dispersing'. It was then that he saw Truman go up to Stalin, and the two men speak together alone with only their interpreters. Churchill's account continued:

> I was perhaps five yards away, and I watched with the closest attention the momentous talk. I knew what the President was going to do. What was vital to measure was its effect on Stalin.
>
> I can see it all as if it were yesterday! He seemed to be delighted. A new bomb! Of extraordinary power! Probably decisive on the whole Japanese war! What a bit of luck!

---

[1] 'P (Terminal) 8th Meeting', 5 p.m., 24 July 1945: Cabinet papers, 99/38.
[2] This message was made public on 26 July 1945. It was rejected by the Japanese Government.

This was my impression at the moment, and I was sure that he had no idea of the significance of what he was being told. Evidently in his intense toils and stresses the atomic bomb had played no part. If he had had the slightest idea of the revolution in world affairs which was in progress his reactions would have been obvious. Nothing would have been easier than for him to say, 'Thank you so much for telling me about your new bomb. I of course have no technical knowledge. May I send my expert in these nuclear sciences to see your expert tomorrow morning?' But his face remained gay and genial and the talk between these two potentates soon came to an end.

As we were waiting for our cars I found myself near Truman. 'How did it go?' I asked. 'He never asked a question,' he replied. I was certain therefore that at that date Stalin had no special knowledge of the vast process of research upon which the United States and Britain had been engaged for so long, and of the production for which the United States had spent over four hundred million pounds in an heroic gamble.[1]

It had been 'anticipated', Churchill told Lord Camrose two weeks later, 'that when he received this information Stalin would express congratulations and then ask if his people might be allowed to get particulars of the design and manufacture of the bomb'. Churchill had decided, Camrose noted, that Stalin 'should then be told that as he had refused in the past to communicate any particulars of new discoveries made by Russian scientists and manufacturers, he would be refused particulars of the new bomb until he had come to a more reciprocal turn of mind. Churchill did not get Truman to say definitely that they would adopt this policy, but thought he would have been able to persuade him in the end. However, Stalin just expressed congratulations and, much to their surprise, did not ask for particulars.'[2]

That night Churchill dined alone with Admiral Mountbatten, who had arrived in Potsdam that afternoon. Churchill told his South-East Asia Commander-in-Chief about the atom bomb, and that the Americans proposed to drop it in early August. 'He advised me to take all necessary steps,' Mountbatten wrote in his diary, 'to complete the capitulation as soon after that date as possible.' Churchill also invited Mountbatten to call on him in Downing Street next time he was in London. 'We will talk about your future,' Churchill told him, 'as I have great plans in store.' 'It was a mournful and eerie feeling,' Mountbatten noted that night, 'to sit there talking plans with a man who seemed so confident that they would come off, and I felt equally confident that he would be out of office within 24 hours.'[3]

That night Churchill had 'an unpleasant dream', telling Lord

[1] Winston S. Churchill, *The Second World War*, volume 6, pages 579–80.

[2] 'Notes of Interview with Churchill at DT Offices, Tuesday, August 7th, 1945': Camrose papers. Lord Camrose was then Chairman of the *Daily Telegraph*.

[3] Mountbatten diary, 24 July 1945: Philip Ziegler, *Mountbatten*, London 1985, page 299.

Moran in the morning: 'I dreamed that life was over. I saw—it was very vivid—my dead body under a white sheet on a table in an empty room. I recognized my bare feet projecting from under the sheet. It was very life-like.' Churchill added: 'Perhaps this is the end.' [1]

At ten o'clock on the morning of Wednesday July 25 Churchill again saw Bierut, to try to resolve the Polish impasse. Hitherto, said Churchill, he and Bierut had 'been on opposite sides, but that he was very glad that an arrangement had now been reached'. Speaking of the 'future development' of Poland, Bierut told Churchill this war 'provided an opportunity for new social developments'. Did this mean, asked Churchill, 'that in the chaos caused by war, Poland was to plunge into Communism? He was opposed to that, but it was of course a purely Polish affair.' According to his ideas, Bierut replied, Poland would be 'far from Communist', living on friendly terms with the Soviet Union and wanting to profit from the Soviet Union's experiences, but not wishing 'to copy the Soviet system'. The Polish nation, Bierut insisted, would not consent to the Soviet system 'since they had different traditions. Even if any attempt were made to impose such a system by force the Polish nation would probably resist. Poland would develop on lines of her own.'

Churchill suggested to Bierut that 'the democratic development of Czechoslovakia before the war had been on sound lines'. Internal developments in Poland, he stressed, were for the Poles to decide, but 'would affect relations between our two countries'. He agreed, however, that there was room for reform in Poland, 'especially in the matter of the great landed estates'.

In reply, Bierut said that Poland's development 'would be based on the principles of Western democracy', and he went on to mention 'the English model', to which Churchill replied that 'he attached particular importance to free elections. Not only one side must be able to put up candidates. There must be free speech so that everyone can argue matters out and everyone can vote.' This, Churchill added, 'had recently been happening in Great Britain. He hoped that Poland too would have such free elections and take pride in them.' As for the Poles returning from abroad, he would do 'all in his power' to persuade them to do so, but they must be enabled to start their life again 'on honourable terms with their fellow countrymen'. Poland must also have courts of law 'independent of the executive'. The latest phase of

[1] Moran diary, 25 July 1945: *The Struggle for Survival*, page 285.

development in the Balkans, Churchill warned, 'had not been towards Sovietization so much as in the direction of police government'. The Western democracies viewed such happenings 'with aversion'. He hoped that there would be 'an improvement in such matters' in Poland. 'Was, for instance,' he asked, 'the NKVD leaving the country?' [1]

'Generally speaking,' Bierut replied, 'the whole Russian army was leaving.' The NKVD 'played no part in Poland at present'. The Polish Security Police were 'independent' and under the control of the Polish Government. Bierut then sought to assure Churchill that 'he shared the Prime Minister's views on elections and democratic life'; Poland 'would be one of the most democratic countries in Europe'. Some '99 per cent of the population were Catholics'. There was 'no intention to limit the development of Catholic sentiments'. The clergy, 'generally speaking', were satisfied with the present conditions.

Churchill then told Bierut: 'Great Britain wanted nothing for herself in Poland but only to see Poland strong, happy, prosperous and free.' Elections should be based on as broad a franchise as possible. 'Not all people had been equal to the terrible events of the German occupations. The strong resisted but many average people bowed their heads. Not all people could be martyrs or heroes. It would be wise now to bring all back into the main stream of political life.'

The elections in Poland, said Bierut, 'would in his view be even more democratic than those in England'. Internal Polish political relations would develop 'more and more harmoniously following the general lines of English political life'. He wished the Poles 'all success', was Churchill's reply.

Turning to the question of Poland's western frontier, Churchill told Bierut that he had been ready to support Polish claims up to the Oder at some points but not along its whole length. Now the Poles were asking too much. In consequence there might be failure to reach agreement: 'We and the Americans might pursue one policy on our side and the Russians another.' That, warned Churchill, 'would have serious consequences'.

The meeting was nearly at an end. He hoped, said Churchill, that Bierut, 'was getting on well with' Mikolajczyk.[2] He had 'always

---

[1] The NKVD was a successor to the CHEKA (Extraordinary Commission) set up by Lenin in 1917 'to combat counter-revolution'; renamed GPU (State Political Administration) in 1922, then OGPU (Unified State Political Administration) in 1924, then NKVD (Peoples' Commissariat of Home Affairs) in 1934, then MVD (Ministry of Internal Affairs) in 1946, then, after Stalin's death, KGB (Committee of State Security).

[2] Stanislaw Mikolajczyk, the Polish Peasant Party leader between the wars, had been Prime Minister of the Polish Government in London in 1943 and 1944. He returned to Poland in 1945; in June he had entered the Provisional Government as Minister of Agriculture and Vice Premier. Not allowed any real responsibility, and fearing a show-down, after being publicly denounced as a traitor, in October 1947 he fled from Poland. He died in Washington in 1966.

pressed' Mikolajczyk to return to Poland. 'We wanted all Poles to return.' He looked to Bierut 'to make the most of his present opportunities to encourage Poles abroad to go back and help to build the free, happy and prosperous Poland which we wished to see'.[1]

The discussion between Churchill and Bierut had lasted fifty minutes: the gulf was clearly unbridgeable between the two men, and between the systems which they represented. The Poland for which Britain had gone to war in 1939 no longer existed.

At eleven o'clock Churchill was back at the Cecilienhof, for the ninth Plenary session. Once more, he urged that Poland's western frontier could not be settled without taking into account the million and a half Germans who were still in the area 'claimed by the Poles'. Truman agreed, warning Stalin that he was 'not prepared to abuse' his wartime presidential powers, which were 'unlimited', by invoking them for purposes 'for which they were not intended'. Churchill, speaking after Truman, emphasized how important for the success of the Conference was the settlement of the Polish question, and the other questions 'bound up with it, such as reparations and the feeding of Germany'. Churchill added:

If the Poles were allowed to assume the position of a fifth occupying Power, without arrangements being made for spreading the food produced in Germany equally over the whole German population and without agreement being reached on a reparations plan or a definition of war booty, it must be admitted that the Conference would have failed. It was his earnest hope that a broad agreement would be reached on this net-work of problems lying at the very heart of their work. So far, however, no progress had been made towards such an agreement.

In reply, Stalin said that a more important question was that of obtaining for the rest of Germany supplies of coal and metals from the Ruhr. This led to a long and stern altercation during which Churchill strenuously opposed using the coal of the Ruhr for the Russian zone of Germany, or for Poland, without any reciprocal arrangement, such as food for the Ruhr. If the miners in the Ruhr did not get food, Churchill argued, they could not produce coal. 'There was still a good deal of fat left in Germany' was Stalin's reply.

Churchill did not accept Stalin's argument, telling the Soviet leader that the British Government would be 'glad' to send coal from the

---

[1] 'A meeting between the Prime Minister and M. Bierut at the Prime Minister's House, Potsdam', 10 a.m., 25 July 1945: Cabinet papers, 99/38.

Ruhr to Poland, 'provided they received in exchange food for the German miners who produced the coal'.

No agreement was reached; only a decision 'to defer consideration of this matter until a later meeting'.[1]

It was 12.15 p.m.; the ninth Plenary session of the Potsdam Conference was over. There seemed to be no need for farewells; both Truman and Stalin expected to see their fellow leader back at Potsdam within forty-eight hours. Churchill hurried back to his villa and then, a few minutes later, was driven to Gatow airfield. At 1.23 p.m. his aircraft took off for Britain.

During nine days of intense negotiation, Churchill had achieved three definite victories: agreement to respect the integrity of the eastern frontier of Turkey, agreement to withdraw all Soviet as well as British and American troops from Persia, and agreement to allow Britain and the United States a part in the occupation of Vienna. Only on Poland – its political future and its frontiers – had Churchill failed to gain the concessions from Stalin for which he had fought so hard, first at Teheran in 1943, and then at Yalta earlier in 1945.

[1] 'P (Terminal) 9th Meeting', 11 a.m., 25 July 1945: Cabinet papers, 99/38.

6
Defeat

A T 2.45 on the afternoon of Wednesday 25 July 1945, Churchill's aircraft landed at Northolt from Berlin. Waiting for him were his wife, his brother, Lady Mountbatten and Jock Colville.[1] On reaching No. 10 Annexe, Churchill was greeted by his son Randolph, and by one of the most senior figures in the Conservative Party, Sir Robert Topping. The decision of the electors would be known within twenty-four hours. At Labour Party headquarters, Colville noted in his diary, 'they expected a Government majority of 30'.[2] This was, however, fifty less than Randolph Churchill's earlier estimate, and Stalin's.

That evening Churchill had an audience with the King, to whom he reported on the Potsdam deliberations so far. He also discussed with the King the proposed visit by President Truman to Britain, and the arrangements for the King and Truman to meet. Churchill then returned to the Annexe, where Beaverbrook was waiting to see him. That night he dined with his wife, his son, his daughter Mary and his brother Jack. Randolph, as Mary Churchill recalled, 'was full of confidence'. But Diana and Duncan Sandys, who came in after dinner, 'were gloomy about Duncan's fate in Norwood'.[3] After dinner they were joined by Brendan Bracken.[4] That night Churchill worked until 1.15 a.m., then went to bed 'in the belief', as he later wrote, 'that the British people would wish me to continue my work'. His account continued:

My hope was that it would be possible to reconstitute the National Coalition Government in the proportions of the new House of Commons. Thus

---

[1] Marian Holmes diary, 25 July 1945: Marian Walker Spicer papers.

[2] Colville diary, 25 July 1945: Colville papers.

[3] Mary Soames, *Clementine Churchill*, page 385. Sandys had been the Member of Parliament for Norwood since the previous General Election in 1935.

[4] Private Office diary, 25 July 1945: Thompson papers.

slumber. However, just before dawn I woke suddenly with a sharp stab of almost physical pain. A hitherto subconscious conviction that we were beaten broke forth and dominated my mind. All the pressure of great events, on and against which I had mentally so long maintained my 'flying speed', would cease and I should fall. The power to shape the future would be denied me. The knowledge and experience I had gathered, the authority and goodwill I had gained in so many countries, would vanish. I was discontented at the prospect, and turned over at once to sleep again.[1]

Churchill worked in bed for only an hour on the morning of July 26. The first telegram which he dictated was to Truman, making plans for the President to fly to Plymouth as soon as the Potsdam Conference was ended, to join the battleship *Augusta* for the voyage back to the United States. Churchill told Truman: 'The King feels he would not like you to touch our shores without having an opportunity of meeting you. He would therefore be in a British cruiser in Plymouth Sound, and would be very glad if you would lunch with him. He would then pay a return visit to *Augusta* before she sailed.'[2]

To the Prime Minister of Australia, Churchill sent news that the Combined Chiefs of Staff, meeting in Potsdam, had agreed that a Commonwealth Land Force and assault shipping, and if possible a small Commonwealth Tactical Air Force, 'should take part in the main operations against Japan'.[3]

At ten o'clock, while Churchill was still in his bedroom, the first results, ten Labour gains over the Conservatives, reached the Map Room which Captain Pim, his map expert for all five years of war, had specially fitted up for him to enable the election results to be followed as they came in. Pim went at once to the bedroom. 'The Prime Minister was in his bath,' Pim later recalled, 'and certainly appeared surprised if not shocked. He asked me to get him a towel and in a few minutes clad in his blue siren suit and with cigar he was in his chair in the Map Room—where he remained all day.'[4]

In the Map Room with Churchill were his daughter Sarah and his brother Jack. Also present were Lord Margesson, Lord Beaverbrook, Brendan Bracken and Jock Colville. Every time there was a Conservative gain, Pim later recalled, 'he offered me a brandy. I think there were only three during the day.'[5] 'After half an hour,' noted

[1] Winston S. Churchill, *The Second World War*, volume 6, page 583.

[2] Prime Minister to President No. 104, Prime Minister's Personal Telegram, T.1244/5, 'Onward' No. 220, 'Personal and Top Secret', 26 July 1945: Churchill papers, 20/222.

[3] Prime Minister's Personal Telegram, T.1246/5, No. 260 to Australia, 'Top Secret and Personal', 26 July 1945: Churchill papers, 20/222. Following John Curtin's death on 5 July 1945, and after a brief interim period, Joseph Chifley had become Prime Minister of Australia (on July 13), a post he was to hold until 19 December 1949.

[4] Sir Richard Pim recollections, typescript: Pim papers.

[5] Sir Richard Pim recollections: in conversation with the author, 1975.

Colville in his diary, 'it was clear that there was going to be a landslide to the left.' [1]

At one o'clock the BBC news confirmed the apparent landslide to Labour. Eden, who was in his Midland constituency, at once telephoned Churchill to commiserate with him. 'Mr Churchill's mood at that moment,' he later recalled, 'was not to resign, but to meet Parliament as a Government and let Labour turn us out.' Eden advised no decision until more returns were in. 'If defeat were then beyond dispute,' he felt, 'it would be better to go at once. The Prime Minister grunted and asked me to get back to London as soon as I could.' [2]

The once-hoped-for Conservative majority of 100, 80 or even 30 had disappeared. The Labour Party, with 393 seats, had won an absolute majority of 146 over all other parties. The Liberals had been reduced to a mere 12. The Conservative seats had fallen from the 585 of the previous General Election in 1935 to 213. The Labour vote, for the first time in British history, was higher than the Conservative vote: 11,995,152 as against 9,988,306. Even as Eden was hurrying southward, Churchill made up his mind to resign.

Shortly after one o'clock, Clementine and Mary Churchill reached the Annexe from Woodford, where at the declaration of the Poll they had heard the returning officer announce that Churchill had been re-elected with a majority of 17,000 over his one opponent, an Independent. [3] On their way to the Map Room, they met Colville, 'looking grave', as Mary Churchill later wrote. 'It's a complete debacle,' he told them, 'like 1906.' [4] In the Map Room, Mary Churchill recalled, 'we found my father, David Margesson (former Chief Government Whip and Minister) and Brendan Bracken; the results were rolling in, showing Labour gain after Labour gain. It was now one o'clock, and it was already quite clear that the Conservatives were defeated. Every minute brought news of the defeat of friends, relations and colleagues; Randolph and Duncan were both out; everyone looked dazed and grave.' [5]

Luncheon was at 1.30; there were three guests, Beaverbrook, Margesson and Bracken, and five members of the Churchill family, Chur-

---

[1] Colville diary, 26 July 1945: Colville papers.

[2] Eden recollections: Lord Avon, *The Eden Memoirs, The Reckoning*, London 1965, page 549.

[3] The voting was: Churchill (Conservative), 27,688; Hancock (Independent), 10,488. The Liberal and Labour Parties had both agreed not to put up a candidate against the Prime Minister. Ten years earlier, at the previous General Election (14 November 1935) Churchill had received 34,849 votes as against 14,430 cast for the Liberal and 9,758 for the Labour candidate, giving him a majority of 20,419.

[4] In 1906 a 268 Conservative majority had been replaced by a 270 Liberal majority (Churchill, elected in 1900 as a Conservative, had been returned in 1906 as a Liberal).

[5] Mary Soames, *Clementine Churchill*, page 386.

chill himself, his wife, his daughters Sarah and Mary, and his brother John.[1] 'We lunched in Stygian gloom,' Mary Churchill recalled. 'Papa struggled to accept this terrible blow.'[2] 'To my dying day,' Lord Margesson wrote to Churchill six years later, 'I shall never forget the courage and forbearance you showed at that most unhappy luncheon after defeat was known. It was a terrific example of how to take it on the chin without flinching.'[3]

There was no longer any doubt that the Labour victory would be a substantial one. 'It may well be a blessing in disguise', was Clementine Churchill's comment. 'At the moment,' replied Churchill, 'it seems quite effectively disguised.'[4]

That afternoon, Churchill's Private Office diary noted: 'Sir Alan Lascelles called to see the Prime Minister and to discuss with him constitutional measures consequent upon the defeat of the Government.' Churchill then sat for a while in a small room next to his Private Secretaries' office. 'Well, you know what has happened?' he asked his doctor. Lord Moran spoke of the 'ingratitude' of the British people. 'Oh no,' Churchill answered him, 'I wouldn't call it that. They have had a very hard time.'[5]

Churchill's mind was made up. He would not seek, as he was constitutionally entitled to do, to remain Prime Minister until the recall of Parliament a few days later, and after the crucial concluding sessions of the Potsdam Conference. 'My dear Attlee,' he wrote from No. 10 Annexe that afternoon, 'In consequence of the electoral decision recorded today, I propose to tender my resignation to the King at seven o'clock this evening. On personal grounds I wish you all success in the heavy burden you are about to assume.'[6]

The gloom at No. 10 Annexe was considerable. At one point, unable any longer to watch the procession of Conservative losses in the Map Room, Mary Churchill crossed the corridor to the small kitchen. There she found Mrs Landemare, Churchill's devoted cook housekeeper. She was making honey sandwiches. 'I don't know *what* the world's coming to,' she exclaimed, 'but I thought I might make some tea.'[7]

---

[1] 'Lunch, Annexe, Thursday July 26th', Clementine Churchill's luncheon book: Lady Soames papers.

[2] Mary Churchill diary, 26 July 1945: Mary Soames, *Clementine Churchill*, page 386.

[3] 'My dear Winston', undated (October 1951): Churchill papers, 2/463.

[4] Winston S. Churchill, *The Second World War*, volume 6, page 583. In a letter to Thomas E. Dewey, defeated presidential candidate in 1948, Churchill wrote of Dewey's 'dignity and poise' with which he received the defeat, and he added: 'Such experiences are not agreeable, as I know all too well myself.' ('My dear Dewey', 'Private', 28 February 1949: Churchill papers, 2/263.)

[5] Moran diary, 26 July 1945: Moran, *The Struggle for Survival*, page 286.

[6] Letter of 26 July 1945: Churchill papers, 20/194.

[7] Lady Soames recollections: remarks at the unveiling of a plaque in the corridor of No. 10 Annexe, 17 July 1986.

At seven o'clock that evening Churchill turned to Richard Pim with the words: 'Fetch me my carriage and I shall go to the Palace and hand in my seals of office.' Pim reflected: 'My carriage! It was his old Humber car.'[1] Leaving the Annexe, Churchill drove to Buckingham Palace, where he tendered his resignation to the King. The King accepted; then offered Churchill the Order of the Garter, the highest order of chivalry. Churchill asked leave to decline. 'For me,' he explained five days later to Sir Alan Lascelles, 'I felt that the times were too sad for honours or rewards,' and he added: 'After all, my great reward is the kindness and intimacy with which the King has treated me during these hard and perilous years which we have endured and enjoyed in common.'[2]

From Buckingham Palace, Churchill returned to No. 10 Annexe, no longer Prime Minister. To those awaiting him he 'confessed', one of them reported a few days later, 'that it was distressing after all these years to abandon the reins of power'. 'But at least, Sir,' someone said, 'while you held the reins, you managed to win the race.' 'Yes,' Churchill replied, 'I won the race—and now they have warned me off the turf.'[3]

That evening Churchill prepared a statement, which was sent to the Press at 8.45, and read out by the BBC newsreaders on the nine o'clock news. The statement read:

The decision of the British people has been recorded in the votes counted to-day. I have therefore laid down the charge which was placed upon me in darker times. I regret that I have not been permitted to finish the work against Japan. For this however all plans and preparations have been made, and the results may come much quicker than we have hitherto been entitled to expect. Immense responsibilities abroad and at home fall upon the new Government, and we must all hope that they will be successful in bearing them.

It only remains for me to express to the British people, for whom I have acted in these perilous years, my profound gratitude for the unflinching, unswerving support which they have given me during my task, and for the many expressions of kindness which they have shown towards their servant.[4]

That night Churchill dined at the Annexe with his family and a few personal friends, among them Brendan Bracken and Anthony Eden.

---

[1] Sir Richard Pim recollections: in conversation with the author, 1975.

[2] 'Most Private', 1 August 1945: Churchill papers, 2/355.

[3] Reported by Harold Nicolson in his diary on 1 August 1945: Nigel Nicolson (editor), *Harold Nicolson, Diaries and Letters 1939–1945*, page 479.

[4] Statement on 10 Downing Street notepaper, initialled 'WSC, 26 vii': Churchill papers, 20/10.

'Dinner was a somewhat muted affair,' Mary Churchill recalled, 'understandably so; with everyone trying to help and say the right thing. My father still maintained his courageous spirit, and I described my mother as "riding the storm with unflinching demeanour...".' Her account continued:

The next few days were, if anything, worse than that dreadful Thursday. After years of intense activity, for Winston now there was a yawning hiatus. The whole focus of power, action and news had been transferred to the new Prime Minister. The Map Room was deserted; the Private Office empty; no official telegrams; no 'red boxes'. True, letters and messages from friends and from countless members of the general public started pouring in, sweet and consoling, expressing love, indignation and loyalty. But nothing and nobody could really soften the bitter blow.[1]

Churchill next said farewell to his three Chiefs of Staff, Brooke, Portal and Cunningham. 'It was a very sad and very moving little meeting at which I found myself unable to say much for fear of breaking down,' Brooke wrote in his diary, and added: 'He was standing the blow wonderfully well.'[2]

After the Chiefs of Staff came the Private Secretaries. 'I went into the Cabinet Room at No. 10,' Paul Beards later recalled, 'and WSC spoke for a few minutes to me. He said: "Mr Attlee is a very nice man and you will be well with him. The Private Office is a most important mechanism in the machinery of the State and it is a little known and most useful experience to serve in it." He then got up and put his hand on my shoulder and said good-bye.'[3]

At noon on July 27 Churchill held a final, farewell Cabinet at 10 Downing Street. 'It was a pretty grim affair,' Eden noted in his diary. 'After it was over I was on my way to the front door when W called me back and we had half an hour alone.' Eden's account continued:

He was pretty wretched, poor old boy. Said he didn't feel any more reconciled this morning, on the contrary it hurt more, like a wound which becomes more painful after first shock. He couldn't help feeling his treatment had been scurvy. 'Thirty years of my life have been passed in this room. I shall never sit in it again. You will, but I shall not,' with more to the same effect.

I replied as best I could that his place in history could have gained nothing by anything he might have achieved in this room in the post-war years. That place was secure anyway. This he accepted and at length we parted.[4]

---

[1] Mary Soames, *Clementine Churchill*, page 387.
[2] Brooke diary, 27 July 1945: Arthur Bryant, *Triumph in the West*, page 481.
[3] Paul Beards, 'Some recollections of WSC in June/July 1945': letter to the author, 27 July 1987. Paul Beards had joined Churchill's Private Secretariat in June 1945.
[4] Eden diary, 27 July 1945: Lord Avon, *The Eden Memoirs*, page 551.

Churchill also told Eden that evening that he wished to recommend him to the King for the Order of the Garter, but Eden declined. 'I have many reasons for this,' Eden wrote on the following day, 'and will not weary you with them—one will suffice, that I could not possibly agree to accept such a distinction after five years service under a Chief who accepts nothing for himself. Anyway the measure of our work together & its memories for me cannot be strengthened by any reward. In short, please let it be forgotten, but don't think me ungrateful.' [1]

Churchill's day was almost over; he was no longer Prime Minister, but for his staff he was still the giant whom they had served through nearly six years of war. 'Mary was in tears,' recalled Miss Layton, 'Mrs C went to bed early, and Mr C remained calm.' [2] 'That night,' Paul Beards later recalled, 'the PM was alone for some time in his room, and I counted several half-finished glasses of whisky and half-smoked cigars. The day that started with high hopes had a falling note.' [3]

As he was about to have his bath, Churchill called for Captain Pim. 'He turned quite grey in his bath,' Pim later recalled. 'I thought he would faint. Then he turned to me and said: "They are perfectly entitled to vote as they please. This is democracy. This is what we've been fighting for."' [4]

'The PM was taking it well,' Brendan Bracken told Admiral Cunningham on July 27, 'and his attitude was to be a support to the "stable men" of the Labour Party so as to curb the "wild men".' [5]

There was one more act of the final scene to be played; that weekend Churchill went to Chequers, no longer Prime Minister, but with what Colville called 'world stupefaction' that this should be so. [6] With him were mostly members of his family: his wife, his brother, his son, his daughters Mary, Sarah and Diana, Lord Cherwell, Brendan Bracken, the American Ambassador, Gil Winant, and, of the wartime staff, Commander Thompson and Jock Colville. Mary Churchill has recalled that last weekend:

It would, in other circumstances, have been a very cosy jolly party; but it was certainly quieter than usual with such a gathering of the family, and although everyone tried to be gay, we were all still rather stunned by the

[1] 'My dear Winston', 28 July 1945: Churchill papers, 2/141.

[2] Elizabeth Nel recollections, 'July/August 1945': letter to the author, 6 November 1984.

[3] Paul Beards, 'Some recollections of WSC in June/July 1945': letter to the author, 27 July 1987.

[4] Sir Richard Pim recollections: in conversation with the author, 1975.

[5] Cunningham diary, 27 July 1945: Cunningham papers.

[6] Colville diary, 27 July 1945: Colville papers.

events of the previous week. Winston made valiant efforts to be cheerful; he played cards, and there was croquet (which he liked watching, especially admiring Clementine's expertise and strategy), and neighbours called in to say their goodbyes. After dinner there were films; Clementine quite firmly went to bed before the cinema; she was exhausted, and always found the film sessions over-long at the best of times.

The hardest moments were when, after the film, Winston came downstairs; normally, then, he would get all the latest news; there might even be a 'box', brought down by despatch rider with some urgent and secret communication. Now there was nothing. We saw with near desperation a cloud of black gloom descend. Tommy and Sarah and I played gramophone records for him: Gilbert and Sullivan (usually top favourites) were unavailing now, but French and American marches struck a helpful note, and finally, 'Run, Rabbit, Run' and 'The Wizard of Oz' had a cheering effect. Finally, very late, he felt sleepy, and we all escorted him upstairs to bed.[1]

'Better days will dawn,' Churchill had written on July 28 to Major Vyvyan Adams, one of the 170 Conservative MPs who had lost their seats.[2] From Randolph Churchill, and his fellow Conservative candidate at Preston, Julian Amery, came a short but poignant telegram: 'We are sorry to have let you down.'[3] To Lord Quickswood, his former best man, and one of the hundreds of friends who wrote to commiserate on the defeat, Churchill wrote from Chequers on July 29:

I must confess I found the event of Thursday rather odd and queer, especially after the wonderful welcomes I had from all classes. There was something pent-up in the British people after twenty years which required relief. It is like 1906 over again. My faith in the flexibility of our Constitution and in the qualities of the British people remains unaltered. We must expect great changes which will be hard for the departing generation to adapt themselves to. The next two years will present administrative difficulties of an unprecedented character, and it may well be that a Labour administration will have a much better chance of solving these than we. I agree with you that their internal stresses will soon become acute.

'I propose,' Churchill added, 'to lead the Opposition and the Party, provided they wish me to, if my present springs of energy do not weaken.'[4]

Churchill's continuing presence at Westminster was certainly in Mountbatten's mind when he wrote, trying to console, on July 29:

[1] Mary Soames, *Clementine Churchill*, page 388.
[2] Letter of 28 July 1945: Churchill papers, 2/566. Adams had held West Leeds since 1931.
[3] Telegram dated 28 July 1945: Churchill papers, 2/551. The two Labour candidates had polled 33,053 and 32,889 votes respectively. Randolph Churchill polled 29,129 votes, and Julian Amery 27,885. The Liberal vote was 8,251, and the Communist vote 5,168.
[4] Letter of 29 July 1945, 'My dear Linky', on 10 Downing Street notepaper: Cecil papers.

'Thank God you are still in Parliament to keep an eye on us all.' Mount-batten had begun his letter: 'My dear Prime Minister (I am afraid I find it impossible after serving directly under you for nearly 4 years to think of you by any other title!)' [1]

That Sunday there were fifteen at dinner at Chequers; 'We drank a Rehoboam of champagne,' Colville noted in his diary. [2] He went on to record Churchill's after dinner remarks:

(1) One must never give way to self-pity.
(2) The new Government had a clear mandate which the Opposition had no right to attack in principle.
(3) The new government would have the most difficult task of any government in modern times and it was the duty of everybody to support them in matters of national interest. [3]

Before going to bed, all those present signed the Chequers Visitors' Book. 'My father signed last of all,' Mary Churchill later recalled, 'and beneath his signature he wrote "Finis".' [4]

There were many reasons for the Conservative defeat, not least the feeling among many voters that they could vote out the Conservative Party, but that Churchill himself would remain Prime Minister. There was also the indisputable fact that Churchill himself, although since 1940 Leader of the Conservative Party, had, for almost a decade before the war, been one of the sternest and most effective critics of the Conservative leaders of that time. 'The main factor in the political landslide here,' Beaverbrook wrote to a friend on July 31, 'lies way back in the years 1938–40. It was about that time that the great mass of middle class opinion in Britain decided to punish the Conservatives. It was unfortunate that the blows intended for the heads of Mr Chamberlain and his colleagues should fall upon Mr Churchill.' A week later Beaverbrook wrote to another friend: 'It was Churchill that I was endeavouring to return to office, and not his party. The unpopularity of the party proved too strong for the greatness of Churchill and the affection in which he is held by the people.' [5]

[1] Letter of 29 July 1945: Churchill papers, 2/560.
[2] A Rehoboam is a bottle holding the equivalent of six ordinary bottles of champagne (a Jeroboam holds four).
[3] Colville diary, 29 July 1945: Colville papers. The champagne, the gift of Lord Melchett, had been brought to Chequers by Randolph: 'we drank the champagne with great delectation,' Churchill wrote in thanks, 'on what was my last night at Chequers'. (Letter of 2 August 1945: Churchill papers, 2/141.)
[4] Mary Soames, *Clementine Churchill*, page 388; Chequers Visitors' Book, 28–30 July 1945 (Chequers Trust).
[5] Letter of 31 July and 8 August 1945: A. J. P. Taylor, *Beaverbrook*, London 1972, page 569.

Not only the people, but their sovereign, had held Churchill in high esteem. 'My heart was too full to say much at our last meeting,' King George VI wrote to Churchill on July 31, and he added: 'I was shocked at the result & I thought it most ungrateful to you personally after all your hard work for the people.'[1] In a second letter that same day, also handwritten, the King wrote:

My dear Winston,

I am writing to tell you how very sad I am that you are no longer my Prime Minister.

During the last 5 years of War we have met on dozens, I may say on hundreds of occasions, when we have discussed the most vital questions concerning the security & welfare of this Country & the British Empire in their hours of trial. I shall always remember our talks with the greatest pleasure & I only wish they could have continued longer.

You often told me what you thought of people & matters of real interest which I could never have learnt from anyone else. Your breadth of vision & your grasp of the essential things were a great comfort to me in the darkest days of the War, & I like to think that we have never disagreed on any really important matter. For all these things I thank you most sincerely. I feel that your conduct as Prime Minister & Minister of Defence has never been surpassed. You have had many difficulties to deal with, both as a politician & as a strategist of war, but you have always surmounted them with supreme courage.

Your relations with the Chiefs of Staff have always been most cordial, & they have served you with a real devotion. They I know will regret your leaving the helm at this moment.

For myself personally, I regret what has happened more than perhaps anyone else. I shall miss your counsel to me more than I can say. But please remember that as a friend I hope we shall be able to meet at intervals.

Believe me

I am

Yours very sincerely & gratefully

George R.I.[2]

Churchill replied in his own hand:

Sir,

I have read w emotion the letter of farewell wh Yr Majesty has so graciously sent me. I shall treasure it all my life.

The kindness & intimacy with which Yr Majesty has treated me during these ever-glorious years of danger & of victory, greatly lightened the burden

[1] 'My dear Winston', from Buckingham Palace, 31 July 1945: Churchill papers, 2/560. The King added: 'When I saw Attlee I asked him who he was thinking of as Foreign Secretary & he told me Dalton. I told him I was astonished at his choice & that Foreign Affairs could be the most important subject for a very long time & I told him to think again & put Bevin there. I would like you to know this fact from me.'

[2] 'My dear Winston', from Buckingham Palace, 31 July 1945: Churchill papers, 2/560.

I had to bear. It was always a relief to me to lay before my Sovereign all the dread secrets and perils wh oppressed my mind, & the plans wh I was forming, & to receive on crucial occasions so much encouragement. Yr Majesty's grasp of all matters of State & war was always based upon the most thorough & attentive study of the whole mass of current documents, and this enabled us to view & measure everything in due proportion.

It is with feelings of the warmest personal gratitude to you, Sir, & devotion to the Crown that I have relinquished my Offices & my cares.

Yr Majesty has mentioned our friendship & this is indeed a vy strong sentiment with me, & an honour which I cherish.

With my humble duty,

I remain Sir,

Yr Majesty's faithful servant & subject,

Winston S. Churchill [1]

At Potsdam on July 28, Stalin pressed the new Prime Minister, Attlee, to explain Churchill's defeat. Attlee did so by an analogy. 'Labour enthusiasts,' he said, 'sometimes acted in a strange way. During meetings they would cheer and applaud a Labour candidate, but when it came to voting they would vote against him. The reverse had happened in this case.' Attlee went on to tell Stalin that 'one should distinguish between Mr Churchill the leader of the nation in war and Mr Churchill the Conservative Party leader. The people wanted a parliament based on a definite programme. Many people looked upon the Conservatives as a reactionary party which would not carry out a policy answering to peace requirements.' [2]

From Potsdam, in a letter to his daughter, Truman contrasted Attlee and Bevin with the former Prime Minister:

I did like old Churchill. He was as windy as old Langer,[3] but he knew his English language, and after he'd talked half an hour, there'd be at least one gem of a sentence and two thoughts maybe, which could have been expressed in four minutes. But if we ever got him on record, which was seldom, he stayed put. Anyway, he is a likeable person, and these two are sourpusses.[4]

On August 1, in the last hours of the Potsdam Conference, Attlee wrote to Churchill to tell him that the Conference was ending 'in a

---

[1] Letter of 3 August 1945, from Chartwell: Royal Archives.

[2] 'Record of Meeting between Prime Minister and Foreign Secretary and Generalissimo Stalin, at Potsdam, July 28th 1945, at 10 p.m.' (those present were Attlee, Bevin and Birse, Stalin, Molotov and Pavlov): Premier papers, 3/430/9, folios 3–6.

[3] William Langer, a Republican Senator from North Dakota.

[4] Letter of 29 July 1945: Monte Poen (editor), *Letters Home by Harry Truman*, New York 1984, pages 194–5.

good atmosphere', and that he would like to let Churchill know 'the broad results' before the publication of the official communiqué. Attlee's letter continued:

We have, of course, been building on the foundation laid by you, and there has been no change of policy.

It was clear, when the Conference was suspended that the vital points were Reparations and the Polish Western Frontier. On the former the Russians were very insistent on their pound of flesh. We were firm on the need for supplies of food etc. from the Eastern zone for the rest of Germany and on not allowing reparations to have precedence over maintaining a reasonable economy in Germany. On Poland the Russians insisted on the Western Neisse and eventually the Americans accepted this. We were, of course, powerless to prevent the course of events in the Russian zone. We have tied the Poles down as closely as we can with specific pledges on elections, press facilities and repatriation of fighting Poles. We therefore agreed on the Western Neisse as the western boundary of Polish administration pending the Peace Conference decisions. Other questions proved soluble when these major matters were disposed of.

Uncle Joe was not in a good mood at the start caused I think by an indisposition which kept him in bed for two days.[1] Thereafter he was in good form. The President was very co-operative. My having been present from the start was a great advantage, but Bevin picked up all the points extremely quickly and showed his quality as an experienced negotiator in playing his hand. I think that the results achieved are not unsatisfactory having regard to the way the course of the war had dealt the cards. I hope you have been able to get some rest. If you would care to come and see me to hear more details I should be delighted.

In his postscript, Attlee told Churchill: 'We have reached a satisfactory agreement on the German Fleet, especially on U-Boats. Of these all are to be sunk except 30 which are to be divided equally between the Three Powers for experimental and technical purposes.'[2]

In thanking Attlee for his letter, Churchill commented on the Potsdam decision to fix the Polish–German frontier as far west as Stalin wished: 'I am sorry about the Western Neisse, and I fear the Russians have laid an undue toll even on the Germany which is not in their zone.' This, Churchill noted, 'was certainly not the fault of the British

---

[1] Churchill, who already knew of Stalin's brief illness, had sent him a get well message. 'Thank you for your telegram,' Stalin replied from Potsdam to London. 'My indisposition was slight and I am again feeling well. Greetings, J. Stalin'. (Telegram sent through the Soviet Embassy, addressed to 'Mr W. Churchill, London': Churchill papers, 2/142.)

[2] 'Most Secret', 1 August 1945: Churchill papers, 2/3. Marian Holmes noted in her diary that night: 'Working for the new PM is very different. He calls us in only when he wants to dictate something. No conversation or pleasantries, wit or capricious behaviour. Just staccato orders. Perfectly polite and I'm sure he is a good Christian gentleman. But it is the difference between champagne and water.' (Marian Holmes diary, 1 August 1945: Marian Walker Spicer papers.)

delegation'. Churchill ended his letter: 'I shall look forward to talking things over with you when the House opens. We have an immense amount of work to do in common, to which we are both agreed and pledged.'[1]

'I am not responsible for Potsdam after I left,' Churchill later wrote to the publisher Victor Gollancz. 'I would never have agreed to the Western Neisse and was saving it up for a final "show-down".'[2]

On August 1 the new Parliament assembled at Westminster. 'Winston staged his entry well,' Henry Channon wrote in his diary, 'and was given the most rousing cheer of his career, and the Conservatives sang "For He's a Jolly Good Fellow". Perhaps this was an error in taste, though the Socialists went one further, and burst into the "Red Flag" singing it lustily; I thought that Herbert Morrison and one or two others looked uncomfortable.'[3]

'There's no doubt about the solid support of the Party,' Churchill later told Lord Moran. 'I've never been cheered like that at any time, and there was no victory to cheer.'[4]

That afternoon, Eden discussed Churchill's future position in conversation with Lord Salisbury and Lord Halifax: '. . . much discussion of leadership & W's future,' Eden noted in his diary. 'Edward has apparently thought that W would retire to write books, make only occasional great speeches & hand over leadership of opposition to me. I told him this was not W's idea at all & then he & Bobbety both urged me to suggest to W acceptance of invitation to New Zealand. I explained how very difficult this was to put from me, but undertook to try tonight. So is Edward who is to see him before dinner.'[5]

From seeing Eden, Lord Halifax went to see Churchill. 'He didn't disguise that it was a bitter blow to him,' Halifax wrote in his diary, 'but was large minded about it all. He said that it was almost impossible to believe that a week ago he had been at Potsdam; the measurement of time seemed to have no relevance. He had for five years had everything through his hands day and night, and it was hard to realize that this had suddenly evaporated.'[6]

That night, Churchill dined alone with Eden, at Claridge's Hotel,

[1] 'Most Secret', 3 August 1945: Churchill papers, 2/3.
[2] Letter of 28 December 1946: Churchill papers, 2/20.
[3] Channon diary, 1 August 1945: Robert Rhodes James (editor), *Chips*, page 409.
[4] Moran diary, 2 August 1945: *The Struggle for Survival*, page 288.
[5] Eden diary, 1 August 1945: Avon papers.
[6] Halifax diary, 1 August 1945: Lord Birkenhead, *The Life of Lord Halifax*, London 1965, page 552.

where Churchill was living, in the penthouse on the sixth floor. Eden noted in his diary:

> W spoke of Max.[1] When W said he supposed he had done us some harm, I said much. He said why? I said because tho' to you he is bottle imp to most of world he is Satan.
>
> He deplored my having been ill & said that as a result he had no one to consult, that if I had been at his side he would not have made mistakes in broadcasts, which is not true, though very generous, because each must say what he thinks. But we agreed that there was anyway a strong leftward undertow.
>
> Although he was most friendly and talked of my being his 'alter ego' he was as obdurate as ever against Jim when I made the suggestion as to vice-chairman. He spoke slightingly of him. I recalled his election result.[2] We argued & he turned the subject to Brendan. We spoke of Hendaye where he will go, & urged B & I to join him. Finally I left him, alone at midnight.
>
> It is a staggering change of fortune from a week ago when at his nod came running secretaries to Chiefs of Staff & behind this was real power. Of course he feels the blow heavily & his pride is hurt. But maybe it is for the best for his reputation in history. For he would not have been happy in his handling of these tangled peace questions, especially at home. History will dub the British people ungrateful, whereas perhaps they were really only wise.
>
> Anyway, whatever my personal feelings & however deeply sorry I feel for Winston at this moment I don't change my view that God takes care of England, and that, even in this, it may later mysteriously so appear.[3]

One letter of good cheer reached Churchill from Bill Deakin, who had been his literary assistant for the three years leading up to the war. 'I was away on tour in Croatia when the news of the election results came through,' Deakin wrote to Churchill from Belgrade, where he was with the British Embassy, and he added: 'The comment of one old lady in Zagreb was "Poor Mr Churchill, I suppose that now he will be shot!"' As to Deakin himself, 'At first I felt very saddened and shocked,' he told Churchill, 'but now realise that this political decision can never in any way reflect upon the greatness of your leadership during our darkest moments. You must be proud of that unbeatable record, which stands for all time.'[4]

[1] Lord Beaverbrook, who had become Lord Privy Seal in the Caretaker Government, replacing Sir Stafford Cripps.

[2] Jim Thomas, Eden's former Parliamentary Private Secretary (and from 1943 Financial Secretary to the Admiralty), had been re-elected for Hereford with a majority of more than 9,000 (virtually no change from the result in 1935).

[3] Eden diary, 1 August 1945: Avon papers. Many years later (it is not clear when) Eden added in pencil to this entry: 'Later, perhaps it did. Labour govt was supported in Bevin's firmness to Russia & building of NATO. Would we have been so supported?'

[4] 'My dear Mr Churchill', 4 August 1945: Churchill papers, 2/560. He had not been shot, Churchill later remarked, but 'sentenced to hard labour'.

To those close to Churchill, the decision of the electorate had been a blow. Sometimes, it was he who sought to console them. Sir Leslie Rowan's wife Judy later recalled how, when her husband told Churchill: 'It was absolutely monstrous how ungrateful the nation was,' Churchill 'just dismissed it', telling Rowan: 'That's politics, my dear, that's politics.' [1]

The shock of the Conservative defeat had been rapidly overtaken by the dramatic events on the world stage. On July 27, following the Japanese rejection of the Potsdam message of the previous day, eleven Japanese cities were warned by leaflets that they would be subjected to intensive air bombardment. Further warnings were given on July 31 and August 5. On August 6 an atom bomb was dropped on Hiroshima. 'It was now for Japan to realize,' Churchill wrote in a message which was made public that day, 'in the glare of the first atomic bomb which has smitten her what the consequences will be of an indefinite continuance of this terrible means of maintaining a rule of law in the world.' [2]

On the day after Hiroshima, Churchill visited Lord Camrose at the *Daily Telegraph* offices in Fleet Street. In his notes of their conversation, Camrose wrote:

Churchill is of the opinion that, with the manufacture of this bomb in their hands, America can dominate the world for the next five years. If he had continued in office he is of the opinion that he could have persuaded the American Government to use this power to restrain the Russians. He would have had a show-down with Stalin and told him he had got to behave reasonably and decently in Europe, and would have gone so far as to be brusque and angry with him if needs be. If the President and his advisers had shown weakness in this policy he would have declared his position openly and feels certain that the American people would have backed the policy on the grounds that it would have been carrying out the Atlantic Charter. [3]

On August 8, two days after Hiroshima, the Soviet Union declared war on Japan, and Soviet troops, already massed on the Manchurian frontier, drove southward in a series of fierce and bloody battles. On August 9 a second atom bomb was dropped, this time on Nagasaki. Two Japanese cities had been all but obliterated. [4]

---

[1] Lady Rowan recollections: in conversation with the author, 9 October 1987.

[2] 'Enclosure II', undated: Churchill papers, 2/3. 'The startling news [of the atom bomb] was, at Winston's express request, broken to an unprepared England by W's statement, drafted last weekend at Chequers, with a preface by Attlee.' (Colville diary, 6 August 1945: Colville papers.)

[3] 'Notes of Interview with Mr Churchill at DT Offices, Tuesday, August 7th, 1945': Camrose papers.

[4] The identified victims of the Hiroshima bomb are given as 138,690 on the Cenotaph at Hiroshima (*New York Times*, 6 August 1985), the Nagasaki death toll as 48,857 (*New York Times*, 10 August 1975).

'It may well be that events will bring the Japanese War to an early close,' Churchill wrote to Attlee on August 10. 'Indeed I hope this may be so, for it means an immense lightening of the load we expected to carry.' [1] That day, Radio Tokyo broadcast an appeal to the Allies to accept the Japanese surrender. 'We have as yet nothing more than the Tokyo broadcast,' Attlee wrote to Churchill later that day, 'but are seeking confirmation. I will let you know as soon as I have news.' The probability was, Attlee believed, that Japan would formally surrender 'in the next 48 hours', and he went on: 'I feel that the probability of the surrender of our last enemy is so great that I must, at once, offer to you, our leader from the darkest hours through so many anxious days, my congratulations on this crowning result of your work.' [2]

On August 14 the Japanese Government accepted the Allied terms. The Second World War was over.

[1] Letter of 10 August 1945: Churchill papers, 2/140.
[2] 'My dear Churchill', 10 August 1945 (from 10 Downing Street): Churchill papers, 2/140.

Part Two
In Opposition

7

'Now there is the tumble!'

IN the aftermath of his resignation as Prime Minister on 26 July 1945, Churchill received several thousand letters from friends, acquaintances and strangers: so many letters that a special secretariat had to be set up to answer them. The typist in charge of the replies, Dorothy Spencer, who worked at Conservative Central Office, was given several thousand printed fascsimile letters, in Churchill's handwriting, to be sent to the members of the public. After six weeks' work, she reported to Churchill's senior secretary, Kathleen Hill, that there were still 5,600 unanswered letters from the British public, 900 unanswered from abroad, and 250 as yet unanswered from the Empire and the United States. All organizations had been answered, and all those sending gifts. 'So far as British individuals are concerned,' Dorothy Spencer explained, 'they are impossible to cope with, with existing staff.'[1] Three weeks later, Dorothy Spencer reported that a further five hundred people had written 'thanking Mr Churchill for the facsimile letter'. As to people with 'axes to grind'—268 in all—and a further 217 'cranks or lunatics', no answer would be sent.[2]

Only those letters which came from people whom he knew were shown to Churchill, one of these being a letter from President Truman, sent from Berlin on White House notepaper. 'My dear Mr Churchill,' he began, 'I could hardly refrain from saying as my predecessor used to say, "Winston". In the short time we were associated here I became a very great admirer of yours. It was a shock to me when I returned from Frankfurt and learned the result of the English elections.' Truman added: 'We miss you very much here, the Secretary of State, Admiral Leahy and I, but we wish you the happiest possible existence from now to the last call and we shall always remember that you held the barbarians until we could prepare.'[3]

[1] 'Letters addressed to Mr Churchill', 11 September 1945: Churchill papers, 2/1.
[2] 'Letters addressed to Mr Churchill since 26th July', 9 October 1945: Churchill papers, 2/1.
[3] Letter of 30 July 1945: Churchill papers, 2/142.

Churchill had left 10 Downing Street that day for his home at Chartwell. 'I am sorry indeed,' he wrote to Truman, 'that our work together has been nipped in the bud, but I cherish the hope that our friendship will continue to ripen, and that there may be occasions when it may be of service to both our countries and to the common causes they pursue.'[1]

Another of those who wrote was Jan Masaryk, the former Czechoslovak Minister in London, with whom Churchill had worked closely during the Munich Crisis of 1938. On July 30 Masaryk returned to Prague after six years in exile in Britain. 'Your leadership saved our civilization,' he wrote, and he added: 'Your friendship to me during the Munich days meant everything to me.'[2] 'I am most grateful to you for your kind letter,' Churchill telegraphed on the eve of Masaryk's return, 'and rejoice to see your country marching back into its old freedom.'[3]

While at Chartwell on August 5, Churchill began to reply to the mass of letters which he had received. To Sir James Grigg, whom he had appointed Secretary of State for War in 1942, he wrote: 'I took a great responsibility in drawing you from your comfortable and solid Civil Service post into the rough and tumble of politics. It has certainly been rough and now there is the tumble!'[4] To Sir Alexander Cadogan he wrote that same day: 'You have indeed played a man's part in this glorious struggle, which we got into in one muddle and have come out of in another. Nevertheless the lustrum will glitter in future times.'[5]

Churchill's letters also revealed a lack of rancour towards individual members of the new Labour Government. Of Grigg's successor as Secretary of State for War, John James Lawson, he wrote, in a letter to Field Marshal Brooke: 'I am sure you will like your new Secretary of State. He is an absolutely true and decent fellow, but he will need all your help and that of the Department.'[6] 'I have by no means lost

[1] 'Private', 30 July 1945: Churchill papers, 2/142.

[2] Letter of 27 July 1945: Churchill papers, 2/533.

[3] 'Telegram to Monsieur Jan Masaryk from Mr Churchill', 29 July 1945: Churchill papers, 2/533.

[4] 'Personal', 5 August 1945: Churchill papers, 2/149. Since 1913 a Civil Servant (at the Treasury), from 1921 to 1930 Grigg had been Principal Private Secretary to successive Chancellors of the Exchequer (including Churchill); from 1930 to 1934, Chairman of the Board of Inland Revenue; from 1934 to 1939, Finance Member of the Government of India; and from 1939 to 1942 Permanent Under-Secretary of State for War.

[5] 'My dear Alex', 5 August 1945: Churchill papers, 2/560. A lustrum is a five-year period (the term was much used by economists, and was frequently used by Churchill from 1924 to 1929, when he was Chancellor of the Exchequer).

[6] 'Private', 'My dear Brookie', 6 August 1945: Churchill papers, 2/140. Lawson had been a Labour MP since 1919. From 1939 to 1944 he had been Deputy Regional Commissioner, Civil Defence Northern Region.

my faith in the British democracy,' he wrote to the Marquess of Salisbury on August 6, 'but ten years is too long between Elections.' [1]

On August 7, during his visit to the *Daily Telegraph* offices in Fleet Street, Churchill 'expressed some doubt' Lord Camrose noted, 'as to whether he would continue to lead the Conservative Party for an indefinite period, but would do so for the immediate future'. Camrose added: 'His disappointment at not being one of those who would shape the future of the European peoples is very deep indeed and he found it difficult at various stages in the conversation to conceal his bitterness at the way the people of England had treated him.' [2]

Those who had been close to Churchill during the war hastened to write to him, as he had already written to them, with words of gratitude and affection. On August 7 the Chief of the Air Staff, Sir Charles Portal, wrote from the Air Ministry:

My dear Winston,
    In thus addressing you I trust that you will not object to my very real feeling of personal affection being allowed to overcome (though it can *never* diminish) the deep respect in which I shall always hold you.
    Thank you so much for the very generous remarks in your letter.
    It is impossible to tell you how much you are missed here & how very dim our world now seems.
    After 5 years of it, one is apt to take the inspiration of great leadership as much for granted as fresh air, and to suffer accordingly when the supply is checked.
    However, nothing can spoil the memory of the great years, and the assurance of your continuing friendship is a powerful antidote to the feeling of sadness with which I now regard some of the blessings of democracy.
    Yours ever
                                                        Peter P [3]

Field Marshal Sir Alan Brooke wrote on August 8:

My dear Winston,
    I hope I am not doing wrong by addressing you by your Christian name? I know you will not look upon it as any lack of respect, anything more formal is so out of keeping with my feelings of affection on my close connection during the past years, that I hope I may be forgiven if I have done wrong.
    It was so *very* kind of you to think of writing to me to let me know that you had written to Mr Attlee about your Potsdam conversation concerning my stopping on as CIGS, and am so grateful to you for your very great kindness in remembering me at such a time. . . .

---

[1] 'My dear Jim', 6 August 1945: Churchill papers, 2/560.
[2] 'Notes of Interview with Mr Churchill at DT Offices, Tuesday, August 7th, 1945': Camrose papers.
[3] Letter of 7 August 1945: Churchill papers, 2/449. Sir Charles Portal used the Christian name Peter.

'I am feeling it hard to adjust myself to new conditions,' Brooke ended, 'and miss the privilege of working for you most awfully.'[1]

On August 9 Brooke sent Churchill a second letter, likewise from the War Office:

My dear Winston,

I have just received your letter of Aug 8 stating that you wished to submit my name to the King for a Barony, and am writing to thank you for this great honour.

The very fact that you say in your letter that it was your 'earnest desire that your three great friends the Chiefs of Staff should received some recognition' gives this distinction quite a special aspect.

I shall always connect it with your wonderful friendship during these momentous years I had the joy and privilege of working for you.

I am not good at expressing myself but would like you to realize how much your kindness & friendship means to me in my life, and how very grateful I am to you for submitting my name for a Barony.

With very many thanks,

Yours ever

'Brookie'[2]

Churchill was already thinking of the future, and of his responsibilities as Party leader. 'In the anxious days that lie ahead,' he wrote to Lord Croft on August 10, 'we shall need a strong and closely-knitted team.'[3]

On the afternoon of Friday August 10, Churchill drove from London to Chartwell, where he was to spend the weekend. With him in the car was Miss Layton. 'Victory over Japan was not yet an accomplished fact,' she later recalled, 'but it hung in the air, and the streets of London, as we left Westminster, were already filling with rejoicing people. Not the same as at VE, but yet there was great relief. He looked at all this. We were somewhere in the neighbourhood of Tower Bridge when he said: "You know, not a single decision has been taken since we left office to have brought this about." I didn't know what to say in consolation, and only muttered something about wasn't it better for him now to have a rest. He looked from the car window, and after a while said "No—I wanted—I wanted to do the Peace too."'[4]

'During these difficult weeks,' Mary Soames has recalled, 'everyone

---

[1] Letter of 8 August 1945: Churchill papers, 2/140.

[2] Letter of 9 August 1945: Churchill papers, 2/208. Sir Alan Brooke took the title Baron (and later Viscount) Alanbrooke.

[3] 'Private', 10 August 1945: Churchill papers, 2/560. Lord Croft (formerly Brigadier-General Sir Henry Page Croft) had been Parliamentary Under-Secretary of State for War from 1940 to 1945. He died in 1947, aged sixty-six.

[4] Elizabeth Nel recollections, 'July/August 1945': letter to the author, 6 November 1984.

they knew seemed to want to help Winston and Clementine. A warm-hearted friend, Audrey Pleydell-Bouverie, who years before, in 1931 after Winston's serious accident in New York, had lent them her house over there, once more came forward with the generous offer of her house in the country, pending Chartwell's rehabilitation.' Clementine Churchill's reply illustrated her feelings: 'Now that again we have suffered another unexpected shock, once more you offer to take us in. It is sweet of you, dear Audrey, and I shall never forget it. But actually I think it is best to struggle into Chartwell and re-adjust our lives.' [1]

On August 14 Clementine Churchill wrote to her daughter Mary from Duncan and Diana Sandys's flat in Victoria, 67 Westminster Gardens: 'My darling Mary, Time crawls wearily along. It's impossible to realize that it is not yet three weeks since your Father was hurled from power. He is lion-hearted about it. We have settled into Westminster Gardens & I shall never forget Duncan & Diana's prompt & generous action in lending it to us.' [2]

On August 13 Churchill's retirement Honours List was published, given to the Press by his last wartime Principal Private Secretary, Leslie Rowan. The three Chiefs of Staff, Brooke, Portal and Cunningham, were each to receive a peerage, and there were honours for the members both of his Private Office and of Lord Cherwell's staff at the Statistical Office. There was a knighthood for Captain Pim, the organizer of the Prime Minister's Map Rooms at No. 10 Annexe, in the underground Cabinet War Rooms, and during the many overseas journeys of the war.[3] There was also a knighthood for Brigadier Jefferis, of Churchill's special inventions section.[4] After the announcement was issued, Leslie Rowan, who was now working for Clement Attlee, wrote to Churchill from 10 Downing Street:

---

[1] Mary Soames recollections, and letter: Mary Soames, *Clementine Churchill*, page 389.

[2] Letter of 14 August 1945: Mary Soames, *Clementine Churchill*, page 389.

[3] Sir Richard Pim was about to be appointed head of the Royal Ulster Constabulary.

[4] Jefferis had first met Churchill (then First Lord of the Admiralty) on 23 November 1939, when, as a Major, Royal Engineers, he submitted a model of a small floating mine for use in German rivers. In 1941 Churchill (as Minister of Defence) brought Jefferis's army experimental establishment under the direct control of the Ministry of Defence. Located ten miles from Chequers, it was the scene of intensive rocket and bomb research. In 1941, at Churchill's suggestion, Jefferis was promoted Lieutenant-Colonel, despite War Office objections that he was only 150th in the list of Majors. A year later, he was promoted Brigadier. In 1945 Jefferis was promoted Major-General and received the KBE. The weapons which he had designed and developed during his first year under Churchill's authority included the Sticky Bomb ($1\frac{1}{2}$ million produced), the Bombard ($1\frac{3}{4}$ million), the Puff Ball (50,000) and the Long Delay Fuse (250,000).

My dear Winston—(if I may call you this once)

I have today given out your retirement list and so, unhappily, done my last task for you. I hoped so much that I might have continued to work for you for many years as your PPS. In the event it was for less than a month. But whatever the future may hold it can hold nothing of which I shall be prouder than that short time.

While I have worked with you I have learnt and gained much, and I cannot find the words to thank you and indeed all your family, for all you have done for me.

Today for me marks the end of a glorious and memorable period, during which one man has brought hope and happiness to more people on the earth than anyone else in all its history. These same people expect the same from you in the future and *I* know they will not be disappointed.

Please call upon me if I can be of any help or service. You know I shall be proud to do it.

Leslie Rowan [1]

One of those who received an honour that August was General Ismay, Churchill's devoted 'Pug' and his principal link with the Chiefs of Staff, for whom Churchill had proposed the Companion of Honour: the award which Churchill himself had received in 1922. 'That I should be a Companion of Honour by your personal recommendation,' Ismay wrote, 'gives me a pride and a pleasure that words cannot express.' His letter continued:

Nevertheless I believe you know what it has meant to me to be allowed to serve you during these last five years and more, and to watch you saving our beloved country. I hope that you also know how utterly desolate and unhappy I have been these last three weeks. Please let me come and see you sometimes.

When you told me that you had recommended me for a Companion of Honour, I was too surprised to even thank you properly. But now that I have joined you in this Companionship, I want to say that there is nothing in the world that I would sooner have. I can still scarcely believe my luck. For this, and for countless other kindnesses during a 'wonderful gallop'—as you yourself described it, I thank you from the very bottom of my heart.

Your most devoted servant

Pug [2]

On August 15 Japan surrendered unconditionally to the Allied Powers. That day, a small crowd gathered round Westminster Gardens, the block of flats in Victoria where Churchill was living, 'to see Papa and cheer him', Clementine Churchill wrote to her daughter Mary, adding that 'he got mobbed in Whitehall by a frenzied crowd'. [3]

[1] 'Private', 13 August 1945: Churchill papers, 2/142.
[2] 'My dear Prime Minister', 14 August 1945: Churchill papers, 2/449.
[3] Letter of 18 August 1945: Mary Soames, *Clementine Churchill*, page 390.

'Now that we have come to journey's end,' Ismay wrote to Churchill on August 15, 'the Chiefs of Staff ask you to accept their warmest congratulations on the completion of the task that you undertook over five years ago, and their heartfelt thanks for the inspiration of your leadership and encouragement. They wish you to know that you are much in their thoughts today.' [1] From General Marshall came a telegram of personal congratulations. 'With the termination of hostilities,' Marshall wrote, 'my thoughts turn to you and the long hard pull up the heights to final triumph of your labour.' [2]

On August 15, the day of the Japanese surrender, the King and Queen opened Parliament. Jock Colville, now briefly Private Secretary to the new Prime Minister, noted in his diary: 'I drove to the House with Mr Attlee through exuberant crowds. Winston received the greatest ovation of all.' [3]

Speaking in the House of Commons on August 16, Clement Attlee paid tribute to Churchill's war leadership. 'In the darkest and most dangerous hour of our history,' he said, 'this nation found in my Right Honourable friend the man who expressed supremely the courage and determination never to yield which animated all the men and women of this country. In undying phrases he crystallized the unspoken feeling of all.' Churchill's 'place in history', Attlee added, 'is secure'. [4]

Churchill also spoke: 'a brilliant, moving gallant speech', Clementine Churchill called it, and she added: 'The new house full of rather awe-struck shy nervous members was riveted & fascinated.' Clementine Churchill commented on this response and the crowds who had cheered her husband on VJ Day:

These friendly manifestations have reassured & comforted him a little. He says all he misses is the Work & being able to give orders.

The crowds shout 'Churchill for ever' & 'We want Churchill'. But all the King's horses & all the King's men can't put Humpty Dumpty together again. [5]

---

[1] 'The Right Hon. Winston S. Churchill, CH, MP', minute dated 15 August 1945: Cabinet papers, 127/50.

[2] 'Restricted', 'Important', IZ 8276, 16 August 1945: Cabinet papers, 127/50.

[3] John Colville, recollections of 15 August 1945: Colville papers. In thanking Sir William Rootes for the loan of an open car on VJ Day, Churchill added: 'It was a great pleasure to me to use it driving through the delighted crowds.' (Letter of 1 September 1945: Churchill papers, 2/140.)

[4] Speech of 16 August 1945: Hansard. Paul Beards, Churchill's Private Secretary, who had gone to work with Attlee in July 1945, later wrote: 'One night at Chequers, a year or two later, at dinner, the conversation turned to the war. One of those present said, "I suppose that the part of WSC in the war has been much exaggerated." The PM turned round and said "There is one man that won the war, and that was WSC".' (Paul Beards, 'Some Recollections of WSC in June/July 1945': letter to the author, 27 July 1987.)

[5] Letter of 18 August 1945: Mary Soames, Clementine Churchill, page 390.

As Leader of the Conservative Party, Churchill could not avoid the demands of his Party, despite his obvious need for a rest. On August 21 he addressed its backbench 1922 Committee. 'He seemed totally unprepared, indifferent and deaf,' Henry Channon wrote in his diary, 'and failed to stir the crowded audience.' [1]

Among the invitations which reached Churchill was one of a particularly personal and pleasant nature: an invitation to return to the lakeside house near Quebec at which he had stayed for a few days' rest after the first Quebec Conference in 1943. His host then, Colonel Frank W. Clarke, offered Churchill and his wife La Cabane as a place for enjoying scenic beauty and complete relaxation. Failing that, he had a house at Miami Beach which he would be pleased to put at their disposal that winter. 'Alas, I do not think we can manage La Cabane and Snow Lake as we cannot cross the Atlantic so soon,' Clementine Churchill wrote to Colonel Clarke on August 21, and she added: 'We have to buy a little London house, try to open up our country home in Kent—which is much dilapidated by six years of unavoidable war neglect—and generally speaking readjust our lives. But your invitation to stay with you in Florida during some part of the winter is most tempting. I think it would do Winston such a lot of good and I should enjoy it so much.' [2]

Writing to her daughter Mary on August 26, Clementine Churchill gave a sad picture of life at Chartwell, and of their personal unhappiness:

I cannot explain how it is but in our misery we seem, instead of clinging to each other to be always having scenes. I'm sure it's all my fault, but I'm finding life more than I can bear. He is so unhappy & that makes him very difficult. He hates his food (hardly any meat), has taken it into his head that Nana tries to thwart him at every turn.[3] He wants to have land girls & chickens & cows here & she thinks it won't work & of course she is gruff & bearish. But look what she does for us. I can't see any future. But Papa is going to Italy & then perhaps Nana & I can get this place straight. It looks impossible & one doesn't know where to start. . . .

In a few days' time, Clementine Churchill added, 'we shan't have a car. We are being lent one now. We are learning how rough & stony the World is.' [4]

Dining at Westminster Gardens on August 31, Jock Colville noted

---

[1] Channon diary, 21 August 1945: Robert Rhodes James, editor, *Chips*, page 412.

[2] 'My dear Colonel Clarke', 21 August 1945: Churchill papers, 2/225.

[3] 'Nana' was Maryott Whyte, Clementine Churchill's 'Cousin Moppet', who in the inter-war years looked after Mary Churchill and was now helping the Churchills to return to Chartwell. Her brother Mark had been killed in action on the Western Front in August 1918.

[4] Letter of 26 August 1945: Mary Soames, *Clementine Churchill*, pages 390–1.

in his diary: 'W spoke sourly of Herbert Morrison. He said that the Administration were making a muddle of demobilization and that Mr George Isaacs, "like Pharaoh, has hardened his heart and has told the people they may not go".' [1]

Before leaving for Italy Churchill dined at Claridge's with his son Randolph and Brendan Bracken. At one point the conversation turned to Churchill's war memoirs, and the necessary legal and contractual preparations for them. Randolph's letter to his father, written later that night, explained why he had left the dinner table:

My dearest Papa

I am more sorry than I can say that I should have provoked you so much tonight. Knowing your prejudice against literary agents I was most careful in all I said to make no mention of them. What I said was that in view of the immense complexity of the whole situation what was wanted was that it should be studied & reported on by one expert. I was not even thinking of a literary agent but of a lawyer. When therefore you started to answer me as if I had suggested a literary agent I tried to explain what it was I had really said. I'm afraid my interruptions must have been very clumsy because I made you extremely angry.

I went away because I cannot bear to have you talk to me like that in front of other people—particularly in front of Brendan on whose account I have always been so grievously wounded.

But I beg you to forgive me & to believe that I was solely concerned to avoid an argument on a subject which I knew to be sterile.

'I do so hope that the sun will shine at Como,' Randolph's letter ended, '& that you will paint some lovely pictures. Your loving son Randolph.' [2]

---

[1] Colville diary, 31 August 1945: Colville papers. Morrison was Lord President of the Council, and Isaacs Minister of Labour and National Service in the new Labour Government. On 7 September 1945 Colville left Attlee's service and returned to the Foreign Office, from which he had been seconded in 1939.

[2] 'My dearest Papa', Claridge's, 31 August 1945: Churchill papers, 1/42. Despite the dispute, Churchill took his son's advice, consulting the solicitor, Anthony Moir, of Fladgate & Co., who in turn consulted the barrister and tax-specialist, Leslie Graham-Dixon.

8

Italian Interlude

O N the morning of 2 September 1945 Churchill flew from London in Field Marshal Alexander's Dakota to Italy, where he was to stay as Alexander's guest in a villa on the shore of Lake Como. He was accompanied by his daughter Sarah, his doctor Lord Moran, his secretary, Elizabeth Layton, his new detective, Sergeant Davies, and his valet, Frank Sawyers.

As he began his holiday journey, Churchill was thinking about what would one day be his war memoirs. Before leaving England, he had arranged for a set of his wartime minutes, specially printed, to be prepared for him. These he now read, contemplating the possible use of them as a part of his war memoirs. 'Never has the world had the history of a gigantic war written by the Napoleon himself,' Mountbatten had written to Churchill at the end of July, and he added: 'If you will do this, posterity will gain something unique.' [1] 'At the moment,' Lord Camrose had noted a week later, 'he has decided that he will not publish his account of the war direction in his lifetime.' But, Camrose added, 'He has voluminous detail inasmuch as every month his own telegrams, decisions and instructions have been put into type by the Government printers, and he reckons that each month's printing is equal to, say, two issues of a weekly review like *The Spectator*.' [2]

Throughout the flight to Italy, Lord Moran noted on September 2, 'Winston remained buried in a printed copy of the minutes which for five years he had sent out month by month to the Chiefs of Staff and the Cabinet. Even during luncheon he went on reading, only taking his eyes from the script to light a cigar.' Moran went on to record Churchill's comment:

'People say my speeches after Dunkirk were the thing. That was only a

---

[1] 'My dear Prime Minister', 29 July 1945: Churchill papers, 2/560.
[2] 'Notes of Interview with Mr Churchill at DT Offices, Tuesday, August 7th, 1945': Camrose papers.

part, not the chief part,' he complained. 'They forget I made all the main military decisions. You'd like to read my minutes, Charles.'

I asked him had they worn well. He smiled comfortably.

'They are mine. I can publish them.'[1]

Unknown to Lord Moran, there were many minutes which Churchill knew he could not publish as he had written them: all those in which there was a reference to the Enigma decrypts, on which so many of his decisions and enquiries had been based, but which had still to remain a closely guarded secret. There was also one minute which Churchill felt should be destroyed altogether, on personal grounds. He had written it in April 1945, criticizing the work of Air Chief Marshal Tedder at Eisenhower's Headquarters. 'I have, in accordance with your instructions,' General Ismay wrote to Churchill that winter, 'destroyed my copy of the minute in question and also my copies of the minutes which the Chiefs of Staff addressed to you on the subject.' Ismay added: 'I will tell the Chiefs of Staff of your wishes, at the very first opportunity, and see to it that any copies that they may have kept of the minutes in question are duly destroyed.'[2]

Churchill reached Lake Como on September 2. On the following day Sarah wrote to her mother, who had not felt well enough to travel: 'I was so distressed to see you so unhappy and tired when we left, and so was he. We never see a lovely sight that he doesn't say: "I wish your mother were here."'

Alexander had seconded an army officer, Major Ogier, to serve as Churchill's ADC during the visit. 'He is a big husky young man,' Sarah told her mother, 'who has been through the entire war, and seen much action. I thought him about 30, but he is only 25—Dunkirk to the Gothic line via Alamein, has physically matured him—but he is extremely youthful to talk to, intelligent, kind and considerate to Papa. They get on like a house on fire.' Sarah and Lord Moran 'sit back

---

[1] Moran diary, 2 September 1945: Moran, *The Struggle for Survival*, pages 291–4.

[2] 'Private', 31 December 1945: Churchill papers, 2/142. On 12 April 1945 Admiral Cunningham, the First Sea Lord and a member of the Chiefs of Staff Committee, noted in his diary: 'A violent memo directed against Tedder by the PM today was considered at COS today in private session.' Cunningham added: 'It is curious that with all his great qualities, when he deals with personalities he gets childish.' (Cunningham diary, 12 April 1945: Cunningham papers.) No copy of the minute itself appears to have survived in Churchill's papers, or in the papers of the Chiefs of Staff. From the first planning in 1943 of the Normandy landings, Tedder had been Deputy Supreme Commander (under Eisenhower) to the Allied Expeditionary Force in North-West Europe.

comfortably', Sarah added, 'while the two boys fight the battles from Omdurman to Alamein!'

On September 3 Churchill had gone painting. The first picture, Sarah told her mother, 'was a success—a luminous lake and boats, backed by a beetling crag, with a miniature toy village caught in the sunlight at its foot'.[1] Churchill's doctor, who was also on this first painting expedition, noted in his diary: 'When he was satisfied that he had found something he could put on canvas, he sat solidly for five hours, brush in hand, only pausing from time to time to lift his sombrero and mop his brow.'[2]

Churchill painted, watched by a small crowd of Italians, most of them children. For them the war was forgotten, Sarah wrote:

Who won it? Who lost it? Who cares? That was last week—this is today. Look! Churchill—Churchill—Hurrah—Hurrah! Both the young and old know him. I was astonished at a bunch of children—the eldest not more than 12 or 13—who looked at us calmly and the eldest said, 'Churchill'. They can't do enough for us, they bring out chairs for us to sit on, towels to dry our hands with, and then retire about 20 yards and sit and watch for hours. Our ADC has the hearty contempt that all the soldiers who have fought them, or been long in Italy have for them. I think he thinks we are too polite with them.

Sarah Churchill added: 'I really think he is settling down—he said last night—"I've had a happy day"! I haven't heard that for I don't know how long!'[3]

Churchill's own first letter from Lake Como was also written on September 3, to his wife:

My darling Clemmie,

This is really one of the most pleasant and delectable places I have ever struck. It is a small palace almost entirely constructed of marble inside. It abuts on the lake, with bathing steps reached by a lift. It is of course completely modernized, and must have been finished just before the War, by one of Mussolini's rich commercants who has fled, whither it is not known. The villa is officially called the Headquarters of the 2nd Division but no one else is here except our party and a very agreeable young officer from the 4th Hussars who has been told off as my aide-de-camp. Every conceivable arrangement has been made for our pleasure and convenience. Sarah and I have magnificent rooms covering a whole floor, with large marble baths and floods of hot and cold water.

Alex is coming here on the 6th for a few days and has suggested I go on with him to Trieste, where there is to be a Tattoo. I am rather doubtful about this, as I do not want publicity or to see strangers. Moreover, here the

[1] Letter of 3 September 1945: Sarah Churchill, *Keep on Dancing*, London 1981, pages 78–9.
[2] Moran diary, 3 September 1945: Moran, *The Struggle for Survival*, pages 294–5.
[3] Letter of 3 September 1945: Sarah Churchill, *Keep on Dancing*, page 79.

weather is delightful, being bright and warm with cool breezes. Yesterday we motored over the mountains to Lake Lugano, where I found quite a good subject for a picture. I made a good beginning and hope to go back there tomorrow, missing one day. I have spotted another place for this afternoon. These lakeshore subjects run a great risk of degenerating into 'chocolate box', even if successfully executed.

Churchill had dictated this letter to Miss Layton. He now added, in his own hand:

I have been thinking a lot about you. I do hope you will not let the work of moving in to these 2 houses wear you down. Please take plenty of rest. With fondest love
Your devoted husband

W [1]

Churchill painted again on September 4, when an officer of the 4th Hussars, Colonel Barne, arrived from Austria with another officer, Lieutenant Tim Rodgers, and a guard of twenty-four men.[2] One of the men, who had recently returned to his unit from Vienna, gave 'a sombre account of that city under the Russians', noted Lord Moran: 'Winston listened in gloomy silence.'[3]

Also at the villa on September 3 was Brigadier Harold Edwards, Consulting Surgeon for the Army in Italy, who had been summoned there by Lord Moran. Edwards later recalled:

... when I entered his large bedroom in the villa, he was lying on his bed, dressed in his famous blue battle suit which later I saw to be finely cut and of nice soft material. I noted (and was thereby able to answer a question I had often asked myself) that his eyebrows were rusty red, and his remaining hair was that non-descript colour between ginger and grey. His pale blue eyes were tired, and that famous chin, and that nose, and straight mouth (inclining from the horizontal) made up the portrait one had seen so often in print and in colour.

He got up from the bed to shake hands and to thank me for coming, looking directly into my eyes, but not smiling. He started to answer a few questions about himself, but he was far more interested in showing Lord Moran and me the results of his labours with the brush. There were two canvases, quite large, perhaps 4 ft × 3 ft. Both were in water colour—one,

---

[1] 'Lake Como', 3 September 1945: Baroness Spencer-Churchill papers.

[2] Colonel Anthony Miles Barne, born 1906, was the former Commander of the Royal Dragoons in North Africa. From November 1944 to April 1946 he served as Commanding Officer of the 4th Queen's Own Hussars, Churchill's old regiment. He was created an OBE in December 1945, and retired from the Army in 1953. Lieutenant A. D. D. Rodgers had been commissioned into the Royal Armoured Corps in 1943.

[3] Moran diary, 5 September 1945: Moran, *The Struggle for Survival*, pages 297–9. Six weeks later Churchill wrote to Sir George Franckenstein, the pre-war Austrian Minister in London: 'I shudder to read the accounts that come to me of the Russian maltreatment of Vienna and the paralysis of Allied assistance.' (Letter of 15 October 1945: Churchill papers, 2/1.)

which was near completion, painted at Lake Lugano and one here at Como. The latter had been done today at a three hours sitting. It seemed a lot of painting for three hours.

Not being anything of a painter, I could not dare be critical, and as I was averse to fulsome praise, I said very little, or turned his questions as to my opinion of the mountains, or the water, with evasive answers. I reminded him of the article he wrote in the *Strand Magazine* of perhaps 20 years ago which he wrote after he first tried his hand at painting. He then had said that painting up to a reasonable standard was easier than he had imagined.

Finally, after perhaps 20 minutes, we returned to the physical infirmity of Winston Churchill—and this time to some purpose. He was very patient with my examination, and having finished it, and made my diagnosis, I was subjected to a cross examination—which was surely a search for knowledge and performed in a kindly way—which for detail & directness would have done credit to a member of the Court of Examiners. It was then that I had an insight into that extraordinary brain (I had much more reason later in the evening to admire it more fully). It was fortunate for me that I knew the subject well.

When we had finished, he twice thanked me for my kindness in coming to see him. I was quite speechless the second time. I felt I owed him so much (as do so many thousands, nay millions) and as he must have endured so much sycophantism I was fearful lest anything I said should be mistaken by him for anything having the slightest flavour of that detestable trait. But thinking back I need not have worried, for anything I said would have been too sincere to have been mistaken for anything but what I really felt: and now he is a private gentleman, axes had no grindstone on which to sharpen.[1]

That night the local British military commander, General Heydeman, came to dine.[2] On this, and many other aspects of his holiday, Churchill reported in full on September 5, in a second letter to his wife:

My darling,

We have had three lovely sunshine days, and I have two large canvasses under way, one of a scene on the Lake of Lugano and the other here at Como. The design is I think good in both cases, and it has been great fun painting them. Today I was going to finish the second of the two, but last night we had a heavy and prolonged thunderstorm and now there are heavy clouds and no sunlight effects.

[1] Harold C. Edwards recollections: in correspondence with the author, 18 November 1968. Born in 1899, Edwards had served in the Royal Engineers in the last years of the First World War. A member of the Court of Examiners of the Royal College of Surgeons from 1931 to 1960, in 1967 he became Vice-President of the Royal College of Surgeons. In 1979 his son, John Hilton Edwards, was appointed Professor of Genetics at the University of Oxford.

[2] Major-General Cecil Albert Heydeman had joined the Queen's Bays in 1909. In the First World War he served as Brigade Major to the South African Brigade (Battle of the Somme), Brigade Major to the 4th Cavalry Division, and in 1919 as Brigade Major to the Rhine Army. In 1940 he formed and commanded one of the two Indian Armoured Divisions. From 1941 to 1943 he had been a Divisional Commander in India. He died in 1967, at the age of seventy-eight.

I cannot describe to you the luxury of this small palace. It is the last word in modern millionairism. It must not be judged as a work of art but simply as a most convenient, up-to-date residence adapted to the lake situation. Doors, windows and shutters all slide or shut with the utmost smoothness and precision. It is nice walking barefoot on the large marble floors or soft carpets. I have a portico at either end of my rooms. The dining room is a striking creation of marble and mirrors, not unduly decorated. There is a large cage with a beautiful parrot of doubtful temper, and another in which twenty canaries chirrup or at night sleep in a long row on their perch. There is a small bathing-pool in the garden which is full of very clear water, but also the lake is only a few yards away. A lift carries you up the 70 or 80 feet from the water to the successive floors of the house. I bathed yesterday for a few minutes after painting at Lake Lugano, but I have not been in the water here.

Alex arrives tomorrow, and I am looking forward very much to seeing him. I cannot say too much for the care and authority which he has bestowed on making my visit pleasant. For instance, I am guarded by the 4th Hussars. 24 men and two officers travelled 400 miles (I blush to say) from Austria to be my personal protectors here, and the Colonel, Barne, arrived also yesterday, a most agreeable man, who, again, has come this enormous distance. On the road he had a motor accident of a most dangerous character which might easily have killed him and the two others on board. The car was gradually forced off the road by a lorry, struck the embankment, went over a 12-foot drop turning twice in the air, to be smashed out of all recognition. The Colonel, his servant and the driver were all unhurt. Fancy what I should have felt if they or any of them had been killed!

However, thank God we are now safely assembled, and I have three 4th Hussar Officers. The men are all picked men, but were very keen to come and are particularly smart and intelligent. My aide-de-camp Major Ogier— he is only 24—is most attentive and tireless in planning painting and bathing expeditions with picnic lunches.[1] Last night General Heydeman, who commands the 2nd Military District, came and dined.[2] This house is nominally his Headquarters, though he has never used it and keeps it for the Field Marshal. He brought with him his Staff Officer, Sir Nigel Mordaunt, who has distinguished himself in the war and is now delighted to return in a few days to the Stock Exchange whence he sprung. He is a friend of Randolph's and spoke very appreciatively of him. He seems quite young to have reached the position of GSO.[3] The General lunched with us after the last war at Sussex Square. He was employed in Palestine, and evidently it was on this subject that I had made contact with him. He is a very able man and has

---

[1] Eight days later Churchill wrote to his wife, about Major Ogier: 'He is a most agreeable and good-looking young man, and takes infinite pains to amuse us and make us comfortable. He has made up his mind to enter politics and fight Driberg in Essex. He is going to become a farmer and set to work for five years to fling him out of the seat. This seems to be a very good idea.' (Letter of 13 September 1945: Baroness Spencer-Churchill papers.)

[2] Heydeman, like Churchill, had gone to school at Harrow.

[3] Born in 1907, Nigel Mordaunt had been a member of the London Stock Exchange since 1929. In 1939 he succeeded his uncle as 13th Baronet. He died in 1979.

managed all the difficult problems of the military occupation, the displaced persons and the relations with the Italians and foreign contingents, Poles, etc., in his area with great success. He is, like his Staff officer, a dyed-in-the-wool Tory, and says the soldiers all voted wrong for two reasons, first, the shortage of cigarettes, and secondly, their belief that a Labour Government would get them out of the Army quicker. Although his name is Heydeman and his extraction German and his appearance Semitic, he served for many years in the Queen's Bays and rose to command that regiment.

An air of complete tranquillity and good humour pervades these beautiful lakes and valleys, which are unravaged by war. There is not a sign to be seen in the countryside, the dwellings or the demeanour or appearance of the inhabitants which would suggest that any violent events have been happening in the world. I am, of course, immediately recognised, even by a small party of young girls right out in the mountains, and everywhere am clapped and cheered, pressed with demands for autographs and so on. The feeling of the population towards the British Army seems very good, and I understand everything works most smoothly. Of course, however, the Italians are very good at making themselves agreeable. They are a handsome race in these mountains, with a great many fair-haired people, both men and women. The children are well-nourished, and nobody seems to have suffered in any way. The Partisans are frequently to be seen in their half-uniform carrying their weapons. I am told that in this part of the country they were very strong and ardent, and that there were hardly any Germans, so that they were also successful. The people have the air of having won the war (if there was a war), and make the V-sign to me with gusto. All they want is a large influx of tourists to make their happiness and prosperity complete. Meanwhile the place of these is supplied by large British, American, New Zealand and South African leave resorts established in all the hotels for officers and men. On the road near this house is painted a large sign 'American Bar—English spoken'.

It has done me no end of good to come out here and resume my painting. I am much better in myself, and am not worrying about anything. We have had no newspapers since I left England, and I no longer feel any keen desire to turn their pages. This is the first time for very many years that I have been completely out of the world. The Japanese War being finished and complete peace and victory achieved, I feel a great sense of relief which grows steadily, others having to face the hideous problems of the aftermath. On their shoulders and consciences weighs the responsibility for what is happening in Germany and Central Europe. It may all indeed be 'a blessing in disguise'.

I imagine to stay here for another fortnight from now, as I have ascertained that this would be welcomed, and thereafter I may stay with Duff and Diana in Paris for two or three days. He has sent me a cordial invitation.

I long to hear from you how you are progressing on your two fronts, and whether Whitbread [1] is continuing to give you satisfaction, and when the

---

[1] Whitbread was one of the bricklayers (the other was Kurn) who had taught Churchill bricklaying between the wars; he continued to do odd jobs about the estate, including whatever painting and repairs were needed.

German prisoners are going to come. I expect to find when I return that all the barbed wire they have collected from the grounds will have been made into an impenetrable defence around the property in order to prevent the premature arrival of milch cows. How are the Beaverbrook chickens? Have they laid any eggs yet? Is there any particular flavour about the eggs that you do not like? I fear you must be very near the end of the lemon-scented magnolias.

The sun is beginning to gleam fitfully through the clouds, so perhaps we are going to have a painting afternoon.

Up to this point, Churchill had dictated his letter to Miss Layton. The rest of the letter was in his own handwriting:

Darling a tiresome thing has happened to me. When I was vy young I ruptured myself & had to wear a truss. I left it off before I went to Harrow & have managed 60 years of rough & tumble. Now however in the last 10 days it has come back. There is no pain, but I have had to be fitted w a truss wh I shall have to wear when not in bed for the rest of my life. Charles got a military surgeon from Rome who flew here & has been in for the last 3 days.[1]

I do hope you are having a good rest & not taking things too seriously. I have still had no letters or papers & have not the slightest idea what is going on.

Always yr loving husband

W

Churchill ended his letter with a postscript. 'Sarah,' he wrote, 'is a joy to all.'[2]

Clementine Churchill's first letter, dated September 4, soon arrived. In it she described her journey from the airport to Woodford, where she was staying until Chartwell was ready to move back to. 'Driving along the road so familiar for twenty years,' she wrote, 'I thought how the War had changed it. Many of the humble but neat little homes were shuttered, all were battered & squalid. In every space, where before had been busy shops & houses, huge menacing Venereal Disease posters were erected. After passing half a dozen of these—suddenly I saw a new design, the picture of an insect (upside down so that you could see his mandibles & count his crawling feet) magnified to 12 feet and across it written "Beware the Common Bed Bug".'[3]

In a second letter, dated September 7, and headed 'Just off to

---

[1] Brigadier Harold Edwards, Consulting Surgeon for the Army in Italy. 'It seems a long time ago that I was basking in the sunshine of the Riviera,' Churchill wrote to Edwards two months later, 'but I am toiling on with the treatment.' (Letter of 2 November 1945: Churchill papers, 2/141.)

[2] 'My darling', 5 September 1945: Spencer-Churchill papers.

[3] 'My darling Winston', 4 September 1945: Churchill papers, 1/41.

Chartwell', Clementine Churchill sent her husband some painting advice. 'I was so much pleased,' she wrote, 'to get your telegram saying that you had achieved some victories in the field of painting. What Fun! Please don't impose on them, but leave well alone!' [1]

Miss Layton's work was far from the wartime scale. She had brought with her to Italy, for Churchill's attention, twenty letters and telegrams which, she later recalled, 'really did need his attention, being from persons such as Queen Mary!', and she added: 'I took these with us to Como, and when we had settled in put them out for him to see. After dallying for many days he finally said: "Oh, you write and thank them and I'll sign"—which is what happened—something which would never have been countenanced previously. This is told you only to illustrate that his whole life and routine and his usual outlook had been thrown off balance by what had happened.' [2]

Among the letters which Miss Layton took to Lake Como was one from Maurice Ashley, Churchill's first research assistant on his Marlborough biography. 'Now that the war is won,' Ashley wrote, 'may I add my voice as that of an ordinary unimportant citizen to those of so many who have expressed their profound gratitude to you for all we owe you? I shall always take pride in the memory that I once served you in a humble capacity.' [3]

Brigadier Edwards had remained at the villa for four days. 'Dinner and after-dinner was (to me) wholly entertaining,' he later recalled. 'I was fascinated by three things—what he said, how he said it, and his changes of expression.' The Brigadier's account continued:

He talked freely of the war—the atom bomb, Stalin (pronounced *Starleen*), *Mister* Bevin, Alex and Monty; Vienna, Greece, Australia; the advantages of a monarchy, of republican America; of casualties in relation to fire power. Of how he would have used gas were England invaded, and of the 'humanity' of gas as a weapon of war. He has a flare for exactness (he was troubled by my remarks about the depredations of the royalists in Greece) and a supreme gift of saying exactly what he means. The glorious hesitancy while he waited to search his mind for the right word, and with which we became familiar in our time of danger, is constantly noticeable. He has the knack of emphasising differences between things by using a qualifying adjective for each, which has an opposite inference.

He is a great European (he confesses—or rather prides himself on this) and a monarchist rather than a Tory. 'The crown,' he said, 'separates pomp from power.' He made the remarkable—but to me wholly understandable—statement that he would prefer to be enslaved (? was that the word—dominated perhaps) by the Germans than the Russians. And thank God, he said, that

[1] 'My darling Winston', 7 September 1945: Churchill papers, 1/41.
[2] Elizabeth Nel recollections, 'July/August 1945': letter to the author.
[3] 'Dear Mr Churchill', 26 August 1945: Churchill papers, 2/140.

the secret of the atom was in the right hands. It will take Russia three years to discover and act upon the discovery. There are, he also said, only two peoples who knew and practised the right way of life. Thank God also that the French didn't accept his offer to become citizens of Britain. It wasn't his idea originally, and he was never keen, but the Cabinet, who were acutely and emotionally distressed by the invasion and the mortification of France, pressed it. But our offer, made in such good faith, would have been misinterpreted by some sections of French opinion as a desire to annex France as a Colony!

India must go. It is lost. We have consistently been defeatist. We have lost sight of our purpose in India. We were now in their debt—was 1200 million the figure?—which we owed to them for the privilege of having saved them from conquest by the Japanese. It was sad about Leros—the Americans would not spare the 'lift' to enable sufficient men (which were available) to make the project successful. Success meant bringing Turkey into the war. Our failure kept them out. They were worried about forty German Divisions. He cannot understand Hitler's prodigal dispersal of troops and his extravagant usage of them. 1200 were sunk (or at least had to swim) in the first attack on Leros. The second 1200 Germans did the trick.

Churchill has the most fascinating chuckle, and his face, when he is pleased with a thought of his, or a situation conjured up by a remark of someone else, wrinkles up like a baby's—like Puck's. His eyes are dull—and the conjunctivae a little red, as though he had had conjunctivitis. They can be hard as he looks at you—or as tender as a woman's—they can weep easily. I believe now the story of how he cried—of how he wept—as described by M. Herriot when he realised all was lost in France. He is emotional—not 'Irishly' so. I think the right description is that he allows himself to react fully and without restraint and without troubling himself about what impression he makes on the onlooker. He is no actor, no poseur.

As I look out of my high window o'erlooking the lake (how beautiful it is in the gathering twilight) I see his launch approaching.

Churchill is pleased to be relieved of his responsibilities: he told me so—in this way. Talking of affairs in Europe, 'I am glad I won't have the responsibility of it.'

Next day—again after dinner he said, 'For the first time I feel this has slipped from me: I am free of the reaction: the void after office (or sense of void) has disappeared.'

He was even more kindly and amicable after dinner the second night. He suggested I read Maeterlinck's Life of the Bee and Life of the White Ant.[1]

On September 6 Alexander arrived at the villa. 'When you see Alex,' Clementine Churchill had written, 'pray give him my respects and admiration.'[2] Alexander was accompanied by his aide-de-camp,

---

[1] Harold C. Edwards recollections: in correspondence with the author, 1968. The Belgian dramatist and poet Maurice Maeterlinck published his *Life of the Bee* in 1901 and *Life of the White Ant* in 1926. He died in 1949, at the age of eighty-six.

[2] Letter of 4 September 1945: Churchill papers, 1/41.

Major Desmond Chichester, who later recalled the drive on the morning of September 7 to a picnic and painting spot on the shore of Lake Como, and how, at the end of the excursion, both Churchill and Alexander 'looked happy and relaxed'. On the drive back to the villa, Chichester added, 'Churchill obviously sensed that I was nervous and very kindly soon put me at my ease. He asked me all sorts of questions—about my own experiences during the war in Italy and prior to that in North Africa.[1] He also kept admiring the countryside and also remarked how pretty some of the Italian girls were! We were in an open car and of course he was frequently recognized on our drive back. There were many shouts of "Viva Churchill" and he cheerfully waved back.' That night, at dinner, Churchill persuaded the young officers to join him in singing Army songs. 'Even Alex joined in,' commented Chichester, 'which was most unusual.'[2]

'During the weekend I was there I painted a picture with him,' Alexander later recalled. 'It was a tremendous business when he painted. First there was an enormous easel, the sort that portrait painters have in their studios. Then there was a small table with whisky and cigars. Then there were the paints. He loved colours, and used far too many. That's why his paintings are so crude. He couldn't resist using all the colours on his palette.' Churchill had 'no illusion' about his paintings, Alexander added. 'He once said to me: "Now don't go out and imagine you are going to paint a masterpiece, because you won't. Go out and paint for the fun and enjoyment of it." That was what he did.'[3]

On September 8 Churchill wrote to his wife again, his third letter in five days:

My dearest one,

Alex and his aide-de-camp, who is the son of Lord Templemore, have left us after staying two nights. I hope Alex will come back again next weekend. He certainly enjoyed himself painting, and produced a very good picture considering it is the first time that he has handled a brush for six years. I have now four pictures, three of them large, in an advanced state, and I honestly think they are better than any I have painted so far. I gave Alex your message and he was very pleased.

The painting has been a great pleasure to me, and I have really forgotten

---

[1] Desmond Chichester, 7th Queen's Own Hussars, had been taken prisoner in 1941, but later escaped. From 1944 to 1945 he was ADC to Field Marshal Alexander (to whom he was later ADC in Canada, where Alexander was Governor-General). Like Churchill and Alexander, he had been educated at Harrow.

[2] Major Lord Desmond Chichester recollections: letter to the author, 23 April 1987.

[3] Field Marshal Earl Alexander of Tunis recollections: in conversation with the author, 28 December 1968.

all my vexations. It is a wonderful cure, because you really cannot think of anything else. This is Saturday, and it is a week since we started. We have had newspapers up till Wednesday. I have skimmed through them, and it certainly seems we are going to have a pretty hard time. I cannot feel the Government are doing enough about demobilization, still less about getting our trade on the move again. I do not know how we are ever to pay our debts, and it is even difficult to see how we shall pay our way. Even if we were all united in a Coalition, gathering all the strength of the nation, our task might well be beyond our powers. However, all this seems already quite remote from me on this lovely lake, where nearly all the days are full of sunshine and the weather bright and cool.

Much better than the newspapers was your letter, with its amusing but rather macabre account of the journey to Woodford. I am longing to hear how our affairs are progressing. I do hope you are not overtaxing yourself with all the business that there is to do. We shall certainly not forget about Mary's birthday; but let me know what you have done about a present.

Considering how pleasant and delightful the days have been, I cannot say they have passed quickly. It seems quite a long time since I arrived, although every day has been full of interest and occupation. I have converted my enormous bathroom into a studio with makeshift easels, and there all this morning Alex and I tried to put the finishing touches on our pictures of yesterday. He has set his heart on buying a villa here on a promontory. I have not seen it inside, but from the outside it looks the most beautiful abode one can possibly imagine, and I understand that inside it is even more romantic, going back to the fifteenth century. He was a little startled when I pointed out to him that no one will be allowed to buy a foreign property across the exchange perhaps for many years.

He begged me to stay on here as long as I like, but I think I shall come back the 18th or 19th. I am doubtful whether I shall stop in Paris. I expect in another ten or eleven days I shall be very keen to get home again. Sarah has been a great joy, and gets on with everybody. She and I both drive the speed-boats. They are a wonderful way of getting about this lake, and far safer than the awful winding roads around which the Italians career with motorcars and lorries at all sorts of speeds and angles.

Charles [1] plays golf most days. There is a very pretty link here, and he has fierce contests with himself or against Ogier. His devoted care of me is deeply touching.

You may be amused to see the elaborate form in which your telegram, which I rejoiced to receive today, was sent.

His dictation over, Churchill continued in his own handwriting:

My Darling I think a gt deal of you & last night when I was driving the speed-boat back there came into my mind your singing to me 'In the Gloaming' years ago. What a sweet song & tune & how beautifully you sang it in all its pathos. My heart thrills w love to feel you near me in thought. I feel so

[1] Lord Moran.

tenderly towards you my darling & the more pleasant & agreeable the scenes & days, the more I wish you were here to share them & give me a kiss.

You see I have nearly forgotten how to write with a pen. Isn't awful my scribbles?

Miss Layton has heard from her 'boy-friend' in S. Africa that she is to go out there (not Canada) immediately if possible to marry him.[1] So she is vy happy. Yesterday the South African officers came from their hotel & took her out to 'water-plane' behind their speed boat. She looked vy handsome whirling along in the water & made three large circles in front of the villa before she tumbled in. Sarah is writing you now. The DB[2] is starting. Always yr loving husband.

W[3]

On September 10 Churchill wrote a letter to his daughter Mary, in the hope that it would reach her in time for her twenty-third birthday, five days later. The letter read:

My darling Mary,

'Many Happy Returns of the Day!' This shd reach you on yr Birthday the 15th: but if it comes earlier or later it carries with it the fondest love of yr Father. I have watched with admiration & respect the career of distinction & duty wh you have made for yourself during the hard years of the war. I look forward in the days that may be left me to see you happy & glorious in peace. You are a gt joy to yr mother & me & we are hoping that vy soon you will be living with us at Chartwell and in our new house in London. It will be lovely having you with us.

Here it is sunshine & calm. I paint all day & every day & have banished care & disillusionment to the shades. Alex came & painted too. He is vy good. Monsieur Montag is coming to comment & guide me in a few days.[4] I have three nice pictures so far, & am now off to seek for another. Sarah is writing you herself.

With all my affection

Your loving Father

Winston S. Churchill

In his postscript Churchill added: 'We will choose a present for you together when you come home.'[5]

On September 11 Churchill urged Alexander to return to Lake Como. The Swiss painter Charles Montag was to arrive in two days'

[1] The 'boy friend' was Frans Nel, a South African Army lieutenant who had been taken prisoner-of-war at Tobruk. They were married that December.

[2] The Dinner Bell.

[3] Letter of 8 September 1945: Baroness Spencer-Churchill papers.

[4] Montag, with whom Churchill had several times painted before the war, was living in Paris as the Swiss representative on the Fine Arts Commission. Born in 1880, he had first met Churchill in the South of France in 1920, and was one of those with whom Churchill had painted, and corresponded about painting, between the wars. He died in 1956.

[5] Letter of 10 September 1945: Lady Soames papers.

time. 'I hope for a heavy concentration on the pigmentorial front,' Churchill telegraphed to Alexander, 'preliminary bombardment beginning 14th and general assault 15th–16th. Essential you should be present on the battlefield and encourage troops to further victories.' The weather conditions were 'favourable', Churchill added, 'and supplies of all kinds ample, especially now that Swiss communications can be opened'.[1]

As well as painting, Churchill was reading; on September 11, having finished Robert Graves's *The Golden Fleece*, he wrote to its author, who had sent it to him as a gift:

It is the stiffest of all your books, but once it gets hold of you, you cannot put it down. I am astonished at the tremendous amount of study and knowledge you have amassed, and how once again you are able to illumine the darkness, in this case profound, and so enable modern eyes to see these old mysteries. For this I am indeed grateful.

Some say that the present day Greeks are only Levantines, or at the best the descendants of the slaves of the Ancient Greeks. But your book shows that their ancestors behaved in exactly the same way as they do now, and that Greek mythology is as tangled as Greek politics.[2]

As on every occasion when Churchill and his wife were apart for more than a few days, their correspondence was a lively exchange of news, opinions and concern. On September 11 Clementine Churchill wrote to her husband from London:

My Darling,

I'm so distressed about the truss—I hope it is comfortable & does not worry you. Did you strain yourself or stretch unduly, and will you now be able to do your exercises which are so potent a preventative of indigestion? Please take great care of yourself.

I have big news. Mary is home from Germany for good & has applied for a position in London or nearby. It's very good of her because she was having a thrilling time in Germany. She asked to be sent home so that she could be near us. And they granted her request. She rang me up from Tilbury, & said 'I'm home for good'. I think she may be demobilized in February—I feel warmed & comforted by her presence.

I'm so happy to see from your letter that you are enjoying the beauty of the Lakes & the comfort & elegance of the Villa. I have had a most amusing letter from Sarah describing her apricot coloured & mirrored bathroom.

Work is progressing rather slowly, but I hope surely, on the Chartwell & London fronts—Whitbread is industrious & thorough & smiling. Max's hens are beautiful & have laid a few (a very few) eggs, of exquisite flavour but of diminutive size—about the size of a pigeon's egg. So we have to give two

[1] 'No. 11', 'Dispatched by telephone', 11 September 1945: Churchill papers, 2/140.
[2] 'My dear Graves', 11 September 1945: Churchill papers, 2/141.

instead of one, to those who are registered with us. But Moppett says, they will get bigger & more numerous presently.

No German prisoners yet till after the Harvest. It will be lovely when the lake camouflage is gone & also the barbed wire.

Your Pal, Damaskinos is here being entertained by Mr Attlee & Crankie.[1] I see Anthony Eden attended the dinner.

I must hurry because your mail is just off. I'm sending 2 bottles of brandy as requested. I hope they are the right sort?

I enclose a cutting from the DT.

Your loving

Clemmie

'Please remember me to Colonel Barne,' Clementine Churchill added. 'Do you remember he came to luncheon at the Annexe & you walked in thinking it was going to be your old friend Reggie Barnes.'[2]

On September 13, after ten days of painting and reading, Churchill dictated his fourth letter to his wife from Lake Como:

My Darling,

The days pass very pleasantly. It takes an hour to an hour and a half by motor-car through winding roads, or speed-boat across the lake, to reach the painting grounds, so we take our lunch with us and have picnics nearly every day. I have six pictures in all, but some are not quite complete. Yesterday evening there was a lovely scene at the far end of the lake and I thought the first go-off was not at all bad. Montag arrives today from Switzerland, and he will be a great help. I am hoping that Alexander will return for the weekend. He enjoyed himself very much when he was here on the 6th. However, I expect he has a great deal of work to do.

The country people are most friendly and in the smallest villages press up clamouring for autographs, which I rarely give. There are masses of children, many very pretty and not at all ill-nourished. Yesterday where I was painting I witnessed the extraordinary spectacle of a tiny tot of about four who pushed a great heavy boat off the shore, and jumped in and punted it about. The strength of this little being in pink cotton seemed a prodigy. Evidently she was a personality in local Italian affairs. She was armed with a small switch, with which she kept her two brothers in order. She declined to come up and make friends with us, but gave me an arch smile from a distance and was

[1] Lieutenant-Colonel Sir Edward Crankshaw, Secretary of the Government Hospitality Fund from 1929 to 1949. From 1920 to 1921 he had been Churchill's Assistant Private Secretary when Churchill was Secretary of State for War. Archbishop Damaskinos had been installed as Regent of Greece as a result of Churchill's dramatic wartime Christmas dash to Athens in 1944. He was also (briefly) Prime Minister, from 17 to 31 October 1945.

[2] 'My darling', 11 September 1945: Churchill papers, 1/41.

finally placated by a piece of chocolate. The beauty and richness of the country makes a great impression upon me.

I have not definitely settled on my plans. The weather is appreciably cooler than when we arrived. There is an autumn nip in the wind. Yesterday was one of the most lovely days we have had, but today is greyish and clouds keep out the sun. I have done absolutely nothing but painting, and have hardly time to read the newspapers when they arrive. I have had a long, charming letter from Duffie, which I will send you. I do not think I will go to Paris on the way home, as he will not be there owing to the Conference of Foreign Ministers, and though he says Diana would welcome me, I think I will choose some other time. I rather plan to leave here between the 18th and 20th. It is possible that I may motor along the Riviera with Major Ogier. There is no difficulty about motor-cars, petrol, food, etc. I could take three or four days from Genoa to Cannes and paint by the way. In this case Sarah, Charles and Miss Layton will come back on the 18th, but you may expect to see me turn up at the Biggin Hill airfield any time after the 22nd or 23rd. I will of course let you know beforehand.[1]

The letter from 'Duffie'—Alfred Duff Cooper—contained the fullest analysis sent to Churchill about the election defeat. The Conservative Party, Duff Cooper wrote, 'were paying for the sins of the past—sins of which you were guiltless—and I only partly guilty. They were paying for Munich and for Hoare-Laval for having failed in those two branches of affairs in which it was believed they could be trusted, the conduct of foreign affairs and the maintenance of defence. After 20 years of hardly interrupted power they turned the country into a war for which they had failed to make the proper preparations. A fearful indictment.' Duff Cooper added: 'The normal swing to the left had been restrained during that period because the middle classes mistrusted the Socialists but after they had seen Socialist Ministers working successfully under your direction and control for five years they lost that distrust and have now definitely adopted the Labour Party as the best alternative, and the party itself has ceased to be a class party.'[2]

Churchill did not entirely agree with Duff Cooper's analysis. What he did feel strongly, as he wrote to the Marquess of Cholmondeley on September 16, was that 'there is a gulf in England (as in France) between the Old world and the New'.[3] But as to the election result, and the reason for the large Labour vote, he was less convinced, replying on September 17:

[1] Letter of 13 September 1945: Baroness Spencer-Churchill papers.
[2] 'My dear Winston', 7 September 1945: Churchill papers, 2/140.
[3] 'My dear Rock', 16 September 1945: Churchill papers, 2/140. The Marquess of Cholmondeley, formerly Earl of Rocksavage, was known to his friends as 'Rock'. In 1913 he had married Sybil Sassoon, sister of Sir Philip Sassoon. Before the war Churchill had often been a guest at their villa in the South of France. Their London house was in Kensington Palace Gardens.

... there are some unpleasant features in this election which indicate the rise of bad elements. Conscientious objectors were preferred to candidates of real military achievement and service. All the Members of Parliament who had done most to hamper and obstruct the war were returned by enormously increased majorities. None of the values of the years before were preserved. The voters have swung back to the mood of the Fulham by-election. The soldiers voted with mirthful irresponsibility. The General here says that the shortage of cigarettes and some questions of leave were the deciding factors. Also, there is the latent antagonism of the rank and file for the officer class, and of course the hopes raised by the Socialists that a vote for Labour would get them out of the Army more quickly.

Churchill's letter continued:

A period not only of great difficulty and hardship but of disillusionment and frustration awaits the country. The new Ministers will not have time or strength for revolutionary measures. They will be dominated by the daily pressure of administration and finance, in both of which they will fail to give satisfaction. We are back at the two-Party system, and must await in a patriotic state of mind the inevitable revulsion.[1]

It had been Churchill's intention, when he flew to Italy on September 3, to return to Britain on September 18. He decided, however, to prolong his holiday, writing to his wife on his last day at Lake Como:

My darling one,

I hope you will not mind my change of plans. The weather has been so good and the prospects seem so favourable that the opportunity of having another four or five days in the sunshine was too tempting to miss. Alexander was delighted that his plane should carry Moran and Sarah home and return for me. Thus it was not necessary for me to curtail my holiday on account of Sarah having to return to her unit and Moran to his business. I did not want to send them home in the ordinary transport plane with perhaps 20 other passengers. All this is now avoided. I plan to go to Genoa tomorrow, and stay two nights there, so as to get two afternoons at a picture, and then on via Nice or Cannes to Marseilles, hoping to get another picture by the way. I am arranging to fly home on the 24th, so as to give plenty of time for the plane to return to bring Alex to England on October 1.

I really have enjoyed these 18 days enormously. I have been completely absorbed by the painting, and have thrown myself into it till I was quite tired. I have therefore not had time to fret or worry, and it has been good to view things from a distance. I think you will be pleased with the series of pictures, eight in all (now nine!) which I have painted. I am sending them home by Sarah, who will give you all our news. I hope you will be able to keep them in their packet till I come, for I am so much looking forward to showing them to you and Mary one by one myself. If of course you cannot bear it, I shall forgive you. I am sure you will consider they are a great

[1] 'My dear Duffie', 17 September 1945: Churchill papers, 2/140.

advance, particularly the later ones. I am confident that with a few more months of regular practice, I shall be able to paint far better than I have ever painted before. This new interest is very necessary in my life.

Montag has just left, having been with us four days. He was most helpful in his comments. I do not entirely agree with his style, and when he paints himself it is disappointing, but he has a vast knowledge and one cannot paint in his presence without learning. I am quite embarrassed by the magnificent outfit of colours and brushes which he brought with him. They must have cost him £50 at least, and he is not at all a rich man. However, we made much of him here and Sarah got up to take him to the station at 7.30 this morning. He was very full of an invitation from 'The Swiss family' for me to go on into Switzerland and paint for a few weeks there. On being pressed, he said it was the Federal Government & the Municipality of Zurich, where he lives. However the Government is shy of making a formal invitation as they cannot measure the political situation in England. This plan was too difficult altogether, because as you realize one cannot take any money abroad, and it is absolutely necessary for one to know at whose cost one is living. It is possible that the Federal Government may send a friendly message inviting us to be their guests at some time in the future. However, the year is getting late now and as I do not return till the 24th we shall have Parliament upon us quite soon. I will however cast about for future expeditions. Sunshine is my quest.

I have made great friends with these two young officers of the 4th Hussars. The Lieutenant, Tim, is a great character, a Southern Irishman and devoted to horses. He will scout on ahead of us on each stage of our journey and find a sleeping-place. We shall come along behind, and stop off at any scene that catches my fancy. My party is now very small. I only have Sawyers and Sergeant Davies. We are all men, so it will not be difficult for us to fend for ourselves along the route. We have every facility in the way of cars.

I send you herewith some nice letters I have received and answered. Duffie's is well worth thinking about. I wonder whether on getting this, if you have decided to entertain Blum yourself, you would not ask him to lunch too. Rock writes a charming letter; alas for his poor old vanished world! However, I am content to vanish with it. Harold Nicolson was prompted by Randolph to send me these very civil remarks. I have signed the cheque for Southon, and enclose it herewith.[1] I am most anxious to see how much progress you have been able to make. But it really does not matter about being ready at any particular date, either Chartwell or the house in London.

Sarah has been a joy. She is so thoughtful, tactful, amusing & gay. The stay here wd have been wretched without her.

Every yr loving husband

W [2]

The 'very civil remarks' which Harold Nicolson had sent were, as Nicolson explained, two 'perfectly authentic expressions of opinion'

[1] Robert Southon, a local builder, had worked at Chartwell for many years.
[2] Letter of 18 September 1945: Baroness Spencer-Churchill papers.

about the General Election.[1] The first was from a young friend of Nicolson who, having a bad stammer, and thus unable to get a commission, was serving as a Corporal in the British Army of the Rhine.[2] This friend had written to Nicolson:

In their futile political arguments they speak of *Labour* collectively, but when they wish to say Conservative they say *Churchill*. And yet when the election results came out there was no rejoicing or even satisfaction. Men who had spent the past weeks with their voices perpetually raised in heated and fantastic obloquy of Mr Churchill sat down and said, half ashamedly—'poor old Basket. Best bloody Prime Minister we ever 'ad. He'd know how to get us out of this mess. Wonder how he feels now. This 'ere Attlee—'e ain't got the touch the same as the old man had. Bugger me, wish I'd known.'

The second comment which Nicolson sent Churchill came, as he explained, 'from a more educated source', Sir Arthur Salter, the war-time shipping expert who had been Chancellor of the Duchy of Lancaster in the Caretaker Government. Unlike Nicolson, who, standing as a National Labour candidate, had lost his seat in the Election to the Labour candidate, Salter, standing as an Independent, had been re-elected. 'He told me about the new House of Commons,' Nicolson told Churchill, and he added:

He said that seldom can any election have returned so large a number of eager, intelligent and somewhat bewildered young Members. 'The whole thing,' he said, 'might have got out of hand had it not been for Churchill. It was not only the speeches that he made on the Address, but his general attitude and the patience with which he has sat in the House and listened to many maiden speeches. He has succeeded in making all these young impatient people realise what centuries of tradition lie behind the House of Commons and has shown to them that when one of the greatest Statesmen in our history can accept electoral defeat without bitterness, and display the utmost deference to the working of the Constitution and the authority of the House itself, then younger Members, however gifted and impatient they may feel, must adopt a similar attitude of discipline and reverence.' He then added the following sentence which I am glad to say much impressed the Americans who were present:—

'One is apt' he said 'to take the word "magnanimity" as some academic expression. Churchill, since July 26, has given it a concrete splendour.'

'I only send you these,' Nicolson added, 'since Randolph told me it might please you.'[3]

[1] Letter of 6 September 1945 ('Dear Mr Churchill'): Churchill papers, 2/142.
[2] Later the British Army of Occupation of the Rhine (BAOR).
[3] Letter of 6 September 1945 ('Dear Mr Churchill'): Churchill papers, 2/142. 'Thank you so much for your kindness in passing to me two such contrasting but agreeable comments,' Churchill replied to Nicolson, and he added: 'I am so sorry you are not in Parliament, where you were one of the best first-class debaters.' ('My dear Harold', 16 September 1945: Churchill papers, 2/142.)

On September 19 Churchill left Lake Como for the Villa Pirelli, on the Mediterranean coast eighteen miles east of Genoa. He was met at the villa by the Commander of the Genoa Sub-Area, Colonel Wathen, who later recalled:

I had never seen him before and the following points struck me. He looked much less tired than one would have expected after six years of war and the fact that he was over 70 years of age. Although his hair was thin it was not entirely grey, he had a boyish pink and white complexion and a merry twinkle in his eyes. He was active in his movements. He was full of thanks for my hospitality and hoped that I had not been inconvenienced. He soon put one at one's ease. On arrival he was *not* smoking a cigar. During his stay, he usually did have one stuck in his face, but as often as not it was out and he used as many matches as a pipe-smoker. He did not smoke more than five or six cigars a day.

As regards drinks he might have had six or seven small whiskies a day, with lots of soda; a brandy after lunch and two after dinner. Field Marshal Alex had given him 100 bottles of Veuve Clicquot; by the time he came to us, four bottles were left and he was very generous at passing them round at dinner. Incidentally, he told me that the Government had allowed him £200 for his holiday expenses.

To my surprise and considerable apprehension the morning after his arrival, Mr Churchill said that he was going to bathe and would I accompany him. We did our best to dissuade him, as there was a bit of swell and the bathing place was rocky. However, he was quite adamant.

We had to go down some 75–100 steps to reach the sea. The cavalcade was headed by Mr Churchill wearing his California hat, a silk dressing gown and bedroom slippers and smoking a cigar. I followed, then came Ogier, Rodgers, Sergt Davies, Mr Sawyers (carrying an enormous towel) and finally two military policemen following at a discreet distance. The cavalcade made several stops to admire the view. Mr Churchill and I were the only two that bathed. He was wearing his pants. He thoroughly enjoyed himself, frisking about like a porpoise. Getting him out was a bit of a problem, owing to the swell and the rocks; we managed, by me pushing from the water and Ogier pulling from the land.

On September 20 Ogier and Rodgers drove to Monte Carlo, to arrange for Churchill's stay there. Colonel Wathen went into Genoa, leaving Churchill busy at his painting:

When I got back I found to my dismay that he had gone off in the car with Sergeant Davies to find somewhere else to paint as the light at the villa had changed and made painting difficult. Apparently he came across a bombed railway viaduct and houses at Recco and started to paint. Inevitably a crowd of small boys appeared and although Sergeant Davies more or less successfully shooed them away a larger crowd gathered and started to boo and shake their fists. The crowd probably didn't recognise him, but didn't take kindly to a foreigner painting their bombed homes. Without any more ado, Mr Churchill packed up and came home. The incident upset him somewhat, but he readily admitted that it was a tactless thing to do and said that he would have been damned annoyed if Hitler started to paint the bomb damage in London.[1]

From Genoa, Churchill travelled westwards, first to Monte Carlo, then to a villa on the French Riviera, put at his disposal by Eisenhower. It was from this villa, at Antibes, that he wrote to his wife on September 24, his letter dictated to an American stenographer provided by Eisenhower:

My darling,

Here is some account of my doings.

We motored in four hours to Genoa through lovely country with a particularly striking view of Pavia over the Ticino River and arrived after dark to find the local British colonel in charge of the district installed in the marble palace which belonged to Pirelli. You remember that little man who makes the tyres and was sometimes helpful in public business in long ago days when I was at the Exchequer. His dwelling, which is reputed to have cost one-hundred-thousand pounds before the war, is half a marble palace and half a Swiss chalet and seems an utterly incongruous structure such as would be built by a prosperous Fascist manufacturer. There it stands on a rocky bluff overlooking the sea and the bathing place where I got a beautiful clear water of the palest green to try to paint. I worked hard for two days at the illusion of transparency and you shall judge when you see the result how far I have succeeded.

The weather was delightful and it seemed to me very foolish to go home on the 24th. We, therefore, sent Tim Rodgers (Lt) and Major John Ogier on ahead to reconnoiter the neutral State of Monaco. Their report was highly pleasing and the manager of the hotel which is only half full was delighted to receive us on reasonable terms. We motored there on the 21st along the coast road which you will remember we traversed together on our return from the Cairo conference in 1921 and where I had the row at Ventimiglia with the French customs officer. Every important bridge over the valleys leading down to the sea has been smashed to pieces by bombing or naval artillery and all kinds of deviations had to be made. Nevertheless in five hours we came through and arrived in the lap of luxury at Monte Carlo. The square in front of the hotel and the Casino is very empty and dead looking but the Monegasques gathered in crowds and welcomed me on every occasion with the greatest fervour.

We had our meals on the veranda facing the Casino but I did not transgress the 80 paces which separated me from that unsinkable institution. Instead we sent Tim in with 2 milles to try his luck on strict instructions how to play and after he had prepared himself by two days of intense thought. After a half hour he returned bringing two other milles with him. He left the town the next day.[2]

---

[1] Colonel Wathen recollections: letter to the author, 8 November 1968.
[2] Letter of 24 September 1945: Spencer-Churchill papers.

Those two days at Monte Carlo, as remembered by Captain
Rodgers, were later vividly recounted:

Early in their stay Tim received an urgent message from Clementine Churchill enjoining him at all costs to prevent Churchill gambling in the casino.
The subject was not raised until four days before their departure, when Churchill remarked that it would be fun to have a flutter. Tim told him that he
had instructions from Clemmie to scotch any such idea. 'Then you shall go
and gamble for me,' was Churchill's rejoinder.

Tim played with great circumspection the whole evening and ended up
£250 to the good. He returned to the hotel and reported to Churchill, who
told him scornfully, 'That's not the way to gamble; I shall have to go down
myself tomorrow and show you how to do it.'

Churchill had taken the bit between his teeth, and Tim knew that further
remonstrance would be useless. The next night Churchill won £3000, but
the night after that he lost it all; and on the final night he lost £7000. On the
morning they were to leave, Churchill wrote a cheque for £7000 and
instructed Tim to hand it to the casino manager with a request that it
should not be presented until Churchill sent word, because foreign exchange
controls made immediate payment awkward. Tim delivered the cheque and
the message. Flourishing the cheque above his head, the manager answered
in theatrical tones, 'Pray tell Mr Churchill that this cheque will never be presented.'

Tim hurried back to the hotel and, as he came into the room, Churchill
asked anxiously, 'Well, what did he say?' 'He said that the cheque will never
be presented.' 'That's much more agreeable,' said Churchill. 'We'll have a
bottle of champagne.' [1]

Churchill's letter to his wife continued with an account of his holiday after Rodgers had left:

General Eisenhower sent his aide-de-camp to see me on arrival, asking me
to come on to his villa at Antibes which was vacant and fully staffed. I
therefore moved in here after two days at Monte Carlo. My two young
officers and I are now in this beautiful place surrounded by every comfort
and assistance. In four or five days I propose to return to Monte Carlo and
to stay there until the 5th or 6th of October when I shall be back to have a
few shadow cabinet meetings and settle the policy of the opposition before
Parliament meets. I wonder whether we shall be able to hold these in the
new house even if the residence is not complete in other respects. The dining
room will be most convenient for that.

I went back to Cap Martin, where I painted a picture which you will
remember and had another go at olive trees with a brightly coloured background gleaming in the sun, but I must return there a third time as yesterday

---

[1] Captain Rodgers recollections: Peter Willett, *Makers of the Modern Thoroughbred*, London
1984, page 249. In 1961 Rodgers, a horse-breeder, was to buy the racehorse High Hat from
Churchill for £80,000.

afternoon there was no sunlight—only warmth and brightness but not enough to cast a shadow which I need for my effect. A relative of Lord Rothermere has acquired his villa where you remember we stayed for a while and his small children who are very nice came out and brought the picture which I painted eight years ago. It is not a patch on what I can do now, although, as you know, I have hardly touched a brush in the interval. Apparently they had been brought up on the picture and were tremendously excited to see the painter.

I have sent you various telegrams all of which I suppose took two or more days to get through. Your telegram saying you could not come out here took 48 hours to reach me and I suppose that mine equally miscarried. Therefore, Alex's airplane came out without the various things I have asked for and hence Major Ogier's visit. He will collect what is wanted and bring it back here. I am sure you will like him very much. I really don't know when you will get this letter although I hope it may go by airplane tomorrow to the military assistant of the CIGS. He should send it to you expeditiously. I am writing full directions otherwise he may direct it to 10 Downing Street where it may be overwhelmed in the enormous post which afflicts a Prime Minister.

When Alex returns home at the end of this month he and Margaret should be invited to lunch with us in the new house. After lunch we will show him the Como pictures together with the new series now developing on the Riviera. He is most anxious to see them. I had his own picture varnished and framed and sent to GHQ. It is quite good and he thoroughly enjoyed the hours spent upon it.

I have all this batch of newspapers now up to the 21st and am wading through them. Also the pilot brought out Sunday's *Observer* of the 23rd with him. I was sure there would be a complete deadlock at the Foreign Ministers' conference, but I hardly expected the Russians to come out so boldly with a demand for one or more of the African colonies of the Italians in the Mediterranean for naval and air bases. Their wish is a strange one and belongs to a very crude and out of date form of Czarist imperialism. In these matters they are about forty years behind the times, and I do not myself see any serious objections to their having these places if they will be reasonable in other directions. All navies, seaborne commerce and overseas naval and air bases are merely hostages to the stronger sea and air power. However, I have no doubt that these demands will cause a great stir. The Bolshevization of the Balkans proceeds apace and all the cabinets of Central, Eastern and Southern Europe are in Soviet control, excepting only Athens. This brand I snatched from the burning on Christmas day. The failure of the conference will of, course, have bad results. The Russians have no need of agreement and time is on their side, because they simply consolidate themselves in all these countries they now have in their grasp.

I regard the future as full of darkness and menace. Horrible things must be happening to millions of Germans hunted out of Poland and Czecho-Slovakia into the British and American occupied zones. Very little is known as to what is happening behind the Russian iron curtain but evidently the Poles and Czecho-Slovakians are being as badly treated as one could have expected.

We shall have to have a two day debate on demobilization and if it be true that the Labor government has thrown over their Zionist policy and mean to adhere to Chamberlain's White Paper there will be a row about that. Curiously enough, in this matter the government will be against their own party and I equally differ from the Tories.

There will be no lack of topic to discuss when we all come together again. Meanwhile this rest and change of interest is doing me no end of good and I never sleep now in the middle of the day. Even when the nights are no longer than 5, 6 or 7 hours, I do not seem to require it. This shows more than anything else what a load has been lifted off my shoulders.

Since I dictated this (to an American stenographer) yr 2nd telegram has come in. I am so glad you think me right to stay. With tender love

Your devoted

W [1]

This letter signed and sealed, Churchill wrote again to his wife that same day:

My Darling,

As communications are so bad Major Ogier (who brings this) decided to fly home today & come back Wednesday. I hope you will meet him & if possible give him luncheon Tuesday. He is a charming man & I have taken a gt liking to him. He will tell you all about our doings & needs.

Naturally I am vy sorry you cd not come out by Alex's plane—It wd have done you good to bask in this mellow sunshine for a spell.

I made a good arrangement w the Manager of the Hotel de Paris Monte Carlo to put my party (3) up at £4.4.0 a head a day *all* included. I cannot describe the kindness & attentiveness w wh we were treated. The food scrumptious—the wines the best. It was like the old days. [2]

We moved in here last night at Ike's request & repeated invitation—this was arranged by a General sent specially from Germany. It is a palatial villa with every comfort & more. I shall stay here about one week & then go back to Monte Carlo Hotel for a few days. I may not be home till the 5th or 6th October. But why shd I not stay here in the sunlight & have a little rest & detachment after all these years of unrequited struggle.

Do make the most of John Ogier. He is a grand man & contemplates farming in Essex with his father and turning Mr Driberg out at the Gen Election. [3] He was an MC, mentioned in desp & 2 wounds. He has only been in

---

[1] Letter of 24 September 1945: Spencer-Churchill papers.

[2] Churchill's previous stay at the Hôtel de Paris in Monte Carlo had been from 28 December 1932 to 3 January 1933. Between 1945 and 1963 he was to stay there on eleven separate occasions.

[3] John Ogier did not stand for Parliament. Tom Driberg, opposed by both a Conservative and a Liberal candidate in 1950, held his seat (polling 20,567 votes as against a combined Conservative and Liberal vote of 22,702).

the army 4 years & is already the trusted sq leader of the 4th Hussars. He has not been home for 4 years & will be seeing his family. He is just off.

Your ever loving

W [1]

It was while he was at the Hôtel de Paris in Monte Carlo that Churchill read a report of a speech by Sir John Anderson, the Shadow Chancellor of the Exchequer, to the effect that 'no reduction in taxation was justified at present'. Churchill at once wrote out a telegram to James Stuart: 'If true, this wd hamper the action of the Opposition & I do not agree with it.' His draft continued: 'I propose to have a meeting of the Shadows early in October to discuss these sorts of large issues. You shd ask our former colleagues to be so obliged as to defer pronouncements till we have met.' [2]

Churchill returned to London in the first week of October. 'I have returned to this country much refreshed,' he wrote to Attlee on October 6, 'but, unhappily, with a cold which I am nursing attentively.' [3] 'I have brought back fifteen paintings,' he wrote to his friend Bendor, Duke of Westminster, 'as a result of these twenty-five days of sunshine.' [4] This was the first letter which Churchill had written from his new London house, 28 Hyde Park Gate.

While Churchill had still been at Lake Como, the Prime Minister had consulted him about a draft message to President Truman about the future control of the atom bomb. In his message, Attlee had proposed asking the United States to make an 'Act of Faith' by offering its atomic knowledge for the benefit of the whole world. 'We must bend our utmost energies,' Attlee wrote, 'to secure that better ordering of human affairs which so great a revolution at once renders necessary and should make possible.' Churchill replied to Attlee, after studying the draft:

I thank you for consulting me about the draft message. I am in general agreement with the sentiments you express and feel with you the appalling gravity of the matter. However the message does not seem to me to make

[1] Letter of 25 September 1945: Baroness Spencer-Churchill papers.

[2] 'To James Stuart from Colonel Warden', 23 September 1945: Churchill papers, 2/1. There is no indication in Churchill's papers that this telegram was ever sent.

[3] Letter of 6 October 1945, 'At Claridge's': Churchill papers, 2/3.

[4] Letter of 7 October 1945, 'My dear Bennie', written from 28 Hyde Park Gate: Churchill papers, 2/142. 'I had great fun painting in Italy and the south of France,' Churchill wrote to Oswald Birley on October 13, 'and was very much relieved to find that I had got no worse through not painting for six years.' ('My dear Oswald Birley', 'Private', 13 October 1945: Churchill papers, 2/146.)

clear what in fact you want the Americans to do. Do you want them to lay their processes before a conference of the United Nations? It would not be easy for them to convene a conference themselves unless they were prepared to share their knowledge and the uranium etc. Do you wish them to tell the Russians? Is this what is meant by (quote) 'An Act of Faith' (Unquote). If so I do not believe they will agree, and I personally should deem them right not to, and will certainly have to say so, if and when the issue is raised in public.

Churchill's letter to Attlee continued:

The responsibility for propounding a world policy clearly rests with the USA. I imagine they have two or three years lead, and will have got still further on at that time. I am sure they will not use their advantage for wrong purposes of national aggrandisement and domination. In this short interval they and we must try to reach some form of security based upon a solemn covenant backed by force viz the force of the Atomic bomb. I therefore am in favour, after we and the USA have reached agreement, of a new United Nations Conference on the subject. I do not however consider that we should at this stage at any rate talk about (quote) 'Acts of Faith' (Unquote). This will in the existing circumstances raise immediate suspicion in American breasts.

With reference to the Anglo-American aspect of atom bomb research since 1941, Churchill told Attlee:

Moreover we have a special relationship with them in this matter as defined in my agreement with President Roosevelt. This almost amounts to a military understanding between us and the mightiest power in the world. I should greatly regret if we seemed not to value this and pressed them to melt our dual agreement down into a general international arrangement consisting, I fear, of pious empty phrases and undertakings which will not be carried out. (See what happened about the submarines.)

Churchill then turned to the question of the bomb as a deterrent, and the control of any international agreement:

Nothing will give a foundation except the supreme resolve of all nations who possess or may possess the weapon to use it at once unitedly against any nation that uses it in war. For this purpose the greater the power of the US and GB in the next few years the better are the hopes. The US therefore should not share their knowledge and advantage except in return for a system of inspection of this and all other weapon-preparations in every country, which they are satisfied after trial is genuine. Evidently we all have to hasten.

'I sympathize deeply,' Churchill ended, 'in your anxieties.' [1]

Attlee accepted the force of Churchill's argument. 'As you will see,'

[1] 'Personal and Secret', 'undated', marked 'show again on return' and 'Keep for Tuesday meeting': Churchill papers, 2/3.

he wrote to him on October 4, 'the beginning of the penultimate paragraph of the original draft has been omitted.'[1] 'I am much obliged to you for sending me a copy of your letter to the President,' Churchill wrote on October 6, and he added: 'I fully recognize the fearful gravity of the problem with which it deals.'[2]

---

[1] 'Secret and Private', 4 October 1945: Churchill papers, 2/3.
[2] 'Personal and Top Secret', 6 October 1945: Churchill papers, 2/3.

9
'Vain repinings'

ON his return to London in October 1945, Churchill received the first of what were to be many hundreds of invitations to lecture. It came through President Truman, and was an invitation to deliver 'a series of three or four lectures' at Westminster College, in the small Missouri town of Fulton. 'This is a wonderful school in my home State,' Truman explained, and he added: 'Hope you can do it. I'll introduce you.'[1] This was the genesis of Churchill's 'Iron Curtain' speech. Another invitation came from Field Marshal Montgomery, to the Alamein Dinner. 'We shall expect a terrific speech from you!' Montgomery wrote.[2]

Churchill accepted both invitations. He also accepted the Freedom of the City presentation at Bancroft School, in his Woodford constituency, an event which took place on October 21. This was his first public appearance after his cold and sore throat, which had prevented him from attending Parliament for more than a week. 'I have not made the progress I had hoped,' he wrote to Sir James Hawkey, his constituency Chairman, on October 18. His letter continued:

My throat is still inflamed and my voice quite incapable of any effort. However I hope the next forty-eight hours will show an improvement and that my vocal cords can be touched up before I start. If I am voiceless on the day, I will, none the less, come and have my speech read out in my presence. I shall only speak for ten or twelve minutes.

I will certainly visit the guests in both the Halls after the Ceremony, but this must not involve any more speechmaking.

'At present I can hardly croak,' his letter ended. 'I am right in myself, as long as I do not get a fresh cold.'[3]

---

[1] Letter of 3 October 1945 from President F. L. McCluer, Westminster College, Fulton, Missouri; with an additional note on the letter, written by President Truman: Churchill papers, 2/230.

[2] 'Dear Mr Churchill', 8 October 1945: Churchill papers, 2/143.

[3] 'My dear Sir James', 18 October 1945: Hawkey papers.

All was well on the day. 'I freely avow to you, my friends,' Churchill told his constituents, 'that it was not without a pang that I found myself dismissed at the General Election from the honourable task of guiding our country.' He had hoped 'that the position I had gained in the world, the experience and knowledge which I had acquired, and the links which had been forged in the fires of war with other lands and leaders might have been of service in this critical time of transition and in the fateful work of trying to revive the life and glory of Europe within the circle of assured world peace'. He had also looked forward to throwing all his 'personal strength', and that of his colleagues, 'into the demobilization of the forces, into the rebuilding of our homes, into the switch-over of our industries to peace-time production, and into the liberation of British genius and energy from the long thraldom of war conditions'. But these, he added, were 'vain repinings'.[1]

On October 23, at the Alamein Reunion Dinner, held at Claridge's, Churchill declared: 'Up till Alamein we survived. After Alamein we conquered.' As for Montgomery—'Monty, as I have for some time been allowed to call him'—he was, said Churchill, 'one of the greatest living masters of the art of war'. Either on the eve of great battles, 'or while the struggle was actually in progress, always I have found the same buoyant, vigorous, efficient personality with every aspect of the vast operation in his mind, and every unit of mighty armies in his grip'.[2] 'I *did* enjoy our reunion at the Alamein Dinner the other evening,' Churchill wrote to Montgomery a few days later. 'It was indeed an honour and a happy occasion for me.'[3]

On October 26 the Canadian Prime Minister, Mackenzie King, lunched with Churchill at Hyde Park Gate. 'He has a marvellous mind,' Mackenzie King noted in his diary, 'ranges from one subject to another with perfect ease and adequate expression.' Churchill told King 'he feared conditions were going to be pretty serious in England as a consequence of the policy of destroying the rich to equalize incomes of all'. He himself 'would have been prepared to take three quarters of the income of wealthy men but he would have left them enough to have an incentive to work'. King also noted Churchill's thoughts on Russia:

He said that Russia was grabbing one country after another—one Capital after another. He said that all these different countries, naming the lot of the Balkans, including Berlin, would be under their control. He thought they should have been stood up to more than they were. I asked him if it was true

---

[1] Speech of 21 October 1945: Churchill papers, 5/1.
[2] Speech of 23 October 1945: Churchill papers, 5/1. There is a recording of this speech in the BBC Written Archives Centre, Library No. LP 25587.
[3] 'My dear Monty', 3 November 1945: Churchill papers, 2/143.

that Stalin had told them at one time that if need be settlements would have to be made by force. He said no, that was not true, though he had had some pretty stiff talks with Stalin. He did not know what was the truth about Stalin's position. Whether he was sick or well. The Government had told him nothing.

He spoke about the Russian regime as being very difficult but said there was nothing to be gained by not letting them know that we were not afraid of them. That they would not thank us for lying down before them at any stage. He said that he had strongly pressed before the war to make no settlements or awards until the armies were holding all the positions they had taken. He stressed very strongly what realists they were. He called them 'realist lizards', all belonging to the crocodile family. He said they would be as pleasant with you as they could be, although prepared to destroy you. That sentiment meant nothing to them—morals meant nothing. They were hard realists, out for themselves and for no one else and would be governed only in that way.

I asked him how they got the money to develop the power they have. He said to me that they had quantities of gold and platinum in Russia. That was one source and they had paid for nothing that had been given to them. He then spoke of the difference between the people and the militarist regime. He said that the militarist regime were a class by themselves and were the controlling factor.

King then told Churchill of the defection in Canada of a leading Soviet spy. This, said Churchill, was 'interesting and most important', and he went on to tell King:

. . . you must remember that with the Communists, Communism is a religion. One could say if one were using an expression that should not be misunderstood that some men would call them Jesuits without Jesus in the relationship. What he meant was that they were using any means to gain an end, that end being the end of Christianity, of Christian purposes. He said that it was impossible to view them in any other than a most realistic way. They were realists to the extreme. He said to me he thought that where men had done what was wrong, the wrong should be exposed but he agreed that it would be better not to do anything without exploring the situation very carefully at first. He strongly approved of the President, Britain and Canada all acting together in the matter. He thought it would be as well to delay action until a careful plan had been worked out but that it should not be allowed to go by default. He felt it was right to talk to the Ambassador but to leave it there would be a mistake. That the world ought to know where there was espionage and that the Russians would not mind that; they had been exposed time and again. He felt that the Communist movement was spreading everywhere and that those who were Communists would do anything for their cause, deceive everybody. They had no religion or religious belief beyond that of what they were seeking in their cause.

He then went on to speak about the US and the UK. He said to me he hoped I would do all I could to keep the two together. I said to him I did not think the British Commonwealth of Nations could compete with the Russian situation itself nor did I think the US could. That I believed that it would require the two and they must be kept together. He said to me, that is the thing you must work for above everything else if you can pull off a continued alliance between the US and Britain. It must not be written, it must be understood. But if you can get them to preserve the Joint Chiefs of Staff arrangement and have plans made to keep the two together you will be doing the greatest service that can be done the world.[1]

Churchill made one more public speech that October, to the boys of Harrow School. In a reference to his own premiership he told them how, as a schoolboy, when 'much attracted' by the kettle-drum:

Again and again I thought 'If I could only get hold of this on one of these fine evenings.' However, there must have been some protecting interest which inspired the authorities in those days, and I was never allowed to have my opportunity. So I gave up that ambition and transferred my aspirations to another part of the orchestra. I thought 'if I cannot have the kettle-drum I might try to be the conductor'; there is a great deal in the gestures at any rate—in those which occur most readily to a politician. At any rate it always seemed to me that that was the part in the orchestra I could play best, always excepting the kettle-drum. That could not be arranged either while I was at Harrow, but eventually, and after a great deal of perseverance, I rose to be the conductor of quite a considerable band. It was a very large band and it played with very strange and formidable instruments, and the roar and thunder of its music resounded throughout the world. We played all sorts of tunes, and we finished up the concert, Sir, with 'Rule, Britannia' and 'God Save the King'.

That 'particular concert' was now over, 'and I was looking for a new orchestra, and thought perhaps that I might find one here'. But if he could 'no longer aspire to keep the position of conductor I at least hoped to find a kettle-drum'.

'This is a time,' Churchill ended, 'when the voice of youth will be welcomed in the world.'[2] It was also a time when several of the defeated Conservative MPs were turning to Churchill, hoping for a message of support in their struggle to return. 'We have made a good start,' wrote Harold Macmillan in seeking one such message, 'but it is not going to be an easy fight. The tide of slop and sentiment is still flowing and the people do not seem to realize the serious condition of

---

[1] Mackenzie King diary, 26 October 1945: J. W. Pickersgill and D. F. Forster, *The Mackenzie King Record*, volume 3, *1945–1946*, Toronto 1970, pages 83–7.
[2] Speech of 31 October 1945: Harrow School archive.

affairs.'[1] In his reply, Churchill told Macmillan, for his constituents: 'We need you very much on the Front Opposition Bench. . . .'[2]

On November 9, as a gesture of support for Macmillan, Churchill drove through the suburbs of Penge and Bromley in an open car, while *en route* for Chartwell, joined by Macmillan from the Crystal Palace to the southern edge of his constituency.[3]

Churchill's work as Leader of the Opposition was centred during these early months of his leadership on the creation of a 'Consultative Committee of the Opposition', or, as it was more popularly known, a 'Shadow Cabinet'. There were to be fifteen members, each with a special area of responsibility: the Committee member responsible for Indian policy was R. A. Butler, to whom Churchill forwarded such letters as he received on the subject of Indian independence.

One problem Churchill dealt with in connection with his Shadow Cabinet was the size of the table in his room in the House of Commons. It would, as Churchill's secretary Mrs Hill explained to Harold Wilson, Parliamentary Secretary at the Ministry of Works, 'seat only eight or nine in comfort'.[4] A larger table had, it appeared, already been installed, but if Churchill wanted 'a yet larger table', Harold Wilson's secretary replied, 'instructions will be given for one to be provided'.[5]

The Shadow Cabinet met every Tuesday at 6 p.m., in Churchill's room at the House of Commons. The first three peers whom Churchill invited to attend were Lord Woolton, Lord Cherwell and Lord Cranborne, to whom he had written in August: 'It will give me great pleasure if you will be one of our regular members.'[6]

Nearly two decades later, Randolph Churchill and Harold Macmillan discussed these early months of Churchill's leadership of the Opposition. Their conversation went as follows:

HM: We met a lot then. He didn't enjoy opposition very much. He took the defeat very well—outwardly.

RSC: Outwardly, but God, he hated it inwardly. I remember him saying to me one day—three months after the election—he was very miserable. He

[1] 'My dear Winston', 'Personal', 30 October 1945: Churchill papers, 2/2. Macmillan, the Conservative MP for Stockton-on-Tees since 1924, and Secretary of State for Air in the Caretaker Government, had been defeated by more than 8,000 votes by the Labour candidate, Captain G. R. Chetwynd, a lecturer for the Workers' Educational Association, and a former officer in the Army Education Corps.

[2] 'My dear Harold Macmillan', 1 November 1945: Churchill papers, 2/2. Macmillan was re-elected to Parliament, at a by-election, by the electors of Bromley, with a majority of more than 10,000 over his Labour opponent, Mrs J. R. Elliott.

[3] Note by Kathleen Hill, 5 November 1945: Churchill papers, 2/2.

[4] Letter of 10 November 1945: Churchill papers, 2/2.

[5] Letter of 20 November 1945: Churchill papers, 2/2.

[6] 'My dear Bobbety', 25 August 1945: Churchill papers, 2/1. Cranborne had been Secretary of State for the Dominions in Churchill's Caretaker Government.

said: 'These people think it silly when the child minds if his toys are taken away from him. But he *does* mind. What I mind is the Boxes.'

HM: He found it difficult to attune himself at first to that House with a great Socialist majority, they'd be in for 20 years, there would never be another Conservative Government. And his speeches, although admirable, were a bit long and not quite attuned to that. And I think he minded that rather. And Attlee developed a rather clever, rather pawky way of answering in 20 minutes, puncturing this tremendous balloon getting off the ground slowly.[1]

Churchill now spent as much time as possible at Chartwell, to which during the war he had been able to make only half a dozen brief visits. Invited with her husband to stay with a cousin in Gloucestershire, Clementine Churchill wrote: 'But he simply won't go visiting,' and she went on to explain: 'After six years, Chartwell is liberated! It's in a sad state but we go down every weekend & struggle amid piles of dusty & mildewed books & are told by the gardener that the garden can *never* be got back!'[2]

Churchill did not intend to allow the gardener's opinion to deter him. Focusing on the problems of the Fish Pool, he set out for those who would have to deal with it what he wanted done, now that German prisoners-of-war were available for the task:

The water will remain at its present level in the two lakes. There should be room for the fish in the upper pool. Every care should be taken to close, by means of wire netting, the pinstock. It does not matter the water going to and fro but I do not want the big fish to escape from the upper pool.

I am afraid of people coming by night and netting the fish crowded in here. Therefore no further efforts should be made to pull any more stakes or brushwood out of the part which is still filled with water.

The Germans should clear all the exposed parts thoroughly of brushwood and debris. Then they should go to the swimming pool, the bottom of which should be quite cleared of debris and camouflage. Next they should go up the sunken trench between the swimming pool and the meadows and clear all the barbed wire from there and cut away the weeds and briars that have grown among it. They should continue to work upwards on the barbed wire till it cuts the road and then take out the barbed wire near Harris's cottage and opposite the tennis ground.

Harris[3] on Sundays, and Whitbread during the rest of the week, should keep a sharp eye to drive away herons. There is no harm in the water being made and kept muddy. We should try every means to procure a drag-net.

[1] Randolph Churchill and Harold Macmillan in conversation, 17 May 1962: Randolph Churchill papers.

[2] Letter of 30 October 1945 (to Captain George Spencer-Churchill): archival collection of F. Bartlett Watt.

[3] The gardener at Chartwell; he was later succeeded by Vincent.

Mr Blayter (?) of Harrods should help, but perhaps there is one in the neighbourhood which could be borrowed. I do not want to buy it if we can get one without. It should be at least 50 yards long.

While the fish are crowded together in this narrow space, it would be as well to give them a few handfuls of food each day.

The pulling out of the last stakes and brushwood in this inundated part of the upper pool could be started on Friday. As soon as I get back I will supervise the pulling out of the fish with the net and the carrying of them in the tins to the garden pool where, of course, as there is no mud, they will have to be fed till they go to sleep for the winter.[1]

Clementine Churchill had never been entirely at ease with the burdens of Chartwell life, and with the need to repair the dilapidations of the five war years those burdens were no lighter. 'Although she acquiesced in the developments at Chartwell,' her daughter Mary has written, 'she derived more worry than pleasure from them. Moreover, she was not really reconciled to the fact that Winston was determined to battle on in politics. She had longed, and she still longed, for him to retire.' Mary Soames added:

All her life her energy had been in excess of her stamina, but like many others, during the crisis years, Clementine had 'kept going': now accumulated exhaustion was catching up on her. Throughout the autumn and winter of 1945 her health was only middling, and she suffered from depression and nervousness. The build-up of her worries, which her fatigue served to enlarge, made her often impatient and irascible with Winston; and he, for his part, could be demanding and unrealistic. These months saw a series of scenes between them. After any quarrel both suffered pangs of remorse, and both were always anxious to make it all up. But these were difficult days for them both.

To add to the difficulties, Churchill's work, whether at Chartwell or in London, and the mass of correspondence which descended upon him, required three full-time secretaries, Clementine Churchill needing a fourth to manage the many requests which also came to her. All this was a strain on the resources at 28 Hyde Park Gate, a strain only relieved when Churchill was offered, during 1946, the freehold of the adjoining house, No. 27. For a while, Mary Soames later recalled, 'Clementine hesitated, as it seemed to her a monstrously extravagant way to acquire more office space—to buy a complete house with a garden! However, it really was the only solution, and No. 27 was duly bought. And eventually Clementine's Scottish prudence was appeased when it was found possible to create a charming maisonette on the top two floors, which was let.'[2]

[1] 'The Fish Pool, Chartwell', 10 November 1945: Churchill papers, 1/30.
[2] Mary Soames recollections: *Clementine Churchill*, pages 397–8.

That November Churchill made a short visit to the French and Belgian capitals. In Paris, on November 12, he spoke of how it was his hope 'that a new and happier Europe may one day raise its glory from the ruins we now see about us. And in this noble effort the genius, the culture and especially the power of France should play its true and incontestable role.'[1] While in Paris, however, staying with the Duff Coopers at the British Embassy, Churchill's thoughts were on the implications of the closest possible relationship with the United States. He had been upset by the reluctance of the British Foreign Office to press for joint Anglo-American control of occupied Japan. 'The question of the administration of Japan,' Churchill had explained to Attlee in August, 'by the American Supreme Commander without any Allied Control Commission was never discussed between me and President Truman. I should strongly have opposed such a suggestion.'[2] Lord Halifax, the British Ambassador in Washington since 1940, now argued in favour of United Nations Trusteeship rather than joint Anglo-American control. To Ernest Bevin, who had sent Churchill the telegrams on this issue, Churchill wrote on November 13, from Paris:

Dear Ernest,
Thank you for sending me the telegrams, which I have duly burnt.

The long-term advantage to Britain and the Commonwealth is to have our affairs so interwoven with those of the United States in external and strategic matters, that any idea of war between the two countries is utterly impossible, and that in fact, however the matter may be worded, we stand or fall together. It does not seem likely that we should have to fall. In a world of measureless perils and anxieties, here is the rock of safety.

From this point of view, the more strategic points we hold in Joint occupation, the better. I have not studied particular islands and bases in detail on the map, but in principle there is no doubt that the Joint occupation greatly strengthens the power of the United States and the safety of Britain. Although the United States is far more powerful than the British Commonwealth, we must always insist upon coming in on equal terms. We should press for Joint occupation at all points in question rather than accept the exclusive possession by the United States. We have so much to give that I have little doubt that, for the sake of a general settlement, they would agree to Joint occupation throughout.

I do not agree with the characteristic Halifax slant that we should melt it all down into a vague United Nations Trusteeship. This ignores the vital fact that a special and privileged relationship between Great Britain and the

---

[1] Speech of 12 November 1945, the French Institute, Paris: Churchill papers, 5/2.
[2] Note by Churchill (to John Peck, for Clement Attlee), 27 August 1945: Churchill papers, 2/2.

United States makes us both safe for ourselves and more influential as regards building up the safety of others through the international machine. The fact that the British Commonwealth and the United States were for strategic purposes one organism, would mean:

(a) that we should be able to achieve more friendly and trustful relations with Soviet Russia, and

(b) that we could build up the United Nations organization around us and above us with greater speed and success. 'Whom God hath joined together, let no man put asunder.' Our duties to mankind and all States and nations remain paramount, and we shall discharge them all the better hand in hand.

Churchill's letter continued:

As you know, I write as a strong friend of the Russian people, and as one of those responsible for the Twenty Years' Treaty with the Soviet Government, to which Treaty I most strongly adhere. The future of the world depends upon the fraternal association of Great Britain and the Commonwealth with the United States. With that, there can be no war. Without it, there can be no peace. The fact that strategically the English-speaking world is bound together, will enable us to be all the better friends with Soviet Russia, and will win us the respect of that realistic State. Strategically united, we need have no fear of letting them come out into the great waters and have the fullest efflorescence as their numbers and their bravery deserve.

The Joint Association of the Great British Commonwealth and the United States in the large number of islands and bases, will make it indispensable to preserve indefinitely the organization of the Combined Chiefs of Staff Committee. From this should flow the continued interchange of military and scientific information and Intelligence, and also, I hope, similarity and interchangeability of weapons, common manuals of instruction for the Armed Forces, inter-related plans for the war mobilization of civil industry, and finally, interchange of officers at schools and colleges.

What we may now be able to achieve is, in fact, Salvation for ourselves, and the means of procuring Salvation for the world.

'You are indeed fortunate,' Churchill ended, 'that this sublime opportunity has fallen to you, and I trust the seizing of it will ever be associated with your name. In all necessary action you should count on me, if I can be of any use.' [1]

'I agree with you about joint bases,' Bevin replied. 'But the difficulty is that we have committed ourselves to the United Nations, and I must keep this aspect in mind.' [2]

---

[1] 'Most Secret', 13 November 1945: Churchill papers, 2/2.
[2] 'Dear Winston', 'Top Secret and Personal', 17 November 1945: Churchill papers, 2/2.

While he was in Paris, Churchill reflected on an aspect of the election campaign which had caused him considerable distress: his inability to influence the decision of the Liberal Party to put up candidates against the Conservatives in as many constituencies as possible. To Lady Violet Bonham Carter, daughter of the Liberal Prime Minister H. H. Asquith, who had been Churchill's personal friend since the first decade of the century, including Churchill's own twenty years as a leading member of the Liberal Party, he wrote on November 14: 'I am forced to say that, in my view, you, and other leading Liberals, have behaved with a complete indifference and detachment to the vital interests of our country, and have sought Party advantage in a reckless and wanton manner.' Churchill added: 'Animal hatred of the Conservative Party, which appears to be the sole remaining theme of Liberalism, certainly did us an immense amount of harm at the late General Election without doing the slightest good to Liberal interests. You may well find that the future will bring great dangers and privations upon us all, for which certainly you will bear a small but quite recognizable responsibility.'

Churchill added: 'I am not animated by any personal sense of soreness at having been dismissed.' [1]

While still in Paris, Churchill received a personal request from a former French Prime Minister, Pierre-Etienne Flandin, to write a letter on his behalf for submission to the court before which Flandin was appearing, on a charge of treason, based upon his support for the Vichy Government in its early days. Churchill's letter read:

Dear Monsieur Flandin,

For many years I regarded you as a strong friend of the Franco-British Entente, and you were the French statesman with whom I had the closest personal contacts before the War. I well remember your visit to me when, as Foreign Secretary, you came early in the morning to my flat in London after the German invasion of the Rhineland in 1936. Although I was at that time out of Office, it was to me that you came first, asking my help, which I gladly promised, in your endeavours to bring about a more decisive joint action between the two countries in view of the gross outrage which Hitler had committed.

In those days, His Majesty's Government were still hoping against hope that the Hitler menace would not materialize in war, and in this hope and wish they were undoubtedly supported by very large majorities of the British and, as far as I could see, the French people. I very much regret that the ideas we had in common at that time could not have been brought into effect, and that a solid front or circle of nations, including those of the Little Entente, was not built up against the ever-growing encroachments of Germany.

[1] 'Private', 13 November 1945 (marked 'Mrs C to see' and 'hold', and never sent): Churchill papers, 2/146.

Afterwards, when the Munich Agreement was made, you sent a telegram to Hitler congratulating him on the peaceful settlement. I did not agree with this for reasons which I gave abundantly in public, but I must admit that the Munich Settlement was supported by very large majorities on both sides of the Channel, not only in the Parliaments but in the countries at large. I did not consider that the differences between us at this time in any way altered our personal relations, or weakened my confidence in you as a French friend of England.

Presently terrible things happened and France, under the overwhelming fury of the German irruption, asked for an Armistice. As an Englishman, I have never reproached the French nation on account of this yielding to dire necessity. My grief was that, although we had done all that we had promised, we had not been able to do more. However we made up for this later on, and in the end, all came right.

When, in the middle of December 1940, I learned that you had joined the Vichy Government, I was glad. I thought to myself, 'here is a friend of England in a high position in the Vichy Government, and I am sure that this will lessen the danger of that Government declaring formal war upon us'. I also thought it only too probable that you would not last long, and that the Germans would have you out. This is exactly what happened, at the beginning of February.

I have heard that in your period of Office, you managed to stop an expedition being sent from Dakar against the Free French centre at Tchad. If this is true, it would seem to me important that the facts should be elicited, because any such expeditions from Dakar would have added greatly to the troubles which General de Gaulle and I were facing together at that rather forlorn and desperate time before the corner had been turned.

Accordingly when later in 1942 and 1943 you were in Algiers, I did not hesitate to enter into friendly relations with you through the medium of my son, Randolph, and I always regarded you as on our side and against the common foe and his collaborators.

Now of course in all this that I have written, I am judging these matters as an Englishman, and not presuming to do so as if I were a Frenchman. You have however asked me, in your danger, to put down what our personal relations have been, and I feel I should be failing in a duty of friendship, which I always try never to do, if I did not set forth the facts as I saw them and felt them at the time. It is for you and your legal advisers to judge whether the reading of this letter will be serviceable to you, or not. So far as I am concerned, I leave the decision entirely in your hands.[1]

Flandin decided to use the letter in his defence: it caused a considerable stir when read out in court.[2]

---

[1] Letter of 14 November 1945: Churchill papers, 2/149.

[2] On 23 January 1946 the charges against Flandin of 'intelligence with the enemy and conspiracy' were dropped, and he was released from custody (he had been in a nursing home since July 1945, and under arrest since 1943). Following his trial he was declared ineligible for Parliament. He died in 1958, at the age of sixty-nine.

From Paris, Churchill travelled to Brussels, where he was met by large and enthusiastic crowds lining the streets and cheering wherever he passed. 'I have never seen such excitement or such enthusiasm,' the British Ambassador, Sir Hughe Knatchbull-Hugessen, later recalled, and he explained:

Presents of all kinds began to pour into the Embassy long before his arrival—cigars, flowers, books, paintings; there was a large work of art in marzipan representing Snow White and the Dwarfs. Crowds assembled and waited for hours. Even in more select gatherings, such as the Palais des Académies where he was made an Associate, people stretched out their hands to touch him as he passed up the hall. In the streets stray remarks were overheard—'Shall I say "Hurrah" in English or French, which do you think he would like best?' and from an old lady who had placed her camp-stool at a street corner—'Now I have seen Mr Churchill, I can die.'

'People broke through the police-cordon,' Knatchbull-Hugessen added, 'dodged the motor-cycle escort which surrounded the car and threw their bouquets into the car if they were not actually successful in handing them to Mr Churchill. One girl leapt on to the running-board, threw her arms round his neck and kissed him fervently.' [1]

While in Belgium, Churchill had to deliver four speeches. Before his visit he had written to Knatchbull-Hugessen, to say that he would be most obliged if the Ambassador could send him drafts for all four speeches. This task had fallen to Cecil de Sausmarez, the First Secretary at the Embassy, who during the war had been Regional Director for the Low Countries in the Political Warfare Executive in London. De Sausmarez later recalled:

My four drafts suffered very different fates.

The first was delivered exactly as I wrote it with only one expression changed ('gilded bars' into 'tinsel bars'). As I had also drafted for my friend the Rector of Brussels University a speech in English conferring the degree, the two fitted together very well and Churchill congratulated the Ambassador on the result of his labours!

The draft for Louvain was considerably cut down though some of the essential facts were retained. I think that, by now, Churchill was becoming rather tired, especially as Brussels was visited that evening by one of its very rare pea soup fogs.

Elated by the tremendous reception which he was receiving everywhere from the Belgian crowds, Churchill abandoned the last two drafts completely and relapsed into what can only be described as 'Franglais'. I remember that he delighted his audience in Brussels by finishing his impromptu address with

---

[1] Sir Hughe Knatchbull-Hugessen, *Diplomat in Peace and War*, London 1949, page 238.

the words 'Vive la Bruxelles', though his opening words at Antwerp 'Je suis très heureux d'être rentré enfin à l'Anvers' must have puzzled many Flemings to whom he appeared to be saying that he was 'very happy to be returning at last upside down'.[1]

On November 16, Churchill spoke at a joint meeting of the Belgian Senate and Chamber. During his speech he explained why, during the war, when Roosevelt had asked him what the war should be called, he had replied, 'The Unnecessary War'. As Churchill explained:

If the United States had taken an active part in the League of Nations, and if the League of Nations had been prepared to use concerted force, even had it only been European force, to prevent the re-armament of Germany, there was no need for further serious bloodshed. If the Allies had resisted Hitler strongly in his early stages, even up to his seizure of the Rhineland in 1936, he would have been forced to recoil, and a chance would have been given to the sane elements in German life, which were very powerful especially in the High Command, to free Germany of the maniacal Government and system into the grip of which she was falling.

Do not forget that twice the German people, by a majority, voted against Hitler, but the Allies and the League of Nations acted with such feebleness and lack of clairvoyance, that each of Hitler's encroachments became a triumph for him over all moderate and restraining forces until, finally, we resigned ourselves without further protest to the vast process of German re-armament and war preparation which ended in a renewed outbreak of destructive war.

'Let us profit at least by this terrible lesson,' Churchill declared; and he added, 'In vain did I attempt to teach it before the war.'

Churchill went on to appeal to his Belgian audience to uphold 'the conception of free democracy', to have above all 'tolerance, the recognition of the charm of variety, and respect for the rights of minorities'. His speech ended with a plea for a 'United States of Europe' which would, he said, 'unify this Continent in a manner never known since the fall of the Roman Empire, and within which all its peoples may dwell together in prosperity, in justice, and in peace'.[2] He made a similar plea, in French, during his speech of acceptance for the Freedom of Brussels.[3]

Returning to London, Churchill hastened to thank Knatchbull-Hugessen for his work in arranging the visit. 'It provided the Belgian people,' Churchill wrote, 'with an opportunity of letting off their ex-

---

[1] C. H. de Sausmarez recollections: letter to the author, 1 September 1986.
[2] Speech of 16 November 1945, Brussels: Churchill papers, 5/2.
[3] Speech of 16 November 1945, Brussels: BBC Written Archives Centre, Library No. 9262–3.

plosive feelings of enthusiasm for the British nation, and I was fortunate enough to be the recipient of these sentiments.' Churchill also thanked the Ambassador for the speech drafts which the Embassy had given him on his arrival. 'All the speeches which were prepared by you or your staff,' he wrote, 'were admirable and, though I did not in every case use them wholly, they formed the foundation upon which it was easy for me to compose the various remarks I made. Will you please thank Mr de Sausmarez for the work he did upon them. It must have been a great labour preparing all these drafts.'

Churchill's visit to Belgium had given him great pleasure. 'My only regret,' he told the Ambassador, 'is that my wife could not be with me to see for herself all that happened.'[1]

Clementine Churchill's health, which so often was not good enough to allow her to accompany her husband on his journeys, was not to prevent her from joining him in his first post-war journey across the Atlantic. Indeed, for Churchill himself that journey was connected with his health. 'My doctor thinks that four or five weeks' rest and recuperation in the sunshine and with sea-bathing, would be good for me,' he explained to President Truman at the beginning of November, 'and the prospect is certainly most attractive.' He had also been invited to visit Mexico—though he feared that the altitude 'might not be particularly good for me'—and Brazil. He had consulted the British Government about such a tour, 'and they inform me', he told Truman, 'they view it with favour'. If he came, it would be a 'great pleasure' to speak at Westminster College, Fulton, Missouri, 'on the world situation, under your aegis'. That was the only public-speaking engagement he had in mind, 'for it would be my respect for you and your wishes'.[2]

In a further letter to Truman three weeks later, Churchill reiterated that he would not make any other public-speaking engagements in the United States, 'certainly not' before Missouri. 'I have had so many colds and sore throats already this winter,' he explained, 'that Lord Moran, my doctor, is very anxious for me to have a month in the warmth and sunshine, and I shall therefore be under medical protection from the many kindnesses which I feel sure will be offered me by my American friends when they hear of my plan.' As for Mexico, he had 'abandoned' that project altogether: 'It would not be good for me,' he explained, 'to live at such a height even for a week or ten days.' Churchill's letter ended:

I shall indeed look forward very much to some talks with you. The United

[1] 'My dear Ambassador', 20 November 1945: Churchill papers, 2/222.
[2] 'Private and Personal', 'My dear Mr President', 8 November 1945: Truman papers.

States has reached a pinnacle of glory and power not exceeded by any nation in the whole history of the world, and with that come not only opportunities literally for saving misguided humanity but also terrible responsibilities if those opportunities cannot be seized. Often and often I think of you and your problems as I did of those of our dear friend FDR. I am most thankful you are there to fill his place.[1]

Churchill's last major speech before his American journey was to the Central Council meeting of the Conservative Party. 'You give a generous welcome,' he began, 'to one who has led you through one of the greatest political defeats in the history of the Tory Party,' and he added: 'It may perhaps be that you give me some indulgence for leading you in some other matters which have not turned out so badly.' He would use 'such facilities as remain to me' to organize an opposition Front Bench in the House of Commons 'of really able, competent, modern-minded men', to carry forward the cause 'of the greatness of Britain', now threatened by a Socialism which, 'if not overcome and defeated, will cramp and press the British nation down to levels we have never contemplated'. His speech ended with a warning of 'fundamental quarrels' soon to come:

It seems impossible to escape the fact that events are moving and will move towards the issue—'The People versus the Socialists'. On the one hand will be the spirit of our people, organised and unorganised, the ancient, glorious, British people, who carried our name so high and our arms so far in this formidable world. On the other side will be the Socialist doctrinaires with all their pervasive propaganda, with all their bitter class hatred, with all their love of tyrannising, with all their Party machinery, with all their hordes of officials and bureaucracy.

'There lies the impending shock,' Churchill declared, 'and we must be ready to meet it as a true People's Party, gathering together all that is vital and healthy in our island life and caring for nothing except the glory, strength, and freedom of Britain.'[2]

Churchill spoke these words of warning two days before his seventy-first birthday. He also was sent that day a letter from Burke Trend, the Private Secretary to the Chancellor of the Exchequer, expressing Treasury reluctance to enable him to transfer £25 sterling to the United States, a transfer which was against the Government's currency regulations. His draft, which he dictated in the third person, read, as if from his secretary:

Mr Churchill desires me to say that he certainly does not seek any personal favours from His Majesty's Government. He thought, however, that his

---

[1] 'My dear Mr President', 29 November 1945: Churchill papers, 2/230.
[2] Speech of 28 November 1945: Churchill papers, 5/2.

family association with the United States had been of public advantage in the war, and might still be of public advantage; and it was on public even more than on private grounds that he wished to make this small symbolic contribution to the rebuilding of the Church of Pompey in which his American forebears are buried.

However, if the Chancellor has finally decided not to allow this personal token of twenty-five pounds to be given by him, he will write to the Syracuse body and explain the circumstances. Mr Churchill presumes he will be permitted to publish or refer to the Treasury letter, and instructs me to say that he does not consider that this particular exercise of arbitrary power is an instance of wise or sensible judgment.[1]

On November 30, Churchill celebrated his seventy-first birthday. 'Seventy-one is a good age,' Montgomery wrote from his headquarters in Germany, 'and you do not want to overdo it.'[2] At Christmas came a letter of greeting from Sir Stafford Cripps, once Churchill's Ambassador to Moscow, emissary to India, and Minister of Aircraft Production; now President of the Board of Trade, and a political opponent. 'May I,' Cripps wrote, 'as an old colleague still imbued with gratitude for all you did for us during the war, send you and Clementine my very best wishes for a happy Christmas and a good New Year.'[3] From King George VI came a photograph of the Buckingham Palace balcony on VE Day, 'our famous "balcony scene"' Churchill called it, signed by the King and Queen, and by the two Princesses, Elizabeth and Margaret. 'This is indeed a magnificent Christmas Card for me,' Churchill wrote, 'and it will ever be preserved in my family as a memorial of a great and joyous day, and also as another instance of the kindness and honour with which Your Majesty has always treated Yr Faithful and devoted servant and subject, Winston S. Churchill.'[4]

Churchill had also written to the King's brother, the Duke of Windsor, that December, to report failure in his attempt to support the Duke's wish to be given some honorary post with the British Embassy in Washington. Churchill also commented, in his letter to the Duke of Windsor, on his own political position. 'The difficulties of leading the Opposition are very great,' he wrote, 'and I increasingly wonder whether the game is worth the candle.' It was only from 'a sense of duty', Churchill added, 'and of not leaving friends when they are in the lurch, that I continue to persevere'.[5]

In mid-December Churchill received a gift from Lord Mountbatten, a surrendered Samurai sword which, Mountbatten wrote, 'I wish you

---

[1] 'Dear Mr Trend', undated (and possibly never sent): Churchill papers, 1/41.
[2] 'Dear Mr Churchill', 3 December 1945: Churchill papers, 2/143.
[3] 'My dear Winston', 21 December 1945: Churchill papers, 2/140.
[4] 22 December 1945: Churchill papers, 2/141.
[5] 'Private', 15 December 1945: Churchill papers, 2/178.

to accept since it was surrendered as a result of the overall victory against Japan of which you were the principal architect'.[1]

There was a second reminder of the war that December, when Churchill read in the newspapers a statement by General Marshall to a Senate Committee that during the war Roosevelt and Churchill had telephone conversations which were 'tapped by the enemy'. Churchill wrote at once to Marshall: 'Of course the late President and I were both aware from the beginning even before Argentia that anything we said on the open cable might be listened in to by the enemy. For this reason we always spoke in cryptic terms and about matters which could be of no use to the enemy, and we never on any occasion referred directly or indirectly to military matters on these open lines.'[2]

Churchill and his wife spent the first post-war Christmas in London. 'It was quietish, but very pleasant,' Mary Soames has recalled, 'with Diana and Duncan, Sarah, myself, Uncle Jack and Aunt Nellie, all mustered. It made a quiet and peaceful ending to a year that had seen such cataclysmic events for the world, and had been full of drama in our own personal lives as well.'[3]

As part of the Christmas festivities, a Churchill family party was held at Hyde Park Gate on December 22. John Carr, a Civil Servant at the Law Courts who had a string marionette show as a hobby, was engaged to perform to the grandchildren. As the show was about to begin, Churchill took his seat in the front row. 'During the show he concentrated on it absolutely,' Carr's daughter Barbara later recalled, 'giving a running commentary, and remarking at the end that he liked the item about a frog and duck "because the frog got away". He also told the children about a butterfly that had hatched out in his room.'[4] On December 24 there was a family dinner party at Hyde Park Gate, and on Boxing Day a visit to the theatre.[5] Then, on December 27, Churchill went to Chartwell for the New Year.

At the end of 1945, Churchill had learned of a plan, conceived by Lord Camrose, to set up a Trust which would purchase Chartwell from him, lease it back to him at a nominal rent, and, on his death, transfer it to the National Trust. Churchill was delighted by the plan, which would give him a good capital sum immediately, and at the

---

[1] 'My dear Mr Churchill', 14 December 1945: Churchill papers, 2/141.

[2] 'Private and Secret', sent through Ambassador Winant, 9 December 1945: Churchill papers, 2/144. The meeting at Argentia, off Newfoundland, the first wartime meeting between Churchill and Roosevelt, had taken place in August 1941.

[3] Mary Soames, recollections: *Clementine Churchill*, page 399. 'Aunt Nellie' was Clementine Churchill's sister Nellie Romilly.

[4] Mrs Barbara Sharpe recollections: letter to the author, 12 January 1982.

[5] Churchill Engagements Calendar, December 1945. The play was Shakespeare's *Henry IV*, Part Two, in which Laurence Olivier played Mr Justice Shallow (that afternoon, in Part One, he had played Hotspur).

same time ensure that Chartwell, as he had created it, would survive his death. On December 29 he wrote to Lord Camrose from Chartwell:

Living at this place in the dying year I have been thinking so much of your noble and princely plan for making Chartwell a national possession, and I feel how inadequate my thanks have been to you for all your kindness. I take it as an immense and precious compliment that you should have conceived this plan with your eminent friends. You may be sure that Clemmie and I will do our utmost to invest the house and gardens with every characteristic and trophy that will make it of interest in the future.

I am now off almost immediately for much needed rest and sunshine on Florida beaches. When I come back the lawyers will have finished their work, and I would venture to suggest that I should be your guest at a dinner of the Trustees, where the formal signing of the deeds can take place and where I can express my thanks personally to each and all of you—But to none more than you, my dear Bill, who have never wavered or varied in your faithful friendship during all these long, baffling, and finally tumultuous years since you took the Chair for me at that luncheon in 1924.[1]

The work of restoration at Chartwell continued unabated. 'While I am away,' Churchill wrote to Robert Southon, the local builder, 'the following things should be done.' He set them out under four headings:

1. *Urgent.* The German prisoners will shortly remove the escape hatch of the air raid shelter in front of Chartwell Manor, and level the ground, etc. This will expose the cellar itself, and it will be necessary for you to make it good by filling in the small space in the roof, and making it water-tight and weatherproof. It is intended to use the shelter itself as a storeroom in the future, and you should yourself consider and decide whether a ventilating shaft is necessary or not. The present one is very unsightly.

2. There is now no chance of the wood for the bookshelves arriving in time for the work in the small library to be done before I leave for America. However I have explained to your carpenter exactly what I want done, and I hope he will be in a position to carry out the work as soon as the wood arrives.

3. The castors for the painting platform are absolutely essential to its use. It is a great burden to me pushing it to and fro across the floor. I trust the castors will be available before my return in March. It is essential that they should work in every direction.

4. There is a great draught in my Study, which in cold weather makes it impossible for me to sit at my writing-table. This draught comes in partly at the big bay window, which requires re-puttying. Opportunity might be taken to do the other windows as well. Still more, according to your carpenter, does the draught come in at the boarding of the roof at this part. It is not necessary to go over the whole roof, as this was done thoroughly ten or

---

[1] 'Private', 'My dear Bill', 29 December 1945: Camrose papers.

twelve years ago. I should be glad however if the spaces between the boards could be puttied up, or otherwise made good.[1]

In the last week of 1945, Churchill took up work again on *A History of the English-Speaking Peoples*, the four-volume work which he had virtually completed on the outbreak of war in September 1939; indeed, he had been working on the final chapter on the night Hitler invaded Poland. Among the historians who had helped him before the war, and were helping him again, was Denis Brogan, Professor of Political Science at the University of Cambridge, and an expert on the history and politics of both the United States and France.

Brogan now sent Churchill his notes on the English political system in the eighteenth century.[2] Churchill read these notes on the last day of 1945.

In the New Year's Honours List for 1946 Churchill was awarded the Order of Merit. His daughter Mary wrote to him at once, on New Year's Day 1946:

My darling Papa,
  Happy New Year!
  I was so proud and excited when I read in the press this morning of yet another distinction which is yours.
  And this letter is to say thank you, very, very much for your generous present to my Church Army Fund.
  I am going to miss you and Mama so much when you go away, but I shall rejoice to imagine you both tossed by star-spangled waves and petted by your friends and kinsmen—the Americans. I hope with all my heart you will find a measure of peace and contentment there, and in this new year.
  I can guess at a small part of your sense of disillusion and frustration in these times which to so many seem the dawn of better times and again to so many the twilight of prestige and greatness and unity.
  To all who love you—and there are so great a number—it is a grief to see you so set aside—and so saddened. The grief is the greater for the little we can do to help you.
  We can only tell you of our unfaltering faith, and burning gratitude and tender love.
  From your proud and ever loving daughter

Mary[3]

'It seems fatuous to congratulate you on accepting the Order of Merit,' Desmond Morton, Churchill's wartime Intelligence adviser,

---

[1] Letter of 5 January 1946: Churchill papers, 1/30.
[2] Professor Brogan's notes, marked 'Read, 31 xii 45': Churchill papers, 8/800. Denis Brogan, who was born in 1901, was knighted in 1963. He died in 1974.
[3] 'My darling Papa', 1 January 1946: Lady Soames papers.

wrote on January 2. 'There is no worldly honour too high for you. The only honour worthy of your deeds will come to you in history, and in the hearts of men who have known you.' [1]

'The OM comes from the King alone,' Churchill wrote to one of those who had congratulated him, 'and is not given on the advice of Ministers. This renders it more attractive to me.' [2]

One of those who had served under Churchill in the war had received no decoration in the Honours List: Marshal of the Royal Air Force Sir Arthur Harris. On January 6, three days before he was to sail for New York, Churchill wrote to Attlee to protest:

I was sorry and very much surprised to see that Marshal of the Royal Air Force Sir Arthur Harris received no decoration in the recent Honours List. No Commander-in-Chief in the Royal Air Force after Lord Dowding bore so heavy a direct burden as he, and none contributed more distinguished qualities to the discharge of his duty. As Minister of Defence I had the opportunity and the duty of watching his work very closely and I greatly admired the manner in which he bore the altogether peculiar stresses of planning and approving these repeated, dangerous and costly raids far into the heart of the enemy's country. For nearly four years he bore this most painful responsibility and never lost the confidence or loyalty of Bomber Command, in spite of the fact that it endured losses equalled only, in severity, by those of our submarines in the Mediterranean.

When we consider also the immense part played by the bombing offensive in shortening the war and thus bringing it to an end before the enemy long-range weapons developed their full potency, nobody can deny its cardinal importance. It was also a grim and invidious task that was laid upon this Air Marshal and which he discharged with unfailing poise and equanimity, although deeply conscious of its grievousness.

'I earnestly trust,' Churchill added, 'that this omission may be repaired before Marshal of the Royal Air Force Harris leaves this country to make his home in South Africa.' [3]

In reply, Attlee stated that had Harris been given an Honour it would have meant either 'increasing the List considerably' beyond its present size, or omitting names whose exclusion 'if his had been included' would have given rise to dissatisfaction and justifiable criticism. Attlee ended: 'I can hold out no hope that the decision which has been taken in this case will be revised'; promotion to Marshal of the Royal Air Force, Attlee insisted, a high rank which was 'so rarely' accorded during the war, 'cannot be regarded as an inadequate

---

[1] Letter of 2 January 1946: Churchill papers, 2/456.
[2] 'Confidential', 4 January 1946: Churchill papers, 2/2.
[3] 'My dear Prime Minister', 6 January 1946: Churchill papers, 2/150.

recognition of his great services'.[1] Churchill's efforts on his friend's behalf had been in vain.[2]

Always concerned that his wife and children might have financial needs which he could not meet, Churchill now embarked upon yet another literary project, the publication in book form of his wartime Secret Session speeches. A new secretary, Elizabeth Gilliatt, had come to take the place of Mrs Hill, who was retiring from secretarial work after being with Churchill for more than nine years, including the whole of his wartime premiership. Mrs Hill stayed on in order to help Miss Gilliatt learn what had to be done, and it was the typing out of the Secret Session speeches which proved to be her first task.[3] For the next nine and a half years Miss Gilliatt was to be a devoted member of the small inner circle which made possible Churchill's mastery of so many spheres of activity. 'He didn't waste a single talent', was Miss Gilliatt's reflection, thirty-one years after those first days at Churchill's side.

Before leaving for the United States, Churchill had one sad personal letter to send. His son's marriage to Pamela Digby had ended in divorce. 'I grieve so much,' Churchill wrote to Pamela's mother, Lady Digby, 'for what has happened which put an end to so many hopes for the future of Randolph and Pamela,' and he wrote, in explanation but without rancour: 'The war strode in however through the lives of millions. We must make the best of what is left among the ruins.'

Everything must now be 'erected', Churchill wrote, upon 'the well being and happiness' of young Winston. Pamela had 'brought him up splendidly'. There must be friendship 'to shield him from the defects of a broken home'. It was a 'comfort', Churchill added, 'that the relations between our families remain indestructible'.[4]

On the afternoon of January 9, Churchill and his wife sailed on board the *Queen Elizabeth* for the United States.

---

[1] 'Private', 9 January 1946: Churchill papers, 2/150.

[2] Many years later, Sir Arthur Harris was to quote Churchill's remark to him, recalling the Battle of Jutland: 'You fought a thousand battles and won most of them. Jellicoe fought one and lost it, and Lloyd George made him an Earl' (Sir Arthur Harris recollections: in conversation with the author, 1 May 1982). On 6 January 1953 Brendan Bracken wrote to Harris of how 'you alone as Commander-in-Chief were able to carry the war into Germany when the soldiers and sailors were unable to strike a blow at Hitler's warriors' (Letter of 6 January 1953: Harris papers).

[3] Elizabeth Gilliatt recollections: in conversation with the author, 12 June 1987.

[4] Letter of 6 January 1946: Churchill papers, 1/41.

10

The Fulton Speech

ON 7 January 1946, two days before Churchill set sail for the
United States, his photograph appeared on the front page of
Life magazine. Wearing his siren suit, cigar in mouth, hat on head, he
was shown standing in his studio at Chartwell, retouching a painting.
'Winston Churchill has played many roles in contemporary history,' the
magazine declared, 'but none more enthusiastically than that of the ama-
teur painter.'[1] Inside were four pages of Churchill's colour paintings.[2]

It was not, however, as a painter, but as an author, that his mind
was focused as the *Queen Elizabeth* sailed westward. He had not yet
decided whether he should write his war memoirs. On board the *Queen
Elizabeth* he therefore continued work on *A History of the English-Speaking
Peoples*. From on board ship, he sent Professor Brogan the typescript of
the medieval section, together with notes specially prepared by a leading medieval historian, Professor Vivian Galbraith. 'I am greatly impressed with the precision and learning of Professor Galbraith's work,'
Churchill told Brogan, 'as I am also with your own.' Churchill added:
'The only service this book of mine can render is to excite the interest
of a large number of people who, once they have escaped from school,
might not otherwise read about these periods at all.' It was therefore
'most necessary that I should not make any mistakes which would
allow critics to discredit the general accuracy of the work'.

Churchill had already incorporated Brogan's notes on Scotland and
Ireland in the Middle Ages, and had corrected the Joan of Arc section
'after reading Anatole France's highly documented study'. He hoped
that Brogan would not think his praise of Joan 'excessive'.[3]

---

[1] *Life*, 7 January 1946, page 9.
[2] 'On the shore of Lake Como'; 'Reflections at St Jean (Cap Ferrat)'; 'Scene in Cannes
Harbour'; 'Villa on the Nivelle (Hendaye)'; 'Olive Grove at La Dragonière'; 'Goldfish Pond
(Chartwell)' and 'Terrace at Chartwell (after a snowfall)'. Luce had founded *Life* magazine in
1936, six years after he had established *Time* magazine.
[3] 'Private', 'On board RMS *Queen Elizabeth*', 10 January 1946: Churchill papers, 4/443.

Among those on board the *Queen Elizabeth* were several hundred Canadian troops, returning home at last after what had been for many of them more than five years overseas. On their last day at sea, Churchill spoke to the assembled troops and crew. His speech, typed out by his secretary Miss Sturdee, was later given to Commodore Bisset, the ship's captain. Churchill told the Canadians:

My friends and shipmates in the *Queen Elizabeth*!

For most of you it is homeward-bound. It has been a good voyage in a great ship, with a fine Captain—or indeed Commodore. We have not got there yet, but I am quite sure he will find the way all right.

At any rate, he has been over the track before, and as I can testify myself, having been several times with him, in those days there used to be U-boats and things like that.

They all seem to have dropped off now and we don't have to worry about them at all. Something has happened.

The seas are clear, the old flag flies, and those who have done the work, or some of it—because the British did some—turn home again, their task accomplished and their duty done.

What a strange, fearful, yet glittering chapter this war has been!

What changes it has wrought throughout the world and in the fortunes of so many families!

What an interruption in all the plans each of us had made! What a surrender of the liberties we prized! What a casting away of comfort and safety! What a pride in peril!

What a glory shines on the brave and true!

The good cause has not been overthrown. Tyrants have been hurled from their place of power, and those who sought to enslave the future of mankind have paid, or will pay, the final penalty.

You Canadians, many of whom served in the Canadian Fifth Division, no doubt have your minds filled with the victorious war scenes of Italy and the Rhine.

But we Englishmen always think of the days of 1940 when the Canadian Army Corps stood almost alone in Kent and Sussex, and the Germans had 25 divisions ready to leap across the Channel and wipe Great Britain out of life and history.

I think about those days, too, sometimes and how fine it was to see everyone, at home and throughout the Empire, moved by the same impulse, so simple, so sublime—'Conquer or die!'

Victory in arms, or in any walk of life, is only the opportunity of doing better on a larger scale and at a higher level.

Do not be anxious about the future! Be vigilant, be strong, be clear-sighted, but do not be worried.

Our future is in our hands. Our lives are what we choose to make them.

The great British Commonwealth and Empire, emerging from the fire once again, glorious and free, will form a structure and an organisation within which there will be room for all, and a fair chance for all.

Churchill's speech continued:

Yesterday I was on the bridge, watching the mountainous waves, and this ship—which is no pup—cutting through them and mocking their anger.

I asked myself, why is it the ship beats the waves, when they are so many and the ship is one?

The reason is that the ship has a purpose, and the waves have none.

They just flop around, innumerable, tireless, but ineffective. The ship with the purpose takes us where we want to go.

Let us therefore have purpose, both in our national and Imperial policy, and in our own private lives.

Thus the future will be fruitful for each and for all, and the reward of the warriors will not be unworthy of the deeds they have done.[1]

Disembarking at New York, Churchill went by train direct to Miami Beach, where he was the guest of Colonel Frank W. Clarke, who in 1943 had been his host in the Canadian lakeland after the Quebec conference.[2]

On January 15, his first day at Miami Beach, Churchill gave a press conference on the patio of Colonel Clarke's house. Asked by newsreel cameramen to say 'ten words' into the microphone, Churchill said: 'I have been asked to say just ten words, but I haven't been told what ten words they should be. The ten that come to my mind are: "The great pleasure I feel in enjoying the genial sunshine of Miami Beach."' According to the report in the *Miami Daily News*:

He was in good humor and answered reporters' questions quietly and distinctly.

In explaining why England required the loan, he said:

'We suffered far more than any other country during the war.

'Some other countries were overrun, but they were not fighting. We were fighting and using up our credit. We borrowed all we could and now we must use all we can get.'

---

[1] Speech notes: Sir James Bisset, *Commodore*, London 1961: first printed in the *Daily Express*, 21 September 1961.

[2] Colonel Clarke, whose family had in 1920 sold their paper mills in Quebec to Lord Northcliffe and Lord Rothermere, had first met Churchill during the General Strike in 1926, and had worked for Churchill on the *British Gazette*. They had met again at the Quebec Conference in 1943, when Churchill had stayed at the Colonel's lakeside cabin for two days of rest and seclusion. Clarke's oldest son, Captain William F. Clarke, had spent nearly four years as a prisoner-of-war of the Japanese. Clarke was a shipowner; many of his ships had served in Allied operations, as hospital ships, supply ships and troopships.

He confessed that the Japanese attack on Pearl Harbor was 'a complete surprise to him'.

'I never thought they would be guilty of such madness,' he said.

He added he wasn't surprised when Germany attacked Russia.

'I did my best to warn Russia,' he added.

Asked if there was any resentment in England toward the United States use of British bases under a 90-year lease, he said emphatically: 'No, we didn't trade those islands for 50 old destroyers. We did it for strategic use by the United States and for your safety and ours.'

The main question at the press conference concerned the four-billion-dollar loan which Britain was asking from the United States. Churchill told the journalists:

We are most anxious to earn our own living and be independent. I'm sure His Majesty's Government would never approve of having the social and economic life of Britain improved at the expense of other countries, particularly when they are now our good friends.

But if we're not given the opportunity to get back on our feet again we may never be able to take our place among other nations.[1]

One of the journalists present, Walter Locke, gave his readers a pen portrait of Churchill in Miami.

A round-faced, round-headed, benevolent, almost jolly gentleman without a vestige of a front! The collar of his shirt spreads open. A soft hat with brim upturned in front gives him a look of genial impishness not incompatible with a brownie or kewpie doll. His hat removed, one wisp of hair serves as a cover to his crown. The humor which has lubricated his life flashes in his face and sparkles on his tongue. Lubricated his life? Who that has fought as he has fought could live at all except a saving humor balanced him? As to pose, he sits slumped, looking never an inch the statesman, this atomic bomb of an Englishman.

'It is a mild quiet voice,' Locke added, 'that runs on pleasantly here under the palms. No hint is given of the fierce growling of the cornered lion of five years ago. He speaks in English, not American. "I 'ave been asked," he says. Between his sentences he keeps the perpetual cigar alight. Had he brought a supply along with him? That, with Havana so near, would be coals to Newcastle.' Locke's account ended:

The interview is over. The Gibraltar of his Britain rises and turns to go. His face, at 71, is chubby, smooth. But the man who fought at Omdurman almost 50 years ago and who has been fighting ever since must surely show somewhere the marks of his struggling years. As he turns his back—the back

[1] *Miami Daily News*, 16 January 1946.

never shown to an enemy—we see in a sagging of the shoulders a sign of
the burdens they have borne. Such, in the flesh, is the giant of the spirit
whose deeds will echo through centuries, a body needing the rest beneath the
southern sun which so richly it has earned.[1]

At Miami, Churchill was helped by two secretaries: his own Miss
Sturdee, who had crossed the Atlantic with him, and Lorraine Bonar,
whom Colonel Clarke had lent to him. On January 17 Lorraine Bonar
wrote to her parents in Canada:

Well, the great man has arrived and he's just wonderful—he entirely cap-
tivated me with his lack of pretentiousness and is really charming to everyone.
I met both him and Mrs Churchill, who is very lovely and charming in
manner as well as appearance, when they arrived from the train and of
course have seen them several times in the house. Today, Mr Churchill and I
had a little chat concerning the goldfish, of which I am keeper. He is very
fond of them and thought that he may try to take some back with him.[2]

In her subsequent letters home, Lorraine Bonar continued to report
on this extraordinary man who had descended into their midst:

Mr C is quite a tease and can't resist sailing through the library a couple
of times a day to tease Miss Sturdee about the time change between England
and Florida. With a twinkle in his eye and a very gruff voice, he says—
'What time is it now in England, Miss Sturdee' and I shake for fear he asks
me as my mind goes completely blank in his presence.

No one, least of all Colonel Clarke, expected the ovation which would be
given to Mr Churchill in the US and we are consistently overwhelmed by it.
We receive an average of 300 letters a day and can't begin to open them, let
alone answer them. Lord Halifax from the British Embassy in Washington had
a secretary flown down to the Consulate in Miami just to take care of the
requests for autographs (Miss Shullemson and then later Georgie Duffield,
who Jo and I enjoy very much). Jo and I are kept busy just taking care of
our bosses and answering letters about gifts that arrive and thank-you notes
etc. I imagine out of the multitude of mail, that Mr C only actually dictates
answers to about 10 per day. The rest, the secretaries handle on their own.[3]

Lorraine Bonar later recalled:

Mr C invariably had a little smile on his face in the house and seemed to
be secretly amused at the fact that he caused such a sensation. He just loved
to shout at the top of his lungs for Miss Sturdee despite the fact that we had
had buzzers installed in his room and maids and telephones, etc. Miss Sturdee
would very calmly reply—'Alright, I'm coming' which really broke me up
because I was so much in awe of him. He wasn't above being very difficult
and contrary and even had his little spats with Mrs Churchill when he

[1] Walter Locke, 'Churchill in Miami': Lorraine Bonar collection of press cuttings.
[2] Letter of 17 January 1946: Lorraine Bonar papers.
[3] Letter, undated: Lorraine Bonar papers.

screamed 'Clemmie' at her from across the hall. Once they went for about two days with only the very necessary speaking between them.

'Millions of words have been written about and by Mr Churchill,' Lorraine Bonar added, 'but one creed that he drilled into us in Miami was "Don't Waste Words" with the result that our letters were very short . . .' [1]

'I hope to find sunshine and painting here,' Churchill wrote from Miami Beach on January 18, to his old friend Sir Hugh Tudor, 'but today it is grey and cold.' In his letter, Churchill recalled the Victorian era in which they had served together in India in the 4th Hussars, reflected on the General Election, and remembered old friends:

I have seen a good deal of the 4th Hussars from time to time during the war. I am their Colonel and I inspected them four times in different theatres during the war. When I went to Como a few months ago, Alexander paid me the compliment of sending a detachment all across Italy to look after me with two very good young officers—quite up to the standard of the old days.

I found it very odd being turned out of power just at the moment when I imagined I would be able to reap where I had sown, and perhaps bring about some lasting settlement in this troubled world. However it may all be for the best as there is no doubt that a Conservative Government would have been very roughly treated by the Left-Wing elements, and strikes and labour troubles would have made our path one of extreme difficulty. I found it none too easy to change over so quickly from a life of intense activity and responsibility to one of leisure in which there is nothing to be looked for but anticlimax. However, luckily I have my painting, into which I have plunged with great vigour, and many other amusements, so that the time passes away pleasantly and rapidly.

What a wonderful thing it is, looking back, to see all we have survived. All the follies that England commits in time of peace did not prevent her true greatness from shining forth in the hour of need. And now, although other perils can be discerned, we may at least say that the German danger is behind us.

I heard from Reggie Barnes the other day. He has not been at all well, but is now about again. [2] Reggie Hoare also is recovered from a serious operation. [3] I also think of Albert Savory, our Number 2. It is forty-five years since he was killed in action, and yet so vivid are the memories and friendships of early youth that I can remember him as if it was but yesterday we were all planning

---

[1] Lorraine Bonar recollections: letter to the author, 14 November 1986.

[2] Reginald Barnes, three years Churchill's senior, had accompanied him to Cuba in 1894, served with him in India, and was later severely wounded in South Africa. He was twice wounded in the First World War, promoted Major-General, and knighted (1919). He died on 19 December 1946.

[3] Reginald Hoare (born in 1865) was one of Churchill's fellow officers in India. He later served in South Africa and on the Western Front, where he was wounded, and promoted Brigadier-General. He died on 14 October 1947.

to win the Cavalry Cup.[1] So strong and lasting also, my dear friend, are my feelings towards you, not only of far-off Bangalore days, but of the great moments of Plug Street and March 21.[2]

Willie Y. Darling is now one of my supporters in the House of Commons. He is a grand fellow, well worthy of the 'Black and Tans'.[3]

Wishing you the best of fortune.[4]

'Papa has not yet settled down to painting,' Clementine Churchill wrote to her daughter Mary on January 18, 'and is a little sad and restless, poor darling. I hope he is going to begin writing something.' Later that day she added: 'The weather has slightly improved and Papa has now started a picture of palms reflecting in the water. I visited him, and draped a knitted Afghan round his shoulders as he was sitting under a gloomy pine tree in a particularly chilly spot.'[5] Four days later Clementine Churchill wrote again:

Papa, thank God, has recovered or nearly so. We had a wretched 36 hours when we telephoned to Lord Moran & the temperature, tho' not very high, simply would not go down & poor Papa was very nervous about himself, & yet very obstinate & would either take no remedies at all or several conflicting ones at the same time.

But today he bathed! & loved it. The weather is now perfect but tropical. Crickets chirp all night—there are lovely flowering hedges of hibiscus pink lemon & apricot. . . . The sea is heavenly—water about 70°.

Papa has learnt a new card game 'Gin Rummy' & plays all day & all night in bed & out of bed. He has started 2 not very good pictures.

Tender love (I must fly Papa is calling). . . .[6]

---

[1] Albert Savory had first met Churchill when they were fellow subalterns at Aldershot. Shortly after Savory was killed in action in South Africa, Churchill wrote to Lady Randolph Churchill (on 1 September 1900): 'Albert Savory was almost the best friend I have at the front, and we lived in the same regiment for $4\frac{1}{2}$ years. I have not been so pained for a long time.'

[2] From January to June 1916 Churchill served as Lieutenant-Colonel Commanding the 6th Royal Scots Fusiliers at Ploegsteert (known to the British troops as Plug Street). In March 1918 he was with General Tudor at the front on the morning of the German breakthrough. In 1920, when Churchill was Secretary of State for War, Tudor commanded the Irregular Forces in Ireland (the 'Black and Tans'). In 1922, when Churchill, as Colonial Secretary, was the Minister responsible for Britain's Palestine Mandate, Tudor was General Officer Commanding the Palestine gendarmerie (known as 'Tudor's lambs'). After his retirement in 1923 he lived in Newfoundland. Three years older than Churchill, he died eight months after Churchill, on 25 September 1965.

[3] William Young Darling, a silk merchant, had served at Gallipoli, at Salonica, and with the 9th Scottish Division on the Western Front. In 1920, when Churchill was Secretary of State for War, he was second-in-command of the Black and Tans. Lord Provost of Edinburgh from 1941 to 1944, he was Conservative MP for South Edinburgh from 1945 to 1957. He died in 1962. In his book *Hades, the Ladies*, published in 1933, Darling described Churchill as 'the most interesting figure in public life to me since Joseph Chamberlain left it', and he called *The World Crisis* a 'great panorama of man's endeavour', adding that 'women do not find a place in its pages except as munitions workers'.

[4] 'As from 5905 North Bay Road, Miami Beach', 18 January 1946: Churchill papers, 2/230.

[5] Letter of 18 January 1946: Mary Soames, *Clementine Churchill*, page 401.

[6] Letter of 22 January 1946: Mary Soames, *Clementine Churchill*, page 401.

While Churchill was at Miami, the first of what were to be hundreds of wartime reminiscences, including recollections of Churchill himself, was published: a series of articles by Eisenhower's naval aide, Captain Harry C. Butcher. These contained copious diary extracts of conversations between Eisenhower and those whom he met, Churchill included. Butcher had no access to the many messages exchanged between Churchill and Eisenhower, nor had he been present at most of their conversations. So he had fallen back, as so many memoir writers were to do, on trivia, stressing for example Churchill's late hours of work, irrespective of the pressure of events or the needs of the war. 'I have skimmed over the Butcher articles,' Churchill wrote to Eisenhower on January 26, 'and I must say I think you have been ill-used by your confidential aide.' Churchill's letter continued:

The articles are, in my opinion, altogether below the level upon which such matters should be treated. Great events and personalities are all made small when passed through the medium of this small mind. Few people have played about with so much dynamite and made so little of it. I am not vexed myself at anything he has said, though I really do feel very sorry to have kept you up so late on various occasions. It is a fault I have and my host here, Colonel Clarke, has already felt the weight of it. It is rather late at my age to reform, but I will try my best.[1]

In reply, Eisenhower assured Churchill that 'I never complained about staying up late. I didn't do it often and certainly I always came away from one of those conferences with a feeling that all of us had gotten some measure of rededication to our common task.'[2]

The memoirs of others were a vexation; but his own war memoirs promised to be the most lucrative venture of his life. While in Miami he asked his pre-war European literary agent, Emery Reves, to come to see him. Reves, who was then in Chicago, flew to New York, took the night train to Washington, then flew down to Miami in a British Embassy plane.[3] Twenty years later, in conversation with Randolph Churchill, Reves recalled that meeting:

During the luncheon I was terribly touched by the fact that in spite of what he had done during the war he remembered everything of our relationship in the pre-war years, and quite sentimentally with tears in his eyes he said to me: 'Everyone wants me to write my memoirs which I may do if I

---

[1] 'Private', 'My dear Ike', 'As from 5905 North Bay Road, Miami Beach, Florida', 26 January 1946: Churchill papers, 2/226. Butcher's book, *Three Years with Eisenhower*, was published later in 1946.
[2] War Department, the Chief of Staff, Washington DC, 30 January 1946: Churchill papers, 2/226.
[3] Among the passengers was Ian Fleming, on his way to Jamaica.

have time. And if I do, I have not forgotten what you have done for me before the war and I shall want you to handle it.'

I was naturally terribly touched because I knew that every American publisher wanted this and every literary agent, and he could have just have had anyone.

He said that for private reasons and financial reasons he was going to carry out the transaction through Lord Camrose because he had to make a capital deal and contractually I should have to deal with Lord Camrose. But that he will arrange all this and he will let me know when and how to contact him or Camrose so for the time being I should keep quiet.[1]

Those who hoped to publish Churchill's memoirs were already active in seeking to stake their claim for when negotiations would begin in earnest. On January 28, *Life* magazine published the first of Churchill's Secret Session speeches. 'It was of course a pig in a poke,' Henry Luce, the owner of *Life*, wrote to Daniel Longwell, its editor, and he added: 'I believe that *Life* has got to buy some such pigs in order to keep a position in the meat market. Also, the prestigious flamflam may make it worth while. Also, it can be worth the space plus the money if, in some sense, Churchill becomes "our author".'[2]

Two weeks later, a Labour MP, Adam McKinlay, asked in the House of Commons about Churchill's intention to publish his war memoirs, and suggesting that 50 per cent of all earnings by former Ministers from books 'based on official documents collected during their term of office' should go to the State. Without mentioning Churchill by name, he asked Herbert Morrison whether he was 'aware or not' of the plan for such a book. McKinlay was asked by the Speaker to withdraw, and did so 'unreservedly', but then went on to ask 'whether it is not the height of vulgarity that these things should be bandied about in the Press for gain?' The altercation continued:

Mr Morrison: Of course, I am not quite sure what is being referred to though I could have a good and intelligent guess, but if it is the publication of certain speeches of the right hon. Member for Woodford (Mr Churchill), they were not State documents.

Mr McKinlay: On a point of Order. I think I have tried to make the point clear. I was not referring to any particular person. I submit through you, Mr Speaker, that I am raising a question of vital principle affecting State documents in this country.[3]

*   *   *

[1] Account by Emery Reves, in conversation with Randolph Churchill, La Capponcina, Thursday 4 August 1966: Randolph Churchill papers.

[2] Letter, undated: quoted in Robert T. Elson, '*Time Inc.*', *The History of a Publishing Enterprise*, New York 1966, volume 2, page 157. Daniel Longwell was appointed Managing Editor of *Life* in 1944. He became Chairman of the Board of Editors in 1953.

[3] *Hansard*, 14 February 1946. McKinlay, a woodworker, had been Labour MP for the Partick Division of Glasgow from 1929 to 1931, and for Dumbarton since 1941.

On January 29 Churchill sent a personal message to Truman. 'It is very kind of you,' he wrote, 'to place a powerful plane at my disposal and I am going to Cuba in it on Friday for a week.' Churchill's letter continued:

I have abandoned my plan of going to Trinidad as it is too long a hop for pleasure-time, but I am examining the possibilities of going to Veracruz, which is on the sea level and where I hear the scenery is very fine for painting. I shall be back here on February 10.

I am very glad to know you are coming along this coast. I will certainly come out and see you on your ship if you would wish it. I need a talk with you a good while before our Fulton date. I have a Message to deliver to your country and to the world and I think it very likely that we shall be in full agreement about it. Under your auspices anything I say will command some attention and there is an opportunity for doing some good to this bewildered, baffled and breathless world.

I have just received a telegram from Harry Hopkins' wife saying that he is failing rapidly. I have a great regard for that man, who always went to the root of the matter and scanned our great affairs with piercing eye.

Churchill ended his letter with a reference to American domestic politics:

Let me congratulate you on what seems to be an improvement in the strike situation. My feeling, as an outsider, has been that there is so much good work and good wages going about at this time that the common interest of the State and the workers is enormous and will prevail, after the inevitable, convulsive movements of post-war readjustment have had their hour.[1]

Churchill's American visit was causing a certain distress in the Conservative Party. 'Personally,' wrote Lord Derby to Lord Beaverbrook on January 29, 'I think it is quite wrong of Winston to have gone abroad at such a time as this and for so long. I admit he wanted a holiday. Still, that he could have taken, but really to be left as we are now without any controlling power in our Party is to my mind bad statesmanship. . . .'[2] Unknown to Lord Derby, Churchill had already intervened, at the request of Conservative Central Office, to persuade J. H. Wooton-Davies not to split the Conservative vote at a by-election. He had done so by telegram from Miami, telling Wooton-Davies: 'I should regard it as a great act of loyalty and magnanimity on your part to stand aside or even to give your full support to the candidate chosen by the Association.' This, Churchill added, 'would

---

[1] 'My dear Mr President', from 5905 North Bay Road, Miami Beach, Florida, 29 January 1946: Churchill papers, 2/158.
[2] Letter of 29 January 1946: Derby papers.

be in full harmony with the service you have rendered to the Party in the past'.[1] On January 29, the day of Lord Derby's complaint, Ralph Assheton telegraphed to Churchill from Central Office: 'Your personal appeal to Wooton-Davies, couched in such persuasive language, has been entirely successful. . . .'[2]

On February 1 Churchill and his wife, joined by their daughter Sarah flew from Florida to Cuba. Asked at a press conference that day for his criticisms of the Attlee Government he declared: 'I do not discuss the government of my country when I am away from there.' As to the General Election results, 'in my country', he said, 'the people can do as they like, although it often happens later that they don't like what they have done'.[3]

Asked to comment on the current war crimes trials at Nuremberg, Churchill told his questioner: 'Terrible evidence has been presented against the accused, and there is no doubt that the trials are just. The guilty have been allowed defence. But I would never have believed in the atrocities committed by them, if I had not seen the evidence which revealed their terrible crimes.'

Questioned about the 'veto right of the Big Powers' at the United Nations, Churchill replied: 'it is a matter of right for them, although I understand that the small countries should also have their rights'. On atomic energy he expressed his hope 'that it would never be used for destructive purposes'.[4]

From London on February 2, James Stuart sent Churchill an account of the first two weeks of Parliamentary business: 'I miss your robust presence very much,' he wrote.[5] In his account, Stuart praised two of the younger Conservative MPs: David Eccles for a speech 'of a high order', and Peter Thorneycroft, who 'spoke very well on the Coal Bill from the Back Benches and seems to be a man who cannot be ignored'.[6]

While enjoying painting and swimming in Cuba, Churchill pondered the speech he was to make at Fulton. 'I am worried about the

---

[1] Telegram 'To Mr Wooton-Davies from Mr Churchill', 5905 North Bay Road, Miami Beach, Florida, 24 January 1946: Churchill papers, 2/8. In the General Election of 1945, Wooton-Davies, who had been elected unopposed for Heywood and Radcliffe in 1940, was defeated by 892 votes.

[2] Western Union telegram, 29 January 1946: Churchill papers, 2/8. The by-election, at Preston, was nevertheless won by Labour (which had won the seat in the General Election).

[3] Commenting ten years earlier on his daughter Sarah's marriage to Vic Oliver, Churchill had remarked: 'She has done what she liked, and now she must like what she has done.' On 8 February 1946 Anthony Eden wrote to Churchill: '. . . England is a good land, or would be if there weren't so many Socialists in it.' ('My dear Winston', 8 February 1946: Churchill papers, 2/6.)

[4] 'Summary of Mr Churchill's Press Conference of Feb. 1st as reported in the Daily Press', Havana, Cuba, 2 February 1946: Churchill papers, 2/231.

[5] 'My dear ex-Prime Minister', 2 February 1946: Churchill papers, 2/8.

[6] James Stuart, Note of 1 February 1946: Churchill papers, 2/8.

way things are going,' he wrote to Eisenhower on February 6, and added: 'There is only one safe anchor; wh both you & I know.' [1]

Even in Havana, Churchill could not avoid the pressures of British Parliamentary life. On February 8 he was sent a telegram from Eden, about criticisms in the House of Commons concerning omissions in the published Yalta agreements, as debated in Parliament in February 1945. One of the omissions, the agreement about Russia coming into the war against Japan, was, Churchill pointed out in a telegram to Eden as soon as he was back in Miami, 'a military secret of the most deadly character which, had it leaked out, might have led to a forestalling Japanese attack on Russia in the Far East'. [2]

At the suggestion of Lord Halifax, Churchill now made a considerable effort on Britain's behalf. The issue was the conditions imposed by the Americans on the new Loan to Britain, which was not to have any of the favourable terms which had earlier applied to Lend-Lease.

On February 17 Churchill sent Attlee an account of his discussion with his American friend Bernard Baruch and Secretary of State James Byrnes. 'I was surprised,' he began, 'that so much importance should be attached to Mr Baruch's attitude as to make the Secretary of State travel 1,000 miles one day and go back the same distance the next, merely for this purpose. However all passed off very pleasantly.' Churchill had been ill for the previous three days, 'but was able to receive them', he told Attlee, 'in my bedroom, where we had a two-hours talk on the Loan and on affairs in general'. Churchill's telegram continued:

Baruch thought it a mistake that interest should be charged for the Loan, that Imperial preference should be brought into it at all and that we should not be able to convert as soon as was proposed. On the other hand he considered that we should specify precisely the object for which we required the Loan. If it was for food or raw material he would gladly have them supplied. He made no objection to machine tools but said that Mr Brand had assured him that we did not require equipment. [3] He repeated continually that there would be no question but that the United States would supply Great Britain with all the food she needed in the transition period. On the other hand, he considered no case had been made out for so large an amount as four billion dollars, and commented adversely upon our heavy dollar credits.

I explained to him that these were more than balanced by the indebtedness we had incurred to India, Egypt, etc. for the war effort. He was opposed to

---

[1] 'Private', 'My dear Ike', 6 February 1946: Churchill papers, 2/226. 'Like you,' Churchill wrote to Wooton-Davies on 10 February 1946, 'I am full of anxiety for the future of the country and of its position in the world.' ('Dear Wooton-Davies', 10 February 1946: Churchill papers, 2/8.)

[2] 'Top Secret', 9 February 1946: Churchill papers, 2/6.

[3] Robert Brand (later Lord Brand) was Chairman of the British Supply Council in North America.

the American Loan being used for repaying or otherwise providing for such debts saying that we had both defended these countries from invasion and ruin, that it was an American interest to see that Britain did not collapse but not an American interest to have her pay her debts to those we had defended. You know well my views on this part of the story.

I was not able to supply particulars of exactly what we wanted the Loan for, but if you like to let me have them in a compendious form, I shall have a further opportunity of showing them to Baruch when I am in New York, who will certainly be mollified by being consulted. He is of course very much opposed to American money being used to make Socialism and the nationalization of industry a success in Britain.

I rejoined that the failure of the Loan at this stage would bring about such distress and call for such privation in our island as to play into the hands of extremists of all kinds and lead to a campaign of extreme austerity, detrimental alike to our speedy recovery and to our good relations. I also explained to him the deficit between export and import and the inevitable delay in building up our export trade which we had completely sacrificed for the common cause. He did not seem convinced but undoubtedly he is most anxious not to be unfriendly to our country, for which he expressed the most ardent admiration.

Churchill ended his telegram with a reference to his forthcoming speech in Missouri:

I am thinking now about my speech at Fulton, which will be in the same direction as the one I made at Harvard two years ago, namely fraternal association in the build-up and maintenance of UNO, and inter-mingling of necessary arrangements for mutual safety in case of danger, in full loyalty to the Charter. I tried this on both the President and Byrnes, who seemed to like it very well. Byrnes said that he could not object to a special friendship within the Organization, as the United States had already made similar special friendships with the South American States. There is much fear of Russia here as a cause of future trouble and Bevin's general attitude at UNO has done us a great deal of good.

The final paragraph of Churchill's telegram concerned Marshal of the Royal Air Force Sir Arthur Harris, the former head of Bomber Command, on whose behalf he had already intervened, but to no avail. Churchill tried once more, telling Attlee:

I ought to let you know that there is a great deal of feeling here among the high officers of the American Air Force about what is thought to be the slighting treatment of Bomber Harris. This will no doubt find expression when he comes here to receive the American Distinguished Service Medal on his way to make his home in South Africa. I am sorry about all this. Honours are made to give pleasure and not to cause anger. Surely you might consider a Baronetcy.[1]

---

[1] 'Private and Personal', 17 February 1946: Churchill papers, 2/210.

Replying on February 25, Attlee thanked Churchill for his talk with Baruch: 'I am sure that you will have done much good.' He also commented on Churchill's outline of what he would say in Missouri: 'I am sure your Fulton speech will do good.' As for Harris and the baronetcy, 'you know better than I do', Attlee wrote, 'the difficulty of keeping a balance both within a service and between services'.[1]

While he was at Miami Beach, Churchill was invited by one of his American cousins, Lillian Jerome, to visit his American ancestors' homes in Pompey and Syracuse. 'I have now decided,' he wrote to his cousin Shane Leslie, 'that, as I am here on doctor's orders for rest and leisure, I cannot add to the few engagements to which I am committed here, much as I should like to visit the place where our ancestors spent so much of their lives, and meet some of our relations.' Churchill added: 'I do not think it would be suitable for me to become a member of the Sons of the Revolution, as we were evidently on both sides then.'[2]

In his first public appearance since he had reached the United States more than a month earlier, Churchill spoke at the University of Miami on February 26, recalling before a crowd of 17,500 in Burdine Stadium the help which the University of Miami had given in 1941 by training cadets for the Royal Air Force before the United States 'became a belligerent'. Upwards of 1,200 cadets, he recalled, 'received here a very high quality of technical, navigational and meteorological training'. They flew five and a half million miles over Florida on instructional courses and, he reminded his audience, 'the majority, indeed a very large majority, gave their lives shortly afterwards for their country and our common cause'.

Speaking of his honorary degree, Churchill told the assembled faculty members and students, as his speech notes recorded:

> I am surprised that in my later life
> I should have become so experienced
>   In taking degrees.
> When, as a school-boy,
>   I was so bad at passing examinations.
> In fact one might almost say
>   that no one ever passed so few examinations
>   and received so many degrees.

---

[1] 'Top Secret', 'Private and Personal', sent to Miami as No. 13 from Ambassador Washington to Consul Miami, 25 February 1946: Churchill papers, 2/210.

[2] 'My dear Shane', 18 February 1946: Shane Leslie papers. Leslie and Churchill were both the grandsons of Leonard Jerome (born in Pompey, Onondaga County, New York State, in 1817, died 1891), great-grandsons of Samuel Jerome, a Militia Sergeant during the American Revolutionary War, and, on their mothers' side, of Major Libbeus Ball, 4th Massachusetts Regiment, who was wounded in 1777. (Genealogical Table: Richard Harrity and Ralph G. Martin, *Man of the Century, Churchill*, New York 1962, page 23.)

From this a superficial thinker might argue
   that the way to get the most degrees
     is to fail in the most examinations.
This would however, ladies and gentlemen, be a conclusion
   unedifying in the academic atmosphere
     in which I now preen myself,
and I therefore hasten to draw another moral
   with which I am sure we shall all be in accord:
namely, that no boy or girl
   should ever be disheartened
     by lack of success in their youth
but should diligently and faithfully
   continue to persevere
     and make up for lost time.[1]

On March 1, while still in Miami, Churchill sent the New York publishers Simon & Schuster the typescript of his wartime *Secret Session Speeches*. In return, the publishers sent him a cheque for $4,035, the American currency equivalent of £1,000.[2] This had been agreed in Miami between Churchill and Marshall Field, the owner of the *Chicago Sun*, who was to serialize the speeches at the time of publication.[3]

On March 3 Churchill left Miami for Washington, where he stayed overnight at the British Embassy. There, he continued to work on his speech for Fulton. His arrival in Washington came only nine days after the State Department had received a telegram from George Kennan, United States Chargé d'Affaires in Moscow, which opened up a quite new perspective on Soviet relations with the West.

Kennan had been asked to comment on a speech made by Stalin on February 9, in which he said that no peaceful international order was possible, that production of iron and steel, 'the basic materials of national defence', must be trebled, and that consumer goods 'must wait on rearmament'. 'Wherever it is considered timely and promising,' Kennan wrote, 'efforts will be made to advance official limits of Soviet power,' and he added: 'For the moment, these efforts are restricted to certain neighboring points conceived of here as being of immediate strategic necessity, such as Northern Iran, Turkey, possibly Bornholm. However, other points may at any time come into question, if and as concealed Soviet political power is extended to new areas. Thus a "friendly" Persian Government might be asked to grant Russia a port on Persian Gulf. Should Spain fall under Communist

---

[1] Speech notes, 26 February 1946: Lorraine Bonar papers.
[2] The value of £1,000 in 1946 had risen by 1987 to £13,410.
[3] M. Lincoln Schuster to Churchill, 4 March 1946: Churchill papers, 4/5.

control, question of Soviet base at Gibraltar Strait might be activated. But such claims will appear on official level only when unofficial preparation is complete.'

Soviet power, Kennan wrote, 'unlike that of Hitlerite Germany, is neither schematic nor adventuristic. It does not work by fixed plans. It does not take unnecessary risks. Impervious to logic of reason, and it is highly sensitive to logic of force. For this reason it can easily withdraw—and usually does—when strong resistance is encountered at any point. Thus, if the adversary has sufficient force and makes clear his readiness to use it, he rarely has to do so. If situations are properly handled there need be no prestige-engaging showdowns.' Gauged against the Western world as a whole, Kennan believed that the Soviet Union was 'still by far the weaker force. Thus, their success will really depend on degree of cohesion, firmness and vigor which Western World can muster. And this is factor which it is within our power to in-fluence.' [1]

As Churchill worked on his speech for Westminster College, it was learned in Washington that, contrary to earlier assurances, the Soviet Government would withdraw only a portion of its troops from north-ern Persia. The remaining Soviet troops would stay there 'pending examination of the situation'. March 2 had been the date which both Bevin and Molotov had accepted in September 1945, at the Council of Foreign Ministers, as that by which the Soviet troops would have left. The Soviet decision not to abide by this date came shortly after the Soviet Government had made it clear in Istanbul that it would like to see the Turkish Government replaced by one more amenable to Soviet wishes. These had hitherto been expressed by Molotov him-self as the cession of the Kars and Ardahan provinces of eastern Turkey, and joint Soviet–Turkish control of the Straits. [2] The mood which Churchill found at the White House was therefore one of alert-ness and uncertainty, reinforced by the telegram from George Kennan. It was not surprising that Admiral Leahy, to whom Churchill showed his speech 'first of all' on March 3, was, as Churchill informed Attlee and Bevin, 'enthusiastic', while Secretary of State Byrnes, to whom he showed it on the night of March 3, 'was excited about it and did not

[1] 'Secret', 22 February 1946: *Foreign Relations of the United States, 1946*, volume 6, Washington 1976, pages 696–707. From 1952 to 1953 George Kennan was in Moscow as Ambassador. Subsequently he wrote several books on Soviet–American relations and Soviet foreign and nuclear policy; his book *Russia Leaves the War* won the Pulitzer Prize in 1957.

[2] Feridun Cemal Erkin, *Les Relations Turco-Soviétiques et la question des Détroits*, Ankara 1968, pages 323–7. The Soviet demand had been made through Erkin himself, then Secretary-General of the Turkish Foreign Ministry. (Feridun Cemal Erkin recollections: in conversation with the author, Ankara, 1969.)

suggest any alterations'.[1] Churchill also telephoned to his son, who was then in New York, to read him the speech in its evolving form. Then, shortly after midday on March 4, he drove to the White House, where both President Truman and Admiral Leahy joined him for the drive to the railway station. The three men then boarded a special train for the twenty-four-hour overnight journey to Jefferson City, Missouri. Three days later, Churchill wrote to Attlee and Bevin of his talks on the train:

The President told me, as we started on our journey from Washington to Fulton, Missouri, that the United States is sending the body of the Turkish Ambassador, who died here some days ago, back to Turkey in the American battleship *Missouri*, which is the vessel on which the Japanese surrender was signed and is probably the strongest battleship afloat. He added that the *Missouri* would be accompanied by a strong task force which would remain in the Marmara for an unspecified period. Admiral Leahy told me that the task force would consist of another battleship of the greatest power, two of the latest and strongest aircraft carriers, several cruisers and about a dozen destroyers, with the necessary ancillary ships. Both mentioned the fact that the *Missouri* class carry over 140 anti-aircraft guns.

I asked about the secrecy of this movement and was told that it was known that the body of the late Ambassador was being returned in a warship but that the details of the task force would not become known before March 15. I feel it my duty to report these facts to you, though it is quite possible you may have already been informed through other channels. At any rate, please on no account make use of the information until you have received it from channels, other than my personal contact with the President.

Churchill commented on what Truman and Leahy had told him:

The above strikes me as a very important act of state and one calculated to make Russia understand that she must come to reasonable terms of discussion with the Western Democracies. From our point of view, I am sure that the arrival and stay of such a powerful American Fleet in the Straits must be entirely beneficial, both as reassuring Turkey and Greece and as placing a demurrer on what Bevin called cutting our life-line through the Mediterranean by the establishment of a Russian naval base at Tripoli.

That night, as the train steamed westward towards the Mississippi, Churchill and Truman played poker. According to another of the players, Clark Clifford, at about 2.30 a.m. Churchill put down his cards and said: 'If I were to be born again, there is one country in which I would want to be a citizen. There is one country where a man knows he has an unbounded future.' When his companions asked Churchill to name the country he replied: 'The USA, even though I

[1] 'Most Secret and Personal', 7 March 1946: Churchill papers, 2/4.

deplore some of your customs.' Which customs, he was asked. 'You stop drinking with your meals,' he replied.[1]

During the morning of March 5, as the train continued westward along the Missouri river, Churchill completed his speech for Fulton. It was then mimeographed on the train, and a copy shown to Truman. 'He told me he thought it was admirable,' Churchill told Attlee and Bevin, 'and would do nothing but good, though it would make a stir.'[2] Speaking of the power and 'ascendancy' of the United States, Churchill had intended to quote a verse of Byron, which he wrote out as follows:

> He who ascends to mountain tops shall find the loftiest
>   peaks most wrapped in clouds and snow.
> He who surpasses or subdues mankind must look down on the
>   hate of those below.
> Though far above the sun of glory shine
> And far beneath the earth and ocean spread
> Round him are icy rocks
> And fiercely blow contending tempests on his naked head and
>   thus reward the toils which to those summits led.[3]

'Not every word in this fits the scene, because the prevailing sentiment of the world towards the United States is not hate but hope,' Churchill had intended to say.[4] But as he read and re-read his notes, Churchill decided to delete the poem and the commentary. There was to be nothing unduly pessimistic or negative in his remarks about his hosts.

Reaching Jefferson City shortly before noon on March 5, Churchill, Truman and Leahy drove to Fulton, a distance of twenty miles, where Dr Franc L. McCluer, the President of Westminster College, was waiting for them, and gave them lunch. Immediately after the lunch, Churchill and Truman headed an academic procession to the college gymnasium. There, to the assembled dignitaries, professors and students of Westminster College, Churchill declared, in words which were broadcast throughout the United States:

I am glad to come to Westminster College this afternoon, and am complimented that you should give me a degree. The name 'Westminster' is somehow familiar to me. I seem to have heard of it before. Indeed, it was at Westminster that I received a very large part of my education in politics,

---

[1] Clark Clifford recollections: Kay Halle (editor), *The Irrepressible Churchill*, London 1985, page 223.

[2] 'Most Secret and Personal', 7 March 1946: Churchill papers, 2/4.

[3] Byron's lines are from *Childe Harold's Pilgrimage*, Canto 3, stanza 45 (first published in 1816). Byron had written 'loudly' (not 'fiercely'), and had set out the lines in verse form (the Spencerian stanza).

[4] 'Speech', notes: Churchill papers, 5/4. In reading this draft, Clementine Churchill had queried the use of the word 'hate'.

dialectic, rhetoric, and one or two other things. In fact we have both been educated at the same, or similar, or, at any rate, kindred establishments.

It is also an honour, perhaps almost unique, for a private visitor to be introduced to an academic audience by the President of the United States. Amid his heavy burdens, duties, and responsibilities—unsought but not re-coiled from—the President has travelled a thousand miles to dignify and magnify our meeting here to-day and to give me an opportunity of addressing this kindred nation, as well as my own countrymen across the ocean, and perhaps some other countries too.

The President has told you that it is his wish, as I am sure it is yours, that I should have full liberty to give my true and faithful counsel in these anxious and baffling times. I shall certainly avail myself of this freedom, and feel the more right to do so because any private ambitions I may have cherished in my younger days have been satisfied beyond my wildest dreams. Let me, however, make it clear that I have no official mission or status of any kind, and that I speak only for myself. There is nothing here but what you see.

Churchill went on to point out that the United States now stood 'at the pinnacle of world power', a 'solemn moment' for the American democracy:

For with primacy in power is also joined an awe-inspiring accountability to the future. If you look around you, you must feel not only the sense of duty done but also you must feel anxiety lest you fall below the level of achieve-ment. Opportunity is here now, clear and shining for both our countries. To reject it or ignore it or fritter it away will bring upon us all the long reproaches of the after-time. It is necessary that constancy of mind, per-sistency of purpose, and the grand simplicity of decision shall guide and rule the conduct of the English-speaking peoples in peace as they did in war. We must, and I believe we shall, prove ourselves equal to this severe require-ment.

What American military men would call the 'over-all strategic con-cept' was clear, Churchill said. 'It is nothing less than the safety and welfare, the freedom and progress, of all the homes and families of all the men and women in all the lands.' To give security to these homes 'they must be shielded from the two giant marauders, war and tyranny'. The 'awful ruin' of Europe and of large parts of Asia 'glares us in the eyes':

When the designs of wicked men or the aggressive urge of mighty States dissolve over large areas the frame of civilised society, humble folk are con-fronted with difficulties with which they cannot cope. For them all is dis-torted, all is broken, even ground to pulp.

When I stand here this quiet afternoon I shudder to visualise what is actually happening to millions now and what is going to happen in this period when famine stalks the earth. None can compute what has been called 'the unestimated sum of human pain'. Our supreme task and duty is to guard the homes of the common people from the horrors and miseries of another war. We are all agreed on that.

Having decided on the 'over-all strategic concept', American military men then always proceeded, Churchill said, to the next step, the method. For the threatened world, this method was the United Nations Organization. 'We must make sure that its work is fruitful, that it is a reality and not a sham, that it is a force for action, and not merely a frothing of words, that it is a true temple of peace in which the shields of many nations can some day be hung up, and not merely a cockpit in a Tower of Babel.' Before the victorious powers 'cast away the solid assurances of national armaments for self-preservation', they must make sure that the temple of the United Nations was built 'not upon shifting sands or quagmires, but upon the rock'.

Churchill proposed, as a first step to strengthen the United Nations, the creation of an international air force. Each State should provide a number of air squadrons, which would be 'directed' by the United Nations. 'I wished to see this done after the First World War,' he explained, 'and I devoutly trust it may be done forthwith.' But, he added:

It would nevertheless be wrong and imprudent to entrust the secret knowledge or experience of the atomic bomb, which the United States, Great Britain, and Canada now share, to the world organisation, while it is still in its infancy. It would be criminal madness to cast it adrift in this still agitated and un-united world. No one in any country has slept less well in their beds because this knowledge, and the method and the raw materials to apply it, are at present largely retained in American hands.

I do not believe we should all have slept so soundly had the positions been reversed and if some Communist or neo-Fascist State monopolised for the time being these dread agencies. The fear of them alone might easily have been used to enforce totalitarian systems upon the free democratic world, with consequences appalling to human imagination.

God has willed that this shall not be and we have at least a breathing space to set our house in order before this peril has to be encountered: and even then, if no effort is spared, we should still possess so formidable a superiority as to impose effective deterrents upon its employment, or threat of employment, by others.

Ultimately, when the essential brotherhood of man is truly embodied and expressed in a world organisation with all the necessary practical safeguards to make it effective, these powers would naturally be confided to that world organisation.

Churchill spoke next of tyranny. 'It is not our duty,' he said, 'at this time when difficulties are so numerous to interfere forcibly in the internal affairs of countries which we have not conquered in war. But we must never cease to proclaim in fearless tones the great principles of freedom and the rights of man which are the joint inheritance of the English-speaking world and which through Magna Carta, the Bill of Rights, the Habeas Corpus, trial by jury, and the English common law find their most famous expression in the American Declaration of Independence.'

If the dangers of war and tyranny were removed, Churchill argued, then there was 'no doubt' that science and co-operation could bring the world, 'in the next few decades', an expansion of material well-being 'beyond anything that has yet occurred in human experience'. There was, however, a 'shadow' which had fallen 'upon the scenes so lately lighted by the Allied victory'. Nobody knew 'what Soviet Russia and its Communist international organisation intends to do in the immediate future, or what are the limits, if any, to their expansive and proselytising tendencies'.

Churchill then spoke of his personal feelings towards Russia, and of the feelings of the British people:

I have a strong admiration and regard for the valiant Russian people and for my wartime comrade, Marshal Stalin. There is deep sympathy and good-will in Britain—and I doubt not here also—towards the peoples of all the Russias and a resolve to persevere through many differences and rebuffs in establishing lasting friendships. We understand the Russian need to be secure on her western frontiers by the removal of all possibility of German aggression. We welcome Russia to her rightful place among the leading nations of the world. We welcome her flag upon the seas. Above all, we welcome constant, frequent and growing contacts between the Russian people and our own people on both sides of the Atlantic. It is my duty however, for I am sure you would wish me to state the facts as I see them to you, to place before you certain facts about the present position in Europe.

The facts as Churchill saw them were these:

From Stettin in the Baltic to Trieste in the Adriatic, an iron curtain has descended across the Continent. Behind that line lie all the capitals of the ancient states of Central and Eastern Europe. Warsaw, Berlin, Prague, Vienna, Budapest, Belgrade, Bucharest and Sofia, all these famous cities and the populations around them lie in what I must call the Soviet sphere, and all are subject in one form or another, not only to Soviet influence but to a very high and, in many cases, increasing measure of control from Moscow. Athens alone—Greece with its immortal glories—is free to decide its future at an election under British, American and French observation.

Churchill then surveyed each of the areas under Russian or Communist control:

The Russian-dominated Polish Government has been encouraged to make enormous and wrongful inroads upon Germany, and mass expulsions of millions of Germans on a scale grievous and undreamed of are now taking place. The Communist parties, which were very small in all these Eastern States of Europe, have been raised to pre-eminence and power far beyond their numbers and are seeking everywhere to obtain totalitarian control. Police governments are prevailing in nearly every case, and so far, except in Czechoslovakia, there is no true democracy.

Turning then to the news which had reached him, and Truman, in Washington, Churchill told his listeners: 'Turkey and Persia are both profoundly alarmed and disturbed at the claims which are being made upon them and at the pressure being exerted by the Moscow Government,' and he added: 'An attempt is being made by the Russians in Berlin to build up a quasi-Communist party in their zone of Occupied Germany by showing special favours to groups of left-wing German leaders.'

Speaking further of Eastern Germany, Churchill pointed out that in June 1945 the American and British armies in Germany had withdrawn, by prior agreement, to a depth at some points of 150 miles along a 400-mile front, 'in order to allow our Russian allies to occupy this vast expanse of territory which the Western Democracies had conquered', and he went on to warn:

If now the Soviet Government tries, by separate action, to build up a pro-Communist Germany in these areas, this will cause new serious difficulties in the British and American zones, and will give the defeated Germans the power of putting themselves up to auction between the Soviets and the Western Democracies. Whatever conclusions may be drawn from these facts—and facts they are—this is certainly not the Liberated Europe we fought to build up. Nor is it one which contains the essentials of permanent peace.

Churchill now urged upon his audience the need for 'a new unity in Europe', from which no nation should be 'permanently outcast'; a 'grand pacification of Europe', he called it, 'within the structure of the United Nations and in accordance with its Charter'. The need for it was, he believed, an urgent one. Even 'in front of the iron curtain', in Italy and in France, in places far from the Russian frontiers, and 'throughout the world', including the Far East, Communist parties or Communist fifth columns 'constitute a growing challenge and peril to Christian civilisation'.

In 1919, Churchill recalled, when he himself was a 'high minister', there were 'high hopes and unbounded confidence that the wars were over, that the League of Nations would become all-powerful', and he went on to declare: 'I do not see or feel that same confidence or even the same hopes in the haggard world at the present time.'

This did not mean that a new war was inevitable, 'still more that it is imminent'. It was because he was sure 'that our fortunes are still in our own hands and that we hold the power to save the future, that I feel the duty to speak out now that I have the occasion and the opportunity to do so'.

Churchill then set out his view of Soviet intentions, and how to contain them, telling his audience:

I do not believe that Soviet Russia desires war. What they desire is the fruits of war and the indefinite expansion of their power and doctrines. But what we have to consider here to-day, while time remains, is the permanent prevention of war and the establishment of conditions of freedom and democracy as rapidly as possible in all countries.

Our difficulties and dangers will not be removed by closing our eyes to them. They will not be removed by mere waiting to see what happens; nor will they be removed by a policy of appeasement. What is needed is a settlement, and the longer this is delayed, the more difficult it will be and the greater our dangers will become.

From what I have seen of our Russian friends and Allies during the war, I am convinced that there is nothing they admire so much as strength, and there is nothing for which they have less respect than for weakness, especially military weakness. For that reason the old doctrine of a balance of power is unsound.

We cannot afford, if we can help it, to work on narrow margins, offering temptations to a trial of strength. If the Western Democracies stand together in strict adherence to the principles of the United Nations Charter, their influence for furthering those principles will be immense and no one is likely to molest them. If however they become divided or falter in their duty and if these all-important years are allowed to slip away then indeed catastrophe may overwhelm us all.

The unity of the Western Democracies: such was Churchill's clear call on that calm Missouri afternoon. But he could not end his appeal without a reference to his own personal position in the pre-war years. 'Last time,' he said, 'I saw it all coming and cried aloud to my own fellow-countrymen and to the world, but no one paid any attention,' and he went on to explain:

Up till the year 1933 or even 1935, Germany might have been saved from the awful fate which has overtaken her and we might all have been spared the miseries Hitler let loose upon mankind. There never was a war in all history easier to prevent by timely action than the one which has just desolated such great areas of the globe. It could have been prevented in my belief without the firing of a single shot, and Germany might be powerful, prosperous and honoured to-day; but no one would listen and one by one we were all sucked into the awful whirlpool.

Churchill then returned to his proposals for the post-war era:

We surely must not let that happen again. This can only be achieved by reaching now, in 1946, a good understanding on all points with Russia under the general authority of the United Nations Organisation and by the maintenance of that good understanding through many peaceful years, by the world instrument, supported by the whole strength of the English-speaking world and all its connections. There is the solution which I respectfully offer to you in this Address to which I have given the title 'The Sinews of Peace'.[1]

No one should underrate, he said, 'the abiding power of the British Empire and Commonwealth', nor of Britain. 'Because you see the 46 millions in our island harassed about their food supply, of which they only grow one half, even in war-time, or because we have difficulty in restarting our industries and export trade after six years of passionate war effort, do not suppose that we shall not come through these dark years of privation as we have come through the glorious years of agony, or that half a century from now, you will not see 70 or 80 millions of Britons spread about the world and united in defence of our traditions, our way of life, and of the world causes which you and we espouse.' This would be Britain's strength, and he ended:

If the population of the English-speaking Commonwealth be added to that of the United States with all that such co-operation implies in the air, on the sea, all over the globe and in science and in industry, and in moral force, there will be no quivering, precarious balance of power to offer its temptation to ambition or adventure. On the contrary, there will be an overwhelming assurance of security. If we adhere faithfully to the Charter of the United Nations and walk forward in sedate and sober strength seeking no one's land or treasure, seeking to lay no arbitrary control upon the thoughts of men; if all British moral and material forces and convictions are joined with your own in fraternal association, the high-roads of the future will be clear, not only for us but for all, not only for our time, but for a century to come.[2]

In London on March 6 *The Times* was critical of Churchill's theme, describing him as 'perhaps less happy' in those passages in his speech in which 'he appeared to contrast "western democracy" and "Com-

---

[1] Churchill had earlier intended to call the speech 'World Peace'. (Letter of 14 February 1946 to Dr F. L. McCluer: Westminster College papers.)

[2] Speech of 5 March 1946: Churchill papers, 5/4; Recording: BBC Written Archives Centre, Library No. T18184. The speech was subsequently printed in Randolph S. Churchill (editor), *The Sinews of Peace, Post-War Speeches by Winston S. Churchill*, London 1948, pages 93–105.

munism".' While western democracy and Communism 'are in many respects opposed', *The Times* asserted, 'they have much to learn from each other, Communism in the working of political institutions and in the establishment of individual rights, western democracy in the development of economic and social planning'.[1]

Churchill's call for Anglo-American unity in the face of the Communist danger also led to protests in the United States, one of them in the *Chicago Sun*, the very paper which, a week earlier, had been so eager to publish his *Secret Session Speeches*. Churchill's object, the newspaper declared, 'is world domination, through arms, by the United States and the British Empire'. 'To be sure,' the *Chicago Sun* added, 'he speaks again of his regard for Russia, and Stalin. But such words are hollow in an address of threat and menace, which would pose the British and American peoples against Russia to win "peace" for a "century" through an alliance of the fortunate of the earth.' These were 'poisonous doctrines'.[2]

Churchill replied at once to this fierce but far from untypical attack, writing to Marshall Field on March 7:

It was a great surprise to me to read in the *Chicago Sun* the enclosed leading article of March 6. I seem to have been under a complete misapprehension about the *Chicago Sun*. I had understood it was an attempt to counter the vicious McCormick propaganda and I greatly admired the public spirit which had led you to make exertions to that end.[3] As the views expressed here are the stock Communist output, I feel it might be an embarrassment to you if your publications were in any way connected with me. I feel this the more because I was about to suggest to you that the 'poisonous' speech I delivered at Fulton should be added to the little volume we have had under consideration, and this will be done in the English edition. I should be much obliged therefore if you would send me back the copy which I sent to you, and which you may have forwarded to your staff.

I must apologize to you for not having followed sufficiently closely the line taken by your newspapers, and for having misled myself so foolishly about them.

I trust our personal relations may remain unaffected.[4]

Having returned by train to Washington, Churchill stayed once more at the British Embassy. It was from the Embassy that he sent a handwritten letter to Truman on March 7:

---

[1] *The Times*, 6 March 1946.
[2] 'Churchill's Call for World Domination', *Chicago Sun*, 6 March 1946.
[3] Robert R. McCormick (1880–1955) had been editor and publisher of the *Chicago Tribune* from 1925, and a persistent advocate of non-intervention and isolationism.
[4] Letter of 7 March 1946: Churchill papers, 4/5.

My dear Harry (you see I am obeying your commands),

I send you a set of my wartime books which you may care to put in your library. They cover a long and stormy period. There are two other volumes which will come to you when they are published in the next few months, namely *Victory* and *Secret Session Speeches*. To these last I shall add the Fulton address.[1]

I enjoyed my journey with you so much and am most grateful for all the kindness you have shown me during my visit to your well-loved country.[2]

Also on March 7, Churchill sent Attlee and Bevin, in the same letter in which he described the journey to Fulton, an account of White House opinion:

Having spent nearly three days in the most intimate, friendly contact with the President and his immediate circle, and also having had a long talk with Mr Byrnes, I have no doubt that the Executive forces here are deeply distressed at the way they are being treated by Russia and that they do not intend to put up with treaty breaches in Persia or encroachments in Manchuria and Korea, or pressure for the Russian expansion at the expense of Turkey or in the Mediterranean. I am convinced that some show of strength and resisting power is necessary to a good settlement with Russia. I predict that this will be the prevailing opinion in the United States in the near future.

As to his Fulton speech, Churchill added: 'Naturally I take complete and sole responsibility for what I said, for I altered nothing as the result of my contact with these high American authorities.'[3]

Throughout the United States, the reaction to Churchill's speech continued to be almost universally hostile. According to the *Nation*, Churchill had 'added a sizeable measure of poison to the already deteriorating relations between Russia and the Western powers'. The magazine added that Truman had shown himself 'remarkably inept' in associating himself with the speech by his presence. 'The United States wants no alliance,' declared the *Wall Street Journal*, 'or anything that resembles an alliance, with any other nation.' According to Pearl Buck, speaking on the following day to the People's Congress of East

---

[1] The text of the Fulton speech was not in fact added to Churchill's *Victory* or *Secret Session Speeches*, but was published two years later, as part of the first volume of his post-war speeches, *The Sinews of Peace*.

[2] 'Private' (signed 'Yours vy sincerely, Winston S. Churchill'), 7 March 1946: Truman papers.

[3] 'Most Secret and Personal', 7 March 1946: Churchill papers, 2/4.

and West Association, 'we are nearer war tonight than we were last night'.[1]

On March 8, at a press conference, Truman not only denied that his presence indicated endorsement of Churchill's ideas, but stated that he had not known in advance what Churchill was going to say. To distance the United States even further from Churchill's warnings, in public at least, Truman instructed Dean Acheson, the Under-Secretary of State, not to attend a reception for Churchill which was being given that week in New York. Ironically, Churchill had spoken at Fulton more than a week after the arrival in Washington of the Kennan telegram, which was to have the effect of changing the concerns and direction of United States foreign policy in exactly the same way as Churchill had envisaged in his speech.

A unified Western defence and the search for an understanding with the Soviet Union; these were to be Churchill's main themes throughout the coming decade, despite Byron's warning of the lack of reward for those who reached the summits—'the hate of those below'.

[1] John P. Rossi, 'Winston Churchill's Iron Curtain Speech: Forty Years After', *Modern Age*, Bryn Mawr, Pennsylvania, Spring 1986. Pearl S. Buck was a popular American writer, author of *The Good Earth* (1933). She had been awarded the Nobel Prize for Literature in 1938.

11
Virginia, Washington, New York

THE reverberations of the Fulton Speech were to be heard for the rest of Churchill's stay in the United States, and beyond. On 8 March 1946, the Secretary of the Navy, James Forrestal, sent Churchill a note of Averell Harriman's opinion: 'I do not think you would find him in any profound disagreement with your observations of last Tuesday.'[1] That day, speaking at Richmond, Virginia, in the presence of General Eisenhower, Churchill reiterated his theme that the English-speaking peoples must be united if democracy was to be preserved, telling the General Assembly of Virginia:

Peace will not be preserved by pious sentiments expressed in terms of platitudes or by official grimaces and diplomatic correctitude, however desirable this may be from time to time. It will not be preserved by casting aside in dangerous years the panoply of warlike strength. There must be earnest thought. There must also be faithful perseverance and foresight. Greatheart must have his sword and armour to guard the pilgrims on their way. Above all, among the English-speaking peoples, there must be the union of hearts based upon conviction and common ideals. That is what I offer. That is what I seek.[2]

On March 9 Churchill spoke again, also at Eisenhower's suggestion, to an informal meeting of senior officers, including Admiral Nimitz,

[1] 'My dear Mr Churchill', 8 March 1946: Churchill papers, 2/226. Two months later the Duke of Windsor wrote to Churchill from the South of France that the 'frankness' of his Fulton speech 'impressed me profoundly'. The Duke added: 'No one but you has the experience to tell the world the true implications of Soviet foreign policy and, being out of office, you were free to do so. That part of your speech, I am glad to say, received overwhelming applause, and even if your reference to an Anglo-American Military Alliance offended in certain quarters of America, I can see no hope of avoiding a third global war in our time unless our two countries can think and act in closer harmony than they used to.' ('Dear Winston', 5 May 1946: Churchill papers, 2/178.)
[2] Speech of 8 March 1946: Churchill papers, 5/4.

General Devers, General Spaatz and General Bradley. Churchill told the gathering, which met in the office of the Secretary of War: 'The prevailing feature of our work together was the intimacy of association. Language is a great bridge. There are many, many ideas we have in common and also in practice: but there was a spirit of loyalty, of good will, of comradeship which never has been seen in all the history of war between Allied Armies, Navies and Air Forces fighting together side by side.' [1]

In London, on March 11, two Labour MPs, Tom Driberg and William Warbey, asked Attlee to 'repudiate' the tone and temper of Churchill's Fulton speech. Attlee declined to do so, telling Driberg and Warbey that Churchill had spoken 'in an individual capacity' in a foreign country, and that neither he, Attlee, nor the British Ambassador to Washington, 'were under any obligation to approve or disapprove' what Churchill had said. Ninety-three Labour MPs thereupon tabled a motion of censure against Churchill. The motion read:

That this House considers that proposals for a military alliance between the British Commonwealth and the USA for the purpose of combating the spread of Communism, such as were put forward in a speech at Fulton, Missouri, USA by the right honourable gentleman the Member for Woodford, are calculated to do injury to good relations between Great Britain, the USA and the USSR, and are inimical to the cause of world peace; and affirms its view that world peace and security can be maintained, not by sectional alliances, but by progressively strengthening the power and authority of UNO to the point where it becomes capable of exercising, in respect of world law order and justice, the functions of a world government.

Among the signatories was Jim Callaghan, elected in 1945, and later Prime Minister; Woodrow Wyatt, who later crossed to the Conservative benches; and the former Independent Liberal, T. L. Horabin, who had stood for Parliament in the spring of 1939 on the slogan that Churchill was 'the only possible man for Prime Minister in this hour of danger'. [2]

That same day, in Moscow, *Pravda* published a full-page denunciation of the Fulton speech, under the headline: 'Churchill rattles the sabre'. After the First World War, it wrote, 'He was the sharpshooter and standard bearer of the anti-Soviet campaign and he was the chief organiser of the armed intervention against the Soviet Union. The British people paid no small price for this extravaganza on the part of English reactionaries who tried by force of arms to impose their will on the young Soviet Republic. It is well known that this escapade was

---

[1] 'Mr Churchill greets Army and Navy Officers', 9 March 1946: Churchill papers, 2/226.
[2] Letter from Horabin to Churchill, 'Dear Sir', 27 March 1939: Churchill papers, 2/358.

a complete fiasco. . . .' Following the events of the Second World War, while Britain and Europe were threatened 'with mortal danger', Churchill had 'become himself again'. It was worth reading his Fulton speech 'so that there should be no doubt as to how false and hypocritical are these phrases on Churchill's lips when he pours out words venomous with poison and hatred about the "expansionist tendencies" of the Soviet Union, about "an iron curtain that has been lowered on to the continent", about the "shadow from the East that has been cast on to the fields so recently illuminated by the victory of the Allies".' The *Pravda* article continued:

Churchill is now speaking out with his old slanders against the Soviet Union, attempting as of old, just as he did twenty or more years ago, to frighten the whole world with the horrors of Soviet 'expansionism' and the threat that this presents to 'real democracy' in the West. With unconcealed malice he talks of Warsaw, Prague, Belgrade, Bucharest, Budapest, Sofia, all of which to Churchill's horror are now in 'the Soviet sphere' and are all not only subject in one form or another to Soviet influence, but are also 'to a significant extent under increasing control from Moscow'.

The *Pravda* article of March 11 went on to warn of the dangers in Churchill's call for 'a special relationship' between Britain and the United States, telling its readers:

What are Churchill's proposals leading to? To create an Anglo-American military alliance that will liquidate the coalition of the three powers and at the same time destroy the United Nations Organisation, by a policy of force. To complete the picture, he openly presents the formula of a 'cordon sanitaire' against the USSR.

Churchill's plans are wide-sweeping but they are clearly not in tune with realistic possibility and realistic circumstances.

He himself knows that he does not have the means to carry out the plans that were born in his stormy fantasies, so Churchill is convulsively grabbing at Uncle Sam's coat-tails in the hope that an Anglo-American military alliance will enable him to follow his plan through. The British Empire, although it is in the role of the junior partner, is continuing its policy of imperialist expansion.

It is very characteristic that Churchill has put his plans forward not in England, but in the United States of America. Obviously Churchill remembers that his first post-war attempt at speculation on the 'Red Menace' during the recent parliamentary elections in England brought him a cruel defeat. Having lost politically in England, Churchill has decided to try his luck in the United States.[1]

From Truman came words of encouragement on March 12. 'The people in Missouri were highly pleased with your visit,' he wrote,

[1] 'Churchill rattles the sabre': *Pravda*, 11 March 1946.

'and enjoyed what you had to say.'[1] Churchill, meanwhile, continued to try to support the British Government's search for a fairer American loan. 'I have just heard from Ben Smith,' Attlee telegraphed to Churchill on March 13, 'of the very helpful remarks which you made at the National Press Club luncheon about the American Loan and I should like to send my warm thanks and appreciation for the friendly line you took.'[2]

In the hope of obtaining the most favourable terms possible for Britain, Churchill held a number of further talks with Bernard Baruch. As a result of their discussions, Churchill telegraphed to Attlee on March 19: 'I do not think he will take any action against the Loan.' This did not mean, Churchill explained, that Baruch's opposition to it had changed, 'but he considers that the Russian situation makes it essential that our countries should stand together. He is of course in full agreement with me on that.' Indeed, Churchill added, 'he spoke last night to me in the sense that he might urge that the Loan should be interest-free as a gesture of unity.'[3]

As to the United Nations Atomic Committee, to which Baruch had been appointed, 'in my opinion,' Churchill told Attlee, this appointment was 'an effective assurance that these matters will be handled in a way friendly to us'. Churchill added: 'There is no doubt that the Soviet aggressiveness has helped us in many directions.'[4]

The discussion at Bernard Baruch's dinner on March 18 had ranged over many topics. One of those present, Elisha Friedman, a leading economist, described some of them in a letter on the following day, in which he complimented Churchill on having spoken with 'the assured touch of a master'. Friedman had been particularly struck by Churchill's statements on Soviet Russia, on the need for Russia 'to join in international co-operation to maintain peace', but, Friedman added, 'you moved me most deeply, when you said you were a Zionist'. Indeed, Friedman continued, Baruch had told him 'that you were

---

[1] 'My dear Winston', 12 March 1946: Churchill papers, 2/158.

[2] 'Personal', No. 514 from British Embassy Washington to Consulate-General New York, 14 March 1946: Churchill papers, 2/4. Sir Ben Smith, who had first been elected a Labour MP in 1923, had served as Minister Resident in Washington for Supply from 1943 to 1945; in 1945 he was appointed Minister of Food.

[3] Speaking in the House of Commons on 12 March 1947, Churchill declared, in defence of his claim that the Conservative Opposition wished to work with Labour in the economic sphere, to the national advantage: 'I, and my leading colleagues, did our utmost, against a good many of our friends here, in our party, to help the Government to obtain the American loan of £1,000 million, in spite of the disadvantageous conditions under which it was offered. I used such personal influence as I had in the United States, as the Chancellor of the Exchequer knows, to clear away American misunderstandings, so far as it is in the power of any private citizen to do any such thing.'

[4] 'Personal and Secret', 19 March 1946: Churchill papers, 2/210.

trying to convert him to Zionism. This was heartening to me, for I have not succeeded in doing so, after thirty years of effort. . . .'[1]

On March 14 it was Stalin's turn to comment on the Fulton speech. He did so by the device of an interview published that morning in *Pravda*. The interview, set out as a series of questions and answers, began:

Q: How do you evaluate Mr Churchill's latest speech in the United States?
A: I consider it to be a dangerous act, calculated to sow the seeds of discord between the allied governments and make collaboration difficult.
Q: Can it be said that Mr Churchill's speech will do harm to the cause of peace and security?
A: Undoubtedly, yes. In fact Mr Churchill is now in the position of a war-monger. But in this Mr Churchill is not alone—he has friends not only in England but also in the USA.

Stalin went on to tell his interviewer:

It must be noted that in this respect Mr Churchill and his friends are strikingly reminiscent of Hitler and his friends. Hitler began the process of unleashing war by pronouncing his racial theories, declaring that only those people whose mother tongue was German could be considered a full-blooded nation.

Now Mr Churchill is starting his process of unleashing war also with a racial theory, declaring that only those people who speak English are full-blooded nations, whose vocation it is to control the fate of the whole world. The German racial theories brought Hitler and his friends to the conclusion that the Germans, as the only full-blooded nation, were destined to rule over other nations. The English racial theories have brought Mr Churchill and his friends to the conclusion that those nations who speak English, as the only full-blooded ones, must rule over the other nations of the world.

In point of fact Mr Churchill and his friends in England and in America are presenting those nations who do not speak English with a kind of ulti-matum: recognize our supremacy over you, voluntarily, and all will be well—otherwise war is inevitable.

But the nations spilled their blood during five years of cruel war for the freedom and independence of their countries, and not in order to change the rule of the Hitlers for the rule of the Churchills. It is most probable therefore that the nations who do not speak English, and who, together, make up by far the largest portion of the population of the world, do not agree to walk into a new slavery.

Stalin also commented on Churchill's assertion that there was 'no

[1] 'My dear Mr Churchill', 19 March 1946: Churchill papers, 2/6.

real democracy' in the Communist countries of Eastern Europe, telling his interviewer:

In England today the government of one party is ruling, the Labour Party, and the Opposition is deprived of the right to take part in the government. This is what Mr Churchill calls 'true democracy'. In Poland, Roumania, Yugoslavia, Bulgaria and Hungary, the government is made up of a bloc of several parties—from four to six parties—while the opposition, if it is more or less loyal, is assured the right to take part in the government. This is what Mr Churchill calls 'totalitarianism, tyranny, police state'. Mr Churchill does not realize into what a ridiculous position he has put himself, with his screaming speeches about totalitarianism, tyranny, police state.

Mr Churchill would like Poland to be ruled by Sosnkowski and Anders, Yugoslavia by Mihailovich and Pavelich, Roumania by Prince Stirbei and Radescu, Hungary and Austria by some king or other of the Hapsburgs and so on. Mr Churchill wants us to believe that these gentlemen from some fascist underground cellar can ensure 'true democracy'. Some 'democracy' Mr Churchill!

Stalin's remarks continued:

Mr Churchill is wandering near the truth when he talks of the growth of the influence of the Communist Parties in Eastern Europe. It must be noted however that he is not quite exact. The influence of the Communist Parties has grown not only in Eastern Europe but in almost every country in Europe where previously the fascists held sway (Italy, Germany, Hungary, Bulgaria, Roumania, Finland), or where the country was under German, Italian or Hungarian occupation (France, Belgium, Holland, Norway, Denmark, Poland, Czechoslovakia, Yugoslavia, Greece, the Soviet Union etc.).

The growth of the influence of the Communists is not just a chance phenomenon. It is a perfectly natural happening. It is because during the difficult years of the rule of fascism in Europe the Communists were the reliable, the daring, the self-sacrificing fighters against the fascist regimes for the liberation of the peoples.[1]

On March 14, while Churchill was still in New York, Henry Luce entertained him to dinner at the Union Club. 'Our eminent guest is doing heavy work in the world,' Luce wrote beforehand to the other guests, and he added: 'Like good working men, he loves his work, no doubt. Nevertheless it is work, and tonight we don't want to overtire him with overtime work. . . . So let every Time Inc'er, as a joint host, try to contribute to Churchill's enjoyment. It will be a success if we get our guest well and happily in the groove of discussion—with him, of course, doing 80 per cent or 90 per cent of the talking.'

In the main reception hall outside the dining room stood an Ameri-

---

[1] 'A correspondent of *Pravda* interviews Comrade J. V. Stalin regarding the speech by Mr Churchill': *Pravda*, 14 March 1946.

can eagle, carved in ice, holding a bowl of caviar in his claws. It was a hot night, and water was already dripping from the eagle's wings. Commented Churchill: 'The American eagle seems to have a cold.' [1]

One of those present at the dinner Charles, J. V. Murphy, described, in an account of the dinner, Churchill's reaction to the *Pravda* onslaught.

One moment the situation was 'a crisis of the most urgent nature, holding real danger for my country'. But on second thoughts he was inclined to regard the Russian reaction as an ill-tempered, crude and typical Communist trick. He pointed out how Moscow, before uttering a word, had waited eight days to judge world reaction and prepare its line; how then the whole apparatus of propaganda had opened up on him, with Stalin himself joining the historians and editorial writers in an orchestra of abuse and vilification. 'This in itself,' he concluded, 'is flattering.' He could not resist making fun of the clumsiness of the process and even at Stalin's heavy-handed attack on him personally. 'You know,' he suggested half seriously, 'if I had been turned loose on Winston Churchill, I would have done a much better job of denunciation.'

The thought gave him pleasure. Brightening perceptibly, he went on to tell how Hitler had attacked him in almost identical terms: 'Warmonger, inciter of wars, imperialist, reactionary, has-been—why, it is beginning to sound almost like old times.' It nettled him to be told that many Americans could not fathom his hostility toward Russia and a suggestion that his attacks were taken by some earnest citizens as Red-baiting brought the almost fierce retort: 'I won't change on that account.' [2]

After dinner, another of those present, John Davenport, asked Churchill whether, in the light of the ominous circumstances outlined in the Fulton speech, it had been wise to make the concessions which had been made at Yalta, in particular those designed to bring the Soviet Union into the final offensive against Japan, a nation, Davenport noted, 'then on the brink of surrender'. Forty years later, Charles Murphy recalled how:

The abruptness of the question stunned the room, Davenport had broken the Luce commandment. Luce jumped to his feet. He said to Churchill, 'Mr Prime Minister, you do not have to answer that question. My colleagues and I had agreed before this meeting that political issues of a controversial character would be avoided. You need not answer the question, and I apologize for the rudeness of my colleague.'

[1] John Davenport recollections: letter of 7 April 1987, communicated to the author. Davenport was a member of the staff of *Fortune* magazine; with Charles Murphy, he had written a book, *The Lives of Winston Churchill*. He was also a member of The Harrison Committee which helped implement the Marshall Plan for Europe. At Westminster College, when presented with a magnificent local ham, Churchill had remarked: 'In this ham, the pig has reached its highest form of evolution.'

[2] Charles J. V. Murphy note: Robert T. Elson, '*The World of Time Inc.*', *The Intimate History of a Publishing Enterprise, 1941–1960*, New York 1973, pages 159–60.

Far from being upset, Churchill thanked Luce and then said, with a bow to Davenport across the table, 'The question is one I welcome.' My recollection is that he went on to say that it went to the heart of the problem of cooperation with the Soviet Union. The slaughter in Europe was ending; now the Allies and the United States in particular faced the terrible task of invading Japan, and the frightful losses the Americans had already experienced in Eye-wo-Jy-ma and O-keenawa were warning of the bloodier campaigns in prospect. It was to reduce these casualties that the Soviet Union was asked to enter the battle against Japan—with whom it had honored a non-aggression pact throughout the war—from the Asian mainland.

Churchill's pronunciation of Eye-wo-Jy-ma brought amusement, and his masterly summing up of the case for the strategy brought handclapping and 'hear hears'. Having gone to the Western Pacific after my return from England I knew that Churchill was mistaken. I decided, though, not to correct him right away, but to wait for an effective moment.

The comment moved on. Churchill answered other questions deftly and wittily. The brandy had taken hold. Then I asked if I might present a question; something the Prime Minister had said troubled me and I was sure that he would not want to leave us with a possible misunderstanding.

My question, as I best remember, was, 'Excuse me, Mr Churchill, but I would like to ask whether, on longer thought, you would hold that the casualties at Iwo Jima and Okinawa really had any influence on the decision to bring the Soviet Union into the Pacific War?'

There was another awkward silence. Churchill stared at me. 'What do you mean? They were terrible battles and anything that could be done to avoid a repetition of such slaughter on the Tokyo Plain had to be done.'

I said, 'Yes, I agree. But are you sure of your dates?'

'What dates?' asked Churchill.

'Yalta,' I said, 'preceded the fighting first on Iwo Jima and then Okinawa. Those battles had not been fought when you met Stalin.'

Much murmuring. Much argument around the table. I knew the dates, roughly. Yalta, 3–12 February; Iwo Jima was invaded some three weeks later;[1] and Okinawa some months later. The upshot of the ransacking of memories produced a judgment that Churchill had indeed been mistaken.

Churchill conceded it. 'I'm glad that I didn't make that mistake on the floor of the House of Commons.'[2]

The altercation was at an end. 'That's the kind of man I like to see on my side of the House' was Churchill's final comment.[3]

[1] Not so; Iwo Jima was invaded on 19 February 1945, only a week after the end of the Yalta Conference. The planning of Iwo Jima had taken place well before Yalta. The invasion of Okinawa began on 1 April 1945 and ended on 21 June 1945.

[2] 'The Churchill Dinner, 1946': notes by Charles J. V. Murphy, 1 April 1987 (subsequently communicated to the author). It was not Churchill, but his American interlocutors, who made the mistake.

[3] John Davenport's recollections, 7 April 1987: communicated to the author by his daughter, Ann Mavroleon.

Soviet troops remained in Persia, despite a second appeal to the United Nations Security Council by the Persian Minister of War on March 15. That day, Churchill was the guest of the Mayor and civic authorities of New York at a reception in the Waldorf Astoria Hotel. 'When I spoke at Fulton ten days ago,' he said, 'I felt it was necessary for someone in an unofficial position to speak in arresting terms about the present plight of the world. I do not wish to withdraw or modify a single word.' Churchill added:

The only question which in my opinion is open is whether the necessary harmony of thought and action between the American and British peoples will be reached in a sufficiently plain and clear manner and in good time to prevent a new world struggle or whether it will come about, as it has done before, only in the course of that struggle.

I remain convinced that this question will win a favourable answer. I do not believe that war is inevitable or imminent. I do not believe that the rulers of Russia wish for war at the present time. I am sure that if we stand together calmly and resolutely in defence of those ideals and principles embodied in the Charter of the United Nations, we shall find ourselves sustained by the overwhelming assent of the peoples of the world, and that, fortified by this ever-growing moral authority, the cause of peace and freedom will come safely through and we shall be able to go on with the noble work—in which the United States has a glorious primacy—of averting famine, of healing the awful wounds of Hitler's war and rebuilding the scarred and shattered structure of human civilisation.

Such an outcome would not come to pass, however, without 'the persistent, faithful and above all fearless exertions of the British and American systems of society'.

Churchill went on to speak of his sympathies and respect for Russia, telling his New York hosts:

I certainly will not allow anything said by others to weaken my regard and admiration for the Russian people or my earnest desire that Russia should be safe and prosperous and should take an honoured place in the van of the World Organisation. Whether she will do so or not depends only on the decisions taken by the handful of able men who, under their renowned chief, hold all the 180 million Russians, and many more millions outside Russia, in their grip.

We all remember what frightful losses Russia suffered in the Hitlerite invasion and how she survived and emerged triumphant from injuries greater than have ever been inflicted on any other community. There is deep and widespread sympathy throughout the English-speaking world for the people of Russia and an absolute readiness to work with them on fair and even terms to repair the ruin of the war in every country. If the Soviet Government does not take advantage of this sentiment, if on the contrary they discourage it, the responsibility will be entirely theirs.

Churchill then suggested a 'very good way' in which the Soviet authorities could 'brush aside any speeches which they dislike'. It was a way which was open to them in the next two weeks. During the war Britain and Russia had signed a solemn undertaking to evacuate their troops from Persia 'by a certain date'. This undertaking had been reaffirmed by Roosevelt, Stalin and himself. 'But we are told that the Soviet Government, instead of leaving, are actually sending in more troops.' Let the matter be 'thrashed out' at the United Nations Security Council in New York, at its meeting on March 25, at which Soviet representatives would be present. 'In this way,' Churchill declared, 'the reign of world law and the international foundations of enduring peace would be immeasurably consolidated.'

The Soviet Union, Churchill pointed out, should not feel 'ill-rewarded' for her efforts in the war. 'If her losses have been grievous, her gains have been magnificent.' In the Far East she had recovered 'almost without striking a blow' all that she had lost to Japan in the Russo-Japanese war forty years earlier. The Baltic States had been 'reincorporated' into Russia. He welcomed 'the Russian flag on Russian ships on the high seas and oceans'. Individual Russians should also be welcomed:

No doubt we all have much to learn from one another. I rejoice to read in the newspapers that there never were more Russian ships in New York harbour than there are to-night. I am sure you will give the Russian sailors a hearty welcome to the land of the free and the home of the brave.

Churchill then turned to the criticisms that had been made, that in the Fulton speech he had advocated a military alliance between Britain and the United States:

I have never asked for an Anglo-American military alliance or a treaty. I asked for something different and in a sense I asked for something more. I asked for fraternal association, free, voluntary, fraternal association. I have no doubt that it will come to pass, as surely as the sun will rise to-morrow. But you do not need a treaty to express the natural affinities and friendships which arise in a fraternal association. On the other hand, it would be wrong that the fact should be concealed or ignored. Nothing can prevent our nations drawing ever closer to one another and nothing can obscure the fact that, in their harmonious companionship, lies the main hope of a world instrument for maintaining peace on earth and goodwill to all men.

The United States stood, Churchill pointed out, 'at the highest point of majesty and power ever attained by any community since the fall of the Roman Empire'. This imposed upon the American people a duty which could not be rejected. 'With opportunities comes responsibility. Strength is granted to us all when we are needed to serve great causes.' The British Commonwealth would stand at America's side 'in powerful and faithful friendship, and in accordance with the World Charter'. Together, he was sure, 'we shall succeed in lifting from the face of man the curse of war and the darker curse of tyranny. Thus will be opened ever more broadly to the anxious toiling millions the gateways of happiness and freedom.' [1]

On March 20 Churchill's visit to the United States came to an end. At his son's suggestion, he gave an interview to Randolph himself; an interview which took the form of notes dictated to Randolph, and then transmitted throughout the world by Jack Bisco, Vice-President of United Press Associations. 'I now fully understand,' Bisco wrote to Churchill two days later, 'why Randolph is such a good newspaper man. He is just a chip off the old block. . . .' [2]

Randolph's first question was how Churchill had enjoyed his trip to America, 'and whether he had benefited by it in health'. Churchill replied: 'I enjoyed it very much. I came here for a rest cure and now I am going home to have a rest after the rest cure.' Asked if the reception given to his Fulton speech had been a surprise to him, Churchill replied:

The Fulton speech was addressed to long-term policies and broad and general themes. Since then, as the result of Soviet troop movements in Persia ordered some time ago, a more difficult and sharper situation has developed. I do not think that this should be beyond the capacity of UNO. Obviously however this is a very important test for the United Nations Organization at the beginning of its career. If it should show itself helpless and futile a most grievous blow will be struck at the instrument upon which the hopes of the world are founded. I share these hopes. A resolute effort must be made by all concerned to prevent the outbreak of future wars. This can only be done by dealing with disputes at an early stage and before the parties concerned have got themselves into positions from which they cannot withdraw.

What had he to say, Churchill was asked, about the recent Soviet proposals to 'defer consideration' of the Soviet withdrawal from Persia until April 10? Churchill replied:

It would be very dangerous to let matters go from bad to worse in Persia and on the frontiers of Turkey and Iraq. It is very easy to raise disorders in those countries. With money, force and inflammatory propaganda, lawful governments may be overthrown, a state of disorder created and a Quisling government installed. But the Security Council of the United Nations must

[1] Speech of 15 March 1946: Churchill papers, 5/4.
[2] 'My dear Mr Churchill', 22 March 1946: Churchill papers, 2/230.

show that it is a reality and not a pretence; that it deals with facts and truth. I trust that we shall not find that the World Organization allows itself to be confronted with a fait accompli. That would greatly add to the difficulties with which we are confronted.

Churchill was then asked his opinion of the efforts of the United Nations 'to get Franco' out of Spain. He answered:

If I were a Spaniard I would not wish to live under his government, but it seems to me that he must be very grateful to the French government in particular for having given him a new lease of life. The Spaniards are proud, morose people with long memories. Their memories even go back to the Peninsular War against Napoleon. They do not like to have their affairs dictated to them by a foreign power. I am sorry the French Government should have yielded to Communist pressure and picked a quarrel with Spain. [There is more freedom in Spain than in any Communist governed country.] [1] Left to themselves the Spaniards will develop increasingly liberal regimes. Moreover it must not be forgotten that Spain has recently had a most deadly and devastating Civil War. Even the extreme left-wing elements in Spain do not wish to renew the carnage which has stricken almost every home in Spain. The underlying feeling in Spain is that too much blood has been shed already in internal quarrels and that it would be better to try and have a little peace and life and even prosperity. The Spaniards will not thank foreigners for telling them that they ought to revolt again, especially when the foreigners assure them that they do not mean to interfere themselves.

In a question which Churchill later asked to be deleted, together with his answer, he was asked what he thought of the Soviet gift of 600,000 tons of grain to France. His answer, as he gave it before asking it to be omitted, read:

I understand the bulk of this grain came from the United States and was meant to nourish the Russian people. It appears it will be transported by American ships to France and Monsieur Thorez has expressed his thanks to Russia for this great help. [2] I hope the French people, with their accustomed wit and shrewdness, will realize the exact character and purpose of this remarkable transaction.

'I suppose we may take it,' Churchill was next asked, 'that you are still an opponent of International Communism?' He replied:

I have never been able to get to like it very much. We must not forget that all the Communists in the world would have seen England sunk for ever beneath the waves by Hitler's Germany, and that it was only when Soviet Russia was attacked that they put themselves in line with the modern world.

[1] Churchill deleted this sentence when he was shown the transcript of his interview.
[2] Maurice Thorez, General Secretary of the French Communist Party since 1930.

I always admire the bravery and patriotism of the Russian Armies in defending their own soil, when it was invaded by Hitler's legions. I have the greatest regard for the Russian people with all their virtues, courage and comradeship. But I made it clear in my broadcast of June 22, 1941, that my support of Russia in no way weakened my opposition to Communism, which means in fact the death of the soul of man.

In answer to the question, how would the fraternal Anglo-American association he suggested differ from the existing relationship, he replied: 'Only by becoming stronger, more intimate, more effective and more mutually conscious.' He was then asked, as the penultimate question, 'Have you any message to give the United States on your departure?', to which he replied:

The United States must realize its power and its virtue. It must pursue consistently the great themes and principles which have made it the land of the free. All the world is looking to the American democracy for resolute guidance. If I could sum it up in a phrase I would say, 'Dread nought, America.'

The last question was about the relationship between Britain and the Commonwealth. 'The underlying unities which prevail among us,' Churchill replied, 'are such as to make us unconquerable.' [1]

'Your interview highly successful,' Randolph Churchill telegraphed to the *Queen Mary* as Churchill and his wife sailed home. 'It was printed verbatim throughout the United States and was front paged in London, Paris, Canada and South America. European interest was particularly marked.' Randolph added: 'I cannot thank you enough for your kindness.' [2] It was indeed a scoop.

On March 22, two days after Churchill sailed eastward from New York, the *Missouri* left New York for Istanbul. That same day, the Soviet Union announced that all Soviet troops would be evacuated from Persia. '*New York Times* attributes changed Russian tactics to your two speeches,' Randolph telegraphed to his father from New York on March 24, 'and to firmer Washington attitude. This view widespread here.' [3] Churchill's 'winged words', James W. Gerard telegraphed to him from New York, 'have contributed in no small degree to the settlement of the affairs of the world and the supremacy of the United Nations'. [4] From Asquith's daughter Violet came further words

[1] 'Press Release on evening of departure from New York', 20 March 1946: Churchill papers, 2/225.

[2] Telegram of 22 March 1946: Churchill papers, 1/42.

[3] Radiogram of 24 March 1946: Churchill papers, 2/8.

[4] 'My dear Sage', 4 April 1946: Churchill papers, 2/226. Gerard had been the United States Ambassador to Germany from 1913 to 1917, and Special Ambassador at the Coronation of King George VI in London in 1937.

of congratulation 'on the truth you spoke at Fulton. It *is the root of the matter whether people wish to recognize it or not,*' and she added: '*Events have powerfully reinforced your words.*' [1]

For Churchill, as for his son, the American visit had been a success. Within the Foreign Office, too, the importance of Churchill's speech had been fully understood. On March 6 Pierson Dixon had written in his diary:

I must say Winston's speech echoes the sentiments of all. None but he could have said it. What he is urging is something more intimate than an alliance between the British Empire & USA; this would represent such overwhelming strength that nobody (ie Russia) could possibly challenge it; thus the peace of the world would be assured; if we fall back on the old balance between the 3 Powers, war is possible. I fear I think it is certain, since Russia will grab & push, relying on our temporary weakness & America's instability. And then the moment will come when—I hope not too late—we & America call a halt.

Dixon added: 'Alas, it is plain that Winston's solution won't work, for the Americans will be too frightened and we shall be too proud.' [2]

On April 16 Churchill asked Dixon to see him in the House of Commons. Dixon noted in his diary:

Went over & saw WSC, who talked for ½ an hour about Russia & America, striding up and down the room, & evidently meditating martial thoughts. He remarked that he had seen a film showing the President 'applauding my Fulton speech in all the most controversial places'. The great American eagle stood immobile, poised, with sharp beak and ready talons; the Russians put a dart in under a wing, another under the tail, & still the bird remained immobile; 'but there is movement in the breast of the bird'. He thought Russian tactics incredibly clumsy, & said that he would tell Stalin so if he saw him. [3]

'I know that it was far from perfect for you,' Sarah Churchill wrote in thanking her father for the trip she had shared with him, 'but you contributed much to the World Cause, quite apart from all you did for poor Old England.' [4]

---

[1] 'Dearest Winston', 29 March 1946: Churchill papers, 2/146. 'International Air Force—yes,' Violet Bonham Carter wrote in a postscript, 'you & I & some others have always favoured that. But who the devil should we be allowed to use it *against* under UNO's peculiar constitution? Portugal & Switzerland perhaps? The veto wld protect the rest.'

[2] Pierson Dixon diary, 6 March 1946: Dixon papers.

[3] Pierson Dixon diary, 16 April 1946: Dixon papers.

[4] 'My darling Papa', 1 April 1946: Churchill papers, 1/42.

12

'Victory bleak and disappointing'

O N 29 March 1946, three days after his return to London, Churchill invited his pre-war literary assistant, Bill Deakin, to lunch with him at Hyde Park Gate.[1] 'He said he was going to write his war memoirs,' Deakin later recalled; 'would I deal with the political and diplomatic side?'[2] Deakin had served in the war behind German lines in Yugoslavia; later he had been a diplomat in Belgrade. Now he was back at Oxford University, teaching again at Wadham College, hoping to educate the generation whose education had been disrupted by the war. But he agreed to return to Churchill's employ at the end of the year, and to help him with his task.

On his return from the United States, Churchill also took on a new secretary, Lettice Marston. Their first encounter involved an historical recollection. In 1909 Churchill had taken a major part in the introduction of the first national insurance scheme, whereby both the employee and the employer made a contribution, as did the State. 'When I joined him,' Miss Marston later recalled, 'he said to me, about stamping my card, "I pay both parts. It's all my fault."'[3]

During his second week back from America, Churchill also saw others, as well as Bill Deakin, who were to be of particular importance to him in planning the massive task; on April 2 he saw his solicitor, Anthony Moir, and his tax adviser, Leslie Graham-Dixon, to discuss the legal and financial aspects. On April 3 he saw Desmond Flower, of the publishing house of Cassell, and on April 4 Lord Ismay, who was to be his principal adviser on all military questions.[4] There were also current military matters on Churchill's mind; on his return to

---

[1] Churchill Engagements Calendar, March 1946: Churchill papers.
[2] Sir William Deakin recollections: in conversation with the author, 15 March 1975.
[3] Mrs Shillingford recollections: in conversation with the author, 2 July 1987.
[4] Churchill Engagements Calendar, April 1946: Churchill papers.

England, he had been asked by Attlee to look at an outline of a possible scheme for a post-war defence organization. 'I hope very much,' Attlee wrote, 'that when you have read this we may have a talk as I should greatly value your views.' [1]

In his reply, Churchill approved the proposed establishment of a Minister to co-ordinate the military supply and research of all three Service departments, but suggested that such a post 'should certainly have the rank and title of Secretary of State'. Churchill also drew Attlee's attention to Lord Randolph Churchill's memorandum on Army and Navy Administration, included in Lord Hartington's Commission of 21 March 1890. Churchill told Attlee:

It is surprising how much was foreseen in this pregnant document, although the machinery therein proposed would not now be suitable. For instance there we find the idea of combination between the Services; the primacy of the fighting chiefs of the Services in formulation of the plans, subject to Cabinet approval; the institution of the new Minister, which you are now about to propose; the assignment to the Minister of the business of supply—'He would as it were set up and carry on a great shop from which the military and naval heads could procure most of the supplies they needed' (here we have a clear foretaste of the Ministry of Munitions); and lastly the presentation of a joint Defence Budget by the new Minister, both to the Cabinet in the first instance and afterwards to Parliament—a project to which I have always attached great importance and which the advent of the Air has made indispensable.

Lord Randolph Churchill's memorandum had been published forty years earlier as an appendix to Churchill's life of his father. 'I am almost sure I presented a copy of this book to the Cabinet Room Library,' Churchill wrote, 'but if this is not so Rowan should telephone and let me know and I will send you one.' [2]

In his letter of March 31 Churchill went on to point out to Attlee that, even with strategy assigned to the Chiefs of Staff 'communicating directly with the Prime Minister and Minister of Defence', the new Minister would still retain 'an enormous sphere':

Especially there is this keeping 'a great shop' which is virtually the Ministry of Supply and Ministry of Aircraft Production in combination. The new Minister would supply the three Services with all they require, except only that warship-building would remain with the Admiralty. The military departments would thus be freed from the making of contracts work, in which they have so often failed. A great deal of coordination has already been achieved

---

[1] 'Personal and Confidential', 'My dear Churchill', 27 March 1946: Churchill papers, 2/29.
[2] 'I have read your father's memorandum with the greatest interest,' Attlee replied; 'he was certainly far ahead of his time.' ('My dear Churchill', 3 April 1946: Churchill papers, 2/29.)

and this should now be finally settled. In making contracts for the three Services the new Minister would be responsible also for using his patronage and power to make sure that expansive capacity was maintained and developed, not only in Government arsenals but in private firms, which would enable the transition to war conditions, or the danger of war, to be smooth and rapid.

Another point raised by Churchill in his letter was the Imperial War College 'where the three Services are taught to work together'. Churchill told Attlee:

I trust that this College, in the founding of which I was concerned after the last war, will not only be maintained but encouraged. There should be a junior course instituted in some way or other for officers of from seven to ten years' service, in order to facilitate what will ultimately arise, namely fusion. If these processes were hurried it would cause all manner of friction, but we should now begin to breed the generation which will achieve it.[1]

On his return from the United States, Churchill read in the British newspapers that the Labour Government was contemplating an alliance with France. Worried about the possibility that a Communist Government might come to power, he wrote at once to Bevin, about the proposed alliance: 'I need scarcely say that I am strongly attached to the idea, having been for so many years in the closest touch with France in all her vicissitudes. However, I ask myself the question whether we should not be well advised to allow the elections in France to take place before this matter is carried through.' There would then be 'a much more representative Government to deal with and it could not be said that we are doing anything to influence the course of the elections'.

Churchill then raised with Bevin the recent elections in Greece. 'Whatever else may or may not be said,' he wrote, 'about the Greek elections, they are surely a great vindication of our policy, both in the Coalition and since, of not allowing Greece to fall into the hands of the Communist Party as the result of an unconstitutional seizure of power. It is quite clear that the Greeks did not wish to be governed by the Communists, who would undoubtedly have seized the Central Government in December 1944 if we had not intervened in full force.' It was now his hope, Churchill added, that it would be 'feasible to bring the British troops home as soon as possible as this will put an end to the suspicion that we are trying to gain some advantage for ourselves in Greek territory'.

His letter signed and sealed, Churchill reopened it to tell Bevin that

. . . when I was staying with Governor Dewey at Albany, he told me that John Foster Dulles, who had just returned from the London UNO Confer-

---

[1] 'My dear Prime Minister', 31 March 1946: Churchill papers, 2/29.

ence, had informed him that, at the Session devoted to the discussion of freedom or free speech, after Mrs Roosevelt had spoken effectively, Vyshinsky made a very impressive and 'terrifying' statement containing such phrases as 'Liberty, in all its forms, is mere weakness' and 'persons who criticize or oppose the governments of their countries should be hunted down, no matter where they are', or words to the above effect. If this speech was made in a public Session, I have not seen any report of it and should be obliged if you would let one of your people send me a copy of it.[1]

Two days later, with the threat of a Communist victory in France still much on his mind, Churchill wrote to his friend Alfred Duff Cooper, the Ambassador to France:

I am naturally most grieved to see France fall again into political fatuity and, of course, if they became definitely Communist, I should consider them ruined for ever. I am hoping that no Anglo-French Alliance will be made until after the Elections. I certainly think we should do all we can to make it clear that we have no sympathy with Communists.

Have you by any chance read the extraordinarily vigorous refusal which the Labour Executive sent to the Communist appeal for affiliation? I could have a photostat made of it if you like, as I think you might certainly find it of value to have it by you. I still nurse the hope that France will shape her destiny in harmony with the two great western democracies.

It will be a gloomy outlook, even if the three-party compromise continues, because the Communists, who give nothing, will not only carry a great number of points, but will infiltrate steadily through their organization and persistency into the Socialist party, already so weak in spirit and character.

The folly of the French action about Franco is patent to the world. They have given Franco a new lease of life and, quite apart from this, it is a great danger when foreign policy, taking the form of closing frontiers and threats of blockade, is decided not on its merits but to meet political balances at a Cabinet table.

'I shall not come to France until after the Elections,' Churchill told Duff Cooper, and he added: 'I hope that even a Communist France will not debar me from Monte Carlo.'[2]

Churchill was also troubled by the extent of Soviet control in East Germany, and the expulsion of several million Germans from the areas annexed by Poland. 'I am afraid your former Russian friends have got all the feeding districts on which Germany lived,' he wrote to his cousin Clare Sheridan on April 19, 'and, with the aid of the Poles, have driven vast masses of helpless Germans into the British and American Zones where there is great scarcity of food.'[3]

*   *   *

[1] 'Private and Personal', 'My dear Bevin', 5 April 1946: Churchill papers, 2/5.
[2] 'Personal and Private', 'My dear Duffie', 7 April 1946: Churchill papers, 2/5.
[3] 'Private', 'My dear Clare', 19 April 1946: Churchill papers, 1/42.

On April 6 a company which had made contact with Churchill while he was in New York, the Sound Scriber Company of America, installed, free of charge, the most advanced machine it had been able to design, equipped with microphones that could pick up Churchill's voice wherever he was—whether in his bed, his bath or his study. It went on recording for several hours without requiring new discs, and it started and stopped from the action of the sound waves.

Walter Graebner, the London representative of Time-Life, was present when the head of the Sound Scriber Company, Mr Gfroerer, went down to Chartwell to test the machine and its user. As a result, he listened in to, and witnessed, the following conversation:

Churchill: What is your day in America like (looking Mr Gfroerer straight in the eye)? What time do you get to your office and when do you stop working?

Gfroerer: I'm at my desk every morning at 8 and leave at 5.30. At noon I have a short break for lunch. We do that five days a week, and sometimes I go around to the office Saturday mornings to read the mail.

Churchill: My dear man, you don't mean it. That is the most perfect prescription for a short life that I've ever heard.

Graebner recalled how Gfroerer, 'a little frightened and somewhat staggered by Churchill's sudden probing into his private life, then confessed that his wife also did not approve of his hours at all, and would certainly be delighted to hear the views of Mr Churchill'. The conversation continued:

Gfroerer: Mrs Gfroerer hates to get up at 6.45 and have breakfast so early. Then she doesn't see me until 6 in the evening. We have dinner early, and by 10 I'm so tired that I fall into bed and am asleep in two minutes. I know I've got to slow down. That's what Mrs Gfroerer is always telling me.

Churchill: You must sleep some time between lunch and dinner, and no half-way measures. Take off your clothes and get into bed. That's what I always do. Don't think you will be doing less work because you sleep during the day. That's a foolish notion held by people who have no imagination. You will be able to accomplish more. You get two days in one—well, at least one and a half, I'm sure. When the war started, I *had* to sleep during the day because that was the only way I could cope with my responsibilities. Later, when I became Prime Minister, my burdens were, of course, even greater. Often I was obliged to work far into the night. I had to see reports, take decisions and issue instructions that could not wait until the next day. And at night I'd also dictate minutes requesting information which my staff could assemble for me in the morning—and place before me when I woke up.

Churchill relit his cigar, poured himself a little more brandy, passed the bottle to Gfroerer and continued:

But a man should sleep during the day for another reason. Sleep enables you to be at your best in the evening when you join your wife, family and friends for dinner. That is the time to be at your best—a good dinner, with good wines (champagne is *very* good), then some brandy—that is the great moment of the day. Man is ruler then—perhaps only for fifteen minutes, but for that time at least he is master—and the ladies must not leave the table too soon.

Gfroerer: I must slow down. My wife has been telling me that for years, but something is always happening at the office. Mrs Gfroerer will agree with everything you've said when I tell her.

Churchill: Do you always get up for breakfast?

Gfroerer: But of course.

Churchill: Your wife too?

Gfroerer: Why, yes.

Churchill: My, my! My wife and I tried two or three times in the last forty years to have breakfast together, but it didn't work. Breakfast should be had in bed, alone. Not downstairs, after one has dressed.

His eyes twinkling, Churchill added: 'I don't think our married life would have been nearly so happy if we both had dressed and come down for breakfast all these years.' [1]

'It was first acclaimed by us secretaries,' Miss Marston later recalled of the recording machine, 'as relieving us of some of the long hours of night dictation.' Indeed, Churchill was so delighted with the device that he dismissed his secretaries for the weekend. They rejoiced at this unexpected change in their routine. [2]

A few days later, Lord Beaverbrook was Churchill's guest at luncheon. Bill Deakin, who was also there, later recalled how after luncheon Churchill took Beaverbrook upstairs to his study and said to him: 'Max, this is the most wonderful machine. We must try it out.' Churchill then strode up and down the study, dictating to the machine, with a microphone pinned to his lapel, attached to a long wire. 'He kept on tripping over the wire,' Deakin added, 'tearing the microphone out of his lapel. The machine had failed. But there were no secretaries to take its place: Churchill had given them the day off. "We don't need to bother secretaries at the weekend any more," he had explained. Now the machine had to go; and the secretaries returned.' [3]

* * *

[1] Walter Graebner recollections: *My dear Mister Churchill*, London 1965, pages 53–6.

[2] Mrs Shillingford recollections: letter to the author, 6 June 1987.

[3] Sir William Deakin recollections: in conversation with the author, 1 July 1987. Denis Kelly, who was soon to join Churchill's team on his war memoirs, later commented: 'Churchill needed a *human* reaction and the machine couldn't provide it.' (Denis Kelly recollections: letter to the author, 14 November 1987).

Churchill had suffered from dizziness while he was in the United States, and, in a talk with Eden, spoke of handing over to Eden the leadership of the Opposition in the House of Commons. A specialist, called in by Lord Moran, had assured him, however, that the dizziness would pass in a few weeks. 'It is already definitely better,' Churchill wrote to Eden on April 7. 'Also I seem to have more strength.' He had therefore decided to remain as Leader of the Opposition at least 'for a while', and he went on to tell Eden: 'I feel sure I can count on your help in an ever-increasing measure and that, when I am not at the House and you are, you will feel that you have perfect freedom of action.' Policy would in any case be 'broadly speaking' regulated by 'the weekly meetings of Shadows'. But Churchill did not intend to remain as Leader indefinitely. 'I am most anxious to handle matters,' he told Eden, 'so as to make the formal transference, when it occurs, smooth and effectual.'

Worried lest Eden would be disappointed not to take over the leadership, Churchill added: 'I look forward to working in all the old confidence and intimacy which has marked our march through the years of storm.' [1] 'You can count on me to play my part' was Eden's reply, but he went on to warn Churchill:

When, however, you write of help 'in an ever-increasing measure' I am bound to reply that I cannot see how this can be worked—It is only the Leader of the Opposition who can guide and father the party in the House, and take the day to day decisions. To do this he must be constantly in the House and in touch with the rank and file of the party. The position is quite different from that when a Leader of the House, with a majority behind him, can act for the Prime Minister. In short there is, I am sure, no room for anything in the nature of a Deputy Leader of the Opposition in the House of Commons.

I do not imagine, after our talk the other night, that this is in your mind; but I think that I ought to let you know what is in mine. [2]

Churchill saw trouble brewing in Eden's handwritten reply, to which he dictated an answer on the following day:

With regard to what you say about there being 'no room for anything in the nature of a Deputy Leader of the Opposition in the House of Commons', I hope this does not mean that you will not continue to act for me when I am away or that you wish to give up presiding over the meetings of the

[1] 'Private and Personal', 'My dear Anthony', 7 April 1946: Churchill papers, 2/6. Churchill also told Eden that he favoured Harold Macmillan as Chairman of the Conservative Party when Ralph Assheton retired, as Macmillan 'would bring a great deal of force and zeal into the business and . . . is certainly one of our brightest rising lights'. Eden replied that he would prefer Lord Woolton for the task.

[2] 'Personal and Private', 'My dear Winston', 10 April 1946: Churchill papers, 2/6.

Chairmen of the Party committees. There ought surely to be room for a second-in-command such as you certainly were before I went abroad. I hope to be able to be at the House every sitting day, except perhaps an occasional Monday, but I should like to have someone who would be willing to act for me should I be called away for any reason. The only engagement I have which will take me out of the country is to visit Holland on Wednesday, May 8. This will mean my absence from the House on Wednesday, Thursday and Friday of that week: I hope, however, to be back on Monday or Tuesday, May 14, at the latest.

'May I presume,' Churchill asked 'that you will take charge on this occasion?' [1]

That evening, while both men were on the front Opposition bench in the House of Commons, Eden assured Churchill that he would be 'very ready' to deputize for him when he was out of the country, as well as to continue to preside over the meetings of the Chairmen of the Party committees. 'Please, therefore,' Eden wrote that night on returning home, 'don't worry about these things. My only point (which I stick to!) is that when you are here there is no room for a Deputy Leader in the House.' [2]

As Churchill's health improved, so did his mood. 'He is in very fine form these days and very tolerant,' Miss Sturdee wrote to John Peck on April 10, and she added: 'He keeps us all dancing about and amused. I don't know that his holiday in America was much of a rest for him, but he seems to have come back refreshed and just as vigorous as ever.' [3] As to Churchill's view of the Labour Government, in his letter to Duff Cooper on April 7 he had written: 'Things are pretty grim here,' but to Lord Halifax he wrote five days later:

It is not so bad over here as one thought it would be from the reports reaching America. The Government seem to me to be learning a good deal from responsibility and contact with events. The Budget is, of course, a 'mark time' affair, but people seem to rejoice at anything now and are even thankful if things get no worse. The Chancellor, who has inherited the mighty revenue gained by the Coalition Government on the impulse of the struggle for life, proposes to lead a lush life upon it and finds a little small change in his pocket for local charities, designed to give him a good name in the neighbourhood. I am very glad the indications of the Loan getting through are so much improved. [4]

Churchill was well enough by the end of April to travel to Scotland, to receive an honorary degree at Aberdeen University, where, on April

---

[1] 'My dear Anthony', 11 April 1946: Churchill papers, 2/6.
[2] 'My dear Winston', 11 April 1946: Churchill papers, 2/6.
[3] 'Personal', 10 April 1946: Churchill papers, 2/228.
[4] 'Private', 'My dear Edward', 12 April 1946: Churchill papers, 2/6.

27, he spoke about 'the needs of a sick world'.[1] Two days later, at Edinburgh, he chose as his theme 'the failure of the Government's "doctrinaire Socialism"'.[2] On May 7 he received the Freedom of Westminster. 'My own life is confused with petty trivialities and ceremonies,' Churchill wrote to his cousin Clare Sheridan that day, 'and one is astonished how little time one has when one has nothing to do.'[3]

During the course of his speech of May 7, Churchill set out a philosophical reflection:

The human story does not always unfold like an arithmetical calculation on the principle that two and two make four. Sometimes in life they make five or minus three; and sometimes the blackboard topples down in the middle of the sum and leaves the class in disorder and the pedagogue with a black eye. The element of the unexpected and the unforeseeable is what gives some of its relish to life and saves us from falling into the mechanical thraldom of the logicians.

Churchill's speech of May 7 contained a strong appeal for a resolution of the international discord which had emerged so sharply in the year that had passed since Germany's defeat. 'The supreme hope and prime endeavour,' he said, 'is to reach a good and faithful understanding with Soviet Russia,' and to do so 'through the agency and organisation of the United Nations'. In this 'patient, persevering, resolute endeavour', Churchill added, 'the English-speaking world and the western democracies of Europe must play their part and move together. Only in this way can catastrophe be averted. . . .'[4]

Churchill was beginning to be concerned about the Labour Government's Imperial policy. India, Egypt and Palestine were the three areas of dispute. On May 1 he had set down his points of difference in

[1] Speech of 27 April 1946: Churchill papers, 5/4. Recording: BBC Written Archives Centre, Library No. 16321. On receiving a copy of the university oration about him, Churchill wrote to the university orator, H. A. Taylor: 'I hope you did not suppose that, when I said that such a eulogy was not good for a man to hear about himself, I was not moved by what you said. I am keeping this record by me and I can only hope that history will not write a different account. However, that may be. But I am none-the-less grateful to you for your extremely kind thoughts.' (Letter of 27 May 1946: Churchill papers, 2/157).

[2] Speech of 29 April 1946: Churchill papers, 5/4.

[3] 'Private', 'My dear Clare', 7 May 1946: Churchill papers, 1/42. Churchill also gave Clare Sheridan some financial advice: 'The purchasing power of money is falling every day. There are other general troubles, but the value of the land and house of Brede will rise proportionately. This is not the time to get rid of real estate. It is wiser to hang on and live on one's capital or selling power of one's tail for a year or two. This is my serious advice. If you have anything solid hold on to it now. We have a very bad time to go through, but England will survive. It would be wrong to take any hasty final decision now.' Churchill added, of his cousin's fears that a Labour Government would destroy her wealth: 'do not try to be a Bolshevik and complain of Bolshevism at the same time.'

[4] Speech of 7 May 1946: Churchill papers, 5/4. Recording: BBC Written Archives Centre, Library No. 9543-4.

a letter to Attlee which, after holding it back for a while, he decided not to send. It gave his thoughts, however, in a succinct form. He began with India:

First, I consider myself committed up to the Cripps Mission in 1942, though you know what a grief this was to me. However the imminence of Japanese invasion of India and the hope which failed of rallying all forces possible to Indian national defence compelled me to take the line I did. But everything stood on the basis of an Agreement between the great forces composing Indian life. If that Agreement is not forthcoming, I must resume my full freedom to point out the dangers and evils of the abandonment by Great Britain of her mission in India.

Secondly, we had always contemplated that a Constitution would be framed on Dominion status and only when that was definitely established should the latent right of a Dominion to quit the Empire or Commonwealth become operative. If, at the present time, you reach immediately a solution of independence, I should not be able to support this. I may add that the dangers of civil war breaking out in India on our departure are at least as great as those which are held by the Anglo-American Commission on Palestine to make a continuance of British or Anglo-American Mandate necessary.

Churchill then turned to Egypt, telling Attlee:

I could not myself support the evacuation of British troops and Air forces from the country. I consider that even if we consent, as may be necessary, to withdraw from Cairo, we must hold the Canal Zone with British troops, though these might be incorporated in an Anglo-Egyptian force specially charged with that duty.

I was very glad to hear that there is no intention to alter the condominium in the Sudan.

Churchill's third point of difference was over Palestine:

I strongly favour putting all possible pressure upon the United States to share with us the responsibility and burden of bringing about a good solution on the lines now proposed by the Anglo-American Commission. If adequate American assistance is not forthcoming, and we are plainly unable either to carry out our pledge to the Jews of building up a national Jewish home in Palestine, allowing immigration according to absorptive capacity, or if we feel ourselves unable to bear single-handed all the burdens cast upon us by the new Commission's report, we have an undoubted right to ask to be relieved of the Mandate, which we hold from the now defunct League of Nations. On the other hand, from a strategic point of view, it would be necessary to treat this matter in conjunction with the situation reached in Egypt about the Canal Zone.

'I earnestly hope,' Churchill added, 'that we shall not find ourselves suddenly confronted with far-reaching and irrevocable decisions in these fields, for it will be a great shock to the British nation to find themselves, all of a sudden, stripped of their Empire and position in the East on the morrow of their victory in the war.'[1]

Writing to Field Marshal Alanbrooke on May 8, Churchill focused on the Government's Egyptian policy:

My dear Brookie,

I am profoundly concerned that you should be associated, as I am told, with the Government's policy of evacuating all British forces, naval, military and air, from Egypt and that your name and technical reputation should be quoted in support of this deadly policy.

There is no way whatever of guarding the Canal, in the sense of keeping it open, except by the permanent presence of British personnel in the Nile Valley. An attempt to bring them in at the last moment would be countered by a Russian threat of bombing Cairo or of precipitating war, and no British Government working for peace, as they always will until the last moment, would dare to take that step. Nor would any Egyptian Government refuse a Russian guarantee that if they remained completely neutral and allowed no foreign troops within their bounds, they would not be in any way molested. A demand upon the Egyptians to sabotage any installations and facilities that may be prepared would no doubt be part of the hostile procedure previous to a declaration of war or to a showdown leading to a British submission.

All idea of America being brought into Palestine to help, on account of their Jewish interests, seems to me also to be destroyed by the Government's policy. How can the United States be expected to send troops or aid to an establishment which will in future be represented as the British *place d'armes* in Palestine, in order to dominate or terrorize Egypt?

I fear you have been sadly misled and that unfair questions have been put to you. You should read carefully what were the questions put to Chatfield and the other Chiefs of the Staff, which resulted in the loss of the ports of Southern Ireland, and brought us to within an ace of destruction.[2]

'You must be upset,' Montgomery wrote to Churchill on May 12, 'at what is happening in Egypt and the way it has been handled. We lack your strong hand on the helm at these times.'[3] 'Danger arises,' Churchill replied, 'when military and political questions are mixed up together and put before Staffs in a confusing way in order to obtain their assent to policies with which on purely technical grounds they would have disagreed.'[4]

*   *   *

[1] 'Private and Personal', 'Hold', 28 Hyde Park Gate, London SW7, 1 May 1946: Churchill papers, 2/42. When eventually sent on 14 May 1946, Churchill deleted the sections on Egypt and Palestine.

[2] 'Strictly Private & Personal', 'At the Royal Palace, Amsterdam', 8 May 1945: Churchill papers, 2/5. This was a reference to 1938, when Neville Chamberlain prevailed upon the Chiefs of Staff to confirm that British control of its naval bases in southern Ireland was not a strategic necessity. The ports were returned to Eire. A year later, they would have provided vital air and sea cover to protect the Atlantic shipping lanes.

[3] 'Private', 'Dear Mr Churchill', 12 May 1946: Churchill papers, 2/143.

[4] 'My dear Monty', 14 May 1946: Churchill papers, 2/143.

On May 8, at the invitation of Queen Wilhelmina, Churchill, his wife, and their daughter Mary travelled to Holland, where, at The Hague, Churchill spoke to the States-General of The Netherlands. During his speech, Churchill spoke of the 'test' of political democracy: 'do the Government own the people or do the people own the Government?' There were seven questions which, if answered, would enable 'the political health and soundness' of any community to be ascertained. These were:

Does the Government in any country rest upon a free, constitutional basis, assuring the people the right to vote according to their will, for whatever candidates they choose?

Is there the right of free expression of opinion, free support, free opposition, free advocacy and free criticism of the Government of the day?

Are there Courts of Justice free from interference by the Executive or from threats of mob violence, and free from all association with particular political parties?

Will these Courts administer public and well-established laws associated in the human mind with the broad principles of fair play and justice?

Will there be fair play for the poor as well as for the rich?

Will there be fair play for private persons as well as for Government officials?

Will the rights of the individual, subject to his duties to the State, be maintained, asserted and exalted?[1]

Churchill ended his speech with a plea for 'the building of a world instrument of security', in which Britain and France, and 'the Western democracies of Europe', would draw together 'in ever closer unity and association'. He would say in Holland, as he had said in Belgium the previous November, 'that I see no reason why, under the guardianship of the world organisation, there should not ultimately arise the United States of Europe, both those of the East and those of the West, which will unify this Continent in a manner never known since the fall of the Roman Empire, and within which all its peoples may dwell together in prosperity, in justice and in peace'.[2]

Churchill, his wife and daughter remained in Holland for five days, 'a pageant of kindness and honour', Churchill wrote to Queen Wilhelmina on his return, 'and I shall never forget the seas of upturned, joyous faces wh welcomed me in the streets of Amsterdam, Rotterdam and Leiden'. To address the States-General, to receive the gold medal of Amsterdam and the degree of Leiden, and to see in Rotterdam crowds whose enthusiasm was 'beyond description', all these were events in his life, he wrote, 'which I rejoice to have experienced'. His letter ended:

[1] Churchill had asked these same questions in a message to the Italian people on 28 August 1944.
[2] Speech of 9 May 1946: Churchill papers, 5/5.

I saw and admired during the long years of war and exile Yr Majesty's dignity, fortitude and inherent authority amid all the misfortunes and disappointments. Now I have seen the Beloved Sovereign restored to her people and surrounded by the truest men and women of the stubborn, valiant Dutch race. I saw stability, comradeship, industry and moral strength on every side. I feel high confidence in the future of the Netherlands under the guidance and inspiration of Yr Majesty's commanding personality. May all our hopes come true.[1]

'I was so delighted to read of the wonderful ovations you received during your visit to Holland,' Lloyd George's widow wrote to Churchill after his return. 'It must have been very gratifying, and a real tonic.'[2]

The differences between the Dutch and British 'at the moment', Churchill wrote to Sir Nevile Bland, the British Ambassador to Holland, 'is that the Dutch were compressed by the war and are now erect and expanding, whereas we, who were blood donors throughout, are now exhausted physically, economically, and, above all, financially, and find victory bleak and disappointing'.[3]

Immediately on his return from Holland, Churchill was present in the House of Commons when Attlee read a statement of the Government's intentions in India: the Indian parties having failed to agree on the earlier British proposals for Dominion Status, new proposals were to be put forward—a machinery whereby the Indians themselves could decide upon the form of Government. 'It will, I hope,' Churchill told the House of Commons, 'be common ground between us that we cannot enforce by British arms a British-made Constitution upon India against the wishes of any of the main elements in Indian life.' The 'main elements', Churchill explained, were the eighty million Muslims of India, the sixty million Untouchables, and the Indian Princely States, each bound to the Crown by separate treaties, and together comprising 'a quarter of the population and a third of the territory of the Indian sub-Continent'.[4] 'Untouchables all over India are grateful to you for your speech in Parliament,' Dr B. R. Ambedkar telegraphed from New Delhi. His telegram continued: 'Future of Untouchables very dark. Entirely depend upon you for safeguarding their interest.'[5]

[1] 'Madam', 18 May 1946: Churchill papers, 2/234.

[2] Letter of 28 May 1946: Churchill papers, 2/152.

[3] 'My dear Ambassador', 19 May 1946: Churchill papers, 2/234. 'Owing to the gifts I have received,' Churchill told the Ambassador, 'I shall evidently have to learn to drink gin. I believe it is quite good once you have the knack of it, provided you keep in practice. At present I remain faithful to whisky.'

[4] Speech of 16 May 1946: *Hansard*.

[5] Telegram of 17 May 1946: Churchill papers, 2/42. The Untouchables, Ambedkar pointed out, had 'no representation in constituent assembly, no representation in the advisory committee, no protection by treaty'. Ambedkar, a member of the Governor-General's Executive Council, was himself an Untouchable and a delegate to the pre-war Indian Round Table Conference in London.

'Your speech on the Government Statement on India,' Walter Monckton wrote from New Delhi on May 18, 'gave great satisfaction to such of the Princes and the Muslim Leaguers as I came across yesterday,' and he added: 'To my mind, the most important point is that we should do all we can to persuade and encourage the principal elements in India to remain attached to the British Empire.' [1]

To the Duke of Windsor, who had protested to Churchill that he was not to be allowed, while in the United States, to be associated in some way with the British Embassy there, Churchill wrote: '. . . we are all under the harrow, and our position in the East is clattering down in full conformity with our financial situation at home.' [2]

The pressures on Churchill to speak were formidable. Replying to an invitation through Lord Cherwell to visit the English-Speaking Union, Churchill wrote: 'I am at what poor Keynes called in the last few weeks of his life "saturation point". It is so easy to put these things down on the card, and so bloody when the day comes round.' [3]

One reason why it had become 'so bloody' for Churchill to speak when the day came round was that he had now begun intensive work on the first two volumes of his war memoirs. On May 3, Henry Luce and Walter Graebner of Time-Life had discussed the American aspects of the war memoirs with Churchill when they came to see him at Hyde Park Gate. On May 6 and again on May 23, Leslie Graham-Dixon and Anthony Moir had given him an account of the financial aspects. [4] Lord Ismay had sent Churchill a year earlier a printed version of the minutes of the Anglo-French Supreme War Council of 1939–40. By the third week of May 1946 Churchill had dictated for Ismay a set of notes on the events leading up to the outbreak of war. 'What absorbing reading they make,' Ismay replied, 'and what prodigious moments they recall.' In return, Ismay sent Churchill his own recollections 'of those acts in the drama at which I was present'. He also sent 'a few pencil amendments as regards dates, times, personalities etc on your own notes'. [5]

---

[1] 'My dear Mr Churchill', 18 May 1946: Churchill papers, 2/42. Sir Walter Monckton had been Solicitor-General in the Caretaker Government of 1945, after which he became Legal Adviser to the Nizam of Hyderabad.

[2] 'Confidential', 'Sir', 19 May 1946: Churchill papers, 2/178.

[3] 'My dear Prof', 19 May 1946: Churchill papers, 2/147. Lord Keynes (John Maynard Keynes) had died on 21 April 1946.

[4] Churchill Engagements Calendar, May 1946: Churchill papers.

[5] 'My dear Mr Churchill', 20 May 1946: Churchill papers, 4/44.

With Ismay as a guide, Churchill knew that he could be certain of a careful, accurate scrutiny of his work, and the bringing in wherever necessary of other experts and helpers. He had also to ensure that he could use the official documents of his premiership. 'My father, Lord Randolph Churchill,' he explained to Attlee that month, 'had a clause in his will enjoining upon his literary executors that no document or State paper relating to the official work of the Offices he had held should be made public without the consent of the Departmental Minister concerned and of the Prime Minister of the day. I have myself incorporated this provision in my own Trust. However, permission ought not to be unreasonably withheld. . . .' Churchill argued that a Prime Minister, 'as responsible head of a British Government, should be free if he wishes to explain and defend his conduct of affairs, and that for this purpose he should be accorded exceptional considerations by the Government of the day'. Lord Baldwin had asked Churchill 'for such facilities' during Churchill's premiership, 'and I thought it no more than common justice', Churchill explained, 'to have them given to him'. Churchill added:

In my own case an unusually large proportion of my work was done in writing, i.e. by shorthand dictation, and there is therefore in existence an unbroken series of minutes, memoranda, telegrams, etc., covering the whole period of my Administration, all of which were my own personal composition, subject to Staff or Departmental checking. I certainly hope that in accordance with the principles laid down these, or many of them, may some time see the light of day in their textual form. These pieces, written at the moment and under the impact of events, with all their imperfections and fallacies of judgment, show far better than anything composed in subsequent years could do, the hopes and fears and difficulties through which we made our way. I am by no means certain that I should wish to publish these documents in my lifetime, but I think they would certainly win sympathy for our country, particularly in the United States, and make them understand the awful character of the trials through which we passed especially when we were fighting alone, and the moral debt owed to us by other countries.

In the United States, Churchill pointed out, there was no Official Secrets Act, and 'at any time partial and misleading disclosures or versions of what took place may be made public'. Two recent books, by Captain Butcher and Ralph Ingersoll, were 'very offensive and disparaging' to Britain, and to Churchill's own personal conduct of the war, and 'many statements are made which are quite untrue and in some cases malicious'. Churchill added: 'I must of course consider my position from time to time in relation to American revelations, but I will naturally consult His Majesty's Government. . . .' [1]

[1] 'My dear Prime Minister', 29 May 1946: Churchill papers, 2/4.

Ralph Ingersoll's book had been particularly offensive, his theme being that Churchill had worked systematically and deviously to ensure that the Normandy landings were to be 'under all-British management'. In 1944, Ingersoll alleged, the Anzio landings had been 'Winston Churchill's own personal undertaking. He had thought of it while recovering from pneumonia in Marrakech.' As for the events of May and June 1945, he wrote, 'We had agreed at Yalta to turn over the Russian sphere in Germany as soon as hostilities were over. Instead, on Churchill's personal persuasion, we rattled a sabre at the Russians across the Elbe for months before we went back to our territory with all the grace of a grudging giver.'[1]

On June 10, Whit Monday, Churchill held the first of what were to be many hundreds of film shows, using a projector and screen installed a week earlier by Ernest Young. The film chosen was *Antony and Cleopatra*; also shown that day were several wartime newsreels in which Churchill appeared. Mrs Young, whom Churchill took to see his butterflies while her husband was finally checking the projector, later recalled:

After the showing of the film we went to a private room to arrange films for future showings. Mr Churchill was very friendly. He was still puzzled by the election results of 1945, but was not bitter. He asked me as an ordinary citizen why I thought the people had gone against him. He told us anecdotes of his visit to Russia.

One of the persons present produced a copy of a message from the King which had been distributed to school children and asked Mr Churchill to autograph it. I spontaneously said 'Why didn't I think of that?' whereupon Mr Churchill took a book from the bookshelves and, after writing in it, presented it to me. I was very moved and said that I would keep it always and then pass it on to one of my children.

'How many children have you?' he asked. When I replied that I had two children, he said 'then you must have another book'. He went to take another copy of *My Early Life*, then changed his mind, saying 'you will not want two copies of the same book', and selected a copy of *Thoughts and Adventures*, which he also autographed and gave to me.[2]

'Of his visit to Russia,' Mrs Young added, 'I remember he said that the Russians eyed each other with suspicion—all eyes following if one of their number went from the room.'[3]

[1] Ralph Ingersoll, *Top Secret*, London and New York 1946, pages 11, 50 and 271. Ingersoll, publisher of *Time* magazine from 1937 to 1939, had served on the General Staff Corps from 1943 to 1945 (serving for a time on Montgomery's staff). He was awarded the Bronze Arrowhead for his part in the Normandy landings, and seven campaign stars.

[2] Mrs E. L. Young recollections: letter to the author, 29 October 1968. Ernest Young had been a cinematograph engineer with Granada Theatres before the war. During the war he worked with Service Film Entertainment. He died in 1950.

[3] Mrs E. L. Young recollections: letter to the author, 26 November 1968.

Work on the memoirs continued without respite: on June 20 Ismay sent Churchill a summary of the Norwegian operations of 1940, based upon the official records.[1] Churchill at once dictated a note of his own recollections. Over the decisive weekend, he recalled, 'Air Vice-Marshal Joubert got very busy in the Admiralty. He represented the Air Ministry in the Admiralty and he certainly exerted himself volubly to emphasise all this cold feet business. I did not forgive him,' Churchill added, 'and a long time passed before he got his feet above water again.'[2] Churchill did not shrink, however, from accepting his own part in the Norwegian campaign. Writing to Ismay about the changes in the Chiefs of Staff Committee structure in April 1940, Churchill wrote: 'I should be very much obliged if I could have the texts and the dates of these changes. I have forgotten all about them except, of course, that I succeeded Chatfield at this time in the co-ordinating work. However, I certainly bore an exceptional measure of responsibility for the brief and disastrous Norwegian Campaign—if campaign it can be called.'[3]

At no moment in the work on his memoirs, despite the time and effort involved, did Churchill put aside the politics or controversies of the day; nor, as Conservative Party Leader and Opposition Leader in the Commons, could he do so. On May 23 he had approved a telegram to Dr Ambedkar, pledging that the Conservative Party would 'do its utmost' to protect the sixty million Indian Untouchables 'whose melancholy depression by their co-religionists constitutes one of the gravest features in the problem of the Indian sub-Continent'.[4] On the following day, speaking in the House of Commons, he urged the maintenance of the 1936 Anglo-Egyptian Treaty, whereby British troops, having left Cairo and Alexandria, would be stationed in the Canal Zone. To withdraw from the zone, he warned, would be similar to giving up the Irish ports in 1938, an event, he said, 'which nearly brought us to our ruin'. At that phrase, 'our ruin', there was laughter on the Labour benches. Churchill, stung, retorted:

I have heard all this mocking laughter before in the time of a former Government. I remember being once alone in the House, protesting against the cession of the Southern Irish ports. I remember the looks of incredulity, the mockery, derision and laughter I had to encounter on every side, when I said that Mr de Valera might declare Ireland neutral. We are seeing exactly

---

[1] Letter of 20 June 1946: Churchill papers, 2/142.

[2] 'Rough Notes on Trondheim Operations: From Memory. For a Guide', 'Personal and Private': Churchill papers, 4/142. Promoted Air Chief Marshal in 1941, Joubert served as Officer Commanding-in-Chief Coastal Command, 1941–42. In 1944 he became Deputy Chief of Staff.

[3] 'My dear P', 26 May 1946: Cabinet papers, 127/50.

[4] 'Priority', drafted 22 May 1946, approved by Churchill on 23 May 1946: Churchill papers, 2/42.

the same sort of thing happening to-day, although I am not so much alone as I used to be. I would hardly have believed it possible that such things could happen twice in a lifetime.[1]

Speaking in the House of Commons on June 5, Churchill returned to the theme of his Fulton speech. 'There was and there still is,' he said, 'an earnest desire to dwell in friendly co-operation with the Soviet Government and the Russian people.' But, he went on,

... there is no use in concealing the fact that the Soviet propaganda and their general attitude have made a profound impression upon this country since the war, and all kinds of people in great numbers are wondering very much whether the Soviet Government really wish to be friends with Britain, or to work wholeheartedly for the speedy re-establishment of peace, freedom and plenty throughout the world.

Across the ocean, in Canada and the United States, the unfriendly Soviet propaganda has also been very effective in the reverse direction to what was intended. The handful of very able men who hold 180 million Soviet citizens in their grasp ought to be able to get better advice about the Western democracies. For instance, it cannot be in the interest of Russia to go on irritating the United States.

There are no people in the world who are so slow to develop hostile feelings against a foreign country as the Americans, and there are no people who, once estranged, are more difficult to win back. The American eagle sits on his perch, a large, strong bird with formidable beak and claws. There he sits motionless, and M. Gromyko is sent day after day to prod him with a sharp pointed stick—now his neck, now under his wings, now his tail feathers. All the time the eagle keeps quite still. But it would be a great mistake to suppose that nothing is going on inside the breast of the eagle.

I venture to give this friendly hint to my old wartime comrade, Marshal Stalin. Even here, in our patient community, Soviet propaganda has been steadily making headway backwards. I would not have believed it possible that in a year, the Soviets would have been able to do themselves so much harm, and chill so many friendships in the English-speaking world.

Churchill then spoke of the Yalta Conference decision, which he had strongly supported, to make Russia's western border the Curzon Line of 1920, telling the House of Commons:

We are not now in the presence of the Curzon Line as the Western frontier of Soviet authority. It is no longer a question of the line of the Oder. So long as Poland is held in control, the Soviet domination, in one form or another, runs from Stettin in the Baltic to the outskirts of Trieste in the Adriatic, and far South of that. The Russified frontier in the North is not the Curzon Line; it is not on the Oder; it is on the Elbe. That is a tremendous fact in European history, and one which it would be the height of unwisdom to ignore.

[1] Speech of 24 May 1946: *Hansard*.

Not only has a curtain descended, from the Baltic to the Adriatic, but behind that, is a broad band of territory containing all the capitals of Eastern and Central Europe and many ancient States and nations, in which dwell nearly one-third of the population of Europe, apart from Russia. At the present moment all this is ruled or actively directed by that same group of very able men, the Commissars in the Kremlin, which already disposes with despotic power of the fortunes of their own mighty Empire. It is here in this great band or belt, if anywhere, that the seeds of a new world war are being sown.

We may be absolutely sure that the Sovietising and, in many cases, the Communising of this gigantic slice of Europe, against the wishes of the overwhelming majority of the people of many of these regions, will not be achieved in any permanent manner without giving rise to evils and conflicts which are horrible to contemplate.

Meanwhile, it was clear from the speech of the Foreign Secretary that the policy of the Soviet Government seems, up to the present, to be to delay all final settlements of peace and to prevent the peoples of Western and Eastern Europe from getting together in friendly, social and economic association, as many of them would like to do.

Churchill spoke next of Poland, the country on behalf of whose independence Britain had gone to war in 1939, and for whose democratic future he had fought so hard, first at Teheran in 1943, then at Moscow in 1944 and finally at both Yalta and Potsdam in 1945:

Poland is denied all free expression of her national will. Her worst appetites of expansion are encouraged. At the same time, she is held in strict control by a Soviet-dominated government who do not dare have a free election under the observation of representatives of the three or four Great Powers. The fate of Poland seems to be an unending tragedy, and we, who went to war, all ill-prepared, on her behalf, watch with sorrow the strange outcome of our endeavours.

There was one aspect of the iron curtain divide which had caused Churchill particular concern:

I deeply regret that none of the Polish troops—and I must say this—who fought with us on a score of battlefields, who poured out their blood in the common cause, are to be allowed to march in the Victory Parade. They will be in our thoughts on that day. We shall never forget their bravery and martial skill, associated with our own glories at Tobruk, at Cassino and at Arnhem. Austria and Hungary are stifled, starved and weighed down by masses of Russian troops.

On this point, Churchill added, the Conservative Opposition agreed with Ernest Bevin 'in all he said'.[1] One had to face reality; and among

[1] 'In the case of Poland,' Bevin had told the House of Commons, 'I suggest that the acid test will be: will she carry out the solemn pledge which the President of the Provisional Government gave me at Potsdam, to have early and free elections?' (*Hansard*, 4 June 1946.)

the facts of the new Europe was that 'two' Germanies were coming into being, 'one organised more or less on the Russian model, or in the Russian interest, and the other on that of the Western democracies'. As to the line of demarcation between them, Churchill pointed out, it 'is not fixed with regard to any historical or economic conditions, but simply runs along the line agreed to when the whole future of the war was highly speculative, and nobody knew to what points armies would be likely to go or what would become of the struggle. It runs along the line to which, a year ago, the British and American Armies voluntarily retired—a 150 mile retreat in some cases, on a 400 mile front—after the Germans had surrendered.'

From the political aspect, Churchill turned to the moral aspect: the obligation, as he saw it, for Britain and America to sustain life within their zones of Germany; not to allow 'chaos and misery' to continue there indefinitely:

Indescribable crimes have been committed by Germany under the Nazi rule. Justice must take its course, the guilty must be punished, but once that is over—and I trust it will soon be over—I fall back on the declaration of Edmund Burke, 'I cannot frame an indictment against an entire people.'

We cannot plan or even dream of a new world or a new Europe which contains pariah nations, that is to say, nations permanently or for prolonged periods outcast from the human family. Our ultimate hopes must be founded—can only be founded—on the harmony of the human family.

So far as it remains in the power of this island people to influence the course of events, we must strive over a period of years to redeem and to reincorporate the German and the Japanese peoples in a world system of free and civilised democracy. The idea of keeping scores of millions of people hanging about in a sub-human state between earth and hell, until they are worn down to a slave condition or embrace Communism, or die off from hunger, will only if it is pursued, breed at least a moral pestilence and probably an actual war.

Churchill then told the House of Commons that the Opposition agreed with the Government that peace would have to be made with Germany, 'or whatever parts of Germany are still in our control', and with Italy, and that if this could not be achieved by inter-Allied discussion at which the Soviet Union was an integral part, then it should be done at the United Nations:

If we are to be told that such a procedure as this would rend the world organisation, and that a line of division, and even of separation, might grow up between Soviet Russia and the countries she controls on the one hand, and the rest of the world on the other, then I say—and I say it with much regret, but without any hesitancy—that it would be better to face that, when all has been tried and tried in vain, than tamely to accept a continued degeneration of the whole world position.

It is better to have a world united than a world divided; but it is also better to have a world divided, than a world destroyed. Nor does it follow that even in a world divided there should not be equilibrium from which a further advance to unity might be attempted as the years pass by. Anything is better than this ceaseless degeneration of the heart of Europe. Europe will die of that.

It was for the survival of Europe that Churchill then voiced his deepest concern; a concern heightened by his recollection of the fate of Europe after 1919. 'Her miseries, confusion and hatreds,' he declared, 'far exceed anything that was known in those bygone days,' and he added:

Let us beware of delay and further degeneration. With all their virtues, democracies are changeable. After the hot fit, comes the cold. Are we to see again, as we saw the last time, the utmost severities inflicted upon the vanquished, to be followed by a period in which we let them arm anew, and in which we then seek to appease their wrath?

We cannot impose our will on our Allies, but we can, at least, proclaim our own convictions. Let us proclaim them fearlessly. Let Germany live. Let Austria and Hungary be freed. Let Italy resume her place in the European system. Let Europe arise again in glory, and by her strength and unity ensure the peace of the world.[1]

'Somehow or other,' wrote Leo Amery in congratulation, 'we must help to rebuild this old home of civilisation which we call Europe, first of all up to the present iron curtain, and eventually, I hope, up to the Curzon Line, which is the real frontier between Europe and Asia.'[2]

Churchill now sought an active part in the establishment of a United Europe, the indispensable first feature of which, for him, was the closest possible accord between Britain and France. The recent French elections and referendum, upholding the Fourth Republic, gave him particular cause for hope.[3] 'I have a feeling of increasing stability in France, and indeed throughout Western Europe,' he wrote to Duff Cooper on June 8, and he added: 'It looks as if the Communist

[1] Speech of 5 June 1946: *Hansard*. Speaking about Spain, Churchill had been unable to resist two digs at Britain's own Labour Government, telling the House of Commons: 'None of us likes the Franco regime, and, personally, I like it as little as I like the present British administration, but between not liking a government and trying to stir up a civil war in a country, there is a very wide interval. It is said that every nation gets the government it deserves. Obviously, this does not apply in the case of Britain.'

[2] 'My dear Winston', 7 June 1946: Churchill papers, 2/145.

[3] On 19 April 1946 the National Assembly approved the Constitution of the Fourth Republic by 309 votes to 249. On May 5 a nationwide referendum upheld the Constitution by 10,670,993 votes to 9,130,784. On June 2, at the polls, the Republican Party, which was committed to the maintenance of the Fourth Republic, emerged as the strongest political Party in France, with a lead of 16 seats over the Communists.

virus is being decidedly corrected. I should have been very hard hit in my feelings to France if the Communist deserter from the French Army in time of war had definitely appeared at the head of the French Government.[1] That would indeed have been a blow.'

Churchill planned to visit France again once the new Government had been formed. He went on to ask Duff Cooper:

I wonder, however, whether you and Diana would care to have me and Clemmie for a few days? If it is in the least inconvenient we can easily stay at the Ritz, I have no doubt, and come to see you from there.

I am anxious to renew my contacts with some of the old crowd who have now, I am glad to see, returned, as well as with Bidault, Herriot and Co. I have not made up my mind about the Ruhr, etc., and should like to understand the French point of view. I am thinking about the invitation from the Mayor of Metz, but if I came over at all on July 14 it would be the procession in the Champs Elysées I should like to see.[2]

Churchill next sought Attlee's approval for his acceptance of the invitation to Metz. It was an invitation which, Churchill explained, would enable him to fulfil an 'engagement' which he had made with General Giraud in North Africa in 1942, at the time of the Allied landings, when he had said to Giraud: 'I give you rendezvous at Metz.' Churchill added, of his proposed visit:

I also think it may do good to Anglo-French relations as I have a very long association with France, even before the last war began.

Let me assure you that my motives are entirely public and that pleasure forms no part in them. In fact it is a great exertion to travel all this way. Still, I think it may be an opportunity of saying a few words of friendship and encouragement to the French, which will reach many homes in France. Therefore, while thanking you for your courtesy, I hope my visit will not be looked upon as a personal favour to me but as a means of furthering the general interest.[3]

To Viscount Cecil of Chelwood, who before the war had supported a request for Churchill to succeed Aristide Briand as President of the Pan-European Union, Churchill wrote on June 9 of his temptation to accept. 'I have a feeling,' he wrote, 'that an immense amount of pro-British sentiment, in Western Europe at any rate, could be evoked by my working in this association, and also that I personally could save

---

[1] Churchill was referring to Maurice Thorez (1900–64). Having been mobilized in 1939, Thorez had left the army and gone underground when the Vichy Government banned the Communist Party for its opposition to the war. In 1945 he was a Minister of State under de Gaulle. From 1946 to 1958 he served as a Deputy in the Assembly; in 1958, when the Communist Party strength in the Chamber dropped to ten, he retained his seat.

[2] 'Private', 'My dear Duffie', 8 June 1946: Churchill papers, 2/237.

[3] 'Private', 'My dear Prime Minister', 2 July 1946: Churchill papers, 2/237.

it from rivalry with the United States of America, and might prevent its having at the outset a needlessly anti-Soviet bias.'

The movement for a United States of Europe, Churchill told Cecil, 'might become very big indeed, and a potent factor for world peace. After all, Europe is the foundation of almost all the glories and tragedies of mankind.' [1]

In reply, Cecil pointed out that the United States of Europe movement, under the guidance of Count Coudenhove-Kalergi, had as its main object 'to restrain Russia, or to protect the rest of Europe from her'. [2] Churchill at once wrote to his son-in-law Duncan Sandys: 'I think it would be a pity for me to join an organisation which had such a markedly anti-Russian bent, but I was not aware that this was Count C.K's conception.' [3]

In the early hours of June 27 Churchill spoke in the House of Commons on the Finance Bill. [4] Later that day, he told Lord Moran that he could now do 'a great deal' without getting tired. Lord Moran noted Churchill's words to him:

Yesterday I dined out and sat talking till two o'clock, and on my way home I saw a light in the Commons and found them sitting. I listened for half an hour, and then I made a very vigorous speech. I don't see why the Government shouldn't be beaten up. They've made an awful mess of this bread business. By August or September there may be no bread in the shops. They are very worried about it. Why, if we'd failed to bring in the wheat we should have been for it.

'A short time ago,' Churchill added, 'I was ready to retire and die gracefully. Now I'm going to stay and have them out. I'll tear their bleeding entrails out of them.' [5]

Churchill reiterated this determination a week later, in conversation with Lord Camrose, who noted in a memorandum of their conversation:

---

[1] 'My dear Bob', 9 June 1946: Viscount Cecil of Chelwood papers.

[2] 'My dear Winston', 19 June 1946: Churchill papers, 2/19.

[3] 'My dear Duncan', 29 June 1946: Churchill papers, 2/23. Count Richard Nicolaus Coudenhove-Kalergi had published his first appeal for a united Europe, Pan-Europa, in Vienna in 1923. He had visited Churchill before the war, at the time of the publication of his book The Totalitarian State Against Man (1938). The founder and Chairman of the Pan-European movement, he published Europe Must Unite in 1940. He visited Churchill in Geneva in September 1946 and at Chartwell in 1946, 1947 and 1950. In 1953 Churchill wrote the preface to his book An Idea Conquers the World. He died in 1972, at the age of seventy-seven.

[4] Speech of 26 June 1946: Hansard.

[5] Lord Moran diary, 27 June 1946: The Struggle for Survival, page 313.

Feels much better than when he returned from America and full of energy. Had intended to retire then but hates 'the enemy' so much that he will stay on to put them out. Would like Anthony to take on the leadership of the Opposition on condition that he, Winston, has the right to 'barge in' on any occasion he wants to. Difficulty of making the arrangement at the moment is that Anthony feels he cannot take the salary while he is a director of public companies, an idea at which Winston scoffs.[1]

One area of the Government's policy on which Churchill had emerged as a leading critic was Palestine. An upsurge in Jewish terrorism had led to a feeling that Britain might have to abandon the Mandate, leaving the Jews and Arabs to their own devices. This Churchill rejected. 'Terrorism is no solution to the Palestine problem,' he wrote to Attlee on July 2, but, he added, 'Yielding to terrorism would be a disaster. At the same time I hold myself bound by our national pledges, into which I personally and you also and your Party have entered, namely the establishment of a Jewish National Home in Palestine, with immigration up to the limit of "absorptive capacity", of which Britain, as the Mandatory Power, was the judge.' Churchill went on to tell Attlee: 'Several of my friends are far from abandoning Partition'—the 1936 plan for two separate States, one Jewish and one Arab—'and I am very much inclined to think this may be the sole solution.'[2]

'We shall not accept any solution,' Attlee replied, 'which represents abandonment of our pledges to the Jews or our obligations to the Arabs....'[3]

Churchill's discussion with Camrose on July 3 had been primarily concerned with two major literary projects: Churchill's war memoirs and his biography. Churchill had decided to establish a Literary Trust, of which his wife, Lord Cherwell and Brendan Bracken were to be Trustees, so that all benefits accruing from the use of his private papers would go to his children and grandchildren. Churchill explained to Camrose that the Trustees would have two tasks, to sell the right to use the wartime papers in the form of Churchill's own war memoirs, and to give the earlier papers to Churchill's son Randolph to write the biography, 'but not', Camrose noted, 'until five or ten years after his death'.

[1] 'Memorandum of Conversation with Mr Winston Churchill, Wednesday, 3rd July 1946': Camrose papers.
[2] 'Private', 'My dear Prime Minister', 2 July 1946: Churchill papers, 2/237.
[3] 'Private', 'My dear Churchill', 4 July 1946: Churchill papers, 2/237.

This scheme had been devised to protect Churchill's archive and literary asset against death duties, Churchill told Camrose, 'but confessed he did not know how'.[1] The person who did know how was Churchill's tax adviser, Leslie Graham-Dixon, to whose talent the scheme owed both its origins and its success. Meanwhile, on June 27, the last volume of Churchill's war speeches was published. Entitled *Victory*, it had been put together for him by Charles Eade, and brought to a conclusion a project begun in 1941 with *Into Battle*.[2]

On July 23 Churchill had received at Chartwell the flag of the Cinque Ports, of which he had been appointed Lord Warden in 1941. On learning from Clementine Churchill's secretary, Miss Hamblin, that the flag had arrived, he noted in red ink:

> Oh frabjous day!
> Callooh!
> Calay!!
> And then he chortled in his joy.[3]

As a souvenir of the war years, Churchill had devised a medallion, inscribed with the words 'The Grand Coalition'; he now sent this medallion to each of the 122 Ministers who had served under him in the National Coalition Government. On July 23 he sent one to the King, explaining to Sir Alan Lascelles: 'It would make an excellent paper weight,' and adding, 'After all, His Majesty saw a great deal of his principal Ministers in those days.'[4] 'I cannot suppose,' wrote Anthony Eden on receipt of his medallion, 'that any of us, even were we to live for more than a hundred years, can ever again know such stupendous times.'[5]

For Churchill, the sending of the medallions brought back memories of deep comradeship. He was, at the same time, troubled by those individuals and institutions whose contribution to the national well-

[1] 'Memorandum of Conversation with Mr Winston Churchill, Wednesday 3rd July 1946': Camrose papers.

[2] The British edition of *Victory* was of 38,000 copies. The American edition, published on 7 August 1946, was of 5,000 copies. The volume was eventually translated into French, German, Finnish, Czech, Spanish, Swedish, Danish and Norwegian.

[3] Note of 23 July 1946: National Trust (Chartwell) Archive. The original note is on display in one of the doorways leading to Churchill's study. The flag itself now hangs in the study. The lines are from Lewis Carroll, *Through the Looking-Glass*. Carroll's spelling had been 'O' and 'Callay', and his last line was: 'He chortled in his joy.' A recording of Churchill's speech on his installation as Lord Warden and Admiral of the Cinque Ports on 14 August 1946 is in the BBC Written Archives Centre, Library No. LP9994.

[4] 'My dear Alan', 23 July 1946: Churchill papers, 2/495.

[5] 'My dear Winston', 9 July 1946: Churchill papers, 2/495. On receiving his medallion six months later, Field Marshal Montgomery wrote to Churchill: 'Under your leadership we went through some very dark days; without your leadership I feel we might have gone under.' ('Dear Mr Churchill', 13 December 1946: Churchill papers, 2/495.)

being he doubted. One of those institutions was *The Times*, which, as he wrote to its proprietor, Colonel J. J. Astor, on July 7, had in its editorial columns during the previous fifteen years 'been a very important adverse factor in the life and strength of the British Empire and Commonwealth'. Churchill went on to explain, in an outburst against the newspaper's editorial columns which in the end he decided not to send:

Time after time they have thrown their immense weight on the wrong side, and such is their power that they have been able again and again to blow away the head of every front or formation which could be made to keep Britain great and strong. Forgive me if I recall some milestones: India, 1930/31; one-sided disarmament, 1931/35; the Anglo-German Naval Treaty, 1935; preparation for war, 1936/39—always the bias against the effort; Munich (but many were in that too); in latter days Greece; India again, and Egypt. I do not deal with the smaller matters of domestic policies because they are so numerous, and in almost every one of them the whole balance has been tilted against the stable continuity of our life and history.

No doubt you will feel all this is very wrong and unkind. I can only tell you that, living my life during all this long period, I have felt a cramping, paralysing influence at work encouraging the subversive forces and weakening our poor island and its life and power in the world. You may well rejoin that the course of events has proved that the nation does not agree with me. All the same, *The Times*, apart from personal courtesies, has been a heartbreak to me and a dire oppression to all the ideas for which I stand.

We are slithering down the drain pretty fast now. Poor old England, with all her sacrifices and all her victories, is sinking to a minor position in the world, but nobody seems to mind, and I have no doubt *The Times* will write a very good leading article on the advantage and moral dignity of Britain taking a back seat.

These views, Churchill added, came 'from the bottom of my heart'.[1]

It was to try to halt that 'slithering down the drain' in the international sphere that, a week later, Churchill spoke, first in Luxembourg on July 14, and on the following day in Metz.[2] His first remarks in Metz were of his personal memories of sixty-three years before, when his father had taken him as a young boy, aged eight, to Paris:

[1] 'Personal and Private', 7 July 1946: Churchill papers, 2/145. One of Churchill's literary assistants, Denis Kelly, has recalled how, in writing about *The Times* in his memoirs, Churchill had dictated the phrase 'though devoid of guile was not devoid of guilt'. He then crossed this out and wrote in its place 'the weighty influence of *The Times*', telling Kelly: 'I don't want to bite against them.' (Denis Kelly recollections: in conversation with the author, 26 January 1987.)

[2] As a souvenir of his Luxembourg visit, Churchill was given a postcard printed specially for the occasion, which both he and the Grand Duchess Charlotte then signed. On the postcard he was described as 'Winston Churchill, Ex-Premier'. (National Trust, Chartwell Archive.) The card itself is now on display in Churchill's study at Chartwell.

It was in the summer of 1883. We drove along together through the Place de la Concorde. Being an observant child I noticed that one of the monuments was covered with wreaths and crepe and I at once asked him why. He replied, 'These are monuments of the Provinces of France. Two of them, Alsace and Lorraine, have been taken from France by the Germans in the last war. The French are very unhappy about it and hope some day to get them back.' I remember quite distinctly thinking to myself, 'I hope they will get them back.'

'This hope at least,' Churchill commented, 'has not been disappointed.' He then spoke of his visit to France in 1907, when he was the guest of the French army at its annual manoeuvres, three years after the signing of the Anglo-French Entente Cordiale:

I was already a youthful Minister of the Crown. In those days the soldiers wore blue tunics and red trousers and many of the movements were still in close order. When I saw, at the climax of the manoeuvres, the great masses of French infantry storming the position, while the bands played the Marseillaise, I felt that by those valiant bayonets the rights of man had been gained and that by them these rights and also the liberties of Europe would be faithfully guarded.

Since then, Churchill reflected, 'the road has been long and terrible. I am astonished to find myself here at the end of it all.' During the ordeal of two generations of Frenchmen he had never neglected anything 'that could preserve and fortify our united action', and he added: 'Never let us part.'

Churchill appealed, at Metz, for a unity of purpose and action between Britain and France. 'Europe must arise from her ruin,' he said, 'and spare the world a third and possibly a fatal holocaust.' In this, he declared, France had a central part:

There can be no revival of Europe with its culture, its charm, its tradition and its mighty power, without a strong France. Many nations in the past have wished and tried to be strong. But never before has there been such a clear need for one country to be strong as there is now for France. When I think of the young Frenchmen growing into manhood in this shattered and bewildered world, I cannot recall any generation in any country before whose eyes duty is written more plainly or in more gleaming characters.

Two hundred years ago in England, the Elder and the greater Pitt addressed this invocation to his fellow-countrymen, torn, divided and confused by faction as they then were. 'Be one people.' That was his famous invocation. And in our island, for all its fogs and muddles, we are one people to-day, and dangers if they threaten will only bind us more firmly together.

Using my privilege as your old and faithful friend, I do not hesitate to urge upon all Frenchmen, worn or worried though they may be, to unite in the task of leading Europe back in peace and freedom to broader and better days. By saving yourselves you will save Europe and by saving Europe you will save yourselves.[1]

'Mary told me Metz was most thrilling,' Sarah Churchill wrote to her father.[2]

Returning from Metz to London, Churchill spoke twice in the House of Commons on July 18. 'Good luck for this afternoon,' Sarah Churchill wrote.[3] His first intervention was on India. Any future constitutional arrangement for India, he insisted, must have the agreement of the Muslims. 'One cannot contemplate,' he warned, 'that British troops should be used to crush Muslims in the interests of the caste Hindus.' Whatever Britain's responsibilities might be, and 'whatever may be the day appointed on which we quit India', the British must not make themselves 'the agents of a caste Government, or a particular sectional Government, in order to crush by armed force and modern weapons another community which, although not so numerous, is numbered at 90 millions'.[4]

Although he was a supporter of India's Muslims, Churchill was not uncritical of the Muslim attitude. He wrote to M. A. Jinnah two weeks later:

As you know, from my public statements, I am very much opposed to the handing over of India to Hindu caste rule, as seems very largely to be intended, and I have always strongly espoused the rights of the Moslems and the Depressed Classes to their fair share of life and power. I feel that it is most important that British arms should not be used to dominate the Moslems, even though the caste Hindus might claim a numerical majority in a constituent assembly. I was, however, surprised to read all the insulting things that were said about Britain at the Moslem Congress in Bombay, and how the Moslems of India were described as 'under-going British slavery'. All this is quite untrue and very ungrateful. It also seems to be an act of great unwisdom on the part of the Moslems. The tendencies here to support the Congress are very strong in the Government party, and you are driving away your friends.

I am sorry to see you taking up an attitude towards Great Britain which cannot be reconciled with your letter to me asking for help. Having got out of the British Commonwealth of Nations, India will be thrown into great confusion, and will have no means of defence against infiltration or invasion from the North.[5]

In his second speech in the House of Commons on July 18, Churchill

---

[1] Speech of 15 July 1946: Churchill papers, 5/7.
[2] 'Darling Papa', undated (18 July 1946): Churchill papers, 1/42.
[3] 'Darling Papa', undated (18 July 1946): Churchill papers, 1/42.
[4] Speech of 18 July 1946: *Hansard*.
[5] 'Private & Confidential', 3 August 1946: Churchill papers, 2/42.

opposed the Government's scheme for the introduction of bread rationing, commenting that he would have hoped that 'there would be time to perfect the existing scheme of bread distribution as far as possible, or make a better scheme. . . .' He had studied the statistics of wheat and flour supply and stocks; statistics which, although he did not say so, he had been sent by Lord Cherwell. Bread rationing, he declared, would be 'a measure of great hardship to the people which nevertheless, for all its cost, appears at once panic-stricken in motive and futile in action'.[1]

At luncheon on July 30 Churchill was the guest of Lord Mountbatten. Sir John Anderson was also present, as was Mountbatten's personal assistant, Alan Campbell-Johnson, who noted down Churchill's comment that, after the First World War, Clemenceau had written a book which he entitled *Le Grandeur et la Misère de la Paix*. 'Now, after this war,' said Churchill, 'it is all "misère" and no "grandeur".'[2]

Churchill also told Mountbatten and his guests that the Japanese war power was as 'the lighting of fire on ice. It did not go deep'. Churchill added that he had 'never hated the Japanese and that his attitude was never to worry about enemies that had just been defeated but only to keep his eye on those to come'. Campbell-Johnson's account continued:

The general tenor of his argument was that the Japanese were nothing like as strong as we thought them to be and that they had been crippled by American power long before the Atom Bomb was dropped.

Mountbatten felt that the Atom Bomb was perhaps the only grounds which the Japanese had for excusing themselves and thereby saving face.

Churchill said that the decision to release the Atom Bomb was perhaps the only thing which history would have serious questions to ask about. 'I may even be asked by my Maker why I used it but I shall defend myself vigorously and shall say—"Why did you release this knowledge to us when mankind was raging in furious battles?"'

Sir John Anderson's comment was—'You cannot accuse your judges.'

Although Churchill did his utmost to show interest in the Japanese war, it was clear from all that he said that his whole being had been absorbed in the war against Germany and he kept on returning to the European Theatre. He said he had had, during the War, no idea that the German atrocities had been on the scale that the Nuremberg evidence had shown them to be and although he had had misgivings about that trial at the beginning, he now felt it was well justified. This was largely because of the grovelling attitude of the defendants.

If he had been in the dock (as indeed he certainly would have been if the War had gone the other way), the line he would have taken was—'We do

---

[1] Speech of 18 July 1946: *Hansard*. Throughout the Second World War, Churchill had successfully opposed the introduction of bread rationing. Despite his renewed opposition in 1946, it was introduced by the Labour Government.

[2] The French title of Clemenceau's book was *Grandeurs et Misères d'Une Victoire*, the English title *The Grandeur and Misery of Victory* (1930).

not recognise the competency of your court. We will await the verdict of the German people, whom we served, in 20 or 30 years time. You won the War; take your vengeance on us in whatever way you like. We do not recognise any authority above the rights of the German State.' But undoubtedly the enormity of the crimes had come as a surprise to the defendants themselves.

During the luncheon, Churchill spoke of the removal of Auchinleck from command of the forces in the Middle East in August 1942. 'Auchinleck kept on looking over his shoulder when he was in the Middle East,' Churchill remarked, 'and assigned a whole Division to Cyprus at a most critical time where it was about as much good to us as if it had been locked up in the Isle of Wight. He kept on worrying about the threat from the Caucasus whereas Churchill told him that his only duty was to protect Cairo from Rommel.' [1]

Within two weeks of his criticisms of the Government for its Indian policy and bread rationing proposals, Churchill spoke again, this time against its Palestine policy. 'Had I had the opportunity,' he said, 'of guiding the course of events after the war was won a year ago, I should have faithfully pursued the Zionist cause as I have defined it'—a Jewish National Home in Palestine—'and I have not abandoned it to-day, although this is not a very popular moment to espouse it.'

Churchill went on to say, however, in support of a remark earlier in the debate by Sir Stafford Cripps:

. . . no one can imagine that there is room in Palestine for the great masses of Jews who wish to leave Europe, or that they could be absorbed in any period which it is now useful to contemplate. The idea that the Jewish problem could be solved or even helped by a vast dumping of the Jews of Europe into Palestine is really too silly to consume our time in the House this afternoon. I am not absolutely sure that we should be in too great a hurry to give up the idea that European Jews may live in the countries where they belong.

I must say that I had no idea, when the war came to an end, of the horrible massacres which had occurred; the millions and millions that have been slaughtered. That dawned on us gradually after the struggle was over. But if all these immense millions have been killed and slaughtered, there must be a certain amount of living room for the survivors, and there must be inheritances and properties to which they can lay claim.

Are we not to hope that some tolerance will be established in racial matters in Europe, and that there will be some law reigning by which, at any rate, a portion of the property of these great numbers will not be taken away from them? It is quite clear, however, that this crude idea of letting all the Jews of Europe go into Palestine has no relation either to the problem of Europe or to the problem which arises in Palestine.

Was Churchill suggesting, interjected the Labour MP Sydney

Silverman, himself a Jew, 'that any Jew who regarded a country in Europe as nothing but the graveyard and cemetery of all his relatives, friends and hopes should be compelled to stay there if he did not want to do so?'

'I am against preventing Jews from doing anything which other people are allowed to do,' Churchill replied, and he added: 'I am against that, and I have the strongest abhorrence of the idea of anti-Semitic lines of prejudice.'

Returning to the creation of a Jewish National Home in Palestine, Churchill told the House of Commons:

I am convinced that from the moment when we feel ourselves unable to carry out properly and honestly the Zionist policy as we have all these years defined it and accepted it, and which is the condition on which we received the Mandate for Palestine, it is our duty at any rate to offer to lay down the Mandate.

We should therefore, as soon as the war stopped, have made it clear to the United States that, unless they came in and bore their share, we would lay the whole care and burden at the feet of the United Nations Organisation; and we should have fixed a date by which all our troops and forces would be withdrawn from the country.

At that time we had no interest in Palestine. We have never sought or got anything out of Palestine. We have discharged a thankless, painful, costly, laborious, inconvenient task for more than a quarter of a century with a very great measure of success.

Churchill then spoke of the upsurge in Jewish terrorist attacks against the British forces in Palestine:

Many people have made fine speeches about the Zionist question. Many have subscribed generously in money, but it is Great Britain, and Great Britain alone, which has steadfastly carried that cause forward across a whole generation to its present actual position, and the Jews all over the world ought not to be in a hurry to forget that. If in the Jewish movement or in the Jewish Agency there are elements of murder and outrage which they cannot control, and if these strike not only at their best but at their only effective friends, they and the Zionist cause must inevitably suffer from the grave and lasting reproach of the atrocious crimes which have been committed. It is perfectly clear that Jewish warfare directed against the British in Palestine will, if protracted, automatically release us from all obligations to persevere as well as destroy the inclination to make further efforts in British hearts. Indeed, there are many people who are very near that now.

These were strong words, the reaction to a recent upsurge of Jewish terrorism in Palestine. Yet Churchill added, by way of caution against allowing such sentiments too easily to prevail: 'We must not be in a hurry to turn aside from the large causes we have carried far.'

Churchill then spoke of the Zionist leader, Dr Chaim Weizmann, with whom he had first shared a platform in Manchester forty years earlier.[1] Here, he felt, was one area of hope for an end to terrorism and the creation of a Jewish National Home:

> There is the figure of Dr Weizmann, that dynamic Jew whom I have known so long, the ablest and wisest leader of the cause of Zionism, his whole life devoted to the cause, his son killed in the battle for our common freedom.[2] I ardently hope his authority will be respected by Zionists in this dark hour, and that the Government will keep in touch with him, and make every one of his compatriots feel how much he is respected here. It is perfectly clear that in that case we shall have the best opportunities of carrying this matter further forward.

Churchill then contrasted the British Government's policy in Palestine with that in India and Egypt:

> The Government are, apparently, ready to leave the 400 million Indians to fall into all the horrors of sanguinary civil war—civil war compared to which anything that could happen in Palestine would be microscopic; wars of elephants compared with wars of mice. Indeed we place the independence of India in hostile and feeble hands, heedless of the dark carnage and confusion which will follow.
>
> We scuttle from Egypt which we twice successfully defended from foreign massacre and pillage. We scuttle from it, we abandon the Canal zone about which our treaty rights were and still are indefensible; but now, apparently, the one place where we are at all costs and at all inconveniences to hold on and fight it out to the death is Palestine, and we are to be at war with the Jews of Palestine, and, if necessary, with the Arabs of Palestine.
>
> For what reason?
>
> Not, all the world will say, for the faithful discharge of our long mission but because we have need, having been driven out of Egypt, to secure a satisfactory strategic base from which to pursue our Imperial aims.

Churchill then proposed a drastic solution: 'action this day', he called it. If the United States was not willing to 'come and share the burden of the Zionist cause', then Britain should give immediate notice 'that we will return our Mandate to the United Nations Organisation and that we will evacuate Palestine within a specified period'.[3]

'I wish indeed,' Dr Weizmann wrote to Churchill on the following day, 'that Fate had allowed you to handle our problem; by now it would probably all have been settled, and we would all have been spared a good deal of misery.'[4]

[1] Churchill and Weizmann were among the speakers denouncing the persecution of Jews in Tsarist Russia at a public meeting in Manchester on 10 December 1905.

[2] Weizmann's son Michael, an officer in the Royal Air Force, had been killed in 1942 while in command of a bomber on anti-U-boat duty over the Bay of Biscay.

[3] Speech of 1 August 1946: *Hansard*.

[4] 'My dear Mr Churchill', 2 August 1946: Churchill papers, 2/8.

Learning, later that month, of British plans to disarm the Jews of Palestine, in an attempt to end terrorist attacks, Churchill wrote to Leslie Rowan at 10 Downing Street, for Attlee to see, that the disarmament of the Jews, 'if effective, carries with it the obligation to protect them from the Arabs'.[1]

For many years Churchill had been unhappy at the designation 'Conservative and Unionist Party' for what had become commonly known as the Conservatives. To Lord Woolton, who had just become Party Chairman, he wrote on August 3 to suggest a new name:

I am increasingly drawn to the idea of 'The Union Party', the members of which would be called Unionists and could call themselves at pleasure 'Conservative Unionists', 'Progressive Unionists', etc. I feel this is the broad high road by which alone the greatness of our Country and Empire can be maintained. 'The Union Party' would stand for the union of the Empire and Commonwealth, the union of men of goodwill, and of every class, opposed to the Socialist doctrinaires, and also to the union or fraternal association of the English-speaking peoples all over the world. 'We all go the same way home.'[2]

Although Leader of the Conservative Party, Churchill never abandoned the radical instincts of his two decades as a Liberal. 'I am opposed to State-ownership of all the land,' he explained to his son Randolph, 'but we must not conceal from ourselves that we should be much stronger if the soil of our country were divided up among two or three million people, instead of twenty or thirty thousand.' Churchill added, by way of explanation: 'Man is a land animal. Even rabbits are allowed to have warrens, and foxes have earths.'[3]

'You have never been a real Tory,' George Bernard Shaw wrote to Churchill in reply to Churchill's birthday greetings, and he went on to explain: 'a foundation of American democracy, with a very considerable dash of author and artist and the training of a soldier, has made you a phenomenon that the Blimps and Philistines and Stick-in-the-muds have never understood and always dreaded.'[4]

Churchill replied to Shaw at once, commenting that he would treasure his letter 'among my extending archives' and hoping that they would be 'enriched by several more as time passes'. His letter continued, with a reference to Shaw's play *Saint Joan*:

[1] 'Private', 'My dear Leslie', 21 August 1946: Churchill papers, 2/46.
[2] 'Private', 3 August 1946: Churchill papers, 2/8. It was Eden who had pressed for Lord Woolton as Party Chairman. Churchill had wanted Harold Macmillan for the task.
[3] 'Private', 'My dear Randolph', 10 August 1946: Churchill papers, 1/42.
[4] 'My dear Churchill', 12 August 1946: Churchill papers, 2/165.

I have always been much stirred by Joan. Anatole France is pretty good about her.[1] She is indeed a gleaming star. I am taking your play about her away with me to read on my 'holiday'. Like you, my work and my holidays are the same.

It must be agreeable to enjoy such a prolonged view of the dissolving human scene and to be perennially rejuvenated by the resilience and permanence of what you have written.

We do not agree about Communism. The impending division or collision will be Communism v The Rest. I read with some sympathy Maeterlinck's *Life of the Bee*. At any rate the bees have preserved the monarchical principle! I am not attracted by 'The soul of the white ant'. To hell with all static ideals of human society. What matters is the behaviour of individuals under an infinitely varying and, we must hope, on the whole improving atmosphere and surroundings.

Do you think that the atomic bomb means that the architect of the universe has got tired of writing his non-stop scenario? There was a lot to be said for his stopping with the Panda. The release of the bomb seems to be his next turning-point.[2]

Churchill's letter to Shaw was written seventeen days after the signing into law by Truman, on August 1, of the McMahon Act, under which the United States could no longer share its atomic secrets with other countries. This Act abrogated the agreement which Churchill and Roosevelt had signed in Quebec on 19 September 1944, which stated that the 'full collaboration' between Britain and the United States in developing atomic power 'for military and commercial purposes' should continue 'after the defeat of Japan until and unless terminated by joint agreement'. The Quebec Agreement had never been made public. It was now set aside to Britain's immediate and subsequent disadvantage. 'I cannot but regret'—Churchill wrote to Eisenhower nine years later—'that you had not the power at the time the McMahon Act was under discussion. If the agreement signed by me and FDR had not been shelved we should probably already have been able to add a substantial reinforcement to your vast and formidable deterrent power.'[3]

---

[1] Anatole France's *Vie de Jeanne d'Arc* had been published in 1908.

[2] 'Private', 'My dear Bernard Shaw', 18 August 1946: Churchill papers, 2/165. In his letter Churchill also asked Shaw: 'Ought we not to try and settle the Irish question? Could we not call it quits in the long tragedy? We succeeded in exercising remarkable forbearance about the Irish ports.'

[3] 'My dear Friend', 'Top Secret', 'Private and Personal', 12 January 1955: Churchill papers, 2/217.

13

Chartwell, 'the Corpse' and the War Memoirs

━━━━

A T Chartwell, Churchill found the time and comfort to enjoy his years of comparative political inaction. Each facet of life in that idyllic setting absorbed him: the lakes, the farms, the livestock, even the insects. Learning that his tortoiseshell butterflies were dying, he noted for Miss Sturdee: 'Ask whether a little pot of honey wd be any good for them.' He also told her that he would leave the cage door open 'on nice days and let them go out among the flowers'.[1]

In 1938 Churchill had been forced by financial difficulties to put Chartwell on the market. Fortunately for him a friend, Sir Henry Strakosch, had enabled him to cover his debts, and to withdraw Chartwell from the market. Now, in the autumn of 1946, he was again feeling financial constraints. He had received £50,000 from Alexander Korda's film company for the film rights of *A History of the English-Speaking Peoples*, a book whose first draft had been completed in 1939, but which still awaited revision and publication. He had sold all his pre-1940 book copyrights to Odhams for £25,000.[2] He had received £5,000 from Henry Luce for the reproduction of some of his paintings in *Life* magazine. Luce had also paid him £12,500 for the publication in book form of his *Secret Session Speeches*. In all, in the bank, he had between £110,000 and £120,000. 'He reckoned,' he told Lord Camrose when they met in London on 7 August 1946, 'that he could not live on less than £12,000 a year.'[3] But he wanted to leave all his earnings on his war memoirs to his heirs. He felt therefore, he explained to Camrose, that he should sell Chartwell, 'and add to his capital that

---

[1] Note and letter of 17 June 1946: Churchill papers, 1/30.
[2] This was the exact sum which Churchill was about to offer his neighbour, Major Marnham, for Chartwell Farm.
[3] From 4 September 1945 Churchill had also drawn £2,000 a year as Leader of the Opposition.

way'. In 1938 he had expected between £20,000 and £25,000 for the house, 'and he thought nowadays he ought to get at least the latter figure'.

Camrose, amazed that Churchill should contemplate selling his beloved Chartwell, proposed that it should be bought 'privately' by friends who would then let him stay in it for the rest of his life, after which it could be maintained as a memorial to him.

'I asked him,' Camrose noted, 'whether he would sell the house for £50,000 with that object in mind. At which he laughed and replied "Yes", adding with one of his characteristic chuckles "and throw in the corpse as well".'

Camrose's account continued:

I told him he could consider the matter settled and that I would undertake to arrange the finance with myself and a limited number of other people. He was rather taken aback by my ready undertaking and thought it might be difficult to achieve. When I told him that the cheque would be forthcoming as soon as the formalities were concluded he seemed very affected.

Later he became very enthusiastic and his mind started working as to how he could help to make the memorial an interesting and permanent one. Said he would leave a lot of papers and documents in the house and was sure Clemmie would co-operate most willingly.

Churchill also told Camrose that 'he had always thought that he would like to be buried at Chartwell and my proposal would make his mind definite on that point'.

Camrose at once set about raising the money: £50,000 for the purchase of Chartwell and a further £35,000 required by the National Trust as an Endowment for its future maintenance. He approached sixteen people. 'Only in two cases,' he noted, 'did a "victim" fail to give an affirmative reply within three minutes of hearing of the scheme. In one of these cases time was requested to "talk to my wife" and the cheque arrived the next morning.' The second hesitation was that of Lord Nuffield, who, Camrose noted, 'was very worried and depressed about the doings of the Labour Government when I spoke to him', and declined to join the scheme. But when Camrose spoke to Lady Nuffield, 'she waxed very enthusiastic about Winston and in due course the cheque came along'.[1]

When news of the National Trust arrangement was made public, Major Marnham, whose farm adjoined Chartwell, and who had cut

---

[1] 'Chartwell', dated (wrongly) 4 August 1946: Camrose papers. Camrose himself subscribed £15,000; he raised £5,000 each from Lord Bearsted, Lord Bicester, Sir James Laird, Sir Hugo Cunliffe-Owen, Lord Catto, Lord Glendyne, Lord Kenilworth, Lord Leathers, Sir James Lithgow, Sir Edward Mountain, Lord Nuffield, Sir Edward Peacock, Lord Portal, James de Rothschild, J. Arthur Rank and Sir Frederick Stewart.

Chartwell Farm's corn, was alarmed. 'I do not think you need be troubled immediately,' Churchill wrote to him, 'about the future of Chartwell as a national possession affecting the amenities at Chartwell Farm. Of course I cannot tell how long I shall live, but the actuarial tables afford a reasonable working basis.' [1]

Churchill remained at Chartwell, whenever possible, making arrangements for the sale and serialization of his war memoirs, and painting. He was also making plans for the publication of a volume of post-war speeches. 'Do you wish to take them all away to Switzerland with you?' asked Miss Sturdee. 'No,' he replied; but he did wish to know how many words they made. [2]

On the day after his talk with Lord Camrose in London, Churchill was back in Kent. Lord Moran, whom he had invited to lunch, noted in his diary:

Winston is happy at Chartwell, as happy as he can be when the world has gone all wrong. I found him in the studio, the walls of which are covered with his canvases. When he had greeted me he climbed on to a big chair on a kind of platform, and surveyed the canvas he was painting, which was at the other end of the square room.

'My desert is too hot,' he said descending from his throne and applying a white paint with a few bold strokes of a fat brush.

I said he had been busy.

'Yes, it gives me something to do—an occupation.' He paused to take in his handiwork. 'And I must have an occupation. Elliott Roosevelt has been writing a foolish book; he attacks me.'

He advanced to the easel and made two or three quick strokes with his brush.

'I don't care what he says,' he added almost absentmindedly and with his eyes glued to his picture. 'He's not much of a fellow. Elliott says I delayed the cross-Channel invasion of Europe for two years.' He turned to me. 'A short time ago I asked Monty whether we could have invaded France before we did. Monty answered: "It would have been madness. We could not have done it without the landing craft."'

Winston seemed to be thinking more of the picture than of Elliott Roosevelt. This was the real Winston, magnanimous, refusing to be ruffled by the small change of politics. The telephone rang. It was Clemmie summoning us to lunch. He put on a waterproof over his boiler suit, and walked very slowly up the slope to the house. I admired the fine setting.

[1] 'My dear Marnham', 17 August 1946: Churchill papers, 1/30. In 1946 the actuarial tables gave a man of seventy-one (Churchill's age at the time) a life expectancy of between eight and ten years. On 20 October 1946 Churchill offered Marnham £25,000 for his farm; this came into Churchill's possession on 1 January 1947. (Churchill papers, 1/32.)

[2] 'Mr Churchill', initialled 'NS', 16 August 1946, and reply in red ink. (Churchill papers, 5/1.) Two days later Miss Sturdee replied that the total came to 89,300 words, of which 50,300 were in the House of Commons. Churchill's first volume of post-war speeches, *The Sinews of Peace*, edited by Randolph Churchill, was published two years later, on 19 August 1948.

'Ah, you should see it when the sun is on the Weald.'

He stood still to get his breath. I asked him how he had been.

'Two nights ago I was arguing with Randolph at two o'clock. We got heated. I bellowed and he counter-bellowed, and I felt things weren't right here.'

He pointed to his heart. I asked him if it was pain. He hesitated.

'No, but I was conscious of my heart; it was like the ghost of what happened at Washington when I tried to open the window. But I'm very well if I keep within my limits. I think I can make plans for some years yet. I feel much better than when I was Prime Minister.'

Winston did not seem to expect me to intervene. When he came to the house he pulled himself wearily, step by step, up to his work-room, where he picked up a little book and asked me if I would like it. I looked over his shoulder at the title: *Secret Session Speeches by Winston Churchill.*

'It has just come from America. I'm very pleased with it.'

At lunch with Clementine Churchill and Lord Moran, Churchill, as Moran noted, 'spoke gloomily of the future'. Moran later sought to reconstruct the conversation:

'You think there will be another war?'

'Yes.'

'You mean in ten years' time?'

'Sooner. Seven or eight years. I shan't be there.'

I asked him if it would be between Russia and her satellite countries and the Anglo-Saxon countries.

'Yes, with France and Scandinavia and Belgium and Holland on our side.'

I wondered how England could take part in an atomic war when she was so small. He said:

'We ought not to wait until Russia is ready. I believe it will be eight years before she has these bombs.' His face brightened. 'America knows that fifty-two per cent of Russia's motor industry is in Moscow and could be wiped out by a single bomb. It might mean wiping out three million people, but they would think nothing of that.' He smiled. 'They think more of erasing an historical building like the Kremlin.'

His cigar had gone out; he fumbled in his pockets for a match.

'The Russian Government is like the Roman Church: their people do not question authority.'

I made some passing reference to Potsdam. 'Ah,' he said sadly, 'that was when the blow fell.'

He said nothing for a little, and then observed, half to himself:

'It was a blow.' [1]

Recalling the recent past was not merely a question of idle or sombre reminiscence. As each new book of memoirs or history was published, such as Elliott Roosevelt's short volume, so Churchill found himself

[1] Moran diary, 8 August 1946: *The Struggle for Survival*, pages 313–15.

returning to the most controversial aspects of the years on which he had himself to write. Hardly a week passed without some such intrusion. Reading a draft account of British bombing policy which Air Marshal Sir Arthur Harris had written for publication, Churchill wrote to Harris's assistant:

Our friend should be very careful in all that he writes not to admit that we ever did anything not justified by the circumstances and the actions of the enemy in the measures we took to bomb Germany. We gave them full notice to clear out of their munition-making cities. In fact, they had very good shelters and protection, and the position of the civilian population was very different from that of London, Coventry, Liverpool, etc. when they were bombed in the second year of the war. I am not quite clear about Dresden. It may be we were asked to do this as part of some large military combination, but I am afraid the civilian losses there were unduly heavy.

All these affairs anyhow are overshadowed by what we did to Japan with the atomic bomb, yet this in a way gave the Japanese a reason for surrender, which in their eyes saved their military honour, & saved Britain & the US several hundred thousand lives.[1]

Two weeks later Churchill was drawn into controversy over the wartime *aide mémoire* known subsequently as the Morgenthau Plan, which had argued in favour of the total destruction of German industry, and the creation of an entirely pastoral or agricultural Germany. In the autumn of 1945, in a book published in the United States, Morgenthau himself had referred, as he had telegraphed to Churchill at the time, to 'the plan for Germany that you and President Roosevelt agreed to and signed at Quebec'.[2] The Morgenthau Plan had at once been denounced as harsh and illiberal, quickly entering history as yet another proof, in particular for the American reader, of Churchill's old-fashioned attitudes. In answer to a question by Robert Sherwood, who was preparing a biography of Harry Hopkins in which the Morgenthau Plan was to be mentioned, Churchill dictated his own version of the event, using the third person:

Mr Morgenthau has since published this *Aide Mémoire* and has represented it as a solemn agreement. It certainly was the result of his persistence and dynamic energy on a hypothetical topic, applied to tired and busy men.

Mr Churchill fully shares President Roosevelt's subsequent dissent from it. It was a great shame to screw this out and hawk it abroad. When one is fighting a terrible foe, savage feelings arise. These were known during the conflict, but must not be allowed to govern thought after victory has been gained.[3]

---

[1] 'Most Private & Confidential' (to W. A. J. Lawrence), 3 August 1946: Churchill papers, 2/150.

[2] Telegram of 9 August 1945: Churchill papers, 2/3.

[3] 'Personal and Confidential', 17 August 1946: Churchill papers, 2/155.

Speaking of the Morgenthau Plan in the House of Commons four years later, Churchill said: 'I must say it never required a Cabinet negative; it never had any validity of any sort or kind.' He added: 'Nevertheless, I must say that I do not agree with this paper, for which I none the less bear a responsibility. I do not agree with it, but I can only say that when fighting for life in a fierce struggle with an enemy I feel quite differently towards him than when that enemy is beaten to the ground and is suing for mercy. Anyhow, if the document is ever brought up to me I shall certainly say, "I do not agree with that, and I am sorry that I put my initials to it." I cannot do more than that.' [1]

While he was at Chartwell that August, Churchill was asked, by both Robert Boothby and Viscount Cecil of Chelwood, to become involved in the question of the South Tyrol, an area of northern Italy lost by the Austro-Hungarian Empire in 1919 and still claimed by Austria. On August 17, Churchill told Boothby that he hoped he had 'some Labour men' on the fact-finding Committee that was being formed. 'I must leave the development of the campaign to you,' he wrote, 'but pray keep me informed. . . .' [2] To Viscount Cecil of Chelwood, Churchill wrote that same day about the Tyrol: 'In the vast confusion of Europe it is indeed a Touchstone,' and he added: 'Such baffling situations as those which now confront us can only be dealt with selectively. One way is to make up one's mind which is the true point of attack on the long front of evil and bewilderment.' [3]

On August 23 Churchill left Chartwell for three weeks in Switzerland, on the shore of Lake Geneva, to paint, work on his war memoirs, and to prepare an address to the University of Zurich. His home was to be the Villa Choisi, owned since 1940 by a Swiss banker, Alfred Kern. [4] With Churchill were his wife, their daughter Mary, and two secretaries, Miss Marston and Miss Gilliatt.

Press reports of Churchill's visit gave a vivid picture; one account, in the Sunday Express, was so graphic that Churchill cut it out. The first section dealt with his security, and his seclusion:

---

[1] Speech of 21 July 1949: Hansard.

[2] 'My dear Bob', 'Private', 17 August 1946: Boothby papers.

[3] 'Dear Bob', 17 August 1946: Boothby papers. On 6 September 1946 Austria and Italy reached agreement on South Tyrol, which was to remain in Italy, with safeguards for its German-speaking population, which was guaranteed equality of cultural, linguistic and economic rights, as well as promises of increased local autonomy and easier movement between the Alto Adige (South Tyrol) and the Austrian Tyrol. The Italian Prime Minister, Alcide de Gasperi, had himself come from this former Austro-Hungarian region, and had sat in the Vienna Parliament for three years before the First World War.

[4] In 1986 the 99-year-old Kern caused a stir in Switzerland by entering into negotiations to sell Choisi and its park for building purposes, and the creation of 220 identical dwellings. (Neue Zürcher Zeitung, 16 August 1986.)

Mr Winston Churchill, Europe's most popular personality, has today become known in Geneva as 'The prisoner of the château'.

From the moment he set foot on Swiss soil at the airport yesterday, for a three weeks' holiday, accompanied by Mrs Churchill and their daughter Mary, he has held the concentrated attention of the Swiss police.

At Château Choisi, on the shores of Lake Leman, scores of armed police patrol the grounds and police speedboats manoeuvre constantly within 50 yards of the shore.

The police have built a nest in a high tree in the château's grounds, from where the look-out man can take stock of the surrounding territory and at the same time watch Mr Churchill's every movement.

Four square miles of territory in and around the château have been marked off as No-man's-land. In this region neither pedestrian nor car is allowed to loiter. Even the gardener has been informed that he cannot receive his family or friends while Mr Churchill is resident there.

The report ended with an account of the pattern and pleasures of Churchill's daily life at Choisi:

Rising early in the morning, he went down to the lake side, followed discreetly by two policemen, to look at the scenery. In the afternoon he was seen with brushes and easel wending his way to the private port to start the first of his pictures of Lake Leman.

Everything has been done, apart from police attention, to give Mr Churchill the best of all holidays. Priceless Louis XIV furniture has been borrowed to furnish the rooms, a bar has been built in one room, with the widest range of aperitives, wines, brandies and champagnes.

A famous chef from St Moritz has been brought in to prepare his meals. New flower beds have been built through the parks of the château.

Mr Churchill has expressed a desire that no official receptions be given while he is holidaying. Tonight, however, he attends the International Horse-riding Exhibition in Geneva.[1]

'We are having a delightful time here,' Churchill wrote to Oliver Stanley on August 29, from his lakeside villa, 'with every comfort and the strictest privacy. I find lots to paint in the garden. . . .'[2] To one of the many local inhabitants who asked to see him at Choisi, Churchill replied: 'I am living here in the most complete seclusion, and am not making any appointments.'[3]

When the weather took a turn for the worse, as it did after the first four days, and outdoor painting became impossible, Churchill painted 'indoors': General Guisan, the officer commanding the Swiss army during the war, had lent Churchill his campaigning tent for this purpose, as well as for his literary work. The approaches to the villa,

[1] *Sunday Express*, 25 August 1946.
[2] Letter sent from the Villa Choisi, Bursinel, 29 August 1946: Churchill papers, 2/357.
[3] Letter of 13 September 1946: Churchill papers, 2/244.

the British Consul-General in Berne informed Ernest Bevin, 'were permanently guarded by Swiss troops and police', keeping away all curious or prying eyes. One visitor to the villa was General Guisan, another Field Marshal Smuts, and a third the man who had arranged for Churchill to stay there, the Swiss painter Charles Montag. The Consul-General's account continued:

Miss Mary Churchill won most flattering notice from the Swiss press by her presence of mind and courage in administering first aid to a man who had just been badly injured in a road accident not far from the Villa Choisi. Towards the end of her stay at the Villa Choisi, Mrs Churchill unhappily damaged her rib through a fall in a motor boat and was unable to join in the public part of Mr Churchill's visit to Switzerland.[1]

Throughout his stay at Choisi, Churchill continued work on his war memoirs, seeking help from those who had participated in the events which he wished to describe. On September 9 he wrote to Field Marshal Alanbrooke, his letter indicative of the care which he was taking:

I have been putting together a few notes about the first battle in France before Dunkirk, and for this purpose have had available, besides my own documents, a very full diary prepared by the Historical Section and also Gort's despatch. I do not gather from either of these exactly when and how your action was fought near the Ypres–Menin road. I always understood this was a most important feature of the successful withdrawal into the Dunkirk perimeter, that you commanded the divisions of Alex and Monty and I think a third division, that you repulsed the enemy on the whole corps front with heavy loss, and that at the same time the four British divisions we were withdrawing from Lille were streaming homewards along the road only a few miles behind your front line. I should be so much obliged if you could give me a note on this, as it has always figured in my mind.

'We have horrible weather here,' Churchill added; 'indeed they say it has never been so bad at this season. However, the villa is very comfortable. I have been playing at "still life" and experimenting in Tempera which is a most amusing medium for preliminary work.'

Reflecting briefly on current affairs, Churchill told Alanbrooke: 'Things do not seem to be very good anywhere. Indeed I could easily find stronger terms in which to describe them.'[2]

Alanbrooke sent Churchill the notes he wanted, twelve pages of them, with maps to illustrate the retreat to Dunkirk. 'I think the

---

[1] No. 494 from Berne, 25 September 1946: Churchill papers, 2/245. The Consul-General was T. M. Snow.

[2] 'Private', 'My dear Brookie', 9 September 1946: Churchill papers, 4/196.

account is fairly correct,' he wrote, 'and is based on a diary I kept at that time.'[1]

Henceforth, many of those to whom Churchill turned for materials and recollections were to send him not only what they remembered, but their actual documents or diary extracts of the time. Among those whose diaries he was sent privately, and which he used in his account, were Sir Stafford Cripps, Alfred Duff Cooper, Lord Moran and Jock Colville.[2]

While he was still at Choisi, Churchill, his wife and daughter Mary were joined for some days by Duncan and Diana Sandys. 'It was a wonderful holiday,' Duncan Sandys wrote on their return to London, '& reminded us so much of the happy time we all had together in Marrakech ten years ago.' As to Churchill's Zurich speech, Sandys wrote, 'I am sure the public in all countries is very much in the mood to listen to what the late pilot has got to say.'[3]

On September 16 Churchill left Choisi for Geneva, where he was to lunch with the President and Committee of the International Red Cross. Before he left Choisi, Clementine Churchill had advised him to visit some of the departments of the Red Cross, as well as lunching with the Committee. 'If you would pay a short visit to one or two of the departments before lunch,' she wrote, 'you would then in your speech be able to refer to what you had actually seen. I think, if you would not find this wearisome, you should include this in your plan (it would not do for me to go alone) because had it not been for the action of the International Red Cross in Switzerland none of our prisoners would have received any parcels at all.' Geneva, Clementine Churchill thought, had been 'the great entrepôt town and practically the whole population worked at the distribution'.[4]

At the time of Churchill's visit, more than a quarter of a million Italian, German and Austrian prisoners-of-war were still in camps under Allied control, visited regularly by delegates from the International Committee of the Red Cross. These included 23,000 Germans in Egypt and nearly 3,000 in Britain.

After noting the 'kindly reception' which he had received in all the villages which he had passed on his drive into Geneva, 'by all classes of the population', Churchill told his hosts:

---

[1] 'My dear Winston', 31 October 1946: Churchill papers, 4/196.

[2] 'I enclose you a few extracts from my confidential diary,' Cripps wrote to Churchill in December 1947, 'dealing with the matter you mentioned to me. Perhaps you will destroy them when you have read them!' ('My dear Winston', 'Personal', 24 December 1947, Churchill papers, 4/19.) Churchill did not destroy the extracts, which date from the summer of 1939; they are printed in full in the relevant document volume of this biography. From Lord Moran came extracts from the diary which he had kept during Churchill's visit to Athens in December 1944.

[3] 'My dear Winston', 15 September 1946: Churchill papers, 1/42.

[4] 'Winston', signed 'Clemmie', dated 'Tuesday 27th': Churchill papers, 2/244.

It has been said that little gratitude was shown to the founders of the International Committee of the Red Cross. I saw in an article that in a large dictionary of European history their names were not even mentioned. But those who know about these things will ever honour M. Dunant, M. Moynier and General Dufour, pioneers in the sixties of the last century. They were all blessed with long life and—if it is a blessing—with old age. They toiled faithfully and enjoyed in their old days the very great results obtained.

We must not underrate them and their work even though their good arguments may often be countered by bad arguments in captivating forms. For instance, it has been objected: How can you humanize war? How can you prevent war? It has been further said: What is this about being impartial? and so on. However, the force of this opposition has faded away before the persistence and perseverance of the pioneers who triumphed by the quality of their spirit already put forward by Rousseau in his famous statement, which elevated the wounded man as something sacred, something apart, detached from all forms of human tragedy and quarrels.

Churchill's speech continued:

In bygone ages, Europe was linked by many ties together; there were the Romans, there was the Empire of Charlemagne, there were the bonds of Christendom, there were aristocratic ties which were cosmopolitan, the great association of reigning houses which in the days of Queen Victoria gave something in common between countries. But all have disappeared this time. There was then chivalry in war, which seemed in a way to disguise its guilt, and was still observed in the wars of the seventeenth and eighteenth centuries.

But all has vanished in this terrible twentieth century. All relations have been shattered between opposing armies; between nations engaged in the war, there has been no point in common. There never has been such a devilish state of destruction of all points of human contact, owing to the character of these two most terrible conflicts in which man has been engaged. One thing however has been preserved and that as a link between the many nations,—not perfectly preserved, but still as a great effective force, namely the work of the International Committee of the Red Cross.

The Red Cross was a platform, the only platform between the lines of battle; men could there meet together and recognize their common humanity, and the value of an international code of law and convention. A great achievement has thus been reached; it is a warrant of the spirit of those who devoted their life to this task, and it is a Swiss achievement—a Swiss achievement primarily, and one which shows that the preservation of a healthy spirit of independence does not necessarily mean absence of interest in the fortune and affairs of others less fortunate.

I am sure I greatly admire the scope of your work. There are days when hope and confidence spring very strongly, and there are days when the sense of disappointment is keen that, so much having been gained, so little results should apparently have been presented. There are days now when you cannot feel as you did after the First War, but the moral factors are in the ascendance and there are no great organized forces which could change the onward march of civilization. But of this I am sure: that no one can be asked to do more than his part, and everyone who has helped this building-up of the International Committee of the Red Cross, working as international guides, will endeavour to preserve all civilized customs which can regulate the affairs and even the quarrels of misguided self-torturing humanity. They will be playing an honourable and valuable part in this world, and may go to sleep with an easy conscience after a good day's work is done.

It was the International Red Cross, Churchill ended, which, while it could not 'spare mankind the consequence of its crimes and follies, may at least mitigate its worst excesses and preserve that spark of human inspiration, without which humanity sinks lower than the animals'.[1]

While he was at the Red Cross headquarters, Churchill was taken to the room in which were the cards listing the addresses of more than two million German prisoners-of-war, for whom the Red Cross had acted as the sole conduit of correspondence. 'This,' he commented, as he looked down on the files from a balcony, 'is the first time that I have had two million Germans at my feet.'[2]

That afternoon Churchill went with his daughter Mary to Berne, where they were put up at the Château de Lohn, the Swiss Chequers. On September 17, in Berne, he was given a luncheon by the Swiss Federal Council and, on September 18, a luncheon by the French Ambassador, after which he left for Zurich.

Churchill's speech at Zurich, on September 19, was an appeal for the creation of 'a kind of United States of Europe'. All that was needed for this, he said, 'is the resolve of hundreds of millions of men and women to do right instead of wrong, and gain as their reward blessing instead of cursing'. Was 'the only lesson of history', he asked, 'that mankind is unteachable?[3] Let there be justice, mercy and freedom. The people have only to will it, and all will achieve their heart's desire.' But where to start? He had a proposal, he said, 'that will astonish you', and he went on: 'The first step in the re-creation of the

[1] 'Address by Mr Winston Churchill on the occasion of his visit to the International Committee of the Red Cross, Geneva', 16 September 1946: Archives of the International Committee of the Red Cross.

[2] Marion Scheinberger recollections: in conversation with the author, Geneva, 19 February 1987.

[3] In 1928 Churchill had written to Lord Beaverbrook (who had just written a history of the politics of the First World War): '. . . what a tale! Think of all these people—decent, educated, the story of the past laid out before them—What to avoid—what to do etc. patriotic, loyal, clean—trying their utmost—What a ghastly muddle they made of it! Unteachable from infancy to tomb—There is the first & main characteristic of mankind.' (Letter of 21 May 1928: Beaverbrook papers.)

European family must be a partnership between France and Germany. In this way only can France recover the moral leadership of Europe. There can be no revival of Europe without a spiritually great France and a spiritually great Germany.'

Churchill ended his Zurich speech with a reference to the atom bomb, and with a warning:

Time may be short. At present there is a breathing-space. The cannon have ceased firing. The fighting has stopped; but the dangers have not stopped. If we are to form the United States of Europe or whatever name or form it may take, we must begin now.

In these present days we dwell strangely and precariously under the shield and protection of the atomic bomb. The atomic bomb is still only in the hands of a State and nation which we know will never use it except in the cause of right and freedom. But it may well be that in a few years this awful agency of destruction will be widespread and the catastrophe following from its use by several warring nations will not only bring to an end all that we call civilisation, but may possibly disintegrate the globe itself.

France and Germany, Churchill concluded, should take the lead together in the 'urgent work' of creating a United States of Europe. At the same time Britain and the British Commonwealth, as well as 'mighty America, and I trust Soviet Russia—for then indeed all would be well'—must be the 'friends and sponsors of the new Europe, and must champion its right to live and shine'.[1]

Churchill's speech showed once again, declared *The Times* on September 20, that he was 'not afraid to startle the world with new and even, as many must find them, outrageous propositions'. Was the remedy Churchill prescribed for Europe's ills 'one to which Europe, in its present situation, will submit', *The Times* asked, and went on to answer its own question: 'It must be admitted that there are few signs of it. Even in western Europe there is little to suggest that the unity so much spoken of, and indeed so much desired, is on the way.' Churchill's speech 'was in fact based on the assumption that Europe is already irrevocably divided between East and West. This is the peril of his argument and of its enunciation at this moment.'

Churchill's call was given 'a still more challenging turn', *The Times* commented, 'by the inclusion of Germany within the unity he postulates'. The 'first practical step' towards European unity was not, *The Times* felt, Churchill's call for a Council of Europe, but something 'more humdrum', which 'may prove to be best directed along the path of economics rather than of politics; such as the recent Franco-British economic agreement, or the proposed economic union between Holland

[1] Speech of 19 September 1946: Churchill papers, 5/8. Recording: BBC Written Archives Centre, Library No. 10253.

and Belgium, or the proposed Economic Commission for Europe'.[1]

From Leo Amery came words of high praise. 'You have indeed lit a torch to give its message of hope to a shattered world,' Amery wrote. 'The French are startled, as they were bound to be, but the idea will sink in all the same. As for the Germans your speech may have been just in time to save them from going Bolshevist. You have done few bigger things, even in the great years behind us.'[2]

'Now that *you* have raised the European question,' wrote the founder of the European movement, Count Coudenhove-Kalergi, 'the Governments can no longer ignore it.'[3]

From Zurich, Churchill returned to London. Then, on September 25, together with his wife, he left once more for Europe, going to Brussels and then to Paris. With Churchill and his wife was their daughter Mary, then aged twenty-four. It was while in Paris that she met for the first time a young officer at the British Embassy, the Assistant Military Attaché, Christopher Soames. Flying home from Paris on September 29, in an aeroplane put at his disposal by the Count of Flanders, the Regent of Belgium, Churchill wrote to him of their meeting in Brussels, and of his own activities in Paris:

Airborne:

Sir,

We enjoyed our visit so much and it was a great pleasure to meet Your Royal Highness and to have such long and interesting talks. I shall often think about all your problems as Regent under these extraordinary conditions and earnestly hope that you will solve them. I am sure the key is duty.

I was painfully affected by all you told me about your brother's singular attitude and behaviour to you in these long tragic years.[4] I have a brother who is five years younger than me and whom I dearly love and have always cherished. I grieve indeed that you have never found the same kindness and protection which Nature decrees.

My visit to Paris was successful. I had long talks at the British Embassy with Byrnes, Bedell Smith and General Smuts. How much we all agree! There has been no publicity to cause embarrassment to Mr Bevin and I have brought my knowledge of the general position up-to-date, and renewed my very intimate American contacts.

'I write this in your beautiful and silent aeroplane,' Churchill added. 'It was indeed kind of you to let it take me home by a triangular

---

[1] 'A Voice from Zurich': *The Times*, 20 September 1946.

[2] 'My dear Winston', 20 September 1946: Churchill papers, 2/18.

[3] 'My dear Winston Churchill', 23 September 1946: Churchill papers, 2/19.

[4] The Regent's brother was Leopold III, King of the Belgians, who had surrendered his army to the Germans in 1940. Thereafter, the Germans had confined him to his palace in Brussels. From 1945 to 1950 he was not allowed even to live in Belgium. Following a referendum in 1950 permitting him to return, there were riots. In 1951 he abdicated in favour of his son.

route. We carry with us very pleasant memories and send you back
our warmest wishes for yourself and your country.'[1]

Back at Chartwell, Churchill returned at once to the work on his
memoirs. Having now dictated his chapters about the battle in France
in 1940, he sent the typescript to the printer, who was responsible for
printing the Government's own confidential documents. As each section came back to him, he proposed to send them to Ismay for his
comments. 'They are of course only very provisional notes,' Churchill
explained, 'and are derived mainly, though possibly incorrectly, from
the Staff Diary which you so kindly sent me. It may interest you to
read them, and make any notes you like in correction or improvement.' However, Churchill added, it would probably be 'several years
before they see the light, and of course they must undergo organised
examination by the young gentlemen I am going to employ'.[2]

Before any 'young gentlemen' were recruited Churchill completed
both the financial and archival aspects of his design. 'I am pressed
from many quarters,' he wrote to the Cabinet Secretary, Sir Edward
Bridges, on September 23, 'to give my account of the British war story
and, without at present making any definite plans, I have been getting
my papers in order and considering the project.'

Churchill then set out what he proposed to do:

I should like to tell the story so far as possible in my own words written at
the time. As you know a great part of my work was done in writing (dictated
typescript) and I should scarcely need to publish any documents other than
those I have composed myself. I should of course not wish to publish any
paper which was not considered in the public interest by the Government of
the day, and I should be quite ready to discuss the omission of any particular
phrase, sentence or passage in any memorandum otherwise unobjectionable.
Moreover I do not expect that any publication can take place for two or
three years and I may not live so long. I should agree to a final revision of
the text in detail by HMG before publication, in case the foreign situation
might be such as to make what is now harmless injurious. This can only be
judged in the future.

I should like to know, without necessarily accepting the view as final,
whether *in principle* there would be any objection to the publication of the
kind of memoranda which are attached to this note. I feel I have a right, if I
so decide, to tell my tale and I am convinced that it would be to the advantage of our country to have it told, as perhaps I alone can tell it. . . .

---

[1] 'Sir', 29 September 1946: Churchill papers, 2/249. Four years later, Churchill wrote to the
Regent, in sending him a specially bound copy of volume 3 of his war memoirs: 'I have the most
pleasant memories of my visits to Brussels, and of painting excursions, and of the kindness with
which I have been treated. But most of all I value our long talks together into the small hours of
the morning. They have given me an enduring picture of a Prince whose resolve was to do his
duty.' (Letter of 30 September 1950: Churchill papers, 2/167.)

[2] 'My dear P', 30 September 1946: Churchill papers, 4/19.

'I should be glad,' Churchill ended, 'to receive the Prime Minister's view upon this matter at his convenience in order that I may consider what course to take.'[1]

Bridges submitted to Attlee a draft reply to Churchill's request, for submission to the Cabinet, and, as Bridges wrote in his covering letter, 'tilted rather gently in favour of acceptance of Mr Churchill's proposal'.[2]

From Paris, Ernest Bevin opposed giving Churchill the right to publish. 'In my view,' he telegraphed to Attlee on October 9, 'the publication of these documents at the moment would be a grave embarrassment to His Majesty's Government and in particular to me as Foreign Secretary. Nothing ought to be written until peace has been finally settled.'[3]

In submitting this telegram to Attlee, Bridges noted that Churchill's original request had contained the sentence: 'I do not expect that any publication can take place for 2 or 3 years.' Bridges added: 'This in substance meets the point, but the reply to Mr Churchill could add that publication cannot take place until after the peace settlement.'[4]

At Cabinet on October 10 Bevin's objections were set aside, and it was agreed to allow Churchill to go ahead 'on the understanding that before any part of his book was published the text would be submitted for final revision on behalf of the Government, in the light of the situation existing at the time'.[5]

On October 10, Churchill received Attlee's acceptance of his plan. He could, Sir Edward Bridges informed him, have whatever access he wished to the archives of his premiership: '100 per cent acceptance,' Bridges wrote, 'with no provisos, other than those which you yourself suggested.' Bridges added: 'you know, I hope, that I and my colleagues in the Cabinet Office will always be ready to give you any help we can over these questions of documents and so forth. It will be our endeavour to be as helpful to you as you have been to us. We are most grateful to you.'[6]

In a second letter on October 10, the Cabinet Office did lay down one proviso, that it would be necessary to consult the United States

[1] 'My dear Edward', 23 September 1946: Premier papers, 8/1321.
[2] 'Prime Minister', 7 October 1946: Premier papers, 8/1321.
[3] Telegram No. 893 from Paris, 'Personal', 9 October 1946: Premier papers, 8/1321.
[4] 'Re attached telegram', 10 October 1946: Premier papers, 8/1321.
[5] Cabinet Conclusions No. 85 of 1946, 'Secret', 10 October 1946: Premier papers, 8/1321.
[6] 'Personal', 'Dear Mr Churchill', 10 October 1946: Camrose papers. The provisos, which Churchill had himself proposed in his letter to Bridges of 23 September 1946, were, as Bridges noted, 'that you would be ready to discuss the omission of any particular phrase, sentence or passage; and also that there should be final review on any particular points and passages by the Government of the day before publication'.

Government 'before publication of any messages to (or from) President Roosevelt'.[1] All was now set for Churchill to begin.

On October 14 he interviewed two potential research assistants, James Joll and Alastair Buchan.[2] 'I went to see him in his room in the House of Commons,' Joll later recalled. 'He asked me whether I had a car, to get to and fro to Chartwell. "His Majesty's Government," he said, "have very kindly placed at my disposal the records of my administration," and he added: "When you see the documents, you will be amazed to see how often I was right."'[3]

In a letter to Lord Camrose on October 15, Churchill explained that the printing of his wartime minutes had so far covered the years 1941, 1942 and 1943. 'I should propose,' Churchill explained, to follow the method 'I used in *The World Crisis*, which itself is modelled on the lines of Defoe's *Memories of a Scottish Cavalier*, namely a thread of personal narrative amusing to the reader, on which are hung the great situations and the necessary documentations.'

Churchill envisaged four or five volumes, 'each with heavy appendices', with the first two volumes finished by the end of 1947, with a view to serialization in 1948, but, as he told Camrose:

I cannot give any guarantee on account of political work which I may have to do. I am certainly not going to be hurried. On the other hand, the amount of original composition already available in the documents which I wrote at the time, is very substantial and of course commands the highest historic interest. This also applies to the documentation of the succeeding books which, if there were four, might come out at yearly intervals.

Should I undertake the task I shall immediately assemble the documentation and have the facts necessary for its setting carefully prepared so that in the event of my being unable to complete the task, the whole corpus and documentation design will be available, and it would be for another author to finish it.[4]

Pushing ahead even before the financial aspects had been worked out, Churchill sent his draft chapters on the Battle of Britain to Air Marshal Sir Keith Park, who had commanded No. 11 Fighter Group during the battle. Park studied Churchill's draft and returned it with many factual corrections. 'Thank you so much for all the trouble you have taken in correcting my notes,' Churchill wrote on October 22. 'It has so greatly helped me in telling this story.'[5]

[1] 'Dear Mr Churchill', 10 October 1946: Camrose papers.

[2] Neither joined Churchill's team; James Joll, who had just begun teaching at New College, where he was soon to become a Fellow, was later Professor of International History at the University of London (1967–81); Alastair Buchan was later Director of the Institute for Strategic Studies (1956–69).

[3] James Joll recollections: in conversation with the author, 7 October 1987.

[4] 'My dear Camrose', 15 October 1946: Churchill papers, 4/57.

[5] 'My dear Park', 22 October 1946: Churchill papers, 4/198.

Whenever Churchill remembered a paper which he had written, but could not find it, he wrote at once to Ismay. 'I am sure you could easily find duplicates for me,' he wrote on October 30 of two such papers, one an essay by Churchill on 'a large-scale combined descent', in 1941 or 1942, 'upon occupied France, in which violence, scale, rapidity and variety of points of impact were to be the main features'.[1]

Ismay sent Churchill all the documents for which he asked, as well as recollections of his own. 'Please send me any notes of your recollections of the incidents in which we were involved,' Churchill wrote on November 4, and he added: 'I have incorporated your Tobruk amendments in my revise.' He was also 'composing a passage' on the lines of a recent lecture by Ismay to the Foreign Policy Association in New York.

'Please remind me of things that occur to you,' Churchill ended. 'It is a great help to have one's memory jogged.'[2]

Churchill's memory was also 'jogged', in a less pleasant sense, each time some other author published an account of the war years. One such account, by Alan Moorehead, printed under banner headlines in the *Sunday Express* on November 10, described how, 'barely a week before D-Day', Churchill had gone down to Montgomery's headquarters to interfere with the plans already agreed by the General Staff 'upon the subject of vehicles and loading priorities'.

'Alan Moorehead in the *Sunday Express* is making a series of untruthful and offensive statements about me and Montgomery,' Churchill telegraphed to Lord Beaverbrook on November 11. 'Today is very bad. I hope you will call for a report. I may have to make a public statement.'[3] That same day Ismay wrote to Churchill:

The only meeting at Montgomery's Headquarters that I can recall is the one which took place at St Paul's School on the 15th May, i.e. three weeks before the invasion, when the King, you and Field Marshal Smuts were present. On that occasion, Sir Humfrey Gale and Sir Miles Graham unfolded the Q Plans and you expressed some doubt as to whether there were not too many vehicles in the initial assault. You did not, however, press the point very far, and I myself certainly left the meeting with the feeling that the plans presented had received your full approval.

I must, however, add that after the meeting was over, you went off to Field Marshal Montgomery's office with him alone, while I talked to some of the Staff outside. I do not know what passed at this private meeting, but I distinctly remember leaving St Paul's building with you and that you did not express any dissatisfaction with the arrangements on the drive home.

[1] 'Private', 'My dear P', 30 October 1946: Churchill papers, 4/19.
[2] 'My dear P', 4 November 1946: Churchill papers, 2/151.
[3] Telegram dated 11 November 1946: Beaverbrook papers.

Ismay had not been content to trust his own memory. As he explained to Churchill:

I have asked the Secretaries at No. 10 to look up your diary and see whether you paid any visits other than the above to Montgomery's Headquarters. They tell me that you attended an exercise called 'Thunderclap' there on 7th April, i.e. two months before D-Day. I did not accompany you on that occasion, but it seems extremely unlikely that any plans came under discussion. [1]

To the editor of the *Sunday Express*, Churchill protested directly on several specific points in Moorehead's article, which were, he said, 'pure invention of a mischievous and offensive character'. Nothing like the incidents described 'ever occurred'. [2] Both the Editor and Moorehead apologized, and the passages were dropped in the book itself. [3]

At the same time that Churchill dealt with historical disputes from 1944, he was steadily working for his own memoirs on the events of 1941. Indeed, on the day that Ismay wrote to him about the D-Day controversy, he also wrote in answer to an earlier enquiry from Churchill about a proposal Churchill had made in April 1941, to send badly-needed tanks to Egypt through the submarine-infested, air vulnerable Mediterranean. Ismay now sent, as he wrote, 'the following local colour' about Churchill's minute of 20 April 1941, concerning this tank move:

At about 11 a.m. on April 20th, you summoned me to Ditchley and read out the minute in question, which you had only just dictated. You told me to take it straight up to London and summon the Chiefs of Staff to discuss it at once. As it was a Sunday, the Chiefs of Staff had to be collected from their country residences, and it was not until 6 p.m. that we got round the table.

Although it is not recorded in the minutes of the meeting, I distinctly remember that the first reactions were—

(a) That the tanks were not available in this country; and
(b) That, even if they were available, the chances of their getting through the Mediterranean were remote, since on the day before entering the Narrows and on the morning after passing Malta they would be liable to dive bombing attack out of range of our shore-based fighters.

---

[1] 'My dear Mr Churchill', 11 November 1946: Churchill papers, 4/351A.

[2] 'Dear Sir', 12 November 1946: Churchill papers, 4/351A.

[3] Churchill had in fact visited Montgomery on 19 May 1944, four days after the meeting at St Paul's and had questioned the loading priorities. Far from Churchill 'interfering in them', these priorities had been persued as planned. 'I may add however,' Churchill wrote in his memoirs, six years after the *Sunday Express* allegations, 'that I still consider that the proportion of transport vehicles to fighting men in the early phase of the cross-Channel invasion was too high and that the operation suffered both in risk and execution from this fact.' (Winston S. Churchill, *The Second World War*, volume 6, London 1952, page 544.)

However, after a very long meeting, opposition petered out, and the Chiefs of Staff were able to report to you at 12 noon the following day the ways and means by which Operation 'Tiger' could be carried out. So far as I remember, they got through unscathed, but this will have to be checked.

'I have now found out,' Ismay noted in the margin, 'that one ship out of the five, *The Empire Song*, was mined and sunk just this side of Malta.' [1]

On November 20 Ismay promised to prepare for Churchill a list of all the code names used in 1940: 'no such list', he pointed out, 'has ever been compiled'. He was also sending a print of the Dakar expedition of 1940, and all the telegrams received by Churchill from the Secretary of State for War during October 1940. [2]

Churchill, having been impressed by an Air Ministry pamphlet on the Blitz, asked Ismay to find out its author. 'This man might be very helpful to me,' Churchill explained, 'in constructing the short but accurate condensation which I must make of this episode.' [3]

The man who 'did most of the work' on the pamphlet, Ismay replied on November 25, 'was Flight-Lieutenant Goodwin, who is now a Professor of History at Jesus College, Oxford'. [4] Churchill at once asked Ismay to contact Goodwin. 'If you think well of him,' Churchill wrote, 'I should like to see him myself in the course of the next month.' [5] In due course, Goodwin provided Churchill with a series of notes on the Blitz; notes which Churchill was to use as the narrative basis for his own account.

Churchill's daily work on his war memoirs was pleasantly interrupted on November 27 when he received a telegram from Lord Camrose to say that Henry Luce, owner of *Life*, had offered $1,150,000 for the serialization of Churchill's war memoirs in the United States. [6] In addition, the Boston publishers Houghton Mifflin would pay $250,000 to publish the memoirs in book form. 'Will phone you in the morning,' Camrose added.

[1] 'My dear Mr Churchill', 11 November 1946: Churchill papers, 4/351A.

[2] 'My dear Mr Churchill', 20 November 1946: Churchill papers, 4/351A.

[3] 'My dear P', 23 November 1946: Churchill papers, 4/19.

[4] 'My dear Mr Churchill', 25 November 1946: Churchill papers, 4/19.

[5] 'My dear P', 28 November 1946: Churchill papers, 4/19. Goodwin lunched alone with Churchill on December 29. After he had left, Churchill gave a sitting to the sculptor Jacob Epstein, for whom he again sat on the following day. (Churchill Engagements Calendar, December 1946.) Among Epstein's earlier works were the tomb of Oscar Wilde in Paris (1909), Lord Fisher (1915), Christ in bronze (1920), the Duke and Duchess of Marlborough (1923), Lord Beaverbrook (1933), Ramsay MacDonald (1934) and Ivan Maisky (1941). He lived near Churchill, at 18 Hyde Park Gate.

[6] Telegram of 27 November 1946: Churchill papers, 4/57.

Thus was brought to a remarkable conclusion the negotiations which Churchill had entrusted to Camrose, and to his pre-war European literary agent, Emery Reves. The money earned as a result of their negotiations was conveyed to the Literary Trust, the arrangements for which were in the process of being worked out by Leslie Graham-Dixon. The terms of the Trust were such as to enable Churchill's children and grandchildren to receive the benefits of his literary labours without the burden of taxation. On December 8 Churchill invited Graham-Dixon and his wife to Chartwell, for a luncheon to mark the successful organization of the Trust.[1] 'Come *please*,' he had written, 'if you can spare the Sunday, at about 12.30 p.m., so that we can have a walk before luncheon.'[2] Six days later, on December 14, Churchill invited Bill Deakin to luncheon at Hyde Park Gate.[3]

It was Deakin who now undertook to co-ordinate the finding, checking, and interweaving of a mass of historical material, both in the Cabinet Office archives and from many scattered published and unpublished sources. Thus was reborn a literary partnership which had already enabled Churchill to complete his biography of the Duke of Marlborough and to write the first version of *A History of the English-Speaking Peoples*. Henceforth, Deakin was to be the guiding hand for the most demanding enterprise of all, the war memoirs. He later recalled:

My main work in 1947, 1948 and 1949 was in the old Ministry of Defence vaults.[4] A room next door to the Map Room. Everything was there in one room. There was a secretary in charge of the files. I worked there. It was very laborious. I was making manuscript notes.

Winston and I would discuss together, alone, a sort of synopsis, which he would think out in his head and discuss with me. I would work into that frame. I would look up what happened. He then would dictate away what he remembered about people. He would also send me to talk to people, as a kind of interpreter. He sent me to talk to General Georges, to discuss the state of the French Army in 1940.

When I would produce a memorandum, this would provoke his personal memory. He would stop completely. No more documents. He would dictate his feelings (when he became First Lord, when he became Prime Minister).

I would go to Chartwell for days at a time. Everything was devoted to his memoirs. He concentrated ruthlessly on this. He saw it as his monument.[5]

---

[1] Churchill Engagements Calendar, 8 December 1946. Graham-Dixon was assisted throughout by Churchill's solicitor, Anthony Moir.

[2] Letter of 3 December 1946: Graham-Dixon papers.

[3] Churchill Engagements Calendar, December 1946: Churchill papers.

[4] These vaults, known during the war as the Central (or Cabinet) War Rooms, housed the War Cabinet and Chiefs of Staff offices, and also a bedroom for Churchill, for periods when the bombing was severe. They have been open to the public since April 1984.

[5] Sir William Deakin recollections: in conversation with the author, 15 March 1975.

14

'Fulton still holds its own!'

ON 5 October 1946 Churchill spoke at the Conservative Party Conference at Blackpool. His speech was a sustained attack on the Labour Government's policy at home and overseas. 'In little more than a year,' he said, 'they have diminished British influence abroad and very largely paralysed our revival at home.' Speaking of the food supply he declared: 'The German U-boats in their worst endeavours never made bread-rationing necessary in war. It took a Socialist Government and Socialist planners to fasten it on us in time of peace when the seas are open and the world harvests good. At no time in the two world wars have our people had so little bread, meat, butter, cheese and fruit to eat.'

The Conservative Party, Churchill commented, was opposed to State control of the means of production, distribution and exchange. It was asked: 'What are your alternatives?' To this he replied: 'A property-owning democracy,' and he went on to explain: 'In this I include profit-sharing schemes in suitable industries and intimate consultation between employers and wage-earners. In fact we seek so far as possible to make the status of the wage-earner that of a partner rather than of an irresponsible employee.'

Churchill then turned to the part which the State should play in setting up 'systems of safeguards' against failure, accident or misfortune. 'We do not seek,' he said, 'to pull down improvidently the structures of society, but to erect balustrades upon the stairway of life, which will prevent helpless or foolish people from falling into the abyss.' His personal part in this linked both the Liberal and Conservative Parties of earlier years:

It is 38 years ago since I introduced the first Unemployment Insurance Scheme, and 22 years ago since, as Conservative Chancellor of the Exchequer, I shaped and carried the Widows' Pensions and reduction of the Old Age Pensions from 70 to 65. We are now moving forward into another vast scheme of national insurance, which arose, even in the stress of war, from a Parliament with a great Conservative majority.

Speaking of the Government's India policy, Churchill told the assembled Conservatives:

The Government of India has been placed—or I should rather say thrust—into the hands of men who have good reason to be bitterly hostile to the British connection, but who in no way represent the enormous mass of nearly 400 millions of all the races, States, and peoples of India who have dwelt so long in peace with one another.

I fear that calamity impends upon this sub-Continent, which is almost as big as Europe, more populous, and even more harshly divided.

It seems that in quite a short time India will become a separate, a foreign and a none too friendly country to the British Commonwealth. . . .[1]

Churchill made no reference at Blackpool to a severe letter of criticism which he had received from Jinnah, about Britain's abandonment of the Muslims of India. Indeed, each of Churchill's speeches on India, in Parliament and in the country, stressed this very aspect. He was therefore angered by Jinnah's charge, which certainly did not apply to him or to the Conservatives. After receiving Jinnah's letter Churchill dictated a reply which he decided not to send, in which he intended to tell the Muslim leader:

. . . it seems to me that your friends should have been careful to distinguish between complaints against the British Party Government of the day and abuse of the British Nation as a whole. Britain has played a noble part in India, and has given India not only effective protection from external attack for many generations, but the British raj is the only form in which the unity of India can possibly be maintained. There is no nation in the world that would voluntarily, in the moment of world victory, quit and cast away so great an Empire. Personally, I hope that wiser counsels will prevail and that India will not put itself outside the shelter of the British Commonwealth of Nations and all the world influence we can command. That is, however, a matter for the Indian elected bodies to settle under Dominion status.

Churchill had intended to end his letter to Jinnah with a wider reflection on Britain's attitude to the end of its Indian Empire:

I do not think we shall lose very much by leaving India at the present time, and that feeling is undoubtedly widespread here. There is a feeling it is a great burden and danger and that we are continually abused by the political classes who, irrespective of race or religion, vie with one another in scolding us. What would happen to India when we have gone is another matter.

---

[1] Speech of 5 October 1946: Randolph Churchill (editor), *Sinews of Peace*, pages 203–5.

Having thought much about these matters, I foresee a period of civil war and anarchy, not only as a result of a struggle between religions, but also, as in China, between Communists and anti-Communists.[1]

Churchill's fear of rampant Communism was not confined to Asia. 'The European situation,' he wrote to Attlee on his return from Blackpool to London, 'has deteriorated gravely. I am informed that the Soviet Government have over 225 divisions on a war footing beyond the Russian frontiers in the occupied territories of Europe. This compares with about 25 British and American divisions, of which some are only Police divisions without artillery.'[2]

'We have entered the atomic age,' Churchill telegraphed that day in a message of tribute to Bernard Baruch. 'At one of their most disorganised moments men have been gifted with supernatural powers. No one knows whether they will use them for prosperity or damnation. We British have our solemn rights but the prime responsibility rests with the United States.'

Bernard Baruch had just been appointed head of the United States Atomic Energy Commission. Because of this, Churchill added, 'all God's children may sleep comfortably in their beds for the next few years'. But during this 'merciful breathing space' there must be worked out 'an august design which will make mankind master of its destiny and will secure to every humble home, in every country, life, liberty and the pursuit of happiness'. It was for Baruch 'to raise this fearful agency above the level of national or material conflict and make it the servant and not the destroyer or the enslaver of the human race'.[3]

When this telegram was read out to the guests assembled to honour Baruch, he told Churchill: 'your name was greeted by great applause'.[4]

To Attlee, who had neither confirmed nor rejected the figures Churchill had sent him of Soviet military strength in Europe, Churchill wrote again on October 10: 'It is clear to me that only two reasons prevent the westward movement of the Russian armies to the North Sea and the Atlantic. The first is their virtue and self-restraint. The second, the possession by the United States of the Atomic Bomb.'[5]

'Life slips away,' Churchill commented to his friend Louis Spears, 'but one fights with what strength remains for the things one cares about.'[6]

---

[1] 'Draft', 'Not sent', 'Dear Mr Jinnah', undated (in reply to Jinnah's letter of 22 August 1946): Churchill papers, 2/46.
[2] 'Private', 'Dear Prime Minister', 6 October 1946: Churchill papers, 2/4.
[3] Telegram of 6 October 1946: Churchill papers, 2/210.
[4] 'Dear Winston', 9 October 1946: Churchill papers, 2/210.
[5] 'Personal & Private', 'My dear Prime Minister', 10 October 1946: Churchill papers, 2/4.
[6] 'Dear Louis', 8 October 1946: Churchill papers, 2/156.

'Winston is in very good fettle,' Brendan Bracken wrote to Lord Beaverbrook on October 16, 'and is determined to continue to lead the Tory Party until he becomes Prime Minister on earth or Minister of Defence in Heaven.'[1] He was also enjoying the leisure of painting in his studio at Chartwell. 'Since I came home,' he wrote to the Swiss paint supplier Willy Sax, 'I have been amusing myself with painting in Tempera, which I find a most delightful medium offering great possibilities both in the ground-work and the finish of pictures, and working in so happily with oil colours in the final stages. I should be much obliged if you could send me in a letter the exact description of the glycerine which you said could be spread upon the colours on the palette to prevent their drying up, and thus avoid needless waste.' Churchill added, with a reference to his meeting with Sax in Switzerland: 'As I told you, I am sure that the use of these colours will give pleasure to very large numbers of people.'[2]

Churchill had now accepted the leadership of the growing movement for a United Europe, the virtues of which he had extolled at Zurich. During late October he prepared a Statement of Aims which he sent to those who questioned him about the need for such a movement. 'In the mechanized world of today,' Churchill declared, 'the small nation States of the past can scarcely hope for political or economic survival as isolated units. The peoples of Europe, or as many of them as are willing to make a start, should come together in order to create an effective European union, not aimed against any other nation but designed to maintain their common peace, to restore their common prosperity and above all to preserve their common heritage of freedom.' The aim was to unite all Europe 'from the Atlantic to the Black Sea'. If, however, the countries of Eastern Europe were 'for the present' unable to join the proposed 'European Federation', then the countries of Western Europe should 'make a start on their own, always leaving it open to the other States to join later as and when they can'. The United States of Europe would be neither dependent on nor

---

[1] Letter of 16 October 1946: Beaverbrook papers.

[2] 'Private', 'Dear Mr Sax', 16 October 1946: Churchill papers, 1/17. On 18 February 1947 Churchill licenced the Soho Publishing Company to reproduce his painting 'Island of Choisi' as a greetings card, in colour. Ten days earlier he had licensed the same company to reproduce 'Still Life' and on 25 November 1948 they were licensed to reproduce his pre-war painting 'Blue Sitting Room, Trent Park, 1934'. In the first four months of 1947 *Life* magazine published sixteen of Churchill's paintings, also in colour.

opposed to the United States of America or the Soviet Union; like them, it would be 'fitted into the structure of the United Nations Organization and subject to the authority of the Security Council'.[1]

To Viscount Cranborne, who had questioned the wisdom of setting up a 'Western bloc' which would serve to perpetuate the division of Europe into East and West, Churchill wrote on October 19:

I am not attracted to a Western bloc as a final solution. The ideal should be EUROPE. The Western bloc as an instalment of the United States of Europe would be an important step, but the case should be put on the broadest lines of a unity of Europe and Christendom as a whole. This conception is free from the vice of dividing Europe into an Eastern Russian-controlled bloc and a Western Anglo-American-influenced bloc. . . .

'Moreover,' he explained, 'without Germany, however sub-divided or expressed, there is no force of nationhood in the West which could hold the balance with the Soviet power.'[2]

Speaking in the House of Commons on October 23, Churchill returned to the theme of Soviet power and Soviet intentions. Eight months earlier, at Fulton, Missouri, 'I said that I did not believe the Soviet Government wanted war. I said that what they wanted were the fruits of war. I fervently hope and pray that the view which I then expressed is still correct, and on the whole I believe it is still correct. However, we are dealing with the unknowable.'

Churchill then raised the question which he had put to Attlee privately at the beginning of October:

Is it or is it not true that there are to-day more than 200 Soviet divisions on a war footing in the occupied territories of Europe from the Baltic to Vienna, and from Vienna to the Black Sea? There is the question which I am asking, and it acquires particular significance in view of the Prime Minister's reference, which I heard only this afternoon in the House, to 'total mobilised forces which may constitute a positive danger to peace'. I am not referring to the armies of satellite Powers which, in Poland, are numerous but reluctant, and in Yugoslavia and Bulgaria are less numerous but more ardent.

I shall be very much relieved if I can be told in the course of to-day's Debate that the figures I have given—which I have not given without prolonged consideration and heart-searching, or without discussion with colleagues—are altogether excessive, and if His Majesty's Government can relieve our anxieties in the matter I am quite ready to accept their statement, but I feel bound to put the question.[3]

---

[1] 'United States of Europe', 'Statement of Aims', undated: Churchill papers, 2/19. Churchill sent a copy of this statement to Lord Citrine on 20 October 1946.

[2] 'Private', 'My dear Bobbety', 19 October 1946: Churchill papers, 2/23. During Churchill's wartime premiership, Viscount Cranborne had been Secretary of State for Dominion Affairs (1940–42 and 1943–45), Secretary of State for the Colonies (1942), Lord Privy Seal (1942–43) and Leader of the House of Lords (1942–45).

[3] Speech of 23 October 1946: *Hansard*.

Churchill's question was answered later in the debate by Hector McNeil, Under-Secretary for Foreign Affairs, who told the House of Commons: 'I am unable to say whether the information of the right hon. Gentleman about the number of Russian divisions in occupied countries between the Baltic and the Black Sea is correct, or what proportion of these divisions is on a war footing; but it is, of course, well known that there are very considerable Russian forces in these countries.' [1]

Speaking in his constituency on October 24, Churchill reiterated his concerns about the strength of Soviet forces in Eastern Europe. [2] To Lord Moran, Churchill spoke of how, if the Russians wished, they could 'march to the Atlantic' in a few weeks, 'practically unopposed'. Churchill added, according to Lord Moran's account: 'They've got forward dumps of arms everywhere. The Swiss are most perturbed. Only the atomic bomb keeps the Russians back. They're making rockets to fire on us when they get to the coast.'

'I doubt whether there could be war,' Moran commented, to which Churchill replied, in agreement: 'I don't think there will be.' [3] But he was determined to discuss the dangers with senior Ministers and, just as in 1936 he had led a delegation to Baldwin, he now asked Attlee to receive a small group of senior Conservatives, himself and Eden among them. 'It is my duty,' Churchill wrote, 'to impart to you certain information which I have received which causes me deep concern, and involves the safety of the country.' In submitting this information, Churchill added, 'I in no way inhibit myself or my colleagues from making it public if we consider this accords with our responsibility. On the other hand, of course, any conversations which may occur or any information which you may think fit to give us would be treated on the principles set out in our correspondence of June 1945.' [4]

Attlee at once agreed to meet Churchill's delegation, and fixed November 5 for the meeting. [5] Before the meeting could take place,

---

[1] *Hansard*, 23 October 1946.

[2] Speech of 24 October 1946: Churchill papers, 5/9.

[3] Moran diary, 24 October 1946: *The Struggle for Survival*, pages 315–16.

[4] 'My dear Prime Minister', 27 October 1946: Churchill papers, 2/29. Three days after sending this letter, Churchill received further information about the strength of the Red Army stationed in Roumania, including the location of seven Soviet divisions marked on a map, and the location of 'airdromes occupied by the Red Air Forces' at the end of July 1946. As to the Soviet divisions, the note commented 'these units are kept in constant move in order to avoid the possible friendly relations between the Russian soldiers and the Roumanian population, as well as to keep the Secret about the strength of this Army of occupation' ('Confidential', 'Russian Troops in Roumania', 30 October 1946: Churchill papers, 2/30). Within a month Churchill was sent a three-page survey of the strength and location of Soviet forces throughout Eastern Europe, together with a map ('Information Recently Received of the Red Army', 20 November 1946: Churchill papers, 2/30).

[5] 'My dear Churchill', 28 October 1946: Churchill papers, 2/29.

Stalin, in reply to a series of questions put to him in Moscow by Hugh Baillie, President of the United Press Associations of America, when asked 'What constitutes today, in your judgement, the worst threat to world peace?', replied: 'Instigators of a new war, in the first place Churchill, and those, his partisans, who think like him in Great Britain and the United States.' Such 'instigators of a new war', Stalin added, 'have to be unmasked and kept in check'.[1]

Churchill was at Chartwell when Stalin's comments reached him. He at once issued a statement to the Press:

I have a regard and respect for Premier Stalin, and always remember all we went through together. I also wish to see the Russian people, who fought so bravely for their native land, safe and glorious and happy. It was always my desire that when the war was won the Soviet Government should play one of the leading parts in the rebuilding of our shattered world.

By the Anglo-Russian Treaty made when I was Prime Minister in 1941, we are bound not to interfere in each other's internal affairs or system of society. Therefore I do not see why we cannot all be friends and help each other, and thus advance the whole basic standard of livelihood of the broad masses of people in every land.

I am glad to see Premier Stalin's statement about Russian forces in the occupied territories he mentions. But even sixty divisions on a war-footing would of course greatly exceed the British and American forces in enemy-occupied Europe.

There followed a sentence which Churchill had written in his original statement but deleted before it was issued to the Press. 'Moreover,' the deleted sentence read, 'Premier Stalin's figures do not include Roumania. Nor of course do they include the heavy Soviet concentrations in the Leningrad and Odessa regions.' The statement, as issued, continued:

I asked His Majesty's Government whether my estimate of 200 divisions applied to the West was excessive, and I asked the question in such a form that it could be answered 'Yes' or 'No'. Considering the difference between 200 divisions and 60 divisions, it ought to have been possible, if I was in error, for a contradiction to be given. None was forthcoming. On the contrary the statement of the Prime Minister and the Under Secretary of State for Foreign Affairs showed only anxiety at the strength of the Soviet mobilized forces.

No one would have been more pleased than I to be told that I was mis-informed. No one will be more pleased if this proves to be the case. It is clearly most important that the facts should be made known. It is difficult to

---

[1] 'Complete text of questions submitted to Generalissimo J. V. Stalin by Hugh Baillie, President of the United Press of America; and Stalin's replies thereby', 29 October 1946: Churchill papers, 2/116.

believe that Allies occupying together enemy territory recently gained with their blood, should not know about the strength of each other's garrisons. Indeed, one would have thought they would have interchanged and shared this information between themselves as a matter of course, and that there would be reciprocal inspection of the forces mobilized in their respective zones. We hear a great deal about suspicions. Nothing sweeps away suspicions like facts, and I consider it my duty to continue to press for the facts.

I should add that my information, which of course is not official information, contemplated a strength of ten thousand men per Soviet division. However, during the last war, American and British divisions sometimes ran as high as forty or fifty thousand men, and thirty thousand would be a fairly good average figure including of course auxiliary services, corps troops and lines of communication. It is not possible to judge the strength of an army unless not only the number of organized divisions are known, but also and at the same time, the total ration strength.

'It seems to me,' Churchill's statement ended, 'that a clearing up of this matter would be highly beneficial from every point of view, and surely the present meetings of UNO should be the occasion for the fullest and fairest disclosure of all military forces that cause anxiety to any of those who fought and won the great victory together.'[1]

In search of a united Western response to any possible Soviet threat, Churchill approached General de Gaulle, although in the war years he had felt unease at the General's apparent flirtation with the Soviets. All that was now put aside. 'I have received from various quarters,' Churchill wrote to de Gaulle, 'disquieting information about the Soviet mobilized strength in the occupied territories of Europe and of the immense disproportion which exists between the Soviet forces and those of their satellite states, on the one hand, and those of the other Allies, on the other hand.' There was very little doubt in his mind, Churchill added, 'that it is in the power of the Soviet armies to advance westward with considerable rapidity. This does not of course prejudge the question of whether they would wish to do so.' Churchill's letter continued:

I have also heard, though this is mere rumour, that you are anxious about the position. In these circumstances I should like to know whether you would agree to send some trusted friend of yours to meet my son-in-law, Duncan Sandys, who was a Minister and a Member of Parliament during my administration. He could come to Paris almost any time.

It seems to me that an interchange of views in strict privacy might be advantageous to both our countries. The method I am suggesting would have the advantage of attracting no attention. However, I shall quite under-

---

[1] 'Press Notice', Chartwell, 29 October 1946: Churchill papers, 2/116.

stand and shall not be in the least offended if you think such a contact inadvisable. . . .[1]

The United States of Europe remained Churchill's hope as a focus for the strengthening of Western democracy. In the second week of November he began to seek seven or eight members for an All-Party Handling Group 'to get a move on here', as he explained to George Hicks, Labour MP for East Woolwich since 1931 and Parliamentary Secretary, Ministry of Works, throughout Churchill's premiership. 'To one with all your experience I do not need to argue the matter,' Churchill wrote. 'I have no doubt that you have been thinking deeply and anxiously about the future and of the part which a United Europe might play in it.' To Hicks, as to each of those to whom he wrote, Churchill added: 'without the resurrection and reconciliation of Europe there is no hope for the world.'[2]

On November 5 Churchill, Eden and a former Secretary of State for War, Oliver Stanley, met Attlee and A. V. Alexander, the First Lord of the Admiralty, who was about to succeed Attlee as Minister of Defence. During the meeting Churchill asked whether it was true 'that the railways in Czechoslovakia were being widened to the Russian gauge'. Attlee promised to make enquiries and, six days later, Alexander sent Churchill a note by the Joint Intelligence Staff.[3] It appeared that in the eastern area annexed by Russia, east of the new frontier, the gauge had been widened, but that west of the now Soviet border town of Cop, within the new Czechoslovak territories, no widening had taken place, except 'for a short distance' and that there had been 'no material change in the Czechoslovak rail network'.[4]

On November 11, as a result of the General Elections in France,

[1] 'Private & Confidential', 'My dear de Gaulle', 1 November 1946: Churchill papers, 2/30. In reply, de Gaulle said he would be glad to receive Duncan Sandys at his home at Colombey. ('Cher Monsieur Churchill', 13 November 1946: Churchill papers, 2/30.)

[2] 'My dear George Hicks', 7 November 1946: Churchill papers, 2/21. Hicks did not accept. 'As the Labour Party stands for the same principle,' he wrote, 'then I should refrain from associating myself with any other group, and should pursue the advocacy of the same idea within the framework of the Labour Party' ('My dear Winston Churchill', 13 November 1946: Churchill papers, 2/21). Those who agreed to serve on the All-Party Handling Group were Lord Citrine 'with Attlee's full approval' (as Churchill told Lord Camrose on 9 November 1946), Sir Archibald Sinclair (Liberal), Oliver Stanley (Conservative), Sir David Maxwell-Fyfe (Conservative), L. S. Amery (Conservative), Robert Boothby (Conservative), Sir Walter Layton (Liberal) and Victor Gollancz, the publisher (and a supporter of the Labour Party). The General Secretary was to be Duncan Sandys.

[3] 'Top Secret', 11 November 1946: Churchill papers, 2/29. Stanley had been Secretary of State for War in 1940, during the last months of Neville Chamberlain's premiership. In 1942 Churchill appointed him Secretary of State for the Colonies.

[4] 'Czechoslovak Railways': Churchill papers, 2/29. There was also ominous information for Churchill three days later, when General Ismay, having spoken to him on the telephone, sent him a further Joint Intelligence Staff Report, dated 14 November 1946, stating that 'the overwhelming Anglo-US naval strength would not necessarily deter Russia from embarking on a major land campaign in Europe should she so desire'. The report also referred to 'the re-organisa-

the Communists were returned, not as a majority, but as the largest single party in the National Assembly. Speaking on the first day of the new session of Parliament on November 12, Churchill referred to this in his survey of the Soviet and Communist position in Europe:

The Prime Minister, at the Mansion House, drew a sombre picture from which I cannot dissent. At the General Election, we were assured that a Socialist or Left-Wing Government would get on especially well with the Soviet Government of Russia, but relations have steadily deteriorated. The British and American Forces in Europe have melted away, as was inevitable in the case of governments resting upon the popular will, after a great victory. The Russian Armies, based on a despotic form of Government, have been maintained in Europe in vast strength, and mostly on a war footing. More than one third of Europe is held under the Russian Soviet control. The Soviet military frontier is on the Elbe, and it is impossible to forecast what the future and the fate of France will be.

Churchill also spoke of the future of Germany, telling the House of Commons:

I am told that Germany must be punished. I ask: When did punishment begin? It certainly seems to have been going on for a long time. It began in 1943, and continued during 1944 and 1945, when the most frightful air bombardments were cast upon German cities, and when the general exhaustion of their life, under the cruel Nazi regime, had drained the last ounces of strength from the German race and nation.

The Nuremberg trials are over, and the guilty leaders of the Nazi regime have been hanged by the conquerors. We are told that thousands yet remain to be tried, and that vast categories of Germans are classed as potentially guilty because of their association with the Nazi regime. After all, in a country which is handled as Germany was, the ordinary people have very little choice about what to do.

I think some consideration should always be given to ordinary people. Everyone is not a Pastor Niemöller or a martyr, and when ordinary people are hurled this way and that, when the cruel hands of tyrants are laid upon them and vile systems of regimentation are imposed and enforced by espionage and other forms of cruelty, there are great numbers of people who will succumb.

I thank God that in this island home of ours, we have never been put to the test which many of the peoples of Europe have had to undergo. It is my hope that we shall presently reach the end of the executions, penalties, and punishments, and that without forgetting the hard lessons of the past, we shall turn our faces resolutely towards the future.[1]

---

tion and re-equipment of the Soviet Army, in particular as regards the mechanisation of infantry formations'. (Report signed 'W. E. Parry, G. W. R. Templer and T. W. Elmhirst', Offices of the Cabinet and Minister of Defence, 14 November 1946: Churchill papers, 2/29.)

[1] Speech of 12 November 1946: *Hansard*.

Lord Ismay later recalled: 'I happened to be with him at Chartwell when the results of the Nuremberg trials of the Nazi war criminals were published. "It shows," he remarked, "that if you get into a war, it is supremely important to win it. You and I would be in a pretty pickle if we had lost."' [1]

From one of the elder statesmen of the Conservative Party, Lord Derby, there was a note of caution, and indeed of complaint, about Churchill's leadership. 'I have heard occasionally from Winston,' Derby wrote to Lord Beaverbrook on November 20, 'and I am not very happy about what I hear. I am afraid he has never really got over that last illness of his which has left him very weak and I do not think he really takes very much interest in things now, except from the point of view of being able to say something which he knows will irritate individual members of the Government, and I am bound to say I think he does that very successfully.' [2]

Churchill's principal concern, that winter, continued to be the size of the Soviet military forces in Eastern Europe. On November 26, when Duncan Sandys set off for France to see General de Gaulle, he took with him a letter from Churchill asking de Gaulle's views on two points, 'for my own personal guidance, and of course in strict confidence'. The first point was Soviet intentions:

First, what do you think about the danger of a Soviet advance westward to the sea? It is evident that they have the power to do it at any time. On the other hand the end might not be so agreeable as the beginning. This was certainly Hitler's experience and it may be a deterrent. Sandys will give you various information which I have received from Continental sources. My own view is that there are over two million Soviet troops in the occupied territories of Europe or in immediate reserve in the Leningrad and Odessa regions. Their exact organisation, mobility and efficiency cannot be accurately measured.

Churchill's second point, relevant to the first, was about the concept of a United States of Europe. 'You will have seen my speech at Zurich,' Churchill wrote, 'and it is my conviction that if France could take Germany by the hand and, with full English cooperation, rally her to the West and to European civilization, this would indeed be a glorious victory and make amends for all we have gone through and perhaps save us having to go through a lot more.'

[1] Ismay recollections: *The Memoirs of General the Lord Ismay*, London 1960, page 157.
[2] 'Personal', 20 November 1946: Derby papers.

Churchill went on to tell de Gaulle that he had watched the course of French politics 'with the closest attention', as de Gaulle no doubt was 'watching ours'. The 'main characteristic' of the Socialist-Labour Government in England, Churchill told de Gaulle, was 'its hatred of Communists and Communism'. In this, he added, 'they will of course be supported by the Conservative Party'.[1]

On November 29 Duncan Sandys drove from Paris to Colombey, where he had lunch with General de Gaulle, and gave him Churchill's letter. On returning to Paris that afternoon, Sandys wrote at once to Churchill:

I showed him the secret report on Soviet troop dispositions. He did not appear to have any detailed information of his own, but was inclined to think that the Russians had appreciably less than 200 Divisions in the Western theatre and were in the process of demobilising a considerable number of their more seasoned troops.

He felt sure that the Russians were, for the present, not ready for war. Their policy was one of opportunism. They were out for anything they could get in the way of additional territory or influence, but they would not, in his opinion, be prepared to go to the lengths of fighting for it. There would doubtless be a succession of diplomatic clashes. The Russians might on occasions overreach themselves. But even so, he did not think this would result in war. Having no public opinion to consider, the Soviet Government would, if they found resistance too great, be quite prepared to retract their demands. In such an eventuality, the Western allies would, in order to avoid war, do everything possible to save the Soviet face.

For these reasons, General de Gaulle considered that until such time as she developed the atom bomb, Russia would be most unlikely to provoke war. However, taking a longer view, he was of opinion that war between the Western Democracies and Soviet Russia was sooner or later a virtual certainty.

As to the idea of a European Federation, 'de Gaulle undoubtedly believes firmly in this project', Sandys reported, 'but his support is hedged around with numerous qualifications'. These arose as a result of disagreements with one of Churchill's main themes at Zurich.

He said that the reference in Mr Churchill's Zurich speech to a Franco-German partnership had been badly received in France. Germany, as a state, no longer existed. All Frenchmen were violently opposed to recreating any kind of unified, centralised Reich, and were gravely suspicious of the policy of the American and British Governments. Unless steps were taken to prevent a resuscitation of German power, there was the danger that a United Europe would become nothing else than an enlarged Germany.

He stressed that if French support was to be won for the idea of European union, France must come in as a founder partner with Britain. Moreover,

[1] 'My dear General de Gaulle', 26 November 1946: Churchill papers, 2/30.

the two countries must reach a precise understanding with one another upon the attitude to be adopted towards Germany before any approaches were made to the latter.

De Gaulle further thought that France should make her support for the policy of European federation conditional upon the settlement of outstanding differences between herself and Britain. A permanent allocation of coal from the Ruhr; consent to the continuance of French military occupation in Germany over a long period and possibly the incorporation of the Northern Rhineland in the French Zone; the establishment of a regime of international control of the Ruhr industries satisfactory to France; a fuller recognition of French interests in Syria; an Anglo-French agreement to adopt a common line towards the Arab countries. 'Voilà mes conditions,' he said.

'In any case,' Sandys added, 'his attention is at present exclusively concentrated upon internal French politics.'[1]

In London, Churchill's United Europe call was receiving a less than favourable response among many Labour Party stalwarts. On November 27 Churchill wrote direct to Attlee:

This is about the United States of Europe. 'Europe must federate or perish!' You very kindly wrote favouring Citrine joining our small Handling Group with which to make a start. With much regret he has come to the conclusion that he ought not to undertake any activities which would cut across the Coal Board. I followed up your advice about Gibson and had an acceptance from him, a copy of which I enclose. I thought I might ask George Hicks, who is not engaged at present, and he expressed a sincere desire to take part. However he said he would have to take 'a few soundings'. As the result of these he felt he ought to decline.

Since then, Churchill told Attlee, the project had been 'bruited about' in *Reynolds News*, a Labour paper owned by the Co-operative movements. Churchill's letter continued:

I cannot think it is contrary to Party interests of any kind that such an all-Party movement should be started. I certainly thought that was your feeling. I hope therefore that no general directions will be given preventing any Members of the Parliamentary Party from taking part in it.

Anyhow I should be very much obliged if you would let me know how the matter stands, because if there were to be a veto on Socialist members joining this organisation, which is an important out-work of your main policy, I should have to make another plan. Personally I should have thought it would have been reasonable to let it stand on the same sort of basis as the New Commonwealth, of which I am British Honorary President. If this is not to be, pray let me know.[2]

Attlee's reply was short, discouraging and negative. He had been

[1] 'Visit to General de Gaulle—November 29th, 1946': Churchill papers, 2/20.
[2] 'Private', 'My dear Prime Minister', 27 November 1946: Churchill papers, 2/18.

'considering' the question with his colleagues. 'While, of course, our members are free to take whatever course seems good to them,' he reported, 'in respect of joining your organisation, it has been suggested that the objects aimed at by the organisation would be better achieved through the United Nations Association rather than through a separate society, the aims of which might be misunderstood and misrepresented.'[1]

Churchill's disappointment at Attlee's reply was heightened that same day when he received, from Attlee, a series of 'Top Secret' reports on the strength and organization of Soviet forces. At the end of the war, he learned from the first of these reports, by the Service Directors of Intelligence, there were about 600 divisions in the Red Army. The post-war reduction in forces was, 'for the present time', being limited at about 500 divisions, and the numbers of armoured brigades, 160 at the end of the war, 'will be increased'. The division of Soviet forces in Europe was also given, including 38 divisions in Germany, 30 in Roumania, 19 in Poland and Czechoslovakia, 17 in Bulgaria and 12 in Hungary. Details were given of the armaments, mobility and training of these divisions, and of the areas of relative strength and deficiency.[2]

Attlee also sent Churchill a note, by the Directors of Plans at the Ministry of Defence, assessing this report on Soviet strength which, while deprecating exaggeration and pessimism, went on to agree with the Service Directors of Intelligence about the 'relative Russian superiority and the practical possibility of a Russian conquest of Western Europe'.[3]

As he had been in 1935, Churchill was worried lest the calculations were based upon a false premise. In 1935 he had been convinced that the Air Ministry was calculating too few German aircraft in each squadron. Now he sought to have his fears allayed about the number of troops in each Soviet division. 'My Swiss figures,' he explained to Attlee, 'were given on the basis of 10,000. I understood you were estimating 15,000.'[4]

---

[1] 'My dear Churchill', 4 December 1946: Churchill papers, 2/18.

[2] 'Information Received on the Red Army', 20 November 1946: Churchill papers, 2/30. 'Report by the Service Directors of Intelligence', 'Top Secret', 14 November 1946: Churchill papers, 2/29.

[3] 'Report by the Directors of Plans', 'Top Secret', 23 November 1946: Churchill papers, 2/29. Signed 'J. F. Stevens, J. H. N. Poett and G. H. Mills'.

[4] 'Secret', 'My dear Prime Minister', 4 December 1946: Churchill papers, 2/29. Attlee replied that the Director of Plans estimated 15,400 troops in each Soviet division. The war establishment of a division, Attlee noted, was indeed 10,000; over and above this were a future 12,000 'average overheads' such as 'Corps Troops, lines of communication, troops etc.' making a total establishment of 22,000. The 'average *strength* of a division was estimated as 70 per cent of the total establishment, i.e. 15,400 men'. ('Secret', 'My dear Churchill', 6 December 1946: Churchill papers, 2/29.)

'If I made the Fulton speech today,' Churchill wrote to Governor Dewey of New York, 'it would be criticised as consisting of platitudes.'[1] Three days later, in a postscript to Colonel Frank Clarke, his host in Florida, Churchill wrote: 'Fulton still holds its own!'[2]

The American Secretary of State, James Byrnes, had appealed publicly for the Russians to reduce their forces from nearly two million to 200,000. Such a proposal, Churchill wrote to Attlee on December 10, was one 'which seems to me admirably conceived, and which we should be right to support'. Churchill added: 'I shall be most grateful if you will let me know when it is achieved, and will make you my public congratulations.'[3]

Revisiting Fulton that autumn, Randolph Churchill wrote in the magazine *Europe Today*: 'Hearing the speech again in the quiet of Dr McCluer's house on the campus at Westminster College, one could not but be struck by the way in which the events of the last seven months have already vindicated what Mr Churchill had to say about Russia. And I could not but be struck by how mild and restrained was his so-called "denunciation" of Russia compared with what we have heard since, not from "private citizens" like Mr Churchill, but from responsible Government spokesmen, like Mr Byrnes, Mr Bevin, and Mr Attlee.' Randolph added: 'Of course the real offence which Mr Churchill committed at Fulton was the crime of leadership. He only said in public what all instructed persons had been saying for many months in private. And today there is hardly a word in the Fulton speech which is not accepted as a political truism. At the time Mr Churchill gave his warning about Russia, most people knew it was warranted by the facts. It was precisely this which made the critics so angry. . . .'

Randolph's article ended:

One fact encouraged me in listening again to this historic speech. One piece of Mr Churchill's advice has already been adopted by Britain's Labour Government. They are standardising Britain's basic weapons on the American pattern. This is a quicker result than Mr Churchill ever got out of Mr Chamberlain's Government before the war, and may perhaps encourage us to hope that the rest of his good advice may be adopted before it is too late.

Looked at in retrospect, the great merit of the Fulton speech was that it focussed attention upon the most critical issue of the hour, dispelled much wishful thinking, and forced all save the most mushy-minded to clarify their

---

[1] 'My dear Mr Dewey', 4 December 1946: Churchill papers, 2/148.

[2] 'My dear Frank', 7 December 1946: Churchill papers, 2/161.

[3] 'Secret', 'My dear Prime Minister', 10 December 1946: Churchill papers, 2/29. Eleven days later Churchill telegraphed to Stalin: 'All personal good wishes on your birthday my wartime comrade' (Telegram of 21 December 1946: Churchill papers, 2/156). 'My warm thanks for your good wishes on my birthday,' Stalin replied (Churchill papers, 2/156).

thought on the Russian issue. In fairness to Mr Molotov and the Kremlin it must be admitted that they too have greatly helped in this valuable process. Indeed the increasingly close relations of Britain and the United States probably owe more to the insolence and intransigence of Mr Molotov than to the persuasive powers of Mr Churchill.[1]

On November 28, two days before his seventy-second birthday, Churchill made his seventh journey to Harrow School, for the school 'Songs', telling the boys: 'You will be going forth into the world, and you may find it, if I may say so, full of problems, more baffling problems than it has ever had before.' It had been said, Churchill added, 'that from every version of success, however great, comes forward something to make a greater struggle necessary'.[2]

The concept of an All-Party group to press for a European Federation having been frowned upon by Attlee, Churchill decided to set up a broad-based non-political group to continue to press for his goal. On December 28 he wrote to Dr Ballard, Moderator of the Free Churches, to explain what he now had in mind:

It is my deep conviction, as I think you know, that if we are to avoid the catastrophe of a third World War we must somehow contrive to bring order out of the chaos in Europe, break down national hatreds and suspicions and foster by every means in our power the essentials of unity and the practice of co-operation.

To attain this end we must arouse the fervour of a crusade. We shall need all our resources of statesmanship and of propaganda. But I believe that if properly presented, there will be a tremendous response from the war-wracked millions of the Continent of which we form a part.

Churchill's letter continued:

I have therefore brought together a few people drawn from all political parties as well as from non-political walks of life who are anxious to set the ball rolling in this country. I have called this small group a 'Steering Committee', for its purpose is not necessarily to set up a new organisation but rather to stimulate those which already exist, as well as individual leaders of opinion who are in sympathy with our aims, into action for the furthering of this specific idea. It is also our intention to encourage the formation of similar groups in as many countries of Europe as possible.

The statement of aims attached to this letter (which is still open to minor amendments) will be published about the middle of January.

[1] *Europe Today*, October 1946.
[2] 'My dear Head Master, Ladies and Gentlemen', 28 November 1946: Churchill papers, 2/336.

The impact of this initiative on public opinion will largely depend on the representative character of those who sponsor it. The sentiments to which we must appeal and the forces which we seek to stir are rooted in the spiritual depths of our fellow men and women. It is therefore essential that from the outset we should have the support of the Churches throughout Europe.

It is in this connection that I venture to bring this matter to your attention. All the signatories of our first declaration will sign in their individual capacities and not as representatives of parties or organisations. I should be deeply grateful if you would consent to add your name.[1]

On the last day of December, in an article entitled *One Way to Stop War*, Churchill put his ideas to a wider public.[2] A few weeks later a manifesto called 'United Europe' was published by a Committee of which he was Chairman.

Churchill also sought to enlist support across the Channel, asking Léon Blum to receive a member of the Committee, Commander Stephen King-Hall, 'a man of singular ability', who was going to be in Paris for several days. 'I greatly hope that a French group can be formed on parallel lines,' Churchill wrote, 'so that Britain and France can keep in touch with each other on the further steps that may be taken.' Churchill ended his letter on a personal note, congratulating Blum 'on the brilliant success of your short administration, which tends to prove that the day of the septuagenarian is not past'.[3]

---

[1] 'Private', 'My dear Dr Ballard', 28 December 1946: Churchill papers, 2/20.

[2] In February 1947 Lord Camrose paid for the printing of 10,000 copies of this article in pamphlet form.

[3] 'My dear Monsieur Blum', 24 January 1947: Churchill papers, 2/18. Blum had been born on 9 April 1872. In 1947 he was President of the Socialist Party of France. He served as Prime Minister from 4 June 1936 to 3 February 1937, from 13 March to 10 April 1938 and from 16 December 1946 to 22 January 1947.

15

' "Scuttle", everywhere, is the order of the day'

A FTER a private visit to Chartwell, Mohammed Ali Jinnah invited Churchill to lunch in London. Churchill declined. It might be wiser, he wrote, 'for us not to be associated publicly at this juncture'. Churchill then wrote out for Jinnah the London address of his secretary Miss Gilliatt, telling the Indian Muslim leader: 'I now enclose the address to which any telegrams you may wish to send me can be sent without attracting attention in India. I will always sign myself "Gilliatt". Perhaps you will let me know to what address I should telegraph to you and how you will sign yourself.' [1]

Speaking on India in the House of Commons on 12 December 1946, Churchill noted that, although it had been several months since the last debate on India, the Indian drama was 'unfolding itself remorselessly'. Nevertheless, the very fact that this new debate was taking place had been 'deplored', albeit in 'moderate terms', by Sir Stafford Cripps. 'But it would be a pity,' Churchill commented, 'if the British Empire in India passed out of life into history, without the House of Commons seeming to take any interest in the affair, and without any record, even in *Hansard*, of the transaction.'

Those who had been 'content' with the course of British policy to India in the previous twenty years had hoped, Churchill pointed out, 'that the desire of many Indians to be rid for ever of British rule and guidance would have brought about a melting of hearts among the vast populations inhabiting the Indian sub-Continent, and that they would have joined together to maintain the peace and the unity of India, and stride forth boldly into their independent future, on which we impose no bar.'

---

[1] 'Private', 'My dear Mr Jinnah', from 28 Hyde Park Gate, SW7 (appending the address 6 Westminster Gardens, Marsham Street, London SW1), 11 December 1946: reproduced in facsimile in *Dawn* (Karachi, Pakistan), 2 April 1981.

Such had not been his views, but 'they are the views of a great number of people'. No such 'melting of hearts' had so far occurred, he said, and he went on to declare that, on the contrary:

... all the facts and all the omens point to a revival, in an acute and violent form, of the internal hatreds and quarrels which have long lain dormant under the mild incompetence of liberal-minded British control. This is the dominating fact which stares us in the face to-day. The House will probably be of the opinion that it is too soon for us to accept this melancholy conclusion, or to regulate our conduct by it. To me, however, it would be no surprise if there were a complete failure to agree. I warned the House as long ago as 1931, when I said that if we were to wash our hands of all responsibility, ferocious civil war would speedily break out between the Muslims and Hindus. But this, like other warnings, fell upon deaf and unregarding ears.

Churchill then drew the attention of the House of Commons to the words of Lord Randolph Churchill in 1886, and to their relevance in 1946:

I have always borne in mind the words my father used when he was Secretary of State for India 60 years ago. He said:

'Our rule in India is, as it were, a sheet of oil spread out over a surface of, and keeping calm and quiet and unruffled by storms, an immense and profound ocean of humanity. Underneath that rule lie hidden all the memories of fallen dynasties, all the traditions of vanquished races, all the pride of insulted creeds, and it is our task, our most difficult business, to give peace, individual security and general prosperity to the 250 millions of people'—

there are now 400 millions—

'who are affected by those powerful forces, to bind them and to weld them by the influence of our knowledge, our law and our higher civilisation, in process of time into one great united people and to offer to all the nations of the West the advantages of tranquillity and progress in the East.'

Having quoted these words of his father, Churchill continued:

That is the task which, with all our shortcomings and through all our ordeals, we have faithfully and loyally pursued since Queen Victoria assumed the Imperial Crown. That is the task which we have now declared ourselves willing to abandon completely, provided that we have such assurance of agreement between the Indian races, religions, parties and forces as will clear us from the responsibility of bringing about a hideous collapse and catastrophe.

'We have no such assurance at the present time,' Churchill commented.

Four months had passed since the Government had invited Jawaharlal Nehru to form a Government, based upon the Congress

Party of which he was the head. By this invitation, Churchill declared, the Government had 'precipitated a series of massacres over wide regions, unparalleled in India since the Indian Mutiny of 1857. Indeed, it is certain that more people have lost their lives or have been wounded in India by violence since the interim Government under Mr Nehru was installed in office four months ago by the Viceroy, than in the previous 90 years, or four generations of men, covering a large part of the reigns of five Sovereigns.' Churchill's speech continued:

This is only a foretaste of what may come. It may be only the first few heavy drops before the thunderstorm breaks upon us. These frightful slaughters over wide regions and in obscure uncounted villages have, in the main, fallen upon Muslim minorities. I have received from high and credible witnesses, accounts of what has taken place, for instance, in Bihar.[1] The right hon. and learned Gentleman gave us his report. What happened in Bihar casts into the shade the Armenian atrocities with which Mr Gladstone once stirred the moral sense of Liberal Britain.[2]

We are, of course, cauterised by all that we ourselves have passed through. Our faculty for wonder is ruptured, our faculty for horror is numbed; the world is full of misery and hatred. What Mr Gollancz, in a remarkable book—which, I may say, shows an evident lack of peace of mind—has called 'our threatened values', do not stir us as they would have done our fathers or our predecessors in this House; nor, perhaps, after all our exertions and in our present eclipse, have we the physical and psychic strength to react against these shocking tidings, as former generations and earlier Parliaments, who have not suffered like us, would certainly have done.

Churchill went on to tell the House of Commons:

The official figure of the lives lost since the Government of India was handed over to the Interim Administration of Mr Nehru is stated at 10,000. I doubt very much whether that figure represents half the total racial and religious murders which have occurred up to date. An outbreak of animal fury has ravaged many large districts, and may at any time resume or spread its devastation through teeming cities and Provinces as big as England or the main British island. It is some comfort to recall, and I was glad that the right hon. and learned Gentleman reminded us of it, that both Muslim and Hindu leaders have joined together to arrest, or at least mitigate this appalling degeneration. I have been informed that it was Mr Nehru himself who gave the order which the Provincial Government of Bihar had been afraid to give, for the police and troops to fire upon Hindu mobs who were exterminating

[1] During Muslim violence against Hindus in Calcutta in August 1946 more than 4,000 Hindus had been killed. Then, as a reprisal, as many as 7,000 Muslims were killed by Hindus in Bihar. On 25 November 1946 Lord Pethick-Lawrence (Secretary of State for India and Burma) had stated in Parliament that during October and November 1946 alone there had been, 6,700 deaths in communal fighting in India.

[2] In fact, in his famous philippic of 1876, Gladstone had denounced the Turkish massacre of *Bulgarians*. The 'Armenian atrocities' did not begin until 1895 (the year after Gladstone's final resignation).

the Muslim minorities within their midst. That was certainly to his credit and may be taken, so far as it goes, as an encouraging sign.

Nevertheless, I must record my own belief, which I have long held and often expressed, that any attempt to establish the reign of a Hindu numerical majority in India will never be achieved without a civil war, proceeding, not perhaps at first on the fronts or armies of organised forces, but in thousands of separate and isolated places. This war will, before it is decided, lead through unaccountable agonies to an awful abridgement of the Indian population. Besides and in addition to this, I am sure that any attempt by the Congress Party to establish a Hindu Raj on the basis of majorities measured by the standards of Western civilisation—or what is left of it—and proceeding by the forms and formulas of governments with which we are familiar over here, will, at a very early stage, be fatal to any conception of the unity of India.

Churchill then spoke of the Muslims and the Untouchables, the minorities which were each in fact an 'entity', telling the House of Commons that, whatever might be the outcome of the divisions in India as a result of the present situation, in which the Muslims under Jinnah had refused to participate in the Constituent Assembly, there was 'one thing' that, whatever happened in India, 'we must not do':

We must not allow British troops or British officers in the Indian Army to become the agencies and instruments of enforcing caste Hindu domination upon the 90 million Muslims and the 60 million Untouchables; nor must the prestige or authority of the British power in India, even in its sunset, be used in partisanship on either side of these profound and awful cleavages. Such a course, to enforce religious and party victory upon minorities of scores of millions, would seem to combine the disadvantages of all policies and lead us ever deeper into tragedy, without giving us relief from our burdens, or liberation, however sadly purchased, from moral and factual responsibility. It is because we feel that these issues should be placed bluntly and plainly before the British and Indian peoples, even amid their present distresses and perplexities, that we thought it our bounden duty to ask for this Debate.[1]

Not India, but Palestine, prompted Churchill's next Parliamentary speech, on 31 January 1947. The subject was recent Jewish terrorism, 'this series of detestable outrages' as Churchill called them.[2] There were those who had argued for reprisals, or at least for a war on the terrorists. Churchill cautioned the House:

[1] Speech of 12 December 1946: *Hansard*.
[2] On 3 January 1947 five British soldiers were injured when their jeeps were blown up by mines. That same day an Arab constable, injured in an earlier attack, died of his injuries. On January 5, Jewish terrorists attacked a railway transport office: no one was hurt. On January 27 Judge Ralph Windham was kidnapped by six armed Jewish terrorists from his court in Tel Aviv (he was released two days later). Shortly before Churchill spoke, the Government had announced the death by terrorism in Palestine in 1946 of 45 British soldiers, 29 members of the Palestine Police Force, 63 Jewish civilians, 60 Arab civilians, and 14 British civilians (including 2 British Jews).

The idea that general reprisals upon the civil population and vicarious examples would be consonant with our whole outlook upon the world of affairs and with our name, reputation and principles, is, of course, one which should never be accepted in any way. We have, therefore, very great difficulties in conducting squalid warfare with terrorists. That is why I would venture to submit to the House that every effort should be made to avoid getting into warfare with terrorists; and if a warfare with terrorists has broken out, every effort should be made—I exclude no reasonable proposal—to bring it to an end.

Churchill also urged the House, as he had done in his previous speech on Palestine, not to turn its back on a Jewish National Home in Palestine:

All my hon. Friends on this side of the House do not agree with the views which I held for so many years about the Zionist cause. But promises were made far beyond those to which responsible Governments should have committed themselves. What has been the performance? The performance has been a vacuum, a gaping void, a senseless, dumb abyss—nothing.

The 'outrageous acts' in Palestine, Churchill pointed out, were being committed by a 'small, fanatical desperate minority'. Of one Jewish terrorist, Dov Gruner, who was under sentence of death, Churchill commented: 'The fortitude of this man, criminal though he be, must not escape the notice of the House.' [1]

Churchill then spoke of the financial aspect of British rule in Palestine:

We are told that there are a handful of terrorists on one side and 100,000 British troops on the other. How much does it cost? No doubt it is £300 a year per soldier in Palestine. That is apart from what I call a slice of the overheads, which is enormous, of the War Office and other Services. That is £30 million a year. It may be much more—between £30 million and £40 million a year—which is being poured out and which would do much to help to find employment in these islands, or could be allowed to return to fructify in the pockets of the people—to use a phrase which has dropped out of discussion now, but which was much in vogue at one time in Liberal circles, together with all sorts of antiquated ideas about the laws of supply and demand by people like Adam Smith, John Stuart Mill, and other worthies of that kind.

One hundred thousand men is a very definite proportion of our Army for one and a half years. How much longer are they to stay here? And stay for what? In order that on a threat to kill hostages we show ourselves unable to

[1] On 1 January 1947 Dov Gruner was sentenced to death for his part in an attack on a police station in Palestine in April 1946, in which an Arab policeman had been killed. He was executed on 16 April 1947, together with three other Jews caught after the flogging of British soldiers by members of a Jewish terrorist group. Gruner had refused to ask for a pardon; hence Churchill's reference to his 'fortitude'.

execute a sentence duly pronounced by a competent tribunal. It is not good enough. I never saw anything less recompensive for the efforts now employed than what is going on in Palestine.

There were those who said that Britain should stay in Palestine because otherwise 'Jew and Arab would be at each other's throats', because there would be civil war. Churchill reflected on this that a civil war was 'very likely indeed', but was this reason 'why we should stay'? and he added:

We do not propose to stay in India, even if a civil war of a gigantic character were to follow our departure. No, that is all brushed aside. We are not going to allow such things to make us stay. We are told to leave the Indians to settle their own affairs by getting a verdict from a body which is unrepresentative and then march out. In Palestine we are told we cannot go, because it would lead to a terrible quarrel between Jews and Arabs and there would be civil war as to who would have the land.

Churchill proposed that, henceforth, the responsibility for Palestine should be borne by the United Nations and not by 'poor, overburdened and heavily injured' Britain. He saw 'absolutely no reason' why Britain should continue to suffer 'all this pain, toil, injury and suffering'; unless the United States was prepared to 'come in with us shoulder to shoulder on a 50 per cent basis on an agreed policy, to take a half and half share of the bloodshed, odium, trouble, expense and worry', then Britain should lay its Mandate at the feet of the United Nations:

Whereas, six months ago, I suggested that we should do that in 12 months I suggest now that the period should be shortened to six months. One is more and more worried and one's anxiety deepens and grows as hopes are falsified and the difficulties of the aftermath of war, which I do not underrate, lie still heavily upon us in a divided nation, cutting deeply across our lives and feelings.

In these conditions we really cannot go on, in all directions, taking on burdens which use up and drain out the remaining strength of Britain and which are beyond any duty we have undertaken in the international field.

I earnestly trust that the Government will, if they have to fight this squalid war, make perfectly certain that the will power of the British State is not conquered by brigands and bandits and unless we are to have the aid of the United States, they will at the earliest possible moment, give due notice to divest us of a responsibility which we are failing to discharge and which in the process is covering us with blood and shame.[1]

'I cannot help being interested in politics,' Churchill told Lord Moran a month later; 'the Government is doing so much harm,' and he added: 'Of course, it's all anti-climax.'[2]

[1] Speech of 31 January 1947: *Hansard.*
[2] Moran diary, 22 February 1947: *The Struggle for Survival*, page 318.

As Churchill had urged, the Cabinet now decided to transfer the Palestine Mandate to the United Nations as soon as possible. This decision was made public by Bevin on February 14. Six days later, Attlee announced that it was his Government's intention, in India, to transfer power to 'responsible Indian hands' not later than June 1948, and that Mountbatten was to succeed Wavell as Viceroy. Churchill was convinced that such a transfer of power was at variance with the 1942 British offer of Dominion Status for India, an offer which, at the time, the Indian Congress Party under Nehru had rejected.

On March 4, in preparation for the debate on the Government's proposals, Churchill received a series of notes from Enoch Powell, dealing with the legality of secession of a country with Dominion Status, and the terms of the earlier rejection by the Congress Party of Dominion Status when offered by Sir Stafford Cripps in 1942. Despite this rejection, Powell pointed out, Churchill had accepted his Secretary of State for India's statement at the time, that despite the Congress rejection, the British Government, as L. S. Amery had expressed it, 'stand firmly by the broad intention of their offer'.[1]

Speaking in the House of Commons on March 6, Churchill argued that the Government had now gone beyond the offer of Dominion Status in two respects. One was the 'total abandonment' by the Government of all responsibility for carrying out its earlier pledges to the minorities and to the depressed classes, as well as to the Indian States. 'All these are to be left to fend for themselves,' he said, 'and fight for themselves as best they can.' The second change concerned agreement between the Muslim and Hindu communities. Such agreement was 'the essence of the Cripps declaration' of 1942. 'It is the Government which has broken away from the agreement. . . .'

During the debate, there was an altercation between A. V. Alexander and Churchill on the subject of the Congress leader, Jawaharlal Nehru:

Referring to Mr Churchill's reference to the Cabinet Mission, Mr Alexander denied that this Mission attempted to formulate a Constitution and force it on the Indians. Mr Churchill had attacked Pandit Nehru, but we had had evidence in the past to recognise Nehru as an experienced and cultured person, and if he and his colleagues were given a fair opportunity to cooperate with the other parties they would bring India through her present difficulties to power, prosperity, and peace.

[1] 'Dear Mr Churchill', 4 March 1947: Churchill papers, 2/43. The Cripps offer had been announced on 11 March 1942. Amery's statement was made in the House of Commons on 30 July 1942. Speaking in the House of Commons on 10 September 1942 Churchill had confirmed that the offer of Dominion Status 'must be taken as representing the settled policy of the British Crown and Parliament'. In 1947 Powell was working at the Conservative Parliamentary Secretariat in London.

Mr Churchill: I certainly have not made any personal attack on Mr Nehru, except to point out that he has good reason to be our bitterest enemy.

Mr Alexander said that for a man of Mr Churchill's great experience to get up in the House and talk about Indian leaders of that kind, with whom we had negotiated and had got closer to than ever before, as if they were existing enemies of this country was a really fatal thing to do.

Nehru's interim Government, Churchill continued, had been 'a complete disaster'. It had been, and remained, a 'critical mistake' to entrust the Government of India in this interim period 'to the leader of the caste Hindus, Mr Nehru'. Mountbatten was being sent out to India as Viceroy with fourteen months to secure a working agreement with Nehru on the future independence of India, in theory still as a Dominion. 'Is he to make a new effort to restore the situation?' Churchill asked:

... or is it merely 'Operation Scuttle' on which he and other distinguished officers have been despatched? One thing seems to me absolutely certain— the Government by the time limit has put an end to all prospect of Indian unity. In my view everyone will start to stake out their claims and prepare to defend them.

These 14 months will not be used for the melting of hearts and the union of Muslim and Hindu all over India. They will be used in preparation for civil war; and they will be marked continually by disorders and disturbances such as are now going on in the great city of Lahore. In spite of the great efforts which have been made by the leaders on both sides to allay them, out of sheer alarm and fear of what would happen, still these troubles break out, and they are sinking profoundly into India, in the heart of the Indian problem.[1]

At this point, Sir Stafford Cripps, as the *Manchester Guardian* reported, was 'smiling cynically'.[2] Churchill at once replied:

... the right hon. and learned Gentleman ought not to laugh. Although of fanatical disposition, he has a tender heart. I am sure that the horrors that have been going on since he put the Nehru Government in power, the spectacle we have seen in viewing these horrors, with the corpses of men, women and children littering the ground in thousands, have wrung his heart. I wonder that even his imagination does not guide him to review these matters searchingly in his own conscience.[3]

The fourteen months' 'limitation', Churchill told the House of Commons, would 'cripple' Mountbatten 'and destroy the prospect of even going through the business on the agenda which has to be

[1] Speech of 6 March 1947: *Hansard.*
[2] *Manchester Guardian,* 7 March 1947.
[3] *Hansard,* 6 March 1947.

settled'. Churchill then quoted a remark by Gandhi—'one of his most scatterbrained observations', he called it—at the time of the Cripps Mission in 1942. Rejoicing in the rejection by Congress of Cripps's offer of Dominion Status once the war was ended, Gandhi had said: 'Leave India in God's hands, in modern parlance, to anarchy; and that anarchy may lead to internecine warfare for a time, or to unrestricted dacoities. From these a true India will arise in place of the false one we see.'

This statement, Churchill commented, was, 'as far as I can see, a statement indistinguishable from the policy His Majesty's Government are determined to pursue'.

Churchill then compared, as he had done in the Palestine debate in January, the Government's policies on Palestine and India. He made the comparison, he said, 'with bewilderment':

There is a time limit for India, but no time limit for Palestine. I must say, that astonished me. Two bottles of powerful medicine have been prepared, but they are sent to the wrong patients. The policy in these two places taken together is incomprehensible. I do not understand how they can have originated from any coherent human brain; and even from a Cabinet which, no doubt, has many incoherencies in it, it is incomprehensible.

Can the House believe there are three or four times as many British troops in little petty Palestine as in mighty India at the present time? What is the idea behind such a thing? What is the point and sense of this distribution of our forces, which we are told are so limited?

I do not know where the sustained effort we are making in Palestine comes from, or what element of obstinacy has forced this peculiar assertion in the midst of general surrender and scuttle of British will-power in Palestine. I do not know where it comes from; but evidently some very powerful Minister has said he is going to have his way in it, and nobody has dared to withstand him. I cannot tell who it is. I have only my surmise.

The sustained effort we are making in Palestine, if applied in India, would have enabled the plan of the Cripps Mission to be carried out, fully discussed with full deliberation and firmness; and we should have kept all our pledges, and we should have gone steadily forward through this crisis.

It is indeed a paradox that the opposite course should be taken, and that here, in India, where such vast consequences are at stake, we are told we must be off in 14 months; whereas, in this small Palestine, with which we have been connected but 25 years, and hold only on Mandate, we are to make all these exertions, and pour out our treasure, and keep 100,000 men or more marching around in circumstances most vexatious and painful to them.

To the surprise of almost everyone present, Churchill then proposed for India the solution he had earlier proposed for Palestine: to 'invoke the aid' of the United Nations. The Government had now agreed 'after six or seven months' delay—a needless delay' to involve the United Nations in Palestine. They should do the same for India:

We are told that we cannot walk out of Palestine because we should leave behind us a war between 600,000 Jews and 1,200,000 Arabs. How, then, can we walk out of India in 14 months and leave behind us a war between 90 million Muslims and 200 million caste Hindus, and all the other tribulations which will fall upon the helpless population of 400 million? Will it not be a terrible disgrace to our name and record if, after our 14 months' time limit, we allow one fifth of the population of the globe, occupying a region nearly as large as Europe, to fall into chaos and into carnage? Would it not be a world crime that we should be committing, a crime that would stain—not merely strip us, as we are being stripped, in the material position—but would stain our good name for ever?

If the Government felt that it was right 'in the case of little Palestine' to lay their difficulties before the United Nations, what 'conceivable reason' could there be, Churchill asked, 'for not following a similar course in the case of this vast sub-Continent of India?' and he went on to ask, of Attlee's Government:

... if they cannot, through their weakness and moral prostration, fulfil their pledges to vast, helpless communities numbered by scores of millions, are they not bound in honour, in decency, and, indeed, in common sense to seek the aid of the wider instruments and authorities? I say that if all practical hopes of Britain's discharging her task have vanished—it is not my view, but it is the prevailing mood; it is the mood of those who are all-powerful to-day—if they have all vanished, then, at least, there is this new world organisation, brought into being by the agonies of two devastating wars, which should certainly not be overlooked or ignored.

He had spoken, Churchill said, 'with a lifetime of thought and contact with these topics'. This was indeed true. More than fifty years had passed since he had been a young soldier in India; more than twenty-five since, in the aftermath of the Amritsar massacre, he had warned the House of Commons against using 'frightfulness' in its dealings with India; more than a decade since, during the India Bill debate, he had tried to persuade the Conservative Party not to be in such a hurry to give up Britain's control over India. Now the days of the British Raj were numbered:

It is with deep grief I watch the clattering down of the British Empire with all its glories, and all the services it has rendered to mankind. I am sure that in the hour of our victory now not so long ago, we had the power to make a solution of our difficulties which would have been honourable and lasting. Many have defended Britain against her foes. None can defend her against herself. We must face the evils that are coming upon us and that we are powerless to avert. We must do our best in all these circumstances and not exclude any expedient that may help to mitigate the ruin and disaster that will follow the disappearance of Britain from the East. But, at least, let us not add—by shameful flight, by a premature hurried scuttle—at least, let us not add to the pangs of sorrow so many of us feel, the taint and smear of shame.[1]

Churchill made a second onslaught on the Government six days later, during a debate on the economic situation. Having won the votes of only 37 per cent of the total electorate, he said, the Labour Party had committed 'a crime against the British State and people' by their Socialist legislation, 'the consequences of which have hampered our recovery, darkened our future and now endanger our very life'. His denunciation of the Government continued:

... mouthing slogans of envy, hatred and malice, they have spread class warfare throughout the land and all sections of society, and they have divided this nation, in its hour of serious need as it has never been divided, in a different way from that in which it has ever been divided in the many party conflicts I have witnessed in the past. In less than two years, our country, under their control, has fallen from its proud and glorious position in the world, to the plight in which it lies this afternoon, and with even more alarming prospects opening upon us in the future.

That is their offence, from which we shall suffer much, and with the guilt and discredit of which their name and the doctrines of their party will long be identified in British homes.

Churchill turned a few moments later to the Government's Palestine policy:

... £82 million since the Socialist Government came into power squandered in Palestine, and 100,000 Englishmen now kept away from their homes and work, for the sake of a senseless squalid war with the Jews in order to give Palestine to the Arabs, or God knows who.

'Scuttle', everywhere, is the order of the day—Egypt, India, Burma. One thing at all costs we must preserve: the right to get ourselves world-mocked and world-hated over Palestine, at a cost of £82 million.

Churchill then spoke of the increase in the number of civil servants under the Labour Government. The 'Socialist ideal', he said, 'is to reduce us to one vast Wormwood Scrubbery', and he went on to explain that at Wormwood Scrubs prison in West London 'there is only one official to every four prisoners, whereas up to the present we have the advantage of only one official to look after every eight wage-earners or producers'.

Contrasting the philosophies of private enterprise and State control, Churchill told the House of Commons:

[1] Speech of 6 March 1947: *Hansard.*

Let every man now ask himself this: Is it the interest of the wage-earners to serve an all-powerful employer—the State—or to deal with private employers, who, though more efficient in business, are in a far weaker position as masters? Is it the interest of the housewife to queue up before officials at public distribution centres, as Socialism logically involves, or to go as a customer to a private shopkeeper, whose livelihood depends on giving good and friendly service to his customers?

Of course, the State must have its plan and its policy. The first object of this plan should be to liberate and encourage the natural, native energies, genius and contrivance of our race, which, by a prodigy, have built up this vast population in our small island, and built up a standard of living which, before the war, was the envy of every country in Europe.

The first object then, is to liberate these energies; the second stage is to guide and aid all the forces that these native energies generate into the right channels. The Government have begun the wrong way round. They have started with control for control's sake on the theory of levelling down to the weakest and least productive types, and thus they have cramped and fettered the life-thrust of British society.[1]

---

[1] Speech of 12 March 1947: *Hansard.*

16

Family, Friends and Fears

I N the winter of 1946, Churchill's daughter Mary became engaged to Christopher Soames, the Assistant Military Attaché in Paris. Born in October 1920, Soames had been educated at Eton and the Royal Military College, Sandhurst, being gazetted 2nd Lieutenant Coldstream Guards in 1939. He had served throughout the war, in the Middle East, Italy and France, being promoted Captain in 1942. It was shortly after his twenty-sixth birthday that he first visited Chartwell. 'Lunch at Chartwell was, for me, such a great awakening,' he wrote to Churchill on November 16, after his return to Paris. 'Please believe me when I say that I had the impression of living for an all-too-short period of time in another world—a world of greatness such as I never believed existed. I took away with me such wonderful memories.'[1] One such memory was of Churchill showing him around Chartwell Farm. When they came to the piggery Churchill scratched one of the pigs and said: 'I am fond of pigs. Dogs look up to us. Cats look down on us. Pigs treat us as equals.'[2]

On 29 November 1946, the day before his seventy-second birthday, Churchill formally sold Chartwell to the National Trust for £43,800. The sum had been collected by the group set up by Lord Camrose less than a month earlier. That same day, Churchill took a lease on the property for fifty years, at a cost of £350 a year.[3]

On the morning of November 30 Churchill awoke to find a magnificent bowl of flowers; it was a birthday gift from the seven secretaries

---

[1] 'Dear Mr Churchill', 16 November 1946: Churchill papers, 1/42.
[2] Lord Soames recollections: Reform Club Political Committee Dinner, 28 April 1981.
[3] Churchill papers, 1/37. Churchill had also to pay the rates. Chartwell was first opened to the public under the auspices of the National Trust on 22 June 1966. In the subsequent twenty years, it was visited by 3,329,073 people. (National Trust, Chartwell, Archive, note dated 27 July 1987.)

who worked for him at Chartwell and Hyde Park Gate.[1] Also on the
bedside table were two double magnums of champagne from General
and Lady Ismay, a white china cat from Leslie and Judy Rowan, a
pot of honey from Sawyers and violets 'from an anonymous donor'.[2]
That night Churchill dined with his family and a few friends, one of
whom, Brendan Bracken proposed Churchill's health. Lord Moran,
who was also presented, noted:

> Winston was much moved when he got up to reply; a big tear gathered be-
> neath his left eye. His emotions are always near the surface, but they are never
> manufactured. He said very simply that it was a comfort to him at the end of the
> journey to have around him those for whom he cared. Then he exclaimed:
> 'But we are the past, and that is done with. Mary is the future.'
> He went on to speak, very shortly, of her coming marriage, and sat down;
> the old man at his affectionate best. Mary said she hoped, with Christopher,
> to found another English home, and went on to speak of what she owed to
> her own home, which would always be the greatest influence in her life.
> When the ladies had retired, Brendan belittled Smuts. Winston retorted:
> 'My faith in Smuts is unbreakable. He is a great man.'
> Later someone referred to Winston's book, when he said:
> 'I should like to put down, without malice and without vanity, what hap-
> pened.'

Moran's account continued:

> The butler came in and asked Winston if he could get the table ready for
> Harry Green, an actor, whose thought-transference stuff had gripped Wins-
> ton. I retired with Green to a room, where he gave me a pencil and paper,
> and asked me to put down some serious thought. He then left the room. I
> wrote, 'Shall I write another book?' and folded the paper up several times.
> When he came back he took it from me, but without undoing it, held it
> against my forehead and repeated what I had written. Winston also retired
> and wrote: 'Shall I go to Chicago in the spring?' He was astounded when
> Green repeated this. Leslie Rowan then went out and asked: 'Shall we be at
> war with Russia within ten years?' Green not only got the words right, but
> went on to say, 'No.' Whereupon Winston pointed out that he was much
> impressed by the fact that he had got Leslie's words right, but he was not at
> all impressed by his views as to whether there would be a war with Russia or
> not. Winston found it easier to swallow magic than the conjurer's claim to
> views, as if ordinary folk ought not to have views at all.

'In the past twelve months,' Moran reflected, 'his spirits have risen
and his vigour has come back. He has put vain regrets away; once

---

[1] 'Thank you so much for the beautiful flowers which I greatly enjoyed receiving when I
awoke this morning' (30 November 1946: Churchill papers, 1/42). The secretaries were Miss
Sturdee, Miss Gilliatt, Miss Marston, Miss Taylor, Miss Hipwell, Miss Graham and Miss
Hamblin (Clementine Churchill's secretary).

[2] 'List of Birthday Gifts, November 30, 1946': Churchill papers, 1/42.

more there is a purpose in life. He is very happy at Chartwell, farming and painting and dictating his book. In short, it has been a year of recovery.'[1]

Things were not so easy for Clementine Churchill, for whom the war years had been a time of considerable strain, and who now had to adjust to the new problems of Hyde Park Gate. 'I am sorry to say,' Churchill wrote to Christopher Soames's father Arthur on December 8, 'that Clemmie has been ordered by her doctor to take at least three weeks rest-cure. She has found life vy strenuous of late, & I want her to be fit for the joyous event to wh we all look forward.'[2]

In a letter to Commander Tommy Thompson on December 15, Miss Sturdee gave a brief sketch of the Churchill family's doings:

> Mrs Churchill's engagements are still in a state of cancellation. Miss Mary is getting all ready for her marriage, although no date has been fixed yet. Mr Churchill got caught in the fog the other night. He walked all the way from Hyde Park Corner to Knightsbridge, got fed up I suppose, and so spent the night at Hyde Park Hotel. But with all these things the world goes on.[3]

Having spent the night at the hotel, Churchill decided to stay there for a while. Miss Marston, summoned to take dictation, later recalled: 'I went there in the morning and found him in bed. He spent the day there. He rather enjoyed it.'[4]

On December 19, Churchill concluded the purchase of a farm adjacent to Chartwell, Parkside Farm. The cost was £10,250, and the farm covered 52 acres, 13½ of them arable, just over 34 of them pasture and leys, and 3 of them woodland. Also included in the sale was the farmhouse, which had been built in 1650, a cottage which was found to be 'beyond repair' when inspected by Churchill's builders, and livestock: eleven cows in milk, six heifers and two bulls, as well as two hives of bees and a tractor.[5] Five days later, Churchill bought Chartwell Farm for £22,545 from Major Marnham.[6] Its twenty-seven head of cattle were valued at just under £2,000 and brought in more than £130 a month in milk sold to the Milk Marketing Board.

Throughout December, Churchill spent as much time as possible at

---

[1] Moran diary, 30 November 1946: *The Struggle for Survival*, pages 316–17.

[2] 'Private', 8 December 1946: Churchill papers, 2/156.

[3] Letter of 15 December 1946: Churchill papers, 2/157.

[4] Mrs Shillingford recollections: in conversation with the author, 1 July 1987.

[5] Sale completed 19 December 1946: Churchill papers, 1/35.

[6] Sale completed 24 December 1946: Churchill papers, 1/32. On 3 January 1947 Churchill accepted £8,000 from Lord Antrim in respect of the Carnlough Estate, which he had inherited in 1921, through the will of Lord Randolph Churchill's grandmother Frances Anne Vane, Marchioness of Londonderry. Will dated 6 July 1864. On the death of her grandson, Churchill had inherited the estate. His net income from it had been £114 (1943), £245 (1944) and £262 (1945). (Churchill papers, 1/18.)

Chartwell. When, in the second week of December, Churchill's cousin Oswald Frewen invited him to luncheon in London, Churchill replied: 'Alas, I cannot make any engagements at the present time. I am pressed with a variety of heavy business, and am looking forward to a complete break at Chartwell until the House reassembles in the latter part of January.' Churchill added: 'It is a great relief to me not to move at all or make any engagements.'[1]

Churchill had of course to go to London for meetings of the Consultative Committee—soon known as the 'Shadow Cabinet'—and for Parliamentary debates. But if possible he spent Mondays and Fridays at Chartwell, as well as weekends.

While he was at Chartwell that December, Churchill received an invitation to visit Australia and New Zealand. In the course of his long life he had never visited either. Canada, South Africa and India were the three principal Commonwealth countries which he had visited. 'Am honoured and touched by your splendid invitation,' he replied, 'and I hope indeed some day I may have the time accorded to me to visit Australia and New Zealand as I have long desired to do. Alas, it is impossible for me to come in the spring of 1947. My work here in leading the Opposition is very heavy and I am not sure that my strength is equal to so long a journey by Air.'[2]

Churchill was never to visit Australia or New Zealand.

At Chartwell on Christmas Day, Churchill's presents included honey from Sir Stewart Menzies, head of the Secret Service throughout Churchill's premiership, two bottles of port from Duncan and Diana Sandys, and a bottle of turpentine from Sir Stafford Cripps. In reply to Christmas greetings from Attlee and his wife, Churchill mentioned that he was 'worrying a great deal' about his war memoirs. 'It is a colossal undertaking,' he told Attlee, 'and I may well collapse before the load is carried to the top of the hill. However, it is a good thing to get a certain amount of material together which, if not history, will still at least be a contribution thereto.'[3]

One of Churchill's worries was that his wife and family would not be properly provided for. To this end Leslie Graham-Dixon and

---

[1] 'My dear Oswald', 19 December 1946: Sir Shane Leslie papers. Oswald Frewen was the son of Churchill's aunt Lady Leslie (Lady Randolph Churchill's sister).

[2] Telegram, undated: Churchill papers, 2/145.

[3] 'Private', 'My dear Prime Minister', 28 December 1946: Churchill papers, 2/145. Financially, Churchill's book was drawing in lucrative contracts: £175,000 for the British book rights, £20,000 (from Sir Keith Murdoch) for the Australian and New Zealand rights, £10,500 for the South African rights and £45,000 (from Emery Reves) for the Foreign book and serial rights. (Letter from Lord Camrose's Private Secretary, 9 January 1947: Churchill papers, 4/57.)

Anthony Moir continued to advise him on the establishment of a Trust most suitable to create an income for his descendants, free from the burden of taxation. 'One had the feeling throughout all those years,' Graham-Dixon later recalled, 'that he was always worried about dying a pauper. He was always conscious of Mrs Churchill's position.' A Chartwell Literary Trust was set up, with Lord Cherwell, Oliver Lyttelton and Brendan Bracken as Trustees, and with Leslie Rowan and Jock Colville as Joint Honorary Secretaries. Graham-Dixon and Anthony Moir continued to call on Churchill whenever advice was needed. Later, Graham-Dixon recalled Churchill's kindnesses, 'His magnanimity always', characterized by a visit to the Studio at Chartwell—'Come and see my daubs'—followed by the gift of a painting. Churchill's phrases, too, were vivid across the years:

> On his son Randolph: 'We have a deep animal love for one another, but every time we meet we have a bloody row.'
> On smoking: 'I never smoke before breakfast.'
> On the war: 'Ah, how I enjoyed those years,' and 'There were times when I could not see my way through.'
> On the post-war aftermath: 'All is now anticlimax.'
> On money: 'How it melts.'
> On death: 'Any man who says he is not afraid of death is a liar.' [1]

During the first week of January, Churchill, at Chartwell, worked on his memoirs. Leslie Graham-Dixon and Anthony Moir were his luncheon guests on January 3, Emery Reves on January 7. Three days later, Bill Deakin, General Ismay and General Pownall were his guests overnight.[2] Pownall, who had returned from the Far East in 1945 after a distinguished military career, now joined Ismay and Deakin in the scrutiny of Churchill's text, and the preparation of extra material on all military aspects.[3]

There were further sittings in January for the sculptor Jacob Epstein, and, on January 5, a gift and some painting advice for his six-year-old grandson, 'little' Winston:

Darling Winston,
Thank you so much for your charming card.

---

[1] Leslie Graham-Dixon recollections: in conversation with the author, 15 March 1982.

[2] Churchill Engagements Calendar, January 1947: Churchill papers.

[3] Pownall, born in 1887, had seen active service in the First World War and on the North West Frontier of India. In 1939 he returned to Britain as Chief of General Staff, British Expeditionary Force. Inspector-General of Home Guard (1940), active service as Commander of British Troops in Northern Ireland (1940–41), Vice-Chief of the Imperial General Staff (1941), Commander-in-Chief Far East (December 1941–January 1942), General Officer Commanding, Ceylon (1942–43) and Persia-Iraq (1943); and Chief of Staff to the Supreme Allied Commander (Mountbatten) in South-East Asia (1943–44). He was knighted in 1945. Known at Chartwell as 'General P'.

I now send you a box of very lovely paints, and some brushes. These paints must only be squeezed out a drop at a time, not more than the size of a pea. You can mix them with water freely, using plenty of water; but they dry and become no good any more in about half an hour. You may use about three times as much of the white tubes; that is to say a blob about equal to three peas, each time you paint a picture.

Do not waste these paints for they are very hard to get and come from abroad.

After you have tried them by yourself I hope you will come down here one afternoon so that I can show you myself how to use them.

With much love,

Your affectionate grandfather,

WSC

PS, You do not need to squeeze out all the colours at once, only two or three at a time as you need them.[1]

In the third week of January, Churchill received a letter from Field Marshal Montgomery, who, as Chief of the Imperial General Staff, had just returned from a visit to the Soviet Union:

When in Moscow, Stalin asked if I ever saw you and made enquiries as to your health. I said you were in first class form.

He then said that you disagreed with him now on political matters, but he would always have the happiest memories of his work with you as the great war leader of Britain; he added that he had the greatest respect and admiration for what you had done during the war years.

I told him that I would tell you of what he had said; he said he would be delighted if I would do so.[2]

'Thank you so much indeed for the message which you have brought from Stalin,' Churchill replied. 'I shall venture to write to him in a similar spirit.'[3] Churchill did so, writing to Stalin ten days later:

My dear Stalin,

I was very glad to receive your kind message through Field Marshal Montgomery.

I always look back to our comradeship together, when so much was at stake.

I was also delighted to hear from Montgomery of your good health. Your life is not only precious to your country, which you saved, but to friendship between Soviet Russia and the English speaking world.[4]

In a sentence which he deleted before sending this letter, Churchill wrote: 'and you can always count on me where the safety of Russia and the fame of her Armies are concerned'. 'About political dif-

---

[1] Letter dated 5 January 1947: Churchill papers, 1/42.

[2] 'Dear Mr Churchill', 21 January 1947: Churchill papers, 2/143.

[3] 'My dear Monty', 23 January 1947: Churchill papers, 2/143.

[4] 'My dear Stalin', from Chartwell, 3 February 1947: Churchill papers, 2/57. Before sending this letter, Churchill replaced the phrase 'English speaking world' with 'Great Britain'. The letter as redrafted was sent to Stalin on 6 February 1947.

ferences,' Churchill had written in a sentence which he also deleted before sending the letter, 'you know I was never good at Karl Marx.'

There was another link between wartime controversies and Churchill's memoirs when, in January 1947, it was alleged in the United States that Churchill had opposed appointing General Marshall as Supreme Commander of the Allied Forces before the Normandy landings. From Washington, the new Ambassador, Lord Inverchapel, reported, as Churchill was told by the Foreign Office on January 23, 'that this rumour, which could easily have an exacerbating effect on day to day Anglo-American relations, is so widely believed that he considers that no unilateral repudiation by His Majesty's Government, any more than a mere undocumented statement by General Marshall at a press conference, would kill it successfully'.[1]

Churchill decided to intervene directly to protect his, and Britain's, reputation. Before he did so, however, he received a letter from Ismay in which the former head of his Defence Office wrote: 'I am as sure as I can be that our refusal to unify the "Overlord" and Mediterranean Commands and put them under one Supreme Commander was the reason that led the President to give up the idea of Marshall and substitute Eisenhower.'[2]

Aware of the difficulties that might arise once the controversy grew, on January 24 Churchill dictated a letter to Miss Gilliatt, to be sent in reply to the Foreign Office concerns:

The salient facts are that Mr Churchill himself proposed to the President that there should be an American Commander for the cross-Channel operation. He understood from the President that it would certainly be General Marshall, and he cordially welcomed this choice. The appointment of an American Commander for the cross-Channel operation eventually called 'Overlord' was of course contingent upon a British Commander in the Mediterranean, but in November 1943 the President proposed that General Marshall should command both theatres.

Mr Churchill could not agree to this for the reasons stated in his telegram to Field Marshal Dill of 5th November, 1943. The matter then remained in abeyance until the Teheran Conference. At this time Mr Churchill still believed that General Marshall would command 'Overlord' and told Marshal Stalin that he thought this was the President's wish. When they got back to Cairo the whole question of a Supreme Commander for the two theatres was

---

[1] J. N. Henderson to Elizabeth Gilliatt, Foreign Office, 23 January 1947: Churchill papers, 2/144. Lord Inverchapel, formerly Sir Archibald Clark Kerr, had been British Ambassador in Moscow from 1942 to 1946.

[2] 'My dear Mr Churchill', 22 January 1947: Churchill papers, 2/144.

discussed by the Combined Chiefs of Staff and the arguments set out by the British Chiefs of Staff were found overwhelming and were accepted.

While these discussions were proceeding on the staff level Mr Churchill still remained under the impression that General Marshall would command 'Overlord' and that Eisenhower would take his place at Washington; and that a British Commander would be nominated by him (Mr Churchill) for the Mediterranean. However, a few days before they left Cairo the President told him that he could not spare Marshall for 'Overlord' and proposed Eisenhower. Mr Churchill immediately accepted this suggestion, having complete confidence in the military attainments of both these great officers.

It was Churchill's 'personal belief', he added, 'that the British refusal to agree to Marshall being Supreme Commander over both theatres made the President feel he could not part with him at Washington, but Mr Churchill did not realise this at the time, and has no proof of it now'.[1]

Churchill's recollection of events scarcely three years old was borne out by Averell Harriman, who told the Associated Press in New York on January 24 that at Teheran 'Mr Churchill urged President Roosevelt' to appoint Marshall as Supreme Commander but that, 'after weighing all the factors', Roosevelt decided that Marshall 'could not be spared from his post in Washington'.[2] Harriman made no reference to Roosevelt's wish for a single Supreme Commander for the two war zones, and the opposition of the British Chiefs of Staff to this idea. This single Commander, Churchill told Leslie Rowan on January 29, 'would have destroyed the whole working of the Combined Chiefs of Staff Committee'.

'It may be that the matter has died down,' Churchill added.[3] This was indeed so: 'Mr Harriman's statement,' telegraphed Lord Inverchapel on January 31, 'has certainly done much to convince more responsible opinion here. Public interest is now dormant. . . .'[4]

As he continued work on the war memoirs, Churchill sought details for many episodes of which he had not first-hand knowledge. One of these was the resignation of Anthony Eden from Neville Chamberlain's Cabinet in 1938. Eager to help, Eden sent Churchill the diary kept at the time by his Principal Private Secretary, Oliver Harvey.[5] Eden also sent Churchill a memorandum by Lord Cranborne, who had

[1] Letter dated 24 January 1947: Churchill papers, 2/144.

[2] 'Harriman Tells How Marshall Won the Praise of Churchill', New York Herald Tribune, Paris, 25 January 1947 (cutting in Churchill papers, 2/144). In 1947 Harriman was United States Secretary of Commerce. Harriman sent this cutting to Churchill, who sent it on to Leslie Rowan, suggesting that Attlee might like to see it.

[3] 'Secret', 'My dear Leslie', 29 January 1947: Churchill papers, 2/144.

[4] No. 643 from Washington to Foreign Office, 31 January 1947: Churchill papers, 2/144.

[5] This was later published as The War Diaries of Sir Oliver Harvey, 1941–1945, edited by his son, John Harvey (London, 1978).

resigned at the same time, summarizing their differences with Chamberlain.[1] On the following day, the Prime Minister's office sent Churchill, as a prelude to possible official publication by Britain, the printed record of the proceedings of the Yalta Conference and the Downing Street file of telegrams dealing with Reparations. 'I hope this will give Mr Churchill what he requires,' Attlee's Assistant Private Secretary, Francis Graham-Harrison, wrote to Miss Gilliatt, 'but if there is anything more that is wanted, please let me know.'[2]

Between 1945 and 1950 Churchill had to send messages to each Conservative by-election candidate; these messages were drafted for him at Conservative Central Office.[3] It was rare for Churchill to change more than a phrase. On January 22, however, in the message for Enoch Powell, Churchill added a whole sentence of his own. It read: 'Thus we hope to create by enterprise & good national housekeeping that property-owning democracy without which individual freedom cannot be enjoyed by the mass of the people.' Churchill also added, to a passage on socialism: 'the fallaciousness of their doctrines and the incapacity of their management'.[4] On a draft message to Colonel H. C. Joel, Honorary Secretary of the Political Committee of the Constitutional Club, Churchill added (the draft had been prepared by Joel himself): 'Our Europe is being cast away.'[5]

On January 29 Churchill went to Buckingham Palace to see the King, who was about to leave for a tour of South Africa, with the Queen and the two Princesses, Elizabeth and Margaret. 'His Majesty would just like to shake you by the hand before he goes,' explained Sir Alan Lascelles.[6]

On February 11 Churchill and his wife were at St Margaret's, Westminster, for the marriage of their daughter Mary to Christopher Soames. The reception was held at the Dorchester. It was a moment of great joy for the Churchill family. 'What a beautiful wedding it

[1] 'Confidential', 'My dear Winston', 19 March 1947: Churchill papers, 4/52. Viscount Cranborne succeeded his father as Marquess of Salisbury on 4 April 1947.

[2] Letter of 20 March 1947: Churchill papers, 2/4.

[3] Some of these candidate messages were drafted by Sir Arthur Young, others by David Stelling, whose pamphlet, *Why I Am a Conservative*, published in July 1943, had become a basic Party handbook.

[4] Message of 22 January 1947: Churchill papers, 2/14. Powell was unsuccessful; he was first returned to Parliament in 1950, for Wolverhampton South-West, with a majority of 691 (20,239 votes, as against a combined Labour and Liberal vote of 23,777, of which Labour received 19,548).

[5] Draft submitted by Colonel H. C. Joel, 21 February 1947: Churchill papers, 2/315.

[6] Note by Miss Sturdee, 27 January 1947: Churchill papers, 2/171.

was,' wrote Churchill's daughter Sarah. 'How beautifully you both walked up the aisle'—Churchill and his daughter Mary—'both so proud of each other.'[1]

Of the inner family circle only Randolph could not be present: he was in the United States, travelling from coast to coast as part of his work as a journalist and lecturer.

Mary and Christopher Soames left London for their honeymoon in Switzerland. In London, a fuel crisis led to electricity cuts of up to five hours a day. 'It is agonisingly cold here,' Clementine Churchill wrote to her daughter, '& in this completely electric house we are feeling the five hour daily switch off. But I got a doctor's certificate for Papa's bedroom as he can really not work in the icy cold. We have pulled his bed near the window so he can see without a lamp.' Clementine added: 'Papa did not go to Chartwell this week-end becos' of the biting cold & I think he has been quite happy here. He sends you his dear love & messages to Christopher.'[2]

On January 29 Churchill had written to his son that, having acquired Chartwell Farm, he wished Randolph to inherit it. Churchill's letter reached Randolph on February 7, four days before his sister's marriage, while he was in Salt Lake City. He replied that same day to say how 'overjoyed' he was at the purchase of Chartwell Farm, and 'more grateful than I can say that you are leaving it to me in your will'. His letter continued:

I long ago decided that I would like eventually to live in the country— and to think that one day I shall be able to do so so close to Chartwell, with all its happy memories & associations, fills me with gratitude & joy.

I have read all you wrote about my present occupations & future plans with careful attention. I am deeply moved by this latest example of the deep interest you have always taken in my welfare. Though I always try & put a brave face on it to the world, & indeed to you, I must own that I am myself far from pleased with my present situation. At the same time I do not take quite so gloomy a view of it as you do.

As you know the only career in which I am seriously interested is politics. For this career I believe I have aptitudes & abilities which are granted to few. This may seem a little arrogant, but I know that if I am ultimately proved right in my belief, then all the credit will be due to yourself for the upbringing & inspiration you have given me. So far my political life has not been a great success. While fully realizing that I have made my full share of mistakes I believe also that circumstances have not so far been propitious. But I am still young & fortune may yet come my way.

I have of course long regretted that I did not 15 years ago take your excellent advice & adopt a legal career. Sloth—my besetting sin—was mainly

[1] 'My darling Papa', 26 February 1947: Churchill papers, 1/42.
[2] Letter of 16 February 1947: Mary Soames, *Clementine Churchill*, page 416.

responsible. Also over confidence, I always expected that political life would suddenly open up for me.

When I came home after the war I was 34. It was too late to think of a career that would require a lengthy preparation. I had a five year old son & felt the need to earn my living as best I could. Of course I have been improvident, but on the whole I do not think the last 18 months of my life have been wasted. I have travelled a great deal & established connections—particularly in the US—which will be valuable to me all my life. My column has taught me habits of industry I never knew before. And my lecturing has given me invaluable practice in public speaking. I agree that it would be more satisfactory at my age if I had a settled career & position in life. But considering all the circumstances (including the war) I still regard these as the formative years of my life. And I think I have learnt more in the last year than in the previous ten!

I am the last person to try to pretend that my life has been as successful as I had hoped it would be by this time. But looking round among my contemporaries I do not feel entirely discouraged. I have long agreed with you that the friendship of England & America is the hope of the future. Against this background I feel I have some credentials that justify a little optimism. There is no Englishman of my age who knows this country as well as I do or who has so many influential American friends. There is no other Englishman of my age who can get his articles regularly printed in the American Press; and there is no-one else alive of any age (except yourself) who could have had the amazing oratorical success I have had on this present tour. This last I would say to no-one but you, whose name I bear & who has made this possible. But I promise you it is the sober truth.

Of course I know how much you would like me to achieve solid success in your lifetime. But you must realize how improbable that is;—even harder for me than for Duncan.

It happens that I have matured (after a premature blossoming) much later than you did. But though I am far from self-satisfied I have confidence that I will eventually make my mark & carry on the tradition. It's very hard however for two generations to carry the same flag simultaneously!

I know how often I have offended you by my clumsy attempts to stand on my own feet, develop my own personality and make my own way in life. I can only hope that I shall later be a worthier & more satisfactory son than I have been in your lifetime.

Please don't expect too much of me now. Believe instead, I beg you, that I have no other ambition than to be ultimately judged an honourable & faithful son. No day passes but that you are constantly in my thoughts & I am grateful that you think so often of me. Give me your confidence & I shall not fail you.[1]

*   *   *

[1] 'My dearest Papa', 7 February 1947: Churchill papers, 1/47. Two weeks later Randolph telegraphed to his father from Grant's Pass: 'Just leaving here to drive to San Francisco through Redwood Highwood as we did in nineteen twenty nine. Fondest love. Randolph.' (Western Union Cablegram, 22 February 1947: Churchill papers, 1/42.)

Churchill now worked on his war memoirs with little respite. From Professor Goodwin, at Oxford, came comments on Churchill's chapters on the Blitz and the Battle of Britain: he had only a few comments to make on what he called Churchill's 'extremely interesting account'.[1] 'I am devoting all my leisure, such as it is, upon the book,' Churchill wrote to Henry Luce on February 19, 'and I have already more than 600,000 words in print.' Churchill continued: 'I am much amused to see all the rubbish that has been published so far in the United States about our affairs. How easily the documents will blow it all away.' He added: 'Whether I shall live to complete these projects, I cannot tell. . . .'[2]

In writing his memoirs, Churchill had to wend his way between much 'rubbish', conflicting recollections, Anglo-American disagreements and personal accusations. But he was not trying to write a history of the Second World War. Bill Deakin later recalled:

Winston's attitude to the war memoirs was 'this is not history, this is my case'. He made it absolutely clear that it was *his* case he was making. It was an anthology—with his own papers—not a history.

It was extremely difficult *not* to put everyone's case. The difficulty was not how to distort his case (which he did not want to do) but how *not* to distort other people's views—while remaining autobiographical and not writing a history.

Norman Brook saw everything.[3] He used to come down quite often to Chartwell. He was a man of limitless integrity. He was of enormous help. He and I would go through everything in detail. He was the most responsible and most learned witness.

Ismay comes after Norman Brook of those who saw everything. Ismay read everything on the military side. He was frequently at Chartwell and at Hyde Park Gate. He loved Winston with a passion. Winston relied on his judgement. He had no military confidant except Ismay. He would love trying out drafts on people whom he regarded as his friends.[4]

Almost every Friday in January, and every Friday in February, Ismay, Pownall and Deakin dined at Hyde Park Gate: working sessions which nothing was allowed to interrupt.[5] But the session on February 21 was overshadowed by the worsening health of Churchill's brother Jack, six years his junior, who had been ill for some time with a weak heart, and was now struck down again. At one luncheon, after his brother had left the room, Churchill turned to Graham-Dixon

---

[1] 'Dear Mr Churchill', 4 February 1947: Churchill papers, 4/198.

[2] 'My dear Mr Luce', 19 February 1947: Churchill papers, 4/25.

[3] Sir Norman Brook was Secretary of the Cabinet from 1947 to 1962 (he was created Baron in 1963, taking the title Normanbrook).

[4] Sir William Deakin recollections: in conversation with the author, 15 March 1975.

[5] Churchill Engagements Calendar, February 1947: Churchill papers.

with the words: 'My dear Jack, every day washed nearer the reef, at which he glares with undaunted eyes.'[1] 'He may not get through this turn' were Churchill's words to Lord Moran on February 22, and he added: 'Jack may go out with the tide.'[2] On the following day, Jack Churchill died.

'There couldn't have been a more perfect relation between two brothers than yours with him,' wrote Sir Edward Marsh, '& I know what he was in your life. I'm so glad he lived to take part in Mary's wedding.'[3] 'The loss of Jack must be almost the worst thing that has ever happened to you, dear Winston,' wrote Sir Archibald Sinclair.[4] 'I should like you to know,' wrote Harold Macmillan, 'how much anything which saddens you causes the sympathy of all your friends and colleagues.'[5]

During the Second World War, Jack Churchill had dined each night at the Annexe in the mess set up specially for Churchill's Private Secretaries. Two of them were among those who sent their condolences. 'It will never be possible to think of our strangely happy life in the Private Office mess at the Annexe,' wrote John Martin, 'without remembering Jack—his unfailing courage and good humour and the overflowing cheerfulness of a gayer and more genial age.'[6] 'Nobody who knew him could have anything but real affection for him,' wrote Jock Colville; 'indeed I never remember hearing an unpleasant word spoken of him, which is a great deal more than I can say of anybody else I know.'[7]

'Deeply grieved to read of Uncle John's death,' Randolph telegraphed from San Francisco.[8] From Rome, Sarah Churchill wrote to her father:

Darling darling Papa,
    The news of Uncle Jack's death grieves me terribly. Not so much for him, as I feel; indeed he so often said to me, it would be but a blessed relief for him when it came, but for you. I know what it will mean for you—how suddenly terribly lonely you will feel—what a large part of your life—what a host of memories he takes with him. I know you loved him dearly, and he adored you, with a love untinged by any hint of envy of the triumphs, excitement and high destiny of your life. Humorous, gentle & patient—and how

[1] Leslie Graham-Dixon recollections: in conversation with the author, 15 March 1982.
[2] Moran diary, 22 February 1947: *The Struggle for Survival*, page 310.
[3] 'My dear Winston', 24 February 1947: Churchill papers, 1/43. Marsh had first met Jack Churchill in 1905, when he became Churchill's Private Secretary.
[4] 'Dear Winston', 24 February 1947: Churchill papers, 1/43. Like Sir Edward Marsh, Sinclair had known Jack Churchill for more than forty years.
[5] 'My dear Winston', 1 March 1947: Churchill papers, 1/43.
[6] 'Dear Mr Churchill', 24 Feburary 1947: Churchill papers, 1/43.
[7] 'Dear Mr Churchill', 27 February 1947: Churchill papers, 1/43.
[8] Western Union Cablegram, 26 February 1947: Churchill papers, 1/42.

we loved him as children! 'God Save the King' or the 'British Grenadiers'
played on his teeth—seemed to me as a child, the height of artistic achievement!

During the war—when I was ill for a bit—I spent some sick leave with
him in Weymouth. It was there I really got to know him. Please do not be
too sad—well if that is impossible—not too lonely.[1]

At Churchill's wedding in 1908, his best man had been Lord Hugh
Cecil, later Lord Quickswood. In 1908, Cecil and Jack Churchill had
already known each other for a decade. In reply to Cecil's letter of
condolence, Churchill wrote:

I feel lonely now that he is not here, after 67 years of brotherly love. I
remember my father coming in to my bedroom at the Vice Regal Lodge in
Dublin & telling me (aged 5) 'You have a little brother.' We have always
been attached to one another, & after his house was blown up in the war he
lived w me at No. 10 or the Annexe.

He had no fear & little pain. Death seems vy easy at the end of the road.

Do you think we shall be allowed to sleep a long time. I hope so. (Ready
to serve if really required.)

The only thing Jack worried about was England. I told him it wd be all
right.[2]

---

[1] 'My darling Papa', 26 February 1947: Churchill papers, 1/42.
[2] 'My dear Linky', 16 March 1947: Quickswood papers.

17

'Our battered shores'

IN March 1947 a new American Ambassador reached Britain, Lewis ('Lew') Douglas. 'A thousand welcomes to our battered shores,' Churchill wrote, 'to which we know you bring a strong breeze of friendship based on knowledge.' The purpose of Churchill's letter was to invite Douglas to The Other Club, for dinner at the Savoy.[1] This dining club, founded by Churchill and F. E. Smith in 1911, and meeting once a fortnight when Parliament was in session, was Churchill's most regular, and most favoured, rendezvous. Henceforth, Douglas was to be a member. 'I am eternally grateful to you,' Douglas wrote after his first dinner, 'for giving me a glimpse of the delights and gaieties so carefully guarded and fostered by the powers of "Impenetrable Mystery".'[2]

Churchill's most frequent visitor that March and April was Bill Deakin, with whom he worked on his war memoirs. On April 1, his wife's birthday, he saw Deakin in the morning, and attended a cocktail party at the Soviet Embassy in the evening. He had already given a small cocktail party of his own at 28 Hyde Park Gate for the delegates from the Supreme Soviet, led by Vassilli Kuznetzov, President both of the Soviet of Nationalities and the All-Union Central Council of Trade Unions. Also in the delegation, which included several Soviet writers and poets, was Mikhail Suslov, described in the official list as 'Political Worker'.[3] Churchill's British guests included Eden, Woolton and Walter Elliot.[4]

[1] 'My dear Ambassador', 19 March 1947: Churchill papers, 2/54.
[2] 'My dear Mr Churchill', 29 March 1947: Churchill papers, 2/54.
[3] Telegram No. 624 from Moscow to the Foreign Office, 5 March 1947: Churchill papers, 2/57. Suslov was to rise within a decade to considerable prominence. Sir William Hayter, British Ambassador to Moscow from 1953 to 1957, later wrote: 'Suslov was the Party's ideologue. A melancholy, bespectacled, schoolmasterish figure, he was sometimes thought to be the leader of a Stalinist opposition to Khrushchev. But he was too totally devoid of personal magnetism ever to aspire to the leadership, and in fact he supported Khrushchev at the time of the "Anti-Party Plot".' (Sir William Hayter, *A Double Life*, page 119.) It was under Brezhnev's leadership of the Party from 1964 that Suslov obtained his greatest prominence.
[4] 'Telephoned to the Press', 10.15 p.m., 25 March 1947: Churchill papers, 2/57.

Churchill also spoke, in the House of Commons, in favour of the Government's National Service Bill, making all men between the ages of eighteen and twenty-six liable for eighteen months' national service.[1] The Bill, he said, 'has evidently been very carefully shaped and considered. We shall do nothing to endanger its passage into law.' There would be criticisms on points of detail, but the Conservatives would be 'careful' to be present 'in good strength' to support the Government when it came to the vote. He wished, however, to make some points about the past. Though he did not say so, it was a past very much in his mind as he worked each day on the pre-war chapters of his war memoirs.

Speaking of Attlee and A. V. Alexander, Churchill told the House of Commons:

. . . it is certainly an irony of fate that the Prime Minister and the Minister of Defence should be the men to bring a conscription Bill before the House now, after two years of peace, when all our enemies have surrendered unconditionally. Why, these were the very politicians who, four months before the outbreak of the war, led their followers into the Lobby against the principle of compulsory military service, and then had the face to accuse the Conservative Party of being 'guilty men'.

I and a handful of others have a right to criticise and censor the lack of preparation for the late war, but the Prime Minister and his friends have no right to do so; the whole effort of their party was designed to make every preparation for defence of the country and resistance to Hitler so unpopular, that it was politically impossible.

Now, in the long swing of events, the Prime Minister and the Minister of Defence, who refused in May 1939 to vote for conscription against Hitler and Nazism, when that was proposed by Mr Hore-Belisha in Mr Chamberlain's Government, come forward in a time of peace and victory, to ask us to support conscription against some other danger, some other dictatorship, which I do not propose this afternoon precisely to define.

This performance this afternoon encourages me. I do not despair of the party opposite. It is never too late to mend; we all may live and learn, and they may live and learn, but the question is whether, when they have learned, we shall still be alive.

Churchill then turned his retrospective glance to the Liberal Party, to its former leader in the House of Commons, Sir Archibald Sinclair, and its current leader, Clement Davies:

I remember well the day when my right hon. Friend, Sir Archibald Sinclair, who is not with us at the moment, marched his followers into the Lobby,

---

[1] The two exceptions were residents in Northern Ireland (to whom the Bill did not apply) and underground coalminers (exempt for five years).

with the Prime Minister and with the Minister of Defence, to vote 'No' to conscription against Hitler and Nazism in the spring of 1939.

In this world of human error and constant variations, usually of an unexpected character, the Liberal Party can range themselves in party doctrine, few but impeccable. They have no need to recur for safety or vindication to that well-known maxim, or dictum, that 'Consistency is the last resort of feeble and narrow minds'. They are quite entitled to say that they have always been against compulsory service. They were against it before the first world war, and, in spite of some considerable pressure from Mr Lloyd George, they were against it after the first world war.

In the interval many things have changed, but here today the Liberal Party are ready to sacrifice themselves in the constituencies, and face any amount of unpopularity, fearless of by-elections, however they may come, and ready at this juncture to stand firm by the old theme and the old flag.

It is no part of my policy to pick unnecessary quarrels with the right hon. and learned Gentleman the Member for Montgomery and those whom he leads, and I shall, therefore, content myself with paying this well-deserved tribute to their rigid and inflexible consistency.

There was no doubt, Churchill reflected, that the passage of the Bill would help 'to sustain our otherwise fading influence in world affairs', and particularly in the United Nations. 'That influence,' he pointed out, 'is being steadily reduced by the policy of the Government, both at home and abroad.' It was 'remarkable', he added, 'that this curious Administration should step aside from its broad downward path to take this single solitary step towards a more hopeful national policy. We welcome the step all the more because of the contrast in which it throws so much else they have done'; and he added a line from *The Merchant of Venice*:

'So shines a good deed in a naughty world.' [1]

The Conservatives honoured their pledge to vote for the Bill: 152 voted for it and only one against. But opposed to the 241 Labour supporters were 72 Labour MPs who opposed it. The Government immediately announced its intention to reduce the period of National Service from eighteen months to one year. It now appears, Churchill declared in a press statement issued from Chartwell on April 5, that 'rather than have trouble with the "tail" of their Party', the Government had 'cast their policy aside'. This 'naked confession' would be 'deeply injurious to the reputation of the Country at this critical time'. His statement continued: 'This is another example of the policy of 'scuttle" before anything that looks difficult or fierce which has

[1] Speech of 31 March 1947: *Hansard*.

characterized the Socialist Government administration, and which in less than two years has reduced us from our Victory Day to our present confusion and disrepute.'[1]

Speaking at the Albert Hall on April 18, at a meeting of the Primrose League, which his father had founded with a group of Conservative friends in 1883, Churchill referred to the National Service Bill, and the way in which A. V. Alexander 'turned round and ran like a hare', as 'a typical example of the infirmity of purpose and lack of moral courage which degrades the character of the Socialist Government'.[2]

Churchill used his platform at the Albert Hall once more to assert the need for a United Europe, and to support him in his invocation 'Let Europe Arise'.[3] It should, however, be made 'absolutely clear', he said, 'that we shall allow no wedge to be driven between Great Britain and the United States of America, or be led into any course which would mar the growing unity in thought and action, in ideals and purpose, of the English-speaking nations, spread so widely about the globe, but joined together by history and by destiny'.[4]

At a meeting of the Conservative Party Defence Committee on April 18, it was decided that the Conservative Party would vote for eighteen months' National Service. This decision was not universally accepted. 'It is true that the Defence Committee took your view,' Harold Macmillan wrote on April 23, 'but, if I may say so, this was largely under the influence of the very strong lead which you gave from the Chair. Moreover, that Committee is naturally very much swayed by professional considerations.' Macmillan's letter continued:

I feel strongly that it would be a very grave error for the Party to be definitely committed by its leaders to the eighteen months. If some members force a division, that will not hurt us. What matters is that we should place all the responsibility on the Government and keep our position open for the election.

[1] 'Press Notice', 6 p.m., Saturday 5 April 1947: Churchill papers, 2/55.

[2] To Lieutenant-General Sir Gifford Martel, who in 1950 advocated an end to National Service, Churchill wrote: 'I am entirely opposed to departing from compulsory national service. Quite apart from the practical aspect, on which I disagree with you, such a step would be profoundly injurious to our moral position in the world and to our country's safety. I am sorry to see you pressing such views, which only darken Counsel' ('My dear General', 14 April 1951: Churchill papers, 2/115). In 1943 Martel had been head of the British Military Mission in Moscow. During the First World War he had been mentioned in despatches five times.

[3] On the previous day, Duncan Sandys had written to Churchill by way of warning: 'I hear that there is a certain amount of feeling among Conservative back-benchers that they have not been taken sufficiently into your confidence about your United Europe movement and that there is, in consequence, a danger that they may become hostile to it.' Sandys added: 'I think, therefore, that it would be very wise if you could, on some occasion in the near future, tell the Conservative 1922 Committee something about our movement and endeavour to secure their goodwill and support.' ('My dear Winston', 17 April 1947: Churchill papers, 2/22.)

[4] Speech of 18 April 1947, Albert Hall, London: Churchill papers, 5/12.

The Conservative Private Members Committee is to discuss this question on Thursday. It may be that you will decide to listen to their views, without taking part yourself. But, if you think it right to express your own opinion, I hope you will not think it disloyal, if I and others of your colleagues do the same.[1]

Macmillan was supported in his doubts by Robert Hudson, who likewise hoped Churchill would not think it 'disloyal' if he opposed making eighteen months the Party view. The conscription issue, Hudson wrote, 'is bound to play an important part at the next Election, and I think, therefore, it is imperative that the Party as a whole should not incur any avoidable unpopularity'. It was not as though 'by voting for eighteen months now' the Conservatives would in fact 'be able to secure the adoption of that term'.[2]

On April 25 Viscount Montgomery joined in the Conscription controversy with a letter to Sir John Anderson, one of Churchill's most senior Conservative colleagues, in which he wrote that if the National Service Bill were delayed, or hung up, 'we are completely sunk'. Regular recruiting had not yet reached 'the figure we need, nor is it likely to for some time'. Montgomery added: 'I do hope that the Conservative Party will lend a hand and not be too troublesome.'[3]

Anderson sent Montgomery's letter on to Churchill, who replied with alacrity:

Thank you for sending me Montgomery's letter. I think he would do much better to keep clear of politics, of which he knows little, and do his duty as a faithful adviser of the Government. We do not require to be lectured by him, especially when so much of his recent conduct is unexplained.

I have, as you may have heard, carried the Conservative 1922 Committee to the support of the advice which I gave to our Shadow Cabinet. It really might be wise for you to hint to Montgomery that he had much better mind his own business and leave politicians to mind theirs. Reading it again, I think his letter most impudent. Thank you for showing it to me all the same.[4]

Churchill's rebukes to Attlee over the Conscription Bill led to a formidable riposte by Attlee on April 24, when the Prime Minister was speaking to the Scottish Trades Union Congress at St Andrews. In his speech, Attlee called Churchill 'the most disastrous Chancellor of the century', and he added:

It was he that brought us back on the gold standard, which led to the

---

[1] 'Private and Confidential', 'My dear Winston', 23 April 1947: Churchill papers, 2/53.
[2] 'My dear Winston', 23 April 1947: Churchill papers, 2/53.
[3] 'My dear Anderson', 25 April 1947: Churchill papers, 2/53.
[4] 'My dear John', 28 April 1947: Churchill papers, 2/53.

crisis in the coal industry from which we are suffering today. He inflicted untold misery on the people of this country. Of course he did not intend this, but he accepted the advice he got from the Bank of England. He sinned, no doubt in all ignorance, but much of our troubles today can be traced back to that error of ignorance and to his simple trust of others in a field where he had little knowledge.[1]

Churchill, who was at Chartwell when Attlee spoke, was alerted to the contents of the speech by the editor of the *Daily Graphic*.[2] He at once issued a reply, which was widely published. It read, in full:

Mr Attlee described me as 'the most disastrous Chancellor of the century'. Yet during my tenure of that Office in the Conservative Government the cost of living declined by at least 18 points while money wages remained stable. This represented a great benefit to the working people of this country. At the same time the number of men and women in the insured trades rose by nearly 600,000. Within two years under a Socialist Government the rate of unemployment has more than doubled.

Mr Attlee made much play with the figure of 2 million unemployed. I must point out that it was under the Socialist Administration of 1929 which followed the Conservative Government that the number of unemployed first passed 2 million.

Mr Attlee referred to my action in bringing this country back to the Gold Standard in 1925. He says that I acted on advice. Indeed I did, on the advice of a Committee appointed by Lord Snowden, the Chancellor in the Socialist Government in 1924, of which Mr Attlee was himself a member. What did Lord Snowden say about our return to the Gold Standard? On the Second Reading of the Gold Standard Bill he said that while the Government had acted with undue precipitancy he and his Socialist colleagues were in favour of a return to the Gold Standard at the earliest possible moment. Later on in December 1926 Lord Snowden wrote an article in the *Financial Times*, in which he said: 'All the facts therefore do not support the impression that the return to gold has been detrimental to industry. The Bank Rate has not been raised; unemployment has not risen; real wages have not fallen; and the price level has been fairly well maintained.'

So far from causing what Mr Attlee calls 'untold misery' the facts as I have said show that while I was the Conservative Chancellor of the Exchequer the real wages of our workpeople steadily and substantially increased.

The return to the Gold Standard was not the only act of my five years' administration of the Exchequer. Old Age Pensions were brought down from the remote age of 70 to 65, and the Widows' and Orphans' Pensions scheme, which was an entirely new departure, was introduced. A great De-rating Act was passed, enabling factories to be set up, without being deterred by heavy

---

[1] *The Times*, 25 April 1947.
[2] Note by Grace Hamblin, 25 April 1947: Churchill papers, 2/4.

rates, in districts where unemployment was rife. A very large sum of money for those days was provided by me for the establishment of the Electric Grid. A succession of reductions in the rate of Income Tax on earned income to married Income Tax payers with children were secured. And finally the tax on tea, which is a heavy burden to the old, the weak and the poor, was repealed.

Mr Attlee accuses me of attacking the Civil Service. This is utterly untrue, and must be a deliberate distortion. What I said, and what I repeat, is that we have now too many officials compared to the number of wage-earners engaged in productive industry. I have the highest regard for our civil servants, with whom I have worked in many offices and for many years. It is no fault of theirs if they are now made too numerous; it is the fault of this Government, that is constantly heaping upon them fresh tasks, many of which are needless and futile.

The overburdening of our administrative machine is one of the greatest mistakes this Government is making. To describe criticism of this mistake as an attack on the Civil Service is an unworthy misrepresentation.

'Mr Attlee must feel himself very hard pressed,' Churchill ended, 'to have to go back nearly a quarter of a century to find excuses for the mismanagement and blunders of which he evidently feels his Government guilty.' [1]

On May 7, in a further debate on the National Service Bill, now amended to a one-year Conscription term, Churchill attacked Attlee and A. V. Alexander with acerbity:

The party on this side of the House have suffered a great deal from the taunt of 'guilty men', which was made great use of at the Election, and which hon. Gentlemen think they can jeer about today. But nothing I have seen in my Parliamentary experience, and I have a right to speak on this matter, has been equal, in abjectness, in failure of duty to the country, and in failure to stand up for convictions and beliefs, to this sudden *volte-face*, change and scuttle of which the Prime Minister and his Minister of Defence were guilty. They may never be called to account in the future for what they are doing now, but it is perfectly certain that, henceforward, we have no foundation to rest upon in respect of defence.

The title of the Minister of Defence should be changed. He should be called the 'Minister of Defence unless Attacked'. What a lamentable exhibition he has made of himself—one which must be deeply injurious to the reputation which he built up for himself during the war, when he had different leadership. [2]

---

[1] Final draft: Churchill papers, 2/4. Published in full in (for example) the *Birmingham Post*, 28 April 1947.

[2] During Churchill's wartime premiership, A. V. Alexander had been First Lord of the Admiralty.

1. 14 May 1945, Churchill and his wife, followed by their daughter Mary, leave St Paul's Cathedral after the Victory thanksgiving service.

2. 26 May 1945, Churchill in his constituency, with his wife, during the election campaign.

3. 16 July 1945, Churchill in Berlin, visiting the ruins of Hitler's Chancellery, followed by his interpreter, Major Birse.

4. 21 July 1945, Churchill on the saluting stand at the Victory Parade in Berlin. With him are (left to right) Lord Cherwell, Field Marshal Montgomery, General Ismay, Field Marshal Alexander, Lord Moran, Anthony Eden and Clement Attlee.

5. 17 July 1945, Churchill, Truman and Stalin at Potsdam.

6. 26 July 1945, Churchill leaves his wartime rooms at Storey's Gate, known as No. 10 Annexe, to go to Buckingham Palace, to resign as Prime Minister.

7. 15 August 1945, Churchill, Leader of the Opposition, goes to St Margaret's Westminster for the thanksgiving service following the defeat of Japan. On Churchill's right, Anthony Eden; on his left, Clement Attlee and Herbert Morrison.

8. 14 July 1946, Churchill at Metz, cheered by the immense crowds which greeted him on all his European journeys in the immediate post-war years.

9. 8 March 1946, Churchill at Williamsburg, Virginia, with his wife and General Eisenhower, two days after his 'Iron Curtain' speech at Fulton, Missouri.

10. 15 July 1946, Randol
and Mary Churchill with th
father, at the American M
tary Cemetery at Nam
Belgium.

11. January 1948, Churchill, Bill Deakin (behind him) and Sarah Churchill,
arriving at Marrakech, where Churchill was to paint and to work on his war
memoirs.

12. 29 April 1947, Churchill in his study at Chartwell, working on the proofs of his war memoirs.

13. May 1948, Churchill with the Duchess of Kent.

14. January 1950, Churchill and his wife on holiday in Madeira.

15. 9 February 1950, Churchill listens as he is introduced by his son Randolph, during Randolph's election campaign at Devonport.

The Government's change of policy because of seventy or eighty adverse votes by their own Party, was, Churchill said, 'a degradation and disreputability of Government which has rarely been seen in this House', and again he turned his sharp tongue against A. V. Alexander:

I must say I am very sorry for the Minister of Defence. His naked, squalid confession that all design, planning and expert advice were thrown aside, although he had received a 300 majority from the House, of which we contributed 152, lowers his position as Minister of Defence, and I am afraid that he will never be able to retrieve what he has lost.

What confidence can we place in his future statements about the defence of the country when it is quite clear that if 70 or 80 pacifists or 'cryptos', or that breed of degenerate intellectuals who have done so much harm, vote against him he is prepared to run away, abandon all his prepared plans, worked out over months, and produce, in 48 hours, anything that can be rushed out to placate his critics.[1]

Two years had passed since the end of the war in Europe. But its repercussions were continuous. 'Am concerned about Kesselring's death sentence,' Churchill telegraphed to Field Marshal Alexander on May 6, on learning that the Commander-in-Chief of the German forces in Italy had been sentenced to be hanged for war crimes.[2] 'Propose to raise question in Parliament,' Churchill added, and he went on to ask: 'Can you do anything?'[3]

It was Attlee who, a week later, advised Churchill to leave the Kesselring matter in abeyance, as the matter was *sub judice*. Provided, Churchill replied, 'there is a suitable interval between an adverse sentence and the execution of the sentence'. Churchill's letter continued: 'It is in my opinion a matter of public policy whether the process of killing the leaders of the defeated enemy has not now exhausted any usefulness it may have had.'[4]

For Churchill, the one source of unmitigated pleasure on the international scene was the presidency of Harry Truman. On February 21

---

[1] Speech of 7 May 1947: *Hansard*. Among the Labour MPs who were critical of Churchill was James Callaghan. Throughout Churchill's speech, he said, 'we have not heard a single word about the substance of this Amendment'.

[2] Field Marshal Alexander was then Governor-General of Canada. Until May 1945 he had commanded the armies in Italy which were in combat with Kesselring's forces.

[3] Telegram sent 6 May 1947: Churchill papers, 2/83.

[4] 'My dear Prime Minister', 14 May 1947: Churchill papers, 2/83. On 30 June 1947 Attlee wrote to Churchill: 'General Harding has now reported that he has decided to confirm the findings of "Guilty" in the case of Kesselring and also in the cases of von Mackensen and Maeltzer who were connected with Kesselring in the same series of incidents. He has however decided to commute the sentences in all three cases to imprisonment for life. This sentence will be promulgated as soon as possible.' (Letter of 30 June 1947: Churchill papers, 2/83.)

Attlee's Government had made clear to the United States its intention to withdraw from its role as protector of Greece and Turkey within thirty-eight days. All the dangers of which Churchill had spoken at Fulton now loomed, but Truman had responded by taking over the role which Churchill had urged upon him a year earlier, introducing a Bill which was to give legal form to what became known as the Truman Doctrine, that the United States would not realize its objectives unless it was 'willing to help free people to maintain their institutions and their national integrity against aggressive movements that seek to impose upon them totalitarian régimes'. This, the Bill added, 'is no more than a frank recognition that totalitarian régimes imposed on free peoples, by direct or indirect aggression, undermine the foundation of international peace and hence the security of the United States'.

'I cannot resist,' Churchill wrote to Truman on May 12, 'after the year that has passed and all that has happened, writing to tell you how much I admire what you have done for the peace and freedom of the world, since we were together.'[1]

Returning as often as he could to Chartwell, Churchill continued with his war memoirs, painted, and busied himself with the final restoration of his property to its pre-war condition. He had found an ally in this task in his new son-in-law, Christopher Soames, who, having returned from honeymoon, was living in a house which Churchill had specially prepared for the young couple, and agreed to look after the farm for him.[2] On April 22, in the first of many notes for his son-in-law, Churchill set out a plan of action:

It is most important to get the water for the walled garden settled. One or two of the German prisoners should help Whitbread unscrew the pipes which we saw yesterday, and the other Germans can work at your drain in the field. There are about 50 good land drains close up to where the new boiler has been dumped in the front of the house, so a beginning could be made at getting some.

After that I want all the prisoners to quit wood cutting and concentrate on opening up the old lead pipe we walked over yesterday, so that new pipes can be laid alongside, then at the last moment disconnect and pull out the

---

[1] 'Private', 'My dear Harry', 12 May 1947: Churchill papers, 2/158. The Bill was passed on 22 May 1947, when the Truman Doctrine came into effect.

[2] Churchill paid Christopher Soames £400 a year to be in charge of Chartwell Farm. He also had the use of the Farm House free of rent, rates, lighting and heating.

lead. (It would not do for the extension for carrying oil to the swimming-pool—it is not big enough.)

Churchill's note to his son-in-law continued:

I do not know how long it will take the Germans to open up the trench. I fear it will not be possible to do it by Friday as I had hoped. Therefore let us aim at Monday for the change-over. Southon[1] should be asked to send his plumbers then. One, or at the out-side two days should see the whole of the pipes laid, and the Germans filling in as they go.

I wonder whether the bothy roof could not be made water-tight by putting a thatch over the present roof. Thus, all the wet would be kept out by the thatch, and the slates would be an added protection and would not have to be broken up. There must be good thatchers about now and I think it would all look very picturesque. Stevens[2] would I am sure, tell you where to get a good thatcher.[3]

Intent on extending his farming activities, on May 23 Churchill bought Bardogs Farm, Toy's Hill, adjacent to Chartwell Farm, for £8,700. It was 94 acres in extent, with a farmhouse, outbuildings and two cottages, and a further 25½ acres rented out at £30 a year in yearly tenancies.[4] The cost of this purchase had come quite easily out of Churchill's literary earnings.[5] Once more, Christoper Soames undertook to supervise the considerable amount of new work that had now to be done.[6]

Churchill's literary work had prospered. On April 14 *Life* magazine and the *New York Times* had published jointly an article by him entitled 'If I Were an American'. *Life* had also published, during the first four months of 1947, colour photographs of sixteen of Churchill's paintings. At the same time, *Life* had bought the American rights to Churchill's *Secret Session Speeches*.

On April 8 the Publisher of *Life*, Andrew Heiskell, and the General Manager of the *New York Times*, General Julius Ochs Adler, flew to London, where, in negotiations with Lord Camrose, and on April 13

---

[1] Southon, the builder from Edenbridge, had been involved with improvements at Chartwell for more than twenty years.

[2] Stevens, a local farmer.

[3] 'Captain Soames', 22 April 1947: Churchill papers, 1/32.

[4] Churchill papers, 1/34. Churchill later told Leslie Graham-Dixon, in a discussion of a possible Dukedom: 'Duke of Bardogs would sound well, and Randolph could be Marquess of Chartwell.' (Leslie Graham-Dixon recollections: in conversation with the author, 15 March 1982.)

[5] On 16 May 1947 Churchill held £94,330 in Securities (including £19,062 Consolidated Stock and £11,285 Union Corporation): Churchill papers, 1/9. As of 20 June 1947 he held £103,000 of Securities. (Churchill papers, 1/16.)

[6] From 1 January 1948 Churchill raised Soames's salary from £400 to £600 a year 'in view of the considerable increase in acreage now under your supervision'. ('My dear Christopher', 'Private', 1 February 1948: Churchill papers, 1/42.)

with Churchill himself, they achieved agreement in principle on the contract for the war memoirs. That contract was signed on April 23. Two days later, a formal announcement was made in London and New York, stating that Churchill's memoirs were to be serialized in the New Year by *Life*, the *New York Times* and the *Daily Telegraph*. 'The fact that so much of Mr Churchill's work was done by him in writing day by day,' Churchill himself added to the announcement before it was issued, 'invests the writing with exceptional interest'.[1]

It was Walter Graebner who kept the staff of *Life* informed of Churchill's progress on his war memoirs. His first report was sent that April:

Churchill does most of his work in bed either at Chartwell or at 28 Hyde Park Gate. Sometimes he'll work in bed all day up till midnight. If he works out of bed it's always in his siren suit. (I don't think I've seen him out of it more than twice—and one of these times was at his daughter's marriage.) He keeps six secretaries busy; they work in shifts so that someone is on hand 16 hours or more a day, seven days a week. One secretary drives with him to and from the country, as Mr Churchill uses this time to dictate. 'I can do about 1,000 words while motoring to Chartwell—never less than 800,' says Churchill. One of his secretaries told me it was hell to take down the dictation going around some of the Kentish curves.[2]

On May 3 two of Churchill's paintings, 'Winter Sunshine' and 'The Loup River, Alpes Maritimes, 1930', were exhibited at the Royal Academy, of which he was an honorary Academician. Six days later, Churchill left for Paris. He had originally intended to wear his Air Commodore's uniform, which he had so often worn during his wartime travels, but Clementine Churchill was able to dissuade him, her letter a masterpiece of tact and firmness:

Winston,

I would like to persuade you to wear Civilian clothes during your Paris visit. To me, air-force uniform except when worn by the Air Crews is rather bogus. And it is *not* as an Air Commodore that you conquered in the War but in your capacity & power as a Statesman. All the political vicissitudes

---

[1] Announcement of 25 April 1947: Churchill papers, 4/57. Churchill's other literary works also flourished. On April 24, the day after the signature of his war memoirs contract (for a million dollars, the sterling equivalent in 1947 of £250,000), he received £600 for an article in the *Daily Telegraph* on the United States intervention in Greece. On May 9 he received a further £1,000 from Emery Reves on account of the foreign rights of this same article, for which a further £518 reached him in August. On July 15 the first fruits of the British sale of his war memoirs arrived: £5,000 from the *Daily Telegraph*. (Accounts, 24 April to 1 December 1947: Churchill papers, 1/7.)

[2] Letter of April 1947: Robert T. Elson, '*Time Inc.*', *The History of a Publishing Enterprise*, volume 2, pages 214–15.

during the years of Exile qualified you for un-limited & supreme power when you took command of the Nation.

You do not need to wear your medals to shew your prowess. I feel the blue uniform is for you fancy-dress & *I* am proud of my plain Civilian Pig.

Clemmie.[1]

Churchill accepted his wife's advice, instructing his valet: 'I shall wear civilian clothes and take no uniform at all.'[2] Before leaving, Churchill invited to Chartwell, and greeted there, members of the Guinea Pig Club, a club consisting of burnt and disfigured air crews. 'I believe it was the highlight of their visit,' wrote Archibald McIndoe, the plastic surgeon who had done so much to heal their wounds.[3]

On his first night in France, on May 9, Churchill dined with the French Prime Minister, Georges Bidault. Then, on May 10, at a ceremony at the Cour des Invalides, he was presented with the Médaille Militaire, and then, driving to the Arc de Triomphe, laid a wreath on the tomb of the Unknown Warrior. That night he dined with the President of the Republic, Vincent Auriol, at the Elysée Palace.

On May 11, a Sunday, Churchill lunched at Chantilly with Duff and Diana Cooper, before flying from Le Bourget to Northolt, and driving straight to Hyde Park Gate.[4] Three days later, at the Albert Hall, Churchill told a meeting of the United Europe Committee: 'we are here to proclaim our resolve that the spiritual conception of Europe shall not die'. Of the plan of action of the United Europe campaign he declared:

We are not acting in the field of force, but in the domain of opinion. We cannot give orders. We can only persuade. We must go forward, step by step, and I will therefore explain in general terms where we are and what are the first things we have to do. We have now at once to set on foot an organisation in Great Britain to promote the cause of United Europe, and to give this idea the prominence and vitality necessary for it to lay hold of the minds of our fellow countrymen, to such an extent that it will affect their actions and influence the course of national policy.

France and Germany would have to be reconciled; it was by an 'act of faith' on the part of France that this could be done, and it was 'by this act of faith alone that France will regain her historic position in the leadership of Europe'.

---

[1] Note, undated, on Chartwell notepaper: Churchill papers, 2/252.

[2] Note of 29 April 1947 (to Miss Marston, for Greenshields): Churchill papers, 2/252.

[3] Letter of 14 May 1947: Churchill papers, 2/304. Working at East Grinstead, McIndoe and his team had pioneered experimental plastic surgery for wounds and burns. Their work had been particularly supported by Mrs Elaine Blond, one of the daughters of the founder of Marks & Spencer.

[4] 'Programme of Mr Churchill's Visit to Paris', 9–11 May 1947: Churchill papers, 2/252.

During his speech, Churchill answered the criticism that advocacy of a United Europe was nothing but 'a sinister plot' against the Soviet Union:

There is no truth in this. The whole purpose of a united democratic Europe is to give decisive guarantees against aggression. Looking out from the ruins of some of their most famous cities and from amid the cruel devastation of their fairest lands, the Russian people should surely realise how much they stand to gain by the elimination of the causes of war and the fear of war on the European Continent.

The creation of a healthy and contented Europe is the first and truest interest of the Soviet Union. We had therefore hoped that all sincere efforts to promote European agreement and stability would receive, as they deserve, the sympathy and support of Russia. Instead, alas, all this beneficent design has been denounced and viewed with suspicion by the propaganda of the Soviet press and radio.

We have made no retort and I do not propose to do so to-night. But neither could we accept the claim that the veto of a single power, however respected, should bar and prevent a movement necessary to the peace, amity and well-being of so many hundreds of millions of toiling and striving men and women.[1]

On May 15 Churchill was at Ayr, where he spoke to the Unionist Associations in Scotland. Referring to the election defeat of 1945 he told his audience of Party faithful:

It was a shocking misfortune that on the morrow of our victory, after we had rendered services for which the whole world should be grateful, we were suddenly struck down and laid low by the arrival in power of a narrow, bigoted, incapable Socialist faction, who, instead of trying to help the country out of its perils and solve its problems, cared above all for the gratification of their Party dogmas and did not scruple to divide our nation as I have never seen it divided before. This is their offence against the State and people, namely that they have used the power that a misguided electorate gave them—an electorate which for ten years had not had a chance to use the franchise—in an unthinking moment, not to forward the national recovery and revival, but to prove what good Party men they are, and thrust their Socialist doctrines upon our Island in its hour of exhaustion.

Churchill went on to speak of the Labour Government's economic policies and their effect on Britain:

Do not underrate, I warn you—and I have given some warnings before—in any degree the gravity of the economic and financial circumstances and distresses into which we are moving. They will be of a greater intensity and severity than any we have known before. There is no victorious country in the world that is being racketed to pieces in the way we are, and there is no

[1] Speech of 14 May 1947: Churchill papers, 2/18.

country, because of its complicated artificial structure, less capable of surviving such maltreatment.[1]

Returning to the theme of foreign policy, on May 20 Churchill declared: 'War is not inevitable, but it would be inevitable if Britain and the United States were to follow the policy of appeasement and one-sided disarmament which brought about the last war.'[2]

From Scotland, Churchill returned to Chartwell, where, on May 14, he met Denis Kelly, a young barrister who had been chosen to catalogue all his papers. Kelly later recalled:

We sat on the first floor in the drawing-room, and I was entranced by a white chestnut tree in full blossom which towered below us. 'A noble vegetable' he remarked, sipping a very weak whisky and soda, and then descended to the basement, unlocked a couple of doors to a cellar beside the central-heating plant and said with a wave of his arm 'Your task, my boy, is to make Cosmos out of Chaos.'

The place was stacked from floor to ceiling with the black, tin deed-boxes used by old-fashioned Victorian solicitors and on the other side of the furnace was a smaller cellar crammed with copies of his books and still more boxes and box-files.

As I began to explore their contents I realised I was handling the personal papers of a man who had experienced and shaped the history of the world in the last fifty years—school notebooks from the age of nine; letters and despatches from the wars in India, the Sudan, Cuba and South Africa; file upon file about the Dardanelles, the Somme and Czarist Russia; secret telegrams from Roosevelt and Stalin—all entangled with the politics between the two World Wars and private family letters and bank-accounts. Everything had been kept and nothing had been thrown away and all were unique and perishable.

Kelly was shocked to find this archival treasure piled next to the roaring oil furnace by which Chartwell was heated. 'He hated a cold house even in mid-summer,' Kelly recalled, adding that the tin boxes were soon replaced by fire-resistant safes. At the same time, at Kelly's suggestion, vital documents were photographed and put in a bank vault. Then began the task of starting a catalogue of the treasure. Working with a single typist, Miss Gemmell, it took Kelly four months to complete this. From time to time, as cataloguing proceeded, key documents would be sent upstairs for Churchill to study.[3]

The technique which Churchill adopted was to send Bill Deakin,

---

[1] Speech of 15 May 1947: Churchill papers, 2/52. Published in pamphlet form as *Trust the People*, Conservative and Unionist Central Office, London, 1947, No. 3874. There is a recording of this speech in the BBC Written Archives Centre, Library No. 16288.

[2] 'Press Statement', 20 May 1947: Churchill papers, 2/58.

[3] Denis Kelly draft memoirs: Kelly papers. Kelly had been recommended to Churchill by Leslie Graham Dixon, in whose Chambers he was then working.

or one of his other assistants, down to the Muniment Room in the basement at Chartwell, to find the document for which he had asked, and bring it up to him. This process was known at Chartwell as 'rummaging'. Churchill would then use the document, often writing on the document itself, or even cutting it up, as a basis for his narrative. Often a document, removed from its file, would be pinned to a sheet of paper, the unwanted parts of it crossed out or cut out and thrown away, and Churchill then wrote a short introduction on it, often in red, or dictated a longer introductory passage to it, or a linking passage to the next document.

It was not from documents alone that Churchill worked, but from his own memory. This memory was sometimes called upon by his former wartime staff. In an article in the *Daily Telegraph* on April 29, Churchill had written of how, at Potsdam, Stalin had asked for a base on the Aegean, at Dedeagatch or Salonica. As far as the official records of Potsdam were concerned, Jock Colville wrote from the Foreign Office to Miss Gilliatt on May 30, 'we have drawn a blank', and he added: 'Since this statement has aroused a good deal of interest we should indeed be grateful if Mr Churchill could himself throw any light on the matter. I know from experience that Mr Churchill's memory is often a good deal more reliable than official records and it may be that Stalin put forward this claim in a private conversation which was not recorded in the official minutes of the Potsdam meeting.'[1]

Churchill was confident in his assertion of Stalin's request. 'Undoubtedly he said it to me in conversation,' he noted on Colville's letter, 'on our last night together at Potsdam—as an alternative to bases in the Straits. But I cannot think the matter of any consequence.'[2]

On May 20 Attlee and Mountbatten, the new Viceroy of India, saw Churchill and his senior Conservative colleagues, to propose an all-Party accord on the Government's final proposals for Indian independence. These were that India should be partitioned into two States, the predominantly Hindu India and the predominantly Muslim Pakistan, both to be granted Dominion status, and both, after a period of time, free if they wished to declare full independence of the Crown. After having this plan explained to them, Churchill and those who shared Churchill's feelings towards India agreed to accept the Attlee

[1] Letter of 30 May 1947: Churchill papers, 2/57.
[2] Note of 10 June 1947: Churchill papers, 2/57.

and Mountbatten proposal. 'I am in a position to assure you,' Churchill wrote to Attlee on the following day, 'that if those terms are made good, so that there is an effective acceptance of Dominion Status for the several parts of a divided India, the Conservative Party will agree to facilitate the passage this Session of the legislation necessary to confer Dominion status upon such several parts of India.'[1]

Leading Conservative and Labour politicians now worked together for the final act of the severance of India from Imperial rule. On May 22, after a further talk with Mountbatten, Churchill suggested to Attlee that Anthony Eden, Sir John Anderson, Harold Macmillan and 'possibly' Lord Simon should meet Mountbatten to clarify several questions on which Churchill had not been able to answer them in detail. 'None of them,' he added, 'so far as I can judge, will affect, in any way, the decision to which we came, which I communicated to you yesterday.' Churchill added: 'I think it would be a pity if these matters were discussed with any but Privy Councillors, and I have most carefully enjoined secrecy upon all my colleagues. I hope therefore that private Members in my Party will not be consulted at this stage. This advice was very agreeable to Mountbatten.'

Churchill hoped that Attlee would give the Conservatives 'timely notice' before any legislation was introduced, 'so that we can consider how things stand'. His letter ended: 'we are at your service if you should wish, at any time, to see us on this matter, which I hope may go forward on a bi-partisan basis.'[2]

On May 26, with Attlee's approval, Mountbatten saw Sir John Anderson, Lord Salisbury, Harold Macmillan, Anthony Eden and Lord Simon, to explain the details of Attlee's partition plan. With Mountbatten was his Chief of Staff, General Ismay, Churchill's friend and wartime adviser. The Conservatives accepted what they heard. Two days later, Mountbatten left for India.

On June 3, in the House of Commons, Churchill stated that if the conditions of the agreement, and 'a period of Dominion Status with perfect freedom to choose' were fulfilled, as they appeared to be by the Government's India proposals, just announced publicly by Attlee, 'then I say that all parties in this House are equally pledged by the offer and the declaration that we have made, and on these points we can only be well assured by the course of events in the next few weeks and months'. Churchill added:

It is quite true that the agreement of the various parties in India has only been achieved on the basis of partition. I gather that is the foundation.

[1] 'Secret', 'My dear Prime Minister', 21 May 1947: Churchill papers, 2/43.
[2] 'My dear Prime Minister', 22 May 1947: Churchill papers, 2/43.

Nevertheless, after a reasonable period of deliberation and responsibility, should all these parties decide to remain within the British Commonwealth of Nations, the theme of the unity of India will be preserved, and the many nations and States of India may find their unity within the mysterious circle of the British Crown, just as the self-governing Dominions have done for so many years after all other links with the mother country, save those of senti-ment, have been dissolved.

It may, therefore, be that through a form of partition, the unity of India may, none the less, be preserved.

If the hopes 'enshrined' in the new plan were borne out, Churchill ended, 'great credit will indeed be due, not only to the Viceroy but to the Prime Minister who advised His Majesty to appoint him'.[1]

Four weeks later, learning that Attlee intended to call the new Bill for India the 'Indian Independence Bill', Churchill wrote at once to protest. 'The essence of the Mountbatten proposals,' he wrote, 'and the only reason I gave support to them is because they establish the phase of Dominion Status.' Churchill's protest continued:

Dominion Status is not the same as Independence, although it may be freely used to establish Independence. It is not true that a community is independent when its Ministers have in fact taken the Oath of Allegiance to the King. This is a measure of grave constitutional importance and a correct and formal procedure and nomenclature should be observed. The correct title would be, it seems to me, 'The Indian Dominion Bill'.

Churchill was willing, he told Attlee, to support the Bill if it were called either 'The India Bill, 1947' or the 'India Self-Government Bill'.[2] Attlee replied, however, that 'owing to the time factor' no change could be made, and he went on to explain why the Bill was not misnamed, even according to Churchill's concept of Dominion Status. Dominion Prime Ministers, he explained, 'constantly stress the point that they are independent States within the British Com-monwealth'. They bore allegiance to the King, who was 'The King of all the Dominions'. The 'insistence on independence', Attlee added, 'does not touch the point of allegiance, but emphasizes the complete freedom of every member of the Commonwealth from control by any other member'. This, indeed, was in Attlee's view 'a most valuable counter to the demand for independence outside the Commonwealth as it shows that this demand can be satisfied within it'. This was, in fact, 'the meaning of Dominion Status'.[3]

The Indian Independence Bill was presented to the House of Com-mons on July 4. It provided that, as of 15 August 1947, 'HM Govern-

[1] Speech of 3 June 1947: *Hansard*.
[2] 'My dear Prime Minister', 'Copy sent to Mr Eden', 1 July 1947: Churchill papers, 2/43.
[3] 'My dear Churchill', 4 July 1947: Churchill papers, 2/43.

ment in the United Kingdom will have no responsibility for the government of any of the territories now included in British India.' Lord Mountbatten was to be Governor-General both of India, and of Pakistan, whose Prime Ministers would be Jawaharlal Nehru and Mohammed Ali Jinnah respectively. Four days later, Churchill was consulted on a matter of the utmost urgency and sensitivity. In anticipation of the transfer of power in India, fixed for August 15, and the creation on that day of two sovereign states, India and Pakistan, the Muslim leader, Mohammed Ali Jinnah, had insisted that his own position from Independence day should be that of Governor-General of Pakistan, nothing less. Jinnah was willing to see Mountbatten remain Governor-General of India, but not of Pakistan, although four days earlier a dual Governor-Generalship had been envisaged under the Indian Independence Bill, with Jinnah and Nehru as the respective Prime Ministers.

Would the Conservative Party accept this unexpected development? It was to seek immediate acceptance, if possible, that General Ismay, Churchill's closest wartime adviser and now Mountbatten's Chief of Staff, had flown to London. On July 8, at Attlee's urging, Ismay travelled to Chartwell to seek Churchill's approval. That night Ismay's Press Officer, Alan Campbell-Johnson, noted in his diary: 'Any expectations Ismay may have had of a difficult interview with the great man were quickly dispelled.' During his talk with Ismay, Churchill 'stressed in particular', Campbell-Johnson wrote, the 'political value' of Mountbatten's role in the months to come 'in mitigating communal tension, preserving the interests of the Princes and strengthening the ties of sentiment between India and the rest of the Commonwealth'. Campbell-Johnson added:

Ismay, much relieved, came back to London post-haste and told Churchill's Conservative colleagues of the interview and message which was relayed to Delhi immediately. This decisive expression of opinion, combining as it did the great man's breadth of view and immediate grasp of essentials with his ability to relate his exact ideas to perfect logic, set everybody's mind at rest.[1]

On July 31, two weeks before Britain was to divest itself of its rule in India, Jewish terrorists in Palestine hanged two British sergeants, as a reprisal for the hanging of two Jews found guilty of terrorist acts.[2]

---

[1] Alan Campbell-Johnson diary, 8 July 1947: Alan Campbell-Johnson, *Mission with Mountbatten*, London 1951, page 132.
[2] On 4 May 1947, as a result of an attack on Acre prison by members of the Irgun and Stern

Four days later Churchill told a West Country Conservative rally, held at Blenheim Palace:

While we have blithely cast away India and Burma, regardless of what may happen in the near future after our slowly-built-up Empire has passed away, the Socialist Government have at all costs clung on to Palestine. Nearly 100,000 British soldiers have been kept in Palestine, and 30 or 40 millions a year of our hard-earned money has been cast away there.

Our sympathies go out to the British soldiers who have endured these unspeakable outrages with so much fortitude and discipline and who are just kept marking time month after month under most false and painful conditions, waiting for the Government to think of some sort of plan or policy. No British interest is involved in our retention of the Palestine Mandate. For nearly 30 years we have done our best to carry out an honourable and self-imposed task.

A year ago I urged the Government to give notice to the UNO that we could and would bear the burden of insult and injury no longer. But the Ministers only gaped in shameful indecision, and they are only gaping still.

Churchill also recalled, in his Blenheim speech, the hostile reaction to what he had said at Fulton a year and a half earlier:

We are told that it is wrong to divide Europe into two parts and into two systems; but this is not our aim and certainly not our fault.

It is true that an Iron Curtain has descended across Europe, from Stettin on the Baltic to Trieste on the Adriatic. We do not wish the slightest ill to those who dwell on the east of that Iron Curtain, which was never of our making. On the contrary, our prosperity and happiness would rise with theirs.

Let there be sunshine on both sides of the Iron Curtain; and if ever the sunshine should be equal on both sides, the Curtain will be no more. It will vanish away like the mists of morning and melt in the warm light of happy days and cheerful friendship.[1]

On August 15 India received its independence. As Churchill had promised, the Conservative Opposition accepted the final legislation

---

gangs, forty-one Irgun and Stern gang prisoners escaped. Two of the attackers, injured in the attack, were later caught and hanged. On July 12 the Irgun seized two British soldiers, Sergeant Clifford Martin and Sergeant Mervyn Paice. On July 31 their bodies were found hanging in an orange grove. A British officer, cutting them down, was wounded by a booby-trap mine set in the ground under the bodies. Martin and Paice were the fifteenth and sixteenth victims of Jewish terrorism that month. The Jewish Agency for Palestine denounced the killings and appealed to the entire Jewish community of Palestine to report what information they could glean in connection with them. It later emerged that Martin's mother was Jewish.

[1] Speech of 4 August 1947: Randolph S. Churchill (editor), *Europe Unite, Speeches 1947 and 1948 by Winston S. Churchill*, London 1950, pages 106–18. 'Warmest congratulations on Blenheim speech,' Randolph Churchill telegraphed from Monte Carlo, 'which ranks with Fulton and Zurich.' (Telegram, 6 August 1947: Churchill papers, 1/42.)

taking India out of the Empire. The civil war between Hindus and Muslims, which Churchill had so feared, and of which he had warned for more than a decade, broke out with fearsome violence. But Churchill accepted that there could be no going back on what had been decided, and no return by the British to India. Like tens of thousands of Britons, he had only his memories now; his went back to the last decade of the nineteenth century. Then, as a young soldier, he had fought on the North-West Frontier to maintain the security and unity of Empire. It was in India that he had first fallen in love, and had ridden on an elephant through Hyderabad with his girl friend, later Lady Lytton, 'the most beautiful girl I have ever seen'.[1] It was in India that he had played in the winning team in the Inter-Regimental polo tournament. In the years that followed, keenly aware of the poverty and divisions of the sub-Continent, he had sought an active, beneficent British policy to alleviate the plight of the Indian masses. To this end, he had been a vigorous opponent of too swift a transfer of power from British to Indian control in the nineteen-thirties. But if, in regard to India, Churchill had only memories, he had also the knowledge that, in one of the great achievements of the post-war world in Europe—the Marshall Plan—he had been a prime mover. On June 12, in introducing his Plan at a News Conference, General Marshall had declared that it was Churchill's call for a United Europe, in his Zurich speech in September 1946, that had influenced Marshall's belief that the European States could work out their own economic recovery, with financial help from the United States.

---

[1] Letter to his mother, 26 October 1896.

18

Britain, 'The vital link between them all'

O N 11 June 1947 Churchill went into hospital in London for a hernia operation. 'Wake me up soon,' he said to the anaesthetist, 'I've got lots of work to do.'[1] He was operated on by Sir Thomas Dunhill, surgeon to three successive Sovereigns.[2] Two days later, while still in hospital, he received a pleasing report from his archival assistant, Denis Kelly, who had now been working at Chartwell for almost a month. 'Cosmos begins to glimmer in the chaos of the muniment room,' Kelly reported, '& I hope soon to be able to submit some short proposals for your consideration.'[3]

While Churchill remained in hospital, a former member of his Map Room staff, Lieutenant-Commander Frank de Vine Hunt, was preparing a 'Legend' to serve as a ready reference for Churchill when he began once more to write his memoirs. 'He is coming home tomorrow in an ambulance,' Clementine Churchill wrote to de Vine Hunt on June 16, 'and will have to spend another fortnight in bed. He will find the "Legend" by his bedside.' The operation had been 'most successful', she added, 'and I believe that it will give him a new lease of life'.[4]

'Papa is getting on splendidly,' Clementine Churchill telegraphed to Sarah Churchill, who was in Brussels, on June 17, 'and comes home this afternoon. He will be in bed another ten days.'[5]

Returning to Chartwell, Churchill was looked after by Nurse Helen Blake. His first visitor, on his first afternoon at home, was Anthony

[1] As reported by Denis Kelly: in conversation with the author, 26 January 1987.
[2] Surgeon to King George V, Sergeant Surgeon to King George VI and Extra Surgeon to Queen Elizabeth II. Born in 1876 and knighted in 1933, Dunhill died in 1957.
[3] Letter of 13 June 1947: Churchill papers, 2/163.
[4] Letter of 16 June 1947: Churchill papers, 2/150.
[5] Telegram, 17 June 1947: Churchill papers, 1/42.

Eden, followed by Bill Deakin. The pattern of visitors for the next week was dominated by those who were helping him with his memoirs: General Sir Henry Pownall and Commodore G. R. G. Allen on June 19, Bill Deakin again on June 20. Allen had agreed to help on all the naval aspects of the work; a naval officer, he was also an expert on the naval history of both world wars.[1] Other visitors included Lord Beaverbrook, Herbert Morrison, Brendan Bracken and Clement Attlee.[2]

On June 22, while Churchill was still recuperating, the *Daily Telegraph* finally agreed to allow him to extend his war memoirs from the originally envisaged length of four volumes to a total of five volumes.[3] Churchill remained in bed, surrounded by many messages and gifts of goodwill: on June 24 he sent a telegram to Lady Anderson to thank her for 'the delicious wild strawberries and cream which I much enjoyed'.[4]

On June 27 Clement Attlee sent Churchill a book, and a handwritten letter:

My dear Churchill,
I was glad to see you looking so well when I saw you this week. When I was recovering from an operation in 1939, you kindly sent me a volume of your speeches which I read with much appreciation. As a very minor practitioner of an art of which you are an *acknowledged* master, I am sending you this volume, not for reading, but only as a tangible expression of my wishes for your speedy and complete restoration to health.

Yours ever

Clement R. Attlee [5]

On July 1, while Churchill was still forced to remain in bed, Denis Kelly delivered a broadside against the memoir writer's habit of

---

[1] George Roland Gordon Allen had entered the Royal Navy as a Sub-Lieutenant in 1911, at the age of twenty. During his naval service he was awarded the DSO, and created CBE. Known to his friends as 'Peter', he had served at the Battle of Jutland in 1916, and, in the Second World War, as Officer in Charge of the landings in Algeria, Chief of Staff to Admiral Troubridge in the capture of Elba, and Senior Naval Officer at Combined Operations Headquarters (from January 1945). He died in 1980, at the age of eighty-nine.

[2] Churchill Engagements Calendar, June 1947: Churchill papers. Beaverbrook lunched on June 18 and Morrison on June 20. Bracken dined on June 21. Attlee called on the afternoon of June 25.

[3] Churchill papers, 1/28. In the event, the memoirs were to run to six volumes (totalling 4,448 pages).

[4] Telegram, 24 June 1947: Churchill papers, 2/145. Earlier in June, Lady Anderson had written to ask whether her first husband, Ralph Wigram, would appear in his war memoirs, or whether they would begin only after Wigram's death in 1936. When Wigram had died, she recalled, Churchill had written of him as the 'Light in the broken lamp'. (Letter of 4 June 1947: Churchill papers, 2/145.)

[5] 'My dear Churchill', 27 June 1947: Churchill papers, 2/145. In 1937 Attlee had published *The Labour Party in Perspective*.

'rummaging'. The initial cataloguing and indexing of the archive was, Kelly wrote, almost complete; this achievement 'will, however, be wrecked within two months if the process known as "rummaging" is allowed to continue. At the same time I realise that you and your staff's freedom of access to the documents must be unfettered, and I have given some thought as to how these apparently conflicting aims can be reconciled'. Kelly's letter continued:

I propose that the following system be instituted: a small pool of deed boxes should be maintained for your personal use in the study at Chartwell and elsewhere and these boxes should on no account be placed in either of the Muniment Rooms. They should be marked with the letter 'P' (standing for 'pool' or 'personal') and in them can be kept the documents which are in use. After having been perused, pruned or destroyed as the case may be, they should be put into one of the pool boxes which will be clearly marked 'documents for return to Muniment Room'. Whoever is appointed in charge of the Muniment Rooms will then be responsible for ensuring that the document, or what is left of it, is returned to the appropriate box under which it has been catalogued and indexed.[1]

On July 7 Churchill learned from the King's Private Secretary that the King had 'given his consent to the betrothal of Princess Elizabeth to Philip Mountbatten'. A special announcement would be made shortly: 'till then it is a profound secret'.[2] 'The young people have known each other for some years now,' the King replied in answer to Churchill's letter of congratulation, '& it is their happiness which we hope for in their married life.' The King added: 'I am so glad to hear from Mrs Churchill that you are progressing well & that you are about again.'[3]

From Princess Elizabeth came a handwritten letter of thanks for Churchill's good wishes:

Dear Mr Churchill,
    I write to send you my sincere thanks for your kind letter of congratulations on my engagement, which has touched me deeply.
    We are both extremely happy, and Philip and I are quite overwhelmed by the kindness of people who have written sending us their good wishes. It is so nice to know that friends are thinking of one at this important moment in

---

[1] 'Mr Churchill', initialled 'DK', 1 July 1947: Churchill papers, 4/57.
[2] 'Private', Buckingham Palace, 7 July 1947: Churchill papers, 2/148. The public announcement was made on 9 July 1947.
[3] 'My dear Winston', Buckingham Palace, 12 July 1947: Churchill papers, 2/171.

one's life, and I would like to thank you once again for being one of the first who have sent their good wishes.

Yours very sincerely

Elizabeth [1]

'The news,' Churchill wrote to the King, 'has certainly given the keenest pleasure to all classes and the marriage will be an occasion of national rejoicing, standing out all the more against the sombre background of our lives.' [2] Four months later, Churchill invited Lieutenant Philip Mountbatten to lunch at Hyde Park Gate. 'He wanted him to realize how serious it was, marrying the heir to the throne,' Miss Marston later recalled. [3] The idea of the meeting, Prince Philip remembered, had come from his uncle, Lord Mountbatten. [4]

While Churchill was ill, several Conservatives, among them R. A. Butler and Harry Crookshank, were working with Hugh Dalton and several other Labour parliamentarians to construct a new Coalition Government. Their plan was to make Ernest Bevin Prime Minister, by-passing Churchill altogether. 'Mrs Rab Butler, at lunch, told me,' Pierson Dixon noted in his diary on July 21, 'Winston would have a rude awakening when there was a Coalition and he was not the Leader.' [5] But neither Eden nor Macmillan would agree to any such manoeuvre.

Also that July, Butler, Crookshank, Lord Salisbury, Lord Woolton and Oliver Stanley asked the Conservative Chief Whip, James Stuart, to tell Churchill that it was in the best interests of the Party if he retired. Later Stuart recalled wrily: 'None of the others present at our private meeting repeated to him the news which they had so kindly invited me to convey.' [6]

The summer of 1947 saw work on the memoirs reach a high pitch of activity. Commodore Allen had been given the task of finding, in

[1] Letter dated 13 July 1947, Buckingham Palace: Churchill papers, 2/171. Three months later, Princess Elizabeth wrote to Churchill to thank him for his wedding gift, the six-volume *The World Crisis*, published between 1923 and 1931, bound in red morocco and tooled and embossed with gold: 'Dear Mr Churchill, I have today received the beautifully bound volumes of your book, for which I would like to thank you very much indeed. I am so delighted to have them, and I really cannot thank you enough for giving me such a lovely wedding present. I am most touched by your very kind thought and by your good wishes, which I very much appreciate. Yours very sincerely Elizabeth.' (Letter of 13 October 1947, Buckingham Palace: Churchill papers, 2/148.)

[2] 'Sir', Chartwell, 16 July 1947: Churchill papers, 2/171.

[3] Mrs Shillingford recollections: in conversation with the author, 2 July 1987.

[4] Prince Philip recollections: letter to the author, 23 June 1987.

[5] Pierson Dixon diary, 21 July 1947: Pierson Dixon papers.

[6] James Stuart recollections: Viscount Stuart of Findhorn, *Within the Fringe, An Autobiography*, London 1967, pages 145–6.

the Cabinet Office, the answers to Churchill's many minutes of the nine months when he was First Lord of the Admiralty. 'These must have been given to me,' Churchill explained to General Pownall, 'and would have been kept with my papers.'[1]

On August 10 Churchill dined with two of the Americans involved in the publication of his war memoirs, Daniel Longwell and Walter Graebner. 'I gave Longwell a set of the proofs of Books I and II,' Churchill told Lord Camrose, 'and also showed him the great mass of official photographs, of which I have about twenty albums. There are also my own scrap books and many detached photographs. Would it not be best for me to send all this to you and for your people to talk it over with Longwell?'[2] This considerable progress with the war memoirs arose from a rigorous work schedule and the devoted help of advisers, secretaries and, from the Muniment Room, Denis Kelly, who later recalled daily work:

The day began at seven o'clock at night. I had to go straight up to his bedroom because he could hear the taxi arrive and was impatient for the latest proofs from London. A grunted 'Good evening, my dear'; a long silence while he poured over the white rectangular pages and then, five or fifty minutes later: 'See you at dinner.' This was a scramble. He had a manservant who filled his bath, laid out his siren suit, and helped him undress and dress. I had less than twenty minutes to unpack, wash, shave, get into a dinner jacket and be at his elbow for a gulp of tomato-juice or sherry. We did this standing up. No slouching in arm-chairs for cocktails and cigarettes.

We ate at opposite ends of the table each with our copy of the current text. Sherry with the soup; champagne with the main course; port with the cheese; brandy with the coffee; each with our pen and scribbling pad, then back to his study where another table flanked with small china figures of Nelson and Napoleon gave a twenty-mile view in day-time of the Weald of Kent. A woman secretary with the evening's letters. 'Yes.' 'No.' 'Regret.' 'Show again tomorrow.'

Then down to the real work of the evening. Silent typewriter behind us to our right; long, hesitant, brilliant dictation; corrections with red pen; re-type. 'Envelope for the printer. Let me see it.' Initials at the bottom left-hand corner; sealed with a damp sponge from an earthenware bowl. ('You can get cancer by licking stamps.') 'Make sure he gets it by the "Davey Jones"—his nickname for the Godfrey Davis car-hire firm—tomorrow morning' and so to bed.

The first time this happened he stuck out his right arm and said: 'Give me a pull.' Siren-suit in beautiful red, black or electric-blue velvet pulled off; flung himself on the bed with legs outstretched; socks and long-underwear removed; totter to the bathroom, sounds of washing. 'Put out the light, dear

---

[1] 'My dear Henry', 19 July 1947: Churchill papers, 4/198.
[2] 'Private', 'My dear Bill', 11 August 1947: Churchill papers, 4/57. In a letter to his wife, Churchill wrote of Longwell and Graebner: 'They brought as goodwill offerings Cigars, Brandy and a ham and lots of Chocolate for you.'

boy,' and then a twenty-minute discourse on the night's work and the work to come, spoken with false-teeth removed. Rush back to my bedroom to scribble it down and serve it up beautifully typed at the appropriate moment, maybe three weeks later, and so, with difficulty, to sleep.

Breakfast was in one's room. He took sixteen newspapers from *The Times* to the *Daily Worker* and every few minutes the manservant would plonk the one he had finished with on your tray so that by ten o'clock you had read all the news, commented on from every angle, and were ready for the morning's work. This restful process took place in the bedroom adjoining his study, with the budgerigar perched on his head or pecking at the proofs—(his name was Toby and Churchill's papers, which were always held together by metal and cord tags because he hated pins, were normally the subject of his attention. He would peck and nibble till the tag fell out and the bundle slid to the floor)—the ginger cat on his lap and Rufus the poodle asleep across his ankles at the foot of his bed.

The first task was to make a contents-table to give the new volume a structure and proportion; the next was to collect the key documents for each chapter; the third was to compose the linking narrative. Each chapter was drafted, printed, re-drafted and reprinted at least half a dozen times and circulated to a group of experts for criticism and comment. The 'master-text' lay side by side on a slope in the study with the documents on a flat shelf beneath them, and at the far right-hand end was the embryo of the next volume to come.

A chapter was usually between five and eight thousand words; the rule was 'chronology is the key to narrative, but subjects break in'; the commandment:— 'Say what you have to say as clearly as you can and in as few words as possible.' The briefs from the naval, military, air and political experts suffered great slaughter with blue pencil for deletions and red pen for additions to clarify the style and achieve the proportion demanded by the chapter and, once printed, were returned to them for further criticism lest the compression and re-shaping distorted their accuracy.

Lunch was of similar dimensions to dinner and was followed by a walk round the estate. First the goldfish, fed by hand with live maggots sent by post in fibre-packed tins; then down by waterfalls to the lake with the black and red New Zealand swans; up to the farm to scratch the pigs' backs, and then to the German prisoners of war felling a dead oak with enormous pride and enthusiasm as he watched from a camp stool. 'Strange how hard they work for you when you defeated their country.'[1] 'Yes, the Germans are strange people. You can lead them to heaven or hell.' And so to his afternoon sleep while we toiled to give him enough work for the evening and until two o'clock next morning.

Denis Kelly's recollections continued:

Churchill never claimed to be a great author. The most he admitted to me was 'the discovery at school that I had this astonishing gift for writing' but

---

[1] On 30 July 1947 Churchill was given three weeks' notice of the withdrawal from his employ of three German prisoners-of-war, Max Schoeps, Emil Offenhauser and Ewald Oster, 'for repatriation' to Germany. (Churchill papers, 1/32.)

he insisted that it is not enough to collect and establish facts, it is not enough to have them checked, corrected and commented upon by experts. What is of equal and, if you are trying to influence peoples and nations, of supreme importance, is how you present them, and he took immense pains in what he called 'dishing them up'.

The first time I drafted a page of his war memoirs was a humbling and instructive experience. He had asked me to condense an expert's account of the German air-attacks on London in the autumn and winter of 1940—the Blitz.[1] The expert's version ran to over one hundred and fifty printed pages and after ten days' effort I managed to reduce it to the three typewritten sheets he required. They seemed quite good till I sat beside him and he pulled out his red pen and slowly and patiently corrected what I had written. My sloppy, verbose sentences disappeared. Each paragraph was tightened and clarified, and their true meaning suddenly stood out.

It was like watching a skilful topiarist restoring a neglected and untidy garden-figure to its true shape and proportions. In the middle of this penitential process he gently turned to me and said: 'I hope you don't mind my doing this?' 'Sir,' I answered, 'I'm getting a free lesson in writing English.' He was visibly moved and from then on we worked in harness. I could at least help by weeding the garden and cleaning the vegetables and the Master Chef knew I would never be offended if he told me to throw them away and start all over again.

The number of those enlisted to help with the war memoirs was considerable. As Denis Kelly later wrote:

There was Mr Wood, the proof-reader. He had spent most of his life proof-reading for Harrap, the publishers who had produced *Marlborough, His Life and Times*, and though long retired, had a ruthless eye for misprints and inconsistencies. He was the same age as Churchill, never smoked or drank, and was so slightly-built that on Mafeking Night the crowd had swept him from Trafalgar Square to St Paul's Cathedral without his feet touching the ground. His presence was dictated by a printer's error which was almost as gross as the famous newspaper account of Queen Victoria 'pissing over Clifton Suspension Bridge to the cheers of her loyal subjects'. In an early volume of his war memoirs Churchill had written: 'The French Army was the *prop* of the French nation.' The printers and publishers produced it as: 'The French Army was the *poop* of the French nation.'

I spotted it at midnight in page-proof and could hardly believe my eyes. It was too near the truth to let it go and the first copies were already coming off the presses. What to do? A very angry telephone message exploded from the author and 'errata slips' had to be inserted in the offending copies—which should now be bibliophiles' treasures.

Thereafter, Mr Wood was an essential member of the team and no error escaped his eye. If Molotov was spelt with a 'v' at page 27 and with an 'f' at page 298, Mr Wood would point it out and ask which was correct. The same

---

[1] This was the account prepared for Churchill by Professor Goodwin.

if a strategic place was mentioned in the text and not on the accompanying map. 'Indefatigable, interminable, intolerable' he might sometimes be, as the author once irritably remarked when overhearing a long telephone discussion between Mr Wood and myself about some obscure problem of punctuation, but by the time he died no fewer—(Mr Wood would have immediately corrected me if I had written 'no less')—than ten volumes had passed through his hands with scarcely a blemish in spelling, syntax or punctuation. He and Sir Edward Marsh had frequent disagreements on this subject—which is often a matter of taste and personal preference rather than strict grammatical rules—but these were usually resolved by Fowler's *Modern English Usage* or by consulting the practices of Gibbon, Macaulay and Carlyle.

Then there was the General—Sir Henry Pownall—and the Royal Navy in the person of Commodore G. R. G. Allen, affectionately referred to in marginal queries as 'Gen P' and 'Comm A'. Churchill was not physically present at the great naval battles and only on the fringe of the Allied advance in Italy in 1944 and the crossing of the Rhine in 1945, and although much could be gleaned from the telegrams sent and received at the time, the reader needed a clear and reliable account based on the latest post-war information.

The briefs of Pownall and Allen filled the gap. Sometimes, of course, they were couched in somewhat technical language and fuller than space allowed—'Dear Comm A can't bear a single one of his ships going to the bottom without it going into my book'—but this was remedied.

Next followed the briefs on specialised subjects—the 'conventional' war in the skies—(Air Chief Marshal Sir Guy Garrod)—and the secret Intelligence battles—(Professor R. V. Jones, Duncan Sandys, Lord Cherwell and many others)—who like all good specialists had vigorous disagreements between themselves, and it was during one of these controversies about who should get credit for doing what that I made some remark about the unfairness of life and received one of the best pieces of advice I have ever had. 'My dear boy,' said 'The Prof', i.e. Lord Cherwell, 'never forget that the object of a Public School education is to teach you at an early age the essential injustice of life.' [1]

Heading Churchill's team as it grappled with myriad past events was Bill Deakin, quiet, self-effacing, devoted to his task and to his master. 'I work all day & night at the book with Bill D,' Churchill wrote to Clementine Churchill, who was on holiday in France, on August 11, 'and it is bounding ahead. I must get the decks cleared for the ensuing battle.' [2]

There was one brief moment of unexpected relaxation, or sport, on August 7, when Churchill joined Christopher Soames for a rabbit shoot. Churchill's detective, Ronald Golding, later recalled:

[1] Denis Kelly recollections: Kelly papers.

[2] 'My darling one', 11 August 1947: Spencer-Churchill papers. Bill Deakin was with Churchill fourteen times between May and August 1947; from May 2 to 4, May 17 to 19, May 23 to 24, May 30 to 31, June 7 to 8, June 17, June 20, June 27, July 5 to 7, July 10 to 11, July 13 to 15, August 6, August 15 and August 26. (Churchill Engagements Calendar, May to August 1947: Churchill papers.)

I remember during wheat harvesting, Mr Churchill's farm manager and others were prepared for rabbit shooting. They had gone the whole morning without bagging a rabbit. About noon, I drove WSC up in a Jeep, by which Mr Churchill always used to get round the farm. We stopped at a field which was almost harvested, with just a small square of wheat in the middle.

Mr Churchill clambered slowly out of the Jeep—he was about 73 years old at the time. Just as he got his feet on the ground there was a shout from the others and a rabbit darted from the centre of the field. In a flash Mr Churchill raised his gun and fired one barrel. The rabbit keeled over dead. It was a wonderful shot, and the usual Churchill luck. The others had been waiting hours for the opportunity.[1]

'In one minute I shot one rabbit with one shot—the first I have fired in nine years!' Churchill reported to his wife four days later. Now he was off to supervise the tidying up of Bardogs Farm, commenting: 'Never did so small a farm harbour such masses of manure.' Churchill also told his wife of a young Labour MP, Raymond Blackburn, who had brought his 73-year-old father down to Chartwell to luncheon. 'He amused me vy much,' Churchill wrote. 'His medical advice for long life is plenty of Champagne & cigars.'

Always anxious, indeed desperate, to see his wife's health improve, Churchill ended his letter of August 11: 'Cast care aside. What we may have to face cannot be worse than all we have crashed through together. I send you my fondest love. You are ever in my thoughts.'[2]

In the autumn of 1947, the Labour Government's intention to nationalize the steel industry seemed to Churchill to offer a focal point for combined Conservative and Liberal action. As he explained to Lord Woolton on August 11: 'The Liberal Party are whole-heartedly with us in our defence of the liberties of the working classes from Socialist serfdom.' That day's *News Chronicle* leading article 'shows clearly that they will oppose the nationalization of steel. In my opinion all this will come to an issue in 1948, and it is my belief that we shall all be together in one line against this vile faction. I hope therefore you will continue to do everything in your power to promote unity of action with the Liberals on the basis of an Independent Liberal Party.' On this being achieved, Churchill added, 'depends the future revival of Britain'. 'Let nothing be done,' Churchill ended, 'to rebuff the growing association.'[3]

[1] Ronald Golding recollections: *Finest Hour*, the Journal of the International Churchill Society, Winter 1981, Number 34.
[2] 'My darling one', 11 August 1947: Baroness Spencer-Churchill papers.
[3] 'Private and Confidential', 'My dear Fred', 11 August 1947: Churchill papers, 2/64.

Writing to his wife on August 13, Churchill sent an amalgam of personal and political news, including that of 'the Mule'—their daughter Sarah—and Julian Sandys, their ten-year-old grandson:

My darling one,

We had a flare-up about the Government's demanding a blank cheque. I send you a few cuttings in case you are not receiving the English papers. I propose to broadcast Saturday night, in a tone of which you will, I think, approve.

It is delicious here. I have just been bathing with Mary and Christopher and Julian. Six new cows have arrived which Christopher bought. They look very fine and will replace the Marnham contingent when it leaves at the end of next month.

Bennie and his new wife came down here yesterday and spent the whole afternoon going round the farm.[1] She is charming and he as sunlit as ever. They were very disappointed you were not here, but he just rang up in the morning and was off to Ireland the next day.

The Marlborough medal has arrived from General Whitaker.[2] It was presented by Queen Anne to him and is probably the only one struck. It is a most magnificent and valuable treasure. I am wearing it at present at the other end of my watch chain.

Everything here is pretty grim and poor little Attlee is hard-pressed. I have no feelings of unfriendliness towards him. Aneurin Bevan is making the running to gain power by extreme left-wing politics. If this proves true, we must certainly expect a political crisis, in addition to the economic collapse, which is worse than ever, and for which the Government have no plan. We had vehement Liberal support against the 'Dictator Bill', including even Samuel, and from the Socialist side, Raymond Blackburn, who I think is going to leave them,[3] and Victor Gollancz.[4] Perhaps you saw his letter in *The Times*. However the House of Lords have decided to meet every three weeks and they have the power to annul any Regulation which the Government decree. Moreover Regulations are not protected, as is Legislation, by

---

[1] 'Bendor', 2nd Duke of Westminster (a friend of Churchill for half a century), and his fourth wife, Anne Winifred Sullivan, whom he had married on 7 February 1947.

[2] Major-General Sir John Whitaker, 2nd Baronet, who had commanded the 7th Guards Brigade in France and Belgium at the outbreak of the Second World War, and was subsequently Director of Military Training, War Office. His son Ben Whitaker was Labour MP for Hampstead from 1966 to 1970, when he was a Junior Minister in Harold Wilson's Labour Government.

[3] Captain Raymond Blackburn had been elected Labour MP for King's Norton in 1945, at the age of thirty. A barrister, and author of a book on the problems and rights of soldiers. Re-elected for Northfield, 1950. Member of the Parliamentary Labour Party group on external affairs. In 1951 he left the Labour Party and became an Independent. He did not stand for Parliament again.

[4] On 4 April 1948 Churchill wrote to General Marshall: 'Mr Victor Gollancz is a well-known publisher of Left-Wing literature and of books against the Conservative Party. He is also a prominent Socialist who has been working cordially with me in our All-Party Organization of the United Europe Movement of wh he is a Vice President, and he has vigorously championed its cause. He puts these questions far above our serious Party differences. In this, as in the treatment of Germany, he has the root of the matter in him.' (Churchill papers, 2/20.)

the Parliament Act. Of course these powers will not be used by us except in extreme cases, but it is a satisfaction to feel that we are not at their mercy.

The harvest is proceeding with tremendous vigour and in perfect weather. Most of the fields are already cut and stooked and some have been put up on tripods. Christopher is very good and at it all day long. The lettuces in the walled garden were sold for £200 though they cost only £50 to grow. Thus it may be that the garden will pay its expenses and even be a contributor to the farm. The Smiths seem very pleased.[1] The hot-houses are dripping with long cucumbers. The grapes are turning black and a continuous stream of peaches and nectarines go to London. I have one a day myself—'le droit du seigneur'.

The book advances rapidly and I do not doubt I shall be free of the first portion, namely till December 31, 1940, by the end of October. It is very necessary to clear the decks as I am sure considerable events impend.

The Mule has promised to come and stay with me for a day or two. I expect her Hollywood film plans will have come to an end through the Government tax on American films. It seems to have been done in the worst possible way—so as to cause the utmost irritation in America and procure a minimum dollar relief for the British nation. They really are awful fools.

Juliet is coming to luncheon on Saturday.[2] Christopher has heard from Lord de L'Isle,—very civil but in a negative sense. He has been philosophical about it. After all one cannot expect plums to drop absolutely ripe into one's mouth and I dare say there are half a dozen people with long, local attachments, in this highly developed constituency.

'Darling,' Churchill added later by hand, 'I have just heard that you are returning 17th instead of 25th. How lovely! I send this to Reims on the chance of catching you. You will find everything bright & happy here. Always yr devoted, W.'[3]

On August 16 Churchill made the Party Political Broadcast of which he was so sure his wife would approve. He began by speaking of his 'grief at the plight into which our country is falling'. The choice which lay before Britain was 'between a system of competitive selection and a system of compulsion':

There is no easy or pleasant road. It will be uphill all the way. But I am sure that it is only by personal effort, free enterprise and ingenuity, with all its risks and failures, with all its unequal prizes and rewards, that anything like forty-seven millions of people can keep themselves alive in this small island, dependent as it is for half its food on selling high-quality goods and rendering necessary services to the rest of mankind.

[1] The Smiths lived at Frenchstreet Farm, Churchill's small market garden. They would sometimes bring the peaches over to Chartwell for his breakfast.

[2] Lady Juliet Duff, only daughter of the 4th Earl of Lonsdale. In 1903 she married Robert Duff of Vaynol Park, Bangor, who was killed in action on 16 October 1914, three weeks after succeeding his father as 2nd Baronet. In 1914 Lady Juliet Duff married Major Keith Trevor, MC. After their marriage was dissolved in 1926, she resumed her former name of Lady Juliet Duff. She died in September 1965.

[3] Letter of 13 August 1947: Spencer-Churchill papers.

I am sure that industrial compulsion and all that follows from it adopted as a peace-time system will result in an ever-diminishing standard of production, standard of living and respect for law; and in an ever-increasing army of officials fastened on the top of us all.

The only path to safety is to liberate the energies and genius of the nation, and let them have their full fruition.

Churchill then recalled his earlier views, and their consistency:

It is forty-one years since, as a young Liberal Minister in Mr Asquith's Government, arguing against this same Socialist fallacy, I said: 'The existing organisation of society is driven by one mainspring—competitive selection. It may be a very imperfect organisation of society, but it is all that we have got between us and barbarism.' I should now have to add, totalitarianism, which indeed is only state-organised barbarism.

'It is all we have been able to create,' I said in days before most of you were born, 'through un-numbered centuries of effort and sacrifice. It is a whole treasure which past generations have been able to secure and to bequeath. Moreover, this system is one which offers an almost indefinite capacity for improvement. We may progressively eliminate the evils—we may progressively augment the good which it contains. I do not want to see impaired the vigour of competition, but we can do much to mitigate the consequences of failure. We want to draw a line below which we will not allow persons to live and labour yet above which they may compete with all the strength of their manhood. We want to have free competition upwards—we decline to allow free competition to run downwards.'

That was my faith as I expressed it more than forty years ago in the same words, and it is my faith to-night. And if there were any country in the world to which these truths apply, it would be to our British Island.

I warn you solemnly, if you submit yourselves to the totalitarian compulsion and regimentation of our national life and labour, there lies before you an almost measureless prospect of misery and tribulation of which a lower standard of living will be the first result, hunger the second, and a dispersal or death of a large proportion of our population the third.

You have not always listened to my warnings. Before the war, you did not. Please pay good attention to this now.[1]

'God bless you,' Lord Altrincham wrote to his former political chief, 'your broadcast last night gave us all a sense of deliverance.' To feel that 'the old pilot' was at hand again was 'manna in the wilderness'.[2] 'I thought your broadcast last night was quite excellent,' wrote Field

---

[1] Party Political Broadcast, 16 August 1947: Randolph S. Churchill (editor), *Europe Unite*, pages 129–34. Recording: BBC Written Archives Centre, Library No. LP 10674.

[2] 'My dear Winston', 17 August 1947: Churchill papers, 2/145. As Sir Edward Grigg, Lord Altrincham had been Joint Parliamentary Under-Secretary of State for War (1940–42) and Minister Resident in the Middle East (1944–45).

Marshal Montgomery, 'balanced, fair, and putting the issue very squarely. I felt I would like to tell this to my old war time chief.' [1]

'It sounded to us out here,' Colonel A. R. Wise wrote from the British Army of Occupation on the Rhine, 'that it was an announcement of the turning point in the battle against Socialism—that the Party had at last reorganised and was ready to take the offensive once more.' [2]

'Congratulations on your speeches and your broadcast,' Sir Edward Marsh wrote from Norfolk, and he added, of the war memoir drafts: 'These admirable chapters have been a delightful occupation on my visit. . . .' [3]

In the last weeks of August, Randolph Churchill prepared to leave on a journey to Australia, New Zealand and Japan. On August 23 Churchill wrote a letter of introduction for his son to General Mac-Arthur. After stating that Randolph had his 'entire confidence', Churchill went on to tell MacArthur with what 'interest and sympathy' he had followed MacArthur's policy and administration in post-war Japan. His letter continued:

In spite of what happened in the war, I have a regard for the Japanese nation and have pondered upon their long, romantic history. To visit Japan is one of my remaining ambitions; but I can hardly hope it will be fulfilled. I am so glad you have been able to raise them up from the pit into which they had been thrown by the military castes, who only had a part of the facts before them. They ought to be our friends in the future, and I feel this wish has been a key to many of your important decisions.

'It would have been very easy to prevent the last war,' Churchill reflected, 'but it is not so easy to cope with the future. The peace and freedom-loving nations must not make exactly the same mistake again. That would be too hard.' [4]

On August 30 Harold Macmillan visited Churchill at Chartwell.

[1] 'Dear Mr Churchill', 17 August 1947: Churchill papers, 2/143.
[2] 'Dear Churchill', 18 August 1947: Churchill papers, 2/54. Wise, elected to Parliament as a Conservative in 1931, had been defeated in the General Election of 1945.
[3] Letter of 18 August 1947: Churchill papers, 4/127.
[4] 'Private and Confidential', 'My dear General MacArthur', 23 August 1947: Churchill papers, 2/153. Churchill also wrote to MacArthur: 'I often think of Lumsden, my Lieutenant-General whom I sent to you, and who lost his life while on your staff. As Colonel of the 12th Lancers he brought the Armoured car into fashion in the disastrous battle we had to fight on the French left before Dunkirk.'

'At present we can only "watch and pray",' Macmillan wrote on the following day. 'But I feel sure that we shall have our chance soon. I hope not too soon.'[1]

Throughout September, Churchill worked on his memoirs, but he took the opportunity of Lew Douglas's return to America on leave to send a handwritten message to Truman, in which he referred to the Marshall Plan which was already, under the guidance of General Marshall, bringing much-needed aid to still war-damaged Europe:

My dear Harry,

As our friend Lew Douglas is going home for a spell, I cannot resist sending by his hand a few lines to tell you how much I admire the policy into wh you have guided yr gt country; and to thank you from the bottom of my heart for all you are doing to save the world from Famine and War. I wish indeed I cd come over & see you & many other friends in the Great Republic. The political situation here requires constant presence. I think there is no doubt that if there were a General Election, the Conservatives wd be returned by a majority. That is however the reason why an Election is unlikely.

You have my warmest good wishes in yr memorable discharge of yr tremendous office, and you can be sure that all the strongest forces in Britain are & will be at yr side if trouble comes.[2]

Replying in his own hand, Truman told Churchill:

The world is facing serious problems and it has been my lot to have to make decisions on a great many of them. Our Russian 'friends' seem most ungrateful for the contribution which your great country and mine made to save them. I sometimes think perhaps we made a mistake—and then I remember Hitler. He had no heart at all. I believe that Joe Stalin has one but the Polit Bureau won't let him use it.

Vyshinsky has assured my re-election I think,[3] although the voters would do me a very great favor if they retired me. No one man can carry the burden of the Presidency and do it right. But I have a good team now.

---

[1] 'My dear Winston', 1 September 1947: Churchill papers, 2/57.

[2] Letter dated 24 September 1947: Harry S. Truman papers.

[3] On 2 October 1947, at the United Nations in New York, Andrei Vyshinsky had urged Russia's veto against the applications of Italy and Finland for membership of the United Nations. On 3 October 1947 *The Times* reported that Vyshinsky had declined an invitation to take part in a radio discussion with Eleanor Roosevelt 'on his recent United Nations resolution' on American 'warmongering'. Three days later, in a speech at the United Nations, Vyshinsky had 'contemptuously rejected' (according to *The Times* on the following day) a compromise proposal by the United States to leave out all references in the United Nations resolution on Greece to Bulgarian, Yugoslav and Albanian complicity in the Greek civil war. Vyshinsky had also said, of Churchill and Greece in 1944: 'By inviting British troops, the Greek Government had violated its country's constitution, and if some delegates regarded Mr Churchill's order to fire on Greek Communists in 1944 as legitimate assistance to a legal Government, he regarded it as an illegal intervention.'

Your Fulton speech becomes more nearly a prophecy every day. I hope conditions will warrant your paying us another visit. I certainly enjoyed your stay here immensely.

You are very kind to me, and I think give me too much credit. But I like it—particularly from you.

May you continue to enjoy health and happiness and a long life—the world needs you now as badly as ever.[1]

The Fulton speech was also on Churchill's mind. In a speech which he recorded in London, to be broadcast at a public dinner in New York in memory of Governor Al Smith, Churchill declared:

We have travelled a long way in opinion since I spoke at Fulton under the auspices of the President eighteen months ago, and many things which were startling or disputable then have now become the foundation of dominant Anglo-American thought.

During all this time the Soviet Government have poured out, through their radio in twenty-six languages, and in all the speeches made on their behalf, an unceasing stream of abuse upon the Western World, and they have accompanied this virulent propaganda by every action which could prevent the world settling down into a durable peace or the United Nations Organization playing its part as a great world instrument to prevent war. Indeed the Conferences at Lake Success—perhaps prematurely named— have become a forum in which reproaches and insults are hurled at each other by the greatest States, hurled at each other for all mankind to hear if they care to listen. But some of them are getting tired.

Churchill then reiterated his view that he did not think the Soviet Union's 'violently aggressive' line was a prelude to war. 'If their minds were set on war,' he said, 'I cannot believe that they would not lull the easy-going democracies into a false sense of security.' Hitler had been a 'master' of this, 'and always, before or during some act of aggression, he uttered soothing words or made non-aggression pacts'. The reason for the violent Soviet language was, he believed, internal, deriving from 'the fourteen men in the Kremlin who rule with despotic power':

If there are only fourteen men, all eyeing one another and deeply conscious of the enormous populations they hold in chains of mind and spirit enforced by terror, it may well be that they think it pays them and helps them to perpetuate their rule by representing to the otherwise blind-folded masses of the brave and good-hearted Russian people, that the Soviet Government stands between them and a repetition of the horror of invasion which they withstood when it came so manfully.

'I devoutly hope,' Churchill added, 'that this view of mine may prove

[1] 'My dear Winston', The White House, Washington, 14 October 1947: Churchill papers, 2/158.

correct.' But the United States and the Western democracies of Europe 'would fail to profit by the hard experiences they had undergone', he added, 'if they did not take every measure of prudent, defensive preparation which is open to them'. His speech ended:

There is no doubt whatever that the Government and the overwhelming mass of the British people, at home and throughout our Commonwealth, if any great issue should arise affecting human freedom, would act with the United States in the same solidarity and fraternal intimacy which has, so lately, given us victory against the combined dictatorships of Germany, Italy and Japan.

I believe that Britain will rise again with even higher influence in the world than she now exercises. I work for the revival of a United Europe. I am sure that the English-speaking world can weather all the storms that blow, and that above all these a world instrument, in Al Smith's words 'to weld the democracies together', can be erected, which will be all-powerful, so long as it is founded on freedom, justice and mercy—and is well armed.[1]

In the last week of September 1947, Churchill began work on the speech which he was to deliver at the Annual Conference of the Conservative Party, to be held in Brighton at the beginning of October. Notes for some of his points, particularly those concerning the Labour Party's economic policy, and the Conservative proposals, were provided for him by Reginald Maudling, a member of the Conservative Party Secretariat.

Churchill had been warned, not only that the speech would be televised, but that the lights would be particularly bright. 'Mr Maudling is finding out for me if the things are as beastly as they sound,' he noted nine days before his speech.[2] That day, Maudling wrote to put his mind at rest: no light would shine into Churchill's face, and there would be no flashes of any kind. 'It might perhaps be wise,' Maudling added, 'to have your notes typed on paper that is matt, as you might get a reflection from the lights from a very smooth surface.'[3]

Before going to Brighton for the Conservative Party Conference, Churchill spoke in his constituency, referring bitterly to the civil war which was then raging in India, where hundreds of thousands of Hindus and Muslims had been killed in savage fighting between the two communities. After reminding his constituents of the warnings which he had given between 1931 and 1935, he added:

[1] Broadcast of 14 October 1947: Randolph S. Churchill (editor), *Europe Unite*, pages 162–6.
[2] Note of 25 September 1947: Churchill papers, 2/59.
[3] 'Dear Mr Churchill', 25 September 1947: Churchill papers, 2/59.

We are of course only at the beginning of these horrors and butcheries, perpetrated upon one another, men, women and children, with the ferocity of cannibals, by races gifted with capacities for the highest culture and who had for generations dwelt side by side in general peace under the broad, tolerant and impartial rule of the British Crown and Parliament. I cannot doubt but that the future will witness a vast abridgement of the population throughout what has, for 60 or 70 years, been the most peaceful part of the world, and that, at the same time, there will come a retrogression of civilization throughout these enormous regions, constituting one of the most melancholy tragedies Asia has ever known.[1]

From Sir James Grigg came a letter of praise, and a question of 'how we can ever recover morally from what we have done in India'.[2]

'I am too grieved with what is happening in India to write more,' Churchill explained to Lord Mountbatten a month later. 'But you always have my good wishes & my admiration for your achievements.'[3]

On October 4 Churchill spoke at Brighton. 'In the present circumstances,' he told his fellow Party members, 'when the consequences of Socialist spite, folly and blundering are about to fall upon every home and business in ever-sharper forms, we can safely say that time is on our side. It does not rest with us when a General Election will take place; but it is quite certain that we should be most imprudent not to be ready for one at any time this year or next.'

Referring again to India, where the civil war continued from day to day with undiminished fury, he spoke of how 'the Socialist Government on gaining power threw themselves into the task of destroying our long-built-up and splendid structure in the East with zeal and gusto, and they certainly have brought widespread ruin, misery and bloodshed upon the Indian masses to an extent no man can measure, by the methods with which they have handled the problem'.

Turning to domestic politics, Churchill castigated the Labour Government. The nationalization of industries, he warned, 'will not make them profitable to the country or satisfactory to the workers'. Speaking of Attlee and Morrison, he declared:

Look at these unhappy men. Two years ago they romped into office as if it was part of our Victory joy-day. Now they are found out, with all their vain assurances. They are exposed. They are in the grim and disagreeable position of having promised blessings and given burdens, of having promised prosperity and given misery, of having promised to abolish poverty and only abolished wealth, of having vaunted their new world and only wrecked the old.

---

[1] Speech of 27 September 1947: Randolph S. Churchill (editor), *Europe Unite*, pages 141–6.
[2] 'My dear Winston', 28 September 1947: Churchill papers, 2/54.
[3] 'My dear Dickie', 'Private', 21 November 1947: Churchill papers, 2/43.

Churchill's final appeal was for the triple combination of the British Commonwealth, the European Union, and 'fraternal association' with the United States: with Britain 'the vital link between them all'.[1]

[1] Speech of 4 October 1947: Randolph S. Churchill (editor), *Europe Unite*, pages 147–61. Recording: BBC Written Archives Centre, Library No. 11178–9.

19

'Grinding and gnawing peace'

WORKING steadily on the first two volumes of his memoirs, Churchill sought advice from, and sent his draft chapters to, those participants in the events he was describing whom he had known, or for whose recollections he felt the need. Replying to Paul Reynaud, the Prime Minister of France during the dark days of June 1940, to whom he had sent the chapter on the fall of France, Churchill thanked him for 'your responsible and concrete comments', which were 'most valuable to me'.[1]

During October, Churchill sent Desmond Morton a copy of the reference which he wished to make of their pre-war association. 'In your letter,' Morton replied, 'you are good enough to say that you think I helped our country. It certainly was my hope and desire, but unfortunately those in power then would not listen to me. Nevertheless I am more than happy to feel that the little I could do for you, either in those pre-war days or during the war, was of any service to you.'

Morton also corrected a biographical error in Churchill's account. 'You might also like,' he wrote, 'to make some slight alteration to the words "unique distinction of having been shot through the heart". I have been told by doctors that that is what occurred, but still remain somewhat dubious about it. Even if it is true it is not unique, since Arthur Sloggett, Director-General of Medical Services in the war of 1914, had a similar experience at Omdurman, and came to see me in hospital in consequence.' Morton also confirmed that Ramsay Mac-Donald, when Prime Minister of the National Government from 1931 to 1934, 'gave me personal permission to talk freely to you, as you state'.[2]

'I have been toiling away at my book about the War,' Churchill wrote to Duff Cooper on October 25, and he added:

---

[1] 'My dear Reynaud', 1 October 1947: Churchill papers, 2/57. This letter was drafted in its entirety by Bill Deakin and signed by Churchill unaltered.
[2] 'My dear Winston', 'Private', 21 October 1947: Churchill papers, 4/141.

So far I have only completed the story of the interval between the wars; but the rest is far advanced up to the end of 1940. There are several chapters in which you are involved, and in which you will certainly be interested. I should be most grateful if you would read them for me, and say if there is anything referring to yourself which you would like omitted. I have quoted a letter or two, but if you prefer it they can be left out. Anything that you care to add by way of enrichment, and any marginal comments you may feel inclined to make, will be welcomed by me.[1]

While Churchill prepared his war memoirs, Randolph had begun editing his father's war speeches. Explaining two payments of £500 each to Randolph in July and August, Churchill noted on November 14: 'both are payments for editing & preparing speeches'.[2]

Churchill's own work now hit a snag: Henry Luce was dissatisfied with the quality of the draft first volume which Churchill had sent him. Luce's main complaint was that there were too many documents breaking up the flow of the narrative ('they mar the architectural sense' were Luce's words) and too little 'analytical insight' (Luce's words again) into why the pre-war years had been a time of vacillation and weakness.[3]

'I have not yet tried to read it through at a run,' Churchill telegraphed to Luce on November 22. 'I hope to do this in the seclusion of Marrakech and in the light of commentaries for which I have asked.'[4] Later that day he wrote to Luce to explain that he was not averse to making changes, but defending his method and his theme:

I have read your letter with great attention, and am in much agreement with what you say. You must remember that so far I have been assembling the material and arranging it in chronological order. I work chapter by chapter and, as I cabled you, have not up to the present attempted to read Book I through at a run. This I shall hope to do in the seclusion of Marrakech and in the light of the commentaries which I have invited from various people. I certainly contemplate the excision of ten to fifteen thousand words, and probably more.

Coming to your first special point; the tale is necessarily told not only from the British, but from my personal, stand-point. It is presented only as a contribution to history. It may well be that Chapters II and III will be compressed into one, and also that Chapter X (Air Defence Research) and Chapter XV (The Rebuilding of the Fleet), which are altogether too technical, will be aborted and redistributed between other chapters and the Appendix. I have carefully kept my eye fresh for the final shaping of the work, although I now have its structure complete in my mind.

[1] 'My dear Duffie', 'Private', 25 October 1947: Churchill papers, 4/141.
[2] Note of 14 November 1947: Churchill papers, 1/19.
[3] 'Dear Mr Churchill', 18 November 1947: Churchill papers, 4/141.
[4] Telegram despatched 22 November 1947: Churchill papers, 4/141.

The above deals to some extent with your second point, and I have no doubt the quotations will be greatly reduced or melded in the narrative. I had not intended Book I to be so lengthy, but the task expanded as I went along.

The third question which you raise, namely why were the leaders so stupid and weak, and why did the nations and peoples of Europe throw up such bad leadership, shall certainly receive an answer. The reason is because in those years there happened exactly what is happening today, namely no coherent or persistent policy, even in fundamental matters, among the good peoples, but deadly planning among the bad. The good peoples, as now, drifted hither and thither, to and fro, according to the changing winds of public opinion and the desire of public men of medium stature to gain majorities and office at party elections from electorates, who were absorbed in earning their daily bread, whose memories were short and whose moods changed every few years.

There was, of course, also the lack of a world instrument of government for the prevention of war. This was largely because the United States abandoned the League of Nations at its birth. The League of Nations made a far better start than the present UNO, and the prospects of peace were brighter ten years after the First World War than they are now, only two-and-a-half years after the Second. But the lack of will-power and conscious purpose among the leading states and former allies drew us upon those slippery slopes of weak compromises, seeking the line of least resistance, which led surely to the abyss.

The same thing is happening now, only with greater speed, and unless there is some moral revival and conscious guidance of the good forces, while time remains, a prolonged eclipse of our civilisation approaches.

The above is the conclusion to be drawn from all this assembly of facts in Book I, and I shall make this abundantly plain before this part of the work leaves my hands.[1]

Simultaneously with work on the memoirs, work on the farm progressed, under the watchful eye of Christopher Soames. On October 21 Churchill sent a second set of instructions to his new son-in-law. One item read:

Friday, we aim at cutting down the big dangerous tree. A fifty yard rope should be provided as otherwise in falling it will destroy two other good trees. It must fall inwards of course. The electric saw will be used.

'In the event of running short of work,' Churchill added, 'please be so kind as to ring me up.'[2]

---

[1] 'My dear Mr Luce', 'Private', 22 November 1947: Churchill papers, 4/141.
[2] 'Chartwell Jobs', 'Captain Soames', 21 October 1947: Churchill papers, 1/32. In a further

On October 22 Churchill took a brief break from his literary and farm pursuits, to drive to London to second the Address of Congratulations to the King and Queen, and to Princess Elizabeth on the forthcoming royal marriage. He began his concluding remarks with a quotation from *Troilus and Cressida*:

'One touch of nature makes the whole world kin,' and millions will welcome this joyous event as a flash of colour on the hard road we have to travel. From the bottom of our hearts, the good wishes and good will of the British nation flow out to the Princess and to the young sailor who are so soon to be united in the bonds of holy matrimony. That they may find true happiness together and be guided on the paths of duty and honour is the prayer of all.[1]

Churchill returned to London for the Debate on the Address, to hear Herbert Morrison attack him over his Palestine policy. 'The amazing thing is,' Morrison said, 'that after condemning us for getting out of India and allowing it to grow to Dominion Status, and having come to the decision about Burma which he says we have flung away, he then goes to Palestine and says, "why didn't you get out of Palestine before?" That is not exactly logical.'

Churchill replied:

The right hon. Gentleman should realise that Palestine is a mandated area, and as he and his colleagues have broken their pledges to the Zionists, there was no moral reason why we should not, & every practical reason why we should, give the Mandate back to the United Nations organisation. There is a great difference between British territory built up and held for generations and a mandate which we accepted.

Churchill went on to tell the House of Commons:

The Government have at last adopted the policy which I urged upon them in the summer of 1946 of laying the Palestine Mandate at the feet of the UNO, and giving a time limit for our evacuation of the country. It is a measure of their inadequacy and of their embarrassment in taking decisions, and of the curious balance of forces in their Cabinet, that more than a year and a half of expense and discredit and waste of our limited military Forces, has been allowed to flow out since then. Yet they came to the same conclusion which should have been taken, with all its consequent saving, nearly 18 months ago.

There is no dispute between us as to policy; we support them in their policy.

---

note to Christopher Soames two weeks later, of work to be done, Churchill ended: 'I see some bonfires in the four cottage gardens. I hope care will be taken not to burn the houses down. A word of caution would be wise.' ('Needed Work', 'Bonfires', 'Captain Soames', 4 November 1947: Churchill papers, 1/32.)
[1] Speech of 22 October 1947: *Hansard*.

It is the delay to which I am drawing attention, and the strange impotence of will and lack of control and leadership which renders these fatal and ghastly compromises, prolonged for month after month, at the present time.

Whoever was responsible for our staying in Palestine with five times the Army we were keeping in India, at a cost of at least £80 million a year, to say nothing of the torturing ordeal of our troops and officers, and world-wide prejudice excited against us, whoever that Minister was, he bears a guilty load.

Speaking of the economic situation, Churchill described Conservative policy as the creation of 'an active, independent, property-owning democracy', and he added: 'our policy is an adequate basic standard, and above that, within just and well-known laws, let the best man win—'

To the laughter that came from the Labour benches at this remark, Churchill replied: 'The crackling of thorns under a pot does not deter me.' [1] He continued:

Ministers may not agree with this, and their followers still cling to the shibboleths which they have learned to substitute for any other more ameliorative mental process, but at least they must admit that here is a policy, a theme, a proposition, a method which reaches into every sphere of human thought and action, and constitutes the division between us, which will be brought one day to the decision of a country far better instructed upon these matters than it was on the last occasion.

It is not nature which has failed us. It is not nature which has failed mankind. It is Governments, which, misled and steeped in folly or perversity, have rejected and squandered the fruits of nature, endeavouring to prevent the normal working of its processes, even though those fruits are presented by the ever more efficient servitors of an ever widening science. The true path is still open if we could only have the wisdom and the courage to enter it. But we shall never enter it by substituting Whitehall planning on anything but the highest and most general level for the native genius and infinitely varied capabilities of our race. [2]

Listening to Churchill's speech was Henry Channon, a Conservative who had never really liked Churchill's attitudes or rhetoric: 'he was magnificent', Channon wrote in his diary on October 29, 'but there were touches of sadness in his patriotic eloquence, and at times I found him almost inaudible. He is ageing. But he impressed and moved the House, and Morrison's reply was, in comparison, weak and cheap.' [3]

Churchill was also vigilant in watching the development of the countries whose independence from Communism he had striven so hard to preserve in 1944 and 1945. Reading of the actions of the Greek

---

[1] 'For as the crackling of thorns under a pot, so is the laughter of the fool' (Ecclesiastes VII: 6).
[2] Speech of 29 October 1947: *Hansard*.
[3] Channon diary, 29 October 1947: Robert Rhodes James (editor), *Chips*, page 415.

Government in crushing a renewed Communist upsurge, he wrote to Sir Orme Sargent, who in 1946 had become Permanent Under-Secretary of State at the Foreign Office: 'We have not of course the same responsibility as we had in those days, but when we remember how many islands there are in which people can be put until things blow over, it seems to me very unwise for the present Greek Government to carry out mass executions of this character and almost reduces us to the Communist level.' [1]

Speaking to the boys at Harrow School on November 4, Churchill commented that the problems of 'blaring and crashing war' had been replaced by those 'of grinding and gnawing peace'. [2]

On November 12, a few moments before he was to deliver a supplementary Budget, Hugh Dalton was responsible for a last-minute leak which was both accidental and trivial. For many Conservatives it seemed a chance to flay the Government, but Churchill would not do so. 'His whole instinct was the generous one,' John Boyd-Carpenter later recalled. 'The Party wanted it raised. He wanted to leave it alone.' [3]

In the House of Commons, Churchill expressed his sympathy with Dalton, and criticized instead the Lobby correspondent who had extracted the budget details from him. 'May I acknowledge,' Churchill asked the House, 'on the part of the Opposition the very frank manner in which the Right Hon. Gentleman has expressed himself in the House and our sympathy with him at the misuse of his confidence which has occurred?' [4] Churchill's generous instinct was not reflected in his Party. 'Determined to hunt,' Pierson Dixon noted in his diary, 'the Conservatives persuaded Winston that it must be raised in the Select Committee. Dalton then insisted on resigning and Attlee accepted.' [5]

Gil Winant, the American Ambassador in Britain for the last four

---

[1] 'My dear Sargent', 'Confidential', 31 October 1947: Churchill papers, 2/54.

[2] 'Mr Moore, Ladies and Gentlemen', 4 November 1947: Churchill papers, 2/336. Among the boys in Churchill's audience were two future Kings, Feisal of Iraq and Hussein of Jordan.

[3] Lord Boyd-Carpenter recollections: in conversation with the author, 25 February 1987. John Boyd-Carpenter had been elected Conservative MP for Kingston upon Thames in 1945. He was to serve first as Financial Secretary to the Treasury and then as Minister of Transport and Civil Aviation in Churchill's second premiership.

[4] Speech of 13 November 1947: Hansard.

[5] Pierson Dixon diary, 13 November 1947: Dixon papers.

years of Churchill's premiership, had committed suicide in the United
States on November 3. In London, a memorial service was to be held
at St Paul's Cathedral on November 19. When Churchill asked his
wife to go, she replied:

My darling Winston,

OF COURSE *I* will go Mr Winant's Service. But I do beg of you to go in
memory of your joint work in the War & of your friendship during these
heart-shaking days. Your absence would strike a chill in the hearts of all his
friends & raise a cynical smile on the lips of those who prefer the Averell
Harriman style.

Clemmie.[1]

Churchill agreed to go, his wife marking the date and time on his
engagement calendar.[2] On the following day, they were both among
the vast concourse in Westminster Abbey for the marriage of Princess
Elizabeth and Lieutenant Philip Mountbatten, RN. 'The Ceremony
itself was beautiful,' Clementine Churchill wrote to a friend, 'and we
went to an Evening Party at Buckingham Palace which was really
gay & brilliant.'[3]

As he prepared for his journey to Morocco, Churchill again saw
Mackenzie King, to whom a year earlier he had spoken of his fears of
Western disunity in confronting Russia. Having heard Ernest Bevin
speak on the previous day of the possibility of an Anglo-American
confrontation with Russia, Mackenzie King asked Churchill, on November 26, 'how America could possibly mobilize forces at this time
for another war'. King recorded Churchill's reply in his diary. The
Americans 'would, of course, begin the attack in Russia itself'. They
had plans 'all laid for this, for over a year'. Churchill added:

What the Russians should be told at the present conference, if they are
unwilling to co-operate, is that the nations that have fought the last war for
freedom, have had enough of this war of nerves and intimidation. We do not
intend to have this sort of thing continue indefinitely. No progress could be
made and life is not worth living. We fought for liberty and are determined
to maintain it. We will give you what you want and is reasonable in the
matter of boundaries. We will give you ports in the North. We will meet you
in regard to conditions generally. What we will not allow you to do is to

<hr />

[1] 'My darling Winston', 12 November 1947: Churchill papers, 1/41.

[2] Engagements Calendar, November 1947: Churchill papers. The service was at 11 a.m. Churchill's other engagements were : Lord Mountbatten (12 noon), lunch with the Danish Ambassador, Shadow Cabinet at 6 p.m., and dinner with the King of Norway at the Norwegian Embassy.

[3] Letter quoted in Mary Soames, *Clementine Churchill*, pages 404–5. Churchill had first met
Princess Elizabeth in 1928, when she was two years old, at Balmoral, describing her to his wife
as 'a character. She has an air of authority & reflectiveness astonishing in an infant'. (Letter of
25 September 1928: Spencer-Churchill papers.)

destroy Western Europe; to extend your régime further there. If you do not agree to that here and now, within so many days, we will attack Moscow and your other cities and destroy them with atomic bombs from the air. We will not allow tyranny to be continued.

Mackenzie King's account continued:

... from Churchill's words, it would seem as if his inside information was to the effect that America was expecting that she might have to act in a short time and had made her plans accordingly. Churchill said he believed if Molotov and Stalin and others were told that this is what would happen, they would yield and put an end to their bluff. He really believed they were hoping to increase their territories as Hitler had sought to increase his by bluff, etc.

Churchill sought, as always, not to despair, but to seek an avenue of hope, as Mackenzie King recorded:

He sat back and said that war can be saved if we stand up to them now. 'I can see as clearly as can be, that, if that stand is not taken within the next few weeks, within five years or a much shorter time, there would be another world war in which we shall all be finished.' His whole face and eyes were like those of a man whose whole being was filled with the belief which he had. He turned to me and he said:

'I told you many, many years before this last war . . . that England would be at war within five years, and that she ran the risk of not possessing our own island at the end of that time. You remember this?' I told him that I indeed remembered it, and had made a memo of it at the time. He said: 'I am telling you now what I see in the future.' [1]

[1] Mackenzie King diary, 26 November 1947: J. W. Pickersgill and D. F. Forster (editors), *The Mackenzie King Record*, volume 4, *1947–1948* (Toronto 1970), pages 112–13.

20
The Dream

I T was in late November 1947, during a meal at Chartwell with his son Randolph and his daughter Sarah, that Sarah asked her father, by way of conversation: 'If you had the power to put someone in that chair to join us now, whom would you choose?' Instead of saying someone like Julius Caesar or Napoleon, Sarah later recalled, Churchill thought for a moment, 'and then he said very simply: "Oh, my father, of course."'

It was then that he told his son and daughter of an incident which had taken place in his studio not long before. They, as Randolph later noted, were 'immensely excited about it', and urged him to dictate an account of it straight away, but he was reluctant to do so. Over the following months, however, he committed the incident to paper.[1] Headed, prosaically, 'Private Article', it became known to his family circle as 'The Dream'. It is published here as Churchill left it, in a locked box, and as it was found by his son nearly twenty years later:

One foggy afternoon in November 1947 I was painting in my studio at the cottage down the hill at Chartwell. Someone had sent me a portrait of my father which had been painted for one of the Belfast Conservative Clubs about the time of his visit to Ulster in the Home Rule crisis of 1886. The canvas had been badly torn, and though I am very shy of painting human faces I thought I would try to make a copy of it.[2]

[1] Randolph Churchill, 'How he came to write it': *Sunday Telegraph*, 30 January 1966, the day on which the full text of 'The Dream' was published in the *Sunday Telegraph*.

[2] Churchill had been sent this portrait by Ian M. B. Stuart, the Headmaster of Portora Royal School, Enniskillen, and a former Master at Harrow, who had found it in an auction room in May 1945. In sending it to Churchill, Stuart noted: 'I asked if the portrait was for sale, and the attendant told me that it had been "put up" the day before, but there had been "no bid"! To cut a long story short I bought it for £1! He wondered why I wanted "such a dirty old portrait" and great was his surprise when I informed that gentleman that I would have gladly paid a good deal of money—as it was a very fine portrait of Lord Randolph Churchill, when he was about 35 years of age. I called a taxi and brought the portrait back with me on the train to Enniskillen!' Stuart added: 'It is unfortunately impossible to have oil paintings cleaned and repaired in Ulster now-a-days, so I had to do the best I could myself and haven't made a bad

My easel was under a strong daylight lamp, which is necessary for indoor painting in the British winter. On the right of it stood the portrait I was copying, and behind me was a large looking glass, so that one could frequently study the painting in reverse. I must have painted for an hour and a half, and was deeply concentrated on my subject. I was drawing my father's face, gazing at the portrait, and frequently turning round right-handed to check progress in the mirror. Thus I was intensely absorbed, and my mind was freed from all other thoughts except the impressions of that loved and honoured face now on the canvas, now on the picture, now in the mirror.

I was just trying to give the twirl to his moustache when I suddenly felt an odd sensation. I turned round with my palette in my hand, and there, sitting in my red leather upright armchair, was my father. He looked just as I had seen him in his prime, and as I had read about him in his brief year of triumph. He was small and slim, with the big moustache I was just painting, and all his bright, captivating, jaunty air. His eyes twinkled and shone. He was evidently in the best of tempers. He was engaged in filling his amber cigarette-holder with a little pad of cotton-wool before putting in the cigarette. This was in order to stop the nicotine, which used to be thought deleterious. He was so exactly like my memories of him in his most charming moods that I could hardly believe my eyes. I felt no alarm, but I thought I would stand where I was and go no nearer.

'Papa!' I said.

'What are you doing, Winston?'

'I am trying to copy your portrait, the one you had done when you went over to Ulster in 1886.'

'I should never have thought it,' he said.

'I only do it for amusement,' I replied.

'Yes, I am sure you could never earn your living that way.'

There was a pause.

'Tell me,' he asked, 'what year is it?'

'Nineteen forty-seven.'

'Of the Christian era, I presume?'

'Yes, that all goes on. At least, they still count that way.'

'I don't remember anything after ninety-four. I was very confused that year. . . . So more than fifty years have passed. A lot must have happened.'

'It has indeed, Papa.'

'Tell me about it.'

'I really don't know where to begin,' I said.

'Does the Monarchy go on?' he asked.

---

job of it—for apart from surface dirt and a small tear—fortunately in the top background—the canvas is in excellent state, and the necessary repairs and reframing could be done easily in London (the original frame wasn't worth sending).' ('Dear Prime Minister', 30 May 1945: Churchill papers, 2/142.) In his letter, Stuart noted that 'over the mantlepiece in my study hangs my late Father's appointment to be an Estates Commissioner for Ireland—at the foot of which—"Given at Our Court at St James's the second day of March 1911 in the First year of our Reign—By His Majesty's Command. W. S. Churchill". Naturally I regard this as my most cherished possession.'

'Yes, stronger than in the days of Queen Victoria.'

'Who is King?'

'King George the Sixth.'

'What! Two more Georges?'

'But, Papa, you remember the death of the Duke of Clarence.'

'Quite true; that settled the name. They must have been clever to keep the Throne.'

'They took the advice of the Ministers who had majorities in the House of Commons.'

'That all goes on still? I suppose they still use the Closure and the Guillotine?'

'Yes, indeed.'

'Does the Carlton Club go on?'

'Yes, they are going to rebuild it.'[1]

'I thought it would have lasted longer; the structure seemed quite solid. What about the Turf Club?'

'It's OK.'

'How do you mean, OK?'

'It's an American expression, Papa. Nowadays they use initials for all sorts of things, like they used to say RSPCA and HMG.'

'What does it mean?'

'It means all right.'

'What about racing? Does that go on?'

'You mean horse-racing?'

'Of course,' he said. 'What other should there be?'

'It all goes on.'

'What, the Oaks, the Derby, the Leger?'

'They have never missed a year.'

'And the Primrose League?'

'They have never had more members.'

He seemed to be pleased at this.

'I always believed in Dizzy, that old Jew. He saw into the future. He had to bring the British working man into the centre of the picture.' And here he glanced at my canvas.

'Perhaps I am trespassing on your art?' he said, with that curious, quizzical smile of his, which at once disarmed and disconcerted.

Palette in hand, I made a slight bow.

'And the Church of England?'

'You made a very fine speech about it in eighty-four.' I quoted, '"And, standing out like a lighthouse over a stormy ocean, it marks the entrance to a

[1] The Carlton Club, of which most Conservative MPs and Peers were members, was bombed on the evening of 14 October 1940. 'I think,' wrote one Club member (Sir Clive Morrison-Bell), on the following day, 'it would take the Prime Minister himself adequately to paint the effect of a high explosive bomb at what might be described as the far end of the room.' Among those present that evening were the Chief Whip (David Margesson), Harold Macmillan and Quintin Hogg, who carried out his father, Lord Hailsham, on his shoulders. The Club premises, in Pall Mall, were too severely damaged to be rebuilt, and new premises were found in nearby St James's.

port wherein the millions and masses of those who at times are wearied with the woes of the world and tired of the trials of existence may seek for, and may find, that peace which passeth all understanding".'

'What a memory you have got! But you always had one. I remember Dr Welldon telling me how you recited the twelve hundred lines of Macaulay without a single mistake.' [1]

After a pause, 'You are still a Protestant?' he said.

'Episcopalian.'

'Do the Bishops still sit in the House of Lords?'

'They do indeed, and make a lot of speeches.'

'Are they better than they used to be?'

'I never heard the ones they made in the old days.'

'What party is in power now? Liberals or Tories?'

'Neither, Papa. We have a Socialist Government, with a very large majority. They have been in office for two years, and will probably stay for two more. You know we have changed the Septennial Act to five years.'

'Socialist!' he exclaimed. 'But I thought you said we still have a Monarchy.'

'The Socialists are quite in favour of the Monarchy, and make generous provisions for it.'

'You mean in regard to Royal grants, the Civil List, and so forth? How can they get those through the Commons?'

'Of course they have a few rebels, but the old Republicanism of Dilke and Labby is dead as mutton. The Labour men and the trade unions look upon the Monarchy not only as a national but a nationalised institution. They even go to the parties at Buckingham Palace. Those who have very extreme principles wear sweaters.'

'How very sensible. I am glad all that dressing up has been done away with.'

'I am sorry, Papa,' I said, 'I like the glitter of the past.'

'What does the form matter if the facts remain? After all, Lord Salisbury was once so absent-minded as to go to a levée in uniform with carpet slippers. What happened to old Lord Salisbury?'

'Lord Salisbury leads the Conservative party in the House of Lords.'

'What!' he said. 'He must be a Methuselah!'

'No. It is his grandson.'

'Ah, and Arthur Balfour? Did he ever become Prime Minister?'

'Oh, yes. He was Prime Minister, and came an awful electoral cropper. Afterwards he was Foreign Secretary and held other high posts. He was well in the eighties when he died.'

'Did he make a great mark?'

'Well, Ramsay MacDonald, the Prime Minister of the first Socialist Govern-

[1] J. E. C. Welldon was the headmaster of Harrow when Churchill was at school there. He was subsequently Bishop of Calcutta (1898–1902), Canon of Westminster (1902–6), Dean of Manchester (1906–18) and Dean of Durham (1918–33). He died in 1937, at the age of eighty-three.

ment, which was in office at his death, said he "saw a great deal of life from afar".'

'How true! But who was Ramsay MacDonald?'

'He was the leader of the first and second Labour-Socialist Governments, in a minority.'

'The first Socialist Government? There has been more than one?'

'Yes, several. But this is the first that had a majority.'

'What have they done?'

'Not much. They have nationalised the mines and railways and a few other services, paying full compensation. You know, Papa, though stupid, they are quite respectable, and increasingly bourgeois. They are not nearly so fierce as the old Radicals, though of course they are wedded to economic fallacies.'

'What is the franchise?'

'Universal,' I replied. 'Even the women have votes.'

'Good gracious!' he exclaimed.

'They are a strong prop to the Tories.'

'Arthur was always in favour of female suffrage.'

'It did not turn out as badly as I thought,' I said.

'You don't allow them in the House of Commons?' he inquired.

'Oh, yes. Some of them have even been Ministers. There are not many of them. They have found their level.'

'So Female Suffrage has not made much difference?'

'Well, it has made politicians more mealy-mouthed than in your day. And public meetings are much less fun. You can't say the things you used to.'

'What happened to Ireland? Did they get Home Rule?'

'The South got it, but Ulster stayed with us.'

'Are the South a republic?'

'No one knows what they are. They are neither in nor out of the Empire. But they are much more friendly to us than they used to be. They have built up a cultured Roman Catholic system in the South. There has been no anarchy or confusion. They are getting more happy and prosperous. The bitter past is fading.'

'Ah,' he said, 'how vexed the Tories were with me when I observed that there was no English statesman who had not had his hour of Home Rule.' Then, after a pause, 'What about the Home Rule meaning "Rome Rule"?'

'It certainly does, but they like it. And the Catholic Church has now become a great champion of individual liberty.'

'You must be living in a very happy age. A Golden Age, it seems.'

His eye wandered round the studio, which is entirely panelled with scores of my pictures. I followed his travelling eye as it rested now on this one and on that. After a while: 'Do you live in this cottage?'

'No,' I said, 'I have a house up on the hill, but you cannot see it for the fog.'

'How do you get a living?' he asked. 'Not, surely, by these?' indicating the pictures.

'No, indeed, Papa. I write books and articles for the Press.'

'Ah, a reporter. There is nothing discreditable in that. I myself wrote articles for the *Daily Graphic* when I went to South Africa. And well I was paid for them. A hundred pounds an article!'

Before I could reply: 'What has happened to Blenheim? Blandford (his brother) always said it could only become a museum for Oxford.'

'The Duke and Duchess of Marlborough are still living there.'

He paused again for a while, and then: 'I always said "Trust the people". Tory democracy alone could link the past with the future.'

'They are only living in a wing of the Palace,' I said. 'The rest is occupied by M.I.5.'

'What does that mean?'

'A Government department formed in the war.'

'War?' he said, sitting up with a startled air. 'War, do you say? Has there been a war?'

'We have had nothing else but wars since democracy took charge.'

'You mean real wars, not just frontier expeditions? Wars where tens of thousands of men lose their lives?'

'Yes, indeed, Papa,' I said. 'That's what has happened all the time. Wars and rumours of war ever since you died.'

'Tell me about them.'

'Well, first there was the Boer War.'

'Ah, I would have stopped that. I never agreed with "Avenge Majuba". Never avenge anything, especially if you have the power to do so. I always mistrusted Joe.'

'You mean Mr Chamberlain?'

'Yes. There is only one Joe, or only one I ever heard of. A Radical turned Jingo is an ugly and dangerous thing. But what happened in the Boer War?'

'We conquered the Transvaal and the Orange Free State.'

'England should never have done that. To strike down two independent republics must have lowered our whole position in the world. It must have stirred up all sorts of things. I am sure the Boers made a good fight. When I was there I saw lots of them. Men of the wild, with rifles, on horseback. It must have taken a lot of soldiers. How many? Forty thousand?'

'No, over a quarter of a million.'

'Good God! What a shocking drain on the Exchequer!'

'It was,' I said. 'The Income Tax went up to one and threepence.' He was visibly disturbed. So I said that they got it down to eightpence afterwards.[1]

'Who was the General who beat the Boers?' he asked.

'Lord Roberts,' I answered.

'I always believed in him. I appointed him Commander-in-Chief in India when I was Secretary of State. That was the year I annexed Burma. The place was in utter anarchy. They were just butchering one another. We had to step in, and very soon there was an ordered, civilised Government under the vigilant control of the House of Commons.' There was a sort of glare in his eyes as he said 'House of Commons'.

---

[1] In 1947 the basic rate of Income Tax was three shillings and sevenpence in the pound.

'I have always been a strong supporter of the House of Commons, Papa. I am still very much in favour of it.'

'You had better be, Winston, because the will of the people must prevail. Give me a fair arrangement of the constituencies, a wide franchise, and free elections—say what you like, and one part of Britain will correct and balance the other.'

'Yes, you brought me up to that.'

'I never brought you up to anything. I was not going to talk politics with a boy like you ever. Bottom of the school! Never passed any examinations, except into the Cavalry! Wrote me stilted letters. I could not see how you would make your living on the little I could leave you and Jack, and that only after your mother. I once thought of the Bar for you but you were not clever enough. Then I thought you might go to South Africa. But of course you were very young, and I loved you dearly. Old people are always very impatient with young ones. Fathers always expect their sons to have their virtues without their faults. You were very fond of playing soldiers, so I settled for the Army. I hope you had a successful military career.'

'I was a Major in the Yeomanry.'

He did not seem impressed.

'However, here you are. You must be over 70. You have a roof over your head. You seem to have plenty of time on your hands to mess about with paints. You have evidently been able to keep yourself going. Married?'

'Forty years.' [1]

'Children?'

'Four.' [2]

'Grandchildren?'

'Four.'

'I am so glad. But tell me more about these other wars.'

'They were the wars of nations, caused by demagogues and tyrants.'

'Did we win?'

'Yes, we won all our wars. All our enemies were beaten down. We even made them surrender unconditionally.'

'No one should be made to do that. Great people forget sufferings, but not humiliations.'

'Well, that was the way it happened, Papa.'

'How did we stand after it all? Are we still at the summit of the world, as we were under Queen Victoria?'

'No, the world grew much bigger all around us.'

'Which is the leading world-power?'

'The United States.'

'I don't mind that. You are half American yourself. Your mother was the most beautiful woman ever born. The Jeromes were a deep-rooted American family.'

'I have always,' I said, 'worked for friendship with the United States, and indeed throughout the English-speaking world.'

[1] Churchill was to celebrate his fortieth wedding anniversary on 12 September 1948.

[2] A fifth child, Marigold, had died in 1921, shortly before her third birthday.

'English-speaking world,' he repeated, weighing the phrase. 'You mean, with Canada, Australia and New Zealand, and all that?'

'Yes, all that.'

'Are they still loyal?'

'They are our brothers.'

'And India, is that all right? And Burma?'

'Alas! They have gone down the drain.'

He gave a groan. So far he had not attempted to light the cigarette he had fixed in the amber holder. He now took his matchbox from his watch-chain, which was the same as I was wearing. For the first time I felt a sense of awe. I rubbed my brush in the paint on the palette to make sure that everything was real. All the same I shivered. To relieve his consternation I said:

'But perhaps they will come back and join the English-speaking world. Also, we are trying to make a world organisation in which we and America will be quite important.'

But he remained sunk in gloom, and huddled back in the chair. Presently: 'About these wars, the ones after the Boer War, I mean. What happened to the great States of Europe? Is Russia still the danger?'

'We are all very worried about her.'

'We always were in my day, and in Dizzy's before me. Is there still a Tsar?'

'Yes, but he is not a Romanoff. It's another family. He is much more powerful, and much more despotic.'

'What of Germany? What of France?'

'They are both shattered. Their only hope is to rise together.'

'I remember,' he said, 'taking you through the Place de la Concorde when you were only nine years old, and you asked me about the Strasbourg monument. You wanted to know why this one was covered in flowers and crape. I told you about the lost provinces of France. What flag flies in Strasbourg now?'

'The Tricolor flies there.'

'Ah, so they won. They had their revanche. That must have been a great triumph for them.'

'It cost them their life blood,' I said.

'But wars like these must have cost a million lives. They must have been as bloody as the American Civil War.'

'Papa,' I said, 'in each of them about thirty million men were killed in battle. In the last one seven million were murdered in cold blood, mainly by the Germans. They made human slaughter-pens like the Chicago stockyards. Europe is a ruin. Many of her cities have been blown to pieces by bombs. Ten capitals in Eastern Europe are in Russian hands. They are Communists now, you know—Karl Marx and all that. It may well be that an even worse war is drawing near. A war of the East against the West. A war of liberal civilisation against the Mongol hordes. Far gone are the days of Queen Victoria and a settled world order. But, having gone through so much, we do not despair.'

He seemed stupefied, and fumbled with his matchbox for what seemed a minute or more. Then he said:

'Winston, you have told me a terrible tale. I would never have believed that such things could happen. I am glad I did not live to see them. As I listened to you unfolding these fearful facts you seemed to know a great deal about them. I never expected that you would develop so far and so fully. Of course you are too old now to think about such things, but when I hear you talk I really wonder you didn't go into politics. You might have done a lot to help. You might even have made a name for yourself.'

He gave me a benignant smile. He then took the match to light his cigarette and struck it. There was a tiny flash. He vanished. The chair was empty. The illusion had passed. I rubbed my brush again in my paint, and turned to finish the moustache. But so vivid had my fancy been that I felt too tired to go on. Also my cigar had gone out, and the ash had fallen among all the paints.

On November 30 Churchill celebrated his seventy-third birthday. 'The years do fly by,' General Marshall wrote from Washington, 'but for you each year seems to offer more and greater opportunities to serve your people and the world.'[1] That night there was a dinner party at 28 Hyde Park Gate, Jock Colville, who was present, noting in his diary:

Winston is in a sombre mood, convinced that this country is destined to suffer the most agonizing economic distress. He says that the anxiety he suffered during the Battle of the Atlantic was 'a mere pup' in comparison. We could only get through if we had the power of the spirit, the unity and the absence of envy, malice and hatred which are now so conspicuously lacking. Never in his life had he felt such despair and he blamed it on the Government whose 'insatiable lust for power is only equalled by their incurable impotence in exercising it'.

'The phrases and epigrams rolled out in the old way,' Colville added, 'but I missed that indomitable hope and conviction which characterized the Prime Minister of 1940–41.'[2]

On December 2 Churchill gave a dinner for Marshall at 28 Hyde Park Gate; among those present were the three former Chiefs of Staff, Alanbrooke, Cunningham of Hyndhope and Portal of Hungerford, as well as two former members of Churchill's Defence Office, Major-

---

[1] 'Dear Mr Churchill', 8 November 1947: Churchill papers, 2/144.
[2] Colville diary, 30 November 1947: *The Fringes of Power*, pages 620–1.

General Sir Leslie Hollis and Major-General Sir Ian Jacob. The other British guest was Anthony Eden.[1] On December 4 Churchill gave the fourth in what had become regular luncheons for Members of Parliament during the Parliamentary session.[2]

It was a week, too, busy with instructions on the war memoirs. After Bill Deakin had been to see him on December 1, Churchill set out his thoughts on the various points which Deakin had put before him, in preparation for their work together at Marrakech. The most recent points had come from Eden's former Private Secretary, Oliver Harvey, and from a former Permanent Under-Secretary of State at the Foreign Office, Lord Vansittart. 'I shall want to take with me the Eden file,' Churchill noted, 'including Oliver Harvey's diary.' Of the conscription issue in 1939, Churchill noted: 'Both Liberal and Labour parties voted against this vital though tardy step. Their objections must be recorded in fairness to the Government.'[3]

Churchill also consulted for his war memoirs the current Permanent Under-Secretary at the Foreign Office, Sir Orme Sargent, who in 1938 had been Assistant Under-Secretary, and a stern critic of the policy of appeasement.

On December 5 Churchill went to Manchester to receive the freedom of the City. In preparation for his speech at Manchester, he was helped by Reginald Maudling, a young member of the Conservative Research Department, who later recalled:

> I remember so well our first meeting. I was sent down to Chartwell, bidden to appear at 4 p.m., and I was duly waiting in his Private Secretary's office. In came the great man, clad in his famous boiler suit. 'Ah, Maudling,' he said, 'I see you have arrived, come and have a whisky and soda. Of course,' he said, after a moment's reflection, 'there is tea if you would prefer it.' I did not prefer it, and my relation with the great man thereby got off to a satisfactory start.[4]

After their meeting, Churchill gave Maudling an outline on which to build, an outline which gave both scheme and theme to his intended speech:

[1] 'Press Notice', 2 December 1947: Churchill papers, 2/144.

[2] '1947', 'Luncheons to Members of Parliament', 'No. 4', 3 December 1947: Churchill papers, 2/63. In all, Churchill gave lunch to 191 Unionist members of Parliament (Note by Elizabeth Gilliatt, 3 February 1948: Churchill papers, 2/63). The sixth Parliamentary lunch was held on 4 February 1948, the seventh on 12 February 1948. The first three lunches had been on November 6, 13 and 27.

[3] 'Some Notes & Reflections after talking to OS and reading Van's Memorandum', initialled 'WSC', 2 December 1947: Churchill papers, 4/141. Vansittart, as Permanent Under-Secretary at the Foreign Office from 1930 to 1938, had shared Churchill's apprehensions about Hitler's intentions; in June 1940 he had been a principal advocate of the Union of France and Britain.

[4] Reginald Maudling recollections: Reginald Maudling, Memoirs, London 1978, page 44.

Artificial Britain.

Our precarious position.

Compare USA and France with Britain's tradition—if all the rest of the world sank beneath the ocean.

Russia.

Impossibility of our getting our living under Socialism. Nothing but thrift, ingenuity, enterprise, good-housekeeping can support this population of 48 million rising to 50, though altering unfavourably among those in the prime of life.

The Lancashire Cotton Trade. How we used to boast in the old days. A mighty industry, built up on a crop grown one end of the world and markets at the other, anchored here by British skill and craftsmanship. The cost of production under State Socialism imposes greater burdens than private industry, running for profits, which profits are in turn corrected by graduated taxation.

Coal. Very glad about the improvement in output, have always considered that the miners have a special claim on account of working 'away from the light of the sun'. Coal problem cannot be considered apart from cost. Look at the increase in the cost of coal which affects every industry, especially transport, which also will now have to support the State management. At the same time interest paid to the railway shareholders. All this is a tax on national production. Expense for management of the coal-mines from centralized departments. Whitehall. How many collieries have added greatly to their cost of management? There can be no question of denationalizing coal. Should some part of the burden of management not be borne by the Exchequer, so as to secure a cheaper fuel for our harassed industries?

Fallacy of an export trade without corresponding importation. Read the Petition of the Merchants of London 1828—a stock Free Trade quotation (Mr Maudling to supply).[1]

Churchill travelled to Manchester with his son-in-law Christopher Soames, two secretaries, Miss Marston and Miss Gilliatt, his detective Sergeant Price, and his new valet, William Greenshields.[2] On the afternoon of December 5 he received the Freedom of the City, and on the afternoon of December 6, accompanied by Maudling, who had

---

[1] 'Ideas for Manchester', undated, marked 'Copy has been sent to Mr Maudling': Churchill papers, 2/60.

[2] In his letter of recommendation (to Sir Strati Ralli) for his valet of the war years and earlier, Sawyers, Churchill wrote: 'Sawyers came everywhere with me in these six and a half tempestuous years, and showed many excellent qualities. He is absolutely honest, capable of attending to a great many personal details as a valet, and always rises to the occasion. In my illnesses he has been very attentive, and he stood up to the bombardment well. He was particularly good in the air journeys which at first had to be made in uncomfortable machines. He waits well at table, and also has an admirable manner with visitors. He has a good memory and always knows where everything is. He is leaving me at his own wish, and I am sorry to lose him.' ('Dear Sir Strati Ralli', 7 June 1946: Churchill papers, 1/65.) In 1952 Greenshields was succeeded by a Swiss valet, Walter Meyer.

helped him in preparing his address, he spoke at King's Hall, Belle Vue—a scene which he recalled in his opening words:

It is almost 40 years since I spoke in Belle Vue. Then there was an open-air meeting, at which Lloyd George, John Burns and I appeared together, and championed many of the great social reforms which have since been carried into law by Liberal or Conservative Governments in which I have served.

It is curious that, while in the days of my youth I was much reproached with inconsistency and being changeable, I am now scolded for adhering to the same views I had in early life and even for repeating passages from speeches which I made long before most of you were born.

Of course the world moves on and we dwell in a constantly changing climate of opinion. But the broad principles and truths of wise and sane political action do not necessarily alter with the changing moods of a democratic electorate. Not everything changes. Two and two still make four, and I could give you many other instances which go to prove that all wisdom is not new wisdom.

Churchill's principal theme was the perils of Socialism; he had, he said, 'a sad and anxious tale' to tell:

I am deeply anxious about our survival in this island as a free, prosperous, civilised community. I am quite sure that Socialism, that is to say the substitution of State control by officials for private enterprise, will make it impossible for 48 millions to live in this island, and that at least a quarter of all who are alive today will have to disappear in one way or another after enduring a lowering of standards of food and comfort inconceivable in the last 50 years.

Emigration, even if practised on a scale never before dreamed of, could not operate in time to prevent this melancholy decline.

Turning to Britain's policy overseas, Churchill once more contrasted, in even more condemnatory tones than before, the Government's policies towards India and Palestine:

Half the British soldiers kept in Palestine under conditions of intolerable provocation would, if they had been stationed in India, have enabled the transference of power and responsibility from British to Indian hands to have been made in a gradual and orderly manner, and would have averted the slaughter of at least a quarter of a million Hindus and Moslems in a series of hideous massacres, the like of which have never stained the British Empire in all its history.

'The blame for these various blunders and calamities', Churchill ended, 'rests upon the Government. . . .'[1]

---

[1] Speech of 6 December 1947: Randolph S. Churchill (editor), *Europe Unite*, pages 210–21.

21
Marrakech, 1947

I N a letter to Duff Cooper at the end of October 1947, Churchill had outlined his plans to go to Marrakech for six or seven weeks, staying at the Hôtel de la Mamounia. 'Because of currency restrictions,' he explained, 'I shall be the guest of my American publishers.' The doctors had recommended 'a sojourn in warmer climates', and the publishers were 'very anxious' to make it possible for him to work 'under the most favourable conditions'. He hoped, too, to paint as well as to write, and to have what he described as 'a complete break with the melancholy drama which is developing over here and will reach its climax in the coming year'.[1]

Duff Cooper was delighted to invite Churchill to his farewell party at the British Embassy in Paris on the way out: 'I don't think there will be a revolution,' he wrote, 'so bring your ball dress and tiara.'[2]

Under the currency regulations then in force, Sir Edward Bridges had explained, 'no foreign exchange is provided, even as pocket money', when a doctor certified that the patient's life would be endangered by not going abroad.[3] Three weeks later, Miss Sturdee informed Churchill that the total cost of staying at the Mamounia would be $6,000, but that this excluded all drinks, car and chauffeur expenses, laundry, telephone and postage.[4] A letter from Walter Graebner, the London representative of Time-Life International, brought Churchill the news that a first payment of $5,000 had been deposited for him in a bank in Marrakech.[5] No breach of the British

---

[1] 'My dear Duffie', 'Private', 25 October 1947: Churchill papers, 4/141.

[2] 'My dear Winston', 6 December 1947: Churchill papers, 2/161.

[3] 'Dear Mr Churchill', 24 October 1947: Churchill papers, 1/68.

[4] 'Mr Churchill', 10 November 1947: Churchill papers, 1/68.

[5] Walter Graebner to Miss Sturdee, 3 December 1947: Churchill papers, 1/68. On 9 December 1947 a further £50 worth of French francs was deposited by Time-Life International for Miss Sturdee. The total Time-Life International payments for the Marrakech visit were $13,600 paid in four instalments (19 November 1947, 1 January 1948, 5 January 1948, and 19 January 1948).

currency regulations was involved in this or in any of the subsequent transactions.

An aircraft was provided free of charge for Churchill and those travelling with him by Silver City Airways, one of whose directors, W. S. Robinson, Churchill had known since the India Bill struggle between 1931 and 1935. 'I need scarcely say how grateful I am for this princely offer,' Churchill wrote, 'and how much it facilitates my wish and need for a short holiday in the sunshine, which the doctors recommend.'[1]

An alternative offer of a holiday had come from Lord Beaverbrook, who offered to be Churchill's host at his villa in the South of France, La Capponcina, and also to accommodate his secretaries and assistants. 'You know I have control of Canadian funds,' Beaverbrook explained; 'I can provide staff & food & drink too & motor.'[2] Churchill replied a month later, in his own hand:

My dear Max,

I must thank you for yr vy kind letter & invitation sent to me on yr departure. I am planning to go to Marrakech (as the guest of *Life*) from December 11 to the end of January, as this gives the best hopes of warmth, sunshine & paintable subjects. This will be I fear my only excursion this year, as the political siren draws me more closely to her ugly talons. Perhaps in the spring & *especially if you were there* I might fly out to yr villa. Anyhow I value yr hospitable offer.

We are struggling along here and making steady progress as a party, tho' not alas as a country.

My operation has proved a complete success & it is a gt relief to be free from all that nuisance.

Once more thanking you.

Yours ever,

W

Churchill's postscript, 'the book advances like an elephant', was a clue to his decision to take the work and his helpers to Marrakech.[3] As he explained to Henry Luce, in the letter in which he had tried to answer Luce's criticisms of the book itself:

'I must warn you that I am increasingly convinced that I cannot finish Book I before the end of January, a month later than I had hoped. I am relying on my seven weeks at Marrakech, free from all distractions, except a little painting, to enable me to present a final picture. I do not think that this delay need affect the making of excerpts for the serials. It will, however, prevent the book publishers beginning pagination before the beginning of February.[4]

[1] 'My dear WS', 'Private', 7 November 1947: Churchill papers, 1/69.
[2] 'My dear Winston', 26 September 1947: Churchill papers, 2/146.
[3] 'My dear Max', 26 November 1947: Beaverbrook papers.
[4] 'My dear Mr Luce', 'Private', 22 November 1947: Churchill papers, 4/141.

Clementine Churchill decided not to go to Morocco; she 'does not feel up to the Marrakech expedition', Churchill explained to Duff Cooper, 'and is going to stay at home'. Churchill would be accompanied by his daughter Sarah, two secretaries, a valet and a detective, as well as by Bill Deakin. 'He is an Oxford don,' Churchill explained, 'who distinguished himself in the war, rising from Second Lieutenant in the Oxfordshire Hussars to Colonel and, in the Foreign Office, to Chargé d'Affaires at Belgrade. He helps me in my book.' [1]

Churchill and his entourage left Northolt on the morning of December 10, together with twenty suitcases, painting materials and 'a certain amount of Book papers'. [2] Further painting materials, 'a dozen soft camelhair brushes all different sizes for use with Tempera', Churchill arranged by telegram to be sent from his supplier Willy Sax, in Switzerland, to the British Embassy in Paris. [3] As well as the book papers sent by air with Churchill, a further selection was sent out separately on December 12, including Commodore Allen's notes on various Admiralty questions in 1939 and 1940.

The first stop was Paris, to join Duff Cooper's Embassy farewell party on the night of December 10. Among the other guests was Odette Sansom, the wartime heroine by whose courage in German concentration camps Churchill had been much moved. 'The star couple', Sarah Churchill wrote to her mother on the following day, 'were Odette and Papa—Papa looked pink and smiling and shy and sweet. He stood irresolute in the middle of the ballroom aglow with his medals and stars—"I would like to dance with you," he said to Odette, "but really I am not very good. Won't you sit down and talk to me for a moment?" . . .' [4]

That night, Churchill slept at the Embassy, flying on to Marrakech on the morning of December 11, and reaching the city late that afternoon, after an eight-hour flight. On the following evening he wrote to his wife:

The flight was perfect in every way and we have been welcomed here in a suitable fashion by the French authorities. The weather is cold out of the sun, but the sunlight is brilliant and warm. I shall have to take much care

---

[1] 'My dear Duffie', 1 December 1947: Churchill papers, 2/161. The two secretaries were Elizabeth Gilliatt and Jo Sturdee. The valet was W. Greenshields, the Scotland Yard detective (as far as Paris) was Sergeant C. S. Price; (from Paris to Marrakech, at Marrakech, and on the return journey) Sergeant G. Williams.

[2] 'Note of Conversation between Mr Churchill, Air Commodore Powell and Wing Commander Arthur', 7 November 1947: Churchill papers, 1/69.

[3] Telegram of 9 December 1947: Churchill papers, 1/19.

[4] Letter of 11 December 1947: Sarah Churchill, *Keep on Dancing*, London 1981, pages 99–100.

about not catching cold. The hotel is well-heated and there is a very distinct change going out of doors in the evening. During the day one can fling the wide windows open, but when darkness falls everything must be shut.

I painted this afternoon for a couple of hours from the roof of the hotel from where there are two or three lovely views and I do not expect to move beyond the precincts for several days. Sarah and Bill have made excursions in the town and in the Arab quarters. The food is excellent and I have made an arrangement with the hotel which will enable me and my party to stay here for 42 days at about two-thirds of the money provided. This leaves a margin for contingencies. Judging from the first start I have made to-day, I think I am going to paint better than I have done before. The days are very short however, for the effect does not come on till 2.30 and it is dusk and chilly at 5. Next week we will try some picnics to places you have seen when I was convalescing here four years ago. 'Flower Villa'[1] has been bought from Mrs Taylor by the nephew of the Marquis de Breteuil. He has invited me to go and paint in his garden but I looked at this very thoroughly when we were there last and did not think much of it and there is just as good a view from the top of this hotel as from his tower. The Atlas are magnificent and as glorious as ever in the evening light.

The Moroccans are enjoying the experience of voting for the first time, but it is clearly understood that the military government is supreme.

England and politics seem very different here. I continue to be depressed about the future. I really do not see how our poor island is going to earn its living when there are so many difficulties around us and so much ill-will and division at home. However I hope to blot this all out of my mind for a few weeks.

I worked hard all the morning on the book and shall begin again after dinner. I did not get my sleep today because we had to entertain to cocktails the four officers of the aeroplane who brought us here so well. They will bring this letter back when they start on Sunday morning.

Tender love my dearest Clemmie. I do hope you will be peaceful & happy, & will often think of yr ever loving.

W [2]

'Am painting from the tower and working night and day,' Churchill telegraphed to his wife two days later. 'Have sent heavy batch of proofs home by returning plane. Weather lovely. Am planning picnic. Hope you like mandarins. Mule in great form. Much love. W.'[3]

'I am happy that the sun is shining with you,' Clementine Churchill wrote to her husband on December 16. 'Here we are muffled in drizzle, *but* it is quite warm and muggy. Whereas I am nervous about the sharp cold which comes down from the Atlas.' She remembered the 'delicious air (like champagne)' and felt that it would do him

---

[1] Churchill's wartime villa and headquarters, it was known as the Villa Taylor during his six-week stay there at the end of 1943 and beginning of 1944.

[2] Letter of 12 December 1947, Hôtel de la Mamounia, Marrakech: Spencer-Churchill papers.

[3] Telegram despatched 14 December 1947: Churchill papers, 1/44.

good, '*if only* you don't catch cold. Please take great pains not to.' He ought, she felt, to come indoors by four o'clock.[1]

Also on December 16, Sarah Churchill sent her mother an account of Churchill's activities:

So far he has not left the hotel, he paints from a high balcony of the new wing of the hotel—and as it has till now been cold, I am glad. But today a sortie is planned—just a small one—to the pink walls. He is inclined to work a little too late. Bill is an enormous help to him—but also a temptation to work on too late at night.

Bill planned to leave Dec 22nd and meet his wife in Paris for Christmas but now great telegrams have been sent to persuade her to come out here for five days so that Bill can stay longer.

The 'girls' and Sergeant Williams and Greenshields are all very good and devoted, and seem happy and thrilled with the place—as indeed they might be, for it is really a terrestrial paradise. The people in the hotel are very nice and do not stare or bother one—with the exception of one man who tried to take photographs of Papa. We ignored several attempts, then Sergeant Williams appeared from behind a palm tree and delivered a little lecture about the rules of a private hotel being respected and the man, crestfallen, packed up his Brownie camera and fled down an olive grove. Sergeant Williams retired majestically behind his palm tree again![2]

Every day some proofs were sent back to England for the printer. 'Warm and brilliant sunshine though days are short,' Churchill telegraphed to his wife on December 18, and he added: 'Much progress with book.'[3] That same day he sent her a full report:

My darling Clemmie,

We have been here a week today. The weather is lovely and increasingly warm. It is always supposed to rain for two or three days at Christmas, but at present the skies are cloudless. At 10 o'clock in the morning it is possible to lie in bed, as I am doing now, with the French windows wide open on to the balcony. I have been working very hard, rather too hard, in fact. My routine is: Wake about 8 a.m., work at Book till 12.30, lunch at one, paint from 2.30 till 5, when it is cold and dusk, sleep from 6 p.m. till 7.30, dine at 8, Oklahoma[4] with the Mule—who was given a credit of £28 and has been completely stripped (I have given her another credit, but she says she will not accept it). At 10 or 11 p.m. again work on the Book. Here I have been rather naughty; the hours of going to bed have been one o'clock, two, three, three, three, two, but an immense amount has been done and Book II is practically finished. I am not going to sit up so late in future.

[1] 'My darling Winston', 16 December 1947: Churchill papers, 1/44.

[2] Letter of 16 December 1947: Sarah Churchill, *Keep on Dancing*, pages 100–1.

[3] Telegram, 18 December 1947: Churchill papers, 1/44.

[4] Commenting on the card game Oklahoma, Churchill told Walter Graebner: 'The degree of thrill that one gets from Oklahoma compared to gin rummy, is in direct proportion to the effect on the nervous system of an attack of delirium tremens and a single whisky and soda.' (Walter Graebner recollections: *My dear Mr Churchill*, page 35.)

The painting has not gone badly but I only have these two and a half short hours of good light. Three daubs are on the way.

We have followed exactly the same routine each day, but I think we shall go for a picnic on Saturday. Yesterday the Comte d'Hauteville and his wife (he is the Colonel commanding the whole of this district with both military and civil powers) came to luncheon with us. They are persons of quality. She looks like a more gracious Eva Keyes. We are going to lunch with them on Sunday. Tonight we dine with the Glaoui. He is the same age as me. He has sent large crates of grapefruit, oranges, and mandarines, and enormous jars of butter, jam, and honey, and a basket of dates. Monsieur Majorelle will be away for another fortnight, but I will then get into contact with him. I have invited Mrs Deakin to come on here for Christmas as this will enable me to keep Bill till at least the New Year.

Comte d'Hauteville is planning a 3 days' excursion for me and Sarah, and the Prof if he comes, after the Deakins leave in the New Year. It is much more ambitious than Taroudant, which he says is only a 'petit Marrakech'. We are to go right through the Atlas Mountains into what he calls wonderful country beyond, in the Sahara Desert, or half desert as it is there. I shall know more about this plan before I decide on it, but certainly it sounds attractive and by then a change of routine may be necessary.

They are very attentive in the Hotel; the only fault has been the bathwater not being hot, but this is being attended to. The food and wine are beyond criticism. Generally I am much settled down and very glad to be here, and to feel that I have a good long spell ahead of me, away from the distraction of British politics, and the sense of gathering gloom in our affairs which oppresses me.[1]

Churchill had dictated this letter. On being given it to sign, he added in his own hand:

Yes I like to rest here, where I combine *rest* & continual occupation. Sarah & Bill find lots to talk about. Do tell me about Chartwell. Dictate me a Chartwell Bulletin, with a supplement by Christopher. I hope you are getting all you want done (Have mercy!), & that Whitbread and Kurn are making progress with the Jacob's ladder.

Tender love my dearest Clemmie & every wish that my heart can signal for yr health & happiness.

Always yr devoted husband

W

Dinner with the Moroccan Arab chieftain, El Glaoui, on December 18 proved to be the highlight of the visit. Churchill asked Sarah to describe it, which she did in a letter to her mother:

I wonder if I can remember all we ate, because it is all we did! A sort of second wind came to us round about the sixth platter of food, and, by then, all shyness of eating with one's fingers having gone, we were plunging merrily ahead as to the manner born. However, we were to learn that all courses are

[1] Letter of 18 December 1947: Spencer-Churchill papers.

not eaten with the fingers, and Papa committed one small social error by plunging his fingers into the centre of a great bowl of what looked like stewed and mashed apples and semolina, only to be handed a spoon! How could one know? The Glaoui gallantly waved away his spoon and plunged too!

Later, somewhere round the tenth course, an ice cream turned up. I am sorry to say that though it was quite clear that this was one of the courses to be eaten with a spoon, Papa was enjoying himself so much that, muttering, 'I simply must', he plunged his fingers into the ice cream. The Glaoui and son luckily were highly amused. . . .

'Wow, darling,' Sarah Churchill ended her account, 'I will write soon to you again. He is happy and well, loves his routine. Today we are off for the first picnic.' [1]

On December 19 Princess Elizabeth's Private Secretary, Jock Colville, who had worked for Churchill during the war, sent a Christmas card from the Princess to Churchill to Hyde Park Gate, with the request that it should be sent to Marrakech 'by the first available means'.[2] Not only the royal Christmas card, but more notes by Commodore Allen, were on the way: 'Scandinavia and Finland', 'Action of R. Plate' and 'The Combat Deepens'.[3] Also on December 20 came a section of proofs which had been read by Sir Edward Marsh and a printer's proof of the chapter entitled 'The Dark New Year'.[4] Further proofs, as well as notes by General Pownall, Professor Savory and Sir Orme Sargent were brought that day by Bill Deakin's wife Pussy.[5]

From Marrakech more proofs were sent back to London almost every day: two chapters, 'The Darkening Scene' and 'The Loaded Pause', going back on the evening of December 22.[6] There was also a telegram for Churchill from Emery Reves: 'Airmailing twenty-one factual corrections.' [7]

A further three proof-read chapters were sent out to Marrakech on December 23, despatched from Charing Cross Post Office at Churchill's urging, 'cos it's open all night—see?' [8]

'Here the sun shines brightly,' Churchill telegraphed to his wife on December 24. 'Sarah and I send you all our fondest love and every good wish for a happy Christmas.' [9] From Chartwell Farm came news,

[1] Letter of 19 December 1947: Sarah Churchill, *Keep on Dancing*, pages 101–3.
[2] Letter of 19 December 1947, Buckingham Palace: Churchill papers, 2/148. The Christmas card did not reach Marrakech until 27 December 1947, on 'Outwards 12'.
[3] 'Outwards 10', despatched 6 p.m., 20 December 1947: Churchill papers, 1/68.
[4] 'Outwards 5', received 10 a.m., 20 December 1947: Churchill papers, 1/68.
[5] 'Outwards 6', arrived 20 December 1947: Churchill papers, 1/68.
[6] 'Inward Bag No. 6', despatched 6.30 p.m., 22 December 1947: Churchill papers, 1/68.
[7] Telegram sent from New York, 22 December 1947, received Marrakech, 23 December 1947: Churchill papers, 1/68.
[8] 'Outwards 15', despatched 8.30 p.m., 23 December 1947: Churchill papers, 1/68.
[9] Telegram despatched 24 December 1947: Churchill papers, 1/44.

via Christopher Soames, that the German prisoners-of-war, after their Christmas holiday, would be coming over daily from their camp without a foreman, but that on 3 January 1948 'they leave for good'.[1]

During December 24 Churchill completed his revision of the first six chapters of his first volume. He at once instructed Miss Marston to have twenty-four copies printed: two to be sent straight back to Marrakech for himself and one for Deakin; one to go to General Pownall for his own use, one for Commodore Allen, one more for Pownall to show to the Secretary of the Cabinet, 'explaining that further instalments will rapidly come to hand', one to Walter Graebner, one to Henry Luce, twelve to Lord Camrose and the *Daily Telegraph*, one to the Oxford philosopher Isaiah Berlin, and three to be kept at Chartwell for office purposes 'and emergencies'.[2]

In his letter to Isaiah Berlin, thanking him 'for all the work you have done', and for his suggestions, Churchill added:

I now send you the first six chapters which, as you will see, have been completely remoulded. I have not yet decided to leave out the political stuff, though I agree it is a little off the track. I should like to know how you think the new first six chapters run. Personally I feel they fit together much better than they did before. However please state exactly what your view is upon them and to what extent your first impressions have been affected by the drastic changes I have made.[3]

After two weeks at Marrakech, the pattern of work and relaxation was well established. Bill Deakin later recalled:

He liked excursions. They were working sessions. Sometimes he would write a piece of his own, without any documents. When I got to Marrakech I found an awful piece about the Spanish Civil War. I said, 'But these weren't your views at the time.'

He shouted at me: 'You God-damn, damn you, you always think you're right.'

At eight in the morning I went into his bedroom as usual. He gave me the galley proofs. He was silent. He didn't say a thing. But he had put in all my points in red ink.

At lunch he said to my wife: 'You must think I'm a horrible old man.'

His mind was fixed on the conduct of the war. Occasionally, late at night, we might talk about the Dardanelles.

The point of the excursions was to work on the galley proofs, not to break into new material. But I would prepare certain things in advance.

'He didn't do very much work,' Deakin added. 'He wanted company. He painted most of the time.'[4]

[1] 'My dear Mr Churchill', 22 December 1947: Churchill papers, 1/45.
[2] 'Miss Marston', 24 December 1947: Churchill papers, 4/57.
[3] 'Dear Mr Berlin', 25 December 1947: Churchill papers, 4/67.
[4] Sir William Deakin recollections: in conversation with the author, 15 March 1975.

It was with a report of his painting that Churchill began his letter of December 24 to his wife, his third long weekly letter since arriving in Marrakech:

My darling Clemmie,

The weather continues to be cloudless and lovely. The air is cold, and in the shade or when the sun goes down it is biting. I am very careful to wrap up warmly and never paint after 5 o'clock. I have five (six now) pictures on the stocks. They are really much better, easier, looser, and more accomplished than those I painted twelve years ago (which I also have with me). I think you will be interested in them. They look much more like the real thing, though none as yet are finished, and there is many a slip.

Yesterday we went for a picnic at Ouriki, where we had three picnics together in 1943/44. Do you remember it? It is an opening of a beautiful gorge in the hills, with great snowy mountains in front and red buildings on either side of the enclosing foothills, and quite a river flowing out of the mountain chain. The whole party went, and I think everybody enjoyed themselves. We are going again in two or three days to the same place so that I can finish my picture.

Bill's wife has arrived and makes herself most agreeable. He has not been quite well, with a slight temperature. I sent him to bed early last night, and today he is normal again.

'It was chicken pox,' Bill Deakin later recalled, 'an absolute disaster, as Churchill was due to go to the southern Atlas mountains. He came into my room to see how I was. He didn't mind the risk of infection. That was typical of him.' [1]

Churchill's letter of December 24 went on:

I continue to be extremely fit, and my existence is strictly divided into sleeping, eating, painting and the Book with a nightly game of Oklahoma with the Mule. We have been here a fortnight tomorrow and so far hardly any letters and not all the bags have come through. I am greatly relieved that the copy I have sent home is all now safely received. Of some parts I had not kept a copy here, and loss would have been a terrible vexation. The progress I have made is immense. Book I is practically finished and so is Book II. I believe they will cease to be burdens on me except for minor corrections by the end of the year. It would have been quite impossible for me to do this work if I had not buried myself here, where every prospect pleases, and only the twenty-four hours are too short. As I have often told you, I do not need rest, but change is a great refreshment.

I am so glad you had such an interesting dinner to meet General Marshall. I think we have made good friends with him. I have long had a great respect for his really outstanding qualities, if not as a strategist, as an organiser of armies, a statesman, and above all a man.

[1] Sir William Deakin recollections: in conversation with the author, 1 July 1987.

Cripps seems to me to be taking a far more responsible view of his duties than his predecessor, the dirty Doctor,[1] did, and his speech about the Royal Grants was courageous and dignified. I do not think the Debate has done any harm. All will be forgotten, and they will get their £5,000 a year extra.[2]

I am also glad that neither the fire nor the burglar did you any harm, and I am delighted to hear of the putting away of the valuables, etc. The great danger is an unoccupied house, or an unoccupied part of a house. It is essential there should be a man and wife at Chartwell. Also the local Police might help. Never mind the expense—a stitch in time saves nine. Lights could be shown here and there after dark. The moment they know the house is empty they have it at their mercy, and in three or four hours there is no ordinary safe or strong room into which they cannot break.

The only incident we have had here has been a crazy French Colonel, who had fought bravely in the war, and is now retired and quite dotty. He is also said to have undesirable political connections and was forbidden by the Colonel commanding the 'Région' to deliver an address in Marrakech. He came here nevertheless, and stayed in the Mamounia, and presented himself a little before midnight to thank me for having given him the Victoria Cross (which is a delusion) and asked for my advice on his various grievances. I received him because I thought he had come from Rabat with some of my proofs which I was expecting to get. When I saw he was a mental case I dismissed him courteously. However, in the meanwhile the French Police had sent on his dossier stating that he was quite mad and queer. On searching his suitcase, which they and Sgt Williams very promptly did, they found a loaded automatic pistol of which they deprived him. He made no complaint. Great vigilance was practised by the French Police, and he was carefully watched during the weekend he stayed here. He prowled about the Hotel till 5 a.m., and the Colonel-Governor got very excited and he was ordered back to Rabat on Monday. I took a friendly farewell of him in the restaurant, and hope I may never see his face again. (No, he turned up at the dance last night.)

I have not given up hopes that Prof may be able to come. The Deakins will probably leave in the early days of January. Montag arrives on the 9th for a week, and Mr Graebner on the 10th. I am hoping the Mule will stick it out with me. Her Jewish friend has arrived at Casablanca and I think they

[1] Hugh Dalton, who held a Doctorate of Science at London University: Cripps's predecessor as Chancellor of the Exchequer.

[2] Speaking in the House of Commons on 17 December 1947, Sir Stafford Cripps had defended the Government's decision to give Princess Elizabeth an additional £25,000 a year (to the £15,000 she already received under the former Civil List Act) as from the day of her marriage, and to give the Duke of Edinburgh £10,000 a year from the day of his marriage, and a further £15,000 a year after her death while any of their children might be Heir Presumptive to the Throne. It was essential, he argued, that the Duke of Edinburgh 'may enjoy a proper degree of independence in financial matters'. Some Labour MPs had tried to reduce Princess Elizabeth's additional income to £20,000. This Cripps stoutly rejected. 'If I can live on £1,000 a year, including expenses,' said William Gallacher (Communist) 'why is it necessary for this couple to have £1,000 a week?' The amendment was defeated by 345 votes to 33: those voting for it included Bessie Braddock, William Gallacher, John McGovern, Ian Mikardo and D. N. Pritt. He hoped, Cripps concluded, 'that we have got through this Debate without anything having been said which will cause any distress to these two young people'.

plan a tour of Fez together. I am sending you the telegrams I have received from Randolph.

Here is a paragraph for your expert mind. The expense for the first week for seven of us was £300, which is a little more than a fiver a day per head. Considering the excellent food, and service of the highest class, and that we have an office and a studio besides our bedrooms, this is not excessive, taking into account the state of the world. They give you enormous helpings, at least four times what one could eat. I have remonstrated about this, but I gather it is not wasted, any more than the Glaoui's banquet, of which Sarah has given you a very full description. I do not eat very much myself, even at lunch, but it is nice to see beef again. £300 for six weeks = £1800. £2,500 in dollars are being supplied, and Miss Sturdee has had a message from Mr Graebner saying that there is plenty more if necessary. I think myself the original figure I mentioned will cover everything.

When you recollect how much it means to all these publishers to get delivery of Volume I by the end of February, and that they would perhaps lose many thousands of pounds and suffer immense inconvenience if I failed them, I feel fully justified in the course I have taken, which results only from the fact of our currency regulations which prevent my using my own money. Moreover, considering that all here is concentrated on the book, I have no doubt our American hosts can make a perfectly valid case for the money to be treated as expenses from the point of view of American Income Tax. If this be so, it will not cost them much.

It is practically certain that I shall not go to America, but come back straight from here on the 19th or 20th. I have telegraphed to Bernie saying I will try to come in the early Spring. It is important for me to go there, not only for large political reasons, but also on the Book. There will be no difficulty in obtaining expenses from the Government for an American visit on an adequate scale. However, I have made no plans.

With fondest love, my sweet & darling Clemmie

Your ever devoted husband,

W[1]

'I came here to Play,' Churchill added in his own hand, 'but in fact it has only been Work under physically agreeable conditions.'

Churchill's reference in his letter to the value for money which his American publishers were receiving was borne out by the amount of work he was doing; his American publishers did not, however, entirely appreciate this. Daniel Longwell, the editor of *Life*, was later to write scathingly, in an internal memorandum, of Churchill's style of work and living while he was on his overseas journeys. 'We've given him $60,000 or $70,000 worth of expense money on those trips to work on the book,' Longwell wrote five years later. 'They did hasten the various books and help their completion—that I know. But this is very

---

[1] Letter of 24 December 1947: Spencer-Churchill papers.

delicate money.' Longwell added: 'However, and this we must keep private, these were very lavish trips. Always some of the family went along to get their holiday. He had his cronies with him; he sent for various people from England. He had the best in food and hotels. We paid for his sort of state dinners to noteworthy folk, and the last expedition to Marrakech presented an expense account I wouldn't want anyone to peer into too far.'

Longwell went on to explain that the money paid could not be cited by Time-Life as payments for the volumes 'because they weren't payments—they were free-will expense gifts. If we so much as breathe they were payments, he'd have to pay income tax on them, and I believe we'd have to pay a retrospective 20 per cent withholding tax.'[1]

On Christmas Eve at the Mamounia Hotel, Churchill gave a party for all those who had come out with him, thereby losing their Christmas at home. 'Last night was a big success,' wrote Sarah, 'and it was sweet of you to dance with all the girls and stay so late. I do hope you are not tired this morning.'[2]

In a letter to her mother, Sarah gave a fuller account of the evening's festivities at the Mamounia:

Papa invited the girls and Sergeant Williams and Greenshields who generally sit in the opposite corner to join us for the evening! We all put on evening dress and Greenshields in a great flutter borrowed a black tie from Bill and we all met in the sitting room for a cocktail, and then we went down in force to the dining room at 10.30. A glittering scene met our eyes. In the short space of the afternoon, they had transformed the large dining room. A gigantic Christmas tree 25–30 feet high had been installed and decorated. The windows were hung with branches laden with oranges, and daubs of white paint on the window panes made it seem that a blizzard was blowing outside—clever idea.

Everyone was 'dolled up'. It was a very international atmosphere—Danes, Swiss, Portugese, Spanish, American—the smattering of English—us, French, and an Italian waiter. When midnight struck, they lowered the lights, and with one accord the International mêlée rose as a man to their feet just on the spur of the moment and looked to Papa. They raised their glasses, and clapped—and 'Vive Churchill' and 'Bravo' echoed round the room.

The band, who had practised hard all afternoon English surprises for us, played 'It's a long way to Tipperary' as the Christmas pudding was brought in. Renewed clappings and murmurs, and Papa stood up very moved and bowed to them all, and received the Christmas pudding as he does a casket

[1] Daniel Longwell to Andrew Heiskell, 10 December 1962: Daniel Longwell papers.
[2] 'Darling Papa', 25 December 1947: Churchill papers, 1/45.

on being given the freedom of a city. Then he got up—I thought he was going—but no.

'Whirl me round the floor once Mule—I think I can manage it.'

This was too much for them—like a famous dance team we took the floor amidst a roar of applause—we were very good—it was a waltz. Then he danced during the evening with Miss Sturdee, Miss Gilliatt and Mrs Deakin—and I was whirled off my feet by Sergeant Williams—who is pretty hot on a rumba (Scotland Yard training is most extensive). I was also whirled by Greenshields, who was too shy at first but ended up the strongest. Papa stayed till two![1]

There was also an episode which Sarah Churchill did not relate to her mother. As she later recalled:

At the party, I had noticed that my father had been attracted by a good-looking fair lady who had sat against the wall with a gentleman; but now that the festivities were in progress she was alone, profiled against the snow-screened window.

My father said, 'Why is she alone?'

'The gentleman had to go back to his family,' I said.

'How do you know that?'

'Don't gentlemen usually go home to their families?'

Immediately he rose to his feet and said, 'Dance me around the floor.'

He danced me around the floor and stopped at the forlorn but proud lady. Looking at her he said, 'You are the Christmas fairy, may I have a dance?'

My job was once again ended. I returned to my seat and he took the lady in his arms. I have no idea what he said, but I can imagine. He never liked to see a beautiful woman alone. When their turn at dancing was done, he left her at her place. Meanwhile, the detectives were wondering if she had been imported as a spy. We never discovered her name, but later received a telegram: 'YOU WILL NEVER KNOW MY NAME BUT I AM PROUD TO HAVE DANCED WITH WINSTON CHURCHILL.'[2]

From Chartwell came news from Clementine Churchill of 'a happy & peaceful Christmas Day' with Mary and Christopher Soames, '& we drank your health & Sarah's before we fell to a fat turkey'.[3]

On December 27 the printer's proofs of the Norwegian campaign arrived, as did Princess Elizabeth's somewhat delayed Christmas card, and a Christmas card from Nurse Blake.[4] But that day Churchill was taken ill. 'I have a slight cold without fever which I am nursing carefully,' he telegraphed to his wife.[5] 'Much better this morning,' he

---

[1] Letter of 26 December 1947: Sarah Churchill, *Keep on Dancing*, page 104.
[2] Sarah Churchill recollections: Sarah Churchill, *Keep on Dancing*, page 104–105.
[3] 'My darling', 26 December 1947: Churchill papers, 1/44.
[4] 'Outwards 12', 6.30 p.m., 22 December 1947, received 4 p.m., 27 December 1947: Churchill papers, 1/68.
[5] Sent 27 December 1947: Churchill papers, 1/45.

telegraphed on the following day. 'No temp, but taking all precautions.' [1] 'Apart from his cough,' Sarah Churchill reported to her
mother, 'he seems well in himself and his colour and appetite are
good and temperature normal.' But she added that she felt the presence of Lord Moran was 'essential to guide and relieve anxiety, else all
benefits of holiday will be spoiled'. [2]

Churchill himself, after discussing his condition with the local doctor,
Dr Diot, telegraphed to his wife, and to Lord Moran on 1 January 1948:

A bad cough in the tubes but not in the lungs has now lasted for six days
without temperature or improvement. Neither Dr Diot nor I could say condition is serious enough to warrant your journey. On the other hand he would be
very glad if you were here. Weather is brilliant but rather treacherous as the air
is exceptionally cold this year. There is a good deal of pneumonia about in the
town. It would be a great comfort if you and Dorothy would come out and I am
sure that you would find it very pleasant. I should be most grateful if you feel
you can come. Arrange journey through Miss Marston. Blood count follows. [3]

'Beloved,' Churchill telegraphed to his wife, 'you will have seen the
various telegrams. There is really nothing to be worried about if
proper care is taken. I am very glad Charles is coming.' [4]

While Lord Moran was on his way, ten chapters were sent back
corrected to the printer, spanning the years 1935 to 1938, in two
separate bags. [5] At the same time, more historical notes were also
arriving from General Pownall, together with material about the
strength of the German Air Force in 1940 from Field Marshal Alanbrooke. [6] Also arriving before the doctor were extracts from *Hansard* in
1938 and 1939, prepared for him by Denis Kelly. [7] There were further
notes from Commodore Allen, and a letter from Sir Stafford Cripps
enclosing his 1939 private diary. [8] On all the material which reached
him, Churchill worked without serious respite, with Bill Deakin at his
side. There was also a pleasing culinary message from Christopher
Soames at Chartwell Farm: 'We have massacred a pig, and have sent
him off to be cured; so you will have a delicious peach and milk fed
bacon and ham for your breakfasts when you return.' [9]

---

[1] Telegram dated 28 December 1947: Churchill papers, 1/45.

[2] Telegram, undated: Churchill papers, 1/45.

[3] Telegram, undated: Churchill papers, 1/45.

[4] Telegram, undated: Churchill papers, 1/45.

[5] 'Inwards bag No. 9', 28 December 1947 and 'Inwards Bag No. 10', 29 December 1947:
Churchill papers, 1/68.

[6] 'Outwards 16', and 'Outwards 18', received 30 December 1947.

[7] 'Outwards 19', received 30 December 1947: Churchill papers, 1/68.

[8] 'Outwards 20', and 'Outwards 21', 29 December 1947: Churchill papers, 1/68.

[9] 'My dear Mr Churchill', 31 December 1947: Churchill papers, 1/45.

World events could not be entirely excluded, even amid the idyll of Marrakech. On December 24 a former Greek partisan general, having previously proclaimed a Soviet Republic of Greece—from the safety of Communist Albania—announced the formation of a Free Greek Government. 'Papa is depressed by events,' Sarah Churchill reported to her mother on December 30; 'he thinks it is very serious and hopes the Americans take decisive action in Greece, and not fall between two stools.' Pussy Deakin, added Sarah, 'is upset about her Roumania'.[1]

On 2 January 1948 Bill Deakin returned to England, taking with him twelve chapters corrected and ready for the printer, covering the last year of peace and the first four months of war.[2] Sent out to Marrakech a day later were Denis Kelly's notes on the Fulham by-election of 1933, where a Labour challenger won a previously Conservative seat.[3] When Lord Moran arrived on January 3, he was not alone: Clementine Churchill had flown out with him. On arrival they were greeted by a Churchill eager to know the worst. 'I had come a long way to help him,' Moran noted, 'and he was all agog to hear my verdict. There was not much amiss, and when I had satisfied him that he had not got pneumonia he seemed to forget all about his illness. He began to come down to the restaurant for luncheon and dinner, and in a day or two had taken up his life just as it had been before he took to his bed a fortnight ago.'[4]

'Mr Churchill's temperature is now normal,' the Press were told that night, 'and his condition is satisfactory.'[5] He was certainly well enough to write, as always in his own hand, to the King to say how pleased he was about the 'satisfactory conclusion' to the recent Debate and Select Committee on the royal grants. Churchill went on to tell the King:

I am vy glad that the Debate & the Select Cte on the Royal Grants had such a satisfactory conclusion. There are always a number of venomous

[1] Letter of 30 December 1947: Sarah Churchill, *Keep on Dancing*, page 106. By August 1948 the Communists had been defeated by the Greek Government. Roumania, however, remained firmly under Communist control. Pussy Deakin was from Roumania; she and Bill Deakin had met in Egypt during the war.

[2] 'Inward Bag No. 11' and 'Inward Bag No. 12', 'Taken by Mr Deakin, noon, January 2, 1948': Churchill papers, 1/68.

[3] 'Mr Churchill', 3 January 1948: Churchill papers, 4/143.

[4] Moran diary, 3 January 1948 (misdated 7 December 1947): *The Struggle for Survival*, pages 321–9.

[5] Communiqué, 3 January 1948: Churchill papers, 1/69.

people in a free country who write spiteful letters & say poisonous things. In the days of Queen Victoria the most violent Republicanism was thought fashionable among those who then constituted the 'Left'. But these never represented the British Nation wh is devoted to our Ancient Constitutional Monarchy the form of which has been enhanced by the ten years glorious reign of Yr Majesty, & wh finds its sure foundation in the people's heart.

Yr Majesty's Ministers, if I may venture to say so, as Leader of the Opposition, behaved in a most becoming manner & all is now settled in accordance with the dignity of the Crown & in its lasting interests.

In signing my Christmas Card I observed that Yr Majesty wrote R instead of RI. I found this vy painful, but I still hope that much will one day return. May God Bless Your Reign is the prayer of Yr Majesty's devoted humble servant & subject.

Winston S. Churchill[1]

On January 4 Churchill agreed to see three British journalists, S. Taylor of Reuters, Archibald Wilson of the *Daily Express* and John Fisher of the *Daily Mail*, who had flown out on the previous day from England, 'where', they told him, 'there has been a great public anxiety about your health'.[2] He also gave them a short statement for publication. 'I am much better,' it read, 'and I am going painting this afternoon. The sunshine will do me good.' Marrakech was, he added, 'one of the most beautiful places in the world'. As to his having 'called Lord Moran out here', this was because 'at my age everyone has to be careful'.[3]

On January 4 Lord Cherwell flew out to Marrakech, bringing with him eight chapters corrected by Sir Edward Marsh. Also reaching Churchill in that first week of January were a set of criticisms from Isaiah Berlin. When Moran's wife Dorothy asked Churchill which year of his life, if he could choose, he would relive, he replied: 1940 every time, every time,' then told those around him: 'I wish certain people could have been alive to see the events of the last years of the war; not many: my father and mother, and FE, and Arthur Balfour, and Sunny. Sunny and I were like brothers. I have stayed for months with him at Blenheim.'[4]

As the comments of his readers continued to reach him at

---

[1] 'Sir', 3 January 1948: Churchill papers, 2/171. In his reply, the King noted that the recent change of Chancellor of the Exchequer (on 13 November 1947), from Hugh Dalton to Sir Stafford Cripps, 'made all the difference' in the acceptance of the grant ('My dear Winston', 11 January 1948: Churchill papers, 2/171). The initials RI (Rex Imperator, Regina Imperatrix) had been used by successive British Sovereigns since 1877, when Queen Victoria had become Empress of India.

[2] Letter of 4 January 1948: Churchill papers, 1/69.

[3] Press notice, *Daily Express*, Paris Office, undated: Churchill papers, 1/69.

[4] F. E. Smith (later Lord Birkenhead) had died in 1930; Sunny, Duke of Marlborough, in 1934; Arthur Balfour (Lord Balfour) in 1930. Churchill's father and mother had died in 1895 and 1921 respectively.

Marrakech, Churchill asked his wife to read through the chapters as each was ready to be sent back to the printer. Her comment was, as Moran noted, 'that he had used initials too much. They would convey nothing to the average reader.' These initials, she felt, should be replaced by the full name of the organization in question.[1] 'He looked up impatiently with a pained expression,' Moran recalled. 'He doesn't really want criticism; he wants reassurance.'[2]

Not reassurance, however, but criticism, had already arrived in a letter from Emery Reves, the burden of which was that the first volume would have to be rewritten almost in its entirety. 'There are too many documents, letters and quotes from speeches in the text,' Reves wrote, and he added: 'Not as if every one of them would not be of importance and interest. But the narrative is so dramatic, so exciting, that one resents the many interruptions, and the average reader will certainly skip most of the documents for the simple reason that he will be anxious to continue reading the narrative.'

Reves suggested that it would be possible for Churchill 'to absorb the greatest part of the documents into the narrative, and either to eliminate the original documents or relegate them to the Appendix'.[3]

Whatever wisdom lay in Reves's criticisms, and they were indeed reiterated in a private letter from Colin Coote to Lord Camrose which Churchill did not see, the verbs 'absorb', 'eliminate' and 'relegate' were not calculated to put Churchill at ease, at the very moment when the first volume was, as far as he was concerned, almost ready to be printed.

Churchill's daughter Sarah, seeing him downcast, wrote to him at once with words of support and encouragement:

Darling Papa,

Forgive me butting in. I understand that perhaps you are a little depressed by the criticism of Reves? This may or may not be true. In any case—Don't listen to too many critics—Each critic criticises from a personal angle. The work is yours—from deep within you—and its success depends on it flowing from you in an uninterrupted stream.

I have made the mistake up to now (you have not I know!) of listening to too many people in my work. The only peace I find faintly credible was when I stopped up my ears and listened to myself.

Now of course—one must have critics—particularly those who can criticise the whole sincerely—not from a small window—A journalist will criticise it as being, say a little ponderous—seeing newspaper headlines and excerpts for weeklies etc. A technical man—for the technicalities—a soldier from the army

---

[1] Initials such as CIGS (Chief of the Imperial General Staff), COS (Chief of Staff).

[2] Moran diary, 7 January 1948 (misdated 7 December 1947: *The Struggle for Survival*, pages 321–9.

[3] 'Dear Mr Churchill', 22 December 1947: Churchill papers, 1/68.

view etc—It is your story, as you moved through, what will one day be history.

You are the best historian—the best journalist—the best poet—shut yourself up and only listen to a very few, and even then, write this book from the heart of yourself—from the knowledge you have—and let it stand or fall by that—it will stand—everyone will listen to your story.

I hate to see you pale & no longer happily preoccupied—Wow Wow Wow darling—

Your darling Mule

Sarah.[1]

Churchill persevered with his readers' points. Isaiah Berlin felt that two at least of the early chapters were 'too episodic and insubstantial to act as an adequate scaffolding to the more tremendous story of the Rise of Hitler, with which the book really gets into a wonderful stride'.[2] Churchill was not averse to this criticism, writing to Lord Camrose on January 4:

A friend of mine, Mr Isaiah Berlin, read Book I at my request and, apart from many points of detail, made the following comment (Enclosure 'A'). Thereafter Sir Norman Brook, the Secretary to the Cabinet who was reading the Book at my desire, made independently a similar comment.

Of course it would be quite easy to cut out and abridge the domestic-political material and throw Chapters 2 and 3 into one.

You will also see that I have reshaped these chapters in the 'Almost Final' edition and I think to some extent have met the criticisms.[3]

From Emery Reves came further criticisms on January 5. Five of the 'highest literary authorities' in the United States were reading the book for the Book-of-the-Month Club. 'I watched them reading,' wrote Reves, 'while they were sitting in my room. They were completely absorbed, but they all skipped the documents and speeches, and said exactly what I indicated to you in my last letter.'[4]

Reves now urged again that '*All* speeches, documents should be integrated into the narrative', quotations 'reduced to a minimum',

---

[1] Undated letter: Churchill papers, 1/45. Colin Coote wrote in his internal *Daily Telegraph* memorandum (to the editor, Arthur Watson): 'I have read the draft of Winston's book. It is, as you say, scrappy in places and, though it contains some very fine passages, I received the definite impression that the writer feels rather tired and hurried. It must, of course, be remembered that it is not merely a narrative, but a record and, therefore, large extracts from official documents, which can have little interest to the general reader, have had to be included. But I do think that the whole book falls rather between the two stools of a narrative and a record. It does not reach the level of absorbing interest maintained throughout by Winston's book on the First World War.' (Letter dated 28 December 1947: Camrose papers.)

[2] Enclosure 'A', undated: Churchill papers, 4/141.

[3] 'My dear Bill', 'Private', 4 January 1948: Churchill papers, 4/141.

[4] The judges were Henry Seidel Canby, Dorothy Canfield Fisher, Christopher Morley, John P. Marquand and Clifton Fadiman.

and both narrative and quotes printed 'in the same type to avoid interruption in one organic text'.[1] Churchill had already replied by telegram to Reves's first letter, that 'There is no question of altering the whole character of work in manner you suggest.'[2] Reves now telegraphed in return on January 6: 'There is no question altering character work, which is superb and unparalleled.' The 'integration' of the documents, Reves added, was a 'purely technical editorial matter' which could be accomplished in a few days with 'minimum alteration in text'. 'Of course,' Reves added, 'I may be altogether wrong.'[3]

Churchill, believing that Reves was wrong, telegraphed to him in reply: 'The "Almost Final" text of Book I should reach you soon. Pray give me your suggestions for cutting documents and speeches. Much has already been done in new text. My method is to tell the tale from current authentic documents where possible. Please reread the whole from the beginning.'

'Have made immense progress out here as you will see,' Churchill added, hoping to reassure Reves.[4] On receiving Reves's second letter he telegraphed again: 'I do not agree with your suggestions, but only that you make them. There is no question of changing the book in manner you suggest.'[5]

Had Reves taken criticism too far, or had Churchill already met his criticisms in the first chapters? 'Five "Almost Final" chapters absolutely perfect,' Reves telegraphed on January 14. 'You have reshaped everything as I would have suggested. If other chapters edited likewise our sole criticism fully met.' Reves was opposed, however, to Churchill's accepting Isaiah Berlin's suggestions. 'Strongly feel excellent chapters II and III should stay unabridged,' he wrote. 'Domestic picture essential for understanding coming events.'[6]

A final telegram from Emery Reves was decisive in an area of utmost importance, the title of the first volume. Churchill had chosen 'Downward Path' as the theme of the years 1931 to 1939. This title, Reves telegraphed, 'sounds somewhat discouraging'. The American and other publishers would prefer a 'more challenging title indicating crescendo events'. Reves suggested 'Gathering Clouds', 'The Gathering

---

[1] 'Dear Mr Churchill', 5 January 1948: Churchill papers, 4/141.

[2] Telegram, undated, from Marrakech to New York: Churchill papers, 4/141.

[3] Received at Marrakech on 7 January 1948: Churchill papers, 4/141.

[4] Telegram, undated, from Marrakech to New York: Churchill papers, 4/141. The phrase 'an immense amount of work' was one Churchill used to describe his efforts at Marrakech, in a letter to Cripps on January 8, thanking him for extracts from his 1939 diary. The weather, Churchill told Cripps, 'though treacherous is lovely'.

[5] Telegram sent on 12 January 1948: Churchill papers, 4/141.

[6] Telegram dated 14 January 1948: Churchill papers, 4/141.

Storm' or 'The Brooding Storm'.[1] The title Churchill chose was 'The Gathering Storm'.

The return of Bill Deakin and his wife to London enabled yet further chapters to be returned to the printer, corrected and revised. 'Papa said last night the Deakins left a very pleasant memory,' Sarah Churchill telegraphed to Deakin on January 9, and she added: 'Thought you would like to know we miss you. . . .'[2]

On January 9 Churchill's Swiss painter friend Charles Montag arrived at the Mamounia as Churchill's guest, followed two days later by Lord Camrose and Walter Graebner, both of whom paid their own way.[3] Lord Cherwell and Lord Moran were still with him. On January 18 they all left Marrakech by air, spending the night at Bordeaux, and reaching London during the morning of January 19. 'Only a line of welcome & joy that you are back—safe & sound,' wrote Violet Bonham Carter that day, and she added: 'What a fright you gave us & what a relief it was to hear you are better. You are badly needed here.'[4]

[1] Telegram received 17 January 1948: Churchill papers, 4/141.
[2] Telegram sent 9 January 1948: Churchill papers, 1/68.
[3] 'Hotel Account', 8 to 14 January 1948: Churchill papers, 1/69.
[4] 'Dearest Winston', 19 January 1948: Churchill papers, 2/146.

22

'My experience, which is unique. . . .'

RETURNING to London on 19 January 1948, Churchill at
once began work on his speech for the Foreign Affairs debate
which began on January 20. When he rose to speak on January 23,
three weeks had passed since the abdication of King Michael of Roumania, and the clear imposition there of Communist rule, as well as an
upsurge in Communist violence in Greece. It was also in the wake of
strong warnings from two leading Ministers, Attlee himself and Herbert Morrison, that Soviet Russia was pursuing a dangerous and expansionist policy. Morrison had gone so far as to speak, twice, of the
risks of war. 'I was much criticised on both sides of the Atlantic,'
Churchill commented, 'for the Fulton speech, but in almost every
detail, and certainly in the spirit and in its moderation, what I there
urged has now become the accepted policy of the English-speaking
world. The language used by the Prime Minister and the Lord President of the Council about Soviet Russia, and about the dangers of a
new war, far exceed in gravity and menace anything which I said at
that time, or, indeed, have ever said on this subject since the war.'

Later in his speech Churchill noted that Ernest Bevin had also
warned of Soviet expansionism; it was therefore wrong to allow the
debate to 'evaporate in benevolent and optimistic platitudes'. His
speech continued.:

We are, after all, the guardians of the ordinary, humble, hard-working
people, not only here at home, but in many lands. It is so little that they ask—
only to get their daily bread by the sweat of their brow and enjoy the simple
pleasures of life which were meant for all and should be denied to none.

'To make a happy fire-side clime
For weans and wife

> There's the true pathos and sublime
> Of human life.' [1]

But now all these millions of humble humans are hustled and harried this way and that, first by nationalistic or imperialistic ambitions or appetites, now by ideological doctrines and hatreds, and all their small lives may be shattered and convulsed, millions at a time, and they may be only regimented up to suffering wounds and unrewarded toil. We, their representatives in this world-famous assembly, have a great responsibility, and we cannot always discharge it by treading easy paths and saying smooth things.

Churchill went on to tell the House of Commons:

I am often asked, 'Will there be war?', and this is a question I have often asked myself. Can you wonder, sir, that this question obtrudes itself upon us when the Lord President of the Council speaks, as he did ten days ago, of the 'risk of war' with Russia—twice, I think, he used that phrase—and speaks of:

'The availability and, if necessary, the readiness of armed force to prevent the outbreak of violence'—and when the Prime Minister says—and I agree with him when he says:

'Soviet Communism pursues a policy of Imperialism in a new form—ideological, economic, and strategic—which threatens the welfare and way of life of the other nations of Europe.'

These are statements from men whose whole lives have been spent in denouncing the dangers of militarism, when they have not been actively engaged in fighting for their lives against tyranny. These are the speeches of Socialists. It is not a question of Jingoism. These are the speeches of Socialists and the Ministers responsible.

Churchill's answer was not to challenge Russia militarily. He was looking, he said, for some policy which would enable war to be avoided. The 'best chance of avoiding war', he felt, was, 'in accord with the other Western democracies, to bring matters to a head with the Soviet Government, and, by formal diplomatic processes, with all their privacy and gravity, to arrive at a lasting settlement'. Even this method would not guarantee that war would not come. 'But I believe it would give the best chance of preventing it, and that, if it came, we should have the best chance of coming out of it alive.' [2]

To give the European States their due weight in future international deliberations, Churchill persevered with his plans to create a United Europe movement. 'I am sorry you did not come into our United Europe movement as one of its founders,' he wrote to Sir Archibald Sinclair in February 1948. 'Great developments have followed,' he added, and went on to explain:

[1] The quotation is from Robert Burns, 'Epistle to Dr Blacklock'. The second line begins 'To weans' not 'For weans'. The third line in fact begins 'That's' not 'There's'.
[2] Speech of 23 January 1948: *Hansard*.

General Marshall said publicly that it was a link in his train of thought, and now Bevin and the whole of HMG are committed to positive action far greater than I had hoped to see in my lifetime. The difficulties about defining the frontiers of United Europe have, for the time being, been settled by the sixteen nations pact, although of course any of the ones inside the Iron Curtain are free to join the club as and when they please or dare. Violet, Walter Layton, Lady Rhys Williams are very staunch regular supporters and attend all my committee meetings. Gollancz and our Socialist members have stuck to their guns in spite of a Party ban. I hope this ban will soon be lifted. There is considerable division in the Socialist Party about it.

'Perhaps you will consider,' Churchill asked, 'whether this all-Party and non-Party movement of a cultural, moral and sentimental character may even now receive your support.'[1]

A conference to advance the cause of United Europe had been called for The Hague in the Spring of 1948. Churchill strove to obtain the Labour Party's participation, but he failed. 'It is felt,' wrote Emanuel Shinwell, the Secretary of State for War, on February 10, after a meeting of the National Executive Committee of the Labour Party, 'that the subject of European unity is much too important to be entrusted to unrepresentative interests.' The presence at the proposed Hague conference of 'private individuals selected by an unknown process robs the congress of any real representative character'.[2] Angered, Churchill spoke of the Hague conference during a Party Political broadcast four days later:

This event has been welcomed by all parties except, of course, the Communists. It has been welcomed by all parties throughout the countries of Western Europe. Alone, the British Labour Party has decided to discourage its members from attending.

When I proclaimed this idea at Zurich in September 1946, I earnestly hoped that it might be at once all-party and above party, but through their petty jealousies and internal divisions, the Government is being drawn into the grave and anti-social error of trying to form an exclusive union of the Socialists of Europe.

By forming in this wide sphere a kind of 'closed shop' they seem to want to repel the aid and support of all other parties and influences in this country and on the Continent. In this behaviour they are only imitating the Communists whom they so loudly condemn.

'We are asking the nations of Europe,' Churchill pointed out, 'between whom rivers of blood have flowed, to forget the feuds of a thousand years and work for the larger harmonies on which the future depends: and yet we in this island, who have so much in common, who have no

---

[1] 'My dear Archie', 'Private', 11 February 1948: Churchill papers, 2/23.
[2] 'My dear Churchill', 10 February 1948: Churchill papers, 2/21.

serious grievances or vendettas to repay, are unable to lay aside even
for the sake of such a cause, even for the sake of a cause on which we
are all agreed, party strife and party prejudices.'[1] 'I listened with
delight—to your broadcast on Saturday night,' wrote Violet Bonham
Carter. 'It was magnificent, & I hope it made them (the Labour
Executive, Shinwell & Co.) feel as uncomfortable as they deserve
to.'[2]

Violet Bonham Carter offered to speak to Sinclair to press him 'to
enter our fold', and on February 19 Sinclair wrote direct to Churchill
to say that 'any small influence I can exert will be used on Liberals &
others in support of your campaign'. Sinclair added: 'Your speeches
& action inspired the Marshall Plan and the development of your
campaign will facilitate its progress.'[3]

On February 21 the Czechoslovak Communists seized power in
Prague. Churchill's friend of the pre-war years, Jan Masaryk, remained as Foreign Minister, the post he had held since 1945. Within
three weeks, however, Masaryk's body was found beneath an open
window of the Foreign Ministry in Prague. To this day it is not known
whether he committed suicide in despair at his failure to halt the
Czech Government's policy of 'Sovietization', or whether he was murdered for being an obstacle to that policy.

Churchill's sense of urgency for a United Europe was heightened
by the events in Czechoslovakia, whose capital was less than seven
hundred miles from London. In a further effort to widen support for
the conference at The Hague, and to prevent a European Socialist
boycott, he wrote to Léon Blum, who had warned in a public article
that Churchill's approval brought with it 'the danger that the European federations would have a character too narrowly Churchillian'
and that the Federalist movement would have 'great difficulty in
emerging from the shadow of a too illustrious name'. In the course of a
six-page reply, Churchill told Blum:

. . . the Conservative Party in Britain have given their full support to Mr
Bevin in the policy of a Western European Union, which he has adopted. No-
one is seeking to deprive him or the British Socialist Government of any credit
which is theirs. The position of a Minister, holding the high executive Office
of Foreign Secretary, is quite different from that of a private person, even if he
has the misfortune to be, to quote your flattering words, 'too illustrious'.

The Minister has executive responsibility and has to act as well as to
speak. There will be great credit for Mr Bevin, and indeed for all, if a good
result is gained and Europe stands aloft once more in splendour.

[1] Speech of 14 February 1948: Randolph S. Churchill (editor), *Europe Unite*, pages 238–44.
[2] 'Dearest Winston', 16 February 1948: Churchill papers, 2/146.
[3] 'My dear Winston', 19 February 1948: Churchill papers, 2/23.

'Those will be unworthy of the occasion,' Churchill warned, 'and fall below the level of events, who allow Party feelings or personal likes and dislikes to hinder the way to the main result.'

Later in this same letter, Churchill told Blum:

I cannot feel that my own initiative has been harmful. You may remember that Mr Marshall at his News Conference on June 12, 1947, disclosed that my advocacy of the United States of Europe had influenced his development of the idea that Europeans should work out their own economic recovery and that the United States should extend financial help.

I feel greatly honoured to have been a link in setting in train the Marshall Plan upon which all our Governments are united and all our hopes depend.

Churchill ended his letter with the wish that he and Blum, in their 'closing years', might find themselves united 'in the march towards what is noble and true'.[1]

Churchill reiterated his support for a United Europe at a meeting of the Central Council of the Women's Committee of the Conservative Party, held at the Albert Hall on April 21, when he also praised the 'active and distinguished part' taken by Ernest Bevin in the establishment of 'an association of material help' between Britain, France, Belgium, Luxembourg and The Netherlands.[2] There could be 'no hope for the world', he said, 'unless the peoples of Europe unite together to preserve their freedom, their culture, and their civilisation founded upon Christian ethics'.

In Italy, the Communist Party had been defeated at the elections. But Czechoslovakia had finally fallen under Communist control. 'There will never be a settled peace in Europe,' Churchill declared, 'while Asiatic Imperialism and Communist domination rule over the whole of Central and Eastern Europe.'

Churchill also spoke to the Conservative women about the abolition of the death penalty:

As I listened the other night in the House to the crazy cheers with which the Socialist backbenchers, in defiance of the advice of the majority of their leading Ministers, swept away the Death Penalty for the wickedest forms of murder at a time when crimes of robbery and violence by armed men have so grievously increased, I could not but wonder if these hysterical, emotional Members could be the same men who regarded the slaughter, as a result of their mistakes and mismanagement, of at least half a million Indians in the Punjab alone, as a mere incident in the progress of oriental self-government.

What a confession of impotence it was that the Prime Minister and the

---

[1] 'My dear Monsieur Blum', 7 April 1948: Churchill papers, 2/18.

[2] On 17 March 1948 conversations initiated by Bevin had reached their conclusion in the signature of a Treaty of mutual assistance between Britain, France, Belgium, The Netherlands and Luxembourg.

Cabinet, who did not dare to stand by their declared convictions of what they thought was right and necessary in the present circumstances, should have cast their duty to the wind and left this grave decision on Capital Punishment to the casual vote of the most unrepresentative and irresponsible House of Commons that ever sat at Westminster.[1]

'I cannot imagine a worse time to abolish the Death Penalty than now, in the height of the outburst of criminality from which we are suffering,' Churchill wrote to a fellow Conservative, Vyvyan Adams, who was in favour of abolition. 'They have of course abolished the Death Penalty in Russia,' Churchill added, 'because they prefer to toil them to death in slavery.'[2]

In early March, Churchill was preparing his speech on the Naval Estimates. In a letter of congratulation to Lord Fraser of North Cape, the new First Sea Lord, he had written of 'a deliberate writing down of our real strength' which had already produced 'damage to our prestige' all over the world, 'and especially, as we have seen, in South America'. Churchill's letter continued:

I am also shocked at the manner in which old battleships, two of which were practically rebuilt in 1939/40, are being scrapped. I believe this policy is also applied to destroyers. When we look back through our experiences in the last war, when the fifty aged American destroyers became one of our main objects of desire, and remember how even the old *Centurion* was ready to play her part in the invasion crisis, it is I am sure a very great mistake to cast all this latent and undefined strength away.

My experience, which is unique, is that the moment war is declared every ship in the basins is a factor of value. To describe the Home Fleet as consisting of one cruiser and four 'battle' (!) destroyers seemed to me most unwise to publish, and also untrue in fact. It would be easy to arrange emergency complements which would enable the battleships we are using for training or target purposes to be recorded as available, if need be, at short notice.[3]

On March 8, during the debate on the Navy Estimates, Churchill spoke of the Soviet navy, which 'has not yet taken shape, except, perhaps, for submarines, about which there should be serious consider-

---

[1] Speech of 21 April 1948: Randolph S. Churchill (editor), *Europe Unite*, pages 293–303.

[2] 'My dear Vyvyan Adams', 2 April 1948: Churchill papers, 2/67. Three months later Churchill spoke in the House of Commons in favour of retaining the death penalty. 'I wonder myself,' he said, 'whether, in shrinking from the horror of inflicting a death sentence, hon. Members who are conscientiously in favour of abolition do not underrate the agony of a life sentence. To many temperaments this is a more terrible punishment—to some at least.' (*Hansard*, 15 July 1948.) The death penalty had been abolished in the Soviet Union in 1947; it was restored in 1950 for treason, espionage and sabotage; and extended to murder in 1954, banditry in 1958.

[3] 'My dear Fraser', 25 February 1948: Churchill papers, 2/149.

ation'. As to the Government's decision to scrap so many battleships, ten in all 'consigned to the scrap heap', he wanted to know if it would not be a better policy 'to make the most of all we have got', reminding the House of Commons:

I have some experience in these matters because twice on the first night of two great wars I have sat in the First Lord's chair at the Admiralty, and well I know how in the hour of crisis one looks around for every item of strength that can be scraped together. A set of short-term half-wits in time of peace may brush away old vessels with all kinds of penny-wise, pound-foolish arguments and, if they have the political power, I have no doubt that they will find many experts to testify that these vessels are useless, especially if the experts have a hope that they are going to get new ones built in their place, which they are not.

But, when war comes, that is not what you feel. Before the second Great War, I think I prevented by speeches in this House the destruction of several ships which a year or two later we found most useful. I remember that very old vessel the *Centurion*, battered by target practice for many years, playing an important part in our plans for resisting cross-Channel invasion, and she was moved to Plymouth for that very purpose. There are such things as 'expendables'. There are occasions on which an old ship structure can perform a great feat of arms, and where it would be wrong to risk an up-to-date capital unit of the Fleet, of which there are nowadays so few that they can be counted on the fingers.

Churchill also spoke scathingly of what he saw as an excessive number of Civil Servants at the Admiralty, 12,500 in all, 8,000 more than at the outbreak of war. This was a 'scandal' which any House of Commons 'worthy of its financial responsibilities should probe, scrub and cleanse'. An equivalent number of men to these extra 8,000, he said, 'differently trained and employed—and, no doubt, much less well remunerated—could man two battleships, four cruisers and ten destroyers, now all laid up'. It was the duty of the House 'to cut into this abuse and excessive tophamper'.

Running through all he had said, Churchill ended: 'I censure the lack of policy and comprehension which in this as in other spheres has led our country down to levels of inefficiency which we have never plumbed before.'[1]

Not only inefficiency, but apparent disloyalty, disturbed Churchill during the spring of 1948. 'I see the *Express* has taken a rather anti-American line since you returned to the helm,' he wrote to Lord Beaverbrook on March 23, 'and I have heard some comments in the House about bias for the Communists and the Russians.' All these differences, Churchill warned, 'are going to become acute and deadly

[1] Speech of 8 March 1948: *Hansard*.

in the future'. The Conservative Party was, as a Party, supporting the Government 'against their extreme-Leftists and "cryptos", because these are matters of life and death of the same order and character as those which developed before the last war. I have not heard of any differences in the Party about the line which we have taken.'[1]

On 17 February 1948 Churchill had written to Herbert Morrison to protest at 'the undue prominence given by the BBC to Communist and neo-Communist speakers'.[2] He had repeated his protest eight days later, when he told an all-Party meeting on political broadcasting 'that undue prominence had been given to the Communist point of view in news and features on the BBC. The Communists were not a party but a conspiracy. It was a mistake, in his view, to treat them on an equality with other Parties, but he would have had no complaint if the Communist point of view had received attention in exact propor-tion to the voting strength of its party membership in the country. As it was, it was given an importance and prominence far beyond its deserts. Mr Churchill then gave instances in support of his claim that, with the exception of Sir Stafford Cripps, Messrs Pollitt and Horner had received more prominence on the BBC than any other politician. He also warned the BBC to be on the lookout for Communist penetra-tion inside their own organisation.'[3]

Churchill reiterated two months later that the Communists 'were enemies of the country and that they were an unconstitutional party; and he thought that the BBC's desire for tolerance of their views rested on a misunderstanding of the nature of the Communist creed. It was not to be expected, if the Communists themselves were in control, that any kind of freedom of expression would be tolerated. His fear was that a nest of Communist sympathisers within the BBC were seeking to organise the propagation of these views.' The Communists, he warned, 'had no respect for truth or tolerance of any kind'.[4]

It was now nearly two years since Churchill's Iron Curtain speech. 'I have very agreeable memories of those days,' he wrote to Colonel

---

[1] Letter of 23 March 1948: Churchill papers, 2/146. It is not clear whether this letter was ever sent.

[2] 'My dear Lord President', 17 February 1948: Churchill papers, 2/38.

[3] 'Draft Minutes of a Meeting held in the Lord President's Room in the House of Commons', 'Confidential', 3.45 p.m., 25 February 1948: Churchill papers, 2/38. The Government repre-sentatives present were Morrison, Wilfred Paling (Postmaster-General) and William Whiteley (Chief Whip). The Opposition representatives were Churchill, Brendan Bracken, Lord Woolton and Patrick Buchan-Hepburn. The BBC was represented by Lord Simon of Wythenshawe (Chairman of the Governors), Sir William Haley (Director-General) and George Barnes (Direc-tor of the 'Spoken Word').

[4] 'Minutes of a Meeting held in the Lord President's Room in the House of Commons', 5.30 p.m., 22 April 1948: Churchill papers, 2/38.

Clarke, his host in Miami, 'and after all Fulton has turned out to be a signpost which hundreds of millions of people have followed.'[1] Three weeks later, on April 17, Lew Douglas, the United States Ambassador in London, reported to Washington that Churchill 'believes that now is the time, promptly, to tell the Soviets that if they do not retire from Berlin and abandon Eastern Germany, withdrawing to the Polish frontier, we will raze their cities'.[2]

Following the Communist take-over in Czechoslovakia in February 1948, Churchill was visited by four Czech refugees. He did his best to help them, writing on their behalf to Ernest Bevin, to Lew Douglas, and to a former member of his Defence Office, Major-General Sir Ian Jacob, who had recently been appointed Director of the BBC Overseas Services. One of the Czechs, Churchill wrote to Jacob, 'told me the BBC is listened to now in Czechoslovakia even more than in the war, but that there is a feeling that the best use of this great opportunity is not being made'.[3] 'I was much impressed with these four Czechs,' Churchill told Douglas, 'and I said I would approach you on their behalf.'[4]

At the beginning of the year, Churchill had submitted the printed proofs of the first volume of his war memoirs to the Cabinet Office, and on January 23 Sir Norman Brook had advised Attlee that although Churchill had made 'faster progress than we expected', there was no Cabinet Office objection to the publication of any of the official documents which he wished to use, including eight War Cabinet papers.[5] 'I agree . . .' noted Attlee, and when he raised the matter in Cabinet three days later, his agreement was endorsed.[6] The Cabinet also rejected the earlier suggestion of Adam McKinlay, the Labour MP who wanted Churchill to pay over 50 per cent of his receipts to the State, Attlee telling his colleagues 'that there were no sufficient grounds for suggesting to Mr Churchill that he should pay over to the

---

[1] 'My dear Frank, 28 March 1948: Churchill papers,2/161.

[2] Lewis Douglas report, 17 April 1948: *Foreign Relations of the United States, 1948*, volume 3, Washington 1974, pages 90–1.

[3] 'My dear Jacob', 25 April 1948: Churchill papers, 2/67. In 1952 Jacob became Director-General of the BBC, a post he held until 1960.

[4] 'My dear Lew', 'Private', 25 April 1948: Churchill papers, 2/67. The four Czechs were Mr Firt, Vladimir Krajina, General Ingr and Mr Stransky (who was married to an Englishwoman, a half-sister of Lord de Clifford). General Ingr had been Commander-in-Chief and Minister of Defence of the Czechoslovak Government in Exile in London during the Second World War.

[5] 'Prime Minister', 23 January 1948: Premier papers, 8/1321.

[6] Notes of 24 and 26 January 1948: Premier papers, 8/1321.

Exchequer any part of his receipts from his book by reason of the fact that it was based largely on information which he had acquired as a Minister and included a number of official documents in respect of which Crown copyright could be claimed'.[1]

Subsequently, Churchill was asked to paraphrase two documents, neither written by him. One was a paper written by the Naval Staff, the other an *aide-mémoire* by the Chiefs of Staff about the Norwegian expedition. In both cases Norman Brook prepared the paraphrases which Churchill used, and obtained Attlee's approval. He also persuaded Attlee to allow a minute by General Hollis on the invasion risk in 1940 to be published, on the grounds that 'Mr Churchill quotes so many of his own documents that there is some danger of his creating the impression that no-one but he ever took an initiative. This chapter as it stands comes near to creating that impression; and the quotation of General Hollis's minute, which gives the views of the Chiefs of Staff at first hand, is a valuable corrective.'[2] On Churchill's behalf, in the months ahead, Attlee wrote to the various Dominion Prime Ministers enclosing extracts which Churchill wished to include from his messages to the Dominions and adding, as drafted by Norman Brook: 'Unless you see objection, I propose to tell Mr Churchill that he is at liberty to reproduce these documents in his book.'[3]

Permission was in every case granted, and on April 19 *Life* magazine began its serialization. Even as Churchill continued his work on later volumes, the first volume received, through these extracts, its American acclaim. Each issue was enriched by illustrations which came not only from Churchill's photographic albums but from pictures sought out by a team of *Life* researchers in New York. One of these researchers, Constance Babington Smith, had been the photo reconnaissance interpreter working at Medmenham who had discovered the German rocket installations at Peenemunde on the Baltic Coast. Churchill called her 'Miss Peenemunde'.[4]

On April 19, the day of the first serialization in *Life*, Bill Deakin dined and slept at Chartwell; he was at Chartwell again on April 24, and dined again four days later.[5]

Churchill now made his final preparations for The Hague, asking

[1] Cabinet Conclusions No. 7 of 1948, 'Secret', 26 January 1948: Premier papers, 8/1321.

[2] 'Prime Minister', 26 February 1948, and note by Attlee, 'I agree', of the same date: Premier papers, 8/1321.

[3] 'My dear Prime Minister', 3 March 1948: Premier papers, 8/1321.

[4] In 1958 Constance Babington Smith published an account of her wartime experiences, *Evidence in Camera, the Story of Photographic Intelligence in World War Two*. In 1961 she published *Testing Time: Man and Machine in the Test Flying Era*. She was subsequently a distinguished biographer, publishing biographies of Amy Johnson (1967), Rose Macaulay (1972), John Masefield (1978) and Iulia de Beausobre (1983).

[5] Churchill Engagements Calendar, April 1948: Churchill papers.

Christopher Soames to come with him as his personal assistant, and writing to Stafford Cripps on April 26: 'I am sorry you are not coming to The Hague. I should have liked to lift this whole business above our Party politics and try to make a real brotherhood of Europe, overriding all national, class and Party frontiers. But I quite understand your difficulties, especially when you have already such a heavy burden to carry.'[1]

The object of the Hague Conference was, as its manifesto proclaimed, to 'affirm the urgent need for close and effective unity among the peoples of Europe'. Among those who accepted invitations were Churchill, Léon Blum, Jean Monnet, Paul Reynaud, Paul-Henri Spaak, Paul van Zeeland, Alcide de Gasperi, and a representative of the Vatican 'whom the Pope proposes to designate'.[2] The 140 British participants included Lady Violet Bonham Carter, Anthony Eden, Commander Stephen King-Hall, Harold Macmillan, Duncan Sandys, twenty-two Labour MPs, seven Liberals and, in all, twenty-three Conservatives, as well as the conductor Sir Adrian Boult and the poet John Masefield.[3]

Churchill began his speech by noting how, since he had spoken in Zurich eighteen months earlier, events had carried the cause of a United Europe 'beyond our expectations'. That cause, he said, could either be 'vital or merely academic'.

If it was academic, it would wither by the wayside; but if it was the vital need of Europe and the world in this dark hour, then the spark would start a fire which would glow brighter and stronger in the hearts and the minds of men and women in many lands.

This is what has actually happened. Great governments have banded themselves together with all their executive power. The mighty republic of the United States has espoused the Marshall Plan. Sixteen European States are now associated for economic purposes; five have entered into close economic and military relationship.

We hope that this nucleus will in due course be joined by the peoples of Scandinavia, and of the Iberian peninsula, as well as by Italy, who should now resume her full place in the comity of nations.

[1] 'My dear Stafford', 'Private', 26 April 1948: Churchill papers, 2/376.

[2] 'European Conference at The Hague, May 7–10, 1948', 'Purpose', undated: Churchill papers, 2/21. Spaak was Prime Minister of Belgium (since 1946) and van Zeeland a former Belgian Prime Minister and Minister for Foreign Affairs.

[3] 'List of Participants to the Congress of Europe from Great Britain': Churchill papers, 2/21. In answer to an appeal in Britain for funds for the United Europe Movement, more than £25,000 was raised, the largest donations being £2,500 from Lord Nuffield, £2,000 from Lord McGowan of Imperial Chemical Industries, and £1,000 each from, among others, Viscount Kemsley (Viscount Camrose's brother), Sir Simon Marks of Marks & Spencer and Sir Archibald Jamieson of Vickers Ltd. (List of Supporters from Lord McGowan's Appeal, 1947, dated 28 May 1948: Churchill papers, 2/22.)

All who have worked and tried their best and especially Ministers in responsible office—we must not forget what their difficulties are—like Mr Bevin, M. Bidault, M. Spaak, and General Marshall and others, have a right to feel content with the progress made and proud of what they have done.

The United Europe movement was not of parties but of peoples. If there was to be rivalry of parties, 'let it be to see which one will distinguish itself the most for the common cause'. Churchill continued:

We shall only save ourselves from the perils which draw near by forgetting the hatreds of the past, by letting national rancours and revenges die, by progressively effacing frontiers and barriers which aggravate and congeal our divisions, and by rejoicing together in that glorious treasure of literature, of romance, of ethics, of thought and toleration belonging to all, which is the true inheritance of Europe, the expression of its genius and honour, but which by our quarrels, our follies, by our fearful wars and the cruel and awful deeds that spring from war and tyrants, we have almost cast away.

This first Congress of Europe, Churchill declared, was a 'dynamic expression of democratic faith, based upon moral conceptions and inspired by a sense of mission'. Mutual aid in the economic field, and 'joint military defence', must both 'inevitably be accompanied step by step with a parallel policy of closer political unity'. Addressing himself further to the central issue of European unity, the political aspect, Churchill told the Congress:

It is said with truth that this involves some sacrifice or merger of national sovereignty. But it is also possible and not less agreeable to regard it as the gradual assumption by all the nations concerned of that larger sovereignty which can also protect their diverse and distinctive customs and characteristics and their national traditions all of which under totalitarian systems, whether Nazi, Fascist, or Communist, would certainly be blotted out for ever.

Churchill then welcomed 'into our midst' the German delegations. For the Congress of Europe, he said, 'the German problem is to restore the economic life of Germany and revive the ancient fame of the German race without thereby exposing their neighbours and ourselves to any rebuilding or reassertion of their military power of which we still bear the scars'.

Churchill then spoke of the aim of United Europe in its human dimension, recalling the efforts of his wartime American partner to set out the objectives of the war itself:

President Roosevelt spoke of the Four Freedoms, but the one that matters most today is Freedom from Fear. Why should all these hard-working families be harassed, first in bygone times, by dynastic and religious quarrels, next by nationalistic ambitions, and finally by ideological fanaticism? Why should they now have to be regimented and hurled against each other by variously labelled forms of totalitarian tyranny, all fomented by wicked men, building their own predominance upon the misery and the subjugation of their fellow human beings? Why should so many millions of humble homes in Europe, aye, and much of its enlightenment and culture, sit quaking in dread of the policeman's knock?

That is the question we have to answer here. That is the question which perhaps we have the power to answer here. After all, Europe has only to arise and stand in her own majesty, faithfulness and virtue, to confront all forms of tyranny, ancient or modern, Nazi or Communist, with forces which are unconquerable, and which if asserted in good time may never be challenged again.

Churchill urged the Congress to resolve, at The Hague, to constitute 'in one form or another' a European Assembly to enable the voice of United Europe 'to make itself continuously heard', and he ended with a peroration reminiscent of his largely unheeded calls to unity in the years before the war:

A high and a solemn responsibility rests upon us here this afternoon in this Congress of a Europe striving to be reborn.

If we allow ourselves to be rent and disordered by pettiness and small disputes, if we fail in clarity of view or courage in action, a priceless occasion may be cast away for ever.

But if we all pull together and pool the luck and the comradeship—and we shall need all the comradeship and not a little luck if we are to move together in this way—and firmly grasp the larger hopes of humanity, then it may be that we shall move into a happier sunlit age, when all the little children who are now growing up in this tormented world may find themselves not the victors nor the vanquished in the fleeting triumphs of one country over another in the bloody turmoil of destructive war, but the heirs of all the treaures of the past and the masters of all the science, the abundance and the glories of the future. [1]

'Your speech at The Hague,' wrote Churchill's Principal Private Secretary of 1940, Eric Seal, 'touches the same high level of vision as those you made in 1940. You were the chief architect of Victory by force of arms over Nazi tyranny. May you be given life and energy to add to these great feats of arms the crowning achievement of the final liberation of Europe by the force of a great idea.' [2]

It was eight years since Churchill had become Prime Minister;

---

[1] Speech of 7 May 1948: Randolph S. Churchill (editor), *Europe Unite*, pages 310–17. Recording: BBC Written Archives Centre, Library No. 12174–5.
[2] Letter of 10 May 1948: Churchill papers, 2/155.

nearly three since he had been dismissed by the electorate. At the age of seventy-three and a half he still had the stamina, and the will, to persevere. His speech at The Hague was proof of an energy which he could still command; and of his broad and inspiring view of the future. 'For myself,' he told an open air meeting in Amsterdam two days later, 'I am not the enemy of any race or nation in the world.' Russians, Germans and Japanese, 'we all understand their toils and sufferings'. It was not against any race or nation 'that we range ourselves. It is against tyranny, in all its forms. . . .' [1]

From The Hague, Churchill travelled to Oslo, where he and his wife were guests of the King of Norway. On May 11 he received an honorary doctorate at the University of Oslo, and spoke of how the rights of the individual could be reconciled with the demands of society in a way to bring 'happiness and peace to humanity'. The 'flame of Christian ethics', he said, 'is still our best guide'. [2] On the following night, at an academic dinner in Oslo, he told the assembled guests:

Human judgment may fail. You may act very wisely, you think, but it may turn out a great failure. On the other hand, one may do a foolish thing which may turn out well. I have seen many things happen, but the fact remains that human life is presented to us as a simple choice between right and wrong. If you obey that law you will find that that way is far safer in the long run than all calculation which can ever be made.

I want to say this to you because that is something my experience has taught me. But I certainly do not want you to understand me to say that I have always done the right thing—I should be ashamed to claim that. But I do have the feeling that one must act in accordance with what one feels and believes, and that we must now keep up old relations in freedom and in peace and move together to establish that happy world which surely the toilers, the hard-toiling masses, have a right to enjoy after all they have suffered. [3]

Twice more Churchill was asked to speak, in the City Hall in Oslo before many thousands of people, and at a dinner given for him by the Norwegian Parliament. 'It was most interesting,' he wrote to his wife on May 14, after the dinner in the Parliament House, which she did not feel well enough to attend, '& I made a fourth speech without

[1] Speech of 9 May 1948: *Europe Unite*, pages 318–21.
[2] Speech of 11 May 1948: *Europe Unite*, pages 325–8.
[3] Speech of 12 May 1948: *Europe Unite*, pages 329–31.

repeating myself. The dinner was a remarkable display of wealth, plenty & elegance. The table was about *5 yards across* & 20 yards long. I will come along later & tell you more.'[1]

While Churchill was in Oslo, his wife urged him not to forget to write to the Dutch Queen, who had so recently entertained him in The Hague. '*Please* write quickly "in your own paw" to Queen Wilhelmina,' Clementine Churchill wrote, 'before memory fades.'[2] Churchill did so, from Oslo. His letter read:

Madam,

After these busy days I am so glad to tell Yr Majesty how much my wife and I enjoyed our visit to Het Loo, and how greatly we felt honoured by Yr Majesty's gracious kindness. I earnestly hope that the rest which Yr Majesty is going to take may soon produce good results, and that the first sign of these will be some more of those beautiful pictures by wh I was so much attracted and impressed.

The Conference at The Hague ended in unanimous agreement upon many important principles and cannot fail to exercise a beneficial effect on Europe. All the delegates expressed their gratitude for the charming hospitality with wh they had been received.

And with every sincere wish and my humble duty,
I remain
Yr Majesty's obedient and devoted servant,

Winston S. Churchill[3]

On May 17 Churchill returned to England. While he had been in Norway, Britain's Palestine Mandate had come to an end. David Ben-Gurion had proclaimed the name and independence of the State of Israel. Immediately, five Arab armies had invaded Israel, seeking to bring a rapid end to the Jewish State in whose evolution, especially in 1921 and 1922, Churchill had played a main and consistent part. On May 21, a week after the establishment of the new State, Randolph wrote to his father that a friend who had returned from Palestine two weeks earlier 'tells me that all the local British commanders believe the Arabs will win unless they make incredibly foolish mistakes'. On the other hand, Randolph reported, 'Wavell told a friend of mine last night that he is convinced the Jews can hold their own.'[4]

From Chartwell, Churchill drafted a press statement which he had intended to telephone to the BBC and the Press Association. It read:

---

[1] 'My darling', 14 May 1948: Spencer-Churchill papers. The words in italics had been underlined by Churchill in the letter itself.
[2] 'Winston', undated: Churchill papers, 2/174.
[3] 'Madam', undated: Churchill papers, 2/174.
[4] 'My dear Papa', 21 May 1948: Churchill papers, 1/45.

As Parliament is not sitting I think it necessary to place on record the deep anxiety that is felt about the policy of the British Government in Palestine.

When I became convinced that all chance of making & enforcing a settlement by partition was lost, I advised the Government in the House of Commons on August 1, 1946, nearly two years ago, to return the Mandate to the United Nations Organisation and quit the country at the earliest moment. More than another year passed before this decision was taken by His Majesty's Government, and during all this period the situation grew steadily worse. On September 27, 1947, the Government accepted the policy of returning the Mandate and leaving Palestine. This was generally supported as the only policy possible in the disastrous conditions which had arisen.

Churchill's statement, which in the end he did not issue, continued:

The renunciation of our responsibilities was in any case a most grave decision. I never conceived it possible that the Government, in carrying it out, would not show the strictest impartiality between Jew and Arab. Instead of this it appears that the Arab Legion, led by forty British officers, armed with British equipment and financed by a British subsidy, has fired on the Jewish quarter of Jerusalem. This is a violation of the impartiality which at the least we were bound to observe. Furthermore Article 1 of the Treaty of Alliance between His Majesty's Government and the Kingdom of Transjordan, signed as recently as March this year, prescribes that 'each of the high contracting parties undertakes not to adopt in regard to foreign countries an attitude which is inconsistent with the Alliance or might create difficulties for the other party thereto'. By not invoking this Article we become in a marked degree responsible for the military action of the Arab Legion.[1]

'I am deeply disturbed about the situation which has arisen in Palestine,' Churchill wrote to Lew Douglas on May 26, 'and at the policy of His Majesty's Government and am proposing to raise the matter in the House of Commons.'[2] Churchill's concern was assuaged, however, two days later when he learned that all British officers in the Arab Legion had been withdrawn from active participation in the attack on Jerusalem. 'It would be amazing in any Government but this,' he told a Scottish Unionist meeting in Perth on May 28, 'that the danger of allowing British officers to be compromised in this way was not seen beforehand.'[3]

Asked by Brendan Bracken to intervene again in debate, Churchill replied: 'I cannot do any more on Palestine. Events must take their course.'[4]

---

[1] 'Press Statement', marked 'Not Sent': Churchill papers, 2/46.
[2] 'My dear Lew', 26 May 1946: Churchill papers, 4/57.
[3] Speech of 28 May 1948: Randolph S. Churchill (editor), *Europe Unite*, pages 339–51.
[4] 'My dear Brendan', 19 July 1948: Churchill papers, 2/46.

23

Writing the Memoirs, 1948

―――――――

AS he continued work on his memoirs, Churchill was sent the diaries of Ulrich von Hassell, one of the anti-Hitler conspirators of July 1944. 'I am very carefully studying the efforts made by the German champions of civilization to save their country,' he wrote to the publisher, Hamish Hamilton, on 24 January 1948, and he added: 'All will be understood by history.'[1]

The Marrakech revisions had now been printed, and had themselves been sent to the critics whose points had led to them. On February 1 Emery Reves telephoned to say that Book I as revised 'is absolutely perfect'.[2] Isaiah Berlin was also more content. 'I have read the latest batch of proofs with close attention,' he wrote, 'and greatly welcome the result—particularly such changes and rearrangements as I have noticed.' More even than the opening chapters, Berlin added, which had seemed to him 'to get off to a slow start', the later chapters now set the 'tempo and the rhythm' for the whole work, which was, more than ever, 'a literary and political masterpiece'.

'You did, I recollect, order me to be quite candid,' Berlin reminded Churchill.[3] Churchill had accepted Berlin's suggestion substantially to recast the second and third chapters. He also accepted advice from Christopher Soames, not to ascribe the Polish seizure of Teschen in 1938 to Polish 'baseness in almost every aspect of their collective life'. 'Was the gallant defence of Warsaw not an aspect of their collective life?' asked Soames, and he added: 'The seizure of Teschen was a vile act perpetrated by the Polish Government. Munich was a despicable act perpetrated by the British Government. But nobody blames the

―――――――

[1] 'Dear Mr Hamish Hamilton', 'Private', 24 January 1948: Churchill papers, 2/376.
[2] 'Mr Churchill', note signed by Chips Gemmell, 1 February 1948: Churchill papers, 4/141.
[3] Letter of 14 February 1948: Churchill papers, 4/141. For his help, Isaiah Berlin received an honorarium of 200 guineas. ('My dear Isaiah Berlin', 27 March 1948: Churchill papers, 4/17.)

British *people* for it.' Churchill agreed to replace 'baseness' by 'faults', and 'collective life' by 'Governmental life'.[1]

While working at his war memoirs, Churchill received from his cousin Sir Shane Leslie a book, still in proof, about their American grandfather, Leonard Jerome. It came as a shock to read something so different in style and content to his own. 'The whole story of the Aylesford divorce is intolerable,' Churchill wrote.[2] 'There are many other references to my father and mother which I have noticed and resent,' he added, and he went on to explain, in a passage which he decided to delete before the letter was sent:

All the society gossip which fills the latter part of the book is, in my opinion, utterly unworthy of your literary reputation. I object very much to any reference being made to my father and mother's financial affairs. If you wish to unfold these petty details of a past generation, I trust you will confine it to your own family. I certainly could not allow any of my letters to appear in such a book.

'I am earnestly hoping,' Churchill ended, 'that you will not think of publishing this book which will do you no good, will only pander to the vulgar and which, in its present form, I could never forgive.'[3]

Shane Leslie promised to make the changes Churchill wished. 'I am afraid my error has lost me your affection,' he wrote.[4] Churchill responded at once, and all was forgiven. 'I am most grateful to you,' he telegraphed, and signed his telegram: 'Affectionately, Winston.'[5] But when the book was published, Churchill was again distressed, writing in rebuke:

I have begun to read your book and want to tell you at once I do not like the Introduction which suggests that I only took the trouble to find out about our Grandfather when I had to do a broadcast for America. Can you not manage to leave me out of this?

It is a pity to make out that the family were engaged in 'unending bewailment' at the loss of their fortunes. They were left much better off than most people.

I have no objection to your quoting, on page 8 of the Introduction, what I actually said on July 15, 1941.[6]

---

[1] 'Mr Churchill', 19 March 1948: Soames papers.

[2] The story of the Aylesford divorce appears, far more fully documented, in the first volume of this biography (by Randolph Churchill), published in 1966, and is completely documented in the companion volumes (edited by Randolph Churchill in 1967).

[3] Letter of 26 March 1948: Churchill papers, 1/44.

[4] 'My dear Winston', 7 April 1948: Churchill papers, 1/44.

[5] Telegram sent 10 April 1948: Churchill papers, 1/44.

[6] Churchill's words about his ancestor, spoken in fact on 16 June 1941 in his broadcast acceptance of an honorary degree at his mother's birthplace, Rochester, in New York State, were: 'here my grandfather, Leonard Jerome, lived for so many years, conducting as a prominent and rising citizen a newspaper with the excellent eighteenth-century title of the *Plain Dealer*.' Chur-

I think the expression on page 14—'the maternal pit from which he was digged'—most unpleasant.

The story attributed to me on page 15 about my Father being remembered as 'Winston's father' is utterly untrue. I never spoke in such disrespectful terms of him. I should have thought the biography I have written proved the reverence with which I regarded him.

Of another reference to the Jerome family in Shane Leslie's book, Churchill wrote to his cousin: 'I doubt whether there is any need to talk about "the corrosion of luxury" on p.22.' [1]

Throughout the years when he was writing his memoirs, Churchill's principal contact with his American publishers was Walter Graebner, with whom he had struck up a friendship after their first meeting in the autumn of 1945. It was Graebner who protected him from the cruder efforts of Time-Life to publicize the memoir-writing process. In reading the draft of an article which Time-Life wished to publish in the spring of 1948, to coincide with the publication of volume 1 in the United States, Graebner telegraphed to New York: 'It is most important that you omit the whole section on trust taxes and salary, as publication of this would wreck our relations. We didn't even read this to Churchill because I know he would have insisted that the whole story be killed.' Graebner added: 'Can you change the title to Churchill at Work? He hates that name Winnie.' Churchill was also 'very annoyed', Graebner reported, 'at the references to the bed and to the table on the stomach, so please delete,' and he ended his telegram: 'If you could work in a sentence some place mentioning Churchill's enormous vitality and intensive work, there would be less chance of a blow-up when he sees the story in print.' [2]

Help and encouragement reached Churchill from participants in the historical events he was describing, first from Sir Robert Vansittart and then from Anthony Eden. 'The sweep of the Munich chapters is tremendous,' Eden wrote, 'and I think unchallengeable.' [3]

Churchill sent a further copy of his as yet unpublished work to the

---

chill added: 'The great Burke has truly said, "People will not look forward to posterity who never look backward to their ancestors," and I feel it most agreeable to recall to you that the Jeromes were rooted for many generations in American soil, and fought in Washington's Armies for the independence of the American Colonies and the foundation of the United States. I expect I was on both sides then. And I must say I feel on both sides of the Atlantic Ocean now.'

[1] 'My dear Shane', July 1948: Churchill papers, 1/44.
[2] Telegram of 2 May 1948: Daniel Longwell papers.
[3] 'My dear Winston', 1 April 1948: Churchill papers, 4/144.

woman with whom he had been in love half a century earlier, Lady Lytton: 'it may amuse you', he wrote, 'to keep these galley proofs'.[1]

Plans were meanwhile being made for Volume 2, and the documents assembled. 'Full justice must be done to the other side,' Churchill minuted to his four principal helpers—'our own secret circle' he called them.[2] In a letter to Lord Ismay about the need to challenge various hostile opinions of the Greek and Western Desert policies in 1941, subjects on which Ismay had provided him with notes, Churchill wrote: 'You must understand that it is no part of my plan to be needlessly unkind to the men we chose at the time, who no doubt did their best.'[3]

At the end of April 1948 Churchill received a second payment from Lord Camrose, £35,000 due on the delivery of his second volume.[4] Three days later Jock Colville, after dining at Chartwell, noted in his diary how he, Mary Soames and her husband Christopher 'saw an exceptionally good film called *To Be Or Not To Be*, and dined most agreeably. Winston, who had been busy all day painting a red lily against the background of a black buddha, switched from art to Operation "Tiger".'[5] This operation, the attempt to send tanks by convoy through the Mediterranean in 1941, was at that moment part of the work in hand at Chartwell, Commodore Allen having just sent Churchill a set of all the original Cabinet papers, telegrams and minutes.[6]

After dinner Churchill talked of the visit he and Colville had made to the Rhine in March 1945. Colville noted:

He was scathing about Monty's self-advertising stunts and said he presumed British soldiers would soon have to be called 'Monties' instead of 'Tommies'.

Speaking of the Anglo-American disputes over the question of a Second Front in the Cotentin in 1942, Winston said, 'No lover ever studied every whim of his mistress as I did those of President Roosevelt.'[7]

---

[1] 'Dearest Pamela', 10 April 1948: Countess of Lytton papers.

[2] Note dated 14 April 1948: Churchill papers, 4/351A. The four recipients were Lord Ismay, General Pownall, Commodore Allen and Bill Deakin. Sets of all the specially printed documents were also sent to Lord Camrose, Emery Reves, Henry Luce, Walter Graebner and Daniel Longwell.

[3] 'My dear Pug', 23 April 1948: Churchill papers, 4/208.

[4] 'Dear Winston', 29 April 1948: Churchill papers, 4/57.

[5] Colville diary, 2 May 1948: *The Fringes of Power*, pages 623–4.

[6] 'Mr Churchill', 'Tanks for the Middle East', 30 April 1948. Churchill had proposed that one ship of the convoy should be diverted to Crete. 'You will see,' noted Allen, 'that the Chiefs of Staffs did not carry out your suggestion for diverting a ship of the convoy to Crete but proposed alternative action which there was little time to carry out.'

[7] Colville diary, 2 May 1948: *The Fringes of Power*, pages 623–4.

Immediately on his return from Oslo, Churchill had invited Bill Deakin to dine and sleep at Chartwell, to plan the next stage of the memoirs. The amount of material to be woven into the narrative was formidable. Five years later, Churchill was to say to his publisher, Desmond Flower: 'Desmond, you must admit I have made a prodigious effort.' [1]

To his four principal memoir helpers, Churchill wrote on May 19, when sending them the first rough chapters of volume 3: 'Please do everything you can to fill them in,' and he added: 'Meanwhile I welcome any aid.' [2] 'I have been much hunted lately,' he explained that day to his neighbour, Major Marnham, 'but am hoping to get a little freedom in June.' [3]

On May 21 Churchill was in Westminster Abbey to unveil the memorial to the Commandos, the Submarine Service, the Airborne forces and the Special Air Service. 'Above all,' he said, 'we have our faith that the universe is ruled by a Supreme Being and in fulfilment of a sublime moral purpose, according to which all our actions are judged. This faith enshrines, not only in bronze but forever the impulse of these young men, when they gave all they had in order that Britain's honour might still shine forth and that justice and decency might dwell among men in this troubled world.' [4]

Churchill's words, wrote Major-General Laycock two days later, were 'words which only you could have composed and spoken. All of us are grateful to you, and, particularly, I think, the mothers and widows whose sorrow you have made easier to bear.' [5]

Returning to his war memoirs, on May 24 Churchill minuted to Bill Deakin, about the notes Deakin had prepared on the coup d'état in Belgrade in April 1941: 'Can we have also a paragraph on Hitler's *fury* at the Yugoslav volte-face? He must have been vy much vexed.' [6]

In a second note to Deakin about the Yugoslav coup d'état, this time concerning the Soviet perspective, Churchill wrote:

---

[1] Desmond Flower recollections: letter to the author, 17 July 1987.
[2] Note (to Lord Ismay, General Pownall, Commodore Allen and Bill Deakin), 19 May 1948: Churchill papers, 4/19.
[3] Letter of 19 May 1948: Churchill papers, 2/153.
[4] Speech of 21 May 1948: Randolph S. Churchill (editor), *Europe Unite*, pages 336–8. Recording: BBC Written Archives Centre, Library No. 11978–9.
[5] Letter of 23 May 1948: Churchill papers, 2/303.
[6] 'Mr Deakin', 24 May 1948: Churchill papers, 4/19. The paragraph as finally published read: 'Hitler was stung to the quick. He had a burst of that convulsive anger which momentarily blotted out thought and sometimes impelled him on his most dire adventures. In a cooler mood, a month later, conversing with Schulenburg, he said, "The Yugoslav *coup* came suddenly out of the blue. When the news was brought to me on the morning of the 27th I thought it was a joke." But now in a passion he summoned the German High Command.' (*The Second World War*, volume 3, London 1950, page 144.)

Now we see them at the moment of the Serb crisis, apparently unconscious of what was loading up against them. One flash of sentiment and that merely a grimace—their expression of goodwill towards Yugoslavia at the moment of its destruction. The only deviation into sentiment from cold-blooded, crafty, unmoral, subhuman calculation of self-interest, all founded on wrong data and stupid & erroneous beyond description.

Here we are at the end of March, 1941, with Hitler massing his forces to destroy Russia, and these foolish commissars, the Kremlin gang, let the whole Balkans go to pieces. Our feeble intervention, such as it was, gained them five weeks in which Hitler lost the necessary time to take Moscow before the winter.[1]

On May 25 Commodore Allen presented Churchill with a chronology and documents of the ill-fated Dakar expedition in September 1940, when he had been much criticized. Allen was sending these materials, he wrote, 'after discussion with the First Sea Lord'.[2] On May 26 Churchill was again in London, where he made a short speech at the laying of a new foundation stone in the House of Commons.[3]

On June 2 the first volume of *The Second World War* was published in the United States. That day, there was a lunch at the Savoy in Churchill's honour, given by the Conservative Party. '"The Boss" was in gentlest of moods,' wrote Henry Channon in his diary, 'and made a mild, almost apologetic speech, which was yet not devoid of point and wit. I was very near to him and watched his easy smile and wet blue eyes that always look as if he had been crying.' During his speech, Channon noted, Churchill made it clear 'that he expects to win the Election "next year", or early in 1950, with a "three-figure" majority. His reception was tepid, but not in the least unfriendly— though gone is the rapture of yesteryear. I think that the Party resents both his unimpaired criticism of Munich, recently published, and his alleged pro-Zionist leanings.'[4]

Clementine Churchill's health continued to give her husband considerable concern; he wanted so much to be able to comfort her, and to be with her when the spells of tiredness and depression overcame her. On June 15, after she had been away for two weeks' recuperation, he wrote to her from Chartwell:

[1] 'Mr Deakin', undated: Churchill papers, 4/19.
[2] 'Mr Churchill', 25 May 1948: Churchill papers, 4/248. From 1946 to 1948 the First Sea Lord was Admiral Sir John Cunningham.
[3] Speech of 26 May 1948: BBC Written Archives Centre, Library No. 11980-1.
[4] Channon diary, 2 June 1948: Robert Rhodes James (editor), *Chips*, page 426.

Darling,

You did promise Sept 12 1908 'To Love, Honour & *Obey*'. Now herewith are *Orders*:

3.15   You come up here to *rest*. EYH will bring you & is waiting[1]
7.30   Dinner
8.30   Journey to 28
9.40   Bed & a *read*
Given at Chartwell GHQ.

The Tyrant[2]

The publication of Churchill's memoirs in the United States had caused immediate offence to many Poles, who resented phrases such as 'ingratitude over the centuries has led them through measureless suffering', 'squalid and shameful in triumph', 'too often led by the vilest of the vile', and 'two Polands: one struggling to proclaim the truth and the other grovelling in villainy'.[3] On July 6 Brendan Bracken sent Churchill these phrases, as sent to him by Count Raczynski, the former Polish Ambassador to London. These passages, noted Bracken, 'deeply offended the Poles in Britain, but they remain deeply devoted to you'.[4]

Churchill at once arranged with Cassell to make sure that these phrases did not appear in the British edition, which was yet to be published. On July 12 Denis Kelly informed him that the corrections had been made.[5] Six days later Churchill wrote to Sir Edward Marsh: 'I am much distressed about this Polish passage and have cut it to rags in the English volume. It was written in a feeling of anger against the behaviour of the present Polish Government and the temporary subservience of the Polish people to them.'[6]

In Britain, Volume 1 of Churchill's memoirs was now being serialized in the *Daily Telegraph*. 'May I say how much I have been enjoying your memoirs in the *Telegraph*,' Lloyd George's widow, formerly Frances

[1] EYH was the registration number of the small car (a Morris) in which Churchill used to be driven around the fields of Chartwell. It is now on display at Longleat, as part of the Churchill collection of the Marquess of Bath.

[2] Letter of 15 June 1948: Spencer-Churchill papers.

[3] All these phrases had first appeared in the *New York Times* serialization on 27 April 1948.

[4] 'My dear Winston', 6 July 1948: Churchill papers, 4/144.

[5] Note of 12 July 1948: Churchill papers, 4/144.

[6] 'My dear Eddie', Private, 18 July 1948: Churchill papers, 4/5. When Churchill's second volume was published, it was the French generals who protested (Gamelin, Weygand, Prioux, and the son of General Billotte). Emery Reves commented: 'It seems that your Memoirs have aroused the aggressive spirit of the French generals which was so sadly lacking in 1939. Perhaps it was a mistake not to publish this second volume at the beginning of the war.' ('Dear Mr Churchill, 23 February 1949: Churchill papers, 4/16.)

Stevenson, wrote on June 23, 'particularly the exposure of pre-war Governments.'[1] As well as writing about past Governments, Churchill continued to seek to expose the Government of the day. He was again helped in preparing his speeches by Reginald Maudling, who later recalled:

I have never met, and I am sure I shall never meet, a man cast in the same mould. Perhaps it was an age of titans—Bob Menzies, for example, or Smuts. Perhaps one is merely deluding oneself in thinking that the personalities then were on a larger scale than one meets today. But whatever the truth or falsehood of the generality, Winston stood alone. There was a power, a vision and a magic about the man which I have encountered nowhere else.[2]

Churchill had agreed that summer to speak to a Conservative fête at Luton Hoo. 'It would be very kind of you,' he wrote to Maudling on June 17, 'to get something ready for me for the Luton Hoo meeting. Of course, the Agricultural Charter will be out in the morning papers, and that will require ten minutes or so. Generally speaking, I should take the Brighton Conference speech as a foundation and make a restatement of our position a year later, which has so much improved from a Party standpoint. I think the broad principles should be reaffirmed. I should like very much to have something of yours to work on.'[3]

Churchill spoke at Luton Hoo on June 26, warning his listeners that there would be 'no recovery from our present misfortunes until the politicians whose crazy theories and personal incompetence have brought us down, have been driven from power by the vote of the Nation'. Once that was done, there would be 'a bound forward in British credit and repute in every land'.[4]

Returning from Luton Hoo, Churchill embarked upon as uninterrupted a summer as he could create, to press ahead with his war memoirs, spurred by the enthusiastic reception of the first volume. He recognized from the start that his was not a definitive account, writing to Eisenhower about some of the controversial episodes of 1943 and 1944 with which he would deal: 'However there are matters on which only another generation can pronounce.'[5]

---

[1] Letter of 23 June 1948: Churchill papers, 2/152. The *Daily Telegraph* extracts appeared daily between 16 April and 17 June 1948. The volume itself was published in Britain on 4 October 1948 (four months after its publication in the United States).

[2] Reginald Maudling recollections: Reginald Maudling, *Memoirs*, London 1978, page 44. Maudling was elected to Parliament in February 1950.

[3] 'My dear Maudling', 'Private', 17 June 1948: Churchill papers, 2/69. Churchill's Engagement Calendars show that in the first six months of 1948 he saw Reginald Maudling on February 12 and February 14 (the day he had to make a political broadcast), and again on June 11 (the day before a Young Conservative rally at the Albert Hall).

[4] Speech of 26 June 1948: Randolph S. Churchill (editor), *Europe Unite*, pages 353–66.

[5] 'My dear Ike', 'Private', 1 July 1948: Churchill papers, 2/48. In his letter, Churchill told Eisenhower: 'The only point about which I was unhappy at the time was your inability to give

In a series of notes to General Pownall, Churchill set out his thoughts and needs for the chapters on the battles in the Western Desert in 1941, and the tank reinforcements sent to Wavell. One such note, intended as a short request, became an historical essay in itself. In thanking Pownall for his various notes, and asking for one 'at your leisure' on operation 'Battle Axe' of 16 to 18 June 1941, Churchill told him:

I exerted myself a great deal to bring about this battle which was the hope I had set before myself all the time in Operation Tiger. Alas, I could not pull it off. Wavell did his very best, but the delays in getting the Tiger Cubs into action were heartrending, and due to petty causes like air coolers etc.

I had hoped to fight this battle before the end of May. Rommel was then at his last impetuous gasp. Every round he had to fire, every can of petrol he had to use were his last heart beats. There he lay at Sollum with a thousand miles of communications behind him and all his hitherto successful bluff remaining to be called. In rear of him was an army with road, rail and sea communications, three or four times as strong and with more than three hundred brand-new tanks. Tobruk lay behind him to menace his life-line and it is incredible to me why this was not achieved.

An extensive battle towards Sollum and a grab on his tail from Tobruk would have spelt utter ruin. I cannot conceive why this could not be done. Rommel's glory was built up on our incompetence just as his armies were sustained by his captures of our petrol and ammunition.

Presently comes the battle of June 18. Wavell tried a great deal. He not only flew up but flew out to the Desert Flank, where our Armoured Division had gone astray, in order to bring it back. Meanwhile General Messervy (I think anyhow there was a Mess in it) retired before he could get back to him.[1] The battle was broken off. Losses were about equal, and thereafter from June 18 to October 15, about four months, nothing was done on this front. This proves how weak Rommel was and how he hung on by his eyelids. All that was necessary, even if the battle was muddled, was to go on fighting him and forcing him to fire his ammunition and use up his petrol. But no. For my sins I appointed the great General Auchinleck, who naturally wanted to play for a sitter no matter what was lost in every other direction.[2]

---

me the help I needed to take Rhodes in the autumn of 1943. I still hold to the view I took then, but I quite understand your difficulties. As you know, I did not agree with "Anvil", which was launched in 1944, as I thought it too far to assist you in your Normandy struggle. As things turned out it was you who helped "Anvil", and not "Anvil" which helped you.'

[1] Major-General Sir Frank Messervy had first commanded the 4th Indian Division, then the 1st Armoured Division, and finally the 7th Armoured Division, in the Western Desert. He subsequently commanded the 7th Indian Division in Burma, at Arakan and at Kohima. He was knighted in 1945.

[2] 'It was always my view that you rated Auchinleck too high,' Montgomery wrote to Churchill on 30 December 1950, and he added: 'I knew him well and remember telling you at Tripoli in February 1943 that he was a poor soldier. He was also a very bad judge of men.' (Letter of 30 December 1950: Churchill papers, 2/173.)

Churchill's letter continued:

These notes may be of some help to you. The moral is that war consists of fighting, gnawing and tearing, and that the weaker or more frail gets life clawed out of him by this method. Manoeuvre is a mere embellishment, very agreeable when it comes off. But fighting is the key to victory.

'I had meant this only to be notes,' Churchill ended. 'I now find I am beginning to write the book. Please forgive me.' [1]

Since June 24, the Soviet occupation forces in Eastern Germany had imposed a road and rail blockade on all movement into and out of Berlin. On July 10, Churchill spoke in his constituency in support of Ernest Bevin's firm response. Bevin, he said, 'was right to speak for a united Britain', except for the Communist fifth column 'and those connected with them', but they had 'no power to make us change our national purpose'. [2] On the day Churchill spoke, President Truman wrote to him from the White House of how Churchill could 'look with satisfaction upon your great contribution to the overthrow of Nazism & Fascism in the World'. Truman added: ' "Communism", so called, is our next great problem. I hope we can solve it without the "blood and tears" the other two cost.' [3]

Churchill's mood was now much influenced by the deepening crisis over Berlin. 'Clare says you were depressed and pessimistic about the Russians and the future,' Churchill's cousin Oswald Frewen wrote on July 20, after talking to his sister Clare Sheridan. [4] That night Churchill was able, at least on the surface, to cast aside care, as Henry Channon witnessed at dinner in a private room at Claridge's:

People stood up and clapped as Winston and Mrs Churchill passed through. We were about twenty-two, and an agreeable party, but not the one that I should myself have given for Winston. Not sufficiently distinguished. I was between my sister-in-law Patsy Lennox-Boyd, who was sweet, and Mrs Churchill, who looked most distinguished: beside her Lady Kemsley seemed almost naked. Winston entered like royalty, and bowed a little and made himself charming. . . .

At the end of dinner the men remained behind and Gomer Kemsley appointed himself spokesman and tried to draw out Winston (I have long known of their hostility). But the great man needed no prompting: he was gay, he was grave, he was witty, he was provocative, and in the highest spirits, but

[1] 'General Pownall', 6 July 1948: Churchill papers, 4/220.
[2] Speech of 10 July 1948: Randolph S. Churchill (editor), *Europe Unite*, pages 368–78. In private, Churchill was less confident about Bevin's resolve. 'The gravity of events makes me anxious,' he wrote to Montgomery. 'I trust we are not approaching another "Munich". For such a crime by a British Government there would be no forgiveness.' ('My dear Monty', 'Private', 18 July 1948: Churchill papers, 2/143.)
[3] 'My dear Winston', 10 July 1948: Churchill papers, 2/158.
[4] Letter of 20 July 1948: Churchill papers, 1/44.

he admitted, indeed insisted, that never before in our history had the position of England been so precarious. . . .

When asked by Gomer if he did not admire Attlee he replied, 'Anyone can respect him, certainly, but admire—no!' [1]

On the following day, July 21, Churchill wrote to Attlee about the feelings of his Conservative colleagues, as the Soviet grip tightened on Berlin, of 'anxiety about the state of our defences and resources, both Britain and Allied, on which of course we have not been given any information'.[2] To Eisenhower, who had decided not to stand for the Presidency that year, Churchill wrote:

I am deeply distressed by what we see now. There can be no stable peace in the world while Soviet Imperialism is rampant and Asia on the Elbe. I am strongly of the opinion that waiting upon events to find the line of least resistance will not provide a means of escape for the poor world and the horrors which threaten it. I feel there should be a settlement with Soviet Russia as a result of which they would retire to their own country and dwell there, I trust, in contentment. It is vital to the future that the moment for this settlement should be chosen when they will realise that the United States and its Allies possess overwhelming force.

'That is the only way,' Churchill added, 'of stopping World War Number Three.'[3]

Churchill referred to Berlin when he spoke in the House of Commons on July 31. His speech was in protest against the Indian Government's attempts to annex the predominantly Muslim state of Hyderabad, and against the British Government's refusal to intervene to uphold the provisions of the Indian Independence Act which guaranteed the independence of Hyderabad as a state. During his speech, in which he clashed angrily with Attlee, Churchill declared, of Hyderabad:

. . . it is at present a sovereign independent State. It has a perfect right, as such, to apply for admission to UNO. It has 17 million inhabitants; it has a long history, and a long corporate identity. Of the 54 Member States of the United Nations, 39 have smaller populations, 20 have smaller territory and 15 have smaller revenue.

We are told that Hyderabad is surrounded by Indian territories, that it is

---

[1] Channon diary, 20 July 1948: Robert Rhodes James (editor), *Chips*, page 429.

[2] 'My dear Prime Minister', 'Secret', 'Urgent', 21 July 1948: Premier papers, 8/871.

[3] 'My dear Ike', 'Private', 27 July 1948: Churchill papers, 2/148. Of Eisenhower's decision not to stand for the Presidency, Churchill wrote: 'my feeling is that you were right not to intervene on this occasion. Because if you had stood as a Democrat, it would have looked like going to the rescue of a party which has so long held office and is now in difficulties. On the other hand if you had stood as a Republican it would have been hard on the party whose President you served. However, luckily there is plenty of time.'

completely land-locked, that it has no access to the sea. But such considerations have nothing to do with the right of independence. Switzerland is completely land-locked, and has no access to the sea, but has maintained its independence for hundreds of years. Austria and Czechoslovakia, also, are States which have no access to the sea, but their independence has never been treated lightly by the British House of Commons.

Since when are the rights of States to independence to be impugned or compromised by the fact that they are land-locked? I say that Hyderabad has an absolutely indefeasible status of independence, and that it is fully entitled to membership of the United Nations organisation if accepted by that body and, still more, is entitled to lay its case before that body and appeal for its support and mediation, especially when a breach of the peace may be involved.

Referring to Berlin, Churchill told the House of Commons:

... a very harsh blockade has been imposed on Hyderabad by the Central Government of India, a blockade which, in many aspects, is similar to that which the Soviet Union are now throwing around Berlin, except that the numbers of helpless people are far greater—17 million compared with $2\frac{1}{2}$ million—and also because several very harsh features have been introduced into it, such as the prevention of the supply of medicines, drugs and hospital equipment. The Prime Minister, as I happen to know from interchanges we have had, contradicts this, but I would suggest that he should search more fully for his facts.[1]

Churchill now prepared for a second journey abroad. Not Morocco, but southern France was his autumn choice. He was intending to publish much that bore on current arguments, such as his instructions to Mountbatten in 1943 to prepare for a cross-Channel landing. He would publish these instructions, he said, 'because our American friends all make out that I was the inveterate foe of any descent on the Continent'.[2]

In terms of sales, volume 1 was doing exceptionally well. More than 600,000 copies of the American edition were likely to be sold by Christmas, he told Sir Norman Brook in mid-August. Cassell, who would publish the British edition in October, 'have got the paper for 200,000 copies'.[3] Financially, other income was coming to him as a result of earlier writings: £10,000 as the second and final payment

[1] Speech of 30 July 1948: Hansard. Indian troops invaded Hyderabad on 13 September 1948. Within a few days an Indian Governor-General had been appointed and Hyderabad incorporated into the Republic of India.
[2] 'My dear Dickie', 4 August 1948: Churchill papers, 2/153.
[3] 'My dear Norman Brook', 'Private', 12 August 1948: Churchill papers, 4/17.

from London Film Productions for the film rights in *Savrola* and *The River War*, both written at the turn of the century: £1,855 from Cassells as outright purchase of a volume of his post-war speeches, *Sinews of Peace*; and £450 for the Dutch rights in his pre-war biography of the 1st Duke of Marlborough.[1]

On August 17 Churchill received a bank draft for one million French francs, from Time-Life International, 'in accordance', as its Paris business manager wrote to one of Churchill's secretaries, 'with the arrangements with which you are familiar'.[2] This once more enabled Churchill to travel abroad free from financial constraints. He left for Aix-en-Provence on August 22, together with his wife, his daughter Mary and his son-in-law Christopher Soames. During Churchill's stay, it was explained in a press notice issued from Chartwell, he would 'continue to work on his War Memoirs', living at Aix as 'the guest of *Life* and the *New York Times*'.[3] Before leaving, Churchill arranged for seven daily newspapers, and four Sunday newspapers, to reach him by air on the day of publication.[4] 'If the situation deteriorated to a point affecting my personal safety,' Churchill wrote to Sir Stuart Menzies, 'I should be very glad if you would send me a message advising me to come home in the following terms: "Zip—Menzies".'[5]

Churchill's last message before setting off was a telegram to Willy Sax in Switzerland, which read: 'Please send six tubes of white tempera to Aix-en-Provence.'[6] 'I hope the sun will shine in Aix,' wrote Jock Colville, in inviting Churchill to his wedding, 'and that you will find many agreeable subjects to paint.'[7]

On the day before leaving for France, Churchill was angered to learn from Attlee that the British Government would not support the establishment of a European Assembly, as proposed by Bidault at The Hague on July 20, and as so strongly urged by Churchill as an essential

[1] Financial note, 12 August 1948: Churchill papers, 1/12.
[2] John R. Snedakar to Lettice Marston, 17 August 1948: Churchill papers, 1/70. The currency allowance at that time for those going abroad was £35 in travellers cheques or foreign currency per person and £5 in English sterling. Churchill received a further 500,000 French francs from Time Life International on September 20. The sterling equivalent in August 1948 of one million French francs was £1,136. This was equal to £14,459 in the purchasing power of 1987. The total Time-Life payments for Churchill's travels in August and September 1948 were $8,444.
[3] 'Press Notice issued 5.30 p.m., August 19, 1948': Churchill papers, 1/70.
[4] Note dated 16 August 1948: Churchill papers, 1/72. The daily newspapers were *The Times*, *Daily Telegraph*, *Daily Express*, *Daily Mail*, *Daily Herald*, *Daily Worker* and *Manchester Guardian*; the Sunday papers were the *Sunday Times*, *Observer*, *Sunday Pictorial*, and *Sunday Dispatch*. There was one weekly, the *New Statesman*.
[5] 'My dear Menzies', 'Private', 19 August 1948: Churchill papers, 2/153.
[6] Telegram of 21 August 1948: Churchill papers, 1/19.
[7] 'My dear Mr Churchill', 13 August 1948: Churchill papers, 2/161.

step towards United Europe. Ernest Bevin's view, Attlee reported, was that 'he could not for the time being commit himself'.[1] Now that the Belgian and French Governments had both proposed 'a practical form of action' by setting up a European Assembly, Churchill replied, 'I venture to hope that His Majesty's Government will find it possible to place themselves more in line with Western European opinion upon an issue which they themselves have already done much to promote.'[2]

---

[1] 'My dear Mr Churchill', 21 August 1948: Churchill papers, 2/18.
[2] 'My dear Prime Minister', 21 August 1948 Churchill papers, 2/18.

24
'Hard, *hard* working wonderful Papa'

ON Sunday 22 August 1948 Churchill left Chartwell for Dover, where he was joined by his wife, who had come from Hyde Park Gate. With them on the boat to Calais were Mary and Christopher Soames, two secretaries, Miss Marston and Miss Gemmell, a detective, and Greenshields the valet, all of whom then travelled by the Blue Train overnight to Marseilles, from where they were driven to Aix-en-Provence, to the Hôtel du Roy René.

The first work telegram was succinct, sent on August 24 by Miss Marston to Miss Gilliatt, who had remained in London: 'Urgently require Reynaud correspondence regarding book.' Work at Aix on the book had already begun. 'Despatching bag one today,' Miss Marston added.[1] Also on August 24, Churchill sent back a series of queries, some to Ismay, some to Pownall and some to Deakin, with a note that Lord Cherwell should be asked to check one of the statistics. In connection with the meetings in France at the time of the German breakthrough, three helpers were given the further instruction: 'My French should be checked.' Also enlisted to help on the correct insertion of the extra materials was Denis Kelly.[2] But Churchill was anxious to receive material from London more quickly than it could reach him. 'Am astonished,' he telegraphed to his helpers on August 25, 'to hear and receive nothing from you.'[3]

Miss Marston's telegram to London also revealed some of the strains of a working holiday. 'Lots of curses as we are trying to get ready for a picnic' was one.[4] And on August 26: 'Things warming up. Keep in touch with Deakin re his coming sooner.'[5] That same day: 'Please

[1] Telegram dated 24 August 1948: Churchill papers, 1/70.
[2] 'Notes on Volume II, Book 3', 24 August 1948: Churchill papers, 1/70.
[3] Telegram dated 25 August 1948: Churchill papers, 1/70.
[4] 'Outwards Bag 3', undated 1948: Churchill papers, 1/70.
[5] Telegram dated 26 August 1948: Churchill papers, 1/70.

send minutes August 1941 soonest.'[1] On August 27 Miss Gilliatt telegraphed back to Miss Marston: 'Deakin leaving Sunday by train.'[2]

On August 26 Churchill telegraphed to Deakin, who was still at Chartwell: 'Could you prepare note, about five hundred words, on my relations with Vichy from armistice to end of year, with any telegrams or minutes of mine including Rougier.'[3]

On August 27 Churchill sent notes to Ismay, Pownall and Commodore Allen, for the checking of dates and figures.[4] That day, Deakin telegraphed to Churchill: 'Final meeting Ismay, Pownall, Allen, Tuesday afternoon.'[5] The Tuesday was August 31; Churchill meanwhile wanted Deakin to be with him, telegraphing on August 26: 'I need your help in checking volume two. How soon can you come?'[6]

Deakin had intended to drive out to Aix-en-Provence a few days later, with Walter Graebner. But Churchill's telegram was now followed by a telephone call. Graebner later recalled its gist:

Churchill: Bill, I am very hard pressed. I want you to come down right away. Take to-morrow's plane and I'll have a car meet you at the airport.

Deakin: I'm so sorry, Sir, but I can't possibly get away that early. I have a lot of work to wind up here at Oxford and can't leave for at least four days. Walter Graebner and I are planning to drive down then if that's all right with you.

Churchill: What's that you say? I can't hear you. I need you down here very much. Get on the plane as fast as you can. We'll arrange everything from this end.

Deakin: But, Sir, I said I can't possibly do it. There is work I must finish up here first.

Churchill: This connection is very bad. I can't hear a word you say. We'll see you to-morrow then, Good-bye.[7]

Bill Deakin left at once, on the afternoon of August 28, reaching Aix on the following morning. At Pownall's suggestion, he had agreed to look up, for inclusion in volume 2, more material from Italian sources, including Count Ciano's diary.[8] This too he did, ever the conscientious as well as devoted researcher.

The only political letter which Churchill wrote while at Aix was to James Byrnes, who had expressed his interest in Churchill's eventual

---

[1] Telegram dated 26 August 1948: Churchill papers, 1/70.

[2] Telegram dated 27 August 1948: Churchill papers, 1/70.

[3] Telegram dated 26 August 1948: Churchill papers, 1/70. Louis Rougier was an alleged emissary from Vichy France who had gone to London in October 1940.

[4] 'Notes on Vol II, Bk 3, Chapter VI', 27 August 1948: Churchill papers, 1/70.

[5] Telegram of 27 August 1948: Churchill papers, 1/70.

[6] Telegram of 26 August 1948: Churchill papers, 1/70.

[7] Walter Graebner recollections: Walter Graebner, *My dear Mister Churchill*, page 47.

[8] 'Mr Churchill' (from General Pownall), 31 August 1948: Churchill papers, 4/196.

account of the Potsdam Agreement, and the Soviet advance into Germany. 'It will be quite a time before I reach my account of the closing phase of the war,' Churchill replied, and he added, in two paragraphs which he decided to delete before the letter was sent:

As you will remember, I was strongly in favour of delaying the American and British withdrawal to the zone agreed with the Russians in 1943 till after there had been a general showdown on the spot and a settlement of all the outstanding problems from Trieste to Korea. I must regard the giving up of the heart of Germany as a terrible event. I think we were quite free to consider the matter in the light of the general situation, after the 'mockery' that was made by the Russians of our agreements at Yalta about Poland.

About Prague; my recollection is that I did my utmost to persuade General Eisenhower to let his two armoured divisions roll into Prague, as they could so easily have done in a few hours. In this also great disasters have followed and no one can measure what will happen in the future.

'We are now confronted,' Churchill ended, in a sentence which he did send, 'with the designs and ambitions of despots as wicked as Hitler and even more absolute. How right you were to stand up firmly to them about Persia in 1945.'[1]

On September 1 Walter Graebner left London for Aix-en-Provence, bringing with him corrected proof pages from Ismay, Pownall and Allen, as well as comments from Professor R. V. Jones on the 'secret' war of the bending of the German aircraft direction-finding beams. Amid work and reflection, Churchill also found time for several excursions to paint. One such excursion was to the Montagne Sainte-Victoire, so beloved of Cézanne, a 'long happy afternoon', Walter Graebner later recalled. But at dinner that night, Churchill at first said little:

Deep in thought for several minutes, he suddenly broke into the conversation around him, and said rather gravely:

'I have had a wonderful life, full of many achievements. Every ambition I've ever had has been fulfilled—save one.'

'Oh, dear me, what is that?' said Mrs Churchill.

'I am not a great painter,' he said, looking slowly around the table. For a few seconds the embarrassment was so complete that no one could bring himself to say anything, and then the party talked of other things.[2]

Some of the telegrams from Aix to London were about Churchill's medicines and paints. 'Send three tubes pink madder from Rober-

---

[1] 'Private and Confidential', Hôtel du Roy René, Aix-en-Provence, 31 August 1948: Churchill papers, 2/146.

[2] Walter Graebner recollections: Walter Graebner, *My dear Mister Churchill*, page 92.

sons . . .' began one of them.[1] But most of the notes and telegrams
concerned the last-minute demands of Volume 2. 'I am sure Reynaud
paid a visit to London either on May 18 or 19, 1940,' Churchill
minuted to Ismay. 'Bill is going to see him shortly and will ask.'
Lord Halifax might recall lunching with Churchill and Reynaud
during that visit 'downstairs at the Admiralty', Churchill added. 'He
could be asked.'[2]

On September 4 Lord Cherwell left London for Aix. He too brought
proofs from the printer and notes from the researchers. Four days
later came a letter from Ismay, in reply to one from Churchill, who
had asked whether, at the Briare meeting at the time of the fall of
France, he had really, as some French writers alleged, insisted that
the French, far from retreating south of Paris, should take the military
offensive. Ismay replied:

I am positive that you did not express any 'considered military opinion' on
what should be done. When we left London, we considered the breakthrough
at Sedan serious, but not mortal. There had been many 'breakthroughs' in
1914–1918, but they had all been stopped, generally by counter-attacks from
one or both sides of the salient.

When you realised that the French High Command felt that all was lost,
you asked Gamelin a number of questions with, I believe, the dual object
first of informing yourself as to what had happened, and what he proposed to
do, and secondly of stopping the panic. One of these questions was—'When
and where are you going to counter-attack the flanks of the Bulge? From the
North or from the South?' But I would be prepared to swear in a Court of
Law that you did not press any particular strategical or tactical thought
upon the Conference. The burden of your song was: 'Things may be bad,
but certainly not incurable.'[3]

That day, in 'Bag 14' from the Roy René to Chartwell, Churchill sent
a letter to Montgomery, 'to be delivered by hand'.[4] It was about the
fate of the German Field Marshals captured by the Allies in 1945,
and still held in custody. Their treatment, Churchill wrote:

. . . has already been severely criticised by the leading newspapers who point
out that they have been held for three years and four months as prisoners of

---

[1] Telegram of 8 September 1948: Churchill papers, 1/70. 'Pink madder unobtainable in England' was the reply (from Miss Sturdee). Churchill at once telegraphed to Willy Sax in Switzerland: 'Please send me three tubes pink madder to Aix.' (Telegram of 9 September 1948: Churchill papers, 1/19.)

[2] 'Lord Ismay', 'Chapter III', 3 September 1948: Churchill papers, 4/19. Reynaud does not appear to have visited London on 18 or 19 May 1940, but Churchill and the War Cabinet did send, on May 18, a special emissary, Sir John Dill, to see him. Dill reported back in writing to Churchill that Reynaud did not want the British forces to withdraw to Dunkirk, but to move southwards towards the defences of Paris.

[3] 'My dear Mr Churchill', 8 September 1948: Churchill papers.

[4] 'Bag 14', despatched 5 p.m., 8 September 1948: Churchill papers, 1/70.

war without any charge being brought against them. They are now to be deprived of their military rank, which is a serious procedure affecting the entire military profession throughout the world. They have been given much more rigorous confinement since they were repatriated to Germany than they had during their long stay as prisoners of war in Great Britain. I am quite sure that their treatment is contrary to the whole spirit of the British Army and also strikes the wrong note for our future relations with Germany.

Churchill's letter continued:

I can assure you that the Conservative Party will press this matter severely in the House of Commons. Unless there are some facts of which we know nothing, I feel, though I have not finally decided, that I shall have to curtail my holiday to come back and challenge this action in the House when it meets on September 14. I must frankly say that I regret very much that you, who have always shown a chivalrous disposition towards the vanquished, should have been involved in all this by the Socialist Government.

'It pains me very much,' Churchill ended, 'to see such bad things done.'[1]

Among those who visited Churchill at Aix-en-Provence was Robert Boothby, who later recalled much talk about the events of 1940 and 1941, as well as about current affairs. As Boothby recalled:

The conversation then turned to the Jews. I said that they were going to win hands down in Palestine, and get more than they ever expected. 'Of course,' he said. 'The Arabs are no match for them. The Irgun people are the vilest gangsters. But, in backing the Zionists, these Labour people backed the winners; and then ran out on them. You were quite right to write to *The Times* protesting against the shelling of Jerusalem.' This brought Christopher Soames in. He said that public opinion at home was pro-Arab and anti-Jew.

'Nonsense,' said Winston. 'I could put the case for the Jews in ten minutes. We have treated them shamefully. I will never forgive the Irgun terrorists. But we should never have stopped immigration before the war.'

He went on to say that he never saw Weizmann because he found him so fascinating that, if he did, he would spend too much of his time talking to him. 'Weizmann gives a very different reason,' I replied. 'What is that?' 'Last time I saw him he said that the reason you would not see him was because, for you, he was "Conscience".' Silence.

The final discussion was about Berlin:

I asked him if he knew what was going on in Berlin. 'No,' he said. 'It might be another Munich. With this difference. We shall be far stronger this time next year. The American Air Force will be three times the size, and their bombs a third bigger. With this advantage, we shall be able to have our holiday in peace!'

'Nevertheless,' he continued, 'I would have it out with them now. If we do

[1] 'My dear Monty', 'Private and Personal', 6 September 1948: Churchill papers, 2/31.

not, war might come. I would say to them, quite politely: "The day we quit Berlin, you will have to quit Moscow." I would not think it necessary to explain why. I am told that they are absolutely certain that we shall behave decently, and honourably, and do the right thing—according to their ideas of our own standards—in all circumstances. With me around, they would not be quite so sure.'[1]

On the evening of September 10, Randolph Churchill left London for Aix, bringing yet more proofs and notes, including more from Ismay and Pownall. Churchill, meanwhile, had gone for a weekend to stay with the Duke and Duchess of Windsor at their villa on Cap d'Antibes. It was there, on September 12, that Churchill and his wife celebrated their fortieth wedding anniversary. In giving her a gift, Churchill wrote, above a drawing of a pig:

My Beloved,
    I send this token, but how little can it express my gratitude to you for making my life & any work I have done possible, and for giving me so much happiness in a world of accident & storm.
    Your ever loving and devoted husband   W[2]

On September 13 Churchill and his wife returned to Aix-en-Provence. 'Antibes was great,' Miss Marston telegraphed to Ismay.[3] That same day, carried by BOAC flight from Marseilles to London, 'Bag No. 16' contained a letter from Churchill to Eden, 'for immediate and personal transmission to him'.[4] In this letter, Churchill urged the strongest possible Conservative protest against India's 'cruel blockade' of Hyderabad. The acquiescence of the Labour Government in this was 'about the most odious of transactions as any in which a British Ministry has ever been implicated'. Churchill then wrote about a possibility of the German Field Marshals being brought to trial, a prospect which 'offends everyone', and he added:

Some of the most extreme Socialists have signed a letter against it. All decent soldiers and military opinion is shocked. I personally feel so strongly about it that I am considering sending a subscription to the defence of these aged generals. That they should have been kept waiting for three and a half years without any charge formulated and should now be brought to trial is deemed indefensible even by *The Times*. Our improving relations with the

---

[1] Lord Boothby recollections: Lord Boothby, *My Yesterday, Your Tomorrow*, London 1962, pages 211–12.
[2] Letter of 12 September 1948: Spencer-Churchill papers.
[3] Telegram of 13 September 1948: Churchill papers, 1/70.
[4] 'Bag No. 16', 12 noon, 13 September 1948: Churchill papers, 1/70.

mass of the German people have been greatly stimulated by the blockade and our efforts to feed the two and a half million Germans in Berlin, will all be set back by the continuance of these trials not only of the field marshals but the interminable and indefinite persecution and hunting-down of individuals; after all, the principal criminals have been punished. You perhaps noticed De L'Isle and Dudley's letter to *The Times*.[1] I am sure every honourable soldier deplores and resents what is being done.

'There was however', Churchill suggested, an explanation 'which you may be able to elucidate behind the scenes, namely that the Russians are demanding that these men should be handed over to them to try, and that we are acting in order to forestall the Soviet demands'.

Churchill then wrote to Eden about the continuing Soviet blockade of West Berlin:

We must naturally ask for a full statement about the position in Berlin. It is obvious that the Kremlin have no intention to come to a friendly all-round agreement. If one cause of quarrel is adjusted another will be fomented. If a four-power conference is arranged on the general question of a treaty of peace with Germany or a united Germany, everyone knows that this will only be a pretext for delay resulting in a deadlock.

'Meanwhile,' Churchill warned, 'we must be careful not to lose the soul of Germany.'

Churchill's next concern was the part which the possession by Russia of the atomic bomb would have on the balance of power. As he told Eden:

I have felt misgivings and bewilderment which is latent but general in thoughtful circles about the policy of delaying a real showdown with the Kremlin till we are quite sure they have got the atomic bomb. Once that happens nothing can stop the greatest of all world catastrophes. On the other hand it must be borne in mind that the American Air Force will be nearly double as strong this time next year as today, that the United States will have a third more atomic bombs and better, and far more effective means of delivery both by airplanes and the bases they are developing, the largest of which is in East Anglia. Therefore while we should not surrender to Soviet aggression or quit Berlin, it may well be that we and the Americans will be much stronger this time next year, and it is very improbable according to my information, that the Soviets should have made the bomb by then. I am not therefore inclined to demand an immediate showdown, although it will certainly have to be made next year.

[1] On 6 September 1948 *The Times* published a letter from a former junior Minister in Churchill's caretaker government, Lord De L'Isle and Dudley (who had won the Victoria Cross during the Second World War), in which he wrote: 'The detention of prisoners-of-war in rigorous confinement for three years after the end of hostilities, the proposed "demilitarization" and trial of the leading commanders of a defeated enemy, upon charges so long delayed and not yet announced, fill me, Sir, with dismay. I fear for the reputation of our country, and I fear for the precedent which is likely to prove not a deterrent but an incitement to further barbarity in war.'

'None of this argument,' Churchill noted, 'is fit for public use.'

Churchill's final theme and concern was the 'extraordinary behaviour' of the Labour Government in not supporting the European
Assembly. France, the United States and the Benelux countries were,
he said, 'astonished' at this obstruction. 'I earnestly hope,' Churchill
ended, 'that this matter may be raised and probed, and that strong
condemnation should be expressed. Conceit, jealousy, stupidity are all
apparent in the behaviour of Bevin and other Socialist leaders concerned.'[1]

From Montgomery came a letter to Aix-en-Provence, sent from
London on September 18, about the German Field Marshals. 'The
facts are,' he wrote, 'that the War Office (Shinwell, myself, and everyone) has always said it is utterly monstrous to deal with the German
Field Marshals and Generals in the war as they are doing.' It was
'entirely a Cabinet decision', Montgomery added, 'and Bevin is at the
bottom of it'.[2]

Volume 2 of the war memoirs was now almost completed. Yet still
more material was reaching Churchill daily from his helpers. On September 20 Ismay sent two recollections of Britain awaiting invasion,
additional to the stories which Churchill himself had included. The
first read:

We went down the front at some small seaside place, where practically
every house was a boarding house which relied on the summer visitors for a
living. It was a miserable rainy day, but all the old women who owned these
boarding houses, and who had temporarily lost their livelihood, turned out
and cheered you wildly and called God's blessing upon you.

The second Ismay recollection was also a vivid one:

I remember that the first visit that you made to the troops was to a Corps
commanded by General Massy and that you made it by car. I well recall
your wrath on this occasion at being taken into the Corps War Room and
introduced to all the staff. You told me that you had not come to see this sort
of thing but to see troops exercising.[3]

On September 20 Clementine Churchill returned to London.

---

[1] 'My dear Anthony', 'Private & Confidential', 12 September 1948: Churchill papers, 2/68.

[2] 'My dear Mr Churchill', 'Private', 18 September 1948: Churchill papers, 2/31.

[3] 'My dear Mr Churchill', 20 September 1948: Churchill papers, 4/196. General Massy, who
had fought in the First World War at Gallipoli and on the Western Front, and had been
Director of Military Training at the War Office from 1938 to 1939, served as a Corps Commander from 1940 until his retirement in 1942.

Churchill himself remained in France, moving his entourage and his work to Lord Beaverbrook's villa, La Capponcina, on the Côte d'Azur. 'I am glad you prolonged your holiday,' Clementine wrote to her husband on September 21, '& are driving slowly along that coast you love so well.'[1]

Further proofs now reached Churchill at La Capponcina, and others were returned by him from La Capponcina to London. On September 24 Churchill had a series of final questions for Deakin about the fall of France. 'I pay a considerable tribute to M. Charles-Roux,' he noted. 'I should like to know a little more about him before letting this go finally.'[2] 'I do hope you are painting lovely gay pictures of sea & air & wind,' Clementine Churchill wrote that day from London.[3]

Churchill was indeed painting, and enjoying his work and holiday so much that he decided not to fly back in Lord Beaverbrook's private plane, but to stay a few more days on the Riviera. 'Divine weather this morning,' he told Beaverbrook in a telephone message to Miss Sturdee, '& I could not bear to tear myself away. I therefore told your aeroplane it need not come and fetch me.' He would move on the next day to the Hôtel de Paris in Monte Carlo, 'where everything is comfortably arranged', but hoped he could still 'come and paint' in Beaverbrook's garden '& keep my tackle in the garden house'.[4]

On September 29, Churchill, now on his final week of holiday work at Monte Carlo, but still sending every day a bag with queries to London, wrote to Deakin about the chapters on the desert victory in 1941. 'I have not yet used the note by Captain Soames,' Churchill pointed out, 'in which the expression occurs "three or four acres of officers and two square miles of prisoners". I cannot find this in my boxes at this moment.' Churchill also asked Deakin to make sure, with Pownall, that they added 'some mention of Wavell's use of the 4th Indian Division which had played its part in the opening battle but was very shrewdly sent off to Abyssinia and made Keren possible.

---

[1] 'My darling Winston', 21 September 1948: Churchill papers, 1/41.

[2] 'Mr Deakin', 24 September 1948: Churchill papers, 4/19. Describing Pétain's formation of a new French Government on the night of June 16, Churchill wrote: 'M. Baudouin, who had already undertaken the Foreign Office, for which he knew himself to be utterly inadequate, was quite ready to give it up. But when he mentioned the fact to M. Charles-Roux, Permanent Under-Secretary to the Ministry of Foreign Affairs, the latter was indignant. He enlisted the support of Weygand. When Weygand entered the room and addressed the illustrious Marshal, Laval became so furious that both the military chiefs were overwhelmed. The permanent official however refused point-blank to serve under Laval. Confronted with this, the Marshal again subsided, and after a violent scene Laval departed in wrath and dudgeon.' (Winston S. Churchill, _The Second World War_, volume 2, London 1949, page 190.)

[3] 'My darling', 24 September 1948: Churchill papers, 1/41.

[4] 'Lord Beaverbrook' (noted down on the telephone by Miss Sturdee), undated: Churchill papers, 2/146.

This is much acclaimed by Wavell's champions, and it seems to me to deserve mention and tribute here.'[1]

One last instruction to Deakin and Miss Sturdee concerned style. He had always given this to the charge of C. C. Wood, the former employee at Harrap when Churchill was writing his four *Marlborough* volumes; indeed, the process of proof-reading for style and punctuation was known in Churchill's circle as 'wooding'. Now the need for it seemed urgent again, as Churchill explained to his assistant and his secretary:

In view of all the piecemeal alterations inserted in Volume II it would be well for Mr Wood to read them through with a fresh eye. I must have a talk with him about commas. I have arranged with Sir Edward Marsh to cut these down as much as possible as they are a nuisance. I have no doubt what principles are correct. I do not want the whole book repunctuated with commas on each side of the 'however's, and 'of course's. Neither do I want my particular spelling of Tsar, etc., to be altered in accordance with modern malpractice.

On the other hand repetitions are best detected by a fresh eye. This also applies to apparent contradictions of one part of the text by another.

Finally of course he should note all obvious inaccuracies, mistakes and misprints. There is no need however for him to go into merit. Nor does he need to go through the documents on which the book is founded.[2]

Churchill returned to England, and to Chartwell, on October 2. Three days later, Clementine Churchill wrote to her husband about the purchase by the Chartwell Literary Trust of a London house for Randolph costing in the region of £14,000, after Randolph had explained to her that 'he intends to marry again, and also that he would like to have room to put up little Winston'. She added: 'If we take Randolph's possible marriage into consideration we must also suppose there might be a baby.'[3] Randolph did get married, that November, to June Osborne; and there was to be a baby, Arabella. The Chartwell Literary Trust bought him a London house, and later, when he decided to live in the country, a house in the country.

On October 5, at Croydon, Churchill spoke at the opening of a new headquarters for 615 Squadron. 'I have been Commodore of this Squadron,' he said, 'since a year before the late war and I have fol-

---

[1] 'Desert Victory', 29 September 1948: Churchill papers, 4/196. Marked by Churchill, 'Done'.

[2] 'Mr Deakin,' 'Miss Sturdee', 29 September 1948: Churchill papers, 4/201.

[3] 'WSC from CSC', 5 October 1948: Churchill papers, 1/45.

lowed with the closest attention its many periods of arduous service, illuminated by brilliant exploits and achievements.' The Auxiliary Squadrons, he said, 'fought in every field', and their record was 'surpassed by none'. Now their part was no less vital. 'Large scale formations,' he said, 'are indispensable to the safety and freedom of any community.' From the Rhine it was possible to carry a 'stream' of pilotless weapons, rockets, to southern England. 'At present the frontier of Asia is upon the Elbe.' Churchill continued:

We should be very foolish to repeat again the mistakes of the past and be drawn under even worse and far less excusable conditions into a life and death struggle for the mere existence of our country.

It is not as if the existence of our country alone was at stake, because the cause of freedom, the resistance to tyranny in all its forms, whatever livery it wears, whatever slogans it mouths, is a world cause, and a duty which every man and woman owes to the human race in all its circumstances.

Churchill then praised the Squadron's recent efforts at recruitment, and urged them to continue those efforts, telling the assembled pilots:

There is no Party question in this. Whatever views we hold, a free country under Party politics, we must always try our utmost, and other people must always try their utmost, to put country before Party. Let us make sure we set the example.[1]

Three days after his visit to Croydon, Churchill travelled by train to Llandudno in North Wales, for a Conservative Party rally, where, on October 9, he spoke, at the Pier Pavilion, telling his audience of several thousand: 'Our minds are oppressed by the accounts of our relations with Soviet Russia.' Britain was confronted with the 'deadly enmity and continued aggression' of the Soviet Government and its 'imprisoned satellites'. No words that he could use 'could surpass the declaration of the Foreign Secretary, Mr Bevin, or of Mr McNeil, the Minister of State. . . .' Russia was heavily armed, and her forces in Europe 'far exceed those of all the Western countries put together'. 'Our Socialist Government,' Churchill pointed out in sarcastic vein, 'who now call upon us in quavering tones to take all kinds of serious half-measures of preparation and precaution, are the same people who assured the electors in 1945 that they alone possessed the secret of dwelling on good terms with Soviet Russia, and who boasted of the underlying affinities and comprehension subsisting between Left-Wing parties and doctrines all over the globe.'

Casting his mind back to the last years of the war, Churchill declared:

[1] Speech of 5 October 1948: Robert Shillingford papers (gramophone recording).

... the gulf which was opening between Asiatic Communist Russia and the Western Democracies, large and small, was already brutally obvious to the victorious War Cabinet of the National Coalition even before Hitler destroyed himself and the Germans laid down their arms.

In fact, as we can all now see, the growing aggressiveness and malignity of the Soviet Government and its complete breaches of good faith at that time should have made both the British and American Governments refrain from dispersing their armies so completely. Nor should they have carried out their great withdrawals in Germany until after there had been a general confrontation along the line upon which the Western and Eastern allied armies had met.

It would also have been wiser and more prudent to have allowed the British Army to enter Berlin, as it could have done, and as many good judges thought would be done, and for the United States armoured division to have entered Prague, which was a matter almost of hours.

He and his 'colleagues of all parties', Churchill added, 'foresaw at that time that the armies of democracy would melt in the sunlight of victory, while the forces of totalitarian despotism could be held together on a gigantic scale for an indefinite time'.

Today, Churchill warned, nothing stood between Europe and 'complete subjugation to Communist tyranny' except the atomic bomb in American possession. The Soviet Union had proposed the internationalization of atomic energy and the outlawing of its military use. For this to be accepted, Churchill argued, they must 'reassure the world', not by words but by action, and he went on to explain what he meant:

Let them release their grip upon the satellite States of Europe. Let them retire to their own country, which is one-sixth of the land surface of the globe. Let them liberate by their departure the eleven ancient capitals of Eastern Europe which they now hold in their clutches. Let them go back to the Curzon Line as was agreed upon in the days when we were fighting as comrades together. Let them set free the million or more German and Japanese prisoners they now hold as slaves. Let them cease to oppress, torment, and exploit the immense part of Germany and Austria which is now in their hands.

We read continually of the blockade of Berlin. The lifting of the blockade at Berlin would be merely the stopping of blackmail. There should be no reward for that.

Let them cease to distract Malaya and Indonesia. Let them liberate the Communist-held portion of Korea. Let them cease to foment the hideous protracted civil war in China.

Above all, let them throw open their vast regions on equal terms to the ordinary travel and traffic of mankind. Let them give others the chance to breathe freely, and let them breathe freely themselves.

None of the other victorious allies, Churchill pointed out, had tried to add 'large territories and populations' to its domain. Britain, indeed, had gone to the opposite extreme 'and cast away her Empire in the East with both her hands'. Let the Russians be content, he said, 'to live on their own and cease to darken the world and prevent its recovery by these endless threats, intrigues and propaganda'. There would be time for 'putting away' the one 'vast, and I believe sure and overwhelming, means of security' which remained in the hands of the United States, 'and which guards the progress of mankind'.

Speaking of the Berlin blockade, then in its third month, Churchill insisted that he would not have allowed the crisis to develop as it had done:

It would have been better to meet, in good time, the blockade of Berlin by counter-measures against Russian shipping, and imports of all kinds, which might be useful for war purposes, than to be driven from the roads, the railways and the canals and left with only the prodigious exertion of what is called the 'Air-Lift' into Berlin, which may at any moment be interrupted by the winter weather or by Soviet action.

Thus we should at a much earlier stage have had something practical to bargain with, and not be reduced to bickering and bluster and a very hard task.

The contest between East and West, Churchill said, was an 'unequal trial of strength, an unfair ordeal'; it was like an endurance contest between two men, 'one of whom sits quietly grinning in his armchair while the other stands on his head hour after hour in order to show how much he is in earnest'.

Churchill then praised 'the wonderful and prolonged efforts' by the American and British Air Forces to feed the $2\frac{1}{2}$ million Germans in Berlin. This 'tremendous, beneficial and humane effort' had, he believed, demonstrated to the Germans in the Western Zones, 'as no words could have done', that the future of Germany 'lies with the European family and with the glory and civilization of the West, to which the German race has still a measureless contribution to make'.

Churchill then made his first public pronouncement against the 'endless trials', as he called them, of Germans 'who were connected with the former Nazi regime'. Now it was the turn of 'these aged German Field Marshals and Generals', he said, to be subjected, 'without the formulation of any charges', to what he considered to be 'a new, prolonged ordeal'. Churchill's criticism of these trials continued:

On every ground soldierly, juridical and humanitarian, it is known to be a wrong and base thing to do. But how foolish, how inane—I might almost say insane—it is to make a feature of such squalid long-drawn vengeance when the mind and soul of Germany may once again be hanging in the balance between the right course and the wrong.

I trust that even now wiser councils may prevail, and also, on the general question of post-war vengeance, I strongly urge our American friends to let bygones be bygones. After all, three years have passed and the principal criminals have suffered the punishments they deserved.

When I survey the misfortune in which Europe is plunged, I admire the wisdom and statecraft which General MacArthur has displayed in his dealing with Japan. He is making it possible for decent Japanese to say 'the future of our country lies with the United States and their sister nation, our old ally, Britain'. That cannot be to the disadvantage of the security of the world.[1]

Churchill's catalogue of criticisms against the Attlee Government was wide-ranging. It began with India, where 'our pledges and obligations to great masses of people who trusted us'—the Untouchables, the Muslims and the Princes among them— had been 'repudiated', and where at least 400,000 people, 'that is to say a larger number than all ours killed in the war', had been 'butchered' in the Punjab alone. Sir Stafford Cripps, 'whose sensitive mind is shocked at the execution of a single murderer for the vilest crimes, treats this frightful holocaust as a mere incident in the process of oriental self-government'. Churchill's criticisms continued:

The orgy of anarchy and murder which I predicted to you in Burma has already come to pass. Alas that we should have to say it.

The Socialists, more than any other Party in the State, have broken their word in Palestine and by indescribable mis-management have brought us into widespread hatred and disrepute there and in many parts of the world.[2]

Southern Ireland, or Eire, is about to cast off the last tenuous association with the Crown, and is apparently expecting Ulster, without whose loyalty we could not have maintained our lifeline into the Mersey and the Clyde

[1] Later that month Churchill wrote to the Court that was about to try the former German diplomat and State Secretary, Baron Weizsaecker: 'I have never met Baron Weizsaecker, but from the impressions I derived and from my subsequent study I think it unworthy of the victors that after more than three years he should be brought to trial for performing his functions as an official in the German foreign office.' (Note of 25 October 1948: Churchill papers, 2/72.) This note is marked by Churchill 'hold', and may never have been sent.

[2] For six months Britain had refused to recognize the new State of Israel, despite both American and Soviet recognition. A memorandum from Marcus Sieff, of Marks & Spencer, which was sent on to Churchill, stressed the danger of Arab extremism against Israel if Britain were to continue not to recognize the new State. In a letter to Churchill on 2 November 1948, Marcus Sieff wrote: 'Many Israeli leaders are anxious to see ties with this country renewed. The present British policy in the UN Assembly vis-à-vis Israel and the Arab States prevents any such rapprochement. Israel could become a bulwark against the spread of Communism in the Middle East. The present Government there has no desire to get tied up with the Eastern bloc; only a continuation of our present foreign policy can force the new State into the Russian orbit.' ('Dear Mr Churchill', 2 November 1948: Churchill papers, 2/46.)

during the war, to be driven out by us against her will from the British Empire.[1]

These, Churchill commented, were 'but some of the misfortunes and tragedies which have befallen us under Socialist misrule on the morrow of our greatest victory and the services we had rendered to all mankind. Once again we have cast away by our folly and inconsequence much that we had gained by our virtue and our valour.'[2]

'I thought your speech at Llandudno was magnificent,' wrote Field Marshal Montgomery on the following day.[3] *The Times* disagreed. Quoting Churchill's statement that 'the western nations will be far more likely to reach a lasting settlement, without bloodshed, if they formulate their just demands while they have the atomic power and before the Russians have got it too', the newspaper commented: 'Put like this, it must seem a dangerously simple solution. Even if it were true—and what Frenchman or Italian would agree?—that it is the atomic bomb which alone prevents the victory of Communism, it is extremely unlikely that just the threat of the bomb would make Russia consent to a settlement on western terms. No great and proud nation will negotiate under duress; Britain and the United States have rightly refused to do so in the case of Berlin. It is unreasonable to suppose that Russia will willingly negotiate on the division of the world under threat of atomic bombardment.' To ask Russia to withdraw from Eastern Europe and to bring an end to Communist agitation and infiltration throughout the world was, *The Times* added, 'infinitely desirable, but Mr Churchill cannot seriously imagine them happening by arrangement. To ask the Communists to give up agitation and revolt is to ask a leopard to change his spots or a tiger to remove his stripes.'[4]

'Only the Communists and *The Times* seem to dislike your speech!', Sarah Churchill wrote to her father on October 11.[5] 'I was really astonished when *The Times* leader was shown to me,' Churchill wrote to Colonel J. J. Astor, 'at the way in which history repeats itself,' and he added that even the *Daily Herald*, the Labour Party newspaper, had not attacked his speech. 'This can only be,' he commented, 'because the Foreign Office have told them that it was helpful to the general position.'[6]

---

[1] On 10 October 1948 the President of the Irish Republic, Eamon de Valera, launched a campaign in Britain under the auspices of the Anti-Partition League of Ireland, declaring the partition of Ireland to be an 'anachronism', and accusing Britain of 'aggression' in Ireland.

[2] Speech of 9 October 1948: Randolph S. Churchill (editor), *Europe Unite*, pages 409–24.

[3] 'Dear Mr Churchill', 10 October 1948: Churchill papers, 2/143.

[4] 'Mr Churchill at Llandudno': *The Times*, 11 October 1948.

[5] 'Darling Papa', 11 October 1948: Churchill papers, 1/45.

[6] 'My dear John', 'Private', 14 October 1948: Churchill papers, 2/145. This letter had been marked 'Put By', and was never sent.

So angered was the Conservative candidate Julian Amery at the attitude of *The Times* towards Churchill's Llandudno speech that he sent the newspaper a magisterial rebuke:

Sir,

Your leading article on Mr Churchill's speech at Llandudno does all that can be done with words to discredit his sombre warning. You seek to dismiss his whole case for firmness backed by the ultimate use of force on the ground that 'no great and proud nation will negotiate under duress'. But are not the blockade of Berlin, and the Civil War in Greece, flagrant acts of 'duress' undertaken or instigated by the Russian Government? When and how is that 'duress' to be removed? It is not for me to formulate on Mr Churchill's behalf the precise demands which he would make the test of Western resolution. But seriously, what prospect is there of any demands however reasonable proving acceptable to the Russians, unless backed by overwhelming 'duress'? Was that not the whole sum and substance of Mr Churchill's speech?

I would further venture the following comments on two other aspects of your criticism. You wrote of the speech: 'If there was in it a lighter note, a rather larger use of stress and emphasis, a somewhat slighter recognition of the responsibility of a great elder statesman and a consequent over-simplification when compared with the famous speeches at Fulton or Zurich or The Hague, the explanation must no doubt be found in the air of Llandudno—and in the cheers of the massed Conservatives who welcomed him so movingly.' Was this intended to suggest that Mr Churchill departed from his prepared text in response to the warm welcome he received? If so, I can assure you as one who sat in the audience with the authorised text of the speech in hand, that he departed at no significant point from his typescript.

As to your attribution to Mr Churchill of 'a somewhat slighter recognition of the responsibility of a great elder statesman . . . when compared with the famous speeches at Fulton or Zurich', I do not recall that either of these speeches struck you as particularly statesmanlike at the time. Those of your readers who care to refresh their memories by looking back at your leading articles of March 6, 1946 and September 30, 1946, will find that your comments on those speeches struck much the same note of deprecation and showed the same unwillingness to face an increasingly inescapable issue as did your more recent comments on the speech at Llandudno.

If so much were not at stake it would be interesting to see whether two years hence you will pay the same tribute to the Llandudno speech as you now afford to the Fulton and Zurich speeches two years after their delivery.[1]

When he spoke in the House of Commons on October 28, during the Debate on the Address, Churchill reiterated many of the points of his Llandudno speech, including his view that Russia should be challenged over the Berlin blockade. He also criticized the continued trials in Germany, which he called 'this lump of folly'. The trial of Baron

---

[1] 'Sir', 12 October 1948: Churchill papers, 2/145. *The Times* did not publish Amery's letter.

Weizsaecker, he added, was 'a deadly error', and he told the House of Commons:

The time has come to stop these denazification trials which are taking place throughout Germany. We run the risk of creating a veritable vested interest among those who are engaged in conducting the vast number of trials which are in process, or liable to come to one. The principal criminals have been executed by their conquerors. There may be some exceptional cases, such as the slaughter of men of the Norfolk Regiment, which was the subject of a trial in Hamburg last week. This it was right to pursue, as one would pursue a common case of murder, even after 15 years had passed before it came to light, but the general process of denazification has gone on far too long and should be brought to an immediate end.[1]

During his speech of October 28, Churchill also spoke of his attitude towards a united Ireland, which in 1921 and 1922 had been the long-term goal of the Irish Treaty into whose negotiation and defence he had put so much time and energy:

I shall always hope that some day there will be a united Ireland, but at the same time, that Ulster or the Northern Counties will never be compelled against their wishes to enter a Dublin Parliament. They should be courted. They should not be raped.

As the Minister responsible for carrying out the Cabinet decisions embodied in the Irish Treaty of 1921 I have watched with contentment and pleasure the orderly, Christian society, with a grace and culture of its own and a flash of sport thrown in, which this quarter of a century has seen built up in Southern Ireland, in spite of many gloomy predictions.

I well know the grievous injury which Southern Irish neutrality and the denial of the Southern Irish ports inflicted upon us in the recent war, but I always adhered to the policy that nothing, save British existence and survival, should lead us to regain those ports by force of arms, because we had already given them up.

In the end we got through without this step. I rejoice that no new blood was shed between the British and Irish peoples. I shall never forget—none of

---

[1] On 2 November 1948 Frederick Elwyn-Jones, Labour MP for Plaistow and a leading jurist, wrote to Churchill about 'some of the allegations being made against Weizsaecker in connection with mass murder'. His letter continued: 'Weizsaecker and his subordinates signed a number of communications to German envoys in foreign countries and to the RSHA, ordering and authorizing the departure from country after country of death transports to the East. On March 20th 1942, for example, Weizsaecker and Woermann informed Eichmann, the RSHA official in charge of Jewish extermination, that there were no objections on the part of the German Foreign Office to the deportation of 6,000 French and stateless Jews to Auschwitz.' 'I won't trouble you with any more examples,' Elwyn Jones ended, 'but I do feel that we shall be rendering little service to democracy or decency if we denigrate the American trial of the men responsible for these abominations.' ('My dear Winston Churchill', 2 November 1948: Churchill papers, 2/72.) The RSHA (Reich Security Main Office) of the SS had been established in 1930; from 1939 its Section IV B4, headed by Adolf Eichmann, supervised the arrest and deportation of Jews throughout Germany, occupied Europe, Axis Europe and North Africa.

us can ever forget—the superb gallantry of the scores of thousands of Southern Irishmen who fought as volunteers in the British Army, and of the famous Victoria Crosses which eight of them gained by their outstanding valour. If ever I feel a bitter feeling rising in me in my heart about the Irish the hands of heroes like Finucane seem to stretch out to soothe it away.[1] Moreover, since the war, great antagonisms have grown up in this world against Communist tyranny and Soviet aggression. These have made new ties of unity of thought and of sympathy between the Irish and the British peoples, and indeed throughout the British Islands, and they deeply stir Irish feelings. The Catholic Church has ranged itself among the defenders and champions of the liberty and the dignity of the individual. It seemed to me that the passage of time might lead to the unity of Ireland itself in the only way in which that unity can be achieved, namely, by a union of Irish hearts.

There can, of course, be no question of coercing Ulster, but if she were wooed and won of her own free will and consent I, personally, would regard such an event as a blessing for the whole of the British Empire and also for the civilised world.[2]

For Churchill, October 1948 was a month of great personal satisfaction in his capacity as an author. 'The reviews of your book,' wrote his daughter Sarah on October 11, 'are almost all unanimously overwhelmed with it—as a literary classic—a personal story—and history. Wow!' and she added: 'Hard, *hard* working wonderful Papa.'[3] In sending Churchill one of his own books on October 22, Maurice Ashley, his literary assistant from 1929 to 1935, wrote: 'I shall always remember with gratitude that I learned more of the art of writing history from working for you than I did from my Oxford professors.'[4]

For Churchill, the sending out of copies of his book was an opportunity, both for the pleasure of authorship and giving, and, on occasion, for making a current political point. Thus on October 29, in

---

[1] Wing Commander Brendan ('Paddy') Finucane, who was born in Dublin in 1920. He was a much decorated fighter pilot with the DSO and DFC and two bars. He shot down 32 enemy aircraft, which put him fifth in the British 'league table' of fighter aces. He was drowned on 15 July 1942 when returning from a sweep over France. His Spitfire was forced to ditch in the sea after being hit by ground fire. The eight Irish winners of the Victoria Cross in the Second World War were: Flying Officer Donald Edward Garland, RAF (who won his VC in Belgium, 12 May 1940); Captain Harold Marcus Ervine-Andrews, East Lancashire Regiment (Dunkirk, 1 June 1940); Acting Captain Edward Stephen Fogarty Fegen, RN (North Atlantic, 5 November 1940); Temporary Captain James Joseph Bernard Jackman, Royal Northumberland Fusiliers (Tobruk, 25 November 1941); Lieutenant-Commander Eugene Kingsmill Esmonde, RN (Straits of Dover, 12 February 1942); Lance-Corporal John Patrick Kenneally, Irish Guards (Tunisia, 28–30 April 1943); Private Richard Kelliher, Australian Military Forces (New Guinea, 13 September 1943); Flight-Lieutenant David Samuel Anthony Lord, RAF (Arnhem, 19 September 1944).
[2] Speech of 28 October 1948: *Hansard.*
[3] 'Darling Papa', 11 October 1948: Churchill papers, 1/45.
[4] Letter of 22 October 1948: Churchill papers, 2/378.

sending a copy of Volume I to the President of Turkey, Ismet Inönü, whom he had met in conference at Adana in 1943, Churchill wrote, of 1948:

As this anxious year unfolds itself I am glad to feel the ties grow stronger which unite the freedom-loving and civilized nations against Bolshevik barbarism. I rejoice that the United States as well as Great Britain are in such close sympathy with Turkey. Our Socialist Government here have put their duty to the cause of world freedom above all party considerations, and from across the Atlantic comes an ever-stronger flow of comradeship and aid. We may therefore face the future together in good heart.

I trust you are keeping the gallant Turkish Army in good order to defend, if need be, your native lands.

You will probably have read some of my speeches from time to time and therefore I hardly need to assure you that I march steadily along the same road against aggression and tyranny, whatever garments they wear or language they speak.

'You very kindly invited me,' Churchill added, 'to come with my paint box to Turkey, and I shall certainly bear this in mind as a future treat for me. Alas, I have many duties here and they do not look as if they would become lighter in the future. Still, if the chance offers, I shall not hesitate to write to you, my valued and honoured friend.'[1]

On November 4 Churchill made his ninth journey back to Harrow since 1940 to join in the school 'Songs'. Referring at one moment to his age, Churchill remarked 'I may say that you would be terrified to know how old I am'.[2]

The election of Harry Truman as President that November gave Churchill much pleasure; on November 8, from Chartwell, he sent the President a handwritten letter of congratulation:

My dear Harry,

I sent you a cable of my hearty congratulations on your gallant fight and tremendous victory. I felt keenly the way you were treated by some of your party and in particular Wallace who seemed to us over here to be a greater danger than he proved. But all this has now become only the background of your personal triumph. Of course it is my business as a foreigner or half a foreigner to keep out of American politics, but I am sure I can now say what a relief it has been to me and most of us here to feel that the long continued comradeship between us and also with the Democratic Party in peace and

[1] 'My dear President Inönü, 29 October 1948: Churchill papers, 2/151.
[2] 'My dear Head Master, Ladies and Gentlemen', 4 November 1948: Churchill papers, 2/336.

war will not be interrupted. This is most necessary and gives the best chance of preserving peace.

I wish you the utmost success in your Administration during this most critical and baffling period in world affairs. If I should be able to come over I shall not hesitate to pay my respects to you.

With kind regards,
Believe me
Your friend,

Winston S. Churchill

Churchill added, in a postscript: 'Mrs Churchill predicted your success and sends her compliments and good wishes to your wife whom she met at Fulton time.'[1]

Churchill continued to work steadily on his war memoirs, enlisting, as hitherto, the help of participants in the events he wished to describe. 'I should like to have your narrative of the Battle as you saw it with the Coldstream,' he wrote to Christopher Soames on November 11, and he went on to explain:

I should like you to put this down from your own recollection. I do not want you to try to write the story of the Battle as a whole, because evidently immense compressions would be required. Seven or eight thousand words is all I can give to the tale. Meanwhile I send you a few papers from my own secret file, and Auchinleck's Despatch. These you might look into as a background and to refresh your memory. I may want them back any day. Meanwhile please keep them under lock and key.[2]

On November 16 Churchill was again in the House of Commons, to lead the Opposition's attack on the Government's Bill to nationalize the Iron and Steel industries. At one point there was both a quotation and an interruption casting back to Churchill's days as a Liberal four decades earlier:

I used to say in bygone days, and I repeat it gladly now, 'Socialism attacks Capital, Liberalism attacks Monopoly.'

Mr Shurmer (Sparkbrook): Is that what the right hon. Gentleman used to say about Conservatives?

Mr Churchill: If I were to try to recall at this moment all the utterances I have made during 50 years of public life, I should trespass unduly on the patience of the House. I therefore confine myself to the citation of such statements as I may consider relevant.

Nationalization and all its methods were, Churchill said, a 'murder-

---

[1] 'My dear Harry', 8 November 1948: Truman papers. 'His defeat of Dewey for the Presidency in 1948,' noted *The Times* in Truman's obituary in 1972, 'was the most unforeseen electoral result this century, and remains to this day the pollster's nightmare.'

[2] 'Christopher', 10 November 1948: Lord Soames papers.

ous theme'; the remarks of Government spokesmen about the control of raw materials by the State were 'about as refreshing to the minor firms as the kiss of death'. The fate of the coal industry was proof of the 'great and costly failure' of nationalization. 'I have always held,' Churchill said, 'that miners, working far from the light of the sun, should have special consideration.' There was then an interruption:

Mr Fernyhough (Jarrow): In 1926?
Mr Churchill: Yes, in 1926 particularly. If the hon. Gentleman perused the story of those negotiations he would see how unjust is his interruption. Forty years have passed since I moved the Second Reading of the Mines Eight Hours Bill. In comradeship with Mr Bob Smillie—I do not know if the hon. Member has ever heard of him, he was a much admired leader in those days—I introduced baths at the pitheads. I greatly admired the spirit of the miners in both wars and regretted that I had to deny so many of them the opportunity of winning distinction on the field to which they ardently aspired.[1]

In mid-November Churchill learned from the King's Private Secretary, Sir Alan Lascelles, that the royal tour to Australia and New Zealand, planned for the following year, would have to be postponed. Examination of the King's left leg had revealed a serious condition of the circulation; so serious that unless great care were to be taken, gangrene, and possibly thrombosis, might appear, and appear quite suddenly.[2] Churchill wrote at once to the King:

Sir,
    It is with sorrow that I learn that Yr Majesty has had to abandon Your visit to Australia and New Zealand. I am sure that the decision is a wise one. I had been concerned to think of the intense and prolonged exertions the tour wd have demanded from both Yr Majesty and the Queen. They wd have killed you by kindness! The distances are enormous and everywhere there wd have been delighted and loyal crowds. One must not underrate the strain of such enjoyable contacts with enthusiastic friends.
    Sir, I trust that the rest and relief will restore yr health, and enable you to add long years to your reign. It has been a time of intense stress and trial. It may well be that history will regard it as 'our finest hour'. I am proud to have been Yr First Minister in all these great adventures. I ever hope in spite of my

---

[1] Speech of 16 November 1948: *Hansard*. Robert Smillie, President of the Miners' Federation of Great Britain from 1912 to 1921, had helped Churchill (then President of the Board of Trade) with the Liberal mines legislation of 1908. Smillie had died in January 1940, at the age of eighty-two.
[2] 'Dear Mr Churchill', 'Top Secret', 19 November 1948: Churchill papers, 2/171.

age to stand at Yr Majesty's side once again. However this may befall, I remain Yr Majesty's devoted and grateful servant

Winston S. Churchill [1]

'I always dreaded this Australian visit,' Churchill wrote to Sir Alan Lascelles, and he added: 'Few human beings could undergo such an ordeal without an immense loss of vitality. Now I trust the King will take things easy, and not be worried about the way things are going. All will come right, and I feel sure his reign will see not only Victory but its Reward.' [2]

From the King himself came a handwritten letter, sent from Buckingham Palace:

My dear Winston,

I must write & thank you so much for your kind letter & for so kindly giving me the beautifully bound copy of your book *The Second World War* Volume 1.

I am very sorry that our tour in Australia & New Zealand has had to be postponed for a while, but I do genuinely feel relief that this malady of mine, which has been aggravated by constant worry & anxiety over the World situation, will keep me at home & will give me a period of rest for a time.

The treatment prescribed by my doctors is already doing me good, & I am benefiting from it to a great degree.

This is really no time for me to go such a long distance from home, as I feel anything may happen in the next 6 months or so.

Thanking you again so very much for your letter.

I am

Yours very sincerely

George R [3]

On November 30 Churchill celebrated his seventy-fourth birthday. Two of those who wrote to him with congratulations had fought with him at Omdurman in 1898 and in South Africa in 1899. 'I never forget our luncheon the day before the battle of Omdurman began,' Churchill replied to Sir Reginald Wingate. [4] And of his soldier friend Angus McNeill, Churchill told Eden: 'He took over the command of the Montmorency Scouts in the Boer War after Montmorency was killed, and I had a very dangerous ride with him.' [5]

---

[1] 'Copy of letter to the King in Mr Churchill's own hand', Chartwell, 22 November 1948: Churchill papers, 2/171.

[2] 'My dear Alan', 'Private', 22 November 1948: Churchill papers, 2/171.

[3] 'My dear Winston', 25 November 1948: Churchill papers, 2/171.

[4] Letter of 30 November 1948: Churchill papers, 2/157.

[5] 'My dear Anthony', 13 December 1948: Churchill papers, 2/49. In his book *London to Lady-smith via Pretoria*, published in 1900, Churchill wrote of De Montmorency: 'In Egypt the name was associated with madcap courage,' but in South Africa 'they talk of prudent skill' (page 232). De Montmorency was awarded the Victoria Cross at the battle of Omdurman in 1898, during the charge of the 21st Lancers in which Churchill also took part. He was killed in action on 24 February 1900.

25

'Poor old Britain . . .'

THREE days before his seventy-fourth birthday, Churchill had, as reported by *Time*, 'donned jodhpurs, fortified himself with rum punch and galloped off to the hounds astride a borrowed horse'.[1] This was indeed so. 'I was glad,' he wrote to the King on 2 December 1948, 'to be able to have a gallop with "The Old Surrey and Burstowe", and not to be tired at all.' Churchill added: 'I trust and pray Yr Majesty's progress is good. I think so much of you Sir in these days and of all you have done and have still to do for our country in these dangerous and depressing times.'[2]

When he spoke in the Foreign Affairs debate on December 10, Churchill congratulated Bevin and his colleagues upon 'the success, surpassing expectation, of the prodigious airlift to feed the people of Berlin'. The airlift had taught the people of Germany 'on the other side of the Iron Curtain', in a way which no speeches, arguments or promises could do, 'that their future lies in ever-closer association with the Western world'.

Referring to the recent elections in Berlin as a proof of 'the resurrection of the German spirit', Churchill spoke of 'a mighty race' without whose effective aid 'the glory of Europe' could not be revived. It was for these reasons, he added, 'that I look forward to the day when all this hateful process of denazification trials and even the trials of leaders or prominent servants of the Hitler regime may be brought to an end. At any rate, I should like to put this point—surely enough blood has been shed. I would not take another life because of the quarrels, horrors and atrocities of the past.'

Churchill then raised the question of the British Government's continual refusal to recognize the State of Israel, telling the House of Commons:

---

[1] *Time* magazine, 13 December 1948.
[2] 'Copy of a letter in Mr Churchill's own hand', 2 December 1948: Churchill papers, 2/171.

The Jews have driven the Arabs out of a larger area than was contemplated in our partition schemes. They have established a Government which functions effectively. They have a victorious army at their disposal and they have the support both of Soviet Russia and of the United States.

These may be unpleasant facts, but can they be in any way disputed? Not as I have stated them. It seems to me that the Government of Israel which has been set up at Tel Aviv cannot be ignored and treated as if it did not exist.

Churchill pointed out that nineteen countries had already recognized Israel, 'and we, who still have many interests, duties and memories in Palestine and the Middle East and who have played the directing part over so many years, would surely be foolish in the last degree to be left maintaining a sort of sulky boycott'.

Then there was Britain's duty to King Abdullah of Transjordan. It was twenty-seven years since Churchill had first proposed and supported his appointment as Emir in Amman. 'We cannot remain indifferent to his fate,' Churchill argued, 'and treat him'—here he turned to the Indian example which still rankled with him—'as we have treated the Nizam of Hyderabad.' But if Transjordan were attacked, Churchill explained, 'and we are drawn in, this might bring us into direct dispute with the United States. After all the good work we did over 20 years in Palestine—and all the progress that was shown there—it would indeed be tragic if the only result we carried away, apart from the hatred and abuse of Jews and Arabs, was a deep divergence on a critical issue between us and the United States.' That indeed, Churchill added, 'would be a sorry reward for all our efforts'.

Britain should send an envoy, Churchill urged, 'without delay' to Tel Aviv.[1]

During the last two weeks of December, Churchill worked again on his memoirs. He had been encouraged by a letter from Noël Coward, who admired in Volume I 'your impeccable sense of theatre which kept bubbling up at unexpected moments. Your "curtain" line after your description of Ribbentrop—at lunch in 1938—"that was the last time I saw him before he was hanged" was quite wonderful.' He admired also in the book 'so much wisdom and dreadful truth and sublime use of words and, strangely enough, so little bitterness'. Coward ended his letter with an apology for his effusive language. 'But I do love my country and its traditions and its language and—to

[1] Speech of 10 December 1948: *Hansard*.

hell with self-consciousness—Thank you deeply and sincerely for your immortal contributions to all three.'[1]

Throughout December, General Ismay and General Pownall prepared historical material for Churchill's scrutiny. He was also helped considerably by Denis Kelly. In explaining to the Chartwell Literary Trust the reasons for paying Kelly £1,200 a year for the next three years, Churchill pointed out how important his assistant's work was 'to the completion of my task in writing the book on which the Trust depends'. This work, Churchill explained, was threefold: the 'normal care of the archives', the 'special and much heavier task of looking out and extracting from them the papers which I require for the book' and help in 'a great deal of the spade work'.[2]

The range of documents put at Churchill's disposal was considerable. Among those who sent him previously unpublished material was the former Permanent Under-Secretary of State at the Foreign Office, Sir Alexander Cadogan, who provided extracts from his diary of the Atlantic meeting of August 1941 between Churchill and Roosevelt. 'I send them to you,' he wrote, 'in the hope that they may at least remind you, if you read them, of some of the lighter moments which the conscientious historian would be inclined to disregard. So forgive any apparent flippancy. This record is only the ragged fringe of great events. . . .'[3]

On December 28 Churchill left England for France. On New Year's Eve he gave a dinner in Paris for the Duke and Duchess of Windsor, before taking the night train south, to Monte Carlo.[4] From the Hôtel de Paris at Monte Carlo, on January 11, he wrote to King Michael of Roumania, in congratulating him on his marriage: 'I earnestly hope that a joyous life may be yours, despite the bitter winds that blow.'[5]

Among those who visited Churchill at the Hôtel de Paris was his daughter Sarah, who brought with her a man with whom she was very much in love. Churchill, unfortunately, took against him, as he had indeed taken against another of Sarah's friends the year before.

[1] 'Dear Mr Churchill', 9 December 1948: Churchill papers, 2/455. Churchill replied by telegram: 'Thank you so much for your charming letter.' (Telegram of 12 December 1948: Churchill papers, 2/455.)

[2] 'Dear Sirs', December 1948: Churchill papers, 4/57. During December 1948 Denis Kelly made five overnight visits to Chartwell, Bill Deakin three and General Pownall one. (Churchill Engagements Calendar, December 1948: Churchill papers.)

[3] 'My dear Winston', 31 January 1949: Churchill papers, 4/225.

[4] Once more, Churchill's journey was paid for by Time-Life, their payments for December 1948 and January 1949 totalled just under $5,000.

[5] Letter of 11 January 1949: Churchill papers, 2/164.

Distressed at her father's behaviour, Sarah wrote to him from the hotel:

Darling Papa,

I am so grieved to have upset your holiday by once again intruding one of my friends upon the scene.

Of course I should after Marrakech last year have known better, but 'hope springs eternal in the human breast', and when Mummie told me I could bring someone I was delighted, and thought that perhaps things would go better this year.

If I live a hundred years I shall never understand your point blank rudeness and unkindness.

Am I not a human being? Can you not call me into your room, tell me you do not like him, and for the love that you say you have for me, extend him just the common courtesy that you do to the maître d'Hôtel or chef d'orchestre, & trust me to see that the visit is terminated quickly. What kind of a position have you put me into now? It is *my* mistake, not his, that he is here. Rightly or wrongly, he *was* invited.

If you think by insulting him, you can change one jot, the opinion I hold of him—you are most sorely mistaken. If you think by insulting him, you will make him go away—you are certainly right, for he is a young man of considerable dignity & spirit. But except for the love I have for both you and Mama, I should leave at once, too, for you have also succeeded in deeply wounding me.

I assure you I shall never again, subject you to any of my friends, nor indeed them, to your contempt.

I do not understand how you can say you love me—when you are so very, very unkind.

I love you very much—nothing can ever change that—but I see now how right I have been to build a life for myself, and arm myself with four good hoofs & a crusty carapace, for the slings & arrows of family life are sharp indeed.

Your loving

Sarah [1]

Randolph Churchill was also to be in dispute with his father when, after his marriage to June Osborne, he asked his mother for details of the family Trust. This had led his father to write to him, refusing to disclose any details. Like his sister Sarah, Randolph set down his grievance in writing:

... I explained to June that under the Trust considerable provision had, I understood, been made for your children and grand-children and that therefore, though I was not in a position to make adequate provision for her, the future of any children we might have would be amply safeguarded.

Now that June is going to have a baby I thought it right & proper to

---

[1] Letter undated, on Hôtel de Paris notepaper: Churchill papers, 1/46.

enquire as to the terms of the Trust under which I have already been a beneficiary. I had understood that your main object in setting up the Trust had been to provide for the future security of your children and grand-children. It seemed to me that one element in that security would be knowledge, at least in general terms of the provisions of the Trust. It is obviously easier to plan one's life in this uncertain world if one is aware as far as possible of the prospects of oneself and one's children.

Like all your children I am immensely grateful to you for the exertions & generosity by which you have contributed so handsomely to our past, present & future welfare. I hope that this letter will make it plain that my request to my mother to acquaint me with the terms of the Trust was not intended in any way as an intrusion into your private affairs. I had merely thought that I had a duty and responsibility to my wife, my son and any children I may have in the future to acquaint myself as far as possible with our prospects. For, naturally, my plans must to some extent depend upon them.

'Please forgive me,' Randolph added, 'if I was at fault.' [1]

Churchill hastened to put his son's mind at rest, informing him of the financial provision that had been made for him, including the promised purchase for him, by the Trust, of a house in the country. 'I am deeply grateful to you,' Randolph replied, '& it is a great comfort to me to know that I shall have this security in my lifetime.' [2]

Churchill found himself, while at Monte Carlo, in the midst of a controversy about Spain. A leading Spanish liberal, and émigré since 1936 from the Franco régime, Salvador de Madariaga, had urged the Western democracies not to admit Spain into the United Nations. Churchill did not approve of this exclusion, to Madariaga's distress. 'It is my belief,' Churchill wrote to his critic, 'that Franco would have already disappeared by now but for the fact that foreign countries have so pointedly identified Spain with him.' Churchill added:

I am sure it is a mistake to punish and insult whole nations. Spain has as much right to be represented on the United Nations Organisation as Russia or Poland, and most civilised people would find it easier to live in Spain than in either of the other two totalitarian countries. I do not propose to live in either. [3]

* * *

[1] 'My dear Papa', 'Private', 25 April 1949: Churchill papers, 1/46.
[2] 'My dear Papa', 12 May 1949: Churchill papers, 1/46.
[3] 'Dear Don Madariaga', 2 January 1949: Churchill papers, 2/27.

While he was still at Monte Carlo, Churchill read extracts which Fitzroy Maclean had sent him of Maclean's memoirs of the war years, and of his meetings with Churchill in connection with the British mission to Tito, of which Maclean had been the head. On January 12 Churchill sent Maclean what he called 'a few casual notes' about the references to himself, notes which show how hard he worked to dispel the many growing myths about himself, but which indicate also that those myths could never be entirely dispelled:

p. 2   I have never worn pyjamas, heavy silk or otherwise, in my life.

p. 3   I have never addressed anyone as 'My boy'.

p. 5   I was much too feeble to paint during this visit of convalescence to Marrakech.

p. 5   Last paragraph of Marrakech, Jan 1944. Why should you dwell on this luxury?

p. 6   We had one dinner, if I remember rightly, at Naples, but certainly not a gargantuan banquet. In any case I did not order the food, it was done by Headquarters in Italy.

p. 6   'his mountain fastness'. Perhaps I am wrong but I thought this was the time when Tito had fled from the mainland and was living under my protection on the island of Vis.

p. 6   'a full scale invasion of the Balkans was no longer contemplated'. No one ever contemplated at any time a full scale invasion of the Balkans. This is one of the silly stories that the Americans have propagated. I never myself contemplated anything but commando and partisan assistance. A movement through the Ljubljana Gap to Vienna was a different story.[1]

On January 12 Churchill left Monte Carlo by night sleeper to Paris. From Paris he went to the British Embassy 'for a bath and coffee' before continuing by train to Calais, boat to Dover, and the car to Chartwell.[2]

While Churchill was at Chartwell, he learned that he had been given permission by the King to wear American Air Force pilot's wings. 'This is a unique honour,' he had explained to Sir Alan Lascelles on January 21, 'held by only three others.'[3]

On January 26 Churchill was in the House of Commons to speak during an emergency debate, following the shooting down by Israeli aircraft of four Spitfires and a Tempest aircraft, which were on a reconnaissance flight over Israeli positions just inside the Sinai borders of Egypt. Two British pilots had been killed.[4]

---

[1] 'My dear Maclean', 'Private and Confidential', 12 January 1949: Churchill papers, 2/163.

[2] Notes on visit to France, 28 December 1948 to 12 January 1949: Churchill papers, 1/73.

[3] Letter of 21 January 1949: Churchill papers, 2/311.

[4] 'Clash between RAF and Israeli Air Forces over Palestine-Egyptian Frontier, 7th January 1949', initialled JSB/FCP, 16 January 1949: Churchill papers, 2/46.

Churchill spoke with passion of Bevin's 'astounding mishandling of the Palestine problem', a mishandling that had been 'gross and glaring'. His first criticism was that Britain had still not accorded recognition to the State of Israel, nine months after that State had been proclaimed in Tel Aviv, and recognized by the United States and the Soviet Union, as well as by more than a dozen other States. 'I am quite sure,' he said, 'that the right hon. Gentleman will have to recognize the Israeli Government, and that cannot be long delayed. I regret that he has not had the manliness to tell us in plain terms tonight, and that he preferred to retire under a cloud of inky water and vapour, like a cuttlefish, to some obscure retreat.' Churchill then set out his answer to Bevin's specific points:

De facto recognition has never depended upon an exact definition of territorial frontiers. There are half a dozen countries in Europe which are recognized today whose territorial frontiers are not finally settled. Surely, Poland is one. It is only with the general Peace Treaty that a final settlement can be made. Whoever said, 'How can we recognize a country whose limits and boundaries are not carefully defined'? I am astonished to find the right hon. Gentleman giving any countenance to it.

What trouble, what inconvenience, what humbling rebuffs should we have avoided if the Foreign Secretary had taken the sincere advice tendered to him from this side of the House. The only reason, or, certainly, one particular reason, offered by him was irrelevant and incorrect. He talked about the mistakes which some countries have made in hastily recognizing Indonesia.

Recognition, or hasty recognition, he thought, would be a bad precedent, but how absurd it is to compare the so-called Republic of Indonesia with the setting-up in Tel Aviv of a Government of the State of Israel, with an effective organization and a victorious army.

Churchill then drew Bevin's attention to a longer time-scale than the events of the previous months and years:

Whether the right hon. Gentleman likes it or not, and whether we like it or not, the coming into being of a Jewish State in Palestine is an event in world history to be viewed in the perspective, not of a generation or a century, but in the perspective of a thousand, two thousand or even three thousand years. That is a standard of temporal values or time values which seems very much out of accord with the perpetual click-clack of our rapidly-changing moods and of the age in which we live.

This is an event in world history. How vain it is to compare it with the recognition, or the claims to recognition, by certain countries, of the Communist banditti which we are resisting in Malaya or of the anarchic forces which the Dutch are trying to restrain in Indonesia.

Many in the Conservative Party, Churchill said, including himself, had 'always had in mind' that the Jewish National Home in Palestine 'might some day develop into a Jewish State'.[1]

Now that the Jewish National Home had come into existence, Churchill told the House of Commons with considerable anger, 'it is England that refuses to recognize it, and, by our actions, we find ourselves regarded as its most bitter enemies. All this is due, not only to mental inertia or lack of grip on the part of the Ministers concerned, but also, I am afraid, to the very strong and direct streak of bias and prejudice on the part of the Foreign Secretary.'

This was a strong accusation against Bevin, which Churchill followed up at once by telling the House: 'I do not feel any great confidence that he has not got a prejudice against the Jews in Palestine.'

Bevin had thought, Churchill said, that the Arab League was stronger in May 1948 'and that it would win if fighting broke out'. He, Churchill, had taken another view:

I certainly felt that the spectacle of the Jewish settlements being invaded from all sides—from Syria, Transjordan and Egypt—and with a lot of our tanks and modern tackle was, on the face of it, most formidable, but I believed that that combination would fall to pieces at the first check, and I adhered to the estimate I had formed in the war of the measure of the fighting qualities and the tough fibre of the Zionist community, and the support which it would receive from Zionists all over the world. But the Foreign Secretary was wrong, wrong in his facts, wrong in the mood, wrong in the method and wrong in the result, and we are very sorry about it for his sake and still more sorry about it for our own.

On the question of Palestine, Churchill continued, Britain now had 'arrayed' against itself the United States, the Soviet Union, the Palestine settlers and Zionist supporters all over the world, without, 'and I want my hon. Friends on this side to realize this', doing the 'slightest service' to the Arab countries with whom Britain had 'very serious obligations', and he continued:

This is a poor and undeserved result of all that we have created and built up in Palestine by the goodwill and solid work of twenty-five years. We have lost the friendship of the Palestine Jews for the time being. I was glad to read a statement from Dr Weizmann the other day pleading for friendship between the new Israeli State and the Western world. I believe that will be its destiny. He was an old friend of mine for many years. His son was killed in the war

[1] In 1937, giving evidence in secret to the Royal Commission on Palestine, Churchill spoke of how, when he was Colonial Secretary in 1922, it had always been his view of the Jewish National Home in Palestine that 'if more and more Jews gather to that Home and all is worked from age to age, from generation to generation, with justice and fair consideration to those displaced and so forth, certainly it was contemplated and intended that they might in the course of time become an overwhelming Jewish State'. (Palestine Royal Commission, notes of evidence, 12 March 1937: Churchill papers, 2/317.)

fighting with us. I trust his influence may grow and that we shall do what we can, subject to our other obligations—because we cannot forget those other obligations—to add to his influence. I hope that later on a truer comprehension of the Zionist debt to this country will revive.

Churchill then spoke of how, after the war, he was sure Britain could have obtained both Arab and Jewish support for a partition scheme, whereby two separate States, one Jewish and the other Arab, would have been set up in Palestine. This led to an interruption by Attlee:

The Prime Minister (Mr Attlee): May I ask the right hon. Gentleman, if he thought that could have been done, why did he not do it after the war? He was in power.

Mr Churchill: No. The world and the nation had the inestimable blessing of the right hon. Gentleman's guidance. I am sure that we could have agreed immediately after the war upon a partition scheme which would have been more favourable to the Arabs than that which will now follow their unsuccessful recourse to arms.

Mr Thomas Reid (Swindon): Agreed with whom? Would it not have led to a major war in the Near East if partition had been pursued?

Mr Churchill: I give my opinion. I am sure we could have made better arrangements for the Arabs at that time—I am not talking of the Jews—than will be possible after there has been this unfortunate recourse to arms. Indeed, the scheme of partition proposed by UNO was better than what they will get now, after their defeat.

Churchill spoke next of the Royal Air Force reconnaissance mission which had come to such a violent end:

This was no high altitude photographic operation. They were to fly low over areas where they knew hostilities were in progress. No warning had been sent to the Israeli forces, but restrictive orders were given to our pilots about not firing their guns except after having been fired upon effectively by others.

The first reconnaissance was sent out on a wholly unnecessary mission, because there was a cease fire that evening. The second reconnaissance was sent out in order to ascertain what had happened to the first, but before the second could have got back the cease fire between Jews and Arabs had already taken place.

'Why expose our Forces, our young men, to such risks as that?' Churchill asked. 'It was in these circumstances that we had to endure the affront and injury for which our two young airmen lost their lives.' Summing up his criticisms of the air episode, Churchill told the House:

Curiosity to know what was going on would certainly not justify doing a thing so improvident as this sortie of aircraft at such a moment. I say it was the quintessence of maladresse of which the right hon. Gentleman and the Prime Minister, who takes the responsibility, were guilty. And now poor old Britain—Tories, Socialists, Liberals, Zionists, anti-Zionists, non-Zionists alike, we find ourselves shot down in an air skirmish, snubbed by the Israeli Government, who said, 'We understand you do not recognize us,' and with a marked lack of support from the international bodies upon which we depend so greatly and whose opinions we value so highly.

Churchill ended by referring to the question of the Arabs of Palestine. The 'whole point' of his own White Paper of 1922 had, he said, been that Jewish immigration was to be free, 'but not beyond the limits of economic absorptive power'. Britain could not have had it said, Churchill continued, 'that newcomers were coming in, pushing out those who had lived there for centuries. But the newcomers who were coming in brought work and employment with them, and the means of sustaining a much larger population than had lived in Palestine and Transjordan. They brought the hope with them of a far larger population than existed in Palestine at the time of Our Lord.' Churchill then spoke of the growth of the population of Palestine since his 1922 White Paper had established that Jewish immigration there was 'of right and not on sufferance':

In twenty-five years the Jewish population of Palestine doubled or more than doubled, but so did the Arab population of the same areas of Palestine.[1] As the Jews continued to reclaim the country, plant the orange groves, develop the water system, electricity and so forth, employment and means of livelihood were found for ever-larger numbers of Arabs—400,000 or 500,000 more Arabs found their living there—and the relations of the two races in the Jewish areas were tolerable in spite of external distractions and all kinds of disturbances. General prosperity grew.

The idea that only a limited number of people can live in a country is a profound illusion; it all depends on their co-operative and inventive power. There are more people today living twenty storeys above the ground in New York than were living on the ground in New York 100 years ago. There is no limit to the ingenuity of man if it is properly and vigorously applied under conditions of peace and justice.

The Government's policy over nearly four years, Churchill concluded, had 'deprived Britain of the credit she had earned, and of the rights and interests she had acquired, and made her at once the mockery and scapegoat of so many States who have never made any positive contribution of their own'.[2]

[1] In 1922 there were approximately 500,000 Arabs and 90,000 Jews in Mandate Palestine; in 1947 there were 1,238,000 Arabs and 650,000 Jews (Arabs as well as Jews having immigrated in considerable numbers into Palestine between 1922 and 1939).
[2] Speech of 26 January 1949: *Hansard*.

Among those listening to Churchill's speech was Marcus Sieff, whose earlier notes had given Churchill a picture of the Israeli perspective and hopes.[1] 'I know from my experience,' Sieff wrote, 'not only here but in the Middle East in the early years of the War, how great was the part you played in the last quarter of a century in constructing the bridges between this country and the Jews of Palestine, and how the name of Britain stood in that community.' The Labour Government's Palestine policy in recent years had 'largely destroyed' those bridges, but now, Sieff wrote, 'you have again given a lead which, if sincerely followed by the Government, will go a long way to restoring those ties to the advantage of the moderate people, be they Gentile, Arab or Jew, and for which all moderate people must be grateful'.[2]

Nine days later, Britain recognized the State of Israel. In answer to a telegram of thanks from Dr Weizmann, who had been elected the eight-month-old State's first President, Churchill replied: 'I look back with much pleasure on our long association,' and he added, in his own hand: 'The light grows.'[3]

Just as the routine of Churchill's work was divided between his war memoirs and Parliament, so the pattern of his domestic life spanned both London and Chartwell, with Chartwell the place he preferred. But London made many claims on his time, not least because of the House of Commons, and his wife did all that she could to make the house a comfortable one. An account of it was set down in January 1949 by a luncheon guest, the Conservative MP Henry Channon:

... set off for Hyde Park Gate, where I found the street enlivened by the presence of a policeman, and three MPs—all too early, like me. We went in, and I was at once struck by the air of elegance and tidiness that the house has. Mrs Churchill greeted me with 'Hello Chips' as did daughter Mary.

Winston soon joined us and was in a rippling mood. He looked small, even diminutive, and his face was as pink as a baby's. Clemmie referred to him as 'Winston darling'. She is obviously devoted to him. He greeted me affectionately and put me next to him at luncheon.

[1] Once ties between Great Britain and the Jews had been re-established, Marcus Sieff had written in his memorandum of 25 October 1948, 'Israel would not then be tempted to drift into the orbit of the Eastern bloc, which will be the almost inevitable result of a continuation of present British policy'. ('Implications of British policy towards Israel', 25 October 1948: Churchill papers, 2/46.)

[2] 'Dear Mr Churchill', 31 January 1949: Churchill papers, 2/46. Churchill received a letter from Marcus Sieff's uncle, Sir Simon Marks. 'I know,' he wrote, 'that our mutual friend Dr Weizmann will be thrilled at the news, and particularly at your remark that "this is a great event in world history".' ('Dear Mr Churchill', 31 January 1949: Churchill papers, 2/163.)

[3] 'My dear Weizmann', 9 February 1949: Churchill papers, 2/46.

The dining-room looks onto the garden. Food excellent—and four bottles of champagne—Winston talked of Southend, and suddenly, to my surprise, burst into an old Southend music hall song of the '80s, singing two verses of it lustily. Finally the conversation got onto politics and last night's debate: he is immensely pleased with the figures and thinks that we may have deflated Bevin a bit.[1]

As a concerned grandparent, Churchill had advice for his grandson Winston, now aged eight and enrolled in a school in Switzerland. The young man should, his grandfather wrote to him, 'learn all you can about the history of the past, for how else can one even make a guess at what is going to happen in the future?'[2]

In a letter to Montgomery which he decided not to send, Churchill pondered the future with a sceptical eye. 'As you know,' he wrote, 'I doubt myself very much whether any defence can be improvised in Europe, apart from the altogether devastating effects of the atomic bomb, and the cutting of the "swathe" between the advancing Russian Armies and the Kremlin and their native land.' Churchill added 'I am not addressing my mind in this letter to the probabilities of war or the reverse, and when it would come. I do not think anyone knows.'[3]

At Chartwell, where he had dictated this letter, Churchill was busy again with his garden and all its delights. 'I am just going out,' he wrote to his son Randolph on February 9, 'to supervise the construction of my new reservoir for the chalk pool. This will give me a reasonable cascade for about five hours.'[4]

The death of relations and contemporaries was now almost commonplace, the cutting of old ties of companionship and conviviality. 'These are indeed sad times,' Churchill wrote to his cousin Lady Londonderry on the death of her husband, whom he had known for more than sixty years. 'How all our old world has crumpled around us!'[5]

* * *

[1] Channon diary, 27 January 1949: Robert Rhodes James (editor), *Chips*, pages 433-4.

[2] 'My dearest Winston', 9 February 1949: Churchill papers, 1/46. To another of his grandsons, Julian Sandys, who had just gone to Eton, Churchill wrote of the far greater 'liberty and responsibility' there than at a state school, and he added: 'Keep your eye on history because a knowledge of the past is the only way of helping us to make guesses at the future.' ('My dear Julian', 11 February 1949: Churchill papers, 1/46.)

[3] 'My dear Monty', marked, 'Do *not* send, WSC', February 1949: Churchill papers, 2/31.

[4] 'My dear Randolph', 'Private', 9 February 1949: Churchill papers, 1/46.

[5] 'My dear Edie', 14 February 1949: Churchill papers, 2/163.

On February 26 Churchill travelled to Brussels, where he spoke to the Council of the European Movement, giving his support to the establishment of a European Court of Human Rights. 'We have the Charter of Human Rights,' he said, 'and we must have a European means of defending and enforcing it. It must not be possible that, within the boundaries of United Europe, such a legal atrocity could be perpetrated as that which has confronted us all in the case of Cardinal Mindszenty.[1] Here you have the crime of religious persecution committed on an innocent man under the direct orders of Moscow, and carried through with all those features of police government with which we are familiar in trials under the Soviets.' There must be means 'by which such events in any of the countries with which we can consort can be brought to the test of impartial justice'. Nor could the supporters of a United Europe 'rest content' with the division of Europe into two parts, 'the free and the unfree'. The Europe 'we seek to unite', he declared, 'is *all* Europe. . . .'[2]

[1] Jozsef Mindszenty, of peasant origin, had become Archbishop of Esztergom and primate of Hungary in 1945, and Cardinal in 1946. An opponent of Communism, he was particularly outspoken against the nationalization of Catholic schools. He was arrested at Christmas 1948, tried, and imprisoned. Liberated during the Hungarian revolution of 1956, he appealed to the United Nations to help his country. When the revolution was crushed, he sought asylum in the American Embassy in Budapest, where he remained for fifteen years. In 1971 the Communist Government allowed him to leave for Rome. In 1974 the Pope retired him against his will from his position as Hungarian primate; he died in Vienna in 1975.

[2] Speech of 26 February 1949: Randolph S. Churchill (editor), *In the Balance, Speeches 1949 and 1950 by Winston S. Churchill*, London 1951, pages 26–30. Recording: BBC Written Archives Centre, Library No. 13917.

26

Peace, and the Atomic Bomb

O N 3 March 1949 Churchill's worries about the financial future of his family were finally assuaged, when Anthony Moir told him that the various Trust arrangements set up over the past three years by Leslie Graham-Dixon were all in order. 'The news I have received from Moir,' Churchill wrote that day to Dixon, 'vindicates the soundness of the advice which you have given me, upon which I have acted. Thank you very much indeed for all your help.'[1] For the first time, an author had been allowed to set his annual literary income into a Trust Fund without it being counted as income as each payment was made by the publishers. From the capital sum, an annual payment was then made to Churchill for his living and literary expenses.[2]

A week after this good news, Clementine Churchill organized the twenty-sixth in the series of lunches at Hyde Park Gate for Churchill to meet Conservative backbenchers. The six who came on that occasion included Fitzroy Maclean.[3] These lunches represented a considerable effort on Clementine Churchill's part to maintain her husband's personal links with members of the Party of which he had now been leader for almost eight and a half years.[4] So concerned was she about his relations with the Party that she intervened to try to persuade him not to go to Jamaica as the guest of Lord Beaverbrook when, later in March, he was about to set off for a month's transatlantic journey, having been invited to speak at the Massachusetts Institute of Technology. Her letter was emphatic:

My Darling,
I am so unhappy over Jamaica & I must seem to you and I fear to Mary & Christopher as a spoil-sport. But as I said to you in my letter yesterday (which I tore up perhaps before you had time to assimilate it) I feel that for you, at this moment of doubt and discouragement among our followers, to

---

[1] 'My dear Graham-Dixon', 3 March 1949: Graham-Dixon papers.

[2] The Trust received £350,000 as its first payment, Churchill being entitled under the arrangement to £20,000 a year.

[3] 'Parliamentary Luncheon No. 26', 10 March 1949: Churchill papers, 2/63.

[4] Churchill had succeeded Neville Chamberlain as Leader of the Conservative Party on 3 October 1940.

stay with Max will increase that doubt & discouragement. It would seem cynical and an insult to the Party.

You often tease me and call me 'pink' but believe me I feel it very much. I do not mind if you resign the Leadership when things are good, but I can't bear you to be accepted murmuringly and uneasily. In my humble way I have tried to help, with political luncheons here, visits to Woodford, attending to your Constituency correspondence. But now & then I have felt chilled & discouraged by the deepening knowledge that you do only just as much as will keep you in Power. But that much is not enough in these hard anxious times.

My Darling—Please take Mary with you to America. It would give her such joy and I think it's most important for her & Christopher to be together & to share every possible experience while they are young and passionate.

I still hope that you may decide against Jamaica but I cannot venture to persuade you. I only know, that feeling as I do, it would be wrong for me to go.

Your loving

Clemmie [1]

Clementine Churchill's argument was effective, and decisive. 'The political situation here is uneasy,' Churchill wrote to Beaverbrook five days later, 'and I do not feel I ought to be away so long.' His family had all very much looked forward, he said, 'to the delights of Montego Bay. But I hope you will give us another chance later on.' [2]

Churchill also asked his daughter Mary to join him, which she did. On March 17, the day before leaving, Churchill gave instructions for various building and repair work at Chartwell while he was away, as well as the purchase of rhododendron plants, and fish for the new pool. 'Report to Miss Hamblin at once,' he wrote to the head gardener, 'any signs of trouble with the goldfish.' The 'most serious need' was more logs. For these, a fallen beech tree should be cut. 'The filling of the wood-shed is most important and must be pushed forward at every possible opportunity.' [3]

On March 18, Churchill, his wife, his daughter Mary and her husband, Miss Sturdee, Miss Gilliatt, the detective and the valet boarded the *Queen Elizabeth* for the transatlantic crossing. 'It is now nearly fifty-five years since I first crossed the Atlantic in the 7,000 ton *Etruria*,'

[1] Letter dated 5 March 1949: Churchill papers, 1/46. Piers Dixon, who married Churchill's granddaughter Edwina in 1960, later recalled: 'Clemmie told me—I think in 1965 or 1966— that she was really a Liberal. Without admitting that she had in recent times voted Liberal, she added that she had never voted Conservative.' (Piers Dixon recollections: notes for the author, December 1987.)

[2] Letter dated 10 March 1949: Churchill papers, 1/78.

[3] 'Vincent', 18 March 1949: Churchill papers, 2/266.

Churchill wrote to B. H. Russell of the Cunard White Star Line, 'and came back in the *Lucania*, which is a long time as human lives go.' [1]

On March 25 Churchill spoke in New York, thanking the American people 'on behalf of Britain and on behalf of Western Europe, of free Europe, as I have some credentials to do—for all you have done and are doing'. The Marshall Plan, he said, was 'a turning point in the history of the world'. Now there was the Atlantic Pact, 'which when Mr Attlee kindly showed it to me before it became public—but after it was settled—I thought it was one of the most important documents ever signed by large communities of human beings and certainly indicates a very considerable advance in opinion as far as the United States of America are concerned. Well, there you are—you're in it now because there's no way out, but still if we pool our luck and share our fortunes I think you will have no reason to regret it.'

What had brought about 'this great change', Churchill asked, 'from the time when I was so scolded three years ago for what I said at Fulton?' No one could possibly have done it but Stalin. 'He is the one.' The men in the Kremlin had deliberately united the free world against them. 'It is, I am sure,' Churchill added, 'because they feared the friendship of the West more than they do its hostility. They can't afford to allow free and friendly intercourse between their country and those they control, and the rest of the world. They daren't see it develop—the coming and going and all the easements and tolerances which come from the agreeable contacts of nations and of individuals. They can't afford it.' The Russian people 'must not see what goes on outside and the world must not see what goes on inside the Soviet domain'.

Churchill then spoke of the meeting in Brussels: 'there were these 30,000 people in this great square at Brussels, and I could feel their anxiety. I could feel, as I spoke, their anxiety—their fear. After all, they haven't got the Atlantic Ocean between them and danger. They haven't even got the Channel and the Channel is pretty good, as we showed you in the last war—and showed others. In ten days—in ten days perhaps the Soviet armour might be in Brussels.' There were these 30,000 people, 'good, faithful, decent people—naturally they know about it all'. While he was speaking to them, he could feel their fear and anxiety, 'but when I spoke of the United States being with us in this matter of European freedom, I felt a wave of hope in this great concourse and I know you will not let them down in regard to any matter in which you have pledged the word of the great Republic'.

The only way to 'deal' with a Communist, Churchill told his New

[1] Letter of 18 March 1949: Churchill papers, 2/263.

York audience, was by having superior force on your side on the matter in question—and they must also be convinced that you will use—you will not hesitate to use—these forces, if necessary, in the most ruthless manner. You have not only to convince the Soviet Government that you have superior force—that they are confronted by superior force—but that you are not restrained by any moral consideration if the case arose from using that force with complete material ruthlessness. And that is the greatest chance of peace, the surest road to peace. Then, the Communists will make a bargain. . . .'

Churchill went on to contrast German Nazism with Soviet Communism. It was his most outspoken denunciation of Communism since his warnings in 1919 and 1920, immediately following the Bolshevik revolution:

We are now confronted with something which is quite as wicked but much more formidable than Hitler, because Hitler had only the Herrenvolk stuff and anti-Semitism. Well, somebody said about that—a good starter, but a bad stayer. That's all he had. He had no theme. But these fourteen men in the Kremlin have their hierarchy and a church of Communist adepts whose missionaries are in every country as a fifth column, and not only a fifth column, in your country, ours, everywhere, and so on, with a feeling that they may be running a risk, but if their gamble comes off they will be the masters of the whole land in which they are a minority at the present time. They will be the Quislings with power to rule and dominate all the rest of their fellow countrymen.

It was 'certain' in his opinion, Churchill insisted, 'that Europe would have been Communized and London would have been under bombardment some time ago, but for the deterrent of the atomic bomb in the hands of the United States. That is my firm belief and that governs the situation today.' [1]

A few days later, in a private conversation with President Truman in Washington, Churchill not only reiterated this point, but urged the President to make plain, and to make public, that the United States would indeed be prepared to use the atomic bomb in order to defend democracy.

From Washington, Churchill travelled by train to Boston, to speak at the Massachusetts Institute of Technology. This was the original invitation which had brought him to the United States, and the speech on which he had worked throughout the transatlantic crossing. President Truman, who was to have been with him, as at Fulton, and was to have stayed with Churchill for two days, was unable at the last moment to come. Churchill at once decided to leave immediately

---

[1] Speech of 25 March 1949: Randolph S. Churchill (editor), *In the Balance*, pages 32–9.

after his speech, abandoning the second day. Clementine Churchill and Randolph were against this change, writing to him jointly:

We hope you do not mind us making the following point. When President Truman ran out of coming here you could perfectly well have decided not to remain for the second day. Very handsomely however, you said you would go through with the original plan, so as to help to make it a success and incidentally to show that your own plans were in no way dependent on President Truman.

Having decided to stay surely you must go through with the programme as planned, even though it is very tiresome? Enormous pains have been taken about the banquet to-morrow night, and it seems that the early hour was inevitable. The country has been combed for the finest food and wines, and we are both sure that it will not be as bad when it happens as it seems in advance.

If you were not to go it would really spoil the whole show.

'A great many of the faculty,' Randolph and his mother added, 'did not have dinner jackets, or their wives long dresses, and they have bought them specially because you are coming to the dinner.'[1]

Churchill accepted this advice. In his speech on March 31, he began by casting his mind, and that of his audience, back to the beginning of the century:

In 1900 a sense of moving hopefully forward to brighter, broader, easier days predominated. Little did we guess that what has been called the Century of the Common Man would witness as its outstanding feature more common men killing each other with greater facilities than any other five centuries put together in the history of the world. But we entered this terrible twentieth century with confidence.

We thought that with improving transportation nations would get to know each other better. We believed that as they got to know each other better they would like each other more, and that national rivalries would fade in a growing international consciousness. We took it almost for granted that science would confer continual boons and blessings upon us, would give us better meals, better garments and better dwellings for less trouble, and thus steadily shorten the hours of labour and leave more time for play and culture. In the name of ordered but unceasing progress, we saluted the age of democracy expressing itself ever more widely through parliaments freely and fairly elected on a broad or universal franchise. We saw no reason then why men and women should not shape their own home life and careers without being cramped by the growing complexity of the State, which was to be their servant and the protector of their rights.

Churchill then turned to the changes brought about by 'the conquest of the air and the perfection of the art of flying':

[1] 'Mr Churchill', initialled 'CSC, RSC' undated: Churchill papers, 2/265.

In the first half of the twentieth century, fanned by the crimson wings of war, the conquest of the air affected profoundly human affairs. It made the globe seem much bigger to the mind and much smaller to the body. The human biped was able to travel about far more quickly. This greatly reduced the size of his estate, while at the same time creating an even keener sense of its exploitable value.

In the nineteenth century Jules Verne wrote *Round the World in Eighty Days*. It seemed a prodigy. Now you can get around it in four; but you do not see much of it on the way. The whole prospect and outlook of mankind grew immeasurably larger, and the multiplication of ideas also proceeded at an incredible rate.

This vast expansion was unhappily not accompanied by any noticeable advance in the stature of man, either in his mental faculties, or his moral character. His brain got no better, but it buzzed the more. The scale of events around him assumed gigantic proportions while he remained about the same size. By comparison therefore he actually became much smaller.

We no longer had great men directing manageable affairs. Our need was to discipline an array of gigantic and turbulent facts.

To this task we have certainly so far proved unequal. Science bestowed immense new powers on man, and, at the same time, created conditions which were largely beyond his comprehension and still more beyond his control. While he nursed the illusion of growing mastery and exulted in his new trappings, he became the sport and presently the victim of tides, and currents, of whirlpools and tornadoes amid which he was far more helpless than he had been for a long time.

Now, after two world wars, a 'fundamental schism' had opened up between Communism and the rest of mankind. 'But we must not despair. We must persevere, and if the gulf continues to widen, we must make sure that the cause of freedom is defended by all the resources of combined forethought and superior science. Here lies the best hope of averting a third world struggle.'

Churchill then turned to the nature of man, and man's ability to rise above the dictates of science:

Laws just or unjust may govern men's actions. Tyrannies may restrain or regulate their words. The machinery of propaganda may pack their minds with falsehood and deny them truth for many generations of time. But the soul of man thus held in trance or frozen in a long night can be awakened by a spark coming from God knows where and in a moment the whole structure of lies and oppression is on trial for its life.

Peoples in bondage need never despair. Let them hope and trust in the genius of mankind. Science no doubt could if sufficiently perverted exterminate us all, but it is not in the power of material forces in any period which the youngest here tonight need take into practical account, to alter the main elements in human nature or restrict the infinite variety of forms in which the soul and genius of the human race can and will express itself.

Churchill ended by reiterating what he had said in New York six days before: that 'thirteen or fourteen men in the Kremlin, holding down hundreds of millions of people and aiming at the rule of the world, feel that at all costs they must keep up the barriers'. Hence the 'cold war' as it was being called in America. Hence the need for the 'prodigious efforts' of the Berlin airlift. Hence the combined 'friendship and anxiety' of those to whom he had spoken in Brussels. Communist Russia was 'something quite as wicked but in some ways more formidable' than Hitler. Hence Churchill's conviction that Europe 'would have been "Communized", like Czechoslovakia, and London under bombardment some time ago but for the deterrent of the atomic bomb in the hands of the United States'.

The 'aim and ideal', Churchill declared, was friendship with Russians everywhere. 'We seek nothing from Russia but goodwill and fair play.' If, however, there was to be a war of nerves, 'let us make sure our nerves are strong and are fortified by the deepest convictions of our hearts. If we persevere steadfastly together, and allow no appeasement of tyranny and wrong-doing in any form, it may not be our nerve or the structure of our civilization which will break, and peace may yet be preserved.'[1]

'Churchill Declares Atom Bomb Alone Deters Russia from War' was the headline in the *New York Herald Tribune* on April 1, while a second headline noted, with terse accuracy: 'Tells Boston Crowd War Can Be Avoided If West Stays United and Tough'.[2]

Churchill's speech had been broadcast to Britain. 'I thought your speech was terrific' was Montgomery's comment.[3]

On April 4, as Churchill was returning to Britain on board the *Queen Mary*, Ernest Bevin, in Washington, signed the North Atlantic Treaty. By this treaty, the United States and Canada joined with eight European countries in a defence organization, the North Atlantic Treaty Organization, soon to be known by its initials, NATO. Two days after the treaty was signed, Truman, in an informal talk to recently elected Members of Congress, said that he would 'not hesitate' to order the use of the atomic bomb if it were necessary for the welfare of the United States and if the fate of the democracies of the world were at stake. He added that he hoped and prayed it would never be necessary to do so; he considered that the signing of the North Atlantic Treaty would prevent the United States from having to make such a decision.[4]

---

[1] Speech of 31 March 1949: Randolph S. Churchill (editor), *In the Balance*, pages 40–51. Recording: BBC Written Archives Centre, Library No. T 13906.

[2] *New York Herald Tribune*, 1 April 1949.

[3] 'Dear Mr Churchill', 'Yrs ever Monty', 9 April 1949: Churchill papers, 2/143.

[4] 'America and the Atomic Bomb', *The Times*, 8 April 1949.

'Presume you saw President's declaration,' Bernard Baruch tele-graphed to Churchill.[1] 'I certainly saw statement you mentioned,' Churchill replied 'and am sure it will help for peace.'[2] 'I was very struck by Truman's remark about the Atomic Bomb,' Churchill wrote to Baruch two weeks later. 'This was indeed what I urged him to make in our short conversation at Washington. It will, I have no doubt, be a help to the cause of peace.'[3]

To Truman himself, Churchill wrote two months later, from Hyde Park Gate: 'I was deeply impressed by your statement about not fear-ing to use the atomic bomb if the need arose. I am sure this will do more than anything else to ward off the catastrophe of a third world war.' Churchill added: 'I have felt it right to speak, as you have seen, in terms of reassurance for the immediate future, but of course I remain under the impression of the fearful dangers which impend upon us. Complete unity, superior force and the undoubted readiness to use it, give us the only hopes of escape. Without you nothing can be done.'[4]

'I am not quite so pessimistic as you are about the prospects for a third world war,' Truman replied from the White House, and he added: 'I rather think that eventually we are going to forget that idea, and get a real world peace. I don't believe even the Russians can stand it to face complete destruction, which certainly would happen to them in the event of another war.'[5]

During his visit to Boston, Churchill had explained to his American publishers, Houghton Mifflin, his need for one more volume of war memoirs, over and above the five already contracted for. Strong op-position to any enlarging of the memoirs had come from Henry Laugh-lin of Houghton Mifflin, as well as from *Life* and the *New York Times*, the principal financial supporters of the project.

Churchill was determined to tell the story on the scale he believed necessary, especially as he had such vast and previously unpublished documentation. He was supported in his wish for a sixth volume by Emery Reves, who, after several hours' conversation with Henry Laughlin at Houghton Mifflin, persuaded the firm to accept Chur-chill's judgement. 'It is my strongest conviction,' Reves wrote to him,

[1] Telegram of 8 April 1949: Churchill papers, 2/210.
[2] Telegram of 14 April 1949: Churchill papers, 2/210.
[3] 'My dear Bernie', 28 April 1949: Churchill papers, 2/210.
[4] 'My dear Harry', 'Private', 29 June 1949: Churchill papers, 2/158.
[5] 'Dear Winston', 2 July 1949: Churchill papers, 2/158.

'that you should write your War Memoirs exactly as you think they should be written.' He himself would pay £10,000 for the foreign rights of the extra volume. So would Lord Camrose, Houghton Mifflin, Cassell and the Dominion newspapers, leaving Luce of *Life* and Sulzberger of the *New York Times* on a limb, but securing for Churchill £50,000, 'sufficient guarantee', Reves wrote, 'for you to construct your work the way you think best'.[1]

The debate between the publishers continued, and was eventually resolved as Churchill wished, while he was on his way back to Britain on the *Queen Mary*. 'It is a floating hotel,' he wrote to his grandson Julian Sandys, 'which rushes along at 33 miles an hour, and is a great credit to our country.'[2] To his pre-war American publisher, Charles Scribner, who had published *The World Crisis*, *A Roving Commission* and *Amid These Storms*, Churchill wrote from on board ship: 'In view of the increased publicity I now command it astonishes me that the books of which you hold the copyright have not had any sale worth speaking of in the United States during or since the war years.'[3]

During the voyage home, Churchill enlisted the help of his son-in-law Duncan Sandys for the preparation of a chapter on 'the tank story' both before and during the war, for inclusion in the third volume of his war memoirs. In warning Sandys that the account must be 'readable and therefore not too technical or suffer from over-detail', Churchill dictated his own single-sentence summary and reflections:

The salient facts are neglect between the wars; failure of the War Office to produce agreed models of medium tanks and to make plans for going into production in the event of war by making jigs and gauges in advance, etc., and briefing firms accordingly, (I complained about this in the House of Commons before the war);

the situation at the outbreak—not even one single armoured division ready when the German attack developed in May, 1940;

my emergency meeting in June or July 1940 at which measures were taken to order 1,000 Churchill tanks (these were to defend England in the event of invasion in 1941, and everything was sacrificed to having something ready by then—there is a report on this meeting available);

the history of the Churchills and the under-gunning;

the troubles about making the models desert-worthy, and my efforts in 1941 to overcome these; the episode of my sending the two first Churchills

[1] 'Dear Mr Churchill', 'Confidential', 1 April 1949: Churchill papers, 4/63. The extent of Churchill's earning power is seen from an offer made to him by Lewis Rosenstiel two months later (at Chartwell) of $25,000 a broadcast for twelve broadcasts a year for three years, to North and South America. (Note of 27 May 1949: Churchill papers, 2/197.)

[2] 'My dear Julian', 5 April 1949: Churchill papers, 1/46.

[3] 'My dear Charles', 5 April 1949: Churchill papers, 4/311. *A Roving Commission* was the American title of *My Early Life*. *Amid These Storms* was the American title of *Thoughts and Adventures*. They had been published in 1930 and 1932 respectively.

out with their technicians to have them made desert-worthy on the spot under the special care of Auchinleck and Oliver Lyttelton, and how this was almost sabotaged;

the real truth about the quality of our tanks in 1941 and 1942;

the superiority of the German methods of tank production, and how discreditable to us it was that they, who were strangers to the desert, seemed to have mastered the difficulties of good staff work beforehand.

Churchill's letter continued:

These points occur to me as I speak, but there must be many more, particularly the origin of the Sherman tank which you mentioned, although that does not eventuate till the American gift in 1942. The tale can be told here as a prelude to the American gift after Tobruk, in 1942. It is no use going beyond 1942 at this period, but there is no reason why you should not foreshadow what happened in later years, and I can work it in in subsequent Volumes. If you will do this, you should consult with Pownall, who will be able to get you access to or copies of all the relevant documents at the Cabinet Offices. When you have got your outline ready we could work the story up together.

'As we all have to earn our living,' Churchill added, 'I hope you will let me pay you a good substantial fee for all your thought and knowledge. We can talk this over. The matter is urgent, as the third Volume will leave my hands finally in the next three or four months, and I should like to have anything you can do for me by the end of June or earlier.' [1]

Also during the voyage home, Churchill declined a request to sign a letter of appeal on behalf of a memorial in London to the Polish war leader General Sikorski. 'Mr Bracken should say I have taken on too much,' he told Miss Gilliatt. [2] Two days later Clementine Churchill sent her husband a short dictated note:

Please forgive me for interfering but do you not think that, as a year ago you gave your consent to head an appeal for the General Sikorski Memorial in London, it would give sorrow and disappointment if you were not able to fulfil your promises. (Moreover you have headed the Masaryk Memorial Fund in London.)

Will you allow Miss Sturdee to ask the General Sikorski Historical Institute to draft a letter of which you would be the principal signatory?

I would not like a letter in connection with one of the great national figures of the Second World War to be signed by a second-rate figure like Sir John Anderson.

Churchill accepted his wife's advice. 'Yes, draft accordingly,' he

[1] 'My dear Duncan', 8 April 1949: Churchill papers, 4/54.
[2] Note of 4 April 1949: Churchill papers, 2/327.

noted on her letter. 'Thank heavens!' Clementine Churchill exclaimed in writing to Miss Sturdee, and she added: 'Please act accordingly.'[1] Churchill duly signed, and indeed headed, the appeal.[2]

Returning to Chartwell, Churchill was confronted with continuing French criticism of his reference to the French generals in 1940. The newspaper *Figaro* had been particularly censorious. One idea he had was to write a special preface for the French and Belgian editions. This he did, encouraged to do so by General Pownall. Churchill's draft preface read:

I have not tried to write the history of these tragic times but only to record what we saw and felt and did from the British angle. When good people are sharing only miseries, there cannot be rejoicing and there must be differences. I have not attempted to describe the stern and forlorn battle fought by the French Army all along the front. That must be left for French historians.

In the confusion and agony of a vast lost campaign nations, armies, divisions, all have their point of view, and as time passes these must be sifted and weighed by the writers for posterity. The facts which I testify are that the French Army was not given a good chance before the war by the politicians or the Chamber, and secondly that it was ripped up by the incursion of the German armour on a scale and in a manner which few of us, whether in office or in a private station, could foresee. Thus for all the bravery of its soldiers and the skill of its commanders its men never had their chance of fighting it out with the Germans, front to front and face to face.

The Belgian Army fought with gallantry and determination, but they were put into the war so late that they could not even occupy their own prepared front lines. These were overrun by the German onslaught. Nevertheless the Belgian Army should tell its own tale of stubborn resistance in the face of overwhelming disasters.[3]

Back in Britain, Churchill wrote to Bernard Baruch of how he would not continue in politics 'but for the fact that I feel it my duty to help the sane and constructive forces in Britain to restore our position in the world'. Restore did not mean turning the clock back, however. On April 28, in the House of Commons, he decided to welcome the

[1] 'CSC to WSC', 6 April 1949: Churchill papers, 2/327.

[2] On 5 July 1949, in the presence of Sir John Anderson, Churchill spoke at the first stone-laying of the Sikorski Institute in London. 'I remember as if it were yesterday,' he said, 'the shock which came to us both—Mr Eden and me—when the news of his sudden, tragic, untoward death came in upon us. The aeroplane crash, taking off at that restricted landing-ground at Gibraltar, where many of us had to go several times, and a great factor—a great figure—fell out of the Allied line of battle.' ('Speech by Mr Churchill', 'Transcribed from Bush House Recording', 5 July 1949: Churchill papers, 2/50.)

[3] 'Preface to the French and Belgian Editions', undated: Churchill papers, 4/16.

decision of the London Conference of Commonwealth Premiers, that India could remain in the Commonwealth as an Independent Republic. 'I shall have to speak briefly on the subject,' Churchill wrote to Lord Salisbury that morning, 'shortly after the announcement has been made to Parliament this afternoon. I have no doubt that it is our duty to do all we can to make a success of the new system. This will, I am sure, be the general view of the Shadow Cabinet, and Buchan-Hepburn reports that the large majority of the 1922 Committee will share it.' Churchill added: 'I am not distributing any bouquets to the Government but there is no doubt they will gain in prestige by what has happened. For us, as a Party, to set ourselves against all the seven Prime Ministers of the Commonwealth would be still more injurious to us. We should immediately be asked, "Are you going to undo what has been done, and in what respects?" And it could be said the Tory Party is resolved to drive India out of the Commonwealth. This would never do.' [1]

It was 'the duty of us all', Churchill told the House of Commons, 'wherever we sit, to try our best to make this new expression of the unity of the world-wide association of States and nations a practical and lasting success, and that that is the course which we on this side of the House intend to steer. I feel that the tides of the world are favourable to our voyage.' Churchill's words of welcome and reconciliation ended:

The pressure of dangers and duties that are shared in common by all of us in these days may well make new harmonies with India and, indeed, with large parts of Asia. We may also see coming into view an even larger and wider synthesis of States and nations comprising both the United States of America and United Europe which may one day, and perhaps not a distant day, bring to harassed and struggling humanity real security for peace and freedom and for hearth and home. [2]

'You were both magnanimous and wise,' wrote L. S. Amery after the debate. [3]

Field Marshal Smuts was distressed that Churchill accepted the

---

[1] 'My dear Bobbety', 28 April 1949: Salisbury papers. Lord Cranborne had succeeded his father as Marquess of Salisbury in 1947. In 1952 Churchill appointed him Secretary of State for Commonwealth Relations (1952) and Lord President of the Council (1952–57). He died in 1972.

[2] Speech of 28 April 1949: *Hansard*.

[3] 'My dear Winston', 29 April 1949: Churchill papers, 2/44. In the personal sphere Churchill was also magnanimous, or tried to be. On April 29 he settled two seven-year covenants so that each of Lord Moran's sons could receive £300 a year free of income tax. 'You have always refused,' Churchill noted, 'to allow me, even when I was a Minister, to make any return to you for all you have done for me.' This was the way in which he felt he could express his gratitude. ('My dear Charles', 'Private and Confidential', 29 April 1949: Churchill papers, 2/163.)

adherence of the Republic of India in the Commonwealth. But Churchill was not to be deflected from his view. 'It is absolutely necessary,' he wrote to Smuts, 'for the Conservative Party to have a policy which is not unfavourable to the new India.' [1] In the message as finally sent to Smuts, Churchill was emphatic in his support for India's new status, telling his friend of nearly half a century:

When I asked myself the question, 'Would I rather have them in, even on these terms, or let them go altogether?' my heart gave the answer, 'I want them in.' Nehru has certainly shown magnanimity after sixteen years' imprisonment. The opposition to Communism affords a growing bond of unity.

No one can say what will happen in future years. I cannot think that any Soviet invasion of India would occur without involving UNO against the aggressor. Therefore the burden of Indian defence no longer falls on us alone. Finally I felt it would place the Crown in an invidious light if it appeared an exclusive rather than an inclusive symbol. For these reasons among others I took my decision which was accepted without protest by the Party. [2]

Not only Smuts from afar, but many Conservatives, reproached Churchill for his acceptance of Republican India, and his hope for its having a part to play, with Britain, in the 'new harmonies' to which he had referred on April 28. One persistent critic was Lord Salisbury, to whom Churchill wrote on May 7:

I consider that the fatal step towards India was taken when Baldwin supported the Ramsay MacDonald plan in 1930 and enforced it upon the Conservative Party in 1931. I and seventy Conservatives—and your Father—resisted this for four long years, and were systematically voted down by the Baldwin–Ramsay MacDonald combination, supported for this purpose, I need hardly say, by the Socialist Party in opposition. Once the Conservative Party cast aside its duty to resist the weakening of the Imperial strength, the gap could not be filled, and from this point we slid and slithered to the position we have reached today. I could not therefore accept any reproach for the present situation from any Conservative who supported the Baldwin and Chamberlain policies.

Churchill's letter continued:

I am glad you realize that the clock cannot now be put back. 'The moving finger writes. . . .' All the same I must admit that the latest developments are not so bad as I thought they would be six months ago, when I made a speech in the House which was the result of much sorrowful heart-searching. I thought then that India would become a hostile, as well as an independent, State. But now the door of hope has re-opened in my mind. The world tides are very favourable, and the next ten years may easily see the development and the growth of strong ties. I do not even think it impossible that the

---

[1] Elizabeth Gilliatt dictation notes, 3 May 1949: Churchill papers, 2/176.
[2] Telegram despatched on 22 May 1949: Churchill papers, 2/176.

Indian people, whose sentimental attachment to the Crown is widespread and deep, may some day accept the full status of Imperial citizenship. Anyhow I am glad no irrevocable gulf has opened.

It is possible, even, that Burma may take a second-class ticket back. This I should welcome. Perhaps you will remember the difficulty I had to get the Party to vote against the Burma Independence Bill. But now, in their tragedy and misery, many Burmese must be turning their minds back to the palmy days of Queen Victoria.

'These may be but the vain dreams of an aged man,' Churchill ended. 'However I cannot despair; still less must you, for whom the future holds many tasks.'[1]

Churchill now worked to finish the third Volume of his war memoirs. 'By sitting up very late several nights,' he informed Bill Deakin on May 5, 'I have finished Volume III, and the last chapters come back from the printer tomorrow.' Churchill asked Deakin to 'look through these closing chapters and let me know of any unintentional omission or duplications on my part'.[2] To Ismay, Pownall, Allen and Deakin, Churchill wrote that he wanted the proofs scrutinized not only by them, but by 'the principal people concerned', including Eden, Wavell, Smuts and Norman Brook, with a view to a final revision in three months' time. Churchill, meanwhile, was 'turning to Volume IV'.[3]

'I am not attempting to write a History of the Second World War,' Churchill explained to a critic of his description of the Belgian surrender in 1940, 'but only to give the story of events as they appeared to me and to the British Government, and to confine myself to expressions of opinion which I made as its opening tragedy unfolded.'[4]

On 12 May 1949 Churchill spoke in the House of Commons in support of the Labour Government's conclusion of the North Atlantic Treaty. The signature of this Treaty came just after Stalin had called off the Berlin blockade. 'I am glad,' Churchill told the House of Commons, 'that the lifting by the Soviet Government of the blockade of

[1] 'My dear Bobbety', 7 May 1949: Salisbury papers.
[2] 'Mr Deakin', 5 May 1949: Churchill papers, 4/19.
[3] 'Lord Ismay, General Pownall, Commodore Allen, Mr Deakin', May 1949: Churchill papers, 4/19.
[4] Letter of 12 May 1949 (to Baron Carton de Wiart): Churchill papers, 4/52.

Berlin has not been taken by him as an occasion for proclaiming that an important peace gesture has been made,' and he went on to explain:

Before the last war, I do remember how, every time Herr Hitler made some reassuring statement, such as 'This is my last territorial demand', people came to me and said, 'There, now, you see how wrong you have been; he says it is his last territorial demand'; but the bitter experience we have all gone through in so many countries, on this side and on the other side of the Atlantic, has made us more wary of these premature rejoicings upon mere words and gestures.

Any deed done by the Soviet Government, Churchill said, 'which really makes for the peaceful and friendly intercourse of mankind', would have its 'immediate response', but 'mere manoeuvres will be watched with the utmost vigilance'. The situation in which Soviet Communism had not only 'vast armies' but also 'a theme, almost a religion', was one which was 'unprecedented and incalculable'. In addition:

Over the whole scene reigns the power of the atomic bomb, ever growing in the hands of the United States. It is this, in my view, and this alone that has given us time to take the measures of self-protection and to develop the units which make those measures possible, one of which is before us this afternoon. I have said that we must rise above that weakness of democratic and Parliamentary Governments, in not being able to pursue a steady policy for a long time, so as to get results. It is surely our plain duty to persevere steadfastly, irrespective of party feelings or national diversities, for only in this way have we good chances of securing that lasting world peace under a sovereign world instrument of security on which our hearts are set.

It was for this reason, Churchill concluded, that the Opposition would support the Government, and cast its votes in favour of the North Atlantic Treaty.[1]

On May 29 Walter Graebner took down to Chartwell five episodes of the film *Crusade in Europe*, a documentary of the Second World War by the March of Time.[2] Graebner later recalled:

Churchill loved it, as it enabled him to relive his grandest years again, and he watched it with the closest attention, tears often rolling down his cheeks and comments on the action continually on his lips. Characteristically he

[1] Speech of 12 May 1949: *Hansard*.
[2] 'Mr & Mrs Graebner for tea, film & dinner', Churchill Engagements Cards, 29 May 1949: Churchill papers. Bill Deakin was also at Chartwell that night.

showed no feeling of triumph over his vanquished enemy. 'Poor fellows, poor, poor fellows,' he would say with generous pity, as towards the end he watched scenes of German prisoners-of-war huddling together in their camps. After the hour and forty minutes it took to run off the five reels, Churchill was calling for more, though it was then 11 p.m.

Graebner's account continued:

That evening provided a good example of Churchill's extraordinary thoughtfulness. It was the custom at Chartwell to invite everyone who lived or worked on the estate to view the movies. Among the group of twenty or thirty was an ex-German prisoner-of-war named Walter, who did odd jobs like wood-cutting and lawn-mowing, and who, from the way he responded to anything Churchill said, was obviously a devoted servant. The March of Time film was not under way more than a few minutes before it was clear that it would not evoke happy memories for a former member of the Reichs-wehr.

Churchill rose from his seat at once, tapped Walter on the shoulder, and motioned him to leave the theatre with him. Later we learned that Churchill's object in going out was to suggest to Walter that perhaps he would prefer not to see the film that evening. Walter, however, returned to the theatre with Churchill and remained till the end.[1]

Guided by R. A. Butler and Harold Macmillan, the Conservative Party prepared for the coming General Election by setting down its policy proposals for social reform without Socialism. Churchill, who in 1908 had argued in favour of a major programme of 'minimum standards' supervised by the State, looked with approval on the new development.[2] When the policy document of 1949 was ready, Harold Macmillan wrote to Churchill to ask if he would write a short preface to it, to make clear that the document not only had Churchill's full endorsement, but was 'inspired' by him. Macmillan added:

You will forgive me—but I am so anxious that you should be known to the *younger* section of the voters (and that means, for this purpose, anyone under 40) not merely as the great war leader, but as the social reformer. Surely with these proposals, the wheel comes full circle? You can appeal to everything which your Father wanted to do and which you helped to ac-

[1] Walter Graebner recollections: Walter Graebner, *My dear Mister Churchill*, pages 37–8.
[2] On 14 March 1908 Churchill wrote to H. H. Asquith, in explaining why he was accepting a Cabinet position in the domestic sphere (President of the Board of Trade, his first Cabinet post): 'Dimly across gulfs of ignorance I see the outline of a policy wh I call the Minimum Standard. It is national rather than departmental. I am doubtful of my power to give it concrete expression. If I did, I expect before long I should find myself in collision with some of my best friends—like for instance John Morley, who at the end of a lifetime of study & thought has come to the conclusion that nothing can be done.' (Asquith papers.)

complish in your Liberal days. Surely this document presents a rallying point
for all reasonable people, of all political affiliations and of none, to oppose
Socialism not with a negative but with a positive policy.

Who is so fitted to present this as yourself? In your life these immense
social changes have taken place and largely with your support and guidance.
The ground won must be consolidated, and then extended; it is in danger of
being lost. Make it clear—especially to the young—what has been (in addition to your record as a War Minister) your life-long work.[1]

Churchill readily agreed to write the preface as Macmillan had
suggested.[2] But his principal concern during the summer of 1949 was
Britain's defence preparedness. On July 13 he had gone with a small
but senior delegation of Conservatives to see Attlee about Soviet military strength and Britain's defence capacity. Among those on the
delegation was Lord Cherwell, who not only provided Churchill with
most of the figures used at the meeting, but drafted the letter which,
when it was over, Churchill signed, and sent to Attlee. The letter
began by expressing 'how disquieted we all were' by the information
which Attlee had given them, and continued:

We cannot reckon upon a 'phoney' war period of seven months next time.
The next war, if there is one, will undoubtedly start with violent air attacks
designed to cripple our fighting potential. We have not yet been informed
about the state of our anti-aircraft defences though I have heard some very
depressing tales about them. But even if our anti-aircraft batteries were in
first-class condition, we must rely for our main defence against air attack
almost entirely upon fighters.

The very small number of our fighters causes us the greatest anxiety. A
total of 415 with only 196 modern jet-fighters would have very little chance
against the 4,800 Russian bombers, supported by 8,000 fighters once the
Russians had reached the Channel, more especially if they can match our
196 jets with 500 of their own. Even if it be true that the Russians have only
100 copies of B29, their 4,700 light-bombers and 3,200 dive-bombers would
be very destructive if they could once achieve mastery of the air over
England.

The night-fighter position is even more serious. Apparently the whole defence of these Islands is entrusted to a handful of 48 obsolescent Mos-
quitoes. . . .

Another point made in the letter concerned Britain's bomber forces:

The weight of our possible counter-offensive is equally disheartening. A
mere 144 heavy bombers could probably scarcely deliver 5,000 tons per

---

[1] 'Dear Winston', 'Personal', 'Yours affectionately, Harold Macmillan', 24 June 1949: Churchill papers, 2/88.

[2] *The Right Road for Britain*, The Conservative Party's Statement of Policy, July 1949.
Foreword by the Rt Hon. Winston S. Churchill, OM, CH, MP, published by the Conservative
Party, London.

month on targets in Russia as against the 50,000 tons per month which we dropped on Germany in the summer of 1944. This would scarcely be a deterrent. Our only hope as usual seems to be the atomic bomb. . . .

The letter continued, as drafted by Lord Cherwell, but as if by Churchill alone:

In all my long experience I can recall nothing parallel to this giving away of our actual means of life. It compares with the struggle about the twenty-five squadrons which the French demanded in 1940. That we steadfastly refused. I earnestly hope that, from now on, every jet-plane we make will be sent at once to the British fighter squadrons and that the necessary number of airfields will have their run-ways extended to take not only British jet-fighters, but the more exacting American planes.

The letter to Attlee ended:

I may add that, considering the very large numbers of Russians who are allowed to circulate in our factories—far more, I am assured, than our police and other agents can supervise—it is very likely that the Soviets had already got the bulk of the information about jet-planes which has to be kept secret from Parliament and other nations.[1]

Churchill sent copies of this letter to Eden, Cherwell and Montgomery. 'That such burdens should bear so heavily on us,' Montgomery had written two weeks earlier, 'when we have been at peace for over four years, is not good,' and he added: 'I hope you keep well. You will have to take us through the next crisis as you did the last. So take care of yourself.'[2]

---

[1] 'My dear Prime Minister', 'Private and Personal', 24 July 1949: Churchill papers, 2/29. At Lord Cherwell's suggestion, for the sake of security, no figures were given in the letter itself, only the letters 'a' to 'p'. A second letter, sent separately, contained the key. I have instated the figures from the key in place of the letters.

[2] 'Dear Mr Churchill', 8 July 1949: Churchill papers, 4/51.

27

Thoughts, and plans, at Seventy-four

I T was while Churchill had been in the United States in the spring of 1949 that the second volume of his war memoirs had been published there, with the sub-title 'Their Finest Hour'.[1] The British edition was published that summer. In thanking Churchill for a copy, Sir Alexander Cadogan wrote of how this volume had moved him even more than its predecessor. 'You would say that you only interpreted the feelings and faith of the British people,' Cadogan added, 'but 80 or 100 musicians may have all the spirit and the skill and the aspiration (if not the inspiration) in the world, and it still takes the genius of the exceptional leader (with a small l) to weld them together into a perfect instrument.'[2]

Even as the letters of thanks for the British edition of Volume 2 were reaching him, Churchill was incorporating the final new material for Volume 3, encouraged by the success of Volume 2. 'The publishers tell me there has been a record sale,' he wrote to Sir Alan Lascelles at the end of June, 'well over a quarter of a million people having bought the book in a single day.'[3]

On July 19 General Pownall sent Churchill a progress report. He had spent 'some time' with Field Marshal Wavell going through the chapters in which Wavell appeared. 'As you will see,' Pownall wrote, 'there is nothing of great moment, indeed his general remark was "on the whole he has been very kind to me".'

Pownall also submitted to Churchill a number of suggestions about the passages dealing with General Auchinleck, 'which if accepted would make the draught less chilly'.[4] As to the Alamein section, it was

[1] Publication day was 29 March 1949 in the United States, and 27 June 1949 in Britain.
[2] 'Dear Winston', 5 June 1949: Churchill papers, 4/51.
[3] 'My dear Tommy', 29 June 1949: Churchill papers, 2/171. The first printing was 276,000.
[4] Churchill's final description of the change of command in November 1941 was: 'Although I cordially approved what had been done in the High Command, I thought it a pity that Auchinleck did not take it over himself instead of entrusting it to one of his staff officers, as yet unproved in the field.' (Winston S. Churchill, *The Second World War*, Volume 3, London 1950, page 510.)

'nearly ready', Pownall reported; 'a last overhaul by the Air Historian is all that remains'.[1]

On July 23 Churchill flew from Biggin Hill to Wolverhampton, where he spoke at a mass rally of Midland Conservatives. On his return that evening he was given an escort of Spitfires by 615 Squadron, of which he was Honorary Air Commodore.[2] That evening Bill Deakin was at Chartwell to dine and sleep, and to work, followed on July 24 by Denis Kelly. As well as continuing his work on the war memoirs, Churchill was planning a holiday in Italy. Walter Graebner, who was present during some of the planning stage, and had already seen Churchill at work during one such excursion, later recalled: 'A recurring problem was to find a hotel big enough, or with enough rooms available, to hold the entire party. And did the windows of all the principal rooms face on to the water? Were there enough telephones? Where was the nearest airport? Could Mr Churchill avoid all public engagements? Would there be adequate local police protection?' Graebner's account continued:

Hotels turned themselves inside out to make Churchill comfortable. The one on Lake Garda, where he stayed only a week, spent millions of lire remodelling an entire wing, replacing much of the furniture, and installing a new motor in a lift that had broken down some years before. Large stocks of Scotch whisky, red and white port and brandy were brought in (Churchill usually took his own cigars and champagne), and a fleet of automobiles was reserved for the duration of the stay.

No matter how far he went, whether by rail or air, Churchill took with him all the equipment for an office, other than tables and chairs. Nothing was left to chance: he wanted an office functioning within an hour or two after his arrival. Crates and black dispatch boxes were filled with typewriters, paper clips, pencils, ink, paper, paste, scissors, pins, envelopes, sealing-wax, seals and string.

The office was always installed near the middle of the Churchill wing, since it functioned as the nerve centre for the entire party. All mail, for example, was delivered to the office, not to the rooms of any individuals. If anyone wanted to find out who was coming to dinner he inquired at the office. All plans for the day were issued through the office. The management of this vital part of the holiday operation was entrusted to two secretaries

---

[1] 'Mr Churchill', 19 July 1949: Churchill papers, 4/351. The 'Air Historian' to whom all air sections were submitted was Denis Richards, Senior Narrator in the Air Ministry Historical Branch from 1943 to 1947, and co-author of the three volume official History of the Royal Air Force in the Second World War, who later recalled how Pownall 'used to come to my Air Ministry rooms in Cadogan Gardens bearing large sheets of printed matter with enormous margins for comment'. (Denis Richards recollections: letter to the author, 16 December 1987.) An historian of the Tudor and Stuart periods, Richards later published a biography of Viscount Portal of Hungerford (1978).

[2] Desmond Bungey log book, 23 July 1949: Bungey papers.

from the London staff, one of whom was available whenever Churchill called between 8 a.m. and 2 a.m.

Equally important was the installation on arrival of a studio where Churchill could paint when inclement weather kept him indoors, and where he could display his works in various stages of completion as the holiday moved along. One large, well-lighted room was set aside for this, and the equipment brought from England included about fifteen frames, several dozen canvases, six or eight easels, and three or four powerful lamps.

There were always about a dozen people in the Churchill entourage. Two were Scotland Yard detectives, who worked twelve-hour shifts each so that Churchill was never left unguarded. Since they were the same team that was assigned to him in England they felt quite at ease in the party, and on painting and picnic excursions they pitched in and helped like everyone else. Also present was a valet, who not only dressed Churchill and looked after his other needs in the bedroom, but squeezed the tube when his master wanted more paint, saw that a fresh cigar was never more than a few feet away, and did hundreds of other little things which added to his comfort.

To help him with his *Memoirs*, as well as to keep him company, Churchill brought relays of historians, researchers and military advisers who were part-time members of his London staff. Sometimes his doctor, Lord Moran, would be invited for a week or ten days even when Mr Churchill was in the best of health. At other times he turned for companionship to someone like Sir Oswald Birley, the portrait painter. . . .[1]

From Gardone, Churchill, his wife and his entourage moved on to Carezza. 'My wife and I are very much enjoying our holiday,' Churchill telegraphed to Graebner on August 6, 'though it was hot at Gardone. Here at Carezza much cooler and most paintable scenery.' Both Lord Ismay and Bill Deakin were with him. 'We have made immense progress volume four.'[2]

Churchill's holiday was not all painting and writing; he had also to prepare a speech for the first meeting of the Council of Europe, to be held in Strasbourg on August 12. 'I do hope all will go well,' his daughter Mary wrote to him on August 9, 'and much will be advanced by the meetings at Strasbourg—I am sure you will be much fêted—but I expect you look forward to escaping again to your lakes and paints.'[3]

Churchill was to lead the Opposition section, and Herbert Morrison the Government section of the British delegation at Strasbourg.[4] The Assembly opened on August 10, Paul-Henri Spaak being elected President. In a nomination for one of the four Vice-Presidents, Herbert

[1] Walter Graebner recollections: Walter Graebner, *My dear Mister Churchill*, pages 72–4.

[2] Telegram despatched 6 August 1949: Churchill papers, 1/77. Churchill's travels in the summer of 1949 were once more paid for by Time-Life, $2,500 in July and $5,763 in August.

[3] Letter of 9 August 1949: Churchill papers, 1/46.

[4] The other Opposition members were Harold Macmillan, Sir David Maxwell-Fyfe, Robert Boothby, David Eccles, Sir Ronald Ross, Duncan Sandys and (for the Liberals) Lord Layton.

Morrison had proposed the Labour Chief Whip, William Whiteley. On reaching Strasbourg, the British Conservative representatives at once objected. 'We put up Layton,' Macmillan noted in his diary, 'and canvassed freely for him. L was terrified and wanted to withdraw. Churchill seized the trembling L during an interval and thundered at him: "If you retire now, I will never speak to you again. You will have betrayed me. You will have betrayed the whole Liberal Party".'

Strongly supporting Layton in the furore that followed were two of the British journalists present, Randolph Churchill and his friend Alastair Forbes. Layton was duly, very narrowly, elected. There was then an adjournment, during which Macmillan escorted Churchill back to his villa, noting in his diary: 'He was so tired that he lay on his bed—fully dressed—but declaring repeatedly, "This is the best fun I've had for years and years. This is splendid. This is really fun."' [1]

That evening there was a public meeting in the Place Kléber, at which Macmillan estimated there must have been nearly 20,000 people present. He added:

Churchill received a tremendous welcome and made an extremely effective speech—written in English, translated into French—and delivered with a better accent than usual. Every part of the huge square was filled. At every balcony and every window were massed spectators—except one. That, of course, was the window of Bevin's sitting-room in the hotel overlooking the square. [2]

Churchill participated with zeal in the deliberations of the Assembly, somewhat to the alarm of the British delegates, as Macmillan described in a letter home:

This extraordinary man, during the early sittings, seemed to come down almost too rapidly to the level of normal political agitation. His intervention in the Layton–Whiteley incident and his several short speeches on the question of the powers of the Assembly to fix its own agenda, were all calculated—perhaps intentionally—to reveal him as a Parliamentarian, rather than as a great international figure. You can imagine that we were all a little alarmed at this. For our pains, we were treated with a firm and even harsh refusal to accept our advice.

He certainly took more trouble to listen to the debates than I have ever known him do in the House of Commons. He walked about, chatted to each representative, went into the smoking-room, and generally took a lot of trouble to win the sympathetic affection of his new Parliamentary colleagues. This was done with much assiduity. He used his villa for entertaining the more important to luncheon and dinner; and he took much trouble over all this determination to charm them as well as impress them. [3]

[1] Macmillan diary, 12 August 1949: *Tides of Fortune*, pages 170–1.
[2] Macmillan diary, 12 August 1949: *Tides of Fortune*, page 174.
[3] Letter, undated: *Tides of Fortune*, page 175.

For four days, Churchill entertained the delegates for lunch and dinner at his villa. 'How he can stand it,' Macmillan noted, 'I cannot imagine. He is entertaining very freely—Americans, French, Belgians, Dutch, Italians—all who can in any way be flattered or cajoled.'[1] On August 15, a holiday, Churchill received the freedom of Strasbourg. 'I think,' Macmillan later recalled, 'he was under the impression that the public holiday was in his honour. When it was explained to him that it was for the Feast of the Annunciation, he seemed rather put out.'[2] 'It took a lot of explaining', was Macmillan's comment nearly four decades later.[3]

In his speech at Strasbourg on August 17, Churchill reiterated that the Council of Europe was intended as 'a European unit' in the United Nations. This Europe, he stressed, was not meant to be a divided one, yet there were ten empty seats:

Ten ancient capitals of Europe are behind the Iron Curtain. A large part of this continent is held in bondage. They have escaped from Nazism only to fall into the other extreme of Communism. It is like making a long and agonizing journey to leave the North Pole only to find out that, as a result, you have woken up in the South Pole. All around are only ice and snow and bitter piercing winds.[4]

We should certainly make some provision for association with representatives of these countries, who are deprived of ordinary democratic freedom but who will surely regain it in the long march of time. This is a matter which should be carefully considered by the Assembly, and I agree with all those, and there are many, who have spoken in favour of setting aside some seats in the Assembly as a symbol or proof of our intention that the Assembly shall some day represent all Europe, or all Europe west of the Curzon Line.[5]

Then, as Harold Macmillan recalled: 'In a dramatic outburst, looking round the hall, he demanded almost fiercely, "Where are the Germans?" He pressed for an immediate invitation to the West

[1] Macmillan diary, 14 August 1949: *Tides of Fortune*, page 174.

[2] Macmillan recollections: *Tides of Fortune*, page 174.

[3] Harold Macmillan recollections: letter to the author, 30 October 1986.

[4] In an article entitled 'The Infernal Twins', published in *Colliers* magazine twelve years earlier, on 3 July 1937, Churchill wrote, of Nazism and Communism: 'I am reminded of the North Pole and South Pole. They are at opposite ends of the earth, but if you woke up at either Pole tomorrow morning you could not tell which one it was. Perhaps there might be more penguins at one, or more Polar bears at the other; but all around would be ice and snow and the blast of a biting wind. I have made up my mind, however far I may travel, whatever countries I may see, I will not go to the Arctic or Antarctic regions. Give me London, give me Paris, give me New York, give me some of the beautiful capitals of the British Dominions. Let us go somewhere where our breath is not frozen on our lips because of the Secret Police. Let us go somewhere where there are green pastures and the shade of venerable trees. Let us not wander away from the broad fertile fields of freedom into these gaunt, grim, dim, gloomy abstractions of morbid and sterile thought.'

[5] Only the Soviet Union, of the European nations, lay east of the Curzon Line.

German Government to join our ranks. Time was passing. There should be no delay. "We cannot part at the end of this month on the basis that we do nothing more to bring Germany into our circle until a year has passed. That year is too precious to lose. If lost, it might be lost for ever. It might not be *a* year. It might be *the* year." '[1]

The arrival of a German delegation 'as a result of our work here this month' would, Churchill told the Assembly, have a 'highly beneficial' result in the cause of world peace and European security.

Churchill ended with a reference to the 'sentimental and moral aspects' of the work of the Strasbourg meeting. 'I hope we shall not put our trust in formulae or in machinery,' he said. It was by the spirit 'that we shall establish our force'. It was by 'the growth and gathering of the united sentiment of Europeanism, vocal here and listened to all over the world, that we shall succeed in taking, not executive decision, but in taking a leading and active part in the revival of the greatest of continents which has fallen into the worst of misery.'[2]

From Strasbourg, Churchill travelled south to Monte Carlo, to continue his holiday, leaving Harold Macmillan to send him a daily report of the discussions. Herbert Morrison's intervention, Macmillan reported on August 19, 'showed complete lack of mastery of the subject or sympathy with the audience'.[3]

At Beaverbrook's villa, La Capponcina, near Monte Carlo, Churchill received and studied a comprehensive set of comments on Volume 4 of his war memoirs; comments sent to him by Emery Reves. 'The volume is superb,' wrote Reves, as a prelude to his points. Of one chapter he wrote: 'Chapter excellent, but ending somewhat flat,' and of another: 'Chapter very good, but ending needs something more exciting.' Reves also sent detailed notes on the final proof version of Volume 3, in which he felt there was 'too much detail' on the military campaigns. Other chapters, however, he wanted to see extended. 'In view of the fact that Roosevelt is dead and Stalin will never publish his documents,' Reves wrote, 'you are the only man who can reveal the decisive issues of the last war.'[4]

For almost a week, Churchill painted, worked on his book, and swam. August 23, as Denis Kelly later recalled, 'had been a happy day. Merle Oberon had been imported by Beaverbrook as a house-guest and we had bathed in hot and windy sunshine from a private

---

[1] Macmillan recollections: *Tides of Fortune*, page 176.
[2] Speech of 17 August 1949: Randolph S. Churchill (editor), *In the Balance*, pages 75–83.
[3] 'Message from Mr Macmillan', 19 August 1949: Churchill papers, 2/75.
[4] Emery Reves to Mr Churchill', 22 August 1949: Churchill papers, 4/351B. Churchill noted, on receiving Reves's letter and notes: 'Miss Sturdee, Please make 4 or 5 copies of this . . .'

beach in Monte Carlo with Churchill turning somersaults in the sea to amuse her.[1] He was broad and well-covered and as we sat afterwards drinking dry martinis in our towels, he suddenly put his weak whisky and soda on the bar, looked at my skinny body and grunted: "Denis, you're a disgrace to the British Empire." '[2]

That evening, Churchill played cards with Lord Beaverbrook until two o'clock in the morning. Getting up from the table, he steadied himself with his hands on the table, and bent his right leg several times, 'as if', so Beaverbrook noted, 'it had gone to sleep'.

'I've got cramp in my arm and leg,' Churchill told Beaverbrook. He began closing and opening his right fist, then went on playing.

That night, Churchill asked Kelly to sit with him while he took his bath; 'he was worried about Beaverbrook's anti-American sentiments', Kelly later recalled. 'He splashed about in the bath, and said to me, 'these people don't know what it's all about.'[3]

When Churchill awoke at about seven o'clock on the morning of August 24, the cramp was still present. 'A little later,' as Beaverbrook noted, 'he found he could not write as well as usual.' Dr Roberts was called in, and at once telephoned to Lord Moran. 'I think Mr Churchill has had a stroke,' he said. 'I would like you to see him as soon as you can.'[4]

Lord Moran flew at once to Nice, taking with him his golf clubs, so that it would not seem that anything was amiss. At Nice airport he was met by Beaverbrook, who told him what had happened. Moran went straight to Churchill's bedroom, where he found the patient awaiting him:

'I am glad you've come; I'm worried.' I could find no loss of power when I examined him; his grip was strong. Later, when he squeezed paints out of their tubes, he could not do it as well as usual. Max had told me that he was not sure whether his speech was affected. Winston was certain that it was not, and there was nothing I could detect. I asked him about his writing. Reaching for his pen, and steadying a bit of paper against a book, he wrote very slowly and carefully:

'I am trying to do my best to make it legible. It is better than it was this morning. W. Churchill.'

He handed me the paper, which shivered as he held it out—I felt he was watching my face as I read it.

[1] Merle Oberon, born Merle Thompson in 1911, was a well-known film star, who in 1939 had married Sir Alexander Korda, the first of her four husbands. She died in 1979.

[2] Denis Kelly recollections: Kelly papers.

[3] Denis Kelly recollections: in conversation with the author, 9 March 1987. It was the only time in ten years that Kelly had been asked to sit with Churchill while he had a bath.

[4] Dr John Roberts, who had been invalided out of the Royal Air Force with a 90% disability pension, practised medicine in Monte Carlo, with permission of the French authorities, on condition that he treated only British patients. Unlike Lord Moran, he kept no diary.

'What has gone wrong, Charles? Have I had a stroke?'

'Most people,' I explained, 'when they speak of a stroke mean that an artery has burst and there has been a haemorrhage into the brain. You've not had that. A very small clot has blocked a very small artery.'

'Will I have another?' he demanded at once. 'There may be an election soon. An election in November is now more a probability than a possibility. I might have to take over again.' He grinned. 'It feels like being balanced between the Treasury Bench and death. But I don't worry. Fate must take its course.'

His memory did not seem to be impaired. He was quite calm, though perhaps a little fearful.

Moran: 'Do you notice anything different?'

Winston: 'Yes, there seems to be a veil between me and things. And there's a sensation in my arm that was not there before.'

Moran: 'What kind of sensation?'

Winston: 'Oh, it's like a tight feeling across my shoulder-blade.'

I told him he had done enough talking and that I would come back later.[1]

Churchill was particularly worried about his signature. 'He kept on practising it,' Miss Gilliatt later recalled, 'asking one again and again, "is it all right?".'[2]

Churchill had intended to return to Strasbourg on August 24, and had invited his fellow Conservatives to dine with him that night. These plans had now to be set aside. 'We got the most exaggerated stories,' Harold Macmillan noted in his diary; 'he had pneumonia, he had had a stroke, he was gravely ill. However, Duncan Sandys came in to me early in the morning, to say that he had talked with him on the phone and he seemed in good form. It seems that he has certainly got a chill, and since Moran is with him, it is probable that he will not be allowed to return here. . . .'[3]

It was announced in the Press that Churchill had 'caught a chill'.[4] The truth of his stroke remained a secret known only to the doctors, and to Lord Beaverbrook. At their urging, Churchill stopped work for three days, but felt well enough on the fourth day to dictate a few letters. 'I have been thinking about what you told me about Lili Marlene coming to your Alamein Reunion,' he informed Montgomery on August 27, and he added: 'I cannot think this would be a good idea and it might excite a lot of unfavourable comment both here and in Germany. I should strongly advise against it.'

Churchill ended his letter to Montgomery with a reference to his health as the public had been informed of it: 'I am laid up here for a

---

[1] Moran notes, 24 August 1949: *The Struggle for Survival*, pages 333–5.
[2] Elizabeth Gilliatt recollections: in conversation with the author, 9 July 1987.
[3] Macmillan diary, 25 August 1949: *Tides of Fortune*, page 179.
[4] Press statement, published in the newspapers on 26 August 1949.

few days as the result of a chill, but am making good progress.'[1] To his former daughter-in-law Pamela, who was staying nearby, he wrote: 'I found it too hot here, especially at nights, but I may be back presently.'[2] From his daughter Sarah, whom he had so upset five months earlier, came a letter from New York, sent on September 3:

My darling Papa,
    I was so terribly relieved to hear that it was only a cold, and that you are now alright again. Darling—I was thrilled by your Strasbourg speech—so was everyone here. I cannot tell you how wonderful it is to move round the world and have people come up to me to wring my hand because of what they know you have done for the world. I wish I could convey to you—all the simple, sincere heart-warming things people say—Everyone here stayed up half a night because you had a cold!! You really must take more care![3]

'I do hope you are really better,' wrote the widow of Admiral Tom Phillips, Lady Phillips, to whom Churchill had sent a copy of his second volume, and she added: 'The whole world I think & we at home were very concerned when we read in the papers you had caught a chill. For all our sakes, in this grim world of today please take care of yourself.'[4]

As he recovered, Churchill reflected on the four years in Opposition: 'four wasted years' he called them one evening with Denis Kelly, at dinner. 'One afternoon,' Kelly also recalled, 'Churchill said to me "Come and have dinner in Monte Carlo tonight." We sat at a balcony table overlooking the street. A French lady in full evening dress passed by, stopped, gasped and curtsied. She could not believe her eyes. Churchill bowed from his chair and I stood up. I realised that he had intended to show the world he was fit and well and had deliberately chosen this most public yet normal way of proving it.'[5]

Lord Moran later recalled:

. . . when some days later he lunched at the Hôtel de Paris, and everyone rose to their feet as he entered and no one noticed anything, he gained confidence. He was, to be sure, irritable at times. Next day, when we dined at another restaurant where the service was slow, he said in tones which carried that he had never been in a worse restaurant. And when an American lady at another table came across and asked him to sign her menu he exploded. Could he not have even his dinner in peace?

Moran's account continued:

[1] 'My dear Monty', 'At La Capponcina, Cap d'Ail', 27 August 1949: Churchill papers, 2/143.
[2] 'Dearest Pamela', 'At La Capponcina, Cap d'Ail', 1 September 1949: Churchill papers, 1/46.
[3] Letter dated 3 September 1949: Churchill papers, 1/46.
[4] 'Dear Mr Churchill', 8 September 1949: Churchill papers, 4/51.
[5] Denis Kelly recollections, typescript, page 34: Kelly papers.

He wanted to get home, but he had misgivings that when he got out of the aeroplane in England the Press would notice that he did not walk straight. He devised a plan—I suspect with Max's assistance—by which the Press would be sent to Northolt while he arrived at Biggin Hill. It seemed a mad thing to do, and would have given rise to all kinds of stories. Eventually I managed to scotch this plan. When, however, we arrived at Biggin Hill and he saw all the photographers with their cameras, he was certain they would notice that something was wrong with his gait, and he waved them away with an angry gesture.[1]

Returning to England on August 31, Churchill felt well enough by September 3 to go to Epsom to see his new racehorse Colonist II, a French-bred grey which had just won its first race under Churchill's colours, running at Salisbury in his first English race. Two weeks later, Churchill invited Colonist's trainer Walter Nightingall to lunch at Chartwell. Nightingall, who in 1948 had obtained the thousandth success of his career, was henceforth to train all Churchill's horses.[2]

On September 18 Churchill went to 11 Downing Street, to be told by Sir Stafford Cripps of the imminent devaluation. Lord Moran noted in his diary:

A little later at Chartwell he said to me: 'I'm not the man I was before this happened. I had to see Cripps at No. 11 about devaluation. It was an act of courtesy on his part. He was cool and debonair, but I was in a twitter.'[3]

As a gesture of thanks to Lord Moran, Churchill now executed a second seven-year Deed of Covenant in favour of Moran's wife Dorothy, for £500 a year, free of tax. 'I hope you will not forbid me to do this,' Churchill wrote, 'and I have taken the necessary steps with the Bank.'[4]

Churchill had intended, before he had been taken ill, to go from the South of France to Switzerland for several days' painting with his painter friends Charles Montag and Willy Sax. Back at Chartwell he painted there instead. 'Please send me six large tubes of "Königsblau hell No. 94" and six of neutral tint,' he telegraphed to Willy Sax on September 17, and he added: 'I was so sorry my plan fell through because of my chill.'[5]

As Churchill recovered at Chartwell, his helpers worked away at

---

[1] Lord Moran recollections: *The Struggle for Survival*, page 335.

[2] Born in 1895, Nightingall had taken over his father's South Hatch stable, in 1926 (and in 1927 had trained fifty-five winners). By 1965 he had trained seventy winners for Churchill in fifteen seasons. He died in 1968. It is said that when Nightingall suggested that Churchill put Colonist II out to stud, Churchill replied: 'To stud? And have it said that the Prime Minister of Great Britain is living on the immoral earnings of a horse?' (Quoted in Kay Halle, *The Irrepressible Churchill*, page 241.)

[3] Lord Moran recollections: *The Struggle for Survival*, page 335.

[4] 'My dear Charles', 16 September 1949: Churchill papers, 2/163.

[5] Telegram of 17 September 1949: Churchill papers, 1/21.

the year 1943 in the war memoirs, with Ismay recalling details of Churchill's determination at Washington in May 1943 to persuade the Americans to follow up the capture of Sicily with the invasion of Italy, 'and knock the Italians out of the war'.[1] As well as submitting all his proof chapters to his helpers, Churchill also showed them to his wife. Her comments were few but outspoken. Reading his strictures on the Admiralty in the draft of Volume 3, she wrote in the margin:

> I am glad you have in this paragraph at last said something generous about the Admiralty. Reading the Chapter up to this point I feared the Admiralty and officers of the Navy might be offended and worse still wounded. You do not print a single reply to your sharp strictures and the reader would conclude you were addressing inert and slothful men. I think you might print one or two answering minutes from the dead Pound.[2]

For some time Randolph Churchill had been agitating for a standard form of writing the dates on letters and documents, preferring the British '6 October 1949' to the American, 'October 6, 1949'. As Churchill took up work again on his war memoirs, Randolph sent him a reasoned proposal for such a standardization. 'Your note about dates is masterly,' Churchill replied on September 22, 'and I have given instructions for it to be universally adopted in any works with which I may burden the public.'[3]

In a letter to Henry Luce on September 23, about the progress of the work, and the need for a sixth volume, Churchill noted that if the Conservatives were to win the election this would not interrupt his progress, as 'I think it very likely in that event that I should offer the leadership to someone else and retire from public life'.[4]

Meanwhile, Churchill had no intention of withdrawing from the political debate; indeed, on September 22 he sent Attlee one of his

---

[1] 'My dear Mr Churchill', 7 September 1949: Churchill papers, 4/362.

[2] Undated notes: Churchill papers, 1/46. Churchill relegated most of his minutes to the Appendix, but without the replies to them.

[3] 'Dearest Randolph', 22 September 1949: Randolph Churchill papers. Randolph Churchill's note read as follows: '6.10.49 means, to an English reader, 6 October 1949. To an American it means 10 June 1949. Even if your readers know which system you are using, many of them will still have to do a lot of counting on their fingers. The compromise adopted in Volume 2 of writing "6. x. 49". is far from clear to American readers and encounters an obvious difficulty for all dates in February: thus 2 Feb. 49 would be written under this system 2.ii.49, which could easily be mistaken for 2 Nov. 49. The whole difficulty can be overcome and an important lead given to others in this matter if you issue a simple blanket instruction that all dates, at the top of memoranda and minutes, should be printed, "6 Oct. 49". When more formality is required 6 October 1949 can be used. *The Times* always prints dates, "October 6th, 1949". Under this system all the numbers come together, instead of being separated by the month, and the "th" merely wastes space and time, and is an unnecessary tribute by the written word to the spoken. *Hansard*, I am glad to say, has long printed the date in the style I recommend.' (Note received at Chartwell on 21 April 1949, signed 'RSC'.)

[4] 'My dear Luce', 'Confidential', 23 September 1949: Churchill papers, 4/25.

strongest letters yet, about the defence situation. 'As I see it,' he began, 'the question is not between short-term and long-term policies, or between isolation and a Grand Alliance. It concerns the physical life of Britain as a unit,' and he continued:

A defenceless Britain can play no part in the defence of Europe. Her power to help in the past has arisen from an integral, insular security. If this falls, all falls. If it endures, all may be defended or regained. Mere contributions, however generous, to European schemes of defence will be useless to Europe if Britain is herself no longer a living military entity. It is certainly not isolationism to set this first objective first. On the contrary it is the only foundation upon which effective help can be given to Europe and to other parts of the Empire.

Churchill then gave an illustration which he was sure would 'help' Attlee to understand his argument:

In 1940 we did everything in human power and ran great risks to help France, sending almost our last divisions abroad, but the one thing we did not ever give way upon was sending the twenty-five fighter air squadrons. This is always considered to have been a cause of our salvation. Distributing 'jets' to Allied European countries or to our Dominions or still more selling them to strangers, while they are so scarce and precious, is in my opinion exactly on a footing with distributing the twenty-five last fighter squadrons in 1940.[1] There would be no objection to a few for training, but to cripple our Air Force and reduce its strength below the safety margin, as has, I am grieved to say, been done, seems to me a terrible event.

Churchill stressed to Attlee that he did not feel that war was imminent, 'but nothing is more likely to bring about a Soviet attack on Western Europe', he wrote, 'than the knowledge that they could not only reach the coast with their ground forces, but could overwhelm, by mass attacks, the air defence of Britain, which would otherwise, in the long run, be fatal to them as it was to Hitler'.

Churchill ended his letter with a reference to a question which had troubled him for some time, the number of 'Russian agents in our midst', telling Attlee:

I was informed some time ago that there were 150 members of the Russian embassy here, excluding the Trade Delegation and its affiliates. The corresponding figure for our representation in Moscow is 85, but varying in ones and twos from day to day. The Russian Trade Delegation here numbers at least 70. In addition to the Russian Trade Delegation there are always up to 20 Russian representatives with firms. These also enjoy diplomatic privileges

[1] The Government had announced the sale of a hundred jet fighter aircraft to the Argentine, where, Lord Cherwell wrote to Churchill, 'they can have no strategic use unless it is against the United States'. (Note, enclosed with 'My dear Winston' of 17 October 1949: Churchill papers, 2/36.)

and are considered attached to the Trade Delegation. These privileges mean in practice unrestricted travel. I am informed that there is no effective watch on persons attached to the Embassy or to the Trade Delegation, either by the police or by MI5. They have not got the necessary numbers for such a task.

I am also informed that in May the Russian figures, including minor attachments, were 236 as against 113 of ours in Russia, and that these figures hold good to-day.

'I am sure,' Churchill's letter ended, 'that if these facts are true there must be a vast number of details about our aircraft and munitions production which are reported to the Soviet, about which the House of Commons is denied all information.' [1]

In sending the King a specially bound copy of his second war memoirs volume, Churchill noted: 'It is a serious task to tell this tale amid gathering political cares, and I am very glad to have got well ahead with it.' He also hoped that the King was 'continually improving in health', adding that 'All will be needed in the anxious days ahead. We may hope they will not be so perilous as those we went through together.' [2]

'I am very worried about the country's present condition,' the King replied, 'though those who should know do not appear to be in the least perturbed, at least outwardly.' [3]

Churchill's concern was reflected in his correspondence; in thanking Truman for an account of Sarah Churchill's acting abilities and their meeting after the theatre, as well as for a signed copy of the programme, Churchill wrote: 'It is pleasant to receive these gestures of friendship at a time when so much is uncertain and when—as I see it—the sky darkens for us all.' [4]

Learning from Attlee that the Anglo-American Combined Chiefs of Staff Organization, which Churchill had so wanted to be continued after the war, was now to be abolished, he wrote at once in protest:

I am very sorry that the Anglo-American Combined Chiefs of Staff Organisation has been abolished. It would have been much better to have preserved it and created an additional and larger organisation to cover the Atlantic Pact Powers. France, without a French army is a liability and not an asset to Great Britain, and there is no reason why our ties with the United States should have been weakened, in form at any rate, to please her.

'I can fully understand the reluctance of our Chiefs of Staff to con-

---

[1] 'My dear Prime Minister', 22 September 1949: Churchill papers, 2/29.

[2] 'Sir', 3 October 1949: Churchill papers, 2/171. Churchill maintained excellent relations with the Royal Family, whose cause he had so often supported. On 15 November he received a telegram from Princess Elizabeth: 'Very grateful for your good wishes to Charles on his birthday' (Telegram from Buckingham Palace, 15 November 1949: Churchill papers, 2/162.) Prince Charles had been born on 14 November 1948.

[3] 'My dear Winston', 'Balmoral Castle', 8 October 1949: Churchill papers, 2/171.

[4] 'Dear Harry', 10 October 1949: Churchill papers, 2/158.

sent to these proposals,' Churchill added, 'and I wonder why they did so.'[1]

The 'situation in Britain today', Montgomery wrote to Churchill later that month, 'is very similar to the situation in the Eighth Army when I took over command in August 1942: Bad leadership, no plan, low morale.'[2]

Churchill was well enough by mid-October to make two substantial speeches, one to the Conservative Trades Union Congress on October 13, the second to the Conservative Annual Conference on the following day. Fortunately for him, both meetings were held in London. Six days later, however, he had to go to Bristol, to deliver the Chancellor's Address at the University's annual honorary degree-giving ceremony. And on October 21 he spoke again, in London, at the Albert Hall, at the fourth Alamein Reunion, using words which electrified his audience of several thousand veterans of the Western Desert:

> Up till Alamein we survived.
> After Alamein we conquered.[3]

For his political speeches, Churchill, who hitherto had been helped considerably by Reginald Maudling, found a new researcher at Conservative Central Office, George Christ. 'I now enclose some extracts,' Christ wrote on October 24, 'from speeches you have made in the past about Conservative Party policy which I think could quite easily be made topical.' He had also 'put down on paper', Christ added, 'a few of my own thoughts which might give you an idea or two'.[4] Churchill also received help from J. P. L. Thomas, who drafted a letter, for Churchill to sign, to the Young Conservative Association. 'I hope the draft will do,' Thomas noted. 'Very good' was Churchill's comment, and he signed the letter unaltered.[5]

[1] 'My dear Prime Minister', 'Confidential', 11 October 1949: Churchill papers, 2/81. 'We shall of course,' Attlee had written to Churchill when sending him the news of the abolition, 'do our utmost to keep alive the spirit underlying the Combined Chiefs Organization and we know it is the Americans' intention to revert to this type of High Command in the event of hostilities.' ('My dear Churchill', 'Personal and Private', 30 September 1949: Churchill papers, 2/81.)

[2] 'Dear Mr Churchill', 20 October 1949: Churchill papers, 9/27.

[3] Speech of 21 October 1949: Churchill papers, 9/27.

[4] Letter of 24 October 1949: Churchill papers, 5/49. Born in 1904, George Christ (his name was pronounced to rhyme with whist and grist) had been Political Correspondent of the *Daily Telegraph* from 1940 to 1945. In 1945 he became the Conservative Party's Parliamentary Liaison Officer, and editor, from 1945 to 1965, of the Conservative Party's weekly newsletter. He died in 1972. 'He was very self-effacing,' Miss Portal later recalled, 'and most amusing. He was always coming out with some witty remark.' (Lady Williams of Elvel recollections: in conversation with the author, 8 July 1987.)

[5] Letter of 7 November 1949: Churchill papers, 2/16.

George Christ quickly became a much-liked member of the inner circle of Churchill's helpers. Later he was to recount one of Churchill's dinner table recollections of the First World War, when Churchill told him of the day when he received the list of survivors of a German ship sunk off the Dogger Bank, in 1914. In the list, Christ recalled, 'he saw the name of Von Tirpitz's grandson, and wrote to tell the Admiral the news, thus cutting out the lengthy delays involved in the normal procedure. He sent the letter via Sweden, he said, and chuckled at the recollection of the scandal which would have arisen if it had come to light that the First Lord had been in communication with the enemy.'[1]

On October 16, Churchill learned from Pownall that the New Zealand War Historian had sent his comments on the chapters about the battle for Crete. These comments were duly incorporated by Pownall and Kelly.[2] Admiral of the Fleet, Lord Cunningham also sent his comments, including criticism of Churchill's account of the failure of the bombardment of Tripoli in 1941. But he considered the rest of the Mediterranean sections, Commodore Allen told Churchill, 'a fair picture of the doings of the Fleet', and expressed his 'great appreciation' to Churchill for showing him these chapters beforehand.[3]

Criticism of Churchill's draft chapters also came from his American publishers, in the form of a three-page letter from Daniel Longwell. 'I am certain you are aware of the fact,' Longwell wrote, 'that some of the Minutes, important as they are, do tend to drag out. Perhaps that is necessary for a rounded out picture, but you said the other day that some of these might have to go back in an appendix.'[4]

After Churchill read Longwell's letter, a message was sent to Walter Graebner that 'the old man was very pleased'. One additional ally in the task of greater readability was Clementine Churchill, as Graebner wrote to Henry Luce:

I think perhaps Mrs Churchill has done more to help than all the rest of us combined. Last night at the end of dinner, completely out of the blue, she said, 'Winston, I have now finished Volume III and I hope you will pay some attention to the little notes I have made in the margins. You must make a great many changes. I got so tired of the endless detail about unimportant battles and incidents. So much of the material is pedestrian.'

---

[1] George Christ recollections: letter to the author, 7 April 1972. In fact, Tirpitz's son Wolfgang, who was Churchill's guest at Chartwell in October 1953.

[2] 'Mr Churchill' (from General Pownall), 16 October 1949: Churchill papers, 4/218. The New Zealand War Historian was Daniel Marcus Davin.

[3] 'Mr Churchill' (from Commodore Allen), 11 October 1949: Churchill papers, 4/218.

[4] 'Dear Mr Churchill', 18 August 1949: Churchill papers, 4/141.

Churchill growled and was annoyed for a few minutes, but then said that he was 'going through it again'. All ended happily with Mrs Churchill throwing napkins at her husband.[1]

In continuing to submit his drafts to the Cabinet Office, Churchill received and accepted several criticisms of content from Norman Brook. On one occasion Attlee himself wrote to Norman Brook, commenting on a reference by Churchill to Australia's 'deep fear' of invasion in December 1941: 'Could you not suggest to Mr Churchill the substitution of "apprehension" for "fear". . . . Attlee added: 'Fear suggests cold fear.'[2] Churchill eventually chose the phrase 'deep alarm'.[3]

Further comments came from Randolph Churchill, to whom his father sent a set of the most recent proofs. 'They are mostly of a minor character,' Randolph noted, 'and could be dealt with by Bill Deakin.'[4] Churchill noted on Randolph's letter, for Denis Kelly: 'Mr K, Go through these with me.'[5]

Churchill's method of starting a chapter was to dictate his thoughts, and to let his helpers discuss them with him. Somewhat unusually for Churchill, one of his dictated notes concerned a hypothetical question, together with his tentative answer:

What would have happened if the Germans had not attacked Russia?
? The air war over Germany in such circumstances.
US + GB against Germany.
Bomb in Canada.
I still believe that we (US + GB) could have won single-handed.
The great contrast between the war as presented to the Russian mind of great masses of men moved and manoeuvred overland and the problem of the Allies which was all sea, amphibious, and air.[6]

The author broke off his labours, briefly, in order to speak about authorship, telling the National Book Exhibition at Grosvenor House, London, on November 2:

Writing a book is an adventure. To begin with, it is a toy, and an amusement; then it becomes a mistress, and then it becomes a master, and then a tyrant. The last phase is that just as you are about to be reconciled to your servitude, you kill the monster, and fling him about to the public.[7]

With the work on Volume 3 having advanced by the beginning of

[1] Letter, undated: Robert T. Elson, '*Time Inc.*', page 215.
[2] Note of 26 October 1949: Premier papers, 8/1321.
[3] Winston S. Churchill, *The Second World War*, volume 4, London 1951, page 4.
[4] 'My dearest Papa', 7 November 1949: Churchill papers, 4/52.
[5] Note by Churchill on Randolph Churchill's letter of 7 November 1949.
[6] 'Miscellaneous', 'War Memoirs 3', 5 October 1949: Churchill papers, 4/351A.
[7] Speech of 2 November 1949: Churchill papers, 5/28. Recording: BBC Written Archives Centre, Library No. 14170.

November to the verge of completion, Churchill instructed his five principal helpers—for Denis Kelly was now added to the quartet of Ismay, Pownall, Allen and Deakin—to sit together with all the readers' points and their own, and to prepare the volume for publication. As he explained to them in a directive on November 8:

I hope your meeting will be fruitful. It seems to me there should be several. I am counting on you to let me have this book free from serious errors of fact. It is already very far advanced in this direction.

I shall be very glad also to have general views about shortening and transferences from chapter to chapter. As soon as I get these chapters back from you I shall start reading Book 6 straight through. I am keeping the last three chapters, as I hope to work on them tonight and tomorrow morning.[1]

From time to time amid this literary labour, current affairs occasioned some comment from the busy writer. When Bernard Baruch advised withholding diplomatic recognition from the newly established Communist Government in China, Churchill replied: 'Diplomatic relations are not a compliment but a convenience. If we recognise the bear why should we not recognise the cub?'[2]

In the Foreign Affairs debate on November 17, Churchill referred to the effect of the British Government's 'belated dismantlement' of German industry while simultaneously encouraging elections in which the Germans could unite against the dismantlement: 'a grotesque piece of mismanagement' he called it. 'The Foreign Secretary, I regret to say,' Churchill continued, 'has succeeded with astonishing precision in securing for our country the worst of both worlds at the same time. It is, indeed, melancholy to find that the fine work of British administration in Germany is blurred over in this way, and needless misunderstandings are created between peoples who, for good or ill, have to live together if the world is to revive.' It was like someone painting, 'with art and labour, a magnificent picture and then, at the moment when it is about to be exhibited, throwing handfuls of mud all over it. Happily, perhaps the mud can be washed off by other hands.'[3]

Speaking on November 28, again in London, at a meeting to advance the cause of European Union, Churchill supported the Labour Government's caveat that Britain could not enter any European econ-

---

[1] 'Lord Ismay, General Pownall, Commodore Allen, Colonel Deakin, Mr Kelly', 8 November 1949: Churchill papers, 4/19.

[2] Telegram sent 15 November 1949: Churchill papers, 2/210. Baruch replied: 'I would not recognise the bear if we had to do it over again nor would I recognise the cub who may grow up to be an even greater bear.' (Telegram sent and received 16 November 1949: Churchill papers, 2/210.)

[3] Speech of 17 November 1949: *Hansard*.

omic system from which the Commonwealth was excluded. He did not believe, however, that this issue would prove an ultimate barrier:

The French Foreign Minister, M. Schuman, declared in the French Parliament this week that 'Without Britain there can be no Europe'. This is entirely true. But our friends on the Continent need have no misgivings. Britain is an integral part of Europe, and we mean to play our part in the revival of her prosperity and greatness.

But Britain cannot be thought of as a single State in isolation. She is the founder and centre of a world-wide Empire and Commonwealth. We shall never do anything to weaken the ties of blood, of sentiment and tradition and common interest which unite us with the other members of the British family of nations.

But nobody is asking us to make such a desertion. For Britain to enter a European Union from which the Empire and Commonwealth would be excluded would not only be impossible but would, in the eyes of Europe, enormously reduce the value of our participation. The Strasbourg recommendations urged the creation of an economic system which will embrace not only the European States, but all those other States and territories elsewhere which are associated with them.

In urging his listeners to support the Strasbourg plan, Churchill emphasized that the basic idea underlying the conception of European Union was the desire to preserve and develop 'the free way of life' of the participating nations. 'This implies,' he said, 'the acceptance of collective responsibility for the defence of liberty and the dignity of man.' [1]

On October 18 Sarah Churchill had married the war artist and photographer Antony Beauchamp. Unfortunately, Churchill and his wife learned of the marriage, which took place in the United States, from the newspapers, journalists having been speedier with the news than Sarah's own telegram. 'The shock and hurt of hearing of the marriage first from the Press,' Sarah's sister Mary has recalled, 'greatly upset both Winston and Clementine—but particularly Clementine, who took it very hard indeed.' [2] Later, however, all was resolved. 'We have made friends with Antony's father and mother,' Clementine Churchill wrote to Sarah on December 20, 'and we had an agreeable luncheon together.' [3]

*   *   *

[1] Speech of 28 November 1949: Randolph S. Churchill (editor), *In the Balance*, pages 151–4.
[2] Mary Soames recollections: Mary Soames, *Clementine Churchill*, page 418.
[3] Letter of 20 December 1949: Mary Soames, *Clementine Churchill*, page 418. Antony Beauchamp's mother was Vivienne, the photographer; on 19 December 1949 Churchill visited her studio in St John's Wood.

On November 30, Churchill celebrated his seventy-fifth birthday. On the following day, at his traditional annual visit to Harrow for the school 'Songs', he told the boys: 'Hard times lie ahead; no easy resting-place is open to us now. We have to march on, not indeed under the enemy's bombardment; but we have to march on under other trials and stresses and toil on up the hill. But if there is any nation which is capable of unbroken effort, it is our British race.' [1]

In the second week of December Churchill was forced to remain in bed with a bad cold. Political correspondence proved impossible for a while, but, from Hyde Park Gate, he still kept a careful watch over the problems of winter at Chartwell, particularly as he intended to return to the South of France at the end of the month. 'Should the Lakes become frozen over during my absence,' he wrote to Christopher Soames on December 15, 'it will be necessary in good time to collect the ten black swans as quickly as possible and keep them in the little yard below the woodshed until there is open water again. They must be kept in their present three separate batches, and will have to be specially fed as they will not be able to graze in the field or from the weeds in the Lakes.' Churchill added: 'will you look after this personally for me?' [2]

A further problem which Christopher Soames was asked to attend to was the improvement of the fox-proof fence. 'For this purpose,' Churchill told him, 'we must buy as much wire netting as we can get. All those men available should work on this, and do the best they can.' [3]

Churchill was well enough to go down to Chartwell himself a few days later, when Sir Archibald Sinclair, his friend of more than forty years and former Second-in-Command in the trenches of the Western Front, was among his guests. In a letter some days later to Lord Beaverbrook, Sinclair reported on his visit, and on his host and hostess:

Clemmie was younger, more active and agile in supervising everything, more exquisitely neat than ever and in excellent queenly looks. Winston was recovering from a very bad cold but he was in grand form—as lively, and incessant, in his conversation as he was in Cabinet in the old days, eating, drinking and smoking as voraciously as ever.

He took me round the farms, showed me short-horns, and Jerseys and then a huge brick hen-house which he had built himself—'Chickenham Palace'. Alongside was a noisome & messy little piece of bare ground—'Chickenham

---

[1] 'Dr Moore, Ladies and Gentlemen, Harrow School', 1 December 1949: Churchill papers, 2/336.
[2] 'Captain Soames', 15 December 1949: Soames papers.
[3] 'Christopher', 24 December 1949: Soames papers.

Palace Gardens'. 'What kind of hens?' I asked. 'Oh, I don't bother about the details,' growled Winston.

He seemed hopeful (after the Gallup Poll & New Zealand but before South Bradford & Australia) but not, I thought, strongly confident about the result of the General Election.[1]

Two and a half weeks before Christmas, Attlee sent Churchill the secret papers about two recent North Atlantic Defence Committee meetings at Washington and at Paris. He wanted, he wrote, to keep Churchill 'as fully informed as possible'.[2] Churchill was pleased to receive them. 'I have read these with attention,' he replied, 'and hope they may prove beneficial to our security. I now return them to you.'[3] Churchill also sent Attlee a letter he had received in his capacity, since 1939, as Honorary Air Commodore of 615 County of Surrey Squadron of the Royal Auxiliary Air Force. 'I have not yet raised in public the serious question of jet fighters, about which we have had some correspondence,' Churchill wrote, 'but I thought I ought to send you this letter which shows how the sale of one hundred jets to the Argentine and other countries of that character affects the Auxiliary Air Force. Will you kindly treat this letter as confidential as it is for your personal information only.'[4]

Churchill and his family spent Christmas at Chartwell: it was twenty-six years since their first Christmas there. The guests on December 27 included Field Marshal Montgomery and his son David, Clare Sheridan and her brother Oswald Frewen, and Brendan Bracken. Also joining his father for the festivities was Randolph, together with his son Winston, and his new wife June.[5]

Churchill had long contemplated a winter holiday. 'Please write soon about Madeira in January,' he had telegraphed on November 19 to Bryce Nairn, the British Consul in Madeira, and had gone on to ask: 'query warm, paintable, bathable, comfortable, flowery, hotels etc. We are revolving plans. Keep all secret. Should so much like to see you both again.'[6]

Madeira it was to be: 'Bill Deakin will land with us,' Churchill

[1] Letter of 19 December 1949: Beaverbrook papers. The New Zealand election of 1949 had been won by Sidney Holland's National Party, which gained 46 seats as against 34 for the Labour Party. South Bradford, a British by-election, was to be won by the Labour candidate, George Craddock, with a 5,346 majority (but with less total votes than the Conservative and Liberal candidates combined). In Australia, the Liberal Country coalition was to defeat the Labour Party at the polls, on 10 December 1949 (and was to do so again in 1955, 1958 and 1961).

[2] 'My dear Churchill', 'Top Secret', 7 December 1949: Premier papers, 8/1160.

[3] 'My dear Prime Minister', 23 December 1949: Churchill papers, 2/29.

[4] 'My dear Prime Minister', 22 December 1949: Churchill papers, 2/29.

[5] 'Chartwell, 1949': National Trust, Chartwell Archive.

[6] Telegram of 19 November 1949: Churchill papers, 1/81.

telegraphed to Nairn on the eve of his departure.[1] Also travelling with Churchill were his wife, his daughter Diana, two secretaries—Miss Gilliatt and Miss Sturdee—and two Special Branch detectives, G. E. Williams and E. A. Davies. On November 29 Churchill had written to F. H. Keenlyside, the Assistant Manager of the Union Castle Mail Steamship Company: 'It was fifty years ago, not fifteen, that I travelled this way before.'[2]

'We are off today,' Churchill wrote to Lord Camrose on December 29; 'a fortnight's sunshine is in our hopes, and some weeks or months, or other things, in our minds.'[3] 1950 was to be Election year.

[1] Telegram of 1 January 1950: Churchill papers, 1/81.
[2] Churchill had left Southampton for South Africa on 14 October 1899, on the *Dunottar Castle*. Reaching Madeira three days later he had written to his mother: 'We have had a nasty rough passage & I have been grievously sick.'
[3] 'My dear Bill', 29 December 1949: Churchill papers, 2/161.

28

An Election Lost

THE New Year of 1950 opened for Churchill in Madeira, at Reid's Hotel, surrounded by his war memoir materials, and in the company of his wife, his daughter Diana, his literary assistant Bill Deakin, Miss Sturdee and Miss Gilliatt. 'May 1950 be a Churchill year,' Deakin wrote to him on January 4.[1] 'Winston is painting in Madeira,' Brendan Bracken wrote to Lord Beaverbrook six days later. 'I spent a day with him before he left. He was in high spirits and seemed to be in remarkable physical health. He ardently hopes to be back in Downing Street at the beginning of Spring. He says if we lose the election he will promptly retire and spend the rest of his life in enjoying himself!'[2]

Churchill had intended to stay in Madeira for several weeks, hoping to make considerable progress on the fourth volume of his war memoirs. But while he was away Attlee announced that a General Election would be held on February 23. His working holiday disrupted, Churchill flew back from Madeira to London on January 12. His wife remained in Madeira. 'We were lucky yesterday,' he telegraphed to her on the morning of January 13, 'with fog which obligingly lifted for half an hour.' Although the flight had been 'most comfortable', he added, 'I still recommend you coming by sea at this time of year.'[3] Later that day he telegraphed again. His 'children' were shooting with the Duke of Westminster and he was therefore alone, but only briefly. 'Anthony lunched with me today,' he reported, 'Rab Butler comes tonight and Woolton tomorrow.'[4]

The discussion at Chartwell centred on the Conservative Party's campaign for the coming election, and on the Party's election manifesto. 'Many thanks for yr kind & inspiring hospitality,' wrote R. A.

---

[1] Letter of 4 January 1950: Churchill papers, 1/80.
[2] Letter of 10 January 1950: Beaverbrook papers.
[3] Telegram despatched 13 January 1950: Churchill papers, 1/47.
[4] Telegram despatched 13 January 1950: Churchill papers, 1/47. The 'children' were Mary and Christopher Soames.

Butler on his return to London, and he added: 'I await further orders.'[1] 'Immersed in politics all day,' Churchill telegraphed to his wife on the evening of January 14. 'Randolph's speeches Devonport magnificent. Liberals have started a candidate to split his votes but we have good hopes.' As to the Conservatives' wider prospects, 'Very hard fight ahead.'[2]

'Hope all has been pleasant,' Churchill telegraphed again to Madeira on January 16. 'Here nothing but toil and moil.'[3]

Churchill took an active part in the preparation of the Conservative Party's election manifesto. Some of his notes and suggestions were written on the blank side of the proof sheets of his war memoirs. Randolph Churchill helped his father with the phrases which might best express the Party's view. 'Incentive' and 'stimulus' were two words Churchill wished to see given prominence in the sections on production and industry. He also tackled the style of the Party's prose. 'It is our intention to initiate consultations with the Unions' became, under Churchill's pen, 'We shall consult with the Unions.'[4]

On January 19, while working on the manifesto, Churchill sent a letter from Chartwell to 28 Hyde Park Gate, to greet his wife's return to London:

My Darling,

Welcome home! And what a pack of toil and trouble awaits you! I have not thought of anything in the week since I returned except politics, particularly the Tory manifesto on which we have had prolonged discussions. One day we were nine hours in the dining room of No. 28.

The Socialists are forcing the Election on to the most materialist lines. All bold treatment of topics in the public interest is very dangerous. The Liberals are running over four hundred candidates, of which at the outside seven will be elected, apart from the six others who are working with us.

The Gallup Polls I showed you on the diagram have taken a big dip. Instead of being nine points ahead we are only three. This I think is due to Christmas and the fact that none of the evils of Devaluation have really manifested themselves yet and are only on the way. How many seats the Liberal 'splits' will cost us cannot be measured. All is in the unknown. However there would be no fun in life if we knew the end at the beginning.

Hawkey is in much better health.[5] I think you will find things locally getting into good order. My Liberal opponent has withdrawn and gone to fight Herbert Morrison at Lewisham. He must be a very pugnacious fellow. We have a new one, but I do not recall his name.

[1] 'Dear Mr Churchill', 14 January 1950: Churchill papers, 2/89.
[2] Telegram despatched at 7.45 p.m., 14 January 1950: Churchill papers, 1/47. Randolph was opposed by Michael Foot (Labour) and A. C. Cann, a former Conservative (Liberal).
[3] Telegram despatched 16 January 1950: Churchill papers, 1/47.
[4] 'This is the Road', draft, 19 January 1950: Churchill papers, 2/89.
[5] Sir James Hawkey was Churchill's constituency chairman.

I have an immense programme but not more than I can carry. The broadcast speech is finished. I am planning to open my speaking campaign in the constituency with an address to the same lot of Headquarters staff and workers that we met the other night, last month. This will enable me to make a nationwide speech on Saturday, January 28.

You will like to see Randolph's admirable opening speech. They now say that Foot is going to bolt to a safer seat. Randolph is coming for the weekend. June is staying in the constituency to electioneer with Arabella.[1]

I was grieved to learn this morning from Christopher that he has a duodenal ulcer. Until he is photographed next week we cannot tell how serious it is. The doctor hopes he will be able to fight. If not, Mary will have to fill the gap.

I am so glad your voyage home was comfortable, but it would have been disastrous if I had not been on the spot here during this difficult week when so many grave decisions had to be taken, not of what to *do*—that would be easy—but of what to *say* to our poor and puzzled people. I am much depressed about the country because for whoever wins there will be nothing but bitterness and strife, like men fighting savagely on a small raft which is breaking up. 'May God save you all' is my prayer.

Come home & kiss me

Your ever loving

W[2]

Churchill made a Party Political broadcast on January 21. The choice before the electorate was, he said, 'whether we should take another plunge into Socialist regimentation, or by a strong effort regain the freedom, initiative and opportunity of British life'. The 'practical question' which would have to be settled by the election was, he reiterated, 'whether we shall take another deep plunge into State ownership and State control, or whether we shall restore a greater measure of freedom of choice and action to our people, and of productive fertility and variety to our industry and trade'.

Churchill than explained the cause, as he saw it, of Britain's economic decline:

The main reason why we are not able to earn our living and make our way in the world is because we are not allowed to do so. The whole enterprise, contrivance and genius of the British nation is being increasingly paralysed by the wartime restrictions from which all other free nations have shaken themselves clear, but these are still imposed upon our people here in the name of a mistaken political philosophy and a largely obsolete mode of thought. Our Government is the only one glorying in controls for controls' sake.

I am sure that a parliament resolved to set the nation free would soon enable it to earn its own living in the world. I am sure on the other hand

---

[1] Arabella Churchill had been born on 30 October 1949.
[2] Letter of 19 January 1950: Spencer-Churchill papers.

that the Socialist policy of equalizing misery and organizing scarcity instead of allowing diligence, self-reliance and ingenuity to produce abundance, has only to be prolonged to be fatal to our British island home.

Referring next both to the Conservatives and to their Liberal allies, the National Liberal Party led by Lord Simon, Churchill declared:

The scheme of society for which Conservatives and National Liberals stand is the establishment and maintenance of a basic standard of life and labour below which a man or a woman, however old or weak, shall not be allowed to fall. The food they receive, the prices they have to pay for basic necessities, the homes they live in, their employment, must be the first care of the State, and must have priority over all other peace-time needs.

Once we have made that standard secure we propose to set the nation free as quickly as possible from the controls and restrictions which now beset our daily life. Above the basic standard there will be free opportunity to rise. Everyone will be allowed to make the best of himself, without jealousy or spite, by all the means that honour and the long respected laws of our country allow.

Later in his broadcast Churchill referred to the dangers of unemployment, which the Labour Party had warned would be one result of a Conservative victory. 'The Conservative and National Liberal Parties,' Churchill said, 'regard the prevention of mass unemployment as the most solemn duty of government. Great difficulties lie ahead when the consequences of devaluation come home to us and when American aid ends. If human brains and will-power can conquer these dangers, we shall, with God's blessing, succeed. It is not the first time we have been through a life and death struggle together.' [1]

As the election campaign proceeded, Churchill received a protest from the Leader of the Liberal Party, Clement Davies, about the use by at least four Conservative associations of the title 'United Liberal and Conservative Association'. In at least two cases no Liberals were present when this Liberal addition to the name was made. In a third case the prospective Liberal candidate was refused admittance to the meeting which set up the new association. 'Is it so much to ask,' wrote Clement Davies, 'that the Conservative Party should fight under its own name, or at least under a name which does not clash with that of another Party which is recognized throughout the world?' Now that Churchill had himself endorsed the label 'Liberal-Conservative', Davies would, he said, give copies of this letter of protest to the Press. [2]

---

[1] Speech of 21 January 1950: Randolph S. Churchill (editor), *In the Balance*, pages 155–60. Two days before his speech, Churchill had received a letter from Lord Simon: 'Every good wish for your Broadcast on Saturday. If you can include a word of appeal and commendation addressed to the "National Liberals", you will put them in good heart' ('Dear Winston', 19 January 1950: Churchill papers, 2/65). Churchill had shown Simon's letter to Reginald Maudling, who was helping him with the broadcast.

[2] 'My dear Churchill', 23 January 1950: Churchill papers, 2/64.

Churchill at once drafted a sustained rebuke:

I thank you for your kindness in writing to me amid your many cares. As you were yourself for eleven years a National Liberal and in that capacity supported the Governments of Mr Baldwin and Mr Neville Chamberlain, I should not presume to correct your knowledge of the moral, intellectual and legal aspects of adding a prefix or a suffix to the honoured name of Liberal. It has certainly often been done before by honourable and distinguished men. There has also been a general custom that at Elections people are free to call themselves—and to some extent their opponents—what they like, and that it is for the electors in each Constituency to judge for themselves about it all. The local Associations in the Conservative Party enjoy a measure of freedom and independence unrivalled in modern political life, and I should certainly not attempt to limit their rights. Indeed, it is natural and proper that Conservatives and Liberals who conscientiously are opposed to Socialism should join together in this crisis in whatever seems to be the most effective way in order to resist the common danger to our country, and to defend so much that is dear to us in our way of life. Thus alone can they give effect to their most sincere convictions. But you have been through all this yourself, and I do not need to dwell upon it further.

Since however you have been good enough to address me, I will venture to draw your attention to the fact that you and your friends do not seem to have any difficulty on the question of nomenclature with the Socialist Party. I have not heard, for instance, of any candidate who is standing as a Liberal-Socialist. The reason is, no doubt, that the two terms are fundamentally incompatible. No one can be at once a Socialist and a Liberal. The establishment of a Socialist State controlling all the means of production, distribution and exchange, is the most complete contradiction of Liberal principles that now exists. I do not therefore expect that you will have to write any letter to Mr Attlee on this point.

Churchill then recalled the reasons for the decline of the Liberal Party, telling Davies:

It is not the Conservatives who have ousted the Liberals from their position as a great Party. The Liberal Government that entered the war in 1914 had 263 Members in the House of Commons. Making such allowances as are possible for Redistribution, it is not I think inaccurate to state that four out of every five Liberal seats have been devoured by the Socialists. I saw a cartoon the other day of a lion with its mouth wide open confronting the Liberal Party. On the lion's stomach was inscribed the word 'Toryism'. This was evidently a mistake on the part of the gifted cartoonist. The true word would have been 'Socialism'. They have not only devoured the bulk of the Liberal Party; they have digested it. Not a trace of their meal remains. Not even a label is hanging out of the Socialist lion's mouth.

Why then should you and your friends and your four hundred candidates always blame the Conservative Party, and do all in your power to help the Socialists? It seems to me that as patriotic men you are taking a grave responsibility by a policy of vote-splitting on a fantastic scale. It is strange political conduct to scheme for the return of minority candidates with whom you disagree, be they Tories or Socialists, at the risk of bringing about a stalemate or deadlock at this anxious juncture.

We hope that responsible and serious minded Liberals will not waste their votes on this occasion, and that the solid strength of the Conservatives and National Liberals will save the country from this danger. But if such a misfortune were to happen the six or seven members you may have in the new Parliament, even if they agreed, would be quite unable to cope with the consequences.

There is a real measure of agreement between modern Tory democracy and the mass of Liberals who see in Socialism all that their most famous thinkers and leaders have fought against in the past. An intense passion of duty unites us in this fateful hour in an honourable freedom in which the undying flame of Liberalism burns.

I hope you and your friends will ponder carefully upon what I have set down, and do not hesitate to write to me again if you think I can be of further service.[1]

In his reply, Davies called Churchill's letter 'facetious and evasive' and deplored the fact that Churchill was prepared to support 'what we Liberals rightly regard as an unworthy subterfuge'.[2] Churchill noted on Davies's letter: 'No further answer.'[3]

Undeterred by the imminence of Polling Day, or the acerbity of the election campaign, Churchill found time on January 24 to send Lord Ismay a three-page note about the presentation of the story of the atomic bomb in the war memoirs. Of his own discussions with Roosevelt on this subject he instructed Ismay: 'An accurate description is required of these negotiations,' and he added:

My general impression is that our scientists were a little ahead of the Americans and at any rate more confident that results could be achieved during the war. What evidence is there of this and who were the men principally concerned?

This matter is of the highest interest and importance. I do not think we have had the information I expected from the United States about information being interchanged. We have not now either got any bombs or the way of making them or, so far as I know, have made any arrangements to have them brought over.

'The whole subject requires most careful statement,' Churchill wrote, and he cautioned: 'We must get the dates and facts right first.' There was of course 'no hurry'.[4]

[1] 'My dear Davies', 25 January 1950: Churchill papers, 2/64.
[2] 'My dear Churchill', 26 January 1950: Churchill papers, 2/64.
[3] Note initialled 'WSC', 26 January 1950: Churchill papers, 2/64.
[4] 'Lord Ismay', 24 January 1950: Churchill papers, 4/299.

During the morning of January 24 Churchill again felt unwell. He at once sent for Lord Moran, as he had during his earlier stroke in the South of France. Moran noted in his diary:

I went at once. He told me:

'About an hour ago everything went misty. There was no warning. I could just read, with difficulty. What does it mean, Charles? Am I going to have another stroke?'

I reassured him:

'You seem to get arterial spasms when you are very tired.'

He looked up sharply.

'You mustn't frighten me.'

In fact, I am more frightened than Winston. This is a grim start to the racket of a General Election.[1]

Churchill's Engagements Calendar records the pace and pattern of this 'racket', amid ill-health, work on the war memoirs, and the needs of the General Election:

January 24, Tuesday		Mr Buchan-Hepburn to Luncheon
		Lord Ismay, General Pownall to dine and sleep
		Mr Deakin to dine and sleep & Mr Kelly
January 25, Wednesday		To London
	1.15	To Luncheon: Lord Woolton, Mr Eden, Col Stanley, Mr Lyttelton, Mr Bracken and Mr Buchan-Hepburn
	3.30	Mr Gerald O'Brien
	5.30	Mr Moir
	10.45	Mr Sandys
January 26, Thursday	10.00	Mr Christ and Mr Maudling
	11.00	Mr Kelly
	3.15	Sir James Hawkey
	5.30	News Film, Pathé Studios, 103 Wardour Street
	8.00	Lady Lytton to dinner
January 27, Friday	10.00	Mr Christ
	1.00	Lord & Lady Salisbury to Luncheon
	3.15	Associated British Pathé Studios, 133 Oxford Street
January 28, Saturday	10.00	Mr Christ
	11.45	Mr Maudling
	7.00	Sir James Hawkey house
	7.30	Woodford County High School
		To Chartwell[2]

[1] Lord Moran diary, 24 January 1950: *The Struggle for Survival*, page 336.

[2] Churchill Engagements Calendar, January 1950. O'Brien, at Conservative Central Office, had the task of informing Churchill of Party opinion.

Churchill was fortunate at this time of illness and electioneering to have his two devoted speech writers, Reginald Maudling and George Christ. When, on January 26, Churchill gave a film interview for newsreel, his remarks had been drafted by Maudling; Churchill read them out as drafted.[1] In preparation that same day for a speech in his constituency, George Christ prepared a note. Churchill asked for it to be redone. 'I am sure you are right,' Christ noted. 'It is not on the level that will be expected of that speech.'[2]

Churchill spoke in his constituency, at the Woodford County School for Girls, on January 28. Appealing to 'our Liberal friends' in Woodford, who had not had a Liberal candidate for sixteen years, he said: 'I earnestly hope that they will set an example to Liberal voters throughout the country by voting according to their consciences and convictions, and according to the long established principles of their party and world Liberalism against the establishment of the Socialist State.'

Much of Churchill's speech was an attack on the nationalization policy of the Labour Government, and a warning of future nationalization to come: the steel industry, whose Act had already been passed but which 'we shall repeal', the cement, sugar and chemical industries, and life insurance.[3] Churchill told his constituents:

Having made a failure of everything they have so far touched, our Socialist planners now feel it necessary to get hold of a few at present prospering industries so as to improve the general picture and the general results. There appears to be no plan or principle in the selection of these industries, except caprice and appetite. It does not matter how well they are now managed, how well they are serving the public, how much they sustain our export trade, how good are the relations between employers and employed. The Socialists just like the look of them, and so they think they will have them. But here you have your vote and your responsibility.[4]

That day, January 28, Churchill was formally adopted as Conservative candidate for Woodford. On February 2 his son Randolph was adopted for Devonport. His son-in-law Duncan Sandys was likewise adopted for Streatham, and his son-in-law Christopher Soames for Bedford.

On February 4 Churchill went to Leeds, to speak at the Town Hall to five thousand people. Again, the main part of his speech was an attack on nationalization, and a declaration that if the Conservatives

[1] Note, 26 January 1950: Churchill papers, 2/99.
[2] Note, 26 January 1950: Churchill papers, 5/10.
[3] The Nationalization Bills which had already passed the House of Commons and come into law were for the Bank of England (29 October 1945), Coal (30 January 1946), Civil Aviation (6 May 1946), Transport (18 December 1946), Electricity (4 February 1947) and Gas (11 February 1948). The Iron and Steel Bill had passed its second reading on 17 November 1948.
[4] Speech of 28 January 1950: Randolph S. Churchill (editor), *In the Balance*, pages 161–9.

were returned to office, they would repeal the nationalization of steel before it came into effect and 'free all other industries from the cloud of oppression and uncertainty under which they lie at the present time by forbidding all further nationalization'. No single broad decision would do more 'to prevent unemployment, to improve our credit, and to lighten and simplify our problems both at home and abroad than the stopping of nationalization'.[1]

On February 8 Churchill was in Cardiff, where he addressed a mass meeting at the Ninian Park Football Ground, where he spoke, inevitably, of Lloyd George:

Mr Lloyd George was a democrat if ever there was one, but he recoiled, like all those who are ready to fight for freedom must recoil, from the fallacy and folly of Socialism. This is what he said about it almost a quarter of a century ago. His words are vivid: they are also prophetic:

'You cannot trust the battle of freedom to Socialism. Socialism has no interest in liberty. Socialism is the very negation of liberty. Socialism means the community in bonds. If you establish a Socialist community it means the most comprehensive universal and pervasive tyranny that this country has ever seen. It is like the sand of the desert. It gets into your food, your clothes, your machinery, the very air you breathe. They are all gritty with regulations, orders, decrees, rules. That is what Socialism means.'

These are the words of Lloyd George. See how they live and ring through the years. He might have said this yesterday. He knew what it would feel like long before it came upon us.[2]

From Cardiff, Churchill travelled to Devonport where, at the Forum Cinema, he spoke in support of his son. Randolph's opponent, Michael Foot, was apparently disconcerted by Churchill's visit. He had been counting on the positive impact of a visit by Aneurin Bevan but, Randolph explained to his father: 'Your visit on the same day will prick this cherished bubble.'[3]

Churchill began his speech at Devonport with two local references from the opening years of the war. Watching him as he spoke were not only Randolph, the candidate, but Randolph's son Winston.

I last visited Devonport when I was First Lord of the Admiralty to welcome home the *Exeter* after her glorious victory in the Battle of the Plate. Alas, the gallant *Exeter*, after all her victories, was to sink in action under the fire of overwhelming numbers of the Japanese fleet, but her name will live for ever, and the memory of those who died for their country and the cause of freedom will long be cherished in Britain and throughout the West Country.

---

[1] Speech of 4 February 1950: Randolph S. Churchill (editor), *In the Balance*, pages 170–80.
[2] Speech of 8 February 1950: Randolph S. Churchill (editor), *In the Balance*, pages 181–9.
[3] 'My dearest Papa', 5 February 1950: Churchill papers, 2/272.

The next time I came to you was on the morrow of one of your worst bombing raids; my wife was with me when we drove through your streets, and I was inspired to see the high morale which everyone in the city and in the dockyards maintained.

We went through a lot in those days together. Let us make sure we do not throw away, by the follies of peace, what we have gained in the agonies of war. Let us make sure that in the exhaustion which follows fighting for the freedom of others we do not cast away the freedom which has made us what we are.

Churchill then spoke about his son, 'a mature, formidable and experienced politician', who had 'done his part' in the war. 'I have a feeling,' said Churchill, 'he is going to come into his own.'[1]

On February 10 Churchill returned to his constituency, where he spoke first at Buckhurst Hill and then, for the second time in the campaign, in Woodford. On February 11 he spoke in Kent, and on February 14, nine days before Polling Day, in Edinburgh. Again he spoke of the perils of nationalization, and of the 'falsehood' of Labour's claim that a Conservative Government would create massive unemployment. Churchill also spoke of Attlee's reaction to a statement Churchill had made during the campaign, about the need to increase the petrol ration:

He described it as 'window dressing', and said I had not given a minute's thought to it. I give a great deal of thought to what I say and to what I do. My task at this election has not been the dressing of windows so much as the undressing of humbugs.

It is curious that, almost at the very moment when Mr Attlee was deriding the idea of an increase in the basic petrol ration at Liverpool, his own Minister of Fuel, Mr Gaitskell, at Harrogate was saying that the prospects of an increased petrol ration were 'not bad'. Talks, he said, were now going on in Washington to see if we could get extra petrol without spending dollars.

'This is important news,' Churchill commented, 'and I am very glad to have extorted it from the Government by the demand which I made for a review of the petrol ration.'

At Edinburgh Churchill also spoke about foreign affairs, and what he described as Bevin's 'many pitiful blunders'. Nevertheless, he added, Bevin had not failed to uphold the main principle 'upon which our life and safety depends, having followed with steadfastness the line I marked out at Fulton of fraternal association with the United States, and the closest unification of our military arrangements. In the Atlantic Pact we have a great instrument making for world peace. In the Brussels Treaty and the building of Western European Union he

[1] Speech of 9 February 1950: Randolph S. Churchill (editor), *In the Balance*, pages 190–6.

has, albeit somewhat sheepishly, given effect to the theme of United Europe.' As to the need for such a policy, Churchill wished to remind his Scottish listeners of how:

While we are all so busy with our internal party controversies we must not forget the gravity of our position or indeed that of the whole world. Soviet Russia—the immensely powerful band of men gathered together in the Kremlin—has ranged itself against the Western democracies. They have added to their dominion the satellite States of Europe; the Baltic States, Poland, Czechoslovakia, Hungary, Bulgaria, Rumania. Tito of Yugoslavia has broken away. Greece has been rescued by the United States, carrying on the task which we began. At the other side of the world the 500,000,000 of China have fallen into the Communist sphere. But Communism is novel and China is old. I do not regard China as having finally accepted Soviet servitude.

Still, when you look at the picture as a whole you see two worlds ranged against one another more profoundly and on a larger scale than history has ever seen before. The Soviet Communist world has by far the greatest military force, but the United States have the atom bomb; and now, we are told that they have a thousandfold more terrible manifestation of this awful power.

When all is said and done it is my belief that the superiority in the atom bomb, if not indeed almost the monopoly of this frightful weapon, in American hands is the surest guarantee of world peace tonight. But for that we should not be talking about all these burning domestic questions that fill our minds, our mouths and our newspapers today.

Churchill's speech continued:

It is my earnest hope that we may find our way to some more exalted and august foundation for our safety than this grim and sombre balancing power of the bomb. We must not, however, cast away our only shield of safety unless we can find something better and surer and more likely to last.

The phrase a 'more exalted and august foundation' was not mere rhetoric. Churchill now revealed his wish for a meeting with the Soviet leaders, coining the word 'summit' for such a meeting, the last one of which had been at Potsdam:

Still I cannot help coming back to this idea of another talk with Soviet Russia upon the highest level. The idea appeals to me of a supreme effort to bridge the gulf between the two worlds, so that each can live their life, if not in friendship at least without the hatreds of the cold war. You must be careful to mark my words in these matters because I have not always been proved wrong. It is not easy to see how things could be worsened by a parley at the summit, if such a thing were possible. But that I cannot tell.

Churchill ended with an appeal that, above the electoral clatter of party politics, no one should 'shut out the hope' that the burden of fear and want 'may be lifted for a glorious era from the bruised and weary shoulders of mankind'.[1] It was his son Randolph who had suggested to him that he should not be inhibited by electoral moods and styles from speaking of such grand themes.

Following Churchill's return from Edinburgh to London, and then to Chartwell, it was rumoured and widely repeated that he had died. He at once issued a statement to the Press: 'I am informed from many quarters,' it read, 'that a rumour has been put about that I died this morning. This is quite untrue. It is however a good sample of the whispering campaign which has been set on foot. It would have been more artistic to keep this one for Polling Day.'[2]

On February 17, within twenty-six hours of his rumoured demise, Churchill made his second Party Political broadcast. In taking 'another plunge in Socialism', he declared, 'we should be absolutely alone in the free and civilized world'; one of the 'chief reasons' which had turned the tide in Europe against Socialism, he said, was 'the utter failure of Socialist Governments to make any effective resistance to Communist aggression and permeation'.

By 'one heave of her shoulders', Churchill told his listeners, 'Britain can shake herself free'. But the opportunity should not be missed. It might not return. And he illustrated his feelings with a story:

I am reminded of the tale of the prisoner in the Spanish dungeon. For years he longed to escape from his bondage. He tried this, he tried that—all in vain. One day he pushed the door of his cell—it was open. It had always been open. He walked out free into the broad light of day. You can do that now on this very Thursday, and what a throng there will be to welcome us back in the forefront of the nations who now regard us with bewilderment and pity, but for whom only a few years ago we kept the flag of freedom flying amid all the winds that blew.[3]

'You gave a great wind up last night,' Lord Swinton wrote in congratulation, and he added: 'I find everywhere devout thankfulness that you have given a lead on Russia.'[4] 'Your intervention about Russia was more than justified,' Lord Cecil of Chelwood, a founder and stalwart of the idea of the League of Nations, wrote a few days later.[5]

Churchill made one more campaign journey, to Manchester on

---

[1] Speech of 14 February 1950: Randolph S. Churchill (editor), *In the Balance*, pages 197–207.
[2] Press notice, 16 February 1950: widely publicized in the newspapers on the following day.
[3] Speech of 17 February 1950: Randolph S. Churchill (editor), *In the Balance*, pages 208–14. Recording: BBC Written Archives Centre, Library No. LP 14447.
[4] 'My dear Winston', 18 February 1950: Churchill papers, 2/101.
[5] 'My dear Winston', 28 February 1950: Churchill papers, 2/95.

February 20, before returning to his constituency for the Election itself on February 23. He then returned to Hyde Park Gate to listen to the election results as they came in throughout the early hours of February 24. With him were several friends, including Lord Salisbury, who described the waiting as 'intensely interesting, if a little anxious, in view of the earlier return'.[1]

Those early returns were discouraging, although Churchill's own news, as that of Christopher Soames, was good. 'Mr Churchill elected in his constituency with eighteen thousand majority,' Miss Sturdee telegraphed to Sarah Churchill, who was in California, and she added: 'Captain Soames in by two thousand. At present Socialists lead by fifteen seats with about 100 results to come.'[2] In a second telegram, Miss Sturdee sent Sarah Churchill the rest of the family electoral news: 'Duncan in with eleven thousand majority. Randolph lost by three thousand.'[3]

'We *were* so sorry about Randolph,' wrote Lord Salisbury. 'He seems to have made a splendid fight, and it would have been grand if he could have thrown out that odious Foot.'[4]

By noon on February 24 it was clear that the Conservatives had failed to overturn the Labour ascendancy, but by only the narrowest of margins. The Labour seats had fallen in number from 393 to 315; the Conservatives had risen from 213 to 298. Labour's overall majority, discounting the Speaker, had dropped to six. The Liberals, as Churchill had anticipated, had fallen, but from twelve to nine, not down to six as he had predicted.

Clement Attlee remained Prime Minister. Churchill, though disappointed, was not dismayed. 'Our vigil the other night,' he wrote to Lord Salisbury, 'was a case of "the evening red, the morning blue".'[5] 'Whatever happens,' he wrote to Sir Alan Lascelles, 'I think that another General Election in the next few months is inevitable.'[6]

'He was disappointed,' Harold Macmillan told Randolph Churchill twelve years later, 'but he carried on.' Randolph Churchill commented: 'Remarkable pertinacity. Ninety-nine people out of a hun-

---

[1] 'My dear Winston', 25 February 1950: Churchill papers, 2/101.

[2] Telegram despatched 24 February 1950: Churchill papers, 1/47.

[3] Telegram dated 24 February 1950: Churchill papers, 1/47.

[4] 'My dear Winston', 25 February 1950: Churchill papers, 2/101. Randolph Churchill had been beaten by the Labour candidate, Michael Foot, who thus entered the House of Commons for the first time; thirty years later he was to become Leader of the Opposition, a position he held from 1980 to 1983. His vote was 30,812, Randolph's 27,329 and the Liberal vote 2,766 (a combined vote against Foot of 30,095). It was Randolph Churchill's fourth failure to be elected to Parliament (in 1940 he had been returned unopposed, according to wartime procedures).

[5] 'My dear Bobbety', 28 February 1950: Churchill papers, 2/101.

[6] 'My dear Tommy', 27 February 1950: Churchill papers, 2/171.

dred would have cleared out, but not he.' 'A lot of people wanted him to clear out' was Macmillan's reply.[1]

Among the Conservative candidates who had been defeated, like Randolph, by only a narrow margin, was Anthony Barber, who, as a pilot in the Royal Air Force, had been captured by the Germans, had taken part in several escape attempts, and, still in captivity, had taken a law degree through the International Red Cross while in prison camp, with first-class honours. He had been beaten, at Doncaster, by a mere 878 votes. In reply to Churchill's telegram to all defeated Conservative candidates, Barber wrote: 'At the next election, which it seems must come before very long, I have not the slightest doubt that we can win here in Doncaster,' and he added:

To most of the young candidates like myself, it was a great inspiration to have a man of your personality and experience at the helm and I hope that you will not consider it either impertinent or commonplace when I say that your leadership since the end of the war has been one of the most vital factors which has brought our Party back to its present position.[2]

Among the successful Conservative candidates was John Profumo, who had been defeated in 1945. 'I hasten to send you my thanks,' he wrote to Churchill in reply to a telegram of congratulations, 'and to take the opportunity of telling you how happy I am to be back in the House once more. I assure you of my loyal support at all times and I look forward to contributing in any possible way towards those duties, which, under your inspiring leadership, must be carried out by our party in these months which lie ahead.'[3]

Many Conservatives were anxious to know what Churchill thought the immediate future would be, and how long a Labour Government could survive with so slender a majority as six. To one such questioner, Lord Salisbury, Churchill drafted a reply which, as so often, he decided not to send:

I think myself that the present Government will probably continue till June, or it may be October, and will pounce at the moment they think best. It may well be however that later in the Session they will be defeated on some important issue in the Commons, because we must carry on the effective opposition and there will certainly be many Divisions. The future therefore is as usual veiled in obscurity. What a bore life would be if it were not. I am personally convinced that we should gain greatly from forming a Govern-

---

[1] Randolph Churchill in conversation with Harold Macmillan, 17 May 1962: Randolph Churchill papers.

[2] 'Dear Mr Churchill', 28 February 1950: Churchill papers, 2/97. Barber was duly elected at Doncaster in the 1951 Election. From 1970 to 1974 he was Chancellor of the Exchequer. He was created a Life Peer in 1974.

[3] 'Dear Mr Churchill', 4 March 1950: Churchill papers, 2/97.

ment, possibly on a wider basis than is now open, and then appealing to the people. I hope you will bear these possibilities in your mind, and I must repeat my quotation of Abe Lincoln: 'Never cross the Fox river till you get to it.'[1]

'One more heave before the year is out,' Churchill wrote somewhat more confidently to Lord Kemsley, in thanking him for the 'invaluable support' his newspapers had given during the Election, 'and we may have a stable Government in Britain'.[2]

Churchill was determined to finish the remaining two volumes of his war memoirs before that 'stable Government' came to pass. Often working late into the night, he dictated his narrative to a new secretary, Miss Portal, straight on to her typewriter. One night, as work progressed, he looked at her and exclaimed: 'I know I am going to be Prime Minister again. I know it.'[3]

---

[1] Letter of March 1950, marked by Churchill, 'Put by': Churchill papers, 2/107.

[2] 'My dear Kemsley', 2 March 1950: Churchill papers, 2/171. Lord Kemsley (the brother of Lord Camrose) was the owner and editor-in-chief of the *Sunday Times* from 1937 to 1959, and owner of the *Daily Dispatch*, the *Daily Sketch* (later renamed the *Daily Graphic*), the *Sunday Chronicle* and the *Empire News*. He also owned the Glasgow *Daily Record*.

[3] Lady Williams of Elvel recollections, in conversation with Piers Dixon, 17 March 1987: Piers Dixon papers. Miss Portal, who had joined Churchill's secretarial team in December 1949, was the niece of both R. A. Butler and Marshal of the Royal Air Force Viscount Portal of Hungerford.

29

'No extinct volcano he'

THE new Parliament opened on 6 March 1950; in his speech on the following day, Churchill spoke of how 'refreshing it was to feel', with an overall Labour majority of only six, 'that this is a Parliament where half the nation will not be able to ride rough-shod over the other half, or to sweep away in a Session what has been carefully and skilfully constructed by generations of thought, toil and thrift. I do not see the Attorney-General in his place, but no one will be able to boast "We are the masters now".'[1]

During his speech, Churchill suggested the need for a debate on the position of the pound and the effect on confidence and credit of the Government's 'bitter hostility to accumulated wealth', even when this hostility was 'held in check in this Parliament by lack of voting strength'. The following altercation then occurred:

> It would be vain to touch in the Debate upon the vast sphere of finance and economics. I ask that an opportunity for a full Debate upon it may be accorded to us in the next fortnight or so.
> Mr H. Morrison indicated dissent.
> Mr Churchill: It will take more than the oscillation of the Lord President's head in this Parliament necessarily to convince us that our desires must be put aside. . . .

Churchill then spoke of the intractability of the political situation as it had developed in the previous five years and as it now reached a virtual Parliamentary stalemate:

> The two sides of the House face each other deeply divided by ideological differences. I have lived through many of the fierce quarrels of the past, about Irish Home Rule, about church or chapel, about free trade and protec-

---

[1] The Attorney-General was Sir Hartley Shawcross. Speaking in the House of Commons during the third reading of the Trade Disputes and Trade Union Bill he had said: 'We are the masters at the moment—and not only for the moment, but for a very long time to come.' (*Hansard*, 2 April 1946.)

tion, which all seemed to be very important at the time. They were, however, none of them, fundamental to our whole system of life and society.

Those who believe in the creation of a Socialist State controlling all the means of production, distribution and exchange, and are working towards such a goal, are separated from those who seek to exalt the individual and allow freedom of enterprise under well-known laws and safeguards—they are separated by a wider and deeper gulf than I have ever seen before in our island.

'We shall certainly not survive,' Churchill warned, 'by splitting into two nations. Yet that is the road we are travelling now, and there is no sign of our reaching or even approaching our journey's end.' [1]

Unknown to Churchill, at the Cabinet on March 9 Clement Attlee told his colleagues that in the event of a Government defeat in the Debate on the Address, 'he was inclined to think that his proper course would be to advise the King to send for Mr Churchill'. In the discussion that followed, however, 'emphasis was laid', the Cabinet minutes reported, 'upon the embarrassments which the Labour Party would face if they went into Opposition in the present Parliament'. [2]

On March 16 Churchill made a further substantial speech during the Defence Debate. He wished first, he said, to touch on the 'disagreeable topic' of recent Ministerial appointments in the military sphere. [3] He then quoted a statement he had made in the House of Commons in December 1948, 'that the Army would be better entrusted to men who are not engaged in the most bitter strife of politics. Nor should the War Office be regarded as a receptacle for Ministerial failures.' The following altercation then occurred:

Mr Shinwell: Would the right hon. Gentleman prefer to appoint his son-in-law to a post?

Mr Churchill: I was not aware that he had been appointed to a high military post.

The Parliamentary Secretary to the Admiralty [Mr James Callaghan]: Anyway, the right hon. Gentleman is the biggest party politician there is.

Mr Churchill: I am merely reading what I said a year and a quarter ago. No doubt it has stung the right hon. Gentleman, but it is really not so much an attack upon him as a criticism of the method of these appointments.

Churchill spoke next about rumours which had been put about, widely, during the General Election, that if the Conservatives were returned to power, men doing National Service 'would all have their

[1] Speech of 7 March 1950: *Hansard*.

[2] Cabinet Meeting No. 9 of 1950, 'Top Secret', 'No Circulation Record', 9.30 a.m., 9 March 1950: Cabinet papers, 128/21.

[3] Emanuel Shinwell had been appointed Minister of Defence (in succession to A. V. Alexander), and John Strachey had succeeded Shinwell at the War Office.

service increased'. This rumour, he said, had been put about 'at Malta and everywhere'. This remark led to a series of Government protests, led by Attlee himself:

The Prime Minister: The right hon. Gentleman is constantly talking about whispering campaigns. There was the ridiculous one which he suggested had been put about that he was dead. No one has heard of these whispering campaigns except the right hon. Gentleman.

[Hon. Members: 'Oh.']

Perhaps the hon. Members on the second Opposition bench will allow me to address their Leader. Unless the right hon. Gentleman can give us some evidence of where these whispering campaigns came from, he should not make charges of this kind. No one here has heard of any of these reports. I am unaware that anyone out in Malta has. It is extraordinary to have these constant suggestions by the right hon. Gentleman about these whispering campaigns being put about.

Mr Churchill: I certainly do not withdraw what I have said. Hundreds of messages and letters were received. Of course, I have not suggested that the Prime Minister himself went about whispering, but that and other statements—

Mr Paget (Northampton): On a point of Order. The right hon. Gentleman has referred to certain documents. Ought not those documents to be available to the House?

Mr Churchill: The hon. and learned Gentleman should learn a little more about our Rules of Order before he raises points of Order. All I can say is that I was very glad to be in a position myself to deny the rumour that I was dead, and I only regret it was not as easy to get upon the track of and kill a great many other falsehoods to which we were subjected. Personally I think it was very shabby for hon. Members and others, if they were engaged in the campaign at all—

[Hon. Members: 'If']—

considering the help that we have given them in supporting National Service, to have taken every advantage that they could as occasion offered.

Hon. Members do not disturb me at all by their indignation. I am only sorry that the topics I have to deal with this afternoon are of a laborious and technical character and do not enable me to stimulate them more vigorously than I shall be able.

Churchill then spoke about the discrepancy between the number of men in uniform and the 'pitiful shortage' of the means to send even small reinforcements abroad at short notice. When his criticisms were met by laughter from the Government benches he replied: 'It is not a thing to laugh at; it is a thing to puzzle at, and to try to find a way to do it. We shall not get through our difficulties by this attempt at geniality when under examination.'

It was a time, Churchill argued, 'to concentrate upon essentials', and he went on to speak about the need to match the Soviet U-boat force, at least by submarines of equal speed and capacity, and by methods, vessels and aircraft which could find them and then destroy them. 'An intense effort should be made,' he said, 'to improve the methods of detecting submerged U-boats from the air', and he added by way of encouragement and exhortation: 'I have seldom seen a precise demand made upon science by the military which has not been met.'

Finally, Churchill spoke of the Air Force, and of the 'enormous numerical strength' of the Soviet air force, telling the House of Commons, in words reminiscent of his warnings and thoughts fifteen years earlier:

If we wish to have that strength which will deter war, or if the worst comes to the worst, enable us to win through, we require far larger numbers of the highest class aircraft than we now possess. Every sacrifice should be made in other branches of defence to make sure that that is not neglected. The highest priority should be accorded to it.

Fortunately and providentially there is the American Air Force, far stronger than ours and of equal quality. We have allowed them to establish in East Anglia a base for their bombing aircraft, the significance of which cannot be lost on the Soviets.

We on this side supported His Majesty's Government in the steps they have taken. If any other party had taken such steps I do not know whether the Socialists in Opposition would have sustained them. Certainly they have not been put to that test. It was certainly a step which in any other period but this strange time in which we live might have led to war.

What has distressed and disquieted me is that those who took it should appear not to be fully conscious of its importance. Our defensive forces in fighter aircraft should be raised and our radar precautions should be raised by our utmost exertions to the highest possible level.

Churchill's speech continued:

We have the jet fighter. This is the product of British genius. There is nothing to surpass it in the world and it is continually improving. I was glad to read in the White Paper, page 5, paragraph 15, the plan for doubling the jet fighter strength of Fighter Command would be completed. I hope that means really 'doubling' and not merely filling up existing squadrons and bringing them up to strength. I was glad to read it for what it was worth. But I cannot understand why a British Government which has established an American base in East Anglia should have allowed anything to diminish the supply of jet fighter aircraft upon which our deterrent against war and our survival should it come might alike depend.

Here again I base myself only upon what has been made public in the newspapers and is common property. The right hon. Gentleman made a reference to jet fighters. British jet fighters have hitherto been for many good but insufficient reasons—and a good reason if insufficient in a matter like this is a bad reason—dispersed and distributed in various quarters. I am content to deal only with those which have been sold to the Argentine, or written-off against what are called 'sterling balances' to Egypt. I do not know how many have been sent or given—for that is what it comes to—to Egypt; but it is already public knowledge that 100 jet fighter aircraft have been sold to the Argentine for little more than £2,000,000.

There is a sense of disproportion about an act like this which passes the frontiers of reason. The Air Force lays before us Estimates for £223,000,000, and yet to gain perhaps little more than £2,000,000 of foreign exchange—which the Liverpool Cotton Exchange could have earned for us in a year; a trifle compared to the vast scale of our expenditure—100 of these vital instruments have been sent away.

Churchill went on to tell the House of Commons that even upon the basis of the facts 'known to the public' he was prepared 'to argue this matter in a little further detail', and he continued:

A wise use of our jet aircraft would have enabled the whole of our Auxiliary Air Force squadrons to be at this moment effectively re-armed. I do not think that those who conduct the Government of the country, although animated I am sure by a sincere purpose, have comprehended this aspect of their problem.

As far as I could understand him this afternoon, the Minister of Defence gave a most extraordinary reason. He said that the Air Force could not afford to buy them; and when I asked why they could not afford to, it was because apparently they had overrun the Estimate agreed with the Chancellor of the Exchequer. But all this is in the same sphere of ministerial responsibility, and money should be saved elsewhere rather than that a vital need of this kind should be denied to the Air Force.

Remembering the reasons which had been given in the years leading up to the war for not proceeding more rapidly with air rearmament, and having so recently set out those reasons and his answers to them in the first volume of his war memoirs, Churchill told the House of Commons:

We shall hear all sorts of excuses about the time it takes to lengthen runways on the airfields, the collection of skilled mechanics, the importance of building up, as the right hon. Gentleman told us, a future clientele of customers abroad, and the like. We have only to think of the total cost of the Air Estimates of £223,000,000 to see what such arguments are worth. We have only to think of the time that has passed since we allowed the Americans to establish their bombing base in East Anglia to see how vain are these excuses for not having taken all the concomitant measures at the same time. If we had strictly safeguarded our jet fighter aircraft of the waste of which I have given only one example—and that because it is public—the whole of our Auxiliary Air Force could have been re-armed by now, and even further aircraft might have been made.

Churchill ended his speech with words of warning and a call for negotiations with the Soviet Union on the basis of strength; a strength now challenged by the recent conviction of Dr Klaus Fuchs for having passed on the secrets of the atomic bomb to Russia.[1] Churchill told his fellow Members of Parliament:

Do not, I beg the House, nurse foolish delusions that we have any other effective overall shield at the present time from mortal danger than the atomic bomb in the possession, thank God, of the United States. But for that there would be no hope that Europe could preserve its freedom, or that our island could escape an ordeal incomparably more severe than those we have already endured. Our whole position in this atomic sphere has been worsened since the war by the fact that the Russians, unexpectedly as the Minister admitted, have acquired the secrets of the atomic bomb, and are said to have begun its manufacture.

Let us therefore labour for peace, not only by gathering our defensive strength, but also by making sure that no door is closed upon any hope of reaching a settlement which will end this tragic period when two worlds face one another in increasing strain and anxiety.[2]

'Winston spoke in the Defence Debate for over an hour,' Henry Channon wrote in his diary, 'and seemed in the highest spirits. No extinct volcano he.'[3]

On March 28 Churchill spoke again in the House of Commons, during the debate on Foreign Affairs. His principal theme was the need for West Germany to take a part in Western defence. There could be 'no hope' for a United Europe without Germany, and there was 'no hope' for Germany except within a free and United Europe. Britain, France and Germany should, by combining together, make 'the core or the nucleus upon which all the other civilized democracies of Europe, bound or free, can one day rally and combine'. Churchill continued:

Woe be it to anyone in the free world, who, by lack of understanding, or by lack of goodwill, or by lack of world hope, or any more flagrant fault or blunder, obstructs or delays this essential combination. There was a time when men thought that the conception of a United States of Europe would be resented by the United States of America, but now we have the American

[1] On 3 February 1950 Dr Klaus Fuchs had been arrested in Britain for betraying atomic bomb secrets to the Soviet Union; he was sentenced on 1 March 1950 to fourteen years' imprisonment. Fuch's arrest was followed by a nine-year American ban on the flow of atomic secrets to Britain. Released in 1959, Fuchs went to East Germany, where he became a Member of the Central Committee of the East German Communist Party. He died on 28 January 1988.

[2] Speech of 16 March 1950: *Hansard*. Churchill was particularly worried at this time that American bomber bases in Britain carrying atom bombs would be the first target of a Russian attack. 'If I were a Russian Commissar,' he told Denis Kelly one evening at dinner, 'I would vote against war. If I was over-ruled, I would say: "The first place we must destroy is the British Isles."' (Denis Kelly recollections: letter to the author, 4 December 1987.)

[3] Channon diary, 16 March 1950: Robert Rhodes James (editor), *Chips*, page 442.

people, with their own heavy burdens to bear, sacrificing themselves and using all their power and authority to bring about this very system. In this lies the hope of the Western world and its power to promote beneficial solutions, perhaps, of what happens in Asia.

'I do not wish,' Churchill told the House, 'to fall into vague generalities. Let me, therefore, express our policy as I see it in a single sentence. Britain and France united should stretch forth hands of friendship to Germany, and thus, if successful, enable Europe to live again.'

Turning to relations with the Soviet Union, and the impact on East–West relations of the atomic bomb, Churchill reiterated his appeal for 'a further effort for a lasting and peaceful settlement' between the Soviet Union and its Western adversaries. As he explained:

There is no doubt now that the passage of time will place these fearful agencies of destruction effectively in Soviet hands, that is to say, where there is no customary, traditional, moral or religious restraint.

Of course, there is an interlude between the discovery of the secret and the effective large-scale production of the article, and that also has to be borne in mind. Of course, the United States have their 'stockpile', as it is called, and it will be only by a gradual process than anything similar can be built up in Soviet Russia.

The atomic bomb, though preponderating, is only one of the factors in the military situation before us, but is the dominant factor. If, for instance, the United States had a 'stockpile' of 1,000 atomic bombs—I take the figure as an illustration merely; I have no knowledge of any sort or kind of what they have—and Russia had 50, and we got those 50, fearful experiences, far beyond anything we have ever endured, would be our lot.

Therefore, while I believe there is time for a further effort for a lasting and peaceful settlement, I cannot feel that it is necessarily a long time or that its passage will progressively improve our own security. Above all things, we must not fritter it away.

Churchill ended his speech by pointing out that man had now conquered 'the wild beasts' and even 'the insects and the microbes'. He had emerged 'in greater supremacy over the forces of nature than he had ever dreamed of before'. He had it in his power to solve 'quite easily' the problem of material existence. There lay before him 'as he wishes', a golden age of peace and prosperity. He had only to conquer 'his last and worst enemy—himself'. With 'vision, faith and courage', Churchill declared, 'it may still be within our power to win a crowning victory for all'.[1]

*   *   *

[1] Speech of 28 March 1950: *Hansard*.

On April 6 Churchill was at Salisbury, where his horse Colonist II finished fourth in the Salisbury Spring Handicap.[1] That night Churchill returned to Chartwell, to continue work on his memoirs, Bill Deakin arriving on April 7 for five days, to be joined on April 11 by General Pownall and Commodore Allen. On April 12 Denis Kelly took over the task of late night working.[2] Four days later, while still at Chartwell, Churchill received the first bound copies of Volume 3 of his war memoirs, subtitled 'The Grand Alliance', and planned for publication in the United States eight days later. 'My dear Harry,' he wrote in his own hand to President Truman from Chartwell on April 16. 'Only our friendship entitles me to send you one of the earliest copies of my new Volume III on the War, & to warn you that you may have to face in future years IV, V & even possibly six. Forgive me.'[3]

Also on April 16, Churchill sent a copy of the new book to Bernard Baruch. 'Herewith another Volume is inflicted on yr good nature,' he wrote, and he added: 'There are more to come in future years, if the world goes on—for me, or for itself. It well may.'[4]

Financially, the book was the most profitable so far; the *Daily Telegraph* paying him £109,000, the equivalent of more than a million pounds in the values of today.[5]

Sixteen months earlier, Clementine Churchill had taken on the strenuous responsibilities and considerable travelling of Chairman of the National Hostel Committee of the YWCA. That April she was forced to take two weeks off to recuperate from her exertions. Her husband, as was his habit, tried to keep her in touch with the events at Hyde Park Gate and Chartwell, writing to her on April 18, as from her Pig:

I am so sorry that you have had disappointing weather. I do hope you have enjoyed the change of scene & the relief of household cares, & that you will come back refreshed. I have passed a peaceful ten days at the Chart, & plunged deeply into my task of finishing Vol. IV. One page leads to another & three new chapters have come to life. I never had a chance to squeeze a tube to any purpose.

Mary & Christopher were a blessing and often came to meals. The days flashed away & now here I am back in 28, w the budget opening upon us, the crisis prowling around the corner, and the Primrose League & Reading Dinner hanging like vultures overhead.

I have thought much about you my sweet darling, and it will be a joy to

---

[1] A photograph of Churchill and Christopher Soames in the paddock, watching Colonist II being prepared for the race, was published in *Sport and Country* on 19 April 1950.

[2] Churchill Engagements Calendar, April 1950: Churchill papers.

[3] Letter of 16 April 1950: Harry S. Truman papers.

[4] 'My dear Bernie', 16 April 1950: Churchill papers, 4/55.

[5] Letter from Anthony Moir of Fladgate & Co. to Miss Sturdee, 5 June 1950: Churchill papers, 4/57. The equivalent of £109,000 in purchasing power for 1987 was £1,180,000.

have you back. Your flowers are growing beautifully on the Chartwell balcony & here the cherry tree is a mass of blossom. All yr arrangements have worked perfectly in yr absence, and no one cd have been more comfortable than yr P.

    With tender love

    Your ever loving husband

W [1]

Enclosed with Churchill's letter was what he had long called, since first writing one for her in 1925, his Chartwell Bulletins, to give her more news. These Bulletins, unlike his letters to her, were dictated:

Before he went to Cannes, Anthony Eden said that the hawthorn had come out early and that this was a sure sign of cold weather. This was the only thing he knew about the weather. Certainly it has turned out true. We have had sunshine and showers but the temperature is very low.

The waterfalls and filters are all running in good order. As coke is off the ration it would be possible to heat the swimming pool this year, but this would mean erecting the chimney again, or at least half of it—eight feet. As the old tree has been cut down there is no cover for it, and I am sure it would offend everyone's eye. Moreover I myself cannot bathe, so I have not done anything about it. Although the pool has not been cleaned out the water is very clear.

All the fish, big and small, and the ten black swans are well and send their compliments. The father swan has fallen in love with one of his daughters, and I think they mean to make a nest on the island. We are watching this most carefully. The other three (outside the Iron Curtain) are friendly with each other, and Papa only comes to be fed. Four of the ten now eat readily from the hand and also pinch my fingers.

On Saturday week I went round the farms with Christopher. I was very much impressed by the improvements made and the tidiness. The overhanging branches have been cut almost everywhere and a large part of the Bardogs and Chartwell Farms have been ditched and hedged. A good plan of cultivation is on foot, approved by Mr Cox [2] who is most helpful. Bardogs, especially the farthest part of it, is immensely improved. The lane one turns down to the right after leaving Bardogs has been completely stripped of its overhanging branches and trees and is now quite open country—a great improvement. There is still a good deal more to be done.

Even greater improvement is taking place in the quality of the two milking herds. At Bardogs there are forty-five calves from a month to eighteen months old. All are pedigree and will be worth far more than their predecessors. There are twelve jerseys in milk, looking very well and pretty. Altogether it is a very fine show up there and works much better now there is a man in charge. Doris [3] and her husband are looking forward to moving into their

---

[1] 'My darling one', 18 April 1950: Spencer-Churchill papers.

[2] Cox was the Agent for Churchill's farms.

[3] Doris Edelson, the daughter of Hill the gardener at Chartwell; she had married the under-gardener.

new cottage. This will be better for all. The shorthorn herd is also steadily improving, and practically all the rubbish has been got rid of. I am considering getting rid of the belties, but have not yet heard from Mr   ?[1] to whom Christopher has written about them. I am sorry to let them go as they are most ornamental and characteristic. But there is no doubt that six or seven milch cows of good quality would save three or four hundred pounds a year of loss.

The little grey pony which is with them comes now when called, at a gallop, three or four hundred yards, to eat a piece of bread—a new feature in my daily peregrinations.

The two filly foals are growing well and strong and will have to be broken in very soon. The brood mare Poetic went to Lord Derby's to have her foal, which is a colt with three white anklets and a white star, said to be very good looking. He is by King Legend and might well be a valuable animal. Poetic will be married this week to Lord Derby's Borealis, and it is thought that this progeny will also be valuable. I may buy another brood mare with a colt foal in order to keep company with the new foal by Poetic.

April 29 will be a big day for us. Colonist II runs in the 'Winston Churchill' Stakes at Hurst Park, and the same day Cyberine, his sister, runs for the first time there too.[2] I hope you will come with me to see these two horses running. So far all this shows a quite substantial profit, and the whole outfit could be sold for two or three times or more what we gave for it. In addition there are twelve hundred pounds of winnings with Wetherby's. Of course I do not expect Colonist II to win the 'Winston Churchill' Stakes. He will meet the best horses in the world there.

Sir Gerald Kelly and the RA Committee picked out of the seven sent to them to choose from, the following four which you may remember: your Carezza sketch (No. 1); the snow scene out of the studio window; a very old one of the Calanque at Cassis, and, to my surprise, Mont Ste Victoire, which was one of our Christmas cards. I think it was better to send in four and not six. The Academy opens on the 27th and I have to speak at the dinner. The pairing difficulty has been arranged.

I have completely turned off politics these last ten days in a struggle to deliver Volume IV in good condition on May 1. This will certainly be achieved. Indeed I am almost at the end of it now. Another two or three mornings and it can go. It is a great relief. If there is no General Election till October I shall hope to have Volume V far enough advanced to earn the fifth instalment. But no one can tell what will happen. Cripps opens his Budget tomorrow and we may get some indication from it about Government tactics.

---

[1] Churchill left a blank and inserted a question mark at this point. 'Belties', or belted cattle, are black cattle of Dutch origin, with a broad band of white round the middle.

[2] Five days earlier, Christopher Soames had written, about Colonist II, to Churchill: 'This will be a very difficult race to win, as he will be competing with the best horses in the world, but bearing in mind the good which the race at Salisbury will have done him, and the fact that he has another fortnight to improve, I am quite sure that he will not be disgraced. He is in my opinion quite good enough to run in such a race, though I do not think it will be a race to bet on him.' ('Mr Churchill', 13 April 1950: Soames papers.)

Various visitors came to lunch or dinner: Lord Woolton, with whom I had a very good talk; Camrose, with whom much was settled, and Randolph, June and little Winston stayed the night. Pamela L came for the weekend which was very agreeable and peaceful. Mary did the honours. Pamela brought with her her little white pekinese, called Puff, who was very sweet and made tremendous friends with Rufus, although both are boys.

I am now on my way to the Duchess of Kent's luncheon and am going up to London thereafter as it is only forty minutes. I shall be alone working with Mr Kelly at the book tonight.

All this week is the Parl and I shall be back at Chartwell Thursday night late.

After talking things over with Christopher I have abandoned the idea of making any further inquiries about that nearby property, and no expense has been incurred. It would be better to buy land which is already let, without reference to how near it is to Chartwell. We shall know more about what to do after the Budget tomorrow. It is quite possible Cripps will have something spiteful in it in order to placate his followers.

I send you a cutting from the *Manchester Guardian* which I thought very interesting about Germany. It is incredible what follies Bevin has committed. No one but he could have managed to quarrel at the same time with Germans *and* French, with Russians *and* Americans, with Arabs *and* Jews. I do not think the poor old creature can last long in office, whatever happens.

Lords Reading and Rennell, having joined the Conservatives was a heavy blow to Violet, who was counting on them in her fight with the Party Committee.[1] On the whole I think the foreign situation is darkening somewhat, and it is thought that this year will see Soviet intensification at least of the 'cold war'. There is nothing we can do about it.

With all my love

W[2]

Two weeks later, after Clementine Churchill's return, there was another gilded luncheon, this time at the Spanish Embassy, at which Churchill and his wife were the guests of honour. Among those present was Henry Channon, who noted in his diary:

A grand luncheon party at the Spanish Embassy, for Winston and Mrs Churchill, both very smiling.

[1] The 2nd Baron Rennell (born 1895) and the 2nd Marquess of Reading (born 1899). Both were the sons of leading Liberal peers. The 1st Baron Rennell had been a Liberal MP from 1928 to 1932. The 1st Marquess of Reading had been a Liberal Cabinet Minister (and from 1921 to 1926 Viceroy of India).

[2] 'Chartwell Bulletin', 18 April 1950: Churchill papers, 1/47. In a handwritten postscript, Churchill told his wife that the Duchess of Kent's luncheon 'went off all right', and he added: 'The Spanish chargé d'affaires, the Wernhers, Sybil Ch, the departing Dutchman, & the Princess Olga. Our hostess was looking beautiful. She paints and gets fun out of it. Otherwise it looks like life in dignified twilight. There were lots of children.' Churchill had known Sybil Cholmondeley for many years; her brother Sir Philip Sassoon, who died in 1939, had been Under-Secretary for Air when Churchill was Secretary of State (1919–21). Princess Olga was the wife of Prince Regent Paul of Yugoslavia (and the sister of Princess Marina, Duchess of Kent).

He came up to me and joked about my party and said 'I am creditably informed that owing to the abundance of your viands and the excellence of your wines, that you almost failed to support me in the Division lobby last night.' He was in the very highest of spirits, and joked with everyone and announced that he, too, had almost been late. 'I was told to be there at 10—a merciful providence got me there at 10 to the hour.'

As we walked towards the dining-room George of Denmark hung politely back and Winston, in a rollicking mood, tried to push him in front of him—to make him pass before him. 'I wouldn't dream of it' George said. 'Don't dream of it: just do it' Winston retorted, and went on prodding.

It was one of Winston's hilarious days (he has silent, truculent ones too) and he had obviously relished last night's frolic in the House. As he left he came up to the Duchess of Kent and apologised for leaving, adding 'The Prime Minister wants to see me: I suppose he will suggest a coalition!!' There was scorn in his voice as he stressed the words 'Prime Minister'.[1]

On April 24 Churchill made his speech on the Budget. It was yet another sustained and detailed criticism of Government policy, quite up to the standard of his two previous speeches on Defence and Foreign Affairs, and covering every aspect of the Budget. 'I always try,' he said, in commenting on the increase in bus and taxi fares, 'especially in a new House of Commons, to study the opinions of those to whom I am opposed, their expressions and moods, so far as I can. I confess I am surprised that hon. Members opposite who hold Socialist conceptions—there are, I believe, some of them—were not shocked at this rise in the bus and taxi fares. Is this not a case of rationing by the purse? Ought they not to ask themselves, on their theories, whether this is not allowing mere money to decide who can ride in a bus or taxi and who has to walk?'

At one point in his speech Churchill referred to a personal episode of 1946:

Four years ago I travelled back from America with Lord Keynes, who had been on a Government mission and was working at the Treasury. I asked him why the then Chancellor of the Exchequer, when reducing the income tax by a shilling, should have made sure that the surtax on these largest incomes was retained at the confiscatory rate of 19s. 6d. in the £. I shall never forget the look of contempt which came over his expressive features, on which already lay the shadow of approaching death, when he replied in a single word 'Hate'.

[1] Channon diaries, 2 May 1950: Robert Rhodes James (editor), *Chips*, pages 443–4. At ten o'clock on the night of 1 May 1950, when the House of Commons divided on the question of the salaries and expenses of the Ministry of Transport, the voting was 278 for the Government and 278 against. The Speaker, 'in accordance with practice', cast his vote with the Government.

Hate is not a good guide in public or in private life. I am sure that class hatred and class warfare, like national revenge, are the most costly luxuries in which anyone can indulge. The present Chancellor has boasted of the number of persons who have net incomes of £5,000 or over a year. He has boasted that it has been reduced from 11,000 before the war to 250 at the present time, and that the number of those over £6,000 has been reduced from 7,000 to 70. These are great achievements. However necessary this extreme taxation was in the war—I was responsible, as Prime Minister, for its imposition—it certainly is not a process which increases the long-term revenue of the nation or its savings.

By way of illustration of his point, Churchill turned to his experiences at Chartwell Farm, giving the House what he called a single illustration which had occurred to him 'the other day, when I was looking at a cow':

Late in life I have begun to keep a herd of cows, and I find that quite a different principle prevails in dealing with cows to that which is so applauded below the Gangway opposite in dealing with rich men. It is a great advantage in a dairy to have cows with large udders because one gets more milk out of them than from the others. These exceptionally fertile milch cows are greatly valued in any well-conducted dairy, and anyone would be thought very foolish who boasted he had got rid of all the best milkers, just as he would be thought very foolish if he did not milk them to the utmost limit of capacity, compatible with the maintenance of their numbers.

I am quite sure that the Minister of Agriculture would look in a very different way upon the reduction of all these thousands of his best milkers from that in which the Chancellor of the Exchequer looks upon the destruction of the most fertile and the most profitable resources of taxation.[1]

'You must have been delighted,' Harold Macmillan wrote to Churchill on April 25, 'with the reception of the speech yesterday and still more pleased with the tremendous press today. It was a privilege to have been present on Sunday during part of its composition.'[2]

At Question Time on April 27 Churchill was again in the House of Commons, to ask the Minister of State at the Foreign Office, Kenneth Younger, whether he did not realize that the President of Israel, Dr Weizmann, and the King of Jordan, King Abdullah, had both been staunch friends to Britain over 'the vicissitudes of 20 or 30 years', and would the Minister not be willing to 'avail himself to the full possibilities of bringing these two eminent men into the closest harmonious contact?' Churchill also asked the Government to reconsider the decision to sell 110 jet aircraft to Egypt, and suggested that the Government might 'discuss with the Egyptian Government the stoppage of

[1] Speech of 24 April 1950: *Hansard*. Tom Williams was Minister of Agriculture (1945–51).
[2] 'Dear Winston', 25 April 1950: Churchill papers, 2/76.

tankers passing through the Canal, which are deeply needed to get the Haifa refinery into working order?'

Younger was noncommittal. Churchill's points were 'under consideration', he said.[1] Ten days later, Dr Weizmann wrote to Churchill from Israel: 'Your kind words about my own long standing association with Britain touched me deeply.' Weizmann added: 'I feel I ought to tell you how impressed I was by your understanding of an aspect of the situation borne out by your reference to arms supplied to Egypt. There is no doubt that the man in the street, as well as the Government here, are anxious and apprehensive. The accumulation of arms in one country only breeds counterpreparations and tends to plunge the nations of this area into a costly armaments race which they can ill afford and only deflects their limited resources from real constructive work.'[2]

There was delight on April 29 when Colonist II won the Winston Churchill Stakes at Hurst Park, and more delight on May 18 when he won the Paradise Stakes; a 'red-letter day', Churchill told a Scottish Unionist meeting in Edinburgh, both for the racecourse victory and because he was again addressing a 'great audience' at the Usher Hall.[3] His themes were the extra taxation imposed in the Budget, the cutback in the Government's house-building programme, the 'utter failure' of nationalization, and the Conservative concept of the relationship between State and citizen. 'We proclaim that the State is the servant and not the master of the people,' he said. 'We reject altogether the Socialist conception of a division of society between officials and the common mass. We repudiate their policy of levelling down to a minimum uniformity, above which only politicians and their agents may rise. We stand for the increasingly higher expression of individual independence.'[4]

Churchill continued to be helped in his speeches during 1950, as he had been in 1949, by George Christ, now Parliamentary Liaison Officer at Conservative Central Office and editor of the Party *Newsletter*. On one occasion, in thanking Christ for his brief, Churchill wrote: 'The fact that I did not use it in no way detracts from the help you gave me. It gave me a rope with which to crawl ashore till I could walk on my own feet up the beach.'[5]

---

[1] *Hansard*, 27 April 1950.
[2] 'Dear Mr Churchill', 7 May 1950: Churchill papers, 2/102.
[3] Churchill's other horse running that day at Hurst Park, Cyberine, finished fourth.
[4] Speech of 18 May 1950: Randolph S. Churchill (editor), *In the Balance*, pages 271–80.
[5] Letter of 27 March 1950: Churchill papers, 2/95.

With the prospect looming of another election in either 1950 or 1951, Churchill had already proposed, in March, the setting up of a committee of the Shadow Cabinet 'to go into all the questions open between Conservatives and Liberals and to see what can be done to secure greater unity among the forces opposed to Socialism'.[1] Speaking on May 16 at a luncheon of the Conservative backbench 1922 Committee, he declared, as set out in his speech notes:

We must obtain Liberal aid both as individuals and if possible as a Party, not by any political deal or bargain, but by proclaiming the fundamental principles on which all those who voted against Socialism agree.

1 State servant not master.
2 Individual right to freedom.
3 No more nationalization. No steel.
4 The right road. United Europe.

As Lord Woolton pointed out there is a great overlap of common doctrine. Those who sincerely agree upon this common doctrine should try their best to help each other as much as they can and to hurt each other as little as they must. I am sure that if we can create this friendly atmosphere very great advantages might be gained and not only for our Party but for our country, and a great responsibility rests upon every one of us during the critical weeks and months that lie before us.

Churchill went on to speak of his own 'great responsibility' as Leader of the Conservative Party, and to offer 'a broad principle of action' which had its place in policy as well as in strategy:

You should try not to quarrel with two at a time. I did not want Mr Bevin to quarrel with Germany and with Russia at the same time. I am very content with the influence we have exerted in the last five years upon foreign policy.

Applied to the domestic sphere, I would rather not, unless we are forced to do so, fight Liberal and Labour at the same time. The little parlour of interested individuals who control what is left of the Liberal Party gives us endless provocation and were guilty, through their partisanship, of a great national disservice at the late election, but it is always better to look forward than to look back.

The word 'appeasement' is not popular, but appeasement has its place in all policy. Make sure you put it in the right place. Appease the weak, defy the strong. It is a terrible thing for a famous nation like Britain to do it the wrong way round.

It would be a mistake for a Party as strong as ours and with our dominant

---

[1] 'Chief Whip', 29 March 1950. Churchill suggested R. A. Butler as the Committee Chairman, with Harold Macmillan, Duncan Sandys and James Stuart as the other members, and he added: 'They would work in the closest concert with Lord Woolton who would come whenever he desired. We must have the whole of this position studied with close attention from the House of Commons' angle.'

responsibility to be provoked into doing anything to antagonise weaker elements from joining in the common struggle with Socialism, provided of course we do not sacrifice the principles or the cause to which we are in honour bound.

I hope you will give me as your Leader the confidence and the sympathy which I require. Your welcome here today has removed the barrier which had risen in my mind, and I hope to come more frequently to the 1922 Committee in the future, and also to see your executive at regular intervals.

'I want a Liberal Party,' Churchill ended, 'as a witness, not one as a makeweight.' [1]

Churchill's return to speechmaking at such frequent intervals was a considerable burden. 'I have had a strenuous pitch,' he wrote to his son Randolph on May 21, 'three speeches and two nights in the train.' [2] And to Lord Beaverbrook he wrote on the following day, of the political and international situation: 'Everything seems vy bloody.' [3]

Just how 'bloody' Churchill felt things to be was made clear in a letter which he sent to Attlee on May 24 in which he warned that 'something between seventy and a hundred divisions, with proportionate armour and air force', would be needed to resist 'a Russian attack on the Western front'. Yet the Western forces had 'barely ten divisions', a proportion of which were dependent on German services for their transport. Given these facts, he was certain that without the 'strong aid' of a German military contingent, 'beginning with five and running up, as American, British and French armies grew, perhaps to twenty divisions, there are no means of offering any effective defence for Western Europe'. At present, Churchill noted, 'the only Germans who are allowed to be trained are the Communists, whom the Russians have been for a long time organizing into an Army on a large scale both inside and outside the Eastern Zone'.

The only thing that keeps the peace is the American possession of the atomic bomb. I see however that General Omar Bradley said that 'in three or four years the Soviets would have a sufficient supply of these to cause a major catastrophe at any time they so decided', or words to that effect. They may not be affected by the same moral restraints as have governed the United States during their phase of unquestioned superiority. At any rate they will have in three or four years both overwhelming military superiority in Europe and a formidable supply of atomic bombs.

We have quite rightly given the Americans a base in East Anglia for the obvious purpose of using the atomic bomb on Moscow and other Russian

---

[1] '1922 Committee Luncheon', 16 May 1950: Churchill papers, 2/99.
[2] 'My dear Randolph', 21 May 1950: Churchill papers, 1/48.
[3] 'My dear Max', 22 May 1950: Beaverbrook papers.

cities. We are therefore a prime target for attack. Our defence against such an attack has been greatly weakened by our sale of jet-fighter airplanes to the Argentine and Egypt as we have read in the newspapers, and no doubt elsewhere to an even larger extent.

In my long experience I have never seen a situation so perilous and strange.

Churchill asked Attlee to agree to a Secret Session of the House of Commons, so that Members of Parliament could have 'some realization of the position'. Were Attlee to 'deny this knowledge to Parliament', Churchill added, 'I think you will be bearing a very exceptional load of responsibility.' [1]

Attlee refused Churchill's request, as he had done once before, in 1948, arguing that the holding of a Secret Session 'would give rise to serious public alarm, and a crop of irresponsible rumours, which neither the Government nor the Opposition would be able to control'. Attlee added: 'I cannot imagine that such a situation could do any service to the countries which are friendly to us; and I feel confident that those which are unfriendly would not fail to exploit it to our disadvantage.' Attlee also argued that if the holding of a Secret Session in time of peace 'gave rise to the widespread public anxiety which I fear, I for my part should find it difficult to resist the pressure which, I feel sure, the Press would bring to bear for some public debate or statement which would enable the public to put matters in their true perspective'.

Attlee then made what he hoped would be regarded as a constructive suggestion:

The suggestion which I put forward—and I ask you to give it your most earnest consideration—is that, instead of expressing your views and your anxieties in debate, even in Secret Session, you should bring some of your friends who share your confidence in these matters to discuss them with me and some of my Cabinet colleagues.

In the course of last year we had several confidential discussions of this kind on the strength of our Armed Forces. At the last of these meetings, on 20th October, you said that you would revise the memorandum which you had presented to us in the light of the information which you had obtained from Ministers in the course of these talks.

May I suggest that those confidential discussions should now be resumed, and that their scope should be widened to cover the more general questions relating to the defence of Western Europe which you raised in your letter of the 24th May? [2]

*   *   *

[1] 'My dear Prime Minister', 24 May 1950: Premier papers, 8/1160.
[2] 'My dear Churchill', 13 June 1950: Churchill papers, 2/29.

At the age of seventy-five, Churchill's burdens of work did not seem to diminish. 'I was so sorry we could not meet,' he wrote to his cousin Clare Sheridan on June 4, 'but I am still the slave of worldly events, and hope to remain so.'[1] That day, in asking Sir Alexander Korda to excuse him from attending the première of *Odette*, to which the King and Queen were going, he wrote: 'My burdens are heavy and holidays are short.' He would be glad, however, if Korda would let him have a copy of the film 'for a show at Chartwell'.[2]

At the time when Churchill was preparing his Secret Session letter to Attlee, Churchill saw the distinguished neurologist Sir Russell Brain. The cause of this consultation was described by Lord Moran in his notes for May 25:

> Winston is quite sure that the tightness over his shoulders has increased. He can't get the stroke out of his mind. To reassure him I called in Russell Brain.
>
> 'The cells in your brain,' he explained, 'which receive sensory messages from your shoulder are dead. That's all. It's a bit of luck that sensation only is affected.'
>
> He seemed relieved by Brain's air of finality, and began talking about his dyspepsia. For ten years he had been 'tortured' by it; then he heard of Cortlandt MacMahon's name.
>
> 'He cured me by his breathing exercises. Why, after his third visit there was an enormous difference in the whole structure of the body.'[3]

Within a month, Lord Moran had introduced Churchill to a second specialist, Sir Victor Negus, consulting surgeon to the Ear, Nose and Throat Department at King's College Hospital. Again Lord Moran's diary explained the cause of the visit, its discoveries, and a moment of unintentional humour:

> Took Winston to Negus for increasing deafness. He found that the higher notes were lost.
>
> Negus: 'You won't be able to hear the twittering of birds and children's piping voices.'
>
> Winston: 'Are you going to hurt me?' He was watching Negus as he fiddled with his tuning forks. 'You must tell me if you are.'
>
> Negus: 'Can you hear a clock ticking in your room?'
>
> Winston: 'I won't have a ticking clock in my room.'[4]

Churchill's concern about his health, his fears of another stroke,

---

[1] 'Dearest Clare', 4 June 1950: Churchill papers, 1/48.
[2] 'My dear Korda', 4 June 1950: Churchill papers, 2/171.
[3] Lord Moran diary, 25 May 1950: *The Struggle for Survival*, page 337.
[4] Lord Moran diary, 21 June 1950: *The Struggle for Survival*, page 338. Churchill had a deep dislike of certain noises, among them hammering, whistling, and ticking clocks.

and his awareness of growing deafness, came at a time when, in the personal sphere, he was also worried about his son's future, following his election defeat. In an attempt to direct Randolph to a profession other than spasmodic journalism, Churchill agreed to pay his son's bank overdraft and election debts.[1] He also gave him some fatherly advice. Randolph accepted the advice with a good will. 'I have thought very seriously,' he wrote, 'about your suggestion of my reading for the Bar,' and he added: 'I will start doing this as soon as the Plymouth Fair is over.' As for the payment of his debts, 'I assure you,' Randolph wrote, 'I shall make a resolute effort to arrange my life more prudently from now on.'[2] 'I am very glad you have decided to read for the Bar,' Churchill replied, 'as soon as the Plymouth Fair is over next week,' and he added, on his own behalf and that of the Chartwell Literary Trustees, who had in fact paid the debts:

Your acceptance of our suggestion of course implies that when you are called to the Bar you will practise and do your best to make a success of this profession. It would be quite possible to combine this, as many do, especially in the early stages, with House of Commons work should you become a Member. I should like to have your assurance that this is so.[3]

Randolph gave his father the assurances he required. But he was never to be called to the Bar. For at that very moment an event was taking place in the Far East which was to draw him away from Britain, and reinstate him as a successful working journalist.

Throughout May and June, Churchill had continued to work on his memoirs, with Bill Deakin and Denis Kelly spending alternate weekends at Chartwell. Sometimes they both came; on Friday June 9 Bill Deakin arrived for the weekend, and on the Saturday Denis Kelly came for the night. That Saturday, Walter Graebner was invited for luncheon. On arrival, he found Churchill 'busily at work on a manuscript in his study'. Graebner's account continued:

'I've done a lot of work,' he told me happily. 'Volume Five is in good shape. It can be called a Property. And I'm getting along with Six, too.' He

---

[1] Randolph Churchill's debts amounted (on 19 June 1950) to £3,324. He also had an unsecured bank overdraft of £980. Of this total indebtedness of £4,304 'about £520', he explained, 'is owed to bookmakers'. Randolph added: 'It is with a deep sense of shame that I set these figures down.' ('My dearest Papa', 19 June 1950: Churchill papers, 1/51.)

[2] 'My dearest Papa', 3 June 1950: Churchill papers, 1/51.

[3] 'My dear Randolph', 6 July 1950: Churchill papers, 1/51. The Chartwell Literary Trust was administered by Lord Cherwell and Brendan Bracken, with Clementine Churchill as Chairman. Neither Churchill nor his wife could benefit from it, only their children and grandchildren.

then jumped up and marched to the long wooden counter along the wall where a complete set of proofs was always kept. 'See,' he said. 'Eighty thousand words in the first book of Volume Five and ninety thousand in the second. If I should fall down dead to-morrow this book could carry my name.'

'But you're in the best of health,' I declared. 'You've not looked better in years.'

'I know,' he answered. 'The important thing is that I live until July 1st. By that time the trust will be five years old, and after that I can die without the Government taking most of it away in taxes. I must be careful about flying until then because I want to be sure the kids are looked after. But after July—hmmm—then I can fly like hell.'

Churchill added: 'I'm getting £35,000 out of Volume Five. That's plenty for me, but nothing of that will be left for the trust. Still the trust has had five whacks at the book already. Not so bad.'[1]

Bill Deakin later recalled the pattern of work as the writing of the memoirs proceeded:

He would stay in bed until just before lunch. He would give me something to do—correcting proofs. He would then dictate his mail to one of the girls. At about eleven he would summon me, and again give me things to do. He would have a bath, get dressed. I would sit at his desk. Then we would go down to lunch.

After lunch he would go for a walk. He would count the swans, count the fish in the lake. Then a nap. Waking at about five he would play bezique with Clementine. I would make myself scarce, I'd go and work in my room.

Between 6.30 and 7 he would sign his correspondence. I'd be in the room. Then we would talk about whatever chapter he was working on. He would read whatever paper he had asked me to write, almost without comment. Then we would change for dinner.

He spent quite a long time at dinner. He really loved that. He would hold forth. One didn't realize it was sometimes a monologue, one was so caught up in it, one felt so much a part of it. He didn't start work again until about eleven. He and I would go upstairs. We would work until 2, or even 3. He would pick up what he had read before dinner; then he would start dictating. He wouldn't look again at what I had written. It was in his head.

As work on the memoirs proceeded night after night, Deakin was struck by what he called 'this enormous power of living for the moment, the most intense concentration I have ever known'.[2] 'He really did go at it hammer and tongs,' Miss Gilliatt later reflected.[3]

---

[1] Walter Graebner recollections: Walter Graebner, *My dear Mister Churchill*, pages 43–4.

[2] Sir William Deakin recollections: in conversation with the author, 1 July 1987.

[3] Elizabeth Gilliatt recollections: in conversation with the author, 12 June 1987.

30

Korea, and the 'Front against Communism'

O N 25 June 1950 reports had been received in London that forces from North Korea had crossed the 38th parallel at a number of points, in the course of an invasion of South Korea. In answer to a question by Churchill on the following day, Attlee stated that at an Emergency Meeting of the Security Council of the United Nations, a meeting called at the request of the United States, a resolution was passed, declaring that the action of North Korea 'constituted a breach of the peace'. The British Government welcomed this resolution, which also urged all States 'to refrain from giving assistance to the North Korean authorities'.[1]

While supporting the Government's firmness about Korea, Churchill was distressed at its failure to send any representatives to Paris, for a Conference on the Schuman Plan, the aim of which was to set up a coal and steel pool for Western Europe. Churchill told the House of Commons:

> Here are the six Powers talking all these matters over among themselves with the United States beckoning encouragement to them from across the ocean. Nothing has done more harm in the United States than the publication in this country of this document—and Britain, although absolutely safe from being committed, finding excuses, elaborate excuses, to keep out of the conference altogether and thus perhaps spoil the hopes of a general settlement. The French have a saying: 'Les absents ont toujours tort'. I do not know whether they learn French at Winchester.[2]

The absence of Britain, Churchill insisted, 'deranges the balance of

[1] *Hansard*, 26 June 1950.

[2] The Chancellor of the Exchequer, Sir Stafford Cripps, had been at school at Winchester, as had the Minister of Economic Affairs, Hugh Gaitskell (who succeeded Cripps as Chancellor on 19 October 1950). Experts gathered at the International Court of Justice in the Hague in February 1985 confirmed privately that *les absents ont toujours tort* 'has no roots in international law'. The practice of the International Court of Justice has indeed, in recent years, been the reverse. In the case of Iceland (fisheries), France (nuclear tests) and Iran (hostages) the Court has made persistent efforts to make allowances for the absentees' supposed position.

Europe' and he added: 'I am all for a reconciliation between France and Germany, and for receiving Germany back into the European family, but this implies, as I have always insisted, that Britain and France should in the main act together so as to be able to deal on even terms with Germany, which is so much stronger than France alone.' Without Britain, the coal and steel pool 'must naturally tend to be dominated by Germany', which would be the 'most powerful' member. This same point, Churchill noted, had been made earlier in the debate by the Labour MP Richard Crossman, and he went on to tell the House:

It would be quite fair to ask me whether I should have welcomed this event even if there were no such thing as this Russian menace, or the Soviet government or the Communist movement in many lands. I should say, 'Yes, certainly.' The unity of France and Germany, whether direct or in a larger Continental grouping, is a merciful and glorious forward step towards the revival of Europe and the peace of the world. The fact that there is a grave Soviet and Communist menace only adds to its value and urgency.

Churchill then appealed once more, as he had done at Zurich, The Hague and Strasbourg, and in the House of Commons in several major debates, for the Goverment to accept the concept of a United Europe and to work towards it:

We must find our path to world unity through the United Nations Organization, which I hope will be re-founded one day upon three or four regional groups, of which a united Europe should certainly be one. By our unique position in the world, Great Britain has an opportunity, if she is worthy of it, to play an important and possibly a decisive part in all the three larger groupings of the Western democracies. Let us make sure that we are worthy of it.

The whole movement of the world is towards an interdependence of nations. We feel all around us the belief that it is our best hope. If independent, individual sovereignty is sacrosanct and inviolable, how is it that we are all wedded to a world organization? It is an ideal to which we must subscribe.

How is it that we have undertaken this immense obligation for the defence of Western Europe, involving ourselves as we have never done before in the fortunes of countries not protected by the waves and tides of the Channel? How is it that we accepted, and under the present Government eagerly sought, to live upon the bounty of the United States, thus becoming financially dependent upon them? It can only be justified and even tolerated because on either side of the Atlantic it is felt that interdependence is part of our faith and the means of our salvation.

The Labour Government's refusal to participate in the Schuman Plan discussions was, Churchill declared, 'a squalid attitude at a time of present stress'. He rejected Sir Stafford Cripps's claim in his speech on the previous day that at no time in British history had the understanding between Britain and France 'been greater than it is today'. 'It would hardly be possible,' Churchill remarked, 'to state the reverse of the truth with more precision.'[1]

It was the Korean War which now began to dominate the headlines of the Western Press. 'When I accepted your invitation,' Churchill told the American Society in London at their Independence Day dinner on July 4, 'I could not foresee that when the date arrived we should once again be brothers in arms, engaged in fighting for exactly the same cause that we thought we had carried to victory five years ago.' But, he continued: 'Tyranny, external or internal, is our foe whatever trappings or disguises it wears, whatever language it speaks or perverts.' It was of 'vital consequence' to the hopes of peace and the unity of the democratic States 'that what the Communists have begun in Korea should not end in their triumph'. If this were to happen, 'a third world war, under conditions even more deadly than now exist, would certainly be forced upon us, or hurled upon us before long'.[2]

On the following day Churchill spoke in the House of Commons in support of a Government motion pledging resistance to 'the unprovoked aggression' against South Korea. 'The Conservative Party,' he said, 'will give their full support to the Government in these matters'; as would the Liberal Party. When Labour MPs interrupted at this point, Churchill called out to them: 'Do not despise help and friendship when it is offered. Neither of us see what else the Government could have done in the circumstances.'[3]

On July 15 Churchill flew from Biggin Hill to Plymouth where, at his son's invitation, he spoke at the Plymouth Fair. After praising the 'daring and skill' with which, in Korea, a handful of American soldiers, 'three or four battalions at most', had fought their delaying action against overwhelming odds, he told his West Country audience:

I still hope that the unities now being established among all the Western Democracies and Atlantic Powers will ward off from us the terrors and unspeakable miseries of a third world war. I wish also that every effort could be made on the highest level to bring home to the Russian Soviet Government the gravity of the facts which confront us all, them as well as us. I do not give

---

[1] Speech of 26 June 1950: *Hansard*.
[2] Speech of 4 July 1950: Randolph S. Churchill (editor), *In the Balance*, pages 309–12.
[3] Speech of 5 July 1950: *Hansard*.

up the hope which I expressed to you five months ago, of a supreme effort to bridge the gulf between the two worlds, if not in friendship, at least without the hatreds and manoeuvres of the cold war. But of this I am sure: that the best hope will be founded upon the strength of the Western Democracies and upon their unwavering will-power to defend the causes for which they stand.

To work from weakness and fear is ruin. To work from wisdom and power may be salvation. These simple but tremendous facts are, I feel, being understood by the free nations better than they have ever been before.[1]

During several of his speeches during the summer of 1950, Churchill had criticized the Government for failing to manufacture a single British atomic bomb. This had led in the Press to several charges of warmongering. In an attempt to make his true position known, Churchill dictated a statement for the Press, casting it in the third person. 'Mr Churchill wishes to make it clear,' he began, 'that he has never urged, nor does he now advise, the large scale manufacture of the atomic bomb in this country, which our danger from air attack renders specially unsuitable.' Nor did he 'criticise the scale of production on which the Government have embarked', or disagree with their policy 'in pursuing experiments and research necessary in the first instance to make a prototype'. But he did consider it 'a matter of complaint that after five-and-a-half years with all the knowledge we had amassed in the course of our joint work with the Americans during the War, we have not succeeded in making a single specimen'. Meanwhile, Churchill's statement continued, the Soviet Government 'which started so far behind has not only solved the initial difficulties but has, it seems, begun regular production'.[2]

During the Defence Debate on July 26, Churchill again appealed for the following day's debate to be turned into a Secret Session. Attlee had already refused to allow such a step, however. 'Considering how evenly the parties are balanced in this Parliament,' Churchill said, 'and that the Prime Minister's party is a minority in the country of nearly 2,000,000 voters, it is much to be regretted that he should adopt such an authoritarian attitude. I cannot think that his decision will be helpful, either to his party, or, what is of far greater importance, to the welfare of the country.'[3]

Churchill spoke of his great regret that Attlee and the Government 'persist in refusing a Debate in Secret or Private Session. It might, I think, have been quite natural and in the public interest that, after hearing a public statement by the Minister of Defence and after some

---

[1] Speech of 15 July 1950: Randolph S. Churchill (editor), *In the Balance*, pages 320–9.

[2] Press Statement, undated: Churchill papers, 2/28.

[3] In the General Election of 23 February 1950 the Labour Party won 13,266,592 votes. The votes cast for other parties totalled 15,766,079 (of which 12,502,567 were for the Conservatives, 2,621,548 for the Liberals and 91,746 for the Communists).

public discussion upon it, we should have gone into Private Session and talked things over among ourselves as Members of the House of Commons.'[1] But it was not to be. 'The fact of the secret session,' Attlee wrote to Churchill on July 26, 'will obviously detract from the value of the public debate and will tend to cause the greatest amount of suspicion and uneasiness both at home and abroad.'[2]

The Prime Minister's letter was not the final word. As the debate opened on July 27 Churchill called out the traditional remark for opening a Secret Session: 'I spy strangers.' The Speaker thereupon put the question to the House 'that strangers do withdraw'. Amid much excitement, MPs filed into the Division Lobby. The result was narrow, but decisive: 295 in favour of a Secret Session, 296 against.

During his speech, Churchill spoke of the preponderance of Soviet military strength: 40,000 Soviet tanks, 6,000 American tanks and 6,000 British tanks. 'In Korea,' he pointed out, 'we have seen how formidable even a few score of tanks can be, and how tough the Russian tanks are.' In Western Europe, Churchill noted, there were twelve Western divisions, of which less than two were armoured, facing 80 Soviet divisions of which between 25 to 30 were armoured. 'The Russians know their own strength,' he said, 'but it is certain that they also know with great precision the Allied weakness and condition. Apart from agents, there are Communists all over Germany who see the troops living among them day after day. . . .' Churchill told the House:

In all that I have said so far, I have only spoken of the Soviet forces with which we are confronted—eight or nine to one against us in infantry and artillery, and probably much more than that in tank formations. I have not mentioned the satellite powers. Poland, under strict Russian control, with a Russian marshal at the head of her forces, has a powerful party army.[3] Czechoslovakia has another army, though less trustworthy, and the arsenals of Skoda, possibly the largest arms plant now in Europe, are steadily pouring out their weapons.

If the facts that I have stated cannot be contradicted by His Majesty's Government, the preparations of the Western Union to defend itself certainly stand on a far lower level than those of the South Koreans. I notice that the right hon. Gentleman[4] said yesterday with candour:

'I will not conceal from the House that the Forces at present available, or in sight, fall a long way short of requirements estimated even on the most conservative basis. There is nothing to be gained by failing to recognize this fact.' It is always, I think, true to say that one of the main foundations of the British sense of humour is understatement, and this appears to be a very excellent example of that fact.

[1] Speech of 26 July 1950: *Hansard*.
[2] 'My dear Mr Churchill', 26 July 1950: Churchill papers, 2/29.
[3] From 1949 to 1956 the Polish Army was commanded by a Soviet Marshal, K. K. Rokossovsky.
[4] Emanuel Shinwell, the Minister of Defence.

Emanuel Shinwell had also told the House of Commons that the Russian military forces were backed by 19,000 aircraft, including jet fighters and bombers of the latest design, a statement which led Churchill to ask:

But, on the Western front, which is the matter which I have most in point at the moment, in fighter and bomber aircraft, how many have they got in full commission? Would 4,000 or 5,000 or 6,000 be too large an estimate?

I should be greatly relieved if the Government were able to answer this question in a reassuring manner. But, considering all we have been told of the Russian strength, I can see no reason why, even under the conditions of a public Session, it should not be answered. But, even if we take it as only 4,000, how many have we got?

We and the Americans and the Western Allies, how many have we got on the Continent—I am not speaking of home forces—to sustain our Armies of perhaps twelve divisions, as stated by M. Reynaud, against eighty or ninety? Here, again, even if we were in Secret Session, I would not ask the Government to state the exact figure, but could they say, for instance, that we have a half, a third, a fourth, a fifth, a sixth, or a seventh of what we know we have to face?

Churchill then spoke of the Soviet submarines. 'I believe it is probably true to say,' he warned, 'that the Russian-Soviet U-boat menace to our trans-ocean Atlantic life-line and world communications, which also comprise all American reinforcements for Europe, would be far more severe than was the German U-boat force in their attacks of 1939 and 1940; and this seemed quite enough then.'

With the same arguments, the same forebodings, and the same forcefulness as fifteen years earlier, Churchill urged the Government to realize the importance of every aspect of defence preparedness, including the deterrent effect of the possession of the atomic bomb. 'We are, of course, dependent upon the United States both for the supply of the bomb and largely for the means of using it,' he said. 'Without it, we are more defenceless than we have ever been. I find this a terrible thought.' In 1940 he 'had good hopes that we should win the battle in the air even at heavy odds and that if we won, the Navy could stave off and repel invasion until eventually vast air power was developed here which would bring us out of our troubles, even if left alone. But now I cannot feel the same sense of concrete assurance.'

Britain's industrial capacity and that of the free world was enormous, Churchill pointed out. Her scientific capacity and technical ability were 'unsurpassed'. There might well still be time to reorganize and develop the 'mighty latent strength' of Britain 'surrounded by her Commonwealth'. But, Churchill continued:

... I warn the House that we have as great dangers to face in 1950 and 1951 as we had ten years ago. Here we are with deep and continuing differences between us in our whole domestic sphere, and faced with dangers and problems which all our united strength can scarcely overcome. It was this that led me to hope that in Private Session the sense of the corporate life of the House of Commons might have asserted itself. But that has been forbidden by the Prime Minister.

Hon. Members: 'By the House.'

It has been forbidden by the Prime Minister, and at his request the House has prevented our meeting together and talking things over among ourselves in secret.

It is with deep grief that I have to say these things to the House, and to reflect that is only five years ago almost to a month when we were victorious, respected and safe.

Churchill ended his speech by offering the Opposition's help to the Government, and explaining why they would do so:

The whole burden does not rest upon the country, nor upon the government of this country.

They have done several important things, like establishing compulsory National Service and the East Anglian American base. They have fostered the closest relations with the United States and our European friends, and they have maintained active resistance to Communism in its various forms.

Nevertheless, I say they bear a fearful accountability. The Prime Minister and his party have had power, men and money never enjoyed before by any Government in time of peace. If they had asked for more Parliament would have granted it to them and we would have given it our full support.

It was with a sense of relief that I felt entitled to say in March that we could accept no responsibility for the present state of our defences. That does not mean that we will not strive to help the Government, in spite of their total lack of consideration for our wishes and point of view, in every measure, however unpopular, which they may propose and which we recognize is aimed solely at securing national survival.[1]

On August 2 Churchill went to see Attlee about British defence preparedness. He was 'much depressed' by his interview, Harold Macmillan noted in his diary four days later. Macmillan added: 'It seems that to scrape together 3,000 men and their equipment for Korea will take two months! Even their anti-aircraft guns can only be obtained by taking some of those now in Lincolnshire defending the American "atomic" bombers.' Attlee had received Churchill courteously, 'but seemed uncertain and baffled by the difficulties and dangers'.[2]

On August 6, Churchill flew from Biggin Hill to Strasbourg, and on the following day attended the opening session of the Consultative

[1] Speech of 27 July 1950: *Hansard*.
[2] Macmillan diary, 6 August 1950, and recollections: *Tides of Fortune*, page 334.

Assembly of the Council of Europe. Then, for four days, in the seclusion of the Villa Merckel, he worked on his speech. 'The seclusion which I found there,' he wrote to Madame Merckel on his return, 'enabled me to work in the privacy and quietness which I much value.'[1]

For those who wished to see the creation of a European Army, much seemed to depend upon what Churchill would say, and how he would say it. On August 8 Harold Macmillan wrote in his diary:

> Mr Churchill will speak—no, he will not—yes, he will. I went round in the morning, before the session. He was in bed and working on a speech. He will speak tomorrow, Thursday; Spaak should be so informed.
>
> The truth is that he is in one of those moods, preparatory to some creative effort, when the artist is anxious, nervous, dissatisfied with himself, and everyone else—a good sign on the whole.[2]

Churchill consulted Macmillan several times on the text of his speech. 'One cannot but admire,' noted Macmillan on August 10, 'his extraordinary attention to detail and desire to perfect and improve.'[3]

Churchill made his speech on August 11, telling the Assembly how 'very glad' he was that the Germans, 'amid their own problems, have come here to share our perils and augment our strength. They ought to have been here a year ago. A year has been wasted, but still it is not too late. There is no revival of Europe, no safety or freedom for any of us, except in standing together, united and unflinching.'

Churchill then warned the delegates that the freedom and civilization of Western Europe lay 'under the shadow of Russian Communist aggression, supported by enormous armaments'. For that reason, there would have to be created, and in 'the shortest possible time', a 'real defensive front' in Europe, and he went on to explain:

> Great Britain and the United States must send large forces to the Continent. France must again revive her famous army. We welcome our Italian comrades. All—Greece, Turkey, Holland, Belgium, Luxembourg, the Scandinavian States—must bear their share and do their best. Courage and unity must inspire us and direct the mighty energies at the disposal of our Governments to solid and adequate measures of defence. Those who serve supreme causes must not consider what they can get but what they can give. Let that be our rivalry in these years that lie before us.[4]

Churchill had spoken for twenty-five minutes, and had moved his resolution in favour of a European Army. 'His speech was impassioned,'

---

[1] Letter of 26 August 1950: Churchill papers, 2/275.
[2] Macmillan diary, 8 August 1950: *Tides of Fortune*, page 215.
[3] Macmillan diary, 10 August 1950: *Tides of Fortune*, page 216.
[4] Speech of 11 August 1950: Randolph S. Churchill (editor), *In the Balance*, pages 347–52. Recording: BBC Written Archives Centre, Library No. 15815.

Macmillan noted in his diary, 'both in manner and matter. The little touches of humour found their mark, although the technique of speaking to an audience the greater part of which is listening to an indifferent translation through earphones is not an easy one. It is really more like a broadcast than a speech. But then the truth is that WSC's broadcasts are speeches.'[1]

At the end of the Strasbourg meeting, Churchill's resolution was passed in favour of the setting up of a European Army.[2] 'This,' Churchill wrote to Truman on August 13, 'is of course to me the fruition of what I have laboured for ever since my speech at Zurich four years ago.' Churchill added, of the decisions and mood of the Council of Europe as he had seen it at Strasbourg:

The ending of the quarrel between France and Germany by what is really a sublime act on the part of the French leaders, and a fine manifestation of the confidence which Western Germany has in our and your good faith and goodwill, is I feel an immense step forward towards the kind of world for which you and I are striving. It is also the best hope of avoiding a third World War.

Churchill's letter to Truman continued:

The only alternative to a European Army with a front against Russian aggression in Europe is, of course, a kind of neutrality arrangement by Germany, France and the smaller countries with the Soviets. This is what the Communists are striving for, and it could only mean the speedy absorption of the neutral European countries by the methods which have subjected Czechoslovakia, as they would be in a sort of no-man's-land between Britain, with its American air-bombing base, and the Soviet armies. They and their cities and junctions might all become involved, especially if these countries were used for the rocket bombardment of Britain.

Although none of us can tell what the Soviet intentions are, I have no doubt that we ought, at this stage, to reject the strategy of holding the Channel and the Pyrenees and strive for the larger hope.

The point however on which I wish particularly to address you is, what will happen to the Germans if they send a substantial contingent—say five or six divisions—to the European Army, in which British and, I trust, Americans will be strongly represented, and the Soviet retaliate by invading Western Germany? Would the United States treat a major aggression of this kind into Western Germany in the same way as it would treat a Soviet attack on France, the Benelux or Britain, or should we let these German people, whom we have disarmed and for whose safety we have accepted responsibility, be attacked without the shield of the atomic deterrent? I should indeed be grateful if I could have your views on this.

[1] Macmillan diary, 11 August 1950: *Tides of Fortune*, page 216.
[2] The vote was 89 for the motion, 5 against, with 27 abstentions, much of the latter consisting of British Labour delegates.

You will note that I said at Strasbourg that if the Germans threw in their lot with us, we should hold their safety and freedom as sacred as our own. Of course I have no official right to speak for anyone, yet after the firm stand you have successfully made about Berlin, I think that the deterrent should be made to apply to all countries represented in the European Army. I do not see how this would risk or cost any more than what is now morally guaranteed by the United States.

Perhaps you will consider whether you can give any indication of your views. A public indication would be of the utmost value and is, in my opinion, indispensable to the conception of a European front against Communism. Perhaps it may be the case that Mr Acheson, or your representative in Germany, has already given an assurance in this respect.

You may perhaps have noticed the unexpected and fortunate fact that the view of the German Delegation, who represent all parties in the German Government, is that Germany should send a contingent to the European Army (say of five or six divisions), but should not have a National Army of her own. I had feared they might take the opposite view, namely, 'let us have a National Army with its own munitions, supplies, and the right to re-arm, and we will then give a contingent to the European Army'. I need not say what an enormous difference this has made to the French view. They and we can get it both ways.[1]

In Strasbourg, Duncan Sandys now worked on the outline of a European Army scheme. He also asked his father-in-law for his thoughts. These Churchill set out on a single sheet:

About the European Army, each country would of course supply divisional units, tactically interchangeable, and the military organization would follow the model of SHAEF. It would seem that about sixty divisions should be formed at once and stationed in Europe with another forty ear-marked as reinforcements for the ninetieth day after general mobilization. However these figures are of course only illustrative. A unified military command, in which all contributors take their proper part, and a civilian Defence Chief responsible to the existing national Governments acting together and/or through the United Nations, are of course indispensable.

Sandys had hoped that Churchill would put forward a specific scheme of his own, but Churchill decided not to do so. 'I think the best plan would be for you to let me have any draft scheme which is being prepared,' Churchill wrote, 'and also to give me a list of questions in which you think I can help. This would be better than my

[1] 'My dear Harry', 13 August 1950: Churchill papers, 2/32. Churchill read a copy of this letter to Lew Douglas in London, who then sent it by telegram to Washington, as he informed Churchill on the following day. ('My dear Winston', 'Top Secret', 14 August 1950: Churchill papers, 2/32.) 'We are living in a tumultuous and uncertain age,' Truman replied non-commitally, 'and I am sincerely hoping that the right decisions may be made by our Government to create a condition that will lead to general world peace.' ('Dear Winston', 18 August 1950: Churchill papers 2/32.)

putting forward a cut and dried plan, even in general outline.' Churchill added: 'I should very much deprecate our getting involved in detail, for we have not the military knowledge or any kind of authority to make a plan.'[1]

On August 17 Macmillan sent Churchill details of the continuing debates at Strasbourg, which now centred upon the machinery whereby pressure could be brought by the European Parliament on the Ministers of the different member countries, without usurping their Ministerial functions. 'I am sure it would be a mistake,' Churchill replied on August 17, 'to get involved in details. Council of Europe can never at this stage in affairs deal with problems which belong to executive Governments. It may point the way and give inspiration. We cannot possibly do better than by our resolution.'[2]

'How terrible it is,' Churchill wrote to de Gaulle on August 22, 'that all we were able to achieve is now plunged in the greatest peril I have ever known, and that is saying a good deal.'[3] 'I am continually oppressed,' Churchill wrote that same day to Sir Norman Brook, 'by the sense of the perils which now surround us,' and he added: 'I am glad you are in a position where you can do much to ward them off. Old or young one can only do one's best.'[4]

On July 29 Randolph Churchill left England for South Korea as a war correspondent for the *Daily Telegraph*. 'Randolph has a considerable political experience in England,' Churchill wrote by hand to General MacArthur, 'and was for five years in the House of Commons. He did not see much of it as he served in the Commandos most of the time, and was an officer in my own regiment, the 4th Hussars (of which he is a reserve member). He has lectured all over the United States, and is fully versed in all forms of public discussion.' Churchill added: 'He was with me at Casablanca and Teheran and heard many very confidential things. I found his discretion impeccable on all these

[1] Note marked 'Telephone the following to Mr Sandys at Strasbourg', 15 August 1950: Churchill papers, 2/32.

[2] Letter of 17 August 1950: quoted in *Tides of Fortune*, pages 218–19. Macmillan has commented: 'At that stage, as indeed in many other aspects of his European policy, Churchill had no clear or well-defined plan. He was then in Opposition, deprived of the vast machinery at the disposal of Ministers. He was an old man trying to give a new lead to the world which he had helped to save. He therefore did not consider this question as a Minister introducing the second reading of a Bill. His purpose was to throw out general ideas and give an impetus towards movements already at work. It was for others to find detailed solutions. Nevertheless, it was clear from his words that he contemplated a system in Europe in which Britain should play a leading role, not merely cheer from the side-lines.' (*Tides of Fortune*, page 217.)

[3] 'My dear de Gaulle', 'Private', 22 August 1950: Churchill papers, 2/169.

[4] 'My dear Norman Brook', 22 August 1950: Churchill papers, 4/24.

serious matters. His outlook is broadly mine; and I therefore feel I may trespass upon you in these days of growing stress by commending him to you as a comprehending admirer of all the work you have done and are doing.' [1]

On the evening of August 23, news reached the *Daily Telegraph* that Randolph had been wounded in Korea: shot in the leg. 'I was extremely sorry to hear this morning about Randolph's injury,' Malcolm Muggeridge, then the paper's Deputy Editor, wrote to Churchill on August 24, 'but relieved to learn that it was not serious.' [2]

Malcolm Muggeridge had gone down to Chartwell on the previous day to discuss current politics. But he had been drawn in, as all visitors were, to the discussion of the Korean War. His journalist's eye was struck by what he saw around him, which his diarist's pen set down:

Churchill walked in suddenly wearing his famous siren suit and smoking a huge cigar—a quite astonishing figure, very short legged, baby faced, immensely thick neck, and oddly lovable. I was expecting tea, but a tray of whiskies and sodas was brought in, and continued to be brought in at intervals. Churchill began by talking about his Memoirs and how he was getting on with them. I told him that he ought now to do the last volume before the intervening ones because it was so essential that he should write an account of Yalta. He agreed that it was essential, but said that to do so would involve so much criticism of the Americans that the political repercussions would be dangerous. Nothing, he said, would convince the Americans of the reality of the Russian danger.

He, Churchill, had wanted Patton to take Prague, and had suggested to the Americans that there should be no Anglo-American withdrawal in Germany until a final agreement had been reached. He wanted a battle conference between himself, Stalin and Truman where the armies met, before there had been any disarmament, and he wanted German arms to be kept handy in case they were required. This proposal, he said, was entirely unacceptable to the Americans. It was not, he went on, the Yalta Agreement which was at fault, but the breaking of the Yalta Agreement: and the moment the Russians began to break it he had done all that lay within his power to induce the Americans to join him in calling them to order.

What has happened about his Memoirs, and why he was so troubled, is that in truth he has lost interest in them and has simply been stringing together masses of documents which he had written in the war. The Ameri-

---

[1] 'My dear General MacArthur', 'Private', 28 July 1950: Churchill papers, 2/173.

[2] 'My dear Mr Churchill', 24 August 1950: Churchill papers, 2/173. Randolph was taken from Korea to the Tokyo Army Hospital. 'When I entered,' the editor of *The Rengo Press*, Togo Sheba, wrote to Churchill, 'he was resting comfortably, his wounded leg above the covers, and was reading a novel. Rather a brusque man, but kind hearted when I began talking to him.' Togo Sheba added: 'You had a narrow escape in the Boer War. So had your son recently. God be with you both!' ('Dear Mr Churchill', 4 September 1950: Churchill papers, 1/48.)

cans, who have paid a huge sum of money for the serial and book rights, have protested. In the course of conversation about them it slipped out that certain chapters had not been written by him at all, and I suspect that he is doing extremely little.

He broke off to speak about his conversation with Attlee concerning the advancement of the summoning of Parliament. Attlee, he said, now takes in at most 50 per cent of what is said to him. He referred scornfully to the fact that Attlee had insisted to him (Churchill) that there was no possibility of taking troops from Hong Kong for Korea and that the Americans were not pressing for the British forces. Both these statements were contradicted the very next day. When I told him that the troops going from Hong Kong were going naked, with no proper equipment and, to all intents and purposes, unarmed except for ammunition, he was even more distressed. He spoke much about his broadcast and started reciting a few bits of it.

He then spoke about the Germans and said it was absolutely essential to re-arm them. He mentioned that he'd been invited to go to Cologne where he was to address a huge gathering, perhaps 30,000, and he believed he would receive a great ovation. He then began walking up and down the room and, in effect, giving the speech he was to give at Cologne—a bizarre spectacle, the great wartime Prime Minister, rather tight, walking up and down reciting his speech which he proposed to give to a German audience from whom he expected warm applause. He obviously still has a great affection for Stalin. 'What a pity,' he said, 'that he has turned out to be such a swine,' and went on: 'Why, he and Truman and Attlee could have governed the world—what a triumvirate! . . .

He took me downstairs to look at his pictures which are really very striking, one room completely covered with them, remarkably vivid colouring. Here he was rather touching. Sitting humped-up in a chair looking at them, he pointed to one which he said was the last he'd done, and added, 'I expect the last I shall ever do.' I made the usual observations about being sure he would do many more etc., but he just paid no attention and sat there seemingly sunk in thought surrounded by these brilliantly coloured pictures. We then went into his study, the walls of which are covered with presentation photographs, and, still thinking about his German speech, showed me a picture of Bismarck which had been given by the German Chancellor to his father. He also showed me a printed notice offering £25 reward for his (Churchill's) capture dead or alive at the time of the Boer War, signed by Kruger. He said, 'It's more than they would offer for me now.'

We strolled out into the grounds, and he showed me the little waterfall he'd made, and explained the difficulty he has in getting sufficient water. He'd been draining his ponds, and had hoped to have the whole operation completed by the time his wife returned, but now she was coming back four days earlier and he feared she would be displeased with it all and that there'd be trouble.

We went along to see his goldfish in a little pool. He sat down in a chair set there specially for him and began to shout, the supposition being that at the sound of his voice the goldfish would assemble. They showed no signs of assembling as far as I could see, but presently an attendant appeared and gave him some maggots which he threw into the water, whereupon the gold-fish did come and started eating them. He said that his whole standing with the goldfish depended on their associating the sound of his voice with the provision of maggots, and he laughed heartily when I said that he was in very much the same situation vis à vis his constituents, that they, too, needed to associate the sound of his voice with a provision of maggots. . . .

'He waved goodbye very cheerfully,' Muggeridge added, 'and I waved back, and drove thoughtfully back to the *Daily Telegraph*.' [1]

'Talking about Yalta and related matters,' Muggeridge wrote to Churchill in his letter of thanks on August 24, 'was, to me, particularly interesting, and if ever you had another hour or two to spare, I should like more than I can say to come and continue the discussion.' [2]

Time, however, was what Churchill did not have. On August 24, in explaining why he could not write a tribute for *The Times* to his friend George Paynter, he explained to the Duke of Westminster: 'Alas, much though I should like to pay my tribute I am beaten down by work al-ready.' [3]

All Churchill's efforts were focused on trying to complete his fourth volume. 'I have had to give up all my holiday,' he explained to his cousin Oswald Frewen, 'and cannot even squeeze a tube. Volume IV is a worse tyrant than Attlee.' [4]

Joining the tyranny of the new volume was the need to answer com-plaints about previous volumes. There was an amendment to be made concerning the campaign in British Somaliland in 1940, of which Chur-chill had written: 'I am far from satisfied with the tactical conduct of this affair, which remains on record as our only defeat at Italian hands.' [5]

This statement, wrote Major-General Chater, 'is very unfair on those who strove hard to defend the Protectorate, and is not wholly true'.[6] Having read the General's detailed account of the campaign which he had conducted, and of the crucial part played in its failure by the collapse of the French forces in French Somaliland on whose

[1] Malcolm Muggeridge diary, 23 August 1950: Malcolm Muggeridge, *Like It Was*, London 1981, pages 408–13.
[2] 'My dear Mr Churchill', 24 August 1950: Churchill papers, 2/173.
[3] Letter of 24 August 1950: Churchill papers, 1/178.
[4] 'My dear Oswald', 22 August 1950: Churchill papers, 2/167. 'I spend a great deal of my time resting in bed,' Churchill explained to Christopher Soames's father, on declining to join him in a pheasant shoot, 'and would not be able to get through all my trials if I were to attempt to renew the sports of former days.' ('My dear Arthur' (Captain Arthur Soames, MC), 15 September 1950: Churchill papers, 2/177.)
[5] Winston S. Churchill, *The Second World War*, volume 2, page 383.
[6] 'Dear Mr Churchill', 27 June 1950: Chater papers.

co-operation the British defence had depended, and impressed by what Chater called 'the failure of the War Office and the Colonial Office to give approval to the proposals for defence, which had to be submitted to them, until it was too late', Churchill agreed to change the offending passage. This was to read, in all subsequent editions: 'I was very much disappointed with this affair, which remains on record as our only defeat at Italian hands. This in no way reflects upon the officers or men of the British and Somali troops in the Protectorate, who had to do their best with what equipment they were allotted, and obey the orders they received.'

'I hope,' Churchill told General Chater, 'this will remove any bad feeling from you and your friends.' [1]

The Dutch had also been offended, by no reference having been made to the activities of Dutch submarines in the Far East in December 1941. At Commodore Allen's suggestion, a letter was sent to Emery Reves, through whom the complaint had been forwarded, that 'Mr Churchill considers that no alteration should be made to his own text in the Book but has no objection to the publication, in the Dutch edition of his Volume III, of an amplifying footnote recording further details of the exploits of Dutch submarines at this time in the Allied cause. He is very sensible of the importance of the part they played both then and later.' [2]

Other memoirs were also a cause for concern; reading the Duke of Windsor's account of the Abdication crisis of December 1936, Churchill was upset by a suggestion that when he had intervened in the House of Commons in December 1936 to ask for more time for the Duke to make up his mind, he had been 'shaken and dismayed' by the hostile reaction. Though 'naturally conscious of the overwhelming opinion of its Members', Churchill wrote to Brendan Bracken, 'that afternoon I addressed a very large gathering of the Conservative Committee on military defence, speaking I think for nearly an hour and was listened to with the utmost attention'. [3]

Out of concern for Churchill, and as an eye-witness, Jock Colville was angered by Michael Foot's review of Churchill's third volume. In his review, Foot wrote, of the events of June 1941 when Hitler invaded the Soviet Union: 'the suggestion that Mr Churchill was anything other than convinced of the Russian inability to withstand the German attack amounts to a downright falsehood.' It was clear from quotations cited for other purposes, Foot added, that Churchill, along with many others, 'grossly under-estimated the Russian powers of resistance, and

[1] 'Dear General Chater', 'Private', 9 July 1950: Chater papers.
[2] 'Volume III, Exploits of Dutch Submarines', 21 July 1950: Churchill papers, 4/54.
[3] 'My dear Brendan', 'Private and Personal', 1 August 1950: Churchill papers, 2/178.

that the main strategy of the war as directed from Downing Street was not altered at all for several months by Hitler's huge plunge eastwards'.[1]

In an indignant letter to Churchill, Colville wrote that he could 'at least provide oral testimony' that Foot was wrong:

> On that Sunday in June 1941 when Hitler invaded Russia, I remember a discussion on this very point at Chequers. Sir John Dill and Mr Winant both thought the Russians could not last six weeks. After everybody had expressed their views, including Mr Eden, Sir Stafford Cripps and Lord Salisbury, I remember your closing the discussion with the following words: 'I will bet anybody here a Monkey to a Mousetrap that the Russians are still fighting, and fighting victoriously, two years from now.'[2] I recorded your words in writing at the time because I thought they were such a daring prophecy, and because it was such an entirely different point of view from that which anybody else had expressed.

'So much,' Colville added, 'for Michael Foot.'[3]

Work on Volume 4 proceeded at a rapid pace that August, when it reached one of the controversial episodes of the war, the Dieppe raid of 1942, for which Churchill had frequently been held responsible. On August 2 Churchill wrote to Ismay that, whereas he had not yet decided what to write about Dieppe, 'we must at least know ourselves exactly what the facts were—namely: did the Chiefs of Staff, or the Defence Committee or the War Cabinet, ever consider the matter of the revival of the operation (a) when I was in England, (b) when I was out of England, or was it all pushed through by Dickie on his own without reference to higher authority?' Churchill's letter continued:

> I must say that I have very little recollection of the matter. I was in favour, as my minutes show, of large-scale raids up to 10,000 on the French coast, but I expected to be consulted on timing and details. Of course if I was out of the country at the time it is a different story. Is there anything on record on this point? I cannot write the tale without being informed on all this.
>
> Of course Dickie would be the authority to consult. He has taken all responsibility upon himself in his speech in Canada, but I cannot believe that he was allowed to do this without higher authority becoming responsible. The question is at what stage was this matter cut from the supreme war direction, or how and where was it put up to them?[4]

Ismay now contacted Mountbatten, who promised, Ismay told Churchill, 'to look through any personal papers he may have and to

[1] *Tribune*, 28 July 1950.
[2] The wager was of a Monkey (£500) to a Mousetrap (a sovereign), or 500:1.
[3] 'Dear Mr Churchill', 'Private and Personal', 3 August 1950: Churchill papers, 2/168.
[4] Minute initialled 'WSC', 2 August 1950: Churchill papers, 4/25.

consult those who were nearest to him at the time'.[1] Meanwhile, Bill Deakin had found a minute by Churchill to Ismay, written four months after the raid, in which Churchill had written:

Although for many reasons everyone was concerned to make this business look as good as possible, the time has now come when I must be informed more precisely about the military plans.

Who made them? Who approved them? What was General Montgomery's part in it? and General McNaughton's part? What is the opinion about the Canadian generals selected by General McNaughton? Did the General Staff check the plans? At what point was VCIGS informed in CIGS's absence?' [2]

At first sight it would appear to a layman very much out of accord with the accepted principles of war to attack the strongly fortified town front without first securing the cliffs on either side, and to use our tanks in frontal assault off the beaches by the Casino, &c., instead of landing them a few miles up the coast and entering the town from the back.[3]

It was clear that such a critical minute could not be published without some sort of explanation or contribution from Mountbatten. But there were problems in obtaining this, as Bill Deakin explained. 'I have spoken to Lord Ismay about Dieppe,' he wrote to Churchill on August 29. 'His frank opinion is that you will get little of value out of Lord Mountbatten who is at the moment playing polo and visiting Naval establishments.' Deakin went on to explain to Churchill:

Mountbatten took the responsibility for the operation and Ismay says that this is the only occasion in the whole War when nothing was put in writing by the Chiefs of Staff about a final operational decision. Six months later there is a minute of a Chiefs of Staff meeting at which Mountbatten stated that he had taken this responsibility himself.[4]

Mountbatten did finally set out for Churchill his own recollections of what had occurred, the principal point of which was that Churchill was '(as ever) the moving spirit' behind the operation. The reason that no records had been kept was 'that you and the Chiefs of Staff agreed to this on account of the extraordinary secrecy'.[5] Churchill decided to omit his minute of 21 December 1942. He wrote to Mountbatten:

[1] 'Mr Churchill', 'The Dieppe Raid', 14 August 1950: Churchill papers, 4/281.

[2] The Vice-Chief of the Imperial General Staff (VCIGS) was Lieutenant-General Sir Archibald Nye. The Chief of the Imperial General Staff (CIGS) was General Sir Alan Brooke.

[3] Prime Minister's Personal Minute, D.224/2, 'Secret', 21 December 1942: Premier papers, 3/256, folio 8.

[4] 'Mr Churchill', 29 August 1950: Churchill papers, 4/281. Deakin added: 'The story of Dieppe as produced by Allen is a bare summary of the operation, in the launching of which you had no direct part, although you knew of the early planning and the ultimate change of code names. If anyone wishes to read the story of Dieppe there is a detailed account in the Canadian Official History.'

[5] 'My dear Mr Churchill', 4 September 1950: Churchill papers, 4/17.

My dear Dickie,

I am very much obliged to you for the pains you have taken and I have accepted practically verbatim your redraft. I must confess that I cannot remember all the details you mention, which is not surprising considering that no written records were kept, and how much was going on. Certainly I wanted a large scale raid in the summer of 1942.[1] Also I was abroad for a fortnight before Zero. But of course the overall responsibility is mine. In these circumstances I am omitting my minute of questions written four months later and the replies thereto.[2]

Churchill's critical minute did not appear in his memoirs.

To accelerate work on the volume, Churchill postponed a holiday he had planned at Biarritz. 'I find it extremely difficult,' he explained to Henry Laughlin of Houghton Mifflin, 'to settle all the corrections, overtakes and cuts to be made in Volume 4 in time for a December publication by Book of the Month.' Laughlin must also realize, Churchill wrote, 'how heavily the public affairs in the international crisis are pressing upon me'.[3]

Towards the end of August, Churchill received some important corrections to the final proofs from Sir Norman Brook. The arrival of these Cabinet Office corrections marked the last major shaping of the text. Not only were these corrections on points of substance, but they involved a careful re-wording of any telegram sent in code, the original wording of which could have enabled hostile codebreakers to penetrate the cypher. 'I am most profoundly grateful to you,' Churchill wrote, 'for all the help you have given me in my seemingly unending toil.' Brook's reconstruction of one of Churchill's chapters 'was a masterpiece'.[4]

Once more Churchill broke off his literary work to prepare, and then to deliver, a Party Political broadcast on August 26. He spoke of the 'many instances of improvidence and want of foresight' with which Britain's affairs were being conducted. One example, he said, was the delay in sending a British expeditionary force to Korea. On June 27, he noted, 'the United Nations called upon their members to defend South Korea against violent aggression from the north. It took the

[1] After '1942' Churchill wrote, in the first draft of this letter: 'and I said to Stalin at Moscow: "It will be like putting one's hand in a bath before getting in to feel how hot the water is", or words to that effect'.

[2] 'My dear Dickie', 'Private', 5 September 1950: Churchill papers, 4/17.

[3] Telegram despatched 4 August 1950: Churchill papers, 4/24.

[4] 'My dear Norman Brook', 22 August 1950: Churchill papers, 4/13. It was Brook who suggested *The Hinge of Fate* as the title for volume 4.

Socialist Government a month to make up their minds whether or not to send an expeditionary force to comply with this request of the United Nations Organization. There was no new fact in the interval. Another month has passed since the decision to send the small force from here was announced, and more than a third month will pass before it can embark on its six weeks' voyage.' He had himself suggested that a small force be sent 'in good time' from Hong Kong. 'I was told this was impossible, but now it has been done.' He also referred once more to the 'astonishing episode' of the sale of several hundred jet fighters to Egypt and the Argentine, 'and actually sending some to Russia at an earlier period when all the time our own Auxiliary Air Force so urgently needed them, and this at the moment when, by establishing the American bomber base in East Anglia—a policy which the Opposition supported on national grounds—we have placed ourselves in the front line of targets in the event of war'.

The Communists, Churchill said, now wanted to ban the atomic bomb 'in the name of peace'. Their real aim, he said, was to have Europe 'naked and at their mercy'. He was sorry, he said, that before the outbreak of the Korean War 'an effort was not made to have a personal talk on the highest level with the leaders of the Soviet Government. I urged this at Edinburgh in February last, but nothing was done and all sorts of things have happened since.' But, he added: 'My eyes are not fixed on Korea, though I admire the American action there, and am glad our men are going to help.' Churchill went on to explain:

There may soon be Communist attacks upon Tibet and Persia. But the supreme peril is in Europe. We must try to close the hideous gap on the European front. If, in two or three years—should that be granted us—we can make a reasonable defence for the free countries outside the Iron Curtain, while at the same time the United States maintains and increases its superiority in the atomic bomb, the best hope will be given for reaching a final peace settlement.

The only way to deal with Communist Russia is by having superior strength in one form or another, and then acting with reason and fairness. This is the plan for the battle of peace and the only plan which has a chance of success.

Here at home the Socialist policy since the war has divided our own people in a needless and painful manner. We lie between two general elections. We have to make our case against each other. But we must never forget that, whatever our party differences may be, we all share the same dangers, and we all, when we wake up, mean to defend the same great causes. I pray we may wake up in time.[1]

---

[1] Broadcast of 26 August 1950: Randolph S. Churchill (editor), *In the Balance*, pages 353-7.

'Your speech was superb!' Lew Douglas wrote from the American Embassy on August 29, and he added: 'Excellent! No fooling!' [1]

On September 12 Churchill spoke in the House of Commons on Defence, in support of a Motion moved by Attlee which sought approval of expenditure in connection with 'the growing dangers to world peace of which the war in Korea is an example'.[2] 'The Prime Minister has appealed to us,' Churchill said, 'for national unity on Defence', and he added: 'This does not mean national unity on mismanagement of Defence.' When Churchill went on to criticize the delays in sending British troops to Korea, and the specific dates on which he had first suggested it, there was a noisy altercation:

The Prime Minister: I cannot quite make out what is the right hon. Gentleman's special point about this date. What is he hanging on the date that is so important? I have told him the facts.

Mr Churchill: I am hanging on the fact that these great matters which are continually before us and before the nation appear to swing about between one day and another, almost upon caprice, at the hands of the Government.

The Prime Minister: The right hon. Gentleman has more experience in conducting military affairs than anyone in this House. He has been accustomed, no doubt, to receiving advice from those who are responsible for running a campaign. The campaign in Korea is being run by the Americans. We respond to their requests, and if the request changes from what it was before it is not the fault of His Majesty's Government. We have responded to the request made to us.

Mr Churchill: No, sir. I do not feel that that is so [Hon. Members: 'Eh.'] I think the Americans are bitterly disappointed. [Interruption.] Why is the Prime Minister's colleague shouting? He does not know anything about it. That is my personal view. I do not mind noise in the least. Please go on, although we gave the Prime Minister a very silent and patient hearing. . . .

Churchill then spoke of a problem on which several leading industrialists had written to him over the past two months, the sale of machine tools to Russia, telling the House of Commons:

The Government have now, according to the broadcast of the Prime Minister, definitely decided that any machine tools, no matter how vital their war potential, which have been ordered by Soviet Russia or its satellites before the British restrictive regulations of eighteen months ago, must, when made, be delivered to Soviet Russia. I have heard a lot of vague language from the

---

[1] 'My dear Winston', 29 August 1950: Churchill papers, 2/32. The friendship between Churchill and Lew Douglas adversely affected the relations between Bevin and the State Department. On September 2 Hugh Dalton noted in his diary: 'Ernie doesn't trust Lew Douglas any more. He thinks he sees too much of Churchill and tells him too much.' (Dalton diary, 2 September 1950: Dalton papers.)

[2] Speech of 12 September 1950: Hansard.

Prime Minister, but I could not see anything which countered or contradicted that quite definite assertion he made in his broadcast.

The Prime Minister: The right hon. Gentleman has not got it quite right.

Mr Churchill: No doubt what I have said is quite true.

The Prime Minister: What I said was that the machinery and tools were being delivered in respect of contracts already entered into, and the statement made in 1949—I think in February—by the President of the Board of Trade to this House was that that was the practice we were following. . . .

The selling of machine tools to Russia, Churchill insisted, 'is wrong and ought to be stopped'. It was 'surprising', he said with bitter irony, 'that the Government, in other directions so prone to retrospective legislation, should find themselves puristically and pedantically hampered in the matter of war materials when an entirely new situation has arisen and become acute'. It was intolerable to think 'that British troops today should be sent into action at one end of the world while we are supplying, or are about to supply, if not actual weapons of war, the means to make weapons of war to those who are trying to kill them or get them killed. I was astonished when I was told what was going on. I was astounded by the attitude that the Prime Minister has taken.'

Churchill then told the House of Commons: 'I should think that the feeling of the great majority of those in this House would be that no more machine tools of a war-making character and no more machines or engines which would be used for war-making purposes should be sent from this country to Soviet Russia or the Soviet satellite nations while the present tension continues.'[1]

After Churchill's speech, a Ministry of Supply official confirmed that several firms in Britain, including Craven Brothers Limited of Manchester, were making machine tools for Russia. Churchill's details on these sales to Russia had in fact come from the Chairman and Managing Director of Craven Brothers, J. R. Greenwood.

The basis of these sales to Russia was the Harold Wilson 1947 Short Term Trade Agreement, which Wilson had negotiated, whereby Britain would pay for its purchase of Russian grain, timber, etc., by selling British machinery to Russia. On September 5 Churchill had received a note from a locomotive manufacturer, Arthur G. Marshall (sent through Harold Macmillan), who wrote: 'Russia had inserted a clause to the effect that if she was unable to agree terms and conditions of contract with British Manufacturers she should have the right of spending the proceeds of the sale of Russian goods in Colonial markets.' Marshall added: 'Russia insisted on prices, terms and conditions from British Manufacturers in this country to which we on our side could not agree, and took advantage of the provision above to

[1] Speech of 12 September 1950: *Hansard*.

purchase rubber, tin, wool etc., from Commonwealth markets, all of these goods being direct munitions of war. She is still continuing this practice.'[1]

'There is no doubt,' Churchill wrote to Greenwood a month later, 'your letter to me had its effect on policy and perhaps on history.'[2]

Later in his speech of September 12, Churchill pressed for the formation 'as fast as possible' of a European army of at least sixty or seventy divisions 'to close what I have called the hideous gap in the protection of Western Europe from a Russian-Communist onrush to the sea. For this purpose every nation still enjoying freedom from totalitarian tyranny should make extreme exertions. Each of the countries ruled by parliamentary democracies must dedicate their quota of divisions.'

Only by the creation of a European Army deployed on 'our gaping Eastern front', Churchill warned, could Britain and Europe 'become free from the present horrible plight in which the American possession of measureless superiority in the atomic bomb is our only safeguard against what might well be the ruin of the world. This will undoubtedly give the Western democracies the best chance of securing the return to the normal relationships of States and nations. Whether we shall have time or not no one can tell.'

In all this, Churchill concluded, there were two factors which Britain could not measure, 'let alone control'. The first was 'the calculations and designs of the Soviet autocracy in the Kremlin', and the second 'the anger of the people in the United States at the treatment they are receiving and the burden they have to bear'.

It was his belief, Churchill said, 'that while American superiority in atomic warfare casts its strange but merciful shield over the free peoples the Soviet oligarchy will be deterred from launching out upon the most frightful of world wars yet waged in this unhappy and distraught world', and he went on to declare:

It may well be that the vast masses of human beings, who ask for so little, but only to be left alone to enjoy the fruits of peaceful toil and raise their children in the hope of a decent and improving future, can still be rescued from the melancholy and frightful fate which has seemed to be, and now seems to be, closing in upon them.

We cannot control, and no one nation can control, the march of destiny, but we can at least do our part. It is because the Motion now before us offers a minor but none the less considerable make-weight to the peaceful settlement of world affairs that we on this side of the House, Conservatives and Liberals alike, will give it our united and resolute support.[3]

[1] 'Anglo-Russian Short Term Trade Agreement, 1947': Churchill papers, 2/110.
[2] 'Dear Mr Greenwood', 10 October 1950: Churchill papers, 2/110.
[3] Speech of 12 September 1950: *Hansard*.

Churchill frequently referred, in his private letters, to his fears. In introducing Lord Camrose to Eisenhower, he wrote: 'It would I am sure be valuable if you could meet him. He knows my views on every aspect of this continually darkening scene.' [1]

On September 14 Churchill received at Hyde Park Gate the Government of Israel's most senior representative in London, Eliahu Elath. In a letter to Dr Weizmann, sent from London on September 17, Elath reported on their meeting:

... the hour was 12.30 p.m., but I found Churchill in bed, with books and newspapers all round him, whisky close at hand, and puffing at a large cigar. He greeted me with the utmost cordiality, said he always received his friends in bed, and offered me a cigar; on my declining it, he pressed a whisky on me, and raising his own glass, drank to the success of Israel. He kept me for an hour, himself doing most of the talking (while smoking incessantly), but also listening with attention to my answers to questions.

He spoke with genuine warmth and admiration of yourself. He said that Providence had blessed Israel by giving us one of the few great men of our time as leader and guide, and in an office for which you were so eminently fitted by your statesmanship and scientific attainments.

The setting-up of our State, he said, ranked as a great event in the history of mankind, and he was proud of his own contribution towards it. He had himself been a Zionist all his life. There was a time when he was afraid that 'Bevin would overshadow Balfour' and that all Britain had done for the National Home would be forgotten. Now there was no reason why Israel should not recognise that Britain was her best friend, and act accordingly. Romantic realists that they were, the British admired the determination and courage which gained Israel her independence, and fully understood the historical significance of the Jewish nation's rebirth.

Churchill was movingly eloquent on the sufferings of the Jews throughout history, as a persecuted people and the faithful guardians of the Biblical heritage. The free Jewish nation, he declared, must preserve close association with the book; Israel must guard the people's spiritual and moral inheritance.

He then made a lightning survey of the world situation, remarking that America's 'large stockpile' of atomic bombs was decisive for the preservation of peace. In this connexion he asked how close are our relations with President Truman and his Government. Dwelling on the subject of the Middle East, he said that, for her own sake and that of the democracies, Israel must lose no time in developing her potential; she must hasten to become a strong political and military factor.

Expressing his pleasure at the fact that we had beaten the Egyptians,

[1] 'My dear Ike', 14 September 1950: Churchill papers, 2/168. Eisenhower was to become Supreme Commander of NATO, with Montgomery as his Deputy Commander, in December 1950.

Churchill remarked that he did not care for any of the Arab States, with the sole exception of Jordan. Abdullah, whom he had placed on the throne, had proved the only reliable and stable ruler of that region.

The Israel Army came in for great praise. He said he admired and respected it; but then he had always believed that the Jews had the moral and physical qualities which would make them the best soldiers of the Mediterranean and the Middle East. Once all his documents saw the light of day, we should realise how he had supported the setting-up of a Jewish force during World War II.

After that he put a number of questions to me. He showed interest in the composition of our Government and the way it works; in the extent of Communist danger in Israel; and in our schemes for agricultural and industrial development, especially in the Negev. He suggested that we make up for natural deficiencies by the use of scientific resources. He offered us his help whenever it was needed.

I have given you an extensive account of the interview, but cannot hope to convey any idea of his verbal felicity, to which, in any case, you are no stranger. You will be amused to hear that his references to the Foreign Secretary were spiced by uncomplimentary adjectives; as for the latter's Palestine policy, he roundly called it disgusting and outrageous.[1]

On September 19 Churchill spoke on the Iron and Steel Bill, moving the motion of regret that this Bill was to come into operation 'during this period of tension and danger thus needlessly dividing the nation on party political issues and disturbing the smooth and efficient working of an industry vital to our defence programme'.

When, during his speech, Churchill said that, in view of the success of the steel industry, there was no need for Attlee to have taken 'this hazardous course at the present moment', several Labour MPs interrupted him. 'I am sorry,' he said, 'that the facts that I am unfolding give so much pain and cause so much confusion, but it only shows the guilty consciences and lack of conviction which prevail on the benches opposite.'

Were the Conservative Party to be returned to power, Churchill declared, it would repeal the existing Iron and Steel Act 'irrespective of whether the vesting date had occurred or not'.[2] This would be its policy if it came into office either before or after another General Election. But nothing would be done to weaken the national defence:

The right hon. Gentleman the other day accused me of being party-

---

[1] Letter of 17 September 1950: Government of Israel archives.

[2] The vesting date, on which the nationalization would come into effect, was later fixed for 15 February 1951.

minded. Everyone would naturally be shocked if a party leader were party-minded! But we are all party-minded in the baffling and unhappy period between election decisions and between parties so sharply divided and evenly balanced. However, the nation may be assured that, whatever the conduct of the present Government and dominant party may be, the Conservative and, I believe, the Liberal Oppositions will not withdraw in any way the aid they have offered and given to all measures for the national defence.

We shall do our utmost to encourage recruiting, and we shall be prepared to accept additional burdens wherever they are shown to be unavoidable. I trust that all Conservatives and Liberals throughout the country will not be deterred by this vicious by-blow from doing their utmost to stimulate production in all its spheres.

After all, there are millions of Conservative and Liberal trade unionists throughout the land, and I say to them from here—and my voice carries some distance—that they must not let themselves be discouraged in their national efforts by the political and party manoeuvres of a fanatical intelligentsia. . . .[1]

On the day after his speech, Churchill set out for the Political Secretary to the Chairman of the Unionist Party in Scotland, Colonel Blair, a 'hypothesis' for which he sought the Colonel's approval that where there was no Liberal candidate in any particular constituency, 'the Liberal vote is not left *undirected*, but receives guidance from the official Liberal Party to vote for the Conservative candidate'. Churchill added: 'I think this will make a decisive difference.'[2]

Towards the end of his speech of September 19, Churchill had urged Attlee not to throw away 'a golden opportunity of serving the whole nation at a crisis in its fate', but to act as Gladstone had once exhorted the Commons: 'Think well, think wisely, think not for the moment but for the days which are to come.'[3] In a letter to Lord Rosebery five days later, in referring again to Gladstone—the 'Grand Old Man'—Churchill wrote: 'What a light was the GOM. It encourages one to act with vigour in public.'[4]

---

[1] Speech of 19 September 1950: *Hansard*.

[2] 'Dear Colonel Blair', 'Confidential', 20 September 1950: Churchill papers, 2/90. Colonel Blair had been Political Secretary to the Chairman of the Unionist Party in Scotland since 1922, and was to hold the post until 1960.

[3] In his closing words to the House of Commons on 8 June 1886, on the second reading of the Government of Ireland Bill, Gladstone declared: 'Think, I beseech you, think well, think wisely, think, not for the moment, but for the years to come, before you reject this Bill.' Despite Gladstone's appeal, the Bill was defeated by 341 votes to 311.

[4] Letter of 24 September 1950: Churchill papers, 2/175.

31

'New, strange, gathering dangers'

ON 1 October 1950 Churchill celebrated a rare anniversary for any politician, the fiftieth anniversary of his first election to Parliament.[1] One letter of congratulations which he received came from Eliahu Elath, the Israeli diplomat, who wrote to him: 'It gives me the utmost pleasure to convey to you congratulations from my Government and the Israel Knesset, to which I add my personal good wishes, on the occasion of your Parliamentary jubilee.' Elath added: 'The people of Israel, for whom democracy is the only conceivable way of life, cherish their own young Parliament, and deeply admire the British House of Commons which has been its model. They look up to you as an illustrious representative of all that is best in British Parliamentary tradition, and wish that you may long continue to adorn the British political scene.'[2]

Honours now came to Churchill in profusion. On October 10 he was in Denmark, to receive an honorary degree of Doctor of Philosophy from Copenhagen University. After listening to a fulsome introduction about being the architect of victory in the Second World War, Churchill commented: 'I was only the servant of my country and had I, at any moment, failed to express her unflinching resolve to

---

[1] On 1 October 1900 Churchill had received 12,931 votes and his Conservative co-candidate 12,522 votes, as against the 12,947 and 12,709 of their Liberal opponents, at the two-member constituency of Oldham. Ironically, in its report on the election on October 2, *The Times* announced that Churchill had been defeated. It apologized on the following day.

[2] 'Dear Mr Churchill', 6 October 1950: Churchill papers, 2/86. Churchill's interest in the State of Israel, then not quite two and a half years old, was expressed in a letter he had written to Dr Chaim Weizmann, its first President, four months earlier. 'I am told by people who have recently visited Israel,' Churchill wrote, 'of the many signs of hard work, courage and foresight on the part of your fellow-countrymen, and of the great progress which is being made in the agricultural and industrial life there.' Churchill added, on a personal note (he had first met Weizmann in Manchester in 1906): 'As always I follow your fortunes with keen interest, and I take this opportunity of sending you my warmest regards and my good wishes for your continued health and strength. I feel that it is under your leadership and guidance that Israel will enjoy prosperity and happiness.' ('My dear Weizmann', 2 June 1950: Churchill papers, 2/102.)

fight and conquer, I should at once have been rightly cast aside.' The words of praise which the Danes had addressed to him, he said, were 'far too complimentary', containing 'much that no man should hear till dead'. Churchill added:

I am very proud and very grateful to receive a Degree of Philosophy from the famous University of Copenhagen. As life unfolds I have been astonished to find how many more degrees I have received than I have passed examinations. I was never very good at those. But now I am treated as if I were quite a learned man. This is a good argument for not being discouraged by the failures or shortcomings of youth but to perservere and go on trying to learn all your life.[1]

In his speech to the Danish Students' Association, Churchill's theme was 'United Europe'. He had been taught during geography lessons as a child, he said, 'that there is a continent called Europe', and after living a long time 'I still believe it is true'. Professional geographers 'now tell us that the Continent of Europe is really only "the peninsula of the Asiatic land mass". I must tell you in all faith that I feel that would be an arid and uninspiring conclusion, and for myself, I distinctly prefer what I was taught when I was a boy.'[2]

On October 12 Churchill flew back from Copenhagen to London. Two days later he was in Blackpool, to speak to the Conservative Party Annual Conference. The kindness of the delegates in giving him a standing ovation when he arrived constituted, he said, 'the bright flash in the serious times in which we live'. There was cause to rejoice, too, at the 'favourable turn' which the war in Korea had taken.[3]

Churchill then spoke of the domestic scene; of the 'undue prolongation' of Party conflict. 'How can Britain do herself justice,' he asked, 'or play her rightful part, whilst this suspense continues?'[4]

From Blackpool, Churchill returned to Chartwell. He was in London again on October 20, to speak at the fifth Alamein reunion. 'How hard it is,' he told the Alamein veterans, 'that destiny compels us after all our victories, to face new, strange, gathering dangers.'[5]

[1] Speech of 10 October 1950: Randolph S. Churchill (editor), *In the Balance*, pages 386–8.

[2] 'Mass Meeting of Students' Association & Danish–British Society, Copenhagen', speech notes, 11 October 1950: Churchill papers, 2/102.

[3] On 15 September 1950 the South Korean, American and Commonwealth forces had broken out of the small perimeter around the southern port of Pusan, in which they had been trapped for several weeks. Two weeks later, United States forces, landing from bases in Japan, captured the South Korean capital of Seoul, and on October 1 South Korean forces crossed the 38th parallel, the former border between North and South Korea, followed closely by United States troops, who crossed the 38th parallel on October 9.

[4] Speech of 14 October 1950: Randolph S. Churchill (editor), *In the Balance*, pages 389–402. At the Blackpool Conference, Hamar Nicholls had organised the shouting of the figure '300,000' for the number of houses which needed to be built. Churchill had accepted this figure as the 'target' in his speech, stating that, even with the need to rearm, 'the Tory Party puts homes for the people in the very forefront of all schemes for our development'.

[5] Speech of 20 October 1950: Randolph S. Churchill (editor), *In the Balance*, pages 403–15.

Awaiting Churchill at Chartwell was a gift from another author which gave him much pleasure, a signed copy of his most recent, and seventieth, book, *Sixteen Self Sketches*. Churchill replied at once:

My dear Bernard Shaw,

Thank you so much for your letter and self sketches. It was a great pleasure to receive them from you and still more to learn of your recovery.

Let me retaliate as only an author can by sending you these few self sketches of a different character.

Perhaps they will persuade you to take up Painting as a Pastime.[1]

Churchill had first met Shaw in his mother's house before the turn of the century, when Lady Randolph Churchill had been editor of a literary magazine, *The Anglo-Saxon Review*.[2] There was another link with that distant past in October, when Lady Lytton wrote to him to remind him that fifty years had passed since Churchill had proposed marriage to her. Churchill replied, on October 20, in his own hand, from Chartwell:

My dearest Pamela,

I put yr lovely letter of October 2 on one side for me to answer above all. Alas the precaution failed. It got among other letters. I have had (as you may guess) an awful time lately—exciting, exhausting, absorbing—and it is not till now that I can tell you how much I cherish yr signal across the years, from the days when I was a freak—always that—but much hated & ruled out, but there was one who saw some qualities, & it is to you that I am most deeply grateful.

Do let us meet again soon. The Parl. will be sitting in November & perhaps you wd come & lunch one day. Clemmie will telephone a plan.

Fifty years!—how stunning! but after all it is better than a hundred. Then there wd not be memory. With my deepest thoughts & love

From Winston[3]

On October 26 the House of Commons returned to its pre-war Chamber in the Palace of Westminster, from which it had been forced nearly ten years before by German bombs.[4] 'I am a child of the House of Commons,' Churchill said after Attlee's opening address, 'and have

---

[1] Letter of 18 October 1950: Churchill papers, 2/176. Shaw died on 2 November 1950. Churchill's book *Painting As a Pastime* had been published in December 1948, consisting of two articles he had written, 'Hobbies' and 'Painting as a Pastime', in the *Pall Mall* and *Strand* magazines in 1925 and 1921 respectively. Both had also been published in his book *Thoughts and Adventures* in 1932. Churchill had also written an article on Shaw in the *Pall Mall* magazine in 1929, subsequently reprinted in *Great Contemporaries* (1937).

[2] Churchill had published one of his own first articles, on the British Cavalry, in the March 1901 issue of his mother's magazine.

[3] 'My dearest Pamela', 20 October 1950: Countess of Lytton papers.

[4] A part of the Palace of Westminster had been damaged on the night of 8 December 1940, during a raid on London in which eighty-five civilians were killed. The debating chamber itself was destroyed during the final attack of the Blitz of 1941, on 10 May 1941, during which night 1,400 civilians were killed, 5,000 houses destroyed and 12,000 people made homeless.

been here I believe longer than anyone. I was much upset when I was thrown out of my collective cradle. I certainly wanted to get back to it as soon as possible.' Churchill ended his remarks:

The Prime Minister said—and said quite truly—that the House of Commons was the workshop of democracy. But it has other claims, too. It is the champion of the people against executive oppression. I am not making a party point; that is quite unfitting on such an occasion. But the House of Commons has ever been the controller and, if need be, the changer of the rulers of the day and of the Ministers appointed by the Crown. It stands forever against oligarchy and one-man power. All these traditions, which have brought us into being over hundreds of years, carrying a large proportion of the commanding thought of the human race with us, all these traditions received new draughts of life as the franchise was extended until it became universal. The House of Commons stands for freedom and law, and this is the message which the Mother of Parliaments has proved herself capable of proclaiming to the world at large.[1]

That evening, when Churchill saw Lord Camrose, he was in reflective mood, telling Camrose that when he had gone down to the House of Commons in May 1941 to see the damage, he had said to his chauffeur, 'I shall never live to sit in the Commons Chamber again.' His chauffeur had written to him recently, reminding him of this remark.

Churchill then spoke of his horse Colonist II, which had won for the second time under his colours on October 12, at Newmarket. Camrose noted:

When he bought Colonist II, Clemmie expressed grave doubts and Miss Sturdee felt so strongly about it that she sent him a note expressing her fear that it would affect his great reputation.

He stayed in bed the whole of 13th October resting 'and not to chance bad luck'.

Perhaps, he said quizzically, Providence had given him Colonist as a comfort for his old age and to console him for disappointments.[2]

[1] Speech of 26 October 1950: *Hansard*.

[2] The racing journals were enthusiastic both about Colonist II and its owner. What was 'really the hot racing news of the moment', declared Sabretache in *Tatler*, was 'this amazing little grey, Mr Winston Churchill's Colonist II, who won the 2¼-mile Jockey Club Cup exactly as he had won all his other races, by grit and determination. Someone suggested to me that his name ought to be changed to "Quintin", because he is such a little bulldog. I do not agree; but if any change were contemplated, what is the matter with a name beginning with a capital "W"? (*The Tatler*, 15 November 1950.) Another press cutting, unidentified, stated: 'The past season will surely go down to history as Colonist's year, for, in truth, this tough and indomitable grey horse has performed miracles. No horse in living memory has put up such a sequence of wins in good-class races in one season. Eight wins (six in succession, ending with the Jockey Club Cup), once second and twice fourth in 11 races, reads like something inspired, and that in truth, was just what this horse seemed to be, by the great spirit of his indefatigable owner': (Churchill press cuttings). On 11 October 1950 Churchill was elected a member of the Jockey Club, to which his father had been elected more than seventy years before.

'Attlee had been very nice,' Churchill told Camrose, 'in naming the Arch in the House of Commons after him. He had expressed the opinion that he thought it ought to be preserved, but had no idea that it should be given his name.'

As to politics, Camrose noted, Churchill 'feels the tide is now running against the Government'.[1]

On October 31, Churchill spoke during the Debate on the Address. At one point, when he was praising Truman's 'prompt initiative' in Korea the previous June, and said he was glad Britain had 'naval forces on the spot, though at the moment I do not know how big they were', there was an interruption:

Mr John Hynd (Sheffield, Attercliffe): The right hon. Gentleman might give his own country some credit.

Mr Churchill: I have never been at all backward in defending the claims and considerations of this country, but I do not think that those claims are well sustained if they are based on a failure to recognize the overwhelming contribution which another country, the United States, have made.

I have not got the actual figures of our contribution at the present time, but when we see what they are I think it will be found that an enormous proportion of the whole burden has been borne by the United States, and that the least we can do would be to accord that country some consideration. We have quite enough real achievements in our record without endeavouring to minimize the legitimate and rightful contributions of great allies towards the common cause which we support.

Some recognition of the United States' efforts should have been contained in the Gracious Speech.

In his speech of October 31, Churchill argued that Attlee must now call an election. 'The House of Commons is not at its best,' he said, 'when Parties are so evenly balanced and on the verge of another appeal,' and he continued:

The increasing rigidity of party discipline deprives debate of much of its value as a means of influencing opinion except out of doors. All kinds of uncertainties are created in every direction; all kinds of animosities and rancours are fed and worked up, on both sides, I fully admit—[Hon. Members: 'Oh.'] Certainly; and I cannot think it good for the country that this should continue. The Prime Minister deliberately tries to increase and prolong this uncertainty.

'Of course it is very natural,' Churchill ended, 'that anyone should

[1] Note by Lord Camrose, 26 October 1950: Camrose papers.

like to feel that he can keep the rest of his countrymen on tenterhooks and that we are always awaiting the moment when he shall give the signal. All I can say is that I am quite satisfied that the right hon. Gentleman is indulging his personal power in these matters in a manner most costly to the community and harmful to all large enduring interests of the State.'[1]

On November 2 Churchill dined at the Other Club, the Club's first meeting since the death in early October of Field Marshal Smuts. In the privacy of the Club, Churchill recalled his friend of more than five decades:

Jan Smuts loved to come here. He planned to meet us during the visit to be paid after the celebrations of his eightieth birthday. Now he is dead. We must feel, in view of his manifold achievements and the place that he held in the world, that we have lost our greatest living member.

I remember when we first met. I was wet and draggle-tailed. He was examining me on the part I had played in the affair of the armoured train—a difficult moment.

At our next meeting at the Colonial Office, I was an under-secretary. The officials were alarmed at the prospect of a young and untried minister encountering this formidable and sinister man, a sort of compound of Molotov and Vyshinsky. Accordingly a large screen was erected in the corner of the room, behind which Eddie Marsh was installed—the idea being that if I said anything dangerous to the state, Eddie could deny that I had said it.

We are right to mark his loss, breaking our rules and customs. Long may his name be honoured and cherished.[2]

Two weeks later, ashamed at having left his letter of condolence for so long, Churchill decided to write to Smuts's widow. 'That morning,' Denis Kelly later recalled, 'he shut himself away in his bedroom. He wouldn't let anyone come near him. He wanted to be alone. Smuts was the last equivalent statesman of his era, the last of his generation with whom he could talk as an equal.'[3] 'Please accept my deepest sympathy in your sorrow and deprivation,' Churchill wrote to Mrs Smuts, and he added: 'I know how vain are words in such sadness, and how much worse it is for those who stay than for those who go. But there must be comfort in the proofs of admiration and gratitude wh have been evoked all over the world for a warrior-statesman and philosopher who was probably more fitted to guide struggling and blundering humanity through its sufferings and perils towards a better day, than anyone who lived in any country during his epoch.'[4]

[1] Speech of 31 October 1950: *Hansard*.
[2] Speech of 2 November 1950: Colin R. Coote, *The Other Club*, London 1971, page 105.
[3] Denis Kelly recollections: in conversation with the author, 11 February 1987.
[4] 'My dear Mrs Smuts', 19 November 1950: Churchill papers, 2/176.

On November 6 Churchill spoke again, on the Housing Amendment of the Debate on the Address. It was a long, detailed and hard-hitting speech, quite remarkable for someone who was within four weeks of his seventy-sixth birthday. 'I had been led to expect,' he said, 'that I was to undergo very unpleasant ordeals on this day. The Prime Minister—he is not here at the moment—expressed his confidence that the Minister of Health would "wipe the floor" with me. As I have only just taken the floor and he has already exhausted his right of speaking, I naturally feel a sensation of liberation and relief. But I cannot feel that this prospect, or the language of the Prime Minister, did justice to the grave issue open between the two parties and still less to the housing problem.'

The suffering caused to millions of people in Britain by the lack of houses was, Churchill declared, 'a tragedy'.

At one point in his speech Churchill referred to the Minister of Health, Aneurin Bevan. 'I do not believe he is as bad as he makes himself out,' he said, and added: 'But I will say this to him. Hate is a bad guide. I have never considered myself at all a good hater—though I recognize that from moment to moment it has added stimulus to pugnacity.' People who had been denied an opportunity in life were deeply embittered, 'but the Minister of Health does not belong to that class'.

One problem which Churchill wished to raise was the weakness of the building trade, on which all depended. His remarks soon led to Labour protests, which Churchill scornfully rejected:

There is no trade in the country which can more readily adapt itself to a static condition than the building trade. They would like a progressive condition but they are quite ready, after the rough time which they have had in the last generation—I have seen it: the first to be called up for mobilization and so on and the first to be turned off when building slackens and so on— [Interruption.] I am the author of the Labour Exchanges and the first Unemployment Insurance Act. I was in these matters years before many hon. Gentlemen opposite were able to take an adult interest in them. I say that they are quite ready, after their experiences, to settle down into a static condition.

The fact that the Government had limited house building to 200,000 new houses in 1951, Churchill insisted—and to that many only as a result of Conservative pressure—'undoubtedly has most evil and discouraging effects'. The 'resolute aim' of the Conservative Party would be to raise the rate of building to 300,000 a year, nor would that be a 'static' limit. 'We shall thrust towards it,' he said, 'with all our life, strength and wit, but once this figure gleams upon our horizon—"forward again" must be the policy and the order.'

It was during this Housing debate that the first public reference took place to Churchill's growing deafness. It came from Churchill himself, when he was answering an accusation made by Lloyd George's daughter Megan that a licence had been granted for the renovation of the Carlton Club:

I speak as a lifelong friend of her father and her family, and I feel that she should have verified the facts before making the statement about the Carlton Club claiming a licence to rebuild the bomb-damaged premises. We have given up all hope of ever rebuilding the Carlton Club and no application for a licence has ever been made. The site is being disposed of. Speaking as one who lived in her father's generation, I do not consider that prefixing the words 'I am informed that' relieves one of all responsibility.

Lady Megan Lloyd George: I am sorry to interrupt the right hon. Gentleman, but when I was informed that that was not the case I withdrew the statement. [Hon. Members: 'No.'] Certainly I did so.

Mr Churchill: I was here at the time but I suffer a little from deafness and did not realize that the charge had been withdrawn.

Lady Megan Lloyd George: I said that I was very glad that it was so and that no licence had been granted.

Mr Churchill: Honour is completely satisfied on both sides.

Churchill ended his speech with two quotations from a poem which the Liberal MP Charles Masterman 'used to repeat to me'.[1] They were by the poet 'and the teacher' William Watson, who, 'speaking of the hard social conditions of the life of the people', asked:

> 'Is there no room for victories here,
> No fields for deeds of fame?'

'But I have found another verse of William Watson,' Churchill told the House, 'which I remembered at the same time':

> 'The England of my heart is she,
> Long hoped, and long deferred,
> That ever promises to be,
> And ever breaks her word.'

Churchill then asked, with passion: 'Why should she always break her word to those who love her so well and defend her safety and honour with their lives? Now is the time, here is the occasion, and this housing issue is the deed to sweep that hard reproach away.'[2]

On November 8, during a short debate on procedure, the Con-

---

[1] Charles Masterman, who had died in 1927 at the age of fifty-three, served as Under-Secretary of State to Churchill at the Home Office in 1919.

[2] Speech of 6 November 1950: *Hansard*.

servatives decided to spring a surprise division, and to defeat the Government by catching it unawares. 'At 4.35 the Bell rang,' Henry Channon noted in his diary:

I woke from my deep siesta in the library and went to vote. As I came through the Chamber, Winston seized me and asked: 'How are the numbers going?' I went back and asked, and heard we were 235 which I told him and, at that very second, Patrick Buchan-Hepburn interrupted saying 'We have won! By six!'

Winston smiled and remarked 'That is some sugar for the birds' and the tellers announced the Government defeat but not—I fear—their downfall. Nevertheless they looked glum and murmured 'Snap division', etc. But there is no question of their resignation.[1]

In his war memoirs, Churchill had reached 1944, and a wealth of material which had led him to decide upon a sixth volume. On October 24 he had sent Bill Deakin 'some rough notes I have put down' about the Greek mutiny of April 1944. More was needed, Churchill added, about 'how the Communist aggression developed in Greece'; the story was important, he explained, 'because it leads up in Volume VI (to come), to my flight with Anthony to Athens on Christmas Eve, 1944, and to all that business there, which was much condemned in England and America at the time, but was afterwards carried through by the British Socialist and American Governments'. Churchill added: 'Thus the theme runs on,' and he ended, by way of encouragement: 'Make the best contribution which you can.'[2]

On November 1 General Pownall sent Churchill copies of the discussions at two meetings, in January 1944, at which the Mulberry Harbour for the Normandy landings had been discussed. 'I will send you a more general paper on the development of Mulberry in a few days' time,' he wrote.[3]

From Emery Reves there came, on November 3, a word of warning about the proposed sixth volume. 'As things stand now it is certain that you will finish and publish Volume V,' Reves wrote, 'but in one year, or in 1952, you may be in office, there may be a war, and you may be unable to publish your story on Yalta. If you would plan to publish this story in a separate book, there would be no harm in

---

[1] Channon diary, 8 November 1950: Robert Rhodes James (editor), *Chips*, page 449.

[2] 'My dear Bill', 24 October 1950: Churchill papers, 4/24. Bill Deakin had recently been appointed Warden of St Antony's College, Oxford, a new foundation.

[3] 'Mr Churchill', 1 November 1950: Churchill papers, 4/333. The meetings were Staff Conference, Chiefs of Staff Committee No. 22 (O) of 1944 (24 January 1944) and Staff Conference, Chiefs of Staff Committee No. 29 (Operations) of 1944 (31 January 1944).

delay, or even in not publishing such a book. But if that story is planned to be the Sixth Volume of your *Memoirs On The Second World War*, there is a danger that this work, which will certainly go down in History as your greatest literary accomplishment, will remain unfinished.'[1]

In the House of Commons on November 13, during a debate on the Council of Europe, Churchill asked Bevin to 'cast his mind back to the year before—to the Hague Congress, at which time he had used his utmost influence to boycott and forbid Socialist members to attend', although, Churchill added, to Conservative cheers, 'I sincerely believe this was a matter very dear to their hearts.' Bevin replied that there had been 'trouble from this so-called European movement, not always in the open, and it had been extremely difficult to carry on negotiations with this kind of semi-sabotage going on behind the scenes'. Angered, Churchill retorted: 'You are the arch saboteur.'[2]

Churchill and his wife had been invited to dine on the following night with Bevin, to say goodbye to the departing United States Ambassador, Lew Douglas. On the day of the dinner, Churchill wrote to Douglas, to whom he had also intended to bring one of his own paintings as a farewell gift:

My dear Lew,

After the incident in the House of Commons last night I do not feel it would be a good thing for us to dine with Mr and Mrs Bevin this evening, as it would be misunderstood abroad and also it would be embarrassing to meet him.

This letter therefore is to bid you and your Wife my affectionate Au revoir.

I am sending round tonight the picture duly signed and packed up.

Yours ever,

W[3]

Speeches in Parliament, invitations elsewhere, literary work at Chartwell, each contributed to what Churchill described to Sir Ivone Kirkpatrick on November 19 as 'the tremendous pressure of work and events that I am subjected to at the moment'.[4] So busy was Churchill that he declined two invitations to meet Queen Juliana of The Netherlands, first at Dover in his capacity as Lord Warden of the Cinque Ports and then at the Guildhall. On the morning of the Guildhall

[1] 'Dear Mr Churchill', 'Private', 3 November 1950: Churchill papers, 4/63.

[2] Speech of 13 November 1950: *Hansard*.

[3] 'My dear Lew', 14 November 1950: Churchill papers, 2/168.

[4] 'My dear Ivone Kirkpatrick', 19 November 1950: Churchill papers, 2/171. Kirkpatrick was then High Commissioner for the British Zone of Germany. Churchill had promised him a painting.

welcome, Clementine Churchill wrote to her husband about this double absence:

My darling,

I am sad that Queen Juliana should have felt hurt in her personal feelings & offended in her National Pride by your absence at Dover. (The Lord Warden of The Cinque Ports is the first person to greet a foreign sovereign visiting these shores.)

I must also take some blame for having too easily agreed (or was it perhaps my suggestion!) that we should not go to the Guildhall to-day & join in the City Welcome. I fear that this smaller defection will be noticed now. It will grieve me if we should lose the affection of Queen Juliana & particularly of her Mother who flew here specially to honour you & to give you the precious casket of Marlborough letters.[1] And you are the God Father of the little half-blind daughter whom they cherish most of all.

Do you think Darling you would wait upon the Queen or if that is impossible, write to her in your own 'paw' & say you are sorry.

Don't say you are too old! because you are as young as a game cock & the whole World knows about the flight from Copenhagen to London & on to Newmarket & Blackpool.

It was just a slip, because you *are* Monarchial No. 1 & value tradition, form and ceremony.

Your Clemmie but with ears & tail drooping.[2]

On November 23 Churchill went to Harrow School for the 'Songs'. 'The years slip by with extraordinary rapidity,' he said, 'or they seem to do so I suppose when you have to count so many. . . .'[3]

On November 24 Churchill sent the King one of the very first copies of the American edition of Volume 4 to reach him. 'This will not be published here till the summer,' he explained.[4] When reading Churchill's volumes, the King replied, 'I always find that my heart beats faster. They remind me so vividly of the days through which we lived & when we were so much together.'[5]

The new volume, wrote Sarah Churchill to her father from New

---

[1] On 9 May 1946 Churchill had been presented by the Dutch Government with a considerable number of letters written by the 1st Duke of Marlborough. His speech of thanks was recorded at the time (BBC Written Archives Centre, Library No. 9625).

[2] Letter of 22 November 1950: Churchill papers, 1/47. On 24 November 1950 Churchill wrote in his own hand to Queen Wilhelmina (Queen Juliana's mother): 'Madam, It gives me gt pleasure to send Yr Majesty the Third Volume of my war memoirs wh has just reached me from the bookbinders. The visit over here of Queen Juliana has been a wonderful success. With my humble duty I remain, Your Majesty's devoted servant, Winston S. Churchill.' (Archives of the House of Orange-Nassau.)

[3] 'Dr Moore, Ladies and Gentlemen', 23 November 1950: Churchill papers, 2/336.

[4] 'Sir', 24 November 1950: Churchill papers, 2/171. Volume 4, 'The Hinge of Fate', was published in the United States on 27 November 1950. The British edition was not published until 3 August 1951. (The American first printing was 70,000 copies, the British 275,000 copies.)

[5] 'My dear Winston', from Buckingham Palace, 26 November 1950: Churchill papers, 2/171.

York, 'is so, so brilliant—vivid, powerful thrilling', and she added: 'It had a great effect here—they loved the wise, measured, truthful account—and I loved your wonderful warm generosity in your unstinted praise of them—giving always credit where credit was due, yet always holding us, and our own, proudly & firmly.'[1]

November 30 was Churchill's seventy-sixth birthday. That day, speaking in the Foreign Affairs debate in the House of Commons, Churchill referred to the 'sour aftermath' of both world wars. But he wished to draw attention to certain differences in the two post-war periods:

After the First War, when the victors had disarmed the Germans and their allies, no powerful organized army remained upon the scene except the French Army. After this war the armed might of Russia has emerged steadily year by year, almost month by month, as a rock shows more and more above an ebbing tide.

The second difference, which arose out of the realization of the first, was that the United States, instead of retiring into isolation, instead of demanding full and prompt repayment of debts and disinteresting herself in Europe and even in the League of Nations, of which she had been one of the founders, has come forward step by step as the knowledge of the situation has dawned upon her and has made the great counterpoise upon which the freedom and the future of our civilization depends.

This fundamental change in the policy of the United States constitutes, in my view, the best hope for the salvation of Christian civilization and democracy from Communist and Russian conquest and control. I hope, therefore, that we shall regard it as our first objective not to separate ourselves in action or in understanding or in sympathy in any degree, however slight, that can be avoided from the United States.

Dangerous as it was to make a prediction, Churchill said, he would make one 'in all good faith, and without official knowledge'. It was this: that 'a major attack by Russia in Europe is unlikely in the near future, and that it will not be provoked or produced by the modest measures of defence now being so slowly, so tardily and ineffectively developed up to the present by the Atlantic and Western Powers. Even if our preparations developed more rapidly, a long period must elapse before they could offset the Russian superiority, even if the Russian strength itself were not increased meanwhile.' It was on this that he founded his hope 'that we still have time', that there was 'still a breathing space for us to pursue the policy of seeking an understanding, and for us also to pursue the essential counterpart and foundation of any such hope, namely, the building up of a more reasonable measure of defensive strength'. Churchill added:

[1] 'Darling Papa', 27 November 1950: Churchill papers, 1/47.

This may be a vain hope. I may live, perhaps, to be mocked at if proved wrong by events. It is, at any rate, the working hypothesis of my thought in these anxious and agonizing times.

Therefore I am in favour of efforts to reach a settlement with Soviet Russia as soon as a suitable opportunity presents itself, and of making those efforts while the immense and measureless superiority of the United States atomic bomb organization offsets the Soviet predominance in every other military respect and gives us the means to talk together in a friendly and dignified manner and, at least, as equals.

It was his hope, Churchill added, that after matters had been 'stabilized' in the Far East, a conference would take place 'which will not merely be like those of which we have had too many in the past, of two sides arguing against each other in the glare of publicity, but that the decisive conversations will take place in confidence, in privacy and even in secrecy, and will be conducted at the highest levels'.

Once again, Churchill put forward, as he had done at Edinburgh six months earlier, the idea of a Conference of the leading Powers at which a genuine and comprehensive peace and reconciliation, or at least a means of living together without imminent danger of war, might be proposed and procured. Such a Conference, he declared at the end of his 'birthday' speech, indeed even the process leading to it, 'gives the best hope of avoiding a third world war, not by appeasement of opponents from weakness, but by wise measures, fair play from strength, and the proof of unconquerable resolve'.[1]

On November 30 President Truman announced at a press conference that he would, if necessary, use the atomic bomb in Korea, where the Chinese had just made a massive and successful counter-attack. Attlee immediately decided to fly to Washington, and, on December 3, the eve of his departure, sent Churchill a 'Top Secret' letter explaining the circumstances in which the clause in the Quebec Agreement of August 1944 'was allowed to lapse' which provided 'that neither the Americans nor ourselves would use the bomb against third parties without each other's consent'. Attlee explained that:

In negotiations after the war the Americans showed themselves most anxious to get rid of this clause and, indeed, of what might be called the political as opposed to the technical provisions of the Quebec Agreement. This was not so much because they wished to escape the obligations of the Agreement, but because its existence put them in a very embarrassing position with Congress. It was, as you know, a secret agreement of which Congress has not been

[1] Speech of 30 November 1950: *Hansard*.

told and it obviously went much further than the normal scope of an Executive Agreement such as the President has power to conclude, nor did they think it practicable to get a treaty embodying its terms ratified by the Senate.

The best solution for them therefore was that it should be allowed to lapse with the exception of those technical provisions providing for interchange of information and sharing of raw materials which were continued under an informal agreement known as the *modus vivendi* concluded in January 1948.

Attlee went on to explain to Churchill that the British Government had been 'equally anxious to get rid of the fourth clause which prevented us from making use of atomic energy for industrial purposes except on terms to be specified by the President'. Attlee's letter ended:

Finally, and most important, we realised that harmony of action in such a vital matter as the use of the weapon must in the last resort depend upon the degree of friendship and understanding prevailing between our two countries and not on any written agreement, one of the original authors of which[1] was no longer alive.

I do not of course for a moment wish to detract from the very great importance to us of the Quebec Agreement during the war. You will remember very well the difficulty you had in getting the Americans to conclude it, and it was a great achievement. But I think you may also agree that in the quite different circumstances of peace the secret war-time agreement no longer had the same character as a binding understanding between the two countries.[2]

From Lord Cherwell came confirmation that, despite Churchill's belief in it, the Quebec Agreement could not long have survived the war. 'After the war of course,' Cherwell explained, 'Congress intervened and passed the McMahon Act, which strictly speaking would have stopped all collaboration. Presumably if the President had tried to oppose it, praying in aid Roosevelt's agreement with you, the agreement would have been declared unconstitutional and ultra vires.' Cherwell added, in support of Attlee's position: 'Broadly, therefore, I do not think the Government can be blamed for negotiating a new agreement after the war. Whether they could have got better terms is another matter. But I am sure America would not have allowed us to assert a veto in perpetuity on her use of the bomb on the strength of the secret agreement between you and Roosevelt.'[3]

On December 14 Churchill again spoke on the international situation, praising Attlee's recent visit to Washington to confer with Truman, although, he commented, 'it seems to me that five years is

---

[1] President Roosevelt.

[2] 'My dear Churchill', 'Top Secret', 3 December 1950: Churchill papers, 2/28.

[3] 'My dear Winston', 6 December 1950: Churchill papers, 2/28. Churchill noted on the top of Cherwell's letter: 'Show to Mr Eden today in H/C.'

rather a long interval'. After welcoming Attlee's statement about Anglo-American unity, Churchill went on to warn of the dangers to Europe of the continued exclusion of Germany from any European defence force:

It is more than nine months since I pointed out that no effective defence of Europe was possible without the armed strength of Germany. The movement of opinion in that direction has been continual, but nothing has been done. No agreement has been reached, and meanwhile Germany lies even more undefended than other European countries under the menace of Communist and Russian aggression.

The months slip quickly away all the time. Several years have already been wasted, frittered away. The overwhelming Russian military power towers up against us, committees are multiplied, papers are written, words outpoured and one declaration succeeds another, but nothing in the slightest degree in proportion to the scale of events or to their urgency has been done.

Churchill then turned to the question of negotiations with the Soviet Union, negotiations which he had already been advocating for many months:

I am strongly in favour of every effort being made by every means, to secure a fair and reasonable settlement with Russia. I should, however, be failing in frankness to the House, and to some of those who agree with me upon this matter, to whom I am much opposed in many ways, if I did not make it clear at this stage that we must not place undue hopes upon the success of any negotiations which may be undertaken.

It is our duty—and a duty which we owe to the cause of peace and to our own conscience—to leave no effort unmade that wisdom and fair play can suggest, and that patience can bring forward. But on this side of the House we have never contemplated that if negotiations failed we should abandon any of the great causes for which we have stood in the past, and for which the United Nations Organization stands today.

Churchill's speech continued:

The declaration of the Prime Minister that there will be no appeasement also commands almost universal support. It is a good slogan for the country. It seems to me, however, that in this House it requires to be more precisely defined. What we really mean, I think, is no appeasement through weakness or fear.

Appeasement in itself may be good or bad according to the circumstances. Appeasement from weakness and fear is alike futile and fatal. Appeasement from strength is magnanimous and noble and might be the surest and perhaps the only path to world peace.

When nations or individuals get strong they are often truculent and bullying, but when they are weak they become better mannered. But this is the reverse of what is healthy and wise.

I have always been astonished, having seen the end of these two wars, how

difficult it is to make people understand Roman wisdom, 'Spare the conquered and war down the proud'. I think I will go so far as to say it in the
original: Parcere subjectis, et debellare superbos.[1] The modern practice has
too often been, punish the defeated and grovel to the strong.

Churchill then addressed himself to the argument 'that we must
never use the atomic bomb until, or unless, it has been used against us
first. In other words, you must never fire until you have been shot
dead.' That, he said, 'seems to me undoubtedly a silly thing to say
and a still more imprudent position to adopt', which would 'certainly
bring war nearer', and he went on to explain:

The deterrent effect of the atomic bomb is at the present time almost our
sole defence. Its potential use is the only lever by which we can hope to
obtain reasonable consideration in an attempt to make a peaceful settlement
with Soviet Russia. If they had superiority, or even something like equality in
this weapon with the United States, I cannot feel any assurance that they
would be restrained by the conscientious scruples or moral inhibitions which
are often so vocal in this country. It would certainly be a poor service to the
cause of peace to free them from all cause of apprehension until they were in
every respect ready to strike.

Soviet power, Churchill argued, could not be confronted, 'or even
placated', with any hope of success 'if we were in these years of tension
through which we are passing to deprive ourselves of the atomic bomb,
or to prevent its use by announcing gratuitously self-imposed restrictions'.[2]

Churchill's speech in support of the Labour Government's foreign
policy was a powerful re-inforcement for Attlee, who, that week, had
finally committed himself to German rearmament. He and Bevin were
now awaiting only Eisenhower's appointment, on December 19, as
Supreme Commander of the North Atlantic Treaty Organization, to
make this new commitment public. Attlee and Bevin had made the
decision to support German rearmament against the wishes of most
of their Cabinet colleagues. They knew however, that despite continuing reluctance inside both the Labour Party and the Foreign Office to
accept German rearmament, they could rely on Churchill to bring
the Conservatives—half the British people—to support the policy and
make it bi-partisan.

---

[1] One of the so-called 'Roman arts', as opposed to Greek virtues, described by Anchises to
Aeneas in the sixth book of the Aenead. This translation, which Churchill often quoted, had
been given to him by his friend F. E. Smith. The phrase can also be translated: 'to impose
civilization peacefully and to beat down the proud'.
[2] Speech of 14 December 1950: *Hansard*.

32

Return to Marrakech, 1950

TURNING from the concerns of world and Parliamentary strife in search of somewhere to paint and to write in sunshine, on 17 December 1950 Churchill left London for Marrakech, and for his much-favoured Hôtel de la Mamounia. With him were General Pownall and Denis Kelly, Miss Sturdee and Miss Gemmell, a detective, Sergeant Murray, and Norman McGowan, the new valet. Also on the expedition was Lord Cherwell, and his valet Mr Harvey.[1]

On his arrival at Marrakech, Churchill was met by the British Consul in Casablanca, Hugh Pullar, who had driven all the way from Casablanca to greet him. At dinner that night, Pullar later recalled, Churchill asked him 'various questions about the Atlas Mountains, how far it was to Timbuktoo(!) and if I could recommend any places where he could paint'.[2]

On December 18 Churchill sent his first telegram home. 'Quiet day,' it read. 'Began picture from hotel. Hope all well. How is Rufus. Many thoughts, W.'[3] On the following day Churchill dictated a full account of the scene:

My darling,
We arrived after a perfect flight, almost to the minute—seven hours. Everything in the hotel is excellent and I have begun two daubs—one from the hotel tower and the other today from our old picnic spot at a slightly different angle. The river is entirely changed. It flows a hundred yards away from where it did, and the dam has been replaced by a bridge which they are still building.

---

[1] Lord Cherwell had long been a vegetarian, to Churchill's puzzlement. But whenever he was at Chartwell or Hyde Park Gate, his needs were catered for with great care. So too on the flight; while Churchill had wine, hot consommé, smoked salmon, fillet of steak, fruit salad, cheese and coffee, Cherwell had, on Churchill's instructions, milk, vegetable soup, egg mayonnaise, spaghetti and cheese, fruit salad, cheese and coffee. (Note of 17 December 1950: Churchill papers, 1/83.)

[2] Hugh Pullar recollections: letter to the author, 15 March 1987.

[3] Telegram despatched 18 December 1950: Churchill papers, 1/83. Rufus was Churchill's poodle, Rufus II, the gift of Walter Graebner, after Rufus I had been run over and killed during the Conservative Party Conference at Brighton in October 1947.

We have six of those rooms on the verandah and everybody, I think, is comfortable. General Juin has come here and is calling upon me this evening as I come back (so punctually) before 4 o'clock from painting by the river. We had a picnic under the olive trees which you will remember.

After General Juin, the Glaoui is coming. He has sent some beautiful honey and other presents.

We have so far made no plans. Monday's papers arrived this morning, Tuesday, so we are up to date. The sun is lovely and warm, but all the time one is aware that the wind is cooler than it ought to be. I wrap up assiduously.

I asked Dr Diot to come to see me in order to see how *he* was getting on. He has been frightfully ill and, after twenty-five years' hard service in Morocco, he has been removed to take charge of the laboratory. He says he has a highly competent successor, to whom he is going to introduce me in case I need him at any time.

The aeroplane and its crew and its two hostesses are settling down, and the crew are in the other hotel. They seemed to be looking forward to their month here so much.

Alas Timbuktoo is 1,500 miles, so it cannot be considered. However the British Consul at Casablanca, a young man, who met me at the airfield here and came to dinner afterwards, says there is a far better trip the other way— left-handed instead of right. When you go through the mountains you come to two lovely native cities with extraordinary springs of blue water and rocky gorges, which seem by all accounts to be most paintacious.

It is six hours' motoring, and then next day six hours more, but there is a good hotel with central heating at each place run by the same management as the Mamounia; so it may be that later on I shall make a dart in that direction. At present I am settling myself down to the idea that time does not count and that Marrakech is the centre of the still existing universe. (Poor Beast). It looks as if a similar stabilization is developing in Korea.[1]

I try to put the world out of my thoughts as much as possible, but somehow, indeed, it intrudes its ugly face from time to time. Somehow, when one detaches oneself, and has a new scene around, the salient points stand out more clearly.

I am asking Diana, and Duncan if he or she or they can come about the 4th or 5th, when the Prof has to go home for the Oxford term. The change has done him good. He had the best night last night for months.

I find it is possible to telephone from here and I have got a call booked through to you tonight between 8 and 9 o'clock—three minutes for 27/-. (Done—it was worth it.)

The book Randolph gave me, *The God that Failed*, is an impressive study of Communist mentality by those who have recovered from the disease.[2]

---

[1] By 31 October 1950 United Nations forces had reached almost to the Manchurian border, North Korea's border with Communist China. On 26 November 1950 Chinese forces, who were already inside North Korea, counter-attacked, and the United Nations forces retreated. Within a few months, the line of battle had stabilized a few miles north of Seoul, half way down the peninsula.

[2] *The God that Failed*, subtitled 'Six Studies in Communism', introduced by Richard Crossman MP, first published in January 1950, was a personal examination by six former Communists of

I shall be delighted to hear your news and also how Rufus is bearing up. I am sure he will soon make friends with Hedy.

All my best love my darling Clemmie

from your ever loving husband

W[1]

'All well here,' Churchill reported to his wife on December 21, but added, less enthusiastically: 'Alas, lumbago.' [2]

On December 22 Clementine Churchill was sent an account of her husband's activities by Miss Sturdee, who had gone with him to help with the secretarial work on the war memoirs:

Mr Churchill settled in at once and seems quite happy. He seems conscious all the time that the climate here can be colder than it looks, and so fortunately there has been no trouble so far about getting him to wrap up well and be home early. . . .

We all had a lovely day at Ourika and picnicked in the same spot. Today is so brilliant and warm again that it has been decided that, after an early luncheon at 12 sharp in the hotel, Mr Churchill should go there again and work on his picture. Sergeant Murray and Norman are going on ahead to set up the apparatus, and General Pownall is going to see that the operation for today is ended in good time.

Lord Cherwell is taking care and says he seems to be better. Alas he is having to make plans to return about the 7th as he is needed then in Oxford. He takes endless photographs. . . .

I expect Mr Churchill has told you all his news. He was so much pleased to be able to talk to you on such a clear line to London the other evening. The most important thing to report really is that Mr Churchill is in good health and happy. He is making quite good progress with the book and is pleased with the two paintings he has started. I think he wishes you were here; but perhaps you will be able to get away later on.

We all think about you all at No. 28 so often. Our thoughts will be with you at home especially on Christmas Day. [3]

On Christmas Day it was Churchill's turn to write again, the first part of his letter being dictated to one of his two secretaries:

---

how they had come to Communism, and how they had been disillusioned by it. The six were Arthur Koestler, Ignazio Silone, Richard Wright, André Gide (presented by Dr Enid Starkie), Louis Fischer and Stephen Spender. Crossman ended his introduction: 'One thing is clear from studying the varied experiences of these six men. Silone was joking when he said to Togliatti that the final battle would be between the Communists and the ex-Communists. But no one who has not wrestled with Communism as a philosophy and Communists as political opponents can really understand the values of Western Democracy. The Devil once lived in Heaven, and those who have not met him are unlikely to recognize an angel when they see one.'

[1] Letter of 19 December 1950, Hôtel de la Mamounia, Marrakech: Spencer-Churchill papers. Churchill kept a carbon copy in his own papers: Churchill papers, 1/83.

[2] Telegram despatched 21 December 1950: Churchill papers, 1/83.

[3] Letter of 22 December 1950: Churchill papers, 1/47.

My darling Clemmie

How would you like to meet me in Paris about the 15th for three or four days? We could go to Bennie's quiet hotel (? Hotel Maurice). There are several people I ought to get into touch with. Besides there are shops, theatres, galleries and restaurants. We would be independent of the Embassy but no doubt they would wish us to lunch and dine there to see some political notabilities. Send me a telegram whether you like this idea or not, so that I can make plans.

I really do not think it would be worth your while to come here. Kelly leaves here on the 3rd or 4th. Diana arrives on the 5th. The Prof wishes to go home on the 8th. Pownall will stay till, say, the 14th, and if the Paris plan comes off will fly back in the big plane with me to Paris. You and I could both go back together in it on the 18th, 19th or 20th from Paris. Bill Deakin will probably come here with his wife somewhere around the 4th or 5th. Also the Graebners but that is their affair with *Life* and the *NY Times*.

We had a great dinner with the Glaoui. The D'Hautevilles came and both Miss Sturdee and Miss Gemmell. Everybody liked shoving their paws into the dish and remembered with pleasure that fingers were made before forks. The Glaoui is as old as I am but quite lively. He pretends to know neither French nor English, but I believe he understands everything that is said at least in French. After dinner there were dances—three troupes of five each with tomtoms, the first Berber females, the second Arab females and the third Berber males. I never saw dancing, music, or the human form presented in such unattractive guise—the women with sullen expressions on their faces, stamping their feet on the floor, the men in the same vogue but more repellent. All were dressed up in quilts and blankets—they looked like bundles of cotton waste. However no one could say it was not highly respectable. The music brays and squawks and tomtoms, and the singing, which was maintained throughout, was a masterly compendium of discords. I have a great regard for the Glaoui who no doubt has endured all this and many other afflictions in his journey through this vale of sin and even more woe.

I have been painting for a few hours every day. We went to Ourika where the river comes out of the mountains, and the pebbles—you know. It is entirely different but I found a good place. On the whole a better landscape than any I have tried of this scene. I went back again three days later, but though the sun shone brilliantly at Marrakech, the clouds round the mountains cut it off just before my effect came. I am hoping to go tomorrow or the next day. Meanwhile I have advanced the picture by working from photographs in the studio. I have one other picture on the stocks. There has been quite a lot of cloud in the air. Today has been grey with hardly a gleam.

Everybody enjoyed themselves very much last night at the Christmas celebrations. I turned up at the hour appointed—a quarter to 12—and was introduced to the company, who loudly applauded to the strains of 'Lillie Marlene'. (I am terrified of this getting into my mind again. I have several antidotes ready.)

The Governor of Gibraltar and his wife are here and they came to luncheon this Christmas Day. Also the British Consul-General at Rabat, Sir Cyril Cane, and his daughter. The Governor, General Anderson, invited me to go to Gibraltar on my way back. I suppose I have seen it ten times, so I did not commit myself. His wife is a magnificent Tory and helped Randolph to oppose Malcolm MacDonald when he stood for the Scottish Islands in the far north after we came back from Marrakech fifteen years ago. (This is my fifth visit here.)[1]

My day is most tranquil and I do absolutely nothing that I do not want to. The food is the best you can get. I have discovered Marennes oysters—excellent. I get at least eight or nine hours sleep. The weather is sharply cool and there are too many clouds. However I hope for a sunshine spell not only in the garden but in the foothills of the Atlas.

We are developing our plan to go to Wowowow, which they are going to call it in future—namely the left-handed excursion over the mountains. But I shall probably wait till Diana arrives as she would like the adventure.

The one thing that has gone best of all is the one thing that is most needful—namely the book. I have been here tonight eight days, and eight chapters of Volume VI, Book 12, have been sent to the Printer. These are largely, in their present stage, stringing together of telegrams, minutes and other documents with their introductions and tail pieces. However Volume VI, though not yet a 'literary masterpiece', at which we must always aim, is nevertheless an important commercial property. Nobody could sort these telegrams but me, who alone know the sequence and the value. I have worked as much as eight hours a day in my bed, which is very comfortable.

I have received two letters from you. I am so glad you have got a new secretary. She certainly seems magnificent, and we shall have two historians in the house. I am very sorry Pennylope is going.[2] I suppose by the time you get this Maria and Christopher will be back in the burry. I earnestly hope that all is well at Chartwell. The little fish, the Black Mollies, the golden orfes in the pools (but they do not eat now), the black swans (I hope the lakes are unfrozen and they can go back to their various domains). All these I think of, and then there is the sulky, illmannered cat and poor, dear Rufus. I hope he had a good howl but I expect he is reconciled by now to my absence.

Much depends for us all upon the impending battle in Korea. I hope they have made a proper defensive line across the peninsula, with mine-fields and barbed wire and machine guns, well posted with a good artillery organized in the rear. They have had three weeks to do this and if they have behaved

---

[1] In volume 4 of his war memoirs (pages 621–2) Churchill wrote, of Marrakech, that it was '"the Paris of the Sahara", where all the caravans had come from Central Africa for centuries to be heavily taxed en route by the tribes in the mountains and afterwards swindled in the Marrakech markets, receiving the returns, which they greatly valued, of the gay life of the city, including fortune-tellers, snake-charmers, masses of food and drink, and on the whole the largest and most elaborately organised brothels in the African continent. All these institutions were of long and ancient repute.'

[2] Penelope Hampden-Wall, Clementine Churchill's London secretary and companion (now Mrs Neville Barwick). She was succeeded by Miss Heather Mason.

in a sensible way they should be able to teach the Chinese the sort of lessons we learned upon the Somme and at Passchendaele. I have bet General Pownall ten shillings to one that, if the Chinese attack, they will be repulsed with heavy slaughter. After all they need not go unless they want to, and we are never likely to run short of Chinese.

Churchill then added, in his own hand:

I hope the tale will please you. I came here to play, but so far it has only been *work* under physically agreeable conditions.

You have my fondest love. I do pray that all is well with all of you. I am looking forward to come home again. But here I have no distraction & can make extensive progress with my mainstay,

Give my love to all & believe me your devoted & ever loving husband

W

PS, My eyes are closing—good night.[1]

With the Korean war much in his mind, on December 27 Churchill sent a New Year telegram to General MacArthur. 'Remembering the Somme and Passchendaele,' he wrote, 'I have many hopes.' As for Randolph's leg wound, Churchill told MacArthur: 'His wound is healed.'[2]

Painting excursions were a special feature of Churchill's life at Marrakech; so too was sketching and drawing at the luncheon table. Denis Kelly later recalled:

He saw warmth and colour in everything around him. At the height of the war in Korea I watched him painting a landscape on the plain which stretches from Marrakech to the Atlas Mountains. The place he had chosen looked uninteresting—the snow-peaks were far away and we were sitting at the foot of a dry gully with a gaunt tree at its head and flanked by sombre rocks and bushes, but as he worked, it came alive. A dab of paint and a leaf on a top branch flicked into focus against the grey sky; some steady brush-strokes and the rocks glowed with their innate colours. It was as if bright sunlight had suddenly infused the winter scene.

It was the same with his manuscripts. By the time a page was ready for re-printing, with deletions in blue pencil, additions in red ink, and the proof-reader's corrections in green, it looked like a paper tapestry.[3]

[1] Letter of 25 December 1950: Spencer-Churchill papers. There is a copy of all but the handwritten section of this letter in Churchill's own papers: Churchill papers, 1/83.
[2] Telegram despatched 27 December 1950 (from Marrakech to Tokyo, via London): Churchill papers, 2/173.
[3] Kelly recollections, typescript: Kelly papers.

Churchill's messages to his wife were full of the enjoyment of his winter hideaway. 'Wow,' he telegraphed on December 26, and he added: 'Clouds and rain. Meow. Love, W.' [1] 'We have left the mountains,' he telegraphed to her on New Year's Day 1951, 'and found a sunlight painting paradise at Tinerhir. You shall come here too. Love, W.' [2] Two days later he telegraphed again: 'Returned safely over mountains last night after really lovely two days. You will have to see that place, which is in French military occupation. Officers most attentive and look forward much to your visit which I promised them. I got two interesting pictures there. Hope all well with you. Tender love, W.' [3]

This flying visit across the mountains was but a brief interlude in a heavy programme of work on the sixth and final volume of war memoirs. On January 3 General Pownall sent Lord Ismay an account of 'how we are getting on here' with the first phase of Volume 6, and the last phase of its still uncompleted predecessor:

Mr Churchill has been working hard on Volume VI, with special reference to the military–political questions right at the end of the war—such as the occupation of Prague, Vienna and so on. Several chapters are in draft print and will be available for inspection when we get back. I have no doubt that later on he will want you to take a hand in all this high-level argument.

Kelly left to-day and Bill Deakin comes the day after tomorrow. Mr Churchill has said he will then turn back to Volume V. I do not know if he has asked you for contributions to the various Conferences in that volume, but they are of course very much up your street. . . .

Pownall's letter ended, after a request for material on the strategic disputes of 1944:

We are having a very good time here, although the weather is a bit uncertain. Mr Churchill is in very good health and heart, and I fancy he will be returning to London about the 20th, but all plans are 'fluid'.

I am due back about the 16th or 17th, and if you agree, I think we might all get together and discuss things to see how we stand and make a plan for finishing off Volume V in rather tidier shape than Volume IV left us when it went to the Printer. [4]

On January 5 Churchill's daughter Diana reached Marrakech, together with Bill Deakin and his Rumanian-born wife Pussy. Three days later, Lord Cherwell returned to London. 'I think his rest out here has been good for his health,' Churchill wrote to Eden, and he

---

[1] Telegram of 26 December 1950: Churchill papers, 1/83.
[2] Telegram despatched 1 January 1951: Churchill papers, 1/47.
[3] Telegram despatched 3 January 1951: Churchill papers, 1/47.
[4] 'Dear Pug', 3 January 1951: Churchill papers, 1/83.

added, of the world affairs which he had not been able entirely to leave behind him:

Naturally I have followed everything in the newspapers, and am as gravely concerned as you must be about our national perils and party puzzles. I do not understand why the Americans could not form a defensive line in Korea after nearly three weeks' breathing space to fortify it.

I cannot get the Somme and Passchendaele out of my head, and I thought that the Chinese might well renew our experience of those days with the added effect of vastly increased modern fire power. It now looks like a retirement on the former perimeter around Pusan. There must be something very wrong in the whole lay-out. I shall look forward to talking all this and other matters over with you.

The only point which it seems urgent for me to make now is that we should on no account approve any separation between our policy and that of the United States on the measures to be taken against China. I see they are bringing a resolution before the United Nations on the point. We should act with them irrespective of anything that Nehru, who is neutral, may do or say. This would involve not only severing diplomatic relations and withdrawing recognition, but also sharing in any blockade measure which may be proposed. Hong Kong no doubt would suffer gravely, but that must be accepted.

It is possible that the Americans might find such face-saving measures a means of getting out of Korea altogether. They can hardly be more humiliated than they are already. Possibly the best solution is, without declaring war on China, to cut her off for the time being from the comity of the United Nations and in this posture await further developments.

I only send this in case the matter may be raised with you by the Government. If you think well of it and are in agreement, it might be right to inform the Government of our position.

On all other aspects I should deprecate any overtures at this time to them. They have no right to ask for sacrifices from others while being unwilling to give up at this crisis their Party Nationalization of Steel. I have no doubt they will do so eventually under the growing pressure of events.

Churchill's letter continued, with a reference to the Festival planned for the summer of 1951: 'I feel increasing doubts about the Festival of Britain now that the United States have declared and are taking vast emergency measures.' His letter, which Lord Cherwell took back to England with him on January 8, ended:

I am going to Paris on the 20th, and shall stop there for two or three days at the Loti to renew my French contacts. I expect to be with you on the 23rd. I have not burdened you with other matters, though I am thinking continually about the very grave situation closing in upon us.

All good wishes, dear Anthony. I hope you are having a rest. I toil night and day at the book and painting. The lack of sunshine hampers the painting, but the book, both Volume V and VI, are leaping ahead.[1]

'Life is very pleasant out here,' Churchill wrote to Ismay on January 11, 'and I have been working hard both on the book and at my painting. The weather however is somewhat capricious, and we have not had our full share of sunshine.'[2] From Lord Cherwell that day came some comments on the chapters he had read while in Marrakech:

... in the chapter recounting the talks at Teheran about the future of Germany it might be well to insert a few hundred words calculated to reduce the painful impression that might be created in that country on reading these discussions. Of course you might omit some parts, but if you did no doubt the Russians would publish them so that matters would not be improved.

The other point which occurred to me was that the telegrams about de Gaulle might require elisions. If he came to power again in France cooperation with him might be even more difficult if he had read some of the comments.

Cherwell also sent Churchill news of the latest political rumours in London: 'a good deal of talk', he wrote, 'about a coalition', and he went on to explain:

... there seems to be an idea in some Government circles that it would be well to get Bevan and the other violent Left-Wingers, who would go into opposition, thoroughly committed to the unpleasant measures rearmament will entail before making any move so that they should not be able to escape responsibility afterwards and attack any coalition which might be formed for having imposed them.[3]

Talk of coalition left Churchill unmoved. He knew that Attlee would never accept such a diminution of power. He also learned while in Marrakech of the result of a secret Gallup Poll which he had asked for six months earlier.[4] The results, he wrote to Lord Camrose at the

[1] 'My dear Anthony', 8 January 1951: Churchill papers, 1/83. In his reply, Eden commented: 'The Korean campaign is completely inexplicable. Apparently the Americans had intended to defend Seoul. They later changed their minds and thought they could hold a line further south. This again they failed to do. One hears rumours that the fighting value of most of the divisions is not very high, the Marines and our troops excepted. Certainly MacArthur's communiqués do not seem calculated to inspire his men. He talks all the time of "large Chinese armies".' ('My dear Winston', 11 January 1951: Churchill papers, 2/112.)

[2] Letter of 11 January 1951: Churchill papers, 1/83. To his grandson Winston, Churchill wrote on his return to London: 'I hope you will not lose your interest in painting because that is a great amusement in after-life, and you seem to me to have real liking for it.' ('My dearest Winston', 5 February 1951: Churchill papers, 1/48.)

[3] 'My dear Winston', from Christ Church, Oxford, 11 January 1951: Churchill papers, 4/52.

[4] Churchill had written to Lord Woolton, the Conservative Party Chairman, in April 1950: 'I think it would be well to have a secret Gallup poll for our own information in the near future, on "How would you vote in a new General Election?" or to that effect. How much do these

end of January 1951, 'were more favourable to the Conservatives even than those of the *Daily Express* Poll announced about a fortnight ago'.[1] A public Gallup Poll in January 1951 gave the Conservatives an 11 per cent lead over Labour, with 44 per cent of the predicted poll, as against 33 per cent for Labour.[2]

On January 7, Clementine Churchill flew out to Marrakech to be with her husband, and to join him in the expeditions into the Atlas Mountains. 'I took the advice you gave me, that first evening,' Churchill wrote to Hugh Pullar a few days after his return to London, 'to take a flip over the Atlas mountains. I like Tinerhir so much that I went there a second time, when Mrs Churchill joined me, and spent a lot of time painting there.'[3]

Walter Graebner had arrived at Marrakech on January 12, and he too had been enlisted, not only to discuss the war memoirs, but to join a picnic excursion on January 14. Later he recalled:

Churchill's picnics were star turns, and he expected all his guests to attend.

Probably no man in the twentieth century organized an outing on such a lavish scale. The site was selected some days in advance, after Mrs Churchill or another person had explored the region with a careful eye on what would make good subjects for Mr Churchill's brush. Sometimes a site fifty miles from the hotel would be chosen.

Departure time was usually at 11 sharp. About two minutes earlier the whole party, with the exception of Churchill, had arranged themselves in their automobiles. The moment Churchill appeared, the cavalcade set forth, and quite a cavalcade it was. First there would be a police car with two or three local policemen. Then the Churchill car would follow, trailed by four or five automobiles bearing the other guests. After them came the food van, containing, as well as the food and drink, a couple of full-sized tables, an adequate number of chairs, Churchill's easel and painting equipment, and

---

polls cost? I understand that Gallup will carry them out when asked. It would be most interesting to see the mood and tendencies of the electorate. Gallup was quite accurate last time. It might well be better to wait until after the Budget is announced, but perhaps meanwhile you will let me know your views.' ('Chairman of the Party', 3 April 1950: Churchill papers, 2/109.)

[1] 'My dear Bill', 'Private', 30 January 1951: Camrose papers.

[2] 'Voting Intentions (Gallup Poll)' in David Butler and Anne Sloman, *British Political Facts 1900–1975*, fourth edition, London 1975, page 205. On 5 February 1951 David Butler wrote to Churchill: 'I should be surprised if an election in the near future would give the Conservatives quite as overwhelming a victory as today's poll would suggest. But, even if all these factors told heavily against them, I should be still more surprised if the Conservatives failed to win an appreciable majority of the votes. A lead of only 2 per cent, I am certain, would be sufficient to give the Conservatives a Parliamentary majority of over 50 seats. A lead of 5 per cent would give them a majority of well over 100 seats.' ('Dear Mr Churchill', 5 February 1951, Churchill papers, 2/109.)

[3] 'Dear Mr Pullar', 3 February 1951: Pullar papers.

Churchill's valet. After that came the detectives, and, often, after that, another detachment of native police.

Churchill preferred fast driving to slow, but the pace invariably set by the local police, who thought their duty was to get Churchill to his destination as quickly as possible, must have frightened him more than once. Careless speed also annoyed him. Once when his driver, racing through the dusty desert in Morocco, struck a sheep, Churchill stopped the car, growled at the driver, sympathized with the shepherd, and gave him 500 francs.

When the picnic site was reached, everything stopped while Churchill looked around for the best place to set up his easel. Sometimes this took fifteen or twenty minutes. Then he went to work, a whisky and soda having been poured for him in the meantime. Twenty or thirty yards away from him the tables were set up and covered with white cloths, the chairs placed and the food laid out. For everyone there was an individually-packed lunch which the hotel had spent the early part of the morning preparing, and which consisted usually of an assortment of chicken breasts, cold roast beef and York ham, rolls and butter, rich cakes, fruit and several kinds of cheese. Champagne flowed copiously throughout the meal, and there was port for the cheese and brandy for the coffee.

But in spite of the sumptuousness of the fare, the police guard, the formal table-setting and the little band of natives that invariably clustered a courteous hundred or so yards away, the picnics were as gay and easy as those of any ordinary large and good-humoured family. There were no guests and polite attendants: with the exception of Mr Churchill, who painted busily away with sublime disregard for the bustle going on behind him, everyone, from Mrs Churchill and assorted elderly peers and generals down, pitched in to help the detectives and Norman the valet, get things in readiness, and everyone hopped up and down from the table as often as he pleased to get what he wanted of food and drink. Everyone laughed, everyone was unbraced.

If the sun got hot, you put your napkin on your head, turban style, and the others would follow suit, joking inordinately at the strange effects produced. If you got even hotter, you could take off your shirt, for all anybody would care.

Gayest and most unbraced of the company was always Churchill, who on picnics became more roguish and ebullient than ever, and delighted in singing old songs, telling slightly *risqué* stories and pressing drink ('It's *white* port, you know. All the ladies must have some because it's only *white* port') on everyone round him.

Graebner's account continued:

At Marrakech he took special delight in a couple of picnic customs which he quickly elevated to the rank of formal ceremonies. One was the drinking of old Indian Army toasts, which he had learned from his friend and assistant, General Sir Henry Pownall, and at the end of every picnic we would solemnly rise and drink the Toast for the Day. On Sundays it was 'To Absent Friends', on Mondays, 'To Men', and so on through 'To Women', 'To Religion', 'To Our Swords', 'To Ourselves', 'To Wives and Sweethearts', to the end of the week.

The other was a verse from Thomas Gray's 'Ode on the Spring', which he gravely recited at each picnic:

> Beside some water's rushy brink
> With me the Muse shall sit and think
> (At ease reclined in rustic state)
> How vain the ardour of the Crowd,
> How low, how little are the Proud,
> How indigent the great.

One night at dinner my wife asked him to repeat the verse to her. 'Oh, no, I couldn't,' he replied firmly. 'I can only say it at picnics.'

After lunch Churchill was left to himself for two or three hours while the others would go off with Mrs Churchill to visit an ancient ruin, inspect a native village or call on a local chieftain. On their return they usually found that in some mysterious manner a large crowd had collected on the picnic ground. They would be standing stock-still in a huge semi-circle behind Churchill, talking only in respectful whispers, while he painted away, completely oblivious to everything except the scene in front of him.[1]

Like all those who were drawn into Churchill's circle, Walter Graebner was entranced by his thoughts and phrases, some of which he later recalled:

'Man hasn't lived until he has acquired the habit of smoking cigars.'

'Stilton and port are like man and wife—they should never be separated.'

'I write a book the way they built the Canadian Pacific Railway. First I lay the track from coast to coast, and after that I put in all the stations.'

On T. E. Lawrence:

'He was a genius. There is nothing that he couldn't have done had he lived—and had me behind him.'[2]

During his last weeks at Marrakech, Churchill spent an afternoon in the studio of a French painter, Jacques Majorelle, who had lived in Morocco for thirty years. 'I was much impressed with his work,' Churchill wrote to his Swiss paint supplier Willy Sax, and he went on to explain what had particularly interested him about Majorelle's technique:

He had turned entirely to tempera, which he generally uses in the powder form. He certainly had produced remarkably vivid colour effects, which I have never seen surpassed. I have not used tempera lately. There is no doubt that, for skies in Morocco, it is far superior to oils. Pray let me know the recipe which you recommend for making it possible to paint with tempera over oil. I think you told me about it. There is rather a severe chemical wash

[1] Walter Graebner recollections: Walter Graebner, *My dear Mister Churchill*, pages 75–8.

[2] Walter Graebner, *My dear Mister Churchill*, various pages. Another phrase recalled by Graebner was: 'The blood of the Communists flows green.'

which, after it has been applied to the oil-painted surface, renders it fit for tempera. Have you got any of this? If so please send me a bottle urgently.

M. Majorelle also showed me a sky of wonderful blue, the intensity of which I had never before seen. I asked him how he got it and he gave me the enclosed description. I got him to come round to my studio at the Mamounia Hotel and he showed me how it worked. He paints the surface in tempera from tempera powder with as much white as is desired. Thereafter he takes natural cobalt powder (such as is the foundation I think of cobalt oil paint) and blows the powder on with a little bulb spray. The result is to leave a number of fresh particles of great brilliance on the surface and really the colour was wonderful to one's eyes. Do you know anything about this? It would seem to me that you might be very well advised to look at M. Majorelle's paintings which are a manifestation of the power of tempera, the like of which I have never seen.

'Will you please send me another outfit of tempera in tubes,' Churchill added, 'like the one you did last time, and please let me have the bill as I have a few francs available.'[1]

On January 20 Churchill flew from Marrakech to Paris, where he dined at the British Embassy. Two former Prime Ministers, Georges Bidault and Paul Reynaud, were among the guests. During the dinner, one of the British diplomats present, William Hayter, heard Churchill say to Reynaud: 'Perhaps you remember that offer of common citizenship I made to France in 1940 when you were Prime Minister. What did you think of it? I was never sure it was a good idea.' Hayter also spent some time that evening trying to interpret to Churchill 'a rather complicated tribute that Bidault, the Deputy Prime Minister, was paying him, without much success, so that in the end poor Bidault put his head in his hands, crying, "Il ne veut pas m'écouter, il ne veut pas m'écouter".'[2]

Churchill was 'convinced', Iris Hayter wrote in her diary, 'that the French would not agree to any German rearmament, and lectured them quite unnecessarily', and she noted how, after dinner, Churchill 'tried to entice Rab to his bedroom to look at political papers. Rab, an old hand, avoided this session which might have lasted till 3 a.m. by saying he must say goodnight to the ladies.'[3]

On the following night Churchill dined at the British Embassy again, when the Prime Minister, René Pleven, was present. William Hayter later recalled how one of the French guests 'brought along a

[1] 'Dear Mr Sax', 'Private', 24 January 1951: Churchill papers, 2/176. As with Churchill's previous working visit to Marrakech, the expenses of his own and his assistants' stay had been paid for by Time and Life, as part of their payment for the American rights of the war memoirs. Life also paid half the bill for the flight.
[2] Sir William Hayter recollections: Sir William Hayter, A Double Life, page 87.
[3] Iris Hayter diary, 20 January 1951: Lady Hayter papers.

copy of Churchill's speeches for Churchill to sign. Looking at it fondly Churchill said, "Anyway we had much the best of the speeches in the last war, that fellow Hitler wasn't up to much in that respect." Later that evening he said, "I could have defended the British Empire against anyone (pause) against anyone (pause), except the British."' [1]

On January 22 another former Prime Minister, the Foreign Minister Robert Schuman, came to lunch. 'Churchill looked very well,' Iris Hayter wrote in her diary, 'and was amusing about "d'accord en principe" being said to mean "no".' Churchill also remarked: 'I never followed the advice of my military staff unless I happened to agree with it.' [2]

That night Churchill dined with Odette Pol Roger, whose champagne, as well as whose company, he always enjoyed. He then took the night train back to London.

---

[1] Sir William Hayter recollections: Sir William Hayter, *A Double Life*, page 87.

[2] Iris Hayter diary, 22 January 1951: Lady Hayter papers. René Pleven was Prime Minister of France from July 1950 to March 1951, and again from August 1951 to January 1952. Georges Bidault had been Prime Minister from June to December 1946 and October to July 1949. Robert Schuman had been Prime Minister from November 1947 to March 1948, and for seven days in September 1948, and was Foreign Minister from July 1948 until January 1953.

33

'Such awful hazards'

FROM the moment of his return to England from Morocco in the last week of January 1951, Churchill plunged back into the politics of perpetual crisis; the Labour Government's majority of six made a General Election likely before the end of the year. Churchill's own concerns were once more dominated by foreign affairs; 'You may be quite sure,' he wrote to Governor Dewey of New York on January 30, 'that whatever misunderstandings may arise from the petty by-play now going on between Mr Attlee's Government and the United States, the "fraternal" association is unbreakable, and in this respect at least things have only to get worse to get better.' [1]

From the Middle East came information, sent once more by Marcus Sieff, of Israel's isolation as far as the supply of oil was concerned, now that the Government of Iraq had 'stopped the supply of crude oil' along its principal pipeline, which reached the Mediterranean Sea at the Israeli port of Haifa. Even if Western oil companies continued to bring in Israel's crude oil requirements by tanker, Sieff wrote, 'and thus Iraqi crude would not go to meet Israel's needs, Iraq would benefit greatly from the increased royalties and employment which would result from the re-opening of the pipeline to Haifa and Great Britain and the Western Powers would get the benefit of what is a very valuable asset, particularly at this present time of International tension'. [2]

'About the Oil,' Miss Gilliatt wrote to Marcus Sieff's private secretary on January 30, 'Mr Churchill feels that the question is how to persuade the Arabs to allow the pipeline to be used.' [3]

On January 31 Churchill received two visitors from Yugoslavia, Milovan Djilas and Vladimir Dedijer, both close associates of Tito,

---

[1] 'My dear Dewey', 'Private', 30 January 1951: Churchill papers, 2/168.
[2] 'Oil Supplies', 18 January 1951: Churchill papers, 2/46.
[3] Letter of 30 January 1951: Churchill papers, 2/46.

and who had made the breach between Yugoslavia and the Soviet Union in 1948.[1] An account of their meeting was sent to Belgrade by the Yugoslav Ambassador, who also sent a copy to Churchill. 'The conversation was confidential, informal and friendly,' the Ambassador noted, and he went on to tell his Foreign Minister:

1. In the conversation Churchill had mentioned Anglo-Yugoslav relations during the war and their deterioration immediately after the war.

2. He has mentioned also the agreement with Stalin on Balkans, among other matters, the agreement 50:50 on Yugoslavia, pointing out that it was not on territorial basis, but the division of influence.

3. Speaking about world situation, Churchill has expressed the opinion that it is possible to achieve an agreement with Stalin but only under the condition that the West is strong enough. He considers that Soviet Union is not yet ready for a war.[2]

Churchill's return to London coincided with an upsurge of political rumours. 'I am inclined to think Attlee will be forced to resign this week,' Henry Channon noted in his diary on February 5, 'which would make an Election almost but not quite inevitable because there is always the possibility that Winston might agree to head a provisional Government for a few months: this is what many of the Labour Members would prefer. Prefer certainly to an Election which would result in their certain defeat and loss of many seats. Probably 80 to 100.'[3]

On February 7 Churchill spoke in the debate on the Iron and Steel industry, eight days before the Bill to nationalize the industry was to come into law. His anger was matched by many interruptions, but he persevered.

It is commonplace to say that the steel industry has served, and is serving, us well. It is expanding production, especially in exports; its prices are cut lower than in almost any other country; it has nearly half a century of peaceful progress and goodwill between the management and the wage earner—a

---

[1] Dedijer, born in 1914, had been a liaison officer to the British mission to Tito during the Second World War. His father, a Serbian officer, had been killed in the First World War. His wife Olga, a surgeon, was killed during a German air attack in 1943. When Djilas was expelled from the Communist Party in 1954, Dedijer, then a member of the Party's Central Committee, defended his right of free speech, and was given a six months' suspended sentence. In 1962 he was a Research Fellow at St Antony's College, Oxford, of which Bill Deakin was Warden. He lived in Belgrade, where in 1982 he published a 'documentary biography' of Tito. In 1954 Djilas published his book *The New Class*, arguing that party oligarchies in Communist States usurp and preserve the class distinctions of the privileged class which they had overthrown. He was imprisoned from 1956 to 1961 and again from 1962 to 1966 (in the same prison in which he had been imprisoned by the Monarchy from 1933 to 1936).

[2] 'Yugoslav Ambassador to Foreign Minister Kardelj', London, 31 January 1951: Churchill papers, 2/114. The Yugoslav Ambassador was Brilej. He sent Churchill this note of the conversation on 23 February 1951, at Churchill's request (the Foreign Office having asked Churchill for a note on the talks, but he had not made one).

[3] Channon diary, 5 February 1951: Robert Rhodes James (editor), *Chips*, page 452.

great measure of common comprehension exists among them today; it has a well defined and established relationship with the State, including the fixing of prices and the direction and emphasis of effort. All this we have achieved here in the British steel industry. It should be taken as a model. Why should it be turned topsy-turvy? Why this industry, of all others, and now, at this time, of all others?

The nationalization of iron and steel, Churchill pointed out, had not been a part of the Labour Party's 1950 manifesto.[1]

Churchill argued that with the Korean War still being fought, with Europe still vulnerable to a Soviet attack, with a declared shortage of soldiers so serious that nearly a quarter of a million men were to be called up from the Reserves, it was a terrible moment to plunge the iron and steel industry 'into deepening confusion'. By proceeding with the Act, 'a cruel discord' had been 'needlessly and wantonly thrust into our anxious and critical affairs'. There would be 'a deep and major injury to the whole process of rearmament'. Turning his attack on to Attlee himself, Churchill asked:

What defence does the right hon. Gentleman suppose that this will give him at the bar of history, or even before his fellow countrymen in the near future, if the British and United Nations' sky continues to darken? I have had my share of responsibilities in public life. While my strength remains I would not shrink from bearing them again.

But it is no extravagance of rhetorical expression if I say that I would rather be banished from public life for ever than be responsible for the action which the Prime Minister is taking in asking the House to vote for the February 15 vesting date tonight. I earnestly trust that Parliament will restrain him.

So tremendous a situation, such awful hazards, such an unworthy contribution—I can hardly believe that the Attlee who worked at my side for more than five years of a life and death struggle is willing to have his reputation injured in this way.

'I am forced to repeat again,' Churchill declared at the end of his speech, 'that should the Conservative Party be successful in a General Election—which cannot be long delayed however tightly and even passionately Ministers may cling to their offices—we shall at once repeal the Steel Act, and adopt the compromise solutions which the Trades Union Congress have themselves set before us.'[2]

It was not in Korea, but in Europe, that Churchill saw the real threat to Western freedom. As he explained to President Truman on

---

[1] To one interrupter Churchill declared: 'I am not at all disturbed by interruptions, having experienced them almost before many hon. Members opposite were born.' When he was interrupted again, by Opposition laughter, he replied: 'Hon. Members opposite will not get out of it all by laughing.'

[2] Speech of 7 February 1951: *Hansard*.

February 12, in congratulating him on 'the most favourable turn' which events in Korea had lately taken, 'I have always hoped that the United States, while maintaining her necessary rights in the Far East, would not become too heavily involved there, for it is in Europe that the mortal challenge to world freedom must be confronted. I express my gratitude to you and to your Country, which I love so well,' Churchill added, 'for the Eisenhower Mission and the far-reaching measures which it implies. In this I see the best hope of world peace, if time is given to us.'[1]

The Conservative leaders now decided to bring a vote of no confidence against the Government, and on February 15 the 'Great Debate' as it was known in Tory circles was opened, by Churchill himself. 'Though he was far from his best,' Henry Channon noted in his diary, 'there were flashes of truth, of argument and of humour.'[2]

Much of the humour came during the frequent interruptions:

Let me now illustrate by a few major examples the mismanagement of our Defence Forces, which is the gravamen of our charge. For this purpose I must go back, to some extent, into the past.

Mr Shurmer (Birmingham, Sparkbrook): Do not go too far back.

Mr Churchill: If I went too far, I should come to that period of complete victory over all our enemies which was at that time thought to be a subject of general rejoicing.

The Minister of Defence [Mr Shinwell] rose—

Mr Churchill: I am not arguing with the right hon. Gentleman.

[Hon. Members: 'Give way.'] I have all the afternoon before me in which to unfold the arguments I wish to make and, consequently, I am not at all restive under interruptions.

[Hon. Members: 'Get on with it.'] I shall not attempt to be hurried at all; I shall take my time in dealing with every interruption, because I feel I have a perfectly legitimate right to unfold this case in my own way.

Churchill's principal points were that the Army, while adequate, was neither substantial nor efficient; that in five and a half years Britain had failed to produce an atomic bomb and had now been 'outstripped by the Soviets in this field'; that 'behind the scenes' the Government had been discouraging the French from their plan of a European Army; and that far too little was being done to meet the danger from Soviet submarines. On this last point, on which the Government had declined to give any estimate of Soviet strength, Churchill told the House:

[1] 'Dear Mr President', 12 February 1951: Churchill papers, 2/28. Eisenhower had been appointed Supreme Allied Commander, European Forces, with the responsibility of integrating the European armies under a scheme, known as the Pleven Plan, devised by the French Minister of Defence (and from July 1950 to March 1951 Prime Minister) René Pleven.

[2] Channon diary, 15 February 1951: Robert Rhodes James (editor), *Chips*, pages 453–4.

Secrecy is used as a shield to cover the Government shortcomings, but I have no doubt that the main facts of our naval construction are well-known to the general staffs of Europe and certainly to the Russians who have many ways of obtaining information about the work going on in our shipyards and dockyards.

We were told by the Parliamentary Secretary to the Admiralty on 25 October that this year's conversion programme of fleet destroyers to anti-submarine frigates had been doubled. That statement was very much on the same lines as those followed in so much of his speech by the Minister of Defence yesterday.

Doubled from what? In this case it has been ascertained, only from the public statements, that they were doubled from three ships to six.[1]

Churchill then took up another point from Shinwell's speech of the previous day:

The Minister of Defence said yesterday that the danger of war had become more acute in the last few months. I follow these matters as closely as I can, and I am not aware of any facts which justify this assertion.

On the contrary, I think that the gigantic measures for rearmament adopted by the United States—the declaration of a state of emergency, 10,000 million dollars additional taxation, twenty-seven months' military service and the appointment of General Eisenhower—have all improved the chances of the rearmament of the free democracies, and the formation of a European front which will be a real deterrent upon Soviet Communist aggression in Europe; they have all improved the chances of this being achieved before the vast American superiority in the atomic weapon has been overtaken by the Russian stockpile.

If any important facts have occurred justifying the statement made by the Minister of Defence about the increased danger of war they should be imparted to the House, if necessary in Secret Session. To make a statement of that kind is to give, I think, a wrong view, apart from causing alarm.

When Churchill's speech was over, and as he sat down, he began 'to search for something', as Henry Channon noted, and in doing so 'fidgetted so much that Gaitskell, who was speaking for the Government, asked what was the matter. Winston rose very gravely and solemnly announced "I was only looking for a jujube".' The House roared with laughter.[2]

---

[1] On 27 July 1950 Churchill had quoted 'reliable naval reference books' which estimated the Russian submarine fleet at 360, divided between the Pacific and the West, of which between 100 and 200 were ocean-going and capable of high speeds. 'These seem to me very large figures,' he had told the House, 'and I am not at all accepting them as final figures, but what is the truth about them? I do not see why the Minister of Defence should not give us his best estimate, considering the information which has been given about other portions of the Russian forces.' (Speech of 27 July 1950: *Hansard*.)

[2] A jujube is a lozenge made of sugar, flavouring and gum, in imitation of the edible, acid, berry-like fruit of the Zizyphus shrub, a member of the buckthorn family. (French, and medieval Latin, *jujuba*; Greek, *zizyphon*.)

As the debate continued, there were those who thought that Attlee might resign 'and that today', as Channon wrote, 'is the last day of this mad, unsatisfactory Parliament'.[1] It was not to be, however; at the Division the Government, supported by six of the nine Liberal MPs, had a majority of twenty-one.

Churchill was disappointed; and disappointed again a few days later when President Truman rejected Churchill's request to make public the original Churchill–Roosevelt agreement of 1944 on the atomic bomb.[2] Churchill wanted this made known because it had acquired, he explained to Truman, 'a new and practical significance from the fact that His Majesty's Government have, with my full support, accorded the United States a most important bombing base in East Anglia, and I have little doubt that Parliament would consider that this base should not be used for the atomic bomb without the consent of His Majesty's Government'. Churchill added: 'I believe that the publication of the original document would place us in a position where this guarantee would willingly be conceded by the United States. This would I am sure strengthen the ties which bind our two Countries together in "fraternal association" and effective alliance. This remains as always the prime object of any policy which I should support.'[3]

As a co-signatory of the 'original agreement', Churchill explained that day to Attlee, 'I have thought it right to communicate myself with the President of the United States, and I trust that he will at least agree that the atomic bomb shall not be used from British bases without our prior consent.'[4]

In declining Churchill's request, and doing so in a handwritten note, Truman left no room for argument:

Dear Winston,
Your personal note, attached to your request for the release of the Quebec Agreement of 1943, is highly appreciated.[5]
I am making a sincere effort to carry out the Atlantic Treaty with my position in the Congress, which might be termed vicious and unfair under present emergency conditions.

[1] Channon diary, 15 February 1951: Robert Rhodes James (editor), *Chips*, pages 453–4.
[2] On 7 February 1951 Miss Marston wrote to Churchill: 'Mr Kelly has not been able to find the document about the Atomic Bomb Agreement, as he says it is not contained in the archives.' (Note of 7 February 1951: Churchill papers, 2/28.)
[3] 'Dear Mr President', 12 February 1951: Churchill papers, 2/28.
[4] 'My dear Prime Minister', 12 February 1951: Squerryes Lodge collection.
[5] Churchill's covering note, in his own hand, read: 'My dear Harry, Forgive me for burdening you with the enclosed, but I feel it my duty to my country to send it to you.' (Letter of 12 February 1951: Churchill papers, 2/28.)

I hope you won't press me in this matter. It will cause unfortunate repercussions both here and in your country, as well as embarrassment to me
and to your government.

The reopening of this discussion may ruin my whole defense program both
here at home and abroad. Your country's welfare and mine are at stake in
that program.

'I hope,' Truman added, 'you are in good health and enjoying life
as much as one can enjoy it in these troublous times.' [1]

On February 20 Churchill was again in the House of Commons
when the House divided in expectation of a close vote. The Labour
majority was eight. 'As I walked in the Smoking Room corridor,'
Henry Channon wrote in his diary, 'I saw Winston, immaculately
dressed, pleased with himself and puffing a cigar, approach: immediately in front of us walked Attlee and Arthur Moyle, his PPS.
There was almost a collision; Winston did not make way (Attlee did,
slightly) but made them one of his little courtly half-bows which he
reserves for people he does not like. I was fascinated; as he passed me
a second later he smiled, winked and passed on.' [2]

As work continued at Hyde Park Gate and Chartwell on the war
memoirs, other memoirs would arrive, mostly from publishers wanting
to know if Churchill had any comments to make or wished any alterations to be made. One such request came from Harrap, who before
the war had published Churchill's four-volume biography of his ancestor John Churchill, Duke of Marlborough, and who were now
about to publish the memoirs of the former American Commander in
Italy, General Mark Clark. On February 13 Miss Sturdee marked the
publisher's copy to show Churchill the references to himself. [3]

Churchill was not at all pleased by what he read. 'I am sure the
General wishes to be friendly in what he writes,' he informed the
publisher, and then set out his complaints:

. . . to English readers much of his tales about his visits to Chequers will be
considered vulgar: they are certainly vitiated by inaccuracy. I cannot accept
many of the statements which he attributes to me, let alone the form in
which they are expressed. I always say 'aren't' instead of 'ain't'.

The bulk of these passages constitutes an abuse of hospitality and intimacy

[1] 'Dear Winston', The White House, 16 February 1951: Churchill papers, 2/28.
[2] Channon diary, 20 February 1951: Robert Rhodes James (editor), *Chips*, page 454.
[3] 'Mr Churchill', initialled 'NS', 13 February 1951: Churchill papers, 1/168.

in conversation and will, I am sure, do no good to the General or his publication over here. It in no way represents the manner in which Americans I received were accustomed to behave. I doubt very much whether the style in which this book is written is palatable in the United States. I am sure it will not be here.[1]

It was too late, the publishers replied, to make any changes beyond 'ain't' to 'aren't'.

Churchill's own literary work was uninterrupted by such vexations. On February 21 General Pownall sent him the first draft of the chapter 'Preparations for Overlord', leading up to the June 1944 Normandy landings.[2] On the following day Commodore Allen sent Churchill his comments on Pownall's notes, and suggested that the part played by Combined Operations in planning the landings 'should take a prominent place'. To this end, he had sent a revised version of Pownall's draft to Mountbatten.[3]

Churchill's work, and his speech plans, were interrupted by a short illness at the beginning of March 1951; a 'localised staphylococcal infection' was the description used in a short press notice issued on March 1, which added that on the advice of Lord Moran and Sir Thomas Dunhill 'he must rest for a few days and will be unable to attend to his duties'.[4] To Lady Lytton, Churchill wrote that same day, from Hyde Park Gate: 'I am laid up with an unexpectedly violent reaction to a penicillin injection which I took. I had a dreadful night with pain and a swollen face. I have, alas, had to cancel the Freedom and the Cutlers' Feast at Sheffield next Monday and Tuesday.'[5]

On March 2 Sir Alan Lascelles telegraphed to say 'how very sorry Their Majesties are to hear that you are not well, and that they hope you will soon have completely recovered'.[6] Churchill was certainly well enough by March 5 to dictate a letter to Lord Trenchard, and to answer Trenchard's suggestion in the House of Lords about the need to strengthen Britain's bomber force. Britain's 'first need in the air', Churchill felt, was not bombers but fighters. 'I would not embark on the bomber programme at their expense,' Churchill wrote, 'until we have at least enough fighters to give us essential protection.' His letter con-

---

[1] 'Dear Mr White', 'Private', 21 February 1951: Churchill papers, 1/168.

[2] 'Mr Churchill', 21 February 1951: Churchill papers, 4/333.

[3] 'Mr Churchill', 'Vol. V, Preparations for Overlord', 22 February 1951: Churchill papers, 4/333.

[4] 'Press Notice', issued to the Press at 2.30 p.m. on 1 March 1951: Churchill papers, 1/47.

[5] 'Dearest Pamela', 1 March 1951: Pamela, Countess of Lytton papers. Churchill also sent Lady Lytton some Christmas cards which had been made in the United States, using his own paintings. 'They had a two million sale over there,' he told her, and he added: 'As they reproduce in over a dozen colours, instead of our three or four, they get very good results.'

[6] 'Mr Churchill', note initialled by Miss Gemmell, 2 March 1951: Churchill papers, 2/171.

tinued, with reference to Trenchard's argument that Britain should follow America's lead in the development of a long-range bomber force:

I am very glad the Americans should develop a long-range bomber, but when you think of our present plight in this country and how easily we could be over-whelmed by mass attack by bombing, we ought surely to have enough fighters to take so heavy a toll of the enemy that he would be deterred from continuing, as he was last time. After this requirement is met, we could throw our effort into bombers.

What would have happened in the last war if we had had twenty per cent more long-range bombers and fifty per cent less fighters? Not only our daily life but our whole fighting power could have been destroyed.

I am also concerned at large-scale paratroop raids—twenty thousand or so—in our present defenceless condition, where our troops are out of the country, or to be sent away, and we have no Home Guard. I do not admit that giving the highest priority to fighters is 'defence'. It is counter-attack of a very high order.[1]

Churchill recuperated at Chartwell, and had several guests, among them Princess Margaret. 'Thank you so much for showing me all your lovely pictures,' she wrote on March 6, 'and all your fascinating treasures of the war. I shall always remember it as being one of the pleasantest afternoons I have ever spent anywhere.'[2]

By mid-March Churchill was back at work on his memoirs. 'I have embodied most of your corrections,' he wrote on some notes by Bill Deakin about the 'strains and stresses' of Churchill's relations with de Gaulle in 1943, agreeing that the revised chapter should be shown to Harold Macmillan for his 'private opinion'.[3]

Illness now forced Ernest Bevin to leave the Foreign Office, where he was succeeded by Herbert Morrison.[4] In a Party Political broadcast on March 17, Churchill paid tribute to Bevin's work since 1945. 'Although I differed from him in his handling of many questions,' Churchill said, 'I feel bound to put on record that he takes his place among the great Foreign Secretaries of our country, and that, in his steadfast resistance to Communist aggression, in his strengthening of our ties with the United States and in his share of building up the Atlantic Pact, he has rendered services to Britain and to the cause of peace which will long be remembered. As his war-time leader I take this opportunity to pay my tribute. . . .'[5]

[1] 'My dear Trenchard', 'Private', 5 March 1951: Churchill papers, 2/117.
[2] 'My dear Mr Churchill', from Buckingham Palace, 6 March 1951: Churchill papers, 2/173.
[3] 'Mr Churchill', and note by Churchill, 'Mr D', 14 March 1951: Churchill papers, 4/311.
[4] The change-over took place on 9 March 1951.
[5] Ernest Bevin died on 14 April 1951. That evening Churchill issued a short statement to the Press: 'I am deeply grieved at the death of my war-time comrade. A valiant spirit has passed from us. He has his place in history.' ('Press Notice', 7 p.m., 14 April 1951: Churchill papers, 2/167.) In 1952 Churchill obtained a DBE for Bevin's widow.

In his broadcast, Churchill spoke of Britain being in 'a position of danger and perplexity'; things were 'bad' abroad and there was more and more division at home. In 1940 the British had been 'a united people'; now 'we are absorbed in party strife'. Since the last election, there had been a Government 'representing a minority of the electors, trying to conduct all our grave and critical affairs without a normal working majority in the House of Commons'. Churchill added:

Parliamentary debate has become largely meaningless. All the time the two great party machines are grinding up against each other with the utmost energy, dividing every village, every street, every town and city into busy party camps. Each party argues that it is the fault of the other. What is certain is that to prolong the process indefinitely is the loss of all.

After all, no nation possesses in common such long gathered moral and social treasures. No nation is more accustomed to practical methods of give and take from day to day, and few countries have at the present time—let me remind you—to look mortal dangers more directly in the face.

Naturally, we all ask the question, are we really to go on all through the spring, summer and autumn with this struggle in Parliament and strife in the constituencies? Democracy does not express itself in clever manoeuvres by which a handful of men survive from day to day, or another handful of men try to overthrow them.

Once it can be seen that a great new situation or great new issues lie before us, an appeal should be made to the people to create some governing force which can deal with our affairs in the name and in the interest of the large majority of the nation.

For Churchill, that 'great new situation' was the situation abroad. When all Britain's enemies had surrendered by 1945 'we thought we had won'; won the right 'to be let alone to lead our own lives in our own way, under our own laws, and give our children a fair chance to make the best of ourselves'. Now, it seemed, 'we are again in jeopardy', and he went on to explain:

We are in a sad, sombre period of world history where no good-hearted, valiant Russian soldier, worker or peasant; no hard-pressed, disillusioned German family; no home in the war-scarred democracies of Western Europe or in our own islands we have guarded so long, so well, or far across the Atlantic in mighty America—no household can have the feeling after a long day's faithful toil that they can go to sleep without the fear that something awful is moving towards them; and this is what has come to us after all our efforts and sacrifices, and come upon us at a time when, but for the thoughtlessness of the free democracies and the organized designs of the Kremlin oligarchy, expanding science, like a fairy godmother, could have opened the gates of the Golden Age to all.[1]

[1] Broadcast of 17 March 1951: Randolph S. Churchill (editor), *Stemming the Tide, Speeches 1951 and 1952 by Winston S. Churchill*, London 1953, pages 29–34.

On March 21 Churchill spoke in the House of Commons on a complaint of privilege, in which he gave his opinion based on his long period as a Member of Parliament, 'far longer even', he said, 'than the Father of the House'.[1] The issue was whether a letter sent by the Member of Parliament for Sevenoaks to the Bishop of Rochester, complaining about the Vicar of Crockham Hill, was a breach of privilege. The Speaker had ruled that it was not, and Churchill argued in considerable detail and with much erudition that the Speaker's ruling should be upheld. To make the writing of the letter in question a breach of privilege, he argued, 'is putting a curb and a burden upon Members'.[2]

On March 25 Churchill sent a full account of his activities to his wife, who was recuperating from illness in Spain. His letter was written from Chartwell, where his daughter-in-law June and his grandson Winston were staying with him:

My darling,

I had a harrying ten days after you left, what with the broadcast, the Privilege case and other trouble in Parliament, and it is pleasant to have ten days at Chartwell. I send you some cuttings about the broadcast, which was generally considered all right. I also send you the speech I made about the Crockham Hill Vicar's Privilege case. It was considered very successful.

Attlee has gone to hospital with a duodenal ulcer, so I sent some flowers from us both, and I thought you would like to see his letter. Also one from Pamela about little Winston. You see he is to go to Ludgrove in May. He is very nice and well-behaved down here now and has a very good pony so that June can take him out riding.

The sun has shone a little in the mornings but it soon clouds over. There has been a frightful lot of rain. Luckily I have plenty to amuse myself with. So far I have not found time to paint. The Book is a gt standby.

Stassen came over here on purpose to press me to go to Philadelphia for the Bi-centenary of Pennsylvania University.[3] Principal leaders of both Demo-

[1] From December 1944 to October 1951 the Father of the House was the Earl of Winterton, who had first been elected to Parliament in 1904. Winterton was a courtesy title. Churchill had been elected in 1900 (but had been out of Parliament from 1922 to 1924).

[2] Speech of 21 March 1951: *Hansard*. As to his own interest in the case, Churchill told the House during the debate, 'I would not, in ordinary circumstances, have attempted—because I do not wish to take up the time of the House unnecessarily—to discuss the local and special aspects of this case, but the circumstances are somewhat peculiar. I dwell in the diocese of the Bishop of Rochester, I am a parishioner of the Vicar of Crockham Hill and I am a constituent of the hon. Member for Sevenoaks. Therefore, it makes for me what is called, in racing parlance, a triple event.' Churchill's local Member of Parliament was Colonel C. E. Ponsonby, who had been Eden's Parliamentary Private Secretary from 1940 to 1945.

[3] Harold Stassen, from 1948 to 1953 President of the University of Pennsylvania in Philadelphia and a former Governor of Minnesota, had been unsuccessful in his attempt to become the Republican Presidential candidate in 1948 (he was again unsuccessful in 1952 and 1964). From 1953 to 1955 he was Director of the Foreign Operations Administration under Eisenhower, and from 1955 to 1958 Special Assistant to the President with Cabinet rank, charged with directing studies on disarmament.

crat and Republican Parties would be there, and there is no doubt that I could make a helpful speech. It would be an advantage with all this Party fighting in the House of Commons to have this outside engagement lying ahead. If I went at all I should fly both ways in one of the best BOAC special airplanes which is offered. The date of the meeting would be May 8, and I should be away altogether for about a week. My decision turns on what precisely is the President's attitude. At present he has sent a message through Stassen that he would like me to dine with him either the night before or the night after the Philadelphia speech. I require more direct evidence of his wishes as I do not want to embarrass him or myself. I send you Bernie's letter which speaks for itself. I should of course only make one address. It is a week of one's life, but might be a week well spent.

The whole place here is just sodden, and we have not been able to do any ploughing. Everything is behind-hand. Everyone else is in a similar plight.

I have fixed it up all right for Violet in Colne Valley, but the voting of the Conservative Association (secret) was very close: 33 to 26. However no conditions were attached and she is going to accept. Once she gets down there and begins making her good speeches against the Socialists I expect all will be well.[1]

With all my love

W[2]

As soon as Clementine Churchill returned to London, a crisis arose in connection with the remaining two volumes of the war memoirs. It concerned C. C. Wood, the proof-reader, who worked each day at 28 Hyde Park Gate in a small studio room. Clementine Churchill wanted that room used for other purposes, as she explained in a note to her husband on April 5:

There are a great many people who call here in connection with your work; for example Brigadier Blunt, Mr Bremridge,[3] Mr Christ, as well as Lord Ismay, General Pownall, Commodore Allen, Mr Deakin and Mr Kelly, all of whom are sometimes here for hours on end. In addition there are odd

---

[1] Violet Bonham Carter, the elder daughter of H. H. Asquith, had stood for Parliament as a Liberal in 1945, and been defeated (at Wells). A Vice-Chairman of the United Europe Movement, and since 1944 President of the Liberal Party, she stood at Colne Valley in 1951, but, despite the absence of any Conservative candidate, was defeated by 2,189 votes (out of 50,000) by the sitting Labour member W. Glenvil Hall, who was Chairman of the Parliamentary Labour Party, and a Labour delegate to the Consultative Assembly at Strasbourg in 1950 and 1951.

[2] 'My darling', 25 March 1951: Spencer-Churchill papers (carbon copy in Churchill papers, 1/47).

[3] Brigadier Gerald Blunt, DSO (1916), OBE (1919), mentioned in despatches (1940), had joined Conservative Central Office in 1949, after a distinguished military career in both world wars and having been Head of Relief Supplies at the Ministry of Supply from 1945 to 1949. He was fairly frequently at Hyde Park Gate during 1951. Mr Bremridge was helping Churchill on the memoirs; he was twice at Hyde Park Gate with Commodore Allen during April. Once, in March, also with Allen, he had stayed overnight at Chartwell.

callers from time to time, who come without notice with matters for the attention of you or your secretaries—e.g. various Town Clerks, the Chief Rabbi (who came the other day) [1] and representatives of organizations of all descriptions. Consequently, as there is no other room available, they are received and interviewed, and work, in either the Library or the Morning Room, sometimes both. This means that when I go downstairs to use these rooms I often find complete strangers there. If the studio were free, all these people could be accommodated there. I do not think it would be suitable for them to use the front room of No. 27 as it is full of your confidential Trust files. It would not be practicable to ask Mr Wood to vacate the studio when necessary, as this would be every few minutes.

You did ask if Mr Wood could remain there for another two months, until Volume V is finished; but then there will be Volume VI and the revises of the previous volumes.

Would you approve of the following letter now being written to Mr Wood? [2]

The letter to Mr Wood, as drafted and signed by Clementine Churchill, read:

I am so very sorry that you find the front room uncomfortable, and while I was away in Spain you mentioned the matter to my Husband who, I think, arranged for you to continue using the studio room until he was able to discuss the subject with me on my return home.

The reasons which I explained to you are, I fear, still valid. We should so much like to be able to find room for all those who do such important work for my Husband, but the numbers are increasing day by day.

It has occurred to me that, if you find the front room rather sunless and oppressive, perhaps you would prefer to work at home. I am sure this could be arranged if that is what you would like best. [3]

Churchill did not want Wood to leave Hyde Park Gate, or to work from his home in distant Golders Green. Realizing her husband's determination, Clementine Churchill offered Wood the room at the front of the house. But this too proved unsatisfactory. As she herself wrote to Churchill, in a dictated note:

With regard to Mr Wood, when I suggested that he should use the front room, I had alas quite forgotten the detectives. They now have nowhere to sit. Do you not really think that with a little politeness and pressure Mr Wood could be asked to do his work in his own house, and come two or three times a week to Hyde Park Gate to hand it over? We are really horribly

---

[1] The Chief Rabbi, Israel Brodie, had brought Churchill a request from President Weizmann of Israel to be present at the opening of the Weizmann Forest.

[2] 'WCS from CSC', signed 'Clemmie', 5 April 1951: Churchill papers, 1/65.

[3] 'Dear Mr Wood', April 1951: Churchill papers, 1/65.

short of room. The Studio is used every day by a succession of people; and as I said, having offered the Front Room to Mr Wood which I regret to say he spurns, we now have nowhere for the detectives. Sergeant Murray was seen sitting outside the Servants' Hall on a laundry basket. It is impossible for the detectives to sit in the Servants' Hall. They would not like it. It is very small; and the Servants would not like it either.

Clementine Churchill added, in her own hand: 'Winston, Please read this.'[1]

Even with these arguments, Churchill did not agree to ask Wood to go. 'I will not have him turned out now,' he minuted. 'We are at the crisis of the book—I use him on the book every hour of the day.'[2]

Financially, the books were doing well. On April 5, at the height of the crisis over Mr Wood, who eventually agreed to work at home, Churchill learned that his literary earnings over the past year had been £35,016. In addition, he had received £2,000 for two new volumes of his war speeches. His Parliamentary salary was only £494, as he had declined to draw either the sum due to him as a former Prime Minister, or his salary as Leader of the Opposition. Expenses were also high, £8,755 for the trainers and jockeys who were looking after his growing stable of horses, and £546 for the purchase of a horse. But these racing expenses were to be almost wholly offset by the bets he had won between August 1949 and September 1951, £7,359 in all.[3]

Churchill also received that summer an advance payment from Time-Life for the fifth volume of his memoirs. The reason, as Daniel Longwell explained to Henry Luce, 'is that his trust fund for Mrs Churchill and family will be five years old July 31st this year. If he lives past that date, all money deposited up to that time will be subject to something like a capital gains tax and not the eighty per cent inheritance tax.'[4] Thus Churchill gained the maximum benefit from the advice which Leslie Graham-Dixon had given him five years earlier.

Ever vigilant in Party matters, on March 30 Churchill complained to the Director-General of the BBC, Sir William Haley, about a discussion series in which politics were debated on the radio between

---

[1] 'CSC to WSC', signed 'Clemmie', undated: Churchill papers, 1/65.
[2] Note dictated by Churchill to Miss Sturdee, undated: Churchill papers, 1/65.
[3] Financial files and notes: Churchill papers, 1/8.
[4] Memorandum of 28 May 1951: Daniel Longwell papers.

Dingle Foot, a Liberal, and Percy Cudlipp, editor of the Labour *Daily Herald*. 'Considering that, as I am told, a very large audience listens to these discussions,' Churchill wrote, 'it is wrong that for four weeks no Conservative representative should speak, and that the common ground between the two selected speakers is hostility to Conservatism. It seems to me that if an undue bias is to be avoided a third person representing Conservative opinion should be introduced into the discussion.'[1]

Haley replied that of thirty-two speakers in all during the period of these radio talks, twelve would be Conservatives. He was 'surprised', Churchill replied, that Haley considered this 'a fair representation for the Conservative Party'.[2]

Sir Stafford Cripps had been forced to give up the Chancellorship of the Exchequer because of ill-health, and had been succeeded in October 1950 by Hugh Gaitskell.[3] On April 10 Gaitskell introduced his first budget. 'I think,' said Churchill, speaking after him, 'I shall be expressing the opinion of the whole House if I pay our compliments to the Chancellor of the Exchequer upon the lucid, comprehensive statement which he has made to us this afternoon, and upon the evident lack of hatred or malice which I felt was apparent while he was unfolding his proposals.'

It was the seventh budget introduced since Labour had come to power. In it, income tax and petrol tax were increased, and a charge introduced in the National Health Service for spectacles and denture work. Speaking of these new taxes and charges, Churchill told the House:

Those who hold that taxation is an evil must recognize that it falls upon this country in a most grievous manner at the present time, continually burdening the mass of the nation and continually clogging—or, at any rate, hampering our efforts.

There is to be an increase of taxation. I am not at all concerned today to examine even cursorily the detailed proposals which the Chancellor has

---

[1] 'My dear Sir William', 30 March 1951: Churchill papers, 2/38.

[2] 'My dear Sir William', 12 April 1951: Churchill papers, 2/38.

[3] In wishing Cripps a speedy recovery, Churchill sent him Volume 4 of his war memoirs, with the note: 'I do hope however you will not burden yourself with reading it if you find it tiring or boring. Still, we have a great story in common of those days we went through together'. ('My dear Stafford', 26 February 1951: Churchill papers, 2/168). Three months later, Churchill gave Mervyn Stockwood a letter to take to Cripps, who was now extremely ill. 'Mr Stockwood tells me he is paying you a visit,' Churchill wrote, 'and so I take the opportunity to send you a few flowers from me and Clemmie. We are so glad to hear of your progress and of the gallant fight you are making'. ('My dear Stafford', 4 June 1951: Churchill papers, 2/168).

made, but taxation is to be increased; it is to be heavier still. Naturally, many people will feel that the issue should be argued out very tensely as to whether other economies in Government expenditure might not have relieved us from the need of applying new burdens and new taxation.

Of course, we know the times are difficult. The Prime Minister told us the other day that the price rises were due to world causes, but almost in the same breath he claimed the whole credit for full employment for his own party. Everything that is bad is due to world events; everything that is good is due to the Socialist Party.

That may be a very comforting theory, but I feel bound to warn the Chancellor of the Exchequer that it is not one which we can adopt as the basis upon which our debates on the Budget and the Finance Bill will be conducted.

The House of Commons should not be led, Churchill warned, 'by the agreeable presentation which the right hon. Gentleman has given us of these proposals into any weakening in our conviction of the grave financial position in which this country stands and of the very heavy drains which have been made, not only upon its accumulated wealth made since the war, but also upon the incentives and resourcefulness by which our future daily bread can be earned'.[1]

In the United States, public opinion had been amazed by President Truman's decision, while the Korean War was still being fought, to dismiss General MacArthur from his command. MacArthur had wanted to bomb air bases inside China. Truman had rejected his advice. Churchill, who planned to cross the Atlantic in May, telegraphed to Truman in accepting a dinner with him at the White House: 'I look forward very much to a talk with you. May I also assure you that your action in asserting the authority of the civil power over military commanders, however able or distinguished, will receive universal approval in England.'[2]

On April 19 Churchill spoke in the House of Commons on Defence, against the appointment of a Supreme Commander in the North Atlan-

---

[1] Speech of 10 April 1951: *Hansard*.

[2] 'Private', telegram despatched through the United States Embassy, London, 11 April 1951: Churchill papers, 2/28. Six weeks later Miss Sturdee wrote to Margaret Nairn (wife of the British Consul in St Paul-Minneapolis, his friend Bryce Nairn), who had invited Churchill to visit them in the United States: 'Mr and Mrs Churchill are so glad you are liking your new life in the United States. You will have seen that their plans for going to Philadelphia at the beginning of this month had to be postponed. Although Mr Churchill was careful not to admit it publicly, this was because of the MacArthur controversy which has been sweeping and splitting the country. He felt that the speech he will deliver at the University of Pennsylvania will be better received when these domestic Party political issues are over'. (Letter of 24 May 1951: Churchill papers, 2/174.)

tic. There were two dangers that could 'menace the defence of free Europe and our own life here', the submarine and the mine. 'Our means of keeping alive,' he said, 'and the power of the United States and of ourselves to send armies to Europe, depend on our mastering these two problems.' Churchill then spoke of his own experiences:

During these two recent wars, as First Lord of the Admiralty or as Minister of Defence, I studied from week to week the hopeful or sinister curves upon the charts, and nothing ever counted more with me than their movements. It is the kind of experience, prolonged as it was, which eats its way into you. The late U-boat war lasted nearly six years.

'To take the control of this process out of Admiralty hands,' Churchill warned, 'would, I am sure, be a grave and perhaps a fatal injury, not only to ourselves, but to the common cause.'

Churchill then spoke in favour of the other recent appointment of a Supreme Commander, that of General Eisenhower, who had become Supreme Commander of the Armies of the Atlantic Powers, telling the House of Commons:

There is no man in the world who can do that job so well. Although the American troops under his command will only be a fraction of the whole of the European forces which are needed—and far less than the French Army which, if France and Europe are to live, must be reborn—yet everyone was contented, and has been more contented every day since his appointment. It was a great shock however to most of the fifty millions in our islands when they learned that a United States admiral was also to be put in command of the Atlantic and of a large proportion of our Fleet employed there.

For some time Churchill had been dismayed by Attlee's acquiesence in the abolition of the Combined Chiefs of Staff Committee, the joint Anglo-American system of consultation which had operated from 1941 to 1945, and which Churchill had hoped would become a basic feature of peacetime Anglo-American relations and defence. Churchill commented:

The Prime Minister told us that he regretted the abolition of the Combined Chiefs of Staff Committee. But why did he not put up a fight about it?

Surely this was an occasion when he might have crossed the Atlantic and had a personal talk with the President on the top level. Keeping the Combined Chiefs of Staffs Committee in existence need not have prevented a co-existent instrument with other Powers on it for the purpose of executing the Atlantic Pact.

Half the misunderstandings which have been so dangerous to Anglo-American relations during the Korean War would, I believe, have been avoided had there been a regular and constant meeting, as there were in the bygone years, between our two Chiefs of Staffs Committees. We cannot afford in the dangers in which we now stand to make mistakes like this.

'By mismanaging these affairs,' Churchill declared, 'the responsible Ministers may bring untold miseries upon the hard-working, helpless millions whose fate lies in their hands.'[1]

Churchill was not alone in these fears. 'I often think of what you said at your last Cabinet meeting on July 28, 1945,' Sir James Grigg wrote to him on April 17, and he added: 'No doubt some then thought that you were being unnecessarily gloomy, though I didn't, and the event has been worse than you forecast. How you must hate watching the dissipation of a great heritage by ignorance, incompetence, downright wickedness!'[2]

On April 21 Aneurin Bevan resigned from the Government in protest against the introduction of Health Service charges in the Budget. These charges, it emerged, were part of the means of paying for the essential new material supplies needed for Defence, which otherwise could not be budgeted for. In his resignation speech two days later, Bevan assailed Attlee and Gaitskell even more than he savaged the Tories. 'I watched Winston while Bevan was speaking,' Henry Channon noted in his diary. 'He sat grinning and dangling his watch chain. He looked like a plump naughty little boy dressed as a grown up.'[3]

Harold Wilson, who also resigned over the Health Service charges, had become President of the Board of Trade at an age even younger than Churchill himself.[4] Through Brendan Bracken, Churchill commiserated with him on his decision, but went on to say that he knew, from his own experience, that it was the wife of the resigning Minister who suffered most. When Wilson conveyed this sympathetic message to Mary Wilson, she burst into tears. So too did Churchill when Wilson passed back to him Mary Wilson's thanks. 'Two days earlier,' Wilson later recalled, 'I had been a minister of the Crown, red box and all. Now I was reduced to the position of a messenger between her and Winston Churchill, each of whom burst into tears on receipt of a message from the other.'[5]

---

[1] Speech of 19 April 1951: *Hansard*.

[2] 'Dear Winston', 17 April 1951: Churchill papers, 2/169.

[3] Channon diary, 23 April 1951: Robert Rhodes James (editor), *Chips*, page 459. Churchill said of Aneurin Bevan, in conversation with Denis Kelly: 'I wish we had someone on *our* side who could speak like this.' (Denis Kelly recollections: notes for the author, 6 December 1987.)

[4] Churchill had become President of the Board of Trade in 1908, at the age of thirty-four. Wilson became President of the Board of Trade in 1947, at the age of thirty-one.

[5] Harold Wilson recollections: Harold Wilson, *Memoirs 1916–1964*, London 1986, pages 119–120; and in conversation with the author, 20 March 1971.

On April 27 Churchill spoke at the Albert Hall to the Primrose League. He was in robust mood, telling the assembed Conservatives:

We are all glad that the Prime Minister has left hospital and can turn from the jigsaw-puzzles of Cabinet shuffling to the urgent tasks which confront him. It is hard on any country when no one is looking after it.

Mr Attlee combines a limited outlook with strong qualities of resistance. He now resumes the direction and leadership of that cluster of lion-hearted limpets—a new phenomenon in our natural history, almost a suggestion I could offer Mr Herbert Morrison for his fun fair [1]—who are united by their desire to hold on to office at all costs to their own reputations and their country's fortunes, and to put off by every means in their power to the last possible moment any contact with our democratic electorate.

This they do in the name not of principle or policy but of party loyalty enforced by party discipline carried to lengths not previously witnessed in our system of representative and Parliamentary Government.

There was one matter on which the resigning Ministers had 'rendered a public service', Churchill declared. They had done so 'by exposing to Parliament the scandalous want of foresight in buying the raw materials upon which our vital rearmament programme depends. Frantic, belated efforts are now, we are assured, being made to repair the evil which resembles, though on a larger scale, and in a more dangerous sphere, the meat, the nuts, the eggs and other muddles with which we are already only too familiar. But for the resignations of these Ministers we should not have known about it until too late.' No more would have been known about the raw material shortage, Churchill added, 'than the Prime Minister knew about the appointment of the American admiral to the supreme command of the Atlantic. What is happening now in raw materials is typical of the way our affairs drift and bump and flop.'

Churchill ended by a promise that the Conservatives would do all in their constitutional power to bring 'this harmful suspense and uncertainty to a speedy end', and he added: 'Be sure you are ready for the call when it comes.' [2]

---

[1] A reference to the Festival of Britain, being built on the South Bank of the Thames in London. It included many whimsical displays, such as an electric-powered pair of 'windscreen' wipers for spectacles.

[2] Speech of 27 April 1951: Randolph S. Churchill (editor), *Stemming the Tide*, pages 64–6.

34

'It is only the truth that wounds'

O N 1 May 1951 Churchill's work on his war memoirs reached a turning point. 'I regard Volume V as finished except for overtakes, American corrections and final reading by me,' he wrote to his five helpers. Any overtake corrections, or other last-minute alterations, would be dealt with by Denis Kelly and must be sent to him. 'From now on we turn to Volume VI.' Each of the helpers would be receiving copies of what had already been done in outline. 'I should be glad,' Churchill wrote, 'if General Pownall would take up the story from the end of Chapter I "The Struggle in Normandy", and describe the salient military events in France and Normandy covering the liberation of France and Belgium.'

Churchill would prefer his helpers to provide him with 'a synopsis and a report', he wrote, 'rather than attempt at present the writing of the chapter'. He recognized that each process involved 'a great deal of work' by the 'Syndicate', as he now called it in racing parlance, and he went on to outline the division of work for the immediate future:

I should be glad if Mr Deakin will bring 'Balkan Policy & Events' along.

I should be glad if Commodore Allen could survey the assembled material that will come in this Volume for 'Burma and the Pacific'. We only want skeletons (5,000 limit) to begin with.

Perhaps Lord Ismay could look after 'The Second Quebec Conference'.

I am asking Mr Sandys to do me a note on the 'Pilotless Bombardment' which I will then send to Sir Guy Garrod. I think we have already got some material of Mr Sandys on this.

Churchill's Volume 6 instructions ended:

It would I am sure be most helpful if the Syndicate could meet early next week after all the circulations have been made, and could discuss this note, which is of course only my first thoughts on approaching our new text. I thought it would be a help if I put this forward as a sort of guide. I welcome all suggestions.[1]

While the 'Syndicate' prepared the materials and outlines for 1944 and 1945, Churchill worked on a speech to the House of Commons on the dispute which had broken out between Britain and the United States over the export of raw materials to China. Churchill supported the American arguments in favour of the ban on such exports, and invited the House of Commons to try to understand their point of view:

The United States have lost nearly 70,000 men, killed, wounded and missing. We know how we feel about the Glosters, and that should enable us to measure the feelings of people in the United States, in many cities, towns and villages there, when the news comes in of someone who has lost a dear one in the fighting overseas.[2] Feelings are tense: very dangerous to distress or to disturb. We can measure these American feelings by our own. They also know that they are bearing virtually the whole weight of the Korean War.

Churchill then spoke, not without a touch of irony, directed against the Government, of the money which the United States had given to Europe. That too, he argued, had to be taken into consideration:

Look at the money they have lent or given to our country during the period of Socialist rule. I doubt whether we should have had the Utopia which we enjoy without their aid. Where should we all be without their assistance in Europe? Free Europe is quite incapable of defending itself, and must remain so for several years, whatever we do. These considerations must be kept in our minds when we discuss these matters of trade, which I consider minor matters, and the different points of friction between us and the United States.

As he had urged in every speech on defence and foreign affairs, Churchill now reiterated during his remarks on trade with China the theme which he felt most deeply, that Britain must work in harmony

---

[1] 'Lord Ismay, General Pownall, Commodore Allen, Mr Bracken, Mr Kelly', 'Vol. VI, Bk I', 'Provisional Note', 1 May 1951: Churchill papers, 4/392.

[2] The Gloucestershire Regiment (the Glosters) won international fame for its epic action during the Battle of the Imjin River in Korea on 22 April 1951, when the 1st Battalion, which was occupying a defensive position covering the route to Seoul, was attacked by overwhelmingly superior Chinese forces. Though cut off, suffering heavy casualities, and running short of ammunition, water and supplies the battalion held out for four days and nights, making a final stand on Hill 235, where it was encircled. Only 46 officers and men out of a total strength of 750 managed to fight their way back to the British lines; the remainder were killed or captured. The battalion commander, Lieutenant-Colonel J. P. Carne, was awarded the VC; other awards included a posthumous VC, three DSOs and six MCs. The battalion's adjutant, Anthony Farrar-Hockley, was one of the DSOs; he gave an account of the fighting and his subsequent experiences as a prisoner of war (he was tortured by the Chinese) in his book *The Edge of the Sword*, published in 1954.

with the United States, and not pick quarrels on relatively minor issues which might endanger that harmony:

Our great danger now is in pursuing a policy of girding at the United States and giving them the impression that they are left to do all the work, while we pull at their coat-tails and read them moral lessons in statecraft and about the love we all ought to have for China.

Churchill urged 'a sense of proportion'; the States of Western Europe needed the United States 'on the grounds of national safety and even of survival'. The Norwegians, Danes, Dutch, Belgians and French lay 'nearer to Soviet power with its mighty armies and satellite States' than Britain.

Their plight is even worse than ours. We at least have the Channel, although even that as a means of safety would, without air superiority, soon depart; and air superiority cannot be obtained by us without the fullest aid from the United States.

Therefore I say that on every ground, national, European and international, we should allow no minor matters—even if we feel keenly about them—to stand in the way of the fullest, closest intimacy, accord and association with the United States.

During his speech, Churchill reminded the House that he had also been opposed to the export of 'high-grade war manufacture, and even machines and machine tools', to Russia or to its satellites. 'The Government denied the charge,' he commented, 'but took steps to stop it.' In the same way 'we ought not', he declared, 'to be exporting any rubber to China at all'. The question 'we have to consider today', he said, 'is whether it is worth while to go on nagging, and haggling, and higgling with the United States over a lot of details, and extremely complex details, and making little progress and creating ill will out of all proportion to any advantages gained by us. The United States have a valid complaint on the admitted fact that rubber is an indisputable strategic material.'

As was now an increasing feature of each major speech by Churchill, the interruptions were frequent and his reaction as sharp as ever:

Mr Harold Davies rose—
Mr Churchill: Perhaps I am going to use the very argument of which the hon. Gentleman is thinking. Anyhow, it is my show at the moment.

Mr Poole (Birmingham, Perry Barr): Do not write down your own country all the time.
Mr Churchill: Will the hon. Member yell it out again?
Mr Poole: I suggested that the right hon. Gentleman should not so continuously write down his own country.

Mr Churchill: There is no better way of writing down your own country than to make boastful and untruthful statements about facts which are known to all.[1]

Mr Shinwell rose—
Hon. Members: Withdraw.
Mr Churchill: Hon. Members will not frighten me by their yelling.

When Churchill quoted Shinwell to the effect that things would go 'better' in Korea following the removal of General MacArthur, a further altercation took place:

Mr Shinwell rose—
Hon. Members: Sit down.
Mr Shinwell: I shall not sit down. May I tell the right hon. Gentleman that he has made a most false statement about me in this House, and that he had no right to make such statements about Ministers?
Mr Churchill: Do not be so nervous about it.
Mr Shinwell: I am not nervous about it. [Laughter.] You should be ashamed of yourself. The right hon. Gentleman has done more harm to this country than anyone.
Mr Churchill: Very helpful, but it is not the right hon. Gentleman who would have any right to teach me my conduct. However, I am sorry to see him so infuriated. The French have a saying that 'it is only the truth that wounds'.[2]

Churchill had been helped in the detailed preparation of his speech on trade with China by the Conservative MP for Bury and Radcliffe, Walter Fletcher, an expert on rubber and Far Eastern affairs, Chairman of a firm of rubber merchants, and twice past Chairman of the Rubber Trade Association. Like Churchill, Fletcher was also a painter who had exhibited at the Royal Academy.[3] 'Thank you for your letter and enclosures of May 8,' Churchill wrote to Fletcher after the debate. 'They were of considerable assistance to me in preparing my speech, and I am so obliged to you for the trouble you took.'[4] Another of

---

[1] This was in relation to the predominantly American contribution and losses in the Korean War.

[2] Speech of 11 May 1951: *Hansard*. According to a report in *The Times*, Shinwell had said: 'It may be that with the removal of General MacArthur the situation would improve'. (*The Times*, 23 April 1951). Later in the debate Shinwell read out a fuller report of what he had said, as reported on 23 April 1951 in the *New York Times*: 'It might be that, with the removal of General MacArthur from the Korean atmosphere, conditions may improve. That we cannot tell. I am bound to say that I regret that the Peiping Government is not more responsive to the suggestions that have been made to negotiate peace in Korea. I think that opportunity has been present for some considerable time, but here again is the opportunity for the United Nations representatives and the representatives of the Peiping Government to gather together to bring this Korean affair to an end.' There was nothing in this statement, Shinwell said, 'that was derogatory to General MacArthur'.

[3] He was also reputed to be, at nineteen stone, the heaviest man in the House of Commons.

[4] 'My dear Fletcher', 12 May 1951: Churchill papers, 2/114.

those who had provided what Churchill called 'valuable notes' for this same speech was Sir Arthur Salter, newly elected Conservative MP for Ormskirk, and Chancellor of the Duchy of Lancaster in Churchill's Caretaker Government.[1]

There was a brief royal and racing interlude from politics on May 14, when Princess Elizabeth invited Churchill to luncheon with her at Hurst Park racecourse, before the Winston Churchill Stakes. Churchill's horse Colonist II was among the runners. Another runner, Above Board, was in the royal colours.[2] Colonist II came in first, closely followed by Above Board. 'Many congratulations on your win,' the King telegraphed that evening from Balmoral Castle.[3] 'I am deeply grateful for Your Majesty's most kind and gracious telegram,' Churchill replied.[4] A week later he wrote to Princess Elizabeth, in his own hand:

Madam,
I must thank Your Royal Highness for so kindly asking me to luncheon with you at Hurst Park last Saturday, and for the gracious congratulations with which you honoured me. I wish indeed that we could both have been victorious—but that would be no foundation for the excitements and liveliness of the Turf.
Believe me Your Royal Highness'
devoted Servant.

Winston S. Churchill [5]

The pleasure of victory on the course was quite offset by news that Clementine Churchill was in need of an operation. After it, she had to remain in hospital for three weeks. It was, Mary Soames later recalled a 'major "repair" operation'—'a major gynaecological operation'; her mother 'suffered all the pain and lowness of spirit which are inseparable from such an operation'.[6] 'I am so sorry to see the news of

---

[1] 'My dear Salter', 14 May 1951: Churchill papers, 2/117. From 1937 to 1950 Salter had been an Independent MP for Oxford University. The University seats had been abolished by the Labour Party, much to Churchill's anger, in 1951.

[2] Colonist II was ridden by T. Gosling, Above Board by W. H. Carr.

[3] Telegram sent at 6 p.m., 14 May 1951: Churchill papers, 2/171.

[4] Telegram despatched on 14 May 1951: Churchill papers, 2/171.

[5] Letter of 20 May 1951: Churchill papers, 2/171. Later that month, Clementine Churchill wrote to Ronald Tree: 'Have you seen about his horse Colonist II? He has won about 10 races in a year & is now entered for the Gold Cup. I do think this is a queer new facet in Winston's variegated life. Before he bought the horse (I can't think why) he had hardly been on a racecourse in his life. I must say I don't find it madly amusing.' (Letter of 28 May 1951: Mary Soames, *Clementine Churchill*, page 428.)

[6] Mary Soames, *Clementine Churchill*, pages 429 and 442.

Clemmie's illness,' wrote Harold Macmillan on May 21, and he added: 'I am sure it must be a source of great anxiety to you.' [1]

On May 18 Churchill was in Glasgow, where he spoke at the Annual Conference of the Scottish Unionist Association. He had been shocked, he said, during the debate in the House of Commons on the supply of raw materials to China, 'to see how much anti-American feeling there was among the Left-wing Government supporters below the Gangway. They showed themselves definitely pro-Chinese, although it is the Chinese who are killing our men and the Americans who are helping us.'

Churchill also spoke at Glasgow of the differences between Labour and Conservative in economic policy, telling his audience, in answer to the frequent question 'What would you do if you came into power?' that:

A Conservative Government would aim at keeping State expenditure within bounds. We believe that a healthy economy depends, as Mr Gladstone used to say, on money being allowed to fructify in the pockets of the people.

For the production we need for the defence programme, for the export trade, and to maintain decent living standards at home, we look to the impulse of individual effort as well as a well-conceived State policy.

We would encourage work and thrift. We shall call a halt to all further nationalization, and rely for increased production on the experience, skill and enterprise of our great industries. Wherever we can we shall restore freedom to those industries which the State has taken over. Iron and steel will become again a great free-enterprise industry, strengthened and aided as the TUC proposed, by a board representing workers, management and the Government. Where industries cannot be restored to the full freedom of competition we intend to do everything possible to lessen the unhealthy grip of Whitehall and revive local initiative and responsibility.

Churchill ended his Glasgow speech, as he now ended every speech to Conservative audiences, with an election alert. 'Be sure you are ready for the call when it comes. Be sure you lay aside every impediment and allow no class or privilege or vested interest to stand between you and your duty to the nation.' [2]

Throughout June 1951, Churchill stayed as much as possible at

---

[1] Letter of 21 May 1951: Churchill papers, 2/112.
[2] Speech of 18 May 1951: Randolph S. Churchill (editor), *Stemming the Tide*, pages 80–9.

Chartwell, where his wife was convalescing after her operation. On June 3 the new American Ambassador, Walter Gifford, and Margaret Truman came to lunch.[1] Churchill gave Miss Truman a painting for her father, to whom he wrote two weeks later:

This picture was hung in the Academy last year, and is about as presentable as anything I can produce. It shows the beautiful panorama of the Atlas Mountains from Marrakech. This is the view that I persuaded your predecessor to see before he left North Africa after the Casablanca Conference. He was carried to the top of a high tower, and a magnificent sunset was duly in attendance.[2]

'I can't find words adequate,' Truman replied, 'to express my appreciation of the beautiful picture of the Atlas Mountains, painted by you. I shall treasure that picture as long as I live and it will be one of the most valued possessions I will be able to leave to Margaret when I pass on.'[3]

On June 4 Churchill left Chartwell for London. He was at Kempton Park on June 5 to watch Colonist II gallop, dined that night at Buckingham Palace, and dined on the following night at the Norwegian Embassy, to meet the King of Norway.[4] On June 7, at the start of two all-night sessions of the House of Commons, he dined at the Other Club, and for twenty-one hours led the Opposition in a series of divisions. 'Churchill stuck it out, much to the delight of the party,' noted Harold Macmillan, 'and voted in every division.'[5] A week later Macmillan wrote again in his diary:

Conscious that many people feel that he is too old to form a Government and that this will probably be used as a cry against him at the election, he has used these days to give a demonstration of energy and vitality. He has voted in every division, made a series of brilliant little speeches; shown all his qualities of humour and sarcasm; and crowned all by a remarkable breakfast (at 7.30 a.m.) of eggs, bacon, sausages and coffee, followed by a large whisky and soda and a huge cigar. This latter feat commanded general admiration. He had been praised every day for all this by Lord Beaverbrook's newspapers; he has driven in and out of Palace Yard among groups of admiring and cheering sightseers, and altogether nothing remains except for Colonist II to win the Ascot Gold Cup this afternoon.[6]

---

[1] In 1918, when Churchill was Minister of Munitions, Gifford was Secretary to the United States Representation on the Inter-Allied Munitions Council. President of the American Telephone and Telegraph Company, he served as Ambassador in London from 1950 to 1953.
[2] 'My dear Harry', 18 June 1951: Squerryes Lodge Archive.
[3] 'Dear Winston', 28 June 1951: Squerryes Lodge Archive.
[4] Churchill Engagements Calendar, June 1951.
[5] Macmillan diary, 7 June 1951: *Tides of Fortune*, page 322.
[6] Macmillan diary, 14 June 1951: *Tides of Fortune*, page 322. Colonist II came second.

On June 8, Churchill lunched with the President's special representative, John Foster Dulles, who wrote to Churchill later that day
about their exchange of views: 'What you say always reflects the ripe-
ness of experience and the vigor of a dynamic faith.' [1] Later that
month, Churchill learned that in the West Houghton by-election some
20,000 votes, or two-thirds of the electorate, had been uncanvassed.
He wrote at once to Lord Woolton:

When I spoke to the Area Agent he said it was thought better not to
disturb the mining areas which comprised between ten and twelve thousand
electors, but only to concentrate on the districts favourable to us. This is the
essence of defeatism.

Surely there was plenty of time for the area to have organized a strong
campaign in these districts? They could not anyhow have done worse. But
the idea that the Conservatives were afraid to show their noses in these areas
must have had a thoroughly bad effect not only on them but throughout the
constituency.

Considering how important by-elections are at the moment it would
surely have been worthwhile for the Area to force the local people into accepting the outside help which you no doubt could readily have afforded.

'I hope,' Churchill added, 'you will go into this matter searchingly
with the area organization and with the local people.' [2]

Churchill was also angered on the domestic front by a *News Chronicle*
poll which announced a 4 per cent Liberal upsurge. 'Of course,' Churchill told Woolton, 'the *News Chronicle* aims at a deadlock between
Liberals and Conservatives with the Liberals holding the balance,'
and he added: 'I do not trust their bona fides and certainly they have
presented the matter in the most depressing way.' [3]

On the morning of June 18 Churchill was the guest at Biggin Hill
of 615 Squadron, of which he was Honorary Air Commodore. After
he had addressed the whole Squadron on parade there was a fly-past;

---

[1] 'My dear Mr Churchill', 8 June 1951: Churchill papers, 2/114. As special representative of
the President, with the rank of Ambassador, Dulles negotiated and signed the United States–
Japanese Peace Treaty, and the Australian, New Zealand, Philippine and Japanese Security
Treaties. From January 1953 to April 1959 he was to be United States Secretary of State.

[2] At the by-election the Labour candidate, Thomas Price, received 25,368 votes, his Conservative opponent, Frank Land, 16,614, a Labour majority of 8,754. In the General Election of
1950 the Labour majority had been 11,858. In the General Election of 1951 it was to rise again
to 10,675.

[3] 'My dear Fred', 'Private', 25 June 1951: Churchill papers, 2/118. The Gallup Poll for June
1951 gave the Conservatives 42 per cent, Labour 36 per cent and the Liberals 9 per cent (as
against 45 per cent, 34 percent and 7 per cent respectively in April 1951).

Churchill then lunched with the station commander, Wing Commander Arthur Donaldson, and the Squadron's officers, who had been called up for the Korean War emergency. Churchill told them:

That you are discharging a duty which is absolutely vital to your fellow-countrymen, all of you, voluntarily joining this organization and keeping it in a state of efficiency which very soon after any lengthy period of training, in peace, will take its place absolutely on equal terms with our regular friends—it redounds to the credit of all of you. And you have well the right to receive the honour and respect of your fellow-countrymen.[1]

On the international front, it was developments in Persia which now excited Churchill's alarm: the nationalization, on May 2, by the new Prime Minister, Dr Mossadeq, of all foreign oil assets in Persia. The chief of these assets was the Anglo-Persian Oil Company's oilfields and refinery at Abadan, in which Churchill himself had secured the British majority holding by negotiation in the summer of 1914.

On June 27 Churchill discussed the Persian crisis with the Shadow Cabinet at luncheon, and with the Conservative Consultative Committee in the evening. At this latter meeting, Harold Macmillan noted in his diary, Churchill spoke 'with great moderation and caution'. Macmillan added: 'It is clear that he thinks there may be a change for the better and that it would be foolish for the Tory Party to "stick its neck" out. This was not to the taste of some of his audience.'[2]

Alarmed not only by the loss of control over this essential source of oil, Churchill telegraphed to President Truman on June 29:

I feel it my duty to add to the representations His Majesty's Government are making to you about Persia my own strong appeal for your help. The question of commercial oil is minor compared to the strategic and moral interests of our two countries and the United Nations. Short of an invasion of Western Europe I cannot think of any Soviet aggression more dangerous to our common cause than for the region between the Caspian Sea and the Persian Gulf to fall under Russian-stimulated Tudeh Communist control.

If this area fell behind the Iron Curtain it would be a serious blow to Turkey, for whom you have made great exertions. Iraq would inevitably follow suit (forgive the metaphor) and the whole Middle East, both towards Egypt and India, would degenerate. Limitless supplies of oil would remove the greatest deterrent upon a major Russian aggression.

[1] Speech of 18 June 1951: Bungey papers. On one occasion the pilots of 615 Squadron made a low-level fly-past over Chartwell on Churchill's birthday. One pilot, Desmond Bungey, later recalled being invited with his fellow officers to Chartwell in 1951: 'We were there for two or three hours and he took us all round the house and grounds, a memorable visit. The proofs of his 4th volume, "The Hinge of Fate", were in his study being annotated, near the tropical fish tanks which he said he used to sit and watch—a soothing influence!' (Desmond Bungey recollections: letter to the author, 22 June 1987.)

[2] Macmillan diary, 27 June 1951: *Tides of Fortune*, page 346.

I see that the Soviets have just paid up eleven tons of gold to Persia, which shows what they think about it all, and may well enable the tottering Mossadeq to carry on for a while.

Now that he has appealed to you I beg you to reply by word and action so as to lighten the burdens which press upon us all.[1]

'I think this message might be very helpful,' Herbert Morrison wrote from the Foreign Office on July 3, 'and I am glad that you sent it.'[2]

Truman's reply, while stating that he shared 'fully' Churchill's view as to the dangers involved in Persia, was otherwise noncommittal and uninformative. 'This matter is being given constant and most careful attention by this Government,' Truman wrote, 'and we are, as you know, in touch with the Government of the United Kingdom concerning all developments.' He hoped, Truman added, that 'counsels of moderation will yet prevail and that a satisfactory solution can be found'.[3] To Attlee, after three discussions at which the leading political figures of both Government and Opposition were present, Churchill wrote on July 9 of 'certain points' which the Conservative leaders, himself, Eden and Lord Salisbury, had tried to make clear. The first was that the Anglo-Iranian personnel 'should be encouraged to remain at their posts in Abadan'. The second was 'that military movements would be continuous so as to secure ample forces, naval, air and army, on the spot to meet any emergency'. The third was 'that if the worst came to the worst, the Government should not exclude the possibility of a forcible occupation of Abadan'.

Churchill's letter ended:

We have urged that the strongest representations should be made to the United States to take positive action in supporting the common interests of the Atlantic Powers, which would be deeply endangered by the Sovietization of the vital area between the Caspian sea and the Persian Gulf, and we are glad to know that there is no question of our asking for mediation.[4]

In his reply, Attlee assured Churchill that, 'In particular, we are keeping up strong pressure on the United States Government and are urging them to give us their full support.' As to the other points, Attlee added: 'I would be very glad to have another meeting with you on this subject early next week, if you would like it.'[5]

While wanting to put pressure on the United States over Persia,

[1] 'President Truman', 'Private and Personal', 'Sent through US Embassy', 5.30 p.m., 29 June 1951: Churchill papers, 2/126.

[2] 'Dear Winston', 'Private', 3 July 1951: Churchill papers, 2/126.

[3] 'Dear Winston', from the White House, Washington, 12 July 1951: Churchill papers, 2/120.

[4] 'My dear Prime Minister', 9 July 1951: Churchill papers, 2/126.

[5] 'My dear Churchill', 12 July 1951: Churchill papers, 2/126.

Churchill was at the same time perturbed by the strong anti-American feeling which he sometimes encountered. Nor was he alone in being upset by this. As he told the House of Commons seven months later:

In July last, when I was a private person, a delegation of the American Senate, which had been sent round many countries, came to London, and during their visit they asked to see me, and I received them in my home.

I was impressed by the fact that this powerful body was greatly disturbed by the anti-American feeling which they thought existed in the House of Commons. So I said to them: 'Do not be misled. The anti-American elements in Parliament are only a quarter of the Labour Party, and the Labour Party is only a half of the House. Therefore, you may say that one-eighth at the outside give vent to anti-American sentiments. The Labour Party as a whole, and the Government of the day, supported by the Conservative Party in this matter, are whole-heartedly friendly to the United States, and recognize and are grateful for the part they are playing in the world and of the help they have given to us.' [1]

On July 3, General Eisenhower spoke, in Churchill's presence, at an English-Speaking Union Dinner in London. His theme was the danger of any neglect of the Western alliance, and the importance of a United Europe within that alliance. 'A healthy, strong, confident Europe,' he said, 'would be the greatest possible boon to the functioning and objectives of the Atlantic Pact.' [2]

Two days later, Churchill wrote to Eisenhower:

My dear Ike,

As I am getting rather deaf I could not hear or follow your speech when you delivered it. I have now procured a copy for which I am arranging the widest circulation in my power.

Let me say that I am sure this is one of the greatest speeches delivered by any American in my life time,—which is a long one,—and that it carries with it on strong wings the hope of the salvation of the world from its present perils and confusions.

What a great conclave we had last night! I had not comprehended the splendour of your speech until I read the text this evening, which I procured only with some difficulty. But I feel that we were close enough together anyhow. I think we ought now to be able to see the way forward fairly clearly, and I believe that events in the next two years are going to be our servants and we their masters.

You will no doubt have seen the interim judgment of the Hague Court on the Persian tangle. I am sure it would be a great help if in accordance with the view you expressed last night when I read you my telegram to the President, you sent something home on the same lines in support from your angle.

[1] Speech of 26 February 1952: *Hansard*.
[2] 'Notes for Address by General Dwight D. Eisenhower', 3 July 1951: Churchill papers, 2/114.

I look forward to seeing you again before many weeks have passed. Meanwhile with all my heart believe me your comrade and friend.[1]

So pleased was Churchill by Eisenhower's speech, when finally he read it, that on the morning of July 5 he instructed Conservative Central Office to make a hundred copies of it 'by noon tomorrow at the latest'. He also sent Central Office his letter to Eisenhower quoted above, for Lord Woolton to see, with the note: 'Make sure it reaches him without an hour's delay.'[2] In sending a copy of Eisenhower's speech to Woolton, Churchill wrote:

This is one of the greatest speeches that has been made by an American for many years. It was scarcely reported at all in the British Press and Ike had to read it so fast on account of the time limit that it was difficult to follow at the moment. It seems to me that it expresses the policy of our Party, and I trust of our country, in the most complete and perfect manner.

I ask you to give directions for the immediate circulation of this speech in every constituency and through every form of organization that you control. I wish that several millions of copies shall be printed, and that it shall become apparent that this is *our* policy, purpose and plan.

'Please telephone me tomorrow at Chartwell on receipt of this letter,' Churchill added.[3]

After listening to Eisenhower's speech, if not hearing it, Churchill had returned to Chartwell, where he at once began, and finished, a book which its author had sent him: C. S. Forester's novel *Lord Hornblower*. On July 5 he wrote to its author:

I read *Lord Hornblower* during twenty-four hours. I have only one complaint to make about it; it is too short. This is the fault which, if I may say so, belongs in my opinion to all your writings on this inspiring topic. You have created a personality which calls back from the past a grand but hard manifestation of the Royal Navy, in its age of glory. The dark side is not concealed, but, after all we fought and conquered not only for Britain against Napoleon, but kept our place among nations to render other services to the whole world in a succeeding century.

'Thank you so much,' Churchill ended, 'for sending me a signed copy which I shall always prize. Please write more about it all.'[4]

---

[1] 'My dear Ike', 5 July 1951: Churchill papers, 2/114. Of Churchill's growing deafness, Henry Channon wrote in his diary in July 1951: 'I watched Winston today, with his hand to his ear, listening to a fellow MP in the Division Lobby. He has this trick of pretending to be deafer than he is, when he wants to shed a bore, or protect himself from importunities.' (Channon diary, 2 July 1951: Robert Rhodes James (editor), *Chips*, page 461.)

[2] 'Mr Pierssené', 'Urgent', 5 July 1951: Churchill papers, 2/114. S. H. Pierssené was the General Director at the Conservative Unionist Central Office.

[3] 'My dear Fred', 5 July 1951: Churchill papers, 2/114.

[4] 'My dear Mr Forester', 5 July 1951: Churchill papers, 2/169.

Churchill returned to London on July 10, to speak at the Royal College of Physicians at the unveiling of a portrait of Lord Moran, commenting to his medical audience on the 'wonderful bevy of new and highly attractive medicinal personalities'. He went on to explain: 'We have M and B, penicillin, Tetramycin,[1] aureomycin, and several others that I will not hazard my professional reputation in mentioning, still less in trying to place in order.'

After expressing his concern about the onward march of science, Churchill referred to 'such awful agencies as the atomic bomb', exclaiming, 'Give me the horse,' and he went on to contrast 'the destructive sciences with the healing arts', telling his listeners:

All that cures or banishes disease, all that quenches human pain, and mitigates bodily infirmity, all those splendid names, the new arrivals which I have just mentioned to you, all these are welcome whatever view you may take of religion, philosophy or politics. Of course it may be said these discoveries only lengthen the span of human life, and then arises the delicate and difficult question, is that a good thing or not? It is a question which presents itself in a blunt form to the rising generation.

For my part I shall not attempt to pronounce because my impartiality might be doubted. I might be thought an interested party. . . .[2]

On July 10 armistice talks opened in Korea; the war was all but over. Almost six years had passed since the Conservative Party had been defeated at the polls and Churchill thrust out of office and out of power. Speaking in his constituency on July 21, Churchill was harsh in his criticisms of the Labour record. Devaluation was 'the child of wild, profuse expenditure'. Rearmament has 'hardly begun'. Nationalization had proved 'an awful flop'. In Persia, and other

[1] Churchill had himself used the anti-biotic Tetramycin. As Dr R. M. B. MacKenna had explained to him three months earlier: 'I am anxious that you should take the tetramycin, although I realize that you may be reluctant to do so, for if boils do form in the armpit they tend to be deep and difficult to cure. The small nodule you showed me this morning is the right phase for the Tetramycin to attack it.' Supplies of Tetramycin, MacKenna added, 'are very short'. ('Dear Mr Churchill', 5 April 1951: Churchill papers, 2/173.)

[2] Speech of 10 July 1951: Randolph S. Churchill (editor), *Stemming the Tide*, pages 90–2. Of Lord Moran, Churchill said: 'His war record is magnificent. In the First World War he won the MC and was mentioned in many dispatches and has Italian decorations—all gained under the hard fire caused by the mistakes of our military experts in the first great struggle with which our generation has been afflicted. In the last war, Charles came with me wherever I went. That puts me in the position of the man who said one night, "I think my companion here ought to have the VC because he has been everywhere I have been." At any rate, we went for a good many long journeys by air at a time when the comforts of air travel had not been developed to the almost perfect state they have now. I do not think a great deal about travelling by air so long as you get there, and he will remember some awkward moments. I am deeply indebted to him.'

countries, 'our Socialist Utopians are getting fed back with their own tail'. The Government, though it deserved 'credit' for its hostility to Communism, was 'bringing it nearer by all they do'. But all was not lost, Churchill said, for there was going to be a General Election 'as soon as we can force these office-clingers to present themselves before their fellow countrymen'. Then, Churchill declared, 'the people will have a chance to express their will'.[1]

Again in London on July 23, Churchill spoke at the Mansion House, in support of a United Europe and a European Army in which Germany would play its part equally with France. 'It was with a deep sense of comfort,' Churchill commented, 'that I saw the representatives of the German Parliament take their seats in the European Assembly at Strasbourg.' The European Movement and the European idea for which it stood had, he said, 'undoubtedly played a large part in bringing nearer the reconciliation of these two foes whose quarrels through the centuries have wrought both them and all of us grievous injuries'. He was sorry only that the British Government had refused an invitation to join in the Paris talks on the Schuman Plan. 'I believe that if a British representative had been there,' he said, 'we might very likely have secured further modifications which would have made it possible for Britain to join in this scheme, either on the same footing as the others or as some kind of associate member. From the Continental standpoint the Schuman Plan is greatly weakened by the absence of Britain—the largest steel and coal-producing nation in Europe.'[2]

The final volume of the war memoirs was now being completed. Help came from many quarters, including Miss Sturdee who, having accompanied Churchill to Yalta as one of his personal secretaries, now set down her recollections for him, including an occasion at Yalta when Sir Charles Portal 'happened to remark that there was no lemon-peel for the cocktails at your villa. The next day a lemon tree, in a large tub and laden with lemons, appeared.'[3]

Prompted by Miss Sturdee's notes, Churchill dictated his own recollections of the journey to Yalta, the course of the discussions there, and, once the conference had ended, the visit to Athens and then his final meeting, as it turned out, with Roosevelt, off Alexandria, and Roosevelt's 'placid, frail aspect'.[4]

[1] Speech of 21 July 1951: Randolph S. Churchill (editor), *Stemming the Tide*, pages 93–7.
[2] Speech of 23 July 1951: Randolph S. Churchill (editor), *Stemming the Tide*, pages 98–100. On the day of this speech, Marshal Pétain died in France at the age of ninety-five.
[3] 'Mr Churchill', 'Yalta Conference', initialled 'NS', 10 May 1951: Churchill papers, 4/362.
[4] 'Notes on Volume VI', undated: Churchill papers, 4/362.

In setting out his own recollections for General Pownall, Churchill asked that in preparing the account of the fighting on German soil in 1945, while there was 'no doubt of the tremendous achievements of the Americans in encircling the Ruhr and forcing all the fortifications on their own front', it should be remembered that 'We did fight also on our front'.[1]

On July 20 Churchill had been sent a comprehensive set of queries, sixty of them in all, for Volume 5 from Austin G. Olney of his American publishers, Houghton Mifflin. 'I think it is better to err on the side of fussiness,' Olney wrote to Denis Kelly.[2] Churchill at once asked Kelly to recheck the chapters which Olney had scrutinized; many of the American's points made possible the avoidance of factual errors of the sort which a disgruntled reviewer would much have enjoyed pouncing upon.[3]

Briefly, current affairs intruded on Churchill's pattern of work when he learned of the assassination of King Abdullah of Jordan, murdered in Jerusalem by a Palestinian Arab. Asked for his comment, Churchill declared: 'I deeply regret the murder of this wise and faithful Arab ruler, who never deserted the cause of Britain and held out the hand of reconciliation to Israel. This is a tragic event.'[4]

Churchill had also to speak in the House of Commons in answer to a speech by Herbert Morrison to the Durham miners, accusing the Conservatives of wanting war. On July 29, a Sunday, Harold Macmillan went down to Chartwell to help co-ordinate Churchill's speech with his own speech winding up the debate. Macmillan later recalled:

With his usual skill he had prepared a great deal of material which would stand whatever might happen in the next twenty-four hours. But he was continually distracted by one of his new hobbies—an indoor aquarium with

---

[1] 'My dear Henry', 9 June 1951: Churchill papers, 4/25.

[2] Letter of 20 July 1951: Churchill papers, 4/342.

[3] For example, Churchill stated that 'nearly four million tons of merchant shipping had been sunk in 1940'. Olney pointed out that Command Paper 6564, Statistics Relating to the War Effort of the UK, published in November 1944, gave the figure as 2,725,000. Or, of the liberation of the Soviet city of Nikopol on 25 October 1943, 'Nikopol did not fall until Feb. 8, 1944'. Or, of the reference in February 1943 to Air Chief Marshal Slessor, Olney pointed out that he was at that time Acting Air Marshal. Or, of a particular air attack described by Churchill as having been carried out 'with no casualities', Olney noted that the Royal Institute of International Affairs *Chronology of the Second World War* 'states Allied losses at 40 airmen and less than 20 planes'. ('Queries for Volume V, Book I': Churchill papers, 4/342.)

[4] 'Mr Churchill comments on the Assassination of King Abdullah of Jordan', 20 July 1951: Churchill papers, 3/166. In March 1921, at a meeting with Abdullah in Jerusalem, Churchill had given him British support as Emir of Transjordan (as well as confirming the throne of Iraq for his brother Feisal). Britain had recognized the complete independence of Transjordan on 22 March 1946 (name changed to Jordan on 17 June 1946). Abdullah was succeeded by his son Tallal, who was subsequently deposed, in 1953, in favour of his own son (Abdullah's grandson) Hussein.

tanks of tropical fish, minute but very lovely. He was quite fascinated by their delicate beauty.

On this occasion he gave me an inscribed copy of Volume IV of his war history, 'The Hinge of Fate'. It was really amazing to realise the amount of work of which this extraordinary man was capable, in spite of his age. Since the war, with its appalling strain, he had fought two General Elections and was about to fight a third; by the Fulton speech he had been the inspiration of the Western rally against Russian aggression; he had launched the European Movement; and he had completed four volumes of his book.[1]

Churchill's speech, Macmillan noted in his diary, was 'one of his most devastating and polished efforts. (It was much improved on the version he had completed on Sunday.) He was in tremendous form and under a mass of chaff and invective covered the only weakness of his position—that is, the brake which he has put during the last six weeks on the more ardent Tory spirits. He thus established a complete ascendancy over the party and indeed over the House.'[2]

During his speech, Churchill criticized the Government for being unwilling to do anything to counter Egypt's refusal to allow ships bound for Israel to go through the Suez Canal. During the debate there were several angry altercations between Churchill and Morrison. At one moment, Morrison declared: 'They are laughing at the right hon. Gentleman behind him,' to which Churchill replied: 'I expect that the right hon. Gentleman wishes that he had such cordial relations with his own backbenchers.' Referring to Morrison's speech to the Durham miners in which he had stated that if the Tories had had their way 'we should have been involved in two wars in the last ten days', Churchill commented: 'how far the right hon. Gentleman dwells below the level of events, and how little he understands their proportion in the discharge of the great office to which he has been appointed.' Morrison's 'main thought in life', Churchill added, 'is to be a caucus boss and a bitter party electioneer. It is tragic indeed that at this time his distorted, twisted and malevolent mind should be the one to which our foreign affairs are confided.' As to the Government's bowing to Persian pressure to evacuate British personnel from the oilfields at Abadan, Churchill warned:

If they use their precarious and divided majority to cast away one of the major interests of the nation, and indeed injure, as I think and I have sought to show, the world cause, if they are found to be guilty of such a course of action now that they are asking of all of us so many sacrifices to carry out the policy of rearmament, then I say the responsibility will lie upon them for this shameful disaster, diminution and impoverishment of our world position;

[1] Macmillan recollection and comment: *Tides of Fortune*, page 347.
[2] Macmillan diary, 30 July 1951: *Tides of Fortune*, page 347.

and we are quite certain that in the long run justice will be done to them by the British people.[1]

Churchill also spoke on July 30 about what he had long considered another of the Labour Government's 'mistakes and miscalculations', the 'winding-up' of the Palestine Mandate in such a way as 'to earn almost in equal degree the hatred of the Arabs and the Jews'. It was Britain's 'weakness', he pointed out later in his speech, which had let Israel suffer through the Suez Canal being closed to Israeli ships.[2]

Speaking of Persia, Churchill supported the Government's policy of seeking conciliation and accepting President Truman's proposal that Averell Harriman should be sent to Persia as a mediator.[3] It was a situation, Churchill said, 'calling, in an exceptional degree, for patience on the basis of firmness'. If there was violence against British personnel, however, 'we must not hesitate to intervene, if necessary by force, and give all the necessary protection to our fellow subjects'.

Frequently during this debate there were again interruptions and altercations, including one with the Foreign Secretary and one with Attlee:

The Prime Minister indicated dissent.

Mr Churchill: The Prime Minister may hold a very different view, but he cannot dismiss an argument or even an assertion by muttering: 'Quite untrue, quite untrue.'[4]

On August 1, Field Marshal Alexander sent his comments on Volume 5, suggesting in the Italian campaign chapters 'a special tribute to the Polish Corps and the French Corps—They were both excel-

[1] Speech of 30 July 1951: *Hansard*.

[2] In April 1951 Churchill had been invited by President Weizmann of Israel to attend the opening of the Weizmann Forest. In declining the invitation, he wrote to the Israeli Minister Plenipotentiary in London, Eliahu Elath: 'As a Zionist since the days of the Balfour Declaration I am much complimented to receive this invitation from so great a world statesman as Doctor Weizmann, whose son fell in the cause of freedom, which we now all labour to defend. It is with much regret therefore that I do not find it possible to come to the ceremony which signifies another stage in reclaiming the desert of so many centuries into a fertile home for the Jewish people. Please convey my warm thanks to the President and express my great regrets.' ('Dear Mr Elath', 9 April 1951: Churchill papers, 2/170.)

[3] Speaking of Averell Harriman, Churchill told the House of Commons: 'He is a man who has a complete grasp of the whole scene and a man of the highest personal capacity.' Churchill added: 'Mr Harriman does not necessarily represent British views. Nevertheless, I believe that the Harriman mission has been helpful and that it has improved, and not lessened, the hopes of eventual agreement. Mr Harriman's exertions have, at any rate, brought the prospects of a resumption of civilized conversations much nearer than they were before.'

[4] Speech of 30 July 1951: *Hansard*.

lent, also to say something about the 3 Indian Divisions', who, Alexander added, 'got on very well with the Italian people'.[1]

All Alexander's factual points, Pownall noted, had been 'taken care of'. As to the Poles and French, Pownall added, 'The trouble is that if one does too much of that sort of thing the poor b——— English feel out in the cold.'[2]

From Emery Reves came a further criticism on Volume 5, on August 2, when he urged 'The elimination of the far too many code names in the text and their replacement by clear language.'[3] Churchill made no comment, and no change. A few days later, however, Reves sent an impressive list of fifty-six points on the first eleven chapters. Kelly, Pownall and Deakin at once set to work on them. 'Reves has sent a long list of suggestions and amendments,' Churchill wrote to Lord Camrose, 'most of which, as usual are extremely good,' and he added: 'I wish he had sent them earlier.'[4]

The private comments of a critic reading the proofs of an as yet unpublished volume were offset on August 3 by the main leading article in *The Times*, which declared that while the text of Volume 4 was filled, as its predecessors had been, with documents 'in great profusion', nevertheless 'the design to which they are moulded is subtly different, revealing that, though the earlier volumes may have marched with the steady pace of a melancholy epic, Mr Churchill's true genius is not epic but dramatic'. *The Times* continued: 'The essence of tragedy lies in reversal of fortune. So also does that of comedy, and Mr Churchill, with the youthful zest which has carried him unfatigued through half a century of public life, here misses no opportunity of picking out the little comic things in the midst of the sorrows and terrors of war.' The review went on: 'The quiet faith in ultimate victory in no way detracts from Mr Churchill's consciousness of the infinite inherent evil of war itself.' Quoting Roosevelt's telegram to Churchill, 'It is fun to be in the same decade as you,' *The Times* concluded: 'Many readers will feel the same sort of exhilaration as they turn the pages of this most graphic and revealing autobiography.'[5]

In its review of the new volume, *The Times Literary Supplement* wrote of how, 'As a chronicler of war, Mr Churchill has, hitherto, been disappointing,' but in 'The Hinge of Fate' 'the methods followed with varying success in its predecessors match the theme. It is a breathtaking book.' The review continued: 'To say that Mr Churchill is a

---

[1] Letter of 1 August 1951 (to General Pownall): Churchill papers, 4/334.
[2] 'Mr Churchill', 3 August 1951: Churchill papers, 4/334.
[3] 'Dear Mr Churchill', 2 August 1951: Churchill papers, 4/334.
[4] 'My dear Bill', 6 August 1951: Churchill papers, 4/11.
[5] 'The Hinge of Fate': *The Times*, 3 August 1951.

romantic, as immortally young as the hero of *Treasure Island*, is not to lose sight of the massive common sense of his judgment at the grimmest moments or his superhuman resilience in facing the ugliest facts squarely and taking tremendous decisions. It is rather to point at one deep source of his strength.' [1]

On the day these encouraging reviews were published, Churchill sent a long letter to his wife, who was recuperating at Hendaye near Biarritz, accompanied by their daughter Mary:

My darling,

We had a rotten day at Goodwood. Nightingall should not have proposed running Colonist only ten days after his effort in the Festival Stakes. He was undoubtedly an overworked horse. Also he lost a shoe early in the race and hurt himself, though not seriously. There is no reproach on him, but undoubtedly his immediate sale value has been reduced. Why Tell, who was only being trained to the racecourse, did not have an experienced jockey put upon her by Nightingall, and when the gate went up, the poor lamb turned the other way and started fifty lengths behind everybody. However both these misfortunes were understood sufficiently for everybody to make polite explanations to me.

The Duke and Duchess of Richmond were most affable. I had not seen him before—he seems a very nice fellow. He was an airman in the war, and has several extremely presentable young boys and girls. [2] Princess Margaret was there, very piano, but she assured me that she had recovered from the German measles.

The Session has ended, thank God, but no one knows what is going to happen next. The uncertainty is a bore, as one cannot make clear-cut plans about the farm, etc.

I am plunged in Volume V, which I am trying to deliver in time for the Book-of-the-Month Club in America, which sells 350,000, to take it for November. They have taken the whole five volumes, and this is a record when you think of the enormous figures involved. The British edition of Volume IV comes out to-day, or rather tomorrow, August 4, and is reviewed in all the papers to-day. I thought you would like to see *The Times* leading article, *The Times Literary Supplement* review, and *The Manchester Guardian* review, which are now enclosed. [3] I am sending a hundred copies of the book to our friends.

[1] *The Times Literary Supplement*, 3 August 1951. The hero of Stevenson's *Treasure Island* (first published in 1838) was Jim Hawkins.

[2] The 9th Duke of Richmond had succeeded his father as Duke in 1935, at the age of thirty-one. From 1941 to 1945 he served as a Flight Lieutenant in the Royal Air Force. He was also President of the British Automobile Racing Club. His wife was the younger daughter of the Rev. Thomas Hudson, Vicar of Wendover, Bucks. They had two sons, Charles Henry, Earl of March, and Lord Nicholas Gordon-Lennox. One of the Duke's 'presentable young girls' was his elder son's wife, whom his son had married on 26 May 1951.

[3] In his review of the fourth volume, A. P. Wadsworth, editor of the *Manchester Guardian*, wrote: 'Though the purple patches are few and the documentation extensive there is no falling off in sweep or in magnanimity. While the author was writing the book half his days were given to fierce political sparring, yet on paper he preserves a proper charity of judgment and the

I am virtually re-writing the early chapters of Volume V as I deal with them. They take four or five hours apiece, and there are twenty in each. You may imagine I have little time for my other cares—the fish, indoors and out-of-doors, the farm, the robin (who has absconded). Still, I am sleeping a great deal, averaging about nine hours in the twenty-four.

Camrose came here the other night to celebrate the five-years consummation of our Literary Trust gift. Randolph and Christopher were there too and all passed off jubilantly. (Camrose has a similar anniversary of his own, though on a much smaller scale.) This of course is the most important thing that could happen to our affairs, and relieves me of much anxiety on your account.

I am dead set on taking the Freedoms of Deal and of Dover in the morning and afternoon of August 15, leaving with Christopher by the ferry after midnight, and expecting to meet you and Maria at the Lotti Hotel in Paris (unless you can make better plans) on the 16th. Then the night train to Annecy. I am sure it would not be well to chop and change now, unless you have some altogether new plans for staying longer at Hendaye.

Here I must mention that Massigli arrived yesterday.[1] He is coming with his wife to Hendaye on August 12, and I think you should offer them some salutation. They are staying at your hotel. Perhaps you would send him a telegram. How clever the French are to get on without a Government, or Prime Minister, or Parliament. All these follies cancel themselves out. The Civil Servants run the show, and the happy land rejoices in the sunshine and complete contempt of politics.[2]

I send you the Hansard of the Debate on Persia, in which I spoke, with this letter and other stuff which I have mentioned, by Randolph who goes forth tomorrow. His visit passed off all right and I think Winston enjoyed himself all right riding at Sam Marsh's and swimming and petting Nicko. He enjoyed going to the races and spotted a winner which no one else had thought of. The reason was because it belonged to the Aga Khan, whose sons were with him in the school at Switzerland. This is as good a reason as any other.

Give my best love to Maria, and please don't get drowned by the billows of the Bay of Biscay.

---

historian's detachment. There could be no greater tribute to the man and the artist.' The review ended: 'The book is a rich quarry into which one could dig endlessly. Some of it—Mr Churchill on post-war plans—might even come in for the next election.' (*Manchester Guardian*, 3 August 1951.)

[1] René Massigli, French Ambassador to Britain from September 1944 to January 1955, and Secretary-General at the Quai d'Orsay from January 1955 to June 1956. A noted Anglophile, in 1938 he was appointed Honorary KBE, in 1950 Honorary GCVO and in 1954 Honorary CH. He died in 1988, at the age of 99.

[2] On 11 August 1951 René Pleven became Prime Minister of France (for the second time), having succeeded (as he had done once earlier, on 12 July 1950), Henri Queuille. On 20 January 1952 Pleven was succeeded by Edgar Faure, who was himself succeeded by Antoine Pinay on 8 March 1952.

The Birleys are arriving at 5 o'clock, and I shall have to sit up in a chair for two hours a day.[1]

Churchill had agreed to sit for Sir Oswald Birley for two hours each day, from August 3 to August 8. 'He used to dictate during the sessions,' Miss Gilliatt later recalled, 'because he could not relax.'[2]

The publication in Britain of Volume 4, 'The Hinge of Fate', though so many months after its publication in the United States, gave Churchill considerable pleasure, especially as it had been so well reviewed. 'How proud and happy you must be,' Clementine Churchill wrote from Hendaye on August 5, 'of the warm and glowing reception of "The H of F".'[3]

Among those to whom Churchill sent the new volume was Jock Colville, who described it, and its predecessors, as 'one of the brightest things in this depressing age'. 'I am glad to see you are having a holiday in France', Colville added, 'before returning to the rigours of the political battle and, very soon I am sure, of No. 10.'[4]

---

[1] 'My darling', 3 August 1951: Churchill papers, 1/49. Churchill's other visitors during those five days included Sir Laurence and Lady Olivier (Vivien Leigh) to lunch on August 5, Denis Kelly on August 6 (for work over the Bank Holiday), Bill Deakin to dine and sleep on August 7 and General Pownall to dine and sleep on August 8. (Churchill Engagements Calendar, August 1951: Churchill papers.)

[2] Elizabeth Gilliatt recollections: in conversation with the author, 9 July 1987. Sir Oswald Birley painted four portraits of Churchill between 1945 and 1951, one of which is in the House of Commons; the portrait which belonged to Lady Birley now hangs at Chartwell. Birley died in May 1952. As well as the official portraits which Birley painted of Churchill there was a joint portrait by Churchill and Birley of Churchill's secretary, Miss Gemmell, signed 'WSC, OB'.

[3] 'My darling Winston', 5 August 1951: Churchill papers, 1/49.

[4] 'My dear Mr Churchill', 11 August 1951: Churchill papers, 4/59.

35

Towards the General Election

BEFORE leaving for France, Churchill gave a cocktail party at Chartwell. 'The Cocktail Party must have been a Wow!' Clementine Churchill wrote from Hendaye. 'I heard 32 bottles of Champagne were consumed among 32 People.'[1] Clementine Churchill's letter continued: 'I hope the tasty tit-bits made by Mrs Landemare were also appreciated,' and she added: 'Christopher says that you both are in love with Vivien Leigh but that he hasn't a look-in!'[2]

'Delighted to hear we shall all meet in Paris,' Churchill telegraphed to his wife on 11 August 1951. 'Longing to see you. Here it is pouring with rain.'[3] 'For Annecy all depends on sun,' Churchill wrote to Lady Lytton explaining his travel plans, 'for I hope to paint as well as toil at the Book—Volume V now going into final print!' Of the outer world, Churchill reflected, to his friend of more than half a century:

I am sure you are happy at Knebworth, but the world is grim, & I am glad we had our lives when we did. I shd be vy doubtful about beginning all over again. Poor India—a hard fate lies before her. Not yr fault or mine anyhow![4]

---

[1] Perhaps it was Pol Roger champagne. Three months earlier, at a dinner at Buckingham Palace, Churchill had written a note on the back of the drinks card to another of the guests, Madame Odette Pol Roger. The note read: 'My dear Odette, If you turn over the page you will see why I write on this paper. I thought you would be interested to see that the King seems to have the same ideas about this as about other important affairs we have dealt with together. Every good wish from your affectionate friend. Winston.' (Note of 8 May 1951: Churchill papers, 2/157.)

[2] 'My darling', 10 August 1951: Churchill papers, 1/49. Mrs Landemare had been Churchill's cook–housekeeper since before the war.

[3] Telegram despatched 11 August 1951: Churchill papers, 1/49.

[4] 'Dearest Pamela', 14 August 1951: Countess of Lytton papers. Churchill had first met Pamela, Countess of Lytton (then Pamela Plowden), in India in 1896, when her father was Resident of Hyderabad. She was seven months older than Churchill. 'I must say that she is the most beautiful girl I have ever seen,' Churchill wrote to his mother after their first meeting, and he added: 'We are going to try and do the City of Hyderabad together—on an elephant. You dare not walk or the natives spit at Europeans—which provokes retaliation leading to riots.' Five years later, when Churchill met her in Canada, he wrote to his mother: '. . . there is no

On August 15 Churchill left England to join his wife at Annecy, in the Haute Savoie, where he worked for a week on his memoirs.[1]

Miss Portal later recalled the work on the book, 'without any young gentlemen', with Miss Marston as the other secretary, and Christopher Soames. 'There were no boxes of papers, because Parliament was in recess. It was just slogging away on the last volume, because he had this premonition that he would be Prime Minister after the next election; a very strong premonition that he would get back. He talked about it all the time.'[2]

Bad weather at Annecy led Churchill to make a move southward. 'Am just off,' he telegraphed to Eden from Annecy on August 22, 'to Venice for a fortnight.'[3] To the neurologist, Russell Brain, Churchill wrote more fully, and in search of medical guidance:

I am going to Venice for a fortnight and there will be beautiful bathing at the Lido. I think it would do me good provided that first, the water is well over 70° and secondly, that I do not plunge in but change the temperature gradually, taking two minutes or more in the process. This is after all only what I do in my bath.

'Will you kindly telegraph your advice to me,' Churchill added, 'at The Excelsior Hotel, Lido, Venice, after you have had a word with Charles.'[4]

Churchill intended to take the train from Annecy to Venice. 'I told him that as the train did not stop at Annecy we would have to drive to Geneva,' Miss Portal later recalled. 'Kindly remember I am Winston Churchill,' he replied. 'Tell the station master to stop the train.' The train was duly stopped.[5]

On Churchill's journey from Annecy to Venice, French Railways transported fifty-five suitcases and trunks, and sixty-five smaller articles. His rooms at the Excelsior Hotel on the Lido were those used shortly before by a royal honeymoon couple—King Farouk of

---

doubt in my mind that she is the only woman I could ever live happily with.' A year later (in 1902) Pamela Plowden married the 2nd Earl of Lytton. Their elder son was killed in 1933 as a result of an aeroplane accident; their younger son was killed in action in 1942 at Alamein.

[1] To cover the expenses of this visit to Annecy, and later to Paris, *Life* paid Churchill $5,000. This was part of his $50,000 advance which had been agreed for the extra, sixth, volume of the war memoirs. (Financial notes: Churchill papers, 1/86.)

[2] Lady Williams of Elvel recollections: in conversation with the author, 7 July 1987.

[3] Telegram despatched 22 August 1951: Churchill papers, 2/122. Eden was then in the United States.

[4] 'My dear Dr Russell Brain', from Annecy, Haute Savoie, 22 August 1951: Churchill papers, 2/167. Brain was knighted in 1952, created Baronet in 1954, and Baron in 1962.

[5] Lady Williams of Elvel recollections: in conversation with the author, 7 July 1987.

Egypt and Queen Narriman. But Churchill almost failed to reach the hotel, as his valet, Norman McGowan, later recalled:

> Anxious to obtain a glimpse of the city as we approached it, he leaned right out of the train window.
>
> I was standing near him, also eager to see a place which was, of course, unknown to me, when the detective wrenched Mr Churchill backwards by the shoulder.
>
> A split second later a concrete pylon carrying the overhead wires of the electric railway flashed past, only about a foot from the side of the train.
>
> My Guv'nor's smiling comment was: 'Anthony Eden nearly got a new job then, didn't he?' [1]

To Annecy, and then to Venice, came a series of telegrams and messages about Volume 5 of the war memoirs, which Houghton Mifflin were about to print. Last-minute queries had been sent in by Sir Norman Brook and Lord Cherwell which Denis Kelly, in charge of the work from the London end, felt the need to put to Churchill. One set of queries came from Austin Olney and Daniel Longwell at *Life*. 'Mr Longwell has cabled,' reported Kelly on August 24, 'that it is important to clear up the date of your visit to the Sphinx with the President, as it affects their illustrations.' This was Kelly's second telegram on this point. Churchill noted: 'I have wired you it is *not* important,' the word 'not' being underlined three times. [2]

Kelly almost panicked at Churchill's reluctance to intrude upon his holiday to deal with these extra points. 'For God's sake,' he noted to Miss Marston on August 24, 'or at any rate for my sake, get Mr C to read Prof's comments carefully. If necessary type them out, as his pencil scribbles will put him off.' Kelly was also worried about the chapter in which the bombing raids on Germany were described. 'Gen P says that Prof writes from memory,' Kelly explained to Miss Marston, '& is often wrong, & if Mr C makes a mess of this chapter there will be a howl from all the widows who had husbands killed in our bomber raids!' [3] Churchill agreed to wait for the comments of Air Marshal Sir Guy Garrod before clearing this chapter for printing, even though this meant it 'may well delay our deliveries'. [4]

To speed up the work, C. C. Wood was summoned to Venice. 'He was the most professional of professionals,' Miss Portal later recalled. 'He was indispensable to the writing of the memoirs.' But he was also 'techy and rude'. Churchill, she added, 'immediately sensed that Mr Wood was being ostracized by us. He therefore went out of his way to

---

[1] Norman McGowan, *My Years with Churchill*, London 1958, page 101.
[2] 'Mr Churchill', 24 August 1951: Churchill papers, 4/342.
[3] 'Office', initialled 'DK', 24 August 1951: Churchill papers, 4/342.
[4] 'Mr Kelly', initialled 'WSC', 27 August 1951: Churchill papers, 4/342.

be nice to him. "If none of you will be nice to him," he said, "I will lunch with him alone."' Miss Portal added: 'He was very much aware of people who were being persecuted by other people.' [1]

From Air Marshal Garrod came the needed casualty figures, the accuracy of which Kelly had felt to be essential, and for which Churchill asked by telegram. [2]

With the arrival of these figures, Churchill's work on Volume 5 was at last complete. 'I presume all the chapters are being given a final proof read for clerical errors,' Churchill wrote to Kelly from Venice on September 3, and he added: 'I am not reading any of them again.' [3] Twelve years had passed since the outbreak of war, the story of which he was now so near to completing.

Other figures reached Venice in the first week of September, a Gallup Poll which revealed a widespread Conservative preference for Eden rather than Churchill as leader. 'The intelligence that Mr Eden was preferred even by a majority of Liberals,' wrote Alastair Forbes in the *Sunday Dispatch*, 'must have been singularly disappointing. For Mr Churchill has been a better friend to the Liberal Party than Mr Eden, and indeed has been much criticised in his own party for his activities in this direction. Only recently many Tory MPs were exceedingly indignant to find a speech by Lady Violet Bonham Carter circularised to them "at the request of the Leader of the Party" and by him warmly commended to their attention.' Forbes went on to give a cautious yet confident picture of Churchill's abilities as he approached his seventy-seventh birthday:

His energy is as fabulous as ever, though he may have to take more pains to conserve it. The hours which he puts in on his literary labours, on top of his political life and his equally strenuous pursuit of leisure, are far longer than those worked by men 30 years his junior.

His great war history with its compendious appendices has revealed to many people for the first time that the greater part of his stupendous wartime achievement was accomplished by means of the dictation of minutes, messages and memoranda, an operation which, like reading, can be as well performed in bed as anywhere else. But it is none the less true that he could

[1] Lady Williams of Elvel recollections: in conversation with the author, 7 July 1987.

[2] The figures were as follows, for total Royal Air Force, American Air Force and Dominion Air Force casualties from 3 September 1939 to 8 May 1945: 75,720 killed in action and 26,872 killed in accidents: a total of 102,592 deaths. 'Total Casualties, RAF, Allies, and Dominions, All Theatres', figures as at 31 May 1947: Churchill papers, 4/342. Of these, the Royal Air Force deaths were 54,796 killed in action (of which 47,609 were bomber and 7,187 fighter command) and 8,000 killed in accidents (almost all of them from Bomber Command).

[3] 'Mr Kelly', initialled 'WSC', 3 September 1951: Churchill papers, 4/342.

not today effectively undertake the task of Premiership without delegating to others a far greater part of its duties than he found it necessary to do during the war.

'If it is true,' Forbes added, 'that he is a big enough man to be willing, in certain special circumstances, to serve under another, it is equally true that in another sense he is far too big a man for such an arrangement to work.' No doubt, as seen from Downing Street, 'Mr Churchill could complete the revolution in Atlantic and European politics and strategy which is so urgently required and which he has been foremost in demanding. But this will have to be done anyway if we are not all to go under.' [1]

Miss Portal later recalled the swimming parties at the Lido. 'The Press waited every morning for Churchill to go swimming. They would call up, "When is he coming?". He also did a lot of painting there. He always took one of us on the painting expeditions, so that he could dictate to us on the launch. Every now and then he would stop painting—if it was too hot—and go on with the book. Work on the book never stopped. He would start work again every night at 10.30 dictating to two or three in the morning.' [2]

Churchill returned to England in the second week of September, spending a few days in Paris during which, on September 10, he was the guest of the British Ambassador, Sir Oliver Harvey, at a dinner in his honour. [3] Among those present were Paul Reynaud, Jean Monnet, and General Stehlin, the Assistant to the French Minister of Defence who was deeply involved in the discussions for a European Army. [4] In an account of the conversation which the Ambassador sent to London, he noted that the European Army was the main topic. During the discussion, Churchill told the Frenchmen present that the present plan differed 'fundamentally' from his original concept. At the time when he had first advocated a European Army the Germans had stated publicly that they desired no national army, though they would contribute to a European Army. The other European States would have retained their national armies, allocating part of them to the European Defence force. 'An army needed spirit and tradition,' Churchill declared. 'The European Army, as at present planned, could only be "a sludgy Amalgam". After years it might develop an *esprit de corps* but time was lacking and we should only have an inefficient and ineffective force.'

[1] 'Mr Churchill and the Premiership', by Alastair Forbes: *Sunday Dispatch*, 2 September 1951.

[2] Lady Williams of Elvel recollections: in conversation with the author, 7 July 1987.

[3] Sir Oliver Harvey had succeeded Alfred Duff Cooper as Ambassador in Paris in January 1948, and was to remain there as Ambassador until April 1954.

[4] 'Programme, Monday 10th September', British Embassy, Paris, 10 September 1951: Churchill papers, 1/86.

Churchill particularly 'deplored', according to the Ambassador's account, 'the disappearance of the French Army which was so identified with the spirit and glories of France. In 1914 France had 120 divisions in the field. Now there would only be 10 French divisions by the end of the year. Surely the right objective was to rebuild a national army of 50 or 60 divisions.' With things as they were 'he could not understand what happened to the annual intake of 220,000 men. Would it not be a much more sensible system to take fewer men and keep them longer in order to obtain more trained soldiers?'

It was Jean Monnet who, as the Ambassador reported, 'bore the main brunt' of the exposition of the French point of view, and who 'stressed that Mr Churchill's original plan was no longer feasible since the Germans were now insistent on receiving equal treatment. If the French retained a national army, then the Germans would insist on having a national army also. This was unacceptable and France must be prepared to sacrifice hers.' This, Monnet argued, the French people were 'more than ready to do'. The defeat of 1940 and the German occupation had left a 'deep mark' on the French character. 'They no longer hankered after national glory, nor did they trust their national army, unassisted, to guard their frontiers. Materially they wanted a larger force to defend them. Spiritually, they were in search of new ideas.'

The French 'were not alone in this', said Monnet. 'The other countries which suffered German occupation, and even the Germans themselves, shared this feeling and there was on the Continent a real and genuine growth of the European mentality.'

Monnet then referred to Churchill's Zurich speech, in which, he recalled, Churchill had suggested 'that France should lead Germany by the hand'. 'That was exactly what France was doing. Both in the Schuman Plan and in the European Army they were seeking to bury the old feuds and rivalries and to fuse, on a basis of equality, the talents and resources of the two countries.'

As Monnet spoke, Churchill 'several times', as the Ambassador noted, 'paid tribute to the skill' with which he made his case, and, when Monnet had finished, said that although he doubted the 'practicability' of the current Pleven Plan for a European Army, 'he would certainly do nothing to obstruct its fulfilment'.

Churchill then spoke about the United States, telling his French guests:

. . . he did not believe that the USA could be counted upon to continue indefinitely with their present scale of rearmament and aid to Europe. In two or three years they would insist on having a show-down, and Russia would then have to withdraw from her present forward positions in Poland and Czechoslovakia, or there would be war. Mr Churchill admitted that it was seven years since he had seen Stalin, and they might have brought a change.[1] Nevertheless, if he were again Prime Minister he would certainly seek a personal meeting in order to see whether some arrangement could not be reached. 'You can't argue with Communists but you can bargain with them.' As an instance of this, Mr Churchill cited the agreement reached in Moscow in 1944 about zones of influence in the Balkans. He suggested that there were concessions we could make. For instance, he would give the Russians access to warm waters by instituting international control of the exits of the Baltic and the Dardanelles. He believed the Russians might gain assurance and be more willing to co-operate with the outside world.[2]

On the following day, September 11, Churchill lunched at the British Embassy with the Ambassador and one other guest, General Eisenhower. Once more, the Ambassador recorded the course of the conversation, with Churchill referring to his talk on the previous night 'with his French friends' and repeating his view that 'the European Army which did not preserve national contingents would have no fighting spirit'. Eisenhower disagreed 'strongly', arguing that it was 'necessary in life sometimes to attempt to do things which appeared impossible'.

Churchill then had what the Ambassador described as 'a long and rather technical discussion with General Eisenhower about French manpower and what in effect happened to the call-up if, as the French maintained, they only produced ten or fifteen divisions'. Churchill pressed strongly the need for a call-up of three years' service 'in limited numbers of one in three of those of military age, the selection being made by lot'. He also told Eisenhower 'that it was more important now to train cadres capable of using the highly complicated weapons of the day rather than embody vast numbers of peasant boys with a year or 18 months' service only'.

Churchill and General Eisenhower agreed, despite their argument, that the French should adopt training camps to undertake the training of troops from their first call-up, 'rather than push them straight into the divisions which would thus be bogged down and quite incapable of combativity owing to having to train their own men'.

The discussion then turned to Eisenhower's wartime deputy, and now his number two again as Deputy Supreme Commander, Allied Forces Europe. As the Ambassador noted:

Mr Churchill observed that he believed Montgomery was co-operating better than in the past. General Eisenhower said that he had mellowed a great deal and they got on extremely well together and indeed their views on the military problems coincided. Montgomery was one who saw everything

---

[1] Churchill had last seen Stalin at Potsdam on 25 July 1945, slightly over six years earlier.
[2] 'Mr Winston Churchill'. 'Dinner at the Embassy', 10 September 1951: Churchill papers, 2/221.

clearly in simple military terms, completely ignoring the political complications of a situation. This however was a very valuable point of view.

For the first time in any formal discussion, Churchill spoke of the German wish to make the smallest possible financial contribution to the cost of the European Army. 'We should certainly not allow ourselves to be blackmailed by the Germans,' he said, and went on to tell Eisenhower and Oliver Harvey what he thought should be said to the Germans:

He would put the position quite squarely to them, either they would participate in the common defence of the West as everybody else or the West would decide to do without them, which would simply mean withdrawing their effective frontier to the Rhine and leaving Germany as No-Man's Land to be bombed and fought over.

The Germans should not think we were asking favours of them. We were in fact merely giving them the opportunity of joining in the Common defence with the rest of us.

He was strongly in favour of letting all the German Generals and Admirals out of prison now, as a gesture before we were forced to do it.[1]

While Churchill had been in Venice he had read the draft of a Conservative Party statement which Lord Woolton had sent him, and which was intended to serve as its 'policy document' for the next election, whenever that might be. 'I like the statement very much,' Churchill replied, 'and think it full of good sense, moderately and lucidly stated. I do not think it can do anything but good, and may do a great deal of good. It reflects great credit on you and Rab and all who have been engaged in preparing it. Pray let him see this letter of mine.'[2]

'It is always a good thing,' Churchill wrote direct to R. A. Butler on September 4, 'to collect thoughts from as many quarters as possible.'[3] To David Eccles, Churchill wrote that same day: 'It is not so much a programme we require as a theme. We are concerned with a lighthouse not a shop window.'[4]

Churchill was back in England in the third week of September.

For some time, plans had been made for a visit to Canada by Princess Elizabeth and the Duke of Edinburgh. But on September 15 the King had to undergo an emergency operation. The Princess had therefore to abandon her planned departure by sea. The operation was a suc-

---

[1] 'Mr Winston Churchill', 'Luncheon at the Embassy (General Eisenhower and myself)', 11 September 1951: Churchill papers, 2/221.

[2] 'My dear Fred', from the Excelsior Palace, Venice Lido, 3 September 1951: Churchill papers, 2/117.

[3] Letter of 4 September 1951: Churchill papers, 2/113.

[4] 'My dear Eccles', 4 September 1951: Churchill papers, 2/117. Eccles had been Conservative MP for Chippenham since 1943, and was one of the most prominent Opposition speakers in Parliament. He was to be Minister of Works from 1951 to 1954 and of Education, 1954 to 1957 and 1959 to 1962. In 1962 he was created Baron and in 1964, Viscount.

cess, but, as the Duke of Edinburgh later recalled, 'the only way we could catch up with the programme was to go by air. To this Churchill was deeply opposed, so it was decided that I should try to persuade him to give his approval. I am glad to say that he eventually did agree, after I had reminded him of his flights across the Atlantic during the war while he was in the rather more responsible position of Prime Minister.'[1]

On September 16, Churchill broadcast an appeal for the Royal Air Force Benevolent Fund. 'By 1945 alas,' he said, 'as our casualty lists told the tale, the few had become the many,' and he added: 'Had it not been for those young men whose daring and devotion cast a glittering shield between us and our foe, we should none of us be sitting at rest in our homes this Sunday evening, as members of an unconquered—and, as we believe, unconquerable—nation.'[2]

On September 20 the news which Churchill had expected for some time now came, in the form of a note from the Prime Minister, as pithy as any he had sent him in the past. 'My dear Churchill,' it read, 'I have decided to have a General Election in October. I am announcing it tonight after the nine o'clock news. Yours sincerely, C. R. Attlee.'[3]

'I am so sorry your holiday should be spoilt almost as soon as begun,' Churchill telegraphed that evening to Eden, who was at Forte dei Marmi, in Italy, on the Mediterranean coast. 'I can carry on here for a week,' he added, 'but shall need you by then.'[4]

At lunch that day, Churchill invited six of his leading colleagues to discuss their election plans.[5] He was 'very conscious', he told them, as recorded by Harold Macmillan, 'of the difficulties which would face any Conservative administration, both at home and abroad. He could not add to his own reputation; he could only hazard it.'[6]

For two days Churchill prepared a series of drafts for the Party Manifesto, which he showed his Shadow Cabinet on September 22. He also, as Harold Macmillan recalled, 'raised an important question of policy'. As Macmillan explained in his diary:

---

[1] Prince Philip recollections: letter to the author, 23 June 1987.

[2] Broadcast of 16 September 1951: Randolph S. Churchill (editor), *Stemming the Tide*, pages 116–17.

[3] 'My dear Churchill', 20 September 1951: Churchill papers, 2/128.

[4] Telegram despatched 20 September 1951: Churchill papers, 2/112.

[5] Those present were Lord Woolton, R. A. Butler, Patrick Buchan-Hepburn, Brendan Bracken, Oliver Lyttelton and Harold Macmillan. (Churchill Engagements Calendar, September 1951: Churchill papers).

[6] Macmillan diary, 20 September 1951: *Tides of Fortune*, page 354.

He felt concern about the Stock Exchange boom and the general feeling which might be created, and exploited, by the Socialists that the Conservative party was that of business and profits and dividends. Something must be done (from the political point of view) to counter this. Could a plan be devised which would be politically advantageous and at the same time economically sound? What about a restoration, in a modified form, of the Excess Profits Tax during this rearmament period? [1]

The General Election campaign had begun; it was the fourteenth General Election in which Churchill had taken part since his first Parliamentary success half a century earlier.

Two days after Attlee announced the impending General Election, fixed for October 25, both he and Churchill were told that the King was to have an operation on his lung. Together with Clement Davies, the Leader of the Liberal Party, they at once sent a message of sympathy to the Queen and the Princesses. 'It is our earnest prayer,' they wrote, 'that His Majesty the King may soon be fully restored to health.' [2] Churchill was also concerned, in view of the King's illness, about the future of Princess Elizabeth. 'I think I ought to let you know,' he wrote to Attlee, 'that in the present circumstances it would be, in my opinion, wrong for the Princess Elizabeth to fly the Atlantic. This seems to me more important than any of the inconveniences which may be caused by changing plans and programmes in Canada. Thank God the operation this morning has so far been successful,' he added, 'but a period of grave anxiety evidently lies before us.' [3]

On September 27 Dr Mossadeq ordered the staff of the Anglo-Persian oil refinery at Abadan to leave Persia within a week. That afternoon, Churchill and Eden went to 10 Downing Street.[4] Later that day Churchill set down what had been discussed:

I told the Prime Minister that we had asked to come because we thought our presence might show the Persians that the Election did not weaken national unity on any measures which might be necessary to deal with the Persian crisis.

He then explained what had taken place and read the telegrams which had passed between him and Truman.

I informed him that if he chose to resist the expulsion of our personnel by force, he would have our support in this matter, which would be treated as entirely outside election politics.

---

[1] Macmillan diary, 22 September 1951: *Tides of Fortune*, page 355.
[2] Message sent on 23 September 1951: Churchill papers, 2/171.
[3] 'My dear Prime Minister', 'Secret', 23 September 1951: Churchill papers, 2/114.
[4] Churchill Engagements Card, entry for 3 p.m., 27 September 1951: Churchill papers.

When the Prime Minister said that he did not interpret his declaration in the House of Commons about refusing to evacuate the nucleus oil personnel as including being pushed out by *force majeure*, I said that knowing him as I did I was very much surprised.

I said that we should of course treat the information he had given us as strictly secret until the events had occurred. It may be indeed that any publication by us of the true position would destroy what slender chance remains of the British and American pressure upon the Shah being effective.

We then departed.[1]

As the election campaign began, Churchill's hopes of victory were muted but firm. 'I think the prospects are very favourable,' he wrote to Lord Kemsley on September 27, 'so long as we do not indulge in over-confidence.'[2] To General MacArthur he wrote that same day of how the Election 'may be of great consequence to the future', and he commented: 'I earnestly hope it may bring all of us on both sides of the Atlantic into the fraternal association for which I have so long worked.'[3]

'I hope you win the "ELECTION",' Churchill's grandson Winston wrote on September 30. 'I am looking forward to going to Plymouth with you.'[4]

On October 2 Churchill made his election address, at Liverpool. Speaking of Dr Mossadeq's order of September 27 to the staff of the Anglo-Persian oil refinery at Abadan to leave for Britain within the week, Churchill declared: 'We have fled the field even before the parleys were completed,' and he added:

Dr Mossadeq can hardly follow us over here. I don't know what would happen if he got loose in Downing Street, but that cannot happen, so the question of whether force should or should not be used to defend our rights or protect our people is settled.

Dr Mossadeq has won a triumph, although at a heavy cost to his own people. He has penetrated the minds and measured accurately the will-power of the men he had to deal with in Whitehall. He knew that with all their cruisers, frigates, destroyers, tank-landing craft, troops and paratroops, sent at such great expense, and all their bold confident statements, they were only bluffing. They were only doing what the Prime Minister calls, 'rattling the sabre'. And the Persian Prime Minister shrewdly chose the moment of the election, knowing what they would be thinking about then.

And so this chapter is finished. The Conservative Party accepts no responsibility for what has happened. Presently it will be my duty and that of my trusted friend and deputy, Mr Anthony Eden, to unfold and expose the

---

[1] Dictated note, undated: Churchill papers, 2/126.
[2] 'My dear Kemsley', 27 September 1951: Churchill papers, 2/171.
[3] 'My dear General MacArthur', 'Private', 27 September 1951: Churchill papers, 2/171.
[4] 'Dear Grandpa', 30 September 1951: Churchill papers, 1/49.

melancholy story of inadvertence, incompetence, indecision and final collapse, which has for six months marked the policy of our Socialist rulers.

Had foresight, alertness and reasonable common sense been shown there need have been no danger of any serious conflict. But all this belongs to the past. We have now only to bear the loss and suffer the consequences.

Churchill then spoke of how Britain's friends seemed 'baffled and downcast' by the way in which 'we seem to have fallen from the high rank we had won'. Britain's enemies 'rejoice to see what they call "the decline and fall of the British Empire"'. The electors would have their opportunity on October 25, Churchill said, 'to show that our enemies are wrong. But do not fail. The chance may not come again.'

Speaking of home policies, Churchill spoke in cautionary vein, telling his Liverpool audience:

Let me make it clear that we do not intend to enter upon this electoral contest on the basis of Utopian promises. We shall not follow the bad example of the Socialist Party at the Election of 1945.

It is evident that this Election has come upon us largely because the Prime Minister foresaw how dark and bleak were the winter months that lie ahead, and felt it good political tactics to cast the burden on to his opponents.

It would be very unwise and also wrong for us who have no special or official knowledge of the exact state of affairs to make all kinds of promises for the immediate future. How can anyone suppose that the results of six years' government, warped by faction and class prejudice and hampered by quite unusual incompetence can be repaired by magic? Evils can be created much quicker than they can be cured. How easy to slide downhill! How toilsome to climb back uphill. Not only have we to face the present conditions, but the tide is still running and may even continue to run against us.

Please remember that, and, this is important, bear witness: I have tonight, at the opening of our campaign, not concealed the hard and grim facts, and that we do not in any way underrate the difficulties with which a new Government will be faced. I do not promise or predict easy times. On the contrary, a new period of effort lies before us, and this effort will require the whole weight and drive of Britain behind it.

As for October 25, it was, said Churchill, 'a day which we must make memorable in our history'.[1]

'Your Liverpool speech was a grand overture,' Lord Swinton wrote two days later.[2]

The Conservative Manifesto, *Britain Strong and Free*, was published on October 3. It included one surprise item, an Excess Profits Levy to be imposed during the period of rearmament. This levy, R. A. Butler later recalled, 'was invented by Churchill himself'. Butler added:

---

[1] Speech of 2 October 1951: Randolph S. Churchill (editor), *Stemming the Tide*, pages 118–27.

[2] 'My dear Winston', 4 October 1951: Churchill papers, 2/130.

'Somewhere at the back of his mind was the memory that when re-armament had got going in the 1930s special measures had been pro-posed to offset any profiteering. What he did not remember was that this so-called "national defence contribution" had been greeted with a Stock Exchange slump, a torrent of protest in the Commons, and devastating criticism by Keynes who dubbed it "a tax on enterprise, growth and youth".'[1]

As the election campaign mounted in intensity, many politicians sought Churchill's advice, or sought to help him. To Sir John Ander-son, who had asked for some 'general lines' for a speech he had to make, Churchill replied: 'You are not a Party politician, for which you may thank God, but nevertheless it is most necessary we should keep in step.'[2] From Harold Macmillan came some suggestions for Churchill himself, with a covering note: 'Dear Winston, Of course you will have thought of all these points, but I venture to send you a contribution in the hope that it may be of use.'[3]

On October 6, Churchill spoke in his constituency, where his main theme was again Persia. Dr Mossadeq, he said, had seen through Attlee's 'bluff'. It was only 'the British people and the world' who were 'taken in' by the tough talk. It was a 'lamentable story', not a policy 'either of resistance to violence or of negotiation. It is simply a case of Ministers drifting from day to day and week to week, unable to make up their minds, until now we have been confronted with a major loss and disaster.' As to the actual results of Attlee's failure to act:

... now it is known that we will not in any circumstances offer physical resistance to violence and aggression on a small scale in these Middle East countries, we must expect that Egypt will treat us more roughly still, and many other evils will come upon us in the near future unless the Ministers who have shown themselves to be utterly incapable are dismissed from power by the electors.

Anyhow, the financial loss is most grave and affects the whole of our posi-tion in the present dollar crisis.

Now that the Abadan refinery has passed out of our hands we have to buy oil in dollars instead of in sterling.

This means that at least 300 million dollars have to be found every year by other forms of export and services. That is to say, that the working people of this country must make and export at a rate of one million dollars more, for every working day in a year. This is a dead loss, which will directly affect our purchasing power abroad and the cost of living at home.

[1] *The Art of the Possible, The Memoirs of Lord Butler*, London 1971, page 155.
[2] Letter of 4 October 1951: Churchill papers, 2/113.
[3] Letter of 6 October 1951: Churchill papers, 5/43.

Churchill then spoke of the *Daily Mirror* question which had caused him considerable distress:

Mr Bartholomew's newspaper, the *Daily Mirror*, coined a phrase the other day which is being used by the Socialist Party whom he supports. 'Whose finger,' they asked, 'do you want on the trigger, Attlee's or Churchill's?'

I am sure we do not want any fingers upon any trigger. Least of all do we want a fumbling finger.

I do not believe that a Third World War is inevitable. I even think that the danger of it is less than it was before the immense rearmament of the United States. But I must now tell you that in any case it will not be a British finger that will pull the trigger of a Third World War. It may be a Russian finger, or an American finger, or a United Nations Organization finger, but it cannot be a British finger.

Although we should certainly be involved in a struggle between the Soviet Empire and the free world, the control and decision and the timing of that terrible event would not rest with us. Our influence in the world is not what it was in bygone days. I could wish indeed that it was greater because I am sure it would be used as it always has been used to the utmost to prevent a life-and-death struggle between the great nations.[1]

On Sunday October 7 Harold Macmillan was Churchill's guest at luncheon. With him he brought a note about what Churchill might say in his forthcoming Party Political broadcast. 'We went through it together,' Macmillan later recalled. 'I felt it would turn out well, and so it did.'[2]

On October 8 Churchill made the first Conservative political broadcast of the election campaign. By 'the qualities of our race', the 'soundness' of Britain's institutions, the 'peaceful progress of our democracy' and the 'very great lead' which had been gained in former generations, Britain had been able to 'withstand and surmount' all the shocks and strains of what Churchill called 'this terrible twentieth century with its two awful wars'. But Britain's 'very existence' would be endangered 'if we go on consuming our strength in bitter party or class conflicts'. What was now needed was a period of several years of 'solid stable administration by a Government not seeking to rub party dogmas into everybody else'.

Churchill then gave an allegorical picture of the difference between the Conservative and Socialist philosophies:

The difference between our outlook and the Socialist outlook on life is the difference between the ladder and the queue. We are for the ladder. Let all try their best to climb. They are for the queue. Let each wait in his place till his turn comes. But, we ask: 'What happens if anyone slips out of his place in

---

[1] Speech of 6 October 1951: Randolph S. Churchill (editor), *Stemming the Tide*, pages 128–30.
[2] Macmillan recollections: *Tides of Fortune*, page 356.

the queue?' 'Ah!' say the Socialists, 'our officials—and we have plenty of them—come and put him back in it, or perhaps put him lower down to teach the others.' And when they come back to us and say: 'We have told you what happens if anyone slips out of the queue, but what is your answer to what happens if anyone slips off the ladder?' Our reply is: 'We shall have a good net and the finest social ambulance service in the world.'

'This is of course,' Churchill said, 'only a snapshot of a large controversy.'

'The human race is going through tormenting convulsions,' Churchill ended. There was 'a profound longing for some breathing space, for some pause in the frenzy', and he went on to ask: 'Why not make a change in this harassed island and get a steady stable Government, sure of its strength, fostering the expansion of our society, making sure of our defences, being faithful to our allies and to the common cause of law and freedom, but seeking as its final and supreme aim that all classes, all nations, friends and enemies alike, can dwell in peace within their habitations?' [1]

Of the effect of Churchill's broadcast, David Butler, an expert on British General Elections, later wrote: 'In his moderation and vigour, in his clarity and technical adroitness in delivery, Mr Churchill gave the best Conservative broadcast of the election, perhaps the best broadcast for any party. It was thought by many to have been his finest personal effort since the war.' [2]

Churchill now spoke almost every day, an exhausting and indeed punishing schedule for a man of almost seventy-seven. On October 9 he gave his election address at Woodford. 'A Bevan-coloured Government,' he said, 'or even a Bevan-tinted Government or tainted (to change the metaphor excusably), might well lead to our still being left in the front-line of danger without our fair share of influence upon the course of events.' He added: 'I warn you solemnly that the mass growth of the Bevan movement inside the Socialist Party, which the Scarborough Conference revealed, may make the return of a Socialist Government a real blow to our hopes of escaping a Third World War.' It would indeed be 'the irony of fate', he said, 'if the peace-at-any-price voters became the means of destroying our prospects of getting safely through the next two or three years of anxiety. It is certain that a vote for Bevanite Socialism is in fact, whatever its intention, a vote which increases the hazard of a world catastrophe. Let us make October 25 a day of liberation from fears, as well as from follies.' [3]

---

[1] Broadcast of 8 October 1951: Randolph S. Churchill (editor), *Stemming the Tide*, pages 131–6.
[2] D. E. Butler, *The British General Election of 1951*, London 1952, pages 66-7.
[3] Speech of 9 October 1951: Randolph S. Churchill (editor), *Stemming the Tide*, pages 137–44.

Churchill spoke again in his constituency on October 12. Angered by Attlee's charge, which many Labour candidates had echoed, that he was putting party before nation in the election, Churchill commented: 'This is ungrateful,' considering that the Conservative Party had supported Attlee 'in every important measure that he has taken for national defence and safety'. In 1950, 'When he proposed the great scheme of spending £4,700 million in three years upon rearmament, we immediately gave him our full support, although if we had suggested that such steps were necessary he and his friends would no doubt have called us warmongers. We also supported him in increasing the compulsory military service from eighteen months to two years, although at the Election of 1950 his party had tried to gain votes by accusing the Tories of this very intention.' Churchill then turned to the question of 'the conduct of Mr Attlee and his own friends' in the years before the war. On 10 November 1935 it was Attlee who had said that the National Government 'is preparing a great programme of rearmament which will endanger the peace of the world', and Morrison had denounced the Government for being 'ready and anxious to spend millions of pounds on machines of destruction'. Churchill commented:

. . . such was the language of the Socialist leaders in the years while Hitler's Germany was rearming night and day. But after all, actions speak louder than words, and the most remarkable event in the Prime Minister's conduct was his leading his party into the Lobby to vote against conscription on 27 April 1939, although this was four weeks after he and his party had welcomed the British guarantee to Poland against German aggression.

And yet later on, when the war was raging, and after it was won, the Labour Party gained great credit by denouncing the Chamberlain Government as guilty men for not having made larger and more timely preparations.

But that Mr Attlee, bearing this load upon his shoulders, should accuse the Conservative Party, on whose support as we now know he has relied in all matters of national importance, of setting party before country, deserves a prize for political impudence.[1]

On October 14 there was an encouraging telephone message for Churchill, which Miss Sturdee took down. It came from Harold Macmillan, who had just completed a week of electioneering, mostly in Lancashire and the Midlands. 'Your broadcast had a profound effect,' Macmillan reported, 'it was perfect. The people seem in a serious mood and prefer to listen to serious arguments.'[2]

[1] Speech of 12 October 1951: Randolph S. Churchill (editor), *Stemming the Tide*, pages 142–5.
[2] 'Mr Churchill', 'Mr Macmillan telephoned the following message to you this morning', initialled 'NS', 14 October 1951: Churchill papers, 2/115.

'We are all *delighted*,' Lord Killearn wrote from Ashford in Kent, 'you are trouncing them as they deserve,' and he added: 'Persia is a marvel of mishandling. So I suspect is Egypt.'[1]

On October 15 Churchill went by train to Huddersfield to speak in support of the Liberal candidate, Lady Violet Bonham Carter, the Conservatives in the Colne Valley having agreed, at his urging, not to oppose her, but to have her as the single anti-Socialist candidate. She was, Churchill said, 'one of the very best speakers, male or female, in this island at this time'. Recalling his own Liberal past—he was for twenty years a member of the Liberal Party and one of the Party's leading lights—Churchill told the Conservatives and Liberals assembled in the Huddersfield town hall to hear him:

I look back with pride to the great measures of social reform—Unemployment Insurance, Labour Exchanges, Safety in the Coalmines, bringing Old Age Pensions down from seventy to sixty-five years of age, the Widows' and Orphans' Pensions—for which I have been responsible both as a Liberal and a Conservative Minister.

I find comfort in the broad harmony of thought which prevails between the modern Tory democracy and the doctrines of the famous Liberal leaders of the past. I am sure that in accord with their speeches and writings, men like Asquith, Morley and Grey, whom I knew so well in my youth, would have regarded the establishment of a Socialist State and the enforcement of the collectivist theory as one of the worst evils that could befall Britain and her slowly-evolved, long-cherished way of life.

As to the Labour Government, there was 'not a field' in which they had acted during the past six years 'in which they have not failed':

In the domestic field we can see the cost-of-living; the disorder of our finances; the vast increases in the cost of Government. All that is apparent.

Abroad they have been false to the cause of United Europe by proclaiming that there should be no United Europe unless it is a Socialist United Europe. They have lost all their influence on the Continent.

It was a wonderful thing, which really ought to be preserved as a model of what not to do, how they managed to excite equally the animosity of the Israelites and the Arabs in the Middle East.

Towards the United States their attitude has been to take everything they can. Indeed they have been maintained upon the bounty of capitalist America, whilst at the same time trying to come the moral superior over them.

'Now is the time,' Churchill ended, 'to break with these follies.'[2]

---

[1] 'Dear Winston', 15 October 1951: Churchill papers, 2/171. Lord Killearn had been (as Sir Miles Lampson) British Ambassador to Egypt from 1936 to 1946. Churchill had stayed with him several times during the war, at conferences in Cairo, or on his way to conferences further east.

[2] Speech of 15 October 1951: Randolph S. Churchill (editor), *Stemming the Tide*, pages 146–51.

'The valley is still aglow with your presence,' Lady Violet Bonham Carter wrote to Churchill three days later, 'and the echoes of your speech are still ringing through it.' It was 'wonderful to think', she added, 'that a week today you may be leading the country again. . . .'[1]

On October 16 Churchill spoke in Newcastle, at the St James's Boxing Hall. If the Conservatives were to be entrusted with the Governing of Britain 'at this crisis in her fate', he said, 'we will do our best for all without fear or favour, without class or Party bias, without rancour or spite, but with the clear and faithful simplicity that we showed in the days of Dunkirk'.[2]

A day later Churchill spoke at St Andrew's Hall, Glasgow. That day, as Egyptian nationalist leaders uttered threatening words about Britain's permanent bases in the Suez Canal Zone, Attlee ordered the 16th British Parachute Brigade from Cyprus to reinforce the Canal Zone. 'It is six months ago,' Churchill wrote for the *News of the World*, 'that I urged the Government to act with America and France in settling these problems in the Middle East. I am glad they have now done that; but it would have been better if they had acted sooner. It might well have averted bloodshed and the serious dangers which now loom ahead.'[3]

Returning from Glasgow, Churchill spent the morning at Hyde Park Gate, where, Walter Graebner recalled, 'He picked up one paper after another, glanced at it quickly to measure the size of the headline, then flung it aside. Every few minutes he would ring for a secretary to demand a later edition. "These all went to press *before* I spoke," he growled. "I want to know what they said *afterwards*."'[4]

On October 23 Churchill was in Plymouth, where his son was a candidate. During his speech on Randolph's behalf, he said, of the Egyptian crisis:

We support the Government's belated policy of firmness in Egypt. If we became responsible we should go on with it firmly and resolutely. But if even six months ago they had taken the advice I gave in Parliament, and approached the problems of the Middle East on the three-Power or four-Power basis, as they have now at last done, how differently might all the Persian and Egyptian situations have been unravelled.

---

[1] 'Dearest Winston', 18 October 1951: Churchill papers, 2/111.

[2] Speech of 16 October 1951: Randolph S. Churchill (editor), *Stemming the Tide*, pages 152–8.

[3] Manuscript note by Churchill for a *News of the World* article published on 21 October 1951 (the rest of the article was drafted in its entirety by George Christ): Churchill papers, 2/129. George Christ also drafted Churchill's messages of 24 October 1951 to the *Yorkshire Post* and the *Liverpool Post*. Both were approved by Churchill unaltered, and sent as drafted. (Messages of 24 October 1951:Churchill papers, 2/117.)

[4] Walter Graebner recollections: *My dear Mister Churchill*, pages 48–9.

He was determined to give the lie, Churchill said, to the 'false and ungrateful charge' that the return of a Conservative Government would increase the likelihood of a world war. If he remained in public life at this juncture he would strive to make an important contribution to the prevention of a third world war and to bringing the peace that every land fervently desired. 'I pray indeed,' he declared, 'that I may have this opportunity. It is the last prize I seek to win.' [1]

From Plymouth, Churchill returned to London. 'I am most grateful to you for all the help you have given us,' he wrote to Lord Beaverbrook on October 24, the day before the Election, and he added: 'I hope we may both take our revenge for 1945.' [2]

On Polling Day the *Daily Mirror* published a photograph of a man with a cigar, in close half-profile, with the caption 'Whose finger on the trigger?' a reiteration of its campaign two weeks earlier to portray Churchill as a warmonger. Churchill at once brought a legal action against the newspaper, its owners and its editor. The result was a full apology. 'Daily Mirror Newspapers Limited,' the apology began, 'and the individual Defendants regret that statements and pictures appearing in the *Daily Mirror* on Polling Day, the 25th October, 1951, were widely understood as making personal reflections on Mr Churchill. The statements and pictures referred to were never intended to suggest that Mr Churchill did not dislike war and the possibility of war as much as the Defendants do themselves.' [3]

The *Daily Mirror* did not keep the Conservatives from power; the 'revenge' of which Churchill had written to Beaverbrook was taken in full measure, with the Conservatives winning 321 seats, as against 295 for Labour. In a bizarre electoral twist, however, more Labour votes were cast than Conservative: 13,948,605 compared with 13,717,538. The Liberals vote dropped substantially, from 2,621,548 in 1950 to 730,556, with the Liberal seats falling from nine to six. Lady Violet Bonham Carter, one of 475 Liberal candidates, failed in her attempt

---

[1] Speech of 23 October 1951: Randolph S. Churchill (editor), *Stemming the Tide*, pages 168–75.

[2] 'My dear Max', 24 October 1951: Beaverbrook papers.

[3] The apology continued: 'The Defendants want to make it clear that they never had the smallest intention of making any imputation against Mr Churchill and they accordingly desire to apologise for having published in their newspaper words and pictures which conveyed this impression. The Defendants are further prepared to pay Mr Churchill's costs and to make a contribution to a charity to be named by him.'

to enter Parliament. 'Am so sorry you were not successful,' Churchill telegraphed to her on October 26. 'It was a gallant fight.' [1]

At Plymouth Devonport, Randolph Churchill was defeated by Michael Foot, in a straight fight, losing by only 2,390 votes. [2] It was his sixth defeat at the Polls. [3] In 1940 he had been elected unopposed.

Churchill's own constituency returned him with an even larger majority than in 1950, 18,579 as against 18,499. His two sons-in-law, Christopher Soames and Duncan Sandys, were both re-elected, for Bedford and Streatham respectively.

On the evening of October 26 a special Court Circular announced:

The Right Honourable C. R. Attlee had an audience of The King this evening, and tendered his resignation as Prime Minister and First Lord of the Treasury, which His Majesty was graciously pleased to accept.

The King subsequently received in audience the Right Honourable Winston Spencer-Churchill, and requested him to form a new Administration. The Right Honourable Winston Spencer-Churchill accepted His Majesty's offer, and kissed hands upon his appointment as Prime Minister and First Lord of the Treasury. [4]

'Thank God,' wrote Field Marshal Montgomery as soon as the news was known. 'At last we have you back again and in charge of the ship. May you stay there for five years and more.' [5]

'May you have health and strength and wisdom to do something to restore Great Britain to the place she once had among the nations,' the Archbishop of York, Cyril Garbett, wrote on October 28. 'This seems at the moment to be the task of supreme importance for the nation and the world.' [6]

'Now you'll be back at Number 10,' wrote Churchill's wartime Secretary of State for War, David Margesson, and he added:

[1] Telegram despatched 26 October 1951: Churchill papers, 2/111. The voting in the Colne Valley constituency was W. G. Hall (Labour, the sitting MP), 26,455; Lady Violet Bonham Carter, 24,266; a Labour majority of 2,189. In the 1950 General Election, Hall had received 24,910 votes, as against a combined vote of 25,480 for his Conservative (15,826) and Liberal (9,654) opponents.

[2] Michael Foot (Labour), 32,158 votes; Randolph Churchill (Conservative and National Liberal), 29,768.

[3] He had previously stood for: Wavertree (by-election) 1935; West Toxteth (General Election) 1935; Ross and Cromarty (by-election) 1936; Preston (General Election), 1945; and Devonport (General Election) 1950.

[4] 'Court Circular', 26 October 1951: Churchill papers, 6/4. According to family custom, there should be no hyphen between Spencer and Churchill; nor, since the first decade of the century, had Churchill used the Spencer in his signature (his usual signature being 'Winston S Churchill'). In 1906 one of his books (*Lord Randolph Churchill*) was by 'Winston Spencer Churchill' and another, *For Free Trade* by 'Winston S. Churchill'. After 1914, only 'Winston S. Churchill' was used.

[5] 'Dear Mr Churchill', 26 October 1951: Churchill papers, 2/463.

[6] Letter of 28 October 1951: Churchill papers, 2/462.

'Wonderful—almost too good to be true. And England will start on her long journey back to greatness. The majority is small, alas. But it's a majority nevertheless. That's what counts!' [1]

'I do hope Winston will be able to help the country,' Clementine Churchill wrote to Ronald Tree on November 4, and she added: 'It will be up-hill work, but he has a willing eager heart.' [2]

[1] 'My dear Winston', undated: Churchill papers, 2/463.
[2] Letter of 4 November 1951: Mary Soames, *Clementine Churchill*, page 429.

Part Three
Second Premiership

36

Prime Minister for the Second Time

W ITHIN hours of becoming Prime Minister on the evening of 26 October 1951, Churchill began the process of forming an administration, combining as he had done in May 1940 the posts of Prime Minister and Minister of Defence. This was not, however, a post which he intended to hold for long, his own choice for it being Lord Portal, former Chief of the Air Staff, and, after Portal had declined, Field Marshal Alexander.[1] Anthony Eden, widely thought to be his fairly imminent successor as Prime Minister, became Foreign Secretary, the third time he had been appointed to this post in sixteen years.[2] Other senior appointments were three 'Overlords' to supervise Government policy—Lord Leathers as Minister for Co-ordination of Transport, Fuel and Power, Lord Woolton as Lord President of the Council, Lord Salisbury as Lord Privy Seal—as well as R. A. Butler as Chancellor of the Exchequer and Sir David Maxwell-Fyfe as Home Secretary.

On that first night of the new administration, Lord Ismay, who from 1940 to 1945 had been head of Churchill's Defence Office, went to bed early. He was fast asleep when the telephone rang, rousing him from his slumbers. As he later recalled:

I was told that Mr Churchill wanted to speak to me. There were many people sitting by their telephones that night, hoping, and perhaps praying, that the new Prime Minister might have something to offer them, but these were problems which were no concern of mine.

[1] Four months later Churchill told the House of Commons: 'On the day when I accepted the late King's Commission to form a Government, I proposed the appointment of Lord Alexander to this office, and His Majesty was greatly attracted by the proposal. It was necessary, however, to obtain the assent of the Canadian Government and to enable them to make all necessary arrangements in due course. I had foreseen this delay, even if Lord Alexander were willing to accept so onerous a task.' Alexander had been Governor-General of Canada since 1946.

[2] Eden was first appointed Foreign Secretary in December 1935 (resigning in February 1938), and again in December 1940 (continuing in the Caretaker Government from May to July 1945).

The conversation was brief. 'Is that you, Pug?' 'Yes, Prime Minister. It's grand to be able to call you Prime Minister again.' 'I want to see you at once. You aren't in bed, are you?' 'I've been asleep for over an hour.' 'Well, I only want to see you for five minutes.'

I put my head under a cold tap, dressed in record time, and was at 28, Hyde Park Gate within a quarter of an hour of being wakened. Mr Churchill was alone in his drawing-room, and told me, without any preliminaries, that he wanted me to be Secretary of State for Commonwealth Relations. I thought that the cold tap had failed to do its work and that I was still dreaming, but Mr Churchill brushed aside my doubts and hustled me into the dining-room, where I found Mr Eden, Lord Salisbury, Sir Norman Brook, and a bevy of secretaries working away on a variety of drafts.

The years rolled back. It was like old times.[1]

Thus Ismay, who only a few weeks earlier had been helping Churchill with the final volume of his war memoirs, now joined the Government.

On October 27 one of Churchill's former Private Secretaries, Jock Colville, having been in London on election night, was at Newmarket for the races, on his way to Scotland for a holiday. He too later recalled the part which the telephone was to play in his future employment:

As I watched the races and contemplated my losses (endemic, as far as I am concerned, on a race-course) an agitated official emerged from the Jockey Club Stand and asked if I was Mr Colville. When I assented, he said, 'It's the Prime Minister wants you on the telephone.' 'Whatever he asks you to do,' advised my innately cautious wife, 'say No.'

I heard a familiar voice: 'Norman Brook tells me you are home on leave. Would you, if it is not inconvenient (but do pray say if it is), take a train to London and come to see me?'

'Tomorrow morning?'

'No, this afternoon.'

Of course I did, and was invited to be the new Prime Minister's Principal Private Secretary.[2]

Scarcely a month earlier, Attlee had appointed a senior Treasury official, David Pitblado, as Principal Private Secretary. When Colville explained that Whitehall might resent Pitblado's replacement by a relatively junior Foreign Office official, Churchill's immediate reaction was: 'Rubbish. Pitblado is doubtless an excellent man, but I must have somebody I know.' In the end a compromise was reached, with the two men being Joint Principal Private Secretaries; indeed, Pitblado, as the existing Principal Private Secretary at 10 Downing Street, was in attendance during Churchill's first weekend at Chart-

---

[1] Ismay recollections: *The Memoirs of General the Lord Ismay*, London 1960, pages 452–3.
[2] Colville recollections: *The Fringes of Power*, pages 631–2.

well as Prime Minister. On October 28, in an attempt to persuade the Liberals to join the Government, Churchill had invited the Leader of the Liberal Parliamentary Party, Clement Davies, to visit him. Pitblado later recalled how, as the talk progressed, Churchill 'was politely gloomy'. At one point the conversation turned to the past:

> Clem Davies: Do you remember speaking at Bradford in 1909?
> Winston: No.
> Clemmie: Yes dear, you must.
> Winston. Ah yes. That was when I was a young Liberal. I must have made a very *truculent* speech.[1]

Clement Davies was offered the Ministry of Education, and said he would like to accept, but must first consult his Liberal colleagues. The discussion with Davies was part of a hectic day. That morning, Churchill had sent a message to Harold Macmillan, inviting him to Chartwell. 'On arrival, at 3 p.m.,' Macmillan noted in his diary, 'I found him in a most pleasant and cheerful mood. He asked me to "build houses for the people". What an assignment!'

Macmillan asked Churchill to explain the existing housing 'set-up' as far as Ministerial responsibilities were concerned. The 'boys' would know, was Churchill's reply. Macmillan added: 'So the boys (Sir Edward Bridges, Head of the Civil Service, and Sir Norman Brook, Secretary to the Cabinet) were sent for—also some whisky.'

Macmillan agreed to become Minister of Housing. 'It was fun,' he noted, 'to join again in the old scenes which reminded me of the wartime Churchill. Children, friends, Ministers, private secretaries, typists, all in a great flurry but all thoroughly enjoying the return to the centre of the stage.'[2]

Macmillan remained at Chartwell, his diary for October 28 giving a graphic account of the continuing Cabinet making:

> Lord Leathers arrives. He is to be Secretary of State for co-ordination of Transport, Fuel and Power. But where is Sir John Anderson? He is to be a viscount and co-ordinate Raw Materials, Supply, etc. Has he been told this? No, not yet. Let's ring him up. So this is done.
> Meanwhile Clem Davies has come and gone. Will he be Minister of Education? He would love this, but what about the Liberal party? He will try to persuade them, but Megan L. George and Lord Samuel will resist. He leaves for the meeting. (We hear later—on the wireless—that the Liberals will not play.)
> Then much talk about junior offices. Harry[3] and Patrick Buchan-Hepburn (who have arrived) are very strong on this. Churchill hardly knows the names—except that Eccles must have a job. And then Ralph Assheton.

[1] Sir David Pitblado recollections: in conversation with the author, 17 July 1987.
[2] Macmillan recollections, and diary for 28 October 1951: *Tides of Fortune*, pages 364–5.
[3] Harry Crookshank.

Then there are other posts to be filled not in the Cabinet, like Postmaster-General, Minister for National Insurance, etc. But what about the Service ministers?

And then the Speaker? Shall it be W. S. Morrison or Hopkin Morris—both good men? And so on.[1]

Walter Elliot, telephoned to be asked if he would become Secretary of State for Education, was not in. As a result, Florence Horsbrugh was appointed, and Elliot was heartbroken.[2]

There was one friend, who had served in Churchill's Coalition Cabinet throughout the war, who had no place in the new administration. For several months, ill-health had forced Brendan Bracken to retire from political life, and to give up his seat in the House of Commons. Churchill offered him a Peerage, which he accepted.[3]

For four days Churchill worked almost without interruption to complete the enormous list of Government office holders: eighty-seven in all.[4] His close friend Lord Cherwell became Paymaster-General. Harold Macmillan was appointed Minister of Housing and Local Government. Among the non-Cabinet posts, the Ministry of Supply went to Churchill's son-in-law Duncan Sandys. Churchill originally intended to appoint Duncan Sandys Secretary of State for War, but Clementine Churchill doubted the wisdom of such a course. 'My darling,' she wrote, after learning of Churchill's intention, 'Do not be angry with me—But first—do you not think it would be wiser to give Duncan a smaller post—Secretary of State for War is so very prominent—then do you think it wise to have him working immediately under your orders as Minister of Defence. If anything were to go wrong it would be delicate and tricky—first of all having to defend your son-in-law & later if by chance he made a mistake having to dismiss him. Forgive me I think only of your welfare happiness and dignity.'[5]

To his Private Office at 10 Downing Street, Churchill brought three of his devoted secretaries, Miss Sturdee, Miss Gilliatt and Miss Portal. The fourth, Miss Marston, working from Hyde Park Gate, was in charge of all secretarial matters relating to the war memoirs, and all

---

[1] Macmillan diary, 28 October 1951: *Tides of Fortune*, page 365. David Eccles became Minister of Works, and W. S. Morrison was appointed Speaker. Neither Ralph Assheton nor Hopkin Morris received office, Assheton being made Chairman of the Select Committee on Nationalized Industries (and created Baron Clitheroe in 1955).

[2] As a consolation, Elliot was made a Companion of Honour, in 1952. After his death in 1958, his wife was created a Life Peer, as Baroness Elliot of Harwood, and for the next twenty years was an active member of the House of Lords.

[3] Brendan Bracken was created Viscount Bracken on 8 January 1952.

[4] Eighteen Cabinet Ministers, nineteen non-Cabinet Ministers, four Law Officers, five members of the Household, thirty-three Junior Ministers, five Junior Lords of the Treasury and three Lords in Waiting.

[5] 'Monday Evening', from Chartwell: Churchill papers, 1/50.

constituency matters.[1] They were to be his personal secretaries, in addition to five male civil servants of the Administrative grade and some twenty 'young ladies' of the regular establishment at 10 Downing Street.[2] For weekends at Chequers or Chartwell, the wartime system of Duty Private Secretaries on a rota basis was abandoned, and arrangements made on an ad hoc basis, with Jock Colville the Private Secretary most usually in demand.

The first Cabinet meeting of Churchill's second Premiership was held at three in the afternoon of October 30, with Churchill in the Chair as Prime Minister and Minister of Defence. The minutes began by recording: 'The Prime Minister welcomed his Cabinet colleagues at their first meeting,' telling them that the composition of his Cabinet would be completed 'later in the day'.

Speaking about the Conservative Party's election pledge to repeal the Labour Government's Iron and Steel Act, 1949, Churchill told his Cabinet that 'urgent consideration' must be given to the means of implementing that pledge, and of restoring the industry to free enterprise. 'If a short, simple Bill would suffice for this purpose,' Churchill said, 'it might be passed into law before Parliament was adjourned for the Christmas recess.' In the discussion that followed, however, it was 'suggested', as the minutes recorded, that the restoration of the industry to private ownership 'was likely to involve complex questions which would take some time to resolve'.

A committee was set up, headed by the new Minister of Health, Harry Crookshank, to report to the Government on what action was needed. A second committee was set up, at Churchill's suggestion, to report on what Hugh Gaitskell's successor as Chancellor of the Exchequer, R. A. Butler, described as the 'progressive deterioration' of the economy in the last weeks of the Labour Government.[3] Churchill then said that it was his wish that 'during the period of rearmament', or for the next three years, whichever ended first, Ministers entitled to a salary of £5,000 a year should draw £4,000 instead. He himself proposed to draw during that period a salary of £7,000 instead of his statutory salary of £10,000. The Cabinet approved these reductions in salary.

Churchill's last point at that first Cabinet concerned British policy

---

[1] Miss Sturdee and Miss Gilliatt were to receive £469 a year each, Miss Portal £405. 'One or more of them,' Miss Sturdee wrote to Churchill in confirmation, 'would always accompany you when you are abroad.' In addition, 'Each would be on duty one night in week.' ('Prime Minister', 25 November 1951: Churchill papers, 1/66.) Miss Gemmell ('Chips' Gemmell) did Clementine Churchill's secretarial work at 10 Downing Street. These secretarial payments were all made out of Churchill's private purse.

[2] The five male civil servants were later reduced to four.

[3] The annual rate of surplus in 1950 had been running at about £350 million for the year; so far in 1951 there was an external deficit of about £700 million for the year.

in Egypt. This policy, he said, 'should now be based on the principle that it was the duty of the United Kingdom Government to keep the Suez Canal open to the shipping of the world, using such force as might be necessary for that purpose. It would be consistent with that principle that oil tankers bound for the refinery at Haifa should be allowed to pass through the Canal.' The oil to Haifa, whose passage had been prevented hitherto by Egypt, was Israel's lifeline.

Eden, while he 'fully endorsed' the principle of what Churchill had said, 'doubted whether it would be expedient to apply it at the moment to the passage of oil tankers bound for Haifa'. What he called 'precipitate action' by Britain regarding the passage of tankers through the Canal on their way to Israel 'would be likely to arouse resentment', if not in Egypt, then 'in some of the other Arab States'.[1]

Churchill's proposed initiative on behalf of Israel, and of unimpeded trade, had failed; the blockade of ships bound for Israel continued.

When the Cabinet met on November 1, it was to hear a plea by R. A. Butler for a drastic reduction in Government expenditure. Churchill endorsed this plea, and suggested that the Treasury should 'call on all Departments' to reduce their expenditure, 'and should suggest specific means of doing so'. In addition, Ministers in charge of Departments should make their own proposals for reducing expenditure. 'By a combination of both these methods,' Churchill commented, 'substantial savings could be secured.' Churchill also proposed to see representatives of the Trades Union Congress 'at an early date', to 'discuss these matters with them'.[2]

That evening Churchill went to the House of Commons to take the oath as a Member of Parliament for the new session. 'At 6.14 Winston came in,' Henry Channon noted in his diary, and he added: 'the Chamber was almost empty, a few attendants, two Whips and a few desultory spectators in the Gallery. The old man, smiling, good-tempered slowly signed his name, beamed and approached the Chair and I heard him apologise to "Shakes" whom he correctly called "Mr Speaker" for being late.[3] He has a new habit of raising his voice. Then, still grinning, he passed through the door. Only four MPs witnessed Winston taking the oath, perhaps for the last time. The light and the atmosphere made it a touching little scene. . . .'[4]

[1] Cabinet Conclusions No. 1 of 1951, 'Secret', 3 p.m., 30 October 1951: Cabinet papers, 128/23.
[2] Cabinet Conclusions No. 2 of 1951, 'Secret', 11 a.m., 1 November 1951: Cabinet papers, 128/23.
[3] W. S. ('Shakes') Morrison had been elected Speaker only a few hours earlier.
[4] Channon diary, 1 November 1951: Robert Rhodes James (editor), *Chips*, page 462.

During his speech for the Debate on the Address, Churchill told the House of Commons: 'What the nation needs is several years of quiet steady administration, if only to allow Socialist legislation to reach its full fruition. What the House needs is a period of tolerant and constructive debating on the merits of the questions before us without nearly every speech on either side being distorted by the passions of one Election or the preparations for another.' Whether they would get that or not was, he added, 'to say the least, doubtful'. He and his Government believed, however, that they were 'capable of coping with whatever may confront us'.

Speaking about the recent abrogation by Egypt, on the day after the Government had been formed, of the 1936 Anglo-Egyptian Treaty, Churchill told the House:

We are resolved to maintain our rightful position in the Canal Zone in spite of the illegal and one-sided Egyptian action over the 1936 Treaty. We shall do our utmost to safeguard the Canal as an international highway, using, of course, no more force than is necessary. Here again I think that time, within certain limits, and restraint and forbearance—not so strictly limited—may give the best chance of the crisis being successfully surmounted.

On the day before his speech, Churchill had sent a telegram to Stalin. 'Now that I am again in charge of His Majesty's Government,' he wrote, 'let me reply to your farewell telegram from Potsdam of August 1945, "Greetings. Winston Churchill".'[1] The 'great hope' in foreign affairs, he now told the House of Commons, was 'to bring about an abatement of what is called "the cold war" by negotiation at the highest level from strength and not from weakness'. Churchill then read out the text of his telegram to Stalin of April 1945.[2] 'That was written more than six years ago,' Churchill commented, 'and, alas, all came to pass with horrible exactitude.' He and Eden held to the idea, Churchill said, 'of a supreme effort to bridge the gulf between the two worlds, so that each can live its life, if not in friendship at

[1] Telegram dated 5 November 1951: Foreign Office papers, 371/94841.

[2] On 29 April 1945 Churchill had said, in the course of a telegram to Stalin: 'There is not much comfort in looking into a future where you and the countries you dominate, plus the Communist Parties in many other States, are all drawn up on one side, and those who rally to the English-speaking nations and their associates or Dominions are on the other. It is quite obvious that their quarrel would tear the world to pieces and that all of us leading men on either side who had anything to do with that would be shamed before history. Even embarking on a long period of suspicions, of abuse and counter-abuse and of opposing policies would be a disaster hampering the great developments of world prosperity for the masses which are attainable only by our trinity. I hope there is no word or phrase in this outpouring of my heart to you which unwittingly gives offence. If so, let me know. But do not, I beg you, my friend Stalin, under-rate the divergencies which are opening about matters which you may think are small to us but which are symbolic of the way the English-speaking democracies look at life.' (Prime Minister's Personal Telegram, T.675/5, No. 2255 to Moscow, 'Personal and Top Secret', 29 April 1945: Premier papers, 3/356/6.)

least without the fear, the hatreds and the frightful waste of the "cold war"'. He had, however, to utter 'a word of caution':

The realities which confront us are numerous, adverse and stubborn. We must be careful not to swing on a wave of emotion from despondency to over-confidence; but even if the differences between West and East are, for the time being, intractable, the creation of a new atmosphere and climate of thought, and of a revived relationship and sense of human comradeship, would, I believe, be an enormous gain to all the nations.

Never must we admit that a Third World War is inevitable. I heard some months ago of a foreign diplomatist who was asked: 'In which year do you think the danger of war will be the greatest?' He replied: 'Last year.' If that should prove true, as we pray it may, no one will deny their salute to the memory of Ernest Bevin, or their compliments to those who worked faithfully with him.

'Let us,' Churchill ended, 'in these supreme issues with party politics far beneath them, move forward together in our united fight as faithful servants of our common country, and as unwearying guardians of the peace and freedom of the world.' [1]

'I thought your speech yesterday was a masterpiece,' Randolph Churchill wrote to his father on November 7, and he added: 'Now that your Government is complete, I would like to congratulate you upon it. Many of the Appointments are imaginative and I am sure the public have been impressed by the marked all round superiority to the previous Government.' [2]

In Cabinet that day, Churchill told his Ministers that he was 'disturbed' at the high cost of British military commitments in Malaya, and suggested that Oliver Lyttelton, the new Secretary of State for the Colonies, should make proposals for remedying it. [3] At the Lord Mayor's Banquet on November 9, Churchill spoke of the Labour Government's legacy, a 'tangled web of commitments and shortages, the like of which I have never seen before'; he hoped and prayed his Government would be granted 'the wisdom and strength to cope with them effectively'. He also spoke of the world scene, where 'Mighty forces armed with fearful weapons are baying at each other across a gulf which I have the feeling tonight neither wishes, and both fear to cross, but into which they may tumble or drag each other to their common ruin'. On the one side were Soviet Russia and the 'Communist satellites, agents and devotees in so many countries'. On the

---

[1] Speech of 6 November 1951: *Hansard*.

[2] 'My dearest Papa', 7 November 1951: Churchill papers, 1/51.

[3] Cabinet Conclusions No. 5 of 1951, 'Secret', 11.30 a.m., 7 November 1951: Cabinet papers, 128/23. The state of insurgency which had existed in Malaya for several months, had been highlighted since 6 October 1951 by the assassination of Sir Henry Gurney, High Commissioner of the Malayan Federation.

other side were the Western democracies gathered around the United States 'with its mastery of the atomic bomb'. Churchill added five sentences which expressed the essence of his philosophy of defence, and of the Anglo-American relationship:

The sacrifices and exertions which the United States are making to deter, and if possible prevent, Communist aggression from making further inroads upon the free world are the main foundation of peace.

A tithe of the efforts now being made by America would have prevented the Second World War and would have probably led to the downfall of Hitler with scarcely any blood being shed except perhaps his own.

I feel a deep gratitude towards our great American Ally. They have risen to the leadership of the world without any other ambition but to serve its highest causes faithfully.

I am anxious that Britain should also play her full part, and I hope to see a revival of her former influence and initiative among the Allied Powers, and indeed with all Powers.[1]

In order to evolve a common Anglo-American policy, Churchill made plans to go to the United States. On November 12 he asked Lord Ismay, Lord Cherwell, Sir Edward Bridges and Sir Norman Brook to consult together about what should be discussed in Washington. 'I feel you all know a great deal about it,' Churchill minuted. 'Presently I will add my own quota.'[2]

Churchill was approaching his seventy-seventh birthday; his mental vigour was unimpaired and his judgement based firmly upon more than half a century of experience in public life. But his health was poor, his deafness growing, his heart weakened by several minor but warning strokes. On November 15 Harold Nicolson noted in his diary that Robert Boothby had been to see Churchill that afternoon, and had told him that Churchill was getting 'very, very old; tragically old'.[3] 'There were many,' Jock Colville later recalled, 'including his wife, who did not think Churchill should return to office a month short of

---

[1] Speech of 9 November 1951: Randolph S. Churchill (editor), *Stemming the Tide*, pages 187–90. Recording: BBC Written Archives Centre, Library No. 17186. Churchill had begun his speech with a joke. 'Though I have very often in the last forty years or so been present at your famous Guildhall banquets to salute the new Lord Mayor,' he said 'this is the first occasion when I have addressed this assembly here as Prime Minister. The explanation is convincing. When I should have come here as Prime Minister the Guildhall was blown up and before it was repaired I was blown out! I thought at the time they were both disasters. But now we are all here together in a union which I hope will bring good luck.'

[2] Prime Minister's Personal Minute, M.37/51, 12 November 1951: Cabinet papers, 21/3057.

[3] Nicolson diary, 15 November 1951: Nigel Nicolson (editor), *Harold Nicolson Diaries and Letters 1945–1962*, volume 3, London 1968, page 212.

his seventy-seventh birthday. At first he himself, as he told me when I rejoined him, intended to remain Prime Minister for one year only, and then hand over to his invariably loyal lieutenant, Anthony Eden, whose courage, energy and integrity, though not always his judgment, Churchill consistently respected.' He just wanted, Churchill told Colville, 'to have time to re-establish the intimate relationship with the United States, which had been a keynote of his policy in the war, and to restore at home the liberties which had been eroded by war-time restrictions and post-war socialist measures'.[1]

'He could be up some days and down the others,' Miss Gilliatt later recalled. 'He was variable. I never thought him too old for what he was doing.'[2]

In the second week of his Premiership, Churchill saw the fruition of the arrangements on which he had embarked five years earlier, to create a special Family Trust whereby all earnings from his war memoirs would go to the benefit of his children and grandchildren without the burden of taxation. His generosity was much appreciated by those of his children who had children of their own. 'It is a great security for them,' his daughter Mary wrote on November 10, on her behalf and that of her husband, 'and an enormous help to us both in providing for them.' There was no way to repay him, she added, 'except by our loving gratitude, which overflows, and trying to show to our children and dependents the same largeness of heart and steadfastness of love which you have always shown to yours'. It was 'hardly in the nature of things', Mary Soames wrote, 'that your descendants should inherit your genius—but I earnestly hope they may share in some way the qualities of your heart'.[3]

From his daughter Diana came another warm note of thanks. 'We are overwhelmed by your generosity to us,' she wrote.[4] 'I think it wonderful,' wrote Randolph in his letter of thanks on behalf of his two children, Winston and Arabella, 'that your marvellous literary industry in the six years after the war should cast its protection round these young lions for so many years to come.'[5]

Churchill returned to the Guildhall on November 19, to welcome Princess Elizabeth and the Duke of Edinburgh after their extremely successful visit to the United States and Canada. 'Madam,' he said, 'the whole nation is grateful to you for what you have done for us and

[1] John Colville recollections: *The Fringes of Power*, pages 632–3.

[2] Elizabeth Gilliatt recollections: in conversation with the author, 12 June 1987.

[3] 'My darling Papa', 10 November 1951: Churchill papers, 1/52.

[4] 'Darling Papa', 15 November 1951: Churchill papers, 1/52. Diana and Duncan Sandys had three children: Julian (born 1936), Edwina (born 1938) and Celia (born 1943).

[5] 'My dearest Papa', 17 December 1951: Churchill papers, 1/51. On 7 November 1951 the *Daily Telegraph* agreed to pay Churchill £60,000 for the sixth and final volume of his war memoirs (£35,000 to be paid in May 1952 and £25,000 in May 1953): Churchill papers, 1/28.

to Providence for having endowed you with the gifts and personality which are not only precious to the British Commonwealth and Empire and its island home, but will play their part in cheering and in mellowing the forward march of human society all the world over.' [1]

Also on November 19, Churchill sent a message to Chaim Weizmann, who two days earlier had been re-elected President of the State of Israel. 'The wonderful exertions which Israel is making in these times of difficulty,' he wrote, 'are cheering to an old Zionist like me. I trust you may work in with Jordan and the rest of the Moslem world. With true comradeship there will be enough for all.' His letter ended: 'Every good wish my old friend.' [2]

At lunch on November 24, at Chequers, the guests included all four members of Churchill's 'book syndicate': General Pownall, Commodore Allen, Bill Deakin and Denis Kelly. On Sunday there was a film, *Antony and Cleopatra*, provided, together with its operator, by Gaumont British.[3] Among the guests that Sunday was Richard Casey, the Australian Minister of Foreign Affairs. Jock Colville, who was also present, noted in his diary:

The Prime Minister said that he did not believe total war was likely. If it came, it would be on one of two accounts. Either the Americans, unable or unwilling any longer to pay for the maintenance of Europe, would say to the Russians you must by certain dates withdraw from certain points and meet us on certain requirements: otherwise we shall attack you. Or, the Russians, realising that safety did not come from being strong, but only from being the strongest, might for carefully calculated and not for emotional reasons, decide that they must attack before it was too late. If they did so their first target would be the British Isles, which is the aircraft carrier.

It was for that reason that Mr Churchill was anxious to convert this country from its present status of a rabbit into that of a hedgehog.

Mr Casey said that there was an ancient Lebanese proverb to the effect that one did not cut a man's throat when one had already poisoned his soup. Mr Churchill said he agreed: it was a matter of supererogation. Mr Casey thought that until the sores in Malaya, Indo-China and the Middle East had been cured, the Russians might consider that the soup was poisoned.[4]

On November 30 Churchill celebrated his seventy-seventh birthday. Churchill's duty Private Secretary that day was David Hunt. That night, after dinner, 'he came down to the Cabinet Room to work just the same', Hunt later recalled, 'and with his usual thoughtfulness in-

[1] Speech of 19 November 1951: Randolph S. Churchill (editor), *Stemming the Tide*, pages 193–4. Recording: BBC Written Archives Centre, Library No. 16988–9.

[2] 'My dear Weizmann', 19 November 1951: Weizmann papers.

[3] 'Chequers Week-end, November 23–26, 1951': Chequers Archive.

[4] Colville diary, 25 November 1951: *The Fringes of Power*, pages 635–6.

vited me to have a drink with him'. Churchill's comment was: 'You've never seen a Prime Minister of seventy-seven before.' [1]

'I have been thinking so much about you—and the momentous task you have embraced,' Sarah Churchill wrote to her father from New York, and she added: 'On paper everything looks very bleak—but I feel, out of a shining & glorious life, this chapter will be one of the most thrilling and deeply satisfying—the last prize, you said. I think it would be more, a fitting reward to those qualities in you which are not so quickly recognized—those of philosopher & humanitarian.'

'I just pray to God,' Sarah added, 'that He will give you life & strength to achieve the last prize for the struggling world. . . .' [2]

Churchill's second speech of his second Premiership was to be on Defence, the subject which had come to dominate his last years in Opposition, and was now to be a principal preoccupation. David Hunt, one of the Private Secretaries who was in attendance at times of speech preparation, has recalled:

One thing was certain: it was all his own work, which was not always the case with other Prime Ministers. Naturally, if it was an important policy speech, there would be suggestions made by the various interested ministries, contributing facts and figures and advice on how they might be presented: if foreign policy was involved the Foreign Office often put forward drafts of whole paragraphs. All this material was recast, often two or three times, so that the final result was phrased in his own characteristic manner.

The process of speech preparation was, Hunt noted, 'semi-public', and he went on to explain:

A Private Secretary would sit beside him. This was partly so that he could be used to check any points on which Churchill felt doubtful, partly to be able to intervene if the speech appeared to be departing too far from the departmental brief and partly because Churchill liked having an audience.

Across the table, or on the other side of the bed if that was where he was working, was a stenographer. She was usually replaced by another every quarter hour or so, not because she could not keep up with the dictation—which in fact was always steady and composed—but so that he could see the typed version of what he had been saying as quickly as possible. He would take a sip of his weak whisky and soda, and perhaps draw on his cigar, and mutter a sentence to himself; he would repeat it, sometimes more than once, varying the choice of words and rolling them round his tongue until he had

[1] Sir David Hunt recollections: *On the Spot, An Ambassador Remembers*, London 1975, page 63.
[2] '*Darling* darling Papa', 25 November 1951: Churchill papers, 1/50.

got them just right, and then dictate them to be taken down. The same business with the next sentence.

This took a long time, quite apart from the fact that the process might be frequently interrupted because new ideas had crossed his mind, or new topics for inclusion which would have to be checked rapidly.

When the whole typescript was completed only the first stage had been reached. Every word was scrutinized, and most of them altered in ink. Occasionally a supplementary paragraph would be dictated. The final version would often be far removed from the original dictation, in the same way as the famous galley-proofs of his books would receive constant alteration in blue, red and green inks until they had to be taken away and reprinted for a further assault.

He went on correcting right up to the last minute, although this delayed the final typing. The form in which the speech was eventually typed was apparently invented by himself; sentences would be split up into their elements and set out in broken lines [1] on small pieces of paper, fastened together at their bottom edges by a tag. The hole through which this passed was made by the familiar instrument which he always called a 'clop', an expression peculiar to him. (Once when he asked for it at Chequers, the Secretary, who had worked for him when he was writing his life of Marlborough, brought him the 14 volumes of *Der Fall des Hauses Stuart* by Onno Klopp.) After the sheets had been strung together he insisted on checking personally that they were in the right order, because once in the past there had been a dreadful mishap and two sheets were misplaced. All this took an immense amount of time, invariably at the last possible minute, and a great deal of fuss.

So when Churchill rose in the House what he had in his hand was not just notes but the whole text of what he intended to say, from the ingenuously bland opening to the resonant peroration. He might at times, if he was not opening the debate, prefix a few extemporary remarks referring to previous speakers, as House of Commons good manners demand, but otherwise he stuck to his text. [2]

'He took great pains on his speeches,' David Pitblado later recalled. 'They were always dictated, so that although he read them, they were the spoken word. They took a long time to prepare, two or three weeks of labour. He would ask Jock and David and me to get pieces from the Government departments. Then there were little bits we would put in. Towards the end they were all thrown out. "This is very good," he would say, "but . . .".'[3]

On 6 December 1951 Churchill spoke in the House of Commons on Defence. Three 'most important' decisions taken by the Labour

---

[1] Sir David Hunt noted at this point: 'The final stage was known in the Private Office as "psalm form" because the speech looked as though it had been printed for singing; I learn from Jock Colville that the description was first applied by Lord Halifax in 1940.'

[2] Sir David Hunt recollections: *On the Spot*, pages 69–70.

[3] Sir David Pitblado recollections: in conversation with the author, 17 July 1987.

Government formed, he said, 'the foundation on which we stand today': the establishment of compulsory National Service, the Atlantic Pact and the creation 'of what, for short, we call NATO', and the 'tremendous rearmament programme' which had enabled Britain to stand 'beyond question second only to the United States in our share of the measures upon which our hopes of a lasting peace are based'. On assuming 'responsibility', he said, the new Government's feeling was that, since the time of the Berlin airlift crisis in 1948, 'the deterrents have increased and that, as the deterrents have increased, the danger has become more unlikely'.

Speaking of the European Army, Churchill made two observations. First, the German Chancellor Dr Adenauer, on a visit to London a few days earlier, had renewed an earlier assurance that the Germans did not press for a national army—'no national army'. Secondly, as far as Britain was concerned, 'we do not propose to merge in the European Army, but we are already joined to it'. British troops were 'on the spot', and through them Britain would try its utmost 'to make a worthy and effective contribution to the deterrents against aggression and to the causes of freedom and democracy which we seek to serve'.

Churchill then spoke of the British manufacture of the atomic bomb. When in Opposition, he had been a critic of the Labour Government, but on coming to power he had learned new facts hitherto kept secret:

Two years ago I commented unfavourably on the fact that the Socialist Government had not been able to make a specimen atomic bomb although they had been trying to do so for four years. When we came into office, we found that a great deal of work had been done, not only on making the crucial materials required for making atomic bombs, but in preparing to manufacture these weapons. I think the House ought to know about that.

Considerable if slow progress has been made. The House will realize that this is not the moment to discuss the British research and manufacture of atomic bombs in detail. All that I will say is that we have taken over the very costly production of the Socialist Government. We have not decided on any important change in policy or principle. We hope, however, in this as in other matters, by different methods of organization and administration to effect some improvements. . . .

There were two regions about which Churchill wished to speak, Malaya and Egypt. 'Dull tragedy rolls forward in Malaya,' he said. No decision had yet been made about policy, but there were some 'brutal statistics' to consider. There were in Malaya over 25,000 British troops, as well as more than 10,000 Gurkhas and 7,000 other soldiers. Added to this there were 60,000 local police in different stages of armament, and many part-time auxiliaries. 'Thus the whole amounts to over 100,000 men employed in a most costly manner.' The total expense of the 'Fighting Forces' was nearly £50 million a year, quite apart from any other 'emergency expenses' falling upon the Malayan Government. 'We are also suffering,' Churchill explained, 'heavy loss in the restriction through terrorism of our tin-mines and rubber plantations. It is said that the bandits, or whatever they should be called, number 3,000 to 5,000, and I do not suppose that their maintenance cost is comparably at all heavy. Certainly it seems some improvement should be made in this theatre of tragedy and waste. . . .'

As to Egypt, Britain would 'do its duty' according to its treaty rights in the Canal Zone, and hoped for an 'increasing measure' of aid from the Egyptian Government 'in preventing mob violence and other forms of lawless and murderous attack'. The British forces in the Canal Zone or within reach of it were, the Government believed, 'strong enough for any work they may have to do'. Time was 'a potent factor', Churchill commented, and he went on to tell the House: 'We certainly propose to use it with patience as well as with firmness.' [1]

Churchill's speech was ended, but when, at the end of the debate, the Secretary of State for War, Anthony Head, rose to wind up for the Government, Churchill rose to his feet, and asking the indulgence of the House for speaking twice, spoke a few personal words about the former Minister of Defence, Emanuel Shinwell:

I should not like—if the House would permit me—the speech of the late Minister of Defence to go without its due and proper acknowledgement from this side of the House. We have our party battles and bitterness, and the great balance of the nation is maintained to some extent by our quarrels, but I have always felt and have always testified, even in moments of party strife, to the Right Honourable Gentleman's sterling patriotism and to the fact that his heart is in the right place where the life and strength of our country are concerned.

Tonight he has made a speech which was the most statesmanlike, if he will allow me to say so, that I have heard him make in this House in those days that we have gone through. He has surveyed the whole field in terms from which I do not think we should differ.

We have our differences, and when we were in Opposition it was our duty to point out the things that we thought were not done right, and it is equally his duty, and that of those who sit with him, to subject us to an equally searching examination. I am so glad to be able to say tonight, in these very few moments, that the spirit which has animated the Right Honourable Gentleman in the main discharge of his great duties was one which has, in peace as well as in war, added to the strength and security of our country. [2]

'The House was stirred,' recalled David Hunt, who had accompanied Churchill to the Commons, and he added:

[1] Speech of 6 December 1951: *Hansard*.
[2] Speech of 6 December 1951: *Hansard*.

Going back in the car to Number 10 after the debate ended Churchill harked back to the subject. 'I am glad I said that about Shinwell,' he said, 'he well deserved it. There's a lot of good in that Shinwell. He's a real patriot. During the war he and Bevan'—and he laid a thunderous emphasis on the second syllable, to be sure of distinguishing his aversion from the admired Ernest Bevin—'were more or less playing the part of the opposition, but I always said there was a great difference between them. When things were going badly for us that Be-van used to look quite pleased but Shinwell looked miserable. Yes, there's a lot of good in Shinwell, and I'm glad I took the chance of saying something about him.'

'Next morning,' Hunt added, 'there was a gracefully-expressed note of thanks from Shinwell, and the first trickle of what became a flood of protests from Conservatives. Churchill had no doubt borne in mind but disregarded the fact that at that time Shinwell was a great bugbear of the party having made, while still in office before the election, a very provocative remark about them which had featured in many large headlines.' [1] For the next week and more, 'letters of complaint continued to arrive, from individuals and from local branches of the party, some violent and some plaintive, as though the writers could not imagine how their hero had fallen into this strange error. Churchill was robustly impenitent, and the more that people protested the more certain he felt that he had spoken well.' [2]

At the Cabinet on December 7, Eden announced that preparations were to be made to introduce Military Government in the Canal Zone, and that if terrorist activities against British troops had not stopped by the time the preparations were completed, 'a stern warning could then be given to the King of Egypt that drastic measures might have to be taken'. [3] A week later, in a minute to Churchill, Eden explained that what he had in mind was 'possible joint UK-French-US action against Alexandria and Cairo'. [4]

'Now the term has begun again,' Churchill told the boys of Harrow at their annual school 'Songs' that afternoon, 'a very severe and hard term, I can assure you. The hours are very long, the lessons are very hard,' nor did he and his colleagues quite know, yet, 'what form the examinations will take'. One of his favourite Harrow songs, he said, was one which he had wanted sung when he came down to the school in 1940. Then, however, it 'could not be found' by the Masters. It

---

[1] Speaking at a Trades Union Conference at Margate on 7 May 1947 Shinwell had declared: 'We know that you, the organized workers of the country, are our friends. ... As for the rest, they do not matter a tinker's curse.'

[2] Sir David Hunt recollections: *On the Spot*, pages 72–3.

[3] Cabinet Conclusions No. 15 of 1951, 'Secret', 12 noon, 7 December 1951: Cabinet papers, 128/23.

[4] 'Egypt', note of a minute of 14 December 1951: Churchill papers, 2/517.

contained lines about the Spanish Armada which he had never forgotten since his own school days:

> But snug in her hive, the Queen was alive
> And Buzz was the word in the Island.[1]

At Cabinet on December 11 Churchill told his colleagues that he intended to visit the United States as soon as possible. It was not his intention, he explained, to ask for financial aid for Britain. He would ask the Americans instead for assistance 'in the form of materials and equipment', for the purpose 'either of assisting our defence programme directly, or of assisting our exports and thus furthering the defence programme indirectly'.[2]

During this Cabinet meeting, Churchill also read out a letter from Montgomery in which the Field Marshal opposed the fusion of the Continental armies into 'a single force under single direction'. The French wanted this, Montgomery explained, because they were 'apprehensive' of the creation of a German national army, but a single direction would make it 'impossible' Montgomery believed, to produce an effective military force. The European Army, he argued, should be made up of units 'maintaining their national character and spirit but integrated under one United Nations Command'. With these views, Churchill said, 'he was in general agreement'.[3]

On December 18, at the end of a two-day visit by Churchill and Eden to Paris, a communiqué was issued which had 'made it clear', Churchill told the Cabinet on the following day, 'that the United Kingdom Government favoured the creation of a European Defence Community, though they could not join it, and that they were ready to associate themselves with it as closely as possible in all stages of its political and military development'. This, Churchill commented, 'should forestall any further suggestion that the delay in securing agreement to the creation of a European Army was due to the unhelpful attitude of the United Kingdom Government'.[4]

During a Party Political broadcast on December 22, Churchill spoke of how, while in Paris, he and Eden had wanted 'our French friends' to feel that Britain meant to be a good friend and ally, 'and that we welcomed the measures which the French have taken to bring Germany into the

---

[1] Speech of 7 December 1951: Churchill papers, 2/336. Churchill also told the boys that when he went on board ship at Arromanches during the Normandy landings in June 1944, and sang these two lines to those on the ship, 'not one of them knew the words'.

[2] Cabinet Conclusions No. 16 of 1951, 'Secret', 11.30 a.m., 11 December 1951: Cabinet papers, 128/23, conclusion 7.

[3] Cabinet Conclusions No. 16 of 1951, conclusion 8.

[4] Cabinet Conclusions No. 18 of 1951, 'Secret', 11 a.m., 19 December 1951: Cabinet papers, 128/23.

new European system and to end their age-long quarrel from which both these valiant races have suffered so much, and have brought so much suffering upon the rest of the world'. This had been his appeal at Zurich in 1946, and he rejoiced at the progress which had been made since then.

Speaking of the economic situation in Britain, Churchill, in a sustained metaphor, appealed for time and patience in the reversal of the Labour Government's economic policy and nationalization of six years:

If a train is running on the wrong lines downhill at sixty miles an hour it is no good trying to stop it by building a brick wall across the track. That would only mean that the wall was shattered, that the train was wrecked and the passengers mangled.

First you have to put on the brakes. The Chancellor of the Exchequer has already done that and the train is coming under control and can be stopped. Then the engine has to be put into reverse. We have to go back along the line till we get to the junction. Then the signalman has to switch the points and the train has to be started again on the right line, which, I am telling you beforehand—please remember it—is uphill all the way. On an ordinary railway this might cause quite a long delay. In the vast complex evolution of modern life and government it will take several years.

'We require at least three years,' Churchill told his listeners, 'before anyone can judge fairly whether we have made things better or worse.'

Churchill also spoke in his broadcast of December 22 about the prospects for war and the maintenance of peace:

At the General Election much party capital was made by calling me 'a warmonger'. That was not true. Now that I am at the head of the Government I shall work ardently in harmony with our allies for peace.

If war comes it will be because of world forces beyond British control. On the whole I do not think it will come. Whatever happens we shall stand up with all our strength in defence of the free world against Communist tyranny and aggression. We shall do our utmost to preserve the British Commonwealth and empire as an independent factor in world affairs. We shall cherish the fraternal association of the English-speaking world. We shall work in true comradeship for and with United Europe.

'It may be,' Churchill ended, 'that this land will have the honour of helping civilization to climb the hill amid the toils of peace as we once did in the terrors of war.' [1]

*   *   *

[1] Broadcast of 22 December 1951: Randolph S. Churchill (editor), *Stemming the Tide*, pages 210–14. Recording: BBC Written Archives Centre, Library No. LP 24417.

Churchill spent Christmas 1951 at Chequers, with his family. His thoughts were much on his American visit, his first there as Prime Minister for more than seven years. 'This is to wish you Bon Voyage,' Randolph Churchill wrote on December 27, in a letter while still at Chequers; 'I am sure you will have a success. It is not the interest of the Administration that any hint of disagreement should emerge. You have much to give & doubtless much to receive.' Randolph added: 'I foresee the British lion being a greater pet than ever!' [1]

[1] 'My dearest Papa', signed 'your loving son, Randolph', 27 December 1951: Churchill papers, 1/51.

37
Transatlantic Journey, January 1952

O N 31 December 1951 Churchill left London by train from Waterloo Station for Southampton, and went on board the *Queen Mary* for his transatlantic voyage, the eleventh time he had set off for the New World.[1] With him were three Cabinet Ministers, Eden, Ismay and Lord Cherwell, as well as the Chief of the Imperial General Staff, Field Marshal Slim, and the First Sea Lord, Admiral Sir Rhoderick McGrigor.[2] That night the ship's anchor was found to be fouled, so that the first night had to be spent on board, moored at the quayside.

That evening Lord Mountbatten, then Fourth Sea Lord, was Churchill's guest at dinner. It was a stormy conversation, as Mountbatten questioned the wisdom of linking Britain irrevocably to American foreign policy, especially if it seemed that the course followed by the Americans was likely to lead to war; 'the one thing that could destroy the present relatively happy and peaceful conditions in this country would of course be a war,' Mountbatten declared. Churchill replied that the only security for Britain was to be found in linking its fortunes entirely with the Americans, and then, as Mountbatten noted in his diary:

He then turned to me and said: 'I think you should be careful about your anti-American attitude. The Americans like you. They trust you. You are one of the few commanders that they would willingly serve under. You will throw all that away if they think you are against them!'

I replied that I was very fond of all my American friends, and that individually I thought they were a charming people; but, taken as a corporate mass, they were immature, and if they were allowed their own way they

[1] His previous journeys had been in 1895, 1900, 1929, 1931, 1941 (twice), 1942, 1943, 1944 and 1946.

[2] The civil servants who accompanied Churchill were Roger Makins (Foreign Office), Norman Brook (Cabinet Office), David Pitblado and Jock Colville (Private Office).

would probably take a course which would not only destroy this country but would ultimately end in the destruction of their own system. . . .

He then said: 'I am very sorry to hear you express such Left-Wing views. I think you should try and avoid expressing any political opinions. Your one value as a sailor is that you are completely non-political. Take care you remain so!'

I pointed out that I had always been completely non-political. . . . I had never been known to make any political remarks, but that I could not see that expressing the hope that he would be able to guide the Americans in such a way that our own country would not be destroyed could possibly be regarded as Left-Wing.

My impressions of this grand old man are that he is really past his prime. He was very deaf and kept having to have things repeated to him. He quoted poetry at great length. He went through the whole of the verses of 'Rule Britannia' and 'It's All Quiet Along the Potomac'. He was very sentimental and full of good will towards me. He kept telling me what a friend he was of mine and of my family.

'I realize,' Mountbatten added, 'that I made myself very unpopular by the views that I expressed that night. But I also believe that he is a big enough man to at least have absorbed the point of view I was putting forward.' [1]

Jock Colville, listening to this altercation, noted in his diary that Mountbatten was talking 'arrant political nonsense; he might have learned by heart a leader from the *New Statesman*. The PM laughed at him but did not, so Pug Ismay thought, snub him sufficiently.' [2]

Among those on board the *Queen Mary* was Lord Moran, who recorded in his notes how he and the other members of the Prime Minister's party had been summoned to his room at ten minutes before midnight, to toast the New Year:

When the clock had struck twelve times the PM, whose thoughts seemed a long way off, pulled himself out of his chair, put down his glass and, crossing his arms, began to shout 'Auld Lang Syne'. When this had been sung he tried to give the note for 'God Save the King'. Then he resumed his seat as if his part in the proceedings had been safely accomplished. After a little the room began to thin—youth went off to dance—till none were left but the Prof, Pug, Slim and Norman Brook. For some time the PM sat lost in his thoughts and no one spoke.

'I cannot tell you,' he said at last, 'how much happier I shall be when I have worked out the substance of what I shall say to Congress. The speech might not come off,' he mused, 'but I shall do my best whatever happens. I feel bewildered in my mind. The three thousand seven hundred millions of pounds which was to be spent on rearmament has gone up to five thousand

---

[1] Mountbatten diary, 31 December 1951: Philip Ziegler, *Mountbatten*, pages 502–3.
[2] Colville diary, 31 December 1951: *The Fringes of Power*, page 637.

two hundred millions. We have not stopped the rise in wages. Anyway, I'm not going to beg.'

He sat glowering at the carpet.

'We shall have to make great sacrifices,' the PM murmured without looking up. Then his face brightened. 'How much would it mean to the country,' he asked, 'if everyone gave up smoking? I would not hesitate to give up my cigars.'

He got up and I went with him to his room.

'I have done very little today,' he said as he kicked off his slippers so that they skidded along the floor. 'I am not so good mentally as I used to be. A speech has become a burden and an anxiety. Tell me, Charles, the truth. Am I going slowly to lose my faculties?'

He asked me to take his pulse; it was rapid and irregular.[1]

As soon as the *Queen Mary* had sailed, Norman Brook wrote to a colleague in the Cabinet Office, 'and the PM found himself without newspapers or telegrams, he at once convinced himself that all activity in Whitehall had stopped. He could not be persuaded otherwise.' Hence a series of insistent demands for news, passed back from ship to shore. 'Once he got here,' Norman Brook added after the *Queen Mary* reached New York, 'he ceased to be so insistent, tho' he hates getting the English newspapers later.'[2]

'During the crossing,' Jock Colville later recalled, 'we worked on our briefs: oh the amount of paper that even a small conference evokes!' It was 'very difficult', Colville added, 'to get the PM to read any of it. He said he was going to America to re-establish relations, not to transact business.'[3] Not everyone had the same impression, however. One of those on board ship was Donald MacDougall, a member of Churchill's Statistical Office during the Second World War. 'I was responsible for preparing Churchill's brief for the economic part of his talks with Truman,' he later wrote, 'and was delighted when, after he had read it, he sent me back a masterly summary in true Churchillian prose.'[4]

The *Queen Mary* reached New York on January 4. Among those waiting to greet Churchill was Leslie Rowan, to whom, when they were alone on the following day, Lord Moran put the question of whether he noticed many changes in Churchill since 1945. Rowan's answer, as recorded by Moran, was unequivocal:

'Oh, yes,' he answered rather sadly, 'he has lost his tenacity; he no longer pushes a thing through. He has lost, too, his power of fitting in all the pro-

[1] Moran diary, 1 January 1952: *The Struggle for Survival*, pages 352–3.
[2] Letter of 10 January 1952: Cabinet papers, 21/3057.
[3] Colville diary: *The Fringes of Power*, pages 636–7.
[4] Sir Donald MacDougall recollections: letter to the author, 22 November 1984.

blems one to another. Of course in the war he would run a pet scheme, but it was always fitted into the whole plan. And he forgets figures. In the war he never did. Why, the other day I mentioned a figure he had used in the House of Commons. "Did I?" he asked, puzzled. Besides, the problems are different now. Questions of economics. He was not brought up on such things.'

I asked Leslie if he had noticed any physical changes. He seemed surprised that I should ask such a question.

'Yes, of course.'

'How?' I persisted.

'Oh, the way he walks—slowly, like an old man. Even his handling of the Press Conference today was different. It was good, of course, but not so good as it used to be in the war.' Leslie smiled. 'But he can still coin phrases. He referred yesterday to the Standing Group who deal with a future war as "Chiefs of Staff vitiated by the intrusion of the French".' [1]

From New York, Churchill flew in the President's plane to Washington, where he was greeted at the airport by President Truman. That night they dined together on board the Presidential yacht *Williamsburg*.[2] The Secretary of State, Dean Acheson, later recalled how:

... with apparent spontaneity and the aid of the Prof and his slide rule, Mr Churchill put on what I was told was a favourite act. He first established from the President the dimensions of the dining saloon of the *Williamsburg*, and then that over a period of sixty years he had consumed on the average a quart of vinous and spirituous liquors a day, some days more, some days less, some not at all, as when he had been a prisoner of war in South Africa or hiding after his escape. If, he asked the Prof, all this liquid were poured into the dining saloon, how high would it rise? His vast disappointment when, instead of drowning us all in champagne and brandy, the flood came only up to our knees provided the high point of the performance.

The first serious discussion of the evening took place on board the *Williamsburg* in the aft saloon, as the dining table was being cleared, with Churchill, Dean Acheson later recalled, giving 'his unfavourable view of Schuman's European Defense Community, which was to be repeated often'. Acheson then described how, that evening, Churchill 'pictured a bewildered French drill sergeant sweating over a platoon made up of a few Greeks, Italians, Germans, Turks and Dutchmen, all in utter confusion over the simplest orders. What he hoped to see were spirited and strong national armies marching

[1] Moran diary, 5 January 1952: *The Struggle for Survival*, pages 354–6.

[2] With Churchill were Eden, Ismay, Cherwell and the British Ambassador to Washington, Sir Oliver Franks. With Truman were the Secretary of State, Dean Acheson, the Secretary of the Treasury, John W. Snyder, the Secretary of Defence, Robert A. Lovett, Averell Harriman and the United States Ambassador to London, Walter Gifford.

together to the defense of freedom singing their national anthems. No one could get up enthusiasm singing, "March, NATO, march on!".'[1]

The President and the Prime Minister then moved below, to the dining room, the table having been cleared, whereupon Churchill gave Truman a survey of the international scene. There was, he said, 'fear in the Kremlin'. The Russians had feared British and American friendship more than their enmity. This was now beginning to change. At the time of the Berlin airlift in 1948 risks had been very great. Now they were a little less. He did not expect a deliberate attack by the Soviet Union in 1952. On the other hand, the Soviet Union had not lost much; since the end of the war 'they had gained half Europe and all China without loss'.

Churchill went on to describe the result of the Korean War and Truman's 'great decision' to commit American forces, as American rearmament. 'Now the free world was not a naked world, but a re-arming world.'

The Americans had complained in strong terms about British trade with China. Truman had reiterated these complaints. Churchill did not belittle American fears of China, telling Truman that he looked upon Hong Kong 'as a little Formosa', and promising to aid the United States 'as far as was possible'. He did not think that China had gone permanently Communist. 'But we had to deal with what was before us.' He therefore 'felt inclined' to give aid in resisting further Chinese aggression. At the same time, he asked the United States to give Britain 'moral assistance' in Persia. 'We must both play one hand there.'

As to Egypt, Britain's position there was not one of imperialism, Churchill told Truman, but of international duty. The proposal of the Four Powers for an international supervisory force on the Suez Canal was 'an act of genius'. He hoped that the United States would be willing to back up this proposal by sending 'a Brigade perhaps, as a symbol' to the Canal Zone. If America would send such a force, 'everything would be cleared up quite quickly. Everyone else would fall in behind this.'[2] The British would then withdraw 'a whole Division or more'. Churchill added, by way of explanation, as Acheson noted:

This one step would indicate such solidarity between us that the Egyptians would stop their unlawful conduct and get on with the four-power discussions. Similarly, in Iran, if we undertook to give financial support to the Iranians, the problem would never be solved. Whereas, if we would stand solidly with the British, the Iranians would come to terms in short order.

[1] Dean Acheson, *Present at the Creation, My Years in the State Department*, New York 1969, pages 763–5.
[2] Note of the conversation between the Prime Minister and the President, 5 January 1952: Cabinet papers, 21/3057.

As Churchill prepared to return to the British Embassy, where he was staying, he said to Dean Acheson: 'Did you feel that around that table this evening there were gathered the governments of the world—not to dominate it, mind you—but to save it?' [1]

When, in the small hours, Churchill returned to the British Embassy, even the sceptical Moran was 'startled', as he wrote, 'to find something like the Winston we had half forgotten. He was full of the evening. "Oh, I enjoyed it so much. We talked as equals."' [2]

Throughout January 6 and 7 the Washington talks centred upon the question of the organization of NATO and its commands. At the first Plenary session, held at the White House on the morning of January 7, Churchill pointed out that Britain had put in hand a re-armament programme for the common cause 'against aggression and the spread of Communism'. Despite rising defence costs and the need for economy at home, it was Britain's intention 'to make the maximum possible contribution to common defence against aggression and Communism'. To do this, however, there was an urgent need of steel; the United States must help Britain here. It was also essential to increase coal production. This would be done by offering special incentives to the miners, by provision of additional houses, and by the introduction of foreign labour. It was not easy, Churchill pointed out, to persuade miners to accept the importation of foreign labour, 'but every effort was being made to do so'.

Turning to the North Atlantic Treaty Organization, Churchill declared: 'The great burden which the United States was bearing on behalf of the free world was a matter of universal admiration.' The United Kingdom would continue to make 'the biggest contribution of which they were capable'. The Second World War had 'swallowed up' Britain's reserves and resources to such an extent that the Government would still have to impose 'restrictions and restraint' upon the fifty million inhabitants of the British Isles. [3]

The British Government, Churchill told Truman, 'is determined to see that the UK with its own resources takes care of its internal problems and difficulties'. He was not in Washington 'to seek aid in order to improve the comfort and welfare of the British people. The British people themselves will accept the necessary sacrifices required by the British internal situation, and the British Government will adopt the necessary measures.' Churchill added: 'This is the UK's form of a declaration of independence.'

[1] 'Talks between the President and Prime Minister Churchill', 5 January 1952, memorandum drafted by Dean Acheson, 'Top Secret', 6 January 1952: Truman papers.
[2] Moran diary, 5 January 1952: *The Struggle for Survival*, pages 354–6.
[3] 'First Plenary Meeting', 11 a.m., 7 January 1952: Cabinet papers, 21/3057.

Churchill went on to tell Truman that he was 'governed' by two principles: 'First, the British Government will submit to Parliament whatever measures are needed for Britain's "internal independence". Second, the UK considers that the defence task against Communist tyranny is a common one and therefore Britain is not abashed to accept help in this field.'[1] He hoped, Churchill concluded, that the 'strength of the West' would now reverse the Soviet fear of the friendship between Britain and America, 'so that they would fear our enmity more than our friendship and would be led thereby to seek our friendship'.[2]

On January 7, Moran noted in his diary:

There was a discussion during luncheon—it went on till half past three—in the course of which Mr Churchill attacked with some heat the decision to give the command of the Atlantic to an American. The CIGS,[3] the First Sea Lord[4] and Pug Ismay in turn urged him to accept the plan; we had got everything, they argued, that really mattered, for in a war the First Sea Lord would really be in control. They were particularly anxious to avoid putting up the back of the American Navy, which had taken criticism from the PM in the most generous spirit, just because it was Mr Churchill.

The British Ambassador to Washington, Sir Oliver Franks, 'interjected in his cool way', noted Moran, 'that it was an issue which only counted on paper'. But Churchill 'would have none of it', telling his advisers:

I realize that England is a broken and impoverished power, which has cast away a great part of its Empire and of late years has misused its resources, but these fellows bungled the U-boat war; and had to come to us for help. America may know far more than our Navy does about combined 'ops' in the Pacific, between their Navy and Air Force, but she knows very little of U-boat warfare. You have urged me to do this fake without any explanation to public or Parliament. I will not do that. It must all come out publicly.[5]

The second Plenary session, held on the afternoon of January 7, discussed Truman's proposal for the 'standardisation of weapons for the free world'; the President felt that a useful start could be made

---

[1] 'Truman-Churchill Talks', 'First Formal Session', 'Top Secret', 11 a.m. to 1 p.m., 7 January 1952: Truman papers.
[2] 'First Plenary Meeting', 11 a.m., 7 January 1952: Cabinet papers, 21/3057.
[3] The Chief of the Imperial General Staff, Field Marshal Sir William Slim.
[4] Admiral Sir Rhoderick McGrigor.
[5] Moran diary, 7 January 1952: *The Struggle for Survival*, pages 356–8.

with the rifle.[1] Churchill disagreed. It was, he said, 'dangerous to change the calibre of a rifle unless a really long period of change was in prospect'. For the moment, when circumstances were 'critical', Britain and the United States would be well advised to continue to operate on the basis of their existing rifles.[2]

Turning to naval matters, Churchill 'declared', as the American note of the discussion recorded, 'that he was not convinced of the need for a Supreme Commander in the Atlantic. He had lived through two world wars without any such arrangement. He insisted that he was not speaking lightly for, indeed, the Atlantic supply line was of vital importance to the UK and if naval affairs in the Atlantic were mismanaged, the UK "would die".' This was 'not true' in the case of the United States, Churchill added, 'which later would still be in a position to land its armies in Europe'.[3]

Churchill then asked the First Sea Lord, Sir Rhoderick McGrigor, to present the case for a British naval commander for the Atlantic. There followed what Colville recalled as 'an embarrassing incident', as the Admiral 'went red in the face, large drops of perspiration appeared on his brow and he was too overawed to do more than stutter a few disjointed words'. At that moment, Field Marshal Slim 'stepped into the breach and presented the naval case coolly and calmly. It was a magnificent tour de force by the representative of another service and it was evident that the Americans were as impressed as we were.'[4] The Americans did not agree, however, to the British proposal; three months later, when the Atlantic Command was formally set up, it was under an American Admiral, Lyndon McCormick.[5]

At the third Plenary meeting, on the morning of January 8, Churchill reiterated that Britain was now in Egypt 'from a sense of international duty and for no other reason'. If the United States could make a contribution to the defence of the Suez Canal Zone, 'the

---

[1] The Americans wanted their .30 rifle to become the standard rifle, replacing in Britain the British .303 rifle.

[2] 'Second Plenary Meeting', 5 p.m., 7 January 1952: Cabinet papers, 21/3057. At one moment during the discussion on the rifle, Field Marshal Slim is said to have commented: 'Well, I suppose we could experiment with a bastard rifle, partly American, partly British,' to which Churchill replied: 'Kindly moderate your language, Field Marshal, it may be recalled that I am myself partly British, partly American.' (Quoted in Kay Halle (editor), *The Irrepressible Churchill*, page 261.) In his war memoirs, Churchill wrote, of Slim's wartime service in Burma: 'The famous Fourteenth Army, under the masterly command of General Slim, fought valiantly, overcame all obstacles, and achieved the seemingly impossible': Winston S. Churchill, *The Second World War*, volume 6, page 538.

[3] 'Truman-Churchill Talks', 'Second Formal Session', 'Top Secret', 5 p.m. to 7 p.m., 7 January 1952: Truman papers.

[4] Colville diary: *The Fringes of Power*, page 638.

[5] The Atlantic Command, 'Saclant', was established on 11 April 1952.

trouble in Egypt would soon be brought to an end, and the British would be able to make more forces available to Europe or to the United Kingdom itself, which was without adequate defences'.

Churchill went on to tell Truman that Britain would support the American proposal of a four-power pact for the Middle East, of Britain, the United States, France and Turkey. He then, as the American minutes recorded, 'stressed the great importance of the four powers all sending token forces to this area. He thought that such a proof of solidarity should bring the difficulties with Egypt very quickly to an end.'

Speaking of the Korean war, Churchill, as the American minutes recorded:

. . . expressed his admiration for the manner in which the United States was carrying virtually the entire load of the West in the Far East. He paid special tribute to American fortitude in the Korea war which had resulted in 100,000 United States casualities. He recognized the peculiar difficulty of prosecuting such a war when the nation as a whole does not consider itself to be directly threatened. He emphasized the United Kingdom's desire to help the United States in every way possible and recognized that in the Far East there could be no UK priority or equality of leadership. The role of leader squarely belonged to the United States and the UK will do its utmost to meet US views and requests in relation to that area.

Churchill went on to tell Truman, Acheson, and the other Americans present that, in his opinion, 'the President's decision to resist in Korea had done more than anything else to reverse the tide in our relations with the Soviets in the postwar period. Indeed, he felt that June 25, 1950 marked the turning point in the danger to the free world of communist aggression, and the United Kingdom was profoundly grateful to the United States for its action.' Had he been in power in June 1950, Churchill continued, 'he would have broken relations with China when the Chinese attacked the UN forces in Korea. However, when he was returned to power the phase of armistice talks had been initiated and he did not think that such a British action would be desirable now because of its possible effect on the negotiations.'[1]

He was 'most anxious', Churchill added, to help the Americans in any way possible 'and would be glad to know where this help was needed'.

When Truman pressed for a more sympathetic British attitude to the Chinese Nationalist Government in Formosa, Churchill agreed

[1] 'Truman–Churchill Talks', 'Third Formal Session', 'Top Secret', 11 a.m. to 1 p.m., 8 January 1952: Truman papers.

that 'in spite of the weakness and corruption of Chiang Kai-shek's régime, it would be wrong to leave his three or four hundred thousand followers in Formosa to be murdered by the Communists'. As to the war in Indo-China, Churchill emphasized the effect of that war on Europe. It was a 'constant drain' on the French Army, with the result that France remained militarily weak in Europe 'and therefore more apprehensive about the arming of Germans'.[1]

One of those present at the Plenary meetings, Evelyn Shuckburgh, noted in his diary, about Truman:

He was quite abrupt on one or two occasions with poor old Winston and had a tendency, after one of the old man's powerful and emotional declarations of faith in Anglo-American co-operation, to cut it off with a 'Thank you, Mr Prime Minister. We might pass that to be worked out by our advisers.' A little wounding.

Shuckburgh's account continued:

Our own side (including AE, Lord Cherwell and Lord Ismay) were a good deal concerned by the PM's readiness to give away our case, both in regard to the Far East and on raw materials. On the latter subject, when we were trying to get steel in return for tin and some other metals, but were known to be unable to meet the Americans over copper, Winston electrified us by himself raising the question of copper, just at the point when agreement was about to be reached without it. He gave quite a little lecture on the need to develop copper production in the British African colonies, and appeared to be under the impression that he was addressing the British Cabinet. The American officials bravely and loyally extracted us from this difficulty.[2]

This misunderstanding took place at the fourth Plenary session, on the evening of January 8. The American minutes recorded Churchill's intervention, and Eden's counter efforts:

Mr Churchill then said that there was plenty of copper in Africa, and the UK should provide the necessary inducements and take the necessary steps to increase production there.

Mr Eden said that this was much more complicated than it might appear. . . .

Lord Cherwell responded that the British government would explore this possibility to the best of its ability. . . .

Mr Churchill again expressed his disbelief that copper production could not be increased in Africa.

Mr Eden reiterated that the task was much more complicated than it sounded and that in any event no copper could be produced immediately. He assured the Prime Minister, however, that the British government would do its best, as furthermore it would be to the UK's own advantage to increase copper production.

[1] 'Third Plenary Meeting', 11 a.m., 8 January 1952: Cabinet papers, 21/3057.
[2] Evelyn Shuckburgh diary: *Descent to Suez, Diaries 1951–56*, London 1986, page 32.

Mr Churchill then referred to nickel.

Mr Fleischmann reported that no request had been made of the UK. . . .[1]

At one point in the discussion that evening, Churchill told the Americans:

Frankly, he did not think that the French were doing their full part towards this European army but that this was due to the fact that they had to fight 'like tigers' to protect their empire in Indochina. Were it not for this, the French could become stronger in Europe and therefore be willing to permit the Germans to become stronger. As it is, we could well lose both France's and Germany's contribution in Europe.[2]

It was the rearming of Germany, and the future of the European Defence Community, which dominated the discussion at the Plenary meeting that afternoon, when Churchill told Truman that Britain would do 'everything possible' to further the formation of a European Army, although she would not participate in a European Federation. The European Army, he said, 'offered the only method of integrating German forces in the defence of Western Europe'. Without the support of the Germans, he doubted if Western Europe could be 'successfully defended'. What was needed was 'loyal' divisions which would fight 'shoulder to shoulder' in the defence of Europe. His one fear was that the 'sacrifice of nationality' which the European Defence Community implied, with its creation of a multi-national force, would damage the loyalty of the soldiers.[3]

The American minutes of the meeting recorded:

Mr Churchill said that what we had to bear in mind was whether or not there would be an army available to meet a Soviet aggression. More important than constitutional and other instruments are divisions available and ready to do their best. At the present time the UK had four divisions on the Continent, this figure including three armored divisions.

The UK is ready to fight and to die. That, in the opinion of the Prime Minister, is the important thing and not the technical arrangements. He saw no reasons why the British divisions could not serve temporarily in the midst of the European forces. That, he considered, was only a tactical matter. Whether or not these divisions are organically a part of the EDC is immaterial. Mr Churchill reaffirmed that the UK would do everything within its power to encourage the European army even though he personally still thought that the 'national spirit element' was most important.[4]

---

[1] Hanley Fleischmann was the senior American expert at the talks responsible for raw material purchases.

[2] 'Truman–Churchill Talks', 'Fourth Formal Session', 'Top Secret', 5.30 p.m. to 7.30 p.m., 8 January 1952: Truman papers.

[3] 'Fourth Plenary Meeting', 5 p.m., 8 January 1952: Cabinet papers, 21/3057.

[4] 'Truman–Churchill Talks', 'Fourth Formal Session', 'Top Secret', 5.30 p.m. to 7.30 p.m., 8 January 1952: Truman papers.

It was during the Washington talks that Churchill and Truman agreed that the atomic bomb would not be used from the American base in East Anglia without British consent. This written agreement, which was made public, stated in a formal manner an earlier verbal and secret understanding between Truman and Attlee.[1] By so doing, it put at rest many fears that had grown in Britain of a unilateral American action which might lead to fearsome reprisals.

On January 9, before leaving Washington for New York, Churchill addressed the staff of the British Embassy, who had assembled in the garden for the occasion. Jock Colville later recalled:

When he walked out on to the terrace for this purpose, he gasped with astonishment. In front of him, filling the entire garden, was a crowd not, as he had expected, of some fifty or sixty people, but, including the wives and children, the best part of a thousand. The service departments in particular were grossly overmanned.

He addressed the huge gathering most affably, but he instructed me to procure a detailed list of the officers attached to the Embassy. I did so when we returned to London and discovered that there were, amongst many others, forty-seven lieutenant-colonels and forty-three wing commanders. Evidently nobody had given thought to reducing the vast staffs established in a war which had ended six and a half years previously.

The Prime Minister then issued a peremptory order, in his capacity as Minister of Defence, and a drastic reduction was effected.[2]

In New York, Churchill was the guest of Bernard Baruch, then aged eighty, at his magnificent apartment on East 66th Street. Baruch and Churchill had become friends before they had ever met, in 1918, when as Minister of Munitions Churchill had negotiated with Baruch by telegram on an almost daily basis about the supply of raw materials, and particularly nitrates, from South America to Britain.[3] Lord Moran, who was present when Churchill and Baruch were reminiscing, noted that only once in the discussion was the 'pleasing harmony' between the two men 'in danger':

[1] Churchill reported on this agreement to the House of Commons on 26 February 1952. Churchill also told the House of Commons on that occasion: 'I was not aware until I took office that not only had the Socialist Government made the atomic bomb as a matter of research, but that they had created at the expense of many scores of millions of pounds the important plant necessary for its regular production. This weapon will be tested in the course of the present year by agreement with the Australian Government at some suitable place in that continent.'

[2] Colville diary: *The Fringes of Power*, page 638.

[3] Baruch was then (1917–18) Commissioner in Charge of Raw Materials, War Industries Board, and subsequently (1918–19) Chairman of the War Industries Board. In 1946 he had been appointed by Truman to be the United States Representative on the Atomic Energy Commission.

Britain ought to be consulted, the PM contended vigorously, before an atomic bomb was sent off from airfields in East Anglia. Baruch at once broke in:

'But a considerable proportion of our bombing personnel are in Britain, and they would in that case be subject to your veto. If that is maintained it might be wise to withdraw them.'

The PM (with some vehemence): 'If the American Government take the line that they need not consult us, then they had better begin removing them now. Have you seen our agreement with Roosevelt?'

Baruch: 'No, I haven't.'

PM: 'It laid down that neither America nor Britain would release bombs without the consent of the other Government.'

Baruch: 'Cadogan made no objection.'

The PM thought the Russians were frightened of us and that there would be no war, but he spoke of October, 1952, as if it might be touch and go. Baruch agreed.[1]

During his two days in New York, Churchill continued the preparation, which he had begun on the *Queen Mary*, for what was clearly to be the culminating point of his American visit, his address to Congress. On January 10 Baruch gathered for him at luncheon, at Churchill's request, three of America's leading journalists, General Adler and Arthur Sulzberger of the *New York Times* and Daniel Longwell of *Life*. His aim, Churchill told Moran, was to 'get the feel' of American opinion before his address. 'We had hardly taken our seats,' Moran added, 'when the PM said without warning':

'What other nation in history, when it became supremely powerful, has had no thought of territorial aggrandizement, no ambition but to use its resources for the good of the world? I marvel at America's altruism, her sublime disinterestedness.'

All at once I realized Winston was in tears, his eyes were red, his voice faltered. He was deeply moved. Sulzberger broke the silence.

'I think, Prime Minister, it was hard-headedness on our part. I mean it was thought out, not emotional. Anyway, I hope it was, because emotion soon passes, whereas a thought-out plan might last. What view is taken in Britain about German unity?'

PM: 'I always felt in the war that we must strike down the tyrant, but be ready to help Germany up again as a friend. I have been doubtful about a European army only because I was concerned with its fighting power. It will not fight if you remove all traces of nationalism. I love France and Belgium, but we cannot be reduced to that level.'

And then the PM began to plead for a token American brigade, or even a battalion of Marines, to be sent to the Suez Canal.

PM: 'Now that we no longer hold India the Canal means very little to us.

[1] Moran diary, 9 January 1952: *The Struggle for Survival*, pages 360–1.

Australia? We could go round the Cape. We are holding the Canal not for ourselves but for civilization. I feel inclined to threaten the Americans that we will leave the Canal if they don't come in.'

General Adler: 'Could not America be invited to send this token force? If this is not done, I doubt if Congress will play.'

PM: 'I want it as a symbol that it is a United Nations project. Stalin was responsible for the United Nations and for the coming together of the two great English-speaking peoples; without him it might not have happened for generations. The architect of the Kremlin "builded better than he knew".

'Since Persia the Egyptians have felt that America would not support Britain. A token brigade would convince them they were wrong.' [1]

From New York, Churchill travelled by train overnight to Ottawa, where he was greeted and entertained by the Governor-General, Field Marshal Alexander. He also spent two hours with General Templer, soon to be appointed High Commissioner of the Malayan Federation, with the task of trying to restore order after the assassination of his predecessor. [2] Templer later gave Lord Moran an account of the conversation:

Winston began: 'I am an old man. I shall probably not see you again. I may be sending you to your death.' When he said this he almost broke down. And then he said to me: 'Ask for power, go on asking for it, and then—never use it.' At the end the PM smiled: 'Here am I talking to you for all this time when I have two speeches on my hands.'

'What is there about this man,' Templer asked Moran, 'which no one else has?' [3]

On January 14 Churchill spoke in Ottawa at a banquet given in his honour by the Government of Canada. He had first come to Canada, he recalled, 'more than fifty years ago, to give a lecture about the Boer War'. Ten years had passed since his last visit at 'an inspiring but formidable moment' in the war when, with the entry of the United States into the struggle, 'the pathway to victory seemed, and in fact was, open and sure'.

Churchill went on to ask his Canadian listeners:

What is the scene which unfolds before us to-night? It is certainly not what we had hoped to find after all our enemies had surrendered unconditionally and the great World Instrument of the United Nations had been set up to make sure that the wars were ended. It is certainly not that. Peace does not

[1] Moran diary, 10 January 1952: *The Struggle for Survival*, pages 361–2. Churchill, now with access to the Government files for 1945 to 1951, had been studying the American Government's failure to join Britain in its protest against the Persian Government's nationalization of the Anglo-Persian Oil Company on 2 May 1951.

[2] Sir Henry Gurney, assassinated on 6 October 1951.

[3] Moran diary, 11 January 1952: *The Struggle for Survival*, pages 363–4.

sit untroubled in her vineyard. The harvest of new and boundless wealth which science stands ready to pour into the hands of all people, and of none perhaps more than the people of Canada, must be used for exertions to ward off from us the dangers and the unimaginable horrors of another world war.

At least this time in visiting you I have no secrets to guard about the future. When I came last time I could not tell what was going to happen, because I could not make it public. This time I do not know. No one can predict with certainty what will happen. All we can see for ourselves are the strange clouds that move and gather on the horizons, sometimes so full of menace, sometimes fading away. There they are. They cast their shadow.

Churchill then spoke of NATO, calling it 'the surest guarantee not only of the prevention of war, but of victory should our hopes be blasted'. Hitherto the North Atlantic Treaty had been regarded 'only in its military aspect', but 'now we all feel, especially since our visit to Washington, it is broadening out into the conception of the North Atlantic community of free nations, acting together not only for defence but for the welfare and happiness and progress of all the peoples of the free world'. For this, a United Europe, and a European Army including Germany, were essential. That did not mean that Britain would become 'a unit in a federated Europe', nor that the British Army, which was already 'in line' on the Continent and which would grow steadily, would be merged 'in such a way as to lose its identity'. But, under the Supreme NATO Commander, Britain stood 'with the United States, shoulder to shoulder with the European Army and its German elements', ready to face 'whatever aggression may fall upon us'.[1]

'Your speech in Ottawa was wonderful,' Sarah Churchill wrote from Washington, where she was staying as the President's guest at Blair House.[2]

On January 15, Churchill travelled by train from Ottawa to Washington. Sir Roger Makins, a senior Foreign Office official who was travelling with him, later wrote:

I recall lunching in the train restaurant car with him, the Prof and Norman Brook. We had the tale, told in many forms, of the Prof, the slide rule and the amount of champagne imbibed by WSC during his lifetime, a result which he found extremely disappointing.[3] The head attendant in the res-

---

[1] Speech of 14 January 1952: Randolph S. Churchill (editor), *Stemming the Tide*, pages 215–19.

[2] 'Darling Papa', 16 January 1952: Churchill papers, 1/50.

[3] 'WSC: "Prof! How many pints of champagne in cubic feet have I consumed in twenty-four years at the rate of a pint a day, and how many railway carriages would it fill?" The Prof (after rapid calculation) "Only a part of one." WSC: "So little time, and so much to achieve."' (Kay Halle, editor, *The Irrepressible Churchill*, page 222.)

taurant car was a Filipino. The PM told him he was a carnivore and would have a steak. An immense hunk of beef was placed before him. The PM looked at it and said, 'I may be a carnivore, but I'm not a glutton.' [1]

After his arrival in Washington, Churchill continued to work on his speech to Congress. The final version proved more troublesome than he had anticipated. As Roger Makins later recalled:

By the time WSC had left for New York and Ottawa (I went with him) it was in pretty good shape, but on the journey some rats got at it, and the revised version was not shown to the Ambassador, Oliver Franks, and myself until 9.00 p.m. on the evening of the 16th January. We read it through hastily and saw that it needed a lot of amendments.

We quickly decided to try to take a couple of points that evening, and we obtained access to the PM in his double bedroom in the Embassy. (The PM was lying prone in one bed, but both beds were made up, apparently so that if he got too hot in the first one he could move to the second!) [2]

In the Prime Minister's speech, Jock Colville later recalled, 'it was essential to refer to Britain's contribution in the Korean War, which had been raging since 1950'.

'If the Chinese cross the Yalu River, our reply will be—what?' Churchill asked.

'Prompt, resolute and effective,' suggested Roger Makins on the spur of the moment.

'Excellent,' said Churchill, writing the words in his speech. [3]

That night, Churchill slept at the British Embassy. But the speech was still not completed. As Roger Makins recalled, of January 17:

Next morning Oliver Franks and I went to see the PM in bed again to take up the remaining points in the speech. Oliver had to go off after a bit, and I was left to argue with the PM. As I am sure you know, he was very obstinate and rough to deal with, especially if a Foreign Service Officer was involved, and it was necessary to be equally obstinate in return. In the end the PM always agreed to meet the objection, but it was a time-consuming operation.

The speech was to be delivered at 12.00 noon and at 11.20 the PM was still in bed arguing with me. However, by that time I had got pretty well all the bugs out of the speech.

'The PM then got up,' Makins added, 'was quickly dressed, and with the assistance of a motor cycle escort, reached the Capitol on time.' [4]

[1] Lord Sherfield (formerly Sir Roger Makins) recollections: letter to the author, 19 June 1987.
[2] Lord Sherfield recollections: letter to the author, 19 June 1987.
[3] Colville diary: *The Fringes of Power*, pages 639–40.
[4] Lord Sherfield recollections: letter to the author, 19 June 1987.

Churchill began his speech by assuring Congress: 'I have not come here to ask you for money to make life more comfortable or easier for us in Britain,' and he added: 'Our standards of life are our own business and we can only keep our self-respect and independence by looking after them ourselves.' During the war Britain had borne her share of the burden 'and fought from first to last, unconquered—and for a while alone—to the utmost limits of our resources'. America's 'majestic obliteration' of all she had given Britain under Lend-Lease 'will never be forgotten by this generation in Britain, or by history'.

Churchill then spoke of China, of British democracy, and of his own presence in the Capitol that morning:

I am by no means sure that China will remain for generations in the Communist grip. The Chinese said of themselves several thousand years ago: 'China is a sea that salts all the waters that flow into it.' There's another Chinese saying about their country which is much more modern—it dates only from the fourth century. This is the saying: 'The tail of China is large and will not be wagged.' I like that one. The British democracy approves the principles of movable party heads and unwaggable national tails. It is due to the working of these important forces that I have the honour to be addressing you at this moment.

After thanking the United States for bearing 'nine-tenths, or more' of the burden in Korea, Churchill went on to welcome American patience in the armistice negotiations. The two countries were agreed, he said—using the words which Roger Makins had suggested to him—'that if the truce we seek is reached, only to be broken, our response will be prompt, resolute and effective'.[1]

Churchill went on to tell Congress:

The vast process of American rearmament in which the British Commonwealth and Empire and the growing power of United Europe will play their part to the utmost of their strength, this vast process has already altered the balance of the world and may well, if we all persevere steadfastly and loyally together, avert the danger of a Third World War, or the horror of defeat and subjugation should one come upon us.

Mr President and Mr Speaker, I hope the mourning families throughout the great Republic will find some comfort and some pride in these thoughts.

---

[1] Colville later commented: 'It was these words with no special significance except to declare that the Allies would react strongly to such an attack, which the Labour Opposition interpreted to mean that an atomic bomb would be used. Such a thought had not crossed Churchill's mind nor, I believe, President Truman's.' (*The Fringes of Power*, page 640). On 29 January 1952 Churchill told the House of Commons that he had thought it better 'to speak in general terms of the action we should take in the event of a breach of the truce, and I used the words, "prompt, resolute and effective". I do not believe they were bad words to use. Certainly, if one is dealing in general terms, they are better than "tardy, timid and fatuous". I certainly did not mean to suggest that the words, "prompt, resolute and effective" represented any new designs or decisions arrived at during our visit.'

Churchill also spoke of the Middle East. It was 'no longer possible' for Britain alone 'to bear the whole burden of maintaining the freedom of the famous waterway of the Suez Canal'. That had become 'an international rather than a national responsibility', one in which Britain, the United States, France and Turkey would have to share with Egypt. There were more than 80,000 British troops in the Canal Zone. Even 'token forces' of the United States, France and Turkey would create 'a symbol of the unity of purpose which inspires us'. Nor did he believe it an exaggeration to state that such token forces 'would probably bring into harmony all that movement by which the Four-Power policy may be made to play a decisive part by peaceful measures, and bring to an end the wide disorders of the Middle East in which, let me assure you, there lurk dangers not less great than those which the United States has stemmed in Korea'.

Churchill also spoke of one other area of the Middle East, where 'there is still some sunshine as well as shadow'. It was a personal perspective which, although not shared by many of those who had travelled with him across the Atlantic, was emphatically his own, but in no way uncritical:

From the days of the Balfour Declaration I have desired that the Jews should have a national home, and I have worked for that end. I rejoice to pay my tribute here to the achievements of those who have founded the Israelite State, who have defended themselves with tenacity, and who offer asylum to great numbers of Jewish refugees.

I hope that with their aid they may convert deserts into gardens; but if they are to enjoy peace and prosperity they must strive to renew and preserve their friendly relations with the Arab world without which widespread misery might follow for all.

Churchill then spoke about the prevention of a third world war, by means of a 'united command' of the strongest possible forces in Europe. The sooner this was done, he said, 'the sooner, also, will our sense of security, and the fact of our security, be seen to reside in valiant, resolute and well-armed manhood, rather than in the awful secrets which science had wrested from nature'.

These secrets, the atomic bomb, constituted 'at present' what Churchill went on to call 'the supreme deterrent' against a third world war, and the 'most effective guarantee' of victory in such a war, and he then set out his own words of advice and warning:

If I may say this, Members of Congress, be careful above all things, therefore, not to let go of the atomic weapon until you are sure, and more than sure, that other means of preserving peace are in your hands. It is my belief that by accumulating deterrents of all kinds against aggression we shall, in fact, ward off the fearful catastrophe, the fears of which darken the life and mar the progress of all the peoples of the globe.

We must persevere steadfastly and faithfully in the task to which, under United States leadership, we have solemnly bound ourselves. Any weakening of our purpose, any disruption of our organization would bring about the very evils which we all dread, and from which we should all suffer, and from which many of us would perish.

Churchill's concluding words were not, however, words of warning, but words that looked forward to a healing of the wounds and a reconciling of the differences:

We must not lose patience, and we must not lose hope. It may be that presently a new mood will reign behind the Iron Curtain. If so it will be easy for them to show it, but the democracies must be on their guard against being deceived by a false dawn.

We seek or covet no one's territory; we plan no forestalling war; we trust and pray that all will come right. Even during these years of what is called the 'cold war', material production in every land is continually improving through the use of new machinery and better organization and the advance of peaceful science. But the great bound forward in progress and prosperity for which mankind is longing cannot come till the shadow of war has passed away.

There are, however, historic compensations for the stresses which we suffer in the 'cold war'. Under the pressure and menace of Communist aggression the fraternal association of the United States with Britain and the British Commonwealth, and the new unity growing up in Europe—nowhere more hopeful than between France and Germany—all these harmonies are being brought forward, perhaps by several generations in the destiny of the world.

If this proves true—and it has certainly proved true up to date—the architects in the Kremlin may be found to have built a different and a far better world structure than what they planned.

Many changes had taken place throughout the world, Churchill said, since his visit in 1941, but there was 'one thing which is exactly the same as when I was here last. Britain and the United States are working for the same high cause'; and he ended: 'Bismarck once said the supreme fact of the nineteenth century was that Britain and the United States spoke the same language. Let us make sure that the supreme fact of the twentieth century is that they tread the same path.'[1]

These were stirring sentiments, but not all those who listened to them were as impressed as they might have been. One of those present, Denis Rickett, the head of the British Treasury and Supply Delegation in Washington, later recalled:

[1] Speech of 17 January 1952: Randolph S. Churchill (editor), *Stemming the Tide*, pages 220–7. Recording: BBC Written Archives Centre, Library No. 17188–91.

The Prime Minister included a reference in his speech to Congress, 'I have not come to ask for Gold but for Steel, not for favours but for equipment.' It did not make the sort of impact left by his famous wartime phrase, 'Give us the tools and we will finish the job.' He worried over the speech until the last moment and seemed to lack spontaneity and inspiration.[1]

Also listening to Churchill's speech from the floor of the Congress were Jock Colville, Viscount Knollys, Economic Minister in the Washington Embassy, and Air Chief Marshal Sir William Elliot, Chairman of the British Joint Services Commission in Washington. They, with other British Embassy people present, 'thought it had had a chilly reception', Colville recalled, 'but we were quite wrong. Congress reacted slowly, but the subsequent praise was generous. . . .'[2] 'It was very moving,' Miss Gilliatt later recalled, 'even if one had been up all night working on it!'[3]

'When it was done,' noted Lord Moran, 'the PM, flushed and happy, was like a man who has been granted a reprieve. He slumped back in the car, gazing vacantly out of the window; his cigar had gone out; he yawned contentedly. It had gone well, he thought; anyway, they had been very kind before he left the Senate.'

'It was a great success, Prime Minister,' were General Marshall's words when he greeted him at the door of the British Embassy.[4]

'Mary and I listened together to your speech with emotion,' Clementine Churchill telegraphed from London. 'We both send our love.'[5] 'Perfect radio reception,' telegraphed Randolph, 'your magnificent, masterly, meaty speech.'[6]

That afternoon Churchill and Truman presided over the fifth and final Plenary meeting of their conference. The subject under discussion was a possible meeting between the Western and Communist leaders. At the present time, Churchill told Truman, he would not be in favour of proposing a meeting with the leaders of the Soviet Union to review the major questions outstanding between Russia and the West. 'A different situation would however arise,' Churchill added, 'at any time the Soviet leaders indicated that they were prepared to make a genuine effort to reach an understanding with the democracies.'

Churchill then spoke of the danger that people would assume, if a summit conference broke down, that 'war would be inevitable'. He would wish to interpose between the breakdown of such a conference

[1] Sir Denis Rickett recollections: letter to the author, 18 July 1987.
[2] Colville diary: *The Fringes of Power*, page 639.
[3] Elizabeth Gilliatt recollections: in conversation with the author, 9 July 1987.
[4] Moran diary, 17 January 1952: *The Struggle for Survival*, pages 366–8.
[5] 'Immediate', 18 January 1952: Churchill papers, 1/51.
[6] Telegram sent 17 January 1952: Churchill papers, 1/51.

and total war an 'intermediate stage' in which there would be 'an intensification of the cold war'. In that stage the democracies would make an intensive effort to bring home to all people behind the Iron Curtain the true facts of the world situation, 'by broadcasting, by dropping leaflets and by all other methods of propaganda which were open to them'. He believed that the leaders in the Kremlin 'would fear such a revelation of the truth to the masses whom they held in their grip'. And it might well be, Churchill added, 'that, under pressure of an intense propaganda campaign on these lines, the conference might be resumed with greater hope of success'. Detailed methods for conducting such a campaign, Churchill proposed, 'might profitably be studied in advance'.[1]

As the discussion continued, the question of the Atlantic Command was raised again. 'There followed,' Dean Acheson later recalled, 'one of Mr Churchill's greatest speeches,' and he went on to give the gist of it:

For centuries England had held the seas against every tyrant, wresting command of them from Spain and then from France, protecting our hemisphere from penetration by European systems in the days of our weakness. Now, in the plenitude of our power, bearing as we did the awful burden of atomic command and responsibility for the final word of peace or war, surely we could make room for Britain to play her historic role 'upon that western sea whose floor is white with the bones of Englishmen'.[2]

Churchill's arguments were in part effective; the United Kingdom Home Command was extended westward to the hundred-fathom line. The final communiqué noted: 'These changes however do not go the full way to meet the Prime Minister's objections to the original arrangements. Nevertheless, the Prime Minister, while not withdrawing his objections, expressed his readiness to allow the appointment of a Supreme Commander to go forward in order that a command structure may be created and enabled to proceed with the necessary planning in the Atlantic area. He reserved the right to bring forward modifications for the consideration of NATO, if he so desired, at a later stage.'

On January 19 Churchill left Washington by train for New York. That night he stayed with Bernard Baruch on East 66th Street, and on the following morning, learning that Sir Roger Makins was about to return to Britain, he wrote out in his own hand a letter to his wife:

My darling,
    Sir Roger Makins is flying home today & I send this line w him to tell you how much you have been in my thoughts & how much I love you.

[1] 'Fifth Plenary Meeting', 3 p.m., 18 January 1952: Cabinet papers, 21/3057.
[2] Dean Acheson recollections: *Present at the Creation*, page 769.

I have just finished what seems to be the most strenuous fortnight I can remember, & I am staying quiet here for 48 hours to recover. I never had such a whirl of people & problems, and the two speeches were vy hard & exacting ordeals. Now I sail for home going on board QM midnight 22.

Beatrice Eden came to dinner last night. She seems as young and attractive as she was when I saw her last 8 or 10 years ago. She gave no intelligible explanations of her mental attitude though she tried vy hard to do so. She says Anthony has no heart—She does not seem to have much herself. She is coming over to England in March. She is a real puzzle.[1]

You will have seen what the papers say about my 'Mission'. The enclosed cutting wh Bernie gave me is fair & informative. I am far from sure about the future in the Far East—or indeed elsewhere. No one can tell what is coming. I still hope we shall muddle along to greater strength.

The Presidential Election is now going to amuse the Americans for the next nine anxious months. They in their turn will have the dose we have swallowed in the last 2 years. But I suppose the Russians have their troubles too. I hope so anyway.

I look forward so much to seeing you next Monday week. Let us dine alone at No. 10. Tender love my darling Clemmie.

Your ever loving husband

W

'Sarah is looking lovely,' Churchill added, '& Miss Truman & she seem to have made good friends.'[2]

On the following day Churchill wrote to his wife again:

Darling,

It is splendid (as I cabled) that you will meet me at Southampton. The arrangements are being made accordingly. It is possible we may have to motor to London as the train may have to wait for the other passengers. I have only one piece of urgent business wh I may have to settle before starting either by train or car. This may settle itself beforehand. The enclosed telegram to Tommy Lascelles will explain the possible urgency.[3]

I have let myself in for a Parade through the streets of New York to the Mayor's Parlour tomorrow (Tuesday) to receive a gold medal. Unfortunately the weather has turned *icy*. (Yesterday warm & muggy.) I have the beginning of a cold. This is a tiresome problem. I shall however have to follow Charles's directions. But if I cancel there will be gt disappointment! Such is life now-

---

[1] Beatrice Eden (Beatrice Beckett) had married Anthony Eden in 1923; the marriage was dissolved by divorce in 1950. She died in 1957. Their elder son Simon had been killed on active service in Burma in June 1945. On 7 June 1952 Eden wrote to his son Nicholas: 'I dined with W on the way here, & stayed the night. He mentioned that your Mummie had dined with him in New York, & that she had been very much moved when he spoke of me, & the work I was trying to do; but he admitted that he didn't think her dislike of politics was any less. He had not told me before because there was no change about politics, but I was much touched at what he told me of your Mummie's feelings towards me. We didn't pretend that they could overcome her aversion to politics.' (Letter of 7 June 1952: Robert Rhodes James, *Anthony Eden*, page 323.)

[2] 'My darling', 20 January 1952: Spencer–Churchill papers.

[3] The King's worsening illness.

adays. I am so glad you reminded me about the Ronnie Trees, I have been so hunted that I had forgotten them, & they have only today returned from Washington. They are coming to dine. [1]

Sarah was really vy good yesterday in the opening, it is all in the Hall brothers Christmas Card Trade Advertisement programme of the Television. She does 4 a month—one of wh is all her own acting. The fee is $2,000 each time! All this may broaden out considerably. She seems vy happy & is looking beautiful.

I shall indeed be delighted to get home. I never remember 3 weeks taking so long to live, although it has been all kindness & compliments.

With fondest love

Your loving husband

W[2]

At midnight on January 22, as planned, Churchill left New York for home. His cold was still not entirely better. 'Started very comfortably,' he telegraphed to his wife from the *Queen Mary* on January 23. 'Temperature normal in the morning. Cold will take another day or two. Am staying in bed almost entirely. Much love, W.' [3]

Reflecting on Churchill's American mission, Lord Moran noted in his diary on January 26, while they were still on board the *Queen Mary*:

What have I learnt about the PM during this American visit that I did not know before? He is still better informed than any of his Ministers on any question affecting the Armed Forces of the Crown. It had taken a long time to settle the Atlantic Command, and his obstinate refusal to yield had provoked even members of his own little party. But in the end he salvaged more out of the dispute than anyone thought possible. British anti-submarine forces were, he argued, the key to action in the Atlantic, and he insisted that our naval staff should retain control of any action fought within the 'hundred-fathom line'—Shinwell, he said with contempt, had never heard of the line.

'Our writ will run in the western approaches; two hundred miles west from Plymouth and the St George's Channel; a hundred and fifty miles from Belfast and the Mull of Kintyre and more than a hundred miles from Scapa Flow.' [4]

'No other man could have achieved so much,' Moran added, 'when the Americans were disposed to give so little.' [5]

[1] Ronald Tree, a Conservative MP from 1933 to 1945 (and from 1940 to 1943 Parliamentary Private Secretary to Brendan Bracken) and his second wife, Marietta. During the war, Churchill had spent many of the full-moon weekends at Tree's house, Ditchley Park, near Oxford, as it was less vulnerable to air attack than Chequers.

[2] 'My darling', 21 January 1952: Spencer–Churchill papers.

[3] Telegram despatched 23 January 1952: Churchill papers, 1/50.

[4] Speaking in the House of Commons on 29 January 1952, Churchill explained: 'The one-hundred-fathom line has many advantages; among others, it broadly corresponds to the limits within which moored mining is profitable and was a very well-known feature in all our affairs in the last war.' (*Hansard.*)

[5] Moran diary, 26 January 1952: *The Struggle for Survival*, pages 370–1.

On January 28 the *Queen Mary* reached Southampton. At the quayside to greet the Prime Minister were Clementine Churchill and Mary; they lunched with him on board ship before returning to London. 'It is splendid that you are safely back' was Randolph's epistolary greeting.[1]

[1] 'My dearest Papa', 28 January 1952: Churchill papers, 1/51.

38

1952: 'A volcanic flash'

ON 29 January 1952, the day after his return to London, Churchill spoke in the House of Commons about his American visit. One aim of the visit, he said, was for the Government to establish 'intimate and easy relations and understandings' with the President and the governing authorities of the United States. He had also felt it important to try to give the impression to the American people 'that we rejoice in their effort to defend the cause of world freedom against Communist aggression and penetration and that we will aid them in this purpose, which is also ours, with all our strength and goodwill'.[1]

A week later, challenged by Labour backbenchers to defend what they claimed was a commitment to the Americans that Britain would use the atomic bomb against China if the Korean War were to flare up again, Churchill was prepared to reveal the 'dramatic fact', as Colville noted, that Attlee's Labour Government had already gone further in committing Britain to bomb China, in certain circumstances, than anyone had supposed, and that he had certainly entered into no new commitments.[2] But this revelation, and with it the trouncing of his Labour Party critics, had momentarily to be postponed. On the morning of 6 February 1952 when Colville arrived early and asked the Private Secretary on duty for the text of the speech, he was told 'there was no need to think of it further'. Edward Ford, the Assistant Private Secretary to the King, had just come from Buckingham Palace to Downing Street to announce that the King was dead.

Colville's account continued:

When I went to the Prime Minister's bedroom he was sitting alone with tears in his eyes, looking straight in front of him and reading neither his official papers nor the newspapers. I had not realized how much the King meant to him. I tried

---

[1] Speech of 29 January 1952: *Hansard*.
[2] Colville diary: *The Fringes of Power*, page 640.

to cheer him up by saying how well he would get on with the new Queen, but all he could say was that he did not know her and that she was only a child.[1]

Churchill at once called a meeting of the Cabinet for 11.30 that morning, and informed them of 'the grievous news'.[2] At a second Cabinet meeting that afternoon, Churchill told his colleagues 'that the new Sovereign was returning to this country by air and was expected to arrive on the following afternoon'.[3] Princess Elizabeth, now Queen, had been in Kenya with Prince Philip, on her way to Australia and New Zealand.

On the morning of February 7 Churchill drove to London Airport to welcome the Queen back to Britain. 'He took me down in the car,' Miss Portal later recalled. 'He was going to broadcast that afternoon. On the way down, he dictated. He was in a flood of tears.'

After welcoming the Queen, Churchill returned to London. During the drive back, he continued to dictate his broadcast. On reaching London, he hurried into his study, whereupon both Jock Colville and David Hunt rushed up to Miss Portal to ask if the broadcast was ready. 'You've got to give him half an hour to finish it,' she told them. 'It was finished,' she later recalled. 'But I wanted them to lay off. He was exhausted.'[4]

Rehearsing the speech at lunchtime, Churchill broke down.[5]

During his broadcast, Churchill spoke of how, when the death of the King had been announced on the previous morning, 'there struck a deep and solemn note in our lives which, as it resounded far and wide, stilled the clatter and traffic of twentieth-century life in many lands and made countless millions of human beings pause and look around them. A new sense of values took, for the time being, possession of human minds and mortal existence presented itself to so many at the same moment in its serenity and in its sorrow, in its splendour and in its pain, in its fortitude and in its suffering.'

Churchill also spoke of the King's final illness:

During these last months the King walked with death, as if death were a companion, an acquaintance, whom he recognized and did not fear. In the end death came as a friend; and after a happy day of sunshine and sport, and after 'good night' to those who loved him best, he fell asleep as every man or woman who strives to fear God and nothing else in the world may hope to do.

The nearer one stood to him the more these facts were apparent. But the

---

[1] Colville diary: *The Fringes of Power*, page 640.

[2] Cabinet Conclusions No. 11 of 1952, 'Secret', 11.30 a.m., 6 February 1952: Cabinet papers, 128/24.

[3] Cabinet Conclusions No. 12 of 1952, 'Secret', 2.45 p.m., 6 February 1952: Cabinet papers, 128/24.

[4] Lady Williams of Elvel recollections: in conversation with the author, 7 July 1987.

[5] Moran diary, 7 February 1952: *The Struggle for Survival*, pages 372–3.

newspapers and photographs of modern times have made vast numbers of his subjects able to watch with emotion the last months of his pilgrimage. We all saw him approach his journey's end.

There were also the war years to speak about, for it was then that Churchill had developed his friendship with the King which was now, and so early in his second Premiership, brought to an abrupt end:

My friends, I suppose no Minister saw so much of the King during the war as I did. I made certain he was kept informed of every secret matter; and the care and thoroughness with which he mastered the immense daily flow of State papers made a deep mark on my mind.

Let me tell you another fact. On one of the days, when Buckingham Palace was bombed, the King had just returned from Windsor. One side of the courtyard was struck, and if the windows opposite out of which he and the Queen were looking had not been, by the mercy of God, open, they would both have been blinded by the broken glass instead of being only hurled back by the explosion.

Amid all that was then going on—although I saw the King so often—I never heard of this episode till a long time after. Their Majesties never mentioned it, or thought it of more significance than a soldier in their armies would of a shell bursting near him. This seems to me to be a revealing trait in the Royal character.

The 'Second Queen Elizabeth' was now ascending the throne, in her twenty-sixth year, the same age, Churchill pointed out, as the first Queen Elizabeth nearly four hundred years before. 'She has already been acclaimed as Queen of Canada,' he said, referring to her recent visit to Canada as princess, and he added: 'we make our claim, too, and others will come forward also; and tomorrow the proclamation of her sovereignty will command the loyalty of her native land and of all other parts of the British Commonwealth and Empire'.

Churchill ended his broadcast with stirring words, telling his listeners throughout Britain, and beyond:

I, whose youth was passed in the august, unchallenged and tranquil glories of the Victorian Era, may well feel a thrill in invoking, once more, the prayer and the Anthem

GOD SAVE THE QUEEN[1]

On February 11, Churchill spoke in the House of Commons on the Motions for Addresses of Sympathy to the Queen, the Queen Mother and Queen Mary. He had been present, he said, on every previous occasion when a Prime Minister had moved such a motion: Balfour on the death of Queen Victoria, Asquith on the death of King Edward

---

[1] Broadcast of 7 February 1952: Randolph S. Churchill (editor), *Stemming the Tide*, pages 237–40. Recording: BBC Written Archives Centre, Library No. MT17176.

VII, and Baldwin on the death of King George V, 'and I shall follow, in what I say, the example of those eminent men'. Churchill continued:

With the end of the Victorian Era we passed into what I feel we must call 'the terrible twentieth century'. Half of it is over and we have survived its fearful convulsions. We stand erect both as an island people and as the centre of a world-wide Commonwealth and Empire, after so much else in other lands has been shattered or fallen to the ground and been replaced by other forces and systems.

When King Edward VII, so long familiar to his generation as Prince of Wales, passed away, both Mr Asquith and Mr Balfour dwelt upon his labours for the cause of peace in Europe, and many called him 'Edward the Peacemaker'. But only four years after his death we were plunged into war by forces utterly beyond our control.

Of Edward VII's son and successor, Churchill told the House of Commons:

King George V succeeded to a grim inheritance; first, to the fiercest party troubles I have ever seen and taken part in at home, and then to the First World War with its prodigious slaughter. Victory was gained, but the attempt to erect, in the League of Nations, a world instrument which would prevent another hideous conflict, failed.

The people of the United States realize today how grievous was the cost to them, in life and treasure, of the isolationism which led them to withdraw from the League of Nations which President Wilson had conceived and which British minds had so largely helped to shape.

It was during the reign of King George VI, however, that the 'greatest shocks' had fallen on Britain. His first three years had been 'clouded by the fears of another world war, and the differences of opinion, and indeed bewilderment, which prevailed about how to avert it'. Then war had come:

The late King lived through every minute of this struggle with a heart that never quavered and a spirit undaunted; but I, who saw him so often, knew how keenly, with all his full knowledge and understanding of what was happening, he felt personally the ups and downs of this terrific struggle and how he longed to fight in it, arms in hand, himself.

Thus passed six more years of his reign. Victory again crowned our martial struggles, but our island, more than any other country in the world, and for a longer period, had given all that was in it. We had victory with honour and with the respect of the world, victor and vanquished, friend and foe alike.

Alas, we found ourselves in great straits from the exertions which we had made, and then there came, in the midst of the ordeals of the aftermath and of the problems which lay about us, a new menace. The surmounting of one form of mortal peril seemed soon only to be succeeded by the shadow of another.

The King felt—as the Leader of the Opposition, who was his first Minister for so long, knows well—the fresh anxieties which thronged up against us and the disappointment that followed absolute triumph without lasting security or peace.

Though deeply smitten by physical afflictions, he never lost his courage or faith that Great Britain, her Commonwealth and Empire, would in the end come through. Nor did he lose hope that another hateful war will be warded off, perhaps to no small extent by the wisdom and experience of the many realms over which he ruled.

After expressing the sympathy of the House of Commons to the Queen Mother, and to Queen Mary, Churchill ended his speech, as he had ended his broadcast four days earlier, by talking about the new Queen, with whose reign 'we must all feel our contact with the future':

A fair and youthful figure, Princess, wife and mother, is the heir to all our traditions and glories never greater than in her father's days, and to all our perplexities and dangers never greater in peacetime than now. She is also heir to all our united strength and loyalty.

She comes to the Throne at a time when a tormented mankind stands uncertainly poised between world catastrophe and a golden age. That it should be a golden age of art and letters, we can only hope—science and machinery have their other tales to tell—but it is certain that if a true and lasting peace can be achieved, and if the nations will only let each other alone an immense and undreamed of prosperity with culture and leisure ever more widely spread can come, perhaps even easily and swiftly, to the masses of the people in every land.

Let us hope and pray that the accession to our ancient Throne of Queen Elizabeth the Second may be the signal for such a brightening salvation of the human scene.[1]

'I thought he was sublime,' Henry Channon wrote in his diary of Churchill's speech; 'so simple and eloquent with his Macaulay phrases pouring out. The attentive House was electrified.'[2]

On February 15 Churchill was among the mourners at St George's Chapel, Windsor, for the King's funeral. 'Distinguished figures were filling up the places in front of the stalls,' reported The Times, adding: 'Only Mr Churchill and General Eisenhower attracted general notice.'[3]

Attached to the Government's wreath was a card which bore the words 'For Valour', the same words as the inscription on the Victoria Cross. 'Lord Athlone told me,' noted Lord Moran, 'that it was in Winston's handwriting. He said the Royal Family loved the words.'[4]

---

[1] Speech of 11 February 1952: Hansard.
[2] Channon diary, 11 February 1952: Robert Rhodes James (editor), Chips, pages 463–4.
[3] The Times, 16 February 1952.
[4] Moran diary, 12 February 1952: The Struggle for Survival, page 373. The Earl of Athlone was Queen Mary's brother; from 1940 to 1946 he had been Governor-General of Canada, and was Churchill's official host at Quebec in 1943 and 1944.

To Bernard Baruch, Churchill had written two days earlier: 'We have sustained a terrible loss in the death of King George VI, who was a devoted and tireless servant of his country, and these are sad days indeed. But I am sure that in his daughter we have one who is in every way able to bear the heavy burden she must now carry.'

In his letter to Baruch, Churchill also wrote of his American visit. Only two weeks had passed since he had returned to London, but the King's death had disrupted the normal pattern of work and of saying thank you. Churchill now sought to rectify this lapse:

I cannot tell you how much it meant to me to be with you, and in such peace and comfort, my dear friend. As you well know, these visits, although I am treated everywhere with the greatest kindness, are a heavy load; and to have a few days in such pleasant company and surroundings does more to refresh and strengthen me than anything else. Thank you so much for all your care for me, and for my party.

My cold has now been vanquished. I worked in bed most of the time on the ship, and did not leave my quarters at all. There was plenty to do, but except for one day, we had a very smooth passage.[1]

Following the King's death there was no respite from the affairs of State. To Eden's suggestion that it might be possible to reach an agreement with Egypt whereby British forces in the Canal Zone could be substantially reduced, Churchill cautioned the Cabinet, on February 14, that 'he did not think we should relinquish it until our forces were replaced by adequate allied forces under a Middle East Command. He therefore suggested that we should make no immediate offer of withdrawal, but should keep this in reserve as a possible means of bringing pressure to bear on our Allies to induce them to share with us the responsibility of defending the international waterway.' Even if satisfactory plans could be made for Four-Power defence of the area with Egyptian co-operation, Churchill commented, 'it would probably be impracticable for us to leave the Zone within a year'.[2]

Four days later, and despite Churchill's caveat, Eden proposed in Cabinet that the Egyptian Government should be offered the base installations in the Canal Zone provided it agreed to make them available in due course to an Allied Middle East Command. Once more, Churchill disagreed with the proposed policy, telling his Cabinet colleagues:

He thought that we should be in a position of dangerous weakness, after we had handed over the installations to the Egyptians, if the Four-Power arrangements did not come into operation at once. He would much prefer

[1] 'My dear Bernie', 13 February 1952: Churchill papers, 2/210.
[2] Cabinet Conclusions No. 17 of 1952, 'Secret', 5 p.m., 14 February 1952: Cabinet papers, 128/24.

an arrangement by which our responsibility was transferred directly to the Middle East Command. It might indeed be best to insist on Four-Power negotiations at the outset and on an agreement by which Egypt would be associated on terms of equality with the other Powers in the Middle East Command as a prior condition of any arrangement affecting the Canal Zone base.

The reason for transferring the base to the Egyptian Government 'in the first instance', Churchill was told, 'was that it was on Egyptian territory and none of the other Powers who would be concerned in a Middle East Command had at present any right to hold or use military property in Egypt'.

Churchill made no comment; or at least none that was recorded.[1] At a further Cabinet meeting that same evening, when Churchill asked for his view to become the Government's policy, Eden 'felt bound to warn the Cabinet', the minutes recorded, that if the negotiations with Egypt were to succeed, 'further concessions' would have to be made, including a 'definite undertaking' that once an Allied Middle East Command was established, 'we would withdraw from Egypt within a specified period' all British land forces not required by the Allied Commander. Again, Churchill made no further recorded protest, or comment. In its conclusions, the Cabinet accepted that 'some further concessions' would have to be made to the Egyptians; but that these should not yet be communicated to the Egyptian Government.[2]

Three days after this Cabinet meeting, in the early evening of February 21, Churchill summoned his doctor to Downing Street. It was an hour after his habitual late afternoon siesta. 'I am glad you have come,' he told him, and went on to explain the reasons for the summons:

I took up the telephone when I woke an hour ago, and I couldn't think of the words I wanted. Wrong words seemed to come into my head, but I was quite clear what was happening and did not say them. This went on for about three or four minutes. Then the operator asked, 'Do you want the Private Office?' What does it mean, Charles? Am I going to have a stroke? If this happened again I'd have to pull out. It might come on in a speech. That would be the end.[3]

Churchill had suffered a small arterial spasm. This, Lord Moran warned Jock Colville on the following morning, 'might be the precursor of an immediate stroke; if not, it was at least a plain warning

---

[1] Cabinet Conclusions No. 18 of 1952, 'Secret', 12 noon, 18 February 1952: Cabinet papers, 128/24.
[2] Cabinet Conclusions No. 19 of 1952, 'Secret', 10 p.m., 18 February 1952: Cabinet papers, 128/24.
[3] Moran diary, 21 February 1952: *The Struggle for Survival*, pages 373–5.

that if the pressure was not relaxed dire results would follow in six months or less'.

Together, Moran and Colville went to see Lord Salisbury for advice. Lord Salisbury's view was, Colville noted, that Churchill 'might go to the Lords, leaving Eden to manage in the Commons', but remaining Prime Minister until after the Coronation, which was planned for May 1953.[1] Lord Moran also left an account of the discussion with Lord Salisbury at his office in Whitehall:

I was shown, with Jock, into Lord Salisbury's room at Gwydyr House. I said my piece: I asked if the Prime Minister's work could be lightened.

'A Prime Minister cannot shed his responsibilities,' Salisbury replied.

Jock thought the Honours List and Ecclesiastical preferment might be done by Salisbury with Harry Crookshank. Perhaps even the Budget proposals could be simplified and summarized a little more before being shown to the PM.

Salisbury: 'Of course, I don't know how far they are peptonized already.'

Jock: 'I hate to be disloyal, but the PM is not doing his work. A document of five sheets has to be submitted to him as one paragraph, so that many of the points of the argument are lost.'

I pointed out that this had happened in the last years of the war when Martin, Rowan and Bridges in turn had complained that he was not mastering his brief.

Salisbury: 'His work seems to vary enormously from day to day.'

Jock: 'Yes, that's true. Only yesterday I simplified something and he burst out, "Can't I read?" He was right on the spot.'

Salisbury: 'Another time in the Cabinet he will talk about something for two and a half hours without once coming to the point.'

Jock: 'Yes, Egypt, for example.'

The real difficulty, I said, was that he hated delegating anything.

Salisbury (sympathetically): 'We are all the same; the more tired we get, the more we seem to feel we must do the thing ourselves.'

As they talked I saw that even if Winston were willing to turn over a new leaf all this tinkering would come to nothing. Then Salisbury said suddenly:

'Of course he ought to go to the Lords—oh, yes, remaining Prime Minister.'

Jock: 'Eden would lead the House and would be virtually Prime Minister. In 1952 no one but Winston could be Prime Minister in the Lords. He would be the grand old man of politics, coming down from time to time and making a great speech to their Lordships.'

Salisbury felt sure he could go to the Lords and remain Prime Minister.

'We are beginning to see light,' he added cheerfully.

My heart leapt; this was a solution that had not occurred to me. But Jock's face had become serious.

'He won't do it,' he said gloomily. 'I did once suggest to him that he should go to the Lords, and thought at first he was taking it seriously, when

---

[1] Colville diary: *The Fringes of Power*, page 642.

he said: "I should have to be the Duke of Chartwell, and Randolph would be the Marquis of Toodledo." I saw that he was laughing at me.'

Salisbury, ruefully: 'No, I am afraid he regards us in the Lords as a rather disreputable collection of old gentlemen.'

Lord Moran and Jock Colville then went on to see Sir Alan Lascelles at Buckingham Palace. Lascelles suggested that Moran should go to Churchill 'and say outright that he should go to the Lords'. But Moran replied that whereas Churchill would listen to him on medical grounds, 'when I began on politics he would switch off'. No one could be thought of with the ability to persuade Churchill to go to the Lords, not even Ismay. 'The King might have done it,' Lascelles said, 'but he is gone.' [1]

Churchill had gone down to Chartwell to recuperate. When Colville telephoned him there on February 23 he suggested that in the coming Defence debate Churchill should leave the Government's speech to Anthony Head, the Secretary of State for War. 'Have you been talking with Charles?' Churchill asked. 'Jock had brazened it out, but he was shaken,' recorded Moran when Colville told him of the incident. [2]

On February 26 the powers of recuperation and the extraordinary determination of this man of seventy-seven were made abundantly clear to those who had known of his arterial spasm and discussed how to send him to the House of Lords. For it was only five days after the attack that Churchill spoke in the House of Commons on Foreign Affairs. To his doctor, he confided later that day that before the speech, 'I seemed to have no wits, and I was very tired and shaky before getting up to speak, but I felt stronger as I got under way.' [3]

This was no ordinary debate, but the vote of censure for which Churchill had been preparing on the evening before the King's death. It was not even an ordinary vote of censure on the Government, but a personal one against Churchill himself, accusing him of wanting to make war on China in order to hasten the end of the Korean deadlock.

This censure was set out by Herbert Morrison, who cited Churchill's Congress pledge of 'prompt, resolute and effective action' as proof of this sinister intention. 'I have hardly ever listened,' Churchill replied, 'from a skilled Parliamentarian—to such a weak, vague, wandering harangue which at no point touched the realities or which was so largely composed of quotations of all kinds, some of his own, and none selected with a view to proving or sustaining any effective case.'

[1] Moran diary, 22 February 1952: *The Struggle for Survival*, pages 375–8.
[2] Moran diary, 23 February 1952: *The Struggle for Survival*, pages 378–9.
[3] Moran diary, 26 February 1952: *The Struggle for Survival*, pages 379–80. Three days later, Churchill told Lord Moran that he had felt 'stupid, dull and muzzy' during the luncheon before his speech, and had wondered 'if I could make a speech at all'. (Moran diary, 29 February 1952: *The Struggle for Survival*, pages 380–1.)

'I must remind the House,' Churchill said, 'that I have never changed my opinion about the danger of our getting involved in China,' and he then exploded his bombshell. 'It was agreed,' he said, in May 1950, 'between the United States Government and the late Socialist Administration that in certain circumstances and contingencies action would be taken not confined to Korea. Only they wished, quite properly in my opinion, that they should be consulted beforehand.'

Nor had the agreement of May been the only one. It had been renewed in a more limited way in September 1950, without even the proviso. The facts were clear from the records which he had consulted: the Labour Government had agreed with the United States that, if heavy air attacks were launched from Chinese bases on United Nations troops in Korea, the air forces of the United Nations, including British aircraft, would undertake retaliatory bombing against those bases. Britain, under Attlee, would have participated in the bombing of China.

In both the May and September 1950 cases, Churchill declared, as Labour MPs were first provoked to indignant outcries of protest and then shocked into silence by these revelations, 'Her Majesty's Government consider that the decision of our predecessors was right and, in my view, in both cases it justifies the words which I used in the United States Congress, namely "prompt, resolute and effective".'

'There was pandemonium,' Nigel Nicolson wrote to his father Harold, and he added: 'I was sitting directly opposite Attlee. He was sitting hunched up like an elf just out of its chrysalis, and stared at Winston, turning slowly white. The Labour benches howled—anything to make a noise to cover up the moment of shock. Winston sat back beaming. Bevan—a most charming, dangerous man—did his best to launch a counter-attack, but it was too late. We had won.'[1]

As Churchill produced the evidence that the Labour Government had been prepared, secretly, to accept the very action they now, but falsely, accused him of planning, he had been pressed to cite the documents on which he based his recital. 'Produce the document and prove it,' demanded Richard Crossman. But equally emphatic protests, including one from Aneurin Bevan, led, through the intervention of the Deputy Speaker, to the ruling that the citing of documents from a previous administration was a breach of privilege.

'I do not understand,' Churchill commented mischievously, as the interruption proceeded, 'why there should be all this fear on the benches opposite,' and he added: 'I am not making a quotation. I am stating a fact.'

[1] Letter of 3 March 1952: Nigel Nicolson, editor, *Harold Nicolson, Diaries and Letters 1945–1962*, volume 3, pages 222–3. Nigel Nicolson had been elected Conservative MP in February 1952.

That fact, devastating in itself, was exploited by Churchill to devastating effect:

As I have already said today, and as I pointed out when I spoke a month ago, it is not possible, while military operations are going on, to state either positively or negatively exactly what those consequences might be. But let me make it clear that we conformed, in principle, to the policy of our predecessors. Indeed, in some respects it might be said that we did not commit ourselves even as far as they had done.

Nevertheless, the action to which we agreed, like that of the Socialist Government before us, fully justified the description which I gave to Congress of being 'prompt, resolute and effective'.

Churchill then spoke of the Conservative Government's policy towards any flare-up of the war in Korea, telling the House that during his and Eden's visit to Washington no changes had been sought, or made, to what the Labour Government had committed Britain. It was 'a fact', Churchill said, 'that we did not discuss the matter further at any conference in Washington with our American colleagues', and he added:

It is absolutely true therefore to say, as in the words of the Opposition Motion, that we adhered to the policy followed by the late Administration with regard to the Korean conflict and the relations between Great Britain and China. It is not true to say that I in any way departed from this position. There is no truth in the suggestion that any secret or private arrangements were made or any change of policy agreed upon, formally or informally, actual or implied, by me or my right hon. friend the Foreign Secretary on these issues during our visit to the United States.

Linking the issue of censure with his wider hopes, Churchill then told the House of Commons that it was the 'design and intent' of the Soviet Union 'and its satellites and all its associates and fellow-travellers in many lands to drive a wedge between the British and American democracies and everything which tends to consolidate the mighty forces of the English-speaking world, upon which the hopes of United Europe also depend'. Anything that secured that unity 'must be considered a service not only to freedom but to peace'.

The prospects of a truce being 'reached and respected' in Korea, Churchill added, would depend to a large extent 'upon the unity between Great Britain and the United States being proved to be not only unbreakable but growing stronger, and the attempts of all who seek to weaken or divide us being repulsed and condemned as they will be tonight by the House of Commons'.[1]

Immediately after his speech, Churchill's doctor advised him 'to go

---

[1] Speech of 26 February 1952: *Hansard*.

home and have a bath and dine before returning to the House'. But Churchill declined this well-meant advice, and hurried to the Smoking Room. 'He really wanted to know what the people thought of his speech,' Lord Moran noted. 'He was excited. His pulse was 112,' and Moran added: 'I have a feeling that the chance of translating him to the Lords is gone.'[1]

In the Smoking Room was Nigel Nicolson, who wrote to his father Harold: 'I was sitting in the smoking-room afterwards with Cranborne when Winston came up to us, with a cigar and a glass of brandy. "It was a great day," he said, "a great triumph, and I am glad that you joined us in time to witness it."'

Of Churchill's appearance during his speech, Nicolson commented: 'How much better he is in the House than on a platform! How he loves it! He is looking white and fatty, a most unhealthy look, you would say, if he were anyone else, but somehow out of this sickly mountain comes a volcanic flash.'[2]

Among those who had heard Churchill speak was his throat doctor, C. P. Wilson, who wrote to him that evening: 'May I say how much I appreciated your masterly address & how glad I was to be present at such a crushing & devastating disposal of your detractors.'[3]

Three days later, Churchill told Lord Moran, with animation: 'We put them on their backs.'[4] It had been a personal triumph. In Cabinet on the day after his speech, Churchill assured his colleagues, who had been worried by the Opposition demand that the Cabinet papers cited by Churchill would have to be laid before the House, that the statement he had made 'had in fact been based on Foreign Office telegrams and despatches, which for this purpose were in quite a different category from Cabinet papers'. As he had not purported, however, to quote the telegrams textually, 'he did not think he was under any obligation to lay them before Parliament'.[5]

In spite of concerns for his ability to deal with details, Churchill was actively seeking many defence initiatives. Since becoming Prime Minister and Minister of Defence he had caused the 249,000 soldiers then in depots and training centres to be organized into effective fighting groups, comprising more than five hundred 'mobile columns', capable, as he later told the House of Commons, 'of giving a good account of

---

[1] Moran diary, 26 February 1952: *The Struggle for Survival*, pages 379–80.

[2] Viscount Cranborne was the elder son of the 5th Marquess of Salisbury, and from 1950 to 1954 Conservative MP for Bournemouth West.

[3] 'Dear Mr Churchill', 26 February 1952: Churchill papers, 1/54. C. P. Wilson was the ear, nose and throat surgeon to the Middlesex Hospital.

[4] Moran diary, 29 February 1952: *The Struggle for Survival*, page 380.

[5] Cabinet Conclusions No. 22 of 1952, 'Secret', 11 a.m., 27 February 1952: Cabinet papers, 128/24.

themselves and of imposing a considerable deterrent upon any airborne adventure by being able to kill or capture the ones who land'. The process had been strengthened by the sailors ashore and the Air Force ground men, 'who also make important contributions'. The weekly reports which he had called for showed 'that morale is high, and that all ranks understand and have welcomed the reality and importance of their new duties, and that they like to feel that they are guarding their homes and their fellow-countrymen, as well as learning or teaching'.

At the beginning of 1952 Churchill had initiated the registration of men for Home Guard duty. By March of that year 30,000 had registered. 'They must be careful not to leave it too late,' he warned that March. 'If war should come,' he explained, 'it will be with violent speed and suddenness, and here at home, with almost all our Regular Army overseas, we must rely to an unusual extent on the Home Guard. Enough resolute men must be armed and ready to aid all the other forms of protection against raids, descents and sabotage.' At first he had felt unable to provide the Home Guard with uniforms, or even with greatcoats or boots, but then 'I decided upon consideration to draw upon our mobilization reserves to the extent necessary to clothe at least the first 50,000'.[1]

Another defence initiative which Churchill had started, drawing upon his experiences in both world wars, was, by 'a severe combing of the tail' of existing regiments, to produce even more Regular Army second battalions.

On February 20 Churchill asked the Chiefs of Staff to ensure that the Falkland Islands were properly defended, and that a detachment of Royal Marines should be sent in a frigate to the vicinity of the islands. 'It will no doubt be easy,' Eden told him, 'to arrange that the Marines are in evidence at Port Stanley from time to time.'[2]

On March 3 Churchill was in the Chair at the first meeting of the Defence Committee of the Cabinet, held in the Prime Minister's Map Room at the Ministry of Defence. On the first question raised, that of the Royal Naval base at Simonstown, Churchill stressed that Britain had 'a legal right of perpetual user on which we could justifiably stand firm', and he added: 'It was strategically necessary for the Royal Navy to have base facilities in Simonstown in any major war, and perhaps more particularly in a war in which South Africa was neutral. Simonstown was an essential link in Imperial communications and there was no obvious alternative to it. He was in favour of taking no fresh initiative in this matter. . . .'

[1] Speech of 5 March 1952: *Hansard*.
[2] Minute No. 18 of 1952 from Secretary of State to Prime Minister, 'Top Secret', 'Defence of the Falkland Islands', 2 March 1952: Churchill papers, 2/517.

16. 26 October 1951, Churchill in his constituency after the declaration of the poll,
about to become Prime Minister for the second time.

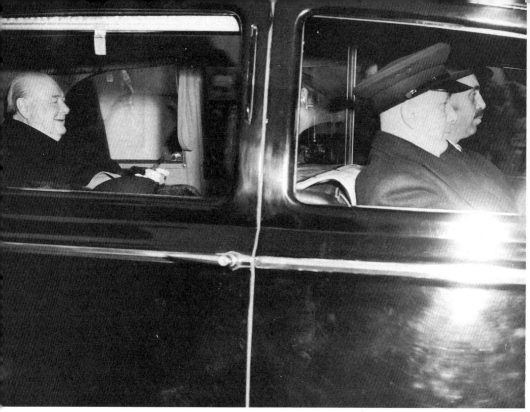

17. 27 October 1951, Churchill leaving Buckingham Palace after a meeting of the Privy Council at which the principal appointments in his new government were approved.

18. 5 January 1952, Churchill in Washington with President Truman, on board the Presidential yacht USS *Williamsburg*.

19. 5 January 1952, on board the USS *Williamsburg*. Eden, Churchill, Dean Acheson and Truman look at a photograph taken at the Potsdam Conference.

20. 30 September 1952, Churchill leaving Balmoral. This photograph of Churchill, the Queen, Princess Anne and Prince Charles was taken by Princess Margaret.

21. 9 January 1953, Churchill reaches Jamaica from Washington, having flown in the Presidential plane. Behind him on the steps are his son-in-law Christopher Soames and his Joint Principal Private Secretary, Jock Colville.

22. 16 April 1953, Churchill outside 10 Downing Street with the Soviet Ambassador to Britain, Andrei Gromyko. Gromyko was later Foreign Minister and subsequently President of the Soviet Union.

23. 10 October 1953, Churchill at Margate, speaking at the Conservative Party Conference, less than four months after his stroke.

24. 4 April 1955, Churchill and his wife say goodbye to the Queen and Prince Philip after the farewell dinner at 10 Downing Street. Two days later, Churchill resigned as Prime Minister.

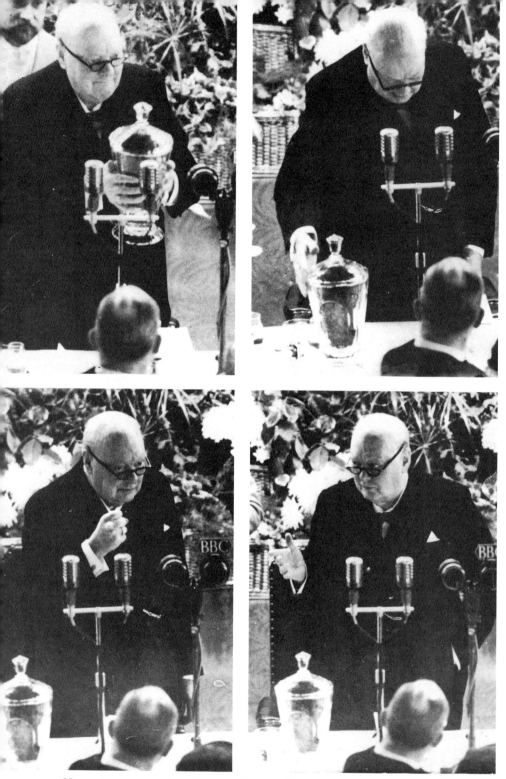

25. 24 November 1955, Churchill speaking at Harrow, six days before his 81st birthday. He had just become the first Freeman of the newly created Borough.

On the wider question of the strategic stockpiles of war reserves, Churchill told his colleagues that he had been 'disturbed by the large demands which were being made by the Admiralty for stocks of fuel oil. On the figures supplied to him the Admiralty seemed to be aiming at stocks greater than those which they had held before and during the last war. It was surprising that this should be thought necessary at a time when there was no hostile Navy in existence comparable with the German Navy, when our own refining capacity had been greatly increased and our fleet of tankers was greater than ever before.' In reply, J. P. L. Thomas, the First Lord of the Admiralty, said that more accurate figures had now been drawn up, showing that the total stocks of fuel oil were lower than in July 1939, at which the Chief of the Air Staff, Marshal of the Royal Air Force Sir John Slessor, noted that 'at the present time we held only four weeks' reserves of jet aviation fuel calculated at intensive rates'.

The discussion then turned to the Middle East. According to Field Marshal Sir William Slim, Chief of the Imperial General Staff, 'to hold the Middle East in war' it was necessary to have a base in Egypt. If British troops were to be withdrawn from the Canal Zone, he added, it might be possible 'to negotiate with Egypt for legal right to station troops in Gaza, for which the consent of neighbouring Israel would also have to be obtained'. Churchill commented that he had 'no wish to see the British Forces evacuated from the Canal Zone, and he still hoped that it might be possible to prevent this. Nevertheless, as the Treaty ran out in 1956, it was prudent to consider alternatives, and he thought that the Chiefs of Staff should work out a detailed plan, with an estimate of the cost, for stationing British Troops in Gaza and Cyprus.'[1]

Despite Jock Colville's earlier suggestion that the task should be left to the Secretary of State for War, on March 5 Churchill introduced the Government's Defence Estimates to the House of Commons. He was, he explained, no longer Minister of Defence, as Field Marshal Alexander had now accepted that office.[2] His own 'first impression' on becoming Minister of Defence the previous October was, Churchill said, 'a sense of extreme nakedness such as I had never felt before in peace or war—almost as though I was living in a nudist colony. When the 6th Armoured and the 3rd Infantry Divisions had left the country in pursuance of orders given or policies decided upon in the days of the late Administration, we had not a single Regular combat formation in the country. . . .'

[1] Defence Committee No. 1 of 1952, 4.30 p.m., 'Top Secret', 3 March 1952: Cabinet papers, 131/12.

[2] Field Marshal Viscount Alexander received his Seal of Office on 1 March 1952. He was created Earl on 11 March 1952.

Churchill then explained the different measures which he had earlier initiated: the 'mobile' columns, the revived Home Guard, and the extra Regular Army battalions. He also spoke of the 'improved patterns' of the Centurion tank 'which are on the way'. This tank, he said, was not only of 'high military value' itself, but 'may also in time become a useful dollar-earning export'.[1]

Churchill now explained an initiative of the Labour Government which he had continued as Minister of Defence, 'active voluntary recruitment' for short-term Regular Army service of three or four years, designed to attract National Service men and those about to be called up to National Service.

Speaking of the Royal Air Force, Churchill said that it was Britain's air power 'which causes me the most anxiety', and he went on to explain:

Deliveries of modern aircraft are seriously behind the original programme, which, in consequence, has had to be revised. As the result, the Air Force, though maintaining its size, is not being re-equipped with modern machines as rapidly as it should be. Our greatest need is for modern aircraft in the squadrons. For example, we have no swept-back wing fighters in service, such as the American F-86 and the Russian MiG-15.

It is true, as the Leader of the Opposition said in our debate last December, that it is not unnatural in this competition of types for one nation temporarily to outstep its rivals. It is rather unfortunate, however, if war should come at a moment when the enemy has a great advantage in modernity. It is not a good arrangement to have the highest class of air pilots and all the personal staffs required and for them to have only second-best weapons to fight with.

The 'late Government', Churchill commented, 'who are so critical in their anticipations of our ability, certainly did not produce good solutions. Here, as in other spheres, our inheritance leaves much to be desired.'

Churchill ended his speech by pointing out that the motives which 'inspired' the Leader of the Opposition, the former Minister of Defence, and the Service Ministers of the Labour Government to embark upon 'this great scheme of rearmament', were creditable to their military zeal, but that it was a scheme 'loosely and hastily framed and declared, and only five months intervened between the £3,600 million plan and its being superseded by that of £4,700 million'. Moreover, he said, they did not take sufficient account of the serious financial situation into which they were moving 'and of which we are today the anxious legatees'. It was a 'curious commentary' on British politics,

[1] Among the foreign sales of Centurion tanks were two contracts from the United States in 1952 and 1954, involving 800 tanks, spares and ammunition for a total of just over $140 million. These tanks were subsequently passed by the United States to Denmark under the Mutual Defence Assistance Programme.

Churchill reflected, that it should fall to a Conservative Government 'in the face of dire financial stress to have to reduce or slow down the military defence programme and expenditure on which the Socialist Government had embarked and to which they had committed the nation'. They had, however, to be 'governed by realities', and while trying their utmost to carry out the programme 'we must not mislead the country into expectations beyond what its life energies can fulfil'.[1]

On March 1, Churchill had handed over his Defence portfolio to Field Marshal Alexander. Although this reduced his own workload considerably, it did not satisfy his doctor. On March 12 Lord Moran wrote direct to Churchill:

My dear Prime Minister,
I have given careful thought to the significance of the little disturbance when you went to the telephone on February 21st. It was of the same nature as the sudden mistiness which you had within a fortnight of the Leeds speech in the 1950 election, namely due to spasm of the cerebral arteries. And these were first cousins of the blocking of a little artery at Monte Carlo in August, 1949. All three point to some instability in the cerebral circulation, which must be increased by excessive mental effort.
On the other hand if it were possible to lighten the load without giving up being Prime Minister, which on medical grounds would not be wise at the moment, then you ought to be able to carry on more or less indefinitely. Of course if you would like confirmation of my interpretation of events, we could get Russell Brain at any time, but they are really capable of no other explanation.
If there is any point that I have not made clear, I will of course come at any time you want. I feel sure that you would like the medical facts put down for your consideration. When I saw Clemmie about your deafness I told her my view.[2]

To strengthen his case Lord Moran took the precaution of writing to Clementine Churchill, enclosing a copy of his letter to her husband.

My dear Clemmie,
There seem to me to be two dangers attendant upon this letter. Firstly, that he may resign, and it is our medical experience that to take a man out of a very active mental life into retirement is often—I might almost say always—accompanied by profound changes. And I would dread them here.
Secondly, that he may just take no notice. In this case we have to remember that it is not really putting the whole case when he talks about dying in harness. What one dreads much more is an attack which leaves him disabled.
I have not the slightest doubt that though there are risks in any course, to remain Prime Minister and to go to the Lords for a year or so is much the safest course medically.

[1] Speech of 5 March 1952: *Hansard*.
[2] 'My dear Prime Minister', 12 March 1952: *The Struggle for Survival*, pages 381–2.

I know it would be a sacrifice on his part, but I am sure it would be best for the Monarch, the country and his successor, and I think the country would look on it as a noble gesture, paving the way for the succession.[1]

Churchill's reaction to Lord Moran's letter was muted. 'He was not angry when he got your letter,' Clementine Churchill telephoned to Moran. 'He just swept it aside.'[2]

'He took it, so I gather, with sang froid' was Colville's comment.[3] Churchill had in fact gone to bed, instead of going to the Commons as he had intended, to listen to the President of the Board of Trade, Peter Thorneycroft.[4] 'But I am under no illusions,' Moran noted. 'We have failed.'[5]

'I got your letter,' Churchill remarked to Moran a few days later, adding, so Moran reported: 'I don't want you to worry. You really needn't. One has to die some time.'[6]

On March 13 Churchill presided as usual over the morning Cabinet, and spoke on two Defence issues. On the Ministry of Defence proposal to sell arms to both India and Pakistan, he warned of the risk 'that these two countries might use the arms supplied to them for war against one another. We should then bear a grave responsibility. And we should not in any event receive any valuable return for these supplies, since their cost would be debited against the sterling balances held by India and Pakistan.'

In deference to the views of Ismay, however, the Cabinet concluded that it should be Britain's policy 'to continue to make limited supplies of equipment available on a scale sufficient to prevent India and Pakistan from turning to United States sources'. It was 'most unlikely', Ismay told his colleagues, that there would be war between India and Pakistan.[7]

Churchill's second suggestion was that priority should be given to the production of a limited number of specified types of defence equipment, 'viz, the latest types of aircraft, ammunition for aircraft, the Radar chain and Centurion tanks'. But both R. A. Butler and Peter Thorneycroft pointed out, speaking from the perspectives of the Treasury and the Board of Trade, that 'if the use of the priority symbol

[1] Letter of 12 March 1952: *The Struggle for Survival*, pages 381–2.

[2] Moran diary, 13 March 1952: *The Struggle for Survival*, page 382.

[3] Colville notes: *The Fringes of Power*, page 642.

[4] Thorneycroft was President of the Board of Trade and a member of the Cabinet throughout Churchill's second Premiership. Churchill's own first Cabinet post (from April 1908 to February 1910) had been as President of the Board of Trade in Asquith's Liberal Government.

[5] Moran diary, 13 March 1952: *The Struggle for Survival*, page 382.

[6] Moran diary, 22 March 1952: *The Struggle for Survival*, page 382. (Reporting a conversation 'A week ago'.)

[7] War did not break out between India and Pakistan until August 1965. It came to an end after fifty days.

were extended to sub-contractors, there would be serious interference with the production of civil supplies, especially in the engineering industry, and consequent loss of production for export which, in the current crisis in our balance of payments, was no less important than defence production'.

His second proposal thus expertly rejected, Churchill then proposed 'the enlargement of the industrial capacity available' for the production of Centurion tanks. But his son-in-law Duncan Sandys, the Minister of Supply, opposed this on the grounds that 'the existing capacity would suffice for the programmes now contemplated; and the creation of additional capacity would conflict seriously with exports'. It was agreed, after discussion, that no further capacity need be provided 'at present' for the production of Centurion tanks.[1] The third of Churchill's three suggestions had been rebuffed.

The Cabinet's ability to out-argue the Prime Minister could not be taken for granted. Lord Alexander later recalled Churchill's method of dealing with his Cabinet, when things were not going entirely his way:

If there was something he wanted done he would set about it very carefully. First he put his proposal, quite simply. Then, if he saw frowns around the Cabinet table, he would turn on the charm. 'This,' he would say, 'is something very close to my heart. It is my deepest wish. For many years I have believed in it, and now. . . .'

If, after all that, we were still frowning he would try a tougher line, exerting his power. 'After all, gentlemen, I *am* Prime Minister. . . .'

When even this failed to work, and we were obviously going to turn it down, he would say: 'Well, the Cabinet is a place for thrashing out ideas. We musn't rush into a decision on this. Why don't we go away—and you can think about what I've said. I'm sure, when you've had time to think it over, you will come round to my view.'

Churchill's ability to defer to his advisers was masked by an outer face of impenetrability. Alexander's recollections continued:

Winston loved argument. Whenever I saw him and Brendan Bracken together they were quarrelling. That's what Winston liked; he hated yes-men—he had no use for them. What he wanted was people who would stand up to him. Winston would put forward some point of view and Brendan would say straight out 'That's all wrong.' Then Winston would question him at length, probing his position.

Once, in Cabinet, when I was Minister of Defence, Winston began running down the Army. I got very angry and burst out: 'That's all nonsense. You don't know anything about the Army . . .' I was very outspoken;

[1] Cabinet Conclusions No. 30 of 1952, 'Secret', 11 a.m., 13 March 1952: Cabinet papers, 128/24.

Winston just grunted. When I had finished my outburst I thought, 'That's done it. I've overstepped the mark.' That same night we were to dine together at a mutual friend's house. I was rather anxious. Winston came up to me, and I began to apologize. Then a smile came over his face—'Dear Boy,' he said, 'you said what you felt had to be said.' And we sat down to dinner. He bore no malice.[1]

Those closest to Churchill knew the extent to which he welcomed argument and could defer to expertise. At Chartwell, on March 15, he saw a special Ministry of Defence film on guided missiles, 'explained', Colville noted, 'by a brilliant man called Mitchell from the Ministry of Supply'.[2] It appeared, Colville added, that these missiles would 'revolutionize' defence in war 'and may go some way to neutralize the atomic bomb'.[3]

Thirty-four years later, Steuart Mitchell, who in 1952 was Controller, Guided Weapons and Electronics, Ministry of Supply, recalled:

We were sitting in a small room fitted for showing films. The front row of seats consisted, on one side of a central gangway, of a huge armchair occupied by Winston: outside it a smaller one occupied by me: and on the other side of the gangway a settee occupied by Lady Churchill and, I think, a secretary.

I had showed him a film of a guided weapon shooting down an aircraft target. On this first showing, I don't think he quite understood what it was he was seeing. So I rewound the film and showed it again.

This time he did understand it and, turning to his wife, said, and I recollect his exact words very clearly:

'Do you see, my dear? Do you understand, my dear? This CONTRAPTION (and you will note he did not say "missile" or "weapon" but "contraption") seeks out the enemy. Smells him out. AND DEVOID OF HUMAN AID ENCOMPASSES HIS DESTRUCTION.'

This to his wife! In ordinary conversation!!

A most astonishing man!![4]

At dinner on Sunday, March 16, Churchill told Colville, as Colville noted in his diary, that he was 'worried about Egypt, where he thinks Eden is throwing the game away; irritated with the Prof, who is being tiresome about atomic matters; and disturbed by the thought that

---

[1] Field Marshal Earl Alexander of Tunis recollections: in conversation with the author, 28 December 1968.

[2] Steuart Mitchell joined the Royal Navy as a cadet in 1916, and in 1918 served in the Grand Fleet in HMS *Hercules*. Inspector of Naval Ordnance, in charge of Admiralty contracts in the United States, 1940–44. Controller, Guided Weapons and Electronics, Ministry of Supply, 1951–56. Subsequently Controller, Guided Weapons Electronics, Ministry of Aviation, 1959–62, and a Member of the National Economic Development Council, 1967–70. He was knighted in 1954.

[3] Colville diary, 15 March 1952: *The Fringes of Power*, page 643.

[4] Sir Steuart Mitchell recollections: letter to the author, 25 October 1986.

the old-age pensioners may suffer in consequence of an otherwise admirable Budget'.[1]

It was not, however, Egypt, atomic matters or old age pensions of which Churchill spoke when the Cabinet met on March 18, but the recent increase in bus and railway fares in the London area. 'These were causing widespread discontent,' he told his colleagues, 'and he wished the public to understand that they resulted directly from the policy of nationalization which had been pursued by the Labour Government.' With this in view he had suggested to the Minister of Transport that he should add, to his reply to a Parliamentary Question by Air Commodore Harvey MP about the withdrawal of special fares for shift workers, a paragraph in the following terms: 'All these rules were made and all those who are enforcing them were appointed by the late Government and they are a definite feature in the nationalization policy. We are considering how and when changes can be made which will secure that workmen working on a night shift can again obtain workmen's travel tickets.'

The Cabinet rejected Churchill's advice, after it had been pointed out to him that 'nothing could be said on behalf of the Government which would reflect upon the impartiality of the Transport Tribunal, which was a judicial body enjoying the powers, rights and privileges of the High Court'. Moreover, the minutes continued, 'it would not be right to imply that the appointment of this Tribunal was one of the features of the nationalization policy adopted by the late Government, for similar functions had been exercised for some time previously by the Railway Rates Tribunal set up under the Railways Act, 1921'.[2]

On March 19 Churchill was in the Chair at the second meeting of the Cabinet's Defence Committee. The meeting had been called to discuss possible 'further aggression' by China in South-East Asia, beyond the confines of French Indo-China. The American Government, explained Field Marshal Slim, wished to 'extend the area of conflict beyond the actual point of aggression' by bombing Chinese ports and lines of communications, by mining Chinese rivers, and by 'instituting a naval blockade of the China coast'. To this proposed course of action, Churchill was vehemently opposed, telling the Defence Committee:

. . . in his view a blockade of China would be futile if it did not include Soviet ports. This would bring about a direct challenge to the Soviet Government, with consequences which no one could foretell. On the other hand, the

[1] Colville diary, 16 March 1952: *The Fringes of Power*, page 643.
[2] Cabinet Conclusion No. 31 of 1952, 'Secret', 11 a.m., 18 March 1952: Cabinet papers, 128/24. At the time of the Railways Act 1921, Churchill had been Secretary of State for the Colonies in Lloyd George's peacetime coalition.

bombing of Manchurian communications or air bases would not, in his judgment, raise the decisive issue. It would be effective in stopping supplies sent
to the Chinese Communist forces in Korea, whether they came by land or
sea. Similarly, air attacks on the communications from China to French
Indo-China delivered from the Philippines might be effective. It would be
silly to waste bombs in the vague inchoate mass of China, and wrong to kill
thousands of people for no purpose.

'This was the view which His Majesty's Government had previously
expressed,' Churchill added, 'and there should be no question of our
departing from it.'

Churchill also pointed out that the return of French regular forces
from Indo-China 'would substantially increase the capacity of Western
Europe to defend itself'. As to the possibility of a direct Communist
threat to the borders of Malaya, Churchill told the Defence Committee:

. . . it was too early to assume the worst. There might be many developments
in the world situation before a real threat to Malaya developed. The Americans, for example, might conclude that the time had arrived for straight
talking with the leaders of the Soviet Union. The result of straight talking
might be an intensification of the cold war, or even the start of open war; on
the other hand, it might lead to a general pacification of the world, including
the Far East and South-East Asia. It would, therefore, be wrong to commit
ourselves at this stage to preparations for the defence of Malaya against a
possible threat in the future. It would, however, be prudent to make plans,
without expenditure of money or resources, on the lines suggested by the
Chiefs of Staff. . . .

These plans included the possibility of help from Australia and New
Zealand for the defence of Malaya, and the support of an anti-Communist Government in Siam. As to any future direct danger of Soviet
power, Churchill commented that he was 'particularly interested in
the number of fast submarines now possessed by the Russians, or likely
to be available to them in the future. The threat from submarines and
mines in the next war would be far greater than any possible threat
from surface ships.' [1]

On Saturday March 22 Churchill returned to Chequers, where the
guests were the Marquess of Salisbury and his wife, Field Marshal
Alexander and his wife, and Mary and Christopher Soames, with
Colville as the duty Private Secretary. On the Sunday, Montgomery

---

[1] Defence Committee No. 2 of 1952, 11.30 a.m., 'Top Secret', 19 March 1952: Cabinet papers,
131/12.

and Lord Cherwell came to lunch. 'Monty, mellow and in good form,' Colville noted in his diary, 'but, as ever, trying to lobby the PM about matters in which he is but slightly interested (this time Greece and Turkey) or on which he hardly thinks Monty an expert.' Colville added:

The PM is angry, almost to breaking point, with the Prof, who is digging in his toes over the control of atomic energy. In the long gallery on Sunday night, after the rest had gone to bed, he told Christopher and me that the programme of the Tory Party must be: 'Houses and meat and not being scuppered.' He didn't feel quite happy about the latter though he does not himself think war probable unless the Americans lose patience. As he subsequently added, perhaps 'not being broke' is going to be our major difficulty and preoccupation.[1]

One day during the week of March 23, while Churchill was at Downing Street, his doctor called on him just as he was about to lie down for his afternoon sleep. Churchill began at once to talk about his health, telling Lord Moran:

'I have noticed a decline in mental and physical vigour. I require more prodding to mental effort.' He smiled. 'I get a good deal of prodding. I forget names. I might even forget yours—people whose names I know as well as my own. I'm as quick at repartee in the House as ever I was. I enjoy Questions there. Do you think I ought to see Brain?'

I replied that it was no use seeing him unless he was ready to take his advice. The PM himself thought it would be a bad thing if he retired now. I said Brain would certainly advise cutting down what he had to do. He protested that he already devoluted a good deal of work. Rab and Anthony, for example, did a lot—and they worked in a broad field. There were others, such as Lord Salisbury. He had worries, of course. He was worried over Egypt, and whether we were going to be blown up, and whether we should be able to solve our financial problems, and about houses and food.

'I'm halfway in my seventy-eighth year, and one can't expect to live for ever. I really don't think you need worry. I soon get tired physically; when I have fed the robin and the swans, and perhaps walked three-quarters of a mile, I have had enough. I dislike standing, except when making speeches.'[2]

Two days after this confession of forgetfulness, Churchill intervened decisively in Cabinet during a discussion of the alarmingly high unemployment in the textile and clothing industries, where 10 per cent of the former workforce was now without work. He was prominent in the decision that, to help bolster production, the armed forces and

---

[1] Colville diary, 23 March 1952: *The Fringes of Power*, pages 643–4.
[2] Moran diary, 23 March 1952: *The Struggle for Survival*, pages 382–3. Lord Moran's date must be wrong, as Churchill was at Chequers throughout March 23.

civil defence services should place their orders for clothing with the manufacturers most hit by the unemployment.[1]

That Churchill's age affected his output and energy there could be no doubt. 'He did not want to talk about Cabinet matters as much as he had done before,' David Pitblado later recalled, and he added: 'One of the jobs was to get him to get through the box. He would take some of that, and then get bored with it.' Nevertheless, Pitblado added, 'it would be wrong to exaggerate the degree to which he'd lost his grip', and he went on to recall:

Each night he read the political part of the papers. It was his contact with the ordinary man. Clemmie had gone to bed. He would come down to the Cabinet room and read the papers. Instructions would be sent out through the duty secretary to this or that Minister. In the morning he would ask the duty secretary of that day, 'What did he say?' 'What did *who* say?' would be the reply, at which Churchill would ask: 'Why can't you men tell each other?' So we found it useful, if we were on duty at night, to come back in the morning.

The night work took place at times in the bathroom, with a sponge on his face. It was a mixture of companionship, and being able at any time to get something moving.[2]

The worries which Churchill had expressed at Chartwell on March 16, that Eden was 'throwing Egypt away', were reiterated in Cabinet on April 1, when he 'expressed his reluctance', the minutes recorded, 'to accept any agreement which involved withdrawing British troops from Egypt until the security of the Suez Canal and the British base was assured by the establishment of an international system backed by sufficient force'.

Eden combated Churchill's view vigorously, telling the Cabinet that under the Four-Power proposals for an Allied Middle East Command, 'which was the only international system which had so far been suggested', none of the other Powers concerned would station forces on Egyptian territory in time of peace; and that he was 'satisfied that no Egyptian Government would conclude an agreement which provided for land forces of the United Kingdom or any other foreign Power to be stationed in Egypt in peace'. The Allied Middle East Command, Eden added, was 'no more than a command structure which, in peace, would be backed in the main by Egyptian land forces and British air forces and base technicians'. This, however, in Eden's view, 'would

---

[1] Cabinet Conclusions No. 33 of 1952, 25 March 1952: Cabinet papers, 128/24. Within nine months the Cabinet learned that as a result of these orders having been placed, unemployment in those industries had been reduced by two-thirds, to 67,000. (Cabinet Conclusions No. 105 of 1952, 16 December 1952: Cabinet papers, 128/25.)

[2] Sir David Pitblado recollections: in conversation with the author, 17 July 1987.

afford a substantial safeguard, since the Egyptians were most unlikely to encroach upon base installations which were maintained under the control of an Allied Command'.[1]

This discussion continued three days later, when Churchill stressed that, in his opinion, 'the first need was to demonstrate to the Egyptian Government and people that we were not to be turned out of the Canal Zone by force or by threats'. Churchill added:

The show of force which we had recently made had produced good results; and he believed that still further advantages might be secured by making it clear that we were not in any hurry to abandon our rights under the existing Treaty. Our second objective should be to convince the United States Government that effective international arrangements would have to be made for safeguarding the security of the Suez Canal after the expiration of the present Treaty. It should be made clear to the Americans that we were not prepared to go on carrying this burden alone, and that they would have to take their share in fulfilling this international obligation. In this lay the best hope of persuading Egypt to join in an international organization which would serve, not merely to protect the Canal, but to safeguard the security of the Middle East.

The Cabinet finally agreed that negotiations with Egypt could be started by Britain alone. At the same time, Britain would press upon Egypt the need to associate herself with an international organization for the defence of the Middle East.[2] Four days later Colville noted in his diary 'trouble with Eden over the Egyptian situation, the PM wishing to take a much stronger line with the Egyptians than Eden does'. Colville added that Eden 'is rather discredited in the PM's eyes at present'.

Since Churchill had become Prime Minister, it had been assumed by many that Eden would succeed him by the end of 1952. 'I don't myself quite see how he can prove a very good successor to Winston,' Colville commented, 'when he has no knowledge or experience of anything except foreign affairs.'[3]

On April 9 Churchill clashed with Eden again in Cabinet, when he warned in connection with Eden's proposals for entering into negotiations with the Egyptians 'that we ought not at the outset of negotiations, of which the purpose was to achieve Five-Power arrangements for the defence of the Middle East as a whole, to appear to accept the suggestion that Egypt was to assume sole responsibility for the defence of the Canal Zone'.

---

[1] Cabinet Conclusions No. 35 of 1952, 'Secret', 11.30 a.m., 1 April 1952: Cabinet papers, 128/24.

[2] Cabinet Conclusions No. 37 of 1952, 'Secret', 11.30 a.m., 4 April 1952: Cabinet papers, 128/24.

[3] Colville diary, 8 April 1952: *The Fringes of Power*, pages 644–5.

In reply, Eden pointed out that that paragraph of the formula to which Churchill objected 'did not go beyond recognizing the right of the two Governments to discuss their respective points of view'. In addition, he welcomed the reference to the arming of Egyptian forces, 'since the Egyptian Army had always been the most co-operative element in the country and it would be wise to invite their continued support'. The paragraph might, however, be amended, Eden volunteered, by deleting the words 'in order that Egypt may fulfil her determined intention to defend this area'. The Cabinet agreed, and Churchill was, for the time being at least, satisfied. [1]

On April 7, at the Honours Committee, Jock Colville wrote in his diary: 'Some of the PM's wishes cause consternation—especially baronetcies for "Bomber Harris" and Louis Spears.' [2] There was further 'trouble' on the following day, Colville noted, with the Ministry of Transport, as 'The PM wants to denationalize road haulage as quickly as possible.' [3]

In the second week of April Churchill was again beset by ill health: a 'miserable cold', he explained to Lord Moran, 'has settled on my chest'. He had hoped to be able to go to Newmarket, where two of his horses were running, but Clementine Churchill had already taken 'a strong line', Miss Sturdee told Lord Moran, that he should not go. 'I told him,' Moran noted, 'there was a risk in going to Newmarket, though the risk was small.' [4]

Churchill deferred to this combined advice, and stayed at Chartwell. On April 16 there was a telephone message for him from Marlborough House: 'Queen Mary is anxious to know how you are and hopes your cold is better.' [5] 'I am getting on all right' was Churchill's reply on April 18. [6] That same day, however, Lord Moran told him that he was 'still full of bronchitis' and that if he did not take care of himself 'it may spread to the smaller tubes'. [7]

[1] Cabinet Conclusions No. 40 of 1952, 'Secret', 11.30 a.m., 9 April 1952: Cabinet papers, 128/24.

[2] Colville diary, 7 April 1952: *The Fringes of Power*, page 644. In 1945 Churchill had urged Clement Attlee to make Harris a Peer. Major-General Spears had been Churchill's friend since they had served together in the trenches of the Western Front in 1915. Both Harris and Spears received baronetcies in 1953.

[3] Colville diary, 8 April 1952: *The Fringes of Power*, page 633. Road Haulage was denationalized under the Transport Act of 6 May 1953.

[4] Moran diary, 16 April 1952: *The Struggle for Survival*, page 384.

[5] Message dated 16 April 1952: Churchill papers, 2/197.

[6] Message dated 18 April 1952: Churchill papers, 2/197.

[7] Moran diary, 18 April 1952: *The Struggle for Survival*, pages 384–5.

Another of those who asked after Churchill's health was the Duchess of Kent. 'Am surviving,' he replied, 'surrounded by the descendants of Your Royal Highness's lilies.' [1]

On April 23 Churchill returned to London, to pay his tribute to Sir Stafford Cripps, who had died two days earlier. Cripps, he told the House of Commons, 'was a man of force and fire. His intellectual and moral passions were so strong that they not only inspired but not seldom dominated his actions. They were strengthened and also governed by the working of a powerful, lucid intelligence and by a deep and lively Christian faith. He strode through life with a remarkable indifference to material satisfaction or worldly advantages.' There were few members in any part of the House, Churchill commented, 'who have not differed violently from him at this time or that, and yet there is none who did not regard him with respect and with admiration, not only for his abilities but for his character'.

Churchill's tribute to Cripps, who had been a member of his wartime Cabinet for two and a half years as Minister of Aircraft Production, continued:

His friends —and they were many, among whom I am proud to take my place—were conscious, in addition to his public gifts, of the charm of his personality and of the wit and gaiety with which he enlivened not only the mellow hours, but also the hard discharge of laborious business in anxious or perilous times. In all his complicated political career he was the soul of honour and his courage was proof against every test which the terrible years through which we have passed could bring.

'Our hearts go out,' Churchill ended, 'to the noble woman, his devoted wife, who through these long months of agony, mocked by false dawns, has been his greatest comfort on earth. To her we express profound sympathy and we trust that she may find some solace in the fact that Stafford's memory shines so brightly among us all.' [2]

Churchill was now well enough to make a second speech, on April 25, at the Royal Albert Hall, to the Primrose League. It was only a short one, however, to introduce the main speaker, Sir David Maxwell Fyfe, the Home Secretary. It was his belief, Churchill told the gathering, 'that in three or four years we shall be able to present to our fellow-countrymen a situation in which world peace will be more secure and British solvency firmly re-established'.

[1] Message dated 20 April 1952: Churchill papers, 2/197. The Duchess of Kent had sent Churchill lilies with their bulbs in 1942. He had planted them at Chartwell, where their descendants survive to this day.

[2] Speech of 23 April 1952: *Hansard*. Churchill also told the House that he had first met Cripps in 1917, when Cripps was managing a small-arms factory, whose 'excellence and efficiency' had been brought to his notice as Minister of Munitions.

Of the now regular late-night sessions, and even all-night sessions in the Commons, some of which had been punctuated by Labour jeers not only at times when Churchill himself rose to speak, but even when he entered or left the Chamber, Churchill declared:

We shall not be turned from our course by their clamour or obstruction. They are themselves most bitterly divided on the main issues of the day and the struggle for the leadership of their party is going on. They try to heal or conceal these differences as much as possible by spitting out their spite upon us. I cannot remember a time—and my experience is a very long one—when public difficulty and party strife have both risen to such heights together.

Very often a common sense of the dangers of the country has caused an abatement of party strife, but in this case we still seem to be living in an electioneering atmosphere, and it is only by long, steady, faithful and skilful administration that we shall get into the cooler and calmer atmosphere—so necessary to enable our country, by natural fruition, to attain its highest expression.

'Here let me say,' Churchill added, 'how much we owe to the Conservative Members of the House of Commons—and I see here my friend Sir Ian Fraser [1]—who, by their regular attendance on all occasions, especially at long night sittings, have enabled us to maintain an average majority double that which we gained at the polls.' [2]

On April 27 Evelyn Shuckburgh noted in his diary a complaint by Eden 'that the Party are more and more concerned about the conduct of the Government, especially Winston's lack of grip and the fumblings of the Leader of the House'. [3] Returning that day to Chartwell, Churchill was again accompanied by Colville, who noted in his diary:

The PM plans to sack Lord Woolton and make 'Mr Cube' (Lord Lyle) Chairman of the Tory Party. [4] He also revealed to me a private project for getting the Queen Mother made Governor General of Australia. We went through the Honours List during the week-end and I was pleasantly surprised to find the PM amenable to my views on most points.

---

[1] Sir Ian Fraser had been blinded in action in the First World War.

[2] Speech of 25 April 1952: Randolph S. Churchill (editor), *Stemming the Tide*, pages 279–81. Two weeks earlier Henry Channon had noted in his diary: 'Could there be any more nauseating performance than that of half a hundred hale young Socialists howling at Mr Churchill, jeering at his pronouncements and even at his entrances and exits into the House, taunting him with his advanced age and growing deafness? The man who may be the wrecker of the Tory Party, but was certainly Saviour of the civilized world? It happened again today. However in the 1922 Committee he had a rapturous reception, and stood the strain of speaking and answering questions well for over an hour.' (Channon diary, 9 April 1952: Robert Rhodes James (editor), *Chips*, page 467.)

[3] Shuckburgh diary, 27 April 1952: *Descent to Suez*, page 41. The Leader of the House was Harry Crookshank.

[4] He afterwards preferred the idea, Colville noted, of Malcolm McCorquodale. But Lord Woolton remained Chairman until July 1955 (after Churchill's resignation). Lord Lyle was the owner of Tate and Lyle, sugar refiners, one of whose regular advertisements featured 'Mr Cube'.

On Sunday evening Lord and Lady Donegall [1] came bringing a Russian film called *The Fall of Berlin*. Russia, it seems, won the war single-handed and now breathes nothing but peace.

I gave Christopher Soames a lecture on not appearing to have too much of the PM's ear. It is dangerous for his future. I like him increasingly, though his manners can be coarse. Brendan Bracken, with whom I had a drink the other day, says that Eden is violent against Christopher. [2]

At the Cabinet on April 29, it was again Egypt which provoked Churchill to intervene, and again Eden who doubted the efficacy of what Churchill proposed. It was his hope, Churchill said, 'that no opportunity would be lost of bringing home to the United States Government our unwillingness to continue indefinitely to carry alone the international burden of safeguarding the security of the Suez Canal'.

While he would continue 'to keep this in mind', Eden replied, 'he was unlikely to make much impression on the United States authorities at the present time, since they were disposed to think that he should have been ready to make further concessions about the Sudan for the purpose of reaching an agreement with the Egyptian Government'. [3]

On April 29 in the United States, at Carnegie Hall, Sarah Churchill read out a message from her father on the fourth anniversary of the independence of Israel. 'As a Zionist from the days of the Balfour Declaration,' the message read, 'I have watched with admiration the courageous effort of Israel to establish her independence and prosperity. May this and future anniversaries be celebrated with growing confidence and good will by Israel's friends throughout the world.' [4] 'Thank you *so* much,' Sarah Churchill wrote to her father from New York on May 1, 'for sending me a message to read at the celebration of Israel's 4th birthday. They were thrilled, and I enjoyed myself, as I found quotes from your speech in 1921 when you planted a tree at the Hebrew University on Mount Scopus—and also from your speech to Congress this year.' [5]

---

[1] The 6th Marquess of Donegall, and his wife Gladys. Donegall, born in 1903, had served from 1939 to 1945 as a British war correspondent.

[2] Colville diary, 27 April 1952: *The Fringes of Power*, page 646.

[3] Cabinet Conclusions No. 47 of 1952, 'Secret', 11.30 a.m., 29 April 1952: Cabinet papers, 128/24.

[4] *New York Herald Tribune*, 30 April 1952. The celebration at Carnegie Hall had been sponsored by the American Zionist Council, an organization of eight national Zionist groups in the United States. According to the Gregorian calendar, Israel was established 14 May 1948. By the Hebrew calendar which Israel uses, however, that founding date was the fifth of Iyar, which in 1952 was from sunset on 29 April to sunset on 30 April.

[5] Speaking to an audience of several thousand Jews on Mount Scopus, Churchill declared (on 29 March 1921): 'We owe to the Jews a system of ethics which even if it were entirely separated from the supernatural would be the most precious possession of mankind worth, in fact, the

Speaking in public, Sarah Churchill added, 'is really quite easy that way!' and she went on to tell her father about a second ceremony at which she had spoken, the unveiling and dedicating of a plaque on the house in Brooklyn, 426 Henry Street, where Churchill's mother had been born in 1854. 'It was a charming ceremony,' Sarah wrote, 'with lovely speeches of tribute to your beautiful Mama and to yourself, and I as proud granddaughter unveiled the plaque with the President of the Borough. About 1000 people crowded into the narrow street & there were lots of children all let out of school for the half day. I thanked them on your behalf & said that I *knew* you would have been touched at their kind tributes to your mother & yourself & would be anxious to see the plaque the next time you visited these shores.'[1]

The first six months of Churchill's premiership had confirmed his ability to be a peace-time Prime Minister, and to act effectively at the age of 77. Even if he was sometimes tired, he presided over, and where necessary controlled, four remarkable men—Anthony Eden, R. A. Butler, Oliver Lyttelton and Harold Macmillan—each of whom administered his portfolio with considerable skill. In particular, Churchill realised that unless Butler could engineer an economic recovery during the first two or three years of his administration, the economic resources needed to re-arm Britain would not be available. Butler's Budget of March 11, the first Conservative Budget since 1940, and described by *The Times* as 'a triumph', had owed much to Churchill's persistent support for his Chancellor of the Exchequer. So well was the Government working under Churchill's leadership, that by May 1952 all public talk of his early resignation had been put aside.

---

fruits of all other wisdom and learning together.' Churchill added: 'Personally, my heart is full of sympathy for Zionism. This sympathy has existed for a long time, since twelve years ago, when I was in contact with the Manchester Jews. I believe that the establishment of a Jewish National Home in Palestine will be a blessing to the whole world, a blessing to the Jewish race scattered all over the world, and a blessing to Great Britain. I firmly believe that it will be a blessing also to all the inhabitants of this country without distinction of race and religion.'

[1] '*Darling* Papa', 1 May 1952: Churchill papers, 1/50. 'This plaque is erected as a memorial to Lady Churchill,' it stated, 'to evidence the esteem in which her son is held by the people of this community.' Not only was Lady Randolph Churchill wrongly named, her year of birth was given as 1850. She was in fact born on 10 January 1854 (her son being born six weeks before her twenty-first birthday).

39

'The zest is diminished'

ON 3 May 1952 Churchill went to the Cup Final, where the cup was retained by Newcastle. He was accompanied on the journey to and from Wembley by Miss Portal, who had to take dictation for the Party Political broadcast which Churchill was to make that night. During the broadcast, he spoke of the Conservative Party's first six months in power; six months which needed to be judged, he said, against the Labour Party's six-year record. This record, 'of extravagance and waste, of over-spending and of living upon American money, had brought us all within sight of a dead stop. National insolvency was what stared us in the face when we took over.' As to the Conservatives, he said, 'we have the will, and I believe we have the power, to continue for another three or four years of steady, calm and resolute Government at home and abroad, making our mistakes—who does not?—but devoting our life-effort to what we believe is the national interest; and we ask to be judged by results and by deeds rather than by words and for a fair time to bring them about'.[1]

May 3 also saw the opening of the sixth successive Royal Academy Exhibition at which paintings by Churchill had been chosen. The four for 1952 were 'On the Var' and 'Cannes Harbour' from the South of France, and 'Ramparts over Rhodes' and 'Sunset over Jerusalem' from his visit to the Eastern Mediterranean in 1934, on Lord Moyne's yacht.[2]

On May 6 Churchill dined at the French Embassy as the guest of the French Ambassador, René Massigli. Anthony Eden and Lord Alexander were the other Cabinet Ministers present. The French visitors included General Juin, former commander of the Free French

---

[1] Broadcast of 3 May 1952: Randolph S. Churchill (editor), *Stemming the Tide*, pages 282–6. A favourite phrase of Churchill was: 'The man who makes no mistakes makes nothing.'

[2] 'List of Works Exhibited at the Royal Academy by Sir Winston Churchill, Hon. RA': Royal Academy archives.

Forces, first in North Africa and then in Italy. 'The PM said Germany must be given fair play,' another of the guests, Jock Colville, noted in his diary. If France 'would not co-operate' in giving Germany fair play, Churchill added, 'we, America and Germany must go forward without her'. What he wanted to see, Churchill told General Juin and the others, was 'British, American, German and French contingents march past him at Strasbourg, each to their own national songs; in creating international unity, national marching songs could play a great part'.[1]

The prospects for a substantial British contingent in Germany itself were challenged in Cabinet on the following morning, when Eden warned that from no later than June 1953 the local cost of the British forces in Germany would no longer be borne by the Germans, but by Britain. These costs were estimated at £130 million a year, and would have a 'serious effect' on the British economy. R. A. Butler was even more perturbed by the situation, emphasizing the 'gravity', and telling his colleagues that Britain's overseas military commitments, in Germany, the Middle East, and the Far East, 'were ten times greater than they had been before the war, when we had the help of the Indian Army in meeting them'. While he believed that the situation 'could be held for the next six months', Butler warned that 'the long-term outlook was very grave'.

After listening to this warning, Churchill uttered a caveat of his own, telling the Cabinet that 'great care must be taken to avoid any public statement which might imply that we were likely to break our pledges to NATO by reducing our forces in Germany'. This, he said, would have 'the gravest possible effects on the whole structure of Western defence and would shock public opinion in the United States'. At the same time, Churchill argued, it was 'essential that the minimum figure for the local costs of the British forces in Germany should be firmly established, and that all unnecessary expenditure should be eliminated'. To this end, he then proposed that a small Committee should be appointed 'to examine these costs and to indicate means by which they might be reduced, say, to £70 million a year'.

The Cabinet agreed to set up such a Committee, with Lord Alexander as Chairman.[2]

On Saturday May 10 Churchill was again at Chartwell. His grandson Winston, who was among the guests, later wrote to say what

---

[1] Colville diary, 6 May 1952: *The Fringes of Power*, page 646–7.

[2] Cabinet Conclusions No. 50 of 1952, 'Secret', 11.30 a.m., 7 May 1952: Cabinet papers, 128/24. The other members of the Committee were Lord Cherwell (Paymaster-General) and Lord Swinton (Chancellor of the Duchy of Lancaster), with representatives of the Foreign Office and the Chancellor of the Exchequer.

'great fun' the visit had been.[1] Churchill replied to this thank-you letter from Downing Street, in his own hand:

My dear Winston,

I was so pleased to get your letter this morning and to learn your news. It was very nice having you at Chartwell though only for a flash; and I hope you were not too tired by the excursion. Tell me how your Master received the book I ventured to send him. I hope he was not offended by my peace offering—though I do not know him.

Please carry on this correspondence with your ever loving grandfather.

　　　　　　　　　　　　　　　　　　　　　　Winston S. Churchill[2]

Churchill also sent a personal letter that week to Lady Lytton. 'I do hope we can meet soon,' he wrote; 'I am much hunted by politics. We are reaping where others sowed. Presently we shall reap our own crop.'[3] At the Cabinet meeting on May 13, Alexander, who had just returned from Paris, spoke of how the French 'seemed obsessed with the logistical difficulties of joint military operations by forces drawing their supplies from different countries, and they had evidently not yet overcome their disappointment at our unwillingness to become full members of the European Defence Community'. Agreement had now been reached, however, Alexander reported, on the practical step of initiating joint staff discussions 'on methods of associating the British forces with the forces of the Community in matters of training, administration and supply'.[4]

In Cabinet two days later, Ismay warned that 'any attempt to create an economic association between Western Europe and the sterling Commonwealth would be likely to prejudice Commonwealth unity'. Indeed, Ismay added, he thought 'it would be dangerous to suggest', as some Ministers had argued, 'that because of our position in Europe, the other Commonwealth countries should cultivate a close association of any kind with the Council of Europe. He feared that the effect of our pressing such a suggestion upon them would be to increase the likelihood that some of them might turn towards the United States.'

Churchill did not entirely accept Ismay's reasoning, telling the Cabinet that, 'while he would certainly deprecate any project for economic association between Europe and the sterling Commonwealth, he saw no reason to discourage other Commonwealth Governments from

---

[1] 'Dear Grandpapa and Grandmama', from Ludgrove School, Wokingham, Berkshire, 11 May 1952: Churchill papers, 1/51.

[2] 'Written in Mr Churchill's own hand', 12 May 1952: Churchill papers, 1/51. The headmaster, young Winston replied, was 'very pleased with the book and thanks you very much for it'.

[3] 'Dearest Pamela', 11 May 1952: Lytton papers.

[4] Cabinet Conclusions No. 52 of 1952, 'Secret', 11 a.m., 13 May 1952: Cabinet papers, 128/25.

showing interest in the work of the Council of Europe'. Political leaders in many Commonwealth countries, Churchill pointed out, had 'welcomed this movement towards European unity, as a valuable factor in preserving world peace; and, as those countries had twice been involved in a world war originating in Europe, they would be ill-advised to disinterest themselves wholly from European affairs'.

The Cabinet concluded, however, that if the proposal for closer association between Western Europe and the sterling area Commonwealth came up for discussion at the forthcoming Committee of Ministers of the Council of Europe, Britain's representative, Eden, should, after pointing out the 'difficulties' of the proposal, 'seek to secure that its further discussion should be adjourned for as long as possible'.[1]

That evening Churchill and his wife gave a dinner at 10 Downing Street for General and Mrs Eisenhower, who were on their way back to the United States, where Eisenhower, giving up his European Command, was to become a Republican candidate for the 1952 Presidential Election. Jock Colville noted in his diary:

There were thirty-two to dinner, including most of the wartime Chiefs and the present Service Ministers—Alexanders, Tedders, Alanbrookes, Portals, Jumbo Wilson, Attlees, etc. Both the PM and Ike made admirable speeches. When Ike left he said that if he were elected he would pay just one visit outside the USA—to the UK—in order to show our special relationship. The atmosphere could not have been more cordial—though things almost started badly with neither the PM nor Mrs C knowing that it was white tie and decorations.[2]

'If I had been given a wish how I would spend my last night in England before saying farewell,' Eisenhower wrote in his thank-you letter, 'I could not have had it fulfilled in all respects so completely as I did at your dinner party last Thursday.'[3]

Another issue which had arisen that week was civil defence. At a meeting of the Defence Committee on May 14, Churchill had deprecated too great an expenditure. 'In general,' he told his colleagues, 'he was disposed to think that very large expenditure could be incurred on civil defence without any proportionate reduction of the military effectiveness of enemy air attack; and, although it would be wise to do enough to create an impression of activity in civil defence, care must be taken to avoid spending large sums of money on measures which would pay no dividend.'[4]

[1] Cabinet Conclusions No. 53 of 1952, 'Secret', 11 a.m., 15 May 1952: Cabinet papers, 128/25.
[2] Colville diary, 15 May 1952: *The Fringes of Power*, page 647.
[3] 'Dear Prime Minister', 22 May 1952: Churchill papers, 2/217.
[4] Defence Committee No. 5 of 1952, 'Secret', 11.30 a.m., 14 May 1952: Cabinet papers, 131/12.

On the evening of Friday May 16, Churchill returned to Chartwell, where he now tried to spend every weekend. 'Alone with PM who is low,' noted Colville, and he added:

Of course the Government is in a trough, but his periods of lowness grow more frequent and his concentration less good. The bright and sparkling intervals still come, and they are still unequalled, but age is beginning to show. Tonight he spoke of coalition. The country needed it he said, and it must come. He would retire in order to make it possible; he might even make the demand for it an excuse for retiring. Four-fifths of the people of this country were agreed on four-fifths of the things to be done.[1]

On Saturday May 17 Colville lunched alone with Churchill, who, he noted in his diary, 'recited a great deal of poetry'. After his afternoon sleep, Churchill then drove with Colville from Chartwell to Chequers. 'On the way,' Colville wrote, 'he dictated notes for a speech. He says he can only dictate in a car nowadays.' The speech was on transport, and Churchill's theme, 'a good one' in Colville's view, that 'the nationalization by the Socialists of only 41,000 vehicles was for doctrinaire, not practical motives, and they need 80,000 people, including 12,000 clerks, to run them'. Private owners of transport for hire to a total of 800,000 had 'been driven to the most uneconomic measures to survive'. When Churchill had finished his dictation he said to Colville: 'It is a great mistake to be too mechanically minded in affairs of State.'

Among those at Chequers that night were Lord Montgomery and Anthony Head. 'The men sat up till 2.30,' Colville added, 'gossiping about strategy and Generals in a lively manner.'[2]

Churchill remained at Chequers throughout Sunday May 17. A heatwave, which had begun on the previous day, now grew even hotter.[3] Once more, Colville recorded in his diary the events of the day:

Worked with W all the morning; sat on the lawn and gossiped most of the afternoon: walked on the monument hill (the whole party went, notwithstanding all the picnickers) after tea. Monty in role of grand inquisitor: how did the PM define a great man? Was Hitler great? (PM said No—he made too many mistakes.) How could PM maintain that Napoleon was great when he was the Hitler of the nineteenth century? And surely the great religious leaders were the real great men? The PM said their greatness was indisputable but it was of a different kind. Christ's story was unequalled and his

---

[1] Colville diary, 16 May 1952: *The Fringes of Power*, page 647.
[2] Colville diary, 17 May 1952: *The Fringes of Power*, pages 647–8.
[3] Between 16 and 19 May 1952 the temperature in southern England rose to as high as 76 degrees Fahrenheit (75 degrees on May 17).

death to save sinners unsurpassed; moreover the Sermon on the Mount was the last word in ethics.[1]

Colville's diary comment of May 16 that Churchill's age was 'beginning to show' was echoed four days later by Brendan Bracken, Churchill's close friend, and Minister of Information during the war, who told Colville he was 'doubtful about W's ability to go on'.[2] But on the following day, speaking in the House of Commons during the Transport debate, Churchill 'made a good impression' on his Private Secretary.[3] During his speech, Churchill remarked of Herbert Morrison that he was 'a curious mixture of geniality and venom'. The geniality, 'I may say after a great many years of experience', was natural to Morrison; the venom 'has to be adopted' in order for him to 'keep on sides' with the Labour backbenchers. As to Morrison's charge that Churchill had been 'cowardly' in leaving the debate to be opened by the new Minister of Transport, Alan Lennox-Boyd, Churchill asked the House, of Morrison:

Does he believe that I am really afraid of opening a debate? Why would I be afraid? I can assure the right hon. Gentleman that the spectacle of a number of middle-aged gentlemen who are my political opponents being in a state of uproar and fury is really quite exhilarating to me. I have not had fifty years' actual service in this House without having got used to the rough-and-tumble of debate.

Churchill continued, still in answer to Morrison's charge:

It was not out of cowardice that I ran away from this position, but because I have great faith in the ability of my right hon. Friend, although he has had such a very short time in this office, to present this extensive case in a masterly form to the House. I, who can speak when I want to or need to, would, I think, have been taking an unfair advantage if I had, as it were, usurped the best place in the debate, and left the Minister, who will fight this matter from the start to the finish, without the opportunity of putting his own stamp on the story and of gaining, as he has done, the confidence and respect of those who now see him in this new office.[4]

During the course of his speech Churchill produced in polished form one of the arguments which Colville had heard outlined during the drive from Chartwell to Chequers:

I am told that the Road Haulage Executive staff of 12,000 which has sprung into being costs more than £6 million a year. I am told that is prob-

---

[1] Colville diary, 18 May 1952: *The Fringes of Power*, page 648.
[2] Colville diary, 20 May 1952: *The Fringes of Power*, pages 648-9.
[3] Colville diary, 21 May 1952: *The Fringes of Power*, page 649.
[4] Alan Lennox-Boyd had succeeded John Maclay as Minister of Transport on 7 May 1952, Maclay having had to resign through ill-health.

ably many times as much money as would be needed if these 41,000 vehicles were allowed once again to be merged in the general system of road transport. The whole of this vast apparatus has been brought into being to manage a twentieth of the road haulage vehicles of the country. This lies upon us as a deadweight and is an unnecessary burden upon our intimate communications which are a vital factor in our economic life. The question we have to ask is, why should this have been done, and, if it has been done, why should it go on?'

Churchill also spoke in the Transport debate about the railways. 'I have never been shocked by the idea of nationalizing the railways,' he said, 'in fact, I believe I proposed it on my own before almost all the Members of the House had even thought about going to Parliament.[1] I am by no means sure I have been right. It is no part of my case that I am always right. Anyhow, we have to face the facts. The railways are and will remain nationalized, and the Tory Party will do their utmost to make them a great, living, lasting success in the vital, though limited, sphere that is open to them.'

As to the Labour Party's declaration that it intended, if re-elected, to renationalize road transport once the Conservatives had denationalized it, Churchill told the House of Commons: 'We believe that in less than the lifetime of this Parliament the benefits of a liberated road transport system, combined with the successful administration of the British Railways, may make it seem a very wrong and foolish thing to renationalize the road transport in a future Parliament. Thus the threat which is now made will be proved to have been vain and idle.'[2]

Churchill also spoke, albeit briefly, in Cabinet on May 22, for which R. A. Butler had circulated a memorandum on Britain's 'economic weakness', of which 'the resources devoted to defence production' were a factor. Commenting on this, Churchill urged upon his colleagues that 'there should be no interference with the special priority accorded to certain types of arms production'. This, Duncan Sandys commented, was a 'limited field'; outside it he, as Minister of Supply, was proceeding on the basis that 'production for defence and for export should rank of equal importance' and that if the Cabinet desired a switch to production for export, the production of 'less essential types' of defence equipment could be slowed down.[3]

Churchill made no further comment. On May 23, a Friday, he

---

[1] As a Liberal, four decades earlier, Churchill himself had frequently proposed the nationalization of the railways, for example, at Dundee on 5 January 1910 and again on 10 December 1918. He had publicly announced his change of mind, however, on 11 March 1924.

[2] Speech of 21 May 1952: *Hansard*.

[3] Cabinet Conclusions No. 55 of 1952, 'Secret', 11 a.m., 22 May 1952: Cabinet papers, 128/25.

spent the whole day at Chartwell. Later he drove up to London to speak at a Tax Inspectors' dinner. But, for almost the first time in a speech-making life of more than half a century, the speech was almost entirely written by someone else: by Jock Colville, who commented on this fact in his diary: 'This is indeed a sign of advancing senility.' [1] A week later Colville noted: 'Mrs Churchill does not think he will last long as Prime Minister.' [2]

Another observer who at this time looked askance on Churchill's moods was Lord Moran. 'He spoke hotly; his detachment had quite gone,' he wrote in his diary on June 3 after a discussion about the BBC. What Churchill had said to Moran was: 'I am against the monopoly enjoyed by the BBC. For eleven years they kept me off the air. They prevented me from expressing views which have proved to be right. Their behaviour has been tyrannical. They are honeycombed with Socialists—probably with Communists.' [3]

There was a moment of personal sadness for Churchill that summer, with the death of his constituency chairman Sir James Hawkey. For a quarter of a century Hawkey had been his guide to all constituency matters, and a staunch supporter. In 1948 Churchill had described him, in Volume 1 of his war memoirs, as 'my ever-faithful and tireless champion' [4] during the Munich crisis, when there had been pressure to replace Churchill by a more appeasement-oriented Member. At Hawkey's funeral, one fellow-mourner later recalled, Churchill 'stood beside the grave in tears'. [5]

In the first week of June, Churchill was among those who, on Horse Guards Parade, watched the Queen at her first Trooping the Colour as Sovereign. He spoke of this event a few days later, when he was the guest of honour at the Press Association's annual luncheon. As he watched 'our young Queen riding at the head of her Guards', he said, 'I thought of the history of the past and the hopes of the future. Not only of the distant past—it is barely ten years since we upheld on our strong, unyielding shoulders the symbols, the honour and even perhaps the life of the free world.' Churchill continued:

Certainly no one of British race could contemplate such a spectacle without pride. But no thinking man or woman could escape the terrible question: on what does it all stand?

It does indeed seem hard that the traditions and triumphs of a thousand years should be challenged by the ebb and flow of markets and commercial

---

[1] Colville diary, 23 May 1952: *The Fringes of Power*, page 649. Colville also noted in this diary entry that what he had written 'wasn't nearly as good as the one I wrote for him in Ottawa'.

[2] Colville diary, 30 May 1952: *The Fringes of Power*, page 649.

[3] Moran diary, 3 June 1952: *The Struggle for Survival*, page 390.

[4] Winston S. Churchill, *The Second World War*, volume 1, London 1948, page 258.

[5] W. E. Tucker recollections: letter to the author, 13 September 1981.

and financial transactions in the swaying world which has sprung up and is growing ever larger around us, and that we have to watch from month to month the narrow margins upon which our solvency and consequently our reputation and influence depend. But fifty million islanders growing food for only thirty millions, and dependent for the rest upon their exertions, their skill and their genius, present a problem which has not been seen or at least recorded before.

In all history there has never been a community so large, so complex, so sure of its way of life, posed at such dizzy eminence and on so precarious a foundation.

Lands and nations whom we have defeated in war or rescued from subjugation are today more solidly sure of earning their living than we, who have imparted our message of Parliamentary institutions to the civilized world, and kept the flag of freedom flying in some of its darkest days.

Churchill's sombre panorama was a reflection not only of his mood, but also of the seriousness of the situation itself, in which Britain still suffered from the economic burden of the war and the harsh reality of post-war international competition and the dominance of the two Great Powers. The days of the Big Three, who had seemed so dominant seven years earlier, were over. Churchill went on to tell his luncheon hosts:

Around us we see the streets so full of traffic and the shops so splendidly presented, and the people, cheerful, well-dressed, content with their system of Government, proud, as they have a right to be, of their race and name. One wonders if they realize the treacherous trap-door on which they stand. I would not say this to you if it was not your duty to expose any facts, however unpleasant, to them. Britain can take it.

To speak like this is not to cry despair. It is the Alert; but it is more than the Alert; it is the Alarm. We have never been beaten yet and now we fight not for vainglory or imperial pomp, but for survival as an independent, self-supporting nation.

It has often been said we were approaching national bankruptcy in October last after our two years' orgy of electioneering, and certainly the figures to prove it can all be produced. But any British Government worthy of the name, called upon to bear the burden, would have taken severe, unpopular measures of one kind or another to ward off the obvious and imminent peril.

In wartime we were confronted with extreme decisions. There was nothing we would not have done for our life and cause. In time of peace happily we work under more limited conditions both in risks and in remedies. The dangers do not present themselves to the mass of the people in the same acute and violent manner as in the days when London was being bombed. Now the crisis is different in form, but as it seems to me, scarcely less fateful.

Moreover there is this outstanding difference between the perils of war and of peace. In war we were united, now in peace we find ourselves torn apart by quarrels which bear no relation to our dangers, and while we brawl along, our thought and action are distracted by a vast superficial process of reciprocal calumniation.

We have to live our life from day to day and give back as good as we get, but I warn you that without an intense national realization of our position in all parties and by all classes, we shall find it very hard to reach that security without which all that we have achieved, all that we possess and all our glories may be cast away.

Churchill ended his remarks by saying that if he was not sure 'that the vital forces in our race, not only in this Island but throughout the British Empire and Commonwealth of Nations, have only to be aroused to conquer, I would not use these harsh words'.[1]

On June 5 Churchill had gone to the races at Windsor with his son Randolph. One of his horses, Non Stop, was running, and came in third. Two other horses of his, Pol Roger and Loving Cup, did well elsewhere.[2] 'The racing season has opened not badly for us' was Churchill's comment to his grandson Winston in a letter on June 12. 'We begin tomorrow our last session of Parliament before the summer holidays,' Churchill added. 'It is a nine-week stretch and I expect there will be a good many late nights.'[3] Even before the session began, there were problems to be confronted in Cabinet, in particular the problem of the rapid growth of unemployment in the textile industry. As well as special measures to meet the situation there, Churchill told his colleagues, the Government 'should make plans well ahead against the possibility of more widespread unemployment as a result of a trade recession'. Early consideration should be given, he said, 'to the measures which might be taken to avert such unemployment, including such public works projects as the reclamation of marginal land, highway development and the construction of a Severn barrage'. This problem, he suggested, should be examined by a small Committee of Ministers, 'who should put constructive proposals before the Cabinet'.

Churchill's idea of public works projects was questioned by R. A. Butler, who warned that 'care would have to be taken to ensure that

[1] Speech of 11 June 1952: Randolph S. Churchill (editor), *Stemming the Tide*, pages 298–300. The phrase 'have only to be aroused to conquer' echoes a phrase Churchill used of the British people in October 1914: 'have only to persevere to prevail'.
[2] On 31 May 1952 Churchill's horse Pol Roger, ridden by E. Smith, finished third in the Katheryn Howard Handicap at Hurst Park. He had started at 4 to 1. On 2 June 1952 Churchill's horse Loving Cup finished third in the Liberty Handicap at Hurst Park. He had started at 6 to 1.
[3] 'My dear Winston', 12 June 1952: Churchill papers, 1/51.

any public works projects, some of which would in any case involve the use of materials badly needed for rearmament and export purposes', did not delay the transfer of workers to the armament and export industries.

As Churchill had suggested, however, a Cabinet Committee was set up, headed by the Chancellor of the Duchy of Lancaster, Lord Woolton, charged with formulating and submitting plans 'for checking any tendency towards widespread unemployment'.[1]

On Friday June 13 Churchill returned to Chartwell, and on the Saturday evening welcomed Lord Cherwell and Bill Deakin as his guests. Deakin brought with him a memorandum explaining the progress which he, Pownall, Allen and Kelly had made on the final volume of the war memoirs. All twenty-seven maps were ready except two which Deakin was obtaining from the Foreign Office. All eight appendices had been checked and Deakin was having 'a final read' over the weekend.[2] Lord Cherwell and Deakin were between them drafting a special 'insertion' on the Morgenthau Plan. One chapter, 'The American Interregnum', had been in part 're-constructed' by Deakin, who would also write in 'a short narrative' on the events leading up to the fall of Trieste in 1945. Pownall, Deakin, Allen and Kelly would meet again in three weeks 'to consider further progress'.[3]

Churchill had reason to be satisfied with the work being done on his behalf to complete his final volume. As for that Saturday night at Chartwell, 'We did little work,' Colville noted, 'but W was in better form than of late, though still depressed.' Colville's account continued:

He told me that if Eisenhower were elected President, he would have another shot at making peace by means of a meeting of the Big Three. For that alone it would perhaps be worth remaining in office. He thought that while Stalin lived we were safer from attack than if he died and his lieutenants started scrambling for the succession.

He also elaborated his theme of 'the commodity sterling dollar'—an international medium of exchange based on the world price of, say, fifteen commodities over a period of three years. This year, for instance, the years chosen would be 1948, 1949, 1950; next year 1949, 1950, 1951; and so on. The Prof said that such a scheme had possibilities if the Americans would lend it their support and their material backing.

[1] Cabinet Conclusions No. 58 of 1952, 'Secret', 11.30 a.m., 10 June 1952: Cabinet papers, 128/25.
[2] The eight appendices were: List of Abbreviations; List of Code-Names; Prime Minister's Directives, Personal Minutes and Telegrams, June 1944–July 1945; the Attack on the South of France; Monthly Totals of Shipping Losses, British, Allied and Neutral, June 1944–August 1945; Prime Minister's Victory Broadcast, 13 May 1945; The Battle of the Atlantic, Merchant Ships Sunk by U-boat, the Last Phase; and Ministerial Appointments, June 1944–May 1945.
[3] 'Prime Minister', 14 June 1952: Churchill papers, 4/24.

'The Prime Minister is depressed and bewildered,' Colville wrote in his diary in the early hours of June 16. 'He said to me this evening: "The zest is diminished."' Colville commented: 'I think it is more that he cannot see the light at the end of the tunnel. Nor can I. But it is 1.30 a.m., approaching the hour when courage and life are at their lowest ebb.'[1] Later that same day Sarah Churchill wrote from New York: 'The newspapers print gloomy things everywhere,' and she added: 'I hope you find some solace, in the comfort that your presence brings.'[2]

Unknown to Churchill, on June 16, while he was at Chequers, four members of the Government met in London at the house of Harry Crookshank, Leader of the House and Lord Privy Seal. The other three were the Commonwealth Secretary, Lord Salisbury, the Scottish Secretary, James Stuart, and the Chief Whip, Patrick Buchan-Hepburn. Even at this moment when the Government was doing well, they sought a change of leadership, and decided to ask Churchill either to resign at once, or publicly to set a date for resignation.[3] Six days after this meeting, and before they had approached Churchill, almost every national newspaper carried reports of rumours that Churchill was about to resign. On the following evening, June 23, one of the four, Patrick Buchan-Hepburn went to see Churchill to give him the views of his fellow malcontents. He was not received with warmth. Nor did Churchill agree to go—or even to give a date for going.[4]

---

[1] Colville diary, 13–15 June 1952: *The Fringes of Power*, pages 650–1.
[2] *'Darling* Papa', 16 June 1952: Churchill papers, 1/50.
[3] Harry Crookshank diary, 16 June 1952: Crookshank papers.
[4] Harry Crookshank diary, 23 June 1952: Crookshank papers.

40

Renewed Vigour

O N 19 June 1952 Churchill was in the Chair when the Cabinet
discussed a report from Lord Alexander, who had just returned
from Korea, and who wanted the British Government to be kept 'more
closely and continuously informed' on military and political developments in Korea. Alexander had proposed the 'integration' of British
officers in the Headquarters of the United Nations Command, while
the United Nations Commander, General Mark Clark, had himself
suggested the appointment of a British Deputy Chief of Staff for Korea.
The Chief of the Imperial General Staff, Field Marshal Sir William
Slim, who was present at the Cabinet, supported Mark Clark's suggestion. Churchill, however, was wary of such a development, telling his
colleagues 'that the United Nations had entrusted the conduct of the
Korean campaign to the United States; and we should be well-advised
to avoid a position in which we shared the responsibility without the
means of making our influence effective'. The difficulties that had
arisen in Korea, Churchill added, 'were political rather than military
and our influence could be exerted most effectively by the Foreign
Secretary in his dealings with the United States Government'.

Churchill's caveat was not accepted; there was, however, 'general
agreement' with Mark Clark's suggestion, which Slim had supported,
for the appointment of a British Deputy Chief of Staff.[1] On the following morning, June 20, Churchill was working on an official memorandum when Lord Moran arrived. The doctor noted:

> He sent out a message: would I make myself comfortable in the drawing-
> room for a few minutes? He would not be long. Then he forgot all about me.
> It might have been an hour later when a secretary discovered me. Winston
> seemed quite upset about it. He had never done this before. He said his
> memory was 'awful'.

[1] Cabinet Conclusions No. 61 of 1952, 'Secret', 11.30 a.m., 19 June 1952: Cabinet papers,
128/25.

I asked him how he had been. He looked up wearily:

'As well as I can be. I'm not what I was—not mentally overflowing. I don't want to dictate a memorandum,' he smiled. 'Of course I have written some quite serious papers.'

I asked him if he had any plans for a holiday.

'What can I do?' he answered a little impatiently. 'I cannot go abroad as the guest of *Life* while I am Prime Minister. I must find some interest.'

'Do you mean your book?'

'Oh no; I must superintend things at Chartwell. I don't mean I am going to cut down trees—I promise you I won't do anything foolish—but I can direct others cutting them down. I don't know why, but I love Chartwell; somehow it's home to me.'

The PM gloomily contemplated the papers on his bed-rest.

'It is a most perplexing time, much worse than the war. All talk and no co-operation. Attlee and his people are behaving badly—currying popularity by attacking America. It's easy to pick out things there to attack in an election year.'

Despite Churchill's growing physical disabilities, Moran wrote, 'there is no weakening of purpose'. As they talked together, Churchill told his doctor of how, a few weeks earlier, 'I told the 1922 Committee that they must trust the Government and that they must trust me too. I said they could be assured that I would not stay if I found I was failing physically or mentally.' Churchill commented: 'They took it all right. There is no movement to get me out. Anthony is absorbed in his work at the Foreign Office. It would be madness to move him.'

Churchill also told Moran, during their talk on the morning of June 20, that his health was 'better than it had been for some time'. He was 'not so stupid in the head in the middle of the day' as he had been five months earlier. The conversation continued:

'Now, Charles, it is nearly three years since the trouble at Monte Carlo. Did you think then that I should be here now?'

He put his hand on my arm.

'You found the pulse good? I can still hold my own in the House. I can put anyone on his back if it is necessary.'

It is no more than the truth. His answers at Question Time in the House of Commons, particularly to Supplementaries, have the old merit of unexpectedness.

'He seemed to want to talk,' Moran commented, 'and rambled on in a way that was not at all like him in the early morning. It became obvious that he wanted to persuade himself that he was fit to carry on.'

'I drink a great deal,' Churchill told his doctor, 'it keeps one going'; then he added: 'Oh, not too much, Charles.' On the previous night,

Moran noted, 'he returned from the "Other Club" hilarious (Camrose took him home) and at Chartwell on Sunday Jock said the PM spoke of his pranks at Sandhurst; Jock had not laughed so much for a long time'.[1]

There was another Chartwell weekend which began later that same morning, Friday June 20. Churchill had no one with him at first but Jock Colville, but in the evening they were joined by Sir Norman Brook. Colville noted in his diary:

After we had fed the fish—indoors and out[2]—and driven away the horses which were eating the water lilies in the lake, we had lunch together.

W greatly exercised by the economic prospects. He said: 'I can assure you it is the most horrible landscape on which I have ever looked in my un-equalled experience.' But when champagne and brandy had done their work he talked of the Chamberlain family—Joe the greatest of the three; Austen, generous and gallant but whose whole work came to nothing; Neville who was not above scheming to ruin Baldwin at the time of the Duff Cooper–Petter[3] election in the St George's Division of Westminster so that Neville might profit by his fall.

After the usual film, Christopher and Mary dined and Norman, who wanted to talk confidentially about the weak position of sterling and suggest changes in the Government, was irked because Christopher would not leave us. However he did tell the PM that Woolton should give up the Home Affairs Committee and that Eden should take it over, relinquishing the FO.

The PM also thinks Eden should have a change but says he is 'Foreign Officissimus' and doesn't want to go.[4]

On June 23 United Nations Air Forces, principally American, carried out the heaviest air attacks of the Korean War, striking at five hydro-electric plants just south of the Yalu River, the border between North Korea and China. On June 24 the British Cabinet discussed the bombing; it might, Churchill told his colleagues, 'give rise to the suspicion that a more aggressive policy was being adopted as a result of the visit of the Minister of Defence'.

Churchill therefore wished to make it clear 'that the decision to

---

[1] Moran diary, 20 June 1952: *The Struggle for Survival*, pages 391–2.

[2] Apart from his outdoor ponds, full of large golden orfe, Churchill established in his working library at Chartwell two tanks of brightly-coloured small tropical fish, each tank supplied with an elaborate oxygen apparatus. 'Feeding the fish,' Colville recalled, 'was a frequent diversion from serious work.' (*The Fringes of Power*, page 651, note 1.)

[3] In 1931 Lord Beaverbrook had put up Sir Ernest Petter as an Empire Free Trade candidate in the previously safe Conservative seat of Westminster St George's. When Lord Rothermere also joined in the attack on the official candidate, Alfred Duff Cooper, Stanley Baldwin told the electors that what the Press proprietors were aiming at was 'power, but power without responsibility, the prerogative of the harlot throughout the ages'. The seat was won by Duff Cooper.

[4] Colville diary, 20 June 1952: *The Fringes of Power*, pages 651–2.

undertake this attack was within the competence of the United Nations Commander and that the United Kingdom Government had not been consulted in advance'. He would stress the fact, he added, 'that this attack did not reflect any change of policy'. It would be 'helpful', also, 'if he could say that similar attacks had taken place in the past'.[1]

At a further Cabinet meeting two days later, Eden told his colleagues that he proposed to make it clear in private conversation with the United States Secretary of State that the British Government 'thought they ought to have been consulted in advance' about the Yalu River bombing, 'and would expect to be so consulted on any future similar occasion'. Churchill agreed that such a communication by Eden 'would be justified', but then, as the minutes recorded, he 'stressed the importance of avoiding any public statement which might be taken to imply that there was any divergence of view on this matter between the Governments of the United Kingdom and the United States'.[2]

On July 1, during a Labour Party Motion of Censure for the Yalu River bombings, Churchill spoke in the House of Commons about the American achievement in Korea. 'Due consideration should be given,' he said, 'to the monumental patience, breaking all previous human records, which has been displayed by the American Government and people in discharging their duty to the United Nations. I defy anyone to show any other historical example which can equal it.' As to the British Government's position, Churchill said:

We in this country are all convinced that it would be a great mistake, with Europe in its present condition, for the United Nations or the United States, which is their champion, to be involved in a war with the Communist Government inside China. I have repeatedly emphasized the danger of such a development.

But do not let us blind ourselves to the terrible cost that is being paid for their patience by the people of the United States. I think we ought to admire them for the restraint which they have practised, instead of trying to find fault with them on every occasion.

There might easily come a time, especially during a Presidential election, when a very sharp reaction of emotion, even of anger, might sweep large sections of the American people, and when any candidate for the Presidency who gave full vent to it would gain a very considerable advantage.

As to the details of the bombing raid near the Yalu, 'As we were

---

[1] Cabinet Conclusions No. 62 of 1952, 'Secret', 11.30 a.m., 24 June 1952: Cabinet papers, 128/25.

[2] Cabinet Conclusions No. 63 of 1952, 'Secret', 11.30 a.m., 26 June 1952: Cabinet papers, 128/25.

not informed,' Churchill said, 'we could not know.' He had already told the House: 'I can only hope that the American people will not suppose that the House of Commons is unfriendly to them or that we are simply naggers and fault-finders.' Yet, although 'technically aimed' at the Government, he added, the censure of the Labour Opposition 'really falls upon the United States'. He was 'sorry' that 'such an attitude should prevail'.

Despite Churchill quoting a strong apology for this 'snafu' [1]—'which word I have had to add to my vocabulary', Churchill remarked—by the American Secretary of State Dean Acheson at a private meeting in Westminster Hall, there was a crescendo of Labour protests not only at the American failure to inform Britain of the bombing, but of the British Government's failure—Churchill's and Eden's and Alexander's—to know anything about it. Churchill told the House, by way of counter-attack:

The former Minister of Defence said at the weekend that nothing like this breakdown in contact ever happened under the Socialist Government, or words to that effect. The most serious mistake that was made in the Korean campaign was the advance by General MacArthur, who has so many fine victories to his credit, not only beyond the 38th Parallel, but beyond the waist of the Korean Peninsula in November 1950.

This involved an enormous scattering of our power and the lengthening of the front, and caused a most fateful setback to the operations of the United Nations. The Chinese were given a deadly opportunity to recover, of which they took full advantage.

But nobody thought of moving a vote of censure on the Government of the day because they had not been consulted by the United Nations Supreme Commander.

Churchill then reiterated his personal attitude to the possibility of a war with China, and his earlier clear statements about such a war:

I was, I think, the first in this House to suggest, in November 1949, recognition of the Chinese Communists. I thought at that time that the Americans had disinterested themselves in what had happened in China, and as we had great interests there and also on general grounds, I thought that it would be a good thing to have diplomatic representation. But if you recognize anyone it does not necessarily mean that you like him. We all, for instance, recognize the right hon. Gentleman the Member for Ebbw Vale [Mr Bevan]. But it is just at the time when things are disagreeable between countries that you need diplomatic relations. But there is one thing which usually severs diplomatic relations, and that is the shedding of blood on a large scale by warlike action.

It is remarkable that in spite of the fact that the Chinese have in no way

[1] *Situation Normal: All Fouled Up.*

responded to our diplomatic gesture and have, on the contrary, treated us
with scorn and have shed the blood of our own soldiers and that of our allies,
we should not only continue—our Government has continued the policy of
the previous Government—to accord them diplomatic recognition; but, if we
followed the advice of the party opposite, we would make it a major effort of
policy to persuade the United States, with their twenty thousand dead, to do
the same while the fighting is actually going on.[1]

'Winston spoke on Korea and the recent bombings,' Henry Channon noted in his diary, 'and the divided Socialists tried to turn the
Debate into a Censure Motion. But the old lion, coolly dressed in
light grey trousers and a short coat, fairly pulverised his attackers;
rarely has he been more devastating; perhaps he is aware of the growing Tory discontent.'[2]

A literary task to which Churchill applied himself in the last week
of June, and a pleasant one, was to read in proof the memoirs of his
cousin by marriage, Consuelo Balsan, born Consuelo Vanderbilt, an
American like his mother, and for more than a decade married to his
cousin 'Sunny' Blandford, subsequently Duke of Marlborough. Her
memoirs, entitled *The Glitter and the Gold*, made, Churchill wrote to
her, 'a very graceful and readable account of a vanished age'. But he
had two critical points to make:

I think the chronology requires a little further study. If you got someone
to put the dates in the margin opposite each event, you could then see where
the pack might be shuffled with advantage. Chronology is not a rigid rule
and there are many occasions when a departure from it is a good thing.
Nevertheless, I think it true to say that chronology is the secret of narrative.

The only serious point that strikes me is your reference to Henry Asquith
and Margot. These, I feel, would cause pain and anger to their children who
are alive, which I am sure you would not like. It would be easy to tone down
the references to Mr Asquith. I would not put in the story of your dining
with him so soon after Raymond was killed in action, nor do I think you will
want to leave in the account of Margot's behaviour when she was your guest
at Eze.

'As I have read so many proofs in earning my own livelihood,' Churchill
added, 'I have marked a few casual corrections which I noticed, but
these are by no means complete. The last chapter makes a very moving
end to your tale, and the title is brilliant. With my best love, Winston.'[3]

[1] Speech of 1 July 1952: *Hansard*.
[2] Channon diary, 1 July 1952: Robert Rhodes James (editor), *Chips*, page 461.
[3] 'My dear Consuelo', 27 June 1952: Churchill papers, 1/50.

At the beginning of July 1952 Clementine Churchill went to Italy, for a holiday and mudbath cure with her daughter Mary. 'Delighted to hear of your safe arrival,' Churchill telegraphed from 10 Downing Street on July 8. 'My very best love to you both. Mind you take it easy darling. I hear Italy is very hot.'[1] 'Yesterday's *Times* has just reached us,' Clementine Churchill wrote to her husband on July 9, 'announcing Eisenhower's initial success at Chicago. I hope it is an augury.'[2]

'All goes well here,' Churchill telegraphed again on July 9. 'Hope not too sizzling with you. Am sending letter out by Sarah on Friday. All my Love W.'[3] This letter was the first of that summer's separation. It was written in Churchill's own hand from 10 Downing Street, and taken out to Italy, as he had promised, by their daughter Sarah:

My darling Clemmie,

Yr '1700' feet letter was vy welcome and I look forward to an account of how you are & what it is all like. I see a picture in the papers wh I enclose. You certainly look 'relaxed'. Are you playing Okla w Mary? I do hope the weather is not too bad. Here it is cooler & cloudy.

Another week of toil is over & I am off to Chartwell in an hour. How I wish I were going to find you there! I feel a sense of loneliness and miss you often, and wd like to feel you near. I love you vy much my dear sweet Clemmie. But I am sure you needed the 'Off Duty' break to recover buoyancy & resilience. I am most anxious to get yr report.

The Shane Leslies come Sat for luncheon & I am polishing off the Lew Douglas's at the same time. I am told he is far from well. Last night Gen Ridgway dined. I think he is a vy good man.

We have changed our Parly. time table, rising July 31, returning October 14 to wind up the Session, reopening the new Session Nov 4 when we shall push the Transport & Steel Bills through. We shall only get a month at Christmas—but it is good to look forward to 10 weeks recess *now*.

It is a vy bleak outlook—with all our might, majesty, dominion & power imperilled by having to pay the crashing Bills each week. I have never seen things so tangled & tiresome. But we must persevere.

I am relieved at Ike's progress over Taft. Once the American election is

---

[1] 'Mrs Churchill', despatched 8 July 1952: Churchill papers, 1/50.

[2] 'My darling Winston', 9 July 1952 (from Grand Hotel and La Plage, Montecatini Terme): Churchill papers, 1/50. On 8 July 1952 *The Times* had a headline: 'General Eisenhower wins an initial victory'. This referred to his victory in procedural disputes over contested delegates at the Republican Convention which had just opened in Chicago. Eisenhower's nomination took place on July 11, at the end of the first ballot, with a total of 614 votes (604 being required for nomination) when the Minnesota delegation switched its support to him from Harold Stassen. Eisenhower's closest competitor was Senator Robert A. Taft, the isolationist from Ohio, who received 500 votes. Taft died on 31 July 1953, only four months after he would have been inaugurated had he won the nomination and been elected President.

[3] Telegram 'read over to switchboard', 9 July 1952: Churchill papers, 1/50.

over we may be able to make real headway. Either Ike or the Democrats wd be all right. A Taft–MacArthur combine wd be vy bad.

I send this scribble by Sarah who is starting today & will send it to you from Rome. She brought Margaret Truman & Mr Snyder's daughter to luncheon two days ago.[1] All went off nicely. I will write again over the week end. Give my love to Mary Marl[2] and believe me always yr devoted loving husband.

W[3]

Ten days later, on July 21, Churchill wrote again, this time from Chartwell. This letter too was in his own hand:

My darling one,

The end of the Session is approaching and will give relief to a vy harsh & worrying strain. Inside our circle we toil continuously at plans to pay our way. The problems are baffling & bewildering because of their number & relationship. What to cut, & all the hideous consequences of the choice. Food, Arms, Housing? or all three? Indeed we were left a dismal inheritance! Beneath all the party malice there is a realization of the facts. But the nation is divided into 2 party machines grinding away at one another with tireless vigour.

Anthony's absence adds to my burdens. He has had a steep dose of jaundice & has lost a stone & a half. His doctor wants him to rest for another week & I am pressing him to do so. Salisbury has been vy tiresome—frail health, private business and combined with these a defeatist frame of mind. However I hope to bring things to a satisfactory close.

It will be a welcome change to have a lull—brief tho that must be.

Bernie comes here next Friday for a long weekend, when I have an important speech to prepare & much to settle: but Mary & Christopher will help & I expect all will pass off well.

The sun is shining & the weather bright & cool. The gardens are lovely. (They are to be opened on the 23rd as you know.) The fish are doing well, (seven baby black Mollies). I have managed to get a good long week-end (Thursday night to Monday afternoon).

Churchill's letter continued:

I am afraid the gt heat of Italy may have been a burden to you my darling. I do hope that when you join with Sarah & Anthony you will not do too much & that cooler breezes will blow. I am expecting you back about August 10. I miss you vy much & am often lonely & depressed. Your sweet

---

[1] John W. Snyder, who in the decisive months of 1941 had been Chairman of the Military Appropriations Sub-Committee of the House of Representatives; in Truman's Cabinet he served as Secretary of the Treasury.

[2] The Duchess of Marlborough, to whom Churchill wrote in August: 'My dear Mary, I am enchanted with the beautiful, sharp little knives you have sent me. They make tough meat seem tender, and tender meat delicious! I am sending you sixpence, so that the knives do not cut our friendship. Yours affectionately, W.' (Letter of 23 August 1952: Churchill papers, 1/52.)

[3] 'My darling Clemmie', 11 July 1952: Spencer-Churchill papers.

letter wh reached me yesterday was a joy. I have been wondering how to draw a Clem Pussy Bird ever since. I enclose a daring attempt. Tender love my dearest.

From your devoted husband

W [1]

Twice more that July Churchill sent his wife a long letter. The first, from 10 Downing Street, was dictated:

Max dined with me at No. 10 the other night. We were alone and I had a very agreeable talk. He is very anxious to order the lift to be got ready to put in, so that whenever it is convenient we can have the carpentering done. I told him of your plan to move my studio upstairs and refit the drawing room as of yore. [2]

I still hold to my plan of closing Chartwell from the end of October until the beginning of May and using Chequers meanwhile for weekends and Christmas. This would be the time to put in the lift & move my studio up.

When Chartwell house is closed it would be convenient to me to have Wellstreet Cottage as a pied à terre, if I come down on Friday or Friday night. Any furniture lacking could easily be taken from my room at Chartwell.

They showed me the plans, which you discussed with the Ministry of Works, for reviving the State Rooms and dining room at No. 10, and I told Jock he might write to you about them. There are a few minor improvements the Ministry of Works suggest. I think it is a brilliant conception and should be done in the public interest, as it is a great pity these rooms are not available for use. We really ought to have them for the Coronation year. Look at all the distinguished people I have had to entertain in our poor little attic. I am sure they are surprised at the difference between the accommodation and the menu.

The only time the changes can be made is during the ten weeks holiday. Once finished, this would not commit you to using them until you felt inclined. There would be no need for more servants, except perhaps one in the kitchen, as the State Rooms would continue to be cleaned as at present.

---

[1] 'My darling one', 21 July 1952: Spencer-Churchill papers.
[2] This lift was installed at Chartwell. It was small, but saved Churchill having to climb the stairs from the ground floor to his study and bedroom.

However I think the structural changes should be made in the Recess and we could stay where we are until you felt able to move down.[1]

The last of the July letters was from Chartwell, and handwritten:

My Beloved One,

No letter yet from remote Cattini.

I send you the enclosed notes on plans. I don't want you to be worried about them. The changes in structure at No. 10 must be begun in the first week of August, but everything can go on as it is at present till you feel like moving down. . . .

Yr letter of 8th has just arrived from London. The temperature seems vy high. I do hope it will not 'sizzle' you for long. Let me know how it goes on.

I have a lot of troubles here with the money shortage & the inevitable cuts. Also *Steel* is not agreed by all. Bobbety[2] is difficult & uncertain. But I expect we shall get away all right for the Ten Weeks interlude—holiday it will not be for your devoted loving Husband.

W[3]

At a meeting of the Defence Committee on July 16, the appointment of the British Deputy Chief of Staff for Korea had been the main item on the agenda. The danger of making this appointment, Churchill told his colleagues, was that the powers and functions of the Deputy Chief of Staff would be misunderstood and misinterpreted, and that the Government would be thought 'to have assumed additional responsibilities for the war in Korea and to have obtained a more powerful influence upon its conduct'. This was 'not at all the case'. If a British Deputy Chief of Staff were appointed, he would be responsible to the United Nations Commander and to him alone. It was therefore 'of the utmost importance that any announcement about this appointment should make these facts unmistakably clear'. If the Government wished to make representations on the conduct of the war in Korea they would do so, 'as at present, direct to the President of the United States on particular occasions or to the United States Joint Chiefs of Staff'.[4]

When the Cabinet met on July 22, Churchill reiterated his criticism of the now imminent announcement of a British Deputy Chief of Staff to the United Nations Commander in Korea. This appointment, he warned, 'would be held to give us more responsibility for the conduct of the operations without any increase in our power to influence it'.

[1] 'My darling one', undated: Spencer-Churchill papers.

[2] Lord Salisbury, who had succeeded Lord Ismay as Commonwealth Secretary in March 1952, following Ismay's appointment as Secretary General of NATO.

[3] 'My beloved one', undated: Spencer-Churchill papers.

[4] Defence Committee No. 9 of 1952, 'Secret', 11.30 a.m., 16 July 1952: Cabinet papers, 131/12.

In reply to Churchill, Eden argued 'that it would be a mistake to abandon the proposal, which had first been put forward by the United Nations Commander himself'. It was agreed that while the appointment should go ahead, the announcement of it should 'make it clear' that the British Government accepted no greater responsibility for the conduct of the war.[1] The British Deputy Commander was to go, not as the representative or nominee of the Ministry of Defence in London, but as the personal deputy to General Mark Clark, in his United Nations capacity as commander of the forces in Korea.

On July 23 the Cabinet were informed that during the previous night King Farouk of Egypt had been deposed by a group of military officers. The officers had made it clear that they would offer organized resistance to any British intervention. In the circumstances, said Churchill, 'any movement of British troops in Egypt should be as unobtrusive as possible'.[2] Four days later, Churchill was shown a telegram from the British Ambassador in Cairo, reporting that there was 'No news of any reaction throughout the country, and I see no reason why we should have any trouble'. Churchill commented: 'They have lost their King!'[3]

Churchill also told the Cabinet of July 23 that in view of the high cost of the rearmament programme, the Supply Department, 'without imposing any general standstill on orders for production in 1953 and later years, should avoid prejudging by any abnormal ordering the decisions which Ministers would have to take in the coming weeks'. The importance of Churchill's cautionary suggestion was underlined by R. A. Butler, who said 'that he must warn the Cabinet that, in his view, it was quite unrealistic to suppose that the country could support the rising burden of defence expenditure'.[4]

When, on the following day, R. A. Butler proposed a cut in the house building programme for 1953, Churchill supported the Minister of Housing and Local Government, Harold Macmillan, in opposing

[1] Cabinet Conclusions No. 71 of 1952, 'Secret', 11 a.m., 22 July 1952: Cabinet papers, 128/25. The British Commonwealth Forces had been commanded since 10 June 1951 by Major-General A. J. H. Cassels. On 27 August 1952, a British officer, Major-General Stephen Shoosmith, was appointed Deputy Chief of Staff, United Nations Forces, Korea.

[2] It was learned later that day that the coup d'état in Egypt had been led by General Neguib. Churchill, concerned about the safety of the British Embassy in Cairo, asked Eden if the staff had arms (Prime Minister's Personal Minute, M.415 of 1952). Eden replied: 'HM Embassy have a variety of small arms including 4 Bren guns, 2-inch Mortars and tommy-guns and tear gas, sufficient to arm the equivalent of two platoons, and a planned operation for their use in emergency' (Minute PM 86 of 1952, Eden to Churchill, 7 August 1952: Churchill papers, 2/517).

[3] Foreign Office telegram of 27 July 1952 and Churchill note of 8 July 1952: Evelyn Shuckburgh, Descent to Suez, page 22 (reproduced in facsimile).

[4] Cabinet Conclusions No. 71 of 1952, 'Secret', 11 a.m., 23 July 1952: Cabinet papers, 128/25.

any cuts. In his view, Churchill told the Cabinet, 'it would be unwise to curtail the housing programme in the critical year 1953'. If the momentum was lost in that year, Churchill added, 'it would be more difficult to achieve the economies planned for 1954 by the use of novel designs'. A few moments later Churchill spoke again: 'it would be wrong', he said, 'to accept any reduction in the housing programme for 1953'. The target of 260,000 houses should be retained, 'but within that target every effort should be made to reduce the use of building labour and imported materials'. Churchill's proposals were accepted, and Macmillan's programme was unharmed.[1]

At the Cabinet on July 29, there was a discussion about a possible amnesty for men who had deserted from the Armed Forces during the Second World War. Churchill told his colleagues:

. . . in his view, it was a grievous thing that, seven years after the end of the war, a large number of war-time deserters should still be living in this country as outcasts and outlaws. After the First World War an amnesty had been granted after four years. He had received many expressions of reproach and indignation from the public on this matter.

On reflection he did not wish to press the suggestion that an amnesty should be declared in connection with the Coronation; but he felt very strongly that the existing position should not be allowed to continue indefinitely. Amnesties had already been granted by Canada, Australia and South Africa; and it was inhuman to condemn so many men to live the lives of outlaws under assumed names.

In the discussion that followed, the Cabinet minutes noted, 'there was some support' for Churchill's view. On the other side, however, 'it was strongly contended that the Government should not, by an amnesty, appear to condone the serious crime of deserting from the Forces in time of war. Some Ministers thought it would be specially dangerous to do this at a time when men were being drafted abroad for operations in Korea and Malaya.'

No conclusion was reached, and it was agreed to resume the discussion 'at a later meeting'.[2]

On July 24 Churchill dined at the Other Club. Lord Altrincham was in the Chair, and those present included Lord Alexander, Duncan

---

[1] Cabinet Conclusions No. 73 of 1952, 'Secret', 11 a.m., 24 July 1952: Cabinet papers, 128/25. Harold Macmillan later recalled: 'From my point of view at any rate, I could always rely on the Prime Minister supporting my housing programme. I certainly never canvassed his support. Yet in the battles which I had with the Treasury and with others of my colleagues on housing matters, I felt that Churchill was always on my side. For he knew as well as I that what ever else might emerge which could throw lustre on the administration or bring political advantage, the one easily measurable and easily ascertainable success would be the progress of the housing campaign.' (*Tides of Fortune*, page 498.)

[2] Cabinet Conclusions No. 74 of 1952, 'Secret', 11.30 a.m., 29 July 1952: Cabinet papers, 128/25.

Sandys, Sir Edward Marsh and Sir Leslie Rowan.[1] These dinners were always a relaxation and a pleasure for him. Three days later, at Chartwell, Lord Rothermere was among the guests, and on July 28 Bernard Baruch. That weekend Churchill worked on the speech he was to make in the House of Commons on July 30, on the economic situation. 'Struggling with speech,' he telegraphed on the morning of July 30 to his wife, who had travelled on to Capri.[2] That morning, when Lord Moran entered Churchill's bedroom, 'the PM threw the morning papers on the floor in great disgust. I knew from the set of the jaw that he was looking for trouble.' Moran asked Churchill if he was rested. 'Yes,' he answered grimly. 'I'll knock hell out of anyone. You would think, from the way Attlee's supporters carry on, that they weren't responsible for the awful mess we found. There will have to be more cuts to keep the country from bankruptcy.'[3]

During the debate Churchill spoke principally of the economy and defence. The defence programmes, he said, 'must be kept within the limits of our economic strength', and he went on to warn, in more general terms, that Britain's financial resources 'are not expanding at the rate we need to enable us to recover in any period which can be foreseen the position which we held before the war'.

Churchill also contrasted the financial basis of defence spending by his administration with that of his predecessor:

As a contribution to the immense new burden of the rearmament plan, we are receiving in this year, 1952, about £175 million from the United States; but this is quite different from the £400 million or £500 million a year enjoyed by the late Government before the arms programme was begun, in loans or gifts from the United States and, to a lesser extent, from Canada and the Commonwealth.

It must never be forgotten that this foreign aid, on which the Socialist Government lived for its whole tenure of power, virtually made good the loss of foreign investments that we suffered at the beginning of the war. Now we are facing the increased burden without having either the one or the other. Now we are striving to repay the American loan with interest.

Churchill then explained that the allocation of raw materials was also a factor in the problems faced by the rearmament programme. 'Our supply of steel and various other metals is limited,' he said, 'and it would be equally foolish for the Government to lay it down that either armaments or exports should have an unlimited call on them

[1] 'Prime Minister', 23 July 1952: Churchill papers, 2/210. Also present were Lord Brabazon, Lord De la Warr, Lord De L'Isle and Dudley, Lew Douglas, Colonel Elliot, General Laycock, Gwilym Lloyd George, Lord Norwich (Alfred Duff Cooper, who had received a Viscountcy from Churchill in 1952), Lord Oaksey, Lord Rothermere, Sir John Salmond and Lord Vansittart.

[2] Telegram despatched 30 July 1952: Churchill papers, 1/50.

[3] Moran diary, 30 July 1952: The Struggle for Survival, pages 392–3.

at the expense of the other.' Demands on these materials by those engaged in manufacturing goods for export had to be 'carefully weighed one at a time—weighed carefully against our individual defence requirements—and we hope and believe that we can, with patience, strike a balance which will build up our defences without endangering our solvency'.

The diversion of resources, whether in the steel industry or in other metal-using and engineering industries, was, Churchill said, 'just as necessary for our military strength as for our daily lives. Not to make it would be to plunge into bankruptcy.'

Churchill then spoke of the future of National Service, where the Government had decided that the intake was to be reduced, but not the two-year period of service:

At this point may I say that I was astonished at the suggestion made by the late Minister of Defence, the right hon. Member for Easington [Mr Shinwell], in a speech at Rugby on 12 July, that the period of compulsory National Service should be reduced from two years to eighteen months. It would hardly be possible to adopt a more improvident course. The fighting units of our Army today are almost all overseas; at least one-half are in the far-off foreign stations of the Middle East, Malaya and Korea, and in all of these there are rather more National Servicemen than Regulars.

The final six months of the two-year service term, Churchill added, 'is of the utmost value', since the National Servicemen's 'efficiency as soldiers will by then have reached its peak'. It was during these last six months 'that a man really begins to gain that degree of training and morale on which so much depends'. To cut the period of service down to eighteen months would be 'dangerous and unthrifty'.

When Churchill went on to assert that Shinwell's motive in now pressing for a six-month reduction in the term of National Service was 'connected with the movement of opinion' in the Labour Party since it had supported, and Shinwell himself 'strongly' supported, the two-year system. There was an immediate protest:

Mr Shinwell: The right hon. Gentleman ought not to have said that. It is disgraceful. He should be ashamed of himself.

The Prime Minister: The French have a saying that it is only the truth that wounds.

Churchill's final criticism in the debate of July 30 was for the last Labour Chancellor of the Exchequer, Hugh Gaitskell:

Yesterday, I was surprised to see the right hon. Gentleman the Member for Leeds, South, standing so smiling and carefree at the Dispatch Box as if he had no responsibility for the shocking and shameful state to which our finances were reduced during his tenure of the Exchequer.

When a Minister has in a single year brought his country from the best position it had held since the war to the verge of bankruptcy, and when he has left to his successors heart-tearing problems to face and solve, I wonder indeed that he should find nothing to do but mock and jeer at the efforts that others make to clear up the confusion and disorder that he left behind him. Indeed, I almost think it is a pity that he ever escaped from Winchester.

Let me also say in answer to him and to that shining star of television, my hon. Friend the Member for Aberdeenshire, East [Mr Boothby], whose rays were turned upon me last night—I very much regret not having heard his speech—that I do not take back a word I said in describing, not the immediate crisis, for that we are dealing with, but the general financial economic position of our country.

My resolve is that the people should realize how different is their position from that of all other Western communities; fifty million of us here standing at a level of civilization not surpassed in the world, and yet barely able to earn our living and pay our way, and dependent for the food of two-fifths of our people on how we can do this in this vast swirling world.

'Tragic it is indeed,' Churchill continued. But his words were at once followed by laughter from the Labour benches. 'Why is there laughter?' he asked. 'Surely it is not a party matter.' Once more the Labour benches interrupted. But Churchill persevered, telling the House, in the concluding words of his speech, amid further Labour cries:

Tragic indeed is the spectacle of the might, majesty, dominion and power of the once magnificent and still considerable British Empire having to worry and wonder how we can pay our monthly bills.

I fully admit I am tortured by this thought and by the processes which I see around me, and I will do everything in my power—[Hon. Members: 'Resign!']—to bring home to the mass of our race and nation the sense of peril and the need for grave and far-reaching exertions.[1]

'Am recovering from speech,' Churchill telegraphed to his wife on the following evening.[2] 'At last we have got hold of the *Daily Telegraph*,' Clementine Churchill wrote from Capri on August 1, 'with a report of your speech which I thought good & necessary.' Clementine commented: 'What atrocious interruptions from the Opposition. Now in the calm of the recess, the alterations you announced will be calmly carried out.'[3]

On July 31 Churchill was in the Chair at a meeting of the Cabinet at which Duncan Sandys argued in favour of deferring National Ser-

---

[1] Speech of 30 July 1952: *Hansard*.
[2] Telegram sent at 6.30 p.m., 31 July 1952: Churchill papers, 1/50.
[3] 'My darling', 1 August 1952: Churchill papers, 1/50. From the Grand Hotel, Capri.

vice call-up for engineer apprentices. He knew, he said, of firms whose production for export was being impeded by a shortage of skilled men. Churchill supported Sandys, telling the Cabinet 'that it was important that some scheme for deferring call-up of engineering apprentices engaged on important export work should be introduced with the minimum of delay'. The Cabinet accepted this advice, and authorized the Minister of Labour to work out the necessary arrangements.[1]

'Session finished,' Churchill telegraphed from 10 Downing Street that August 1 to his wife, and he added: 'Off to Chartwell. Nellie coming.[2] I need rest. . . .'[3] From Chartwell on August 4 Churchill sent his wife a handwritten account of the first few days of his Recess holiday:

My darling one,

With intense relief I have got back here with 10 weeks before Parl meets again. The last month has been vy trying. But now we have a chance to survey the scenes and to try to make better plans. We have saved about £125 m from the torturing exchange and have taken another step to solvency. It seems hard indeed that we shd get no credit for saving the country from Bankruptcy. And even that will require prolonged vigilance. Anthony Eden is back & I have felt his absence vy much. He looks thin & is I fear frail. Still we shall have a holiday—or at least a change.

Rain has come & the arid fields are freshened. Yr croquet lawn is the greenest spot for miles. The Magnolia is just beginning its beautiful crop. I see a wealth of buds & several are trying to climb in to my window. Yr garden is looking lovely & so is yr terrace. I think you will be pleased with all you see.

Nellie cd not come on account of Giles & the baby. But I have Randolph & Arabella (the latter in the Tower room). The Prof is here & is full of thought & wisdom. Patrick[4] sleeps this Sunday night.

On my way down here from London I went to a cocktail party given by Betty at her Chelsea house. The Q Mother was there also Princess Margaret & Diana DC & her son Julius & his fiancée to whom he will be married on Tuesday.[5] She seems vy beautiful. They are going to the Lac de Garde (that auberge across the lakes wh Diana likes so much). I advised Correzze if it

---

[1] Cabinet Conclusions No. 75 of 1952, 'Secret', 11.30 a.m., 31 July 1952: Cabinet papers, 128/25. The Minister of Labour was Sir Walter Monckton.

[2] Clementine Churchill's sister, Nellie Romilly.

[3] Telegram despatched 1 August 1952: Churchill papers, 1/50.

[4] Patrick Buchan-Hepburn, the Government Chief Whip.

[5] John Julius Cooper, then in the Foreign Office, married, on 5 August 1952, Anne, eldest daughter of Sir Bede Clifford, a former Governor-General of the Bahamas, Governor of Mauritius, and Governor of Trinidad and Tobago. In 1954 he succeeded his father (Alfred Duff Cooper) as Viscount Norwich and in 1964 resigned from the Foreign Office to embark upon a distinguished writing and television career. His mother, Lady Diana Cooper, died in 1986.

were too hot on the lakes. I am sending him 2 vols of Marlborough as a token.

The row between Attlee & Bevan is flaring up vy nicely & it is a pleasure to see the newspapers full of Socialist splits instead of only our shortcomings. It was vy disreputable of the Opposition leaders not to vote for their own German Treaty to wh they were pledged in the plainest terms.

Duncan has done vy well & is recognised by all to have his position as a leading figure on our side.

It is too hard for any horses to be galloped, but we hope to have some races in Sept & Oct. The fish (indoor & out) are well & pretty. I feed them all myself. The labour is not unwelcome, after too much politics.

Darling I thought yr letter about Tiberius & the ants most interesting. I expect you have really enjoyed yr stay at Capri. It certainly sounds lovely. I look forward to yr report on the Blue Grotto.

Forgive these disjointed scribblings wh I send by the bag to meet you in Rome on Tuesday.

I love you so much & miss you & long for yr return. We will just do nothing but sit & purr.

Your ever loving & devoted husband

W

Give much love to Sarah [1]

While Churchill was at Chartwell and his wife at Capri, he took Jock Colville and his wife to see *The Innocents*, the stage version of Henry James's *The Turn of the Screw*. 'He got a great welcome,' Colville noted, 'but embarrassed us by being unable to hear and asking questions in a loud voice.'

Among those at Chartwell that weekend was Churchill's niece, Clarissa, the daughter of his brother Jack. She had just become engaged to Anthony Eden, and Churchill was planning that the wedding celebrations should take place at 10 Downing Street. 'W feels avuncular to his orphaned niece,' Colville wrote in his diary, 'gave her a cheque for £500, and told me he thought she had a most unusual personality.' [2]

The wedding of Clarissa Churchill and Anthony Eden took place on August 14. Churchill and his wife then gave the wedding reception luncheon at 10 Downing Street. 'We are still so overcome by your overwhelming kindness,' they telegraphed to Churchill and his wife that evening, 'which has made this the most perfect day for us. Thank

---

[1] 'My darling one', 4 August 1952: Spencer-Churchill papers.

[2] Colville diary, 11 August 1952: *The Fringes of Power*, page 653. In 1987 the purchasing power of £500 had risen to £5,000.

you and bless you both.' [1] 'We too have enjoyed it so much,' Churchill replied. 'All good luck, Winston and Clemmie.' [2]

On Sunday August 17 there was another family celebration, the christening of Churchill's grandson Jeremy Soames in Westerham Church. On the following evening Churchill and his wife took Mary and Christopher Soames, and Jock and Meg Colville, to see *The Yeomen of the Guard* at Streatham. 'The PM,' noted Colville, 'was received with immense acclamation by the audience.' [3]

Churchill's vision had in no way declined with age. On the afternoon of August 19, at Lord Beaverbrook's request, he saw the Prime Minister of Newfoundland, Joseph R. Smallwood, who explained to him an ambitious plan to harness the 245-foot-high Grand Falls on the Hamilton River in Labrador to the potential of electric power. Churchill listened to what Smallwood had to say, and then declared: 'This is a grand imperial concept but not imperialistic.' He then turned to Jock Colville, who was present, with the words: 'Jock, whom do we know in the City of London?' It so happened that Colville had lunched that day at New Court, so he replied: 'Rothschilds.' 'Good,' was Churchill's instant answer, 'they shall do it.'

Having decided both to support the electric power project and to guide it towards the best possible source of investment, Churchill began to pace up and down the Cabinet room, in which the meeting had taken place, singing the refrain from the Lord Chancellor's Nightmare Song, in Gilbert and Sullivan's *Iolanthe*:

> 'and the shares at a penny were ever so many
>   and issued by Rothschilds and Baring
>   and just as a few were allotted to you, you awoke
>   with a shudder despairing'.

Churchill himself eventually became a shareholder in Brinco, the company established to harness the water power of the Hamilton River. He always kept an interest in the fortunes of the company, and was briefed from time to time by Edmund de Rothschild. 'It is high time the Hamilton Falls wore a bridle' was Churchill's comment to Jock Colville. [4]

---

[1] 'Mr and Mrs Churchill', 14 August 1952: Churchill papers, 2/216.
[2] Note in Churchill's handwriting, 14 August 1952: Churchill papers, 2/216.
[3] Colville diary, 15–18 August 1952: *The Fringes of Power*, page 653.
[4] Edmund de Rothschild, 'Brinco: The Early Days', in *The Atlantic Advocate*, July 1967. 'There is an interesting postscript to the story,' writes Edmund de Rothschild. 'When Churchill died Premier Smallwood telephoned me and asked if he should come over from Canada and attend the funeral. I said yes, and together we joined the huge throng paying their last respects at his lying-in-state in Westminster Hall. Both of us were very moved as we walked out into the cold

In the Cabinet room on the following day, August 20, Churchill and his Cabinet colleagues discussed the need for a tax-free educational allowance for the children of officers and men in the Armed Forces who, as regular soldiers or as National Servicemen, were liable to be moved frequently from one place to another, whether at home or abroad. The object of these allowances, explained the Minister of Defence, Lord Alexander, and the Secretary of State for War, Anthony Head, was to enable Service parents to send their children to boarding schools.

During the discussion, it was Churchill who pointed out 'that Service parents were not alone in this difficulty: all middle-class parents were finding it increasingly difficult to send their children to boarding schools by reason of the high level of taxation'. The proposal for a tax-free educational allowance, 'though it might cost a small amount of money, raised a large question of principle. Was it right that the effects of high taxation should be mitigated, by tax-free allowances, for particular sections of the community who were paid by the State? Should not the Government aim rather at reducing taxation to a level which would enable people to meet their obligations out of taxed incomes?'

Churchill was supported in his line of argument by R. A. Butler, himself a former Secretary of State for Education in Churchill's wartime administration, who agreed 'that he could not consider in isolation the difficulties which Service parents found in providing boarding education for their children'. Members of the Colonial Services had 'similar difficulties', on which he had recently been approached by the Colonial Secretary. Representations had also been made to him on behalf of the public schools, regarding 'the difficulties of middle-class parents generally'. The solution might be found to lie, said Butler, not in the grant of tax-free allowances to public servants, 'but rather in some form of income-tax relief in respect of expenditure on children's education'.[1]

That weekend at Chartwell, foreign policy dominated the political talk. 'There is a slight drama' was how Jock Colville expressed it in his diary, and he went on to explain:

January wintry sunshine. I took the Premier by the arm and said: "Mr Premier, we have a lot of unfinished business to do." Smallwood did not reply immediately—he then said "mmm—yes—may be—let them be called the Churchill Falls", and thus they bear this name today, all 5,255 million kilowatts!' (Edmund de Rothschild recollections: letter to the author, 9 July 1986.)

[1] Cabinet Conclusions No. 77 of 1952, 'Secret', 3.30 p.m., 20 August 1952: Cabinet papers, 128/25.

W had persuaded Truman to join with him in sending a message, signed by them both, to Mossadeq in Teheran about the Persian oil question. W himself did it and the FO and oil people agreed. It is the first time since 1945 that the Americans have joined with us in taking overt joint action against a third power. Fear of ganging up has hitherto prevented them.

But Anthony Eden, completing his honeymoon in Lisbon, is furious. It is not the substance but the method which displeases him: the stealing by Winston of his personal thunder.

Moreover, should Eisenhower be elected President of the USA in November—an event thought to be decreasingly probable—there will be further trouble on this score, because W has several times revealed to me his hopes of a joint approach to Stalin, proceeding perhaps to a congress in Vienna where the Potsdam Conference would be reopened and concluded.

If the Russians were unco-operative, the cold war would be intensified by us: 'Our young men,' W said to me, 'would as soon be killed carrying truth as death.' [1]

For several years Churchill had been concerned about the scale and severity of the War Crimes trials and sentences, especially against senior German army officers. On August 23 he sent a minute to Selwyn Lloyd, the Minister of State at the Foreign Office, suggesting that the time had come to release the 'several hundred former army officers still being held prisoner'.[2] Only fifteen former German army officers were now being held, Anthony Eden answered on Lloyd's behalf six days later. Only four of these, he wrote, could be described as having held high command, and several of the fifteen were former SS men. Eden added:

There is therefore no possibility of our releasing 'several hundred' war criminals, as you suggest. The majority of the prisoners now remaining in our hands are real thugs, convicted on charges of ill-treating or killing Allied prisoners-of-war or persons held in concentration camps. Dr Adenauer has said that he does not want us to let such criminals out. The clemency cases which it is now my distasteful responsibility to consider are therefore mostly those where the prisoner was almost certainly a ruffian but where the evidence admits of some doubt.

Were he to go 'further than this', Eden added, 'I should not only be

---

[1] Colville diary, 22–25 August 1952: *The Fringes of Power*, pages 653–4.

[2] Prime Minister's Personal Minute, M.452 of 1952, 23 August 1952. Selwyn Lloyd had been appointed Minister of State at the Foreign Office on 30 October 1951, a post which he held until 18 October 1954.

doing wrong, but I should be doing what Dr Adenauer has specifically asked me not to do.'[1]

There was another issue troubling Churchill in the third week of August, on which he sought action from both the Foreign Office and the Ministry of Defence: the use by the Americans in Korea of the napalm bomb. Churchill had already sent a message to General Omar N. Bradley in Washington expressing his 'confidence' that every effort would be made to avoid needless loss of life and suffering by the use of napalm bombs in crowded areas.[2] On August 22 Churchill informed Alexander that Britain should take 'no responsibility' for any use of napalm in crowded areas.[3]

On August 26 Churchill's luncheon guests included David Sarnoff, the Chairman of the Radio Corporation of America, just back from a visit to Israel. Returning from Chequers to London, Sarnoff reported on the conversation to the Israeli Ambassador, Eliahu Elath, who telegraphed to the Foreign Ministry in Tel Aviv:

According Sarnoff Churchill showed much interest asking many questions different aspects Israel's life including personalities especially PM. He agreed importance strengthening Israel every respect as 'good and reliable investment' for western democracies.

Explaining Britain's economic difficulties prevent her doing much for Israel, Churchill promised nondiscrimination including military supplies. He stressed HMGs interest Israel Arab peace and declared his support idea non-aggression pact but remained vague about what they could do to promote it.

Expressing satisfaction Egypt's defeat by Israel, Churchill said he had 'not much use' for Egyptians and had little faith their capacity put own house in order. He is ready however give Neguib his chance and prepared wait another three months in hope of situation clearing before taking final decision further policy towards Egypt and related problems.

Churchill said American Mideastern policy could be useful and effective only if USA Govt agrees send token force Suez and take full share British responsibilities area he complained his repeated suggestion this effect been rejected by Washington.

[1] 'Confidential', PM 104 of 1952, 29 August 1952: Churchill papers, 2/513. To a further query from Churchill about those war criminals who had been released (Prime Minister's Personal Minute, M.477 of 1952), Eden replied: 'What I have done is what the Germans asked for. They wanted the men let out and did not mind if it was parole or not.' ('Private', PM 114 of 1952, 10 September 1952: Churchill papers, 2/517.)

[2] Telegram No. I.J. 20 of 3 July 1952. From 1949 to 1953, Bradley was Chairman of the United States Joint Chiefs of Staff.

[3] Prime Minister's Personal Minute, M.449 of 1952, 22 August 1952.

On general situation Churchill said did not expect Russia start world war and would like discuss general settlement personally Stalin. Suggested Sarnoff on return USA should use influence promote better understanding USA Britain especially on Middle East.

'Sarnoff highly pleased conversation,' Elath added, 'feels Churchill sincerely friendly Israel and ready help us.' [1]

Anthony and Clarissa Eden were among Churchill's guests at Chartwell from August 25 to August 29; at lunch on August 29 Lord Moran and Denis Kelly were also present. Churchill talked during luncheon 'of many things', his doctor noted, 'ending with his views on the duties of family life. He did not think that celibacy, as imposed by the Roman Catholic Church on priests, could be right. I reminded him how he had been impressed during the election by the other-worldliness of some Roman priests who had come to see him.'

'Kelly here is a Roman,' Churchill interrupted, afraid that Moran might say something unguarded, and went on to tell his guests: 'God is the Supreme Creator. He is good—but I am not certain about a future life after death.' [2] Churchill added: 'Chassez la nature et elle reviendra au galop.'

On another occasion Churchill told Denis Kelly: 'If I were offered the governance of the Universe, I might perhaps accept. If I were offered the black velvet curtains of eternal sleep, I might not decline.' [3]

[1] Telegram sent 27 August 1952: Israel Government Archive.
[2] Moran diary, 29 August 1952: *The Struggle for Survival*, page 393.
[3] Denis Kelly recollections: in conversation with the author, 11 April 1987.

41

Towards Seventy-Eight, and Beyond

As August 1952 came to an end, Churchill planned to go on holiday for two weeks at Lord Beaverbrook's villa, La Capponcina, on the French Riviera. 'To be lent a villa,' wrote the Queen, 'sounds the perfect way to spend a peaceful few days.'[1] 'I can always fly back for a day to these toils,' he telegraphed to Beaverbrook at the end of August.[2]

Those 'toils' in the first week of September included the line Britain was to take over Korea at the forthcoming United Nations General Assembly. Eden was against any British support for a resolution which might lead to the breaking off of relations with China. 'Proceed as you propose,' Churchill minuted, 'but don't let us fall out with the US for the sake of Communist China.'[3]

At the last Cabinet meeting before his holiday, held on the afternoon of September 4, Churchill spoke about the housing programme and the economic situation in Britain. He had noticed reports, he said, of landlords abandoning their property because they were unable to keep it in repair. Could these houses not be 'purchased by the State for a small sum', and then turned over to the Ministry of Housing for repair. This would then add to the total living accommodation provided by the housing programme. Unfortunately, he was told, a large number of the houses which were being abandoned by their landlords 'were beyond repair and ought to be pulled down'.

Commenting a few moments later on the dispute in the engineering industry, concerning overtime and piecework wages, Churchill ex-

---

[1] 'My dear Prime Minister', 30 August 1952: Squerryes Lodge Archive.
[2] Telegram despatched 1.30 a.m., 28 August 1952: Churchill papers, 2/211.
[3] Minute of 3 September 1952 (on Eden's minute PM 108 of 1952, of 1 September 1952): Churchill papers, 2/517.

pressed his hope 'that a settlement would be found by which the employers would agree to some small increase in wages'.[1]

On September 6 Churchill went to his constituency, where he spoke of his wish for Conservative wage-earners, 'of whom we have so many millions', to join their Unions 'and take an active interest in their work'. This had been a theme of his for twenty-five years, since his own time as Chancellor of the Exchequer between 1924 and 1929.[2] That same day, at the Farnborough Air Display, a prototype de Havilland 110 disintegrated during flight; thirty people were killed and sixty-three injured. To the test pilot Neville Duke, who had carried on with the display with his squadron, of which Churchill was Honorary Air Commodore, Churchill wrote on the following day: 'It was characteristic of you, and of 615 Squadron, to go up as you did yesterday after the shocking accident. Accept my salute.'[3]

On September 9 Churchill left London for the South of France. With him were his wife and two of his secretaries, Miss Gilliatt and Miss Portal. There were also two detectives, and a valet. 'Just a line to wish you a happy & sunny holiday with lots of painting,' Sarah Churchill wrote from her home in London, and she added: 'You *do* deserve it—Wow.'[4] On the day he left, Churchill was sent a letter from Desmond Morton, thanking him for Volume 5 of the war memoirs. 'I cannot help declaring my conviction,' Morton wrote, 'that in the circumstances of those days of which you treat, there is no single occasion on which you could have done other than you did. Your critics after the event—and they are but few—are pitifully unaware of the limitations placed sometimes upon your better judgement by persons and events beyond your control. This book, as indeed the earlier volumes, should enlighten them if they are men of good will.' Morton ended: 'Thank you again, and for Heaven's sake, or at least for that of this country, do look after yourself.'[5]

Among those to whom Churchill had sent a copy of Volume 5 was Queen Elizabeth the Queen Mother. 'I trust Your Majesty will accept this token,' he wrote, 'as an expression of my devotion and respect.'[6] 'It is as thrilling and as splendid as the volumes that preceded it,' the

---

[1] Cabinet Conclusions No. 78 of 1952, 'Secret', 3.30 p.m., 4 September 1952: Cabinet papers, 128/25. On 21 October 1952 the engineering employers offered a 7s. 4d. a week increase to adult male workers. This was accepted by the miners on 7 November 1952. On 26 November 1952 the employers and the unions agreed to an increase of 6s. 5d. for adult female workers, and smaller increases for young women.

[2] Speech of 6 September 1952: Randolph S. Churchill (editor), *Stemming the Tide*, pages 331–8.

[3] 'My dear Duke', 7 September 1952: Churchill papers, 2/185.

[4] 'Darling Papa', 8 September 1952: Churchill papers, 1/50.

[5] 'Dear Winston', 9 September 1952: Churchill papers, 4/62.

[6] 'Madam', 9 September 1952: Squerryes Lodge Archive.

Queen Mother replied, 'and I am very grateful to you for thinking of me. I sometimes wonder whether Providence was kinder to us than we realised, when she provided you with TIME to write this wonderful history of those glorious & anguished years of War.' The Queen Mother added that she was glad Churchill was to be at Balmoral on his return from France, 'for it was always the King's ambition to get you there. He particularly wanted to hang your photograph with other Prime Ministers, & I hope that it will now occupy a place of honour in the Ministers' room!' [1]

Churchill remained at La Capponcina for two weeks. 'I hope the sun shines,' Eden telegraphed on September 13.[2] It did; as well as painting, and some swimming, Churchill worked on the 1945 chapters of Volume 6, dictating for Bill Deakin a note of one of the themes which had still to be worked up into a section for the book. The note read:

> The death of President Roosevelt. How did it reach me? How soon did I speak to Parliament? What did I say? Opening interchanges with Truman. His wish that I should come over and have a long talk with him. I felt unable to leave London at this juncture. I wish indeed I had done so. The interim. Three months of Roosevelt's failing health. Three months before Truman could form his own views. Roosevelt's great error in not having a deputy ready to succeed, who knew everything. I had never before, to my recollection, seen Truman; yet he was Vice-President, and the man who would succeed a chief already failing in strength. These six months were the most eventful.[3]

Writing to Deakin on September 15, Churchill commented on one of the telegrams from Roosevelt which he intended to quote, from Roosevelt to Stalin: 'It looks as if the President had told Marshall to draft a severe reply, and then wrote this last sentence in himself. If so it is probable that it was the last powerful impulse of his life.' [4] As to Deakin's suggestion for some more narrative in the chapter in which that telegram was to appear, Churchill wrote: 'It reads very well and the telegrams tell their own tale far more impressively than any narrative however good.' [5]

While Churchill was at Cap d'Ail, Lord Mountbatten, with the Mediterranean Fleet, put in at Villefranche; Churchill at once invited the Mountbattens to dine at La Capponcina. After the women

---

[1] 'My dear Mr Churchill', 30 September 1952: Squerryes Lodge Archive.

[2] PM 115 of 1952, 13 September 1952: Churchill papers, 2/517.

[3] Note, undated: Churchill papers, 4/390.

[4] In fact, the whole of this telegram had been drafted by General Marshall; even the strong sentence which had so impressed Churchill.

[5] 'Mr Deakin', 15 September 1952: Churchill papers, 4/365. Six weeks later work on volume 6 was advanced to the point where, as Churchill wrote to Deakin, there would be 'no more group work' on it. 'Thank you very much indeed,' Churchill added, 'for all your help to me during these past years. I greatly value the work you have done.' ('My dear Bill', 25 October 1952: Churchill papers, 4/24.)

had left the table, Churchill and Mountbatten remained alone. 'With tears in his eyes,' Mountbatten wrote to his daughter, 'he kept repeating how much he had loved me, that he had quite forgotten and forgiven me about India, that I had had a wonderful career and was on the threshold of an even finer career, the country needed me, etc. Quite embarrassing.' [1]

On the following day Churchill attended the Préfet's dinner for the Fleet and was prevailed on to speak. *'Est-ce que je vous fais de la peine quand j'assassine vos genres?'* he asked his host. [2]

To the writer Peter Quennell, whom he met during his stay at La Capponcina, Churchill commented, of his second Premiership: 'It's likely to be my last innings. So it had better be a good one!' As to Churchill's paintings, Quennell noted: 'Like all artists, good or bad, I suspected, he was sometimes plagued by doubts, and felt the sad discrepancy between what he had envisaged and the results he had produced. So splendidly confident in everything else he did, here he needed our support, and hovered about us almost anxiously, showing picture after picture, while he awaited the words of appreciation that were often difficult to find.' [3]

Churchill returned to London from the South of France on September 25. Five days later Lord Moran noted in his diary:

The PM was back from his holiday at Monte Carlo and says he feels better for it; he has more vigour. 'I had no money to gamble at the tables, but I did three pictures while I was away, and worked five hours every day at my book.'

In France he got a second wind. He said to me today:

'The Government position is stronger than it was a year ago. I have not yet decided when to resign. It might do me no good when the curtain is down.' [4]

On the morning after his return from France, Churchill was in the Chair for a meeting of the Cabinet. Commenting on a report by Ismay that the United States 'continued to insist' that Britain could not be associated in any way with the Council established under the Tripartite Treaty between Australia, New Zealand and the United States, and that the Governments of Australia and New Zealand had ac-

---

[1] Letter of 19 September 1952: Philip Ziegler, *Mountbatten*, page 512. Mountbatten, after his period as Governor-General of India, had resumed his naval career, as Commander-in-Chief, Mediterranean Fleet.

[2] Campbell-Johnson narrative: Philip Ziegler, *Mountbatten*, page 512. 'Does it hurt you when I murder your genders?'

[3] Peter Quennell, *The Wanton Chase*, page 108.

[4] Moran diary, 30 September 1952: *The Struggle for Survival*, page 393.

cepted the American view, Churchill told his colleagues that 'he greatly regretted the Australian acquiescence in this attempt by the United States to usurp our special position in relation to Australia and New Zealand, particularly when he recalled our promise in the late war that we would divert our forces from the Middle East if Australia were attacked by Japan'. He was 'disposed', he said, to send personal messages about this to the Prime Ministers of Australia and New Zealand and possibly also to the Australian Foreign Minister.[1]

Speaking of the situation in Persia on September 30, Churchill commented on the divergence of views between Britain and the United States as to how to negotiate with Dr Mossadeq about compensation for the nationalized oilfields. Britain should do all in its power, he said, 'to maintain a joint Anglo-American pressure on the Persian Government, though in the last resort he had no means of preventing the United States Government from financing Dr Mossadeq in the hope of preventing Persia from going Communist'.[2]

'I am going to Balmoral tomorrow,' Churchill told Lord Moran on September 30. 'I felt I ought to see the Queen. I have not seen her for two months.'[3]

On the morning of October 1, Churchill was in the chair at a meeting of the Cabinet. Any legislation amending the Rent Restriction Acts, he told his colleagues, 'must be so designed as to bring no financial benefits to landlords'. It must also be 'made evident', he said, that the Government 'had no other purpose than to increase the number of habitable houses'. The Labour Party itself, he noted, had in a recent pamphlet admitted that the controlled rents of some houses did not provide an income sufficient to maintain the property in a state of repair, and that tenants would benefit from some amendments of the Acts 'which would enable a proportion of the rent to be spent on the improvement or maintenance of a dwelling'.[4]

From London, Churchill flew north to Scotland, where, from October 1 to 3 he was the guest of the Queen at Balmoral. 'I accompanied the Prime Minister to Balmoral,' Jock Colville later recalled, 'where

[1] Cabinet Conclusions No. 81 of 1952, 'Secret', 11 a.m., 26 September 1952: Cabinet papers, 128/25.
[2] Cabinet Conclusions No. 82 of 1952, 'Secret', 5 p.m., 30 September 1952: Cabinet papers, 128/25. The Cabinet Office spelling of Dr Mossadeq was Dr Musaddiq, one of several variants in use at that time.
[3] Moran diary, 30 September 1952: *The Struggle for Survival*, page 393.
[4] Cabinet Conclusions No. 83 of 1952, 'Secret', 11 a.m., 1 October 1952: Cabinet papers, 128/25.

he went in his capacity as Prime Minister at his own suggestion. The Queen and Prince Philip, who had a very young party staying with them, may have been a little reluctant, but the visit went off well and was in the event enjoyed by both sides, although Winston (aged nearly seventy-eight and not having touched a gun for years) complained to me on the way home that he thought he should have been asked to shoot!' [1]

While Churchill was in Scotland, a new Private Secretary arrived at 10 Downing Street from the British Embassy in Paris, Anthony Montague Browne, a former fighter pilot who in 1945 had won the Distinguished Flying Cross. He was twenty-nine years old. 'When I arrived at No. 10,' he later recalled, 'nobody was expecting me. I was hospitably put up at No. 10 and my first introduction to life there was being telephoned in the early hours of the morning to be told by an Admiral that our first nuclear bomb experiment had been a success. He suggested that I should wake the Prime Minister at Balmoral and inform him, but even at this early stage I concluded that this would be imprudent!' [2]

Having returned to London, Churchill wrote on October 4 to the Queen, in his own hand, from 10 Downing Street:

Madam,

I thank Yr Majesty for the vy pleasant visit to Balmoral to wh I was so graciously invited. It will rank in my memory with other agreeable occasions when I have had the honour of being the guest of yr Father, yr Grandfather and yr Great-Grandfather in these Highland scenes. I hope I may have in due course one of the photographs wh Princess Margaret took of my leave-taking from you and yr children. I was keenly impressed by the development of Prince Charles as a personality since I last saw him at Windsor. He is young to think so much. He and his sister must be a great joy to you and their Father. I was also glad to have such good talks with the Duke about the Navy, Flying, Polo and Politics. It gave me gt pleasure to go and see Your Majesty's Mother in her remarkable abode. [3]

'I venture, Madam,' Churchill ended, 'to send w this letter the bound copy of my Volume V which—alas!—was only just too late for me to bring.' [4]

On October 9 Churchill left London for the Conservative Party Conference at Scarborough, accompanied by his wife and Christopher Soames. Randolph Churchill, who had hoped to join his parents on the train journey north, did not do so, writing to his father that morning:

---

[1] Colville recollection: John Colville, *The Fringes of Power*, page 654.

[2] Anthony Montague Browne recollections: letter to the author, 10 March 1987. The experiment had been at Monte Bello Island, off the north west coast of Australia.

[3] The 'remarkable abode' was Birkhall, the house on the Balmoral estate which has been The Queen Mother's Aberdeenshire home since the summer of that year.

[4] 'Madam', 4 October 1952: Squerryes Lodge Archive.

Your office twice rang me up to find out what train I was taking for Scarborough. I naively supposed that this was so that we might, if convenient, go on the same train. But when I rang you up you made it vy plain that you did not want me on the same train as yourself. I have since learnt that this was not due to a desire for privacy for composing your speech (as you told me) but obviously for sheer distaste for my presence in your entourage.

In these circumstances you will scarcely be surprised to learn that I am not coming to Scarborough.[1]

Like each successive, and often strident, tiff between father and son, the storm eventually passed away, leaving affectionate calm. But in the period of dispute, the letters passing between the two men, the one nearly seventy-eight, the other forty-one, could be strongly phrased and strenuously argued. To his son, Churchill sent a short but amicable reply:

My dear Randolph,

I was so sorry that you did not feel able to come to Scarborough. When, in response to your call, I telephoned you, I thought it was all settled and that you would be with us at nine o'clock. You could also have seen the Woodford delegation the next day, and we could have come back together. I am always nowadays much worried while making up a speech, and wished to be as much alone as possible on the journey down.

I am very much concerned about your health. What doctors are you consulting? If I were you I should have a thorough cure, even if it took a couple of months. There must be effective remedies nowadays. Pray let me know about this.

Your loving Father,

WSC[2]

This letter, apparently innocuous and indeed friendly, touched in Randolph a chord of unhappiness so deep that he poured out his soul in reply. His letter, an angry yet at the same time loving one, expressed all the anguish which had tormented him in his relationship with his father for so much of his adult life:

My dear Papa,

Thank you for your letter. You seem to be indifferent to my reasons for not coming to Scarborough. I certainly do not wish to labour them. But I don't want them to be overlooked, still less to be misunderstood.

In your letter you say 'I am always nowadays much worried while making up a speech, & wished to be alone on the journey.' I can't actually recall any occasion when I have disturbed you when composing. Anyway, much though I rejoice in being in your company, particularly on great political outings, I

---

[1] 'My dear Papa', 9 October 1952: Churchill papers, 1/51.
[2] 'My dear Randolph', 16 October 1952: Churchill papers, 1/51.

have long abandoned any thought of ever proposing my presence to you either at your home or in public.

But—since there is no point in my writing to you at all unless I am frank—may I say that it has been a growing source of grief to me that ever since you first became Prime Minister you have repeatedly made it clear to me—& to others—that you no longer have that same desire for my company in private or in public which between 1923 & 1940 was the chief delight & pivot of my existence.

I recognize that when we are together these days I often say things of a provocative character. I assure you that I often try hard to avoid this. But I, who was once honoured by an intimacy with you which few have experienced, find it impossibly hard to sit at your table & prattle platitudes. Instead I attempt a paradox & in the place of the tolerant comprehension I knew, my portion is snubs & insults, flouts & jeers, cries of 'shut-up' which you never address to anyone else & which no-one else would ever address to me. And all of this, mark you, when we are talking on an abstract topic like politics.

I have said that I know that I often say provocative—& needlessly provocative—things. (Such is often the tendency of spirited children with their parents.) Often, too, I indulge in cynicism & irony—doubtless in a clumsy fashion. But where, except at your table & at your feet did I learn to think that these were the most enjoyable vehicles of political talk & that levity & frivolity & unexpected heterodoxy were the proper terms in which the tiny minority who are interested in politics, to the exclusion of all else, should discuss their own peculiar brand of 'shop'?

I realize too that you regard me as a failure & that you cannot disguise this view entirely successfully from other people. Failure is of course a relative term & I should have thought that if you ever had time to cast an eye over the children of your political contemporaries you could scarcely regard my failure as absolute. My view for what it's worth, is that I am not a failure in any terms. Perhaps I will be, but I haven't started yet. In any case the love of one friend for another cannot be affected by worldly success or failure.

What happened about Scarborough would not have been significant or important except that it followed on a score of similar, though partially veiled, incidents in the last few years. I have no wish to recall them. But when one is repeatedly disregarded, rejected & snubbed by the person one loves most in the world one's sensitivity forms a scar tissue of pride & arrogance which seems to protect the injury, not only from others, but (by self-deception) from oneself. But there are some calculated, cold-blooded, open rebuffs which only those of the meanest spirit can overlook.

If we are ever to be friends again (and I cherish this hope above all others in this world) you must, please, understand what you did to me last week. For otherwise you cannot possibly understand the basic cause of my unhappiness & disenchantment which make me in your eyes, & in those of many others, such an awkward customer.

It would never have occurred to me to suggest that I should journey with you to Scarborough. (Fifteen years ago I would have; but those golden days of our friendship & instinctive understanding are now nothing but precious memories—more irrevocably etched in my mind than any other experience.) Of course if you had proposed it I should have been overjoyed. But when one afternoon I came home to find that your office had twice telephoned to ask what train I was taking to Scarborough my heart was filled with joy. Fool that I was, the idea never brushed my mind that the only purpose of the enquiry was to ensure that we should travel on separate trains. (And, what is so droll is that if you had not been at such pains to arrange this it would have happened anyway: I have never been a gate-crasher.)

So, the following morning I rang you up. You were busy & called me back a few moments later. I asked you what train you were taking. After first establishing that you understood that I was taking the three o'clock, you said that you were taking the two o'clock. You added that I should not change my plans as you wished to be alone to work on your speech. I naturally accepted this. But I'm bound to say that I felt dunched. 'In my Father's House there are many mansions.' There's also lots of room in a private car; and still more on an express train.

This was a pretty hard knock. For apart from my own feelings this odious situation was inevitably apparent to three other members (at least) of our family & also to your secretaries—not to speak of mine. But an additional laceration was to be drawn across the wounds of my pride. I was soon to learn that your desire for privacy (which you think worth repeating, even after this event, in your letter) was nothing of the sort. It was a simple desire for my absence.

Since I have never, & especially not in recent years, ever tried to thrust myself upon you this was for me a bitter moment in which, willy nilly, I had to face & accept something which had been creeping up on me for twelve years & which now could only be disregarded by a supreme act of moral cowardice.

I have no boats to burn. They have all mouldered, it seems, on the beaches long ago. I don't pretend to be an acute judge of human nature or character—least of all of my own. But of this I am sure: I have changed much less in the last ten years than you have.

In one thing I have never changed or faltered—my absolute love, devotion & loyalty to you. At this moment I love you more than any man or woman I have ever met. I don't think that anything you could say or do to me or anyone else could make more than a dent in the wholehearted admiration I have for you & which, despite everything, has grown with the years.

Can't you understand the maladjustment, the frustration, yes even (recently) the jealousy that urges the bile of resentment when one's love is scorned as worthless & the person one loves scarcely troubles to hide from friend or foe the indifference or hostility which he feels?

All this permeates the fabric of our relationship. Usually a father & son get on well; (it is an easier relationship than marriage) &, if their interests happen to lie in the same direction, the relationship is that of partners. (Before the war this was virtually achieved.) Now all is changed to a horrible degree. And nothing will be improved by humbug.

Frankly I see no point in our continuing to meet as we have done since the war. The situation is only aggravated when we meet, as we do, occasionally, formally, half-heartedly, almost as a duty & with manifest misgiving on both sides.

What is odd, which I don't think you have noticed—I think Mamma has—is that both before & since the war we have always got on much better in public than in private. The very few times we have been on a jaunt together since the war—Metz, Luxembourg, Strasbourg, Plymouth—never a cross word. It is not for nothing that I coined the 'mot' about myself: 'Randolph should never be allowed out in private.'

I believe that a single episode with Anthony Eden in the Mediterranean (about which you were much too busy to understand the psychological background) has convinced you that I am wholly unfit to be in your company when persons of consequence are present. You assume that the rows we have in private would inevitably be duplicated in an even more painful fashion if outsiders were there. In fact this is the contrary of the truth.

I am confident that you will not do me the injustice of interpreting the foregoing as a plea to be invited to meet your colleagues. Many of them I meet most harmoniously & some of them are my close friends.

But the fact that I am *never* invited when you have any official guests shows the world as well as myself how low a view you take of me. God knows, I don't wish to come to your table, either when you are alone or with company, on the basis that it is a painful duty for you—a doubtful treat for me.

I should not repine if I only saw you five or six times a year provided that on those occasions you showed me, as in earlier days, your trust & affection which, with all my faults, I do not think I have deserved to forfeit.

From the time I was a school-boy I have followed your fortunes in good times & bad. Except for money, over which you have always been supremely generous, I don't think I have ever asked you for anything. I ask something now: that you should try to understand me as I am (and not as you imagine I am or think I ought to be): that you should try once more to show me the love & trust which you brought me up to expect & value above all else in this life; & that if these two requests are too hard of fulfilment you will at least believe that not one word in this letter is intended as a reproach or even a self-justification. The only object of this excruciating exercise has been to try to explain to you some of the reasons for the wayward conduct & profound unhappiness of

Your devoted son,

Randolph

'It is wrong of me,' Randolph wrote in his postscript, 'to impose so long a letter on you. I can only hope that it is not so difficult to read as it was to write.' [1]

*   *   *

[1] 'Personal', 'My dear Papa', 16 October 1952: Churchill papers, 1/51. Jock Colville writes, of the relationship between father and son: 'It is a sad tale, for they loved each other; but they could never meet without quarrelling. Originally it was Randolph who used to start it: latterly it was Winston.' (Sir John Colville: letter to the author, 12 May 1987.)

In his Scarborough speech, the preparation of which owed much to a member of the Conservative Research Department, John Biggs-Davidson, Churchill reviewed the first year of his Government. In his concluding words he struck a defiant note, telling the Conference: 'Let us march forward with our sturdy lions, jaunty lions—yes, unconquerable lions—enrolling our members as we go. So many people believe in us and vote for us who remain silent between elections. We need the encouragement and help of their declared fellowship in our grand design to restore Britain to freedom and to reviving fame.'

One of Churchill's themes in his Scarborough speech had been the need for constant Government vigilance over the economy. The Government's finances, he said, had been 'heavily strained by years of reckless extravagance and waste'.[1] Three days later, with the problems of expenditure much on his mind, Churchill told his Cabinet colleagues 'that some means must be found of preventing the capital expenditure of local authorities from exceeding the provision made for it in the Budget'.[2] Another initiative which Churchill took that week was to invite three Trade Union leaders to a party at Downing Street. As a result of this, noted the Leader of the House, Harry Crookshank, there were 'eyebrows raised' among the Conservative guests.[3]

That evening, October 14, Churchill spoke at a dinner for General Ridgway, Eisenhower's successor as Supreme Commander in Europe. 'We all hate and fear war,' he declared, in the presence of, among others, Field Marshals Alexander and Montgomery, and he went on to tell the guests, and General Ridgway:

Let me tell you why in my opinion, and it is only an opinion, not a prophecy, a third World War is unlikely to happen. It is because, among other reasons, it would be entirely different in certain vital aspects from any other war that has ever taken place. Both sides know that it would begin with horrors of a kind and on a scale never dreamed of before by human beings. It would begin by both sides in Europe suffering in this first stage exactly what they dread the most. It would also be different because the main decisions would probably come in the first month or even in the first week.

The quarrel might continue for an indefinite period, but after the first month it would be a broken-backed war in which no great armies could be moved over long distances. The torments would fall in increasing measure upon the whole civilian population of the globe, and Governments dependent upon long distance communications by land would find they had lost their power to dominate events.

[1] Speech of 11 October 1952: Randolph S. Churchill (editor), *Stemming the Tide*, pages 339–49.
[2] Cabinet Conclusions No. 85 of 1952, 'Secret', 11 a.m., 14 October 1952: Cabinet papers, 128/25.
[3] Harry Crookshank diary, 15 October 1952: Crookshank papers.

These, Churchill said, were 'only a few of the grave facts which rule our destinies'.[1]

When the Cabinet met after Churchill's return from Scarborough, one item on the agenda was Egypt. On this occasion, Harold Macmillan later recalled, 'Winston had not read the brief and did not want—rightly—to quarrel with Eden in Cabinet. So he raised the question of the Derby butler murder.' This was the shooting, on October 9, by Lord Derby's footman, of Lady Derby, who, although grievously injured in the neck, survived. Both the butler, and the under-butler, were killed.

Churchill had read an account of the assault in the *Daily Mail*; when he mentioned it to the Cabinet, he discovered that the Home Secretary, Sir David Maxwell-Fyfe, knew nothing about it. Churchill at once called for a copy of the *Daily Mail* to be brought in, and read out the article to his Cabinet. He then questioned Maxwell-Fyfe on the whole issue of hanging, following which he asked R. A. Butler, as Chancellor of the Exchequer, to tell the Cabinet how much it cost to keep a man in prison; 'all this', Macmillan commented, 'to avoid getting on to the Egypt item—and so to an early lunch'.[2]

Two weeks later, when Egypt was raised in Cabinet again, Churchill was ready to speak, and did so with a certain optimism. He 'still hoped', the minutes recorded, 'that it might be possible to persuade the United States to take some share of the responsibility for safeguarding the Suez Canal as an international waterway, so that we could hand over our responsibilities in Egypt to an international organisation in which the United States and ourselves would both play some part'.[3]

On October 15, as the first year of Churchill's Premiership drew to an end, the Queen commissioned a bust of Churchill for Windsor Castle: 'the choice of yourself as sculptor', Sir Owen Morshead wrote that day to Oscar Nemon, 'commends itself to the Prime Minister, who is prepared to give you a sitting in order that the final touches may be added to the model which you have already done from life'.[4]

---

[1] Speech of 14 October 1952: Randolph S. Churchill (editor), *Stemming the Tide*, pages 350–1.

[2] Harold Macmillan recollections: in conversation with the author, 25 June 1981.

[3] Cabinet Conclusions No. 91 of 1952, 'Secret', 11 a.m., 29 October 1952: Cabinet papers, 128/25. 'You have often told me,' Eden had minuted to Churchill eight days earlier, 'that you had some hopes of Neguib.' These hopes had already led, Eden noted, to the release of fifteen 'obsolescent jet aircraft' to Egypt. ('Personal and Secret', PM 125 of 1952: Churchill papers, 2/517.)

[4] Letter of 15 October 1952: Royal Archives. Sir Owen Morshead was the Librarian at Windsor Castle.

On November 13 Churchill gave Nemon two separate sittings; 'he was very sympathetic in his approach to my task', Nemon informed Morshead three days later, 'and gave me a very warm reception'.[1] A week later Nemon wrote again to Morshead:

. . . the progress of my work depends on this most unpredictable sitter. On Sunday for instance I moved to Chequers where I had a very pleasant contact in a relaxed setting. He said to his Lordly guests that the honour which has befallen him at the hand of the Queen has touched him more than if she had bestowed upon him the Order of the Garter! So you were right, he is deeply moved and is very proud to be immortalized in company with his great ancestor the first Duke of Marlborough.[2]

When the bust was completed, it was placed in the Queen's Guard Chamber at Windsor Castle.

26 October 1952 marked the end of the first year of Churchill's second Premiership. Throughout that year, Harold Macmillan later recalled, 'the Prime Minister maintained remarkable vitality', and he went on to explain:

There was hardly a Cabinet, however serious the situation, without some gem. For instance, after two hours on a long and difficult issue, the only relief came when a Minister said 'I have tried to put the case fairly.' 'A very dangerous thing to do,' growled Churchill.

On another occasion he was concerned at the cost of keeping a criminal lunatic in Broadmoor, which had arisen from a verdict of 'guilty but insane' on a young footman. He had already made the reflection that it was encouraging to note that even in these degenerate days there were still houses where it was possible to shoot a brace of butlers. He was now pressing the Home Secretary as to the cost of keeping this unhappy man in detention. 'What could you do it for?' he asked. 'A monkey a year?' I reflected that it must have been many years since this expression had been used at the Cabinet table.

In the course of another rather dreary session we were given an account of some disturbances in Bechuanaland arising out of the decision regarding Seretse Khama. After the story had been told and the Minister had informed us of what he proposed to say, Churchill summed up the situation as follows: 'Indeed a terrible position. An angry mob, armed with staves and stones, inflamed by alcohol, and inspired by Liberal principles.'

On another occasion he was puzzled, or affected to be, by an argument about the difference between short and long-term interest rates. 'I recall, as a boy, entering into a transaction with a Mr Attenborough about my gold watch. I do not recall any such pedantic distinctions.'[3]

[1] Letter of 16 November 1952: Royal Archives.
[2] Letter of 24 November 1952: Royal Archives.
[3] Macmillan diary, 10 June 1952: *Tides of Fortune*, page 391. A 'monkey' was £500. Macmillan added: 'At a later date, in connection with the Korean War, the Dean of Canterbury, known as

On November 1 Queen Elizabeth The Queen Mother made her first visit to Chartwell, having taken the salute at an inspection, with Churchill, of his and her squadrons at Biggin Hill. The weather there, she later recalled, was 'rather inclement' and the planned fly-past of elements of the squadrons had to be cancelled. The Queen Mother also remembered 'what an enjoyable occasion it was and the kindness of her host and hostess', added to which it was 'a great treat' to her after lunch when Churchill showed her his paintings.[1]

Neville Duke remembered how, on the occasion of the Queen Mother's visit to Biggin Hill, 'all those around Churchill were wearing medals but not he. He was quite upset.' Duke added: 'He was also weak on service ranks. I was introduced to the Queen Mother as "the Commodore Duke"—with much tittering from my assembled pilots.'

Duke added, of his other meetings with Churchill:

In my time we visited Chartwell on two occasions—he seemed to get great pleasure in showing his study with his many mementoes and photographs of very, very distinguished persons. He did tend to assume that I was on christian name terms with past Marshals of the RAF and that no age gap existed!

He was most interested in future aviation developments—he got me in some trouble with the Air Staff by requesting my views—on one sheet of paper I expect—expanding the idea of rocket propelled fighters. A thorny subject at the time but the idea seemed to appeal to him. He also wanted to know, on another occasion, why a parachute could not be deployed by a helicopter, should the engine fail, and thus float down in safety![3]

On November 2 there was a huge explosion on Eniwetok Atoll in the Pacific; two weeks later, it was announced in Washington that the United States had successfully tested 'thermo-nuclear weapons'. No further details were made public. Not even Churchill was informed that this was in fact a hydrogen bomb.

Returning to London on November 3, Churchill listened as R. A. Butler set out in the House of Commons the Government's policies for

---

the "Red Dean", had been making foolish accusations about "germ" warfare. His allegations had caused wide-spread indignation at home and overseas. The very word Canterbury clothed him with a spurious authority, but he could not be removed.' Churchill remarked, of the Dean: '"At home, he does not matter. In the East, they would surely say 'they are afraid of this holy Fakir, so they wish to silence him'. Of course, these ecclesiastics would be better employed in preparing us for a better world and even in facilitating our safe arrival there!—but we can do nothing against the Dean."'

[1] Sir Martin Gilliat: letter to the author, 12 March 1987.
[2] Neville Duke recollections: letter to the author, 20 July 1987.

the year to come. 'I thought your speech set the Government off on the new Session not only with gallantry,' Churchill wrote to Butler, 'but, as a result of your peroration, with colours high and hearts aglow. Now we will take the hurdles as they come.'[1]

Churchill himself spoke in the Debate on the Address on November 4. There were many debts to repay, he said; the economic future held 'many risks and many unknowable factors'; the only way to provide for this was by 'an all out effort to increase our exports'. To foster conditions under which that could be 'most easily and most swiftly achieved' would be the Government's 'primary endeavour'.[2] Ever-vigilant, as his father had been before him, in the matter of military spending, on November 5 Churchill told the Defence Committee of the Cabinet that he was 'not yet satisfied that every possible reduction had been made in administrative and ancillary services, or that the three Services were obtaining the best value for their expenditure'.[3]

In the world 'which has grown so much vaster all around us and towers up above us', Churchill told the boys of Harrow School on November 7, 'we in this small Island have to make a supreme effort to keep our place and station, the place and station to which our undying genius entitles us'.[4]

On November 4, to the delight of the Republican Party, General Eisenhower was elected President of the United States. Churchill telegraphed at once to the President-elect: 'I send you my sincere and heartfelt congratulations on your election. I look forward to a renewal of our comradeship and of our work together for the same causes of peace and freedom as in the past.' He was, Churchill added, also sending Eisenhower a letter.[5] Eisenhower replied on the following day: 'Dear Winston, Thank you very much for the typically generous sentiments expressed in your cable. I shall look forward to receiving your letter and I too look forward to a renewal of our cooperative work in the interests of a free world. Ike.'[6]

'For your private ear,' Churchill told Colville about Eisenhower's success, 'I am greatly disturbed. I think this makes war much more probable.'[7] Such fears gave Churchill a new sense of mission: to stay on as

---

[1] 'RAB', 3 November 1952: Churchill papers, 2/181.

[2] Speech of 4 November 1952: *Hansard*. It was during this speech that Churchill told the House of Commons: 'Personally, I am always ready to learn, although I do not always like being taught.'

[3] Defence Committee No. 11 of 1952, 'Top Secret', 11.30 a.m., 5 November 1952: Cabinet papers, 131/12.

[4] Speech of 7 November 1952: Churchill papers, 2/336.

[5] Telegram of 5 November 1952: Eisenhower papers.

[6] Telegram of 6 November 1952: Eisenhower papers.

[7] Colville diary, 9 November 1952: *The Fringes of Power*, page 654.

Prime Minister until he could bring about, by his own exertions, a reconciliation of the two Great Powers. This aim, more than any other consideration, was the underlying motive of his remaining years of power.

Colville was also a witness of the strain upon Churchill of the once manageable routine of daily work, writing in his diary:

He (W) is getting tired and visibly ageing. He finds it hard work to compose a speech and ideas no longer flow. He has made two strangely simple errors in the H of C lately, and even when addressing the Harrow boys in Speech Room last Friday what he said dragged and lacked fire. But he has had a tiring week, with speeches, important Cabinet decisions, etc., so that I may be unduly alarmist.[1]

On November 10, the day after this 'tiring week', Churchill spoke at the Lord Mayor's Banquet at the Guildhall, the speech being televised live as he spoke. Of the efforts being made by Robert Schuman and Konrad Adenauer, for 'their remarkable wisdom and their courage' in reconciliation, and in linking their two countries with the deterrent strength of NATO, Churchill declared, echoing the sentiments of his Zurich speech of six years earlier: 'There can be no effective defence of European culture and freedom unless a new Germany, resolved to set itself free from the ghastly crimes of Hitlerism, plays a strong and effective part in our system.' Any man in Germany or France or Britain 'who tries to hamper or delay that healing process is guilty of undermining the foundations upon which the salvation of all mankind from war and tyranny depends'. Time alone, Churchill added, could prove 'whether final success will reward these earnest, faithful efforts. Terrible would be the accountability of those in any country who, for petty, narrow, or selfish ends, weakened the common cause by stirring bygone passions, hates and tragedies.'

During his speech at the Guildhall, Churchill also praised the new Government in Egypt, as he had done earlier to Eden, telling his listeners, and viewers throughout Britain:

In July there was a revolution in Egypt rather similar to that of the young Turks in Turkey many years ago, as a result of which a distinguished Egyptian soldier became, for the time being, virtually a military dictator. I have visited Egypt at frequent intervals under varying circumstances during the last fifty-four years. I am bound to say that I felt much sympathy with the new hope aroused by General Neguib, that the shocking conditions of the Egyptian peasantry under the corrupt rule of former Egyptian Governments would be definitely improved.

We are anxious to help the new Government and to negotiate with them on friendly terms. We understand their point of view and we hope they will understand ours.

[1] Colville diary, 9 November 1952: *The Fringes of Power*, page 654.

We are not in Egypt for imperialist motives or self-seeking mastery or advantage, but in the common interests of all nations and to discharge what has become an international rather than a national responsibility, and we have no intention of being turned from our duty.

I hope indeed that negotiations may reach a happy conclusion, as they may well do if only they are inspired by a sense of mutual responsibility and seek the preservation of interests most important to the peace and safety, not only of Egypt, but of the whole anxious area of the Middle East.[1]

Churchill then spoke of Egypt's neighbour, Israel, whose first President, Dr Chaim Weizmann, had died on the previous day:

There is another country I must mention at this moment. Those of us who have been Zionists since the days of the Balfour Declaration know what a heavy loss Israel has sustained in the death of its President, Dr Chaim Weizmann. Here was a man whose fame and fidelity were respected throughout the free world, whose son was killed fighting for us in the late war, and who, it may be rightly claimed, led his people back into their promised land, where we have seen them invincibly established as a free and sovereign State.[2]

Among those listening to Churchill's speech was James de Rothschild, a Zionist and a personal friend. In 1921 his wife Dorothy had been Churchill's host in Jerusalem. Immediately after watching Churchill's speech on television, he wrote from his home in London:

My dear Winston,

Or perhaps on this occasion I should prefer to say my dear Prime Minister.

I have just listened to you and watched you on our TV set and I feel that I really must write and tell you how enchanted I was with your appearance and with what you said.

I have not seen you in action now for nearly 7 years (save perhaps at the Jockey Club meeting) and seven years is a cycle in man's life.

But my dear Winston, you have not changed, the same voice, the same appearance, the same fire and the same cool logic.

I was particularly touched and want to thank you personally for what you said about Weizmann; it will mean a lot to the many thousands & tens of thousands of Jews, it will mean a lot to those who are their friends, also perhaps to those who like them less.

Yours affectionately

Jimmy[3]

---

[1] On 14 November 1952 the Egyptian Cabinet issued a decree conferring supreme powers on General Neguib for six months.

[2] Speech of 10 November 1952: Randolph S. Churchill (editor), *Stemming the Tide*, pages 361–5. Weizmann had been born in the Grodno Province of Tsarist Russia on 27 November 1874, three days before Churchill. They had first met in Manchester in 1906.

[3] 'My dear Winston', 10 November 1952: Churchill papers, 2/197.

Churchill's seventy-eighth birthday was approaching. To a telegram of congratulations from Prince Bernhard of The Netherlands which reached him on November 3 he had replied: 'Alas I have not yet reached the distinction of 78 years and shall not do so until November 30! I shall however carry forward Your Royal Highness's good wishes to that date. . . .'[1] It was now nearly sixty years since the death of Churchill's father, a fact which was in his mind on November 10, when he learned of the death of R. A. Butler's father. Churchill wrote at once, in his own hand:

My dear Rab,
I send you my condolences on the death of your Father.
I know what it was to me to lose my Father, although I had seen him so little. I revered and admired him from a distance, except for a few glittering occasions. I have striven to vindicate his memory.
But you had the comfort and joy of long years of mature intimacy. And he the even greater satisfaction to a parent of watching the unfolding of your career.
Time rolls along, but I feel both you and he had been blessed by Fortune.[2]

During a Cabinet meeting on November 11, Churchill spoke of the Ministry of Transport's wish to build a second London airport at Gatwick: 'he was by no means convinced', he told his colleagues, 'that it would be right for the Government to reaffirm and make known for a second time their decision to develop Gatwick Airport before allowing local interests to express their views through some form of public enquiry'.[3]

At the Cabinet meeting on November 20 it was the question of a possible return to corporal punishment that drew Churchill's comments. He had already, at the end of October, drawn the Cabinet's attention to the strength of the views expressed in the debate in the House of Lords on the previous day in favour of restoring corporal punishment as a penalty for crimes of violence. He thought it would be 'unwise', Churchill had told his colleagues then, for the Government 'to close their minds to the possibility of restoring this penalty if the case for doing so were fully established and public opinion hardened in favour of it. There had been a great increase in crime and the prisons were overcrowded: the problem of prison administration would be eased if, through having discretion to impose corporal punishment,

---

[1] 'Sir', 3 November 1952: Churchill papers, 2/180.
[2] 'My dear Rab', 10 November 1952: Churchill papers, 2/181. While working on his war memoirs, Churchill told Denis Kelly: 'I had only four intimate conversations with my Father.' (Denis Kelly: in conversation with the author, 11 April 1987.)
[3] Cabinet Conclusions No. 95 of 1952, 'Secret', 11.30 a.m., 11 November 1952: Cabinet papers, 128/25.

the courts sentenced fewer offenders to long terms of imprisonment.'[1]

Corporal punishment had been abolished by the Labour Government in 1948. The suggestion before the Cabinet on November 20 was that a Royal Commission, or possibly a Departmental Committee, should be appointed to make a further enquiry into the question. Churchill was 'not attracted', he said, by that suggestion, telling his colleagues that he would prefer that the Government 'should hold themselves free to introduce legislation restoring corporal punishment if at any time it became clear that there was a sufficient body of public support for this course to make it possible to pass the necessary legislation through Parliament'. Corporal punishment, if it were reintroduced, said Churchill, 'should be available as a penalty for all crimes of violence or brutality; and he did not exclude the possibility that this penalty might be reintroduced on an experimental basis, for a period of not more than five years, at the end of which it could be seen whether there had been an appreciable decrease in the crimes for which it was made available'.

If a plebiscite could be held on this question, Churchill added, the majority of the people of this country might, he thought, be found 'to be in favour of reintroducing this penalty'.

It was finally decided to let Members of Parliament express their opinion by means of a free vote.[2]

At a final Cabinet that month, on November 25, the issue on which Churchill spoke was that of the American forces in Britain. The Secretary of State for Air, Lord De L'Isle and Dudley, was afraid, he said, that the creation of 'American communities in Britain' with their higher standard of living 'might cause criticism and discontent among the English communities in the neighbourhood'. Churchill did not belittle this fear, or discuss it, but he did urge his colleagues to realize that the presence of United States forces in the United Kingdom 'was an essential feature in the cold war' and that it was possible for that reason to defend 'the provision of reasonable amenities' for the American forces. Churchill added: 'Continuous effort should be made to preserve friendly relations between the United States forces in this

[1] Cabinet Conclusions No. 89 of 1952, 'Secret', 11 a.m., 23 October 1952: Cabinet papers, 128/25.

[2] Cabinet Conclusions No. 99 of 1952, 'Secret', 11.30 a.m., 20 November 1952: Cabinet papers, 128/25. The relevant Home Office file on the Cabinet's decision of 20 November 1952 has not been preserved. When, however, on 13 February 1953, Wing Commander Eric Bullen moved the reading of the second Criminal Justice (Amendment) Bill, seeking to reintroduce corporal punishment as a sentence available to the Courts, the Home Secretary, Sir David Maxwell Fyfe, after speaking against the Bill on behalf of the Government, announced that members on his side of the House would be given a free vote. The Bill was rejected. Corporal punishment as a disciplinary sanction in prisons, remand centres and Borstal institutions was abolished by the Criminal Justice Act 1967.

country and their English neighbours and he would be glad to hear
from the Secretary of State for Air what was being done for this purpose.'[1]

For those who had worked with Churchill in the Second World
War, and now saw him again after some lapse of time, the inexorable
effects of the passing of time were clear. Sir Ian Jacob, Military Assistant Secretary to the War Cabinet from 1940 to 1945 and now Deputy
Secretary to the Cabinet, later recalled:

I remember one occasion in 1952 when I was having lunch with Churchill
in the flat in which he then lived on an upper floor of No. 10. As we sat
down he heard a noise outside the window. He got up and looked out over
the courtyard behind the old Treasury building in Whitehall. In the corner
of this yard was a large heap of coke, and the noise was caused by a man
who was taking coke in a wheelbarrow from a lorry which was standing
outside the arched entrance to the courtyard and adding it to the pile. The
Prime Minister looked at this, and remarked that it would have been more
sensible to have brought the lorry into the courtyard and to have emptied it
directly on to the heap.

Ten years before he would have summoned a stenographer then and there
and would have sent a Minute on the subject to the Minister of Fuel and
Power (who quite probably was not the right person): 'Pray tell me why . . .'
The fact that he sat down again and went on with his lunch without doing
anything showed me that he was no longer the same man as he had been.[2]

On November 28 Evelyn Shuckburgh recorded in his diary the
most recent twist in the succession debate. 'PM has told Clarissa he
wants to give up,' Shuckburgh noted. 'She says he is looking for an
opportunity and Anthony must be gentle with him. Must let him go
to America. Today he begged Anthony to let him go "as privately as
possible". "Only one speech." AE is tempted. It might be the way
out. But Winston is worried that AE is so deep in foreign affairs and
not preparing.'[3]

On November 30 Churchill celebrated his seventy-eighth birthday.
'May your celebration be filled with joy,' President-elect Eisenhower
and inspired devotion to your country and mankind.'[4] That day,

[1] Cabinet Conclusions No. 100 of 1952, 'Secret', 11 a.m., 25 November 1952: Cabinet papers,
128/25.
[2] Sir Ian Jacob recollections: Sir John Wheeler-Bennett (editor), *Action This Day, Working
With Churchill*, London 1968, pages 187–8.
[3] Shuckburgh diary, 28 November 1952: *Descent to Suez*, page 62.
[4] 'Dear Winston', signed, 'as ever, Ike Eisenhower', Commodore Hotel, New York, 25 November 1952: Churchill papers, 2/217.

Colville took Churchill and his wife, together with Mary Churchill and Miss Portal, to lunch; a private celebration of the sort Churchill always liked, with a small group of people he knew well.

On 2 December 1952 Churchill summoned his doctor to Downing Street. The reason was not some sudden illness of his own, but the illness of Arthur Deakin, the Trade Union leader. Churchill wanted to know what could be done for him. Two other trade unionists, Tom O'Brien and Will Lawther, had told Churchill how worried they were. 'The PM's friendliness to the trade-union leaders is an obvious move,' Lord Moran noted in his diary, 'but their response to his advances is interesting. They know, when they dine with him at No. 10, that it will do them no good in the Party. But they cannot help liking him. He doesn't seem to them at all like other Tories. I remember that Ernie Bevin had a great affection for "The old man".'

During their talk that morning, Moran asked Churchill how he himself felt. 'Oh,' he replied 'as well as I shall ever be.' [1]

Churchill was certainly well enough on December 4 to take the Chair at a Cabinet meeting to which six Commonwealth Prime Ministers, and two Ministers of Finance, had been invited, on the eve of the Commonwealth Economic Conference.[2] It was for him a 'unique experience and privilege', Churchill said, 'to preside over a Cabinet meeting attended by so many Prime Ministers. . . .' They should be encouraged, he said, amid the 'many grave problems' confronting them, 'by the knowledge that their combined influence was capable of affecting the course of world events'.

It was Eden who gave the guests a survey of the world scene, but twice Churchill intervened with points of his own. The first time was when Eden was speaking of the importance of the formation of a European Defence Community, in order to avoid the need to admit the German army as a 'national army' in the forces of NATO. While he 'agreed that this should be our policy,' Churchill interjected, 'he would not be unduly disturbed if the present plans for a European Defence Community were not carried into effect. It had still to be shown that an international army could be an efficient instrument in spite of differences of language and weapons between the participating

[1] Moran diary, 2 December 1952: *The Struggle for Survival*, pages 394–5. Arthur Deakin, who was sixteen years younger than Churchill, died on 1 May 1955.

[2] The Prime Ministers were L. S. St Laurent (Canada), Sidney Holland (New Zealand), Dudley Senanayake (Ceylon), Robert Menzies (Australia), Khwaja Nazimuddin (Pakistan) and Sir Godfrey Huggins (Southern Rhodesia). The two Finance Ministers were N. C. Havenga (South Africa) and Sir Chintaman Deshmukh (India).

contingents.' He also doubted 'whether the soldier in the line would fight with the same ardour for an international institution as he would for his home and his country'.

Later, when the Finance Minister of India, Sir Chintaman Deshmukh, spoke of the importance of not extending the Korean War to China, Churchill intervened to say that he agreed 'that it would be a grave mistake to take any course which would widen the area of conflict in Korea. It was the considered policy of the United Kingdom Government that these operations should be confined within the frontiers of Korea itself.'[1]

Later that day, Churchill went to the House of Commons, to announce that, for financial reasons, expenditure on defence production would have to be curtailed. The debate was a Labour Opposition no-confidence motion on the Government's conduct of economic policy, the 'incompetence' of which the motion deplored. 'Not only have Her Majesty's Government been the victors in over 250 Divisions,' Churchill commented, 'but they have had throughout these Divisions a majority almost double what it is on paper. Is that incompetence?' And he went on to ask the House:

Was it due to incompetence that the business for last week was finished at the time originally proposed, or that the business for this week will be disposed of with equal precision?

On the contrary, our success, which has been the cause of so much anger, is due not only to the competence of the Ministers concerned but to the vigour and exertions of a united party.

Another of the charges in the no-confidence motion was that the Government's economic measures were not related 'to the needs of the nation'. Churchill told the House: 'On the contrary, we should never have faced the trouble and burden of this legislation if we were not convinced that not only were we redeeming our pledges—and who would have mocked us if we had not done so?—but that we were notably improving the conditions on which the fertility and prosperity of our trade and production depends.'

To continuous Labour interruptions, Churchill remarked: 'I am finishing in a minute: I will not keep hon. Members under such a vocal strain for too long. I do not want to make them so hoarse that they cannot even continue the debate.'

Churchill ended his speech with an expression of confidence in the Government's economic policy, and an attack on the Opposition for having been a disruptive force in debate after debate:

[1] Cabinet Conclusions No. 102 of 1952, 'Secret', 11.30 a.m., 4 December 1952: Cabinet papers, 128/25.

If we can show that a Government, even with a majority as moderate as our own, can in fact do several years' good and faithful work, we shall have rendered an historic service to Parliamentary government. We are much encouraged by what has happened so far and by the failure of the Opposition to mask their own internal feuds by uniting in hysterical and violent abuse of their opponents. Their conduct throughout this Parliament in our opinion has been reprehensible in a high degree. Far from moving a Motion of censure on Her Majesty's Government, they should shake and shiver in their shoes with shame.[1]

On December 7 Anthony Eden was at Chequers. Returning to London, he was asked by Evelyn Shuckburgh 'how he got on'. Shuckburgh noted in his diary:

He said to Winston that he must know something of his plans. PM made a solemn Winstonian speech to the effect that his intention was, when the time came, to hand over his powers and authority with the utmost smoothness and surety to Anthony. AE said, yes—but the point was when would that be? A whole minute of silence, then, 'Often I think there are things I could say, speeches I could make more easily if I were not Prime Minister.' Then another long silence. AE said the position regarding leadership in the House could not be maintained. Crookshank not competent. But the net result was no clear indication.[2]

At a meeting of the Defence Committee on December 11, there was discussion about the future of the Suez Canal Zone. 'The Americans should be made to understand,' Churchill told his colleagues, 'that we could not support indefinitely the burden of keeping 70,000 soldiers in the Canal Zone,' and he added: 'other countries must be made to share this burden.'

Churchill was concerned with a wider issue than Egypt or even the Middle East. 'The speed,' he said, 'with which operations would move in the next war had an effect upon the value of retaining a large and elaborate base in the Canal Zone.'[3]

In Cabinet on December 18, Churchill returned to his suggestion that an amnesty could soon be declared for wartime deserters. The Coronation was, for him, an obvious time to choose for the amnesty. He found 'great difficulty', he told his colleagues, 'in accepting the arguments against a general amnesty for deserters'. It was not in the national interest, he said, 'that these men should continue to live the lives of outcasts and outlaws. Nearly eight years had passed since the end of the war, and he could not accept the view that

[1] Speech of 4 December 1952: *Hansard*. The Opposition Motion of Censure was defeated by a majority of 24.
[2] Shuckburgh diary, 8 December 1952: *Descent to Suez*, page 66.
[3] Defence Committee No. 12 of 1952, 'Top Secret', 5.30 p.m., 11 December 1952: Cabinet papers, 131/12.

desertion should never be condoned. The national rejoicing at the time of the Coronation would provide a suitable occasion for an act of mercy towards these men.'

Several Ministers opposed Churchill's argument, the Service Ministers, supported by some others, expressing 'the firm conviction that an amnesty for deserters would be taken as implying that desertion in war was no longer regarded as the most serious of military crimes, and would lead to increased desertion from the Armed Forces at a time when very large numbers of men were serving overseas in circumstances which imposed the most disagreeable duties upon them'. The small number of deserters involved, not more than 2,000, did not 'justify the risk to the genuine discipline of the Forces'.

The Ministers who put forward this view were clearly, as the subsequent discussion showed, in a minority. Summing up the discussion, Churchill noted that 'the balance of the opinion in the Cabinet seemed to be in favour of recommending that Her Majesty should grant some form of amnesty for men who had deserted from the Armed Forces in the war as a special act of clemency in the year of her Coronation'. He would, he said, 'take steps to ascertain informally' whether the Queen would wish such an act of clemency 'to be associated directly with her Coronation'.[1]

Four days later, on December 22, the Cabinet was told of an attempt by Saudi Arabia to extend its influence into the territories of the Trucial Sheikhdoms in the Persian Gulf. These Sheikhdoms, including Oman and Dubai, were traditionally a part of the British sphere of Middle Eastern influence. A cruiser, a frigate, twelve Royal Air Force armoured cars and one squadron of Vampires could be concentrated in the area in 'about a month', the Cabinet were told. Churchill was not at all satisfied with this. It was 'clear', he said, 'that as an immediate step there should be some concentration of British forces in the area. He hoped that it would be possible to send in stronger forces than those suggested in the discussion. At the same time measures should be put in hand to build up the local levies, and the Colonial Secretary should examine the suggestion that the Aden Levies should

---

[1] Cabinet Conclusions No. 106 of 1952, 'Secret', 11.30 a.m., 18 December 1952: Cabinet papers, 128/25. The three Service Ministers were J. P. L. Thomas (First Lord of the Admiralty), Lord De L'Isle and Dudley (Secretary of State for Air), and Anthony Head (Secretary of State for War). The Minister of Labour and National Service was Sir Walter Monckton. On 23 February 1953 Churchill told the House of Commons: 'Her Majesty's Government have decided that ... as a special measure which will not be regarded as a precedent for the future, there will be no further prosecutions of members of the Armed Forces who deserted from the Services between 3rd September, 1939, and 15th August, 1945.' Churchill added: 'any men who are awaiting trial or serving sentences for desertion during the 1939–45 war will be released from custody.'

also be used.' This concentration of forces, Churchill added, should take place 'as unobtrusively as possible'.[1]

Two quarrels were patched up in the weeks before Christmas 1952, both of which had been a cause of distress to Churchill. The first was with Robert Boothby, his Parliamentary Private Secretary from 1925 to 1929, whose indiscretion in 1939 in supporting economic restitution to refugee Czechs, to one of whom he was in debt, had led to his Ministerial eclipse. Boothby had long felt that Churchill could have done more then to help him; but it had been a matter of Parliamentary and not political censure. In the second week of December, Churchill invited Boothby to dine at Chartwell. It was the first time in nearly fifteen years that they had been together in close friendship. Churchill had already supported Boothby's nomination as one of the British delegates to the European Assembly at Strasbourg. All was now reconciled. On December 14 Boothby wrote to the man he had once so fervently admired and followed:

Dear Prime Minister,

I feel impelled to write you a line to say what a very great privilege and pleasure it was for me to dine once again at Chartwell in your company. It took me back to the old care-free days when I was your Parliamentary Private Secretary, and there seemed to be no cloud on the horizon; and on to the fateful days when the cloud was no bigger than a man's hand, and there was still time to save the sum of things.

It was in November 1934 that you invited me to be one of the six signatories of the amendment to the Address which declared that 'the strength of our national defences, and especially of our air defences, is no longer adequate to secure the peace, safety and freedom of Your Majesty's faithful subjects', and to speak in the subsequent debate. I shall be proud of that as long as I live. They are all flinging mud at old Baldwin now, but in those days you were almost alone in facing the facts and telling the truth. The battle was lost, and with it our civilisation; but it is good to have taken part in it on the right side, and under your leadership.

I do hope I am not now the cause of any embarrassment to you. I have had a long and hard struggle for survival, but I see the light at the end of the tunnel; and, thanks to you, I have been able to do some work at Strasbourg which may one day bear fruit. I have no grievances.

All good wishes for Christmas and the New Year

from Yours Ever

Bob [2]

---

[1] Cabinet Conclusions No. 107 of 1952, 'Secret', 4 p.m., 22 December 1952: Cabinet papers, 128/25.

[2] 'Dear Prime Minister', 'Personal', 14 December 1952: Churchill papers, 2/181.

The second quarrel patched up that December was the one which had broken out between Churchill and his son at the time of the Scarborough Conference two months earlier. On December 13 Randolph wrote to his father about the next volume of his father's post-war speeches, which, volume by volume, Randolph had been editing.[1] Randolph now set out for his father the proposed titles for the new book, as suggested by the publishers, Cassell. These included 'Stemming the Tide', 'Fight for Survival', 'Against the Stream', and 'Shouldering the Burden'.

'None of them are very inspiring,' Randolph added, 'but I thought the last the best. Perhaps you can suggest something better?'[2]

On the following day Randolph wrote again, in his own hand:

My dearest Papa,

Further to my letter of yesterday I have stumbled upon what I believe to be a much better title for the book:

'Uphill All The Way'

It is a phrase from the first broadcast you made after the last Election. It admirably describes the task of the nation & of HMG.

The sentence which could be printed on the fly-leaf is as follows:—

'. . . the train has to be started again on the right line, which, I am telling you beforehand—please remember it—*is uphill all the way*.'

Your loving son

Randolph[3]

Churchill replied at once, all hint of quarrel gone:

Dearest Randolph,

Thank you for your letters of December 13 and 14. I rather think 'Stemming the Tide' is the best, but 'Shouldering the Burden' is a good second. Let us have a word about it when we meet at the children's party on Friday.

'Uphill all the way' is a cry of pain.

Your loving Father,

WSC[4]

In the week before Christmas, the reconciliation between father and son was complete, marked by a substantial cash gift. 'My dearest Papa,' Randolph wrote on December 21, 'your princely Christmas present fills me with gratitude which I scarcely know how to express.

---

[1] *The Sinews of Peace*, published on 19 August 1948; *Europe Unite*, published on 3 February 1950 and *In the Balance*, published on 18 October 1951.

[2] 'My dearest Papa', signed 'Your loving son, Randolph', 13 December 1952: Churchill papers, 1/51.

[3] 'My dearest Papa', 14 December 1952: Churchill papers, 1/51.

[4] 'Dearest Randolph', 15 December 1952: Churchill papers, 1/51. The title eventually chosen was *Stemming the Tide*, published on 25 June 1953. There was one further volume, also edited by Randolph Churchill, *The Unwritten Alliance, Speeches 1953 to 1959*, published on 27 April 1961.

It is immensely welcome not only on material grounds but as a renewed expression of your affection. Thank you from the bottom of my heart. Your loving son, Randolph.'[1] When, two months later, Randolph Churchill sent his father one of the first copies of his own first book, *The Story of the Coronation*, Churchill replied at once by telegram: 'Thank you so much dear Randolph for sending me a copy of your most interesting and timely book. I hope it will have a great success.'[2]

Christmas 1952 was celebrated by the Churchill family at Chequers; on Boxing Day there was a family expedition to Kempton Park races.[3] At luncheon that day, Randolph and his son, Duncan Sandys and his two daughters, and Mary Soames, her two sons and her daughter, were Churchill's guests, together with his former principal secretary, Mrs Hill, and her son Richard.[4]

On December 27 Churchill received a handwritten letter from the Queen, who was then at Sandringham, thanking him for the 'beautifully bound' copy of Volume 4 of the war memoirs. She also congratulated him on the success of his horse Pol Roger at Kempton Park on the previous day, and hoped that after his visit to the United States he would have a 'peaceful time in the sun' in Jamaica. The Queen ended her letter with best wishes for the New Year, 'which I trust will see us surmount many of our difficulties successfully'.[5]

[1] 'My dearest Papa', 21 December 1952: Churchill papers, 1/51. Marked, on Churchill's instruction, 'Mrs Churchill to see' and 'Seen, CSC'.

[2] Telegram despatched 22 February 1953: Churchill papers, 1/51.

[3] 'Christmas Programme', Chequers Engagement Lists, 1952: Churchill papers.

[4] 'Meals Lists', 1952: Churchill papers. Mrs Hill had joined Churchill's staff as his first residential secretary in 1936. In 1986 Richard Hill succeeded to a baronetcy, becoming 10th Baronet. The 1st Baronet, Sir Hugh Hill, MP for Derry, was created a Baronet in 1779.

[5] 'My dear Prime Minister', 27 December 1952: Squerryes Lodge Archive.

42

Return to the United States

FROM the moment of Eisenhower's election as President, Churchill was determined to visit him in the United States. This visit, however, even when described by Churchill primarily as a holiday, met with an objection from his doctor, who wrote from his consulting rooms in Harley Street on 13 December 1952:

I gathered yesterday that there were plans for a journey at the end of the month. I think a holiday is very much indicated. What I am not happy about is the long flight. It is true that just as warm water reduces the risk of bathing, so a pressurized cabin does mitigate the effects of flying. Nevertheless in our present state of knowledge of the relations between the circulation in the superficial vessels under the skin and the deep circulation, we just don't know the precise risk. In the event of any slight circulatory weakness drugs can be given which, if they are given at once, help considerably. One could use these in the air but because of the above-mentioned uncertainty one would be happier using them on the ground.

'Is it at all possible,' Lord Moran added, 'to arrange a holiday which avoids these uncertainties?'[1]

'Thank you very much for your letter,' Churchill replied. 'I think I will take a chance, as the visit is not official in any way.'[2] He travelled, however, by sea.

On the morning of December 30, during a Cabinet discussion on Egypt, Churchill gave his Cabinet colleagues an account of what he hoped, as far as Egypt was concerned, to achieve during his American visit. He would, he said, 'point out to General Eisenhower that, although we had no intention of evacuating Egypt under duress, it was beyond our strength to maintain permanently a force of 70,000 men in the Canal Zone. He would press for some effective assistance from the United States in this area.'

On another aspect of the Government's Egyptian policy, Churchill told his colleagues 'that he had been surprised to learn that it was

---

[1] 'My dear Prime Minister', 13 December 1952: Churchill papers, 1/54.
[2] 'My dear Charles', 29 December 1952: Churchill papers, 1/54.

proposed to allow the Egyptians to draw £10 million of their blocked sterling balances at the beginning of 1953. He had hoped that, as had been done twelve months previously, this release would be delayed and held as a useful card in negotiations over the Sudan and over defence. He had certainly expected that this would be fully discussed in Cabinet before any decision was made.'

Replying to this criticism, R. A. Butler pointed out that the release of sterling balances to Egypt was controlled by the Sterling Releases Agreement made with the Egyptian Government by the Labour Government in July 1951. Under this Agreement £5 million could be released whenever Egypt's free sterling holdings totalled less than £45 million. These holdings were now down to a figure of £6 million.

Butler went on to say that a 'refusal to honour the Agreement or to allow any drawings from sterling balances would shake world confidence in sterling and was incompatible with the position of the United Kingdom as the banker for the sterling area'. It was, moreover, 'of importance to United Kingdom trade that the economy of Egypt, which was now in a perilous condition, should receive some support and, even though Egypt would pay for United Kingdom imports with these sterling balances, that was better than the cessation of all trade'. The matter had not been brought to Cabinet, Butler explained, 'since it had been regarded by both the Treasury and the Foreign Office as the routine working of a contractual arrangement'.

Churchill was not at all satisfied with this answer, telling his colleagues 'that he found it difficult to regard this as a routine matter. The releases already made had not improved the attitude of the Egyptian Government towards the United Kingdom; and, while it was right that international agreements should be kept, it was possible to make exceptions where the other party to an agreement had repudiated a treaty as Egypt had done.'

Churchill's protest was to no avail, the Cabinet deciding that £10 million of Egypt's blocked sterling balances would be released in January 1953 'in accordance with the Sterling Releases Agreement of July 1951'.[1]

At 7.30 that evening, Churchill, his wife, his daughter Mary and her husband, and Jock Colville, left Waterloo Station by boat train for Southampton. 'We dined on the train,' Colville noted in his diary, 'and talked of many things, from the War of 1812 to the future of Pakistan.'[2] At 9.45 that night Churchill and his travel companions went on board the *Queen Mary*, which sailed at 10.15 on the following

---

[1] Cabinet Conclusions No. 108 of 1952, 'Secret', 11.30 a.m., 30 December 1952: Cabinet papers, 128/25.
[2] Colville diary, 30 December 1952: *The Fringes of Power*, page 657.

morning. 'I worked with the PM for most of the morning,' Colville noted. That evening the newly appointed Ambassador to Washington, Sir Roger Makins, was Churchill's guest at dinner. Colville noted, of the dinner conversation:

The PM said he thought the recent treason trials in Prague, with so many Jews among the condemned, indicated that the Communists were looking towards the Arab States, Persia and North Africa and were deliberately antagonising Israel. He also said he would preach to Eisenhower the vital importance of a common Anglo-American front 'from Korea to Kikuyu and from Kikuyu to Calais'.[1]

Churchill spent New Year's Day 1953 on board the *Queen Mary* sailing westward. That evening, Colville noted in his diary, he said that if Colville lived his normal span 'I should assuredly see Eastern Europe free of Communism'.[2] He also told Colville that 'Russia feared our friendship more than our enmity'. Recalling the Anglo-American strategic dispute of 1945, Churchill told his Private Secretary that, 'owing to Eisenhower winning the Presidency he must cut much out of Volume VI of his War History and could not tell the story of how the United States gave way, to please Russia, vast tracts of Europe they had occupied and how suspicious they were of his pleas for caution'. Churchill added:

The British General Election in June 1945 had occupied so much of his attention which should have been directed to stemming this fatal tide. If FDR had lived, and had been in good health, he would have seen the red light in time to check the American policy: Truman, after all, had only been a novice, bewildered by the march of events and by responsibilities which he had never expected.[3]

On the evening of January 2, alone with Churchill in the Verandah Grill, Colville put to him some thirty questions which he might be asked at the press conference which was being arranged on arrival in New York. 'He scintillated in his replies,' noted Colville, who listed three of them:

Qn: What are your views, Mr Churchill, on the present stalemate in Korea?
Ans: Better a stalemate than a checkmate.
Qn: How do you justify such great expenditure on the Coronation of your Queen, when England is in such financial straits?
Ans: Everybody likes to wear a flower when he goes to see his girl.

---

[1] Colville diary, 31 December 1952: *The Fringes of Power*, pages 657–8.
[2] Colville died in 1987, when the States of Eastern Europe were still communist, though in varying degrees of change.
[3] Colville diary, 1 January 1953: *The Fringes of Power*, page 658.

Qn: Is not British policy in Persia throwing Persia into the hands of the Communists?

Ans: If Britain and America refuse to be disunited, no ill can come.

'And there were many others as good or better,' Colville added. 'I wished so much I had had a microphone.'[1]

At 8.15 on the morning of January 5 the *Queen Mary* docked in New York. 'Pandemonium let loose,' noted Colville, 'Mr Baruch, high dignitaries, low officials, Embassy people, pressmen swarmed on board.' The expected press conference for which Churchill had prepared during the voyage was held in the Verandah Grill. Churchill answered the questions well, Colville noted, 'but perhaps less well than the night before last'.

From the *Queen Mary*, Churchill and his wife went to Bernard Baruch's apartment, where Churchill had stayed the year before. At five o'clock that afternoon General Eisenhower arrived. There were still fifteen days to go before he became President. 'Well, the one thing I have so far learnt in this damned game of yours,' he told Churchill, 'is that you have just got to have a sense of humour.'

Churchill and Eisenhower spent two hours alone together, before being the guests at a small dinner party given for them by Baruch, in his apartment. Sarah Churchill was also present, and Colville, who noted the evening's conversation in his diary:

Winston said that a protoplasm was sexless. Then it divided into two sexes which, in due course, united again in a different way to their common benefit and gratification. This should also be the story of England and America.

Ike talked about Cleopatra's Needle (how the Egyptians raised it), the charm of the Queen, the intelligence of the Duke of Edinburgh, and a few war-time indiscretions.

After dinner I listened to the PM and the President elect talking: Winston made one or two profound observations. For instance, 'I think you and I are agreed that it is not only important to discover the truth but to know how to present the truth'; and (apropos of the recent treason trials in Czechoslovakia) 'That they should think it good propaganda is what shows the absolutely unbridgeable gulf between us.'

To an after-dinner plea by Baruch for an acceleration of the process of European unity, Churchill commented: 'It may be better to bear an agonising period of unsatisfactory time. You may kill yourself in getting strong enough.'[2]

On January 6 Churchill had a long talk with John Foster Dulles and the new American Ambassador to London, Winthrop Aldrich.

---

[1] Colville diary, 2 January 1953: *The Fringes of Power*, page 658.
[2] Colville diary, 5 January 1953: *The Fringes of Power*, pages 659–60.

Churchill's advice to the new administration was to do nothing 'for some four months', and he quoted to them a favourite proverb, 'The trees do not grow up to the sky.' The Americans, said Churchill, should let events in many places, Korea, Persia and Egypt for example, take their course, and then 'see where we found ourselves'.[1]

Churchill's visit was receiving favourable coverage in the American Press. On January 7 *The Times* reported, from its Washington correspondent: 'It was generally remarked that he looked younger and in better health and was more communicative than on his last trip a year ago.'[2] That day, Churchill visited his mother's birthplace, at 426 Henry Street, Brooklyn, the house on which his daughter Sarah had unveiled a plaque eight months earlier.

Churchill had a second meeting with Eisenhower on January 7, which he reported in a telegram to Eden and Butler on the following day:

Eisenhower opened yesterday with much vigour about direct contacts with Stalin. I was quite welcome to go myself if I thought fit at any time. He thought of making it plain in his inauguration speech that he would go to, say, Stockholm to meet him, if Stalin were willing. Evidently he did not want Britain. 'That would involve asking France and Italy.' I said would he not be wiser to keep to generalities in his inauguration speech and wait till he could survey the whole scene at leisure, and have all official information, before taking plunges. There was no battle going on, and as a General he could afford to wait for full reconnaissance reports. This applied to everything. The election was over; he had four years certain power. Why be in too great a hurry?

He seemed much impressed by this line of argument, but I do not know what he will do. He and others around him are still in their electioneering mood and thinking in headlines and pronouncements. To him and the others I have urged, 'take a few months to get into a calmer atmosphere and learn the facts'. They are not kept informed by State Department. Neither Eisenhower nor Dulles had seen the American message about Persia. Both were steadied by its evident complexity and care. Baruch, who has a good deal of influence, talks in the same strain to them.

Churchill's telegram continued:

Dulles promised me no action would be taken in Korea without consulting, or at least telling, us beforehand. He spoke of 'the fall' as the time when they might make a considerable concerted effort to end the stalemate. Dulles will come over and have full talks with us about all these plans, for which I promised careful unprejudiced consideration.[3]

---

[1] Colville diary, 6 January 1953: *The Fringes of Power*, page 660.

[2] Despatch of 6 January 1953: *The Times*, 7 January 1953.

[3] Washington telegram No. 34, paragraphs 1 and 2, 'Immediate', 'Top Secret', 8 January 1953: Premier papers, 11/422.

Two aspects of Churchill's discussion with Eisenhower were later reported by Colville to Evelyn Shuckburgh, who noted in his diary:

Ike asked if Winston saw any objection to his meeting Stalin alone. Winston said, 'I would have objected strongly during the war when our contribution in forces was about equal. Now I don't mind. But don't be in a hurry. Get your reconnaissance in first.' Winston seems to have been unfavourably impressed with the brashness and impatience of the Republican leaders.

According to Jock, he spoke once of his own plans, only to say, 'I think Anthony should have it, but I have not decided when.' [1]

On the evening of January 7 Churchill dined with Bernard Baruch to meet Governor Dewey. Later they were joined by Dulles. In his telegram to Eden and Butler, Churchill gave an account of the discussion:

Dewey proposed a scheme for a Pacific Treaty between all Pacific powers including the Philippines, Formosa, and the like, excluding (repeat excluding) Great Britain. I said I would denounce such a plan scathingly. Dulles then gave a long account of the negotiations leading up to the Anzus Treaty, and how the Labour Government had made no objection to it at all. I explained our point of view. Dewey, who is thoroughly friendly, then said that if I objected so strongly, he would let his baby, i.e. the Pacific Treaty, die. In fact I could consider it dead. On the spur of the moment he said that an alternative plan might be for the United Kingdom and the United States to make a joint declaration (comparable to our guarantee to Poland in 1939) that if Communist China attempted to occupy Indo-China, Burma or any other countries in the Pacific Area, we and the Americans would declare war.

'I tell you all this,' Churchill added, 'to show you the rough weather that may well lie ahead in dealing with the Republican Party who have been twenty years out of office; and I feel very sure we should not expect early favourable results. Much patience will be needed.' [2]

One of those present at the dinner, Jock Colville, also noted that Dulles had declared, without prevarication, that he thought it would be 'most unfortunate for Churchill to return to Washington in February'. Then, Colville wrote:

He explained that the American public thought W could cast a spell on all American statesmen and that if he were directly associated with the economic talks, the fears of the people and of Congress would be aroused to such an extent that the success of the talks would be endangered.

W took this very reasonable statement ill, but Christopher and I both took pains to assure Dulles afterwards that we thought he was absolutely right.

[1] Shuckburgh diary, 16 January 1953: *Descent to Suez*, page 74.
[2] Washington telegram No. 34, paragraph 3 and 4, 'Immediate', 'Top Secret', 8 January 1953: Premier papers, 11/422.

Irritated by this, W let fly at Dewey after dinner and worked himself into a fury over certain Pacific Ocean questions. Christopher and I again applied soft soap subsequently. We told Dewey that a sharp debate was the PM's idea of a pleasant evening and assured him that he would only have spoken thus to a man whom he trusted and looked upon as a friend.

But, alas, this was not so. W was really worked up and, as he went to bed, said some very harsh things about the Republican party in general and Dulles in particular, which Christopher and I thought both unjust and dangerous. He said he would have no more to do with Dulles whose 'great slab of a face' he disliked and distrusted.[1]

Churchill's New York visit was at an end. On the morning of January 8 he flew in the President's aircraft to Washington, where he stayed at the British Embassy. That afternoon he called on Truman at the White House, and in the evening was Truman's host at a dinner at the British Embassy. Sir Roger Makins, who was present, later recalled: 'I well remember the discussion between WSC and Truman about how they would be received at the gates of heaven after having authorised the dropping of the atomic bomb. They faced this occasion with considerable sangfroid, WSC commenting, "I think we are entitled to assume that the Almighty will apply the principles of the English Common Law."' Makins added: 'The PM was in rollicking form and the dinner was a huge success.'[2]

Jock Colville, who was also present, recorded in his diary some of the dinner conversation, once Churchill and Truman 'decided to hold the table':

There was some talk about Stalin. Truman recalled how at Potsdam he had discovered the vodka Stalin drank for toasts was really weak white wine, and how when WSC had said the Pope would dislike something, Stalin had answered 'How many divisions has the Pope?' W said he remembered replying that the fact they could not be measured in military terms did not mean they did not exist.

After dinner Truman played the piano. Nobody would listen because they were all busy with post-mortems on a diatribe in favour of Zionism and against Egypt which W had delivered at dinner (to the disagreement of practically all the Americans present, though they admitted that the large Jewish vote would prevent them disagreeing publicly). However, on W's instructions, I gathered all to the piano and we had a quarter of an hour's presidential piano playing before Truman left.

The departure of the President, Colville noted, led to no gap in the discussion:

---

[1] Colville diary, 7 January 1953: *The Fringes of Power*, pages 661–2.
[2] Lord Sherfield recollections: letter to the author, 19 June 1967.

When he had gone, the political wrangle started again, this time between W (unsupported) and Dean Acheson (supported by Harriman, Bedell Smith and Matthews).[1] The main bones of contention were the European Defence Community, which the PM persists in describing as 'a sludgy amalgam' infinitely less effective than a Grand Alliance of national armies, and the situation in Egypt where Acheson and Co. have far greater hopes of General Neguib (our last hope, they say) than has W.[2]

The Americans, apart from Truman and Marshall, stayed till 1.00 a.m. I had an uneasy feeling that the PM's remarks—about Israel, the EDC and Egypt—though made to the members of an outgoing administration, had better have been left unsaid in the presence of the three, Bradley, Bedell Smith and Matthews, who are staying on with Ike and the Republicans.[3]

'I have had a dreadful flurry of business in New York and Washington,' Churchill wrote two days later to Lord Cherwell, 'both with Republicans and Democrats,' and he added: 'There are lots of difficulties ahead.'[4]

On the morning of January 9 Churchill flew from Washington to Jamaica, for the holiday leg of his transatlantic journey. The flight was so rough that both Colville and Christopher Soames were worried about the effect of the bumps on Churchill. 'However,' noted Colville, 'he ate a huge steak for lunch and had his usual brandy and cigar, so I concluded he must be looking worse than he felt.'

On reaching Jamaica, Churchill drove to a house near Ocho Rios where he was to stay. Its name was Prospect, and it had been lent to him by Sir Harold Mitchell, a former Vice-Chairman of the Conservative Party. 'Now I am resting,' Churchill wrote to Lord Cherwell on January 10, 'in this pleasant but rather warm and today cloudy Island.'

Much on Churchill's mind during his Jamaican visit was a topic on which he was writing in the final volume of his war memoirs, the moment at which he had learned, in 1945, of the first successful

---

[1] Dean Acheson was the outgoing Secretary of State. 'Doc' Matthews was a senior State Department official. General Bedell Smith, who had been Eisenhower's Chief of Staff in 1944 and 1945, was, like Matthews, an influential figure in the State Department. Averell Harriman was a leading Democrat and Truman supporter. General Bradley was Chairman of the Joint Chiefs of Staff.

[2] One of the British officials present during these discussions, Denis Rickett, later recalled that Churchill 'had no enthusiasm' for the European Defence Community. 'Acheson in particular,' he added, 'was disappointed and felt confirmed in the view he had expressed a year before that the Churchill Government were "men of yesterday not of the future".' (Sir Denis Rickett recollections: letter to the author, 18 July 1987.)

[3] Colville diary, 8 January 1953: *The Fringes of Power*, pages 663–4.

[4] 'My dear Prof', 10 January 1953: Churchill papers, 4/379.

American test of the atomic bomb, in New Mexico. As he examined his archival material, he realized that the Americans had failed to give him any prior information about the imminence of the test. This, he felt, had inadvertent but serious political repercussions. As he wrote to Cherwell, who had been his principal adviser then on the atomic bomb, and was helping him with his narrative now by sending him a note of the events leading up to the New Mexico test:

Can you let me have a record of the progress made in the last three or six months before the experiment in the Mexican Desert? What did the Americans tell us? I do not recollect that the Cabinet or the Defence Committee were ever informed that matters were so imminent.

You have added 'British consent to the use of the weapon had been given on July 4.' When was this decided by the Cabinet? What was the actual detailed procedure by which this decision was taken? I am not making a case about this in any critical sense, but I really must know the details.

Had I known that the Tube Alloys were progressing so fast it would have affected my judgment about the date of the General Election.

'Please consult Norman Brook,' Churchill added, 'and let me have the best information you can awaiting me on my return. We will have a talk about it then.' [1]

On Sunday January 11 Lord Beaverbrook was Churchill's guest at luncheon and, as Colville noted, 'spoke very disparagingly of Anthony Eden'. That evening Churchill drove for drinks to another house on the Island, Roaring River, the Jamaican home of Lord Brownlow. 'The PM,' noted Colville, 'who last night said he would give £10,000 to be back at Chartwell, is cheering up a bit.' [2]

At dinner *en famille* at Prospect on the following night, Churchill said, of Eisenhower, that he was 'a real man of limited stature'. That, Colville noted, 'about sums the new President up'. [3]

Churchill worked at his war memoirs, correcting on January 13 the last three chapters of the final volume, which he gave to Colville to take back to England on the following day. Churchill and his wife remained in Jamaica. It was in Jamaica that Churchill learned of the death, on January 13, of his friend and former Private Secretary, Sir Edward Marsh, who had joined him at the Colonial Office in 1905, and remained at his side in every Cabinet post he held for the next twenty-five years. 'All his long life was serene,' Churchill wrote in

---

[1] 'My dear Prof', 'Secret', 10 January 1953: Churchill papers, 4/379.
[2] Colville diary, 11 January 1953: *The Fringes of Power*, page 664.
[3] Colville diary, 12 January 1953: *The Fringes of Power*, pages 664–5.

tribute, 'and he left that world I trust without a pang and I am sure without a fear.'[1]

On 19 January 1953, while Churchill was still in Jamaica, Evelyn Shuckburgh found Eden 'very depressed this evening. He doesn't think the Old Man will ever go.'[2] Ten days later, Churchill returned by air to London. Eden immediately went to see him. They quarrelled at once, about the policy to be pursued towards Egypt. Speaking of appeasement, Churchill told Eden bitterly that he never knew 'that Munich was situated on the Nile'.[3]

On January 30 Churchill spoke in the Jerusalem Chamber at Westminster Abbey, in support of an appeal to raise a million pounds from a million people, for the Abbey's restoration. 'We have one gift already,' he said, 'the Queen is our first subscriber.' The monuments and the stonework of centuries, Churchill pointed out, were 'falling into decay'. The 'soot of London' had to be cleaned away to prevent the stones from crumbling. 'Our generation,' he warned, 'would indeed be held to shame by those who come after us if we failed to preserve this noble inheritance.'[4]

Having spoken in the Jerusalem Chamber, Churchill returned to 10 Downing Street for a discussion about Egypt and the Sudan. Six Cabinet Ministers were present: Eden, Alexander, Lyttelton, Crookshank, Swinton and Macmillan.[5] Churchill told his colleagues:

... he had been reviewing the general state of our relations with the new Egyptian Government and he was strongly of the opinion that we should now show greater firmness in all our negotiations with them. When

[1] Undated note, on 10 Downing Street notepaper, signed 'Winston S. Churchill': Churchill papers, 2/204. Published as 'Mr Churchill's tribute', *The Times*, 14 January 1953.

[2] Shuckburgh diary, 19 January 1953: *Descent to Suez*, page 74.

[3] As reported by Jock Colville to Evelyn Shuckburgh, Shuckburgh diary, 29 January 1953: *Descent to Suez*, page 75.

[4] Speech of 30 January 1953: *The Times*, 31 January 1953, reprinted in Randolph S. Churchill (editor), *The Unwritten Alliance, Speeches 1953 to 1959 by Winston S. Churchill*, London 1961, pages 1–2. Recording: BBC Written Archives Centre, Library No. 18738. Michael Mayne, Dean of Westminster, writes: 'The Senior Chorister presented the first pound from Her Majesty The Queen and we have Sir Winston's pound note, in the Library here, framed and in a sealed envelope.' The Dean adds: 'Within a few days of the launching of the Appeal there was the east coast flood disaster and the Lord Mayor of London set up an immediate relief fund. This put a damper on the Abbey Appeal, and it was decided that the Appeal activities should be suspended in favour of the Lord Mayor's Appeal. In April the Abbey Appeal was revived.' (Dean of Westminster: letter to the author, 17 November 1986.) In November 1953 Churchill made a further appeal from 10 Downing Street. The target was reached in May 1954.

[5] Respectively Secretary of State of Foreign Affairs, Minister of Defence, Secretary of State for the Colonies, Lord Privy Seal, Secretary of State for Commonwealth Relations, and Minister of Housing and Local Government.

General Neguib had first come to power it had seemed right to adopt a more conciliatory attitude, and even to offer some concessions, in the hope of strengthening his position. Recently, however, his public utterances had become increasingly hostile towards this country; and it was now evident that he was seeking to retain his political influence by pandering to those sections of Egyptian opinion which demanded the early and unconditional evacuation of British troops from Egypt.

Churchill then set out his view of what should be done:

The time had come to make it clear that we were not prepared to make concessions in order to appease these sections of the Egyptian public.

As regards the Sudan, we should not lightly cast away all the benefits which British administration had conferred on the Sudanese people; nor should we allow the Sudanese to be trapped by Egyptian promises which were unlikely to be fulfilled. We should take our stand on the argument that it should be left to a properly elected Sudanese Parliament to decide how far the Sudanese people still required the safeguards provided by the special powers of the Governor-General and the continued assistance of British officials.

If the Egyptians were 'unwilling to accept this solution', Churchill added, 'negotiations for an Anglo-Egyptian agreement could be broken off: this was as good a ground as any on which to break off the talks'.

Speaking of the defence negotiations, Churchill told his colleagues, 'we should take our stand on the 1936 Treaty and keep our troops in the Canal Zone until 1956. If an attempt were made to dislodge us by force we could doubtless give a good account of ourselves. And if there were widespread disorders in Egypt, we could no doubt do something to protect the lives of the British communities in Cairo and Alexandria.'[1]

On the following day, January 31, Churchill discussed with Eden, Alexander, Crookshank and Macmillan what the Government should do to reinforce the British troops in Khartoum if the negotiations with Egypt broke down. If there were to be a 'show of force', Churchill said, 'we should run less risk of trouble if we were able to make a demonstration of overwhelming strength; and for that reason he would prefer that two battalions rather than one should in those circumstances be sent to Khartoum, in addition to the squadron of aircraft which had been suggested. He believed that, apart from steadying the situation in the Sudan, a demonstration of that kind might have a salutary effect on General Neguib.'[2]

*   *   *

[1] 'Secret', 'Minutes of a Meeting held at 10 Downing Street, SW1', 4.15 p.m., 30 January 1953: Cabinet papers, 130/83.

[2] 'Secret', Minutes of a Meeting held at 10 Downing Street, SW1', 12.30 p.m., 31 January 1953: Cabinet papers, 130/83.

In the weeks leading up to the Coronation, Churchill found himself in dispute with Gwilym Lloyd George, the Minister of Food, who wished to continue with chocolate and sweet rationing.[1] Churchill wanted the rationing abolished before the crowds gathered in London for the Coronation, from all over Britain and abroad. Lloyd George warned, however, that if the ration were abolished, it might lead to a chaotic shortage of sugar. Churchill was emphatic, and on February 5 the ration was abolished. Within six months, there was a glut of sugar.

For Churchill, and for his family, the Coronation was to be particularly memorable. 'I am glad indeed,' he wrote to Lord Portal on February 2, 'that Winston is to be your Page at the Coronation and am delighted that you should have invited him. Randolph is to be a Gold Staff Officer so that, thanks to you, there will be three generations of my family in the Abbey.'[2]

Churchill's return to London coincided with a request from the Liberal Party for the introduction of proportional representation. Speaking to his Cabinet colleagues on February 3, Churchill said that, in his view, 'there might be a case at some later stage' for considering the introduction of proportional representation in the larger cities. But the experiences of other countries, he pointed out, suggested that proportional representation 'increased the difficulties of securing stable government'. The present time, he added, 'was certainly not a favourable moment for experiments in electoral reform'.

The Cabinet agreed; Churchill would 'give no encouragement', it noted, to Liberal Party proposals for 'experiments in electoral reform'.[3]

Also at this Cabinet, the text had been approved of the final details of a proposed Anglo-Egyptian Agreement on the Sudan. In essence, Britain was to relinquish the control which she had exercised in diminishing degree since Kitchener's victories over the Mahdi in 1898; victories in which Churchill had participated as a cavalry officer, and about which he had written in 1899 in his first substantial book,

[1] Started on 26 July 1942, the rationing of chocolate and sweets had been suspended in April 1949 but reintroduced in August 1949. Sugar rationing had been abolished on 5 October 1952. Eggs were decontrolled on 26 March 1953. Cheese, butter and margarine rationing did not end until 8 May 1954, meat rationing not until 3 July 1954. Gwilym Lloyd George was the second son of David Lloyd George; in 1957 he was created Viscount Tenby.

[2] 'My dear Peter', 'Confidential', 2 February 1953: Churchill papers, 2/195.

[3] Cabinet Conclusions No. 6 of 1953, 'Secret', 11 a.m., 3 February 1953: Cabinet papers, 128/26.

The River War. Despite Eden's strong endorsement of the agreement, Churchill opposed it, telling his Cabinet colleagues at an early evening Cabinet on February 11 that he doubted whether Eden's proposals 'would command a sufficient measure of support in the Conservative Party'. Churchill added:

He feared that the proposed Agreement would be represented as an ignominious surrender of our responsibilities in the Sudan and a serious blow to British prestige throughout the Middle East. He believed that it would be sharply criticised by the Press. It seemed likely to involve the Government in serious political difficulties, which would doubtless be exploited to the full by the Opposition. He would, therefore, prefer, that no decision should be taken until early in the following week, by which time it would be easier to forecast the probable reaction of public opinion in this country.

From the discussion that followed it was clear that Churchill was in a minority. The Agreement on the Sudan, it was pointed out, 'was the logical outcome of the long-standing promise to confer on the Sudanese people the rights of self-government and self-determination. The expectation had been held out to the Sudanese that they would achieve self-government by the end of 1952.' It was against this background, Churchill was told, 'that the terms of the proposed Agreement would have to be defended to public opinion in this country'.

As to Churchill's wish for a delay, it was pointed out that apart from the 'risk' that the Egyptians might withdraw some of the concessions which they had made, 'it was in our interests that the negotiations should not be drawn out any longer; for it was most desirable that the Sudanese elections should be held before the onset of the rainy season, and this could not be done unless the preliminary arrangements were completed by the end of February'.

'Nothing would now be gained by delay' was the general feeling; the most that Churchill was able to secure was a delay of four hours, during which Eden would explain the proposed Agreement to a meeting of Government supporters 'interested' in foreign affairs; a meeting to be held at 9.30 that same evening. But once Eden had reported back to the Cabinet on the results of that meeting, 'a final decision' would be taken.[1]

At a meeting of the Defence Committee that morning, Churchill had warned of what he saw as the danger, when Neguib had concluded an agreement on the Sudan, that 'he would do his utmost to be rid of all British forces in Egypt, so that he would then be free to exert pressure upon the Sudan by bribery and other means to seek unity with Egypt'. Churchill added:

---

[1] Cabinet Conclusions No. 9 of 1953, 'Secret', 6.30 p.m., 11 February 1953: Cabinet papers, 128/26.

He thought it necessary that we should have some positive plans to defeat military action by the Egyptians against our forces in the Canal Zone and some means by which we could negotiate from strength a further agreement with Egypt about the base. He suggested that we might insist that the cost of removal from the Canal Zone should be charged against Egypt's sterling balances. If this point were maintained, Egypt would be more ready to conclude an agreement which did not entail this financial burden. He thought also that the least sign of military activity, whether by the Egyptian Army or by guerilla forces against us, would be sufficient justification for rounding up and disarming that part of the Egyptian Army which was located in the Sinai Peninsula. This would be an effective card in negotiations, and would carry with it far fewer disagreeable responsibilities and commitments than the occupation of Cairo and Alexandria, which would inevitably lead to action against mobs and bloodshed among civilians.[1]

The full Cabinet met again at 10.40 that night, when Eden and the Chief Whip, Patrick Buchan-Hepburn, reported that, in the private meeting of Conservative Members of Parliament an hour earlier, Eden's explanation of the Anglo-Egyptian Agreement on the Sudan 'had removed many of the misunderstandings which had been current in the Party, and had gone a long way towards allaying the anxieties mentioned in the Cabinet's discussion earlier in the day'. Although many of those present 'continued to be uneasy about the situation, they now recognised that the course which the Government was proposing to follow was the most satisfactory of the alternatives now open to them'. The meeting had, so the Cabinet were told, been well attended; 'and it was clear at the end that, in the light of the explanations which had been given, the main body of Government supporters in the House of Commons would be prepared to accept the policy which the Foreign Secretary proposed to follow'.

Churchill made no recorded comment, and when Eden asked the Cabinet to endorse the final text of the Agreement, it did so without dissent.[2]

On February 17 the Cabinet discussed the terms of a defence agreement with Egypt, based upon a phased withdrawal of British troops from Egypt, but the maintenance of a military base in the Canal Zone 'under conditions which would enable us and our Allies to have immediate use of it in war'. It was also proposed that under the defence agreement there would be a joint Anglo-Egyptian organization for the air defence of Egypt, the participation of Egypt in a

[1] Defence Committee No. 2 of 1953, 'Top Secret', 11.30 a.m., 11 February 1953: Cabinet papers, 131/13.
[2] Cabinet Conclusions No. 10 of 1953, 'Secret', 10.40 p.m., 11 February 1953: Cabinet papers, 128/26. This meeting, like the one at 6.30 p.m., was held in Churchill's room in the House of Commons.

Middle East Defence Organization, and a programme of military and economic assistance to Egypt by the United Kingdom and the United States.

The question that now arose was by what procedure the negotiations for this agreement should proceed. Churchill told his colleagues that in his view 'the first need was to assure ourselves that we should have the full sympathy and support of the United States Government in the approach which we were proposing to make. We were not asking them to give us any military assistance in Egypt at the present time: we ourselves had ample forces there to deal with any situation which might arise. But they should understand that we were not prepared to be bullied or cajoled into withdrawing our troops from Egypt unless we secured in return satisfactory alternative arrangements. . . .'

The terms submitted by Eden, Churchill added, if taken together, would form 'a settlement which we could accept; but they must be taken as a whole and we should not be prepared to see them whittled away in the course of negotiation'.

Both Eden and Swinton 'warmly supported' Churchill's proposals.[1]

In the United States, Eisenhower had declared that China, which had been increasingly supporting the North Koreans, could no longer be considered free from possible American counter-attack. On February 2 Eisenhower explained to Churchill the reasons for this declaration. Churchill replied five days later:

I hope you believe that I understand all the reasons that led to your declaration. If it had been necessary, I would have explained to the House of Commons the distress of millions of Americans whose relations are under fire in Korea because of the prolonged stalemate, and the apparent association of the United States Seventh Fleet with the security of the Communist country that is firing on them. I feel it in my bones, and it grieves and stirs me every day. If you could find time to read Anthony's speech, which I enclose, you will see how earnestly he put this aspect before the House; and there was no doubt that it is fully accepted by all except perhaps an eighth of the Members, and most of them would come into line on a grave issue.

What I do hope is that where joint action affecting our common destiny is desired, you will let us know beforehand so that we can give our opinion and advice in time to have them considered. Now that you are in the saddle and can deal with long term policies, this ought to be possible. Anthony and I are resolved to make our co-operation with the United States effective over

---

[1] Cabinet Conclusions No. 12 of 1953, 'Secret', 11 a.m., 17 February 1953: Cabinet papers, 128/26. Viscount Swinton had succeeded the Marquess of Salisbury as Commonwealth Secretary on 24 November 1952.

the world scene. I am sure that you will not hesitate to tell him frankly all your thoughts on these matters when you see him. He will know mine.[1]

On February 19 Churchill's doctor found him reading George Orwell's *1984*. 'Have you read it, Charles?' he asked. 'Oh, you must. I'm reading it for a second time. It is a very remarkable book.' Churchill's worry that day was about his eyes; he wanted Moran to suggest a new eye specialist. 'I have stuck to Juler for so long,' he said, 'because he did discover the ingrowing eyelashes when no one else did.[2] At that time my eyes were so bad I could not read, even official documents. But he is stumped now, and we must change the bowling.'[3] Five days later Churchill had to see his doctor again; he had spat up a little blood on the previous day. 'So this morning,' Moran noted, 'I packed him off, vigorously protesting, to be X-rayed. I am sure nothing will be found, for he is just now in terrific form.'

Since their journey together to the United States at the end of 1951, Churchill seemed, noted Moran, 'to have taken a new lease of life', and he went on to record some of Churchill's remarks that February 24:

'I'm much better than I was a year ago,' he said gaily. 'I can bite now, really hard.' And he snapped his jaws together. 'After our trip to America I was in poor form. Gladstone lived to be eighty-eight; I might go on another eight years. If I do it will be very tiresome for those who manage my finances. Things are already getting very complicated. You see, Charles, during the war I retired from business, but by the end of the war I had become notorious; and all sorts of things, such as film rights and for the copyright of my books, gave me quite a bit of capital. For the first time in my life I was quite a rich man. But the income-tax people take it all. I let Hyde Park Gate for £2,000 a year—2,000 sixpences.'[4]

Life expectancy was not merely on Churchill's mind as a casual thought; he had even asked his solicitor, Anthony Moir, to look into the actuarial tables. 'According to the latest available Mortality Tables,' Moir wrote on February 26, 'a man aged 78, in good health, has 5·926 years expectation of life.'[5] Moir's work for Churchill was

---

[1] 'My dear Ike—if I may so venture', 'Personal and Confidential', 7 February 1953: Eisenhower papers. Churchill had lunched with Dulles in London on 4 February 1953.

[2] Frank Juler, CVO, a leading ophthalmologist, was Surgeon-Oculist to King George VI's Household from 1936 to 1952, and from 1952 Extra Surgeon-Oculist to Her Majesty's Household. He died in 1962.

[3] Moran diary, 19 February 1953: *The Struggle for Survival*, pages 400–1.

[4] Moran diary, 24 February 1953: *The Struggle for Survival*, pages 401–3. For the highest rate of unearned income, income tax was 19*s*. 6*d*. in the pound (97·5 per cent).

[5] Letter of 26 February 1953, 'Confidential': Churchill papers, 1/28. Churchill was to *exceed* that expectation by nearly seven years.

comprehensive. On one occasion Churchill told Miss Portal, in connection with all correspondence concerning the film and other ancillary rights of his books: 'You are in charge of the mechanical rights. What I mean is, you always talk to Mr Moir. . . .'[1]

Financially, as Churchill had explained to Lord Moran, he had become a rich man. During March 1953 various agreements for the sixth volume of his war memoirs were concluded, bringing him a total sum of £63,726, with a further $28,000 still to come from Time-Life.[2]

On March 5 Churchill introduced the Government's Statement on Defence to the House of Commons, pointing out: 'What is called the cold war—which is not a legal term—continues. What we are faced with is not a violent jerk, but a prolonged pull. We must create forces which can play a real part as a deterrent against aggression and also can afford some measure of defence should war come.'

Churchill spoke during the debate of the situation when he had come into office sixteen months earlier. 'I was startled and concerned,' he said, 'with the condition of home defence, especially against large-scale attacks by paratroops. I felt naked as I had not felt at any time in the recent war. We had moved, or it had been decided to move, all our divisions out of the island. I did not cancel these movements, and, therefore, I accept inherited responsibility.'

Important measures had been taken; the Home Guard had been revived and revitalized. More than 450 mobile columns had been formed. But 'still the fact remains', Churchill said, 'that we have not got a single combat division in this country. This is another aspect of what I said just now: our whole formed or regularly organized Army is abroad. This shows how great is the need to improve our fighting strength at home. No one country is voluntarily running the risks to which we have subjected ourselves.'

Churchill then spoke of the measures being taken to manufacture arms. Before he did so, however, he indulged in a short tease:

I must now warn the House that I am going to make an unusual departure. I am going to make a Latin quotation. It is one which I hope will not offend the detachment of the old school tie and will not baffle or be taken as a slight

---

[1] Lady Williams of Elvel recollections: in conversation with the author, 29 July 1987.
[2] The Volume 6 agreements were (a) serialization, South Africa £2,300, Australia £4,000, Canada £7,100, *Daily Telegraph* £15,000, and foreign serialization through Emery Reves £5,100; and (b) book rights, Cassell UK £8,000, Houghton Mifflin USA £17,826, and European book rights through Emery Reves £4,400. The total value of these and the Time-Life payment of $28,000 was the equivalent of £667,000 in 1987.

upon the new spelling brigade. Perhaps I ought to say the 'new spelling squad', because it is an easier word. The quotation is, '*Arma virumque cano*', which, for the benefit of our Winchester friends, I may translate as 'Arms and the men I sing'. That generally describes my theme.

Mr Hugh Gaitskell (Leeds, South): Should it not be 'man', the singular instead of the plural?

The Prime Minister: Little did I expect that I should receive assistance on a classical matter from such a quarter. I am using the word 'man' in a collective form which, I think, puts me right in grammar.

Let me now come to arms, about which I believe there is no classical dispute.

The Government, Churchill insisted, was making the 'absolute maximum' effort on defence of which it was capable. Any further 'substantial diversions' of British resources from civil to military production would, he warned, 'gravely imperil our economic foundations and, with them, our ability to continue with the rearmament programme', and he added: 'There are a frightful lot of things we are all agreed about.' As to the continuing export of arms to Commonwealth and Western European countries, Churchill told the House:

Let me emphasize that these exports of arms are over and above, not what we want, but the maximum expenditure which we are financially able to afford for the re-equipment of our own Forces.

We should like to rearm some of our own formations more rapidly, but we do not withhold modern weapons from our own troops in order to sell them to other countries. In so far as there is retardation apart from technical delays, it is because we cannot afford to spend more on ourselves.

'This is a serious and unpleasant fact,' Churchill added, 'which I do not hesitate to state to the House.' [1]

Churchill spoke to the Defence Committee on two other items of defence policy on March 6. Asking whether helicopters could not be used against the Mau Mau rebels in Kenya he 'stressed the importance', as the minutes of the meeting recorded, 'of making a display of air power over the heads of the Mau Mau. The more often they saw an aircraft overhead, the more they would feel that all their movements were under observation.' In connection with a danger closer to home, a possible Soviet parachute attack on Britain, Churchill asked:

Would it be practicable for a potential enemy, from existing bases, to drop something of the order of 20,000 parachutists in this country? What warning might we expect? At what points were parachutists most likely to be dropped? It might be assumed that, in order to get the benefit of surprise, the enemy

[1] Speech of 5 March 1953: *Hansard*.

might be ready to launch such an attack even in circumstances in which the troop-carrying aircraft could not make a safe return. This study should be made under three possible hypotheses: (i) a surprise attack without notice; (ii) an attack during the first three days of war; and (iii) an attack after the end of the first week of war.[1]

Worried during the early months of 1953 about some aggressive Egyptian action against the British forces stationed in the Canal Zone, Churchill wrote to Eisenhower in February 18, after talking to Alexander:

Alex assures me that our forces in the Canal Zone are in ample strength to resist any attack, and even if necessary, in order to prevent a massacre of white people and to rescue them, to enter Cairo and Alexandria, for which all preparations have been for some time at nine–six hours notice. Moreover, nearly half the effective Egyptian Army, about 15,000 men, stands on the Eastern side of the Canal watching Israel. They could be easily forced to surrender perhaps indeed merely by cutting off supplies. As for Egypt herself, the cutting off of the oil would, as you know, exercise a decisive effect.

Churchill explained: 'There is therefore no question of our needing your help or to reinforce the 80,000 men we have kept at great expense on tiptoe during the last year. The advantages of our working together on the lines agreed with your predecessors are so great that a successful result might be achieved without violence or bloodshed and without exposing you to any military obligation.'[2]

Britain was not going to be 'knocked about with impunity' Churchill told Eisenhower a week later, 'and if we are attacked we shall use our concentrated strength to the full'. He added: 'It seems to me that you might be standing with us in the approach to Neguib on the lines on which we have agreed bring about a peaceful solution in the truest harmony with the military and moral interests of the anti-Communist front. This is no question of British Imperialism or indeed of any national advantage to us, but only of the common cause.'[3]

Eisenhower declined to accept Churchill's proposal for a joint Anglo-American approach to Egypt. 'You have decided,' Churchill wrote to him six weeks later, 'that unless invited by Neguib, who like all dictators is the servant of the forces behind him, we cannot present a joint proposal. We therefore have to go on alone.'[4]

---

[1] Defence Committee No. 4 of 1953, 'Top Secret', 11.30 a.m., 6 March 1953: Cabinet papers, 131/13.

[2] 'My dear Friend', 'Private and Confidential', 18 February 1955: Premier papers, 11/1074.

[3] 'Prime Minister to President Eisenhower', signed 'Your much older friend, Winston', 'Personal and Confidential', 25 February 1953: Premier papers, 11/1074.

[4] 'My dear Friend', 5 April 1953: Premier papers, 11/1074.

43

Stalin's Death

ON 5 March 1953 Josef Stalin died in Moscow: Churchill's war-time colleague and adversary, whose 'betrayal' of Yalta had, in Churchill's view of the world, poisoned the prospects of any post-war partnership, and led inexorably to the creation of the Iron Curtain between East and West. 'Regret and sympathy', was, however, the message which Churchill sent to Moscow. 'The PM feels that Stalin's death may lead to a relaxation in tension,' Lord Moran wrote in his diary on the following day. 'It is an opportunity which will not recur,' Moran noted, 'and with Anthony away he is sure he can go straight ahead.' Moran added: 'He seems to think of little else. He is much incensed by the *Daily Mirror*'s remarks about Stalin and describes it as "dancing on his tomb".[1] The *Mirror*, for its part, complains of Mr Churchill's "crocodile tears".'[2]

Eden's absence was in connection with the Egyptian negotiations; he was in Washington attempting to win American support for Britain's defence plan. When the Cabinet met on March 9 it was Egypt, not Stalin's death, which brought it together. The news was good: a series of telegraphic reports from Eden in Washington, to the effect that Eisenhower had agreed that the next stage of the defence negotiations with the Egyptian Government 'should be undertaken in Cairo by an Anglo-American team comprising military as well as diplomatic representatives of the two Governments'.

'His anxieties had been relieved,' Churchill told the Cabinet, 'by the assurances which the Foreign Secretary had been able to obtain in his final interview with President Eisenhower. He was specially glad to know that the President appreciated the need for keeping the vital

[1] 'Mr Churchill, the Prime Minister, sends his "regret and sympathy",' reported Cassandra in the *Daily Mirror* on March 6, under the headline 'Crocodile Tears', and he went on to write; 'I am made of much more callous stuff. I have no regret for Mr S. I have no sympathy for Mr S.' Cassandra was Bill (later Sir William) Connor.
[2] Moran diary, 7 March 1953: *The Struggle for Survival*, page 403.

depots and installations in the base under British supervision and command.' If this point were stressed, Churchill added, if the Americans were 'reminded that the five proposals were to be treated as interdependent parts of a single settlement', and if it was clearly understood that no modification of the British conditions for a settlement would be made 'without the concurrence of both the British and American military representatives', Eden could, Churchill thought, 'be authorised to make final arrangements for a joint Anglo-American approach to the Egyptian Government on the basis which he had discussed with the President'.[1]

'Look forward to your return,' Churchill telegraphed to Eden on March 11. 'Hope you are not working too hard. . . .'[2] That same day Churchill telegraphed to Eisenhower:

I am sure that everyone will want to know whether you still contemplate a meeting with the Soviets. I remember our talk at Bernie's when you told me I was welcome to meet Stalin if I thought fit and that you intended to offer to do so. I understand this as meaning that you did not want us to go together, but now there is no more Stalin I wonder whether this makes any difference to your view about separate approaches to the new regime or whether there is a possibility of collective action. When I know how you feel now that the personalities are altered I can make up my own mind on what to advise the Cabinet.

Churchill's telegram continued:

I have the feeling that we might both of us together or separately be called to account if no attempt was made to turn over a leaf so that a new page would be started with something more coherent on it than a series of casual and dangerous incidents at the many points of contact between the two divisions of the world. I cannot doubt you are thinking deeply of this which holds the first place in my thoughts. I do not think I met Malenkov but Anthony and I have done a lot of business with Molotov.[3]

Churchill's telegram crossed with a letter from Eisenhower, sent through the United States Embassy in London, which effectively dashed Churchill's hopes of a Three-Power meeting. Eisenhower wrote:

At our meeting in New York, I by no means meant to reject the possibility

[1] Cabinet Conclusions No. 17 of 1953, 'Secret', 10 p.m., 9 March 1953: Cabinet papers, 128/26.
[2] Telegram No. 170 to New York, 'Immediate', 'Top Secret', 11 March 1953: Premier papers, 11/422.
[3] Telegram No. 171 of New York, Prime Minister's Personal Telegram, T.62/53, 'Immediate', 'Top Secret', 11 March 1953: Premier papers, 11/422. Malenkov was Stalin's successor as Secretary General of the Communist Party of the Soviet Union; he had retained Molotov as his Foreign Minister.

that the leaders of the West might sometime have to make some collective move if we are to achieve progress in lessening the world's tensions.

However, even now I tend to doubt the wisdom of a formal multilateral meeting since this would give our opponent the same kind of opportunity he has so often had to use such a meeting simultaneously to balk every reasonable effort of ourselves and to make of the whole occurrence another propaganda mill for the Soviet.[1]

On March 15 Churchill had to answer an invitation from Lord Beaverbrook to be his guest again at La Capponcina. He decided to decline, writing to his friend and former War Cabinet colleague:

My dear Max,

You very kindly invited me to Cap d'Ail for the Easter holidays, and it would have given me the greatest pleasure to come, especially if you were there as host. However, I fear I cannot manage to get away from England. In the first place I have two horses running on Easter Saturday and two more on Easter Monday whose fortunes are of great interest to me. But more seriously the Budget comes on immediately after the recess and this affects our affairs so much that I feel bound to be in constant touch with Rab, so I am going to stay at Chartwell with a number of grandchildren. I do hope you will give me another invitation later in the year.

The lift is in full working order and I am sure it will be a great relief to me if I go on living. Thank you so much for your very kind thought and for the care and skill with which it has been carried into effect.

Do not fail to let me know when you come to England for there are lots of things I want to talk about. We seem to have been having a pretty rough time lately. Hardly a week passes without some unusual misfortune. The Larne packet, the floods,[2] the poor soldiers and their wives flying to Jamaica.[3] The new Soviet Government shooting down our airplane and killing six men.[4] Neguib, Mussadiq and all the rest. However I am going to welcome Tito on Monday. I hope you are enjoying yourself too.

Yours ever

Winston [5]

---

[1] 'Dear Winston', 'Top Secret', 12 March 1953: Premier papers, 11/422.

[2] On the night of 31 January 1953, more than 260 people lost their lives in floods that followed the bursting of sea defences over a large part of the East Coast. In The Netherlands, there were 1,355 known deaths from the same floods. On the night of the storm the Larne–Stranraer mail-ferry *Princess Victoria* foundered off the coast of County Down, with the loss of 128 lives.

[3] On 2 February 1953 a York transport aircraft belonging to the London firm Skyways, on charter to the War Office, crashed on a trooping flight between Britain and Jamaica. On board were six crewmen and thirty-three passengers: soldiers with their wives and children, including several tiny babies. All were lost. On 12 March 1953 the Government announced the suspension of all North Atlantic trooping operations (usually three to four a month) using York transport aircraft. It was by York that Churchill had often flown during the Second World War.

[4] On 12 March 1953 a Royal Air Force Lincoln bomber on a routine training flight from Yorkshire was shot down near the border of the British and Russian Zones of Germany, while flying along the Hamburg–Berlin air corridor. Six of the crew were killed and one wounded. The Russians claimed that the bomber had strayed into their air space.

[5] 'My dear Max', 15 March 1953: Beaverbrook papers.

Churchill did welcome Tito to London.[1] On March 24 he was in the House of Commons for the debate on the establishment of an African Federation of Commonwealth African States. But the debate was continually interrupted by the buzz of rumour that Queen Mary was dying. 'Winston came into the Chamber,' Henry Channon noted, 'so did Ralph Verney, and the dreadful official announcement was expected at any moment. Christopher Soames darted in and out. Then there was a détente, as we gathered that the story was untrue.'

In the early evening, Churchill was summoned to Buckingham Palace by the Queen. Then, shortly after 10.30, he returned to the Chamber, 'and looked solemn', Channon noted, 'as he whispered to the Speaker'.[2] But the debate, which at that moment was being wound up by Henry Hopkinson, went on for its final half-hour, until the Division, in which the Government received a majority of 44. Then, at 11 o'clock, Churchill rose and, moving the adjournment of the House, announced that Queen Mary was dead. She was eighty-five years old.

On March 25 Churchill moved the Address of Sympathy to the Queen on the death of her grandmother. 'It may sometimes have been thought,' he said, 'that Queen Mary, brought up in an age of conventions more rigid than those that now find acceptance, was intolerant of the changes which she lived to see. This was far from the truth. One of the most remarkable qualities she possessed was her lack of prejudice, and the welcome which she spontaneously gave to young people and to new ideas.'[3]

Churchill also broadcast to the nation on the death of Queen Mary, telling his listeners, and tens of thousands who watched the newsreel:

How few of you listening to me to-night can recall a time without Queen Mary, and even those who never saw her will feel a deep and sincere pang at the passing of this last link with Queen Victoria's reign. When she was born Napoleon III ruled in France and Palmerston had only recently ceased to be Prime Minister of this country. Railways were comparatively new; electric light and the internal combustion engine were unknown. She knew Gladstone and Disraeli; her grandfather was the son of George III. Yet she lived into this atomic age, through the two fearful wars, which cast almost all the thrones of Europe to the ground, and rent but also transformed the world.

---

[1] 'Tito seems full of commonsense,' Churchill wrote to Eisenhower on March 19. 'He is definitely of the opinion that the death of Stalin has not made the world safer, but he believes that the new regime will probably feel their way cautiously for some time and even thinks there may be divisions among them. Malenkov and Beria, he says, are united but Molotov is not so closely tied.' (Prime Minister's Personal Telegram 71 of 1953, 'Top Secret', 19 March 1953: Premier papers, 11/1074.)

[2] Channon diary, 24 March 1953: Robert Rhodes James (editor), *Chips*, page 472.

[3] Speech of 25 March 1953: *Hansard*.

Churchill's broadcast continued:

The chasm which scientific invention and social change have wrought between 1867 and 1953 is so wide that it requires not only courage but mental resilience for those whose youth lay in calmer and more slowly-moving times to adjust themselves to the giant outlines and harsh structure of the Twentieth Century. But Queen Mary did not cling to the insubstantial shadows of what had been. She moved easily through the changing scenes. New ideas held no terrors for her.[1]

'Your speech and your emotion,' Sarah Churchill wrote to her father from New York, 'were very moving. I hated to see you sad & sombre.'[2]

Two days after his speech and broadcast about Queen Mary, Churchill spoke at a Commonwealth Parliamentary Association luncheon, in the presence of the Queen. The setting was a magnificent one, St Stephen's Hall, Westminster, and it was with that hall in mind that Churchill began. 'In this hall of fame and antiquity,' he said, 'a long story has been unfolded of the conflicts of Crown versus Parliament, and I suppose we are most of us within a hundred yards of the statue of Oliver Cromwell. But those days are done. The vehement passionate moral and intellectual forces that clashed in tragic violence three hundred years ago are now united. It is no longer a case of Crown versus Parliament, but of Crown and Parliament.'

There were now 'fifty or sixty Parliaments under one Crown', Churchill pointed out, and he added: 'It is natural for Parliaments to talk and for the Crown to shine. The oldest here will confirm that we are never likely to run short of Members and of Ministers who can talk. And the youngest are sure they will never see the Crown sparkle more gloriously than in these joyous days.'

Churchill ended his remarks on both a personal and a patriotic note, telling the assembled members of so many of the Commonwealth Parliaments, as well as the House of Commons and the House of Lords:

I suppose it is because I have served Her Majesty's great-grandfather, grandfather, father, and now herself, that I have been accorded the honour of expressing our thanks this afternoon to her for her Royal presence here. Well do we realize the burdens imposed by sacred duty upon the Sovereign and her family. All round we see the proofs of the unifying sentiment which makes the Crown the central link in all our modern changing life, and the one which above all others claims our allegiance to the death. We feel

[1] Broadcast of 25 March 1953: Randolph S. Churchill (editor), *The Unwritten Alliance*, pages 24-5. The speech notes from which Churchill spoke are in the Churchill papers, 2/197. I have made one minor amendment to the printed version, using these notes.

[2] 'My darling Papa', 26 March 1953: Churchill papers, 1/50.

that Her Gracious Majesty here with us to-day has consecrated her life to all her peoples in all her realms. We are resolved to prove on the pages of history that this sacrifice shall not be made in vain.[1]

With the last volume of his war memoirs now in the final proof stage, on March 28 Churchill sent a copy to Sir Alan Lascelles for permission to publish two messages which he had sent to King George VI. He had held the whole volume back, he explained to Lascelles, 'until after the Presidential election in the United States, and since then I have gone over it again and taken out any critical references to General Eisenhower which, now that he is President, might conceivably damage Anglo-American relations'. Stalin's death, Churchill added, 'has now removed my last remaining doubts about the expediency of publishing this volume, and I hope to bring it out in the autumn'.[2]

The Queen gave her permission for the two letters to be published, but felt that a reference by Churchill to the London and Lublin Poles was 'rather rough on the Poles' and wondered whether it ought not, 'in the interests of international amity, to be toned down a bit'.[3] Churchill did as suggested.[4]

Churchill also wrote to Eisenhower on March 28, telling the President:

My dear Ike,

The sixth and last volume of my *History of the Second World War* was finished before I took office again & will be ready for publication, here and in the United States, towards the end of this year. It deals with the period from the launching of 'Overlord' down to the Potsdam Conference—a period of almost unbroken military success for the Allied arms but darkened by forebodings about the political future of Europe which have since been shown to have been only too well founded.

[1] Speech of 27 March 1953: Randolph S. Churchill (editor), *The Unwritten Alliance*, pages 26–7. Churchill had served as Under-Secretary of State for the Colonies, President of the Board of Trade and Home Secretary during the reign of Edward VII, the Queen's great-grandfather. Under her grandfather, George V, he had been First Lord of the Admiralty, Chancellor of the Duchy of Lancaster, Minister of Munitions, Secretary of State for War and Air, Colonial Secretary and Chancellor of the Exchequer. Under her father he had been First Lord of the Admiralty and, twice, Prime Minister.

[2] 'My dear Alan', 28 March 1953: Churchill papers, 4/63.

[3] 'My dear Prime Minister', 'Personal and Private', 30 March 1953: Churchill papers, 4/63.

[4] The original sentence read: 'The day before yesterday was "All Poles Day". Our lot from London are as Your Majesty knows, a decent but feeble lot of fools but the delegates from Lublin seem to be the greatest villains imaginable. They could hardly have been under any illusions as to our opinion of them' (Telegram No. 2935 from Moscow to the Foreign Office, Moscow Conference 'Hearty' Series No. 114, 'Top Secret', 16 October 1944: Cabinet papers, 120/165). These two sentences were amended in Churchill's book to: 'The day before yesterday was "All Poles Day". Our lot from London are, as Your Majesty knows, decent but feeble, but the delegates from Lublin could hardly have been under any illusions as to our opinion of them' (Winston S. Churchill, *The Second World War*, volume 6, page 209).

I am thinking of releasing it in the autumn.

It contains, of course, a good many references to yourself, and I am writing to ask whether you would like to see these before the book comes out. I know that nothing which I have written will damage our friendship. But, now that you have assumed supreme political office in your country, I am most anxious that nothing should be published which might seem to others to threaten our current relations in our public duties or impair the sympathy and understanding which exist between our countries. I have therefore gone over the book again in the last few months and have taken great pains to ensure that it contains nothing which might imply that there was in those days any controversy or lack of confidence between us.

There was in fact little controversy in those years; but I have been careful to ensure that the few differences of opinion which arose are so described that even ill-disposed people will be unable now to turn them to mischievous account.

I think therefore that you can be confident that the publication of this final volume will do nothing to disturb our present relationship. And I can imagine that, in these first few months of your new responsibilities, you will not find much time to turn back to those 'far-off things and battles long ago'. If, however, you would prefer to have seen, before publication, those passages which refer directly to yourself, I will gladly have the extracts made and sent to you.

Yours ever

W[1]

That same day, March 28, in the hope of trying to revive the idea of a Three-Power Summit, even at the level of Foreign Ministers, Churchill sent Eden a draft message which he wanted to send to Molotov. The message read:

Greetings.

I was so glad to learn from Eden about your action in seeking the release of British diplomatists captured in North Korea. You have also suggested reciprocal release of wounded and resumption of talks at Panmunjon. All this is agreeable to our minds and we are talking to our American friends about it.

What I should like to see most of all would be for you and Eden, who have had so many long and famous contacts for our two countries, to have another friendly and informal meeting. This might perhaps be at Vienna. I also wondered whether it might not arise out of any broader political aspects of the talks between General Chuikov and Kirkpatrick about arrangements to prevent another aeroplane disaster.

Such talks however they originated might lead us all further away from madness and ruin, but even if nothing much came out of it I can't see that any of us would be worse off.

[1] 'My dear Ike', 'Private and Personal', 28 March 1953: Churchill papers, 4/52. The letter was sent on 9 April 1953 (Eisenhower papers).

Churchill asked Eden, after sending him the draft letter to Molotov: 'Let me know what you think about this sort of approach. I do not want an interview between Gascoigne and Molotov, but between Molotov and you. At a later stage if all went well and everything broadened I and even Ike might come in too.'[1]

A week later, Churchill helped Eden draft two telegrams, one from Eden to Molotov, the other from Churchill to Eisenhower. Eden's telegram to Molotov began:

Sir A. Gascoigne has already told you how pleased Her Majesty's Government and I are at the action you have taken about the British civilian internees in North Korea, in response to my appeal to you.

I am encouraged by this to ask myself whether there are further questions directly arising between our two Governments on which progress might now be made.[2]

Churchill's telegram to Eisenhower read:

Anthony and I have been thinking a good deal as we know you have also about the apparent change for the better in the Soviet mood. I am sure we shall be in agreement with you that we must remain vigilantly on our guard and maintain all that process of defensive rearmament from which any real improvement must have resulted. We think, as I am sure you do also, that we ought to lose no chance of finding out how far the Malenkov régime are prepared to go in easing things up all round. There seem certainly to be great possibilities in Korea and we are very glad of the steps you have taken to resume Truce negotiations.

For our part we are sending our Ambassador back to Moscow with instructions to try to settle with Molotov a number of minor points which concern Britain and Russia alone and have caused us trouble in the last few years. None of these are of major importance: they include such matters as the recent Soviet notice of intention to terminate the Temporary Anglo-Soviet Fisheries Agreement of 1930, the cases of certain individual British subjects in Russia, exchange rates and restrictions on movements. Talks on them may give us some further indication of the depth of the Soviet purpose. We shall of course gladly keep your people informed of how we progress.

It may be that presently the Soviets will make overtures for some form of direct discussion of world problems whether on a Four Power basis or in some other manner. I assume of course that we shall deal in the closest collaboration with any such overtures if they are made.[3]

Eisenhower's reply was not as enthusiastic as Churchill had hoped.

[1] 'Most Private', 28 March 1953: Premier papers, 11/422. Churchill told Eden: 'If it is Mol, you go. If it is Mal, it's me.' Sir Alvary Gascoigne had been British Ambassador in Moscow since 1951.

[2] Telegram No. 171 to Moscow, 'Secret', sent 8 April 1953: Premier papers, 11/422.

[3] Prime Minister's Personal Telegram, T.76/53, No. 1531 to Washington, 'Secret', 'Personal and Private', sent 5 April 1953: Premier papers, 11/422.

'This whole field is strewn with very difficult obstacles, as we all know,' the President wrote, 'but I do think it extremely important that the great masses of the world understand that, on our side, we are deadly serious in our search for peace and are ready to prove this with acts and deeds and not merely assert it in glittering phraseology. This presupposes prior assurance of honest intent on the other side.'[1] On April 11 Churchill telegraphed to Eisenhower in reply:

I believe myself that at this moment time is on our side. The apparent change of Soviet mood is so new and so indefinite and its causes so obscure that there could not be much risk in letting things develop. We do not know what these men mean. We do not want to deter them from saying what they mean. Hitherto they have been the aggressors and have done us wrong at a hundred points. We cannot trade their leaving off doing wrong against our necessary defensive measures and policies which action demands and has procured.

Nevertheless, great hope has arisen in the world that there is a change of heart in the vast, mighty masses of Russia and this can carry them far and fast and perhaps into revolution. It has been well said that the most dangerous moment for evil governments is when they begin to reform. Nothing impressed me so much as the doctor story.[2] This must cut very deeply into communist discipline and structure. I would not like it to be thought that a sudden American declaration has prevented this natural growth of events.

All this comes to a particular point upon Korea. I was hoping that at least we should secure at this juncture a *bona fide*, lasting and effective truce in Korea which might mean the end of that show as a world problem. Indeed, if nothing more than this happened everyone would rejoice. I hope that you will consider what a tremendous score it would be for us all if we could bring off this truce. It seems to me very unlikely that the terms you require for a later political settlement of Korea as set out in your statement would be accepted as they stand by the other side. I fear that the formal promulgation of your five points at this moment might quench the hope of an armistice.

Churchill's telegram ended:

Anthony and I have in mind important comments we could make on your text, but we are not putting them forward now as we hope that our arguments will persuade you to bide your time. We cannot see what you would lose by waiting till the full character and purpose of the Soviet change is more clearly defined and also is apparent to the whole free world. I always like the story of Napoleon going to sleep in his chair as the battle began, saying 'Wake me when their infantry column gets beyond the closest wood.'[3]

[1] 'Dear Winston', 'Personal and Secret', 6 April 1953: Eisenhower papers.
[2] Stalin's accusation, shortly before his death, that fourteen doctors (almost all of them Jewish) were plotting to kill him and the leading members of the Government in the Kremlin. Following Stalin's death, the doctors were released.
[3] 'Message from the Prime Minister to the President', 11 April 1953: Eisenhower papers.

On April 12 Churchill telegraphed to Eisenhower again:

It would be a pity if a sudden frost nipped spring in the bud, or if this could be alleged, even if there was no real spring. I do not attempt to predict what the Soviet change of attitude and policy, and it seems to me of mood, means. It might mean an awful lot. Would it not be well to combine the re-assertions of your and our inflexible resolves with some balancing expression of hope and that we have entered a new era. A new hope has, I feel, been created in the unhappy, bewildered world. It ought to be possible to proclaim our unflinching determination to resist Communist tyranny and aggression and at the same time though separately, to declare how glad we should be if we found there was a real change of heart and not let it be said that we had closed the door upon it.[1]

'I agree with the tenor of your comments,' Eisenhower replied, 'and shall certainly strive to make my talk one that will not freeze the tender buds of sprouting decency, if indeed they are really coming out.'[2]

At Cabinet on April 1, Churchill had spoken of the renewed armistice negotiations in Korea. The proposal now made by the Chinese Communist Government, he said, for an exchange of sick and wounded prisoners, 'and their apparent readiness to consider thereafter arrangements for the disposal of other prisoners of war, was a welcome step towards breaking the present deadlock and might be an indication of a genuine desire to conclude an effective armistice in Korea'. The British Government should be 'careful', Churchill added, 'not to appear to discourage such overtures as these, though we should continue to handle them with all due caution'.

Churchill also spoke to the Cabinet of April 1 about Eden, who, after recurring bouts of illness, was forced to remain out of action. He intended, Churchill said, to comment in the House of Commons that afternoon, 'on the patience and foresight which the Foreign Secretary had shown, since assuming office, in all the negotiations which he had undertaken, in the United Nations and elsewhere, with a view to achieving an effective armistice in Korea'.[3]

On April 4 Eden learned that he would have to be operated on for the removal of gallstones. Six days later he wrote to his son Nicholas of the 'tiresome operation' he would soon have to undergo, 'not dangerous', he explained, and added: 'All is well otherwise, except that W

[1] 'Personal and Secret', 12 April 1953: Premier papers, 11/1074.
[2] Telegram dated 13 April 1953: Eisenhower papers.
[3] Cabinet Conclusions No. 24 of 1953, 'Secret', 11 a.m., 1 April 1953: Cabinet papers, 128/26.

gets daily older & is apt to ring up & waste a great deal of time. Between ourselves, the outside world has little idea how difficult that becomes. Please make me retire before I am 80!' [1]

As acting Foreign Secretary, Churchill now took over from Eden the continuing negotiations for a defence agreement with Egypt, negotiations for which Eden had so successfully secured a unity of Anglo-American requirements and conditions. He was 'anxious', Churchill told the Cabinet on April 14, that these conditions 'as formulated in the intructions which were to have served as the basis for the proposed Anglo-American approach, should be plainly stated to the Egyptians at an early stage; and he preferred on this account that there should be a formal opening of negotiations which would be distinct from normal diplomatic exchanges'. His conversations with General Robertson, he said, had confirmed him in this view. [2] He had therefore 'instructed our negotiations to proceed on the basis that it was the Egyptians who desired to resume the negotiations; that the discussions should begin with a formal meeting at which both sides would state their views; and that our case should be developed on the lines indicated in the instructions which had been drawn up for the purpose of the proposed Anglo-American approach'.

Churchill also told the Cabinet that he was intructing the British negotiators 'to do their utmost to secure Egyptian agreement to the proposal that British troops retained in the base installations in the Canal Zone should wear uniform and carry personal arms'. He thought it 'specially important' that these men should not be left unarmed 'and open to arrest by Egyptian police if, for instance, trouble arose about the Sudan'. If they wore uniform and carried personal arms 'they could not be molested by the Egyptians without military action which would constitute an act of war'. [3]

That afternoon, Churchill was present in the House of Commons when R. A. Butler introduced the second Budget of Churchill's peacetime administration. Three days later, in Glasgow, on April 17, he told a meeting of Scottish Conservatives:

Last Tuesday I went to the House of Commons to hear the Budget. It was a memorable occasion. It was the first Budget since the war without any new taxes. The Chancellor of the Exchequer, Mr Butler, gave a full account of

---

[1] Letter of 10 April 1953: Robert Rhodes James, *Anthony Eden*, London 1986, page 362.

[2] General Sir Brian Robertson was Commander-in-Chief Middle East Land Forces from 1950 to 1953. He was created Baron in 1961. In 1944 and 1945 he had been Chief Administrative Officer to Field Marshal Alexander in Italy; and from 1949 to 1950, United Kingdom High Commissioner for Germany.

[3] Cabinet Conclusions No. 26 of 1953, 'Secret', 11.30 a.m., 14 April 1953: Cabinet papers, 128/26. The Cabinet approved the instructions which Churchill was sending.

the improvement in our world position; how much further we were from national bankruptcy than a year ago and still further than eighteen months ago.

The 'culminating point', Churchill noted, was when Butler perpetrated 'his most insulting and malevolent deed', taking sixpence off the income tax. 'I never take pleasure in human woe,' Churchill said, 'and yet I must confess I wish you had been there with me to see the look of absolute misery and anger which swept across the crowded faces opposite. Sixpence off the income tax! Class favour to over thirty millions of people. What shocking Tory reaction. Only nine shillings in the pound left for the income tax collector!'

Towards the end of his Glasgow speech, Churchill turned to the international situation, and in particular to the future of Russia since Stalin's death nearly six weeks earlier. 'Suddenly mighty events far beyond our control,' he said, 'but in harmony with our highest hopes, have made their mark on the life of the world. New men have obtained supreme power in Moscow and their words and gestures, and even to some extent their actions, seem to betoken a change of mood. We cannot yet tell what this means. We cannot measure how deep is their purpose or where the process they have set on foot will lead them,' and he went on to ask:

Is there a new breeze blowing on the tormented world? Certainly sudden hopes have sprung in the hearts of peoples under every sky. We live in a time when science offers with blind prodigality to mankind the choice between a golden age of prosperity and the most hideous form of destruction.

When at the end of the war eight years ago the three victorious powers met in Berlin all this lay before us. I could not understand why Soviet Russia did not join with the Western Allies in seeking a just and lasting treaty of peace. Instead this immense branch of the human family was led into the morasses of measureless ambition for the triumph and expansion not only of Communist doctrines but of Communist control.

It was only gradually that the Western world became aware of their new danger and several hard years had to pass before they even began to regain their united power. Many grievous things have happened to many valiant and ancient nations and heavy burdens of toils and fear have been laid upon the backs of mankind.

Now it may be that another chance will come. Perhaps indeed it has come. We cannot tell. The future is inscrutable. But as so often happens the path of duty is clear. We must not cast away a single hope, however slender, so long as we believe there is good faith and goodwill.

Churchill ended his Glasgow speech with an appeal for the 'abiding fellowship and brotherhood' of the English-speaking world, 'headed and sustained by the giant power of the United States', for in that fellowship, he said, 'the best hopes reside both for securing peace today and for the broadening future of mankind'.[1]

Churchill's Cabinet colleagues were sceptical as to how far Soviet policy might change. On the day that Churchill was speaking in Glasgow, the Atlantic Committee of the Cabinet, meeting in London, concluded that the conciliatory measure of the new Soviet leaders 'might well prove more dangerous to Western cohesion and to the building and maintenance of the military and economic strength of the West than the bludgeoning xenophobia displayed by Stalin'. The final decision: 'We must avoid being lulled into a sense of false security.'[2] This sense of unease was later reiterated by the new British Ambassador in Moscow, Sir William Hayter, who reported that the new Soviet Government 'talks of co-existence, but they visualize it as the co-existence of the snake and the rabbit. The only real change is of method.' Hayter added: 'Malenkov seems to have concluded that Stalin's methods were too rough. Other and more subtle methods of weakening the West are henceforth to be adopted.'[3]

In the House of Commons, Churchill continued to be the butt of Labour outcries and insults. On one occasion he made an unexpected response: 'When Winston got up to leave the Chamber,' Henry Channon noted in his diary on April 23, 'the squawking Socialists rudely shouted "Good night" at the old man. The PM, surprised, turned and, with his little mocking bow, blew kisses to the Opposition, who were somewhat startled by this response.'[4]

On April 12 Anthony Eden was operated on in the London Clinic. The operation, a relatively simple and normally successful one, went wrong. A second operation was needed, to try to repair the damage. In the event, the damage done by the first operation proved irreparable. The body poisons that pass through the bile duct to be expelled from the body would now, as his official biographer has explained, 'seep into his system, causing high fevers. . . .'[5]

By contrast to Eden's grave illness and continuing ill-health, Churchill seemed to have recovered entirely from the setbacks of a year earlier. 'What have you done with your man?' Lord Swinton had

[1] Speech of 17 April 1953: Randolph S. Churchill (editor), *The Unwritten Alliance*, pages 28–35.

[2] Atlantic (Official) Committee of the Cabinet, 'Conclusion of Foreign Office Paper on Recent Developments in the USSR', 17 April 1953: Cabinet papers, 134/766.

[3] Moscow Telegram of 24 November 1953: Foreign Office papers, 371/106527.

[4] Channon diary, 23 April 1953: Robert Rhodes James (editor), *Chips*, page 474.

[5] Robert Rhodes James, *Anthony Eden*, page 363.

asked Lord Moran on April 23. 'He is full of energy and doing well too'; and on April 24 Lord Moran noted in his diary:

This morning Winston is in good heart.

'I'm really wonderfully well, Charles. Everyone around me is going down. Anthony will be away for months. His doctors are divided, and they are saying that he may have to have another operation. There would not be any danger, but they would like to get him in better condition before anything is done. I have asked him to go to Chequers. Anthony would like to keep an eye on things at the Foreign Office, but I won't let him. I cannot deal with a sick man.'

I knew that this was the PM's way of telling me that he meant to go on with the Foreign Office all the time Anthony was away.

'You could no doubt do this for a short time as an emergency measure,' I told him, 'but to burden yourself with the FO for an indefinite period, perhaps for months, is surely not wise.'

'Oh, I like it,' he answered. 'It doesn't add as much work as you think. You see, I've got to keep an eye on foreign affairs at any time. Yes. I have been hunted. I am making my speeches out of my head at present. They seem to go all right.' [1]

Since the death of Stalin on March 5, Churchill had been alert to any possible change of mood in Soviet policy. After sending the British Ambassador in Moscow a series of points relating to individual cases, Churchill explained: 'These various minor points were raised by us in order mainly to gain some sort of contact.' [2] On April 16 Churchill had spoken to the former Soviet Ambassador to Washington, Andrei Gromyko, who was on his way from the United States to Moscow, to take up the post of First Deputy Minister for Foreign Affairs. 'The conversation was confined to generalities,' Jock Colville wrote later that day to Eden's Private Secretary, Evelyn Shuckburgh, 'and nothing of any substance was said by Mr Gromyko apart from a broad wish that the present improvement in the situation should continue. Mr Churchill gave Mr Gromyko a bound copy of one of his books.' Colville added: 'After Gromyko left Mr Churchill telephoned the American Ambassador in order to tell him of the visit and to ask him to assure the United States Administration that it had been purely formal in nature and had no other significance.' [3]

From Washington, without any prior consultation with London,

[1] Moran diary, 24 April 1953: *The Struggle for Survival*, page 404.
[2] Note of 30 April 1953, headed 'PM to Amb., Moscow': Premier papers, 11/422. The Ambassador (Sir William Hayter's predecessor) was Sir Alvary Gascoigne.
[3] Letter of 16 April 1953: Premier papers, 11/422.

Eisenhower announced that he was willing to consider discussions with the Soviet Union on points of substance. It was, Churchill told the House of Commons on April 20, a 'bold and inspiring initiative'. It was 'too soon', Churchill added, 'to consider any relaxation of our efforts for collective defence', but, he went on, 'I trust that nothing will be said here or elsewhere which will check or chill the processes of good will which may be at work and my hope is that they may presently lead to conversations on the highest level, even if informal and private, between some of the principal Powers concerned.'[1] To Eisenhower, Churchill telegraphed at once:

I should like to know what you think should be the next step. Evidently we must wait a few days for their reply or reaction. It is not likely that the Soviets will agree about the release of the Satellites or a unified Korea. There will, however, be a strong movement here for a meeting between Heads of States and Governments. How do you stand about this? In my opinion the best would be that the three victorious Powers, who separated at Potsdam in 1945, should come together again. I like the idea you mentioned to me of Stockholm. I am sure the world will expect something like this to emerge if the Soviets do not turn your proposals down abruptly.

'If nothing can be arranged,' Churchill's telegram ended, 'I shall have to consider seriously a personal contact. You told me in New York you would have no objection to this. I should be grateful if you would let me know how these things are shaping in your mind.'[2]

At the Cabinet on April 28, Churchill drew his colleagues' attention to a newspaper report that Molotov, the Soviet Foreign Minister, had spoken in favour of the conclusion of a 'peace pact' between the Soviet Union, the United States, Britain, France and Communist China. If there was to be any such meeting of the Great Powers, Churchill commented, 'he would prefer that it should be limited to the Soviet Union, the United States and the United Kingdom, who could take up the discussion at the point at which it had been left at the end of the Potsdam Conference in 1945'. It was in any event 'unlikely', he thought, 'that the United States Government would be willing to be represented at any such meeting which included representatives of Communist China'.

In discussion it was pointed out that proposals for a Five-Power peace pact 'had formed part of Communist propaganda for some time past' and that Molotov had done no more than endorse a proposal to this end submitted by the Congress of the Peoples for Peace, 'which was a Communist-controlled organisation'. More significance could

[1] Speech of 20 April 1953: *Hansard*.
[2] Prime Minister's Personal Telegram, T.101/53, 'My dear Friend', signed 'Yours ever, Winston', 'Immediate', 'Secret', sent 21 April 1953: Premier papers, 11/422.

have been attached to his statement if it had been made, of his own initiative, 'in an official offer to the other Governments concerned'.

The Cabinet agreed that it would be 'premature' to draw any conclusions from what Molotov was alleged to have said, and that it would be 'unnecessary for the Government to volunteer any public statement about it at this stage'.[1]

On April 29 Eden had his second operation. It was a dangerous one; so dangerous that he nearly died. When it was over, it had become clear that he might never be a healthy man again. In despair, he envisaged a third operation, in Boston. Churchill, deeply shocked at what had happened, and aware of the expense of an operation in the United States, wrote to Anthony and Clarissa Eden on May 21:

> After Shuckburgh had brought me the news I saw Horace Evans and Cattell on Tuesday night on the question of Anthony going to Boston in about a month. I had asked Lord Moran to come to advise me not on the medical aspects of the case but on the policy as it affected the medical profession. He took a day to think things over and then wrote the enclosed paper which is sagacious. On the whole I think his conclusion was that Anthony's decision should turn on whether he felt he would like a change of doctors and environment. He considers Cattell outstanding in every way though equally competent men exist in England.

Churchill's letter continued:

> As I have been asked to express a view I would say this: If Anthony feels he would like the new man I will try to arrange for Cattell to come over here to do the operation and stay at least a fortnight. There is a Prime Minister's Fund which can be used in exceptional cases so the expense need be of no worry to you. If however Cattell cannot manage to operate anywhere but in his own setting at Boston and if Anthony feels a strong inclination to using him I recommend he should not hesitate to cross the Atlantic travelling by sea.
>
> All my love to both of you.[2]

---

[1] Cabinet Conclusions No. 29 of 1953, 'Secret', 11.30 a.m., 28 April 1953: Cabinet papers, 128/26.

[2] Letter of 21 May 1953: Churchill papers, 2/216. Lord Moran's note read: 'The Prime Minister has consulted me on one point, namely whether the operation on Mr Eden should be done in Boston or in London. I have advised him as follows:— Travelling especially by boat should not entail fatigue for the patient, and is really not a contradiction to the operation taking place in Boston. As to the relative merits of the surgeons in London and in Boston, Mr Cattell is a surgeon of the highest possible repute, and specially skilled in this kind of operation. He is known both in England and in America and is admired for his judgment and skill and for his attractive personality. Mr Eden could not possibly be in better hands. On the other hand two at least of the London surgeons are, I should say, equally skilled in this branch of surgery. I had in mind Mr Maingot and Mr Julian Taylor. If there is any difference between them it would probably be found to lie in the very large number of cases of this kind which Mr Cattell has operated on. I have said nothing of the effect on public opinion of a decision to have the operation in Boston, as others are more competent to appraise this than I am. Where the pros and cons as between London and Boston are so even, I think the patient's own opinion is of the first importance and might very well decide the issue.' (Note of 19 May 1953: Churchill papers, 2/216.)

Eden decided to go to Boston. To make this possible financially, Churchill arranged for Conservative Party funds to be put at Eden's disposal.

On Sunday April 26 Churchill held a Staff Conference at Chequers, with Lord Alexander, General Sir John Harding, Air Chief Marshal Sir William Dickson and Sir William Strang.[1] When the meeting was over, Harding and Dickson prepared a note for Churchill of what had been decided. 'You reaffirmed,' they wrote, 'your decision that no reinforcements from Malta or elsewhere should be sent to the Canal Zone without reference to you. Orders to that effect had already been sent to Commanders-in-Chief, Middle East. They will not be changed without reference to you.' It was also agreed that the British Commanders-in-Chief, Middle East, 'should not be held responsible for the safety of British subjects beyond their control in Egypt'. The three other conclusions were as follows:

Sudan

You decided that in the event of serious trouble in Egypt which the Cabinet might conclude amounted to a state of war, we should at once reinforce Khartoum with two Infantry battalions and appropriate air forces, disarm the Egyptian battalion there, and resume full control of the Sudan.

Malaya

You accepted the CIGS's view that the Songkhla (Singora) position is the best for the defence of Malaya against invasion by land. You agreed that Her Majesty's Government must seize and hold that position immediately if the security of Malaya on the landward side was in danger as a result of events in Indo-China or Siam. The plan should be prepared in detail now.

Indo-China

You decided that in view of possible developments in Egypt, and our many commitments elsewhere, we could not afford to dissipate any of our resources, or prejudice the mobility of our air and land forces by lending any of our limited air transport resources to the French for use in Indo-China. This may, however, require reconsideration by the Cabinet at a later stage.[2]

These subjects were elaborated on three days later, at a meeting of the full Defence Committee, when Churchill said that he hoped 'we should not have to embark' on the 'difficult and dangerous' operation of trying to safeguard British subjects in Egypt. 'If we had to undertake it,' he said, 'we should do so only if the Egyptians had first attacked us in the Canal Zone. In the event of our having to undertake opera-

---

[1] Harding was Chief of the Imperial General staff, Dickson, Chief of the Air Staff, and Strang, Permanent Under-Secretary of State at the Foreign Office.

[2] Defence Committee No. 26 of 1953, 'Top Secret', 'Conclusions of a Staff Conference held by the Prime Minister at Chequers', Sunday, 26 April 1953: Cabinet papers, 131/13.

tions against hostile mobs in Egypt, full use should be made of tear gas, adequate stocks of which should be maintained in the Canal Zone.' As to the Sudan, Churchill told his colleagues that 'firm action' there might 'offset the damage to our prestige in the Middle East which would result from an unsatisfactory solution in Egypt.' He therefore considered that 'we should be ready at short notice to re-inforce Khartoum, to disarm the Egyptians, and to resume full control of the country, thereupon proceeding with the elections as quickly as possible.'

The Defence Committee of April 29 also discussed the first group of ex-prisoners-of-war exchanged in Korea. Of the thirty-two who were expected to arrive in Britain on May 1, five were believed to be pro-Communist and one to have 'co-operated actively with the Com-munists', broadcasting over Peking Radio and writing letters to the *Daily Worker*. Alexander thought that they might be intercepted on their return, but Churchill told his colleagues:

. . . it would be preferable to take no action at all against the five men on their return to the United Kingdom. Nor should anything be done about the man suspected of having co-operated actively with the Communists except to provide evidence in order to discredit him if he started airing his views in public. People in this country could be relied upon to treat with contempt any subversive activities that these men might indulge in. It would be useful, however, to obtain full details concerning their families and general way of life in case it subsequently became necessary to take any action against them. As regards the larger number of pro-Communist ex-prisoners of war that might eventually return to the United Kingdom, we could decide what was best to be done in the light of our experience in dealing with the first five such men.[1]

In the immediate aftermath of the Second World War, King George VI had been disappointed when Churchill declined the Order of the Garter. With Queen Elizabeth's accession to the throne, the matter was raised again, between the Queen's Principal Private Secretary, Sir Alan Lascelles, and Churchill's Principal Private Secretary, Jock Colville. Recounting these events twelve years later, Colville recalled how, in 1952:

Sir Alan Lascelles told me that the King had been greatly disappointed that Mr Churchill had declined the Garter. Did I think there was any possi-bility of his now accepting it? I said I would find out what he thought and I took the opportunity of dining with Mr and Mrs Churchill to sound him out.

[1] Defence Committee No. 7 of 1953, 'Top Secret', 11.45 a.m., 29 April 1953: Cabinet papers, 131/13.

The reactions of the two were very different. Mr Churchill said that he always felt that it had been discourteous of him to refuse the Garter. And what is more, that as the 1st Duke of Marlborough's father had been Sir Winston Churchill, he felt that he himself would not mind being Sir Winston.[1] And that the Garter had a special appeal. Mrs Churchill disliked the idea very much because she didn't want to give up being Mrs Churchill.

However after a great deal of discussion at dinner—I hadn't of course said that the offer was likely to be remade—it was agreed that the importance was to keep the name Winston Churchill and whether it was Mr Winston Churchill or Sir Winston Churchill didn't matter; and there was no doubt that Mr Churchill was particularly attracted by the thought of the 1st Duke of Marlborough's father. In the end he said he thought that if he were offered it he might well reconsider his view. I so informed Sir Alan Lascelles.[2]

It had not been easy for Churchill to make up his mind, as Sir Norman Brook later recalled:

... he would have preferred to keep unchanged the name by which he had always been known and to remain plain 'Mr Churchill'. Though he had always been avid for medals, he was not interested in titles. This was why he was reluctant for so long to accept the offer of the Garter. He would have liked, characteristically, to have it both ways, to accept the Garter but retain the 'Mr'.

During the long period when he was struggling with this dilemma, he once said to me: 'I don't see why I should not have the Garter but continue to be known as Mr Churchill. After all, my father was known as Lord Randolph Churchill, but he was not a Lord. That was only a courtesy title. Why should not I continue to be called Mr Churchill as a discourtesy title?'[3]

'I will tell you a secret,' Churchill had said to his doctor on April 24, before he and his wife left London to dine with the Queen at Windsor Castle. 'You musn't tell anyone. She wants me to accept the Garter.' He had refused it once before, he said, but then 'the Prime Minister had a say in it. Now only the Queen decides.'[4]

Churchill accepted the Queen's offer, becoming Sir Winston Churchill, and adding KG to his already imposing list of initials, OM, CH, MP. The congratulations from family and friends were exuberant. From his cousin Lord Ivor Churchill came a letter to say 'what joy my father would have derived from the lustre you have shed upon the family name', and he added: 'No one estimated your potentialities

[1] The 1st Duke of Marlborough's father, Winston Churchill, had entered Parliament in 1661 and was in 1664 one of the original members of the Royal Society. Knighted in 1664, he was the author of a book, *Divi Britannici*, which Churchill described in his life of Marlborough as 'a substantial and erudite volume ... universally unread', which explored the principle of the Divine Right of Kings from 'the Year of the World 2855' to the time of writing. It was published in 1675.

[2] 'Mr Jock Colville: Reminiscences', 8 June 1965: Randolph Churchill papers.

[3] Lord Normanbrook recollections: Sir John Wheeler-Bennett (editor), *Action This Day*, page 45.

[4] Moran diary, 24 April 1953: *The Struggle for Survival*, page 404.

more highly than he and a favourite theme of his was to speculate upon your chances of attaining political immortality.'[1]

'Thank you so much dear Ivor,' Churchill replied. 'I loved yr father & I rejoice in yr friendship.'[2]

'Why have you not congratulated me, you pig?' Churchill telegraphed to Brendan Bracken, now Viscount Bracken, a few days later.[3] 'Message for former mister from faithful chela,' Bracken replied by telegram on May 4, 'Dear Sir, recovering from shock. But give me notice of canonisation. Love, Brendan.'[4]

One letter of congratulation came from Lady Lytton, whose husband Victor had likewise been a Knight of the Garter. Churchill replied at once, in his own hand:

Dearest Pamela,

Thank you so much for yr lovely letter. No congratulations were more welcome than yours. I took it because it was the Queen's wish. I think she is splendid.

I am sorry that the Garter stirs poignant memories in yr mind of dear Victor and valiant Antony. You have indeed had fearful blows to bear in life. Still courage and beauty have conquered all.

I do hope yr recovery is now complete. I did not like the cough when I came to see you, but how lively you were, in yr charming home!

With my best love,

Yours devotedly

W[5]

On May 2, Pierson Dixon lunched with Churchill at 10 Downing Street, noting in his diary:

In AE's absence he has taken charge of the FO, and is taking a lively interest in its day to day work. He usually spends Friday night at Chartwell, coming up to Downing St for lunch and a sleep, and down to Chequers for dinner.

We lunched alone with a Private Secretary (Jock Colville). The PM was wearing a very well cut boiler suit in blue serge with a white pin-stripe. We lunched in the small dining-room. The lunch lasted for $3\frac{1}{4}$ hours. A varied and noble procession of wines with which I could not keep pace—champagne, port, brandy, cointreau: W drank a great deal of all, and ended with two glasses of whisky and soda. The champagne was Pol Roger 1928 which he

[1] 'My dear Winston', 26 April 1953: Churchill papers, 1/53.

[2] Draft telegram, undated, Churchill papers, 1/53. Lord Ivor Churchill's father was Churchill's cousin 'Sunny', 9th Duke of Marlborough, who had died in 1934.

[3] Draft telegram, undated, Churchill papers, 1/53.

[4] Telegram sent from Leicester on 4 May 1953: Churchill papers, 1/53. It was Stanley Baldwin, Rudyard Kipling's cousin, taking a leaf from Kipling's *Kim*—who 'acted as Chela to the Lama'—used to refer to Brendan Bracken as Churchill's 'faithful Chela' (a Hindu retainer, follower, pupil or disciple). It is also spelt Cheyla and Chelah.

[5] 'Dearest Pamela', 3 May 1953: Lytton papers.

said he liked more than any other; he had managed to buy up most of the stocks in London.

Churchill made the following points to Dixon:

Indo-China. The Communists invaded Laos, one of the Associate States, last month. Should its King be advised to leave the capital Luang Prabang? W complained that he had been able to remain ignorant about these outlandish areas all his life; it was hard that they had come to tease him in his old age.

Persia. I was explaining a point, and mentioned Musaddiq. He interrupted me. 'I call him Mussy Duck.'

The FO telegrams too verbose and too many of them. The Ambassadors should be made to encypher their reports themselves. The FO too prone to appease.[1]

On May 6 the Defence Committee met to discuss the measures needed to maintain Britain's position in Egypt 'in the context of the breakdown of the current defence negotiations'. The Committee also considered a memorandum by the Chiefs of Staff on the part which Israel might play in the British schemes for the defence of the Middle East, especially against any Soviet threat.[2] As Churchill explained to his colleagues, 'the Chiefs of Staff were anxious to secure the co-operation of Israel in the defence of the Middle East, not only on account of its geographical position, but because the Israelis were potentially the best military material in the area. A Military Mission had visited Tel Aviv in October 1952 and had had exploratory talks with the Israelis. The Chiefs of Staff wished to have further discussions with them, but considered that before doing so it was necessary to secure American agreement to our policy, as we should have to look to the United States to finance the equipment of Israeli forces and defence works.'

Churchill went on to tell the Defence Committee that the Chiefs of Staff 'therefore asked for authority to hold secret discussions with the Americans with the object of securing their support for the general policy proposed in their memorandum', and he added:

This was largely based on the strategic requirements in a war with Russia, and it was therefore proposed that the Israelis should make their major fighting contribution in the air. Israel would be reluctant to establish anything but a balanced force, since their main preoccupation was the defence of their soil against invasion by their neighbours. Moreover, the fear of stronger Israeli forces would constitute a useful deterrent against Egyptian aggressive aspirations and the possibility of such forces being built up would be a useful factor in our present negotiations with the Egyptian Government.[3]

---

[1] Pierson Dixon diary, 2 May 1953: Pierson Dixon papers.
[2] Chiefs of Staff Memorandum No. 21 of 1953.
[3] Defence Committee No. 8 of 1953, 'Top Secret', 11.30 a.m., 6 May 1953: Cabinet papers, 131/13.

On May 13 the Defence Committee met again; once more its discussion was dominated by the need to maintain Britain's position in Egypt in the event of a military move against the British forces in the Canal Zone. Plans for Operation 'Rodeo', a full-scale British military intervention, were now complete, but Churchill doubted if they were yet needed. The recent Egyptian military movements, he said, 'did not necessarily imply a hostile intent. They appeared to be deploying their troops defensively to counter "Rodeo". He thought that the Egyptians might not use their armed forces against us unless and until we had entered the Delta. He considered that, if we were to arrest any of the German leaders of the Muslim Brotherhood gangs, we should detain them and not merely expel them from the Canal Zone.' Churchill warned:

. . . the latest intelligence from Egypt confirmed him in the view that it would be unwise to undertake Operation 'Rodeo' prematurely; for it would involve a wide dispersal of our limited forces. However, if civilians were murdered in Cairo or Alexandria, a new situation would have arisen; a situation in which we should presumably have strong outside support for vigorous action. The Prime Minister said that he wished to be informed of the detailed plans for the defence of Her Majesty's Embassy in Cairo against a mob attack.[1]

Having decided to have his third operation in Boston, Eden planned to fly there on June 9. Before he left, and while he was still in the London Clinic, Churchill telegraphed from Lingfield racecourse: 'Am putting two pounds each way Gibraltar and one pound to win Prince Arthur for you, but don't get too excited.'[2] In the event, Prince Arthur lost, losing Eden a pound, but Gibraltar came third at 6 to 1, winning him a pound: 'i.e.,' Churchill reported, 'no profit no loss.'[3] More successful was the Queen, whose horse won. 'Madam,' Churchill telegraphed, 'my sincere congratulations with my humble duty though this was not a matter on which I felt called upon to tender advice.'[4]

Churchill returned to Chequers from Lingfield, and on the following day received the Queen's reply. 'Most grateful for your kind message of congratulations,' it read. 'Sorry you were not in closer attendance.'[5]

[1] Defence Committee No. 9 of 1953, 'Top Secret', 11.30 a.m., 13 May 1953: Cabinet papers, 131/13.
[2] Telegram despatched 12.15 p.m., 16 May 1953: Churchill papers, 1/156.
[3] Note of 18 May 1953: Churchill papers, 1/156. Although Eden had made no profit, Churchill was up £100 (£1,000 in 1987).
[4] Telegram despatched by telephone from Lingfield racecourse, 3.15 p.m., 16 May 1953: Churchill papers, 2/180.
[5] Telegram received at Chequers by telephone, 12.45 p.m., 17 May 1953: Churchill papers, 2/180. Aureole, owned by the Queen and ridden by W. H. Carr, won the Derby Trial Stakes at Lingfield Park on 16 May 1953 (having started at 2 to 1). In the same race, Churchill's horse Prince Arthur, ridden by E. Smith, finished fifth (he started at 7 to 1).

44

The Call for a Summit

I N replying to Churchill's appeal of 21 April 1953 for a possible meeting with the Soviets, Eisenhower had once more been cautious, even negative. 'Premature action by us in that direction,' he told Churchill, 'might have the effect of giving the Soviets an easy way out of the position in which I think they are now placed. We have so far seen no concrete Soviet actions which would indicate their willingness to perform in connection with larger issues. In the circumstances we would risk raising hopes of progress toward an accommodation which would be unjustified.'[1] Undeterred, Churchill telegraphed to Eisenhower on May 4 with the text of a message which he wished to send direct to Molotov. Churchill's proposed message to Molotov read:

I had hoped you and Eden might soon be having a talk about things as you know each other so well, but his unfortunate illness will prevent this for some time. I wonder whether you would like me to come to Moscow so that we could renew our own war-time relation and so that I could meet Monsieur Malenkov and others of your leading men.

Naturally I do not imagine that we could settle any of the grave issues which overhang the immediate future of the world, but I have a feeling that it might be helpful if our intercourse proceeded with the help of friendly acquaintance and goodwill instead of impersonal diplomacy and propaganda. I do not see how this could make things worse. I should of course make it clear I was not expecting any major decisions at this informal meeting but only to restore an easy and friendly basis between us such as I have with so many other countries.

Do not on any account suppose that I should be offended if you thought the time and circumstances were unsuitable or that my thought and purpose would be changed. We have both of us lived through a good lot. Let me know how you and your friends feel about my suggestion.[2]

Eisenhower and Dulles were not willing to see this message sent:

---

[1] 'Dear Winston', 'Top Secret', 25 April 1953: Eisenhower papers.
[2] 'Personal and Confidential', 4 May 1953: Eisenhower papers.

'We would advise against it,' Eisenhower telegraphed to Churchill on May 5, and he added:

You will pardon me, I know, if I express a bit of astonishment that you think it appropriate to recommend Moscow to Molotov as a suitable meeting place. Uncle Joe used to plead ill health as an excuse for refusing to leave territory under the Russian flag or controlled by the Kremlin. That excuse no longer applies and while I do not for a minute suggest that progress toward peace should be balked by mere matters of protocol, I do have a suspicion that anything the Kremlin could misinterpret as weakness or over-eagerness on our part would militate against success in negotiation.

In my notes to you of April twenty-fifth I expressed the view that we should not rush things too much and should not permit feeling in our countries for a meeting between heads of states and governments to press us into precipitate initiatives. I feel just as strongly now as I did ten days ago that this is right, and certainly nothing that the Soviet Government has done in the meantime would tend to persuade me differently. . . . [1]

Churchill was distressed by Eisenhower's reasoning, replying that same day:

According to my experience of these people in the war we should gain more by goodwill on the spot by going as guests of the Soviets than we should lose by appearing to court them. This was particularly the case when Anthony and I spent a fortnight in Moscow in October 1944. I am not afraid of the 'solitary pilgrimage' if I am sure in my heart that it may help forward the cause of peace and even at the worst can only do harm to my reputation. I am fully alive to the impersonal and machine-made foundation of Soviet policy although under a veneer of civilities and hospitalities. I have a strong belief that Soviet self-interest will be their guide. My hope is that it is their self-interest which will bring about an easier state of affairs.

None of the four men who I am told are working together very much as equals, Malenkov, Molotov, Beria and Bulganin, has any contacts outside Russia except Molotov. I am very anxious to know these men and talk to them as I think I can frankly and on the dead level.

Churchill's telegram ended:

It is only by going to Moscow that I can meet them all and as I am only the head of a Government, not of a State, I see no obstacle. Of course, I would much rather go with you to any place you might appoint and that is, I believe, the best chance of a good result. I find it difficult to believe that we shall gain anything by an attitude of pure negation and your message to me certainly does not show much hope. [2]

Churchill was determined to persevere with what he saw as an

---

[1] 'Dear Winston', 'Top Secret', 5 May 1953: Eisenhower papers.
[2] Telegram of 5 May 1953 (received 7 May 1953): Eisenhower papers.

avenue of hope. May 10 marked the thirteenth anniversary of Churchill's wartime Premiership. On the following day, May 11, he spoke in the House of Commons in the Foreign Affairs debate. With Eden in a nursing home awaiting the ordeal of a third operation, it fell to Churchill to present the panorama and prospects for a world still uncertain of how it would be affected by Stalin's death two months earlier, and to indicate where hope might be found.

Speaking of a proposal put forward by the Communist bloc, that the stalemate in the Korean truce negotiations should be the subject of an arbitration by five Powers, Poland, Czechoslovakia, Switzerland, Sweden and India, Churchill said that there was at present 'no reason known to me' to assume that this proposal 'may not form the basis of an agreement, provided always that it is put forward by the Communists in a spirit of sincerity'.

Churchill then turned to Europe, and back to the immediate aftermath of the Second World War eight years earlier. 'If our advice had been taken by the United States after the Armistice with Germany,' he said, 'the Western allies would not have withdrawn from the front line which their armies had reached to the agreed occupation lines until agreement had been reached with Soviet Russia on the many points of difference about the occupation of enemy territories, of which the occupation of the German Zones was, of course, only a part. Our view was not accepted and a wide area of Germany was handed over to Soviet occupation without any general settlement among the three victorious Powers.'

At Potsdam, Churchill cautioned, 'the Russia of Stalin took a very hostile line to the Western allies'. Then, after Potsdam,

> Stalin found himself resisted from a very early stage by the firmness and tenacity of the late Ernest Bevin, who marshalled and rallied democratic sentiment strongly against this new movement of Russian Soviet ambitions. All the tragic and tremendous events of the last eight years followed in remorseless succession. As the result, the immense and formidable problem of Germany now presents itself in an entirely different aspect.

Eastern Germany had fallen into 'great misery and depression', with a 'powerful and well-armed, Soviet-organised, Communist German military force of over 100,000 men'. As to Western Germany, under Dr Adenauer, 'the wisest German statesman since the days of Bismarck', Churchill told the House of Commons:

> Strong as is our desire to see a friendly settlement with Soviet Russia, or even an improved *modus vivendi*, we are resolved not in any way to fail in the obligations to which we have committed ourselves about Western Germany.
>
> Dr Adenauer is visiting us here in a few days, and we shall certainly assure him that Western Germany will in no way be sacrificed or—I pick these

words with special care—cease to be master of its own fortunes within the agreements we and other NATO countries have made with them.

Churchill then turned to what he called the 'supreme event' of recent months, 'the change of attitude and, as we all hope, of mood which has taken place in the Soviet domains and particularly in the Kremlin since the death of Stalin'.

It was the Government's policy, Churchill declared, 'to avoid by every means in their power doing anything or saying anything which could check any favourable reaction that may be taking place and to welcome every sign of improvement in our relations with Russia'.

The British Government had been 'encouraged', Churchill said, 'by a series of amicable gestures' on the part of the new Soviet Government. These had so far taken the form 'of leaving off doing things which we have not been doing to them'. It was therefore difficult to find 'specific cases' with which to match Soviet actions. He wanted nevertheless to make some 'general observations', which he hoped would be studied 'with tolerance and indulgence'. It would, he thought, 'be a mistake to assume that nothing can be settled with Soviet Russia unless or until everything is settled. A settlement of two or three of our difficulties would be an important gain to every peace-loving country.' For instance, peace in Korea, or the conclusion of an Austrian treaty: 'these might lead to an easement in our relations for the next few years, which might in itself open new prospects to the security and prosperity of all nations and every continent'.

Churchill went on to explain:

Therefore, I think it would be a mistake to try to map things out too much in detail and expect that the grave, fundamental issues which divide the Communist and non-Communist parts of the world could be settled at a stroke by a single comprehensive agreement. Piecemeal solutions of individual problems should not be disdained or improvidently put aside. It certainly would do no harm if, for a while, each side looked about for things to do which would be agreeable instead of being disagreeable to each other.

Above all, it would be a pity if the natural desire to reach a general settlement of international policy were to impede any spontaneous and healthy evolution which may be taking place inside Russia. I have regarded some of the internal manifestations and the apparent change of mood as far more important and significant than what has happened outside. I am anxious that nothing in the presentation of foreign policy by the NATO Powers should, as it were, supersede or take the emphasis out of what may be a profound movement of Russian feeling.

Churchill's appeal for a new approach to the Soviet Union, for such it was, continued:

We all desire that the Russian people should take the high place in world affairs which is their due without feeling anxiety about their own security. I do not believe that the immense problem of reconciling the security of Russia with the freedom and safety of Western Europe is insoluble. Indeed, if the United Nations Organization had the authority and character for which its creators hoped, it would be solved already.

The Locarno Treaty of 1925 has been in my mind. It was the highest point we reached between the wars. As Chancellor of the Exchequer in those days I was closely acquainted with it. It was based upon the simple provision that if Germany attacked France we should stand with the French, and if France attacked Germany we should stand with the Germans.

The scene to-day, its scale and its factors, is widely different, and yet I have a feeling that the master thought which animated Locarno might well play its part between Germany and Russia in the minds of those whose prime ambition it is to consolidate the peace of Europe as the key to the peace of mankind. Russia has a right to feel assured that as far as human arrangements can run the terrible events of the Hitler invasion will never be repeated, and that Poland will remain a friendly Power and a buffer, though not, I trust, a puppet State.

He wanted to 'make it plain', Churchill said, that 'in spite of all the uncertainties and confusion in which world affairs are plunged', it was his belief 'that a conference on the highest level should take place between the leading Powers without long delay'.

Such a conference, Churchill emphasized, 'should not be overhung by a ponderous or rigid agenda, or led into mazes and jungles of technical details, zealously contested by hordes of experts and officials drawn up in vast, cumbrous array', and he went on to expound further what he had in mind:

The conference should be confined to the smallest number of Powers and persons possible. It should meet with a measure of informality and a still greater measure of privacy and seclusion. It might well be that no hard and fast agreements would be reached, but there might be a general feeling among those gathered together that they might do something better than tear the human race, including themselves, into bits.

The Russians, said Churchill, 'might be attracted, as President Eisenhower has shown himself to be, and as *Pravda* does not challenge, by the idea of letting the weary, toiling masses of mankind enter upon the best spell of good fortune, fair play, well-being, leisure, and harmless happiness that has even been within their reach or even within their dreams', and he concluded:

I only say that this might happen, and I do not see why anyone should be frightened at having a try for it. If there is not at the summit of the nations the will to win the greatest prize and the greatest honour ever offered to mankind, doom-laden responsibility will fall upon those who now possess the power to decide. At the worst the participants in the meeting would have established more intimate contacts. At the best we might have a generation of peace.[1]

Churchill's speech was widely applauded. People were looking for a way ahead, out of the constrictions of the Cold War. Eden was then on his sickbed. Later he remembered having been shocked, writing in his diary a year and a half later:

It must be long in history since any one speech did so much damage to its own side. In Italy, as de Gasperi openly stated to Winston, & I believe elsewhere, it lost de Gasperi the election, i.e. his gamble for an increased majority. In Germany, Adenauer was exasperated. Worst of all it probably cost us EDC in France. At any rate, the whole summer was lost in wrangling. The speech was made without any consultation with the Cabinet, & I fear that the *Economist* is only too right in saying this week that it was playing party politics. Nutting[2] fought all he could against it. I, of course, never saw it at all, but W is not to blame for this for I was much too ill. He knew well though what I should have thought of it.[3]

Despite Eden's criticisms, Churchill persevered. He had made the speech, Colville recalled, 'wholly contrary to Foreign Office advice, since it was felt that a friendly approach to Russia would discourage the European powers working on the theme of Western Union'. Selwyn Lloyd, however, the Minister of State at the Foreign Office, 'was personally enthusiastic about it', Colville wrote, 'as were most of the Tories and the Opposition'. Colville added: 'I thought it a states-manlike initiative and knew it to be one which was entirely his own.'[4]

What mattered to Churchill was to try to bring together, in the post-Stalin era, some element of hope in an atomic age. An indication of the difficulties involved in the new approach came, however, eight days later, when Churchill reported to the Cabinet on the 'slow progress' of the armistice talks in Korea, and the growing impression that the United States authorities 'were adopting an unduly stiff attitude towards the proposals put forward by the Chinese'. In this connection, he drew the Cabinet's 'special attention' to a message from the British

---

[1] Speech of 11 May 1953: *Hansard*. 'Although there had been heads of government meetings before,' William Randolph Hearst wrote on the eve of the Eisenhower–Macmillan Camp David summit of 1959, 'Churchill's term "Summit"'—as used by him on 11 May 1953—'was first used for the top level talks at Geneva in July 1955.' ('Origin of "Summit"', *New York Journal-American*, 22 March 1959.)

[2] Anthony Nutting, Joint Parliamentary Under-Secretary of State for Foreign Affairs. In October 1954 he was appointed Minister of State at the Foreign Office; he resigned in 1956 in protest at the Suez landings.

[3] Eden diary, 27 November 1954: Robert Rhodes James, *Anthony Eden*, page 365.

[4] Colville recollections: *The Fringes of Power*, page 667.

Ambassador in Washington, 'from which it appeared that the opposition to some of the Chinese proposals had come mainly from Syngman Rhee, the President of the South Korean Republic'. The fact that South Korean troops 'now outnumbered the United Nations forces in Korea' was, the Ambassador stressed, a reason why the objections raised by Syngman Rhee 'must be given due weight'.

The consideration, said Churchill, 'must be taken into account in any assessment of the conduct of the armistice negotiations'.[1]

On May 14, three days after Churchill's 'Summit' speech, he had to address his mind to a worsening situation in Egypt. In the defence negotiations, he told the Cabinet, a 'deadlock' had been reached over the arrangements for technical supervision of the base installations in the Canal Zone. As a result, 'the negotiations were in effect suspended'. Meanwhile, Churchill warned that 'provocative speeches were being made by Egyptian Ministers and sporadic attacks on British troops and property in the Canal Zone were increasing'. It was known, he said, that about a thousand members of the Muslim Brotherhood had been organized into parties of fifty, 'each under German leadership', for the purpose of undertaking 'sabotage and guerilla activities' in the Canal Zone. The Cabinet's Defence Committee had considered the situation, Churchill explained, 'and had authorised certain precautionary measures, including the despatch of some reinforcements from Malta'. It would, however, be 'unwise', he felt, as did the Defence Committee, to launch the operation for protecting British lives and property in Cairo and Alexandria 'unless civilians in those cities were clearly seen to be in imminent danger'.[2]

Following Churchill's call on May 11 for a Summit Conference, the French Prime Minister, René Mayer, alarmed lest France be excluded, had approached Eisenhower direct, to suggest a pre-Summit meeting of the United States, Britain and France. On May 20 Eisenhower telephoned Churchill, to ask that France be included in the next meeting of Western powers, given the importance of the French position in Indo-China, and in NATO.[3] Churchill agreed, suggesting Bermuda as the meeting place. But a French political crisis delayed any decision from Paris for more than three weeks.

---

[1] Cabinet Conclusions No. 32 of 1953, 'Secret', 11.30 a.m., 19 May 1953: Cabinet papers, 128/26.
[2] Cabinet Conclusions No. 31 of 1953, 'Secret', 12 noon, 14 May 1953: Cabinet papers, 128/26.
[3] Note by the Office of the Staff-Secretary, White House, 21 May 1953: Eisenhower papers.

On May 23 General Bedell Smith and Sir Roger Makins had discussed a possible United States approach to Moscow, to help the Korean negotiations then proceeding at Panmunjon. Churchill at once wrote to Eisenhower:

I don't know how it all passed but since the matter has been discussed I hope you won't mind my giving you my opinion. I think it would be a pity for the United States to make an approach to Moscow at this juncture and that it would only be taken by them as a sign of weakness. You are the overwhelmingly powerful figure in the ring and we are supporting you in your effort to make the Communists accept.[1]

'I asked him this morning how he was weathering the racket,' Lord Moran noted in his diary on May 28, after a visit to Churchill at Downing Street. 'Yes, it is a racket,' Churchill replied, 'and I'm getting older. I miss Anthony. He's going to Boston on the 5th of June in a special Canadian aircraft for his operation. Poor fellow.' Churchill added: 'The Cabinet is very helpful. They have confidence in me.'[2]

Churchill's voice in Cabinet was primarily for caution and conciliation. When Oliver Lyttelton spoke of the Mau Mau gangs in Kenya, the threat which the larger gangs posed to the smaller Home Guard posts in the Colony, and the system of emergency assizes that had been set up to deal with criminal charges 'under a slightly simplified procedure', Churchill advised 'that care should be taken to avoid the simultaneous execution of any large numbers of persons who might be sentenced to death by these courts'. Public opinion in Britain, he said, 'would be critical of anything resembling mass executions'.[3]

On June 1 Churchill spoke with the Turkish Prime Minister, Adnan Menderes, and his Foreign Minister, Professor Fuat Köprülü, who gave him the text of a conciliatory telegram which they had just received from Molotov. The telegram stated that despite Soviet claims in 1945 to Turkish territory in eastern Turkey, and military control of the Bosphorus and Dardanelles, 'Molotov now wished to assure the Turkish Government that these demands no longer formed part of Soviet policy and should be considered as withdrawn'. What did Churchill think of this, the Turkish Prime Minister asked him, to which Churchill replied, as he at once informed Eisenhower:

[1] 'Private and Personal Message from the Prime Minister to President Eisenhower', 'Secret', 29 May 1953: Eisenhower papers. 'I look back with dark memories,' Churchill added, 'to all that followed inch by inch upon the United States's withdrawal from the League of Nations over 30 years ago. Thank God you are at the helm.'
[2] Moran diary, 28 May 1953: *The Struggle for Survival*, pages 404–5.
[3] Cabinet Conclusions No. 33 of 1953, 'Secret', 12 noon, 21 May 1953: Cabinet papers, 128/26.

I said that it showed how wise Turkey had been to join the NATO front. The Turkish Prime Minister replied that this was exactly the impression he and his colleagues had sustained. I then said that of course it might be either part of a plan to divide the allies or, as we should all hope, part of a new Soviet policy to have a detente and easier relations all round.

The course for all of us seemed simple, namely, while welcoming any improved change of heart, to hold firmly together and to our present policy.

He appeared to agree cordially with this.[1]

In the last week of May 1953, all Britain had begun its celebrations for the Coronation of Queen Elizabeth II. Churchill's mind was full of memories—he had served as a soldier in the armies of Queen Victoria, and had written in his histories about the first Queen Elizabeth and Queen Anne. At a reception given before the Commonwealth Parliamentary Association luncheon on May 27, he told an American schoolboy, James C. Humes, then at Stowe on an English-Speaking Union Scholarship: 'Study history, study history. In history lie all the secrets of statecraft'.[2] At the luncheon which followed the reception, Churchill told the assembled guests, who included the Queen and the Duke of Edinburgh:

In our island, by trial and error, and by perseverance across the centuries, we have found out a very good plan. Here it is: The Queen can do no wrong. But advisers can be changed as often as the people like to use their rights for that purpose. A great battle is lost: Parliament turns out the Government. A great battle is won—crowds cheer the Queen. We have found this a very commanding and durable doctrine. What goes wrong passes away with the politicians responsible. What goes right is laid on the altar of our united Commonwealth and Empire. Here today we salute 50 or 60 Parliaments—and one Queen.[3]

That evening Churchill gave a pre-Coronation dinner party at 10 Downing Street, 'resplendent in his Garter', Colville noted, 'with the diamond star that belonged to Castlereagh'.[4]

---

[1] 'Message from the Prime Minister to the President', received 4 June 1953: Eisenhower papers.

[2] James C. Humes recollections: James C. Humes, *Churchill, Speaker of the Century*, London 1980, page vii. Humes later worked as a speechwriter at the White House for three Presidents.

[3] Speech of 27 May 1953: *The Times*, 28 May 1953. Recording: BBC Written Archives Centre, Library No. 19066.

[4] Colville diary, 31 May 1953: *The Fringes of Power*, pages 713–14. Robert, Viscount Castlereagh, 2nd Marquess of Londonderry, Foreign Secretary at the time of the Napoleonic Wars, committed suicide in 1822. His niece, Lady Frances Anne Emily Vane, married the 7th Duke of Marlborough in 1843; she was Churchill's great-grandmother.

The Coronation was to take place on June 2. Much concerned that all should go well on the day, Churchill asked his staff to sleep that night at Downing Street. 'He was very tired when the day came—' Miss Portal later recalled, 'almost reluctant to go.' [1] But go he did, in a closed two-horse carriage with Clementine Churchill at his side.

Despite glowering skies and heavy squalls, the procession returning from the Abbey to Buckingham Palace delighted the hundreds of thousands who watched it in the streets, and millions more who watched it on television. Churchill's carriage was cheered almost as loudly as that of Queen Salote of Tonga. Queen Elizabeth II, resplendent in her crown and Coronation robes, was, of course, the focal point of all eyes.

Wearied by the exertions of the day, Churchill left the return procession on its way back to the Palace, turning his carriage from the procession into Downing Street.

That evening the Queen spoke on the radio to her people, her broadcast introduced by Churchill himself. The words 'gracious' and 'noble', he said, 'are words familiar to us all in courtly phrasing. To-night they have a new ring in them because we know they are true about the gleaming figure whom Providence has brought to us, and brought to us in times where the present is hard and the future veiled.' [2]

On the afternoon of June 3, Churchill was in the Chair at the opening meeting of the Commonwealth Prime Ministers at 10 Downing Street. The object of the meeting, he said, 'was to see how best the members of the Commonwealth should dispose of affairs which concerned them all. Their cherished ideals of freedom and peace were threatened and the facts of the world situation must be faced. He felt that members of the Commonwealth should be able to get round any points of difficulty which lay between them and that unity would grow among them.' Eight Prime Ministers were present to hear Churchill speak: St Laurent of Canada, Menzies of Australia, Holland of New Zealand, Malan of South Africa, Nehru of India, Mohammed Ali of Pakistan, Senanayake of Ceylon and Huggins of Rhodesia. His principal words to them concerned Soviet foreign policy, the official minutes of the meeting recording his remarks, and his hopes:

... after Stalin died he had been struck by the hope that a change had occurred in Russia. He was not particularly impressed with the changes in external policy which had so far manifested themselves, but the repudiation of the doctors' arrest had seemed to him significant. It meant that the whole Russian people had to think on one day the opposite to what they had been required to think on authority the day before. He did not pretend to know the extent of any changes in Soviet policy, but he felt that if all held together in the anti-Communist front and strengthened their unity no risk would be run in trying to ascertain how important these changes were and to reach some settlement with Russia. We should do all we could to avoid a drift into war when perhaps there had been a change in Soviet policy, and he had already advocated making quite sure that the Soviet Government had no intention of changing their policies before the steps now taken by them were disregarded.

So long as the members of the Commonwealth were united, they could retain their influence on the policy of the United States, to whom the free world owed so much, and he believed that they would be able to carry the United States with them in seeking a period of detente, about which he was not without hope.

Churchill continued with words about the deterrent power of the atomic bomb, both military and political, and of the need to seek negotiations with the new Soviet leaders:

The Soviet Government must have their own anxieties about a future war. Though they had the power to overrun much of Western Europe they must know that their central government machinery, their communications and their war potential would be shattered by atomic attack. A future war would differ from any experienced before, for both sides would suffer at the start the worst that they both feared. When he spoke of accumulating deterrents against Russia, he did not mean deterrents against Russian people but deterrents against the Communist regime. The development of atomic warfare would deter the regime, since it would face them with the certain loss of power to wage modern war within a few months of its start. The mighty ocean of land in Russia and Siberia would quickly become uncontrollable and, once the peoples realised that they were free to do as they liked and could no longer be controlled by the central machinery of Soviet Government, they might show their preference for living happily by themselves without allegiance to a unified Soviet state.

There therefore seemed to be no risk in seeking to find out what lay behind the policy of the new Soviet regime. If their actions were a trick to deceive the rest of the world, this would quickly be discovered, but there should be a sincere examination of what he hoped was a new situation. The effort should be made even if there was a risk that it might not succeed. The British people would not fight in a future war with a good conscience if they thought that there had been a possibility of a change in the Soviet attitude which had not been followed up.

Churchill ended his remarks by telling the Commonwealth Prime Ministers:

... in making this examination of Soviet intentions and policies he was willing to risk disappointment, diplomatic rebuff or accusation of being a false prophet. The members of the Commonwealth should hold together and try to find out what the signs amounted to. The best way to proceed seemed to be, as he had suggested in his recent speech, to have an informal talk with the Soviet leaders. This would not be a conference to settle every point of difficulty, but there might be some settlements which would lead to an easier period and there could be further talks as time went on. Time should be allowed to play its part. The free countries had time to wait so long as they did not weaken in their resolve.

To Dr Malan, who asked what it was the Soviets were afraid of, Churchill replied 'that the Russians could not possibly be afraid that the Western Allies could overpower them on the ground, since Soviet forces were vastly greater than those of the West. But the Kremlin undoubtedly did fear the results of the use by the Western Allies of the overwhelming atomic power in the hands of the United States.'

The Canadian Prime Minister said that he hoped the Bermuda Conference would lead to a meeting with the Soviet Union. A meeting with the Russians, Churchill replied, 'with the object of "building bridges and not barriers" was the right aim, but it would be necessary first to persuade the President of the United States that such a meeting without conditions was desirable. The present attitude of the United States Government was that, before such a meeting was held, the Russians must at least give more positive evidence that they were prepared to move nearer to our point of view. In any event he believed a personal meeting with the President of the United States was the only satisfactory method for reaching the desired measure of agreement.' [1]

The Commonwealth Prime Ministers met again on the afternoon of June 4, with Churchill again in the Chair. Speaking of the Korean truce, he warned the Prime Ministers 'that if the truce did break down there would probably be a demand by the United States for a vigorous impulse to active operations and this would have to be considered if and when it arose'. It must be remembered, he added, 'that the United States bore nineteen-twentieths of the military and financial burden of the United Nations in the Korean war. There were, however, certain indications of a slight easing in the general situation; for example, Chou En-lai had sent a friendly telegram concerning Her Majesty's coronation.' [2]

In answer to Sir Robert Menzies, who was afraid that the United

[1] Prime Ministers' Meeting No. 1 of 1953, 'Meeting of Commonwealth Prime Ministers', 'Secret', 3 p.m., 3 June 1953: Cabinet papers, 133/135.

[2] Chou En-lai was Prime Minister of Communist China from 1949 until his death in 1976, at the age of seventy-eight. He was also Foreign Minister from 1949 until 1958.

States might soon decide 'to step up operations' in Korea in order to 'reach a conclusion', Churchill replied that

. . . he was confident that our contacts with the United States were such that they would take no big step without first consulting us. Although our contribution to the United Nations forces in Korea was small when compared with that of the United States, the United States set considerable store by our moral support of their actions and were exceedingly sensitive to our criticisms. They were likely to afford us far more consultation than our contribution entitled us to, if we wielded our considerable influence with tact and friendliness.

He thought it 'not unlikely', Churchill added, that the United Nations 'would follow the policy adopted by the United States, since the latter were bearing so very high a proportion of the burden of the war, more particularly if genuine efforts for peace had failed and in view of the fact that the war had been begun by North Korea'. Churchill continued:

One great world fact had emerged from the Korean conflict; the United States was now the most heavily armed nation in the world. Russia undoubtedly possessed far greater armies than the United Kingdom and Western Europe and could, if she wished, advance a long way across Western Europe; but she would be immediately exposed to a blasting attack on her communications, arsenals, oil-fields, railways and bridges. In such circumstances, the Kremlin would no doubt think twice before unleashing a war.

Later in the discussion, after Nehru had said that India 'would be prepared to play her part in accordance with her capacity and policy', Churchill told the Conference 'that he was hopeful that the Indian Government would be prepared to allow four to five thousand troops to go to Korea. It was a great compliment to India that more than any other country in the world she found herself trusted by both sides; she should not now hold back. At the same time it was out of the question to allow her to bear the whole financial burden, and she would find that we were ready to give her our support.' There was now, however, Churchill added, 'more hope of a settlement. If these hopes were disappointed, courage still remained.'

Churchill's final remarks at this second meeting concerned Burma, where as many as 12,000 Chinese nationalist forces were in action against the Burmese. 'We have been conscious of the problem of the Chinese Nationalist troops in Burma for a long time,' Churchill said and he added: 'We would be very glad to see them leave Burma and we should do all we could to get them out.' [1]

[1] Prime Ministers' Meeting No. 2 of 1953, 'Meeting of Commonwealth Prime Ministers', 'Secret', 3 p.m., 4 June 1953: Cabinet papers, 133/135.

On the afternoon of June 5 the Commonwealth Prime Ministers held their third meeting, at 10 Downing Street as before, and with Churchill once again in the Chair. The principal subject under discussion was Egypt. The Suez Canal, he said, 'was not now so important for our strategy as it used to be, for we had lived without it for three years in the last war and the character of a future war would be such that atomic attacks against Russia would precede any Russian invasion of Africa across the Sinai peninsula or any attempt at domination of the Near East. It might well be that after the first few months of war there would be a change in the strength of the two sides which would make it difficult for the Russians to conduct war over long distances.' Britain must, nevertheless, secure the maintenance of the Canal and of the Canal Zone base. His remarks continued:

The United Kingdom was accused by some of pursuing imperialist or colonialist policies in Egypt. We had a proud imperial and colonial record of which we were not ashamed, but it was unfair to apply these adjectives to our policy in Egypt. British troops were in Egypt for international reasons, in the interests of the free world, to maintain the waterway of the Suez Canal and to secure the base. Without the base an effective defence of Africa could not be assured.

After we abandoned Abadan the Egyptians had started to insist upon British withdrawal from Egypt, and when General Neguib seized power these demands increased in violence. . . .

Churchill then reiterated the British proposals of November 1952, which had been the basis of Britain's negotiations with Egypt: it was Britain's intention, he explained, 'that the 7,000 troops whom we wished to maintain in Egypt to take care of the base should be armed with personal weapons only for their own defence; they would not be in any sense an organised military force capable of offensive action. These proposals entailed no impairment of Egyptian sovereignty and would relieve the United Kingdom of the immense burden of maintaining 80,000 men in the Canal Zone at a cost of some £50 millions a year. Nothing less than these proposals would secure the interests of the Commonwealth and of the North Atlantic Treaty Organisation in the Eastern Mediterranean.'

Churchill then told the Commonwealth Prime Ministers of the current situation:

General Neguib was now being pressed by the Egyptians to show how he would make good his promises to drive us out of Egypt. We were sticking to our proposals, which we had agreed with the United States, but were willing to resume discussions at any time. We wanted no control of Egypt, but we must see that the Canal and the base were protected. We would be only too glad to remove our troops and so reduce our financial burden, but we were not going to accept any solution of the problem at the expense of British humiliation: there was no question of yielding to an ultimatum.

It was in the interests of the United States to maintain the waterway of the Suez Canal and to secure the base for the protection of the Middle East but, though they supported our intentions and Mr Dulles had been not unhelpful, they had been unwilling to brush aside Egyptian objections to their participation in the discussions.

Britain's only wish, Churchill insisted, was 'to discharge international functions with no affront to Egyptian sovereignty'. If any other country 'was willing to help us in discharging these functions, we would be very glad to share our burden: but we would not be ordered out of Egypt and in the meantime we would wait and see'.

In answer to a warning by the Prime Minister of Pakistan, Mohammed Ali, that Russia might take advantage of Britain's dispute with Egypt in order to obtain an influence throughout the Arab world, Churchill sought to give assurances that the Arab world need not regard Britain as hostile, telling the Conference that:

. . . he could give complete assurance that Her Majesty's Government had nothing but good feelings towards the Arab world, and indeed our record supported this; for example, we had supported the attainment of freedom from French control by both Syria and the Lebanon and we had the closest possible ties with Transjordan, where General Glubb and the Transjordan Frontier Force provided great security. We also had very good relations with Iraq and had originally been responsible for establishing the present dynasty there. At the same time we would not allow Israel to be crushed by the Arab countries surrounding her, though equally we certainly should not support Israel aggression against the Arabs.

All we desired was that Israel should have her rightful chance to live in peace and be accorded fair play.

As to the question of the Palestinian Arabs who had been refugees since 1948, Churchill 'agreed', as the minutes recorded, 'that until the question of the 900,000 Arab refugees was settled this problem would remain a festering sore and as soon as the immediate difficulties had been overcome every effort must be made to reach a solution of it'.[1]

That evening, June 5, Churchill and his wife were hosts to the Queen at a banquet at Lancaster House. It was the Foreign Secretary's banquet, given by the Churchills as Eden was still in his nursing home awaiting his flight to Boston. The tables, wrote Colville,

[1] Prime Ministers' Meeting No. 3 of 1953, 'Meeting of Commonwealth Prime Ministers', 'Secret', 3 p.m., 5 June 1953: Cabinet papers, 133/135.

'were bright with the Duke of Wellington's famous Ambassador's Service of gilt plate, the walls and the rooms were decorated by Constance Spry with flowers. Over 150 people sat down to dinner.' Colville added:

WSC was in his full dress of Lord Warden of the Cinque Ports, the Duke of Edinburgh in naval full-dress which had been temporarily revived for the Coronation, and almost everybody resplendent in seldom-seen uniforms and jewels. After it was over we drove down the illuminated Mall—an unforgettable sight—to a reception at Buckingham Palace where again unwonted brilliance reigned.

On June 6 Churchill was at the Derby, where, in the presence of the Queen, he saw Gordon Richards, on Pinza, win his first Derby, beating the Queen's horse Aureole. Three days later Churchill and his wife were hosts at 10 Downing Street at a dinner for the Commonwealth Prime Ministers. Among those present was Queen Salote of Tonga who, Colville noted, 'stole the show'.[1]

Work continued amid these entertainments; on June 8, Churchill was in the Chair at the fourth meeting of the Commonwealth Prime Ministers, held in the Cabinet Office. The discussion centred upon the communiqué which was to be issued at the end of the Conference. Speaking about Egypt, Churchill said 'that evidence of the support of the whole Commonwealth for the present British proposals would be a powerful inducement to the Egyptians to resume negotiations. If, on the other hand, the Egyptians felt that there was disunity between members of the Commonwealth, there was a grave danger that the Egyptians would persevere in obstinacy and resort to bloodshed. He was, therefore, most anxious that something positive should be included in the communiqué. If nothing more than platitudes could be said, then it would be better to say nothing at all.' In reply to a remark by Nehru that there was a 'conflict of fears' in Europe between those who feared Soviet aggression and those who feared a 'resurgence of German militarism', Churchill replied that 'a German army in some form or other was an essential part of an effective defensive system for Western Europe. What the Soviet Union would like to see was a united Germany forming a vacuum in the middle of Europe. That was a proposition which would have to be resisted. The plight of Czechoslovakia was evidence enough of the dangers of this type of solution.'[2]

---

[1] Colville diary, 5, 6 and 9 June 1953 ('Written later in June'): *The Fringes of Power*, pages 715–16.

[2] Prime Ministers' Meeting No. 4 of 1953, 'Meeting of Commonwealth Prime Ministers', 'Secret', 11.30 a.m., 8 June 1953: Cabinet papers, 133/135.

On the afternoon of June 9 the Commonwealth Prime Ministers held their fifth and final meeting. It was held at 10 Downing Street, with Churchill in the Chair. Churchill hoped for Commonwealth support for British policy in Europe, telling the Prime Ministers that 'this was a critical time for Europe and it was very important that the Meeting should express the hope that the European Defence Community would be established at the earliest possible date. He agreed with Mr Menzies that a mere reference to a review of recent developments in Western Europe would be inadequate. The European Defence Community would make a great contribution to the united effort of the democracies to secure Western Europe, and if the Meeting could not give a clear expression of their hopes the cause of peace would suffer.'

The Prime Ministers agreed to give their support in the final communiqué to the establishment of the European Defence Community 'at the earliest possible date'. They also 'recognized the international importance of the Suez Canal and of the effective maintenance of the military installations in the Canal Zone'. In further support of Churchill's arguments in relation to an early meeting with the Soviet Union, they 'agreed that no opportunity should be lost of composing, or at least easing, the differences which at present divide the world. But they recognized that the democracies must maintain their strength and exercise unceasing vigilance to preserve their rights and liberties.' Thanking the Prime Ministers for their expressions of 'a united opinion', Churchill told them:

The nations of the world had the power to tear themselves in pieces in a matter of months. If we could stave off these dangers we would give to the toiling millions the chance of reaping the fruits of science in a larger, safer and better way of life than had ever before been offered or dreamed of. We had done something to bring about a better world which would cast off fear and make the proper use of the gifts which nature had provided.

The 'sole object' of the talks, Churchill added, had been 'to benefit mankind'.[1]

On Friday June 12, Churchill went down to Chartwell. On the following day, Sir Alan Lascelles came to tell him of Princess Margaret's wish to marry the recently divorced Peter Townsend. Churchill's first reaction after Lascelles had left was to say, as Colville

[1] Prime Ministers' Meeting No. 5 of 1953, 'Meeting of Commonwealth Prime Ministers', 'Secret', 2.30 p.m., 9 June 1953: Cabinet papers, 133/135.

noted, 'that the course of true love must always be allowed to run smooth and that nothing must stand in the way of this handsome pair. However, Lady Churchill said that if he followed this line he would be making the same mistake that he made at the abdication.'[1]

That weekend, Churchill telegraphed to Eisenhower:

I look forward to a good talk about Egypt when we meet. I should have no objection to your advising the Egyptians to resume the talks, provided of course they were not led to believe that you were whittling us down, or prepared to intervene in a matter in which the whole burden, not nineteen-twentieths but repeat the whole burden, falls on us.

If as the result of American encouragement at this juncture or a promise or delivery of arms, Dictator Neguib is emboldened to translate his threats into action, bloodshed on a scale difficult to measure beforehand might well result, and for this we should feel no responsibility, having acted throughout in a sincere spirit for the defence not of British but of international or inter-Allied interests of a high order.'[2]

On June 16 Churchill learned that Eden's doctor, Horace Evans, had told Lord Moran that Eden was 'not too good; his future is uncertain'.[3] Churchill saw no reason to give up the plan to go to Bermuda, for a conference between Britain, France and the United States to discuss the upkeep of military forces in Europe, an indispensable preliminary to his hoped-for Summit. On June 19 Churchill wrote to Eisenhower: 'I have absolute confidence in American goodwill and fair play,' but he added, of the continuing French hesitations about going to Bermuda:

These recurring delays are very painful to me and very bad for world affairs. You and I have quite a lot of things which concern us both on which our public agreement would be helpful all round. Could we not both tell the French that we two shall be meeting on July 8, and hope they will join us? This would enable me to receive you at any time convenient to yourself on the 7th with the guard of honour of the Welch Regiment which I have brought from Jamaica.[4] The conference could start the next day the 8th. Such a message would I believe help to clinch matters in the French Chamber.

'Every day's delay before we meet is unfortunate,' Churchill warned Eisenhower, 'and it would be a disaster if our meeting did not take

---

[1] Colville note of late June 1953: *The Fringes of Power*, page 716.
[2] Telegram No. 2377 to Washington, 'Secret', 'Personal and Private', 12 June 1953: Premier papers, 11/1074.
[3] Moran diary, 16 June 1953: *The Struggle for Survival*, page 406.
[4] In fact, the 1st Battalion, The Royal Welch Fusiliers (the Welch Regiment was then in Hong Kong).

place. Uncertainty and bewilderment are growing in Europe every day, and Adenauer's election draws near.'[1]

On June 20 Churchill worked in the Cabinet Room for over an hour and a half with Selwyn Lloyd. Pierson Dixon, who was also present, noted in his diary: 'Mentally he is more alert than he was towards the end of the war. As always, he did all the work himself in the sense of dictating the telegrams himself after reaching his decision.'[2]

Churchill was now in the final stages of planning for this decisive journey. On June 21, in sending Eisenhower a note of those who would accompany him to Bermuda, he wrote, of Lord Cherwell: 'He explains things to me I cannot otherwise understand.'[3] Two days later, on June 23, Churchill telegraphed to Eisenhower again, in further anticipation of their Bermuda meeting:

I am holding three battalions and an artillery regiment at short notice in Hong Kong 'to reinforce General Mark Clark's army in any action that may be required of them by the United Nations'. Let me know whether you would like this made public.[4]

That day, June 23 Lord Moran noted in his diary:

When I saw the PM today he seemed played out—as he was at Cairo before the Carthage illness.[5] I thought his speech was slurred and a little indistinct. Twice I had to ask him to repeat what he had said.

He said the Foreign Office was very hard work. I asked him must he really carry the burden of the FO until the autumn? He said he must.

I told him I was unhappy about the strain, that it was an impossible existence and that I hoped he would find he could do something about it. He grunted and picked up some papers.

'Before I left No. 10,' Moran added, 'I sought out Pitblado to tell him that I was worried about things.'[6]

That night Churchill was host at 10 Downing Street for a dinner in honour of the Italian Prime Minister, Alcide de Gasperi. It was to be Churchill's last official function before leaving for Bermuda a week later, in HMS *Vanguard*.

[1] 'My dear Friend', 'Secret and Personal', 19 June 1953: Eisenhower papers. The German elections took place on 6 September 1953, when Adenauer's coalition increased its number of seats.

[2] Pierson Dixon diary, 20 June 1953: Pierson Dixon papers.

[3] 'Following for President from Prime Minister', 'Secret', received in Washington 5.53 p.m., 21 June 1953: Eisenhower papers.

[4] 'Following private and personal from Prime Minister to President Eisenhower', signed 'Kindest regards, Winston', received in Washington 8.20 p.m., 24 June 1953: Eisenhower papers.

[5] Churchill had been taken ill in Cairo in December 1943; he had worsened in Carthage, telling his daughter Sarah: 'If I die, don't worry—the war is won.' (Sarah Churchill recollections: in conversation with the author, 25 May 1981.)

[6] Moran diary, 23 June 1953: *The Struggle for Survival*, pages 406–7.

45

Stroke

AT the end of the dinner for the Italian Prime Minister on 23
June 1953, Churchill made a short speech, 'mainly', Jock Colville later recalled, 'about the Roman conquest of Britain!' [1] A 'brilliant little speech', Colville told Lord Moran, 'all about Caesar and the
Legions'. [2]

The time had come to leave the dining table. Churchill rose, to
lead his guests into the drawing room. Then, after taking a few steps,
he slumped down into the nearest chair. Sitting on the chair next to
him was Lady Clark, the wife of the art historian Sir Kenneth Clark;
he had known them both since before the war. [3] Turning to her, and
taking her hand, he said, as she later recalled: 'I want a friend,' and
he added: 'They put too much on me. Foreign Affairs. . . .' [4]

Churchill's voice trailed off. Alerted by his wife, Sir Kenneth Clark
went up to Churchill's daughter Mary, 'to tell me', as she later wrote,
'that my father was not feeling well and was sitting down at the other
side of the room. I, of course, immediately went over to him and there
was a woman sitting beside him.' [5]

Unknown to the Clarks, or to Mary Soames, Churchill had suffered
a massive stroke. It was clear however that something was wrong.
When Christopher Soames told Lady Churchill that her husband was
'very tired', she replied at once: 'Oh, we must get him to bed then.'

---

[1] Colville recollections: *The Fringes of Power*, page 668.

[2] Churchill had written his own description of the Roman conquest of Britain in *A History of
the English-Speaking Peoples*, completed in 1939.

[3] Of a dinner party in London in 1938, Kenneth Clark wrote: 'At about 1.30 a.m. Mr
Churchill rose to leave us. He went out into a deserted Portland Place, the pavement glistening
with heavy rain, so that it looked like a canal. Mr Churchill's car was waiting, and he told the
chauffeur to take him to Westerham. "Good heavens," said Jane, "you're not going all that
way." "Yes, my dear, I only come to London to sock the Government or to dine with you."'
(Kenneth Clark, *Another Part of the Wood, a A Self-Portrait*, London 1974, page 273.)

[4] Sir Kenneth Clark recollections: Kenneth Clark, *The Other Half*, London 1977, page 128.

[5] Lady Soames recollections: letter to the author, 8 October 1987.

'We must get the waiters away first,' Soames warned. 'He can't walk.'

It was Lord Moran who reported these words, having been told them by Jock Colville when he was summoned to Downing Street on the following morning. As Colville was giving Moran this account of what had happened at the de Gasperi dinner, Soames himself joined them. Moran noted:

He mentioned that the PM's speech was indistinct; it was difficult to understand what he said. Jock added that others had noticed the PM's plight.

'I think they thought he had had too much to drink.'[1]

'I only realised my father's plight a short time later,' Mary Soames subsequently recalled, 'as I was busy entertaining the guests.' Then, as she wrote,

Christopher told me to try and 'guard' him from the people, as he was having difficulty with his speech; I did my best, but it was not very easy; my father looked unhappy and uncertain and was very incoherent. Christopher managed to convey to Signor de Gasperi that Winston was very much over-tired, and the Italian Prime Minister, with kind understanding, soon took his leave, the other guests following his example. A few had noticed the slur in Winston's speech and his unsteadiness, but attributed it to his having had a little too much to drink; nobody guessed the real reason—that he had sustained a stroke.[2]

At No. 10 on the following morning, Lord Moran listened to what had happened at the dinner, and then to Colville's view of the situation:

Jock was sure his speech was affected; the articulation was only distinct when he made an effort. When I was satisfied that I should get no more out of them, I went to his room.

'Ah, Charles, I thought you would never come.'

I could see that the left side of his mouth sagged; it was more noticeable when he spoke. I got him out of bed to see how he walked.

He asked me to open the door of his wardrobe, which is lined with a long mirror; he wanted to see for himself how he got on. He was not very steady on his feet, and once I jumped to his side, thinking he would fall. When he was back in bed he said: 'I would not like to walk to my seat in the House of Commons with members watching. What has happened, Charles? Is it a stroke?'

It was indeed a stroke. The circulation in his head was 'sluggish', Moran explained to him. 'There was a spasm of the small artery. It belonged to the same family as the incident at Monte Carlo in August 1949.'

[1] Moran diary, 23 June 1953: *The Struggle for Survival*, pages 406–7.
[2] Mary Soames, *Clementine Churchill*, page 434.

Sir Russell Brain was summoned to examine Churchill. When Brain had completed his examination, Churchill announced that he intended to go to the House of Commons that afternoon, to answer the questions addressed to him as Prime Minister, as well as those addressed to the absent Eden. That very day, Eden, in Boston, was having his third operation. Moran's account continued:

I told him he must not go to the House for Questions. He argued about this, saying he liked Questions. Then he sent for Jock and asked him how many questions there were; which were for him and which were addressed to the Foreign Secretary. Were they important?

'Oh, bring them and let me see.'

While Jock was out of the room I felt I must act before he committed himself. I said I could not guarantee that he would not get up in the House and use the wrong word; he might rise in his place and no words might come. He listened in silence. When Jock came back he read the Questions. 'They are not very important,' Jock added, and the PM seemed to agree. Finally, he said abruptly that he would not go to the House.[1]

That morning the Cabinet met at 10 Downing Street. Churchill insisted on presiding, 'even though', as Colville later recalled, 'his mouth was drooping badly and he found it difficult to use his left arm.' R. A. Butler told Colville afterwards 'that he only noticed that the Prime Minister was curiously and unexpectedly silent as he allowed the items to go forward without much comment from himself.'[2] Harold Macmillan noted a week later: 'I certainly noticed nothing beyond the fact that he was very white. He spoke very little, but quite distinctly. I remember that he called to me, "Harold, you might draw the blind down a little, will you?" I also noticed that he did not talk very much.'[3]

At lunch on June 24 there were no guests, 'only', as Mary Soames recalled, 'my mother, Christopher and myself—which was fortunate, as by that time Winston was extremely tired, and once more had difficulty in getting up from his chair'.[4]

On the following day, June 25, Lord Moran noted in his diary after a morning visit to Downing Street to see his patient, who was in bed:

No improvement in his speech, and he is, if anything, more unsteady in his gait.

'I don't feel like managing the world'—there was a long pause—'and yet never have they looked more like offering me it. I feel, Charles, I could do

[1] Moran diary, 24 July 1953: *The Struggle for Survival*, pages 408–9.
[2] 'Mr Jock Colville, Reminiscences', 8 June 1965: Randolph Churchill papers.
[3] Harold Macmillan, diary entry for 2 July 1953: *Tides of Fortune*, page 516.
[4] Mary Soames, *Clementine Churchill*, page 434.

something that no one else can do. I was at the peak of my opportunities, exchanging friendly messages with Malenkov and Adenauer.'

'You meant to send them messages?'

'No, I have done that already. I have stretched out a hand to grasp the paw of the Russian bear. Great things seemed within my grasp. Not perhaps world peace, but world easement. I feel I could have changed the bias of the world. America is very powerful, but very clumsy. Look at this Syngman Rhee business. I could have made her more sensible.'

Churchill was about to attend that morning's Cabinet meeting. But Moran noted that as he talked, his speech 'was becoming blurred and more difficult to follow. He lay back on the pillow as if he were too tired to go on.' Moran's account continued:

Once more I pressed him not to attend the Cabinet, and when he became obstinate I said that the left side of his mouth dropped and I did not want him to go among people until he was better. They would notice things, and there would be talk. After I had gone Christopher took up the good work; and the PM in the end gave up the idea and left about noon for Chartwell.[1]

During the drive to Chartwell, Churchill gave Jock Colville 'strict orders not to let it be known that he was temporarily incapacitated and to ensure that the administration continued to function as if he were in full control'. By the evening, however, as Colville later recalled, 'his physical powers had deteriorated considerably and, if I remember right, he was more or less paralysed in the whole of his left side. By the following day, Friday, he was almost completely paralysed.' Lord Moran was so alarmed when he came down to Chartwell later that day that he told Colville 'he did not think the Prime Minister could possibly live over the weekend'.[2] Colville later recalled:

Meanwhile Sir Winston who was perfectly coherent mentally told me that he didn't wish anybody at all to know what had happened or to be informed that he was ill. Nevertheless it occurred to me rather forcibly that the accepted successor, Mr Anthony Eden, was at that moment on the operating table in Boston, where he was having a serious abdominal operation, and that, if indeed Lord Moran were right and the Prime Minister were to die over the weekend, a very serious constitutional problem would present itself.

And so, in defiance of the Prime Minister's orders I rang up Sir Alan Lascelles, the Queen's private secretary, on the telephone on the scrambler and told him what had happened. I said that the Queen must be prepared, so shortly after her Coronation, to be faced with the necessity of appointing a new Prime Minister on Monday morning.

We discussed the matter at great length and decided that it would be unfair to Eden to send for Butler and in the circumstances the only possible

[1] Moran diary, 25 June 1953: *The Struggle for Survival*, pages 409–10.
[2] 'Mr Jock Colville, Reminiscences', 8 June 1965: Randolph Churchill papers.

solution would be to ask Lord Salisbury, although a peer, to form a caretaker Government on the express understanding that he would retire when Mr Eden was well enough to form a new Government.[1]

Colville at once informed Clarissa Eden of this decision; that if, as appeared likely, Churchill had to resign, the advice of Lord Salisbury and R. A. Butler to the Queen would be for a Caretaker Government headed, as Eden was ill, by Lord Salisbury, the Lord President of the Council, who would not take the title of Prime Minister, but would act as head of the Government until Eden was well enough to take over.[2]

Lord Moran's account of the situation that Friday evening makes clear how grave it had become:

'Look, my hand is clumsy,' the PM said as I entered his room at Chartwell.

Transferring his cigar to his left hand, he made a wavering attempt to put it to his lips.

'It is so feeble. Hold out your hand, Charles.'

And with that he tried to touch the tips of my fingers with the corresponding fingers of his own hand.

'I'm not afraid of death, but it would be very inconvenient to a lot of people. Rab is very efficient up to a point, but he is narrow and doesn't see beyond his nose. If Anthony were standing by the door there, and I was here, and a telegram was given to him involving a decision, well, in nine cases out of ten we should agree.'

When he had done I examined his left hand and arm. There was some loss of power in the left grip—and this had developed since yesterday, three days after the onset of the trouble. I do not like this, the thrombosis is obviously spreading. He knew that his hand was weaker, and he complained, 'I am having great difficulty in turning over in bed.'

'Two days ago,' he reflected, 'I wanted to take the Cabinet. Now I couldn't. I have scratched Bermuda. It will not come out until Ike replies to my telegram.' He handed me the telegram he had sent to Ike.[3]

Churchill's telegram to Eisenhower read: 'You will see from the attached medical report the reasons why I cannot come to Bermuda. I am as bad as the French, thinking that the conference should be postponed.' Meanwhile, Churchill added, Lord Salisbury could fly to Washington 'at any time convenient to you in the next fortnight and would put our point of view and establish the intimate Anglo-American contact which is the keystone of our policy. Then, too, let me know your reaction. No announcement will be made till tomorrow.'[4]

[1] 'Mr Jock Colville, Reminiscences', 8 June 1965: Randolph Churchill papers.
[2] Letter of 26 June 1953: Robert Rhodes James, *Anthony Eden*, page 368.
[3] Moran diary, 26 June 1953: *The Struggle for Survival*, pages 410–10.
[4] 'Message from the Prime Minister to President Eisenhower', 26 June 1953: Eisenhower papers.

Eisenhower replied at once: 'I am deeply distressed to learn that your physicians have advised you to lighten your duties at this time and that consequently you will be unable to come to Bermuda for our talks. I look upon this only as a temporary deferment of our meeting. Your health is of great concern to all the world and you must, therefore, bow to the advice of your physicians.' [1]

On the day that Eisenhower was informed that the Bermuda Conference would have to be postponed, R. A. Butler was summoned to Chartwell. On arriving at Sevenoaks by train he was handed a letter from Jock Colville, dated the previous day, which read:

> I write, very sorrowfully, to let you know quite privately that the PM is seriously ill and that unless some miracle occurs in the next 24 hours there can be no question of his going to Bermuda and little, I think, of his remaining in office.
>
> You must have noticed what befell him after the de Gasperi dinner on Tuesday. It was a sudden arterial spasm, or perhaps a clot in an artery, and he has been left with great difficulty of articulation although his brain is still absolutely clear. His left side is partly paralysed and he has lost the use of his left arm. He himself has little hope of recovery.
>
> His courage and philosophic resignation are beyond praise and admiration and Lady Churchill, too, is heroic.
>
> I have not as yet told anybody but a few of his intimate friends and among his colleagues yourself, Lord Salisbury and the Prof—though I am keeping Tommy Lascelles fully informed. Therefore although the PM certainly wants you to know the position, I hope you will keep the whole matter strictly private for the time being. I will let you know how things progress. [2]

Shortly before R. A. Butler arrived at Chartwell, Lord Moran had drawn up a medical bulletin which he wished to issue to the public. Sir Russell Brain, whom he consulted, signed it with him. The bulletin, as Moran had composed it, read:

> For a long time the Prime Minister has had no respite from his arduous duties and a disturbance of the cerebral circulation has developed, resulting in attacks of giddiness. We have therefore advised him to abandon his journey to Bermuda and to take at least a month's rest.

This bulletin was never issued; when Moran showed it later that day to R. A. Butler, and also to Lord Salisbury, they persuaded Churchill to accept a less precise, and less alarming, form of words. The new bulletin, signed by the two doctors and issued to the Press, read:

> The Prime Minister has had no respite for a long time from his very arduous duties and is in need of a complete rest. We have therefore advised him to abandon his journey to Bermuda and to lighten his duties for at least a month.

[1] Telegram dated 26 June 1953: Eisenhower papers.
[2] Letter of 25 June 1953: *The Art of the Possible, The Memoirs of Lord Butler*, pages 169–70.

'If he dies in the next few days,' Lord Moran noted in his diary 'will Lord Salisbury think his change in the bulletin was wise?'[1]

Those who knew of Churchill's stroke feared that, despite the doctors' bulletins, news of it might become public at any moment. 'So I wrote urgently,' Colville later recalled, 'and in manuscript to three particular friends of Churchill, Lords Camrose, Beaverbrook and Bracken, and sent the letters to London by despatch rider. All three immediately came to Chartwell and paced the lawn in earnest conversation. They achieved the all but incredible, and in peace-time possibly unique, success of gagging Fleet Street, something they would have done for nobody but Churchill.'[2]

On June 26 the Queen sent Churchill a letter in her own hand:

My dear Prime Minister,

I am so sorry to hear from Tommy Lascelles that you have not been feeling too well these last few days.

I do hope it is not serious and that you will be quite recovered in a very short time.

Our visit here is going very well and Edinburgh is thrilled by all the pageantry. We have been lucky in having fine weather, but I fear that it is now raining after a thunderstorm.

With all good wishes,

Yours very sincerely,

Elizabeth R[3]

'The PM himself was thrilled by this letter,' Moran noted.

Churchill replied at once. He recalled, wrote Moran, 'the circumstances in which he had been stricken down; he spoke of his plight as he lay in bed as if it had happened to someone else; he told Her Majesty that he was not without hope that he might soon be about and able to discharge his duties until the autumn, when he thought that Anthony would be able to take over'.[4]

In London, Brendan Bracken had bought Churchill a wheelchair, which he brought down to Chartwell on June 27. That same morning, Lord Moran returned to Chartwell. His patient was certainly no better. 'I'm getting more helpless,' he said. 'I shall soon be completely paralysed on my left side.' It was now clear, Churchill added, 'that we made the right decision in abandoning Bermuda'.

Moran's diary entry for June 27 continued:

I got him out of bed, but he could hardly stand.

Last night I noticed that he was dragging his left leg. Now it is obvious

---

[1] Moran diary, 26 June 1953: *The Struggle for Survival*, pages 410–11.
[2] Colville recollections: *The Fringes of Power*, page 669.
[3] Letter of 26 June 1953: quoted in Lord Moran, *The Struggle for Survival*, page 414.
[4] Letter, undated: quoted in Lord Moran, *The Struggle for Survival*, page 414.

there is some loss of power, so that the foot drops and the toes catch the carpet. He cannot walk now without two people helping him, though in his wheel-chair he can propel himself from room to room. He paused before his portrait in the blue drawing-room:

'It is the picture of a very unhappy man, painted after the Dardanelles by Orpen. He thought I was finished.'[1]

Mary Soames, at Chartwell on June 27, wrote in her diary that day: 'Saw Papa—felt wretchedly gloomy. There are nurses now, and he cannot walk, or use his right hand much. In the afternoon he had a fall—but beyond the jolt—no damage.'[2]

Randolph and June Churchill also went down to Chartwell that Saturday. 'I do want you to know how much I am thinking of you,' Randolph wrote to his mother after his return to London, 'at this sad and difficult time. I thought you were magnificent on Saturday & doing everything possible to maintain Papa's morale. So long as that persists, no miracle is impossible. . . .'[3]

'Today he is gayer,' Mary Soames noted on Sunday June 28. Lord Moran had told her 'there is a distinct improvement'. It was so difficult, she added, to know what to tell people when they telephoned, 'Because when he's down, we're down. And when he's cheerful our spirits, too, revive.' As for Clementine Churchill, 'Mama is truly marvellous—tender, considerate, thinking of everyone's comfort. Unblinded by hope or fear—she teaches us all.'[4]

That Sunday, Churchill felt well enough to sit at the head of the table at luncheon. To Beaverbrook, who was his main guest, he said: 'I think we ought to let the House have a free vote on sponsored television.' As to his plans for a summit, the plea of May 11, he commented: 'I'm not taken in by the Russians, but before the British people are committed to another long struggle, I wanted to be sure there was nothing in their recent change of attitude.'

Lord Moran's account of the luncheon of June 28 continued:

He spoke with tears in his eyes. Then his face lit up and for a little time something of the old vigour of speech came back while Max poured out his soft talk. But I could see the PM was getting very tired and that it was time to break up the party. Clemmie had arranged that he should be carried to the swimming-pool to see the grandchildren bathe, but he asked me to take him back to bed. He insisted on getting out of his chair, and we helped him to his room; his good foot coming down on the passage with a noisy stump,

---

[1] Moran diary, 27 June 1953: *The Struggle for Survival*, pages 411–12. A copy of this portrait hangs in the Hall at Churchill College, Cambridge. The original is in the possession of Churchill's grandson, Winston S. Churchill MP.

[2] Mary Soames diary, 27 June 1953: *Clementine Churchill*, page 435.

[3] Letter, undated: *Clementine Churchill*, page 436.

[4] Mary Soames diary, 28 June 1953: *Clementine Churchill*, page 435.

while the toes of his left foot dragged along the carpet. When we were alone he slumped upon the bed.

'A week ago I was thinking of running the world—and now—' He shrugged his shoulders. 'When I sit still I feel quite well.'

He looked ruefully at his foot, and then he remembered I had told him that other arteries—what doctors call the collateral circulation—would take on the work of the blocked vessel.

'The blood ought to be getting round the back streets by now. What have you to say about that, Charles?'

I brought Max to say goodbye, warning him to stay only a few minutes, and then rejoined Clemmie. She told me Winston had said to her: 'I hope I shall either improve or get worse.'

Churchill's sense of humour had not deserted him. 'Today I have knocked Christie off the headlines,' he told Beaverbrook, 'except in the *Empire News*.' John Christie was on trial, suspected of murder of at least six women. At dinner, Brendan Bracken was a guest. 'He can draw the PM out,' noted Moran, 'and has a kind of explosive cheerfulness which seems to help. The PM said that he had only read one book in the first six months of the war—*Journey to the Western Isles of Scotland*, by Dr Johnson. He admired Johnson. Then Brendan got out of him that he went to the Atlantic Charter Meeting with E. M. Forster's *A Passage to India*.' [1]

Reverting to Churchill's hopes for a summit, Moran wrote that night in his diary:

The fear of another war has occupied men's thoughts since the end of the last war. And in their hearts they feel that the PM can do more than anyone else to avert another catastrophe. Winston knows that he is speaking, not for the Tory Party, but for the whole country, and as he watches the slow spread of this creeping paralysis, he is haunted by the lost opportunity. He realizes that little men are tied to their texts, that he alone can break down the wall of suspicion which shuts off Russia from the West.

When Brendan had gone he rang a bell:

'Bring me the Queen's letter and my reply. I want you to see, Charles, what I can still do.' [2]

That day Field Marshal Montgomery wrote to Churchill: 'My very dear Winston, I am greatly distressed that you are not too fit. Do get well and return to steer the ship. There is much to be done. . . .' [3]

Jim Thomas, who went down to see Churchill at Chartwell on June 28, reported to Eden that for Churchill 'active life is over'. [4] 'However,' Jock Colville later recalled, 'by Monday morning, the Prime Minister,

---

[1] In fact, with one of C. S. Forester's Hornblower books.
[2] Moran diary, 28 June 1953: *The Struggle for Survival*, page 412–4.
[3] 'My very dear Winston', 28 June 1953: Churchill papers, 2/143.
[4] Letter of 29 June 1953: Robert Rhodes James, *Anthony Eden*, page 368.

instead of being dead, was feeling very much better.' Colville added: 'He told me that he thought probably that this must mean his retirement, but that he would see how he went on, and that if he had recovered sufficiently well to address the Tory party at their annual Meeting in October at Margate, he would continue in office.' [1]

At the Cabinet meeting at 10 Downing Street on June 29, R. A. Butler told his colleagues that the Prime Minister 'was suffering from severe over-strain and was in need of a complete rest'. His doctor had advised him to 'lighten his duties' for at least a month. No mention was made in the minutes of a stroke, but, as Harold Macmillan later recalled, R. A. Butler, after describing the visit which he and Lord Salisbury had made to Chartwell, 'revealed to us what we had only surmised—the nature of his illness. It was a terrible shock to us all. Although the story was told simply and discreetly, many of us were in tears or found it difficult to restrain them.' [2]

Butler then told the Cabinet that Churchill would continue to receive during his absence 'the more important official papers', and that decisions 'on major questions of policy' would be referred to him. Lord Salisbury, the Lord President of the Council, would assist Churchill 'in the conduct of foreign policy', with Selwyn Lloyd, as Minister of State, handling the 'day-to-day business' of the Foreign Office. [3]

As soon as she learned of her father's illness, Sarah Churchill flew back from New York. When she and her husband Antony Beauchamp reached Chartwell, on Monday 29 June, Churchill was much improved, in the eyes of those who had seen him each day since his stroke; but for Sarah it was a shock to see him. 'She was distressed,' Mary Soames wrote in her diary. 'It made one realize how used to it we have become, and how *low* we were—for today we feel almost gay—he seemed so improved.' But of course, she added, 'it is only comparative'. [4]

At Chartwell on June 29 Churchill had another close friend to lunch, Lord Cherwell. Once more Lord Moran was a witness to the conversation, and to his patient's improved mood:

The Prof to luncheon. He has developed diabetes. When he asked the PM how he was, Winston answered with a touch of levity:

'I eats well and sleeps well and drinks well, but when I get alongside any business I go all of a tremble. I could do without smoking but not without my liquor; that would be a sad impoverishment.' His face became grave. 'It is extraordinary between night and morning that I should go like this—a bundle of old rags.'

[1] 'Mr Jock Colville, Reminiscences', 8 June 1965: Randolph Churchill papers.
[2] Harold Macmillan, *Tides of Fortune*, page 514.
[3] Cabinet Conclusions No. 37 of 1953, 12 noon, 29 June 1953: Cabinet papers, 128/26.
[4] Mary Soames diary, 29 June 1953: *Clementine Churchill*, page 436.

Among the dinner guests on June 30 was Sir Norman Brook. 'Winston likes him, and they talked for a long time,' noted Moran. It was Brook and Jock Colville who asked the questions. Churchill told them of the mutiny over demobilization at the end of the First World War:

They came to him at the War Office and said that this was a serious mutiny. The soldiers were dissatisfied with the regulations for demobilization; they felt it was not being done fairly. They had gathered on the Horse Guards Parade, and things looked ugly. Winston asked: 'How many troops have we to deal with them?' They answered, a battalion of the Guards and three squadrons of the Household Cavalry. 'Are they loyal?' Winston asked. 'We hope they are,' was the doubtful answer. 'Can you arrest the mutineers?' 'We are not certain.' 'Have you any other suggestions?' They had none. 'Then arrest the mutineers.' He stood watching from a window over the parade ground. He expected firing to break out any minute. But the mutineers allowed the Guards to surround them.

We asked the PM what he did when the mutineers were under arrest.

PM: 'Oh, I changed the system of demobilization overnight: the first to join was the first to be demobilized, and any man with a wound stripe or a decoration could go when he wished. This removed their strong sense of injustice. It was one of the best things I did.'

Moran's account of the evening continued:

Once more he told how one of our tanks at the end of an engagement had to surrender to the Germans, and how the Germans saluted them and complimented them on their courage in the fight.

'That is how I like war to be conducted,' the PM said.

'I'm finished,' he said sadly, 'but a week ago I had big plans. My influence everywhere had never been greater. Nehru and Adenauer were very friendly. Of course I knew that I was taking risks by my advances to the Russians. I might have taken a big toss.'

'Alas,' Moran wrote, 'he will keep thinking of what might have been,' and he added, of the sixth volume of Churchill's war memoirs:

He had given the final volume of the book to Norman Brook to read. He questioned him now about it. Would anything in it cause offence to the Americans? 'If I am going to die, then I can say what I like and take the view that I believe to be right. But if I live and am still Prime Minister, then I must not say things which will anger Ike.' [1]

Fifteen years later, Sir Norman Brook recalled:

He was in a wheelchair. After dinner, in the drawing-room, he said that he was going to stand on his feet. Colville and I urged him not to attempt this, and, when he insisted, we came up on either side of him so that we could catch him if he fell. But he waved us away with his stick and told us to stand

---

[1] Moran diary, 29–30 June 1953: *The Struggle for Survival*, pages 414–15.

back. He then lowered his feet to the ground, gripped the arms of his chair, and by a tremendous effort—with sweat pouring down his face—levered himself to his feet and stood upright. Having demonstrated that he could do this, he sat down again and took up his cigar.

'It was a striking demonstration of will-power,' Norman Brook reflected. '"In defeat: defiance": he refused to accept defeat: as he had done for the nation in 1940, so he did for his own life in 1953. He was determined to recover.'[1]

In the weeks before Churchill recovered, Christopher Soames and Jock Colville shared the burden of work. 'We realised that however well we knew his policy and the way his thoughts were likely to move,' Colville later wrote, 'we had to be careful not to allow our own judgement to be given Prime Ministerial effect.' To have done so, Colville added, 'as we could without too great difficulty, would have been a constitutional outrage'.[2]

On June 30 two messages sent to Churchill gave a flavour of the hundreds that were arriving with every post. The first was from the Labour MP Richard Crossman. 'Allow me to send you my personal good wishes for a speedy recovery,' Crossman wrote. 'Your one-man battle has been cheered on by some of your bitterest domestic opponents. We *all* need you back.'[3] The second message was from the Queen. 'Our thoughts are much with you,' she wrote, 'and I hope that by the time we return you will be fully restored to health. We do not forget that you overwork for us.'[4]

'I am so sorry to be the cause of upsetting so many plans,' Churchill wrote to Eisenhower on July 1, and he went on to explain:

I had a sudden stroke which as it developed completely paralysed my left side and affected my speech. I therefore had no choice as I could not have walked with you along the Guard of Honour of the Welch Regiment complete with their beautiful white goat, whose salute you would I am sure have acknowledged. Four years ago, in 1949, I had another similar attack and was for a good many days unable to sign my name. As I was out of office I kept this secret and have managed to work through two General Elections and a lot of other business since. I am therefore not without hope of pursuing my theme a little longer but it will be a few weeks before any opinion can be formed.[5]

---

[1] Lord Normanbrook recollections: Sir John Wheeler-Bennett (editor), *Action This Day*, pages 43–4.
[2] Colville recollections: *The Fringes of Power*, pages 668–9.
[3] Letter of 30 June 1953: Churchill papers, 2/183.
[4] Telegram despatched at 2.10 p.m., 30 June 1953: Churchill papers, 2/197.
[5] 'My dear Ike', 'Most Secret and Personal', 1 July 1953: Premier papers 11/1074.

46

Recovery

THE speed with which Churchill was able to regain his grasp of events, and to attend to the problems which were most pressing and urgent, was remarkable. In this he was helped by the discretion and skill of three men, his Principal Private Secretaries, Jock Colville and David Pitblado, and his son-in-law Christopher Soames. It was the 33-year-old Soames, the only Member of Parliament of the three, who, quite unobtrusively, took a hundred decisions in Churchill's name, without once breaching the trust which such a heavy responsibility involved.

One of the first matters which had to be resolved in those early days of recovery was Eisenhower's request that all references to him in the final volume of Churchill's war memoirs must be submitted to General Bedell Smith for scrutiny. On July 1, in a letter to Bedell Smith from Chartwell, Churchill enclosed the chapters which dealt with the strategic differences between Britain and the United States in 1944 and 1945. 'These differences cannot be wholly concealed or glossed over,' he wrote. 'They belong to history. And the final judgment on them will be made by the historians of the future.' Meanwhile, Churchill added, 'I hope you will think that I have handled them fairly and with no intent to prejudge the verdict of history. These differences did not then disturb my respect and regard for the President, and the publication of this account of them will not, I think, lead others to misjudge or under-rate the confidence and mutual trust on which our current relationships are founded.' [1]

---

[1] Letter of 1 July 1953: Churchill papers, 4/52. Churchill ended his letter with a short personal postscript. 'There is a point which you will both like in Chapter IV,' he wrote, and went on to explain: 'Your relationship to your Chief and his to you was a model. See page 10.' In his war memoirs, Churchill wrote of the British opposition to the South of France attack: 'Bedell Smith, on the contrary, declared himself strongly in favour of this sudden deflection of the attack, which would have all the surprise that sea-power can bestow. Eisenhower in no way resented the views of his Chief of Staff. He always encouraged free expression of opinion in council at the summit, though of course whatever was settled would receive every loyalty in execution.' (*The Second World War*, volume 6, page 61.)

From General Marshall in Virginia came words of 'concern, affection and sympathy' on July 1, and an added note: 'I am the more concerned because I have seen you ill or convalescing and you are a bad patient to hold down to a careful regime. Please do be careful, a patient in the full meaning of the word. You are too vastly important to the world to take any risks.'[1] That day, Lord Moran noted:

Christopher, finding the PM bright-eyed and alert, said encouragingly: 'You are going to get quite well.'
PM: 'Yes, but I don't know how much difficulty I'll have in getting back my position.'
'You see,' Christopher added dryly, 'he has not given up hope of a comeback. I don't know what Clemmie will say.'[2]

On July 2 Harold Macmillan was invited to dine at Chartwell. 'My first impressions were of astonishment', he recalled, 'that a man who had suffered such a calamity could show such gaiety and courage. During dinner, and until he went to bed, just after 11 p.m., his talk seemed much the same as usual. The atmosphere was not oppressive, but almost lively.'[3]

Lord Moran, who was also present, wrote in his diary:

Winston spoke of death. He did not believe in another world; only in 'black velvet'—eternal sleep. He kept taking up different subjects and then dropping them, almost at once, as if he could not be bothered to go deeply into anything. He spoke of some African chiefs drinking beer, armed with staves, inflamed with alcohol and inspired by liberal principles—the old love of words—and then of Buddhism, 'a Tory religion'. He used not to believe in rationing or in any other device which would lead to bureaucracy, but Sam Hoare had converted him. He drifted on. Lord Rosebery had written a vivid account of Gladstone's last Cabinet. 'By comparison,' Winston concluded, 'my reign has been considerate and reasonable.'[4]

'I could see his state,' Macmillan noted in his diary, 'a sick but a very gay man.' As to the political aspects of the discussion, Macmillan noted Churchill's concern that the future of European unity was in the balance awaiting the German elections and the French decision on the Defence Community. 'But he did not despair. He hoped the Americans would agree to talk with the Russians.'[5]

'I was so delighted to find you so well & in such good form,'

[1] 'My dear Mr Prime Minister', 1 July 1953: Churchill papers, 2/144.
[2] Moran diary, 1 July 1953: *The Struggle for Survival*, page 417.
[3] Harold Macmillan recollections: *Tides of Fortune*, page 515.
[4] Moran diary, 2 July 1953: *The Struggle for Survival*, pages 417–8.
[5] Macmillan diary, 2 July 1953: *Tides of Fortune*, page 515.

Macmillan wrote to Churchill four days later, and he added: 'Take care of yourself, for we need you very much.'[1]

Churchill was careful not to exert himself unduly. 'After the visitors had gone,' Jane Portal later recalled, 'he would retire to his bed and read his novels. He had this ability to switch off and concentrate on something else. He was totally absorbed by the novels. The dictation stopped. Jock and Christopher did the boxes. Miss Gilliatt and I were there to run the office.' Miss Portal added: 'It was extraordinary that the Press did not get hold of the story. One woman journalist who came to the door almost forced her way in. . . .'[2]

The conversation as Churchill convalesced was often on his own political future. Moran noted on July 3:

I went with him to his room. As he got into bed he smiled at me mischievously:

'There will be a bloody row if I get well. And it does not seem impossible.'

Franklin Roosevelt had been dead seven years, he reflected.

'I always looked up to him as an older man, though he was eight years my junior.'

In Churchill's bedroom was a print showing the leaders of Lloyd George's victorious First World War coalition. Moran's attention had been caught by it. Churchill saw his curiosity.

'It was painted by Sir James Guthrie,' the PM explained. 'I never heard of him either before or since, but it is a fine composition.[3] I like it. Arthur Balfour is the key figure. Guthrie has put me in the centre of the picture; it is a little out of focus, for I was in low water then.'

He rose and walked across the room to the picture. There were sixteen men in it.

'I'm the only one left alive,' he reflected.[4]

July 4, Moran noted, was a 'good day', with Churchill 'full of spirits'. He could now walk a short distance unaided. That evening, at dinner, there was more talk of Churchill's political future, which Lord Moran recorded:

During dinner his retirement in October came up.

'I shall do what is best for the country.'

Clemmie: 'Of course, dear, I know you will.'

PM (with a whimsical smile): 'Circumstances may convince me of my indispensability.'[5]

---

[1] Letter of 6 July 1953: Churchill papers, 2/220.
[2] Lady Williams of Elvel recollections: in conversation with the author, 29 July 1987.
[3] Sir James Guthrie, a Member of the Royal Institute of Oil Painters and the Royal Scottish Water-Colour Society, had died in 1930, at the age of seventy-one.
[4] Moran diary, 3 July 1953: *The Struggle for Survival*, pages 419–21.
[5] Moran diary, 4 July 1953: *The Struggle for Survival*, pages 421–2.

That day, Jock Colville wrote to Clarissa Eden of a 'remarkable improvement' in Churchill's condition. The prospect of a Caretaker Government, Colville added, had receded.[1]

On July 5 Field Marshal Montgomery came to lunch and stayed for dinner. At one point in the discussion Montgomery asked Churchill 'What is our policy in Korea?' In his diary, Moran noted Churchill's reply:

PM: 'If I were in charge I would withdraw the United Nations troops to the coast and leave Syngman Rhee to the Chinese. But the American public would not swallow this. Korea does not really matter now. I'd never heard of the bloody place till I was seventy-four. Its importance lies in the fact that it has led to the rearming of America. That may have saved the peace of the world. And Indo-China, too, does not really matter. We gave up India. Why shouldn't France give up Indo-China?'

Monty (demurring): 'Indo-China matters strategically. If Indo-China goes, Siam goes too. And then Malaya would be in danger.'

PM: 'We could hold the Isthmus.'

Monty: 'Yes, perhaps we might.'

PM: 'It's Germany, not Korea, that matters.'[2]

On July 6 Sir William Strang came to Chartwell, to discuss foreign policy. 'Today we should have been at Bermuda,' Churchill commented, and he added, of the movement for European unity of which his own Strasbourg speech in 1950 had been a clarion call: 'The punch seems to have gone out of the movement. I should have said things to the French no one else could say. They want the best of all worlds—not to fight in the war, but to remain a great power.'

The French, pointed out Strang, had put their 'blood and fortune' into Indo-China.

That evening Churchill recited to Lord Moran a poem by Longfellow, 'King Robert of Sicily'. Moran noted in his diary:

He went on and on without apparently hesitating for a word. I asked him when last he had read the poem. He answered: 'About fifty years ago.' 'Wait a moment,' I said, and went in search of a copy of Longfellow. When I found it and had taken it to his room, I said:

'I believe your memory is as good as ever it was, but I want to be sure.'

I asked him to repeat the lines while I checked the words from the text. Wanting to come out with credit, he entered into the spirit of the test.

Churchill recited the poem again, all thirty-four lines. 'This', Moran wrote, 'may perhaps give critics pause, if the day should come when he is harshly judged for sticking to his post. Here and there he got a

[1] Letter of 4 July 1953: Robert Rhodes James, *Anthony Eden*, page 368.
[2] Moran diary, 5 July 1953: *The Struggle for Survival*, pages 422–4.

word wrong: priests became monks and lamps candles; perhaps half a dozen words out of three hundred and fifty. The stroke has not touched his memory. I told him so. He brightened and smiled.'

Moran added: 'He is confiding in no one, but he means to carry on if he is able, and the question whether he will be able is hardly ever out of his head. This is his secret battle. There are moments when he does not want to do anything, when a dreadful apathy settles on him and he nearly loses heart. But he always sets his jaw and hangs on.' [1]

On July 7 Lord and Lady Salisbury were Churchill's guests at dinner. 'For two hours,' noted Moran, 'the PM expounded his views on the international situation, until the acting Foreign Secretary was fully briefed for his visit to Washington; and this the PM did without obvious fatigue.' [2]

The only talk of resignation came, albeit briefly and by allusion, on July 8. Stanley Baldwin had been host to the King and Queen at dinner before he resigned, Churchill remarked at dinner, adding that he 'would like to follow that precedent'. [3] On the next day, however, came words of encouragement to go on, from his daughter Sarah. 'I wish I could do something more than just love,' she wrote, 'to help you regain completely your strength. But it is joyful & merciful to know that you will. I know it is slow. Be patient.' Sarah added:

The improvement in the 8 days I have been home has been miraculous. Try not to fret—I know that although you have laid aside your work—you have much on your mind but remember the most important thing is your health—remember how deeply you are loved & needed not only by the world—but by us—including your loving and devoted Mule. [4]

On July 10 Anthony Eden, who was recuperating in the United States after his third operation, wrote to Churchill to say how 'heartening' it had been for him 'to hear steadily improving reports of your progress from Jock & Harold Macmillan'. He and his wife had felt 'wretchedly far away during this time', he added, '& want so much to get home and to see you again'. As to his own health, 'I am really gaining strength, even though weight takes a little time to come back.'

That day it had been announced in the Press that Lavrenti Beria, head of the Soviet Ministry of International Affairs, and one of the four Deputy Prime Ministers appointed on Stalin's death, had been

---

[1] Moran diary, 6 July 1953: *The Struggle for Survival*, pages 424–6.
[2] Moran diary, 7 July 1953: *The Struggle for Survival*, page 426.
[3] Moran diary, 8 July 1953: *The Struggle for Survival*, pages 426–7.
[4] '*Darling* Papa', 9 July 1953: Churchill papers, 1/50.

dismissed for 'anti-Party and anti-State activities'.[1] 'The Beria development is intriguing,' Eden told Churchill, and he added: 'Cannot be
injurious to us anyway, as far as I can see, which is not very far in this
obscure scene.'[2]

The dismissal of Beria was also being discussed at Chartwell on July
10, when Churchill told his doctor:

Beria—Siberia. Strange things are happening there. It is very significant
and supports the line I have taken. The Russians were surprisingly patient
about the disturbances in East Germany. The aggressive party in the Kremlin
must have said: 'You see what comes of giving in, this is the result of concessions.' But they had not the power to arrest Malenkov. At a conference of
the Big Four he would have welcomed me particularly.

Churchill's eyes then 'dilated', his doctor noted, and 'he spoke
eagerly', still on the theme of the Summit conference for which he had
called three months earlier:

I would have met them more than halfway. It might have meant a real
UNO, with Russia working with the rest for the good of Europe. We would
have promised them that no more atomic bombs would be made, no more
research into their manufacture. Those already made would be locked away.
They would have had at their disposal much of the money now spent on
armaments to provide better conditions for the Russian people. I trust the
opportunity may not slip away. I have not give up hope of attending a Four
Power Conference in, say, September. Do you think, Charles, I shall be fit
by then?[3]

Churchill's mind was focusing more and more, despite his tiredness,
on the prospects for a summit, and the dangers posed for a summit by
a prior meeting of Foreign Ministers, as now proposed by France and
supported by America. After a further visit to Chartwell, R. A. Butler
told his Cabinet colleagues on July 13 that Churchill had considered
the most recent telegrams showing French and American preference
for a meeting of Foreign Ministers, and thought that it was important
that the agenda for such a meeting, and its composition, 'should not
be so rigid as to exclude the possibility that Heads of Government
might attend in the later stages and that the scope of the agenda
would then be widened'.[4]

On the following day, July 14, Churchill told Lord Moran:

[1] After being tried for treason, Beria was executed.
[2] 'My dear Winston', 10 July 1953: Churchill papers, 2/216.
[3] Moran diary, 10 July 1953: *The Struggle for Survival*, pages 428–30.
[4] Cabinet Conclusions No. 42 of 1953, 'Secret', 11.30 a.m., 13 July 1953: Cabinet papers, 128/26.

'I am disappointed with events in America. They've bitched things up. The Foreign Ministers are to meet in the autumn: Bidault, Dulles and Molotov.'

He lapsed into thought. At length he said:

'I'm turning over in my mind saying something serious to Ike. I want to make clear to him that I reserve the right to see Malenkov alone. It's no good seeing the Russians after the Foreign Ministers have drawn up agreements.'

He went indoors to telephone to Rab, to tell him of his misgivings, but I do not know if Rab was able to console him.[1]

Churchill's recovery was accelerated, and Churchill enlivened, by the summit prospect and by the difficulties in its path. On July 16 Lord Moran, entering Churchill's bedroom after breakfast, found his patient 'speaking with vigour' into the telephone, and noted of the Chartwell end of the conversation:

'I have never allowed my private communications to the President to be submitted to anyone, in the war or since.'

He paused and listened.

'Oh, I have no objection to Lord Salisbury seeing my message. Yes, show it to him. Tell him I wish him to see it before it goes. Tell him I think he has done very well in the circumstances—no, in face of great difficulties, in face of Bidault and Dulles. Ike ought to know I do not agree—Oh, I agree of course, but that I do not approve of what has been done about the Four Power Conference.'[2]

On July 17 Churchill sent Eisenhower his first message since informing him of his illness. It was once more on the theme which had dominated all his exchanges with the President: a possible meeting with the Soviet leaders and those of Britain, the United States and France. His telegram read:

Please consider at your leisure whether it might not be better for the Four-Power Meeting to begin, as Salisbury urged, with a preliminary survey by the Heads of Governments of all our troubles in an informal spirit. I am sure that gives a much better chance than if we only come in after a vast new network of detail has been erected. Moreover, Bidault made it pretty clear he wanted this meeting to break down in order to make a better case for EDC before the French Chamber, whereas it would have been a great advantage to go plus EDC with friendly hands in strong array.

Above all, I thought that you and I might have formed our own impression of Malenkov, who has never seen anybody outside Russia. After this preliminary meeting we might have been able to set our State Secretaries to work along less ambitious, if more hopeful, easier lines than we now propose.

---

[1] Moran diary, 14 July 1953: *The Struggle for Survival*, pages 433–6.
[2] Moran diary, 16 July 1953: *The Struggle for Survival*, pages 436–7.

I am very sorry I was not able to make this appeal to you personally as I had hoped.

Churchill ended his telegram with news of his health. 'I have made a great deal of progress,' he reported, 'and can now walk about. The doctors think that I may be well enough to appear in public by September. Meanwhile, I am still conducting business. It was a great disappointment to me not to have my chance of seeing you.'[1]

On Sunday July 19 R. A. Butler was Churchill's dinner guest at Chartwell. Colville, who was with Churchill, noted in his diary: 'W much improved in powers of concentration.' Butler had brought the speech he intended to make in the Foreign Affairs debate. Churchill, noted Colville, 'sparkled at dinner; after dinner he went carefully and meticulously through Rab's speech'.[2]

Butler too had been impressed, telling Lord Moran that he was 'astonished by the progress he had made in the course of a week'. It became plain, Moran wrote, that Butler 'did not rule out a comeback', and he added: 'The PM beamed at me. "They say I was very good with Rab." His voice became stronger. "I am again a forceful animal. I could kick people around this morning." As to what the Government's line would be in the debate, "Oh", Churchill answered, "they are going to stick by my statement of May 11."'[3]

That statement, with its appeal for a summit with the Soviet Union, continued to disturb the Americans. On July 21 Churchill was brought a letter from Eisenhower, who wrote:

In the first place let me say how greatly I rejoice at the report of a great improvement in your health. Your own country, and indeed the whole world, can hardly spare you even in semi-retirement, and I rejoice that you expect to emerge in full vigour in September.

I have a feeling that it is dangerous to talk generalities to the Russians unless and until their proposals for Germany and Austria show that we can depend on them. I like to keep talks informal with those I can trust as friends. That was why I looked forward so much to Bermuda. But I do not like talking informally with those who only wish to entrap and embarrass us. I would prefer, at any rate in the first instance, to leave the initial approach to the Foreign Ministers on limited and specific lines.

[1] 'Personal', 'Message to President Eisenhower from the Prime Minister', 17 July 1953: Eisenhower papers.
[2] Colville diary, 19 July 1953: *The Fringes of Power*, page 671.
[3] Moran diary, 20 July 1953: *The Struggle for Survival*, page 438.

'I greatly look forward to your re-appearance in September,' Eisenhower added.[1]

While Churchill was convalescing at Chartwell, more and more guests were invited to luncheon. One of them, Walter Graebner, later recalled:

Rumours of all kinds had been flying around London about his health, so I did not know quite what to expect as I waited with two other luncheon guests for him to enter the drawing-room to greet us. At 1.30 he shuffled in, perhaps a little less surefooted than usual, but otherwise gay and smiling happily. He was wearing one of his zip or siren suits, a greyish-blue flannel with a pin stripe. A minute or two later we went into lunch.

As he poured champagne into my glass he said: 'My illness, though it should have been mortal, never prevented me from having a square meal and a pint of champagne to go with it.' Later he said that for a time he had lost the use of both legs, and that one arm was partially paralysed.

He was anxious to know how I thought he appeared, and when I told him that I couldn't detect any big change he seemed pleased, and boasted proudly: 'This decaying carcass can still bring fame to anything, so long as it's not overworked.' He was particularly worried about his speech which had developed a slight huskiness. 'I will decide in the next few weeks whether to stay on the job or not,' he announced, then, with eyes twinkling, added: 'It's easy enough to get out, but it's a devil of a lot harder to come back in once you're out.'

In the later afternoon he asked me to go with him for a walk in the gardens. Though it was then five o'clock and the afternoon was getting cold and damp, there were forty or fifty people standing on a little hillock outside the gates waiting to catch a glimpse of the great man as he emerged. They cheered loudly, and Churchill responded with the familiar broad smile and 'V' sign.

We fed the goldfish, and then we sat down on a bench from which we could see the whole Weald of Kent unfold towards the sea. From time to time Rufie brought a ball which he asked his master to throw for him, and in between throws Churchill thought aloud about the future. 'I must be sure that I can master the House of Commons. I'm not worried about anything else, but if I can't master the House I must not go on.'[2]

On July 21 Churchill was well enough to deal with Bedell Smith's comments on the South of France versus Italy strategic conflict of 1944, of which he had written in draft for his war memoirs. He was

---

[1] 'Dear Winston', signed 'With warmest regards, Ike', quoted in Lord Moran's diary entry for 21 July 1953: *The Struggle for Survival*, pages 447–8.

[2] Walter Graebner recollections: *My dear Mister Churchill*, pages 17–18.

prepared to make changes, 'though it is not possible for me', he explained to Norman Brook, 'to conceal my aversion to "Anvil".' It gave him 'much pleasure', Churchill added, 'to address this letter with my own hand'.[1] There was also good news from Norman Brook on the following day: the Queen had given Churchill permission for the publication of all the War Cabinet documents which he wished to include in the volume, as well as his two messages to the King.[2]

On July 22 Lord Camrose went down to Chartwell to discuss the final volume. But Churchill was not as well as he had been for the previous few days. 'Found the PM in poor form,' Moran noted. 'Speech very slurred, and he is walking badly.' Seeing the state Churchill was in, Camrose told Moran: 'He will never go back to the House.' But Moran was not so pessimistic, noting in his diary:

Only once was there a glimpse of the Winston we have known. He began quoting poetry—Pope—and for a little time his manner became animated, his voice strong, his eye alert. Camrose was astonished at his memory. The PM's thoughts went back to his nursery days: he was very happy with his old nurse, till he was sent to 'penal servitude'. That was his description of his life at his prep school at Brighton, where he was from his eighth to eleventh year. He said that at the school there were volumes of *Punch*, and that he would pore over them and their story of what had happened in recent history.

Then his thoughts came back with a jerk to the present. He could not get out of his head the opportunity that had been lost at Moscow. Dulles was 'clever enough to be stupid on a rather large scale'.

He sat brooding; at last he looked up.

'I made an exhibition of myself today. I get maudlin. It seems a feature of this blow. Why am I like this, Charles? I'll have to go. The trouble is, it is easy to go, but it's not so easy when you find them doing things you don't approve of.'[3]

'I have not enjoyed July,' Churchill added. 'I have not had much fun.'

On July 24 Churchill's horse Gibraltar III won at Kempton Park. From the Rock of Gibraltar itself came a telegram of congratulation, signed 'Governor'.[4] That day, Jock Colville was at Chartwell, noting in his diary:

Lunched alone with W at Chartwell. He is now amazingly restored, but

[1] 'My dear Norman Brook', 'Private', 21 July 1953: Churchill papers, 4/392. 'Anvil' was the code name for the South of France landing.

[2] 'My dear Prime Minister', 22 July 1953: Churchill papers, 2/217.

[3] Moran diary, 22 July 1953: *The Struggle for Survival*, page 441.

[4] Telegram of 24 July 1953: Churchill papers, 1/93. The Governor and Commander-in-Chief, Gibraltar, was General Sir Gordon MacMillan, a former commander of the 51st Highland Division (The Netherlands and Germany, 1945) and General Officer Commanding Palestine (1945–8).

complains that his memory has suffered and says he thinks he probably will give up in October or at any rate before the Queen leaves for Australia in November. Still very wrapped up with the possibility of bringing something off with the Russians and with the idea of meeting Malenkov face to face. Very disappointed in Eisenhower whom he thinks both weak and stupid. Bitterly regrets that the Democrats were not returned at the last Presidential Election.[1]

'The more I think of it,' Evelyn Shuckburgh wrote in his diary that day, 'the more I disapprove of WSC fostering this sentimental illusion that peace can be obtained if only the "top men" can get together. It seems an example of the hubris which afflicts old men who have power, as it did Chamberlain when he visited Hitler.'[2]

Later that day Churchill was well enough to travel from Chartwell to Chequers. A month had passed since his stroke, two and a half months since his call for a Summit in his speech of May 11. It was of this, on reaching Chequers, that he spoke to Lord Moran:

When I went to his room to see if he was tired he began at once about the Russians. He said they had refused to work with us in Europe.

PM: 'The Americans were simple-minded to expect them to do anything else. They want the Kremlin to give up the part of Germany they themselves gave up to Stalin.'

Moran: 'What is the next step?'

PM: 'Perhaps I may take it if I can learn to walk properly. Would you come with me to Moscow? I knew you would, my dear Charles. We have travelled a good many miles together.'

I wonder where it will end. Sir Russell Brain, a careful, prudent physician, puts the PM's chance of coming back alive from a trip to Moscow as low as fifty-fifty. Excitement might bring on another stroke, or at any rate leave him unable to play his part when he got there. But if he knew the odds I am sure he would take them.[3]

'Brain thinks he may recover 90 per cent physically,' Moran noted in his diary on the following day, 'but he is less certain about his

[1] Colville diary, 24 July 1953: *The Finges of Power*, page 672.

[2] Shuckburgh diary, 24 July 1953: *Descent to Suez*, page 91. Shuckburgh added: 'Even if you do believe in the theory, surely you should keep this trump card in your hand for emergency and not play it out at a time when there is no burning need, no particularly dangerous tension (rather the reverse) and your opponents are plunged in internal struggles and dissensions. It is hard to avoid the conclusion that WSC is longing for a top-level meeting before he dies—not because it is wise or necessary but because it would complete the pattern of his ambition and make him the Father of Peace as well as of Victory. But it would do no such thing unless he were to make sacrifices and concessions to the Russians which there is no need to make, in return for a momentary and probably illusory "reduction of tension". After that splendid achievement he would die in triumph and we should all be left behind in a weaker position than before.'

[3] Moran diary, 24 July 1953: *The Struggle for Survival*, pages 442–3.

ability to concentrate. He doubts whether he will be alive in a year's time.'

Churchill's own plans were now evolving with determination. Although he accepted Moran's advice not to hold a Cabinet meeting at Chartwell early in August, he was looking forward to two events. 'October 10,' he explained to Moran, 'is the annual Party meeting at Margate, and I must make a speech then or get out.' Pointing to his forehead: 'I feel there is a small bit of the brain which has been affected by this business and may, if I use it too much, crack. Of course I know it's pure imagination—not scientific medicine.'

The second event, the summit, was the predominant reason for his wishing to remain Prime Minister, even though he knew the effect this would have on Eden, who had now returned from America, and expected to be asked to succeed Churchill by the end of the year. Churchill told Moran:

'Eden is coming on Monday. Perhaps it would be better, Charles, if I saw him alone. It is a delicate business. You might come in the late afternoon and stay to dinner. I don't think I shall commit myself when I see Anthony. I don't like being kicked out till I've had a shot at settling this Russian business.'

He leant towards me:

'You realize, Charles, I'm playing a big hand—the easement of the world, perhaps peace over the world—without of course giving up proper means of defence. If it came off, and there was disarmament,' he lisped in his excitement, 'production might be doubled and we might be able to give to the working man what he has never had—leisure. A four-day week, and then three days' fun. I had my teeth in it. I have become so valuable that they would allow me to do it in my own way. I must be right, of course—but I need not be busy—others would do the work.

'What is happening in Germany is very important. You've not seen it in the papers? It was in the *Telegraph*. The Germans are taking my line. They want a Locarno. America must be ready to attack Germany if she should attack Russia, while if Russia is the aggressor America would declare war on her.'

The thought of this better world, where the United Nations would at last keep the peace, left him in tears. He could not speak for some time. Then with an effort he took refuge in levity:

'I am trying, Charles, to cut down alcohol. I have knocked off brandy'— the coming sally made him smile—'and take Cointreau instead.' [1]

Anthony Eden came to Chequers on Monday July 27, 'thin and frail', Colville noted, 'after his three operations, but in good spirits'. Colville added: 'He is, of course, thinking above all of when he will

[1] Moran diary, 25 July 1953: *The Struggle for Survival*, pages 443–4.

get the Prime Ministership, but he contrived to keep off the subject altogether today and to talk mainly of foreign affairs. He thinks the fall of Beria three weeks ago may have been a defeat for moderation. The signs, flimsy though they be, do seem to point that way.'[1]

That day, while Churchill and Eden were at Chequers, the Korean War came finally to an end, with the signing of an armistice agreement at Panmunjon. The prospects for Churchill's summit had certainly not receded thereby. That evening, after dinner, he told Lord Moran: 'I had a greater opportunity before the blow than I ever had since I became a Member of the House of Commons—if only, Charles, I had the strength, I'm a sort of survival. Roosevelt and Stalin are both dead. I only am left. People say: "He means us well, all this is within his reach." ' Churchill went on to tell his doctor:

'Before I lead the British people into another and more bloody war, I want to satisfy my conscience and my honour that the Russians are not just play-acting. I believe they do mean something. I believe there has been a change of heart. I have talked with two Popes. What do you think we talked about? Bolshevism!'[2]

I asked him why Roosevelt had been so friendly to Stalin. But he did not answer my question. It is not easy to draw him out. He thought that the hydrogen bomb accounted for a certain arrogance in the Americans. He did not want them to be arrogant.[3]

On July 29 Adlai Stevenson, the defeated Democratic candidate in the 1952 Presidential Election, went to Chequers for lunch with the now rapidly recovering Prime Minister. His progress was certainly giving pleasure to his staff and secretaries. On July 30, Moran noted:

The PM seems to have more energy. Miss Gilliatt says he is clamouring for work. That, of course, is an exaggeration, but it does mean that he is willing to look at some papers which the private office has collected. He himself is sure that he is gaining ground, though he made this cryptic remark:

'I have a feeling I am only half in the world. It is a curious feeling. Adlai Stevenson lunched here yesterday. I like him.'[4]

Churchill remained at Chequers throughout the August Bank Holiday. His children Randolph, Mary and Sarah were there, as well as Eden and Clarissa. Colville, who was also present, noted in his diary that Eden 'was burning with the big question-mark: "When do I take

---

[1] Colville diary, 27 July 1953: *The Fringes of Power*, page 672. On the following day Lord Moran noted in his diary: 'I asked the PM whether he had discussed with Anthony what was going to happen in October about the succession. Was Anthony in a patient frame of mind? "Oh, he didn't mention it," the PM answered, "and I didn't expect he would." ' (Moran diary, 28 July 1953: *The Struggle for Survival*, page 447.)

[2] Churchill had visited Pius XI in 1925 and Pius XII in 1944.

[3] Moran diary, 27 July 1953: *The Struggle for Survival*, pages 445–6.

[4] Moran diary, 30 July 1953: *The Struggle for Survival*, pages 447–8.

over?"' but that he 'looked very frail and probably realizes he must first prove he will be fit to be PM himself'.[1]

The Chequers weekend showed how poor was the health of both Churchill and Eden. Lord Salisbury, who was also present, reported to Shuckburgh that he had formed 'a poor impression' of Eden's health, finding him 'fragile'. Eden meanwhile reported on his return to London 'that the PM himself said he was very tired and feeling worse, but that his "ménage" came in like attendants in an oriental court, flattering him and assuring him that he was perfectly all right and fit to carry on for ever'.[2]

The principal international concern that Bank Holiday was Britain's 'attitude to Russia', as Colville noted in his diary:

Winston is firmly hoping for talks which might lead to a relaxation of the Cold War and a respite in which science could use its marvels for improving the lot of man and, as he put it, the leisured classes of his youth might give way to the leisured masses of tomorrow. Eden is set on retaining the strength of NATO and the Western Alliance by which, he believes, Russia has already been severely weakened.

W is depressed by Eden's attitude (which reflects that of the FO), because he thinks it consigns us to years more of hatred and hostility. Still more depressing is that Lord S says he found Eisenhower violently Russophobe, greatly more so than Dulles, and that he believes the President to be personally responsible for the policy of useless pinpricks and harassing tactics the US is following against Russia in Europe and the Far East.

On Sunday August 2 Churchill went from Chequers to Windsor, where he had an audience of the Queen. When it was over he told Colville 'that he had told her his decision whether or not to retire would be made in a month when he saw clearly whether he was fit to face Parliament and to make a major speech to the Conservative Annual Conference in October'.[3] I am making continual progress,' Churchill informed Eisenhower on August 3, 'and have almost got back my full mobility.'[4]

Reflecting on the importance of the Party Conference to his future as Prime Minister, Churchill told Moran on August 5:

The party meeting is on October 10; Anthony may not be fit by then. He looked very frail when he was here; and I thought he seemed subdued. It would not be fair to Anthony to let Rab take it. Of course, everything depends on whether I can face October 10. I could not walk up the floor of the House of Commons at present. You must help me, Charles.

---

[1] Colville diary, 31 July–4 August 1953: *The Fringes of Power*, pages 672–3.
[2] Shuckburgh diary, 4 August 1953: *Descent to Suez*, pages 94–5.
[3] Colville diary, 31 July–4 August 1953: *The Fringes of Power*, pages 672–3.
[4] 'Top Secret', No. 3102 to Washington, 3 August 1953: Premier papers, 11/1074.

It was also at Chequers that August 5 that Churchill told his solicitor, Anthony Moir, that Randolph 'was to be his biographer'. [1]

On August 8, six weeks after his stroke, Churchill, Lord Salisbury, Butler, and the head of the Foreign Office, Sir William Strang, met to discuss the Soviet reply to a Three-Power note inviting the Soviet Union to a conference of Foreign Ministers. Jock Colville, who was present, noted in his diary:

The PM took the meeting in the Hawtrey room, the first time he has presided at a meeting since the Cabinet on the morrow of his stroke. The line he had proposed was accepted: namely to ask the Americans a lot of questions and leave them the burden of drafting the answer: this in spite of contrary and long-winded drafts prepared by the FO.

The old man still gets his way: usually because it is simple and clear, whereas the 'mystique' of the FO (as Selwyn Lloyd calls it) tends to be pettifogging and over detailed.

After the meeting we had a most agreeable luncheon party, the PM in sparkling mood. He said that all his life he had found his main contribution had been by self-expression rather than by self-denial. And he has started drinking brandy again after a month's abstinence.

Apart from his unsteady walk, the appearances left by his stroke have vanished, though he still tires quickly. However Lord Moran told me he thought there might be another stroke within a year. Indeed it was probable. [2]

Churchill's resilience and determination were equally remarkable. 'The nurse telephoned this morning,' noted Lord Moran on August 9, 'that yesterday, when Sir Winston was playing croquet, he hit the ball hard, and then, hurrying after it, became very short of breath—he was cyanosed, she added. But Jock said he was in fine form at night, hilarious in fact, and kept them up until one o'clock.' [3] Three days later, after Churchill had been examined at 10 Downing Street by Sir Russell Brain while on his way from Chequers to Chartwell, Moran wrote:

As we drove away, Brain said:

'Probably in a month's time he will be as well as he ever will be. I doubt whether he will be able to re-enter public life. If the Prime Minister goes to the Party meeting on October the 10th he might become emotional, or he might get very tired and walk away from the platform very badly, or he might even forget what he meant to say.' [4]

---

[1] Moran diary, 5 August 1953: *The Struggle for Survival*, pages 448–9. Randolph Churchill was to take up his task eight years later, in 1961, and to publish two volumes of his father's biography, *Youth* (1963) and *Young Statesman* (1966), together with two companion sets of documents.

[2] Colville diary, 6–9 August 1953: *The Fringes of Power*, pages 674–5.

[3] Moran diary, 9 August 1953: *The Struggle for Survival*, page 450. Cyanosis is a blueness or lividness of the skin owing to the circulation of imperfectly oxygenated blood.

[4] Moran diary, 12 August 1953: *The Struggle for Survival*, pages 450–1.

On August 12, less than a year after the United States had secretly exploded the first hydrogen bomb—deceptively called a 'thermo-nuclear weapon'—on Eniwetok, Malenkov announced that the United States no longer had a monopoly of the thermo-nuclear bomb. The primacy of Russia in Churchill's thoughts, and as a motive for remaining Prime Minister, was evident to those closest to him. 'Much talk about Russia,' Colville noted on August 12 in summary of the previous two days at Chequers, and he added: 'the PM still inclining to think we should have another shot at an understanding. He said, "We must not go further on the path to war unless we are sure there is no other path to peace."' [1]

While Churchill was returning from Chequers to Chartwell, Harold Nicolson was at the BBC Television studios at Lime Grove, London, filming his television obituary of Churchill. 'We go through it five times,' he notes, 'before we get it right.' [2] That day, having reached Chartwell, the much alive if weary Churchill dictated a progress report to Lord Beaverbrook, who had invited him to the South of France in October:

My dear Max,
You will be glad to know I am making continual progress, and have strong hopes of being able to do the Margate Conference on October 9 and attend the House of Commons when it meets. I have not been able to make up my mind about my plans for going abroad, being content to live one day after another at Chartwell or Chequers. The last week has been lovely. It is rather necessary for me to be on the spot at a time when so much, including my own small affairs, hangs in the balance.

For your eye alone: I have not absolutely excluded the idea of going to Washington in the last fortnight in September if progress continues good. There are a lot of things I might say in a talk with Ike. [3]

Two days later, Brendan Bracken wrote to Beaverbrook of their ailing friend:

Bless him. He now thinks that the fractional measure of moderation induced by illness has well-nigh renewed his youth. Retirement is not in his vocabulary. Such defeatist trash is not for him! He must be ready to act for Butler when his days of convalescence come. And Swinton may need a rest.... [4]

To use Churchill's 'favoured and hallowed peroration', Bracken added,

---

[1] Colville diary, 11–12 August 1953: *The Fringes of Power*, page 675.

[2] Nicolson diary, 12 August 1953: Nigel Nicolson (editor), *Harold Nicolson Diaries and Letters 1945–1962*, volume 3, page 244.

[3] 'My dear Max', 'Private and Personal', 12 August 1953: Churchill papers, 2/211.

[4] Viscount Swinton, Secretary of State at the Commonwealth Relations Office, was ten years younger than Churchill.

there was 'a "plentiful abundance" of opportunities for an energetic Prime Minister'. 'Cheering beyond all telling,' he commented, 'is this marvellous recovery.' [1] That weekend Colville noted in his diary: 'PM coming round towards resignation in October. Says he no longer has the zest for work and finds the world in an abominable state wherever he looks. Greatly depressed by thoughts on the hydrogen bomb. He had a nightmare on Thursday, dreaming that he was making a speech in the House of Lords and that it was an appalling flop. Lord Rothermere came up to him and said, "It didn't even *sound* nice."' [2]

On August 14 Churchill and his wife received, through Sir Alan Lascelles, an invitation to be the Queen's guests at Doncaster races and then at Balmoral. It was, Churchill wrote to the Queen that day, a 'delightful prospect'. His letter continued:

We shall indeed look forward to coming to Doncaster to see the Leger and to coming to Balmoral afterwards. My doctors think I am progressing steadily and I have every hope of being able to be in close attendance. Alas I have no horses to run. Today Pigeon Vole has a good chance at Newbury; but he is entered only for the *Newmarket* Leger (I did not know there was such a thing). All my loyalties will be devoted to Aureole.

'What a fearful blow to the famous Greek Islands!' Churchill ended. 'The only consolation is that it cannot be blamed upon us.' [3]

Those who worked closest to Churchill were impressed by his steady recovery. 'After a while,' Sir David Pitblado later recalled, 'he got back to another plateau. He certainly had not become incompetent to run the country. He was still anxious for things to happen, for work. At the weekend he would still get restless if nothing came in.' Pitblado added: 'At Chartwell, he loved his films. He liked sentimental films. In conversation at dinner, he was very good about the real past, what a young man could do with a fiver in 1885.' [4]

On the evening of August 15 Oliver Lyttelton dined at Chartwell. 'He cheered me up,' Churchill told Lord Moran, 'he's an agreeable

---

[1] Letter of 14 August 1953: Beaverbrook papers.

[2] Colville diary, 14–15 and 17 August 1953: *The Fringes of Power*, page 675. Colville added, of his master: 'He made a good pun at luncheon on Monday. We were talking about a peerage for Salter, who is to be removed from the Ministry of Materials. Christopher asked whether he could not also get rid of Mackeson from Overseas Trade, but said he didn't merit a peerage. "No," said W, "but perhaps a disappearage."'

[3] 'Madam', 14 August 1953: Squerryes Lodge Archive. A series of earthquakes earlier in August had devastated the Greek islands of Cephalonia (Kephallenia) and Zante (Zakynthos).

[4] Sir David Pitblado recollections: in conversation with the author, 17 July 1987. 'I enclose a photo of myself', Churchill wrote to his mother in October 1885 (aged 10) 'and ask if you will

personality.' Churchill added: 'I was depressed, not only about myself, but about the terrible state of the world. That hydrogen bomb can destroy two million people. It is so awful that I have a feeling it will not happen.' Churchill still did not know that the Americans had actually exploded a hydrogen bomb already. He only knew that such a bomb was being developed.

Churchill also spoke to Moran on August 16 of his hopes for a summit. In his hand as he spoke were the proofs of his war memoirs dealing with the Balkan 'spheres of influence' agreement which he and Stalin had made in Moscow in October 1944. Churchill told Moran:

> Read that. We made an arrangement with Stalin in the war about spheres of influence, expressed in percentages. Rumania, Bulgaria, Greece and so on. Here they are in print. Read the last paragraph. It seems rather cynical, I said to Stalin, to barter away the lives of millions of people in this fashion. Perhaps we ought to burn this paper. "Oh, no," said Stalin, "you keep it." We did that, Charles, on the spot in a few minutes. You see, the people at the top can do these things, which others can't do.[1]

Churchill planned to go to London on August 18 for a meeting of the full Cabinet, the first such meeting since his stroke eight weeks earlier. 'I am taking the Cabinet tomorrow,' he told his doctor with some pride. But Lord Moran was not impressed, writing in his diary:

> I said I was sorry he had made that decision. He ignored my remark. I want to gain time for him. His plan for meeting Malenkov has so far helped him to face the uncertainty of this wretched, drawn-out illness, but for the moment at any rate he has lost faith in his Moscow visit, and the real struggle for survival is only beginning. He sees clearly certain tests he must pass if he is to stay in public life.[2]

The Cabinet met on August 18, at 5 p.m., with Churchill again in the Chair. Speaking of the renewed negotiations for a defence agreement with Egypt, he suggested that the British delegation in Cairo should be 'reminded that we still hoped that firm dealing would result in better agreement than that now proposed'. Commenting a few moments later on a Foreign Office draft which stated that a peace treaty with Germany could only be negotiated with a 'free all-German Government' which was already 'enjoying freedom of action in internal and external affairs', Churchill told his Cabinet:

---

be so kind as to send me the sum of half a quid or 10 bob if you know what that is. I want to get 2 doz more.' 'We will not have a Christmas tree this year,' he wrote to his mother in December 1887, 'But I think a good 3 guinea Conjuror and a Tea and amusements and games after tea would answer better. You see, the Conjurer for 3 guineas gives "ventriloquism" and an hour's good conjuring which always causes some amusement.' Later that month he wrote: 'Auntie Leonie and Auntie Clara both gave me 10/-, which I am to spend on a theatre.'

[1] Moran diary, 16 August 1953: *The Struggle for Survival*, pages 451–3.
[2] Moran diary, 17 August 1953: *The Struggle for Survival*, pages 454–5.

If a unified Germany were allowed to achieve this degree of freedom before the conclusion of a peace treaty she would have nothing further to gain from such a treaty except the rectification of frontiers. Was this consistent with her unconditional surrender in 1945? Germany was still, after all, a defeated, divided and occupied country. Would it not be wiser to omit the words which referred to 'freedom of action in internal and external affairs'?

Churchill's suggestion was accepted; the words would be omitted 'unless', as the Cabinet minutes recorded, 'it were found that similar words had been used, without qualification, in earlier statements. . . .' [1]

The meeting had gone well. When it was over, Norman Brook told Lord Moran 'that he did not think any of the PM's colleagues noticed anything different from an ordinary Cabinet'. Norman Brook added: 'Winston let other people talk more than usual perhaps—he certainly talked less himself. No one noticed anything strange in his speech, and he walked to his seat much as he usually does.' Brook added: 'He has dipped his foot in water, and it wasn't cold; he wants to go on. This isn't the moment to make decisions about retiring.' [2]

On the morning of August 19 Churchill saw the British Ambassador to Moscow, Sir Alvary Gascoigne. 'He said that Beria's fall is a good thing,' Churchill reported to Lord Moran. Beria and Malenkov 'were great friends, but Beria was thrown to the wolves without a moment's hesitation. They are like wild beasts. There has been no change of heart in Russia, but she wants peace.' [3]

Churchill was also planning a new literary venture, or rather the completion of an old one. In September 1939, on the night when war began, Churchill had finished the first draft of a four-volume history of the English-speaking peoples from the earliest times to the death of Queen Victoria, a total of a million words. Now he planned to polish and publish; it was Lord Moran who, Denis Kelly recalled, had said to Churchill after his stroke: 'Take up something that will calm your mind,' whereupon Brendan Bracken remarked: 'Well why not finish *A History of the English-Speaking Peoples*.' [4]

Churchill took Bracken's advice, helped by a group of young historians whom he gathered together under the aegis of Brendan Bracken's

[1] Cabinet Conclusions No. 49 of 1953, 'Secret', 5 p.m., 18 August 1953: Cabinet papers, 128/26. This was not only Churchill's first Cabinet since his stroke, but Eden's first Cabinet after an even longer gap.
[2] Moran diary, 18 August 1953: *The Struggle for Survival*, pages 455–6.
[3] Moran diary, 19 August 1953: *The Struggle for Survival*, pages 456–7.
[4] Denis Kelly recollections: in conversation with the author, 11 April 1987.

friend and wartime assistant Alan Hodge, editor of the monthly magazine, *History Today*.[1] During their talk on August 19, Churchill told Moran, with a smile: 'I've been living on the *Second World War*. Now I shall live on this history. I shall lay an egg a year—a volume every twelve months should not mean much work.'[2]

Together with Bracken, Hodge went to see Churchill at Downing Street, where they found the Prime Minister in the Cabinet Room reading Sir Walter Scott's novel *Quentin Durward*, set in fifteenth-century France.[3] It was agreed that Hodge would now take charge of the planning and co-ordination of whatever extra work was needed, much as Bill Deakin had done for the war memoirs.

On August 19 Churchill returned to Chartwell: 'he looked dazed and grey', recalled Mary Soames. Eight weeks had passed since his stroke. 'Nearly all of us who saw him constantly,' his daughter added, 'could not believe that his recovery would be complete enough for him to wrestle again with public life.'[4]

That August, Walter Graebner returned to Chartwell; it was a day on which Churchill was working with both Commodore Allen and Kelly on the final revisions to the war memoirs' account of the battle of Leyte Gulf, at which the United States had broken the naval power of Japan. Graebner later recalled:

Work began at the luncheon table after the second bottle of champagne was emptied and cigars were lighted. 'Now let's get down to it,' Churchill said. We were still sitting there at a quarter to five, Churchill having gone over every word in the manuscript to make sure that he understood the full story of the battle and that he had related it clearly and in his best words.

'In the years that I knew him,' Graebner added, 'his mind was never sharper than on that grey August afternoon in 1953.'[5]

When, on August 21, Churchill saw Lord Moran again, both the Summit and the History were in his mind, as Moran recorded:

I asked him whether he intended to go to America to see Ike in September. He thought for a moment.

'I think I'd rather go and see the Russians. The country will be very disappointed if I give up trying to get the Russians in a friendly mood.'

Alan Hodge, a young historian, had lunched with him. Together they had looked through some of his first volume on *A History of the English-Speaking Peoples*. He sighed.

'I wish I could write as I did ten years ago. Though they say the sixth

---

[1] The other editor was Peter Quennell. The magazine itself was owned by Bracken.
[2] Moran diary, 19 August 1953: *The Struggle for Survival*, pages 456–7.
[3] Jane Aiken Hodge recollections: in conversation with the author, 3 July 1987.
[4] Mary Soames recollections: Mary Soames, *Clementine Churchill*, page 436.
[5] Walter Graebner recollections: *My dear Mister Churchill*, page 70.

volume of my book, which I call *Triumph and Tragedy*, is the best of the lot—more meat in it. Of course, the Americans will like it, because there is a lot about them. They are sometimes too confident. I have to tell them that.'[1]

Churchill still did not know whether he would be well enough to go to the Margate Conference in October. The two doctors whom he consulted in the last week of August, Sir John Parkinson, Cardiologist to the London Hospital, and Sir Russell Brain, both doubted if he could manage it. Brain wondered if he would ever be able to make speeches in public again, or even to answer questions in the House of Commons. 'I reminded Brain,' noted Lord Moran, 'that the PM was rather a law to himself. The second day after the stroke he insisted on walking about, where others at a like stage would be lying in bed; his will-power may well have called into play what he calls the back streets, and we doctors term the collateral circulation. Brain agreed this had no doubt helped him.'[2]

At three on the afternoon of August 25 Churchill was in the Chair at the second full Cabinet since his stroke. It too was at 10 Downing Street. Five days earlier, Dr Mossadeq had been arrested in Teheran, and two days later the Shah had returned to his capital. After Lord Salisbury had given details of the overthrow of the Mossadeq government and the establishment in its place of a firmly anti-Communist government headed by General Zahedi, to whom the Americans proposed to give financial assistance, Churchill commented that 'in present circumstances it would be easy for the Americans, by the expenditure of a relatively small sum of money, to reap all the benefits of many years of British work in Persia. He therefore hoped that the task of supporting General Zahedi's Government might be undertaken on an Anglo-American basis.'

Only R. A. Butler disagreed with Churchill's suggestion, telling the Cabinet that he would 'deprecate any hasty offer of a loan to General Zahedi. It could be repaid only in oil; and the Anglo-Iranian Oil Company, having developed other sources of supply, were now less interested in securing a resumption of the flow of oil from Persia.' It would be 'premature', Butler added, 'to offer a loan to a Government which had not yet resumed diplomatic relations with us. And we might find it embarrassing to be lending money to Persia when we were obliged to refuse applications for development loans from friendlier countries in the Middle East and even from our partners in the Commonwealth.'

Despite Butler's caution, the Cabinet did not reject Churchill's point

---

[1] Moran diary, 21 August 1953: *The Struggle for Survival*, pages 457–9.
[2] Moran diary, 25 August 1953: *The Struggle for Survival*, pages 459–60.

of view. Lord Salisbury was therefore instructed to 'consider further', with Butler, 'the possibility of rendering some financial assistance to the new Persian Government, and to ascertain what were the intentions of the United States Government in this regard'.

Speaking about the continuing negotiations in Cairo, Churchill praised those conducting them, who had 'done well', adding that they 'should be encouraged to maintain the firm attitude which they had shown'.[1]

The Cabinet meeting of August 25 ended shortly before seven o'clock. Churchill's working day was far from over, however. As Norman Brook later told Moran, at seven o'clock:

'I understand the PM went to his room and, calling for the proofs of *Triumph and Tragedy*, worked on them until dinner-time. Swinton and Rab dined with him and did not leave him until one o'clock. From three in the afternoon until one o'clock in the morning,' said Brook, summing up, 'the PM was in continuous debate on intricate matters of government.'

I told Brook I could add a postscript to his report. I found him at nine o'clock this morning, breakfasting, and right at the top of his form. He looked up brightly as I came into the room.

'I notice I am clear-headed in the mornings now—a great improvement. Even the irritation of my skin vanished when this other business came, as if the Deity felt I could not play with two toys at the same time. I feel 90 per cent—at any rate 80 per cent—of what I was.'

'Pitblado gave me his view,' Moran added. 'He was surprised by the PM's grip of things.' Pitblado told Moran: 'He showed no signs of flagging at one o'clock this morning—indeed, I made up my mind we were going to have a very late night working at papers. At present he seems in pretty good form.'[2]

During the evening of August 26, Churchill had dictated a note to Denis Kelly, as a result of his reading of the proofs which he had called for before dinner. On the following day, he returned from Downing Street to Chequers. There too, the last-minute work on his memoirs went on, interspersed with politics, as Moran recorded on September 1:

It was half-past seven in the evening when I arrived at Chequers and found him in bed correcting proofs.

'I was frightfully well this morning,' he began, 'quite like old times. Now I feel flat. I have had to make a lot of small corrections in the book. I had left out any mention of Bernie Baruch, and I had to correct this and then fit in what I had written to the text. And all the time the bloody telephone kept

---

[1] Cabinet Conclusions No. 50 of 1953, 'Secret', 3 p.m., 25 August 1953: Cabinet papers, 128/26.

[2] Moran diary, 26 August 1953: *The Struggle for Survival*, pages 459–62.

ringing and I had to break off to talk about the reshuffle I am making of the Government.' [1]

Later, Moran asked Churchill at what time he had gone to bed on the previous night. 'He admitted he had talked with Harold Macmillan and Anthony till a quarter to two,' Moran noted. That night, after dinner, Moran and Clementine Churchill waited for the Prime Minister to join them for cards. Moran wrote:

When the PM did not come back, I went after him and found him dictating to a secretary. I told him that he was overtired and ought to go to bed. In a few minutes he rose wearily, swayed as if he might fall and walked unsteadily to his room. There he plopped down on his bed and rang for Walter.

'I'm going to bed,' he grunted. [2]

Churchill having taken on the burden of foreign policy while Eden slowly recovered his health, the Foreign Office was now a main area of his concern. On August 27 Evelyn Shuckburgh noted in his diary:

All this week we are trying to conduct our foreign policy through the PM who is at Chartwell and always in the bath or asleep or too busy having dinner when we want urgent decisions. He had to be consulted about drafting points in the reply to the Soviets; about every individual 'intelligence' operation (which he usually forbids for fear of upsetting the Russians); about telegrams to Persia and Egypt. We are constantly telephoning minutes and draft telegrams down to Chartwell. After many minutes and arguments he has consented not to insist upon a full-scale naval visit to Sebastopol. This idea occurred to him as a means of offsetting British and American naval visits to Turkey which the Russians have complained about.

There were 'inspired stories' in the evening papers, Shuckburgh added, 'that the PM is engaged in forming a new Government for the autumn with AE as a sort of Deputy—described in the *Standard* as "Personal Assistant to Sir Winston" and Leader of the House. Monckton is tipped for Foreign Secretary, mainly because he has recently lunched at Chartwell.' [3]

Churchill's recovery was thought to be in jeopardy, not only by his doctors but by his wife, if he were to proceed with his plans to go, first to the races at Doncaster, and then on to Balmoral. On the evening of September 2 Clementine Churchill, who had injured herself in a fall and was still at Downing Street, telephoned to Chequers to

---

[1] On September 3 Churchill brought in Gwilym Lloyd George as Minister of Food, Sir Thomas Dugdale as Minister of Agriculture and Fisheries, and Florence Horsburgh, the first Conservative woman Cabinet Minister, as Minister of Education.

[2] Moran diary, 1 September 1953: *The Struggle for Survival*, pages 463–5. Walter Meyer was Churchill's Swiss valet, the successor to William Greenshields.

[3] Shuckburgh diary, 27 August 1953: *Descent to Suez*, pages 99–100. Eden, having returned to England for a few days at the end of July, had left for further recuperation.

express her opposition to both these visits, and there were strong words between them. Later that evening Churchill telephoned from Chequers to apologize to her. She replied on the following morning:

My darling Winston,

It was sweet of you to ring me up last night & to say loving & forgiving words to me.

I would like to persuade you to give up Doncaster & Balmoral.

First Doncaster. You will be watched by loving but anxious & curious crowds. It would be rather an effort to keep up steady walking. It may be a longish way to the Paddock & there will be much standing about. Altho' you sit in the Queen's Presence in intimate Court Circles, if you sat in public when she was standing it would be noticed.

Then Balmoral. You are improving steadily though slowly, but I fear you are not up to a night in the train and so on yet. And you don't want to have a set-back before the Margate Speech; but rather you must husband your strength for that important event, & for Parliament.

Doctor Barnett who has just been to see me (& diagnoses cracked ribs) says that the improvement in you will (or may if not arrested by fatigue) continue for 2 years.[1]

Writing from Chequers on September 5, Clementine Churchill told Mary and Christopher Soames:

I am sad about Papa; because in spite of the brave show he makes, he gets very easily tired & then he gets depressed—He does too much work & has not yet learnt how & when to stop. It just tails off drearily & he won't go to bed. He is making progress, but now it is imperceptible. If no set-back occurs the improvement can continue for 2 years.

I expect you have seen from the newspapers the tremendous 'va-et-vient' of ministers. Papa enjoys it very much. Incidentally they are even more tired than he is by the sitting over the dinner table till after midnight![2]

Among the telegrams which Churchill dictated on September 7 was one to Neville Duke: 'Many congratulations on your achievement.'[3]

On September 8 Churchill returned to Downing Street, for the third Cabinet since his stroke. The principal discussion was again about Egypt, where the defence negotiations were nearing completion. Great care, Churchill warned, would be needed in presenting any such agree-

---

[1] 'My darling Winston', from 10 Downing Street, 3 September 1953: Churchill papers, 1/50.

[2] Letter of 5 September 1953: Mary Soames, *Clementine Churchill*, page 437.

[3] Telegram of 7 September 1953: Churchill papers, 2/185. That day, Neville Duke had broken the world air speed record in a Hawker Hunter flying at an average speed of 727 miles an hour. Churchill lunched with Duke on September 10, telling Lord Moran on the following day: '"Neville Duke lunched with me yesterday. He is very able. I should be quite happy to have him in the Cabinet. But he might not be able to get a seat and"—with a smirk—"he mightn't turn out to be a Conservative."' (Moran diary, 11 September 1953: *The Struggle for Survival*, pages 470–3.) In the Second World War, as a fighter pilot, Duke had shot down twenty-eight enemy aircraft.

ment to Parliament. The omission of any reference to freedom of transit through the Suez Canal would, he said, 'certainly attract criticism, as it was the popular belief that this was the main purpose of our military base in the Canal Zone'.

The discussion then turned to a proposal by the Chiefs of Staff for emergency measures to be put into force 'at very short notice' should the Egyptian Government 'stimulate hostile activities against British troops' in the Canal Zone. If the situation 'did in fact deteriorate', Churchill commented, 'it might well be desirable to issue a formal warning to the Egyptian Government, and at that point it might also be necessary to authorize the Commanders-in-Chief in the Middle East to put in hand widespread security measures; but this situation could be faced when it arose'. If the situation deteriorated 'so rapidly', however, 'that a full Cabinet could not be summoned to consider it', he would 'take upon himself the responsibility for giving the necessary instructions'. It should 'not be forgotten', Churchill added, that there were economic and financial sanctions which could be applied to Egypt 'without having recourse to active intervention by British forces'. Above all, 'it was open to us to block Egypt's sterling balances and to control the flow of oil to Cairo'.

Another question which the Cabinet of September 8 was called upon to consider was whether Britain should support the admission of China to the United Nations. Through John Foster Dulles, the Americans had indicated their distaste for such an initiative, and now the Joint Parliamentary Under-Secretary of State for Foreign Affairs, Anthony Nutting, suggested that Britain ought to take no steps which would make it difficult for her to abstain from voting on the proposal. Churchill 'strongly endorsed' Nutting's proposal, telling the Cabinet:

... it would be unwise to subject Anglo-American relations, so soon, to a second strain comparable to that which arose from our proposal that India should be a member of the Political Conference on Korea. We should be well-advised to go to great lengths to avoid any further cause of Anglo-American misunderstanding at the present time. It was natural that, after all the losses and suffering which they had endured in the Korean war, the Americans should now feel reluctant to see Communist China take her seat in the United Nations: and we should make due allowance for the strength of this feeling, which was not likely to be influenced by considerations of logic or expediency.

A final point on which Churchill spoke on September 8 was to welcome a Commission of Enquiry into a strike which had just been called by the Electrical Trades Union. It was in his view 'important', Churchill told his Cabinet colleagues, 'that there should be a full public exposure of the new and sinister techniques adopted by this

Union, in calling out on strike selected workers in undertakings of special importance to the national economy. These innovations might with advantage be debated in the House of Commons, when Parliament re-assembled, even though the strike was then over.'[1]

Greeting his doctor at 10 Downing Street that afternoon, Churchill's first words were: 'I have taken a step forward, Charles. This morning's Cabinet was a considerable advance on the first two.' Churchill added: 'Of course, I am tired now.' R. A. Butler, who was with Churchill at No. 10, 'agreed in such a way'. Moran noted 'that I felt the PM had really done the Cabinet well'. Moran's account continued:

When I left them I had a few words with Pitblado. I asked him whether the PM had made a good impression on his week-end visitors. Pitblado pondered for a little.

'I think,' he said, 'Head and Macmillan left probably without making up their minds. The PM was older, but, on the other hand, I don't think they felt he must necessarily give up. Of course, the Chief Whip is different; he sees so much of him.'

'Do his colleagues want him to carry on?' I asked.

Pitblado hesitated:

'I think Eden would be happy if he knew when the PM was going to retire, even if it was April. Something definite, that's what he wants. Rab is probably quite happy; he may be in a better position now than he would be if the PM resigned, and he has demonstrated that he is of Prime Ministerial timber.

'I have an idea, gathered from little things, that the PM is not certain himself what to do, but that his present intention is to carry on. Of course, this trip north may help; if anything goes wrong he may decide not to go on.

'As for his colleagues, they are bound to be influenced by what happens. If he can sail through the Party Meeting on October 10 and carry on in the House as before I don't think anyone will stir a finger. It is, after all,' Pitblado added, 'because he has so obviously been master of the House of Commons and has dealt so effectively with the Opposition since he became Prime Minister that the Party has been so docile.'[2]

After their meeting in the Cabinet Room in August, Churchill had sent the printed proofs of the first part of *A History of the English-Speaking Peoples* to Alan Hodge, to whom he wrote on September 11:

Of course I cannot give the necessary attention to this project until my burdens in other directions are lightened and I do not yet know when that

---

[1] Cabinet Conclusions No. 51 of 1953, 'Secret', 11.30 a.m., 8 September 1953: Cabinet papers, 128/26.
[2] Moran diary, 8 September 1953: *The Struggle for Survival*, pages 468–70.

will be. The final grasping of Volume I, of which I sent you a copy, is not a work which can be combined with my present duties. I should however like you very much to interest yourself in the enterprise and I shall look forward to another talk with you and with Brendan.

I have today put together what has been written on the Tudor period, with which I am far from content. If you will kindly piece it together I will have it reprinted for what it is worth. It can then be a basis for further study. You could also note any omissions which exist, but it is not worth spending time upon.

Meanwhile I send you a paper on the story of the Common Law with which a great deal of pains was taken at the time, and is I believe a good factual authority. I should be glad if you would look it through and consider whether the part applicable to Volume I, namely to the end of Galley 627, would be better interleaved reign by reign or period by period, or whether it should not be woven into a general chapter of its own. I am afraid it is one to which many readers would not devote the necessary attention. The theme of the growth of our Common Law, which is the inheritance of the English-Speaking Peoples as a whole, must however run through the story. It will take some art to tell this story to others than lawyers who know much of it already.

'It will be of great interest to me,' Churchill added, 'to absorb myself in this work without the violent emotions which filled the years 1938/9, and I hope I may have your company and perhaps that of some of your friends in browsing about these extensive pastures.' [1]

On September 11, disregarding his wife's advice, Churchill went by train to Doncaster, to watch the St Leger from the royal enclosure, as the guest of the Queen. When the Queen appeared in the box, Churchill told his doctor four days later, 'I kept back, but when she came out and said to me, "They want you," I went into the box, and when I appeared I got as much cheering as she did.'

From Doncaster, Churchill travelled north in the royal train to Balmoral, where, on the Sunday, he accompanied the Queen to Crathie Kirk, where he had last worshipped, with King Edward VII, forty-five years before. Then he had been President of the Board of Trade. 'What an innings he has had!' commented Lord Moran. 'Now there were long avenues of people,' Churchill told his doctor on his return to London, 'and they raised their hands, waving and cheering, which I was told had never happened before.' Churchill added, about his Margate speech of October: 'I think I shall be all right on the 10th. I have important things to say that concern the country.' [2]

On the morning of September 16 Churchill was in the Chair at Cabinet, where Harold Macmillan outlined an ambitious scheme for

---

[1] 'Dear Mr Hodge', 'Private and Confidential', 11 September 1953: Churchill papers, 4/27.
[2] Moran diary, 15 September 1953: *The Struggle for Survival*, pages 472–3.

enabling house repairs to be undertaken by local authorities as well as by private landlords. This scheme, noted R. A. Butler, 'offered little relief to the budgetary position. But it was to go ahead.' 'Unless this vital question of repairs were tackled,' Churchill told his colleagues, 'the new housing programme would lose much of its value.' The policy should be pushed through 'as rapidly as possible', he added, 'so that its beneficial effects could be seen at an early date'.[1]

That afternoon, at a second Cabinet, the imminent defence agreement with Egypt was under review. It 'might well be', Churchill said, 'that, in spite of all our efforts, it would not prove possible to reach an acceptable agreement with the Egyptians; if this should happen, we must not flinch from the consequences'. If, on the other hand, an agreement was finally concluded, 'we must make sure that we reaped the full advantages to be derived from it, including the greatest possible reduction in our military forces in the Middle East'.[2]

Between the two Cabinets, Churchill had lunched with the Irish President, Eamon de Valera, his adversary of earlier years. 'A very agreeable occasion,' Churchill told his doctor, and he added: 'I like the man.'[3]

On the following evening, Moran sought out Christopher Soames, and questioned him about Churchill's future, noting of Soames's reply:

He told me that the family felt that Winston ought to retire, but he had told them that it was selfish of them to want him to resign if he could help the country. Christopher questioned me about the PM's future. But I see quite clearly,' he continued, 'that he will do what he wants to do. You have more influence with him than anyone, but of course that's not very much.' And Christopher smiled on me benignly.

'You remember, Charles, when he was in bed, and it was uncertain whether he would come through, he used Anthony's illness as an excuse when he said he would have to carry on. I told you then, you remember, that if he hadn't this excuse he would find another. Well, now that Anthony's quite well enough to lead he just says: "I'm not going to retire. I shall carry on."'

---

[1] Cabinet Conclusions No. 52 of 1953, 'Secret', 11.30 a.m., 16 September 1953: Cabinet papers, 128/26.

[2] Cabinet Conclusions No. 53 of 1953, 'Secret', 5 p.m., 16 September 1953: Cabinet papers, 128/26.

[3] Moran diary, 16 September 1953: *The Struggle for Survival*, pages 473–4. Denis Kelly later recalled one of Churchill's favourite stories—'he used to adore telling it'—'British bomber over Berlin, caught in the searchlights, flak coming up, one engine on fire, rear-gunner wounded, Irish pilot mutters, "Thank God Dev kept us out of this bloody war."' (Denis Kelly: letter to the author, 7 June 1987.)

Soames also told Moran that, during Churchill's journey north, 'the Queen told Miss Gilliatt that the improvement he had made since she last saw him was astonishing'.[1]

On September 17 Churchill left London for two weeks in the South of France, accompanied by Christopher and Mary Soames, and Miss Portal. They stayed at Lord Beaverbrook's villa at Cap d'Ail. 'All is beautiful & sunlit here,' Churchill wrote to his wife on the following day, in his own hand. His letter continued:

There is a sense of peace & quiet. Nothing but yr presence is lacking. The children swim & I have plunged into *Coningsby*.[2] I am going to have a smack at a canvas this afternoon. There is no scarcity of official papers—but I know how to meld them into an easy existence as Honorary Mayor of Cap d'Ail!

Fondest love Darling. Do not worry about anything for a space, but think again about coming here when the children leave.

I have written to the Queen & send you a copy (secret)

With all my love

Your loving husband [Drawing of a pig]

W[3]

Churchill's first letter from Cap d'Ail had been his letter to the Queen, also written in his own hand:

Madam,

I must express to Yr Majesty the keen pleasure which my wife and I derived from our Northern journey, and still more for the kind and gracious thought that led to its being planned. Balmoral was indeed a happy scene of youth and joy—all the brighter on the background of Premonition.[4] But there will be many Legers in which the Royal colours will claim their due.

I am now here in warm sunshine and the delightful villa built by the dressmaker, Molyneux, with much taste and care, and I shall not often leave its garden where I am installing my painting tackle, and reading for the first time (!) *Coningsby*.

The sense of crisis in Security and Finance which oppressed me when two

---

[1] Moran diary, 16 September 1953: *The Struggle for Survival*, pages 473–4. Miss Gilliatt was the daughter of Sir William Gilliatt, Consulting Gynaecologist to the Queen.

[2] *Coningsby, or The New Generation*, a political novel by Benjamin Disraeli, published in 1844, twenty-four years before he first became Prime Minister. (Churchill's only novel, *Savrola*, was published forty years before his first Premiership.) The 'heroes' of *Coningsby* were Tadpole and Taper, they were: 'great friends. Neither of them ever despaired of the Commonwealth.' Among the much-quoted phrases from *Coningsby* were: 'No Government can be long secure without a formidable Opposition,' 'Almost everything that is great has been done by youth,' 'Man is only truly great when he acts from his passions,' and 'Youth is a blunder; Manhood a struggle; Old Age a Regret.'

[3] 'Darling', Cap d'Ail, 18 September 1953: Spencer-Churchill papers.

[4] Premonition had won the St Leger on 12 September 1953.

years ago I was asked by your dear Father to form a Government has subsided into a tangle of detail in which there lie many difficulties, tho, if my
judgment is right, no grave immediate dangers.

Commenting on the Queen's Commonwealth tour, to the Pacific
islands, and to Australia, Churchill added: 'The opportunity is well
chosen for the Royal Visit to what will some day be a mighty State
and is already a rampart of our island home and Monarchy.' [1]

From Cap d'Ail, Jane Portal wrote to her uncle, R. A. Butler:

The PM has been in the depths of depression. He broods continually whether
to give up or not. He was exhausted by Balmoral and the Cabinets and the journey. I sometimes feel he would be better engaged on his History of the English-
Speaking Peoples which is already very remarkable. He greatly likes your messages telling him all the news and you are in high favour. He is preparing a
speech for the Margate conference but wonders how long he can be on his pins
to deliver it. He has painted one picture in tempera from his bedroom window. [2]

On September 21 Churchill wrote to his wife, in his own hand:

My darling one,
The days pass quickly & quietly. I have hardly been outside the garden,
& so far have not had the energy to paint in the sunlight hours. Maugham
who lunched yesterday said that we had left it late in the year to come here.
But the climate is mild and cheerful, but for one downpour & thunderstorm.

I do not think I have made much progress, tho as usual I eat, drink & sleep
well. I think a great deal about you & feel how much I love you. The kittens
are vy kind to me, but evidently they do not think much of my prospects. I
have done the daily work and kept check on the gloomy tangle of the world,
and I have dictated about 2,000 words of a possible speech for Margate in
order to try & see how I can let it off when it is finished to a select audience.
I still ponder on the future and don't want to decide unless I am convinced.

Today I went into Monte Carlo and bought a grisly book by the author of
All Quiet on the Western Front. It is all about concentration camps, but in good
readable print, wh matters to me. [3] It is like taking refuge from melancholy
in horror. It provides a background. I have read almost ¾ of *Coningsby*, but
the print was faint and small. I am glad I did not have to live in that
artificial society of dukes & would-be duchesses with their Tadpoles &
Tapers. I think it wd be interesting to write a short condensed account of the

[1] 'Madam', Cap d'Ail, 18 September 1953: Squerryes Lodge Archive.
[2] Jane Portal letter: *The Art of the Possible, The Memoirs of Lord Butler*, page 171. Owing to
Eden's illness, Butler had been presiding at Cabinet between Churchill's stroke and August 18,
effectively as Deputy Prime Minister.
[3] The author was Erich Maria Remarque, born in Germany in 1898, and twice wounded in
the First World War. He published *All Quiet on the Western Front* in 1929. A million copies were
sold in Germany in its first year, it was translated into thirty-two languages, and turned into a
film (subsequently banned in Germany and Austria). In 1933 the book was among those publicly
burnt by the Nazis in Berlin. Remarque lived in Switzerland from 1938; there, in 1952, he wrote
Spark of Life, a novel about conditions in the concentration camps. He died in 1970. He had
been born Kramer, but reversed his name for his pseudonym.

Victorian political scene. There were so many Governments & so many swells jostling each other for the minor jobs of Court & Office. No doubt we picked the best period to wander in.

Esmond came to luncheon yesterday and was vy friendly & not a bit vexed about poor Randolph's performance—published *verbatim* as you have no doubt seen in the Bevanite rag.[1] Kitty L has been quite ill and cannot yet walk.[2] I shall try to go to see her—though I don't relish the prospect of all those steps! O'Brien the TUC President has been here today. He is a sensible man and I gave him a good dose of Tory Democracy—quite as good a brand as your Liberalism.[3]

Forgive this scrawl in bed with a tiny Biro. I can do better, but I so rarely write with my own paw. *Please continue to love me* or I shall be vy unhappy. I suppose you and Nellion[4] will now be off to Stratford to enjoy *Richard III* & *Twelfth Night*. I doubt if I shall stay much beyond the present week. Write me about it all. I long to hear from you. Burn this scribble. It is worse than I really am.

Ever your loving & as yet unconquered

PS, Once more all my love & with a better pen—like the one you gave UJ & he told he always wrote in pencil. If Beria has escaped he will be much better value than Mrs Maclean![5]

W[6]

[1] Esmond Harmsworth, son of the 1st Viscount Rothermere, who in 1940 had succeeded his father as 2nd Viscount. At a Foyle's literary luncheon in honour of Hugh Cudlipp's book *Publish and Be Damned* (a history of the *Daily Mirror*) Randolph, instead of the customary speech of praise for the book, launched into a ferocious attack on the book, its author and the 'gutter' press, suggesting that it would be appropriate, in Coronation Year, to appoint, from among the Fleet Street proprietors and writers, a Pornographer Royal and Criminologist Extraordinary. 'By far the strongest candidate for the new office,' Randolph declared, was Lord Rothermere's editor of the *Sunday Dispatch*, Mr Charles Eade. In his speech, Randolph had made a point of singling out Lord Rothermere by name. One of the reasons why the London press was so bad, he claimed, was because Fleet Street acted on the principle of Dog Don't Eat Dog (or, as he often phrased it, 'Son-of-a-bitch Don't eat Son-of-a-bitch'.) Randolph added, in his speech: 'This handful of wealthy men have formed a cartel to immunise themselves from anything said against them.'

[2] Lady Katherine Lambton, daughter of the 10th Duke of St Albans and widow of Major-General Sir William Lambton (who had died in 1939). She died in 1958, at the age of eighty. Churchill did go to see her, despite the steps.

[3] Tom O'Brien, born in 1900, had lied about his age in order to join the Army in 1915; he had served at the Dardanelles. General Secretary of the National Association of Theatrical and Kine Employees from 1932, and a Member of the TUC General Council from 1940, in 1945 he had been elected to Parliament as a Labour member. He was knighted in 1956, and died in 1970. In December 1953 he publicly offered the good wishes of the TUC to Churchill for his trip to the United States.

[4] Nellion: Clementine Churchill's sister, Nellie Romilly.

[5] On 16 September 1953 the Foreign Office confirmed that Mrs Melinda Maclean, whose husband Donald had disappeared in 1951, when he was head of the American Department at the Foreign Office, was herself missing from Geneva, where she had been living for the past year. Her husband, together with Guy Burgess, had disappeared on 25 May 1951. On 21 September 1953 it was announced that she had been seen on the Vienna train. She subsequently joined her husband in Moscow. Beria had not escaped; on 10 July 1953 Malenkov announced that he had been 'dismissed'. In fact, he had been shot (this was announced only in December).

[6] 'My darling one', 21 September 1953: Spencer-Churchill papers.

On September 22 Mary Soames wrote to her mother from La Capponcina:

> Papa is in good health—but alas, low spirits—which Chimp and I are
> unable to remedy. He feels his energy and stamina to be on an ebb tide—He
> is struggling to make up his mind what to do. I'm sure you know the form—
> you have been witnessing it all these months. . . .
>
> He thinks much of you & wonders what you are doing. . . .
>
> Chimp & I are having a lovely time—bathing—reading—cards & we love
> being with Papa—Only we yearn to be able to do more than be the mere
> witnesses (however loving) of his sadness.[1]

'Have at last plunged into a daub,' Churchill telegraphed to his wife
on September 23. 'Hope you have got my letter. Much love, W.'[2]

'I hope you are having a happy holiday & recharging your batteries,' Randolph Churchill wrote to his father on September 23.[3]
'Am recharging,' Churchill replied.[4] On September 23 Jock Colville
and his wife flew out to La Capponcina, where they relaxed in the
sun while Churchill, accompanied by his detective Sergeant Murray,
himself an artist, 'spent hours painting the rocks and pine trees'.[5]

In his diary, Colville noted the discussion and concerns of the next
six days:

> Winston cannot make up his mind whether or not to go on as PM. On the
> whole he inclines to do so or at any rate to see what he can do. He certainly
> wants to, but is a little doubtful of his capacity to make long speeches. He
> thinks he will take the big one he has to make on October 10th, at the
> Conservative Conference at Margate, as the test. His conversation at Cap
> d'Ail was of little else, apart from the tragedy that the Bermudan Conference
> had not taken place and the desirability of him and Eden meeting Malenkov
> and Molotov face to face.[6]
>
> Eden, of course, longs for him to go; and Patrick Buchan-Hepburn, with
> whom I had a talk before going to France, thinks there will be trouble in the
> House and in the Conservative Party if he does not.[7]

On September 25 Churchill sent his wife a third handwritten account of his holiday:

My darling,

Mary & Christopher leave now & will carry this to you. I shall follow on
the 30th. It was vy nice talking on the telephone to you tho' I found it so

[1] Letter dated 22 September 1953: Mary Soames, *Clementine Churchill*, page 438.

[2] Telegram despatched 23 September 1953: Churchill papers, 1/50.

[3] 'My dearest Papa', 23 September 1953: Churchill papers, 1/51.

[4] Telegram despatched 26 September 1953: Churchill papers, 1/51.

[5] Colville recollections: *The Fringes of Power*, page 677.

[6] On 12 September 1953 Nikita Khrushchev had been appointed First Secretary of the Central
Committee of the Communist Party of the USSR, and effective ruler of the Soviet Union.

[7] Colville diary, September–October 1953: *The Fringes of Power*, page 679.

difficult to hear. The weather was perfect yesterday but today is cloudy. I have taken the plunge in painting and certainly feel the necessary vigour & strength to be as bad as I used to be. This is a relief because it is a gt distraction and a little perch for a tired bird.

We had the Minister of the Interior here yesterday and about 20 local notables & gave them & their wives champagne.[1] It went off all right. The Minister said he was for a German Army. I think their Govt feels stronger now that Guy Mollet, & the Socialists have rallied to EDC. But there is not much life in the Latin Republics. Nothing cd be more comfortable than this villa, and all arrangements are perfect. I have only left the garden twice, and the days pass vy quickly. I continue to revolve my fate. As usual there seems to be something to be said on both sides. It is rather like a Home Secretary pondering about his own reprieve.

I am so glad you are going down to Chartwell tonight. Do write me the news about it all—including the little yellow cat, with whom I thought I was making progress thanks to grouse.

I do hope my darling you have found the interlude restful and pleasant. I must admit I have had a good many brown hours. However the moment of action will soon come now.

I wish you were here for I can't help feeling lonely.

Your ever loving husband

W

[sketch of pig]

PS, I have begun Père Goriot in French.[2]

On September 26 no painting was possible. 'Alas another rainy day' was Churchill's telegraphic report to his wife.[3] 'Mary almost swallowed by an octopus,' Churchill telegraphed that day to Lord Beaverbrook, 'but the chameleon in the dining room caught two flies at dinner last night. Jock and Meg have arrived. All having a lovely time and most comfortable.'[4] In a letter to Beaverbrook, he wrote:

I have been reading for amusement the first volume of my History of the English-Speaking Peoples written fifteen years ago. I think it will entertain you one of these days. Certainly there has always been plenty going on. On the whole I think I would rather have lived through our lot of troubles than any of the others, though I must place on record my regret that the human race ever learned to fly.

Churchill went on, 'on serious matters', to suggest that Beaverbrook be 'careful' about his opposition to a German army. As Churchill

[1] The French Minister of the Interior was Léon Martinaud-Déplat. He was succeeded in June 1954 by François Mitterand.

[2] 'My darling', Cap d'Ail, 25 September 1953: Spencer-Churchill papers. Le Père Goriot by Balzac was published in 1834, one of Balzac's studies of Parisian life. The novel centres around Goriot, a retired vermicelli manufacturer, who gave away his money in dowries for two ungrateful daughters.

[3] Telegram despatched 26 September 1953: Churchill papers, 1/50.

[4] Telegram despatched 26 September 1953: Churchill papers, 2/211.

explained: 'Although armies are no longer the instruments by which the fate of nations is decided, there is certainly going to be a German army and I hope it will be on our side and not against us. This need in no way prevent, but may on the contrary help, friendly relations with the bear.' [1]

Churchill's rereading of *A History of the English-Speaking Peoples* followed a critical reading done for him by Alan Hodge. Writing to Hodge from La Capponcina, Churchill set out his views on how the book might be recast:

Hitherto after the opening chapters the story has been classified under titles of the reigns of Kings. This was how we learned it at school. Of course it is not in accordance with the scale and temper of the work. Before reprinting this first book reshaped as you have suggested, we should consider only using monarchs for chapter heads when they represent some great phase or turning point in history.

I should like to have a chapter 'Alfred The Great', but it would have to include much more than his reign to make it big enough. 'The Normans' should cover the four Sovereigns commonly associated with them. 'The Angevins' come next. 'Magna Carta' should surely have a chapter. 'The Plantagenets' come next, but in their case they will be too long for a cycle. They must evidently be broken up into three or four. 'The Hundred Years War' also seems a good title. 'Simon De Montfort' or 'The Dawn Of Parliament' seems better than several Kings. 'The Wars Of The Roses' or 'York And Lancaster' is another good title and seems about to match the scope of the chapter required. All this requires much study and consideration.

Churchill's letter continued:

In this story we are keeping alive the famous dramatic incidents and only hesitating to produce cameos of detail when they are worth it. We are recording the march of events in what is meant to be a lively, continuous narrative. We are primarily concerned with the social and political changes which occur, especially with those which have left their marks on today. All this was in my mind when I collected the material and tried to tell the story. The theme is the History of the English-Speaking Peoples as viewed by the modern eye.

'I am so glad you feel on the first reading there is not much to be done,' Churchill told Hodge, and he added: 'We must discuss the whole of this when I get home and make a plan for a provisional reprint. I shall look forward to seeing you.' [2] 'It was so exciting when he went back to that,' Miss Portal later recalled. [3]

---

[1] 'My dear Max', 'At La Capponcina, Cap d'Ail', 26 September 1953: Churchill papers, 2/211.

[2] Letter dated 'September 1953', La Capponcina: Churchill papers, 4/27.

[3] Lady Williams of Elvel recollections: in conversation with the author, 29 July 1987.

Churchill returned from the South of France on September 30. That same day he approved the final preface to the final volume of his war memoirs. 'The original text was completed nearly two years ago,' the preface, as drafted by Denis Kelly, explained. 'Other duties have since confined me to general supervision of the processes of checking the statements of fact contained in these pages and obtaining the necessary consents to the publication of the original documents.' Churchill continued: 'I have called this volume *Triumph and Tragedy* because the overwhelming victory of the Grand Alliance has failed so far to bring general peace to our anxious world.'[1]

More than eight years had passed since Churchill's first efforts to tell the story which was now completed. 'We were alone in the great hall at Chequers after dinner,' Denis Kelly later recalled. 'He took almost twenty minutes looking over the final draft preface, especially the sentences describing the ending of the war. At one point, I had written: "Nazi Germany was occupied and partitioned." He said, "the word you want is *crushed*".'[2]

---

[1] Preface dated 30 September 1953: *The Second World War*, volume 6, page ix. The volume was published in the United States on 30 November 1953 (60,000 copies) and in Britain on 26 April 1954 (200,000 copies).

[2] Denis Kelly recollections: in conversation with the author, 15 March 1987. The sentences as published read: 'Between the Anglo-American landings in Normandy on June 6, 1944, and the surrender of all our enemies fourteen months later tremendous events struck the civilised world. Nazi Germany was crushed, partitioned, and occupied; Soviet Russia established herself in the heart of Western Europe; Japan was defeated; the first atomic bombs were cast.'

47

Staying On: 'I may . . . have an influence'

O N the morning of 1 October 1953, two days after his return
from France, Churchill saw Anthony Eden to discuss both
Eden's own future and the future of Churchill's initiative for a great-
power summit. Eden noted in his diary:

Made it clear to W that I was ready to serve in any capacity, but he made
it evident he wanted me to stay on at FO. Asked him about plans & he said
he wanted to try himself out, first in Margate & then in the House. Have
some doubts as to how that will go physically. Some talk of international
situation & he seemed to accept conclusion that latest Soviet answer showed
little desire for talks at any level (but he admitted he hadn't read it!). We
also spoke of Bobbety's desire for younger men in govt & told him this was
[a] widespread complaint. He made no comment, but clearly doesn't want
any changes now.

That evening, Churchill dined with Eden, Lord Salisbury and
R. A. Butler. The talk was 'almost entirely on Foreign Affairs', Eden
noted in his diary, and he added:

It was difficult at times. W didn't like my lack of enthusiasm for May 11th
speech. He kept emphasizing its popularity to which I replied that I was not
contesting that. Later Bobbety pulled him up very sharp—even angrily—
when the former thought his loyalty to W had been impugned. I had to
make it clear that I did not regard four power talks at the highest level as a
panacea. He maintained that in the war it was only the Stalin Roosevelt
Churchill meetings that had made our Foreign Secretaries' work possible. I
said this was not so, nor was it true that to meet without agenda was the best
method with Russians. I believed they like to have an agenda which they
could chew over well in advance. Our most productive meeting with them
had been with Hull at Moscow in 1943 before Teheran when we had used
just these methods about Second Front, creation of UNO, Austria etc. This

had led to Teheran meeting. Anyway the important question was 'what next?' On this W appeared to have no ideas.

'A depressing evening' was Eden's final comment.[1]

On October 2, Churchill presided at the first Cabinet meeting since his return from France. It was the much-debated, long-negotiated defence agreement with Egypt that dominated the agenda. The Egyptians had refused absolutely to include a reference to freedom of transit through the Canal. They were also challenging the right of British troops in the base to wear uniform. And they had challenged the British view that the base should become available in the event of United Nations' action to resist aggression elsewhere.

Most Cabinet Ministers now opposed further concessions. Churchill, as the minutes noted, 'agreed that we should make no further attempt to compromise with the Egyptians'. Government supporters, he said, 'would find it difficult to accept the concessions already made, but they would be more likely to regard them favourably if it could be explained, when Parliament reassembled, that we had informed the Egyptians of our final terms for a settlement and that we were holding firmly to these'.[2]

'It was a great pleasure to me,' Churchill wrote to Eden after his own return once more to Cabinet that evening, 'to see you in your place today, and I am sure it was right that you should resume your high office on Monday as we have arranged.' Churchill also told Eden, of the transfer of the Foreign Office back to Eden from Lord Salisbury, who had borne the day to day responsibilities in Eden's absence:

I hope you will not overwork yourself by trying to read up all the back papers, and that you will take over from Bobbety in a leisurely way. I am sure he will be delighted to help, and he certainly has got his teeth into the detail. I think also the machine is working very well. For some time I have been watching it very carefully, and have had the feeling that we are getting into a smoother period in international affairs. The important thing for you (and me) is to make a good impression on the Margate Conference and upon Parliament when we meet. I hope you will give first place in your thoughts to your speech next Thursday, and I should myself much like to see any draft beforehand so as to shape my own remarks accordingly. I also think that when Parliament meets there will have to be a Foreign Affairs Debate which may well take a couple of days. In this case I would speak either the first or the second day as you wished, and I think it would be very good for Nutting to wind up. I am sure we have got a thoroughly good case if we all stand together.[3]

For the next week, Churchill prepared his Margate speech, and

[1] Eden diary, 1 October 1953: Robert Rhodes James, *Anthony Eden*, page 371.

[2] Cabinet Conclusions No. 54 of 1951, 'Secret', 11.30 a.m., 2 October 1953: Cabinet papers, 128/26.

[3] 'My dear Anthony', 'Private', Chartwell, 2 October 1953: Churchill papers, 2/216.

practised it. Then, on October 9, he travelled to Margate. His speech on the following day was a remarkable success: a tribute not only to his powers of recovery, but to his determination to continue in office until, as he told Colville after his speech, the Queen had returned from her Commonwealth Tour in May 1954.[1]

Churchill spoke at Margate for fifty minutes, without losing his place or his concentration, standing throughout. Speaking of the trade unions, and the 'important part' they played in British life, Churchill told the assembled Conservatives: 'We are not seeking to bring them into the Conservative Party, but we are asking—I have asked for some time—we are asking all Conservative wage earners to join trade unions and take an effective part in their daily work.' He had often said 'that the trade unions should keep clear of both parties and devote themselves solely to industrial matters. At the present time, however, I must admit they are doing very useful work where they are in restraining the featherheads, crackpots, vote-catchers, and office-seekers from putting the folly they talk into action.'

Later in his speech, Churchill referred to his appeal of May 11 for a summit. He had 'not spoken since', he said, adding that it was 'the first time in my political life that I have kept quiet so long', and he went on to recall the theme of that speech:

I asked for very little. I held out no glittering or exciting hopes about Russia. I thought that friendly, informal, personal talks between the leading figures in the countries mainly involved might do good and could not easily do much harm, and that one good thing might lead to another as I have just said.

This humble, modest plan announced as the policy of Her Majesty's Government raised a considerable stir all over the place and though we have not yet been able to persuade our trusted allies to adopt it in the form I suggested no one can say that it is dead.

Churchill continued, in defence of his May suggestions:

I still think that the leading men of the various nations ought to be able to meet together without trying to cut attitudes before excitable publics or using regiments of experts to marshal all the difficulties and objections, and let us try to see whether there is not something better for us all than tearing and blasting each other to pieces, which we can certainly do.

Churchill then addressed his audience on the part which Germany had in the scheme which he so wished to see come about:

The interests of Britain and of Europe and of the NATO alliance is not to

[1] Colville diary, October 1953: *The Fringes of Power*, page 679. The Queen was to leave for Australia on 23 November 1953.

play Russia against Germany or Germany against Russia, but to make them both feel they can live in safety with each other in spite of their grievous problems and differences. For us who have a very definite part in all this, our duty is to use what I believe is our growing influence both with Germany and with Russia to relieve them of any anxiety they may feel about each other.

Personally I welcome Germany back among the great Powers of the world. If there were one message I could give to the German people as one, a large part of whose life has been spent in conducting war against them or preparing to do so, I would urge them to remember the famous maxim: 'The price of freedom is eternal vigilance.' We mustn't forget that either.

Churchill's final reference to his May speech was in answer to those of his critics who had taken up his reference to the Locarno Agreements of 1925, and had argued that Locarno was an absurd precedent, having failed so conspicuously to prevent war. Churchill had no doubt as to the relevance of Locarno, or the reason for its failure:

When in this same speech I spoke about the master thought of Locarno I meant of course the plan of everybody going against the aggressor, whoever he may be, and helping the victim large or small. That is no more than the United Nations was set up to do. We are told the Locarno Treaty failed and did not prevent the war. There was a very good reason for that. The United States was not in it. Had the United States taken before the First World War or between the wars the same interest and made the same exertions and sacrifices and run the same risks to preserve peace and uphold freedom which I thank God she is doing now, there might never have been a First War and there would certainly never have been a Second. With her mighty aid I have a sure hope there will not be a third.

From this defence of his May speech, and of the need for a summit, Churchill went to his peroration. He had practised it a great deal in the previous week: to his wife, to Lord Moran, and to Colville. Now, as he spoke it, he realized that his speech had succeeded, that he had reached its end without incident, and that he had held the attention of his audience. The peroration was personal, and concerned his remaining as Prime Minister:

One word personally about myself. If I stay on for the time being bearing the burden at my age it is not because of love for power or office.

I have had an ample share of both. If I stay it is because I have a feeling that I may through things that have happened have an influence on what I care about above all else, the building of a sure and lasting peace.

Let us then go forward together with courage and composure, with resolution and good faith to the end which all desire.[1]

[1] Speech of 10 October 1953: Randolph S. Churchill (editor), *The Unwritten Alliance*, pages 57–67.

When Churchill's speech was over, Lord Moran was told that evening by Churchill's Private Office, the members of the conference gathered in little groups in the passages and in the streets. 'There had been all kinds of rumours in the country. They wanted to know if they were true. Was it a fact that he had had a stroke? Was he finished? They went to Margate to settle finally whether he was fit to go on. Now they could see for themselves and hear for themselves. And there could be no doubt about the answer. "He is not a bit changed, after all; he is still in good shape," said one. "I guess the Old Man will be with us next year," said another.'[1] 'It was a terrific ordeal,' Miss Portal later recalled. 'Everyone was watching him for frailty. It was a triumphant achievement to get through that.'[2]

That evening Churchill told Lord Moran: '"Now I can sit back and get others to do the work," and he added: "I may have to say something in the Suez debate, but I shall put Anthony in front. It's his business. If he likes this policy of scuttle in Egypt he must defend it." The PM repeated: "It's his affair." He spoke with distaste.'[3]

On October 11 Colville dined with Churchill at Downing Street. 'W was elated by his success,' Colville noted in his diary, 'but more tired than one might have hoped.'[4] The talk of his imminent resignation had still not entirely died down. That evening Lord Moran recorded Colville's comment: '"The Queen's going away from the country complicates things. The PM says that if he is going to retire he will do so soon, so as to give the new PM time to settle in before the Queen leaves the country. But he won't," said Jock smiling.'

Moran also had some talk that evening with Churchill, about the continuing negotiations for an Anglo-Egyptian agreement:

He hates the policy of 'scuttle' which the Foreign Office and Anthony have persuaded him to accept about the Suez Canal, but tries to console himself with the fact that the eighty thousand troops can be used elsewhere, and that it will mean a substantial economy. The Foreign Office, he thinks, 'is an excellent institution for explaining us to other countries, but when its head is weak it seems to spend its time seeking agreements abroad at our expense.[5]

---

[1] Moran diary, 11 October 1953: *The Struggle for Survival*, pages 482–3.
[2] Lady Williams of Elvel recollections: in conversation with the author, 29 July 1987.
[3] Moran diary, 10 October 1953: *The Struggle for Survival*, pages 476–81. Eden was convinced that, on both economic and military grounds, there was now no point in keeping a large British base in the Suez Canal Zone. He was opposed in the Conservative Party by what was called the Suez Group, an informal but active constellation of backbenchers in which Julian Amery was a leading light. The Cabinet, however, supported Eden, with the result that the Anglo-Egyptian agreement on the withdrawal of British troops from the Canal Zone was signed in Cairo on 27 July 1954.
[4] Colville diary, 11 October 1953: *The Fringes of Power*, page 680.
[5] Moran diary, 11 October 1953: *The Struggle for Survival*, pages 482–3.

In Cabinet on October 13, Churchill spoke of the recently dismissed Prime Minister of British Guiana. No great harm could be done, he said, 'if Mr Jagan came to this country and were seen to be associating with Communists here; but it would hardly be appropriate for the Colonial Secretary to receive him immediately after he had been dismissed from office'.[1]

Later that day Churchill wrote to his wife, who was in France:

My darling,

I do hope you are enjoying yourself. The French are not pleased with me; nor indeed did I expect them to be.[2] But I don't think they will revenge themselves on you. The Pug will certainly approve. Duffie will be adverse.

The Kitten is behaving admirably & with its customary punctilio! Rufus is becoming gradually reconciled. Generally the domestic situation is tranquil.

French St Farm has been bought by Cromer[3] for ten thousand. This is a gt relief to me. The Nobel Literature prize is said to be worth £11,000. I don't think the Swedish Amb wd have rung up asking for an appointment at 4 p.m. on Thursday afternoon to announce the award to me unless he was pretty sure it wd be all right. However we must not count our chickens before they are hatched.

Dulles–Bidault arrive Thursday. I am giving D dinner that night & B luncheon on Friday. Five or six only. Then Chartwell for Sunday.

I was lonely last night but Pitblado dined. I am reading *The Dynasts* & getting into it.[4]

A long good Cabinet this morning. It is curious how much less formidable things look round the Cabinet Table, than they do in the newspapers.

With all my love my beloved Clemmie from

Your devoted husband

W

[1] Cabinet Conclusions No. 57 of 1953, 'Secret', 11.30 a.m., 13 October 1953: Cabinet papers, 128/26. In October 1953 self-government had been suspended in British Guiana for six months, to prevent Communist subversion of the Government. Four years later, in 1957, as a result of a General Election, Dr Cheddi Jagan was returned to power. In 1962, however, following severe riots in protest against Dr Jagan's drastic budget proposals, British troops were called in to restore order.

[2] A reference to Churchill's Margate speech of October 10, where he had welcomed Germany 'back among the great Powers of the world'.

[3] The 3rd Earl of Cromer, Managing Director of Baring Brothers and Company Limited, who had succeeded his father as Earl on 13 May 1953. From 1961 to 1966 he was Governor of the Bank of England. His wife was the younger daughter of Churchill's friend Esmond Harmsworth, 2nd Viscount Rothermere. Following the purchase of French Street Farm (also known as Frenchstreet Farm), Westerham, Lord Cromer lived there. In 1899, as the frontispiece of his book *The River War*, Churchill had published a photograph of Lord Cromer's grandfather, the 1st Earl (British Agent in Egypt from 1883–1907).

[4] *The Dynasts* by Thomas Hardy, first published in three parts in 1903, 1906 and 1908, was an epic drama, dominated by the ironies and disappointments of life and love, describing the struggle of man against the force—neutral and indifferent to his sufferings as Hardy conceives it—that rules the world.

'I am writing in bed after a good sleep,' Churchill wrote in a post-script, '& Camrose is coming to dinner.'[1]

At the Defence Committee meeting on October 14, held at 10 Downing Street, J. P. L. Thomas, the First Lord of the Admiralty, argued that in order to limit naval expenditure in 1955 to £369 millions, the Treasury target, it would be impossible to maintain many of the ships of the reserve fleet. He was 'shocked', Churchill commented, 'to hear that the Admiralty were prepared to scrap these ships, particularly the four battleships. In the "broken-backed" warfare which was likely to succeed the first atomic phase of a future war, these ships would probably be able to fulfil a valuable role. The more modern vessels on either side might well be lost in the opening phase and a situation might easily arise in which these older ships might be able to hold their own against anything left in active service on the enemy's side.' Churchill added:

If this asset were now improvidently thrown away, we should be ignoring many of the lessons of the last war. The old rifles which had been put in store in 1919 had been an invaluable asset after Dunkirk: some of the heavy guns for which the Army had had no use after the first war had provided the batteries at Dover which fired across the Channel in the second war; the 50 obsolescent destroyers which we obtained from the United States in 1940 had been a timely accession to our naval strength, apart from the political value of the transaction. He understood that the saving which would be secured by scrapping the ships listed in the Appendix to D (53)47 would be only about £1 million a year. There must be more acceptable methods of securing an economy of that order. It would, for example, be preferable to reduce the man-power carried on Admiralty Vote A.

The Admiralty, Churchill concluded, 'should consider alternative measures by which a comparable saving could be secured'.

The next item on the Defence Committee agenda on October 14 was the 'likelihood of general war with the Soviet Union' in the period up to the end of 1955. The Chiefs of Staff had concluded war was 'on the whole' unlikely.[2] Churchill agreed; he thought that the possibility of a major war 'had receded slightly', and he went on to tell his colleagues:

He was not shaken in this opinion by Russia's recent support of Yugoslavia in the Trieste dispute; this, he thought, was designed solely for the purpose of undermining the domestic position of Marshal Tito within Yugoslavia. At the same time he thought it would be unwise to give any wide currency to this appreciation by the Chiefs of Staff. In particular, he deprecated the suggestion that it should be communicated to the United States authorities—it was unnecessary for us to do anything which might encourage them to re-

---

[1] 'My darling', 13 October 1953: Spencer-Churchill papers.
[2] Chiefs of Staff Memorandum No. 45 of 1953.

duce the level of their defence expenditure. And public statements by Ministers about the likelihood of war should be made sparingly and with caution.

Speaking of the proposal to station a British armoured brigade in Jordan, Churchill urged that it should be 'made clear' to Israel 'that the presence of our armoured force in Jordan would not represent any threat to their interests but would, in fact, provide a stabilising influence in that area'.[1]

At a meeting of the Cabinet on October 15, Churchill supported Eden and Salisbury, albeit reluctantly, over new proposals for the Anglo-Egyptian treaty. Some Conservatives, he said, 'would be disposed to suggest that, sooner than accept an agreement on these lines, we should have sought to maintain our position in Egypt by force; and they would probably argue that, if a drastic military solution had been sought, it would have been possible thereafter to reduce the strength of the British garrison in Egypt to a figure well below the present level'. He was himself inclined to think, Churchill said, that this course could not have been followed 'unless the Egyptians had committed some flagrant acts of provocation which would have justified us in proceeding on the basis that something equivalent to a state of war had arisen in Egypt'. If Britain had taken strong military action in a situation short of that, however, she would have 'lacked the support of the United States Government; and, if the dispute had been referred to the United Nations, we could not have expected that a decision would have been given in our favour'.

Matters having now gone as they had, Churchill continued, 'he was prepared to agree that it might be the wiser course to seek an agreement on principles on the lines which the Cabinet had now approved. This should, however, be presented to the Egyptians as our last word; and he was anxious that no final agreement should be reached with them until Parliament had reassembled and Ministers had had an opportunity of explaining privately to Government supporters the situation which had now been reached.' It was of great importance, Churchill argued, 'that Ministers should have that opportunity of preparing the way for the agreement, if it was to be concluded, and doing their utmost to reduce the risk of its being subjected to damaging criticism by their own supporters'.[2]

On Friday October 16 Churchill learned that he had been awarded the Nobel Prize for Literature. As he prepared to leave London for Chartwell, he wrote to his wife:

[1] Defence Committee No. 13 of 1953, 'Top Secret', 11.30 a.m., 14 October 1953: Cabinet papers, 131/13.
[2] Cabinet Conclusions No. 58 of 1955, 'Secret', 11 a.m., 15 October 1953: Cabinet papers, 128/26.

My darling one,

I am just off to Chartwell, but come back Sunday to give the Foreign Ministers a final luncheon. Their talks seem to be going all right, but there are a lot of tiresome things happening, & next Tuesday the Parlt meets again to help us.

It is all settled about the Nobel Prize. £12,100 free of tax. Not so bad!

I think we shall have to go to Stockholm for a couple of days in December & stay with the King & Queen there.

I am writing in the Cabinet room & the little cat is holding the notepaper down for me. I miss you vy much. One night I had dinner in bed as I did not want anyone but you for company. I do hope you are enjoying yourself and finding the days interesting.

I am dining with Mary tonight & tomorrow and she lunches with me on a chicken pie on Saturday. Pamela C lunched w me yesterday.[1] How agreeable she is! I had not seen her for years. She told me she had seen you at dinner at the Pugs.

Tender love my darling from Yr devoted husband

W[2]

Those close to Churchill were delighted by his recovery. It was nearly four months since his stroke. 'When I think of how you looked when I arrived back in England,' Sarah Churchill wrote to her father on October 19, 'and of the long, long months of climbing back to the top of the hill, I cried with pride,' and she added: 'If you try to measure wisely the strain you put on yourself, you will still find that you are a day's march ahead of anyone. *Please, please measure the strain*.'[3]

On October 20 Clementine Churchill returned to London from France. It was the day on which her husband was to go to the House of Commons for the first time since his stroke, to answer Prime Minister's Questions. Awaiting her when she reached London was a short, handwritten letter:

My darling,

Welcome Home! I am resting in bed, before my H of C reappearance & many questions. I am following the Margate plan including a 'Moran' wh he advised.[4]

I do hope you have got the better of yr cold. If I am asleep when you

---

[1] Pamela Churchill, from whom Randolph had been divorced in 1945. She later married, first, the American film agent and producer Leland Hayward, then Roosevelt's wartime emissary to Churchill, Averell Harriman.

[2] 'My darling one', 16 October 1953: Spencer-Churchill papers.

[3] 'Darling, *darling* Papa', from Los Angeles, 19 October 1953: Churchill papers, 1/50. The words in italics were underlined by Sarah Churchill in her letter.

[4] A 'Moran', or 'Lord Moran', was a stimulant, in pill form, prescribed for Churchill by Lord Moran.

arrive, it wd be good of you to leave me till 2.30 when I dress for the House at 3. Questions 3.15. But probably I shall be awake longing to see you.
Tender love

W [1]

Churchill took the pill which Lord Moran had advised, went to the Commons, and answered his questions. Henry Channon, who had driven to Westminster with Mary Churchill, wrote in his diary: 'We saw Winston's long-awaited (and some prophesied never-to-be) return acclaimed. He seemed self-confident, though a touch deaf in spite of his hearing-aid, but apparently more vigorous than before.' Channon added: 'But I doubt whether he can carry on for long. The added strain of the House of Commons will be too much.' [2]

On the following day Lord Moran noted in his diary:

There appears to be general agreement that the PM was quite himself in the way in which he handled Questions. Harvie Watt, who was his parliamentary secretary during the war, thought he had done it very well: 'much better than I expected', while the lobby correspondent of the *Manchester Guardian*, whose sharp eyes do not miss much, was satisfied that Mr Churchill had not suffered any change since he was last on view at Westminster. [3]

And when he announced that he had gone back on a firm pledge to the House of Commons—the pledge to restore the University seats—it seemed to be merely the recording of an act of statesmanship.

I asked him: 'Did it tire you jumping up and down for nearly a quarter of an hour answering supplementaries?'

'Oh, no, not at all; but it did make me rather short of breath.'

He picked up the *Guardian*, but when I rose to go he half put it down as he said:

'Thank you, Charles, I hope you got no harm yesterday coming out to see me. You hit the bull's eye with the pill.' [4]

On October 23 Clementine Churchill asked to speak to Lord Moran. 'He promised me he would retire when Anthony was fit to carry on,' she told him, 'and now when Anthony is perfectly fit he just goes on as before.' Her tone was grave as she continued, though her pride in her husband, as Moran noted, 'struggled through the clouds of irritation'. She told Moran, as he set it down in his diary:

'You know, Christopher is very fond of Winston, and he has promised to tell me if his stock falls in the House of Commons. He has given me his word that I shall be told if they want to get rid of him. But the trouble is, Charles, that his

[1] 'My darling', 20 October 1953: Spencer-Churchill papers.
[2] Channon diary, 20 October 1953: Robert Rhodes James (editor), *Chips*, page 478.
[3] From 1945 to 1975 the *Manchester Guardian* Lobby correspondent was Francis Boyd, who in 1956 published a biography of R. A. Butler. He was knighted in 1976.
[4] Moran diary, 21 October 1953: *The Struggle for Survival*, page 484–5.

stock has actually risen, until they say it has not been so high for a long time.

'Do you know what I mean by the 1922 Committee? They are very Right. Well, when they met to discuss Egypt the Chief Whip wanted Winston to open the discussion. But he refused. Anthony ought to open, Winston insisted. And then at the end he got up and gave them a tremendous wigging. They knew that he was not a Little Englander, but he told them bluntly we simply could not afford to stay in Egypt. He looked to them for support in a difficult situation, not for that kind of carping. They were tremendously impressed. The old lion could still issue from his den, and when he did his growl was as frightening as ever.'

She laughed at the thought.

'They cannot make it out at all, Charles. They have heard all kinds of rumours about a stroke and paralysis, and now he seems in better form than ever. They described how he strode up a long corridor in the House of Commons, swinging his arms as if he was twenty.' [1]

Helped by Christopher Soames, Churchill prepared for a meeting of the Cabinet at which the Ministry of Food and the Ministry of Agriculture would each present its own side of a dispute over how best to abolish State trading in meat in the period before the establishment of a new Meat Marketing Board. By the time the Cabinet met on October 27, Churchill was sufficiently master of the complexities of the dispute to give his approval to the plan put forward by the Minister of Food. That plan, he told his Cabinet colleagues, 'was in accord with the general theme of the Government's policy for relaxing controls and restoring free markets, and abandoning State trading and bulk purchase'. At the same time, he said, it would honour the Government's guarantees to the farmers by way of an Exchequer subsidy 'based on the two principles of deficiency payments and buttress prices'. The farmers could insist that the Government should carry out these guarantees; 'but it was for the Government to determine by what methods they should do so'. He himself preferred 'that the public should pay through taxation such sums as were required to ensure the stability of British agriculture, and that the prices which, as consumers, they paid for home-produced food should be left to be determined by the operation of a free market'. [2]

On October 28 Churchill was in the Chair at a meeting of the Defence Committee, when he strongly opposed an Admiralty plan to end the entry of thirteen-year-old cadets into the Royal Navy. The earliest entry, said J. P. L. Thomas, should be at eighteen. Churchill told his colleagues, as the minutes recorded:

---

[1] Moran diary, 23 October 1953: *The Struggle for Survival*, pages 485–6.

[2] Cabinet Conclusions No. 61 of 1953, 'Secret', 11 a.m., 27 October 1953: Cabinet papers, 128/26.

... he was deeply perturbed by the Admiralty proposal to limit the cadet entry to eighteen-year-olds. Life in the Royal Navy was quite different from that in the other two Services; the naval officer was required to spend much of his life afloat in conditions of discomfort, and his efficiency depended on his having a true sense of vocation. By entering cadets at thirteen, this extremely important vocational atmosphere was created.[1] The educational aspect was not so important.

He had himself introduced the special entry at the age of eighteen. It was successful because there was a steady stream of boys who had had a strong naval stamp put on them from their earliest days and were carried through by their intense vocational feelings. He still favoured the mixed entry; but in his opinion, restriction of entry to cadets of eighteen would be striking a death blow to the Royal Navy.[2]

At Churchill's request, it was agreed to postpone the decision, but three weeks later, after learning that the Board of Admiralty were 'unanimously in favour' of making seventeen and a half the minimum age, he agreed that 'he would not press his view further'.[3]

At Cabinet on October 29, it was the future of the Home Guard that was under discussion. To disband it, said Sir David Maxwell-Fyfe, would have a 'discouraging effect' on recruitment to the civil defence services, which were 'seriously under-strength'. It was 'clearly the view of the Cabinet', Churchill commented when all those Ministers who wanted to had spoken, 'that the Home Guard should be retained', and he added: 'The decision to retain it should be announced boldly.'[4]

On November 3 Churchill made his first Parliamentary speech since his stroke. It was by all accounts a masterpiece of presentation and persuasion; spoken without the hesitations or even loss of contact with the occasion which his doctors had earlier feared. Where Margate had been a public triumph, this was a Parliamentary one.

Commenting on Attlee's demand that the House of Commons should exercise control over the development of atomic energy, Churchill said: 'we must not forget that when he was in office his Government spent more than £100 million without ever asking the House to

---

[1] Entry at thirteen had existed in the Royal Navy since 1676.
[2] Defence Committee No. 14 of 1953, 'Top Secret', 11.30 a.m., 28 October 1953: Cabinet papers, 131/13.
[3] Defence Committee No. 16 of 1953, 'Secret', 11.30 a.m., 18 November 1953: Cabinet papers, 131/13.
[4] Cabinet Conclusions No. 62 of 1953, 'Secret', 11.45 a.m., 29 October 1953: Cabinet papers, 128/26.

be aware of what was going on. No doubt having been in office such a short time as we have, we have not yet learned all the tricks of the trade.' In the following week the question of atomic energy being dealt with under Government authority by a corporation would be laid before the House. Both a White Paper and an Order in Council would be issued. 'They will give the House a very great deal of information,' Churchill commented, 'upon a subject which, I must warn hon. Gentlemen, means quite hard reading, if one has to undertake a great deal of it.'

As to Attlee's criticism of the three Government 'Overlords'[1] whom Churchill had appointed in October 1951, but who were in fact no longer to exist as Ministerial supremos, Churchill told the House:

I had no experience of being Prime Minister in time of peace and I attached more importance to the grouping of Departments so that the responsible head of the Government would be able to deal with a comparatively smaller number of heads than actually exists in peace-time. I think we had great advantage—although it may not be believed opposite—from the services of the three noble Lords, who did their very utmost to help forward the public service. On reflection, I have thought it better to revert to the proposal which the right hon. Gentleman himself recommended, namely, to hush it all up and manage it in the Cabinet.

Speaking of the maximum five-year period between elections under the current Quinquennial Act, Churchill noted that two years had passed since the last election, and went on to ask: 'When are we going to have another?' He then answered his own question, telling the House: 'It is always difficult to foresee, and rash to forecast, the course of future events. Still, for practical purposes, one has to try from time to time to weigh the probabilities and make the best guess one can. I do not hesitate to say that, viewing the political scene as it appears to me, it looks as if a General Election is further off this afternoon than it did two years ago.'

It was forty-eight years earlier, Churchill reminded the House, when he had moved the Bill, under the Ten Minute Rule, to establish the quinquennial period, instead of the septennial one then in existence. The quinquennial period, he said, seemed to him to strike 'a happy medium between Parliaments which last too little and Parliaments which last too long'. One had also to consider 'that elections exist for the sake of the House of Commons and not that the House of Commons exists for the sake of elections'. Churchill added, still on this theme:

... I have fought more elections than anyone here, or indeed anyone alive in

[1] The three 'Overlords' appointed in October 1951 were Viscount Woolton (Lord President of the Council), the Marquess of Salisbury (Lord Privy Seal) and Lord Leathers (Co-ordinator of Transport, Fuel and Power, an office abolished on 3 September 1953).

this country—Parliamentary elections—and on the whole they are great fun.[1]
But there ought to be interludes of tolerance, hard work, and study of social
problems between them. Having rows for the sake of having rows between
politicians might be good from time to time, but it is not a good habit of
political life. It does not follow that we should get further apart by staying
longer together.

I am not suggesting that our goal is a coalition; that, I think, would be
carrying good will too far. But our duties, as we see them, are varied and
sometimes conflicting. We have to help our respective parties, but we have
also to make sure that we help our country and its people.

Churchill then spoke of nationalization, of housing, and of farming.
The Government's aim in agricultural policy, he said, was to try to reverse if not abolish the tendency to state purchase and state marketing.
'We hope instead,' he said, 'to develop individual enterprise founded
in the main on the laws of supply and demand and to restore to the
interchange of goods and services that variety, flexibility, ingenuity,
and incentive on which we believe the fertility and liveliness of economic life depend.' Britain had now reached a point 'when the end of
war-time food rationing, with all its rigid, costly features and expensive
staff, is in sight. For our farmers, the abandonment of controls will
bring great opportunities.'

The last section of Churchill's speech dealt with Foreign Affairs.
Two important events had taken place since the Labour Government
had been in power which might have 'actually modified the harshness
of the scene' of 1950 and 1951, when 'our Socialist Government, with
the full support of the Conservative Opposition, were marching with
our American allies in a vehement effort to meet the Soviet menace':

... The fighting in Korea has shifted from the trenches to the tables. We do
not know yet what will emerge from these stubborn and tangled discussions.
But whatever else comes, or may come, as a result of the Korean war, one
major world fact is outstanding. The United States have become again a
heavily armed nation.

The second world event has been the death of Stalin and the assumption
of power by a different regime in the Kremlin. It is on the second of these
prodigious events that I wish to dwell for a moment. Nearly eight months
have passed since it occurred and everywhere the question was, and still is
asked, did the end of the Stalin epoch lead to a change in Soviet policy? Is
there a new look?

Churchill went on to try to answer his own questions:

I should not venture to ask the House, or any outside our doors to whom

[1] Churchill had fought Parliamentary elections in 1899, 1900, 1905, 1908 (twice), 1910
(twice), 1918, 1922, 1923, 1924, 1929, 1931, 1935, 1945, 1950 and 1951; seventeen in all, over a
period of fifty-two years.

my words have access, to adopt positive conclusions on these mysteries. It may well be that there have been far-reaching changes in the temper and outlook of the immense populations, now so largely literate, who inhabit 'all the Russias', and that their mind was turned to internal betterment rather than external aggression. This may or may not be a right judgment, and we can afford, if vigilance is not relaxed and strength is not suffered again to dwindle, to await developments in a hopeful and, I trust, a helpful mood.

The only really sure guide to the actions of mighty nations and powerful Governments is a correct estimate of what are and what they consider to be their own interests.

Applying this test, I feel a sense of reassurance. Studying our own strength and that of Europe under the massive American shield, I do not find it unreasonable or dangerous to conclude that internal prosperity rather than external conquest is not only the deep desire of the Russian peoples, but also the long-term interest of their rulers.

He had hoped to discuss all this at Bermuda with Eisenhower, but had been 'prevented by conditions beyond my control'. Now it was possible that the four Foreign Secretaries would meet; 'we earnestly hope it may take place soon'. If it led to improvements, those very improvements 'might again lead to further efforts on both sides'.

There was one more 'dominant event' which had happened in the past two years, of which Churchill wished to speak: something which had developed 'so prodigiously in this period that I can treat it as if it were a novel apparition which has overshadowed both those I have mentioned'. He was referring to the 'rapid and ceaseless developments of atomic warfare', and to 'the hydrogen bomb'. Once more, Churchill was not speaking about the actual hydrogen bomb test of the previous November, of which he still had no knowledge, but about the research which everyone knew to be in progress. His speech continued:

These fearful scientific discoveries cast their shadow on every thoughtful mind, but nevertheless I believe that we are justified in feeling that there has been a diminution of tension and that the probabilities of another world war have diminished, or at least have become more remote. I say this in spite of the continual growth of weapons of destruction such as have never fallen before into the hands of human beings. Indeed, I have sometimes the odd thought that the annihilating character of these agencies may bring an utterly unforeseeable security to mankind.

He then explained why this thought had come to him:

When I was a schoolboy I was not good at arithmetic, but I have since heard it said that certain mathematical quantities when they pass through infinity change their signs from plus to minus—or the other way round— [Laughter.] I do not venture to plunge too much into detail of what are called the asymptotes of hyperbolae, but any hon. Gentleman who is interested can find an opportunity for an interesting study of these matters.

It may be that this rule may have a novel application and that when the advance of destructive weapons enables everyone to kill everybody else nobody will want to kill anyone at all. At any rate, it seems pretty safe to say that a war which begins by both sides suffering what they dread most—and that is undoubtedly the case at present—is less likely to occur than one which dangles the lurid prizes of former ages before ambitious eyes.

It was a remarkable vision, and a hopeful one. With it, Churchill came to his conclusion, telling the House of Commons:

I offer this comforting idea to the House, taking care to make it clear at the same time that our only hope can spring from untiring vigilance. There is no doubt that if the human race are to have their dearest wish and be free from the dread of mass destruction, they could have, as an alternative, what many of them might prefer, namely, the swiftest expansion of material well-being that has ever been within their reach, or even within their dreams.

By material well-being I mean not only abundance but a degree of leisure for the masses such as has never before been possible in our mortal struggle for life. These majestic possibilities ought to gleam, and be made to gleam, before the eyes of the toilers in every land, and they ought to inspire the actions of all who bear responsibility for their guidance. We, and all nations, stand, at this hour in human history, before the portals of supreme catastrophe and of measureless reward. My faith is that in God's mercy we shall choose aright.[1]

From Churchill's opening sentences, Henry Channon noted in his diary, it had been immediately clear that he was making 'one of the speeches of his lifetime'. Channon added: 'Brilliant, full of cunning and charm, of wit and thrusts, he poured out his Macaulay-like phrases to a stilled and awed house. It was an Olympian spectacle. A supreme performance which we shall never see again from him or anyone else. In 18 years in this honourable House I have never heard anything like it.'

Churchill left the Chamber and walked, unaided, to the Smoking Room, and, Channon noted, 'flushed with pride, pleasure, and triumph sat there for two hours sipping brandy and acknowledging compliments. He beamed like a school-boy.'[2]

Neither Channon, nor any of those who crowded around the triumphant speaker, realized that he was recovering from a stroke; one which had led most of those who knew of it, including the doctors, to conclude that he would never speak in the House of Commons again. 'That's the last bloody hurdle,' were Churchill's words to Lord Moran

[1] Speech of 3 November 1953: *Hansard*.
[2] Channon diary, 3 November 1953: Robert Rhodes James (editor), *Chips*, page 479.

on returning to his room in the House of Commons, and he added: 'Now, Charles, we can think of Moscow.' Churchill went on: 'Your pill cleared my head. Now I can turn to other things. You do not realize, Charles, how much depends on the Russians. I must see Malenkov. Then I can depart in peace.' [1]

Churchill's thoughts now focused on when, and how, his Russian visit could be arranged. On the following morning he told Moran:

'Before I can go to see Malenkov the President must agree.[2] This is very secret. I may go to the Azores. It would take Ike ten hours to fly there—or perhaps to Heaven. Only six hours for us. The *Vanguard* would be waiting for us there to provide accommodation. Of course it depends on Ike's other commitments. There will be a deadlock with the Russians, and Dulles will not be against the Azores once he sees no possibility of himself meeting Molotov.'

'When would you go?'

'Oh, perhaps in the middle of December. I might go by sea. I don't want to go to Washington as long as there is a waddle in my walk.' [3]

Moran himself was buoyed up by his patient's recovery. 'The more I think of Tuesday's effort in the House,' he wrote to Churchill from Harley Street on November 6, 'the more astonishing it seems from every angle.' [4] Churchill's 'complete authority over the Commons', declared *The Times*, 'is one of the most important political factors in the new round of the Parliamentary contest that is now beginning'. [5]

In the first week of November 1953, Churchill's hopes of moving forward fairly rapidly towards a summit were set back by the Soviet Union's negative response to a Four-Power meeting of Foreign Ministers. He did not despair, however, of moving forward to his goal by some other means. On November 5 he telegraphed to Eisenhower:

My dear Friend,

The Soviet answer puts us back to where we were when Bermuda broke down through my misfortune. We are confronted with a deadlock. So why not let us try Bermuda again? I suggest four or five days during the first fortnight in December.

We could then take stock of the whole position and I think quite a lot of people will be pleased that we are doing so. If you want the French, I am quite agreeable and it would be a good opportunity to talk to them about EDC, which surely we ought to get settled now. I hope you would bring

---

[1] Moran diary, 3 November 1953: *The Struggle for Survival*, pages 492–4.

[2] Although Khrushchev was already effective ruler of the Soviet Union, this was not yet appreciated in the West, where Malenkov still seemed the man at the helm.

[3] Moran diary, 4 November 1953: *The Struggle for Survival*, pages 495–7.

[4] 'My dear Prime Minister', 6 November 1953: Churchill papers, 1/54.

[5] *The Times*, 4 November 1953.

Foster. Anthony is all for it and would come with me. It would be worth trying to make Laniel come with Bidault.

All the arrangements were very carefully worked out last time, and it only takes a word of command to put them all on again.

Let me know how this strikes you. I really think there will be serious criticism if we are all left gaping at a void.

Winston [1]

In his reply two days later, Eisenhower agreed that there might be 'considerable value in a good talk between us', but went on to tell Churchill: 'It would be necessary of course to avoid creating a false impression that our purpose in meeting is to issue another invitation to the Soviets. There is nothing to be gained by showing too much concern over their intransigence and bad deportment and I believe that instead of relating our meeting to any Soviet word or act, past or future, we should merely announce that we are meeting to discuss matters of common interest.' [2]

Within forty-eight hours, Eisenhower had accepted in principle Churchill's invitation to meet at Bermuda on December 4. 'I am bringing my paintbox with me,' Churchill telegraphed on November 8, 'as I cannot take you on at golf,' and he added: 'They say the water is 67 degrees which is too cold for me.' [3]

At the Cabinet on November 9, while noting the 'unsatisfactory tone' of the Soviet response, Churchill told his Cabinet colleagues that he nevertheless thought it would be 'valuable' if the Heads of Governments of the United States, United Kingdom and France could meet, with their Foreign Ministers, 'to review the possibility of breaking the existing deadlock and to discuss the urgent problems which were of common interest to the three countries'. He had therefore suggested to Eisenhower 'that the project of the Bermuda Meeting, which he had been obliged to postpone in July, should now be revived'.

The President had 'favoured this plan', Churchill told the Cabinet, 'though he was unable to give a final answer until his Secretary of State returned to Washington. An invitation had therefore been sent to the French.' It now seemed likely, Churchill added, that 'definite agreement would be reached within the next 24 hours to hold this Tripartite Meeting in Bermuda from 4th–8th December'. [4]

---

[1] Prime Minister's Personal Telegram No. 266 of 1953, 'Personal and Private', sent as Telegram No. 4538 to Washington, 'Emergency', 'Decypher Yourself', 'Top Secret', 5 November 1953: Premier papers, 11/418.

[2] 'Top Secret', 7 November 1953: Premier papers, 11/418.

[3] Prime Minister's Personal Telegram No. 269 of 1953, 'Personal and Private', No. 4636 to Washington, 8 November 1953: Premier papers, 11/418.

[4] Cabinet Conclusions No. 64 of 1953, 'Secret', 12 noon, 9 November 1953: Cabinet papers, 128/26.

That evening Churchill spoke at the Lord Mayor's Banquet in the Guildhall, an occasion on which it was customary to speak about foreign affairs. The world was in 'an awful muddle now', he said. Many people thought 'that the best we can do is to get used to the cold war like eels are said to get used to skinning'. He said nothing about his own plans to begin the summit process by a meeting with Eisenhower in Bermuda; but he did set out his thoughts on Anglo-American relations:

. . . Some people say their worry is about Anglo-American relations. I do not share their anxieties. After all we are both very free-speaking democracies and where there is a great deal of free speech there is always a certain amount of foolish speech. But any rude things we say about each other are nothing compared to what we both say about ourselves. It would be a pity if we thought about each other in terms of our local bugbears and matched one against the other.

'Let us stick to our heroes, John Bull and Uncle Sam,' Churchill advised. 'They never were closer together than they are now; not only in sentiment but in common interest and in faithfulness to the cause of world freedom.' It was in fact 'the growing unity and brotherhood between the United States and the British Commonwealth of Nations that sustains our faith in human destiny'.

Churchill also told those present at the Lord Mayor's Banquet: 'Another old saying comes back to my mind which I have often found helpful or at least comforting. I think it was Goethe who said, "The trees do not grow up to the sky." I do not know whether he would have said that if he had lived through this frightful twentieth century where so much we feared was going to happen did actually happen. All the same it is a thought which should find its place in young as well as old brains.' [1]

By November 12 all plans for the Bermuda meeting had been completed, the public announcement that it would take place having been greeted by an outburst of anger in the Soviet press. Churchill telegraphed that day to Eisenhower:

I am very glad it is all settled about Bermuda and I share your hopes that we shall not spend all our time on parade. The table, I presume, should be round.

I agree with you that there is no point in the Soviet complaint about 'collusion'. I always thought allies were expected to 'collude' and I have always had a great dislike for the expression 'ganging up' which has several times got seriously in my way. All the same I am, as I said last time in Parliament, hoping we may build bridges not barriers.

[1] Speech of 9 November 1953: Randolph S. Churchill (editor), *The Unwritten Alliance*, pages 79–82.

I should like to bring Lord Cherwell with me as I want to talk over with you our 'collusion' on atomics, etc. Indeed it might strengthen the impression to which I gathered you were favourable, that our meeting was not simply an incident in the recent correspondence with the Soviets. He can always slip across to Washington after we have had a talk if you thought it convenient for him to see more of your people.

I plan to fly with Anthony the night of the 1st via Gander to Bermuda and we shall have a whole day to recuperate before receiving you on the 4th. The Welch Fusiliers with their Goat will form your Guard of Honour. The barbed wire to protect us from assassins or journalists is still standing as it was.[1]

In the weeks ahead, Churchill studied the notes which Jock Colville and Sir Norman Brook had prepared, as a basis of the Bermuda talks. He also dictated some notes of his own. On the question of trade with the Soviet Union, he wrote: 'If we are to make the full contribution we seek to do to the strength of NATO, we must refresh and extend our overseas trade in Russia. We can find a fertile field. I am therefore for the widest possible trade with the Soviets in everything except actual weapons.'[2]

One aspect of Britain's strength in the world, it was clear to both Conservative and Labour alike, was the maintenance of National Service. Speaking in the House of Commons on November 16, Churchill reflected: 'I believe I myself in my young days spoke of the foul tyranny of conscription. Little did I believe that I should live to see not only Liberals but Radicals, and not only Radicals but Socialists, voting for compulsory service, not only in time of war but actually after victory and in time of peace.' This showed, he said, 'how the force of events bites deeply into all our thoughts, principles, and prejudices, and, of course, we have lived through the most extraordinary convulsions recorded in human experience. There is no doubt at all that they have left their mark on all our minds in an almost irresistible fashion.'

He 'by no means' excluded the possibility of a reduction in the two-year term, Churchill told the House, but 'this was not the time even to toy with the idea of change'. 'I by no means exclude the possibility of change,' Churchill reiterated, 'but this is by no means the time for us to advertise and ventilate that all over Europe and the United States.'

Churchill then explained why he felt any reduction of the term of National Service would, at that moment, be dangerous:

---

[1] Prime Minister's Personal Telegram, No. 273 of 1953, 'Personal and Private', Telegram No. 4736 to Washington, 'Immediate', 'Decypher Yourself', 'Top Secret', 12 November 1953: Premier papers, 11/418. Lord Cherwell had actually resigned from the Cabinet on the previous day, but continued to be Churchill's close confidant.

[2] 'Trade', 3 December 1953: Premier papers, 11/418.

... our policy at present might be defined as, 'Peace through strength', but a change of this character, small as it would be, though it might be understood in its proper proportion by hon. Members in all parts of the House, would have the effect abroad of being thought to be the beginning of a policy of 'Conciliation by weakness', which we regard as most dangerous to peace. Certainly that would do us immense harm both ways.

The Communist world might say, 'There, the NATO forces are breaking up. The British have introduced the thin end of the wedge. Why should we make concessions when we have only to persevere to win?'

And the greatest of our allies, the one without whom the safety of the free world would be doomed, might be quite needlessly disquieted. I do not want to dwell on that too much.[1]

At a meeting of the Cabinet on November 17, Churchill was able to report that, following a recent visit by Lord Cherwell to the United States, 'the Americans had now agreed to exchange information with us and with the Canadians on the effects of the explosion of atomic weapons of all types'. He also argued, during the Cabinet discussion on the recent tension between Jordan and Israel, that he was 'inclined to think that this particular source of trouble concerned the United Nations more than it concerned the United Kingdom'. To send a small British force to Jordan, as Jordan wished, 'might merely provoke Israel'. If Britain 'had to intervene at all', he said, 'it would be better to use overwhelming force which could provide an effective deterrent'.[2]

'Now the FO wants a war with Israel,' Churchill told his doctor on the following morning, and he added: 'Ernie Bevin apparently made a treaty with Jordan. I don't want war.'[3] 'We should be careful,' Churchill reiterated in Cabinet on November 19, 'to avoid a situation in which British troops became engaged in hostilities between Israel and Jordan.'[4]

On the evening of November 17 Churchill had given a dinner at Downing Street for members of the Jockey Club. The Duke of Gloucester had been among the guests. To Lord Moran, who was worried about the strain on Churchill of so many events, Churchill remarked that at the Jockey Club dinner General Baird, 'who is ninety-four, got up the stairs all right and made a short speech'.[5]

---

[1] Speech of 16 November 1953: *Hansard*.

[2] Cabinet Conclusions No. 67 of 1953, 'Secret', 11.30 a.m., 17 November 1953: Cabinet papers, 128/26.

[3] Moran diary, 18 November 1953: *The Struggle for Survival*, page 498.

[4] Cabinet Conclusions No. 68 of 1953, 'Secret', 11.30 a.m., 19 November 1953: Cabinet papers, 128/26.

[5] Moran diary, 18 November 1953: *The Struggle for Survival*, page 498. General Baird (Brigadier-General Edward William Baird) had been a member of the Jockey Club since 1894. He had won the St Leger with Woolwinder in 1907. He died in 1956.

Defence and the road to the summit were not only inextricably linked in Churchill's mind, but were frequently mentioned by him in different ways and on diverse occasions. One such occasion was the presentation of the Freedom of the City of London to Clement Attlee on November 20, when Churchill said, in the course of his congratulatory remarks, that during his six years as Prime Minister Attlee had 'played the leading part in the formidable and costly rearmament programme including the establishment of National Service in time of peace and the culture of the atomic bomb which have enabled the nations of the free world to confront Communist aggression and perhaps clear the way for safer and smoother times'.[1]

One subject to be discussed at Bermuda was mentioned in Cabinet on November 26: the still unresolved treaty with Egypt. It was not primarily the future of the Canal Zone base which 'seriously disturbed' some of the Government's supporters, Churchill explained; 'they were concerned that British troops should remain in Egypt to ensure the right of free transit through the Suez Canal. They would find it difficult to support any agreement which failed to safeguard the use of the Canal as an international waterway.' At Bermuda, he and Eden would seek to secure 'a firm promise of American support', in a fresh approach to the Egyptian Government, should the negotiations break down altogether.[2]

On November 27 Churchill returned for the fourteenth consecutive year to Harrow, for the school 'Songs'. It was with 'high hopes', he said, that he came to the school that afternoon 'and cast out upon the future expectations that we shall make good all along the line'.[3]

Churchill was at Downing Street on November 30, his seventy-ninth birthday. On receiving a message of congratulations from the Queen and the Duke of Edinburgh, who were already on their tour of the Commonwealth, he replied at once: 'I am deeply honoured by the kind telegram I have received from Your Majesty and the Duke of Edinburgh. I do hope the sun shines and the seas are smooth.'[4]

[1] Speech of 20 November 1953: Randolph S. Churchill (editor), *The Unwritten Alliance*, pages 89–90.
[2] Cabinet Conclusions No. 72 of 1953, 'Secret', 11 a.m., 26 November 1953: Cabinet papers, 128/26.
[3] Speech of 27 November 1953: Churchill papers, 2/336.
[4] 'Lane No. 2', 30 November 1953: Churchill papers, 2/467. The Queen and the Duke of Edinburgh had left England on 23 November 1953, going first by air to Bermuda and then to Jamaica, where they boarded S.S. *Gothic* to sail to the Pacific. On 30 November 1953 they were at Cristobal, Panama, where they attended a Presidential reception.

That morning Churchill was in the Chair at a Cabinet meeting at which, during a discussion of where the British troops then in Egypt would be redeployed once the treaty with Egypt was signed, he spoke of the 'cardinal importance' of obtaining American agreement to 'a joint Anglo-United States plan which would effect the best disposition of forces in support of the North Atlantic Treaty Organization and would reassure public opinion in the United Kingdom'.[1]

Also on his seventy-ninth birthday, Churchill wrote to Henry Luce at *Life*. One request which Churchill had was for more funds in connection with the serialization of the final volume of his war memoirs, which Luce had taken on only with reluctance. As Churchill wrote:

You will I am sure not mind my saying that I certainly think in equity a further payment should be made by *Life* and the *New York Times* for the serials of Volume VI. This has undoubtedly proved a feature of first rate importance to you, and had I not been able to complete my tale, or had I compressed it into five volumes, you would have had, I suppose, to have paid a large sum of money to someone else to fill the gap. I must however repeat my thanks for the hospitality which you accorded me at Marrakech and elsewhere in the currency difficulties from which we suffer so much in England.

The main aim of Churchill's letter to Luce was to explain his plans for the completion of *A History of the English-Speaking Peoples*. The four volumes had, he explained, been completed 'before the outbreak of the Second World War'. But 'more recasting and additions' were required. One section was a 40,000-word account of the American Civil War. 'I took great pains about this,' Churchill wrote, 'and have visited, as you know, nearly every battlefield in the United States.'[2]

If he was 'still at work' when the revisions were completed, Churchill wrote, he would consider 'the appropriate finale'. But, he explained to Luce, 'As far as the serials are concerned (in contrast to the perfecting and completion of an historical survey) I do not think that your interests would suffer if I did not live to see the end myself.'[3]

---

[1] Cabinet Conclusions, No. 73 of 1953, 'Secret', 12 noon, 30 November 1953: Cabinet papers, 128/26.

[2] This section was published in the four-volume work; it was also published separately, in London, as *The American Civil War*, on 23 March 1961, when 10,000 copies were printed. A further 5,000 copies were issued two months later. As well as the original text from the four-volume work, Civil War photographs had been added by the publisher, Cassell. Churchill had visited many Civil War battlefields in October 1929, writing in *Colliers* that he was 'astonished' by the many traces of the fighting which still remained after more than 70 years: 'The farmhouses and the churches still show the scars of shot and shell; the woods are full of trenches and rifle pits; the larger trees are full of bullets. Before the War Museum in Richmond still flies a tattered rebel flag. If you could read men's hearts, you would find that they, too, bear the marks.'

[3] 'My dear Luce', 'Private and Confidential', 30 November 1953: Churchill papers, 4/28.

48

The Bermuda Conference,
December 1953

AT midnight on 1 December 1953 Churchill left London by
air for Bermuda. It was a long flight, the first landing, because
of strong headwinds, being at Shannon, before flying on to Gander in
Newfoundland, then south to Bermuda.

Churchill was accompanied by one Cabinet Minister, Anthony
Eden, by the Cabinet Secretary, Sir Norman Brook, by his two Principal Private Secretaries, David Pitblado and Jock Colville, as well
as by Lord Cherwell, Lord Moran, Christopher Soames, and several
Foreign Office officials. 'Lunched at a table for four,' Lord Moran
noted during the flight, 'the Prof and the PM on one side, Anthony
and I opposite. After greeting Anthony cheerfully, Winston took up
his book, *Death to the French*, by C. S. Forester, and kept his nose in
it throughout the meal.'

After the lunch Christopher Soames brought Churchill some notes
connected with the coming conference, 'but Winston', wrote Lord
Moran, 'did not seem at all keen on work'. Moran added: 'We were
bumping on the edge of a storm, and possibly his mind went back to
the night in February, 1943 when we were crossing the Atlantic and
were struck by lightning. His flying memories are not at all happy,
and however he may hide it, he is full of apprehension.' [1]

After seventeen hours' flying, Churchill's party reached Bermuda.
Churchill was driven from the airport to the Mid-Ocean Golf Club,
which was to be his home for the week of the Conference. On the
morning of December 3 he went back to the airport to receive the
French Prime Minister, Joseph Laniel, and his Foreign Minister,
Georges Bidault. 'Last time this conference was proposed,' Jock
Colville noted in his diary, 'the French could not form a Government

---

[1] Moran diary, 2 December 1953: *The Struggle for Survival*, pages 501–2. It was in May 1943,
flying from Newfoundland to Gibraltar, that Churchill's flying boat had been struck by lightning.

and the meeting had to be postponed week after week until just as we were packing to leave the PM had his stroke.'

That night Churchill dined with Lord Cherwell, Lord Moran, Sir Norman Brook, Christopher Soames, Pitblado and Colville, his inner circle for the duration of the Bermuda visit. 'The PM got going well after dinner,' Colville wrote, 'but the room was too small and we were all but perishing from the heat. The PM said, "It may be that we are living in our generation through the great demoralisation which the scientists have caused but before the countervailing correctives have become operative."' [1]

Lord Moran also recorded some of the dinner table conversation on December 3, dominated as it was by the shadow of the hydrogen bomb:

PM: 'We have been living in a time when at any moment London, men, women and children, might be destroyed overnight.'

I was glad to turn the conversation.

'But does Russia want war?'

PM: 'I believe it is not in her interest to make war. When I meet Malenkov we can build for peace.'

Moran: 'Then who is making difficulties?'

PM: 'Ike. He doesn't think any good can come from talks with the Russians. But it will pay him to come along with us. I shall do what I can to persuade him. I might stay longer here than I meant, at any rate if I could persuade Ike to stay too. He is the key man in this business.'

Moran: 'I thought Dulles was.'

He took no notice of my remark.

PM: 'I would not hesitate to go on to Washington if that was necessary. I think, Charles, I could manage it. I don't feel old, though I have some of the disabilities of old age. My outlook on things has not changed. It is exactly what it was. In the mornings I feel the same as I always did, but I have become torpid in the middle of the day. You ought to be able to think out some line of action which would help me. This old carcass of mine is a bloody nuisance.' [2]

On Friday December 4 Churchill returned to the airport to greet Eisenhower and Dulles, then lunched alone with Eisenhower. 'This greatly disturbed Dulles and Eden,' wrote Colville, 'who neither of them trust their chief alone.' [3]

The first topic, raised by Eisenhower, was Korea. Expecting that the Chinese and North Koreans might again seek to challenge the existing lines, he told Churchill that 'if there were a deliberate breach of the Armistice by the Communists' the United States 'would expect to strike back with atomic weapons at military targets'. She would

[1] Colville diary, 3 December 1953: *The Fringes of Power*, page 682.

[2] Moran diary, 3 December 1953: *The Struggle for Survival*, pages 503–4.

[3] Colville diary, 4 December 1953: *The Fringes of Power*, pages 682–4.

not expect to bomb cities 'but would attack areas that were directly supporting the aggression'. Churchill did not object, telling Eisenhower, as the minutes recorded, that he 'quite accepted this', and that Eisenhower's statement of American policy 'put him in a position to say to Parliament that he had been consulted in advance and had agreed'.

Speaking of those countries over which either Britain or the United States could assert their influence, Eisenhower wanted each case to be 'considered on its merits as to who should take the lead and as to who might play the role of "moderator"', and said 'that it was not necessary always openly to appear to present a consolidated front'. Churchill, in reply, 'argued for the united front approach'. Speaking of the United States policy not to recognize Communist China, Eisenhower 'urged a closer alignment of UK policy with the US'. Replying, Churchill said that he had originally opposed recognition of Communist China 'but that this had now become an established fact which would be difficult to alter'. As for trade with China, which the United States had embargoed and wished to see embargoed in the future, Churchill told Eisenhower that he 'looked upon trade as a means of achieving the desired results' of keeping the Chinese nose 'above water'. The Chinese were gradually getting stronger, he said, 'but need trade'.

There was further disagreement in regard to Churchill's suggestion that, if the French continued to 'balk' the European Defence Community, it might be possible to create it without France, or to bring Germany into NATO, or, 'if the French vetoed this, establishing a new treaty arrangement with Germany'. The President, as the American notes of the meeting recorded, 'indicated skepticism concerning this'.

On the question of a Foreign Ministers' meeting with the Soviet Union, there 'seemed agreement', the minutes recorded, 'that there should be a meeting as promptly as possible, preferably early in January'. Churchill then suggested that if the meeting were to be held in Berlin it might alternate between the two sectors, telling Eisenhower that he felt 'we should always keep the "door open" to the Russians'. Eisenhower was not so enthusiastic, emphasizing 'that he would not participate in the Heads of Government meeting until at a Foreign Ministers meeting the Soviets had shown evidence of good faith'.[1]

After his meeting with Eisenhower, Churchill walked with Christopher Soames and Jock Colville to the beach where, Colville noted, 'the PM sat like King Canute defying the incoming tide (and getting his feet wet in consequence) while C and I bathed naked and I swam out to fetch Winston some distant seaweed he wished to inspect'.

[1] 'Memorandum of Conversation', 'Participants: President Eisenhower, Prime Minister Churchill', 'Top Secret', Bermuda, 4 December 1953: Eisenhower papers.

The first Plenary meeting of the Bermuda Conference opened that afternoon at five o'clock. There were several 'memories of former conferences', Jock Colville noted in his diary. 'The Big Three', Churchill, Eisenhower and Laniel, 'first sat on the porch in wicker chairs and were photographed in a manner reminiscent of Teheran. Then, when the conference started, all the lights fused and we deliberated by the light of candles and hurricane lamps as in Athens at Christmas 1944.' [1]

For this first meeting, Eisenhower, Churchill and Laniel, together with Dulles, Eden and Bidault, initially met in restricted session, without their advisers. The meeting was opened by Churchill, who 'rejoiced to think', as the minutes recorded, that they had met together 'and expressed his pleasure at being present at this long-projected meeting'. He had 'long hoped', he said, 'to open the proceedings', and as a first action he would like to ask the President of the United States, as the Chief of State, to take the chair to preside at future meetings'. This, Eisenhower agreed to do. Churchill then asked, 'not as a sign of personal indulgence but rather as an indication of the informal nature of the talks, if he might have permission to smoke'. The President replied that, 'in his first ruling as chairman, he granted this permission'.

Eisenhower then proposed a pool of atomic energy materials, through a United Nations authority. The United States might 'put in' 1,000 kilogrammes, the Soviet Union 200 and Britain 40. 'Thereafter details could be worked out between the interested parties as to how much could be made available to the scientists of the world for practical purposes.' In reply, Churchill said he would like his answer to be 'as helpful and suggestive as possible', but that he felt there would be 'a great difficulty in drawing a line between atomic energy commercial information and atomic energy military information'. Such a line had, however, already been drawn 'in general terms'.

Eisenhower intended to make his proposal public in four days' time, on December 8. 'It would be very nice,' Churchill commented, 'if mankind could share the blessings from this subject without suffering from the disadvantages of its curses. That was as he understood the general line or tendency by which the President would be governed in making his statement. Thus, he would view it with favour.' [2]

---

[1] Colville diary, 4 December 1953: *The Fringes of Power*, pages 682–4.

[2] 'Memorandum of Conversation', 'Bermuda Meeting', 'Restricted Session of Heads of Government and Foreign Ministers', 'Top Secret', 'Strictly Limited Distribution', 5 p.m., 4 December 1953: Eisenhower papers.

Eisenhower then suggested that for a discussion of the Soviet position, the remaining members of the delegation should be invited to join them.[1] It was then Bidault who asked, in a forceful speech, if the changes in Soviet policy since the death of Stalin were more in 'manner, atmosphere and attitude' than 'fundamental policy changes'. Eisenhower then asked Churchill if he would like to 'present a paper, make a presentation or supplement the discussion by any method which he desired'. Churchill had not prepared any paper; but he did have an appeal to make for the possibility that the change since Stalin's death was more than a matter of atmosphere, telling the Conference:

... in his view the great question, the supreme question, which must underlie our judgment in a dozen spheres was 'is there a new look, is there a new Soviet look?' Had there been a deep change in the mighty entity we call the Soviet Union? Had there been such a change since the death of Stalin? Several things M. Bidault had said gave reason for belief that this was so. Other considerations set forth by M. Bidault indicated that there had been no change of heart but an ingenious variation of tactics.

It must of course have come as a great shock to the Kremlin when at the end of the war they thought they had the future at their feet but then found that, owing to the initiative and gigantic strength of the United States, the thing for which they had been hoping and even had been planning was no longer possible, confronted as they were by the immense process in which the conferences were taking part today. The free world was rearming and facing their extensive movements and ambitions. This must have come as a great shock to them. It was easy to see that at the end of 1945 or at the beginning of 1946 they might have thought that they had only to press forward to carry Communism and behind it Soviet imperialism to the shores of the Atlantic and far and wide across the Pacific world. Then they had found that this was not so.

It was profoundly difficult to judge what they had felt but at any rate, when the Stalin regime passed away, they must have thought that an opportunity had come for re-considering the situation. It was quite clear that they would face a struggle if they continued on a course of aggression, infiltration and undermining.

He did not think that it was in any way 'extraordinary', Churchill continued, that in reviewing the new circumstances of the world situation, 'the Kremlin had come to the conclusion that the thoughts they might have had after Potsdam might require profound re-consideration'. This was a first reason why he 'might be inclined to answer the question as to whether there was a new look in the affirmative'. A second reason, he said, was the economic conditions of the Russian people. Churchill told the Conference, as the American notes recorded:

[1] The British participants who joined Churchill and Eden at this point were Sir Norman Brook, Sir Pierson Dixon, Sir Frank Roberts, John Colville and Evelyn Shuckburgh.

The hopes of a Communist utopia which had been dangled before the eyes of millions had not been borne out. At the disposal of the Soviet leaders at any moment were enormous opportunities for improving the material situation of their population. He found it reasonable to believe that these two facts (1) opposition from the United States and (2) the need for economic hope, may well have brought about a definite change in Russian policy and outlook which may govern their actions for many years to come.

Therefore, on the question of a new look he would answer 'let us make sure that we do not too lightly dismiss this possibility'. Confrontation by the Western world abroad and economic and other internal troubles at home might well have led to a definite change.

We should, however, be very careful of two dangers, first to be thrown off our guard, and second, to exclude altogether the possibility that there may have been a real change. If there had been a change, it was due, if not entirely at least mainly, to the strength and unity of the Western allies. If they had gathered to consider whether they should weaken that or to allow themselves to be divided, they would have indeed come to a dangerous pass.

Churchill then set out the philosophy which had guided his attitude to foreign affairs and defence for more than forty years:

The only hope for a better state of affairs lay in the maintenance of Western strength and unity and a clear resolute determination to defend the cause of freedom by all means at hand. If this gathering were being held to find ways to reduce our defenses, that would be an extreme act of criminal folly but if we were resolved to continue our preparation with the utmost vigor and perseverance—if we are, then this second question whether there was any reality in a Russian change was one that could be examined within limits and it should find its part in a general survey of the scene, once we had convinced them that there was no hope of dividing the allies.

We should not repulse every move for the better. There should not be a question of finding a reason full of suspicion for giving evil meaning to every move of the Soviets. That might be so if we were considering lessening our precautions but we might afford to look shrewdly and delicately at the new scene which the Russians presented.

It was 'not merely those around the table' at Bermuda who had to be convinced, Churchill warned, 'but also our peoples', that no bona fide Soviet movement 'towards a "detente" or effort for improvement had been rebuffed or cast aside without consideration'. Britain, the United States and France 'should be on the look out for any sign of improvement in the situation'. Thus, he explained, 'we could guard our people and hope for a real improvement in the situation'. The note it would be right to strike 'was that we have a two-fold policy—of strength, and readiness to look for any hope of an improved state of mind, even if it were necessary to run a slight mental risk. This would give us great strength.'

Churchill went on to tell Eisenhower and Laniel that he:

... felt sure that the British Parliament and people were willing to make every exertion to maintain the unity and strength of the North Atlantic Treaty alliance. Nothing could make it easier to rally and sustain our peoples than the fact that we have not brushed aside anything which would give us assurance or hope of a better state of affairs. Therefore, he was anxious that contacts be considered.

The Soviets were more afraid of infiltration now than we were—infiltration behind the iron curtain if he might use the word. This was feared by what was bad in the Kremlin. If infiltration takes place, it could do us no harm. Trade was a vehicle of infiltration and the best way in which ordinary people and countries could earn their livelihood. We had nothing to fear from that and he would like to see such contacts improved and trade increased and the process of infiltration developed.

He would not be in too much of a hurry to believe that nothing but evil emanates from this mighty branch of the human family or that nothing but danger and peril could come out of this vast ocean of land in a single circle so little known and understood.

Churchill then spoke of the need to open relations with Russia, within the limits of realism:

Contacts, infiltration, trade leading to greater prosperity, reassurance that they would not have another dose of Hitler—and they had a right to this— and at the same time make it clear that we do not regard the position of the satellites nor admit that such a position could be permanent or tolerable but saying that we do not intend to use world war efforts to alter this. Time and patience must play their part. Such are the ideas I would venture. While hope springs eternal in the human heart, there is never an occasion where hope should be so modest and restrained. We are not attempting to heal the world or banish danger for that would be far beyond our powers.

Churchill's final plea was graphically recorded by the United States note takers:

'Encourage, encourage,' Sir Winston repeated, 'the world by stimulating prosperity and getting people in a more agreeable state of mind. This might well carry us through a period of years to a time when a much better scene will come. I would finish where I had begun.' This would only be possible if combined as he had depicted, we continued in a strong and resolute manner to perfect our defenses and organisation so that we would not risk throwing away all that had been gained so far and did not undo the great work already achieved. If mitigation of our work were contemplated, he would not ask for consideration of the other thought.

Standing together indivisible and growing stronger, we might be entitled to cherish the hope that we could come to the end of our difficulties having preserved the peace of the world.[1]

---

[1] 'Bermuda Meeting', 'Tripartite, Heads of Government', 'Plenary Session', 'Plenary Minutes 1', 'Secret', 6 p.m., 4 December 1953: Eisenhower papers.

To the amazement of the British participants, Eisenhower then replied 'with a short, very violent statement, in the coarsest terms', depicting the Soviet Union as 'a woman of the streets'.[1] He believed, he said, 'that Sir Winston meant that we should examine to see if the dress were a new one or merely an old patched one', and he added:

If we understood that under this dress was the same old girl, if we understood that despite bath, perfume or lace, it was still the same old girl, on that basis then we might explore all that Sir Winston had said if we might apply the positive methods of which M. Bidault had spoken. Perhaps we could pull the old girl off the main street and put her on a back alley. He did not want to approach this problem on the basis that there had been any change in the Soviet policy of destroying the Capitalist free world by all means, by force, by deceit or by lies. This was their long-term purpose. From their writings it was clear there had been no change since Lenin.

'If he had misinterpreted the Prime Minister,' Eisenhower added, 'he would be happy if Sir Winston would correct him,' whereupon he adjourned the Conference.[2]

Commenting on Eisenhower's remarks, Jock Colville noted in his diary:

I doubt if such language has ever before been heard at an international conference. Pained looks all round.

Of course, the French gave it all away to the press. Indeed some of their leakages were verbatim.

To end on a note of dignity, when Eden asked when the next meeting should be, the President replied, 'I don't know. Mine is with a whisky and soda'—and got up to leave the room.[3]

That night Churchill dined with Eden and Cherwell, before returning to his room, where he was joined by Soames and Moran. 'He told us,' Moran noted, 'that the Press had got a full account of the first meeting and were making a great story of the division of opinion between the PM and the President about Russia. The PM seemed put out; he did not know that the Press would be informed in this way.'[4]

On Saturday December 5 the British delegation met to discuss the previous afternoon's Plenary meeting, and the meeting for that afternoon. 'Everybody greatly perturbed,' noted Colville, 'by the American attitude on (a) the prospects, (b) their action, in the event of the

[1] Colville diary, 4 December 1953: *The Fringes of Power*, pages 685–7.

[2] 'Bermuda Meeting', 'Tripartite, Heads of Government', 'Plenary Session', 'Plenary Minutes 1, 'Secret', 6 p.m., 4 December 1953: Eisenhower papers.

[3] Colville diary, 4 December 1953: *The Fringes of Power*, pages 685–7.

[4] Moran diary, 4 December 1953: *The Struggle for Survival*, page 505.

Korean truce breaking down. This question has such deep implications that it is undoubtedly the foremost matter at the conference—
though it has to be discussed behind closed doors with the Americans.'
No atomic matters, Colville added, 'can be talked about to the French
who are very sensitive at having no atomic piles or bombs. The PM,
Ike, Lord Cherwell and Admiral Strauss discussed the matter in the
President's room from 11.30 till lunch-time.'[1]

Strauss, the Chairman of the United States Atomic Energy Commission, took a longhand note of the discussion, a copy of which was
preserved by the President. The meeting opened with a reference by
Churchill 'to his concern at the cessation of full scale co-operation between the US and UK which had prevailed during the war. He made
a plea for its resumption.' Churchill also pointed out that British planes
were being 'designed and built' with no proper knowledge of the characteristics of American atomic weapons 'if they might ever be called upon
to deliver them'; he hoped 'as a minimum' that the weight, dimensions
and ballistics of the American weapons could be supplied to Britain.

Eisenhower's reply remains a secret.[2] Churchill then told Eisenhower that Britain, having concluded 'successful weapons tests' of
atomic weapons, was 'now embarked upon weapon production'; the
first weapon had 'recently been delivered to the RAF'. Lord Cherwell
then explained that Britain was 'not intending to do any work on
hydrogen bombs', as she felt able to get sufficient destructive power of
one and possibly two megatons from 'boosted fission weapons', and
that in Britain's view 'few targets needed a larger yield'. At this point
Eisenhower spoke of his belief that atomic weapons 'were now coming
to be regarded as a proper part of conventional armament and that
he thought this a sound concept'. Strauss noted at this point: 'Sir Winston concurred.'

When Churchill told Eisenhower that he felt 'that there should be
more freedom of information between the two countries on discussion
of intelligence concerning enemy weapons and capabilities', Eisenhower expressed himself as 'sympathetic to this idea'. The aim of this
meeting, it was agreed, was to facilitate a climate 'for closer working
relations' on matters of atomic weapons.[3]

The second Plenary meeting was held that afternoon. 'Very heavy
work here,' Churchill telegraphed to his wife just before it began, and
he added, 'No sunshine today.'[4] 'Although this is my first letter,'

[1] Colville diary, 5 December 1953: *The Fringes of Power*, page 684.
[2] Admiral Strauss's note was only declassified on 15 April 1986; several portions of it, however,
were exempted from declassification by a National Security Council letter of 15 April 1986.
[3] 'Meeting held 11.30, lasting until 12.45 (noon) with Sir Winston Churchill, Lord Cherwell,
the President and Admiral Strauss', 'Top Secret', 5 December 1953: Eisenhower papers.
[4] 'Priority', 2 p.m., 5 December 1953: Churchill papers, 1/50.

Clementine Churchill wrote that day from Downing Street, 'I have been thinking of you constantly since you flew away at mid-night on December the 1st,' and she added: 'A telegram has just come from you saying that the work is "heavy". I do pray that it will also be fruitful.'[1]

Clementine Churchill's letter crossed with a further telegram from her husband. 'Much disappointed to have no word from you,' it read. 'I have telegraphed every day but am very hard pressed. Love W.'[2]

The meeting on the afternoon of December 5 was dominated by a discussion of the European Defence Community. If the French refused to ratify the Community, the American administration was prepared to turn its back on Europe. But Bidault, with all the goodwill at his command, could not bring his own people into line.

In an attempt to persuade the French not to abandon the European Defence Community, Churchill suggested that the Conference should look 'at what was wanted, what was the hope of the EDC'. Its object was to form a 'fighting front' with an army. There was, he believed, 'nothing to prevent such a front from being formed under a unified command with whatever resources could be gathered at present'. Churchill went on to tell Eisenhower and Laniel that 'when he had been active in starting this idea in Europe of an EDC or European army, he had thought of it in terms of a grand alliance with all nations standing in line together under a unified command. All sorts of questions arose in connection with an army of a federation of Europe. Three years had been lost on complicated details and the only thing that had come out of it was the EDC Treaty.'

The treaty itself, Churchill felt, was a 'great improvement' on earlier editions. It included an idea of which he approved, the creation of separate national military units—divisions each with its national uniform and identity. The previous idea 'of making an army in a few years of people talking different languages, armed with different weapons', Churchill added, 'was indeed forlorn': even companies and battalions would have been of different nationalities. Churchill continued, in support of the divisional scheme:

There could be no doubt that the division is the minimum that is workable. He would, therefore, refrain from making the criticisms he used to make when he had been independent. Personally, he preferred a national presentation of armies bound by a grand alliance. The present army would be the best that could be obtained with a unified command. We would be prepared to take our part with our troops in line in sections chosen for occupation.

---

[1] 'My darling Winston', 5 December 1953: Churchill papers, 1/50.
[2] Telegram despatched 6 December 1953: Churchill papers, 1/50.

Immense sections would be undefended except by flank attacks. We would be prepared to take our part and submit to the Supreme Commander.

Churchill then pledged Britain to support the EDC proposals. 'He would do all he could,' he said, 'for the defence of the West. British troops could be ordered to any part of the front. If a war were to break out and one who did not know were looking at the forces of the West in action, he could not tell whether they were operating as EDC or as a grand alliance. The troops could be moved about at will.' Of French objections to German participation in the army scheme, Churchill told the Conference:

. . . an immense amount of mutual energy had been expended in raising new and complicated problems. Three years had been completely wasted in getting what was absolutely necessary for a good strong German army. We ought to have had it three years ago. Under EDC, this could be done with the consent of the German Government with safeguards against nationalistic excesses. It contained great advantages. It should not be let slip away but we might have to return to the plan of a grand alliance under NATO. We must have a Germany army.

There was no use in talking of the defence of Europe against Russia without Germany. It was not possible to allow this immense no man's land of Germany to remain utterly undefended. The Germans wanted to defend it and they ought to have effective means of defense. If this contribution were made within the framework of EDC, it would be the most satisfactory solution in the view of our French friends.

We could not go on for three more years without a German army. We must have this German army; even with it the front would still be thinly held. But it would be a deterrent to the Soviets and he would beg his French friends to do their utmost.

Churchill then expressed his appreciation of the efforts which Bidault himself had made to bring about the participation of Germany in the European Army. 'If, however, this were to prove impossible in the next few weeks, eight or ten,' he warned, 'then he would be bound to say that he would propose to make a new version of NATO achieving the same hope as EDC, with controls over the German army by the NATO organization so as to make it quite clear that this army could not be used against France or to precipitate war to regain the Eastern lost territories. . . .' These Eastern territories, he said, 'were far more prominent in the German mind than the old stories of Alsace-Lorraine which are now in the German mind "vieux jeu" compared to the Eastern and Western Neisse'. He therefore 'earnestly hoped' that Laniel and Bidault, 'his French friends', would realize that unless the European Defence Community 'that they had shaped so carefully, could come in at once, we ought to establish an arrangement under NATO that would give us at once 12 German divisions, all battleworthy. Otherwise, we could not undertake this burden as it would present us with an insoluble problem. And we must do this or admit complete failure.'

It was necessary, Churchill told Laniel and Eisenhower, for the Russians to know that the military arrangements of the European Defence Community 'were going to be kept'. He had spoken on the previous day of a 'detente', but he did not advocate detente 'at the expense of jeopardizing our situation'. To reinforce this firmness, Churchill assured the Conference:

The United Kingdom would stand in line and obey the Supreme Commander. It would contribute to the utmost and do everything it could to make its contribution strong and effective. If there is anyone who cannot now come in to join the line of battle in preparation for these dangers, let him then stay out.

Nothing could affect the dominating fact that British and US troops would stand in line with their French comrades and their comrades of the Benelux and that they could be moved as required. To go on waiting would only weaken us from every point of view. It was wrong to think that we could effectively direct the future of Germany with this question unsettled and the Russians closely interested, though without wickedness, in preventing the creation of any Germany military force.

He hoped it would be 'clearly understood', Churchill declared, that if France could not come to a decision about German participation, 'it would not prevent the formation of a German army as soon as possible incorporated into NATO with all the safeguards that could be arranged'. Such a German army, he felt, 'would fight loyally and effectively in defence of the West. If there were traitors then those who remained would close lines and stand together. Germany would then become a no man's land subject to bombing, atomic and otherwise.'

It would make 'no difference' to the strength of the European Defence Community, Churchill told Laniel and Bidault, 'if the British were called partners—with EDC but not in it. The greater part of British armed forces were there. Some countries had comfortable armed forces at home. The British had not a single brigade in the United Kingdom.' The British were already 'doing their utmost'. He would not be prepared 'to advise his fellow countrymen to undertake more'. Nor could he go forward with the British plans to participate in the European Defence Community 'if it should cause any delay in the formation of a German army'. The matter was not one on which Churchill was prepared to delay, or to obstruct, and he told the Conference, in an appeal directed at the Frenchmen present:

He was sorry to have to speak in this way and he would not do it if he did not feel that it were in the interest of France, as well as the United Kingdom. For 40 years, he had been intimately associated with the valiant efforts of his French comrades to face these perils. He knew well the fearful losses they had sustained in the First World War and their great efforts in the Second World War. He understood the brilliant and valiant efforts of the resistance. . . .

At this point, the American minutes noted, 'the Prime Minister's voice choked and tears came to his eyes'. He 'knew well', Churchill continued, 'the gallant part that M. Bidault and M. Laniel had played in this resistance and this had won for them the gratitude of the free world. He must beg his French friends to understand that we must go on with EDC, or have in NATO a German army with a minimum of delay. Much preliminary work had been done and in a few years a substantial German contribution could be available. This would tend to check the Russians as it was the thing they feared most.' [1]

After the second Plenary meeting Churchill spoke to Eisenhower about a possible meeting with the Chinese. 'Meeting the Chinese,' he said, 'does not necessarily imply recognizing them for any purpose other than identification. In war there are often parleys between enemies while they are in fact still fighting (cf the campaign of 1814). This is quite distinct from approval of the actions and policy of the other side or their recognition in the diplomatic sense.' [2]

That evening Churchill, Eisenhower, Eden and Dulles dined alone, the French being excluded because the purpose of the meeting was to evolve a common atomic strategy, without which no summit could possibly succeed, certainly not without a unified Anglo-American stance, and strength.

The 'grim conversations' at that dinner, as Colville learned later that night, were about the future action to be taken in the event of a breach of the truce in Korea. Eisenhower reiterated what he had told Churchill on the previous day, that America was prepared to use the atomic bomb. 'Eden was most particularly disturbed by this,' Colville noted, 'and by the effect on public opinion in England.' Churchill too now 'strongly resisted' Eisenhower's suggestion.

On the morning of Sunday December 6, Colville added, 'everybody was in rather a state' as a result of the previous evening's discussion, which, he added, 'far outstrips in importance anything else at the conference'.

As to the previous day's impasse over the European Defence Com-

---

[1] 'Bermuda Meeting', 'Tripartite—Heads of Government', 'Plenary Session', 'Plenary Minutes 2', Secret, 5 p.m., 5 December 1953: Eisenhower papers.

[2] 'Note (Summary of the Prime Minister's remarks)', initialled 'JRC' (Jock Colville), 5 December 1953: Premier papers, 11/418.

munity, the Americans were now putting the onus of an agreement on Britain, saying that 'it is the British who must satisfy the French Chamber of Deputies by guaranteeing to leave their troops on the continent for a defined number of years or even by actually joining the EDC. Thus it is we who are to suffer on account of French weakness and obduracy.' The 'obvious answer' to that, Colville noted, was '(i) we will keep our troops on the Continent as long as the Americans agree to do so, (ii) we could not possibly get our Parliament and people, or the Commonwealth, to accept our actual membership of EDC.'

That morning Churchill accepted a suggestion by Eden, that the British must make clear to Eisenhower that they did not accept his atomic bomb proposals in so far as they concerned the United States being 'free to use the atomic bomb' in certain circumstances. Eisenhower was going to set out these proposals in a speech to the United Nations. Churchill and Eden then drafted a statement to that effect, which Churchill gave to Colville, to take to the President, so that Britain's reservations could be made clear in the President's speech.

Colville took the British statement to Eisenhower, recording Eisenhower's comment 'that whereas Winston looked on the atomic weapon as something entirely new and terrible, he looked upon it as just the latest improvement in military weapons. He implied that there was in fact no distinction between "conventional weapons" and atomic weapons: all weapons in due course became conventional weapons.' This, Colville wrote, 'represents a fundamental difference of opinion between public opinion in the USA and in England'.

Eisenhower also proposed, in his United Nations' speech, to refer to the 'obsolete Colonial mould' which was now over, or being broken. After lunch that day, Churchill persuaded Eisenhower to remove this 'obnoxious phrase', as Colville called it, from his speech. More significantly, Churchill persuaded Eisenhower to substitute for the United States being 'free to use the atomic bomb' a phrase about the United States 'reserving the right to use the atomic bomb'. The central theme of Eisenhower's proposal, the control of atomic energy by an international body, was very much acceptable to Churchill. It seemed a way back from the brink.

During the afternoon of December 6, the Foreign Ministers sent Dr Adenauer the text of their proposed reply to the Soviet Government, accepting a conference of Foreign Ministers at Berlin in January. Neither Eisenhower nor Churchill had been shown this text before it was sent off. Colville noted in his diary:

W remonstrated strongly with Eden and wanted to have left out the reference to German reunification, on the grounds that you couldn't confront the Russians at Berlin with both our determination that Western Germany should be an armed member of EDC *and* a demand that Eastern Germany be united to it.

Eden enlisted the support of Dulles (even heavier and more flabby now than last January) and after pointing out that German reunification had figured in all the previous notes, and that Adenauer expected it, they won their case.

'In the confusion,' Colville added, 'Frank Roberts, who was in a state of fury with the PM, was mistaken by the latter for one of Dulles' advisers and treated to a homily as such.' [1]

The third Plenary meeting, held on the afternoon of December 6, was again dominated by the European Defence Community problem. The French, increasingly isolated since the Conference began, were now alone. Churchill begged them not to become bogged down by earlier disputes and disagreements with Germany on France's eastern frontier, and especially by French concern over the future of the Saar, about which Bidault had spoken with considerable passion. [2] He had thought, Churchill said, that the heads of Government 'were really going to talk about the EDC with the thought of the salvation of the French. He did not feel we should be mixed up with a few fields in the Saar valley. We should maintain a sense of proportion.' Churchill added:

EDC had been a French proposal and her allies and friends had been doing all they could to help her out. This project had delayed for more than three years the formation of a German army, without which there could be no safety for anyone in Europe. A critical point had been reached where EDC would either be ratified by France or not.

He hoped that the French would consider what the consequences might be before they made a final decision. He had hoped, that if the French were unwilling or unable because of parliamentary difficulties to ratify EDC, Ger-

---

[1] Colville diary, 6 December 1953: *The Fringes of Power*, pages 685–7. Frank Roberts was Deputy Permanent Under-Secretary of State at the Foreign Office (from 1951 to 1954). He was knighted in 1953.

[2] Since 1947 the Saar had experienced economic union with France and a measure of local autonomy. By 1951, however, the Saarlanders were complaining of French exploitation. In May 1953 the French had concluded a preliminary agreement with the Saar Landtag which was interpreted by the Saarlanders as a step towards Europeanizing the region, and resented by the growing number of Saarlanders who wished to be an integral part of Germany. In a debate in the Chamber of 19 November 1953 Laniel insisted that he was seeking a Franco-German agreement over the Saar as a preliminary to reconciliation with Germany in the EDC. This was turned down by Adenauer. In January 1957 the Saar became one of the German Federal Länder recognizing that France had mineral extraction rights valid until 1981. In October 1959, as part of the Adenauer-de Gaulle reconciliation, France accepted the economic integration of the Saar into the German Federal Republic.

many would be brought in by a rearrangement or broadening of the NATO organization. He was not at all sure from what he had heard the President say that this might appear to be a good plan to the United States.

It might be that EDC would be cast aside improvidently at this vital and perilous moment and that the NATO organization might not be reorganized in order to achieve the purpose of EDC. He hoped that before the French Parliament would take a final decision they would see the dark possibilities ahead if the US would withdraw from its policy of direct aid and giving to Europe.

It was certain that British troops could not stay any longer than the Americans (as long, no longer). If US troops were withdrawn from France, it would expose Britain to mortal danger. No other country was doing in peace time what they were. They had two-year military service and not a single brigade in the UK. With the development of aircraft in a few months, they might be faced with a heavy paratroop attack in the UK. If the US were unable to continue their effort, if EDC were rejected, the British would then have to do their utmost to fight to the death in their own island and this they would not hesitate to do to the best of their ability.

He begged and implored his French friends not to let a few fields in the Saar valley come between the life and death of the flaming spirit of France and the break up of the great structure on which so many hopes had been founded.

Churchill now warned the French of what he saw as the ultimate danger of not admitting a German force to the European Defence Community. If the EDC were rejected, he said, and NATO 'put aside as not being feasible', something which could only provide a 'peripheral' defence would be found; this 'would indeed be a frightful disaster, for Europe could be quickly undermined and suborned by the Russian Communist advance and then, if a general war followed, it was very likely that they would never succeed in reviving the civilization and culture of Western Europe and of France'. With stern emphasis, Churchill 'stressed the importance of preventing another world war, the preliminary of which would probably extinguish the culture, civilization and freedom of Western Europe. He could not understand how the seriousness of this was not realized.' Then, as the minutes of the Conference recorded:

He urged that the awful peril be not underrated. He pointed out that Germany would be totally disarmed, at the mercy of Russia at any moment, and that the British themselves might expect to be shattered but thank God they still had the Channel which had stood them in such good stead.

M. Bidault interrupted to say that France did not.

All the more reason, said the Prime Minister, why France should support EDC which might well become for France what the Channel was for the UK. He knew that there was no fault on M. Bidault's part but, if the French

Parliament rejected EDC, he would view the future more somberly than at any time in World War II.

He earnestly hoped this would not happen. EDC should be first and last but if that failed, he would beg the President and his associates to consider some way of achieving the same result through changes in NATO. If this fails the British would stay only so long as the United States.

Eisenhower supported Churchill's plea to Bidault. If no German national army were to be allowed, he warned, he did not see how a European defence policy could be brought about.

The discussion of the European Defence Community had taken up the whole meeting. Other issues must not, however, be crowded out of the agenda, Churchill insisted. He wanted there to be a discussion as soon as possible about Egypt. 'Herein,' he explained, 'the interests of the UK were entirely in accord with those of France. In comparison with the terrible matters they had been discussing, this might seem like a small matter but they had 80 thousand men in this area who might come into action next week or soon thereafter if attacked.' He was not asking 'for physical support in favouring a solution', Churchill added, 'but he felt it would be helpful if the Middle East thought that the US and UK were thinking in the same way, seeking no advantage of imperial power but finding a way to discharge their duty to NATO and to the civilization of the world'.[1]

That night Churchill told Colville that 'he and Ike had agreed to treat forcing through the ratification of EDC as a combined military operation'.

A more serious problem would arise, however, if the European Defence Community did not go through, for in that eventuality, Colville noted, 'the Americans do not agree with the PM that Germany must be invited to join NATO. On the contrary they talk of falling back on "peripheral" defence, which means the defence of their bases stretching in a crescent from Iceland via East Anglia, Spain and North Africa to Turkey.' This, Churchill told Colville, 'would entail France becoming Communist-dominated (and finally going the way of Czechoslovakia) while the Americans sought to rearm Germany sandwiched between the hostile powers of Russia and France'.

If France refused to accept the European Defence Community, Colville noted, 'the PM intends to go all out to persuade the Americans to work for the Germany-in-NATO alternative'.

The possibility of America using the atomic bomb against China perturbed Churchill far more than the problems of the European Defence Community or the Middle East. 'I have been feeling for the past

---

[1] 'Bermuda Meeting', 'Tripartite—Heads of Government', 'Plenary Session', 'Plenary Minutes 3', 'Secret', 5 p.m., 6 December 1953: Eisenhower papers.

forty-eight hours,' he told Colville on the night of December 6, 'that all our problems, even those such as Egypt, shrink into insignificance by the side of the one great issue which this conference has thrown up.' [1]

The problem of Egypt dominated the fourth Plenary meeting, which was held at noon on December 7, when Churchill told the Conference: 'The great waterway of the Suez Canal was a question of world interest. He felt that there was a need to take every precaution to preserve it against neglect or obstruction. He was not considering the closing of the Canal by bombing by hostile nations. That would be difficult with the improved facilities. He did feel that an attempt should be made to consider the Suez Canal on an international basis. It was as worthy of dignity and respect as the Panama Canal.' Anything along the lines of an international force 'would steady the whole Middle East', that was 'all he was asking'. If Britain could obtain assurances from Eisenhower or Dulles 'with the authority that they carry', such assurances 'could have moral support in the negotiations now going on, that might lead to a reasonable conclusion and avoid what was not impossible, namely a lot of fighting'.

What he 'did not want', Churchill warned, was that, with 80,000 British troops and Air Force units in Egypt, troops might be arrested by the local troops 'or something else done which would constitute a military action and might lead to actual war'. [2]

Early on the afternoon of December 7, Churchill read the communiqué which it was intended to issue as soon as the Conference ended. It was the Russian aspect which disturbed him, as he minuted to Eden:

I can find nothing in this communiqué which shows the slightest desire for the success of the Conference or for an easement in relations with Russia. We are to gang up against them without any reference to the 'Locarno' idea. The statement about Europe ends with the challenge about a united Germany in EDC or NATO, for which Russia is to give up the Eastern Zone. Many people would think that we were deliberately riding for a fall. Perhaps we are.

'I understand,' Churchill added, 'this draft is to be submitted to us at 5 p.m., and I hope it will be understood that it is only a draft.' [3] 'I am doing my best with it,' Eden replied, 'without much success.' [4]

[1] Colville diary, 6 December 1953: *The Fringes of Power*, pages 685–7.
[2] 'Bermuda Meeting', 'Tripartite—Heads of Government', 'Fourth Plenary Session', 'Plenary Minutes 4', 'Secret', 12 noon, 7 December 1953: Eisenhower papers.
[3] Prime Minister's Personal Minute No. 330 of 1953, 7 December 1953: Premier papers, 11/418.
[4] Note by Eden initialled 'AE' and Prime Minister's Personal Minute No. 330 of 1953.

That afternoon, at the fifth Plenary meeting, Churchill spoke first of the continuing French struggle in Indo-China, contrasting it with Britain's own withdrawal from India six years earlier:

... he would like to pay his heartfelt compliments to France for her valiant effort to preserve her empire and the cause of freedom in Indo-China. He greatly admired her exertions and was sorry insofar as his own country was concerned that they had not been able to match these efforts on the vast sub-continent of India. This was a colossal disaster which he had lived to see and would leave its imprint on the future. He might not live to see it, but many of those around the table would realize what a great misfortune it was when Great Britain cast away her duties in India. He admired France and envied the record she had established under such difficult conditions.

He also felt impelled to say how much he admired the splendid work of France in North Africa and in Tunisia. He had often been there and had been struck by the wonderful manner in which the French cherished and nourished the civilization they had implanted. He earnestly hoped that all the powers allied with France would endeavour to lend their moral support and aid in the difficult task which she had undertaken with so much skill and resolution. The British had a small but costly preoccupation in Malaya. There the situation was improving and they had not the slightest intention of wavering in their effort. He only wished to pay this tribute to France. He felt it was a great mistake to suppose that the ancient powers of Europe had not made a contribution to the progress of these races in Asia and that all they had done was obsolete and that it was good that it had passed away. He said he hoped that France would courageously persevere in her efforts.

'Dark days lie ahead in Asia,' Churchill continued, 'as a result of those who thought that they could do without the guidance and aid of the European nations to whom they owed so much. He would say no more on this subject. He knew it was not a popular thing at present but he had done his utmost for it all the days of his life.'

As to the struggle in South-East Asia, Churchill said, he 'wished only the best of good fortune to France and to express his gratitude to the United States for giving aid to Indo-China and this aid will be found to have been farseeing'.

It was Bidault who then asked the Conference if it could discuss the problem of assurances in regard to European security, and the part which relations with the Soviet Union would play in this. As this was a clear reference to Churchill's desire for détente, Churchill set out his arguments in favour of the policy which he had come to Bermuda to assert, telling the Conference:

... there was great difficulty in finding something which would please the Russians – which he was anxious to do—because they have already taken everything they could lay their hands on and now we were looking around to find something they had not taken and could not. This was a great pity.

When the Second World War was in its late phases he had been profoundly impressed with the deep grievance and passionate desire of the Soviets for effective protection against another Hitler or something like it, and he had felt the deepest sympathy with that anxiety. If they had not been carried away by victory, something much better for all would have been feasible.

Looking around after they have treated us so badly in the last few years, he still thought one ought not to fail to do for them what was just or express willingness to do it. He would hope that full assurances could be given them not only to the effect that our organization was an absolutely defensive one in nature, but that if they were wrongfully attacked, we should aid and support them. He felt this note should be struck. He had tried to strike it some months ago and it was still audible. We should do something to reassure them.

Such was Churchill's argument in favour of an attempt at détente, but he did not neglect the aspect with which the French, and the Americans, were so concerned. Reassuring the Russians, he said, 'was a minor thing compared to the need of maintaining our unity and self-defence. We should give them the feeling that what was right and just when they were behaving well had not ceased to be right and just at a time when we might believe that they were inclined to behave badly. He felt this note should be struck and played upon.' Churchill added: 'It would be very difficult to make any arrangement if we could not do anything of interest to them. They ought to have freedom of access to the broad waters.' He had 'never contemplated that we should commit ourselves to recognizing the present state of affairs in the satellites. We should try to make clear that we would not try to end this by violence but by allowing time, patience and perhaps good fortune to work. That was the note he would like to see.' Churchill then told the Conference:

In the draft communiqué there were nine notes of strength and unity for a strong front. He felt we could afford to strike one note which, at any rate, would give the sense that we wished them no harm and would feel it our duty to help them if they were maltreated or assaulted, that we would instantly play our part on their side as intended if they were right. He felt it would be well to use such language now. He was sure it would now be welcomed on the other side by the governments at least. It might help to alleviate the suffering and tyranny which prevails.

He had read many phrases in the communiqué on one side, and few on what he called Locarnoism or reassurances. The other way would make the balance better and provide steady and continuous improvement. He recognized all the way through that this was only a very small counterpoise to the main effort which must absorb all our energies and brains.[1]

---

[1] 'Bermuda Meeting', 'Tripartite—Heads of Government', 'Fifth Plenary Session', 'Plenary Minutes 5', 'Secret', 5.30 p.m., 7 December 1953: Eisenhower papers.

The sixth and final Plenary meeting was held that night. On the question of Egypt, Churchill was unable to persuade the Americans to support Britain's position that for the troops withdrawn from Egypt there must be a joint Anglo-American plan of redeployment within the NATO strategic defence system. On the question of negotiations with Russia, too, the principal object and driving force of Churchill's transatlantic journey, he was unable to persuade Foster Dulles to change his mind, telling Lord Moran on the night of December 7:

'. . . it seems that everything is left to Dulles. It appears that the President is no more than a ventriloquist's doll.'

He said no more for a time. Then he said:

'This fellow preaches like a Methodist Minister, and his bloody text is always the same: That nothing but evil can come out of meeting with Malenkov.'

There was a long pause.

'Dulles is a terrible handicap.' His voice rose. 'Ten years ago I could have dealt with him. Even as it is I have not been defeated by this bastard. I have been humiliated by my own decay. Ah, no, Charles, you have done all that could be done to slow things down.'

When I turned round he was in tears. That was the last I heard of Moscow while we were at Bermuda.[1]

One important aspect of the Bermuda meeting concerned the future of Anglo-American co-operation in the sphere of nuclear policy. On December 7 Churchill wrote to Eisenhower, from the Mid-Ocean Club, to summarize what had been decided:

We agreed, did we not, that Admiral Strauss and Lord Cherwell should compile a White Paper of the documents, and their linking together, which constitute the story of Anglo-American relations about the Atomic Bomb. You and I will then consider and discuss whether it will be helpful or not to publish. Personally I think it will be. We both desire a fuller interchange of intelligence and the fact that secrecy is evaporating through growth of knowledge between us, and alas between both of us and Soviet Russia, makes it desirable that we two should make the best joint progress we can.

'Your speech,' Churchill added by way of encouragement, 'will, I think, encourage the new atmosphere.'[2]

On the morning of December 8 Churchill went to see Eisenhower on another serious concern, the Egyptian problem. He was anxious for the Americans to stop sending arms to Egypt, telling Eisenhower, as he later told Colville, 'that the Americans sending arms to Egypt after January 1st would have no less effect in the UK than the British

---

[1] Moran diary, 7 December 1953: *The Struggle for Survival*, pages 507-9.
[2] 'President from Prime Minister', 'Secret', initialled 'WSC', 7 December 1953: Eisenhower papers.

sending arms to China would have in the USA'. The President, said Churchill, 'took this seriously'.

It was their last meeting at Bermuda. Eisenhower left before lunch to return to the United States, where, that same day, he placed before the United Nations a set of proposals for the international control of atomic energy.

At Bermuda on December 8, the French delegation lunched with Churchill, before making its own departure. 'W said to Bidault,' Colville recorded, 'that if he had been rough on the French it was not because he loved them less than formerly, but because he wanted to urge them to save themselves and not, in consequence of refusing EDC, to force the Americans to fall back on a "peripheral" defence of Europe.' [1]

On December 9 Churchill remained at Bermuda with the British delegation. 'I hope,' his wife had written on the previous afternoon, 'that now the heavy work of the Conference is over you will have a little sunshine & rest before flying home.' It was very hard, she added, 'to judge by the newspapers what has been achieved. The general impression is that the French have been as tiresome, obstructive & odious as usual,' and she added: 'I am sure you were right to insist on this meeting.' [2]

Clementine Churchill was flying that evening to Stockholm, with her daughter Mary, to receive the Nobel Prize for Literature on her husband's behalf.

When Lord Moran saw Churchill after breakfast on December 9, his patient told him 'he had had some twitching in his foot' and would have 'an easy day'. The Governor would drive him round the island in the morning, and he had promised to inspect the Bermuda troops in the afternoon. At dinner that night, Lord Ismay, Secretary General of NATO, was also present. Moran recorded some of the discussion, which centred upon Britain's defences against a Russian attack:

> Pug felt the strength of the Russians had been exaggerated. In the event of war they would have long lines of communication, and would always be looking back over their shoulders at Poland and the other satellite countries. The PM agreed they were probably not so strong as people thought, but even if they were only a third as strong we had no real defences in Europe to hold them back.

---

[1] Colville diary, 8 December 1953: *The Fringes of Power*, pages 688–9.
[2] 'My darling', 2 p.m., 8 December 1953: Churchill papers, 1/50.

As long as this discussion went on the PM remained alert and interested. He was particularly scornful of the lack of proportion shown in the allocation of the House's time for debate—two days for TV and only one day for foreign affairs and atomic war. He might be out of date, but to him it sounded fantastic.[1]

Churchill decided to dictate a letter to R. A. Butler on this subject. 'He rang for a secretary to take it down,' Moran noted, 'but there was no one in the private office and no one in the Foreign Secretary's office. Everyone, it appeared, had gone bathing by moonlight. The PM became very irritable. He would never again bring only two private secretaries to a conference. At this point Anthony volunteered to take down the PM's words, and it was in this manner that the letter took shape.'[2]

On the morning of December 10, Colville found Churchill 'in a cantankerous frame of mind'.[3] It was time to go home. But the aircraft was not due to come until the evening. After lunch, as Moran recorded, Churchill went by car to the beach, where 'leaning on his stick and on a detective, he descended a steep sand dune. At the bottom there was a rock, about twice a man's height. Up this, to everybody's amazement and consternation, he proceeded to crawl. We got him down eventually and pulled and pushed him up the dune. At the top he stood getting his breath, perspiring profusely.'

Having recovered his breath, Churchill then 'insisted', Moran noted, on driving to the aquarium eight miles distant. 'Christopher said I was against it,' Moran added. 'The PM had done enough.' But Churchill 'dismissed such counsels of weakness and climbed into his car. . . .'[4]

At eight o'clock that evening Churchill left Bermuda by air for Britain. He reached London at 11.30 on the following morning, December 11. While he had been spending his final day in Bermuda, Clementine Churchill was in Stockholm accepting the Nobel Prize for Literature on his behalf.[5]

There were those who thought that Churchill should have been awarded the Nobel Prize for Peace. Ironically, the prize for literature came on the day of his greatest disappointment since the war, to build at Bermuda a path to the Summit which, as he had envisaged it, would also have been a path to peace.

---

[1] On 25 March 1954 the House of Commons passed the second reading of the Television Bill, which set up independent television in Britain.

[2] Moran diary, 9 December 1953: *The Struggle for Survival*, pages 510–11.

[3] Colville diary, 10 December 1953: *The Fringes of Power*, pages 689–90.

[4] Moran diary, 10 December 1953: *The Struggle for Survival*, pages 511–12.

[5] On 11 December 1953 the prize, £12,093, was paid into his account at Lloyds Bank, 6 Pall Mall. 'I should like to add my congratulations and best wishes,' wrote his Bank Manager, A. L. Ball. (Letter of 11 December 1953: Churchill papers, 1/14.)

On his return from Bermuda, Churchill found that many Conservative MPs were deeply uneasy about the course of the Egyptian negotiations. They feared that Britain was abandoning her one remaining position of strength in the Middle East. On December 16, before a luncheon meeting of the backbench 1922 Committee, Churchill explained to the Cabinet that he would do his utmost 'to assure Government supporters generally that the Government's policy in the negotiations was not in any way based on fear of what the Egyptians might do but on a realistic appraisal of our own interests, and he could appeal to them to have faith that the Government would continue to handle the situation with firmness and cool judgement'.[1]

The meeting itself went well. 'There were two hundred members of the Committee present,' Churchill told Lord Moran that night, 'one of our largest meetings. They were very friendly, singing "For He's a Jolly Good Fellow". I think they took what I said to them, it was quite plain spoken. I was very firm, telling them that we should not be deterred from doing what we thought was right, either by the violence of our enemies or even by the eloquence of our best friends.' Churchill added: 'I dominated and conquered the committee. I spoke for twenty-five minutes. I did not prepare anything. I did not give it ten minutes' thought. Some of the Tories had been very worked up about Suez. . . .'[2]

On December 17 Churchill spoke in the House of Commons. His opening words reflected one of his remarks at Bermuda. 'The curious fact,' he said, 'that the House prefers to give two days to the television White Paper and only one day to foreign affairs may be noted by future historians as an example of a changing sense of proportion in modern thought.' It was, however, 'also a proof of how great a measure of agreement exists between our established parties on the present handling of foreign affairs'.

Speaking first about Egypt, Churchill reiterated that, despite 'a constant stream of minor outrages' on British troops in the Canal Zone. 'We remain convinced, however, that it is in our interests, military and financial, to procure a replacement of our forces in North Africa and the Middle East.'

Turning to the Bermuda Conference, and his hopes for an eventual meeting with the Russian leaders, Churchill told the House of Commons that he had used the opportunity of the Conference 'to emphasize the view which I expressed here on 11 May that the Soviet Union is entitled to assurances against aggression after what she

---

[1] Cabinet Conclusions No. 78 of 1953, 'Secret', 6.45 p.m., 14 December 1953: Cabinet papers, 128/26.
[2] Moran diary, 16 December 1953: *The Struggle for Survival*, page 513.

suffered at Hitler's hands. I think I was successful in impressing upon my colleagues at Bermuda the justice and the advantage of such a course, even though Russian strength is so vast.' It was his hope that from the Foreign Ministers' meeting planned for January 4, 'there may emerge some means of providing the Russians with a sense of security arising from other facts than mere force. The whole world is in need of that.' [1]

In regard to French hostility to the European Defence Community, Churchill sought on December 19 to put Eisenhower's mind at rest. 'If EDC is repudiated by the French,' he wrote, 'I still think some variant of NATO will be necessary. After all, this meets the French objection to being in a European association alone or almost alone with a much more powerful Germany. I think you would find it very difficult to make and get a good plan on the "empty chair" basis.' [2]

Of Eisenhower's proposal of December 8, for the international control of atomic energy, Churchill told the House of Commons:

I consider this speech of the President as one of the most important events in world history since the end of the war. A few weeks ago, I spoke to the House about the ever-increasing destructive power which has now come into human hands, and also about the almost limitless material benefits which science can for the first time give to a peaceful age.

As I meditated on the President's proposals, limited though they are in scope, and shrouded in technicalities as they are for laymen, I could not help feeling that we were in the process of what might prove to be a turning point in our destiny.

I fervently hope that the Soviet Government will not ignore this beam of light through much darkness and confusion. I am sure of the sincerity and altruistic good-will by which it was inspired, and I trust that they will advance with confidence, to which their own strength entitles them, along a path which certainly leads in the direction of expanding the welfare and calming the fears of the masses of the people of all the world. [3]

In his search for an early summit, Churchill did not dismiss out of hand the American hesitations. 'American anxiety about Russian rearmament must be borne in mind,' he wrote to Richard Stokes, Labour MP for Ipswich. 'We cannot get through without them.' [4]

In the last week of December, Churchill saw the Soviet Ambassador, Yakov Malik, who was returning briefly to Moscow. [5] 'I impressed two things on him,' Churchill telegraphed to Eisenhower. 'Firstly that

---

[1] Speech of 17 December 1953: *Hansard*.

[2] 'My dear friend', 19 December 1953: Eisenhower papers.

[3] Speech of 17 December 1953: *Hansard*.

[4] Letter of 21 December 1953: Churchill papers, 2/199. Stokes had been Minister of Works, 1950–51 and Minister of Materials, 1951. From 1914 to 1918 he had served with the Royal Artillery, winning the MC and bar, and the Croix de Guerre.

[5] Malik was Soviet Ambassador in London from 1953 to 1960. From 1968 to 1976 he was the Permanent Soviet Representative at the United Nations.

your atomic proposal was not a mere propaganda move but a sincere attempt to break the deadlock and, though on a small scale, might well achieve invaluable results and also open fruitful contacts. Secondly, there was no chance of splitting the English-Speaking world, though we use our common language to argue about a lot of things.'

Churchill also sent Eisenhower his thoughts on the new French President, René Coty, and his attitude:

Coty has for long been a keen supporter of European movements and has frequently spoken in favour of the European Defence Community. I think we might easily have got someone worse. Anyhow no one can now say that Foster's outspoken warning, which I supported, has done any harm. It seems that in France in order to get on you have to be unknown. It is different in our two democracies where a certain amount of publicity is not necessarily always a drawback.[1]

At a meeting of the Cabinet on December 29, R. A. Butler had proposed the release of a further £5 million to Egypt. Failure to do so, he said, would, under the terms of the 1951 Anglo-Egyptian agreement, 'involve a direct breach of an international agreement and a consequent loss of confidence in sterling. He would prefer that the £10 millions should also be released on 1st January.'

Churchill, speaking next, said that he was 'most reluctant to see this money paid to Egypt at a time when she was showing such hostility to us. He was particularly embarrassed at the thought that this should be done when, with the Foreign Secretary's concurrence, he had been pressing the President of the United States to delay the grant of economic aid to Egypt.' If Britain now released sterling balances, Churchill said, as proposed by Butler, 'we might lay ourselves open to the reproach that we were trying to win from the Egyptians favours which we wished to deny to the United States'.

In the discussions that followed, Eden supported Butler. The American administration, he said, 'would appreciate the difference between the two transactions. We should be repaying the debt in accordance with an international agreement; but the United States were being asked to postpone giving new money for development projects in Egypt which would bring benefits to American engineering contractors. He agreed with the Chancellor of the Exchequer that to withhold the promised instalments of Egypt's sterling balances might lead to a loss of confidence in sterling.' It might 'in particular', Eden added, 'prompt other Arab countries, notably Kuwait, to withdraw sterling balances which were not governed by any formal agreement'.

---

[1] 'Top Secret', signed 'Winston', undated: Eisenhower papers. Coty was President of France from 24 December 1953 to 21 December 1958, when he was succeeded by General de Gaulle.

Churchill was out-argued and overruled; it was agreed to release the £5 million in accordance with the terms of the agreement. As to the continuing defence negotiations with Egypt, here Churchill's views were supported by his colleagues. The time had now come, he said, 'to bring to a head the defence negotiations with Egypt', and he suggested that 'unless the Egyptian Government agreed in the very near future to accept our latest proposals, we should declare that after a specified date these proposals would lapse and we should regard ourselves as free to make our own plans. We should then begin to carry out a vigorous and effective redeployment of our forces in the Middle East.' It was Eden, however, who warned the Cabinet that if Britain withdrew from Egypt without an agreement, 'we should have lost the right of return and might have weakened our influence with other Arab states'.[1]

At Chequers on Christmas Day 1953, Churchill gave his wife a gift of money. 'My darling Beloved Clemmie,' he wrote, 'I hope you will ask Brendan to invest this for you. It may come in handy on some Christmas I shall not see.' And of their Christmas festivities he wrote: 'How wonderfully you have organised it all this time! With all my fondest love, your devoted husband, W.'[2]

That day, at noon, Churchill received a letter from the Queen, written a week earlier on board SS *Gothic*, then approaching Fiji. 'We have followed with interest,' the Queen wrote, 'the news of the Bermuda Conference and all it implies for the good of the world. I hope you are satisfied with the way it went and I trust you did not find it too strenuous.'[3] Churchill replied seven days later, in his own hand:

Madam,

On Christmas Day at noon precisely I received Yr Majesty's most kind and gracious letter and photograph. My wife and I cherish this token of Yr Majesty's thought, and memento of our most pleasant visit to Balmoral (and the Leger!).

Today I have the belief that the New Year starts well and good hopes that its end may be better still. If this shd prove true it will be largely due to the sparkle, youth and unity which the amazing exertions of Yr Majesty and the Duke are making for the sake of our world-wide but hard-pressed combination. My only misgiving is lest too much may be drawn from You by the love and admiration of your subjects in so many lands.[4]

[1] Cabinet Conclusions No. 81 of 1951, 'Secret', 3 p.m., 29 December 1953: Cabinet papers, 128/26.
[2] 'My darling Beloved Clemmie', 25 December 1953: Spencer-Churchill papers.
[3] 'My dear Prime Minister', SS *Gothic*, at sea, 16 December 1953: Squerryes Lodge Archive.
[4] 'Madam', Chartwell, 1 January 1954: Squerryes Lodge Archive.

49

'Unimaginable horrors'

T H E seventy-nine-year-old Prime Minister, victim of a stroke in
June 1953, was now expected to retire at some time in 1954. At
one point it was the Queen's return from Australia in May that seemed
the appropriate or at least the likely moment. 'I had a long yarn with
our friend at lunch & continued at dinner time,' Brendan Bracken
wrote to Lord Beaverbrook on 30 December 1953. 'He intends to give
up before June—in fact he thought of resigning before Parliament
meets next month.' Bracken added: 'I think this decision is quite definite. Though his health is not worse & he gets through a lot of work,
the desire for office has diminished rapidly. I shd think he will spend
next winter in Bermuda. He plans to write another book and to polish
up another, hurriedly put together before the war but still unpublished. This shd be a good earner.' [1]

Despite the setback of the Bermuda Conference, Churchill had no
intention of abandoning his hopes of a summit meeting with the Russians. When, in the first week of January 1954, Eden reported on an
American plan to give military aid to Pakistan, and link it with 'the
initiation of some military collaboration' between Pakistan and
Turkey, Churchill, while not opposed to such a military association
'on its merits', felt that the timing was wrong. It was, he said, 'highly
undesirable that this project should be announced immediately before
the Four-Power Meeting in Berlin. It could do nothing for the moment
to increase the military strength of the West, and it was bound to be
regarded by the Soviet Government as a provocative gesture.'

The announcement at this moment of such a military association
and military aid was likely, Churchill said, 'to increase Soviet
suspicions of American intentions and might even be taken to imply
that the Americans were not anxious to reach any agreement at the
Four-Power Meeting'. Public opinion, in Britain and abroad, 'had high

[1] Letter of 30 December 1953: Beaverbrook papers.

hopes of that Meeting; and, if it led to nothing, the responsibility for the breakdown should be clearly seen to rest with the Soviet Government'. Britain at any rate, Churchill argued, 'should have no part in any action or announcement in advance of the Meeting which seemed calculated to impair what chances it had of producing satisfactory results'. These arguments 'should be forcibly presented to the United States Government'.[1]

In Cabinet on January 18, during a discussion of what goods should or should not be exported to the Soviet Union, and to what extent this list should be co-ordinated with the United States, Churchill spoke in favour of 'increased trade' with the Soviet bloc. Such trade, he said, 'would mean, not only assistance to our exports, but greater possibilities for infiltration behind the Iron Curtain. Determined efforts should be made,' he added, 'to persuade the United States Government to accept a new policy in this matter.' The policy which he suggested, Churchill went on to explain, 'was that we should in future deny to the Soviet *bloc* only goods of direct military value, and should no longer seek to prevent the export of goods which would help merely to strengthen their industrial economy'. The existing lists 'should at once be revised on that basis'.[2] At a meeting of Ministers on January 25, Churchill added that 'practical prospects of increased trade' with the Soviet bloc 'might prove a valuable factor in negotiations with the Soviet Union if the political discussions in Berlin proved abortive'.[3]

Churchill's plan did not find favour with Eisenhower, who two months later indicated that 'while the United States Government were prepared to go some way in contracting and simplifying these controls, he felt that the United Kingdom proposals went further than public and Congressional opinion in the United States would be able to accept'. In particular, Eisenhower considered that the controls should continue to extend 'to equipment and materials which were of high value to the Soviet war potential, and that quantitative restrictions should be retained as part of the mechanism of control'.[4]

Churchill's search for a new policy towards the Soviet Union went much wider than the question of trade. The search for 'friendly relations' with Russia, he explained to Eden on January 27, was not contradictory 'to forming the strongest combination possible against

---

[1] Cabinet Conclusions No. 1 of 1954, 'Secret', 3 p.m., 7 January 1954: Cabinet papers, 128/27.

[2] Cabinet Conclusions No. 3 of 1954, 'Secret', 3.30 p.m., 18 January 1954: Cabinet papers, 128/27.

[3] 'East/West Trade', 1st Meeting, 'Secret', 4.30 p.m., 25 January 1954: Cabinet papers, 130/99.

[4] Cabinet Conclusions No. 22 of 1954, 'Secret', 11.30 a.m., 24 March 1954: Cabinet papers, 128/27.

Soviet aggression. On the contrary it may well be true that the Russians can only be friends and live decently with those who are as strong or stronger than they are themselves.'[1]

Another area in the sphere of Foreign Affairs over which Churchill kept a vigilant eye was the relationship between the State of Israel and its Arab neighbours. When, in the third week of January 1954, the Egyptian Government announced that it would intensify its blockade of Israel, including preventing Israeli ships, or even ships bound for Israel, from using the Suez Canal, Churchill told his Cabinet that such a blockade would lead to increased 'interference' with the passage of ships through the Suez Canal and the blacklisting by Egypt of many ships of all flags trading with the Levant. The Israeli Government were proposing to raise the matter in the Security Council 'and had asked whether they could count on our support and that of the United States Government'. He hoped 'we should give prompt and effective support to the Israel Government in this matter'. In Parliament members of all parties would welcome 'an initiative designed to assert the rights of free transit through the Canal; and it would be convenient if we could transfer the emphasis, in our current differences with Egypt, from the Base to the Canal'.

Commenting on this, Eden told the Cabinet that it should realize 'that the Egyptian Government had legal grounds for their action, in that their war with Israel had not legally been terminated. It was therefore desirable that we should not take any public position in this matter until we had assured ourselves that we should have the support of some of the other maritime Powers.' The Cabinet then 'invited' Eden to try to enlist the support of those maritime Powers for the protest which Israel proposed to make in the Security Council.[2]

When nothing had been achieved in this regard after five days, Churchill raised the matter again, stressing at the Cabinet of January 26 'the importance of upholding the right of international passage through the Suez Canal and the Parliamentary advantages of putting this issue in the forefront of our differences with Egypt'. He hoped, therefore, 'that no effort would be spared in enlisting the support of leading maritime Powers for the protest which Israel wished to make in the Security Council against the Egyptian decision to intensify the blockade'.[3]

[1] Prime Minister's Personal Telegram, T.9 of 1954, 27 January 1954: Premier papers, 11/665.
[2] Cabinet Conclusions No. 4 of 1954, 'Secret', 11.30 a.m., 21 January 1954: Cabinet papers, 128/27.
[3] Cabinet Conclusions No. 5 of 1954, 'Secret', 11.30 a.m., 26 January 1954: Cabinet papers, 128/27.

Churchill's call to support Israel came at a time when the Egyptian defence treaty was nearing its conclusion. At Cabinet on January 28 Churchill asked whether, with a force of 10,000 as allowed by the proposed treaty, Britain could 'hold both ends of the Canal so that we could safeguard the rights of free navigation and also preserve our power to control the supply of oil to the Delta'. In reply, Alexander was emphatic that 'with this small number of troops we could not hope to defend the whole Base area or secure rights of navigation through the Canal against open hostilities by the Egyptian army'. The Egyptian army was, he added, believed to be short of ammunition and therefore unable to sustain hostilities 'for any length of time'. On the other hand, Alexander noted, 'hatred and bitterness were powerful factors in sustaining the morale of an army and it could not be assumed that the Egyptians would not fight well. In these circumstances the best military course would be to hold a perimeter round Suez, including one airfield.'[1]

'It was evident,' Churchill told the Cabinet six days later, 'from the record of a conversation between Gamal Abdul Nasser[2] and a member of Her Majesty's Embassy that the Egyptians felt that time was on their side and that it was of no advantage to them to conclude an agreement. Our interests, on the other hand, were ill-served by a protraction of the negotiations, which would prevent us from making progress with the re-deployment of our forces. . . .'[3]

Randolph Churchill, preparing himself to be his father's biographer, now sent him a further book which he had written, a short study of Blenheim Palace. 'I should think the book will be popular,' Churchill replied, 'with the growing company who like to look at the contrast between the past and the clatter of the present.'[4] Randolph now wrote again, to say that he was 'getting down in earnest' to a biography of the 17th Earl of Derby, and asking for letters and materials from Churchill's own files.[5] Churchill gave him the materials he wanted, and Randolph set about writing the book which he hoped would convince his father that he would make a good biographer.

[1] Cabinet Conclusions No. 6 of 1954, 'Secret', 11.30 a.m., 28 January 1954: Cabinet papers, 128/27.

[2] Colonel Gamal Abdul Nasser, founder of the Free Officers Movement which had overthrown the monarchy and brought Neguib to power in July 1952, had been Deputy President to Neguib since 1953 as well as Minister of the Interior. In April 1954 he became Prime Minister of Egypt. He succeeded Neguib as President seven months later.

[3] Cabinet Conclusions No. 7 of 1954, 'Secret', 11.30 a.m., 3 February 1954: Cabinet papers, 128/27.

[4] 'My dear Randolph', 9 January 1954: Churchill papers, 1/51.

[5] 'My dearest Papa', 12 January 1954: Churchill papers, 1/51.

On January 1 Churchill's friend of four and a half decades, Viscount Norwich, formerly Alfred Duff Cooper, died at the age of sixty-four. 'Diana was greatly touched that you came to Duff's Memorial Service,' Randolph told his father, 'and was much pleased that she ran into you.' [1]

The death of friends was now a frequent occurrence in Churchill's life. But his own vitality still seemed remarkable. On January 21 Lord Moran noted the following conversation in his diary. After Churchill had told him he was 'getting anxious' about his chest, he went on:

'But my walking is better. I can stride up the Lobby of the House of Commons quite briskly if I put my mind to it. You know, Charles, I am less keen than I was on the political scene. I don't know where I am.'

I asked him if he had any speeches hanging over him.

He grinned.

'Well, I ought to have. I told Woolton that I had been reading *The Dynasts* for hours on end. He wondered how I found the time. I explained that I didn't bother about other things as much as I used to do.'

Winston continued: 'The *Manchester Guardian* is very fair to me. Did you see what their Parliamentary Correspondent said?' [2] Then, testily. 'You don't read the papers, Charles. He wrote that there was clearly no physical reason why the Prime Minister should put off his harness at this particular moment.'

He handed me the paper. I read that, while other Ministers snoozed or looked vacant when not answering their own Questions, the PM's mind was always active. But the truth is that he no longer follows the course of events as he did. He reads a novel or plays bezique with Clemmie, or sometimes just potters.

Moran's diary continued:

He showed me a scar on his right arm.

That's where I gave some skin for grafting to Dick Molyneux after the battle of Omdurman—it hurt like the devil. His death is in today's paper.' [3]

---

[1] 'My dearest Papa', 12 January 1954: Churchill papers, 1/51.

[2] In 1953 the Parliamentary correspondent (or 'sketch writer') of the *Manchester Guardian* was Harry Boardman (who had been the paper's Lobby correspondent and sole Parliamentary representative during the war). When, at the end of Churchill's second premiership, he was invited to Churchill's room in the House of Commons, it was taken by his fellow Parliamentary correspondents to be a signal honour. He died in 1958. His book *The Glory of Parliament* was published two years later, edited by Francis Boyd, who wrote, of the 'unusual' visit to Churchill's room: 'Boardman was very flattered by Churchill's invitation and very discreet about it. "We just had a talk", was all he would say to me. The Press Gallery assumed that Churchill had offered Boardman some kind of honour, but if he did Boardman must have refused it. Boardman was regarded 'by some colleagues', Boyd added, 'as Churchill's fugleman among the daily press'. (Sir Francis Boyd recollections: letter to the author, 4 October 1987.)

[3] Major the Hon. Sir Richard F. Molyneux, KCVO, third son of the 4th Earl of Sefton. He had died on 20 January 1954. Born a year before Churchill, he had served on the North-West Frontier of India, in the Sudan, at the battle of Omdurman (1898), in South Africa (1899-1900)

The PM grinned. 'He will take my skin with him, a kind of advance guard, into the next world.'[1]

When, six days later, Lord Stanhope wrote to Churchill to ask if he could give his uniform of the Warden of the Cinque Ports to the National Maritime Museum, Churchill noted for his Private Secretary, Anthony Montague Browne: 'The uniform is worn out & I am not yet dead.'[2]

He was certainly not yet dead: on January 31 Lord Thurso wrote to Lord Beaverbrook of how, at the Other Club on January 28, 'we were all talking noisily with Winston at his gayest'. Thurso added:

Marigold and I spent the night at No. 10 and I saw Winston again the next morning. Neither at night nor in the middle of his morning's work was there any trace of tiredness—still less of weakness or lethargy. The newspaper accounts of his dominance over the House of Commons are not misleading. He still radiates gaiety & power and his authority is unimpaired. If & when he retires I imagine that the Socialists will not be slow to force an election.[3]

On February 1 Churchill spoke in the House of Commons on the new Army rifle. At one point, when he was explaining that the rifle, chosen and recommended by both the War Office and the Ministry of Defence, had seemed to him to embody many important characteristics, there was an interruption:

Mr James Callaghan (Cardiff, South-East): Have the Americans accepted it?

The Prime Minister: As hon. Gentlemen on that side of the House are always looking round in every controversy, even in this one about rifles, to try to find fault with the Americans, I suppose if I were to say that the Americans had accepted it, the hon. Gentleman would regard it as a further argument against the rifle.

There were many further interruptions, so malicious in their tone and content that Churchill was provoked to declare, in the final moments of his speech: 'I wish to conclude. I would have concluded long ago but for the extraordinary rowdiness and malice with which I have been received. I do not ask for any favours of any kind from hon. Gentlemen opposite, but I must say I think they show themselves

---

and on the Western Front (1914–15). On 22 January 1945 Molyneux had written to Churchill recalling the day in 1898 when Churchill had given a piece of his own skin in order to heal Molyneux's wound. 'I never mention and always conceal it,' Molyneux wrote, 'for fear people might think I was bucking.' 'Thank you so much, dear Dick,' Churchill replied. 'I often think of those old days, and I should like to feel that you showed the bit of pelt. I have frequently shown the gap from which it was taken.'

[1] Moran diary, 21 January 1954: *The Struggle for Survival*, pages 521–2.

[2] Note of 27 January 1954: Churchill papers, 2/342.

[3] Letter of 31 January 1954: Beaverbrook papers. Lord Thurso (formerly Sir Archibald Sinclair), Churchill's friend of forty years, had been his second-in-command in the trenches in 1916.

very unsuited to have calm judgement on a complicated matter of this kind. . . .' [1]

The malice had been particularly evident in the remarks by a Labour MP, Woodrow Wyatt, who declared, of the Government's claim that the new rifle had been adequately tested: 'It may be that there has been a lot of rather partial testing, a partial presentation of this case by those concerned to please the Prime Minister in this matter.' [2] Both Anthony Head and Churchill, he said, were in this matter 'lacking in patriotism'. Nor, added Wyatt, did Churchill understand the point about standardization of ammunition: 'He has shown a weakness quite unworthy of him towards the United States and their determination not to have a British weapon.' As to the American rifle, Wyatt added: 'The Prime Minister said it was nicer to use on manual exercises. If the right hon. Gentleman thinks that future wars will be won by PT squads demonstrating manual exercises with the rifle, that is the most childish argument we have heard advanced against the British rifle.'

Wyatt's remarks were consistently hostile. A few moments later he said : 'if the Prime Minister had ever bothered to examine the British rifle properly, which is something he has not troubled to do. . . .' and later: 'The Prime Minister wants to meet the new jet age with the butt end of a rifle.'

At one point in the debate, as tempers rose on the Labour benches, Churchill remarked: 'I am not at all alarmed by being shouted at. In fact, I rather like it.' [3]

In Cabinet on February 3, Churchill made his first intervention on a question which had begun to loom on the political horizon, the possibility of legislative restrictions on coloured immigration from the Commonwealth. The 'rapid improvement of communications', he said 'was likely to lead to a continuing increase in the number of coloured people coming to this country, and their presence here would sooner or later come to be resented by large sections of the British people'. It might well be true, however, Churchill added, 'that the problem had not yet assumed sufficient proportions to enable the Government to take adequate counter-measures'. [4]

[1] Speech of 1 February 1954: *Hansard*. The new rifle, which was chosen in place of the traditional .303 and the .280 which the Labour Government had adopted in April 1951, was the Belgian FN (Fabrique Nationale) rifle. Churchill himself fired the FN rifle at a makeshift range at Chequers, watched by General Pownall and Denis Kelly.

[2] Woodrow Wyatt had been Parliamentary Under-Secretary of State and Financial Secretary at the War Office from May to October 1951.

[3] *Hansard*, 1 February 1954. Following Churchill's return to the House of Commons after his stroke in 1953, it was Woodrow Wyatt who had risen at question time to say: 'May I ask the Prime Minister whether he is aware that the House of Commons is a duller place without him?'

[4] Cabinet Conclusions No. 7 of 1954, 'Secret', 11 a.m., 3 February 1954: Cabinet papers, 128/27.

The call for Churchill's resignation, which had become a regular one in the pages of the *Daily Mirror*, now spread more widely. Churchill's friends rallied to his support. 'I believe that your presence here,' Bracken wrote to Beaverbrook in the aftermath of the debate on February 1, 'will be an encouragement to our old friend who inevitably passes through long periods of depression.'[1] On February 4 Lord Moran wrote in his diary:

The PM rose, went over to a table and, opening *Punch*, handed it to me.

'They have been attacking me. It isn't really a proper cartoon. You have seen it?

'Yes, there's malice in it. The *Mirror* has had nothing so hostile. Look at my hands—I have beautiful hands.'

It was true. Those podgy, shapeless hands, peering out from a great expanse of white cuff, were not his. I was shocked by this vicious cartoon; there was something un-English in this savage attack on his failing powers. The eyes were dull and lifeless. There was no tone in the flaccid muscles; the jowl sagged. It was the expressionless mask of extreme old age. Under this venomous drawing was inscribed this caption:

'Man goeth forth unto his work and to his labour until the evening.'

On the opposite page the editor of *Punch*, Malcolm Muggeridge, supported this attack on Churchill's decline in an effusion entitled: 'A story without an Ending'. It was full of spleen. Writing ostensibly of a Byzantine ruler, Belisarius, he wrote:

'By this time he had reached an advanced age. . . . His splendid faculties . . . began to falter. The spectacle of him thus clutching wearily at all the appurtenances and responsibilities of an authority he could no longer fully exercise was to his admirers infinitely sorrowful, and to his enemies infinitely derisory.'[2]

So it had come to this. Winston was hurt. Then, with an effort, he seemed to pull himself together.

'*Punch* goes everywhere. I shall have to retire if this sort of thing goes on. I must make a speech in a fortnight's time,' Winston continued; 'it is necessary when things like this happen.'[3]

On February 9 Churchill was in the Chair at a meeting of the Defence Committee. Defence expenditure was rising, and the two-year period of National Service would have to be maintained. He had 'no doubt', Churchill said, 'that we must maintain our defence effort; and

---

[1] Letter of 10 February 1954: Beaverbrook papers.

[2] Muggeridge's article ended: '. . . unless a subsequent discovery elucidates the matter further, we shall never know how Belisarius's dilemma was resolved. Did he linger on in power until the authority he would not relinquish fell of itself from his nerveless hands? Did his timid associates at last summon up their resolution to press upon him a retirement he deserved but would not voluntarily undertake? Or did his own splendid historical sense and devotion to his country's interests induce him to make his exit from the public stage before the glory of being its best ornament had departed'. (*Punch*, 3 February 1954.)

[3] Moran diary, 4 February 1954: *The Struggle for Survival*, pages 522–3.

we were in fact doing so. No other country had imposed two years' national service and undertaken so many commitments overseas that it had no formations available for the defence of its own territory.' A few moments later, Churchill told his colleagues:

. . . he had been encouraged by the statement in a speech by the Supreme Allied Commander, Europe, to the effect that the Soviet Army was in no position to launch an attack upon Western Europe without further concentration of forces in the forward areas. Would not this involve large and obvious troop movements? If so, it should mean that we could expect a period of alert, during which we should have the opportunity to make further attempts to prevent a war and at the same time to press on with vigorous preparations for it.[1]

In the second week of February Churchill worked to advance the cause of an even wider conference once the Berlin meeting of Foreign Ministers was over. At Berlin, however, Dulles had put forward a proposal which Selwyn Lloyd described to the Cabinet on February 10 as 'unduly restricted in its scope', and likely to make a meeting of Heads of Government impossible. Churchill did not despair, however, telling the Cabinet that even if 'small results' were obtained from Berlin 'there would still be hope that something better might be obtained from a Five-Power Meeting, and it would be a point gained if the United States and the Chinese People's Government sat down at the same conference table'. For these reasons, Churchill told his colleagues, 'he thought the Cabinet might tell the Foreign Secretary that he should do his best to secure a Five-Power meeting, and that he need not feel obliged to defend every detailed argument used by the French and the Americans on particular points, though he should maintain the unity of the three Western Powers on all issues of principle'.[2]

From Eisenhower too came a warning of Russian intentions which did not make Churchill's self-imposed task any easier; a reiteration of Eisenhower's stark characterization of Russia during the Bermuda Conference. 'It is a bitter disappointment,' Clementine Churchill wrote to her husband on February 13, 'but, alas, I fear he is right about the Russian menace.' Her letter continued:

But if only America were not so unsympathetic & indeed unhelpful to us—over Egypt, India in the past, & now the clumsy suggestion to Pakistan—we could go all in with her more easily.

I wish you could see 'Ike'.[3]

[1] Defence Committee No. 3 of 1954, 'Top Secret', 11.30 a.m., 9 February 1954: Cabinet papers, 131/14. The Supreme Allied Commander, Europe, was General Gruenther, who in 1945 had been Deputy Commander of the United States Forces in Austria.
[2] Cabinet Conclusions No. 8 of 1954, 'Secret', 11 a.m., 10 February 1954: Cabinet papers, 128/27. Selwyn Lloyd had been Minister of State at the Foreign Office since October 1951.
[3] 'Winston', 13 February 1954: Churchill papers, 1/50.

On February 17 a further and extraordinary reason to see Eisenhower arose; for on that day Sterling Cole, the Chairman of the Joint Congressional Committee on Atomic Energy, announced in a public speech that America had for more than a year possessed, and had successfully tested, a bomb more powerful by far than an atomic bomb: a 'hydrogen bomb'. Churchill read the text of Sterling Cole's speech in the *Manchester Guardian*. 'I was astounded,' he told the House of Commons five months later, 'by all that he said about the hydrogen bomb and the results of the experiments made more than a year before by the United States at Eniwetok Atoll.' Churchill's speech continued:

Considering what immense differences the facts he disclosed made to our whole outlook for defence, and notably civil defence, depth of shelters, dispersion of population, anti-aircraft artillery, and so forth—on which considerable expenditure was being incurred—I was deeply concerned at the lack of information we possessed, and in view of all the past history of this subject, into which I do not propose to go today, I thought I ought to have a personal meeting with President Eisenhower at the first convenient opportunity.

'Very little notice was taken over here at first of Mr Sterling Cole's revelations,' Churchill commented, 'but when some Japanese fishermen were slightly affected by the radioactivity generated by the second explosion at Bikini, an intense sensation was caused in this country. . . .'[1] By the revelations of February 17, Churchill told the House of Commons a year later, 'the entire foundation of human affairs was revolutionized, and mankind placed in a situation both measureless and laden with doom'.[2]

Churchill had already taken steps to find a date when it would be convenient for Eisenhower to see him.

At the Cabinet on February 22, Eden reported on the Four-Power Meeting in Berlin. One of its 'most noticeable features', he said, 'had been the extreme rigidity of the Soviet attitude towards European problems. There had been no yielding, even in Austria, where it might have been thought that the Russians could gain some public approval at little cost.' There was no doubt, Eden said, 'that the Russians were genuinely alarmed by the development of United States bases throughout the world and by the large programme of aircraft construction in Western Europe'.

The one result of the conference was that the Russians now wished for a Five-Power conference in Geneva, with Communist China as the fifth Power. Churchill told his colleagues that he was 'not surprised or

[1] Speech of 12 July 1954: *Hansard*.
[2] Speech of 1 March 1955: *Hansard*.

disappointed' by the results of the Four-Power Meeting. The agreement to hold a Five-Power meeting at Geneva 'meant that negotiations on Far Eastern problems would be continued'. In Europe, the Russian attitude should help the French Parliament to proceed with ratification of the European Defence Community. Churchill added, in seeking to draw the most positive conclusions possible from the Berlin meeting: 'Public disappointment at the lack of political argument on Europe would be greatly offset if we could secure American agreement to an expansion of East/West trade. It would be evidence that we were continuing to try to find peaceful means of living side by side with the Soviet Union.'[1]

Churchill's ability to work did not seem to diminish. Even his doctor had become aware of that, noting in his diary on February 23, of a conversation with one of Churchill's Private Secretaries, who agreed with the doctor 'that perhaps I saw the PM at his worst, usually in the early morning'. The Private Secretary went on to tell Lord Moran:

Last night the PM worked on his speech from ten-thirty until midnight, with a Foreign Office expert, making some very good points and directing the argument. Then he went over questions for today and finally read the early editions of the morning papers. He went to bed about a quarter to one. He was really as alert as before his illness. He is generally like that in the evenings.[2]

The speech which Churchill was preparing with such care was his report to the House of Commons on the Berlin Conference. He began by a tribute to Ernest Bevin, and 'other leaders of the Labour Party', during what he described as 'the crisis which Russian ambition and aggression after the war produced', and he added: 'It has helped us to keep our heads above water.'

Speaking of the 'subjugated States' of Eastern Europe—Poland, Czechoslovakia, Roumania, Bulgaria and Hungary—Churchill told the House of Commons:

Time may find remedies that this generation cannot command. The forces of the human spirit and of national character alive in those countries cannot be speedily extinguished, even by large-scale movements of populations and mass education of children. Thought is fluid and pervasive, hope is enduring and inspiring. The vast territorial empire and multitudes of subjects, which the Soviets grasped for themselves in the hour of Allied victory, constitute the main cause of division now existing among civilized nations.

[1] Cabinet Conclusions No. 10 of 1954, 'Secret', 4 p.m., 22 February 1954: Cabinet papers, 128/27.
[2] Moran diary, 23 February 1954: *The Struggle for Survival*, pages 527–8.

On the other hand, Stalin's use of his triumph has produced some other results which will live and last, and which certainly would not have been seen in our time but for the Soviet pressure and menace.

No one but Stalin, nothing but the actions of Russia under his sway, could have made that alliance and brotherhood of the English-Speaking peoples, on which the life of the free world depends, come so swiftly and firmly into being. Nothing but the dread of Stalinized Russia could have brought the conception of United Europe from dreamland into the forefront of modern thought.

Nothing but the policy of the Soviets and of Stalin could have laid the foundations of that deep and lasting association which now exists between Germany and the Western world, between Germany and Britain and, I trust, between Germany and France.

These are events which will live and which will grow while the conquests and expansion achieved by military force and political machinery will surely dissolve or take new and other forms.

Churchill then recalled his speech of the previous May, when he had suggested, as he reminded the House, 'a small meeting between the heads of Governments without agenda, without Press, without communiqués, where full and frank talks could be indulged in and where the principals would not be oppressed by the ordeal—and it is an ordeal which few have experienced and no one should underrate— of playing on the world stage with every word studied, weighed, and analysed, with every word liable to be misrepresented, torn from its context and used by vast, highly-organized machinery for propaganda purposes'. He had thought, he added, that 'a simpler, more primitive meeting, at any rate as a preliminary', would be the best way 'of finding an answer to the question which everyone was then asking, but which few of us here are asking today: Has there been a significant change in Russian policy since the death of Stalin?'

He thought then, Churchill said, and he still thought, 'that any meeting with the Soviet Goverment under the new régime was better than no meeting at all'. The Berlin meeting, although rightly described by Eden as a 'disappointment', had nevertheless been 'very remarkable'; new contacts had been established 'at various levels between important men'; indeed, Churchill added:

I believe it to be true that personal relations and comprehension of each other's point of view were improved as the great debate proceeded.

So far from the conference having proved a failure or a disaster it has actually made the discussion of all these questions less delicate and less dangerous than it was. Further meetings between those concerned are in no way prevented. Nay, one meeting which seemed hopelessly barren has been fixed. At Geneva, on 26 April, all the Powers directly concerned in the Far East will meet together.

This will include the meeting in high level conference of Communist China and the United States of America.

The Geneva meeting was, Churchill said, 'one outstanding hopeful result' of the Four-Power Meeting in Berlin. Although no treaty had been signed in Berlin, as had been hoped, 'to secure the liberation of Austria', the door was not finally closed. He had tried to see the problem as Russia saw it, and was hopeful that a bargain would eventually be made, 'though I hope', he added, 'that it will not be thought I deceive myself or try to lead the House into foolish or vain ideas'.

Churchill then set out what had always been his theme, and would remain his object for the months, and even years, ahead:

Patience and perseverance must never be grudged when the peace of the world is at stake. Even if we had to go through a decade of cold-war bickerings punctuated by vain parleys, that would be preferable to the catalogue of unspeakable and also unimaginable horrors which is the alternative. We must not shrink from continuing to use every channel that is open or that we can open any more than that we should relax those defensive measures indispensable for our own strength and safety.

There was, Churchill argued, 'no contradiction' between the policy of building up the defence strength of the free world against Communist pressure 'and against potential armed Soviet aggression', and trying at the same time 'to create conditions under which Russia may dwell easily and peacefully side by side with us all', and he ended: 'Peace is our aim, and strength is the only way of getting it. We need not be deterred by the taunt that we are trying to have it both ways at once. Indeed, it is only by having it both ways at once that we shall get a chance of getting anything of it at all.'[1]

Churchill's speech was a clear indication both that he had not given up working for his summit, albeit now at some more distant date, and that he was still master of his faculties and his subject. He had also to deal with the urgent matters of Government as they thrust themselves upon him and his Cabinet. On March 1, as soon as he and his colleagues had learned from Eden of riots in Khartoum, following the arrival there of General Neguib from Egypt, Churchill told the Cabinet that he hoped it would give 'serious consideration' to the possibility of sending British troops to Khartoum. This, he said, could help to preserve law and order and ensure 'that the progress of the Sudanese people to self-government was not hampered by outbreaks of violence'. Churchill added:

Two battalions and two RAF squadrons could easily be sent in from the Canal Zone. They could arrive by air within a few days and could be quar-

---

[1] Speech of 25 February 1954: *Hansard*.

tered in some convenient cantonment in the city. There would be no difficulty in keeping them supplied by air. Such a force would be in a position to repel any attempted invasion from Egypt by cutting the railway line across the desert. The move would be a useful preliminary to the re-deployment of our forces in the Canal Zone, and would give us control of one important strategic point.

Eden undertook to examine Churchill's suggestion 'urgently', but went on to point out that a 'relevant' consideration would be the extent of the Governor-General's continuing responsibility for law and order 'and his duty, as the servant of both the Governments sharing the condominium, to seek assistance when he needed it from both the United Kingdom and the Egyptian Government'.[1] It was 'unlikely' Eden added, 'that any hostile move would be made from Egypt if British battalions were sent to Khartoum; but it was not to be assumed that their arrival would be welcomed by the Sudanese—even by the Mahdi's supporters or by those sections of the population which were favourable to the British'.[2]

Churchill reiterated his call for 'a programme of positive action' towards Egypt. 'Thus,' he explained to the Cabinet on March 15, 'we might break off the defence negotiations and embark on a definite plan of re-deployment.' An armoured brigade could be sent at once from Libya to the Canal Zone. A brigade could be sent to Khartoum 'in order to demonstrate in a practical manner our determination to ensure the independence of the Sudanese and to protect them from Egyptian interference'. The troops remaining in Egypt could be re-deployed 'in the manner best calculated to ensure their safety'. Meanwhile 'we should do our utmost to promote effective multilateral action by the maritime Powers to assure the right of international passage through the Canal'. He would like, he added, 'to examine a plan of this kind in greater detail with the Foreign Secretary and the Minister of Defence'.

In reply, Eden told the Cabinet that, 'while he would be ready to consider an alternative policy on these lines, he was not convinced that the arrival of a British brigade in Khartoum would be welcomed by any of the political parties in the Sudan'. There was at the moment, he said, 'no real justification for such a move, although there might be

[1] The Anglo-Egyptian administration of the Sudan had been established in 1899. The agreement with Britain signed by Neguib on 12 February 1953 acknowledged the right of the Sudan to self-determination, and gave the population the right to choose (in 1955) between independence and union with Egypt. On 19 December 1955 the Sudanese parliament voted unanimously for complete independence. This was agreed by Britain and Egypt twelve days later, and an independent republic was proclaimed on 1 January 1956.

[2] Cabinet Conclusions No. 13 of 1954, 'Secret', 6.30 p.m., 1 March 1954: Cabinet papers, 128/27.

if the Governor-General found it necessary to declare a constitutional emergency'.[1]

At Cabinet on March 22, Churchill accepted an American initiative to continue with the Anglo-Egyptian talks on a tripartite basis, with a view to setting up an Anglo-American civilian organization for the maintenance of the Canal Base. He would have 'preferred', he said, 'a definite rupture of the negotiations' and unilateral action by Britain to redeploy the 80,000 British troops in the Zone, sending most to Cyprus or Libya, and leaving 15,000 in the Canal Zone between Ismailia and Port Said. But the American initiative, made by Dulles through Eden, should 'now be worked out', though without 'any final commitment'.[2]

Within a month, Churchill was suggesting to the Cabinet a joint Anglo-American declaration on the maintenance of security in the Middle East. 'We should not need to ask the Americans to provide either forces or money,' he explained. An international agreement, a 'firm' Anglo-American declaration, 'would be a sufficient guarantee of the security of the area and of the right of international passage through the Suez Canal, and no great show of force would be required'. It was 'not easy', Eden commented, 'to create a system of collective defence in the Middle East', but he promised to 'examine the possibility of putting forward practical proposals.'[3]

On March 1 the United States exploded a second hydrogen bomb, at Bikini Atoll in the Pacific. This time, news of it was at once made public. On the following day, in the House of Commons, Churchill defended the increase in British forces and preparedness in Europe, within the NATO forces, now commanded by General Gruenther of the United States, who was preparing a scheme to meet a possible Russian surprise attack. Such a scheme, Churchill told the House of Commons, 'cannot be any menace to the safety of Russia, but it is a great pad and interruption to the horrible dangers that dwell with us night and day if we think about things, and nothing must be done to deprive us of that'.

As to the situation in which such preparations were needed, it was not only 'critical', Churchill said, but 'very complicated', and he

---

[1] Cabinet Conclusions No. 18 of 1954, 'Secret', 5.30 p.m., 15 March 1954: Cabinet papers, 128/27.
[2] Cabinet Conclusions No. 21 of 1954: 'Secret', 5.30 p.m., 22 March 1954: Cabinet papers, 128/27.
[3] Cabinet Conclusions No. 29 of 1954, 'Secret', 11.30 a.m., 15 April 1954: Cabinet papers, 128/27.

added: 'All is in flux—political, economic, and, above all, scientific; all is in flux. Uncertainties, acting and reacting on each other, dominate the scene.' His reflections continued:

When I was a subaltern in India about sixty years ago, and was endeavouring to improve my education, I read a passage in Schopenhauer. It stuck in my mind. I will repeat it to the House, because it a little applies to the general situation.

'We look upon the present as something to be put up with while it lasts and serving only as the way towards our goal. Hence most people, if they glance back when they come to the end of life, will find that all along they have been living ad interim.'[1]

Everyone can weigh the truth of these words of the pessimistic philosopher, but there is no doubt that they very accurately describe the mood of the leaders of many countries, especially the military leaders, on the present position in defence.

No sweeping, clear-cut, wholesale decisions are possible. The changes in the types of weapons are so rapid and continuous that if war should come at any time in the next decade, all the countries engaged will go into action with a proportion—a large proportion—of obsolete or obsolescent equipment, and they will fight each other with this as well as they can on the ground, in the air, and on the sea.

Changes there must be, but it is inevitable that the changes should be gradual, because you must go on living from day to day all the time you are improving. You have to go on living and trying to improve at the same time. It is very hard.[2]

Churchill's stamina amazed even his doctor, who noted on March 4:

He rang me up in the evening after the Cabinet. He had taken a pill which he called the 'Lord Moran' in the morning; did this mean he could not take my 'special' pill in the afternoon? Would they clash? Not being able to get hold of me, he had taken a chance. 'You see, I had five hours on end.' I asked him if he was very weary. 'Not at all. Now I am going out to dinner with the American Ambassador.' This astonishing creature obeys no laws, recognizes no rules.[3]

On March 12 Churchill dined with R. A. Butler, who recorded in his diary Churchill telling him over dinner: 'I feel like an aeroplane at the end of its flight, in the dusk, with the petrol running out, in search of a safe landing.' The 'only political interest he had left', Churchill told Butler, 'was in high-level conversations with the Russians. He would then be glad to retire to Hyde Park Gate to finish his *History of the English-Speaking Peoples*.'[4]

---

[1] This quotation is to be found in A. Schopenhauer, 'Additional Remarks on the Doctrine of the Vanity of Existence', *Parerga and Paralipomena*, volume 2, Oxford 1974, page 285.

[2] Speech of 2 March 1954: *Hansard*.

[3] Moran diary, 4 March 1954: *The Struggle for Survival*, page 529.

[4] Butler diary, 12 March 1954: *The Art of the Possible, The Memoirs of Lord Butler*, page 173.

In the second week of March, Churchill wrote to Eisenhower about the hydrogen bomb revelations which Sterling Cole had made on February 17. In his letter, Churchill pondered this development both in its historical perspective and in its meaning for the future:

There is no difference between us upon the major issues which overhang the world, namely, resistance to Communism, the unity of the free nations, the concentration of the English-Speaking world, United Europe and NATO. All these will and must increase if we are to come through the anxious years and perhaps decades which lie ahead of hopeful but puzzled mankind.

On the day that the Soviets discovered and developed the Atomic Bomb the consequences of war became far more terrible. But that brief tremendous phase now lies in the past.

An incomparably graver situation is presented by the public statements of Mr Sterling Cole at Chicago on February 17. I have discussed these with my expert advisers. They tell me that the 175ft displacement of the ocean bed at Eniwetok Atoll may well have involved a pulverization of the earth's surface three or four times as deep. This in practice would of course make all protection, except for small Staff groups, impossible. You can imagine what my thoughts are about London. I am told that several million people would certainly be obliterated by four of five of the latest H bombs. In a few more years these could be delivered by rocket without even hazarding the life of a pilot. New York and your other great cities have immeasurable perils too, though distance is a valuable advantage at least as long as pilots are used.

Another ugly idea has been put in my head, namely, the dropping of an H Bomb in the sea to windward of the Island or any other seaborne country, in suitable weather, by rocket or airplane, or perhaps released by submarine. The explosion would generate an enormous radio-active cloud, many square miles in extent, which would drift over the land attacked and extinguish human life over very large areas. Our smallness and density of population emphasize this danger to us.

Mr Cole further stated that Soviet Russia, though perhaps a year behind the United States, possessed the know-how and was increasing its production and power of delivery (or words to that effect). Moreover after a certain quantity have been produced on either side the factor of 'over-taking', 'superiority', etc., loses much of its meaning. If one side has five hundred and the other two hundred both might be destroyed. A powerful incentive to achieve surprise would be given to the weaker—what about Pearl Harbour? His natural fears would prey upon his moral and spiritual inhibitions (if indeed he was so encumbered).

When I read Mr Cole's widely reported speech, I was surprised that its searing statements attracted so little comment. The reason is that human minds recoil from the realization of such facts. The people, including the well-informed, can only gape and console themselves with the reflection that death comes to all anyhow, some time. This merciful numbness cannot be enjoyed by the few men upon whom the supreme responsibility falls. They have to drive their minds forward into these hideous and deadly spheres of thought.

All the things that are happening now put together, added to all the material things that have ever happened, are scarcely more important to the human race. I consider that you and, if my strength lasts, I cannot flinch from the mental exertion involved.

I wondered, pondering on your letter, whether this was the background which had forced you to express yourself with such intense earnestness. I understand of course that, in speaking of the faith that must inspire us in the struggle against atheistic materialism, you are referring to the spiritual struggle, and that like me, you still believe that War is not inevitable. I am glad to think that in your spirit, as in mine, resolve to find a way out of this agony of peril transcends all else.

I entirely agree with Mr Cole's remark that in this matter 'It is more sinful to conceal the power of the atom than to reveal it'. This would not of course mean one-sided imparting of secret knowledge. But perhaps we have now reached, or are reaching, the moment when both sides know enough to out-line the doom-laden facts to each other.

Of course I recur to my earlier proposal of a personal meeting between Three. Men have to settle with men, no matter how vast, and in part beyond their comprehension, the business in hand may be. I can even imagine that a few simple words, spoken in the awe which may at once oppress and inspire the speakers, might lift this nuclear monster from our world.

Churchill ended his letter by reiterating his belief in the importance of talks with the Soviet Union:

It might be that the proposals which you made at Bermuda and which are accepted by the Soviets for parleys on this subject could, without raising the issue formally, give a better chance of survival than any yet mentioned. The advantage of the process you have set in motion is that it might probe the chances of settlement to the heart without at the same time bringing nearer the explosion we seek to escape.[1]

The problems of world peace, and those of the Conservative leader-ship, both pressed on Churchill that week. On March 11 Churchill asked to see Eden to talk, so Eden told Shuckburgh, about 'the future of the Government'. Shuckburgh noted in his diary, of Eden:

Great excitement. He said he had been expecting it, because Rab has at last succeeded in getting the Old Man to see the Budget problem, and the need for a plan for elections, etc. On return, he told me as follows, strictly in secret and no one else to know. PM said he had decided to resign in May—or end of summer at the latest (depending on his health).

His only concern is to hand over as smoothly and effectively as possible to AE. He will not resign his seat in the House, but remain as a backbencher. As to timing, Harold Macmillan had told him it would be awkward for Ministers now steering Bills through the House if the change came before

---

[1] 'My dear Friend', 'Most Secret and Confidential', dated, 'March 1954': Eisenhower papers.

the summer recess. He recognized that this was nonsense when AE said so.

They then discussed the question of the Budget and elections. PM asked AE whether he thought election should be this year or next. AE replied (as he had said he would) that he would like to have the option. PM had seemed impressed by this 'which showed that I had thought the matter over'. They both agreed that it was better not to decide until much nearer the autumn; it would not do to appear to be taking a snap election before the economic difficulties of next year set in; but perhaps the socialists would demand an election in the event of a change from Winston to Eden, in which case AE might well decide to have one this autumn. But that means WSC must go in May at the latest, so as to give him six months in office.[1]

There seemed to be no end to the Prime Minister's resilience. 'Jock said this morning,' noted Lord Moran on March 12, 'that the PM had not been in such good form for years.' But when Moran went in to see him, 'he looked up at me without a smile and said sadly, "It casts a shadow over your work when you are going to give it up so soon."'[2]

When that resignation would be was a question being asked in many places: at Westminster, at Conservative Party headquarters, in Eden's entourage, in the Press. 'I'm going to resign at the end of June,' Churchill told his doctor on March 19, and he added: 'They have all been so nice. That's what gets me. If they had attacked me I could have snarled back. I don't want to be selfish.'[3]

In the privacy of his diary Harry Crookshank wrote on March 22 that the Prime Minister was 'ga-ga'.[4] Four days later, on March 26, Lord Moran noted that Miss Portal had described him as 'quite perky'. Pondering the question of resignation, Churchill told his doctor that day: 'It may sound egotistical, but I don't know what the boys will do when I go.' His concern was continually with the hydrogen bomb. The 'bloody invention', as he called it, would do harm 'to society and to the race'.[5]

According to newspaper reports on March 26, the United States hydrogen bomb explosion on March 1 had been three times more powerful than the scientists themselves had expected. 'In other words,' Evelyn Shuckburgh noted in his diary, 'it was out of control,' and he added: 'Very great excitement everywhere about it, as if people began to see the end of the world. AE went over to talk to the PM, who was on the whole quite sensible—unlike *The Times* leader of this morning which proposes an immediate Churchill—Malenkov meeting as a sort of desperate throw.'[6]

[1] Shuckburgh diary, 11 March 1954: *Descent to Suez*, page 145.

[2] Moran diary, 12 March 1954: *The Struggle for Survival*, pages 529–30.

[3] Moran diary, 19 March 1954: *The Struggle for Survival*, page 530.

[4] Crookshank diary, 22 March 1954: Crookshank papers.

[5] Moran diary, 26 March 1954: *The Struggle for Survival*, pages 530–1.

[6] Shuckburgh diary, 26 March 1954: *Descent to Suez*, pages 153–4.

Churchill wrote at once to Eisenhower, who had meanwhile been critical of Britain's growing trade with the Soviet Union and Eastern Europe:

While doing all that is possible to increase our joint strength and unity, I am anxious to promote an easement of relations with Soviet Russia and to encourage and aid any development of Russian life which leads to a wider enjoyment by the Russian masses of the consumer goods of which you speak and modern popular amenities and diversions which play so large a part in British and American life. I hope that this process will lead to some relaxation of the grim discipline of the peoples of this vast land ocean of Russia and its satellites. Moreover, trade means contact and probably involves a good deal of friendly infiltration which I think would be to our advantage from every point of view, including the military.

I am, of course, opposed to exportation to Russia of weapons or military equipment in a direct form, but I do not think this principle should be used to ban so many items because they might be used for military purposes in a secondary or subsequent stage. Any advantage given by this would only be on a small and almost trivial proportion of Russian armaments, for the whole scale of East/West Trade is small and we should be dealing only with a percentage of a percentage. I do not think this ought to stand in the way of the widening of commercial intercourse so long as only conventional forms of equipment are concerned. On the contrary I believe that even in this limited military sphere we should, I think, gain as much or almost as much as we should lose.

Over and beyond that there are those hopes of a broadening of Russian life and relaxation of international tension which may lead to the re-establishment of a peaceful foundation for the tormented and burdened world.

Churchill's letter continued:

How minute do all these military considerations, arising out of trade so limited, appear compared to the Hydrogen Bomb and the rapid progress the Soviets are said to be making with it. There is the peril which marches toward us and is nearer and more deadly to us than to you. We may be sure that whatever raw materials or equipment are available to the Russians, whether from their own resources or from imports, the first priority will be given to nuclear expansion, just as at a former stage in Germany guns counted before butter. I fear, therefore, that even a total prohibition of all East/West trade would not impede the physical progress of these fearful forces. On the other hand there is the hope that the sense of easement may render more fruitful those tentative yet inspiring conceptions of which you told me at Bermuda and with which your letter of March 19, which I received yesterday and to which I will reply later, also so pregnantly deals.

I have not hampered this expression of my most anxious thought by ex-patiating on the well known arguments about British trade in the present economic phase. I will merely mention the headings. If the United States will not let us pay for her goods by rendering reciprocal services and make a reasonable proportion of things your people want or might be attracted by, as is our deep desire, the present deadlock must continue. As the old tag says, those who do not import cannot export. I have learned all about these difficulties from my political youth up and am making no complaint. 'Off shore' purchase is a Godsend, but you are still in the position of having to give away on a vast scale with generosity and human patriotism what we should like to earn by hard work and mental exertion. The arrival of Germany and Japan in the world market makes it necessary that we should open out our trade in every possible direction for we have to keep 50 million people alive in this small island as well as maintaining the greatest armaments next to your own in the free world.

As the proportions of our trade with Russia must in any case be on a minor scale for many years, I cannot rate the commercial aspect so highly as I do those I have mentioned above.[1]

On March 30 Churchill wrote to Lord Beaverbrook about the hydrogen bomb and the *Daily Express*: 'I think the *Express* took a very sensible line about not trying to forbid the United States to proceed with their hydrogen experiments. A breach with them might well be fatal to world peace and to our survival, for they could quite easily go on alone and we are far worse placed geographically.' Churchill added: 'I grieve that you continue to oppose so violently the rearmament, under proper limits, of Western Germany. It is going to happen anyway and it is better to have them on our side than against us.'[2]

That day, in the House of Commons, Churchill answered Labour criticisms that it was the duty of the British Government to use its influence to persuade the United States to abandon the current hydrogen bomb tests, or at least to bring them under some form of international control. The Government, he said, and he repeated this in Cabinet on the following day, 'were not prepared to make any such representations to the United States Government or to take any other action which might impede American progress in building up their overwhelming strength in nuclear weapons, which provided the greatest possible deterrent against the outbreak of a third world war'.

It was now clear, however, Churchill told the Cabinet, that, 'in view of the public anxiety which these experiments had aroused, the House of Commons should be given an early opportunity for a full debate on this question'. The Cabinet endorsed his view.[3]

The Cabinet met twice on March 31. According to Evelyn Shuckburgh, the two meetings had been made necessary because of Churchill's behaviour:

---

[1] 'My dear friend', 27 March 1954: Eisenhower papers.
[2] 'My dear Max', 'Private', 30 March 1954: Churchill papers, 2/192.
[3] Cabinet Conclusions No. 23 of 1954, 'Secret', 11.30 a.m., 31 March 1954: Cabinet papers, 128/27.

A terrible Cabinet, slow, waffling and indecisive, which had to be continued in the afternoon. WSC sending messages to Eisenhower every half an hour about the hydrogen explosions—not with the object of stopping them, or affecting them in any way, but in order to be able to give the impression in the House that he (or, to be fair, the country) plays a large part in arrangements for these tests.

Even Soames is exasperated with him, and the disclosure that we have had facilities to watch the explosions may mean the end of the co-operation we have had, sub rosa, from Strauss.[1] No arguments of this sort affect the Old Man, who vents his feelings by sending peevish telegrams to Roger Makins.

AE says, not for the first time, 'This simply cannot go on; he is gaga; he cannot finish his sentences.'[2]

The Cabinet of March 31 also discussed a plan drawn up by the Chiefs of Staff, for British military assistance to Jordan in the event of Jordanian hostilities with Israel. This plan, explained Lord Alexander, 'involved the invasion of Israel by British forces from the south'. Should it be communicated to the Jordanians? he asked. In reply, the Chief of the Imperial General Staff, Field Marshal Sir John Harding, said that the Chiefs of Staff did not wish to disclose the plan to the Jordanians. He was 'much relieved' to hear this, Churchill commented, adding that 'leakage of such a plan would have very grave consequences'. Later in the discussion, Eden proposed that Churchill should send a message to the Prime Minister of Israel, 'reminding him of our obligations under our Treaty with Jordan and urging him to avoid any provocative action'.[3]

On April 1 the *Daily Mirror*, in its leading article 'Twilight of a Giant', declared that the 'exposure of the myth of Winston as a post-war leader is now complete'. There were demands in Parliament, it wrote, that Britain should give a lead to the world 'in facing the horror-bomb problem', by talking 'straighter and harder' to the United States. What was Churchill's reply, the newspaper asked, and it answered its own question: 'Old and tired, he mouthed comfortless words in the twilight of his career. His battles are past.' The editorial ended: 'This is the Giant in Decay.'

'For the first time since Parliament reconvened last autumn,' the *New York Times* had written, 'Sir Winston appeared unsure of himself

---

[1] Admiral Lewis Strauss, Chairman of the United States Atomic Energy Commission from 1953 to 1958.

[2] Shuckburgh diary, 31 March 1954: *Descent to Suez*, pages 156–7.

[3] Cabinet Conclusions No. 23 of 1954, 'Secret', 11.30 a.m., 31 March 1954: Cabinet papers 128/27.

and tired. This was not the Churchill of two years ago and was only a shadow of the great figure of 1940.'[1] Triumphantly, the *Daily Mirror* printed this comment on its back page, under the headline, 'What America says about Churchill now'.[2] The *New York Times* report had gone on to state that the contrast with 1940 'was all the more marked when Foreign Secretary Anthony Eden rose from his seat beside Sir Winston to answer a question and divert some of the pressure from the Prime Minister. Mr Eden was precise, confident and clear.'[3]

Churchill was to speak on the hydrogen bomb in Parliament on April 5. 'He thinks he will put Attlee on his back on Monday,' Norman Brook told Lord Moran, and he added: 'and I daresay he will'. Brook also told Moran, on the question of Churchill's retirement, that the Conservatives were thinking of a General Election in the autumn of 1955, and the 'one thing that is definite and fixed is the PM's declaration that he will not lead the Party in another election'.[4]

On April 2, while Churchill was preparing his hydrogen bomb speech, Sir Gerald Kelly came to Chartwell to choose some of Churchill's paintings for the Royal Academy summer exhibition. He chose four: 'The Dead Sea from the Mount of Olives', painted in 1921; 'Cassis near Marseilles', painted in 1920; an undated scene 'near Venice'; and a sketch, a view in the Atlas mountains, done in 1950.[5] The Venice painting, Kelly wrote later that day, 'I thought extremely lovely.'[6]

Although Churchill's stroke of June 1953 had never been made public, he made no secret of it in private, telling Gerald Kelly, as they looked at a particular painting: 'I painted that before my stroke.' 'For a man who has had a seizure,' the Lord Chancellor, Lord Simonds, told Moran on April 3, 'he seems wonderfully well.'[7]

On April 5 Churchill made his much-awaited speech on the hydrogen bomb. 'We are all naturally concerned,' he said, 'at the prodigious experiments which are being carried out in the Pacific, but I do not think there will be any difference between us that we would rather have them carried out there than in Siberia.'

---

[1] *New York Times*, 31 March 1954.

[2] *Daily Mirror*, 1 April 1954.

[3] *New York Times*, 31 March 1954.

[4] Moran diary, 1 April 1954: *The Struggle for Survival*, pages 531–2.

[5] 'List of Works exhibited at the Royal Academy by Sir Winston Churchill, Hon RA.': Royal Academy archive.

[6] 'My dear Winston', 2 April 1954: Churchill papers, 2/345. Sir Gerald Kelly was President of the Royal Academy of Arts. The exhibition opened on 1 May 1954. Churchill's paintings were proving an excellent source of income. On 1 February 1954 he received £4,440 for the reproduction of several of his paintings which had been used by Hall Brothers (later Hallmark Cards) of Kansas City, for use as postcards. He received a further £4,462 from Hall Brothers on 7 February 1957, and £4,436 on 4 February 1958. (Churchill papers, 1/26.)

[7] Moran diary, 3 April 1954: *The Struggle for Survival*, pages 532–3.

The gulf in power between the conventional high-explosive bomb in use at the end of the war with Germany and the atomic bomb as used against Japan, he said, was smaller than the gulf in power between the atomic bomb and the hydrogen bomb. 'No words I could use,' Churchill commented, 'are needed to emphasize the deadly situation in which the whole world lies. These stupendous facts, although at present to our advantage, glare upon the human race.'

The first American hydrogen bomb explosion, Churchill noted, had taken place on 2 November 1952, the first Soviet hydrogen bomb explosion on 12 August 1953. Churchill reflected: 'To us in this over-crowded island and to the densely populated regions of Europe, the new terror brings a certain element of equality in annihilation. Strange as it may seem, it is to the universality of potential destruction that I feel we may look with hope and even confidence.'

Churchill then addressed himself to the criticisms which had been made of Britain's failure to obtain a specific joint authority over the use of the bomb. The Americans, he pointed out, 'are acting entirely within their rights as agreed between them and the late Government. I am always ready to bear responsibility where I have power, but if there is no power there can be no responsibility. Whether we like it or not that is the position which we found when we came into office two and a half years ago.'

This had been the agreement made while the Labour Party was in power. Yet the Member for Devonport, Michael Foot, had said on television on April 2: 'I am attacking the British Prime Minister, the British Foreign Secretary, and the British Government because of their failure to demand from the Americans full information about this bomb.' This, Churchill pointed out, 'is only one of the attacks made in the Press and on the public platform by members of the party opposite'.

Churchill then read out to the House of Commons, with President Eisenhower's permission, the text of the Quebec Agreement of 1944 between Churchill himself and Roosevelt. The agreement began by stating that Britain and the United States 'will never use this agency against each other', and it continued with a pledge 'that we will not use it against third parties without each other's consent'. Churchill continued:

Such was how things stood when the Socialist Government came into office. Any changes that have taken place from that position in the interval are their responsibility and not mine. Her Majesty's Government is bound by them nevertheless.

When we think of the importance which attaches to Clause 2 of the original Agreement I have read, namely: 'That we will not use it against third parties without each other's consent,' and also to the provision for the constant interchange of information it seems odd that the hon. Member for Ebbw Vale [1] was an important member of the Government which agreed to abandon these all-important provisions and precautions. I hope he will be specially helpful now.

I do not say that there were not many reasons and facts operative at the end of the War which were different from those during its course. But considering that the abandonment of our claim to be consulted and informed as an equal was the act of the Socialist Administration I feel they have no grounds for reproaching their successors with the consequences.

As a result of what had been decided upon by the Attlee Government, Britain had, Churchill pointed out, 'no means but friendly persuasion of inducing the Americans either to desist from their series of experiments, even if we desired them to, or to supply us with secret information about them and generally in the atomic sphere, if their law permits it'. [2]

At Churchill's accusation that Labour had abandoned the Quebec Agreement, thereby creating the very situation which the Labour benches were criticizing, there was, Lord Moran observed from the Peers' Gallery, 'a disorderly scene' with shouts of 'Withdraw' and 'Resign' so raucous that it was difficult to hear what Churchill was saying. One Labour MP went so far as to call out to Churchill: 'The Right Honourable Gentleman is dragging us down to the gutter,' and another: 'This is disgraceful,' while Bessie Braddock interrupted to tell Churchill: 'Get out!'

Lord Moran noted in his diary:

The Prime Minister struggled on: 'Now let me say only—' Mrs Braddock: 'You have said too much. The Right Honourable Gentleman should look at the faces behind him.' And indeed the Tories were in poor shape: they could not manage a single cheer for their leader; they sat mute. Sir Robert Boothby, white-faced, rose from the Tory benches and walked out of the Chamber. The Opposition cheered wildly this apparent mark of dissatisfaction with his leader. [3]

Nothing could be 'more disastrous to peace', Churchill continued, as the Labour interruptions died down, than for the House of Commons during this particular debate 'to rouse needless antagonism in Congress or throughout America'. Nothing could be more disastrous to the survival of Western Europe and the safety of Britain 'than a grave dispute between Britain and the United States'.

[1] Aneurin Bevan, Labour MP for Ebbw Vale since 1929; Minister of Health, 1945–51 and Minister of Labour and National Service, 1951. After his death in 1960, Michael Foot became MP for Ebbw Vale, and, subsequently, Bevan's biographer.

[2] Speech of 5 April 1954: *Hansard*. In this speech, Churchill also re-iterated his appeal, first made in the House of Commons on 11 May 1953, for a meeting between the Soviet and Western leaders.

[3] Moran diary, 5 April 1954: *The Fight for Survival*, pages 534–8.

Churchill then referred to a newspaper article published by Richard Crossman, Labour MP for East Coventry, on the previous day, in which Crossman wrote: 'On Monday, when the H-Bomb will be debated, Sir Winston must tell Mr Eisenhower and Mr Dulles that they can either scrap their new H-Bomb strategy and join with Britain in the plan for high-level talks or else face the prospect of "going it alone".' Churchill commented:

If this line of thought were adopted, it seems almost certain that 'the agonizing re-appraisal' of which Mr Dulles spoke (in another connection) would follow. The United States would withdraw from Europe altogether, and, with her three-quarter circle of hydrogen bases already spread around the globe, would face Russia alone. I cannot doubt that war in these circumstances would be nearer than it is to-day when the anxiety of the United States, to their abiding honour, is so largely centred upon the safety and freedom of Western Europe and the British Isles.

As to a British 'declaration of neutrality', of which many Labour supporters were in favour, Churchill believed it to be a 'delusion' that this would make Britain 'immune from Russia' and he went on to explain his line of thought. 'The very inferiority of Russia in atomic and hydrogen weapons,' he asserted, 'would make it necessary for them to use to the utmost their enormous preponderance in conventional warfare.' A simultaneous counter-attack by Russia on Western Europe 'would be the only form of immediate reprisal, and of securing hostages, which the Soviet Government could take. Although we still have the Channel, the British Isles would be laid open to every conceivable form of air attack.'

Churchill then spoke, as he had done almost a year earlier, on May 11, of the possibility of a summit meeting; one which would now have a different 'topic', particularly since Eisenhower's United Nations speech proposing a new consultative and co-operative machinery for the industrial atomic sphere. Churchill told the House of Commons:

... if Russia, the British Commonwealth, and the United States were gathered round the table talking about the commercial application of atomic energy, and the diversion of some of their uranium stockpile, it would not seem odd if the question of the hydrogen bomb, which might blow all these pretty plans sky-high, cropped up, and what I have hoped for, namely a talk on supreme issues between the Heads of States and Governments concerned, might not seem so impossible as it has hitherto.

There were, Churchill concluded, 'two main aims' of British policy: 'One is to lose no opportunity of convincing the Soviet leaders and, if we can reach them, the Russian people, that the democracies of the West have no aggressive design on them. The other is to ensure that until that purpose has been achieved we have the strength necessary to deter any aggression by them and to ward it off if it should come.'[1]

'It is my faith that if we work together,' Churchill declared in a broadcast to the University of New York, in accepting an honorary Doctorate of Law on April 7, 'there are no problems we cannot solve, no dangers which we cannot ward off from ourselves, and no tangles through which we cannot guide the freedom-loving peoples of the world.'[2]

Such was Churchill's faith; but the reaction to his hydrogen bomb speech of April 5 had been markedly critical.

'Seldom has Sir Winston Churchill found himself in such an unhappy plight,' *The Times'* Parliamentary correspondent reported on April 6, 'and seldom has the Opposition so vociferously flung reproach and indignation at his head. Cries of "Resign" and other epithets burst about him in a tumult which drowned much of what he was trying to say.' The 'virulence of the attack', *The Times'* correspondent continued, 'for once did not stimulate him to combat. It seemed to rob his voice of resonance and left him ploughing doggedly through this section of his speech.'

'The Prime Minister's sense of occasion is usually one of his greatest strengths in the House of Commons,' *The Times'* leading article began, and it went on: 'It deserted him sadly yesterday.'[3]

'The business of the House was not to cry over spilt milk,' the leading article in the *Manchester Guardian* on April 6 declared, 'but to demonstrate our unity in the present and our sense of responsibility for the future. It was to discuss seriously what the Powers should do to avert the worst of wars and to control, if possible, the worst of weapons. Sir Winston may well have been stung by the reception he got at question time a week ago and by some of the comments made since then. But it is hard to escape the thought that he must have exaggerated these attacks and misjudged the occasion. And that is a great pity.'[4] The *Manchester Guardian's* verdict on Churchill's speech: 'He had blundered.'[5]

Even to many Conservatives, Churchill's speech had seemed too partisan, too much an attempt, indeed, to 'put Attlee on his back'. 'Things didn't go as well as I expected,' Churchill told his doctor on

[1] Speech of 5 April 1954: *Hansard*.

[2] Broadcast of 7 April 1954: Randolph S. Churchill (editor), *The Unwritten Alliance*, pages 137–9.

[3] *The Times*, 6 April 1954.

[4] 'Strange Debate', *Manchester Guardian*, 6 April 1954.

[5] 'Premier Provokes Bomb Storm', *Manchester Guardian*, 6 April 1954.

the following day, and he added: 'When one gets old one lives too much in the past. I ought to have told the House that I was very happy the Opposition had come round to my view that the Heads of the three States ought to meet, instead of . . .'

Churchill was silent for a while, lost in thought, then told Moran:

You see, Charles, I felt it was an extraordinary act of folly on the part of Labour to throw away the Quebec agreement. For years I have wanted it published. I was irritated that we had been relegated to a position where we had no say in things. Besides, I thought that what I said might have some effect on America. But there is truth in what the *Manchester Guardian* says this morning, that it's no use crying over spilt milk.

Moran's account continued:

I asked him if he had been upset by the hostility of the Labour benches. 'Oh, no,' he answered at once, 'I felt very well. After my speech I went to the Smoking Room and had a nice talk.' He pondered a while. 'I can see I must leave it alone,' he said sadly. 'Anthony did extremely well. It gives me confidence that he can control things so well. It was his best speech since his illness.'

He got out of bed and shuffled into the bathroom. I picked up *The Times* and read that the Prime Minister's 'sense of occasion had deserted him sadly' yesterday; he was responsible that 'the proceedings had degenerated into a sterile, angry and pitiful party wrangle'. There was a feeling, not confined to the Labour Press, that by his inept handling of the debate he had played into the hands of those who insist that he is no longer fit to be First Minister of the Crown.[1]

Churchill's speech of April 5 was 'the first time', Anthony Montague Browne later recalled, 'that I realised unmistakably how much his powers had waned. In days gone by he would have put aside his notes and devastated the opposition because he had the strongest case. It was a put-up job. Afterwards Anthony Eden told me, when I met him outside the Prime Minister's room at the House, that two Ministers had advised him not to salvage the Prime Minister in his winding up. He, to his everlasting credit, rejected this advice.'[2]

The speech of April 5 proved a turning-point in the view which people held of Churchill's capacity. There was an 'overwhelming impression', Evelyn Shuckburgh noted in his diary, 'that the PM has made a real bloomer, and exposed his aged feebleness to the House'.[3]

On April 8 Churchill returned to the House of Commons, but not to speak: 'I thought he looked terribly old,' Shuckburgh noted:

AE says he thinks the poor old boy must be going to have another stroke quite soon—that he is ashen grey and taking nothing in. He said to AE

---

[1] Moran diary, 6 April 1954: *The Struggle for Survival*, page 538.
[2] Anthony Montague Browne recollections: notes for the author, 24 March 1987.
[3] Shuckburgh diary, 5 April 1954: *Descent to Suez*, pages 159–60.

wasn't it 'splendid news' that *Izvestia* has called for a cease-fire in Indo-China, to which AE says he replied: 'Don't you see it is a trap; there is no line there; it is a trap and they would overrun the whole place'—and the old boy was quite crestfallen.[1]

Two weeks later, Evelyn Shuckburgh noted in his diary, after a conversation with Jock Colville:

Jock also said that the PM had been impressed with the way AE had faced a hostile House in defending him (WSC) over the Quebec agreement, and was more disposed on account of this to consider him fit to succeed. I expressed astonishment at this, and Jock added, 'Oh, but he has not been at all sure that the Government could hold together if he were to retire.'

AE's comment on what I told him of this was that Whitsun is the last date his colleagues will stand. If the Old Man doesn't go then, the Government will break up—several of them will resign. We shall see.[2]

In 1954 Whit Sunday fell on June 6.

Churchill's conversation frequently turned during April to the twin issues of meeting the Russians and the horrors of the hydrogen bomb. On April 8, when Duncan and Diana Sandys and Lord Moran were dining with him, Moran recorded the following discussion:

And then Malenkov's name came up.[3] Mary and Christopher had lunched with the Soviet Chargé d'Affaires and they gathered that Malenkov would welcome a meeting with the Prime Minister. Winston seemed to wake up.

'I feel better. I feel quite different.'

He began to talk with vigour.

'They will say, of course, that I may get a snub. I don't care. What does a snub matter if you save the world?'

Then he said with an air of finality:

'I shall not relinquish office until I meet Malenkov.'

'Where,' I broke in, 'would you see him?'

'Oh, there would be no difficulty. Ike said once that he would like to meet Malenkov at Stockholm. I could join the Russians there. It would be a great thing if he came out of Russia to meet me.'

He did not think the Russians would object to a meeting outside Russia on grounds of amour propre:

'At my age, with death at my shoulder, the Kremlin cannot speak of jealousy. They know I have nothing to gain. I would pop over to America

[1] Shuckburgh diary, 8 April 1954: *Descent to Suez*, page 161.

[2] Shuckburgh diary, 21 April 1954: *Descent to Suez*, page 167.

[3] On 27 April 1954 Malenkov was re-elected Premier by the Supreme Soviet of the USSR.

first, to make it all right with them. I know them so well, they would not think I was up to dirty work.'

If the Geneva conference failed, Churchill added, 'I shall pick up the bits.' If it triumphed, 'I shall go to meet Malenkov to exploit the victory.'[1]

On April 12 it was the hydrogen bomb which led Churchill to say to his doctor: 'I am told that if a thousand hydrogen bombs were exploded the cumulative effect on the atmosphere might be such that the health, and even the lives, of the whole human race would be affected.' Churchill added: 'I would like to know if that is true. I want it investigated. If it proved true there might be in the world a new common interest in preventing these explosions.'[2]

'In the course of a few bewildering years,' Churchill told a Royal Academy banquet two weeks later, 'we have found ourselves the masters—or indeed the servants—of gigantic powers which confront us with problems never known before. It may be that our perils may prove our salvation. If so this will depend upon a new elevation of the mind of man which will render him worthy of the secrets he has wrested from nature.'[3]

Reconciliation with Russia was again Churchill's theme when he spoke at the Albert Hall on April 30, at the annual meeting of the Primrose League, to introduce that year's main speaker, Harold Macmillan. Britain should 'establish relations with Russia', he said, which in spite of all distractions and perils will convince the Russian people and the Soviet Government that we wish them peace, happiness, and ever-increasing, ever-expanding prosperity and enrichment of life in their own mighty land and that we long to see them play a proud and splendid part in the guidance of the human race'. The 'foundation of all', he added, 'is our friendship and brotherhood with the United States of America, whose exertions and sacrifices since the War ended will long shine in history, and without whose unrivalled power chaos or subjugation might overwhelm us all'.[4]

Churchill had decided to try to accelerate the process of reaching a summit with the Soviets by a visit to Eisenhower. On April 22 he set out what he had in mind. 'My dear Friend,' he began, 'I am told that you will be in Washington between May 20 and May 24 before you receive the Emperor of Abyssinia. I should very much like to have some talks with you. I would stay at the Embassy and probably a

[1] Moran diary, 8 April 1954: *The Struggle for Survival*, pages 539–41.
[2] Moran diary, 12 April 1954: *The Struggle for Survival*, page 542.
[3] Speech of 28 April 1954: Randolph S. Churchill (editor), *The Unwritten Alliance*, pages 140–1.
[4] Speech of 30 April 1954: Randolph S. Churchill (editor), *The Unwritten Alliance*, pages 142–4.

night or two with Bernie.' Churchill added that in a month's time 'We shall know more than we know now about several things—mostly tiresome,' and he ended: 'I should keep the plan secret till the last moment. Do you like the idea? All good wishes, Winston.' [1]

An immediate threat of an escalation of war came in the last week of April, from the Far East where, in Indo-China, French forces surrounded at Dien Bien Phu appealed to America and Britain for help.

On Sunday April 25 Churchill held two emergency meetings with the Ministers 'immediately available' to consider an urgent proposal put forward that day by the United States Government, for a joint Anglo-American military intervention in Indo-China. It was Eden who, at these meetings, recommended that Britain 'should decline' to be associated 'with any immediate declaration of intention to check the expansion of Communism in South-East Asia' or to join in any 'precipitate military intervention' in Indo-China. Churchill had no doubt, he told the Cabinet three days later, that Eden 'had been right' in his recommendation.

On April 26, Churchill told Eisenhower's representative, Admiral Radford: 'The British people would not be easily influenced by what happened in the distant jungles of SE Asia; but they did know that there was a powerful American base in East Anglia and that war with China, who would invoke the Sino-Russian Pact, might mean an assault by Hydrogen bombs on these islands.' Churchill went on, as the record of the conversation noted, 'to impress on Admiral Radford the danger of war on the fringes, where the Russians were strong and could mobilise the enthusiasm of nationalist and oppressed peoples. His policy was quite different: it was conversations at the centre. Such conversations should not lead either to appeasement or, he hoped, to an ultimatum; but they would be calculated to bring home to the Russians the full implications of Western strength and to impress upon them the folly of war.' [2]

On Tuesday April 27, the French Ambassador to London went to Downing Street with a message for Churchill from Laniel, the French Prime Minister, 'urging reconsideration of this decision'. But Churchill had felt 'obliged', he told the Cabinet on April 28, 'to reject this further appeal'. To try to influence the British policy makers, a French military officer had come specially from Paris to ask the Chiefs of Staff

---

[1] 'My dear Friend', 'Private & Personal', 'Top Secret', 22 April 1954: Premier papers, 11/666. Eisenhower's reply was unhelpful: 'The United States and Britain,' he wrote, 'seem to reach drastically different answers to problems involving the same set of basic facts.' (Telegram, 26 April 1954: Eisenhower papers.)

[2] 'Top Secret', 'Record of a conversation at dinner at Chequers, Monday, April 26, 1954': Premier papers, 11/645.

to give British air support to the embattled French forces in Indo-China. But the Chiefs of Staff 'adhered to their opinion', Churchill told the Cabinet, 'that air intervention of the kind proposed would not be effective in saving the garrison at Dien Bien Phu'.[1]

On the Sunday, Eden had flown to Geneva for an Anglo-Franco-American conference on Indo-China. At the conference, he maintained the British position of non-intervention. 'It is no good putting in troops to control the situation in the jungle,' Churchill explained to Lord Moran on April 28. 'Besides,' he added, 'I don't see why we should fight for France in Indo-China when we have given away India.'[2]

On April 26 the final volume of Churchill's war memoirs, 'Triumph and Tragedy', was published in Britain. Among those who wrote to him about it was Brendan Bracken, his friend of more than thirty years:

I ought to know something about your capacity for work as I have had plenty of opportunities of witnessing it since the far-off days when you were living at Hosey Rigg and rebuilding Chartwell. Having read the last volume of the six which you have had to write in the intervals of leading the Opposition and the Government, I can only say that there never was and never will be such an animal as WSC. I think I could pass an examination in all the volumes you have sent me from time to time: the last is the best.

'Your children and grandchildren,' Bracken added, 'have every reason to bless you for undertaking this Herculean labour for them.'[3]

'Looking back,' Churchill wrote to Desmond Flower of Cassell on May 12, 'it seems incredible that one could have got through all these six volumes and I suppose two million words.'[4] 'The concluding pages,' wrote his wartime Principal Private Secretary, John Martin, on receiving his copy of the volume from Churchill, 'recalled to me the memory of how, when at the height of the Blitz of 1940, I said that I should like to survive "to see the end of the film", you answered that "the scenario of history has no end".'[5]

---

[1] Cabinet Conclusions No. 30 of 1954, 'Secret', 11.30 a.m., 28 April 1954: Cabinet papers, 128/27.

[2] Moran diary, 28 April 1954: *The Struggle for Survival*, pages 543–4.

[3] 'My dear Winston', 3 May 1954: Churchill papers, 2/212. Bracken had been created Viscount in 1952.

[4] 'My dear Desmond', 12 May 1954: Churchill papers, 4/24.

[5] 'Dear Prime Minister', 25 April 1954: Churchill papers, 2/193. In 1940 John Martin was number two to Eric Seal in Churchill's Private Office; he succeeded Seal as Principal Private Secretary in 1941.

50

To Resign or Not to Resign

WITH Eden in Geneva receiving daily press coverage for his leading part in the conference on Indo-China, it was inevitable that once again the question of when Churchill would resign emerged as a focus for political speculation. He himself still spoke of July as the probable, or at least possible, month of departure. Yet his personal relations with most of his Ministers remained warm and affectionate. 'You have the power,' Harold Macmillan wrote to him on 29 April 1954, in thanking him for the final volume of his war memoirs, 'of inspiring loyalty & gratitude in all those who have had the privilege of serving you.' [1]

Among Churchill's guests at Chartwell that May was Lady Violet Bonham Carter, who later wrote to a friend:

He was going through a Valley of Decision, or rather of indecision, about the time when he should relinquish power and I felt that he was in great agony of mind. I urged him, rightly or wrongly, to stay on. He said to me: 'You know you and Beaverbrook are the only two people who really want me to stay.' (If this is true I think it is the first time I have ever held the same opinion as Beaverbrook about anything!) [2]

'W may yet delay his departure from his high place,' Brendan Bracken wrote to Lord Beaverbrook in May 1954, and he went on to explain that Churchill 'alone has the capacity to hold on to excitable Uncle Sam's coat-tails'. No one could foretell, Bracken added, 'what the US may do in fulfilling its declared intentions of going to all lengths to prevent a Communist domination of Indo-China which may quickly spread over all SE Asia'. [3]

It was Indo-China which now replaced Egypt as the focus of international concern. At Geneva, Eden had made it clear to the Ameri-

---

[1] Letter of 29 April 1954: Churchill papers, 2/220.
[2] Letter of 6 July 1954: Gilbert Murray papers. The friend was Gilbert Murray, the philosopher and classicist.
[3] Letter dated only 'Sunday', May 1954: Beaverbrook papers.

cans, as Selwyn Lloyd told the Cabinet on May 3, that pending the outcome of the negotiations at Geneva, Britain 'must decline to be drawn
into the war in Indo-China or even into promising moral support for
measures of intervention of which the full scope was not yet known'.

He was sure, Churchill told the Cabinet, that Ministers 'would endorse the policy' which Eden was pursuing. At the same time, he
warned, 'it must be recognised that the fall of Dien Bien Phu, which
now seemed inevitable, would afford great encouragement to Communists throughout the world'. Britain 'must seek to counter its effects
by pressing forward, as soon as the Geneva Conference was over, the
efforts to establish an effective system of collective defence for South-
East Asia and the Western Pacific'.[1]

Dien Bien Phu fell on May 7.

On May 14 Churchill went to the Needles to join the Royal Yacht
Britannia as it brought Queen Elizabeth and the Duke of Edinburgh
back from their Commonwealth tour.[2] 'He and I and his valet climbed
up a gangway from a naval launch,' Jock Colville later recalled, and
he added: 'Quite a remarkable achievement by W.'[3]

Together, Churchill and his Sovereign stood on the bridge of *Britannia* as she sailed up the Thames. 'One saw this dirty commercial river
as one came up,' the Queen later recalled, 'and he was describing it as
the silver thread which runs through the history of Britain.' Churchill
saw things, the Queen added, 'in a very romantic and glittering way;
perhaps one was looking at it in a rather too mundane way'.[4] The
Duke of Edinburgh, Churchill commented to his doctor on the following day, 'knew all about its history'.[5]

On May 17, in the House of Commons, Churchill moved an Address
of Welcome to the Queen on her safe return. During the royal tour, he
said, 'Even Envy wore a friendly smile,' and he added: 'I assign no limits
to the reinforcement which this Royal journey may have brought to
the health, the wisdom, the sanity and hopefulness of mankind.'[6]

Churchill did not speak of Envy only in a poetic or romantic sense.
Half a century earlier he had been a pioneer of Liberal social reform

---

[1] Cabinet Conclusions No. 31 of 1954, 'Secret', 5 p.m., 3 May 1954: Cabinet papers, 128/27.

[2] The tour had begun on 23 November 1953.

[3] Sir John Colville: notes for the author, 1987.

[4] Her Majesty Queen Elizabeth II recollections: *The Queen and Commonwealth*, television
programme, produced by Peter Tiffin, transmitted on 22 April 1986.

[5] Moran diary, 15 May 1954: *The Struggle for Survival*, pages 547–9.

[6] Speech of 17 May 1954: *Hansard*.

and an advocate of minimum standards below which no one should be allowed to fall. Now, in May 1954, shortly before the Queen's return, he had told the Cabinet that in his view 'priority in further social progress should be accorded to improvement of the position of old-age and war-disability pensioners'.[1]

On May 20 Clementine Churchill left England for Aix-les-Bains to seek a cure for her neuritis, which was causing her much suffering. On May 22 Churchill wrote to her in his own hand:

My darling Clemmie,

I am so glad yr journey was so swift & smooth, & I await with eagerness yr account of all the arrangements.

Here all is well but hard. I have no less than 3 speeches next week—

Payment of MP's on wh I have got my way (not without miaouings): The women's meeting at the Albert Hall & a debate on Friday about the atomic agreement wh I published. That is indeed a packet.

Anthony has at last decided to come & all is in train.

Do let me know about yr treatment & how it occupies & helps you.

Mrs Dean Acheson has sent me one of her pictures, wh she promised 3 years ago. Patrick says it is quite good.[2] Oddly enough it is a scene in Antigua, wh you have taken under yr protection. I am just off to Chequers & will write to you tomorrow.

With all my love & prayers for yr restoration to full health & strength.

Your ever loving husband

W

'Have you seen,' Churchill added, 'they have a new disease "atrophic rhinitis". I hope I shall escape it.'[3]

That weekend, Churchill wrote to Eisenhower, in a letter which was not shown to the Cabinet:

My dear Friend,

I am planning to leave for Washington on the 17th arriving 18th as outlined in our telegrams of May 13 and 15, and shall be at your convenience at the British Embassy for a few days thereafter. I think the announcement might be fitted in with Geneva as soon as possible, perhaps even this week. If you still like the idea, I will suggest the text of the communiqué.

---

[1] Cabinet Conclusions, No. 32 of 1954, 'Secret', 11.30 a.m., 5 May 1954: Cabinet papers, 128/27.

[2] Patrick Buchan-Hepburn, the Chief Whip, himself a very good artist.

[3] 'My darling Clemmie', from 10 Downing Street, 22 May 1954: Spencer-Churchill papers. Dr Michael Dunnill, Consultant Pathologist at the John Radcliffe Hospital, Oxford, writes: 'Atrophic rhinitis is a rather nonspecific condition that follows a variety of nasal disorders but is not in itself infectious.' (Letter to the author, 23 January 1987.)

The main and obvious topic is interchange of information about atomics, etc., and the progress for your great design to develop its harmless side. Apart from that we will talk over anything that crops up. For instance, I should like to reinforce Malaya, and Egypt is my first reserve. With your support a sound and dignified arrangement should be possible. I sincerely hope you will be able to postpone sending the Egyptians any aid until you and I have had our talks.

'It seems to me,' Churchill's letter ended, 'that our meetings in the easy informal manner that we both desire may be a help in brushing away this chatter about an Anglo-American rift which can benefit no-one but our common foes.' [1]

On May 25 Churchill wrote again to his wife. This time his letter was dictated. His daughter Diana, his friend Lady Salisbury, and the Edens had been his guests:

Darling,

The weekend at Chequers was a great success. Diana admirable. Jock in particular was enormously impressed with his long talk with her. Betty [2] came over and played Bezique with me. I thought this was what she had played last time, but of course it was then Oklahoma, and she had not played Bezique for years. However she had very good cards and held her own. Anthony and Clarissa enjoyed themselves, but poor Clarissa is, as you probably know, too ill to go back to Geneva. The Doctors have diagnosed duodenal trouble.

I had very good talks with Anthony and we are in pretty close agreement on the Geneva issues, though of course I want to be very careful not to have a break with the Americans. They are the only people who can defend the free world even though they bring in Dulles to do it. There are still hopes of a practical, minor result with an armistice or ceasefire for the local situation. Why are you angry with Bidault? He does not seem to have done anything wrong and is very friendly to us.

We all came up to London after dinner on Sunday, and Monday was Payment of Members in the House. It all worked out as I wished and had planned. The Tory Party are said to be very angry but they seem quite friendly in the Smoking Room and considering they were free to do whatever they liked and get paid a monkey for it, I think they will get over any moral sulkiness.

I am trying to have the debate on Friday about the Quebec Agreement, (about which there was that row in the House) withdrawn as Attlee made a special and public appeal to me in the House to do so. It is really up his street and I am quite content to leave it there.

This really is an intensely busy week. Today after all the excitement of Payment of Members, in which I avoided speaking, I have had Billy Graham

---

[1] 'My dear Friend', signed 'Every good wish, Winston', 'Message from the Prime Minister to the President', 'Top Secret', 24 May 1954: Eisenhower papers.

[2] Lady Salisbury, born in 1897, the eldest daughter of Lord Richard Cavendish, and the wife of the 5th Marquess of Salisbury, whom she had married in 1915.

for half-an-hour, to see me. He made a very good impression and his latest triumph has been to convert the Archbishop of Canterbury. I advised him not to allow mundane considerations to bulk too largely in his mission, and to stick to the spiritual side. I think he finds anti-Communism a pretty good ally to salvation in the United States. After this quite agreeable meeting I had the Duke of Windsor to luncheon, who looked very well and made himself most agreeable. The American historians are bringing out some beastly documents in their eighth Volume, but they will do no harm and I expect it is only put in to add some sensationalism to what would otherwise be a boring book.[1]

Talking of War historians, I have an overwhelming case against the Admiralty historian.[2] He belongs to the type of retired Naval Officers who think that politicians should only be in the Admiralty in time of War to take the blame for naval failures and provide the Naval Officers with rewards in the cases of their successes, if any.

Thursday, alas, I have to address the Women at the Albert Hall—Mrs Emmet in the Chair.[3] This is a toil which lies ahead of me and I do not conceal from you that original composition is a greater burden than it used to be, while I dislike having my speeches made for me by others as much as I ever did.

Churchill's letter continued:

Alas, I have had two bits of bad luck. The black swans have hatched out and there is only one alive and swimming about with its parents. One dead one has been retrieved. Vincent has no idea what has happened to the other four. Perhaps they were stolen by somebody who was prowling around. The fox was certainly not guilty. However even one is very attractive riding on its Mamma's back.[4]

The other piece of bad luck is more serious; 'Red Winter' the Irish horse in whom I have a half share has a chill and is probably unfit to run in the £6,000 race which was one of our principal fixtures next Thursday. I suppose she got to hear that I had to go and address the Women and was offended.

[1] Volume 8 of *Foreign Relations of the United States, 1940* dealt with the Duke of Windsor's contacts with German diplomats in Lisbon, in 1940.

[2] The naval historian Captain Stephen Roskill, later a fellow of Churchill College, Cambridge, author of the multi-volume official history, *War at Sea*, in which he wrote, of the sinking of the *Prince of Wales* and *Repulse*: 'It is beyond doubt that Churchill initiated the idea of the two ships going East, and that the First Lord and the First Sea Lord, Mr Alexander and Admiral Pound, strongly opposed it at many meetings of the Defence Committee and Chiefs of Staff Committee ... In the end Alexander and Pound gave way.' (Roskill, *The War At Sea*, volume 1, pages 553-9.)

[3] From 1951 to 1954 Mrs Emmet was Chairman of the Conservative Women's National Advisory Committee. In 1955 she became Chairman of the National Union of Conservatives, and was elected to Parliament. She was created a Life Peer in 1964.

[4] Denis Kelly later recalled how, to protect his swans, Churchill 'installed a revolving search-light and a device which went bang every few minutes. Before going to bed he would draw back the curtain to see if his deterrents were functioning.' (Denis Kelly: in conversation with the author, 25 March 1987.)

As I have now got out of the debate on Friday on the Quebec Agreement I am able to go to Kempton and I have invited Randolph and June. From Kempton I go down to Chartwell. Maria has just arrived from Frinton where she has had very harsh weather but where the children enjoyed the beach and Jeremy wants to plunge into the sea. She and Christopher are dining tonight and everything is going most smoothly in the household.

'I have used Miss Portal to put this down for me,' Churchill added, explaining the reason for his having dictated the letter, 'as I could not possibly have written it with my own hand during these exceptionally busy days. I enclosed it in my letter as a bulletin.'[1]

On May 27 Churchill spoke to the mass meeting of Conservative women at the Albert Hall. His speech lasted for more than forty minutes, a considerable achievement for a man of seventy-nine and a half. It was his belief, he said, 'that we may live to see—or you may—the awful secrets which science has wrung from nature serve mankind instead of destroying it, and put an end to the wars they were called forth to wage'.[2]

'All well here,' Churchill telegraphed to his wife later that day. 'Albert Hall speech was great success.'[3] Churchill had spoken of the controversial issue of an increase in the pay of Members of Parliament—an increase to which many, perhaps a majority, of Conservatives in the constituencies were opposed.[4] He began cautiously, telling his women listeners: 'And now when I speak about our institutions I come to a point where I ought to be rather careful. And here I am going to ask you a favour. I probably will not be asking you many more. It is not to change your opinion but only to consider mine in a friendly spirit. Of course you know what I am coming to. It is this payment of Members. I would like you just to hear what I have to say.'

Churchill then set out the arguments in their most serious constitutional and ideological aspect:

I am sure it is a very bad thing to have the tremendous affairs and responsibilities of the State discharged by men, a large number of whom are themselves seriously embarrassed. It is remarkable that six Conservatives and six Socialists on the Committee studied this question impartially and came to the same conclusion, namely, that there was real and widespread hardship.

---

[1] 'Darling', from 10 Downing Street, 25 May 1954: Spencer-Churchill papers.
[2] Speech of 27 May 1954: Randolph S. Churchill (editor), *The Unwritten Alliance*, pages 147–52.
[3] Telegram despatched 27 May 1954: Churchill papers, 1/50.
[4] On 24 May 1954, following a Report of the Select Committee on Members' Expenses, the House of Commons had voted by 280 votes to 166 to raise the Members' allowance by £500 a year, above the existing £1,000 salary. R. A. Butler's proposal for a variable expense allowance of up to £500 a year was defeated by 276 votes to 205. The motion for an increase had been put by George Thomas (Labour) and seconded by Robert Boothby (Conservative).

But I do not think myself we ought to regard this matter as one of compassion to individuals. That may be a worthy and important factor, but I am not thinking of individuals. I am thinking of the institution.

I have spoken to you of the pressures and strains we are under in the modern world. Great provinces have gone from us, stern rivals and competitors have sprung up on every side. But the institutions which this island, free for a thousand years from invasion, has developed within itself, win it a measure of respect and power which we cannot afford to cast away. There is the constitutional monarchy. There is the free system of law and justice and the ancient judicature which are honoured all over the world, particularly in the great republic of the United States without whom I warn you there is no path through our perils; and there is Parliament and the House of Commons.

When I think that our ancient and famous Parliament, which has so proudly confronted our foes for centuries, is now the most harassed and poorly sustained assembly of its kind among all the Parliaments of the civilized world, of which it has been the cradle and is still the model, I am convinced that a long-term and far-seeing view should be taken of these problems, and that Conservatives who are capable of doing so will be helping all or many of those causes that they cherish so dearly in their hearts.

'I have said I am not asking for your agreement,' Churchill added. 'But I do ask for your patient consideration of the facts which I venture to give to you and the course which I have not hesitated to advise.' [1]

On the day after his speech, Churchill sent his wife a full account of his activities. Payment of Members had become the controversial issue of the hour:

The weekend party as I told you was most successful, and Diana was a great help. It was followed by a busy week. There is a real row in the Tory Party about the payment of Members, and there is no doubt it is very unpopular. Although it was quite certain that the so-called three Party resolution had a majority in the House, there is still much difference and confusion about the method, and Rab is much puzzled to know which way to steer. The more the Conservatives talk and squabble about it, the greater the publicity and the damage.

At the Women's Conference on Wednesday, there was an outburst, and the one poor lady (an MP's wife) who pleaded the case for the increase was not only interrupted but *booed*, a procedure unusual at women's meetings. When I went to the Albert Hall the next day (yesterday) I tackled the question and was received with the utmost goodwill and respect, though they did not like it. I took an awful lot of trouble making up my speech, and it certainly went over most successfully. I spoke for 42 minutes, and was not at all tired (through taking one of Charles's tablets).

Mrs Emmet, who was in the Chair, does not like Lord Woolton. I had suggested to her and him that he might move the Vote of Thanks to the

[1] Speech of 27 May 1954: Churchill papers, 5/54.

Chair at the end, in case my speech did not last long enough. She does not like him and nipped the organ in with a very prompt National Anthem so he was not able to speak at all. He took it very well, and nobody noticed it except the two or three who were in the know. I am sending you the best report that is available. There is so much going on that the papers are very congested. I was very glad to get it over, and have nothing now until the Constituency on the 26th of June.

The 17th is still my date for the aeroplane. Anthony will come too, and we are both invited to stay at the local place (wh will make things easier). I use those terms because one never can be sure what happens to letters in foreign countries in these highly civilised times. Anthony is doing very well at Geneva and seems to be entirely wrapped up in his task. Naturally he longs to have something to show at the end of it all. It will be very necessary to make sure that we do not have a rift. But I think it is going all right.[1]

Churchill broke off his letter at this point. He continued it later that day:

I began dictating this going down to Kempton where 'Prince Arthur' was running. He was said to have a very good chance, and he certainly galloped ahead of all the others for three-quarters of the way. He then continued to go on at the same or even a faster pace, but the mass overtook him and he came in only fourth. He certainly looks beautiful and has a very long stride: It is thought now he may do better over two miles than over one and a half, and he will run that distance in a race at Ascot. Audrey Pleydell-Bouverie turned up on the racecourse, having come over from Paris to see her horse run.[2] She was very confident of it. It ran second and as I backed it both ways I was no loser. Randolph and June also came and I think enjoyed themselves.

'L'Avengro' is still reported to be galloping well. I am going to the Derby on Wednesday; if we are able to finish Cabinet at about 12.45 p.m., there seems to be a general desire on the part of my colleagues to go, and Rab is making a feature of it.

The police have now made a report on the death or disappearance of the cygnets. They say the criminals were carrion crows. The one survivor is said to be very well, and I hope to see him tonight riding on his Mamma's back. The big red fish in the garden pool are threatening to spawn, and I have got the Zoo expert coming over tomorrow to advise how best we ought to handle this very difficult problem. Max is coming to lunch tomorrow, and Violet is coming to stay the weekend. She was giving away prizes at a school about 20 miles from Chartwell, and was delighted to come. Mary and Christopher will, as you know, be staying in the house, and Sarah and her husband are coming over to

[1] Churchill noted at this point of his letter: 'I put this in a plain envelope not to attract attention.'

[2] Audrey James, former wife of the American department store millionaire Marshall Field. In 1931, after Churchill had been knocked down by a car in New York, she had lent him and Mrs Churchill her New York house in which to recuperate. In 1938 she married Major Peter Pleydell-Bouverie, Chairman of the *Western Gazette* and Director of the *Bristol Evening Post*.

lunch on Sunday. We have lots of films and I hope some of them will be good.

The *Recorder* has collapsed & R has been taken on for his weekly article on Press by *Truth*.

I have only given one luncheon party, of eight. It was in honour of Odette, whom Randolph located. He and June came, and so did Christopher and Mary, and I persuaded Betty [1] to come for, I think, her first outing, apart from Chequers. She can get about on her crutches, though with much difficulty, and of course the lift was indispensable. The party was said to be very pleasant.

Otherwise I have dined & lunched with Christopher or Jock for company, and played a good deal of Bezique. Christopher had a lesson this morning & I shall soon see if he is a good pupil. I am writing in my bed at Chartwell after having a little sleep. I will write to you again Sunday & in the meanwhile send you all my fondest love.

Your ever loving husband

W

'15 stone exactly on yr machine,' Churchill noted in his postscript, 'but rather battered & vy sore eyes.' [2]

Three days later, on May 31, Churchill wrote again:

My darling,

We had a jolly weekend. Mrs Landemare distinguished herself as usual. Violet made herself most agreeable, and Mary made everything go well. Sarah came down for luncheon and dinner yesterday and Antony [3] for dinner. We had three films, of which one, with Danny Kaye, was very lively and laughable, the second *Idiot*, a terrible Russian story, very effectively presented, and the third an American attempt at the same sort of thing, very grim and ghastly, as if there was nothing in life but infidelity, murder and suicide.

Things are not going too well at your place (G) [4] though there is still a hope of producing something. The Frogs are getting all they can for nothing, and we are getting nothing for all we can. I think my aeroplane journey may be very necessary. Meanwhile at home the MPs' salaries or expenses, because the choice is still open, causes much concern, and I am motoring up now to see the Executive of the 1922 Committee. (It turned out all right. 2 hours.)

I think we have made the best possible arrangements for the spawning. The Zoo man fully approved. Vincent has planted a lot of little flowering water weeds in the shingle amongst the stepping stones in the shallow part, offering the big fish attractive glades for their approaching honeymoon. During the Whitsun holiday I am going to take the little ones out of the spring pool and put them in the top one of all. I am sure the cold water has

---

[1] Lady Salisbury. The Odette for whom the luncheon was given was Odette Pol Roger.
[2] 'My darling', 28 May 1954: Spencer-Churchill papers.
[3] Sarah's husband, Antony Beauchamp.
[4] Geneva, thirty-five miles north of Aix-les-Bains.

kept them back enormously compared to the others, which are really beautiful, and little more than two years old.

The garden and the lawns are looking lovely, but the poor pink rhody was
sold a pup by that unnatural spring in February which brought so many
pink flowers low. Your wisteria trees on the other hand are magnificent.
The real injury of the cold weather is to the gunnera. I doubt if it will be half
the ordinary size.

There is no doubt that the weekend at Chartwell did me a lot of good. I
feel much less tired than when I wrote to you last Friday, although I have
had to do a lot of paper work and read a lot of telegrams in the interval. The
weather has been queer—48 hours' real heat between 70 and 80, then down
to between 50 and 60, and cloudy; and now today, of course, when one is
motoring up to London, brilliant sunshine, though cool.

I am longing to get your next letter, and hope you will have some encouraging results to report.

Churchill's letter ended:

I got back here (No. 10) at 6 p.m. after the '22' meaning to play Bezique.
But vy sensibly I went to sleep instead. Christopher is dining. Duncan flies to
USA tonight.

All my love my dearest one. I think of you often amid the daily cares.
Your ever loving husband.

W

[Sketch of a pig][1]

'The glorious first of June is cold and dull,' Churchill telegraphed
to his wife on Tuesday June 1. 'Hope all is going well. Much love,
W.'[2] Four days later he wrote to her, of the events of Wednesday
June 2, an 'active day' he called it:

Cabinet till 12.20 p.m. Six or eight Ministers wanted to go to the Derby
and I said they were 'under starter's orders'. I went and lunched with the
Derbys. It is wonderful how she has got over her terrible wounds. I could see
no trace whatever on her neck of the bullet which so nearly severed her
jugular vein.[3] I saw Sydney, who is very gay and valiant. Rab confided to
me that he had bad news. I do not write it.[4]

---

[1] 'My darling', 31 May 1954: Spencer-Churchill papers.
[2] Telegram despatched 1 June 1954: Churchill papers, 1/50.
[3] Churchill's second reference to the occasion when Isabel, wife of the 18th Earl of Derby, was
sitting alone in the dining room at Knowsley one evening, and the footman appeared with a
gun and attempted to murder her. There appeared to be no motive; the footman was found
guilty but insane. Both the butler and the under-butler had been killed when they came into the
room following the shooting. 'Churchill was sympathetic,' Jock Colville later recalled, 'but shared
the general surprise that in the 1950s anybody, even Lord Derby, still had an *under*-butler.' (Sir
John Colville, recollections: letter to the author, 6 July 1987.)
[4] Sydney Elizabeth Butler, R. A. Butler's wife, the daughter of Samuel Courtauld, was gravely
ill; she died on 9 December 1954.

In the evening we had a further two hours Cabinet about the MPs' Pay, about which there is a tremendous row in the Tory Party.[1] Rab takes a vehement view that we should conform to the free vote of the House, but the general feeling is overwhelming that there should be a compromise. The disadvantage of this is that the Opposition will get about three-quarters of what the House voted. This they will take and at the same time feel free to throw all the blame on us, saying, as they will be able to do with truth, that it was *our* scheme.

After that I presided as Colonel at the Fourth Hussars Balaclava centenary dinner. They were all very devoted. Ogier and Tim Rodgers were both there.[2]

On June 5 Churchill was in the Chair at a long and wide-ranging Cabinet. When Eden, reporting on the progress of the Geneva talks, said that neither the Americans nor the French had yet established any contact with the Communist representatives, whereas he, Eden, had met both Molotov and Chou En-lai, Churchill approved Eden's stance, telling the Cabinet 'that the chance of preserving world peace should not be prejudiced by irrational American inhibitions against making any contact with Communist representatives'. Eden should not, said Churchill, 'be deterred by fear of such misrepresentations from continuing to follow the methods which he had adopted in the hope of securing a successful outcome from the Conference. He should, however, be on his guard against the greater danger that the negotiations might be fruitlessly prolonged while the Communists improved their military position in Indo-China.'

Churchill also told the Cabinet of June 5 that he had suggested to President Eisenhower that he might pay 'a short visit' to Washington, for informal talks on matters 'of current concern' to the two Governments. Eisenhower had suggested that Eden accompany Churchill, and that they should arrive in Washington on June 18.

He thought it important, Churchill said, 'that this opportunity for personal discussions with the President should not be missed. He was specially concerned to take advantage of the President's willingness to discuss the problems created by the development of the hydrogen bomb, and for that purpose he proposed that Lord Cherwell should accompany him to Washington.' The other matter which he was

---

[1] Churchill had dictated 'tremendous' about the row in the Tory Party (Churchill papers, 1/50). When he re-read the letter before signing it, he inserted the world 'petty' after it in his own hand.

[2] 'My darling one', 5 June 1954: Spencer-Churchill papers. In September 1945, these two officers, Major Ogier and Lieutenant Rodgers, had been seconded to look after him by Field Marshal Alexander, at Lake Como, during Churchill's first overseas holiday after the General Election defeat of 1945, Ogier as his ADC and Rodgers as Commander of the twenty-four-man guard.

'specially anxious to pursue with the President', Churchill explained, 'was the possibility of securing some fresh American initiative which would enable us to reduce our military commitment in Egypt'.

When the Washington arrangements had been made, Churchill added, it had seemed 'reasonable to assume' that the Geneva Conference would be over by June 18. 'This now seemed less likely; but it would be unfortunate if this opportunity for personal talks with the President had to be forgone because of the prolongation of the Geneva Conference.'

Eden, who spoke next, said that it would be 'difficult' for him to go to Washington on June 18 if the negotiations at Geneva had not then been concluded. 'It would create a bad impression if he appeared to abandon the Conference for the sake of two or three days' discussions in Washington.' He was, however, 'reluctant to suggest that the Prime Minister should on this account postpone his proposed visit; for personal talks between the Prime Minister and the President at this juncture might yield valuable results'. On the other hand, Eden warned, 'an embarrassing situation might arise if, while the Prime Minister was in Washington, the Geneva Conference broke down and strong political pressures developed in the United States in favour of military intervention in Indo-China'.[1]

Also on June 5, the Cabinet discussed a proposal by Eden to support the Trucial Sheikhs in the Persian Gulf against the United States oil company Aramco, which had sent an oil prospecting party over the Saudi Arabian border into territory 'where the Trucial Sheikhs claimed jurisdiction'. Eden added: 'There was good reason to believe that very substantial amounts of oil might be found in this area, and it was vital to British interests that the American company should not establish a claim to work it. They had no rights in the area, and it was known that their action in prospecting there would not be supported by the United States Government.' He had therefore proposed 'that this prospecting party should be removed from the area, if necessary by force'.

Churchill, while agreeing with Eden 'that this party should be removed from the area', was, he said, 'reluctant to authorise the use of fire-arms—especially as the British force immediately available seemed to be much smaller in numbers than the intruders. He would have preferred to wait until the prospecting party could be confronted with overwhelming forces, so that recourse to violence might be avoided.'

---

[1] According to Macmillan, Churchill's colleagues 'were considerably alarmed at the idea of his going off on his own accompanied only by Lord Cherwell' and decided: 'If the Geneva Conference was over, Eden should go too. If it was not over, Churchill's visit should be postponed.' (*Tides of Fortune*, page 530.)

He would be 'quite ready', Eden replied, 'to consider how his proposed instructions could be modified so as to reduce the risk of personal injury to United States citizens'. It might be 'helpful', Eden added, if Churchill 'could also send a personal message to President Eisenhower asking him to use his authority to recall this prospecting party'.[1]

This Churchill agreed to do. A draft message was prepared by Selwyn Lloyd, and sent by Churchill as drafted.

In his letter to his wife on June 5, Churchill noted that June 5, like June 2, had been a 'lively' day:

Anthony returned and gave us a full account of the gloomy and confusing prospects at Geneva, where the French are paralysed and the Americans very difficult. The Communists are playing their winning hand with civility. A crisis may arise around Hanoi in the latter half of June. This causes complications with that other date I mentioned to you—the 17th. We shall know more in a week. It may well be that the Conference will end in time for Anthony to come with me. We had a two hours Cabinet on this sombre situation before going on to the more squalid but not less bewildering trouble of MPs' Pay.

Churchill's letter continued:

I then rushed off to Hurst Park where we had decided at the last moment to run Prince Arthur in the Winston Churchill Stakes. Premonition, who you will remember in the Leger, was 10 to 1 on, and the *Evening Standard* described Prince Arthur as 'only fit for a handicap'. However we hoped that he would do better over the longer distance of two miles than one-and-a-half. He certainly did.

Premonition is of course one of the best long distance horses alive and we were 25 to 1. However Prince Arthur gave a performance which restored his reputation and value. For one thrilling second a hundred yards from home he took the first place; he was third, but even that paid his expenses for a good many months (£144.5.0.).

It was very exciting and I was very glad to have gone. An awful row arose between the 1st and 2nd, resulting from a Photo Finish between Premonition and her pacemaker which is in the same stables as the Queen used. The pacemaker looked like winning, whereas everything had been staked on the favourite, so the jockey of the pacemaker has been brought before the Stewards for having checked his horse to let the favourite win. One can make too much pace.

I am now on my way back to Chartwell. Christopher came up to see the race and has returned from Frinton. The weather has turned definitely warmer though it has been raining heavily most of the afternoon. (Today, Sunday, cloudy, rainy, windy, bloody.) The children at Frinton have enjoyed themselves enormously and Maria consented to let Christopher come back and look after me. We have a film *Cyrano de Bergerac* tonight.

---

[1] Cabinet Conclusions No. 39 of 1954, 'Secret', 11 a.m., 5 June 1954: Cabinet papers, 128/27.

I have forgotten the story but I believe it is good. (It was worth seeing.) [1]

I stay at Chartwell till Tuesday when I come again to Hurst Park to see Pigeon Vole run in a smallish race; he has a good chance of winning. [2] Thereafter an Audience and then an English-Speaking Union Dinner with a nine minutes broadcast. I have to come up again for the Trooping of the Colour on the 10th.

Pamela L. came to luncheon on Friday before going to the Fourth of June at Eton to see Grandchildren and the fireworks. She sent you many messages. Her form of arthritis is in the left side and comes on in very sharp pain but only at intervals. She takes potent drugs. I am arranging for her to come to the Trooping of the Colour and bring a Grandchild. She came last year and asked if I could manage it. I am sure it can be arranged.

I have got a new weighing-machine. It stands next to yours in my bathroom. It says I am 14 stone and a half compared to the previous version of 15 stone on your machine and 15 stone & a ½ on the broken-down one at Chartwell. The two in London are to be tested on Tuesday next and if your machine is proved to be wrong you will have to review your conclusions and I hope abandon your régime. I have no grievance against a tomato, but I think one should eat other things as well. [3]

On June 6, a Sunday, Churchill added a postscript to his letter of the previous day; a further report, in his own hand, after he had learned that Clementine Churchill would be home the following weekend:

Darling, I rejoice you are coming home on Saturday for a Chequers weekend. Miss Marston arranged with Mrs Hill that the Chequers cook & kitchen maid shd come down here to Chartwell and cook all this week for me, so that I was able to give Mrs Landemare 9 days' complete holiday. She was not vy well, and was delighted.

Diana, Celia & Edwina are coming to luncheon. Alas the weather! Also the father swan has got out of his pen and is now on the bottom lake. His wife & child are looking for him, & he tried hard to return. We were vy anxious lest he flies off too. I am going to get up and see what can be done. These anxieties are grievous.

Always your everloving husband

Winston

His weight, Churchill added in a postscript, was '14½ (subject to confirmation)'. [4]

*   *   *

[1] Denis Kelly later recalled how, after each film show, 'there would be a short silence, then he would give a little verdict on the film, before we all went up to work. After watching *Wuthering Heights* his only comment was "What terrible weather they have in Yorkshire."' (Denis Kelly recollections: in conversation with the author, 25 March 1987.)

[2] Pigeon Vole came fourth at Hurst Park on 8 June 1954.

[3] 'My darling one', 5 June 1954: Spencer-Churchill papers.

[4] 'Darling', 6 June 1954: Spencer-Churchill papers.

Churchill had made no reference in his letters to his wife of June 2 or June 5 to the anxieties which Eden had expressed to him concerning the date of Churchill's eventual retirement. Pressed to set a date by the Party, and aware of his own ill-health, Churchill had spoken to Eden about handing over the Premiership to him at some time in July, after his return from the meeting with Eisenhower in Washington. Eden, unhappy about the July date, had been to see Churchill to explain why he would prefer an even earlier date, if possible before the end of June, as soon as possible after Churchill's return from the United States. On June 7, Eden wrote to Churchill, in his own hand:

My dear Winston,

Thank you for listening so patiently to the problems of July. As it seems to me, a new administration must have the chance once formed to face Parliament for, I would suppose, at least two weeks before the recess begins.

If it cannot do this, it will not be able to prove itself or receive the vote of Parliament. Moreover if the new govt has not been endorsed by Parliament, its authority to take decisions during the recess could be challenged with some justification.

I realize that this may be a more difficult time-table for you. It occurs to me that someone like Norman Brook, who is familiar with such problems, might perhaps write out a programme under your direction, which we could then look at together. There is also the point that any new administration should have a fair chance of contact with its officials before the holidays.[1]

Churchill replied four days later, in his own hand. His letter did not bring the answer, or the comfort, Eden had hoped for:

My dear Anthony,

I am not able to commit myself to what you suggest in your letter of June 7. I am increasingly impressed by the crisis and tension which is developing in world affairs and I should be failing in my duty if I cast away my trust at such a juncture or failed to use the influence which I possess in the causes [of Peace through Strength] [2] we both have at heart.

Before I can judge the issue I must see what emerges from [my] our talks [with Eisenhower] in Washington and how they affect the various schemes I have in mind. [and I cannot therefore at this juncture settle on any definite date] I am afraid this may entail a longer period than your letter contemplates. It will not I hope extend beyond the autumn which you mentioned to me as an alternative when we talked in the Cabinet Room last week.

I am most anxious to give you the best opportunity to prepare for an election at the end of 1955 and to establish the repute and efficiency of your administration.

I have however to offer wider reasons than this to history and indeed to the nation.

[1] 'My dear Winston', 7 June 1954: Churchill papers, 6/4.

[2] This, and the next three phrases in square brackets, were deleted by Churchill, and replaced by the words that follow them, before the letter was re-written and sent.

My personal regard and affection for you will ever weigh with me. I am always ready to talk these matters over with you with all the frankness which our friendship makes possible between us.[1]

Four days after writing this letter to Eden, Churchill discussed his retirement date, and Eden's succession, with Lord Moran, who noted in his diary:

'I'm not thinking of retiring, at any rate till September. I have written to Anthony that I do not intend to resign at present. I don't know if he has accepted it. He'd better.' The PM looked very grim. 'Could I tell them,' he added as an afterthought, 'that you thought I was as well as before the stroke?'

I advised him not to use the expression 'stroke'.

'But I like the word,' he said obstinately. 'Of course I know that I'm nearly eighty and that I may get another stroke any day. My heart may stop at any time, but my health is certainly no excuse for evading all these great issues, just because one doesn't know the answers. I'm not going to quit. It would be cowardice to run away at such a time. No,' he said with great emphasis, 'I shall certainly not retire when any day anything might happen.

'It is not'—and his voice rose—'as if I were making way for a strong young man. Anthony seems to be very tired. I detect strain in his telegrams. Sometimes he sends three thousand words in one day—and there is nothing in them. For instance, he wanted to change all the arrangements that have been made with Ike. He said Dulles had been very difficult and had attacked him. They showed me the account of what had happened, but it had to be pointed out to me how it could be taken as an attack on Anthony.

'Why, one of the incidents,' the PM said scornfully, 'happened a quarter of a century ago. I said I would not change my plans.'

There was a pause and then the PM said quietly: 'He submitted. Look up my May 11 speech, Charles, and you'll see how I gave a warning that nothing can come of these talks at a lower level. They go on, day after day, endlessly. The Foreign Office keeps on splitting hairs. There is no one to say: "Bloody well go and do it." When I read what had happened at Geneva I felt a great sense of defiance. It was just like the war.'[2]

Eden was not alone in wanting Churchill's resignation to take place within weeks rather than months. On the day after his remarks to Lord Moran, Churchill saw Harold Macmillan, to whom he explained why he wished to stay on certainly until September. Macmillan was not convinced, writing to Churchill on June 18. His letter, dictated to a secretary, was marked 'Private and Confidential':

Dear Prime Minister,

I have thought a great deal about the matter which you mentioned to me after the dinner on Wednesday. It was indeed kind of you to take me into your confidence. I appreciate this very much.

---

[1] 'My dear Anthony', 11 June 1954: Churchill papers, 6/4.
[2] Moran diary, 15 June 1954: *The Struggle for Survival*, pages 555–6.

But I must tell you frankly that, in my view, if a new administration is to be formed during this year, it would be a very great advantage for Ministers to be installed in their new offices before and not after the summer holidays. Indeed, I think this is really essential. Otherwise, we shall really waste two or three very precious months.

Of course, there may be developments in the international sphere which would override these considerations. You and Anthony must judge these.

I need hardly say that I am not in the least concerned with my own position. But if someone is to take on my job, the sooner he can start the better. And this applies all round.

Once more, I must tell you how much I appreciate serving you and the support and confidence which you have shown me.

Yours very sincerely

Harold Macmillan[1]

Churchill replied to Macmillan in his own hand, on a single sheet of Downing Street notepaper:

Dear Harold,

I received yr letter yesterday morning.

I do not think it ought to have been written except in yr own hand.

I was well aware of your views.

Yours sincerely,

Winston S. Churchill[2]

Political commentators, even astute political journalists, knew nothing of these sharp exchanges. 'Now that he is on his last lap,' Hugh Massingham had written in the *Observer* on June 6, 'Sir Winston seems to have acquired an ascendancy over his Cabinet that he certainly did not have during the early days of his administration.'[3] On June 20, the day of Churchill's letter to Macmillan, Massingham wrote again in his political column, on the subject of Churchill's future, that there was 'no reason, at least in theory, why he should not lead his party at another General Election'.[4]

[1] 'Dear Prime Minister', 'Private and Confidential', 18 June 1954: Churchill papers, 6/4.
[2] 'Dear Harold', 20 June 1954: Churchill papers, 6/4.
[3] *Observer*, 6 June 1954.
[4] *Observer*, 20 June 1954.

51
Summer 1954: Return to Washington

As he prepared for his American journey, the third of his peace-time Premiership, Churchill spoke, at a dinner given by the English-Speaking Union to welcome General Gruenther to England, of the 'unwritten alliance', as he called it, 'which binds the British Commonwealth and Empire to the great republic of the United States'. It was, he said, 'an alliance far closer in fact than many which exist in writing. It is a treaty with more enduring elements than clauses and protocols. We have history, law, philosophy, and literature; we have sentiment and common interest; we have a language which even the Scottish Nationalists will not mind me referring to as English. We are often in agreement on current events and we stand on the same foundation of the supreme realities of the modern world.'

Churchill then told the English-Speaking Union, the Duke of Edinburgh, who was the guest of honour, and General Gruenther, of his feelings about the 'duty and interests' of both East and West. The duty and interests of both, he said, were 'that they should live in peace together and strive untiringly to remove or outlive their differences'. Churchill warned: 'Humanity stands today at its most fateful milestone. On the one hand science opens a chasm of self-destruction beyond limit. On the other hand she displays a vision of plenty and comfort of which the masses of no race have ever known or even dreamed.'

While the Western world preserved 'at great sacrifice and cost' its military strength, it must never lose sight, he stressed, 'of the importance of a peaceful and friendly settlement of our differences with Russia', and he added: 'What a vista would be open to all if the treasure and toil consumed on weapons of destruction could be devoted to simple and peaceful ends.'[1]

---

[1] Speech of 8 June 1954: Randolph S. Churchill (editor), *The Unwritten Alliance*, pages 153–5.

'I look forward to those talks between you and me,' Churchill telegraphed to Eisenhower on June 10. They were talks, he added, 'which we had always considered an essential part of the vital cooperation of the English-Speaking world. I feel that we have reached a serious crisis in which the whole policy of peace through strength may be involved.'[1]

On June 14 Churchill was at Windsor for the Garter ceremony and service, and was installed as a Knight. He also had an Audience of the Queen. On the following day his friend Lord Camrose died. He was four and a half years younger than Churchill, and had been Churchill's closest adviser on the finances of his memoirs, and on the transfer of Chartwell to the National Trust. Before the war, Camrose had published Churchill's fortnightly articles after Lord Beaverbrook had dropped them, just after Munich. 'His work remains as a living monument,' Churchill wrote in his own hand to Lady Camrose on June 16, 'which will long endure for the good of our hard-pressed country. But the gap so unexpected must be a terrible agony to his nearest and dearest.' 'One comfort at least,' Churchill added, 'is its very suddenness; and to old people it must seem a blessing that the pain and worry of a lingering death was spared him.'[2]

On June 16, at a meeting of the Defence Policy Committee of the Cabinet, Churchill and his Defence Ministers agreed to a dramatic development in Britain's nuclear policy: the production of a British hydrogen bomb, to be built in Britain. This decision was so secret that it was not communicated to the Cabinet. It formed, however, the basis of Churchill's preparations for Washington, and also for Ottawa. Five days after the decision had been made, Churchill set out for Eisenhower what he thought their imminent Conference could seek to achieve now that the French Government had decided to 'clear out' of Indo-China:

I have thought continually about what we ought to do in the circumstances. Here it is.

There is all the more need to discuss ways and means of establishing a firm front against Communism in the Pacific sphere. We should certainly have a SEATO[3] corresponding to NATO, in the Atlantic and European sphere. In this it is important to have the support of the Asian countries. This raises the question of timing in relation to Geneva.

[1] 'My dear Friend', 'Top Secret', 10 June 1954: Eisenhower papers.
[2] 'My dear Lady Camrose', 16 June 1954: Churchill papers, 2/213.
[3] South East Asia Treaty Organization. It was eventually established, in Manila, on 8 September 1954, between Britain, the United States, Australia, New Zealand, Pakistan, France, Thailand and the Philippines.

In no foreseeable circumstances, except possibly a local rescue, could British troops be used in Indo-China, and if we were asked our opinion we should advise against United States local intervention except for rescue.

The SEATO front should be considered as a whole, and also in relation to our world front against Communist aggression. As the sectors of the SEATO front are so widely divided and different in conditions, it is better, so far as possible, to operate nationally. We garrison Hong Kong and the British Commonwealth contributes a division to Korea. But our main sector must be Malaya. Here we have twenty-three battalions formed into five brigades. You are no doubt aware of the operation contemplated in the event of a Communist invasion from Siam. I will bring a detailed plan with me. Alex, who I understand is coming over in July, will discuss it with your Generals.

The question is whence are we to draw reinforcements. There are none at home; our last regular reserves are deployed. It would be a pity to take troops from Germany. On the other hand we have what are called 80,000 men in the Egyptian Canal Zone, which means 40,000 well-mounted fighting troops. Here is the obvious reserve.

Now is the time the Middle East front should be considered together by the United States and Britain. I had hoped more than a year ago that the United States would act jointly with us in negotiating an agreement with the Egyptian military dictatorship in accordance with the terms already agreed between the British and American staffs. It was, however, felt at Washington that America could not go unless invited. The negotiations therefore broke down. Since then there has been a deadlock though the area of dispute is limited.

As time has passed, the strategic aspect of the Canal Zone and base has been continually and fundamentally altered by thermo-nuclear developments and by a Tito-Graeco-Turco front coming into being and giving its hand to Iraq and by America carrying NATO's finger-tips to Pakistan. I like all this improvement in which you and the power and resources of the United States have played so vital a part.

These events greatly diminish the strategic importance of the Canal Zone and base, and what is left of it no longer justifies the expense and diversion of our troops, discharging since the war, not British but international purposes. As far as Egypt is concerned, we shall not ask you for a dollar or a marine. I am greatly obliged by the way you have so far withheld arms and money from the Egyptian dictatorship.

The general theme of completing and perfecting in a coherent structure the world front against Communist aggression, which I suppose in current practice could be described as NATO, MEATO[1] and SEATO, is of course one, but only one of the topics I am looking forward to talking over with you.

---

[1] MEATO (also known as METO), the proposed Middle East Treaty Organization. It was eventually set up, as the Baghdad Pact, in February 1955, between Turkey and Iraq, joined later that year by Britain, Pakistan and Persia, and known (after the withdrawal of Iraq in July 1958) as CENTO (Central Treaty Organization).

Churchill's letter continued:

The other two have long been in my mind. One is better sharing of information and also perhaps of resources in the thermo-nuclear sphere. I am sure you will not overlook the fact that by the Anglo-American base in East Anglia we have made ourselves for the next year or two the nearest and perhaps the only bull's-eye of the target. And finally I seek, as you know, to convince Russia that there is a thoroughly friendly and easy way out for her in which all her hard-driven peoples may gain a broader, fuller and happier life.[1]

On June 22 Churchill was in the Chair at the last Cabinet meeting before he left for the United States and Canada. No mention was made of the decision to build a British hydrogen bomb. Churchill did tell his Ministers, however, that one of his aims in Washington would be to persuade the President to support the building up 'of a defensive front against Communist aggression throughout the world'.

Churchill explained his reasoning on the basis of the problems created by the imminent British withdrawal from Egypt. While he 'accepted', he said, the military argument 'for re-deploying our forces in the Middle East, he continued to be impressed by the political disadvantages of abandoning the position which we had held in Egypt since 1882. This was bound to be deplored by certain sections of Conservative opinion, and the resulting political situation would not be made easier by the developments which were taking place in the Sudan.' He believed, however, he told the Cabinet, that Britain's withdrawal from Egypt 'could be made more palatable to public opinion in this country if it could be presented as a part of a comprehensive Anglo-American plan for building up a defensive front against Communist aggression throughout the world'. He hoped that the talks in Washington 'might result in a declaration foreshadowing the creation of a collective defence system in South-East Asia which would displace, or at least reduce the importance of, the ANZUS Pact, from which the United Kingdom had been excluded'. Such a development would, he believed, 'be welcomed by those sections of public opinion in this country which would be most disturbed by the surrender of our position in Egypt'. Churchill added: 'A close Anglo-American association in the Middle East, parallel with that created in the Atlantic and proposed for South-East Asia, would help to mitigate the political effects of our proposed withdrawal from Egypt.' He also considered that Britain's willingness to conclude a defence agreement with Egypt would be 'a useful bargaining counter' in the talks in Washington. He did not wish to be committed, he said, to resuming the Egyptian

---

[1] 'Message from the Prime Minister, received 6.30 p.m., Monday, June 21, 1954', 'Top Secret': Eisenhower papers.

negotiations before he had 'explored' in Washington 'the extent to which the United States could be persuaded to support us in the negotiations, or even to be associated with us in them'.

Eden was totally opposed to Churchill's suggestion. He was 'doubtful', he said, 'whether the Americans would be willing to join us in the proposed negotiations with Egypt—or, for that matter, whether their direct association with the negotiations would make it easier to reach a satisfactory agreement'. America's influence with the countries of the Middle East, Eden added, 'was not greater than ours: indeed, our own influence in the Middle East as a whole might be damaged if we seemed to be unable to settle our differences with Egypt without American help'.

Churchill reiterated his argument, believing, as he told the Cabinet, 'that some tactical advantage would be lost in the forthcoming discussions in Washington if it were known at the outset that we were now ready to resume those negotiations'. He would prefer, he said, 'to keep this issue open until the whole field of Anglo-American co-operation had been explored in the Washington talks'.

Eden did not accept Churchill's argument, and spoke of how 'his purpose' as Foreign Secretary could be equally met 'by intimating to the Egyptian Government, before he left for Washington, that he had noted their efforts to maintain order in the Canal Zone and that he hoped that conditions there would continue to improve for, as they had already been informed, the defence negotiations could not be resumed while conditions of disorder prevailed in the Zone'.[1]

On this disputatious note, Churchill and Eden prepared to leave for Washington. They flew together from London on the evening of June 24. 'Primarily,' noted Colville during the flight, the purpose of the journey was 'to convince the President that we must co-operate more fruitfully in the atomic and hydrogen sphere and that we, the Americans and British, must go and talk to the Russians in an effort to avert war, diminish the effect of Cold War and procure a ten years' period of "easement" during which we can divert our riches and our scientific knowledge to ends more fruitful than the production of catastrophic weapons.'

Owing to Anglo-American disagreement over South-East Asia, however, as 'reflected very noticeably at the Geneva Conference', the meeting had become 'in the eyes of the world (and the Foreign Secretary) an occasion for clearing the air and re-creating good feeling'.[2]

Once more Churchill was travelling westward across the Atlantic, in search of agreements which would lead him, and the world in

[1] Cabinet Conclusions No. 43 of 1954, 'Secret', 11 a.m., 22 June 1954: Cabinet papers, 128/27.
[2] Colville diary, 25 June 1954: *The Fringes of Power*, pages 691–2.

which he was still a leader, from the fear of nuclear war to the dreams of an age of plenty for all mankind. He had, as always, confidence in his ability to argue his case, and to retain his grip on events. 'Winston was particularly cheerful,' Lord Moran noted during the flight, 'looking incredibly young, his face pink and unlined, his manner boyish and mischievous. Anthony had been to Wimbledon, and his face was reddened by the sun, but he looked tired. He told us that he had found the six-hour sessions at Geneva very fatiguing, especially when he was in the chair. Winston did not appear much interested in his account of Geneva. Perhaps, in the plane, he had difficulty in hearing what Anthony was saying.'[1]

After nine hours' sleep in the aircraft—a Stratocruiser flying at 12,000 feet—and a short stop at Gander, Churchill reached Washington on the morning of Friday 25 June 1954, where he was met by Vice-President Richard M. Nixon and John Foster Dulles. At the airport, before being driven into Washington, he spoke a few words to the American people, the microphones having been set up for him. As typed out in the aeroplane in speech form, they began:

> I have had a very comfortable journey
>   fm my Fatherland
>   to my Mother's Land.
>
> I have come with Anthony Eden to talk over
>   a few family matters
>
>   and try to make sure
>   there are no misunderstandings
>
> The English Speaking family or Brotherhood
>   is rather a large one
> & not entirely without a few things
>   and if we work together
>   we may get along all right ourselves
>
> and do a lot to help our neighbours,
>
> some of whom—
>   on both sides of the Iron Curtain—
> seem to face
>   even greater problems
>   than we do ourselves.[2]

---

[1] Moran diary, 24 June 1954: *The Struggle for Survival*, pages 558-60. In addition to Churchill, Eden, Colville and Moran, the other passengers in the party were Lord Cherwell, Sir Edwin Plowden, Sir Harold Caccia, Denis Allen, Anthony Rumbold and Christopher Soames, as well as what Colville called 'an unusually small body of ancillaries'.

[2] 'PM's speech on landing at Washington from Canopus', 25 June 1954: Churchill papers, 5/54. In reading line ten of his speech, Churchill said 'and not entirely without a few things *here and there*'.

From the airport Churchill, Eden and Christopher Soames were then driven to the White House, their home for the duration of the visit. 'W at once got down to talking to the President,' noted Colville, and he added: 'The first and vast surprise was when the latter at once agreed to talks with the Russians—a possibility of which W had hoped to persuade the Americans after long talks on Indo-China, Europe, atoms. . . .' On all these topics, Colville noted, 'the first impressions were surprisingly and immediately satisfactory while the world in general believes that there is at this moment greater Anglo-American friction than ever in history and that these talks are fraught with every possible complication and difficulty'.[1]

At this luncheon, held in the President's office, the conversation was wide-ranging. 'Among the subjects discussed,' the White House minutes recorded, 'were Germany, France, Guatemala, the Hapsburg and Ottoman Empires, the Kerensky Government in Russia, African colonies, the French position in North Africa, Indo-China, the Oppen-heimer case, the internal problem of Communism, the Boer War, World War II, the relationship of Communist China to Russia, the EDC and NATO and the Locarno Pact.' Before leaving the luncheon table, the minutes noted, Eisenhower 'suggested that whereas it seemed unnecessary to have any fixed agenda, it might be useful to have set down certain key words, such as Egypt, Locarno, etc., as a checklist for discussion in order to make sure that no important topic was overlooked. The President also raised the question of the possible desirability of setting up special joint study groups to report back to the two governments their findings and recommendations on various vexing problems.' To this, Churchill agreed.[2]

Ten minutes after the luncheon ended, there was a further dis-cussion, lasting two hours, at which Churchill asked for 'the possibility of high level talks with the Soviets' to be added to the agenda. Eisen-hower surprised Churchill by saying that he had no objection to such a discussion. Churchill thereupon 'suggested a first "reconnaissance in force" perhaps by himself to see if anything promising developed'. He would be 'interested', he explained, 'in finding out what sort of a man Malenkov was and noted that he had never been outside his own country'. Churchill added that he believed 'there was a deep underly-ing demand on the part of the Russian people to enjoy a better life, particularly after suffering oppression for more than fifty years'.

---

[1] This, and all subsequent Colville diary extracts for Churchill's 1954 Washington visit are taken from Colville diary, 25 June—3 July 1954: *The Fringes of Power*, pages 692–6.

[2] 'Churchill–Eden Visit', 'Memorandum of Conversation', 'Secret' 25 June 1954: Eisenhower papers. Present at the luncheon were Eisenhower, Dulles, Churchill and Eden, as well as one American and one British civil servant (the latter Sir Harold Caccia).

Churchill then turned to the question of Egypt, hoping to secure American participation in a new Anglo-Egyptian agreement. The American minutes recorded his appeal:

The Prime Minister embarked on a prolonged and rather emotional discussion of Egypt. He said the situation must be avoided in which people would think that the United States had driven the UK out of Egypt. He agreed that the strategic importance of the Suez Canal had declined due to the atom bomb and the development of the Balkan Pact.

He recalled, however, that there were more than 50,000 British graves in Egypt or just across its frontiers. He said that the treaty which Anthony had negotiated twenty years before had been unilaterally denounced. This was cheating and he asked what faith could be placed in such people who represented at best a military intrigue and dictatorship.

He said that they must clearly understand that they would receive neither arms nor aid from the United States until they reached agreement and that these would be cut off if they broke any agreement. He said he wanted our guarantee to sustain and support any agreement reached.

Both Dulles and Eisenhower agreed that 'some arrangement could be worked out' under which American aid to Egypt could be suspended if the Anglo-Egyptian agreement were 'violated'. At this point, the discussion turned to South-East Asia, with Churchill telling Eisenhower and Dulles 'that he was anxious to take some of the weight off the United States in its presentation of an anti-Communist front'. Churchill added, however:

. . . that England would never accept going to war in Indo-China. He doubted that the United States would either. He felt, however, that the British could take the major responsibility for the Kra Peninsula line which could be held by sea and air with some ground forces. All of these plans, he said, Lord Alexander would go into with our military people when he came over next month.

He went on to say that in building the front against Chinese aggression he hoped that the Colombo powers would find it possible to join in SEATO as well as the Philippines. He said there was no basic conflict between such a treaty and Eden's idea of a Locarno guarantee of a Geneva settlement.

Turning briefly to the Middle East, Churchill made the remark that it was 'oilism and not colonialism which was evil in the world today'.[1]

There was then a discussion on atomic matters; an examination of the British request for a 'broadening of provisions' for exchange of atomic information. The minutes of part of this discussion are still secret.[2] According to the minutes which can be studied:

[1] 'Churchill–Eden Visit', 'Memorandum of Conversation', 'Top Secret', 3 p.m.–5 p.m., 25 June 1954: Eisenhower papers.

[2] National Security Council letter, 16 April 1986 (attached to the declassified section of the 'Memorandum of Conversation', CEV SPEC-1'), 'Top Secret', White House, 25 June 1954: Eisenhower papers.

In response to a question from the Prime Minister, the President indicated that he felt the US position in the thermo-nuclear field at the present time was several times that of the Russians.

The talk then turned to the possibility of a moratorium of H-bomb experimentation and there appeared to be general agreement that it would be unwise in light of the difficulty of detection and possible concealment of the size of any explosion. There was some further discussion of the dangers which now faced the world as a result of the portability of the bomb.[1]

There was a short adjournment; then, at five o'clock, the discussion on Egypt resumed, with Churchill reiterating 'his feeling that the United States interest in this matter should be so great' that America would be willing to endorse the Anglo-Egyptian agreement, and, as Eden added, 'support freedom of transit' through the Suez Canal. But Eisenhower replied, somewhat negatively, 'that he did not understand what the Prime Minister expected us to do. We could not very well join the negotiations and sign the agreement unless we were asked by both parties to do so.'

A few moments later, both Churchill and Eden 'stressed their desire that we make it clear to the Egyptians that continued assistance from the United States was dependent upon Egyptian fulfilment of their agreement with the British'. It was 'generally agreed', the American notes of the meeting continued, 'that this would be the case and that it should be accomplished in a manner which would not indicate to the Egyptians in advance distrust that they would in fact not live up to the agreement'.[2]

When would he go to Russia, Lord Moran asked Churchill as he was dressing for dinner. 'It might be in July,' Churchill replied.[3]

That evening, June 25, Eisenhower gave a dinner for Churchill to meet the American Cabinet—Eden and Dulles were also present. On the following morning Churchill spent several hours with Eisenhower, 'again', Colville noted, 'to his satisfaction'. It was at this meeting that Churchill told Eisenhower of the decision to manufacture a British hydrogen bomb, and to do so in Britain.

Churchill's next talk with Eisenhower, on June 26, lasted from 9.30 in the morning until just before noon, when the two men walked together to the President's Office in the West Wing. 'I remember being here in this room,' Churchill remarked, 'when I visited President

[1] 'Churchill–Eden Talks', 'Memorandum of Conversation, CEV SPEC-1', 'Top Secret' White House, 25 June 1954: Eisenhower papers.
[2] 'Churchill–Eden Visit', 'Memorandum of Conversation', 'Top Secret', 5 p.m., 25 June 1954: Eisenhower papers.
[3] This, and all subsequent Moran diary extracts for Churchill's 1954 Washington visit are taken from the Moran diary, 25 June–3 July 1954: *The Struggle for Survival*, pages 560–74.

Roosevelt and I had a press conference. The room was absolutely full. They (the newsmen) could not see me; I had to stand on a chair.' Among those to whom Churchill was introduced was Sherman Adams, a former Governor of New Hampshire, who had become Chief of the White House Staff in 1953. Of his talk with Eisenhower, Churchill told Adams: 'I have had a delightful talk with the President. We have many topics in common besides the business in hand.'

Eisenhower then introduced Churchill to the other members of his White House staff with the words 'these people keep me on the straight and narrow path'. Churchill remarked: 'To enable you to put your hand exactly where you want it,' and he added: 'In the last twenty-five years of peace and war, things have gotten ten or fifteen times more complicated. The problems I have now to face are much greater in numbers and complexity than they used to be.' Speaking of the respective British and American systems, Churchill commented: 'You have one safety valve—that is your 48 states. You must be able to dump a lot on to them. I have given serious consideration to the advisability of the return to the heptarchy.'

During their conversation, Churchill asked Eisenhower how many Communists there were in the United States. The President replied that there were 25,000, 'that we knew where they were, in emergency could pick them up'. The discussion turned to the principal purpose of Churchill's visit:

The President then brought up the topic of 'reconnaissance' in force which the Prime Minister had referred to in conversation the previous night (i.e., a meeting of the leaders of Soviet Russia, Great Britain and the United States).

The President would not agree to a meeting anywhere under the present Soviet rule, but did not object to Churchill's suggestion of either Stockholm or London.

The President tried to urge the Prime Minister to (1) make the first move through diplomatic channels, and (2) include France. As to the first, the Prime Minister feels he can approach the matter obliquely, either through Malik or directly to Malenkov, by saying something to the effect, 'How would you feel if you were asked to go to a Big Three meeting?' etc. The President tried to stress that opportunity should not be given to Malenkov to 'hit the free world in the face'.

There was a brief discussion about Communist China: 'Of admittance to the UN, Churchill said, "My line about recognition is that there has got to be peace first." The President said that if they would withdraw to their own borders, release our prisoners, and say they would observe propriety in international relationships, he would consider using his influence to obtain recognition.' The conversation then returned to the main theme of the visit:

The President (going back to the question of meeting) thought it ought to be stressed that meeting would be concerned only with European affairs. Churchill thought that he could ask that Russians sign Austrian treaty. About this he said, 'It is a dream; if I were a Russian I should think it would be good politics.'

President went on to say that with the Communists we could do certain things. None of these men are allowed to work in places working on confidential contracts for the government, but there is a weakness in our law. Suppose a man worked in a power plant supplying power to this same factory—nothing to outlaw that.

President said we had tried a number of Communists for conspiracy to destroy government by force, and added that it is a rather laborious process. President went on to say that it has been held by our courts that to be a Communist is prima-facie evidence that you have agreed to destroy the government by force and that you are taking orders from outside our government.

Churchill said in Britain they had about 40,000 Communists. Eisenhower said that in his own mind he forgives anyone who was trying to make friends with Communists up to the time of the Berlin Airlift. He believes that anyone who was at least fairly friendly with the Communists from '33 to '46, should not be viewed with alarm. It was a policy of our government at that time to try to win over the Russians.

The talk between the two leaders now ranged over several related issues, returning again and again to the question of a conference with the Russians:

Talk veered to discussion of Oppenheimer.[1] President said Oppenheimer himself had testified that he was approached to sell secrets in 1943; but that within the past six months Oppenheimer had had dinner twice with that same man. Churchill asked if that had been made public. Eisenhower said it was in testimony but press had not featured it. He said, 'It isn't that anyone believes that Oppenheimer is really disloyal—but when you have a Communist brother and a Communist wife—etc. We don't want to hurt his reputation.'

Churchill said: 'We have really in a way an advantage. The Labour Party has taken violent line against them. Many men in the Labour Party are very careful not to go too far. Our Labour Party is very sensible. Attlee and Morrison have a very great deal of courage and have come forward in favour of Germany's rearmament.' Eisenhower said: 'We have got to do something before we lose Adenauer.' Some discussion of Bonn Agreement (could not hear as too many people were talking).

[1] J. Robert Oppenheimer; from 1943 to 1945, as Director of the Los Alamos Scientific Laboratory in New Mexico, he was the man principally responsible for the development of the American atomic bomb. From 1946 to 1952 he was Chairman of the General Advisory Committee to the United States Atomic Energy Commission (of which Churchill's friend Bernard Baruch was a member).

Churchill: 'I personally feel that if the French would not or could not do EDC, we ought to try and see if we could get some safeguards against another Hitler—on the part of NATO.'

President asked group if they would like to hear letter from President Coty; and he read it.

Churchill said that when he came to see Truman two years ago, he telegraphed Molotov about the trip; he did not inform him of this trip because he considered the 'old friendship' basis so different.

Eisenhower suggested that the matter be talked over with Eden and Dulles. He again suggested ordinary diplomatic channels, but Churchill did not agree to that. He suggested Sir Winston might use as excuse his age, but Sir Winston did not agree to that.

At this point the President also said he would think favourably of The Hague as a meeting place.

Churchill does not want to inquire until he returns to England, of course; thinks he can find out 48 hours after his return.

About nations to be asked, Churchill said: 'Two is company; three is hard company; four is a deadlock.'

Churchill implied that he was going to turn things over to Anthony Eden some time before their elections in fall of '55.

Some discussion of salaries of Members of Parliament and of Congress; and of their own financial situations.

Referring again to primary subject of conversation, Churchill's tentative inquiry about Big Three meeting, he said, 'I swear to you that I will not compromise you in the slightest.'

The President suggested again the matter be talked over with Foster Dulles. He said this was one field where he was completely inexperienced in the kind of negotiations, and he was therefore unsure as to exactly what was right thing to do. The President: 'I am not afraid to meet anybody face to face to talk to him, but the world gets in a habit of expecting a lot.' He said he could conceive of going to the first day of such a conference meeting and coming home, leaving the Vice-President and Foster Dulles there, and then perhaps going back for the last five days of such a conference. . . .

At the end of their discussion, Eisenhower read a British memorandum on atomic matters. His comment: 'We will give you everything we have got on that.' Eisenhower then suggested that Churchill might want to speak a little on Egypt, Iran and Trieste at a luncheon for legislative leaders; at that, the conversation was at an end.[1]

At lunch on June 26 Churchill met the leaders of Congress 'and', Colville wrote, 'according to his own account, addressed them afterwards with impromptu but admirable eloquence!' It was the same room, Eisenhower told those present, in which Churchill had presided over a meeting of the Combined Chiefs of Staff during the war.

[1] 'Saturday, June 26, 1954': Eisenhower papers.

Despite the increased complexities of the modern age, Churchill told his listeners, 'a way could be found through the difficulties by the use of two important factors: One—Time—Do not throw away time. There are lots of things that seem impossible but it can be worked out given time; and two—Vigilance—Eternal vigilance that is needed to guard the freedom of the world against the intolerable philosophy of Communism.' Churchill added:

Communism uses any motive, sordid or violently belligerent, to gain its end. Actually, it is only another form of aristocracy or bureaucracy seeking control of millions of people and digging itself in. Communism is a tyranny which will be difficult to overthrow, but let us of the free world make sure that we make every sacrifice to keep it from ourselves and to keep it from being foisted, by force or ignorance, upon the human race.

Churchill then told the American legislators:

... the gathering would probably like to hear his viewpoint on some detailed matters. He said that conferences of this kind were vitally important, that meeting jaw to jaw is better than war.[1]
He realized how complicated the problems were and said that each problem could not be thrashed out to the last inch. But it was important to have consenting minds at the summit to back up the conference table. Otherwise, the conference may go on forever.

It was 'true perhaps', Churchill commented, 'that America could stand alone in the world, particularly with its advantage in thermonuclear matters. Such a stand, however, would be very unwise. He added that the United States, even at the height of its present power, has not attempted to acquire territory and that made him very proud of his blood connections.'

After criticizing the French for having 'dilly-dallied' over the European Defence Community, Churchill told his American listeners that 'in creating lines of defense for freedom there is NATO, there could be METO and SEATO. These could be welded into effective defense units and is a task which both the United States and the United Kingdom must work at steadily. There is no doubt that you must be strong if you care about peace. Peace through strength is necessary.' Churchill continued his remarks, as recorded by the White House stenographer, by saying that:

... he was very glad to come over here; that he had thought about it two months ago and had contemplated coming over to stay at the Embassy for a discussion of exchange of information on thermonuclear matters but that it

---

[1] On 30 January 1958 Harold Macmillan, speaking in Canberra, echoed Churchill's words with the phrase (frequently but wrongly attributed to Churchill himself), 'Jaw–jaw is better than war–war.'

had been put off from week to week. Finally the President had invited him to come to the White House and stay there as a guest and he wanted to say he had never had a visit to Washington so agreeable and pleasant as this one.

We could not have met at a better time. There is a great underlying friendship between us, and the agreement and unity expressed to the world by just being here and talking frankly about our difficulties is vitally important. It will add to our combined strength and will help maintain the peace of the world.

Churchill ended by telling the legislators that he and Eisenhower 'had been talking for twelve years now about the problems of the day, that they had got to know each other and that as far as he was concerned, the President was one of the few people from whom the Prime Minister derived pleasure in talking to him. Thank God you have him at the head of your country and that your country is at the head of the world. There is more need for forceful and valued service to show the way to peace with honour.' [1]

Lord Moran, who spoke to Churchill about his luncheon speech, noted in his diary:

He felt his speech to about thirty members of Congress had gone well. It was quite unprepared, 'Unpinioned on the wing.' He asked Christopher what reports had come in from the 'Congress ferret'. But it appeared that the ferret had not yet returned. However, Hagerty, the President's Press Secretary, said the speech had made a great impression on all the Congressmen, and had gone with a swing. The PM seemed much relieved. He complained that the English papers were badly informed. He exclaimed impatiently:

'Why, they draw a picture of Anthony and me meeting angry and unsympathetic Americans, the exact opposite of the truth. I have never known them so friendly.'

He picked up the *Manchester Guardian*.

'Look at this in a sober journal. It speaks of a "bleak background". That is all wrong. I feel in my bones things are getting better and better.'

'Premier and Mr Eden on way to US' had been the *Manchester Guardian* headline on June 25, followed by: 'Bleak Background for Talks, American Bitterness'. The article continued: 'Rarely, says our Washington Correspondent, has a visit taken place against a background of more critical and bitter comment. This is largely due to Mr Eden's failure to mention Mr Dulles by name when he spoke on South-east Asian policy in the Commons on Wednesday. Mr Eden's omission is interpreted as a snub to the Secretary of State.' [2]

The afternoon of June 26 was spent in conference at the White

---

[1] 'Notes on remarks by the President and the Prime Minister at the Congressional Luncheon at the White House, Saturday afternoon, June 26, 1954': Eisenhower papers.
[2] *Manchester Guardian*, 25 June 1954.

House. 'Good progress,' Colville wrote, 'this time on Egypt. The PM elated by success and in a state of excited good humour. In the middle of the afternoon meeting, while Christopher and I were sipping high-balls and reading telegrams in his sitting-room, he suddenly emerged and summoned us to go up to the "Solarium" with him so as to look at a great storm which was raging.' Colville added: 'I can't imagine anybody else interrupting a meeting with the President of the United States, two Secretaries of State and two Ambassadors just for this pur-pose.'

The Russian visit project, Colville noted, 'has now been expanded (by the President, so the PM says) to a meeting in London, together with the French and West Germans, at the opening of which Ike himself would be present'.

'To hold off the threat of war until it is no longer worthwhile for anyone to break the peace,' Lord Moran wrote in his diary, 'that is the only thing left to him now, his one consuming purpose.' Moran added: 'He does not underrate the difficulties of his task. America does not trust the Soviet Union. She cannot forget Stalin's duplicity; she cannot believe that a Russian promise is worth the paper it is written on.'

That night Churchill again dined with Eisenhower at the White House. At eleven o'clock he asked the President if he might be excused; he must make up the six hours' sleep he had lost through the time zones. For Churchill and his party, it was the London equivalent of five o'clock in the morning as they went to bed.

Talks continued at the White House throughout Sunday June 27, interrupted in the morning by a Presidential showing of *White Heron*, a two-hour film of the Queen's Commonwealth tour. 'The Russian project,' noted Colville in his diary, 'has shrunk again as Dulles has been getting at the President.' But Churchill was 'still determined' to meet the Russians himself, 'as he has now an assurance', Colville added, 'that the Americans won't object'.

Dulles was not only seeking to influence the President. Shortly after midday on June 27 he had a private talk with Churchill at the White House. His own note of it makes clear just how wide was the gulf between his position and Churchill's:

Sir Winston spoke of the possibility of his having a high-level meeting with the Russians, which might perhaps be preliminary to a three-power meeting. He said he had in mind possibly going to Stockholm to see whether there were 'consenting minds' which would make it profitable to have a three-power meeting. He referred to the President's suggestion that the President might make a brief personal appearance at such a meeting, but that in the main it would have to be carried by me, possibly with the Vice-President taking the President's place.

I pointed out to Mr Churchill that it was extremely dangerous to have such a meeting unless it would have positive results. An illusion of success would be bad, and also an obvious failure would be bad and might create the impression that the only alternative was war.

I asked Churchill what concrete accomplishment would be possible and he said an Austrian treaty. I said I thought we had gone very far with Molotov in trying to get an Austrian treaty and I was skeptical about the possibility of getting it by his 'method.

I pointed out that if Mr Churchill should make an exploratory mission alone, it would not be looked upon well in this country, and also we might have to make it clear that Mr Churchill was in no sense speaking or acting for the United States. Sir Winston said he fully understood this. On the other hand, he would be going not in any sense as an intermediary between the United States and the Soviet Union, but representing the spirit and purpose of 'our side'. I urged that the matter be very carefully weighed before any positive decision was made.[1]

That evening Churchill and Eden were again the guests of the President for dinner. The other Americans present included Dulles, Bedell Smith, and Winthrop Aldrich, the American Ambassador to London. The three other Englishmen were Roger Makins, Christopher Soames and Jock Colville, who wrote in his diary:

Very gay dinner, during which the PM and the President spoke highly of the Germans and in favour of their being allowed to rearm. The President called the French 'a hopeless, helpless mass of protoplasm'. Eden took the other line, with some support from Dulles, and ended by saying he could not be a member of any Government which acted as Ike and Winston seemed to be recommending.

After dinner we adjourned to the Red Room and worked collectively and ineffectively on the draft of a Declaration—a kind of second Atlantic Charter—which the PM and the President propose to publish. It seems to me a very messy affair.

The PM went to bed at 12.00 elated and cheerful. He has been buoyed up by the reception he has had here and has not as yet had one single afternoon sleep. His sole relaxation has been a few games of bezique with me. Roger Makins said he never remembered a more riotous evening.

On the morning of June 28 Churchill and Eisenhower met again to discuss the joint Declaration which they intended to issue, 'in which', Colville noted, 'the PM had suddenly espied some Dulles-like anti-colonial sentiments'. On the American draft, the 'right of self-determination' was therefore changed to the 'principle of self-determination', and the phrase 'capable of sustaining self-government and independent existence' reduced to 'capable of sustaining an

[1] 'Memorandum of Conversation with Mr Churchill at the White House, Sunday, June 27, 1954, 12.30 p.m.', 'Top Secret': Eisenhower papers.

independent existence'. Churchill personally struck out the phrase 'unhappy plight' in relation to 'formerly Sovereign states now in bondage', replacing it with the words 'unwilling subordination'.[1]

In their own talks, Eden and Dulles had covered Indo-China, the European Defence Community and Egypt. As soon as the Declaration had been approved, Churchill went to the Washington Press Club, where he lunched, and then answered written questions that were handed in to him. One question concerned the tension between Egypt and Israel, and Churchill's own attitude towards Israel. He replied:

I am a Zionist. Let me make that clear. I was one of the original ones, after the Balfour Declaration, and I have worked faithfully for it.

I think it a most wonderful thing that this community should have established itself so effectively, turning the desert into fertile gardens and thriving townships, and should have afforded a refuge to millions of their co-religionists who had suffered so fearfully under the Hitler, and not only Hitler, persecution. I think it's a wonderful thing.[2]

Of the Allied intervention against Bolshevik Russia in 1919, Churchill told the assembled journalists: 'If I had been properly supported in 1919, I think we might have strangled Bolshevism in its cradle, but everybody turned up their hands and said, "How shocking!".'[3]

Churchill's answers, noted Colville, were given 'with his best verve and vigour. Everybody greatly impressed by the skill with which he turned some of the more awkward.' Churchill was so pleased by his reception, Colville wrote, 'that when I leant over to collect his notes he shook me warmly by the hand under the impression that I was a Senator or pressman endeavouring to congratulate him'.

'Press Club was tremendous success,' Christopher Soames telegraphed to Clementine Churchill that afternoon. 'He showed great vigour and they showed great affection.'[4]

Colville's account of June 28 continued:

After lunch the PM and Eden drove to the Embassy, whither they move their headquarters this afternoon. I played bezique with a highly contented Winston (in spite of the fact that I won 26,600 in one solitary game), but at 6.00 he was still fresh enough to address, first, the Commonwealth Ambassadors and after them the British press representatives.

This was followed by a huge dinner at the Embassy, from which I mercifully escaped. I dined at the Colony restaurant. Meanwhile at the Embassy

[1] 'Declaration', draft, undated: Eisenhower papers.

[2] This section of Churchill's remarks was published by the Government of Israel in a press statement on 24 February 1955.

[3] Speech of 28 June 1954: Premier papers, 11/1015. Extracts recorded: BBC Written Archives Centre, Library No. 22256–7.

[4] 'Following for Lady Churchill from Captain Soames', 28 June 1954: Churchill papers, 1/50.

the PM was holding forth about the Guatemala revolution (a current event) and, according to Tony Rumbold, making the Foreign Secretary look rather small in argument (the FS being all for caution and the PM being all for supporting the US in their encouragement of the rebels and their hostility to the Communist Guatemalan régime).

Lord Moran was also present during the discussion about Guatemala, noting in his diary that Pierson Dixon, Britain's representative at the United Nations, had opposed American intervention in Guatemala in support of anti-Communist forces, following the revolution there on June 18. America was 'grossly inconsistent', Dixon argued, to support in Guatemala the kind of interventionist policy which she had condemned as immoral when practised by the Soviet Union in Greece or Korea. Moran's note continued with Churchill's reply:

'A great principle only carries weight when it is associated with the movement of great forces.'

It was important, he said, to keep a sense of proportion.

Raising his voice: 'I'd never heard of this bloody place Guatemala until I was in my seventy-ninth year.'

'Come now, Winston,' Anthony interposed mildly.

The PM took no notice. 'We ought not,' he continued, 'to allow Guatemala to jeopardize our relations with the United States, for on them the safety of the world might depend.'

'But, Prime Minister, this is a moral issue,' Bob persisted. 'It is surely a question of right and wrong.'

The PM gave a great snort. Bob Dixon got very red in the face, but he seemed unable to stop arguing with Winston, though you don't have to be a diplomatist to sense how unprofitable such an argument can be. Every sentence began 'But, Prime Minister'.

Anthony listened demurely, though it was plain he was on Dixon's side. From time to time Roger Makins gave a great guffaw. At last I said that, without taking sides, I thought there would be general agreement that Guatemala was not sufficiently important to allow it to interfere with the night's rest. I got up, and Lady Makins, who had joined the party, backed me up.

Winston was wide awake and reluctant to go to bed. Everybody else had risen, but he remained slumped on the couch. At last he levered himself out of his seat, and I took him to his room. 'You know, Charles,' he expostulated, 'I feel very lively; I don't know whether it is the magnetism of this country or your pills.'

As he went to bed, Churchill talked to Colville, telling him 'that Anthony Eden was sometimes very foolish: he would quarrel with the Americans over some petty Central American issue which did not affect Great Britain and could forget about the downtrodden millions in Poland'.

On the morning of Tuesday June 29 Churchill went to see

Eisenhower to finalize the Declaration of Principles. 'In that declaration,' Churchill told the House of Commons two weeks later, 'we affirmed our comradeship with one another; we offered the hand of friendship to all who might seek it sincerely; we reasserted our sympathy for and loyalty to those still in bondage; we proclaimed our desire to reduce armaments and to turn nuclear power into peaceful channels; we confirmed our support of the United Nations and of subsidiary organizations designed to promote and preserve the peace of the world; and we proclaimed our determination to develop and maintain in unanimity the spiritual, economic, and military strength necessary to pursue our purposes effectively. These are the principles which we share with our American friends.' [1]

'I think we have broken the backbone of our difficulties,' Churchill telegraphed to his wife on June 29. 'I am very well.' [2]

In addition to the Declaration of Principles, Churchill and Eisenhower also signed a communiqué in which they announced their agreement that the German Federal Republic 'should take its place as an equal partner in the community of Western nations where it can make its proper contribution to the defence of the free world', and they added: 'We are determined to achieve this goal. . . .' [3]

From the White House, Churchill went to the British Embassy for lunch. Dean Acheson was one of the American guests, also Sterling Cole, Chairman of the Atomic Energy Commission, whose speech of February 17 had been the catalyst of British nuclear policy, and reinforced Churchill's determination to visit the United States. The agreement reached on nuclear policy remains, however, a secret to this day. [4]

'After lunch,' Colville noted in his diary, 'the PM became jocular. He said that if he were ever chased out of England and became an American citizen, he would hope to be elected to Congress. He would then propose two amendments to the American Constitution: (i) that at least half the members of the US Cabinet should have seats in Congress, (ii) that the President, instead of signing himself Dwight D. Eisenhower a hundred times a day should be authorised to sign himself "Ike".'

At 3.30 that afternoon Churchill left Washington by air for Ottawa, seen off, as he had been welcomed, by Nixon and Dulles. 'I played bezique with the PM most of the way,' wrote Colville.

After a flight lasting two hours and fifteen minutes, Churchill

[1] Speech of 14 July 1954: *Hansard*.

[2] 'Following for Lady Churchill from the Prime Minister', 29 June 1954: Churchill papers, 1/50.

[3] The West German Army came into existence on 12 November 1955.

[4] 'Secret', 'Final', 'Declassified 16 July 1985', 'Portions Exempted' (from Declassification), National Security Council letter of 29 April 1985: Eisenhower papers.

reached Ottawa. At the airport he broadcast a short message, 'written by me', Colville noted in his diary. That night, at the Château Laurier Hotel, he gave a dinner for the Canadian Prime Minister, Louis St Laurent, and his Minister of Defence, Clarence Howe. Lord Cherwell was also present, and, as Colville noted, 'a most secret subject' was discussed: the British decision to become the third nation in the world to build a hydrogen bomb.

On the morning of Wednesday June 30 Churchill, Eden and Cherwell were present at a meeting of the Canadian Cabinet. At noon Churchill addressed the press correspondents. 'He did not do it as well as in Washington,' wrote Colville, 'but it went down all right.'

Churchill had only one serious speech to make, a broadcast to the Canadian people. 'The PM would spend most of the afternoon reading the English newspapers,' Colville wrote, 'so that he started his broadcast (to which I contributed a few sentences) very belatedly, recorded it after we were supposed to have left for the Country Club and in consequence made everything late throughout the whole evening.' During his broadcast, Churchill spoke of how 'I have been all over Canada in my time and I have most vivid pictures in my mind of many places from Halifax to Kicking Horse Valley and further on to Vancouver'. One of the only important places he had not visited was Fort Churchill, 'which was named after my ancestor, John Churchill, 1st Duke of Marlborough'.

Britain and the Commonwealth, Churchill declared a few moments later, 'do not fear the future while we advance hand in hand together and in company with the United States'.[1]

Churchill then left the hotel for the Country Club, where he was to be the dinner guest of the Canadian Prime Minister. 'As his car drove off,' wrote Lord Moran, 'there was loud cheering, and I could see that Winston was greatly moved.' At dinner, Colville noted, Churchill made 'a moving speech'. He was, wrote Moran 'full of life and fun and beamed on everyone'.

From the Country Club, Churchill drove with Eden to the airport, where a Canadian aircraft was waiting to fly them to New York. 'I played bezique,' Colville noted of the flight, 'with a somewhat tired but very triumphant PM.'

Reaching New York after midnight, Churchill was driven to the Hudson River docks, where he boarded the *Queen Elizabeth*. It was one o'clock in the morning. The ship remained that night moored to the quayside. In the morning, as Colville noted, 'a milling crowd' came on board to see Churchill, among them Bernard Baruch and

[1] 'Prime Minister's Broadcast on leaving Canada', 30 June 1954: Churchill papers, 5/54.

Antonio Giraudier, 'a Cuban who keeps Winston supplied with cigars and brandy at home'.[1] At noon the *Queen Elizabeth* sailed down the Hudson River and out into the Atlantic.

The return voyage was made uncomfortable because, with broken ice having moved further south than usual, the *Queen Elizabeth* had to sail along the southern Gulf Stream, a hot and indeed oppressive time. But Churchill now fixed his thoughts upon the summit for which he had first argued in public more than a year earlier, and to which, in Washington, Eisenhower had given his consent. 'The PM told me this morning,' Colville noted in his diary on July 2, 'he was decided on an expedition to Russia, where he would ask freedom for Austria as an earnest of better relations.'

For Eden, who was also on board, there was another priority, however, as Colville noted:

Anthony Eden, who has only come back by sea because he wants to talk over future plans and to get a firm date for Winston to hand over to him, is feeling bashful about choosing the right moment and last night consulted me about this.

I thought, and said, how strange it was that two men who knew each other so well should be hampered by shyness on this score.

This morning the opportunity came and W tentatively fixed September 21st for the hand-over and early August for the Moscow visit.[2]

According to Lord Moran's diary entry for July 4, Churchill spoke during that day of September 18 as the day on which he would retire. He also told Moran that he would not go to Moscow for the summit, but to Vienna, 'to try to persuade the Russians to sign an Austrian Treaty'. Then, if that came off, people would 'whoop with joy', and he might go on to Moscow for a 'courtesy visit', perhaps, he told Moran, 'staying forty-eight hours'.[3]

Back in his cabin, Churchill then dictated to Colville 'a long telegram' to Molotov proposing talks with the Soviet leaders 'in which

---

[1] At Chartwell, Denis Kelly later recalled, Churchill 'used to have a census of the cigar population' (Denis Kelly recollections: in conversation with the author, 25 March 1987). Most of these cigars had been provided by Giraudier. 'Sir Winston Churchill has a friend of some fifteen years' standing called Monsieur Antonio Giraudier,' Anthony Montague Browne explained to the Foreign Office ten years later, and he added: 'He was a Cuban who fled from the Castro régime, and now lives at Palm Beach and Nassau, and has I believe taken Spanish nationality. He is a genuine friend of Sir Winston. . . .' (Letter of 20 July 1964: Churchill papers, 2/524.) He was also extremely generous in providing Churchill's secretarial staff with brandy and scent.

[2] Colville diary, 2 July 1954: *The Fringes of Power*, pages 697–8.

[3] Moran diary, 4 July 1954: *The Struggle for Survival*, pages 574–7.

the US would not, indeed, participate but could, W thought, be counted on to do their best with their own public opinion'.[1]

Of his telegram to Molotov, Churchill informed Eisenhower:

After referring to my speech of May 11, 1953 for a top level Meeting of the Big Three, and to the statements I have made from time to time in the House of Commons, that if this were impossible I would seek to make a contact myself with the Soviet Government, I put the question, how would they feel about it. I should like to know this, I said, before we make any official proposal, or considered such questions as the time and place. I went on, 'I should be very glad if you would let me know if you would like the idea of a friendly Meeting, with no Agenda and no object but to find a reasonable way of living side by side in growing confidence, easement and prosperity. Although our Meeting, wherever held, would be simple and informal and last only a few days, it might be the prelude to a wider reunion where much might be settled. I have, however, no warrant to say this beyond my own hopes. I ask you to let me know, as soon as you can, what you and your friends think.'[2]

'You did not let any grass grow under your feet' was Eisenhower's comment when Churchill sent him the text of his message to Molotov. Eisenhower added: 'When you left here, I had thought, obviously erroneously, that you were in an undecided mood about this matter, and that when you had cleared your own mind I would receive some notice if you were to put your program into action. However, that is now past history and we must hope that the steps you have started will lead to a good result.'[3]

Colville's account of the voyage continued:

We all had a gay luncheon in the PM's dining-room, but after luncheon the fun began over the Molotov telegram. Eden went on deck to read; Winston retired to his sitting-room and had the telegram shortened and amended. He asked me to take it to Eden and to say he now intended to despatch it.

Eden told me he disliked the whole thing anyway: he had been adding up the pros and cons and was sure the latter (danger of serious Anglo-American rift, effect on Adenauer and Western Europe, damage to the solid and uncompromising front we have built up against Russia, practical certainty that the high hopes of the public would be shattered by nothing coming of the meeting) far outweighed the pros.

However, what he really disliked was Winston's intention of despatching the telegram without showing it to the Cabinet. Why couldn't he wait till we were home and let AE deliver the message to Molotov when he saw him at Geneva? Would I tell W that if he insisted, he must do as he wished but that it would be against his, Eden's, strong advice.

[1] Colville diary, 2 July 1954: *The Fringes of Power*, pages 697–8.
[2] Telegram, Churchill to Eisenhower, 'Top Secret', 'Private and Personal', undated: Eisenhower papers.
[3] 'Dear Winston', 7 July 1954: Eisenhower papers.

I imparted this to W who said it was all nonsense: this was merely an unofficial enquiry of Molotov. If it were accepted, that was the time to consult the Cabinet, before an official approach was made. I represented, as strongly as I could, that this was putting the Cabinet 'on the spot', because if the Russians answered affirmatively, as was probable, it would in practice be too late for the Cabinet to express a contrary opinion.

W said he would make it a matter of confidence with the Cabinet: they would have to choose between him and his intentions. If they opposed the visit, it would give him a good occasion to go.

I said this would split the country and the Conservative Party from top to bottom. Moreover if he went on this account, the new administration would start with a strong anti-Russian reputation.

After a great deal of talk Eden was sent for and eventually agreed to a compromise which put *him* 'on the spot'. The PM agreed to send the telegram to the Cabinet provided he could say that Eden agreed with it in principle (which of course he does not). Eden weakly gave in.

'I am afraid the PM has been ruthless and unscrupulous in all this,' Colville added, 'because he must know that at this moment, for both internal and international reasons, Eden cannot resign—though he told me, while all this was going on and I was acting as intermediary, that he had thought of it.' [1]

July 3 saw cooler Atlantic breezes, but no cooling of moods. 'Saw Eden this morning,' Colville noted in his diary, and he added: 'Got the impression that he was aggrieved with W which I don't find surprising. W, on the other hand, complains to me that he was trapped into sending the telegram to the Cabinet, had forgotten it was the weekend, and now he wouldn't get a reply till Monday. So he telegraphed to Rab saying that he assumed the telegram had already gone on to Moscow.'

By evening, the crisis seemed over. Churchill was now 'quite reconciled to the Cabinet having been consulted about the Molotov telegram', Colville noted, 'because Rab had telegraphed suggesting only one or two small amendments and had appeared generally satisfied with the main idea. So everybody went to bed happy and W and I played bezique, to my great financial advantage (six grands coups!) till nearly 2.00 a.m.' [2]

During July 3 Churchill received a telegram from his daughter Sarah and her husband in the United States. 'Bon voyage,' they wrote, 'it was a dazzling success with great impact on public opinion.' All

[1] Colville diary, 2 July 1954: *The Fringes of Power*, pages 697–8.
[2] Colville diary, 3 July 1954: *The Fringes of Power*, pages 698–9.

the reactions to his visit, they added, 'indicate you were at peak form'.[1] At sea, July 4 passed calmly, with Churchill reading Harold Nicolson's book *Public Faces* and 'greatly impressed', as Colville noted, 'by the 1932 prophecy of atomic bombs'.[2] At lunch with Churchill, Gavin Astor[3] and Christopher Soames, Colville found Churchill 'in splendid form, describing the heart trouble he developed in consequence of dancing a *pas seul* after dinner at Blenheim some fifty years ago, elaborating the desirable results which would come from re-establishing the Heptarchy in England (so as to ease the pressure on Parliament) and teaching Gavin, a non-smoker, to smoke cigars'.

All went well on July 4 until evening, when, as Colville noted, a 'blood row' developed between Churchill and Eden. The two men were dining with Lord Moran and Christopher Soames. Half an hour before midnight Colville went down to see how their dinner party was getting on. His diary record continued:

Everybody very jovial when suddenly Miss Gilliatt brought me a telegram from Roger Makins about the effects in America of a speech made by Senator Knowland, who has evidently implied that we have been pressing the Americans to let Red China into UNO and has said that if this happens, the United States will leave the Organisation.

Eden read the telegram first and said that he objected to HMG saying anything in reply to Knowland: it looked as if we minded. The PM then read it and wanted to issue a statement from this ship to the effect, first, that the matter had not been seriously discussed during the Washington talks and secondly that there was no question of our recognising Red China while she was still in a state of war with the United Nations.

Eden said that if we made any such statement it would destroy all chance of success at Geneva: we ought to keep entry into UNO as a reward for China if she were good. The PM looked grave: he had not realised, he said, that what Knowland said was in fact the truth—Eden *did* contemplate the admission of China into UNO while a state of war still existed.

Eden got red in the face with anger and there was a disagreeable scene.

'They both went to bed,' Colville added, 'in a combination of sorrow and anger, the PM saying that Anthony was totally incapable of differentiating great points and small points (a criticism that has an element of truth in it).'[4]

---

[1] Telegram of 3 July 1954: Churchill papers, 1/50.

[2] Churchill had himself prophesied a super-bomb eight years before Nicolson, in an article 'Shall We All Commit Suicide', *Nash's Pall Mall*, September 1924.

[3] Gavin Astor, son of the Proprietor of *The Times* (Lord Astor of Hever). Served as Chairman of *The Times* Publishing Company Limited from 1959 to 1966, succeeding his father as 2nd Baron Astor of Hever in 1971. He lived at Hever Castle, only a few miles from Chartwell. In 1945 he married Lady Irene Haig, younger daughter of Field Marshal Earl Haig.

[4] Colville diary, 4 July 1954: *The Fringes of Power*, pages 699–700.

On the morning of July 5, Colville found Churchill 'still grave and depressed' over the Knowland question. Eden, however, having slept late, 'seemed to have recovered his equanimity and was cheerful'. In the early evening, after playing bezique with Colville, Churchill gave a small cocktail party for fellow passengers, with Eden as his co-host. Colville's account of the day continued:

We all dined in the PM's dining-room. It was a most amicable occasion, last night's differences resolved and the PM saying that provided AE always bore in mind the importance of not quarrelling violently with the Americans over Far East questions (which affected them more than us) a way ought certainly to be found of bringing Red China into the United Nations on terms tolerable to the USA.[1]

'Winston was in his most benign mood,' noted Moran. 'He did not avoid delicate subjects; he seemed to be able to talk about them with Anthony's full approval. A topic, which last night was full of perils, was now touched so lightly that it was seen, as it were, in retrospect in a spirit of amused detachment. His words, to be sure, were not very different from those he used last night, but he seemed to have now only one purpose in his mind—to smooth over the changing of the guard.'

Moran's account continued:

To Anthony, Winston talked as father to son, as if he were only concerned for his future happiness. Speaking very earnestly, he implored him not to quarrel with America, whether China was or was not a member of the United Nations. He spoke of himself as a link with Queen Victoria, and it was surely the historian who impressed on Anthony that influence depends on power.

'Up to July 1944 England had a considerable say in things; after that I was conscious that it was America who made the big decisions. She will make the big decisions now.'

Winston said this with an air of finality.

'We do not yet realize her immeasurable power. She could conquer Russia without any help. In a month the Kremlin would be unable to move troops. The Americans would become enraged—violent. I know them very well. They might decide to go it alone. That was what Dulles meant when he talked about an agonizing reappraisal of policy. Without their help, England would be isolated; she might become, with France, a satellite of Russia.'

Winston's voice broke, and his eyes filled with tears.

On Christopher Soames's initiative, a magnificent dinner had been arranged, and Churchill's mood matched the relaxed atmosphere of a feast among friends. Moran wrote:

[1] Colville diary, 5 July 1954: *The Fringes of Power*, page 700.

It was late now, but Winston's gaiety and good humour had spread to his guests, and there was no thought of bed. The old man bubbled merriment. Then he went back to the First War—always a sign with Winston that the weather is set fair.

Anthony began reciting Persian poetry, rather shyly and without confidence. Winston was astonished and excited. 'But Anthony, I did not know you could speak Persian. I had no idea you had this gift. It is extraordinary. When did you learn this language?'

I reminded Winston that Anthony had taken his Final Schools at Oxford in Oriental languages, and got a First in them. Winston knew nothing of this. Why should he? He had nominated Anthony to succeed him, but that did not mean that before he did so he had ferreted out all the facts of his life.

Anthony began writing in Persian the names of those round the table, but Winston's interest in Persian poets soon began to flag. He beamed round the table; the dinner, he said, had been very agreeable, he hoped a year tonight the same people might meet and dine together.

'You, Anthony,' Churchill added, 'will be able to give the party at No. 10.' 'No,' Eden replied. 'Whatever happens I will be your guest.' [1]

---

[1] Moran diary, 5 July 1954: *The Struggle for Survival*, pages 577–9.

52
Disputes on the Road to Moscow

═══════

AT nine o'clock on the morning of 6 July 1954 the *Queen Eliza-beth* reached Cherbourg, and just before five o'clock that after-noon docked at Southampton. On the following day, first Eden and then Churchill informed the Cabinet of what had been agreed upon at Washington. Concerning Egypt, the provision of American aid to Egypt would, Eden explained, 'be conditional on Egyptian fulfilment of any agreement relating to the Canal Zone base and that the United States would support publicly the principle of free transit through the Suez Canal'. Conditions in the Canal Zone had, Eden noted, 'im-proved considerably of late, and this made it easier to propose a re-sumption of negotiations'. The British negotiators 'would be instructed to aim at an agreement to last for twenty years and to cover the case of aggression against Persia as well as Turkey. . . .'

This American commitment, Churchill commented, 'would in-crease the chances that the Egyptian Government would abide by the terms of any agreement we might reach with them'. In spite of his earlier doubts, Churchill told the Cabinet, he was now 'satisfied' that the withdrawal of British troops from Egypt could be fully justified on military grounds. 'Our requirements in the Canal Zone,' he explained, 'had been radically altered by the admission of Turkey to the North Atlantic Treaty Organisation and the extension of a defensive Middle Eastern front as far east as Pakistan. Furthermore, the advent of thermo-nuclear weapons had greatly increased the vul-nerability of a concentrated base area and it would not be right to continue to retain in Egypt 80,000 troops who would be better placed elsewhere.'

It was 'also relevant', Churchill added, with severe practicality, that the conditions in the Canal Zone 'were damaging both to the morale of the Forces and to recruitment'.

The Cabinet were then told—the minutes do not say whether by Churchill or Eden—'of a proposal that the Prime Minister might meet M. Malenkov, with a view to exploring the possibility of arranging a meeting of Heads of Governments of the United States, United Kingdom and Soviet Union'.

There was some discussion on the proposed Churchill–Malenkov meeting, recorded separately from the 'Secret' minutes and still secret thirty-four years later.[1] The secrecy was dictated, at least in part, by Lord Salisbury's vehement opposition to the proposed meeting; so vehement that he threatened to resign if the meeting were to go ahead.

This contentious subject having been strongly aired, Churchill then told the Cabinet of the decision by the Defence Policy Committee three weeks earlier, before he had left for the United States, that Britain should adjust its atomic weapons programme 'to allow for the production of hydrogen bombs in this country'. This decision had hitherto been kept from the full Cabinet. His talks in Washington and Ottawa had been conducted, Churchill said, 'on the basis that we should produce hydrogen bombs'. He therefore 'suggested' that the Cabinet 'should now formally approve the proposal that hydrogen bombs should be produced in this country' and that it should 'endorse the preliminary action which had already been taken to this end'.

In explaining why the hydrogen bomb should become a part of Britain's defence arsenal, Churchill told the Cabinet:

... we could not expect to maintain our influence as a world Power unless we possessed the most up-to-date nuclear weapons. The primary aim of our policy was to prevent major war; and the possession of these weapons was now the main deterrent to a potential aggressor.

He had no doubt that the best hope of preserving world peace was to make it clear to potential aggressors that they had no hope of shielding themselves from a crushing retaliatory use of atomic power.

For this purpose the Western Powers must provide themselves, not only with a sufficient supply of up-to-date nuclear weapons, but also with a multiplicity of bases from which a retaliatory attack could be launched. They must put themselves in a position to ensure that no surprise attack, however large, could wholly destroy their power of effective retaliation.

It was these considerations, Churchill concluded, which in his view made it 'essential' that Britain should manufacture hydrogen bombs in the United Kingdom 'so as to be able to make our contribution to this deterrent influence'.

---

[1] A note in the Cabinet papers at the Public Record Office, Kew, states that the record of this discussion, forming a Confidential Annex to the Cabinet Conclusions, has been retained by the Cabinet Office. The note is dated 3 October 1984, shortly before the Cabinet Conclusions for 1954 were opened to public scrutiny. The record was still closed in 1988.

Speaking after Churchill, Lord Salisbury said that he accepted 'the strategic argument outlined by the Prime Minister'. But the Lord Privy Seal, Harry Crookshank, pointed out that the Cabinet 'had had no notice that this question was to be raised' and he hoped they would 'not be asked to take a final decision on it until they had had more time to consider it'. It was then agreed to resume the discussion 'at a later meeting'.[1]

The discussion on the hydrogen bomb was to resume on the following morning. Meanwhile the disagreement about Churchill's proposed visit to Malenkov, which had provoked Lord Salisbury to threaten to resign, led to a dispute which clouded the afternoon and evening of July 7. Lord Swinton, who tried to act as an intermediary together with Lord Simonds, approached Jock Colville, asking him to explain all the circumstances of the plan to meet Molotov, or indeed Malenkov, 'for the information', and as Lord Simonds thought, 'possible intervention' of the Queen herself. Colville noted in his diary:

Salisbury both dislikes the Russian project and objects to the PM's action in approaching Molotov without consulting and obtaining the agreement of the Cabinet. Lord Swinton has represented to him, first that this is the 'end of a voyage' with Winston and that a similar case is therefore unlikely to occur; secondly, that his (Lord Salisbury's) resignation will do great harm to Anglo-American relations because it will be greatly played up by those who, like Senator Knowland, will cry out against the Russian talks and will be represented as a revolt by Lord Salisbury against an anti-American move on the part of Winston and Eden.

'Also, of course,' Colville noted, Lord Salisbury's resignation would be 'highly embarrassing to Eden,'[2]

That evening Churchill's hopes of a meeting with the Russians were dramatically enhanced by a telegram which reached him from Moscow, from Molotov himself. The telegram read, as received:

I express my gratitude for your important message handed to me by Ambassador Hayter on the 4th July.

It is with interest that the Soviet Government got acquainted with this message, the importance of which is quite clear. You may be sure that your initiative will find here favourable attitude which it fully deserves especially in the present international situation in general.

Your idea about a friendly Meeting between you and Premier G. M. Malenkov as well as the considerations expressed by you regarding the aims of such a Meeting, have met with sympathetic acknowledgement in Moscow. Mr Anthony Eden's participation in such a Meeting who is closely connected

---

[1] Cabinet Conclusions No. 47 of 1954, 'Secret', 11.30 a.m., 7 July 1954: Cabinet papers, 128/27.

[2] Colville diary, 7 July 1954: *The Fringes of Power*, page 701.

with the development of the relations between our countries, is, of course, accepted as quite natural. We feel that such a personal contact may serve to carrying out a broader Meeting on the highest level, if it is accepted by all the parties which are interested in easing the international tension and in strengthening peace.

I deem it necessary to express to you the general opinion of the leading political statesmen in Moscow. They have often recalled about our friendly relations during the war and about the outstanding role which you personally played in all that. Once again you have rightly reminded of this time. One may ask why during the years of war there existed between our countries the relations which had a positive significance not only for our peoples but for the destinies of the whole world, and why such relations cannot be developed in the same good direction now.

'As to us,' Molotov ended, 'we are striving to this end and we are regarding your message from this point of view.'[1]

As soon as Molotov's telegram reached him, Churchill telegraphed a copy of it to Eisenhower. 'I should like to know how this strikes you,' Churchill wrote, and he added: 'We have many pleasant and enduring memories of our visit to the White House.'[2]

When the British Cabinet met on the morning of July 8, Churchill made no immediate reference to Molotov's telegram, the first item on the agenda being to resume the discussion on the hydrogen bomb. In answer to a question about the 'financial commitment' involved, the Cabinet were informed that the net additional cost of adjusting the programme so as to allow for the production of thermo-nuclear bombs 'would not be very substantial'. The capital cost should not exceed £10 million, and the thermo-nuclear bombs would be made in lieu of atomic bombs at a relatively small additional production cost. Much of the material needed for the production of the new type of bomb, it was explained, would have been required for the production of atomic bombs, and there would be a substantial degree of flexibility in the programme, since atomic bombs could be converted into thermo-nuclear bombs. In terms of explosive power the thermo-nuclear bomb 'would be more economical than the atomic bomb'.

Several further questions were then asked, by Ministers not named in the minutes. Might we not wish to prevent the manufacture of thermo-nuclear bombs in Western Europe, particularly in Germany? Would it be easier for us to prevent this if we ourselves refrained from producing these weapons? Some of our other defence preparations were already based on the assumption that we should not engage in major war except as an ally of the United States: could we not con-

---

[1] Telegram of 7 July 1954: Eisenhower papers.
[2] 'Dear Friend', 'Private and Personal', 'Top Secret', 7 July 1954: Eisenhower papers.

tinue to rely on the United States to match Russia in thermo-nuclear weapons?

In reply it was pointed out 'that the strength of these arguments was weakened by the fact that we had already embarked on the production of atomic weapons'. There was 'no sharp distinction' in kind 'between atomic and thermo-nuclear weapons', and, as Britain was already engaged in the manufacture of this kind of weapon, 'it was unreasonable that we should deny ourselves the advantage of possessing the most up-to-date types'.

Eden then told the Cabinet 'that our power to control the production of thermo-nuclear weapons in Western Europe would not in his view be weakened by the fact that we ourselves were making these weapons'.

A third, moral, question was then recorded in the minutes: 'Was it morally right that we should manufacture weapons with this vast destructive power? There was no doubt that a decision to make hydrogen bombs would offend the conscience of substantial numbers of people in this country. Evidence of this was to be found in the resolutions recently passed by the Methodist Conference in London.'

In reply the point was again made 'that there was no difference in kind between atomic and thermo-nuclear weapons; and that, in so far as any moral principle was involved, it had already been breached by the decision of the Labour government to make the atomic bomb'.

It was also argued that the moral issue would arise, not so much on the production of these weapons, but on the decision to use them; and that the resolution of the Methodist Conference was directed mainly against the use of atomic weapons. The further point was made that, if Britain was ready to accept the protection offered by United States use of thermo-nuclear weapons, 'no greater moral wrong was involved in making them ourselves'.

A series of arguments was then put forward, again without any name or names being mentioned, in favour of a British hydrogen bomb. No country could claim to be a leading military Power, it was asserted, 'unless it possessed the most up-to-date weapons', and the fact must be faced that, 'unless we possessed thermo-nuclear weapons, we should lose our influence and standing in world affairs'. Strength in thermo-nuclear weapons would henceforward provide the most powerful deterrent to a potential aggressor; 'it was our duty to make our contribution towards the building up of this deterrent influence. It was at least possible that the development of the hydrogen bomb would have the effect of reducing the risk of major war.' At present 'some people thought that the greatest risk was that the United States might plunge the world into war, either through a misjudged intervention in Asia or in order to forestall an attack by Russia. Our best chance of preventing this was to maintain our influence with the United States Government; and they would certainly feel more respect for our views if we continued to play an effective part in building up the strength necessary to deter aggression than if we left it entirely to them to match and counter Russia's strength in thermo-nuclear weapons.'

A final doubt concerned 'the feasibility of keeping secret, for any length of time, a decision to manufacture thermo-nuclear weapons in this country'. It was therefore suggested, again by an unnamed Minister or Ministers, 'that thought should be given to the question how a decision to manufacture these weapons could best be justified to public opinion in this country and abroad'.

The Cabinet minutes then noted that it had 'emerged from the discussion that there was general support in the Cabinet for the proposal that thermo-nuclear bombs should be manufactured in this country'. Some Ministers asked, however, 'that there should be a further opportunity for reflection before a final decision was taken'. Meanwhile, it was agreed 'that there should be no interruption of the preliminary planning which had already been put in hand'.

The Cabinet then agreed to resume their discussion of this question 'at a further meeting before the end of July'.[1]

The Cabinet of July 8 then returned to the issue of Churchill's proposed Anglo-Soviet summit: a 'bilateral meeting with M. Malenkov' was how Churchill described it. He was waiting to learn, he said, if Eisenhower approved. So far, the response from the White House had not been so favourable as he had expected. Churchill also 'made it clear' to the Cabinet that he would 'not be disposed' to accept an invitation to meet Malenkov in Moscow. He had suggested, in seeking Eisenhower's support, that either Stockholm or Vienna should be the meeting-place.

The friendly reply from Molotov, non-committal but not ruling out a meeting, encouraged Churchill to persevere. Commenting in Cabinet on criticisms that had been made privately the previous day, Churchill admitted that some of his colleagues 'might think that the Cabinet should have been consulted before he had sent to M. Molotov the personal and private message embodied in Foreign Office telegram to Moscow No. 873'. It had been his practice, however, he explained, 'both during the war and since the present Government took office, to exchange personal messages with Heads of Governments and more particularly with the President of the United States. Most of these

[1] Cabinet Conclusions No. 48 of 1954, 'Secret', 11.30 a.m., 8 July 1954: Cabinet papers, 128/27.

messages had been seen before despatch by the Foreign Secretary, who could always suggest that reference should be made to the Cabinet if he thought this necessary.' He therefore hoped 'that he would continue to enjoy the confidence of his colleagues in continuing a practice which, in his opinion, had proved beneficial in the conduct of public affairs'.

Churchill's hope was not rewarded, Lord Salisbury stating 'that he was glad that this opportunity had been given to discuss the constitutional aspects of this matter'. He did not contest the right of a Prime Minister to determine policy. 'But, if a Prime Minister took a decision of policy which involved the collective responsibility of the whole Government without prior consultation with his Cabinet colleagues, any of his colleagues who dissented from the decision might thereby be forced to the remedy of resignation.' The message which Churchill had sent to Molotov, 'though framed as a personal enquiry, was in his opinion an important act of foreign policy; and it would have been preferable that the Cabinet should have been given an opportunity to express their views on it before it was sent'.

The second critic of Churchill's method was Harry Crookshank. He also regarded Churchill's message to Molotov, the minutes noted, 'as an important act of policy, on which the Cabinet should have been consulted. For, although it was presented as a personal enquiry, it was bound to commit the Government to some extent to the view that this was an opportune moment for a meeting of the kind suggested.' For his part, Crookshank added, 'if his view had been sought, he would have been inclined to advise against making such an approach at the present time'.

Churchill intervened to suggest 'that a distinction could be drawn between an informal enquiry and a formal proposal for a meeting. The latter could clearly not have been made without the approval of the Cabinet. But he had not thought that the Cabinet would be in any way committed by a personal and preliminary enquiry; and he had understood that the Foreign Secretary, whom he had consulted, was of the same opinion.'

Eden then came to Churchill's defence, telling the Cabinet that a draft of the message to Molotov had in fact been sent to R. A. Butler, and that it had been in Eden's mind when sending it 'that the Chancellor would bring it to the notice of his Cabinet colleagues'. But Butler did not support Eden and Churchill, telling the Cabinet:

. . . the draft had reached him during the afternoon of Saturday, 3rd July, when he was in Norfolk. The telegram embodying it had been addressed to him personally, and copies had at that stage been shown only to senior

officials in the Foreign Office and to the Prime Minister's Private Secretaries at
10 Downing Street.

There was nothing in the telegram to suggest that the views of the Cabinet
were being invited. Indeed, before he had been able to despatch his own
comments, which he had formulated after discussion with senior Foreign
Office officials, a further telegram had been received from the Prime Minister
enquiring whether the message had been transmitted to Moscow. This had
confirmed his view that he had not been expected to invite the views of other
Cabinet colleagues—and it would in any event have been very difficult for
him to do so when Ministers were dispersed at the week-end.

Many Cabinet Ministers were shocked by Butler's recital of these
facts. Lord Salisbury, speaking next, pointed out that Churchill's message to Molotov had been despatched to Moscow on July 4. But
Churchill and Eden had arrived back in London on July 6, 'and could
then have held full consultation with their Cabinet colleagues'. Was
the message 'so urgent', Salisbury asked, 'that its despatch could not
have been delayed for three days?'

Churchill sought once more to defend what he had done, and at
the same time to make an apology, telling the Cabinet that 'in his
anxiety to lose no opportunity of furthering the cause of world peace,
he might have taken an exaggerated view of the urgency of the matter.
There had seemed no reason to delay what he regarded as a personal
and informal enquiry which could not commit his colleagues.'

Lord Swinton now spoke; he too was critical of Churchill's action.
A Prime Minister 'was certainly free to conduct unofficial personal
correspondence with Heads of other Governments,' he said. 'But,
equally, in such correspondence a Prime Minister would take care
to avoid committing the Cabinet to any act of policy without their
prior approval. The practical question was whether any particular
message, sent in the course of such personal correspondence, had the
effect of committing the Cabinet. Though it was clear that this had
not been intended on the present occasion, had it produced this
effect?'

Lord Salisbury now spoke again, telling the Cabinet that 'in his
opinion the Cabinet's freedom of action had to some extent been limited by the message which the Prime Minister had sent'. When the
Cabinet came to take a decision on the substance of the issue, 'they
might wish to decide that it would be preferable not to go forward
with this project for a meeting with M. Malenkov. But, if they so
decided, and if the Russians then chose to give publicity to the messages exchanged between the Prime Minister and M. Molotov, the
public would be left with the impression that the Prime Minister had
wished to arrange such a meeting but had been deterred from doing

so by his Cabinet colleagues.' That consideration, Salisbury warned, 'might now influence the Cabinet's eventual decision'.

Oliver Lyttelton now spoke. He too was reluctant to endorse Churchill's initiative. It 'could not be denied', he felt, that as a result of Churchill's message to Molotov 'it was now more difficult for the Cabinet to decide that this was not an appropriate moment for a bilateral meeting of the kind suggested in that message. Nevertheless, he thought it was still open to the Cabinet to decide not to proceed further with this project.'

Sensing a lifebelt thrown into a stormy sea, Churchill at once agreed with Lyttelton. 'It might well be,' he said, adding a further retreat of his own, 'that, when President Eisenhower had replied to his further message, he would be convinced that it would be preferable not to proceed further with this project.' In that event 'he would not feel obliged to give M. Molotov any detailed reasons for this decision. It would suffice to thank him again for his cordial message and to say that we did not think it practicable to proceed further with this project at the present time. This, however, must be left for consideration in the light of a further expression of the President's views.'

The Cabinet then agreed, as the minutes recorded, 'to resume their discussion of this question when President Eisenhower had replied to the further message which the Prime Minister now proposed to send him'.[1]

Churchill's message to Eisenhower read:

Dear Friend,

I hope you are not vexed with me for not submitting to you the text of my telegram to Molotov. I felt that as it was a private and personal enquiry which I had not brought officially before the Cabinet I had better bear the burden myself and not involve you in any way. I have made it clear to Molotov that you were in no way committed. I thought this would be agreeable to you, and that we could then consider the question in the light of the answer I got.

Much grass has already grown under our feet since my telegram to you of May 4, 1953. I should be grateful if you would glance again at our correspondence of that period. I have of course stated several times to Parliament my desire that a top level meeting should take place and that failing this I did not exclude a personal mission of my own. I have never varied, in the fourteen months that have passed, from my conviction that the state of the world would not be worsened and might be helped by direct contact with the Russia which has succeeded the Stalin era. However, as you say this is now past history.

---

[1] Cabinet Conclusions No. 48 of 1954, 'Confidential Annex', 'Top Secret', 11.30 a.m., 8 July 1954: Cabinet papers, 128/27.

I thought Molotov's reply was more cordial and forthcoming to what was after all only a personal and private enquiry than I had expected. It strengthens my view that the new government in the Kremlin are both anxious about the thermo-nuclear future and secondly, attracted by the idea of a peaceful period of domestic prosperity and external contacts. This is certainly my view of what is their self-interest. I was struck by the fact that they did not suggest a meeting in Moscow but respected my wish to leave the time and place entirely unsettled. Of course it would be much better to have even the two power meeting about which I enquired in Stockholm or Vienna or Berne and if the Cabinet decide to go forward with the project a margin of six or eight weeks would be open to us for fitting the timing into the movement of events both at Geneva and in Indo-China.

It is on all this that I most earnestly seek your advice, while being willing to bear the brunt of failure on my own shoulders.[1]

'Of course I am not vexed,' Eisenhower replied, and he added:

Personal trust based upon more than a dozen years of close association and valued friendship may occasionally permit room for amazement but never for suspicion. Moreover, I cannot too strongly emphasize to you my prayerful hope that your mission, if you pursue it, may be crowned with complete success. My appreciation of the acute need for peace and understanding in the world certainly far transcends any personal pride in my judgments or convictions. No one could be happier than I to find that I have been wrong in my conclusion that the men in the Kremlin are not to be trusted no matter how great the apparent solemnity and sincerity with which they might enter into an agreement or engagement.[2]

As soon as Eisenhower's telegram reached him, Churchill replied with further arguments in favour of a summit:

Dear Friend,

I am very much relieved by your kind telegram which reassures me that no serious differences will arise between our two governments on account of a Russian excursion or 'solitary pilgrimage' by me. I feel sure that you will do your best for me in presenting it to the United States public. I accept the full responsibility as I cannot believe that my American kinsmen will be unanimous in believing I am either anti-American or pro-Communist.

I do not intend to go to Moscow. We can only meet as equals and though Stockholm which you mentioned to me before you took office, or Vienna, are both acceptable, Anthony has proposed what I think is the best, namely, Berne. If Malenkov will come to Berne when Geneva is over, Molotov could meet him there and Anthony and I could have a few talks on the dead level.

My idea is to create conditions in which a three-, or perhaps with the French, a four-power conference might be possible, perhaps, as I said to you,

[1] 'Dear Friend', 'Message from the Prime Minister to the President', received 8 July 1954: Eisenhower papers.
[2] 'Dear Winston', sent 8 July 1954: Eisenhower papers.

in London early in September. For this I feel, and I expect you will agree, that Russian deeds are necessary as well as words. I should ask them for a gesture or as better expressed, 'an act of faith' after all Stalin's encroachments in Poland, Czechoslovakia, Korea, etc. which ruptured Anglo-American war-time comradeship with them, and created the world-wide union of the free nations, of which NATO is the first expression and METO and SEATO are coming along. The sort of gesture I should seek at Berne would be, as I think I mentioned to you, an undertaking to ratify the Austrian Treaty in which *all* their conditions have been agreed, and to liberate Austria and Vienna from Russian military domination. Surely also it would be a help if they would accept your atomic theme which you told us about at Bermuda and afterwards proposed to UNO.

But I am not asking any promise from you that even if the above gesture were attained you would commit yourself to the three- or four-power conference in London, but naturally my hopes run in that direction.

Of course all this may be moonshine. The Soviets may refuse any meeting place but Moscow. In that case all would be off for the present, or they will give nothing and merely seek, quite vainly, to split Anglo-American unity. I cherish hopes not illusions and after all I am 'an expendable' and very ready to be one in so great a cause.

I should like to know your reactions to what I have set out above before I formally ask the Cabinet to propose to the Soviets the two-power meeting as described.[1]

On July 9 there was further Cabinet criticism of Churchill's Soviet initiative. If the Indo-China negotiations at Geneva were to result in an agreement 'from which the United States Government expressly dissociated themselves', several Ministers declared, it was 'arguable that a bilateral meeting between the Prime Minister and M. Malenkov would at that moment give the impression that an even wider breach was being created between the United Kingdom and the United States'. On the other hand it was 'arguable', according to other Ministers, also unnamed, 'that in those circumstances—and, perhaps even more, if no agreement of any kind were reached at Geneva—it would be reassuring to public opinion throughout the world that a further opportunity was being created for discussions with the Soviet Government which might yet avert the danger of world war'. In either event, it was pointed out, 'it seemed clear that a final decision must await the outcome of the resumed negotiations at Geneva'.

Churchill still did not feel that all was lost for his summit hopes, suggesting that Eden 'should take the opportunity, while at Geneva, to make it clear to M. Molotov that this project could not proceed

---

[1] 'Dear Friend', 'Message from Prime Minister to the President', 9 July 1954: Eisenhower papers.

further until the outcome of the Geneva Conference was known. He might also put to him the advantages of Berne as a possible meeting-place.'

For Eden, the dangers of a 'Churchill' summit were the lack of any fixed agenda, and the problem of 'the questions which the Russians were likely to raise', and he went on to ask the Cabinet how the Russians would react, 'for example, to the suggestion that they should give an undertaking to ratify the Austrian Treaty? Were they not likely to counter this by pressing the suggestion for a European security guarantee which they had put forward at the Berlin Meeting—a suggestion which, as Ministers would remember, was designed to prevent the establishment of a European Defence Community.' As an alternative to the creation of that Community, Eden warned, 'they would probably suggest that a united Germany should be admitted to the North Atlantic Treaty Organisation, and that the Organisation should thereafter be widened to include the Soviet Union'. As regards the project for 'a broader meeting', Britain must be prepared for the Russians to press the suggestion that this should be on a five-Power basis, 'including Communist China'.

Further thought should be given to all these questions, Eden proposed, 'while he was in Geneva'. Whereupon the Cabinet agreed 'to resume their discussion of these matters at a later meeting'.[1]

On July 12, in the House of Commons, Churchill gave an account of his American journey. He had never, he said, had 'a more agreeable or fruitful visit than on this occasion', or the feeling 'of general goodwill more strongly borne in upon me'. As to the discussion of 'current atomic and hydrogen problems', it would not, said Churchill, 'be in the public interest for me to make any detailed statement upon what passed. I can only say that there was cordial agreement that both our countries would benefit from a wider latitude both in co-operation and in the exchange of knowledge.'

Churchill made no reference to Britain's decision to manufacture the hydrogen bomb, or to Eisenhower's approval of that decision. He did speak of the storm caused by Senator Knowland's charge that one aim of Churchill's visit had been the admission of Communist China to the United Nations, against America's wishes. British policy on the subject of the admission of Communist China to the United Nations, Churchill told the House of Commons, 'has been unchanged

[1] Cabinet Conclusions No. 49 of 1954, 'Confidential Annex', 'Top Secret', 12.30 p.m., 9 July 1954: Cabinet papers, 128/27.

since 1951 when the right hon. Gentleman the Member for Lewisham, South [Mr H. Morrison], then Foreign Secretary, stated that His Majesty's Government believed that the Chinese People's Government should represent China in the United Nations but that, in view of the Government's persistence in behaviour inconsistent with the purposes and principles of the Charter, it appeared to His Majesty's Government that consideration of the question should be postponed.'

That, Churchill reiterated, 'was the policy of the late Government and it has been the policy of the present Government, reaffirmed in July last by the Chancellor of the Exchequer'.

Churchill then recalled how Eden, in his speech just before their departure to the United States, in speaking about the relations of the Communist and free worlds, 'used the remarkable phrase "peaceful co-existence"', and he added: 'This fundamental and far-reaching conception certainly had its part in some of our conversations at Washington, and I was very glad when I read, after we had left, that President Eisenhower had said that the hope of the world lies in peaceful co-existence of the Communist and non-Communist Powers, adding also the warning, with which I entirely agree, that this doctrine must not lead to appeasement that compels any nation to submit to foreign domination.'

What a 'vast ideological gulf' there was, Churchill commented, 'between the idea of peaceful co-existence vigilantly safeguarded, and the mood of forcibly extirpating the Communist fallacy and heresy. It is, indeed, a gulf. This statement is a recognition of the appalling character which war has now assumed and that its fearful consequences go even beyond the difficulties and dangers of dwelling side by side with Communist States.' [1]

On July 13 Churchill received the answer to his request to Eisenhower about the proposed meeting with Malenkov. At the Cabinet that morning, Churchill reported Eisenhower's view 'that this project would not create any difference between the Governments of the United States and the United Kingdom or alter his confidence in the Prime Minister's dedication to the principles which had united the two countries in time of peril and now constituted the best guarantee of world peace. Though he feared the effect on public opinion in the United States, he would do his best to mitigate any immediate unfavourable reaction.'

Churchill also told the Cabinet of July 13 that Eisenhower had 'welcomed the Prime Minister's statement that he would not be willing to meeting M. Malenkov except on a basis of full equality'. He had

[1] Speech of 12 July 1954: *Hansard*.

also been 'reassured by the Prime Minister's insistence that the Soviet Government should give proof of their sincerity by deeds as well as words'; and he had agreed 'that it would help to re-establish public confidence if the Russians would undertake to ratify the Austrian Treaty and to co-operate in the Atomic Bank Plan'.

With understandable satisfaction, Churchill told the Cabinet 'that he was gratified by the terms and the tone' of Eisenhower's message.

In Geneva, Eden had already raised with Molotov the prospect and nature of a Churchill–Malenkov meeting. Molotov had 'recognised', the Cabinet were told, 'that this project of a bilateral meeting could not proceed further until the outcome of the Geneva Conference was known'. As regards the choice of meeting-place, Eden 'had rejected a tentative suggestion by Molotov that the meeting might take place within the Soviet Union, and had suggested London or, as an alternative, Berne'. Molotov had replied 'that his Government had not yet considered questions of time and place, but he would now communicate with them on this and would let the Foreign Secretary have their views in due course'.

The Cabinet were told that Eden 'had deduced from this interview that, if it were finally decided to pursue this project, we need not exclude the possibility of persuading the Russians to accept London, or alternatively Berne, as the place for a meeting'.

For Churchill, Eden's report was a hopeful sign that his dream might still become a reality: 'he would not ask the Cabinet to reach decisions on this matter', he said, 'until after the Foreign Secretary had returned from the Geneva Conference'.[1]

Lord Salisbury was not alone in feeling that Churchill's idea, and his actions, had been at variance with both constitutional procedure and the needs of the international situation. 'Things came to a head today', Colville noted in his diary on July 16, 'at any rate within 10 Downing Street', and he went on to explain:

Before luncheon Harold Macmillan came to see Lady Churchill and told her that the Cabinet was in danger of breaking up on this issue. When he had gone she rang me up and asked me to come and see her. I in fact knew more about the situation than she did and since she proposed to 'open' the matter to Winston at luncheon, I suggested I should stay too.

She began by putting her foot into it in saying that the Cabinet were angry with W for mishandling the situation, instead of saying that they were trying to stop Salisbury going. He snapped back at her—which he seldom does—and afterwards complained to me that she always put the worst complexion on everything in so far as it affected him.

[1] Cabinet Conclusions No. 50 of 1954, 'Top Secret', 11.30 a.m., 13 July 1954: Cabinet papers, 128/27.

However, he did begin to see that Salisbury's resignation would be serious on this issue, whereas two days ago when I mentioned the possibility to him he said that he didn't 'give a damn'.

On the other hand it became clear that he had taken the steps he had, without consulting the Cabinet, quite deliberately. He admitted to me that if he had waited to consult the Cabinet after the *Queen Elizabeth* returned, they would almost certainly have raised objections and caused delays.

As Churchill saw it, Colville wrote, the 'stakes in this matter were so high', and the possible benefits 'so crucial to our own survival', that Churchill was prepared to adopt 'any methods to get a meeting with the Russians arranged'.[1]

On July 23, a week after this confrontation at Downing Street, the 'summit' crisis reached a stormy climax at a Cabinet meeting following the end of the Geneva Conference and Eden's return to London. The Cabinet must now decide, Churchill said, what further communications should be made to Molotov. It was his hope that his colleagues would agree to a draft telegram which he had prepared after discussion with Eden. 'This suggested,' Churchill explained, 'that it would be useful if, before an official proposal was made, agreement could be reached informally about the time and place for a meeting.' The draft telegram proposed that the meeting between Churchill and Malenkov should not take place 'before the early part of September, and that it should be held in Berne, Stockholm or Vienna'. It also 'threw out the suggestion that other Ministers, besides the Prime Minister and the Foreign Secretary might attend'.

It might now be 'convenient', Churchill told his Cabinet colleagues, that he should carry the summit procedure a stage further 'on a personal basis', and he asked whether the Cabinet would be 'content' for him to send such a 'personal and private' message.

In the discussion that followed Churchill's request, it was argued, as the minutes recorded 'that such a communication, though expressed as a personal message from the Prime Minister, must now be regarded as engaging the collective responsibility of the Cabinet. Since the Prime Minister's return the Cabinet had been fully consulted on this matter—indeed this was stated in the draft message—and any further communication must be taken as an expression of the Government's view.'

There was then a further discussion of the constitutional propriety of Churchill having sent the original message to Molotov on July 3. When, in the 'course of' his return from Washington, Churchill ex-

---

[1] Colville diary, 16 July 1954: *The Fringes of Power*, pages 701–2. These methods apparently included a possible appeal 'over the heads of his Cabinet colleagues to the conscience of his countrymen'. (Sir John Colville recollections: Anthony Seldon, *Churchill's Indian Summer*, page 407.)

plained, 'he had reached the conclusion that the time was ripe for suggesting such a meeting, he had thought it better that he should himself take the responsibility for making the first informal approach to the Soviet Government'. Churchill then defended his action in some detail, telling his colleagues of his motives in approaching Molotov without first consulting the Cabinet:

He had thought it would be preferable that the Cabinet should not be in any way committed at that stage, and that he should first explore the possibility on a purely personal basis. He had thought, and still thought, that it was perfectly proper for him to do this without prior consultation with the Cabinet. For the idea of such a meeting was not novel. It had been mentioned in his speech in the House of Commons on 11th May, 1953. More recently, in the debate in the House of Commons on 5th April, 1954, the Government had accepted an Opposition motion welcoming 'an immediate initiative' by the Government to bring about a meeting between the Prime Minister and the Heads of the Administrations of the United States and the Soviet Union.

Churchill then drew the Cabinet's 'particular attention' to a statement by Eden in winding up the debate of April 5, 'that when the Government thought there was the least chance of such a meeting being fruitful they would not hesitate to go for it', and he commented:

In the light of this it had seemed natural that he should explore the possibility of proceeding with a project which, as his colleagues well knew, had been in his mind for some time past; and he was not prepared to admit that there was anything unconstitutional in the course which he had taken in making his preliminary approach to M. Molotov on a purely personal basis.

Before sending his message he had discussed the matter fully with the Foreign Secretary and had gained the impression that, while he would not himself have initiated this project, he did not disapprove it.

Churchill went on to say that if Eden had disapproved of his message to Molotov 'he could have insisted that the matter should be referred to the Cabinet'. Eden at once replied that it 'had been his view' that the Cabinet should be consulted before the message was sent, 'and he had made this clear to the Prime Minister at the time'.

R. A. Butler then stated that when he had received the draft of Churchill's proposed telegram to Molotov, 'he had understood that it had been sent to him for his personal comments only'. It would have been 'possible, though very difficult', Butler insisted, 'for him to have consulted the Cabinet at that stage, and he must accept personal responsibility for having decided not to do so'.

Churchill now spoke strongly in his own defence. He would 'not be prepared to abandon the practice,' he said, 'which he had followed for many years, of conducting personal correspondence with Heads of other Governments, and he could not accept the view that the despatch of his original message to M. Molotov involved any constitutional impropriety'.

He was 'sure', Churchill added, 'that there were many good precedents' for his message to Molotov, an action 'in which preliminary enquiries or *pourparlers* had been carried out by a Prime Minister or a Foreign Secretary without prior consultation with all members of the Cabinet. Indeed, there must have been many occasions on which a Prime Minister or a Foreign Secretary had taken far more decisive action than this without the knowledge of all members of the Cabinet.'

Harold Macmillan, who spoke next, suggested that the Cabinet 'should now look to the future rather than to the past'. But he wished to state nevertheless that he shared Lord Salisbury's view that Churchill's message to Molotov 'was an important act of foreign policy which engaged the collective responsibility of the Cabinet and that the Cabinet should have been consulted before it was sent'. The Cabinet should now, however, discuss what action should be taken 'in the situation which had now been reached'.

Lord Salisbury then set out the reasons for his opposition to a meeting between Churchill and Malenkov. There were those, he said, who believed that the 'greatest threat' to world peace came from Russia. He himself believed 'that the greater risk was that the United States might decide to bring the East/West issue to a head while they still had overwhelming superiority in atomic weapons and were comparatively immune from atomic attack by Russia'. During that period, the 'supreme object' of British policy should be to preserve the 'unity and coherence' of the Western Alliance, and he went on to ask: 'Could we expect the Americans to respect the unity of that Alliance if, with- • out their agreement, we embarked on bi-lateral discussions with the Russians? Was there not a great risk that they would thereby be encouraged to pursue independent policies and to take less account of our views on international affairs?'

In reply to Lord Salisbury's criticisms, Churchill said that his message to Molotov 'had not been sent without any consultation with the United States Administration. While he was in Washington he had held many informal talks with President Eisenhower about the prospects of arranging a three-Power or four-Power meeting at the highest level, and he had also mentioned to him and to Mr Dulles the possibility that he might propose a bi-lateral meeting with M. Malenkov as a personal reconnaissance with a view to a later meeting on a broader basis. Although he had not said anything about the timing of such a bi-lateral meeting, they certainly had known that it was in his mind.'

It was now Eden's turn to voice his criticisms of a Churchill–Malenkov meeting, telling the Cabinet: 'He did not himself believe that any good would come from a bi-lateral meeting with the Russians at the present time'. On all the main topics for discussion, he said, 'there was no prospect that any agreement could be reached'. The proposals which the Russians were likely to put forward at such a meeting 'were quite unacceptable to us', Eden said; and he gave as examples 'their plan for the abolition of atomic weapons, their own security plan for Europe and the demand that the Chinese People's Government should at once be recognised as the proper representatives of China in the United Nations'.

'On the other hand,' Eden continued, Churchill was 'most anxious to make a personal attempt to discover, by conversation with the Russian leaders, whether a three-Power or four-Power meeting at the highest level would help to preserve world peace, and was convinced that some result might be achieved by this personal contact with the Russian leaders'. Eden continued:

As the Prime Minister, with all his long experience, felt so strongly that the attempt was worth making, the Foreign Secretary was ready to acquiesce—so long as the meeting was not held on Russian soil. For his part, therefore, he had not wished to raise objections to the despatch of a further message to M. Molotov in the terms of the draft which the Prime Minister had read to the Cabinet. But he agreed that, before any such message was sent, it would be wise to study the announcement which the Soviet Government had issued that morning on the results of the Geneva Conference.

If the Russians were about to intensify their propaganda about the aggressive intentions of the United States, it might be more difficult to go forward with this project at the present time. It might be expedient that we should take the line that we could not attend a meeting with the Russians while they continued to use their propaganda machine for violent attacks on the policy of our American ally.

For this reason he suggested that the Cabinet might defer their decision until he had had an opportunity to study more closely the announcement by the Soviet government to which the Lord President had drawn attention.

Lord Salisbury's doubts, and Eden's caution, were reflected in the Cabinet Conclusions. A decision would be postponed until the following week, to 'consider the significance' of the new Soviet statement. It was also argued, before the Cabinet came to an end, that any further message which Churchill sent to Molotov 'would be sent after full discussion by the Cabinet and would engage the full collective responsibility of Ministers'. In any event, the minutes of the meeting recorded, 'the Government would certainly be held responsible by public opinion, whatever the form of the correspondence'.[1]

When the Cabinet met three days later, on the morning of July 26, Churchill withdrew his proposal to meet Malenkov. Since their last meeting there had been a Soviet proposal, made publicly two days earlier, for an early conference of all European Governments to consider the establishment of a system of collective security in Europe. 'This created a new situation,' he said. Although the Soviet motive was probably to influence the French against the establishment of the European Defence Community, he was 'satisfied', Churchill told the Cabinet, 'that he could not proceed with his proposal for a bi-lateral meeting with the Russians while this suggestion of a much larger meeting of Foreign Ministers was being publicly canvassed'. He had therefore prepared a revised draft of his proposed message to Molotov 'indicating that the larger meeting which the Soviet Government had now publicly proposed did not seem to accord with the plan for an informal bi-lateral meeting which he had previously had in mind, and asking whether this Soviet proposal was intended to supersede his plan'.

The discussion which followed was a short one; nobody pressed Churchill to continue with his Malenkov plan.[2] Churchill's last great foreign policy initiative was at an end.

On July 27 the much-debated Anglo-Egyptian agreement was signed in Cairo. British troops were to withdraw from the Suez Canal Zone. More than seventy years of British presence and control were at an end. In the House of Commons two days later, Captain Waterhouse, a Conservative backbencher, denounced the agreement as an act of surrender. 'In this piece of paper,' he said, waving the agreement in his hand, 'we have got all that is left of eighty years of British endeavour, thought and forethought.' Then, turning towards Churchill, he declared: 'It must be grave indeed for him now, to have to take this decision.'

A Labour MP, Major Paget, then accused Churchill of having held up the agreement for as long as possible, by encouraging Conservative back bench opposition to it. Churchill, angered, told the House of Commons, with reference to the impact of the hydrogen bomb on defence:

---

[1] Cabinet Conclusions No. 52 of 1954, 'Confidential Annex', 'Top Secret', 11 a.m., 23 July 1954: Cabinet papers, 128/27.

[2] Cabinet Conclusions No. 53 of 1954, 'Confidential Annex', 'Top Secret', 11.30 a.m., 26 July 1954: Cabinet papers, 128/27.

How utterly out of all proportion to the Suez Canal and the position which we held in Egypt are the appalling developments and the appalling spectacle which imagination raises before us.

Merely to try to imagine in outline the first few weeks of a war under conditions about which we did not know when this Session commenced, and about which we had not been told—merely to portray that picture and submit it to the House would, I am sure, convince hon. Gentlemen of the obsolescence of the base and of the sense of proportion which is vitally needed at the present time, not only in military dispositions but in all our attempts to establish human relationships between nation and nation.[1]

Churchill had spoken for four minutes; a mere 121 words. He had said no more than the Secretary of State for War, Anthony Head, had said in opening the debate. 'Why then,' asked Lord Moran in his diary, 'was the PM's intervention so effective?' and he went on to answer his own question:

The answer is to be found, I think, in the fact that Winston is a poet. And it is because he is a poet that he could do what Head, with his logic, had failed to do. He could open the eyes of the House to the appalling spectacle of the first few weeks of the next war. When hydrogen bombs were falling on London, what happened at a base at Suez would not, he thought, matter a great deal.

Before he sat down he had restored to the House a sense of proportion, so that they were able to measure the importance of Suez against the incredible calamities of a war of annihilation.[2]

'If I never speak again in the House,' Churchill told his doctor on the following day, 'I can say I have done nothing better.'[3]

Despite Churchill's success in Parliament, a growing number of Cabinet Ministers who felt that the time had come for him to step down, their feelings sharpened by the controversy in Cabinet over the message to Molotov. These Ministers were prepared to put their demands direct to Churchill. Eleven years later Jock Colville recalled, in a conversation with Randolph Churchill:

Harold Macmillan, deputed by a small committee which had decided that your father should go, came to see your mother one morning and said that Rab Butler and he and Lord Salisbury and Patrick Buchan-Hepburn had been discussing the future of the Tory Party and had felt that it was in the interests of the Party and the country that your father, much as they loved him, should now give way to Anthony Eden.

Your mother received Harold Macmillan in her bedroom one morning and when he left she rang me up in great distress and asked me to come and

[1] Speech of 29 July 1954: Hansard.
[2] Moran diary, 29 July 1954: The Struggle for Survival, pages 582–5.
[3] Moran diary, 30 July 1954: The Struggle for Survival, pages 585–6.

see her and she told me what he had said. I said: 'I thought that you yourself felt that Sir Winston should go' and she replied: 'Yes I do indeed, but I don't wish to be told that by Mr Harold Macmillan.' However, obviously it was her duty to tell the Prime Minister what Macmillan had said and she would be very glad if I would come and lunch with them because she would like to have somebody else present when she told him what would clearly displease him very much.

I accordingly lunched with the Prime Minister and Lady Churchill and after a somewhat embarrassing start she told him in detail what Harold Macmillan had said. The Prime Minister reacted somewhat mildly, to her great surprise and also to mine, and merely said to me: 'When you have finished your fish would you be so kind as to tell the Minister of Housing and Local Government I should be glad if he would come and tell me in his own words what he feels rather than tell my wife.' And so I went next door and rang up and asked Mr Macmillan to come and see the Prime Minister at 4 o'clock.

Colville's account continued:

After luncheon the Prime Minister reverted to a war-time habit of going to have a sleep. This was astonishing because he had long given up that practice. I went down to my desk and proceeded to work. At about a quarter past three the telephone rang and the Prime Minister was speaking: 'I think it would be nice if we were to have a game of bezique at half past three. Would you ask the servants to have the table put out and meet me in Clemmie's sitting room at half past three?' So before half past three I was there, very much surprised because, although I was used to playing bezique later in the evening, never before had I been bidden to do so at half past three in the afternoon. The Prime Minister, contrary to all practice, was on time, in fact he arrived at 29 minutes past three. A game of bezique took 20 minutes, a fact which he constantly referred to and indeed he often timed one.

At half past three sharp we sat down to play. I won. At ten minutes to four, the Prime Minister said he would like to have another game—that he wished to have his revenge. I pointed out that there was hardly time because Mr Macmillan would be arriving at four o'clock. He said 'Never mind, let us have another game, I must have my revenge' and so we started. At four o'clock a messenger came in and announced that Mr Macmillan had arrived; and so the Prime Minister asked the messenger to have him shown up at once. When he came in Sir Winston said he hoped that he might be forgiven if he finished this game of bezique because it really was intolerable he was so unlucky that I had won the last game, that I had had three grand cops as he called them and that it was essential that he should win back the fortune that he had lost. It amounted I think to about £1. So the game went on and for ten minutes the Prime Minister kept up a running commentary on the course of the game and on the extraordinary good fortune that I was having.

He offered Mr Macmillan a whisky and soda, he gave him a cigar and he carried on this running talk. Mr Macmillan was getting obviously more and more embarrassed and I noticed him sitting closer and closer to the edge of the sofa. At ten minutes past four the game finished and I again had won. The Prime Minister said that he must pay me. This was very surprising because we kept a washing book and it was very contrary to all practice for me to be paid at the end of any one game which I had won.[1] However he insisted on sending for his personal secretary who brought down his cheque book and his pen. When the pen arrived he said it was the wrong pen and that he must have his gold pen as it was the only one he could use. This was very surprising as only the night before the gold pen had not been working properly and he had demanded to have the one which the unfortunate secretary had in fact brought him. I began to smell a rat at this stage. Then there was a long discourse about how much I owed him. I said it was £2. 5s. od. and he announced that it was £2. 2s. od. We had a wrangle about this and Mr Macmillan became more and more embarrassed while the talk went on. Eventually the cheque was signed and I was paid off and at about 20 past four, he said that he believed that perhaps Mr Macmillan wanted to talk to him about some matter of political importance and would I be so good as to leave the room.

I left the room telling the messenger that I wished to be informed immediately when the Minister of Housing and Local Government had left. Ten minutes later the messenger came into my office and said that Mr Macmillan had gone. I rushed upstairs and found the Prime Minister still sitting at the bezique table and saying: 'I cannot understand what all the fuss was about, why Clemmie was making such a fuss. He really had nothing to say at all. He was very mild and I don't know what all the fuss was about.'[2]

Meanwhile, the question of when Churchill would retire found echoes even in his family circle. 'WSC is a marvel & a mystery,' Mary Soames noted in her diary on July 29, 'and none of us *really* know what his intentions are—Perhaps he doesn't himself!'[3] A week later, in a letter to Eisenhower, Churchill set out what he felt his intentions were in the international sphere:

One has to do one's duty as one sees it from day to day and, as you know, the mortal peril which overhangs the human race is never absent from my thoughts. I am not looking about for the means of making a dramatic exit or of finding a suitable Curtain. It is better to take things as they come. I am however convinced that the present method of establishing the relations between the two sides of the world, by means of endless discussions between Foreign Offices, will not produce any decisive result.

The more the topics of discussion are widened, the more Powers concerned,

---

[1] Sir John Colville writes: 'A "washing-book" is (or was) the running account of gains and losses, e.g. if you were staying with friends and played some games of chance two or three evenings running you would not pay till the last evening. In the case of WSC he always kept our 'washing book' with the cards and (since he generally lost!) paid up about once a month!' (Sir John Colville: letter to the author, 6 October 1987.)

[2] 'Mr Jock Colville, Reminiscences', 8 June 1965: Randolph Churchill papers.

[3] Mary Soames diary, 29 July 1954: Mary Soames, *Clementine Churchill*, page 450.

& the greater the number of officials and authorities of all kinds involved, the less may well be the chance of gaining effective results in time or even of using time to the best advantage.

I have, as you know, since Stalin's death hoped that there could be a talk between you and me on the one hand, and the new Leaders of Russia, or as they might be, the Leaders of a new Russia, on the other. It will seem astonishing to future generations—such as they may be—that with all that is at stake no attempt was made by personal parley between the Heads of Governments to create a union of consenting minds on broad and simple issues. This should surely be the foundation on which the vast elaborate departmental machinery should come into action, instead of the other way round.

Fancy that you and Malenkov should never have met, or that he should never have been outside Russia, when all the time in both countries appalling preparations are being made for measureless mutual destruction. Even when the power of Britain is so much less than that of the United States, I feel, old age notwithstanding, a responsibility and resolve to use any remaining influence I may have to seek, if not for a solution at any rate for an easement. Even if nothing solid or decisive was gained no harm need be done. Even if realities presented themselves more plainly, that might bring about a renewed effort for Peace. After all, the interest of both sides is Survival and, as an additional attraction, measureless material prosperity of the masses. 'No,' it is said. 'The Heads of Governments must not ever meet. Human affairs are too great for human beings. Only the Departments of State can cope with them, and meanwhile let us drift and have some more experiments and see how things feel in a year or two when they are so much nearer to us in annihilating power.'

Now, I believe, is the moment for parley at the summit. All the world desires it. In two or three years a different mood may rule either with those who have their hands upon the levers or upon the multitude whose votes they require.

Forgive me bothering you like this, but I am trying to explain to you my resolve to do my best to take any small practical step in my power to bring about a sensible and serious contact.

In his letter to Eisenhower of August 8 Churchill also commented on a long letter Eisenhower had sent him, highly critical of British Colonialism. As Churchill wrote:

I read with great interest all that you have written me about what is called Colonialism, namely: bringing forward backward races and opening up the jungles. I was brought up to feel proud of much that we had done. Certainly in India, with all its history, religion and ancient forms of despotic rule, Britain has a story to tell which will look quite well against the background of the coming hundred years.

As a matter of fact the sentiments and ideas which your letter expresses are in full accord with the policy now being pursued in all the Colonies of the British Empire. In this I must admit I am a laggard. I am a bit sceptical about universal suffrage for the Hottentots even if refined by proportional representation. The British and American Democracies were slowly and painfully forged and even they are not perfect yet. I shall certainly have to choose another topic for my swan song: I think I will stick to the old one 'The Unity of the English-Speaking peoples'. With that all will work out well.[1]

The emphasis in Churchill's work was now almost entirely on Foreign Affairs. In the domestic sphere he knew that he could rely upon a strong Ministerial team. Of the sixteen Cabinet ministers whom he had appointed in October 1951, eleven were still in his team three years later. By the standards of any of the peace-time premierships through which he himself had lived and served between 1900 and 1940, his own had proved astonishingly stable.

---

[1] 'My dear Friend', 'Private & Secret', signed 'Please believe me always your sincere friend, Winston S. Churchill', 8 August 1954: Eisenhower papers. In this last phase, 'all will work out well', Churchill echoed a phrase he had first heard in South Africa fifty-four years earlier, which he often quoted, and which expressed his philosophy of politics and life: 'Alle sal reg kom', 'All will come right'. A favourite phrase of President Steyn, Churchill had used it in February 1938 in his letter to Eden, on Eden's resignation from Neville Chamberlain's Cabinet. 'He also,' notes Sir David Hunt, 'used it in a Christmas telegram to Dr Malan in December 1951. He dictated it in fact in Dutch; I was on duty and corrected it to Afrikaans. He was indignant but I stood my ground, having learnt Afrikaans. As always when opposed by someone who he thought knew what he was talking about, he gave way.' (Sir David Hunt: notes for the author, 20 December 1987.)

53

'No intention of abandoning my post'

W ITH the ending of his Malenkov meeting plans, Churchill had one more decision still to make: the date of his resignation. In May he had proposed June, in June he had intimated July, and in July he had settled for September. That August, with Parliament in recess, Churchill had time and leisure to make up his mind. 'I am at Chartwell now,' he wrote to his grand-daughter Arabella on 9 August 1954. 'It is raining every day, but I have always been able to feed the fish and the black swans.'[1] 'Here it hardly ever stops raining,' he telegraphed that same day to Clementine Churchill, who was at Ste Maxime in the South of France, and he added: 'My cold continues but all well.'[2] On the following day he wrote again, in his own hand, his news almost entirely of Chartwell:

My darling,
 Last night your dear letter arrived. I was delighted to read the word 'heavenly' applied to the weather. I feel you have sunshine. Here we have hardly had a gleam. Pouring rain, dull skies are our only fare, abundant but unpleasant! But *you* have sunshine.
 I hope you find Rhoda[3] a good companion. Fancy bathing in the open sea! Has she done any painting? Do you play cards?
 Here I stay in bed most of the time and only go out to feed the fish. Gabriel gets on vy well with everyone except his yellow rival.[4] He is vy friendly to me & Rufus and most attractive. My cold has now gone down on to my chest & turned into a cough, and Charles (who comes nearly every day) watches it vigilantly. I fear I have passed it on to Christopher, but I am

---

[1] 'Darling Arabella', 9 August 1954: Churchill papers, 1/51.
[2] Telegram of 9 August 1954: Churchill papers, 1/50.
[3] Lady Birley, widow of the painter Sir Oswald Birley, who had died in 1952.
[4] Gabriel was Lady Churchill's Siamese cat.

giving him my remedies as well. I dined at the Farm last night & he and Mary came here after. I have had to avoid Charlotte Clementine for more than a week, so as not to make her an untimely gift.[1]

One gets no consolation at this moment from the animal world. All the Chartwell rabbits are dead & now the poor foxes have nothing to eat, so they attack the little pigs and of course have eaten a few pheasants. It is said they will perish & migrate & that then there will be no one to cope with the beetles and rats. Christopher paints a gloomy picture.

On the other side the Swans are well & the Zoo man came down yesterday to clip their wings so that they cannot fly away if they dislike what is going on around them.

Christopher and I have jointly invested nearly £1000 in 8 Swedish 'Landrace' pigs: out of wh he expects to make a fortune. They live at Bardogs and have remarkable figures.

Their hams are much admired—and there are only about 1200 of them in our Pig population of 5 millions. The Boar is said to be worth 4 or 6 hundred £s, & in two years we hope to make a fortune. As they can be kept on what is called 'a herd basis', they will not be income but a capital gain!

There was also news about Clementine Churchill's sister Nellie, who was suffering from cancer. 'The hospital say they are satisfied w her progress under the rays,' Churchill reported. His letter continued:

I do nothing, and enjoy it. It is nice having no plans except what one makes from day to day, & better still hour to hour. I see a few people at lunch and play a good deal of bezique w Christopher & Jock. I hold my own more or less.

Randolph has just rung up. He has returned & will come to lunch tomorrow or perhaps dine & sleep. Alexander Korda comes to lunch today, & Rab to dinner on Friday 13th (Blenheim day). I fear he has got anxieties. Jane P keeps me informed.[2]

My darling one I brood much about things, and all my moods are not equally gay. But it does cheer my heart to think of you in the sunlight and I *pray* that Peace & Happiness may rule yr soul. My beloved darling come back soon refreshed & revived, & if possible bring the sun with you as wide as your lovely smile.

W [3]

On August 19 Clementine Churchill returned to England. Awaiting

---

[1] Charlotte Clementine Soames, born on 17 July 1954, Mary and Christopher Soames's fourth child.

[2] Jane Portal, Churchill's secretary, was R. A. Butler's niece. Butler's wife was dying of cancer (she died on 9 December 1954).

[3] 'My darling', 10 August 1954: Spencer-Churchill papers.

her was a letter in her husband's own hand, with all the latest family, Chartwell and political news:

Welcome Home, My Darling,

I do hope you have got real good as well as pleasure out of yr trip. We await you tonight with eagerness. All is well here except the weather.

I lunched yesterday with Mary & the children. They are a wonderful brood. Jeremy is a portent. I have not seen his like before. It is a lovely home circle and has lighted my evening years.

Gabriel is much more at home and I feed him personally twice a day. He is quite friendly with Rufus, but it is an armed neutrality wh prevails with the yellow cat.

We bought another Indian pig for £300 on Tuesday at a sale where many of them were sold for £700 or more. A litter fetches £2000. Christopher is much excited about it all and may well be on a good thing. Mr Cox who takes a sober view predicted that prices at the sale wd average about £80. Actually they averaged £290!

Mr Mendès-France (I have got a better pen) proposed himself to look in here on his way back from Brussels on Sunday or Monday. He will land at Biggin Hill and I shall tell 615 Squadron to provide a Guard of Honour. I have been most anxious to meet him as he is a new fact in France.[1] I am so glad you will be here.

Osbert Peake came to dine & sleep last night and Christopher and I had 4 hours vy informative talk w him about OAP, which is the dominant feature of next year's Cons Programme. 7/6 a week addition wd be an event of first importance (most secret) and they say the people are quite content to lick a few more stamps (10d). This sort of approval wd enable us to restore all and more than the Six Years of Socialist misrule took in *real value* from the Old & Poor.

Peake hates Old people (as such) living too long and cast a critical eye on me. He told about his Father who was stone blind for 20 years and kept alive at gt expense by 3 nurses till he died *reluctantly* at 91: and of course the Death Duties were ever so much more than they wd have been if he had only been put out of the way earlier. I felt vy guilty. But in rejoinder I took him in to my study and showed him the 4 packets of proofs of the History of the E S Peoples wh bring 50,000 dollars a year into the island on my account alone. 'You don't keep me, I keep you.' He was rather taken aback. I think he will play a large part in this coming year. He has some vy important ideas about Insurance. I think I may put him & his office in the Cabinet on account of the pre-eminence of the OAP in our decisive year. (Secret).[2]

---

[1] Pierre Mendès-France had become Prime Minister of France in June 1954, and was to remain Prime Minister until February 1955.

[2] The Ministry of Pensions and National Insurance became a Cabinet post on 18 October 1954. Osbert Peake (later Viscount Ingleby) died in 1966, aged sixty-eight. The National Insurance Act, introduced by Peake on 1 December 1954, increased all pensions, including Old Age Pensions, war pensions and insurance benefits by 23% (although the individual's contributions rose by only 17%). Six million people were beneficiaries of the increase, including four and a half million retired people.

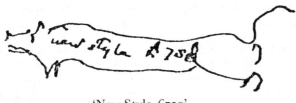

'New Style £750'

Bedell Smith has resigned at Washington not about policy but to gain Health & Wealth. I hope he will succeed. Longing to see you my Beloved.

Your devoted husband

Winston[1]

There were times when Churchill's work intruded into his private life. One such episode occurred a few days after his wife's return, at 10 Downing Street, when he was dictating to Miss Portal. As Churchill explained, in a letter of apology and affection:

My darling & beloved Clemmie,

Do forgive me for my lapse this morning. I was preoccupied with dictating a message to Ike. I only wanted the Portal not to go back to the office but wait in the next room while we had a talk. I was enraptured by yr lovely smile of greeting, & longing to kiss you. And this I spoiled by my clumsiness & gaucherie. I cherish your morning comings & I beseech you to be noble & generous as you always are to your thoroughly penitent & much ashamed, but loving & hopeful,

W

'You have been so bright and splendid here,' Churchill added, 'and I have thanked God to see you much stronger.' His postscript ended: 'I will try to do better.'[2]

On August 12 there had been an unexpected intrusion into Churchill's holiday mood: the news that Attlee and Bevan were to visit both Moscow and Peking. 'There would have been an outburst of joy if I'd seen Malenkov,' Churchill told his doctor. 'Now Attlee has done it.'[3] More serious by far, however, that August, was Churchill's decision, made at the beginning of the month, not to hand over the Premiership to Eden in September. Eden was disturbed at what would be his own electoral chances in the autumn of 1955 if Churchill were to remain Prime Minister until the spring of 1955, leaving Eden, as Churchill proposed, to be in charge of domestic policy. 'I don't think

---

[1] 'Welcome Home, My Darling', 19 August 1954: Spencer-Churchill papers.

[2] 'My darling & beloved Clemmie', 25 August 1954: Spencer-Churchill papers.

[3] Lord Moran diary, 12 August 1954: *The Struggle for Survival*, page 590.

you understand what a gap your departure must make,' Eden wrote to Churchill from Austria on August 10, and he went on to explain:

If there isn't sufficient time for the new Government to make its own name for itself in advance of the general election, then it will have no chance of survival. It will be hard enough anyway. But at least a year, beginning with a Party Conference, seems to me the minimum.

This is not, I am sure, a selfish view, nor a personal one, though I am convinced that it is correct and that there is no escape from it. As, however, we are both so much concerned, I hope you won't hesitate to talk to any of our colleagues about it while I am away. I know that this is what they would like.[1]

The Party Conference was to be held at Blackpool in October; such was Eden's new change-over date. But Churchill did not accept it, and in taking up Eden's suggestion that he talk over the date with 'any of our colleagues', Churchill argued for remaining at the helm until the early months of 1955. The first colleague invited down to Chartwell was R. A. Butler, to whom Churchill showed a draft of a letter to Eden, making clear that October would not be a possible change-over date. On his return home, Butler wrote to Churchill:

First, many thanks for a very pleasant evening. Second. Thank you for letting me see a copy of your letter to Anthony. I think this puts your own decision against the background of world events in the best way possible. But of course it will come as a shock to him. I comment only because you asked me and not in order to approve or disapprove any action you think fit, or to interfere in yr relations with Anthony.

I am glad that no reference is made to the Election. I could not bring myself to agree now to any idea of an early election. I cannot yet forecast my Budget. I have not got enough saving on 'Defence' & it is only now being realised what burdens we are carrying.

Up till now you have always expressed yourself in favour of a long delay before an Election & have even mentioned early 1956. You have also warned me always of the snare & delusion of 'popular' budgets, quoting your own tea duty reaction![2]

---

[1] 'My dear Winston', 10 August 1954: Churchill papers, 6/4.

[2] As Chancellor of the Exchequer in Stanley Baldwin's Conservative administration (1924–29) Churchill had abolished the tax on tea. On 13 April 1929 Churchill had written to King George V, of his nearly completed Budget: 'Mr Churchill still has in hand a surplus of £10,300,000. He proposes to spend £6.2 million of this in the total, immediate and he trusts final abolition of the duty on Tea. No tax will be retained even against foreign Tea, as this is the tea drunk by the poorest people who otherwise would be the only ones left out of the benefit. Tea will go down by 4d a pound. There has been a tea duty in existence ever since the reign of Queen Elizabeth, and Mr Churchill is glad to think that your Gracious Majesty's reign should witness its removal. The ladies who are to take so important a part in our political affairs may recognise that it is right to raise £6 million as we are doing from the taxes on Silk and thus be able to remit the tax on Tea.' Female suffrage had just been extended to all women between the ages of 21 and 30. In the General Election on 30 May 1929 the Conservatives were defeated.

I feel sure however that you do not mean to decide now on the Election or on the Leadership at the Election.[1]

On the following day, Churchill sent Butler a revised draft of his letter to Eden. 'Please have a look at this version,' he wrote. 'I hope it is the final edition and I wonder whether you think it worse or less bad than its precursor.'[2]

Butler replied on August 18:

Dear Prime Minister,

I value your confidence in asking me to look at your second epistle to Anthony. Since last Summer at the time of your severe illness we have all accepted that Anthony is to be your successor. I have therefore a loyalty to him which you realise that I must be careful not to abuse.

Up till my visit to you last Friday I thought you would hand over to your successor this Autumn leaving him time to mobilise his forces, his programme and public opinion.

You have now thought over the situation and have introduced a new argument, which you fortify with your experience, namely that you distrust the outlook for 'fag-end' successor Governments. This is an important argument; and no doubt in order to give it its full force, your second draft omits detailed description of the type of reconstituted Government which you envisage and leaves this as well as the detailed timetable of the changeover until you have talked to Anthony. I think this is right. . . .

'How we shall resolve all this,' Butler added, 'I don't yet see, but you may be sure that I shall from now on expend a fund of understanding on your arguments and shall evaluate at its priceless worth the boon of your strength and experience in handling world events.'[3]

On August 24 Harold Macmillan was at Chartwell. 'Churchill was in a relaxed and amiable mood,' he later recalled, adding that in the course of the luncheon, which lasted until 4 p.m., 'after a certain amount of desultory discussion about Soviet policy, EDC, NATO, Adenauer's position, the French confusion, and the like, we got to the real point. He had now made up his mind not to resign in September as had been the original plan. He reminded me that I had protested against this as being too late to allow for a successful Government to be formed before the end of the year. He therefore made it clear that he proposed to stay as long as he could.'[4]

Churchill then gave Macmillan a number of arguments in favour of staying on, which Macmillan noted in his diary:

First, he (and he alone in the world) might be able to steer through the

---

[1] 'Prime Minister', 16 August 1954: Churchill papers, 6/4.
[2] 'My dear Rab', 17 August 1954: Churchill papers, 6/4.
[3] 'Dear Prime Minister', 'Personal', 18 August 1954: Churchill papers, 6/4.
[4] Macmillan recollections: *Tides of Fortune*, page 539.

complications of Foreign Policy and international problems. He had a unique position. He could talk to anybody, on either side of the Iron Curtain, either by personal message or face to face. Having now fully recovered his health, he could not abandon [his] commission. . . .

Secondly, a 'fag-end' government, formed at the end of a Parliament, could never succeed. Such brilliant figures as Lord Rosebery and Arthur Balfour had been swept away, in spite of their talents and their charm, when they had to succeed to Gladstone and Salisbury. It would be much better for Eden if he (Churchill) were to go on till the Election. Or, perhaps, it might be wise to let Eden become PM just before the Election. That could be decided later.

Thirdly, he was PM and nothing could drive him out of his office, so long as he could form and control a Government and have the confidence of the House. This continual chatter in the lobbies and the press about his resignation was intolerable. It arose, of course, from his illness last year. But he was now recovered. Naturally, like any man of nearly 80, who had had two strokes, he might die at any moment. But he could not undertake to die at any particular moment! Meanwhile, he did not propose to resign.[1]

'Naturally, all this did not pour out in a single flood of rhetoric,' Macmillan recalled. 'There were pauses, questions and silent broodings, and I had to make appropriate remarks at intervals in order to encourage him to tell the whole story. When he pressed me for my opinion, I thought it right to give it sincerely and truthfully.'[2]

Macmillan's opinion was very much in favour of an early changeover. His arguments, as he set them out in his diary, were as follows:

(i) there was no reason to suppose that the foreign problems were temporary or passing;

(ii) that there were arguments the other way about the 'fag-end' administration. We needed a new impetus and a new theme. Anthony Eden might give us these. It was impossible for him.

(iii) Since he had repeatedly told everybody that he proposed to resign this autumn, it was he who was responsible for this widespread (even general) assumption. He had said farewell to the Women's Party Conference at the Albert Hall this summer.

But much more important, he had many times in the last few months told Anthony that he was on the point of 'handing over'. First he had told him the Queen's return, that is May; then he had said, July; finally, in a letter, written on June 11th (which I had seen), he had categorically told Eden that he would resign the Premiership in September. Anyway, what had he now said to Eden?[3]

Churchill then explained to Macmillan what he now had in mind.

[1] Macmillan diary, 24 August 1954: *Tides of Fortune*, pages 539–40.
[2] Macmillan recollections: *Tides of Fortune*, page 540.
[3] Macmillan diary, 24 August 1954: *Tides of Fortune*, page 540–1.

He, Churchill, would remain Prime Minister and Eden would become Deputy Prime Minister and Leader of the House of Commons, responsible for the 'home front'. Eden would 'speak in the country', he would take control of the Conservative Party machine, he would plan the programme for the next General Election. He would, Churchill said, 'be, as it were, to use an analogy of commerce, the managing director', while Churchill remained as Chairman.

'I replied frankly,' Macmillan recalled, 'that I thought this decision would be a severe shock to Eden and that he would be much more likely to wish to stay at the Foreign Office. At any rate, I urged him not to let things drift but to bring them to a head. We really must settle, and within a few weeks, what was to be done and how we were to plan our work.' [1]

In the light of this discussion, Churchill revised yet again his letter to Eden. 'Here is the final edition,' he wrote to Butler on August 25. 'I think it is the best. Thank you so much for your help.' [2] 'Can I say, Charles,' Churchill had asked his doctor immediately after Macmillan's visit, 'that you think I am able to bear the burden?' [3]

The first paragraph of Churchill's letter to Eden was deleted in the letter as sent. The paragraph read:

It is certainly no easier to see ahead in world politics than when we last talked. The Attlee–Bevan meeting with Malenkov is a new event which must be weighed and measured as it deserves. We have yet to hear about their visit to China which I consider far more dangerous from the American point of view. Chou En-lai's threats last week about 'determined Chinese action to liberate Formosa' may easily be deemed grave at Washington. I approved some strong telegrams, which Kirkpatrick had drafted, to Mendès-France not to dawdle or whittle away EDC, but I do not expect any result. It is a terrible example of the domination of impotence. [4]

Churchill's letter made clear that he intended to remain Prime Minister until a General Election in November 1955. 'He hated sending it,' Miss Portal later recalled. [5] The letter read, as finally sent:

My dear Anthony,

I have been pondering over your letter of August 10 but thought it better to wait till you came back before replying.

I am sorry you are not happy about home affairs. We have both had a hard fifteen months. During the first part of them I was much grieved and

---

[1] Macmillan recollections: *Tides of Fortune*, page 541.
[2] 'My dear Rab', signed 'Yours ever, W', 'Private', 25 August 1954: Churchill papers, 6/4.
[3] Moran diary, 24 August 1954: *The Struggle for Survival*, page 593.
[4] 'My dear Anthony', draft letter, August 1954: Churchill papers, 6/4. Sir Ivone Kirkpatrick was Permanent Under-Secretary of State at the Foreign Office from 1953 to 1957.
[5] Lady Williams of Elvel recollections: in conversation with the author, 29 July 1987.

troubled by your illness and the uncertainty as to whether and when you could return. Since these fears have happily passed away, I have been oppressed by a series of suggestions that I should retire in your favour. I have done my best to discharge the Commission I hold from Crown and Parliament, and I am glad to say that I have not missed a single day in control of affairs, in spite of a temporary loss of physical mobility a year ago. Now I have good reports from my doctors, and I do not feel unequal to my burden.

I have no intention of abandoning my post at the present crisis in the world. I feel sure that with my influence I can be of help to the cause of 'peace through strength', on the methods of sustaining which we are so notably agreed. I trust therefore I may count on your loyalty and friendship during this important period, although it will not, as I hoped in my letter to you of June 11, be ended by the autumn.

At another level, coming to Party affairs, I have reflected long and deeply on the domestic scene by which we are confronted. The dominant fact is that the changes in the rating valuations are said to make it overwhelmingly desirable to have the election before November, 1955. It does not seem to me that the brief spell which remains till then gives the best chance to the Party or offers a propitious outlook to my successor. Certainly he would court a very heavy responsibility which in fact rests on me. He would have to present in twelve or thirteen months the impression of something new and different which would spread the sense of improvement. But we must ask ourselves whether this is likely in the prevailing circumstances. It is certain that one half of the country, instead of judging the new Government fairly on its merits, will on the contrary make it their target for electioneering abuse and for unfavourable comparisons.

Woolton, whom as Party Chairman I have consulted, tells me that he has already expressed the opinion that such a procedure would be bad electoral tactics. Looking at the scene impartially, as I try to do when I am in a good humour, it seems to me that it might be wiser not to attempt, with the restricted resources available, to conquer the hearts of an audience the majority of whom are hostile Party men. Fag-end Administrations have not usually been triumphant. I can remember Rosebery after Gladstone and AJB after Salisbury. Both were brushed aside in spite of their ability, experience, and charm.

When our Cabinets resume regularly in September, we shall be concerned both with the severe pruning of the Estimates, on which the hopes of the Budget depend, and also with The Queen's Speech for what will be our final Session. There is not much margin of money, and the array of Bills which have so far been paraded do not seem attractive. Departmental legislation occupies Parliamentary time, but rarely wins the mead of popular applause, most rarely from the Conservative Party.

Moreover—need we forget it—the present Government have not got a bad record, with Rab's and Harold's solid and memorable achievements and your own skill at the Foreign Office. Prosperity, Homes, Employment, Solvency, and 'Peace through Strength', is a theme both simple and majestic. This will, I trust, be made good by the 1955 Budget, saved up from last year, which we are trying so hard to sustain. Apart from this and earlier in the year the one obvious and outstanding task on which our domestic fortunes turn is the humane and large-scale handling of Old Age Pensions and kindred subjects. All this is a natural climax, and not a new venture.

As to the election, I ought to bear the responsibility for the past and leave to my successor a fair start and the hope of the future. We can discuss in detail the mechanism and timing by which such a transition could most effectively be achieved. I would in any case stand as a Conservative at the Polls.

I fear a great many of our colleagues will be abroad on their holidays during September, and certainly the Cabinet work before the new Session will be exacting. One thing stands forth. There must be a thorough reconstruction of the Government. This in itself will end the uncertainty which has arisen from your physical afflictions and my own.[1]

'Harold thought I ought to send it,' Churchill wrote to his wife on August 25. 'It has gone. The responsibility is mine. But I hope you will give me your love.'[2] 'On this basis,' Churchill wrote to Macmillan, 'we can certainly plan the future and arrive at what you so aptly described as a prospectus and not a sample.'[3]

'Thank you for your letter of yesterday,' Eden wrote from the Foreign Office on August 25, 'and for telling me of your changed plans since our conversations and your letter of June 11.' The problem was, Eden added, 'not a personal one for any of us, but how the government is to be carried on and the future of the party best assured'.[4] 'Of course we must try to make the best plans possible to win the Election and to save the world,' Churchill replied on August 26, and he added: 'They are not necessarily opposed. I shall be glad to have a talk with you tomorrow at noon at No. 10, if this would be convenient.'[5]

'I told Swinton of your intentions,' Christopher Soames wrote from Yorkshire. 'He was much interested and said that events were moving so fast he thought you should stay.' Swinton also advised the appointment of someone 'to take a firm grip on Home Affairs'. Swinton's choice was Macmillan. As to Churchill remaining Prime Minister, 'he thought your decision would be well received on the whole by your colleagues,' Soames reported, 'though some & notably AE would be disappointed'. Soames added: 'I long to know how your talk with Anthony went.'[6]

[1] 'My dear Anthony', final draft dated 24 August 1954: Churchill papers, 6/4.

[2] 'My darling one', signed 'Your ever loving W', 25 August 1954: Churchill papers, 1/50.

[3] 'My dear Harold', 'Private', 25 August 1954: Churchill papers, 6/4.

[4] 'My dear Winston', 25 August 1954: Churchill papers, 6/4.

[5] 'My dear Anthony', 26 August 1954: Churchill papers, 6/4.

[6] 'Wow', 'Personal and Private', signed 'Yours very affectionately, Chimp', undated: Churchill papers, 6/4.

On August 27 Churchill and Eden met to discuss their exchange of letters. Before the discussion, Eden spoke to R. A. Butler and Harold Macmillan, at their request, noting in his diary:

Rab said that he had been much embarrassed, that he had a double loyalty to W & to me & had told W so. He was convinced that W was determined to stay. Neither pretended that this was nationally desirable. The issue was what to do.

Rab clearly wanted me to consider whether I could take over Home front & leadership of the House. This he urged would make me PM in everything but name. Harold did not conceal his concern at attempting to carry on with W as he now is. Nor did I. The reshuffle was merely a device to enable him to carry on longer while doing even less. He would then do nothing except interfere with FO. This might have disastrous results. We all agreed that it was essential to have a meeting of a number of colleagues soon.

We were all pretty gloomy but friendly. A disagreeable feature of this whole business is that in the reshuffle I am sure we will find W actuated by animus against Bobbety, Harry Crookshank & perhaps the Lord Chancellor.[1]

Eden then walked from the Foreign Office to 10 Downing Street to see Churchill. Eden's diary continued:

Interview opened stiffly. He paid various compliments about FO documents since my return. I did not respond. Eventually we got to the point. He asked me what I thought of the position. I said 'I have your letter, you have mine, what more is there to say?'

He then launched into a long rigmarole as to how he felt better (he didn't look it & his argument was often confused—for instance when later he discussed whether I should stay at FO or lead the House he gave the arguments for one in support for the other). He also argued that this was a bad time for him to go; not possible for the new administration to make its mark in the last year. This was Woolton's view too. Unfortunate I had been ill when he had his stroke last year. Now better wait until he fell ill again, or nearer the election when he would give me all the help he could.

I said I had explained what I thought many times. If I was not fit to stand on my own feet now & choose an administration now, I should probably be less so a year from now. The Govt was not functioning well & this was putting a heavy strain on all his senior Ministers. These were able men but there was no co-ordination.

Of course he didn't like this & said he had never missed a day since his illness. I said that wasn't the point. There was no co-ordination on home front & Cabinets dragged on far too long. There was much argument about this which got us nowhere. I said that I would have been glad of the chance to take over a year ago, but it meant less to me now, & would mean less still next year if I were still there.

[1] Lord Simonds, Lord Chancellor since October 1951, was replaced by Viscount Kilmuir on 18 October 1954. On retirement, Simonds was created Viscount.

I added that I envied Oliver & would like to do as he had done.[1] He replied that the Party would never forgive me if I did, that they were counting on me, etc. I was young. It would all be mine before sixty. Why was I in such a hurry? Anyway if I felt like it he would be ready for me to take over Leadership of House and home front. I showed no enthusiasm and felt none.

He said there was another alternative, that I might lead a rebellion of five or six Ministers. But that would be very grave. I said of course it would & he knew perfectly well that I was the last person to want to do this after our many years of work together.

Then there was some emotion, after which I said I would like to talk it all over with political colleagues together. He didn't like this much, but eventually agreed as long as it was a discussion of reconstruction and not of his resignation (it wasn't put like that, but that is what it amounted to).[2]

Churchill had offered Eden a choice: the Foreign Office or the home front. For his part, Eden had deferred to Churchill's wish to remain Prime Minister. 'I was deeply touched this morning,' Churchill wrote to Eden later that day, 'by your kindness to me.'[3]

Two days later, in Cabinet, Churchill announced his intention not to resign. That afternoon, Christopher Soames telephoned Churchill from Scotland, to ask how the Cabinet had gone. It had 'all gone well' was Churchill's reply. 'We are so glad,' Mary Soames wrote at once to her mother, and she added: 'I'm sure indecision was the worst of all possible climates to live in for everyone—& liable to breed unrest. I'm afraid Papa's decision to stay must in some ways be a blow to you—I only hope that you are feeling better from yr neuritis & more rested, and that the winter ahead will not be too burdensome.'[4]

'I was so glad,' Duncan Sandys wrote to Churchill on August 31, 'to hear from you last night about your decision to carry on. This will, I am sure, be almost universally welcomed here and abroad.'[5]

On August 29, with the crisis over the succession resolved, as it seemed, to his satisfaction, Churchill dictated a letter to Bernard Baruch, in which he reflected on his failed summit initiative, France,

[1] Oliver Lyttelton, the Secretary of State for the Colonies since 1951, had decided to leave active politics, going to the House of Lords on 9 September 1954 as Viscount Chandos. He was subsequently Chairman of Associated Electrical Industries (AEI), a Director of Imperial Chemical Industries (ICI), Chairman of the National Theatre Board, President of the Institute of Directors, a Trustee of the National Gallery and a Trustee of Churchill College, Cambridge. Aged 62, he was four years older than Eden, and had only entered politics, at Churchill's request, in 1940 (as President of the Board of Trade).
[2] Eden diary, 27 August 1954: Robert Rhodes James, *Anthony Eden*, pages 385–6.
[3] 'My dear Anthony', 27 August 1954: Churchill papers, 6/4.
[4] Letter of 29 August 1954: Mary Soames, *Clementine Churchill*, page 450.
[5] 'My dear Winston', 'Private', 31 August 1954: Churchill papers, 6/4.

America, his political future and, still dominating his thoughts, the hydrogen bomb:

My dear Bernie,

The Kremlin did not turn out to be particularly keen on the visit and though the issue of the rendezvous being on neutral ground was never mentioned I have no reason to believe they liked the idea. I should certainly not go to Moscow. My hope, as you know, was to have talks which might lead to a larger Top Level meeting at a later date. That I have a very good British warrant in pursuing this matter you can judge from the resolution *unanimously* passed by the House of Commons last Session, a copy of which I enclose.

I am also on pretty strong ground about EDC, etc. It is now ten months since I addressed the Conservative Party Annual meeting and I cannot express our policy today better than in repeating what I said then. The French Chamber with its extraordinary constitution has enabled an indefinite stalemate to be maintained, greatly to the injury of our vital interests in the attitude of Germany.

I was glad to hear again about Jimmy Byrnes. I liked what I saw of him personally very much as I remember with pleasure your and his visit to me when I was ailing at Miami. I cannot think he treated us very fairly over the Atomic Bomb by not letting the Congressional Committee see the text of my Agreement with FDR,—a memorable document of undoubted American constitutional validity. However we are now going on all right on our own after losing several years and spending a lot.

You will, I am sure, be glad to hear that I am not thinking of retirement at the present time. I feel earnestly I still have something to contribute to the cause of 'Peace through Strength'. I am sure that I shall always get a fair hearing in my Mother's Land. I have seemed to gather vigour as this year has progressed and can do a long and thorough day's work especially if I get a good sleep in the middle of the day. I am not however trying any of your equestrian or high-diving exercises at the present time though I am most envious. Still, we have never been rivals.

I doubt if I shall leave England except for a week or two before the end of the holidays, and after that the Party and the Parl resume their sway.

My mind is continually oppressed by the thermo-nuclear problem, though I still believe it is more likely to bring War to an end than mankind.

Mind you let me know if there is any prospect of your coming over here.

Yours ever

W [1]

At a meeting of the Cabinet on August 27, Churchill was critical of the possible sale of up to sixty British helicopters to the Argentine,

---

[1] 'My dear Bernie', 'Personal and Private', 'Top Secret', 29 August 1954: Churchill papers, 2/210.

allegedly for crop spraying. 'He did not himself feel sure,' Churchill told the Cabinet, 'that the helicopters the Argentines now wanted would not in fact be used to our detriment.' It was agreed that not more than ten helicopters should be sold; if the Argentines later wanted to place a larger order, 'the matter should be considered again by the Cabinet'.[1]

On the last day of August 1954 the French Assembly rejected the European Defence Community by 319 votes to 264. 'The throwing out of EDC,' Churchill told his doctor, 'is a great score for the Russians.'[2] This decision, Churchill told the Cabinet on September 1, 'had put the German Government into a strong tactical position vis-à-vis Germany's Western Allies' and had, in his view, presented them 'with a rare opportunity to restore Germany's moral standing and expose the failure of France to rise to the needs of the hour'.

If Adenauer were to issue, 'promptly, spontaneously and without waiting for demands on Germany to be formulated, a generous public declaration to the effect that the German Government would not seek to derive advantage from the predicament now facing her partners in the Western Alliance', Churchill suggested, 'and that she continued to recognise that her contribution to Western defence must remain subject to limits acceptable to her partners, this would be likely greatly to further her cause, besides reassuring her neighbours'.

Churchill had it in mind, he said, to address a personal message to Adenauer immediately, 'urging him to consider making a declaration on these lines'. But Eden, while saying that he would 'welcome a message in this sense' from Churchill to Adenauer, added that 'the suggested terms of such a public declaration should, in his view, be kept as general as possible'. Support for Eden's view was expressed by other Cabinet Ministers also, 'on the ground that, by issuing a detailed declaration of Germany's intentions, Dr Adenauer might prompt French comment to the effect that German declarations were not enough and that her undertakings must be formally embodied in any agreement which might be evolved'.[3]

---

[1] Cabinet Conclusions No. 57 of 1954, 'Secret', 3.30 p.m., 27 August 1954: Cabinet papers, 128/27.

[2] Moran diary, 2 September 1954: *The Struggle for Survival*, page 596.

[3] Cabinet Conclusions No. 58 of 1954, 'Secret', 3 p.m., 1 September 1954: Cabinet papers, 128/27.

Churchill was now determined to encourage Germany to make her contribution to the new Europe. On September 3 he telegraphed to Adenauer:

It seems to me that at this critical juncture a great opportunity has come to Germany to take her position among the leaders of free Europe. By a voluntary act of self-abnegation she could make it clear that in any new arrangement as a substitute for EDC she would not ask for a level of military strength beyond that proposed in the EDC plan or to be agreed with her partners in western defence. This would invest the new Germany with a moral dignity and respect far more worth having than merely claiming the right to create as many divisions as she chose or as anybody else and plunging into an endless legalistic argument on the subject. This might well be expressed in terms in no way derogating from the equal and honourable status of the Germany Federal Republic and would indeed open a new chapter by the very fact that the decision was taken on the initiative of Germany herself.

'I beg you to think this over,' Churchill ended, 'as coming from one who after so many years of strife has few stronger wishes than to see the German nation take her true place in the worldwide family of free nations.' [1]

To Eisenhower, in a telegram on September 9, Churchill reported on Eden's imminent journey in search of a co-ordinated European defence policy:

We are all agreed that an 8-power meeting of allies, plus Canada, would be the right move now and prefer it to the 16 NATO powers proposal, which might well follow it, and we should like very much to have it in London which is a big and well known place and has stood by the Thames for quite a long time without having a conference of this kind. Anthony, who knows all the continental personalities involved from long experience, feels that he could smooth out difficulties, queries and objections, of which there are no lack, better by personal contacts than by the interminable interchange of coded messages and arguments. He is, therefore, at the desire of the Cabinet, proposing to start on a flying circuit of Brussels, Bonn, Rome and Paris to see what he can do.

Churchill ended: 'We shall keep you and Foster fully and punctually informed.' [2] Three days later he was able to telegraph to Eisenhower again, to report that the Belgian, Netherlands and Luxembourg Foreign Ministers were 'attracted by the suggestion which Anthony laid before them of modifying the Brussels Treaty so as to admit Germany and Italy. We want of course to keep this idea secret until we can put it to the French.' [3] On September 18, Churchill telegraphed to Eisenhower again:

---

[1] 'Top Secret', 3 September 1954: copy, Eisenhower papers.
[2] 'My dear Friend', 'Top Secret', received 9 September 1954: Eisenhower papers.
[3] 'My dear Friend', 12 September 1954: Eisenhower papers.

Foster lunched with me and Anthony today and we had an agreeable and helpful talk. As you know, EDC was very different from the grand alliance theme I opened at Strasbourg in August, 1950. I disliked on military grounds the Pleven European army plan which began with mixing races in companies if not platoons. At that time when I saw you in Paris I was talking of it as a 'sludgy amalgam'.

However, when I came to power again I swallowed my prejudices because I was led to believe that it was the only way in which the French could be persuaded to accept the limited German army which was my desire. I do not blame the French for rejecting EDC but only for inventing it. Their harshness to Adenauer in wasting three years of his life and much of his power is a tragedy. Also I accepted the American wish to show all possible patience and not to compromise the chances of EDC by running NATO as a confusing rival.

All this time I kept one aim above all others in view, namely a German contribution to the defence of an already uniting Europe. This, I felt, was your aim too, and I am sure we both liked the plan better when the intermingling was excluded from all units lower than a division. But it was to get a German army looking eastward in the line with us that commanded my thought, and also I felt yours, with all its military authority. Although the French have rejected EDC I do hope and pray that you and I will still keep the German contribution as our No. 1 target and also to get them on our side instead of on the other.[1]

At one point during the Cabinet of September 1, Alexander had spoken of South African demands that the naval base at Simonstown 'should now be handed over to the Union of South Africa'. Churchill, in opposing the giving up of the base, told his colleagues 'that he was reluctant to contemplate any transaction which would be presented as yet another surrender of the rights and responsibilities of the United Kingdom'. The 'political pressure engendered by the colour problem', Churchill added, 'might lead South Africa at some time to sever her ties with the United Kingdom and the rest of the Commonwealth'. Indeed, he felt that this consideration 'might underlie the Union's desire to have the base handed over to her'.[2]

He recognized, Churchill told the Cabinet at a further discussion of Simonstown a week later, that the significance of the base from a defence point of view was 'largely symbolical', but he would find it hard, he said, 'to reconcile himself to its surrender, which would dishearten those elements in South Africa who remained steadfast in

---

[1] 'My dear Friend', 18 September 1954: Eisenhower papers.

[2] Cabinet Conclusions No. 58 of 1954, 'Secret', 3 p.m., 1 September 1954: Cabinet papers, 128/27.

their loyalty to this country and were sadly in need of encouragement at the present time'.[1]

Churchill now addressed himself to a letter which Eisenhower had written to him on August 20, to suggest that the United Nations might be asked to examine the question of Cyprus, where the movement for union with Greece had gained a violent momentum, as well as considerable international support. 'A simple test,' Churchill wrote to Eisenhower on September 18, 'is to compare the conditions prevailing in Cyprus with those in the Greek Islands and particularly in Rhodes since the Greeks took them over from the Italians. Cyprus has never known more rapid progress while in the others there is a grievous decline.' Churchill added:

It cannot be disputed that our claim against the inscription of this question affecting our own external affairs is justified by the Statutes and spirit of UNO. If any such item were discussed by the Assembly, we would of course walk out. Injury would be done to that institution of which the United States and Britain and her Commonwealth are the main pillars. Cyprus would acquire utterly disproportionate publicity and be magnified by the enemies of the English-Speaking world on both sides of the ocean.[2]

On October 5 Churchill congratulated Eden on the satisfactory conclusion of the Nine-Power Conference. 'The influence of the United Kingdom in international affairs,' he said, 'had been greatly strengthened by the settlement which had been reached, and would be still further enhanced by the agreement on Trieste which was due to be signed in London that day.'[3]

By the Nine-Power Agreement, Germany was enabled to contribute to the defence of Europe without, as Churchill explained a month later at the Guildhall, becoming 'a threat to French security'. This, he added, was the result of the 'energy and initiative' of Anthony Eden.[4]

At Chequers during September, Churchill wandered one evening with some of his colleagues into his wife's parlour. The result was a

---

[1] Cabinet Conclusions No. 59 of 1954, 'Secret', 3 p.m., 8 September 1954: Cabinet papers, 128/27.

[2] 'My dear friend', 18 September 1954: Eisenhower papers.

[3] Cabinet Conclusions No. 63 of 1954, 'Secret', 11 a.m., 5 October 1954: Cabinet papers, 128/27. The Free State of Trieste, set up in 1947, was to return to Italy, less one small strip which was joined to Istria (which had been de-facto a part of Yugoslavia since 1945).

[4] Speech of 9 November 1954: Randolph S. Churchill (editor), *The Unwritten Alliance*, pages 192–5.

petition which began with the drawing of a cat, and was signed with a second cat:

A Petition from the CAT
The 'White Parlour' is the ladies' Bower & the private sitting room of the Wife of the Prime Minister.
   Would it be possible for the Prime Minister when he confabulates with men to use:—
1) 'The Prime Minister's Study' (opposite dining-room)
   or
2) the Long Gallery upstairs?

Churchill wrote in the margin, over the drawing of a mouse: 'I was only trying to catch a fat mouse for the Cat. I will not trespass again. W.'[1]
   Among the guests at Chequers was Graham Sutherland, who was painting a portrait to be presented to Churchill on his eightieth birthday. On September 1 Clementine Churchill wrote to her daughter Mary:

Mr Graham Sutherland is a 'Wow'. He really is a most attractive man & one can hardly believe that the savage cruel designs which he exhibits, come from his brush. Papa has given him 3 sittings & no one has seen the beginnings of the portrait except Papa & he is much struck by the power of his drawing.[2]

'He used to dictate while he was sitting,' Miss Portal later recalled, and she added: 'Sutherland would not let him see it. He would scribble on a piece of paper and say "this is what it is going to be". But he wouldn't let us see the picture itself.'[3] Each time Sutherland left Chequers, the portrait was covered up. When he finished, it was taken away, still unseen.

   Among Churchill's visitors that summer was Walter Graebner, who later recalled:

. . . he talked a little of his exhausting life as a peacetime Prime Minister. 'In many ways I had an easier time of it during the war,' he said. 'Then, if we won a battle, we simply began preparing for the next. If we lost one, it was the same. We always knew exactly where we stood, and we had the power to act as we thought best. Now everything is different. There is so much patter, patter, patter, chatter, chatter, chatter, it's a wonder anything ever gets done.'

[1] Exchange of notes, September 1954: Mary Soames, *Clementine Churchill*, page 442.
[2] Letter of 1 September 1954: Mary Soames, *Clementine Churchill*, page 445.
[3] Lady Williams of Elvel recollections: in conversation with the author, 29 July 1987.

'That same afternoon,' Graebner added, 'Churchill indicated to me for the first time that he was seriously thinking of retiring.'

Somehow he led the conversation round to holidays, saying: 'I've been thinking a lot about Marrakech lately. I don't believe there's a better place to go to.' When I agreed, and said that in my opinion February was the best month there, he looked at me in the teasing way that was characteristic of him and said: 'Do you mean the best month for me to retire?'[1]

Still unwilling to contemplate resignation before the autumn of 1955, Churchill now tried to persuade Eden, if possible, to take over the Home Front. On August 30 he had set out his arguments:

My dear Anthony,

I am glad you are weighing the issue carefully. There is of course the argument that with Foreign Affairs in their present condition and your long association and deep knowledge of them as well as your prestige and connections in the external sphere, a choice in favour of the Home Front might be deemed unduly Party or parochial-minded. On the other hand as Deputy Prime Minister and Leader of the House of Commons you would have immense influence over Foreign Affairs in the Cabinet. Since we are agreed instinctively on nearly everything that crops up as well as upon the main foundations of our policy I do not think you would feel any sense of deprivation if Harold relieved you of the immense burden of daily drudgery and frequent absences which your detailed and thorough control of the Foreign Office involves. It may well be that the most fateful decade in our history lies before us. During this period the political pre-eminence of the Unionist Party may be greatly helped by your study and control of the Home Front. On the whole I feel that this would be a right choice. By all means let us discuss it dispassionately at our meeting.

When do you think it should take place? I see no harm in waiting till the week beginning Sunday 12: say Tuesday and Wednesday? We could have a Cabinet on one of the days and intimate talks on both. Let me know what you think of this and also who you think should be invited. I should have thought Rab, Harold, Patrick and James Stuart would be the nucleus[2] and we can add one or two if we need them. Personally I think Philip would be helpful. He has written to me that he hopes his own Office will not be changed in the reconstruction. Walter Monckton would be good also. It is not possible I feel to bring in Ministers personally affected by the major questions (except in the case of Harold which presents no difficulty). Indeed I feel the fewer the better, and in the first instance You, Me, Rab and Harold would be best. Let me know what you think.

[1] Walter Graebner recollections: *My dear Mister Churchill*, pages 18–19.
[2] R. A. Butler, Harold Macmillan, Patrick Buchan-Hepburn and James Stuart.

'It is not my intention,' Churchill ended, 'nor in your interest to weaken in any way the constitutional position of the Prime Minister in regard to the advice he tenders to The Crown on Ministerial appointments. Nevertheless I should be quite willing to talk over the reconstruction in a small circle and then when we get to the lower ranks bring in Patrick and James.'[1]

Included in Churchill's list of names were those Ministers who could be relied upon to support him in staying on, or at least not to combine against him. 'Philip' was his friend Lord Swinton, who had been brought into the Cabinet just under a year earlier. Excluded from the list of those to be consulted were four senior Cabinet colleagues on whom he could not always rely: Salisbury, Kilmuir, Crookshank and Woolton.

'W came to luncheon with Clemmie,' Eden noted on September 10. 'He was in very poor shape & complained of dizziness caused by reading in the car.' Eden's diary continued:

Had further talk with Patrick & Harold. They were gloomy at the prospects of the Party if W remained & a little inclined to complain, perhaps rightly, that I had made things too easy for him. I am quite clear that Ministry of Defence gambit is impossible & told them so. They were keen to press for departure on birthday. I don't think we can succeed, but no harm in trying.[2]

On the following day, September 11, Eden wrote in his diary:

Woke up at seven, finished my box & wrote to W & Harold. W will not like the letter but I had to tell him that no scheme of reconstruction so far devised was any good if the Govt was to function & we were to have best chance of winning next election. Both Harold & Patrick were insistent that I should write this because W is now merely fiddling with names of juniors & all the old men in Cabinet are still to stay. But it isn't easy for an 80 year old to sack a 70 year old.[3]

'I have in mind,' Eden wrote to Churchill on September 11, 'not only the present working of the Govt—unfortunate as that is—but how to give ourselves the fairest chance to win the next general election upon which we are all convinced that so much depends, at home &

---

[1] 'My dear Anthony', 'Secret & Private', 30 August 1954: Squerryes Lodge Archive.
[2] Eden diary, 10 September 1954: Robert Rhodes James, *Anthony Eden*, page 387.
[3] Eden diary, 11 September 1954: Robert Rhodes James, *Anthony Eden*, page 388. Churchill would be eighty on 30 November 1954. Of his 'younger' colleagues who were in their seventies that August, Lord Simonds was 72, Lord Woolton 71 and Lord Swinton 70. Simonds retired that October.

abroad. I am sure that we are not doing it by any of the present plans.'[1]

Two weeks later, with no decision yet in sight, Eden again saw Churchill, at Churchill's own request, as Eden noted in his diary:

Then over to talk to W at his request. It took time but amounted to very little. He seemed inclined to [the] view I couldn't leave FO at present reshuffle. I said I wasn't eager to do so. But if I stayed there until a week or so before General Election I wouldn't have chance to make any impression home front. Silence on this.[2]

On September 26 Eden wrote again. He was reluctant, he said, to remain at the Foreign Office 'until within a few weeks of the general election', and he went on to explain: 'If I am to lead the party then, this doesn't seem to me to give time or opportunity for any leadership, or to develop any theme.'[3] Churchill replied at once, and in his own hand:

My dear Anthony,

I like yr thought of my calling for all Ministers' resignations. It looks more *thorough* and also avoids invidious exceptions which cause pain. I am looking for precedents if any there be. The Queen will not return to London before October 11.

Meanwhile we have the 9 Power Conference and the week after there is our Party Conference—with a *speech* from me!

I am glad you think you may be able to decide about the FO when your Conference is over, and perhaps after this week. That wd be a great simplification. Of course I shall welcome any advice you may give about the changes and I fully agree with what you say about their importance to the future fortunes of the Party.

I wish you all success in your gt task at Lancaster House. I have a feeling that the chances are improving.

There is quite a lot going on!

Yours ever

W[4]

Four days later, Eden telephoned Macmillan, 'rather distressed', Macmillan noted in his diary: 'he says he cannot go on unless Churchill will agree to some definite date to the handover. He wants me to tell him this which I agreed to do.'[5] That same day, October 2, Macmillan wrote to Churchill, his letter marked 'Typed at home':

[1] 'My dear Winston', 11 September 1954: Squerryes Lodge Archive.
[2] Eden diary, 22 September 1954: Robert Rhodes James, *Anthony Eden*, page 389.
[3] 'My dear Winston', 26 September 1954: Churchill papers, 6/4.
[4] 'My dear Anthony', 28 September 1954: Churchill papers, 6/4.
[5] Macmillan diary, 2 October 1954: Macmillan papers.

I am grateful to you for taking me into your confidence yesterday. May I do the same?

I can quite see that there are difficulties about making more sweeping changes in the Government at this moment.

But I feel that the most important thing now is Anthony's position. This is vital.

After all that has happened, I hope you will find it possible to come to a clear and definite arrangement with him about the date of the hand-over.

He must know this and have a fair run on his own before the Election. Otherwise I fear we may lose him now, as well as the Election, when it comes.[1]

Churchill would make no decision. But he strove to maintain friendly relations with Eden, writing to him on October 5 in his own hand:

My dear Anthony,

I am so sorry for yr chill—perhaps it is a Parthian shot by Mendès-France! You are quite right to stay in bed and rest. We have a hard week before us and I don't suppose there will be much time or strength on Friday night. I worry more than I used about speeches. But if you and Clarissa are coming back by train *after* the Conference is over we cd dine together—a small party in my saloon and then an unhurried talk afterwards.

Everyone is singing yr praises—none more heartily than your sincere friend.

W[2]

On October 8 Churchill went to Blackpool, accompanied by Christopher Soames and Jock Colville, with Miss Portal and Miss Gilliatt as his secretarial team. A year earlier, many of the delegates at the Party Conference had assumed that they were listening to Churchill's last speech as leader. But when he spoke to them on October 9, he was not only in better health and form, but gave no indication whatsoever that this would be his last Party Conference at their helm. After nearly three years in office, he said, 'We survey the scene without complacency but, I admit, with growing confidence.'

Churchill made no reference at Blackpool to his own destroyed hopes of a summit. He did however refer to Attlee's visit to Moscow, telling the delegates:

I am sorry that Mr Attlee did not have more success on his trip abroad, but even our football team came a cropper in Moscow[3] and they never

[1] 'Dear Prime Minister', 'Private and Confidential', 2 October 1954: Squerryes Lodge Archive.

[2] 'My dear Anthony', 5 October 1954: Squerryes Lodge Archive.

[3] On 5 October 1954 Moscow Dynamo had beaten Arsenal 5–0.

meant to go to China. They did not, of course, represent the full strength of Britain and that may apply to Mr Attlee's team also. Certainly the politicians said several things which were not helpful to our affairs, but we are all very glad they came back safely and we hope they will do better next time.

He had been leader of the Conservative Party now, he said, for fourteen years; he was 'supposed to be acquainted' with its guiding aims and principles. These were 'the maintenance of freedom, national and individual, in accordance with the well-tried laws and customs of our island'; the development of a 'property-owning democracy'; profit-sharing and co-partnership schemes in industry 'thus enabling workers to become owners of a share in their work and giving them an interest in its fortune'; the stimulation of thrift and savings; and the maintenance of 'those basic standards which are dictated by the humanities, and below which no one must fall', basic standards which the Party would seek the means to raise 'progressively as the years go by'. [1]

The Conference, commented the *Observer* on the following morning, 'was endlessly delighted with him'. As for speculation about when he would retire, 'At any rate for the moment,' the paper added, 'the rank and file seem content that he should go in his own time and how he pleases.' [2] But other observers were less certain of the success of the speech or the willingness of the delegates to wait. 'Christopher had gone down among the delegates,' noted Lord Moran on October 10, 'and sensed that it was not what the PM's hearers wanted. There was an election, not too far off now, and the Party was frankly worried; the public-opinion polls showed them to be doing none too well.' Moran added, after talking to Soames and Colville, that Churchill 'seemed to have lost touch with the rank and file' and he went on to explain:

They had gone to Blackpool hoping for news; what they wanted to hear from the Prime Minister was when he intended to retire. This uncertainty about the leadership was not doing the Conservatives as a party much good. And all they were told was that there was quite enough for both Mr Churchill and Mr Eden to do at the present time. In this mood what was more natural than that the delegates should look for signs in the old man that would confirm their feeling that the time had come for him to go.

Someone had noticed that he said 1850 when he meant 1950 (he had made the same mistake in the Cabinet), while others thought he looked tired and that his delivery was a little slow and rather halting at times. As long as

---

[1] Speech of 9 October 1954: Randolph S. Churchill (editor), *The Unwritten Alliance*, pages 181–91.

[2] *Observer*, 10 October 1954.

he made the Opposition look small the Party would be quiet and let him carry on, but he ought to know that only success could justify his lingering on the stage.

However, if those who listened to the Prime Minister had doubts, he himself had none. 'The Tories as a party,' he once complained to me, 'aren't responsive,' but he did not feel like that at Blackpool. When I went to his room and asked him what had happened, he replied:

'Oh, it was a huge success. I was not at all tired at the end. The pill was wonderful. I felt exactly as I did twenty years ago when I could work the whole bloody day like any other man. Tell me, Charles, does it do very much harm to the constitution? It gives me great confidence.'

For a time he seemed a long way off, and then he looked up: 'While Anthony has this French business on his hands how could he give it all up and take on my job?'[1]

From Blackpool, Churchill had gone straight to Chartwell, telephoning Harold Macmillan to ask him to join him there. 'Churchill has won on every point,' was Macmillan's comment in his diary.

Churchill was to remain Prime Minister 'without any commitment written or verbal as to date', and he went on to note 'with what skill and tenacity Churchill had played his hand, refused to see us except separately—he has played off one against the other and has come off triumphant'.[2]

At Chartwell on October 10, Churchill made a particularly attractive offer to Macmillan; eight days later, when he reshuffled his Cabinet, Macmillan replaced Lord Alexander as Minister of Defence. With Duncan Sandys becoming Minister of Housing and Local Government, Selwyn Lloyd, the Minister of State at the Foreign Office, succeeded Sandys as Minister of Supply. The national Press on October 18 was not particularly impressed by the changes. 'I hope,' Churchill wrote to his wife that day, 'you will find time & energy to look through the enclosed cuttings from the country Press. They give a more widely representative view of the national opinion than do the London papers,' and he added: 'They are certainly encouraging. I send them up to you at once.'[3]

Churchill ended his letter: 'Nil desperandum Teucro duce et auspice Teucro.'[4]

As well as bringing Duncan Sandys into the Cabinet, Churchill

---

[1] Moran diary, 10 October 1954: *The Struggle for Survival*, pages 603–4.
[2] Macmillan diary, 10 October 1954: Macmillan papers.
[3] 'My darling', 18 October 1954: Spencer-Churchill papers.
[4] 'With Teucer as leader and Teucer as guardian there is no need to despair' (Horace, *Odes*). The next four lines read: 'For unswerving Apollo has promised us a new Salamis, in a land we are yet to know. O noble heroes who have endured with me even worse misfortune than this, now banish care with wine. For tomorrow we embark on the mighty sea.'

had also brought in Osbert Peake as Minister of Pensions and National Insurance, and Sir David Eccles as Minister of Education. Both men, like Sandys, could be relied upon to support him in Cabinet, and to benefit from his support.

Among the new Ministerial appointments was that of the Financial Secretary to the Treasury, John Boyd-Carpenter, as Minister of Transport, his first Ministerial appointment. Boyd-Carpenter later recalled how Churchill's vigour was undiminished despite his stroke of 1953, and despite his age. 'In the mornings, while I was still shaving, he would telephone to draw my attention to some Transport matter which he had read in the morning paper.'[1]

Boyd-Carpenter was among Churchill's guests at 10 Downing Street on October 27, to welcome the Prime Minister of Japan to Britain.[2] Similar grand functions were not infrequent; on November 24 there was one for the Prime Minister of Ceylon,[3] when Lord De L'Isle and Dudley was among the guests. He too later recalled Churchill's continuing vigour, despite age and ailments. 'Deep down,' he recalled, 'there was always a fire burning, a deep fire of wisdom and experience. And he could still be a fountain of energy—of mind and spirit. In Cabinet there were often long silences, and bullying. Then he could take you to the heights.'[4]

Churchill was at Chartwell when the Cabinet changes were announced. That weekend he worked on the proofs of his unfinished pre-war magnum opus, *A History of the English-Speaking Peoples*. On October 16 Churchill sent Mr Wood for his final scrutiny the set of proofs which had been first scrutinized by Professor Brogan eight years earlier.[5]

One announcement which gave Churchill pleasure was that Anthony Eden was to become a Knight of the Garter. 'It was the Queen's suggestion,' Churchill told Lord Moran on October 21. Moran added: 'A broad grin appeared as he told me of a cartoon by Low in yesterday's *Manchester Guardian*. Set in the year 1984, Low's cartoon showed a youthful Churchill, complete with a full head of hair, addressing three old men, two of them on sticks, one in dressing gown and slippers, under the caption: "Prime Minister Churchill making his 27th Cabinet reshuffle,

---

[1] Lord Boyd-Carpenter recollections: in conversation with the author, 24 February 1987.

[2] Dinner List, 27 October 1954: Spencer-Churchill papers.

[3] Luncheon List, 24 November 1954: Spencer-Churchill papers.

[4] Lord De L'Isle and Dudley recollections: in conversation with the author, 13 July 1987. After one outburst, Lord De L'Isle later recalled, Churchill turned to him with a smile and said: 'My dear, don't be alarmed.'

[5] 'Mr Churchill', note of 3 August 1946, marked by Denis Kelly, 'Sent to Printers, 16 October 1954': Churchill papers, 4/443.

telling Macmillan, Eden and Butler they have to go. Too old. Winston, who has grown progressively younger since his eightieth birthday, gives a half promise that he will resign on reaching the age of fifteen." [1] Winston thought it a good idea that at eighty a man should get younger every year. The smile vanished. "But it won't happen,' he muttered glumly.' [2]

On Octber 24, Churchill told Moran he had accepted an invitation to talk to the Scottish Conservatives. 'Thinking he meant in the immediate future,' Moran wrote, 'I asked innocently, "What date?" He hesitated. Then he grinned. "May 20th."' [3] Two days later, on October 26 Mary Soames noted in her diary: 'How fantastic it now seems that one actually thought & believed that Papa must retire! He is in full flight now—having re-shuffled his government.' [4]

[1] 'Low's Crystal Ball', 'Things to Come': *Manchester Guardian*, 20 October 1954.
[2] Moran diary, 21 October 1954: *The Struggle for Survival*, pages 605–6.
[3] Moran diary, 24 October 1954: *The Struggle for Survival*, pages 607–8.
[4] Mary Soames diary, 26 October 1954: Mary Soames, *Clementine Churchill*, pages 450–1.

54
Prime Minister at Eighty

———

NOVEMBER 1954 was to see Churchill's eightieth birthday; at the beginning of the month Cassell published a book of tribute by his friends, *Winston Churchill, Servant of Crown and Commonwealth*. To Lady Violet Bonham Carter, one of the contributors, Churchill wrote on November 4: 'It seems that after all these years you still believe me to be a glow-worm. That is a compliment which I find entirely acceptable.' [1] 'As you know,' he wrote to another of the contributors, Sir John Rothenstein, 'I do not pretend to any merit as an artist, but it is nonetheless gratifying that those who do know about pictures should even think my efforts worth writing about.' [2] And to Lord Samuel, his colleague in Asquith's Liberal Cabinet before the First World War, he wrote of 'that famous Government in which we both served before the world of our youth was shattered'. [3]

The past was much recalled during that birthday month; but Churchill, speaking at the Guildhall on November 9, also spoke of the future, and did so with optimism. 'We might even find ourselves in a few years,' he said, 'moving along a broad, smooth causeway of peace and plenty instead of roaming around on the rim of Hell.' [4]

Churchill had spoken at the Guildhall 'with plenty of vigour', wrote Lord Moran, but he went on to note that 'there were some awkward pauses'. Even when reading a speech, his invariable method, 'he seems', Moran added, 'to lose his concentration, as if he were bored with it, and only wanted to get to the end'. One of Churchill's secretaries told Moran, so he recorded: 'He would play bezique instead of getting on with the speech. It was never properly prepared. That

[1] 'My dear Violet', 4 November 1954: Churchill papers, 2/423.
[2] Letter of 4 November 1954: Churchill papers, 2/423.
[3] Letter of 4 November 1954: Churchill papers, 2/423.
[4] Speech of 9 November 1954: Randolph S. Churchill (editor), *The Unwritten Alliance*, pages 192–5. Recording: BBC Written Archives Centre, Library No. MT 21402.

was why there were those dreadful pauses; he was not familiar with the script.'[1]

Thousands of letters, and hundreds of gifts, had already begun to arrive at 10 Downing Street in anticipation of Churchill's eightieth birthday. On November 10 Lord Moran noted in his diary:

He spoke very simply of the kindness of everybody. 'I am humbled,' he said, 'by what is being said. Look at that,' and he pointed to a letter from two old-age pensioners, with a postal order for 5s. 'I have had it framed.' A boy had sent six penny stamps. 'I have not deserved all this.'

This was not conventional modesty—indeed, Winston has never been a modest man in the usual sense. It was not the Englishman's instinctive response when praised, but rather a deep human response to a profoundly moving experience.[2]

On November 12 Churchill made his fifteenth successive visit to Harrow for the school 'Songs'. 'Make quite sure you do not bring politics into private life,' he told the boys. 'You must not let the ordinary flow and ebb of political affairs interfere with loyalty and friendship.' Churchill added: 'Although I have been here fifteen times, it is my intention to come a sixteenth time'.[3]

On November 22 Clementine Churchill opened a Churchill House for old people at Sevenoaks. 'One of the old lady residents gave me this blotter for you,' she wrote to her husband on the following day, and she went on to explain: 'It seems that 500 old ladies live in the 47 Churchill Houses sprinkled up & down the country. Each of the residents contributed towards this list. Wow!' Her letter was signed, 'Your devoted old Clem-Pussy Bird', and she added: 'The "waiting list" for a room in a "Churchill House" is over 7,000.'[4]

The 'beautiful silver blotter', Churchill wrote to Miss D. E. Richardson, one of the organizers of the Churchill Houses, 'will be constantly on my desk, and will be a reminder to me of the good-will so kindly expressed in the message of greetings inscribed on it.'[5]

---

[1] Moran diary, 10 November 1954: *The Struggle for Survival*, page 608.

[2] Moran diary, 10 November 1954: *The Struggle for Survival*, page 608.

[3] Speech of 12 November 1954: Churchill papers, 2/336.

[4] 'Winston', 23 November 1954: Churchill papers, 2/423.

[5] 'Dear Miss Richardson', November 1954: Churchill papers, 2/423. The blotter is today (1988) on the desk in Churchill's library at Chartwell. The inscription reads: 'To the Right Hon. Sir Winston Churchill, KG, OM, CH, MP, on his 80th birthday, 30th November, 1954, with affectionate greetings from the tenants of all Churchill Houses, Church Army Housing.' The blotter's silver knob is engraved with the initials 'WSC'. Among the other eightieth birthday gifts on display at Chartwell are a silver dish from the grandchildren, Nicholas, Emma, Jeremy, Charlotte, Julian, Edwina, Celia, Winston, Arabella (inscribed 'To Grandpapa, 30th November, 1954', the dish has the name of all the grandchildren and is on the study desk); a silver shako from Officers of the 4th Queen's Own Hussars (Museum Room); a black and white engraving of Westerham after a drawing by G. Shepherd presented by friends in Westerham and Crockham

On November 23 Churchill spoke at Woodford at the presentation of a portrait of his wife. He used the occasion to speak on Foreign Affairs. In May 1953, he said, 'I advocated that we, with our allies, should work towards closer contact with Russia in order to make sure whether that great people had undergone any important change of mood and outlook under their new leadership. This is still my purpose. Our policy is Peace through Strength.'[1]

So far, so good; but Churchill then spoke of an episode in 1945 which had hitherto been secret. 'Even before the war had ended,' he said, and while the Germans were surrendering in their hundreds of thousands to the Western Allies, 'I telegraphed to Lord Montgomery directing him to be careful in collecting the German arms, to stack them so that they could easily be issued again to the German soldiers whom we should have to work with if the Soviet advance continued.'

The Times, quoting these words, was indignant. Did Churchill imagine for a moment, it asked, 'that the Western democracies, hating the Hitler régime with a hatred greater than anything they had known, would understand and accept the use of Hitler's defeated soldiers to set a military barrier against the forces they still welcomed as victorious allies?

'What on earth made him say it,' *The Times* continued. Considering that the object of his speech was to urge an accommodation with the Soviet Union, 'How much greater the pity that he threw in his ill-timed remark. It certainly will not help to convince the Russians that the Western Powers are straightforward in their declarations of peace today. Nor, by suggesting that we were ready to use Nazi-indoctrinated troops in 1945, will it help the cause of West German rearmament now.' Churchill himself, *The Times* noted, had been the leader 'both in the expressions of hatred for the Hitler régime and in the testimonials of valour and comradeship towards the Russians. Could he have expected memories and emotions to fade overnight?' As for using German troops against Russia in 1945, *The Times* concluded: 'The idea was unrealistic at the time; it is unwise to come out with it now.'[2]

The indignation of *The Times* was offset, however, by the philosophic calm of the *Manchester Guardian*. Churchill could hardly have foreseen, it wrote, that when he told his constituents 'this little anecdote', he would be denounced by 'the oddest of Press choruses', *The*

Hill (Ante-room); and an alloy cast of the Duke of Windsor by Mme Haas (Main stairs). (Jean Broome, Curator, Chartwell: letter to the author, 3 November 1986.)

[1] Speech of 23 November 1954: Randolph S. Churchill (editor), *The Unwritten Alliance*, pages 196–7.

[2] 'Why?' *The Times*, 24 November 1954.

Times, the *Daily Herald*, the *Daily Mirror*, and the *Daily Worker*, whose 'common link' seemed to be the wish 'to force him out of office'.[1]

Churchill weathered the storm, and continued with a punishing schedule of public speeches. Three days after speaking at Woodford, he was at Bristol, to speak, as Chancellor of Bristol University, at the conferment of degrees. During his visit he thanked the students for the birthday gift of an eighteenth-century silver salver 'on a day when if you look at the papers, I am supposed to be in a bit of a scrape'. 'For their part,' noted Lord Moran, the students 'had no feeling that he was an old man; on the contrary, he seemed to be one of themselves, and two thousand young voices shouted their joy and approval. The same puckish humour marked his approach to their seniors.'[2] For the degree ceremony, Churchill wore, as he had done in 1929, and again in 1941, the robe which his father had worn as Chancellor of the Exchequer in 1886. It was 'most carefully preserved by my mother', Churchill told the assembled university dignitaries, 'until I had the opportunity of wearing it as Chancellor of the Exchequer myself, but also as Chancellor of this University. The alterations which had to be made are really not by any means fundamental.'

'Today,' Churchill pointed out in his speech at Bristol, was 'nearly as far removed from the Second World War as we were from the Treaty of Versailles on the day I became your Chancellor. Once again the country has regained a large measure of its lost prosperity. Once again we are trying to establish a rule of law for the world under the auspices of most of the great nations.' In the case of the post-1945 developments, Churchill added, 'we have the measureless advantage denied us in the days after the First World War, the measureless advantage that the United States is the principal champion and servant and member of the United Nations Organization. Had that happened twenty years before we might indeed have had a very different story to tell.'[3]

Among those at Bristol when Churchill spoke was Sir Oliver Franks. 'I saw him at Buckingham Palace a few days before,' Franks told Moran, 'sitting on the sofa, apparently too weary to listen to anybody; his face was white and like a mask, his body had flopped, he seemed a very old man who had not long to live. But at Bristol he was pink, his expression was full of animation and his eyes twinkled.'[4]

* * *

[1] *Manchester Guardian*, 24 November 1954.

[2] Moran diary, 28 November 1954: *The Struggle for Survival*, pages 611–12.

[3] Speech of 26 November 1954: Randolph S. Churchill (editor), *The Unwritten Alliance*, pages 198–200. Recording: BBC Written Archives Centre, Library No. LP 27556.

[4] Moran diary, 28 November 1954: *The Struggle for Survival*, page 612.

The repercussions of Churchill's Woodford speech reached Moscow, where *Pravda* described his German arms proposal of 1945 as a 'betrayal'. On November 29, the day before his birthday with all its celebrations, Churchill was troubled by the harm he might have done, telling Lord Moran:

'I'm worried about this stupid mistake of mine. I was quite certain it was in my book, otherwise I would never have said what I did. And now it seems there wasn't a telegram, after all. Anyway, no trace can be found of it. I must have thought better of it. My speech ought, of course, to have been checked.'

He sat for some time glowering at his feet. 'If my slip has done harm with the Russians I may pull out sooner than I intended. Take my pulse, Charles.' It was 82. When I had reassured him he brightened up a little. 'The *Daily Mirror* had declared a truce for tomorrow, They have sent £1,000 to my birthday fund. I am to be given a cheque for £140,000 tomorrow. All this leaves me very humble; it is more than I deserve.'

Montague Browne told me that the PM was worried about the Russians; he would like to be sure that his speech has done no harm at the Kremlin. 'That's all he cares about. He didn't seem at all depressed by the criticisms of his speech until he read what appeared in *Pravda* yesterday.'

I asked Montague Browne about the telegram. It appears that Pownall was asked three years ago to check this telegram and concluded the PM must have decided at the last moment not to send it. I asked if Labour would be able to make capital out of the speech. 'They can and will,' he replied.

'As I left,' Moran added, 'the doorway of No. 10 was blocked by an immense birthday cake which two men were trying to lever into the hall without injuring any of the eighty white candles.'[1]

'You have been, and are, such an inspiration to our people,' the Queen Mother wrote in congratulation, 'and we are all *very* proud of you.'[2]

No Prime Minister since Gladstone had been in office at eighty. No Member of Parliament other than Churchill had been elected at the turn of the century, in the reign of Queen Victoria. Fifty-six years had passed since Churchill had charged with the Lancers at Omdurman; forty-nine years since he had entered Campbell-Bannerman's Government as Under-Secretary of State for the Colonies; forty-four years since he had become a Privy Counsellor.

From the royal family he was to receive a set of four silver wine

[1] Moran diary, 29 November 1954: *The Struggle for Survival*, pages 612–13.
[2] Letter of 27 November 1945, from Clarence House: Churchill papers, 2/425.

coasters, engraved with the cyphers of those who had joined to give the gift: the Queen and the Duke of Edinburgh, the Queen Mother, Princess Margaret, the Duke and Duchess of Gloucester, the Princess Royal, the Duchess of Kent, Princess Alice and the Earl of Athlone. The list of the donors was written out by the Queen in her own hand, with the added note: 'To Sir Winston Churchill with every good wish.' [1]

Parliament, to mark Churchill's eightieth birthday, presented him with the portrait painted by Graham Sutherland. As well as the portrait, Churchill was honoured with an illuminated book signed by virtually every Member of Parliament. The presentation took place in Westminster Hall on the morning of November 30. Churchill had seen the finished portrait about two weeks before it was to be presented, taking, as his daughter Mary later recalled, 'an instant loathing to it', and she added:

He felt he had been betrayed by the artist, whom he had liked, and with whom he had felt at ease, and he found in the portrait causes for mortal affront. Clementine too was shocked by it—she thought it was a cruel and gross travesty of Winston, showing all the ravages of time, and revealing nothing of the warmth and humanity of his nature. They were both deeply disturbed by it, but when she realised the violence of Winston's reaction—to the extent that he even considered refusing to accept the picture, she threw her influence into calming his wounded sensibilities, and tried to make him concentrate on the feelings which the commissioning of this portrait represented, to which indeed he was very much alive, and to which he paid warm and heartfelt tribute in his speech. But all this made a great and emotional upset behind the scenes in the days prior to the presentation. [2]

'The portrait,' Churchill told the assembled Members of Parliament and Peers, 'is a remarkable example of modern art. It certainly combines force with candour.' 'There was a little pause,' noted Lord Moran, 'and then a gust of laughter swept the hall.' [3]

Attlee, in his tribute to Churchill, described him as 'the most distinguished member of the Parliamentary family'. He had overcome the 'handicap' of being the son of a distinguished father. He had become a 'vigorous, even obstreperous back-bencher'. He came not to bury Caesar, Attlee said, but to praise him, and he added: 'Caesar indeed—for you have not only carried on war but have written your own commentary.' Attlee also recalled Churchill's reforms of the prison system, his 'full share' in the Liberal social reforms of the Lloyd

---

[1] Buckingham Palace, 30 November 1954: Spencer-Churchill papers.

[2] Mary Soames recollections: Mary Soames, *Clementine Churchill*, page 446. After Churchill's death, Clementine Churchill gave instructions for the portrait to be destroyed.

[3] Lord Moran diary, 30 November 1954: *The Struggle for Survival*, pages 614–16.

George era, and his 'winged words' in the attacks on the House of Lords in 1910. Then there was the Dardanelles, 'the only imaginative strategic idea of the war. I only wish that you had had full power to carry it to success.' He had also urged the adoption of the tank, 'the only new tactical weapon of first importance in that war'.

Attlee's survey of Churchill's career included the 1930s. 'You did not go to the back benches but dug in on the front bench below the gangway, prepared for offence and defence against all opponents. Once again, the wiseacres said, "Churchill is finished," but they had not reckoned on your remarkable powers of resilience. You did not choose to play the role of Achilles sulking in his tent; you appeared instead as Cassandra, and like her, your warnings were not believed.' In 1940, he had been recognized by all as 'the daring pilot in extremity through the storm that had struck, whom Britain required. Those days are fresh in our memory.'[1]

In his reply, Churchill spoke of the book with which he had been presented as 'the most striking example I have ever known of that characteristic British Parliamentary principle cherished in both Lords and Commons: "Don't bring politics into private life"', and he added: 'It is certainly a mark of the underlying unity of our national life which survives and even grows in spite of vehement party warfare and many grave differences of conviction and sentiment. This unity is, I believe, the child of freedom and fair play fostered in the cradle of our ancient island institutions, and nursed by tradition and custom.'

He was most grateful, Churchill said, for Attlee's 'magnanimous appraisal' of his 'variegated career'. He had to confess, however, that the ceremony 'and all its charm and splendour may well be found to have seriously affected my controversial value as a party politician. However, perhaps with suitable assistance I shall get over this reaction and come round after a bit.'

Churchill and Attlee had been the only two Prime Ministers of Britain in the last fourteen years. 'There are no other Prime Ministers alive,' Churchill pointed out. The monopoly which he and Attlee had 'of the most powerful and disputatious office under the Crown all this time is surely the fact which the world outside may recognize as a symbol of the inherent stability of our British way of life. It is not, however, intended to make it a permanent feature of the Constitution.'

Referring to Attlee's comment that Churchill's wartime speeches had expressed the will not only of Parliament but of the whole nation, Churchill told those gathered to pay him tribute, of the British people in the war years:

[1] Speech of 30 November 1954: *The Times*, 1 December 1954.

Their will was resolute and remorseless and, as it proved, unconquerable. It fell to me to express it, and if I found the right words you must remember that I have always earned my living by my pen and by my tongue.

It was a nation and race dwelling all round the globe that had the lion's heart. I had the luck to be called upon to give the roar. I also hope that I sometimes suggested to the lion the right places to use his claws.

I am now nearing the end of my journey. I hope I still have some services to render. However that may be and whatever may befall I am sure I shall never forget the emotions of this day or be able to express my gratitude to those colleagues and companions with whom I have lived my life for this superb honour they have done me.[1]

Jock Colville, who was present, described Churchill's speech as one of 'wit and fire', noting how 'The puckish humour, the calculated asides, the perfectly modulated control of voice, and that incomparable moral sturdiness made him look, and sound, years younger than his true age'. Colville added: 'Tributes poured in upon him and Lady Churchill from throughout the world as well as from their fellow countrymen. Even to someone as egotistical as Churchill this volume of gratitude and praise genuinely surprised and moved him.'[2]

That afternoon, Churchill went to Buckingham Palace where the Queen presented him with the Royal Family's gift. Later, seated in an armchair at 10 Downing Street with his wife beside him, he took part in a television programme which began with greetings from many friends and colleagues. Then Churchill spoke. 'I am fortunate indeed,' he said, 'to have met these men and women and to have worked with them in the years of struggle through which we have passed. I am grateful that modern science has enabled me upon my birthday to receive in this amazing manner their friendly greetings and good wishes.'[3]

That night, in response to repeated calls from the crowd in Downing Street, Churchill stood for a minute in one of the first-floor windows of No. 10, 'repeatedly giving his "V" sign'.[4]

Among Churchill's eightieth birthday gifts was a large silver goblet from the German Chancellor, Dr Adenauer. 'I am high on the list of your admirers as a statesman and as a patriot,' Churchill wrote in his letter of thanks, and he added: 'I did not send my congratulations on your electoral victory, because I always try to keep out of other people's politics.'[5] To the Queen, Churchill wrote on December 3 in his own hand:

[1] Speech of 30 November 1954: *The Times*, 1 December 1954. Recording: BBC Written Archives Centre, Library No. 20761–2.

[2] Jock Colville recollections: *The Fringes of Power*, page 391.

[3] Television broadcast, 30 November 1954: *The Times*, 1 December 1954.

[4] *The Times*, 1 December 1954.

[5] 'Secret', 1 December 1954: Churchill papers, 6/6.

Madam,

I am deeply grateful for Your Majesty's gracious gift to me on my birthday wh is a source of intense pleasure and pride to me and my wife. We have already taken these beautiful coasters into daily use and they are greatly admired by all who have seen them. I was much honoured by the presence of so many members of Your Majesty's family and am writing to thank them for their participation and for their initials.

I am also much obliged to Your Majesty for letting me have the vacant subscription to Aureole. I shall buy the most suitable mare I can find in the December sales and hope for the future.

Madam I am still overcome by the kindness—far beyond my deserts—wh I have received from the highest and the humblest in the land. From the latest accounts it looks as if this mood might soon change in certain quarters: but I have confidence that I shall enjoy Your Majesty's favour as long as I live. At least that is my cherished hope.

And with my humble duty,

I remain

Your Majesty's faithful and devoted servant

                                        Winston S. Churchill[1]

It was the Sutherland portrait that was proving the least acceptable present. 'I think it is malignant,' Churchill told Lord Moran. Nor did Moran entirely disagree. 'There is, to be sure, plenty of power and vigour and defiance in the coarse features that Graham Sutherland has drawn,' he wrote, 'but they do not belong to Winston Churchill. Look again at him as he is in life. Take your eye away from the fleshy folds of the jowl and look again at the bony structure of the lower jaw. It is delicate, almost feminine, in its contours; where there is massive moulding, in the brow and skull, the artist has given us only an egg-shell.' The lips too, Moran added, 'though they often pout, are delicately moulded; in short, the coarseness of the face in the portrait is only part of the artist's romantic conception of a man of wrath struggling with destiny. It is not Winston Churchill.'[2]

Two months later, Churchill was approached by Salvador Dali with a request to do a further portrait. 'Lady Churchill thinks you should on no account agree to be painted by Dali,' Miss Gilliatt wrote to Churchill. In Clementine Churchill's view, Miss Gilliatt added, Dali 'is extremely futuristic, much more so than Graham Sutherland'.[3] When, a few weeks after the presentation of the Sutherland portrait, President Eisenhower asked Churchill if he would be willing to sit for an American artist, Churchill replied: 'I need hardly say I shall be greatly honoured to be one of your subjects in an artistic sense. Al-

---

[1] 'Madam', 3 December 1954: Churchill papers, 2/475.

[2] Moran diary, undated, but printed between the entries for 3 and 5 December 1954: *The Struggle for Survival*, pages 620–2.

[3] Note of 8 March 1955: Churchill papers, 2/185.

though my experiences as a model have not been altogether agreeable lately I submit myself with great confidence to your well-balanced love of truth and mercy.'[1]

One present which Churchill received had been a public subscription, one pound per person. 'I am indeed proud,' Churchill wrote to Lord Leathers, one of the sponsors of the subscription, 'that over three hundred and fifty thousand people should have responded.' The question arose as to what should be done with the sum which had been raised. Churchill told Leathers, in regard to the donors:

> The great majority of these have, I understand, expressed their wish that their gift should be personal to me. Others would like them to be devoted to charitable purposes, to use the legal term, in which I take an interest. This also is very agreeable to me. I have long had an idea of building a small museum at Chartwell in which many things of personal interest could be displayed including numbers of my pictures and the Trophies which have been given me. This building would also include sanitary accommodation and one or two resting-rooms needed by visitors to Chartwell who would also have access to the House when that has been handed over to the National Trust to whom it now belongs.
>
> Apart from this I have long been associated with the Church Army enterprise which is called The Churchill Homes for Elderly People.
>
> But if further Funds were at my disposal I should like to encourage the study and use of the English language in the Public Schools and other educational establishments. I have my own ideas based on my own experience for inculcating the writing of good and simple English and also for stimulating the learning of famous passages of English prose and poetry by heart. It is not possible for me to give thought and care to these plans at present, but it would be a great pleasure to develop them if sufficient resources were placed at the disposal of the Trust.[2]

'I have had a very hard time this last three weeks,' Churchill wrote to Lord Quickswood on December 8, and he added: 'Kindness can be as exacting as nagging and I have had both harmony and discord rolling over each other inside my octogenarian nut.'[3] His 'prevailing mood', Churchill wrote, was 'to have received kindness utterly beyond my deserts'. But he was determined to complete one last literary task, *A History of the English-Speaking Peoples*, telling Quickswood:

> It will take four volumes. I lay one egg a year and will amuse myself with

[1] 'My dear Friend', 'Private and Personal', 12 January 1955: Eisenhower papers. The rest of this four-page letter remains classified, under a National Security Council ruling of 5 February 1986.

[2] 'My dear Fred', 'Private and Confidential', 15 January 1955: Churchill papers, 2/422.

[3] Quickswood, formerly Lord Hugh Cecil, had been Churchill's best man in 1908 and, earlier, one of a group of fellow rebels ('Hughligans') within the Conservative Party. Born five years before Churchill, he died in December 1956.

polishing and improving each in turn. It encourages me to see how good and tense your thought is although you are five years ahead of me, and I wonder whether it would amuse you to read the first volume which is practically in its final stage? I am therefore sending you down the first half-dozen chapters to read in your leisure. Please let me know whether you would like some more. The volume itself goes down to the Battle of Bosworth.[1]

From Emery Reves, who was to handle the foreign translations of the new book, Churchill received one of his more magnificent birthday gifts, '80 Magnums of your beloved golden liquid'.[2] Churchill also received a budgerigar, Toby, who arrived in the third week of December. 'I do hope you will like him,' Toby's donor, Mrs Dido Cairns—Christopher Soames's sister—wrote on December 14. 'I am sure he will not take long to get to know you, especially if you allow him to perch on the rim of your Brandy glass. He will enjoy doing this.'[3] 'We have received Toby in great state,' Churchill telegraphed in reply three days later. 'Thank you so much.'[4]

Churchill's delight at the eightieth birthday gifts and congratulations seemed to give him a new vigour. 'Mama has collapsed with fatigue and a streaming cold,' Mary Soames wrote in her diary, 'and we all feel flat and stale and tired—WSC is fresh as a daisy, and enjoying mulling over his presents and letters!'[5]

On the day after Churchill's eightieth birthday, Emanuel Shinwell had made a sustained attack on him in the House of Commons, deriding the Montgomery telegram to which Churchill had referred at Woodford. To have spoken as he did at Woodford, Shinwell declared, was 'I would say—putting it very mildly and without using strong language, however much one might be tempted—it was a most unfortunate and inopportune prelude to a four-Power conference'.

The 'whole point', Shinwell told the House of Commons, was whether Churchill in fact sent such an order to Montgomery 'to collect and stack surrendered German arms so that they could easily be issued again to the German soldiers with whom we should have to work if the Soviet advance continued'. Such had been Churchill's quotation from the telegram when he spoke at Woodford a week earlier. Had Churchill in fact, asked Shinwell, 'contemplated rearming German troops in order to fight the Russians in certain eventualities?'

---

[1] 'My dear Linky', 8 December 1954: Churchill papers, 2/196.
[2] 'My dear Sir Winston', 6 November 1954: Churchill papers, 2/475.
[3] 'Dear Sir Winston', signed 'Dido', 14 December 1954: Churchill papers, 2/423.
[4] Telegram despatched 17 December 1954: Churchill papers, 2/423.
[5] Mary Soames diary, 3–5 December 1954: Mary Soames, *Clementine Churchill*, page 447.

When the criticism had burst on the morning after Churchill's Woodford speech, he had said that the controversial telegram had been published in Volume 6 of his war memoirs. But, said, Shinwell, it was not there. 'I cannot find in his book,' Shinwell added, 'any reference to the rearming of the surrendered Germans' and he went on to ask:

Why this omission from these memoirs? Why at this late stage—nine years after—is that signal disclosed? What was the purpose of the disclosure—that remarkable revelation? What was the intention? Was the intention to seek an understanding with the Russians? Was this the overture or part of the symphony? The right hon. Gentleman, no doubt, will give us his version of the matter.

In his reply, Churchill said that he had been under the 'rooted impression' that the telegram had been published in his war memoirs. It had not, and 'I express my regrets to the House for what I said last week'. Shinwell had asked for the text of the telegram. 'Indeed,' Churchill said, 'I should be very glad to give that to the House— when I find it. It may well be that I never used these precise words in a telegram'—a telegram which, 'it may be', was never sent at all. 'At any rate,' Churchill added, 'it has not been traced in the official records, though a search of the utmost extent has been made, and is still continuing.' Churchill then told the House of Commons:

No Cabinet assent was sought for this particular telegram. It was only of precautionary character, and, if it were sent at all, it went only as one of scores of similar messages which were passing at the time about the German surrender. Anyhow, if there is any question of responsibility, and if there is any telegram and any question of responsibility for it, I accept it for myself.

When I come to the facts of what I did in 1945, of what I intended to do—certainly it was in my mind; I am not making any concealment of that— of the motives animating them, I have no misgivings. In those days of victory, the thought which filled my mind was that all the efforts we had made to free Europe from a totalitarian regime of one kind might go for naught if we allowed so much of Europe to fall into the grip of another totalitarian regime from the East.

This is the theme of the sixth volume of my book. This was the tragedy which came on us in our hour of triumph. The realization of it filled many of the messages which I sent at that time. I sent an awful lot at different levels. I may easily have been in error as to any particular one. The attitude of our Russian allies at that time gave ample grounds for this fear. We had taken up the sword in 1939 on behalf of the independence of Poland. What was happening to Poland in 1945? What has happened to it since?

I also had at this time the gravest anxieties about the fate of Denmark. The time of this is about the first fortnight in May, 1945. If the Soviet forces had overrun Denmark, they would have controlled the Baltic, with all that that involves. In such circumstances, the same kind of situation would have arisen as that which, four years later, compelled the Western world to create NATO, to contemplate the EDC arrangements, and now to sign the London and Paris Agreements.

The situation which we faced in May, 1945, was grave and threatening. I can find no better words to describe it than those which I used in my telegram of 12 May to President Truman, the telegram which I have called the Iron Curtain telegram.

Churchill then read out to the Commons his telegram to Truman of 12 May 1945, in which he had asked the President: 'What will be the position in a year or two, when the British and American Armies have melted and the French has not yet been formed on any major scale, when we may have a handful of divisions, mostly French, and when Russia may choose to keep two or three hundred on active service?' Churchill had gone on to say, of the Russians: 'An iron curtain is drawn down upon their front.'

It was the final paragraph of this telegram to Truman, however, which Churchill described during his speech on December 1 as expressing the feelings which 'governed my thoughts' in May 1945. The paragraph read:

Surely it is vital now to come to an understanding with Russia, or to see where we are with her, before we weaken our armies mortally or retire to the zones of occupation. This can only be done by a personal meeting. I should be most grateful for your opinion and advice. Of course, we may take the view that Russia will behave impeccably, and no doubt that offers the most convenient solution. To sum up, this issue of a settlement with Russia before our strength has gone seems to me to dwarf all others.

No trouble could have arisen with the Soviets in May 1945, Churchill told the House of Commons, 'unless they had continued their advance to a point at which they forced the breaking out of a new war between Russia and her Western allies. To prevent such a disaster, it might have been a help to warn them that we should certainly in that case rearm the German prisoners in our hands, who altogether, including those in Italy, numbered two and a half million.' In that sense, the telegram to Montgomery, even if it did not exist, was in general spirit 'not contrary to my thoughts'.

Churchill's defence continued:

I am not unduly disheartened by any Russian reaction to what I said last week. *Pravda*, like the *Daily Worker*, can always be turned on or off at will. In my recent thoughts I have always tried to measure what are the true Russian interests at this present time in history. There lies the key. Personally, I believe their interest is in peace and plenty. *The Times* newspaper, to which the right hon. Gentleman referred, in the very full report that it gave of my speech, omitted altogether in any of the editions I have seen the references I made to Soviet Russia which were intended to balance the other statements so fully printed. I suppose they were preoccupied with their leading article.

There is, however, a very good report in the *Manchester Guardian* which I hope the House will forgive me quoting—hon. Members have been very indulgent when I have been quoting so much of myself—because I should like to give publicity to it. This is what I said at Woodford on 23 November. It ought to be read with what *The Times* had already quoted:

'But meanwhile another great event has happened. Stalin died, and the new men sharing power together are at the head of Russia. It was in May last year that I advocated that we, with our allies, should work towards closer contact with Russia in order to make sure whether that great people had undergone any important change of mood and outlook under their new leadership. This is still my purpose.'

'In fact,' Churchill declared, 'that is the only explanation of my presence here to-day. It is still my purpose.' [1]

'I made a goose of myself at Woodford' was Churchill's private comment to his doctor. [2] Not every reaction to the Woodford gaffe was hostile, however. A Labour Peer, Lord Stansgate, told the House of Lords on December 1: 'I believe, and I think the great bulk of the people in this country believe, that the greatest measure of defence we can have is that the Prime Minister should retain his position until his meeting with the Russians takes place.' [3]

On December 7 Churchill wrote to Eisenhower, to thank him for two birthday messages. His letter was yet another appeal for a summit meeting of the great Powers:

My dear Friend,

I am so sorry that the pressure upon me of events both large and small has been so unceasing that I have not replied other than by telegrams to your last three most kind letters, including the two about my birthday. I am so grateful to you for all that you wrote. Our comradeship and friendship were forged under hard conditions, and stood the test of war and aftermath. They always remain for me a possession of inestimable value. Thank you so much.

About the present and future. I think our two countries are working together even more closely than I can ever remember. They certainly need to do so. I greatly admired your speech on Thursday last about China in the teeth of the brutal maltreatment of your airmen. In my view China is not

---

[1] Speech of 1 December 1954: *Hansard*.

[2] Moran diary, 1 December 1954: *The Struggle for Survival*, pages 618–19.

[3] *Hansard*, 1 December 1954. One of Lord Stansgate's sons was Anthony (Tony) Wedgwood Benn, who later renounced his father's peerage.

important enough to be a cause of major hazards. Many people over here exaggerate the power and importance of China as a military factor, and talk about six hundred million Chinese who, we are told, have all become Communists.

I am old-fashioned enough to look to Steel as a rather decisive index of conventional military power, and of manufacturing and communication capacity. Crude steel output in 1953 of the non-Soviet world was 182.2 million tons, and that of the total Soviet bloc 51.7 million tons. Of this China contributed 1.7 million tons. I have had a number of other principal metals examined from this viewpoint and enclose a list, (A).

These figures seem to me to deserve taking into account when thinking about the power to conduct modern war of the six hundred million Chinese now said to exist. It may be a different picture in a decade. When I was young I used to hear much talk about 'the Yellow Peril'.

I am thinking of course only on a 'conventional' basis. But you have no reason to be worried about the nuclear balance. It is Soviet Russia that ought to dominate our minds. That is one of the reasons for my pleasure at your speech and the profound sense of proportion which it revealed.

I still hope we may reach a top level meeting with the new regime in Russia and that you and I may both be present. We can only contemplate this on the basis of the London Agreement and a united NATO. In spite of the tyrannical weakness of the French Chamber I still hope for ratification by all Powers in the first few months of the New Year. It is in the hope of helping forward such a meeting that I am remaining in harness longer than I wished or planned.

'I hope,' Churchill added, 'you will continue to look to it as a goal in seeking which we could not lose anything and might gain an easier and safer co-existence—which is a lot. When I had my last Audience with The Queen she spoke of the pleasure with which she would welcome a State visit by you to London. This might be combined in any way convenient with a top level meeting. Anyhow, please keep it high in your mind among your many cares and hopes.' [1]

On both December 6 and December 15 Churchill had been in the Chair at Cabinet meetings at Downing Street, but he made no recorded intervention at either of them. [2] He had not been present at five other Cabinets that month, leaving Eden to preside.

For those Ministers who supported Eden in wishing Churchill to

---

[1] 'My dear Friend', 'Top Secret', 'Personal and Private', 7 December 1954: Eisenhower papers.
[2] Cabinet Conclusions Nos 82 and 87 of 1954, 'Secret', 5.30 p.m., 6 December 1954, and 11.30 a.m., 15 December 1954: Cabinet papers, 128/27.

stand down altogether, the possibility of Churchill's resignation now seemed remote. 'Churchill refuses to go and there is no likelihood of his changing his mind,' Harold Macmillan noted in his diary in the second week of December.[1]

After the Cabinet of December 15 Churchill gave a Christmas staff party at No. 10. Marian Holmes, one of his wartime secretaries, who had also been invited, later recalled:

We were standing in a corner exchanging news with former colleagues of mine when Jock Colville led the Prime Minister over to us and we shook hands with him.

At Mr Colville's prompting, Mr Churchill reminisced about war-time days, the journeyings abroad and in particular the excitements of the December 1944 Conference in an Athens torn by civil war. Mr Churchill looked totally exhausted.

After he had left us, I commented on this and was told he had had a particularly full day. There had been a Cabinet meeting in the morning, Parliamentary Questions in the House in the afternoon, and the early evening Audience with HM The Queen at Buckingham Palace.[2]

On December 23 Churchill went to Chequers, where all nine grand-children had gathered for the Christmas festivities. Also with him was his new friend Toby, of whom he wrote to Mrs Cairns before leaving for Chequers that he was 'settling in very happily and is giving me a lot of enjoyment'. Churchill added: 'He has a blue cage and green cage and has stayed the weekend at Chartwell and will come with me to Chequers tomorrow to spend Christmas. He is quite delightful and friendly and already sits on my glass and even my spectacles.'[3]

At Chequers on Christmas Day, Churchill gave his wife a gift of cash. 'My Beloved Darling,' he wrote in a short covering letter:

Buy yourself something you
like out of this and
keep the rest for a
Christmas without a

All my love

Winston[4]

[1] Macmillan diary, 11 December 1954: Macmillan papers.
[2] Marian Walker Spicer recollections: letter to the author, 23 October 1986.
[3] 'My dear Dido', 22 December 1954: Churchill papers, 2/423.
[4] 'My Beloved Darling', 25 December 1954: Spencer-Churchill papers.

On December 29 Churchill wrote to Lady Lytton: 'We have had a family gathering of all our nine grandchildren & their parents which has been vy pleasant but also exacting.' [1]

There was much now that was proving exacting. 'Towards the end of 1954,' Sir Norman Brook later recalled, 'there were signs that he would not be able to carry on for very much longer,' and he added:

He could still rise to the great occasion, by an effort of will and a modest use of the stimulants prescribed by his doctor. But in the daily round of his responsibilities he no longer had the necessary energy, mental or physical, to give to papers or to people the full attention which they deserved.

He was reluctant to take the final step of naming a date for his resignation. In part, I believe, he was influenced by the thought that resignation of office would also mean the end of his connection with Parliament. For him, Parliament meant the House of Commons: he had no wish to take an honorific position in the House of Lords. [2]

---

[1] 'Dearest Pamela', 29 December 1954: Lytton papers.
[2] Lord Normanbrook recollections: Sir John Wheeler-Bennett (editor), *Action This Day, Working with Churchill*, pages 44–5.

55

Decision to Resign

W ITHIN three weeks of Churchill's eightieth birthday,
Anthony Eden renewed his pressure for a date to be set for
Churchill's resignation. On 21 December 1954 he went to see Chur-
chill, to put the matter to him directly, noting in his diary:

Set out for No. 10 at 9.30. Found Clemmie there with W. She was charming & worried at my colour. W said he supposed I had been living too well
in Paris. Then when Clemmie had gone after a long pause he said 'What do
you want to see me about?' in his most aggressive tone.

I said that he had had my letter and said he should be ready to discuss it.
And slowly the argument began. At first he would have nothing. All was as
well as possible. There was no hurry for an election or for him to hand over,
the end of June or July would do very well.

Laboriously I explained first that the new administration should have a
chance to establish itself with the public. This gave us none. Second that it
would place me in a much stronger position if I could take over in a month
when an election was possible. Then, if my authority or mandate was challenged I would have the option either to fight it out in Parliament or to
say very well let the country judge, & go to the country. This I could not do
in July.

He wasn't much interested in this but when I had made it quite clear that
I was not interested either in taking over at the end of June he eventually
agreed to meeting at 3 p.m. with the people I chose. But it was all most
grudging. There was much rather cruel 'divide et impera'. For instance, he
asked me how I got on with Harold. I said 'very well, why?' He replied 'Oh,
he is very ambitious.' I laughed.[1]

When a group of senior Cabinet Ministers met Churchill on the
afternoon of December 22, it was 'a very painful affair', Harold Mac-

---

[1] Eden diary, 21 December 1954: Robert Rhodes James, *Anthony Eden*, page 392. In 1965
Eden noted that 'This was the only occasion I recall when Winston warned me about a colleague.'

millan noted in his diary.[1] Nominally at least, the object of the meeting was to discuss the date of the next General Election. In fact, however, Macmillan added, it was 'to discuss how long Churchill should stay. He now suggests July 1955. Eden is in despair.'[2] According to Eden's own account of the meeting:

After a certain amount of further desultory conversation & explanation of value of an option to a new Govt, W rounded on me and said it was clear we wanted him out. Nobody contradicted him. Earlier he had said that I had made no difficulty about end of July last year. I replied that he had first said Queen's return if not sooner. End of July had been an afterthought.

At the end W said menacingly that he would think over what his colleagues had said & let them know his decision. Whatever it was he hoped it would not affect their present relationship with him. Nobody quailed. James said afterwards to me that it had been painful but absolutely necessary. He had to be told he could not pursue a course of 'such utter selfishness'.

Eden was later joined in his room at the Foreign Office by Lord Salisbury and Harold Macmillan, noting in his diary:

We gloomily surveyed the scene. It was clear to us that Rab would give no help. I said that I had said my say & they agreed that no more could be expected of me. Therefore they would try to hold a meeting without W or me of the remaining colleagues before Christmas. Bobbety charged himself with this task & later Rab assured him that he would attend and only wished to be helpful.

What the result of all this may be I cannot tell except that the old man feels bitterly towards me, but this I cannot help. The colleagues are unanimous about drawling Cabinets, the failure to take decisions, the general atmosphere of 'après moi le déluge' & someone had to give a heave.[3]

Before that 'heave' could be given, Churchill and Eden clashed in Cabinet, in the first week of 1955, over Eden's attitude to a railway dispute which was threatening to lead to strike action. On January 6 Eden noted in his diary: 'W & I had rather a sharp altercation at Cabinet. He attacked me for having been bellicose from the start & added "You'll get your strike alright."' There was also much talk, Eden noted, at a private luncheon with Churchill 'about the handing over'. That afternoon, R. A. Butler told Eden that he would like the handover to be at the end of the Commonwealth Conference, 'but that Easter was more probable'.[4]

---

[1] The Ministers present were Anthony Eden, Lord Salisbury, Lord Woolton, R. A. Butler, Harry Crookshank, James Stuart and Harold Macmillan.

[2] Macmillan diary, 22 December 1954: Macmillan papers.

[3] Eden diary, 22 December 1954: Robert Rhodes James, *Anthony Eden*, pages 392–4.

[4] Eden diary, 6 January 1955: Robert Rhodes James, *Anthony Eden*, page 395. The Commonwealth Conference was due to end in mid-February; Easter Sunday was on April 10.

On January 7 Churchill asked Macmillan to come to see him at 10 Downing Street. It was midday. 'He had just got up and seemed very tired,' Macmillan noted in his diary. The two men discussed 'a large number of defence problems', but, Macmillan added, with the exception of those concerned with air policy, Churchill 'did not seem to "connect" very much'. At luncheon Churchill 'cheered up' and was 'very charming throughout', telling Macmillan that he 'would go on until Easter anyway'.

Listening to Churchill talk, Macmillan had the impression that 'all this was trailing his coat, hoping to be contradicted'.[1]

Two days later, on January 9, Macmillan saw Lord Moran, who told him that he 'really thought Churchill could not go on much longer'. Indeed, Moran told Macmillan, Churchill himself now 'seemed reconciled to a life out of Office'.[2] According to Moran's account of this same conversation, Macmillan declared: 'Winston ought to resign. He didn't interfere in my housing, just left it all to me. But since I became Minister of Defence I have found that he can no longer handle these complicated matters properly. He can't do his job as Prime Minister as it ought to be done. He does not direct. Of course he is still tough and he isn't bothered with principles like Salisbury.' Macmillan added, according to Moran: 'When the moment comes Winston will have to decide how he goes; he has missed so many curtains, when he could have gone with everyone applauding, that it won't be as easy now.'[3]

'Harold's intervention has left a bruise,' Lord Moran noted in his diary on January 20, and he added: 'The PM had come to depend on him and counted on his support if it came to a row. After all, it was Harold who had encouraged him to hang on. Winston called him the Captain of the Praetorian Guard. And now he has gone over to the other camp.'[4]

Churchill now made up his mind to fix a date for his retirement, but to do so privately, telling only the inner circle of his closest friends. 'During the winter months,' Colville noted that March, 'alone with him at the bezique table or in the dining-room, I listened to many disquisitions of which the burden was: "I have lost interest; I

---

[1] Macmillan diary, 7 January 1955: Macmillan papers.
[2] Macmillan diary, 9 January 1955: Macmillan papers.
[3] Moran diary, 9 January 1955: *The Struggle for Survival*, pages 626–7.
[4] Moran diary, 20 January 1955: *The Struggle for Survival*, pages 627–8.

am tired of it all". So he finally decided to go at the beginning of the 1955 Easter Recess.'[1]

That year, the House of Commons was to rise for the Easter Recess on April 7.

News of Churchill's decision remained a tightly guarded secret, except among his intimates. On January 17 Brendan Bracken confided to Lord Beaverbrook: 'Our friend, under no pressure from Clemmie, Eden or other ministers, intends to depart before July. He says, without any sign of regret, that it is time he gave up. His only wish now is to find a small villa in the South of France where he can spend the winter months in the years which remain to him.'[2]

---

[1] Colville notes, 29 March 1955: *The Fringes of Power*, pages 704–7.
[2] Letter of 17 January 1955: Beaverbrook papers.

56

The Challenge of the Hydrogen Bomb

DESPITE his decision to resign, which was kept a close secret, Churchill was determined to make a final effort to pursue a summit; to go beyond the now acceptable pattern of meetings of Foreign Ministers, to the gathering of Heads of State and Prime Ministers on the wartime pattern, but with a peacetime purpose. 'I have for some time felt a strong desire,' he wrote to Pierre Mendès-France on 12 January 1955, 'to establish a direct personal contact with the new leaders of the Soviet Government such as might lead to a fruitful Four-Power Conference.' These thoughts, Churchill added, had received 'a rude check when the Soviets requested a Four-Power meeting of the Foreign Secretaries, apparently with the object of stimulating opposition in the French Chamber to the Ratification of EDC'. Then had come the London Conference, and following that the Paris Agreements, all at the level of Foreign Ministers. He was aware of the requirement that the EDC treaty had still to pass the Conseil de la République 'and of the many opportunities for uncertainty and delay which still remain'. His letter continued:

I still hold most strongly to my conviction that a Top-Level Meeting might be productive of real advantages if the time and circumstances were well chosen. This view was, as you know, expressed in a unanimous resolution by the House of Commons last year. I cannot feel however that at this juncture any negotiation with the Soviets about a Four-Power Meeting, even though conditional on the Agreements having been previously ratified, would help our common cause. Weakness makes no appeal to the Soviets. To mix up the process of ratification with what might well follow soon afterwards would very likely dilute both Firmness and Conciliation. The sooner we can get our united ratification the sooner the Top-Level Four-Power Conference may come.

Churchill went on to tell Mendès-France:

Although we have every sympathy with you in your difficulties and admiration for your exertions, the fact should be accepted that I and my colleagues are wholeheartedly resolved that there shall be no meeting or invitation in any circumstances which we can foresee between the Four Powers, either on the Foreign Secretaries' level or on that of the Heads of Governments, until the London–Paris Agreements have been ratified by all the signatories. In this we are in the closest accord with the United States. I cannot believe there is the slightest chance of any change of attitude on this point in either of our two countries. Indeed I fear that an indefinite process of delay may well lead to the adoption of other solutions which are certainly being studied on both sides of the Atlantic.

I, myself, am very much opposed to the withdrawal of all American and British troops from the continent. You may count on me to oppose to the best of my ability the strategic conception known as 'peripheral'. On the other hand I should feel bound, whether as Prime Minister or as a Private Member, to support the policy known as 'The Empty Chair', although this would involve large changes in the infra-structure of NATO, both military and political. I feel that the United States with their immense superiority of nuclear weapons and acting in association with Great Britain, the British Commonwealth and the German Federal Republic, will be strong enough, at any rate during the next few years, to afford to the Benelux countries and our other Allies for whom we have a deep regard, and also the German Federal Republic to whom we are bound in honour, a definite and substantial security based on physical and moral deterrent power.

In this breathing space much may be achieved. But having ever since 1910 worked and fought with and for France, for whose people I have a deep affection, I should feel the utmost sorrow to see her isolated and losing her influence with the rest of the free world.

'I hope indeed,' Churchill added, 'that it will fall to you to preserve your country from this evil turn of fortune.' [1]

In pursuit of his final goal, a summit at which he would represent Britain and guide the Great Powers to agreement, Churchill also wrote on January 12 to President Eisenhower:

My dear Friend,

I waited to answer your letter of December 15 until the vote had been taken in the French Chamber and after that our Governments were in such complete accord that I let the days slip by. There are still opportunities open to the French obstructors for making serious delays. Anthony and I are in full agreement with you that there can be no Four Power Conference of any kind until ratification is complete, and we feel of course that everything reasonable in our power should be done to press for a definite decision. I suppose they could, if they chose, spread the whole process out for four or five months.

[1] 'My dear Monsieur Mendès-France', 'Private and Personal', 12 January 1955: Churchill papers, 6/6.

I am sure you will agree that this would be a most improvident way of wasting the ever-shortening interval of time before the Soviets have developed their nuclear strength, including delivery, though not to anything approaching equality with you, to what is called 'saturation point', namely the power to inflict mortal injury upon the civilized structure of the free world.

Britain will, of course, be stronger in two or three years in nuclear weapons. I visited some of our secret establishments last week, and was struck by their progress and prospects, both in the atomic and in the hydrogen sphere ('sphere' is apposite in more senses than one). We are making atomic bombs on a steadily increasing scale, and we and our experts are confident that we have the secret, perhaps even with some improvements, of the hydrogen bomb. I am very glad that the difficulties about the 'fittings' which you promised me at Bermuda have been solved, and that your officers have been over here talking to ours. Thank you very much.

Looking back and knowing your views throughout the story, I cannot but regret that you had not the power at the time the McMahon Act was under discussion. If the agreement signed between me and FDR had not been shelved we should probably already have been able to add a substantial reinforcement to your vast and formidable deterrent power. We have, however, through Attlee's somewhat unconstitutional exertions in making vast sums available for nuclear development without disclosing the fact to Parliament, mastered the problems both of the atomic and the hydrogen weapons by our own science independently. The inevitable delay must, however, be regarded as a severe misfortune to our common cause from which your convictions would have saved it.

'I feel pretty sure,' Churchill ended, 'that you and I were thinking separately on the same or similar lines—as we have done before.'[1]

In his reply two weeks later, Eisenhower reflected on the wider implications of Churchill's search for a summit:

I am certain there is nothing to be gained in that situation by meekness and weakness. God knows I have been working hard in the exploration of every avenue that seems to lead toward the preservation and strengthening of the peace. But I am positive that the free world is surely building trouble for itself unless it is united in basic purpose, is clear and emphatic in its declared determination to resist all forceful Communist advance, and keeps itself ready to act on a moment's notice, if necessary.[2]

At the Cabinet meeting on January 31, Churchill supported the American position towards China, telling his colleagues that if the United States 'took a firm stand on a reasonable position, it seemed

---

[1] 'My dear Friend', 'Top Secret', 'Private and Personal', 12 January 1955: Churchill papers, 2/217.

[2] 'Dear Winston', signed 'As ever, Ike', 'Top Secret', The White House, Washington, 25 January 1955: Churchill papers, 2/217.

unlikely that the Chinese Communists would press their claims to a point at which they ran the risk of provoking general hostilities with the United States'.[1]

In Cabinet on February 15, Eden said that the United States would not be able to command 'the support of large sections of world opinion' if they publicly committed themselves to a policy which might involve them in giving 'active support' to the Chinese Nationalists in the islands of Quemoy and the Matsus, just off the coast of Communist China. Churchill commented that

... it suited the Communists' purpose to divide Western opinion on this question, and the United States Government would be falling into an obvious trap if they made a public declaration which had the effect of dividing that opinion still further. Peking's threats to seize Formosa by force were idle words: in fact it would be quite impossible for the Chinese Communists to mount an effective attack against Formosa in the face of United States opposition.

'It was, therefore,' Churchill added, 'both unnecessary and unwise for the United States Government to make any public declaration implying they paid serious attention to these threats.'[2] 'You know how hard Anthony and I have tried to keep in step with you,' Churchill warned Eisenhower on February 15, 'and how much we wish to continue to do so. But a war to keep the coastal islands for Chiang would not be defensible here.' Churchill added: 'Anthony and I deeply desire to do our utmost to help you and our strongest resolve is to keep our two countries bound together in their sacred brotherhood.'[3]

The Russian 'hope', Churchill wrote to the Queen five days later, 'is to divide Britain and the United States by words. They find "Formosa" a very useful word.' Nevertheless, Churchill added, the situation about the offshore islands 'is more than ever full of danger', and he ended: 'It is a great anxiety, but nothing like what we should feel if there were no United States.'[4]

On February 1 Clementine Churchill's sister Nellie died of cancer; she was sixty-six years old. For many months Churchill had kept her company on her visits to Chartwell and Chequers. Nellie's death

---

[1] Cabinet Conclusions No. 8 of 1955, 'Secret', 11.30 a.m., 31 January 1955: Cabinet papers, 128/28.

[2] Cabinet Conclusions No. 13 of 1955, 'Secret', 11.30 a.m., 15 February 1955: Cabinet papers, 128/28.

[3] 'My dear Friend', Prime Minister's Personal Telegram No. 6 of 1955, Washington Telegram No. 697 15 February 1955: Premier papers, 11/1074.

[4] 'Madam', 20 February 1955: Churchill papers, 6/6.

26. Churchill at Chartwell, with his dog Rufus.

27. Churchill at Chartw[ell] a few days after his 8[0th] birthday, with his racehor[se] 'Gibraltar'.

28. 15 February 195[5] Churchill leaving 10 Dow[n]ing Street, having lunch[ed] with Anthony Eden, his su[c]cessor as Prime Minister.

29. 18 May 1956, Churchill with British officers at the Headquarters of Northern Army Group, Celle, West Germany.

30. Churchill, his daughter Sarah, and his host Emery Reves, at Reves' villa, La Pausa, in the South of France, a photograph taken in 1956.

31. Churchill at La Pausa.

32. Churchill at La Pausa, working on the proofs of his last literary task, *A History of the English-Speaking Peoples*.

33. 13 September 1958, Churchill, his wife, his son Randolph and Randolph's daughter Arabella, on the Churchills' Golden Wedding anniversary, celebrated at Lord Beaverbrook's villa, La Capponcina, in the South of France.

34. 6 May 1959, Churchill with President Eisenhower at Gettysburg, during a private visit by Churchill, aged 84, to the United
States. Detective Sergeant Murray is standing behind them.

35. Anthony Montague Browne, a
photograph taken on board the *Queen
Mary* when he was on his way to New
York to sign on Churchill's behalf the
contract for the film *Young Winston*.

36. 27 July 1959, Churchill on board Aristotle Onassis' yacht *Christina*, off Capri.

37. Churchill at Chartwell, playing bezique with Lady Churchill's cousin, the Hon. Sylvia Henley.

38. Churchill's coffin leaves St Paul's Cathedral; on the steps, Lady Churchill and Randolph Churchill followed by Churchill's daughters Sarah and Mary, and by his grandson Winston and son-in-law Christopher Soames. The spot on which Christopher Soames stands is the one on which Churchill himself is seen walking on 14 May 1945, in the first photograph in this volume.

was a culmination of personal blows for Churchill and his wife, including their daughter Diana's nervous breakdown just over a year earlier, and the break-up of the marriage between Sarah and Antony Beauchamp. These were heavy burdens to bear, amid the continuing uncertainties of illness and the unremitting pressure of public life.

In the first and second weeks of February 1955 Churchill was host to the Commonwealth Prime Ministers at their conference in London. In answer to a suggestion in a letter from James de Rothschild that Israel, then approaching its seventh year of independence, should be admitted to the Commonwealth, Churchill minuted to Eden: 'This is a big question. Israel is a force in the world & a link w the USA.' [1]

On February 2 the Queen gave a dinner at Buckingham Palace for the Commonwealth Prime Ministers. 'Last night Attlee came up to me at the Palace,' Churchill told Lord Moran. 'I could see he was quivering, and then he fainted in my arms. I'm not very strong, but with Mrs Attlee's help I got him on to a couch. Poor Attlee, he is getting old; he is seventy-two. A lot of people saw it happen.'

Lord Moran asked Sir Norman Brook, David Pitblado and others how Churchill was getting on at the Conference. When he was saying a 'set piece' to the full assembly, sitting down, they replied, 'he mumbled and havered, but on the less formal occasions he was wonderfully impressive'. Moran also wanted to know Churchill's view of the Indian Prime Minister, noting in his diary on February 3:

I asked the PM about Nehru. He said to me: 'I get on very well with him. I tell him he has a great role to play as the leader of Free Asia against Communism.' I was curious to know how Nehru took this. 'Oh, he wants to do it—and I want him to do it. He has a feeling that the Communists are against him, and that,' Winston added with a grin, 'is apt to change people's opinions.' [2]

At a Cabinet meeting on February 17, Ministers were warned of an 'alarming' natural increase of Indian communities in the African colonies and elsewhere. In some colonies 'this was already giving rise to racial tension'. Churchill did not want, however, to do anything 'which might give offence to the Indian Government'. As he explained:

[1] Note initialled 'WSC', 9 February 1955. James de Rothschild had also written in his letter of 'our stay in Jerusalem in 1921' and he added: 'You then laid the foundations of the Jewish State by separating Abdullah's Kingdom from the rest of Palestine. Without this much-opposed prophetic foresight, there would not have been an Israel today.' ('My dear Winston', 1 February 1955: Churchill papers, 2/197.)

[2] Moran diary, 3 February 1955: *The Struggle for Survival*, pages 630–1.

India was in a position to exercise a moderating influence in Asia; and it was specially important at the present time that she should maintain the closest possible association with us in the handling of the major international problems of the day. It need not be assumed that in all Colonies Indian communities would prove an embarrassment to us: in some they might even be a balancing factor. Thus, although the problem should be carefully watched, precipitate action should be avoided.[1]

Four days later Churchill wrote to Nehru:

I am so much obliged to you for sending me the fascinating book of paintings taken from the Ajanta Caves. The reproductions are beautifully executed and I am indeed happy to possess such a wonderful book. It also gives me great pleasure that it should have come from you, and that our personal relations, after all that has happened, are so agreeable. I hope you will think of the phrase 'The Light of Asia'. It seems to me that you might be able to do what no other human being could in giving India the lead, at least in the realm of thought, throughout Asia, with the freedom and dignity of the individual as the ideal rather than the Communist Party drill book.

'I am so glad,' Churchill ended, 'your Sister is in so important a position over here.'[2]

During the Commonwealth Conference the visiting Prime Ministers had been informed of Britain's decision to manufacture the hydrogen bomb. The Government would be 'embarrassed', Churchill told the Cabinet on February 4, 'if there were any premature disclosure of this decision, and he had thought it right that the Cabinet should have an opportunity of considering whether an official announcement should be made in advance of the publication of the Defence White Paper'. He himself was satisfied 'that public reception of this decision would be less favourable if it were announced in isolation; and he would much prefer that it should be made public in the White Paper in the context of the Government's defence policy as a whole'.

It was agreed to make the announcement on February 17, as part of the Defence White Paper.[3] Meanwhile, on February 8, the Soviet leader, Malenkov, fell from power, and was replaced by Marshal Bulganin and Nikita Khrushchev.

*   *   *

[1] Cabinet Conclusions No. 15 of 1955, 'Secret', 11.30 a.m., 17 February 1955: Cabinet papers, 128/28.

[2] 'My dear Nehru', 21 February 1955: Churchill papers, 6/6. Nehru's sister, Mrs Pandit, was Indian High Commissioner in London.

[3] Cabinet Conclusions No. 9 of 1955, 'Secret', 5 p.m., 4 February 1955: Cabinet papers, 128/28. The Defence White Paper was issued on 1 March 1955 as Command Paper No. 9391.

Churchill's decision to resign 'before July', which Brendan Bracken had reported to Lord Beaverbrook on January 17, had remained a secret even from the Cabinet. It was not until a month later, after a Cabinet meeting on the morning of February 17, that Harold Macmillan, having written in his diary that Churchill was in a 'very merry mood', added: 'I think now he has taken the final decision to go. He is resigned to it and has begun to plan a future and quite agreeable life for himself.' At one point during the Cabinet discussion, the question had arisen of the future lay-out of Parliament Square, and to a possible redesign and enlargement. This, Churchill remarked, would be 'a good subject for a politician in retreat'. This, Macmillan added, was the first time that Churchill had referred in Cabinet to a period when he would no longer be Prime Minister.[1]

In the second week of February the Shah of Persia was in London on a state visit. On February 18 Churchill was among those invited to luncheon at Buckingham Palace to meet him. After lunch, Prince Charles and Princess Anne were brought in to meet the guests. One of those present, Eden's Principal Private Secretary, Evelyn Shuckburgh, noted in his diary:

The little princess was fascinated by Winston, who sat slumped in his chair, looking just like the Sutherland portrait.

I was drawn into some talk with him, and he said the FO was 'riddled with Bevinism' on Middle East questions, i.e. anti-Jewish. He had heard (from James de Rothschild) that the Israelis would like to join the British Commonwealth. 'Do not put that out of your mind. It would be a wonderful thing. So many people want to leave us; it might be the turning of the tide.'

I congratulated him on the success of the Commonwealth Prime Ministers Conference. He said, 'I have worked very hard with Nehru. I told him he should be the light of Asia, to show all those millions how they can shine out, instead of accepting the darkness of Communism. But you ought to let the Jews have Jerusalem; it is they who made it famous.' He also said that large numbers of the refugees ought to be settled in the Negev. I'm not sure whether he was aware that this is something the Israelis are resisting.[2]

On February 21 Churchill was the host at 10 Downing Street to the Shah of Persia and Queen Soraya.[3] Three days later he received the Israeli Ambassador, Eliahu Elath, who presented him with a portfolio of woodcuts of Old Jerusalem as an eightieth birthday gift from the Prime Minister and Government of Israel as 'a small token of Israel's admiration and enduring gratitude for the man who saved the

---

[1] Macmillan diary, 17 February 1955: Macmillan papers.

[2] Shuckburgh diary, 18 February 1955: *Descent to Suez, Diaries 1951–56*, page 251.

[3] Luncheon List, 21 February 1955, 10 Downing Street: Spencer-Churchill papers.

world from Nazi domination, thus securing for all its peoples—Israel among them—the renewed hope of peace, freedom and progress'. [1]

Returning to his Embassy, Elath telegraphed to his Foreign Minister:

This afternoon I presented your gift to Churchill at 10 Downing Street. It was obvious that the words of the dedication moved him more than the pictures themselves. The state symbol made a great impression on him and he asked various questions about the menorah and its traditional origins. [2] While looking at the pictures I told him about the fate of the Jewish Quarter in the Old City. He asked what had happened to the Western Wall. [3] In the course of the conversation he inquired about painting in Israel.

I refrained from raising any political issue but he himself began to speak about his part in the Balfour Declaration and about his Zionism. He asked if I had read his statement to the press in Washington last year—a statement which, he said, was absolutely spontaneous, being a reply to an unexpected question by one of the journalists.

He mentioned his friendship with Weizmann. He said that he has been and remains our friend. He took joy in the establishment of our State and expressed his confidence in its splendid future. He went on to say: you are a nation of ideals and that is the greatest thing in the life of both the community and the individual. He added that he admires the fact that we have absorbed so many refugees and that we have succeeded in developing the land and conquering the wilderness.

I thanked him for his words, pointing out how much you and the Government would appreciate what he said. In the course of my remarks I noted that we could do more than we have hitherto done if only the necessary conditions were created by ensuring our security in the region. I said there was no other state in the Middle East whose democratic social structure and fidelity to the principles of freedom were greater than ours, and that seemed to us a firm basis for the continuation and reinforcement of our traditional friendship with Britain.

Churchill interrupted by saying that a few days earlier he had received an interesting letter on this subject from James de Rothschild and he—Churchill—recognises our problems. He wants us to know that he will continue to see to it that no evil befalls Israel. I replied that these are difficult times for the world and our need for help from our friends is greater now than ever before.

The Ambassador's telegram continued:

I was in his room about a quarter of an hour. At the end of the conversation he remarked that he would confirm receipt of the gift and would express his

[1] Press release, 24 February 1955: Government of Israel Archive.

[2] The menorah, or candelabrum; a seven-branched candelabrum which, according to the Bible, was a prominent feature of the Tabernacle erected by the Children of Israel in the wilderness, as well as in the Temple of Jerusalem. In 1948 it was chosen as the official symbol of the State of Israel.

[3] The Western Wall is commonly called the 'wailing' wall. From 1948 until 1967 Israeli Jews were forbidden access to it, and to the entire Old City, by the Jordanian authorities.

thanks to you in writing. The gift would take its place among all the others he received for his birthday and he was happy that future generations would thereby know that the sons of the prophets dwelling in Zion were among his many well-wishers from all over the world. He was alert throughout the conversation and looked stronger than he did the last time, when we visited him. . . .

The Ambassador added that, on leaving, Churchill's secretary commented that 'as was customary, the conversation would remain secret and not a word of it may be published'.[1]

Churchill's Cabinet colleagues were still suspicious of his true intentions. On February 25 R. A. Butler told Macmillan: 'Winston is now trying to run out of his engagement to Anthony.'[2] On the following day, as Churchill's guest at Chartwell, Macmillan found the Prime Minister 'in very mellow mood and very charming, but weak and old'. Churchill told his visitor that 'he would not leave on a note of trouble or failure'. He wished to hear the next budget 'as PM', a suggestion with which Macmillan agreed. The budget was set for March 28. As for the actual day on which Churchill would resign, 'he has in mind April 5', noted Macmillan, and he added: 'We shall really miss him if he really does go—which I doubt.'[3]

In the last week of February, Churchill made plans to give a farewell dinner at 10 Downing Street on April 4, for the Queen. 'I do not think we shall have to go down to the dug-out in the midst of our proceedings,' he wrote to Sir Michael Adeane on February 28, 'as we several times had to do in those bygone days.'[4] The secret of the dinner was well kept.

There remained one major speech to be made in the House of Commons, on the Defence White Paper, in which Parliament and the world were to be told that Britain was to build its own hydrogen bomb. Churchill spent a total of twenty hours preparing this speech, which he wanted to contain both a warning and a way forward in the new era. 'He dictated it all himself,' Miss Portal later recalled.[5]

[1] Telegram of 24 February 1955 to Moshe Sharett: Government of Israel Archive.
[2] Macmillan diary, 25 February 1955: Macmillan papers.
[3] Macmillan diary, 26 February 1955: Macmillan papers.
[4] Letter of 28 February 1955: Churchill papers, 6/6.
[5] Lady Williams of Elvel recollections: in conversation with the author, 29 July 1987.

It was on March 1 that Churchill introduced the Defence White Paper to Parliament, speaking of how 'We live in a period, happily unique in human history, when the whole world is divided intellectually and to a large extent geographically between the creeds of Communist discipline and individual freedom, and when, at the same time, this mental and psychological division is accompanied by the possession by both sides of the obliterating weapons of the nuclear age.'

The antagonisms of the 1950s were, Churchill said, as deep as those of the Reformation, and its reactions which led to the Thirty Years' War. 'But now,' he noted, 'they are spread over the whole world instead of only over a small part of Europe. We have, to some extent, the geographical division of the Mongol invasion in the thirteenth century, only more ruthless and more thorough. We have force and science, hitherto the servants of man, now threatening to become his masters.'

It was owing to the 'breakdown in the exchange of information' with the United States in 1946, Churchill pointed out, that Britain had started, under Attlee's leadership, and in the utmost secrecy, to make its own nuclear weapons. By Attlee's initiative, he said, 'we have made our own atomic bombs', and he continued: 'Confronted with the hydrogen bomb, I have tried to live up to the right hon. Gentleman's standard. We have started to make that one, too. It is this grave decision which forms the core of the Defence Paper. . . .'

There was 'no absolute defence against the hydrogen bomb', Churchill told the House of Commons, nor was there any method in sight 'by which any nation, or any country, can be completely guaranteed against the devastating injury which even a score of them might inflict on wide regions', and he went on to ask:

What ought we to do? Which way shall we turn to save our lives and the future of the world? It does not matter so much to old people; they are going soon anyway; but I find it poignant to look at youth in all its activity and ardour and, most of all, to watch little children playing their merry games, and wonder what would lie before them if God wearied of mankind.

The best defence would of course be bona fide disarmament all round. This is in all our hearts. But sentiment must not cloud our vision. It is often said that 'facts are stubborn things'. A renewed session of a sub-committee of the Disarmament Commission is now sitting in London and is rightly attempting to conduct its debates in private. We must not conceal from ourselves the gulf between the Soviet Government and the NATO Powers, which has hitherto, for so long, prevented an agreement. The long history and tradition of Russia makes it repugnant to the Soviet Government to accept any practical system of international inspection.

A second difficulty lies in the circumstances that, just as the United States, on the one hand, has, we believe, the overwhelming mastery in nuclear weapons, so the Soviets and their Communist satellites have immense superiority in what are called 'conventional' forces—the sort of arms and forces with which we fought the last war, but much improved.

The problem now confronting the Great Powers was, Churchill said, to devise 'a balanced and phased system of disarmament', which at no period enabled any one of the participants to enjoy an advantage 'which might endanger the security of the other'. There was a widespread belief 'throughout the free world', Churchill added, 'that, but for American nuclear superiority, Europe would already have been reduced to satellite status and the Iron Curtain would have reached the Atlantic and the Channel', and he went on to tell the House of Commons:

Unless a trustworthy and universal agreement upon disarmament, conventional and nuclear alike, can be reached and an effective system of inspection is established and is actually working, there is only one sane policy for the free world in the next few years. That is what we call defence through deterrents. This we have already adopted and proclaimed. These deterrents may at any time become the parents of disarmament, provided that they deter. To make our contribution to the deterrent we must ourselves possess the most up-to-date nuclear weapons, and the means of delivering them.

Churchill was careful in his speech to talk of the 'Soviets' and 'Soviet' Communism. 'The House will perhaps note,' he said, 'that I avoid using the word "Russia" as much as possible in this discussion,' and he went on to explain: 'I have a strong admiration for the Russian people—for their bravery, their many gifts, and their kindly nature. It is the Communist dictatorship and the declared ambition of the Communist Party and their proselytizing activities that we are bound to resist, and that is what makes this great world cleavage which I mentioned when I opened my remarks.'

To nuclear attack, Churchill went on, 'continents are vulnerable as well as islands'. Hence the 'enormous spaces and scattered population' of Soviet Russia was, with the advent of the hydrogen bomb, 'on an equality or near equality of vulnerability with our small densely populated island and with Western Europe'. The hydrogen bomb, 'with its vast range of destruction and the even wider area of contamination, would be effective also against nations whose population, hitherto, has been so widely dispersed over large land areas as to make them feel that they were not in any danger at all'.

The power and value of deterrents was 'well understood', Churchill pointed out, 'by all persons on both sides—I repeat "on both sides"—who have the power to control events'. That was why he had hoped 'for a long time' for a top-level conference 'where these matters could be put plainly and bluntly from one friendly visitor to the conference to another'. Then, he added, 'it may well be that we shall, by a process of sublime irony, have reached a stage where safety will be the sturdy shield of terror, and survival the twin brother of annihilation'.

Churchill still believed that, as he told the House, 'mercifully, there is time and hope if we combine patience and courage', and he ended:

The day may dawn when fair play, love for one's fellow men, respect for justice and freedom, will enable tormented generations to march forth serene and triumphant from the hideous epoch in which we have to dwell. Meanwhile, never flinch, never weary, never despair.[1]

Churchill's powers, commented the *Sunday Times*, 'as he has so brilliantly demonstrated, are still of the highest order'.[2]

'He spoke for three quarters of an hour,' noted Lord Moran, who was present in the Peers' Gallery, 'and his voice at the end was as strong as at the beginning. The speech held the House, though he seemed more concerned with his theme than with its effect on members.' When Churchill left the Chamber, Moran followed him to his room in the House of Commons:

The door opened and O'Brien[3] came in; he keeps the PM in touch with political opinion and with the Press. Winston turned to him eagerly:
'How did they take it? Good. I thought they might like what I said.'
He was still all agog to find out the response of the House. He seemed to be bottling up his excitement, and I noticed that he was out of breath. 'If you never made another speech,' said Christopher—and he seemed just as excited as the PM—'that was a very fine swan-song.' Winston's face fell.
'I may not make many more speeches in the House,' he said gloomily.
He turned to Jock and told him to have his frock-coat sent over from No. 10; he was going to see the Queen.
He caught my eye.
'It's all right, Charles, of course I'm tired, but not too tired. In fact, I'm very well. I had to do it alone; no one could do it for me. Shinwell said there was nothing original in my speech. I don't know why he should say that,' Winston complained in an injured voice. 'I couldn't—'
At that moment Clemmie came into the room and I slipped away.[4]

---

[1] Speech of 1 March 1955: *Hansard*. The advice in Churchill's peroration, one historian has written, 'may be considered his legacy to the nation' (Anthony Seldon, *Churchill's Indian Summer*, London 1981, page 439).
[2] *Sunday Times*, 6 March 1955.
[3] Gerald O'Brien was Chief Press Officer at the Conservative Central Office.
[4] Moran diary, 1 March 1955: *The Struggle for Survival*, pages 633–7.

'I was glad to see,' Churchill wrote to Eisenhower on March 4, 'from reports of your interview with the Press that we are in such good agreement about the H Bomb and all that. All went very well in the House of Commons. Considering we only have a majority of sixteen, the fact that the Opposition vote of censure was rejected by 107 votes was a remarkable event and entitles me to say that our policy of "Defence through deterrents" commands the support of the nation.'[1]

'He could still make a great speech,' Jock Colville noted a month later, 'as was proved in the defence debate on March 1st. Indeed none could rival his oratory or his ability to inspire.' But, Colville added:

... he was ageing month by month and was reluctant to read any papers except the newspapers or to give his mind to anything that he did not find diverting.

More and more time was given to bezique and ever less to public business. The preparation of a Parliamentary Question might consume a whole morning; facts would be demanded from Government departments and not arouse any interest when they arrived (they would be marked 'R' and left to moulder in his black box); it was becoming an effort even to sign letters and a positive condescension to read Foreign Office telegrams.

And yet on some days the old gleam would be there, wit and good humour would bubble and sparkle, wisdom would roll out in telling sentences and still, occasionally, the sparkle of genius could be seen in a decision, a letter or a phrase.

But was he the man to negotiate with the Russians and moderate the Americans? The Foreign Office thought not; the British public would, I am sure, have said yes. And I, who have been as intimate with him as anybody during these last years, simply do not know.[2]

The Defence debate continued on March 2, when Aneurin Bevan, in urging talks with Russia, claimed that Churchill had not gone to Bermuda to advance those talks, because the United States had refused to allow them. In answering Bevan, Churchill made the first public reference to his stroke, to an amazed House of Commons.

It was 'absolutely wrong', Churchill declared, 'to suggest that the course that we have followed here has been at the dictation of the United States', and he added: 'I prepared in every way to go over to see the President. However, I was struck down by a very sudden illness which paralysed me completely, physically. That is why I had to put it all off.'[3]

---

[1] 'My dear Friend', 'Message from the Prime Minister to the President', 4 March 1955: Eisenhower papers.

[2] Colville notes, written on 29 March 1955: *The Fringes of Power*, pages 704-7.

[3] Speech of 2 March 1955: *Hansard*.

57

'A new chance'

ON 8 March 1955 Churchill lunched with Anthony Eden. 'It seems settled,' noted Harold Macmillan on the following day, 'Winston will resign on April 5.'[1] On the day of his lunch with Eden, at which, at last, the date was fixed for the Cabinet as well as for the Queen, Churchill received a welcome gift from his friend Lord Chandos, two new hearing aids. 'I am sure they will help me immensely,' he dictated in reply, and then added in his own hand: 'Looking forward to seeing and *hearing* you soon.'[2] Resignation no longer seemed to hold any terror for the man who could still hold the attention of the House or unfold a vision of a better world. 'I have lost interest; I am tired of it all' had been the burden of his remarks to Jock Colville during the winter months. Churchill had also spoken to Colville of Eden's 'hungry eyes'.[3]

On March 11 Churchill left London by car for Chequers. On the way out of London he stopped at the London Zoo to see two animals which had been given to him as gifts, Rota the lion and Sheba the leopard.[4] Once at Chequers, Churchill settled down to bezique with Colville. But hardly had they begun their by now familiar and frequent game than a minute arrived from Anthony Eden, commenting on a telegram just received at the Foreign Office from Sir Roger Makins in Washington.

The Makins telegram, No. 539 from Washington, described, as Colville noted, 'various manoeuvres suggested by the Americans for inducing the French to ratify the London–Paris Agreements which have taken the place of the European Defence Community as the basis of Western European Defence'. These included a suggestion that Eisenhower should go to Paris on 8 May 1955, the tenth anniversary of

---

[1] Macmillan diary, 9 March 1955: Macmillan papers.

[2] Letter of 8 March 1955: Churchill papers, 6/6.

[3] Colville notes written on 29 March 1955: *The Fringes of Power*, pages 704–7.

[4] Rota had been given to the Zoo in February 1943, Sheba in October 1953. Rota died on 18 June 1955 and Sheba on 21 November 1955.

VE Day, 'and solemnly ratify the agreements in company with President Coty, Adenauer and Sir Winston Churchill'.[1]

There was also a sentence in the telegram, which Colville did not mention in his diary, that Eisenhower might be prepared, at Paris, to 'lay plans for a meeting with the Soviets in a sustained effort to reduce tensions and the risk of war'.[2]

As Colville later recalled, Churchill 'did not take in the implications at once' of what Eisenhower was proposing. That night, however, Lord Beaverbrook came to dinner, 'the first time for many months', Colville noted, 'and it was not until he had gone that W re-read the telegram and the somewhat discouraging and disparaging minute which accompanied it'.

Churchill suddenly saw, in Eisenhower's willingness to meet him and President Coty in Paris, and to use that meeting to make plans for a meeting with the Soviets, an opportunity to revive his own grand design. But it would mean remaining Prime Minister for at least a month beyond his still secret April resignation date. 'Of course,' Churchill told Colville, the possibility of a Paris meeting 'meant all bets were off: he would stay and, with Eisenhower, meet the Russians. I pointed out that no suggestion of meeting the Russians was made, but he brushed this aside because he saw a chance of escape from his increasingly unpalatable timetable.'[3]

Such was Churchill's view when he went to bed on the night of March 11. Nor had he changed his mind when he awoke on March 12. That morning he dictated a minute to Eden, which he then signed and sent. It read, in full:

1. Makins' tel. no. 539 is of prime importance. It is the first time President Eisenhower has responded to my appeals beginning on May 11, 1953 and has shown willingness to visit Europe in person and after securing ratification of the London and Paris Agreements, to 'lay plans for a meeting with the Soviets in a sustained effort to reduce tensions and the risk of war.' This proposal of a meeting of Heads of Governments which he would attend himself must be regarded as creating a new situation which will affect our personal plans and time-tables.

2. It also complicates the question of a May Election to which I gather you are inclining. Your proposed last sentence of your paragraph 7 might be dangerous as it seems to suggest that the Party politics of a snap Election to take advantage of Socialist disunity would be allowed to weigh against a meeting of the Heads of Governments which would give a chance to the world of warding off its mortal peril. The British national reaction to this would not be favourable.

---

[1] Colville notes, written on 29 March 1955: *The Fringes of Power*, pages 704–7.
[2] Washington telegram No. 539: Foreign Office papers (Eden archive).
[3] Colville notes, written on 29 March 1955: *The Fringes of Power*, pages 704–7.

3. It would I think be wrong to assume that the French Senators or the French people would be disdainful of a procedure which would accord to France the leading position in Europe. Certainly it seems unwise to adopt personal estimates of when they would regard honourable treatment as flattery or factual appraisal of consequences as threats. Anyhow we should not allow such estimates to be the main factor in our decisions upon the tremendous issues which have now been opened by the President and Dulles.

4. The magnitude of the Washington advance towards a Top Level Meeting is the dominant fact now before us and our reply must not underrate it or fail to encourage its development.

5. I shall be most interested to see the actual draft of what you propose to say. I presume you are circulating Makins' tel. no. 539 to the Cabinet who must be consulted. Meanwhile a cordial interim message should be sent for Makins to deliver.

'It may well be this is what you have in mind,' Churchill ended.[1]

Eden replied at once. He was clearly far from pleased:

1. I have your message to-day.

2. I was not aware that anything I had done in my public life would justify the suggestion that I was putting Party before country or self before either.

3. I am circulating the telegram to our colleagues as you suggest. I must ask that we discuss it at an early Cabinet; at latest Monday morning.

4. I will send no reply to Dulles' message meanwhile.[2]

Churchill was not deterred in his new zeal for a summit by Eden's reply; when it reached him that same day he answered it immediately:

Your paragraph 2. Nothing in my minute suggested or was intended to suggest that you were putting Party before country or self before either. What I meant, and mean, is that the last sentence of paragraph 7 of your minute PM/55/21 would be taken to imply a snap Election in May. This would in any case rouse a Party struggle of intense bitterness. That our treatment of the Eisenhower–Dulles proposal was in any way associated with our electoral schemes, and this became known, as it well might, would certainly be made the grounds for a Socialist charge that we had discouraged a Top Level approach to the international problem for reasons connected with our Party tactics. That is why I deemed the sentence dangerous in this context.

I am distressed that you should have read a personal implication, which I utterly repudiate, into a discussion of policy. There are enough difficulties already without misunderstanding between you and me after all these years.[3]

---

[1] 'Secretary of State for Foreign Affairs', 12 March 1955: Churchill papers, 6/4.
[2] 'Prime Minister', 12 March 1955: Churchill papers, 6/4.
[3] 'Foreign Secretary', 12 March 1955: Churchill papers, 6/4.

Churchill returned to London on the evening of Sunday March 13, when he and Norman Brook dined with Colville at the Turf Club. That same day, Macmillan noted in his diary that, as a result of the Makins telegram, Churchill, in a conversation with Eden, 'immediately withheld his offer to go on April 5'.[1] On the following morning the Cabinet met to discuss the Makins telegram. 'It was proposed,' the Cabinet were told, 'that President Eisenhower should come to Paris in order to exchange the instruments of ratification with the Heads of Governments of the United Kingdom, France and Germany. This, it was suggested, would also give an opportunity to make plans for a Meeting with the Soviet Government, in pursuance of the policy of the Western Powers to ease international tension and to reduce the risk of war.'

Eden then told the Cabinet that Dulles had previously suggested that, if the French delayed unduly their ratification of the Paris Agreements, 'other means' would have to be found of emphasizing the independence of Western Germany. It seemed likely, therefore, 'that the primary purpose of this new plan was to ensure French ratification of the Paris Agreements'. It should not be assumed, Eden warned, that it was certain to have this effect on the French; 'and it might be doubtful whether the Germans would appreciate the choice of the tenth anniversary of VE-Day as the most suitable date for a ceremonial exchange of ratifications of the Paris Agreements'.

A 'more important consideration' in Eden's view, however, was the effect which the announcement of this plan might have on the Soviet Government. 'If it were announced before the French Senate debated the Agreements,' Eden feared, 'the Russians were likely to counter it by a public declaration that, if the French ratified the Agreements, they would decline the proposed invitation to a Four-Power Meeting.'

If the 'primary purpose' of the Paris meeting was to prepare the way for a Four-Power Meeting, Eden said, 'he would wish to give it his support'. But he felt nevertheless that 'if that were its object', it would be 'more likely to produce results if both the announcement and the invitation were withheld for some time after the ratification of the Paris Agreements'. He would like also to know 'what kind of Four-Power Meeting was envisaged by the Americans'. There was nothing in the Makins telegram, he said, to suggest that they had in mind a Meeting of Heads of Governments. 'Indeed, the subjects suggested for preliminary discussion by the four Foreign Ministers implied that what the Americans had in mind was a continuation of the Berlin Conference—though, for the resumption of those discussions, no further preparation by the Western Powers was necessary.'

[1] Macmillan diary, 12 March 1955: Macmillan papers.

The 'main question' for the Cabinet to consider, Eden told his colleagues, 'was whether an early announcement of the plan outlined by Mr Dulles was likely to further our primary purpose of securing a fruitful Four-Power Meeting with the Russians. He himself doubted whether it would improve the prospects of securing such a Meeting.'

Churchill then spoke in favour of the Paris meeting, and of the summit that might follow it. He attached 'primary importance', he said, 'to the President's willingness to come to Europe for the purpose of making plans for a Four-Power Meeting with the Russians. This was a new and significant initiative, and we should welcome it. We should certainly say nothing to discourage it.'

Many people, both in Britain and elsewhere in Western Europe, would, Churchill said, 'have high hopes that such a visit would make a significant contribution towards the preservation of world peace. Even though it might be true that the primary purpose of the plan was to ensure French ratification of the Paris Agreements, it would give us an opportunity to discuss with the President means of securing a fruitful Meeting with the Russians. We should therefore be ill-advised to brush it aside or deny ourselves the chance of turning it to good account.'

In its conclusion, the Cabinet tried to reach a compromise between Churchill's enthusiasm and Eden's caution. 'Precipitate action' on the lines proposed by Dulles, the minutes noted, 'though it might help to ensure French ratification of the Paris Agreements, was not likely to improve the prospects for a Four-Power Meeting with the Russians which might produce fruitful results. Indeed, it was more likely than not that the Russians would decline an invitation issued in the circumstances envisaged in this plan.' On the other hand, the minutes continued, 'much good might come from a visit to Europe by President Eisenhower; and we should certainly do nothing to discourage the initiative which he had shown in suggesting it'. Many of the difficulties which had been mentioned in the Cabinet's discussion could be avoided, the Cabinet concluded, 'if any immediate announcement of his plans could be confined to a statement that he was willing to come to Europe later in the summer—perhaps in June'.[1]

Was it the mention of June, rather than May, which then led to an outbreak by Eden? On the previous night both Norman Brook and Colville had urged Eden to 'stick entirely to the merits of the American proposal'. But as the discussion in Cabinet proceeded, Colville noted that Eden 'raised the personal issue, and W, in the face of silent and embarrassed colleagues, said coldly that this was not a matter on which

---

[1] Cabinet Conclusions No. 23 of 1955, 'Secret', 10 Downing Street, 12 noon, 14 March 1955: Cabinet papers, 128/28.

he required guidance or on which Cabinet discussion was usual'.[1]

One of the Ministers present at the Cabinet meeting of March 14, Harold Macmillan, noted in his diary how 'the atmosphere was queer', and that those Ministers present who were 'in the know' about April 5 'were very unhappy'. It was when Churchill had mentioned Eisenhower's possible visit to London 'in June' that Eden had said, slowly and deliberately: 'Does that mean, Prime Minister, that the arrangements you have made with me are at an end?'

Churchill seemed 'rather staggered' by Eden's question, Macmillan added, and 'mumbled something' about 'the national interest', 'this has been my ambition. . . .' whereupon Eden interjected: 'I have been Foreign Minister for ten years.[2] I am not to be trusted?'

At this point in the discussion, Lord Salisbury, who was not among those who had been told about the April 5 resignation date, commented acerbicly: 'It seems certain facts are not known to all of us' and urged that the whole Cabinet should be informed. Churchill refused. 'I cannot assent to such a discussion,' he said. 'I know my duty and will perform it. If any member of the Cabinet dissents, his way is open.'[3]

The ensuing days, Colville recorded two weeks later, were 'painful', and he added: 'W began to form a cold hatred of Eden who, he repeatedly said, had done more to thwart him and prevent him pursuing the policy he thought right than anybody else. But he also admitted to me on several occasions that the prospect of giving everything up, after nearly sixty years in public life, was a terrible wrench.[4] He saw no reason why he should go: he was only doing it for Anthony. He sought to persuade his intimate friends, and himself, that he was being hounded from office.'[5]

On March 15 Churchill wrote to his wife about the tension in Cabinet:

Most Secret
Burn or Lock up

My darling Clemmie,

The Cabinet met for the purpose of approving the answer to be sent to the long Makins telegram I showed you. However, Anthony had been unable to compose a draft and we had a wandering talk over the whole field, at the end of which he asked whether this made any difference in the planned date on which we had agreed.

[1] Colville notes, written on 29 March 1955: *The Fringes of Power*, pages 704–7.

[2] The ten years were: December 1935 to February 1938, December 1940 to July 1945 and October 1951 to March 1955.

[3] Macmillan diary, 14 March 1955: Macmillan papers.

[4] Churchill had made his first public speech, at a Conservative Party rally at Claverton Manor near Bath on 26 July 1897, nearly 58 years before this stormy Cabinet.

[5] Colville notes, 29 March 1955: *The Fringes of Power*, page 706.

I pointed out that it was unprecedented to discuss such matters at Cabinet, and most of the Ministers seemed very embarrassed. I made it clear that I should be guided by what I believed was my duty and nothing else, and that any Minister who disagreed could always send in his resignation.

The poor Cabinet, most of whom knew nothing about the inner story, seemed puzzled and worried. Of course, as you know, only one thing has influenced me, and that is the possibility of arranging with Ike for a top level meeting in the near future with the Soviets. Otherwise I am very ready to hand over responsibility. I thought this Makins message offered a new chance, and that is why I am testing it.

'Thus the Cabinet ended,' Churchill wrote, 'and I had to concentrate on my speech.' [1]

Speaking in the House of Commons a few hours after the Cabinet at which he had again looked forward to a summit with the Russians, Churchill answered a vote of censure moved by Attlee, critical of the Government's efforts to secure world peace, and calling for a Three-Power Conference of Britain, the United States and the Soviet Union. Churchill could say nothing of the Makins telegram, or the Cabinet discussion on it—a discussion which had been set to continue the following day. But he did tell the House of Commons that he felt France and Germany should no longer be dissociated 'from the tasks of resolving the fears and disputes which beset Europe and the world today'. Only to mention Three Powers, Churchill commented, 'would give serious offence', and at a time when France 'is taking, or about to take, decisions important to her welfare and also to the policy which both parties in the House have supported'.

Churchill also told the House of Commons on March 14:

Earnestly as I desire to get a peaceful arrangement for co-existence brought about with Russia, I should regard it as an act of insanity to drive the German people into the hands of the Kremlin and thus tilt into Communist tyranny the destiny of mankind. Moreover, the only safe policy for us to pursue is, as we have often stated, peace through strength. Without unity there can be no strength. For the Western Powers to abandon EDC and have nothing to put in its place in Europe would have presented us divided and in vacuity before the mighty Communist oligarchy and dictatorship and its satellites.

Weakness makes no appeal to Moscow. To mix up the process of ratification with what might well follow soon afterwards would very likely dilute both firmness and conciliation. The sooner we can get our united ratification settled, the sooner the top-level Four-Power—it may be Five-Power—conference may come. On the other hand, it might well be that one retreat would lead to another and, far from assuaging differences, would stimulate further aggression from the East and slowly arouse the reluctant anger of the West.

[1] 'My darling Clemmie', 15 March 1955: Spencer-Churchill papers.

We went through all this in the years before the war, which I remember only too well. Therefore, we felt that we must on no account allow our earnest desire to bring about a top-level conference of great Powers to expose us to the charge of having thrown doubt and disarray into the ranks of NATO.

It was for this reason that, once the European Defence Community had become an unresolved issue, the Government had 'no choice but to suspend for the time being' the proposals which Churchill had made to Molotov for a meeting in 1954. Since then, Malenkov had been replaced by Marshal Bulganin, and new initiatives might be possible. 'I have tried very hard,' Churchill added, 'to set in motion this process of a conference at the top level and to bring about actual results. Although I do not pretend to measure what the recent changes in the Soviet oligarchy imply, I do not feel that they should in any way discourage us from further endeavours.'

As to the United States, 'My feeling is,' Churchill told the House, 'that the wish of the United States for peace grows stronger at the same pace as their capacity for war. They give great consideration to our views. They show marked respect for our experience of the European scene. But this very attention which they pay to what we advise is accompanied by serious irritation of their public opinion at anything they take to be unfair criticism.'

Churchill ended his speech of March 14 with an appeal which bore directly on what he knew to be the plan for a possible summit meeting, and which he so hoped to see come to pass:

No President of the United States has ever had the knowledge and experience of Europe and of the very group of problems now confronting us as is possessed by President Eisenhower, and I do hope that nothing will be said on this side of the Atlantic, and particularly in this House, which will raise new inhibitions in American minds against the freedom of his personal movements.

I still believe that, vast and fearsome as the human scene has become, personal contacts of the right people in the right place at the right time may yet have a potent and valuable part to play in the cause of peace which is in our hearts.[1]

'The Opposition was in a pitiable plight,' Churchill wrote to his wife on the following day, and he added: 'A majority of 30 when one only has 16, on a Vote of Censure, is remarkable.'[2]

Not long after Churchill's speech, the American Ambassador, Winthrop Aldrich, brought to the Foreign Office a dampening message

---

[1] Speech of 14 March 1955: *Hansard*.
[2] 'My darling Clemmie', 15 March 1955: Spencer-Churchill papers.

from Washington. It was at once sent across to 10 Downing Street. This message, Churchill told his wife, was 'to the effect that Ike was not willing himself to participate in a meeting with Russia. Whether this referred to a top level meeting at a later date or not is still uncertain. It may only apply to the immediate meeting of the Four Powers referred to in the Makins note, but this I understand is to be, like all the other failures, upon the Foreign Office level.'

Churchill's letter continued:

We are now going to meet again today to settle the answer to America. Of course, if it is clear that Ike will not in any circumstances take part in the near future in a top level meeting, that relieves me of my duty to continue and enables me to feed the hungry. This will soon settle itself.

I had a nice talk with Bobbety after the Cabinet, and I told him that the 9th in any case was on, but the date of return would have to be settled later.[1] He quite understood. I think it probable, however, that Ike will be negative and obstinate, in which case I should be free. We must see how things go on today, but it may be there will be further delays. Anyhow we are working on the basis of the 9th as planned.[2]

When the Cabinet met on March 15, Eden presented a draft reply to Dulles which 'set out', the Cabinet minutes noted, 'some of the main difficulties which the Cabinet had seen in the specific plan outlined by Mr Dulles, and suggested that these might be avoided if the President were to announce, before the French debates on the ratification of the Paris Agreements, his willingness to visit Europe some time later in the summer, perhaps in June?' It was also suggested in Eden's proposed telegram that the announcement of such a visit need not be linked specifically with the ratification of the Paris Agreements: 'it could refer more generally to the easing of international relations in Europe and the possibility of a top level Four-Power Meeting with the Russians'.

He attached 'particular importance', Churchill told the Cabinet, 'to the reference to a top level meeting with Russians'. This should ensure 'that the United States Government would make it plain whether they envisaged a meeting of Heads of Governments of the Four Powers or further meetings of Foreign Ministers in continuation of the Berlin Conference'.

The Cabinet then authorized Eden to send a message to Dulles in the terms of the draft.[3]

---

[1] It had been agreed that Lord Salisbury would go to Washington on April 9 to put the case for a top level meeting to the Americans.

[2] 'My darling Clemmie', 15 March 1955: Spencer-Churchill papers.

[3] Cabinet Conclusions No. 24 of 1955, 'Secret', 10 Downing Street, 11 a.m., 15 March 1955: Cabinet papers, 128/28. Eden's telegram to Dulles was sent as Foreign Office to Washington No. 1057.

On the morning of March 16 the Cabinet was told of a further telegram from Sir Roger Makins 'reporting the preliminary views of the United States Secretary of State on the message which the Foreign Secretary had sent to him in pursuance of the Cabinet's decision of the previous day'. According to Makins, Dulles 'was to discuss the matter further with President Eisenhower. It seemed unlikely, however, that either of them was contemplating an early Four-Power Meeting with the Russians.'[1] For Churchill, the news was a cruel blow. 'Churchill made a gesture of disappointment,' Macmillan noted in his diary. It did mean, however, as Macmillan wrote, that 'The Cabinet crisis is over.'[2]

On the following day Macmillan lunched with Churchill and Montgomery. 'PM seems rather low,' Macmillan noted. 'It is now certain that the crisis of indecision is over.'[3]

All remained set for resignation on April 5, unless from Washington or Moscow were to come some exceptional invitation or prospect of a summit. 'From his own point of view,' Mary Soames told Lord Moran on March 17, 'it would have been better if he had gone on till he dropped in his tracks, but his colleagues would not agree to that. He is terribly flat, but when he resigns I think his "lust for life" will keep him going. If his big speech on the hydrogen bomb had been made a hundred years ago nothing more would have been expected of him for a long time. Now it's different. Something else blows up without warning; there is no respite. It's the detail that gets Papa down.'[4]

'From now till the "day",' Mary Soames wrote in her diary on March 19, 'it will be hard going. He minds so much. It is sad to watch—Mama too feels it—she said "It's the first death—& for him, a death in life."'[5]

On March 20 the *Sunday Express* announced that Churchill was about to resign; it was the first that the public had heard of it. 'You will find the PM very depressed,' Miss Portal told Lord Moran on the following day, and she explained: 'He has given up reading the newspapers and sits about staring into space.' He did find time, however, to look at Randolph Churchill's newly published book *Churchill: His Life in Pictures*, telling Jock Colville, who asked him if he liked it: 'It can't do any harm,' and adding: 'My vanity led me to spend two hours looking through it—I didn't go to bed until one forty-five. Perhaps'—and

[1] Cabinet Conclusions No. 25 of 1955, 'Secret', 10 Downing Street, 11.30 a.m., 16 March 1955: Cabinet papers, 128/28.
[2] Macmillan diary, 16 March 1955: Macmillan papers.
[3] Macmillan diary, 17 March 1955: Macmillan papers.
[4] Moran diary, 17 March 1955: *The Struggle for Survival*, page 640.
[5] Mary Soames diary, 19 March 1955: Mary Soames, *Clementine Churchill*, page 451.

here he smiled—'the public will not be as interested in it as I was.'[1]

On March 22 President Eisenhower sent Churchill a letter from the White House. It made no reference to the Paris meeting or the possible summit. Instead, it referred to a reference in Churchill's most recent letter to him that he was soon to withdraw from active political life. 'I echo your hope,' Eisenhower wrote, 'that the impending divergence of our lives will apply to political occasions only. Indeed, I entertain the further hope that with greater leisure, you will more often find it possible to visit us in this country—after all, we do have a fifty percent share in your blood lines, if not in your political allegiance.'[2]

Churchill's possible resignation was again headline news on March 23, when the *Manchester Guardian* declared: 'Cabinet urging Premier to resign. His health said to be retarding his work.'[3]

Lord Moran was indignant. The *Manchester Guardian* was 'usually so friendly,' he said. But Churchill understood more about the newspaper than his doctor did. 'Oh, this was not their Parliamentary correspondent,' he said, referring to Harry Boardman whose work he much admired, 'it was their Lobby correspondent', a reference to Francis Boyd, who, Churchill insisted, had based his information on a conversation 'with one Conservative MP. "One", he repeated scornfully.'

'If I dug in I don't think they could make me go,' Churchill told Lord Moran that morning, and he added, as Moran noted: '"But I like Anthony so much and I have worked with him so long. And he wants to be Prime Minister terribly. Several times he has tried to bring on an election because he thought it would get me out." A wry smirk spread over the PM's face. "He might succeed in getting me out and fail to get himself in."'[4]

At Cabinet on March 23 Churchill made only a brief comment, pointing out that as ten years had passed since Lloyd George's death, he proposed to invite the House of Commons to present an address to

[1] Quoted in Moran diary, 21 March 1955: *The Struggle for Survival*, page 640. The book *Churchill: His Life in Pictures* was Randolph Churchill's first gift to this author, when he joined Randolph's research team in 1962.

[2] 'Dear Winston', 'Top Secret', 22 March 1955: Churchill papers, 2/217. The reason for the secrecy of Eisenhower's letter was his explanation of why the United States Government was publishing the transcripts of the Yalta discussions. 'Of course both Foster and I have been unhappy about the affair of the Yalta papers,' he wrote, and went on to explain: 'Actually we had hoped that we had made adequate arrangement for an indefinite postponement of the appearance of the documents; an unexplained leak finally put the State Department in the position that it had either to release the papers publicly or to allow one lone periodical a complete scoop in the matter. As for myself, you know how earnestly I have argued that no matter what else might happen, really good international friends cannot ever afford to be guilty of bad faith, one towards the other. I pray that you do not consider that any such thing was intended in this case.'

[3] *Manchester Guardian*, 23 March 1955.

[4] Moran diary, 23 March 1955: *The Struggle for Survival*, pages 641–2.

the Queen 'praying that a monument to his memory be erected in the Palace of Westminster'. The Cabinet endorsed this proposal.[1] 'PM seems rather low,' Macmillan noted in his diary, 'and resigned to his decision and I do not anticipate any more crises.'[2]

'I do think of you so much darling Mama,' Mary Soames wrote to her mother on March 24, 'especially during these last days of Papa's public life—It must seem like the end of a long, long journey, full of harassments & trials—& triumphs & bitter-sweet joys and anxieties. But what a story! And I know it would not have been such a splendid one if you had not been there.'[3]

On March 25 Churchill received a note from his wife, who was at Chequers with him; it was the last note she was to write to him while he was Prime Minister, and it concerned their arrangements for saying goodbye:

Winston,

This week-end will be the last that we shall spend and sleep at Chequers. We shall want to say Goodbye to everybody here and I am sure you will like to say something to them.

Next week-end we had planned to spend in London because of the Birthday party you are giving for me on Friday April the 1st, and because the Queen is coming to dinner on the Monday, and of course I should want to be all that day in London trying to make the arrangements as perfect as possible. I wonder if you would like to come down to Chequers to lunch on Sunday the 3rd, after which we could make our farewells, and then go back to Downing Street? If you liked we could ask a few people to dinner there on Saturday the 2nd and again on Sunday the 3rd.

I am sending you this minute so that you have time to consider it before we meet here tomorrow evening.

Clemmie[4]

On March 26 Churchill drove from Chequers to Woodford, to open the Sir James Hawkey Memorial Hall, named after his Constituency Chairman and champion of the inter-war years. Clementine Churchill did not feel well enough to accompany him on this cross-country journey. Returning to Chequers that evening, he was saying his farewells on March 27 when he learned that the new Soviet leader, Marshal Bulganin, had spoken favourably of Four-Power talks. At first he did not allow this fact to lead to any change of plan; he would resign on

---

[1] Cabinet Conclusions No. 26 of 1955, 'Secret', 10 Downing Street, 11.30 a.m., 23 March 1955: Cabinet papers, 128/28.

[2] Macmillan diary, 23 March 1955: Macmillan papers.

[3] Letter of 24 March 1955: Mary Soames, *Clementine Churchill*, page 451.

[4] 'Prime Minister from CSC', 'Winston', written at Chequers, 25 March 1955: Churchill papers, 1/50.

April 5 and go at once to Sicily. He had already decided not to take Lord Moran with him on this journey, and on March 28 he explained why:

My dear Charles,

As I mentioned to you the other day it would in my opinion be a mistake for me to inflict upon you the burden of coming out with me to Sicily. At this particular time it would give the appearance that I had resigned through ill-health, which is not true. At the same time there is no doubt that I need a rest and sunshine, so I hope you will sign the very simple paper which the Bank of England requires for an addition to the normal currency. As you may not be familiar with this, I send you the new form which is of course entirely private.

Perhaps you will let me know how many of the minors I ought to take. I thought about two a week. I think it very likely I shall be back during the first week of May and anyhow I am sure you would come to my aid in case anything goes wrong; but I feel quite well thanks to your attention and all I need at present is agreeable occupation and an occasional sight of the sun.[1]

On March 28 Churchill was in the House of Commons to move the motion for an address to the Queen for a statue of Lloyd George. 'Ten years is long enough,' he said, 'to allow partisan passions, whether of hatred or enthusiasm, to cool, and not too long to quench the testimony of contemporary witnesses.' He would not, however, 'conceal' his personal opinion, and he went on to tell the House: 'David Lloyd George was a House of Commons man. He sat here for one constituency for fifty-five years. He gave sparkle to our debates. He guided the House through some of its most critical years, and without the fame and authority of the Mother of Parliaments he could never have rendered his services to the nation.' As for where the monument should be, Churchill added, Lloyd George himself 'might have liked it to be as near this Chamber as possible'.[2]

That evening Churchill dined with R. A. Butler, to discuss the forthcoming Budget. Suddenly, and in conjunction with what Butler said of the economic problems, Marshal Bulganin's favourable comment about a possible Four-Power meeting took on a new light. When Butler had gone, Colville noted on the following day, Churchill told Colville 'that there was a crisis: two serious strikes (newspapers and docks); an important Budget; the date of the General Election to be decided; the Bulganin offer'. Colville added:

---

[1] 'My dear Charles', 'Private', 28 March 1955: Churchill papers, 1/89.

[2] Speech of 28 March 1955: *Hansard*. Lloyd George's statue was unveiled on 18 December 1963 by the then Prime Minister, Sir Alec Douglas-Home. It stands in the Members' Lobby at the entrance to the Chamber. Also at the entrance to the Chamber is a statue of Churchill by Oscar Nemon unveiled on 1 December 1969. The toe of Churchill's statue is shiny: it is said that a Tory member touches the toe before making a speech. Also in the Members' Lobby are statues of Asquith, Attlee, Balfour and Joseph Chamberlain (the only non-Prime Minister).

He could not possibly go at such a moment just to satisfy Anthony's personal hunger for power. If necessary he would call a party meeting and let the party decide. This latter threat was one he had made during the March 11th–15th crisis and I had said that it would indeed make an unhappy last chapter to his biography if it told how he had destroyed the party of which he was the leader. However, I took all this to be late-night fantasy, a rather pathetic indication of the grief with which he contemplated the approach of his political abdication.

It was not. In the morning he was coldly determined not to go. He sent for Butler and despatched him as an emissary to Eden to say that the proposed timetable must be changed. As for me, I preached to Tony Rumbold that for Eden 'Amiability must be the watch-word'. The Prime Minister thrived on opposition and show-downs; but amiability he could never resist.

Tonight he and Lady C dine with the Edens who are giving a supposedly farewell dinner in their honour. During the day AE has at least had the good sense not to say or write anything.[1]

Before the dinner party of March 29, Churchill had an Audience of the Queen. He told her, Colville noted, that 'he thought of putting off his resignation. He had asked her if she minded and she said no!'

The dinner party with Eden had been 'agreeable', Churchill told Colville.[2] At the Cabinet on March 30, however, Churchill 'insisted on discussing the date of an election', Macmillan noted in his diary, and he added: 'If he resigns next week, it is for the new PM to decide. He is still finding it difficult to give up power.' For Eden and Macmillan it still seemed that April 5 was ever to remain a date without certainty; but later on March 30 Eden told Macmillan that Churchill was 'prepared to stick' to the April 5 plan, with his farewell Cabinet to be held on April 3, the day before the farewell dinner for the Queen.[3]

Churchill had come to the conclusion, Colville noted, that 'he did not really think there was much chance of a top-level conference and that alone would be a valid reason for staying'.

At 6.30 that evening Churchill saw Eden and Butler to tell them his decision. He would resign, he said, as planned, in a week's time, on April 5. Before the meeting he told Colville: 'I have been altered and affected by Anthony's amiable manner.' Colville added: 'This proved to me that the advice I had given was right and I am sure that the result, though pathetic, is in the best interests of all.'[4]

---

[1] Colville notes, 29 March 1955: *The Fringes of Power*, pages 704–7.

[2] Colville notes, post 30 March 1955: *The Fringes of Power*, pages 707–9.

[3] Macmillan diary, 30 March 1955: Macmillan papers. Churchill was said to have told Eden, on this occasion: 'Of course, if there is an election I shall stand at Woodford—*probably* as a Conservative'.

[4] Colville notes, written shortly after 30 March 1955: *The Fringes of Power*, pages 707–9.

R. A. Butler later recalled:

Anthony and I were invited into the Cabinet room. Winston made a slip by asking me to sit on his right, but then corrected himself and beckoned to Anthony. We all gazed out over Horse Guards Parade. Then Winston said very shortly, 'I am going and Anthony will succeed me. We can discuss details later.'

The ceremonial was over. We found ourselves in the passage where Anthony and I shook hands.[1]

When the meeting with Eden and Butler was over, Colville commented: 'W was a sad old man.' Churchill asked him to dine with him that night but Colville could not; he had a friend's twenty-first birthday party to go to. 'All he said was,' Colville wrote, '"What an extraordinary game of bezique we had this afternoon. I got a thousand aces the very first trick and yet in the end you rubied me."'[2]

---

[1] R. A. Butler recollections: *The Art of the Possible, The Memoirs of Lord Butler*, pages 176–7.
[2] Colville notes, written shortly after 30 March 1955: *The Fringes of Power*, pages 707–9.

58

Resignation

O N the morning of 31 March 1955, Churchill asked Sir Michael Adeane to inform the Queen that he would resign as Prime Minister on April 5. Adeane replied that same afternoon:

Dear Prime Minister,

The Queen was having her portrait painted this morning but I was able to deliver your message just before luncheon.

Her Majesty said at once that she was most grateful to you telling her privately of your intention and that I was to emphasize in replying to you that she fully understood why it was that when she received you last Tuesday there still seemed to be some uncertainty about the future.

She added that I must tell you that though she recognized your wisdom in taking the decision which you had, she felt the greatest personal regrets and that she would especially miss the weekly audiences which she has found so instructive and, if one can say so of State matters, so entertaining.[1]

On the evening of April 1 Churchill gave a birthday party at 10 Downing Street for his wife; she was seventy years old. 'Winston looked tired and old' was Lord Moran's comment, and he added that it was 'pleasant to see the Attlees at the most intimate family parties at No. 10, and Clemmie kissing Mrs Attlee'.[2] On the following day, a list was made of the numbers of letters received at 10 Downing Street during the week ending April 2:

> 'Lunatics', 76
> Requests for autographs, photographs, 45
> Requests not to retire, 42
> Foreign letters, 33
> Congratulations and good wishes, 30
> On the atom bomb and H-bomb, 21.[3]

[1] 'Dear Prime Minister', 'Secret', Buckingham Palace, 31 March 1955: Churchill papers, 6/4.
[2] Moran diary, 1 April 1955: *The Struggle for Survival*, pages 643–4.
[3] Note: Churchill papers, 6/7.

On April 2 Churchill received an 'Eyes Only, Top Secret' letter from Eisenhower, which had been sent from the White House on March 29. In it Eisenhower urged British support in the struggle against Communism in the Far East. The letter ended:

Two decades ago we had the fatuous hope that Hitler, Mussolini and the Japanese war lords would decide, before we might become personally involved, that they had enough and would let the world live in peace. We saw the result.

Yet the Communist sweep over the world since World War II has been much faster and much more relentless than the 1930 sweep of the dictators. I do believe that all of us must begin to look some of these unpleasant facts squarely in the face and meet them exactly as our Grand Alliance of the 40's met our enemies and vanquished them.

You and I have been through many things where our judgments have not always been as one, but, on my part at least, my admiration and affection for you were never lessened. In this long experience, my hope is rooted that the two of us may bring up some thought or idea that could help us achieve a personal concord that could, in turn, help our two governments act more effectively against Communists everywhere.[1]

On April 3 Churchill dictated his reply. It was typed out on 10 Downing Street notepaper, on the Prime Minister's embossed stationery. It was never sent. But it was among Churchill's last letters as Prime Minister:

My dear Friend,

I have to thank you for your two memorable letters of March 22 and 29. By the time you get this very inadequate reply I shall have resigned my Office as Prime Minister and relinquished my direction of British policy. Anthony Eden and I have long been friends and lately even related by marriage; but quite apart from personal ties I feel it is my duty, as Leader of the Conservative Party, to make sure that my successor has a fair chance of leading the Conservatives to victory at the next Election, which, under the Quinquennial Act, falls at the end of October 1956. The choice of the date is indeed one of extraordinary complication, in to which Luck and Hazard enter on a remarkable scale. I feel that the decision should be taken by the man whose fortunes are governed by the result. It will in many ways be a disaster to most of the causes with which we are both concerned if the Socialist Party in its present feebleness and disarray should again obtain what might be a long lease of power in Britain. I do not feel sure that our national vitality and wisdom would survive the event and the impression it would make on the world. At any rate I did not feel that I ought to overhang the situation unless I were prepared to lead the Party in the Election myself. This at my age I could not undertake to do. Hence I have felt it my duty to resign.

[1] 'Dear Winston', 'Eyes Only—Top Secret', The White House, Washington, 29 March 1955: Churchill papers, 2/217.

To resign is not to retire, and I am by no means sure that other opportunities may not come upon me to serve and influence those causes for which we have both of us worked so long. Of these the first is Anglo-American brotherhood, and the second is the arrest of the Communist menace. They are, I believe, identical.[1]

A newspaper strike made it almost certain that Churchill's resignation would receive no public coverage. But there was one avenue of such coverage, television, which could be used. At the suggestion of Winifred Crum Ewing, head of the Conservative Television and Film Department, Churchill agreed to make a three-minute television test at Conservative Central Office.

The three-minute test showed Churchill at a desk. 'I am sorry to have to descend to this level,' he said, 'but there is no point in refusing to keep pace with the age.' Churchill added: 'It is to one person, one person only, to judge what is to happen to it. I am that one.'

Churchill then recited a poem from *Punch* about the ducks in St James's Park. As he spoke the words of the poem, which he knew by heart, his eyes were closed. When Winifred Crum Ewing went down to Chartwell to show Churchill the result, he remarked: 'I should never have appeared on television.' The film was never shown.[2]

The time had come to arrange for Eden to succeed him both politically and physically. 'The following are my ideas about our changing guard,' Churchill wrote on April 2. Even the Prime Minister's goldfish had to be taken into account:

Cabinet, Tuesday at noon—Parliamentary business and Foreign Affairs, after which I will say what I am going to do. We might then go upstairs to the pillared room and have a photograph taken. There is supposed to be one, Norman Brook says, of every Cabinet.

I shall not attend the House on Tuesday. I am expecting to arrange 4.30 as the time of my Audience. I understand that my Successor will be summoned to the Palace probably about noon on Wednesday, when he will become responsible.

On Wednesday afternoon at 4 p.m. I am having a Staff party for the typists and messengers and some others from No. 10, and a party from Chequers. I shall leave for Chartwell before 6 p.m. Clemmie has various household things to settle, and would be proposing to join me Thursday evening.

I am arranging that the Cabinet Room and offices shall be at my Successor's disposal (I hope yours) if you want a Cabinet, from Thursday onwards. As far as the residential quarters are concerned, it will take about a week to have all our stuff cleared out, and as Easter intervenes, it would seem convenient that Miss Hamblin, my Wife's Secretary, should have till, say,

---

[1] 'My dear Friend', April 1955, marked '? not sent': Churchill papers, 2/217.

[2] 'Churchill's secret test by television', the *Independent*, 30 October 1986; recollections of Humphry Crum Ewing: in conversation with the author, 8 July 1987.

the 20th to do this. Thereafter the whole building will be at your disposal, but I expect you will be a few days getting the house in order before you can move in.

I am going now to Sicily on the 12th. I understand you have been planning a meeting at Chequers for the weekend after this; we have a good deal of stuff of our own to remove from there, but this can be done thereafter. I hope there will be no hurry about the fish, as I have to arrange for their removal, care and reception, which is all a complicated business.[1]

On April 4 Churchill and his wife gave their farewell dinner at 10 Downing Street for the Queen and the Duke of Edinburgh. Among the guests were not only Clement Attlee, Herbert Morrison, and their wives, but also Anne Chamberlain, Neville Chamberlain's widow. Churchill's after-dinner speech that evening was his last as Prime Minister. The notes from which he spoke have survived, set out, as were so many of his speeches, in the 'speech form' or 'psalm form', as his secretariat called it, which he had used for more than half a century:

> Your Royal Highness,
>
> Your Grace,
>
> My Lords, Ladies and Gentlemen.
>
> I have the honour
> 　of proposing a Toast
> 　　wh I used to enjoy drinking
> 　　　during the years
> 　　　　when I was a Cavalry
> 　　　　　　　　　Subaltern
>
> in the Reign
> 　of Your Majesty's
> 　　Great-great-Grandmother,
> Queen Victoria.
>
> Having served in office or in Parlt
> 　under the four Sovereigns
> 　　who hv reigned since those days,
>
> I felt,
>
> with these credentials,
>
> tt in asking
> 　Your Majesty's gracious permission,
>
> I should not be leading
> 　to the creation of a precedent
> 　　wh wd often cause inconvenience.

[1] 'Secretary of State for Foreign Affairs', 2 April 1955: Churchill papers, 6/4.

Madam,

I should like to express
the deep and lively sense
of gratitude
which we

and all your peoples

feel to you
and to His Royal Highness
the Duke of Edinburgh

for all the help and inspiration
we receive
in our daily lives

and which spreads
with ever-growing strength
throughout the British Realm
and the Commonwealth
and Empire.

Never have we needed it more
than in the anxious
and darkling age
through wh we are passing

and which we hope
to help the world to pass.

Never have the august duties
wh fall upon the British Monarchy
been discharged
with more devotion

than in the brilliant opening
of Your Majesty's reign.

We thank God
for the gifts he has bestowed upon us

and vow ourselves anew
to the sacred causes

and wise and kindly way of life
of wh Your Majesty
is the young, gleaming champion.[1]

Churchill then raised his glass to lead his guests in the loyal toast,
'The Queen.'

---

[1] 'PM's Speech at Dinner to The Queen, No. 10 Downing St', 4 April 1955: Churchill papers,
5/57. The letters 'tt' were Churchill's usual speech-form abbreviation for 'that'.

The guests departed, the Queen being escorted to the door, and to her car, by Churchill and his wife.[1] Finally Churchill was alone. 'I went up with Winston to his bedroom,' Colville later recalled. 'He sat on his bed, still wearing his Garter, Order of Merit and knee-breeches. For several minutes he did not speak and I, imagining that he was sadly contemplating that this was his last night at Downing Street, was silent. Then suddenly he stared at me and said with vehemence: "I don't believe Anthony can do it."'[2]

Among the letters of thanks which Lady Churchill received after the dinner party was one from Prince Philip:

Dear Lady Churchill,

This is a most inadequate note of thanks for the perfectly delightful dinner on Monday.

It was such a friendly and happy occasion that I find it hard to realize that it must have been rather a sad moment for you.

I do hope that your holiday in Sicily will do you good and that when you come back your arm will be fully recovered.

Again many thanks for a charming evening.

Yours sincerely,

Philip[3]

At noon on April 5 Churchill held the last Cabinet of his career, almost fifteen years after the first Cabinet of his wartime administration, and almost fifty years since he had first sat in Cabinet. The Cabinet minutes recorded his final words:

The Prime Minister said that he intended to submit his resignation to Her Majesty at an audience that afternoon. His resignation would carry with it the resignation of the whole Administration. Other Ministers need not tender their resignations to The Queen, but they should regard their offices as at the disposal of his successor. Meanwhile they should carry on the necessary administration of their Departments until a new Government was formed. Ministers of Cabinet rank who were not members of the Cabinet would be so informed at a meeting which he was holding later in the day. Junior Ministers would be similarly informed by letter.

The Prime Minister said that it remained for him to wish his colleagues all good fortune in the difficult, but hopeful, situation which they had to face. He trusted that they would be enabled to further the progress already made in rebuilding the domestic stability and economic strength of the United Kingdom and in weaving still more closely the threads which bound together

---

[1] An event witnessed by the author, who had left school three days earlier, and was about to go into the Army as a National Serviceman (on 14 April 1955).

[2] Colville notes, 'Written shortly afterwards, but not dated': *The Fringes of Power*, pages 707–9.

[3] 'Dear Lady Churchill', Buckingham Palace, 6 April 1955: Spencer-Churchill papers.

the countries of the Commonwealth or, as he still preferred to call it, the Empire.

It was Anthony Eden, so soon to succeed Churchill, and so long in waiting for that day, who spoke the valedictory words:

The Foreign Secretary said that his Cabinet colleagues had asked him to speak on this occasion on behalf of them all. It therefore fell to him to express their sense of abiding affection and esteem for the Prime Minister and their pride in the privilege of having served as his colleagues. He himself had enjoyed this privilege for sixteen years, others for varying shorter periods; but all, whatever the length of their service, had the same strong feelings of affection for him. If in a succeeding Government they met with success, this would be largely due to the example which he had shown them: if they did less well, it would be because they had failed to learn from his experience and skill as a statesman. They would remember him always—for his magnanimity, for his courage at all times and for his unfailing humour, founded in his unrivalled mastery of the English language. They would always be grateful for his leadership, and for his friendship, over the years that had passed; and they would hope to enjoy in future his continuing interest and support in their endeavours.[1]

Churchill's final words to those Ministers not in the Cabinet made a strong impact on those who heard them. 'He wished to make two points,' Lord De L'Isle and Dudley later recalled: '"Man is spirit", and "Never be separated from the Americans"'.[2]

One further problem remained to be resolved between Churchill's farewell dinner on April 4 and his resignation. This was the question of whether or not he would be offered a dukedom. His Audience of the Queen had been arranged for April 5. As Jock Colville recalled ten years later, it was he, Colville, who had suggested to Sir Michael Adeane that, in Colville's words:

... when the Prime Minister resigned, since he was quite different from any other Prime Minister, it would be quite appropriate if he were offered a dukedom. To which the reply was that no more dukedoms would ever be given except to Royal personages. However it did seem appropriate. Could I give the undertaking that the Prime Minister would refuse it?

I said I would take some soundings. So on the next possible occasion I asked Sir Winston what would happen if when he resigned the Queen were to offer him a dukedom? To which he said nothing would induce him to accept it. First of all what could he be Duke of? Secondly even if he were Duke of Westerham, what would Randolph be? He could only be Marquis of

[1] Cabinet Conclusions No. 28 of 1955, 'Secret', 10 Downing Street, 12 noon, 5 April 1955: Cabinet papers, 128/28.
[2] Viscount De L'Isle recollections: in conversation with the author, 13 July 1987.

Puddleduck Lane which was the only other possession he had apart from Chartwell. And thirdly, and quite seriously, he wished to die in the House of Commons as Winston Churchill. He therefore told me that even if this un- likely event came to pass he would certainly decline it.

I rushed to the telephone and rang up Sir Michael Adeane and said that he could safely tell the Queen the dukedom could be offered.

Accordingly when Sir Winston went to Buckingham Palace on 5 April 1955, to resign, the dukedom was duly offered.

I was greatly disturbed because as I saw the Prime Minister going off in his frock coat and his top hat and knowing as I did that he was madly in love with the Queen—and this was clear from the fact that his audiences had been dragged out longer and longer as the months went by and very often took an hour and a half, at which I may say racing was not the only topic discussed,—I was rather alarmed that sentimental feelings might indeed make him accept at the last moment. In which case I knew that both the Queen and Sir Michael would be very angry with me for having given this pledge.

When he returned from his audience the first thing I said to him as we sat in the Cabinet room was 'How did it go?' With tears in his eyes he said 'Do you know, the most remarkable thing—she offered to make me a Duke.'

With trepidation I asked what he had said. 'Well you know, I very nearly accepted, I was so moved by her beauty and her charm and the kindness with which she made this offer, that for a moment I thought of accepting. But finally I remembered that I must die as I have always been—Winston Chur- chill. And so I asked her to forgive my not accepting it. And do you know, it's an odd thing, but she seemed almost relieved.' [1]

Churchill declined the dukedom; and the Queen accepted his resigna- tion. She also wrote that day to Lady Churchill, from Buckingham Palace:

Dear Lady Churchill,

This is just a line to try and express our thanks for such a delightful evening at No. 10 last night.

It was a most interesting and friendly party and we enjoyed it all greatly. I hope we did not stay too late and tire you all out completely! Though I don't think it was intentional that your kind invitation to dinner should be a farewell occasion, in fact it could not have been more perfectly arranged, coming just before today's resignation.

I hope you will both now have time for rest and relaxation in the sun in Sicily.

With renewed thanks

Yours sincerely Elizabeth R [2]

Returning to 10 Downing Street, Churchill dictated his own ac- count of his last Audience as Prime Minister:

---

[1] 'Mr Jock Colville: Reminiscences: Stour', 8 June 1965: Randolph Churchill papers.
[2] 'Dear Lady Churchill', Buckingham Palace, 5 April 1955: Spencer-Churchill papers.

I tendered my resignation to The Queen, which Her Majesty accepted. She asked me whether I would recommend a successor and I said I preferred to leave it to Her. She said the case was not a difficult one and that She would summon Sir Anthony Eden.

After some further conversation Her Majesty said She believed that I wished to continue in the Commons but that otherwise She would offer me a Dukedom. I said that I would like to go on in the Commons while I felt physically fit but that if I felt the work was too hard I would be very proud if She chose to reconsider Her proposal.

I expressed my deep gratitude to Her Majesty for Her Kindness.[1]

On the morning of April 6, Churchill received his last document at 10 Downing Street, a note by Anthony Montague Browne about the economies achieved in the Cyprus Headquarters under the most recent set of proposals.[2]

Churchill's second Premiership was over. That afternoon he gave a tea party for the staff at No. 10, about a hundred people in all, Private Secretaries, telephonists, messengers and drivers, and was later, as he left, cheered by the staff who lined both sides of the corridor leading from the Cabinet Room to the front door. Then, for the last time as Prime Minister, he drove away from Downing Street. With him, the newspapers later reported, was 'an unknown woman'. This was Miss Gilliatt, his secretary since 1945. 'I was very sad,' she later recalled. 'I had wished he could die in office.'[3]

On reaching Chartwell that afternoon, Churchill found a small crowd of well-wishers and journalists waiting there to greet him. How did it feel not to be Prime Minister, he was asked by one of the journalists. 'It's always nice to be home,' he replied.[4]

Churchill's resignation had come at the end of the second week of a national newspaper strike; with the result that it obtained neither the news coverage nor the valedictory acclaim which it would otherwise have attracted. From Lord Camrose's son Seymour came a letter to say 'how distressing it has been that the *Daily Telegraph* has not been able to pay the immense tribute to yourself which we should have liked to have done. My father would have been very sad.'[5] 'I am so

---

[1] Undated note: Churchill papers, 2/197.

[2] 'Sir Winston Churchill', initialled 'AMB', 6 April 1955: Churchill papers, 6/4. Of the existing Army and Air Force personnel of 958, a total of 245 were to be cut, once the Army had put aside the 'temporary increase' needed 'to deal with the stockpiling of equipment moved from the Canal Zone, and a building programme covering Jordan, Libya and Cyprus'.

[3] Elizabeth Gilliatt recollections: in conversation with the author, 9 July 1987.

[4] Mary Soames, *Clementine Churchill*, page 453.

[5] 'Dear Sir Winston', 7 April 1955: Churchill papers, 2/481A.

sorry that the *Daily Telegraph* tribute was never published,' Churchill replied. 'It would I am sure have gone far beyond what I deserve. But that might have been expected by the oldest correspondent of the *Daily Telegraph* alive.'[1]

On April 8 Churchill received his first letter from Anthony Eden written from 10 Downing Street, and telling him that the General Election was likely to be on May 26. It was the deterioration of Britain's financial position, Eden explained, that was 'the disagreeable reality which pushes us towards a May Election', and he added: 'As you know I have been tempted to try to show that we can be a good Administration for at least six months before appealing to the Country but I am increasingly compelled to take account of these distasteful economic factors.'[2]

At Chartwell, on April 7, Churchill began to work again on the 1939 proof sets of *A History of the English-Speaking Peoples*, chapter 1 of which opened in 55 BC. Thus, within forty-eight hours of his retirement, he had found a new focus of activity. He also asked Miss Sturdee to rejoin his staff in order to help him answer the many hundreds of letters which he had received on his retirement. Then, on April 12, his sixth day of retirement, he left Chartwell for a two-week holiday in Sicily with his wife. 'This is just to send the warmest love from us both to you & to Clemmie,' Anthony Eden wrote from Chequers, 'with every good wish for the journey and for sunshine and a happy holiday. . . .'[3]

As he boarded the plane for Sicily, Churchill was handed a letter. It was from the Queen, written in her own hand at Windsor Castle, and read:

My dear Sir Winston,

I need not tell you how deeply I felt your resignation last Tuesday, nor how severely I miss, and shall continue to miss, your advice and encouragement.

My confidence in Anthony Eden is complete and I know he will lead the Country on to great achievements, but it would be useless to pretend that either he or any of those successors who may one day follow him in office will ever, for me, be able to hold the place of my first Prime Minister, to whom both my husband and I owe so much and for whose wise guidance during the early years of my reign I shall always be so profoundly grateful.

In thanking you for what you have done I must confine myself to my own experience, to the comparatively short time—barely more than three years—

---

[1] 'My dear Seymour', 24 April 1955: Churchill papers, 2/481. Churchill's first article for the *Daily Telegraph* had appeared on 6 October 1897 ('On the Indian Frontier, by a Young Officer').

[2] 'My dear Winston', 'Private and Personal', 10 Downing Street, 8 April 1955: Churchill papers, 2/216.

[3] 'My dear Winston', 11 April 1955: Churchill papers, 2/216.

during which I have been on the throne and you have been my First Minister. If I do not mention the years before and all their momentous events, in which you took a leading part, it is because you know already of the high value my father set on your achievements, and you are aware that he joined his people and the peoples of the whole free world in acknowledging a debt of deep and sincere thankfulness.

During the more recent years you have had to face the Cold War and with it threats and dangers which are more awe-inspiring than any which you have had to contend with before, in war or peace. By your foresight and by your shaping of our destiny you have, if it were possible to do so, enhanced the admiration in which you are held, not only here but throughout much of the world, and you know that you will take with you into retirement a deep fund of affectionate goodwill.

For my part I know that in losing my constitutional adviser I gain a wise counsellor to whom I shall not look in vain for help and support in the days which lie ahead. May there be many of them.

My husband and I so much enjoyed the dinner party at No. 10 Downing St last Monday—neither of us will ever forget it.

We send our best wishes to you and to Lady Churchill for your time in Sicily and we look forward to seeing you on your return and frequently in the future.

With my deepest gratitude for your great services to my Country and to myself,

I am, yours very sincerely

Elizabeth R [1]

Churchill replied to the Queen's letter on April 18, from Sicily:

Madam,

I was honoured and cheered by Your Majesty's most gracious letter, which was given to me as I boarded the aeroplane for Sicily. I have since read it often with renewed pleasure and it will always be one of my most treasured possessions.

I deem myself extremely fortunate to have been Your Majesty's adviser in the first three years of what, I pray, may be a long and glorious epoch in our history. I have tried throughout to keep Your Majesty squarely confronted with the grave and complex problems of our time. Very soon after taking office as First Minister I realized the comprehension with which Your Majesty entered upon the august duties of a modern Sovereign and the store of knowledge which had already been gathered by an upbringing both wise and lively. This enabled Your Majesty to understand as it seemed by instinct the relationships and the balances of the British constitution so deeply cherished by the mass of the Nation and by the strongest and most stable forces in it. I became conscious of the Royal resolve to serve as well as rule, and indeed to rule by serving.

I felt also the impact of a new personality upon our unfolding history. Our

[1] 'My dear Sir Winston', 11 April 1955: Squerryes Lodge Archive.

Island no longer holds the same authority or power that it did in the days of Queen Victoria. A vast world towers up around it and after all our victories we could not claim the rank we hold were it not for the respect for our character and good sense and the general admiration not untinged by envy for our institutions and way of life. All this has already grown stronger and more solidly founded during the opening years of the present Reign, and I regard it as the most direct mark of God's favour we have ever received in my long life that the whole structure of our new formed Commonwealth has been linked and illuminated by a sparkling presence at its summit.

I am most deeply grateful for all that Your Majesty writes in approval of my work and conduct during those opening years of Your Reign, and for all the kindness with which I and my Wife have been treated by Your Majesty and The Duke of Edinburgh. His Royal Highness's remarkable qualities are making an ever-deepening impression upon the minds of people of all classes and Parties.

I feel that Your Majesty is right to put complete confidence in Anthony Eden, who has given proof of his character and capacity in great office over so many years. There was no-one to whom I should have found it easier to hand over my duties. I shall do all I can to support him in his difficult and anxious task.

Churchill ended his letter with a description of his life in retirement:

The historical atmosphere of Syracuse grows perceptibly upon me and my companions here as the days pass. Our hotel rises out of the sinister quarries in which six thousand Athenian prisoners of war were toiled and starved to death in 413 BC, and I am trying to paint a picture of a cavern's mouth near the listening gallery whose echoes brought secrets to the ears of Dionysius. All this is agreeable to the mental and psychological processes of laying down direct responsibility for the guidance of great affairs and falling back upon the comforting reflection 'I have done my best'.[1]

---

[1] 'Madam', 18 April 1955: Squerryes Lodge Archive.

Part Four
Final Decade

59

In Retirement

FOR two weeks, Churchill and his wife stayed at the Villa Politi at Syracuse. 'I am glad to be freed from responsibility which was not in every case accompanied by power,' he wrote to Bernard Baruch on 14 April 1955, 'and have not yet made any plans concerning the new freedom. It is very nice to reach a milestone in the journey on which I may sit and rest.' Churchill added: 'Of course all our plans are affected by the uncertainty about the Election, which I expect to go home to fight in the Woodford constituency in the first week of May, when I imagine the dissolution will be announced, but all is still unsettled, as it ought to be in any well-constructed human society.' [1]

Churchill had declined Lord Moran's offer to accompany him to Sicily. With him instead he took two friends, Lord Cherwell, whom he had known for thirty-five years, and Jock Colville, who had been a member of his Private Office for more than eight years of the past fifteen. One day, in conversation with Cherwell and Colville, Churchill expressed his deep regret that he had not taken up, while he was Prime Minister from 1951 to 1955, the recommendations made by Cherwell and others concerning Britain's failure to produce technologists in sufficient numbers. Cherwell and Colville replied that it was still not too late, and the idea was born of an institution in Britain similar to the Massachusetts Institute of Technology in the United States, at which Churchill had spoken in 1949. It was Colville who offered to raise the money; on his return to England, he began the long and at times almost daunting process which was to lead, within five years, to the establishment of a new college, Churchill College, at Cambridge. [2]

On April 24, a few days before returning to England, Churchill set out for his wife the secretarial scheme which he envisaged for his new

[1] 'My dear Bernie', Villa Politi, Syracuse, Sicily, 14 April 1955: Churchill papers, 2/210.
[2] Colville notes, undated (written in the summer of 1955): *The Fringes of Power*, pages 707–9.

life in retirement while remaining a Member of Parliament. His note began with a philosophic quotation:

Schopenhauer has said 'We look upon the present as something to be put up with while it lasts, and as a means of helping us towards our goal. Most people when they get to the end of their life find they have lived throughout ad interim.' Such is the view of the pessimistic philosopher.

When we get home on Tuesday night we shall soon find ourselves in the General Election. I shall ask Miss Sturdee and Mrs Shillingford to help till the end of May. (Mrs Shillingford anyhow does the work of the Constituency.) If an additional shorthand writer is required to typewrite speeches many good ones are available. It is necessary to wait till the result of the Election is known before making plans. If we win, I shall hope for a long spell abroad. If, on the contrary, we are beaten, a new and more difficult situation will arise.

We really must wait and see what happens. Meanwhile Miss Hamblin will, I hope, continue to do exactly what she is doing now. I was hoping Miss Wood could give me half her time.[1]

After the present deluge of correspondence has been disposed of, and time does a lot, I must look out upon a prospect of a vast reduction in letters which have to be answered and a continuing decline in quantity. The 'English-Speaking Peoples', which is to be my main work, does not require new composition but is almost entirely revision and done by hand.

I am quite agreeable to a junior being engaged.[2]

On his last day in Sicily, in thanking Dean Acheson for his letter of good wishes, Churchill referred to 'the important work we did together in the baffling years that followed our victory'.[3] 'Being an old and old-fashioned animal,' he wrote to Earl De La Warr that day, 'I am no enthusiast for the TV age, in which I fear mass thought and actions will be taken too much charge of by machinery, both destructive and distracting.'[4]

To the Duchess of Kent, Churchill also sent thanks for her letter 'on my departure from power', and he added: 'The red lilies which you sent me when I was ill in 1942 have brought a healthy and buoyant posterity. This year was, I think the best crop we have yet had. They always remind me of Your Royal Highness's kindness.'[5]

Another letter which Churchill dictated on his last day in Sicily was to Lord Rothermere, who had been one of the Press Lords most determined not to give in to Trade Union pressure, even if it meant, as it did, the newspaper strike which had, among other ills, prevented

[1] Miss Heather Wood was Clementine Churchill's London secretary.
[2] 'To CSC from WSC', 24 April 1955: Churchill papers, 1/55.
[3] Letter of 27 April 1955: Churchill papers, 2/179.
[4] 'My dear Buck', 27 April 1955: Churchill papers, 2/184.
[5] 'Madam', 27 April 1955: Churchill papers, 2/197.

national coverage of Churchill's resignation. Churchill told Rother-mere:

I am so glad that the National Press has resumed its strong and active life. I missed it very much, but I feel sure you were right in the course you took. I am sure that the spectacle of four Socialists, at the head of seven hundred unskilled, highly paid men, being able to inflict this vast and far-reaching injury upon the nation with its cruel hardships on many sides, cannot be reconciled with any process of democracy. I believe it has made a deep impression upon the nation, and I hope the new Parliament will consider basically the new problems which have come to us as the examples of the malignant activities of Communism.

'We are having beautiful weather in Sicily on the day of our depar-ture,' Churchill added. 'Otherwise the gleams of sunshine have been few and far between. The Sicilians regarded our disappointment with characteristic shrewdness, "We are very glad to see him here, but what a pity he should have thought it necessary to bring his English weather with him." Now I expect they will say, "Thank God he has taken it away."'[1]

On his return to London, Churchill stayed for a few days at the Hyde Park Hotel, in Room 708 looking down over Hyde Park. There, on April 27, he showed his doctor two of the paintings he had done in Sicily. 'I painted with great vigour,' he told Lord Moran. 'What mat-tered was that I found I could concentrate for three hours—I got interested in it, and was always late for luncheon. I played a lot of cards with Jock.'[2]

'Welcome home,' Harold Macmillan, the new Foreign Secretary, telegraphed to Churchill that day.[3]

Among the letters waiting for Churchill in London was one from R. A. Butler, who had remained as Chancellor of the Exchequer in Eden's Government. 'It was very nice of you to write to me in all the hurry of the Budget days,' Churchill replied, 'and give me such a good account.' The only point on which he would have differed, Churchill added, 'was the half-measure about the purchase tax easements in the cotton trade. Now that you cannot think of a quota any more because of India's favourable reactions to its disciplinary menace, would it not be possible to go the whole hog—or perhaps it would be better to say the "whole little pig"—about the purchase tax? This is my only sugges-tion.'

Churchill's letter ended: 'I hope we shall meet soon. I am not coming to the House during this Parliament. Everybody feels you

[1] 'My dear Esmond', 'Private', 27 April 1955: Churchill papers, 2/197.
[2] Moran diary, 27 April 1955: *The Struggle for Survival*, pages 652–3.
[3] Telegram, 27 April 1955: Churchill papers, 1/90.

have been a pillar of strength to my Administration. I should like to record once again my warmest thanks to you for your services.' [1]

Among the hundreds of well-wishers who had written to Churchill at the end of his Premiership was Sir Charles Taylor. Twenty years earlier, Taylor had been one of the young Conservative MPs who had supported Churchill over India. 'I well remember,' Churchill replied, 'our association in the effort to keep India within the circle of the Crown,' and he added: 'Nothing that has happened since has made me regret that we did our best.' [2]

Having accompanied Churchill to Sicily, to help guide the new plan of work and secretarial help, and to set the first steps towards what was to become Churchill College, Jock Colville now said good-bye to Churchill for the last time in an official capacity. On April 29 he wrote from his home in the country to the man in both of whose Premierships he had served with ever-increasing responsibilities:

My Dear Winston,
Since you bid me address you like this, I take you at your word.
First let me thank you for your kindness in taking me to Sicily, at no cost to myself. Though it is not an island for which I have developed any notable affection, I certainly have a very highly developed one for those I went with and my memories are not of the grey skies but of Lady Churchill and you, with whom the North Pole or Katmandu would be enjoyable.
But what I really want to say, and that is much more difficult, is that my official association with you, which began fifteen years ago, has meant more to me in every way than anything else ever has or can in my future career. To have been at Downing Street in the summer and autumn of 1940 is something on its own, and yet no month or year since then, whether during the war or in your second administration, has ever seemed an anticlimax to those great days; and I suspect I shall become a famous bore on the subject to my descendants as the years go by, because it will always seem to me that the years I spent with you were the really important years of my life.

'I am coming up to London for the night on Tuesday,' Colville added, 'and will call upon you either that afternoon or on Wednesday morning to pay my respects and to be of any service.' [3]

On April 30 the Royal Academy summer exhibition opened, with two Churchill paintings among the latest showings: 'Bottlescape' and 'Sunset at Roehampton'. It was the ninth successive year in which his talents as a painter had been open to public view. [4]

---

[1] 'My dear Rab', signed 'Your sincere friend', 28 April 1955: Churchill papers, 2/481 A.

[2] 'My dear Charles', 27 April 1955: Charles Taylor papers. Taylor had entered Parliament in 1935, at the age of twenty-five. Knighted in 1954, he remained in Parliament until 1974.

[3] 'My dear Winston', 29 April 1955: Churchill papers, 1/66.

[4] 'List of Work Exhibited at the Royal Academy by Sir Winston Churchill, Hon. RA': Royal Academy archive.

Back in Britain, Churchill found a political ferment from which he was excluded. 'Jock was upset,' noted Lord Moran on May 4, 'because Winston had come back anxious to help in the election, only to find he was not wanted.' Colville told Moran that Churchill 'had not been asked to do any broadcasting'. According to Norman Brook, it was Eden who, while 'quite friendly' to Churchill, 'didn't want to be regarded as Winston's nominee for the Premiership'.[1]

Churchill had, however, been invited to make a number of speeches, including one for his son-in-law Christopher Soames at Bedford, one at Walthamstow and another at Woodford. On May 4 he wrote to Lord Rothermere to enlist his help. 'I have for a long time been impressed,' Churchill wrote, 'with the Leading Articles in the *Daily Mail*, which I am told are written by Mr Murray. I wondered whether he would care to give me privately a little help in one or two of the speeches I have to make.' Churchill added: 'A little reinforcement would be most welcome.'[2]

'This is my nineteenth contest,' Churchill wrote to Bernard Baruch on May 8, 'so that I cannot say it is either a novelty or a pleasure.'[3] 'He does not share Jock's resentment that he was not invited to take part in the Tory campaign on the air,' Lord Moran noted three days later. 'Quite the contrary, for he thinks it very reasonable that the broadcasts should be reserved for "responsible ministers". He talked about a good Conservative majority that would give Anthony a fine start.'[4]

One champion of Churchill as the election campaign progressed was the *Manchester Guardian*. In its leading article on May 11, headed 'The Man Who Was', it took Eden to task 'for so pointedly ignoring the man whom he succeeded and to whom personally he owed so much. Sir Winston had been dropped as if he had become a liability; there was not a single reference to him in Sir Anthony's early speeches.' After all, the newspaper asked, 'would Sir Anthony be Prime Minister at all if Sir Winston had not nursed him for the succession?' And it went on to give its own explanation of 'this lack of generosity. Sir Anthony had to show himself as the new, strong, self-sufficient leader standing on his own feet'.[5]

Churchill did not belittle Eden's point of view: 'One has to think of

[1] Moran diary, 4 May 1955: *The Struggle for Survival*, pages 653–4.

[2] 'My dear Esmond', 4 May 1955: Churchill papers, 2/137. George McIntosh Murray, a *Daily Mail* leader writer, died in 1970, at the age of seventy. Churchill continued to be helped in his speeches by George Christ, who went to see him on May 7, May 14 and May 16 (Churchill Engagements Calendar, May 1955: Churchill papers).

[3] Letter of 8 May 1955: Churchill papers, 2/210.

[4] Moran diary, 11 May 1955: *The Struggle for Survival*, pages 654–5.

[5] *Manchester Guardian*, 11 May 1955.

one's successor,' he wrote to his friend Major-General Sir Hugh Tudor, in explaining why he had resigned when he did, 'and make sure that he has a fair chance—both for his own sake and that of his party'.[1] 'I think things are going well,' Churchill wrote to Beaverbrook on May 12, and he added: 'I am so glad about the Big Four talks.'[2]

There was a break from politics on May 15, when Alan Hodge lunched with Churchill for their first discussions since Churchill had left Downing Street, on the renewed work now needed to revise and polish *A History of the English-Speaking Peoples*. Churchill was to enjoy Hodge's company, and that of his wife Jane, until his last years. On one occasion, when Hodge made rather heavy weather of reaching forty, Churchill commented: 'You will find being eighty a more interesting experience.' For the Hodge family this became a watchword, as did Churchill's recommendation of cream, because it 'cushions the nerve ends'.[3]

Speaking at Woodford on May 16, Churchill stressed how, since October 1951, 'From the brink of national bankruptcy we advanced to a greater prosperity than we have ever known before.' He also spoke scathingly of Attlee's call for a reduction in the length of National Service. 'Fancy,' he said, 'at this time, when all hopes are centred on the forthcoming conference with Russia, when we know that the strength of Britain is that she seeks peace for its own sake and not merely to avoid the burdens or dangers for which duty calls; fancy, when the meeting of the Big Four at the summit holds the first place in all our thoughts and hearts, the Leader of the Socialist Party feeling himself compelled to try to gain popularity in his Party and votes in the election by saying something which might give the impression to the Communist world that Britain is on the run.'

The aim of the Four-Power Conference was 'a reduction of armaments fair and square all round', including the call-up period. Nothing would be more likely to make that meeting fail 'than for Britain to go to such a conference whining that she cannot bear the expense or burden'.

It was two years ago 'almost to a day', Churchill pointed out, that he had spoken, as both Prime Minister and acting Foreign Secretary, in favour of a summit meeting with Stalin's successors. He con-

---

[1] 'My dear Hugh', May 1955: Churchill papers, 2/201.

[2] 'My dear Max', 12 May 1955: Beaverbrook papers. The Big Four talks, between the British, American, French and Soviet Foreign Ministers, were held in Geneva in July and August 1955.

[3] Jane Aiken Hodge recollections: letter to the author, 6 July 1987. More than a year had past since Alan Hodge had begun work, corresponding from his office at *History Today* in Bracken House and working at his home in Wimbledon.

gratulated Eden and his Government on the 'good fortune' of their efforts to bring about 'the policy for which I have faithfully striven'. Eisenhower's earlier rejection of the summit plan had been overcome. Britain, France and the United States would go to the meeting 'strong and united, seeking the peace of the world, the welfare of all mankind and that period of relaxed tension, disarmament, and all-round prosperity which is within our reach and may soon be within our grasp'.

Churchill ended this, his first public speech since his resignation as Prime Minister:

I have been a lifelong opponent of Communism which I am convinced is a fallacious philosophy, fatal to individual and democratic liberty and imposing itself by the tyrannical rule, either of dictators or oligarchies working through a numerous hierarchy of officials or would-be officials. But this is an internal issue for the Russian people to settle for themselves.

At this juncture, the British electors have the great opportunity of casting their votes in favour of the sincere effort for a friendly way of living between States great and small which has now to be made and nations all over the world are waiting on tenterhooks to see if Britain will rise to the occasion.

In this terrible twentieth century, our country has played an honourable and famous part. Britain is regarded as being territorially unambitious, wise, and sober and, above all, morally and physically fearless and unconquerable. Let us make sure we do not cast away by casual or careless behaviour the reputation upon which both our influence in the world and our safety depend.[1]

On the following day, May 17, Churchill spoke at Bedford in support of his son-in-law Christopher Soames. Speaking of the new situation created by the hydrogen bomb, Churchill told his son-in-law's potential electors: 'This is no time for panic. It is indeed the moment for calm, prudent, clear-headed, resolute behaviour. Above all, this is the time for talking things out in a fair and friendly manner with other people who have the same, or indeed far greater dangers to face than we have.' Churchill added: 'I am for a top-level conference at the Summit. I have worked for it for two years. Let us do our best for our fellow-men, and let us put our trust in God. All will come right.'[2]

'Thank you so much for coming to our meeting,' Christopher Soames telegraphed to Hyde Park Gate later that day. 'Everyone is rejoicing at its success and you gave new life to our workers and supporters.'[3]

---

[1] Speech of 16 May 1955: Randolph S. Churchill (editor), *The Unwritten Alliance*, pages 251–6.

[2] Speech of 17 May 1955: Randolph S. Churchill (editor), *The Unwritten Alliance*, pages 257–61.

[3] Telegram received 18 May 1955: Churchill papers, 2/137.

Churchill now decided to challenge an assertion which was being made by Attlee, that production had risen considerably faster under the previous Labour Government than under the Conservatives. Churchill sought R. A. Butler's advice on how to answer this, and received the answer from Butler's Private Secretary, Robert Armstrong. 'The period of the Labour Government's term of office,' Armstrong wrote, 'and particularly the earlier years of it, covered the period of de-mobilisation and restrictions, when there was a large return of man-power into industry, and switch from defence to civil production. It would therefore have been not merely surprising but disgraceful if there had not been a considerable increase in production in those years.'

Although, under the Conservatives, production fell in 1952, the causes of this fall, Armstrong pointed out, were 'inherent in the econ-omic crisis which the present Government found when it came into office'. By the end of 1952 inflation had been checked, the balance of payments strengthened, and production brought back on its upward trend. Since then, Armstrong noted, 'production has been rising by $6\frac{1}{2}\%$ a year, which is just as good as what was achieved by the Labour Government'.[1]

On May 19 Churchill spoke at Walthamstow, a constituency in which the Labour candidate had won in October 1951 because a Liber-al candidate had split the vote.[2] The defeated Conservative was John Harvey, a former Chairman of the Young Conservatives in Churchill's own nearby constituency. Liberals, Churchill declared, should not 'sacrifice the fundamental principles of Liberalism in upholding the rights of the individual against the State' by so using their vote 'as to send a Socialist candidate to Parliament'.[3]

'Your visit to Walthamstow tonight,' Harvey telegraphed, 'was of the greatest possible value and is sincerely appreciated by us all.'[4]

On May 23 Churchill spoke once more in his own constituency, warning the electors of the dangers of apathy. 'Do not be lulled with a false sense of security,' he said, 'by the broad sense of agreement which we feel exists among our fellow-countrymen, or think in terms of mass

[1] 'Sir Winston', 17 May 1955: Churchill papers, 2/135. From 1970 to 1975 Armstrong was Principal Private Secretary to the Prime Minister, from 1979 Secretary of the Cabinet, and from 1983 Head of the Home Civil Service. He was knighted in 1978, and retired with a peerage at the end of 1987.

[2] The Labour victory had been by 1,020 votes. A total of 2,814 votes had been cast for the Liberals. The Conservative candidate had received 18,016 and the Labour candidate 19,036 votes. In 1955 John Harvey won the seat for the Conservatives.

[3] Speech of 19 May 1955: Randolph S. Churchill (editor), *The Unwritten Alliance*, pages 262–5. Recording: BBC Written Archives Centre, Library No. LP 22109.

[4] Telegram received 20 May 1955: Churchill papers, 2/137.

effects, averages, and Gallup Polls.' Every man or woman who had a vote was, he said 'responsible for recording it according to what he really believes is for the nation's good. Apathy, complacency, illness, chatter or indifference may often be faults. On Thursday they will be crimes.'[1]

This was Churchill's last speech of the campaign. Two days later he wrote to Sir Norman Brook: 'It is very agreeable to feel that the election will be over in forty-eight hours. I think we have got a very good chance of winning a working majority.'[2] 'I am looking forward to the end of the Election,' Churchill wrote to Bernard Baruch on Polling Day. 'Although I have not taken a full part in it,' he added, 'I have found the work quite sufficient.' If the Conservatives were to gain 'a majority of fifty or more', as he hoped, 'I propose to take a good long rest at Chartwell, and then perhaps in the autumn I shall try some painting somewhere in the South of France'. Churchill's letter ended: 'I have at the moment a great desire to stay put and do nothing.'[3]

The election results were a triumph for the Conservatives, who obtained a majority of fifty-nine over all other Parties. Unlike the Election of 1951, where the actual Labour vote had been larger than that of the Conservative victors, the Conservatives now polled an absolute majority: 13,286,569 votes as against 12,404,970 for Labour. 'This big vote must be gratifying to you,' Lord Beaverbrook wrote to Churchill on May 27, and he added: 'The result is due to your wise & far seeing foreign policy & your sound administration at home.'[4]

Also on May 27, Sir Norman Brook wrote to Churchill from the Cabinet Office:

Dear Sir Winston,
    You have been much in my thoughts during this Election, and I should like to send you my sincere congratulations on its result. For it is a most remarkable testimony to the record and achievement of your Government over the past $3\frac{1}{2}$ years. The real issue was whether the people were content with the Government they had had. And it is very evident that they were. The drop in the Labour vote is surely significant. I am sure you must be gratified by the way things have gone.
    I have not forgotten my promise to keep you informed of what goes on. During the Election nothing much has happened in Cabinet circles: but now that Government is about to be resumed, I shall have things to tell you.[5]

[1] Speech of 23 May 1955: *The Times*, 24 May 1955. Recording: BBC Written Archives Centre, Library No. LP 22109.
[2] Letter of 25 May 1955: Churchill papers, 2/184.
[3] 'My dear Bernie', 26 May 1955: Churchill papers, 2/210.
[4] 'My dear Winston', 27 May 1955: Churchill papers, 2/137.
[5] 'Dear Sir Winston', 27 May 1955: Churchill papers, 2/181.

'You certainly have a right to be proud of the Election result,' Harold Macmillan wrote from the Foreign Office on May 31. 'It was a wonderful tribute to the success of your last administration.' During the past three and a half years, Macmillan added, despite 'such a weak Parliamentary position', with so many internal and external difficulties, 'under your leadership, we got through triumphantly'.[1]

Churchill's mood after the Election was benign. On May 29, at Chartwell, Lord Moran recorded Miss Gilliatt's comment: 'He has been so good tempered. Even when he had three speeches on his hands and we were looking out for storms, there was never a cross word. You know, Lord Moran, how he dislikes a new secretary. Now he has two, and he has been so sweet to them. This morning I was unpunctual, but when I said I was sorry, well, you heard how kind he was.'[2]

Churchill's two new secretaries were Miss Doreen Pugh and Miss Gillian Maturin. It was intended that they should remain until the correspondence generated by the Election had cleared, a matter, it was thought, of three or four weeks. In the event, Miss Maturin stayed for three and a half years and Miss Pugh for nearly ten. Both girls were amazed, as Lord Moran had been, by Churchill's mood. Both realized, as Miss Pugh later recalled, 'how shattering it was for him to retire. We were both overcome', she added, 'by how sweet he was.'[3]

On May 30, at Chartwell, Churchill was in a reflective mood, and a kindly one, as Lord Moran noted:

. . . he spoke in loving praise of Mary and of her record in the war. It had been a great happiness to him to watch her lovely family growing up at Chartwell. He hoped Christopher would be given office; he would run a department perfectly well.

He spoke of a British Butterfly Society.

'It would aim at increasing their numbers, and it would educate young people to be kind to them. When I was a small boy at school we were given nets and encouraged to massacre butterflies. When they were caught they were pinned on a board, and boys competed with boys in the number of species on their board. There were Tortoiseshells and Red Admirals and Peacocks. Something, too, could be done about suitable plants for the caterpillars.'

He looked at the budgerigar perched on my fingers.

'Out of that small body is produced the mechanism that made all those feathers in that pattern. All the machinery in the world could not do that.'[4]

---

[1] Letter of 31 May 1955: Churchill papers, 2/220.
[2] Moran diary, 29 May 1955: *The Struggle for Survival*, pages 657–8.
[3] Doreen Pugh recollections: in conversation with the author, 18 June 1987.
[4] Moran diary, 30 May 1955: *The Struggle for Survival*, pages 659–60.

While at Chartwell, Churchill worked each day on the corrections to his *A History of the English-Speaking Peoples*, sending his amendments to Alan Hodge to check, and then to the printer. 'Please look at it over the weekend,' he wrote on May 26 of the second chapter of Volume 1, 'and make sure it is with the printers as soon as possible.' Churchill added: 'We can discuss the outstanding points later on. I should be glad of any comments in the meantime.'[1] That same day, Churchill sent Hodge a note on a point that was troubling him:

Page 6 and its neighbours seem to me worthy of expansion. Is it to be suggested that William knew what he was doing and planned a balanced society, or did it all simply happen as the result of his actions? Was he a man capable of comprehending these issues, or did he simply try to build up his own power? Was there an aim? Was there a design? Or did it simply work out that way?

'I should like to talk it over with you,' Churchill continued, 'and perhaps you will let me know if there is any interesting literature upon the subject. I do not remember who helped me on this period sixteen years ago. Perhaps Bill Deakin will remember. I should write to him if you thought that would help.'[2]

Five days later, Churchill told Lord Moran:

'This morning I did three hours on the book. Oh, it was simple, just rearrangement, and picking out an unnecessary passage here and there. It's thinking and composing I find difficult.'

Ringing for a secretary, he said he would like to see a list of his horses. For a long time he stood looking over the Weald, his eye feasting on the different shades of green in the evening light. At last he turned to me and said: 'I bought Chartwell for that view.'[3]

A strike of railway engine drivers and firemen had begun on May 29; so serious was the strike in disrupting the movement of food, and especially of meat, that a search had begun for National Servicemen who might be able to drive the trains. On May 30 Eden wrote to Churchill:

My dear Winston,
I am getting a little sunshine at Chequers today. Until now I have had to devote all my time to the railways dispute.
First let me thank you again for all that you did in the Election. I think that the result has fully justified the decision to hold it now. I have not forgotten that you were in favour of that decision.

---

[1] 'My dear Hodge', 26 May 1955: Churchill papers, 4/27.
[2] 'Note', 26 May 1955: Churchill papers, 4/27.
[3] Moran diary, 31 May 1955: *The Struggle for Survival*, page 660.

The strike situation both in the docks and on the railways is very disturbing. We shall have to try to find some ways of preventing these inter-union squabbles being carried to these lengths. At the same time we must try to carry the Trade Union movement with us. This should be possible since the TUC are very properly extremely worried themselves. Unhappily their authority is limited.

We are taking the necessary emergency measures and a State of Emergency will be proclaimed and the necessary Regulations made tomorrow. These Regulations have to be laid before Parliament and approved within seven days, and for this reason and also because Parliament will want to discuss the situation if the strike goes on, I fear we shall have to bring forward the formal Opening of Parliament and The Queen's Speech to Friday, June 10. We shall be discussing this with the Opposition Leaders tomorrow. This unfortunately gives us less time to prepare The Queen's Speech and we are at work upon it this week.

I am not thinking of reconstructing the Government at all for the present. For one thing I haven't time, and it might be better to make changes just before the Summer Recess so as to have the new team well in the saddle when Parliament resumes in the Autumn.

Our exchanges about the Four-Power Conference are continuing. The President has suggested that the top-level meeting should be held either around July 20 or towards the end of August. The latter date would give more time for preparation and make it more easy to have a rather longer meeting but we do not want to appear to be holding back. The French seem to prefer August to July.

Eden's letter continued:

I have of course been very happy to include in my Birthday Honours recommendations the names which you sent me from Sicily. The only exception is the Prof. You know how much I like him and that I value all the help which he has given us but I am not making many recommendations for peerages and none for any award higher than a barony. You gave the Prof a CH only two years ago and he is still helping us in the atomic world and indeed in other ways. I will be prepared to consider him again for a Viscountcy a little later.[1]

I should have been happy to recommend Miss Davies[2] for a DBE, but she herself has asked that this recommendation should not be made, since she feels herself amply rewarded by the CBE, with which her predecessor, Miss Watson, retired at the end of the war. It is of course a source of deep and

---

[1] On April 21 Churchill had written to Eden from Sicily to ask him to propose to the Queen, for the Birthday Honours List, that Lord Cherwell be made a Viscount. 'He has given great services to the State,' Churchill wrote, 'and as a Cabinet Minister he took no salary. He has no heir.' Churchill added that he had 'already mentioned' Lord Cherwell's name to the Queen ('My dear Anthony', 'Confidential', 21 April 1955: Squerryes Lodge Archive.) Cherwell was created a Viscount in 1956.

[2] In 1939 Neville Chamberlain's closest adviser, Sir Horace Wilson, had his own secretary at 10 Downing Street, Miss Gwen Davies. She continued to work for Churchill throughout the Second World War and again from 1951 to 1955 (having also worked for Clement Attlee from 1945 to 1951).

continuing pleasure to her to know that you wished her to be recommended for this signal honour.

Clarissa and I send our love to you both, and hope that you will come and have a meal with us when you are next in London.[1]

Churchill replied to Eden on the following day:

Firmness in the strike is vital. It can only be based on patience at the outset. The national response may be overwhelming. You are indeed wise to try to get the TUC with you. A few days more or less should be borne. The timing of the strike by its leaders so as to hit the holiday makers will be judged very cruel. Personally, I have always had a great liking for engine drivers, and am astonished at their behaviour. Perhaps they are pained themselves. Increased tension may be a necessary phase.

I did not like the idea of a Christmas strike, but now the weather is less severe and it should be faced. I am sure you will be supported. Of course, there are great numbers of potential volunteers and it is not so very hard to drive an engine with safety and three quarters efficiency. This, however, would raise grave issues with the TUC.

I shall come to the House for the formal opening, and having tried a good many, I shall try to get the corner seat below the gangway.

I think you are very wise not to reconstruct the Government in a hurry or a crisis.

I do not see much difference between August and July. I was sorry I could not persuade Ike to test the Malenkov 'New Look' in 1953. Khrushchev has the Army in a way that Malenkov did not, so that if there is a 'New Look' it may be more fruitful. I do not think the Russian Army wants war. There is no such thing as military glory now. Soldiers would be safer than civilians, though not so comfortable as in time of peace. Surveying the scene from my detached position, I feel the corner will be gradually turned, and that the human race may be subjected to the tests of extreme prosperity.

I am sorry about the Prof. It would, of course, have been attributed to me. I could, I believe, have had a resignation list of my own, had I tried. The matter, however, is not one to which I attach much importance, and the Prof certainly much less.

I congratulate you on the manner you fought the election. You did not seem to me to put a foot wrong, and one is a centipede on such occasions.

NOW, however, may be the appointed hour. All good luck.

I have put my thoughts on paper as I am sure you would like me to do.

All good wishes

Yours ever

W [2]

---

[1] 'My dear Winston', signed 'Yours ever, Anthony', 10 Downing Street, 30 May 1955: Churchill papers, 2/216.

[2] 'My dear Anthony', 31 May 1955: Churchill papers, 2/216.

60

'Determined to persevere'

ON 1 June 1955, the Glorious First of June in Britain's historical annals, Churchill worked at his history with Alan Hodge and Denis Kelly, with whom he planned to continue throughout the summer. Work was halted, however, on the following evening, when Churchill suffered a spasm of the artery. For several days he was affected in little ways: knocking over his coffee cup, finding difficulty in writing in his own hand, and even holding his cigar in his mouth. When Lord Beaverbrook came to lunch, Churchill told his doctor on June 2, 'I kept dropping my cigar and Max kept picking it up.' He also had difficulty walking, for often, as he did so, noted Lord Moran, his right leg 'shot out unsteadily in the air'.[1]

Lord Moran spent the night at Chartwell. In the morning Churchill felt better, but all was still not well, as Moran noted:

He fiddled clumsily for his pen on the table by his bed, and began writing his name. Nine times he wrote with great care and deliberation 'Winston Churchill'. Opposite the fourth of these signatues he scribbled 'No noticeable improvement' and at the bottom of the sheet of paper '20% down'. Just then Kirkwood appeared with his breakfast.[2] I was poring over his signature when he said:

'This is the thing to look at, what I'm doing now.'

He was holding out his cup at arm's length.

'Pretty good, Charles.'

When he had put down the cup his attention wandered, and his right arm made a sudden purposeless and uncontrolled movement, upsetting the cup, so that his fingers ended in the coffee. Looking up, as if he wanted to say, 'There, you see, that's what I do,' he gave his dripping fingers a rueful look.[3]

*   *   *

[1] Moran diary, 2 June 1955: *The Struggle for Survival*, pages 660–61.

[2] Kirkwood was the valet who had succeeded Walter Meyer. He was himself succeeded by Sheppard.

[3] Moran diary, 3 June 1955: *The Struggle for Survival*, pages 662–4.

The engine drivers' strike had continued, but their Union had not been supported by the National Union of Railwaymen. There were more than two thousand engine drivers in the Forces, Randolph told his father on June 3. 'I think they ought to be used' was Churchill's reply.[1]

On June 8 Churchill was well enough to be driven to London for the opening of Parliament. 'Attlee was very kind to me when I took my seat in the House,' he told Lord Moran, who went on to note in his diary:

It appears that when a Member caught sight of Winston advancing up the floor—he was not very steady on his feet—he cried in his excitement, 'Churchill.' At that, before anyone could check it there was an unashamed clapping of hands in the public gallery, while all the Members crowding the benches waved their order papers, cheering madly. Where would he take his seat? It could only be in the seat below the gangway alongside the Treasury Bench. It was from this seat that he had warned the nation of its danger in the years before the war. Members must have wondered what was passing through his head at that moment—the rush of memories.

When they thought of him their feelings welled over into little signals of affection. Mr Shinwell gaily beckoned him to come over to the Labour benches. And then, when no Member dared trust himself to speak, Mr Attlee rose from his seat and, quickly crossing the floor, took Winston by the arm pushing him forward in front of him towards the table. Sir Winston must take the oath before him; while the whole House, seeing what was being done, rose to applaud.

Herbert Morrison, who was following Attlee, touched Winston affectionately on the back, and Winston, turning round, grasped Morrison's hand and shook it warmly. Then he signed the roll of members, writing his name for the thirteenth time in the roll of the Parliaments of Great Britain, very carefully, very deliberately—no doubt he had in mind what had happened at Chartwell.[2]

Churchill was now recovered from his spasm of June 2, and made plans to see as much of Alan Hodge and Denis Kelly as possible to move forward with the History. On June 2 he had sent them both his thoughts and instructions about the first volume. He had now re-read chapter 7 which had lain unaltered for nearly twenty years. He was not entirely satisfied with what he read, noting of page 9 of that early chapter:

We are talking very freely about Henry III's son Edmund. Something more should surely be inserted about the new King Henry III. He succeeded as a minor at 9. I do not notice any reference to his definitely succeeding to

[1] Moran diary, 3 June 1955: *The Struggle for Survival*, pages 662–4.
[2] Moran diary, 9 June 1955: *The Struggle for Survival*, page 667.

the throne. He is planning an expedition in 1229 to take an army to France and quarrelling with Hubert de Burgh. We are now on page 9 learning of his son Edmund for the first time. At least a paragraph must record his early years on the throne and his development as a ruler. How old was Edmund in October 1255? He had already been on the throne 39 years.

'Do not delay reprinting,' Churchill told his assistants, 'but please meditate upon strengthening the structure of the fact that he is King.'[1]

On June 15 Churchill learned from Harold Macmillan that he could retain the services of one of his former Private Secretaries, Anthony Montague Brown. 'Please make all use of him you can for as long as you wish,' Macmillan wrote.[2] 'I am lending you to Winston because he needs somebody,' Macmillan told Montague Browne, and he added: 'In the nature of things it will only be a year or two.'[3] In fact, for nearly another ten years, Montague Browne was to be Churchill's constant and devoted Private Secretary and guide, to the very end.

'From 1955,' Mary Soames later recalled, 'until my father drew his last breath, Anthony was practically never absent from his side. What was private life for my father when he retired? The whole world trod to 28 Hyde Park Gate. When we went abroad it was to call upon kings and presidents and prime ministers, to address great assemblies. The mail poured in. My father's business affairs, and his private life, Anthony really masterminded and managed, advised and helped. His knowledge, his professional know-how, his devotion to my father was one of the major factors in the last ten years of my father's life.'[4]

On June 20, at Harold Macmillan's persistent urging, Churchill saw the Burmese Prime Minister, U Nu, who had asked to see Churchill, despite a cooling of Anglo-Burmese relations. Hence Macmillan's keenness on the meeting. 'Herewith brief notes on U Nu prepared by the FO for your talk this afternoon,' wrote Montague Browne on the morning of the meeting, enclosing some suggestions of what Churchill might say to his visitor.[5] U Nu had been Prime Minister of Burma since 1948; one of those accompanying him was his Private Secretary,

[1] 'Mr Hodge and Mr Kelly', 12 June 1955: Churchill papers, 4/27.
[2] Letter of 15 June 1955: Churchill papers, 2/220.
[3] Anthony Montague Browne recollections: letter to the author, 22 October 1986.
[4] Lady Soames, speech of 25 September 1985: *Finest Hour*, Journal of the International Churchill Society, Issue No. 50, Winter 1985–6.
[5] 'Sir Winston Churchill', 20 June 1955 and 'Visit of U Nu, Prime Minister of Burma, Note for Sir Winston Churchill': Churchill papers, 2/131.

U Thant.[1] 'I was glad to see U Nu,' Churchill wrote to Macmillan ten days later, 'and much admired his celestial baby's face (?). The query is confidential.'[2]

On June 21 Churchill returned to London to speak at the Guildhall, at the unveiling of his statue. 'I confess,' he said, 'that like Disraeli I am on the side of the optimists. I do not believe that humanity is going to destroy itself. I have for some time thought it would be a good thing if the leaders of the great nations talked privately to one another. I am very glad that this is now going to happen.'[3]

The statue was the work of a Yugoslav Jewish refugee, Oscar Nemon, for whom Churchill had sat in the spring of 1954, when the Queen had asked for a bust of Churchill to place with Nelson and Wellington in the library at Windsor. 'I greatly admire the art of Mr Nemon,' Churchill said, and he admired too 'this particular example', which seemed to him 'such a very good likeness'.[4]

While Nemon had sculpted Churchill, Churchill had himself turned sculptor, and, as Nemon worked, had made a clay model of Nemon which Nemon later cast. 'I beg you not to underrate the artistic value of this work,' Nemon wrote, 'which would be considered by any expert as outstanding for a first attempt.'[5]

On June 30, from Chartwell, Churchill wrote a long letter to Pamela Lytton, who had been unable through illness to be at the Guildhall. The letter was written entirely in his own hand:

My dearest Pamela,

It was sweet of you to write me yr letter about the Guildhall, but I am indeed sorry for the cause wh prevented you from coming. I do pray that you are better & free from pain. I have just heard that you are back at Knebworth so I hope for the best.

I put yr letter aside when I got it, as I do my most important or cherished communications, and, as alas often happens, one trifle after another put me off from day to day, with renewed resolve & continued deferment. Do forgive me for I have wanted to write to you every single day and I am ashamed at myself.

[1] U Nu had been imprisoned by the British for sedition in 1940. From 1948 to 1958 and again from 1960 to 1962, he was Prime Minister of Burma. Imprisoned for seven years after the military coup of 1962, he left Burma for India. U Thant had been brought into Government by U Nu in 1948, becoming a Burmese delegate at the United Nations in 1952. From 1962 to 1971 he was Secretary-General of the United Nations. A devout Buddhist, he sought to apply the principles of detachment and concentration to the solving of international problems.

[2] 'My dear Harold', signed 'Yrs ever, W', 30 June 1955: Churchill papers, 2/131.

[3] Speech of 21 June 1955, manuscript notes: Churchill papers, 5/58. Recording: BBC Written Archives Centre, Library No. 22086. The phrase 'talked privately' he replaced when he spoke with the phrase 'talked freely to one another without too much formality'.

[4] Speech of 21 June 1955: Randolph S. Churchill (editor), *The Unwritten Alliance*, pages 266–8.

[5] 'Dear Sir Winston', 5 May 1955: Churchill papers, 2/195. The head of Nemon, Churchill's only work as a sculptor, is now in the Studio at Chartwell.

I wish you could have been at the show. It is the last engagement I have, and I am vy chary of adding to them. I have a protracted desire to avoid the public kindness. But this Guildhall statue was certainly worth the worry these things take me now. I am getting much older now the stimulus of responsibility & power has fallen from me, and I totter along in the shades of retirement.

They now tell me you are 'a little better today'. I do trust indeed that this is a real gain.

Clemmie & I wd love to come to The Manor House one day. Alas she is suffering a great deal of pain from her neuritis, & for the last 3 weeks has been a complete invalid with her broken wrist and the shock of her fall. I spend my days between Chartwell & 28, with the Book as my main task.

This tardy letter is meant to carry you my love and every good wish. Please send me a line to say how you are and that you forgive my stupid delay.

Your ever loving
and devoted

W

'Excuse the scrawl,' Churchill added. 'It is due to age!' [1]

That day, writing to Harold Macmillan, Churchill commented about Anthony Montague Browne: 'AMB is a great help to me in my official and semi-official aftermath.' [2]

Churchill's work at Chartwell was centred increasingly on his History. On June 23 both Alan Hodge and Denis Kelly had been invited to dine and sleep. Hodge lunched again on June 30, and July 4. 'Immense drafts were turned in by J. H. Plumb and other historians and worked over by Churchill and Alan,' Jane Hodge later recalled, 'with Churchill', she added, 'totally in command.' As for Denis Kelly, she recalled: 'Churchill felt kindly towards him, and didn't want him left out; that was the sort of person he was. He was enormously caring.' Jane Hodge added: 'He had a real personal relationship. Alan told him all his troubles. He listened. When Alan was ill, the telephone rang. It was Churchill on the line.' [3] 'He so loved Alan,' Churchill's secretary Miss Pugh later recalled, and she added: 'He so admired Alan's use of words.' [4]

When, on July 4, Lord Moran went to Chartwell to see how Churchill was feeling, he found him dictating to a secretary, nor was the work to be all that easily interrupted, Moran wrote in his diary:

[1] 'My dearest Pamela', 30 June 1955: Churchill papers, 1/56.
[2] Letter of 30 June 1955: Churchill papers, 2/131.
[3] Jane Aiken Hodge recollections: in conversation with the author, 3 July 1987. Alan Hodge was also with Churchill on June 9, June 14, June 30, July 4, July 6 (with Denis Kelly), July 9, July 14, July 28 (with Denis Kelly), August 2, August 7, August 11, August 15 to 18 and August 28. (Churchill Engagements Calendar: Churchill papers.)
[4] Doreen Pugh recollections: in conversation with the author, 18 June 1987.

'May I just finish these notes for my book?'

While he dictated I glanced at a pile of books by his bed.—G. M. Trevelyan's *History of England*; J. R. Green's *Short History of the English People*; *The Later Plantagenets*, by V. Green; *War in the Middle Ages*, by Oman. 'Do you read all these books?' I asked.

'Oh, no, I'm not rewriting my book. But when a difficult point arises I fatten my own account by referring to them.' 'Now,' said Winston to the Secretary, 'run away.'

'You are staying at your country home?' he enquired. I explained that I was on my way to London and that Violet Bonham Carter was in the car. He said he would like to see her. She asked him about his book.

'That is all that concerns me now,' he replied. 'Though I'm going up to London this afternoon to vote in the House.'

She asked him what was being debated; he smiled: 'It's a three line whip, that's all I can tell you.' [1]

'I feel I am entitled to take a good rest down here,' Churchill wrote a week later to Lewis Rosenstiel of New York, who sent him regular supplies of whisky and cigars. [2]

On July 11 Churchill invited the Oxford historian A. L. Rowse to lunch with him at Chartwell. Rowse noted in his diary:

Before lunch I was summoned up to his bedroom, and there, at last, was the so familiar face, much aged: that of an old man who had gone back to his baby looks. The eyes a cloudy blue, a little bloodshot, spectacles on snub nose, a large cigar rolled round in his mouth. He had been at work—'I like work.' Beside the bed a small aluminium pail for cigar-ash; before him, stretching right across the bed, a tray-desk, on which were the long galleys of his *History of the English-Speaking Peoples*.

He welcomed me with a touch of old-fashioned exaggerated courtesy, as if the honour were his that the professional historian had come to see him. I returned the compliment, sincerely meant, that he had beaten the professionals at their own game, that his *Marlborough* was an historical masterpiece along with Trevelyan's *Age of Queen Anne*. He said that, now that he had some time, he was rereading the *History* he had written before the war, but he wasn't satisfied with it. However, there were people who would read it on account of his 'notoriety'. . . .

Rowse then read the revised chapters on Henry VII and Henry VIII, while Churchill got dressed. Rowse waited in the dining room:

The figure all the world knew then entered: striped blue zip-suit, blue velvet slippers with WSC worked in gold braid, outwards, in case anybody didn't know who was approaching. He led me to the window to look at his

[1] Moran diary, 4 July 1955: *The Struggle for Survival*, pages 674–5.

[2] Letter of 12 July 1955: Churchill papers, 2/197. Rosenstiel was head of the largest distillers in the United States, and a friend of Brendan Bracken. He had first met Churchill in the South of France in 1922.

beautiful mare cropping with her foal below—I think, Hyperion, out of whom by someone I didn't take in. He soon saw that I hadn't come to talk horses, even if I could; we looked away down the valley, 'up which the planes came', he said. The memory of 1940, when the Germans had everything their own way, was still vivid.

The two men lunched together. During their discussion, as Rowse noted,

Winston spoke with gallantry of Mrs Chamberlain—'wonderful woman: twenty years, and she's quite unchanged'. I responded that I was glad he had asked her to his Farewell Dinner at 10 Downing Street, and delighted that he had asked the Attlees and Morrisons. 'That was not much after five years of comradeship in war,' he said feelingly. He added that the new Mrs Herbert Morrison was a strong Tory, though they were not advertising the fact. . . .[1]

'Winston spoke kindly of Dalton,' Rowse noted, 'and said that of all the letters he had received on leaving office in 1945, his was the nicest. I told him of Dalton's admiration for the weekly talks he used to give the Cabinet, to strengthen morale in the worst days of 1940, and that Dalton used to go away and write them down.' The talk continued:

Winston told me quite candidly of the severe stroke he had, said that he couldn't feed himself—and yet managed to hold on to office. He talked about the Labour Party, with no animus or opposition: all that had dropped away with the years. He did not speak like a party-man, indeed he never had been a mere party-politician, had sat loosely to party-ties. I noticed that he referred to the Tories, not as 'we' but as 'they'—as if he sat on some Olympus above the party struggle, as indeed he did. He had made that most difficult walk in life, crossing the floor of the House of Commons, not once but twice—'I have never had any objection to the rat, as such.' When Jowitt awkwardly left the Liberal Party to become Labour's Lord Chancellor, Winston said with a twinkle: 'He has disgraced the name of rat.'

Speaking of social inequalities and private enterprise, Churchill told Rowse: 'There should be minimum standards beyond which people should not be allowed to fall—and beyond that, Free Run!' Turning to the post-war world, Churchill exclaimed: 'If only I had more time—to make peace.' Rowse noted: 'Now, enormously ambitious as he was about his place in having won the war, he had longed to be the man to end the Cold War with Russia.'

That afternoon, Churchill walked with Rowse in the garden, talking history, then returned to his study for more history. Having said his goodbyes, Rowse noted: 'It was infinitely sad and touching. One may

---

[1] Herbert Morrison had just married, as his second wife, Edith Meadowcraft.

never see or hear him again. At any moment the last stroke may come.'[1] But Churchill's work and strength were not yet over.

On July 13 Churchill sent a specially designed silver V-sign to 113 former members of his staff and the establishment at 10 Downing Street, including the cleaners, electricians, telephonists, messengers and carpenters. Among the recipients were his pre-war and wartime secretary Kathleen Hill, who was the Curator at Chequers, and Jock Colville, who wrote on July 17: 'I treasure the silver V-sign, commemorating your Second Administration, and am placing it on my watch-chain as an object to be very especially prized.' Colville added: 'I hope that during the last week of July or any time in August you will let me know if you feel the need of either companionship or Bezique, and I will be at your disposal.'[2]

Also thinking of Churchill at this time was President Eisenhower, who was about to leave the United States for the Four-Power summit talks at Geneva. Before leaving, he wrote to Churchill from the White House:

Dear Winston,

Soon Anthony and I will be meeting with the French and the Russians at Geneva. As you know, I feel sure that the Western nations could not, with self-respect, have earlier consented to a Four Power Summit meeting. Yet I cannot escape a feeling of sadness that the delay brought about by the persistently hostile Soviet attitude toward NATO has operated to prevent your personal attendance at the meeting.

Foster and I know—as does the world—that your courage and vision will be missed at the meeting. But your long quest for peace daily inspires much that we do. I hope that in your wisdom you will consider that we there do well; certainly we shall do the best of which we are capable in the opportunities we may encounter at Geneva.

Personally I do not expect, and I hope the people of this country and of the world do not expect, a miracle. But if we can inch a little closer to the dream that has been yours for these many years, if together at the meeting table we can create a new spirit of tolerance and perhaps, in concert, come to the realization that force and the threat of force are no longer acceptable in dealings among nations, we shall gain much that will help us in the long and complicated processes that must come after the Summit meeting.

As I leave Washington, my thoughts are with you. . . .[3]

Churchill replied at once:

My dear Friend,

I am deeply grateful to you for your letter and the thought that prompted you. I was touched by what you said when I resigned, and I had two of your

[1] A. L. Rowse, *Memories of Men and Women*, London 1980, pages 1–18.
[2] 'My dear Winston', 17 July 1955: Churchill papers, 1/66.
[3] 'Dear Winston', signed 'Your old friend, Ike', 15 July 1955: Churchill papers, 2/217.

letters with me at the time which I had not answered. What often happens is that one puts on one side the most important features in one's correspondence in order to do justice to them in the reply, and then keeps putting them off from day to day for less important things. I can only beg you to forgive, as I am sure you will, my neglect.

It is a strange and formidable experience laying down responsibility and letting the trappings of power fall in a heap to the ground. A sense not only of psychological but of physical relaxation steals over one to leave a feeling both of relief and denudation. I did not know how tired I was until I stopped working.

I cannot help, however, feeling satisfied with the way things have turned out. I am fortunate to have a successor whose mind I know and whose abilities are of the highest order. I had to consider the interests of the Party I have led for fourteen years and I was convinced that this was the time to ask the verdict of the nation on what we had done in three years of office. Moreover, I have for a long time felt that at my age I should not be justified myself in leading in the election when I could not feel any assurance that I could carry out in an effective manner any new programme to which I pledged myself. I was very pleased with the result, and, indeed, on the whole I feel that we Changed Guard at Buckingham Palace at the right time and in the right way.

I am very glad that the meeting 'at the summit' is now to take place, and I will gladly do anything in my power from a distance and a private station to help it to a good result. I have never indulged in extravagant hopes of a vast, dramatic transformation of human affairs, but my belief is that, so long as we do not relax our unity or our vigilance, the Soviets and the Russian people will be increasingly convinced that it is in their interests to live peaceably with us. There is a strong reaction from the post-war mood of Stalin. Abundance for hundreds of millions is in sight and even in reach. These processes of growth require time, and one improvement can easily lead to another.

I do not relish the idea of 'saturation' in the nuclear sphere. If, however, that is accompanied by the undoubted fact that a full scale nuclear war means not the mastery of one side or the other but the extinction of the human species, it may well be that a new set of deterrents will dominate the soul of man.[1]

On June 15 Sir John Rothenstein informed Churchill that the Board of Trustees of the Tate Gallery 'would welcome the inclusion in the collection of an example of your work as a painter'.[2] 'I have been dwelling with much pleasure on your letter,' Churchill replied, in inviting Rothenstein to lunch at Chartwell, and offering him the painting 'The Loup River, Alpes Maritimes'.[3] Rothenstein later recalled:

---

[1] 'My dear Friend', signed 'Yrs always, W', 18 July 1955: Churchill papers, 2/217.
[2] Letter of 15 June 1955: Churchill papers, 1/25.
[3] Letter of 5 July 1955: Churchill papers, 1/25.

The morning I arrived at Chartwell, his country house in Kent, no car stood in front of the house, and from the hall no sound was heard. Upon a table reposed by itself an object made familiar by innumerable photographs: a wide-brimmed grey painting-hat. I was contemplating this celebrated object with respect, as though it were the hat of a King sent on some ceremonial occasion to represent him, when I heard soft padding steps approach, and presently, dressed in his sky-blue siren-suit and shod in soft black slippers on which his initials were worked in gold, there appeared Mr Churchill benignly welcoming.

At large parties the noise, the movement and the emanations of a number of personalities blur our impressions: it now seemed to me as we walked about the house that I was seeing my host for the first time. At such gatherings I had never sufficiently noted the fine wood-ash whiteness of his skin, the largeness of his light blue eyes, how quick to smile at the laughable yet how quick too to steady and to harden in the contemplation of serious matters. Nor had I noticed how uniquely at ease he was in the world, this relaxed man dressed for convenience and comfort.

Before lunch we briefly visited his studio, a long narrow room brightly lit by high windows on one side and at the far end. Upon a long narrow table that stood lengthwise to the room were placed tidily arranged rows of clean paint tubes; beside this table was a great terrestrial globe, a present, he told me, from the American army. But for this globe, there was throughout the whole house a conspicuous absence of any display of trophies, historic battle orders and the like. The suggestion was mooted not long since that Chartwell should one day be preserved as a museum. If it were left in its present state there would be little to remind the visitor of the fabulous career of its former owner; if it were filled with appropriate exhibits it would give a wholly false impression of his manner of living.

During our first visit to his studio Mr Churchill told me that he would be grateful for any criticism of his painting I might care to make. 'Speak, I pray, with absolute frankness' he said as we went into lunch. As soon as we sat down he began to speak of Sickert. 'He came to stay here and in a fortnight he imparted to me all his considered wisdom about painting. He had a room specially darkened to work in, but I wasn't an apt pupil, for I rejoice in the highest lights and the brightest colours.' Mr Churchill spoke with appreciation of Sickert's knowledge of music halls, and he sang a nineteenth century ballad he had learnt from him, not just a line or two, but right to the end. 'I think the person who taught me most about painting was William Nicholson. I noticed you looking, I thought with admiration, at those drawings upstairs he made of my beloved cat.'

During lunch his most memorable remark did not concern painters or painting. Upon his enquiring why I had declined his offer of a cigar, I replied that every man should possess one virtue: the only one I could certainly claim was that I did not smoke; to which he instantly replied 'There is no such thing as a negative virtue. If I have been of any service to my fellow men, it has never been by self-repression, but always by self-expression.' Back in the studio fortified by a bottle of champagne, his invitation to give my opinion of his work without reserve seemed less alarming. In the course of the afternoon we must have looked at every one of the numerous paintings in the studio and the few others that hung in various other parts of the house.

Mr Churchill was so genial and so exhilarating a companion that before I had been with him a few hours the notion of speaking with absolute frankness seemed as natural as it had earlier seemed temerarious. My first detailed criticism of one of his paintings had an unexpected, indeed a positively start-ling result. I offered the opinion, with regard to a landscape—a wood on the margin of a lake—that the shore was too shallow, too lightly modelled and too pale in tone to support the weight of the heavy trees with their dense, dark foliage, so that, intead of growing up out of the earth they weighted it down.

'Oh' Mr Churchill said, 'I can put that right at once; it would take less than a quarter of an hour,' and he began to look out the appropriate brushes and colours. 'But this painting, surely' I said 'must be among your earliest.' 'I did it about twenty years ago' he conceded. 'Well then,' I protested 'surely it's impossible for you to recapture the mood in which you painted it, or indeed your whole outlook of those days.' 'You are really persuaded of that' he grumbled, abandoning the notion of repainting with evident reluctance. This was the first of several occasions when I had to persuade him to desist from repainting an early work in consequence of some criticism of mine. If pride could be exorcized by a single experience (which, alas, being a rank weed it cannot) my own would have been exorcized by the spectacle of 'the greatest human being of our times prepared to act so confidently upon my advice. 'If it weren't for painting,' Mr Churchill observed as we left the studio, 'I couldn't live; I couldn't bear the strain of things.' [1]

On July 19 Churchill received a letter from Eden, who had reached Geneva and begun the negotiations which Churchill had so wanted to initiate. Eden told his former chief:

Our proceedings have opened on rather a quiet note like the general elec-tion. It is too early to tell what the week may bring. The Russians are polite in private talk, so far as we have had any, and moderate in tone in public. However, most of what they said today was the mixture as before. We have all the bears to dinner tomorrow.

Eden added that Eisenhower 'seems to be in good heart and not too unhappy to find himself here'. [2]

On his return from Geneva, Eden wrote to Churchill again. At one

[1] 'Mr Churchill, The Artist', undated: Churchill papers, 2/175.
[2] 'Dear Winston', 'Secret', sent through 10 Downing Street, 19 July 1955: Churchill papers, 2/216.

private talk with Bulganin, Khrushchev and Molotov, he reported, 'they showed greater interest in our security than they had in open session'.[1] Four days later, Churchill went up to London to lunch with Eden at 10 Downing Street. Eden 'was not particularly optimistic', Churchill told Lord Moran, but had told Churchill that the Russians had been 'simple, friendly and natural'. As Churchill gave Moran an account of his London visit, Moran was shocked by how difficult Churchill found it to complete a sentence; 'more than once,' Moran noted, 'I could not follow what he was trying to say.'[2] Three days earlier Mary Soames had noted in her diary, of her father: 'He just seems slower and sleepier every day. . . .'[3]

On August 4 Churchill accompanied his wife to London Airport to see her off to Switzerland. 'It sent me off happy,' she wrote from Suvretta House, St Moritz, on the following day, 'in my laborious effort to regain my health.' The doctor of the Spa, she added, was going to see if he could smooth her neuritis away 'with some magic peat or pine baths'.[4] That same day Churchill wrote to his wife from Chartwell, in his own, and much steadier hand; but it had nevertheless not been an easy letter to write:

Darling,

Monty came to lunch today. He was vy amusing & made most thorough inquiries about you. I told him all there was to tell. We all went down to the Pool with Jeremy [5] who was a gt success.

I am eagerly awaiting news of you & hope to receive some on Monday. It may well be that you will have a set back for a few days and that then the attacks of pain will lessen. Several people have told me that they have had *arthritis* and after a bit it has worn off & so why shd not *neuritis* do the same? Anyhow do not Despair. I beg you not to do that. I am *sure* you will find a remedy. I know it may be hard, but you have valiant blood.

This is the third letter I have tried to write to you and always failed. I love you so much and am determined to persevere.

It will be easier when I have one of your own dear letters to begin on.

Always your loving husband

W [6]

On August 8 Churchill wrote again, also in his own hand:

[1] 'My dear Winston', 25 July 1955: Churchill papers, 2/216.
[2] Moran diary, 29 July 1955: *The Struggle for Survival*, pages 680–1.
[3] Mary Soames diary, 26 July 1955: Mary Soames, *Clementine Churchill*, page 454.
[4] 'My darling', signed 'Your devoted Clemmie', 5 August 1955: Churchill papers, 1/55.
[5] Jeremy Bernard Soames, Churchill's grandson (born on 25 May 1952).
[6] 'Darling', 5 August 1955: Spencer-Churchill papers.

My darling,

I was so glad to get your letter & to learn the details of yr journey. I had been waiting eagerly for it. Now it has come I take up my pen to answer aided by Toby who is sitting on the sheet of note paper insisting on lapping the ink from my pen in order to send you a personal message. He has come down here greatly improved and there is no doubt that he knows I am writing to you and that he wishes to join in. He is a wonderful little bird. He pecked and scribbled with his beak and what I have written so far is as much his work as mine. He has gone back to his cage now (by my bedside) so perhaps I may write better. (I have also had my pen refilled.)

Monty evidently enjoyed himself and has given me a letter to send you. He has asked to come on Sunday 11th September. You may well be here & *high time too*. You will find a lot of changes which I hope you will like. (Toby is back again on my hand.) This is really a joint message so I make him sign it.

I have had Hodge down for a couple of days & in a quarter of an hour expect Bill Deakin. I must bring him along if I can. I am dividing him with Nemon who comes at about 4.

I can't harden my heart to get rid of the old van, & am going to keep it for a bit, so as to let the secretaries & Miss Hamblin do some of their short trips for a while. (Toby is back.) But you can settle when you come home.

My dearest one you have all my love. Do write to me & don't give up hope.

Your ever devoted husband

W [1]

Bill Deakin was helping Churchill and Hodge to organize whatever extra material was needed for the History. Further help came that autumn from Joel Hurstfield, an expert on the Tudor period, who offered on August 10, in response to a request from Churchill, to give 'any further assistance' Churchill might require. [2]

From Clementine Churchill came news, on August 10, that her health was much improved. Churchill wrote at once, again in his own hand:

Darling,

Your letter of the 8th has reached me this morning. I am enchanted that you feel better. This is really good news after only three days. Let me know what the local doctor says after his blood tests, and also what he prescribes. I am sure it is a good thing to take all opinions which are authoritative on a question like this—but whether you act upon them is another matter. Still the remedies proposed *may* be harmless & fit in with the regime of the Spa. And there is always the chance of hitting the bull's eye. There are so many cures or alleviations.

[1] 'My darling', 8 August 1955: Spencer-Churchill papers.
[2] Letter of 10 August 1955: Churchill papers, 4/27.

You must be popping up and down a lot to drop down 5000 feet to lunch with Mildred Gosford. I have a distinct recollection of her—tho I do not suppose I shd recognise her. It must have been a wonderful drive, and how amusing to meet the friends of girlhood!

I have been working at my book & Christopher and Mary have made all sorts of plans to fill in the 11 days (wh begin tomorrow) which I am bound to say seems attractive. Violet is coming here for Saturday. Today we have the Ismays. He tells me that his sinus is much better since he had his teeth pulled out & that perhaps he will not have to have another operation. But about this I will write in my next.

Anthony & Cleopatra have chosen the 10th September for their visit and Christopher will be available. They only stay one day. I do hope you will be back flourishing. Monty lunches on the 11th September & I am trying to persuade them not to go till after lunch.

Tender love my dearest Clemmie

Your devoted husband

W

A few tiny bites on the margin of the letter clearly called for an explanation. 'Toby has signed,' Churchill noted.[1]

On August 9 Mary Soames reported to her mother: 'Darling Papa really does seem in distinctly better form these last five days. He was awfully worried & low about you, & I think knowing you had safely arrived & having had a letter—he feels much better about everything.'[2]

On August 11 it was Churchill's turn to report to his wife on his continuing social life. 'Christopher,' he wrote, 'has made some good arrangements for me.' Not only was Violet Bonham Carter coming to lunch that week, so too, on the Sunday, were Earl and Countess De La Warr, and Lady Juliet Duff on the following Sunday.[3] On August 13 Churchill wrote again, heading his letter 'Blenheim Day':

My darling,

I am getting quite festive, Violet is staying with me today & tomorrow: I have asked Pamela, who proposed herself, to come on Thursday 18th & Juliet for the weekend of the 27th, when Lord & Lady De La Warr[4] are coming to lunch. This is a record.

Violet made herself vy agreeable last night and argued a great deal about her Papa, the Liberal Party & all that. Mr Hodge, who has now gone to retrieve his family, was thrilled. I am to have a string of painters (to whom I

[1] 'Darling', 10 August 1955: Spencer-Churchill papers.

[2] Letter of 9 August 1955: Mary Soames, *Clementine Churchill*, page 456.

[3] 'My darling', signed 'Your ever devoted husband, W', 11 August 1955: Spencer-Churchill papers.

[4] Lord De La Warr, the 9th Earl, had been Chairman of the National Labour Party from 1931 to 1943, and Postmaster-General throughout Churchill's second premiership. In 1920 he had married Diana, daughter of Captain Henry Gerard Leigh, 1st Life Guards.

shall give a fleeting glimpse) next week & Mr Laughlin who comes over from Ireland to talk 'Book'. There are others filling in the intervals.[1]

My plans were deranged by Meg & Jock. Jock was smitten by appendicitis & had to have an operation on the 11th. He has come through all right, but it was vy sudden & unwarned.

Now I want to hear your news. I am expecting a letter with a full account of yr progress. What a wonderful thing it will be if you have had *less* neuritis and *fewer* injections! It is a week & 2 days since you left. In the meantime I can do no more than hope.

With all my love
Your devoted husband

W [2]

On August 17 Churchill dictated a letter to his wife; the first letter since she had left for St Moritz which he had not written by hand:

My darling,

I am still awaiting your reply to my telegram before sending any further chapters. If, as I suppose, you have the first revise with you up to the end of 'The Saxon Dusk', it will be easy to send some of the early chapters of William the Conqueror, etc. from a later revise, and then Mary can bring the rest when she comes. I expect to hear from you today. But I should like you to read it in sequence, and to have the latest edition.

I am so glad you like it, and what you say about it is a great encouragement to me. I have read Volume 1, which includes Books I, II, and III, three times now, and have, I think, a good deal improved it. I am delighted at what you say about helping a lot of people to read history, and that it will have results which may be compared with *Painting as a Pastime*.

I am still waiting anxiously for further reports on the new treatment. It sounds very hopeful. Do not hesitate to prolong your stay for another week if the doctor thinks it will do good.

I will write you again later in the day. Mr Laughlin, the Canadian publisher, who is a very nice man, is coming to lunch.

Churchill added, in his own hand, 'with all my love, your devoted W' and a postscript: 'Montague Browne is just off & we have to post in London to catch the Air Mail.'[3]

On August 20 Churchill received a letter from his wife, to say that there had been a definite improvement in her health. She also told

---

[1] The painters who came were Max Nauta, who had been commissioned by the Dutch Government, and Edward Halliday. The sculptor Oscar Nemon, who had done a sitting early in August, came again on August 23. The 'others' included Emery Reves, Anthony Montague Browne and Alan Hodge. (Churchill Engagements Calendar, August 1955: Churchill papers. Max Nauta's sittings were on August 15, 22 and 29; Edward Halliday's on August 16.)

[2] 'My darling', 13 August 1955: Spencer-Churchill papers.

[3] 'My darling', 17 August 1955: Spencer-Churchill papers (carbon copy in Churchill papers, 1/55). Henry Laughlin was in fact an American, the head of Houghton Mifflin, Churchill's American publishers.

him about an elderly American widower she had met, Lewis Einstein, who had strong views on the impropriety of Britain's rejection of Greek demands for Cyprus. On receiving his wife's letter, Churchill replied at once, once more in his own hand:

My darling,

Mary comes home to-day & stays with me. She leaves on Monday & will bring you all the news. Pamela cd not come for the weekend, but Randolph is coming with little Winston; but June is abroad.

Your letter dated 18 has just reached me. It tells me what I wanted. There has been a definite improvement during the fortnight. This is anyhow to the good, and I feel you are right to postpone yr return. I have only one engagement—the 7th (the Cinque Ports) which I wd not recommend you to attempt, & have duly prepared them. So that if you feel you want a day or two more you cd take them. On the other hand it wd be very nice to have you here from the 5th onwards.

Anthony & Clarissa are coming on the 10th—sleep the night and remain till after luncheon on 11th, when Monty lunches. They leave in the afternoon.

I shd be a bit stiff with Einstein.[1] We *saved* Greece from being inside the Iron Curtain by our personal exertions. Cyprus has never had any pledge from us that she wd be handed over to the Greeks who have never had her. Although I do not say that this is a decisive argument, we have embarked upon a clearance plan for Egypt which is based upon our base in Cyprus, & we are not likely to choose this moment (above all others) to compromise it. The Greek revilings leave me quite cold—or indeed hot me up. I will see if I can put something more down for Mary to bring.

Tender love my dearest one. I am struggling along with my book—much bucked up by yr approval—

All my love & many kisses

Your devoted & loving husband

W

'I go out harvesting every day in the new Land Rover.'[2]

On August 20 Churchill was joined at Chartwell by his daughter Mary, his son Randolph and Randolph's son Winston. 'We had a very pleasant dinner (after a bathe wh I witnessed),' Churchill wrote to his wife on the following day, 'and saw a vy good film.' Randolph was 'vy pleasant', Churchill wrote, 'and likes his house, in which he is now established, "very much"'.[3]

---

[1] Lewis Einstein, an American living in Paris. In 1912 his step-daughter Marguerite Christine Ralli had married the 11th Marquess of Tweeddale. In 1915 Einstein had served in the United States Embassy at Constantinople. Two years later he published *Inside Constantinople, A Diplomatist's Diary during the Dardanelles Expedition*.

[2] 'My darling', 20 August 1955: Spencer-Churchill papers.

[3] 'My darling', signed 'Your devoted husband, W', 21 August 1955: Spencer-Churchill papers. Randolph's new house was Stour, East Bergholt, Suffolk, his home from 1955 until his death in 1968.

Randolph had been shocked on that first evening to find his father in a rather miserable mood. On the following morning he wrote, to cheer him, a note which he headed 'Pensées matinales et filiales (presque lapidaires)'. The note read:

Power must pass and vanish. Glory, which is achieved through a just exercise of power—which itself is accumulated by genius, toil, courage and self-sacrifice—alone remains. Your glory is enshrined for ever on the unperishable plinth of your achievement; and can never be destroyed or tarnished. It will flow with the centuries.

So please try to be as happy as you have a right and (if it is not presumptuous for a son to say it) a duty to be. And, by being happy, make those who love you happy too.

All on one sheet of paper!

With devoted love,

Randolph [1]

On August 24 Churchill spoke to his wife on the telephone. 'I'm just going to start out on the new chapters you have sent me,' she wrote to him a few moments later. 'I love your book,' and she added: 'Darling Winston take care of yourself.' [2]

Among the very few letters which Churchill dictated that August was one to his friend Major-General Sir Hugh Tudor. 'I am indeed enjoying the period of comparative leisure,' Churchill wrote, 'and it is a real relief for me to be freed from the burdens of Prime Minister. The worst thing about it is that when you let all these responsibilities drop you feel your power falls with the thing it held.' [3]

In his wife's absence, Churchill dined with Montague Browne for seventeen evenings. 'Those seventeen evenings alone with him,' Montague Browne later recalled, 'were utterly fascinating'—a revelation of 'the nimbleness and diversity of his mind—even at the age of 80'. Montague Browne added:

He told me that when he was a boy his great ambition was to play the cello, and when he was in his teens he felt he ought to go into the church. 'I wonder what would have become of me then?' he asked. I suggested he would have crossed the floor and become Pope. He wasn't particularly amused at the time!

Actually he rarely went to church. When he was approached about this, he said he was not a pillar of the church but a buttress—he supported it from the outside.

[1] Note dated 21 August 1955, on Chartwell notepaper: Churchill papers, 1/56.
[2] 'My darling', 24 August 1955: Churchill papers, 1/55.
[3] 'My dear Hugh', 25 August 1955: Churchill papers, 2/201.

In answer to a question of his final opinion of Lawrence of Arabia, he said, 'He had the art of backing uneasily into the limelight. He was a very remarkable character, and very careful of that fact.'

I asked him what he had thought during his celebrated cavalry charge at Omdurman, when the 21st Lancers had gone headlong into a gully filled with quite unexpected and extremely bad-tempered dervishes. He said, 'It was very stimulating, but I did think "Suppose there is a spoil-sport in the hole with a machine gun?"' [1]

On August 27 Churchill and Christopher Soames went to Windsor races, where one of Churchill's horses 'won a good victory', as Churchill reported to his wife. 'Although we have not sold anything this year,' he noted, 'there is every prospect of balancing the racing account.' 'Racing gave him great pleasure,' Miss Pugh later recalled. 'Thanks to Christopher Soames, he did enjoy it. If he had a win he would always share it, he would always give us a gift—a tenner. It was quite a lot in those days.' [2]

In a letter on August 28, Churchill also sent his wife two more chapters of his History. 'I am so glad you like the book,' he wrote. 'I am much encouraged by it. You now have the whole of Book II, ending with "The Black Death", which reduced the population of the world by at least a third at a time when it was certainly not over-crowded. Let me know how you get on, for there is a third Book included in the volume, which is, I think, a good one.' [3]

On September 7 Churchill spoke in Hastings at the presentation of his portrait as Warden of the Cinque Ports. 'When you approach the end of a long life,' he said, 'there is a comfort in looking back on the past, and belonging to an institution of such age and dignity.' [4] Among his visitors to Chartwell in the second week of September were Anthony and Clarissa Eden. 'Clarissa and I much enjoyed our visit,' Eden wrote on his return to Chequers, 'and my talks with you about our problems. Whatever else happens they will always be there in some form.' [5]

On September 15, Churchill travelled to the South of France, to Lord Beaverbrook's villa at Cap d'Ail. There, joined by his wife, and by Mary and Christopher Soames, he painted in the warm autumn sun, writing to Beaverbrook on September 18:

[1] Montague Browne recollections, speech to the International Churchill Society, London, 25 September 1985: *Finest Hour*, Journal of the International Churchill Society, Issue No. 50, Winter 1985–6.

[2] Doreen Pugh recollections: in conversation with the author, 18 June 1987. The value of a tenner was £90 in 1987.

[3] 'My darling', 28 August 1955: Spencer-Churchill papers.

[4] Speech of 7 September 1955: Randolph S. Churchill (editor), *The Unwritten Alliance*, page 270.

[5] 'My dear Winston', 12 September 1955: Churchill papers, 2/216.

My dear Max,

We are all spreading out beautifully. The Soames are in your jolly little house, which has everything they can want. I wish they were going to stop longer. I have begun painting that other daub half way down the wall and I shall still have another try at it. Everything is going as well as it can, and I look forward to a delightful rest. Clemmie has taken another good turning, and I hope she may get a real break.

There are so far as I can see no lizards, but there are two cats with whom we have made friends, or sort of friends. The violet heather looks lovely. Thank you so much for lending me this beautiful place.[1]

'I have been very well,' Churchill wrote to Lord Moran on September 26, 'and have lived an idle life except at the Book and painting. I have taken one minor so far since arriving, in two parts. Memory lags and tickles tease. I eat, drink and sleep well.' Churchill added: 'I am sorry about Ike. He will be a great loss.'[2]

Churchill's work on his History included a first attempt at a preface. On September 30 he sent this back to London, with an instruction to Alan Hodge and Denis Kelly: 'Print it at once, and see they get to work at it first thing on Monday morning.' Churchill added, for he never liked to work alone: 'It would be very nice if one or both of you could come out about the 10th of October as my guests. There is an excellent hotel in Cap d'Ail.'[3]

After three weeks at La Capponcina, Churchill was in a relaxed and contented mood, writing to Beaverbrook on October 6:

My dear Max,

We have had a very pleasant three weeks here, and Clemmie is better. The Chef is excellent, and the garden lovely. I have painted another picture, and so far I have not spoiled it, which is something.

We dined with the Préfet des Alpes Maritimes the other night, and I was glad to feel myself sincerely in a mood to congratulate France on clearing out of the United Nations *pro tem* and also on not going to Russia *now*. I am getting a bit tired of this Nehruism, and I gather you are too. The Americans must have learned a lot.

Mr Billmeir of Lloyds has lent us a very convenient 200-ton yacht which awaits our beck and call.[4] Clemmie is delighted with it, and I went to San Remo yesterday. Bur really I very rarely leave the garden which I like so much.

I think of you in your *cold, bleak, winter-ridden country* with wonder and

---

[1] 'My dear Max', signed 'Yours always, Winston', 18 September 1955: Beaverbrook papers.

[2] 'My dear Charles', 26 September 1955: Churchill papers, 1/54. Eisenhower had suffered a coronary thrombosis. 'If I were in Ike's shoes,' Lord Moran replied, 'I should count it no more than a provisional notice to quit' ('My dear Winston', 3 October 1955: Churchill papers, 1/64).

[3] 'Mr Hodge and Mr Kelly', 30 September 1955: Churchill papers, 4/27.

[4] Jack Billmeir, a self-made millionaire ship-owner, Chairman of the Stanhope Line, lent Churchill his motor yacht *Aronia* for cruises up and down the French Riviera coast.

admiration that you have made this sacrifice for me. But perhaps you like to do it. That would only make it better.

Clemmie sends her love.

Yours always,

Winston[1]

In London, Alan Hodge and Bill Deakin had almost completed reading the proofs of the first volume of Churchill's History. 'Nothing arises with which we should trouble you,' Hodge wrote to Churchill on October 10. As neither he nor Deakin felt expert on the period, they had consulted Robert Carson of the British Museum to scrutinize 'dates and names and facts'. Hodge added: 'He has fished patiently but not caught more than five or six sprats, the biggest of which is that Constantius, on page 29, was not born at York but died there. It is reassuring to know that he has found so little to question.'[2]

Churchill was so enjoying his holiday in the South of France that he began to contemplate an even longer stay than he had originally intended. As he explained to Beaverbrook on October 10, 'Life at your Villa is so pleasant and peaceful that I wonder whether you could keep me longer than the 31st October. I could then fly over for my engagements in England in November and December, and return to this sunshine world.'[3]

On October 15 Clementine Churchill returned to London, leaving her husband to his paintings and his History. Both Alan Hodge and Denis Kelly flew out to help, as Churchill had hoped they would, while Anthony Montague Browne supervised such general correspondence as had to be attended to. On October 20 Churchill wrote to his wife, the first part of his letter dictated:

My darling,

Today it is raining, and the prophets predict at least two days of similar weather. There is no doubt you were well advised to leave when you did.

I have been working at the book. I hope that Miss Pugh gave you the ninth and tenth sections. You must not judge by the end. It is incomplete, and I have not looked at it (except 'The Great Republic') for fifteen years. There is, however, plenty of time, as it is not required till October 1958.

I have bidden Hodge and Kelly to lunch each day, and dined alone with Anthony. We have been to the Casino on two occasions, and so far I am £90 to the good, (never having staked a fiver). I think, however, I shall probably go again as no mention of it has appeared.

[1] 'My dear Max', 6 October 1955: Beaverbrook papers.

[2] 'Dear Sir Winston', 10 October 1955: Churchill papers, 4/26. In 1955 Robert Carson was Assistant Keeper, and from 1978 to 1983 Keeper of the Department of Coins and Medals at the British Museum. He published three volumes, *Principal Coins of the Romans*, in 1978, 1980 and 1981.

[3] 'My dear Max', 10 October 1955: Churchill papers, 2/211.

I am perplexed at Max not answering. Ten days have passed. If by the end of the week no reply by letter or telegram is received, I shall return to England on the 31st. There is no doubt I am in better health.

I will keep you informed by telegram. The posts often take three or four days. You seem to be having stormy weather.

Churchill added in his own hand:

Tell me what yr doctor said. Are you not making slow but sure progress? I think so much of you and all your kindness to your poor [sketch of a pig]. I am looking forward to a letter from you when the post comes tomorrow. You have been gone 5 days. But I expect you will say 'where is yours'. The common difficulty is that there is little to tell.

All my love & many kisses,
Your ever loving husband

W[1]

On October 23 Christopher Soames sent Churchill an account of the politics back at home. 'The Conference was not very exciting,' he wrote, 'though your telegram was well received. Anthony got a good cheer, but there is a widespread feeling that the Government hasn't got a firm enough grip of affairs—there is too much drift and not enough evidence of decision on many outstanding problems.'[2]

Churchill planned to stay in the South of France until November 15. He also contemplated a visit to the Bahamas, telegraphing his wife on October 24: 'Max says weather Nassau perfect and offers us Pancake House fully staffed which he owns. He lives at Aitken House in Nassau which is his also. I think it would be very nice for first two months of New Year let me know what you think about it. I am most anxious to receive doctor's report and to hear how you feel.' Churchill added: 'There is no news here. Weather is not cold and quite pleasant.'[3]

Among the requests which reached Churchill while he was in the South of France was one from Sir Gerald Kelly, asking if the Royal Academy could mount an exhibition of Churchill's paintings which were then at Chartwell.[4] 'Thank you for your kind suggestion,' Churchill replied, 'but I do not contemplate such a display in my lifetime.'[5]

On October 26 Churchill dictated a short letter to his wife:

My darling,
The weather is very pleasant—bright and calm. The only change is that it

---

[1] 'My darling', 20 October 1955: Spencer-Churchill papers.
[2] 'My dear Sir Winston', 23 October 1955: Churchill papers, 1/56.
[3] Telegram sent 24 October 1955: Spencer-Churchill papers.
[4] Letter of 25 October 1955: Churchill papers, 1/24.
[5] Letter of 2 November 1955: Churchill papers, 1/24.

has become a little cooler. I am very glad that Sarah is coming out again on Friday. She will have your room. Anthony MB is going home for a week on Sunday next, and it will be very nice to have Sarah with me.

I am going to invite Bill Deakin to spend a prolonged weekend also. He has been working a great deal at the book. I am reading the volume to be delivered in the first fortnight of November through again. This will be my final. I think it is all right, and will in three or four days turn to the re-read of Volume II.

As regards my correspondence with Max, which I forwarded to you on Monday, he showed himself most kind and obliging, and if on reflection you are still for it I will accept for January and February. I think the fortnight's voyage will do you good, though I will not commit myself finally at this stage whether or not to save time by flying. It is only twenty-two hours, and I am not a good sailor. How many tons is the *Caronia*? However, we can talk this over when I get back on the 15th November. I will, however, write and accept Max's invitation to Pancake House.

I am bidden tomorrow to lunch with Reves and Madame R at the St Pol Restaurant, which I believe is where you went the other day, and I will look at the Matisse Chapel after lunch.

On being given this letter to sign, Churchill added three more pages in his own hand:

Darling your doctor's account is very vague. Perhaps Sarah will bring me details. I send this letter by Hodge & Kelly who are returning home today, so it will reach you tonight, i.e. quicker than a telegram. I am certainly better & am sure I shall be able to do the speeches all right—within the limits. I have a fine set of notes from Christ. The dinner shd be easy.[1]

I hear from Christopher that you are going to spend the weekend at Chartwell & that they are 'meeting' you. This seems a good idea. The time passes fairly quickly here. I have been every night to the Casino! & not a word in the Press, & am still playing on my winnings. When they stop I shall stop too.

Darling one I think of you so much & of how we are to lead a happy life. I was quite content with Nov. 15 as my date for going home. It will be interesting to get in touch with political affairs again.

I am so glad you like the Nassau plan.

Sarah will bring me news of Diana. I have some now. She is vy dear to me.

I am afraid this is a vy discursive letter, but I know you will receive it with kindness & I hope pleasure.

Always my tender love my dear one & many many kisses.

Your devoted husband

W[2]

---

[1] Churchill had five speeches to give on his return to England: in his Constituency (on November 18), at Harrow (November 24), to the Young Conservatives (December 5), at the Drapers Hall (December 7) and at a Mansion House dinner (December 16).

[2] 'My darling', 26 October 1955: Spencer-Churchill papers.

'Sarah is back and great fun,' Churchill reported to his wife from La Capponcina on October 30. He also told her of how, on the previous day, he had been taken 'to see a villa here which has been empty for twenty years, in a vast forest exactly above Monte Carlo, which would have much to recommend it if I were twenty years younger and everything else was the same'. Churchill added: 'You need not have any anxiety that I shall commit you to anything,' [1]

The search for the 'Dream Villa' continued; on November 9 Sarah Churchill wrote to her mother: 'we have been going to see villas (mostly monstrous!) with vague plans of buying—don't worry—he would never without you—I don't think he even wants to really—but he does love the sun so. . . .' [2]

On November 9 Churchill sent a last letter to his wife before returning to England, and to a speech which he had agreed to make in his constituency. 'I have no doubt about getting through all right,' he wrote. He and Sarah, together with his daughter Diana and Anthony Montague Browne, were engaged in reconnoitering houses, but without any result. Do not be alarmed therefore by anything you read in the *Nice-Matin*.' Churchill's letter ended: 'Darling one I think so much of you & hope & trust you are making progress. I love you vy much my dearest Clemmie & feel sure you reciprocate these sentiments wh spring from my heart. Your devoted husband, W.' [3]

Churchill's final days at La Capponcina were occupied with work on his History. His proof reader, C. C. Wood, had flown out to the South of France, and revealed all sorts of problems. 'It seems to me very stupid,' Churchill wrote to Alan Hodge about one of them, 'that the works of celebrities like Caesar and Tacitus should be unquotable except with their translators' names. Surely anyone has a right to translate Caesar himself, and the numbers of words are very small.' Then there was the preface which he had written for the first volume. 'Reves has given me back the amended text which I proposed of the Preface,' Churchill told Hodge. 'He has had lengthy telephonings with French, German, Italian and Scandinavian publishers, showing what they want for their editions. I am quite willing to cut out "of the English-Speaking peoples" at the bottom of the first page in the foreign editions.' Churchill added: 'Mr Literary Wood made me feel that a vortex might break out in the detailed final correction of the First Volume which could be avoided if he were out here. [4] The posts are

---

[1] 'My darling', 30 October 1955: Spencer-Churchill papers.
[2] Letter of 9 November 1955: Mary Soames, *Clementine Churchill*, page 460.
[3] 'My darling', 9 November 1955: Spencer-Churchill papers.
[4] C. C. Wood was known as 'Mr Literary Wood' to distinguish him from 'Mr Accountant Wood' (James Wood) Churchill's accountant for many years.

very tardy. As a matter of fact it will be better to settle things in England, which we will do next week.'

'I have a speech of modest dimensions,' Churchill warned Hodge, 'which a little overhangs me till Friday, 18th, but I will see you on Tuesday morning and you could tell me how things are going.'[1]

In a further note to Hodge, on November 12, Churchill commented on the problems posed by trying to calculate the numbers involved in the early medieval battles. On one of his pages it stated that 'seven hundred vessels' had carried seven thousand men: a mere ten men per ship. This, Churchill commented, 'is absurd', and he added:

I expect myself that the seven thousand men were warriors in character and substance, and that they had eight or ten thousand more armed dependents. However, this cannot be proved, and modern historians are trying to cut down the numbers in all the battles.

Let me know what your solution is. Later on, in the Battle of Towton, another instance occurs, where the Lancastrian fugitives, although now put at a very small number, are able to dam the stream and make bridges with their bodies. I should think myself there were fifty thousand men at Towton.[2]

Churchill's mind was continually ranging over the themes and episodes of his volumes, often linking what they said with more modern moments. As he explained to Alan Hodge and Denis Kelly in connection with the period immediately before the Norman Conquest of 1066: 'The contacts between Normandy and England were very close during the last twenty years of the reign of Edward the Confessor. Westerham Church is built with stone from Ouistreham, where we landed in 1944 in Normandy, and the name of Westerham as well as the stone may have come from there.' Churchill added: 'It is no use introducing, as on page 3, an epitome of the history of Normandy, which had already been playing a great part in our affairs, and was itself nearly a hundred years old.'[3]

On his return to England in the second week of November 1955, Churchill was greeted by a friendly letter from the Prime Minister:

My dear Winston,

Welcome home. I hope that you have had plenty of sunshine.

We have had our troubles, economic and otherwise, but are battling through. Geneva was not good. The Bear would only move backwards. The question

[1] 'My dear Hodge', La Capponcina, Cap d'Ail, 10 November 1955: Churchill papers, 4/27.

[2] 'Mr Hodge', 12 November 1955: Churchill papers, 4/27.

[3] 'Mr Hodge, Mr Kelly', undated,: Churchill papers, 4/27.

is what we should do next. I am inclined to think that there should be no further meeting of Foreign Secretaries until we have had a go at Bulganin and Khrushchev as our guests here in April.

Ike is recovering but I am afraid it will be a little time yet before he can do serious business again.[1] Adenauer is also better but I fear not too stalwart. You can imagine how we have missed them both.

Do let us know when you will be in London and come and have a quiet meal with us.

Clarissa and I send all love to you both.

Yours ever

Anthony[2]

'I have watched with attention your battle,' Churchill replied, 'and it seems to me that you are getting along pretty well.' He had a speech to make in his constituency, Churchill added, 'and this hangs over my head in a disproportionate manner'.[3]

Churchill was helped in preparing his speech by Christopher Soames and Randolph Churchill. 'I am not going to make a long speech tonight,' he told his constituents, 'because the purpose of this gathering is to dine and dance. I have, however, put a few notes on paper, because I have always been a bit shy of the really extemporary speech ever since I heard it said that an extemporary speech was not worth the paper it was written on.' It was on December 5, he said, at the Young Conservative Rally, that he would 'unfold my thoughts about the political situation and the problems that assail us'.[4]

On November 24 Churchill made his sixteenth consecutive visit to Harrow for the school 'Songs'. It was, he said, 'a very agreeable gathering that we have here and I hope it may long continue. I will certainly come as long as I am here available on duty.' That night there was to be an all-night sitting in the House of Commons, Churchill explained, so that 'some of my colleagues here who have come down' would have to go back to London for the debate. 'But I am going to take advantage of the Chief Whip's courtesy to go to bed.'[5]

---

[1] On 1 October 1955, a week after President Eisenhower had suffered his heart attack, *The Times* reported that a White House doctor 'who first saw no reason why the President should not run again, has now said in a television interview that, having seen something of the strain involved in the Presidency, he would personally not wish to do so if he were in General Eisenhower's place'. On November 11 Eisenhower returned to the White House, having been recuperating in Denver. That day, a leading article in *The Times* reported that, 'providing there is no setback, Americans will have the feeling that, at least where major matters are concerned, the President is in circulation again'.

[2] 'My dear Winston', 13 November 1955: Churchill papers, 2/216.

[3] 'My dear Anthony', 15 November 1955: Churchill papers, 2/216. On 30 December 1955 Edward Heath had succeeded Patrick Buchan-Hepburn as Chief Whip.

[4] Speech of 18 November 1955: Randolph S. Churchill (editor), *The Unwritten Alliance*, pages 273–4.

[5] Speech of 24 November 1955: Churchill papers, 2/336.

Churchill had decided to return to the South of France in the New Year, rather than go to the Bahamas as Beaverbrook had suggested. He had, he explained to Beaverbrook on November 26 'became increasingly attracted to the Riviera, which is so handy to get at and avoids long journeys. You have been so kind to me, and the nine weeks I spent as your guest were so pleasant and peaceful that, as perhaps you have seen, I have been looking about for a dwelling of my own where we could be neighbours.' Churchill went on to explain:

I am now exploring two retreats. The late French Premier, or was he President, Tardieu, found a place in the mountains behind Mentone about ten miles inland, which they would sell furnished, I believe, for 27 million francs, which is approximately £27,000. Tardieu built this place.[1] He guillotined the mountain to make a flat space and built upon the summit a rather jumbled house, which I think a little alteration might make acceptable to me.

Another place which seems suitable is in the Eze curve, called Château St Laurent. The proprietor came to see me yesterday. He has already got a villa on the peninsular Saint Jean Cap Ferrat, and is quite willing to rent St Laurent to me for, say, a couple of years, with the option to buy at the end. This would in any case give me the opportunity of looking around.

'Of course,' Churchill added, 'neither of these is as nice as yours. But I do not want to take advantage of your kindness and generosity, or abuse the hospitality you have so abundantly given me.'[2]

As Churchill approached his eighty-first birthday, he agreed, at Eden's request, was to try to persuade R. A. Butler to accept Eden's offer of the Leadership of the House of Commons without combining it with any departmental office. 'I had a long talk with Rab yesterday,' Churchill wrote to Eden on November 27, 'and I advised him to accept. . . .' It was true, Churchill had told Butler, that in wartime a seat in the War Cabinet gained by the addition of a departmental position, 'but in Peace', Churchill said, 'it is only a burden'. By this argument, Churchill told Eden, 'He seemed convinced.'[3] Churchill added, of the wider international scene: 'I think you will have to review your invitation to the Russians in the light of Khrushchev's Indian exhibition; but April is still a long way off.'[4]

'The bears are certainly behaving ill,' Eden replied; 'perhaps it

---

[1] André Tardieu, who had died in 1945, was three times, though briefly, Prime Minister of France, from November 1929 to February 1930, March to December 1930, and February to June 1932. He was never President.

[2] 'My dear Max', 26 November 1955: Beaverbrook papers.

[3] Butler, who had been Leader of the House of Commons since 7 April 1955, continued to combine this Office with that of Chancellor of the Exchequer until 20 December 1955, when he became Lord Privy Seal, a non-Departmental Cabinet position.

[4] 'My dear Anthony', 'Secret', 27 November 1955: Churchill papers, 1/56. The Soviet leader was in India, where he was vigorously denouncing Capitalism and the West.

would do the British public no harm to see them so. But, as you say, we don't fortunately have to decide on that yet.'[1]

On November 30 Churchill celebrated his eighty-first birthday. 'My husband and I send you our warmest congratulations and best wishes for your birthday,' the Queen telegraphed that day.[2] From Eisenhower came a gold medallion as 'a token of America's enduring gratitude'. The English-Speaking peoples, wrote the President, 'and the entire world, are the better for the wisdom of your counsel, for the inspiration of your unflagging optimism and for the heartening example of your shining courage. You have been a towering leader in the quest for peace, as you were in the battle for freedom through the dark days of war.'[3]

'Your letter has moved me more than I can tell you,' Churchill replied on November 30, and he added: 'As you know, it is my deepest conviction that it is on the friendship between our two nations that the happiness and security of the free peoples rests—and indeed that of the whole world. Your eloquent words have once more given me proof, if it were needed, that you share my own feelings and reciprocate my personal affection.'[4]

On December 5 Churchill spoke at Woodford to the Young Conservatives. The draft had been provided by Jock Colville, who noted: 'I have not put in any percentages!'[5] Speaking of the new mathematical calculators which enabled addition and multiplication 'at a rate and on a scale we could not have been taught at school', Churchill warned: 'I am all for your using machines, but do not let them use you.'[6]

Two days after speaking at Woodford, Churchill spoke at the Drapers' Hall, London, in accepting the first Williamsburg Award by the Trustees of the preserved and reconstructed Virginia township and

[1] 'My dear Winston', 29 November 1955: Churchill papers, 2/216.
[2] Telegram, 30 November 1955: Churchill papers, 4/483A.
[3] 'Dear Winston', sent from Gettysburg, 26 November 1955: Churchill papers, 2/217. The citation on the medallion read: 'Presented to Sir Winston Spencer Churchill by President Dwight D. Eisenhower on behalf of his millions of admiring friends in the United States for courageous leadership and in recognition of his signal services to the defense of freedom in which cause his country and the United States have been associated in both peace and war.'
[4] 'My dear Friend', 30 November 1955: Churchill papers, 2/217.
[5] Letter of 24 November 1955: Churchill papers, 5/49.
[6] Speech of 5 December 1955: Randolph S. Churchill (editor), *The Unwritten Alliance*, pages 275-9.

memorial of Colonial Williamsburg. 'No more fascinating gleam exists of a vanished world,' he said, 'embodying as it does the grace, the ease, and the charm of bygone colonial days.' Churchill added:

The horizons of life are dark and confused, but I think that most of us here have the sort of feeling that we shall not go far wrong if we keep together. I am very glad to learn that Sir Anthony Eden and the Foreign Secretary, Mr Harold Macmillan, whom we are all so glad to see here tonight, are going over in the New Year for another talk about all those tiresome and difficult matters in which our common interests are involved. They will talk about them on foundations strong, and ever growing stronger, and which will never be broken by force or the threat of force.

As for himself, Churchill said, he was by blood half American, 'and on my mother's side I have the right to enjoy the early memories of Colonial Williamsburg as much as anyone here. I delight in my American ancestry. . . .'

Churchill had been presented at the ceremony with a town crier's bell, modelled on one from Colonial days. 'Its silver tone is gentle,' he said. 'I shall ring it whenever I feel there is duty to be done.' [1]

'Eighty-one is an awful age,' Churchill wrote on December 9 to Lady Juliet Duff.[2] On December 12 he spent nearly four hours in the House of Commons listening to the debate, but on the following day he told his doctor: 'I keep losing my memory. I could not remember Anthony's name today.' [3] On December 16 he had yet another speech to give, his fifth since his return from France. It was at the Mansion House, London, to receive the Freedom of Belfast and Londonderry. It was 'indeed remarkable', he said, 'that the three Field Marshals whom we have with us today, the most celebrated soldiers we had in the War, "Brookie", "Alex", and "Monty", should all be Irish. They certainly adorn the record which Belfast and Londonderry have made of famous men across the centuries.' As to his own part in the war, 'I am glad,' he said, 'you think I did my duty. . . .' [4]

[1] Speech of 7 December 1955: Randolph S. Churchill (editor), *The Unwritten Alliance*, pages 280–1.

[2] Letter of 9 December 1955: Lady Juliet Duff papers. Lady Juliet Duff was seventy-four; she died in September 1965.

[3] Moran diary, 13 December 1955: *The Struggle for Survival*, page 687.

[4] Speech of 16 December 1955: Randolph S. Churchill (editor), *The Unwritten Alliance*, pages 282–4. Recording: BBC Written Archive Centre, Library No. 22632–3.

61

New Strength, and a New Book

O N 15 December 1955, Churchill introduced Laurence Olivier
to the Other Club; on the following day Olivier wrote to him
of 'sharing in the joy of your company last night'.[1] On December 17
Churchill went to his son Randolph's house, Stour, in Suffolk, where
he spent two nights; Clementine Churchill joined him there for the
day on December 18. Returning to London for a night, Churchill
went on to Chartwell for the last two weeks of December, where Alan
Hodge joined him twice for work on the history, revising and polishing
the second volume, 'The New World'.

On December 20, Churchill's first day back at Chartwell, Christopher Soames was appointed Under-Secretary of State for Air. 'Yes, it
will be very interesting at this time,' Churchill told Lord Moran a
week later. 'England may be indefensible. But I think we may be able
to make other countries indefensible.'[2] As to his own plans, Churchill
told Moran on December 20: 'I'm going to France on January 11.'
'Permanently?' asked the doctor. 'Well, semi-permanently,' replied
Churchill with a smile.[3]

Churchill spent Christmas 1955 at Chartwell with his family. On
January 2 Montgomery came for the night, on January 5 Jock Colville
and two days later Lord Cherwell. On January 6 Churchill telegraphed to Beaverbrook about his holiday plans. He would stay with
Emery Reves 'at the Chanel Villa' until the end of February, and
would be 'searching for a habitation' of his own.[4]

The 'Chanel Villa' had been built for Coco Chanel in the early
1920s by Churchill's friend Bendor, Duke of Westminster. Emery
Reves and Wendy Russell, who were soon to be married, had lived in

---

[1] Letter of 16 December 1955: Churchill papers, 2/343.
[2] Moran diary, 28 December 1955: *The Struggle for Survival*, page 688.
[3] Moran diary, 20 December 1955: *The Struggle for Survival*, pages 687–8.
[4] Telegram despatched 6 January 1956: Churchill papers, 2/211.

it since 1950, and knew it by its original name, La Pausa. It was an idyllic villa in an idyllic spot, high above the Riviera, with magnificent views down to the sea, surrounded by its own olive grove. 'We should be very glad to accept your kind invitation to stay at La Pausa,' Churchill had written to Reves on December 4, 'and I should like to come out for the latter half of January and all February, provided that you will let me pay for the housekeeping. Lady Churchill has some obligations over here and will come out later. During this period I shall hope to arrange something permanent in the neighbourhood, either by rent or purchase.' Purchase from a French proprietor, Churchill added, 'will be very difficult on account of the Treasury regulations'.[1]

'I have some unfinished daubs,' Churchill telegraphed to Beaverbrook on January 8, 'which I hope I may go to Capponcina to complete while staying with Reves.'[2]

Clementine Churchill remained in England that winter. In January she had to go into University College Hospital for a complete overhaul, for three or four days. While she was in hospital she was unlucky enough to catch an infection, and was forced to remain in hospital for three weeks. From La Pausa, in long hand-written letters, Churchill kept her posted with his news and views. His first letter was sent on January 15:

My dear One,
   I have been worried by your sore throat & temperature; but Drs Barnett & Rosenheim have reassured me, & now I learn they are taking a normal course. If not I will return. I also rang up Maria whose promised morning telegram I await.
   We have had so far nothing but clouds & rain. So I have not left this luxurious house & have passed the time mainly in bed revising the Book. They predict a gleam of sunshine this afternoon.
   Rab came to dinner with the Birkenheads,[3] but the occasion gave little opportunity for serious talk. Randolph has arrived and is staying with the Onassis on the monster yacht.[4] He had a dangerous voyage, but seems vy well. I do hope you will get back to 28 soon. Toby awaits you there expectantly & Rufus shd be in Vincent's care.[5] The presence of one & the absence

---

[1] 'My dear Reves', 4 December 1955: Reves papers.

[2] Telegram despatched 8 January 1956: Churchill papers, 2/211.

[3] The 2nd Earl of Birkenhead, son of Churchill's close friend 'FE' Smith. Born in 1907, he succeeded his father as 2nd Earl in 1930. His wife Sheila was the daughter of another of Churchill's friends, the 1st Viscount Camrose. In 1944 Lord Birkenhead had served with the Yugoslav partisans together with Randolph Churchill.

[4] The 'monster yacht' was the *Christina*, formerly the Canadian frigate *Stormont*, converted in 1953 at the Howaldt Werke in Kiel to a luxury yacht, in time for Onassis's first Christmas aboard in 1954.

[5] Victor Vincent, the head gardener at Chartwell.

of the other shd make the house perfect for what I hope will form a short rest-cure.

Reves told me last night he intended to marry Wendy soon—but privately. She is a charming hostess and asked me to carry my respects to you. All is vy quiet here.

You have all my love, my Darling & I pray for your early cure. Wendy's mother had arthritis and was cured after 4 years of woe.

Your loving husband

W[1]

On January 16, at La Pausa, Churchill authorized a major financial transaction, his purchase of 10,000 Brinco shares, at three dollars each, as part of the first public issue in the Hamilton Falls hydro-electric project in Canada. 'It is high time the Hamilton Falls had a bridle,' he wrote that day to Colville.[2] That evening, January 16, Aristotle Onassis was one of the dinner guests at La Pausa. The day after the dinner party, Churchill sent his wife a full report:

My darling,

All the children go home today by one route or another. Arabella & Celia were both vy sweet to me. Diana will give you accounts. She seems vy well & mistress of herself. Randolph brought Onassis (the man with the big yacht) to dinner last night. He made a good impression upon me. He is a vy able and masterful man & told me a lot about whales. He kissed my hand!

I have passed another morning in bed at the Book. I had a peep outside yesterday, but today the sun has definitely begun to shine & I shall take a walk in the garden after luncheon. We dine with Rab on Wednesday next.

I am so grieved & worried by the news that your throat has not cleared up entirely and that you had a temperature. Dr Rosenheim is a regular informant & he gives me full accounts twice a day. He says the arthritis is better & that his new treatment of it is answering.

My dear One I would so much like to kiss you now. I send you my love by this. You see I have written it by my own paw & no one has seen it. The children will take it home.

All my love
Your devoted

W[3]

Later that same day, Churchill wrote again:

---

[1] 'My dear One', La Pausa, Roquebrune, Alpes-Maritimes, 15 January 1956: Spencer-Churchill papers.

[2] Letter of 16 January 1956, La Pausa: Churchill papers, 1/105. Sixteen months later Colville informed Churchill that Brinco shares were changing hands at six dollars and more, 'which means that you have doubled your capital' (Letter of 30 May 1957: Churchill papers, 1/108).

[3] 'My Darling', 17 January 1956, La Pausa: Spencer-Churchill papers.

My darling,

I have so much pleasure & relief at hearing good news of you. Things sound so bad and to be at a distance is vy trying. But this morning when I was awakened at half past nine to hear from Doctor Rosenheim that your temperature was normal I was filled with joy.

I have passed the time since I arrived three quarters in bed & come down to meals. Reves & Wendy are most obliging. They ask the guests I like and none I don't. A few people have written & so we had last night Daisy Fellowes & her young man Hamish Edgar. Daisy was vy sprightly.[1] I remember meeting her in 1918 when she was the Princess de Broglie in Paris. She is wonderfully well maintained & kept us all agog. Her young man is coming to play bezique with me this afternoon at 4.

Arthur Soames has also written and he & his wife[2] are to dine tonight. On Wednesday we all go to lunch or dinner with RAB as the weather (which is unbroken clouds) permits. Thursday we are going to paint still-life & garden according as the sun shines.

My darling one I send you all my love. We have devised a means of getting the airplanes to carry the letters by making them into packages. I hope therefore this will reach you today.

  With all my heart
  Your loving husband

                                                                  W

Churchill added at the bottom of this letter: 'Own paw.'[3]

On January 18 Churchill left La Pausa for the first time in a week, to lunch in Monte Carlo with R. A. Butler. On the following day Butler was at La Pausa to paint. 'He is a bit anxious,' Churchill wrote to his wife, 'I reassured him,' and he added: 'I shall have to get my paints out. I have not touched them yet.' It was also the first day of blue sky, at least 'in small patches'. Churchill's letter continued:

I have been working in bed at the Book & have almost finished Volume II. I don't think there will be any difficulty about my retirement, so that anything more I do can be stored in yr hands—if indeed I last so long.

I thought well of Onassis & perhaps I will go and inspect his yacht, wh he wants me to do vy much.

(A gleam of sunshine) Perhaps it portends the Spring. But I am not dependent on the weather except for painting. The days pass by quickly. My cough continues. I always hate having to get up.

---

[1] Marguerite Séverine Philippine, daughter of the 3rd Duc Decazes and de Glücksbierg. Known as 'Daisy,' in 1910 she married Prince Jean de Broglie (who was killed in action in 1918); hence her nickname 'the Imbroglio'. In 1919 she married the Hon. Reginald Ailwyn Fellowes, second son of the 2nd Baron de Ramsey, whose wife Lady Rosamond Spencer-Churchill was Churchill's aunt (his father's sister). Her villa in the south of France was Les Zoraïdes. She died in December 1962.

[2] Mrs Audrey Sloane-Stanley, Arthur Soames's third wife, whom he had married in 1948.

[3] 'My darling', 17 January 1956, La Pausa: Spencer-Churchill papers.

'It is quite audible talking on the telephone when you feel fit for it,' Churchill ended. 'I should love to hear your dear voice.'[1]

Two days later Churchill sent his wife a further account of his activities and plans, including the possible permanent employment of Anthony Montague Browne:

My darling,

It is raining again! We have not had a sunshine day since I arrived—only a few fitful gleams. All the same the time has passed pleasantly. I don't get up till one thirty and have a two hours nap in the afternoon. I shd think I average 10 hours sleep a day, & the Book occupies my leisure. The final chapter of Vol II goes off today. I am content with it.

I was so much relieved at your increasing good news, & I hope you will soon be home again. Anthony goes back tomorrow (Sunday) & wd like vy much to come to see you to give you a full account. I am vy much inclined to take him on. From what Norman Brook said I am sure I can deduct his salary from the literary expenses, & also that he can be 'seconded' so as not to leave the service or lose pension rights for two or three years. He is vy companionable & means eventually to choose another career. He is out flying now in Onassis' airplane.[2] It will be his first flight in his own hands for *seven* years. However there is a pilot & (I hope) dual control.

We are going after luncheon to look at a house wh can be let furnished & in good order for several months at a time, & is said to have many attractions. I shall not commit you to anything permanent. I feel however that I am a burden here as they both mean to stay on—Nothing could exceed Wendy's kindness & they repulse with vigour all suggestions that they want me to go—even after February. Wendy will look after the housekeeping and she is a marvel at this. Do not have any worries. Everything will be temporary & I shall not be committed beyond a couple of months.

I am inviting Diana to come out here during AMB's absence. She said she would like to come & I think the scene & setting will do her good.

My darling one I love you dearly

Your devoted husband

W

PS Anthony's air trip was a 'fiasco' (his own expression). The plane wd not get off the ground. So there was no accident. He is back & the motor car will take this letter. It shd reach you tonight.[3]

'It is very quiet and peaceful here,' Churchill wrote to Edward Heath

---

[1] 'My darling One', La Pausa, 19 January 1956: Spencer-Churchill papers.

[2] Having joined the Oxford University Air Squadron as an undergraduate in 1941, Montague Browne served in the Royal Air Force from 1942 to 1945, flying fighter bombers, mainly in Burma, and being awarded the Distinguished Flying Cross. He returned to university in 1945, joining the Foreign Office in 1946.

[3] 'My darling', La Pausa, 21 January 1956: Spencer-Churchill papers.

on January 22, 'though we have had no sunshine so far. It is I fancy on the way.'[1]

On January 22 Churchill sent his wife a further account of his plans:

Darling,

Anthony leaves this morning and bears this. I am going to make him head of my private office. He will be 'seconded'. He will preserve his pension rights & can go back to the FO at any time. I can with Treasury sanction include his salary in my expenses. I am sure this is a good arrangement.

We went to look at a house yesterday—beautifully situated but in disrepair. I have been made so comfortable here and Wendy is so kind & charming that I am not hurrying renting another house. She persists in begging me to stay, saying in her husband's presence that I have done everything for him & that they never can repay etc. At any rate I shall stay until March. They are keeping a lovely room for you & are most eager you shd try it. Anyhow think it over during your rest cure at 28.

I am telegraphing to Diana to come out for ten days. She will be able to give you a full report.

My dear one I am planning to talk on the telephone to you as I want to hear your voice & to tell you how much I love you.

Your loving husband

W

PS Weather still warm & sultry.[2]

'Her Majesty and the Duke of Edinburgh hope that you are finding some sun—' Sir Michael Adeane wrote from Buckingham Palace on January 24, 'there is not much here—and desire me to send you their best wishes. May I please send you my own?'[3] Enclosed with Adeane's letter were details of the Queen's tour of Nigeria, on which she was about to embark. Churchill wrote at once to the Queen, in his own hand:

Madam,

It is very kind of Your Majesty to think of me at this hour of departure and to send me such interesting information about the journey to Nigeria. I had thought a great deal about it myself and all the exertions and sacrifices Your Majesty makes for the public interest. I have not troubled Your Majesty with a letter amid so much business, and that this gracious message should reach me from Yourself and the Duke gives me the keenest pleasure. May God protect Your Majesty and bring You both back safely to our shores.

I am looking forward to sending the first copy of the History of the English-

[1] La Pausa, 22 January 1956: Churchill papers, 2/129.
[2] 'Darling', La Pausa, 22 January 1956: Spencer-Churchill papers.
[3] 'Dear Sir Winston', Buckingham Palace, 24 January 1956: Churchill papers, 2/532.

Speaking Peoples, which will come out in April and occupies my time meanwhile, to Your Majesty.

And with my humble duty,

remain

Your Majesty's devoted servant,

Winston S. Churchill[1]

'I am working hard at the third volume,' Churchill wrote four days later to Bill Deakin, 'and hope to make the Marlborough part more interesting.'[2]

The amount of work that Churchill did was in no way onerous. On January 25 he wrote to Field Marshal Montgomery: 'We have not had one day of sunshine since arriving here, but I am very comfortable and idle.'[3] That day there was a pleasing telegram from Eden, who was about to leave London for his first visit to the United States as Prime Minister. 'On setting out on this journey which we have made so often together,' Eden wrote, 'I want to tell you how much I am thinking of our past experiences.'[4]

On January 26 Churchill wrote again, in his own hand, to his wife, enclosing the Queen's message and a copy of his own reply. 'I pray she may come safely home,' he wrote. 'She works hard!' At last he could report to his wife that there was 'blazing sunshine'. But from his daughter Diana he had learned that Clementine's illness had been compounded:

She gave me a gloomy account of the University College hospital, & said you got a touch of '*pneumonia*' there. Between morning & night the doctor decided not to telegraph for me because you or they had shaken it off. These are disconcerting things to hear. I am sure it is much better to be ill at home & not get all the local illnesses wh the hospitals exist to cure.

Darling one take care of yourself. Do no work that does not amuse you. Make no plans for the present. I thought Diana's visit might—if all goes well—give you time to look round. If not I will come home & see you, & fly out again. They are vy nice people here & Wendy is charming.[5]

Churchill had hoped that as soon as his wife was better, she would join him and their daughter Diana at La Pausa. She decided instead to go by sea to Ceylon with her cousin, and closest friend, Sylvia Henley. On January 30 Churchill wrote from La Pausa:

My Darling,

Assuming you have made up your mind to start with Sylvia on the 17th, I

---

[1] 'Madam', La Pausa, 26 January 1956: Churchill papers, 2/532.

[2] 'My dear Bill', La Pausa, 30 January 1956: Churchill papers, 4/27.

[3] 'My dear Monty', La Pausa, 25 January 1956: Churchill papers, 4/27.

[4] Foreign Office Telegram to Nice, No. 2 of 25 January 1956, 'Confidential': Churchill papers, 2/216.

[5] 'My darling', La Pausa, 26 January 1956: Spencer-Churchill papers.

shall come home on the 10th to see you off and return here about the 20th—
probably with Montague Browne.

I had hoped to persuade you to come and convalesce out here and that
you would meet Wendy who is a vy charming person. But I feel that with
Sylvia & the Ceylon sun your plan is a good one, and the weather here in
February is vy half & half. (Today & yesterday unfit for human consump-
tion) and once you have got through the Bay of Biscay you will have a good
convalescent cruise. Be vy careful about Ceylon & do not treat it like England.

Give me warning of any change because my plans depend on yours my dearest
One. I spend the days mostly in bed, & get up for lunch and dinner. I am being
taken through a course of Monet, Manet, Cézanne & Co by my hosts who are
both versed in modern painting and practise in the studio—now partly an office
with Miss Maturin. Also they have a wonderful form of gramophone wh plays
continuously Mozart and other composers of merit and anything else you like on
10-fold discs. I am in fact having an artistic education with vy agreeable tutors.

Darling unless I hear to the contrary we meet on the 10th at 28.

All my love

Your devoted husband

W[1]

'Winston has been so happy with you both,' Clementine Churchill
wrote to Wendy Russell from Hyde Park Gate on February 3. 'I wish
so much I could meet you,' she added, 'but this must be deferred. The
doctors feel I shall not be well until I have gone to a really hot climate.
You can imagine how I look forward to a few days with Winston
before I sail. I am looking forward to seeing his paintings.'[2]

On February 4 Churchill wrote again:

My darling,

I have not been out for a week & for the last 3 days have not even been on
the verandah. This is not because the weather is bad. The last three days
have been cold (comparatively) but you would call them bright and sunny.
The truth is that I stay a gt deal in bed and have taken (when I get up) to
painting Cézanne. I will bring you 2 or 3 home with ease.

My hosts are vy artistic, they paint & they collect. More than that they
delight in the famous painters of Europe & I am having an education in art
wh is beneficial. Also they play Mozart & others on these multiplied gramo-
phones. I am responsible for the few guests who come. Wendy is vy hard
working as well as gay. She organizes the household & they seem to be
devoted to her. I take them out every few days to give the servants a rest.
Wendy has undertaken the outfitting & repairs of any house I may want.
But I have decided to do what they wish and stay here through March. So
there is no hurry. In fact, *except for the Book*, I am idle & lazy.

---

[1] 'My Darling', La Pausa, 30 January 1956: Spencer-Churchill papers.

[2] 'My dear Mrs Russell', 3 February 1956: Reves papers. Wendy Russell was not yet married
to Reves.

My hope is that in April you will change ships at Suez & look in here for the Easter holidays. You wd like it & yr room awaits you.

Darling One I send you all my love & many kisses.

Your ever loving husband

W

[Sketch of a pig]

Torpid & recumbent.

'I was enchanted by your voice & miaouw on the telephone,' Churchill added. 'You gave me the impression of having got round the corner. I look forward so much to seeing you on the 10th.' [1]

On February 6 Churchill dined with Onassis on the *Christina*. It was his first visit to the yacht on which he was later to spend so many relaxing days, the days of old age, unhampered by ceremony or publicity. But on that first visit, Onassis's biographer has written, 'a swarm of photographers and newsmen were there to get their pictures and file their stories, touching off the legend of a remarkable friendship. Churchill, who had difficulty getting up the gangplank, was visibly upset by the presence of so many cameras.' [2]

As he prepared to return from La Pausa to London, Churchill also made plans to return immediately afterwards to the South of France. Emery Reves and Wendy had proved the perfect hosts. 'They have devoted themselves to my comfort in every conceivable way,' Churchill wrote to his wife on February 8, '& the month has passed vy comfortably.' Churchill added:

I have learned a lot I did not know about modern painters & musicians, & at their sincere request I shall come back here & not take a living place for March.

We dined with the Onassis on their yacht two nights ago. He is an extraordinary man. He wanted to lend us the yacht to go to Ceylon! It is the most beautiful structure I have seen afloat. I did not accept.

My darling I shall see you soon. The sun is shining & the wind has dropped. We are going to luncheon at a café on a pinnacle. [3]

On February 10 Churchill returned to London. Hardly had he reached England than, as he later telegraphed to Lord Rosebery, 'the downfall of snow occurred which enveloped our house at Roquebrune'. [4] For many hours, La Pausa had been cut off from the outside world.

On February 11 Churchill wrote to Wendy Russell from Hyde Park Gate:

[1] 'My darling', La Pausa, 4 February 1956: Spencer-Churchill papers.
[2] Peter Evans, *Ari, The Life and Times of Aristotle Socrates Onassis*, London 1986, page 158.
[3] 'My darling', La Pausa, 8 February 1956: Spencer-Churchill papers.
[4] Telegram to Lord Rosebery, 19 February 1956: Churchill papers, 2/197.

My dear Wendy,

We arrived safely after an adventurous journey. Lady Churchill is really much better, but needs rest, quiet and hot weather. I have gone over the idea of our meeting her at Suez in Onassis' yacht, and found both her and Mrs Sylvia Henley attracted by it. There is no need of any decision yet, so please observe the strictest secrecy. When I come out again on the 23rd, we will talk it all over together.

There is deep snow here, but the roads are kept open, and I got back from Chartwell in record time. You have had very unusual experiences, but I feel pretty sure that they will all be swept away by the time I come back.

I will write you again shortly. It was very nice having a month under your care, and I am certainly the better for it, although I get older as the days pass.

Write and tell me about things.

Thanking you so much for all your kindness & hospitality,

Believe me,

Yours sincerely,

Winston S. Churchill[1]

Awaiting Churchill when he reached London was another offer from Lord Beaverbrook, asking him to come as his guest to the Bahamas. But Churchill had now set his sights on remaining in the South of France. 'I am set on the Riviera,' he telegraphed to Beaverbrook on February 13, 'and shall be staying with Reves the bulk of March and April pending finding a permanent residence.' Then, with some of the properties he had already looked at in mind, he added: 'We shall be neighbours.'[2]

At Chartwell on February 13, Lord Moran asked Churchill about his painting while at La Pausa. 'He showed me a copy of a painting by Cézanne that he had taken from a book,' Moran noted. 'I asked him why he had chosen this particular picture to copy. "I like it," he answered, "because of the contrast between the red and the green."' Churchill also told Moran that he would go to the House of Commons that Thursday to vote in favour of hanging. 'I am a hanger,' he told his doctor. 'It is one of the forms of death of which I have no horror, I never thought about breaking my neck out hunting.'[3]

The hanging vote took place on February 16. In a free vote, hanging

---

[1] 'My dear Wendy', 11 February 1956: Reves papers.

[2] Telegram to Lord Beaverbrook, Nassau, Bahamas, 13 February 1956: Churchill papers, 2/211.

[3] Moran diary, 13 February 1956: *The Struggle for Survival*, pages 689–90. In *My Early Life*, Churchill wrote: 'Young men have often been ruined through owning horses or through backing horses, but never through riding them; unless of course they break their necks, which, taken at a gallop, is a very good death to die' (Winston S. Churchill, *My Early Life*, London 1930, page 59).

was abolished by forty-six votes; 292 MPs, including Churchill, voting to retain capital punishment, and 246 opposing it.[1]

Although Churchill supported the death penalty, he had reservations about its use. In August 1950, for example, he had written to the then Home Secretary, Chuter Ede: 'I think I ought to let you know that as a former Home Secretary I feel that the execution of three British soldiers for the murder of one person goes beyond what I believe to be the usual practice. Perhaps you would consult recent precedents at the Home Office. It must be very rare that as many as three should suffer when only one pulled the trigger. Justice is usually, though not always, satisfied with life for life, but three seems to me most severe.'[2]

On February 18 Clementine Churchill left Britain for her sea voyage to Ceylon. 'All quiet at Chartwell,' Churchill telegraphed to her on the following evening, and he added: 'Am probably not going back this week as La Pausa is still frozen.'[3]

From Clementine Churchill came a wireless telegram on February 23: 'Lovely voyage but still very cold. We have just been inoculated against typhoid, cholera, etc. Thinking of you. Love, Clemmie.'[4] 'Have postponed return to Roquebrune till weather there improves,' Churchill telegraphed to his wife on the following day. 'Hope now go next week. Love, W.'[5] 'Am returning Roquebrune Thursday,' Churchill telegraphed again on February 26, and he added: 'Cannot catch you with letters before Colombo. Love, W.'[6]

On February 27, shortly before leaving London for La Pausa, Churchill wrote to his wife, in his own hand, from 28 Hyde Park Gate:

My darling One,

It is hard to catch you with a letter with your different ports of call, so I have telegraphed. I do hope you are *both* feeling better and that the Indian Ocean has been warm. As you voyage southwards you carry my thoughts with you. I got yr second letter this morning and this reply shd reach you at Colombo according to the Post Office.

---

[1] *Hansard*, 16 February 1956. Those in favour of retaining capital punishment included Eden, Macmillan, R. A. Butler and Edward Heath. Those against included Hugh Gaitskell, Harold Wilson and James Callaghan. Hugh Gaitskell had succeeded Clement Attlee as Leader of the Labour Party in December 1955, following Attlee's resignation (when he was created Earl Attlee). According to the resolution that was passed, the death penalty 'no longer accords with the needs or the true interests of a civilized society'.

[2] 'My dear Ede', 26 August 1950: Churchill papers, 2/102.

[3] Telegram despatched 9.30 p.m., 19 February 1956: Churchill papers, 1/55.

[4] Telegram of 23 February 1956: Churchill papers, 1/55.

[5] Telegram despatched 24 February 1956: Churchill papers, 1/55.

[6] Telegram sent to Lady Churchill, Passenger *Himalaya*, care Peninsular, Aden, 26 February 1956: Churchill papers, 1/55.

I love you so much and envy you yr three weeks in Ceylon. I hope the High Commissioner will make things go smoothly.

I spent the long weekend at Chartwell mostly alone. It was not fit for more than one peep out. I walked however round the ponds—3 inches of ice, and down to the Farm. Mary & Christopher had the Fords staying with them & they all came to dine & see the film on Saturday.[1] It was a vy good one, *The Four Feathers*, with lots of good pictures of the battle of Omdurman. These stirred my memory, though accuracy was not achieved.

I had made all arrangements for going back to Roquebrune on Monday, March 5, but Reves telephoned to say that the weather was now beautiful & the temperature 70 (here it is 35°). I therefore altered my plans which are now to set out on March 1 from London Airport with Diana & AMB to La Pausa. If no fresh snowfall recurs I shall start accordingly. I thirst for warmth, and Chartwell even with Mary & Christopher & Dido[2] does not make up for the sunny landscape my window reveals. The thaw however seems to have begun here too, & will I trust continue.

I came back this morning to attend the Debate on foreign affairs which are in a fog. Tomorrow & Wednesday Defence is the subject. I shall vote with the Government. Chandos is dining with me & I hope for a little Bezique.

You are quite right to go first of all to the Galle Face Hotel, they tell me in the House, and push out to the Lavinia afterwards.

I will write about your landing at Marseilles & bringing Sylvia with you to stay for a few days at La Pausa. I do hope she likes Vol. I. She is I am sure a good judge.

Tender love my darling Clemmie from yr old & battered [sketch of pig] Your devoted husband

W[3]

The very first bound pre-publication copies of Volume one of *A History of the English-Speaking Peoples* had just reached Churchill; Lord Chandos was the first person to receive a copy, on February 29, followed on March 1 by Eden, Butler, Mary and Christopher Soames, Randolph and June Churchill, Denis Kelly and Alan Hodge. A week later, copies were sent to Bill Deakin, Diana Sandys and Lord Ismay.[4] The volume, entitled 'The Birth of Britain', was formally published on April 23, with a massive first printing of 130,000 copies followed within a month by a second printing of 30,000 copies.[5] 'You see how

---

[1] Edward Ford was Assistant Private Secretary to the Queen from 1952 to 1967. He was knighted in 1957. His wife Virginia was the daughter of Lord Brand.

[2] Dido Cairns, Christopher Soames's sister.

[3] 'My darling One', 27 February 1956: Spencer-Churchill papers.

[4] 'List of people who have been given copies of Volume I, *ESP*': Churchill papers, 4/67.

[5] Followed by further reprints of 20,000 (January 1957), 10,000 (August 1957), 9,750 (January 1958), 5,000 (February 1959), 3,475 (August 1960), 5,000 (April 1962), 5,000 (October 1964) and 5,000 (February 1965). The American edition was reprinted four times up to September 1958 (3 April 1956, 19 April 1956, 21 February 1958 and 15 September 1958). (Frederick Woods, *A Bibliography of the Works of Sir Winston Churchill, KG, OM, CH*, London 1963, revised 1969, page 136.)

easily it opens,' Churchill told his doctor on February 29, 'it is not necessary to break the back of the book to keep it open. I made them take away a quarter of an inch from the outer margins of the two pages and then add the half inch so gained to the inner margin. Look at it, Charles. It lies open like an angel's wings.' [1]

'It is a thrilling and moving panorama of events,' Mary Soames had written to her father when she had first read the proofs, and she added: 'I think people will be thrilled when it is published, and full of admiration and amazement at its author!' [2]

Immediately following the arrival of the first copies of his book from the printer, Churchill flew back to France, and to La Pausa. On arrival, he gave copies of the book to Wendy Russell, to his Detective, Sergeant Murray, and to Lord Beaverbrook. To his wife, Churchill wrote on March 2, again in his own hand:

My darling,

Here I am, with Diana & Anthony, in gt comfort but nursing a sore throat with the aid of Dr Roberts who is I think a good man. (I had him last time you will remember.) Meanwhile you shd have reached Colombo & I hope are already safely ensconced. I await a letter. They tell me the posts take 3 or 4 days, which is pretty good—but it leaves *me* in an hour.

I had an interesting time in London, & saw a lot of Christopher & Maria & also of the PM. He is having a hard time & the horizon is dark whichever way one looks. The Defence debate was an awful flop. 12 millions to be evacuated according to Walter Monckton and what they do when the wind changes (as it is sure to do in 3 weeks): the condition of the air force: the state of the Navy: all vy disturbing. WM was not good at this difficult task— to which he is completely new; and Nigel Birch was deservedly shouted down. [3]

Christopher goes into action next Monday & will I trust establish himself. He has a gt chance.

I give you my impressions gained in my corner seat, which is most respect-fully kept open for me by Hinchingbrooke, and wh I fill at the critical moment. [4]

I have brought Toby out here! He can go home whenever I choose. There is no restraint in England now, so I took him along. He is a bit subdued, but I think it is only the change of scene. (He had a peck at this, but it did not come off.)

Pamela L has had to go into the University College Hospital for an opera-

---

[1] Moran diary, 29 February 1956: *The Struggle for Survival*, pages 691–2.

[2] Letter sent from Suvretta House, St Moritz, Saturday 27 September 1955: Churchill papers, 1/56.

[3] Nigel Birch was Secretary of State for Air.

[4] Viscount Hinchingbrooke, son of the 9th Earl of Sandwich, was a Conservative MP from 1941 to 1962. He succeeded to the Earldom in 1962, but two years later he disclaimed his peerage for life, to be known as Victor Montagu.

tion on Monday. She has written me but the letter is still in the French post. Mary is finding out and will telephone to me. Operations unexpected are anxious at eighty.

I must close this letter now my dearest Clemmie.

Your ever loving husband

W [1]

While Churchill was at La Pausa, he received, through the British Consul-General in Nice, a series of Foreign Office telegrams, on Harold Macmillan's intructions. 'I am so much obliged to you for your courtesy in making this arrangement,' Churchill wrote to the Foreign Secretary, Selwyn Lloyd, in March 1956. 'It is of considerable help and interest to me.' [2]

There were a number of occasions when Churchill was in contact with the Foreign Office. On being asked to subscribe to an ornamental candelabrum to be set up outside the Israeli Parliament building in Jerusalem, as a gift from Britain, Churchill was told by Montague Browne after he had consulted with the Foreign Office: 'There would be no political objection to your subscribing to this fund if you wished.' Montague Browne added: 'We are not very happy that the Israeli Parliament should have set itself up in Jerusalem, which is supposed to be an international city, but this is rather a fine point.' [3] Churchill became a subscriber.

While Churchill was at La Pausa, Alan Hodge sent him notes, prepared by the Oxford historian Alan Bullock, for the late nineteenth-century section of Churchill's History. 'Sir Winston is now beginning to think that he might well write 1870 onwards himself,' Montague Browne wrote to Hodge on March 4, 'as he has such a close acquaintance with the period, both from his own early life and from the work he did for *Lord Randolph*.[4] He is ruminating on getting me to delve further into 1763–1815, but quite on what lines I do not yet know. So for the moment I am marking time.' [5]

On March 6, in a letter to Bernard Baruch, Churchill commented on Baruch's report that he still rode on horseback: 'I am sure I could ride, but I have not done so for five years.' As to Baruch's assertion that Churchill would in a few years be accorded the opportunity 'of righting the world', Churchill replied that he was 'not so sure', adding:

---

[1] 'My darling', La Pausa, 2 March 1956: Spencer-Churchill papers.

[2] 'My dear Selwyn Lloyd', La Pausa, March 1956: Churchill papers, 2/194. Lloyd had become Foreign Secretary on 20 December 1955.

[3] 'Sir Winston', initialled 'AMB', 4 March 1956: Churchill papers, 2/341.

[4] Churchill's two-volume biography of his father, *Lord Randolph Churchill*, was first published on 2 January 1906.

[5] 'Private', La Pausa, 4 March 1956: Churchill papers, 4/26.

However, if an emergency arises during the time I am hanging about the guardroom, I hope you will consider that I have not failed.

Personally, I think that the Soviets will exploit their peaceable policy another five or six years during which the United States is on duty. But we have made sufficient progress, though greatly hampered by the McMahon Act, to be able at the end of that time to send them back, whatever they choose to send us. It is on this that I rely for the safety of the world and the impossibility of war.[1]

'It is tough going here,' Eden wrote from 10 Downing Street in thanking Churchill for his Volume 1, 'but we are surviving.'[2]

On March 11 Churchill sent his wife a substantial budget of news, in his own hand:

My Darling.

I was so glad to get yr letter of the 5th & to realize that we are only 5 or 6 days apart.

Pamela L had a kidney taken out, wh is a shock at 79 and I was astonished to hear that the doctors said that she wd be able to go home in 12 days! I hope she will not have a relapse.

Now the weather has clouded over again here & I have hardly been out of doors since I arrived. Perhaps it is saving up for yr landing on April 5 at Marseilles. The Reves will be delighted to put you & Sylvia up. I must get back by the 12th as I have to preside at the Albert Hall Primrose League on the 13th. It is vy comfortable here & Wendy makes herself most agreeable. I work in bed at the book every morning & Kelly is at the hotel & Alan Hodge relieves him on the 15th. This is the way to get the job finished I am sure.

I brought Toby out here with me and I have arranged for him to have 2 female companions. He did not take much interest in them & seems to prefer me. He is sitting at my side & my conscience feels easier. Diana is staying now till the 13th and Christopher & Mary are planning to come out on the 27th. And we can make arrangements all to go home together after the Easter Recess. However if this does not attract you I shall have done my best.

I am vy glad that the 'Zoo' is so attractive, but I think it wd be better not, repeat NOT, to bring more than three 30 inch elephants to Chartwell!

I enclose a cutting from the MG. It happened the day after I left. It was a silly thing to say.[3]

---

[1] 'My dear Bernie', La Pausa, 6 March 1956: Churchill papers, 2/210.

[2] 'My dear Winston', 11 March 1956: Churchill papers, 4/67.

[3] On 6 March 1956 the London Correspondent of the *Manchester Guardian*, Gerard Fay, a friend of Churchill's son Randolph, reported: 'Of course, there has been a revival of the Anti-Eden movement, and Mr Randolph Churchill has been feeding it more fuel in the "Evening Standard". He recalls that at the time of the Washington conference he reported that no substantial results had come from the meetings between Sir Anthony and the President "because no joint plan had emerged for coping with the deadly situation in the Middle East". He was told how unkind it was to say such disagreeable things about a Prime Minister who was "doing his best". Mr Churchill does not doubt that Sir Anthony was doing his best, "and this", he thunders, "is

Best & fondest love
Your devoted husband

W

I have had a cough & sore throat but am recovered thanks to Dr Roberts & Penicillin.[1]

From the Mount Lavinia Hotel, Ceylon, Clementine Churchill replied that she did not feel able to leave the ship at Marseilles in order to join her husband for a while at La Pausa, but would go straight back to London. 'Fundamentally I am better,' she explained, 'but I have had 2 set-backs.' For this reason she felt the need of 'an uninterrupted voyage home', and would await her husband 'either at Hyde Park Gate or Chartwell'.[2] Before his wife's letter could reach him, Churchill had written to her again. Anthony Montague Browne had now been seconded to him on a permanent basis.

My darling One,
No news from Ceylon by letter or telegram! I do hope this is because you and Sylvia are enjoying yourselves.

Here all is peaceful & the weather 'mezzo tint'—I spend most of my time in bed. Tonight Pug Ismay & his wife with M. de Starch[3] are coming for dinner. Both Kelly & Alan H are at their hotel working hard. I see them every morning. K goes home today with Book VIII, in a finished condition. I am still house-hunting on the basis of renting not buying; and I bear in mind that you must not be burdened with more housekeeping. I hope to have some proposals to put before you when we meet. When!

Christopher & Mary come out on the 27th; & Nonie[4] on the 19th (for 5 days).

This is the last letter that will reach you before you sail for home.

Toby is flourishing. He sends you his best love. I have got him 2 females—blue for company who are ensconced in a large separate cage. *Nothing* has or will occur. He is vy cool about them. (He made this blot and has been

why I am sure there has got to be, and quickly, a change in the occupancy of 10 Downing Street".' (*Manchester Guardian*, 6 March 1956). On the following day the London Correspondent added: 'There have been some ironical musings on the question of whether Mr Churchill's chances of selection for a safe party seat are rather worse than before or whether, in some circumstances they might not be rather better. It is also asked, of course, whether or not as a political journalist he writes with any special knowledge of what his father might be thinking at the moment. Whichever is the case he has certainly stirred up plenty of gossip with his latest article.' (*Manchester Guardian*, 7 March 1956.)

[1] 'My Darling', La Pausa, 11 March 1956: Spencer-Churchill papers.

[2] 'My darling', Ceylon, 16 March 1956: Churchill papers, 1/55.

[3] André de Staercke was the Belgian Ambassador to NATO, and a close friend of Prince Charles, the Belgian Regent from 1945 to 1950.

[4] Noel Evelyn Montague Browne (née Arnold-Wallinger). She had married Anthony Montague Browne in 1950 (marriage dissolved in 1970). In 1981 she married Sir Edmund Sargant, a former President of the Law Society.

lapping the ink from my pen.) How he knows I am writing to you I cannot tell.

Darling my fondest love

W

PS I enclose a paper to show what I am considering now. It was written by AMB who is a wonderful addition.[1]

'Your March 16 letter received this morning,' Churchill telegraphed to his wife on March 21. 'Am much disappointed. Shall be home 11th. Writing Aden. Bon voyage. Love, W.'[2]

With the pre-war proofs of an essentially finished book to be re-read and recast, work on the History was not too onerous a task. At one moment Churchill found himself re-reading the section on the Congress of Berlin of 1878. Putting his finger on a particular sentence, he turned to Denis Kelly with the words: 'I'm alive now.'[3]

At La Pausa, Churchill called upon the local doctor, Dr Roberts, for whatever medical help was needed; he was being much troubled by a skin irritation. He made no reference to his skin problem, however, when he wrote to his wife on March 23, but only to her continuing ill-health. His letter was sent to meet her ship at Aden:

My Darling,

It is comforting to think of yr ship paddling Home, & that we plan to dine together on the 12th of April at 28. Your buoyant telegram gave me joy. I am so glad you had a successful visit to Ceylon. I fear you are not yet clear of pain. Also, we must continue our search for a cure.

I lunched with W Somerset Maugham on Wednesday & he told me he was going to a watering place just north of Venice in May where the ancients took mixed baths & often shook off the different varieties of neuritis in bygone days. I will bring home the details. The cure takes 12 days & it might be worth trying. All say it is vy pleasant to undergo, & return to Venice afterwards.

Give my love to Sylvia. I hope she has benefited by the voyage.

Longing to see you my dearest one, with all my love

Your devoted

W[4]

'Hope you are having a pleasant voyage,' Churchill telegraphed to his wife on March 24. 'It never leaves off raining here.'[5]

To Edward Heath, Churchill wrote on March 24 that he did not wish to be paired 'in favour of the Malta decision on Monday', and

[1] 'My darling One', La Pausa, 17 March 1956: Spencer-Churchill papers.

[2] Telegram from La Pausa, 21 March 1956: Churchill papers, 1/55.

[3] Denis Kelly recollections: in conversation with the author, 25 March 1987.

[4] 'My Darling', La Pausa, 23 March 1956: Spencer-Churchill papers.

[5] Telegram of 24 March 1956, from La Pausa, to Lady Churchill, passenger *Stratheden*: Churchill papers, 1/55.

he went on to explain: 'I am convinced this is a wrong and mistaken thing to do, and it will inflict lasting injury upon the character of the House of Commons.' [1]

April 1 was Clementine Churchill's seventy-first birthday. '"Many Happy Returns of the Day"' he wrote to her on March 26, and he added: 'I wrote this to reach you at Port Said on April 1.' His letter continued:

I hope you have had a pleasant voyage, & that Sylvia has shared your progress. The weather here has been detestable; but the company is vy quiet & friendly. I am sorry you will not join us, but I cannot promise anything like the shining blue skies of the Riviera. We have had a bout of rain, & I fear great distress will fall upon all engaged not only in flower growing but also in large scale agriculture.

Once more my best wishes for your Birthday. May you long enjoy life & hope.

Your ever loving husband.

W [2]

'Many happy returns of the day,' Churchill telegraphed to Port Said on March 31, and he added: 'Do think over whether you will come on here from Marseilles. We can go home together by air on 10th or 11th. Love, W.' [3]

At the end of March Alan Hodge returned to London, after two weeks working at La Pausa on the final volume of the History. 'The hospitality of La Pausa is a thing I shall always remember with delight,' he wrote to Churchill from London on March 27, and he added:

One of the best pieces of reconstruction you have done on your History was this time accomplished. Book Nine is taking splendid shape, and the alternation of interest between England, America and France is most impressively planned. The chapters you gave me to bring back have gone to press. The new printers are quick at their work; it is encouraging to have the

[1] 'My dear Heath', La Pausa, 24 March 1956: Churchill papers, 2/129. The Malta Round-Table Conference had recommended the admission of Malta Members of Parliament to Westminster, in order to meet the demand from Malta itself for greater powers and eventual independence. On 26 March 1956 the Secretary of State for the Colonies, Alan Lennox-Boyd, stated that he 'could not recommend to the House that they should increase the powers of the Maltese Government and Parliament' unless he could be 'sure of safeguarding the United Kingdom's own interests and imperial responsibilities in Malta'. Malta became independent in September 1964.

[2] 'My darling', La Pausa, 26 March 1956: Spencer-Churchill papers.

[3] Telegram to Lady Churchill, Passenger *Stratheden*, Cape Peninsular, Port Said, from La Pausa, 31 March 1956: Churchill papers, 1/55.

fresh Revise coming in daily. Shortly I hope to submit to you a piece on Wellington and the Peninsular War.[1]

Churchill's second visit to La Pausa, and the sight of him at the Casino in Monte Carlo, had led to considerable press comment, on which, at the beginning of April, Bernard Baruch made a somewhat caustic comment. 'I see from your holograph note,' Churchill replied, 'that you have been reading the tales they tell of Monte Carlo. I had no win, but came out quits after three days' play, which was not bad.' Most of the newspaper reporters, Churchill added, 'put in fairy-tales about Onassis. He is a friendly kind of man, but I did not depend on his invitation to go there.'[2]

On April 6, while Churchill was at Roquebrune, his wife reached Marseilles, on board the *Stratheden*. 'Welcome darling,' he telegraphed to her that morning. 'I will talk to you on the telephone at 10 a.m. Love, W.'[3] When they spoke, Churchill asked his wife to join him for four days at La Pausa. She promised to consider it, then telegraphed to him from the *Stratheden*: 'So sorry darling but cannot sort and repack crumpled and inadequate clothes so am making straight for home all my love, Clemmie.'[4]

On April 11 Churchill flew back from the South of France to London. His wife was still on her way to London by sea. The visit to La Pausa had been a tonic. 'It was wonderful to see Winston looking so well as he did in the setting of your lovely home,' Christopher Soames wrote to Wendy and Emery Reves—now married—on April 20, and he added: 'It seems that he has taken on new strength. You looked after him with such care and affection, and he was so happy with you.'[5]

'For the last three weeks,' Miss Pugh told Lord Moran, 'he seemed twenty years younger, and now he is as happy as a child to be home again at Chartwell.'[6]

The work at Chartwell centred on the History. 'Your comments are most valuable,' Churchill wrote to the Tudor historian A. L. Rowse on April 12, 'and it is very good of you to have devoted so much time to my affairs.'[7] Churchill also prepared to speak at the

[1] 'Dear Sir Winston', 27 March 1956: Churchill papers, 2/189.
[2] 'My dear Bernie', 15 April 1956: Churchill papers, 2/210.
[3] Telegram of 6 April 1956, La Pausa: Churchill papers, 1/55.
[4] Telegram (Lettre Radiomaritime) sent at 9 a.m., 7 April 1956: Churchill papers, 1/55.
[5] 'My dear Wendy and Emery', 20 April 1956: Reves papers.
[6] Moran diary, 11 April 1956: *The Struggle for Survival*, page 693.
[7] 'My dear Rowse', 12 April 1956: Churchill papers, 4/28.

Albert Hall, to the Primrose League. ' "Welcome Home" ,' he wrote
to his wife on April 13, having driven up to London. 'I long to see &
kiss you. You will find me putting the finishing touches on my speech.
I hope you will approve of Miss Hamblin's plan for a long weekend at
Chartwell. Your ever loving husband, W.' [1]

On the evening of April 13 Churchill spoke at the Albert Hall, as
Grand Master of the Primrose League, to introduce the principal
speaker, the Colonial Secretary, Alan Lennox-Boyd. He had spent
three days preparing what to say. His speech lasted seven minutes. Of
the United States, Churchill declared: 'I do not share the view of
those who think that they have failed in their duty, or will fail in their
duty if the moment comes. They are a wise and experienced people.
They learn from history. They know well that both the great wars
which have darkened our lives and dishevelled the world could have
been prevented if the United States had acted before they began to
prevent them.'

Now a similar case had arisen, Churchill pointed out, 'though on a
much smaller scale'. Egypt and Israel were 'face to face'. It was 'perfectly sure' that the United States, as well as Britain, would intervene
'to prevent aggression by one side or the other'. The moment for this
would probably never come, but, Churchill warned, 'it may come,
and come at any moment'. If Israel was to be 'dissuaded from using
the life of their race to ward off the Egyptians until the Egyptians
have learnt to use the Russian weapons with which they have been
supplied', he argued, 'and the Egyptians then attack, it will become
not only a matter of prudence but a measure of honour to make sure
that they are not the losers by waiting'. [2]

'I should like you to know,' wrote Eliahu Elath, the Israeli Ambassador, later that day, 'with what deep gratification my Government
and the people of Israel will receive your friendly references to our
country in your speech to the Primrose League to-day.' Elath added:
'Our own heartfelt appreciation will, I know, be shared by all friends
of Israel everywhere. We shall all hope and pray that these words,
coming from you, will have their effect on those, in London and in
Washington, in whose hands now lie the crucial decisions on the matters to which you referred, including that of the supply to Israel of
adequate arms for her self-defence.' [3]

The Middle East was one of the subjects to which Churchill referred
in a letter which he wrote to Eisenhower on April 16. 'I am so glad

[1] 'My Darling', 13 April 1956: Spencer-Churchill papers.
[2] Speech of 13 April 1956: Randolph S. Churchill (editor), *The Unwritten Alliance*, pages 285–7.
[3] 'Dear Sir Winston', 13 April 1956: Government of Israel Archive.

that you recognise so plainly the importance of oil from the Middle East,' Churchill told the President. 'When I was at the Admiralty in 1913 I acquired control of the Anglo-Persian Company for something like £3,000,000, and turned the large fleet I was then building to that method of propulsion. That was a good bargain if ever there was one.'[1] Churchill then turned to the current confrontation between Egypt and Israel. 'I am sure that if we act together,' he wrote, 'we shall stave off an actual war between Israel and Egypt,' and he went on to tell Eisenhower:

I am, of course, a Zionist, and have been ever since the Balfour Declaration. I think it is a wonderful thing that this tiny colony of Jews should have become a refuge to their compatriots in all the lands where they were persecuted so cruelly, and at the same time established themselves as the most effective fighting force in the area. I am sure America would not stand by and see them overwhelmed by Russian weapons, especially if we had persuaded them to hold their hand while their chance remained.

Churchill also wrote in his letter of April 16 about the imminent arrival in Britain of Marshal Bulganin and Nikita Khrushchev, who had recently, in a speech to the Communist Party Congress, denounced Stalin and Stalinism in terms of contempt and derision. Churchill commented:

Our Russian guests are expected this week, and we shall soon see whether anything material results. We have only forty or fifty thousand professional Communists in this country, but I suppose the people as a whole will treat them on the Malenkov lines.

They have made an extraordinary volte-face about Stalin. I am sure it is a great blunder which will markedly hamper the Communist Movement. It would have been easy to 'play him down' gradually without causing so great a shock to the faithful.

Stalin always kept his word with me. I remember particularly saying to him when I visited Moscow in 1944, 'You keep Roumania and Bulgaria in your sphere of influence, but let me have Greece.' To this bargain he scrupulously adhered during months of fighting with the Greek Communists. I wish I could say the same about the Greeks, whose memories are very short.

Churchill also wrote to Eisenhower of the failure of the United States to share its hydrogen bomb secrets with Britain. 'This is past now so far as the main secret is concerned,' Churchill reflected, 'but we have lost two or three years in having to work it out for ourselves.' His letter continued:

[1] Under the Anglo-Persian Oil Agreement of June 1914, for which Churchill had been responsible as First Lord of the Admiralty, the British Government received 51 per cent of the profits of all oil produced by the Anglo-Persian Oil Company, as well as first use of the oil for the Royal Navy. Britain's 51 per cent share of the profits paid, in interest alone, for the cost of all battleships built after 1914.

I do not think, however, that a world war is likely to develop in the next decade. Till then we are, of course, defenceless against a Russian attack. After that or a lesser period we shall be able to say to the Russians, 'If you kill twenty or thirty million Englishmen, we have made unbreakable arrangements to kill double that number of Russians in the next few days.' The creation of such a situation would certainly be the end of nuclear war, except, of course, for accidents, which all nations have an equal interest in preventing.[1]

Churchill ended his letter to Eisenhower with a budget of literary and personal news:

I venture to send you a copy of my forthcoming book *A History of the English-Speaking Peoples*. The whole thing is finished now. I am afraid the Americans do not come into this volume, because it was only

> 'In fourteen hundred and ninety-two
> Columbus over the ocean flew.'

I am so glad to be able to tell you that Clemmie has returned from Ceylon far better than when she went. The monotony of the voyage, although cold and stormy, had good effects.

Let me finish by saying how relieved I am to hear of your recovery, and my admiration for the courage and stamina which enable you to face the ordeal of another term.[2]

April 23 marked the formal publication of the first volume of Churchill's history. Among the copies which Churchill inscribed were the first two which he had specially bound, for the Queen and the Queen Mother. 'I am much touched,' the Queen wrote from Sandringham on April 28 in her own hand, 'that you should send me a copy of the first volume. . . . I look forward keenly to reading it and the subsequent volumes—I have already heard great praise for this first one.'[3] Queen

---

[1] Eisenhower disagreed with Churchill's conclusion, writing to him in reply: 'I do not fully share your conclusion that an end to nuclear war will come about because of realization on both sides that by using this weapon an unconscionable degree of death and destruction would result. I do think it might tend to reduce very materially the possibility of *any* war; but I think it would be unsafe to predict that, if the West and the East should ever become locked up in a life and death struggle, both sides would still have sense enough not to use this horrible instrument. You will remember that in 1945 there was no possible excuse, once we had reached the Rhine in late '44, for Hitler to continue the war, yet his insane determination to rule or ruin brought additional and completely unnecessary destruction to his country; brought about its division between East and West and his own ignominious death.' ('Dear Winston', The White House, Washington, 27 April 1956: Churchill papers, 2/217.)

[2] 'Dear Ike', signed, 'Believe me, Yours always, W', Chartwell, 16 April 1956: Eisenhower papers. On 15 February 1956 *The Times* reported that President Eisenhower's physicians had reached the 'considered conclusion' that there was 'no medical reason why he should not continue an active life in the White House for a second term'. The doctors added that Eisenhower 'should be able to carry on an active life satisfactorily for another five to ten years'.

[3] 'My dear Sir Winston', 28 April 1956: Squerryes Lodge Archive.

Elizabeth The Queen Mother, in her letter of thanks, described it as a 'glorious book'.[1]

Churchill also sent a copy to Attlee, who wrote in thanks: 'I am glad that you did full justice to the Wessex kings. What they did is often underrated.'[2] 'It is a delight to read this book,' Jawaharlal Nehru wrote from New Delhi, 'and I am very grateful to you for sending it.'[3] But from Aristotle Onassis came a somewhat bizarre note of criticism, sent from Monte Carlo:

. . . I was sad to notice an omission, which knowing full well the pleasure you derive from free comment, I should like to take the liberty to point out to you here. There is no mention in the opening chapters of your book of the great old neighbour and compatriot of mine—Pytheas the Massaliot, the historian and explorer who discovered Britain long before Caesar landed there.

I am afraid, too, that the Hellenic (in its wider sense) contribution to the fundamentals of British civilisation and culture is either ignored altogether or submerged in the ostentatious grandeur (not glory) of Rome.[4]

Among those who had scrutinized Churchill's text was Dr J. H. Plumb, History Tutor at Christ's College, Cambridge. 'I was deeply touched by your kind and generous gesture in sending me a copy of your great work,' he wrote, 'which I shall treasure as long as I shall live. After the little that I had done to help, I did not expect so noble a gift.' From what he had read so far, Plumb added, 'it is clear that the book possesses the great qualities which we have come to expect from your heart and mind—the same grandeur in the writing of history as in the making of it'.[5]

'I wish our school history books had been as vivid and absorbing,' wrote Miss Sturdee.[6] 'I started reading it last night in bed,' wrote the Duchess of Marlborough, 'and I suddenly looked at the clock and saw it was 2.15 a.m.'[7] The preface, wrote G. M. Trevelyan from Cambridge, 'is a noble piece and will I have no doubt be read by people on both sides of the Atlantic for generations to come'. The time would come, Trevelyan added, 'when they will stop reading us professional

---

[1] 'My dear Sir Winston', 7 July 1956: Squerryes Lodge Archive.

[2] 'My dear Winston', signed 'Yours ever, Clem', 21 April 1956: Churchill papers, 4/67.

[3] 'My dear Sir Winston', 22 September 1956: Churchill papers, 4/67.

[4] 'My dear Sir Winston', 9 May 1956: Churchill papers, 4/67. Pytheas of Massilia (Marseille), a pioneering Greek geographer and explorer, lived more than 300 years before Caesar's conquest of Britain (at about the time of Alexander the Great). His writings are lost, but several important fragments survive, quoted by later authors, including Pliny the Elder and Strabo. According to these fragments, Pytheas, sailing from Cadiz, had circumnavigated Britain, visiting Belerium (Land's End) and Ictis (either St Michael's Mount in Cornwall, or the Isle of Wight). These facts were discussed in detail in Paulys, *Realencyclopädie der Classischen Altertumswissenschaft*, Stuttgart, 1901, volume 24, pages 314–66.

[5] 'Dear Sir Winston', 22 April 1956: Churchill papers, 4/28.

[6] 'Dear Sir Winston', 24 April 1956: Churchill papers, 4/67.

[7] 'My dear Winston', Blenheim Palace, 23 April 1956: Churchill papers, 4/67.

historians but not you'. Churchill's treatment of Richard III, Trevelyan wrote, was 'exactly right. There has been so much nonsense
written about him on both sides, and you steer an even course.' [1]

'I now have your earliest and your latest book—' G. M. Young
wrote from All Souls College, Oxford, 'Charles Dilke's copy of the
Malakand Field Force and The Birth. And what a world of experience
and reflexion lies in between!' [2] 'I greatly admire your amazing industry and courage,' wrote the eighty-year-old Lord Hankey, 'in
taking up again a task, begun before the war, which even a whole-
time historian might approach with hesitation. But it is not your first
Labour of Hercules!' [3]

From Sir Desmond Morton came memories of 'the beginnings of the
book at Chartwell before the last war', and he added: 'I remember too
talks then and even later, during the war itself, when in your own forceful and inimitable way, you professed with deep sincerity your conviction that the forging of a closer link between the peoples of the British
Empire and the United States was an end to be sought above all others
in this area, if progress and decent living were to be won for the
human race.' 'You at least,' Morton added, 'have done your utmost
to guide our destinies towards that end and you have not failed.' [4]

A cloud in those relations had risen, suddenly and darkly, over
America's reluctance to support Britain in the Middle East, as the
crisis with Egypt grew. Alarmed by the American attitude, Churchill
had sent Eden a letter he had received from Eisenhower, in which the
President wrote, in connection with the essential 'co-ordination' between the two countries' policies, that 'the different political climates
in the two countries, the need that politicians feel to have themselves
re-elected even at the cost of demagoging against a friend, and differing
national policies that go back sometimes a long way into history, all
combine to make very difficult the kind of cooperation of which I
speak and which I believe is, in the long run, a vital necessity'. [5]

On receiving this letter, Eden showed it to Sir Norman Brook. A
few days later Eden wrote to Churchill:

I have now been able to study Ike's letter more carefully. I confess that I
find it rather puzzling. I am not at all sure what the middle part of it is
intended to convey. His intention may, however, have been to explain why it
is that, although they are willing to work closely with us in discussing common

---

[1] 'Dear Churchill', 23 April 1956: Churchill papers, 4/67.
[2] 'Dear Sir Winston', 25 April 1956: Churchill papers, 4/57. *The Story of the Malakand Field
Force* had been published on 14 March 1898.
[3] 'Dear Winston', 27 April 1956: Churchill papers, 4/67. There were in all twelve Labours of
Hercules.
[4] 'My dear Winston', 23 April 1956: Churchill papers, 4/67.
[5] 'Dear Winston', The White House, Washington, 29 March 1956: Churchill papers, 2/217.

policies for the Middle East, it is difficult for them to admit publicly that they are doing so—especially in an election year. There has been an unhappy revival of that phrase 'no ganging up' and we have strongly protested against it. Their unwillingness to let it be known that we are at one on this important issue diminishes the influence which each of us could exercise in the area. It also puts a considerable strain on our relations. We shall, however, survive this. I am resolved that we shall not be divided from our American friends over this crucial issue, however much we may be provoked by the outbursts of American columnists in support of Nasser.

Churchill's answer to Eisenhower, Eden added, 'was very good. I am, as always, most grateful to you for your help.' [1]

During the visit of Bulganin and Khrushchev to Britain, Churchill was Eden's guest at 10 Downing Street to meet the Soviet leaders. 'I sat next to Khrushchev,' he told his doctor. 'The Russians were delighted to see me. Anthony told them I won the war.' [2]

At the end of April, Churchill made plans to return to La Pausa for the first two weeks of June, when his wife, after a visit to Paris, would join him. In telling Wendy and Emery Reves of this plan, Churchill added: 'Let me thank you once more for your kindness and hospitality to me during my ten weeks with you. You certainly made up for the weather. *Indeed* I passed a peaceful and happy time under the shelter of your palatial roof.' [3]

The pleasure which the first volume of Churchill's history had given his friends continued to be reflected in their enthusiastic letters of thanks. One such letter, from Brendan Bracken, recalled the somewhat stormy evolution of the project:

What a history your history has had! I remember my unavailing efforts to soothe the savage breast of the elder Flower when he was unreasonably demanding delivery at what he called the 'due date'. A better negotiator, dear Bill Camrose, suppressed his caterwaulings. Then came Korda and afterwards the resurrection of the faded old proofs. [4] And now happily the book is

---

[1] 'My dear Winston', 10 Downing Street, 21 April 1956: Churchill papers, 2/216.
[2] Moran diary, 22 April 1956: *The Struggle for Survival*, pages 694–5.
[3] 'My dear Wendy & Emery', 30 April 1956: Reves papers.
[4] During the Second World War, at the suggestion of Sir Newman Flower's son Desmond, the film director Sir Alexander Korda had bought the film rights of *A History of the English-Speaking Peoples*, so that Churchill could receive his final payment for a work that had been due for delivery in 1939, but whose publication had been indefinitely postponed. In the autumn of 1954 the proofs of the version which Korda had bought were found. This was after the corrected proofs of an earlier version of volumes I and II had already been re-set. This 'New Discovery', as it was known, was itself then re-set, dated 30 November 1954, and became the basis of the final version.

launched and the back broken of most of the work required to produce three more volumes.[1]

By a sad irony, on May 3 Churchill unveiled a memorial to Lord Camrose in St Paul's Cathedral. 'In dark and uncertain times,' he said, 'no man could be more steady and persevering. During the war his unfaltering confidence helped to sustain all those who knew him.' To his friends 'and to the causes in which he believed he was steadfastly loyal'.[2] There was another strange link with Lord Camrose on May 5, when one of the two paintings chosen for the Royal Academy summer exhibition opened that day was his 'Marrakech, 1950', painted when Camrose had been his guest in Morocco.[3]

Churchill now prepared for his first visit to Germany since 1945, his second since 1932, in order to receive in Aachen the Charlemagne Prize. 'That he, the chief architect of Germany's downfall, should be their guest excites him,' noted Moran on May 3. 'But he is bothered by his speech for Aachen.'[4]

On May 9 Churchill flew from London to Aachen, where he was given a short reception at the aerodrome before being driven to his hotel, where he dined quietly and without any ceremony. On the following morning he was driven to the Town Hall where, at noon, he walked up the outside stairs, and was carried up the remainder in a sedan chair. Inside the Town Hall he was presented with the Charlemagne Prize. It was sixteen years to the day since he had become Prime Minister in the war against Germany.

Churchill's aim in his acceptance speech at Aachen was twofold: to urge upon the Germans a receptiveness to any possible relaxation in Soviet policy, and at the same time to warn them not to be too hasty in their desire for reunification. With these themes in mind, Montague Browne had drafted the speech, which Churchill then delivered.[5] 'It was his own idea,' Montague Browne later recalled, and he added: 'It struck a chill.'[6]

From Aachen, Churchill went to Bonn, where he saw Chancellor Adenauer. The Aachen themes had not been at all those which the Chancellor had hoped to hear. For the next three days Churchill visited British army bases and spoke, impromptu, on six occasions. Dinner with the British troops at Celle was 'a tremendous success',

[1] 'My dear Winston', signed 'Yours ever, Brendan', 1 May 1956: Churchill papers, 4/67.
[2] Speech of 3 May 1956: Randolph S. Churchill (editor), The Unwritten Alliance, page 288.
[3] 'List of Works Exhibited at The Royal Academy by Sir Winston Churchill, Hon. RA': Royal Academy archive. The other painting was 'Sir John Lavery's Studio, 1920'.
[4] Moran diary, 3 May 1956: The Struggle for Survival, page 695.
[5] Speech of 10 May 1956: BBC Written Archives Centre, Library No. 22603.
[6] Anthony Montague Browne recollections: in conversation with the author, 14 July 1987. Three years earlier, Lord Moran had written in his diary: 'His generous heart seems, as the days

Montague Browne remembered. 'The soldiers were so nice to him. It was very much his atmosphere.' [1] On the afternoon of May 13 Churchill flew back to Biggin Hill, escorted by fighters of 615 Squadron. [2] 'Altogether the visit leaves a pleasant memory in my mind,' he wrote to Eisenhower, 'and I was glad to see that in spite of the march of time I can still do four days continuous toil.' [3]

In his diary, Lord Moran noted Churchill's continuing literary efforts. He did not refer, however, to a more personal matter between him and his patient. That summer, Churchill renewed the deed of covenant under which, for the previous seven years, both Lord Moran's sons had received an annuity. 'The money has been a tremendous help to us,' Lord Moran's son John Wilson wrote on July 11, 'in setting up with our family, and if anything should happen to my father it would enable us to make sure that my mother was provided for.' [4] From Lord Moran too came a letter of thanks. 'I am writing this,' he explained, 'because when talking to you I can never put into words what I so deeply feel.' [5]

At Chartwell, Churchill worked on the final volume of his History. Would it come 'right up to the present?' Lord Moran had asked him on June 19. '"No, no," he replied. "I stop in Victoria's reign. I could not write about the woe and ruin of the terrible twentieth century." (Sadly) "We answered all the tests. But it was useless."' [6]

---

pass, to be flushed with kindly thoughts about all mankind, even about the Germans. He has always admired them, they are a great people. He admired their Army, and would have liked, he once said, to go to Germany to appeal to young Germans to wipe out the disgrace of Hitler and of the cruel murder of the Jews.' (Moran diary, 27 July 1953: *The Struggle for Survival*, page 446.)

[1] Anthony Montague Browne: notes for the author, 24 March 1987.
[2] Desmond Bungey, log book, 13 May 1956: Bungey papers.
[3] Letter marked 'not sent', May 1956: Churchill papers, 2/217.
[4] 'Dear Sir Winston', 11 July 1956: Churchill papers, 1/54.
[5] 'My dear Winston', undated ('Friday'); Churchill papers, 1/54.
[6] Moran diary, 19 June 1956: *The Struggle for Survival*, page 699.

62

'A temple of peace'

A T the end of May 1956 Churchill returned yet again to the South of France, for a two-week holiday at La Pausa. Clementine Churchill joined him there, as did their daughter Sarah. On June 4 Clementine Churchill returned to London, leaving Churchill and Sarah at La Pausa. 'I send you both my thanks for your kindness to me,' Clementine Churchill wrote to Wendy Reves on June 7, '& for the affection and care you lavish upon Winston.'[1] Churchill and Sarah remained at La Pausa for another ten days. On their return to London they telegraphed to Wendy and Emery: 'Arrived safely armed with memories of another delightful visit to Pausaland. Thank you so much.'[2] Eight days later, Churchill wrote to Wendy Reves:

Dear Wendy,

I have now been home a week, and it has passed so slowly because of the many things we had to do that it might have been a fortnight. My horse, First Light, did not distinguish himself at Ascot, and my other horse, Le Pretendant, runs on Saturday, when, alas, I have to be in my Constituency.[3] Mr Truman is coming to luncheon on Sunday—a family gathering, plus Max.

Although we had a wonderful reception when we arrived, and gleaming sunlight gilded the scene, we only just got home before there was a thundershower. Since then the weather has been beneath contempt for this time of year: two or three hours of sunshine in the early morning, and cloud and rain storms for the rest of the day. I am now going down to Chartwell under grey skies.

I wonder what luck you and Emery have had. It certainly has been a very disappointing year for weather.

I have made no plans as yet for the future, but I will write to you as soon as I do.

I have been asked many questions about the princely couple who

[1] 'My dear Wendy', 7 June 1956: Reves papers.
[2] Telegram dated 14 June 1956: Reves papers.
[3] Le Pretendant was the winner of the Churchill Stakes at Ascot on 23 June 1956.

entertained us to their first official luncheon, and have replied giving them both a good character.

Give Emery my regards. I hope the proofs are reaching him punctually. I am toiling at them and I hope to make an end of the Second Volume by the weekend.

Thank you both once more for your delightful hospitality. The warmth of your welcome and your kindness made my stay most memorable. I am so grateful to you for all the trouble you took—not least in preparing for me such a beautiful and sunny room.

Yours ever

Winston S. Churchill [1]

For the second two weeks of June and all of July, Churchill stayed at Chartwell, with the exception of a brief racing excursion to Germany. As he wrote on July 30 to his wife, who was then in St Moritz, his letter dictated:

My darling One,

Christopher was quite right in his judgment about flying. He rang up the proper authorities and was told that the clouds, which were 6,000 feet in England, were 3,000 feet in the neighbourhood of Düsseldorf. We started amid gusts, which the plane encountered with a few bumps, and reached our destination in one hour and fifty minutes. Immediately after our departure a really frantic hurricane of rain and wind broke on Chartwell and the neighbourhood. This stripped many branches off trees, and there is quite a mess for the gardeners to clear up. One of the front gates was blown down.

We were received with the utmost courtesy in Düsseldorf, and were all invited to luncheon with the Stewards at the hotel. I cannot imagine why Nightingall thought we could win this race, only on German interested assurances we would have a walk-over.[2] The French horses were quite good. The paddock was invaded by the mob, who pressed around our horse, causing him to stream with sweat long before he even got to the course. We had a ten minutes hail and rain storm before the race, which made the ground even more boggy than it was after the heavy rain. As you know, Le Pretendant's form largely depends on hard ground, but here he was slipping all over the place. The Irish horse ridden by Lester Piggott was just behind us at the tail.

It all passed off very pleasantly, however. The Germans paid the expenses, and the Ambassador met us and accompanied us all the time.[3] His wife is in Scotland. He asked after you. I must confess I thought you would be all right in the big aeroplane, though I was a little worried about the prospects

---

[1] 'Dear Wendy', 22 June 1956: Reves papers.

[2] Walter Nightingall was the trainer of Churchill's horses.

[3] Sir Frederick Hoyer Millar, the last British High Commissioner in Germany (1953–55) was also the First British Ambassador to West Germany (1955–57). In 1931 he had married Elizabeth van Swinderen.

of our flight in a six-seater. But I fear you had a very bumpy journey—
perhaps even worse than we had.

On July 26, President Nasser of Egypt had nationalized the Suez
Canal, following the withdrawal of British and American funds to finance the Aswan Dam. In his letter of July 30, Churchill told his wife:

I am on my way to the Royal luncheon, and afterwards am going to the
House. Eden says he wants to see me, as he has much to tell. Personally, I
think that France and England ought to act together with vigour, and if
necessary with arms, while America watches Russia vigilantly. I do not
think the Russians have any intention of being involved in a major war. We
could secure our rights in the Arab world, and France has every reason to
resent Nasser's attitude and action in Algeria.

I do hope you will take a good rest & acquire height usage, and will
recover from the bumpy journey and the long and very tiring motor drive.

With all my love

Your ever devoted husband

W [1]

'I fear,' wrote Clementine Churchill to her husband, 'that AE will
wait for America who for the third time will arrive on the scene very
late,' and she added: 'I hope you may be able to influence him.'
Clementine went on: 'I think Monsieur Mollet is being very brave.
What do you think of digging a second Canal?' [2]

That same day Lord Moran noted in his diary:

Winston is very angry about Nasser's seizure of the Suez Canal.
Moran: 'Nasser is not the kind of man to keep his job for long?'
Winston: 'Whoever he is he's finished after this. We can't have that malici-
ous swine sitting across our communications.' (He said this with something of
his old vehemence.) 'I saw Anthony on Monday. I know what they are
going to say. Anthony asked me to treat it as a matter of confidence.'
Moran: 'What will the Americans do?'
Winston snapped: 'We don't need the Americans for this.'
Moran: 'Will you speak in the House?'
Winston: 'I might. I shall dictate something and see how it goes.'

Churchill was working, he told Moran, on the American Civil War
section of his History. 'I read four or five books on it,' he explained,
'before I dictated anything.' [3]

On August 3 Churchill wrote again to his wife, this letter once
more a dictated one:

[1] 'My darling One', from 28 Hyde Park Gate, 30 July 1956: Spencer-Churchill papers. Carbon
copy in Churchill papers, 1/55.

[2] 'My darling', Palace Hotel, St Moritz, 1 August 1956: Churchill papers, 1/55. Guy Mollet
was Prime Minister of France from January 1956 to June 1957.

[3] Moran diary, 1 August 1956: *The Struggle for Survival*, page 702.

My darling One,

Your letter of the 1st arrived the morning of the 3rd, which is pretty good. Tomorrow is the 4th of August, a date which used to be very memorable in our minds. I was away from Chartwell when Sir Richard Lloyd-Roberts was killed by the fall of the old walnut a few miles away.[1] There are dangers everywhere, even in the safest places. Lester Piggott, was, I think, in the same position as we were, completely messed up by the boggy ground. I do not feel that Le Pretendant has lost his pace, but it will take him a month to recover.

Give my regards to Mr Einstein.[2] I am very glad he has turned up to give you company. August, from which we had hoped so much, has so far lived up to the reputation it inherited from July. I wish indeed I could spend a day or two with you. This is not meant to be ungrateful for the two hours of sunshine I have had tonight. I do hope you will continue to gain strength and to eat up your bruises. I will inquire about Lord Birdwood. The original must be very old, if he is still alive.[3]

I am pleased with the policy being pursued about Suez. We are going to do our utmost. Anthony told me everything, and I even contemplated making a speech, but all went so well in the Thursday debate that this would have been an unnecessary hazard. As I am well informed, I cannot in an unprotected letter tell any secrets, but I feel you may rest assured that there will be no ground of complaints on what we try to do. The French are very sporting, and it is nice to feel they are working with us, and that we and the Americans are both agreed. We have taken a line which will put the Canal effectively on its international basis, and will also make it secure until long after 1968. Anthony has told my Anthony to keep himself fully informed from Downing Street, and I am actually reading large bundles of telegrams from day to day.

Violet is coming to spend the night of Bank Holiday with me, and thereafter I have Juliet on Friday the 11th. I propose to ask Pamela for the following week.[4] It is Bernie Baruch's 87th birthday on Sunday the 19th. Randolph has gone off to America after giving me a dreadful beating up about supporting such a Government as this. I took the brunt of it off myself by a film, and he was astonished the next morning (Wednesday) when he saw the newspapers, which I could not reveal to him until they were published. There is only one opinion in the House of Commons, and this fully covers the use of force as and when it may be necessary.

[1] Sir Richard Lloyd-Roberts had been killed on 29 July 1956. Aged seventy-one, he had been one of the civil servants responsible for Labour Exchanges following Churchill's introduction of Labour Exchanges before the First World War. From 1927 to 1948 he was Chief Labour Officer of Imperial Chemical Industries. Knighted in 1951, from 1952 he was a Member of the Industrial Disputes Tribunal.

[2] The American whom Clementine Churchill had befriended on her travels.

[3] Clementine Churchill had asked whether a letter in *The Times* signed 'Birdwood' was from the Field Marshal Birdwood whom they had known, or from his son. It was from Field Marshal Birdwood's son, his father having died on 17 March 1951, at the age of eighty-six.

[4] Violet Bonham Carter, Lady Juliet Duff and Pamela Lytton.

Churchill added, in his own hand: 'My dearest Clemmie do persevere in getting back yr strength & we can make some plans together. With all my love. Your devoted husband W' [sketch of pig].[1]

'I am indeed relieved,' Clementine Churchill replied, 'that you are satisfied with the policy pursued by Great Britain & France over Suez,' and she added: 'I don't include America because I'm afraid she will hang fire in the back-ground.'[2] 'I listened to Anthony last night,' she wrote again on August 9. 'It was hard to hear but I'm afraid I was disappointed by what I *did* hear. There was no inspiration.'[3]

On August 5 Harold Macmillan dined with Churchill at Chartwell, noting in his diary: 'I said that unless we brought in Israel it couldn't be done. Surely if we landed, we must seek out the Egyptian forces, destroy them and bring down Nasser's government. Churchill got out some maps and got quite excited.'[4]

Churchill decided to give Eden his own view of what should be done, and of what should be avoided. In strictest secrecy, he therefore set off by car on August 6, the Bank Holiday Monday, from Chartwell to Chequers. Taking Miss Pugh with him, he dictated as they drove, then stopped the car in a lay-by so that Miss Pugh could type out what he had done. 'He was awfully pleased with it,' she later recalled, 'and told Eden proudly, "I've prepared a little note." He said I had typed it in the car.'[5] The note read:

The military operation seems very serious. We have a long delay when our intentions are known. The newspapers and foreign correspondents are free to publish what they choose. A censorship should be imposed.

In a month it should be possible for at least 1,000 Russian & similar volunteers to take over the cream of the Egyptian aircraft and tanks. This might expose us to much more severe resistance. I was not used readily to accept from the Air Force numbers of aircraft which could be used by us from various stations. For instance, it seems to me unreasonable not to use at least 100 Canberras in Cyprus alone, and generally to follow the principle of 'more than enough'.

The more one thinks about taking over the Canal, the less one likes it. The long causeway could be easily obstructed by a succession of mines. We should get much of the blame of stopping work, if it is to be up to the moment of our attack a smooth-running show. Cairo is Nasser's centre of power. I was very glad to hear that there would be no weakening about Libya on account of the [   ][6] Prime Minister etc., but that the armoured divisions,

[1] 'My darling One', Chartwell, 3 August 1956: Spencer-Churchill papers.
[2] 'My darling', Palace Hotel, St Moritz, 5 August 1956: Churchill papers, 1/55.
[3] 'My darling', Palace Hotel, St Moritz, 9 August 1956: Churchill papers, 1/55.
[4] Harold Macmillan diary, 5 August 1956: quoted in the *Sunday Times*, 4 January 1987.
[5] Doreen Pugh recollections: in conversation with the author, 18 June 1987.
[6] Handwritten word, unclear in the original (added while the car was in motion).

properly supported by air, with any additional forces that may be needed, would be used.

On the other side a volte face should certainly free our hands about Israel. We should want them to menace and hold the Egyptians and not be drawn off against Jordan.[1]

In her letter of August 9, Clementine Churchill had also wanted to know 'why Israel has not been bidden to the Conference'.[2] In his reply, which he sent on August 11, Churchill tried, amid his other views and thoughts, to answer her:

My darling One,

The weather is awful. We had one lovely day, not a cloud from dawn to dusk, and I hoped it marked a decided turn. Since then we have not had a gleam, and lots of rain.

Like you, I am anxious about the situation in the Middle East. I suppose why they did not bring Israel in was that they were afraid she would become uncontrollable. But she is there in the background, and I have no doubt that if it comes to war she will join in. One can never be quite sure whether a number of 'volunteers' will not be mixed up with the Egyptians, who manage the Russian aeroplanes and tanks. There is no doubt that this would involve hard fighting, but I think we will have enough troops on the move.

Naturally I am worried about this pow-wow, which was to have finished by the end of August at the latest. I do not see myself how it is to be closured and wound up, and I am not sure that Selwyn Lloyd is the man. However, there is nothing for it but to go on with the programme. The President is quite right in saying that if he stays out America will balance Russia.

The unity of Islam is remarkable. There is no doubt that Libya, to whom we have paid £5,000,000 a year, like Jordania, to whom we paid £10,000,000 or more, are whole-heartedly manifesting hostility. You will be home before anything serious happens. I shall go up to London next Wednesday to see my Optician about my left eye, which is very bloodshot, and will take occasion to make some contacts then. I have not worried Anthony since I saw him.

Christopher has been to Paris, but comes back today. I rather gather that Maria follows a little later.

I am so glad you are having sunshine. It is indeed dreary gazing out through rain-spotted windows on the grey mists that wrap the Weald of Kent. I have been reading about Disraeli, because I must have a chapter on Disraeli and Gladstone to come after the American Civil War Book.

I hope to have good news for you about MGM (Metro-Goldwyn-Mayer). It appears that I retained the television and film rights and that they are just my ordinary property. This makes a great difference. I will explain it all to you when we meet.[3]

---

[1] 'Note by Sir Winston', 'Private', 6 August 1956; Churchill papers, 2/130.

[2] 'My darling', Palace Hotel, St Moritz, 9 August 1956: Churchill papers, 1/55.

[3] The book in question was *My Early Life*, published in 1930, by Thornton Butterworth in England and by Scribner's in the United States (with the title *A Roving Commission*). It had been republished in the United States by Scribner's in 1939, and in England by Macmillan in 1941.

Juliet is coming to luncheon to-day and will stay till Monday. If I remember right she plays Bezique.

In a handwritten postscript, Churchill added: '4 p.m. Juliet is here, & she has brought the new book with her & sends you lots of love. We are sitting in yr rose garden wh is really *hot*. All my love, Yr devoted husband, W' [sketch of pig].[1]

At Chartwell, Denis Kelly had been helping with the History. 'I felt refreshed & fortified by my stay at Chartwell,' he wrote to Churchill on August 10, after his return to London, '& will go "all out" to help finish the book by Christmas.'[2] Anthony Montague Browne was also enlisted to help with the book, preparing for Churchill the section on the rise of Germany. A proud author, Churchill told Montague Browne, as the work progressed: 'It is nice to see yourself in print.'[3]

On August 14 Churchill sent his wife another letter, in which the Suez crisis dominated, but his literary work also had a place:

My darling One,

I enclose you a cutting which I tore from today's *Mirror*. It is a pretty odious piece of money-grubbing. Nevertheless I expect it represents at least a large minority of the country. I think it may be a reflection of Harold Macmillan's views. He expressed them fairly frankly to me last week. They point to the futility of taking the Canal and having a hundred thousand troops to find to guard it, instead of what he favours, if need be going for Cairo and the Egyptian state.[4]

The Russians have come over with a delegation of fifty—the numbers being picked, according to AMB, to proselytize the rest of the Conference. I really don't see how they (HMG) will be able to cope with the clatter of voices and get the thing wound up by the end of August. You will be home in plenty of time for the *fun*, if any.

To-day it is cloudy, but bright, and I am sitting on a seat in the garden dictating a letter to Miss Maturin, who sends you her regards.

I had Miss Thorson of the MGM down here yesterday. She is a really clever woman.[5] The negotiations are settled in principle on the basis of seventy

---

[1] 'My darling One', Chartwell, 11 August 1956: Spencer-Churchill papers. The dictated portion of this letter is also in Churchill papers, 1/55.

[2] Letter of 10 August 1956: Churchill papers, 1/143.

[3] Anthony Montague Browne recollections: in conversation with the author, 14 July 1987.

[4] On 14 August 1956 the front page of the *Daily Mirror* warned Eden that 'If he allows himself to be goaded into rash deeds by his own bold words, by the din from the sabre-rattlers and gunboat diplomats, or by applause from France, he will find himself in a position that could be resolved in one way only—*His Own Resignation as Prime Minister*.' The newspaper declared: 'Nothing that has yet happened over the Suez Canal justifics war or the threat of war,' and it went on to tell its readers: 'Sir Anthony Eden's desire or intention to overthrow Nasser as Egypt's leader is blatantly unrealistic. Eden cannot talk to Nasser in 1956 as Churchill talked to Mussolini in the 1940s.'

[5] Marg Thorson was assistant head of the story department of Metro-Goldwyn-Mayer, based at the MGM studio in Culver City, California; later she became head of the department.

thousand down, and God knows how many millions in the future as a result of fifty per cent of the profit. The extraordinary thing is that it is practically certain that this fifty-year-old story is my own property and not taxable.

I have to make arrangements for reading four or five minutes from the text. Miss T worked up a good extract, which I considered and polished this morning, and which I will deliver on Saturday next in my study. I think it is all very good, and will unfold it to you at better length when you arrive.

Mary says she had a long and lovely letter from you. She has come back to look after her brood, and is dining with me tonight. Christopher is wrapped up in his office duties, as you can imagine.

All my love

Your devoted husband

W [1]

'I am very glad that France and England are acting together,' Churchill wrote to Odette Pol Roger on August 14, and he added: 'Nasser is at the bottom of many of your troubles in Algeria.' [2]

On August 15, when Churchill wrote again to his wife, it was clear that his film hopes for *My Early Life* had been dashed. As for the Suez crisis, Eden had decided to resolve it by force:

My darling One,

I came up to London today and had a lunch to which I invited Christopher, Nigel Birch and Antony Head. [3] We talked over all our affairs. I think it would be very difficult to arrive at a good result. After lunch I received the Lions deputation who gave me 'Rusty'. [4] They are an interesting body of charitable intentions. They gave me a beautiful plaque which I will have put on the cage. I send you a letter which will explain them.

What I have to tell you about is the downfall of my hopes about the film. Apparently, I sold it in 1941 to the Warner Brothers for £7,500! They have done nothing about it all the time, and when we asked Nicholl Manisty if there was any record of any truck with them, they said 'No'. However, yesterday afternoon they wrote a letter saying they had found a document

---

[1] 'My darling One', Chartwell, 14 August 1956: Spencer-Churchill papers. The carbon copy is in Churchill papers, 1/55.

[2] Letter of 14 August 1956: Churchill papers, 2/395.

[3] Nigel Birch, the Secretary of State for Air (1955–7) was subsequently Economic Secretary to the Treasury. A Conservative MP from 1945 to 1970, in 1970 he was created Baron Rhyl. Antony Head, the Secretary of State for War (1951–6) was later Minister of Defence. A Conservative MP from 1945 to 1960, in 1960 he was created Viscount. British High Commissioner to Nigeria (1960–3) and Malaysia (1963–6).

[4] Rusty, a young male lion at London Zoo, had been presented to Churchill, to replace Churchill's lion Rota, who had been put to sleep in June 1955 at the age of seventeen. Rusty died in 1960. Lions Clubs International, who presented Rusty, had been founded in 1917, with their headquarters in the United States, and consisted of professional and business groups devoted to community service and the promotion of better international relations, being particularly noted for their work for the deaf and blind, and their international youth exchange programme.

which coupled with the American records make it quite clear that I had no possession. It was very careless of Nicholl Manisty not to give an answer, and of course Moir and all my people were misled. This seemed such a good thing and so simple that I am sorry that it falls to the ground. It was after all only an additional resource, but none the less it is a disappointment.[1]

I brought Rufus up today and sent him to Miss Lobban who has shaved him beautifully. He looks as good as ever. There is no doubt the doctor made a great cure of him. He put a $2\frac{1}{2}''$ needle in his broken left jawbone, which now seems to work perfectly, though of course he has no teeth. He eats good meals, and I think I may look forward to a reasonable prolongation of his life.[2]

They begin the conference tomorrow, and I imagine that very considerable difficulties will still encroach upon them. The Grenadier Guards are leaving today! What a tangle. However this is settled, I expect we must look to Israel for the next move.

'My dearest,' Churchill added in his own hand, 'I have been absorbed all day with difficult points ranging from War to my financial affairs. I long to see you & am so glad it will be a week tomorrow. Your loving & devoted husband, W.'[3]

Even as he awaited his wife's return from Switzerland, Churchill was planning his next visit to the South of France. Once more it was to La Pausa that he intended to go, writing to Wendy Reves on August 16:

My dear Wendy,

I was very sorry you could not visit this country with Emery. It would have been very jolly to see you again. Emery will have told you about my present plans, which remain to visit you about the middle of September. I hope that the Egyptian situation will not develop in a way to delay or prevent it. I don't see why it should. I look forward to coming back to Pausaland again, and will do the same thing about the motorcar and Mario if that can be arranged.

I have been toiling at the book, but have not made the progress I expected. I hope, however, that it will all be finished by the end of January. Five months.

I am sorry that the Princess[4] did not reply to your flowers. Did you make

---

[1] It was a disappointment that was eventually to pass; Warner Brothers having agreed to give Churchill back the film rights to *My Early Life*, and MGM having decided not to go ahead with the film, in 1960 Anthony Montague Browne negotiated its sale to Carl Foreman, of Columbia Pictures, for £100,000 (against a percentage of the gross). It was eventually made, with the title *Young Winston*. 'I handed the cheque to him,' Montague Browne later recalled. 'It thrilled him. He sent for his cheque book and proposed giving me a quarter—£25,000. Knowing his true financial situation, I declined. But it shows how he retained these generous instincts.' (Anthony Montague Browne recollections: in conversation with the author, 6 October 1987.)

[2] This was Rufus II, the original Rufus having been run over and killed while Churchill was at the Conservative Party Conference at Brighton in October 1947.

[3] 'My darling One', 28 Hyde Park Gate, 15 August 1956: Spencer-Churchill papers. The carbon copy of the dictated section is in Churchill papers, 1/55.

[4] Princess Grace of Monaco (formerly Grace Kelly, the actress).

it clear that they came from you and not from me? She wrote a very nice letter in answer to mine. She may be tripping over the irregularity. It makes it difficult for people in formal surroundings.

Clemmie has gone to St Moritz. She had a painfall fall before leaving. She thought it was only bruises, but knee and ankle have been afflicted by a torn muscle, and she is unable at present to walk. She is coming back here on Thursday next.

The weather is disappointing. When June failed, I hoped for July. When July disgraced itself, my thoughts turned to August. We have had the most curious changes of weather. Sometimes the most beautiful day without a cloud in the sky, but nearly always succeeded by periods of rain and gales. I wonder what sort of weather you are having and whether the lavender has fulfilled your courageous hopes?

'Christopher's official work,' Churchill told Wendy Reves, 'takes him up to London a great deal, & Mary has her brood, but I can live a solitary life without great discomfort.'[1]

On August 16, at Chartwell, Lord Moran asked Churchill for his views of the Suez crisis. 'Winston is not so sure that Nasser can be written off,' Moran wrote. 'He is worried about Suez. He still argues that if we invade the Canal we need not stay there; when Nasser gave in we would get out. "Anthony," said Winston, "wants me to speak on Suez in the House—he would like me to speak from the box." He shook his head. "I shall not do that. Anthony says I must be told everything."'[2]

In a 'Top Secret and Personal' letter, sent from 10 Downing Street on August 17, Anthony Eden explained his hopes and feelings:

We are only at the beginning but there are some encouraging elements. Most important of all, the Americans seem very firmly lined up with us on internationalisation. Secondly, there are signs that the Middle Eastern States who are also oil producers, e.g. Iraq, Persia, and Saudi-Arabia, are in varying degrees opposed to Nasser's plans. In other Arab States demagogy howls in support of Nasser.

Preparations about which I spoke to you are going forward with some modifications, which should lead to simplification of our plan should the need arise. I am sure that you will think this all to the good.

It is difficult to judge about public opinion. The left-wing intellectuals and some liberals are all out against us. The BBC is exasperating me by leaning over backwards to be what they call neutral and to present both sides of the case, by which I suppose they mean our country's and the Dancing Major's.

---

[1] 'My dear Wendy', Chartwell, 16 August 1956: Reves papers. Churchill signed this letter 'Yours vy sincerely, W.'

[2] Moran diary, 16 August 1956: *The Struggle for Survival*, pages 703–5.

I am, however, seeing Jacob this afternoon. He and nearly all the seniors have been away on leave. I hope we can improve on past performances.[1]

Bob Menzies has been very helpful and it would help me if you would tell him so when you see him. I will keep you posted.

'I was sorry to be away on Monday,' Eden added, 'but I needed a few hours off. I am very fit now.'[2]

On August 23 Clementine Churchill returned to England from St Moritz. 'Welcome my darling,' he wrote to her from Chartwell to greet her at the airport. 'I am so glad you are safely home. Maria brings this with all my love, W.'[3]

Churchill continued with his plans to return to La Pausa. 'We are having characteristically anti-harvest weather here,' he wrote to Emery Reves on August 24, adding, hopefully: 'I suppose you are having sunshine in Pausaland?'[4] 'The only thing that might alter my plans,' he wrote to Wendy Reves on September 4, 'will be WAR. In that case I should have to attend Parliament, and whatever sittings may be necessary.'[5]

For three weeks Churchill and his wife were together at Chartwell and Hyde Park Gate. On September 12, their wedding anniversary, Churchill sent her a note: 'My darling One, Some flowers to salute our 48th anniversary! All my love, W.'[6] Four days later, Lord Moran noted in his diary: 'Found Winston playing bezique with Clemmie, a happy picture. They insisted on stopping the game, and Clemmie went off to bring Dorothy[7] in to tea.' The discussion turned to Suez:

Winston: 'I don't like the way things are going. After the first debate in the House I came away encouraged, even elated. When there was danger to

[1] Sir Ian Jacob was Director-General of the BBC from 1952 to 1960 (in 1946 he had been Controller of European Services, and from 1947 to 1952 Director of Overseas Services, BBC). From 1939 to 1946 he had been Military Assistant Secretary to the War Cabinet, and in 1952 Chief Staff Officer to the Minister of Defence and Deputy Secretary (Military) to the Cabinet. Sir Ian Jacob writes: 'There certainly was difficulty between Eden and the BBC, because Eden thought that we should not give prominence to Gaitskell & his political friends.' Jacob adds: 'Eden seems to have misunderstood the type of neutrality the BBC was upholding—it was not neutrality in regard to Nasser—it was neutrality between the British parties. As the nation and the Parliament was divided in their views of how to deal with the Canal affair, we had to reflect that division.' (Sir Ian Jacob: letter to the author, 2 July 1987.)

[2] 'My dear Winston', 'Top Secret and Personal', 10 Downing Street, 17 August 1956: Churchill papers, 2/216.

[3] Note of 23 August 1956, Chartwell: Spencer-Churchill papers.

[4] 'My dear Emery', 24 August 1956: Reves papers.

[5] 'My dear Wendy', 4 September 1956: Reves papers.

[6] 'My darling One', 12 September 1956: Spencer-Churchill papers.

[7] Lord Moran's wife.

the country the Opposition seemed behind the Government, and Gaitskell showed himself capable of playing an Englishman's part. But the second debate undid all the good; in fact, it did a good deal of harm. Gaitskell went back on things—the feeling in his party was too strong for him. I want our people to take up a strong point on the Canal with a few troops and to say to Nasser: "We'll get out when you are sensible about the Canal."'

He was silent for a time. Then he said sadly: 'I am afraid we are going downhill.' The fallen state of Britain troubles him more than his own parlous condition.

At tea, Moran noted, 'Clemmie invoked my aid to get Winston to persevere with a hearing aid. She got up and, speaking into his ear, said playfully: "It's just a question of taking a little trouble, my dear. Quite stupid people learn to use it after a short time." His eye twinkled as he put his hand affectionately on hers. He is flying to France tomorrow.'[1]

'I will re-visit Pausaland,' Churchill had written to Wendy Reves in his letter of September 4. 'I hope I may bring Montague Browne with me,' he added, 'and I shall indeed look forward to finding you and Emery safely ensconced in the villa.'[2]

On September 17 Churchill flew to the South of France. 'The weather is beautiful—sunny yet cool,' he wrote to Lord Cherwell two days later in urging him to fly out and join him. 'The sooner you come the better,' he added.[3]

While Churchill was at La Pausa, Eden sent him a letter commenting on the continuing crisis at Suez. 'I am not happy at the way things are developing here,' Eden wrote, with reference to opposition inside Britain, 'but we are struggling hard to keep a firm and united front in these critical weeks,' and he added: 'Firm is even more important than united.' He had been assured by Foster Dulles 'that the US is as determined to deal with Nasser as we are—but I fear he has a mental caveat about November 6. We cannot accept that.'[4]

Churchill's first letter to his wife during this September holiday was sent on September 19:

My darling,

It is all very bright and peaceful here. The air is cool yet the temperature is warm, and in the sun of course it is very hot. Since the beginning of the month they have not had a rainy day. So far I have not moved from the house and the verandah, but we are going to the Château de Madrid for luncheon to-day.

[1] Moran diary, 16 September 1956: *The Struggle for Survival*, pages 705–6.
[2] 'My dear Wendy', 4 September 1956: Churchill papers, 2/532.
[3] 'My dear Prof', La Pausa, 19 September 1956: Churchill papers, 2/214.
[4] 'My dear Winston', 10 Downing Street, 21 September 1956: Churchill papers, 2/216. Eden had proposed the setting up of a Canal Users' Association, which would enforce free passage of the Suez Canal from 6 November 1956. This deadline was rejected by the United States.

They are asking the Prof out here, and I hope he will come. I have not done a stroke of work, but have read about three-quarters of *Tono-Bungay*.[1] Yesterday the Kemsleys came to luncheon.[2] I found him very friendly and agreeable.

Dr Roberts has examined me and finds me in very good health. I have started resolutely on the Baruch hearing aid, and am getting very used to wearing it. I can even hear the bird talk when I am alone.

I do hope your improvement has been continuous. The recovery seemed almost miraculous, and it was a joy to me to see you getting better every day.

My dear One all my love

W[3]

Five days later Churchill learned that his wife would not after all be joining him. He at once dictated a further progress report of his life at La Pausa:

Here all is peaceful and I am glad to say that the whole book team is hard at work.

Thank you so much for dealing with poor Ivor's funeral.[4]

I am wearing Bernie's hearing-aid every day when in company and I find it a great relief. It is complete and in perfect order and I think I shall get used to the habit of using it. I quite agree that it is a necessity.

I have not tried any painting yet, although there has been plenty of sunlight. The Prefect and his wife are coming to dine on Thursday next. So far we have had no strangers as company.

I had a letter from Anthony thanking me for the cigars, and incidentally showing a robust spirit. I am so glad they are going to the Security Council immediately. I see he is to be in Paris tomorrow or the next day. I must say I am very glad the burden does not rest on me.

I stay in bed all the morning, and am very pleased with the way the book is getting on, and I think you will be both pleased and surprised at the way the work is going.

---

[1] First published in 1909, H. G. Wells's novel *Tono-Bungay* described English society in dissolution in the latter part of the nineteenth century, and the advent of a new class of rich. In 1909, Churchill had been a leading public critic of excessive wealth, telling an audience at Leicester on 4 September 1909: 'If we carry on in the old happy-go-lucky way, the richer classes ever growing in wealth and in number, the very poor remaining plunged or plunging ever deeper into helplessness, hopeless misery, then I think there is nothing before us but savage strife between class and class, and the increasing disorganisation with increasing waste of human strength and human virtue.'

[2] James Gomer Berry, 1st Viscount Kemsley, Chairman of Kemsley Newspapers Ltd, and Editor-in-Chief of the *Sunday Times*, from 1937 to 1959. In 1947 he married, as his second wife, Pamela, elder daughter of Lord Richard Wellesley. Lord Kemsley was the brother of Churchill's friend Lord Camrose, who had died in 1954.

[3] 'My darling', La Pausa, 19 September 1956: Spencer-Churchill papers.

[4] Lord Ivor Spencer-Churchill, who had died on 17 September 1956, was the son of Churchill's first cousin, the 9th Duke of Marlborough. He died a month before his fifty-eighth birthday, leaving a widow, and a son aged two and a half.

Churchill added, in his own hand:

My darling One,

It is such a pleasure to receive your letters—the handwriting is so strong and you can dash them off with a vigour wh shows that your tumbles and their consequences are now steadfastly relegated to the background.

I must say I am attracted by this neighbourhood & am cherishing the idea of La Dragonière when I have ended my visit here, in the opening days of November.[1] If all my plans work out and I can return in January—(I shall know next week) we shall have a large canvas to paint and we must try to fit ourselves into the design with the utmost pleasure & company.

My tender love

Your devoted husband [Sketch of pig]

W

Toby sends his salutations
wh I enclose. . . .[2]

Among those who were helping Churchill with the nineteenth-century chapters of his History was a young history don at University College, Oxford, Maurice Shock. 'It would be very nice,' Churchill telegraphed to him on September 25, 'if you could spend the weekend with Alan at his hotel as my guest. I should like to meet you very much. I can get you a seat on the plane Friday or Saturday.'[3]

Maurice Shock came as bidden, and worked with Alan Hodge and Churchill for three days. On October 2 Shock flew back to London, taking with him a letter from Churchill to his wife:

My Darling,

Just cannot think what I meant by 'princely gift'. Perhaps when I get to Chartwell I may find something in the early letters of the muniment room which will reveal it.

It continues to be lovely here. We have had, since the electric storms reduced the tension, four lovely days and have no reason not to hope for more.

You do not say anything in your letters to me about how your health is faring. Has the pain gone completely away from the leg, and does it come back to the shoulder? I will telephone again in a day or two.

Here all goes very quietly. The Château de Madrid is closed for two months' holiday and we have the chef to cook for us. The food is therefore excellent, though as you know I do not eat so much as I used to. I have done a great deal of work at the book and not painted yet. Mr Shock, who brings this letter this afternoon, has done me a very good note on the first Gladstone and Disraeli chapter, and I look forward to receiving another fertile wodge in a fortnight. He is a very nice young man, and I am glad to have had him at the hotel for the week-end. There are only three more chapters in the last

---

[1] La Dragonière was Lord Rothermere's villa on Cap Martin.

[2] 'My dearest' and 'My darling One', La Pausa, 24 September 1956: Spencer-Churchill papers.

[3] Telegram sent 6.30 p.m., 25 September 1956: Churchill papers, 4/28.

book to be composed after which there will only be bits and pieces and final revise. I am keeping the printers and my whole outfit very busy.

The Prof arrived last night. It was nice of him to face this journey. He is having a dreadful fight with Duncan, and the papers, particularly the *Spectator*, are making it as bad as they can. I cannot see what right D has to use his powers to stir up all this trouble.[1]

I also enclose a very nice letter I have had from poor Ivor's widow.[2] I have answered it myself, but perhaps you will keep it for me till I return.

I never heard a word from anyone about Collusion running last Saturday, though I see now that he was not placed.

With all my love

Your devoted husband

W[3]

On October 4 Sir Norman Brook sent Churchill an account of 'developments in the Suez situation', in the course of which he wrote:

The Americans have certainly not been helpful. It is clear now that we should have been in a much better position here, and should have had a much less divided public opinion, if we had gone to the Security Council at the time when Parliament met. This, as you know, is what we ourselves would have preferred to do. But we were restrained by the Americans who urged us most strongly to hold our hands and give room for the trial of their plan of 'the users' association'. At that stage they presented this plan as a practical means of bringing the issue to a head. But the Second London Conference, at which this plan was discussed, was much less successful than the first—and by the end of it most of the 'teeth' had been removed from that plan. Now, at his latest Press Conference, Dulles has gone so far as to say that it never had any teeth at all. His other statements at the Press Conference have been very far from helpful. And I doubt if he has made matters any better by the alterations which he has made today in the official transcript of the record. His statements about colonialism and about our differences 'on fundamental issues' must surely have the effect of encouraging Nasser—and perhaps the Russians too.

Our best hope of bringing Nasser to his senses was to preserve a firm front among the Western Powers—and particularly between the United States,

---

[1] As Minister of Housing and Local Government (since 18 October 1954), Duncan Sandys had given his strong support to the scheme for a relief road to be built across Christ Church Meadow, Oxford. 'A storm has finally burst over Oxford,' the *Spectator* had reported on 28 September 1956, 'where town and gown have been set in uproar. . . .' Lord Cherwell was one of the principal opponents of the road, advocating in its place a tunnel, to avoid scarring the meadow. Such a tunnel could be built, its supporters argued, for £2 million. Twice, on October 23 and October 30, Sandys challenged the tunnel scheme in the House of Commons, arguing that it would cost £7 million, a sum that made it too expensive, and citing expert opinion in support of his claim.

[2] Lady Ivor Spencer-Churchill's son Robert was two years old at the time of his father's death.

[3] 'My Darling', La Pausa, 2 October 1956: Spencer-Churchill papers.

France and ourselves. I fear that, during the last week or so, the Western position has been seriously weakened by public statements made in the United States. This at any rate is the PM's view—and I am sure that it will be held even more strongly by the French.

You may like to know that the PM was deeply impressed by the youth and vigour of M. Mollet's Government. He says that they are by far the best French Government he has seen since the war. Over Suez they are tough and uncompromising. He believes that we may be at the beginning of something like a renaissance of strength in France.

We have had no indications yet what course the discussions in the Security Council are likely to take. It seems inevitable, however, that we should be pressed to accept negotiation in some form or other. We do not think it will be possible to reject out of hand all suggestions for negotiation. Possibly the most acceptable form for us would be direct negotiation between ourselves, the French and the Egyptians. It is too early to say how these discussions will go. . . .[1]

It was Gaitskell's 'determined speech' two months earlier, Churchill told his wife on October 5, which was 'responsible to a large extent for the Government committing themselves by large troop movements', and he added: 'It would be very hard to use force now.'[2]

Progress on his History continued. 'There are only two or three chapters to do,' Churchill reported.[3] 'My next chapter is progressing,' Maurice Shock wrote that day from Oxford. 'I will send it to you as soon as it is fit to be seen.'[4]

On October 7 Nonie Montague Browne joined Churchill and her husband in the South of France. 'Sir Winston called for his paints,' she noted in her diary three days later, 'and the canvas, and a bowl of flowers—and said to me, "Paint!"'[5]

In the second week of October, Churchill learned that his son Randolph had won a libel action against the *People* newspaper, for having described him as a 'paid hack'. 'I feel ashamed and mortified by Randolph's Libel Action,' Clementine Churchill had written on October 9, before the result was known.[6] But when Churchill wrote back three days later, Randolph had been victorious, and there was also hope of victory on the turf:

---

[1] 'Dear Sir Winston', 'Top Secret and Personal', Cabinet Office, 4 October 1956: Churchill papers, 2/181.
[2] On October 22, at a villa on the outskirts of Paris, Selwyn Lloyd, Guy Mollet and David Ben-Gurion concluded a plan which was to involve an Anglo-French military landing at Port Said on November 5. Some form of 'Port Said option' had been in Eden's mind since August.
[3] 'My dear One', La Pausa, 5 October 1956: Spencer-Churchill papers.
[4] 'Dear Sir Winston', 5 October 1956: Churchill papers, 4/28.
[5] Nonie Montague Browne diary, 10 October 1956: Lady Sargant papers.
[6] 'My darling', 28 Hyde Park Gate, 9 October 1956: Churchill papers, 1/55.

My dearest One,

I am so glad you and Mary are going to see the horse run on Saturday. I hope it will not rain and that Le Pretendant will fulfil our hopes. You might tell Christopher to send me a telegram, or better still ring me on the telephone, whatever happens.

The weather is very good. Yesterday was one of the finest days I have seen out here. I invited hosts and guests to lunch with me at the Vistaero, which is really a most beautiful villa perched on a peak from which you can look down a thousand feet or more. We came home and I went for my usual daily walk in the garden. Wendy was taken ill, having, it is presumed, eaten something, but today she has recovered.

I plan to come home on the 22nd, and am looking forward so much to seeing you . Toby sends his love, but has not given me any overt sign which I can enclose.

I admit I was astonished that Randolph won his action, and at the damages.[1] It is quite true that he is not a 'paid hack', but I did not think that a jury would draw so firmly the very refined distinction between his vocabulary and the *People*'s. He seems to have acquitted himself well in the box. I have written him a letter of congratulation.

I was so glad to hear from your own lips that you have made a recovery from the many evils which haunted you. I do hope it will last.

With my fondest love
I remain
Your devoted husband

W[2]

On October 15 Churchill wrote again, in his own hand. His horse had won, defeating the Queen's horse:

My darling,

The time has passed vy quickly & I am now within a week of coming home—five weeks to a day it will be. It has been a vy pleasant spell, quiet and peaceful. I wish you had come for a week or so. I have not decided anything about a permanent residence or indeed anything except read the papers.

I have begun painting one picture—a large long one of the view to the Eastward; and have progressed so well that after three days it is still an attraction to me. Today it rains, but there is hope of clearing in the afternoon.

Sarah is coming on Thursday & the prospect gives gt pleasure all round. I am going to speak to her on the telephone in an hour or so. Do you know the Baroness Jean de Rothschild, she is a gt friend of Wendy's, and I think an agreeable woman. *She plays Bezique.* Her husband—a Vienna Rothschild—is 72 and she about thirty years younger. She leaves on Wednesday when Sarah arrives.

I hope the Queen was not too vexed at being beaten. It was just as well I

---

[1] Randolph Churchill was awarded £5,000 damages, with costs.
[2] 'My dearest One', La Pausa, 12 October 1956: Spencer-Churchill papers.

wasn't there as there wd have been embarrassing cheers and counter-cheers. I agreed to let the colt go to the USA yesterday on Christopher's advice.

The book is going to be finished in time; but I have not heard so far from the Revenue. The man who dealt with my affairs says that there is a good deal of holiday making just now.

I am so glad to have your good reports confirmed by Sarah who says you are vy well. I look forward so much to seeing for myself. My dearest,

With all my love

Your devoted husband

W

Churchill ended his letter of October 15 with the drawing of a pig 'resting'.

'Anthony E made a good speech at the conference,' Churchill added, with a reference to the Conservative Party Conference at Llandudno.[1] It was the first Party Conference Churchill had not attended for eleven years.

Churchill's thoughts were still on a permanent house in the South of France, or at least a villa in which he would not have to impose on the hospitality of Emery and Wendy Reves, unstinted though their hospitality was. One possibility was made all the more attractive by a suggestion of Aristotle Onassis, as Montague Browne explained:

The villa is situated on a promontory above Monte Carlo Beach about 100 ft above the sea. The property comprises practically the whole of the point except the Western seaboard which belongs to the Monte Carlo Beach Hotel. It is isolated, but within a few minutes of the centre of Monte Carlo, and in undoubtedly one of the best positions one could find on the coast. The villa is in very bad condition and war-damaged, and the garden is overgrown.

The Société des Bains de Mer, the company which controls the Casino, the Hôtel de Paris, the Beach Hotel, etc., own the villa. They have for some time been proposing to reconstruct it as a luxury annex to the Beach Hotel or something similar. Mr Onassis, who is the largest single shareholder in the company, has made the following proposal:

The Company must in its own interest reconstruct the villa or else raze it and build something new on the site. They would like to erect the new building to the specifications of Sir Winston, and let it to him furnished for

[1] 'My darling', La Pausa, 15 October 1956: Spencer-Churchill papers.

his lifetime at a rent to be agreed—probably £1500 a year. (Various figures were mentioned, but £1500 a year seemed the most likely.) The reconstruction would probably cost the Company in the neighbourhood of £40,000–£50,000. Their preliminary proposal is that it should be rebuilt as a one-storey 'colonial' type house with five-seven bedrooms. When Sir Winston no longer required the property it could be modified without much difficulty to meet the Company's requirements as a Hotel. Staff and if necessary cooking could be provided from the Beach Hotel which is a few minutes away.

At first sight there do not seem to be many snags. But the possible ones are:—

1 The point is exposed and in rough weather extremely windswept.
2 The railway passes behind the point (but further away than is the case at La Capponcina).
3 The point is somewhat overlooked by houses on the hill behind, though from a distance.
4 In high summer one might be disturbed by noise from the Beach Hotel swimming pool which is below the house on the West side.
5 It would take ten to twelve months to reconstruct the house or build a new one.[1]

Nothing came of this plan; and Churchill remained at La Pausa, entertained when he wanted to be, working when he wished to, and painting when the mood took him.

Churchill's kindness in October led him to write a letter to the Secretary-General of the Roumanian Communist Party, in which he asked him to intercede on behalf of Bill Deakin's father-in-law, Liviu Popescu-Nasta, who had been sentenced in 1950 to twenty years' imprisonment, and was then dangerously ill and paralysed in a prison hospital.[2] It was Deakin's hope, Churchill wrote, 'that the Roumanian government would consider allowing the family as a whole to join him and his wife in England so that he could assume full care and responsibility'. Churchill added: 'I consider that, on humanitarian grounds alone, this is an entirely correct request, and earnestly hope that you will feel able to give it every due consideration.'[3]

In mid-October Alan Hodge returned to London with his wife Jane, who wrote to Churchill on October 12 that when her daughters asked her where she had been, 'I shall tell them I have been visiting the world's kindest great man.'[4]

---

[1] Undated note: Spencer-Churchill papers.

[2] Popescu-Nasta, a newspaper editor, and confidant of the pre-war Roumanian Foreign Minister, Nicolae Titulescu, had been imprisoned by General Antonescu's Government during the Second World War for his pro-British stance. He was subsequently imprisoned by the Communists. The Secretary-General of the Roumanian Communist Party in 1956 was Gheorge Gheorghiu-Dej, the head of the Roumanian Communist Party from 1945 until his death in 1965.

[3] 'Dear Secretary-General', October 1956: Churchill papers, 2/184. Churchill's letter was to no avail; Liviu Popescu-Nasta died in prison two years later.

[4] 'Dear Sir Winston', 13 October 1956: Churchill papers, 2/189.

On October 17 Churchill was sent an account of the Suez crisis from Frederick Bishop, Eden's Principal Private Secretary, set out for him in a letter to Anthony Montague Browne:

On the whole the Prime Minister was satisfied with the outcome of the debate in the Security Council. Of course, it was not easy to decide what form of resolution was best, to be consistent with the line which the Prime Minister wished to take in his speech after the Party Conference at Llandudno, and it was even harder to carry the French with us in formulating such a resolution, particularly as Mr Dulles and the Secretary-General [1] had also to be considered. As it came out, with considerable emphasis on the 18 Power proposals, it was about right. The fact that the Russians vetoed it was a help rather than a disadvantage from the political point of view.

We have tried to make it clear that we regard the Security Council as having taken the matter only a very little way forward towards a settlement. The fact that Mr Dulles and President Eisenhower welcomed the resolution 'with a prayer of thanksgiving in their hearts' does not seem to have misled people here, at any rate, into undue optimism.

Immediately the Foreign Secretary returned, the Prime Minister and he decided to accept an invitation from the French Prime Minister to go over to Paris to talk about the next steps. The Prime Minister is only just back, but there seems no doubt that, broadly speaking, we and the French still see eye to eye about how to carry the matter forward. Probably our diplomatic attitude will be to repeat that it is up to the Egyptians to put forward practical proposals to seek a settlement in accordance with the principles agreed at the Security Council; until they do, we stand by the 18 Power proposals as the best basis.

But this straightforward diplomatic picture is now overlaid with the complicated situation between Iraq, Jordan and Israel. Seemingly the Jordanians are unwilling to take the risk that the Israeli assertion that the entry of Iraqi troops into Jordan would be regarded by them as an aggression may be more than a bluff, and the Iraqi troops are held near the frontier. It may be that, because of our part in all this and our assurances to Jordan, Britain will now be seen to be of more value to the Arab States than Egypt. On the other hand, if the result of these movements has been to make Western help more suspect in Arab eyes, the position of the Government of Jordan may be endangered, and even Nuri may be affected. But the latter seems safe enough at present. On the whole, the events of the last few days seem to have made the cracks in Arab solidarity a little more evident.

I think that that is all, to date. Needless to say, the precautionary measures are being fully maintained. The Prime Minister's repetition that no responsible Government could undertake in the present circumstances that force will never be used, is becoming more widely appreciated, as the limitations of the United Nations are demonstrated, for example by Russia's use of the veto last Saturday. [2]

[1] The Secretary of the United Nations (1953 to 1961), Dag Hammarskjöld.
[2] 'Secret', 10 Downing Street, 17 October 1956: Churchill papers, 2/130.

In sending this letter on to Churchill, Montague Browne wrote in his covering letter that 'Bishop's only addition orally was to say that military action was "by *no* means ruled out"'.[1] Five days later, unknown to Churchill, and to all but a handful of senior civil servants and Eden, the Foreign Secretary, Selwyn Lloyd, flew to Paris for a secret meeting with the French Prime Minister Guy Mollet and Foreign Minister Christian Pineau, together with the Israeli Prime Minister David Ben-Gurion, and the Israeli Defence Minister Moshe Dayan.[2] At this meeting, it was agreed to launch a joint Anglo-French and Israeli military attack on the Suez Canal.

At La Pausa, Churchill had suffered what seemed to be a black-out on October 20, falling down, and losing consciousness for about twenty minutes. It was in fact a stroke. 'Sir Winston has had an attack of cerebral spasm,' Dr Roberts wrote to Lord Moran five days later. During the attack he had lost the use of his right leg, his right arm and the left side of his face.

Dr Roberts went on to give an encouraging report of the events since October 20. 'He has made very good progress,' Roberts wrote, 'and has even been out in the garden.'[3]

On October 28 Churchill was well enough to fly back to Britain. On the following morning Lord Moran wrote to him, as he waited to see him:

My dear Winston,

I was a little worried last night because Dr Roberts in his letter of October 25 to me said you were on (1) a vitamin, (2) a fat diminished diet and (3) aminophyline.

Aminophyline is a depressant of the circulation and directly contraindicated. However, from what I can gather you are not taking aminophyline now. The diet, the vitamins and the papaverine are all right: anyway they will do no harm, though I doubt if they will do any good. But I didn't want any depressant of the circulation used. Brain agrees about *not* using aminophyline. I shall be back Wednesday evening and could see you 9 p.m. with Brain. This will suit Brain. If you would rather see him alone, he will I'm sure fit in.

There has never been any question that the Anticoagulants are dangerous so the regulation time does not arise. Cholesterol is a long time consideration. There are the blood tests he suggested. I shall not wake you.

Yrs, Charles[4]

[1] 'My dear Sir Winston', 'Secret', 17 October 1956: Churchill papers, 2/130.

[2] Also present from Israel was a senior civil servant of the Defence Ministry, Shimon Peres, later (1984–6) Prime Minister of Israel.

[3] 'Dear Lord Moran', 25 October 1956: Churchill papers, 1/54.

[4] 'My dear Winston', 9.15 a.m., 29 October 1956: Churchill papers, 1/54.

'I am so grateful for your goodness to and your care of Winston,' Clementine Churchill wrote to Wendy and Emery Reves on October 30, and she added: 'He stood the journey very well. He thinks a great deal of the happy, sunny six weeks he spent at La Pausa.'[1] That same day Churchill wrote to Wendy, who was then on her way to the United States:

My dear Wendy,

Thank you so much for all your hospitality. Pausaland was really a temple of peace. There is not much elsewhere.

I send this letter to catch you before you leave, and shall be delighted with any answer you may care to give me on board the boat on Wednesday night. I shall not go to Chartwell until Friday.

I look forward very much to seeing you again. Please remember me to your Mother.

Churchill added, in his own hand: '& tell her how much I appreciated her references to me, with much love, Yours always, W'.[2]

Three weeks later, Churchill's letter was returned. He wrote again, to New York:

My dear Wendy,

I was dismayed to have returned to me today the letter which I sent to you on board the *Queen Elizabeth*. I am so very sorry that it missed you, and hasten to send it on now. You must have thought me very unappreciative of all your kindness.

I hope that you are enjoying your stay in America and that we shall meet in January.

Yours ever,

W[3]

On October 30, as Churchill recovered from his second stroke in three and a half years, Israeli forces attacked Egypt in the Sinai desert, destroying the Egyptian army, occupying the Straits of Tiran, and reaching within a few miles of the Suez Canal. Following a twelve-hour Anglo-French ultimatum to Egypt, insisting that an Anglo-French force 'move temporarily' to the Suez Canal, British bombers struck at Egyptian airfields, while British troops set sail on the long journey from Malta towards Port Said, at the Canal's northern end.

On November 3, as the British forces were still on their way to Egypt, Churchill issued a public statement giving 'the reasons that lead me to support the Government on the Egyptian issue'. In spite of all the efforts of Britain, France and the United States, he wrote, 'the

---

[1] 'My dear Emery & Wendy', 30 October 1956: Reves papers.
[2] 'My dear Wendy', 30 October 1956: Reves papers.
[3] 'My dear Wendy', 21 November 1956: Reves papers.

frontiers of Israel have flickered with murder and armed raids'. Egypt, 'the principal instigator of these incidents', had 'rejected restraint'. Israel, 'under the gravest provocation', had 'erupted against Egypt'. Britain intended 'to restore peace and order' to the Middle East, 'and I am convinced that we shall achieve our aim'. Churchill was also 'confident', he added, 'that our American friends will come to realize that, not for the first time, we have acted independently for the common good'.[1]

Churchill's message was published in the Press on the morning of November 5, at the very moment when British and French paratroops, in advance of the forces still on their way by sea, landed at the northern end of the Suez Canal, capturing Port Said.

'My dear Winston,' Eden wrote to Churchill, 'I cannot thank you enough for your wonderful message. It has had an enormous effect, and I am sure that in the US it will have maybe an even greater influence.' Eden added: 'These are tough days—but the alternative was a slow bleeding to death.'[2]

'Thank you for your kind words,' Churchill replied. 'I am so glad it was a help.[3]

On the morning of November 6, the seaborne forces of Britain and France finally reached Port Said, landed, and advanced southward along the Canal. Later that same day, however, as the culmination of a week of intense American pressure, augmented by the refusal of many of Eden's own colleagues to support him, Eden agreed to a ceasefire.[4] On the following day, November 7, in unveiling a statue to Field Marshal Smuts in Parliament Square, Churchill declared, with Nasser's triumph much in mind:

Today, among the many clamours and stresses of the world, we are beset by a narrow and sterile form of the vast and sometimes magnificent force of nationalism. To Smuts, great patriot though he was, this shallow creed would have been distasteful and alien. His own qualities transcended nationality.[5]

On November 20 Jock Colville dined with Churchill at 28 Hyde Park Gate. The eventual withdrawal of the Anglo-French forces had been accepted by Eden as the one condition on which the United States would continue to support Britain.

Nine years later Colville recalled his conversation with Churchill:

[1] *Manchester Guardian*, 5 November 1956.
[2] 'My dear Winston', 10 Downing Street, 5 November 1956: Churchill papers, 2/216.
[3] 'My dear Anthony', 'Yours ever, W', 5 November 1956: Churchill papers, 2/216.
[4] Those Ministers most opposed to continuing the military operation were Harold Macmillan, R. A. Butler, and Lord Salisbury.
[5] Speech of 7 November 1956: Churchill papers, 2/347.

I told him that my step-grandmother, Peggy Crewe[1], to whom he was devoted, made what I thought was quite an amusing remark. I had said to her 'What we really need now is a Charlotte Corday' to which she replied 'What on earth induces you to suppose that Colonel Nasser ever has a bath?' Winston, who liked Peggy very much, was highly amused by this and said this was in the best Rosebery tradition of witticism.

I then said to him: 'If you had been Prime Minister would you have done this?' And he said to me: 'I would never have dared, and if I had dared, I would never have dared stop.'[2]

We discussed the violent fury of the United States and the hurt feelings of indignation of Eisenhower and of Washington generally. And I said to Winston: 'Why don't you write a letter to Eisenhower pointing out that the enemy are not the British but the Russians,' which he said he would do, and we discussed this at length and he said: 'You are no longer my private secretary, but would you go away and draft a letter for me to write to General Eisenhower?'

So I went back to my office in the city and did so and sent it round by special messenger. He altered it as he thought fit and he sent it off to the General through the US Embassy.[3]

The theme of the letter, as first drafted by Colville, then substantially redrafted by Montague Browne, and finally accepted by Churchill, was that whatever the arguments put forward in Britain and in the United States 'for or against Anthony's action in Egypt', it would now be an act of folly, 'on which our whole civilisation would founder', to let events in the Middle East come between the two countries. The only country who would gain from that would be the Soviet Union.[4]

In his reply, Eisenhower asserted that Nasser was 'a tool, possibly unwittingly, of the Soviets, and at the back of the difficulties that the free world is now experiencing lies one principal fact that none of us can afford to forget. The Soviets are the real enemy of the Western world, implacably hostile and seeking our destruction.' As to Britain's action during the Suez crisis, Eisenhower told Churchill that it was 'not only in violation of the basic principles by which this great combination of nations can be held together, but that even by the doctrine of expediency the invasion could not be judged as soundly conceived and skillfully executed'. His hope was 'that this one may be washed

[1] Lady Margaret Primrose, younger daughter of the 5th Earl of Rosebery, who had married the 1st Marquess of Crewe (then Baron Crewe) as his second wife, in 1899. She died in 1967.

[2] Anthony Montague Browne later recalled that Churchill had said to him after Suez: 'I would never have dared to do it without squaring the Americans, and once I had started I would never have dared stop' (Anthony Montague Browne recollections: notes for the author, 24 March 1987). Sir David Pitblado later commented that, once the breach with the United States had become evident, 'Winston would have appeared in Washington' (Sir David Pitblado recollections: in conversation with the author, 17 July 1987).

[3] 'Mr Jock Colville: Reminiscences: Stour', 8 June 1965: Randolph Churchill papers.

[4] 'My Dear Ike', 'Private and Personal', sent on 23 November 1956: Churchill papers, 2/217.

off the slate as soon as possible and that we can then together adopt other means of achieving our legitimate objectives in the Middle East. Nothing saddens me more than the thought that I and my old friends of years have met a problem concerning which we do not see eye to eye, I shall never be happy until our old time closeness has been restored.' [1]

Churchill sent a copy of Eisenhower's letter to the Queen. 'It is most interesting to learn his appreciation of the situation,' she wrote in reply, 'and I hope it means that the present feeling that this country and America are not seeing eye-to-eye will soon be speedily replaced by even stronger ties between us.' The Queen added, on a personal note: 'I must take this opportunity to thank you most sincerely for sending me the second volume of your book, which I am most delighted to have.' [2]

'Would to heaven that you were twenty years younger,' Desmond Morton wrote to Churchill on November 22, 'you could ensure the healing of the rift between us and the great English-speaking Republic. . . .' [3]

Morton's letter had been prompted by the arrival of the second volume of Churchill's History, entitled 'The New World', which was formally published on November 26. Three days earlier, Eden, urged by his medical advisers to take a rest, had flown to Jamaica. The Prime Minister's departure was discussed by Churchill and Lord Moran on November 26:

Moran: 'What made Anthony leave the country?'
Winston: 'I am shocked by what he did, and I'm an Anthony man.'
Winston said this as if it had hurt him, adding in a low tone: 'I should not have done half the work he has been doing. I'd have got others to do it. He let them wake him up at all hours of the night to listen to news from New York—our night is their day.'
Moran: 'Will Anthony be able to take over when he returns from Jamaica?'
Winston (hesitating): 'I am very doubtful. I'd like to see Harold Macmillan Prime Minister, but they may ask Lord Salisbury. I cannot understand why our troops were halted. To go so far and not go on was madness.'

'A lot of people,' Moran added, 'are wishing you had been in charge.' But Churchill shook his head. 'I am not the man I was. I could not be Prime Minister now.' [4]

Churchill had several meetings that week with Emery Reves, who was full of plans to bring out an abridged version of the war memoirs. [5]

---

[1] 'Dear Winston', 'Top Secret', 27 November 1956: Squerryes Lodge Archive.
[2] 'My dear Sir Winston', 30 November 1956: Squerryes Lodge Archive.
[3] 'Dear Winston', 22 November 1956: Churchill papers, 4/67.
[4] Moran diary, 26 November 1956: *The Struggle for Survival*, pages 709–10.
[5] Three months later, Churchill formally waived his rights to approve any abridgement in advance. ('Dear Mr Reves', 20 February 1957: Reves papers.)

On November 30 Reves left for New York. With him he took a letter from Churchill to Wendy, dated November 29:

Dear Wendy,

Emery leaves by the *QE* tomorrow afternoon. He has been most companionable to us during his short stay in London. He visited us at Chartwell for a weekend, and I think he enjoyed himself.

I am looking forward very much to coming out in January to Pausaland. I gathered from what Emery said that you very likely would not be able to receive me before, perhaps, the 15th. If this should be so, let me know in good time. Otherwise, expect me about the 3rd, and may I bring Anthony Montague Browne with me? We have had a stirring fortnight between England and America, but I think it is all calming down now. At any rate, I do not think that these great affairs will interfere with the pleasant company we keep.

Let me know if you ever got the letter I sent to you for your voyage. I thought I was so clever, but it appears that we did not address it right.

I am looking forward very much to our meeting again.

Yours ever,

W[1]

On November 29, at luncheon at Hyde Park Gate, Colville again asked Churchill what he thought of the Suez operation. It was, he replied, 'the most ill-conceived and ill-executed imaginable'.[2] A week later, Field Marshal Montgomery wrote to Churchill: 'In all my military experience I have never known anything to have been so "bungled" as the Suez affair. You would not have handled it that way. Nor would you have gone off to Jamaica. Under such conditions the captain of the ship does not go sea bathing—he dies on the bridge.'[3]

On December 6 Churchill discussed Suez once more with Lord Moran, telling him:

'. . . I have been turning the Suez episode over in my mind. Of course, one can't tell what one would have done, but one thing is certain, I wouldn't have done anything without consulting the Americans.'

Moran: 'Why didn't Anthony go ahead?'

Winston: 'When things become known it will turn out, I think, that Anthony has been bitched, and that he wanted to go on and complete the

---

[1] 'Dear Wendy', 29 November 1956: Reves papers.

[2] Colville recollection of 29 November 1956: *The Fringes of Power*, page 721. Talking about Eden to Leslie Graham-Dixon, Churchill later commented: 'Faced with a great evil he made a great error' (Leslie Graham-Dixon recollections: in conversation with the author, 15 March 1982). Graham-Dixon and his wife lunched with Churchill on 4 January 1957.

[3] Letter of 6 December 1956: Churchill papers, 2/143. Randolph Churchill earned Eden's life-long opprobrium for writing to the *Manchester Guardian* that the disastrous position of Britain at Suez was like that of the Germans at Stalingrad. 'But even Hitler did not winter in Jamaica'.

military operation. When the Cabinet wouldn't let him he tried to resign, but they told him that he would split the Conservative Party.'[1]

For Churchill, the Suez crisis led to a resolve to act in a personal capacity in one particular sphere. 'After Suez,' Clementine Churchill wrote to Harold Wilson nine years later, 'he specifically set out to mend fences with the United States, and I believe that he had a marked effect in the ensuing years, both by his visits, speeches and talks with major American figures, and also by his public messages.' Clementine Churchill added:

In other directions, too, he sought to improve our situation, for instance, by his persistent friendly references to Russia being part of Europe. (After his Charlemagne Prize speech at Aachen in 1956, there were, I am told, some of the first indications of the post-Stalin thaw.) During his many visits to France, and elsewhere in his travels, he sought to leave the impression of Britain's friendship and benevolent influence in the world. And I do not think that he was without success.[2]

On 30 November 1956 Churchill celebrated his eighty-second birthday, amid continuing congratulations for the second volume of *A History of the English-Speaking Peoples*. 'I like it even better than the first,' wrote G. M. Trevelyan.[3] The third and fourth volumes were almost done, Maurice Shock preparing material at Oxford, and A. P. Thornton of Aberdeen University reading the chapter on the Indian Empire and the section on the Indian Mutiny. Thornton had made 'a number of useful suggestions', Alan Hodge wrote to Anthony Montague Browne, 'which have been adopted and passed by Sir Winston'.[4]

Two days before his eighty-second birthday, Churchill had presented the first Duff Cooper Literary Award to Alan Moorehead, author of *Gallipoli*. The ceremony took place in the house next to Churchill's in Hyde Park Gate, that of Sir Roderick Jones, the Proprietor of Reuters. Harold Nicolson noted in his diary:

I find all Duff's special friends there—all somewhat aged in appearance. Then Winston comes in with Clemmie. He is very tottery and is helped to a chair. I say a few introductory words, and then Winston reads from a piece of paper his bit about Duff. He hands the prize to Moorehead, who replies in excellent terms.

---

[1] Moran diary, 6 December 1956: *The Struggle for Survival*, page 710.
[2] 'Private and Confidential', 15 February 1965: Churchill papers, 1/144.
[3] 'Dear Winston', 29 November 1956: Churchill papers, 4/67
[4] 'My dear Anthony', 19 December 1956: Churchill papers, 4/28. Shock was paid £200 for his drafts, Thornton £25 for his suggestions.

Meanwhile Winston has drunk his glass of champagne and says to me, 'I think I should like to say a little more.' So up he gets and adds a few charming impromptu words.[1]

It was nearly two years, Churchill told those assembled for the award, 'since Duff died, but his memory is cherished in our hearts, and it is agreeable to reflect that when all of us in this room are ourselves no more, the annual bestowal of this prize will keep his memory bright in the field of literature which he did so much to adorn'.[2]

Among those at the prize-giving ceremony was 'Atticus' of the *Sunday Times*. The public had recently been worried, he wrote, that the announcements of Churchill's 'chills' concealed 'something more grievous'. Atticus added:

I can reassure them. He is a trifle bowed, his steps are shorter and his hair is whiter, but it is still the Winston we knew, with that vitality, that quick, humorous eye, the splendidly theatrical affectations in the speech and those short gestures of the right hand, like someone flinging down a pack of cards.

After reading his brief, graceful address in that voice that, particularly in these times, brings a lump to the throat, Sir Winston rose again to thank his hostess and to wish Mr Moorehead—'more good fortune in his further literary campaigns than, er, attended the, er, campaign that formed the subject of his, um, prize-winning book'.[3]

On the late afternoon of 9 January 1957 Churchill received a handwritten letter from Anthony Eden, sent from Sandringham, where he had been to see the Queen:

My dear Winston,

I have heavy news about health. The benefit of Jamaica is not significant. More troubling is that over Christmas & the New Year I have had a return of internal pain, which, apart from its fatiguing effect, worries the doctors in relation to my past operation.

In short they say firmly (and I have refused to accept one opinion & this is outcome of 3 apart from my own doctor) that I am endangering my life—& shortening it—by going on. This in itself, as you will know, would not influence me. What is troublesome is that the immediate result is a gradually increasing fatigue. In short I shall be less & less able physically to do my job as weeks go by.

This seems to me an impossible position, the more so since they give me little hope that I can continue as I am doing without collapse until Easter, & virtually no hope, if I attempt to go on, until the end of summer.

Bobbety & Norman Brook both agree that it will be of no use for me to drag on for such a short period of time.

---

[1] Nicolson diary, 28 November 1956: Nigel Nicolson (editor), *Harold Nicolson Diaries and Letters*, volume 3, page 321.

[2] Speech, 28 November 1956: Churchill papers, 2/190.

[3] 'Atticus' column, *Sunday Times*, 2 December 1956.

I am very sad, but I did not want you to know by any hand but mine.
Yours always

Anthony

'I expect this to be announced about 6.30 p.m.,' Eden added.[1]

'Darling,' Churchill wrote at once to his wife, 'Poor Anthony has just sent me this. You will have the secret for about an hour. Keep the letter to give me. Let no one see it again.'[2]

That evening Eden's resignation was made public. But, Anthony Montague Browne later recalled, 'there was no move from the Palace to consult the old man. He was very reluctant to be drawn in. He didn't want to do it. He was at Chartwell. Anthony Eden wanted the old man to come up to London. He declined to come. I prompted Adeane. He *ought* to be seen to go to the Palace.'[3]

On January 10, Churchill was summoned to the Palace by the Queen. Had he remembered to take his top hat, asked Christopher Soames. 'Oh, yes,' Churchill replied, 'but it's getting very shabby; as there may be more than one of these consultations in the future I must get a new one.'[4]

On January 10 Sir Michael Adeane consulted Lords Salisbury, Waverley and Chandos, and also Churchill, who had come specially up to London. Chandos later recalled that all four, 'Quite independently of each other, recommended Macmillan over Rab.'[5] That same day Harold Macmillan kissed hands on his appointment as Prime Minister. On the following night, he dined with Churchill at Hyde Park Gate.[6]

Eden decided to go with Clarissa to New Zealand to recuperate. Churchill wrote at once to wish him luck. On January 17 Eden replied from Chequers:

My dear Winston,
   Thank you so much for your letter and also for the very kind message you sent me. We have carefully weighed the advantages and disadvantages of this journey, but the doctors seem convinced that it is best to get away to entirely different surroundings. We hope to have a real rest at the other end in a lovely house near Auckland by the sea which Holland has found for us, and then perhaps, on to the Barrier Reef before we finally come home. I so look forward to seeing you then.

[1] 'My dear Winston', Sandringham, Norfolk, 9 January 1957: Churchill papers, 2/216.
[2] 'Darling', signed 'Your own ever loving Winston', Chartwell, 9 January 1957: Churchill papers, 2/216.
[3] Anthony Montague Browne recollections: notes for the author, 24 March 1987.
[4] Moran diary, 12 January 1957: *The Struggle for Survival*, page 710.
[5] Lord Chandos, in conversation with Piers Dixon, 28, 29 and 30 July 1967: Piers Dixon papers.
[6] Churchill Engagements Calendar, January 1957.

I am naturally very sad that this had to be at this time, but with the doctors all lining up one behind the other I am quite sure that there was no choice.

'Nor have I felt in these last days,' Eden added in his own hand, 'that the decision was wrong, odious as it was.'[1]

Churchill was also about to embark upon a journey: a return journey to La Pausa. 'A very bientôt,' he telegraphed to Wendy and Emery Reves on January 13.[2]

'I have come down here to my friends and the sun,' he wrote to Bernard Baruch on January 18, and he added: 'My History is rapidly nearing its completion.'[3]

On January 18 Christopher Soames was appointed Parliamentary and Financial Secretary at the Admiralty. The news of this was the opening subject of Churchill's first letter to his wife from La Pausa:

My darling One,

I have been worrying about Christopher. There is no doubt that the naval appointment will be promotion, which gives him the spokesmanship in the House of Commons and all that flows from that. I am afraid the Navy is to be shockingly cut, and it may be trouble will arise over that.

We arrived here very smoothly, and I have done nothing ever since. Today is lovely sunshine, the air chilly, but the sun warms everything. I aimed at getting up before lunch, and am now sitting dressed on the terrace enjoying the sunshine in an overcoat.

Wendy was delighted to have Sarah, and addressed her on the telephone in a decisive manner. She is coming, I think, either tomorrow or the next day. Wendy would also like to have Mary at the same time as AMB & Sarah, and I think she will arrange this for the beginning of February. I gave her your lovely present, which was a touching scene. She put a powder puff inside, and is using it regularly now. She will have written to you herself on this.

I had a telephone message from Brendan to say that Bernie was seriously ill, so I have both telegraphed and written. He has never lost interest in life, a kind of long latent joie de vivre, which I have not been able to acquire.[4]

I have started to read *Brave New World*.[5] My 'boys' arrive today, and dine tonight.[6] I have no doubt I shall succeed in finishing the job by the end of the month.

I think you are absolutely right to try and see the effect of freeing yourself from drugs, but I am most anxious to know how things proceed.

---

[1] 'My dear Winston', 'Personal', signed 'Love from us both, yours always, Anthony', 17 January 1957: Churchill papers, 2/216.

[2] Telegram sent 13 January 1957: Reves papers.

[3] La Pausa, 18 January 1957: Churchill papers, 2/210.

[4] Baruch outlived Churchill, dying on 20 June 1965, aged ninety-four.

[5] Aldous Huxley's *Brave New World* was first published in 1932. In 1958 he was to publish *Brave New World Revisited*.

[6] The 'boys' were Alan Hodge and Denis Kelly.

Churchill added, in his own hand: 'Do let me know how you get on. Tender love my Darling, Your ever devoted husband, Winston. PS I have got an aurist coming with Dr Roberts tomorrow & am going to have a good try to work a cure.' [1]

It was on a medical theme that, eight days later, Churchill wrote to Lord Moran from La Pausa:

My dear Charles,

Thank you so much for sending me the ear chart and report. I will let you know developments.

The French seem to have an outfit of very good effective remedies, all made up as popular medicines. For instance, I enclose you a specimen of a white lozenge which Dr Roberts gave me at once and urged me to use with freedom in order to provoke sleep after luncheon. One (a quarter) is certainly effective. It gave about two hours' sleep. Roberts said these lozenges were widely used, and there was no sort of complaint about them locally. He advised me try a half at night instead of the reds. I cross-examined him as well as I could about the effect on lowering the blood pressure. This he said is much less than the red, though he recognised the evil. I certainly had a good night without red or yellow. My blood pressure is 80–140 this morning, and the pulse 67.

'Here,' Churchill added, 'we are getting quite a lot of sunshine, and my Book is rapidly nearing completion.' [2]

All authors receive letters from contented readers who also notice the occasional error. One such letter reached Churchill at La Pausa from Mrs Joan Ronald. 'On page 50,' she wrote, 'you mentioned that Jane Seymour was "about twenty-five" (i.e. in 1533) while on page 56 you say "and when she died, still aged only twenty-two. . ." (i.e. in 1537). My husband and I feel that she must have had (like yourself!) the secret of perennial youth!' [3]

On January 20 Emery Reves informed Churchill that the only work still to be done on volume 3 and 4 of his History was the proof reading for spelling and punctuation. 'However,' Reves added, 'Mr Wood can no doubt do this job without your spending any time on it.' Reves also reported that an epilogue was needed for the abridgement of the war memoirs, and that he, Reves, offered £20,000 for 10,000 words. 'I believe this is the highest amount ever paid for a manuscript,' Reves wrote, '£2 per word.' It would have to be done in seventeen days. 'With Hodge, Kelly and Anthony being around,' Reves pointed out,

---

[1] 'My darling One', La Pausa, 18 January 1957: Spencer-Churchill papers.
[2] 'My dear Charles', La Pausa, 26 January 1957: Churchill papers, 1/54.
[3] 'Dear Sir Winston', Inverness, 20 January 1957: Churchill papers, 4/28.

'they could submit you a draft of the Preface within 2–3 days. I think that in 8–10 days it could be completed.'[1]

Churchill accepted this generous offer; the epilogue was written as Reves suggested, and in time.[2] The £20,000, paid under the arrangements devised by Churchill's tax expert, Leslie Graham-Dixon, was not taxable.

On January 21 Churchill awaited at La Pausa for his daughter Sarah. Before she arrived, he wrote to his wife, in a dictated letter:

My darling Clemmie,

Thank you so much for your delightful and informative letter which reached me yesterday, Monday. The Aurist took two large pieces of wax out of my ears, and I certainly hear more clearly since then. He is awaiting the technical report that the people who examined me in England must have made. I am sure French medicine is much ahead of English. I had a sore throat which was cured immediately by a box of tablets Dr Roberts produced out of his bag, and I cannot find any minor ailment that the French have not got a ready cure for. Another cure which meets all needs is a small pill taken after lunch to provoke sleep. A quarter of it sends me to sleep for two hours in the afternoon, whereas the English version failed completely. (It is said to be perfectly harmless & widely used.) They have adopted all the modern dodges and in a moment produce them from their wallet. There must be at least half a dozen common afflictions which are driven off in this easy way.

'We hope that Sarah will come tomorrow,' Churchill ended his letter. 'They are very fond of her here, and look forward much to seeing her. I am doing a good deal of work, and I think I shall have the book finished in time. If not, there is at least one extra week to spare in February.'

That night Sarah Churchill reached La Pausa, bringing news that Clementine Churchill would join them in due course. 'The skies are clouded today,' Churchill wrote in a postscript to his letter of January 21, '& it may be the week's perfect weather is about to pass. But it will soon return & bring you with it—*I hope*.'[3]

On January 24 Churchill sent his wife a handwritten letter, with financial news of considerable importance to her:

[1] 'To Sir Winston Churchill', 'Confidential', La Pausa, 20 January 1957: Churchill papers, 1/7.

[2] The single volume *The Second World War*, with an epilogue on the years 1945 to 1957, was published by Cassel on 5 February 1959, extracts from the epilogue having been published in the *Daily Telegraph* from 21 to 24 April 1958 and in *Look* on 29 April 1958. The edition had been prepared almost entirely by Denis Kelly, whose initials 'DK' appeared at the foot of the acknowledgements.

[3] 'My darling Clemmie', La Pausa, 21 and 22 January 1957: Spencer-Churchill papers.

My darling,

I send you herewith the notification from Lloyds that they have bought me £29,900 odd of shares immune from duty at my death. I hereby give it to you as I promised & hope you will long live to enjoy it.

I have asked Lloyds to let you know that I wish to make the transfer to you; and you consult Moir upon any steps you shd take to bring it under your effective control as soon as possible.

I am vy glad to be able through my own exertions to testify in this way my love & gratitude to you.

Your ever-devoted husband,

Winston S. Churchill [1]

'I have been so hunted with winding up these proofs of the book,' Churchill wrote to his wife on February 3, 'and other things before the date when I return, and I have not been able to write to you as I should wish.' Sarah was 'a great pleasure'. He would be coming back to London on February 13, for three days, and hoped, as did Emery and Wendy Reves, that she would come out with him when he returned on February 16. 'It is foggy today,' Churchill added, 'but I hope it will clear. I have had vy good weather till the last two days.' [2]

During his stay at La Pausa, Dr Roberts had continued to give Churchill white pills in place of his 'reds'. Lord Moran, however, was scathing about Roberts's ignorance of the barbiturate sleeping pill which Churchill had been taking for so long:

My dear Winston,

The reds that you have taken for a long time contain one and a half grains of seconal and nothing else. The white lozenge which you have sent me, is precisely the same, namely one and a half grains of seconal and nothing else. The lozenge is therefore exactly the same as a 'red' only the red coating was not added.

To confirm this I took the lozenge to the head dispenser at St Mary's. He knew these lozenges and was familiar with the fact that in France seconal is not always coated red. He confirmed that the lozenges were 'reds' in everything but colour.

To be quite sure we rang up Roussel, the manufacturers of these white lozenges, and they confirmed that the white are identical with the reds.

I can only suppose that Roberts does not know what is in them as he suggested using them 'instead of the reds at night', and also said that the effect in lowering the blood pressure was 'much less than the red'. I imagine if Roberts knew he was really using a 'red' after luncheon he would hesitate to use a drug depressant to the circulation, in a dose of one and a half grains, twice in the twenty-four hours. . . .

[1] 'My darling', La Pausa, 24 January 1957: Spencer-Churchill papers.
[2] 'My darling One', La Pausa, 3 February 1957: Spencer-Churchill papers.

'In case Roberts might get a stroke,' Moran added, 'perhaps it might be wise not to show him this letter.' [1]

'For three days only a shaft of sunshine,' Churchill wrote to his wife on February 6. 'However we are still gay, for it will give a better chance later on. . . .' He was looking forward to 'finishing up the book—it is nearly ended. I hope you like what you have read of it.' [2]

That week, in London, Lord Alanbrooke's diaries were published with a copious and critical commentary by Arthur Bryant. No single book gave a more distorted picture of Churchill's war leadership, or would provide for many years to come so much material for critical, hostile and ill-informed portrayals of Churchill in the war years. Alanbrooke sent Churchill a copy of the book, *The Turn of the Tide*, with a fulsome, and at the same time embarrassed and apologetic dedication:

To Winston from Brookie
With unbounded admiration, profound respect, and deep affection built up in our 5 years close association during the war.

Some of the extracts from my diaries in this book may contain criticisms, and references to differences between us. I hope you will remember that these were written at the end of long and exhausting days, often in the small hours of the morning, and refer to momentary daily impressions.

These casual day to day impressions bear no relation to the true feelings of deep-rooted friendship and admiration which bound me so closely to you throughout the war.

I look upon the privilege of having served you in war as the greatest honour destiny has bestowed on me. [3]

'The more I read *The Turn of the Tide*,' Lord Ismay wrote to Churchill a month after the book's publication, 'the more certain I am that Bryant has done Brookie an injury almost as grievous as Henry Wilson's widow did to her husband.' [4]

---

[1] 'My dear Winston', 4 February 1957: Churchill papers, 1/54. Dr Michael Dunnill writes: 'Seconal is a barbiturate and in fact is sodium quinal-barbitone. Today it is usually given as an orange capsule. The side effects of this drug include drowsiness, dizziness, unsteady gait, and hypersensitivity skin reactions—particularly in the elderly' (letter to the author, 23 June 1987). Churchill did indeed suffer at this time from skin irritation.

[2] 'My dearest One', La Pausa, 6 February 1957: Spencer-Churchill papers.

[3] Inscription in *The Turn of the Tide*, dated 'Feb 57': Churchill papers, 2/519, with a note that the book was in Churchill's study at Chartwell.

[4] Letter of 5 March 1957: Churchill papers, 2/190. Field Marshal Sir Henry Wilson had been Chief of the Imperial General Staff from February 1918 to February 1922. In June 1922 he was assassinated by an IRA gunman on the steps of his London home. His diaries were published five years after his death in a two-volume edited edition which nevertheless showed him to have been an active opponent, to the point of disloyalty, of many of the policies of the Government he was supposed to be serving. In the *Dictionary of National Biography* (Oxford 1937, page 916), H. de Watteville wrote of Wilson: 'The publication of his diaries in 1927, full of violently expressed prejudices and mistaken opinions, was followed by the appearance of further literature which went a long way to shatter belief in the superiority of his military talents. It was recognized that he was at heart a politician rather than a soldier.'

'My dear Brookie,' Churchill wrote, generously as usual, to Alan-brooke from La Pausa. 'Thank you for sending me a copy of your book,' and he added: 'On the whole I think that I am against publishing day to day diaries written under the stress of events so soon afterwards. However, I read it with great interest, and I am very much obliged to you for what you say in your inscription.' [1]

By February 10 Churchill had completed the work on his History, and had written the epilogue to the single-volume edition of his war memoirs. 'You have worked so hard and done so well,' Sarah Churchill wrote to him two days later. '*Do* take today as easily as possible.' Sarah added:

> You have 'The Journey' *to-morrow*—Lunch with Mr Macmillan and the Other Club the *next* day and Mr Moir on Friday morning and then the journey *back* on Saturday Wow—you are so well at the moment—it would be silly to spoil it. *Please* rest this afternoon and try not to read too much to-day so as to rest the pore eye!
> Love—love—love—
> *don't* bite me. [2]

Sarah Churchill signed her letter, as so often to her father, with the head of a mule.

While preparing the single-volume edition of his war memoirs, Churchill had decided to refer in the preface to the acts by Jewish terrorists which had so marred the last three years of the Palestine Mandate. 'I wrote a phrase,' recalled Anthony Montague Browne, 'to the effect that these were acts of black ingratitude to their saviours which would always be a blot on the creation of Israel. Emery Reves took exception to this but W insisted that it should go in. He said, "The Jewish people know well enough that I am their friend". . . .' [3]

The sentences as published read: 'Few of us could blame the Jewish people for their violent views on the subject. A race that has suffered the virtual extermination of its national existence cannot be expected to be entirely reasonable. But the activities of terrorists, who tried to gain their ends by the assassination of British officials and soldiers, were an odious act of ingratitude that left a profound impression.' [4]

While still at La Pausa, Churchill received from Emery Reves a note about the attitude of the United States to Israel: following the

---

[1] 'My dear Brookie', La Pausa, 12 March 1957: Churchill papers, 2/179.
[2] 'Darling Papa', 12 February 1957: Churchill papers, 1/56.
[3] Anthony Montague Browne recollections: notes for the author, 24 March 1987.
[4] Winston S. Churchill, *The Second World War and an Epilogue on the Years 1945 to 1957*, London 1959, pages 953–73.

Israeli occupation of the Sinai peninsula in 1956, the American Government was demanding the immediate and unconditional withdrawal of Israeli troops, and was threatening sanctions. 'If,' Reves wrote, 'there has been since 1949 a state of belligerence, as Egypt asserts, then how can the occupation of the Sinai Peninsula in November be called "aggression"? Under the circumstances of belligerency the move of Israeli troops was an offensive, and certainly nations at war have the right to take the offensive and to attack. Under the theory of Israel and Egypt having been belligerents since 1949 the occupation of the Sinai Peninsula is legally the same operation as was the Anglo-American landing in Normandy. An offensive but not "aggression" in the sense of the UN Charter.' [1]

From La Pausa, Churchill sent Reves's note to Harold Macmillan, with a covering letter:

This seems to me to contain a point of real substance. It has been written by Reves, who you know is an Israelite. I do not see myself the answer to it on principle, and I hope it will influence your mind.

I am astonished at Eisenhower and America's State Department. [2]

From Eisenhower's 'last message to me', Macmillan replied, 'it seemed that the United States administration have abandoned the idea of simply voting for sanctions against Israel and are now thinking in terms of a solution giving reasonable guarantees.' [3]

Churchill flew back from La Pausa to London February 13. 'Arrived safely,' he telegraphed to Emery and Wendy Reves on February 14, and he added: 'Am having dinner in bed.' [4] That day he saw Lord Moran at 10, Alan Hodge and Denis Kelly at 11.30, and Christopher Soames at 12.45, before lunching alone, with Harold Macmillan. 'It seemed strange for me to be entertaining at No. 10,' Macmillan wrote in his diary. 'He has aged, but he is still very well informed and misses little that goes on.' [5] That night, Churchill presided at dinner at the Other Club, in the Pinafore Room in the Savoy.

---

[1] Note by Emery Reves, undated: Squerryes Lodge Archive.

[2] 'My dear Harold', 24 February 1957: Squerryes Lodge Archive.

[3] 'Dear Winston', 27 February 1957: Squerryes Lodge Archive. On Easter Sunday 1957 Anthony Eden wrote to Churchill from hospital in Boston: 'We have been surprised at the extent of the support for us over Suez, this from Republicans as well as Democrats. But I don't feel that this will for a moment influence Dulles in his pursuit of Arab favours at the cost of French, British or Israeli interests. As long as he is there we shall get no effective support or even whole-hearted sympathy in any negotiation over the canal or anything else. We delude ourselves, if we think otherwise. Ike may protest that he means well, may be he does, but he don't count much more than Pétain did. Laval did the work.' ('My dear Winston', Easter Sunday 1957: Squerryes Lodge Archive.)

[4] Telegram dated 14 February 1957: Reves papers.

[5] Harold Macmillan diary, 14 February 1957: Macmillan papers.

On February 15 his schedule was no less hectic, but lunch was a quiet one with Jock and Lady Margaret Colville, and dinner with Randolph. Then, on the following morning, after only two full days in London, he flew back to La Pausa.[1] Clementine Churchill was with him. When, in the second week of March, she returned to London, Churchill stayed on at La Pausa for a further week. His first letter to her after her return, written entirely in his own hand, concerned a painting, and oil:

Darling,

I have tried to make the best arrangements possible to convey this letter to you to-day. It is Sunday, and the Préfet & Madame le Préfet are coming for luncheon. I have made up my mind to give him the picture of the swans, & I shall tell him that you chose it for him. They have quite fallen in love with it. Alas such is generosity; we must do our duty. But really it is vy beautiful, & I hate parting with it, I never thought anything of it while it hung for years in my bedroom at 28. Now it is a wrench. But I think he will like it & show it to lots of people. I hope so anyhow. Voilà![2]

Yesterday we were given lunch by Onassis at the Château de Madrid, & we ate a whole large tin of caviare, which must have cost him a fortune. (He has one at present.) As his wife was held up at St Moritz by snow she could not reach us till after the meal. So his sister came as hostess. She looked vy nice. Her teeth were much admired. The conversation centred on politics & Oil. I reminded him that I had bought the Anglo-Persian for the Admiralty forty or fifty years ago and made a good profit for the British Government, about 3 or 4 hundred millions! He said he knew all about it. All this reminded me of poor Hopkins[3]—but I think we did it together. I enjoy the credit.

Darling One, all passes peaceably & quietly here. Toby has just flown on to the page I have written, and thrown it on the floor.

What a lovely letter you sent me by Anthony! It was a duck. I feel all over of a purr when I read it through. I send you in return my most tender love my dearest Clemmie.

Your devoted and ever loving husband [sketch of pig]

Winston

On March 12, Churchill added in a postscript, 'I am going to look at a house. But none shall be bought without your approval.'[4]

[1] Churchill Engagements Calendar, February 1957: Churchill papers. Churchill's other engagements on February 15 included his doctor Lord Moran, his accountant Mr Wood, his solicitor Anthony Moir, his literary assistants Alan Hodge and Denis Kelly, his daughter Mary Soames, his son-in-law Duncan Sandys, Nonie Montague Browne and Lord Cherwell.

[2] Two years earlier, Churchill had written to his friend Louis Spears: 'I am very shy about giving my pictures outside the family circle. They are like children to me, often very badly behaved but still regarded.' ('Dear Louis', 31 December 1954: Churchill papers, 2/199.)

[3] Sir Richard Hopkins, a young Treasury official in 1913, when Churchill was the Minister responsible for negotiating the Anglo-Persian Oil Agreement. In 1927 Churchill, then Chancellor of the Exchequer, appointed Hopkins Controller of Finance and Supply Services at the Treasury. Hopkins had died in 1955.

[4] 'Darling', La Pausa, 11 March 1957: Spencer-Churchill papers.

Churchill's next two letters were about this house which he had found. The first was dictated:

My Darling,

I have been giving a good deal of thought to finding a suitable dwelling out here, and I think I have hit upon one. It is one of three detached in a cul-de-sac of four at the base of Cap Martin. It comprises an acre of ground, and is on the sea facing west. I was very much struck with the convenience of the house. I could live on the ground floor and no lift would be necessary. The layout is really well considered. There are five master bedrooms and four, perhaps five servants'. It was a surprise to find anything so close to Pausaland. The house is unpretentious but most compactly planned. I asked Wendy and Emery to go and see it next day. There is no doubt they are very much impressed with it, and so was Sarah. The price put on it is 30,000,000 francs, or £30,000, but I have every reason to believe it could be had much cheaper. My own feeling is that an offer of, say, £16,000 cash down might certainly lead to purchase at, say, £20,000.

We have looked at a great many houses, and Anthony has gone this afternoon for a preliminary exploration of Cannes and Mougins possibilities. All these seem to be much dearer. This also applies to others of the many I have looked at at Cap Ferrat and in the Nice region. We will go on with our explorations, and bring you home a comprehensive report.

Churchill added in his own hand:

The weather is vy cloudy & windy, & rather cold. What a contrast to what you are having in England! Pug Ismay & his wife are coming to dine tonight—they are staying with Daisy,[1] but they have full liberty & so Wendy does not have to worry about asking them.

    Always your loving & devoted

                                                     W

Under this sketch, Churchill had written: 'meant to be lying down!'[2]

Two days later Churchill wrote again, in his own hand:

Darling—Here is a damnable thing—the House I wrote to you about was offered by the agents at *thirty* million francs but now that my name is mentioned to the owner—a swindling Italian prince, he has put it up to *forty-seven*

[1] Daisy Fellowes.
[2] 'My Darling', La Pausa, 15 March 1957: Spencer-Churchill papers.

million. Of course I will not touch it on these terms. So we are all at sea again.

Anthony is off today to look at 2 Houses at Cannes. There is one at 25 million and one all on one floor. But I do not like the idea of Cannes vy much.

It is vy nice to think I shall be home again in 60 hours, Darling one I look forward to living with you so much.

Tender love from

Winston

A vy small one but black & smudged [1]

Among those who had come out to La Pausa was Churchill's publisher, Desmond Flower, who later recalled how Wendy Reves 'spent the whole time ribbing WSC unmercifully, and he loved it. It was a very happy occasion.' [2]

Churchill's last letter of his visit was again written in his own hand:

My darling One,

Here I have found another swift & trustworthy Aide-de-camp—Mr Desmond Flower, the head of Cassel—who came to dine last night, & will be in London tomorrow. He will take this letter to you tomorrow, & assumes full responsibility for its delivery. I trust him with the mission. He leaves his hotel to go to the Paris plane at 10.30. It is now 10.7, & the car is waiting. There is therefore just time for me to write and tell you that I love you dearly, & that I am looking forward to the 22nd when I trust I shall have dinner & tell you all the news.

I have been reading the short stories of W. Somerset Maugham. They are quite good, & have so far interested me that I am nearly late for lunch & dinner every day. I have no other news except that I visited 2 houses yesterday & am sure they wd not commend themselves to your eye. I am going to persevere & will make an extensive report.

The sun is shining, the air & sky are clear & warm. You have my fondest love, my darling, your ever devoted husband.

W [3]

Churchill flew back to Britain on March 22. 'You will be glad to hear,' he wrote to Emery Reves five days later, 'that three cygnets had been born to the black swans, and so far are all alive and thriving.' In thanking Reves for 'all your hospitality', Churchill added: 'I am afraid I have been a great burden to you.' [4]

Churchill's last days at La Pausa had been clouded by the distress of Wendy Reves at rumours of unkind remarks spoken about her by Daisy Fellowes in conversation with Lady Churchill. As soon as he

[1] 'Darling', La Pausa, 17 March 1957: Spencer-Churchill papers.
[2] Desmond Flower recollections: letter to the author, 12 June 1987.
[3] 'My darling One', La Pausa, undated: Spencer-Churchill papers.
[4] 'My dear Emery', London, 27 March 1957: Reves papers.

reached Chartwell, Churchill hastened to try to put Wendy's mind at ease, writing to her in his own hand:

My dear Wendy,

I had a vy pleasant journey home; & find all smiling here.

I talked to Clemmie &, as I told you, there is no foundation for her having made friends with Daisy F, or indeed for the slightest goodwill between them. They met at table—nothing more. Clemmie was astonished that you thought her manner to you had hardened during the last few days of her visit. She was concerned that you shd have imagined this. Do put it out of yr mind my dear.

With all my love & best wishes
I remain
Ever yours

W

Churchill added: 'The White Rabbit arrived with Miss Maturin. We had great fun with it. I shall take gt care of it & treat it vy kindly.' [1]

On March 29, Jock Colville flew to the United States to try to raise interest, and funds, for what he called 'Winston's and my technological scheme' for a university college in Churchill's name. [2] Shortly after his return, Colville had lunch with Lord Moran, who wrote in his diary:

I asked Jock which of Winston's gifts had been of most value to the country in the war. He said at once:

'Winston's capacity for picking out essential things and concentrating on them.'

It came into my mind that Norman Brook singled out the same quality. 'What next?'

Jock needs a good deal of jogging to make him communicative. He pondered, but nothing happened. At last he added:

'I think his great moral courage. If something went wrong he would patiently start again at the beginning. And his vivid imagination. It was always coming to his help in the war. His magnanimity of course, and his power of inspiring everyone he met.'

Jock grinned and went on ruefully:

'He always got his way. He could persuade anybody to do anything. When he asked me to be his secretary for the second time I was determined to refuse. I knew exactly how the interview would go, and I had thought out

---

[1] 'My dear Wendy', undated, Chartwell: Reves papers. Lord Boothby later recalled of Churchill at this time: 'Once he rang up a friend of mine, who had a villa in Monte Carlo, and said that he would like to come to lunch. My friend was rather apprehensive, and invited Mrs Fellowes, the Singer sewing-machine heiress, who had known him for many years, to help him out. Soon after lunch began, he closed his eyes and appeared to pass out. Mrs Fellowes then said to her host: "What a pity that so great a man should end his life in the company of Onassis and Wendy Reves." Suddenly, to their horror, one eye opened, and Churchill said: "Daisy, Wendy Reves is something that you will never be. She is young, she is beautiful and she is kind." Then the eye closed again.' (*Boothby, Recollections of a Rebel*, London 1978, page 65.)

[2] Sir John Colville, *The Fringes of Power*, page 723.

what I should say at each turn. I would have my excuses ready. But ten minutes later I came out of the room his secretary.'

'I see all that. But, Jock, you must admit that Winston's judgment was often wrong.'

Jock was not going to admit anything of the kind.

'More than once during the war Winston would come to the right decision when everyone else was on the other side.'

'Give me an example.'

'Oh,' said Jock, 'sending the Armoured Division to Egypt in 1940 when it was obvious to us all that we needed it at home in case of invasion. And his refusal to allow any more pilots and aircraft to fight in the Battle of France; everyone wanted to send them to France. But if Winston had given way we should have lost the Battle of Britain.' [1]

During April, Churchill went with his wife to Suffolk, to visit once more the house at East Bergholt which their Trust had bought for Randolph. Its name was Stour, and there Randolph was to live until his death eleven years later. It was his determination, he told his friends, to remain at Stour and to write his articles and books from there; and in due course to fulfil his one remaining ambition, to write a life of his father.

Returning to Chartwell, Churchill invited Harold Macmillan to dine with him on April 25. 'He was in good form,' Macmillan wrote in his diary, 'though getting very deaf. Nor does he say much now, for the first time he listens. All this is rather sad—for the fight has gone out of him. He is a very charming, courteous old man.' [2]

Churchill now made plans to return again to La Pausa. He was eager to get away as soon as possible, and for as long as possible, but his racing interests were a problem for him, as he explained in a letter which he dictated for Wendy Reves, who was then in Paris:

I have been thinking over my affairs here, and particularly the racing. They take so very long settling which days to run the horses. It will either be Friday, the 17th of May, that I cd come or Sunday, the 19th, and I will telegraph and let you know as soon as it is settled. May I bring Anthony with me?

I hope you would be able to put me up for nearly a month. I have to be back on the 16th of June, as I have undertaken to sponsor Pug Ismay at Windsor in his reception of the Garter. He is delighted to have this honour, and asks me whether I will do my part.

[1] Moran diary, 16 April 1957: *The Struggle for Survival*, pages 723–4.
[2] Harold Macmillan diary, 25 April 1957: Macmillan papers.

Do let me know whether the dates I have mentioned will fit in with your plans. I have heard from Max, and he is established at Capponcina. I hope friendly relations continue and that all is well.

I am so glad you went to the Louvre and saw the Queen. I am told it was a brilliant function.[1]

'I look forward so much to seeing you again,' Churchill added in his own hand, signing his letter: 'Yours ever devotedly, W.'[2]

On May 3 Churchill spoke once more in the Albert Hall, at the annual meeting of the Primrose League. 'For good or ill,' he said, 'new and disturbing powers are falling into the hands of mankind. They may bring an unsurpassed blessing or a senseless and meaningless wholesale destruction. We must hope that man's wisdom will match his widening knowledge.'

Speaking of Suez, and of Eden, Churchill said: 'We all deplore the illness which struck down Sir Anthony Eden a few months ago. We rejoice to read the better accounts of his progress and we all wish him a speedy restoration to full health and strength. Our party, as indeed our country, owes him its gratitude for a lifetime of work upon the causes we all serve. Indeed,' Churchill added, 'those who at home and abroad attacked the resolute action which, in company with our French allies, he took last autumn, may now perhaps have reason to reconsider their opinions. I do not think that the attitude then adopted by the United Nations has been helpful either to the free world or to the cause of peace and prosperity in the Middle East.'[3]

'Thank you so much for your speech,' Anthony Eden telegraphed from the United States, 'which has I am sure exactly hit the mood of second thoughts which now prevails here. It has had of course an excellent reception here.'[4]

On May 4, at the Royal Academy, Churchill was an exhibitor for the twelfth consecutive year, with the painting 'Black Swans and Chartwell'.[5] That night, he attended the Royal Academy banquet, where he was cheered loudly by a crowd in the courtyard when he arrived. Harold Nicolson, who was present, noted in his diary: 'On the wall in

---

[1] The Queen was in Paris between 8 and 11 April 1957, the highlights of her visit being a State Banquet on the 8th, lunch at Versailles and a reception at the British Embassy on the 9th, and a dinner and reception by the French Government at the Louvre on the 10th. She also laid a wreath at the Tomb of the Unknown Soldier beneath the Arc de Triomphe.

[2] 'My dear Wendy', April 1957: Reves papers.

[3] Speech of 3 May 1957: Randolph S. Churchill (editor), *The Unwritten Alliance*, pages 293-5. Recording: BBC Written Archives Centre, Library No. LP 23617.

[4] 'Sir Winston', telegram sent via the Foreign Office, marked by Anthony Montague Browne: 'Seen by Sir Winston and Lady Churchill', 5 May 1957: Churchill papers, 2/216.

[5] 'List of Works Exhibited at the Royal Academy by Sir Winston Churchill, Hon. RA': Royal Academy archive.

one of the rooms there is a monstrous caricature of him by Ruskin Spear RA which makes him look like a village dotard from the Auvergne. The dinner is far better than last time, and there is un-stinted champagne, port and brandy. Winston sits there looking very old. . . .' [1]

Among Churchill's guests at Chartwell that weekend was his grand-son Winston, then at Eton, and hoping to go to Oxford. A week later Churchill wrote to him:

My dear Winston,
I believe that next year you are hoping to go to Christ Church. I am glad about this, because it is one of the finest colleges in Oxford.

I have been making inquiries, and I hear that the competition is keen and the examination stiff. It will therefore mean *sustained work* if you are to be successful. I do hope you will be, my dear Winston.

Ever your loving grandfather,

Winston S. Churchill

Having dictated this letter, Churchill underlined the words 'sustained work'. He then added in his own hand: 'PS, you will see by the nibbled edges that Toby, who is watching, wishes to be remembered. I'm sure that he shares my view. Don't let over-confidence lead to neglect. This might compromise your entry into the serious aspects of life—now opening before you. WSC.' [2]

'When I had dinner at Chartwell the other evening,' Churchill's grandson replied, 'the Prof told me that I would have to work very hard to get into Oxford,' and he added: 'I am enjoying your third volume of the English-Speaking Peoples; it is so much easier reading than the History books we read at school and your vivid description brings it all to life.' [3]

'I am off to Roquebrune tomorrow morning,' Churchill wrote back on May 18, and he added: 'Toby is already there.' [4]

---

[1] Nicolson diary, 4 May 1957: Nigel Nicolson (editor), *Harold Nicolson, Diaries and Letters*, volume 3, page 334.

[2] 'My dear Winston', 11 May 1957: Squerryes Lodge Archive. Churchill's grandson was successful, becoming an undergraduate at Christ Church, and subsequently graduating with a BA degree in Modern History.

[3] 'Dear Grandpapa', Eton College, 14 May 1957: Churchill papers, 1/56.

[4] 'My dear Winston', 18 May 1957: Squerryes Lodge Archive.

63

Travels and Reflections

O N 18 May 1957 Churchill returned to the South of France, for four weeks at La Pausa. While he was there, the guest once more of the hospitable Wendy and Emery Reves, he sent his wife regular handwritten accounts of his holiday. The first was dated May 21:

Darling,

We arrived and all is well. To-day the skies are without a cloud & the temperature is warm. Toby as you can see sends his love & salute. I am going to get up and paint in half-an-hour. Yesterday was not quite so good, but still pleasant. Great progress has been made in & with the garden, and the lavender covers almost all. Sarah & AMB are very happy & will write you for themselves. The cold & clouds of England are left behind.

Wendy was obviously disappointed to learn that you wd not come, but could see you at Capponcina in September. I was exhausted yesterday and slumbered well.

Your visit to me the night before I left was vy precious. Do not let the idea that I am 'mean' to you tear your mind. As a matter of fact I take every lawful opportunity of passing money to you in a way which will avoid the 67% toll which the State will almost certainly take at my death & will continue to do so as long as I am able. Your life of devotion & kindness to me has made my own one both happy & successful. (Toby is busy and attentive.) I am weary of a task wh is done & I hope I shall not shrink when the aftermath ends.

My only wish is to live peacefully out the remaining years—if years they be. But you, dearest one, have the twilight of a glorious spell upon you in all probability. So be happy & do not let misconceptions of me darken & distort your mind.

With all my love and many kisses X X X

I remain

Your loving husband

W [1]

---

[1] 'Darling', La Pausa, 21 May 1957: Spencer-Churchill papers.

Churchill's second letter was undated:

My Darling,

Your delightful letter has just arrived.

Alas rain & clouds kept us all indoors yesterday, but Welsh Abbot's victory by six lengths brightened the afternoon. Wendy has had a cold but is now recovering and is most kind and agreeable. She & Sarah paint flowers all day in the hall & I have (two days ago) begun a large outdoor picture which I think you may like when it is finished, I am occupied with *I Claudius* which is quite readable.[1] The days pass smoothly & pleasantly.

How vy interesting is your account of the lunches at the French Embassy & at home to the Rowans! I shd have enjoyed being there! But I envy you your forthcoming visit to Hatfield with the meeting with Adlai Stevenson. He is vy well thought of in English political circles & I hope he will run again for the Presidency; but that is a long time yet.

I am sending this letter to Hatfield. Give my love to Betty[2] & tell her I am playing a gt deal of Bezique. Emery has learned to play it vy well. We have had a gt number of vy small games for vy small stakes (1/−) in which Anthony joins. I do not know whether skill predominates *yet*.

Darling one do write again and tell me about Hatfield and Adlai. I shall be home again in two weeks (14th June). I hope Christopher will come as planned. The weather *must* improve by then.

With all my love

I remain

Your loving & devoted husband

                W

'The whole party here send you their salutations,' he added.[3]

On May 28 Churchill wrote again:

My darling,

I expect & hope that you had an interesting Sunday & that you will tell me all about it & Adlai Stevenson when you have time. I am vy glad the Frogs are trying to form a solid Government in France & that Guy Mollet will be the head of it.[4]

It has been sullenly cloudy with winds & rain for four days running & I am waiting to finish my picture of the verandah through the olive trees impatiently. I see the Doctor every few days, but not with any definite cause. Dr Roberts is a vy nice fellow and he looks me over with a reassuring air which has a beneficial effect.

I send you a cheque for £400 wh I beg you to cash & keep. It is a part of my policy to send you money from time to time of reasonable sums which can be considered insurance from the death duties of 67 percent.

---

[1] *I Claudius*, by Robert Graves, later turned into a successful television series.

[2] Lady Salisbury.

[3] 'My Darling', La Pausa, undated: Spencer-Churchill papers.

[4] Guy Mollet, who had succeeded Edgar Faure as Prime Minister of France on 31 January 1956, was himself succeeded by Maurice Bourgès-Manoury on 11 June 1957.

Randolph's birthday! I sent him a message, and will send him a present if you will look around & let me have it when I come home on the 14th.

Christopher is coming out here on the 7th, having I hope witnessed the victory of Holiday Time which runs on the 6th, & of which he has hopes.[1]

With love & kisses XXX

from your devoted husband,

W

'I hope you will enjoy your visit to Ireland,' Churchill ended. 'I wd like to go there. I believe they would be nice to me.'[2]

In his letter of June 1 Churchill wrote:

My darling,

I am vy glad to hear about yr visit to Hatfield & the conversation with Adlai. His succession to Ike wd no doubt be popular in England. But it is the Americans who have to choose!

Now I write to you on another glorious 1st of June. The weather is a little better & I painted for $2\frac{1}{2}$ hours yesterday. Today I give a luncheon to the company & the Billmeirs who start tonight in their yacht for Corsica.

Wendy seemed unhappy at our going to the Capponcina in September, but cheered up when I said it was only for a month & I wd come back afterwards.

You will have gone to Ireland before I write again in all probability. I hope you will enjoy yr stay there, let me know about the Irish people, I am worried about them, they come to England in large numbers instead of building up their own country.

The weather improves every minute and we lunch at the Château de Madrid. I will deliver suitable messages to our guests from you.

Thank you for going to see Pamela at Knebworth. It is a picturesque estate.

What fun it was winning two races in one day! Quite an event for a beginner. Christopher is vy clever about horses & the stud has become numerous & valuable: & pays for itself so far.

Always your loving husband

W[3]

Churchill's next letter was dated June 5, 'Derby Day':

Darling,

Your fourth letter has just arrived. I telegraphed to Randolph on his Birthday & was vy glad when he thanked me for the garden chairs along with you. He recognised they were a joint present. But I can claim no credit for it.

I am absorbed in *Wuthering Heights*. There is no doubt it deserves its fame. One can see it is a good book, I am $\frac{3}{4}$ of the way through.

---

[1] 'Holiday Time was to have run, but did not. It was Welsh Abbot which therefore ran for Churchill on June 6, coming second in the Great Surrey Foal Stakes.

[2] 'My darling', La Pausa, 28 May 1957: Spencer-Churchill papers.

[3] 'My darling', La Pausa, 1 June 1957: Spencer-Churchill papers.

Here we have mainly clouds & I spend my mornings in bed. But in the occasional gleams I have painted 2 landscapes which are worth bringing home to show you.

Christopher comes the day after tomorrow (Friday) & I am looking forward to seeing him and hearing his news. We are going to lunch in Italy today at the Restaurant across the frontier. Did you go there—I forget. I would rather stay at home. The Prefect is coming. His wife is still in Paris. They are both coming by Sunday next when Christopher will have joined us.

I read what you say about Clarissa & Anthony and agree with it. They bear their lot with courage.

Here is a letter from the Governor of the West Indies which I think you will like to read.[1] He has had a rough time. But I do not think we shd make it worse. Poor Patrick! They will get along all right. But it was a chilling episode.

The French are dawdling & dithering over their new Government & their large deficit. Algeria is a shocking situation. I think 15 days has lasted long enough. The politicians must be enjoying their 'Crisis'. I hope they will pull through & beat the Algerian terrorists.

I envy you your heat wave. The world has become as muddled as its people about the weather, and it is a relief to find the shelter of Victorian Literature, when the alternative wd be to stare out at really bloody prospects from the windows.

I hope you have had *rain* or will have it as the ground is reported shockingly hard & stiff—good for my horses on the whole.

My dearest one, I love you from a gloomy background I fear. The one thing that cheers me this morning is the new bath of wh you write. I shall look forward to wallowing in it.

Tender love my darling. Your devoted husband.

W

PS Anthony[2] has returned from his cruise with the Billmeirs. He flew back from Corsica (of which he gives good account) in a plane lent him by Onassis, & piloted by him.

WSC[3]

In the second week of June 1957 Churchill returned to England from La Pausa, his first public appearance being at the Garter ceremony at Windsor. 'It must have been awfully hot in all your robes,' wrote his grandson Winston from Eton.[4]

On June 22 Churchill was at Ascot, to see his horse Le Pretendant run; 'but he did not do quite as well as I had hoped', he told his

---

[1] The Governor-General of the Federation of the West Indies was Lord Hailes, formerly Patrick Buchan-Hepburn. In 1929 he had been Churchill's Private Secretary for several months, before entering Parliament.
[2] Anthony Montague Browne.
[3] 'Darling', La Pausa, 5 June 1957: Spencer-Churchill papers.
[4] 'Dear Grandpapa', 19 June 1957: Churchill papers, 1/56.

grandson.[1] Le Pretendant had come third. On the following day Churchill wrote to Wendy Reves, in his own hand:

My dear Wendy,

I waited till you had got to Paris before writing.

All is well here & your visit on the 20th is greatly looked forward to. I really enjoyed my last stay at Pausaland in spite of the clouds and cold, & the pictures are much admired. It will be a great pleasure to show you this place which I have done a lot to over many years.

We found wonderfully hot weather on arrival but now there is a distinct change although the sun shines brightly. It was stifling & sultry, & the Garter show took place on the hottest day of all. The next day when we were showing the gardens to the YWCA it poured!

I went to Ascot yesterday with Christopher to see the Pretendant run, but he did not repeat his success of last year in this race—The Churchill Cup—named after a relation who had a fine record in The Turf & is now dead.

Thank you so much for all the trouble you took to make our visit a success. You had no need to worry over the weather. Banish all such thoughts.

With much love,

Believe me,

Yours always,

W[2]

'Winston is well,' reported Christopher Soames to his hosts at La Pausa, '& wanting to go racing constantly—in fact more often than the horses do!'[3]

Churchill hoped very much to see Eden and his wife in London, and had invited them to lunch at Hyde Park Gate. But on June 23 Eden wrote from his home near Salisbury that his British doctor, Sir Horace Evans, and the American surgeon 'are firm that I must stay quiet here this summer'. Journeys to London, or to Chartwell, 'are beyond my strength at present'. Eden told Churchill that he was:

...much encouraged by increasing American understanding of our Suez action. *New York Times* so much better than our own which seems to have returned to the Dawson appeasement days.[4] In view of this Canadian & US attitude it seems to me important that we should not renege on what we have done, or we should lose the respect we are still gaining. I have told Harold that this is my view and that Socialists have more cause to wish to forget their Suez conduct than we.

[1] 'My dear Winston', 23 June 1957: Churchill papers, 1/56.
[2] 'My dear Wendy', Chartwell, 23 June 1957: Reves papers.
[3] 'My dear Wendy & Emery', Admiralty, 26 June 1957: Reves papers.
[4] On 23 May 1937 Geoffrey Dawson, editor of *The Times*, had written to Lord Lothian: 'I should like to get going with the Germans. I simply cannot understand why they should apparently be so much annoyed with *The Times* at this moment. I spend my nights in taking out anything which I think will hurt their susceptibilities and in dropping in little things which are intended to soothe them.' (Lothian papers.)

But enough of politics. I find it pleasant to read again—books not news-papers. When we have a little more room for documents and papers, I may feel disposed to try my hand at some account of the Thirties. You have always told me what a good companion the writing of a book can be.[1]

Churchill replied on June 26 that he had met Horace Evans at Ascot 'and was glad to hear all he said about you. You should nurse your strength.' Churchill added: 'Do let me know if there is any way in which you think I can be of help.' His letter ended:

I am getting older with every day that passes, but I still hope to see us get the better of Nasser. I am sure it would be a very good thing for you to write a book about the 30s, and you will find plenty of material. But there is no reason why this should be the end of the story which you have to tell, and I am sure it will be good all through.[2]

The following week, Churchill dined at 10 Downing Street as the guest of Harold Macmillan.

On July 3 Lord Cherwell died. He was seventy-one, the same age as Clementine Churchill. Since 1920 he had been Churchill's close friend; since Lord Birkenhead's death in 1930 his closest friend. 'I do not think we ever disagreed on general matters,' Churchill wrote to Alan Lennox-Boyd that day.[3] 'Darling Papa,' Mary Soames tele-graphed from Bath, 'I know how much you must be feeling the Prof's death. Loving thoughts from Mary.'[4] 'Without you,' wrote Jock Colville, 'the Prof might have been a great scientist, but he could never have been what he was or achieved what he did. In a sense, indeed, you created him and the result gave his friends untold satisfaction and his country immeasurable service.'[5]

Churchill went to Oxford for his friend's funeral. Roy Harrod, who met Churchill at Christ Church in order to take him to his seat in the Cathedral, recalled in his memoirs:

We paused on the lawn of Tom Quad and I explained our plan for a brief rest. 'But I must go to the grave,' he said. Lady Churchill asked him if he was sure that he would want to do anything more after the funeral service was over; the cemetery was a couple of miles away. 'I must go to the grave,' he reiterated firmly and simply.

As we came up the aisle of Christ Church Cathedral the congregation rose

[1] 'My dear Winston', 23 June 1957: Churchill papers, 2/216.
[2] 'My dear Anthony', 26 June 1957: Churchill papers, 2/216.
[3] 'My dear Alan', 3 July 1957: Churchill papers, 2/214.
[4] Telegram, 4 July 1957: Churchill papers, 2/214.
[5] 'My dear Winston', 9 July 1957: Churchill papers, 2/182.

spontaneously to their feet. After the service he drove to the cemetery. He walked in the procession up the cemetery path. He walked beyond the path, advancing over the difficult tufts of grass, with unfaltering, but ageing, steps, onward to the graveside of his dear old friend.[1]

That same week, Churchill spoke in his constituency. 'I am so happy,' he said, 'to see that our relations with our American partner are being restored to their normal warm temperature. Make no mistake. It is in the closest association with our friends in the Commonwealth, America, and NATO that our hopes of peace and happiness lie. Neither we nor they can afford estrangement.' To rely solely on the United Nations, he added, 'would be disastrous for the future'.[2]

On July 9 Churchill spoke again, at a United Europe meeting at Central Hall, Westminster. Although he had said he would speak 'impromptu', Montague Browne wrote, 'I nevertheless submit a few very banal lines'.[3] 'My message to Europe today,' Churchill said, in words which he added to Montague Browne's draft, 'is still the same as it was ten years ago—unite. Europe's security and prosperity lie in unity.'[4]

On July 16, Churchill went to see *Titus Andronicus*. It was, he wrote to Vivien Leigh, 'a great presentation', and he added: 'I was too far away to hear, but I very much enjoyed the evening, and especially seeing you again.'[5] A week later, Churchill and his wife went by train from London to Salisbury, to visit Eden at his home. 'It was very kind of you and Clemmie to come to see us yesterday,' Eden wrote on July 25. 'Your visit gave us so much pleasure. I enjoyed every moment of it. I can only hope that you were both not too exhausted when you got back to London.'[6]

Back in London, on July 25 Churchill was at the Other Club, where he said, in tribute to his friend Lord Cherwell: 'He was a man individual in character, of great courage both moral and physical.'[7]

On July 31 Churchill spoke at the Guildhall, at a dinner given by the Law Society for the American Bar Association. It was his third speech that month. Once more, Montague Browne prepared the draft.

[1] R. F. Harrod, *The Prof, A Personal Memoir of Lord Cherwell*, London 1959, page 276.
[2] Speech of 6 July 1957: Randolph S. Churchill (editor), *The Unwritten Alliance*, pages 296–9.
[3] 'Sir Winston', 8 July 1957: Churchill papers, 2/131.
[4] Speech of 9 July 1957: Randolph S. Churchill (editor), *The Unwritten Alliance*, page 300.
[5] 'My dear Vivien', 18 July 1957: Churchill papers, 2/195.
[6] 'My dear Winston', 25 July 1957: Churchill papers, 2/216.
[7] Remarks of 25 July 1957: Colin R. Coote, *The Other Club*, page 105.

Speaking of the United Nations, Churchill said: 'There are many cases where the United Nations have failed. Hungary is in my mind. Justice cannot be a hit-or-miss system. We cannot be content with an arrangement where our new system of international laws applies only to those who are willing to keep them.' [1]

'What an excellent speech you made to the American lawyers,' Eden wrote on the following day. [2]

On August 8 Churchill and his wife lunched with Harold Macmillan at Downing Street. 'Winston was in pretty good form,' Macmillan wrote in his diary, 'and remarkably quick either on very old questions (where his memory is most attentive) or on very new ones (which he has not had time to forget). He was splendidly indignant about Lord Altrincham's (Ned Grigg's son) foolish attack on the Queen in the *National Review* and the TV.' [3]

In August 1957 Sarah Churchill suffered a personal blow of great severity: the suicide of her husband Antony Beauchamp. Although they had been separated for nearly two years, Beauchamp's death came, as Mary Soames has written, 'as a tremendous shock to her; and suicide leaves such a cruel legacy of unanswered and unanswerable questions'. [4] Courageously, Sarah returned to America, to work in television drama, living alone in a house at Malibu, just north of Los Angeles.

On October 14 the third volume of Churchill's *A History of the English-Speaking Peoples* was published in London, entitled 'The Age of Revolution'. The very first copy reached him from his publisher, Desmond Flower, on August 30. 'I hope that you will like it,' Flower wrote. He also asked Churchill what title he wanted for the fourth and final volume, and suggesting, instead of 'The Nineteenth Century' as it stood then, calling the book 'The Great Democracies'. [5] 'It is not for me,' Churchill replied, 'who has retired, to decide upon the ques-

---

[1] Speech of 31 July 1957: Randolph S. Churchill (editor), *The Unwritten Alliance*, pages 301–3.

[2] 'My dear Winston', 1 August 1957: Churchill papers, 2/216.

[3] Harold Macmillan diary, 8 August 1957: Macmillan papers. John Grigg, the son of the 1st Baron Altrincham, had renounced his father's peerage. Edward Grigg, his father, a former Liberal MP, and Churchill's last wartime Minister Resident in the Middle East, had died in 1955.

[4] Mary Soames, *Clementine Churchill*, page 464.

[5] 'Dear Sir Winston', 30 August 1957: Churchill papers, 4/26. Desmond Flower was then the Literary Director of Cassell & Company Ltd. 'The Great Democracies' was published on 14 March 1958.

tion of the title of Volume IV, but I think the change you propose is a great improvement.'[1]

The theme of retirement marked the end of Churchill's active literary life. 'I have now retired from literature,' he had written to Bernard Baruch at the beginning of the month, 'and am endeavouring to find ways of spending pleasantly the remaining years of my life.'[2]

At the beginning of September 1957 Churchill and his wife went to Lord Beaverbrook's villa at Cap d'Ail for three weeks. Lady Birley was also a guest. On September 7 the National Trust adviser on historic buildings, James Lees-Milne, and his wife Alvilde were invited to luncheon. William Somerset Maugham was also present. Lees-Milne noted in his diary that, after the ladies had left the table:

. . . we talked of obituary notices in *The Times* and I told him that the writers of obituaries were sent their contributions after an interval of ten years or so to add paragraphs, if the subject was still alive, for which they were paid an extra fee. This seemed to amuse him.

He told Willie that had he won the 1945 election he would have been obliged to give India self-government under the pledge made by the pre-war Conservative Government and this would have much gone against the grain with him. He said he was all for leaving India to stew in her own juice now, but he added with a twinkle, 'I am now merely a retired, and tired old reactionary.'[3]

'The weather has been excellent on the whole,' Churchill wrote to Beaverbrook on September 11, 'and I have managed to do a little painting.' He had hardly left Beaverbrook's villa, except for lunch with Wendy and Emery Reves at Roquebrune, 'and a few visits to the Casino, with indifferent fortune'. As for international affairs, 'I do not care for the look of things in the Middle East,' Churchill wrote, and he added: 'By their action on Suez the Americans have put an end to the chance of using anything but words and money, and they are not always enough.'[4]

On September 15 James and Alvilde Lees-Milne returned to La Capponcina for drinks, Lees-Milne noting in his diary:

Sir Winston sitting slumped in an arm chair in the middle of the room, to whom we talked in turns. Alvilde told him how much she was impressed by Neville Shute's book *On the Beach*, which he too has read. He said he was sending it to Khrushchev. She said, why not also send it to Eisenhower. Sir W's retort:

[1] 'My dear Desmond', 31 August 1957: Churchill papers, 4/26.
[2] Letter of 1 August 1957: Churchill papers, 2/519.
[3] James Lees-Milne diary, 7 September 1957: Lees-Milne papers.
[4] 'My dear Max', La Capponcina, 11 September 1957: Churchill papers, 2/211.

'It would be a waste of money. He is so muddle headed now.' The 'now' is significant. He said to Montague Browne: 'I think the earth will soon be destroyed by a cobalt bomb. I think if I were the Almighty I would not recreate it in case they destroyed me too the next time.'[1]

'All is well out here,' Montague Browne wrote to a friend on September 21, 'and the weather excellent. Sir Winston paints and visits the Casino, and my Wife and I potter about with Lady Churchill and swim. In between times swarms of people descend on us or we on them.'[2]

On October 1 Churchill moved from the Cap d'Ail to Roquebrune. 'Today you moved to Pausaland,' his daughter Sarah wrote from California, and she added: 'I know you will be well settled at Pausa—I hope the weather is good this time, so you can enjoy the garden more.'[3] A few days later Churchill wrote to his wife, who had returned to London. Like each of the letters of that visit, it was entirely in his own hand:

My darling,

I am definitely better this morning, & am going out to inspect the new Pink House.

The race I won yesterday was worth £1,154 wh is above the level of ordinary prizes. I am so glad you saw it on TV. It is beautiful weather here, but 2 or 3 degrees colder than at Capponcina.

I have started a new picture of flowers painted indoors and am about to get up for the purpose. They are awfully kind here.

And Wendy received yr messages with satisfaction and sends suitable ones in return.

All my love my dearest.

Your devoted husband

W

I am reading *The Third Eye* wh promises well.[4]

On October 7 Churchill wrote to his wife again:

Yesterday (Sunday) we went over to Mortola &, after an excellent luncheon, we were inspired to visit your favourite house.[5] The owners were most agreeable. The poor lady was charming & crippled though she be. She had *not* known of your visits though this would have delighted her. She knows you from of old. You did not tell me she had offered to lend you her

---

[1] James Lees-Milne diary, 15 September 1957: Lees-Milne papers.

[2] La Capponcina, 21 September 1957: Churchill papers, 2/180.

[3] 'My very darling Papa', Malibu, California, 1 October 1957: Churchill papers, 1/55.

[4] 'My darling', La Pausa, undated: Spencer-Churchill papers.

[5] La Mortola was the nineteenth-century English house and garden created by Sir Thomas Hanbury in 1867. 'The gentle climate of La Mortola,' writes Francesca Greenoak, 'opened vast possibilities for experimenting with plants never before grown in Europe: under the supervision of Sir Cecil Hanbury, who developed his father's work, the number of species reached an astonishing 6,300' (*The Times*, 7 March 1987). Sir Cecil Hanbury's widow left La Mortola to the University of Genoa.

house & grounds in 1945—but we were about to start for Marrakech. I felt vy sorry for her. She was absolutely charmed to see me.

I clambered up to the square terrace, & we all sat and talked. She had sent her conveyance. It was Queen Victoria's special Chair, in which I was wheeled about from the top to the bottom (the sea) & the bottom to the top, & saw everything, accompanied by the whole family—husband, son, son's wife and my own party. (The Reves had to go back from the house because Wendy had terribly high heels but they enjoyed themselves vy much with all they saw.) It is indeed a wonderful spot.

I am sorry to say that Anthony MB has to return on the 11th as his mother is to be seriously examined for heart trouble. Monty arrives on the same day for a week-end,

> With tender love
> my dearest one
> Your ever loving husband
>
> W [1]

On October 11, while Churchill was at La Pausa, both Chartwell Farm and Bardogs Farm were sold for £37,500. It was the end of the farming activities which had given Churchill so much pleasure; and another milestone on the long, slow road of age and time.

On October 4 the Soviet Union launched the first earth satellite. Overnight the success of this little 'Sputnik' became a cause of concern throughout the Western world. On October 11, a week after the launching, Churchill wrote to his wife from La Pausa:

> The satellite itself etc. does not distress me. The disconcerting thing is the proof of the forwardness of Soviet Sciences compared to the Americans. The Prof was as usual vigilant and active. Plenty of warnings were given but we have fallen hopelessly behind in technical education, & the tiny bit we have tends to disperse & scatter about America & the Dominions. This is the mechanized age, & where are we? *Quality & of the Front rank* indeed we still possess. But numbers are lacking. The necessary breeding ground has failed. We must struggle on; & looking to the Union with America.
>
> After inviting Christopher & Mary to come out in Anthony's place, Wendy has asked Diana, who seemed quite pleased to come. We are going to luncheon in the Onassis Yacht to day.
>
> I have painted two (2) pictures, one is rather good.
> Tender love & many kisses XX
> from your devoted husband
>
> W [2]

---

[1] 'My darling', La Pausa, 7 October 1957: Spencer-Churchill papers.
[2] 'Darling', La Pausa, 11 October 1957: Spencer-Churchill papers.

'It makes me happy that Winston is painting again,' Clementine Churchill wrote to Wendy Reves from Chartwell on October 12, '& I feel that both you and Emery are great stimulators.'[1]

While Churchill was at La Pausa, Clementine Churchill also wrote to Lord Beaverbrook, to say how sorry she was that they could not take up Beaverbrook's offer to be his guests that winter in the Bahamas. In the course of her letter she commented that the Graham Sutherland portrait of Churchill, presented to him by Parliament in November 1954, 'will never see the light of day'. Clementine Churchill went on to explain to Beaverbrook, who was a friend of Sutherland: 'This gift which was meant as the expression of the affection and devotion of the House of Commons caused him great pain & it all but ruined his 80th birthday.' It 'wounded' her husband 'deeply', she added, that this 'brilliant' painter 'with whom he had made friends while sitting for him should see him as a gross & cruel monster'.[2]

What Clementine Churchill did not tell Beaverbrook was that, on her own initiative, she had burnt the painting more than a year earlier; a secret revealed to the public only in her daughter Mary's biography.[3] Churchill's own artistic efforts had flourished. 'I have done some painting in the garden,' he wrote from La Pausa to his grandson Winston on October 18, 'and also completed two flower studies in my room.'[4] Churchill also wrote that day to his wife:

Darling,

We had a slip-up in organization wh arose from the strike of Electric & Gas workers on the 16th & the Communist Demonstrations of the 17th. The first caused some inconvenience; the second was a flop. Otherwise all has run smoothly, and my vy pleasant visit will end on Monday.

I took Mrs Lees-Milne & my hosts out to lunch yesterday at the Vistaero (on the spike of the hills) and I think it went all right. Mrs LM is quite interesting and revives memories of my old friend Tom.[5]

Wendy had an alarm of Flu yesterday but temperature had dropped to normal this morning after American medicine. I hope I am not going to plunge into an epidemic myself on return. I am going to paint this morning after ending *The Black Arrow* wh I have entirely forgotten.[6]

Looking forward to seeing you on Monday, ever your loving husband.

W[7]

---

[1] 'My dear Wendy', Chartwell, 12 October 1957: Reves papers.

[2] Letter of 13 October 1957: Beaverbrook papers.

[3] Mary Soames, *Clementine Churchill*, page 501.

[4] 'My dear Winston', La Pausa, 18 October 1957: Squerryes Lodge Archive.

[5] Alvilde Lees-Milne's father, General Sir Tom Bridges, who had lost a leg at Passchendaele. In 1938, in the foreword to Bridges' memoirs, Churchill noted that the two men had 'soldiered together' in the Boer War.

[6] *The Black Arrow*, an historical novel by Robert Louis Stevenson, first published in 1888.

[7] 'Darling', La Pausa, 18 October 1957: Spencer-Churchill papers.

In the third week of October, Churchill returned to London. 'As always after my visits to you,' he wrote to Wendy Reves, 'I retain happy memories of your many kindnesses and the great hospitality that you and Emery always show to me. My stays in your beautiful home are delightful episodes, and I feel the better for the sun and light.' Churchill added:

Clemmie is well, but has to have an operation on her foot which will keep her in bed for about ten days. She sends you her love.

The October weather here is warm and pleasant, but there is a widespread influenza epidemic which is affecting everybody, including our own household.

I trust that you have good news of your Mother. Let me know when you are going to America. As you know, it would give us all great pleasure if you and Emery came to see us at any time.

With all good wishes
Your affectionate friend,

W [1]

On October 25 Churchill went to Harrow School for the annual 'Songs'. 'Songs,' he said, 'are a companion with whom you can walk through life, and it may be that you will find that they are as good a companion as any....' [2] 'I am now back in London,' he wrote to Lord Beaverbrook at the beginning of November, 'and contemplating our usual autumn weather.' An operation on Clementine Churchill's foot had been successful, 'but she is laid up for the time being'. [3]

On reaching London, Churchill had sent out copies of the third volume of his History to his friends. 'I am already embarked,' wrote Eden on November 4, 'and enjoying the opening chapters of the voyage; it is grand writing and proud reading.' Eden then turned to an issue close to his and Churchill's concerns throughout both their peacetime Premierships. 'I suppose that our American friends now regret,' he wrote, 'that the numerous attempts you and I made to break down the barriers of the McMahon Act, or find a way round them, all failed.' Eden added: 'As late as January 1956 I made a further attempt with Eisenhower. Much was promised, but scarcely anything performed.' Repeated reminders, Eden told Churchill, 'met with excuses—Congress, the impending elections etc. etc. And now we are, the Russians know, many laps behind.' [4]

On November 6 Churchill went to St Paul's Cathedral for the unveiling of a memorial to his friend of more than sixty years, Sir Ian

---

[1] 'My dear Wendy', Chartwell, 28 October 1957: Reves papers.
[2] Speech of 25 October 1957: Churchill papers, 2/336.
[3] 'My dear Max', November 1957: Churchill papers, 2/211.
[4] 'My dear Winston', 4 November 1957: Churchill papers, 2/216.

Hamilton.[1] On November 7 he dined with the Queen at Buckingham Palace. On November 8 Brendan Bracken was his guest at Chartwell; they watched the film *The Bridge on the River Kwai*.[2] On November 10 Emery Reves was at Chartwell to choose some of Churchill's paintings for an exhibition in the United States, at Kansas City. Four days later Churchill wrote to Wendy Reves, who was then on board the *Queen Elizabeth* at Cherbourg:

Dearest Wendy,

I was so sorry that you were not able to come to Chartwell with Emery. We had a very busy afternoon examining and choosing pictures. They are very nearly ready for the show, and I think they are not a bad lot.

Clemmie had an operation to her foot. It had been giving her pain for forty years, and we hope it is going to be entirely successful. She cannot, however, put it to the ground for another day or two, having had a fortnight in bed. We are all off to Chartwell tomorrow.

Emery will explain to you where we stand over the cruise.[3] First I want to be invited, and then we must see how to make things fit it. I am looking forward to spending February and March in Pausaland, and have written to tell the President[4] that I shall not be with him till April. He replied most graciously.

I hope indeed you will have a smooth voyage, and will arrive refreshed and calm with a conquered ocean at your tail.

'I send my best love to you,' Churchill added in his own hand, 'and I hope you will have a refreshing touch of the USA, & *not* too cold. Ever your loving friend, W.'[5]

While he was at Buckingham Palace, Churchill had told the Queen that he intended to be present, as he had been almost every year since 1920, at the Armistice Day ceremony at the Cenotaph.[6] Four days

---

[1] General Sir Ian Hamilton, twenty-one years Churchill's senior, had died in 1947. Churchill had first served with him on the North-West Frontier of India in 1897. In July 1915, on the eve of the second main Gallipoli battle, Churchill had written to Hamilton (the Commander-in-Chief of the forces at the Dardanelles): 'Well done & with good luck, or mistakenly done & with bad luck, if done in the end it will repay all losses & cover all miscalculations in the priceless advantage wh will rise for the Allied cause.'

[2] Among the other films that Churchill watched in November 1957 were *The Wages of Fear*, *The Ten Commandments* and *The Snows of Kilimanjaro*.

[3] Aristotle Onassis had invited Churchill to be his guest on *Christina*, on which he was first to cruise in September 1958.

[4] René Coty, President of France from December 1953 to December 1958 (when he was succeeded by Charles de Gaulle).

[5] 'Dearest Wendy', London, 14 November 1957: Reves papers.

[6] It was as Secretary of State for War and Air that Churchill had attended the first Cenotaph ceremony in 1920.

earlier he had received a letter from Sir Michael Adeane in which he wrote: 'The Queen desires me to tell you that she gladly excuses you from any obligation that you may feel to be present. Indeed Her Majesty hopes that you will not take the smallest risk to your health by prolonged exposure to November weather which this ceremony entails.'[1]

Moved by the Queen's consideration, Churchill nevertheless attended the ceremony.

On 30 November 1957 Churchill was eighty-three years old. From Beaverbrook came another invitation to La Capponcina. 'I am however engaged to go in January and February to La Pausa,' Churchill replied, 'and I fear that I should upset the Reves if I changed.'[2]

Sarah Churchill had hoped to come over from the United States for Christmas with her parents. But as Churchill explained to her on December 12, Clementine Churchill was not well: according to her doctor she was 'in a state of nervous tension and fatigue and we want to avoid anything that adds to the strain'. He therefore hoped Sarah would 'defer coming over until you join me at Pausaland'—where he would be from mid-January—'and visit London on our return'.[3]

That December, President Eisenhower visited Europe, but not Britain. 'It would have given me great pleasure,' Churchill wrote to him on December 16, 'if you had been able to include this little island in your tour, and we should not have been behindhand in showing you what we think and feel about you.'

Churchill also told Eisenhower that he had personally 'gone through all the business' of looking out thirty-five paintings for the exhibition of his paintings to be held in Kansas City. 'I do hope,' he added, 'they will be considered worthy of the honour you have done them, and I hope myself to come to Washington in the closing half of April.'[4]

'Here, I am attending very regularly at Parliament,' Churchill wrote to Wendy Reves on December 18, 'though I do not listen to many of the debates,' and he added, in his own hand: 'I vote.'[5]

---

[1] 'My dear Sir Winston', 'Personal and Confidential', Buckingham Palace, 7 November 1957: Churchill papers, 2/127.

[2] 'My dear Max', 28 Hyde Park Gate, 4 December 1957: Beaverbrook papers.

[3] Letter dated 12 December 1957: Churchill papers, 1/55.

[4] 'My dear Ike', 'Personal', signed 'Yrs always, Winston', 16 December 1957: Churchill papers, 2/217.

[5] 'Dearest Wendy', 'Your loving friend, Winston', London, 18 December 1957: Reves papers.

As planned, Christmas was a quiet one. The gifts that year from relatives and friends included some C. S. Forester books from Randolph, a box of handkerchiefs from Christopher and Mary Soames, a bottle of cognac 'older than 1878' from Anthony and Clarissa Eden, a book of Osbert Lancaster's cartoons from Violet Bonham Carter, a case of Israeli oranges from President Weizmann's widow Vera, and a Virginia ham from Bernard Baruch.[1]

To Eden's gift, Churchill and his wife reciprocated with a hock 'of that superb 1921 vintage', as Eden wrote in thanks.[2]

For the first two weeks of 1958, Churchill and his wife remained at Chartwell, their only guests being Christopher and Mary Soames, and Sylvia Henley. On January 13, as Churchill prepared to leave for La Pausa, Emery Reves telephoned to say that the villa's entire central heating system had burst.[3] 'So sorry to hear of your bad luck,' Churchill telegraphed that same day. 'I will stay at the Hôtel de Paris until you are ready for me, and hope you will both come to lunch and dinner with me continuously.'[4] 'Heath told me I could go away,' Churchill explained to James Stuart, 'which was very kind of him.'[5]

As Churchill flew to Monte Carlo together with Montague Browne and Sergeant Murray, the British, and indeed world, press gave front-page prominence to the arrest of Sarah Churchill in Los Angeles, on a charge of drunkenness. Refusing at first to say who she was, she was initially held in prison as 'Jane Doe'. Eight hours after her arrest, she was released on bail. On January 16 she pleaded guilty, and was fined fifty dollars.

From La Pausa, Churchill dictated a letter to his wife on January 18; he had taken with him a fur muff, to help warm his hands:

My darling,
The muff is a great success here. I use it at all meals, and on the whole it achieves its purpose. It is vy cold.

We had Onassis to dinner on Thursday night, and I in no way committed myself or you to a voyage. It all went off very pleasantly. I have spent the greater part of my days in bed, but sit for a couple of hours in the sunshine from 2.30 till 4.30. It is very pleasant & bright.

I agree with you that Sarah got out of it as well as she could. I sent her the following telegram, of which I hope you will approve: 'Let me know your plans. Congratulations and love from Papa.' I will keep you informed of any

[1] 'Christmas Presents Received 1957': Churchill papers, 2/441.
[2] 'My dear Winston', 2 January 1958: Churchill papers, 2/216.
[3] 'Sir Winston', initialled 'DP', 13 January 1958: Churchill papers, 1/149.
[4] 'Telegram to Mr Reves', 13 January 1958: Churchill papers, 1/149.
[5] 'My dear James', La Pausa, 17 January 1958: James Stuart (Viscount Stuart of Findhorn), *Within the Fringe, An Autobiography*, London 1967, page 117. Edward Heath was then Chief Whip (and later, from 1970 to 1974, Prime Minister).

correspondence with her. Personally I hope she will find it possible to come here as soon as she has finished her local engagements.[1]

I think the Edens would like to come, and therefore we must fit things in good time, as space is limited and I think the Reves would like to make plans for the latter part of February.

We had another lovely day today—the third running, and for the moment the prospects are good. I hope you will find it possible to come, if only for a few days. Wendy is very well, and has put on weight without impairing her figure in any way. She has written to you.

I have been reading a Russian novel, which has made a great impression in America as it is critical of the Russian world and yet the author has apparently been permitted by the Russian government to publish it and print an edition of thirty thousand copies for Russian use.[2] This is a step in the right direction, and we should watch it with attention.

The Dynevors are coming to dinner tomorrow.[3] I have not heard anything about Christopher's father, who, as you know, has been far from well.[4] I will pick my way through these complications.

I shall send this letter off tomorrow, Sunday, and am told it ought to reach you on Monday.

He had just received a letter from Sarah, Churchill added in his own hand. 'She has arranged to come in the first week of February.'[5]

'How I wish Winston would paint *before* luncheon instead of *after*,' Clementine Churchill wrote to Wendy Reves on January 20 from London, and she added: 'I'm so afraid of his catching cold when the sun begins to decline at about 3.30.'[6]

On January 22 Churchill wrote to his wife again, in his own hand:

My darling Clemmie,

No word from Sarah yet; but I assume she adheres to the 3rd or 4th as the date of her arrival here. The sun shines every day and I hope to begin painting *indoors* fairly soon. At present I am dawdling in bed till lunch, but I agree with what you write in yr letter to Wendy that the mornings are the best. Today we are going to

---

[1] To one of Sarah Churchill's friends in the United States, who had helped her during the incident of her arrest, Churchill later wrote from La Pausa: 'My Daughter, Sarah, has told me how very kind and staunch you have been, and what this has meant to her both professionally and personally. I hope you will accept my most warm thanks for what you have done. It is very helpful to me to know that Sarah has such good friends in America.' (Letter to Albert McCleery, La Pausa, 8 February 1958: Churchill papers, 1/56.)

[2] *One Day in the Life of Ivan Denisovitch* by Alexander Solzhenitsyn.

[3] Charles Arthur Uryan Rhys, 8th Baron Dynevor, a Conservative MP from 1923 to 1929 and 1931 to 1934, had married, in 1934, Arthur Soames's former wife Hope Mary Woodbine Parish. Their only son, Richard Charles Uryan Rhys, succeeded his father as 9th Baron in 1962 (in 1959 he married the only child of the painter Sir John Rothenstein). The 8th Baron's father, Walter, had been an Assistant in the Ministry of Munitions in 1917 and 1918, when Churchill was Minister of Munitions.

[4] Arthur Soames died on 6 July 1962.

[5] 'My darling, 18 January 1958: Spencer-Churchill papers.

[6] 'My dearest Wendy', London, 20 January 1958: Reves papers.

lunch at the Château de Madrid, wh shd be good both for food and sunlight.

I get a bad report of the weather at home, tho I shd like to be in Parlt for the Thorneycroft debate, and I nearly came home for it. Laziness however decided my conduct.

Toby is brisk and kind and sends you messages. He flits into Wendy & is much encouraged. He spends the bulk of his mornings on my bed table.

I send you my best love, and hope you will come out soon.

With my deepest affection always

Your loving husband

W[1]

On January 23 Churchill wrote again, once more in his own hand:

My darling Clemmie,

I have started painting again: *indoors* for the snow is on the hills all round. Flowers arranged by Wendy is the subject & she has painted for three days herself just from memory. It is much better to have a model. The sun shines brightly & today I got up before luncheon and sat in the porch.

Not a word from Sarah! She really ought not to neglect her trusted friends. They do not know when to expect her & the house only holds three! I am sending her a telegram which I trust will be effective. Randolph sent me a nice one but telling nothing about her movements.

My darling—I love you so much. You are a sweet 'Clemmie Cat'. I would like so much to give you my loving kisses. My heart goes with this scrawl.

Your affectionate husband

W[2]

On January 25 Clementine Churchill reported to her husband that, according to the *Daily Mail*, '1,221 persons visited your Exhibition in one day at Kansas City and that this is a record.'[3] The exhibition, arranged by Joyce Hall of Hallmark cards, was the first exhibition devoted solely to Churchill's paintings. Clementine Churchill added: 'I was disquieted by the report (in the *News Chronicle*) that you were indisposed & very tired, but so relieved that it was baseless.'

So disquieted had Clementine Churchill been, not only by this rumour, that she spoke about it to Anthony Montague Browne, who wrote to Detective Sergeant Murray:

Lady Churchill is rather worried by the amount that gets into the Press when Sir Winston is at La Pausa—false rumours about his health today, and in the past details of his day-to-day life. You know the sort of thing I mean. Can you throw any light on where this comes from? Do you think it is any of the staff there, or the police at the gate?

'I should be most grateful if you could drop me a line about it,'

[1] 'My darling Clemmie', La Pausa, 22 January 1958: Spencer-Churchill papers.
[2] 'My darling Clemmie', La Pausa, 23 January 1958: Spencer-Churchill papers.
[3] 'My darling', 28 Hyde Park Gate, 25 January 1958: Churchill papers, 1/55.

Montague Browne added, 'as Lady Churchill is most distressed, and has asked me to do what I can to stop it.'[1]

On January 27 Churchill wrote to his wife again, also in his own hand, on notepaper which Wendy Reves had designed:

My dearest One,

This is the new paper wh the Reves have at last invented. You will recognise the gate wh is of an attractive design.

What an interesting letter you have written me, wh I have just got. I thought Moran was making a mistake when I read what he wrote, & I do not wonder he has had a bad reaction.[2] The doctors are not a happy tribe just now.

I was delighted you had fixed a date for your visit to La Pausa. It is still a long way off! But I will wait with patience. Wendy was vy pleased too. She looks forward so much to seeing you.

The pictures seem to have got off all right at Fulton, though the hurricane made it difficult for those interested to get there. I don't think it will do any harm either to me or them.

I shall be interested to see the result of repainting my study, & think you are quite right to close Chartwell till I come back—bringing I hope summer with me.

Your loving and devoted husband,

W

'Toby is sitting on the paper,' Churchill added.[3]

At the end of January, Eisenhower invited Churchill to visit the United States. 'It will be a very short visit,' Churchill wrote in a dictated letter to his wife on January 31, 'only a week, of which three and a half days will be spent at the White House and the rest with Bernie, either in New York or at his country place. I do hope you will be able to come with me, but I shall quite understand if you feel that a double flight across the Atlantic is more than the experience will be worth. I hope and trust, however, that you will come.' Churchill added: 'I am sitting here in the garden under the balcony. We have only had one cloudy day, and all the rest have been lovely and sunny

[1] 'Private', 24 January 1958: Churchill papers, 1/143. The alternative to this letter, Montague Browne later recalled, 'was to have him sacked, which would have distressed WSC who was fond of him'. The letter was sent, and Murray remained. (Anthony Montague Browne recollections: notes for the author, 24 March 1987.)

[2] As inflation led to a demand for an increase in the pay of National Health doctors, a leading article in *The Times* on doctors' pay declared, on 5 January 1957: 'adjustment in the long run is unavoidable unless services are to be curtailed.' Lord Moran took issue with this: in one of several letters in which he criticized any pay increase for doctors, he wrote: 'I trust that in spirit of the pledges they have received they will have the good sense to see that when the cost of living goes up they cannot always expect a rise in pay.' What was needed, Moran added, 'even more than higher pay, is some change in the machinery for arbitration'. This particular letter was published in *The Times* on 19 February 1957.

[3] 'My dearest One', La Pausa, 27 January 1958: Spencer-Churchill papers.

and really not cold. I expect March will be very warm out here, and I am keeping it un-planned.'[1]

Joined at La Pausa by his wife, and by his daughter Sarah, Churchill and his wife gave Sarah all the comfort they could. 'Thank you both,' she wrote to her mother a month later, 'you and Papa, for being so gentle and understanding.'[2]

On February 11 Churchill received a letter from Eden, regretting that he could not come out to La Pausa, but explaining he was 'embedded in documents and beginning to put thoughts down on paper' for his memoirs of the inter-war years. 'The world news seems to me to get steadily darker,' Eden wrote, and he commented: 'Perhaps that is how retired politicians often view events.'[3] 'I can only agree with you,' Churchill replied, 'that the world picture seems to grow progressively blacker,' and he added in his own hand: 'Let me know when you can come out here.'[4]

On February 17 Churchill was invited to lunch by Aristotle Onassis, on his yacht. Then, as Emery Reves later told Lord Moran:

> About three o'clock Winston expressed a wish to go to the Rooms at Monte Carlo to have a little gamble. Reves suggested that they might play chemin-de-fer on the yacht instead. They played for high stakes and drank more alcohol than usual. Winston got very excited. As the afternoon wore on it was noticed that he was very white and tired. About seven o'clock Reves ventured to remind him that they had been invited for lunch. Was it not time to go home? Winston grumbled that Reves was breaking up the party. When they got home, Winston seemed 'all in'.[5]

On the following night Dr Roberts telephoned to Lord Moran: 'Sir Winston was feverish and coughing.' It was in fact bronchial pneumonia. 'SIR WINSTON ILL' was the banner headline across all eight front-page columns of the *Daily Mail* on the following morning. 'I would say Sir Winston has a chill,' Dr Roberts told the Press. 'The weather is so changeable here.'[6]

On the morning of February 19 Lord Moran flew to Nice. 'I found him shivering violently,' he noted, 'his teeth chattering. A rigor on the third day meant that the infection was spreading. I decided to change the anti-biotic. . . .'[7] On February 21 Montague Browne told Churchill that he had heard from Buckingham Palace that the Queen

[1] La Pausa, 31 January 1958: Churchill papers, 1/55.

[2] Letter of 12 March 1958: Mary Soames, *Clementine Churchill*, page 465.

[3] 'My dear Winston', 'Personal', 11 February 1958: Churchill papers, 2/216.

[4] 'My dear Anthony', signed 'Yrs ever, W', La Pausa, 14 February 1958: Churchill papers, 2/216.

[5] Lord Moran diary, 19 February 1958: *The Struggle for Survival*, page 732.

[6] *Daily Mail*, 19 February 1958.

[7] Moran diary, 20 February 1958: *The Struggle for Survival*, page 732.

was being kept closely informed of Churchill's news, 'but that the Palace much like to hear from here direct'. [1] At Montague Browne's suggestion, a telegram was sent to the Queen that same day: 'My Wife and I are deeply grateful to your Majesty for your most kind inquiries.' [2] From the President of Turkey came a telegram on February 23: 'Following course of your illness with great concern. Wish you speedy recovery from depths of my heart. Ismet Inönü.' [3]

In the last week of February it was announced that Churchill was on the mend. 'Delighted you are so much better,' Lord Alanbrooke telegraphed on February 25. 'Every wish for rapid recovery, Brookie.' [4] Two days later the Prime Minister, Harold Macmillan, and the Leader of the Opposition, Hugh Gaitskell, telegraphed jointly: 'At Question Time today whole House asked that a message of congratulations should be sent to you on your recovery, conveying the warm good wishes of us all.' [5]

After thanking Macmillan, Gaitskell and the House of Commons on the following day, Churchill added: 'I hope soon to be once more in my seat.' [6]

From Brendan Bracken came a letter on February 27:

My dear Winston,

I am pleased and relieved beyond all telling by the news of your rapid recovery.

If you were to write a book on 'Health Without Rules' it would outsell all your other books and would soar above the fantastic sales of Mary Baker Eddy's Science and Health With Key to the Scriptures. It is claimed by Christian Scientists that this book has already sold 50 million copies, but as Madam Baker Eddy only attained the trifling age of 62, your book would be a much more 'authoritative guide to the best means of attaining long life'.

As the Inland Revenue would take away any profits you would derive from such a masterpiece, this must remain one of the great unwritten books of our age. [7]

'How happy I am that you fooled the doctors, just as I did,' Truman wrote from his home in Independence, Missouri, and he added: 'I know that you will soon be back in Churchillian flying trim.' [8]

---

[1] 'Sir Winston', initialled 'AMB', 21 February 1958: Churchill papers, 1/60.
[2] Telegram of 21 February 1958 (drafted by Montague Browne and approved by Churchill): Churchill papers, 1/60.
[3] Telegram received 23 February 1958: Churchill papers, 1/60. Churchill and Inönü had last met at Adana in Turkey in January 1943.
[4] Telegram sent 25 February 1958: Churchill papers, 1/60.
[5] Telegram received 27 February 1958: Churchill papers, 1/60.
[6] Telegram dated 28 February 1958: Churchill papers, 1/60.
[7] 'My dear Winston', 27 February 1958: Churchill papers, 1/60.
[8] Message dated 28 February 1958: Churchill papers, 1/122. Vice-President Nixon also wrote to wish Churchill well. The news of Churchill's recovery, Nixon wrote, was 'the kind of encouraging good news all of your friends want to hear!' (Office of the Vice-President, Washington, 24 February 1958: Churchill papers, 1/60.)

The 'flying trim' was not to be. 'I had been making good progress,' Churchill wrote to Eisenhower in March, 'but I have had a setback, which will mean that I have to take things quietly for a time.' He had been 'so much looking forward' to seeing Eisenhower, and he hoped 'it will still be possible to make a rendezvous later in the year'.[1]

On March 7 Churchill was well enough for Lord Moran to feel able to fly back to England. He was also well enough, on March 8, to sign four letters, inviting Lord Weeks, Lord Godber, Sir Alexander Fleck and Lord Chandos to become Trustees 'of the new College we hope to set up in Cambridge'.[2] 'He has made a good recovery,' Clementine Churchill wrote that day to a friend, 'but is rather depressed, and suffering from the effects of the anti-biotics.' She was hopeful however that they would be back in England 'in about a fortnight's time'.[3]

'My illness came on all of a sudden,' Churchill wrote to Lady Lytton on March 12, 'but the doctors were quite ready to grapple with it.' He proposed returning to England on the following Tuesday 'if nothing goes wrong'.[4] 'How charming of you to send me the case of delicious champagne,' he wrote to Odette Pol Roger on March 15. 'It is making my recovery most cheerful and pleasant.'[5]

Churchill continued to hope that he could go to the United States in April, but on March 15 Clementine Churchill wrote to Mary Soames:

Papa, for the first time, shews hesitation about going to America—
I think Alas—he feels definitely weaker since his illness—He certainly made a marvellous recovery, but without the mass use of antibiotics he would have sunk and faded away. . . . If Papa does go to America . . . would you go with him in my place? I don't feel strong enough, I am ashamed to say; but I think a member of his family should go. . . .

Of course—I hope he won't go—If he does not make one or two speeches & television appearances, the visit will be a flop as regards the American People—who . . . want to see and hear him. Then if he lets himself be persuaded to make public appearances it will half kill him. Monty, the dear creature, has just arrived & thinks Papa is crazy to contemplate the idea. . . .[6]

Montgomery's visit to La Pausa, Clementine Churchill added three days later, had been 'a great tonic'.[7]

[1] 'My dear Ike', La Pausa, March 1958: Churchill papers, 2/277.
[2] La Pausa, 8 March 1958: Churchill papers, 2/571. Churchill signed as Chairman of the Trustees. The Cambridge Trustees already appointed were Lord Tedder (Chancellor of Cambridge University), Lord Adrian (Vice-Chancellor), Professor Downs (Master of Christ's), Sir Alexander Todd and Sir John Cockcroft.
[3] La Pausa, 8 March 1958: Churchill papers, 1/60.
[4] La Pausa, 12 March 1958: Churchill papers, 1/60.
[5] 'My dear Odette', La Pausa, 15 March 1958: Churchill papers, 1/60.
[6] Letter of 15 March 1958: Mary Soames, *Clementine Churchill*, page 465.
[7] Letter of 18 March 1958: Mary Soames, *Clementine Churchill*, page 465.

A luncheon had been arranged at Hyde Park Gate for the Churchill College Trustees, to be held on March 28. But as he prepared to return to London, Churchill suffered two further bouts of fever. On March 21, a week before the luncheon was to take place, the Trustees were informed by Montague Browne that Churchill had been advised by his doctors 'not to return to London until the weather is warmer'.[1] From Harold Macmillan came a letter on March 22, from 10 Downing Street:

Dear Winston,

I have been told that you have postponed your return to this country for a few days. I am sure this is wise and will give you a much better chance of coming back really fit. The weather here has been very cold. I need hardly say that I greatly look forward to seeing you some time after you come back for a talk. You will have read that I am going to see Ike in June.

It was good of you to let me know about Churchill College, and I read what you said about it with great interest. It is an exciting development. I am told that the University Grants Committee are to consider the question of the grant to be given round about the end of the month, and I have asked to be kept informed.[2]

On March 24, after speaking on the telephone to Dr Roberts and Clementine Churchill, Lord Moran flew back to Nice. 'It had been noticed that Winston was yellow,' Moran noted in his diary, 'but this was thought to be due to the antibiotic I had prescribed. In fact, he is suffering from obstructive jaundice, caused either by a stone or by an infection of the bile passages. I shall be glad when we get him back to England.'[3]

From England came news, in a letter from Lady Eden, that Eden had succumbed again to a severe bout of fever. 'I am indeed sorry to hear that Anthony has been ill again,' Churchill wrote to his niece on March 25. 'Do let me know how he progresses. I myself have had a slight setback but I hope soon to be about again and back in England.'[4] To Harold Macmillan, who had written to ask if the Americans could now publish in their diplomatic documents series five telegrams which Churchill had sent to Roosevelt in 1943, Churchill replied, on March 27: 'I do not claim any right of veto on the publication of these telegrams. On the other hand, I think that the timing is important, even today. It seems to me unhelpful to draw attention to our suspicions of de Gaulle at a time when he may still have services to render to France. Could it not be deferred for rather longer?'[5]

[1] La Pausa, 21 March 1958: Churchill papers, 2/571.
[2] 'Dear Winston', 22 March 1958: Churchill papers, 2/220.
[3] Moran diary, 24 March 1958: *The Struggle for Survival*, pages 733-4.
[4] La Pausa, 25 March 1958: Churchill papers, 1/60.
[5] 'My dear Harold', 'Confidential', La Pausa, 27 March 1958: Churchill papers, 2/220. 'De Gaulle has a great chance', Churchill told Lord Moran in May. 'He is on top. They have all

On April 1, Clementine Churchill was seventy-three. Two days later, after a final examination by Dr Roberts, Churchill was judged well enough to make the two-and-a-half-hour flight back to Britain. At Nice airport he met Lord Beaverbrook. 'I saw Winston for fifteen minutes or more,' Beaverbrook wrote to Bracken. 'He was certainly clear in mind and I do hope that by this time he is strong in body.'[1]

'Welcome home,' wrote Eden in a handwritten message to greet Churchill on his arrival at Chartwell. 'I am so glad that you have so completely routed the whole army of germs, virus and other foes.'[2] On April 4, from Chartwell, Churchill telegraphed to Wendy Reves: 'Never said goodbye to you darling Wendy. Now send you my love. So does Clemmie. Feel very well. Winston.'[3]

Illness recurred, however; on April 10 Churchill was not well enough to go to the gallop trials of one of his horses, and, on his doctor's advice, he stayed in bed all day, with a pain over his lower ribs.[4] On the following day, his doctor noted, 'he was feverish all day'.[5] 'I have another attack with temperature,' Churchill wrote in his own hand to Beaverbrook on April 11, 'and am under full medical treatment. How bloody!'[6] That same day he dictated a letter to Wendy Reves:

My dear Wendy,
We got back here after a smooth, swift voyage, and for a week I had no fault in my temperature or anything else. Now it has gone up a bit and I am having a small attack similar to the last one.

I am afraid my illness must have been an awful burden to you, but certainly one could not have had a nicer place to be ill in than your beautiful room. I know no other surroundings which leap ahead of health and weather, whatever they may be.

I was so sorry not to see you to say goodbye. It just came on to rain at that moment.

Do let me know when you will be coming over here. There are all sorts of rumours about what the summer in England will be. So far I cannot believe that there is going to be any at all. But at all events do let us know when you are coming and we shall look forward to seeing you.

As I expect you will have seen in the papers, I have decided to cancel my visit to Ike. This is a great disappointment, but it may come off later on.

---

submitted to him. It may purge French politics.' As for the Algerian Committee of French settlers and soldiers, 'they will bloody well try to make trouble', Churchill told Moran, 'but they won't succeed' (Moran diary, 19 May 1958: *The Struggle for Survival*, page 741). General de Gaulle was returned to power as Prime Minister on 2 June 1958.

[1] Letter of 6 April 1958: Beaverbrook papers.
[2] 'My dear Winston', 2 April 1958: Churchill papers, 2/216.
[3] Telegram received at Roquebrune on 4 April 1958: Reves papers.
[4] Moran diary, 10 April 1958: *The Struggle for Survival*, page 734.
[5] Moran diary, 11 April 1958: *The Struggle for Survival*, page 734.
[6] 'My dear Max', Chartwell, 11 April 1958: Beaverbrook papers.

Meanwhile I hope that you and Emery will have an agreeable journey in Europe and that you will recover from your fatigue. I am so grateful to you for all you did. We are all much in your debt for your hard work, care and hospitality.

'Your affectionate W', Churchill added in his own hand.[1]

Churchill remained in bed, with jaundice, and in some pain, for seven days. On April 16 he was well enough to leave his bedroom and dine with his wife and doctor. 'I recalled to Winston,' Lord Moran noted in his diary, 'how after his stroke in 1953 he had recited the first fifty lines of "King Robert of Sicily" with only two mistakes. He tried to repeat the feat, but only succeeded in recalling a line or two. 'My memory,' he said sadly, 'is much worse; in the last nine months it seems to have deteriorated.'[2]

On April 17 Jock Colville dined at Chartwell, to give Churchill a progress report about the coming public appeal for £3,500,000 for the new Cambridge college. Churchill was to open the fund with a gift of £25,000.

'Our friend Winston is, of course, a medical marvel,' Brendan Bracken wrote to Lord Beaverbrook on April 21, and he went on to explain: 'He had disregarded all the normal life-lengthening rules and has witnessed, doubtless with regret, but with some complacence, the burial of most of his doctors, save Charles. But the sun is Churchill's greatest life-maintainer and the lack of it has probably played some part in creating his present condition.'[3]

Although he seldom spoke in public now, Churchill still sent the occasional message to public meetings. For the annual Albert Hall meeting of the Primrose League at the end of April 1958, a meeting which he had hitherto addressed in person, he was given a draft message prepared by George Christ. 'It seems a good one,' Montague Browne told him.[4] Churchill sent it unaltered, except for deleting the adjective 'vast' in the phrase 'every member of your vast audience'.[5]

'I have had a further setback,' Churchill wrote to Princess Alice on April 22, 'but am now making good progress.'[6] Two days later he felt well enough to dine at the Other Club, where Harold Macmillan found him 'quite alert', telling Lord Moran: 'he talked a lot and seemed to hear pretty well, that is if no one else is talking at the same time.' Churchill had also gone to the House of Commons: 'When I met

[1] 'My dear Wendy', London, 11 April 1958: Reves papers.
[2] Moran diary, 16 April 1958: *The Struggle for Survival*, pages 736–7.
[3] Letter of 21 April 1958: Beaverbrook papers.
[4] 'Sir Winston', initialled 'AMB', 22 April 1958: Churchill papers, 2/368.
[5] 'I am so sorry that I cannot be with you. . . .': Churchill papers, 2/368.
[6] 'Madam', 22 April 1958: Squerryes Lodge Archive.

him in the Lobby,' Macmillan told Moran, 'he seemed very frail.'[1]

At Chartwell, Churchill spent much of his time reading. *Tom Jones* was one of the books he read after his return from France. Another was Georgette Heyer's *An Infamous Army*, 'a good solid account of the three months in Brussels before Waterloo', Churchill told his doctor.[2] Another was *Rob Roy*. He was also sent the first chapters of Lord Ismay's memoirs, in their typescript form. 'He could not put them down,' noted Lord Moran.[3] 'My dear Pug,' Churchill wrote on May 23, 'Thank you so much for sending me the opening salvo of your Memoirs. I found it most interesting, and so did Clemmie.' Churchill added: 'I look forward to more.'[4]

While Churchill had been in France, the fourth and final volume of *A History of the English-Speaking Peoples* was published, entitled 'The Great Democracies'.[5] The book had been given 'a very prominent display' in the local bookshop, his grandson Winston wrote from Eton on April 29, and he added: 'I have so far read the first five chapters and find it easy reading. It has very great clarity and forthrightness, and is much more interesting to read than other books which I have read covering such a long period.'[6] 'I have already dipped, out of order,' wrote Eden on April 29, 'into the American Civil War, superbly told.'[7]

'I am afraid that Sir Winston's budgerigar has taken a small bite out of Volume II,' Churchill's secretary Miss Pugh wrote to Mary Soames, about a four-volume set being sent to Lord Mountbatten for his eldest grandson, Norton Knatchbull, and she added: 'I do hope that Lord Mountbatten will not mind.'[8] Toby's bite, Mountbatten wrote to Churchill, 'will add to its historic significance.'[9]

On May 6 Churchill gave a luncheon at Chartwell for the Churchill College Trustees, as well as for Lord Knollys, the co-ordinator of the appeal for funds, and Jock Colville. 'It was an interesting and pleasant occasion,' Knollys wrote to Churchill two days later, and he added: 'I was glad to be able to report that the Appeal had begun so promis-

[1] Moran diary, 27 April 1958: *The Struggle for Survival*, pages 739–40.

[2] Moran diary, 27 April 1958: *The Struggle for Survival*, pages 739–40.

[3] Moran diary, 19 May 1958: *The Struggle for Survival*, page 741.

[4] 'My dear Pug', 23 May 1958: Churchill papers, 2/190.

[5] Publication day was 14 March 1958, and 150,000 copies were printed.

[6] 'Dear Grandpapa', 29 April 1958: Churchill papers, 156.

[7] 'My dear Winston', 29 April 1958: Churchill papers, 2/216.

[8] Doreen Pugh to Mary Soames, 19 May 1958: Churchill papers, 2/194.

[9] Letter of 22 May 1958: Churchill papers, 2/194.

ingly.'[1] A week later, on May 15, it was announced publicly that Churchill College, Cambridge, was to be founded, and that Churchill would head the College Trustees.

To make Churchill's increasing deafness more bearable, in the first week of May, Sir Victor Negus installed a wiring system in the dining room at Hyde Park Gate, similar to one which had earlier been set up for him in the House of Commons. 'When all was ready,' Lord Moran noted on May 8, 'Clemmie produced Winston. He was able to hear what she said, even when she spoke in a low voice, and was ready to admit that this was a great advance. Before he left the room he told Negus to go ahead with the wiring.'[2]

During the course of a year, Churchill now received several hundred requests for the reproduction of his paintings. He was always reluctant to do so. Guided by Montague Browne, who had to deal with all such requests, literary and artistic, Churchill agreed on May 17 that the Medici Society could reproduce his painting 'Menton from La Pausa, 1957', subject to the Society making payments in respect of royalties to the British Empire Cancer Campaign, of which Churchill was a patron. Later he also allowed his painting 'Cap d'Ail' to be reproduced on similar terms, the sum paid being £212 to the Cancer campaign.[3]

On May 29 the leading technical university in Israel, the Technion at Haifa, opened a new auditorium, which Churchill had agreed could be called the Churchill Auditorium. Representing him at the opening ceremony was his daughter Sarah. 'They love you very much,' she wrote, 'and the auditorium was designed to honour your achievements and exist as a constant reminder of your courage and inspiration.'

On her arrival in Israel, Sarah Churchill had gone to Jerusalem, where she met the Prime Minister, David Ben-Gurion, reporting to her father:

Mr 'BG' as they call him, was great fun and easy to talk to. He only wanted to know about you—Were you well? What were you doing? What do you like to do? How did you find time to write 'all those books'? How did you plan your day—then—and now? What recreation did you take? Did you play chess? Bridge? Poker? etc. etc. His face glowed like an eager schoolboy's. It became solemn & sad when he reminded me he had had serious differences of opinion with you in the past—But he said after thinking a moment—'One cannot change the past—one must try to change the future.'

[1] 'My dear Sir Winston', 8 May 1958: Churchill papers, 2/571. Lord Knollys was Chairman of Vickers.

[2] Moran diary, 8 May 1958: *The Struggle for Survival*, pages 740–1. Sir Victor Negus, who had been knighted in 1956, was Consulting Surgeon to the Ear, Nose and Throat Department, King's College Hospital, London, and a leading laryngologist. Among his nine books were the *The Mechanism of the Larynx* (1929) and *Comparative Anatomy and Physiology of the Nose* (1958). He died in 1974, at the age of eighty-seven.

[3] Note of 17 May 1958: Churchill papers, 1/24.

He wants you to come to Israel if physically possible, and he will take us all to the desert—his beloved Negev—from which he is convinced he can still squeeze some asset. He doesn't wear a tie—he can't hear enough about you. In himself—he is a humble spirit.[1]

Since his return from France at the beginning of April 1958, Churchill was looked after, at both Chartwell and Hyde Park Gate, by two nurses; they were to be his helpers for the remaining years of his life. In addition, a young male nurse, Roy Howells, had just been given the task of looking after him both in England and during his travels; Howells was to remain with Churchill for nearly six years.

Jane and Alan Hodge were among those invited to Hyde Park Gate to lunch with Churchill that summer. There could be many moments of silence, unexpected activities, and philosophic reflections. Jane Hodge later recalled how, on one occasion, 'he made me stand on a chair to look at a painting of Blenheim which he felt I hadn't studied close enough'. On another occasion, while sitting by the fire with Alan Hodge, Churchill remarked: 'Curious to imagine oneself a log—reluctant to be consumed—yet obliged *eventually* to give way.' [2]

This sombre reflection came at the time when Churchill had learned that Brendan Bracken was dying of cancer: he visited him in the Westminster Hospital on June 27; this was one of the last meetings of two friends whose friendship spanned thirty-five years. 'Brendan was very animated,' Churchill told Lord Moran later that day. 'I was a quarter of an hour with him, and he talked all the time—good sense. He had a rubber tube hanging from his mouth. They feed him through it. Why do they do that, Charles?' When Lord Moran explained that Bracken's gullet was obstructed, Churchill was silent for a while, then asked Lord Moran: 'The surgeons can do nothing for his kind of cancer?' [3]

That afternoon Churchill saw Alan Hodge, then went to Blenheim, where he and his wife celebrated the fiftieth anniversary of their engagement. It was in a pavilion in the park at Blenheim that Churchill had proposed to Clementine in 1908. Among the guests at this celebratory weekend was the historian A. L. Rowse, who noted in his journal:

Winston and Clemmie appeared, Clemmie all billowing gown and broadened out with age. I was shocked to see how much he had aged, much more feeble, another illness will puff him away—or possibly without. Unsteady on his feet he took a low seat, beaming happily, contentedly around, saying

[1] 'Darling Papa', 'In the plane, en route for Rome', 30 May 1958: Churchill papers, 2/369.
[2] Jane Aiken Hodge recollections: in conversation with the author, 3 July 1987. The phrase about the log was quoted by Alan Hodge's friend Peter Quennell in his book *The Wanton Chase* (page 185). Jane and Alan Hodge lunched with Churchill on 11 May 1958; Lord Beaverbrook was the other guest. Hodge was with Churchill again on the afternoon of June 27.
[3] Moran diary, 27 June 1958: *The Struggle for Survival*, page 742.

nothing, kissing the children goodnight. It was sad to see him: still the centre of all our attention, the embers of a great fire, all the force gone. Very deaf now and rather impenetrable, apparently he had asked for me to sit beside him at dinner, the ladies' talk being like 'the twittering of birds' to him.

We went into dinner, he on the Duchess's right, I next to him. She was very good at managing him, but we were reduced, as with the very old, to treating him like a child. He spent much of the time holding her miniature dachshund in his arms, at one point offering it some of the delicious lobster mousse on a fork: the expression of disgust was charming to see, little velvet paws hanging limply down, head drawn back, nose averted. 'Darling,' said the old man, always sentimental about animals.

Not that he has become senile: he is still capable of a good phrase, an echo of his former power. Someone asked whether he would be attending church tomorrow. 'At my age,' he replied, 'I think my devotions may be attended in private.'

Rowse's account continued:

He still could make single comments, rather than command an argument. He thought the failure of the new French constitution to provide for an interim dissolution of the Chamber a mistake. Similarly of the statutory limitation upon American Presidents to two terms of office. This led to a long disquisition in the American manner by the Duke's son-in-law, the Duke obviously impatient, Winston all bland courtesy. (He couldn't hear it.)

Indeed it was the most touching thing to observe—all force gone after these strokes, now all contentment and old-world courtesy. He was still compos mentis: he had won £21 off the Duchess at bezique that evening, and during the weekend had cleaned her out of £50 altogether. He takes his own cards, case and spectacles around with him, laid out ceremoniously upon a red velvet cloth. Upstairs in his bedroom he had brought his love-bird in a cage—boyish, troublesome, lovable as ever. To everyone's surprise he demanded water: 'Oh, I drink a lot of water—the doctor tells me to—along with everything else.' [1]

Clementine Churchill returned to London. 'I like to think of you having a peaceful time at Blenheim,' she wrote on July 2, 'varied with fierce exciting Battles at Bezique.' [2]

On July 15 a rebellion in Iraq led to the murder of the King and his family, and of the Prime Minister, Nuri al-Said, whose body was dragged through the streets of Baghdad. In Lebanon, President Chamoun appealed for support from the United States. Within hours, American carrier-borne troops landed in Beirut. Churchill's immediate response was to support the American action, and to prepare a speech for Parliament. He at once told Harold Macmillan of his intention, and then dictated a few introductory remarks, which read:

[1] A. L. Rowse, *Memories of Men and Women*, pages 22–3.
[2] Letter of 2 July 1958: Churchill papers, 1/135.

I have not troubled the House with any remarks since I left Office three and a half years ago. Nor should I do so now if circumstances did not warrant it. I have a feeling that the events which have recently taken place in the Middle East are of a different order from anything which has occurred, and that they confront us with the need of scanning the whole field with a gravity not unworthy of the moral and material issues which they naturally excite.[1]

There followed four pages of handwritten notes, which began:

> Outrage Embassy Bagdad.
> 　　What are we going to do?
> *America & Britain* must work together,
> 　　reach *Unity* of purpose.
>
> The complications which the problem presents
> 　　can be cured if, & only *if*,
> 　　　　they are dealt with by united forces
> 　　& common principles
> 　　　　not merely increase of strength.
> When we divide we lose.
> 　　It is not primarily a question of material force.
> *Anthony Eden & Suez*.
> 　　He was *right*.
> These recent events prove him so.
> 　　It may be that his action was *premature*.

Churchill then intended to speak about the American landings in Lebanon. His notes continued:

> It wd be too easy to mock USA
> We should refrain
> The Lebanon is part of the ME
>
> Comparisons are often dangerous
> 　　& still more often futile.
>
> This is no time for our
> 　　trying to balance a long account.
>
> The accounts are balancing themselves.
>
> I do not want to take points off the US
> 　　& point the finger of scorn at them
>
> How easy to say
> 　　Look at the US & compare them with us at Suez.
>
> *We were right.*
>
> Chamoun—a good friend to this country.[2]

---

[1] Dictated notes, undated: Churchill papers, 2/129.

[2] In 1956, Camille Chamoun, the leader of the Maronite Christians, had been a passionate opponent of Nasser, having secretly encouraged Britain in its efforts at that time.

What is really foolish is for two nations like
   England & USA
to search for points of difference

No case for picking a quarrel with USA
A clear conscience—
   We have no need for self-reproach.

Churchill's notes ended:

The Middle East is all *one*
   One problem
The US have entered the Lebanon.
They are in every way justified.
They do not need our material or military help
If they did, I am assured they wd receive it.[1]

'I spent an hour or two thinking over what I would say,' Churchill wrote to Harold Macmillan on July 15, 'and came to the conclusion that I had nothing worth saying. I will turn up to support you in the Lobby. Forgive my change of plan.'[2]

On July 16, guided by Montague Browne, Churchill wrote to the President of the English-Speaking Union of the United States, to approve a plan to raise money for Anglo-American educational purposes 'and to name the fund after me'. Churchill added: 'I am very much complimented that you should wish to do this, and I think that the educational concept is most commendable, in particular if emphasis can be placed on the technological side.'[3] From this letter was born the Winston Churchill Memorial Trust, whose travelling fellowships were, in the years to come, to enable men and women 'in all parts of the Commonwealth and the United States to further their professional education through overseas study and travel'.[4]

On July 18, and again on July 30, Churchill visited Brendan Bracken in hospital. Then, on July 31, he returned to the South of France, as Lord Beaverbrook's guest at La Capponcina. 'Very hot and very fine,' he telegraphed to his wife on August 1, and he added:

---

[1] Handwritten notes, undated: Churchill papers, 2/129.

[2] 'My dear Harold', 15 July 1958: Churchill papers, 2/129. In 1921, at the Cairo Conference, Churchill, then Colonial Secretary, had established the Emir Feisal as ruler of Iraq (and his brother Abdullah as ruler of Transjordan).

[3] Letter from Churchill to Arthur Houghton Jnr, 16 July 1958: English-Speaking Union archive.

[4] Appeal proposal, as agreed at a meeting at the Pacific Union Club, San Francisco, on 14 November 1962, attended by, among others, the Duke of Edinburgh, Field Marshal Lord Alexander and Lord Baillieu (R. A. L. Morant, *The Winston Churchill Memorial Trust, Origins and Development*, Canberra, January 1983). The number of Travelling Fellowships awarded by the Winston Churchill Memorial Trust from the inauguration of the scheme in 1966 to the end of 1987 was 2,173.

Have done nothing at all except order some thin clothes. The Onasses are dining tonight. Otherwise all tranquil. Max has passed the day on his boat. I have remained ashore. Pamela lunched with us looking admirable and leaves for Venice tonight. Take my love to Maria & Christopher and the rest of the family and accept my fondest thoughts from a completely idle

W [1]

On August 7 Churchill was sent a letter from Harold Macmillan:

Dear Winston,

I hope you are having better weather than we are. We have had very poor days since you left.

I called to see Brendan last week. He is certainly very gallant and talked as well and gaily as ever.

We are rather disappointed that the summit meeting did not come off. It seems as if Khrushchev was much more impulsive than Stalin and, if possible, even more crooked. However, since I cannot go in one direction, I have decided to go in another.

Yours ever

Harold [2]

On August 8 Churchill went from La Capponcina to La Pausa for luncheon. On his return he telegraphed to Wendy and Emery Reves: 'Equally intoxicated by sunflowers and brandy. Love Winston.' [3] To Clementine Churchill, her husband wrote that day, in his own hand:

Darling,

The days pass monotonously but pleasantly & quickly. More than a week has gone since I arrived. I have done nothing but play bezique with Anthony—seven games a day!—and have won thirty shillings.

Max & Dalmeny [4] go out in their boat, wh is a flat bottomed contrivance and enables them to face rough weather. I have not accompanied them. They go along the coast, 5 or 6 hours a day, and seem to enjoy it—I think it is a bit risky—although the sea is calm & the sun shines bright. You will have to try it when you arrive.

I brought Daisy Fellowes to the Villa & we lunched together. She is vy well preserved. Lady Derby is also here & they are trying to get her for dinner again at this moment. She is vy nice and seems to have recovered from the stormy episodes of which you know.

It is vy hot & beautiful, & time passes swiftly. I *long* to have you here & I am sure you would find it agreeable, 'Toby' is on my bed at the moment & I have had a large cage constructed which serves as an exercise ground for him.

[1] Telegram despatched 1 August 1958: Churchill papers, 1/55.
[2] 'Dear Winston', 10 Downing Street, 7 August 1958: Churchill papers, 2/220.
[3] Telegram despatched from Cap d'Ail, 8 August 1958: Reves archive.
[4] Neil Archibald Primrose, Lord Dalmeny, son of the 6th Earl of Rosebery. He succeeded his father as Earl in 1974.

Before he had finished this letter, Churchill learned that Brendan Bracken had died that day. His letter continued:

We have been deeply moved by Brendan's death—but I am sure it was best for him. His will about no memorials for him made us resist a return journey tomorrow wh we had contemplated.

Darling one I am eagerly looking forward to seeing you. I rejoice that the doctors give a good report, & that progress continues steady to the eye.

This is an awful scrawl, but I write in bed & have almost lost the art of legibility.

Always your loving & devoted husband.

W [1]

'You will miss Brendan so much,' Clementine Churchill wrote from Chartwell on August 9, 'and so will Max. Please give him a message of sympathy.' [2] 'I have thought much of you also since Brendan died,' Mary Soames wrote on August 12. 'You and Max must indeed grieve for such a friend as he was.' [3] 'I know how much you loved Brendan,' Jock Colville wrote on August 11, 'and what this breach with the happier past will mean to you. You of course were everything to him and whenever I have seen him in the last few weeks he has scarcely spoken of anybody else.' [4]

Bracken was only fifty-eight years old. He had been born when Churchill was already a Member of Parliament. 'Like Sir Winston and Lord Beaverbrook,' wrote Randolph Churchill in an obituary in the *Evening Standard*, 'he had a magnanimity which transcended all pettiness and bitterness.' [5]

Churchill had known Bracken for as long as he had known Lord Cherwell, whose death a year earlier had been an equally severe blow; both men had supported him during the wilderness years before the war. Both had served under him in the war years. He had confided in both, and had enjoyed their company and companionship in good times and bad, and above all at the end of those long, difficult days, when uninhibited friendship enabled the tension and toil of war to be relaxed, at least for a few brief moments. On August 23 Churchill wrote from La Capponcina to Harold Macmillan:

My dear Harold,

Only two days ago I received your letter of August 7. Meanwhile, the end had come. He was one of my best friends and a man whose sterling qualities

---

[1] 'Darling', La Capponcina, 8 August 1958: Spencer-Churchill papers.
[2] Letter of 9 August 1958: Spencer-Churchill papers.
[3] 'Darling Papa', 12 August 1958: Churchill papers, 1/55.
[4] 'My dear Winston', 11 August 1958: Churchill papers, 2/212.
[5] Randolph Churchill, 'This was Bracken, Man of Mystery': *Evening Standard*, 8 August 1958.

we all admired. They talk of starting a memorial for him, but I do not think that a scholarship for some university would meet the case. Have you any ideas?'[1]

Churchill ended his letter with a reference to the international scene. 'I have followed as well as I can,' he wrote, 'the tangled negotiations with Khrushchev. I am very glad you are giving your mind to the job, and let me congratulate you on the remarkable response that the whole nation now gives to your conduct of power.'[2]

Churchill intended to remain at La Capponcina until the last week of September, then to accept an invitation from Aristotle Onassis, first made the previous November, to go on a cruise. In thanking Beaverbrook for his 'kindness' in making him so welcome at Cap d'Ail, Churchill wrote, on September 5, with feline news. 'I must tell you,' he wrote, 'the remarkable story about the white cat. I gave him supper last night, and the next thing I knew half an hour later was that he had brought a beautiful rat he had killed, and laid it at *my* feet. The incident was so remarkable and personal that it should be recorded.'

In his letter to Beaverbrook, who had just left for Canada and the United States, and had written to thank Churchill for having been his guest, Churchill went on in more intimate vein: 'I am very glad that you liked my companionship. It has now become very feeble, though none the less warm.' Beaverbrook's letter had made him realize, Churchill wrote, 'that the ties we formed so many years ago and strengthened in the days of war have lasted out our lifetime'.[3]

---

[1] In his will, Brendan Bracken had given instructions that he wanted no memorial, and that all his papers should be destroyed. The papers were destroyed. On the initiative of Jock Colville, however, £30,000 was raised from Brendan Bracken's friends to build the reading room at Churchill College, Cambridge, Bracken's only public memorial. Bracken himself endowed an altar in a side-chapel in the monastery of the Benedictine monks at Ampleforth.

[2] 'My dear Harold', 'Personal', La Capponcina, 23 August 1958: Churchill papers, 2/220.

[3] 'My dear Max', La Capponcina, 5 September 1958: Churchill papers, 2/211.

64

'The closing days or years of life'

======

FRIDAY 12 September 1958 would mark the Golden Wedding of Churchill and his wife; in the first week of September they learned that their four children would give them, as a Golden Wedding gift, an avenue of golden roses in the garden at Chartwell. As this could not be planted until late in October, or flower until the following year, they had decided to present their parents with a large illuminated vellum book, in which there would be a dedication, a list of the twenty-eight varieties of roses to be planted, a plan of the proposed avenue, and twenty-eight watercolour paintings of each rose, each done by a different British artist.[1]

The Golden Wedding was celebrated at La Capponcina: 'one of Winston's horses, Welsh Abbot, had enough sense of occasion', Mary Soames recalled, 'to win a race at Doncaster'.[2] Randolph Churchill and his daughter Arabella were the two members of the family present to join the celebrating couple at La Capponcina that day: they had flown out with the Golden Rose book. From London, Sarah Churchill wrote that day to her father: 'I wonder if you know how many people share in the joy & pride of today? And what another aspect of radiance you both have shed upon daily life by the way you have led your private lives.'[3]

No interviews were given to the Press, and no public ceremony undertaken. But the public response was such that Mary Soames wrote to her mother a week later: 'What moving and touching tributes! I

---

[1] These artists included Paul Maze, Duncan Grant, John Nash and Augustus John. Others who agreed to paint a rose were Cecil Beaton, R. A. Butler, the 1st Earl of Birkenhead's widow Margaret, and Randolph Churchill's friend Natalie Bevan. (Natalie Bevan, 'The Golden Story of the Golden Roses': *Woman's Own*, 31 January 1959.)

[2] Mary Soames, *Clementine Churchill*, page 466.

[3] Letter of 12 September 1958: Mary Soames, *Clementine Churchill*, page 466.

felt so proud & so gratified that your great achievements, & all your long years together should receive the praise due. You see now what you both together mean to hundreds & thousands of people.'[1]

On September 22, Churchill left the South of France on the yacht *Christina* for a Mediterranean cruise, as the guest of Aristotle Onassis. Comfort was the main aspect of life on board *Christina*, every aspect of which was adapted to pleasure and relaxation. Here, on this first of what were to be eight cruises, Churchill was able to find a gentle repose, with no demands made upon him. Roy Howells, who accompanied Churchill on the cruise, later recalled:

On board the yacht the usual card games were played. Bezique was the favourite and each time the cards came out so did Sir Winston's special green velvet table cover which he took everywhere. For some reason he also took with him a maroon cover. It was widely reported at the time that Onassis and his guests played for high stakes but in actual fact it was only a penny a point.

Howells's account continued:

Onassis' yacht was extremely luxurious, even down to the gold bath taps made in the form of dolphins. It had its own small hospital and a laundry run by a Greek husband and wife who managed to do dry cleaning in record time. There were telephones in every bedroom, each of which had its own bathroom. Air-conditioning was fitted throughout and the owner had gone to enormous expense to have a Cretan mosaic dance-floor converted at the touch of a switch to a swimming pool. The salon had gold and silver ashtrays in the form of sea shells and the salon centre piece was one of Sir Winston's landscapes.

Each night a film would be shown. Howells later wrote:

Strangely enough the yacht, with all its gadgets, had only one film projector. This meant that at the end of every reel there was a short interval while the new reel was put on. A general discussion about the film used to ensue and any parts that Sir Winston had missed, or could not understand, were filled in by his host. The films went on until about midnight, everyone usually turning in at about 1 a.m.

During the day, Howells added, the 'more energetic guests would swim, but Onassis was usually to be found sitting on the deck cross-legged near Sir Winston's chair, listening to his views'.[2]

The cruise of September 1958 ended at Gibraltar, where, Churchill wrote to Beaverbrook on October 10, 'we were very well received by everybody, including the apes'.[3] 'Everybody' included the Governor

[1] Letter of 19 September 1958: Mary Soames, *Clementine Churchill*, page 466.
[2] Roy Howells recollections: *Simply Churchill*, London 1965, pages 31–2.
[3] 'My dear Max', 10 October 1958: Churchill papers, 2/211.

of Gibraltar, his ADC John Crookshank, and the crew of HMS *Eagle*. John Crookshank later recalled 'looking down from the bridge of the aircraft carrier *Eagle* as she moved to her berth at Gibraltar, on to the quarter deck of Aristotle Onassis' yacht *Christina* which was lying at a mooring in the harbour, and seeing Sir Winston looking up at the great warship with a look of pride on his face'. The officers and men, he added, 'looking down at the diminutive figure on the yacht's quarter-deck were aglow with pride and excitement. . . .' [1]

Once home, Churchill made a special journey to Worthing, to see his daughter Sarah in the part of Rose in Terence Rattigan's play, *Variations on a Theme*. 'He sat with his party in the third row,' Roy Howells later recalled, 'and I remember him turning to a man sitting near him and saying, "Don't worry, the cigars will not come out during the performance."' [2]

In the first two weeks of October, Churchill went three times to the races, to watch his own horses run, once at Lingfield and twice at Ascot. On October 7 he wrote to Wendy Reves:

My dear Wendy,

I am looking forward so much to coming out to Pausaland again. I thought you would not mind my delaying the visit a little, because I wanted very much to see my horses run at Ascot on Saturday. But I will come on Sunday morning, and I am delighted to hear of the good weather you are enjoying. Here we have a change for the better, though much qualified. I have got out of the Royal dinner party to which I had promised to go on the 20th, so that I can stay till the end of the first week in November. It will be nice sitting in front of your lavender.

Yours affectionately,

Winston [3]

On October 12 Churchill returned to La Pausa. Two days later he wrote to his wife, in his own hand:

My darling One,

Yesterday, Monday, was a perfect day. Today begins not quite so good— it is cloudy, but I think it will improve. We shall see. All is peace & quiet here. It is six months—so they calculate—since I was last here. They all send appropriate messages. I am passing the morning in bed—reading a book about ancient Greece wh is rather good. Tomorrow I shall try to paint, and Murray is getting the outfit ready.—But I am doubtful, inert & lazy.

I wonder what you will be doing & when you will set off for Chartwell. Would you give some food to the fish? They are vy appreciative. And the black swans. I never visited them this time. It was too wet for the car, & I do not care about walking—much.

[1] John Crookshank recollctions: letter to the author, 9 June 1977.
[2] Roy Howells recollections: *Simply Churchill*, page 33.
[3] 'My dear Wendy', London, 7 October 1958: Reves papers.

You have all my fondest love my dearest. The closing days or years of life are grey and dull, but I am lucky to have you at my side. I send you my best love & many kisses.

Always your devoted

W

'We had Onassis to dinner last night,' Churchill added. 'He was vy lively.'[1]

On October 22 Churchill wrote to his wife again, his letter dictated from La Pausa:

My darling,

The days pass quickly and peacefully here. We see a few old friends at meals. The papers seem to hold no news. The most interesting thing we have is Dr Galleazzi-Liza who Emery tells me came to see him two years ago when the Pope was in excellent health and proposed to sell him for an enormous sum of money the aftermath of his illness. Emery scornfully refused him, but was not at all surprised at what has occurred. He, Emery, had intended to expose the man, but it has all come out without his being called upon to intervene. I think he will be made an example of.

We are going to lunch with the Onasses tomorrow on their yacht, and I will deliver your beautifully framed photograph to Mrs O, and give her suitable messages from you.

We are examining the possibility of going to lunch next Sunday upon the *Randolph*, an American aircraft carrier. They have the idea that they can pick us up in one of their special helicopters and drop us on the ship itself. We have invited the Captain and his wife to lunch on Friday to look into the possibilities. I have never been in a helicopter, and would like to make a voyage which would certainly save a great deal of toil.

I shall look forward to reading Monty's book when you have done with it. He seems to have stirred the waters up a little bit. I am personally keeping myself from reading a copy, and have not indulged in the *Sunday Times* serials.[2]

Darling, I have found very little to say, but I am enjoying myself very much, and my health is pronounced by Doctor Roberts to be much better than it was two years ago.

Always your loving husband,

Winston

PS I am delighted that you will come to Paris. Shall I make arrangements through the Embassy for you to stay there the night before, (November 5)? It may be that Anthony will already have worked this out for you. I have not been in Paris for five years.

W[3]

---

[1] 'My darling One', La Pausa, 14 October 1958: Spencer-Churchill papers.

[2] Montgomery had just published his memoirs.

[3] 'My darling', marked in Churchill's own hand 'Personal', La Pausa, 22 October 1958: Spencer-Churchill papers.

'I hope you have been having a lovely time at Roquebrune,' Jock Colville wrote on October 29, 'and that the helicopter was fun!'[1]

On November 6 Churchill left La Pausa for Paris. On his last night Wendy Reves prepared a special meal for him, and with it a special menu:

Déjeuner d'Au-Revoir

—

Soup Galiwag

—

Rôti de Boeuf Maniakapoo

—

Tarte Waligag

—

Café

—

WOW!!!

The wines which accompanied this feast were a 1947 Dom Pérignon champagne, and a 1906 brand Fine Champagne brandy.[2]

From Roquebrune, Churchill flew to Paris, where on November 6 he was decorated by de Gaulle with the Croix de la Libération, the highest award given to those who had served with the Free French forces, or with the Resistance. He was much moved by this honour, and in the garden of the Hôtel Matignon where the ceremony took place, with his son present as a newspaper reporter, he spoke a few words of thanks in English. 'I have often made speeches in French,' he said, 'but that was wartime, and I do not wish to subject you to the ordeals of darker days.' Churchill then recalled how, when he had seen de Gaulle 'in the sombre days of 1940, I said, "Here is the Constable of France,"' and he added: 'How well he lived up to that title!' 'The future,' Churchill ended his remarks, 'is uncertain, but we can be sure that if Britain and France, who for so long have been the vanguard of the Western civilization, stand together, with our Empires, our American friends, and our other allies and associates, then we have grounds for sober confidence and high hope. I thank you all for the honour you have done me. Vive la France!'[3]

'Winston looked so well & happy when we met in Paris,' Clementine Churchill wrote to Wendy Reves on November 11, 'thanks to his

---

[1] 'My dear Winston', 29 October 1958: Churchill papers, 2/212. Colville had written to seek Churchill's support for an appeal to raise £25,000 to build 'a worthy memorial' for Brendan Bracken. Churchill subscribed £1,000. This was for the reading room at Churchill College, Cambridge.

[2] Menu, 5 November 1958: Reves papers.

[3] Speech of 6 November 1958: Randolph S. Churchill (editor), *The Unwritten Alliance*, page 306. Recording: BBC Written Archives Centre, Library No. LP 24659.

happy time with you and your glorious weather.'[1] On his return to London, Churchill wrote to Wendy Reves:

My dear Wendy,

Our visit to Paris and de Gaulle's reception were a brilliant success, as you may have gathered from the wireless. But that in no way lessened my gratitude to you for all your kindness to me during my stay at Pausaland. It was really most delightful, and I think that our helicopter journey to the giant American ship was an exhilarating incident. I must say I admired your courage at close quarters to the machine, and I am sure that on patriotic grounds you must have enjoyed this day above all others. For my part, all the days were pleasant, and it was particularly nice being so much alone with you and Emery. Thank you so much for your hospitality and goodwill.

If you should decide to come to England, kindly let me know. If, however, you carry out your interesting plans, don't forget to give my love to your Mama. If in the course of my wanderings I should include America, I shall look forward to seeing her and you. But I think that on the whole I shall avoid a winter visit to the United States. We have not made up our minds about the future, but we will do so in the next fortnight. Here we have had lovely weather, and Chartwell has been looking its best with autumn leaves.

Clemmie sends all her best wishes to you and Emery.

With much love

Yours ever,

W[2]

Returning to London, Churchill became, as he wrote to Lord Beaverbrook on November 14, a 'regular attendant' of the House of Commons 'on the three inside days of the week' and was wondering 'whether I can screw myself up to make a speech'. He was going to have a 'preliminary' speech in his constituency, 'which is very quiet'.[3]

Among Churchill's evening excursions after his return from France was a dinner at the Other Club, the first to be held since Brendan Bracken's death. After dinner he spoke about his friend. 'Since we last met,' he said, 'we have suffered a great, a swingeing blow. Brendan has gone. He had been Honorary Secretary of the Other Club for twenty-one years and a member for five years before that. We can all remember how in dark times his spirit, his charm and wit were able to rise superior to personal sorrow or grave events.' Churchill added: 'He bore his illness with courage and patience. Now he is no more, and we all feel the poorer for his loss.'[4]

---

[1] 'My dear Wendy', London, 11 November 1958: Reves papers.

[2] 'My dear Wendy', London, November 1958: Reves papers.

[3] 'My dear Max', 14 November 1958: Churchill papers, 2/211.

[4] Remarks recalled seven days later by Anthony Montague Browne, in a letter to Jock Colville, 27 November 1958: Churchill papers, 2/343.

On November 27 Churchill was driven to Harrow School; it was the eighteenth time, he said, that he had heard the tunes and sung the words which 'have inspired my actions and my life'.[1] Three days later, he was eighty-four.

Under Montague Browne's guidance, and with constant advice from Jock Colville, Churchill continued to guard his investments, which in 1958 were in excess of £60,000 in share value.[2] On December 4, in thanking the financier Thomas Hazlerigg for the regular reports of Rea Brothers Ltd, Churchill wrote: 'It is very helpful to me that you should keep me informed in this way.'[3] Among the regular monthly payments which Churchill made during 1958 were £600 to his wife, £40 to his daughter-in-law Pamela, and £1 to his former cook housekeeper, Mrs G. Landemare.[4]

Since 1945 Churchill had also sent £5 a year to Munuswamy, his former servant of Bangalore days in 1894 and 1895. Munuswamy's last letter was to be sent from Bangalore in May 1959, but he had collapsed and died while dictating it to his wife. 'Do you wish to send his Widow a message and a final present?' asked Montague Browne. 'Yes,' Churchill replied, and a further £5 was sent.[5]

Montague Browne later recalled how Churchill had himself suggested 'that there were a whole host of Munuswamys, the original having died many years ago!'[6]

On December 21 General de Gaulle was elected President of France. Churchill at once asked Montague Browne to draft a message for de Gaulle. Its final sentence read, as drafted: 'May your tenure of this great office be one of peace and prosperity.' Churchill amended this in his own hand to read: 'May your tenure of this great office be one of Peace that none regrets and of prosperity that all enjoy.'[7]

---

[1] Speech of 27 November 1958: Churchill papers, 2/336.

[2] By 8 January 1960 the value of Churchill's share holdings had risen to £77,227: the equivalent of £623,700 in 1987.

[3] Letter of 4 December 1958: Churchill papers, 1/108. Churchill had held stocks in Rea Brothers since 1929, when he had been appointed a director of W. Cory & Son, coal factors, merchants and lightermen, who had a controlling interest in Rea. For ten years he had earned £1,000 a year as a director, resigning his directorship on entering the government in September 1939.

[4] Financial notes, 1958: Churchill papers, 1/3.

[5] 'Sir Winston', initialled 'AMB', 1 June 1959: Churchill papers, 2/194.

[6] Montague Browne recollections: notes for the author, 24 March 1987.

[7] 'Draft message to General de Gaulle', sent by telegram via the Foreign Office, 22 December 1958: Squerryes Lodge Archive.

Before speaking in his constituency, as he had told Lord Beaverbrook he would, Churchill spoke first at a meeting of his Constituency Party workers specially convened for him at the Kensington Palace Hotel, one minute's drive from Hyde Park Gate. His speech, drafted, as his Paris and Harrow speeches had been, by Montague Browne, noted the death in Iraq of the King, his uncle, and his Prime Minister, Nuri Pasha. 'These three men,' he said, 'were most loyal servants of their country and true friends of their allies. They were swept away in the convulsion of the Arab peoples that is still going on. I trust that counsels of peace and moderation will prevail, and that the Arab peoples and Israel will get the long period of prosperity and peaceful development they need.'

During his speech, Churchill also spoke of how 'We all fervently wish' for the success of France, under 'my old friend and wartime colleague' de Gaulle, in restoring the French economy, 'which is potentially so prosperous'.[1]

Merely to speak these words in public was a courageous effort for a man of eighty-four, in uncertain health.

On 7 January 1959 Churchill and his wife left London for Marrakech, where they stayed for just over five weeks. Jock and Lady Margaret Colville and Lady Monckton flew out with them to Marrakech as Churchill's guests, in an Olympic airliner provided especially by Onassis for the flight. 'When we arrived,' Colville later recalled, 'there was an enormous Guard of Honour provided by the King of Morocco, but Winston, aged 84, pulled himself together, strode down the steps of the airliner and inspected the whole Guard of Honour without showing any signs of age or illness.'[2]

After his return to England, Colville wrote to Churchill, on January 26: 'Meg and I loved our stay at Marrakech, every minute of it, and are more than grateful to you for including us in such an agreeable party. We left with sorrow and are still pining for that delectable view of the Atlas, for our nightly games of poker and for the pleasure of your company. The whole excursion was entirely delightful.' Colville went on to give Churchill news of the latest developments concerning Churchill College:

We had a very successful Press Conference about Churchill College yester-

---

[1] Speech, 6 January 1959: Randolph S. Churchill (editor), *The Unwritten Alliance*, pages 307–10.

[2] Sir John Colville recollections: letter to the author, 12 November 1986.

day. The press turned up in force, sending leading representatives (for instance Colin Coote himself came to represent the D.T) and Lord Weeks handled them admirably.[1] As far as I can see only *The Times*—which has all along been captious and tiresome—published a disquieting article.[2] Having seen the long-haired and insalubrious reporter whom they sent, I was certainly not surprised. Great stress was laid by Lord W on your anxiety to get the college operating before it was completed and on the plans for doing this.[3]

On the day that Colville wrote this letter, Sir John Cockcroft, the physicist, was appointed by Churchill as the first Master of the new college.[4]

On the day the Colvilles left, Clementine Churchill wrote to her daughter Mary, 'poor Papa fell into the doldrums—He is better now & has started a picture from the terrace outside his bed-room.' Her letter continued: 'Thank God Papa is blooming in his health. His memory fails a little more day by day & he is getting deafer. But he is well.'[5]

On February 17 Churchill spent his last night at Marrakech before joining Aristotle Onassis's yacht for a second cruise, this time to the Canary Islands and along the Moroccan coast. His dinner guests on that last night ashore were Ari and Tina Onassis and Margot Fonteyn.[6] Nonie Montague Browne was also on board. In her diary she recorded the progress of the cruise: Lanzarote on February 20, and Santz Cruz on February 21, where, after a tour of the island by car, Spanish dancers, including children, came on board after dinner to entertain them.

February 22 saw *Christina* at Las Palmas and February 26 at the Moroccan port of Agadir, scene of the European political crisis of 1911 which had helped to propel Churchill into Ministerial responsibility for the naval defence of Britain. On February 27 *Christina*

[1] Lord Weeks, the Chairman of Vickers Ltd. from 1948 to 1956 and of Vickers Nuclear Engineering; in 1940 he had been Brigadier General Staff, Home Forces, and in 1941 Director-General of Army Equipment.

[2] On 26 January 1959 *The Times* University correspondent reported from Cambridge that on the previous day Churchill College had been recognized as an 'approved foundation'. It added, however, that the undergraduate newspaper *Varsity* had published the result of what it called a survey of undergraduate opinion made during the week, 'which showed a slight balance against the proposal'.

[3] 'My dear Winston', 26 January 1959: Churchill papers, 1/91.

[4] John Cockcroft, born 1897, Director of the Atomic Energy Research Establishment, Harwell, from 1946 to 1958. Knighted 1948. Order of Merit 1957. Master of Churchill College, Cambridge from 1959 until his death in 1967. It had been agreed that Churchill himself should appoint the first Master and that subsequently it should be a Crown appointment.

[5] Letter of 28 January 1959: Mary Soames, *Clementine Churchill*, page 468.

[6] Note dated Marrakech, 17 February 1959: Churchill papers, 1/91.

was at sea, reaching Tangier on the following day, where Bryce Nairn and his wife came on board; Churchill had known them since his illness in North Africa in 1944.[1]

Churchill returned to London from his cruise on March 2. 'The weather was on the whole kind,' he wrote to Lady Violet Bonham Carter, 'and I painted one or two pictures.'[2]

The return to London was brief, from the early evening of March 2 to the morning of March 6, but it was busy in the extreme. On March 3 Churchill saw his solicitor, Anthony Moir, in the morning, lunched with Randolph, and spent the afternoon and evening in the House of Commons. On March 4 he first saw the dermatologist, Dr R. M. B. MacKenna, and then Lord Moran, spent part of the afternoon at the Royal Academy, went on to the House of Commons where he saw Harold Macmillan, returned to Hyde Park Gate for a meeting of the Churchill College Trustees, then went to see Gilbert and Sullivan's *The Gondoliers* with Jock and Lady Margaret Colville. On March 5, after a second meeting with Anthony Moir, he went down to Chartwell, returning to London that evening for dinner at the Other Club. The dinner had been the principal purpose of his return to London.[3]

'He did thrive on to-ing and fro-ing,' Miss Pugh later recalled. 'He thrived on the contrast, being very lackadaisical, then remarkably active. If he came back for three days he would do ever so much, and go back refreshed.'[4]

On the morning of March 6 Churchill flew from London to Nice, and returned to La Pausa. Two days later he sent his wife a dictated account of his arrival:

Clemmie, Beloved One,

I arrived in due course and was met by the Préfet and Emery Reves. I found Nice and Roquebrune and all between wrapped in fog and shrouded impenetrably by clouds. Rain poured on my unfortunate meeters who had to wait three quarters of an hour while the delayed landing took place. However, they all seemed pleased to see me, and Emery drove me on here as quick as he could.

We had a second day of rain yesterday, but today, Sunday, all is bright, although more storms are predicted passing along the coast in our direction. I have not been out so far, but unless a shower intervenes I shall do so before lunch.

Wendy, who came to meet me, was delighted to get your letter, and she will no doubt answer it herself. She has presented me with a gold clip which holds attached to my coat a white napkin. I think you will like this when you

---

[1] Nonie Montague Browne diary, February 1959: Lady Sargant papers.
[2] Letter of 5 March 1959: Churchill papers, 2/520.
[3] Churchill Engagements Calendar, March 1959: Churchill papers.
[4] Doreen Pugh recollections: in conversation with the author, 18 June 1987.

see it, as it prevents food from dropping on my clothes. In fact it is the very thing which you would have suggested yourself.

Today they are all voting all over France and I presume, though I do not know, that de Gaulle will triumph.[1]

I sent for Dr Roberts and he is dealing with all my ticklings which have come back in a very tiresome fashion.

On being given his letter to sign, Churchill added in his own hand:

My darling,

I think a great deal about you & your troubles. I hope for a letter soon to tell me about Sarah. I think they treated her vy roughly at Liverpool & roused her fiery spirit. I hope she will convince you that her affliction is a part of the periodic difficulties which are common to women at the change of life, & above all that she will persevere at her profession.

I am so sorry for the burden this rests on you & hope that staying with Mary & Christopher will relieve your troubles. Dearest my thoughts are with you. It all falls on you: 'Poor lamb!'. With all my love I remain a wreck (but with its flag still flying) & send you my best love and many kisses. I await your letter.

I found Toby safely here & he just got on my elbow to remind me that I must mention him in writing to you, or he wd be offended.

Your loving husband

Winston[2]

Churchill ended the page with eight kisses.

Churchill's letter referred to Sarah Churchill's arrest in Liverpool. After an evening on stage, she had tried to find her way back to her hotel, muddling the Adelphi which she knew and the Lord Nelson which she did not. Those who found her—'slightly distracted', as she recalled—instead of calling for a taxi, called for the police. She was taken to court, fined £2, and dismissed. The case was blown up mightily by the Press.[3] Of Anthony Montague Browne, who did what he could to help, Clementine Churchill wrote, on March 10: 'He is a good friend.'[4]

On March 13 Churchill wrote to his wife, his letter dictated to Miss Pugh:

My darling,

I have been thinking about the Sarah incident and I have come to the

---

[1] In the municipal elections which took place throughout France on 9 March 1959 there was a considerable, but in power terms ineffectual, swing from the Gaullists to the Communists. In Paris the Communist percentage of the vote rose from 19.5 (in November 1958) to 27.7. De Gaulle, who had become President in December 1958, remained as President until his death in June 1969.

[2] 'Clemmie, Beloved One' and 'My darling', La Pausa, 8 March 1959: Spencer-Churchill papers.

[3] Sarah Churchill, *Keep on Dancing*, page 179.

[4] Letter of 10 March 1959: Churchill papers, 1/135.

conclusion that it went off as well as could be expected. I am very glad that Sarah is to do another three weeks in the provinces, and I hope she will realise how much it means to her if she can clear her reputation by good behaviour in the future.

I hope your dinner with the Cholmondeleys went off as expected and that you were victorious in bezique.

We have been invited to go to the Palace for luncheon on Monday and all three have accepted. Tomorrow, Saturday, we lunch with the Préfet. The day after we shall go on board the yacht, and on Friday we lunch with Daisy Fellowes.

'It is fine today though misty,' Churchill added in a shaky hand. 'I have spent long hours in bed. Toby has just bitten off the flicks of blue which he sends you with his love, and mine dearest. Your loving husband, Winston.' [1]

The 'Palace' invitation was to Monaco, to lunch with Prince Rainier and Princess Grace. The other guests, Miss Pugh told Churchill, would be the Queen of Spain, Emery and Wendy Reves, 'and a few officials of the Palace'. [2] On the morning of the lunch Churchill again dictated a letter to his wife from La Pausa with news of his activities:

We are off this morning at 12.30 for lunch with the Prince at the Palace. The Queen of Spain is to be there.

We have had two days of brilliant weather, and I walked each day in the garden. Yesterday Paul Maze and his wife came to lunch. He talked a good deal about painting, and will come and paint with me. I found it too cold to go on painting yesterday morning, but I will try again tomorrow. It is not quite so bright today.

I think it will be best to put the celebrations of your Birthday off until Sunday, April 12, at Chartwell. I choose Sunday because then Sarah will be able to come. Also it will give me more time to make the necessary arrangements after I return on Monday the 6th. Let me know if this will be convenient.

Tender love my darling
Your affectionate loving

W [3]

Painting was Churchill's principal activity at La Pausa that month. He had known the painter Paul Maze since their first meeting on the Western Front in 1916; they had been painting together in Normandy in August 1939, when Churchill, learning that war was imminent,

[1] 'My darling', La Pausa, 13 March 1959: Spencer-Churchill papers.
[2] 'Sir Winston', initialled 'DP', 12 March 1959: Churchill papers, 1/149.
[3] 'Dearest Clemmie', La Pausa, 16 March 1959: Spencer-Churchill papers.

had hurried back to London.[1] Painting now provided Churchill with solace and pleasure. More than thirty years earlier, in an article for the *Strand* magazine, he had written:

One by one the more vigorous sports and exacting games fall away. Exceptional exertions are purchased only by a more pronounced and more prolonged fatigue. Muscles may relax, and feet and hands slow down; the nerve of youth and manhood may become less trusty. But painting is a friend who makes no undue demands, excites to no exhausting pursuits, keeps faithful pace even with feeble steps, and holds her canvas as a screen between us and the envious eyes of Time or the surly advance of Decrepitude. Happy are the painters, for they shall not be lonely. Light and colour, peace and hope, will keep company to the end, or almost to the end, of the day.[2]

From London, Clementine Churchill sent her husband full and regular reports. The main news while he was at La Pausa was of an exhibition of Churchill's paintings at the Royal Academy, his first one-man show in Britain, and, after Kansas City, the second of his painting career. 'Your pictures are attracting such big crowds,' she wrote. 'Up to last night 38,397 persons had seen them. This was in 13 days,' and she added: 'Tomorrow, Ted Heath the Chief Whip is coming to luncheon.'[3] To his wife, Churchill wrote in the last week of March, after Montague Browne had reached La Pausa:

Clemmie darling,

I am getting better slowly from a curious illness which has lasted a whole week mostly spent in bed. Anthony brought me news & relief & will tell you about it. I come home in a week and will occupy myself with your Birthday celebrations which are fixed for the 12th.

The entertainment here of the Prince & Princess was a great success, and we had yesterday Ari and Tina.

With all my love

Your loving husband,

W[4]

It was on March 24 that Prince Rainier and Princess Grace had lunched at La Pausa. Three days later, on Good Friday, Lord Beaverbrook had been the guest, and on March 28, Onassis. On Easter Monday, March 30, the former French Prime Minister, Paul

---

[1] In 1934, in his Introduction to Paul Maze's war memoirs, *A Frenchman in Khaki*, Churchill wrote: '.. we have the battle-scenes of Armageddon recorded by one who not only loved the fighting troops and shared their perils, but perceived the beauties of light and shade, of form and colour, of which even the horrors of war cannot rob the progress of the sun.' Maze was often in England between the wars, taking up residence in England in 1940. In 1950 he married (as his second wife) Jessie Lawrie; she figures in many of his finest paintings and pastels.

[2] *Strand* magazine, December 1921–January 1922; reprinted in Winston S. Churchill, *Thoughts and Adventures*, London 1932.

[3] Letter of 25 March 1959: Churchill papers, 1/135.

[4] 'Clemmie darling', 29 March 1959, La Pausa: Spencer-Churchill papers.

Reynaud, came to lunch.[1] Nearly twenty years had passed since Churchill's dramatic visits to France, amid the onward march of the German army, to try to support Reynaud's efforts not to give in to the less audacious members of his Cabinet and surrender.

The first week of April, Churchill left La Pausa for several excursions: to lunch with Onassis and Paul Maze at the Château de Madrid on April 1, to lunch with Somerset Maugham on April 2, and to dine with Lord Beaverbrook on April 3. Two days later, on April 5, at La Pausa, President Coty was the luncheon guest. On April 6, the day on which Churchill was to fly back to London, Onassis came to see him at eleven o'clock, and Beaverbrook for lunch.[2]

Churchill reached London on the afternoon of April 6. That evening, after seeing Lord Moran and Dr MacKenna, there was a family dinner party. Family matters were also in Churchill's mind two days later, on April 8, when his former Principal Private Secretary, Sir Leslie Rowan, came to dinner, and 'was able to report to him', as Rowan later recalled, 'that I had carried out his instructions to the letter'. These instructions, given to Rowan during the war, a few months after his marriage, had arisen during the following conversation:

'How many children have you?'

'None, sir,'—in a rather surprised tone of voice, in view of my recent marriage.

'Oh, and how many do you propose to have?'

'We have not come to any final view on that yet, sir. But how many should we have?'

Without any hesitation, Churchill replied: 'You should have four.'

I could not leave it at that, so I asked: 'Why?'

Again, without any hesitation: 'One to reproduce your wife, one to reproduce yourself, one for the increase in population, and one in case of accident.'[3]

Following his return to London, Churchill began to prepare for a considerable ordeal, a speech in his constituency. A week before he was to give it, he suffered a small stroke. On April 15 he was examined by Sir Russell Brain, who advised him to cancel any speaking plans, if he had them. Churchill told Brain about his constituency speech, fixed for April 20, then added: 'I cannot cancel it without giving a reason.

[1] Churchill Engagements Calendar, March 1959: Churchill papers.

[2] Churchill Engagements Calendar, April 1959: Churchill papers.

[3] Sir Leslie Rowan recollections: Sir John Wheeler-Bennett (editor), *Action This Day*, page 264. Churchill himself had four children before 1920: Diana (born 1909), Randolph (born 1911), Sarah (born 1914) and Marigold (born 1919). Following Marigold's death in 1921, at the age of 2¾, he had a fifth child, Mary (born 1922).

I should have to tell them about this, and I could not then take part in the election. Macmillan has asked me to take some part. What does it matter if I do break down?'[1]

On April 16 Churchill invited his Constituency Chairman, Alderman Forbes, to lunch. 'Being eighty-four,' Forbes later recalled, 'Sir Winston wished to make sure that he was correct in offering himself as a candidate at the forthcoming General Election.' Forbes added: 'He graciously asked me to reassure him that by so doing he was not blocking any aspirations I had in that direction. He received that assurance. . . .'[2]

That same night, Churchill dined at the Other Club, a tenacious gesture, even a defiant one, for someone so recently in pain and unable to speak properly. 'Winston scarcely spoke to the man on his left,' Sir Hartley Shawcross told Lord Moran on the following day, having himself been told it by Lord Goddard, 'and when something was said to him he seemed to connect for perhaps one or two sentences and then rang off.'[3]

As he was determined to do, on April 20, only four days after this Other Club dinner, and a week after his attack, Churchill was driven to Woodford to speak in his constituency. 'It is a long time since I have made a speech in public,' he began. Speaking slowly and in a voice at times barely audible, he noted that in a recent speech at Leipzig, Nikita Khrushchev had referred to him as the author of the Cold War. 'I am certainly responsible,' he said, 'for pointing out to the free world in 1946, at Fulton in America, the perils inherent in complacently accepting the advance of Communist imperialism. But apart from this, my conscience is clear. It was not Britain,' Churchill went on to explain, 'who in 1939 so cynically compounded with Hitler, and later so greedily devoured the half of helpless and hapless Poland, while the Nazis took what was left. It is not Britain who has advanced her frontiers, absorbing many sovereign peoples who had made great contributions to civilized history. On the contrary, I suppose we are the only nation who fought throughout the war against Germany, and who, far from receiving any reward, have greatly diminished in our tenure on the surface of the globe.'

Churchill went on to say, in a speech prepared for him by Montague Browne:

But we are very willing to forget old scores. I seek, and have always sought, nothing but peace with the Russians, just as after the War I did my utmost

---

[1] Moran diary, 15 April 1959: *The Struggle for Survival*, page 749.

[2] Alderman Forbes recollections: letter to the author, 6 July 1987. Forbes served as Churchill's Constituency Chairman from 1956 to 1961.

[3] Moran diary, 17 April 1959: *The Struggle for Survival*, page 749.

to bring Germany back into the circle of the European family. Both Russia and England have all to gain and nothing to lose from peace. The Soviets hope that the doctrines of Karl Marx may eventually prevail. We on our side trust and believe that, as the mild and ameliorating influence of prosperity begins at last to uplift the Communist World, so they will be more inclined to live at ease with their neighbours. This is our hope. We must not be rigid in our expression of it; we must make allowances for justifiable Russian fears; we must be patient and firm.[1]

Many years earlier, before the Second World War, when asked by a friend what he had said in a particular speech, Churchill had replied: 'I sang my usual song.' Now, though he could no longer write the speeches in which he had sought to guide the post-war world, he could still speak the words whose meaning was central to his convictions of the previous fifty years.

At the end of his speech, which had lasted for twenty-two minutes, Churchill told his constituents that he was ready once again to offer himself as their candidate. This announcement was received 'with tumultuous applause'.[2]

As Churchill came off the platform he turned to Montague Browne with the words: 'Now for America.'[3] A few days later he decided to write to Wendy Reves, his letter drafted by Montague Browne:

I have been so far from well since I returned that I have had the greatest difficulty in getting through my various functions. The one in the Constituency was certainly the most severe, but I managed it all right after all. I am now better, and am going to America to stay with the President on the 4th of May.

It was so nice of you to have me out there and I shall propose myself again some time to you and Emery.

Churchill then wrote at the beginning of this letter 'My dear Wendy', replaced 'out there' by 'at Pausaland', and added in his own shaky hand: 'With all good wishes my dear Wendy & best of love. Your own devoted W.'[4]

On April 23, as he had made clear to Montague Browne, Churchill made his plans for a visit to the United States, informing Bernard Baruch that he would arrive in Washington on May 4, go to New York on May 8 and return to London on May 10. 'Clemmie is still not well,' he added, 'and will not be accompanying me.' His 'whole party' would be Anthony Montague Browne, Sheppard his valet, and

---

[1] Speech of 20 April 1959: Randolph S. Churchill (editor), *The Unwritten Alliance*, pages 311–15. This speech has been misdated in *The Unwritten Alliance*, having been inadvertently dated a month earlier.

[2] Mary Soames, *Clementine Churchill*, page 475.

[3] Moran diary, 20 April 1959: *The Struggle for Survival*, page 750.

[4] 'My dear Wendy', 28 Hyde Park Gate, April 1959: Reves papers.

Sergeant Murray of Scotland Yard.[1] That same day, Montague Browne wrote to Baruch:

You will have had by the same post Sir Winston's letter about the visit. I should tell you for your strictly private information that Sir Winston has not been very well, and we were in doubt as to whether he should go. However, he is determined to visit America again, so that is that! I know that you will safeguard him from fatigue as much as possible.

If it can be arranged for him to have a bell that rings in Sheppard's room, this is the best arrangement, as he needs him at quite frequent intervals.[2]

Montague Browne also wrote that day to Lord Nicholas Gordon-Lennox, 2nd Secretary at the British Embassy in Washington:

I think that the Ambassador should know that Sir Winston has not been well lately, and we have all hoped that he would cancel his visit. However, he is resolutely determined not to do this, so we are making the best of it and endeavouring to minimise fatigue.

As you know, he is declining all invitations outside the programme you have so kindly arranged for him. He is not making any speeches, and although I have no doubt that he can cope with the remarks on arrival at either New York or Washington, we would like to keep them to a minimum. In particular, it would be best for him not to be over-run with the Press at both places on arrival. Washington, the terminal point, would seem to be the logical place for him to be greeted and say a few words.

We hope that it will be possible for there to be no speeches at the luncheons or dinners. Of course, Sir Winston is almost certain to get up at the end of the meal and say a few sentences of thanks to his hosts.

We should like, if possible, to minimise the amount of walking he has to do, and in particular the climbing of stairs. Sheppard, his valet, is a trained nurse, and looks after him very well. Perhaps it could be arranged for a bell to ring from Sir Winston's bedroom to Sheppard's?

I do not know if diet hints are any help to you? If they are, Sir Winston has no particular dislikes and enjoys good cooking! He likes on the whole to drink a still white wine at luncheon, and champagne at dinner.

I leave it to you to pass on as much of all this as you see fit to the White House, and I hope it does not sound too imperious to our hosts.[3]

On the day before his departure, Churchill asked to see Lord Moran. After their discussion, Moran wrote to Churchill:

My dear Winston,

I was rather sad when you said this morning that you wished that you were not going on this trip. I expect you feel that this visit is only worth while if you can do it really well. But I believe that this is still possible.

[1] 'My dear Bernie', 23 April 1959: Churchill papers, 2/298.
[2] 'Private and Confidential', 23 April 1959: Churchill papers, 2/298.
[3] 'Private', 23 April 1959: Churchill papers, 2/298.

Any doubts I have had are not concerned with any vascular accident or emergency; after all it is good odds against anything of that kind happening. I only wonder if you will be in such good form that people in the States will say: 'I'd like to remember him like that.'

I am sure it is possible to tune your circulation so that you will be in such form. I say this because your circulation still responds to 'Minors' if used at the right time, and when it is safe to use them judging from the pulse tension—perhaps using more 'Minors' than we have done hitherto. So far we have used the 'Minors' only before speeches etc. But I had it in mind to use them to keep you in top form throughout your visit (which is short enough to make that possible).

I was pretty certain that 'Minors' so used would make the difference between your visit being an outstanding success and merely one where your form might be compared sadly with what they remembered in former times.

That is why I was very sorry when you decided not to take me. I have learnt so much about your circulation in the last nineteen years and what can be done to tone it up that I believe I could have made the difference. I wanted you so much to bring off this trip so that people would talk of it as a wonderful thing in itself and not just talk of your former visits. I wanted them to say how marvellous it was that in your eighty-fifth year you were so much 'on the spot' and plainly in a state when you could give Ike the advice he so obviously needs.[1]

'I hear,' Moran noted in his diary on May 4, 'he went off in good heart. He has a feeling that for the moment he is on the map again. Perhaps, after all, life is not quite over.'[2]

On May 5 Churchill was in Washington, where President Eisenhower had invited him to stay at the White House. That day he wrote to his wife, in his own hand, on White House stationery:

My dearest Clemmie,

Here I am. All goes well & the President is a real friend. We had a most pleasant dinner last night, & I caught up my arrears of sleep in (11) *eleven* hours. I am invited to stay in bed all the morning & am going to see Mr Dulles after luncheon. Anthony will send you more news. I send my fondest love darling.

Your loving husband

W[3]

At dinner that night, Churchill read the short speech which Montague Browne had prepared for him. 'To come across the Atlantic

[1] 'My dear Winston', 2 May 1959: Churchill papers, 1/54.
[2] Moran diary, 4 May 1959: *The Struggle for Survival*, page 750.
[3] 'My dearest Clemmie', The White House, Washington, 5 May 1959: Spencer-Churchill papers.

and to see so many friends and so many elements in the union of our peoples,' he said, 'has been a great and memorable joy to me.'[1]

On the morning of May 8 Montague Browne telegraphed Lord Moran from Washington, to say that there was 'a black bit' at the end of Churchill's finger. It was the size of a pea.[2] This 'pea' was a small area of gangrenous tissue; showing that the arterial supply to the finger had been gravely affected; yet another warning sign of the progressive failure of the circulation. Old and unwell though Churchill was, two of those whom he saw were far more sick. Foster Dulles, whom he found emaciated, was to die of cancer two weeks later. General Marshall was unable to speak at all; he had recently had a stroke.[3]

On May 5, and again on May 6, Churchill lunched with Eisenhower at the White House, the Foreign Office having provided him with a brief. In a report to Sir Harold Caccia two weeks later, Montague Browne set out what was discussed:

The conversation, which was of a very general nature, ranged much over personalities, with the President returning more than once to how wounded he had been by Field Marshal Montgomery's television interview.[4] He said that he was willing to believe that the Field Marshal had been seduced by Ed Murrow, whom he described as 'a snake', but that it was really too much that Lord Montgomery, who had repeatedly invited himself to stay at the White House, should make a personal attack of this nature. He added that when he had been appointed Supreme Commander of Overlord, Sir Winston had told him that he could sack any British officer who proved difficult, but that he had not exercised this right in the case of Field Marshal Montgomery!

Sir Winston succeeded to a great extent, I think, in smoothing the ruffled feathers, but it was surprisingly evident how affected the President is by personal criticisms levelled at him from abroad. He also referred with asperity to attacks on him in the British Press, and for someone in his position seemed surprisingly thin-skinned.

[1] 'Sir Winston's Speech at the Dinner at the White House', 5 May 1959: Churchill papers, 2/298. Among the fifty-two guests at the dinner were the United States Ambassador to the United Nations, Henry Cabot Lodge, Secretary of Defense McElroy, Mr Speaker Raeburn, the Senate Majority Leader Lyndon Johnson, the head of the CIA Allen Dulles, the former United States Ambassador to London Lew Douglas, the former Secretary of State James Byrnes, Bernard Baruch, and the British Ambassador Sir Harold Caccia. ('Dinner at the White House', 7.30 p.m., 6 May 1959: Churchill papers, 2/298).

[2] Moran diary, 8 May 1959: *The Struggle for Survival*, pages 750–1.

[3] Marshall died on 16 October 1959, two months before his seventy-ninth birthday.

[4] On 28 April 1959 the Columbia Broadcasting System televised an interview with Montgomery by Edward R. Murrow and Charles Collingwood, in which Montgomery, in a criticism of President Eisenhower, said that soldiers should stay out of politics. 'The same man can't do both', he said. He was also critical of Eisenhower's 'stated intention' not to attend a summit meeting unless he was sure it would have some results. On the day that this interview (which had been filmed earlier at his home in Hampshire) was broadcast in the United States, Montgomery arrived in Moscow for a meeting with Khrushchev. (*The Times*, 29 April 1959).

The President spoke warmly of the Prime Minister. He said, 'That's a man you can really do business with. And he's quick, too.' He went on to speak unfavourably of the French in general, and General de Gaulle in particular. He clearly has a paternal feeling for the NATO military machinery, dating no doubt from his tenure at SHAPE, and he thought that the French might well wreck it. He spoke of Algeria and General de Gaulle's illogical position in maintaining that it was an internal French affair, and at the same time seeking NATO endorsement of the French position and policy there. From there the President launched into a disquisition on the position of colonial countries in Africa. This was on the classical American line of 'give it to them before they take it' and seemed greatly to over-simplify the problems.

Sir Winston raised with the President the question of discrimination against British contractors and the trend towards protection to the detriment of our exports, as mentioned in the Foreign Office brief. The President appeared sympathetic, but said that he had a difficult time in selling the desirability of a liberal American policy in this direction. He added that he had heard that the President of the Board of Trade was going to offer the Russians a five-year credit scheme, and that this would break the NATO front on the subject. If we did this the Dutch or probably the West Germans would want to follow suit. He was then working on a message to us about it. This has of course resolved itself since.

Montague Browne's report continued:

During the three days we were in the White House the President showed an affectionate care and consideration for Sir Winston and spent a great deal of time with him. He looked well and seemed alert. He said that he is troubled by deafness, but this was not apparent. His working day seems to be from about half-past eight in the morning until luncheon. In the afternoon, when he was not with Sir Winston, he seemed either to be resting or taking light exercise.

The President spoke with what seemed relief of the approach of the end of his tenure. I do not think that this was assumed. In general he seemed rather less than optimistic, but perhaps this was caused by Mr Dulles' decline, which was much in his mind. At one point he concluded his remarks about the future of NATO with approximately these words: 'The big question is, will the West have the endurance and the tenacity and the courage to keep up the struggle long enough?' (Mr McElroy spoke in rather similar terms to Sir Winston and hinted to him that Great Britain was not pulling its weight in defence matters. I did not hear this conversation, but Sir Winston said that the sense of it was quite clear.)

To sum up, the President seemed relaxed, healthy and following a régime that was light enough to keep him so. His outlook seemed on the melancholy side, and it did not appear that his mind was receptive to ideas differing from those he already held.[1]

Together, Churchill and Eisenhower went to the President's farm

[1] 'Private and Confidential', 21 May 1959: Churchill papers, 2/298.

at Gettysburg. As a token of his visit, Churchill gave Eisenhower one of his paintings, 'Valley of the Ourika and Atlas Mountains', which Eisenhower subsequently put in the Oval Office 'so that', he explained, 'I may display it proudly to each and every visitor there.'[1] Later, during a talk with the Embassy staff in Washington, 'an intrepid person', as Lord Nicholas Gordon-Lennox later recalled, started to ask Churchill about the animals he had seen at Eisenhower's farm, whereupon Churchill 'was surprisingly able to say precisely how many of each had been shown to him. Except for the pigs: for some reason he had not (he said) been allowed to see these.'[2]

On the way to the airport at the end of his visit, Churchill turned to Sir Harold Caccia with the words: 'I hope you will give the Prime Minister a good report of my visit; and say that I behaved myself.'[3]

At the British Embassy, Churchill's presence had been a source of excitement. 'Your visit here,' Lady Caccia wrote to him on May 14, 'was an enormous pleasure to us.' The Ambassador's daughter Clarissa had just announced her engagement to an Oxford undergraduate and former Guards officer, David Pryce-Jones. 'It added greatly to her pleasure,' Lady Caccia wrote, 'that we should have had a telegram from you.'[4]

On his return to London, Churchill lunched with Harold Macmillan at 10 Downing Street. Professor Rob, to whom he had shown his finger that morning, had said that there was a risk if he went out to lunch or dinner in the near future, but that the risk was small. What was the risk, Churchill asked? 'If you don't rest you might lose the hand,' Rob replied.[5] On the following day Moran noted in his diary: 'With a smirk Winston announced his intention of attending Max's annual dinner tonight. He asked Rob what were the odds that this would make his finger worse. Rob replied fifty-fifty.'[6]

Rob's fear was that if Churchill did not rest, his circulatory problems would get worse, even to the extent of another stroke. Alcohol, too, could precipitate a further circulatory crisis.[7]

[1] 'Dear Winston', signed 'As ever, Ike', The White House, 26 May 1959: Churchill papers, 2/217.

[2] Lord Nicholas Gordon-Lennox recollections: letter to the author, 19 October 1987.

[3] Lord Nicholas Gordon-Lennox, recollections of a conversation with Sir Harold Caccia: letter to the author, 19 October 1987.

[4] 'Dear Sir Winston', British Embassy Washington, 14 May 1959: Churchill papers, 2/298. David Pryce-Jones was subsequently a writer, novelist and historian.

[5] Moran diary, 13 May 1959: The Struggle for Survival, page 752. Professor Charles Rob was Professor of Surgery at London University, and a former Consultant Vascular Surgeon to the Army.

[6] Moran diary, 14 May 1959: The Struggle for Survival, page 752.

[7] The crisis passed; within three months the black (necrotic) area had fallen off; the rest of the finger remained healthy.

Churchill went to the dinner, a meeting of Beaverbrook's 1940 Club. Harold Macmillan was also there. From London, Churchill returned in the third week of May to Chartwell. There, and at Hyde Park Gate, he was visited on a number of occasions by Professor Rob, who gave him advice on his circulatory problems. Rob later recalled:

I told him that I had just been offered a position in Rochester, New York, and I was thinking of going there. He then said to me, 'You know some of my ancestors came from that area, you may not know it, but I am descended from a Seneca Indian squaw who was an ancestor of my mother's.' We then talked about the Indians in this area and I have a feeling that he thought he was descended from some enormous chief who had gone around scalping people and winning great battles against other tribes. Of course there was no evidence for this, but it made a nice fantasy for him to think about this Indian ancestor. . . .

He was, I thought, an alert, very interesting and somewhat deaf man, whose age, about 84 or 85, was in good health and mentally still exceptional. I thought he was bored by his retirement. . . .[1]

Churchill had almost given up painting now; in his five weeks at Marrakech he had only painted two pictures. Reading had become his leisure companion; on May 26, when Lord Moran went down to Chartwell, he found him reading Macaulay's essay on Milton.[2]

In the third week of June, Churchill went to the races at Ascot. Then, on the evening of July 22 he rejoined Aristotle Onassis on *Christina* for a cruise in Greek and Turkish waters. Among the other guests was Churchill's doctor Lord Moran, Anthony Montague Browne and his wife Nonie, Umberto Agnelli of Fiat, and Maria Callas. The cruise took them to Capri, where Gracie Fields was invited to dine on board, and after dinner sang some of her most famous songs for Churchill, as well as making up a song especially for him, 'We're glad to see you aboard.'[3]

On July 26 *Christina* sailed past the smoking volcano of Stromboli; two days later she sailed through the Gulf of Corinth. 'If you were an animal, what animal would you be?' Onassis asked Churchill on one occasion. 'A Tiger' was Churchill's reply. 'And you, Ari, what animal would you choose to be?' Churchill asked. 'Your canary, Toby,' Onassis answered.[4]

As *Christina* sailed in Greek waters, the Greek Prime Minister, Constantine Karamanlis, came to dinner, as did Sir Roger Allen, the British Ambassador to Greece. On the evening of August 4 *Christina* sailed

[1] Professor Charles Rob recollections: letter to the author, 17 November 1986.
[2] Moran diary, 26 May 1959: *The Struggle for Survival*, pages 752–3.
[3] Nonie Montague Browne diary, 25 July 1959: Lady Sargant papers.
[4] Peter Evans, *Ari, The Life and Times of Aristotle Socrates Onassis*, London 1986, page 178.

through the Dardanelles, past the Gallipoli peninsula to the Sea of Marmara and Istanbul, where the Patriarch Athenagoras was invited on board to meet Churchill.

The passage of the Dardanelles had been made after Churchill had gone to bed 'because', as Nonie Montague Browne later recalled, 'they knew it would upset him'.

For this part of the cruise, Churchill was joined by his daughter Diana. 'He liked to sit on deck,' Nonie Montague Browne later recalled. 'He would come on deck at about noon. He would have a dry martini and spoonfuls of caviar. We would be a long time over lunch—cigar, brandy, coffee. Then he would sit in the sun. Before dinner he would rest. Lord Moran would not let him swim. "Oh no," he would say, "you may get a chill."' [1]

Returning through the Dardanelles, *Christina* sailed to Mount Athos, Delos and Mykonos. At lunchtime, Churchill, inspired by the encounter with Gracie Fields, would sing 'Daisy, Daisy' and other music hall favourites. During a discussion of Eisenhower's reluctance either to support or to sack one of his aides, accused of financial impropriety, Churchill remarked: 'You must either wallop a man or vindicate him.' [2]

On August 13 *Christina* returned to Monte Carlo: 'The cruise to Greece and Turkey was a great success,' Churchill wrote to his grandson Winston. 'We visited Constantinople and met the Turkish Prime Minister and Foreign Minister, and the Greek Prime Minister dined with us near Athens.' [3]

In the third week of August, Churchill was invited by Eisenhower to meet him during the President's visit to London. 'As Sir Winston is well installed here,' Montague Browne wrote from La Pausa to Eisenhower's Naval Aide, Captain Peter Aurand, 'and Lady Churchill will be in hospital in England at the time, it seems best for him to stay and not return for so short a time.' [4] That same day, at La Capponcina, Churchill dictated a letter to his wife:

Darling One,

We have been overwhelmed by weather and I expect you have had a dose of the same. Immediately after breakfast, from a grey sky, rain began to drip—and pour and everything became sopping, and all who showed a nose out of doors were sopped. I remained in bed and watched the patter from my verandah ledge. I certainly saw more rain in those few hours than we have seen since we sallied forth from London. This letter is at present confined to weather conditions, for these are the only ones which constitute my outlook.

[1] Lady Sargant recollections: in conversation with the author, 21 July 1987.
[2] Peter Evans, *Ari*, page 182. 'Ari' was an affectionate abbreviation for Aristotle.
[3] 'My dear Winston', La Pausa, 28 August 1959: Squerryes Lodge Archive.
[4] La Pausa, 22 August 1959: Churchill papers, 2/217.

Max and I dined together alone last night, and were entertained—or I was—by the lizards on the wall, who each got their fly before they went to bed.

The white cat has just put head and shoulders in the room where I am at present dictating my letter to you. I think you will find it will reach you before you go to the hospital. I send you all my fondest love and trust indeed that things may go well with you in a graver ordeal than I am likely to encounter inside any limits I can foresee.

'Best of all good fortune in the operation,' Churchill wrote in his own hand, '& tender love forever, Your devoted, Winston.'[1]

'I am sure you will be very happy at "Pausa Land"', Clementine Churchill wrote to her husband from Chartwell on August 23, and she added: 'Please give Wendy my love and my greetings to Emery.'[2] Learning that the Prime Minister of Israel, David Ben-Gurion, was in the South of France, Churchill invited him to lunch at La Pausa. 'I deeply appreciate your kind invitation,' Ben-Gurion replied, 'which to my regret arrived too late, when I was already on the high seas on my way back to Israel.' Ben-Gurion added: 'I need hardly assure you that I should have been delighted to accept the invitation, if only it had found me still in France. Like many others in all parts of the globe, I regard you as the greatest Englishman in your country's history and the greatest statesman of our time, as the man whose courage, wisdom and foresight saved his country and the free world from Nazi servitude.' Churchill was also, wrote Ben-Gurion, 'one of the few men in the free world to realize the true character of the Bolshevik regime and its leaders. . . .'

Ben-Gurion went on to write of the dangers inherent in trusting even the post-Stalin leaders of Russia, telling Churchill:

. . . I am very doubtful whether any serious change in the Communist attitude towards non-Communist countries will come about through the Khrushchev–Eisenhower talks, the Foreign Ministers' conference in Geneva, or a Summit Conference. I am gravely apprehensive that all these meetings and talks are meant solely to lull the free world to sleep and weaken its consciousness of the imperative need for unity, solidarity and constant readiness. And it appears to me that you are one of the few men among the world's leaders who are capable of standing in the breach. . . .[3]

Churchill wrote in reply:

I will reflect carefully on what you say. For myself, I believe that your view may perhaps be on the melancholy side. However, there is no doubt

[1] 'Darling One', La Capponcina, 22 August 1959: Spencer-Churchill papers. Clementine Churchill was about to be operated on for a drooping eyelid, the result of a painful and prolonged attack of shingles.

[2] Chartwell, 23 August 1959: Churchill papers, 1/135.

[3] 'Dear Sir Winston', Jerusalem, 3 September 1959: Churchill papers, 2/128.

that we should be well advised to bear in mind the possibilities you discussed.

I often think of your Country, and I view with admiration the way in which you are undertaking your great tasks. I trust that we shall have another opportunity of meeting before long. . . .[1]

Churchill also sent Ben-Gurion's letter to Harold Macmillan. 'Apart from his judgement on world events,' Churchill wrote, 'it is interesting as an indication of the way his own thoughts are moving.'[2]

At the end of August, Churchill returned to England. At La Pausa, the day before Churchill left, Emery Reves was taken ill with coronary thrombosis. From Chartwell, Churchill dictated a letter to Wendy:

My dear Wendy,

I am so grieved at the bad news about Emery, but I hope that six or eight weeks will enable him to recover. It is a lucky thing your Mother is with you. She ought to be a comfort to you in these difficult days.

Here we have beautiful weather every day and we might almost be at Pausaland. Clemmie is home from the hospital. We both read your letters with deep interest, and feel a great deal for you in all your anxiety and care.

It was always great fun and pleasure coming to Pausaland, and taking my daily walks with you.

'I hope we shall have some more,' Churchill added in his own hand. 'Yours ever, W.'[3]

A few days later Churchill wrote again, to Emery Reves, his letter once more a dictated one:

My dear Emery,

You and Wendy are much in my thoughts, and I do hope that you are continuing to make good progress.

Here the Election is approaching its climax and I am gradually drawn into it more and more. I think however, on the whole, that our chances are still good, though not so good as they ought to be. However, in another week we shall know for certain. Indeed you may not get this letter before the results come in. I have had two charming letters from Wendy and hope the rest she has taken amid her anxieties will do her lasting good.

It was a great disappointment to me not to come out again to Pausaland. We have, however, had enchanting weather here and not a day on which the sun has not shone brightly.[4]

There was good news about the plans being made for Churchill

[1] 'My dear Prime Minister', 'Private', 11 September 1959: Churchill papers, 2/128.
[2] 'My dear Harold', 'Private and Confidential', 9 September 1959: Churchill papers, 2/128. At the end of October, Anthony Eden wrote to Churchill: 'I am troubled about the future of Israel, where the Arab boycott seems to be meeting with some success.' ('My dear Winston', 'Personal', 31 October 1959: Churchill papers, 2/517).
[3] 'My dear Wendy', Chartwell, 4 September 1959: Reves paper.
[4] 'My dear Emery', September 1959: Churchill papers, 2/532.

College that September. The Duke of Edinburgh had accepted the Visitorship.[1] In London, too, Churchill was, after all, able to meet Eisenhower again.

The General Election to which Churchill had wished to make his contribution was called for Thursday October 8. 'Everyone up here is in good heart,' Harold Macmillan wrote to Churchill on September 28, in returning to him Ben-Gurion's letter, and he added: 'in spite of what the newspapers say we have not yet given up hope! Indeed, we are calmly confident.'[2]

On September 29 Churchill went to Woodford, for his adoption meeting as Conservative candidate. Sixty years had passed since he had first stood, at Oldham, in the Conservative cause.[3] Since his election for Epping in 1924, he reminded his constituents, 'We have had eight victories running.' If everyone played his part, he was sure 'we shall increase our score' on Election Day.[4] In a second speech that day, prepared for him by Anthony Montague Browne, Churchill told his constituents that out of the 'deadlock' caused by the confrontation of the nuclear and conventional capacity of the Great Powers there was only one way forward, 'disarmament', applied not only to nuclear but to all kinds of weapons, freely accepted by all nations, and 'guaranteed by effective international control'. Churchill added: 'In recent months I have seen signs of hope. The proposals which Mr Khrushchev put forward recently in New York are no different in essential purposes from the plans which Mr Macmillan and his colleagues tabled to be examined by the new United Nations Committee to which Russia has assented. That is a step forward. But much remains to be done. We must above all resist any temptation to rush into agreements which do not provide a workable system of inspection and control. Not to be firm on this principle would be a fatal error.'[5]

[1] 'Dear Montague Browne', from Rear-Admiral Christopher Bonham Carter, 2 September 1959: Churchill papers, 2/571.

[2] 'Dear Winston', 'Private and Confidential', 28 September 1959: Churchill papers, 2/128.

[3] On Polling Day at Oldham, 6 July 1899, Churchill was narrowly defeated, receiving 11,477 votes as against 12,976 for the leading Liberal candidate (in a two-member constituency). The second Liberal received 12,770 votes, the other Conservative 11,499. The *Manchester Guardian* of 7 July 1899 reported that Churchill 'looked upon the process of counting with amusement. A smile lighted up his features, and the result of the election did not disturb him. He might have been defeated, but he was conscious that in this fight he had not been disgraced.' After his defeat, Churchill received a letter from A. J. Balfour. 'Never mind,' Balfour concluded, 'it will all come right; and this small reverse will have no permanent ill effect upon your political fortunes.' Churchill was then twenty-four years old.

[4] Speech of 29 September 1959: Randolph S. Churchill (editor), *The Unwritten Alliance*, pages 318–22.

[5] Speech of 29 September 1959: Randolph S. Churchill (editor), *The Unwritten Alliance*, pages 323–7.

'We are much engaged with the Election,' Churchill wrote to Emery Reves that day, and he added: 'I am making some speeches in my Constituency.' His letter was sent from Chartwell. 'I am conducting my campaign,' he explained, 'from Chartwell where we are still having the most beautiful weather.'[1] From Chartwell, on October 4, Churchill wrote to thank Beaverbrook for a bottle of 1928 champagne which he had brought him: 'I enjoyed it much and it does not seem to have lost any of its sparkle, in spite of its great age.'[2]

On October 6 Churchill spoke again, at Walthamstow, for his friend and neighbouring Member of Parliament, John Harvey.[3] It was the only speech of the campaign which he made outside his own constituency. Three days later, the Conservatives were returned to power for the third consecutive time, and with an increased majority. Harold Macmillan remained Prime Minister, with an overall majority of a hundred MPs. 'The Election has gone very well,' Churchill wrote to Emery Reves, 'and I think we can look forward to a period of stability at home.'[4] 'The Election has given us a majority of a size that is surprising,' he wrote that same day to Wendy Reves, 'and which will I think enable us to run our affairs in a stable way for some time to come. I myself am back in the House once more.'[5]

Churchill's own majority, though a substantial 14,000, was down. 'It may well be,' his daughter Mary has written, 'that the feelings of discontent among some of his own supporters were reflected in this result.'[6]

On October 17 Churchill flew from Biggin Hill to Cambridge, a half-hour flight to save a three-and-a-quarter-hour road journey, in order, as Montague Browne had explained, 'to plant the oak tree (and thereby "lay the foundation stone") of your College at Cambridge. . . .'[7] Lady Churchill accompanied her husband, as did Montague Browne. They were met at the airport by Sir John Cockcroft, and were to lunch at King's College before going on to the site of Churchill College. Among those present at the tree planting was Frank Cousins, head of the Transport and General Workers' Union, who had

---

[1] 'My dear Emery', 29 September 1959: Reves papers.

[2] 'My dear Max', Chartwell, 4 October 1959: Beaverbrook papers.

[3] John Harvey, born in 1920, had contested St Pancras North in 1950 and Walthamstow East in 1951. From 1954 to 1956 he was Chairman of the Woodford Conservative Association, and from 1955 to 1966 Member of Parliament for Walthamstow East. In 1974 he became Director of Burmah Oil Trading Ltd.

[4] 'My dear Emery', 14 October 1959: Reves papers.

[5] 'My dear Wendy', 14 October 1959: Reves papers.

[6] Mary Soames, *Clementine Churchill*, page 476. There is a recording of Churchill's speech after his re-election: BBC Written Archives Centre, Library No. LP 25671.

[7] 'Sir Winston', initialled 'AMB', 29 September 1959: Churchill papers, 2/571.

given £50,000 to Churchill College to build a library as a memorial to Ernest Bevin. 'Mr Cousins, as you know,' Montague Browne had explained, 'is Chairman of the Trades Union Council and has been on the Left wing of it.' [1]

Montague Browne had prepared, as was now his task, a speech for Churchill to make. Together, they had discussed and shaped it. One passage, as read by Churchill in the 'speech form' he always used, was about the most recent development in the world of science and technology, rockets that could reach the moon:

> Let no one believe
>   that the lunar rockets,
>
>   of which we read in the Press,
>
>   are merely ingenious bids
>   for prestige.
>
> They are the manifestation
>   of a formidable advance
>   in technology.
>
> As with many vehicles
>   of pure research,
>
>   their immediate uses
>   may not be apparent.
>
> But I do not doubt
>   That they will ultimately reap
>   a rich harvest
>   for those who have the
>   imagination and power
>   to develop them,
>
>   and to probe ever more deeply
>   into the mysteries of the universe
>   in wh we live. [2]

After his speech, Churchill attended a short meeting of the College Trustees, where he learned that the donations so far subscribed, including one from the Transport and General Workers' Union, and another from the Amalgamated Engineering Union, amounted to just over £3 million. This sum would enable the Trustees to proceed with

---

[1] 'Sir Winston', initialled 'AMB', 15 October 1959: Churchill papers, 2/571.

[2] Speech notes, 17 October 1959: Churchill papers, 2/571. There is a recording of the speech: BBC Written Archives Centre, Library No. LP 25718 (copy in the Churchill College Archive).

the building of the College, leaving a further million to be raised 'for the final equipment and adequate endowment'.[1]

'Your speech at the tree planting was very much appreciated,' Sir John Cockcroft wrote to Churchill on the following day.[2] 'The way in which the University has welcomed the new College is most heartening,' Churchill wrote to Noël Annan, the Provost of King's, on October 21, 'and I know how much you have done personally.'[3]

On October 22, while at Hyde Park Gate, Churchill was again taken ill, becoming briefly unconscious, and on regaining consciousness feeling dazed, 'as if', he told Montague Browne, 'he had been turned upside down'.[4]

Sir Russell Brain, who saw Churchill later that day, and again on October 23, thought it was a mild form of epilepsy, the 'petit mal' from which both Caesar and Napoleon suffered, and a not uncommon sequel, as Moran noted, 'to a sluggish cerebral circulation'.[5] When Moran went to see his patient on October 24, he found him playing cards, and once more reading, as Moran thought, the book he had seen him with last, Tolstoy's *War and Peace*. Moran noted in his diary:

Found Winston playing bezique with Clemmie as if nothing had happened. 'He is much better,' she said, watching Winston as he collected the cards. I asked him if he could detect any difference between his condition before the attack and now. He hesitated.

'If there is any difference it is for the worse.'

'In what way?' I persisted.

'It's not really a headache, but . . .'

I helped him out. 'Muzziness?'

'Yes, muzziness. Shall I have another attack?'

I asked him how he was getting on with his book.

'There's not much in it,' he grunted.

'You don't think Tolstoy makes out his case about Napoleon?'

His face lost its vacant expression and lit up in amusement. 'Oh, I put him on one side in order to read the second volume of the bloody diaries. Tolstoy must wait until I see what Brooke has to say.[6] I was told that the second

[1] 'Press Release for Sunday Papers', 18 October 1959: Churchill papers, 2/57. Jock Colville later told Mary Soames that Clementine Churchill 'had used her influence to ensure that Churchill College, Cambridge, would open its doors to women. At one of the early meetings of the Trustees, Winston had said that "My wife thinks women should be admitted to Churchill . . . and I think so too." Churchill College thus became the first college in either Oxford or Cambridge to receive women students on the same terms as men, living in the same college.' (Mary Soames, *Clementine Churchill*, page 470.)

[2] 'Dear Sir Winston', 18 October 1959: Churchill papers, 2/571.

[3] 'My dear Annan', 21 October 1959: Churchill papers, 2/571.

[4] Moran diary, 22 October 1959: *The Struggle for Survival*, pages 759–60.

[5] Moran diary, 23 October 1959: *The Struggle for Survival*, page 760.

[6] The second volume of Alanbrooke diaries, edited by Arthur Bryant, had just been published, entitled 'Triumph in the West 1943–1946'.

volume was worse than the first, full of venom, but as far as I have read I don't find it so. I had forgotten, my dear, that I called you a bloody old man. I apologize to you,' he said gravely.[1]

As he approached his eighty-fifth birthday, Churchill's powers of recuperation remained considerable. When one visitor brought with him an old picture-postcard of a house party with the King of Portugal, with Churchill in it. 'Winston was thrilled,' noted Lord Moran, 'and talked about each member of the party in turn. This went on till half past three.'[2]

On October 30 Churchill returned to Woodford, to hear Montgomery speak at the unveiling of a statue to Churchill, and to reply to Montgomery's remarks. In many undeveloped areas of the world, he said, 'former systems of government are being thrown aside, and new nations are rising. We wish them well. We may watch them anxiously and take a justifiable pride in true progress there.' As for Britain and its future, he said. 'Let us not lose heart. Our future is one of high hope.'[3]

On November 9, from Chartwell, Churchill wrote to La Pausa:

My dear Wendy,

You are often in my thoughts. I do trust that Emery is continuing to make good progress, and that you yourself are feeling much better and stronger again now. Such anxiety as you have endured is indeed wearing. I hope that the outlook at Pausaland is becoming daily brighter.

Here, all is well. The new Parliament has taken up its duties, and I go to the House a good deal. We are at Chartwell at the weekends, of course. It has been a wonderful autumn, and the trees here are beautiful.

Sarah is touring in a new play called *The Night Life of a Virile Potato*. It seems to be meeting with considerable success, and we hope very much that it will get to London.

Yours ever,

W[4]

Despite his age and infirmities, Churchill continued to carry out the tasks which had become traditional. On November 12 he returned

---

[1] Moran diary, 24 October 1959: *The Struggle for Survival*, page 760.

[2] Moran diary, undated: *The Struggle for Survival*, page 760. The guest was Rupert Gunnis. The house party had been at Blenheim Palace, as an entertainment given in 1908 by the Queen's Own Oxfordshire Hussars for King Manoel of Portugal. The photograph is reproduced in volume 2 of this biography, facing page 274. Among those in it are Churchill's brother Jack and his wife Gwendeline, and Churchill's bride to be, Clementine Hozier. This is the only known photograph of Churchill and his wife taken together before their marriage.

[3] Speech of 31 October 1959: Randolph S. Churchill (editor), *The Unwritten Alliance*, pages 331–2.

[4] 'My dear Wendy', Chartwell, 9 November 1959: Reves papers. In the carbon copy of this letter in Churchill papers, 2/532 the words 'and steady' were deleted from the phrase 'good and steady progress' as first dictated, or drafted.

yet again to Harrow School for the annual 'Songs', and even spoke a few words. Those who took part in the occasion, he said, 'will feel that they have perpetuated a glorious memory which will long continue to give strength to those who have it.'[1]

Churchill's strength was ebbing, albeit slowly. On November 17, while going to lunch with Lord Beaverbrook, he had an attack of giddiness when getting out of his car, and would have fallen heavily but for the speed with which his chauffeur, Bullock, caught him. At the luncheon, which went ahead, Churchill had difficulty in finding the words he wanted.

To Churchill's disappointment, he had to cancel a dinner at 10 Downing Street at which the German Chancellor, Konrad Adenauer, was to be the guest. But Adenauer so wanted to see him that he asked if he could come to Hyde Park Gate, where the two men met on the afternoon of November 18.

Of the meeting between Churchill and Adenauer, Clementine Churchill told Lord Moran: 'The first quarter of an hour he was hesitant and his voice was not very strong, though his answers were all sensible. Then he blossomed. His voice got stronger, and he asked a lot of intelligent questions. They talked a lot about the Summit Conference. Adenauer does not trust Khrushchev. He wants to keep Russia out of everything. I think, Charles, it went off very well.'[2]

'We read with anxiety that you were indisposed,' Wendy Reves wrote to Churchill on November 19, 'and as you know—we telephoned to find out the facts from Anthony. I felt elated to hear that you had just received Adenauer and that you were better. I should know by now that you are stronger than all, an exception to every rule. . . .'[3]

On November 30 Churchill celebrated his eighty-fifth birthday. That afternoon he went to the House of Commons, where Hugh Gaitskell, Leader of the Opposition, rose amid cheers to ask: 'I hope that it will be in order, Mr Speaker, if I offer to the rt hon. Gentleman, the Member for Woodford (Sir Winston Churchill) our warmest congratulations and best wishes and affectionate greetings, on his 85th birthday.' The Leader of the House, R. A. Butler, added: 'May I support the Leader of the Opposition, Sir, and on behalf of the whole House include in the rt hon. Gentleman's and hon. Friends' offer our most heartfelt good wishes to my rt hon. Friend.'

Deeply moved, Churchill rose and replied: 'May I say that I most gratefully and eagerly accept both forms of compliment.'[4]

---

[1] Speech of 12 November 1959: Churchill papers, 2/336.
[2] Moran diary, 18 November 1959: *The Struggle for Survival*, page 762.
[3] 'Dear, dear Sir Winston', La Pausa, 19 November 1959: Churchill papers, 2/532.
[4] *Hansard*, 30 November 1959. The Speaker (since 21 October 1959), was Sir Harry Hylton-Foster.

'Tomorrow is your birthday, dear,' Wendy Reves had written from La Pausa on November 29, 'and I know it will be a joyous one. I cannot believe that you will be eighty-five. So young in heart you are to me.' [1]

From Lord Beaverbrook, Churchill received champagne, from Lord Moran caviar. To mark the eighty-fifth birthday, Dr Adenauer sent a print of Bonn besieged by Churchill's ancestor John Churchill, 1st Duke of Marlborough. 'I trust the citizens do not bear me any inherited illwill!' Churchill replied. [2] On December 15 Churchill told his solicitor, Anthony Moir, that he wanted to be buried, not at Chartwell, but at Bladon, next to his father and mother. [3]

'I am so sorry to have left your letters unanswered,' Churchill wrote to Emery Reves on December 29, 'but I have not been very well.' If his doctor would allow him to travel, he added, he would go to Monte Carlo on January 2, to stay at the Hôtel de Paris. [4] He did indeed go to Monte Carlo. 'Here the weather is superb,' Churchill wrote to Colville from Monte Carlo on 9 January 1960. He had been confined to his bed for two days, with a slight infection, 'but am much better now'. [5] He was certainly well enough, by January 10, to express his support for Alan Hodge as a member of the Other Club, and to assert his unwillingness to consider two other candidates, one nominated by Lord Winterton, the other by Beaverbrook. Not to have one of the candidates, Montague Browne explained to Churchill, 'is perhaps a rebuff to Lord Beaverbrook, one of the oldest members of the Club, who put him forward'. [6]

Montague Browne argued in vain. Churchill had not been disposed 'to hear any arguments', he reported to Colville, 'about the embarrassing position of Lord Winterton or the rebuff to Lord Beaverbrook. So there we are.' [7]

'We are down here in the hope of sun,' Churchill wrote to Lady Lytton on January 14, 'but at the moment there is snow and sleet.' [8] Two days later Montague Browne wrote to Sir Norman Brook:

---

[1] 'My dear', signed 'Your Devoted Wendy', La Pausa, 29 November 1959: Churchill papers, 2/532.

[2] 'My dear Chancellor', 5 December 1959: Churchill papers, 2/443.

[3] Moran diary, 16 December 1959: *The Struggle for Survival*, page 764. Bladon was the parish church of Blenheim.

[4] 'My dear Emery', 29 December 1959: Reves papers.

[5] Monte Carlo, 9 January 1960: Churchill papers, 1/108.

[6] 'Sir Winston', initialled 'AMB', 10 January 1960: Churchill papers, 2/343.

[7] Monte Carlo, 'Private', 10 January 1960: Churchill papers, 2/343. Colville, elected to the Other Club in 1956, had succeeded Brendan Bracken as one of the Honorary Secretaries. In 1960 Peter Thorneycroft, Edward Heath, Viscount Hinchingbrooke, the Duke of Northumberland, Lord Rothschild and John Profumo were elected to the Club; in 1961 Alan Hodge, Bill Deakin, Selwyn Lloyd and Lord Home.

[8] Monte Carlo, 14 January 1960: Churchill papers, 1/136.

The Press in London have been very much stirred up by what they believe to be Sir Winston's imminent death, and in consequence Monte Carlo is full of journalists. However, I am glad to be able to tell you that on the whole Sir Winston seems much better. He had a day or two in bed with a mild recurrence of the infection he suffered in London (liver or gall bladder), but is now about again and, apart from melancholy and boredom, is more alert than I have seen him for a long time. Of course, one may be proved wrong tomorrow, but it does not look like it at the moment.

The weather has been deplorable for the last week, and there are not sufficient entertaining people down here to provide the little visits that Sir Winston welcomes more out here than in England. Lord Beaverbrook has left, but Onassis is very attentive, and Sir Winston is fond of him and amused by him. Incidentally, the Press reports that Sir Winston is Onassis' guest are incorrect. Sir Winston pays his way.

Lady Churchill is in excellent spirits and health, and the 'penthouse' in which we live on the top of the Hôtel de Paris is very agreeable in spite or because of its featureless luxury.[1]

Churchill returned to London on February 10. Eleven days later he learned of the death of Lady Mountbatten, whom he had known since she was a child. 'I couldn't bear to live without Clemmie,' he told Mountbatten. 'She's been everything in life to me. I don't know how you're going to carry on.'[2]

Churchill remained in England for less than a month, going to the races at Epsom and Lingfield with Christopher Soames, on February 22, attending the House of Commons again for a three-line whip on March 1, and dining at the Other Club on March 3. On March 8 he left England again, by air, for Gibraltar, where, accompanied by Lord Moran, he was to join *Christina*. A violent storm over southern Spain forced the plane to land at Tangier, to which *Christina* hurried. Subsequently all went well. On March 21 *Christina* reached Barbados, where Churchill was welcomed by the Governor-General Sir John Stow, who later recalled:

Having gone aboard Onassis's yacht, I was taken over to talk with the great man who was sitting, looking out to sea, puffing a cigar. He was wearing a large Stetson hat. Luckily Onassis was available to make Churchill hear—in fact, he was the only member of the household who seemed able to do so.

Soon we were summoned to lunch at which Lady Churchill, Onassis and the Montague Brownes were present. Churchill started by asking searching questions about the habits of the flying fish, which was on the menu. Luckily I was fairly well informed on the subject but I doubt whether my replies were heard or understood.

---

[1] 'Private and Confidential', Monte Carlo, 16 January 1960: Churchill papers, 5/321.

[2] 'Winston': *Sunday Mirror*, 17 April 1966 (reporting Lord Mountbatten's remarks to the Winston Churchill Society, Edmonton, Alberta, Canada).

As lunch progressed and the afternoon wore on, Churchill seemed to mellow under the influence of some excellent brandy. 'You should have one of these cigars, Governor,' he commanded me and who was to disobey? Later it seemed unlikely that Churchill would come ashore that afternoon and all security precautions and police were stood down.

He promised, however, to come ashore the following day. . . .

Sir John Stow's recollections continued:

Churchill was as good as his word and after inspecting a Police Guard of Honour he entered my car, and after he had declined to sit as Guest of Honour on the right, we were driven through the streets of Bridgetown.

As was to be expected, in an island considered more British than Britain herself, Churchill, with Trinity yachting cap at a jaunty angle, received a tumultuous welcome from the people and appeared to be really touched. No one could fail to be deeply moved at the sight of the greatest Englishman then alive passing the Nelson monument at the head of Broad Street in Bridgetown and there was a touch of history as he gravely saluted the statue.

Although he returned to Bridgetown late in the evening, he insisted on signing the visitor's book at Government House. Onassis accompanied him in an open car and alone seemed to be able to make him hear and do things. Onassis was firmly of the opinion that some blankets should be provided to protect the great man against the wind and in spite of every kind of objection from his guest, he wrapped him lovingly in several blankets for the journey back to the yacht.

Although Churchill was very hard of hearing there were occasions when I was accompanying him by car on which he made extremely lucid and penetrating enquiries. As we passed through the outskirts of Bridgetown, for instance, he commented on the number of white Barbadians, called for an estimate of their number in the island, and an account of their contribution to the community and representation in the House of Assembly. Having been given the answers he proceeded to ask 'supplementaries' as if he was teasing a Government minister from the Opposition benches.[1]

Churchill returned to the yacht. While it was still off Bridgetown, Sir John Stow wrote to him:

Your visit to Bridgetown and your drive through the streets has given intense joy and satisfaction to thousands of people here and will long be remembered especially by the school children.

The people of Barbados (known as Little England) are intensely loyal to the Throne and the spontaneous enthusiasm which was shown today reflects their admiration of you, Sir, as the embodiment of the fighting spirit of Britain.[2]

It was books which now occupied most of Churchill's active hours: for the cruise that March he had with him, among twenty-three books

[1] Sir John Stow recollections: typescript, pages 6–7.
[2] 'Dear Sir Winston', Government House, Barbados, 22 March 1960: Churchill papers, 1/153.

which Montague Browne had chosen, A. P. Herbert's novel of the Dardanelles, *Secret Battle*, Jane Austen's *Mansfield Park*, Joseph Conrad's *Arrow of Gold*, Graham Greene's *A Gun for Sale* and Jack London's *Call of the Wild*.[1] One day, at lunch, when Onassis said to Churchill, 'You are in meditative mood, not talkative,' Churchill replied: 'My mind is very empty all day.'[2] Old age, as he had earlier told Lord Moran, had become 'a feeble substitute for life'.[3]

On March 21 *Christina* reached Trinidad. On the following day, at Tobago, Churchill went ashore and was 'driven through the beautiful island', Nonie Montague Browne noted in her diary.[4] On March 25 *Christina* reached St Lucia, and on the following day Antigua. 'We put on a full Beating Retreat Ceremony,' the Governor of Antigua, Ian Turbott, later recalled, 'complete with Police Band, etc. etc., in the Dockyard. Sir Winston sat through most but, of course, stood up for God Save the Queen.' Turbott added: 'He was very emotional, tears streaming down his eyes and as we sat together in this very romantic and historic harbour he asked me again and again to tell him of the history of the Dockyard and of its Restoration and "Re-Opening".'

At luncheon at Clarence House, musical entertainment was provided by a steel band. During luncheon, Churchill questioned Turbott in detail about the reasons why Nelson had chosen to anchor at the harbour entrance. 'Rowing was good for the sailors' had been one of Nelson's reasons.

At dinner on *Christina*, Turbott recalled, Churchill 'rather enjoyed startling some guests when they asked him something by loudly saying "No" (to any question at all), and then he would turn to me and say in his deep voice "I didn't hear the proposition—even if I did it is better to say no to start with".'[5]

On March 28 *Christina* reached the French island of Martinique, where Churchill dined at the Prefecture and was given a display of local singing and dancing. Three days later the yacht was off St Thomas where, on the following day, Churchill went ashore for a drive through the island.[6] Among those living on St Thomas was the American novelist Herman Wouk, who noted in his diary how, at the waterfront, Churchill 'waved his big floppy hat and made the "V" sign when I led a cheer for him'. Wouk added: 'I saw the greatest

[1] 'Books for Sir Winston on cruise', March 1960: Churchill papers, 1/153.
[2] Moran diary, 23 March 1960: *The Struggle for Survival*, page 769.
[3] Moran recollections: *The Struggle for Survival*, page 770.
[4] Nonie Montague Browne diary, 22 March 1960: Lady Sargant papers.
[5] Sir Ian Turbott recollections: letter to the author, 3 August 1987.
[6] Nonie Montague Browne diary, March–April 1960: Lady Sargant papers.

living human being of our time, a man who will stand with Caesar and Napoleon when the years have rolled away.' [1]

From St Thomas, *Christina* sailed for Puerto Rico, where, at dinner on board, Churchill was 'greeted by a steel band'. [2] On the following evening, April 2, he flew back to London, reaching Hyde Park Gate on the afternoon of April 3; that night Onassis, his cruise host, was his guest for dinner.

Following his return from the West Indies, Churchill embarked upon a busy three days. On April 4 he dined at the Other Club, on April 5 at a banquet in Buckingham Palace, and April 6 at the French Embassy, where General de Gaulle was the guest of honour, having previously called on him at Hyde Park Gate. [3] There followed a quiet month, with family and friends, films in the evening, a visit to Epsom with Christopher and Mary Soames on April 19, and Macmillan as his dinner guest on the following night. [4] It was a time of sombre reflection. It was during 1960, at dinner alone with Jock Colville, that Churchill recited two stanzas which Colville wrote down 'because', he later recalled, 'I thought he was applying the words to himself'. [5] 'Winston was in a dreamy, contemplative mood,' Colville later wrote. 'I had never heard him quote those poems before—which interested me as I know all his usual poetic quotations very well.' [6]

> 'All is over: fleet career,
> Dash of greyhounds slipping thongs,
> Flight of falcon, bound of deer,
> Mad hoof-thunder in our rear.
> Cold air rushing up the lungs,
> Din of many tongues.'

'He paused a minute,' Colville later recalled, 'and then he went on':

> 'We tarry yet, We are toiling still,
> He is gone and he fares the best.
> He fought against odds, he struggled up hill,
> He has fairly earned his season of rest.' [7]

[1] Herman Wouk diary, 1 April 1960: Wouk papers.
[2] Nonie Montague Browne diary, April 1960: Lady Sargant papers.
[3] Churchill Engagements Calendar, April 1960: Churchill papers.
[4] Churchill Engagements Calendar, April 1960: Churchill papers.
[5] Colville recollections: *Footprints in Time*, London 1976, page 281.
[6] Sir John Colville recollections: notes for the author, October 1987.
[7] The poems were both by Adam Lindsay Gordon. The first stanza from Gordon's 'The Last Leap', read (in the original: 'All is over: brief career, / Dash of greyhound, slipping thongs, / Flight of falcon, leap of deer, / Cold air rushing up the lungs, / Sound of many tongues.' The second stanza from Gordon's 'Gone' should have read: 'We tarry on; We're toiling still; / He's gone and he fares the best, / He fought against odds and he struggled up hill; / He has earned his season of rest.'

65

Good Times and Bad

I T had long been Randolph Churchill's ambition to write a full-scale biography of his father. To show that he was capable of doing it, he had written a single-volume biography of the 17th Earl of Derby, *Lord Derby 'King of Lancashire'*. On 20 April 1960 Harold Macmillan, at dinner with Churchill, had told him his view of Randolph's book, which, Macmillan told Randolph two days later, 'pleased him very much'. In Macmillan's view, the book constituted 'an absolutely first class account of the politics of some thirty or forty years', admirably written and 'well documented'.[1]

Randolph was thrilled by Macmillan's praise, and when next he saw his father told him about this unexpected endorsement, and asked if he could now finally be entrusted with the task of the Churchill biography. Following a conversation at Chartwell between Churchill and Anthony Montague Browne, on May 22 Montague Browne prepared a draft letter appointing Randolph as his father's biographer.[2] The draft, approved by Lady Churchill, was signed by Churchill and sent to his son. Randolph was to be the official biographer, but was to defer his writing until after Churchill's death. Nor was anything to be published until 'at least' ten years after Churchill's death.[3] Randolph replied on May 24, four days before his forty-ninth birthday:

Dearest Papa,

Your letter has made me proud and happy. Since I first read your life of your father, thirty-five years ago when I was a boy of fourteen at Eton, it has always been my greatest ambition to write your life. And each year that has passed since this ambition first started in my mind, has nurtured it as your heroic career has burgeoned.

---

[1] 'Dear Randolph', 10 Downing Street, 22 April 1960: Randolph Churchill papers.

[2] 'Sir Winston', initialled 'AMB', 22 May 1960: Churchill papers, 2/619.

[3] 'My dear Randolph' (typed), signed in Churchill's own hand 'Yr affectionate father, WSC', 'Private and Confidential', 23 May 1960: Churchill papers, 2/619.

When the time comes, you may be sure that I shall lay all else aside and devote my declining years exclusively, to what will be a pious, fascinating and I suppose, a remunerative task.

Thank you again from the bottom of my heart for a decision which, apart from what I have already said, adds a good deal to my self-esteem and will, I trust, enable me to do honour in filial fashion, to your extraordinarily noble and wonderful life.

Your loving son

Randolph [1]

Churchill's family and closest friends watched his decline with infinite sadness. At times it was almost unbearable to see so great a life in such a reduced and ever dwindling span. 'I love you so much, darling Papa,' wrote Mary Soames on July 7, 'and hate it that life should be such a poor, pale thing for you now. But I hope you feel as beloved as you are—You & Mama mean so much to so many people. . . .' [2]

During May, Churchill gave the Queen one of his paintings, a scene of Wilton near Salisbury, where, between the wars, he had been a regular guest at Whitsuntide; indeed that festival had been known there as Winstontide. On May 11 the Queen wrote in her own hand from Buckingham Palace to thank Churchill for his gift. 'Philip and I are so thrilled,' she wrote, 'to have one of your pictures for our gallery—we do thank you most sincerely for this very kind gesture, and we do appreciate having such a delightful picture with a gloriously peaceful English summer scene. What a truly lovely place Wilton is and you have captured the feeling and pleasure of being there so well that all can feel it too.' [3]

That June, Churchill felt strong enough to attend the annual Garter ceremony at Windsor, the last occasion on which he was to do so. On July 10 he flew to Venice, to return to the calm comfort of *Christina*. It had been intended to cruise in the Baltic, and for Churchill and his wife to visit Leningrad, which she had seen and so admired in 1945. But the announcement on May 5 that an American spy plane, the U2, had been brought down over the Soviet Union, and the consequent break-up on May 16, of the Khrushchev–Eisenhower Summit in

---

[1] 'Dearest Papa', Stour, East Bergholt, Suffolk, 24 May 1960: Churchill papers, 2/619.

[2] Letter of 7 July 1960: Churchill papers, 1/136.

[3] 'Dear Sir Winston', 11 May 1960: Squerryes Lodge Archive. The picture hangs today in the Private Apartments at Windsor.

Paris, made such a destination impolitic.[1] Instead, on July 14, Churchill and his wife were at the Adriatic port of Split, where they went ashore to visit President Tito. Two days later the British Ambassador to Yugoslavia, Sir Michael Creswell, telegraphed to the Foreign Secretary, Selwyn Lloyd:

President Tito's reception of Sir Winston was cordial in the extreme and he was obviously extremely touched to be able again to meet Sir Winston, whom he had not seen since his own state visit to London in 1953. Their conversation was concerned principally with war-time memories; and current topics were only touched upon lightly.

In answer to a question from Sir Winston, Tito said that he was on the whole an optimist as regards the world situation, as he was convinced that none of the Great Powers would take it upon themselves to cause the world cataclysm which would result from a war with modern weapons.[2]

From Split, *Christina* sailed southward to Dubrovnik and the Gulf of Kotor, then on to Corfu, and through the Corinth Canal, reaching Athens on July 19. From Athens the cruise continued to Crete, where Nonie Montague Browne noted in her diary: 'A lot of men and women in Greek costume came on board to greet Sir Winston.'[3] Churchill went ashore twice: once, at Canea, as the guest at a dinner given by the Greek Liberal leader, Sophocles Venizelos, and on the following day, at Heraklion, when he was driven to see the ruins at Knossos.[4]

On July 22 *Christina* was at Rhodes, sailing on through the Greek islands to reach Athens again on July 28. After six more days of leisurely cruising, during which Diana Churchill joined her father, he flew back to London by Comet on August 4.

On August 15 Churchill asked Montague Browne to telegraph to Wendy Reves, to ask if he could come back to La Pausa in early September, for about ten days. 'Much want to see you both,' the telegram ended.[5] Unfortunately, as Emery Reves explained in a long letter to Churchill, he and his wife had felt, after Churchill's previous stay at the Hôtel de Paris rather than at La Pausa, 'that we had done something, or behaved in a manner which prevented you from returning to us'. Wendy Reves was now ill, upset by the 'intrigues' which had sought to destroy their friendship with Churchill. 'There is a

---

[1] On learning of the cancellation, Ivan Glasgov, of the Soviet Embassy in London, 'expressed the hope that Sir Winston would come to Russia another time'. (Anthony Montague Browne to Ian Samuel, 19 October 1961: Churchill papers, 2/508).

[2] Telegram No. 77 from Belgrade to the Foreign Office, 'Confidential', 16 July 1960: Churchill papers, 1/152. In 1937 Michael Creswell, then a young diplomat just returned from Berlin, had brought Churchill disturbing news of German intentions towards Austria.

[3] Nonie Montague Browne diary, 20 July 1960: Lady Sargant papers.

[4] Roy Howells, *Simply Churchill*, page 55.

[5] Telegram approved by Churchill and sent on 15 August 1960: Churchill papers, 2/532.

certain way,' Reves wrote, 'of disregarding other people's feelings which drives sensitive human beings to the border of insanity.' In October they would go to New York.[1]

'Winston showed me Emery's letter, which had grieved him,' Clementine Churchill wrote to Wendy Reves on September 23. 'He was surprised and sorry that you should feel the way you do.' As far as the Churchills were concerned, 'there were no intrigues; and we are all deeply grateful for the hospitality we have enjoyed with you'. They would go to Monte Carlo. 'We hope you will come to luncheon with us one day at the Hôtel de Paris.'[2]

On September 28 Churchill returned to the Hôtel de Paris, for a few weeks' holiday with his wife and Montague Browne. Two days before leaving London, he was the guest of honour at a dinner to celebrate the publication of the memoirs of his wartime Defence Office head and friend, Lord Ismay.[3]

The South of France revived Churchill's spirits, as it had often done in the past. On October 6 he wrote to Lord Beaverbrook, who was in Canada, of how he had been painting at La Capponcina on two days, and sitting in the sun 'in your beautiful garden' on the third. The holiday was being punctuated, however, by heavy storms.[4] 'The weather here has been patchy,' Montague Browne wrote to Jock Colville a week later, 'but Sir Winston has managed to get some painting and has begun three pictures. He also goes daily to the Casino!'[5] The only sadness was the disappearance of Toby the budgerigar, Churchill's constant companion for several years, who flew away one morning and was never seen again.

Wendy Reves was now leaving La Pausa for the United States with her husband. On October 9 Churchill wrote to her, from the Hôtel de Paris:

My dear Wendy,

I am so sorry to hear that you were vexed with me, and I cannot allow you to leave for America without telling you that the months I spent at your charming house were among the brightest in my life, and I shall always think of them as such.

I hope that you will carry with you to the New World my sincere and warmest thanks and affection.

Yours ever,

Winston S. Churchill[6]

---

[1] 'My dear Sir Winston', La Pausa, 21 August 1960: Churchill papers, 2/532.

[2] Letter of 23 September 1960: Churchill papers, 2/532.

[3] Note in Churchill papers, 2/526. The others present at this dinner were General Pownall, Lord Cunningham of Hyndhope, Lord Alexander, Sir Alan Lascelles, Sir Edward Spears, Lord Portal, Sir Robert Laycock, Colin Coote, Sir Ian Jacob and Jock Colville.

[4] 'My dear Max', Hôtel de Paris, Monte Carlo, 6 October 1960: Beaverbrook papers.

[5] Hôtel de Paris, Monte Carlo, 13 October 1960: Churchill papers, 2/343.

[6] 'My dear Wendy', Hôtel de Paris, Monte Carlo, 9 October 1960: Reves papers.

Learning that President de Gaulle was to be in Nice, Churchill expressed a wish to call on him. On the evening of October 22 he, Lady Churchill, and Montague Browne spent half an hour with the President. Four days later, Montague Browne sent an account of the meeting to the Earl of Home's Principal Private Secretary:

The President asked Sir Winston whether, had he been Prime Minister, he would have gone to the General Assembly. From the way the question was phrased he obviously expected and hoped for the answer 'No'. Sir Winston replied that he had not considered the question in the light of conditions then existing, but that he did not believe that Mr Khrushchev and the anti-Whites should be allowed to have it all their own way without being answered, and he entirely supported the Prime Minister.

'In general,' Montague Browne concluded, 'the President seemed weary but relaxed and calm. His manner throughout the visit was charming and affectionate to Sir Winston.' [1]

On his return to England, Churchill dined at the Other Club on November 3. At Churchill's suggestion, Harold Macmillan was in the chair. Churchill had also given his support to eight proposed new members, among them two recently appointed Ministers, John Profumo and Edward Heath, and the historian Sir John Wheeler-Bennett. [2]

A week later, Churchill was yet again at the Harrow School 'Songs'. In what was to be his last speech in public, he told the boys: 'I am always very glad when the day comes round for me to turn up here.' [3] Five days later Churchill slipped in his wife's room when he went to say goodnight to her, breaking a small bone in his back. 'All the people in America are distressed to hear of your accident,' Eisenhower telegraphed on November 17, 'None more so than I.' [4] 'I was so very sorry to read about Winston's accident,' the Duchess of Kent wrote to Lady Churchill on November 17, '& want to send you these few lines just to say I am thinking of you & realize what an anxious time this is for you. I do pray that he is not suffering & that he will soon be better.' [5]

A series of bulletins issued by Lord Moran and Professor Seddon

---

[1] 'Confidential', to A. C. I. Samuel (Principal Private Secretary to the Secretary of State for Foreign Affairs, 1959–63), 26 October 1960: Churchill papers, 2/523. On 27 July 1960 the Earl of Home had succeeded Selwyn Lloyd as Foreign Secretary, and Selwyn Lloyd had become Chancellor of the Exchequer.

[2] Letter of 11 August 1960 (to Jock Colville): Churchill papers, 2/343. John Profumo had been appointed Secretary of State for War, and Heath Lord Privy Seal, on 27 July 1960.

[3] Speech of 10 November 1960: Churchill papers, 2/336.

[4] 'Dear Winston', 17 November 1960: Churchill papers, 1/61.

[5] 'Dear Clemmie', Kensington Palace, 17 November 1960: Spencer-Churchill papers.

kept the public informed of Churchill's condition. 'Sir Winston has had rather a disturbed night,' the bulletin for November 10 reported, 'but his spinal injury is progressing satisfactorily and is giving no anxiety.' [1] 'Sir Winston did not have a very good night,' the bulletin of November 19 declared, 'but the pain of his injury is less.' [2]

On November 23 Churchill was introduced to Piers Dixon, who had just become engaged to his grand-daughter, Edwina Sandys. [3] As Dixon noted in his diary:

It had not been intended that I should meet Winston. However after lunch Lady C suddenly came down to say that he wanted to see me. Edwina was with him. I was very nervous and did not know what to say and, when I did have anything to say, I shouted, partly because I was so nervous and partly because I knew he was deaf.

He had a little bird which jumped on to Edwina and then on to me and pecked at my right eyelid. I took this gesture to be a mark of approbation not only from the bird but from the whole house. Winston was smoking a cigar, half sitting up in bed, winding and unwinding his hands. Edwina was, I think, very shocked by his condition. She said later that he had never looked so ill. She left almost immediately. She was very worried.

I stayed for a bit and sat down by his bedside. I am afraid I did almost all the talking. I said some silly platitudes about being pleased to be marrying his grand-daughter. I tried hard to think of non-platitudinous but suitable things to say; that I was exactly ten years older than Edwina. Winston replied 'I am ten years older than my wife.' [4]

Piers Dixon entered the family circle, with all its joys and sadness, noting after Churchill's death how, during 1960, Churchill had said to his daughter Diana: 'My life is over but it is not yet ended.' [5]

On November 23, after feeling unwell at lunchtime, Churchill had two visitors during the afternoon, Beaverbrook at 4 p.m. and Onassis at 6 p.m. [6] That same day, Lord Moran told Professor Seddon that

[1] 'Bulletin No. 3', 18 November 1960: Churchill papers, 1/61.

[2] Bulletin of 19 November 1960: Churchill papers, 1/61.

[3] Piers Dixon (born in December 1928) was the son of Sir Pierson Dixon, British Ambassador to France from 1960 to 1965, and formerly, during Churchill's second Premiership, Deputy Under-Secretary of State at the Foreign Office. From 1970 to 1974 Piers Dixon was Conservative MP for Truro (and from 1972 to 1974 Vice-Chairman of the Conservative Backbenchers' Finance Committee). His marriage with Edwina Sandys was dissolved in 1973. They had two sons, Mark, born in 1962, and Hugo, born in 1963.

[4] Piers Dixon notes for 23 November 1960 (written on 4 December 1960): Piers Dixon papers. Edwina and Piers Dixon were married on 22 December 1960. Twenty-two years after Churchill's death, Edwina, an artist who was awarded the MBE in 1983 for her services to British trade (for organising the Britain Salutes New York Festival) commented: 'I am often asked what it was like to be in the shadow of such a great man; I answer that it was not being in his shadow, it was basking in his sunlight.' (*London Portrait*, November 1987).

[5] Piers Dixon diary, 17 January 1965: Piers Dixon papers.

[6] Churchill Engagements Calendar, November 1960: Churchill papers.

that he appeared to have suffered a mild stroke.[1] The dinner at the Other Club on November 24 had to take place without him, but he was well enough, while having to stay in bed, to receive a number of visitors: both Beaverbrook and Onassis came to see him again on November 24, Sarah Churchill, 'little' Winston and Onassis on November 25, and Diana Sandys, Violet Bonham Carter and Edward Heath on November 26. On November 28 he saw Emery Reves in the afternoon, and Lord Beaverbrook on the following afternoon.[2]

November 30 was Churchill's eighty-sixth birthday. For the first time since his mild stroke a week earlier, he was able to get up, to lunch with his wife, his daughters Sarah and Mary, and his grandson Winston. After lunch his third daughter, Diana, called to see him, followed by Lord Montgomery.[3] Another visitor that day was Lord Beaverbrook, who gave Churchill a clock.[4] 'Thank you heartily for this remarkable gift,' Churchill wrote two days later, 'And thank you also dear Max for coming to see me.'[5]

A new President had been elected in the United States, John F. Kennedy. In a letter to Consuelo Balsan, formerly Duchess of Marlborough, Churchill wrote: 'Kennedy certainly has tremendous tasks before him,' and he added: 'I had a friendly exchange of messages with him after his election.'[6]

Churchill spent Christmas 1960 and the New Year of 1961 at Chartwell. 'I have been following with close interest,' he wrote to President de Gaulle on January 10, 'events in France and Algeria culminating in the Referendum. I now write to congratulate you on the outcome. It is, if I may say so, a triumph for your policies and for you personally. It is heartening to see that the French people continue so rightly to express their confidence in you.'[7]

At Stour, Randolph Churchill had begun work on his father's biography, issuing his 'Directive No. 1' on 1 February 1961, whereby he appointed the writer and journalist, Michael Wolff, to assume control of the organization, research and preparation 'of all the documents and books necessary for the accomplishment of the enterprise.'[8]

---

[1] Professor Seddon's medical notes, 23 November 1960: Churchill papers.

[2] Churchill Engagements Calendar, November 1960: Churchill papers.

[3] Churchill Engagements Calendar, November 1960: Churchill papers.

[4] '86th Birthday', 'Gifts', 30 November 1960: Churchill papers, 2/445.

[5] 'My dear Max', 28 Hyde Park Gate, 3 December 1960: Beaverbrook papers.

[6] Letter of 2 December 1960: Churchill papers, 1/80.

[7] 'My dear President', 'Private and Confidential', 10 January 1961: Squerryes Lodge Archive. On 8 January 1961 a referendum in France and Algeria approved De Gaulle's Algerian policy of seeking to suppress the French rebellion there. The rebellion itself collapsed at the end of April.

[8] 'Directive No. 1', 1 February 1961: Martin Gilbert papers. It was in March 1962 that Randolph Churchill invited me to join his team of researchers; I did so in October 1962, and remained on the team, with only a short interruption, until the summer of 1967. Randolph died in June 1968.

That February, it became clear that Clementine Churchill would need a prolonged rest, and indeed medical treatment; she was suffering, her doctor wrote, from 'nervous fatigue, depression and anxiety state', and would have to go into hospital. 'There,' her doctor wrote, 'she will be insulated from everything and will undergo a course of sedation followed by rehabilitation.'[1] Randolph Churchill, meanwhile, had begun to dictate a series of notes about his father's work and friendships, and on February 10 he lunched with his father and mother at Hyde Park Gate. Later that day Randolph set down a note of their conversation:

After lunch, when WSC and I were alone, he suddenly said 'Do you realise I have now been out of office for five years?' I replied 'Well, that's a very dreadful thing, but don't forget that between the wars you were out of office for ten years, so there is nothing to worry about.' He grinned.

He was looking far better than last time I saw him and was looking forward to his journey to Monte Carlo tomorrow and to his cruise in about three weeks time with Aristotle, starting at Gibraltar, whither they will fly, and going on to the West Indies.

He said that he had never met either Gladstone or Disraeli, but that he had seen quite a lot of Harcourt.

He agreed that I should be allowed to have Lord Randolph's papers. He seemed interested in the progress we were making with the book, and agreed that it might be quite a good idea to have the appendix volumes.

WSC said originally that he thought it was mad for me to go off to the Sahara, but later agreed that he saw the point of it. Later he said 'You will make quite a fine show for yourself about the book' and then added 'but don't give up about politics.' I said 'Well, I am happy with the book and my garden, and we might let politics skip a generation. Perhaps Winston might get interested.'[2]

That February, Churchill received an unexpected telegram. It was from the Queen and Prince Philip, then on tour in Pakistan. 'We both send you our best wishes from Malakand,' they wrote.[3] It was here, in the remote wild countryside of the former North-West Frontier of India, that Churchill had fought in the army of the Queen's great-great-grandmother.[4]

---

[1] Letter from Dr J. W. Barnett, 24 February 1961: Churchill papers, 1/135.

[2] Randolph Churchill notes, 10 February 1961: Randolph Churchill papers. Randolph's son Winston contested the Gorton Division of Manchester at a by-election in November 1967; he was Conservative MP for Stretford, Lancashire, from 1970 to 1983, and for Davyhulme, Manchester, since 1983. From 1976 to 1978 he was Conservative Party front bench spokesman on defence, and from 1979 to 1983 Vice-Chairman of the Conservative Defence Committee.

[3] Telegram of 7 February 1961: Churchill papers, 2/532.

[4] In 1897, as a Lieutenant in the 4th (the Queen's Own) Hussars, Churchill had fought with the Malakand Field Force. He had subsequently published a book, *The Story of the Malakand Field Force, An Episode of Frontier War*, his first book, published in London on 14 March 1898. The book was based in part on a series of letters which he had written for the *Daily Telegraph*

ON BOARD S/Y «CHRISTINA»

Mar 20

My Darling Clemmie,

Here is a line to keep us posted
in my own handwriting — all done
myself! And to tell you how
much I love you. We have travelled
ceaselessly over endless seas —
Quite smoothly for weeks on and
and now here we are — within
a few days of meeting Ari and his
family. This is the moment for me
to show you that I still possess
the gift of writing & continue to use
it. But I will not press it too far
Ever your devoted
W.

On March 9 Churchill flew to Gibraltar again, and once more joined *Christina*. Among those on board were Anthony and Nonie Montague Browne, and their seven-year-old daughter Jane. Reaching the West Indies two weeks later, on March 20 Churchill wrote to his wife, the first letter in his own hand for nearly two years:

My darling Clemmie,

Here is a line to keep us posted in my own handwriting—*all done myself!* And to tell you how much I love you: We have travelled ceaselessly over endless seas—*quite smoothly* for weeks on end and now here we are—within a few days of meeting *Ari* and his family. This is the moment for me to show you that I still possess the gift of writing & continue to use it. But I will not press it too far.

Ever your devoted

W [1]

On March 22 *Christina* reached Port of Spain, Trinidad. 'Sir Winston was cheered by the people on the quay,' Jane Montague Browne noted in her diary, as he set off that afternoon for a drive around the island. [2] At Port of Spain, Churchill was welcomed by the Governor-General of the Federation of the West Indies, Lord Hailes, formerly Patrick Buchan-Hepburn, who in 1929 had been his Private Secretary, and later, in his second Premiership, Chief Whip. 'I have never seen such crowds and such enthusiasm in Port of Spain,' Hailes wrote to Churchill three weeks later, 'and it was very moving to see Negro, Indian and Chinese alike with the same expression on their faces— sheer delight and above all, *gratitude*. In fact I found it so moving that I had to think of other things to avoid shedding tears.' [3]

On March 25 Churchill telegraphed to his wife from on board *Christina*:

Leaving today for Becquia to see Anthony and Clarissa. We have had pleasant meetings with Patrick and Diana Hailes and I see Harold this afternoon. The weather is hot and my cold has now gone. I do trust you are feeling better and hope for good news of you. Tender love

Winston [4]

---

during the course of the campaign, entitled 'The War in the Indian Highlands, by a Young Officer'. These letters, fifteen in all, were published in the *Daily Telegraph* between 6 October and 6 December 1897.

[1] 'My darling Clemmie', 'On board s/y *Christina*', 20 March 1961: Spencer-Churchill papers.

[2] Jane Montague Browne diary, 22 March 1961: Jane Hoare-Temple papers. Jane Montague Browne was subsequently a schoolgirl at Tudor Hall, Banbury; after completing secretarial school she became a secretary in advertising. In 1978 she married Piers Hoare-Temple, a barrister.

[3] 'Dear Sir Winston', Trinidad, 21 April 1961: Churchill papers, 1/155.

[4] 'Lady Churchill', telegram, *Christina*, 25 March 1961: Spencer-Churchill papers.

'We stayed on the boat,' Jane Montague Browne noted in her diary, 'and Sir Winston went to visit Mr Macmillan.'[1] On March 31 Churchill telegraphed again to his wife:

Have had agreeable voyage in Grenadines and Anthony and Clarissa lunched on board. We are now bound for Jamaica and Haiti. If convenient for you I propose to fly home on April 13. We will travel via New York which is shortest air route.

Love

Winston[2]

April 1 was Clementine Churchill's seventy-sixth birthday.

Five days later, *Christina* reached the Bahamas. 'After tea we all visited Nassau,' Jane Montague Browne noted in her youthful diary. 'It was pretty. We drove round in cars. Sir Winston too.'[3]

From the West Indies, *Christina* sailed slowly up the Atlantic coast of the United States. Off Cape Hatteras it ran into what Anthony Montague Brown later recalled as 'a most tremendous storm', and he added: 'The old man was quite excited about the storm. To see it, he sat on a piano, in the games room, held down by four sailors.'[4] On reaching New York's Hudson River, *Christina* made fast at a mid-river buoy off the West 79th Street boat basin. At midday, Adlai Stevenson, the United States Ambassador to the United Nations, arrived by launch as one of the luncheon guests.[5]

After lunch, Churchill sat on deck watching the *Queen Mary* leaving the Cunard pier for a transatlantic voyage. That night Bernard Baruch was his guest at dinner. 'It will be good to see my old friend again,' Baruch told the reporters as he boarded the launch. 'He's a wonderful young man at eighty-six.'[6]

During dinner, Montague Browne received a message to call 'Operator 18' in Washington, to take 'a top priority call'.[7] It was President Kennedy, asking if Churchill would like to fly down to Washington in the Presidential aeroplane 'and spend a couple of days with me'. Montague Browne had to make an immediate decision. He did so, explaining to Kennedy that Churchill could no longer undertake such a journey.[8]

Churchill was due to fly back to London on April 13, but fierce

[1] Jane Montague Browne diary, 25 March 1961: Jane Hoare-Temple papers.
[2] 'Lady Churchill', telegram, *Christina*, 31 March 1961: Spencer-Churchill papers.
[3] Jane Montague Browne diary, 6 April 1961: Jane Hoare-Temple papers.
[4] Anthony Montague Browne recollections: in conversation with the author, 14 July 1987.
[5] *New York Times*, 13 April 1961.
[6] *New York Herald Tribune*, 13 April 1961. Baruch himself was ninety (having been born on 19 August 1870).
[7] *Newsweek*, 24 April 1961.
[8] Anthony Montague Browne recollections: in conversation with the author, 14 July 1987.

winds, reaching fifty miles an hour, made it impossible for him to be transferred from *Christina*. That night *Christina* moored at the dockside, when Bernard Baruch was once more Churchill's guest at dinner. On the following morning Churchill left the yacht for the airport, stopping briefly at Baruch's apartment so that the two men could drive to Idlewild Airport together.

Churchill reached London on the evening of April 14. 'I am glad to say,' Montague Browne reported to Eden a month later, 'that he is in good health and spirits, and that Lady Churchill on the whole is a good deal better.'[1] 'I too found our cruise delightful,' Churchill wrote to Nonie Montague Browne in answer to her thank-you letter, and he added: 'The fact that you and Jane were with us added very much to my pleasure.' Following the disappearance of Churchill's budgerigar Toby in Monte Carlo, Nonie Montague Browne had given him a new one. 'Byron,' he reported, 'is settling down well in his new home, and is in good spirits.'[2]

Six weeks after his return to London, Churchill received a request from the Prime Minister of Israel, David Ben-Gurion, for a meeting. He agreed, and on June 2 received the man whom he had just missed in the South of France, and whom Sarah had so enjoyed meeting in Israel. At the meeting, Ben-Gurion was accompanied by his Private Secretary Yitzhak Navon, and by the Israeli Ambassador to London, Arthur Lourie.

The conversation between Churchill and Ben-Gurion lasted about twenty minutes, Montague Browne reported to the Foreign Office later that day. Ben Gurion had told Churchill 'that in his view Iraq would "survive" and be strong enough to contain her own Communists'. He was 'more doubtful about the survival of Jordan which hung on the life of one brave man, to wit, the King'. Ben-Gurion also told Churchill 'that Egypt was slowly preparing for war, that they had twenty and possibly more MIG 19 fighters which were better than anything the Israelis had, and about 200 Russian Army and Airforce instructors'. He added that he had asked Harold Macmillan 'to make available suitable weapons to deal with the air side'.[3]

Yitzhak Navon later recalled the subsequent conversation:

Churchill said that he was always a friend of the Jewish people and Zionism,

---

[1] Letter of 16 May 1961: Churchill papers, 2/517.

[2] 'My dear Nonie', 26 April 1961: Lady Sargant papers.

[3] 'Confidential', 2 June 1961: Churchill papers, 2/506. Letter to M. J. Wilmshurst, Lord Home's Assistant Private Secretary.

and Ben-Gurion responded with expressions of admiration for his friendship and his stand during the Second World War as a leader of the free world which was saved, thanks to him. He told of his stay in London during the Blitz and the impressions he gained of the courageous stand of the British people.

Churchill related en passant, that he had written an essay on Moses. Ben-Gurion expressed great interest and requested to receive a copy.

At the end of the meeting Churchill turned to Ben-Gurion and said: 'You are a brave leader of a great nation.' Ben-Gurion thanked him emotionally and responded with expressions of appreciation.[1]

After Ben-Gurion had gone, Churchill asked Montague Browne to look out a copy of his essay on Moses. It had been published in book form in 1932, in *Thoughts and Adventures*. Both men then read it. 'I have read *Moses*,' Montague Browne wrote to Churchill on June 3, 'and I agree that it is not up to your literary level. However, you promised it to Mr Ben-Gurion, and you may therefore wish to send him a copy of the book with a short letter. I submit a draft.'[2] To the Israeli Ambassador, Arthur Lourie, Montague Browne sent both book and letter. 'As you will see from the letter,' he told the Ambassador, 'Sir Winston does not think very much of the essay himself!'[3]

The letter, drafted by Montague Browne and signed by Churchill, noted that Churchill had re-read the essay and 'would not particularly wish it to be remembered as one of my literary works'. It also expressed the hope 'that we shall have another opportunity of meeting again' and sent Ben-Gurion 'my earnest good wishes for the great tasks in which you are engaged'.[4] The meeting, replied Arthur Lourie, 'was a moving occasion also for those of us who accompanied Mr Ben-Gurion to the talk'.[5]

That summer, Churchill returned to the Hôtel de Paris at Monte Carlo. Once more he kept his wife informed of his daily life in three handwritten letters, each written with difficulty, and, almost for the first time in his long life as a letter writer, undated:

My darling One,

I write, as I promised to salute you with love and kisses. You will recognise the handwriting, for it is my own. It is a feat.

We got here all right, and I am sitting up in bed looking at the view, which you know so well. The sun is shining brightly and perhaps it will continue to shine. I hope so.

---

[1] Yitzhak Navon recollections: letter to the author, 6 July 1987. In 1982 Navon became President of the State of Israel; he was subsequently (from 1986) Minister of Education and Culture.

[2] 'Sir Winston', initialled 'AMB', 3 June 1961: Churchill papers, 2/506.

[3] Letter of 4 June 1961: Churchill papers, 2/506.

[4] 'My dear Prime Minister', 'Private', 4 June 1961: Churchill papers, 2/506.

[5] 'Dear Mr Montague Browne', 9 June 1961: Churchill papers, 2/506.

I am going out for a drive this afternoon in the mountains and look forward to it.

I send you this letter with all my love and hope you will like to get it.

All my kisses.

Yours ever

W

My darling,

We seem to have only just arrived after our dashing start, but the weather is lovely, and even better than we left behind us. The Prefect met us and was all over us with good will. We sailed off through to Monte Carlo & arrived in time for an excellent dinner. Since then we have had the best weather by night & day. Each day better than the last.

I send you my best love & wish I could have persuaded you to join us.

With many kisses

Yours devotedly,

Winston

My darling,

I am writing you a letter with my own paw, from lovely sunshine. We are all going to bask in it from the balcony. I hasten to send you this assurance of my devotion. How I wish you were here.

Tender love

W[1]

'I think Sir Winston is bored,' Anthony Montague Browne wrote to Lord Beaverbrook on June 12. 'There is nobody about at all,' and he added: 'Today we took the liberty of going to sit in the sun in your garden at La Capponcina. It was beautiful and peaceful.' [2]

On his balcony at the Hôtel de Paris, overlooking Monte Carlo and the wide expanse of the Mediterranean, Churchill had difficulty lighting his cigars. 'How very kind of you,' he wrote to Nonie Montague Browne on June 19, 'to send me the special matches. They are most successful, especially on the terrace where there is often a breeze.' Churchill added: 'We are having a pleasant stay down here, and the weather is now excellent. Yours ever, W.' [3]

On June 25 Churchill wrote to his wife on Hôtel de Paris notepaper, in his own hand:

My darling Clemmie,

I am looking forward a great deal to coming home. We have had wonderful weather here, but you seem to have had a fine show too. There is nothing like England when it chooses to be good. I am most eager to get back & to sit in the sunlight.

[1] Undated letters, Hôtel de Paris: Spencer-Churchill papers.

[2] Hôtel de Paris, Monte Carlo, 12 June 1961: Churchill papers, 2/519.

[3] 'My dear Nonie', Hôtel de Paris, 19 June 1961: Lady Sargant papers.

Here we have had a jolly time. Every day we have ranged the country & climbed some new fortress. There is no lack of these, & the French are proud of their defences in this much fought over land.

I have *not, so far*, visited the Casino. But I think I will go before I go.

Tender love my darling. I am longing to kiss you.

You are a sweet duck.

Winston [1]

Returning to Hyde Park Gate at the beginning of July, Churchill was asked if he would visit Churchill College in October for the laying of the foundation stone. 'I think October 14 would be all right,' Montague Browne wrote to the College Bursar, Major-General J. R. C. Hamilton, on July 5, 'but you will perhaps understand if subsequent events make it impossible for Sir Winston to attend. Moreover, I fear that he would not be able to make a speech—but you probably did not expect one.' [2]

To D. McCormack Smyth, a Canadian graduate who had invited Churchill to the college to address the Advanced Students there, Montague Browne replied, on July 6: 'For your strictly private information, his health is somewhat uncertain, and we have to be very careful not to make too many engagements for him, as they tire him much, particularly if it involves meeting a large number of people.' [3]

On Sunday July 16 Lord Beaverbrook lunched at Chartwell, bringing with him his friend Lady Dunn. [4] Both Churchill and his wife were there to entertain them. 'Clemmie and I greatly enjoyed seeing you and Lady Dunn last Sunday,' Churchill wrote on July 20, 'and I do hope that we shall meet again before long.' Since the lunch, Beaverbrook had sent Churchill Alan Clark's book on the First World War, *The Donkeys*, 'which I am reading with interest', Churchill added. [5]

On August 12 Lord Montgomery and Piers Dixon were among Churchill's guests at Chartwell. [6] On the following day, Piers Dixon noted in his diary:

After the guests had left, for the first time one was able—largely at Monty's prompting—to get some ideas from him. These included the opinion that:

[1] 'My darling Clemmie', Hôtel de Paris, Monte Carlo, 25 June 1961: Spencer-Churchill papers.

[2] 'Private', 5 July 1961: Churchill papers, 2/571.

[3] 'Private', 6 July 1961: Churchill papers, 2/576. Twenty-two years later, McCormack Smyth was a founder member of the Churchill Society for the Advancement of Parliamentary Democracy, based in Toronto, Canada (President, F. Bartlett Watt).

[4] Marcia Anastia Christoforides (known as Christofor), the widow of Sir James Dunn. She married Lord Beaverbrook, as his second wife, on 7 June 1963.

[5] 'My dear Max', initialled by Churchill 'W', 20 July 1961: Beaverbrook papers.

[6] Churchill Engagements Calendar, 12 August 1961: Churchill papers.

1. French had been a greater man than Haig in the first world war.

2. Balfour had been the best leader we had had in this century. Lloyd George had not been as good. Baldwin had been a poor leader. Chamberlain had been better than Baldwin, in fact quite good.

At this point Winston suddenly became his old self. With a twinkle in his eye and with great strength of voice, he said, 'But then you see I am prejudiced. The first thing he did when the war started was to ask me to join his government.' [1]

On August 16 Randolph Churchill lunched with his father, bringing with him the American girl, Kay Halle, whom he had once, thirty years earlier, hoped to marry. 'This is what I remember,' she later wrote, 'of that last visit to Chartwell with Randolph':

On our arrival their pony had first escaped through the open gate and the head farmer was rushing out to recover it. Churchill was sitting grinning over the escape and saying he hoped the pony was having fun outside before he is recaptured and returned home.

During lunch I sat next to the Great Man, at his right, and he rose with his glass of hock and turning to me he said, 'Kay, let us drink to your *great* President, and—and ours.' I think it was his delicate way of expressing his fervent wish for a union of Great Britain and the United States as a beginning for a Union of *all* the Democracies.

Later, that afternoon, he said that he felt the Commonwealth System of his country was an example to follow, as he described it, each member country in the British Commonwealth is completely independent but they are united under the symbol—*The Crown*. He hoped that soon we would follow & our symbol would be *The Union*. He believed that if *all* the democracies were to join together it could become a great force in helping to solve our multiple world problems.

Before Randolph and I departed for London we sat in the garden with Sir Winston & his lovely Clemmie and he praised our Constitution as one of the finest political documents but, 'I think our Parliamentary system of Government is a cut ahead of yours. In our system if you win a war the Queen or King is cheered; if you lose it, Parliament fails.' Then looking at me with that look in his eyes which he saw into the far off future, he said, 'Kay, you know I love your country—half mine—but I warn it from becoming stripped bare by the curse of plenty.' [2]

Among Churchill's visitors at Chartwell in August was Alan Hodge, who had been invited with his wife and two daughters on Sunday August 20. Two days later Hodge wrote in thanks:

... my daughters were entranced by the opportunity of meeting you. They will be telling their grandchildren about the occasion many years hence.

My older girl felt she had had such an exciting day that she went to bed as

[1] Piers Dixon diary, 13 August 1961: Piers Dixon papers.

[2] Kay Halle recollections: letter to the author, 12 June 1987.

soon as we got home, in order to recollect her impressions in tranquillity. The younger one, with the red head, stayed up and played a hand of bezique with me. It seemed very appropriate.[1]

On August 21 Churchill flew back to Nice, and to the Hôtel de Paris at Monte Carlo. His grandson Winston, now an undergraduate at Christ Church, Oxford, was also with him. To his wife, Churchill wrote during this August visit, in his own hand:

My dearest Clemmie,

Here is a letter in my own paw. All is vy pleasant and the days slip by. We are steadily wiping off old friendship's debts with lunches & dinners. I find it vy hard to write a good letter and wonder at the rate with which my friends accomplish their daily tasks. It is amazing they can succeed so well.

But now here I have written what is at least the expression of my love Darling. When I was young I wrote fairly well, but now at last I am played out. You have my fondest love.

Your devoted

Winston

PS I am daily astonished by the development I see in my namesake. He is a wonderful boy. I am so glad I have got to know him.[2]

While he was at the Hôtel de Paris, Churchill was invited by Emery and Wendy Reves to lunch or dine at La Pausa.[3] 'Dear Wendy and Emery,' he replied, 'alas I cannot lunch or dine before my departure as you so kindly suggest. All good wishes, Winston.'[4]

On his last Sunday in Monte Carlo, September 3, Churchill decided to visit La Capponcina. Beaverbrook's housekeeper was 'out for a few hours', Montague Browne explained to Beaverbrook in a letter, 'and so Sgt Murray climbed over your wall and let the car in. I hope you will excuse this breaking and entering of your property?'[5]

'I had a most agreeable stay,' Churchill wrote to Aristotle Onassis on his return to London, 'and I would like to tell you again how grateful I am to you for all the arrangements you have made and which the Société des Bains de Mer so effectively carry out, to make my stays at the top of the Hôtel de Paris so easy and pleasant.'[6]

'Sir Winston is very well,' Montague Browne wrote to Lord Beaverbrook on September 23, 'and more alert intellectually than for some time. He asks me to put to you this question: Is the French Canadian

---

[1] 'My dear Sir Winston', 22 August 1961: Churchill papers, 2/526.
[2] 'My dearest Clemmie', August 1961: Spencer-Churchill papers.
[3] Telegram of 1 September 1961: Churchill papers, 1/149.
[4] Telegram of 2 September 1961: Churchill papers, 1/149.
[5] Letter of 23 September 1961: Churchill papers, 2/519.
[6] 'My dear Ari', 8 September 1961: Churchill papers, 1/148.

population of Canada going to outnumber the British Canadian, and if so, when, and what are the results going to be?'[1]

Also on September 23, Montague Browne asked Churchill if he wanted to send a message to David Ben-Gurion on his seventy-fifth birthday. 'You have *not* done so in previous years,' Montague Browne pointed out.[2] The two men had now met, however, and Churchill decided that he did want to send a message. 'On your 75th birthday,' the message read, 'I send you my congratulations and good wishes.'[3] Ben-Gurion replied to Churchill's telegram:

My dear Sir Winston,

I was deeply moved to receive your greeting on the occasion of my birthday, and rejoiced to see that you still remember such trifles. It recalled to my mind the few unforgettable moments I spent with you at the beginning of June, and I cherish as a precious possession your book of essays, which includes that on Moses.

I hold you in esteem and affection, not only—not even mainly—because of your unfailing friendship to our people and your profound sympathy with its resurgence in our ancient homeland. Your greatness transcends all national boundaries.

I happened to be in London, from the beginning of May till September 1940, and I heard the historic speeches in which you gave utterance to the iron determination of your people and yourself to fight to the end against the Nazi foe. I saw you then not only as the symbol of your people and its greatness, but as the voice of the invincible and uncompromising conscience of the human race at a time of danger to the dignity of man, created in the image of God. It was not only the liberties and the honour of your own people that you saved.

If your advice had been taken in the last year of the war, the grave crisis over the question of Berlin, which has aroused the apprehensions of the civilized world, would never have arisen, and some of the East European countries would have remained within the bounds of Western Europe.

Your words and your deeds are indelibly engraved in the annals of humanity. Happy the people that has produced such a son.

In profound admiration and esteem.

David Ben-Gurion[4]

'I have not failed to give Mr Ben-Gurion's letter to Sir Winston, to whom it afforded much pleasure,' Montague Browne informed the Israeli Ambassador on October 12.[5] Two days later Churchill wrote direct to Ben-Gurion, at his desert home in the Negev: 'My dear Prime Minister, I am indeed obliged to you for your graceful and charming letter. It gave me great pleasure to read what you said, and

---

[1] Letter of 23 September 1961: Churchill papers, 2/519.
[2] 'Sir Winston', initialled 'AMB', 23 September 1961: Churchill papers, 2/506.
[3] Telegram sent 27 September 1961: Churchill papers, 2/506.
[4] 'My dear Prime Minister', from Sde Boker, 2 October 1961: Churchill papers, 2/506.
[5] Letter to Arthur Lourie, 12 October 1961: Churchill papers, 2/506.

I would like to assure you again of my very warm good wishes both for the State of Israel and for you personally.' [1]

On October 14 Churchill was to fly from Biggin Hill to Cambridge to lay the foundation stone of Churchill College. Unfortunately, he could not do so. 'The journey,' explained Montague Browne to the Bursar, 'even if we lay on an aircraft, is quite a long and tiring one, and although Sir Winston is much better than he was some months ago, I do not think he feels quite up to this public occasion when, whatever the arrangements, he would think himself bound to make a brief speech.' [2]

On 18 October 1961, Churchill dined with Anthony Eden, who three months earlier had been created Earl of Avon. The two men talked of the situation in Ghana. 'I find,' wrote Churchill to Harold Macmillan on the following day, 'that he shares the increasing perturbation with which I view the Queen's forthcoming visit there.' Churchill went on to explain to the Prime Minister:

I have the impression that there is widespread uneasiness both over the physical safety of the Queen and, perhaps more, because her visit would seem to endorse a regime which has imprisoned hundreds of Opposition members without trial and which is thoroughly authoritarian in tendency.

I have little doubt that Nkrumah would use the Queen's visit to bolster up his own position.

No doubt Nkrumah would be much affronted if the visit were now cancelled and Ghana might leave the Commonwealth. I am not sure that that would be a great loss. Nkrumah's vilification of this country and his increasing association with our enemies does not encourage one to think that his country could ever be more than an opportunist member of the Commonwealth family.

'Is it too late,' Churchill asked, 'for the Queen's plans to be changed?' [3]

Macmillan replied that same day, from Admiralty House, where he was living while 10 Downing Street was being repaired from damages some of which dated back to the Blitz. [4] It was 'a great tragedy', Macmillan wrote, that the Queen's visit to Ghana 'did not take place

[1] 'My dear Prime Minister', 'Private', 14 October 1961: Churchill papers, 2/506.

[2] Letter of 25 September 1961 (to Major-General J. R. C. Hamilton): Churchill papers, 2/571.

[3] 'My dear Harold', 'Private and Confidential', 19 October 1961: Churchill papers, 2/508.

[4] As First Lord of the Admiralty, Churchill had lived at Admiralty House from November 1910 to 1915 and again from September 1939 to May 1940. He had also lived there as Prime Minister from 10 May to 20 June 1940, to give Neville Chamberlain time to leave 10 Downing Street without rush.

when it was originally planned over a year ago, for then things were calm. Unfortunately, it had to be postponed owing to The Queen's baby.[1] Now there is this dilemma to which you refer.' Macmillan also told Churchill: 'I need hardly say that Her wish is to go. This is natural with so courageous a personality.'[2]

The Queen's visit did take place: from 9 to 20 November. 'Sir Winston is well,' Montague Browne wrote to Lord Beaverbrook on November 16, 'but rather bored with events, and disturbed by the international scene and notably by the Queen going to Ghana and thus endorsing Nkrumah's corrupt and tyrannical regime.'[3]

On October 31 Churchill was present at Westminster for the State Opening of Parliament. On the following night he went with his wife to Quaglino's restaurant for the coming out dance of their grand daughter Celia Sandys. 'The occasion was marked,' Roy Howells later recalled, 'by the attendance of practically every member of the Churchill family. Sir Winston, who has seen many a dance step come and go, lightly tapped his foot in time with the music, the Twist. It was the first time it had been played at a debutante dance in London. . . .'[4]

Churchill did not get to bed that night until 2 a.m. On the following day, after lunch at Hyde Park Gate, he again went to the House of Commons, and in the evening to the Savoy, for a dinner of the Other Club. But he no longer felt strong enough to go to 'Songs' at Harrow.

On November 30 Churchill was eighty-seven.[5] That night Lord Beaverbrook dined with him at Hyde Park Gate. 'I think you know,' Churchill wrote to him two days later, 'how much your friendship has meant to me over the years.'[6]

Immediately after his birthday, Churchill flew once more to Nice, and once again took up residence in the Hôtel de Paris at Monte Carlo. To his wife, who had remained in England, he wrote in his own hand, over two pages:

[1] Prince Andrew (subsequently Duke of York) had been born on 19 February 1960.

[2] 'Dear Winston', 'Private and Confidential', Admiralty House, 19 October 1961: Churchill papers, 2/508.

[3] Letter of 16 November 1961: Churchill papers, 2/519.

[4] Roy Howells recollections: *Simply Churchill*, page 74.

[5] His gifts included a case of Pol Roger champagne, 1943, from Madame Pol Roger; eight woodcock from the former head of his Map Room, Sir Richard Pim; goldfish from Lady Juliet Duff; brandy from Harold Macmillan, young Winston and his mother Pamela, Jock and Meg Colville, Edwina and Piers Dixon, and Celia and Julian Sandys; woolly boots from Anthony and Nonie Montague Browne; violets from Lady Violet Bonham Carter; cigars from Onassis; gloves from Mary Soames; and an Owl and Pussycat book and calendar from Lady Lytton. ('87 Birthday', 'Gifts', 30 November 1961: Churchill papers, 2/446.)

[6] 'My dear Max', 28 Hyde Park Gate, 2 December 1961: Beaverbrook papers.

My darling,

Here I am with a pen in my hand & a full sheet of paper before me. I believe I could write a whole letter jobbed in a strong hand together without difficulty; and I think I will take this business up again.

We are now half way through our journey & are already counting the days when the red bricks of Chartwell will shine before us. I am a shocking scribbler & the more I try to write a letter the worse it looks.

I love you vy much indeed my darling Clemmie but I think I have lost the art of writing & when the page is finished I am quite ashamed of all my remaining efficiency as an author, but I am sure you will like to receive this.

Many kisses XXXX

Winston [1]

On December 13 Churchill returned to England, where he spent Christmas at Chartwell. On Boxing Day his guests were two grand-children, Julian and Celia Sandys, their mother Diana, as well as Clementine Churchill's cousin Sylvia Henley, and Edward Heath. 'I have been daily at Chartwell,' Montague Browne wrote to Beaver-brook on 8 January 1962, 'and find Sir Winston physically well enough, but in low spirits and without energy or interest.' [2] 'Sir Winston has been rather low and depressed for some time,' Montague Browne wrote to Lord Ismay a week later, 'and taking very little interest in affairs. But in the last two days he seems brighter.' [3]

On January 24 Churchill dictated a letter to Lord Beaverbrook, about the resignation of Neville Chamberlain from Churchill's War Cabinet in 1940, and on the reasons why Chamberlain had remained in the War Cabinet after Churchill became Prime Minister. He had already asked Montague Browne to explain to Beaverbrook, who was writing a history of British politics in 1940, that Chamberlain had not been forced out in any way. To Beaverbrook, Churchill wrote:

My dear Max,

Anthony has shown me your correspondence about Chamberlain's final resignation. Thank you for what you say about not carrying passengers. I like this compliment, and you yourself were certainly never a passenger!

When Chamberlain's health deteriorated, he offered me his resignation without any prompting from my side. We parted on friendly terms and as

[1] Undated letter, marked by Lady Churchill 'Monte Carlo, December 1961': Spencer-Chur-chill papers.

[2] Letter of 8 January 1962: Churchill papers, 2/519.

[3] Letter of 16 January 1962: Churchill papers, 2/526.

far as I knew he never bore me the slightest animosity. That was why I caused Anthony to write to you.

I do hope all goes well with you. I am contemplating coming out to the South a little later in the Parliamentary Session, and of course your being out there is the greatest inducement to me to come.

Yours ever,

W [1]

A few days later, Churchill wrote to the Queen:

Madam,

At the conclusion of the first decade of your Reign, I would like to express to Your Majesty my fervent hopes and wishes for many happy years to come. It is with pride that I recall that I was your Prime Minister at the inception of these ten years of devoted service to our country.

With my humble duty,
I remain,
Your Majesty's faithful
subject and servant,

Winston S. Churchill [2]

The Queen replied on the following day, from Buckingham Palace, in her own hand:

My dear Sir Winston,

I was most touched to receive your letter of good wishes on the tenth anniversary of my succession.

I shall always count myself fortunate that you were my Prime Minister at the beginning of my reign, and that I was able to receive the wise counsel and also friendship which I know my father valued so very much as well.

Yours very sincerely,

Elizabeth R [3]

Churchill now made plans to go on a further cruise with Aristotle Onassis, starting from Monte Carlo on April 5, and visiting Libya, Lebanon and Greece. 'I fear much, however,' Montague Browne wrote to one of Macmillan's Private Secretaries, Philip de Zulueta, 'that Sir Winston will insist on visiting Israel. I had thought that our host, Mr Onassis, would have been debarred from going there because of his oil interests and his relations with the Arab countries, but I find that this is not so. I will do what I can to persuade Sir Winston not to go to Israel, but I cannot guarantee it in view of his long association with Israel and his outspoken feelings as a Zionist.'

Montague Browne added: 'I will let you know how things develop,

[1] 'My dear Max', 24 January 1962: Beaverbrook papers.
[2] 'Madam', 5 February 1962: Churchill papers, 2/532.
[3] 'My dear Sir Winston', 6 February 1962: Squerryes Lodge Archive.

and possibly as a last resort the Prime Minister might consider writing to Sir Winston if it is thought that it would be really harmful for Sir Winston to stop in Israel.'[1]

On March 14, as the time for Churchill's cruise approached, Montague Browne wrote to Beaverbrook of how 'his hearing has deteriorated further in the last six months'.[2]

On April 4 Churchill was ready to go on his cruise. 'At present,' Lord Moran wrote to Onassis's brother-in-law, Professor Theodore Garofalides, 'Sir Winston is in pretty good form.'[3] As cruise reading, Montague Browne had selected twenty books for him, among them Glubb Pasha's *War in the Desert*, Jane Austen's *Persuasion* and *Northanger Abbey*, and Robert Graves's *Claudius the God*, and *Count Belisarius*.[4]

With Churchill as guests of Onassis on the cruise were Bill Deakin and his wife Pussy, Professor Garofalides and his wife, Anthony Montague Browne, his wife and eight-year-old daughter Jane, and, to accompany Churchill, Roy Howells and Sergeant Murray. 'As you know,' Montague Browne had written to the British Ambassador in Beirut, Sir Moore Crosthwaite, on March 22, 'Sir Winston is now eighty-seven and his vigour and hearing have very much deteriorated. He would not expect any unusual facilities or attentions, and any official ceremonies would be undesirable. What has happened in the past on our cruises, of which there have been about eight, is that on arrival at a capital city we have continued to live on board the yacht, and Sir Winston pays brief visits to the shore usually lasting not more than an hour or two each.' Churchill usually dined and lunched on the yacht, Montague Browne explained, 'and he and our host would, I know, be very pleased if you would come and dine and perhaps bring one or two suitable local dignitaries if you saw fit'.[5]

Churchill flew to Nice on April 6, sailing that same day from Monte Carlo, and content to sit on deck in the spring sun of the Mediterranean. 'Sir Winston is increasingly disinclined,' Montague Browne wrote to Beaverbrook on April 25, 'to go ashore at the points we visit.'[6] 'Please let me know how you are,' Churchill wrote to his wife in his own hand during this long voyage, and he added, 'I do hope you are getting on & will soon be thriving again. Yours ever, Pig.'[7]

Returning from the cruise to Monte Carlo, Churchill went once more to the Hôtel de Paris. Then, at the end of April, he flew back to

---

[1] 'Private and Confidential', 23 February 1962: Churchill papers, 1/155.
[2] Letter of 14 March 1962: Churchill papers, 2/519.
[3] Letter of 4 April 1962: Churchill papers, 1/155.
[4] 'Books for Cruise, April 1962': Churchill papers, 1/155.
[5] 'Private and Confidential', 22 March 1962: Churchill papers, 1/155.
[6] Letter of 25 April 1962: Churchill papers, 2/519.
[7] 'Darling', undated: Spencer-Churchill papers.

Britain, spending May mostly at Chartwell, with visits to London to dine at the Other Club on May 10 and to celebrate Lord Beaverbrook's eighty-third birthday on May 25, at a dinner party given by Lord Rothermere. Churchill remained at Chartwell that June, with an excursion to Cherkley on June 3 to lunch with Lord Beaverbrook. On June 26 he made his first journey that month to London, en route to the airport, for a return to the Hôtel de Paris at Monte Carlo, accompanied by Montague Browne, Roy Howells, and a New Zealand nurse, Miss Robin Powell.

On June 27, Churchill's first full day back at Monte Carlo, he spent the afternoon in Beaverbrook's garden at La Capponcina. Then, early on the morning of June 28, in his hotel bedroom, he slipped off the edge of his bed, breaking his hip. He stayed where he fell, out of reach of his bell, making himself as comfortable as he could. When Miss Powell found him an hour later, she at once sent for Howells. 'I found him lying on the floor in his bedroom,' Howells later recalled, 'covered by a blanket and with his head propped up by a mound of pillows. He seemed reasonably calm and, smiling benignly, said, "I think I've hurt my leg." When it came to suffering pain I knew he was remarkably strong.' [1]

Howells telephoned at once to Dr Roberts, who, arranged for Churchill to be X-rayed with the portable apparatus in the hotel. He was then taken to Monaco hospital, where an extensive plaster cast was applied, enclosing his left leg, his stomach and his lower chest.

'When I went to see him,' Montague Browne later recalled, 'he sent everyone out of the room and said to me, "I want to die in England." I relayed this to No. 10. Harold Macmillan sent an RAF Comet to pick him up in Nice. The Monte Carlo doctors were furious and said that I was killing him.' [2]

Churchill was flown back to London on June 29. On arrival in London, while lying flat on his back, he gave a V-sign from his stretcher. At the airport he was met by Clementine Churchill, Lord Moran and the orthopaedic surgeon, Philip Yeoman; he was then driven by ambulance to the Middlesex Hospital. 'He was cheerful and not distressed,' noted Professor Seddon when his patient arrived, 'and, in particular, he said he had no pain in the back.' [3]

The operation to pin Churchill's hip was a success. Two days later he was lifted from his hospital bed into an armchair. There was no more pain.

Churchill remained at the Middlesex for three weeks. Each evening,

---

[1] Roy Howells recollections: *Simply Churchill*, page 87.
[2] Anthony Montague Browne recollections: notes for the author, 24 March 1987.
[3] Professor Seddon, medical notes, 29 June 1962: Seddon papers.

after dinner, Professor Seddon joined his illustrious patient for coffee, noting in his diary:

When I arrived the coffee, brandy and cigars appeared. Sir Winston poured the coffee himself and always asked whether I preferred white or brown sugar. Then the brandy. Incidentally (I had no idea what he was like in his younger days) I have never met anyone who could make a modest dose of cognac last so long.

The big ceremonial was choosing the cigar, about four boxes were placed on his bed tray. Each was opened and he pawed through the cigars to find one that was exactly right; he sniffed them, he rolled them between his fingers and listened to them. What good that did defeated me, because he was deafer than me. I think I smoked these great cigars on three evenings. Then I gave up: they were just too big, and I asked if I might light a pipe instead. He agreed but added—about the cigars—'You're still young: it's simply a matter of experience.'

Sometimes we talked. He waxed enthusiastic about Marrakech and painting there. I said I had been once, and even done a little painting. On several evenings the Rank Organization sent a man in with a projector and a film that they thought might appeal to him. Maybe I was in on two film sessions, but can remember only one: *Sink the Bismarck*. I think I watched the Grand Old Warrior as much as the movie. He never took his eyes off it, and they lit up. He sat upright and his usually pale face flushed. His cigar went out: he just held it: his mouth opened in rapt attention. Winston was fighting the battle over again.[1]

The newspapers followed Churchill's progress with concern, asking each of his visitors for some comment. 'He is extremely robust,' Christopher Soames told the waiting journalists on July 10, 'Talking to him, he seems in splendid form.'[2]

On the afternoon of July 11, Randolph Churchill went to the Middlesex Hospital to see his father, noting that night:

He was, considering everything, looking well; he was sweetly affectionate, absent-minded and bloody minded. His great grievance was a metal tent over his left foot (to keep the sheet and counterpane from pressing on his left leg). He asked for the nurse, whom I got, and said to her: 'Couldn't you take this damn thing away?' She said 'No' and withdrew. A little later he said with great pathos to me 'Wouldn't even you take it away?' I did, and then regretted it and went out and called the nurse who came back and replaced it rather violently, hurting one of his toes in doing so. All nurses are madly in love with doctors and obey their orders unthinkingly. WSC's hope of living is in his will power and not in the skill of doctors however experienced and devoted.

If he continues to be frustrated in small matters he will blow up and die.

[1] Professor Seddon, 'A personal note': Seddon papers.
[2] *The Times*, 11 July 1962.

A little later, Sergeant Murray, the detective, poked his nose round the door and WSC said 'Won't you take this thing away?' 'No, Sir Winston' said that disciplined man 'the nurses say you must keep it there.'

I was with him for forty minutes and as I have been told that it was a good thing for him to wiggle his toes and move his left ankle, I tickled his toes through the counterpane. He wriggled them with great effect and when the counterpane was removed I looked at his toes. They were still as beautifully shaped as ever and the nails were exquisitely manicured.

He did not seem to want me to leave. When I said 'Would you like me to come and see you again?' he reacted more brightly and coherently than at any time during our talk:—He said 'Next time you come to see me I hope I will receive you in the House of Commons.' [1]

On July 20 Churchill had two visitors at the Middlesex Hospital. The first was Eisenhower, the second, Harold Macmillan. 'He has certainly made a wonderful recovery' Macmillan noted in his diary. 'He was sitting up, reading a novel of C. S. Forester. He seemed very cheerful and quite talkative. He strongly approved the reconstruction of the Government. He had watched Ministers from his corner seat, and thought many of them pretty indifferent.' [2]

Macmillan was now preparing Britain's bid to enter the European Economic Community. That week Churchill's granddaughter Edwina called on Churchill at the hospital. 'The day before,' noted Piers Dixon, 'Montgomery had been to see him and emerged from his meeting to announce that Winston was against our going into the Common Market. Winston told Edwina that Monty's behaviour was "monstrous".' [3]

On August 21 Churchill was well enough to leave hospital, and on the following day he signed a letter of thanks to the ambulance driver and his assistant 'for the skill and care with which they brought me home. . . .' [4] Two days later, Randolph Churchill called to see his father at Hyde Park Gate; that evening he set down a note of their discussion:

When I arrived at Hyde Park Gate shortly before 1 o'clock I first put the Disraeli writing desk into my car and then went in for luncheon at about 1.10 p.m. WSC greeted me with the words: 'You're dreadfully late.'

I told him that Dr Johnson had said that a ship was like a prison only with the added danger of being drowned. 'A hospital' I said 'is like a prison only

[1] 'RSC Reminiscences', 7.30 p.m., 11 July 1962: Randolph Churchill papers.

[2] Harold Macmillan diary, 20 July 1962: Macmillan papers. In wide-ranging Cabinet changes on 13 July 1962, Macmillan appointed R. A. Butler First Secretary of State, Reginald Maudling Chancellor of the Exchequer, Humphrey Brooke Home Secretary, Julian Amery Minister of Aviation, Duncan Sandys Colonial Secretary, Peter Thorneycroft Minister of Defence and Sir Edward Boyle Minister of Education.

[3] Piers Dixon notes (written on 10 April 1963): Piers Dixon papers.

[4] 'Dear Mr Richardson' (Superintendent of Ambulance Services), 22 August 1962: Churchill papers, 1/62.

with the added risk of being murdered.' WSC enjoyed this very much and said, a little surprised, 'Did you think of that?'

I told him about the difficulties we had encountered in trying to trace a record of his baptism. He said 'I hope you'll not waste your time in searching out complicated meticulous facts about me.' I replied 'I hope you don't want us to get these facts wrong.' He saw the point.[1]

The house at Hyde Park Gate was now altered so that Churchill did not have to use the stairs, and a bedroom and bathroom created on the ground floor of No. 27. In No. 28 a lift was installed from the ground floor to the dining room on the lower ground floor, which also enabled Churchill to have access to the garden in which, Mary Soames had recalled, 'he loved to sit'.[2] His life became one of minimum disruption or demands. 'He is seeing very few people,' Montague Browne wrote to Sir Shane Leslie, his first cousin who had wanted to visit him, 'as he tires easily.'[3]

'Sir Winston is doing tremendously well,' Miss Pugh wrote to Emery Reves on September 4, 'and has even walked, with assistance, down the steps into the garden here. He is delighted with his new bedroom. . . .'[4] To Clementine Churchill, in October 1962, Churchill wrote in his own hand:

Darling,

I hope you are going on well & that we may come together again tomorrow. I have found it quite lonely & will rejoice to see us joined together in gaiety and love. Dearest one I place myself at your disposal & intend to take a walk in the park hand in hand with many Kisses

ever loving

W[5]

Churchill now dined and played bezique with a rotating trio of players: his wife, her cousin Sylvia Henley, and his friend of many years, the Marchioness of Cholmondeley. By this means, Clementine Churchill could have what her daughter called a 'night off' from time to time, going to the theatre or dining out quietly with friends.[6] 'He is in fairly good spirits,' Montague Browne wrote to Beaverbrook on October 15, 'and is in many ways intellectually better than before his accident, but his mobility is not increasing and he is very bored.'[7] To

[1] 'RSC Reminiscences', 23 August 1962: Randolph Churchill papers. At Chartwell, Churchill had worked for many years at an upright desk which had belonged to Benjamin Disraeli. From 1962 until his death in 1968, Randolph Churchill was to use this desk at Stour for reading aloud from letters and documents which were to be included in the Churchill biography.

[2] Mary Soames, *Clementine Churchill*, page 477.

[3] Letter of 30 August 1962: Churchill papers, 2/527.

[4] Letter of 4 September 1962: Churchill papers, 4/26.

[5] 'Darling', undated letter marked 'October 1962': Spencer-Churchill papers.

[6] Mary Soames, *Clementine Churchill*, page 478.

[7] Letter of 15 October 1962: Churchill papers, 2/519.

Churchill's cousin Roger Frewen, who asked to call at Hyde Park Gate, Montague Browne explained on October 30: 'Sir Winston asks me to send you his good wishes and to say that he hopes you will excuse him if he does not see you on this occasion. Since his accident he is living very quietly and only sees an extremely small number of his oldest friends. I am sure that you will understand.'[1]

On November 1 Churchill was able to take the chair at the Other Club. 'It was at this dinner,' Colin Coote later recalled, 'that, with the exception of the Executive Committee, members were surprised by the appearance of a new member from abroad, Mr Aristotle Onassis. This was due to Churchill's gratitude for hospitality on board Mr Onassis' yacht, and the Club thought fit to share in this feeling.' Selwyn Lloyd, who was among those present, later told Coote how 'Mr Onassis sat between him and Churchill. The latter was then very deaf, which made it even more difficult to "get through to him". But Mr Onassis had a remarkable capacity for making him understand a conversation. The result was that, with this odd interpreter, Selwyn Lloyd had quite a substantial talk about the Middle East.'[2]

'In a room full of people,' Montague Browne later recalled, 'he would just withdraw into silence. People assumed he was gaga. But with someone he knew, he would talk normally. One did not even have to raise once's voice.'[3] One of Churchill's dinner guests in his last years, Robert Boothby, later recalled:

Lady Churchill was ill in bed, so we were alone. It was a difficult evening because he was pretty far gone. He did not want to talk about the war. I tried to arouse his interest by a reference to the Battle of Jutland, but all he said was: 'I used to know a lot about that—now I have forgotten.'

Finally he repeated, with a rather sad look, something that he had said to me long ago: 'The journey has been well worth making—once.'

'And then?' I asked.

'A long sleep, I expect: I deserve it.'[4]

[1] Letter of 30 October 1962: Churchill papers, 2/523. Churchill's luncheon guests in the last week of October had been the Marchioness of Blandford (on October 24), Lady Juliet Duff and Anthony Montague Browne (October 25), Lady Violet Bonham Carter (October 26), Dr and Mrs James (October 27), Edward Heath (October 28), Anthony Montague Browne (October 29), Christopher and Mary Soames (October 30) and Lord Montgomery and Sylvia Henley (October 31). Diana Churchill had dined with her father on October 27 and October 28. On November 1 Churchill went to the Other Club with Bill Deakin (Churchill Engagement Calendar, October 1962: Churchill papers). Dr Robert James was the Headmaster of Harrow from 1953 to 1971. The Marchioness of Blandford was Tina, formerly the wife of Aristotle Onassis. She had married Churchill's cousin, the Marquis of Blandford, in October 1961, leading Churchill to remark: 'So, Ari, we are related at last!'

[2] Colin R. Coote, *The Other Club*, page 110.

[3] Anthony Montague Browne recollections: in conversation with the author, 14 July 1987.

[4] Boothby, *Recollections of a Rebel*, page 65.

66

Last Years

O
N 30 November 1962 Churchill was eighty-eight. 'On this happy day for all of us,' telegraphed the Duchess of Kent, her daughter, and her daughter's fiancé Angus Ogilvy, 'we send you our affectionate congratulations and best wishes.' The telegram was signed 'Marina, Alexandra and Angus'.[1] 'I am so much touched by the kind message you have all sent me,' Churchill replied, and he added: 'Clemmie and I have been thinking of you since we heard the happy news and we wish Princess Alexandra and Angus the greatest joy.'[2]

On December 6 Churchill was again determined to leave Hyde Park Gate for the Other Club. 'This time,' Roy Howells later recalled, 'the worst smog of the year swirled round the Savoy and quite a few members decided that conditions were too bad for them to attend; but not the founder member.' Howells added:

With his black hat set at a rakish angle, the honourable member for Woodford announced to his household, 'Of course I must go.' There were some doubtful looks but he had his way as usual and he determinedly climbed into his car which gradually groped its way through the smog to the Savoy. He was so keen to be present that he was the second member to arrive! Only eleven members of the club attended that night. It really was a most remarkable recovery.[3]

[1] 'Priority', Buckingham Palace, 30 November 1962: Spencer-Churchill papers.
[2] Telegram sent 30 November 1962, to Kensington Palace: Spencer-Churchill papers. Angus Ogilvy, son of the 7th Earl of Airlie, married Princess Alexandra of Kent on 24 April 1963. The 5th Earl of Airlie was his great-grandfather and Clementine Churchill's grandfather.
[3] Roy Howells recollections: *Simply Churchill*, pages 104–5.

That Christmas, at the family luncheon, Roy Howells and Nurse Powell were among Churchill's guests, as was Lord Moran.[1]

For Churchill's family, 1963 was for Churchill a year of serene yet sad decline. 'Sir Winston,' explained Montague Browne to Sir Frank Roberts, British Ambassador to Germany, 'though physically well, has been somewhat lethargic and indifferent to events.'[2]

On February 20 Lady Violet Bonham Carter dined with Churchill at Hyde Park Gate. 'I see him & spend an afternoon or evening with him,' she wrote eight days later to this author, 'about once every ten days—& feel his mind drifting further & further away alas! Remembering it as I do in its full glory I am agonized. But thank Heaven he is beyond the reach of agony—though not of boredom.' Lady Violet added: 'It is a comfort to feel that I can still meet some of the needs that still remain.'[3]

There were other regular and pleasant distractions. 'He attended the meeting of the Other Club and much enjoyed it,' Montague Browne wrote to Beaverbrook on February 21, 'though he finds it extremely difficult to hear, and his hearing aid only increases the confusion of many people speaking.'[4]

There were times when Churchill wanted to send a letter, and asked Montague Browne to draft it for him; or when Montague Browne realized that Churchill would wish to send one, and prepared the draft. On March 5 one such letter was sent to Beaverbrook, thanking him for his book on *The Fall of Lloyd George*, calling it 'a most remarkable work' both of entertainment and of 'enormous value to the historian'. Churchill signed this letter with the 'W' that had been customary for many decades for his closest friends.[5]

On April 1 Clementine Churchill was seventy-eight. A week later

---

[1] Churchill Engagements Calendar, December 1962: Churchill papers. Churchill now had two female nurses, Miss Powell and Glenda McAlpin, from Australia. When Miss McAlpin left to visit Switzerland in 1963, she was replaced by Miss Ann Huddleston from Yorkshire. Miss Powell was succeeded by Miss Wendy Bunford, from Surrey.

[2] Letter of 13 February 1963: Churchill papers, 2/533.

[3] Lady Violet Bonham Carter recollections: letter to the author, 28 February 1963. Lady Violet had previously lunched with Churchill on February 9, was to lunch with him again on March 12, and dine on March 14.

[4] Letter of 21 February 1963: Churchill papers, 2/519.

[5] 'My dear Max' (typed), signed in Churchill's hand, 'W', 28 Hyde Park Gate, 5 March 1963: Beaverbrook papers.

Churchill wrote to her as he had done every year for fifty-five years, a birthday letter in his own hand:

My darling One,

    This is only to give you my fondest love and kisses *a hundred times repeated*. I am a pretty dull & paltry scribbler; but my stick as I write carries my heart along with it.

    Yours ever & always

W[1]

My darling one,

This is only to give you my fondest love and kisses a hundred times repeated,

I am a pretty dull & paltry scribbler; but my stick as to write carries my heart along with it.

Yours ever & always,

W

---

[1] 'My darling One', dated in Clementine Churchill's hand 'April the 8th 1963': Spencer-Churchill papers.

On April 8, at the instigation of Kay Halle, Churchill received Honorary Citizenship of the United States, an honour apparently granted only once before, to La Fayette.[1] Two days later he received a letter from the Prime Minister:

Dear Winston,

I gave a dinner last night for General Lemnitzer. He used to be American Deputy to Field Marshal Alexander in the Mediterranean Campaign and is now the Supreme Allied Commander in Europe. Field Marshals Alexander and Harding, Lord Mountbatten and General Strong all came. We and others present unanimously agreed to send you a message recalling the days when we worked together under your leadership. We wished also to express our delight at your versatility which allows you to combine being a loyal British subject with being a good United States' citizen.

Yours ever

Harold Macmillan [2]

Also on April 10, Churchill agreed to a suggestion, put before him by Montague Browne, that 'Your College', as he called it, should name one of their boats 'Sir Winston Churchill'.[3]

It was during April that Churchill was pressed, albeit discreetly, both by his wife and by Christopher Soames, to announce that he would not contest the coming General Election. Jock Colville had already taken up the question of a grant of honorary Membership of the House for Churchill, discussing it with Macmillan, and with the Leader of the Opposition, Harold Wilson.[4] But Churchill would not agree not to stand for re-election, even after the urgency of a decision was put to him by Mrs Moss of his Divisional Executive when she was invited specially to Hyde Park Gate, with her husband, for luncheon on April 10. On the following day, Churchill left London for Monte Carlo.

Once more Clementine Churchill remained in England, to spend Easter with her daughter Mary and her family. Churchill was accompanied to Monte Carlo by Anthony and Nonie Montague Browne. He stayed, as he had done for some time now, at the Hôtel de Paris. On being invited to dinner with Beaverbrook at La Capponcina on April 15, he declined. 'I felt rather tired,' he explained on the following day, 'and it seemed better to dine in bed. . . .'[5]

---

[1] The Marquis de La Fayette (1757–1834), a French citizen, had entered the service of the United States as a Major-General in 1776. Seized at Britain's request at Bordeaux, he escaped from custody, subsequently leading his troops against the British throughout the American Revolutionary War.

[2] 'Dear Winston', Admiralty House, 10 April 1963: Churchill papers, 2/539.

[3] 'Sir Winston', initialled 'AMB', 10 April 1963: Churchill papers, 2/571.

[4] Letter (from Montague Browne to Christopher Soames), 'Private and Confidential', 18 February 1963: Churchill papers, 2/514.

[5] 'My dear Max', typed letter, signed by Churchill with the initial 'W', Hôtel de Paris, Monte Carlo, 15 April 1963: Beaverbrook papers.

On April 19 Nonie Montague Browne returned to England, taking with her a letter from Churchill to his wife. 'My darling One,' he wrote in his own hand. The rest of the letter was dictated. One sentence read: 'I wish I had you with me, and I do hope you will not write it off as a gone concern.' [1]

From Clementine Churchill came a letter, also dated April 19, from Hyde Park Gate, in which she expressed her hope that her husband was 'thinking carefully' about a letter Christopher Soames had written him, urging him not to stand again for Parliament. 'He read it to me before he despatched it,' she wrote, '& I agree with all he says.' She added: 'I don't see how you can stand next year without campaigning & fighting for your seat. And it would be kind to let your Executive Council know now, before they became too restive.' [2]

Churchill remained at Monte Carlo for two weeks. On April 21 Wendy and Emery Reves called to see him. But when they invited him to lunch at La Pausa he declined. 'I hope you will understand me,' he wrote, 'if I do not come out for luncheon at the present time. It does seem to suit me better to rise late and have luncheon here.' Churchill added: 'I much enjoyed seeing you yesterday.' [3]

On April 24 Lady Churchill was at Westminster Abbey for the marriage of Princess Alexandra of Kent and Angus Ogilvy. On the following day she was at London Airport, to welcome back her husband from Monte Carlo. 'Sir Winston is very well,' Montague Browne told the Press. 'He enjoyed a good holiday.' [4]

From London Airport Churchill was driven to Chartwell. On the following morning he received a letter from his wife, who had been unable to leave London because of a throat infection, reminding him of the urgency of a decision on not standing for Parliament at the next election. 'You know your Chairman, Mrs Moss, is coming to luncheon today hoping for a decision,' Clementine Churchill wrote, and she added: 'Don't forget that you promised your Executive that you would at the next General Election make way for a younger man.' [5]

This second luncheon with Mrs Moss was as indecisive as the first, and no decision was reached. But on May 1 Churchill made up his mind. 'I am much relieved,' Clementine Churchill wrote to Christopher Soames, 'as the situation at Woodford was becoming increasingly uneasy. . . .' [6]

At last a public announcement was made: Churchill would not

[1] 'My darling one', Hôtel de Paris, Monte Carlo, 19 April 1963: Spencer-Churchill papers.
[2] 'My darling Winston', 28 Hyde Park Gate, 19 April 1963: Spencer-Churchill papers.
[3] 'My dear Wendy and Emery', Hôtel de Paris, Monte Carlo, 22 April 1963: Reves papers.
[4] 'Sir Winston Flies Home', The Times, 26 April 1963.
[5] Letter of 26 April 1963, from 28 Hyde Park Gate: Churchill papers, 1/135.
[6] Letter of 1 May 1963: Mary Soames, Clementine Churchill, page 484.

stand for Parliament at the next election. His family were relieved, yet saddened at the same time. Mary Soames has written, of this period of her father's life:

But now not only was Winston physically less strong, but mentally he had become more lethargic. Gradually the silences became longer, and he was content to sit gazing into the fire, finding faces in the quivering glow; or in the two summers that were left to him he would lie on his 'wheelbarrow' chair contemplating from the lawn the view of the valley he had loved for so long. If he were not in good form, meals could be conducted in almost total silence. He rarely initiated a subject, and his deafness was an added and most daunting barrier to communication. But he hated to be alone, and indeed he hardly ever was. Sometimes after a long silence he would put out a loving hand, or say apologetically: 'I'm sorry I'm not very amusing today'—which wrung one's heart. He still loved to play bezique, but the games were now more drawn out, and he sometimes became confused with the score. This natural, but infinitely sad decline, was slow and uneven. There would be bright clear spells, and then dull and rather hazy days. Life held little for him now, and after the announcement in May 1963 that he would not contest the approaching election, the last stimulus was taken from his life.[1]

On May 13 Churchill was given a luncheon in the House of Commons, and spoke a few words, even reciting a short poem from memory. 'It was a great occasion for us all,' wrote Harold Macmillan on the following day, and, referring to a poem which Churchill had quoted, he added: 'If you could find the poem about the ducks I would be very glad to have it.' Macmillan added: 'I hope you enjoyed the set-to I had with the Leader of the Opposition. It was quite in the good old-fashioned style of knockabout.'[2] Churchill replied:

My dear Harold,
Thank you so much for your agreeable letter. I much enjoyed seeing you at luncheon too. But, alas, no one can find the poem about the ducks: it does not seem ever to have been put on paper. Though I think that it appeared in *Punch* at about the turn of the century. I am so sorry.
Yours ever

W[3]

On May 24 Churchill learned that Beaverbrook had been taken ill. He at once wrote, entirely in his own hand, what was to be the last of many hundreds of letters to his friend of nearly six decades:

[1] Mary Soames, *Clementine Churchill*, page 478.
[2] 'Dear Winston', signed 'Yours ever, Harold', Admiralty House, 14 May 1963: Churchill papers, 2/528.
[3] 'My dear Harold', typed, signed in Churchill's hand, 'W', 18 May 1963: Churchill papers, 2/528. The poem, one of Churchill's favourites, was about a tramp in St James's Park who was jealous of the ducks because people fed *them* with bread and not *him*.

Dear Max,

I am so sorry that you are ill. I hope you will get better & have a happy Birthday.

Yours ever and always

W [1]

On June 21 Churchill returned to Monte Carlo, and to *Christina*. It was to be his last cruise. Both Randolph and his son Winston were on board, as were Anthony and Nonie Montague Browne, and Jock and Meg Colville, who left the yacht when it reached Sardinia. Randolph flew back from Corfu. Churchill's grandson remained for the rest of the voyage. *Christina* reached Athens on June 30. After a further cruise in Greek waters, Churchill flew back to London on July 4. Sad news awaited him. Fifteen months earler, Sarah Churchill had married for the third time, and happily as never before, Henry Audley, the 23rd Baron Audley. 'Winston,' as Mary Soames recalled, 'although now rather too old to really "take in" new personalities, rejoiced for Sarah in her new-found happiness, as did we all.' [2] But on July 3, Lord Audley had been struck down by a massive coronary and died.

On the day after Churchill's return, his detective, Sergeant Murray, in an attempt to cheer him, told Churchill that he was sure that his constituents would like him to stand again. 'This is not the case,' Clementine Churchill wrote to Murray on July 6, and she added: 'They all honour and respect Sir Winston, but they realize that he could not fight an Election, and the Executive Council, numbering ninety persons representing the whole Association, were relieved to receive Sir Winston's letter saying he did not intend to stand at the next General Election.' Clementine Churchill's letter continued:

What you said upset Sir Winston, which is sad. Although I do not believe that you wished to distress him, your uninformed comment was in fact most unhelpful. Naturally, his decision was made after consultation in a number of quarters, and the matter is settled and a prospective candidate has been adopted. Would you therefore be so kind as not to say anything like this to him again?

You may like to know that the new candidate is coming to make Sir Winston's acquaintance on Saturday, July 13, when I am giving a Garden Party for the Executive Council. [3]

On July 29 Churchill was able to go to the House of Commons, where Members marvelled at his tenacity but were shocked by his

---

[1] 'Dear Max', 28 Hyde Park Gate, undated: Beaverbrook papers.

[2] Mary Soames, *Clementine Churchill*, page 479.

[3] 'Sergeant Murray', 'Private', initialled 'CSC', 6 July 1963: Churchill papers, 1/143.

frailty. On August 1 Jock Colville dined; two days later Montgomery came for three nights.[1] Then, on August 12, Churchill again suffered a mild stroke.

The details of Churchill's health were kept a closely guarded secret, and he was well protected by his family and by Montague Browne from all outside pressures. Only to Lord Beaverbrook was an account sent of the problems and of the dangers. For Churchill was now almost entirely confined to bed. 'He cannot get up very much,' Montague Browne explained to Beaverbrook on August 23, 'as when his foot is lowered to the ground it becomes discoloured, indicating that the impediment in the circulation is still there.' Montague Browne added that Churchill was 'mentally much better than he was, and it is a great pity that his physical condition does not march with it'.[2]

Among those who visited Churchill regularly that summer, and who tried to be of good cheer, was Field Marshal Montgomery. 'But, as you know,' he wrote to Mary Soames on September 1, 'he can't now read a book or a paper; he just lies all day in bed doing nothing.' Montgomery added:

This has been a great strain on Clemmie, and she finally collapsed under it all and took to her bed the day after you and the children looked in on your way to France. She really is worn out. Winston dislikes being left alone all day with his nurses, and dislikes having meals alone; Clemmie found it a strain having to talk loudly to make him hear.

Since I have been here I have been with him all day, trying to interest him in things and showing him photographs of us two in the war. He is now definitely on the mend. He will recover. My view is that Clemmie is now the problem; she is worn out and needs rest. . . .[3]

Clementine Churchill was certainly in need of rest. But Churchill was not as confined to his bed as Montgomery reported. 'He is now getting up every day,' Montague Browne informed Beaverbrook on September 3, 'and seeing a film after dinner.'[4]

Among Montague Browne's tasks at this time was to attend a specially constituted Government Committee, code-named 'Hope Not', to plan for Churchill's State Funeral. The Committee was chaired by the Duke of Norfolk. 'WSC knew I was attending meetings of the "Hope Not" Committee,' Montague Browne later recalled, 'but only once commented. He said "Remember, I would like lots of military bands at my funcral." He got nine!'[5]

---

[1] Churchill Engagements Calendar, July–August 1963: Churchill papers.
[2] Letter of 23 August 1963: Churchill papers, 2/519.
[3] Letter of 1 September 1963: Mary Soames, *Clementine Churchill*, pages 479–80.
[4] Letter of 3 September 1963: Churchill papers, 2/519.
[5] Anthony Montague Browne recollections: notes for the author, 24 March 1987.

It was to Montague Browne that Churchill owed much of the calm that now surrounded him. It was a relationship which, from afar, many people envied. Churchill's daughter Mary later spoke of it in understanding tone: 'People might have thought they would have liked to be in Anthony's shoes. But the day came when my father, although much beloved and venerable, was past his wonderful prime, was declining in energy and ability. He still wanted to take his part in affairs, but he needed help. He needed a wise friend, and a knowledge-able one, who would guard his reputation, who would guard every step he took.'

'Long after it was really fun to serve my father,' Mary Soames added, 'Anthony remained to bear the burden of the day, to be his friend and support throughout his sadder, declining years.'[1] 'And now,' she recalled, 'in these last two years, the pace of life for Winston was very slow: it was like a broad, weary river, gently meandering on. Sometimes he seemed quite content: even though he might not say very much, one knew he was glad one was there. But sometimes he withdrew a great distance from us—and who knows what thoughts or images moved across the screen of his consciousness from the long saga of his life, so crowded with events and people?'[2]

When Churchill woke up at Chartwell on September 12, a letter was waiting for him from his wife. It read:

> My darling Winston
> To-day we have
> been married 55 years
> September the 12th 1908
> September the 12th 1963
> Your loving
> Clemmie[3]

Clementine Churchill went to rest and recuperate at Hamsell Manor, Mary Soames's house in Kent, not far from Chartwell. 'How-ever,' Montague Browne told Montgomery on September 26, 'she is still feeling rather low.' Churchill, in contrast, 'has improved con-siderably, not so much physically as in hearing and morale'. When Macmillan visited Churchill on September 25, Montague Browne

---

[1] Lady Soames, speech to the International Churchill Society, London, 25 September 1985: *Finest Hour* (Journal of the International Churchill Society, Issue No. 50, Winter 1985–6).

[2] Mary Soames, *A Churchill Family Album*, London 1982, caption 412.

[3] 'My darling Winston', 12 September 1963: Churchill papers, 1/135.

added, 'he was in particularly good form and talked more than he has for a long time'.[1]

Encouraged by Churchill's improvement, Montague Browne arranged for a series of dinner guests, among them Norman Brook, Jock Colville, Leslie Rowan and Alan Hodge. On the occasional evening when he was by himself, Churchill saw a film. 'Your Grandmother is unwell,' Churchill wrote to his grandson Winston on September 30, 'and is having a rest cure in Westminster Hospital, so I am alone and it would be very nice if you would come and see me. . . .'[2] 'Young' Winston went, on October 4; he was then twenty-three years old and already embarked upon a journalistic career. With him he brought a box of cigars as a gift.

On September 30 Clementine Churchill had written to say that she would spend the next weekend with her husband at Chartwell. 'I shall be delighted to see you again,' he wrote—his letter dictated—'and hope that it will mark a sign of a truly bright time and give me a few days which, like others in their time, will be sweet and happy.'[3]

When the weekend was over, Clementine Churchill returned to the Westminster Hospital. 'Sir Winston,' reported Montague Browne to Montgomery, 'is physically much the same, with perhaps a slight improvement. He is depressed by Lady Churchill's absence, but he is mentally clear and alert.'[4]

On October 13 Harold Macmillan announced his resignation as Prime Minister. Ill health was the cause: an imminent prostate operation. After five days of intense political activity, a close monitor of which was Randolph Churchill, the Earl of Home emerged as Prime Minister, taking office, and reverting to commoner status as Sir Alec Douglas-Home, on October 18.

Within twenty-four hours, this political drama was quite eclipsed in the Churchill household by the tragic suicide of Diana Churchill. She was fifty-four years old. Clementine Churchill was still in the Westminster Hospital when her daughter died. Churchill was at Hyde Park Gate. 'The lethargy of extreme old age dulls many sensibilities,' Mary Soames has written in a moving passage, 'and my father only took in slowly what I had to tell him: but he then withdrew into a great and distant silence.'[5]

'You are much in our thoughts,' telegraphed the new Prime Minister, Sir Alec Douglas-Home. 'We are so sorry, so very sorry,' read the

---

[1] Letter of 26 September 1963: Churchill papers, 2/529.
[2] Letter of 30 September 1963: Churchill papers, 1/136.
[3] Letter of 30 September 1963: Churchill papers, 1/135.
[4] Letter of 8 October 1963: Churchill papers, 2/529.
[5] Mary Soames recollections: Mary Soames, *Clementine Churchill*, page 481.

telegram from Wendy and Emery Reves. There were a myriad other messages, from de Gaulle, from Anthony Eden, from Paul Reynaud and from Pamela Lytton.[1]

Neither Churchill nor his wife was well enough to go to their daughter's funeral. Both went, however, to the Memorial Service held on October 31 at St Stephen's Walbrook in the City of London, the crypt of which housed the headquarters of the Samaritans organization for which Diana had worked.

After Diana's Memorial Service, Clementine Churchill went once more to stay at Hamsell Manor with her daughter Mary. Churchill stayed at Chartwell. Then, on Thursday November 28, two days before his eighty-ninth birthday, he went to the House of Commons, entering the Chamber in a wheel-chair. 'He was greeted with a warm cheer,' reported the *Yorkshire Post*, 'and Sir Alec Douglas-Home gave up his own Front Bench seat to welcome him, sitting by his side for a brief chat.'[2] That night Churchill dined at the Other Club.[3]

On November 30 Churchill was eighty-nine. 'My dear Clemmie,' wrote Lord Beaverbrook that day to Clementine Churchill, 'What a burden you have borne over so many years—and with what charm & dignity. How much the Nation & the World owe to you for all your labours. And on this *89th birthday*, I send you this message. Many many intimates sending Winston messages of love & devotion will think of you. Max.'[4]

In London, Jock Colville continued to work at the idea of making Churchill a Life Member of the House of Commons. But Sir Alec Douglas-Home gave a negative answer. 'I think that the decision is unimaginative of the powers that be,' Jock Colville wrote to Montague Browne on December 9, 'and apart from giving great pleasure to Sir Winston, it would give great pleasure to the country.'[5] Montague Browne replied two days later: 'It is perhaps appropriate that those responsible for our own "very rapidly closing twilight" should not wish to honour the setting sun. So I suppose we must await a Socialist Government who may treat him more honourably than his "friends". It would not be the first time.' Montague Browne added: 'Funnily enough, at the French Embassy last night Anthony Wedgwood Benn raised the matter with me and spoke of a Bill which would "allow Sir Winston to sit in the House". Whether this is the same as Life Membership, I do not know. In any case, we can only wait on events. . . .'[6]

[1] Letter and telegrams on Diana Churchill's death: Churchill papers, 1/139.
[2] *Yorkshire Post*, 29 November 1963.
[3] Churchill Engagements Calendar, November 1963: Churchill papers.
[4] Letter of 30 November 1963: Mary Soames, *Clementine Churchill*, page 487.
[5] Letter of 9 December 1963: Churchill papers, 2/514.
[6] Letter of 11 December 1963: Churchill papers, 2/514.

The New Year of 1964, Churchill's ninetieth year, opened with still more news of his powers of survival. 'Sir Winston has basically been on a decline,' Montague Browne wrote to Beaverbrook on January 17, 'but in the last two or three days he has suddenly staged one of the astonishing come-backs with which he has so often surprised us. Last night, for instance, he talked to me clearly and connectedly about the Prime Minister's speech in the House, to which he had listened. So one simply cannot tell, but I do rather wish that he would not go to the House, so that people will remember him from his great days.' [1]

On January 21 Churchill returned to the House of Commons; two days later he dined at the Other Club. On February 20 he was again in the Commons, where a young Conservative MP, Sir John Langford-Holt, helped him to walk from the Lobby to his seat. That evening, he dined once more at the Other Club. At Hyde Park Gate, a small circle of friends continued to keep him company. [2] 'Sir Winston is well,' Montague Browne wrote to Beaverbrook on March 11, 'but a little down and apathetic.' [3] On April 18 Churchill received a note from his wife:

Winston,

The Government and the Members of the Opposition have been thinking what would be the best way of marking the end of your time in Parliament. They propose that you should be given a Vote of Thanks. This would be passed unanimously by the House, and then a special Committee consisting of the Prime Minister, the Leader of the Opposition and the Leader of the Liberal Party would wait upon you here at Hyde Park Gate to hand you a copy of the Resolution.

Would you be agreeable to this?

Clemmie [4]

'Winston has seen this,' Clementine Churchill noted on the bottom of her copy of this note, and on the following day she informed Montague Browne:

Yesterday afternoon I gave Winston this little note. At first he seemed to pretend not to understand it, but later on he said he thought it would be very suitable. You will notice that I have carefully left out any suggestion that he could possibly be in the House when the Vote of Thanks is proposed. I did not show him the wording of the Resolution.

Later on in the afternoon he seemed very sad and depressed. [5]

[1] Letter of 17 January 1964: Churchill papers, 2/519.

[2] Churchill's dinner guests in February 1964 were Jock and Lady Margaret Colville, Sylvia Henley, Alan and Jane Hodge, Sir Leslie and Lady Rowan, Lord and Lady Normanbrook and Randolph Churchill. His luncheon guests that month were Harold Macmillan, and Randolph Churchill's director of researches on the Churchill biography, Michael Wolff.

[3] Letter of 11 March 1964: Churchill papers, 2/519.

[4] 'Winston', 18 April 1964: Churchill papers, 2/514.

[5] 'Private', 19 April 1964: Churchill papers, 2/514.

It was, however, a depression that could, and did, pass. 'We came to the same conclusions,' Miss Pugh recalled, about herself and Miss Maturin, 'about how he enjoyed contrasts, and after a quiet, perhaps low time, he would come right up.' Shortly after Easter, she noted, it snowed, 'but the first sunny day after that, he was out in the garden at Chartwell at 10.45 a.m.' [1]

On April 25 Churchill left Hyde Park gate by car to go to the Ashcroft Theatre, Croydon, where he saw his daughter Sarah play the leading part in the play *Fata Morgana*. 'He found it very difficult to follow and said so,' Piers Dixon noted in his diary. 'But the difficulty was not surprising since at best it was a complicated play, and in addition, he had been brought in half-way through.' [2]

Apart from two more visits to the House of Commons, this was Churchill's last appearance in public.

Churchill returned to the House of Commons on June 4. 'You will remember,' Miss Pugh reminded him on the following day, 'that Mr Harold Wilson, the Leader of the Opposition, spoke to you in the House yesterday. He had just returned from Russia, and he brought with him good wishes to you from all the Soviet leaders, and particularly Mr Mikoyan.' [3] On June 6, the twentieth anniversary of the Normandy landings, Churchill wrote to Wilson: 'I am so much obliged to you for bringing me the agreeable messages from the Russians. What you said reminded me of my own visits there in days gone by. Thank you very much,' and he signed his three initials, 'WSC'. [4]

Churchill was also able to sign 'WSC' on a letter to Robert Menzies on June 7, thanking him for sending a new pair of swans for Chartwell, to replace those killed by foxes during the severe months of 1962–1963. 'I often reflect on our long comradeship,' the letter ended, 'and I hope that I shall see you when you are over here.' [5]

On June 5 the formal opening of Churchill College had taken place, with the Duke of Edinburgh, the College Visitor, presiding over the ceremony. As Churchill was no longer able to attend such a long event, he was represented by Clementine Churchill, and by many members of his family. Randolph Churchill, recovering from a lung operation, and breaking off his work on the Churchill biography, drove from Stour to Cambridge for the ceremony.

[1] Doreen Pugh recollections: letter to the author, 22 June 1987.
[2] Piers Dixon diary, 25 April 1964: Dixon papers.
[3] 'Sir Winston', initialled 'DP', 5 June 1964: Churchill papers, 2/513.
[4] 'My dear Wilson', signed 'WSC', 6 June 1964: Churchill papers, 2/513.
[5] 'My dear Bob', signed 'WSC', 7 June 1964: Churchill papers, 1/59.

On 9 June 1964 Churchill's friend of nearly six decades, Max Beaverbrook, died of cancer at the age of eighty-five. 'My darling Papa,' wrote Sarah Churchill, whose own husband had died a year earlier, 'I grieve for you. No-one can give back the golden years of friendship. But remember, you have taught me a lot about that. I love you dearly. Your Sarah.'[1]

On June 10 *The Times* published a short message, as if from Churchill, which read: 'I am deeply grieved at the loss of my oldest and closest friend, who served his country and his causes valiantly and was the most loyal and devoted of comrades.'[2] Lady Violet Bonham Carter at once protested to Montague Browne that this message broke Churchill's political silence, a silence which had been tacitly in effect for some time. The phrase 'most loyal and devoted of comrades' was, she said, clearly a political one. Montague Browne replied:

Sir Winston was deeply and obviously moved at Lord Beaverbrook's death, and in the last years no-one had been closer to him. He had spent weeks staying with Lord Beaverbrook, and their mutual visits were as regular as their health allowed. Lady Churchill and I both felt that it would be a most marked omission if Sir Winston did not send a message on this occasion.

In one sentence it is very difficult to sum up a friendship. But Lord Beaverbrook was his oldest (male) friend: he met him six years before he met Bernie, and saw far more of him. In recent years Lord Beaverbrook was one of the very few whose visits consistently caused Sir Winston to light up, and certainly in my time with him, now going back twelve years, he confided in him as much as anyone both on personal and political matters.

Sir Winston told me several times that if Britain had been invaded in 1940 and we had had to fall back north of the Thames, he would have ruled Britain with a triumvirate of himself, Beaverbrook and Ernest Bevin; (this is of course strictly private). Once it was decided to send a message, it would have been impossible to hedge and qualify the deep and undoubted affection which Sir Winston felt for Lord Beaverbrook.[3]

There was a moment of real pleasure for Churchill on June 27, when his grandson Winston married Minnie d'Erlanger. Churchill was too frail to go to the wedding or to the reception, over which Randolph presided; instead, the couple went to him at Hyde Park Gate. In a letter to his mother later that same night, the bridegroom described that visit:

I paid a visit on Grandpa C who has been ill for the last ten days, but today he was in spanking form. He was sitting looking at a book of sculpture in the garden of 28 HPG. It was a lovely sunny afternoon and he greeted me

---

[1] 'My darling Papa', 10 June 1964: Churchill papers, 1/135.
[2] 'Death of Lord Beaverbrook', *The Times*, 10 June 1964.
[3] 'Private and Confidential', 15 June 1964: Churchill papers, 2/520.

with the words: 'Congratulations and happiness.' He looked at me for a while, then returned to brooding over his book. After a few minutes he looked up and seemed surprised that I was there. After fixing me with his eye for a second or two he asked me if I would come to his room with him. His nurse & I helped him to his room. He got into bed and demanded his cheque-book. This was brought by a secretary (but no pen). He browsed through the counterfoils (perhaps to see how much things cost today) and then asked for his pen. I gave him mine and he began writing. The secretary reappeared, glanced at what he was up to and announced that she would write it out. Having done this she presented it to him for his signature. He pondered over it for a while and then barked 'No!'

The secretary then disappeared to consult Lady C, reappeared and proceeded to write out a second cheque. Again—rather more gruffly—he pronounced 'NO!' Then he took his pen and set about inserting another 'o'. The secretary protested and asked if he wouldn't like to leave the whole matter to another day when he was feeling better. He was adamant. Eventually the secretary was prevailed upon to do as she was told and write a third cheque. This one he appeared to like the look of better and in a slow but steady hand he put his name to it. Then with a smile of triumph on his face he passed it to me, sitting at his bedside.[1]

The cheque was for £1,000. At Randolph's urging, Churchill also gave his grandson four of his own paintings.[2]

Politicians still hoped to seek Churchill's views in support of their own, or to ask him for general guidance on points of common concern. But it could no longer be. 'It is now widely known,' Montague Browne wrote to Lord Kilmuir on July 1, 'that Sir Winston is no longer capable of formulating considered opinions on difficult matters, nor of marshalling the arguments to support them. . . .'[3]

On July 27 Churchill went to the House of Commons for the last time. It was more than sixty years since his first day as a Member. Once more, Sir John Langford-Holt was with him in the Chamber:

During Question Time he seemed anxious to know whether anybody was talking about him. He was aware that a Motion expressing the Commons' gratitude to him is due to be moved tomorrow, and was concerned that he should not miss any reference to himself. I sat with him for about an hour in the Smoking Room. He says he is going down to Chartwell tomorrow so this is probably the last time the great old man will be with us.

'There's a very large crowd waiting for him out in Parliament Square,' Langford-Holt added.[4] On the following afternoon the Prime Minis-

[1] Letter of 27 June 1964, written at 3 a.m.: Pamela Harriman papers.
[2] Churchill papers, 1/136.
[3] 'Private and Confidential', 1 July 1964: Churchill papers, 2/512.
[4] Sir John Langford-Holt diary, 27 July 1964: Langford-Holt papers.

ter, Sir Alec Douglas-Home, accompanied by the Opposition Party Leaders, Harold Wilson and Jo Grimond, and the Leader of the House, Selwyn Lloyd, together with the two elders of the house, Sir Thomas Moore and Emanuel Shinwell, and the Clerk Assistant, David Lidderdale, called at Hyde Park Gate to present Churchill with a Resolution which had just come before the House. The Resolution, which had been passed unanimously, read:

That this House desires to take this opportunity of marking the forthcoming retirement of the right honourable Gentleman the Member for Woodford by putting on record its unbounded admiration and gratitude for his services to Parliament, to the nation and to the world; remembers, above all, his inspiration of the British people when they stood alone, and his leadership until victory was won; and offers its grateful thanks to the right honourable Gentleman for these outstanding services to this House and to the nation.

Churchill then spoke a few words of thanks, after which the visitors were given champagne.[1] 'Clementine had asked some of us children to be present with her,' Mary Soames later recalled, 'to witness this rather sad, muted occasion. But it made a dignified end to a long, proud chapter.'[2]

A General Election was now imminent. As Montague Browne had earlier explained to Violet Bonham Carter, no messages were going to be sent under Churchill's name; the Beaverbrook message had been one of condolence and nothing more. But in September the situation changed, as Montague Browne explained:

. . . Sir Winston is going to send two short messages, one to his successor candidate and the other to the Prime Minister: they have both been cut to the bone.

I am strengthened in my feeling that this is the right course by an incident yesterday. Sir Winston, who, as you know, fluctuates very much in his awareness of events, was particularly good at luncheon. He was asked, 'You have been asked to send messages supporting the Conservative party in the General Election to your successor candidate and the Prime Minister. Do you wish to do so or not?' He replied very clearly, 'Yes, I will do it.' With this, I am content that brief messages of general support of the Conservative government are right.[3]

Montague Browne also defended the general issuing of letters over

---

[1] 'Sir Winston and Lady Churchill', initialled 'AMB', 22 July 1964: Churchill papers, 2/514.
[2] Mary Soames recollections: Mary Soames, *Clementine Churchill*, page 485.
[3] 'Strictly Private', 25 September 1964: Churchill papers, 2/520.

Churchill's signature, telling Violet Bonham Carter, who had denounced this practice with some ferocity:

I really do not think you should have used the word 'forgery' to me. Sir
Winston has had things drafted for him for many years, even when he was
Prime Minister. If they represent his views, and he signs them, they are not
'forgeries'. These messages, of the briefest and most general support for the
Conservatives, fulfil this condition: Sir Winston undoubtedly supports the
Conservatives.[1]

Montague Browne was a wise, conscientious and thoughtful friend
and adviser; not only with such correspondence as remained, a fitful
fragment of former days, but with financial guidance. On September
28, for example, he explained to Churchill why, in his opinion, it
would be 'unwise' to invest further in a particular company. Churchill
agreed, declining as a result to take up a rights issue.[2]

Unexpectedly, Violet Bonham Carter came back into Churchill's
life, less than a month after her altercation with Montague Browne. 'I
spoke to Lady Violet Bonham Carter on the telephone,' Miss Pugh
noted for Churchill on October 22, 'and found that she has had more
heart trouble, and has been in bed for nearly a month. She hopes
soon to be better and able to come and see you again, and sent you
her love. Would you like to send her a telegram?' Miss Pugh appended
a draft telegram which read: 'Dearest Violet I am so sorry you are not
well. Hope I may see you soon, Winston.'

Churchill agreed to the telegram as drafted.[3]

On Thursday 15 October 1964, at the first General Election since
1900 which Churchill had not contested, the Conservative Party was
narrowly defeated and a Labour Government formed, headed by
Harold Wilson. But for Churchill, this was an event almost beyond
the dwindling span of his attention. 'After he ceased to be a Member
of Parliament, which did, I know, depress him,' Miss Pugh later wrote,
'it was touching how Sir Winston started having the record player in
the afternoons. He played Gilbert and Sullivan and military marches,
and really did his best to get some pleasure out of them. And in those
last months, when he could not concentrate so well on reading, he did
a lot of looking at books of pictures.'[4]

Those whom Lady Churchill, Montague Browne and Miss Pugh

[1] Postscript to letter of 25 September 1964: Churchill papers, 2/520.
[2] Financial notes, 28 September 1964: Churchill papers, 2/520.
[3] 'Sir Winston', initialled, 'DP', and telegram signed 'Winston', 22 October 1964: Churchill
papers, 2/520.
[4] Miss Doreen Pugh to Randolph Churchill, 'Personal', 11 May 1966: Pugh papers. On the
day before the British General Election, Alexei Kosygin had succeeded Nikita Khrushchev as
Soviet Prime Minister.

knew Churchill liked to see, were regularly invited to Hyde Park Gate to lunch or to dine. If Churchill did not always speak to his guests, he was nevertheless well aware of their presence, and anticipated their arrival with obvious pleasure. On October 13 Sir Leslie and Lady Rowan were his guests at dinner. 'It was sad to see such a great man become so frail,' Lady Rowan later recalled.[1] The Rowans were to be Churchill's last guests at Chartwell. A few days later he returned to London; he was never to see his beloved Chartwell again.

In London, Churchill continued to see those with whom he could feel at ease; Alan and Jane Hodge were his dinner guests on October 21. The Churchills were now back in London, Miss Pugh wrote to Bill Deakin a week later, 'so do not forget,' she added, 'when you are in London, that Sir Winston and Lady Churchill would much like you to suggest coming for a meal. They are both well, and Sir Winston really in very good form at the moment.'[2]

Churchill now seldom left Hyde Park Gate, but he did ask to be taken to the Other Club at the Savoy Hotel, where he was in the company of those who had known him well, and who understood that if he did not speak more than a few words, or even if he were silent, it was a source of pleasure to him to be with them. That month, he dined at the Other Club on November 5. The guests invited to Hyde Park Gate likewise gave him pleasure; among them, that November, were Anthony Eden, Harold Macmillan and Violet Bonham Carter.[3]

On November 15, Piers and Edwina Dixon went to Hyde Park Gate. During their visit they asked Churchill to inscribe a copy of his biography of his father for them.[4] Churchill signed his name in full:

On November 29, the day before Churchill was ninety years old, a small crowd of well-wishers gathered in Hyde Park Gate; 'carefully dressed and looking benevolent', Mary Soames later recalled, 'Winston appeared at the open window of the drawing-room so that the Press could take some birthday photographs. The little crowd of well-wishers cheered and clapped and sang "Happy Birthday to You".'

Mary Soames's account continued:

[1] Lady Rowan recollections: in conversation with the author, 9 October 1987.
[2] Letter of 28 October 1964: Churchill papers, 4/458.
[3] Churchill Engagements Calender, November 1964: Churchill papers.
[4] Piers Dixon diary, 15 November 1964: Piers Dixon papers.

Before luncheon on the actual day Clementine arranged for all his secretarial, nursing and domestic staff to gather in his bedroom to drink his health
in champagne. She took this opportunity to thank them all for their loyal
and devoted care. Clementine's present to him was a small golden-heart
enclosing the engraved figures '90'. It was to hang on his watch-chain, and
joined the golden heart with its central ruby 'drop of blood' which had been
her engagement present to him fifty-seven years before. During the afternoon
the Prime Minister called to bring Winston good wishes from the Cabinet.

That evening there was the usual hallowed family dinner party: Randolph,
Sarah, myself and Christopher; Winston and Minnie, and Arabella, Julian
Sandys, Edwina and Piers Dixon, Celia Kennedy (Sandys); and Cousin
Sylvia. The only guests not members of the family were Jock and Meg Col-
ville, and Anthony and Nonie Montague Browne. Monty had been invited
but was himself ill in hospital.

The house glowed with candlelight and flowers, and we were united yet
one more time in drinking first Winston's health and then Clementine's. But
this birthday evening had for us all a poignant quality—he was so fragile
now, and often so remote. And although he beamed at us as we all gathered
round him, and one felt he was glad to have us there—in our hearts we knew
the end could not be far off.[1]

That evening Churchill was again taken to the window to acknowledge the cheers and singing of the crowd. The curtains were opened
and then, Piers Dixon wrote, 'He raised his hand in the V-sign.'[2]

On Churchill's eightieth birthday in 1954, Montague Browne told
Sir Henry d'Avigdor-Goldsmid, there had been 30,000 messages. 'This
time it will be even more.'[3] There were, in fact, 70,000, involving a
massive temporary staff to send the cyclostyled acknowledgements.

Messages actually signed or approved by Churchill personally were
now extremely infrequent. On December 4 a telegram was sent with
his approval to Violet Bonham Carter, who had just been created a
Life Peer. The telegram read: 'Warmest congratulations dearest
Violet, Winston.'[4]

A very small circle of friends continued to join Churchill for luncheon and dinner. On December 8, encouraged to do so by Miss
Pugh, Bill Deakin had come to lunch, and on December 10 it was
Deakin, towards whom Churchill felt a strong bond of affection, who
accompanied Churchill to the Other Club. It was to be the last Club
dinner which Churchill attended, fifty-four years after the first.[5] One

[1] Mary Soames, *Clementine Churchill*, page 488.

[2] Piers Dixon, letter to his father, 6 December 1964: Pierson Dixon papers.

[3] Letter of 23 November 1964: Churchill papers, 2/609.

[4] Telegram sent 4 December 1964: Churchill papers, 2/609.

[5] The first meeting of the Other Club was on 18 May 1911. Those present had included
Churchill, Lloyd George, F. E. Smith (later Lord Birkenhead), and J. L. Garvin.

of those present, Colin Coote, later recalled: 'It had become increasingly difficult to awake the spark, formerly so vital; and all that could be said was that he knew where he was and was happy to be there. With that his colleagues had to be, and were, content.'[1]

Montague Browne now made plans to go on recuperative leave. He had not been well for some time, and planned a long sea voyage. 'It is my first long leave for twelve years,' he explained in a private letter to Antonio Giraudier on January 5, and he added: 'Sir Winston is well, and sends you his very good wishes for the New Year. . . .'[2] A week later, on January 12, Montague Browne wrote again: 'It looks now as though my plans will have to be put in cold storage as, for your private ear, Sir Winston is not well.'[3]

On January 10 Churchill had suffered a massive stroke. A few days later, news of it was made public, and a nationwide mood of melancholy found echoes throughout the world. On Sunday January 17 the Queen attended morning service at St Lawrence's Church, Castle Rising, Norfolk, at which prayers for Churchill were offered. That Sunday there was a large congregation at Westminster Abbey, where Dr Coggan, the Archbishop of York, told the congregation: 'Again and again he has found the right words for the right occasion, and rallied faltering nations in the hour of trial.'[4]

On Friday January 22 it was announced that Harold Wilson had cancelled two broadcasts he was to have made at the weekend about his first '100 days of dynamic action' in view of the public concern at Churchill's illness. On January 23, Dr Ramsey, the Archbishop of Canterbury postponed a visit he was to have made to Birmingham. 'Sir Winston has had a restful day,' a bulletin, the seventeenth in eleven days, declared, 'but there has been some deterioration in his condition.'[5]

Churchill's children, Randolph, Sarah and Mary were at his bedside each day; Clementine Churchill sat with him for many hours throughout the day and long into the night. For fourteen days he lay in a coma. Then, shortly after eight o'clock on the morning of Sunday January 24, he died.

[1] Colin R. Coote, *The Other Club*, page 110.
[2] Letter of 5 January 1965: Churchill papers.
[3] Letter of 12 January 1965: Churchill papers.
[4] 'Ground Lost by Sir W. Churchill', *The Times*, 18 January 1965.
[5] *The Times*, 23 January 1965.

Epilogue

MEN and women wept when they heard the news of Churchill's death. Nearly ten years had passed since his last months as Prime Minister, a quarter of a century since his 'finest hour' in 1940. He had died seventy years to the day after his father, Lord Randolph Churchill, the man whose respect and approval he would have so liked to have won, but who had not lived long enough to see even the earliest phases of his son's remarkable career.

The outpouring of sorrow was matched by the volume of messages of condolence. President de Gaulle sent a letter to the Queen, in which he wrote, of his former colleague, ally and adversary: 'In the great drama he was the greatest of all.' From Moscow, the new Soviet Prime Minister, Alexei Kosygin, sent a message that the Soviet people 'remember the untiring efforts of Sir Winston Churchill in the years of the war against Hitlerite Germany'. In a broadcast on the night of January 24, Harold Wilson declared: 'Now his pen and sword are equally at rest. The tempestuous, restless vitality of a man who would have scorned the ease of a peaceful retreat, has ended today in quiet, in peace, in stillness.' The Leader of the Opposition, Sir Alec Douglas-Home, in his broadcast, declared: 'Personally he had an abundance of two of the greatest qualities: the first, humanity, and the second, loyalty.'

Harold Macmillan also broadcast that night. Although, he said, Churchill had managed 'with characteristic courage, to take and to give something worthwhile even in the last stages of his life, yet each time that I have seen him in recent months, I have felt that he was waiting—waiting patiently, hopefully, manfully, for his release'.[1]

At 2.35 on the afternoon of January 25 it was announced in the House of Lords, by the Lord Privy Seal, Lord Longford, that a message had been received from the Queen. 'Confident in the support of

[1] *The Times*, 25 January 1965.

Parliament for the due acknowledgement of our debt of gratitude and in thanksgiving for the life and example of a national hero,' it concluded, 'I have directed that Sir Winston's body shall lie in State in Westminster Hall and that thereafter the funeral service shall be held in the Cathedral Church of St Paul.'

That afternoon in the House of Lords, Earl Attlee, Churchill's deputy Prime Minister from 1940 to 1945 and then his successor, said of him: 'He had sympathy, incredibly wide sympathy, for ordinary people all over the world. My Lords, we have lost the greatest Englishman of our time—I think the greatest citizen of the world of our time.'

Also in the House of Lords, the Earl of Avon—formerly Anthony Eden—suggested the establishment of a Churchill Day 'connected with some day in that summer of 1940 when Churchill's leadership, and this country's will to resist, whatever the cost, both expressed themselves so gloriously. They could then be enshrined together for as long as our calendar endures.' In her maiden speech in the House of Lords, Lady Asquith of Yarnbury—formerly Lady Violet Bonham Carter—said: 'It is hard for us to realize that that indomitable heart to which we all owe our freedom and our very existence, has fought its last long battle and is still.' [1]

On January 27 Churchill's coffin was taken from Hyde Park Gate to Westminster Hall, so near to the scenes of his Parliamentary struggles and triumphs. Despite bitter winds, more than three hundred thousand people filed past during the lying-in-state. 'One saw,' Richard Crossman noted in his diary, 'even at one o'clock in the morning, the stream of people pouring down the steps of Westminster Hall towards the catafalque. Outside, the column wound through the garden at Millbank, then stretched over Lambeth Bridge, right round the corner to St Thomas's Hospital. As one walked through the streets one felt the hush and one noticed the cars stopping suddenly and the people stepping out into the quietness and walking across to Westminster Hall.' [2]

'Early on the Saturday morning,' Harold Wilson later recalled, 'the last of the three hundred thousand who had filed past the bier in Westminster Hall came through. I had arranged, as a parliamentary tribute to Sir Winston, that in place of the rota of soldiers who mounted guard in Westminster Hall, three party leaders—Prime Minister, leader of the Opposition and leader of the Liberal Party—together with Mr Speaker, should mount guard for a short period.

[1] *Hansard*, 25 January 1965.
[2] Crossman diary, 30 January 1965: *The Diaries of a Cabinet Minister, 1964–1970*, London 1975.

This we did late on the Friday evening. The four of us, in full morning dress, took up our positions at the corners of the catafalque.'[1]

At 9.45 on that morning of January 30, after Big Ben had struck the quarter-to and was then silenced for the day, Churchill's coffin was taken from Westminster Hall, enfolded in a Union flag, the Order of the Garter resting on it, out into New Palace Yard, followed by Lady Churchill, Randolph, Sarah, Mary, other members of the family, and Anthony Montague Browne. A guard of honour presented arms, joined in its salute by the boys of Harrow School Combined Cadet Force. Watched by many Members of Parliament and Peers, the coffin was lowered on to a grey gun-carriage. Lady Churchill and her two daughters then entered a carriage provided for them by the Queen.

Slowly the gun-carriage proceeded down Whitehall on its journey to St Paul's Cathedral, Randolph Churchill, Christopher Soames and the other male mourners following it on foot, Lady Churchill and her daughters in the carriage, the coffin escorted by the Household Cavalry, and by the bands of the Royal Artillery and the Metropolitan Police.

Reaching St Paul's, Churchill's coffin was carried up the steps and into the Cathedral by eight Grenadier Guardsmen, watched by Churchill's family. Inside St Paul's the congregation was headed by the Queen who, as Churchill's daughter Mary has written, 'waiving all custom and precedence, awaited the arrival of her greatest subject'.[2]

At St Paul's, a congregation of three thousand—family, friends, public figures, foreign statesmen, Kings and Presidents—joined in the prayers, as tens of millions watched on television or listened over the radio which had once carried Churchill's own messages of determination and hope. It was a service charged with emotion, 'all his hymns being sung, everybody singing', as Miss Sturdee later recalled.[3]

Others who, as the service proceeded, could recall episodes in Churchill's long story, included Paul Reynaud, to whose side he had hurried three times in 1940, as France fell to the German onslaught; and Dwight D. Eisenhower, whom he had known both as Supreme Commander of the Allied Forces, and as President. Also in the congregation, from overseas, were four Kings and one Queen—Juliana of The Netherlands—fifteen Heads of State, and Marshal Koniev of the Soviet Union.

Among the Britons who joined in the prayers and hymns were three

[1] Harold Wilson, *The Labour Government 1964–1970, A Personal Record*, London 1971, pages 170–1. The four were Harold Wilson, Sir Alec Douglas-Home, Jo Grimond and Sir Harry Hylton-Foster. Hylton-Foster, a former Solicitor-General, had been Speaker since 1959; he died that September, aged 60.
[2] Mary Soames, *A Churchill Family Album*, London 1982, caption 416.
[3] Lady Onslow recollections: in conversation with the author, 16 July 1987.

former Prime Ministers, one of them, Attlee, frail and weak, and several Field Marshals, Marshals of the Royal Air Force and Admirals of the Fleet who had been among Churchill's principal lieutenants during the Second World War—the sympathy of all, amid the ceremonial, going out to Lady Churchill and the members of the Churchill family. The service ended with the sounding of the Last Post and the Reveille by trumpeters high up in the Whispering Gallery, round the inside of the dome. 'For the first time,' Richard Crossman noted in his diary, 'a trumpet had room to sound in a dimension, a hemisphere of its own.'[1] For each of the three thousand members of the congregation, it was a moment of sublime emotion.

The service over, the family mourners left the Cathedral, followed by the Queen and Prince Philip, who, with the other dignitaries, watched in silent tribute the departure of the coffin on the next stage of its journey, first through the streets of the City, to Tower Pier, to be taken on the deck of the Port of London Authority launch *Havengore*.

As the launch prepared to move upstream, cranes on the other side of the river dipped in solemn salute. Then as *Havengore* sailed under the bridges of the Thames, a fly-past of aircraft in boxes of four broke the silence, a tribute to the man who had been a pioneer in the creation of the air forces of Britain more than half a century earlier.

From Festival Pier, the coffin was taken to Waterloo Station, and then by train, drawn by the Battle of Britain class locomotive 'Winston Churchill', to Long Handborough, the station nearest to the churchyard at Bladon. A single wreath lay on the coffin during the journey: a wreath of iris and daffodils from Churchill's daughter Sarah, who was not well enough to make this final journey. One of those on the train was Churchill's wartime Private Secretary, Sir Leslie Rowan. 'On that last journey by train from Waterloo to Bladon,' he later wrote, 'after the great crowds of London, two single figures whom I saw from the carriage window epitomised for me what Churchill really meant to ordinary people: first on the flat roof of a small house a man standing at attention in his old RAF uniform, saluting; and then in a field, some hundreds of yards away from the track, a simple farmer stopping work and standing, head bowed, and cap in hand.'[2]

After a short private service, Churchill was buried next to his father, his mother and his brother Jack in Bladon churchyard, less than a mile from his own birthplace, Blenheim Palace. Among the wreaths

---

[1] Richard Crossman diary, 30 January 1965: *The Diaries of a Cabinet Minister, 1964–1970*.
[2] Sir Leslie Rowan recollections: Sir John Wheeler-Bennett (editor), *Action This Day, Working with Churchill*, page 265.

at the graveside was one of red roses, red tulips and red carnations, with the inscription: 'To my darling Winston, Clemmie'. Another wreath, of white flowers, had an inscription in the Queen's handwriting: 'From the Nation and the Commonwealth. In grateful remembrance. Elizabeth R'.[1]

Randolph Churchill, returning to his home in Suffolk, continued with the work he had begun four years earlier, of writing his father's biography. Others too, in the days and months to come, recalled the qualities which they had seen and admired. The last forward entry in Churchill's engagements calendar, the only entry marked for February, had been the next fortnightly meeting of the Other Club, fixed for February 4. Two weeks later, at the Other Club meeting on February 18, Harold Macmillan told those who had seen so much of Churchill in his last years: 'We knew it must come; and none who loved him could wish for a long delay. The moment a giant dies, we forget the last few years, and go back in our memory to the days of his prime and his power. This Club looks back over fifty years; and for more than a quarter of a century he has been our supreme member.' Macmillan added: 'Our finest hour and our greatest moment came from our work with him.' Lord Chandos, the other speaker that evening, recalled Churchill the Club member, and the statesman:

He enjoyed a good dinner. He made jokes at the expense of all but at the cost of none. He enjoyed a conflict of ideas, but not a conflict between people. His powers were those of imagination, experience, and magnanimity. Perhaps not enough has been made of his magnanimity. He saw man as a noble and not as a mean creature. The only people he never forgave were those, who, in the words he so often used, 'fell beneath the level of events'.

The memory of his conversation at the Other Club, which meant such a great deal to him in his life, lightens the darkness of this occasion.[2]

Fifty years earlier, in 1925, on another dark occasion, Churchill had written to his wife, on the death of her mother:

An old and failing life going out on the tide, after the allotted span has been spent and after most joys have faded is not a cause for human pity. It is only a part of the immense tragedy of our existence here below against which both hope and faith have rebelled. It is only what we all expect & await. . . .[3]

[1] *The Times*, 31 January 1965.
[2] Speeches of 18 February 1965: Colin R. Coote, *The Other Club*, pages 111–12.
[3] Letter of 22 March 1925: Spencer-Churchill papers.

'I am weary of a task which is done,' Churchill had written to his wife in 1957, 'and hope I shall not shrink when the aftermath comes.'

In 1938, when Churchill was sixty-four, he had written of the death of his ancestor the 1st Duke of Marlborough:

> The span of mortals is short, the end universal; and the tinge of melancholy which accompanies decline and retirement is in itself an anodyne. It is foolish to waste lamentation upon the closing phase of human life. Noble spirits yield themselves willingly to the successively falling shades which carry them to a better world or to oblivion.[1]

Churchill was indeed a noble spirit, sustained in his long life by a faith in the capacity of man to live in peace, to seek prosperity, and to ward off threats and dangers by his own exertions. His love of country, his sense of fair play, his hopes for the human race, were matched by formidable powers of work and thought, vision and foresight. His path had often been dogged by controversy, disappointment and abuse, but these had never deflected him from his sense of duty and his faith in the British people.

Churchill had been a man of great kindness and compassion. On being asked after the First World War, by a French municipality, to devise the wording for its war memorial, he had proposed:

'IN WAR: RESOLUTION

IN DEFEAT: DEFIANCE

IN VICTORY: MAGNANIMITY

IN PEACE: GOODWILL'

Churchill's wording had been rejected, but the spirit behind it was for him an animating one.[2] 'It is hardly in the nature of things,' his daughter Mary had written to him in 1951, 'that your descendants should inherit your genius—but I earnestly hope they may share in some way the qualities of your heart.'

In the last years, when power passed, to be followed by extreme old age with all its infirmity and sadness, Churchill's children expressed to him in private the feelings which many of his fellow countrymen

---

[1] Winston S. Churchill, *Marlborough, His Life and Times*, volume 4, London 1983, page 648. The Duke of Marlborough had died eight days before his seventy-second birthday.

[2] These words now stand in the opening pages of each volume of Churchill's war memoirs, under the heading: 'Moral of the Work'.

also felt. In August 1955, four months after the end of his second Premiership, his son Randolph wrote to him:

Power must pass and vanish. Glory, which is achieved through a just exercise of power—which itself is accumulated by genius, toil, courage and self-sacrifice—alone remains. Your glory is enshrined for ever on the unperishable plinth of your achievement; and can never be destroyed or tarnished. It will flow with the centuries.

So please try to be as happy as you have a right and (if it is not presumptuous for a son to say it) a duty to be. And, by being happy, make those who love you happy too.

Such was a son's encouragement. From his daughter Mary had come words of equal solace nine years later, when at last his life's great impulses were fading. 'In addition to all the feelings a daughter has for a loving, generous father,' she wrote, 'I owe you what every Englishman, woman & child does—Liberty itself.' [1]

---

[1] Letter of 8 June 1964: Churchill papers, 1/136.

Maps

The withdrawal of the Western Allies, July 1945

2   Eastern Europe and the 'Iron Curtain'

SWEDEN

DENMARK

Baltic Sea

Danzig
(Gdansk)

Kiel Canal

Kiel

EAST
PRUSSIA

Swinemünde
(Swinoujscie)

P O M E R A N I A

Stettin
(Szczecin)

POLAND

Berlin

Potsdam

G E R M A N Y

WEST   EAST

SAXONY

Oder

Elbe

Western Neisse

Lodz

S I L E S I A

Breslau

Oder

Eastern Neisse

Elbe

C Z E C H O S L O V A K I A

.. ..   Poland's western frontier 1919 to 1939

....   Poland's western frontier
since 1945

▬▬ ▬▬ ▬▬   The partition of Germany, 1945

⸺ · ⸺ · ⸺   Other international borders, 1945

0		miles	150
0		kilometres	250

3   Poland's western frontier

Baltic Sea

LITHUANIA

Vilna

Minsk

Königsberg

EAST

PRUSSIA

Masurian Lakes

Grodno

Bialystok

U. S. S. R.

Vistula

Brest-Litovsk

Warsaw

Bug

Pripet marshes

Lodz

Lublin

VOLHYNIA

Vistula

SILESIA

Cracow

Przemysl

Lvov

WESTERN GALICIA

EASTERN GALICIA

oil fields

CZECHOSLOVAKIA

Poland's frontier with the Soviet Union from 1921 to 1939

Poland's eastern frontier since 1945

Poland's frontiers with Germany before 1939

Other international borders, 1945

The 'Curzon Line' 1920

The 'Molotov - Ribbentrop', 1939

| 0 | miles | 150 |
| 0 | kilometres | 250 |

© Martin Gilbert 1988

4   Poland's eastern frontier

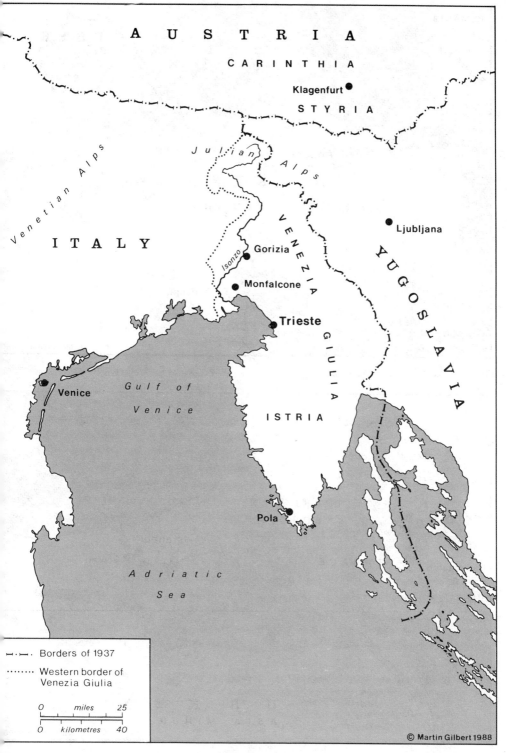

A U S T R I A

C A R I N T H I A

Klagenfurt ●

S T Y R I A

Julian *Alps*

Venetian Alps

I T A L Y

● Ljubljana

V E N E Z I A

Isonzo Gorizia ●

Monfalcone ●

Trieste ●

Y U G O S L A V I A

G I U L I A

Gulf of
Venice

● Venice

I S T R I A

Adriatic
Sea

Pola ●

—·—·— Borders of 1937

·········· Western border of
Venezia Giulia

O ⊢—————⊣ 25
miles

O ⊢—————⊣ 40
kilometres

5   Venezia Giulia

6 Turkey and the Straits

7 The Dardanelles and the Bosphorus

Churchill's European journeys

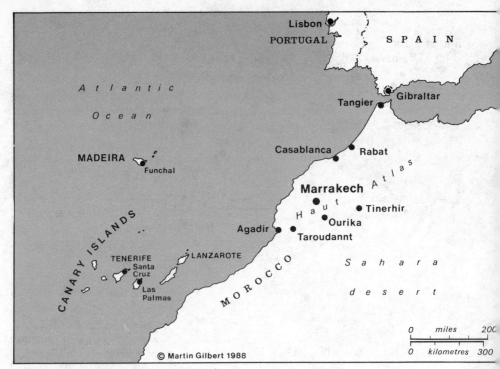

9 Marrakech and the Canary Islands

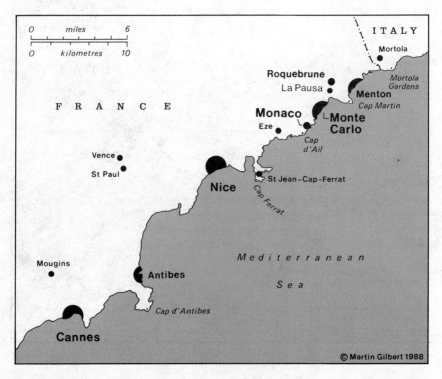

10 The French Riviera

Index

Compiled by the author

A Frenchman in Khaki (Paul Maze): Churchill's introduction to, 1288 n.1

A Gun for Sale (Graham Greene): 1310

A History of the English-Speaking Peoples (Winston S. Churchill, 4 volumes, 1956–8): Churchill's work on, 177, 180, 255, 274, 847 n.2, 876–7, 883–4, 887, 891, 915, 958, 1044, 1066, 1077–8; Churchill renews work on, 1126, 1132, 1136, 1141, 1144, 1145–6, 1148–9, 1161, 1162, 1163, 1165, 1166, 1173, 1174, 1175, 1176, 1177–8, 1179; the first volume published, 1183–4, 1193, 1196–7; continuing work on, 1187, 1188, 1189–90, 1190, 1200, 1201, 1205, 1212–13, 1214; the second volume published, 1223, 1225; 'rapidly nearing completion', 1228, 1229–30, 1233, 1241; the third volume published, 1249–50, 1254; the fourth volume published, 1267

A Passage to India (E. M. Forster): 854

A Roving Commission (Winston S. Churchill, 1930): 469, 1204 n.3

Aachen (Germany): Churchill speaks in (1956), 1197, 1225

Abadan (Persia): 617, 618, 624, 639, 642, 840

Abdication Crisis (1936): 549, 844

Abdullah, King of Transjordan (later Jordan): 449, 527, 558, 623, 1093 n.1, 1272 n.2

Aberdeen: Churchill speaks at (1946), 228–9

Acheson, Mrs Dean (Alice Stanley): 977

Acheson, Dean: 206, 544, 675–6, 677, 680, 692, 741, 793, 1010; and the 'baffling years', 1132; *photograph 19*

Achilles: Churchill declines to emulate (1930s), 1074

Acre (Palestine): 335 n.2

Adams, Governor Sherman: 1001

Adams, Major Vyvyan: 112, 401

Adana Conference (of 1943): 444, 1262 n.3

Adeane, Sir Michael (later Baron): 1097, 1117, 1123–4, 1177, 1227, 1255–6

Aden: use of troops from, 782

Adenauer, Dr Konrad: 666, 756–7, 774, 829–30; 'exasperated', 832; his election 'draws

Adenauer, Dr Konrad—*continued*
near', 844; and 'friendly messages', 849, 856; and a proposed Four-Power conference (at Berlin), 929–30; to be supported, 1003; and Churchill's desire for a Summit with the Soviets, 1013; 'desultory discussion' about, 1047; and the French rejection of the European Defence Community, 1055–6; French 'harshness' to, 1057; Churchill 'high on the list' of admirers of, 1075; and a possible Paris meeting, 1103; unwell, 1168; Churchill meets (in Bonn), 1197; Churchill meets (in London), 1306; a gift from, 1307

Adler, General Julius Ochs: 327, 684, 685

Admiralty House (Whitehall): 1330

Adrian, Baron: 1263 n.2

Adriatic Sea: 6, 16, 200, 238, 239

Aegean Sea: 91, 332

Aga Khan, the: 628

Agnelli, Umberto: 1297

Airlie, 7th Earl of: 1340 n.2

Aix-en-Provence (France): 424, 426–9

Aix-les-Bains (France): 977

Alamein, Battle of (1942): 133, 479–80, 492

Alamein Reunion Dinner: 160, 486, 492, 561

Alanbrooke, Field Marshal Viscount (*for earlier index entries see* Brooke, Field Marshal Alan): 231, 262–3, 373, 389, 551 n.4, 728, 1171; his diaries published, 1232–3; his good wishes, 1262

Albania: 45, 76, 77, 80, 351 n.3, 390

Albert Hall (London): Churchill speaks at (1947), 321, 329; (1948), 400–1; (1951), 607–8; (1954), 972, 977, 979–81, 1048; (1956), 1190–1; (1957), 1240; (1958), 1266

Aldrich, Winthrop: 790, 1007, 1109–10

Alexander, A. V. (later 1st Viscount): 19, 20, 23, 283, 298–9, 319, 321, 324–5, 516 n.3, 979 n.2

Alexander, Field Marshal Sir Harold (later 1st Viscount Alexander of Tunis, subsequently 1st Earl): 5, 7–8, 11–12, 14, 16–17, 28–9, 45, 57, 60, 81, 91, 93 n.2, 94, 98, 815 n.1;

Alexander, Sir Harold—*continued*
and Churchill's visit to Lake Como, 132,
134, 137, 141–2, 144–5, 146, 148, 151, 154,
185, 985 n.2; and an historical query, 262,
625–6; and war crimes, 325; and Churchill's
second Premiership, 653, 685, 709, 711,
713–14, 716, 724, 726, 727, 728, 737, 741,
755, 757, 769, 796, 821, 822; and Egypt,
804, 946; and Jordan, 964; and Malaya,
994, 999; at the Other Club, 748; succeeded
by Harold Macmillan, 1065; and Churchill's retirement years, 1171, 1272 n.4,
1343; *photograph 4*
Alexander, Lady (Margaret, Countess): 154,
716
Alexandra, Princess: 1340, 1344
Alexandria (Egypt): 237, 668, 796, 799, 804,
826, 833
Algeria: 1201, 1206, 1245, 1264 n.5, 1295, 1318
Alice, Princess: 1073, 1266
All Quiet on the Western Front (E. M. Re-
marque): 887
Allen, (Sir) Denis: 997 n.1
Allen, Commodore G. R. G.: his work on
Churchill's war memoirs, 339, 341, 345,
383, 389, 415, 416 n.2, 417, 427, 428, 474,
493, 495, 522, 549, 551 n.4, 597, 601, 609,
663, 735, 877
Allen, Sir Roger: 1297
Almighty, the: and English Common Law,
792; and the cobalt bomb, 1251
Alsace-Lorraine: 247, 926
Altrincham, 1st Baron (formerly Sir Edward
Grigg): 349, 1249
Amalgam: a 'sludgy', 634, 793
Amalgamated Society of Locomotive En-
gineers and Firemen (A.S.L.E.F.): fails to
receive Trade Union support (1955), 1145
Ambedkar, Dr B. R.: 233, 237
American Civil War, the: 371, 1201, 1204,
1267
American Indians: and Churchill's ancestors,
1297
American Zionist Council, the: 723 n.4
Amery, Julian: defeated (1945), 112; defends
Churchill, 441; and Egypt, 897 n.2; enters
Cabinet (1962), 1337 n.2
Amery, L. S. ('Leo'): 241, 267, 283 n.2, 298,
472
Amid These Storms (Winston S. Churchill,
1932): 469
Amman (Jordan): 449
Amnesty (for Second World War deserters):
748–9, 781–2
Ampleforth Abbey: a memorial to Bracken in,
1275 n.1
Amsterdam (The Netherlands): 232, 409

An Infamous Army (Georgette Heyer): 1267
Anders, Lieutenant-General Wladzyslaw: 212
Anderson, Lady (later Viscountess Waverley)
(formerly Ava Wigram): 339
Anderson, Sir John (later 1st Viscount
Waverley): 36, 59, 60–1, 66 n.5, 156, 249,
322, 471 n.2; and India, 333; 'second-rate',
470; and the 1951 General Election, 642;
and Churchill's second Premiership, 655;
for subsequent index entry see Waverley,
Viscount
Anderson, General Sir Kenneth: 580
Andrew, Prince (later Duke of York): 1331
Anglo-Egyptian Agreement (Sterling Balances
Agreement, 1951): 941–2
Anglo-Egyptian Agreement (1953–4): negotia-
tions for, 796, 897, 900, 998–9, 1000; signed,
897 n.2, 1036
Anglo-Egyptian Treaty (1936): 237, 659, 796
Anglo-French Union (1940): 364 n.3
Anglo-German Naval Treaty (1935): 246
Anglo-Persian Oil Company, the: 617, 639,
685 n.1, 878, 1192, 1235
Anglo-Soviet Fisheries Agreement (1930): 812
Anglo-Soviet Treaty (of 1942): 281
Annan, Noël (later Baron): 1304
Anne, Princess (later The Princess Royal):
1095; *photograph 20*
Anne, Queen: 347, 835
Annecy (France): 628, 630, 631
Antigua (British West Indies): 977
Anti-Semitism: 'the strongest abhorrence of',
251; and Hitler, 464
Antonescu, General Ion: 76, n.1, 1217 n.2
Antonov, General Alexei: 92
Antony and Cleopatra (film): 236, 663
Antrim, 13th Earl of: 306 n.6
Antwerp (Belgium): Churchill's Mission to
(October 1914), 856
Anzio Landings (Italy) (1944): 236
Appeasement: 6, 331, 467, 529, 574; and
Egypt (in 1953), 795, 796; and 'conversations
at the centre', 973; and 'co-existence', 1030
Arab countries: and an 'Anglo-French' agree-
ment, 287; 'obligations of', to Britain, 455;
and Onassis, 1333
Arab League, the: 455
Arab Legion, the: 411
Arab peoples: Churchill's appeal to (1958):
1283
Arab refugees: 'a festering sore', 841
Arab States, the: 557–8, 658, 689, 788, 942;
and their boycott against Israel, 1300 n.2
Arab world, the: 841, 1201
Arabs (of Palestine): 244, 252, 253, 295–7, 302,
411, 430, 449, 456–7, 525, 623, 625, 646, 841
Ardahan (Turkey): 75, 91, 195

Argentia (Canada) (Conference, 1941): 175
Argentine, the (Argentina): 490 n.1, 498, 519, 531, 553, 1055
Armistice Day: ceremony, 1255–6
Armstrong, (Sir) Robert (later Baron): 1138
Arnhem, battle for (1944): 239
Arnold, General H. H.: 70 n.2
Arromanches (Normandy): 669 n.1
Arrow of Gold (Joseph Conrad): 1310
Arthur, Wing-Commander: 378 n.2
Ashley, Maurice: 140, 443
Asia: 'on the Elbe', 422, 436; and a United Europe, 521; and the new geography, 561; Europe's contribution to, 934; a possible 'misjudged intervention', 1023–4; Nehru's role in, 1093
Asquith, H. H. (later 1st Earl of Oxford and Asquith): 349, 476 n.2, 601 n.1, 646, 698, 699, 742, 1068, 1114 n.2, 1157
Asquith, Margot (later Countess of Oxford and Asquith): 742
Asquith, Raymond: killed in action (1916), 742
Asquith of Yarnbury, Baroness (Violet Bonham Carter): and Churchill's 'last long battle', 1361
Assheton, Ralph (later 1st Baron Clitheroe): 10, 37, 38, 227 n.1, 656
Associated British Pathé Studios (London): 506
Associated Electrical Industries (AEI): 1053 n.1
Astor, Gavin (later 2nd Baron): 1015
Astor, Colonel J. J.: 246, 440
Aswan Dam, the (Egypt): 1201
Athenagoras, the Patriarch: 1298
Athens (Greece): British experience in (1944–5), 16, 154, 263 n.2, 568; 'free to decide', 200; recollections of, 919, 1083
Athlone, 1st Earl of: 700, 1073
Atlantic, the, Battle of (1941–3): 363, 735 n.2
Atlantic Charter, the: 25, 1007
Atlantic Ocean, the: and the Soviet Union, 7, 277, 278, 463, 540; 'I feel on both sides of', 413 n.6; 'life line' of, 540; the problem of the Command in, 678–9, 692, 694; Soviet thoughts concerning, frustrated, 920; and American nuclear superiority, 1099
Atlantic Pact, the: *see index entry for* North Atlantic Treaty Organization (NATO)
Atomic Age, the: 808, 832
Atomic Bank Plan, the: 1031
Atomic Bomb, the: 'a plop', 59, 62, 66, 85–6, 90, 100–1, 119, 140–1, 156–8; and Churchill's Fulton speech, 199; and Japan, 249, 259, 892; and the 'architect of the universe', 254; and Moscow, 258, 530; and United

Atomic Bomb—*continued*
Europe, 266; and 'God's children', 277; and Switzerland, 280; and Russia, 286, 432, 437, 440, 459, 464, 467–8, 520, 521, 530, 553, 575, 595, 959; and Truman, 467–8; and the United States, 475, 510, 540, 556, 557, 572, 595, 611; 'our only hope', 478; and Churchill's war memoirs, 505, 793–4; made in Britain, 538; and the Quebec Agreement (of 1943), 572–3, 595–6, 1054, 1091; 'the only lever', 575; and the march of science, 621; and the policy of Churchill's peacetime Premiership, 666, 683, 688 n.1, 689–90, 717; and Korea, 688 n.1, 928; 'the supreme deterrent', 689, 837; tested, by Britain, 764; 'no more' to be made (following a Summit), 863; and Attlee, 914; and French sensitivity, 924; discussed at Bermuda (December 1953), 924, 929, 932–3, 936; discussed in Washington (June 1954), 999; a prophesy of (1932), 1015; and morality, 1022; letters about, 1117; *see also index entry for* Hydrogen Bomb
Atomic Energy: 437, 904–5, 919, 937, 940–1; and the Bermuda proposals, 960, 968, 1028; and the 'Atomic Bank Plan', 1031; British work on, 1091
Atomic Secrets: 'evaporating', 936; and the possible exchange of, 999–1000
Atomic Warfare: 'ceaseless developments' of, 907; and the priorities of the House of Commons, 938
Atomic Weapons: exchange of information on, 913; their possible use, in Korea, 917–18; discussed at Bermuda, 924, 929
'Atticus': and Churchill's 'vitality', 1226
Attlee, Clement (later 1st Earl): and the 1945 General Election, 9, 19–20, 36, 52, 53 n.4, 54–6, 110, 115, 150; and Potsdam, 27, 43, 47–8, 60, 66 n.4, 79, 81, 85, 92, 108, 115–16, 125; as Prime Minister (1945–51), 114 n.1, 129, 146, 164, 564; Churchill's letters to, 119–20, 156, 157–8, 191–2, 195, 196, 197, 205; his letters to Churchill, 120, 157–8, 193, 222; and the atomic bomb, 156–8, 572–3, 914, 1091, 1098; and honours, 718–9, 192, 193, 720 n.2; and Churchill's Fulton speech, 195, 196, 197, 208; and defence, 222, 277, 489–90, 530, 538–9, 541, 554, 575, 592, 606, 914; and German re-armament, 574, 575; and India, 229–30, 233, 298, 332–5, 422; and Egypt, 229–30, 647; and Palestine, 229–30, 244, 253, 456; and Churchill's war memoirs, 235, 269, 404–5, 494, 548; and Churchill's European travels, 242; and United Europe, 287–8, 424–5; a gift from, 307; and National Service, 319, 322, 324, 914, 1136; attacks

Attlee, Clement—*continued*
Churchill's record, 322–3; and Churchill's illness (1947), 339; Churchill's criticisms of, 354–5; and Russia, 396, 477–8, 530; and the Berlin blockade, 422; and NATO, 463, 498, 606; and the 1950 Election, 500, 504, 509–10, 512, 517; and the 1950–1 Labour Government, 516, 526, 558, 559, 564, 584, 591; and the Korean war, 535, 547, 554, 705; in the House of Commons, 596; 'assailed' (by Bevan), 607; the 'limited outlook' of, 608; and Persia, 618, 642; an altercation with, 625; and the 1951 General Election, 638–9, 645; resigns (1951), 649; Churchill's guest (1952), 728; and Bevan, 753; and atomic energy, 904–5; Churchill's praise for, 914, 1003; and the hydrogen bomb debate (1954), 965; and the Quebec Agreement (1943), 978; in Moscow and Peking, 1045, 1049, 1063; and Churchill's 80th birthday, 1073–4; unwell, 1093; and a vote of censure (1955), 1108; a statue of, 1114 n.2; at Lady Churchill's 78th birthday party, 1117; at Churchill's farewell dinner, 1120, 1150; Churchill's attacks on (1955), 1136, 1138; 'very kind to me', 1145; succeeded by Gaitskell, 1182 n.1; a gift from Churchill to, 1194; and Churchill's death, 1361, 1363; *photographs 4, 7*
Attlee, Mrs (Violet Millar) (later Countess): 1117, 1120, 1150
Auchinleck, General Sir Claude: 250, 420, 445, 470, 479
Audley, 23rd Baron: marries Sarah Churchill, 1346
Augusta, USS: 106
Auld Lang Syne (song): 673
Aurand, Captain Peter: 1298
Aureole (The Queen's horse): 826, 842, 874, 1076
Auriol, Vincent: 329
Auschwitz (concentration camp): 442 n.1
Australia: 13, 140, 307, 371, 446, 494, 498; and the atomic bomb, 683 n.1, 764 n.2; and Malaya, 716; and the Queen Mother, 722; amnesty in, 748; defence of, 762–3, 993 n.2; Churchill's war memoirs in, 802 n.2
Australia, New Zealand and the United States Pact (ANZUS): 762–3, 791, 995
Austria: 5, 11, 14, 25, 43, 81, 82, 239, 241, 423; and the Tyrol, 260; and the Soviet Union, 437; and a possible Treaty for, 830, 1002, 1012, 1028, 1029, 1031; and Summits, 893, 1028, 1031; and the Berlin Conference (of 1954), 952, 955; and German intentions towards (in 1937), 1314 n.1
Austro-Hungarian Empire: 260

Avon, 1st Earl of (Anthony Eden): 1330, 1350, 1357; and Churchill's death, 1361; *photographs 4, 6, 19, 28*
Aylesford divorce, the (1876): 413
Azores, the: a possible meeting at, 909

BBC, the: Churchill's protest about, 403; and Czechoslovakia, 404; Churchill against the 'monopoly' of, 732; and the Suez Crisis (1956), 1208–9
Babington Smith, Constance: 405
Baghdad (Iraq): murders in (1958), 1270
Baghdad Pact, the: 994 n.1
Bahamas, the: a possible visit to (1956), 1164, 1165, 1181; (and 1957), 1253
Baillie, Hugh: 280–1
Baillieu, Baron (Clive Baillieu): 1272 n.4
Baird, Brigadier-General Edward William: 913
Baldwin of Bewdley, 1st Earl (Stanley Baldwin): 235, 280, 473, 504, 699, 739, 824 n.4, 862, 1046 n.2; 'a poor leader', 1327
Balfour, A. J. (later 1st Earl): 367, 391, 557, 698, 699, 1048, 1050, 1114 n.2, 1301 n.3, 1327
Balfour Declaration, the (of 1917): 625 n.2, 689, 723, 775, 1008, 1096, 1192
Balkan Pact, a: in prospect, 994, 999
Balkans, the: 154, 160, 417, 453, 591, 609, 636, 875, 994, 999
Ball, A. L.: 938 n.4
Ball, Major Libbeus: 193 n.2
Ballard, Rev. Frank Hewett: 290
Balmoral (Scotland): 362 n.3; Churchill's visits to (1952), 763–4; (1953), 874, 880, 881, 884, 886, 887; Churchill recalls his visit to, 942
Balsan, Consuelo (Consuelo Vanderbilt): 742, 1318
Baltic Sea, the: 67, 75, 200, 238, 239, 279, 636; and 'anxieties' about the control of (1945), 1080; Churchill's intended cruise to (1960), 1313
Baltic States, the: 216, 510
Balzac, Honoré de: 890 n.1
Bangalore (India): 186, 1282
Bank of England, the: 323
Barbados: Churchill's visit to (1960), 1308–9
Barber, Anthony (later Baron): 513
Bardogs Farm (Chartwell): purchased (1947), 327; worked, 523; sold (1957), 1252
Barne, Colonel A. M.: 135, 137, 146
Barnes, George: 403 n.3
Barnes, Sir Reginald ('Reggie'): 146, 185
Barnett, Dr J. W.: 881, 1173, 1319 n.1
Bartholomew, Harry Guy: 643
Baruch, Bernard ('Bernie'): 191–2, 193, 210–

Baruch, Bernard—*continued*
11, 277, 341, 468, 471, 495, 522, 601; his friendship with Churchill, 683; and the atomic bomb, 684, 1003 n.1; Churchill the guest of, 683, 692, 693, 789, 790, 791, 806, 973; Churchill's letters to, 701, 1053–4, 1131, 1135, 1139, 1185–6, 1190, 1228, 1250; stays with Churchill, 744, 749, 1202; sees Churchill, 1011; and Churchill's war memoirs, 879; a gift from, 1211, 1257; and Churchill's penultimate visit to America (1959), 1291–2, 1294 n.1; and Churchill's last visit to America (1961), 1322, 1323
Bath (England): Churchill speaks at (1897), 1107 n.4
Battle of France, the (1940): 1239
Baudouin, Paul: 434
Beards, Paul: 110, 129 n.4
Bearsted, 2nd Viscount: 256 n.1
Beaton, (Sir) Cecil: 1276 n.1
Beauchamp, Antony: 496, 983, 1092, 1249
Beaverbrook, 1st Baron ('Max'): and the 1945 Election, 21, 34, 36–7, 46, 57, 65, 93, 105, 106, 113, 118, 739 n.3; and Russia, 77; chickens from, 139, 145; Lord Derby's complaint to, 189; at Chartwell, 226, 982, 1269 n.2; at Downing Street, 745; at Chequers, 1103; a book by, published (1928), 265 n.3; a protest to, 271, 963; letters to, about Churchill, 278, 285, 500, 1087–8; and Churchill's illnesses, 339, 852, 1265, 1266; Churchill's letters to, 377, 402–3, 462, 530, 807–8, 872, 890, 1254, 1265, 1275, 1277, 1281, 1302, 1326, 1331, 1332–3, 1341, 1343; Churchill stays at villa of, 434, 484–5, 759, 886–91, 1161–3, 1250–1, 1272–7, 1315; Churchill visits the villa of, 1325, 1328, 1335; and 'an insult', 461–2; his newspapers, 615; and electric power, 754; and Eden, 794; and Churchill's stroke (1953), 853, 854; and Churchill's path to resignation (1953–5), 943, 950, 975, 1095; and Munich (1938), 993; and Churchill's years of retirement (1955–65), 1136, 1139, 1144, 1168–9, 1172, 1173, 1181, 1184, 1199, 1240, 1253, 1254, 1256, 1265, 1266, 1269 n.2, 1275, 1277, 1281, 1288, 1289, 1299, 1305, 1307, 1308, 1317, 1318, 1331, 1334, 1338, 1341, 1347, 1351; Churchill lunches with (1962), 1335; Churchill's last letter to (1963), 1345–6; his message to Lady Churchill (1963), 1350; dies (1964), 1353
Bed Bug, the Common: 'Beware', 139
Bedford (England): Churchill speaks at (1955), 1137
Beirut (The Lebanon): American troops land at (1958), 1270

Belfast (Northern Ireland): Freedom of, 1171
Belgium: 94, 212, 232, 258, 266–7, 400, 425; 'stubborn resistance' of (in 1940), 471; and the defence of Europe (1950), 542; and Churchill's war memoirs, 609; Churchill's visit to (1945), 170–1
Belgrade: 118, 200, 209, 221, 378, 416
Belties (Dutch cattle): at Chartwell, 524
Benelux (Belgium, The Netherlands and Luxembourg): 927, 1090
Ben-Gurion, David: 410, 1214 n.2, 1219, 1268–9, 1299, 1301; Churchill's meeting with (1961), 1323–4; an exchange of messages with (1961), 1329–30
Benn, Anthony Wedgwood ('Tony'): 1081 n.3, 1350
Beria, Lavrenti: 808 n.1, 828, 862–3, 870, 876, 888
Berlin: conference in (1945), 26, 42–5, 60–104; in the 'Soviet sphere', 200, 201, 404, 437; blockade of, 421, 423, 430–1, 431–2, 437, 438, 440, 441, 448, 467, 474; the blockade recalled (in 1951), 666, 676, 1002, 1329; a possible new summit conference in (1953), 918; a Four-Power Foreign Ministers Conference to be held in (1954), 929–30, 940, 943–4, 951; results of the Conference in, 952–3, 1029
Berlin, (Sir) Isaiah: 383, 391, 393, 394, 412
Bermuda: a possible Conference at, 833, 838, 844, 850–1, 851, 852, 861, 889, 907, 909–10, 914; Conference at, 916–37; repercussions of, 938–42; and atomic energy, 919, 937, 940–1, 960, 962; and Churchill's stroke, 1101
Berne (Switzerland): 265, 1027, 1029, 1031, 1032
Bernhard of The Netherlands, Prince: 775–6
Bevan, Aneurin: 347, 508, 566, 584; resigns (1951), 607; 'tinted . . . tainted', 644; Churchill's 'aversion' to, 668; and a 'counterattack', 705; recognition of, 741; and Attlee, 753; and the Quebec Agreement (of 1943) on the atomic bomb, 967; in Moscow and Peking, 1045, 1049; his criticisms, 1101
Bevan, Mrs Robert (Natalie) (later Mrs Sam Barclay): 1276 n.1
Beveridge, Sir William (later Baron): 36
Bevin, Ernest: and the 1945 Election, 19, 20, 24; and Potsdam, 66 n.4; Foreign Secretary, 114 n.1, 118 n.3, 192, 195, 239, 421, 448, 529; and Churchill's political future (in 1947), 341; one of two 'sourpusses', 115; *Mister*, 140; Churchill's letters to, 166–7, 195, 196, 197, 205, 223; and Churchill's visits to Switzerland (1946), 262; and to Paris (1946), 267; and Churchill's war mem-

Bevin, Ernest—*continued*
oirs, 269; and Soviet Russia, 289, 362; and Western European Union, 399, 400, 407, 425, 433, 569; and Czechoslovakia, 404; and the German Field Marshals, 433; and the Berlin blockade, 448; and Palestine, 297, 454–5, 557, 558; and Jordan, 913; 'deflated a bit', 459; and NATO, 467; and Germany, 495, 574, 575; 'many pitiful blunders' of, 509; 'incredible . . . follies' of, 525; and Churchill's relationship with Lew Douglas, 554 n.1; the 'arch saboteur', 569; dies (1951), 598; his memory saluted, 660; 'admired', 668; his 'affection' for Churchill, 779; 'firmness of, tenacity' of, 829; Churchill's tribute to, 953; and 'Bevinism', 1095; a memorial to, 1303

Bevin, Mrs Ernest (Florence) (later Dame): 569, 598 n.5

Biarritz (France): 552

Bicester, 1st Baron: 256 n.1

Bidault, Georges: 50, 242, 329, 407, 424; Churchill dines with, 588; and the path to the Summit, 863, 864; in London, 898; to go to Bermuda, 910, 916; at Bermuda, 919, 920, 923, 925, 926, 930–4, 937; 'very friendly to us', 978

Bierut, Boleslaw: 94–7, 101–3

Big Ben (London): silenced (30 January 1965), 1362

Biggin Hill (airfield) (Kent): 147, 480, 488, 537, 541, 616–17, 772, 1198, 1302, 1330

Biggs-Davidson, (Sir) John: 769

Bihar (India): 294

Bikini Atoll (Pacific Ocean): hydrogen bomb exploded at, 957

Bill of Rights, the (1689): 200

Billmeir, Jack: his yacht, 1162, 1244, 1245

Billotte, General Gaston: 418 n.6

Birch, Nigel (later Baron Rhyl): 1184, 1206

Birdwood, Lord (Christopher Birdwood, 2nd Baron): 1202

Birdwood, Field Marshal Lord (William, 1st Baron): 1202

Birkenhead, Dowager Countess of (Margaret) (widow of the 1st Earl): 1276 n.1

Birkenhead, Countess of (Sheila) (wife of the 2nd Earl): 1173

Birkenhead, 1st Earl of (F. E. Smith): 1247

Birkenhead, 2nd Earl of: 1173

Birkhall (Aberdeenshire): a 'remarkable abode', 764

Birley, Sir Oswald: 481, 629, 1042 n.3

Birley, Lady (Rhoda Birley): 629, 1042, 1250

Birmingham Post, the: 324 n.1

Birse, Major A. H.: 63, 74, 115 n.2; *photograph* 3

Bisco, Jack: 217

Bishop, (Sir) Frederick: 1218

Bismarck, Otto von: 547, 690

Bisset, Commodore (Sir) James: 181

Black Sea, the: 75, 91, 278, 279, 280

'Black and Tans', the: 186

Blackburn, Raymond: at Chartwell, 346; opposes his own party, 347

Blackpool: Party Conference at (1946), 275; Churchill speaks at (1950), 561, 570; Party Conference at (1954), 1046, 1063–5

Bladon Churchyard: Churchill wishes to be buried at, 1307; Churchill buried at, 1363

Blair, Colonel P. B.: 10–11, 559

Blake, Nurse Helen: 338, 388

Bland, Sir Nevile: 233

Blandford, Marchioness of (Tina): 1339 n.1

Blandford, Marquess of (son of the 10th Duke): 1339 n.1

Blenheim Palace: Churchill's speech at (1947), 336; Lord Randolph 'asks' about, 369; Randolph Churchill's book on, 946; an incident at (in 1904 or thereabouts), 1015; Churchill visits (1958), 1269–70

Blessing, a: 'in disguise', 108

Bletchley: and honours, 18

'Blimps and Philistines': 253

Blitz, the (the London Blitz): 273, 315, 344, 562 n.4, 1324; and 'the scenario of history', 974; and 10 Downing Street, 1330

Blond, Mrs Elaine: 329 n.3

Blum, Léon: 4, 149, 291, 399–400, 406

Blunt, Brigadier Gerald: 601

Boardman, Harry: 947, 1112

Boer War, the: Churchill's escape during, 56; Lord Randolph's 'concern' about, 369, 371; Churchill recalls, 447, 998; Churchill's 'narrow escape' in, 546 n.2; Churchill wanted 'dead or alive' during, 547; Churchill a prisoner-of-war during, 675; Churchill's lectures on, 685; 'soldiering together' in, 1253 n.5

Bolsheviks: and Bolshevism, 229 n.3; 'barbarism' of, 444; discussed with two Popes (1927, 1944), 870; 'in its cradle', 1008

Bombay (India): 248

Bonar, Mrs Lorraine: 184–5

Bonham Carter, Lady Violet (later Baroness Asquith of Yarnbury): 168, 219–20, 395, 398, 399, 525, 601, 633; Churchill speaks for, 646–7; fails, 648–9; at Chartwell, 975, 982, 983, 1149, 1157, 1202; and a 'glow-worm', 1068; a gift from, 1257, 1331 n.5; Churchill's letters and messages to, in retirement, 1285, 1356, 1358; lunches and dines with Churchill, 1339 n.1, 1341, 1357; a protest from, 1353; an explanation given to,

Bonham Carter, Lady Violet—*continued*
1355–6; *for subsequent index entry see*, Asquith of Yarnbury, Baroness
'Boniface': 18
Boothby, (Sir) Robert (later Baron): 260, 283 n.2, 430–1, 481 n.4, 661; a 'shining star', 751; Churchill's renewed friendship with, 782–3; his protest, 967; and payment of Members of Parliament, 980 n.4; and Churchill's years in retirement, 1238 n.1, 1339
Bordeaux (France): 57, 59, 1343 n.1
Bornholm (Denmark, Baltic Sea): 194
Bosphorus, the (Turkey): 834
Bosworth, Battle of (1485): 1078
Boult, Sir Adrian: 406
Bourgès-Manoury, Maurice: 1243 n.3
Boyd, (Sir) Francis: 902, 947 n.2, 1112
Boyd-Carpenter, John (later Baron): 361, 1066
Boyle, Sir Edward (later Baron Boyle of Handsworth): 1337 n.2
Brabazon of Tara, 1st Baron (John Moore-Brabazon): 749 n.1
Bracken, Brendan (later 1st Viscount): becomes First Lord, 23; and Syria, 31; and the 1945 Election, 34, 36–7, 57, 105, 106, 107, 109, 111; Churchill's friendship with, 118, 131, 305, 339, 470, 713, 723, 730, 824, 852, 854, 873–4, 950, 1228; and Sir Arthur Harris, 179 n.2; and Churchill's Literary Trust, 244, 308, 533 n.3, 974; his letters about Churchill, 278, 500; in Opposition, 403 n.3, 506; and Palestine, 411; and Churchill's war memoirs, 418, 549, 610 n.1, 974; at Chartwell, 498; created Viscount, 656; doubts Churchill's 'ability to go on', 730; and Churchill's stroke (in 1953), 852; and Churchill's History, 876–7, 884, 943, 1196–7; and Churchill's path to resignation (1953–5), 943, 950, 975, 1087–8, 1095; and Churchill's health, 1262, 1265, 1266; dying (1958), 1269, 1272, 1273; dies (1958), 1274; 'one of my best friends', 1274–5; memorials to, 1275 n.1, 1280 n.1; Churchill's tribute to, 1281
Braddock, Bessie: 385 n.2, 967
Bradford (England): a 'truculent' speech at (1909), 655
Bradley, General Omar N.: 208, 530, 757, 793
Brain, Sir Russell (later 1st Baron): 532, 631, 711, 717, 848, 851, 868–9, 872, 1219; and Churchill's stroke in 1959, 1289–90; continues to see Churchill, 1304
Brand, W. H. (later 1st Baron): 191
Brave New World (Aldous Huxley): 1228
Brave New World Revisited (Aldous Huxley): 1228 n.5
Brazil: 172

Bread rationing: 248–9
Bremridge, Mr: 601
Breslau (Silesia): 88
Breteuil, Marquis of: 379
Brezhnev, Leonid: 318 n.3
Briand, Aristide: 242
Briare (France): 429
Bridges, Sir Edward (later 1st Baron): 37, 38, 66 n.4, 268–9, 376, 655, 661, 703
Bridges, General Sir Tom: 1253
Brighton: Conservative Party Conference at (1947), 353, 354–5, 419; Churchill at school at (1883), 867
Brilej, Jože: 591
Bristol (England): Churchill speaks at, 492, 1071
Britain, Battle of (1940): 315, 1239; and the locomotive 'Winston Churchill', 1363
Britain: 'genius of', 52; 'can take it', 733
Britain Strong and Free (1951): 641
Britannia (HM Royal Yacht): 976
British Butterfly Society, a: a scheme for, 1140
British Commonwealth, the: and Russia, 162, 167; its structure, 182; its strength, 203, 219; and the United States, 216–17, 353, 354, 911, 1248, 1327; and *The Times*, 246; and India, 248, 276, 334, 471–2; and United Europe, 266, 495–6, 690, 727–8; and machine tools for Russia, 555–6; and the Korean war, 561 n.3, 993; and Princess Elizabeth, 662–3; arms sales to, 803; 'united', 835; conference of Prime Ministers (1953), 836–41, 842–3; and coloured immigration, 949; and Israel, 1093, 1095; and the Crown, 1121, 1128; and an educational fund, 1272; and Ghana, 1330; a wreath from (in 1965), 1364
British Empire Cancer Campaign: Churchill's help to, 1268
British Guiana: 898
British Lion, the: 'a greater pet than ever', 671
British Somaliland: campaign in (1940), 548
Brodie, (Sir) Israel (Chief Rabbi): 602
Brogan, (Sir) Denis: 177, 180, 1066
Brook, (Sir) Norman (later 1st Baron Normanbrook): and Churchill's war memoirs, 315, 393, 404–5, 423, 474, 494, 552, 632, 794, 867, 879; and Churchill's 'sense of perils', 545; and Churchill's second Premiership, 654, 655, 661, 672 n.2, 673, 674, 686, 739, 823; and Churchill's stroke (1953), 856, 857, 876; and the Bermuda Conference (December 1953), 912, 916, 917, 920 n.1; and Churchill's powers (1954), 965, 1084, 1093; and Churchill's retirement, 989, 1119, 1135; and the Makins telegram (1955), 1105, 1106; and Churchill's years of retire-

Brook, (Sir) Norman—*continued*
ment (1955), 1139, 1176, 1195, 1213–14, 1307, 1349, 1351 n.2; and Eden's resignation (1957), 1226; and Churchill's 'gifts', 1238; *for subsequent index entry see* Normanbrook, 1st Baron

Brooke, Field Marshal (Sir) Alan (later 1st Viscount Alanbrooke): 18, 39, 51, 56, 70, 110, 124, 125–6, 127; *for subsequent index entries see* Alanbrooke, Field Marshal Viscount

Brooke, Humphrey (later Baron Brooke of Cumnor): 1337 n.2

Brown, Ernest: 20

Brussels (Belgium): Churchill's speech in (1945), 170–2; Churchill re-visits (1946), 267; Churchill's speech in (1949), 460, 463, 467

Brussels Treaty (1948), the: 509–10, 1056

Brutinel, Brigadier-General Raymond: 57

Bryant, (Sir) Arthur: 1232, 1304 n.6

Buchan, Alastair: 270

Buchan-Hepburn, Patrick (later 1st Baron Hailes): 403 n.3, 472, 506, 638 n.5, 752, 799, 977; and the question of Churchill's resignation, 736, 889, 1037, 1060, 1061; succeeded by Edward Heath, 1177 n.1; in the West Indies, 1245; *for subsequent entry see* Hailes, 1st Baron

Bucharest (Roumania): 97, 200

Buchenwald (Germany): 17, 31

Buck, Pearl S.: 205

Buckingham Palace: Churchill goes to, to resign (1945), 22–3; first Caretaker Government Privy Council meeting at (1945), 27; Churchill lunches at, 36; Churchill goes to, to resign again (1945), 109; Churchill goes to, to say goodbye to the King, 312; and the Socialists, 367; Churchill dines at (1951), 615, 630 n.1; a grave message from, 696; bombed (1941), 698; 'unwonted brilliance' at, 842; Churchill at, seeming 'a very old man', 1071; Churchill receives a gift at, 1075; and the Commonwealth Conference (1955), 1093; and a banquet for the Shah, 1095; and Churchill's resignation (1955), 1124, 1152; Churchill dines at (1957), 1255; Churchill attends a banquet at (1960), 1311

Budapest (Hungary): 76, 200, 209, 460 n.1

Buddhism: 'a Tory religion', 859

Bulganin, Marshal Nikolai: 828, 1094, 1109, 1113, 1114; and the Geneva Summit (1955), 1154–5, 1168; in Britain (1956), 1192, 1196

Bulgaria: 25, 76, 90–1, 97–8, 212, 288, 351 n.3, 510, 874; 'subjugated', 953; and the Moscow Conference (of 1944), 1192

Bullen, Wing Commander Eric: 777 n.1

Bullock (Churchill's chauffeur): 1306

Bullock, Alan (later Baron): 1185

Bunford, Miss Wendy: 1340 n.4

Bungey, Desmond: 480 n.2, 616 n.1

Burgess, Guy: 888 n.5

Burke, Edmund: 240, 413 n.3

Burma: 3, 302, 359, 369; 'down the drain', 371; battles in (1942–5), 420 n.1, 609; 'anarchy and murder in', 439; and the British Commonwealth, 474; General Slim in, 679 n.2; and China, 791; Chinese Nationalist troops in, 839

Burns, John: 375

Burns, Robert: quoted, 396–7

Busch, Field Marshal Ernst: 14, 15

Butcher, Captain Harry C.: 187, 235

Butler, David: 585 n.2, 644

Butler, Sir Montagu: dies, 776

Butler, R. A. (later Baron Butler of Saffron Walden): and the 1945 General Election, 9; and the Shadow Cabinet, 163; and Churchill's political future (1947), 341; and the 1950 General Election, 476, 500–1; and Miss Portal, 514 n.3; and the 1951 General Election, 529 n.1, 637, 638 n.5, 641–2; and Churchill's second Premiership, 657, 658, 670, 712, 717, 724, 726, 731, 734–5, 747–8, 755, 770, 772–3, 787, 807, 815–16, 1050; his first budget (1952), 724; and Churchill's stroke (1953), 848, 849, 850–2, 852, 855, 863, 864, 865; and Churchill's recovery, 872, 873, 879, 883, 887, 893, 938, 958; and the Conservative succession, 871, 883, 1037, 1046–7, 1049, 1050, 1052, 1060, 1066, 1084, 1086, 1097, 1115; his father's death, 776; his wife's illness and death, 984; and Egypt, 787, 941; and Persia, 878; and payment of Members of Parliament, 980 n.4, 981, 985; and the Molotov telegram (of July 1954), 1014, 1024–5; and Churchill's Summit hopes, 1032; at Chartwell, 1043; and the 1955 Budget, 1114, 1133; and Churchill's resignation, 1115–16; a 'pillar of strength', 1133–4; and the 1955 General Election, 1138; and Churchill's retirement years (1955–65), 1169, 1174, 1175, 1183, 1276 n.1; and hanging, 1182 n.1; and Suez, 1221 n.4; and Eden's resignation (1957), 1227; and Churchill's 85th birthday, 1306; and Cabinet changes (1962), 1337 n.2

Butler, Mrs R. A. (Sydney Butler): 341, 984, 1043

Byrnes, James ('Jimmy') (United States Secretary of State, 1945–7): 71, 80, 90, 191, 192, 195–6, 205, 267, 289, 428; 'I liked what I

Byrnes, James ('Jimmy')—*continued*
saw of him', 1054; sees Churchill (1959), 1294 n.1
Byron: a budgerigar, Toby's successor, 1317, 1323
Byron, Lord: 197

Cabinet Defence Committee (1951–5): 708–9, 715–16, 728, 746, 773, 781, 798–9, 803–4, 821–2, 824–5, 833, 899, 903–4, 950–1
Caccia, Clarissa (later Clarissa Pryce-Jones): 1296
Caccia, Sir Harold (later Baron): 997 n.1, 1294, 1296
Caccia, Lady (Nancy): 1296
Cadogan, Sir Alexander: 46, 50, 52, 61, 65, 74, 79, 90, 124, 450, 479, 684
Caesar, Julius: 846, 1194, 1304, 1311
Cairns, Mrs Dido: and Toby, 1078, 1083; at Chartwell, 1183
Cairo (Egypt): 230, 231, 237, 668, 796, 799, 804, 825, 833, 875; and Nasser, 1203, 1205
Cairo Conference, the (1921): 1272 n.2
Calais (France): and a 'common-front', 788
Call of the Wild (Jack London): 1310
Callaghan, James ('Jim') (later Baron Callaghan of Cardiff): 208, 325 n.1, 516, 594, 948, 1182 n.1
Callas, Maria: 1297
Camp David (Maryland USA): a Summit at (1959), 832 n.1
Campaign of 1814, the: parleys while fighting in, 928
Campbell-Bannerman, Sir Henry: 1072
Campbell-Johnson, Alan: 249, 335
Camrose, 1st Viscount ('Bill'): 100, 119, 125, 132, 175–6, 514 n.2, 563, 564; and Churchill's war memoirs, 188, 244, 270, 273, 307 n.3, 327–8, 342, 383, 392, 393, 415 n.2, 469, 626, 628, 1196; and Churchill's political future, 243–4; and Churchill's Literary Trust, 244–5; and Chartwell, 255–6, 304; and United Europe, 291 n.1; at Marrakech, 395, 1197; and Churchill's visit to Madeira (1950), 499; visits Chartwell, 525, 867; 'knows my views', 557; at the Other Club, 739; and Churchill's stroke, 852; dines with Churchill, 899; dies, 993; recalled, 1125, 1196; Churchill's tribute to, 1197
Camrose, Lady (widow of 1st Viscount): 993
Camrose, 2nd Viscount (Seymour Berry): 1125
Canada: 13, 49, 161, 199, 307; troops from, Churchill's speech to (1946), 181–2; and a Churchill interview, 219; and the Soviet Union, 238; 'still loyal', 371; and NATO, 467; and the atomic bomb, 494; Churchill's

Canada—*continued*
visit to (1952), 685–6; the 'Queen of', 698; amnesty in, 748; and Churchill's war memoirs, 802 n.2; and atomic weapons, 913; and Western defence, 1056; and the Suez Crisis, 1246
Canadian Army, the: 6
Canal Zone (Egypt): 230, 237, 252; reinforced, 647; Britain's 'rightful position' in, 659, 667; and the need for 'drastic measures', 668; and the defence of, 676, 679–80, 684, 689, 701–2, 709, 781, 786, 796, 799, 804, 815, 821, 825, 833, 840–1, 843, 881–2, 893; British troops to withdraw from (1954), 897 n.2, 914, 939, 945, 994; and the Sudan riots (1954), 956, 957; and 'thermo-nuclear developments', 994; and the future of, 995–6, 1019; equipment moved from, 1125 n.2
Canby, H. S.: 393 n.4
Cane, Sir Cyril: 580
Cann, A. C.: 501 n.2
Cap d'Ail (French Riviera): 434, 484–5, 759, 886; Churchill's retirement visits to, 1161–3, 1250–1, 1272–7, 1315, 1325, 1328, 1335
Cap d'Antibes (French Riviera): 431
Cap Martin (French Riviera): 153–4, 1212 n.1
Cape of Good Hope, the (South Africa): 685
Capital Punishment: 400–1
Capitalism: denounced, 1169 n.3
Capri (Italy): Clementine Churchill at, 749, 751, 753; Churchill visits, 1297
Cardiff (Wales): Churchill speaks at (1950), 508
Carinthia (Austria): 5
Carlton Club, the (London): 366, 567
Carlyle, Thomas: 345
Carne, Lieutenant-Colonel J. P.: 610 n.2
Caronia, SS: 1165
Carr, Barbara (Mrs Sharpe): 175
Carr, John: 175
Carr, W. H.: 613 n.2, 826 n.4
Carroll, Lewis: 245 n.3
Carson, Robert: consulted, 1163
Carthage (Tunisia): Churchill's illness at (1943), 845
Carton de Wiart, Baron (of Belgium): 474 n.4
Casablanca (Morocco): 576, 577
Casablanca Conference (1943): 545, 615
Casey, Richard (later Baron): 663
Caspian Sea, the: 617, 618
Cassandra: Churchill compared with, 1074
Cassell (Publishing House): 221, 418, 423–4, 469, 784, 802 n.2, 1068, 1230 n.2, 1237
Cassels, Major-General A. J. H.: 746 n.1
Cassino, Monte (Italy) (battle for, 1944): 239
Cassis (France): 524

Castlereagh, Viscount (2nd Marquess of Londonderry): 835
Catholics: in Poland, 102
Cattell, Dr Richard: 820
Catto, 1st Baron: 256 n.1
Caucasus, the: 250
Cecil of Chelwood, 1st Viscount (Lord Robert Cecil): 242, 243, 260, 511
Celle (West Germany): Churchill at, 1197–8; *photograph 29*
Central Treaty Organization (CENTO): 994 n.1
Centurion, HMS: 401, 402
Cézanne, Paul: 428
Chamberlain, Anne (Mrs Neville Chamberlain): 1120, 1150
Chamberlain, Austen: 739
Chamberlain, Joseph ('Joe'): 186 n.3, 369, 739, 1114 n.2
Chamberlain, Neville: 21, 39 n.1, 113, 155, 231 n.2, 283 n.3, 289, 311–12, 319, 504, 739, 1041 n.1, 1142 n.2; and 'hubris', 868; 'in fact quite good', 1327; at 10 Downing Street (in 1940), 1330 n.4; 'We parted on friendly terms', 1332
Chamoun, President Camille: 1270, 1271
Champagne: 'and water', 116 n.2
Chandos, 1st Viscount (formerly Oliver Lyttelton): 1102, 1183, 1227, 1263; his tribute to Churchill (1965), 1364
Chanel, Coco: her villa, La Pausa, 1172–3
Channon, Henry ('Chips'): 11, 34, 36, 117, 130, 360, 417, 421, 458–9, 520, 525–6, 568, 591, 594, 595, 596, 607, 620 n.1; and Churchill's second Premiership, 658, 700, 722 n.2, 742, 808, 817, 902, 908
Charlemagne, Empire of: 264
Charlemagne Prize, the: Churchill receives, 1197, 1225
Charles, Prince (later Prince of Wales): 491 n.2, 764, 1095; *photograph 20*
Charles-Roux, M.: 434
Charlotte, Grand Duchess, of Luxembourg: 246
Chartwell: Churchill at (in 1945), 20, 58, 126, 130, 163, 164–5, 175–7; (in 1946), 180, 225–6, 245, 255–60, 268, 278, 281, 304, 306–7; (in 1947), 308, 313, 315, 320, 323, 326–7, 328, 331–2; 'dilapidated', 130; plans for (1945), 138–9, 139, 144, 145, 149; and the National Trust, 304 n.3, 993, 1077; and some royal lilies, 721 n.1; writing the war memoirs at, 331–2, 338–40, 342–5, 405, 416; Churchill's 'dream' at, 364–372; a burglary at, 385; a pig 'massacred' at, 389; (in 1948), 435, 444; (in 1949), 453, 459, 462, 471, 488, 497–8, 498; (in 1950), 506, 511, 522, 532,

Chartwell—*continued*
533, 546–8, 561, 580; (in 1951), 596, 598, 614–15, 617 n.1, 623–4, 629, 630; and Churchill's second Premiership (1951–5), 654–6, 704, 714, 720, 722–3, 726–7, 728, 730, 732, 735, 738, 743, 745, 749, 752–3, 753, 755–6, 772, 783, 794; (in 1953), 807, 824, 843, 844; and Churchill's stroke (1953), 849–57, 858–68, 873, 874, 877; and Churchill's recovery at, 880; Churchill's frequent return to (1953–5), 900–1, 980, 982–4, 987–8, 1042–5, 1066, 1119; the rebuilding of (1922–4) recalled, 974; a museum at, 1069 n.5, 1077; Toby at, 1083; and Churchill's musings about a Dukedom, 1123–4; Churchill's home during his years of retirement (1955–59), 1125, 1126, 1139, 1140, 1141, 1147, 1148–51, 1152–4, 1160–1, 1172, 1181, 1182, 1183, 1190–1, 1198, 1199, 1200, 1203, 1205, 1208, 1209, 1220, 1227, 1239, 1241, 1255, 1257, 1265, 1276, 1278, 1281, 1285, 1287; sale of farms at, 1252; and the 1959 Election campaign, 1302; and Bladon, 1307; and Disraeli's desk, 1338 n.1; a gift of swans for, 1352; Churchill's last visits to (1959–64), 1305, 1318, 1326–7, 1327–8, 1332, 1335, 1344, 1349, 1352, 1354; Churchill's last guests at (1964), 1357; Churchill looks over the lake at, *photograph 26*; Churchill with a racehorse at, *photograph 27*
Chartwell Farm: purchased (1946), 306; an integral part of Chartwell, 313, 358, 527; sold (1957), 1252
Chater, Major-General Arthur Reginald: 548–9
Chatfield, Admiral of the Fleet Lord (1st Baron): 231, 237
Chavasse, Rt Rev. Christopher Maude, Bishop of Rochester: 600
Chequers (Official country residence of the Prime Minister): Churchill at, 9, 10, 11, 20, 24, 32, 46, 49–50, 111–13; Attlee at, 129 n.4; recollections of, 596; and Churchill's second Premiership, 663–4, 665, 670, 716–17, 729, 730, 745, 785, 821, 824, 868, 869–70, 879, 892, 942, 977, 978, 1058–9, 1102; Churchill sculpted at, 771; Eden at, 781, 978; Toby at, 1083; Churchill's last week-end at (1955), 1113; a farewell to the staff at, 1119; Eden planning a meeting at, 1120; Eden at, as Prime Minister, 1141; Churchill's journey to, during the Suez Crisis (1956), 1203
Cherwell, 1st Baron (later 1st Viscount): 34 n.2, 46, 50, 62 n.2, 66 n.5, 80, 111, 163, 234, 244, 249, 308, 345; at Marrakech, 381, 395, 576, 577, 578, 579, 582, 583; and

Cherwell, 1st Baron—*continued*
Churchill's war memoirs, 426, 429, 584, 632; and defence, 477, 478, 490 n.1; and the Chartwell Literary Trust, 533 n.3; and the atomic bomb, 573, 717, 794; and Churchill's second Premiership, 656, 661, 672, 673, 681, 714, 717, 726 n.2 735, 752, 793; and 'a favourite act', 675, 686, 686 n.3; and the 'sterling-dollar', 735; to accompany Churchill to Bermuda, 844–5; and Churchill's stroke (1953), 851, 855; accompanies Churchill to Bermuda (December 1953), 912, 913, 916, 917, 924, 936; and Churchill's visit to Washington and Ottawa (1954), 985, 986 n.1, 997 n.1, 1011; with Churchill in Sicily (1955), 1131; and honours, 1142, 1143; and Churchill's retirement years, 1172, 1210, 1211, 1213, 1235 n.1, 1241; dies (1957), 1247–8; Churchill's tribute to, 1248; *photograph 4*

Chetwynd, Captain G. R.: 163 n.1

Chiang Kai-shek: 681, 1092

Chicago (Illinois, USA): and Eisenhower, 743

Chicago Sun, the: 204

Chichester, Major (Lord) Desmond: 142

'Chickenham Palace' (at Chartwell): 497

Chifley, Joseph (Prime Minister of Australia): 106

Childe Harold's Pilgrimage (Byron): 197

China (Communist, or 'Red' China): 3, 63, 277, 437; recognition of, 495, 741–2, 918, 1002; 'old', 510; and Korea, 577 n.1, 581, 583, 584 n.1, 696, 704, 706, 715, 739–40, 741–2, 759, 800, 814, 832, 861, 917; and export of raw materials to, 610–11, 614, 676; and the Soviet Union, 676, 688, 715, 739; and South-East Asia, 791; and a possible Summit, 820; and the United Nations, 882; and the Bermuda Conference, 918; and trade with, 918; and a possible meeting with, 928, 951, 952, 954; and the atomic bomb, 932–3; and the hydrogen bomb, 973; a possible 'front against', 999; and its admission to the United Nations, 1015, 1016, 1029–30, 1035; and Formosa, 1049, 1092; its 'power and importance' exaggerated, 1081–2; and the United States, 1091–2

Choisi (Switzerland) (near Bursinel): Churchill stays at (1946), 260–3, 278 n.2

Cholmondeley, Marchioness of (Sybil): 147 n.3, 525 n.2, 1338

Cholmondeley, 5th Marquess of: 147, 149, 1287

Chou En-lai: 838, 1049

Christ, George: helps Churchill with his speeches, 492–3, 506, 507, 528, 601, 647, 1135 n.2; helps Churchill in retirement, 1165, 1266

Christendom: and a United Europe, 279

Christian civilization: 'peril' to, 201; 'salvation of', 571

Christian ethics: 'our best guide', 409

Christian society: and Southern Ireland, 442

Christianity: 'with a tomahawk', 18; and Communism, 161

Christie, John: on trial, 854

Christina, S.Y.: 'the monster yacht', 1173 n.4, 1180, 1181; Churchill's first cruise on (1958), 1277–8; Churchill's second cruise on (1959), 1284–5; Churchill's third cruise on (1959), 1297; Churchill's fourth cruise on (1960), 1308–11; Churchill's fifth cruise on (1960), 1313–14; Churchill's sixth cruise on (1961), 1321–3; Churchill's seventh cruise on (1962), 1333–4; the hospitality of, recalled, 1339; Churchill's eighth and final cruise on (1963), 1346; *photograph 36*

Chronology: 'the secret of narrative', 742

Chronology of the Second World War (Royal Institute of International Affairs, 1947): 623 n.3

Chuikov, General V. I.: 811

Chungking (China): 30

Church of England, the: 366–7

Churchill, Arabella: 435, 502, 662, 752, 1042, 1069 n.5, 1174, 1358; *photograph 33*

Churchill, Clementine (later Baroness Spencer-Churchill): in Russia 3–4, 5, 9, 64–5; and the 1945 General Election, 10, 32, 47, 107, 108, 111–12, 127, 129; and Churchill's resignation (1945), 23, 24; her letters to her husband (1945–55), 37–8, 139–40, 141–2, 145–6, 380–1, 388, 434, 435, 461–2, 470, 489, 570, 629, 630, 691, 751, 924–5, 937, 951, 1059, 1069, 1113, 1155, 1160; advice of, to her husband, 197 n.4, 328–9, 461–2, 465, 470–1, 489, 570, 601–2, 602–3, 656, 844, 880–1, 884; accompanies her husband, 57–9, 128, 172, 184–5, 186, 190, 219, 242, 260, 261, 263, 362, 390, 409, 421, 426, 428, 462, 465, 481, 498, 500, 525–6, 585–9, 764, 836, 841, 1115; joins her husband, 105, 695, 1335; her daughters' letters to, 133, 381–2, 390, 889, 1053, 1113, 1157, 1166, 1276–7; and her husband's gambling, 153, 1165; and Chartwell, 164, 165, 256, 257, 497; unwell (1946), 306; (1947), 346; (1948), 417; (1950), 522; (1951), 600, 613–14, 627; (1954), 977; (1955), 1113, 1148, 1155, 1173; (1956), 1178, 1208; (1957), 1254, 1255, 1256; (1959), 1291, 1298; 1299 n.1; (1961), 1319; (1962), 1339; (1963), 1347, 1348, 1349; and the January freeze (1947), 313; and her husband's illnesses, 338, 340, 711–12, 732, 1061, 1263, 1316–17;

Churchill, Clementine—*continued*
and her husband's war memoirs, 345; 489, 493–4; at Westminster Abbey, 362; unable to accompany her husband, 378; 'devoted' to her husband, 458; and her daughter Sarah, 451, 496; and the Chartwell Literary Trust and her financial future, 308, 535 n.3, 974; and her husband's financial gifts, 1282; and her husband's horseracing, 563, 613 n.5, 720; and her husband's second Premiership (1951–5), 650, 655, 656, 657 n.1, 661–2, 711–12, 714, 718, 720, 728, 823, 844; and her husband's stroke (1953), 846, 848, 851, 853, 854, 859, 860; and her husband's recovery, 880, 880–1, 947; and her husband's decisions to resign, or not to resign, 887, 902–3, 1037–9, 1085, 1088, 1111; and her husband's overseas journeys, 1008; protestations to, 1031, 1037–9; and Graham Sutherland, 1059, 1073, 1076, 1253; and the death of her sister Nellie Romilly, 1092; and her 78th birthday, 1117; and her husband's resignation (in 1955), 1119, 1120, 1122, 1124; and her husband's decision not to stand again for Parliament (in 1963), 1343, 1344–5, 1346; her 'charm and dignity', 1350; with her husband in retirement (1955–65), 1131–2, 1161–3, 1172, 1199, 1235, 1238, 1247, 1248, 1250, 1251, 1261, 1269, 1304, 1306, 1308, 1314, 1315, 1316, 1326, 1355, 1357; and Churchill College, Cambridge, 1304 n.1, 1352; her husband's letter, in 1925, on the death of her mother, 1364; her letters and messages to her husband, in retirement (1955–65), 1182, 1190, 1201, 1203, 1204, 1209, 1214, 1270, 1288, 1299, 1344, 1348, 1351; and the Suez Crisis (1956), 1201, 1203–4, 1225; and her husband's work in retirement, on behalf of Britain, 1225; 'I couldn't bear to live without', 1308; her husband's death, 77 n.1, 1362–4; 'my darling Winston', 1364; *photographs, 1, 2, 9, 14, 24, 33, 38*

Churchill, Diana: *see index entry* Sandys, Diana

Churchill, Lady Gwendeline ('Goonie'): 1305 n.2

Churchill, Lord Ivor (son of the 9th Duke of Marlborough): 823–4

Churchill, John Strange ('Jack'): 49, 50, 105, 175, 370; dies, 315–17; in an old photograph, 1305 n.2; his brother buried near, 1363

Churchill, Marigold: 370, 1289 n.3

Churchill, Mary: in 1945, 3, 4, 9, 32, 47, 53, 57–8, 59, 128, 130, 143, 145, 148; at Potsdam, 61, 66; and the General Election of 1945, 105, 107–8, 109, 111–12; accompanies her father, 232, 248, 260, 261, 262, 263, 265;

Churchill, Mary—*continued*
Churchill's letters to, 144; her letters to her father, 177, 481; her recollections, 165, 496; her letters to her mother, 186; engaged, 304; 'the future', 305; married, 312–13; *for subsequent index entries see* Soames, Mary (later Lady)

Churchill, Pamela (later Mrs Averell Harriman): 179, 487, 901, 1282, 1331 n.5

Churchill, Lady Randolph: 186 n.1, 307 n.1, 499 n.1, 562, 724, 790, 874 n.4

Churchill, Lord Randolph: 222, 235, 293, 306 n.6, 321, 364 n.2; and his son's 'dream', 365–72; Churchill's biography of, 414; and Bismarck, 547; and the Jockey Club, 563 n.2; Churchill's conversations with, 776 n.2; and a 'discourtesy' title, 823; his robes, 1071; his archive, 1319; and his son's death, 1360

Churchill, (the Hon.) Randolph S.: at Chequers, 11, 20, 30, 34 n.2; and the 1945 Election, 39, 46–7, 50, 62, 74 n.3, 105, 107, 112, 148; and his father's last weekend at Chequers (1945), 113 n.3; and the years of Opposition (1945–51), 163–4; letters and telegrams to his father, 131, 336 n.1, 386, 451–2, 465, 489, 533, 660, 662, 671, 691, 695, 764–5, 765–8, 784, 889, 947, 1159–60, 1259, 1365; talks with his father, 196; appreciative talk of, 137; and Flandin, 169; the first marriage of, 179; conversations of, about his father, 163–4, 187–8; and his uncle Jack's death, 316; interviews his father (1946), 217–19; and his father's biography, 244, 413 n.2, 872, 946, 1037, 1239, 1312–13, 1318, 1319, 1338, 1364; his father's letters to, 253, 459, 489, 530, 765, 784, 946; and his father's published speeches, 257 n.2, 357; at Chartwell, 258, 364, 498, 525, 628, 752, 983, 1327; writes about his father, 289–90, 1111–12, 1112 n.1; and his sister Mary's marriage, 313; and a legacy, 313–14, 435; 'Marquess of Chartwell', 327 n.4; 'Marquess of Toodledo', 704; his Far Eastern journey (1947), 350; and Palestine, 410; travels with his father, 431, 465, 482, 734; disputes with his father, 451–2, 764–8, 783–4; and his father's war memoirs, 489, 494; and the 1950 Election, 501, 502, 507, 511, 512; advises his father, 511; his father speaks for, 508–9, 537, 647–8; leaves for Korea, 545; wounded, 546, 581; gifts from, 577; his political future, 580 (1950–1); defeated (1951), 649; at Chequers, 785, 870; at the Coronation, 797; and his father's stroke (1953), 853; his independent activities, 888, 1214, 1215; his literary work, 946; with his father at the races, 979, 982; and the engine drivers' strike, 1145; and his

Churchill, Randolph S.—*continued*
father's years of retirement (1955–65), 1168, 1172, 1173, 1183, 1235, 1285; and Eden, 1186, 1224 n.3; and the Suez Crisis (1956), 1202; and the *People*, 1214, 1215; at East Bergholt, 1172, 1239, 1244; gifts from, 1257; and the death of Brendan Bracken, 1274; and his father's illness (1962), 1336–7; at Hyde Park Gate (1962), 1337–8; on *Christina*, 1346; and Macmillan's resignation, 1349; and his father's last year, 1351 n.1, 1357; and his son's wedding, 1353, 1354; and his father's last illness, 1359; and his father's funeral, 1362–3; *photographs 10, 15, 33, 38*
Churchill, Mrs Randolph (June Osborne): 498, 525, 600, 853, 979, 982, 983, 1159, 1183
Churchill, Sarah (later Mrs Antony Beauchamp, subsequently Lady Audley): her letters and telegrams to her father, 35–6, 220, 248, 312–13, 316–17, 392–3, 440, 443, 450–1, 487, 570–1, 664, 684, 723, 724, 736, 760, 809, 862, 901, 1014, 1233, 1251, 1268–9, 1276, 1353; her Electoral advice, 39, 40; with her father, 50, 106–8, 111–12, 132, 133–4, 139, 143, 144, 145, 148, 149, 190, 348, 364, 378–95, 694, 789, 1165, 1358; and her father's illnesses, 338, 855; 'a joy to all', 139; 'a great joy', 143; the 'Mule', 348; her acting, 491, 694, 1305; her marriage (1949), 496, 1092; and the 1950 Election, 512; messages from her father, 723, 1256, 1257; carries a letter, 743, 744; at Chequers, 870; at Chartwell, 982, 983; at La Pausa, 1199, 1215, 1216, 1228, 1230, 1231, 1236, 1243, 1261; her sorrows, 1249, 1257, 1259, 1286–7, 1346; her plays, watched by her father, 1278, 1352; visits her father, 1318; marries Baron Audley, 1346; and her father's last illness, 1359; and her father's funeral, 1362, 1363; *photographs 11, 30, 38*
Churchill, Mrs Winston (Minnie D'Erlanger): 1358
Churchill, Sir Winston (knighted, 1664): 823
Churchill, (Sir) Winston Leonard Spencer:
his last months as wartime Prime Minister, 3–22; head of the Caretaker Government, 23–109; Leader of the Opposition, 112–649; peacetime Prime Minister, 649–1125; in retirement, 1125–1359; funeral, 1360–6;
his speeches, **in 1897**, Bath (26 July 1897), 1107 n.4; **in 1909**, Leicester (4 September 1909), 1211 n.1; **in 1910**, Dundee (5 January 1910), 730 n.1; **in 1918**, Dundee (10 December 1918), 730 n.1; **in 1921**, Jerusalem (29 March 1921), 723 n.5; **in 1944**,

Churchill, (Sir) Winston L. S.—*continued*
House of Commons (14 December 1944), 92; **in 1945**; Whitehall (9 May 1945), 4; broadcast (13 May 1945), 12–13; House of Commons (15 May 1945), 15; Woodford (26 May 1945), 24; broadcast (4 June 1945), 32–4; broadcast (13 June 1945), 39–41; House of Commons (14 June 1945), 43–4; broadcast (21 June 1945), 48; broadcast (30 June 1945), 51–2; Walthamstow (3 July 1945), 53–4; House of Commons (16 August 1945), 129; Woodford (21 October 1945), 160; Royal Albert Hall, London (23 October 1945), 160; Harrow (31 October 1945), 162; Paris (12 November 1945), 166; Brussels, twice (16 November 1945), 171; London (28 November 1945), 173; **in 1946**, crossing the Atlantic (13 January 1946), 181–2; Miami, Florida (26 February 1946), 193–4; Fulton, Missouri (5 March 1946), 197–203; Richmond, Virginia (8 March 1946), 207; New York (15 March 1946), 215–17; Aberdeen (27 April 1946), 228–9; Edinburgh (29 April 1946), 229; City of Westminster (7 May 1946), 229; The Hague (9 May 1946), 232; House of Commons (16 May 1946), 233; House of Commons (24 May 1946), 237–8; House of Commons (5 June 1946), 239–41; House of Commons (26 June 1946), 243; Metz (15 July 1946), 246–8; House of Commons (18 July 1946), 248; House of Commons (18 July 1946, second speech), 248–9; House of Commons (1 August 1946), 250–2; Geneva (16 September 1946), 263–5; Zurich (19 September 1946) 265–6; Blackpool (5 October 1946), 275–6; House of Commons (23 October 1946), 279; Woodford (24 October 1946), 280; House of Commons (12 November 1946), 284; Harrow (28 November 1946), 290; House of Commons (12 December 1946), 292–5; **in 1947**, House of Commons (31 January 1947), 295–7; House of Commons (6 March 1947), 298–9; House of Commons (12 March 1947), 210 n.3, 302–3; House of Commons (31 March 1947), 319–20; Albert Hall (18 April 1947), 321; House of Commons (7 May 1947), 324–5; Albert Hall (14 May 1947), 329–30; Ayr (15 May 1947), 330–1; House of Commons (3 June 1947), 333–4; Blenheim (4 August 1947), 336; broadcast (16 August 1947), 348–9; Woodford (27 September 1947), 353–4; Brighton (4 October 1947), 354–5; (14 October 1947), 352–3; House of Commons (22 October 1947), 359; House of Commons (29 October 1947), 359–60; Harrow (13 November 1947), 361;

Churchill, (Sir) Winston L. S.—*continued*
Manchester (6 December 1947), 375; **in 1948**, House of Commons (23 January 1948), 396–7; broadcast (14 February 1948), 398–9; Albert Hall (21 April 1948), 400–1; House of Commons (8 March 1948), 401–2; The Hague (7 May 1948), 406–9; Amsterdam (9 May 1948), 409; Oslo (11 May 1948), 409–10; Oslo (12 May 1948), 409–10, 411; Westminster Abbey (21 May 1948), 416; House of Commons (26 May 1948), 417; Perth (28 May 1948), 411; Luton Hoo (26 June 1948), 419; Woodford (10 July 1948), 421; House of Commons (30 July 1948), 422–3; Croydon (5 October 1948), 435–6; Llandudno (9 October 1948), 436–40; House of Commons (28 October 1948), 443; House of Commons (16 November 1948), 445–6; House of Commons (10 December 1948), 448–9; **in 1949**, House of Commons (25 January 1949), 453–7; Brussels (26 February 1949), 460; New York (25 March 1949), 463–4; Boston, Massachusetts (31 March 1949), 465–7; House of Commons (28 April 1949), 472; House of Commons (12 May 1949), 474–5; House of Commons (21 July 1949), 260; Strasbourg (17 August 1949), 483, 484; London (13 October 1949), 492; London (14 October 1949), 492; Bristol (20 October 1949), 492; Albert Hall (21 October 1949), 492; London (2 November 1949), 494; London (28 November 1949), 495–6; Harrow (1 December 1949), 497; **in 1950**, broadcast (21 January 1950), 502–3; Woodford (28 January 1950), 507; Leeds (4 February 1950), 507–8; Cardiff (8 February 1950), 508; Devonport (9 February 1950), 508–9; Edinburgh (14 February 1950), 509–11; broadcast (17 February 1950), 511; House of Commons (7 March 1950), 515–16; House of Commons (16 March 1950), 516–20; House of Commons (28 March 1950), 520–1; House of Commons (24 April 1950), 526–7; House of Commons (27 April 1950), 527–8; Edinburgh (18 May 1950), 528; House of Commons (26 June 1950), 535–7; London (4 July 1950), 537; House of Commons (5 July 1950), 537; Plymouth (15 July 1950), 537–8; House of Commons (26 July 1950), 538–9; House of Commons (27 July 1950), 539–41, 595 n.1; Strasbourg (11 August 1950), 542; broadcast (26 August 1950), 552–3; House of Commons (12 September 1950), 554–5, 556; House of Commons (19 September 1950), 558–9; Copenhagen (10 September 1950), 561; Blackpool (14 October 1950), 561, 566 n.1; Albert

Churchill, (Sir) Winston L. S.—*continued*
Hall (20 October 1950), 561; House of Commons (26 October 1950), 562–3; House of Commons (31 October 1950), 564–5; London (2 November 1950), 565; House of Commons (6 November 1950), 566–7; House of Commons (13 November 1950), 569; Harrow (23 November 1950), 570; House of Commons (30 November 1950), 571–2; House of Commons (14 December 1950), 573–5; **in 1951**, House of Commons (7 February 1951), 591–2; broadcast (17 March 1951), 598–9; House of Commons (21 March 1951), 600; House of Commons (10 April 1951), 604–5; House of Commons (19 April 1951), 605–7; Albert Hall (27 April 1951), 607–8; House of Commons (11 May 1951), 610–13; Glasgow (18 May 1951), 614; Biggin Hill (18 June 1951), 617; London (10 July 1951), 621; Woodford (21 July 1951), 621–2; Mansion House (23 July 1951), 622; House of Commons (30 July 1951), 624–5; broadcast (16 September 1951), 638; Liverpool (2 October 1951), 640–1; Woodford (6 October 1951), 642–3; broadcast (8 October 1951), 643–4; Woodford (9 October 1951), 644; Woodford (12 October 1951), 645; Huddersfield (15 October 1951), 646; Newcastle (16 October 1951), 647; Glasgow (17 October 1951), 647; Plymouth (23 October 1951), 647–8; House of Commons (6 November 1951), 659–60; Guildhall, London (9 November 1951), 660–1; Guildhall, London (19 November 1951), 662–3; House of Commons (6 December 1951), 665–7; Harrow (7 December 1951), 668–9; broadcast (22 December 1951), 669–70; **in 1952**, Ottawa (14 January 1952), 685–6; Washington DC (17 January 1952), 688–90; House of Commons (29 January 1952), 688 n.1, 694 n.4, 696; broadcast (7 February 1952), 697–8; House of Commons (11 February 1952), 698–700; House of Commons (26 February 1952), 619, 683 n.1, 704–7; House of Commons (5 March 1952), 707–8, 709–11; House of Commons (23 April 1952), 721; Albert Hall (25 April 1952), 721–2; broadcast (3 May 1952), 725; House of Commons (21 May 1952), 730–1; London (1 June 1952), 732–4; House of Commons (1 July 1952), 740–2; House of Commons (30 July 1952), 749–51; Woodford (6 September 1952), 760; Scarborough (11 October 1952), 769; London (14 October 1952), 769–70; House of Commons (4 November 1952), 772–3; Guildhall (10 November 1952), 774–

Churchill, (Sir) Winston L. S.—*continued*
5; House of Commons (4 December 1952), 780–1; **in 1953**, Westminster Abbey (30 January 1953), 795; House of Commons (5 March 1953), 802–3; House of Commons (25 March 1953), 808; broadcast (25 March 1953), 808–9; St Stephen's Hall, Westminster (27 March 1953), 809–10; Glasgow (17 April 1953), 815–16; House of Commons (20 April 1953), 819; House of Commons (11 May 1953), 829–32; broadcast (2 June 1953), 836; Margate (10 October 1953), 895–6; House of Commons (3 November 1953), 904–8; Guildhall (9 November 1953), 911; House of Commons (16 November 1953), 912–13; London (20 November 1953), 914; Harrow (27 November 1953), 914; House of Commons (17 December 1953), 940; **in 1954**, House of Commons (1 February 1954), 948–9; House of Commons (25 February 1954), 953–5; House of Commons (2 March 1954), 958; House of Commons (5 April 1954), 965–9; House of Commons (7 April 1954), 969; Royal Academy, London (28 April 1954), 972; Albert Hall (30 April 1954), 972; House of Commons (17 May 1954), 976; Albert Hall (27 May 1954), 980–1; London (8 June 1954), 991–2; Washington DC (airport) (25 June 1954), 997; Washington DC (Capitol) (26 June 1954), 1003–5; Washington DC (Press Club) (28 June 1954), 1008; broadcast, Canada (30 June 1954), 1011; House of Commons (12 July 1954), 952, 1030; House of Commons (14 July 1954), 1010; House of Commons (29 July 1954), 1036–7; Blackpool (9 October 1954), 1064; Guildhall (9 November 1954), 1058, 1068; Harrow (12 November 1954), 1069; Woodford (23 November 1954), 1070; Bristol (26 November 1954), 1071; Westminster Hall (30 November 1954), 1074–5; London, television broadcast (30 November 1954), 1075; House of Commons (1 December 1954), 1079–81; **in 1955**, House of Commons (1 March 1955), 952, 1098–1100; House of Commons (2 March 1955), 1101; House of Commons (14 March 1955), 1108–9; House of Commons (28 March 1955), 1114; 10 Downing Street (4 April 1955), 1120–1; Woodford (16 May 1955), 1136–7; Bedford (17 May 1955), 1137; Walthamstow (19 May 1955), 1138; Woodford (23 May 1955), 1138–9; Guildhall (21 June 1955), 1147; Hastings (7 September 1955), 1161; London (18 November 1955), 1168; Harrow (24 November 1955), 1168; Wood-

Churchill, (Sir) Winston L. S.—*continued*
ford (5 December 1955), 1170; Drapers' Hall, London (7 December 1955), 1170–1; Mansion House (16 December 1955), 1171; **in 1956**, Albert Hall (13 April 1956), 1191; St Paul's Cathedral (3 May 1956), 1197; Aachen (10 May 1956), 1197; London (28 November 1956), 1225–6; **in 1957**, Albert Hall (3 May 1957), 1240; Woodford (6 July 1957), 1248; Central Hall, Westminster (9 July 1957), 1248; Savoy Hotel, London (25 July 1958), 1248; Guildhall (31 July 1957), 1248–9; Harrow (25 October 1957), 1254; **in 1958**, House of Commons notes, never delivered (15 July 1958), 1270–2; Hôtel Matignon, Paris (6 November 1958), 1280; Savoy Hotel (20 November 1958), 1281; Harrow (27 November 1958), 1281; **in 1959**, Kensington Palace Hotel, London (6 January 1959), 1283; Woodford (20 April 1959), 1290–1; Washington DC (The White House) (5 May 1959), 1293–4; Woodford (29 September 1959), 1301; Woodford (29 September 1959, second speech that day), 1301; Walthamstow (6 October 1959), 1302; Woodford (9 October 1959), 1302 n.6; Cambridge (17 October 1959), 1303; Woodford (31 October 1959), 1305; Harrow (12 November 1959), 1306; **in 1960**, Harrow (10 November 1960), 1316
his travels overseas,
   to Germany (Potsdam), 60–104; (Aachen, Bonn and Celle), 1197–8; (Düsseldorf), 1200
   to France (Bordaberry), 57–9; (Monte Carlo), 151–6, 450–3, 1190, 1307–8, 1315–16, 1324–6, 1328, 1331–2, 1334–5, 1343–4, 1346; (Paris), 166, 168–9, 267, 328–9, 376, 378, 453, 588–9, 634–7, 1280; (Metz), 246–8; (Annecy), 630–1; (Aix-en-Provence), 426–31, 431–3; (Cap d'Antibes, Le Croë), 431; (Cap d'Ail, La Capponcina), 434–5, 484–8, 759, 886–92, 1161–6, 1250–1, 1272–7; (Strasbourg), 481–4; (Roquebrune, La Pausa), 1172–80, 1184–90, 1199, 1210–20, 1228–34, 1235–7, 1242–5, 1251–4, 1257–65, 1273, 1278–80, 1285–9, 1298–1300
   to Italy (Lake Como), 132–50; (Villa Pirelli), 150–1; (Lake Garda), 480–1; (Venice), 631–4; (Syracuse, Sicily), 1126–8, 1131–2; (La Mortola), 1251–2;
   to Belgium (Brussels), 166, 170–2, 267, 460
   to the United States (Miami, Fulton, New York), 180–89, 191–219; (New York, Boston), 462–71; (New York, Washington), 672–95; (New York, Washington), 786–93; (Washington), 997–1010; (Washington and

Churchill, (Sir) Winston L. S.—*continued*
Gettysburg), 1291–6; (Hudson River, New York), 1322–3
  to Cuba (Havana), 190–1
  to The Netherlands (The Hague), 232–3, 405–9
  to Luxembourg, 246
  to Switzerland (Villa Choisi), 260–3; (Geneva), 263–5; (Zurich), 265–7
  to Morocco (Marrakech), 376, 378–95, 576–88, 1283–4
  to Norway (Oslo), 409–10
  to Madeira, 500–1
  to Denmark (Copenhagen), 560–1
  to Canada (Ottawa), 685–6, 1010–11
  to Jamaica, 793–5
  to Bermuda, 916–38
  on board *Christina*, 1277, 1284–5, 1297–8, 1308–11, 1313–14, 1321–2, 1334, 1346
his letters to his wife,
  in **1945**, 66, 134–5, 136–9, 139–40, 142–4, 146–7, 152–6; in **1947**, 347–8, 378–9, 380–1, 384–6, 417–18, 501–2; in **1948**, 431; in **1950**, 522–5, 576–8, 579–81, 582; in **1951**, 600–1, 627–9; in **1952**, 692–3, 693–4, 694, 743–4, 744–5, 745–6, 746, 749, 751, 752–3; in **1953**, 886, 887–8, 889–90, 898, 901, 901–2, 924, 925, 942; in **1954**, 977, 981–3, 983–5, 987–8, 1010, 1042–3, 1044, 1045, 1059, 1083, 1107–8, 1109–10; in **1955**, 1155–9, 1161, 1163–6; in **1956**, 1174, 1175, 1175–6, 1176, 1177, 1178, 1178–9, 1179–80, 1180–1, 1182–3, 1184–5, 1186–9, 1190, 1191, 1200–1, 1202–3, 1204–5, 1205–6, 1206–7, 1209, 1210–12, 1212–13, 1214–16, 1216–17; in **1957**, 1227, 1230–1, 1232, 1235–7, 1242–5, 1253; in **1958**, 1257–8, 1258–9, 1260, 1273–4, 1278–9; in **1959**, 1285–6, 1286–7, 1288, 1298–9; in **1961**, 1320 (facsimile), 1322, 1324–5, 1325–6, 1328, 1331–2 (facsimile signature); in **1962**, 1334, 1338; in **1963**, 1341–2 (facsimile), 1344, 1349
in Cabinet, Cabinet Committee and at Staff Conferences,
  in **1945**, 17; in **1951**, 657–8, 658, 660, 668, 669; in **1952**, 697, 701–2, 707, 708, 712–13, 715, 715–16, 718, 718–19, 719–20, 726, 727, 727–8, 728, 731, 734–5, 737, 739–40, 740, 746, 746–7, 747, 748, 751–2, 759–60, 762–3, 763, 769, 770, 773, 776, 776–7, 777, 779–80, 781, 781–2, 782, 786–7; in **1953**, 795–6, 796, 797, 797–8, 798–9, 799, 799–800, 803–4, 805–6, 814, 815, 817, 819–20, 821, 821–2, 824–5, 825, 832–3, 833, 834, 875–6, 878–9, 881–3, 884–5, 885, 894, 898, 899–900, 900, 903, 903–4, 904, 910, 913, 914, 915, 939, 941–2; in **1954**, 943–4, 944, 945,

Churchill, (Sir) Winston L. S.—*continued*
  945–6, 946, 949, 950–1, 951, 952–3, 956, 956–7, 957, 963, 964, 973, 975–6, 976–7, 985–7, 994–6, 1018–20, 1021–13, 1023–6, 1028–9, 1030–1, 1032–6, 1036, 1055, 1057, 1057–8, 1058, 1082; in **1955**, 1091–2, 1092, 1093–4, 1094, 1105–6, 1110, 1110–11, 1112–13; during Churchill's illness (1953), 855, 863
books by,
  A History of the English-Speaking Peoples: 117, 180, 255, 274, 874 n.2, 876–7, 883–4, 887, 891, 915, 958, 1044, 1066, 1077–8, 1126, 1136, 1141, 1144, 1145–6, 1148–9, 1161–3, 1165–6, 1173–9, 1183–4, 1187–90, 1193, 1196–7, 1200, 1201, 1205, 1212–14, 1223, 1225, 1228–30, 1233, 1241, 1249–50, 1254, 1267; *A Roving Commission*: 469, 1204 n.3; *Great Contemporaries*: 562 n.1; *London to Ladysmith via Pretoria*, 447 n.5; *Lord Randolph Churchill*, 1185 n.4, 1357; *Marlborough, His Life and Times*: 344, 424, 435, 596, 1149; *My Early Life*, 236, 469 n.3, 1181 n.4, 1204 n.3, 1206, 1207 n.1; *Painting As a Pastime*, 562 n.1, 1158; *Savrola*, 424, 886 n.2; *The American Civil War*, 915 n.2; *The River War*, 424, 797–8, 898 n.2; *The Second World War* (volumes 1–6, 1948–54), 417, 447, 569, 829 n.1, 1230 n.2; the 'moral' of, 1365; *The Story of the Malakand Field Force*, 1195, 1319 n.4; *The World Crisis*, 186, 270, 341 n.1, 469; *Thoughts and Adventures*: 236, 469 n.3, 562 n.1, 1324
  see also index entries for: Atomic Bomb, British Commonwealth, Chartwell, Communism, Conservative Party, General Election, House of Commons, Labour Government (1945–51), Labour Party, NATO, Painting, Summit, United Nations, War memoirs
Churchill, Winston ('little' or 'young' Winston): 30, 179, 308–9, 459, 498, 508, 525, 584 n.2, 600, 628, 640; one of the 'young lions', 662; at Chartwell, 726–7, 1159; his grandfather's letters to, 727, 734, 844, 1241, 1245–6, 1298, 1349; at the Coronation, 797; and a portrait of his grandfather, 853 n.1; a gift from, 1069 n.5, 1331 n.5; advice to, 1241; his letter to his grandfather, 1267; and politics, 1319; 'a wonderful boy', 1328; on *Christina*, 1346; marries, 1353–4; at Hyde Park Gate, 1358; at his grandfather's funeral, *photograph 38*
Churchill Arch, the: 564
Churchill College, Cambridge: 853 n.1, 1131, 1134, 1238, 1263, 1264, 1266, 1267–8, 1283–4; and Brendan Bracken, 1275 n.1; Churchill visits (1959), 1302; and Clementine Churchill, 1304 n.1; and Chur-

Churchill College, Cambridge—*continued*
chill's last years, 1326, 1330, 1343; formal opening of, 1352
Churchill Day, a: proposed, 1361
Churchill and the Admirals (Roskill): 979 n.1
Churchill: His Life in Pictures (Randolph Churchill): 1111–12
Churchill Houses (Churchill Homes for Elderly People): Clementine Churchill opens, 1069; funds for, 1077
Churchill's Indian Summer (Seldon): 1100 n.1
Ciano, Count Galeazzo: 427
Citrine, 1st Baron (Walter Citrine): 279 n.1, 283 n.3, 287
Civil Service, the: 302–3, 324, 402
Clarence, Duke of (son of King Edward VII): 366
Claridge's Hotel (London): Churchill lives at (1945), 117–18; Churchill dines at, 131, 421; Alamein dinner at, 160
Clark, Alan: 1326
Clark, Sir Kenneth (later Baron): 846
Clark, Lady (wife of Sir Kenneth Clark): and Churchill's stroke, 846
Clark, General Mark Wayne: 596–7, 737, 747, 845
Clark, Colonel Frank W.: 130, 182, 184, 187, 289, 404
Clarke, Captain William F.: 182 n.2
Class warfare: 527
Claudius the God (Robert Graves): 1334
Claverton Manor (Bath): 1107 n.4
Clemenceau, Georges: 249
Clifford, Clark: 196
Coal: 374, 446, 507 n.3
Coalition: a plan for (to replace Churchill) in 1947, 341; 'carrying good will too far', 906
Cobalt Bomb, the: 1251
Cockcroft, Sir John: 1263 n.2, 1284, 1302, 1304
Cocks, Seymour: 43
Coggan, Dr Donald (Archbishop of Canterbury) (later Baron): 1359
Cold War, the: 510, 660, 802; and United States forces in Britain, 777; and Churchill's search for a Summit, 832, 871; and 'unimaginable horrors' as the alternative to, 955; 'its threats and dangers', 1127; Churchill's hopes, to have ended, 1150; and an answer to Khrushchev, 1290
Cole, Sterling: and the hydrogen bomb, 952, 959–60, 1010
Colliers magazine: 483 n.4, 915 n.2
Collingwood, Charles: 1294 n.4
Colombo Powers, the: 999
Cologne (Germany): 547
Colonist II (Churchill's racehorse): 488, 522, 524, 528, 563, 613, 615, 627

Columbia Pictures Inc.: 1207 n.1
Colville, (Sir) John ('Jock'): in 1945, 15, 19, 20–1, 22, 34, 50, 52, 56, 57–9, 105, 106–7, 111, 129, 130–1; in 1946, 263; in 1947, 308, 316, 332, 372, 382; in 1948, 415, 424; in 1950, 549–50; in 1951, 629; and the first two months of Churchill's second Premiership (October–December 1951), 654, 657, 661–2, 662, 663, 665; and Churchill's Private Office (in 1952), 672 n.2, 673, 674, 679, 683, 687, 688 n.1, 691, 696–7, 702–4, 709, 712, 714, 716–17, 720, 722–3, 726, 728, 729–30, 735–6, 739, 745, 753, 754, 763–4, 773–4, 787–9; (in 1953), 789, 791–5, 818, 822–3, 824, 832, 835, 841–2, 844, 857, (in 1954), 976, 983, 984 n.3; and Churchill's health, 730, 732, 774; and Churchill's stroke, 846–57, 858, 860–1, 862; and Churchill's recovery, 865, 867–8, 869–70, 870–1, 872, 873, 896, 961; and Churchill's decisions to resign or not to resign (1953–5), 868, 871, 874, 889, 895, 897, 971, 1032, 1037–9, 1087, 1102, 1106–7, 1114–15, 1116; with Churchill overseas (1953–4), 890, 938; and the Bermuda Conference (December 1953), 912, 916, 917, 918, 919, 923, 923–4, 928–30, 932–3, 936, 937; and the Washington Conference (June 1954), 996, 998, 1000, 1003, 1006, 1007, 1008–9, 1009, 1010–11, 1012–16; and the last nine months of Churchill's Premiership (1954–5), 1020, 1031–2, 1037–9, 1063, 1064, 1075, 1083, 1101, 1105, 1111; and Churchill's resignation, 1122; and Churchill's retirement, 1131, 1134, 1135, 1151, 1158, 1170, 1172, 1174, 1221–2, 1224, 1235, 1238–9, 1266, 1267–8, 1280, 1282, 1283–4, 1285, 1315, 1331 n.5, 1343, 1347, 1349, 1350, 1351 n.2, 1358; and the death of Lord Cherwell, 1247; and the death of Brendan Bracken, 1274, 1275 n.1, 1281 n.4; on *Christina*, 1346; *photograph 21*
Colville, Lady Margaret ('Meg'): 754, 889, 890, 1158, 1235, 1285; a gift from, 1331 n.5; on *Christina*, 1346; among Churchill's last dinner guests, 1351 n.2; at Hyde Park Gate, 1358
Common Law, the: the 'growth of', 884
Common Man: 'the Century of', 465
Commonwealth Conference, the (1955): 1086, 1093–4
Communism: and democracy, 12, 24–5; 'a religion', 161; and Churchill's Fulton speech, 199–204; and 'the death of the soul of man', 218–19; and France, 223, 224, 241–2, 1286 n.1; and Germany, 240; '*versus* the rest', 254; and India, 276–7, 473, 1093, 1094; and the Labour Party, 286; in Greece, 360–1, 396,

Communism—*continued*
568; and Russia, 371; and Italy, 400; and
the BBC 403, 732; and Truman, 421; 'our
next great problem', 421; and Israel, 439
n.2, 558, 788; and the atomic bomb, 440,
464; and 'the rest of mankind', 466; and 'a
theme, almost a religion', 475; and the Polar
ice, 483; and China, 510, 1082; and the
Korean war, 537; and Persia, 617; and rearmament, 677, 678; and the Arab States, 788;
'measureless ambition' of, 816; and Laos,
824; and Soviet thoughts in 1945, 920; and
the need for 'resistance to', 959; in South-
East Asia, 973–4, 975; and 'Free Asia', 1093;
and a 'comprehensive' Anglo-American
plan, 995; and the United States, 1001–2;
the 'intolerable philosophy' of, 1004; 'fallacy
and heresy' of, 1030; 'darkness' of, 1095; 'discipline' of, and 'individual freedom', 1098;
and 'the destiny of mankind', 1108; Eisenhower's fears concerning, 1118; and the
need to arrest the 'menace' of, 1119; 'malignant activities' of, 1133; and de-Stalinization 1192; the 'imperialism' of, 1290; and
the effect of 'prosperity' on, 1291; and Iraq,
1323
Como, Lake (Italy): 131, 132–50, 185, 985 n.2
Congress of Berlin, the (1878): 1188
Coningsby (Benjamin Disraeli): 886, 887
Connor, (Sir) William ('Bill'): 805 n.1
'Conquer or die!': 181
Conservative Central Office: 312
Conservative Consultative Committee: 617
Conservative Party, the: and 1945 General Election, 6, 9, 10, 34, 35, 56, 65, 113, 115, 147,
168; in Opposition, 130, 173, 189, 253, 275,
403, 475, 487, 559; and India, 276, 472, 473,
1250; and the General Election in prospect
(1947–50), 351; at Brighton (1947), 353, 354–
5; gives a lunch for Churchill, 417; and
German Field Marshals, 430; and Palestine,
454–5; and Churchill's friendship with Beaverbrook 461; and the 1951 General Election, 500–12, 592, 599, 643–8, 657; and the
Korean war, 537; and housing, 566; and the
BBC, 603–4; and Persia, 617, 640; and
Anthony Eden, 633, 821; Churchill's broadcast for (May 1952), 725; and the railways,
731; and the Sudan, 798, 799; and Churchill's
call for a Summit, 832; and Buddhism, 859;
and the pressure for Churchill to resign, 889,
961, 1037, 1049, 1050, 1052; and the Trade
Unions, 895; and Egypt, 939; and Churchill's
hydrogen bomb speech (April 1954), 967;
and 'loyalty', 975; 'angry', 978; and payment
of Members of Parliament, 978, 980–2, 985;
Churchill's leadership of, 1064, 1065, 1118; a

Conservative Party—*continued*
'Hughligan' in, 1077 n.1; and the 1955 General Election, 1115 n.3, 1118, 1139, 1152; and
a Television film of Churchill, 1119; 'they',
1150; and the Suez Crisis (1956), 1225, 1240;
and the General Election of 1964, 1355, 1356
Constable of France, the: Churchill's tribute
to, 1280
Constantinople (Istanbul): 91, 98, 195
Constitution of the United States, the: 24–5;
and the British Parliamentary system,
1327
Consultative Committee of the Opposition (*see
index entry for* Shadow Cabinet)
Cooper, Alfred Duff (later 1st Viscount
Norwich): 138, 147, 149, 166, 224, 228,
241–2, 263, 329, 376; and Churchill's war
memoirs, 357; his farewell party, 378; his
successor, 634 n.3; and Neville Chamber-
lain, 739; *for subsequent index entries see*
Norwich, 1st Viscount
Cooper, (Lady) Diana: 138, 147, 166, 242,
329, 752, 947
Cooper, John Julius (later 2nd Viscount
Norwich): 752
Coote, (Sir) Colin: 392, 1284, 1315 n.3, 1339,
1358
Cop (Czech-Soviet border): 283
Copenhagen (Denmark): Churchill speaks in
(1950), 560–1, 570
Corday, Charlotte: 1222
Corfu: 7
Coronation, the (of 1953): and an Amnesty,
748–9, 781–2; and rationing, 797; celebra-
tions of, 835–6
Corporal Punishment: 776–7
Cosmos: and Chaos, 331, 338
Cotentin Peninsula (France): 415
Coty, René: 941, 1003, 1102–3, 1255
Coudenhove-Kalergi, Count Richard: 243,
267
Council of Europe, the: 481–4, 541–3, 545,
569, 727–8
Count Belisarius (Robert Graves): 1334
Cousins, Frank: 1302–3
Coventry (England): 259
Coward, (Sir) Noël: 449–50
Cox, Mr (at Chartwell): 523, 1044
Craddock, George: 498 n.1
Cranborne, Viscount (later 5th Marquess of
Salisbury): 163, 279, 311–12
Cranborne, Viscount (later 6th Marquess of
Salisbury): 707
Crankshaw, Sir Edward: 146
Crathie Kirk (Balmoral): Churchill worships
at, 884
Cream: 'cushions the nerve ends', 1136

Creswell, Sir Michael: 1313–14
Crete: 415 n.6, 493
Crewe, Marchioness of ('Peggy') (widow of the 1st Marquess): 1222
Criminal Justice Act, the (1967): 777 n.1
Cripps, Sir Stafford: 40, 49, 118 n.1, 174; helps Churchill with his memoirs, 263, 389, 394 n.4; and India, 292, 298, 299, 439; a gift from, 307; as Chancellor of the Exchequer, 361, 385, 391, 488, 519, 524, 525, 535 n.2, 604; and the BBC, 403; and United Europe, 406, 536–7; in June 1941, 550; Churchill's tribute to (1952), 721
Crockham Hill, Vicar of: 600
Croft, 1st Baron (Sir Henry Page Croft): 126
Cromer, 1st Earl of (Sir Evelyn Baring): 898 n.2
Cromer, 3rd Earl of: 898
Cromwell, Oliver: 809
Crookshank, Harry: 9; and Churchill's political future (in 1947), 341; and Churchill's second Premiership, 655, 657, 703, 722, 769, 781, 795, 796; and the question of Churchill's resignation, 736, 961, 1052, 1061, 1086 n.1; and the hydrogen bomb, 1020; and a dispute on the road to the Summit, 1024
Crookshank, John: 1277–8
Crossman, Richard: 536, 577 n.2, 705, 968; and Churchill's lying in State, 1361; and Churchill's funeral, 1363
Crosthwaite, Sir Moore: 1334
Crown, the: and Parliament, 809
Croydon: Churchill's visit to (1964), 1352
Crum Ewing, Winifred: 1119
Crusade in Europe (film): 475
Cuba: Churchill's visit to (1946), 189, 190–1; Churchill's visit to (1894), 331
Cudlipp, Hugh (later Baron): 888 n.1
Cudlipp, Percy: 604
Cunliffe-Owen, Sir Hugo: 256 n.1
Cunliffe-Owen, Mrs: 58
Cunningham, Admiral of the Fleet Sir Andrew (later 1st Viscount Cunningham of Hyndhope): 5, 11, 42, 43, 46, 70 n.2, 89, 90, 92, 110, 111, 127, 133 n.2; Churchill's guest, 373; and Churchill's war memoirs, 493; and Ismay's memoirs, 1315 n.3
Cunningham, Admiral (later Admiral of the Fleet) Sir John: 417
Curtin, John (Prime Minister of Australia): dies (1945), 106 n.3
Curzon Line, the: 82–3, 87, 88, 95, 96, 238, 241, 437, 483
Cyberine (Churchill's horse): 524, 528 n.3
Cyprus: 250, 647, 957, 1058, 1125, 1159, 1203, 1221
Cyrano de Bergerac (film): 987
Cyrenaica: 88

Czechoslovakia: 14, 25, 32, 82, 90, 102, 154–5, 201, 212, 283, 288, 399, 400, 404, 423; 'communized', 467, 510, 539, 543, 635, 932, 1028; trials in (1952), 789; and Korea, 829; 'plight of', 842, 953

D-Day (Normandy Landings of 1944): 271–2
Daily Dispatch, the: 514 n.2
Daily Express, the: 391, 402, 424 n.4, 585; and the hydrogen bomb, 963
Daily Graphic, the: 323, 369
Daily Herald, the: cited, 47 n.3; 424 n.4, 440, 604, 1070–1
Daily Mail, the: 391, 424 n.4, 770, 1135, 1259, 1261
Daily Mirror, the: 643, 648, 805, 888 n.1; calls for Churchill's resignation (1954), 950, 964–5; critical, 1070–1; and a truce, 1072; 'money-grubbing' in, 1205
Daily Sketch, the: 514 n.2
Daily Telegraph, the: 328, 332, 339, 383, 393 n.1, 418, 424 n.4, 522, 545, 546, 548, 662 n.5, 750, 802 n.2, 869, 1230 n.2; and Churchill's resignation (1955), 1125–6; and Churchill College, Cambridge, 1284; Churchill's writing for (1897), 1319 n.4
Daily Worker, the: 343, 424 n.4, 822, 1070–1, 1080
Dakar Expedition (1940): 273, 417
Daladier, Edouard: 4
Dali, Salvador: 1076
Dalmeny, Lord (later 7th Earl of Rosebery): 1273
Dalton, Hugh (later Baron): 27, 114 n.1; Chancellor of the Exchequer, 210 n.3, 228, 230, 250, 385; and Churchill's political future (in 1947), 341; resigns, 361, 391; recalled, 526, 815, 1150; and Lew Douglas's relations with Churchill, 554 n.1
Damascus (Syria): 30–1, 36
Damaskinos, Archbishop: 146
Danube River, the: 91
Dardanelles, the (Turkey): 67, 75, 89, 91, 98, 195, 196, 331, 383, 636, 834, 853, 1255 n.1; 'the only imaginative strategic idea', 1074; Churchill sails through (1959), 1298
Darling, William Young: 186
Davenport, John: 213–14
'Davey Jones': 342
Davies, Clement: 319, 320, 503–5, 639; at Chartwell, 655
Davies, Detective-Sergeant E. A.: 132, 149, 151, 498
Davies, Miss Gwen: 1142
Davies, Harold: 611
Davies, Joseph: 24, 26
Davin, Daniel Marcus: 493

Dawn (Karachi): 292 n.1

Dawson, Geoffrey: 1246 n.4

D'Avigdor-Goldsmid, Sir Henry: 1358

Dayan, Moshe: 1219

De Clifford, 26th Baron: 404 n.4

De Gasperi, Alcide: 260 n.3, 406, 832, 845, 846, 847, 851

De Gaulle, General Charles (later President): 169, 242 n.1; Churchill's letter to (1946), 282–3, 285–6; and 'all we were able to achieve', 545; and Churchill's war memoirs, 584, 598; and the Saar, 930 n.2; 'he may still have services to render', 1264; Churchill decorated by (1958), 1280, 1281; becomes President, 1282, 1283; and the municipal elections (of 1959), 1286; and Algeria, 1295; in London (1960), 1311; sees Churchill in Nice (1960), 1316; Churchill's letter to (1961), 1318; a message from (1963), 1350; and Churchill's death, 1360

De La Warr, 9th Earl: 749 n.1, 1132, 1157

De La Warr, Countess (Diana): 1157

De L'Isle and Dudley, 6th Baron (later 1st Viscount De L'Isle): 348, 432, 749 n.1, 777, 782 n.1; and Churchill's 'continuing vigour', 1066; and Churchill's resignation, 1123

De Valera, Eamon: 237, 440, 885

De Vine Hunt, Lieutenant-Commander Frank: 338

Deakin, Arthur: ill, 778–9

Deakin, Captain (later Sir) F. W. ('Bill'): works with Churchill on his war memoirs, 45 n.1, 118, 221, 226, 274, 308, 315, 318, 331–2, 339, 345, 356 n.1, 373; works with Churchill at Marrakech, 378–95; continues work on the war memoirs, 405, 415, n.2, 416, 426; works with Churchill at Aix, 427–9, 434, 435; further work by (1948–50), 450 n.2, 474, 475 n.2, 480, 481, 488, 494, 495, 498, 500, 522, 534, 551, 568; at Marrakech again (1951), 582; continues work on the war memoirs (1951–2), 601, 609, 626, 629, 629 n.1, 663, 735, 761; and Churchill's History, 877, 1141, 1156, 1163, 1165, 1178, 1183; Warden of St Antony's College, Oxford, 568 n.2, 591 n.1; Churchill helps, 1217; elected to the Other Club, 1307 n.7; on *Christina*, 1334; Churchill's guest, 1339 n.1, 1357, 1358; *photograph 11*

Deakin, Mrs ('Pussy') (later Lady): 381, 382, 384, 388, 390, 395, 582; on *Christina*, 1334

Deal (Kent): Freedom of, 628

Death Duties: 1044

Death to the French (C. S. Forester): 917

Death Penalty, the: 400–1

Decrepitude: the 'surly advance' of, 1288

Dedeagatch (Greece): 93, 332

Dedijer, Vladimir: 590–1

Dedijer, Olga: killed (1943), 591 n.1

D'Erlanger, Minnie: marries Churchill's grandson Winston, 1353; *for subsequent index entry see,* Churchill, Mrs Winston (Minnie)

Defoe, Daniel: 270

Demobilization: a crisis over (in 1918), 856

Denmark: 212; Churchill's visit to (1950), 560–1; sale of tanks to, 710 n.1; 'anxieties about (in 1945), 1079–80

De-rating Act, the (1928): 323–4

Derby, the (horserace): 366, 842

Derby, 17th Earl of: 189, 285, 524; Randolph Churchill's book on, 946, 1312

Derby, 18th Earl of: 984

Derby, Countess of (Isabel) (wife of the 18th Earl): 770, 984, 1273

Der Fall des Hauses Stuart (Onno Klopp): 665

Deshmukh, Sir Chintaman: 779

Destiny: 'the march of', 556

Devaluation: 501, 621

Devonport (England): 501; Churchill speaks at (1950), 508–9

Devers, General Jacob L.: 208

Dewey, Governor Thomas E.: 223, 289, 445 n.1, 590, 791, 792

D'Hauteville, Comte: 381, 579

Dickson, Air Chief Marshal Sir William: 821

Dictionary of National Biography, the: 1232 n.4

Dien Bien Phu (Indo-China): 973–4, 976

Dieppe Raid, the (of 1942): 550–2

Digby, Lady (wife of the 11th Baron): 179

Dilke, Sir Charles: 367, 1195

Dill, Field Marshal Sir John: 310, 550

Dionysius of Syracuse: recalled, 1128

Diot, Dr: 389, 577

Disarmament Commission, the (1955): 1098

Disarmament Proposals, the (1959): 1301

Disraeli, Benjamin (1st Earl of Beaconsfield): 366, 371, 808, 886 n.2, 1147, 1204, 1212, 1319; his desk, at Chartwell and Stour, 1338 n.1

Ditchley Park (Oxfordshire): 272, 694 n.1

Divi Britannici (Sir Winston Churchill): 823 n.1

Dixon, Piers (son of Sir Pierson Dixon): marries Churchill's granddaughter Edwina (1960), 1317; at Chartwell (1961), 1326–7; a gift from, 1331 n.5; at Croydon, 1352; at Hyde Park Gate, 1357, 1358; his notes, 1337, 1337 n.2

Dixon, Mrs Piers (Edwina) (formerly Edwina Sandys): 1331 n.5, 1337, 1357, 1358

Dixon, (Sir) Pierson: 65, 78, 80, 220, 341, 361, 824, 844, 920 n.1, 1009

Djilas, Milovan: 590–1
Doenitz, Grand Admiral Karl: 14, 15
Dogger Bank (battle of, 1914): 493
Donaldson, Wing Commander Arthur: 617
Doncaster (England): Churchill invited to, 880, 881, 884
Donegall, 6th Marquess of: 723
Dorchester Hotel (London): 312
Douglas, Lewis ('Lew'): 318, 351, 404, 411, 544 n.1, 554, 569, 743, 749 n.1, 1294 n.1
Douglas-Home, Sir Alec (formerly 14th Earl of Home, subsequently Baron Home of the Hirsel): 1114 n.2, 1227 n.5, 1307 n.2; becomes Foreign Secretary, 1316, 1323; becomes Prime Minister, 1349; gives up his seat, to Churchill, 1350, 1351; presents Churchill with a Resolution, 1355; and Churchill's death, 1360; mounts guard, 1361–2
Dover (Kent): 569, 570, 628
Dowding, Air Chief Marshal Lord (1st Baron): 178
Downs, Professor Brian Westerdale: 1263
'Dream Villa': the search for, 1166, 1168, 1173, 1216–17, 1235, 1236–7, 1251
Dresden: bombed (1945), 259
Driberg, Tom (later Baron Bradwell): 137 n.1, 155, 208
Duff, Lady Juliet: 348, 1157, 1171, 1205, 1331 n.5, 1339 n.1
Duff, Robert: 348 n.2
Duffield, Georgie: 184
Dufour, General: 264
Dugdale, Sir Thomas: 880 n.1
Duke, Squadron Leader Neville: 760, 772, 881
'Duke of Bardogs': 'would sound well', 327 n.4
'Duke of Chartwell': a bizarre prospect, 704
'Duke of Westerham': and Churchill's musings, 1123
Dulles, Allen: 1294 n.1
Dulles, John Foster: 223–4, 616, 790–1, 792, 827–8, 841, 863, 864; 'stupid on rather a large scale', 867; and the Soviet Union, 871; and China, 882; in London, 801 n.1, 898; and a possible Summit, 909, 917, 1034–5; at Bermuda, 919, 928, 930, 933, 936, 941; at Berlin, 951; and Egypt, 957; and the hydrogen bomb, 968; and the defence of 'the free world', 978; and Eden, 990; and the Washington Conference (June 1954), 997, 999, 1000, 1003, 1005, 1006–7, 1010; and an 'agonizing reappraisal', 1016; to be kept informed, 1056–7; and the Makins' telegram (1955), 1104, 1106, 1110–11; and the Yalta papers, 1112 n.2; and the Four-Power talks (1955), 1151; and the Suez Crisis

Dulles, John Foster—continued
(1956), 1210, 1213, 1218; Churchill sees (in 1959), 1293, 1294, 1295
Dunant, Henri: 264
Dunhill, Sir Thomas: 338, 597
Dunkirk evacuation (1940): 262, 350 n.4, 647, 899
Dunn, Lady (later Lady Beaverbrook): 1326
Dunn, Sir James: 1326 n.4
Dunnill, Dr Michael: 977 n.3, 1232 n.1
Dunottar Castle, RMS: 499 n.1
Düsseldorf (Germany): Churchill's visit to (1956), 1200
Dynevor, 8th Baron: 1258
Dynevor, Lady (Hope): 1258

Eade, Charles: 245, 888 n.1
Eagle, HMS: 1278
Eagles: 'silent', 18
East Anglia: United States air bases in, 432, 518, 519, 520 n.2, 530, 541, 543, 553, 683–4; and a 'peripheral defence', 932; and China, 973; a 'bull's-eye of the target', 995
East Prussia: 91–2, 96
Eastern Germany (East Germany): 201, 224, 288, 404, 421, 437, 520 n.1, 530, 829, 863, 929–30, 933
Eccles, (Sir) David (later 1st Baron, subsequently 1st Viscount): 190, 481 n.4, 637, 656, 1065
Economist, the: and Churchill's call for a Summit, 832
Eddy, Mary Baker: 1262
Ede, Chuter (later Baron Chuter–Ede): 1182
Edelson, Doris: 523
Eden, Anthony: Churchill's messages and telegrams to (1945), 5–6, 16, 24–5, 26, 28 n.2, 30, 45; (1948), 447; (1951), 582–3, 631; and the General Election of 1945, 6, 10, 14, 20 n.4, 23, 45, 49, 52–3, 107, 109, 110, 117–18, 190 n.3; and the General Election of 1950, 506; and the General Election of 1951, 638; at Chequers, 50, 870, 978; at Potsdam, 60, 61, 65, 66 n.4, 71, 78, 90, 93 n.2; declines the Garter, 111; in Opposition (1945–51), 146, 191, 226–7, 633; and Churchill's political future (in 1947), 341; and Churchill's illnesses, 226–7, 338–9, 703; and the Leadership of the House of Commons, 226–8, 244; a medallion for, 245; and defence, 280, 283, 478; and Churchill's war memoirs, 311–12, 373, 414, 474, 550, 568; and the Other Club, 318; and India, 333, 431; dines with Churchill, 373; and Berlin, 432; and the Soviet Union, 432, 862–3, 871, 1254; and Sikorski's death, 471 n.2; and the 1950 Election, 501; and the weather, 523, 761; and

Eden, Anthony—*continued*
 the atomic bomb, 573 n.3; and Persia, 618, 639, 640–1, 756; and Churchill's second Premiership, 653, 654, 662, 673, 681–2, 717, 724, 726, 728, 739, 756, 779–80, 795, 800; and Egypt, 668, 701, 714, 718, 719–20, 747, 770, 796, 797–800, 805–6, 893, 900, 903, 941–2, 995; his illnesses (1952), 744; (1953), 814, 817, 818, 820, 826, 829, 832, 834, 841, 844; 848, 849, 871, 880, 885; (1956), 1223; (1957), 1246–7; (1958), 1264; and Korea, 706, 740, 741, 747; and the Falkland Islands, 708; marries Clarissa Churchill, 753–4; and war crimes, 756–7; at Chartwell, 758; and Randolph Churchill, 768; and the succession, 778, 781, 791, 795, 869–70, 870 n.1, 870–1, 833, 889, 893, 903, 960–1, 964, 971, 989–90, 1017, 1037, 1045–53, 1060–6, 1084–7, 1097, 1102, 1106–8, 1115; Churchill's letters and messages to (1953–5), 790, 893, 944–5, 989–90; and Beaverbrook, 794; and the Sudan, 797–8, 955–7; and Churchill's Summit hopes, 811–12, 832, 869, 870, 1013–14, 1020–1, 1031, 1032–6; and Suez, 897; and Churchill's stroke (1953), 850, 852, 854, 862; and Churchill's 'plans', 893; and Churchill's recovery, 897; and the Bermuda Conference (December 1953), 912, 914, 916, 917, 923, 928, 929, 929–30, 933; at Bermuda, 938; and Foreign policy (1953–5), 943, 944–5; in Berlin, 952, 954; at Geneva, 973–4, 975–6, 985; and the hydrogen bomb, 961; and the hydrogen bomb debate (1954), 970; and Israel, 964; contrasted with Churchill, 965; and Churchill's visit to Washington (1954), 982, 985, 989, 996–7; and the Washington Conference (June 1954), 997–1010; and China, 1015–16, 1092; his gifts, 1017; 'all will come right', 1041 n.1; and a Churchill message to Adenauer (1954), 1055–6; his Foreign Policy praised, 1058, 1063; receives the Garter, 1066; presides at Cabinet, 1082; and the dispute over the Makins Telegram (1955), 1103–8; and Churchill's resignation, 1115–16, 1118, 1119–20, 1123, 1126, 1128; becomes Prime Minister, 1126, 1135, 1135–6, 1137, 1164; his letters to Churchill (1955–65), 1141–3, 1154; Churchill's letters to (1955–65), 1143; and Churchill's retirement years (1955–65), 1143–4, 1157, 1161, 1167–8, 1169–70, 1171, 1178, 1183, 1184, 1186, 1196, 1248, 1249, 1254, 1261, 1267, 1300 n.2, 1323; and hanging, 1182 n.1; and an Anti-Eden movement, 1186 n.3; and the Suez crisis (1956), 1195–6, 1201, 1202, 1203–4, 1205 n.4, 1206, 1208–9, 1209 n.1, 1210, 1211, 1213–14,

Eden, Anthony—*continued*
 1218–19; 1220–2, 1240, 1246; a 'good speech' by, 1216; in Jamaica, 1223, 1226–7; to resign (1957), 1226–7, 1227–8; Churchill's tribute to '1957), 1240; his 'courage', 1245; a gift from 1257; *for subsequent index entries see*, Avon, 1st Earl of

Eden, Beatrice: 51, 693

Eden, Clarissa (later Countess of Avon): 753–4, 758, 778, 820, 850, 860, 1063; at Chequers, 870, 978; sends her love, 1143, 1168; at Chartwell, 1157, 1161; and her husband's resignation, 1227; her 'courage', 1245; a gift from, 1257; and her husband's recurring illness, 1264

Eden, Nicholas (later 2nd Earl of Avon): 693 n.1, 814

Eden, Simon: killed in action (1945), 51, 693 n.1

Edgar, Hamish: 1175

Edinburgh (Scotland): Churchill speaks at (1946), 229; Churchill speaks at (1950), 509, 528; his speech recalled, 553, 572; 'pageantry' in, 852

Edmondson, Sir James: 34 n.4

Edward VII, King: 698, 699, 764, 810 n.1, 884

Edwards, Brigadier Harold: 135–6, 139, 140–1

Edwards, Professor J. H.: 136 n.1

Egypt: 67, 191, 229, 230, 231, 252; and *The Times*, 246; and Churchill's war memoirs, 272; 'scuttle' in, 302; and Israel, 455, 557, 624, 757, 824–5, 945–6, 1008; sterling balances of, 519, 786–7, 799, 882, 941; jet aircraft for, 527–8, 531, 533; arms sales to, 936; danger to, 617; and the Persian crisis (of 1951), 642; and the continuing crisis with (1951–2), 646, 647, 657–8, 659, 666, 667, 676, 679–80, 689, 701–2, 703, 709, 714, 717, 718, 719–20, 723; under Neguib, 747, 770, 774–5, 781, 786–7, 790, 793, 795–6; a 'diatribe' against, 792; and the Sudan, 797–800, 955–6; and the continuing crisis with (1953), 805–6, 814–15, 821–2, 824–5, 833, 840–1, 842, 844; negotiations in (1953–4), 875, 879, 880, 881–2, 885, 893, 897, 903, 914, 915, 939, 941; discussed at Bermuda, 932, 933, 936; and the United States, 951; British troops in (1954), 978, 986, 993–4, 994–6; discussed at Washington (June 1954), 998–9, 1000, 1006, 1008, 1019; and Cyprus, 1159; and the crisis with Israel (1956), 1191, 1192, 1195–6; and the Suez Crisis (1956), 1201, 1203–4, 1205, 1205, 1207, 1208, 1209–10, 1211, 1213–14, 1218, 1220–2; and Sinai, 1234; 'preparing for war' (1961), 1323

Eichmann, Adolf: 442 n.1

Eighth Army, the: in 1942, 492

Einstein, Lewis: 1158–9, 1202

Eire: 12, 231, 237, 254 n.1, 368, 439, 442–3, 1244

Eisenach (Germany): 7, 30, 45

Eisenhower, General Dwight D. (later President): 7, 17, 43, 46, 152, 153; his Naval Aide's book, 187; and Churchill's visit to the United States in 1946, 190–1, 207; and the Quebec Agreement (of 1944), 254; and an historical controversy, 310–11, 419; and Churchill's search for 'a settlement' with Russia, 422, 806–7; and Prague, 428; Churchill's letters and telegrams to (1950–55), 557, 619–20, 773, 800, 804, 814, 844, 857, 871, 977–8, 993–4, 1039–41, 1056–7, 1081–2, 1090–1, 1092, 1118–19, 1151–2; his letters to Churchill (1952–5), 773, 973, n.1, 1112, 1118, 1151; his Mission (in 1951), 593, 594; becomes NATO Supreme Commander, 574, 575, 606, 636–7; and the funeral of George VI, 700; dines with the Churchills (1952), 728; seeks the Presidency, 735, 743, 756; becomes President, 773, 778, 787; and Egypt, 786, 805–6; Churchill's visit to (1953), 788, 789–93; 'of limited stature', 794; and North Korea, 800, 834, 838–9; and Egypt, 804, 844; and Churchill's war memoirs, 810–11, 856–7, 858; and Churchill's Summit hopes, 811–14, 818–19, 827–8, 831, 838, 864–5, 871, 923, 1039–40, 1109–11; and France, 833; 'overwhelmingly powerful', 834; 'stupid and weak', 868; and Turkey, 834–5; and the proposed Bermuda Conference, 844–5, 850–1, 907; and a proposed Paris conference (1955), 1102–3; Churchill's plan to meet (1953), 873, 909–10; and the Bermuda Conference (December 1953), 917–37; and atomic energy, 940; and trade with the Soviet Union, 944; and the hydrogen bomb, 959–60, 962–3, 964; and the hydrogen bomb debate (House of Commons, 1954), 966; and Churchill's continuing wish for a Summit (1954–5), 972, 972–3, 1012–13, 1026–8, 1030–1, 1108, 1143; and Churchill's Washington journey (1954), 977–8, 985–6, 989, 993, 998–1010; and Cyprus, 1058; and Churchill's 'experiences as a model', 1077; and the Makins telegram, 1103–5; and the Yalta papers, 1112 n.2; and Communism, 1118; and the Four-Power talks (Geneva, 1955), 1151, 1154; taken ill, 1162, 1168; and Churchill's years in retirement, 1170, 1191–3, 1198; and the Suez Crisis (1956), 1195–6, 1204, 1218, 1222, 1222–3, 1234; 'muddle headed', 1251;

Eisenhower, General Dwight D.—continued
and Eden, 1254; and Churchill's American plans (1957–8), 1256, 1260–1, 1263; and Churchill's last American visit (1959), 1293–6; 'wallop...or vindicate', 1298; Churchill meets (1959), 1301; and the Paris Summit (1960), 1313; and Churchill's accident (1960), 1316; at Churchill's funeral (1965), 1362; photographs 9, 34

Elath, Eliahu: 557, 560, 625 n.2, 757, 758, 1095–7, 1191

Elbe River, the 7, 236, 238, 284, 422, 436

Electric Grid, the: 324

Electrical Trades Union: strike of, 882–3

Elizabeth, Her Royal Highness Princess: 174, 312, 340–1, 359, 362, 382, 385, 388, 491 n.2, 613; and her father's illness, 637–8, 639; her trans-Atlantic journey, 662; for subsequent index entries see Elizabeth II, Her Majesty Queen

Elizabeth, Her Majesty Queen (later The Queen Mother): 129, 174, 359, 446, 532, 698, 700, 722, 752, 760–1, 862; at Chartwell, 772; a gift from, 1073; a gift to, 1193, 1193–4

Elizabeth I, Queen: 'snug in her hive', 669; Churchill writes about, 835; and the Tea Duty (abolished by Churchill in 1929), 1046 n.2

Elizabeth II, Her Majesty Queen: accedes to the Throne, 697, 698, 700, 701; and Churchill's illnesses, 712; her first Trooping the Colour, 732; her letters to her Prime Minister, 759, 785, 852, 942; her letters and telegrams to Churchill after his resignation, 1126–7, 1170, 1223, 1319, 1333; and Churchill's visit to Balmoral (1952), 763–4; Churchill's letters and messages to, 764, 874, 886–7, 914, 942, 1076, 1092, 1127–8, 1177–8, 1223, 1262, 1333; commissions a bust of Churchill, 770–1, 1147; and the Coronation, 788, 835–6; her 'charm', 789; and the Westminster Abbey appeal, 795; Churchill speaks in the presence of, 809–10; and Churchill's war memoirs, 810, 867; and Churchill's History, 1193; and the Order of the Garter (for Churchill), 822–3; and horse-racing, 826, 842, 874, 987, 1215; Churchill and his wife hosts to, 841; and Churchill's stroke (1953), 849, 850, 852, 854, 886; Commonwealth Tour of, 868, 914, 943, 1006, 1086; and Churchill's decisions to resign, 871, 895, 897, 943, 1086, 1097, 1115; invites Churchill to Balmoral, 874, 884, 886; invites Churchill to Doncaster, 880, 881, 884; and the 'silver thread', 976; Churchill's Audiences of, 988, 993, 1082, 1083, 1101, 1115, 1119, 1123–5; and Churchill's Summit

Elizabeth II—*continued*
hopes, 1020; and a Cabinet re-shuffle, 1062;
a gift from, 1073, 1075, 1076; and the Commonwealth Conference (of 1955), 1093; and
a monument to Lloyd George, 1112–13,
1114; and a dinner at 10 Downing Street
(April 1955), 1097, 1113, 1115, 1120–2; and
Churchill's resignation, 1117, 1122–5,
1126–8; and an honour for Lord Cherwell,
1142 n.1; in Paris 1240; and a 'foolish
attack' on, 1249; Churchill dines with
(1957), 1255; and the Armistice Day ceremony (1957), 1255–6; and Churchill's pneumonia (1958), 1261–2; and the gift of a
painting, 1313; her visit to Ghana, 1330–1;
'so courageous a personality', 1331; her 'ten
years of devoted service', 1333; and Churchill's last illness, 1359; and Churchill's
death, 1360–1; and Churchill's funeral,
1362–3; a wreath from, 1364; *photographs 20,
24*

Elliot of Harwood, Baroness (Katherine
Elliot): 656 n.2
Elliot, Walter: 318, 656, 749 n.1
Elliot, Air Chief Marshal Sir William: 691
Elmhirst, T. W.: 283 n.4
Elwyn-Jones, (Sir) Frederick (later Baron):
442 n.1
Emmet, Mrs (Evelyn Violet Elizabeth) later
Baroness Emmet of Amberley): 979, 981–2
Empire News, the: 514 n.2, 854
Empire Song, MV: sunk (1941), 273
Engine Drivers' Strike (1955): 1141, 1142;
firmness in, 'vital', 1143, 1145
England: 'will survive', 229; 'would be all
right', 317
English Channel, the: 'the strategy of holding',
543, 611; God thanked for, 931; and the hy-
drogen bomb, 968; and American nuclear
superiority, 1099
English Common Law: and the Almighty, 792
English-Speaking Union, the: 234, 619, 835,
988, 992; and an educational fund, 1272
Enigma decrypts, the: 18, 133
Eniwetok Atoll (Pacific Ocean): 772
Entente Cordiale, the (1904): 247
Envy: wears 'a friendly smile', 976
Epstein, Jacob: 273 n.5, 308
Eritrea: 88
Erkin, Feridun Cemal: 195 n.2
Ervine-Andrews, Captain H. M.: 443 n.1
Esmonde, Lieutenant-Commander E. K.: 443
n.1
Ethics: and the Jews, 723 n.5; and the Sermon
on the Mount, 729–30
Eton College: 459 n.2
Etruria, SS: 462

Europe Today: 289
Europe Unite (Randolph S. Churchill, editor):
783 n.2
European Army, a: 542, 543, 544, 547, 556,
573–4, 593, 622, 634, 636–7, 666, 669, 682,
684, 686; discussed at Bermuda, 925–6
European Assembly, the: 408, 424–5, 433, 622
European Court of Human Rights, the: 460
European Defence Community (EDC): 669–
70, 675–6, 682, 727, 789 n.2, 793, 832, 843,
859, 864, 890, 909; discussed at Bermuda,
918, 925–8, 928–32; continued French hostility to, 940; a French supporter of, 941;
discussed at Washington (June 1954), 998,
1003, 1008; and the French, 1004, 1036,
1049, 1054, 1055–7, 1089; and the Berlin
Conference (1954), 1029; 'desultory dis-
cussion' about, 1047; not a 'grand alli-
ance', 1057; and the 'anxieties' of 1945,
1080; and the London-Paris Agreements
(1955), 1103; and the suspending of any
Summit, 1109
European Economic Community (EEC, or
Common Market): 1337
European Federation, a: 682
European Union: the cause of, 495–6
Evans, Sir Horace: 820, 844, 1246–7
Evening Standard, the: 880, 987, 1186 n.3, 1274
Excess Profits Tax: proposed, 639, 641–2
Exeter, HMS: 508

Fadiman, Clifton: 393 n.4
Falkland Islands, the: to be defended, 708
Farouk, King of Egypt: 631–2, 668; deposed
(1952), 747
Farrar-Hockley, Captain (later General Sir)
Anthony: 610 n.2
Faure, Edgar: 628 n.2, 1243 n.3
Fata Morgana (stage play): 1352
Fate: and Palestine, 252
'Father of Peace', the: 868 n.2
Feast of the Annunciation, the: 483
Fegen, Captain E. S. F.: 443 n.1
Feisal, Emir (later King) of Iraq: 361 n.2, 623
n.4, 1272 n.2; murdered, 1270, 1283
Fellowes, Daisy: 1175, 1236, 1237, 1238 n.1,
1273
Female Suffrage: 368
Fernyhough, E.: 446
Festival of Britain, the: 583, 608
Field, Marshall: 194, 204, 982 n.2
Fields, Gracie: 1297, 1298
Fifth Column: and the Kremlin, 464
Figaro, le: 471
Fiji: 942
Financial Times, the: 323
'Finis' (in 1945): 113

Finland: 97, 212, 351 n.4

Finucane, Wing Commander Brendan ('Paddy'): 443

First Light (Churchill's horse): 1199

First World War: deaths in, 28; 'a ghastly muddle', 265; 'fearful' French losses in, 928; Churchill reads an account of, 1326; Churchill's proposed wording, on a memorial for, 1365

Fischer, Louis: 577 n.2

Fisher, Dorothy C.: 393 n.4

Fisher, Dr Geoffrey (Archbishop of Canterbury) (later Baron): 979

Fisher, John: 391

Fiume (Rijeka): 45

Flanders, Count of (Regent of Belgium): 267

Flandin, Pierre-Etienne: Churchill defends, 168–9

Fleck, Sir Alexander: 1263

Fleet Street (London): the successful 'gagging' of, 852

Fleischmann, Hanley: 682

Fletcher, Walter: 612

Flower, (Sir) Desmond: 221, 416, 974, 1196 n.4, 1237, 1249

Flower, Sir Newman: 1196

Fonteyn, (Dame) Margot: 1284

Foot, (Sir) Dingle: 603–4

Foot, Michael: 501 n.2, 502, 508, 512, 549–50, 649, 967 n.1; and the hydrogen bomb, 966

Forbes, Alastair ('Ali'): 482, 633–4

Forbes, Alderman Donald L.: 1290

Ford, (Sir) Edward: 696, 1183

Ford, Lady (Virginia): 1183

Foreign Relations of the United States: 979 n.1

Foreman, Carl: 1207 n.1

Forester, C. S.: 620, 854 n.1, 917, 1257, 1337

Forrestal, James: 207

Formosa (Taiwan): 676, 680–1, 1049, 1092

Forster, E. M.: 854

Fort Churchill (Canada): 1011

Fortune: Churchill 'blessed' by, 776

Four-Power Conference: (of Foreign Ministers, at Berlin, 1954), 929–30, 940, 943–4, 951, 952–3, 1029; (of Prime Ministers and Heads of State, Geneva, 1955), 1136–7, 1142, 1151, 1154–5

Four-Year Plan (of economic recovery): 34, 36, 39–40

Fox River: Lincoln's advice concerning, 514

France: 'weak and difficult', 6; its rescue, 12; and Italy, 14, 29, 42; and Syria, 30–1; and union with Britain (1940), 141; 'peril' in, 201; and Spain, 218; Communist influence in, 223, 224, 241–2; and a 'United States of Europe', 232, 266, 285, 286, 291, 330, 520; Churchill's early visits to (1883 and 1907),

France—continued
247; and Churchill's war memoirs, 271; and a 'Franco-German partnership', 286, 520–1, 536–7, 954; and a European Assembly, 425; assistance for (in 1940), 490; and NATO, 491; and nuclear tests, 535 n.2; and European defence, 542, 593, 622, 634–5, 636–7; and the European Defence Community (EDC), 669–70, 682, 727, 859, 918, 925–8, 928–32, 940, 1036, 1054, 1055, 1057; and the Middle East, 680; 'a friend', 684; and a 'new unity', 690; Churchill gets a 'second wind' in, 761–2; and a possible Summit, 790, 833, 863, 1027–8; and Locarno, 831; and the Bermuda Conference, 844, 909–10, 918–19, 920, 925–37; and Indo-China, 861, 934, 973–4; and Egypt, 932–3; and Russia, 1016; and the Four-Power talks (1955), 1137; and the Suez Crisis (1956), 1201, 1202, 1203, 1206, 1213–14, 1220–2, 1240; and Algeria, 1245, 1318; and de Gaulle, 1264; and Churchill's Croix de la Libération, 1280; 'proud' of her defences, 1326

France, Anatole: 180, 253

Franckenstein, Sir George: 135 n.3

Franco, General Francisco: 78–9, 218

Frankfurt (Germany): 123

Franks, Sir Oliver (later Baron): 675 n.2, 678, 1071

Fraser, Sir Ian: 722

Fraser of North Cape, Admiral of the Fleet Lord (1st Baron): 401

Freedom from Fear: 407

French Embassy, London: 3

French, Field Marshal Sir John (later 1st Viscount French of Ypres): 1327

French Resistance (1940–45): 'brilliant and valiant efforts' of, 928

Frenchstreet Farm (formerly Parkside Farm): an integral part of Chartwell, and its market garden, 348; sold (1953), 898

Frewen, Clara (Churchill's aunt): 874 n.4

Frewen, Oswald (Churchill's nephew): 307, 421, 498, 548

Frewen, Roger (Churchill's nephew): 1338–9

Friedman, Elisha: 210–11

Friendship: the 'debts' of, 1328; the 'golden years' of, 1353

Fuchs, Dr Klaus: 520

Fulham By-election (1933): 148, 390

Fulton (Missouri): 159, 172, 189, 190, 193, 197–203; reactions to Churchill's speech at, 204–6, 207–17, 219–20, 220; Churchill pursues theme of, 238, 279, 289, 326; recalled, 336 n.1, 352, 396, 441, 445, 463, 464, 509, 624, 1290

Gabriel (the cat, at Chartwell): 1042, 1044
Gaitskell, Hugh: 509, 535 n.2, 594; succeeds Cripps, 604; 'assailed', 607; succeeded by R. A. Butler, 657; his 'legacy', 750–1; 'assistance' from, 803; 'the worst . . . since Dr Dalton', 815; and hanging, 1182 n.1; and the Suez Crisis (1956), 1210, 1214; his good wishes, 1262, 1306
Galbraith, Professor Vivian: 180
Gale, Sir Humfrey: 271
Galicia: 96
Gallacher, William: 385 n.2
Galleazzi-Liza, Dr: 1279
Gallipoli (Alan Moorehead): 1225–6
Gallipoli Campaign (1915): 307, 433 n.3, 1255 n.1
Gallipoli Peninsula (Turkey): 1298
Gallup Polls: 33, 498, 501, 584, 585, 616 n.3, 633, 1138–9
Gambling (at Monte Carlo): 153
Gamelin, General Maurice: 418 n.6, 429
Gandhi, Mahatma: 299–300
Garbett, Cyril (Archbishop of York): 649
Garda, Lake (Italy): 480
Garland, Flying Officer D. E.: 443 n.1
Garofalides, Professor Theodore: 1334
Garrod, Air (Chief) Marshal Sir Guy: 345, 609, 632, 633
Garvin, J. L.: 1358 n.4
Gascoigne, Sir Alvary: 812, 818, 876
Gatwick (Sussex, England): proposed airport at, 776
Gaza (Egypt): 709
Gemmell, Miss ('Chips'): 331, 426, 576, 579, 629 n.2, 657 n.1
General Election: (of 1945), 6, 9, 10, 14, 19–24, 32–6, 46–59, 62, 65, 68, 74, 79, 92, 93, 100, 105–19; reflections on, 125, 147–8, 149–50, 160, 168, 185, 190, 236, 284, 330, 788; in prospect (1947–50), 351, 417, 476–7, 486, 489, 499, 500; campaign for (1950), 501–12; in prospect (1950–1), 513–14, 524, 529, 553, 558, 564, 584–5, 590–1, 591, 592, 595, 621–2, 624, 637; campaign of (1951), 639, 640–8; campaign of (1951) recalled, 670; in prospect (from 1953), 905, 948, 965, 991, 1046–51, 1061, 1063, 1103, 1104, 1114–15, 1115 n.3, 1118, 1126, 1131, 1132, 1135; won by the Conservatives (1955), 1138–9, 1143, 1152; (of 1959), 1300, 1301–2; (of 1964), 1343, 1344–5, 1346, 1355, 1356
Geneva: Churchill speaks in (1946), 263–5; possible conference at, 952–3, 954–5; Conference at (on Indo-China), 972, 973–4, 977, 978, 982, 985, 987, 996–7, 1015, 1027, 1028; and Locarno, 999; a Four-Power Confer-

Geneva—*continued*
ence at (1955), 832 n.1, 1136–7, 1151, 1154–5, 1168
George III, King: 808
George V, King: 698, 699, 764, 810 n.4, 1046 n.2
George VI, King: 12, 21–2; Churchill lunches with, 36, 46; information sent to, 66 n.4; Churchill's audiences of, 105, 312; and Truman, 106; and Churchill's resignation (1945), 108; and a Garter for Eden, 111; 'shocked', 114; and honours, 126, 178; and VJ Day, 129; a medallion for, 245; letters to Churchill from, 174, 447, 570, 613; mentioned, 219 n.4, 236; and the Normandy Landing preparations, 271; and India, 334; and his daughter's engagement, 340–1, 359; and Churchill's 'dream', 366; Churchill's letters to, 390–1, 446–7, 448, 491, 570; ill, 446–7, 638, 639, 693; and 'a unique honour', 453; and possible advice from Attlee, 516; sees *Odette*, 532; and Odette Pol Roger's champagne, 630 n.1; and Churchill's second Premiership, 649, 653 n.1; dies, 696–8; recalled, 699–700, 701, 761, 764; and Churchill's war memoirs, 810, 867; and the Order of the Garter (for Churchill), 822; and Baldwin's resignation, 862; Churchill recalls, 886–7; Churchill's friendship with, recalled, 1333
George of Denmark, Prince: 526
Georges, General Joseph: 274
Gerard, James W.: 219
German Federal Republic: to be an 'equal partner', 1010; the 'equal and honourable status' of, 1056; and the United States, 1090; *see also* Western Germany
Germany: defeat of, 4, 12, 14, 17–18, 229; war criminals of, 20; 'responsibility of, needed, 31; Churchill's instructions concerning, 59; and the Potsdam conference, 64, 66–7, 71–2, 77, 82–5, 90, 91–2, 103; and Churchill's Fulton speech, 201; and pre-war appeasement, 202–3; and Nazi crimes, 240, 249–50, 284, 431–2; bombing of, 259, 284, 477–8, 632, 633 n.2; and the Morgenthau Plan (of 1944), 259; and United Europe, 266, 267, 279, 285, 286–7, 330, 407, 483–4, 536–7; treatment of, 347 n.4; the 'giving up of the heart of' (in May 1945), 428; fate of Field Marshals from, 429–30, 431–2, 438–9, 637, 756; divided, 437, 448; and the Labour Government in Britain, 495, 574; and reconciliation with France, 536, 622, 775, 954; and a National Army, 544, 547, 573–4, 666, 669, 842, 890; and Churchill's war memoirs, 584; defence of, as part of a Western Euro-

Germany—*continued*
pean defence scheme, 634–5, 636–7; and the European Defence Community, 682, 684, 686, 1054, 1055–7, 1108; and a 'new unity', 690; and British military policy (1952), 726; fears of 'resurgence' of militarism in, 842; 'matters' (as opposed to Korea), 861; and a possible new Locarno, 869; and unconditional surrender (in 1945), 876; '*crushed*' (in 1945), 892; and Russia, 895–6, 1108, 1197; and the Bermuda Conference discussions, 925–30, 932, 933; and NATO, 932; and trade competition, 963; rearmament of, 963, 1003, 1007; and the hydrogen bomb, 1021; and the need 'to get them on our side', 1057; and the defence of Europe, 1058, 1108; Churchill visits (1956), 1197–8, 1200; Churchill's hopes for (recalled in 1959), 1290

'Gestapo': and the British Labour Party, 32–3, 35

Gfroerer, Mr: at Chartwell, 225–6

Gfroerer, Mrs: the private life of, 225–6

Ghana (formerly the Gold Coast): 1330–1

Gheorghiu-Dej, Gheorge: 1217 n.2

Gibbon, Edward: 345

Gibraltar: 69, 183, 195, 580, 916 n.1; Churchill 'well received' at, 1277–8; Churchill unable to join *Christina* at, 1308; Churchill joins *Christina* at, 1319, 1321

Gibraltar (Churchill's horse): 826, 867; *photograph 27*

Gibson, C. W.: 287

Gide, André: 577 n.2

Gifford, Walter: 615, 675 n.2

Gilbert, Martin: a gift to, 1112 n.1; an eyewitness, 1122; joins Randolph Churchill's research team, 1318 n.8

Gilbert and Sullivan: 112, 1356

Gilliatt, Elizabeth: 179, 260, 292, 305 n.1, 310 n.1, 312, 332, 373 n.2, 374, 378 n.1, 388, 426, 427, 462, 470, 486, 498, 500, 534, 629; and Churchill's second Premiership, 656, 657 n.1, 662, 691, 760, 860, 870, 886, 1015, 1063, 1076; and Churchill's resignation, 1125; and Churchill's mood in retirement, 1140

Gilliatt, Sir William: 886 n.1

Giraud, General Henri: 242

Giraudier, Antonio: 1011–12, 1358

Gladstone, W. E.: 23, 294, 559, 614, 801, 808, 859, 1048, 1050, 1072, 1204, 1212, 1319

Glaoui, the: 381, 382, 386, 577, 579

Glasgov, Ivan: and Churchill's cancelled cruise to Leningrad, 1313

Glasgow: Churchill speaks at (1951), 614, 647; (1953), 815–16

Glendyne, 2nd Baron: 256 n.1

Glory: 'alone remains', 1160, 1365

Gloucester, Duchess of (Alice): 1073

Gloucester, Duke of (brother of King George VI): 913, 1073

Gloucestershire Regiment (the Glosters): in Korea, 610

Glubb, General (Glubb Pasha): 841, 1334

God: 'takes care of England', 118; and totalitarianism, 199; and the users of the atomic bomb, 249; and the 'scenario' of the universe, 254; his 'children' and the atomic bomb, 277; and Mankind, 1098

Godber, 1st Baron: 1263

Godfrey Davis (Car Hire): 342

Goebbels, Dr Joseph: 7 n.1

Goethe, J. W.: 911

Gold Standard (1925): 323

Golden Age: its gates not yet opened, 599

Golding, Ronald: 345–6

Gollancz, Victor: 117, 283 n.2, 294, 347, 398

Goodwin, Flight-Lieutenant (later Professor): 273, 315, 344 n.1

Gordon-Lennox, Lord Nicholas: 627 n.2, 1292, 1296

Gorizia (Italian-Yugoslav border): 8

Gort, Field Marshal 1st Viscount: 262

Gosford, Mildred: 1157

Gosling, Tommy: 613 n.2

Gothic, SS: at Cristobal, 914 n.4; near Fiji, 942

Grace of Monaco, Princess (Grace Kelly): 1207–8, 1287, 1288

Graebner, Walter: at Chartwell, 225, 475–6, 533–4, 866, 877; at Hyde Park Gate, 234, 647; describes Churchill at work, 328; and Churchill's war memoirs, 342, 376, 414, 415 n.2, 427, 428, 493; recalls Churchill's remarks, 380 n.4, 1059–60; at Marrakech, 385, 386, 395, 579, 585–7; in Italy, 480–1; and Rufus II, 576 n.3

Graham, Billy: 978–9

Graham, Sir Miles: 271

Graham, Miss: 305 n.1

Graham-Dixon, Leslie: 131 n.2, 221, 234, 245, 274, 307–8, 327 n.4, 461, 1224 n.2

Graham-Harrison, Francis: 312

Grant, Duncan: 1276 n.1

Graves, Robert: 145, 1243 n.1, 1334

Gray, Thomas: quoted, 587

Great Contemporaries (Winston S. Churchill, 1937): 562 n.1

Greatheart: 'must have his sword', 207

Greece: 6, 25, 67, 76, 78, 91, 140, 145, 146 n.1; and Churchill's Fulton speech, 196, 200, 212; and Communism, 223, 360–1, 390, 396, 441; and *The Times*, 246; in 1947, 326; and Churchill's visit to, 1944, 351 n.3, 568; in 1941, 415; 'rescued', 510; and the defence

Greece—*continued*
of Europe, 542, 994; and Field Marshal Montgomery, 717; and the 1944 'spheres of influence' discussion, 875, 1192; a dispute concerning, 1158–9

Green, Harry: 305

Green, John Richard: 1149

Green, Professor V.: 1149

Greenoak, Francesca: 1251 n.5

Greenshields, William (Churchill's valet): 329, 374, 378 n.1, 380, 387, 388, 880 n.2

Greenwood, J. R.: 555

Grenadier Guards: leave for the Mediterranean (1956), 1207; and Churchill's funeral (1965), 1362

Grey of Falloden, 1st Viscount (Sir Edward Grey): 646

Grigg, Sir Edward (later 1st Baron Altrincham): 34–5; *for subsequent index entries see* Altrincham, 1st Baron

Grigg, Sir James (P. J.): 30, 60, 124, 354

Grigg, John: Macmillan 'indignant' about, 1249

Grimond, Jo (later Baron): 1351, 1355; mounts guard, 1361–2

Gromyko, Andrei: 238, 818; *photograph 22*

Gruenther, General Alfred M.: 957, 992

Gruner, Dov: 296

Guatemala: 998, 1009

Guildhall (City of London) the: 569, 570, 661, n.1; Churchill speaks at (1951), 660–1, 662–3; (1952), 774–5; (1953), 911; (1954), 1058, 1068; Churchill at the unveiling of his statue at, (1955), 1147, 1148; Churchill speaks at (1957), 1248

Guisan, General: 261, 262

Gunnis, Rupert: 1305 n.2

Gurkhas, the: in Malaya, 666; recruitment of, 803

Gurney, Sir Henry: assassinated (1951), 660 n.3, 685 n.2

Guthrie, Sir James: 860

Gwydyr House (Whitehall): 703

Haakon VII, King (of Norway): 362 n.2, 409, 615

Habeas Corpus (1689): 200

Hagerty, Jim (Eisenhower's Press Secretary): 1005

Hague, The: conference at (1948), 398, 399, 405–9, 410; referred to, 424, 441, 536, 569; International Court of Justice in, 619; a possible Summit at, 1003

Haifa (Israel): ships needed at, 527–8; and oil, 590, 658

Haig, Field Marshal 1st Earl: 1327

Haile Selassie, Emperor of Abyssinia: 80, 972

Hailes, 1st Baron: 1321

Hailes, Lady (Diana): 1321

Hailsham, 1st Viscount: 366 n.1

Haley, Sir William: 403 n.3, 603–4

Halifax, 1st Earl: 8, 14, 117, 166, 184, 191, 228, 429; and 'psalm form', 665 n.1

Hall Brothers: and Churchill's paintings, 965 n.6

Hall, W. Glenvil: 601 n.1, 649 n.1

Halle, Kay: at Chartwell (1961), 1327; and Churchill's Honorary Citizenship (of the United States), 1343

Halliday, Edward: 1158 n.1

Hamblin, Grace: 4 n.1, 245, 305 n.1, 323 n.2, 462, 1119; and Churchill's retirement, 1132, 1156, 1191, 1220

Hamburg (Germany): a trial in (1948), 442

Hamilton, Hamish: 412

Hamilton, General Sir Ian: 1254–5

Hamilton, Major-General J. R. C.: 1326, 1330

Hamilton Falls (Labrador): bridled, 1174

Hamilton River (Labrador): 754

Hammarskjöld, Dag: 1218

Hampden-Wall, Penelope (later Mrs Neville Barwick): 580

Hanbury, Sir Cecil: 1251 n.5

Hanbury, Lady (E. D. C. Symons-Jeune): 1251–2

Hanbury, Sir Thomas: 1251 n.5

Hancock, A.: 107 n.3

Hanging: a free vote on, 1181–2

Hankey, 1st Baron: 1195

Hanoi (Indo-China): 987

Hanover, Kingdom of: 28

Hansard: 292, 389, 489 n.3

Hapsburgs, the: 212

Harcourt, 1st Viscount (Lewis Harcourt): 1319

Harding, General Sir John (later Field Marshal 1st Viscount): 821, 964, 1343

Hardy, Thomas: 898, 947

Harmsworth, Esmond (2nd Viscount Rothermere): 898 n.2

Harrap (Publishing House): 344, 435, 596

Harriman, Averell: 207, 311, 362, 625, 675 n.2, 793, 901 n.1

Harris (the gardener at Chartwell): 164

Harris, Marshal of the Royal Air Force Sir Arthur ('Bert'): 51, 178–9, 192–3, 259, 720

Harrod, Sir Roy (R.F.): 1247–8

Harrow: Churchill receives Freedom of (1955), 1168; *photograph 25*

Harrow School: 139, 142 n.1, 162, 290, 361, 364 n.2, 444, 497, 668–9, 773, 774, 914, 1069, 1168, 1254, 1282, 1305–6, 1316, 1339 n.1; its 'salute', 1362

Hartington, Marquess (later 8th Duke of Devonshire): 222

Harvard University (Boston, Massachusetts, USA): 192

Harvey, Air Commodore A. V.: 715

Harvey, John: Churchill speaks for (1955), 1138; (and in 1959), 1302

Harvey, Mr (Lord Cherwell's valet): 576

Harvey, (Sir) Oliver (later 1st Baron Harvey of Tasburgh): 311, 373, 634, 635, 636–7

Hassell, Ulrich von: 412

Hastings (England): Churchill speaks at (1955), 1161

Hate: 'not a good guide', 526–7

Havana (Cuba): 190–1

Havenga, N. C.: 779 n.2

Havengore (Port of London Authority launch): and Churchill's funeral, 1363

Hawkey, Sir James: 3, 159, 501, 506, 732, 1113

Hayter, Lady (Iris Hayter): 588, 589

Hayter, (Sir) William: 78, 318, n.3, 588, 817, 1020

Hayward, Leland: 901 n.1

Hazlerigg, Thomas: 1282

Head, Anthony (later 1st Viscount): 667, 704, 729, 755, 782 n.1, 883, 949, 1037, 1206

'Health Without Rules': a proposed book, 1262

Hearst, William Randolph: 832 n.1

Heath, Edward: 1177, 1182 n.1, 1188–9, 1257, 1288, 1307 n.7, 1316; at Chartwell, 1332; Churchill's lunch guest, 1339 n.1

Heaven: a possible 'Minister of Defence' in, 278

Hegarty, Jim: 992 n.2

Heiskell, Andrew: 327, 387 n.1

Hell: the 'rim' of, 1068

Hendaye (France): 627, 628, 629, 630

Henderson, J. N.: 310 n.1

Henley, the Hon. Sylvia: 1178, 1179, 1183, 1186, 1187, 1188, 1189, 1257, 1332, 1338, 1339 n.1, 1351 n.2, 1358; *photograph 37*

Heptarchy, the: 1015

Hercules: his labours, and Churchill's, 1195

Herriot, Edouard: 141, 242

Heydeman, Major-General C. A.: 136–8

Heyer, Georgette: 1267

Hicks, George: 283, 287

Hill, Sir Hugh: 785 n.5

Hill, Mrs Kathleen: 57, 123, 163, 179, 785, 988, 1151

Hill, (Sir) Richard: 785

Hinchingbrooke, Viscount (son of 9th Earl of Sandwich) (later Victor Montagu): 1184, 1307 n.7

Hindus (of India): 248, 291–5, 298–9, 301, 332, 337, 353–4, 375

Hippopotamus: and London, 4; and Churchill, 59

Hipwell, Miss: 305 n.1

Hirohito, Emperor (the Mikado): 68, 75

Hiroshima (Japan): 119

History: and the 'United band of friends', 27; and the 'ungrateful' British people, 118; Churchill's 'secure' place in, 129; and the atomic bomb, 249; the 'only lesson of', 265; 'All will be understood by', 412; 'Keep your eye on', 459 n.2; and 'your greatest literary accomplishment', 569; Attlee 'at the bar of', 592; and Ernest Bevin, 598 n.5; contains 'all the secrets of statecraft', 835; its scenario 'has no end', 974; 'wider reasons' to be 'offered to', 989; the United States 'learn from', 1191

History Today: 877, 1136 n.3

Hitler, Adolf: 7 n.1, 8, 61, 64, 79, 80, 141, 152, 437; and appeasement, 168–9, 171, 202; and Churchill's History, 177; his 'warriors' bombed, 179 n.2; Churchill 'reminiscent' of (according to Stalin), 211; his attacks on Churchill reminiscent of Stalin (according to Churchill), 213; effect of 'Hitler's war', 215; invasion of Russia by, 218–19, 549–50; his 'experience' recalled, 285; and the Conscription debate of 1939, 319, 320; 'had no heart at all', 351; created 'false sense of security', 352; pre-1939 apprehensions about, 364 n.3; his 'fury', 416–17; despots 'as wicked as', 428; 'prominent servants' of, 448; 'no theme', 464; 'last territorial demand' of, 475; and air bombardment (1941–5), 490; his speeches not 'up to much', 589; and rearmament in the 1930s, 645; and his possible 'downfall' without bloodshed (in the 1930s), 661; 'made too many mistakes' to be great, 729; 'ghastly crimes' of, 774; and the 'terrible events' of 1939, 831; and Chamberlain's 'hubris', 868; 'another dose of' to be avoided, 922; Soviet desire for 'protection against' in the future, 935, 940; 'safeguards' needed against 'another', 1003; and the Jews, 1008; and the 'use' of his defeated soldiers, 1070; the 'disgrace' of, 1197 n.6; and the division of Germany (in 1945), 1193 n.1; and Eden, 1224 n.3; and the Nazi-Soviet Pact (1939), 1290

Hoare, Brigadier-General Reginald ('Reggie'): 185

Hoare, Sir Samuel (later 1st Viscount Templewood): 859

Hoare-Laval Pact, the (1935): 147

Hoare-Temple, Piers: 1321 n.2

Hodge, Alan: helps Churchill with his History, 876–7, 883–4, 891, 1136, 1141, 1144, 1145–

Hodge, Alan—*continued*
6, 1148, 1156, 1157, 1158 n.1, 1162, 1163, 1165, 1166, 1167, 1172, 1183, 1185, 1187, 1189, 1212, 1217, 1225; one of 'my boys', 1228, 1229, 1234, 1235 n.1, 1269; and the Other Club, 1307; at Chartwell, 1327–8; and Churchill's last years, 1349, 1351 n.2, 1357

Hodge, Mrs Alan (Jane Aiken): 1136, 1148, 1217, 1269, 1351 n.2, 1357

Hodge, Jessica Mary (later Mrs Orebi-Gan): 1327

Hodge, Joanna Marrack: 1328

Hogg, Quintin (later Baron Hailsham of St Marylebone): 366 n.1

Holiday Time (Churchill's horse): 1244

Holland, Sidney: 498 n.1, 779 n.2, 836, 1227

Hollis, Major-General (later Lieutenant-General) Sir Leslie: 373, 405

Holmes, Marian: 61, 116 n.2, 1083

Home Guard, the: 598, 708, 710, 802, 834, 904

Home Rule: 'Rome Rule', 368; and the 'fierce controversies' of the past, 515

Hong Kong: 547, 553, 583, 676, 845, 994

Honorary Citizenship (of the United States): 1343

Hopkins, Harry: 4, 189, 259

Hopkins, Sir Richard: 1235

Hopkinson, Henry: 808

Horabin, T. L.: 208

Hore-Belisha, Leslie (later 1st Baron): 319

Horner, Arthur: 403

Horsbrugh, Florence (later Baroness): 656, 880 n.1

Hosey Rigg ('Cosy Pig'): near Chartwell, 974

Hôtel de Paris (Monte Carlo): 434, 450, 487, 1257, 1307, 1308, 1314, 1315, 1324, 1328, 1331, 1334, 1335, 1343

Hottentots, the: and universal suffrage, 1040

Houghton Mifflin (publishing house): 273, 468, 623, 632, 802 n.2, 1158 n.3

House of Commons, the: Churchill speaks in (15 December 1944), 92; Churchill's speeches in (1945), 12–13, 15, 39–41, 129; (1946), 233, 237–8, 239–41, 243, 248, 248–9, 250–2, 279, 284, 292–5; (1947), 295–7, 298–9, 210 n.3, 302–3, 319–20, 324–5, 333–4, 359, 359–60; (1948), 396–7, 401–2, 417, 422–3, 443, 445–6, 448–9; (1949), 260, 453–7, 472, 474–5; (1950), 515–16, 516–20, 520–1, 526–7, 527–8, 535–7, 537, 538–9, 539–41, 595 n.1, 554–5, 556, 558–9, 562–3, 564–5, 566–7, 569, 571–2, 573–5; (1951), 591–2, 600, 604–5, 605–7, 610–13, 624–5, 659–60, 665–7; (1952), 668 n.1, 683 n.1, 694 n.4, 696, 698–700, 704–7, 707–8, 709–11, 721, 730–1, 740–2, 749–51, 772–3, 780–1;

House of Commons—*continued*
(1953), 802–3, 808, 819, 829–32, 904–8, 912–13, 940; (1954), 948–9, 953–5, 958, 965–9, 969, 976, 1010, 1030, 1036–7, 1079–81; (1955), 952, 1098–1100, 1101, 1108–9, 1114; (1958), 1270–2 (never delivered); Churchill's 'patience' in, 150; and the Laski controversy, 48; and Poland, 73; and Italy, 89; and the Yalta documents, 191; mistakes in, to be avoided, 214; and the Council of Europe, 482; Leadership of, 226–8, 1169; an interview in, 270; and India, 292, 422–3, 472; its 'vigilant eye', 369; its 'responsibilities', 402; rebuilding of, 417; and independent States, 422; and German Field Marshals, 430; pre-war warnings in, 469; 'moods' of, 526; Churchill's 'ascendancy' over, 624; a possible secret session in, 531, 538–9, 540, 541, 594; and Randolph Churchill's future, 533; and the Abdication Crisis (of 1936), 549; and Israel, 560; returns to Palace of Westminster, 562–3; 'not at its best', 564; and 'party strife' (1951), 599; and 'anti-American elements' in, 619; preparation for a speech in, 664–5; Churchill makes 'a good impression' in, 730; not 'simply naggers', 741; Churchill's 'simple errors' in (1952), 774; and Korea, 800; and the death of Queen Mary, 808; and Churchill's stroke (1953), 847, 848, 866, 871, 878, 885; Churchill's return to, 901, 902, 903, 904–8; and University seats, 902; and atomic energy, 904; Churchill's 'authority' in, 909; priorities of, 938, 939; Churchill's presence in (after his stroke), 947, 948, 969–70; and the payment of Members, of, 978, 980–2; a vote of censure in (1955), 1108; and Lloyd George, 1114; Churchill would 'like to die in', 1124; a tribute from (and from the House of Lords), 1073–5, 1253; and Churchill's retirement years (1955–65), 1143, 1145, 1149, 1168, 1171, 1181–2, 1256, 1266–7, 1268, 1281, 1285, 1305, 1308, 1331, 1337; and Malta, 1188–9, 1189 n.1; and the Suez Crisis (1956), 1202, 1208, 1209; a message from (1957), 1262; a speech never delivered in (1958), 1271–2; and Churchill's 85th birthday (1959), 1306; possible Honorary Membership of, 1343, 1350; Churchill not to stand for again (1963), 1343, 1344–5; Churchill given a luncheon in (1963), 1345; Churchill's last visits to (1963), 1346–7, 1350, 1351, 1352; Churchill's final visit to (1964), 1354

House of Lords, the: and Churchill's dream (1953), 874; and a tribute from (and from the House of Commons), 1253

Household Cavalry, the: at Churchill's funeral, 1362

Housing policy: 36, 40–1, 53–4, 566, 568; and Churchill's second Premiership (1951–5), 717, 748, 759, 763, 884–5

Howe, Clarence: 1011

Howells, Roy: 1269, 1277, 1278, 1331, 1334, 1335, 1340

Hoyer Millar, Lady (Elizabeth): 1200

Hoyer Millar, Sir Frederick: 1200

Hozier, Lady (Blanche): her death (in 1925), 1364

Huddersfield (England): Churchill speaks at (1951), 646–7

Huddleston, Miss Ann: 1340 n.4

Hudson, Robert: 322

Huggins, Sir Godfrey: 779 n.2, 836

'Hughligans': Churchill a member of, 1077 n.1

Hull, Cordell: 893

Humanity: 'at its most fateful milestone', 992

Humes, James C.: and history, 835

Humpty Dumpty: and the 1945 General Election, 129

Hungary: in 1945, 25, 76, 97, 212; in 1946, 239, 241, 288; in 1950, 510; in 1954, 953; in 1956, 1249

Hunt, (Sir) David: 663–4, 664–5, 665, 667–8, 697, 1041 n.1

Hurstfield, Joel: 1156

Hussein, King, of Jordan: 361 n.2, 623 n.4, 1323

Huxley, Aldous: 1228 n.5

Hyde Park Hotel (London): 306

Hyderabad: 337, 422, 431, 630 n.4

Hyderabad, Nizam of: 234 n.1, 449

Hydrogen Bomb, the: first explosion of (November 1952), 772; Soviet challenge to, 873; its imminence feared, 874, 875; 'a diminution of tension', 907; and London, 917; Britain 'not intending to do any work on', 924; details of, made public, 952, 959–60, 961, 962; a further explosion of (March 1954), 957; Churchill's speech on (1954), 965–71; need for measures to control, 972; and East Anglia, 973; Britain to build, 993, 995, 1000, 1011, 1019, 1021–3, 1029; the defence of the Canal Zone, 994, 1037; a possible moratorium on experiments with, 1000; British work on, 1091, 1094, 1097; Churchill explains reasons for manufacture of, 1098–1100; letters about, 1117

Hylton-Foster, Sir Harry: and Churchill's 85th birthday (1959), 1306; mounts guard (1965), 1361–2

Hynd, John: 564

I Claudius (Robert Graves): 1243

Iceland: and fisheries, 535 n.2; and a 'peripheral defence', 932

Idiot (a film): 983

Imperial Chemical Industries (ICI): 1053 n.1

Imperial War College: 223

In the Balance (Randolph S. Churchill, editor): 783 n.2

In the Gloaming (song): recalled, 143

Into Battle (Randolph S. Churchill, editor): 245

Income Tax: 324, 369, 815–16

India: 67, 141, 191, 229, 230; Churchill's recollections of, 185–6, 337, 958; the path to Independence of, 233–4, 237, 248, 252, 276, 292–5, 298–302, 332–5, 336–7; the conflict over, recalled, 1134, 1250; and The Times, 246; and Palestine, 297, 300–1; civil war in, 353–4, 375, 400–1; 'down the drain', 371; and Hyderabad, 422, 431; 'pledges . . . repudiated', 439; and the British Commonwealth, 472; and Communism, 617; 'not your fault or mine', 630; and the Suez Canal, 684–5; arms sales to, 712, 803; Mountbatten 'forgiven' about, 762; and the Korean War, 839; and France in Indo-China, 861, 934; a 'colossal disaster' in, 934; and the United States, 951; and the story Britain has to tell, 1040; emigration from, 1093–4

India Bill: debates on (1935), 301, 377

Indian Independence Bill (1947): 334–5, 422

Indian Mutiny (1857): 294

Indo-China: 3, 663, 681, 682, 715, 716, 791, 821, 824, 833, 861, 934, 971; and the Geneva Conference (1954), 973–4, 975–6, 985, 986, 1027, 1028; and the French decision to leave, 993, 998

Indonesia: 454

Ingersoll, Ralph: 235, 236

Ingr, General: 404, n.4

Inönü, President Ismet: 443–4, 1262

Inside Constantinople (Einstein): 1159 n.1

International Court of Justice (The Hague): 535 n.2, 619

Inverchapel, 1st Baron: 310, 311

Iolanthe (Gilbert and Sullivan): 754

Iraq: 217, 590, 623 n.4, 841; and a Western defence plan, 994; and Suez, 1218; rebellion in (1958), 1270–2; and Communism, 1323

Ireland, Republic of (Eire): see index entry for Eire

Irgun Zvai Leumi: 335 n.2; 'vilest gangsters', 430

Irish Treaty (of 1921): 442

'Iron Curtain': 7, 45, 97, 154, 200, 201, 238,

'Iron Curtain'—*continued*
404, 448, 483, 553, 617, 690, 805; a means of breaching (trade), 922, 944; 'neighbours . . . on both sides of', 997; and Churchill's 'unique position', 1048; and the telegram to Truman of April 1945, recalled, 1080; held back from the Atlantic and the Channel, 1099; and Greece, 1159; at Chartwell, 523

Iron and Steel Act (1948): 445–6, 507 n.3, 558–9, 591–2, 614; to be repealed (1951), 657

Isaacs, George: 131

Islam: the 'unity' of, 1204

Isle of Wight: 250

Ismailia (Egypt): 957

Ismay, General Sir Hastings (later 1st Baron) ('Pug'): 46, 66 n.5, 90, 128, 129, 133; and Churchill's war memoirs, 221, 234–5, 237, 268, 271–3, 308, 315, 415, 426, 427, 428, 429, 431, 433, 450, 474, 481, 488–9, 495, 505, 506, 550–1, 582, 584, 601, 609; and defence, 283 n.4; and Churchill's second Premiership, 653–4, 661, 672, 673, 681, 712, 727, 762; becomes Secretary General of NATO, 746 n.2; his friendship with Churchill, 305, 704, 1157; 'will certainly approve' (of the Margate speech), 898; and India, 333, 335; and Russia, 937; and Churchill's years of retirement, 1183, 1187, 1232, 1236, 1239, 1267, 1315, 1332; *photograph 4*

Ismay, Lady (Laura Kathleen Clegg): 305, 1187, 1236

Isonzo, River: 5, 17

Israel, State of: declared (1948), 410; its place in the Middle East, 439 n.2, 448–9; and a Parliamentary debate (1949), 453–8; Churchill drinks 'to the success of', 557; a message from, 560; and Jordanian-Israeli reconciliation, 623; and the right of passage through the Suez Canal, 624, 625, 658; 'wonderful exertions' of, 663; 'achievements' of founders of, 689; 'courageous efforts of', 723; Churchill's view of place of, in Middle East, 757–8; 'invincibly established as a free and sovereign State', 775; 'deliberate' antagonism of, 788; and the crisis with Egypt (1953–6), 804, 824–5, 945–6, 1191, 1192, 1195–6, 1203, 1204, 1208, 1218, 1219, 1220–2; 'should have her rightful chance', 841; and British arms to Jordan, 900; and British troops for Jordan, 913; and British assistance to Jordan, 964; 'a force in the world', 1093; and the separation of Transjordan from Palestine, 1093 n.1; and the British Commonwealth, 1093, 1095; a gift from, 1096; Churchill contributes to a gift to, 1185; and

Israel, State of—*continued*
terrorism (1945–8), 1233–4; and Sinai, 1234; and 'counsels of peace and moderation', 1283; Churchill 'often' thinks of, 1300; Eden troubled about 'the future' of, 1300 n.2; Churchill's 'good wishes' to, 1330; Churchill's 'long association' with, 1333–4

Israelites (the Jews of Palestine): 646

Istria: 15–17, 42, 44–5, 1058 n.3

Italian Somaliland: 88

Italy: and France, 12, 29, 42; and Potsdam, 62, 80, 88, 97; Churchill's visit to (1945), 132–52; 'peril' in, 201; and the South Tyrol, 260; and Russia, 351 n.3; and Communism, 400; Churchill's visit to (1949), 480–1; and Churchill's war memoirs, 489; and the Council of Europe, 542; and a possible summit, 790

Iwo Jima, battle of (1945): 214

Izvestia: and a 'trap', 971

Jackman, Captain J. J. B.: 443 n.1

Jacob, Lieutenant-General Sir Ian: 373, 404, 778, 1209, 1315 n.3

Jagan, Dr Cheddi: 898

Jamaica: 461, 785; Churchill visits (1953), 793–5; Eden in (1956), 1223, 1224, 1226

James, Henry: 753

James, Dr Robert: 1339

James, Mrs Robert ('Bobby'): 1339

Jamieson, Sir Archibald: 406 n.3

Japan: 3, 8, 9, 10, 12, 13–14, 15; and the British General Election of 1945, 19, 21, 33; preparations for the defeat of, 59, 106; and the Potsdam Conference, 63–4, 68–9, 75, 86, 90, 92–3, 94, 99–100, 119, 191; the atomic bombs on, 119, 249, 259, 966; Victory over, 126, 128, 138, 174–5, 196, 892 n.2; post-war administration in, 166-7, 439: and Russia, 216; and HMS *Exeter*, 508; and the first hydrogen bomb tests, 952; the trade competition of, 963

Jeanne d'Arc (French warship): 31

Jefferis, Brigadier (later Major-General Sir) Millis: 127

Jellicoe, Admiral of the Fleet 1st Earl: 179 n.2

Jerome, Leonard: 193 n.2, 413

Jerome, Lillian: 193

Jerome, Samuel: 193 n.2

Jerusalem: 411, 430, 623, 775, 1095, 1096, 1185, 1268

Jesuits: and Communism, 161

Jesus Christ: his story 'unequalled', 729–30

Jet aircraft: (sale of) 490, 498, 518–19, 527–8, 531, 553; and Soviet air strength, 540

Jewish Agency, the: 251, 335 n.2

Jews, the: 89, 230, 244, 250–3; in Palestine, 295–7, 302, 411, 430, 449, 454–8, 525, 625, 646; in Israel, 689, 1192; their ethical system 'the most precious possession of mankind', 723 n.5; and the Prague trials (1952), 788; and Jerusalem, 1095; 'cruel murder of', 1197 n.6; 'I am their friend', 1233; Churchill 'always a friend of', 1323

Jinnah, M. A.: 248, 276, 292, 335

Joan of Arc (St Joan): 180, 253

Jockey Club, the: Churchill elected to (1950), 563 n.2; and Churchill's Joint Principal Private Secretary, 654; meetings at, 775; Churchill's dinner for, 913

Joel, Colonel H. C.: 312

John, Augustus: 1276 n.1

'John Bull': one of 'our heroes', 911

Johnson, the Very Rev. Hewlett (Dean of Canterbury): 771 n.3

Johnson, Lyndon B. (later President): 1294 n.1

Johnson, Mabel: 4 n.1

Johnson, Dr Samuel: 'admired', 854; adapted, 1337–8

Joll, James: 270

Jones, Professor R. V.: 345, 428

Jones, Sir Roderick: 1225

Jordan, Hashemite Kingdom of: 527, 558, 623 n.4, 663, 841, 900; Churchill opposes British military support for, 913; and a British plan of support for, 964; Army work in, 1125 n.2; and the Suez Crisis (1956), 1204, 1218; its 'survival', 1323

Joubert de la Ferté, Air Vice-Marshal (later Air Chief Marshal) Sir Philip: 237

Journalists: at Potsdam, 71

Journey to the Western Isles of Scotland (Dr Johnson): 854

Jowitt, 1st Earl: 1150

Juin, General Alphonse: 577, 725–6

Jujube, a: Churchill looking for, 594

Juler, Frank: 801

Juliana of The Netherlands, Queen: 569–70, 1362

Julius Caesar: 364, 1073, 1166

Jutland, Battle of (1916): 179 n.2, 1339

Kalinin, Mikhail Ivanovich: 63

Karamanlis, Constantine: 1297

Kars (Turkey): 75, 91, 195

Katmandu (Nepal): 1134

Kaye, Danny: 983

Keenlyside, F. H.: 498–9

Kelliher, Private Richard: 443 n.1

Kelly, Denis: helps Churchill with his war memoirs, 226 n.3, 246 n.1, 331, 338–40, 342–5, 389, 390, 418, 426, 450, 480–1; 'a disgrace to the British Empire', 485; and 'four

Kelly, Denis—*continued*
wasted years', 487; and further work on Churchill's memoirs (1949–53), 493–5, 506, 522, 525, 533, 576, 579, 581, 601, 609, 623, 626, 629 n.1, 632, 663, 735, 877, 879, 892; and work on Churchill's History (1953–58), 876, 1066 n.5, 1144, 1145–6, 1148, 1162, 1165, 1167, 1183, 1186, 1187, 1188, 1205, 1228, 1229, 1230 n.2, 1234, 1235 n.1; and a Soviet Commissar, 520 n.2; and the death of Smuts, 565; and the Quebec Agreement (1943), 595 n.2; and Aneurin Bevan, 607 n.3; and 'the black velvet curtains of eternal sleep', 758; and Churchill's memories of Lord Randolph, 776 n.2; and a favourite story, 885 n.3; at Chequers, 949 n.1; and Churchill's swans, 979 n.3; and *Wuthering Heights*, 988 n.1; and cigars, 1012 n.1

Kelly, Sir Gerald: 524, 965, 1164

Kemsley, Countess (Edith) (wife of 1st Viscount): 421

Kemsley, Countess (Lady Hélène Hay) (wife of 2nd Viscount): 1211

Kemsley, 1st Viscount: 406 n.3, 421–2, 514, 640, 1211

Kenilworth, 1st Baron: 256 n.1

Kennan, Goerge: 194–5, 206

Kenneally, Lance-Corporal J. P.: 443 n.1

Kennedy, President John F.: 1318, 1322, 1327

Kensington Palace Hotel (London): Churchill speaks at (1958), 1283

Kent, Duchess of (Marina): 525, 526, 721, 1073, 1132, 1316, 1340; *photograph 13*

Kenya: Kikuyu of, 788; Mau Mau in, 803–4, 834

Keren (Abyssinia): capture of, 434

Kern, Alfred: 260

Kesselring, Field Marshal Albert: 325

Keyes, Lady (Eva Keyes): 381

Keynes, 1st Baron (J. M. Keynes): 234, 526, 642

Khartoum (Sudan): 796, 821, 822; riots in, 955–6

Khrushchev, Nikita S.: 318 n.3, 889 n.6, 909 n.2, 1095, 1143; and the Geneva Summit (1955), 1154–5, 1168; in India, 1169; in Britain (1956), 1192, 1196; and *On the Beach*, 1250; 'impulsive', 1273; 'tangled negotiations' with, 1275; Churchill answers (1959), 1290; Montgomery visits (1959), 1294 n.4; and Summit talks, 1299, 1306; and disarmament, 1301; and the Paris Summit (1960), 1313; should 'not be allowed' to have it all his own way, 1316; succeeded by Kosygin (1964), 1356 n.4

Kiel Canal: 67, 75, 91

Kikuyu (of Kenya): 788
Killearn, 1st Baron: 646
Kilmuir, 1st Viscount (formerly Sir David Maxwell-Fyfe): 1052 n.1, 1061, 1354
Kim (Kipling): 824 n.4
King Canute: 918
King, Fleet Admiral Ernest J.: 14, 70 n.2, 81-2
King Robert of Sicily (Longfellow): 861, 1266
King, W. Mackenzie: 49, 160-2, 362-3
King-Hall, Commander Stephen: 291, 406
Kipling, Rudyard: 824 n.4
Kirkpatrick, Sir Ivone: 569, 811, 1049
Kirkwood (Churchill's valet): 1144
Kislova, Lidya: 4 n.1
Kitchener of Khartoum, Field Marshal 1st Earl: 797
Klopp, Onno: 665
Knatchbull, Norton (later Lord Romsey): a gift to, 1267
Knatchbull-Hugessen, Sir Hughe: 170-2
Knebworth (Hertfordshire, England): 630
Knebworth, Viscount (Antony Lytton) (son of 2nd Earl of Lytton): killed in action at Alamein, 824
Knollys, 2nd Viscount: 691, 1267-8
Knossos (Crete): Churchill visits ruins at (1960), 1314
Knowland, Senator William F.: 1015-16, 1020, 1029
Koestler, Arthur: 577 n.2
Kolesnikov, Dr: 4 n.1
Koniev, Marshal Ivan: at Churchill's funeral, 1362
Königsberg (East Prussia): 83, 89, 92, 96
Köprülü, Professor Fuat: 834
Korda, (Sir) Alexander: 255, 485 n.1, 532, 1043, 1196 n.4
Korea: 205, 428, 437; war in, 535, 537, 539, 541, 552-4, 561, 564, 572, 577, 580-1, 583, 584 n.1, 592-3, 605, 606, 610, 612 n.1, 617; armistice in, 621; results of war in, 676; American 'fortitude' in, 680; and the Yalu river, 687, 688; and the Middle East, 689; 'deadlock in', 704-5; British forces in, 737, 746-7, 748, 750, 993; use of napalm bomb in, 757; and China, 759; and the 'Red Dean', 771 n.3; possible extension of operations in, 779-80: (in 1953), 790, 790-1; renewed negotiations in, 813, 814, 822, 829, 830, 832-3, 834, 838-9; 'does not really matter now', 861; armistice in, 870; American losses in, 882; one 'major world fact' from, 906; and the possible use of atomic weapons, 917-18; and Stalin's 'encroachments', 1028

Kosygin, Alexei: 1356 n.4, 1360
Kra Peninsula (Malaya): 999
Krajina, Vladimir: 404 n.4
Kremlin, the (Moscow): 239, 258, 290, 352, 417, 432, 459, 463, 464, 467, 510, 556, 599; 'fear' in, 676; the 'architect' of, 685; the 'architects in', 690; 'fear ... of truth' in, 692; alleged plot against, 813 n.2; and Western 'weakness', 828; 'change' in mood of, 830; 'would no doubt think twice', 839; the 'aggressive party' in, 863; and a 'different regime' in, 906; and a 'great shock' to (after 1945), 920; infiltration feared by what was 'bad' in, 922; 'cannot speak of jealousy', 971; 'unable to move troops', 1016; and Churchill's Summit hopes, 1027, 1054; and Churchill's Woodford speech (1954), 1072; and 'co-existence', 1108
Kruger, President Paul: 547
Kuwait: 981
Kuznetzov, Vassili: 318

La Capponcina (Cap d'Ail, French Riviera): 377, 434, 484-5, 759, 761-2, 886-91, 1161-3, 1240, 1242, 1250-1, 1256, 1272-7, 1299, 1315, 1328, 1335, 1343; Churchill's Golden Wedding at, *photograph 33*
La Dragonière (French Riviera): 1212 n.1
La Fayette, Marquis Marie-Joseph: 1343
La Mortola (Italian Riviera): Churchill visits, 1251-2
La Pausa (Roquebrune, French Riviera): Churchill to stay at, 1172-3; Churchill's first stay at, 1173-80, 1181, 1182, 1183; Churchill's second stay at, 1184-90; Churchill's third stay at, 1199-1200; Churchill's fourth stay at, 1210-19, 1220; Churchill's fifth stay at, 1228-1234; Churchill's fifth stay at (continued), 1235-7; Churchill's sixth stay at, 1242-5; Churchill's seventh stay at, 1251-4; Churchill's eighth stay at, 1257-65; Churchill lunches at, 1273; Churchill's ninth stay at, 1278-80; Churchill's tenth stay at, 1285-9; Churchill unable to stay at (1960), 1314-15; Churchill unable to visit, 1328, 1344; Churchill at, *photographs 31, 32*
Labouchere, Henry ('Labby'): 367
Labour Exchanges: 'I am the author of', 566; 'I have been responsible for', 646; and Sir Richard Lloyd-Roberts, 1202 n.1
Labour Government (of 1945-51): and Russia, 118 n.3; and India, 230, 375, 431, 439; and bread rationing, 249 n.2; and Egypt, 230; and Palestine, 230, 375, 430, 439, 458, 625; and Communism, 286; and defence, 289, 436, 610, 665-6, 914; its economic policies attacked, 330-1, 354-5, 507,

Labour Government—*continued*
614, 670; and nationalization, 445–6, 507, 529, 558, 583; and German Field Marshals, 430; and the European Assembly, 433, 622; 'misrule' of, 439–40; and NATO, 118 n.3, 474, 575; and European Union, 495–6; and the United States, 536, 646; and Korea, 552–3, 705, 706; 'defeat but not . . . downfall' of, 568; and Greece, 568; and German rearmament, 574; supported by the Liberals, 595; and 'party strife' (1951), 599; and Persia, 624–5, 640–1; 'legacy' of, 660, 725, 744; 'most important' decisions of, 665–6, 666; and the atomic bomb, 683 n.1, 914, 966, 1023; and the ANZUS pact, 791; and Russia, 953
Labour Government (of 1964–70): 1356
Labour Party, the: and the 1945 Election, 9, 10–11, 19, 20–1, 34, 35, 51, 52, 54–5, 115, 150; in Opposition, 28; and the 'Gestapo', 32–3; and Potsdam, 47–8; the 'stable men' of, 111; in power (1945–51), 147, 155; and United Europe, 287, 398; a 'crime' by, 302; and Conscription (in 1939), 373, 645; and Palestine, 430; and the 1950 General Election, 501–12; and German rearmament, 575, 963, 1003; and 'anti-American elements', 619, 948; and re-nationalization, 731; and Korea, 740; and National Service, 750, 912; 'splits' in, 753; and housing, 763; and a motion of no-confidence, 780, 781 n.1; and Conservative 'incompetence', 780; and the Soviet Union, 953; and payment of Members of Parliament, 980; 'very sensible', 1003; and Churchill's Woodford speech (1954), 1072, 1078–81; 'disunity' in (1955), 1103; 'feebleness' of, 1118; defeated (1955), 1139; 'no animus' against, 1150; and the Suez Crisis (1956), 1210, 1246
Lahore: 299
Laird, Sir James: 256 n.1
Lake Success (Conferences at): 352
Lambton, Lady Katherine ('Kitty'): 888
Lancaster, (Sir) Osbert: 1257
Land, Frank: 616 n.2
Landemare, Mrs G. (Churchill's housekeeper): 108, 631, 983, 988, 1282
Langer, Senator William: 115
Langford-Holt, Sir John: 1351, 1354
Laniel, Joseph: 910, 916, 919, 922, 925–8, 973
Laos: 824
Lascelles, Sir Alan: 108, 109, 245, 312, 446, 447, 453, 479, 512, 597, 693, 704, 810, 822, 823, 843–4, 874; and Churchill's stroke (1953), 849, 852; and a dinner for Churchill (1960), 1315 n.3
Laski, Harold: 47–8, 52

Laughlin, Henry: 468, 552, 1158
Laval, Pierre: 434 n.2
L'Avengro (Lavengro) (Churchill's horse): 'galloping well', 982
Lawrence, T. E. ('Lawrence of Arabia'): 587, 1161
Lawrence, W. A. J.: 259
Lawson, John James: 124
Lawther, Will: 779
Laycock, Major-General Sir Robert: 416, 749 n.1, 1315 n.3
Layton, Elizabeth (later Mrs Nel): 111, 126, 132, 135, 140, 144, 147
Layton, Sir Walter (later 1st Baron): 283 n.2, 398, 481 n.4
Le Père Goriot (Balzac): 890
Le Pretendant (Churchill's horse): 1199, 1200, 1202, 1215, 1245–6
League of Nations, the: 171, 201–2, 230, 358, 511, 571, 699, 834 n.1
Leahy, Fleet Admiral William D.: 86, 124, 195–6
Lease-Lend (Lend-Lease): 67–8, 90, 93–4, 191, 688
Leathers, 1st Baron (later 1st Viscount): 256 n.1, 653, 655, 905 n.1, 1077
Lebanon, the: 841, 1271–2
Leeds (England): Churchill speaks at (1950), 507–8
Lees-Milne, Alvilde: 1251, 1253
Lees-Milne, James: 1250–1
Leger, the (St): 366
Leicester (England): Churchill speaks at (1909), 1211 n.1
Leiden (The Netherlands): 232
Leigh, Vivien (Lady Olivier): 629 n.1, 630, 1248
Lemnitzer, General Lyman L.: 1343
Lenin, V. I.: 'poor . . . hungry', 18; 'no change since' (according to Eisenhower), 923
Leningrad (USSR): 281, 285; Churchill's proposed visit to (1960), 1313
Lennox-Boyd, Alan (later 1st Viscount Boyd of Merton): 730, 1189 n.1, 1191, 1247
Lennox-Boyd, Lady Patricia (Patsy): 421
Leopold III, King of the Belgians: 267
Leros (Aegean Sea): 141
Leslie, Lady (Leonie Leslie): 307 n.1, 874 n.4
Leslie, Sir Shane: 193, 413–14, 743, 1338
Leyte Gulf (battle of): 877
Liberal National Party, the: 19, 20
Liberal Party, the: 19, 21, 23–4, 33, 35, 51, 56; 'reckless and wanton', 168; and social reform, 275, 976–7, 1073–4; and National Service, 319–20; and nationalization of steel, 346; opposes Conservatives, 347; and

Liberal Party—*continued*
Conscription (in 1939), 373; 'betrayed' (at Strasbourg), 482; and the 1950 Election, 501, 503–5, 512; defectors from, 525; and the 1951 Election, 529, 530, 559; and the Korean war, 537; and defence, 559; supports Labour Government, 595; prefers Eden to Churchill, 633; Churchill's 'pride' in, 646; and electoral reform, 797; and Lord Jowitt, 1150; and a discussion at Chartwell, 1157

Liberal principles: and Bechuanaland, 771
'Liberal-Conservative': 503–5
Liberalism: 'attacks Monopoly', 445; and 'Tory Democracy', 888; its 'fundamental principles', 1138
Liberty: 'mere weakness' (Vyshinsky's view), 224; Socialism 'the very negation of', 508
Libya: 956, 957, 1125 n.2, 1203, 1204
Lidderdale, David: 1355
Life magazine: 180, 188, 255, 273, 278, 327, 386, 405, 424, 468, 469, 579, 588 n.1, 631 n.1, 632, 684, 738, 915
Life of the Bee (Maeterlinck): 141, 254
Life of the White Ant (Maeterlinck): 141
Lincoln, President Abraham: 514
Lincolnshire (England): anti-aircraft guns in, 541
Lisbon (Portugal): 979 n.1
Literary Trust (Chartwell Trust): 244–5, 274, 308, 435, 450, 451–2, 461, 533, 603, 628, 974, 1239; and 'the qualities of your heart', 662; and Churchill's 'Herculean labour', 974
Lithgow, Sir James: 256 n.1
Little Entente, the: 168–9
Liverpool (England): bombed, 259; Churchill speaks at (1951), 641
Liverpool Post, the: 647 n.3
Ljubljana Gap, the: 453
Llandudno (Wales): Churchill speaks at (1948), 436–7, 440, 441
Llewellyn, J. J.: 9–10
Lloyd, Selwyn: 756, 832, 844, 855, 872, 951, 976, 987, 1056, 1185, 1314; and the Suez Crisis (1956), 1204, 1214 n.2, 1218, 1219; and Macmillan's Premiership, 1227; elected to the Other Club, 1307 n.7, 1339; becomes Chancellor of the Exchequer, 1316 n.1; Leader of the House of Commons, 1355
Lloyd George, David (1st Earl Lloyd-George of Dwyfor): 41 n.2, 179 n.2, 375, 508, 567, 860; his era recalled, 1073–4; and a 'monument to his memory', 1112–13, 1114; and Balfour, 1327; and the Other Club, 1358 n.4
Lloyd George, Gwilym (later 1st Viscount Tenby): 797, 880 n.1

Lloyd George, (Dame) Megan: 567, 655
Lloyd-George of Dwyfor, Countess (Frances Stevenson): 233, 418
Lloyd-Roberts, Sir Richard: killed, 1202
Lloyds Bank: 1231
Lobban, Miss Bella: 1207
Locarno Treaty, the (of 1925): 831, 869, 896, 933, 935, 998, 999
Locke, Walter: 183–4
Lodge, Henry Cabot: 1294 n.1
London (England): a 'hippopotamus', 4; and a Churchill interview, 219; bombing of, 259, 733; increase in bus and railway fares in, 715; and the hydrogen bomb, 917, 959, 1037; and a possible Summit in (1954), 1031; and a possible NATO Conference in (1954), 1056; agreement on Trieste signed in (1954), 1058
London Agreement, the (1954): 1080, 1082, 1090
London to Ladysmith via Pretoria (Winston S. Churchill, 1900): 447 n.5
London-Paris Agreements (1955): 1102–3, 1105, 1106, 1110
Londonderry (Northern Ireland): Freedom of, 1171
Londonderry, Marchioness of (Frances) (Lord Randolph Churchill's grandmother): 306 n.6
Londonderry, Marchioness of (Helen) (widow of 7th Marquess): 459
Londonderry, 7th Marquess of: dies (1949), 459
Londoners (in 1945): praised, 4
Long Handborough (near Bladon): 1363
Longfellow, Henry W.: 861
Longford, 7th Earl of: 1360
Longwell, Daniel: 188, 342, 386–7, 415 n.2, 493, 603, 632, 684
Look magazine: 1230 n.2
Lord, Flight Lieutenant David S. A.: 443 n.1
Lord Derby 'King of Lancashire' (Randolph S. Churchill): 946, 1312
Lord Hornblower (C. S. Forester): 620
'Lord Moran', a (also a 'Moran'); a stimulant, 901, 902, 908–9, 981
Lord Randolph Churchill (Winston S. Churchill, 1906): 1185 n.4, 1357
Lord Warden of the Cinque Ports, the: 569, 570, 842
Lothian, 11th Marquess of: 1246 n.4
Lourie, Arthur: 1323, 1324, 1329
Lovett, Robert A.: 675 n.2
Loving Cup (Churchill's horse): 734
Low, David: a cartoon by, 1066
Luang Prabang (Laos): 824
Lübeck (Germany): 6, 45

Lucania, SS: 463

Luce, Henry: 188, 212–14, 234, 255, 273, 315, 377, 383, 415 n.2, 469, 489, 493, 603, 915; criticism from, 357

Lugano, Lake: 134, 135, 136

Lumsden, Lieutenant-General Herbert: 'my Lieutenant-General', 350 n.4

Luxembourg: 400, 542, 768

Lvov (Eastern Galicia): 96 n.1

Lyle, 1st Baron: 722

Lyttelton, Oliver (later 1st Viscount Chandos): 308, 470, 506, 638 n.5; and Churchill's second Premiership, 660, 724, 795, 834, 874–5, 1026; leaves active politics, 1052; *for subsequent index entries see* Chandos, Viscount

Lytton, Countess of (Pamela Lytton) (widow of 2nd Earl): 337, 414–15, 506, 525, 562, 597, 630, 727, 824, 988, 1084, 1244; Churchill's letters to, in retirement, 1147–8, 1263, 1307; unwell, 1185, 1186; at Chartwell, 1202; a gift from, 1331 n.5; a message from, 1350

Lytton, 2nd Earl of (Victor Lytton): 631 n.4, 824

MEDO (Middle East Defence Organization): 799–800

MI5: 490–1

McAlpin, Glenda: 1340 n.4

MacArthur, General of the Army Douglas: 350, 439, 545, 581, 584 n.1, 605, 612, 741, 744

Macaulay, Lord: 345, 367, 700, 908

McCleery, Albert: Churchill thanks, 1258 n.1

McCluer, Dr Franc L.: 159 n.1, 197, 289

McCormack Smyth, D. (later Professor): 1326

McCormick, Admiral Lyndon: 679

McCormick, Robert R.: 204

MacDonald, Malcolm: 580

MacDonald, Ramsay: 356, 367–8, 473

MacDougall, (Sir) Donald: 674

McElroy, Neil H.: 1294 n.1, 1295

McGovern, John: 385 n.2

McGowan, 1st Baron: 406 n.3

McGowan, Norman (Churchill's valet): 38 n.3, 576, 578, 585–6, 632

McGrigor, Admiral Sir Rhoderick: 672, 678, 679

McIndoe, (Sir) Archibald: 329

MacKenna, Dr R. M. B.: 621 n.1, 1285, 1289

Mackensen, Field Marshal Eberhard von: 325 n.4

Mackeson, H.: 874 n.2

McKinlay, Adam: 188, 404

Maclay, J. S. (later 1st Viscount Muirshiel): 730 n.4

Maclean, Donald: 888 n.5

Maclean, Mrs Donald (Melinda Maclean): 888

Maclean, (Sir) Fitzroy: 453, 461

MacMahon, Cortlandt: 532

McMahon Act, the (of 1946): 254, 573, 1091, 1186, 1254

MacMillan, General Sir Gordon: 867

Macmillan, Harold (later 1st Earl of Stockton): and the 1945 Election, 20; his by-election (in 1945), 162–3; and the years of Opposition (1945–51), 163–4, 227 n.1, 253 n.2, 321–2, 333, 350–1, 476, 527, 555; and Churchill's political future (1947), 341; and the death of Jack Churchill, 316; and the death of Brendan Bracken, 1274–5; at Chartwell, 350–1; at the Carlton Club (1940), 366 n.1; at the Other Club (1960–5), 1316; and United Europe, 406, 481–4; at Strasbourg, 481–4, 486; returns to Strasbourg, 542–3, 545; and the 1950 Election, 512–13; and the 1951 Election, 529 n.1, 638–9, 642, 643, 645; and defence, 541; and Churchill's war memoirs, 598; his letters to Churchill, 613–14; his diary descriptions of Churchill, 615, 623–4; and Persia, 617; and the formation of Churchill's administration (1951), 655–6, 656; and housing, 748, 884–5; and Churchill's second premiership, 724, 748 n.1, 770, 771, 795, 796, 972, 986 n.1, 1050; and Churchill's stroke (1953), 848, 855, 859, 862; and Churchill's recovery, 880, 883; and the question of Churchill's resignation (1954), 960–1, 990–1, 1037–9, 1047–9, 1051, 1052, 1060, 1061, 1062–3, 1066, 1083, 1084, 1085–6, (1955) 1087, 1095, 1095, 1097, 1102, 1107, 1111, 1113, 1115; becomes Minister of Defence, 1065; and Churchill's years of retirement (1955–65), 1133, 1140, 1146, 1146–7, 1148, 1171, 1185, 1233, 1235, 1290, 1300, 1301, 1337, 1343; and Randolph Churchill's 'trial' biography (of Lord Derby), 1312; 'loyalty and gratitude of', 975; and 'Jaw-jaw', 1004 n.1; and Churchill's Summit hopes, 1031–2, 1034; and hanging, 1182 n.1; and the Suez Crisis (1956), 1203, 1205, 1221 n.4, 1223, 1246; becomes Prime Minister (1957), 1227, 1234; wins the General Election (1959), 1302; sees Churchill in retirement, 1239, 1247, 1249, 1266–7, 1297, 1321–2, 1343; his good wishes, 1262; and Churchill College, Cambridge, 1264; and the publication of wartime telegrams, 1264; and Iraq, 1270, 1272; and Israel, 1323; and the Queen's visit to Ghana, 1330; a gift from, 1331 n.5; sends a Comet, 1335; finds Churchill 'very cheerful', 1337; Churchill's

Macmillan, Harold—*continued*
last letter to, 1345; his last meetings with Churchill, 1348–9, 1351 n.2, 1357; resigns (1963), 1349; and Churchill's death, 1360; his tribute to Churchill, 1364

McNaughton, General Andrew George: 551

McNeil, Hector: 280, 436

McNeill, Angus: 447

Madariaga, Salvador de: 452

Madeira (Churchill's visit to, 1950): 498–9, 500–1

Maeltzer, General: 325 n.4

Maeterlinck, Maurice: 141, 254

Magna Carta, the: 200, 891

Mahdi, the: 797

Maingot, Rodney: 820

Majorelle, Jacques: 381, 587, 588

Makins, Lady (Alice) (later Lady Sherfield); 1009

Makins, (Sir) Roger (later 1st Baron Sherfield): 672 n.2, 686–7, 692, 788, 792, 834, 964, 1007, 1009, 1015; his 'telegram No. 539', 1102–1104, 1110–11

Malakand (North-West Frontier, India): 1319

Malan, Dr Daniel François: 836, 838, 1041 n.1

Malaya: 437, 454, 660, 663, 666–7, 685, 716, 748, 750, 821, 861; Britain's 'costly preoccupation' in, 934; Churchill's desire to 'reinforce', 978; Britain's 'main sector', 994

Malenkov, Georgy: Stalin's successor, 806, 808 n.1, 812, 817, 827, 828, 849, 863, 864, 868; and the Soviet hydrogen bomb, 873; and a possible Summit, 875, 889, 909, 917, 936, 961, 971, 972, 998, 1002, 1019, 1010, 1023, 1027, 1030–1, 1032, 1034, 1036, 1040, 1042; and the Soviet 'heart', 876; and Beria, 888 n.5; and Attlee's visit to Moscow (1954), 1045, 1049; falls from power (1955), 1094, 1109; and Khrushchev, 1143

Malik, Yakov: 940–1, 1002

Malta: 517, 821, 833, 1188–9, 1189 n.1

Mamounia, Hôtel de la (Marrakech): Churchill stays and works at, 376–95, 576–88

Manchester (England): Churchill speaks in (1947), 373–4; Churchill meets Weizmann in (1906), 560 n.2

Manchester Guardian, the: 299, 424 n.4, 525, 627, 902, 947, 952; and Churchill's hydrogen bomb speech (1954), 969, 970; and the Washington talks (June 1954), 1005; a cartoon in, gives pleasure, 1066; and Churchill's Woodford speech (November 1954), 1070–1, 1081; and the call for Churchill's resignation, 1112; and Eden's 'lack of gen-

Manchester Guardian—*continued*
erosity', 1135–6; and Randolph Churchill, 1186, 1224 n.3; and Churchill's first electoral contest (1899), 1301 n.3

Manchuria: 205

Mankind: 'Unteachable', 265; its 'weary shoulders', 511; and an 'unforseeable security' (the Hydrogen Bomb), 907; and atomic energy, 919; and the 'awful secrets' of science, 980; and God, 1098; and Communism, 1108

Manoel, King (of Portugal): 1305

Mansfield Park (Jane Austen): 1310

Mansion House (London): Churchill speaks at (1951), 622; 1165 n.1; (in 1955), 1171

March, Earl of (son of 9th Duke of Richmond): 627 n.2

Margaret, Her Royal Highness The Princess, (later Countess of Snowdon): 174, 312, 598, 752, 764; a gift from, 1073

Margate: Conservative Party Conference at (1953), 855, 869, 871, 873, 878, 881, 884, 887, 889, 893, 894–5; Churchill speaks at, 895–7; and the French 'not pleased with me', 898; and 'the Margate plan' (a pep pill), 901; Churchill speaking at, *photograph 23*

Margesson, 1st Viscount (David): 34, 46, 53, 106, 107, 108, 366 n.1, 649

Marks, Sir Simon (later 1st Baron): 406 n.3, 458 n.2

Marlborough, Duchess of ('Duchess Fanny'): 835 n.4

Marlborough, Duchess of (Mary Marlborough): 369, 744, 1194, 1270

Marlborough, 1st Duke of (John Churchill): Churchill's biography of, 274; letters of, 570; Churchill 'proud' to be in company with, 771; his father's knighthood, 823; a port named after, 1011; and the citizens of Bonn, 1307; a 'Noble spirit', 1365

Marlborough, 7th Duke of (Churchill's grandfather): 835 n.2

Marlborough, 8th Duke of ('Blandford'): 369, 823–4

Marlborough, 9th Duke of ('Sunny'): 391, 742, 824 n.4, 1211 n.4

Marlborough, 10th Duke of ('Bert'): 369, 1270

Marlborough, His Life and Times (Winston S. Churchill, 4 volumes, 1933–8): 344, 424, 435, 596, 1149

Marlene, Lili (Lillie): 486; her song, 579

Marmara, Sea of (Turkey): 93

Marnham, Major: 255 n.2, 256, 257 n.1, 307, 416

Marquand, John P.: 393 n.4

'Marquis of Chartwell': a possibility, 327 n.4

'Marquis of Puddleduck Lane': and Randolph Churchill, 1123–4

'Marquis of Toodledo': a bizarre prospect, 704

Marrakech (Morocco): 57, 236, 263, 357, 373; Churchill works on his war memoirs at (1947–8), 376–95, 412; and Sarah Churchill, 451; 1944 in, recalled, 453; Churchill returns to (1950–1), 576–88; Churchill 'thinking a lot about' (1954), 1060; Churchill returns to (1959), 1283–4; Churchill's enthusiasm for, 1336

Marsh, Sir Edward ('Eddie'): 316, 345, 350, 382, 391, 418, 435, 565, 749; dies (1953), 794–5

Marshall, Arthur G.: 555

Marshall, General of the Army George C.: 61, 69, 70 n.2, 75, 86, 129, 175, 310, 347 n.4; his Plan for Europe, 337, 351, 398, 400, 407; his message to Churchill (1947), 372; dines with Churchill, 373, 793; dines with Mrs Churchill, 384; congratulates Churchill, 691; and Churchill's war memoirs, 761; and Churchill's stroke, 858; sees Churchill (in 1959), 1294

Marshall Plan, the: 337, 351, 399, 400, 406, 463

Marston, Lettice (Mrs Shillingford): 221, 226, 260, 305 n.1, 306, 329 n.2, 341, 373, 374, 383, 389, 424 n.2, 426–7, 431, 595 n.2, 631, 632, 656, 988; for subsequent index entry see Shillingford, Mrs Robert

Martel, Lieutenant-General Sir Gifford: 321 n.2

Martin, Sergeant Clifford: killed (1947), 335

Martin, (Sir) John: 3 n.3, 37–8, 46, 51, 316, 703; and the 'scenario of history', 974

Martinaud-Déplat, Léon: 890

Marx, Karl: 310, 371, 1291

Mary, Her Majesty Queen: 140, 698, 700, 720; dies (1953), 808; Churchill's tributes to, 808–10

Masaryk, Jan: 124, 399

Masaryk Memorial Fund: 470

Masefield, John: 406

Masirah Island: 28 n.1

Mason, Miss Heather: 580 n.2

Massachusetts Institute of Technology (MIT): 461; Churchill's speech at (1949), 464–8; and Churchill College, Cambridge, 1131

Massigli, René: 628, 725

Massingham, Hugh: 991

Massy, Lieutenant-General H. R. S.: 433

Masterman, Charles: 567

Masurian Lakes (East Prussia): 96

Matsu Island (Formosa Strait): 1092

Matthews, 'Doc': 793

Maturin, Miss Gillian: 1140, 1179, 1205, 1238, 1352

Mau Mau (in Kenya): 803–4, 834

Maudling, Reginald: 353, 373–4, 375, 419, 492, 503 n.1, 506, 507, 1337 n.2

Maugham, W. Somerset: 1188, 1237, 1250, 1289

Mavroleon, Ann: 214 n.2

Maxwell-Fyfe, Sir David: 50, 283 n.2, 481 n.4; and Churchill's second Premiership, 653, 721, 770, 777 n.1, 904; for subsequent index entries see Kilmuir, 1st Viscount

Mayer, René: 833

Mayne, the Very Rev. Michael (Dean of Westminster): 795 n.4

Maze, Mrs Paul (Jessie): 1287

Maze, Paul: 1276 n.1, 1287–8, 1289

Meat Marketing Board, the: 903

Melchett, 2nd Baron: 113 n.3

Memories of a Scottish Cavalier (Defoe): 270

Menderes, Adnan: 834–5

Mendès-France, Pierre: 1044, 1049, 1063, 1089

Menzies, Robert ('Bob'): 419, 836, 838–9, 843, 1209; Churchill receives a gift of swans from, 1352

Menzies, General Sir Stuart ('C'): 18–19, 307, 424

Merchant Navy: Second World War deaths in, 28 n.1

Merchant of Venice (Shakespeare): 320

Merckel, Madame: and her villa, 542

Messervy, General Sir Frank: 420

Methodist Conference, the (1954): and atomic weapons, 1022

Metro-Goldwyn-Mayer (MGM): 1204, 1205–6

Metz (France): Churchill to visit, 242; Churchill's speech at (1946), 246–8; Churchill's son recalls, 768

Meyer, Walter (Churchill's valet): 374 n.2, 880, 1144 n.2

Mexico: 172

Miami (Florida): Churchill's stay at (1946), 182–94

Miami Daily News, the: 182

Michael, King (of Roumania): 76, 396, 450

Middle East Treaty Organization (MEATO or METO): 994, 1004, 1028

Middlesex Hospital (London): Churchill a patient in (1962), 1335–7

Mihailovitch, General Dragolub: 212

Mikardo, Ian: 385 n.2

Mikolajczyk, Stanislaw: 102

Mikoyan, Anastas: Harold Wilson brings Churchill a message from (1964), 1352

Mill, John Stuart: 296
Mills, Air Vice-Marshal G. H.: 288 n.3
Mindszenty, Cardinal Jozsef: 460
Mines Eight Hours Bill (1908): 446
Minimum Standard, a: Churchill's proposal
    for (1908), 476 n.2
Missouri, USS: 196, 219
Missouri River, the: 197
Mitchell, Sir Harold: 793
Mitchell, (Sir) Steuart: 714
Mitterand, François: 890 n.1
Modern English Usage (Fowler): 345
Mohammed (Chaudri) Ali: 836, 841
Mohammed Reza Pahlevi, Shah of Iran: 640,
    878, 1095
Moir, Anthony: 131 n.2, 221, 234, 308, 461,
    506, 522 n.5, 801-2, 872, 1207, 1231, 1233,
    1235 n.1, 1285, 1307
Mollet, Guy: 890, 1201, 1214, 1218, 1219,
    1243
Molotov, Vyacheslav: 71, 89, 92, 115 n.2, 195,
    290, 344, 363, 565, 808 n.1; and Churchill's
    hopes for a Summit, 806, 811-12, 812, 819-
    20, 827-8, 863, 889, 909, 1109; at the
    Geneva Conference (1954), 985; a courtesy
    to, 1003; Churchill's telegram to (July
    1954), 1012-13, 1014; and Churchill's con-
    tinuing Summit hopes (1954-5), 1020,
    1023-7, 1028, 1031, 1032-6, 1037; and the
    Geneva Summit (1955), 1154-5
Molyneux (the dressmaker): 886
Molyneux, Major the Hon. Sir Richard: dies
    (1954), 947
Monaco: 152
Monckton, Sir Walter (later 1st Viscount
    Monckton of Brenchley): 234, 752, 782 n.1,
    880, 1060, 1184
Monfalcone (Italy): 8
Mongol hordes: 371
Monkey, a (£500): 550 n.2
Monnet, Jean: 406, 634, 635
Montag, Charles: 144, 146, 149, 262, 385, 395,
    488
Montagne Ste Victoire (near Aix-en-
    Provence): 524
Montague Browne, Anthony: joins Churchill's
    Private Secretariat (1952), 764; Churchill's
    notes for, 948; and Churchill's hydrogen
    bomb speech (1954), 970; his notes and let-
    ters (1954-65), 1012 n.1, 1125; and Chur-
    chill's Woodford speech (1954), 1072; and
    Churchill's early retirement years (1955),
    1146, 1148, 1158, 1160-1, 1163, 1165, 1166;
    (1956), 1176, 1177, 1179, 1183, 1184, 1185,
    1187, 1188, 1197-8, 1205, 1207 n.1, 1210,
    1218, 1219, 1221, 1222 n.2, 1224, 1225;
    (1957), 1227, 1228, 1229, 1233, 1235 n.1,

Montague Browne, Anthony—*continued*
    1236, 1237, 1239, 1242, 1243, 1245, 1248,
    1251, 1252; (1958), 1257, 1259-60, 1261-2,
    1264, 1266, 1268, 1272, 1273, 1279, 1281
    n.4; his guidance, 1282, 1283, 1290, 1293,
    1301; 'a good friend', 1286; and Churchill's
    last years (1959-65), 1288, 1291-2, 1294,
    1302, 1303, 1307-8, 1310, 1314, 1315, 1316,
    1321, 1322, 1323, 1325, 1326, 1328-9, 1330,
    1331, 1332, 1333-4, 1334, 1335, 1338-9,
    1339 n.1, 1341, 1343, 1344, 1347, 1350; and
    Churchill's penultimate visit to the United
    States (1959), 1291-6; and Churchill's last
    visit to the United States (1961), 1322; and
    the Churchill biography (to be written by
    Randolph Churchill), 1312; and Churchill's
    meeting with Ben-Gurion (1961), 1323,
    1324; 'a wise friend', 1348; and Churchill's
    last year, 1351, 1353, 1354, 1355, 1357,
    1358-9; and Churchill's funeral, 1362; *photo-
    graph 35*
Montague Browne, Jane (later Mrs Hoare-
    Temple): 1321, 1322, 1334
Montague Browne, Mrs Anthony ('Nonie')
    (later Lady Sargant): 1187, 1214, 1235 n.1,
    1251, 1284, 1297, 1298, 1308, 1310, 1314,
    1321, 1323, 1325, 1331 n.5, 1334, 1343,
    1344, 1358
Monte Carlo (Monaco): 152-3, 155, 224,
    434, 450, 452, 453, 484, 485, 487, 711,
    739, 762; and Churchill's stroke (1953),
    847; Churchill's visits to (from 1953), 887,
    1166, 1190, 1261, 1298, 1307, 1308, 1319,
    1324, 1328, 1331, 1333, 1334, 1335, 1343-
    4, 1346; and Churchill's search for a villa,
    1216
Montgomery, Field Marshal Sir Bernard
    (later 1st Viscount Montgomery of Ala-
    mein): 31, 59, 60, 81, 140, 160, 174; and
    Egypt, 231; a medallion for, 245 n.5; at
    Chartwell, 257, 498, 861, 1172, 1326-7; and
    an historical enquiry, 262; a protest on
    behalf of, 271; visits Stalin, 309; and
    National Service, 322; letters to Churchill
    from, 349-50, 440, 467, 478, 492, 649; 'self-
    advertising' of, 415 and General Auch-
    inleck, 420 n.2; and German Field Mar-
    shals, 429-30, 433; Churchill's letters to,
    459, 486-7; and the Dieppe raid (1942),
    551; becomes Eisenhower's deputy (1950),
    557 n.1; 'mellowed', 636-7; 'mellow', 717;
    and the European Army, 669; at Chequers,
    729; hears Churchill speak, 769; 'Do get
    well', 854; and a controversial telegram
    (1945), 1070, 1078, 1080; lunches with Chur-
    chill, 1111, 1155, 1156, 1159, 1339 n.1;
    Churchill's praise for, 1171; Churchill's let-

Montgomery, Field Marshal—*continued*
ters to, in retirement, 1178, 1224; 'the dear creature', 1263; his book, 1279; Eisenhower wounded by (1959), 1294; at Woodford (1959), 1305; and Churchill's last years, 1318, 1337, 1347, 1348, 1349; *photograph 4*

Montgomery, David (later 2nd Viscount Montgomery of Alamein): 498

Montmorency, De: 'madcap courage . . . prudent skill', 447

Montreux Convention, the (1936): 75, 91

Moore, Sir Thomas: 1355

Moorehead, Alan: 271–2, 1225–6

'Moran', a (also a 'Lord Moran'): a stimulant, 901, 902, 908–9, 981

Moran, 1st Baron (formerly Sir Charles Wilson): his diary quoted (in 1945), 41, 58, 93, 100–1, 108, 117, 132–3, 133, 135; (in 1946), 243, 257–8, 280, 305–6; (in 1947), 297, 316; (in 1948), 390, 392; (in 1949), 485–6, 487–8; (in 1950), 506, 532; (in 1952), 673–4, 674–5, 677, 678, 683, 684–5, 685, 691, 694, 697, 700, 702–4, 707, 717, 720, 732, 737–9, 749, 758, 762, 779; (in 1953), 801, 802, 805, 817–18, 823, 834, 844, 845, 847–57, 859, 860–4, 913; accompanies Churchill, 57, 132, 135, 139, 143, 147, 148, 390, 391, 395, 481, 485–6, 487–8, 673, 694, 916, 917, 937–8, 996, 1005, 1006, 1009, 1011, 1016–17, 1308; advises Churchill medically, 227, 506, 532, 597, 693, 702–4, 707, 711–12, 778, 786, 1042, 1292–3; helps Churchill with an historical enquiry (Greece, 1944), 263; Churchill's letters to, 389, 472 n.3, 1114; Churchill's speech about, 621; and Eden's illness (1953), 820, 834, 844; and Churchill's stroke (1953), 847–57, 859, 860–4, 867, 868–73, 875, 876, 879–80, 881 n.3, 883; and Churchill's 'innings', 884; and Churchill's recovery, 896, 897, 908–9, 939, 947–8, 953, 958, 965; and the problem of Churchill's resignation, 885, 902–3, 950, 961, 990, 1049, 1066–7, 1087, 1111, 1112; and Churchill's pep pills ('Morans'), 901, 902, 908–9, 958; and Churchill's hydrogen bomb speech (of April 1954), 967, 969–70, 972; and Churchill's Suez Canal intervention (of July 1954), 1037; and Churchill's desire to meet the Russians, 971–2; and Indo-China, 973–4; and Churchill's last year as Prime Minister (1954–5), 976, 1055, 1064, 1067, 1068 9, 1071, 1072, 1073, 1076, 1087, 1093, 1100, 1117; not to accompany Churchill (April 1955), 1114; and Churchill's years of retirement (1955–65), 1133, 1135, 1140, 1144, 1145, 1148–9, 1155, 1162, 1171, 1172, 1181, 1183–4, 1190, 1196, 1197, 1198, 1201,

Moran, 1st Baron—*continued*
1208, 1209–10, 1219, 1223, 1224–5, 1229, 1231–2, 1234, 1235 n.1, 1238–9, 1260, 1261, 1263, 1264, 1266, 1266–7, 1268, 1269, 1285, 1289, 1290, 1292–3, 1294, 1296, 1297, 1298, 1304–5, 1305, 1306, 1307, 1308, 1310, 1317, 1317–18, 1334, 1340; *photograph 4*

Moran, Lady (Dorothy Moran): 389, 391, 488, 1209

Morawski, Edward: 94

Mordaunt, Sir Nigel: 137

Morgenthau, Henry, Jr.: 259

Morgenthau Plan, the (1944): 259–60, 735

Morley, Christopher: 393 n.4

Morley, John (later 1st Viscount): 476 n.2, 646

Morocco: Churchill's visits to, 376–95, 576–88, 1283–4

Morris, (Sir) Rhys Hopkin: 656

Morrison, Mrs Herbert (Edith Meadowcroft) (later Lady Morrison of Lambeth): 1120, 1150

Morrison, Herbert (later Baron Morrison of Lambeth): and the 1945 Election, 19, 20, 36, 40; and the Labour Government (of 1945–50), 117, 131; and the General Election (1950), 501; and the Labour Government (of 1950–51), 515, 608, 623, 624; and Churchill's war memoirs, 189; and Churchill's illness, 339; Churchill's criticisms of, 354, 359; and Russia, 396, 397; Churchill protests to, 403; at Strasbourg, 481–2, 484; succeeds Bevin, 598; and Persia, 618; 'twisted and malevolent', 624; and a motion of censure, 704; his 'venom', 730; his 'courage', 1003; and China, 1030; at Churchill's farewell dinner, 1120, 1150; touches Churchill 'affectionately', 1145; *photograph 6*

Morrison, W. S. (later 1st Viscount Dunrossil): 656, 659

Morrison-Bell, Sir Clive: 366 n.1

Morshead, Sir Owen: 770, 771

Morton, (Sir) Desmond: 34 n.2, 177–8, 356, 760, 1195, 1223

Moscow (USSR): Clementine Churchill in, 3–4; 'control of', over Eastern Europe, 200; 'pressure' exerted by, 201, 209; and 'a single bomb', 258; a message from (1947), 309; attack on (1941), 417; and the Berlin blockade, 431; and Cardinal Mindszenty, 460; and East Anglia, 530; a recollection of (1942), 552 n.1; Stalin dies in (1953), 805; 'new men' in power in, 816; Churchill's proposed visit to, 828; danger of giving a 'sign of weakness' to, 834; an 'opportunity lost' at, 867; Churchill still wishes to visit (1953), 868, 908, 936; Churchill does not want a

Moscow (USSR)—*continued*
  Summit in (1954), 1023, 1027, 1028, 1054; Attlee visits (1954), 1045, 1063; 'weakness makes no appeal to', 1108
Moscow Conference (October 1944): 86, 239, 636, 828, 875, 1192
Moses: Churchill's essay on, 1324, 1329
Moss, Mrs Charles (Doris): 1343, 1344
Mossadeq, Dr Mohammed (also Mussadiq): 617, 639, 640, 642, 756, 763, 807, 824; overthrown (1953), 878
Mother of Parliaments, the: 563
Mount Scopus (Jerusalem): Churchill plants a tree on (1921), 723
Mountain, Sir Edward: 256 n.1
Mountbatten, Countess (Edwina): 105; her death (1960), 1308
Mountbatten, Admiral of the Fleet 1st Viscount (later 1st Earl Mountbatten of Burma): 3, 100, 112–13, 132, 174–5; Churchill lunches with, 249; and India, 298, 299, 332–5, 354; and his nephew's engagement, 341; and Churchill's war memoirs, 423, 550–2; and Churchill's second Premiership, 672–3; visits Churchill at Cap d'Ail, 761–2; and a gift, 1267; and his wife's death, 1308; a message from, 1343
Mountbatten, Lieutenant Philip: 340–1, 359, 362; *for subsequent index entries see* Philip, Prince, Duke of Edinburgh
Mousetrap, a (a sovereign): 500 n.2
Moyle, Arthur: 596
Moyne, 1st Viscount: 725
Moynier, M.: 264
Muggeridge, Malcolm: at Chartwell, 546–8; and an attack on Churchill, 950
Mulberry Harbour, the: 568
Munich Crisis (of 1938): 124, 147, 169, 246, 414, 417, 421 n.2, 430, 732; and the River Nile (in 1953), 795; and hubris (in 1953), 868; and Lord Beaverbrook, 993
Munuswamy (Churchill's former servant): 1282
Murdoch, Sir Keith: 307 n.3
Murphy, Charles V.: 213–14
Murray, Detective-Sergeant Edmund: 576, 578, 586, 603, 889, 1184, 1257, 1259–60, 1278, 1328, 1334, 1337, 1346; *photograph 34*
Murray, George McIntosh: 1135
Murray, Professor Gilbert: 975 n.2
Murrow, Edward R.: 1294
Muslim Brotherhood, the: leaders of, 825, 833
Muslims (of India): 233–4, 248, 291–5, 298–9, 301, 332, 337, 353–4, 375, 439
Mussolini, Benito: 14, 79, 134, 1205 n.4

'Mussy Duck': 824
My Early Life (Winston S. Churchill, 1930): 236, 469 n.3, 1181 n.4, 1204 n.3, 1206, 1207 n.1

NKVD: in Poland, 102
Nagasaki (Japan): 119
Nairn, Bryce: 57, 498, 605 n.2, 1285
Nairn, Mrs Bryce (Margaret): 57, 58, 59, 605 n.2
Napoleon Bonaparte: no history by, 132; Spanish memories of, 218; a small china figure of, 342; and a question at Chartwell, 364; Britain's fight against, 620; his greatness questioned, 729; one of Churchill's favourite stories of, 813; and 'petit mal', 1304; and Churchill, 1311
Napoleon III, Emperor: 808
Narriman, Queen (of Persia): 632
Nash, John: 1276 n.1
Nash's Pall Mall magazine: 562 n.1, 1015 n.1
Nasser, Colonel Gamal Abdul: 946, 1196, 1201, 1203, 1206, 1208, 1210, 1213, 1222, 1247
Nation, the: 205
National Health Service, the: 53, 604, 1260 n.2
National Insurance: 53
National Insurance Act (1954): 1044 n.2
National Liberal Party: 503–5
National Review, the: 1249
National Security Council, the: material still classified by, 924, 1077 n.1
National Service: 516–17, 518, 541, 666, 710, 750, 751–2, 755, 912–13, 914, 950–1, 1136
National Service Bill (1947): 319, 321, 324–5
National Trust, the: 175, 256, 304 n.3, 993, 1077
National Union of Railwaymen, the: does not support engine drivers (1955), 1145
Nationalization: 445–6, 507, 529, 558, 583, 591–2, 621, 656 n.1, 715, 720, 731, 906
Nauta, Max: 1158 n.1
Naval Expenditure: Churchill 'shocked' by certain cuts in, 899
Navon, Yitzhak (later President): 1323–4
Nazimuddin, Khwaja: 779 n.2
Nazis (and Nazism): *see index entry for* Hitler, Adolf
Negev, the (Israel): 1095, 1269, 1329
Neguib, General Mohammed: 747 n.2, 757, 770 n.3, 774, 775 n.1, 793, 795–6, 804, 807, 840–1, 844, 955; succeeded by Nasser, 946 n.2
Negus, Sir Victor: 532, 1268
Nehru, Jawaharlal: 294, 298–9, 335, 473, 583, 836, 839, 842, 857; in London (1955), 1093,

Nehru, Jawaharlal—*continued*
1094; and Communism, 1094, 1095; and
'Nehruism', 1162; a letter from, 1194
Neisse River, the (Eastern Neisse): 88, 926
Neisse River, the (Western Neisse): 82, 88, 95,
116, 117, 926
Nel, Elizabeth (formerly Elizabeth Layton):
38 n.3, 144 n.1
Nel, Frans: 144
Nelson, Horatio: his dictum, 31; a small china
figure of, 342; his bust, 1147; and Antigua,
1310
Nemon, Oscar: 770–1, 1114 n.2, 1147, 1158
n.1
Nepal: 803
Netherlands, The: 212; Churchill's visit to
(1946), 232–3; and a third world war, 258;
and United Europe, 266–7, 542; and Churchill's war memoirs, 549
'Never Despair': 466, 733, 1155
New Commonwealth, the: 287
New Delhi (India): 233, 234, 335
'New Look', the: and the Soviet Union, 920,
923, 1143
New Statesman, the: 424 n.4, 673
New York (USA): 196, 212, 214–15, 216, 219;
and Tel Aviv, 457; Churchill's speech in
(1949), 463–4, 467; and the Arctic regions,
483; Churchill visits (1952), 674, 683–5,
693–4; and the hydrogen bomb, 959; Churchill's broadcast to (1954), 969; Churchill's
brief visit to (1954), 1011; and the Suez
Crisis (1956), 1223; a final visit to (1961),
1322–3
New York Herald Tribune, the: 467
New York Times, the: 219, 327, 328, 424, 468,
469, 579, 612 n.2, 684, 915; finds Churchill
'only a shadow', 964–5; and the Suez Crisis,
1246
New Zealand: 13, 117, 307, 343, 371, 446, 493,
498; and Malaya, 716; defence of, 762–3,
993 n.2
Newcastle (England): Churchill speaks at, 647
Newcastle United: retains Football Association
Cup, 725
Newfoundland: 916 n.1
Newmarket (England): 570
News Chronicle, the: 346, 616, 1259
News of the World, the: 647
Newsletter: 528
Newspaper Strike, the (1955): 1125, 1132–3
Nice-Matin, the: 1166
Nicholl Manisty (solicitors): 1206–7
Nicholls, Hamar: 566 n.1
Nicholson, Sir William: 1153
Nicolson, (Sir) Harold: 49, 149–50, 661, 705,
707; records Churchill's obituary (1953),

Nicolson, (Sir) Harold—*continued*
873; Churchill a reader of, 1015; and an
Award ceremony (1956), 1225–6; and a
'monstrous caricature', 1240–1
Nicolson, Nigel: 705, 707
Niemöller, Pastor Martin: 284
Nigeria: a Royal visit to, 1177
Nightingall, Walter: 488, 627, 1200
Nikopol (South Russia): 623 n.3
Nile Delta, the: 946
Nile River, the: and the Munich Crisis (of
1938), 795
Nile Valley, the: 231
Nimitz, Fleet Admiral Chester W.: 207–8
Nine-Power Agreement (1954): 1058, 1062
1984 (George Orwell): 801
Nixon, Vice-President (later President) Rich-
ard M.: 997, 1010, 1262 n.8
Nkrumah, President Kwame: his 'vilification'
of Britain, 1330; 'corrupt and tyrannical',
1331
Nobel Prize for Literature, the: 898, 900, 901,
937, 938
Non Stop (Churchill's horse): 734
Norfolk, 16th Duke of: 1347
Normanbrook, Lady (Ida Mary): 1351 n.2
Normanbrook, 1st Baron: 1351 n.2 (*for earlier
index entries see* Brook, Sir Norman)
Normandy Landings (June 1944): 236, 271, 419
n.4, 568, 597, 609, 669 n.1, 892 n.2; and the
Norman Conquest (of 1066), 1167; and the
Sinai, 1234; twentieth anniversary of, 1352
North Atlantic Treaty Organization (NATO,
formerly the Atlantic Pact): formation of,
118 n.3, 463, 467, 474, 475, 491, 498, 509,
574, 595, 598, 619, 666, 676, 677; 'broadening out', 686; and the Atlantic Command,
692; and British forces in Germany, 726;
Lord Ismay becomes Secretary General of,
746 n.2; and Franco-German friendship,
774; and Germany, 829–30, 895–6, 918,
926–8; and France, 833, 940; and Turkey,
835, 1018; and the Suez Canal, 840, 915;
and Egypt, 932; and British trade with
Russia, 912; and National Service (in Britain), 913; and Britain, 922; and Russia, 957,
959, 1029, 1082, 1098; proposed extensions
of (SEATO, METO), 993–4; discussed at
Washington (June 1954), 998, 1003; and
the defence of freedom, 1004, 1248; and a
possible Summit with the Soviets, 1028;
'desultory discussion' about, 1047; and Western defence, 1056, 1090; and the 'anxieties'
of 1945, 1080; danger of 'disarray' in, 1109;
and the Four-Power talks (1955), 1151; and
trade with Russia, 1295
North Cape, the: 77

North Korea: 535, 561 n.3, 577 n.1, 739, 800, 811, 812, 917
North Pole: 483, 1134
North Sea, the: 7, 277
Northanger Abbey (Jane Austen): 1334
Northcliffe, 1st Viscount: 182 n.2
Northolt (London): 488
Northumberland, 10th Duke of: 1307 n.7
North-West Frontier (of India): 337
Norway: 212
Norwegian Campaign (1940): 237, 388
Norwich, 1st Viscount (Alfred Duff Cooper): 749 n.1, 898, 947, 1225, 1226
Nuclear Strength: and 'saturation point', 1091, 1152
Nuclear Tests; (in 1945), 59; (by France), 535 n.2, (by Britain), 764; (by the United States), 772, 952, 959–60
Nuclear Weapons: 'a definite and substantial security', 1090; American 'mastery' in, 1098–9; and the Iron Curtain, 1099
Nuffield, Countess: 256
Nuffield, 1st Viscount: 256, 406 n.3
Nuremberg War Crimes Trials: 190, 249, 284, 285
Nuri-al-Said, Pasha: and Suez, 1218; murdered, 1270, 1283
Nutting, (Sir) Anthony: 832, 882, 894, 1221
Nye, General Sir Archibald: 551 n.2

Oaks, the: 366
Oaksey, 1st Baron: 749 n.1
Oberon, Merle: 484–5
O'Brien, Gerald: 506, 1100
O'Brien, (Sir) Tom: 888
Observer, the: 154, 424 n.4; and Churchill's 'ascendancy', 991; and the Blackpool Conference (1954), 1064
Oder River, the: 82, 83, 87, 95, 102, 238
Odessa (USSR): 281, 285
Odette (film): première of, 532
Odhams (Publishing House): 255
O'Dwyer, William (Mayor of New York): 214
Offenhauser, Emil: 343 n.1
Ogier, Major John: 133, 137, 147, 151, 152–3, 152, 154, 155, 985
Ogilvy, Angus: 1340, 1344
Oil: a dispute over, 986; and 'oilism', 999; and the Middle East crisis (1956), 1191–2; and Churchill's initiative (in 1914), 1235; and Onassis, 1333
Okinawa: Japanese resistance ends on, 44, 86; recalled, 214
Old Age Pensions: 275, 323, 646, 977, 1044, 1051
Oldham (England): Churchill elected at (1900), 560 n.1, 1301

Olga, Princess: 525 n.2
Oliver, Vic (former husband of Sarah Churchill): 190 n.3
Olivier, (Sir) Laurence (later Baron): 175 n.5, 629 n.1, 1172
Olney, Austin G.: 623, 632
Oman, Carola: 1149
Omdurman, Battle of (1898): 133, 183, 447, 1072; and 'a spoil-sport in the hole', 1161; a film of, 'stirred my memory', 1183
On the Beach (Neville Shute): 1250
Onassis, Aristotle ('Ari'): 1173, 1174, 1175, 1176, 1180, 1181, 1190, 1235, 1238 n.1; an historical criticism from, 1194; and Churchill's search for a villa, 1216–17; his generosity, 1245; his yacht, and his hospitality, 1253, 1261, 1275, 1277, 1318, 1319; dines at La Pausa, 1257, 1279, 1288; dines at La Capponcina, 1273; Churchill lunches with, 1289; Churchill's first cruise with (1958), 1277–8; Churchill's second cruise with (1959), 1284–5; Churchill's third cruise with (1959), 1297–8; 'very attentive', 1308; Churchill's fourth cruise with (1960), 1308–11; dines with Churchill in London, 1311; Churchill's fifth cruise with (1960), 1313–14; and Churchill's sixth cruise with (1961), 1321–3; Churchill thanks, 1328; a gift from, 1331 n.5; and Churchill's seventh cruise with (1962), 1333–4; at the Other Club, 1339; 'related at last!' (1961), 1339 n.1
Onassis, Tina: 1235, 1273, 1279, 1284, 1288; *for subsequent index entry see* Blandford, Marchioness of (Tina)
One Day in the Life of Ivan Denisovitch (Solzhenitsyn): 1258
One Way to Stop War (Winston S. Churchill, article by, 1947): 291
'Operation "Hope Not"': 1347
'Operation Rodeo': 825
Operator 18: a message from, 1322
Oppenheimer, J. Robert: 998, 1003
Order of the Garter, the: Churchill declines (1945), 109, 822; and Eden, 111, 1066; and a bust at Windsor, 771; Churchill 'resplendent' in, 835; Churchill wearing, 1122; and Ismay, 1239; and the Garter ceremony, 993, 1245, 1246, 1313; on Churchill's coffin, 1362
Order of Merit, the: 177–8, 1122
Orpen, (Sir) William: 853
Orwell, George: 801
Osborne, June (later Mrs Randolph Churchill): 435, 451; *for subsequent index entries see* Churchill, Mrs Randolph
Oslo (Norway): Churchill's speeches in (1948), 409–10

Oster, Ewald: 343 n.1

Other Club, the: 318, 565, 615, 739, 748, 948, 1235; Churchill's tribute to Lord Cherwell at, 1248; Churchill's presence at, in his last years, 1266–7, 1281, 1285, 1290, 1308, 1311, 1316, 1331, 1339, 1340, 1341, 1350, 1351, 1357; Churchill's nominees for, 1307; Aristotle Onassis at, 1339; Churchill's last excursion to (10 December 1964), 1358; tributes to Churchill at (18 February 1965), 1364

Ottawa (Canada): Churchill's visit to (in 1952), 685; his speech at, recalled, 732 n.1; Churchill's visit to (in 1954), 1010–11, 1019

Ouistreham: and Westerham, 1167

Pacific Ocean, the: 3, 6, 75, 214; defence plans for, 791–2; a threat to, averted, 920; hydrogen bombs exploded in, 772, 957

Pacific Union Club (San Francisco): 1272 n.4

Paget, General Sir Bernard: 30–1, 36

Paget, Reginald (Baron Paget of Northampton): 517, 1036

Paice, Sergeant Mervyn: killed (1947), 335

Painting: Churchill's relaxation (in 1945), 57–8, 134–7, 140, 142, 143, 144–5, 146, 148–9, 151–2, 153–4, 156; (in 1946), 180, 186, 190, 255, 257, 261, 262, 268 n.1, 278, 306; (in 1947), 308, 308–9, 327, 381, 383, 384; (in 1948), 424, 428, 429, 444; (in 1949), 481, 488; (in 1950), 548, 562, 569, 576, 577, 579, 581, 585, 585–7; (in 1951), 597 n.5, 598, 600, 615, 630, 634; (in 1952), 725, 762, 772; (in 1953), 887; (in 1954), 965; (in 1955), 1128, 1133, 1134, 1139, 1152–4, 1173; (in 1956), 1179, 1181, 1214, 1215; (in 1957), 1251, 1255, 1256; (in 1958), 1258, 1259, 1268; (in 1959), 1284, 1285, 1287–8, 1296, 1297; (in 1960), 1315; a gift of (1964), 1354; Churchill 'too feeble' to embark on (1944), 453; and a reference to the Labour Government's policy in Germany, 495

Painting As a Pastime (Winston S. Churchill, 1948): 562 n.1, 1158

Pakistan: 332, 712, 787, 803, 943, 951; and SEATO, 993 n.2, 994; and MEATO, 994 n.1, 1018

Palace of Westminster, the (London): 562

Palestine (British Mandate): 137, 186 n.2, 229, 230, 231, 244, 250–3, 300–1, 302, 335–6, 359–60, 375, 439; and Nazi crimes, 250; and the State of Israel, 410–11, 430, 453–9; and hatreds 'in equal degree', 625; and Transjordan, 1093 n.1; for subsequent index entries see Israel, State of

Palestine Royal Commission (1936): 455 n.1

Palestine White Paper (of 1922): 457

Palestine White Paper (of 1939): 155

Paling, Wilfred: 403 n.3

Palmerston, Viscount: 808

Panama: the Queen at (1953), 914 n.4

Panama Canal, the: and Suez, 933

Panda, the: 254

Pandit, Mrs Vijaya Lakshmi: 1094

Pan-European Union: 242

Panmunjon (Korea): talks at, 811, 834, 870

Paris: Churchill speaks in, 166; and a Churchill interview, 219; Churchill visits (1946), 267; and Marrakech, 578; Churchill decorated by de Gaulle in (1958), 1280, 1281; and the Communist vote (1959), 1286 n.1; and a disrupted Summit (1960), 1313

Paris Agreements (London–Paris Agreements, 1955): 1102–3, 1105, 1106, 1110

Park, Air Vice-Marshal (later Air Chief Marshal) Sir Keith: 270

Parkinson, Sir John: 878

Parkside Farm (near Chartwell): purchased (1946), 306

Parliament Square (London): future lay-out of, discussed, 1095

Parrots: 'begin to jabber', 18

Parry, W. E.: 283 n.4

Passchendaele, Battle of (1917): 581, 583, 1253 n.5

Pathé Studios (London): 506

Patton, General George S.: 546

Paul, Prince Regent (of Yugoslavia): 525

'Pausaland' (La Pausa, French Riviera): Churchill's love of, 1207, 1208, 1210, 1220, 1224, 1236, 1246, 1251, 1255, 1256, 1278, 1291, 1299, 1300, 1305; photographs 31, 32

Pavelitch, Ante: 212

Pavlov, Vladimir (Stalin's interpreter): 74, 115 n.2

Paynter, Brigadier-General Sir George: dies (1950), 548

Peacock, Sir Edward: 256 n.1

Peake, Major George Herbert: 1044

Peake, Osbert (later 1st Viscount Ingleby): 1044, 1065

Pearl Harbor: 68, 183, 959

Peck, (Sir) John: 49–50, 81, 166 n.2, 228

Peenemünde (Pomerania): 405

Peking (China): Attlee and Bevan visit (1954), 1045; and Formosa, 1092

Peking Radio: 822

People, the: a libel action against, 1214, 1215

Peres, Shimon: 1219 n.2

Persia (Iran): 67, 194–5, 201, 205, 214–15, 216, 217, 428, 535 n.2, 553; crisis in (1951),

Persia (Iran)—*continued*
617–18, 619, 622, 624, 625, 628, 639, 640, 642, 646, 685; and the need for 'assistance' in, 676; an Anglo-American joint message to, 756; and the Communists, 788, 788–9; in 1953, 790, 824, 878, 880; and the Baghdad Pact, 994 n.1; and Egypt, 1018

Persian Gulf, the: 194, 617, 618, 782; a crisis in, 986–7

Persuasion (Jane Austen): 1334

Perth (Scotland): Churchill speaks in, 411

Pétain, Marshal Philippe: 434 n.2, 622 n.2

Pethick-Lawrence, 1st Baron: 294 n.1

Petter, Sir Ernest: 739

Pharaoh: and Herbert Morrison, 131

Philip, His Royal Highness The Prince, Duke of Edinburgh, *for earlier index entries see* Mountbatten, Lieutenant Philip: 385 n.2, 638, 662, 697, 764, 789, 842, 914, 942, 976, 992; a gift from, 1073; dines at 10 Downing Street, 1120–22, 1127; his 'remarkable qualities', 1128; a message from, 1177; and the Winston Churchill Memorial Trust, 1272 n.4; accepts Visitorship of Churchill College, Cambridge, 1300–1; his message from the Malakand, 1319; presides over the formal opening of Churchill College, 1352; at Churchill's funeral, 1363; *photograph 24*

Philippines, the: 716, 993 n.2, 999

Phillips, Lady (widow of Admiral Sir Tom Phillips): 487

Phillips, Admiral Sir Tom: 487

Pierssené, (Sir) Stephen: 620 n.2

'Pigeon Vole' (Churchill's horse): 874, 988

Piggott, Lester: 1200, 1202

Pigs: 'used to find olives', 18; 'treat us as equals', 304

Pim, (Sir) Richard: 61, 106, 109, 111, 127, 1331 n.5

Pinay, Antoine: 628 n.2

Pineau, Christian: 1219

Pinza: wins the Derby, 842

Pirelli, Arnaldo (Italian industrialist): his villa, 150, 152

Pitblado, (Sir) David: and Churchill's second Premiership, 654–5, 665, 672 n.2, 718, 845; and Churchill's stroke, 858, 874, 879, 883; and Churchill's recovery, 898; and the Bermuda Conference, 916, 917; and Churchill's performance (in 1955), 1093; and the Suez Crisis (1956), 1222 n.2

Pitt the Elder (Lord Chatham): 247

Pius XI (Achille Ratti), Pope: 870

Pius XII (Eugenio Pacelli), Pope: 792, 870

Plain Dealer, the: 413 n.6

Plate, Battle of the River (1939): 508

Pleven, René: 588–9, 593 n.1, 628 n.2

Pleven Plan, the: 593 n.1, 635, 1057

Pleydell-Bouverie, Mrs Audrey: 127, 982

Pleydell-Bouverie, Major Peter: 982 n.2

Ploegsteert ('Plug Street', Belgium): 186

Plowden, Sir Edwin: 997 n.1

Plumb, (Sir) John (J.H.): 1148, 1194

Plymouth (England): Churchill speaks at (1950), 537; (1951), 647–8

Poetic (Churchill's horse): 524

Poett, J. H. N.: 288 n.3

Pol Roger, Madame Odette: 589, 630 n.1, 983, 1206, 1263, 1331 n.5

Pol Roger (Churchill's horse): 734, 785

Pola (Pula): 8, 28–9, 42–3

Poland: political future of, 5, 6, 7, 8, 14, 25, 44; discussed at Potsdam, 63, 72–4, 82–5, 86–8, 94–7, 101–3; Germans 'hunted out' of, 154, 224; the night of the invasion of (in 1939), 177; and Churchill's Fulton speech, 201, 212; Soviet 'control' over, 238, 239, 279, 288, 510; and Churchill's war memoirs, 412–13, 418, 810; and Yalta, 428; and Spain, 452; its frontiers 'not . . . settled', 454; its army, 539; and a 'show-down', 635; and the British guarantee of 1939, 645, 791; and Korea, 829; to be a 'buffer', 831; 'subjugated', 953; and Stalin's 'encroachments', 1028; its fate (in 1945), 1079

Policeman's knock: 'dread of', 408

Polling Day: (in 1945), 57; (in 1950), 511, 512; (in 1951), 648–9; (in 1955), 1139; (in 1964), 1356

Pollitt, Harry: 403

Pompey (USA): 174, 193

Ponsonby, Colonel Charles Edward: Churchill a constituent of, 600

Poole, Cecil: 611

Poole, Oliver (later 1st Baron): 1221

Pope, Alexander, 867

Popescu-Nasta, Liviu: 1217

Popiel, Karol: 96

Port Arthur: 67

Port Said (Egypt): 957, 1214 n.2, 1220–1

Port Stanley (Falkland Islands): 708

Portal, Marshal of the Royal Air Force Sir Charles ('Peter') (later Viscount Portal of Hungerford): 70 n.2, 110, 125, 126, 480 n.1; Churchill's guest, 373; and Jane Portal, 514 n.3; and Churchill's war memoirs, 622; and Churchill's second Premiership, 653, 797; and a dinner for Churchill (1960), 1315 n.3

Portal, Jane (later Lady Williams of Elvel): 492 n.4, 514, 631, 632–3, 634; and Churchill's second Premiership, 656, 697, 724, 760, 802, 836, 860, 886, 887, 891, 897, 961, 980, 1043, 1045, 1049, 1059, 1063, 1097, 1111

Portal, 1st Viscount (Wyndham Portal): 256
n.1
Portugal: 220 n.1
Potsdam Conference (1945): preparations for,
42–5; Churchill reaches, 60–1; sessions of,
62–103; Churchill leaves, 104; after Churchill's departure, 108, 115, 119; and Poland,
239; 'when the blow fell', 258; recollections
of, 332, 428, 636 n.1, 792, 829; a possible
renewal of (1952), 756, 819; and Churchill's
war memoirs, 810; and the Kremlin's
thoughts after, 920
Pound, Admiral of the Fleet Sir Dudley: 489,
979 n.2
Powell, Air Commodore: 378 n.2
Powell, Enoch: 298, 312
Powell, Miss Robin: 1335, 1340
Pownall, General Sir Henry: 308, 315, 339, 341–
2, 345, 382, 383, 389, 415 n.2, 416 n.2, 420,
426, 427, 428, 431, 434, 450, 470, 471, 474,
479, 480 n.1, 493, 495, 506, 522, 568; accompanies Churchill to Marrakech, 576, 578,
581, 582, 586; and the continuing work on the
war memoirs, 597, 601, 609, 623, 626, 629,
n.1, 632, 663, 735; at Chequers, 949 n.1;
and Churchill's Woodford speech (1954),
1072; and a dinner for Churchill (1960),
1315 n.3
Prague (Czechoslovakia): 124, 200, 209, 399,
428, 437, 546, 582; trials in, 788
Pravda: criticisms of Churchill in (1946), 208–
9, 211–12, 213; and a possible Summit
(1953), 831; and Churchill's Woodford
speech (1954), 1072, 1080
Premonition (Churchill's horse): 886, 987
Price, Detective-Sergeant C. S.: 374, 378 n.1
Price, Thomas: 616
Primrose League, the: 321, 366, 607, 721, 972,
1186, 1190–1, 1240, 1266
Prince Arthur (Churchill's horse): a bet on,
826; 'the mass overtook him', 982; further
hopes for, 987
Prince of Wales, HMS: 979 n.2
Princess Royal, The (sister of King George
VI): 1073
Princess Victoria (ferry boat): sinks, 807
Prioux, General R.: 418 n.6
Prisoners-of-war: 60, 98, 138–9, 475–6, 513;
at Chartwell, 146, 164, 176, 326–7, 343,
383, 476; Churchill's speech concerning,
263–5; and Korea, 822; in antiquity, 1128
Pritt, D. N.: 385
Profumo, John: 39, 513, 1307 n.7, 1316
Providence: and Israel, 557; and Churchill's
old age, 563; and Princess Elizabeth, 662–3;
and Churchill's war memoirs, 761; and a
'gleaming figure', 836

Pryce-Jones, David: 1296
Public Faces (Harold Nicolson): 1015
Publish and Be Damned (Hugh Cudlipp): 888
n.1
Puck: and Churchill, 141
Pugh, Miss Doreen: 1140, 1148, 1161, 1163,
1190, 1203, 1267, 1285, 1287, 1338, 1352,
1356, 1358
Pullar, Hugh: 576, 577, 585
Punch: and Churchill's schooldays, 867; a hos-
tile cartoon in, 950; a poem in, recalled,
1119
Punjab, the: 400, 439
Pusan (Korea): 561 n.3, 583
Pyrenees, the: 'the strategy of holding', 543
Pytheas of Massalia: 1194

Quaglino's Restaurant (London): 1331
Quebec Agreement, the (of 1944, on the
atomic bomb): 157, 254, 572–3, 595, 684,
1091; and the hydrogen bomb debate (of
1954), 966, 967, 970, 978; a special debate
on (1954), 978, 979; and James Byrnes,
1054
Quebec Conference, the (of 1943): 130, 182 n.2
Quebec Conference, the (of 1944): 259
Queen Elizabeth, RMS: 179, 180–2, 462, 1011–
12, 1018, 1032, 1220, 1224, 1255
Queen Mary, RMS: 219, 467, 469, 672–4, 684,
693, 694–5, 787–9, 1322
Quemoy Island (Formosa Strait): 1092
Quennell, Peter: 3, 762, 1269 n.2
Quentin Durward (Walter Scott): 877
Queuille, Henri: 628 n.2
Quickswood, 1st Baron (formerly Lord Hugh
Cecil): 112, 317, 1077–8
Quinquennial Act, the (of 1911): 905, 1118
Quislings, the: and the Kremlin, 464

RSPCA: 366
Raczyński, Count Edward: 418
Radescu, General Nicolae (Roumanian Prime
Minister): 212
Radford, Admiral A. W.: 973
Radley, Major Arthur Farrand: si monumentum
requiris, circumspice
Raeburn, Mr Speaker (Sam): 1294 n.1
Railways Act (1921): 715
Rainier of Monaco, Prince: 1287, 1288
Ralli, Sir Strati: 365 n.2, 374 n.2
Ramsey, Dr Arthur Michael (later Baron),
(Archbishop of Canterbury): 1359
Randolph, USS: 1279, 1281
Rangoon (Burma): 3
Rank, J. Arthur (later 1st Baron): 256 n.1
Rat: the name of 'disgraced', 1150
Rationing: gradual abolition of (1953–4), 797

Rattigan, (Sir) Terence: 1278
Rea Brothers Ltd: 1282
Reading, 1st Marquess of: 525 n.1
Reading, 2nd Marquess of: 522, 525
Rearmament: in Germany, 574; in Britain 'hardly begun', 621; and an Excess Profits Tax, 639; and the Korean War, 676; and Communism, 677, 688; and Butler's 1952 Budget, 724; plans for, 749; under Labour, 914; and the Free World (since 1945), 920; by Russia, 940; by Western Germany, 963, 1003, 1007, 1070
Recorder, the: 983
Red Air Force, the: 280 n.4
Red Army, the: 25, 76, 84, 88, 280 n.4, 288
Red Cross, the, International Committee of: Churchill's speech to (1946), 263–5; helps a prisoner-of-war, 513
'Red Menace': 209
Red Winter (a racehorse): 'offended', 979
Reid, Thomas: 456
Remarque, Erich Maria (Erich Kramer): 887 n.3
Rengo Press, the (Tokyo): 546 n.2
Rennell, 1st Baron: 525 n.1
Rennell, 2nd Baron: 525
Reparations: 312, 343 n.1
Repulse, HMS: 979 n.2
Reuters: 391, 1225
Reves, Emery: and Churchill's war memoirs, 187–8, 273–4, 307 n.3, 308, 382, 392, 393–4, 412, 415 n.2, 418 n.6, 468–9, 484, 568–9, 626, 802 n.2, 1078, 1158 n.1; and Churchill's retirement years (1955–65), 1165, 1166, 1172–3, 1174, 1175, 1180, 1181, 1183, 1190, 1196, 1199, 1200, 1208, 1209, 1210, 1220, 1223, 1224, 1228, 1229–30, 1233, 1234, 1237, 1254, 1255, 1256, 1257, 1260, 1266, 1279, 1285, 1300, 1302, 1307, 1314–15, 1328, 1338, 1350; learns bezique, 243; taken ill, 1300; Churchill's last meeting with, 1344; *photograph 30*
Reves, Wendy (Wendy Russell): Churchill bidden to lunch with, 1165; Churchill the guest of, 1172–3, 1174, 1175, 1176, 1177, 1179, 1180, 1184–90, 1210–20, 1228–34, 1235–7, 1238 n.1, 1251–4, 1257–65, 1278–80, 1285–9; Churchill lunches with, 1273; Churchill's letters and telegrams to, 1180–1, 1196, 1199–1200, 1207–8, 1209, 1210, 1220, 1224, 1228, 1234, 1238, 1239–40, 1246, 1254, 1255, 1256, 1265–6, 1273, 1278, 1281, 1291, 1300, 1302, 1305, 1315, 1328, 1344; Clementine Churchill's letters to, 1220, 1253, 1258, 1280–1, 1315; her letters and messages to Churchill, 1306, 1307, 1350; unwell, 1314–15; Churchill's last meeting with, 1344

Reynaud, Paul: on VE day (1945), 3; and Churchill's war memoirs, 356, 426, 429; and United Europe, 406; and Western European defence, 540; Churchill dines with (1951), 588, 634; Churchill lunches with (1959), 1288–9; a message from (1963), 1350; at Churchill's funeral (1965), 1362
Reynolds News: 287
Rhee, Syngman: 833, 849, 861
Rhine River, the: 91, 181, 345, 436, 637, 1193 n.1
Rhineland, the (Germany): 87, 168, 171, 287
Rhinoceros, 'a great' (and London): 4
Rhodes (Italy, later Greece): 419 n.4, 1058
Rhys Williams, (Lady) Juliet: 398
Ribbentrop, Joachim von: 449
Richard III (Shakespeare): 888
Richards, Denis: 480
Richards, (Sir) Gordon: 842
Richardson, Mr (Superintendent of Ambulance Services, Middlesex Hospital): 1337
Richardson, Miss D. E.: 1069
Richmond (Virginia, USA): Churchill speaks in, 207; Churchill's visit to (1929), 915 n.2
Richmond, Duchess of (wife of 9th Duke): 627
Richmond, 9th Duke of: 627
Rickett, Sir Denis: 690–1, 789 n.2
Ridgway, General Matthew B.: 743, 769
Ritz Hotel (Paris): 242
Rob, Professor Charles: his medical advice, 1296; Churchill's talks with, 1297
Rob Roy (Sir Walter Scott): 1267
Robersons (artists' suppliers): 429
Roberts, Field Marshal 1st Earl: 369
Roberts, Sir Frank: 920 n.1, 930, 1341
Roberts, Dr John: 485, 1184, 1188, 1211, 1219, 1229, 1230, 1231–2, 1243; and Churchill's illnesses (1958), 1261, 1264, 1265, 1286, 1335; and Churchill's recovery, 1279
Robertson, General Sir Brian: 815
Robinson, W. S.: 377
Rochester (New York State): 413 n.6, 1297
Rodgers, Lieutenant (later Captain) A. D. D. ('Tim'): 135, 149, 151, 152, 153, 985
Rokossovsky, Marshal Konstantine K.: 539
Roman Catholic Church, the: and Russia, 258; and liberty, 443; and celibacy, 758
Roman Empire, the: and the United States, 216; and a 'United States of Europe', 232
Romilly, Giles (son of Nellie Romilly): 752
Romilly, Nellie: 175, 752, 888, 1043; dies (1955), 1092
Rommel, Field Marshal Erwin: 250, 420
Ronald, Mrs Joan: 1229
Roosevelt, Eleanor: 224, 351 n.3
Roosevelt, Elliott: 257, 258

Roosevelt, President Franklin D.: remembered, 4, 8, 61, 69, 70, 79, 88, 157, 171, 173, 175, 216, 407, 415; and the Morgenthau Plan, 259; and Churchill's war memoirs, 269–70, 331, 450, 484, 505, 622, 626, 632, 761; and an historical controversy, 310–11; and the Quebec Agreement (of 1943), 254, 572–3, 595, 684, 966, 1054; and the 'fatal tide' (in 1945), 788; 'dead seven years', 860, 870; and Summits, 893; and a Press Conference, 1001; and the publication of wartime documents, 1264

Rootes, Sir William: 129 n.2

Rosebery, 5th Earl of: 859, 1048, 1050, 1222 n.1

Rosebery, 6th Earl of: 559, 1180

Rosenheim, Dr: 1173, 1174, 1175

Rosenstiel, Lewis: 469 n.1, 1149

Roskill, Captain Stephen: 979 n.1

Ross, Sir Robert: 481 n.4

Rota (the lion): Churchill visits, 1102; his successor, 1206 n.4

Rothenstein, Sir John: 1068, 1258 n.2; at Chartwell (1955), 1152–4

Rothermere, 1st Viscount: 154, 182 n.2, 749, 874, 888 n.1, 1132–3, 1135, 1212 n.1, 1335

Rothschild, Edmund de: 754

Rothschild, Mrs James de ('Dollie'): 775

Rothschild, James de ('Jimmy'): 256 n.1, 775, 1093, 1095, 1097

Rothschild, Baroness Jean de: 1215

Rothschild, 3rd Baron (Victor): 1307 n.7

Rothschilds, the: 754

Rotterdam (The Netherlands): 232

Rougier, Louis: 427 n.4

Roumania: 25, 76, 79, 97–8, 212, 281, 288, 390, 875; 'subjugated', 953; and the Moscow Conference (of 1944), 1192

Round the World in Eighty Days (Jules Verne): 466

Rousseau, Jean Jacques: 264

Rowan, Lady (Judy Rowan): 118, 305, 1243, 1351 n.2, 1357

Rowan, (Sir) Leslie: 10, 118–19, 127–8, 222, 253, 305, 308, 311, 703; and Churchill's visit to the United States (1952), 674–5; at the Other Club, 749; and Lady Churchill, 1243; and Churchill's wartime instructions, fulfilled by 1959, 1289; and Churchill's last years, 1349, 1351 n.2, 1357; and Churchill's funeral, 1363

Rowse, A. L.: at Chartwell, 1149–51; and Churchill's History, 1190; at Blenheim, 1269–70

Royal Academy, the: 328, 615, 965, 972, 1134, 1164, 1197, 1240, 1285, 1288

Royal Air Force Benevolent Fund, the: Churchill's appeal for, 638

Royal Albert Hall (London): see index entry for Albert Hall

Royal Navy, the: and the 13-year-old cadet entry, 903–4

Royal Society, the: 823 n.1

Royal Welch Fusiliers, the: 844 n.4

Rozanov, Vasiliy: 7 n.1

Rufus I (Churchill's poodle): 343, 1207 n.1

Rufus II (successor to Rufus I): 576, 866, 898, 1042, 1044, 1173, 1207; photograph 26

Ruhr, the (Germany): 87, 103, 242, 287, 623

Rule Britannia (song): 673

Rumbold, (Sir) Anthony: 997 n.1, 1009, 1115

Run, Rabbit, Run (song): 112

Russell, B. H.: 462–3

Russell, Edwin F. (Lieutenant, US Navy): 1270

Russell, Wendy (later Reves, Wendy): Churchill's first meeting with (1955), 1165; for subsequent index entries see Reves, Wendy

'Russian peril', the (in 1945): 6

Russian Trade Delegation (in London): 490–1

Russo-Japanese War (1904–5): 216

Rusty (Churchill's lion): 1206

Saar, the: future of, 930, 931

Sackville-West, Vita: 49

St Antony's College (Oxford): 568 n.2, 591 n.1

Saint Joan (George Bernard Shaw): 253

St Laurent, Louis Stephen: 779 n.2, 836, 1011

St Moritz (Switzerland): a chef from, 261

St Paul's Cathedral (London): Thanksgiving Service in (1945), 11; memorial services in (1947), 361–2; (1956), 1197; (1957), 1254–5; and Churchill's funeral (1965), 1361, 1362–3

St Paul's School (London): and an historical dispute, 271–2

St Stephen's Hall, Westminster: Churchill speaks in, 809–10

Salisbury, Marchioness of ('Betty') (wife of the 5th Marquess): 506, 716, 862, 978, 983, 1243

Salisbury, 3rd Marquess of: 367, 1048, 1050

Salisbury, 4th Marquess of: 124–5

Salisbury, 5th Marquess of ('Bobbety'): 117, 333, 472, 473, 506, 512, 513, 550, 618; and Churchill's political future (1947), 341; and Churchill's second Premiership, 653, 703–4, 707 n.2, 716, 717, 744, 746, 800 n.1, 905 n.1; and Churchill's possible resignation (1952), 736; and Churchill's stroke (1953), 849–50, 851, 852, 855, 862, 871, 872; and Churchill's wish for a Summit (1953–5),

Salisbury, 5th Marquess of—*continued*
864, 1019–20, 1024–6, 1031, 1034, 1035–6,
1110; and Persia, 878–9; and the pressure
for change at home, 893, 1037, 1086, 1107;
and Eden's illness (1953), 894; and Egypt,
900; and the succession crisis (1954–5),
1052, 1061; and the Suez Crisis (1956), 1221
n.4, 1223, 1226; and the succession crisis
(1956), 1227

Salmond, Marshal of the Royal Air Force Sir
John: 749 n.1

Salonica (Greece): 332

Salote of Tonga, Queen: 836, 842

Salter, Sir Arthur (later 1st Baron): 150, 613,
874 n.2

Samaritans, the: and Diana Churchill, 1350

Samuel, A. C. I. (Ian): 1316 n.1

Samuel, 1st Viscount (Herbert Samuel): 347,
655, 1068

San Francisco (USA): 10, 13, 47, 68, 314 n.1,
316

San Remo (Italian Riviera): Churchill visits,
1162

Sandhurst (Royal Military Academy): recalled, 739

Sandys, Celia: 662 n.4, 988, 1069 n.5, 1174;
the coming out dance of, 1331; at Chartwell,
1332; at Hyde Park Gate, 1358

Sandys, Diana (Diana Churchill): 50, 57, 105,
127, 263, 307, 498, 500, 577, 579, 580, 662,
971, 978, 988, 1092; 'very dear to me', 1165;
with her father, in his retirement, 1174,
1176, 1177, 1178, 1183, 1184, 1186, 1252,
1298, 1314, 1317, 1332, 1339 n.1; dies
(1963), 1349–50

Sandys, Duncan (later Baron Duncan-
Sandys): and the 1945 Election, 9, 39, 57,
105, 107, 127; and the 1950 Election, 506,
507, 512; and the 1951 Election, 529 n.1,
649; and the move for a United Europe,
243, 321 n.3, 406, 481 n.4, 486, 544; and
Churchill's letter to de Gaulle (1946), 282,
283 n.1, 285–6; Churchill's guest, 50, 263,
577, 785, 971; at the Other Club, 749; a gift
from, 307; and Randolph, 314; and Churchill's war memoirs, 345, 469–70, 609; and
Churchill's second Premiership, 656, 713,
751–2, 753, 984, 1053, 1065; and Lord Cherwell, 1213; and Churchill's years of retirement, 1235 n.1, 1337 n.2

Sandys, Edwina: 662 n.4, 988, 1069 n.5; marries Piers Dixon (1960), 1317; *for subsequent
index entries see*, Dixon, Mrs Piers

Sandys, Julian: 347, 459 n.2, 469, 662 n.4,
1069 n.5, 1332, 1358

Sansom, Odette (later Odette Hallowes): 378

Sargent, Sir Orme: 5, 14, 43, 361, 373, 382

Sarkisov, Professor: 4 n.1

Sarnoff, David: 757–8

Sassoon, Sir Philip: 147 n.3, 525 n.2

Satan: and Beaverbrook, 118

'Saturation' (in the nuclear sphere): 1091,
1152

Saudi Arabia: 782, 986

Sausmarez, Cecil de: 170–2

Savory, Albert: 185–6

Savory, Professor Sir Douglas: 382

Savoy Hotel (London): 318, 417

Savrola (Winston S. Churchill, 1900): 424, 886
n.2

Sawyers, Frank (Churchill's valet): 50, 132,
149, 151, 305, 374 n.2

Sax, Willy: 278, 424, 429 n.1, 488, 587

Saxony (Germany): 88

Scandinavia: and the unity of Europe, 542

Scarborough (England): Churchill speaks at
(1952), 764, 769

Schoeps, Max: 343 n.1

Schopenhauer, Artur: quoted, 958, 1132

Schulenburg, Count Werner von der: 416
n.6

Schuman, Robert: 496; his Plan, 535, 675;
Churchill lunches with, 589; Churchill
praises, 774

Schuman Plan, the: 535, 622, 635; and the
European Defence Community, 675–6

Schwerin von Krosigk, Count Lutz: 7

Science and Health (Mary Baker Eddy): 1262

Scott, Sir Walter: 877

Scribner, Charles: 469

Seal, (Sir) Eric: 408, 974 n.4

Sebastopol (Crimea): 880

Second World War, the: deaths in, 28;
France's 'great efforts' in, 928; and the
Soviet desire for 'protection against another
Hitler', 935

Secrecy: 'a shield', 594

Secret Battle (A. P. Herbert): 1310

Secret Police, the: 483 n.4

Secret Session, a (of the House of Commons):
Churchill proposes, 531, 538–9, 540, 541,
594

Secret Session Speeches (compiled by Charles
Eade, 1946): 179, 194, 204, 205, 255, 258,
327

Security Council, the: 279, 534, 945, 1211,
1213–14, 1218

Sedan (France): 429

Seddon, Professor (Sir) Herbert: 1317, 1335,
1336

Seldon, Anthony: quoted, 1100 n.1

Senanayake, Dudley: 779 n.2, 836

Seoul (Korea): 92, 561 n.3, 584 n.1

Seretse Khama: 771

Service vote, the: and the 1945 Election, 57, 150

Seymour, Horatia: 56

Shadow Cabinet, the (1945–51): 156, 163, 227, 307, 472, 529, 617

Sharett, Moshe (formerly Shertok): 1096, 1097 n.1

Shaw, George Bernard: 253, 254 n.1, 562

Shawcross, Sir Hartley (later Baron): 515, 1290

Sheba, Togo: 546 n.2

Sheba (the leopard): Churchill visits, 1102

Shepherd, G.: 1069 n.5

Sheppard (Churchill's valet): 1144 n.2, 1291, 1292

Sheridan, Clare: 224, 229, 421, 498, 532

Sherwood, Robert: 259

Shillingford, Mrs Robert (Lettice Marston): 1132

Shinwell, Emanuel (later Baron): 398, 399, 433, 516, 519, 539, 540, 593–4, 612; Churchill's tribute to, 667–8; and 'a tinker's curse', 668 n.1; and the 'hundred-fathom line', 694; and National Service, 750; and Churchill's Woodford speech (1954), 1078–9; critical, 1100; and a signal 'of affection', 1145; at Hyde Park Gate (1964), 1355

Shock, Maurice: 1212–13, 1214, 1225

Short Term Trade Agreement (of 1947): 555

Shuckburgh, (Sir) Evelyn: 681, 722, 778, 781, 791, 795, 818, 820, 868, 880, 920 n.1; and the question of Churchill's resignation (1954–5), 960–1, 964, 970–1; and the hydrogen bomb, 961; and a talk with Churchill (1955), 1095

Shullemson, Miss: 184

Shurmer, Peter: 593

Shute, Neville: 1250

Siam (Thailand): 716, 821, 861, 994

Siberia: 30, 837, 863, 965

Sicily: battle for (1943), 489; Churchill's retirement journey to (1955), 1114, 1120, 1122, 1124, 1126, 1127–8, 1131–3, 1134; and Lord Cherwell, 1142

Sieff, (Sir) Marcus (later Baron Sieff of Brimpton): 439 n.2, 458, 590

Sikorski, General Wladyslaw: 470

Silesia: 84, 88, 96

Silone, Ignazio: 577 n.2

Silverman, Sydney: 250–1

Simon, 1st Viscount (Sir John Simon): 333, 503

Simon of Wythenshawe, 1st Baron: 403 n.3

Simonds, 1st Baron (later 1st Viscount): 965, 1020, 1061 n.4

Simonstown (South Africa): 708, 1057–8

Sinai Peninsula, the: 799, 840, 1220, 1234

Sinclair, Sir Archibald (later 1st Viscount Thurso): 17, 20, 23–4, 27, 49, 283 n.2, 316, 319–20, 397, 399; at Chartwell, 497–8; for subsequent index entries see Thurso, 1st Viscount

Sink the Bismarck (film): 1336

Sir Winston Churchill: a boat named (1963), 1343

Siren-suit: 342

Sixteen Self Sketches (George Bernard Shaw): 562

Škoda works (Czechoslovakia): 539

Slessor, Air Chief Marshal Sir John: 623 n.3, 709

Slim, Field Marshal Sir William (later 1st Viscount): 672, 673, 678, 679, 709, 715, 737

Sloggett, Arthur: 356

Smallwood, Joseph R.: 754

Smillie, Robert ('Bob'): 446

Smith, Adam: 296

Smith, (Governor) Al: 352, 353

Smith, General Walter Bedell: 267, 793, 834, 858, 866–7, 1007; resigns (1954), 1045

Smith, Sir Ben: 210

Smith, Eph: 734 n.2, 826 n.4

Smith, F. E. (later 1st Earl Birkenhead): 318, 391, 1247, 1358 n.4

Smuts, Field Marshal Jan Christian: 14, 26–7, 262, 267, 271, 305, 419, 472–3, 474; dies (1950), 565; Churchill's tribute to, 1221

Smuts, Mrs (Sybella): 565

Snedakar, John R.: 424 n.2

Snow, T. M.: 262

Snowden, Ethel (later Countess): 7 n.1

Snowden, 1st Viscount: 323

Snyder, John W.: 675 n.2, 744 n.1

Socialism: and private enterprise, 302–3; the 'fallacy' of, 349; the 'battle against', 350; 'folly and blundering' of, 354; 'burdens' of, 374, 375; 'attacks Capital', 445; and a 'positive policy' against, 476–7; and 'tyranny', 508; and 'levelling down', 528; and the 1951 Election, 529, 643–4

Sofia (Bulgaria): 97, 200, 209

Soames, Captain Arthur: 306, 548 n.4, 1175, 1258

Soames, Mrs Arthur (Audrey): 1175

Soames, Charlotte: 1043, 1069 n.5

Soames, Captain Christopher (later Baron): (in 1946), 257, 304, 305, 306; marries Mary Churchill, 313; takes charge of Chartwell Farm, 326–7, 358; out shooting, 345, 500 n.4; at Chartwell, 347, 348, 358, 381, 382, 388, 389, 497–8, 522, 523–5, 628, 739, 980, 982, 983, 987, 1043, 1183; with Churchill, 374, 406, 424, 426, 430, 462, 631, 754, 764,

Soames, Captain Christopher—*continued*
787, 792, 793, 872 n.2, 886, 889, 916, 917,
918, 984, 1006, 1007, 1015, 1063, 1064,
1100; advice from, 412; and Churchill's war
memoirs, 434, 445; and the 1950 Election,
502, 507, 512; in his 'burry', 580; re-elected
(1951), 649; and Churchill's peacetime Premiership (1951–5), 716, 717, 723, 739, 744,
764; and Churchill's stroke (1953), 846–7,
848, 857, 858–9, 860, 885, 889; and Churchill's eventual resignation, 902, 1051, 1053;
his help to Churchill, 903; 'exasperated',
964; and Malenkov, 971; and Churchill's retirement years (1955–65), 1135, 1157, 1161,
1164, 1165, 1168, 1172, 1183, 1184, 1186,
1187, 1190, 1200, 1206, 1208, 1215, 1228,
1234–5, 1243, 1245, 1252, 1311, 1336, 1339
n.1, 1343, 1344, 1358; Churchill speaks for
(1955), 1137; Churchill's praise for, 1140;
and Churchill's horses, 1244, 1246, 1308; a
gift from, 1257; and his father-in-law's funeral, 1362–3; *photographs 21, 38*
Soames, Emma: 1069 n.5
Soames, Jeremy: 754, 980, 1044, 1069 n.5,
1155
Soames, Mary (Mary Churchill) (later Lady):
married, 313; at Chartwell, 347, 388, 522,
739, 901, 980, 982, 983, 1043, 1044, 1140,
1183; at Chequers, 870; accompanies her
father overseas, 424, 426, 462, 787, 886, 889,
890; accompanies her mother, 627, 743, 937;
her mothers stays with, 1286, 1348, 1350; at
Hyde Park Gate, 458; and the 1950 Election, 502; in her 'burry' 580; her letters and
messages to her father, 662, 1184, 1247,
1274; and her father's second Premiership
(1951–5), 716, 739, 744, 754, 785, 1039; and
her father's stroke (in 1953), 846, 847, 848,
853, 855, 877, 889; and Malenkov, 971; and
her father's decision not to resign (1954),
1053, 1067; and her father's decision to
resign (1955), 1111; and the Sutherland portrait, 1073, 1253; and her father's 80th birthday, 1078; her father's pride in, 1140; and
her father's years in retirement (1955–65),
1146, 1155, 1157, 1158, 1159, 1161, 1183,
1184, 1185, 1186, 1187, 1206, 1208, 1235
n.1, 1252, 1267, 1276, 1284, 1302, 1311,
1338, 1339 n.1, 1345, 1346; and the death
of her sister Diana, 1349, 1350; a gift from,
1257, 1331 n.5; and her father's last illness,
1359; and her father's funeral, 1362; and the
'qualities of your heart', 1365; and 'Liberty',
1366; *photographs 1, 10, 38*
Soames, Nicholas: 1069 n.1
Solzhenitsyn, Alexander: 1258
Somme, the (Battle of, 1916): 331, 581, 583

Songkhla (Malaya): 821
Soraya, Queen (of Persia): 1095
Sophie, Queen (of Spain): 1287
Sosnkowski, General Kazimierz: 212
South Africa: 307, 312, 331, 708, 748, 802 n.2,
1057–8
South America: 219, 401
South Bradford (by-election, 1949): 498
South East Asia Treaty Organization
(SEATO): 993–4, 999, 1004, 1028
South Korea: 535, 537, 539, 545, 553, 561 n.3,
833
South Pole, the: 483
South Tyrol: dispute concerning, 260
Southon, Robert (the builder at Chartwell):
149, 176, 327
Soviet Embassy, London: 3, 318
Soviet Union: troop advances of (May 1945),
5–6, 11, 30, 32, 43, 201, 428, 892 n.2; Churchill's 'deep anxiety' concerning, 6–7; and
understanding with, 'the only hope of the
world', 9; and the Russian people, 12, 25,
281, 1099; and Japan, 13–14, 119, 167, 191;
fears of, 20, 192; ambitions of, 24, 26, 32,
45, 154, 194–5; and Istria, 44–5; and the
Potsdam Conference (1945), 62–103, 829;
to be 'a great power on the sea', 75, 77; and
Turkey, 90–1; and Poland, 94–7, 101–3,
279; and Italy, 154; Churchill's worries concerning, 160–2, 238–9; Churchill's warning
to (1941), 183; and Churchill's Fulton
speech, 200–2, 208–9, 215–16, 220; Churchill's calls for an 'understanding' with, 229;
Churchill recalls his visits to, 236; and the
United States, 258; and United Europe,
266, 278–9, 330; military strength of, 277,
279, 280, 281–2, 284, 285–6, 288, 289, 477–
8, 518, 530, 539, 540, 571, 574, 592, 594,
710, 937, 940, 1098–9; need for 'friendship'
with, 309; uses veto, 351; 'abuse' from, 352;
need to end 'bluff' of, 362–3; Britain 'worried' about, 371; Attlee and Morrison criticize, 396, 397; and the Death Penalty, 401;
Churchill's call for a 'settlement' with, 422;
and the Berlin blockade, 421, 423, 431–2,
437, 438; its possession of the atomic bomb,
432, 520, 521, 575, 593, 959; 'enmity' of,
436; and Austria, 437, 1002; and Palestine,
449, 454; and Spain, 452; and NATO, 118
n.3, 463, 957, 1029; and need for 'strong'
nerves, 467; and 'complete destruction', 468;
and 'mere manoeuvres', 475; representatives
of, in Britain, 490–1; and the defence of
Western Europe, 490; and an historical
query, 494; 'grave ... menace' of, 536; and
the Korean War, 537–8, 539, 553, 715–16,
834; and the European Army, 542, 556;

Soviet Union—*continued*
Churchill's confidence in (in 1941), 550; and British jet aircraft, 553; sale of machine tools to, 554–5, 611; need for the 'widest possible' trade with, 912, 944, 953, 962; and Yugoslavia, 591; and Persia, 617–18; Churchill's warnings concerning, 624, 660–1; Churchill's wish to begin discussions with, 636; and a 'finger on the trigger', 643; and a 'poisoned' soup, 663; and China, 676; 'to seek our friendship' (1952), 678; 'there would be no war', 684, 758; and the slow road to a Summit, 206, 691, 806–7, 811–14, 816, 818–19, 827–8, 830–1, 836–8, 838, 843, 849, 853, 873, 893, 895, 909–10, 918, 936, 943, 968, 971–2, 972–3; its possible 'troubles', 693; and the democracies, 706; and a possible parachute attack by, 804; an aircraft shot down by, 807; and Eastern Germany, 829–30; and the Arab world, 841; fears of 'aggression' of, 842; and the hydrogen bomb, 873, 966, 968, 1000, 1021–3, 1192–3; no change in 'heart' of (after Stalin's death), 876; and British intelligence operations, 880; and Germany, 895–6, 928, 933; and the receding likelihood of war (1953), 899; 'not in her interest' to make war, 917; Churchill's 'hopeful and . . . helpful' mood concerning, 907; and the Bermuda Conference (December 1953), 911, 918, 919, 920–3, 933; and atomic energy, 919, 940; and atomic secrets, 936; Churchill's desire for 'easement in relations' with, 933; Churchill 'anxious' to please, 934; entitled to 'assurances', 939–40; Churchill and Eisenhower in conflict over, 920–3, 951; 'genuinely alarmed', 952; and eastern Europe, 953; Churchill urges an 'easement' of relations with, 962–3; and the hydrogen bomb debates (1954 and 1955), 965–71, 1098–1100; and Churchill's continuing hopes for a Summit and settlement with (1954–5), 992, 995, 1012; military weakness of, 1016; an 'important change of mood' in, 1070; and Churchill's Woodford speech (1954), 1079–81; 'ought to dominate our minds', 1082; 'weakness makes no appeal to', 1089; its 'hope . . . to divide', 1092; and 'conventional forces', 1098–9; and the danger of giving a false impression to, 1136; and a possible 'New Look', 1143; and the Geneva Summit (1955), 1151, 1154–5, 1168, 1169–70; policy of (in 1956), 1186; and Egypt, 1191, 1323; and de-Stalinization, 1192; and the Suez Crisis (1956), 1201, 1203, 1204, 1213, 1218, 1222; 'the real enemy' (Eisenhower), 1222; launches the first earth satellite, 1252; and British trade

Soviet Union—*continued*
with, 1295; and disarmament proposals (in 1959), 1301; and Adenauer's Germany, 1306
Spaak, Paul-Henri: 406, 407, 481, 542
Spaatz, General Carl A.: 208
Spain: 78–9, 195–6, 218, 452, 601, 602; in history, 692; and a 'peripheral' defence, 932
Spanish Civil War, the (1936–9): 383
Spanish dungeon, a (a tale of): 511
Spark of Life (E. M. Remarque): 887
Spear, Ruskin: 1240–1
Spears, Brigadier-General Sir Edward Louis: 277, 720, 1235 n.2, 1315 n.3
Spectator, the: 132, 1213
Spencer, Dorothy: 123
Spencer-Churchill, Captain George: 164
Spencer-Churchill, Lord Ivor: dies (1956), 1211, 1213
Spencer-Churchill, Lady Ivor (Betty): 1213
Spencer-Churchill, Robert: 1213 n.2
Spencer-Churchill, Lady Rosamond: 1175 n.1
Spender, (Sir) Stephen: 577 n.2
Sphinx, the (Egypt): 632
Split (Yugoslavia): Churchill's visit to (1960), 1313
Sport and Country: 522 n.1
Spry, Constance: 842
'Sputnik': launched, 1252
Staercke, André de: 1187
Stalin, Joseph Vissarionovich: no more to be said to, 5; and Poland, 8; Clementine Churchill's letter to, 9; and the future of Europe, 12; and Istria, 15; and a future conference (in 1945), 24, 26, 44; at Potsdam, 62–104, 115, 116, 119, 792; and the British election of 1945, 74, 105, 115; Churchill's messages to, 116 n.1, 289 n.3, 309–10, 659; *Starleen*, 140; 'stiff talks' with, 161; urges rearmament, 194; and Churchill's Fulton speech, 200, 204, 211–12, 213, 220; and Japan, 214; and Persia, 216; Churchill's 'friendly hint to', 238; criticizes Churchill, 280–1; has 'happiest memories' of Churchill, 309; and an historical controversy, 310; and Churchill's war memoirs, 331, 332, 484, 546, 761, 810; has a 'heart', 351; his 'bluff', 363; 'despotic', 371; and NATO, 463; and Berlin, 474; in 1942, 552 n.1; in 1945, 546, 547; 'such a swine', 547; and Yugoslavia, 591; a possible 'personal meeting' with, 636; and 'a supreme effort to bridge the gulf', 659–60; 'responsible' for Anglo-American unity, 685; the West 'safer from attack' during lifetime of, 735; Churchill's hopes of a joint Anglo-American 'approach' to, 756; Churchill's hopes of a discussion with, 758, 790, 806;

Stalin, Joseph Vissarionovich—*continued*
dies (1953), 805; and the 'doctors plot', 813; aftermath of death of, 816, 830, 836, 906, 920, 954, 1026, 1040, 1081, 1152; 'bludgeoning xenophobia' of, 817; recalled, 828, 868, 870; and 'spheres of influence' (1944), 875; and Summits (1943–5), 893; and the United States, 1006; his encroachments (1945–8), 1028; 'always kept his word with me', 1192; and Khrushchev, 1273; *photograph 5*

Stalingrad (USSR): Clementine Churchill's visit to, 65

Stalingrad, Battle of (1942): 1224 n.3

Stallard (Lord Derby's butler): shot, 770, 984

Stanhope, 7th Earl: 948

Stanley, Oliver (later 8th Baron Stanley of Alderley): 10, 261, 283; and Churchill's political future, 341; and the General Election of 1950, 506

Stansgate, 1st Viscount: 1081

Starkie, Dr Enid: 577 n.2

Stassen, Harold: 600, 743 n.2

State Funeral: planned (1963), 1347; in London (1965), 1362–3

Steel: nationalization of, 346, 507, 529, 583; an urgent need of, 677; and Gold, 691; denationalization of, 746; needs of, 750

Stehlin, General: 634

Stelling, David: 312 n.3

Stemming the Tide (Randolph S. Churchill, editor, 1953): 784 n.3

Sterling Releases Agreement (1951): 787

Stern Gang, the (in Palestine): 335 n.2

Stettin (Szczecin): 88, 200, 238

Stevens (a farmer): 327

Stevens, J. F.: 288 n.3

Stevenson, Adlai: 870, 1243, 1244, 1322

Stevenson, Robert Louis: 1253 n.5.

Stewart, Sir Frederick: 256 n.1

Steyn, President Martinus: 1041 n.1

'Stick-in-the-muds': 253

Stimson, Henry: 62, 69, 85–6

Stirbei, Prince: 212

Stirling, David: 30

Stockholm (Sweden): a possible summit in (1953), 790, 819, 971, 1002, 1023, 1027, 1032; and Churchill's Nobel Prize for Literature, 901, 937, 938

Stockwood, Mervyn (later Bishop): 604 n.3

Stokes, Richard: 940

Stormont, HMCS: converted, 1173 n.4

Stour (East Bergholt, Suffolk): Randolph Churchill 'established' in (1955), 1159; Churchill visits (1955), 1172, 1239; Randolph Churchill's work at, 1318, 1338 n.1, 1352, 1364

Stow, Sir John: 1308–9

Strachey, John: 516 n.3

Straits, the (the Bosphorus and Dardanelles): 332

Strakosch, Sir Henry: 255

Strand Magazine, the: 136, 562 n.2; and 'the painters', 1288

Strang, Sir William (later 1st Baron): 821, 861, 872

Stransky (a Czech exile): 404 n.4

Strasbourg (France): 371; Churchill's visit to (1949), 481–4; and the 'dignity of man', 496; Churchill's speech recalled, 536; Churchill returns to (1950), 541–2, 544; Churchill hopes for (1952), 726; Churchill's son recalls, 768; Churchill recalls (1953), 861; and the theme of a 'grand alliance', 1057

Stratheden, SS: 1189 n.3, 1190

Strauss, Admiral Lewis L.: at Bermuda, 924, 936; and atomic co-operation, 964

Strong, Major-General Sir Kenneth: 1343

Stuart (Lord Derby's under-butler): shot, 770, 984

Stuart, Ian M. B.: 364 n.2

Stuart, James (later 1st Viscount Stuart of Findhorn): 9, 10–11, 23, 51, 156, 190, 529 n.1; and Churchill's political future (1947), 341; and the possibility of Churchill's resignation (1952), 736; and the succession crisis (1954–5), 1060, 1061, 1084, 1086; and Churchill's retirement years, 1257

Sturdee, Jo (later Lady Onslow): 57, 181, 184, 228, 255, 257, 305 n.1, 306, 376, 378 n.1, 386, 388, 429 n.1, 434, 435, 462, 470, 471, 484 n.4, 498, 500, 512, 522 n.5, 563; accompanies Churchill to Marrakech, 576, 578, 579; and an unflattering book, 596; her continuing secretarial work, 603 n.2, 605 n.2, 645, 656, 657 n.1, 1132; and Churchill's History, 1194; and Churchill's funeral, 1364

Subasic, Dr Ivan: 79

Sudan, the: 230, 723, 787, 795–6, 797–8, 821, 822; crisis in (1954), 955–6, 995

Suez Canal, the: and Israeli shipping, 527–8, 624, 625, 658; British bases on, 647; need to 'safeguard', 659; and a possible international force on, 676, 684–5, 689, 719, 723, 757, 770, 840–1, 843, 881; and future 'free transit' through, 914, 945, 957, 1000, 1018; and future 'neglect or obstruction' of, 933; and the Conservative Party, 939; and the atom bomb, 999; and the hydrogen bomb, 1037; nationalized, 1201, 1202, 1203, 1205, 1210; to be attacked, 1219; attacked, 1220–2

Suez Crisis, the (of 1956): 1195–6, 1201–4,

Suez Crisis—*continued*
1205, 1208, 1209–10, 1211, 1213–14, 1220–2, 1223–5, 1240, 1246, 1250
Suez Group, the: 897 n.2
Sulzberger, Arthur Ochs: 469, 684
Summit, a: proposed (1950), 510, 572; proposed again (1951), 636; and 'a supreme effort to bridge the gulf', 659–60; and the slow road towards, 691; 'would have another shot at', 735; Churchill's 'hopes of' (1952–4), 756, 758, 790, 806–7, 827–9, 830–2, 833, 836–8, 849, 853, 854, 857, 859, 863, 867, 868, 871, 877, 889, 893, 895, 908–9, 909–10, 918, 920–3, 943, 954–5, 958, 967 n.2; and the hydrogen bomb, 960, 962, 968, 971–2, 972, 973, 992; and the 1944 'spheres of influence' discussion, 875; discussed at Washington (June 1954), 998, 1000, 1001, 1003, 1006–7; Churchill's continuing hopes for (1954–5), 1012, 1013, 1019–28, 1030–6, 1039–40, 1089–92, 1101, 1103–11, 1137; Churchill's reflections on, 1143, 1152; held at Geneva (July 1955), 1154–5; Ben-Gurion's doubts concerning, considered by Churchill 'on the melancholy side' (1959), 1299; Adenauer's doubts concerning, 1306; and the U2 spy plane (1960), 1313
Summits: and the 'hate of those below', 197, 206
Sunday Chronicle, the: 514 n.2
Sunday Dispatch, the: 424 n.4, 633, 888 n.1
Sunday Express, the: 260–1; 'very bad', 271–2; and Churchill's resignation, 1111
Sunday Pictorial, the: 424 n.4
Sunday Telegraph, the: 364 n.1
Sunday Times, the: 424 n.4, 514 n.2, 1100, 1211 n.2, 1226, 1279
Sunshine: 'my quest', 149
Supreme Being, a: and a 'sublime moral purpose', 416
Supreme War Council, the (1940): 234
Survival: 'the interest of both sides', 1040; the 'twin brother' of Annihilation, 1100
Suslov, Mikhail: 318
Sutherland, Graham: 'a "Wow"', 1059; Churchill 'betrayed' by, 1073, 1076; his portrait of Churchill, and Churchill himself, 1095; his portrait 'will never see the light of day', 1253
Sweden: 84, 829
Swinemünde (Swinoujscie): 82
Swinton, 1st Viscount (later 1st Earl): 34 n.4, 511, 641, 726 n.2, 795, 800, 817–18, 873, 879; and Churchill's Summit hopes, 1020, 1025; and the succession crisis, 1051; aged 70, 1061 n.4

Switzerland: 73, 220 n.1, 257; Churchill's visit to (1946), 260–7; 'perturbed', 280; Intelligence from, 288; independence of, 423; and Korea, 829
Syracuse (Sicily): 1128, 1131
Syracuse (USA): 193
Syria: 30, 36, 50, 287, 455, 841

Tacitus: to be quoted, 1166
Taft, Robert A.: 743–4
Tallal, King of Jordan: 623 n.4
Tangier: 1308
Tanks: in the Second World War, 469–70
Tardieu, André: 1169
Tatler, the: 563 n.2
Taylor, Sir Charles: 1134
Taylor, H. A.: 229 n.1
Taylor, Julian: 820 n.2
Taylor, Miss: 305 n.1
Taylor, Mrs: and 'Flower Villa', 379
Taylor, S. (of Reuters): 391
Tedder, Air Chief Marshal Sir William (later Marshal of the Royal Air Force, 1st Baron): 133, 728, 1263 n.2
Teheran (Persia): the return of the Shah to (1953), 878
Teheran Conference (1943): 42, 57, 71, 87, 88, 95, 104, 239, 311, 545, 584, 893; Bermuda 'reminiscent' of (1953), 919
Tel Aviv (Israel): 449, 454
Television: and the House of Commons, 853, 938, 939; and Churchill's 80th birthday, 1075; and Churchill's resignation, 1119; Churchill 'no enthusiast for', 1132; and a 'foolish attack' on the Queen, 1249; and Churchill's American journey (1958), 1263
Templemore, 4th Baron: 142
Templer, General (later Field Marshal) Sir Gerald: 283 n.4, 685
Tennyson, Alfred Lord: 13 n.1
Terrorism: 'no solution', 244; in Palestine, 251, 295–6, 335–6, 430, 1233; in Algeria, 1245
Teschen (Czechoslovakia): seized (1938), 412–13
Teucer: 'no need to despair' with, 1065
Thames River, the: a 'silver thread', 976; and a possible conference, 1056; and Churchill's funeral, 1363
The American Civil War (Winston S. Churchill, 1961): 915 n.2
The Anglo-Saxon Review: 562
The Black Arrow (R. L. Stevenson): 1253
The Bridge on the River Kwai (film): 1255
'The Crown': a symbol, and 'The Union', 1327
The Donkeys (Alan Clark): 1326

The Dynasts (Thomas Hardy): 898, 947

The Edge of the Sword (Farrar-Hockley): 610 n.2

The Fall of Berlin (film): 723

The Fall of Lloyd George (Lord Beaverbrook): 1341

The Fight for the Tory Leadership (Randolph S. Churchill): 1226 n.5

The Four Feathers (film): 1183

The Glitter and the Gold (Consuelo Balsan): 742

The Glory of Parliament (Harry Boardman): 947 n.2

The God that Failed (Richard Crossman, editor): 577

The Golden Fleece (Robert Graves): 145

The Gondoliers (Gilbert and Sullivan): 1285

The Innocents (stage play): 753

The Labour Party in Perspective (Clement Attlee): 339 n.5

'The Light of Asia': Nehru cast as, 1094, 1095

The Mechanism of the Larynx (Sir Victor Negus): 1268 n.2

The Mikado (Gilbert and Sullivan): Churchill's love of, 58

The New Class (Djilas): 591 n.1

The Night Life of a Virile Potato (stage play): 1305

The Queen and Commonwealth (Television documentary film): 976 n.4

The Right Road for Britain (Conservative Party pamphlet): 477 n.2

The River War (Winston S. Churchill, 1899): 424, 797–8, 898 n.2

The Second World War, (Winston S. Churchill, six volumes, 1948–54): 417, 447, 569, 892 n.1, 1230 n.2; the 'moral' of, 1365; *see also index entry for* War memoirs

The Sinews of Peace (Randolph S. Churchill, editor): 205 n.1, 257 n.2, 424, 783 n.2

The Snows of Kilimanjaro (film): 1255 n.2

The Story of the Coronation (Randolph S. Churchill): 784

The Story of the Malakand Field Force (Winston S. Churchill, 1898): 1195, 1319 n.4

The Ten Commandments (film): 1255 n.2

The Third Eye (Lobsang Rampa): 1251

The Times: cited, 7, 20 n.4, 48–9; critical, 203–4; criticized, 246; and Churchill's call for a United Europe, 266–7; one of sixteen newspapers, 343; letters to, 347, 432; and Vyshinsky, 351 n.3; one of eleven newspapers, 424 n.4; and Palestine, 430; and the German Field Marshals, 431–2; and the atomic bomb, 440; rebukes to, 440, 441, 489 n.3; Churchill too busy to write for, 548; an error in, 560 n.1; and Emanuel Shinwell, 612 n.2; and Churchill's war memoirs, 626, 627; and

The Times—continued
the funeral of George VI, 700; and Butler's 1952 Budget, 724; and Eisenhower, 743; and Churchill's visit to the United States (1953), 790; and Churchill's tribute to Sir Edward Marsh, 795 n.1; and Churchill's 'authority' (in 1953), 909; urges a Summit (1954), 961; and Churchill's hydrogen bomb speech, 969, 970; and Churchill's Woodford speech (1954), 1070, 1081; and Eisenhower's illness (1955), 1168 n.1, 1193 n.2; and the Suez Crisis, 1246; and Germany (in 1937), 1246 n.4; obituary notices in, 1250; and National Health doctors' pay, 1260 n.2; 'captious and tiresome', 1284; and the death of Beaverbrook, 1353

The Times Literary Supplement: 626–7

The Turn of the Screw (Henry James): 753

The Turn of the Tide (Bryant-Alanbrooke): 1232

The Unwritten Alliance (Randolph S. Churchill, editor): 784 n.3

The Wages of Fear (film): 1255 n.2

The Wanton Chase (Peter Quennell): 1269 n.2

The World Crisis (Winston S. Churchill, 1923–31, 5 volumes): 186, 270, 341 n.1, 469

The Yeomen of the Guard (Gilbert and Sullivan): 754

Third World War, a: 6, 290, 422, 543; not inevitable, 643, 660, 692; and a future Labour Government, 644; Churchill 'would strive' for prevention of, 648, 688; 'unlikely to happen', 769; and the Kremlin, 839; and the United States, 896; the probabilities of 'diminished', 907

Thomas, George (later 1st Viscount Tonypandy): 980 n.4

Thomas, J. P. L. ('Jim'): 118, 492, 709, 782 n.1, 854, 899, 903

Thompson, Commander C. R. ('Tommy'): 50, 111, 306

Thompson, Detective-Inspector W. H.: 37–8, 57, 59

Thorez, Maurice: 218, 242

Thorneycroft, Peter (later Baron): 190, 712, 1227, 1259, 1307 n.7, 1337 n.2

Thornton, A. P.: 1225

Thorson, Miss Marg: 1205–6

Thoughts and Adventures (Winston S. Churchill, 1932): 236, 469 n.3, 562 n.1, 1324

Thurso, Countess of (Marigold): 948

Thurso, 1st Viscount (formerly Sir Archibald Sinclair): 948

Tibet: 553

Timbuktoo (Sahara): 576, 577

Time: 'should be allowed to play its part', 838; 'Do not throw away', 1004; the 'envious eyes' of, 1288

Time magazine: 188 n.2, 236, 448, 588 n.1

Time-Life Incorporated: 386–7, 414, 424 n.2, 450, n.4, 802

Tiran, Straits of: 1220

Tirpitz, Grand Admiral Alfred von: 493

Tirpitz, Lieutenant Wolfgang: 77, 493

Tito, Marshal Iosip Broz: 5, 8, 11–12, 16, 17, 25, 28–9, 34 n.2, 42, 44–5, 76, 453; 'has broken away' from Russia, 510; visits London (1953), 807–8; and a defence 'front', 994; meets Churchill (1960), 1313–14

Tito, Madame (Jovanka Budisavljevic): 1314

Titus Andronicus (Shakespeare): 1248

To Be Or Not To Be (a film): 415

Tobruk, Battle for (1942): 144 n.1, 239, 271, 420, 470

Toby (Churchill's budgerigar): 1078, 1083, 1140, 1156, 1173, 1184, 1186, 1187, 1215, 1235, 1241, 1242, 1259, 1260, 1267, 1273, 1286, 1297; flies away, 1315; his successor (Byron), 1317, 1323

Todd, Sir Alexander: 1263 n.2

Togliatti, Palmiro: 577 n.2

Tokyo (Japan): 92, 120, 214

Tolstoy, Lev: 1304

Tom Jones (H. Fielding): 1267

Tono-Bungay (H. G. Wells): 1211

Tooting Bec (London): an incident in, 56–7

Topping, Sir Robert: 105

Tower of Babel, the: 199

Townsend, Group Captain Peter: 843–4

Towton, Battle of (1461): 1167

Trade: a 'vehicle' to pierce the Iron Curtain, 922

Trade Disputes and Trade Union Bill (1946): 515 n.1

Trade Unions: and the Conservative Party, 895; and the newspaper strike (of 1955), 1132–3

Trades Union Congress (TUC): and a compromise, 592, 614; and national expenditure, 658; its leaders at Downing Street (1952), 769; and the engine drivers' strike (1955), 1142, 1143

Transjordan Frontier Force, the: 641

Transjordan, Kingdom of: 411, 449, 455, 457; *for subsequent index entries, see* Jordan

Travis, Commander (Sir) Edward: 19 n.1

Treasure Island (R. L. Stevenson): 627

Treasury Bench, the: 'and death', 486

Tree, Marietta (Mrs Ronald Tree): 694

Tree, Ronald: 613 n.5, 650, 694

Trenchard, Marshal of the Air Force 1st Viscount: 597–8

Trend, (Sir) Burke (later Baron): 173–4

Trevelyan, G. M.: 1148–9, 1194–5, 1225

Trevor, Major Keith: 348 n.2

Trieste: 6, 45, 134, 200, 238, 428, 735, 899; agreement reached on (1954), 1058

Trinidad: 189

Tripoli (Libya): 196, 420 n.2, 493

Tripolitania: 88

Troilus and Cressida (Shakespeare): 359

Troubridge, Rear-Admiral Sir Thomas: 339 n.1

Trucial Sheikhdoms, the: 782, 986

Truman, President Harry S.: Churchill's telegrams to (1945), 4–5, 6–7, 26, 106, 124, 1080; and Venezia Giulia, 11–12, 15, 29, 42; and Russia, 14, 16, 24, 26, 161, 331; and Potsdam, 42, 61–94, 99, 104; and a conference that never was (May 1945), 546; and the atomic bomb, 59, 99–100, 254, 464, 468; and East Prussia, 92; and Japan, 166; his letters to Churchill, 183, 158, 351–2, 421; Churchill's letters to, 204–5, 351, 444–5, 468, 491, 522, 543–4, 592–3; and Churchill's 1946 American journey, 172–3, 189, 192, 196–7, 201, 204–5, 206, 209–10, 220; and Churchill's 1949 American journey, 464–5; and defence, 325–6, 543–4; and Communism, 421; and NATO, 467–8; and Israel, 557; and the Korean War, 564, 592–3, 605, 688 n.1; and the European Army, 573–4; and the Quebec Agreement (of 1944), 595–6; and Persia, 617–18, 625, 639, 756; Churchill's visit to (1952), 674, 675–83, 691–2, 696, 1003; and Churchill's war memoirs, 761; 'a novice' (in 1945), 788; Churchill's dinner with (1953), 792; at Chartwell (1956), 1199; a message from, 1262; *photographs 5, 18, 19*

Truman Doctrine, the (1947): 326

Truman, Margaret: 615, 693, 744

Trust the People (pamphlet, 1947): 331 n.1

Truth: and Communists, 403; and 'death', 756

Truth: 983

Tudor, Major-General Sir Hugh: 185–6, 1135–6, 1160

Tunisia: France's 'splendid work' in, 934

Turbott, (Sir) Ian: 1310

Turf Club, the: 366

Turkey: 67, 75, 89, 90–1, 98, 141, Soviet pressure on (1946), 194–5, 190, 201, 205, 217; in 1947, 326; after 1948, 444, 617, 834–5; and the defence of Europe, 542; and the defence of the Middle East, 680, 689, 943, 994; and Field Marshal Montgomery, 717; and a Soviet complaint, 880; and 'peripheral' defence, 932; and Egypt, 1018

Twelfth Night (Shakespeare): 888

Twentieth Century: 'harsh structure' of, 809;
'terrible', 1137, 1198

Twist, the (a dance): 1331

Tyranny: 'the same road against', 444; and
Socialism, 508; 'our foe', 537

U2 (spy plane): and Churchill's intended
cruise to Leningrad, 1313

U-boats: and Eire, 12

UJ (Uncle Joe): Stalin, as known to many in
Britain: 888

U Nu: Churchill receives, 1146–7

U Thant: Churchill receives, 1146–7

Ukrainians, repatriation of: 98

Ulster: at the time of the Home Rule crisis of
1886, 364, 365, 368; expectations, in 1948,
439–40, 443

'Uncle Sam': one of 'our heroes', 911

Unconditional Surrender (of Germany, in
1945): 876

Unemployment (Cabinet Committee on): 735

Unemployment Insurance: 275, 566, 646

United Europe: the search for the creation of,
241, 242–3, 247–8, 278–9, 285–7, 290–1,
321, 329–30, 337, 355, 397–401, 405–9;
Council of, established, 460; and a 'wider
synthesis', 472; and the Labour Government, 495–6, 510; and Germany, 520; and
a Liberal–Conservative consensus, 529;
Churchill's continuing appeals for (1950–1),
536–7, 622; Churchill's warning concerning,
under Labour, 646; 'essential', 686; and the
wider free world, 959; and Europe's 'security and prosperity', 1248

United Nations Association, the: 288

United Nations Atomic Committee, the: 210

United Nations Organization (UNO), the:
establishment of (1945), 5–6, 13, 52, 69, 192;
and Italy, 62; and China (in 1945), 63; and
the atomic bomb (in 1945), 157; and Japan,
166; veto powers in, 190; and Churchill's
Fulton speech, 199, 201, 203; its ideals to be
defended, 215, and Persia, 217, 817, 'peculiar constitution' of, 220 n.1; and a discussion on free speech, 223–4; need to work
through, 229, 240–1; and Palestine, 251,
297, 300, 359, 411, 456; and the Israel-
Jordan conflict, 913; and Soviet military
strength, 282; and India, 300–1, 422, 473;
and defence, 320; Soviet activity in, 351 n.3;
hopes for, 352; and the League of Nations,
358; and Spain, 452; and Hungary, 460 n.1;
and the Council of Europe, 483; and the
Korean War, 535, 552–3, 577 n.1, 583, 705,
737, 739, 746–7, 759, 814, 833, 838, 839,
861; and the 'path to world unity', 536; and
'great causes', 574; and the darkening sky,

United Nations Organization—continued
592; and a 'finger' on the trigger, 643; and
the Suez Canal, 685; the hopes for (in 1945,
as seen in 1952–3), 685, 831, 869, 896; and
a Summit, 863, 893; and China (1953), 882,
1002, 1015, 1016, 1029–30, 1035; and
Egypt, 894; and atomic energy, 937, 1028;
supported, 1010; and Cyprus, 1058; and
the United States, 1071; and France, 1162;
'limitations' of, 1218; and the Suez Crisis
(1956), 1218, 1221, 1240; not to be relied
on solely, 1248; has 'failed', 1249; and disarmament, 1301

United States of America, the: 'magnanimous
deeds' of, 4; troop withdrawals of, 5–6, 11,
30, 32, 43, 201, 428, 437, 546, 829; troops
of, in Istria, 16, 29, 44–5; ideology of, 24–5;
'common people' of, 32; Britain's 'safety'
and, 45, 69; and Lend-Lease, 67–8, 191; and
the atomic bomb, 85–6, 119, 156–8, 432,
437, 438, 464, 467, 475, 505, 510, 520, 540,
553, 556, 557, 572, 661, 689–90, 924; and
the post-war control of Japan, 166–7; and
past mistakes of (between the wars), 171,
358, 834 n.1; Churchill's first post-war journey to (1946), 172–4, 179, 180–219; Churchill's second post-war journey to (1949),
462–9; and Britain's indebtedness, 191–2,
210; and Churchill's Fulton speech, 198–9,
209–10, 220; 'its power and its virtue', 219;
and Palestine, 230, 231, 251, 297, 449, 454;
and Zionism, 792; and Israel, 824–5, 1093,
1235; and Egypt, 804; and the Soviet
Union, 238, 258; and Western Europe,
242–3, 606; and United Europe, 266, 278–9,
321, 355, 400, 520–1, 635–6, 636–7; and
Churchill's war memoirs, 269–70, 315, 418,
423, 878; and the Truman Doctrine, 326;
and appeasement, 331; need for 'solidarity'
with, 353; Churchill's belief in friendship
with, 370; and NATO, 463, 467, 677; and a
'wider synthesis', 472; and the need for 'fraternal association' with, 509, and Greece,
510, 568; and the Schuman Plan, 535; the
'bounty of', 536; and the Korean War, 553,
561 n.3, 564, 583, 593, 610, 612 n.1, 706,
737, 739–40, 861, 906, 928; and 'Christian
civilization', 571; and air defence, 597–8;
and Ernest Bevin, 598; and China, 610, 611,
614, 740–2, 951, 1015, 1016, 1049, 1091–2;
and Persia, 618–19, 676, 763; and 'our hopes
of a lasting peace' (1951), 666; and Egypt,
668, 676, 679–80, 719, 723, 757, 770, 781,
786, 800, 805–6, 814–15, 840–1, 900, 914,
915, 936, 951, 957, 993–6, 1018; Churchill's
first journey to, during his second Premiership (January 1952), 669, 671, 672–95;

United States of America—*continued*
'altruism' of, 684; 'grievous . . . isolationism' of, 699, 896; and British defence policy, 710, 749; and the ANZUS (Australia, New Zealand, United States) Pact, 762–3; and the 'cold war', 777; Churchill's second journey to (1952), during his peacetime Premiership, 786–93; need for a 'common . . . front' with, 788, 800–1; 'giant power' of, 816; and the British Commonwealth, 837, 991; and Churchill's wish for a Summit, 859, 863, 868, 1026–8, 1028–9, 1034–6, 1039–40, 1109; and the hydrogen bomb, 873, 952, 959–60, 961, 965–71, 1021–3, 1192–3; the 'massive shield' of, 907; and the Bermuda Conference (December 1953), 909–14, 917–37; and Churchill's History, 915; and atomic energy, 919; and the use of the atomic bomb against China, 932–3; and Indo-China, 934, 973–4, 975–6; and a 'provocative gesture', 943; and Labour Party criticisms of, 619, 948; and a new British army rifle, 948–9; 'unhelpful', 951; and Soviet fears, 952; the 'unrivalled power' of, 972; and Saudi Arabia, 986; 'I am sure I shall always get a good hearing in', 1054; and the United Nations, 1071; and the security of Europe, 1090; and the Four-Power Conferences (1955), 1137; 'on duty', 1186; 'wise and experienced', 1191; and the Suez Crisis (1956), 1192–3, 1195–6, 1201, 1202, 1204, 1210, 1213–14, 1220–2, 1222 n.2, 1224, 1225, 1246, 1250; and Churchill's work to 'mend fences' with, 1225, 1248; and the Soviet 'Sputnik', 1252; Churchill's proposed visit to (1957–8), 1260–1, 1263, 1281, 1291; and the Lebanon, 1270–2; and an educational fund, 1272; Churchill's penultimate visit to (1959), 1291–6; Churchill's last visit to (1961), 1322; Churchill's reflections on the Government of (1961), 1327; Churchill's Honorary Citizenship of (1963), 1343
United States Atomic Energy Committee: 277, 1003 n.1
United States Embassy, London: 3
'United States of Europe': Churchill's call for, 171, 232, 265–7, 278–9, 285, 287, 400, 520
Universal Suffrage: and the Hottentots, 1040
Universe, the: 'Poor Beast', 577
Untouchables, the (of India): 233, 237, 294, 439
Utopias (or 'nightmares'): 34, 40, 48–9, 610, 622, 641; 'dangled before the eyes of millions', 921

V-sign: 1301, 1358

VE Day (Victory in Europe Day, 8 May 1945): 3–4; 'cashing in on', 9; brings 'no respite', 15; 'confusion' since, 321, 354; the tenth anniversary of, imminent, 1103, 1105
VJ Day (Victory over Japan Day, 15 August 1945): 128–9
Vancouver (Canada): 1011
Vanguard, HMS: 845, 909
Vansittart, 1st Baron: 373, 414, 749 n.1
Variations on a Theme (Terence Rattigan): 1278
Varsity: 1284 n.2
Vatican, the: 460 n.1
Venezia Giulia: 5, 7–8, 11–12, 42
Venice (Italy): Churchill visits (1951), 631–4
Venizelos, Sophocles: 1314
Verne, Jules: 466
Verney, Ralph: 808
Versailles, Treaty of (1920): 1071
Veuve Clicquot (champagne): 151
Vichy Government, the: 169, 427
Victoria, Queen: 264, 293, 344, 366, 370, 371, 391, 474, 698, 808, 835, 876; Churchill 'a link' with, 1016, 1072, 1120, 1319; and the 'power' of Britain, 1127–8; and Churchill's History, 1198; her special chair, 1252
Victoria Cross, the: 443 n.1, 447 n.5, 621 n.2
Victorian Literature: 'the shelter of', 1245
Victory: and 'its Reward', 447
Victory (compiled by Charles Eade, 1946): 205, 245
Vienna (Austria): 6, 25, 43, 81, 82, 135, 140, 200, 279, 453, 582; and a possible Summit conference in, 756, 811, 1023, 1027, 1032; and 'Russian military domination' of, 1028
Vigilance: and Communism, 1004
'Vigilantes': 60–1
Vilna: 96
Vincent, Victor (the gardener at Chartwell): 164 n.3, 979, 983, 1173
Vis, Island of (Adriatic Sea): 453
Vistula River (Poland): 83
Vivienne (the photographer): 496 n.3
Vyshinsky, Andrei: 76 n.1, 224, 351, 565

Wadham College (Oxford): 221
Wadsworth, A. P.: 627 n.3
Wall Street Journal, the: 205
Wallace, Henry A.: 444
Walthamstow (London): Churchill speaks at (1955), 1138; (and in 1959), 1302
War Crimes Trials: 190, 249, 284, 285, 429–32, 438–9, 441–2, 448, 756
War in the Desert (Glubb Pasha): 1334
War Disability Pensions: 977, 1044 n.2
War memoirs: planning of, 221, 234–7, 257, 268, 318, 331–2, 339–40, 342–5, 256–8, 364;

War memoirs—*continued*
work on, at Marrakech, 376–96; work on
(in 1948), 404–5, 412–17, 418–21, 423–4,
426–8, 429, 433–4, 435, 449–50; work on (in
1949), 468–70, 474, 479–80, 484, 488, 491,
493–5; work on (in 1950), 500, 505–6, 522,
524, 546, 550–2, 568–9, 570, 583–4; work
on (in 1951), 596–7, 598, 600, 601, 608–9,
617 n.1, 622–3, 624, 625–7, 627–9, 630,
632–3, 654; work on (in 1952), 735, 761, 785;
(in 1953), 788, 793–4, 810–11, 856–7, 858,
866–7, 877, 877–8, 879, 892; (in 1954), 974;
and Churchill's Woodford speech (1954),
1078–9; the 'moral' of, 1365
War and Peace (Tolstoy): 1304
War at Sea (Roskill): 979 n.1
Warbey, William: 208
Warner Brothers: 1206, 1207 n.1
Warsaw (Poland): 44, 200, 209
Washington DC (USA): Churchill's visits to
(1946), 194–6, 204; Churchill unwilling to
visit (1953), 909; a possible visit to (1953),
912, 917; Churchill's visit to (1954), in pros-
pect, 977, 982, 985–6, 989, 994–6; and the
Suez Crisis (1956), 1222 n.2; Churchill's
visit to (1959), 1293–4
Waterhouse, Captain Charles: 1036
Wathen, Colonel A. H. G.: 151–2
Watson, Arthur: 393 n.1
Watson, Miss E. M.: 41, 1142
Watson, William: quoted, 567
Watt, F. Bartlett: 164 n.2, 1326 n.3
Watt, Colonel Sir George Harvie: 902
Watteville, H. de: 1232 n.4
Wavell, Field Marshal 1st Viscount (later 1st
Earl): 298, 410, 420, 434–5, 474, 479
Waverley, 1st Viscount (formerly Sir John
Anderson): 1227
Weakness: 'makes no appeal to Moscow', 1108
Weeks, 1st Baron (General Sir Ronald): 1263,
1284
Weizmann, Dr Chaim: 252, 430, 455, 458,
527, 528, 557; Churchill's letter to (1950),
560 n.2; a request from, 602 n.1, 625; Chur-
chill's message to (1951), 663; Churchill's
tribute to (1952), 775; Churchill recalls his
'friendship' with, 1096
Weizmann, Flight-Lieutenant Michael: killed
in action (1942), 252, 455–6, 625 n.2, 775
Weizmann, Vera: 1257
Weizsaecker, Baron Ernst von: 439 n.1, 441–2
Welldon, Dr J. E. C. (later Bishop): 367
Wellington, 1st Duke of: 842, 1147
Wells, H. G.: 1211 n.1
Welsh Abbot (Churchill's horse): victorious,
1243, 1244 n.1, 1276
Wernhers, the: 525 n.2

Wessex, Kings of: 'justice' done to, 1194
West Houghton (by-election): 616
Western European Union: 399
Western Germany (West Germany): 520,
829–30, 929–30; rearmament of, 963; to be a
'free partner' in the community of Western
nations, 1010; formation of Army of, 1010
n.3; and trade with Russia, 1295; want 'to
keep Russia out of everything', 1306
Westminster (London): Churchill receives
Freedom of (1946), 229
Westminster Abbey (London): 362, 795, 797,
836, 1359
Westminster College (Fulton, Missouri): 159,
172, 195, 197, 213 n.1
Westminster, Duchess of (Anne): 347
Westminster, 2nd Duke of ('Bendor'): 156, 347,
500, 548, 579; his villa La Pausa, 1172–3
Westminster Hall (London): a private meeting
in, 741; Churchill's 80th birthday ceremony
in, 1073–5; and Churchill's Lying in State,
755 n.4, 1361–2
Weygand, General Maxime: 418 n.6
Wheeler-Bennett, Sir John: 1316
Whitaker, Ben: 347 n.2
Whitaker, Major-General Sir John: 347
Whitbread and Kurn (bricklayers): 138, 145,
164, 327, 381
White City (London): crowds at, 46
White Heron (film): 1006
Whitehall (London): used euphemistically,
and critically, 360, 374, 614; 'activity' in,
seems to stop, 674
Whiteley, William: 482
Why Tell (Churchill's horse): 627
Whyte, Mark: killed in action (1918), 130 n.3
Whyte, Maryott ('Nana') ('Moppett'): 130,
145
Widows' (and Orphans') Pensions: 275, 323,
646
Wigram, Ralph: 339 n.4
Wilhelmina of The Netherlands, Queen: 232–
3, 410, 570 n.2
Williams, Detective-Sergeant G. E.: 378 n.1,
380, 385, 387, 388, 498
Williams, Tom: 527
Williamsburg (Virginia): Churchill's message
to, 1170–1
Williamsburg (the Presidential Yacht): 675–7
Wilmshurst, M. J.: 1323 n.3
Wilson, Archibald: 391
Wilson, Dr C. P.: 707
Wilson, Harold (later Baron Wilson of Rie-
vaulx): 163, 347 n.2; and the sale of
machine tools to Russia, 555; resigns (1951),
607; against hanging, 1182 n.1; Clementine
Churchill's letter to, about her husband's

Wilson, Harold—*continued*
  work for Britain after 1955, 1225; and Churchill's last years, 1343, 1352, 1355; becomes Prime Minister (1964), 1356; calls at Hyde Park Gate, 1357; and Churchill's last illness, 1359; and Churchill's death, 1360; mounts guard, 1361–2
Wilson, Field Marshal Sir Henry: 1232 n.4
Wilson, Sir Horace: 1142 n.2
Wilson, John (later 2nd Baron Moran): 1198
Wilson, Mary (later Lady Wilson of Rievaulx): 607
Wilson, President Woodrow: 699
Wilton (near Salisbury): a painting of, by Churchill, a gift to the Queen, 1313
Winant, Gilbert ('Gil'): 111, 175 n.2, 361–2, 550
Winchester College (Hampshire): 535, 751, 803
Windham, Judge Ralph: 295 n.2
Windsor Castle: Churchill at, 57, 1245; a bust of Churchill commissioned for, 770; Churchill accepts the Garter at, 823; Churchill's audience at, after his stroke, 871; Churchill installed as a Garter Knight at, 993
Windsor, Duchess of (Wallis Simpson): 431, 450
Windsor, Duke of (formerly King Edward VIII): 174, 207 n.1, 234, 431, 450, 549, 979, 1069 n.5
'Winnie': 'He hates that name', 414
Winstanley, Harold: shoots Lady Derby, 770, 771, 984
Winston Churchill (locomotive): and Churchill's funeral, 1363
Winston Churchill Memorial Trust: its origins, 1272
Winston Churchill, Servant of Crown and Commonwealth (1954): 1068
'Winston Club' (at Potsdam): 81
Winston S. Churchill (by Randolph S. Churchill): 872 n.1
Winterton, 6th Earl: 1307
Wise, Colonel A. R.: 350
Wizard of Oz (film): 112
Woermann, Ernst: 442 n.1
Wolff, Michael: 1318, 1351 n.2
Wolmer, Viscount (later 3rd Earl of Selborne): 27
Wolverhampton (England): Churchill speaks at (1949), 480
Wood, Charles Carlyle: 344, 345, 435, 601–3, 632–3, 1066, 1166, 1229
Wood, Miss Heather: 1132
Wood, James ('Mr Accountant Wood'): 1166 n.1, 1235 n.1
Woodard, Peter: 53

Woodford (Churchill's constituency): Churchill speaks in (1950), 509; (1951), 644–5; (1952), 760; (1954), 1070–1, 1072, 1078–81; Churchill to stand at (1955), 1115 n.3, 1131, 1135, 1136–7; Churchill speaks in (1955), 1170; Churchill speaks in (1957), 1248; (in 1959), 1290–1, 1301, 1305; Churchill's decision not to stand again for (1963), 1343, 1344–5, 1346, 1355
Woolton, 1st Baron (later 1st Viscount; subsequently 1st Earl): 163, 227 n.1, 253, 318, 346, 403 n.3, 500, 506, 525, 529, 584 n.4, 620; and Churchill's political future (1947), 341; and by-elections in 1951, 616; and the 1951 General Election, 637; and Churchill's second Premiership, 653, 722, 735, 739, 905 n.1, 947, 981, 1050, 1061, 1084, 1061 n.4
Woolwinder: wins St Leger (1907), 913 n.5
Wooton-Davies, J. H.: 189, 191 n.1
Work (and Play): 386
World, the: 'rough and stony', 130
World Cause, the: 220
World Organization (later the United Nations Organization): 8, 13, 26, 215, 217–18
'Wormwood Scrubbery': and Socialism, 302
Worthing (England): Churchill visits (1958), 1278
Wouk, Herman: 1310–11
Wright, Richard: 577 n.2
Wuthering Heights (book by Jane Austen): 1244
Wuthering Heights (film of the book): 988
Wyatt, Woodrow (later Baron): 208, 949

Yalta Agreements, the (1945): 5, 6, 74, 98, 191, 546, 805
Yalta Conference, the (1945): 42, 63, 71, 82, 86, 95, 104, 213, 236, 238, 239, 312, 428, 546, 548, 569, 622; papers of, published (1955), 1112 n.2
Yalta Declaration, the (1945): 79, 88
Yalu River, the (Korean–Chinese border): 687, 739–40
'Yellow Peril', the: 1082
Yeoman, Dr Philip: 1335
Yorkshire Post, the: 647 n.3, 1350
Young, Sir Arthur: 312 n.3
Young, Mrs E. L.: 236
Young, Ernest: 236
Young, G. M.: 1195
'Young Turks': and General Neguib, 774
Young Winston (film): 1207 n.1
Yugoslavia: and Venezia Giulia, 11–12, 15, 44–5; independence of, 14, 25, 76, 79, 212, 279; and the Second World War, 221; and Greece, 351 n.3; and Hitler's 'fury', 416–17;

Yugoslavia—*continued*
'has broken away', 510; Churchill's visitors from, 590–1; and the Soviet Union (in 1953), 899; and Trieste, 1058 n.3; Churchill's cruise to (1960), 1313–14
Younger, (Sir) Kenneth: 527, 528

Zahedi, General: 878
Zeeland, Paul van: 406
Zhukov, Marshal Georgy: 92
Zionism (and Zionists): 155, 210–11, 250, 251–2, 296, 359, 417, 430, 455–7, 557, 625

Zionism—*continued*
n.2, 663; Churchill's messages and statements concerning, 663, 723, 775, 1008; a 'diatribe' in favour of, 792; Churchill speaks of, 1096; 'I am, of course, a Zionist', 1192; Churchill 'always a friend of', 1323; Churchill's 'outspoken feelings as', 1333
Zulueta, (Sir) Philip de: 1333
Zurich (Switzerland): Churchill's speech at (1946), 265–7, 285, 286; the speech recalled (1947), 336 n.1, 337, 398, 406, 441, 536, 543, 635, 670